# VISUAL DICTIONARY

# Visual Dictionary

ENGLISH · FRENCH · GERMAN · SPANISH

OXFORD UNIVERSITY PRESS

*Oxford University Press, Great Clarendon Street, Oxford OX2 6DP*
*Oxford New York*
*Athens Auckland Bangkok Bombay*
*Calcutta Cape Town Dar es Salaam Delhi*
*Florence Hong Kong Istanbul Karachi*
*Kuala Lumpur Madras Madrid Melbourne*
*Mexico City Nairobi Paris Singapore*
*Taipei Tokyo Toronto*
*ans associated companies in*
*Berlin Ibadan*

*Oxford is a trade mark of Oxford University Press*



*British Library Cataloguing in Publication Data*
*Data available*

*Library of Congress Cataloging in Publication Data*
*Data available*
*ISBN 0-19-863145-6*

*3 5 7 9 10 8 6 4*

*Created and produced by QA International*
*a division of les Éditions Québec/Amérique inc.*
*329, rue de la Commune Ouest, 3e étage, Montréal (Québec), Canada, H2Y 2E1*
*Tél: (514) 499-3000 fax: (514) 499-3010*
Printed in the United States of America

**EDITORIAL STAFF FOR THE ORIGINAL EDITION**

Jacques Fortin - *Publisher*
Jean-Claude Corbeil - *Editor-in-chief*
Ariane Archambault - *Assistant Editor*
François Fortin - *Illustrations Editor*
Jean-Louis Martin - *Art Director*

**COMPUTER GRAPHIC ARTISTS**

Jacques Perrault
Anne Tremblay
Jocelyn Gardner
Christiane Beauregard
Michel Blais
Rielle Lévesque
Marc Lalumière
Stéphane Roy
Alice Comtois
Jean-Yves Ahern
Benoît Bourdeau

**COMPUTER COPYEDITING**

Daniel Beaulieu
Yves Ferland

**RESEARCH EDITOR**

Serge D'Amico

**PAGE SETUP**

Pascal Goyette
Lucie Mc Brearty
Martin Langlois

**PRODUCTION**

Tony O'Riley
Marie Duclos
Éric Hince

**GRAPHIC DESIGN**

Emmanuel Blanc

# ACKNOWLEDGMENTS

The creators of the original edition would like to acknowledge the contribution of the following people and organisations:

A.C. Delco
Aérospatiale (France)
Aérospatiale Canada (ACI) Inc.
Air Canada (Linguistic Policy and Services)
Amity-Leather Products Company
Animat Inc.
Archambault Musique
International Association of Lighthouse Authorities (Marie-Hélène Grillet)
Association des groupes d'astronomes amateurs (Jean-Marc Richard)
Atlas Copco
Atomic Energy of Canada Ltd. (Pierre Giguère)
Bell Canada
Bell Helicopter Textron
Bellefontaine
Benoît, Richard
Beretta
Black & Decker
Bombardier Inc.
Boutique de harnais Pépin
British Hovercraft Corporation Ltd. (Division of Westland Aerospace)
C. Plath North American Division
Caloritech Inc.
Cambridge Instruments (Canada) Inc.
CAMIF (Direction relations extérieures)
Canada Billard & Bowling Inc. (Bernard Monsec)
Canadian National (Information and Linguistic Services)
Canadian Kenworth Company
Canadian Coleman Supply Inc.
Canadian Liquid Air Ltd.
Canadian Curling Association
Canadian Coast Guard
Canadian Broadcasting Corporation (Gilles Amyot, Pierre Beaucage, Claude L'Hérault, Pierre Laroche)
Carpentier, Jean-Marc
Casavant Frères Limitée (Gilbert Lemieux)
Centre de Tissage Leclerc Inc.
Chromalox Inc.
Clerc, Redjean
Club de tir à l'arc de Montréal
Club de planeur Champlain
Collège Jean de Brébeuf (Paul-Émile Tremblay)
Collège militaire royal de Saint-Jean
Communauté urbaine de Montréal (Bureau de transport métropolitain)
Complexe sportif Claude-Robillard
Control Data Canada Ltd.
Cycles Performance
David M. Stewart Museum (Philippe Butler)
Department of National Defence of Canada (Public Relations)
Detson
Direction des constructions navales (Programmes internationaux) (France)
Distributions TTI Inc.
Energy, Mines and Resources Canada (Canada Centre for Remote Sensing)
Environment Canada (Atmospheric Environment Service, Gilles Sanscartier)
FACOM
Fédération québécoise des échecs
Fédération québécoise de tennis
Fédération québécoise de luge et bobsleigh
Fédération québécoise de canot-camping
Fédération québécoise de boxe olympique
Fédération québécoise de badminton
Fédération québécoise d'haltérophilie
Fédération québécoise d'escrime
Fédération de patinage de vitesse du Québec
Festival des Montolfières du Haut-Richelieu
Fincantieri Naval Shipbuilding Division
Fisher Scientific Ltd.
Ford New-Holland Inc.
Gadbois, Alain
GAM Pro Plongée
G.E. Astro-Space Division
G.T.E. Sylvania Canada Ltd.
General Electric Canada Inc. (Dominion Engineering Works, Mony Schinasi)
General Motors of Canada Ltd.
GIAT Industries
Government of Canada Terminology Bank
Gym Plus
Harrison (1985) Inc.
Hewitt Equipment Ltd.
Hippodrome Blue Bonnets (Robert Perez)
Honeywell Ltd.
Hortipro
Hughes Aircraft Company
Hydro-Québec (Centre de documentation, Anne Crépeau)
IBM Canada Ltd.
Imperial Oil Ltd.
Institut de recherche d'Hydro-Québec (IREQ)
International Telecommunications Satellite Organization (Intelsat)
International Civil Aviation Organization (IATA)
Jardin Botanique de Montréal
John Deere Ltd.
Johnson & Johnson Inc.
La Maison Olympique (Sylvia Doucette)
La Cordée
Le Beau Voyage
Le Coz, Jean-Pierre
Lee Valley Tools Ltd.
Leica Camera
Les Manufacturiers Draco ltée
Les Instruments de Musique Twigg Inc.
Les Équipements Chalin ltée
Les Appareils orthopédiques BBG Inc.
Leviton Manufacturing of Canada Ltd.
Liebherr-Québec
Manac Inc.
Manutan
Marcoux, Jean-Marie
Marrazza Musique
MATRA S.A.
Matra Défense (Direction de la communication)
Mazda Canada
Médiatel
Mendes Inc. (François Caron)
Michelin
MIL Tracy (Henri Vacher)
Ministère des transports du Québec (Sécurité routière, Signalisation routière)
Monette Sport Inc.
Moto Internationale
National Oceanic and Atmospheric Administration (NOAA) — National Environmental Satellite and Information Service (Frank Lepore)
National Aeronautics and Space Administration (NASA)
Nikon Canada Inc.
Northern Telecom Canada Ltd.
Office de la langue française du Québec (Chantal Robinson)
Ogilvie Mills Ltd. (Michel Ladouceur)
Olivetti Systems and Networks Canada Ltd.
Ontario Hydro
Paterson Darkroom Necessities
Petro-Canada (Calgary)
Philips Electronics Ltd. (Philips Lighting)
Philips Electronics Ltd. (Scientific and Analytical Equipment)
Pierre-Olivier Decor
Planétarium Dow (Pierre Lacombe)
Plastimo
Port of Montreal (Public Affairs)
Pratt & Whitney Canada Inc.
Quincaillerie A.C.L. Inc.
Radio-Québec
Remington Products (Canada) Inc.
Russell Rinfret
Rodriguez Cantieri navali S.p.A.
S.A. Redoute Catalogue (Relations extérieures)
Samsonite
Secretary of State of Canada (Translation Bureau)
Shell Canada
SIAL Poterie
Smith-Corona (Canada) Ltd.
SNC Defence Products Ltd.
Société Nationale des Chemins de Fer français (S.N.C.F.) (Direction de la communication)
Société de transport de la Communauté urbaine de Montréal
Spalding Canada
Spar Aerospace Ltd. (Hélène Lapierre)
St. Lawrence Seaway Authority (Normand Dodier)
Sunbeam Corporation (Canada) Ltd.
Swimming Canada
Teleglobe Canada Inc. (Roger Leblanc)
Telesat Canada (Yves Comtois)
The Coal Association of Canada
The British Petroleum Company p.l.c. (Photographic Services)
Thibault
Tideland Signal Canada Ltd.
Transport Canada (Montreal Airports, Gilbert L'Espérance, Koos R. Van der Peijl)
Ultramar Canada Inc.
United States Department of Defense (Department of the Navy, Office of Information)
Université du Québec à Montréal (Module des arts, Michel Fournier)
Université du Québec (Institut national de la recherche scientifique, Benoît Jean)
Varin, Claude
Via Rail Canada Inc.
Viala L.R. Inc. (Jean Beaudin)
Ville de Montréal (Bureau du cinéma; Service de l'habitation et du développement urbain; Service de la prévention des incendies, Robert Gilbert, Réal Audet; Service des travaux publics)
Volcano Inc.
Volkswagen Canada Inc.
Volvo Canada Ltd.
Water Ski Canada
Weider
Wild Leitz Canada ltée
Xerox Canada Inc.
Yamaha Canada Music Ltd.

Oxford University Press would like to acknowledge the contribution of Enrique Gonzalez Sardinero and Robin Sawers.

**This world-renowned dictionary is the first comprehensive visual dictionary in full colour. Covering some 600 subjects, it identifies more than 25,000 terms by the use of thousands of detailed and accurate illustrations. The dictionary lets you see, at a glance, the vocabulary of a subject in not one, but four, languages: English, French, German, and Spanish.**

## A PICTURE/WORD DICTIONARY

The *Visual Dictionary* closely links pictures and words.

The pictures describe and analyze today's world: the objects of everyday life, our physical environment, the animal and vegetable life that surrounds us, the communication and work techniques that are changing our lifestyles, the weapons that preoccupy us, the means of transportation that are breaking down geographical barriers, the sources of energy on which we depend, etc.

Illustrations play a specific role in our dictionary: they serve to define words, enabling dictionary users to "see" immediately the meaning of each term. Users can thus recognize the objects they are looking for and, at a single glance, find the corresponding vocabulary.

The *Visual Dictionary* provides users with the words they need to accurately name the objects that make up the world around them.

The terms in the dictionary have been carefully selected from current documents written by experts in each area. In case of doubt, the vocabulary has been studied by specialists in the corresponding field and cross-checked in encyclopedias and language dictionaries. We have taken these precautions to ensure the accuracy of each word and a high level of standardization.

## A DICTIONARY FOR ONE AND ALL

The *Visual Dictionary* is aimed at all persons who participate in one way or another in contemporary civilization and, as a consequence, need to know and use a great number of technical terms from a wide range of fields.

It thus addresses the needs and curiosity of each and every one of us. It is not designed only for specialists.

The depth of analysis varies according to the subject. Rather than arbitrarily providing a uniform breakdown of each subject, the authors have acknowledged that people's degrees of knowledge differ from one field to another, and that the complexity of the topics dealt with varies widely. For example, more people are familiar with clothing and automobiles than with atomic energy or telecommunications satellites, and find the former subjects simpler than the latter. Another aspect of the same problem is that, in describing human anatomy, we are obliged to use medical terminology, even though the terms seem more complicated than those for fruits and vegetables. In addition, our world is changing: photographic vocabulary, for example, has become much more complicated due to camera automation. Similarly, although microcomputer fans are familiar with computer terminology, the field remains a mystery for much of the rest of the population.

The *Visual Dictionary* allows for these phenomena, and reflects the specialized vocabulary commonly used in each field.

## AN EASY-TO-CONSULT DICTIONARY

People may use the *Visual Dictionary* in several different ways, thanks to the List of Chapters (page xxxi), the detailed table of contents (page xv), and the index (page 833).

Users may consult the dictionary:

**By going from an idea to a word**, if they are familiar with an object and can clearly visualize it, but cannot find or do not know the name for it. The table of contents breaks down each subject according to an easy-to-consult, stratified classification system. The *Visual Dictionary* is the only dictionary that allows users to find a word from its meaning.

**By going from a word to an idea**, if they want to check the meaning of a term. The index refers users to the illustrations, which provide the names for the individual features.

**At a glance**, by using the List of Chapters. The coloured page edges help users find the chapters they are looking for.

**For foreign language equivalents**, by browsing through the book or going into depth for particular themes. The objects of the modern world are clearly identified at a glance in four languages.

**For sheer pleasure**, by flipping from one illustration to another, or from one word to another, for the sole purpose of enjoying the illustrations and enriching their knowledge.

## A DICTIONARY WITH A DIFFERENCE

We are all familiar with several types of dictionaries and encyclopedias. It is not always easy, however, to grasp their distinguishing features. The following overview highlights the main differences between the *Visual Dictionary* and other reference works.

**a) Language dictionaries**

These dictionaries describe the meanings given by speakers to the general vocabulary of their language.

They provide two major types of information: headwords (vocabulary), and a list of the meanings of each term (dictionary entries).

The vocabulary, which comprises all of the words covered by lexicographical descriptions, constitutes the framework of the dictionary. For consultation purposes, the headwords are arranged in alphabetical order. Generally speaking, the vocabulary includes common, contemporary language, archaic words useful for understanding the texts or history of a civilization, and a certain number of widely used technical terms.

Each dictionary entry provides an itemized, semantic description of the corresponding headword. Generally, the entry indicates the part of speech for the headword, its etymology and its various meanings, as well as the word's social usage (familiar, colloquial, vulgar, etc.) according to criteria that, even today, remain somewhat "impressionistic."

In general, language dictionaries are classified according to their target users and the number of terms in the vocabulary, which, in addition to nouns, includes all other parts of speech (verbs, pronouns, adjectives, adverbs, prepositions, conjunctions, etc.). A 5,000-word dictionary is intended for children, one with 15,000 words is suitable for schools and a 50,000 word dictionary covers the needs of the general public.

**b) Encyclopedic dictionaries**

In addition to the information included in language dictionaries, encyclopedic dictionaries provide details about the nature, functioning, and history of things, thus enabling laymen with solid general knowledge and specialists to understand the scope of a word. They devote much more space to technical terms, and reflect current scientific and technological developments. Generally speaking, pictures play an important role in illustrating the text. The size of encyclopedic dictionaries varies according to the breadth of the vocabulary, the length of the entries, the emphasis placed on proper nouns and the number of fields of specialization covered.

**c) Encyclopedias**

Unlike the preceding category of reference works, encyclopedias do not deal with language. They are devoted to providing scientific, technical, occasionally economic, historical and geographic descriptions. The arrangement of the entries varies, as all classification systems are valid: alphabetic, conceptual, chronological, by field of specialization, etc. The number of different encyclopedias is virtually unlimited, given the fragmentation of civilization into multiple categories. There is, however, a distinction between universal encyclopedias and specialized encyclopedias.

**d) Specialized lexicons and vocabularies**

These works usually address specific needs created by scientific and technological progress. They focus on ensuring efficient communication through precise, standardized terminology. They vary in all respects: the method of compilation, the authors' approach to the subject matter, the scope of the vocabulary, the number of languages, and the means of establishing equivalents in the various languages (i.e., by simple translation or by a comparison of unilingual terminologies). Specialized lexicography has become an area of intense activity. The number of works is multiplying in all sectors and in all language combinations.

**e) The *Visual Dictionary***

The *Visual Dictionary* is a terminology-oriented dictionary. It is aimed at providing members of the general public with the specific terms they need, in their own or another language, to name the objects of daily life, and helping them grasp the meaning of words through illustrations. The dictionary is an ideal tool for both second-language and mother tongue vocabulary building. Grouped together in interlocking categories, the various elements are interdefined. The dictionary is thus organized according to chapters, subjects, specific objects, and features of these objects. Depending on a person's degree of familiarity with a given chapter, the terminology may seem simple or technical. The fundamental goal, however, is to provide non-specialists with a coherent analysis of useful, necessary vocabulary for each subject.

The *Visual Dictionary* is not an encyclopedia, for at least two reasons: rather than describing objects, it names them; in addition, it avoids listing all the objects in a given category. For example, rather than enumerating the various types of trees, it focuses on a typical representative of the category, and examines its structure and individual parts.

It may even less be considered a language dictionary: like other terminological works, it contains no written definitions and covers only nouns and, in particular, noun phrases.

Nor may it be seen as a compendium of specialized vocabularies, as it avoids terminology used only by specialists, focusing instead on more widespread terms—at the risk of being considered simplistic by experts in specific fields.

The *Visual Dictionary* is the first terminology-oriented dictionary to group together in a single volume the thousands of technical and not-so-technical terms most commonly used in our society, where science, technology, and their end products are part of everyday life.

This is the editorial policy that has guided us in creating this dictionary. Consequently, the number of words it contains does not have the same significance as for a language dictionary, for several reasons: in keeping with our editorial policy, we have deliberately chosen to limit the number of words; unlike conventional dictionaries, this work focuses exclusively on nouns, the most significant words in the language, to the exclusion of adjectives, verbs, prepositions, etc.; and finally no one is sure exactly how to count compound terms!

### COMPUTER-PRODUCED ILLUSTRATIONS

The illustrations in the *Visual Dictionary* have been created by computer from recent documents and original photographs.

The use of computers has given the illustrations a highly realistic, almost photographic look, while allowing to highlight the essential features corresponding to the vocabulary. The graphic precision of the *Visual Dictionary* is one of the main sources of its excellence as an encyclopedic and lexicographical reference tool.

In addition, thanks to computers, we have been able to improve the accuracy of the lines joining objects to their names, thus enhancing the clarity of the link between words and the things they describe.

### CAREFULLY ESTABLISHED VOCABULARY

In creating the *Visual Dictionary*, we have used the method of systematic and comparative terminological research, which is standard practice among professionals who prepare works of this type.

This method comprises several steps, which follow one another in a logical order. The following paragraphs provide a brief description of each of these steps.

**Field delimitation**

First of all, on the basis of our objectives, we defined the scope and contents of the proposed work.

We began by choosing the chapters we felt it necessary to cover. We then divided each chapter into fields and sub-fields, taking care to abide by our editorial policy and avoiding overspecialization and the temptation to cover all subjects in detail. This step resulted in a working table of contents, the dictionary framework, which guided our subsequent steps and was refined as the work progressed. The detailed table of contents is the end result of this process.

**Documentary research**

In keeping with our production plan, we assembled pertinent documents likely to provide us with the required information about words and concepts in each subject matter.

In order of reliability, our documentary sources were as follows:

• Articles and books by experts in the various fields, written in their native language, with an acceptable degree of specialization. Translations of such texts provide revealing information about vocabulary usage, but must be used with due caution;

• Technical documents, such as national standards or the guidelines of the International Standard Organization (ISO), product instructions, technical documents provided by manufacturers, official government publications, etc.;

• Catalogues, commercial texts, advertisements from specialized magazines and major newspapers;

• Encyclopedias, encyclopedic dictionaries, and unilingual language dictionaries;

• Unilingual, bilingual, and multilingual specialized vocabularies and dictionaries. The quality and reliability of these works, however, must be carefully assessed;

• Bilingual and multilingual language dictionaries.

In all, we consulted four to five thousand references. The selected bibliography included in the dictionary indicates only the general documentary sources consulted, and does not include specialized sources.

**Sifting through the documents**

A terminologist went through the documents for each subject, in search of specific concepts and the words used to express them by different authors and works. Gradually, a framework was established, as the terminologist noted the use of the same term for a given concept from one source to another, or, on the contrary, the use of several terms for the same idea. In the latter case, the terminologist continued his research until he was able to form a well-documented opinion of each competing term. All of this research was recorded, with reference notes.

**Creation of a multilingual terminology base**

The English terminology is based on standard British usage; the French terminology on the European French norm; and the Spanish terminology on Castilian usage. The norm for German terminology reflects the criteria used by major German publishing houses. Nothing in this dictionary is the result of translation; all languages have been prepared by renowned specialists and verified by major dictionary houses. Because of this, errors frequently found in other multilingual dictionaries based exclusively on a translation approach have been avoided.

**Creation of terminological files**

The preceding step enabled us to assemble all of the elements for our terminological files.

Each concept identified and defined by an illustration has been paired with the term most frequently used to describe it by the leading authors or in the most reliable sources. Where several competing terms were found in the reference material, following discussion and consensus between the terminologist and the scientific director, a single term was chosen.

**Terminological variants**

Frequently, several words may be used to designate virtually the same concept.

We dealt with such situations as follows:

• In some cases, a term was used by a single author or appeared only once in our documentary sources. We retained the most frequently used competing term.

• Technical terms are often compound words with or without a hyphen, or several-word expressions. This results in at least two types of terminological variants:

**a)** The compound technical term may be shortened by the deletion of one or more of its elements, especially where the meaning is clear in the context. The shortened expression may even become the normal term for the concept. In such cases, we retained the compound form, leaving users the freedom to abbreviate it according to the context.

**b)** An element of the compound term may itself have equivalents (most often synonyms from the commonly spoken language). We retained the most frequently used form.

Variants may stem from the evolution of the language, without terminological consequences. We therefore retained the most contemporary or well-known form.

#### TERMINOLOGICAL APPROACH

A few comments about the terminological approach, as compared to the lexicographical approach, are in order.

Language dictionaries have a long history. They are familiar reference works, used by most people since early school age, with a well-established, widely known and accepted tradition. We all know how to consult a dictionary and interpret the information it provides—or fails to provide.

Terminological dictionaries are either very recent or intended for a specialized public. There is no solid tradition to guide those who design and produce such works. Although specialists know how to interpret dictionaries pertaining to their own fields, given that they are familiar with the terminology, the same cannot be said for the layperson, who is confused by variants. Finally, whereas language dictionaries have to a certain extent established standard word usage among their users, specialized vocabularies are characterized by competing terms in new fields of specialization.

Users of a reference work such as the *Visual Dictionary* should take into account these elements in assessing this new type of reference tool.

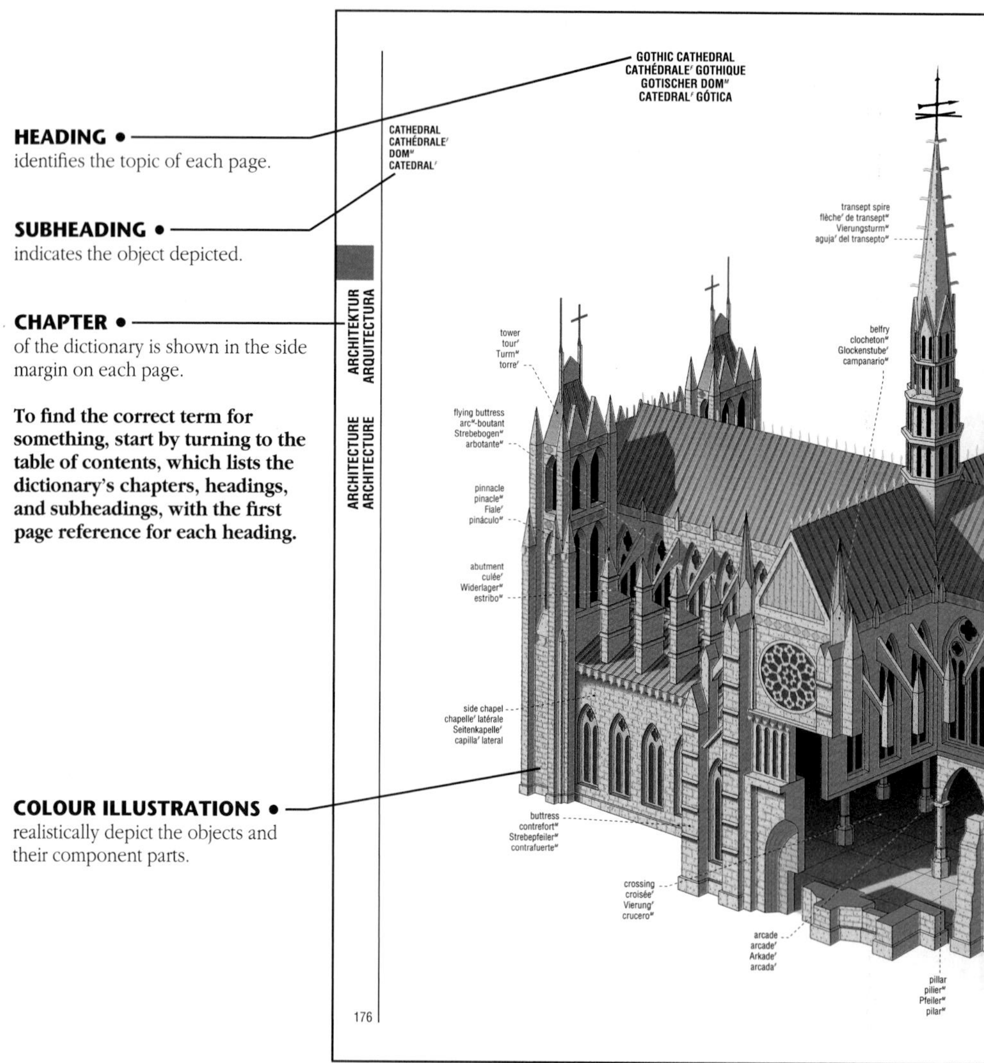


**HEADING •**
identifies the topic of each page.

**SUBHEADING •**
indicates the object depicted.

**CHAPTER •**
of the dictionary is shown in the side margin on each page.

**To find the correct term for something, start by turning to the table of contents, which lists the dictionary's chapters, headings, and subheadings, with the first page reference for each heading.**

**COLOUR ILLUSTRATIONS •**
realistically depict the objects and their component parts.

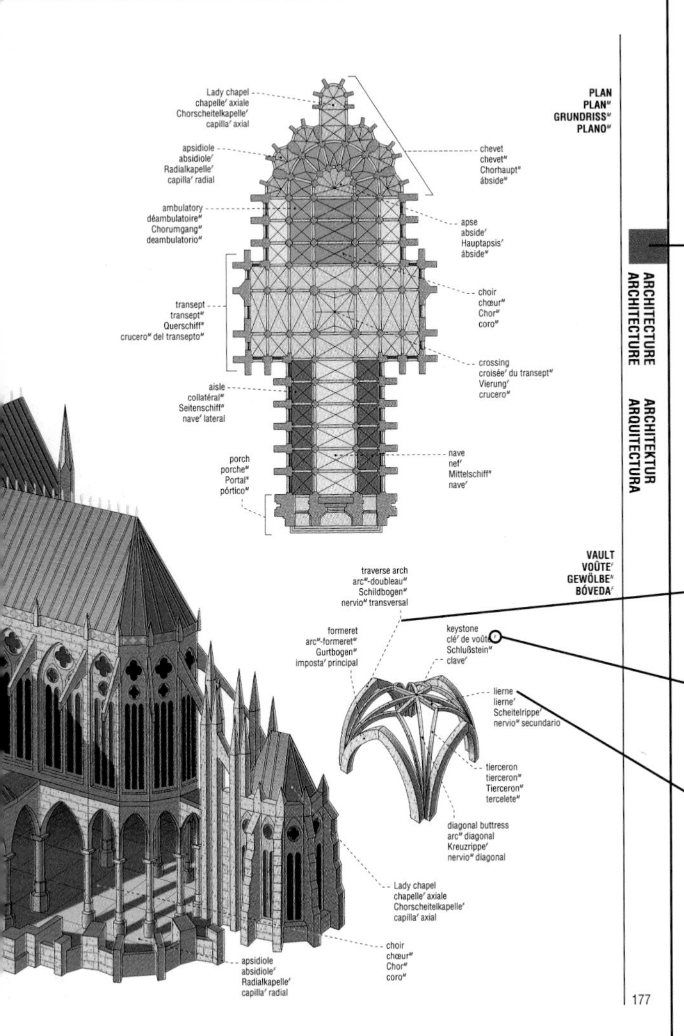


**• COLOURED TAB**

on the edge of the page corresponds to the chapter as shown in the List of Chapters. This colour-coding allows you to find, at a glance, the subject you are looking for.

**• DOTTED LINES**

link the terms with the objects they describe.

**• INDICATION OF GENDER**

f: feminine
m: masculine
n: neuter

**• TERMS**

are included in the index, with references to all pages on which they appear.

**To see an illustration depicting a term that you know, consult the index.**

**DICTIONARIES**

- *Gage Canadian Dictionary.* Toronto: Gage Publishing Limited, 1983, 1313 p.
- *The New Britannica/Webster Dictionary and Reference Guide.* Chicago, Toronto: Encyclopedia Britannica, 1981, 1505 p.
- *The Oxford English Dictionary.* Second edition. Oxford: Clarendon Press, 1989, 20 vol.
- *The New Shorter Oxford English Dictionary*, 1994, 2 vols.
- *Concise Oxford Dictionary*, 1995, 1673 p.
- *The Oxford Illustrated Dictionary.* Oxford: Clarendon Press, 1967, 974 p.
- *Oxford American Dictionary.* Eugene Ehrlich, et al. New York, Oxford: Oxford University Press, 1980, 816 p.
- *The Random House Dictionary of the English Language.* Second edition. New York: Random House 1983, 2059 p.
- *Webster's Encyclopedic Unabridged Dictionary of the English Language.* New York: Portland House, 1989, 2078 p.
- *Webster's Third New International Dictionary.* Springfield: Merriam-Webster, 1986, 2662 p.
- *Webster's Ninth New Collegiate Dictionary.* Springfield: Merriam-Webster, 1984, 1563 p.
- *Webster's New World Dictionary of American Language.* New York: The World Pub., 1953.

**ENCYCLOPEDIAS**

- *Academic American Encyclopedia.* Princeton: Arete Publishing Company, 1980, 21 vol.
- *Architectural Graphic Standards.* Eighth edition. New York: John Wiley & Sons, 1988, 854 p.
- *Chamber's Encyclopedia.* New rev. edition. London: International Learning System, 1989.
- *Collier's Encyclopedia.* New York: Macmillan Educational Company, 1984, 24 vol.
- *Compton's Encyclopedia.* Chicago: F.E. Compton Company, Division of Encyclopedia Britannica Inc., 1982, 26 vol.
- *Encyclopedia Americana.* International Edition, Danbury: Grolier, 1981, 30 vol.
- *How It Works, The Illustrated Science and Invention Encyclopedia.* New York: H.S. Stuttman, 1977, 21 vol.
- *McGraw-Hill Encyclopedia of Science & Technology.* New York: McGraw-Hill Book Company, 1982, 15 vol.
- *Merit Students Encyclopedia.* New York: Macmillan Educational Company, 1984, 20 vol.
- *New Encyclopedia Britannica.* Chicago, Toronto: Encyclopedia Britannica, 1985, 32 vol.
- *The Joy of Knowledge Encyclopedia.* London: Mitchell Beazley Encyclopedias, 1976, 7 vol.
- *The Random House Encyclopedia.* New York: Random House, 1977, 2 vol.
- *The World Book Encyclopedia.* Chicago: Field Enterprises Educational Corporation, 1973.

**ASTRONOMY**
celestial coordinate system ..... 3
Earth coordinate system ..... 3
solar system ..... 4
*planets and moons, orbits of the planets*
Sun ..... 6
*structure of the Sun, phases of the Moon*
Moon ..... 7
*lunar features*
solar eclipse ..... 8
lunar eclipse ..... 8
seasons of the year ..... 8
galaxy ..... 9
comet ..... 9
*Hubble's classification*
constellations of the northern hemisphere ..... 10
constellations of the southern hemisphere ..... 12
astronomical observatory ..... 14
*telescope, observatory*
radio telescope ..... 15
*altazimuth mounting*
planetarium ..... 16
Hubble space telescope ..... 16

**GEOGRAPHY**
profile of the Earth's atmosphere ..... 19
configuration of the continents ..... 20
structure of the Earth ..... 22
section of the Earth's crust ..... 22
earthquake ..... 23
cave ..... 24
volcano ..... 25
glacier ..... 26
mountain ..... 27
ocean floor ..... 28
*mid-ocean ridge, topographic features, abyssal plain, continental margin*
wave ..... 30
common coastal features ..... 30
ecology ..... 31
*structure of the biosphere, food chain, pollution of food on and in the ground, pollution of food in water, atmospheric pollution, hydrologic cycle*
precipitations ..... 36
*stormy sky, classification of snow crystals*
meteorology ..... 38
*weather map, station model, wind*
international weather symbols ..... 39
*fronts, cloud amount, present weather*
meteorological measuring instruments ..... 40
*measurement of sunshine, measurement of rainfall, measurement of temperature, instrument shelter, measurement of air pressure, measurement of wind direction, measurement of wind strength, measurement of humidity, measurement of snowfall, measurement of cloud ceiling*
weather satellite ..... 42
*geostationary satellite, orbit of the satellites, polar-orbiting satellite*
clouds and meteorological symbols ..... 44
*high clouds, clouds with vertical development, middle clouds, low clouds*

climates of the world ........ 45
*tropical climates, temperate climates, polar climates, continental climates, subtropical climates, highland climates, subarctic climates*
desert ........ 46
cartography ........ 47
*hemispheres, grid system*
remote detection satellite ........ 48
*Radarsat satellite, map projections, political map, physical map, urban map, road map*

**PLANT KINGDOM**
mushroom ........ 55
*structure of a mushroom, edible mushrooms, deadly poisonous mushroom, poisonous mushroom*
types of leaf ........ 56
*leaf margin, leaf, compound leaves, simple leaves*
structure of a plant ........ 57
conifer ........ 58
*branch, types of leaves*
structure of a tree ........ 59
*tree, cross section of a trunk, stump*
structure of a flower ........ 60
*types of inflorescence*
grape ........ 61
*steps to ripeness, vine stock, bunch of grapes, vine leaf*
fleshy fruits: berry fruits ........ 62
*section of a berry, section of a raspberry, section of a strawberry, principal types of berry*
fleshy stone fruits ........ 63
*section of a stone fruit, principal types of stone fruit*
fleshy pomes ........ 64
*section of a pome, principal types of pome*
fleshy fruits: citrus fruits ........ 65
*section of a citrus fruit, principal types of citrus fruit*
dry fruits: nuts ........ 66
*section of a hazelnut, section of a walnut, principal types of nut, husk*
various dry fruits ........ 67
*section of a follicle, section of a silique, section of a legume, section of a capsule*
tropical fruits ........ 68
*principal types of tropical fruit*
vegetables ........ 69
*fruit vegetables, inflorescent vegetables, section of a bulb, bulb vegetables, tuber vegetables, root vegetables, stalk vegetables, pulses, leaf vegetables*
herbs ........ 74

**ANIMAL KINGDOM**
insects and spiders ........ 77
butterfly ........ 78
*caterpillar, chrysalis, hind leg*
honeybee ........ 80
*worker, foreleg (outer surface), middle leg (outer surface), hind leg (inner surface), mouthparts, worker, queen, drone, honeycomb section, hive*
gastropod ........ 83
*snail, principal edible gastropods*
amphibians ........ 84
*frog, life cycle of the frog, eggs, tadpole, principal amphibians*
fish ........ 86
*morphology, gills, anatomy*

crustacean .......... 90
*lobster, major edible crustaceans*
mollusc .......... 92
*oyster, principal edible molluscs*
univalve shell .......... 94
bivalve shell .......... 95
*dorsal view, left valve*
reptile .......... 96
*venomous snake's head, rattlesnake, shell, turtle*
types of jaw .......... 98
*rodent's jaw, carnivore's jaw, herbivore's jaw*
principal types of horn .......... 99
principal types of tusk .......... 99
types of hoof .......... 99
horse .......... 100
*morphology, gaits, skeleton, plantar surface of the hoof, horseshoe, hoof*
deer family .......... 105
*deer antlers, principal kinds of deer*
dog .......... 106
*morphology, dog's forepaw*
cat .......... 107
*cat's head, extended claw, retracted claw*
bird .......... 108
*morphology, head, egg, wing, contour feather, principal types of bill, principal types of foot*
bat .......... 112
*bat's head*

**HUMAN BEING**

plant cell .......... 115
animal cell .......... 115
human body .......... 116
muscles .......... 120
*anterior view, posterior view*
skeleton .......... 122
*anterior view, posterior view*
blood circulation .......... 124
*circulation diagram, heart, principal veins and arteries*
male genital organs .......... 127
*sagittal section, spermatozoon*
female genital organs .......... 128
*egg, sagittal section*
breast .......... 129
respiratory system .......... 130
digestive system .......... 131
*large intestine, small intestine*
urinary system .......... 132
nervous system .......... 133
*peripheral nervous system, central nervous system, lumbar vertebra, chain of neurons, sensory impulse*
sense organs: touch .......... 136
*skin, finger, hand*
sense organs: hearing .......... 138
*parts of the ear, auditory ossicles, auricle*
sense organs: sight .......... 140
*eye, eyeball*
sense organs: smell .......... 141
*external nose, nasal fossae*

senses of smell and taste ... 142
*mouth, sagittal section, dorsum of tongue, taste sensations*
teeth ... 144
*human denture, cross section of a molar*

**FARMING**
tractor ... 147
farmstead ... 148
farm animals ... 150
principal types of cereal ... 152
bread ... 153
steps in soil cultivation ... 154
*ribbing plough, manure spreader, tandem disc harrow, cultivator, seed drill, flail mower, rake, hay baler, combine harvester, forage harvester, forage blower*

**ARCHITECTURE**
traditional dwellings ... 165
architectural styles ... 166
*doric order, ionic order, corinthian order*
Greek temple ... 168
Roman house ... 170
mosque ... 172
types of arch ... 174
*semicircular arch, types of arches*
gothic cathedral ... 175
Vauban fortification ... 178
castle ... 180
roofs ... 182
city centre ... 184
cross section of a street ... 186
town houses ... 187
theatre ... 188
*stage*
office building ... 190

**HOUSE**
reading plans ... 193
*elevation, site plan, mezzanine floor, first floor, ground floor*
exterior of a house ... 196
structure of a house ... 198
*timber frame, roof truss, foundations*
wood flooring ... 200
*wood flooring on cement screed, wood flooring on wooden base, wood flooring types*
stairs ... 201
door ... 202
*exterior door, types of door*
window ... 203
*structure, types of window*
heating ... 204
*fireplace, slow-burning stove, chimney, fire irons, forced warm-air system, electric furnace, types of outlet, pumped hot-water system, gilled-tube radiator, boiler, oil burner, humidifier, hygrometer, floor-level electric convector, convector heater, auxiliary heating, heat pump, room thermostat*
air conditioning ... 214
*ceiling fan, room air conditioner*
plumbing system ... 215

pedestal-type cesspit pump ........ 216
septic tank ........ 216

**HOUSE FURNITURE**

table ........ 219
*principal types of table*
armchair ........ 220
*principal types of armchair*
seats ........ 222
side chair ........ 223
*types of chair*
bed ........ 224
*bed linen*
storage furniture ........ 225
*armoire*
window accessories ........ 228
*types of curtain, types of pleat, types of heading, curtain pole, curtain track, traverse rod, roller blind, Venetian blind*
lights ........ 232
*incandescent light bulb, fluorescent tube, tungsten-halogen bulb, energy saving bulb, adjustable lamp, track lighting, chandelier*
glassware ........ 237
crockery ........ 238
cutlery ........ 239
*principal types of knife, principal types of fork, principal types of spoon*
kitchen utensils ........ 242
*types of kitchen knife, for straining and draining, for grinding and grating, set of utensils, for opening, for measuring, baking utensils*
coffee makers ........ 247
*automatic filter coffee maker, vacuum coffee maker, percolator, cafetière with plunger, Neapolitan coffee maker, espresso coffee maker*
cooking utensils ........ 248
*wok set, fish kettle, fondue set, pressure cooker*
domestic appliances ........ 250
*blender, hand mixer, hand blender, table mixer, beaters, food processor, discs, lemon squeezer, ice cream maker, juice extractor, kettle, toaster, deep fryer, waffle iron, microwave oven, griddle, refrigerator, extractor hood, electric cooker, steam iron, coffee mill, tin opener, dishwasher, washing machine, electric tumble dryer, hand vacuum cleaner, cylinder vacuum cleaner, cleaning tools*

**GARDENING**

pleasure garden ........ 263
tools and equipment ........ 264
*impulse sprinkler, revolving sprinkler, hose trolley, watering can, hedge trimmer, motorized ground auger, wheelbarrow, hand mower, trimmer, power mower, chainsaw, Rotavator*

**DO-IT-YOURSELF**

carpentry: tools ........ 275
*claw hammer, nail, ball-peen hammer, mallet, screwdriver, spiral screwdriver, screw, plane, hacksaw, handsaw, slip joint pliers, water pump pliers, mole wrench, washers, adjustable spanner, bolt, nut, electric drill, hand drill, brace, auger bit, twist drill bit, G-clamp, vice, router, pillar drill, circular saw, table saw*
building materials ........ 286
*basic building materials, covering materials, insulating materials, wood, board, wood-based materials*

lock ........ 290
*mortise lock, tubular lock*
masonry ........ 291
*mason's trowel, caulking gun*
plumbing: bathroom ........ 292
*toilet*
plumbing ........ 294
*bib tap, ball-type mixer, disc mixer, cartridge mixer, sink with waste disposal unit, geyser*
plumbing: examples of branching ........ 298
*washing machine, dishwasher*
plumbing ........ 299
*plumbing tools, mechanical connections, transition fittings, fittings*
ladders and stepladders ........ 302
*stepladder, extension ladder, platform ladder*
painting accessories ........ 304
*spray gun, scraper, paintbrush, paint roller*
soldering and welding ........ 305
*soldering gun, arc welding, cutting torch, welding torch, oxyacetylene welding, pressure regulator, butt welding, blowtorch, striker*
welding: protective equipment ........ 308
electricity ........ 309
*lampholder, American plug, European plug, electrician's tools, multimeter, tester screwdriver, inspection light, multipurpose tool, combination pliers, wire stripper, fuse box, fuses*

**CLOTHING**

features of historical costume ........ 315
men's clothing ........ 319
*raincoat, trench coat, duffle coat, overcoat, windcheater, parka, double-breasted jacket, waistcoat, single-breasted jacket, belt, braces, trousers, shirt, necktie, underwear, briefs, vest, socks*
sweaters ........ 326
*V-neck cardigan, knit shirt*
gloves ........ 327
headgear ........ 328
*trilby, hunting cap, cap, balaclava, rainhat*
women's clothing ........ 330
*types of coat, pea jacket, raglan, pelerine, cape, suit, types of dress, types of skirt, types of pleat, types of trousers, types of blouse, waistcoats and jackets, types of pockets, types of sleeves, types of collars, necklines and necks, hose, underwear, bra, nightwear*
children's clothing ........ 349
*hooded towelling robe, plastic pants, frilly pants, blanket sleepsuit, high-back dungarees, sleepsuit, babygro, training set, dungarees with crossover back straps, snowsuit*
sportswear ........ 352
*running shoe, training suit, exercise wear*
shoes ........ 354
*parts of a shoe, principal types of shoe, accessories*

**PERSONAL ADORNMENT**

jewellery ........ 361
*earrings, necklaces, cut for gemstones, brilliant cut facets, precious stones, semiprecious stones, rings, bracelets, pins, charms*
manicure ........ 365
*manicure set, manicuring implements, nail clippers*

make-up ..... 366
*lip make-up, eye make-up, sponges*
hairdressing ..... 368
*illuminated mirror, hairbrushes, combs, haircutting scissors, notched double-edged thinning scissors, notched single-edged thinning scissors, hair roller, hairstyling accessories, curling iron, styling brush, hair dryer*

**PERSONAL ARTICLES**
dental care ..... 373
*toothbrush, electric toothbrush*
razors ..... 374
*electric razor, cut-throat razor, double-edged razor, shaving brush*
umbrella and stick ..... 375
*umbrella, telescopic umbrella, stick umbrella*
spectacles ..... 376
*parts of spectacles, bifocal lens, frames, principal types of spectacles*
leather goods ..... 378
*attaché case, briefcase, bottom-fold document case, calculator/cheque book holder, credit card wallet*
handbags ..... 380
*satchel bag, shoulder bag, accordion bag, drawstring bag*
luggage ..... 382
*travel bag, vanity case, suit carrier, luggage trolley, suitcase, weekend case, trunk*
smoking accessories ..... 384
*cigar, cigarette, cigarette packet, pipe, pipe tools, book of matches, matchbox, gas lighter, ashtray*
writing instruments ..... 389
*fountain pen, communications, ballpoint pen*
photography ..... 390
*cross section of a reflex camera, camera back, single-lens reflex (SLR) camera, lenses, lens accessories, photographic accessories, electronic flash, tripod, still cameras, films, exposure meter, spotmeter, slide projector, projection screen, slide, developing tank, negative carrier, enlarger, developing baths, print washer*
stereo sound system ..... 400
*system components, loudspeaker, tuner, amplifier, cassette, cassette tape deck, record, turntable unit, compact disc, compact disc player*
dynamic microphone ..... 406
headphones ..... 406
radio: studio and control room ..... 407
portable sound systems ..... 408
*personal radio cassette player, portable CD radio cassette recorder*
video camera ..... 409
television ..... 410
*television set, picture tube, remote control, videocassette recorder, studio and control rooms, production control room, studio floor, camera*
mobile unit ..... 415
satellite broadcasting ..... 416
telecommunications by satellite ..... 417
telecommunication satellites ..... 418
*examples of satellites, Eutelsat II, launching into orbit*
communication by telephone ..... 420
*telephone answering machine, telephone, telex, fax machine, types of telephone, telecommunication terminal, pay phone*

**ROAD TRANSPORT**
car ..... 425
*types of bodywork, body, bucket seat, rear seat, door, lights, dashboard, instrument panel, windscreen wiper, disc brake, drum brake, tyre, belted radial tyre, wheel, petrol engine*
types of engine ..... 436
*four-stroke engine, two-stroke engine, diesel engine, rotary engine, radiator, turbo-charged engine, sparking plug, exhaust system, battery*
trucking ..... 440
*tractor unit, articulated lorry with trailer, semitrailer, flatbed*
motorcycle ..... 442
*crash helmet, instrument cluster*
snowmobile ..... 445
bicycle ..... 446
*power train, accessories*
caravan ..... 449
*trailer caravan, camper*
road system ..... 450
*cross section of a road, principal types of interchange, cloverleaf*
service station ..... 453
*petrol pump, service station*
fixed bridges ..... 454
*types of beam bridge, types of arch bridge, types of arch, suspension bridge, cable-stayed bridges*
movable bridges ..... 457
*swing bridge, floating bridge, single-leaf bascule bridge, lift bridge, transporter bridge*

**RAIL TRANSPORT**
high-speed train ..... 458
types of passenger coach ..... 460
*open-plan coach, sleeping car, restaurant car*
passenger station ..... 462
railway station ..... 464
marshalling yard ..... 465
railway track ..... 466
*rail joint, rail section, railway track, remote-controlled points, manually-operated points*
diesel-electric locomotive ..... 468
goods van ..... 470
*bogie van, container, coupling*
level crossing ..... 471
types of goods truck ..... 472
underground railway ..... 474
*underground station, bogie and track, underground train, passenger car*

**MARITIME TRANSPORT**
four-masted bark ..... 478
*masts and rigging, sails*
types of sail ..... 482
types of rig ..... 482
anchor ..... 483
*ship's anchor, types of anchor*
navigation devices ..... 484
*sextant, liquid compass, echo sounder, echo sounder probe*
maritime signals ..... 486
*lighthouse lantern, lighthouse, cylindrical buoy, high focal plane buoy*
maritime buoyage system ..... 488

*cardinal marks, buoyage regions, operational pattern of marks by night, daymarks (region B)*
harbour ..... 490
canal lock ..... 492
hovercraft ..... 492
ferry ..... 494
container ship ..... 494
hydrofoil boat ..... 495
cruiseliner ..... 496

**AIR TRANSPORT**
long-range jet airliner ..... 498
types of tail unit ..... 498
types of wing ..... 499
flight deck ..... 500
turbofan engine ..... 501
airport ..... 502
*passenger terminal, runway, ground airport equipment*
helicopter ..... 508

**SPACE TRANSPORT**
rocket ..... 509
space shuttle ..... 510
*space shuttle at takeoff, space shuttle in orbit*
spacesuit ..... 512

**OFFICE SUPPLIES**
stationery ..... 515
office furniture ..... 520
calculator ..... 523
*pocket calculator, printing calculator*
electronic typewriter ..... 524

**OFFICE AUTOMATION**
configuration of an office automation system ..... 526
*input devices, communication devices, data storage devices, output devices*
basic components ..... 528
*personal computer (view from above), video monitor, floppy disc, mini-floppy disc, hard disc drive, keyboard, mouse, dot matrix printer*
photocopier ..... 532
*control panel*

**MUSIC**
traditional musical instruments ..... 535
*zither, mandolin, lyre, balalaika, banjo, accordion, bagpipes, Jew's harp*
musical notation ..... 537
*staff, clefs, time signatures, scale, intervals, note values, rest values, accidentals, ornaments, chord, other signs*
musical accessories ..... 539
*music stand, tuning fork, quartz metronome, metronome*
keyboard instruments ..... 540
*upright piano, upright piano action*
organ ..... 542
*organ console, flue pipe, reed pipe, mechanism of the organ, production of sound*
stringed instruments ..... 544
*violin, bow, violin family, harp, acoustic guitar, electric guitar*
wind instruments ..... 548

*saxophone, woodwind family, reeds, trumpet, brass family*
percussion instruments ..... 552
*drums, snare drum, kettledrum, triangle, tambourine, xylophone*
electronic instruments ..... 555
*synthesizer, electronic piano*
symphony orchestra ..... 556
examples of instrumental groups ..... 558

**CREATIVE LEISURE ACTIVITIES**
sewing ..... 561
*sewing machine, foot control, presser foot, needle, tension block, bobbin case, pin cushion, tracing wheel, scissors, lining fabrics, pattern, fasteners, hook and eyes, fabric structure, snap fastener, buckle, zip fastener*
knitting ..... 567
*knitting needles, crochet hook, stitch patterns*
knitting machine ..... 568
*needle bed and carriages, latch needle, tension block*
bobbin lace ..... 570
*pillow, bobbin*
embroidery ..... 571
*frame, hoop, cross stitches, flat stitches, couched stitches, knot stitches, loop stitches*
weaving ..... 572
*low warp loom, heddles, shuttle, high warp loom, bobbin winder, ball winder, warping frame, diagram of weaving principle, basic weaves, other techniques*
fine bookbinding ..... 577
*bound book, gathering, trimming, sawing-in, sewing, board cutter, sewing frame, pressing, standing press, backing, backing press, backing hammer, covering, bookbinding leather*
printing ..... 580
*relief printing, intaglio printing, lithographic printing*
relief printing process ..... 581
*inking slab, equipment, etching press*
intaglio printing process ..... 582
*equipment*
lithography ..... 583
*levigator, lithographic press, equipment*
pottery ..... 584
*turning, tools, coiling, turning wheel, slab building, electric kiln, firing*
wood carving ..... 586
*steps, accessories, types of tools, principal types of carving blade*
painting and drawing ..... 588
*principal techniques, equipment, supports, airbrush, drawing board, accessories, useful liquids*

**TEAM GAMES**
baseball ..... 595
*catcher, batter, bat, baseball, fielder's glove, field*
cricket ..... 598
*cricket player, cricket ball, bat, wicket, field, pitch*
association football ..... 600
*footballer, football, playing field*
American football ..... 602
*American football player, protective equipment, football, scrimmage, offence, defence, playing field for American football, playing field for Canadian football, scrimmage in Canadian football*

rugby ........ 606
*field, rugby ball*
field hockey ........ 607
*playing field, hockey ball, stick*
ice hockey ........ 608
*rink, puck, player's stick, goalkeeper, ice hockey player*
basketball ........ 610
*court, basketball, basket*
netball ........ 611
*court, netball*
handball ........ 612
*court, handball*
volleyball ........ 613
*court, volleyball, net*
tennis ........ 614
*court, net, tennis ball, tennis player, tennis racket*
squash ........ 616
*squash ball, squash racket, international singles court*
racquetball ........ 617
*racquetball racket, racquetball, court*
badminton ........ 618
*badminton racket, shuttlecock, court, net*
table tennis ........ 619
*table tennis bat, table, types of grip*
curling ........ 620
*curling stone, curling brooms, rink*

**WATER SPORTS**
swimming ........ 621
*competitive course, starting block, crawl stroke, breaststroke, butterfly stroke, backstroke start, backstroke*
diving ........ 624
*diving apparatus, starting positions, flights, entries, forward dive, backward dive, armstand dive, twist dive, reverse dive, inward dive*
water polo ........ 626
*playing area, goal, water polo ball*
scuba diving ........ 627
*scuba diver*
sailing ........ 628
*sailing boat, points of sailing, upperworks, traveller*
sailboard ........ 631
rowing and sculling ........ 632
*sculling (two oars), rowing (one oar), sculling boats, rowing boats, types of oar*
water skiing ........ 633
*types of ski, twin skis, slalom ski, figure ski, types of handle*

**AERIAL SPORTS**
ballooning ........ 634
*balloon, basket*
sky diving ........ 635
*sky diver*
paragliding ........ 636
*canopy*
hang gliding ........ 637
*hang glider*
gliding ........ 638
*glider, cockpit*

**WINTER SPORTS**
alpine skiing ..... 640
*alpine skier, safety binding, ski boot*
cross-country skiing ..... 642
*cross-country skier, cross-country ski*
luge ..... 643
bobsleigh ..... 643
skating ..... 644
*figure skate, hockey skate, speed skate, skate guard*
snowshoe ..... 645
*Michigan snowshoe*
roller skate ..... 645

**EQUESTRIAN SPORTS**
show-jumping ..... 646
*show-jumping course, obstacles*
riding ..... 648
*rider, saddle, bridle*
types of bit ..... 650
*snaffle bit, curb bit*
horse racing ..... 651
*jockey, stand and track*
harness racing ..... 652
*standardbred pacer*

**ATHLETICS**
track and field athletics ..... 654
*arena, starting block, high jump, pole vault, throwing apparatus, hammer, javelins, shot, discus*
gymnastics ..... 659
*vaulting horse, asymmetrical bars, springboard, balance beam, trampoline, rings, horizontal bar, pommel horse, parallel bars*
weightlifting ..... 662
*weightlifter, two-hand snatch, two-hand clean and jerk*
fitness equipment ..... 663
*weight trainer, barbell, exercise cycle, stepper, rowing machine, dumbbell, handgrips, ankle/wrist weight, skipping-rope, twist bar, chest expander*

**COMBAT SPORTS**
fencing ..... 666
*parts of the weapon, fencing weapons, piste, target areas, fencer, positions*
judo ..... 668
*judo suit, mat, examples of holds*
boxing ..... 669
*ring, boxing gloves, bandage, gumshield*

**LEISURE SPORTS**
fishing ..... 670
*fly rod, artificial fly, fly reel, open-face spinning reel, spinning rod, fishhook, spinner, fishing wear, accessories, terminal tackles*
billiards ..... 673
*carom billiards, English billiards, pool, snooker, table, bridge, billiard cue*
golf ..... 676
*course, golf ball, types of golf club, wood, iron, golf clubs, golf glove, head cover, golf shoe, golf trolley, golf bag, electric golf cart*
mountaineering ..... 680
*mountaineer, hammer axe, descender, piton, tubular ice screw, chock, carabiner, ice-axe*

bowls and petanque ........ 682
*green, delivery*
bowling ........ 683
*bowling ball, types of pins, set-up, lane*
archery ........ 684
*arrow, archer, target, compound bow*

**CAMPING**
camping ........ 685
*two-person tent, family tent, ridge tent, principal types of tent, bed and mattress, sleeping bags, Swiss army knife, cooking set, cutlery set, propane or butane appliances, two-burner camp stove, single-burner camp stove, heater, lantern, tools*
knots ........ 691
cable ........ 692
*short splice, twisted rope, braided rope*

**INDOOR GAMES**
card games ........ 695
*symbols, standard poker hands*
dominoes ........ 695
chess ........ 696
*chessboard, types of move, men*
go ........ 697
backgammon ........ 697
*board, major motions*
game of darts ........ 698
*dartboard, dart, playing area*
video entertainment system ........ 699
dice ........ 699
roulette table ........ 700
*American roulette wheel, American betting layout, French roulette wheel, French betting layout*
fruit machine ........ 702

**MEASURING DEVICES**
measure of temperature ........ 705
*thermometer, clinical thermometer, bimetallic thermometer, room thermostat*
measure of time ........ 706
*stopwatch, mechanical watch, digital watch, analogue watch, sundial, grandfather clock, weight-driven clock mechanism*
measurement of weight ........ 708
*beam balance, steelyard, Roberval's balance, spring balance, bathroom scales, electronic scales, analytical balance*
measurement of pressure ........ 710
*barometer/thermometer, sphygmomanometer*
measurement of length ........ 711
*tape measure*
measurement of distance ........ 711
*pedometer*
measurement of thickness ........ 711
*micrometer caliper*
watt-hour meter ........ 712
*exterior view, mechanism*
measure of angles ........ 713
*bevel square, theodolite, protractor*

measurement of seismic waves ........ 714
*detection of seismic waves, amplification of seismic waves, transcription of seismic waves, visualization of seismic waves*

**OPTICAL INSTRUMENTS**
electron microscope ........ 717
*cross section of an electron microscope, electron microscope elements*
binocular microscope ........ 718
telescopic sight ........ 718
prism binoculars ........ 719
magnetic compass ........ 719
reflecting telescope ........ 720
refracting telescope ........ 721
lenses ........ 722
*converging lenses, diverging lenses*
radar ........ 722

**HEALTH AND SAFETY**
first aid kit ........ 725
first aid equipment ........ 726
*stethoscope, hospital trolley, syringe, stretcher*
wheelchair ........ 727
walking aids ........ 728
*forearm crutch, underarm crutch, sticks*
ear protection ........ 729
*ear plugs, safety earmuff*
eye protection ........ 729
*safety glasses, safety goggles*
head protection ........ 729
*hard hat*
respiratory system protection ........ 730
*respirator, half-mask respirator*
safety jacket ........ 730
feet protection ........ 730
*safety boot*

**ENERGY**
coal mine ........ 733
*open-pit mine, opencast strip mine, jackleg drill, pithead, pneumatic drill, underground mine*
oil ........ 737
*drilling rig, rotary system, production platform, offshore drilling, Christmas tree, crude-oil pipeline, fixed-roof tank, floating-roof tank, road tanker, tanker, tank wagon, refinery products*
electricity ........ 746
*hydroelectric complex, cross section of a hydroelectric power station, embankment dam, gravity dam, arch dam, buttress dam, tidal power plant, generator unit, Francis runner, Kaplan runner, Pelton runner, steps in the production of electricity, pylon, electricity distribution, overhead connection*
nuclear energy ........ 758
*nuclear power station, gas-cooled reactor, heavy-water reactor, pressurized-water reactor, boiling-water reactor, fuel handling sequence, fuel bundle, nuclear reactor, production of electricity from nuclear energy*
solar energy ........ 768
*solar cell, flat-plate solar collector, solar-cell system, solar furnace, production of electricity from solar energy, solar house, Trombe wall*

wind energy ........ 773
*windmill, post mill, horizontal-axis wind turbine, vertical-axis wind turbine*

**HEAVY MACHINERY**
fire prevention ........ 777
*hand lamp, ladder and hose strap, fireman's helmet, fireman*
fire engine ........ 778
*pumper, fire hose, nozzle, dividing connector, fire hydrant wrench, aerial ladder truck, portable fire extinguisher, pike pole, percussion bar, fireman's hatchet, hook ladder*
heavy vehicles ........ 782
*backhoe loader, bulldozer, scraper, grader, tipper truck, hydraulic shovel*
material handling ........ 786
*tower crane, truck crane, gantry crane, forklift truck, wing pallet, box pallet, hydraulic pallet truck*

**WEAPONS**
Stone Age weapons ........ 791
*Gallic warrior, Roman legionary*
weapons in the age of the Romans ........ 791
armour ........ 792
*armet*
bows and crossbow ........ 793
*modern bow, bow, arrow, crossbow*
thrusting and cutting weapons ........ 794
arquebus ........ 795
*flintlock*
submachine gun ........ 795
automatic rifle ........ 796
light machine gun ........ 796
revolver ........ 797
pistol ........ 797
hunting weapons ........ 798
*cartridge (rifle), rifle (rifled bore), cartridge (shotgun), shotgun (smooth-bore)*
seventeenth-century cannon ........ 800
*muzzle-loading cannon, cross section of a muzzle-loading cannon, firing accessories, projectiles*
modern howitzer ........ 802
mortar ........ 803
*modern mortar, seventeenth-century mortar*
hand grenade ........ 804
bazooka ........ 804
recoilless rifle ........ 804
tank ........ 805
submarine ........ 806
frigate ........ 808
aircraft carrier ........ 810
combat aircraft ........ 812
*in-flight refuelling*
missiles ........ 814
*structure of a missile, principal types of missile*

**SYMBOLS**
heraldry ........ 817
*parts of a flag, flag shapes, shield divisions, examples of partitions, examples of ordinaries, examples of charges, examples of metals, examples of furs, examples of colours*
signs of the zodiac ........ 820
*fire signs, earth signs, air signs, water signs*

safety symbols ..... 821
*dangerous materials, protection*
common symbols ..... 822
road signs ..... 824
*major North American road signs, major international road signs*
fabric care ..... 829
*washing, drying, ironing*
common scientific symbols ..... 830
*mathematics, geometry, biology, chemistry, miscellaneous*
diacritic symbols ..... 832
punctuation marks ..... 832
examples of currency abbreviations ..... 832

**ENGLISH INDEX** ..... 833
**FRENCH INDEX (INDEX FRANÇAIS)** ..... 863
**GERMAN INDEX (DEUTSCHES REGISTER)** ..... 895
**SPANISH INDEX (ÍNDICE ESPAÑOL)** ..... 927

## LIST OF CHAPTERS

1 **ASTRONOMY**

17 **GEOGRAPHY**

53 **PLANT KINGDOM**

75 **ANIMAL KINGDOM**

113 **HUMAN BEING**

145 **FARMING**

163 **ARCHITECTURE**

191 **HOUSE**

217 **HOUSE FURNITURE**

261 **GARDENING**

273 **DO-IT-YOURSELF**

313 **CLOTHING**

359 **PERSONAL ADORNMENT**

371 **PERSONAL ARTICLES**

387 **COMMUNICATIONS**

423 **TRANSPORT**

513 **OFFICE SUPPLIES**

533 **MUSIC**

559 **CREATIVE LEISURE ACTIVITIES**

593 **SPORTS**

693 **INDOOR GAMES**

703 **MEASURING DEVICES**

715 **OPTICAL INSTRUMENTS**

723 **HEALTH AND SAFETY**

731 **ENERGY**

775 **HEAVY MACHINERY**

789 **WEAPONS**

815 **SYMBOLS**

833 **INDEXES**

## ASTRONOMY ASTRONOMIE
## ASTRONOMIE ASTRONOMÍA

**SUMMARY**

CELESTIAL COORDINATE SYSTEM ..... 3
EARTH COORDINATE SYSTEM ..... 3
SOLAR SYSTEM ..... 4
SUN ..... 6
PHASES OF THE MOON ..... 6
MOON ..... 7
SOLAR ECLIPSE ..... 8
LUNAR ECLIPSE ..... 8
SEASONS OF THE YEAR ..... 8
COMET ..... 9
GALAXY ..... 9
CONSTELLATIONS OF THE NORTHERN HEMISPHERE ..... 10
CONSTELLATIONS OF THE SOUTHERN HEMISPHERE ..... 12
ASTRONOMICAL OBSERVATORY ..... 14
RADIO TELESCOPE ..... 15
HUBBLE SPACE TELESCOPE ..... 16
PLANETARIUM ..... 16

## CELESTIAL COORDINATE SYSTEM
## COORDONNÉES$^{F}$ CÉLESTES
## KOORDINATENSYSTEM$^{N}$ DER HIMMELSKUGEL$^{F}$
## COORDENADAS$^{F}$ ASTRONÓMICAS

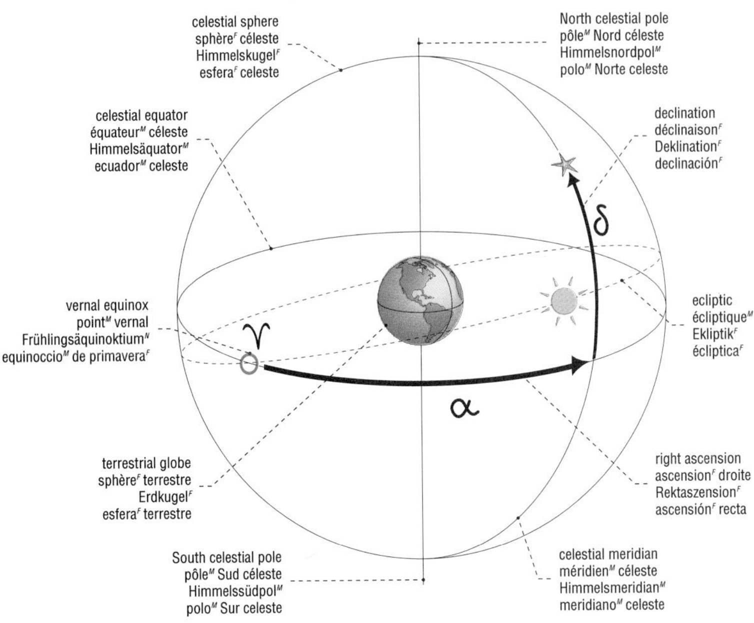


## EARTH COORDINATE SYSTEM
## COORDONNÉES$^{F}$ TERRESTRES
## KOORDINATENSYSTEM$^{N}$ DER ERDKUGEL$^{F}$
## COORDENADAS$^{F}$ GEOGRÁFICAS

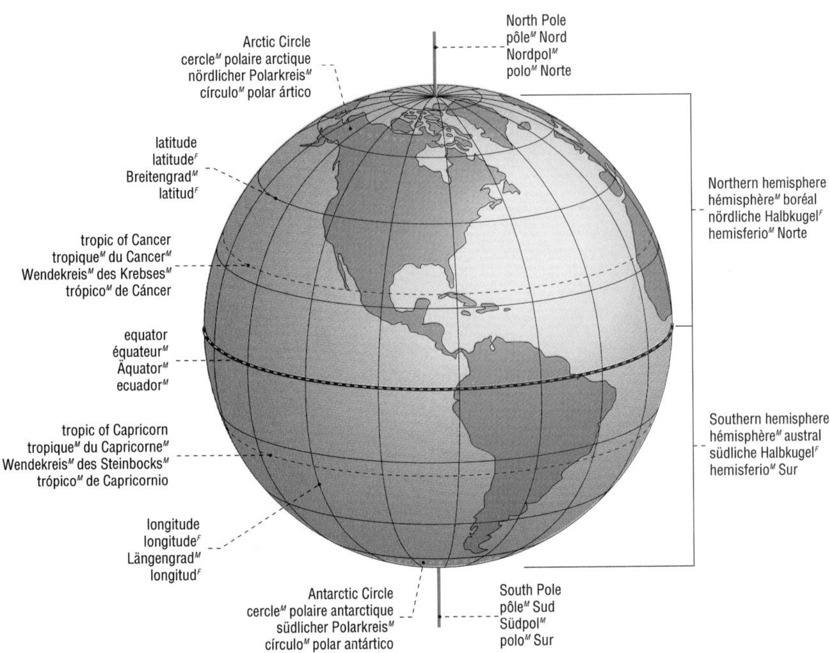

# SOLAR SYSTEM
# SYSTÈME[M] SOLAIRE
# SONNENSYSTEM[N]
# SISTEMA[M] SOLAR

## PLANETS AND MOONS
## PLANÈTES[F] ET SATELLITES[M]
## PLANETEN[M] UND MONDE[M]
## PLANETAS[M] Y LUNAS[F]

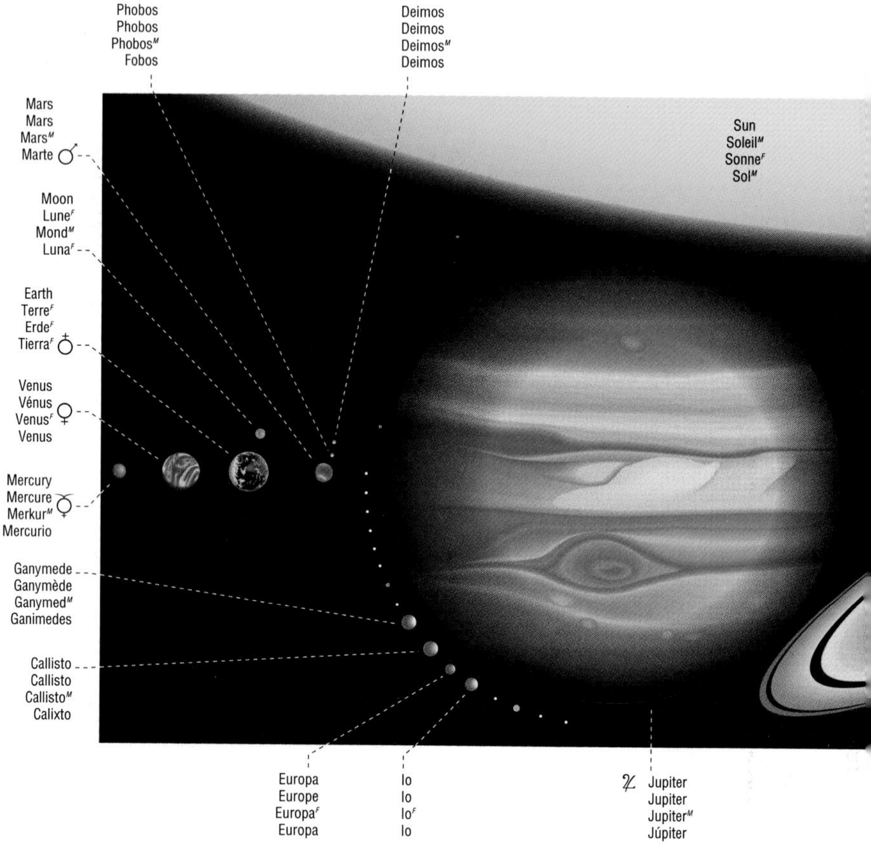

Phobos
Phobos
Phobos[M]
Fobos
Deimos
Deimos
Deimos[M]
Deimos
Mars
Mars
Mars[M]
Marte ♂
Sun
Soleil[M]
Sonne[F]
Sol[M]
Moon
Lune[F]
Mond[M]
Luna[F]
Earth
Terre[F]
Erde[F]
Tierra[F] ♁
Venus
Vénus
Venus[F] ♀
Venus
Mercury
Mercure
Merkur[M] ☿
Mercurio
Ganymede
Ganymède
Ganymed[M]
Ganimedes
Callisto
Callisto
Callisto[M]
Calixto
Europa
Europe
Europa[F]
Europa
Io
Io
Io[F]
Io
♃ Jupiter
Jupiter
Jupiter[M]
Júpiter

## ORBITS OF THE PLANETS
## ORBITES[F] DES PLANÈTES[F]
## UMLAUFBAHNEN[F] DER PLANETEN[M]
## ÓRBITAS[F] DE LOS PLANETAS[M]

asteroid belt
astéroïdes[M]
Asteroidengürtel[M]
zona[F] de asteroides[M]

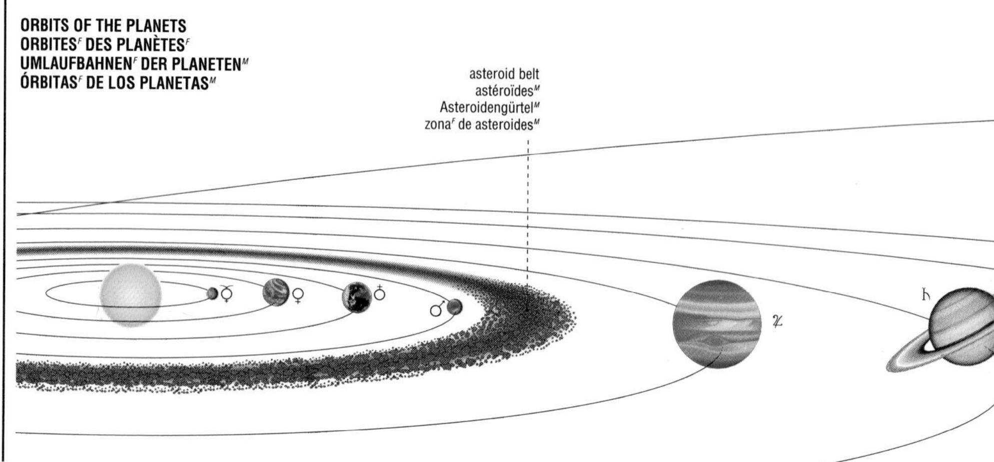

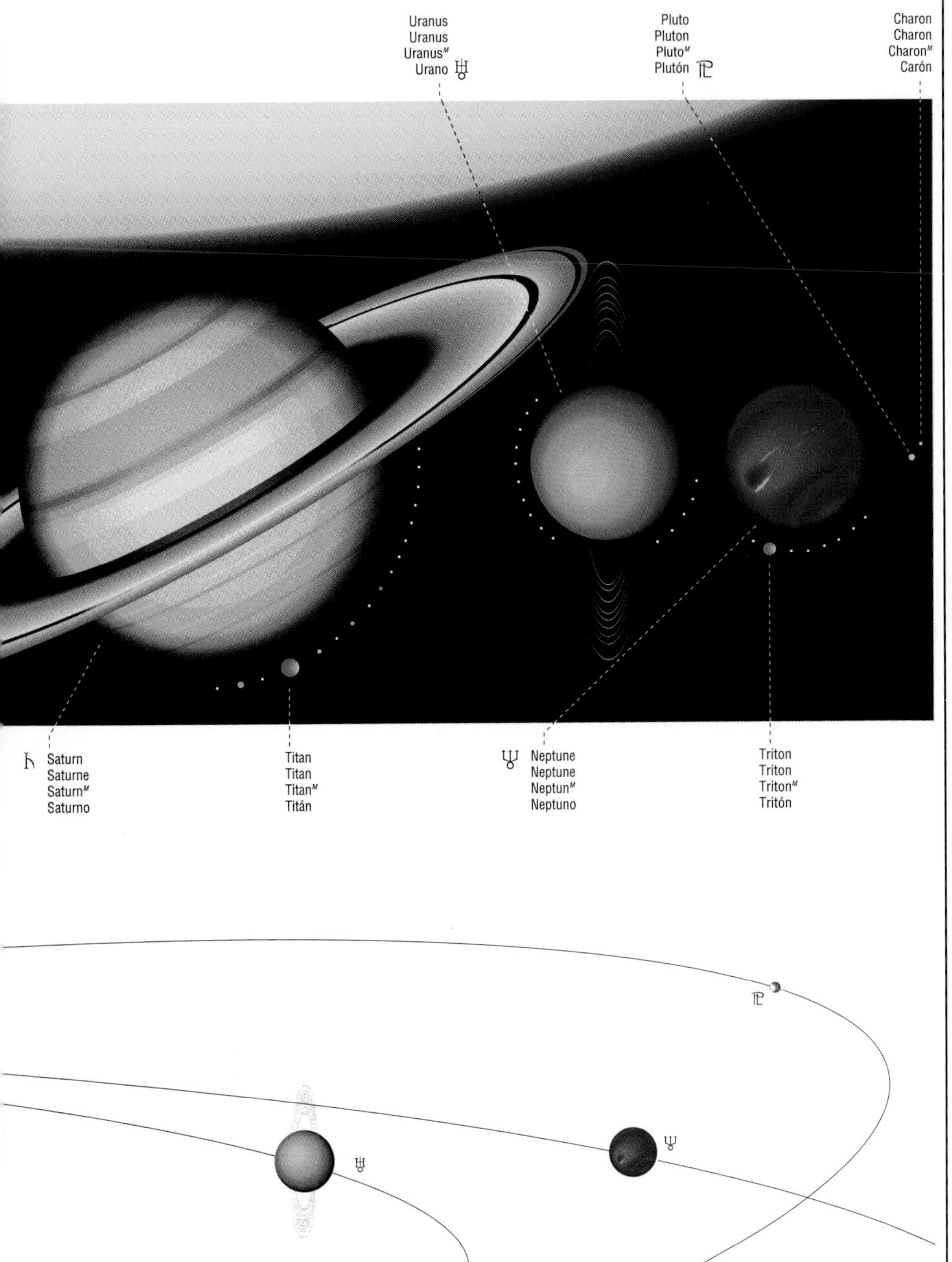
Uranus
Uranus
Uranus[M]
Urano ♅
Pluto
Pluton
Pluto[M]
Plutón ♇
Charon
Charon
Charon[M]
Carón
♄ Saturn
Saturne
Saturn[M]
Saturno
Titan
Titan
Titan[M]
Titán
♆ Neptune
Neptune
Neptun[M]
Neptuno
Triton
Triton
Triton[M]
Tritón
♇
♅
♆

# SUN
# SOLEIL[M]
# SONNE[F]
# SOL[M]

## STRUCTURE OF THE SUN
## STRUCTURE[F] DU SOLEIL[M]
## STRUKTUR[F] DER SONNE[F]
## ESTRUCTURA[F] DEL SOL[M]

photosphere
photosphère[F]
Photosphäre[F]
fotosfera[F]

spicules
spicule[M]
Spikulen[F]
espículas[F]

chromosphere
chromosphère[F]
Chromosphäre[F]
cromosfera[F]

corona
couronne[F]
Korona[F]
corona[F]

convection zone
zone[F] de convection[F]
Konvektionszone[F]
zona[F] de convección[F]

radiation zone
zone[F] de radiation[F]
Strahlungszone[F]
zona[F] de radiación[F]

core
noyau[M]
Kern[M]
núcleo[M]

flare
éruption[F]
Flare[M]
erupción[F]

faculae
facule[F]
Fackeln[F]
fáculas[F]

sunspot
tache[F]
Sonnenfleck[M]
mancha[F] solar

filament
filament[M]
Filament[N]
filamento[M]

prominence
protubérance[F]
Protuberanz[F]
protuberancia[F]

granulation
granulation[F]
Granulation[F]
granos[M] de arroz[M]

## PHASES OF THE MOON
## PHASES[F] DE LA LUNE[F]
## MONDPHASEN[F]
## FASES[F] DE LA LUNA[F]

new moon
nouvelle Lune[F]
Neumond[M]
Luna[F] nueva

new crescent
premier croissant[M]
Mondsichel[F] (zunehmender Mond[M])
creciente[M]

first quarter
premier quartier[M]
Halbmond[M] (erstes Viertel[N])
cuarto[M] creciente

waxing gibbous
gibbeuse[F] croissante
zunehmender Mond[M]
quinto[M] octante

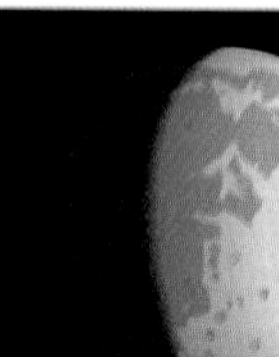

# MOON
# LUNE$^{F}$
# MOND$^{M}$
# LUNA$^{F}$

## LUNAR FEATURES
## RELIEF$^{M}$ LUNAIRE
## OBERFLÄCHENFORMATIONEN$^{F}$ DES MONDES$^{M}$
## SUPERFICIE$^{F}$ LUNAR

bay
baie$^{F}$
Bucht$^{F}$
bahía$^{F}$

cliff
falaise$^{F}$
Felsen$^{M}$
risco$^{M}$

ocean
océan$^{M}$
Ozean$^{M}$
océano$^{M}$

lake
lac$^{M}$
See$^{M}$
lago$^{M}$

sea
mer$^{F}$
Meer$^{N}$
mar$^{M}$

mountain range
chaîne$^{F}$ de montagnes$^{F}$
Bergkette$^{F}$
cordillera$^{F}$

crater
cratère$^{M}$
Krater$^{M}$
cráter$^{M}$

wall
rempart$^{M}$
Wand$^{F}$
muro$^{M}$

cirque
cirque$^{M}$
Kar$^{N}$
circo$^{M}$

full moon
pleine Lune$^{F}$
Vollmond$^{M}$
Luna$^{F}$ llena

waning gibbous
gibbeuse$^{F}$ décroissante
abnehmender Mond$^{M}$
tercer$^{M}$ octante

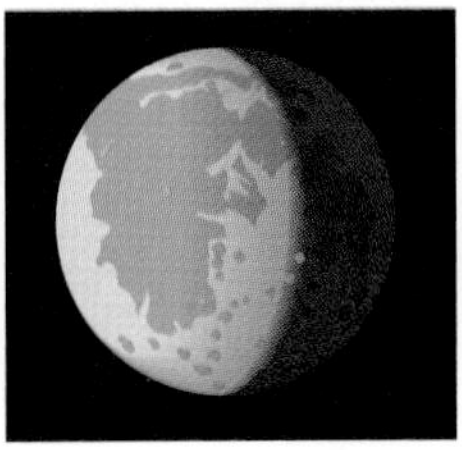

last quarter
dernier quartier$^{M}$
Halbmond$^{M}$ (letztes Viertel$^{N}$)
cuarto$^{M}$ menguante

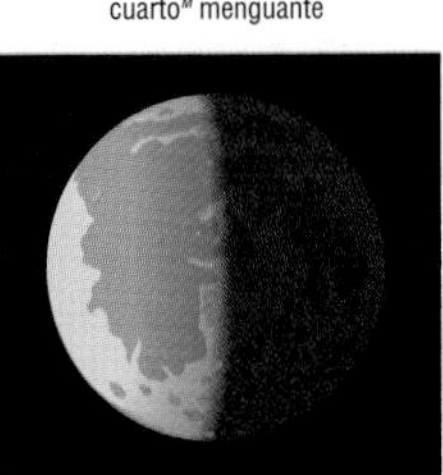

old crescent
dernier croissant$^{M}$
Mondsichel$^{F}$ (abnehmender Mond$^{M}$)
menguante$^{M}$

## SOLAR ECLIPSE
## ÉCLIPSE[F] DE SOLEIL[M]
## SONNENFINSTERNIS[F]
## ECLIPSE[M] DE SOL[M]

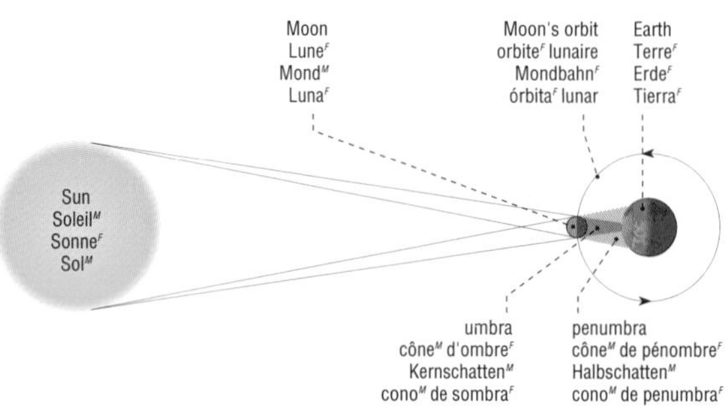


### TYPES OF ECLIPSES
### TYPES[M] D'ÉCLIPSES[F]
### FINSTERNISARTEN[F]
### TIPOS[M] DE ECLIPSES[M]

total eclipse
éclipse[F] totale
totale Finsternis[F]
eclipse[M] total

annular eclipse
éclipse[F] annulaire
ringförmige Finsternis[F]
eclipse[M] anular

partial eclipse
éclipse[F] partielle
partielle Finsternis[F]
eclipse[M] parcial

## LUNAR ECLIPSE
## ÉCLIPSE[F] DE LUNE[F]
## MONDFINSTERNIS[F]
## ECLIPSE[M] DE LUNA[F]

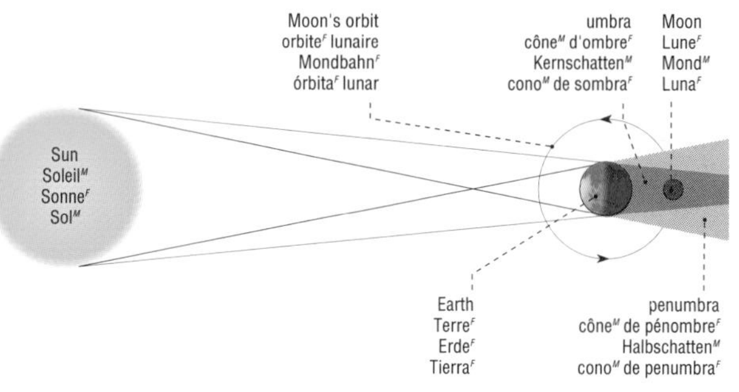


### TYPES OF ECLIPSES
### TYPES[M] D'ÉCLIPSES[F]
### FINSTERNISARTEN[F]
### TIPOS[M] DE ECLIPSES[M]

partial eclipse
éclipse[F] partielle
partielle Finsternis[F]
eclipse[M] parcial

total eclipse
éclipse[F] totale
totale Finsternis[F]
eclipse[M] total

## SEASONS OF THE YEAR
## CYCLE[M] DES SAISONS[F]
## JAHRESZEITEN[F]
## ESTACIONES[F] DEL AÑO[M]

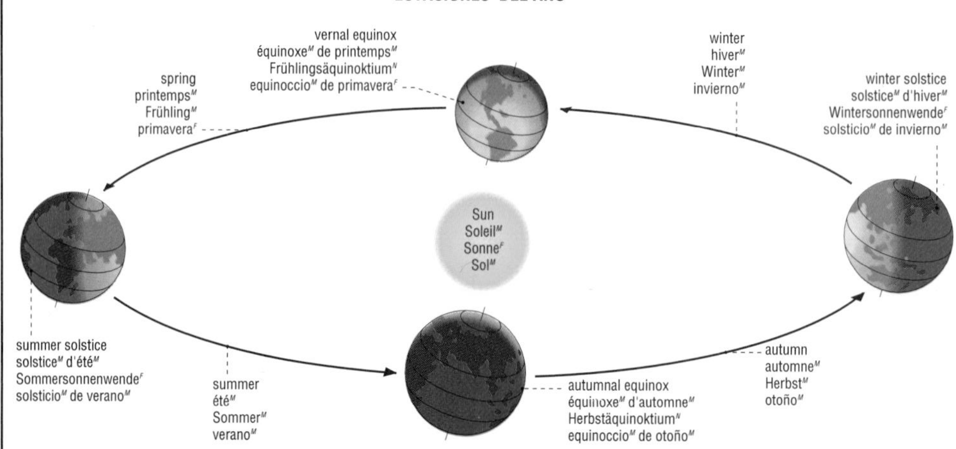

## COMET
## COMÈTE[F]
## KOMET[M]
## COMETA[M]

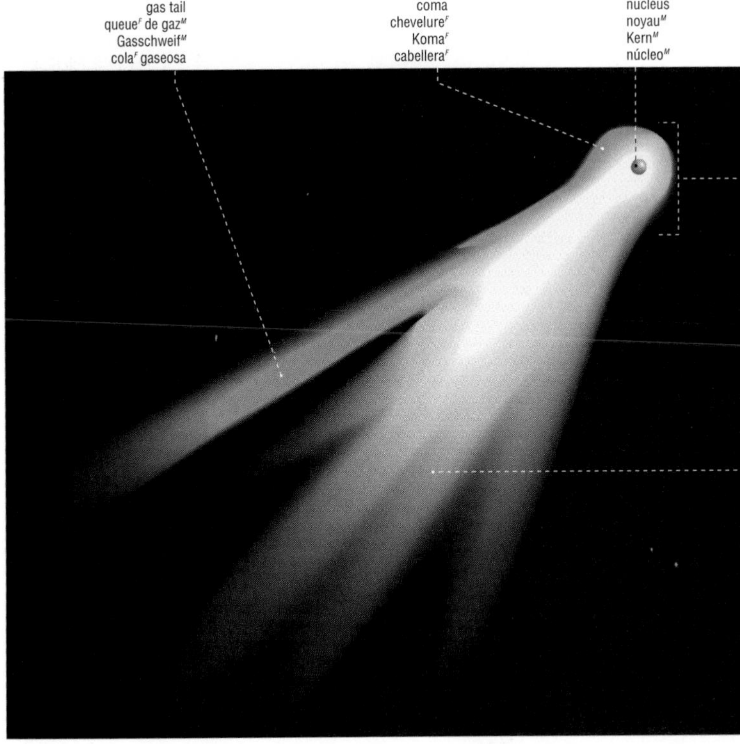


## GALAXY
## GALAXIE[F]
## GALAXIE[F]
## GALAXIA[F]

### HUBBLE'S CLASSIFICATION
### CLASSIFICATION[F] DE HUBBLE
### HUBBLESCHE KLASSIFIKATION[F]
### CLASIFICACIÓN[F] DE HUBBLE

spiral galaxy
galaxie[F] spirale
Spiralgalaxie[F]
galaxia[F] espiral

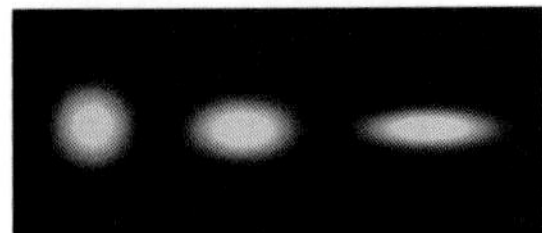

elliptical galaxy
galaxie[F] elliptique
elliptische Galaxie[F]
galaxia[F] elíptica

lenticular galaxy
galaxie[F] lenticulaire
linsenförmige Galaxie[F]
galaxia[F] lenticular

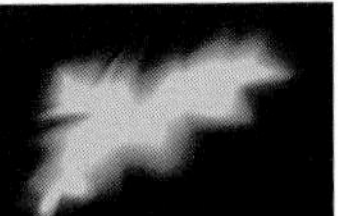

irregular galaxy
galaxie[F] irrégulière
unregelmäßige Galaxie[F]
galaxia[F] irregular

barred spiral galaxy
galaxie[F] spirale barrée
Balkenspiralgalaxie[F]
galaxia[F] espiral con barras[F]

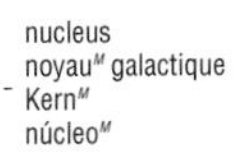

# CONSTELLATIONS OF THE NORTHERN HEMISPHERE
CONSTELLATIONS[F] DE L'HÉMISPHÈRE[M] BORÉAL
KONSTELLATIONEN[F] DER NÖRDLICHEN HALBKUGEL[F]
CONSTELACIONES[F] EN EL HEMISFERIO[M] BOREAL

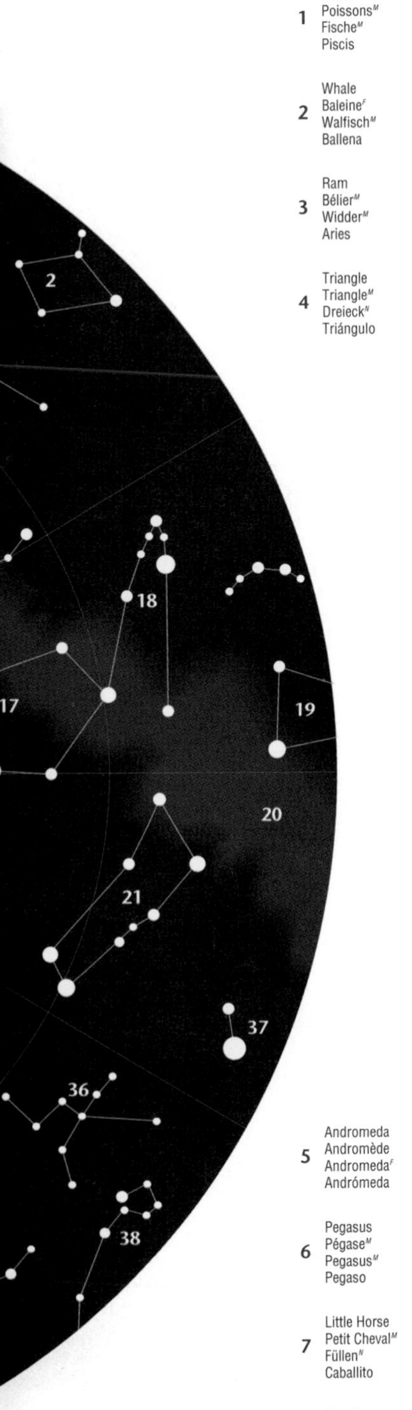


**1** Fishes
Poissons[M]
Fische[M]
Piscis

**2** Whale
Baleine[F]
Walfisch[M]
Ballena

**3** Ram
Bélier[M]
Widder[M]
Aries

**4** Triangle
Triangle[M]
Dreieck[N]
Triángulo

**5** Andromeda
Andromède
Andromeda[F]
Andrómeda

**6** Pegasus
Pégase[M]
Pegasus[M]
Pegaso

**7** Little Horse
Petit Cheval[M]
Füllen[N]
Caballito

**8** Dolphin
Dauphin[M]
Delphin[M]
Delfín

**9** Eagle
Aigle[M]
Adler[M]
Aguila

**10** Arrow
Flèche[F]
Pfeil[M]
Saeta

**11** Swan
Cygne[M]
Schwan[M]
Cisne

**12** Lizard
Lézard[M]
Eidechse[F]
Lagarto

**13** Cepheus
Céphée
Kepheus[M]
Cefeo

**14** Cassiopeia
Cassiopée
Cassiopeia[F]
Casiopea

**15** Giraffe
Girafe[F]
Giraffe[F]
Jirafa

**16** Perseus
Persée
Perseus[M]
Perseo

**17** Charioteer
Cocher[M]
Fuhrmann[M]
Cochero

**18** Bull
Taureau[M]
Stier[M]
Tauro

**19** Orion
Orion
Orion[M]
Orión

**20** Milky Way
Voie[F] lactée
Milchstraße[F]
Vía Láctea

**21** Twins
Gémeaux[M]
Zwillinge[M]
Géminis

**22** Lynx
Lynx[M]
Luchs[M]
Lince

**23** Pole Star
étoile[F] Polaire
Polarstern[M]
Estrella Polar

**24** Little Bear
Petite Ourse[F]
Kleiner Bär[M]
Osa Menor

**25** Dragon
Dragon[M]
Drache[M]
Dragón

**26** Harp
Lyre[F]
Leier[F]
Lira

**27** Hercules
Hercule
Herkules[M]
Hércules

**28** Serpent Bearer
Ophiucus
Schlangenträger[M]
Serpentario

**29** Serpent
Serpent[M]
Schlange[F]
Serpiente

**30** Northern Crown
Couronne[F] boréale
Nördliche Krone[F]
Corona Boreal

**31** Herdsman
Bouvier[M]
Bärenhüter[M]
Boyero

**32** Berenice's Hair
Chevelure[F] de Bérénice
Haar[N] der Berenike[F]
Cabellera de Berenice

**33** Hunting Dogs
Chiens[M] de chasse[F]
Jagdhunde[M]
Lebreles

**34** Great Bear
Grande Ourse[F]
Großer Bär[M]
Osa Mayor

**35** Little Lion
Petit Lion[M]
Kleiner Löwe[M]
León Menor

**36** Crab
Cancer[M]
Krebs[M]
Cáncer

**37** Little Dog
Petit Chien[M]
Kleiner Hund[M]
Can Menor

**38** Water Monster
Hydre[F] femelle
Nördliche Wasserschlange[F]
Hidra

**39** Lion
Lion[M]
Löwe[M]
Leo

**40** Virgin
Vierge[F]
Jungfrau[F]
Virgo

## CONSTELLATIONS OF THE SOUTHERN HEMISPHERE
## CONSTELLATIONS^F DE L'HÉMISPHÈRE^M AUSTRAL
## KONSTELLATIONEN^F DER SÜDLICHEN HALBKUGEL^F
## CONSTELACIONES^F DEL HEMISFERIO^M AUSTRAL

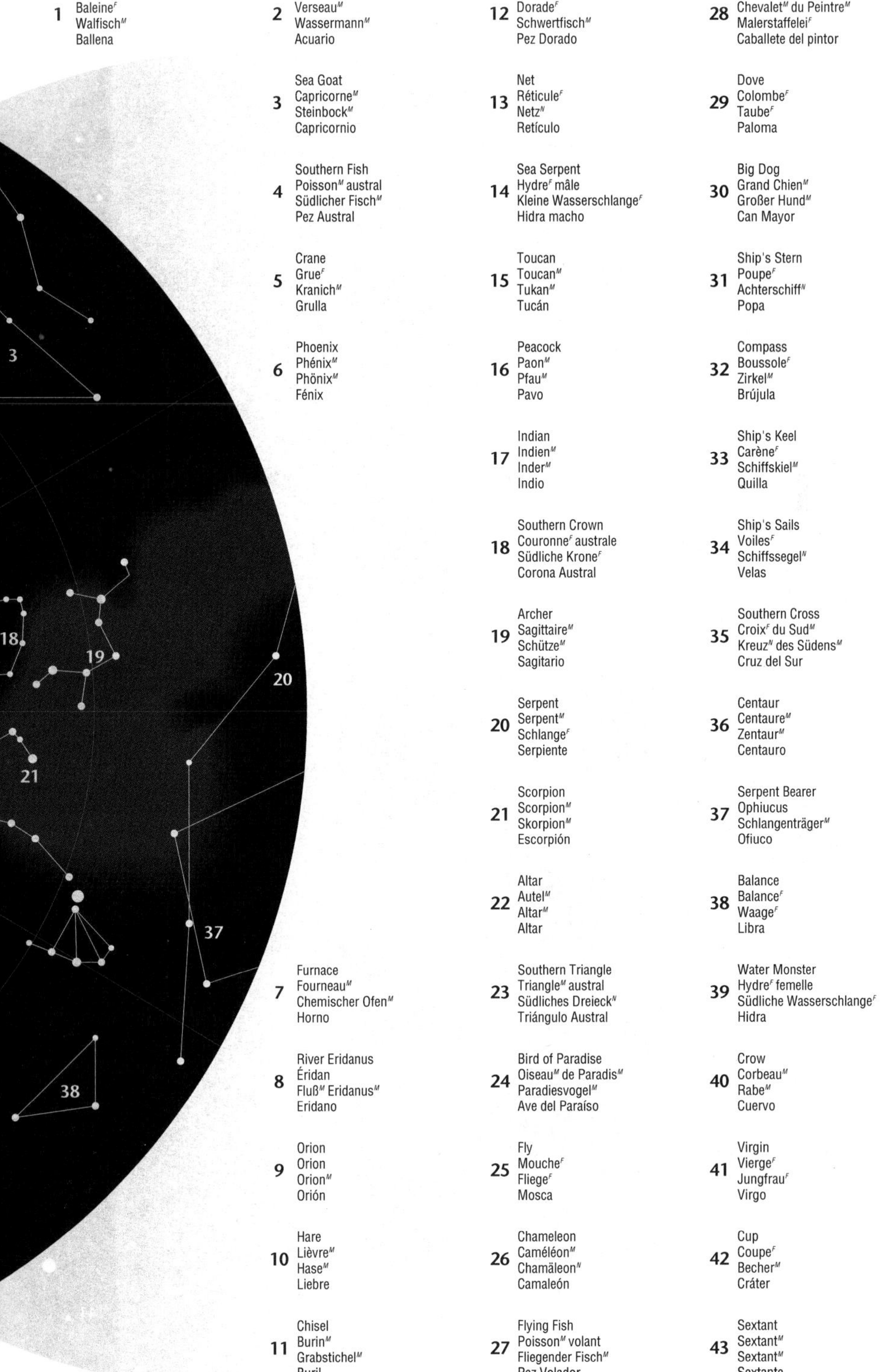


1 Whale
Baleine[F]
Walfisch[M]
Ballena

2 Water Bearer
Verseau[M]
Wassermann[M]
Acuario

3 Sea Goat
Capricorne[M]
Steinbock[M]
Capricornio

4 Southern Fish
Poisson[M] austral
Südlicher Fisch[M]
Pez Austral

5 Crane
Grue[F]
Kranich[M]
Grulla

6 Phoenix
Phénix[M]
Phönix[M]
Fénix

7 Furnace
Fourneau[M]
Chemischer Ofen[M]
Horno

8 River Eridanus
Éridan
Fluß[M] Eridanus[M]
Eridano

9 Orion
Orion
Orion[M]
Orión

10 Hare
Lièvre[M]
Hase[M]
Liebre

11 Chisel
Burin[M]
Grabstichel[M]
Buril

12 Swordfish
Dorade[F]
Schwertfisch[M]
Pez Dorado

13 Net
Réticule[F]
Netz[N]
Retículo

14 Sea Serpent
Hydre[F] mâle
Kleine Wasserschlange[F]
Hidra macho

15 Toucan
Toucan[M]
Tukan[M]
Tucán

16 Peacock
Paon[M]
Pfau[M]
Pavo

17 Indian
Indien[M]
Inder[M]
Indio

18 Southern Crown
Couronne[F] australe
Südliche Krone[F]
Corona Austral

19 Archer
Sagittaire[M]
Schütze[M]
Sagitario

20 Serpent
Serpent[M]
Schlange[F]
Serpiente

21 Scorpion
Scorpion[M]
Skorpion[M]
Escorpión

22 Altar
Autel[M]
Altar[M]
Altar

23 Southern Triangle
Triangle[M] austral
Südliches Dreieck[N]
Triángulo Austral

24 Bird of Paradise
Oiseau[M] de Paradis[M]
Paradiesvogel[M]
Ave del Paraíso

25 Fly
Mouche[F]
Fliege[F]
Mosca

26 Chameleon
Caméléon[M]
Chamäleon[N]
Camaleón

27 Flying Fish
Poisson[M] volant
Fliegender Fisch[M]
Pez Volador

28 Painter's Easel
Chevalet[M] du Peintre[M]
Malerstaffelei[F]
Caballete del pintor

29 Dove
Colombe[F]
Taube[F]
Paloma

30 Big Dog
Grand Chien[M]
Großer Hund[M]
Can Mayor

31 Ship's Stern
Poupe[F]
Achterschiff[N]
Popa

32 Compass
Boussole[F]
Zirkel[M]
Brújula

33 Ship's Keel
Carène[F]
Schiffskiel[M]
Quilla

34 Ship's Sails
Voiles[F]
Schiffssegel[N]
Velas

35 Southern Cross
Croix[F] du Sud[M]
Kreuz[N] des Südens[M]
Cruz del Sur

36 Centaur
Centaure[M]
Zentaur[M]
Centauro

37 Serpent Bearer
Ophiucus
Schlangenträger[M]
Ofiuco

38 Balance
Balance[F]
Waage[F]
Libra

39 Water Monster
Hydre[F] femelle
Südliche Wasserschlange[F]
Hidra

40 Crow
Corbeau[M]
Rabe[M]
Cuervo

41 Virgin
Vierge[F]
Jungfrau[F]
Virgo

42 Cup
Coupe[F]
Becher[M]
Cráter

43 Sextant
Sextant[M]
Sextant[M]
Sextante

# ASTRONOMICAL OBSERVATORY
# OBSERVATOIRE[M] ASTRONOMIQUE
# STERNWARTE[F]
# OBSERVATORIO[M] ASTRONÓMICO

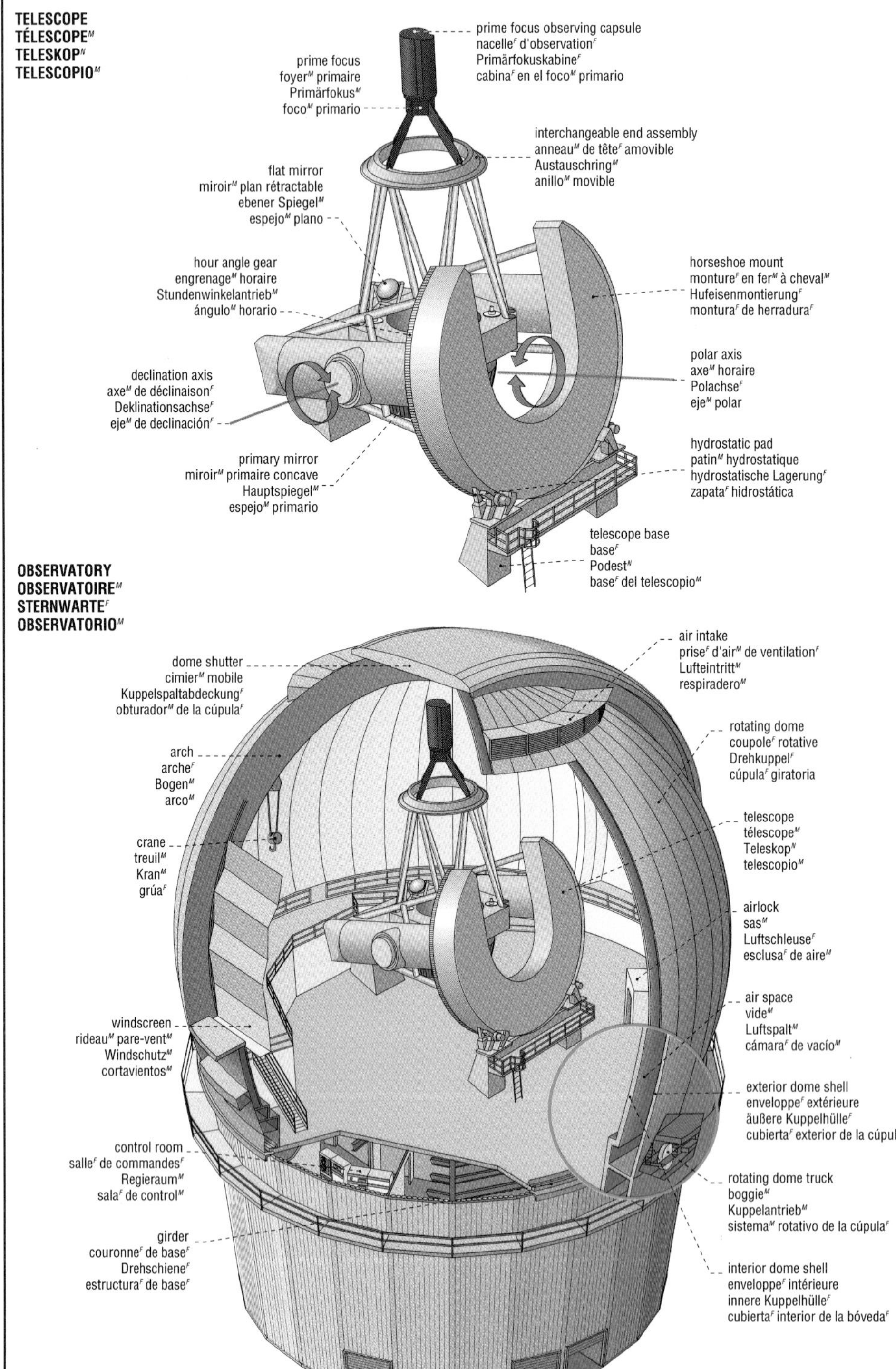

# RADIO TELESCOPE
# RADIOTÉLESCOPE[M]
# RADIOTELESKOP[N]
# RADIOTELESCOPIO[M]

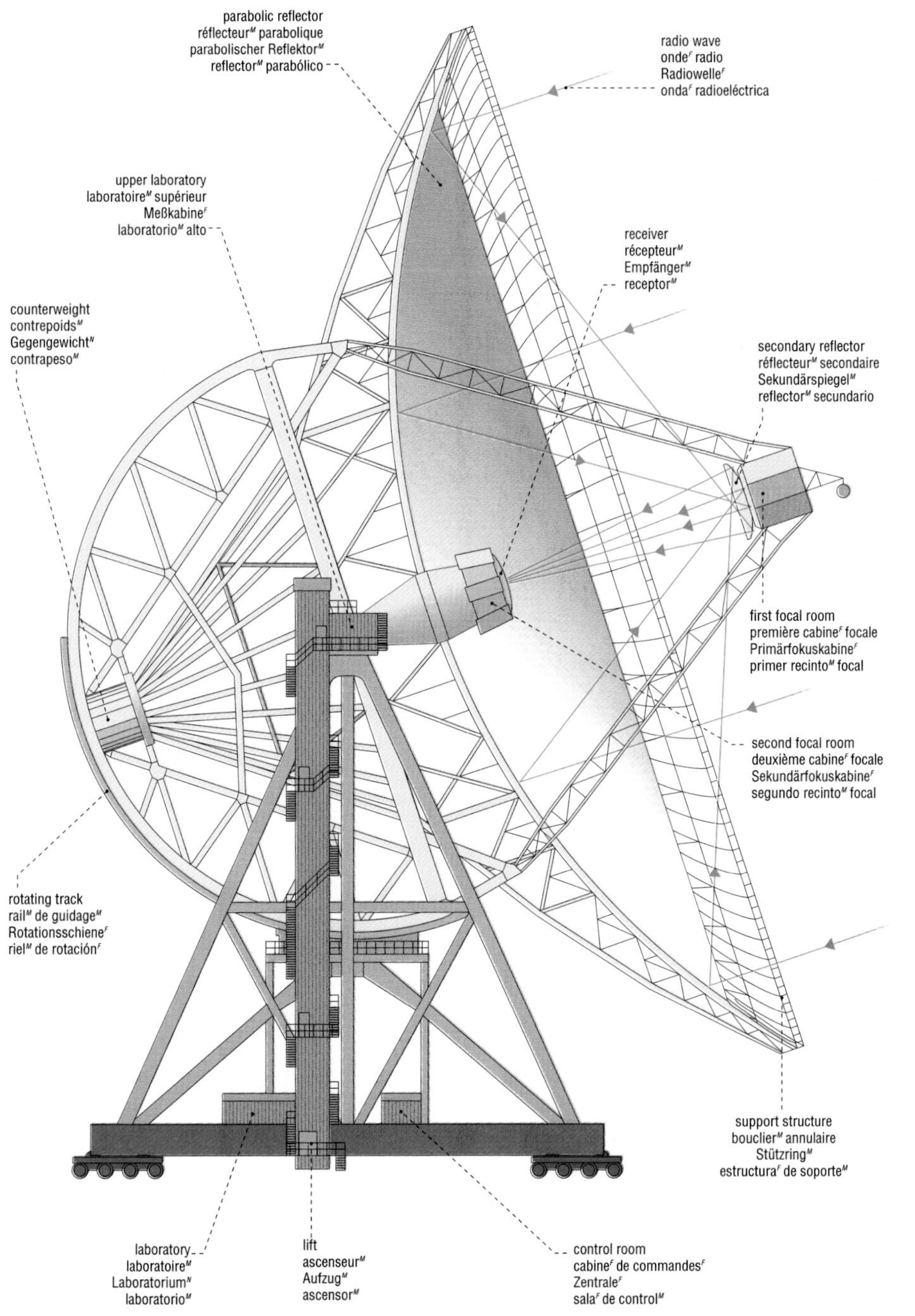

## HUBBLE SPACE TELESCOPE
## TÉLESCOPE[M] SPATIAL HUBBLE
## HUBBLE RAUMTELESKOP[N]
## TELESCOPIO[M] ESPACIAL HUBBLE

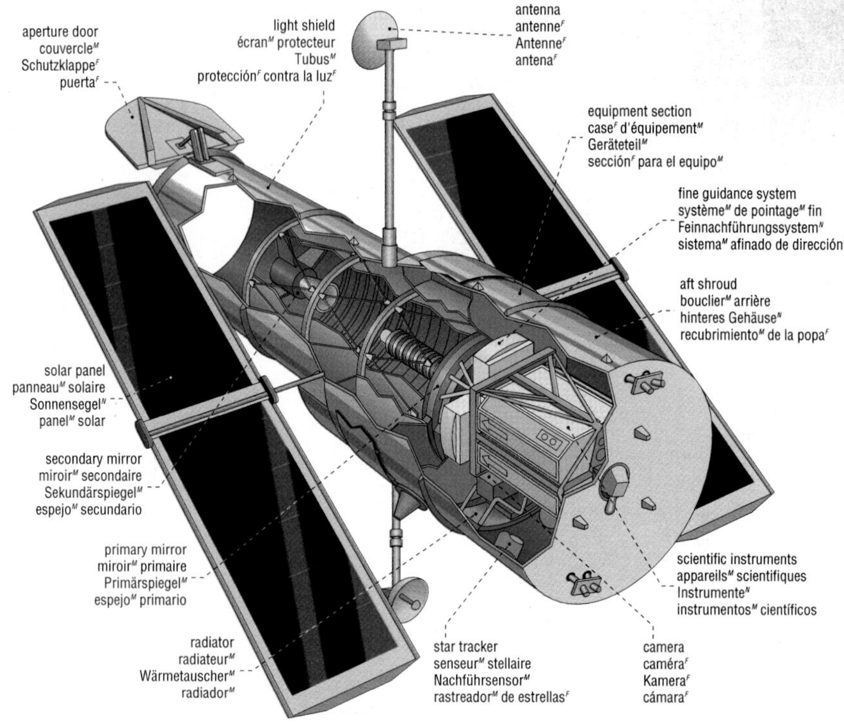


## PLANETARIUM
## PLANÉTARIUM[M]
## PLANETARIUM[N]
## PLANETARIO[M]

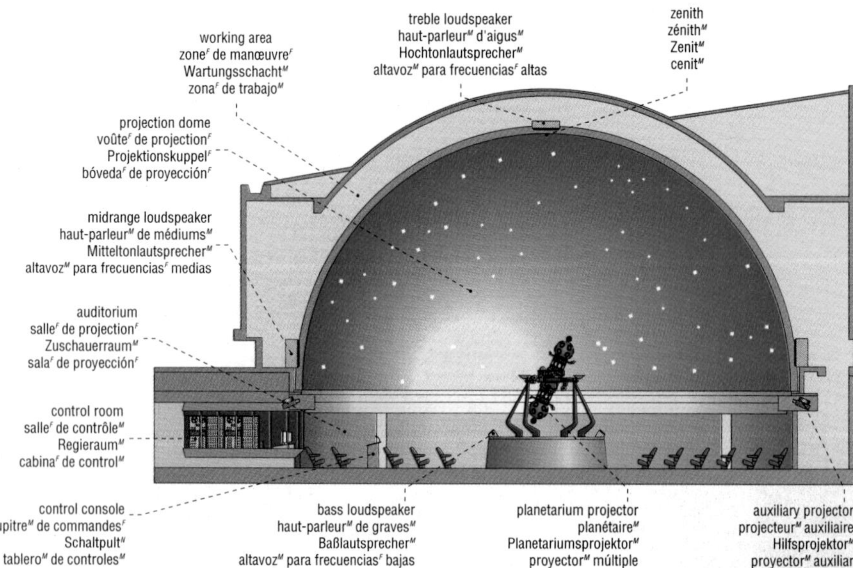

Pinehurst
Burlington
Reading
Lynnfield
Wakefield
Stoneham
Woburn
Winchester
Lexington
Medford
Melrose
Malden
Saugus
Lynn Harbor
Arlington
Everett
Revere
Belmont
Somerville
Chelsea
Cambridge
Newton
Boston
Boston Harbor
Brookline
Quincy Bay
Quincy
Dedham
Milton
Braintree
Islington

SUMMARY

PROFILE OF THE EARTH'S ATMOSPHERE ........ 19
CONFIGURATION OF THE CONTINENTS ........ 20
STRUCTURE OF THE EARTH ........ 22
SECTION OF THE EARTH'S CRUST ........ 22
EARTHQUAKE ........ 23
CAVE ........ 24
VOLCANO ........ 25
GLACIER ........ 26
MOUNTAIN ........ 27
OCEAN FLOOR ........ 28
WAVE ........ 30
COMMON COASTAL FEATURES ........ 30
ECOLOGY ........ 31
PRECIPITATIONS ........ 36
METEOROLOGY ........ 38
INTERNATIONAL WEATHER SYMBOLS ........ 39
METEOROLOGICAL MEASURING INSTRUMENTS ........ 40
WEATHER SATELLITE ........ 42
CLOUDS AND METEOROLOGICAL SYMBOLS ........ 44
CLIMATES OF THE WORLD ........ 45
DESERT ........ 46
CARTOGRAPHY ........ 47
REMOTE DETECTION SATELLITE ........ 48

## PROFILE OF THE EARTH'S ATMOSPHERE
## COUPE[F] DE L'ATMOSPHÈRE[F] TERRESTRE
## PROFIL[N] DURCH DIE ERDATMOSPHÄRE[F]
## CORTE[M] DE LA ATMÓSFERA[F] TERRESTRE

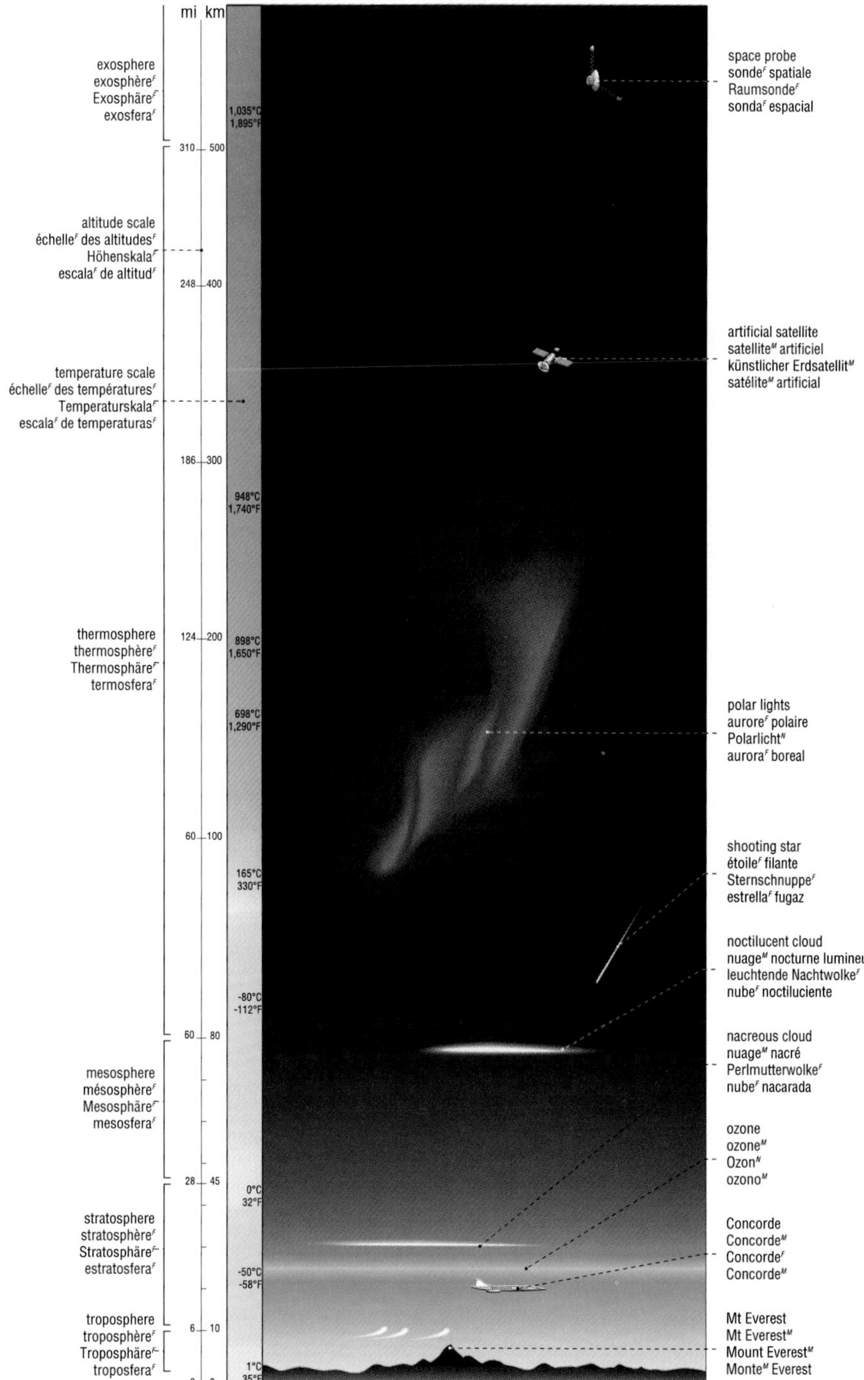

## CONFIGURATION OF THE CONTINENTS
## CONFIGURATION^F DES CONTINENTS^M
## KONFIGURATION^F DER KONTINENTE^M
## CONFIGURACIÓN^F DE LOS CONTINENTES^M

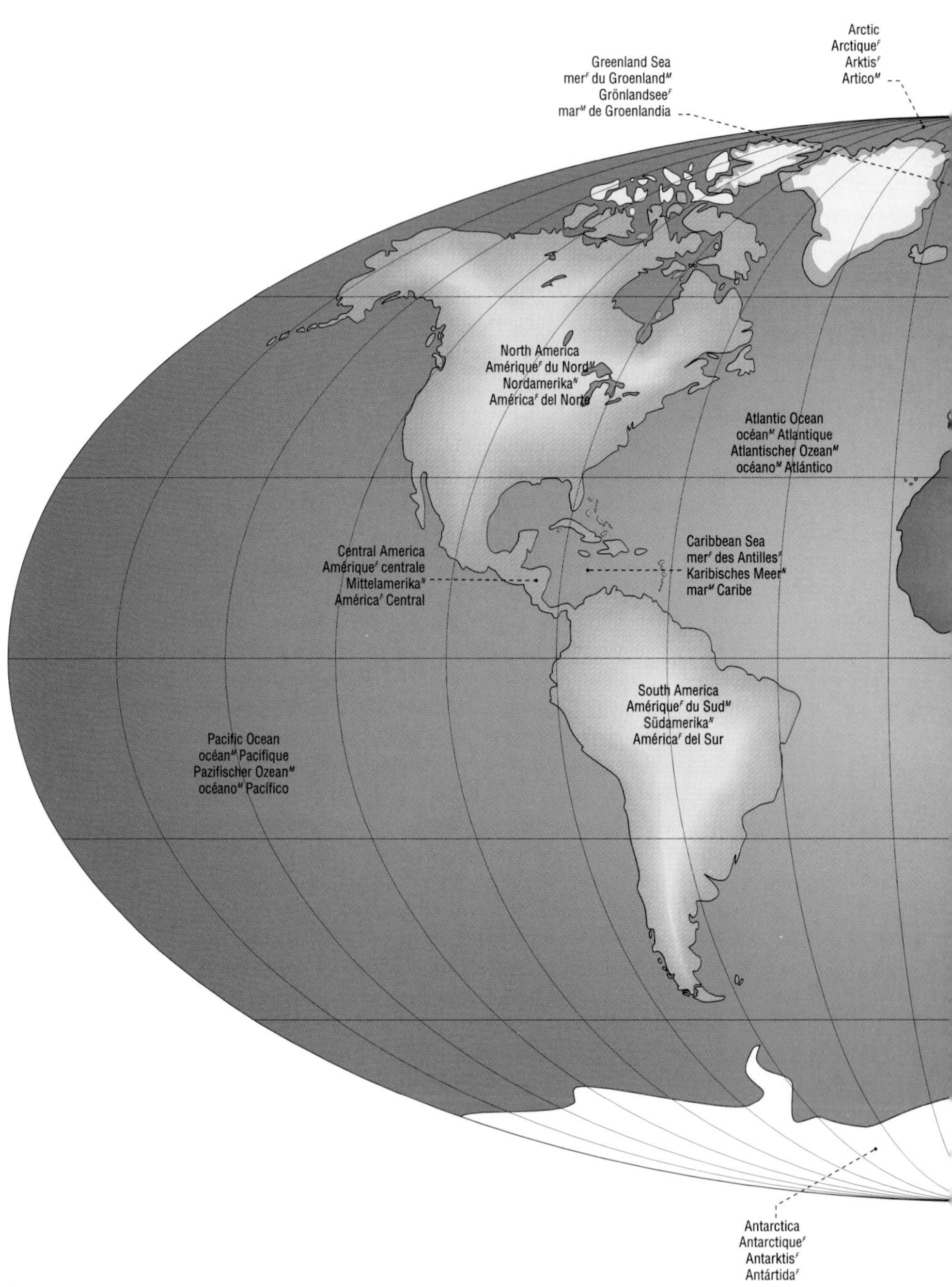

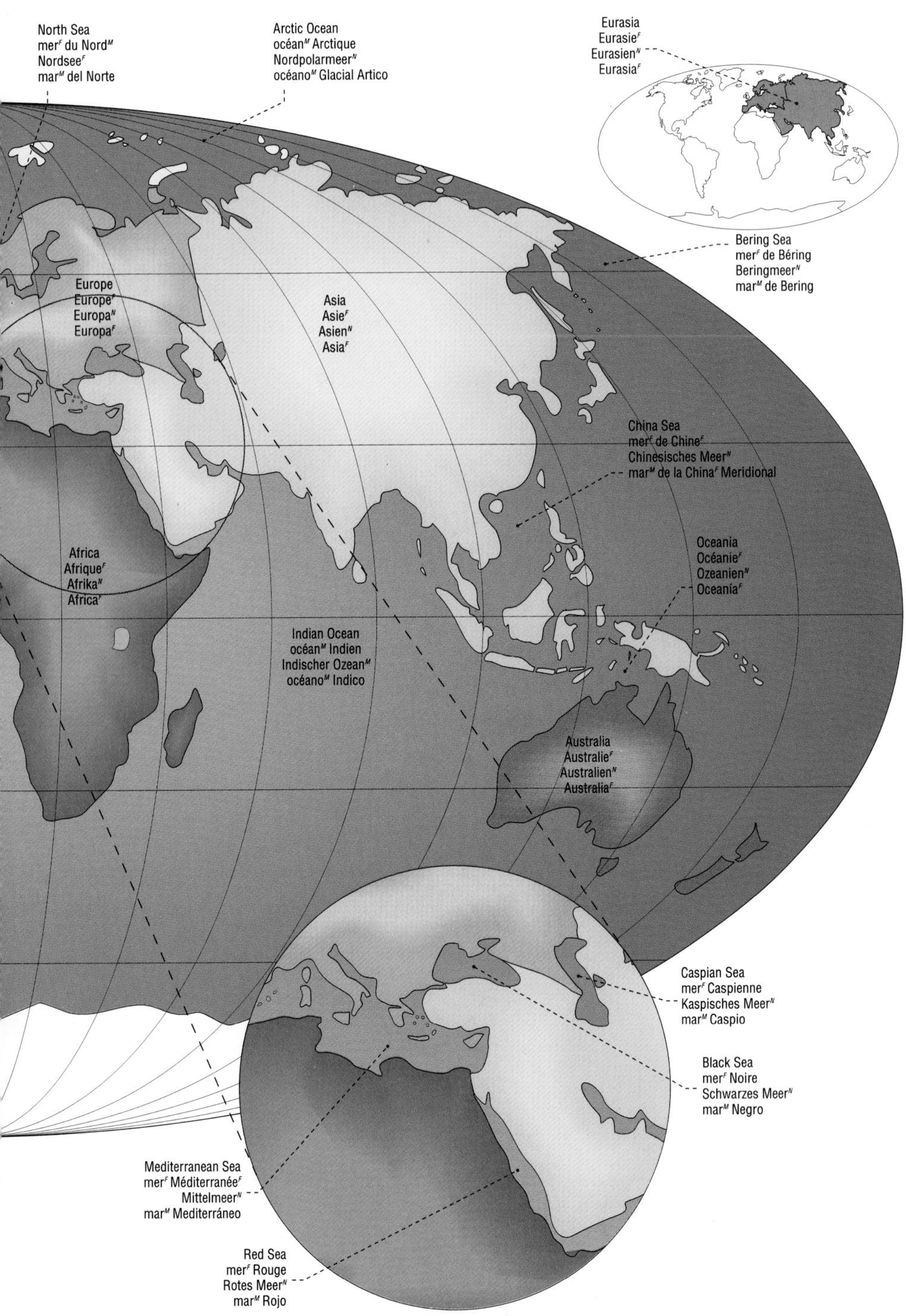
North Sea
mer$^{F}$ du Nord$^{M}$
Nordsee$^{F}$
mar$^{M}$ del Norte
Arctic Ocean
océan$^{M}$ Arctique
Nordpolarmeer$^{N}$
océano$^{M}$ Glacial Artico
Eurasia
Eurasie$^{F}$
Eurasien$^{N}$
Eurasia$^{F}$
Bering Sea
mer$^{F}$ de Béring
Beringmeer$^{N}$
mar$^{M}$ de Bering
Europe
Europe$^{F}$
Europa$^{N}$
Europa$^{F}$
Asia
Asie$^{F}$
Asien$^{N}$
Asia$^{F}$
China Sea
mer$^{F}$ de Chine$^{F}$
Chinesisches Meer$^{N}$
mar$^{M}$ de la China$^{F}$ Meridional
Africa
Afrique$^{F}$
Afrika$^{N}$
Africa$^{F}$
Oceania
Océanie$^{F}$
Ozeanien$^{N}$
Oceanía$^{F}$
Indian Ocean
océan$^{M}$ Indien
Indischer Ozean$^{M}$
océano$^{M}$ Indico
Australia
Australie$^{F}$
Australien$^{N}$
Australia$^{F}$
Caspian Sea
mer$^{F}$ Caspienne
Kaspisches Meer$^{N}$
mar$^{M}$ Caspio
Black Sea
mer$^{F}$ Noire
Schwarzes Meer$^{N}$
mar$^{M}$ Negro
Mediterranean Sea
mer$^{F}$ Méditerranée$^{F}$
Mittelmeer$^{N}$
mar$^{M}$ Mediterráneo
Red Sea
mer$^{F}$ Rouge
Rotes Meer$^{N}$
mar$^{M}$ Rojo

## STRUCTURE OF THE EARTH
## STRUCTURE^F DE LA TERRE^F
## STRUKTUR^F DER ERDE^F
## ESTRUCTURA^F DE LA TIERRA^F

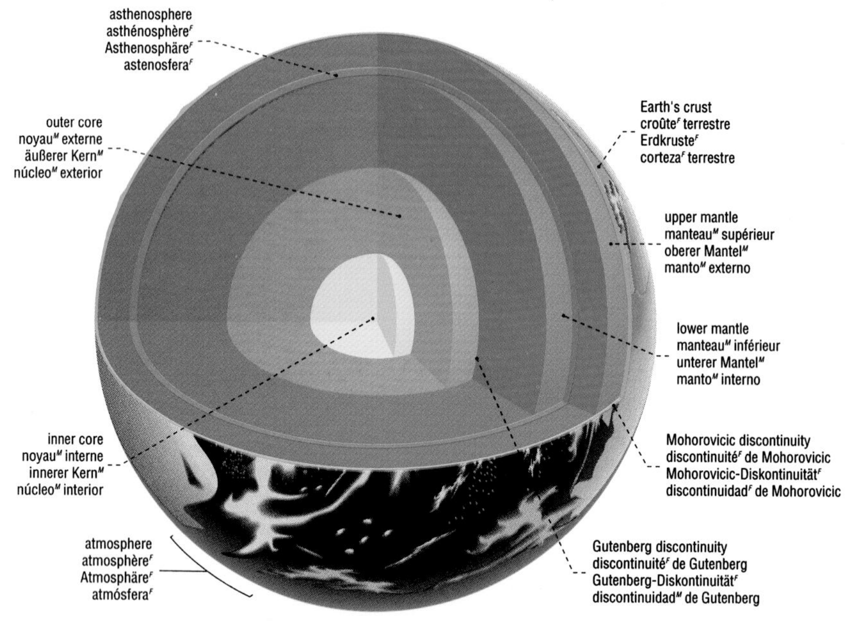


## SECTION OF THE EARTH'S CRUST
## COUPE^F DE LA CROÛTE^F TERRESTRE
## SCHNITT^M DURCH DIE ERDKRUSTE^F
## CORTE^M DE LA CORTEZA^F TERRESTRE

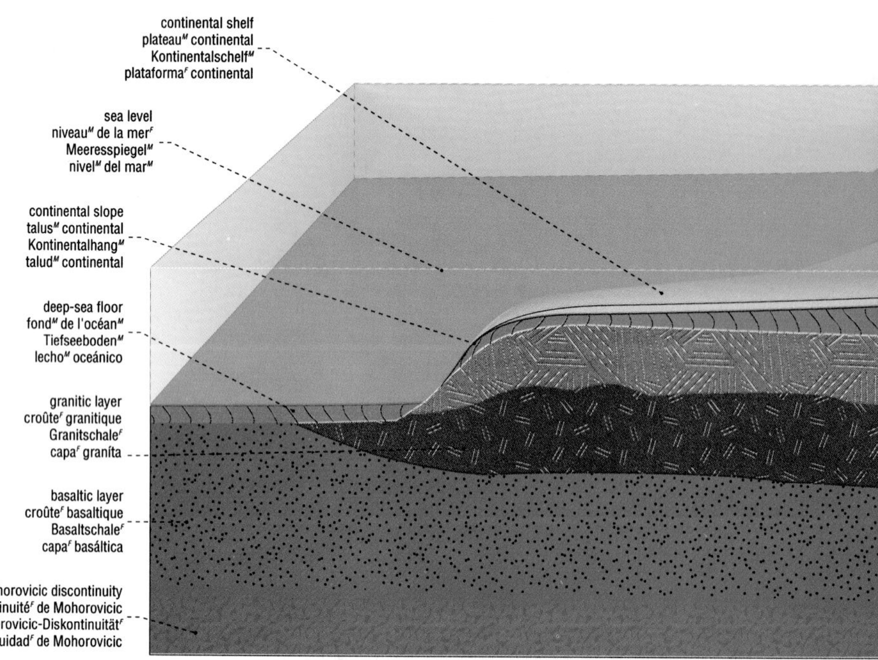

# EARTHQUAKE
# SÉISME[M]
# ERDBEBEN[N]
# TERREMOTO[M]

isoseismal line
ligne[F] isosiste
Isoseiste[F]
línea[F] isosísmica
epicentre
épicentre[M]
Epizentrum[N]
epicentro[M]
Earth's crust
croûte[F] terrestre
Erdkruste[F]
corteza[F] terrestre
depth of focus
profondeur[F] du foyer[M]
Herdtiefe[F]
profundidad[F] del hipocentro[M]
focus
foyer[M]
Herd[M]
hipocentro[M]
fault
faille[F]
Verwerfung[F]
falla[F]
seismic wave
onde[F] sismique
seismische Welle[F]
onda[F] sísmica

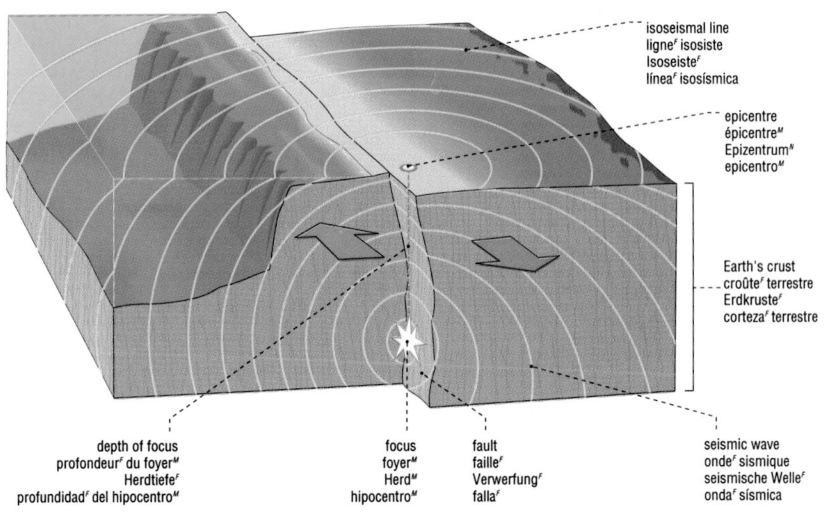

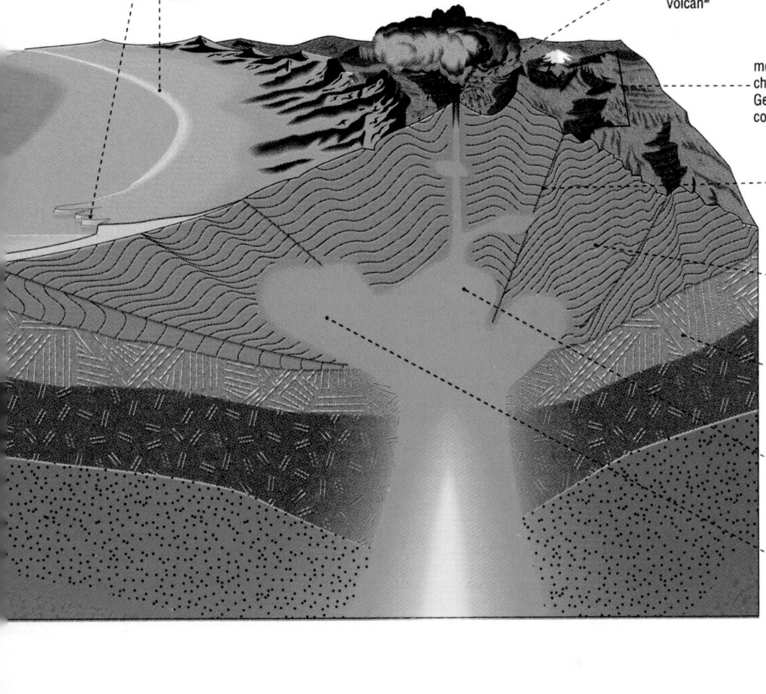

cliff
falaise[F]
Kliff[N]
acantilado[M]
beach
plage[F]
Strand[M]
playa[F]
volcano
volcan[M]
Vulkan[M]
volcán[M]
mountain range
chaîne[F] de montagnes[F]
Gebirgskette[F]
cordillera[F]
fault
faille[F]
Verwerfung[F]
falla[F]
sedimentary rocks
roches[F] sédimentaires
Sedimentgesteine[N]
rocas[F] sedimentarias
metamorphic rocks
roches[F] métamorphiques
metamorphe Gesteine[N]
rocas[F] metamórficas
igneous rocks
roches[F] ignées
Eruptivgesteine[N]
rocas[F] ígneas
intrusive rocks
roches[F] d'intrusion[F]
Intrusivgesteine[N]
rocas[F] intrusivas

# CAVE
# GROTTE[F]
# HÖHLE[F]
# GRUTA[F]

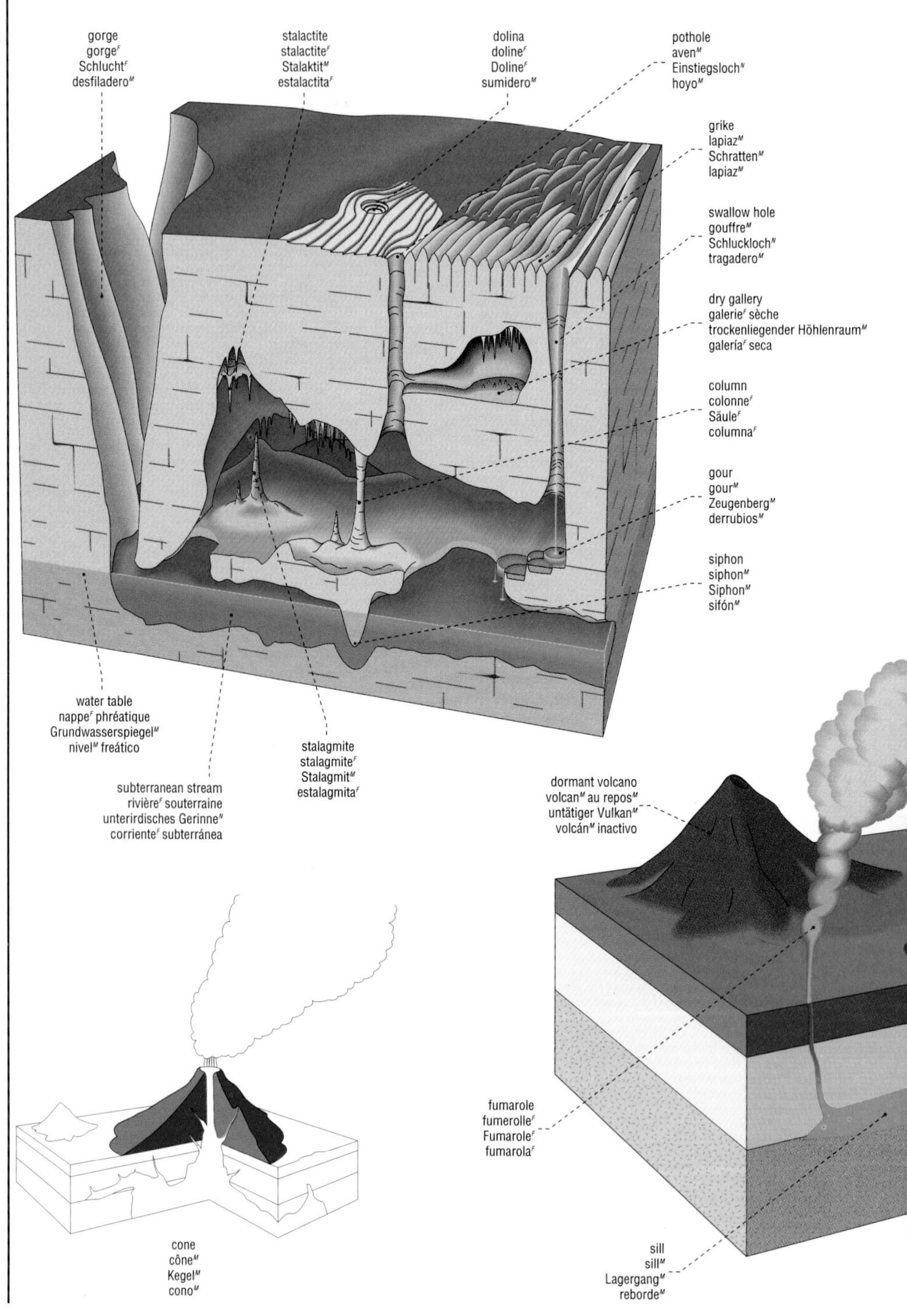

# VOLCANO
# VOLCAN[M]
# VULKAN[M]
# VOLCÁN[M]

## VOLCANO DURING ERUPTION
## VOLCAN[M] EN ÉRUPTION[F]
## VULKAN[M] MIT AUSBRUCHSTÄTIGKEIT[F]
## VOLCÁN[M] EN ERUPCIÓN[F]

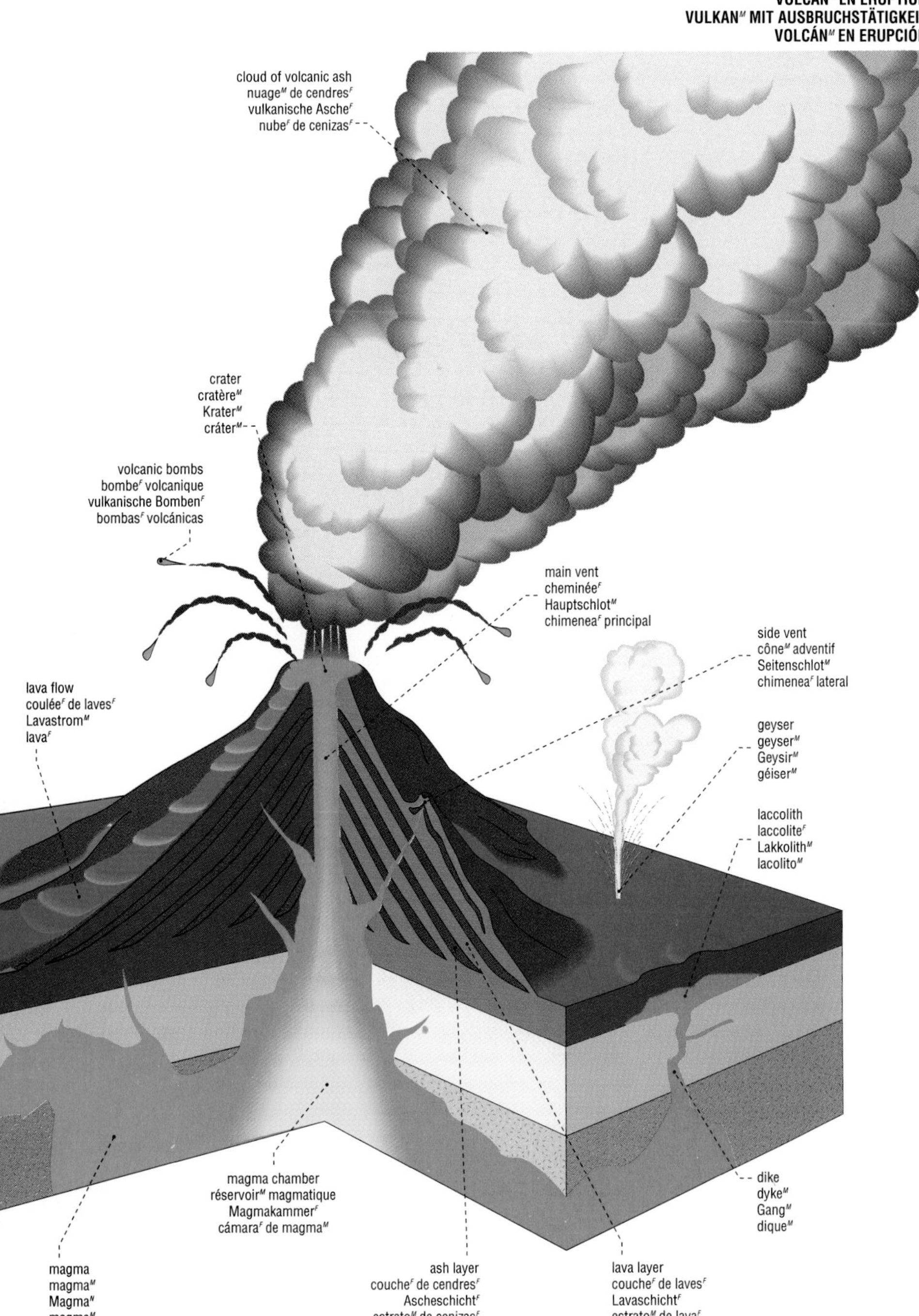

# GLACIER
## GLACIER[M]
## GLETSCHER[M]
## GLACIAR[M]

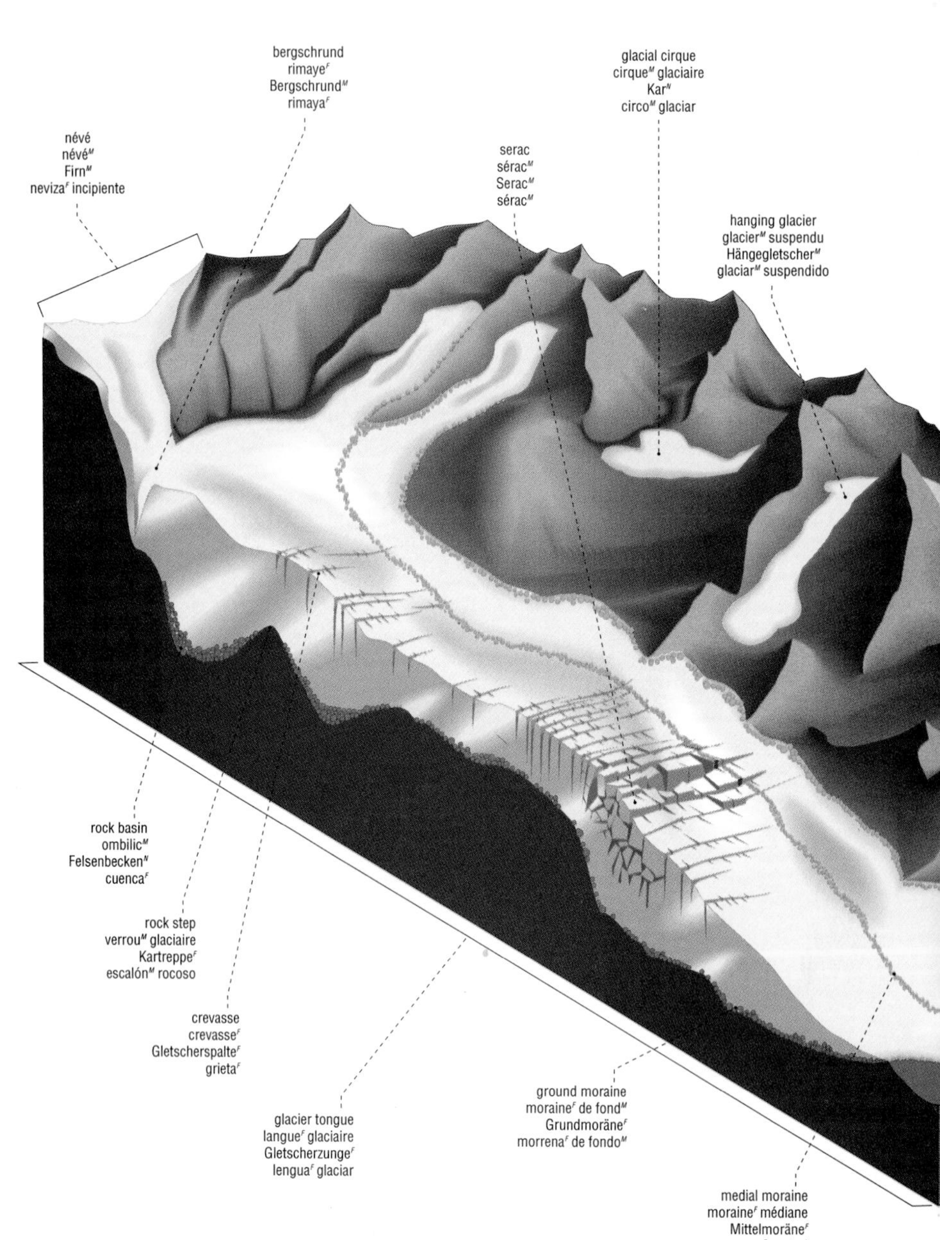

# MOUNTAIN
# MONTAGNE^F
# BERG^M
# MONTAÑA^F

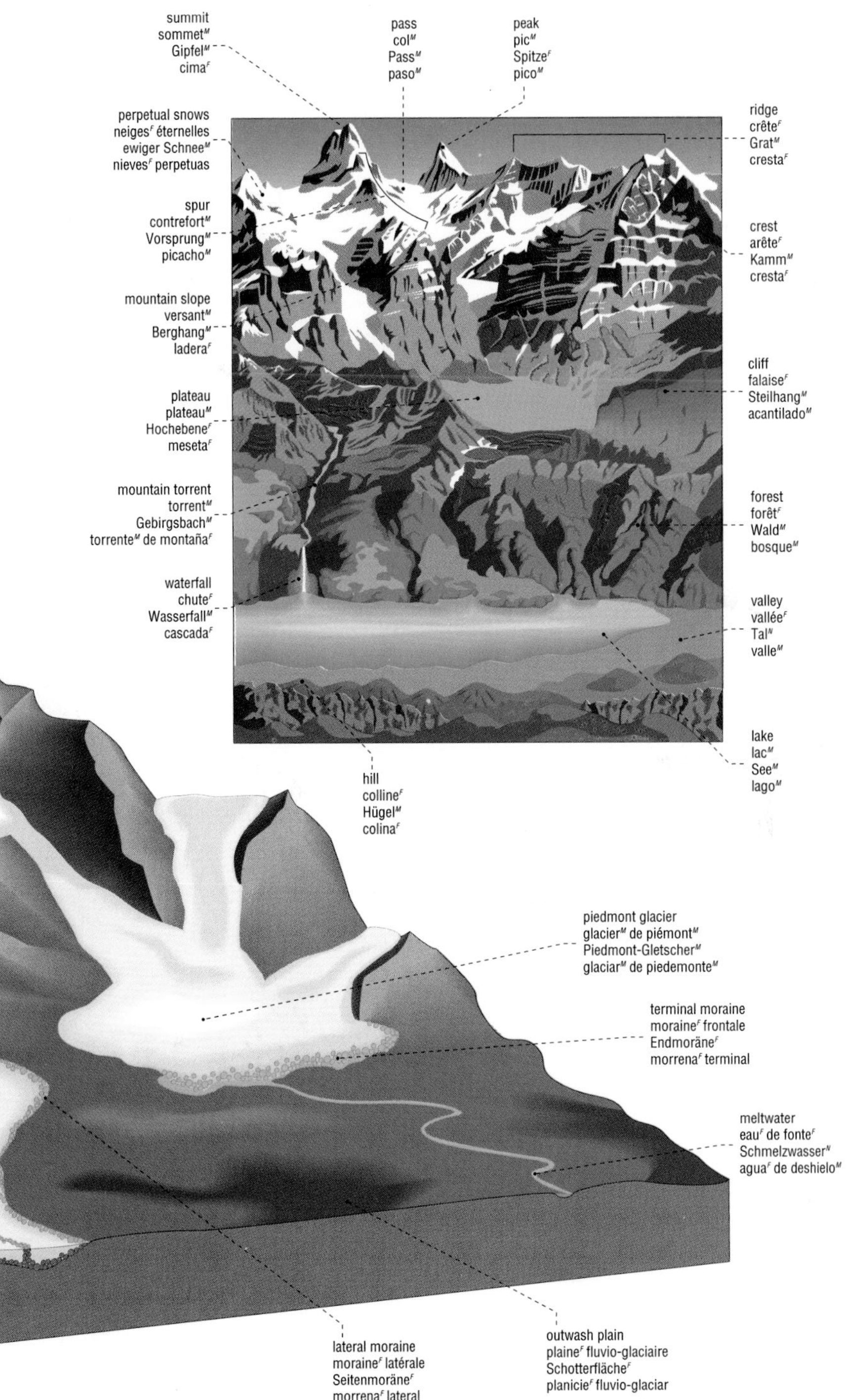

# OCEAN FLOOR
# FOND^M DE L'OCÉAN^M
# MEERESGRUND^M
# LECHO^M MARINO

## MID-OCEAN RIDGE
## DORSALE^F MÉDIO-OCÉANIQUE
## OZEANISCHER RÜCKEN^M
## DORSAL^F OCEÁNICA

## TOPOGRAPHIC FEATURES
## ÉLÉMENTS^M TOPOGRAPHIQUES
## TOPOGRAPHISCHE MERKMALE^N
## CONFIGURACIÓN^F TOPOGRÁFICA

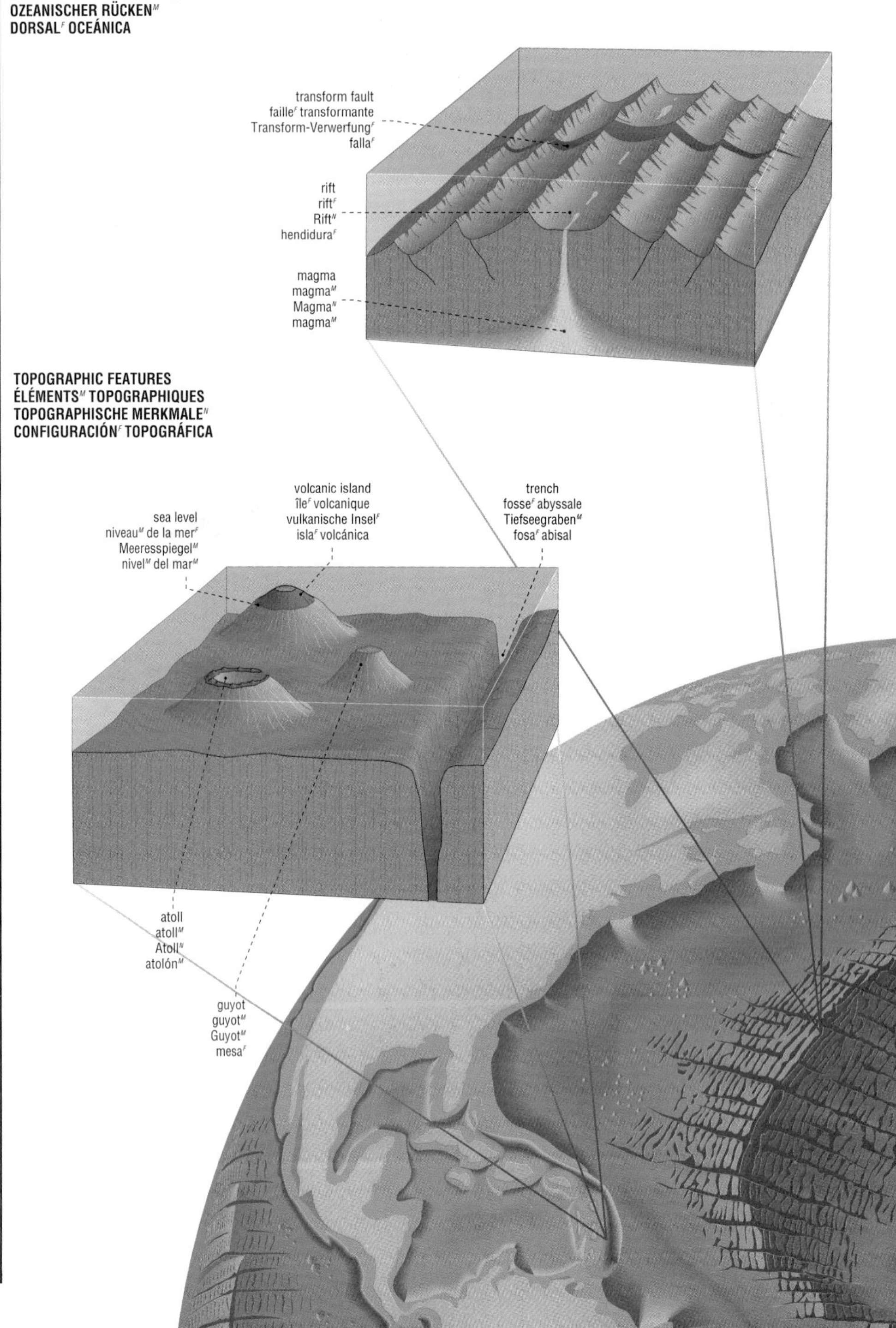

**ABYSSAL PLAIN**
**PLAINE^F ABYSSALE**
**TIEFSEE-EBENE^F**
**LLANURA^F ABISAL**

**CONTINENTAL MARGIN**
**MARGE^F CONTINENTALE**
**KONTINENTALRAND^M**
**CUENCA^F OCEÁNICA**

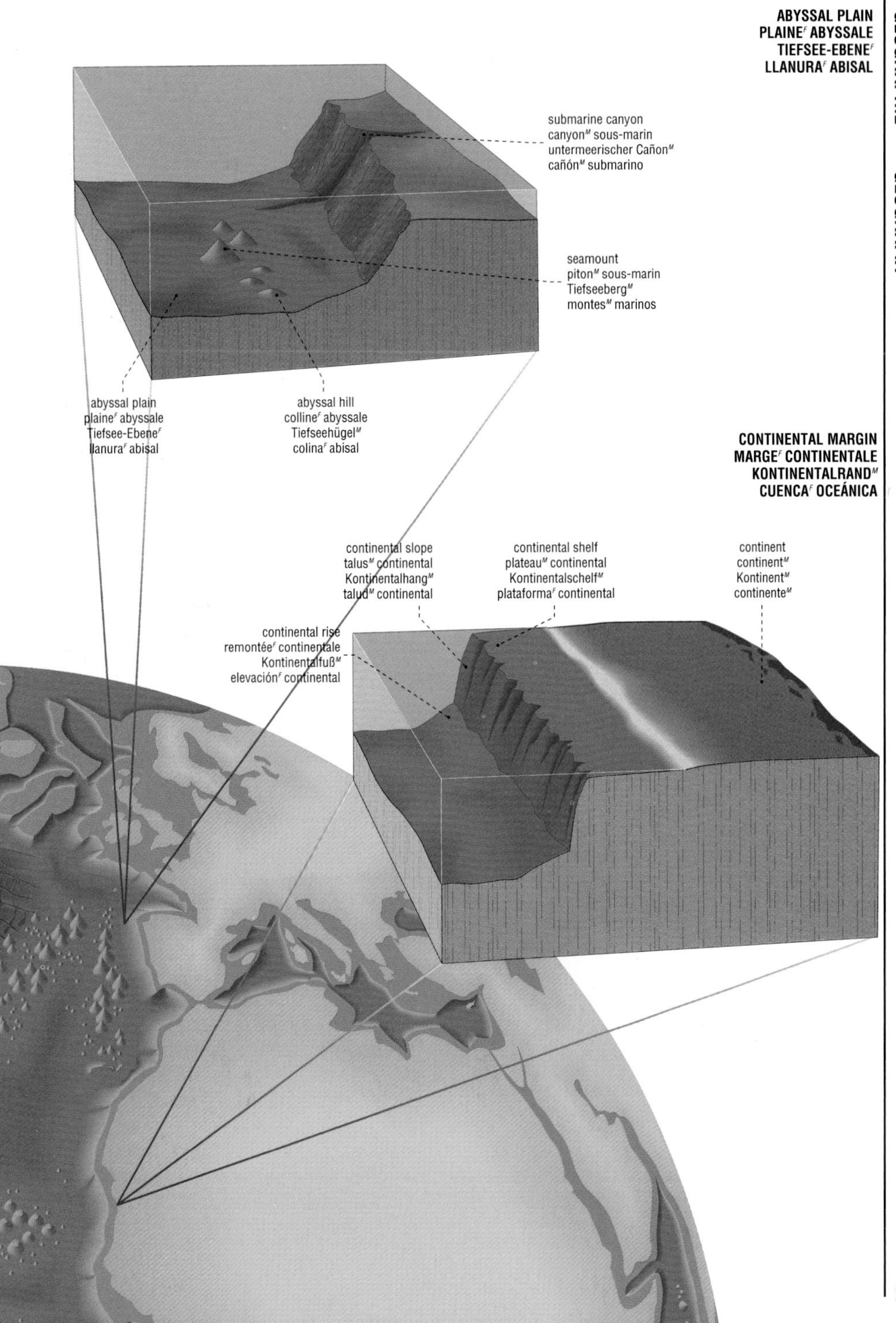

## WAVE
## VAGUE[F]
## WELLE[F]
## OLA[F]

breaker
vague[F] déferlante
Brecher[M]
rompiente[M]
crest
crête[F]
Kamm[M]
cresta[F]
progressive wave
vague[F] d'oscillation[F]
Oszillationswelle[F]
ola[F] de oscilación[F]
wave length
longueur[F] de la vague[F]
Wellenlänge[F]
longitud[F] de la ola[F]
foam
écume[F]
Schaum[M]
espuma[F]
trough
creux[M]
Tal[N]
seno[M]
still water level
niveau[M] d'équilibre[M]
Stillwasserspiegel[M]
nivel[M] de equilibrio[M] del agua[F]
wave height
hauteur[F] de la vague[F]
Wellenhöhe[F]
altura[F] de la ola[F]
shore
côte[F]
Ufer[N]
costa[F]
translation wave
vague[F] de translation[F]
Translationswelle[F]
ola[F] de translación[F]
wave base
base[F] de la vague[F]
Wellenbasis[F]
base[F] de la ola[F]
sandbank
banc[M] de sable[M]
Sandbank[F]
banco[M] de arena[F]

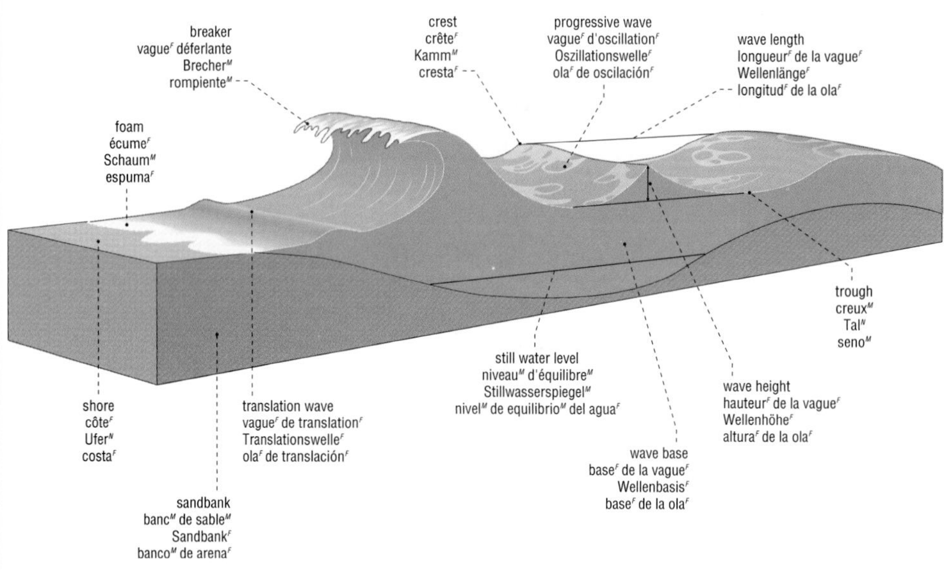

## COMMON COASTAL FEATURES
## CONFIGURATION[F] DU LITTORAL[M]
## KÜSTENFORMEN[F]
## CONFIGURACIÓN[F] DEL LITORAL[M]

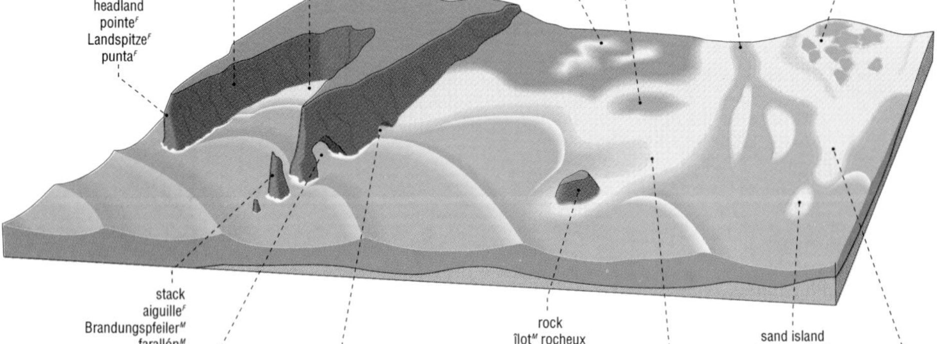

beach
plage[F]
Strand[M]
playa[F]
lagoon
lagune[F]
Lagune[F]
laguna[F]
dune
dune[F]
Düne[F]
duna[F]
cliff
falaise[F]
Kliff[N]
acantilado[M]
salt marsh
marais[M] salant
Salzsumpf[M]
salina[F]
estuary
estuaire[M]
Flußmündung[F]
estuario[M]
headland
pointe[F]
Landspitze[F]
punta[F]
stack
aiguille[F]
Brandungspfeiler[M]
farallón[M]
rock
îlot[M] rocheux
Felsen[M]
roca[F]
sand island
île[F] de sable[M]
Sandinsel[F]
isla[F] de arena[F]
cave
grotte[F]
Höhle[F]
socavón[M]
natural arch
arche[F] naturelle
Brandungstor[N]
arco[M] natural
tombolo
tombolo[M]
Nehrung[F]
tómbolo[M]
spit
flèche[F] littorale
Landzunge[F]
barra[F]

# ECOLOGY
# ÉCOLOGIE^F
# ÖKOLOGIE^F
# ECOLOGÍA^F

## STRUCTURE OF THE BIOSPHERE
## STRUCTURE^F DE LA BIOSPHÈRE^F
## STRUKTUR^F DER BIOSPHÄRE^F
## ESTRUCTURA^F DE LA BIOSFERA^F

atmosphere
atmosphère^F
Atmosphäre^F
atmósfera^F
lithosphere
lithosphère^F
Lithosphäre^F
litosfera^F
hydrosphere
hydrosphère^F
Hydrosphäre^F
hidrosfera^F

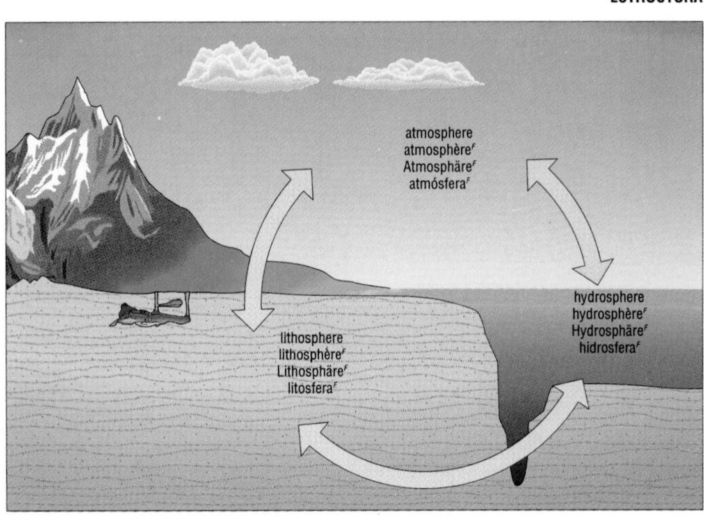

## FOOD CHAIN
## CHAÎNE^F ALIMENTAIRE
## NAHRUNGSKETTE^F
## CADENA^F ALIMENTICIA

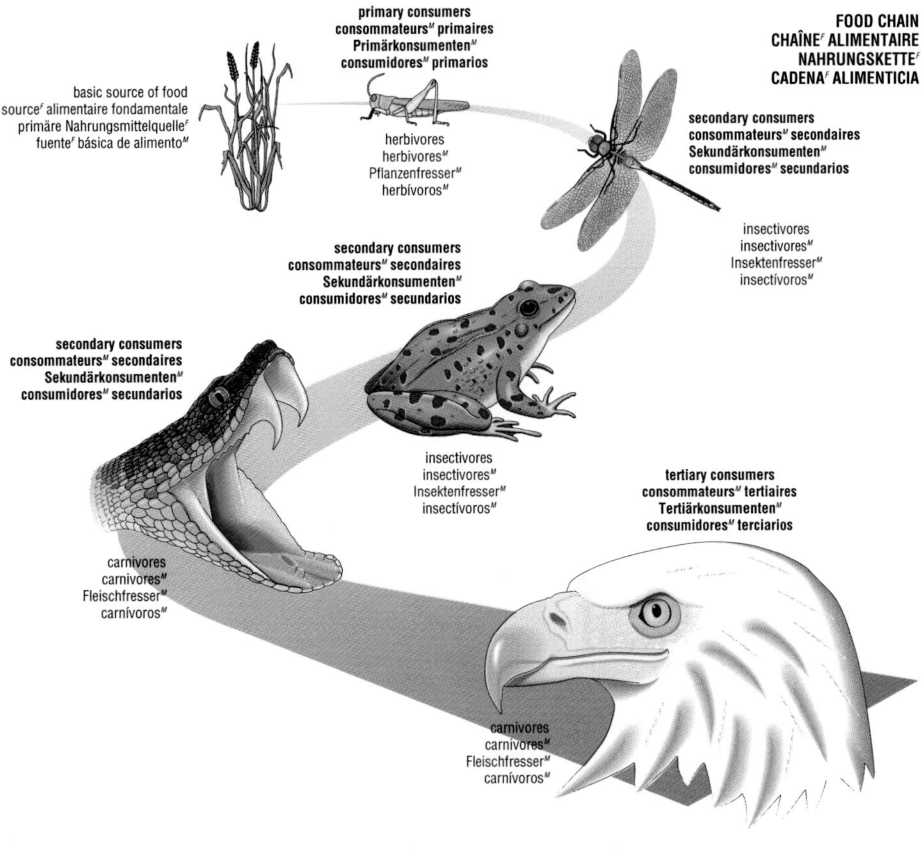

basic source of food
source^F alimentaire fondamentale
primäre Nahrungsmittelquelle^F
fuente^F básica de alimento^M
primary consumers
consommateurs^M primaires
Primärkonsumenten^M
consumidores^M primarios
herbivores
herbivores^M
Pflanzenfresser^M
herbívoros^M
secondary consumers
consommateurs^M secondaires
Sekundärkonsumenten^M
consumidores^M secundarios
insectivores
insectivores^M
Insektenfresser^M
insectívoros^M
secondary consumers
consommateurs^M secondaires
Sekundärkonsumenten^M
consumidores^M secundarios
insectivores
insectivores^M
Insektenfresser^M
insectívoros^M
secondary consumers
consommateurs^M secondaires
Sekundärkonsumenten^M
consumidores^M secundarios
carnivores
carnivores^M
Fleischfresser^M
carnívoros^M
tertiary consumers
consommateurs^M tertiaires
Tertiärkonsumenten^M
consumidores^M terciarios
carnivores
carnivores^M
Fleischfresser^M
carnívoros^M

# ECOLOGY
# ÉCOLOGIE[F]
# ÖKOLOGIE[F]
# ECOLOGÍA[F]

## POLLUTION OF FOOD ON AND IN THE GROUND
## POLLUTION[F] DES ALIMENTS[M] AU SOL[M]
## SCHADSTOFFBELASTUNG[F] IM BODEN[M]
## CONTAMINACIÓN[F] DE ALIMENTOS[M] EN LA TIERRA[F]

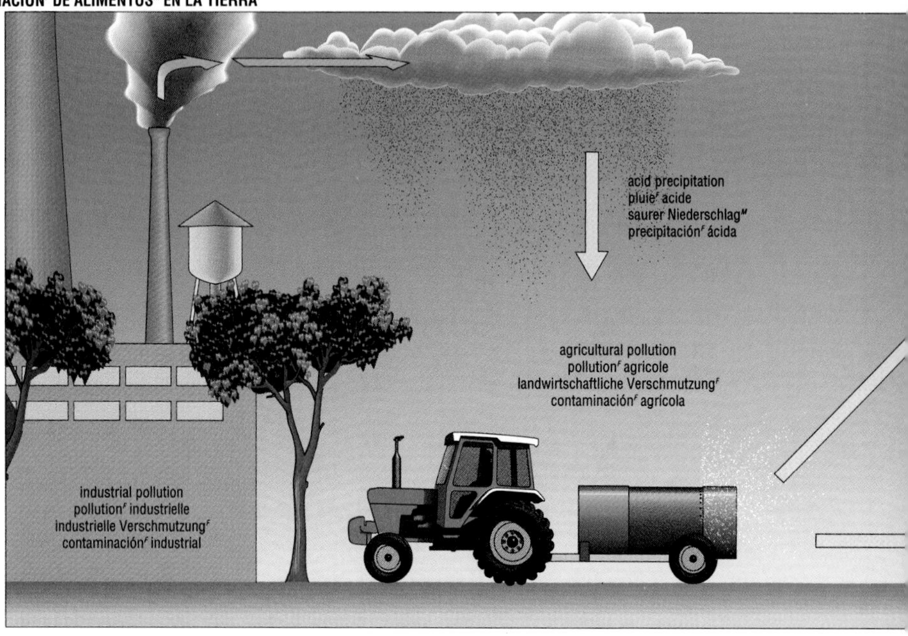


## POLLUTION OF FOOD IN WATER
## POLLUTION[F] DES ALIMENTS[M] DANS L'EAU[F]
## SCHADSTOFFBELASTUNG[F] IM WASSER[N]
## CONTAMINACIÓN[F] DE ALIMENTOS[M] EN EL AGUA[F]

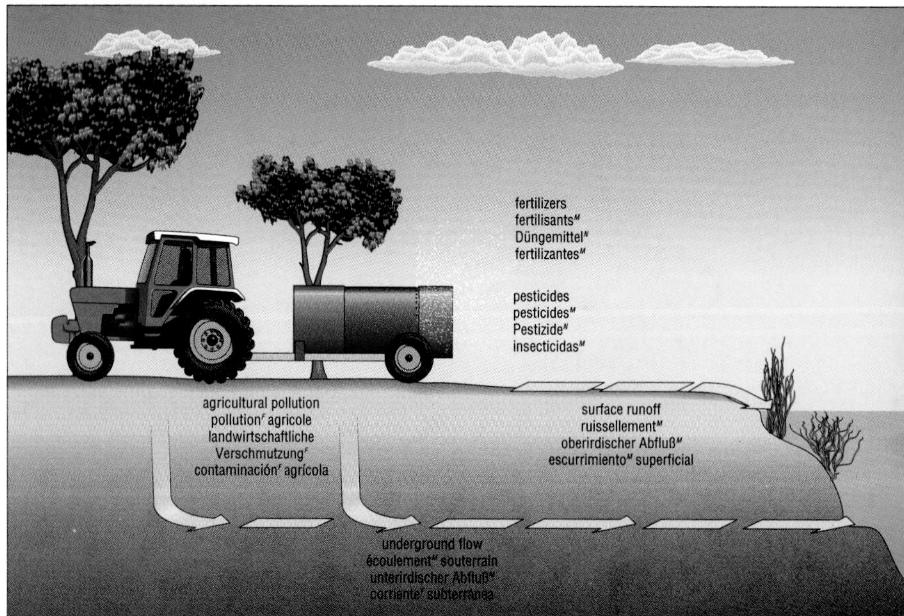

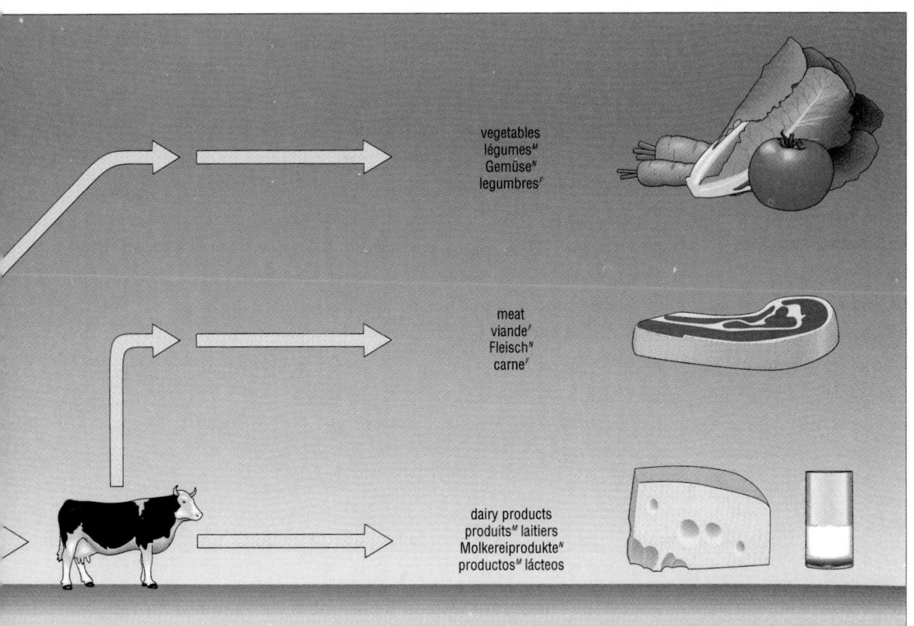
vegetables
légumes[M]
Gemüse[N]
legumbres[F]
meat
viande[F]
Fleisch[N]
carne[F]
dairy products
produits[M] laitiers
Molkereiprodukte[N]
productos[M] lácteos

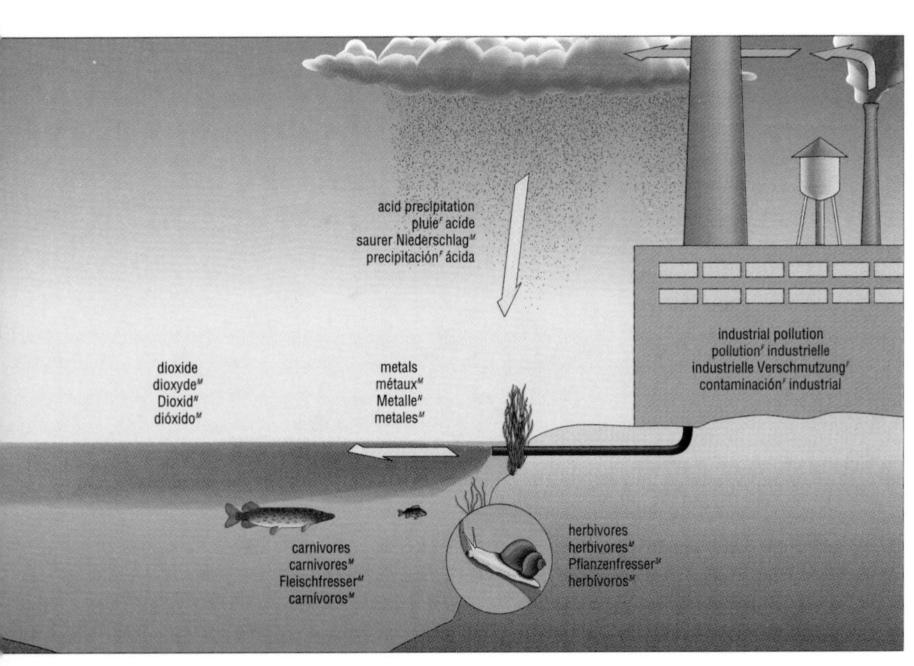
acid precipitation
pluie[F] acide
saurer Niederschlag[M]
precipitación[F] ácida
industrial pollution
pollution[F] industrielle
industrielle Verschmutzung[F]
contaminación[F] industrial
dioxide
dioxyde[M]
Dioxid[N]
dióxido[M]
metals
métaux[M]
Metalle[N]
metales[M]
carnivores
carnivores[M]
Fleischfresser[M]
carnívoros[M]
herbivores
herbivores[M]
Pflanzenfresser[M]
herbívoros[M]

# ECOLOGY
# ÉCOLOGIE^F
# ÖKOLOGIE^F
# ECOLOGÍA^F

## ATMOSPHERIC POLLUTION
## POLLUTION^F DE L'AIR^M
## ATMOSPHÄRISCHE VERSCHMUTZUNG^F
## CONTAMINACIÓN^F ATMOSFÉRICA

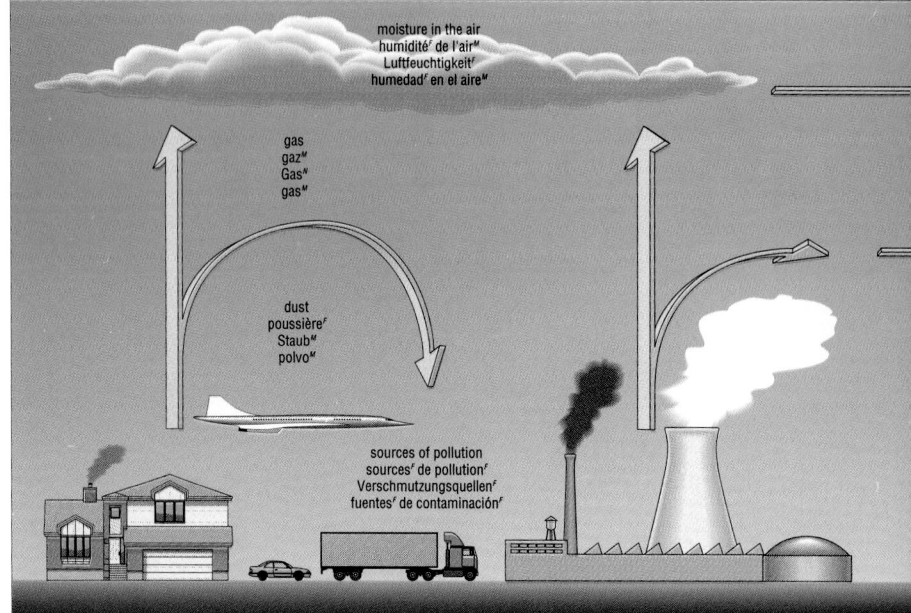


## HYDROLOGIC CYCLE
## CYCLE^M DE L'EAU^F
## WASSERKREISLAUF^M
## CICLO^M HIDROLÓGICO

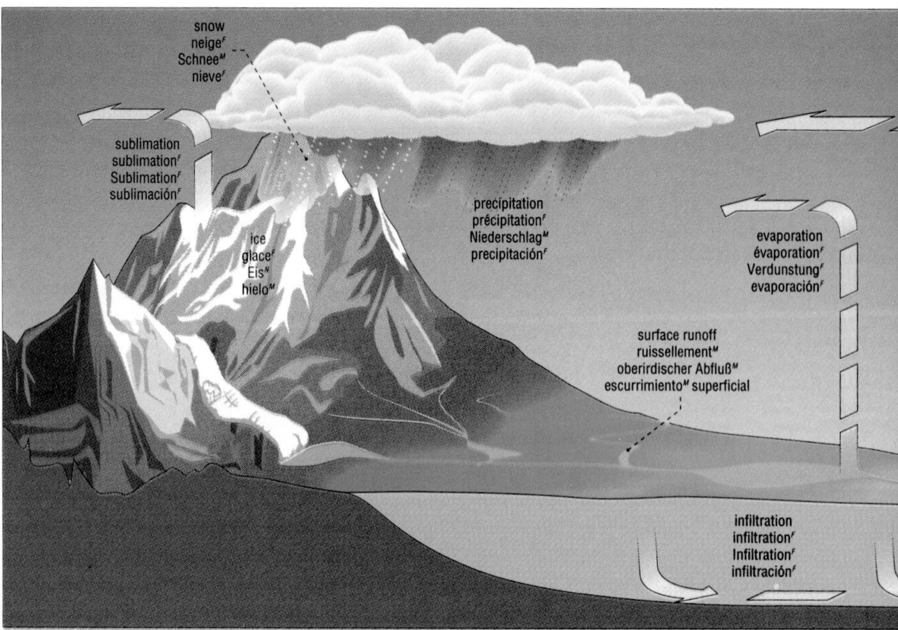

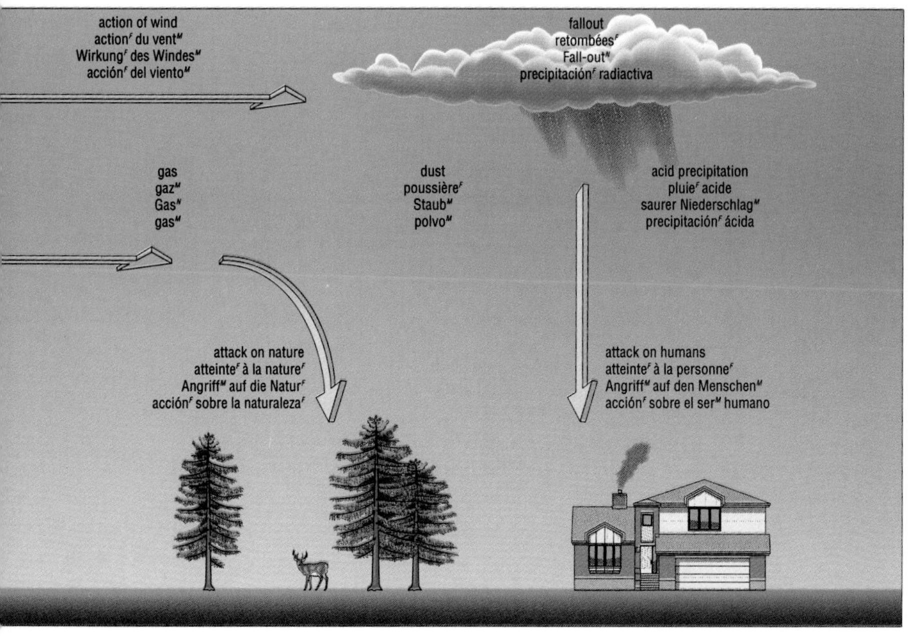
action of wind
action[F] du vent[M]
Wirkung[F] des Windes[M]
acción[F] del viento[M]
fallout
retombées[F]
Fall-out[M]
precipitación[F] radiactiva
gas
gaz[M]
Gas[N]
gas[M]
dust
poussière[F]
Staub[M]
polvo[M]
acid precipitation
pluie[F] acide
saurer Niederschlag[M]
precipitación[F] ácida
attack on nature
atteinte[F] à la nature[F]
Angriff[M] auf die Natur[F]
acción[F] sobre la naturaleza[F]
attack on humans
atteinte[F] à la personne[F]
Angriff[M] auf den Menschen[M]
acción[F] sobre el ser[M] humano

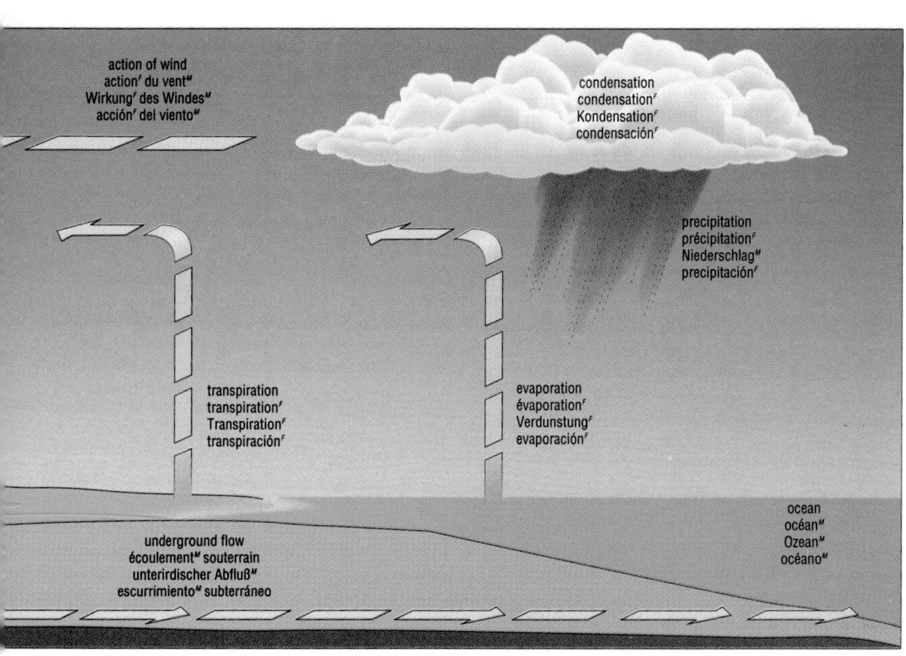
action of wind
action[F] du vent[M]
Wirkung[F] des Windes[M]
acción[F] del viento[M]
condensation
condensation[F]
Kondensation[F]
condensación[F]
precipitation
précipitation[F]
Niederschlag[M]
precipitación[F]
transpiration
transpiration[F]
Transpiration[F]
transpiración[F]
evaporation
évaporation[F]
Verdunstung[F]
evaporación[F]
ocean
océan[M]
Ozean[M]
océano[M]
underground flow
écoulement[M] souterrain
unterirdischer Abfluß[M]
escurrimiento[M] subterráneo

# PRECIPITATIONS
# PRÉCIPITATIONS[F]
# NIEDERSCHLÄGE[M]
# PRECIPITACIONES[F]

## STORMY SKY
## CIEL[M] D'ORAGE[M]
## STÜRMISCHER HIMMEL[M]
## CIELO[M] TURBULENTO

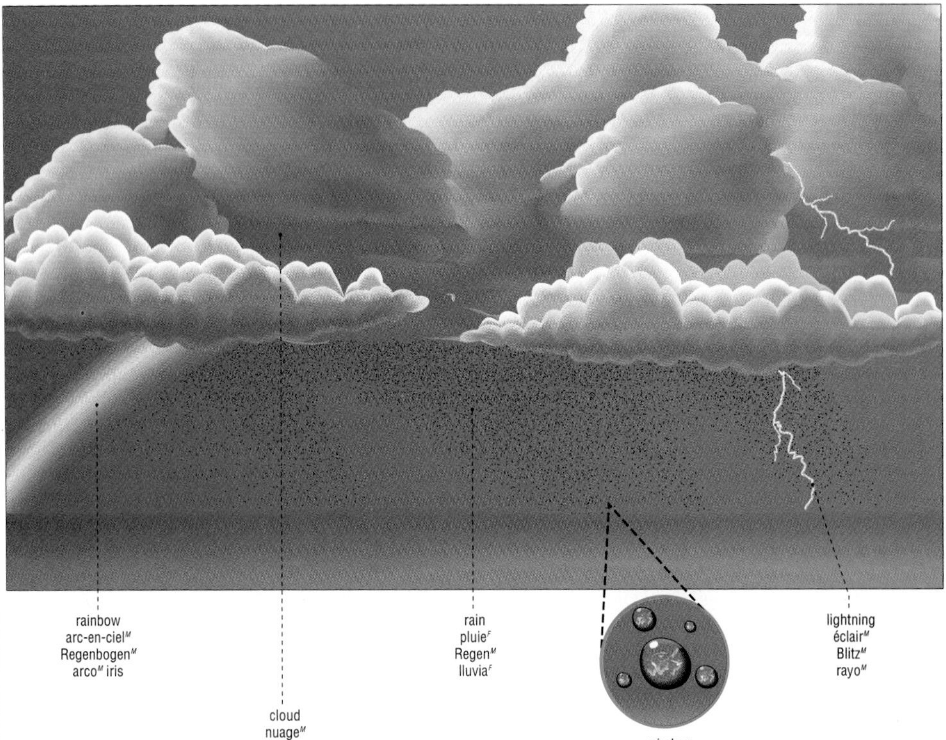

rainbow
arc-en-ciel[M]
Regenbogen[M]
arco[M] iris
cloud
nuage[M]
Wolke[F]
nube[F]
rain
pluie[F]
Regen[M]
lluvia[F]
raindrop
goutte[F] de pluie[F]
Regentropfen[M]
gota[F] de lluvia[F]
lightning
éclair[M]
Blitz[M]
rayo[M]

## CLASSIFICATION OF SNOW CRYSTALS
## CLASSIFICATION[F] DES CRISTAUX[M] DE NEIGE[F]
## KLASSIFIKATION[F] VON SCHNEEKRISTALLEN[M]
## CLASIFICACIÓN[F] DE LOS CRISTALES[M] DE NIEVE[F]

plate crystal
plaquette[F]
Plättchen[N]
plaquita[F] de hielo[M]
stellar crystal
étoile[F]
Stern[M]
estrella[F]
column
colonne[F]
Säule[F]
columna[F]
needle
aiguille[F]
Nadel[F]
aguja[F]
spatial dendrite
dendrite[F] spatiale
räumlicher Dendrit[M]
dendrita[F] espacial

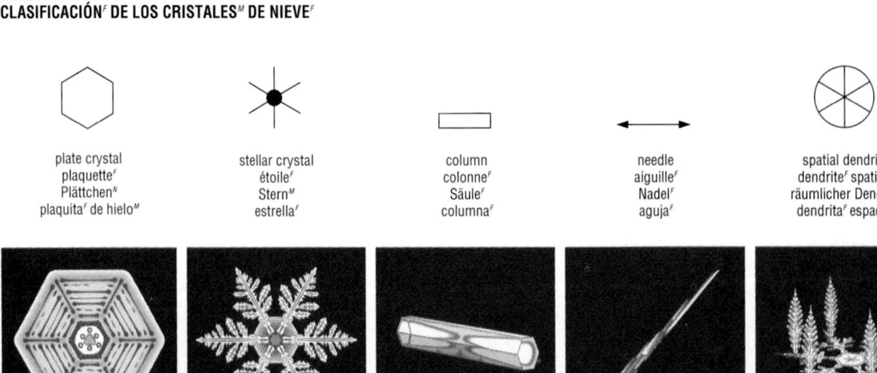

mist
brume[F]
Dunst[M]
neblina[F]

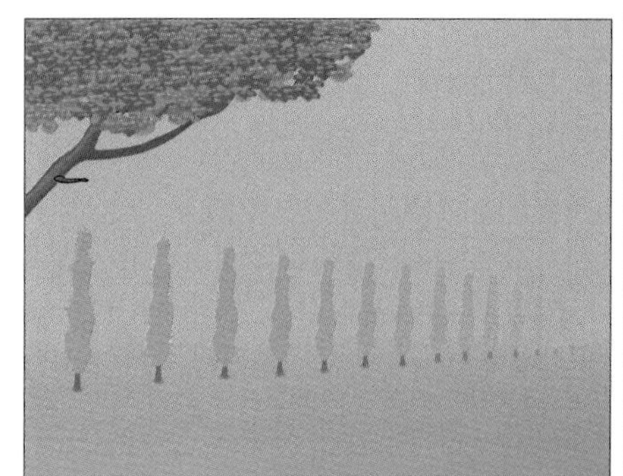

fog
brouillard[M]
Nebel[M]
niebla[F]

dew
rosée[F]
Tau[M]
rocío[M]

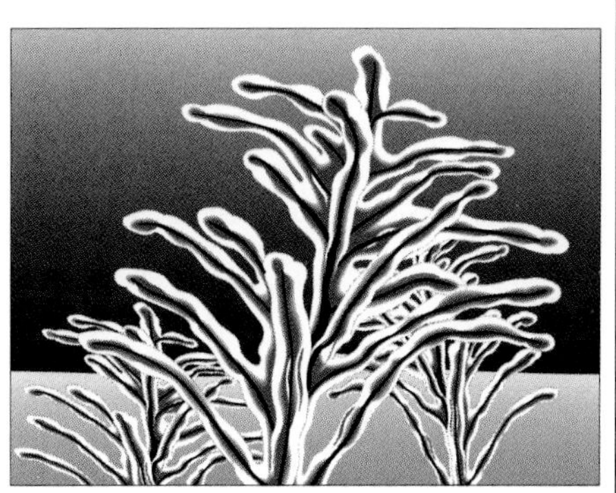

glazed frost
verglas[M]
Rauhreif[M]
escarcha[F]

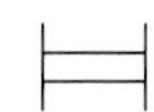

capped column
colonne[F] avec capuchon[M]
bedeckte Säule[F]
columna[F] con capuchon[M]

irregular crystal
cristaux[M] irréguliers
irreguläres Aggregat[N]
cristales[M] irregulares

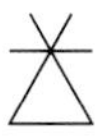

snow pellet
neige[F] roulée
Reif- und Frostgraupel[F]
copo[M] de nieve[F]

sleet
grésil[M]
Eiskörnchen[N]
cellisca[F]

hail
grêlon[M]
Hagel[M]
granizo[M]

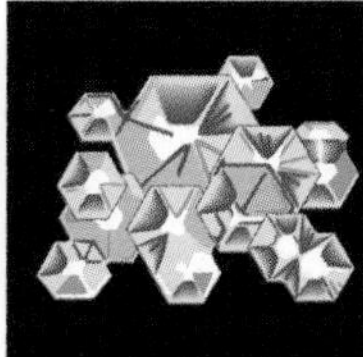

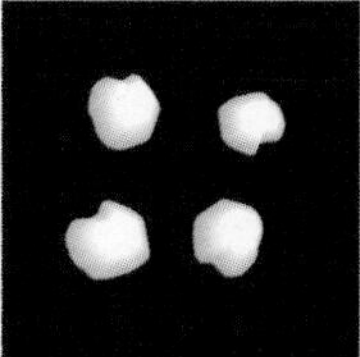

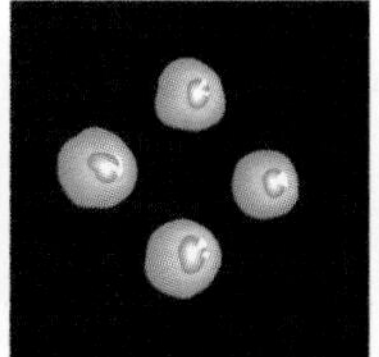

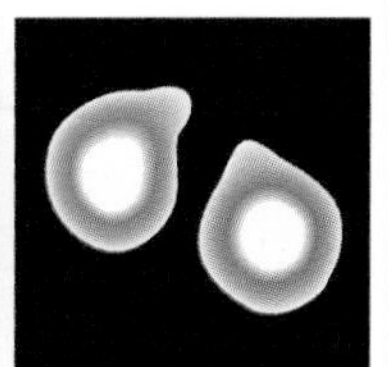

# METEOROLOGY
# MÉTÉOROLOGIE[F]
# METEOROLOGIE[F]
# METEOROLOGÍA[F]

## WEATHER MAP
## CARTE[F] MÉTÉOROLOGIQUE
## WETTERKARTE[F]
## CARTA[F] DEL TIEMPO[M]

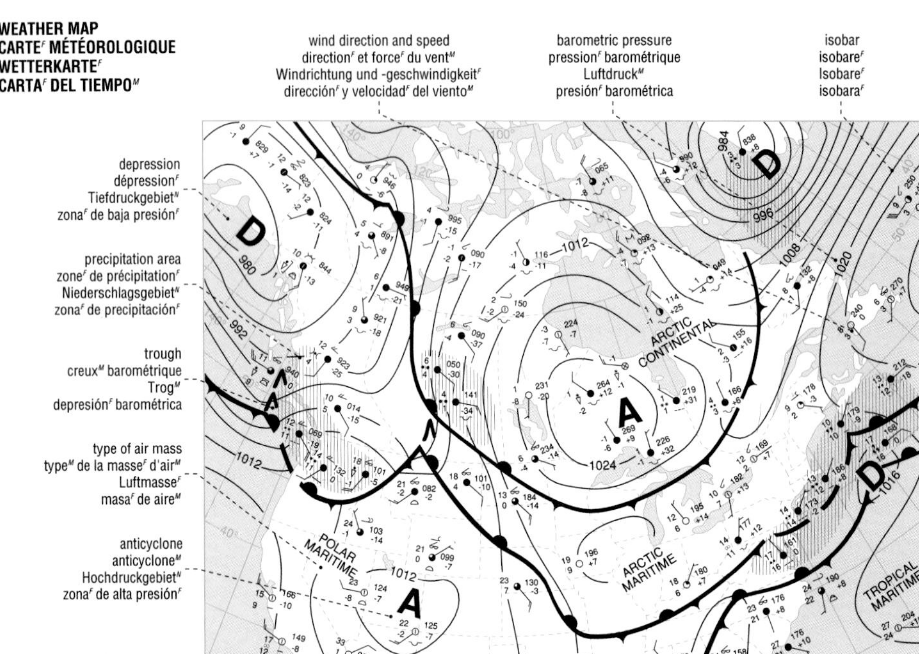


## STATION MODEL
## DISPOSITION[F] DES INFORMATIONS[F] D'UNE STATION[F]
## STATIONSMODELL[N]
## MODELO[M] DE CLAVE[F]

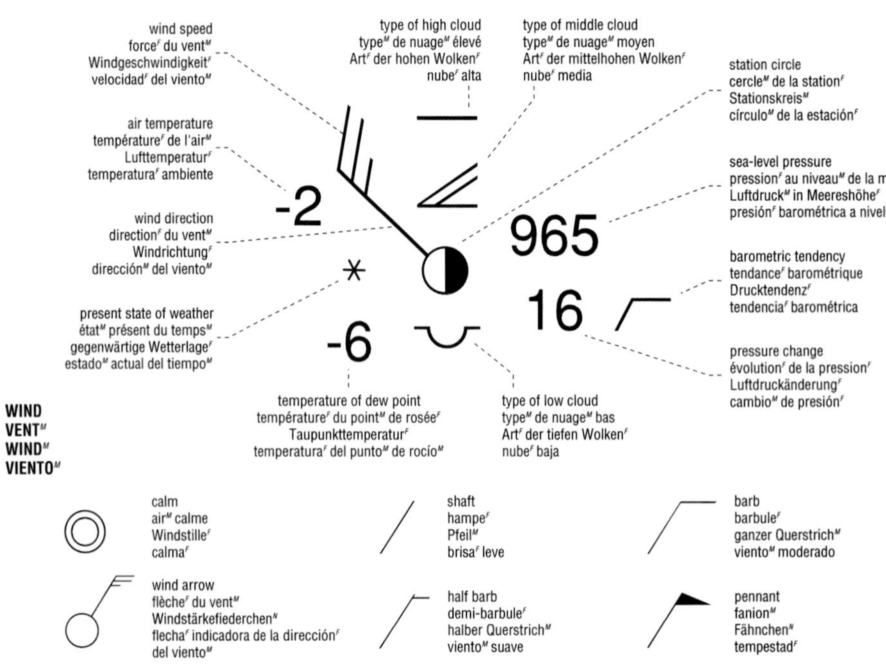

# INTERNATIONAL WEATHER SYMBOLS
# SYMBOLES[M] MÉTÉOROLOGIQUES INTERNATIONAUX
# INTERNATIONALE WETTERSYMBOLE[N]
# SÍMBOLOS[M] METEOROLÓGICOS INTERNACIONALES

## FRONTS
## FRONTS[M]
## FRONTEN[F]
## FRENTES[M]

surface cold front
front[M] froid en surface[F]
Kaltfront[F] am Boden[M]
frente[M] frío de superficie[F]

surface warm front
front[M] chaud en surface[F]
Warmfront[F] am Boden[M]
frente[M] cálido de superficie[F]

occluded front
front[M] occlus
Okklusion[F]
frente[M] ocluido

upper cold front
front[M] froid en altitude[F]
Höhenkaltfront[F]
frente[M] frío en las alturas[F]

upper warm front
front[M] chaud en altitude[F]
Höhenwarmfront[F]
frente[M] cálido en las alturas[F]

stationary front
front[M] stationnaire
stationäre Front[F]
frente[M] estacionario

## CLOUD AMOUNT
## NÉBULOSITÉ[F]
## BEDECKUNGSGRAD[M]
## NUBOSIDAD[F]

clear sky
ciel[M] clair
wolkenloser Himmel[M]
despejado

scattered cloud
ciel[M] à nébulosité[F] dispersée
Himmel[M] mit vereinzelten Wolken[F]
nubes[F] dispersas

very cloudy sky
ciel[M] très nuageux
stark bewölkter Himmel[M]
muy nublado

overcast sky
ciel[M] couvert
bedeckter Himmel[M]
completamente nublado

cloudy sky
ciel[M] nuageux
bewölkter Himmel[M]
medio nublado

slightly covered sky
ciel[M] peu nuageux
heiterer Himmel[M]
ligeramente nublado

obscured sky
ciel[M] noir
nicht angebbar (z.B. wegen Nebel[M])
obscurecido por contaminación[F]

## PRESENT WEATHER
## MÉTÉORES[M]
## METEORE[M]
## FENÓMENOS[M] ATMOSFÉRICOS

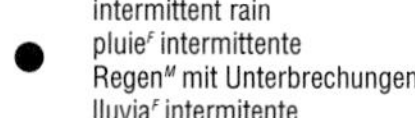
intermittent rain
pluie[F] intermittente
Regen[M] mit Unterbrechungen[F]
lluvia[F] intermitente

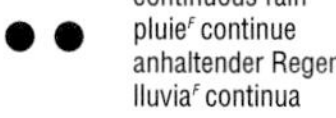
continuous rain
pluie[F] continue
anhaltender Regen[M]
lluvia[F] continua

intermittent drizzle
bruine[F] intermittente
Sprühregen[M] mit Unterbrechungen[F]
llovizna[F] intermitente

continuous drizzle
bruine[F] continue
anhaltender Sprühregen[M]
llovizna[F] continua

intermittent snow
neige[F] intermittente
Schnee[M] mit Unterbrechungen[F]
nieve[F] intermitente

continuous snow
neige[F] continue
anhaltender Schnee[M]
nieve[F] continua

rain shower
averse[F] de pluie[F]
Regenschauer[M]
chubasco[M]

snow shower
averse[F] de neige[F]
Schneeschauer[M]
chubasco[M] de nieve[F]

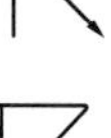
thunderstorm
orage[M]
Gewitter[N]
tormenta[F]

heavy thunderstorm
orage[M] violent
starkes Gewitter[N]
tormenta[F] eléctrica

sandstorm or dust storm
tempête[F] de sable[M] ou de poussière[F]
Sand- oder Staubsturm[M]
tormenta[F] de polvo[M]

tropical storm
tempête[F] tropicale
tropischer Sturm[M]
tormenta[F] tropical

hurricane
ouragan[M]
Orkan[M]
huracán[M]

slight drifting snow at ground level
chasse-neige[F] faible basse
leichtes Schneetreiben[N]
acumulación[F] baja de nieve[F] liviana

heavy drifting snow at ground level
chasse-neige[F] forte basse
starkes Schneetreiben[N]
acumulación[F] baja de nieve[F] pesada

sleet
grésil[M]
Schneeregen[M]
aguanieve[F]

hail shower
averse[F] de grêle[F]
Hagelschauer[M]
granizada[F]

squall
grain[M]
Bö[F]
borrasca[F]

freezing rain
pluie[F] verglaçante
Eisregen[M]
lluvia[F] helada

smoke
fumée[F]
Rauch[M]
humo[M]

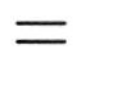
mist
brume[F]
Dunst[M]
neblina[F]

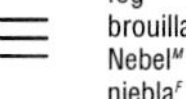
fog
brouillard[M]
Nebel[M]
niebla[F]

# METEOROLOGICAL MEASURING INSTRUMENTS
# INSTRUMENTS$^{M}$ DE MESURE$^{F}$ MÉTÉOROLOGIQUE
# METEOROLOGISCHE MESSINSTRUMENTE$^{N}$
# INSTRUMENTOS$^{M}$ DE MEDICIÓN$^{F}$ METEOROLÓGICA

## MEASUREMENT OF SUNSHINE
## MESURE$^{F}$ DE L'ENSOLEILLEMENT$^{M}$
## MESSUNG$^{F}$ DES SONNENSCHEINS$^{M}$
## MEDICIÓN$^{F}$ DE LA LUZ$^{F}$ SOLAR

**sunshine recorder**
**héliographe$^{M}$**
**Sonnenscheinautograph$^{M}$**
**actinómetro$^{M}$**

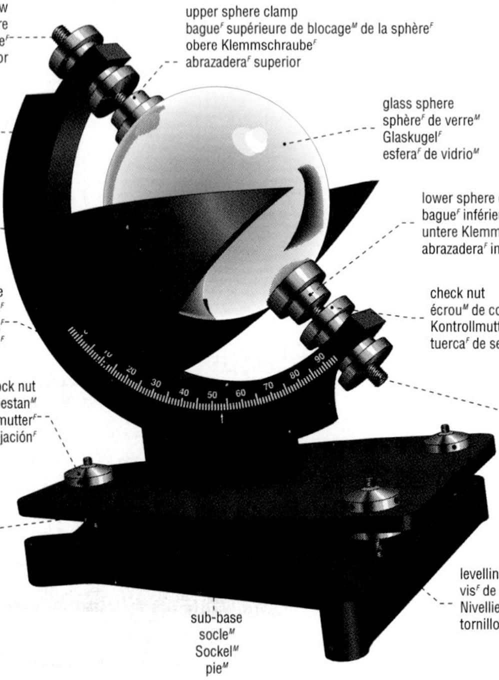

upper support screw
vis$^{F}$ de support$^{M}$ supérieure
obere Halterungsschraube$^{F}$
tornillo$^{M}$ de soporte$^{M}$ superior
upper sphere clamp
bague$^{F}$ supérieure de blocage$^{M}$ de la sphère$^{F}$
obere Klemmschraube$^{F}$
abrazadera$^{F}$ superior
sphere support
support$^{M}$ de sphère$^{F}$
Kugelhalterung$^{F}$
soporte$^{M}$ de la esfera$^{F}$
glass sphere
sphère$^{F}$ de verre$^{M}$
Glaskugel$^{F}$
esfera$^{F}$ de vidrio$^{M}$
card support
porte-cartes$^{M}$
Halterung$^{F}$ für die Registrierkarten$^{F}$
caja$^{F}$
lower sphere clamp
bague$^{F}$ inférieure de blocage$^{M}$ de la sphère$^{F}$
untere Klemmschraube$^{F}$
abrazadera$^{F}$ inferior
latitude scale
échelle$^{F}$ de latitude$^{F}$
Breitengradskala$^{F}$
escala$^{F}$ de latitud$^{F}$
check nut
écrou$^{M}$ de contrôle$^{M}$
Kontrollmutter$^{F}$
tuerca$^{F}$ de seguridad$^{F}$
lock nut
écrou$^{M}$ à cabestan$^{M}$
Gegenmutter$^{F}$
tuerca$^{F}$ de fijación$^{F}$
lower support screw
vis$^{F}$ de support$^{M}$ inférieure
untere Halterungsschraube$^{F}$
tornillo$^{M}$ de soporte$^{M}$ inferior
base plate
base$^{F}$
Grundplatte$^{F}$
placa$^{F}$ base$^{F}$
levelling screw
vis$^{F}$ de nivellement$^{M}$
Nivellierschraube$^{F}$
tornillo$^{M}$ nivelador
sub-base
socle$^{M}$
Sockel$^{M}$
pie$^{M}$

## MEASUREMENT OF RAINFALL
## MESURE$^{F}$ DE LA PLUVIOSITÉ$^{F}$
## MESSUNG$^{F}$ DES REGENFALLS$^{M}$
## MEDICIÓN$^{F}$ DE LA LLUVIA$^{F}$

**direct-reading rain gauge**
**pluviomètre$^{M}$ à lecture$^{F}$ directe**
**selbstschreibender Regenmesser$^{M}$**
**pluviómetro$^{M}$ de lectura$^{F}$ directa**

collecting funnel
entonnoir$^{M}$ collecteur
Sammeltrichter$^{M}$
colector$^{M}$
measuring tube
éprouvette$^{F}$ graduée
Meßrohr$^{N}$
tubo$^{M}$ medidor
levelling screw
vis$^{F}$ de réglage$^{M}$ du niveau$^{M}$
Nivellierschraube$^{F}$
tornillo$^{M}$ nivelador
tightening band
collier$^{M}$ de serrage$^{M}$
Schelle$^{F}$
banda$^{F}$ de tensión$^{F}$
support
support$^{M}$
Ständer$^{M}$
soporte$^{M}$
container
récipient$^{M}$
Behälter$^{M}$
recipiente$^{M}$ de vertido$^{M}$

**rain gauge recorder**
**pluviomètre$^{M}$ enregistreur**
**Niederschlagsschreiber$^{M}$**
**pluviómetro$^{M}$**

recording unit
appareil$^{M}$ enregistreur
Aufzeichnungsgerät$^{N}$
unidad$^{F}$ de grabación$^{F}$

collecting vessel
récipient$^{M}$ collecteur
Auffanggefäß$^{N}$
recipiente$^{M}$ de acumulación$^{F}$

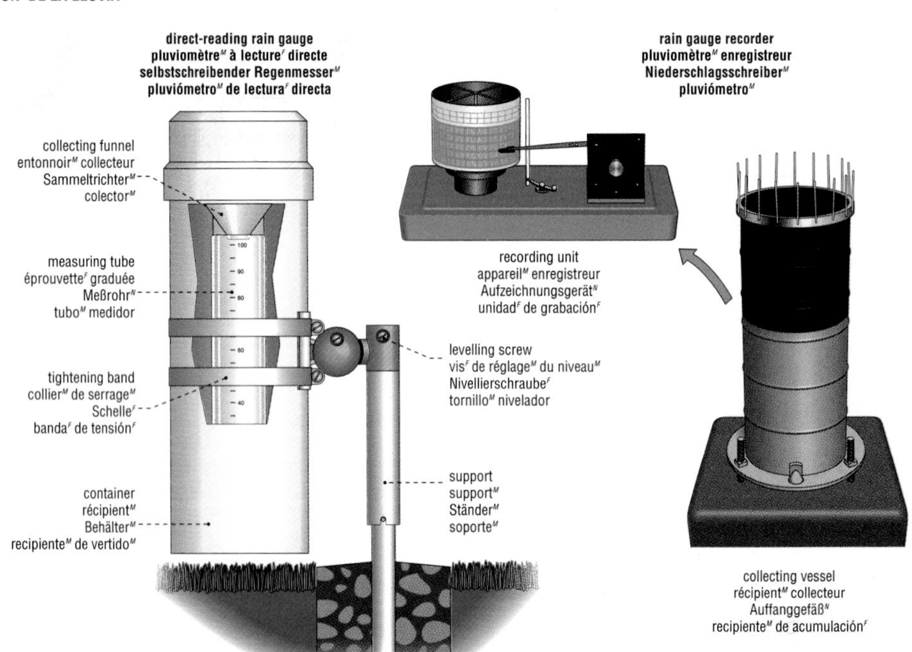

## MEASUREMENT OF TEMPERATURE
## MESURE[F] DE LA TEMPÉRATURE[F]
## MESSUNG[F] DER TEMPERATUR[F]
## MEDICIÓN[F] DE LA TEMPERATURA[F]

minimum thermometer
thermomètre[M] à minima[M]
Minimumthermometer[N]
termómetro[M] mínimo

maximum thermometer
thermomètre[M] à maxima[M]
Maximumthermometer[N]
termómetro[M] máximo

## INSTRUMENT SHELTER
## ABRI[M] MÉTÉOROLOGIQUE
## WETTERHÜTTE[F]
## CASETA[F] DE INSTRUMENTOS[M] METEOROLÓGICOS

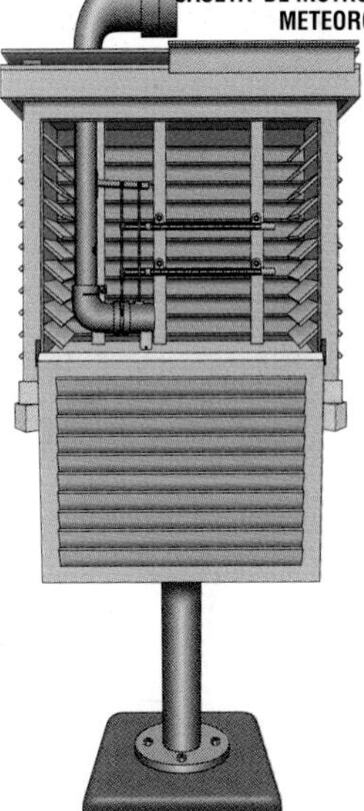

## MEASUREMENT OF AIR PRESSURE
## MESURE[F] DE LA PRESSION[F]
## MESSUNG[F] DES LUFTDRUCKS[M]
## MEDICIÓN[F] DE LA PRESIÓN[F] DEL AIRE[M]

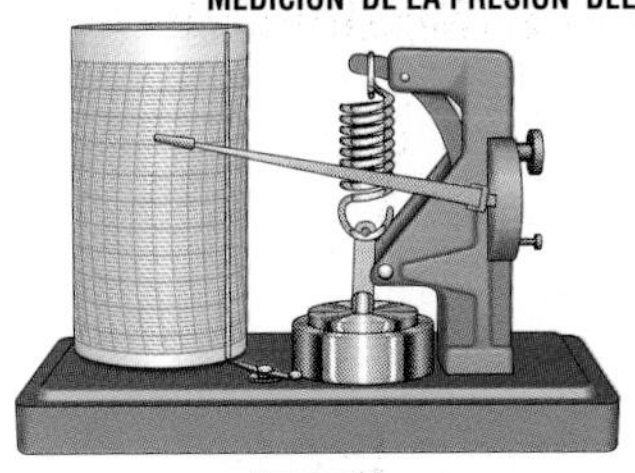

barograph
baromètre[M] enregistreur
Barograph[M]
barógrafo[M]

mercury barometer
baromètre[M] à mercure[M]
Quecksilberbarometer[N]
barómetro[M] de mercurio[M]

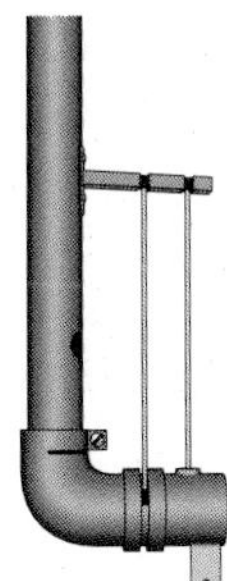

psychrometer
psychromètre[M]
Psychrometer[N]
psicrómetro[M]

## MEASUREMENT OF WIND DIRECTION
## MESURE[F] DE LA DIRECTION[F] DU VENT[M]
## MESSUNG[F] DER WINDRICHTUNG[F]
## MEDICIÓN[F] DE LA DIRECCIÓN[F] DEL VIENTO[M]

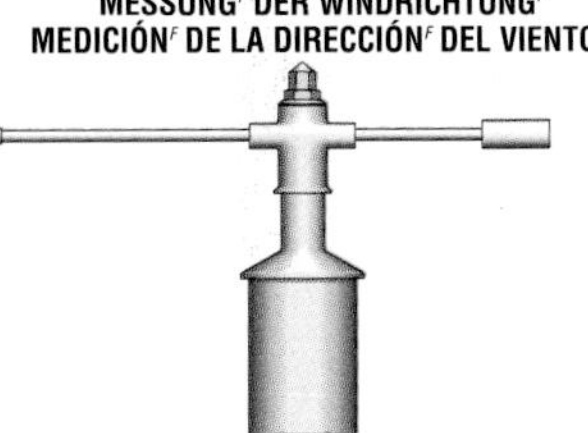

wind vane
girouette[F]
Windfahne[F]
veleta[F]

## MEASUREMENT OF WIND STRENGTH
## MESURE[F] DE LA VITESSE[F] DU VENT[M]
## MESSUNG[F] DER WINDSTÄRKE[F]
## MEDICIÓN[F] DE LA FUERZA[F] DEL VIENTO[M]

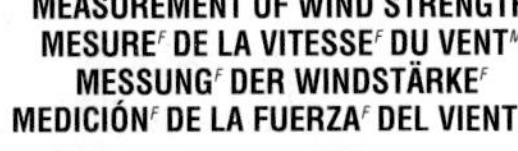
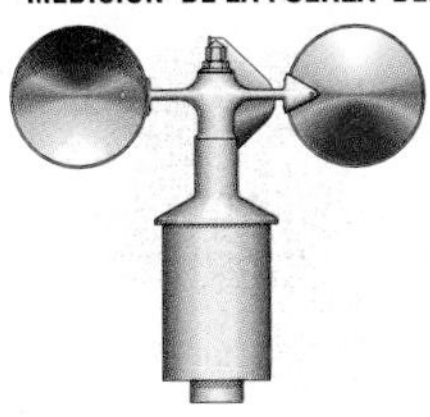

anemometer
anémomètre[M]
Anemometer[N]
anemómetro[M]

## MEASUREMENT OF HUMIDITY
## MESURE[F] DE L'HUMIDITÉ[F]
## MESSUNG[F] DER LUFTFEUCHTIGKEIT[F]
## MEDICIÓN[F] DE LA HUMEDAD[F]

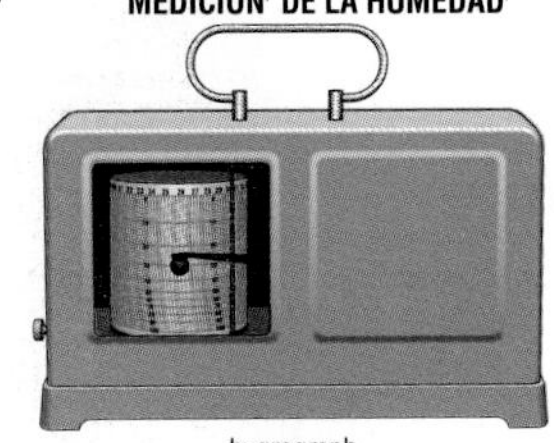

hygrograph
hygromètre[M] enregistreur
Hygrograph[M]
higrógrafo[M]

## MEASUREMENT OF SNOWFALL
## MESURE[F] DE LA NEIGE[F]
## MESSUNG[F] DES SCHNEEFALLS[M]
## MEDICIÓN[F] DE NEVADAS[F]

snow gauge
nivomètre[M]
Schneemesser[M]
nivómetro[M]

## MEASUREMENT OF CLOUD CEILING
## MESURE[F] DE LA HAUTEUR[F] DES NUAGES[M]
## MESSUNG[F] DER WOLKENHÖHE[F]
## MEDICIÓN[F] DE LA ALTURA[F] DE LAS NUBES[F]

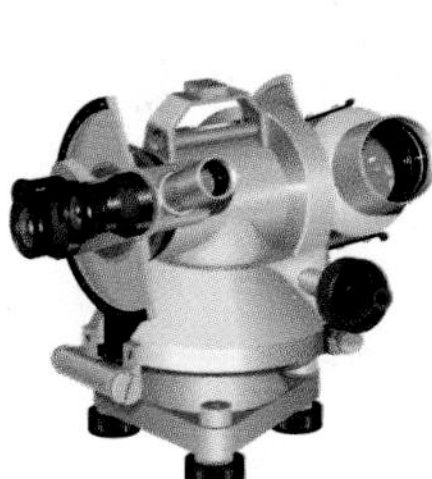

theodolite
théodolite[M]
Theodolit[M]
teodolito[M]

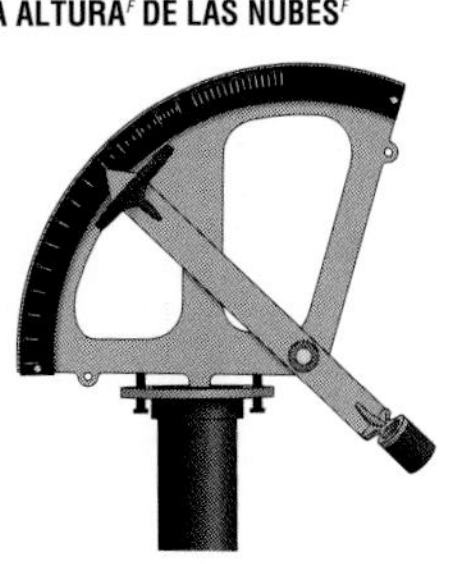

alidade
alidade[F]
Alhidade[F]
alidada[F]

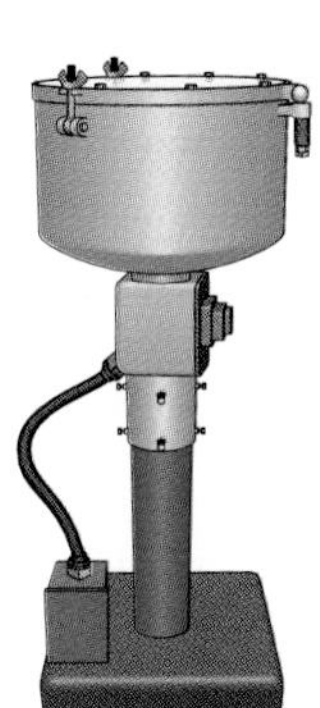

ceiling projector
projecteur[M] de plafond[M]
Wolkenhöhenmesser[M]
proyector[M] de altura[F] máxima

# WEATHER SATELLITE
# SATELLITE[M] MÉTÉOROLOGIQUE
# WETTERSATELLIT[M]
# SATÉLITE[M] METEOROLÓGICO

## GEOSTATIONARY SATELLITE
## SATELLITE[M] GÉOSTATIONNAIRE
## GEOSTATIONÄRER SATELLIT[M]
## SATÉLITE[M] GEOESTACIONARIO

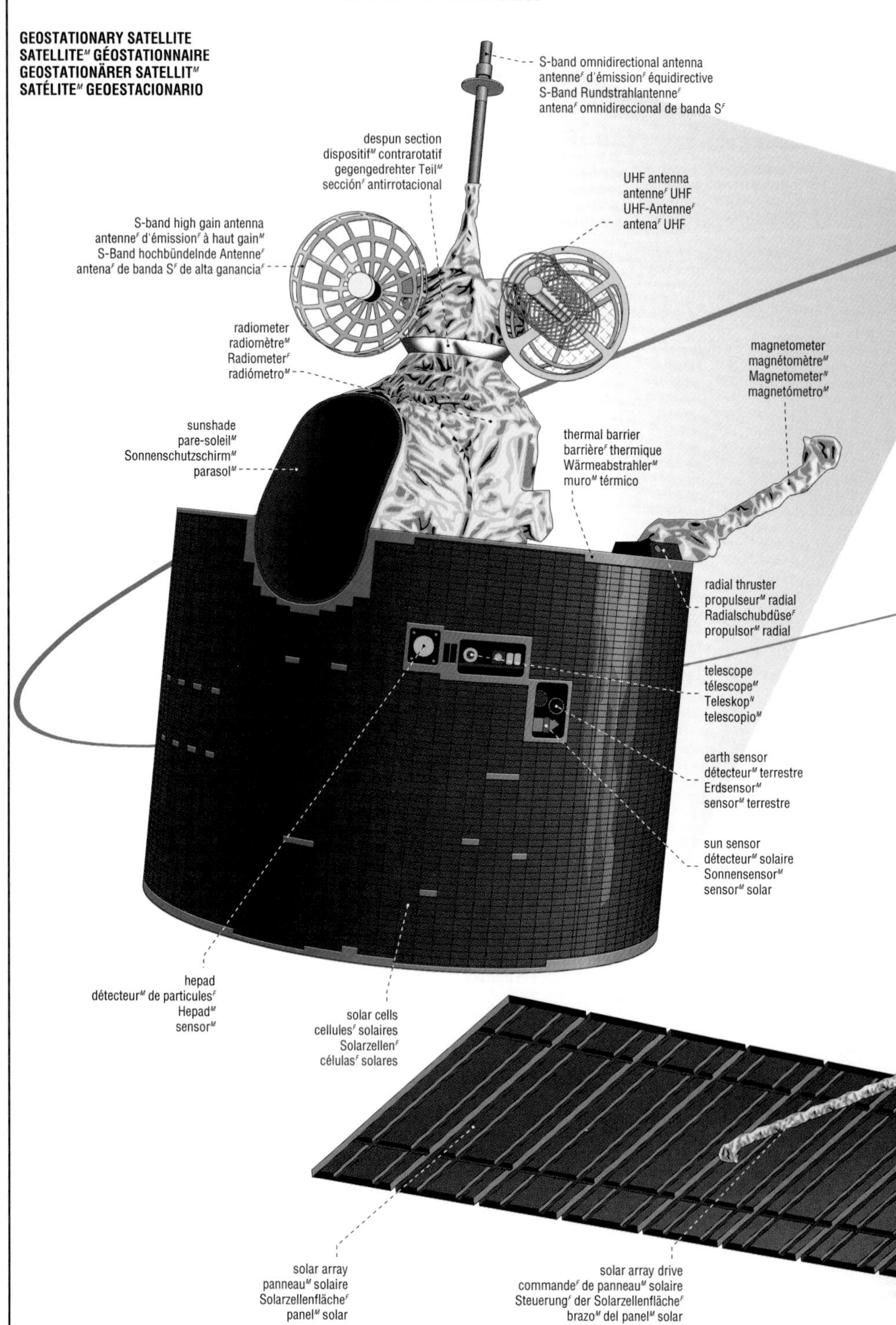

## ORBIT OF THE SATELLITES
## ORBITE^F DES SATELLITES^M
## UMLAUFBAHN^F DER SATELLITEN^M
## ÓRBITA^F DE LOS SATÉLITES^M

## POLAR-ORBITING SATELLITE
## SATELLITE^M À DÉFILEMENT^M
## POLARUMLAUFENDER SATELLIT^M
## SATÉLITE^M DE ÓRBITA^F POLAR

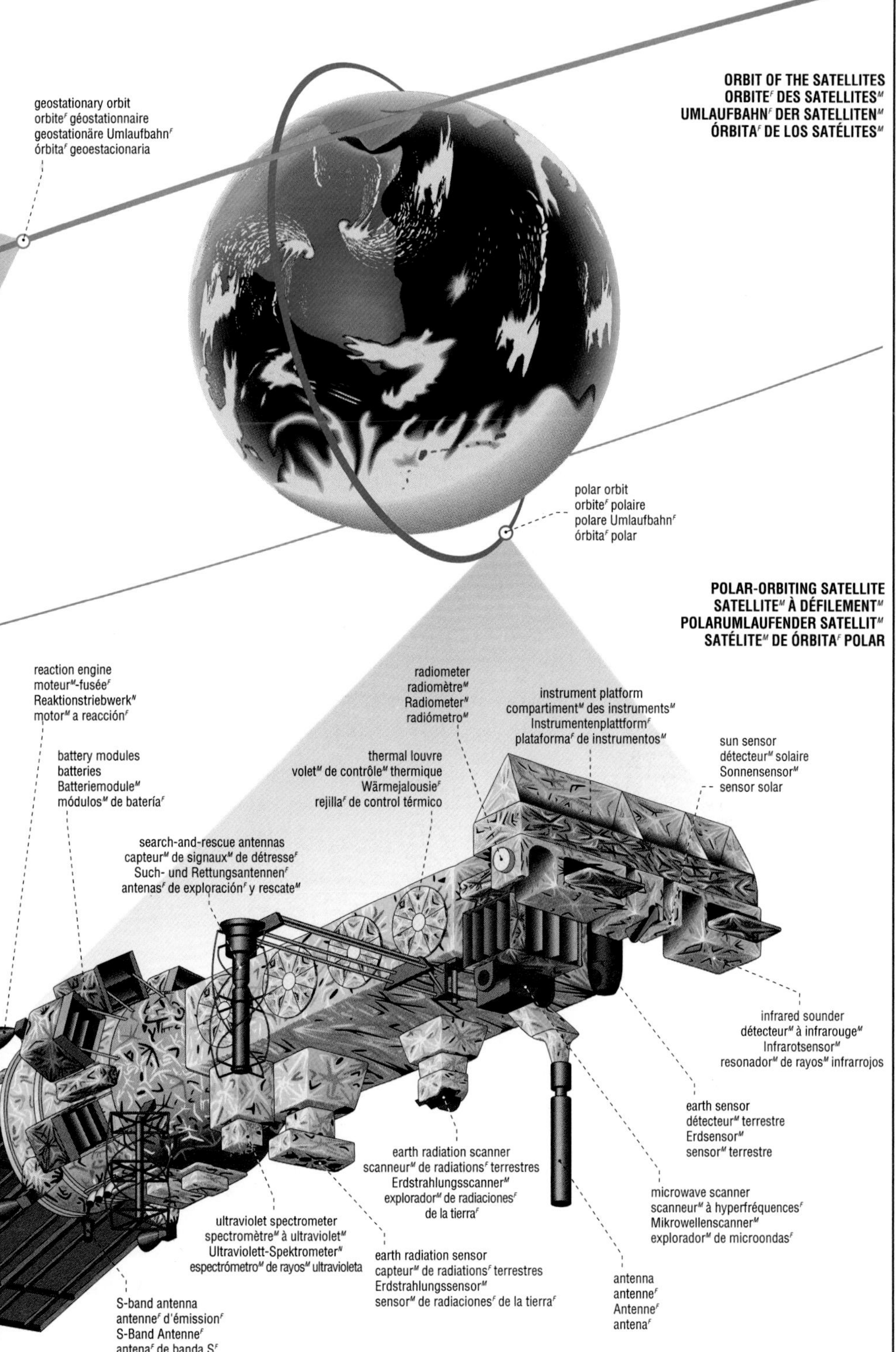

# CLOUDS AND METEOROLOGICAL SYMBOLS
# NUAGES[M] ET SYMBOLES[M] MÉTÉOROLOGIQUES
# WOLKEN[F] UND METEOROLOGISCHE SYMBOLE[N]
# NUBES[F] Y SÍMBOLOS[M] METEOROLÓGICOS

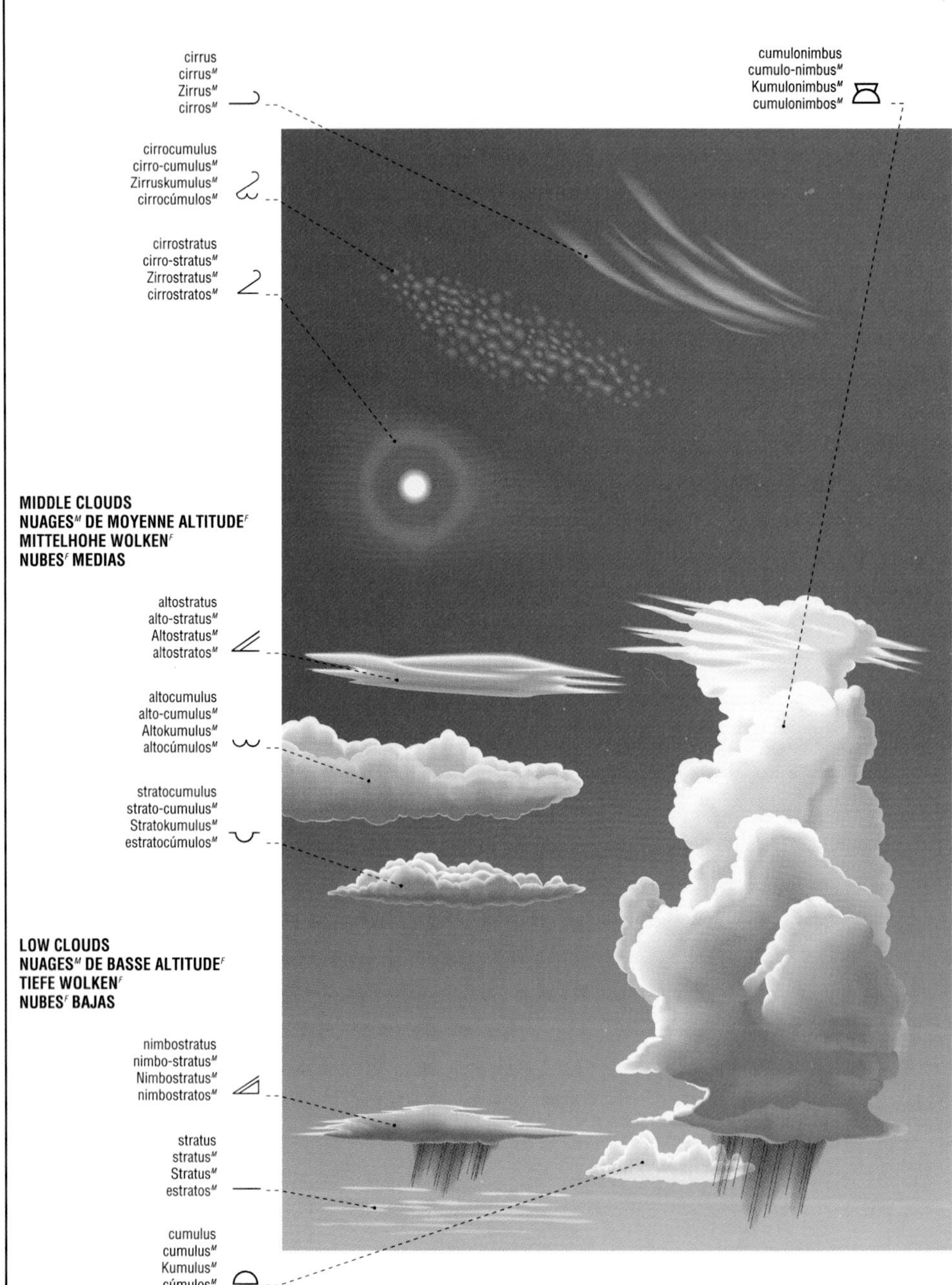

# CLIMATES OF THE WORLD
# CLIMATS[M] DU MONDE[M]
# KLIMATE[N] DER WELT[F]
# CLIMAS[M] DEL MUNDO[M]

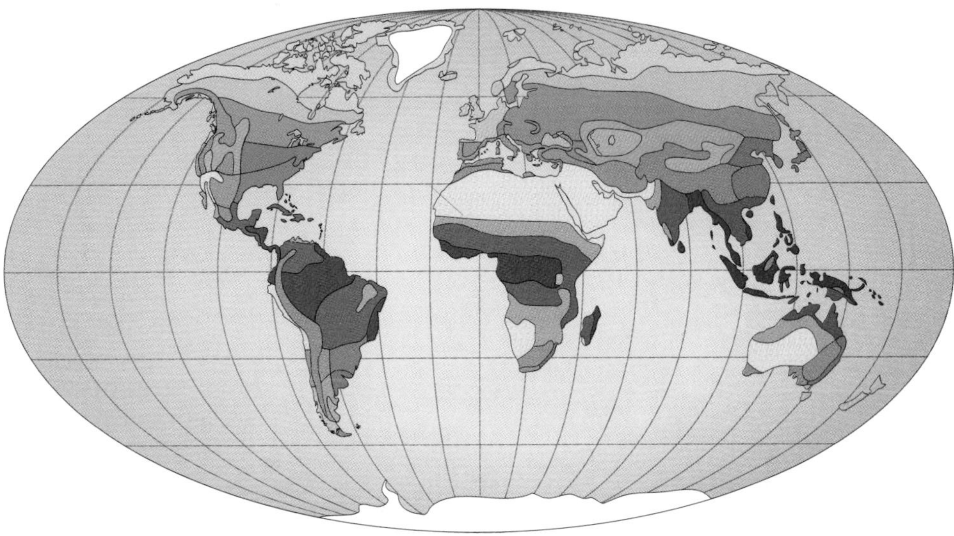

## TROPICAL CLIMATES
## CLIMATS[M] TROPICAUX
## TROPISCHE KLIMATE[N]
## CLIMAS[M] TROPICALES

tropical rain forest
forêt[F] tropicale
tropischer Regenwald[M]
tropical lluvioso

tropical savanna
savane[F]
tropische Savanne[F]
sabana[F]

steppe
steppe[F]
Steppe[F]
estepario

desert
désert[M]
Wüste[F]
desértico

## CONTINENTAL CLIMATES
## CLIMATS[M] CONTINENTAUX
## KONTINENTALKLIMATE[N]
## CLIMAS[M] CONTINENTALES

dry continental - arid
continental aride
kontinental-trocken - trocken
continental seco-árido

dry continental - semiarid
continental semi-aride
kontinental-trocken - halbtrocken
continental seco-semiárido

## TEMPERATE CLIMATES
## CLIMATS[M] TEMPÉRÉS
## GEMÄSSIGTE KLIMATE[N]
## CLIMAS[M] TEMPLADOS

humid - long summer
humide, à été[M] long
feucht - langer Sommer[M]
húmedo de verano[M] largo

humid - short summer
humide, à été[M] court
feucht - kurzer Sommer[M]
húmedo de verano[M] corto

marine
océanique
maritim
marítimo

## SUBTROPICAL CLIMATES
## CLIMATS[M] SUBTROPICAUX
## SUBTROPISCHE KLIMATE[N]
## CLIMAS[M] SUBTROPICALES

Mediterranean subtropical
méditerranéen
mediterrane Subtropen[F]
subtropical mediterráneo

humid subtropical
subtropical humide
feuchte Subtropen[F]
subtropical húmedo

dry subtropical
subtropical sec
trockene Subtropen[F]
subtropical seco

## POLAR CLIMATES
## CLIMATS[M] POLAIRES
## POLARKLIMATE[N]
## CLIMAS[M] POLARES

polar tundra
toundra[F]
Polartundra[F]
tundra[F]

polar ice cap
calotte[F] glaciaire
Eiskappe[F]
hielos[M] perpetuos

## HIGHLAND CLIMATES
## CLIMATS[M] DE MONTAGNE[F]
## HOCHLANDKLIMATE[N]
## CLIMAS[F] DE ALTA MONTAÑA[F]

highland climates
climats[M] de montagne[F]
Hochlandklimate[N]
climas[M] de alta montaña[F]

## SUBARCTIC CLIMATES
## CLIMATS[M] SUBARCTIQUES
## SUBARKTISCHE KLIMATE[N]
## CLIMAS[F] SUBÁRTICOS

subarctic climates
climats[M] subarctiques
subarktische Klimate[N]
climas[M] subárticos

# DESERT
# DÉSERT^M
# WÜSTE^F
# DESIERTO^M

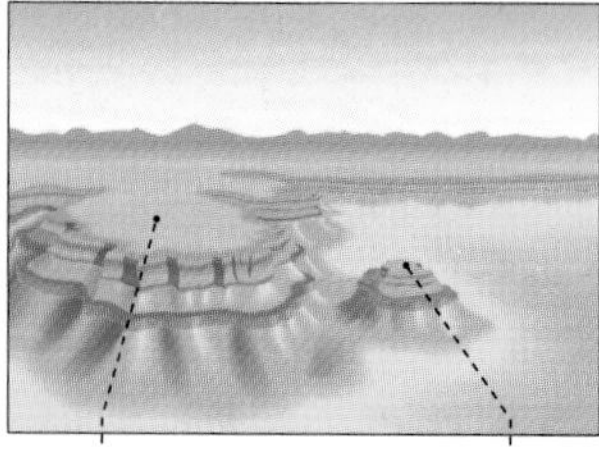

rocky desert
désert^M de pierres^F
Steinwüste^F
desierto^M rocoso

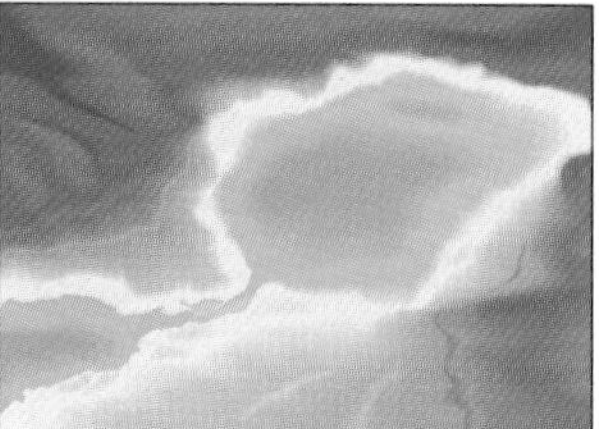

salt lake
lac^M salé
Salzsee^M
laguna^F salada

sandy desert
désert^M de sable^M
Sandwüste^F
desierto^M arenoso

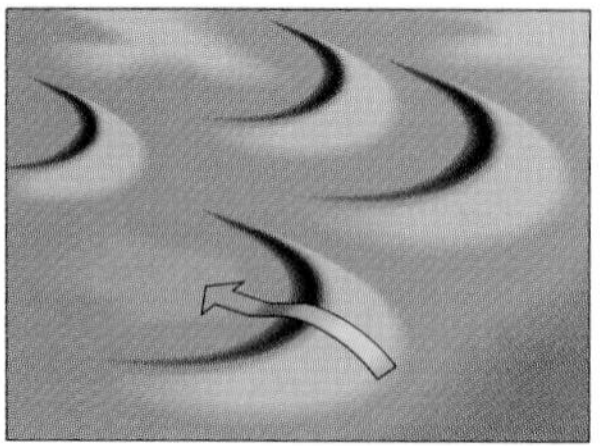

crescentic dune
dune^F en croissant^M
Sicheldüne^F
barjana^F

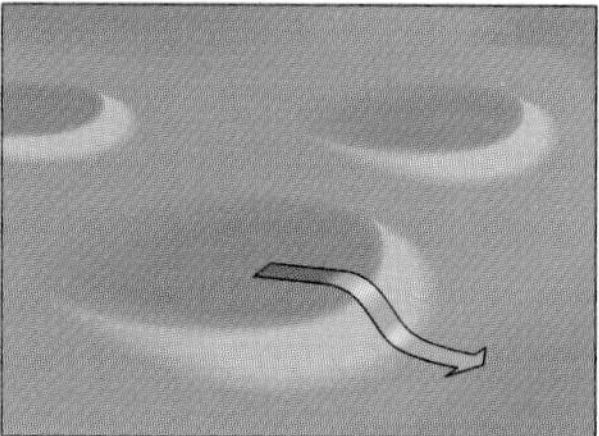

parabolic dune
dune^F parabolique
Parabeldüne^F
duna^F parabólica

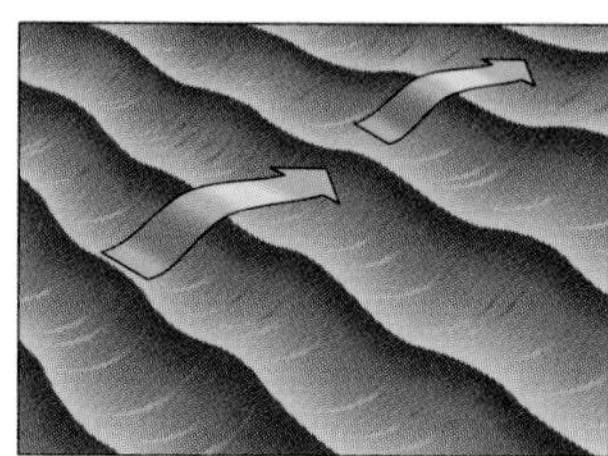

transverse dunes
dunes^F transversales
Querdünen^F
dunas^F paralelas

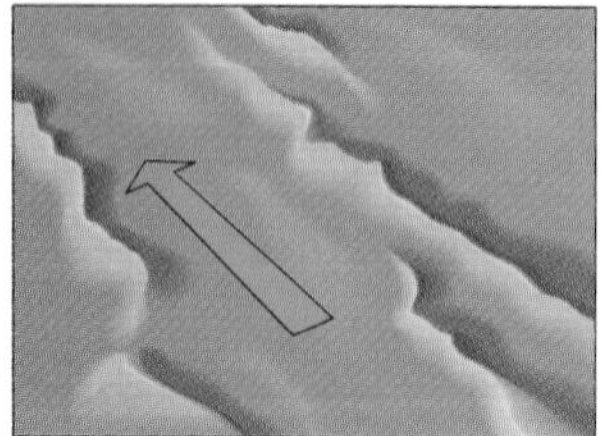

chain of dunes
cordon^M de dunes^F
Dünenzug^M
cadena^F de dunas^F

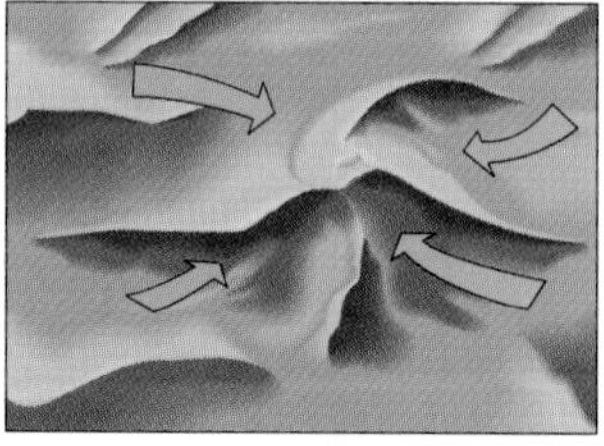

complex dune
dune^F complexe
komplexe Düne^F
duna^F compleja

longitudinal dunes
dunes^F longitudinales
Längsdünen^F
dunas^F longitudinales

# CARTOGRAPHY
# CARTOGRAPHIE[F]
# KARTOGRAPHIE[F]
# CARTOGRAFÍA[F]

## HEMISPHERES
## HÉMISPHÈRES[M]
## HEMISPHÄREN[F]
## HEMISFERIOS[M]

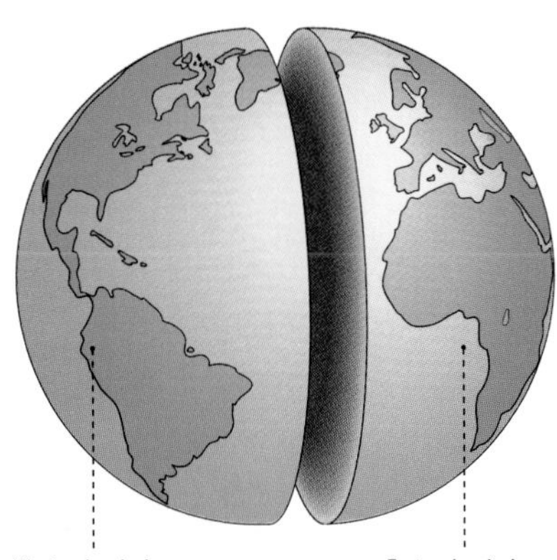


Northern hemisphere
hémisphère[M] Nord
nördliche Hemisphäre[F]
hemisferio[M] Norte

Southern hemisphere
hémisphère[M] Sud
südliche Hemisphäre[F]
hemisferio[M] Sur

## GRID SYSTEM
## DIVISIONS[F] CARTOGRAPHIQUES
## GRADNETZ[N]
## SISTEMA[M] DE REJILLA[F]

**lines of latitude**
**latitude[F]**
**Breitengrade[M]**
**líneas[F] de latitud[F]**

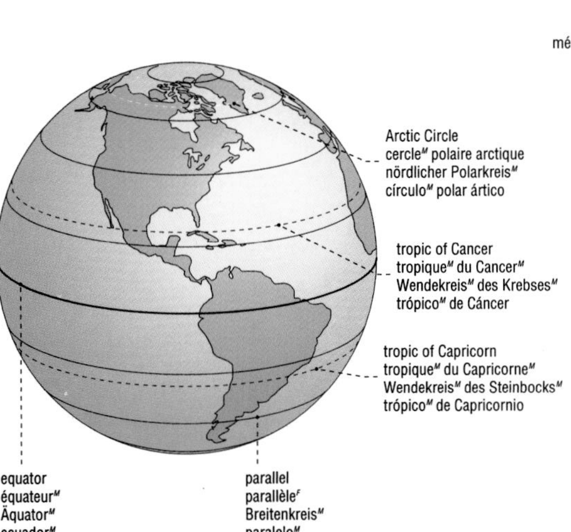


**lines of longitude**
**longitude[F]**
**Längengrade[M]**
**líneas[F] de longitud[F]**

prime meridian
méridien[M] de Greenwich
Nullmeridian[M]
meridiano[M] principal

Western meridian
méridien[M] ouest
westlicher Meridian[M]
meridiano[M] occidental

Eastern meridian
méridien[M] est
östlicher Meridian[M]
meridiano[M] oriental

# REMOTE DETECTION SATELLITE
# SATELLITE$^{M}$ DE TÉLÉDÉTECTION$^{F}$
# ERDERKENNUNGSGEODÄTISCHER SATELLIT$^{M}$
# SATÉLITE$^{M}$ DE DETECCIÓN$^{F}$ A LARGA DISTANCIA$^{F}$

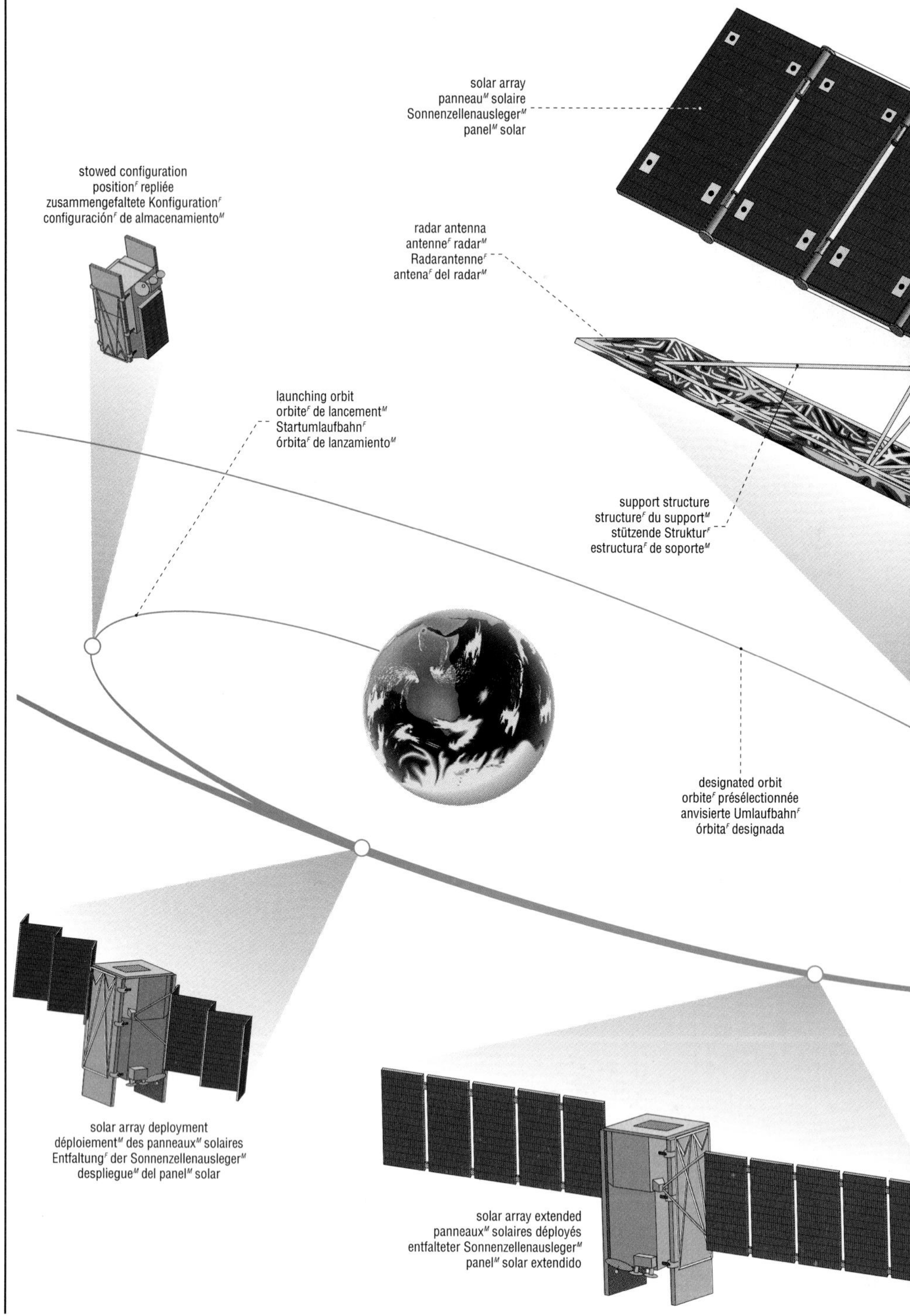

## RADARSAT SATELLITE
## SATELLITE[M] RADARSAT
## RADARSAT[M]
## SATÉLITE[M] RADARSAT

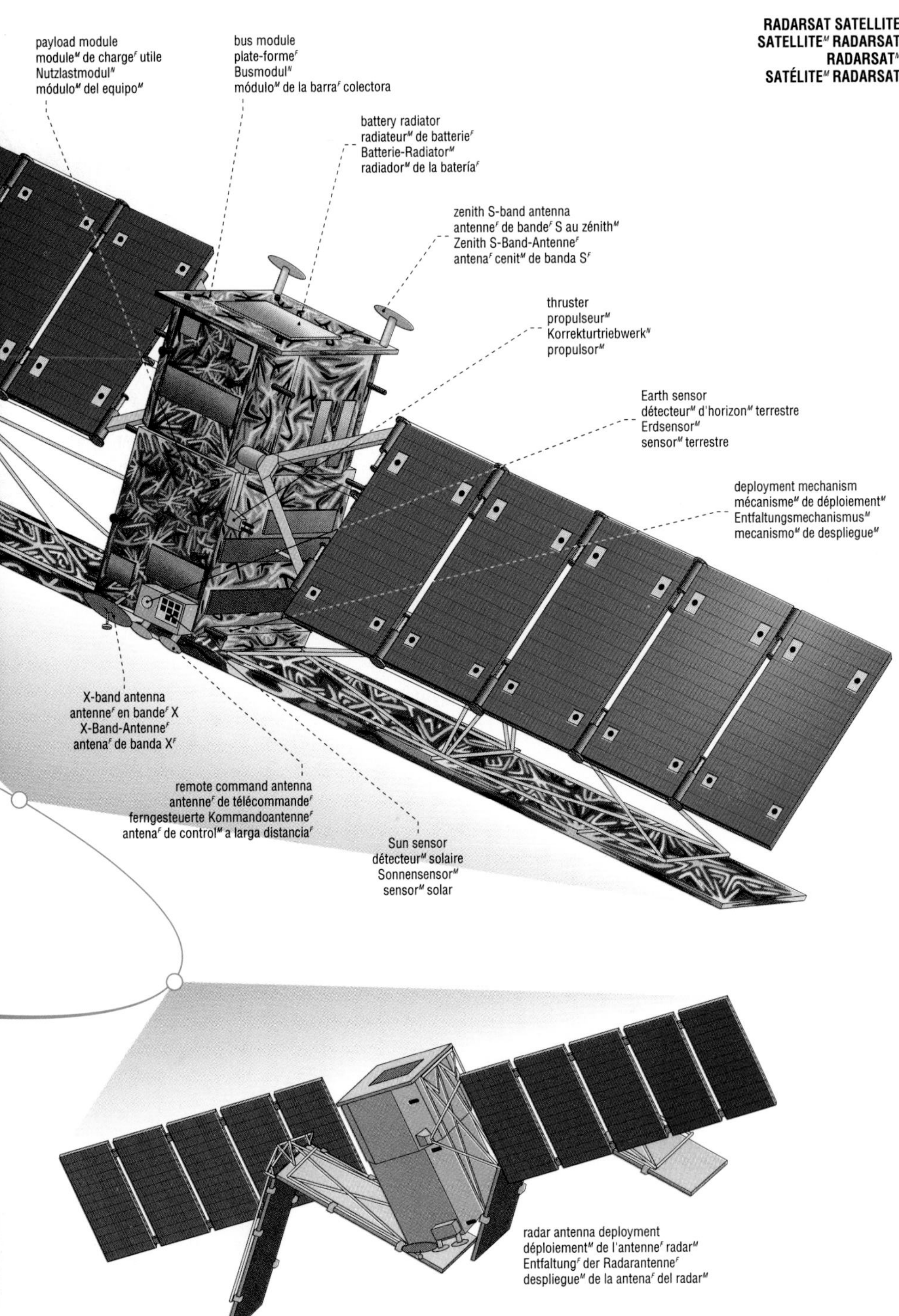

# CARTOGRAPHY
# CARTOGRAPHIE[F]
# KARTOGRAPHIE[F]
# CARTOGRAFÍA[F]

## MAP PROJECTIONS
## PROJECTIONS[F] CARTOGRAPHIQUES
## KARTENNETZENTWÜRFE[M]
## PROYECCIONES[F] DEL MAPA[M]

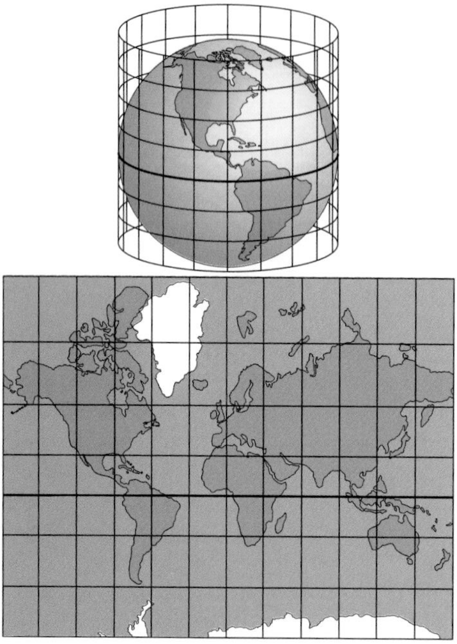

cylindrical projection
projection[F] cylindrique
Zylinderprojektion[F]
proyección[F] cilíndrica

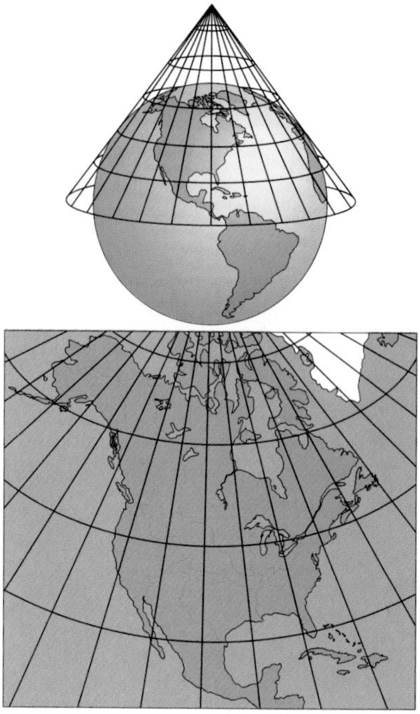

conic projection
projection[F] conique
Kegelprojektion[F]
proyección[F] cónica

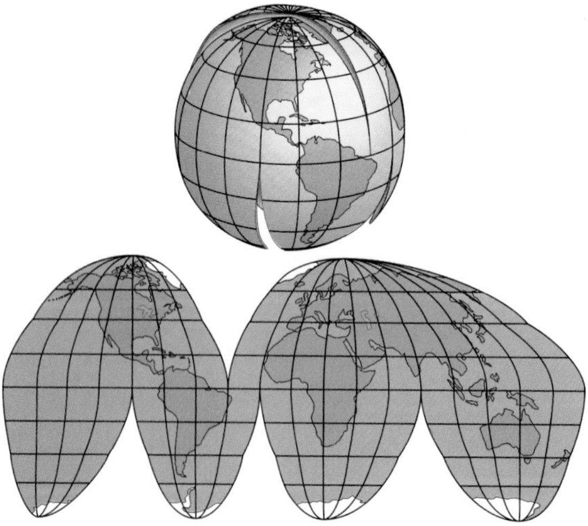

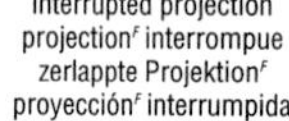

interrupted projection
projection[F] interrompue
zerlappte Projektion[F]
proyección[F] interrumpida

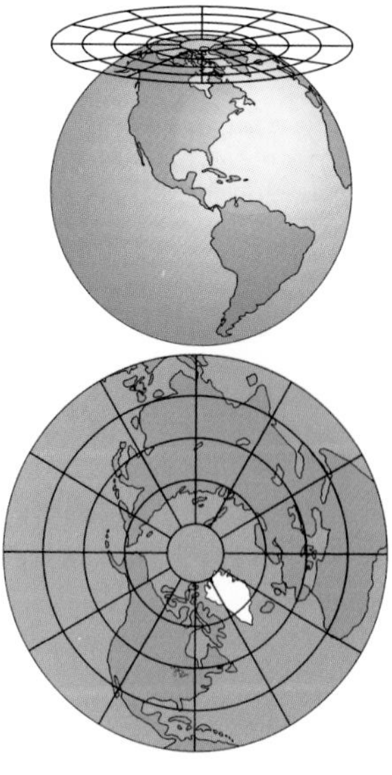

plane projection
projection[F] horizontale
Azimutalprojektion[F]
proyección[F] plana

## POLITICAL MAP
## CARTE$^{F}$ POLITIQUE
## POLITISCHE KARTE$^{F}$
## MAPA$^{M}$ POLÍTICO

internal boundary
division$^{F}$ territoriale
innere Grenze$^{F}$
frontera$^{F}$ interna

province
province$^{F}$
Provinz$^{F}$
provincia$^{F}$

frontier
frontière$^{F}$
Staatsgrenze$^{F}$
frontera$^{F}$ internacional

country
pays$^{M}$
Land$^{N}$
país$^{M}$

city
grande ville$^{F}$
Stadt$^{F}$
ciudad$^{F}$

capital
capitale$^{F}$
Hauptstadt$^{F}$
capital$^{F}$

state
état$^{M}$
Bundesstaat$^{M}$
estado$^{M}$

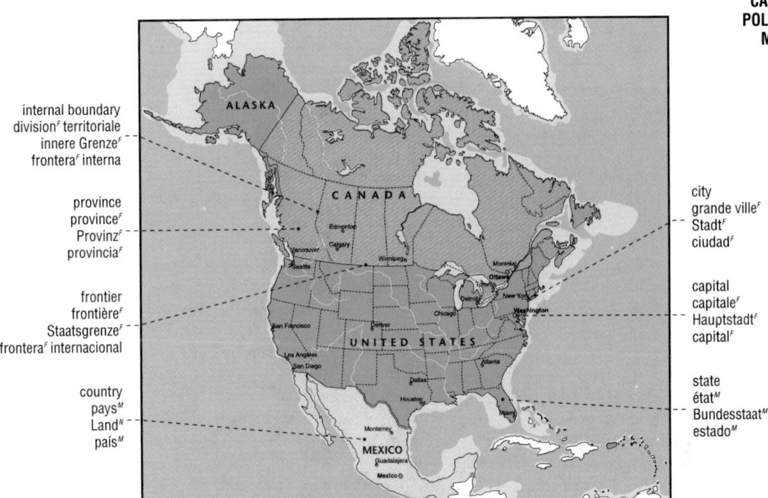

## PHYSICAL MAP
## CARTE$^{F}$ PHYSIQUE
## LANDSCHAFTSKARTE$^{F}$
## MAPA$^{M}$ FÍSICO

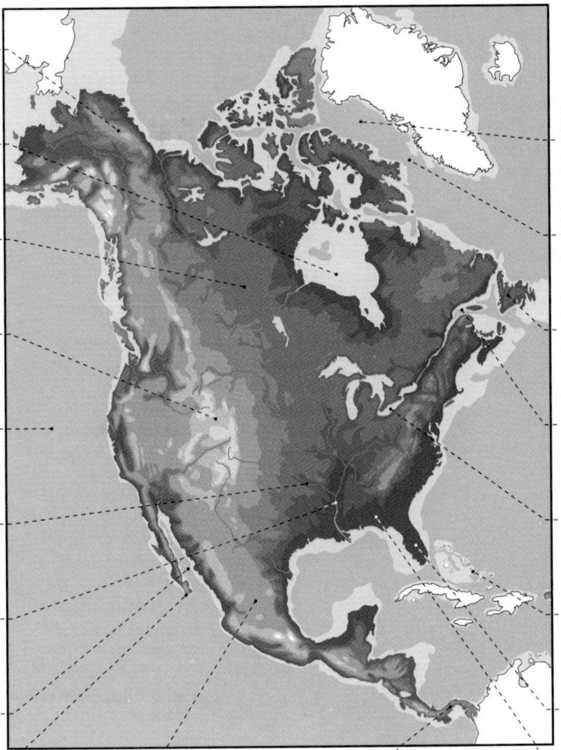

mountain range
chaîne$^{F}$ de montagnes$^{F}$
Gebirgskette$^{F}$
cadena$^{F}$ de montañas$^{F}$

bay
baie$^{F}$
Bucht$^{F}$
bahía$^{F}$

prairie
prairie$^{F}$
Prärie$^{F}$
llanura$^{F}$

massif
massif$^{M}$ montagneux
Gebirgsmasse$^{F}$
conjunto$^{M}$ de montañas$^{F}$

ocean
océan$^{M}$
Ozean$^{M}$
océano$^{M}$

river
rivière$^{F}$
Fluß$^{M}$
río$^{M}$

river
fleuve$^{M}$
Fluß$^{M}$
río$^{M}$

gulf
golfe$^{M}$
Golf$^{M}$
golfo$^{M}$

sea
mer$^{F}$
Meer$^{N}$
mar$^{M}$

strait
détroit$^{M}$
Meerenge$^{F}$
estrecho$^{M}$

island
île$^{F}$
Insel$^{F}$
isla$^{F}$

estuary
estuaire$^{M}$
Flußmündung$^{F}$
estuario$^{M}$

lake
lac$^{M}$
See$^{M}$
lago$^{M}$

archipelago
archipel$^{M}$
Archipel$^{M}$
archipielago$^{M}$

peninsula
péninsule$^{F}$
Halbinsel$^{F}$
península$^{F}$

cape
cap$^{M}$
Kap$^{N}$
cabo$^{M}$

plateau
plateau$^{M}$
Plateau$^{N}$
meseta$^{F}$

isthmus
isthme$^{M}$
Landenge$^{F}$
istmo$^{M}$

plain
plaine$^{F}$
Ebene$^{F}$
planicie$^{F}$

# CARTOGRAPHY
# CARTOGRAPHIE$^{F}$
# KARTOGRAPHIE$^{F}$
# CARTOGRAFÍA$^{F}$

## URBAN MAP
## PLAN$^{M}$ URBAIN
## STADTPLAN$^{M}$
## MAPA$^{M}$ URBANO

suburbs
banlieue$^{F}$
Vororte$^{M}$
suburbios$^{M}$

ring road
boulevard$^{M}$ périphérique
Ringstraße$^{F}$
ruta$^{F}$ circular

avenue
avenue$^{F}$
Allee$^{F}$
avenida$^{F}$

city boundary
limite$^{F}$ de la ville$^{F}$
Stadtgrenze$^{F}$
límite$^{M}$ de la ciudad$^{F}$

park
parc$^{M}$
Park$^{M}$
parque$^{M}$

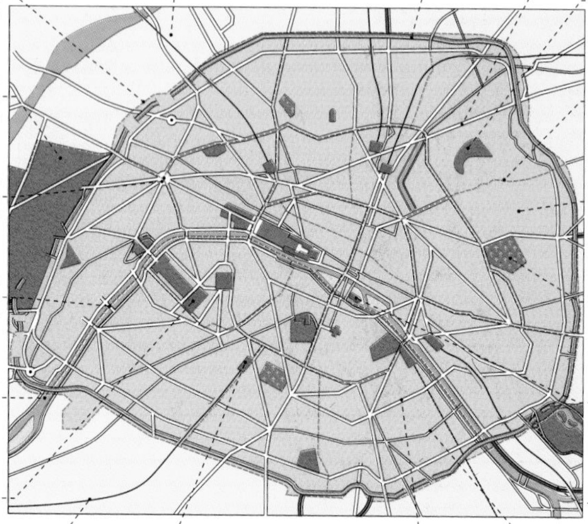

woods
bois$^{M}$
Wald$^{M}$
bosques$^{M}$

district boundary
limite$^{F}$ d'arrondissement$^{M}$
Stadtteilgrenze$^{F}$
límite$^{M}$ de distrito$^{M}$

roundabout
rond-point$^{M}$
Kreisverkehr$^{M}$
rotonda$^{F}$

district
arrondissement$^{M}$
Stadtteil$^{M}$
distrito$^{M}$

bridge
pont$^{M}$
Brücke$^{F}$
puente$^{M}$

cemetery
cimetière$^{M}$
Friedhof$^{M}$
cementerio$^{M}$

river
fleuve$^{M}$
Fluß$^{M}$
río$^{M}$

monument
monument$^{M}$
Denkmal$^{N}$
monumento$^{M}$

public building
édifice$^{M}$ public
öffentliches Gebäude$^{N}$
edificio$^{M}$ público

motorway
autoroute$^{F}$
Autobahn$^{F}$
autopista$^{F}$

railway
chemin$^{M}$ de fer$^{M}$
Eisenbahn$^{F}$
línea$^{F}$ férrea

railway station
gare$^{F}$
Bahnhof$^{M}$
estación$^{F}$ del ferrocarril$^{M}$

boulevard
boulevard$^{M}$
Boulevard$^{M}$
bulevar$^{M}$

street
rue$^{F}$
Straße$^{F}$
calle$^{F}$

## ROAD MAP
## CARTE$^{F}$ ROUTIÈRE
## STRASSENKARTE$^{F}$
## MAPA$^{M}$ DE CARRETERAS$^{F}$

motorway
autoroute$^{F}$
Autobahn$^{F}$
autopista$^{F}$

road
route$^{F}$
Straße$^{F}$
carretera$^{F}$

motorway number
numéro$^{M}$ d'autoroute$^{F}$
Autobahnnummer$^{F}$
número$^{M}$ de la autopista$^{F}$

road number
numéro$^{M}$ de route$^{F}$
Straßennummer$^{F}$
número$^{M}$ de la carretera$^{F}$

rest area
aire$^{F}$ de repos$^{M}$
Rastplatz$^{M}$
área$^{F}$ de descanso$^{M}$

airport
aéroport$^{M}$
Flughafen$^{M}$
aeropuerto$^{M}$

service area
aire$^{F}$ de service$^{M}$
Raststätte$^{F}$
área$^{F}$ de servicio$^{M}$

point of interest
curiosité$^{F}$
Sehenswürdigkeit$^{F}$
punto$^{M}$ de interés

ring motorway
autoroute$^{F}$ de ceinture$^{F}$
Umgehungsstraße$^{F}$
carretera$^{F}$ de circunvalación$^{F}$

national park
parc$^{M}$ national
Nationalpark$^{M}$
parque$^{M}$ nacional

secondary road
route$^{F}$ secondaire
Nebenstraße$^{F}$
carretera$^{F}$ secundaria

scenic route
parcours$^{M}$ pittoresque
landschaftlich schöne Strecke$^{F}$
ruta$^{F}$ pintoresca

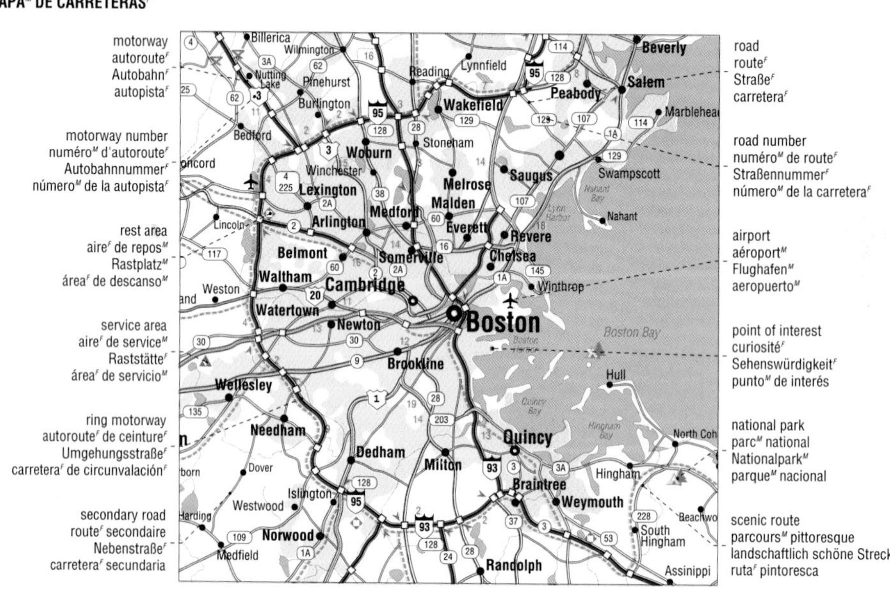

PLANT KINGDOM
RÈGNE VÉGÉTAL

PFLANZENREICH
REINO VEGETAL

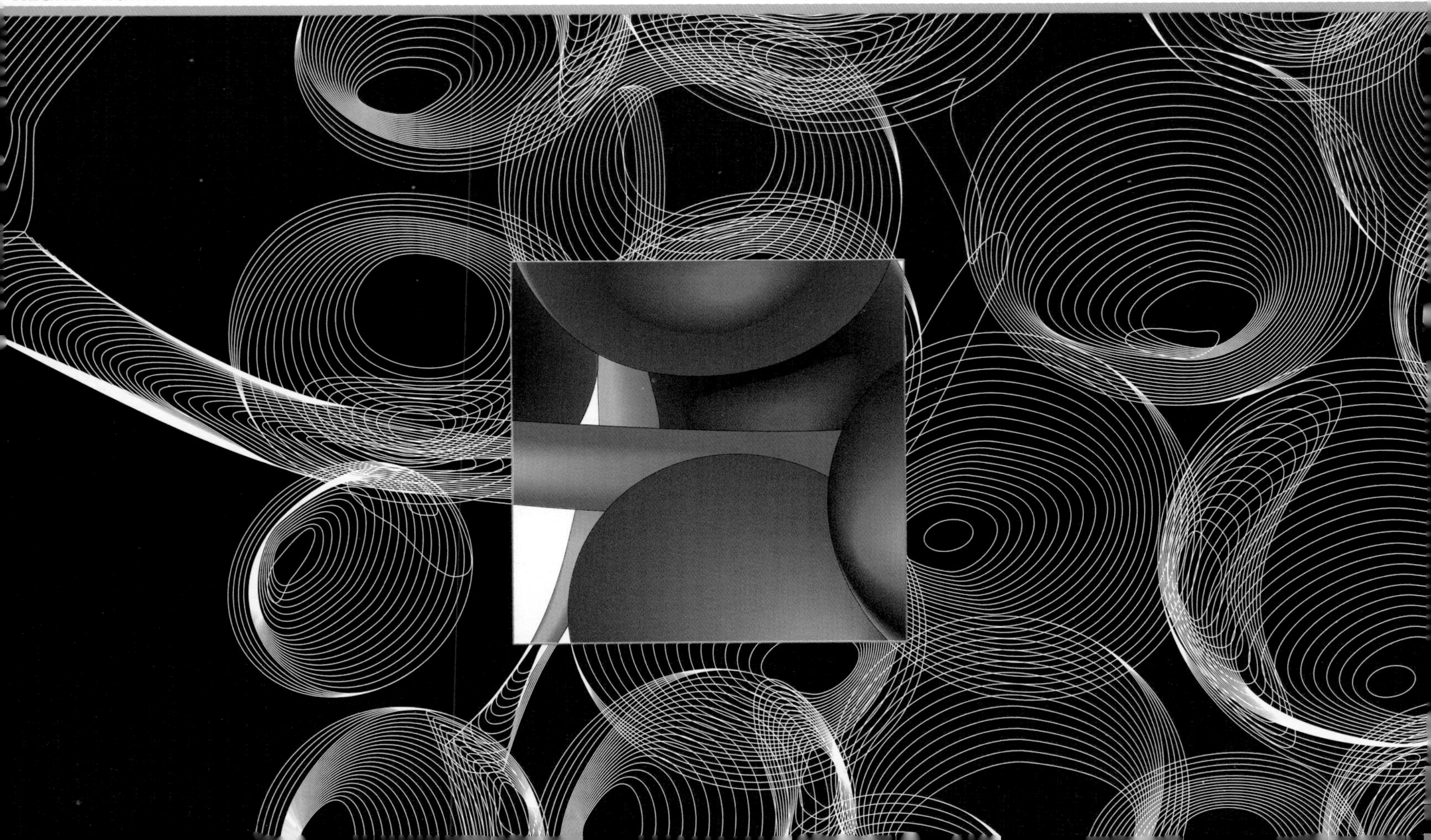

## SUMMARY

MUSHROOM ........ 55
TYPES OF LEAF ........ 56
STRUCTURE OF A PLANT ........ 57
CONIFER ........ 58
STRUCTURE OF A TREE ........ 59
STRUCTURE OF A FLOWER ........ 60
GRAPE ........ 61
FLESHY FRUITS: BERRY FRUITS ........ 62
FLESHY STONE FRUITS ........ 63
FLESHY POMES ........ 64
FLESHY FRUITS: CITRUS FRUITS ........ 65
DRY FRUITS: NUTS ........ 66
VARIOUS DRY FRUITS ........ 67
TROPICAL FRUITS ........ 68
VEGETABLES ........ 69
HERBS ........ 74

# MUSHROOM
# CHAMPIGNON[M]
# PILZ[M]
# HONGO[M]

## STRUCTURE OF A MUSHROOM
## STRUCTURE[F] D'UN CHAMPIGNON[M]
## AUFBAU[M] EINES PILZES[M]
## ANATOMÍA[F] DE UN HONGO[M]

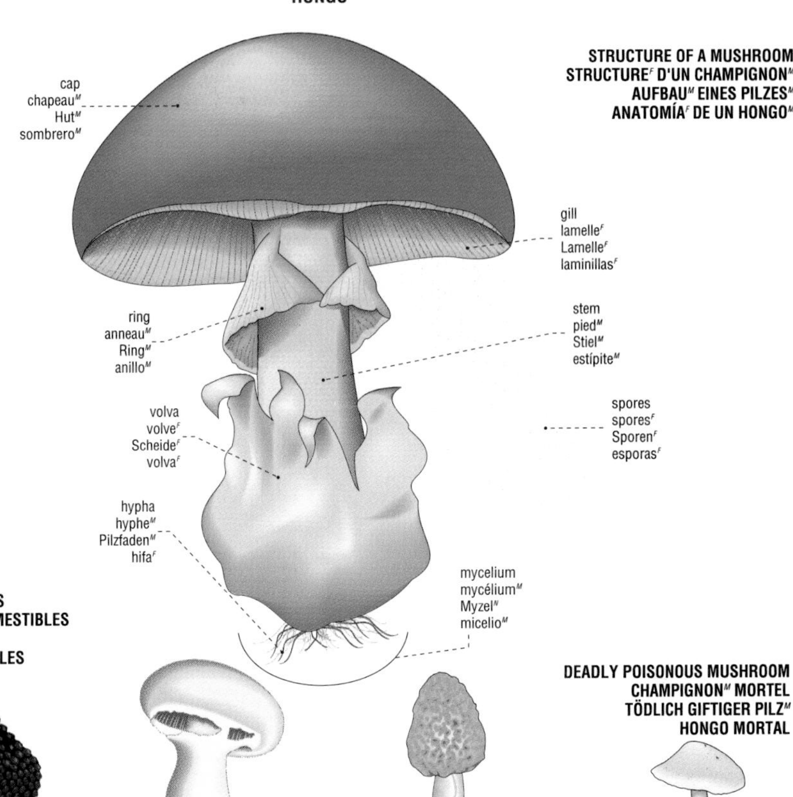


## EDIBLE MUSHROOMS
## CHAMPIGNONS[M] COMESTIBLES
## SPEISEPILZE[M]
## HONGOS[M] COMESTIBLES

truffle
truffe[F]
Trüffel[F]
trufa[F]

cultivated mushroom
champignon[M] de couche[F]
Zuchtchampignon[M]
champiñón[M] (Agaricus campestris)

morel
morille[F]
Morchel[M]
morilla[F] (Morchella esculenta)

royal agaric
oronge[F] vraie
Kaiserling[M]
amanita[F] real

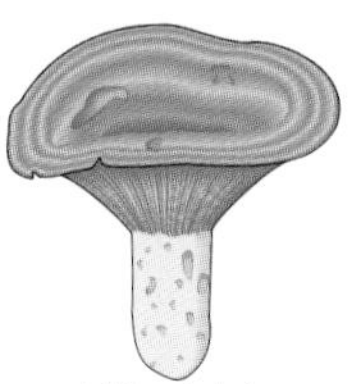

delicious lactarius
lactaire[M] délicieux
echter Reizker[M]
mízcalo[M] (Lactarius deliciosus)

green russula
russule[F] verdoyante
grasgrüner Täubling[M]
gorroverde[M]

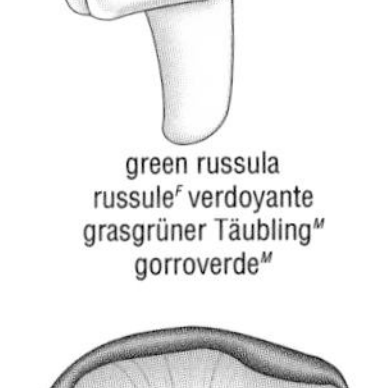

chanterelle
chanterelle[F] commune
Pfifferling[M]
cantarela[F]

boletus
cèpe[M]
Steinpilz[M]
boleto[M]

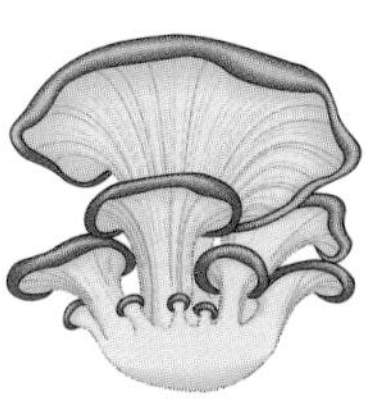

oyster mushroom
pleurote[M] en huître[F]
Austernseitling[M]
sabañón[M]

## DEADLY POISONOUS MUSHROOM
## CHAMPIGNON[M] MORTEL
## TÖDLICH GIFTIGER PILZ[M]
## HONGO MORTAL

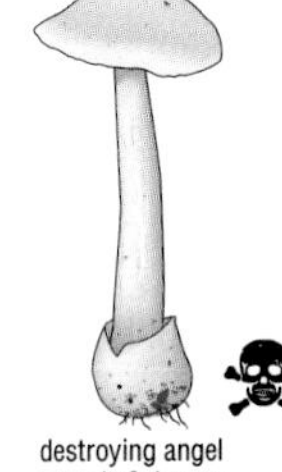

destroying angel
amanite[F] vireuse
Knollenblätterpilz[M]
ángel[M] de la muerte[F]

## POISONOUS MUSHROOM
## CHAMPIGNON[M] VÉNÉNEUX
## GIFTPILZ[M]
## HONGO[M] VENENOSO

fly agaric
fausse oronge[F]
Fliegenpilz[M]
amanita[F] de las moscas[F]

## TYPES OF LEAF
## TYPES^M DE FEUILLES^F
## BLATTFORMEN^F
## LA HOJA^F SEGÚN SU LIMBO^M

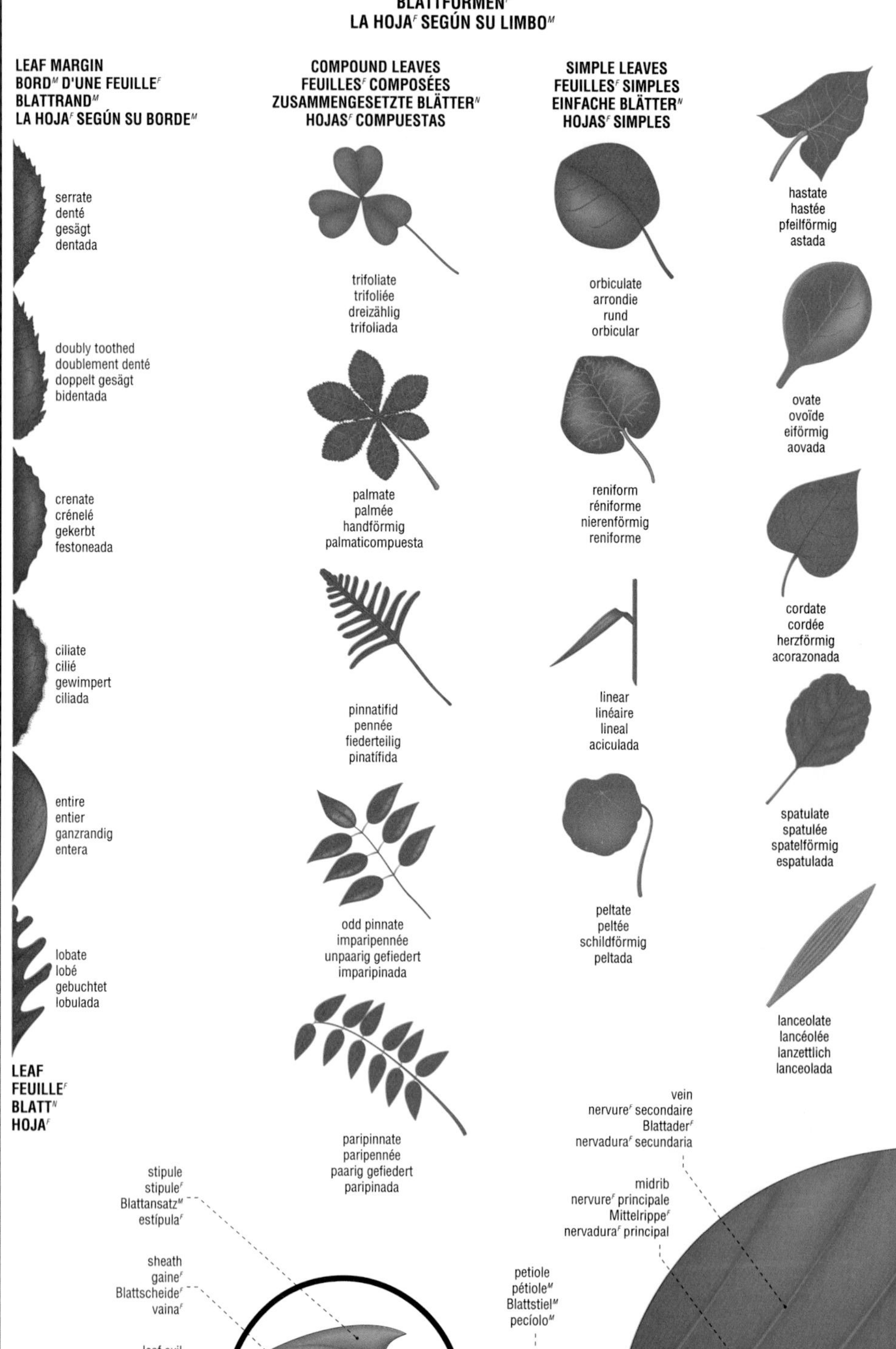

# STRUCTURE OF A PLANT
# STRUCTURE[F] D'UNE PLANTE[F]
# AUFBAU[M] EINER PFLANZE[F]
# ANATOMÍA[F] DE UNA PLANTA[F]

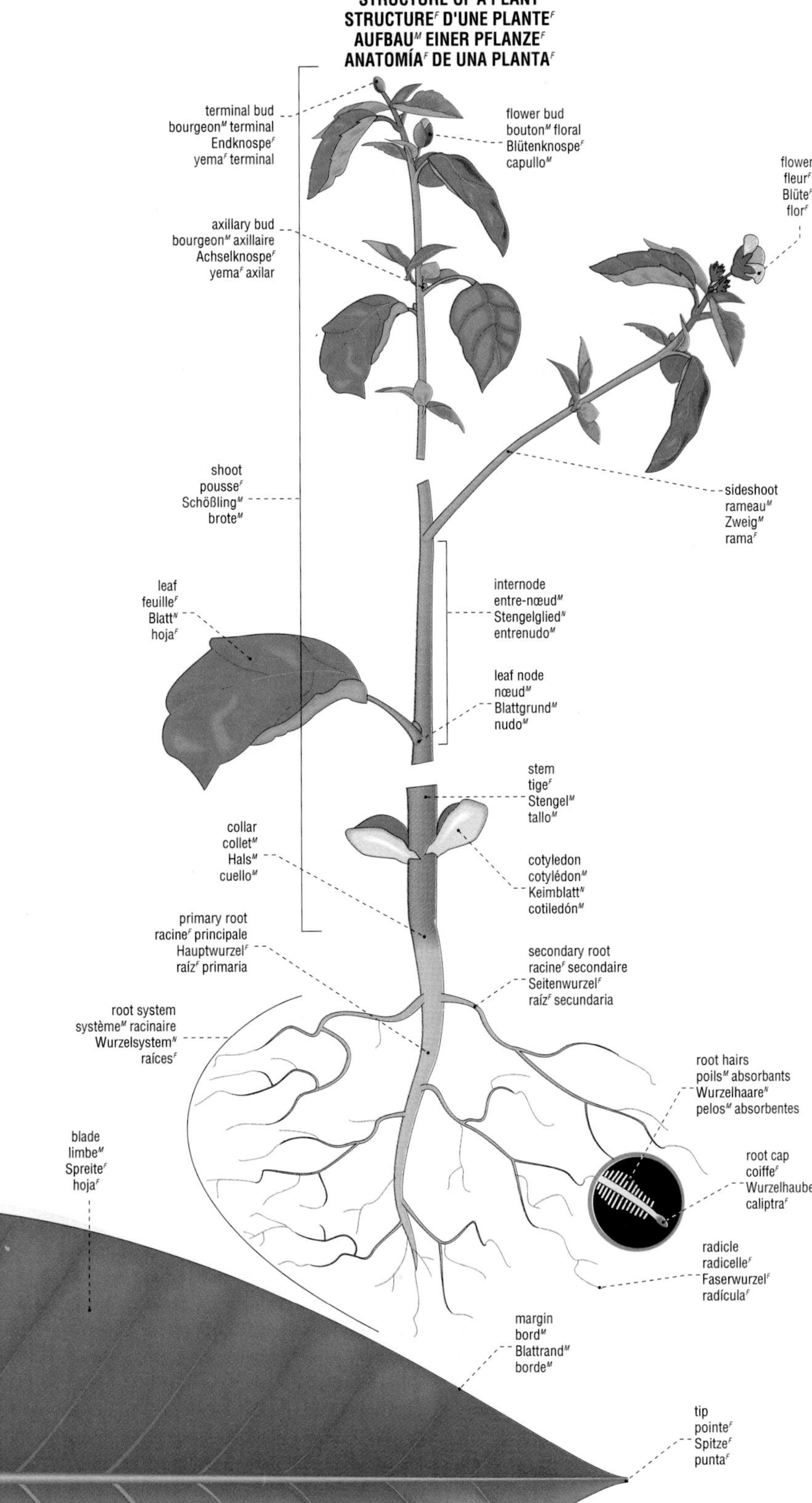

# CONIFER
# CONIFÈRE[M]
# NADELBAUM[M]
# CONÍFERA[F]

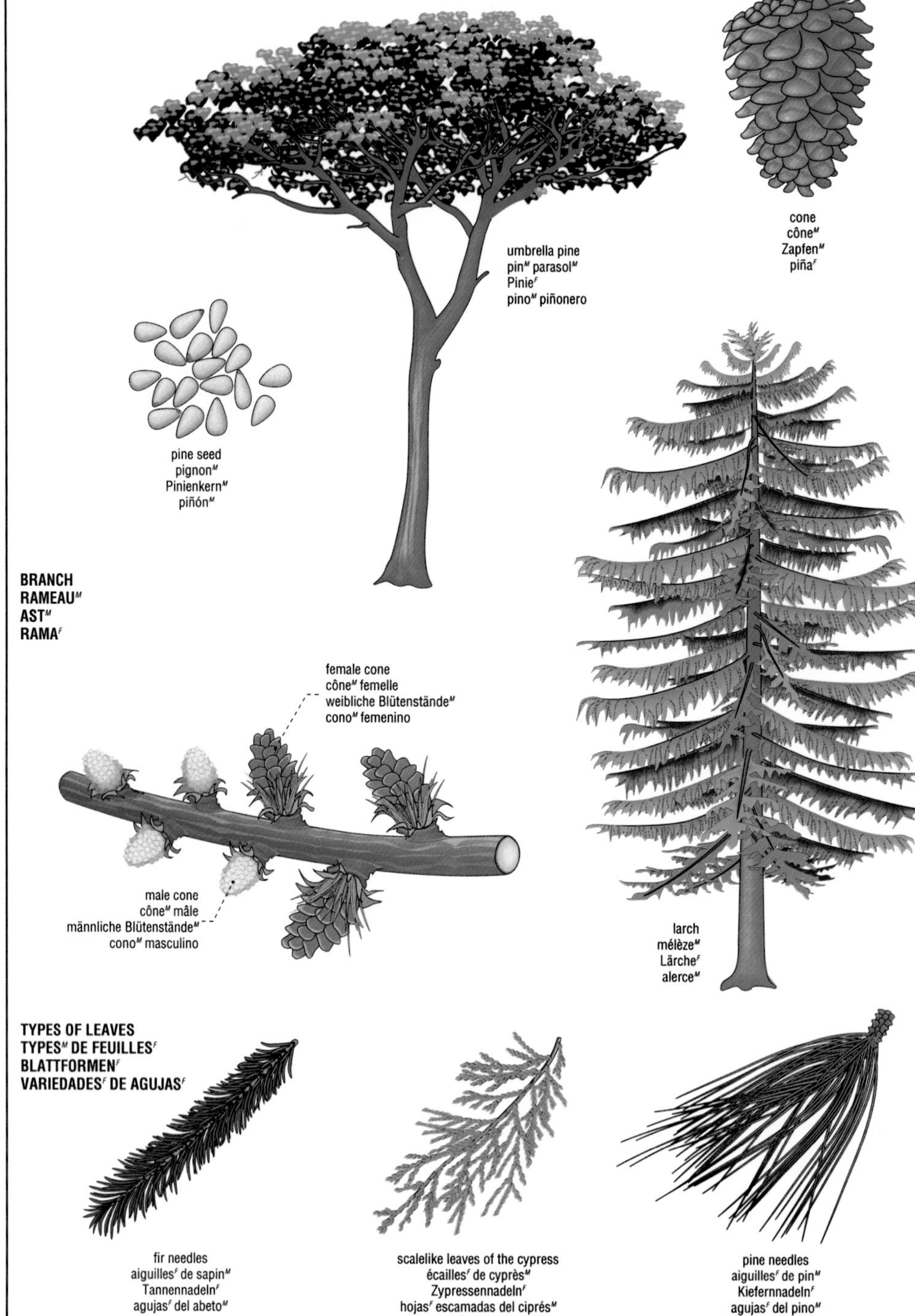

## STRUCTURE OF A TREE
## STRUCTURE[F] D'UN ARBRE[M]
## AUFBAU[M] EINES BAUMES[M]
## ANATOMÍA[F] DE UN ÁRBOL[M]

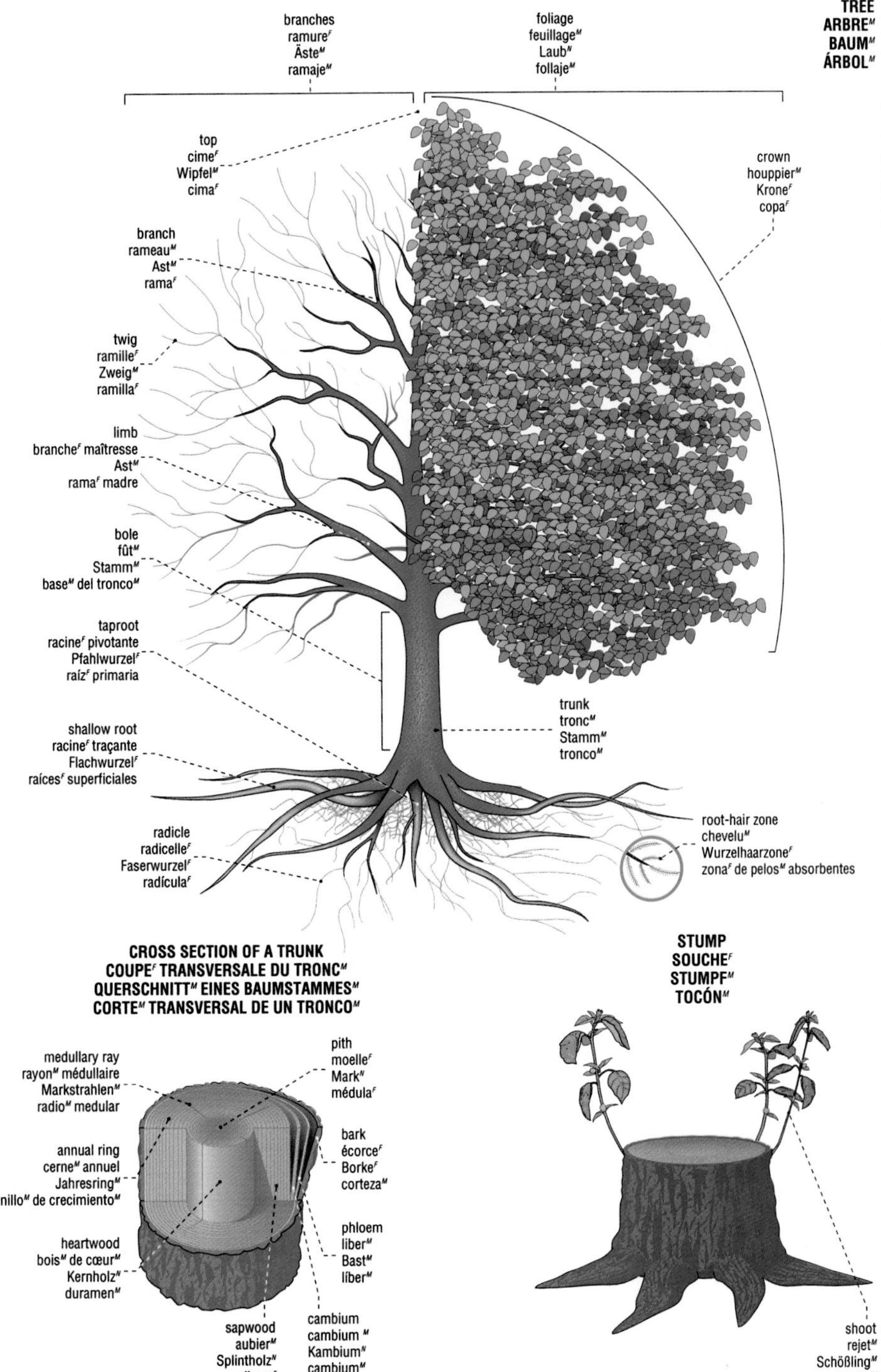

## STRUCTURE OF A FLOWER
## STRUCTURE[F] D'UNE FLEUR[F]
## AUFBAU[M] EINER BLÜTE[F]
## ANATOMÍA[F] DE UNA FLOR[F]

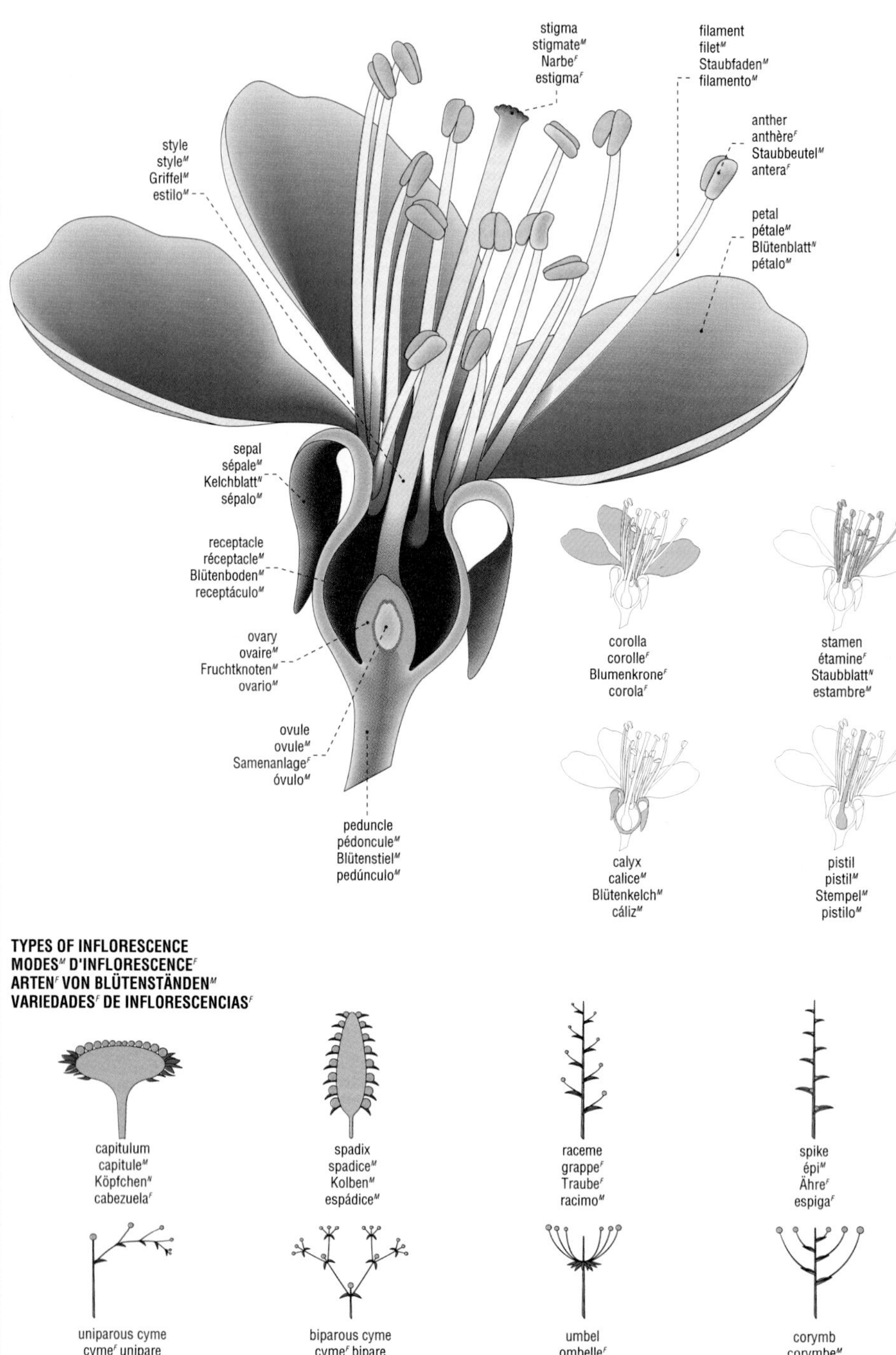

# GRAPE
# VIGNE$^{F}$
# REBE$^{F}$
# UVA$^{F}$

## STEPS TO RIPENESS
## ÉTAPES$^{F}$ DE MATURATION$^{F}$
## STUFEN$^{F}$ DER REIFE$^{F}$
## ETAPAS$^{F}$ DE LA MADURACIÓN$^{F}$

flowering
floraison$^{F}$
Blüte$^{F}$
en flor$^{F}$

fruiting
nouaison$^{F}$
Fruchtbildung$^{F}$
fructificación$^{F}$

ripening
véraison$^{F}$
Reifeprozeß$^{M}$
proceso$^{M}$ de maduración$^{F}$

ripeness
maturité$^{F}$
Vollreife$^{F}$
maduración$^{F}$ completa

## VINE STOCK
## CEP$^{M}$ DE VIGNE$^{F}$
## REBSTOCK$^{M}$
## SARMIENTO$^{M}$

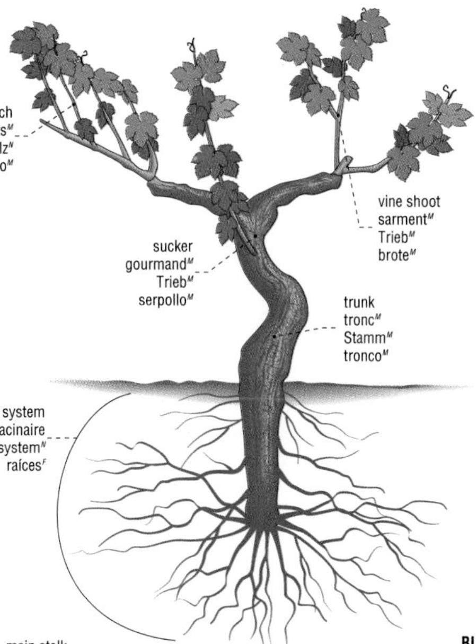

fruit branch
branche$^{F}$ à fruits$^{M}$
Fruchtholz$^{N}$
rama$^{F}$ con fruto$^{M}$

vine shoot
sarment$^{M}$
Trieb$^{M}$
brote$^{M}$

sucker
gourmand$^{M}$
Trieb$^{M}$
serpollo$^{M}$

trunk
tronc$^{M}$
Stamm$^{M}$
tronco$^{M}$

root system
système$^{M}$ racinaire
Wurzelsystem$^{N}$
raíces$^{F}$

## BUNCH OF GRAPES
## GRAPPE$^{F}$ DE RAISINS$^{M}$
## TRAUBE$^{F}$
## RACIMO$^{M}$ DE UVAS$^{F}$

main stalk
axe$^{M}$ principal
Hauptstiel$^{M}$
tallo$^{M}$ principal

tendril
vrille$^{F}$
Weinranke$^{F}$
zarcillo$^{M}$

peduncle
pédoncule$^{M}$
Blütenstiel$^{M}$
pedúnculo$^{M}$

branch
rameau$^{M}$
Fruchtholz$^{N}$
ramificación$^{F}$

grape
raisin$^{M}$
Weintraube$^{F}$
uva$^{F}$

## VINE LEAF
## FEUILLE$^{F}$ DE VIGNE$^{F}$
## WEINBLATT$^{N}$
## HOJA$^{F}$ DE LA VID$^{F}$

terminal lobe
lobe$^{M}$ terminal
Endlappen$^{M}$
lóbulo$^{M}$ terminal

upper lateral sinus
sinus$^{M}$ latéral supérieur
oberer seitlicher Einschnitt$^{M}$
seno$^{M}$ lateral superior

upper lateral lobe
lobe$^{M}$ latéral supérieur
oberer seitlicher Lappen$^{M}$
lóbulo$^{M}$ lateral superior

lower lateral sinus
sinus$^{M}$ latéral inférieur
unterer seitlicher Einschnitt$^{M}$
seno$^{M}$ lateral inferior

petiolar sinus
sinus$^{M}$ pétiolaire
Blattstieleinschnitt$^{M}$
seno$^{M}$ del pecíolo$^{M}$

lower lateral lobe
lobe$^{M}$ latéral inférieur
unterer seitlicher Lappen$^{M}$
lóbulo$^{M}$ lateral inferior

# FLESHY FRUITS: BERRY FRUITS
# FRUITS[M] CHARNUS: BAIES[F]
# FLEISCHIGE FRÜCHTE[F]: BEERENOBST[N]
# FRUTOS[M] CARNOSOS: BAYAS[F]

## SECTION OF A BERRY
## COUPE[F] D'UNE BAIE[F]
## QUERSCHNITT[M] EINER BEERE[F]
## CORTE[M] DE UNA BAYA[F]

**GRAPE**
**RAISIN[M]**
**WEINTRAUBE[F]**
**UVA[F]**

**popular terms**
**termes[M] familiers**
**gebräuchliche Bezeichnungen[F]**
**términos familiares**

**scientific terms**
**termes[M] techniques**
**wissenschaftliche Bezeichnungen[F]**
**términos técnicos**

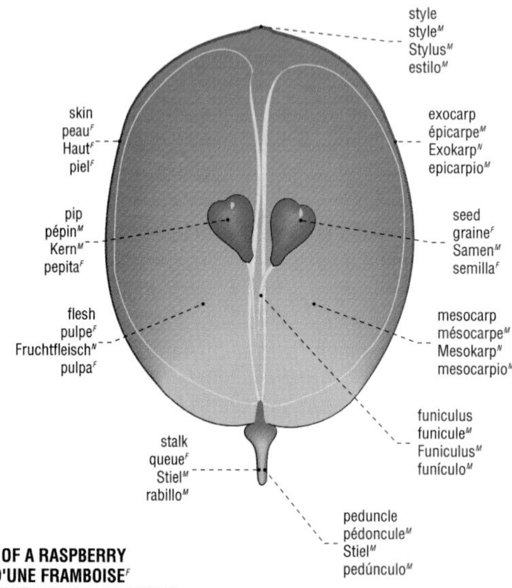


## SECTION OF A RASPBERRY
## COUPE[F] D'UNE FRAMBOISE[F]
## QUERSCHNITT[M] EINER HIMBEERE[F]
## CORTE[M] DE UNA FRAMBUESA[F]

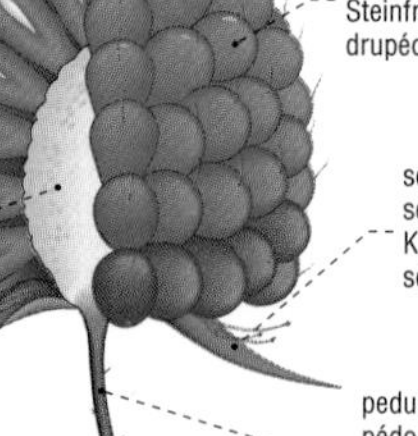


## SECTION OF A STRAWBERRY
## COUPE[F] D'UNE FRAISE[F]
## QUERSCHNITT[M] EINER ERDBEERE[F]
## CORTE[M] DE UNA FRESA[F]

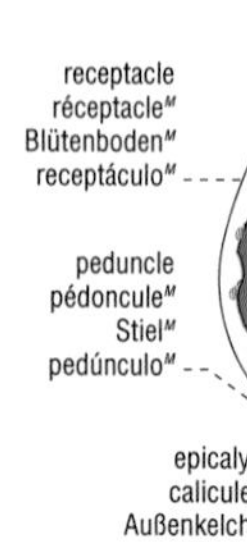


## PRINCIPAL TYPES OF BERRY
## PRINCIPALES VARIÉTÉS[F] DE BAIES[F]
## DIE WICHTIGSTEN BEERENARTEN[F]
## PRINCIPALES VARIEDADES[F] DE BAYAS[F]

blackcurrant
cassis[M]
schwarze Johannisbeere[F]
grosella[F] negra

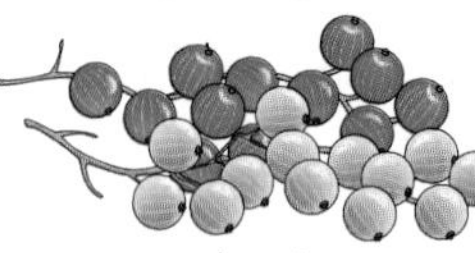
redcurrant
groseille[F] à grappes[F]
Johannisbeere[F]
grosella[F]

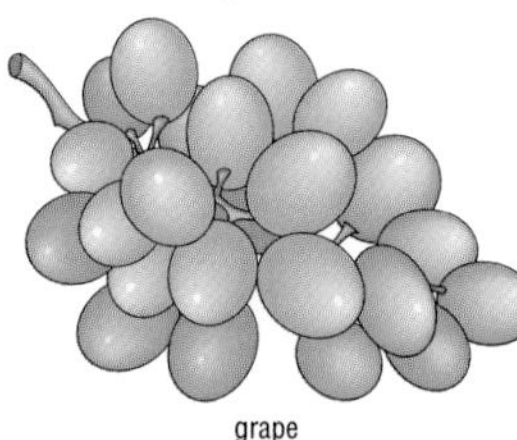
grape
raisin[M]
Weintraube[F]
uva[F]

gooseberry
groseille[F] à maquereau[M]
Stachelbeere[F]
grosella[F] espinosa

blueberry
myrtille[F]
Heidelbeere[F]
arándano[M]

huckleberry
airelle[F]
amerikanische Heidelbeere[F]
ráspano[M]

cranberry
canneberge[F]
Preiselbeere[F]
arándano[M] agrio

# FLESHY STONE FRUITS
# FRUITS[M] CHARNUS À NOYAU[M]
# STEINOBST[N]
# FRUTOS[M] CARNOSOS CON HUESO[M]

## SECTION OF A STONE FRUIT
## COUPE[F] D'UN FRUIT[M] À NOYAU[M]
## QUERSCHNITT[M] EINER STEINFRUCHT[F]
## CORTE[M] DE UN FRUTO[M] CARNOSO CON HUESO[M]

**PEACH**
**PÊCHE[F]**
**PFIRSICH[M]**
**MELOCOTÓN[M]**

**technical terms**
**termes[M] techniques**
**wissenschaftliche Bezeichnungen[F]**
**términos técnicos**

peduncle
pédoncule[M]
Stiel[M]
pedúnculo[M]

exocarp
épicarpe[M]
Exokarp[N]
epicarpio[M]

mesocarp
mésocarpe[M]
Mesokarp[N]
mesocarpio[M]

endocarp
endocarpe[M]
Endokarp[N]
endocarpio[M]

seed
graine[F]
Samen[M]
semilla[F]

seed coat
tégument[M] de la graine[F]
Samenmantel[M]
tegumento[M] de la semilla[F]

style
style[M]
Stylus[M]
estilo[M]

**usual terms**
**termes[M] familiers**
**gebräuchliche Bezeichnungen[F]**
**términos familiares**

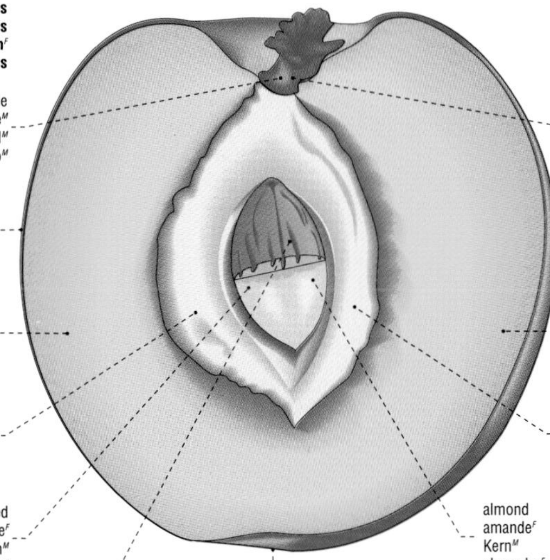

stalk
queue[F]
Stiel[M]
rabillo[M]

skin
peau[F]
Haut[F]
piel[F]

flesh
pulpe[F]
Fruchtfleisch[N]
pulpa[F]

stone
noyau[M]
Stein[M]
hueso[M]

almond
amande[F]
Kern[M]
almendra[F]

## PRINCIPAL TYPES OF STONE FRUIT
## PRINCIPALES VARIÉTÉS[F] DE FRUITS[M] À NOYAU[M]
## DIE WICHTIGSTEN STEINOBSTSORTEN[F]
## PRINCIPALES VARIEDADES[F] DE FRUTOS[M] CARNOSOS CON HUESO[M]

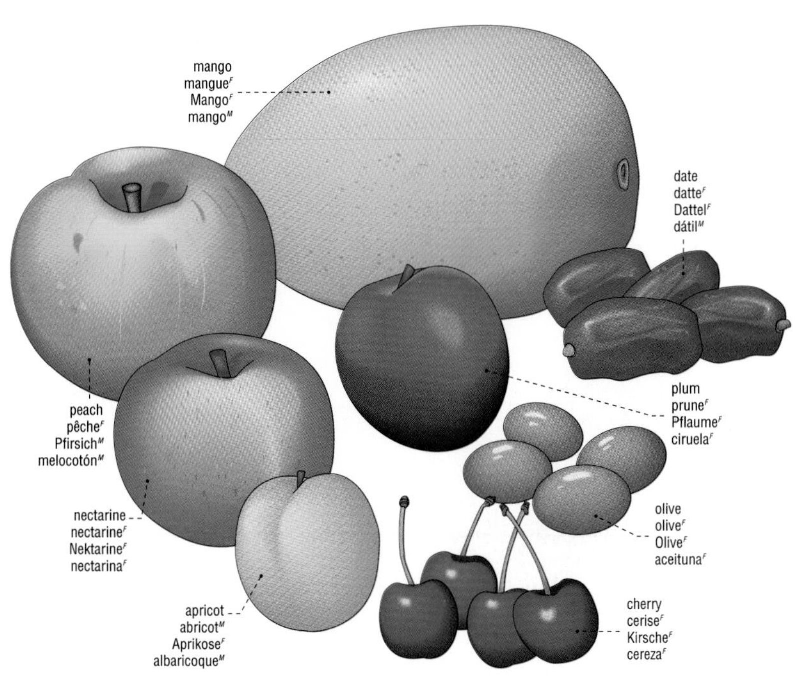

# FLESHY POMES
# FRUITS[M] CHARNUS À PÉPINS[M]
# KERNOBST[N]
# FRUTOS[M] CARNOSOS CON SEMILLAS[F]

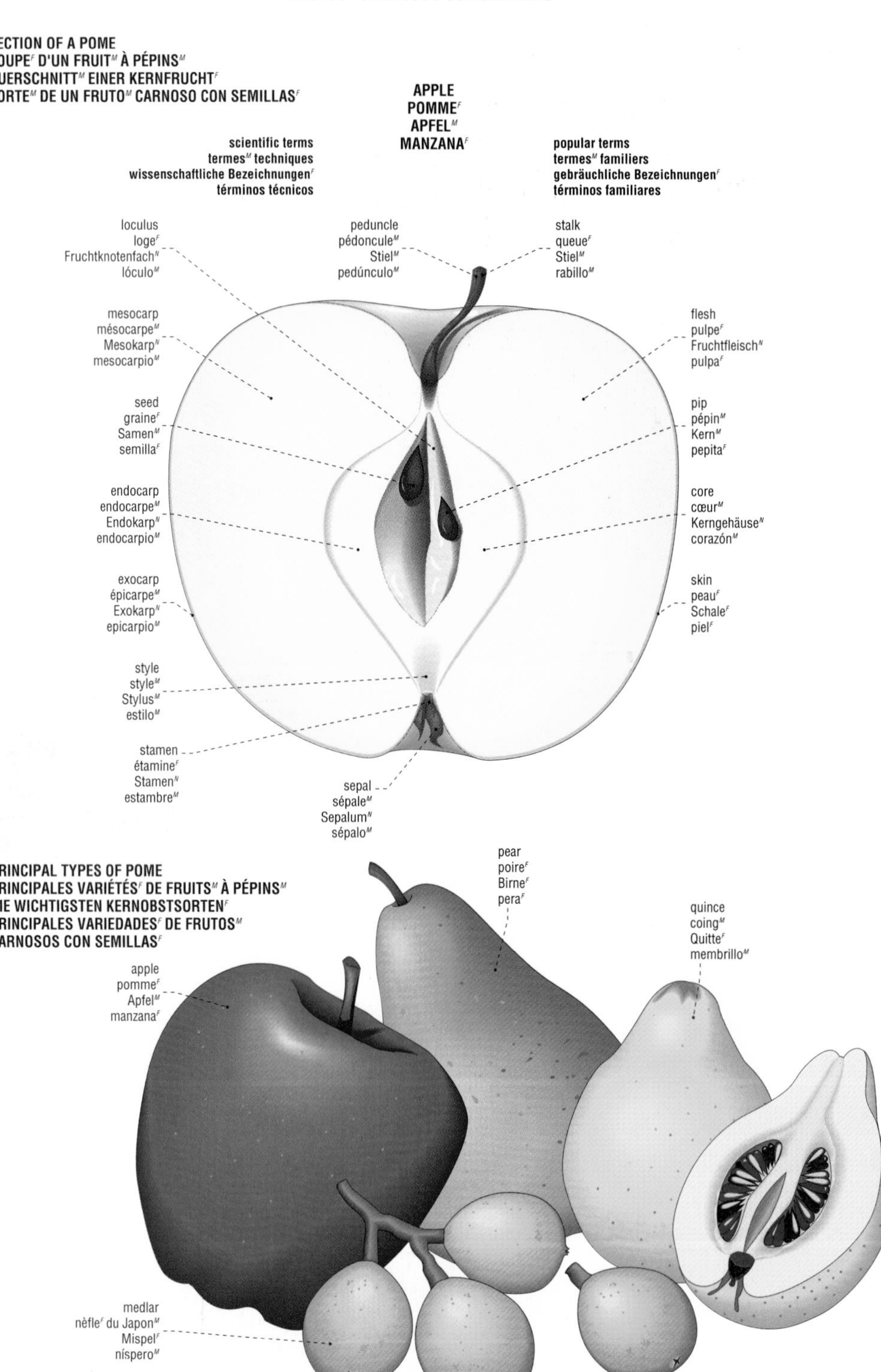

# FLESHY FRUITS: CITRUS FRUITS
# FRUITS[M] CHARNUS: AGRUMES[M]
# FLEISCHIGE FRÜCHTE[F]: ZITRUSFRÜCHTE[F]
# FRUTOS[M] CARNOSOS: CÍTRICOS[M]



## ORANGE
## ORANGE[F]
## ORANGE[F]
## NARANJA[F]

## SECTION OF A CITRUS FRUIT
## COUPE[F] D'UN AGRUME[M]
## QUERSCHNITT[M] EINER ZITRUSFRUCHT[F]
## CORTE[M] DE UN CÍTRICO[M]

**scientific terms**
**termes[M] techniques**
**wissenschaftliche Bezeichnungen[F]**
**términos técnicos**

wall
cloison[F]
Scheidewand[F]
membrana[F]

seed
graine[F]
Samen[M]
semilla[F]

juice sac
loge[F]
Fruchtfach[N]
celdilla[F]

mesocarp
mésocarpe[M]
Mesokarp[N]
mesocarpio[M]

pericarp
péricarpe[M]
Perikarp[N]
pericarpio[M]

**popular terms**
**termes[M] familiers**
**gebräuchliche Bezeichnungen[F]**
**términos familiares**

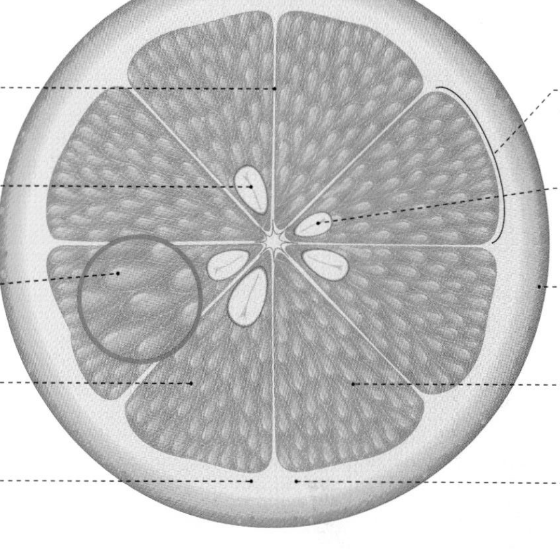

segment
quartier[M]
Spalt[M]
gajo[M]

pip
pépin[M]
Kern[M]
pepita[F]

peel
zeste[M]
Schale[F]
piel[F]

pulp
pulpe[F]
Fruchtfleisch[N]
pulpa[F]

rind
écorce[F]
Fruchtwand[F]
corteza[F]

## PRINCIPAL TYPES OF CITRUS FRUIT
## PRINCIPALES VARIÉTÉS[F] D'AGRUMES[M]
## DIE WICHTIGSTEN ZITRUSFRÜCHTE[F]
## PRINCIPALES VARIEDADES[F] DE CÍTRICOS[M]

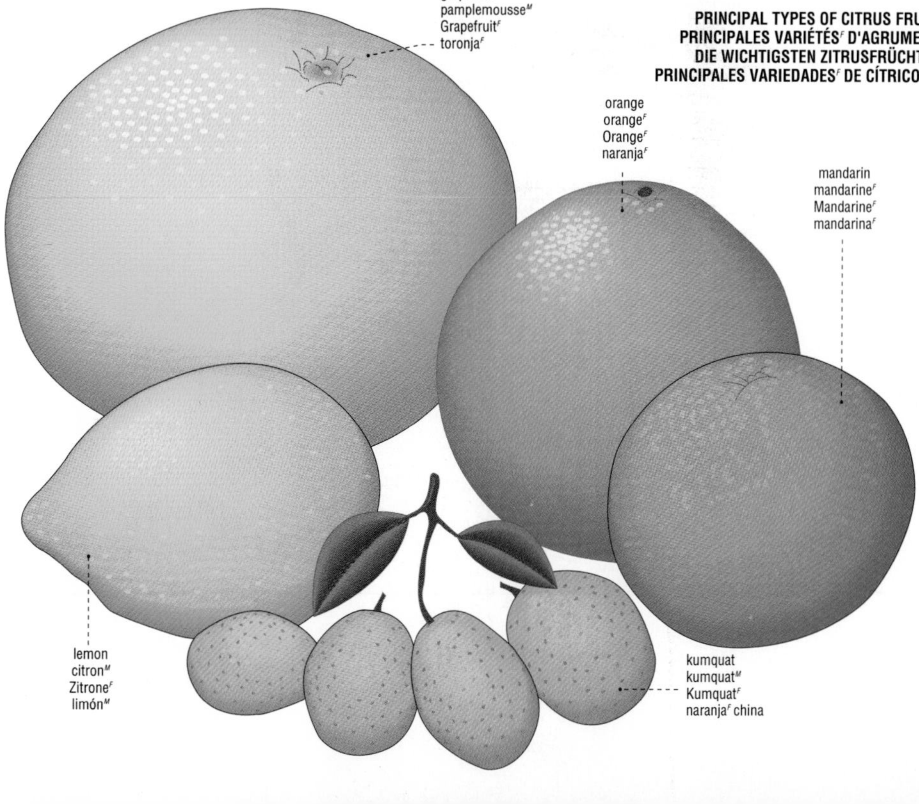

grapefruit
pamplemousse[M]
Grapefruit[F]
toronja[F]

orange
orange[F]
Orange[F]
naranja[F]

mandarin
mandarine[F]
Mandarine[F]
mandarina[F]

lemon
citron[M]
Zitrone[F]
limón[M]

kumquat
kumquat[M]
Kumquat[F]
naranja[F] china

# DRY FRUITS: NUTS
# FRUITS[M] SECS: NOIX[F]
# TROCKENFRÜCHTE[F]: NÜSS[F]
# FRUTOS[M] SECOS: OLEAGINOSOS

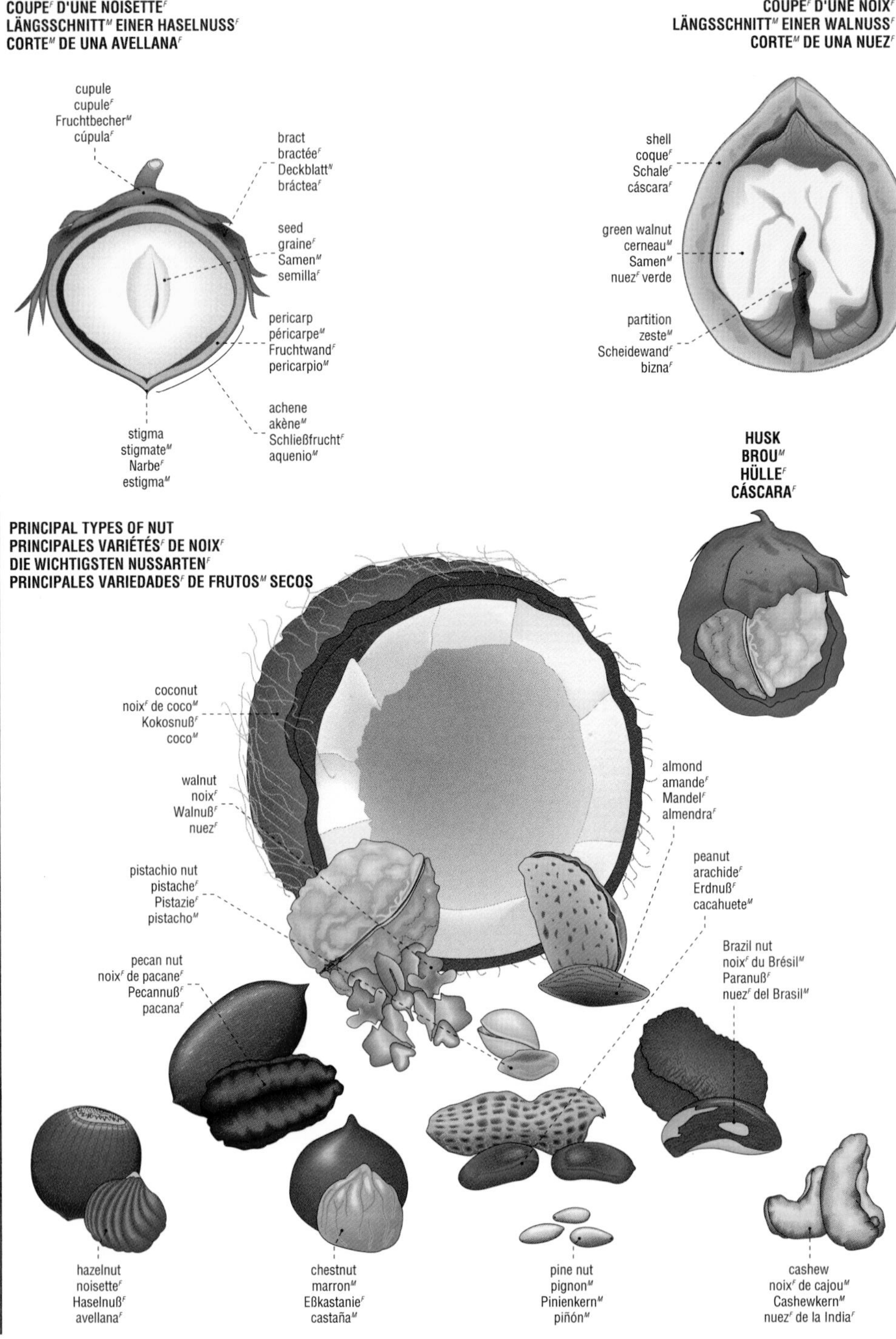

# VARIOUS DRY FRUITS
# FRUITS[M] SECS DIVERS
# VERSCHIEDENE TROCKENFRÜCHTE[F]
# FRUTOS[M] SECOS: DEHISCENTES

## SECTION OF A FOLLICLE
## COUPE[F] D'UN FOLLICULE[M]
## QUERSCHNITT[M] EINER FRUCHTKAPSEL[F]
## CORTE[M] DE UN FOLÍCULO[M]

**star anise**
**anis[M] étoilé**
**Sternanis[M]**
**anís[M] estrellado**

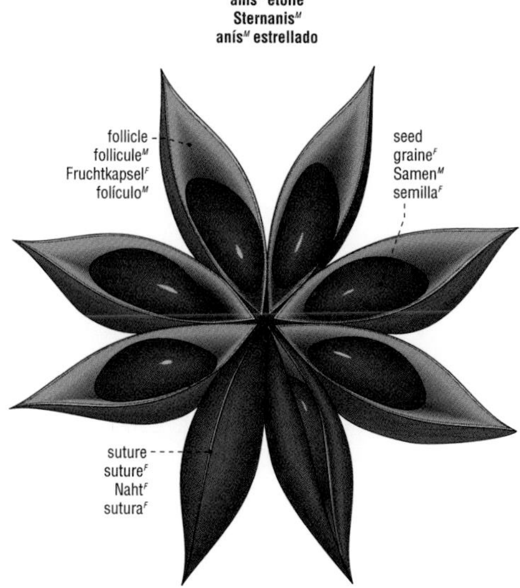


## SECTION OF A SILIQUE
## COUPE[F] D'UNE SILIQUE[F]
## LÄNGSSCHNITT[M] EINER FRUCHTSCHOTE[F]
## CORTE[M] DE UNA SILICUA[F]

**mustard**
**moutarde[F]**
**Senf[M]**
**mostaza[F]**

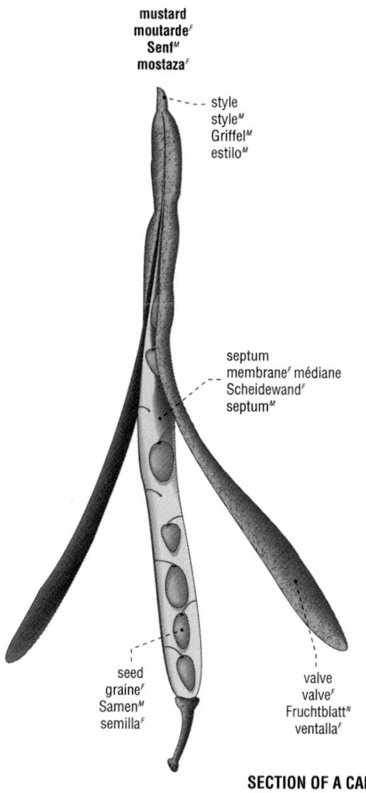


## SECTION OF A LEGUME
## COUPE[F] D'UNE GOUSSE[F]
## LÄNGSSCHNITT[M] EINER HÜLSENFRUCHT[F]
## CORTE[M] DE UNA LEGUMBRE[F]

**pea**
**pois[M]**
**Erbsenschote[F]**
**guisante[M]**

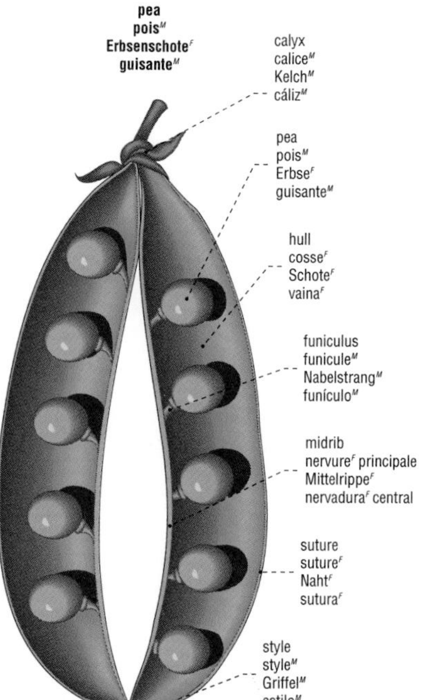


## SECTION OF A CAPSULE
## COUPE[F] D'UNE CAPSULE[F]
## LÄNGSSCHNITT[M] EINER KAPSEL[F]
## CORTE[M] DE UNA CÁPSULA[F]

**poppy**
**pavot[M]**
**Mohn[M]**
**amapola[F]**

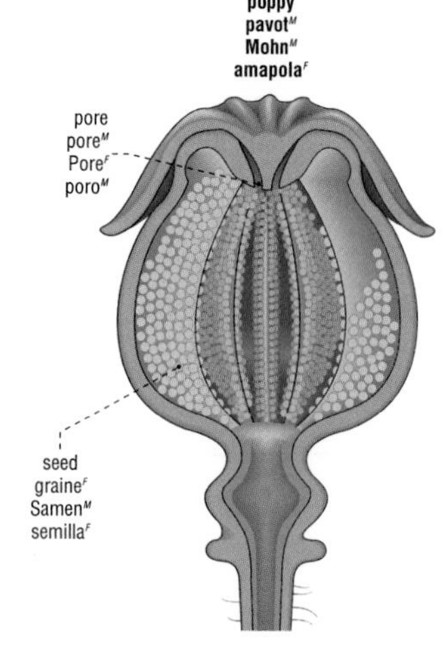

# TROPICAL FRUITS
# FRUITS[M] TROPICAUX
# SÜDFRÜCHTE[F]
# FRUTAS[F] TROPICALES

## PRINCIPAL TYPES OF TROPICAL FRUIT
## PRINCIPAUX FRUITS[M] TROPICAUX
## DIE WICHTIGSTEN SÜDFRÜCHTE[F]
## PRINCIPALES VARIEDADES[F] DE FRUTAS[F] TROPICALES

# VEGETABLES
# LÉGUMES[M]
# GEMÜSE[N]
# HORTALIZAS[F]

## FRUIT VEGETABLES
## LÉGUMES[M] FRUITS[M]
## FRUCHTGEMÜSE[N]
## FRUTOS[M]

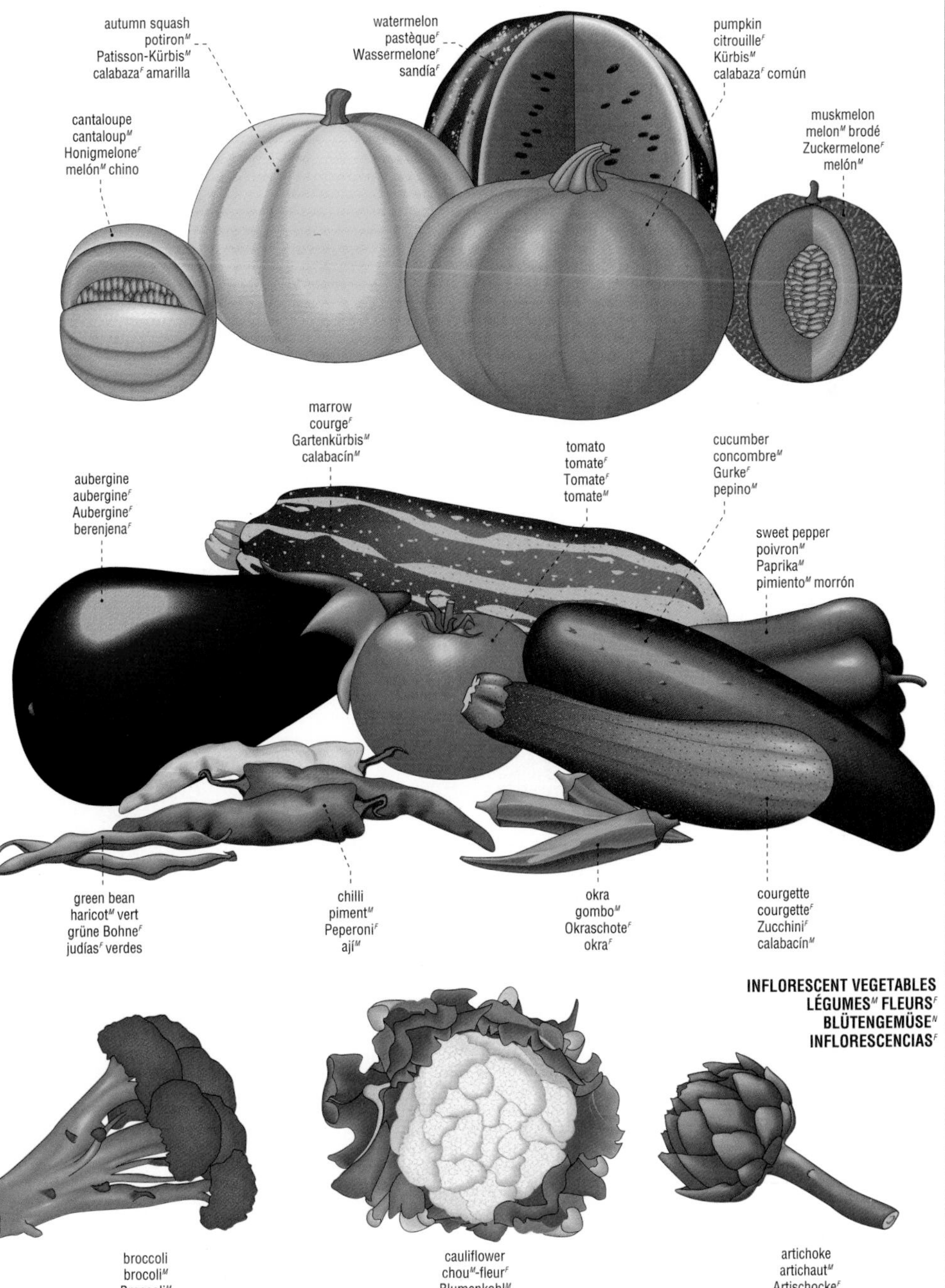

# VEGETABLES
# LÉGUMES
# GEMÜSE
# HORTALIZAS

## SECTION OF A BULB
## COUPE D'UN BULBE
## LÄNGSSCHNITT EINER ZWIEBEL
## CORTE DE UN BULBO

## BULB VEGETABLES
## LÉGUMES BULBES
## ZWIEBELGEMÜSE
## BULBOS

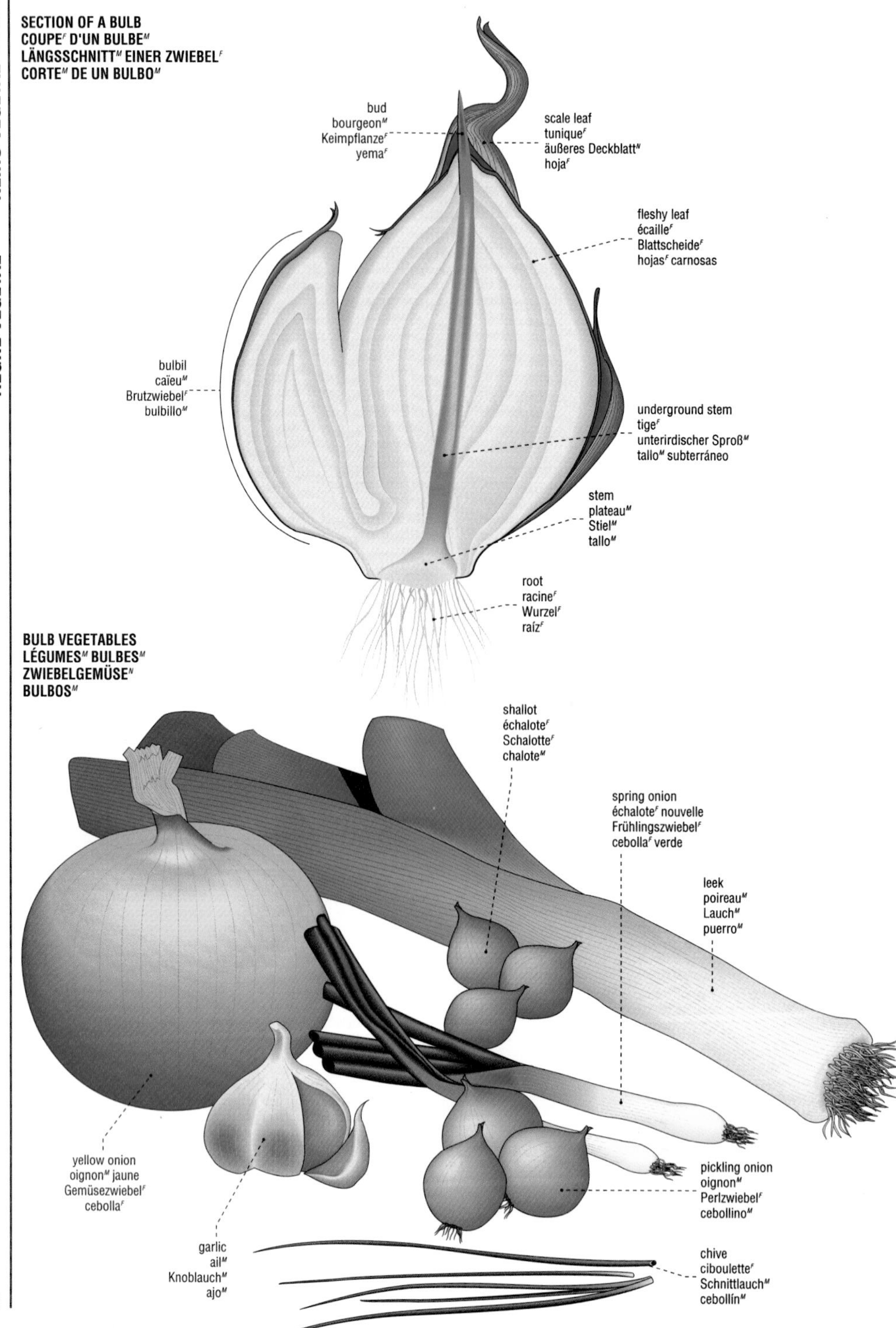

# VEGETABLES
# LÉGUMES[M]
# GEMÜSE[N]
# HORTALIZAS[F]

## TUBER VEGETABLES
## LÉGUMES[M] TUBERCULES[M]
## KNOLLENGEMÜSE[N]
## TUBÉRCULOS[M]

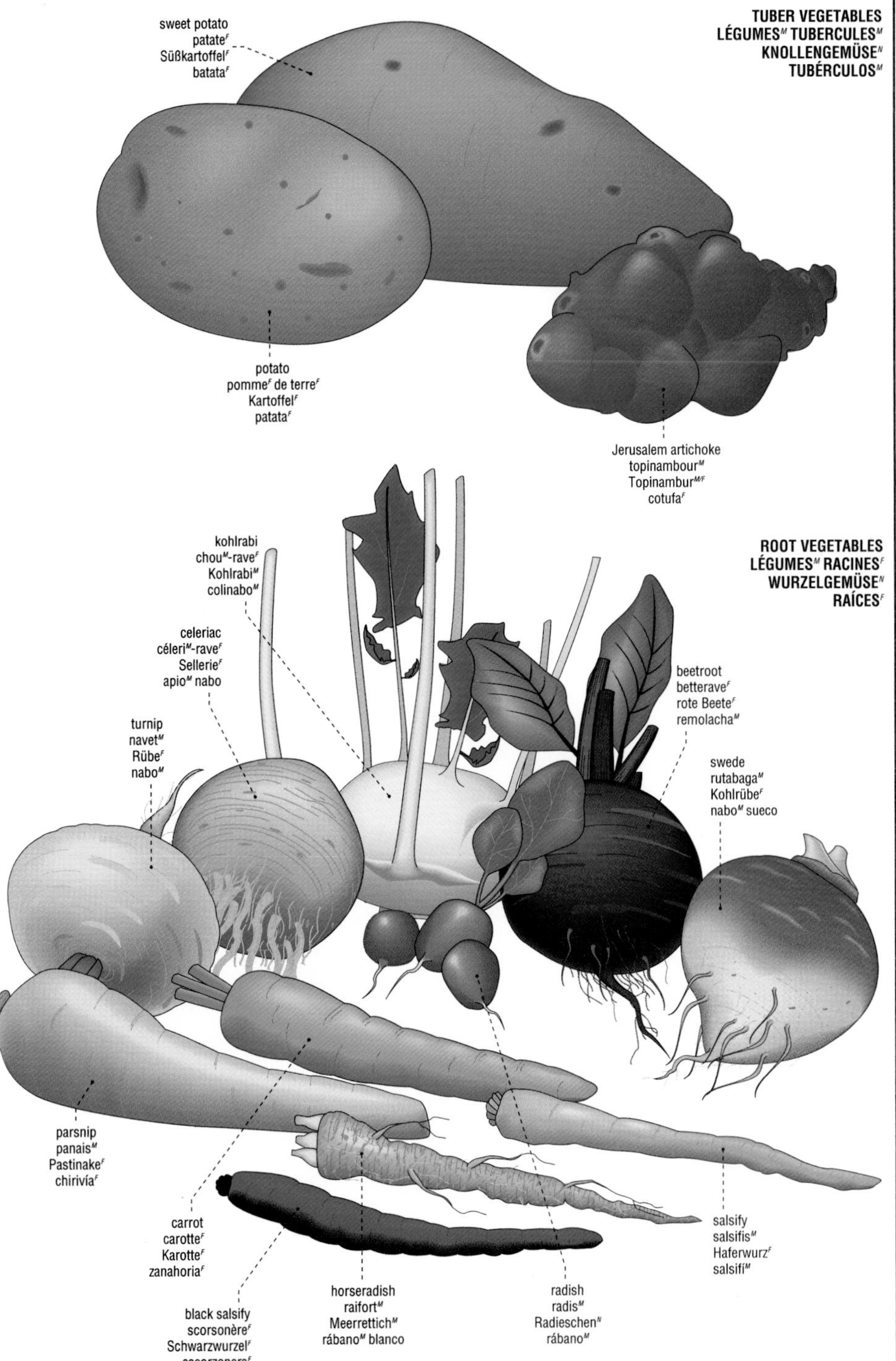

# VEGETABLES
# LÉGUMES[M]
# GEMÜSE[N]
# HORTALIZAS[F]

## STALK VEGETABLES
## LÉGUMES[M] TIGES[F]
## STENGEL- UND SPROSSENGEMÜSE[N]
## TALLOS[M]

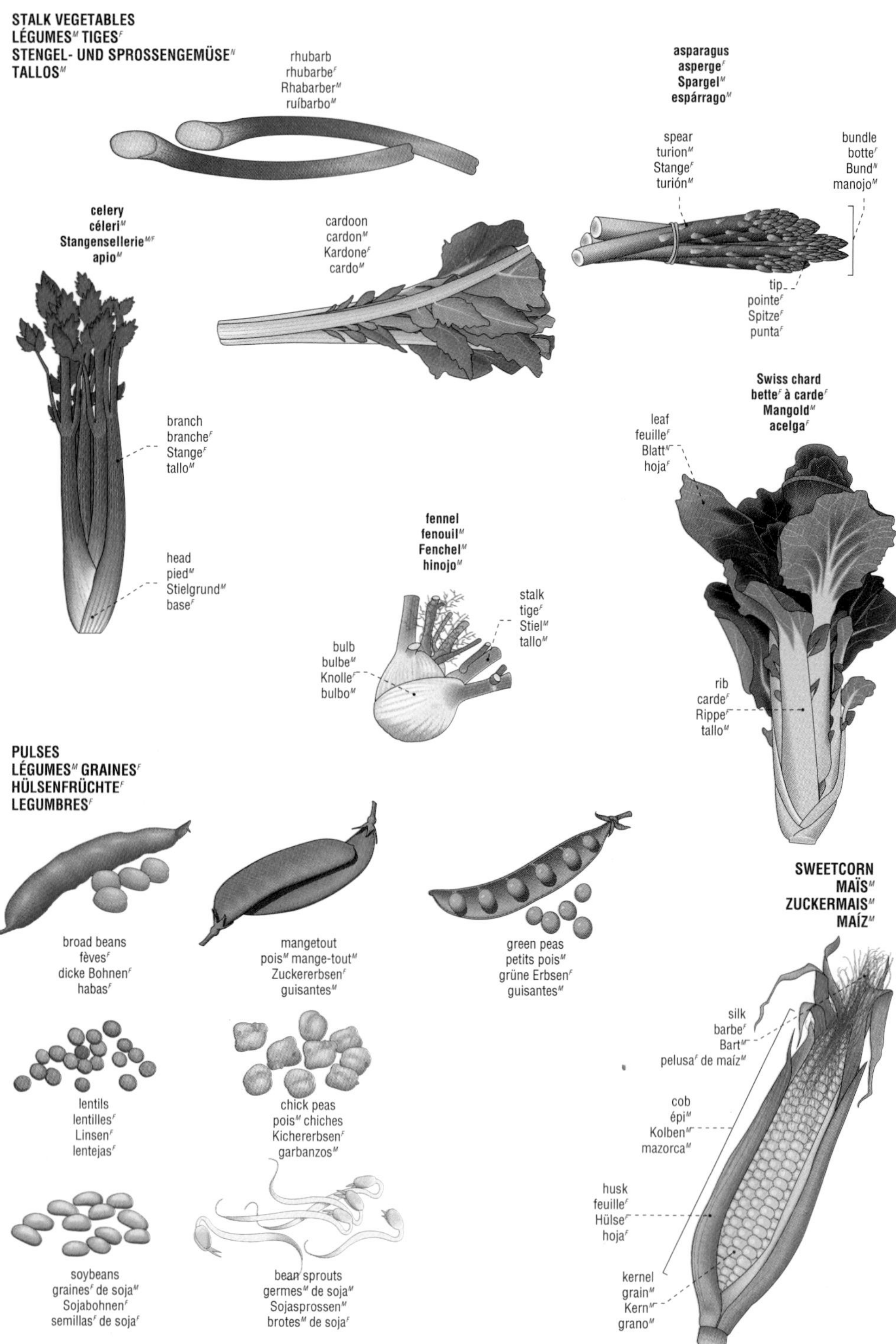

# VEGETABLES
# LÉGUMES[M]
# GEMÜSE[N]
# HORTALIZAS[F]

## LEAF VEGETABLES
## LÉGUMES[M] FEUILLES[F]
## BLATTGEMÜSE[N]
## VERDURAS[F] DE HOJAS[F]

corn salad
mâche[F]
Feldsalat[M]
colleja[F]

watercress
cresson[M] de fontaine[F]
Brunnenkresse[F]
berro[M]

chicory
endive[F]
Chicorée[M/F]
achicoria[F]

Brussels sprouts
choux[M] de Bruxelles
Rosenkohl[M]
coles[F] de Bruselas

curly kale
chou[M] frisé
Grünkohl[M]
col[F] rizada

vine leaf
feuille[F] de vigne[F]
Weinblatt[N]
hoja[F] de parra[F]

garden sorrel
oseille[F]
Garten-Sauerampfer[M]
acedera[F]

spinach
épinard[M]
Spinat[M]
espinaca[F]

curly endive
chicorée[F]
krause Endivie[F]
escarola[F] rizada

broad-leaved endive
scarole[F]
glatte Endivie[F]
escarola[F]

cos lettuce
romaine[F]
Romagna-Salat[M]
lechuga[F] romana

dandelion
pissenlit[M]
Löwenzahn[M]
diente[M] de león[M]

white cabbage
chou[M] pommé blanc
Weißkohl[M]
repollo[M]

cabbage lettuce
laitue[F] pommée
Kopfsalat[M]
lechuga[F] francesa

green cabbage
chou[M] pommé vert
Kohl[M]
repollo[M] verde

Chinese cabbage
chou[M] chinois
Chinakohl[M]
col[F] de China[F]

# HERBS
# FINES HERBES$^{F}$
# KRÄUTER$^{N}$
# HIERBAS$^{F}$ AROMÁTICAS

dill
aneth$^{M}$
Dill$^{M}$
eneldo$^{M}$

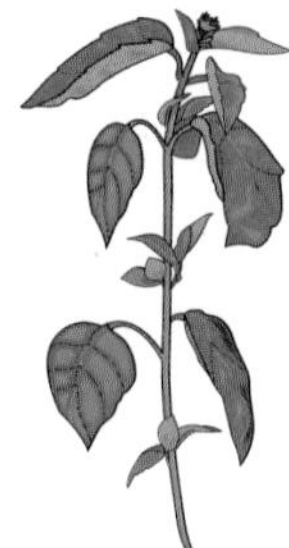

basil
basilic$^{M}$
Basilikum$^{N}$
albahaca$^{F}$

borage
bourrache$^{F}$
Boretsch$^{M}$
borraja$^{F}$

chervil
cerfeuil$^{M}$
Kerbel$^{M}$
perifollo$^{M}$

coriander
coriandre$^{F}$
Koriander$^{M}$
cilantro$^{M}$

tarragon
estragon$^{M}$
Estragon$^{M}$
estragón$^{M}$

hyssop
hysope$^{F}$
Ysop$^{M}$
hisopo$^{M}$

bay
laurier$^{M}$
Lorbeer$^{M}$
laurel$^{M}$

lovage
livèche$^{F}$
Liebstöckel$^{M/N}$
ligústico$^{M}$

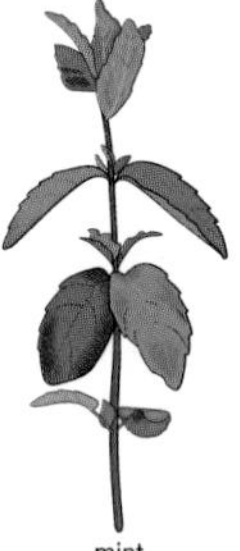

mint
menthe$^{F}$
Minze$^{F}$
hierbabuena$^{F}$

oregano
origan$^{M}$
Oregano$^{M}$
orégano$^{M}$

parsley
persil$^{M}$
Petersilie$^{F}$
perejil$^{M}$

rosemary
romarin$^{M}$
Rosmarin$^{M}$
romero$^{M}$

savory
sarriette$^{F}$
Bohnenkraut$^{N}$
ajedrea$^{F}$

sage
sauge$^{F}$
Salbei$^{M}$
salvia$^{F}$

thyme
thym$^{M}$
Thymian$^{M}$
tomillo$^{M}$

# ANIMAL KINGDOM
# RÈGNE ANIMAL
# TIERREICH
# REINO ANIMAL

## SUMMARY

INSECTS AND SPIDERS ........ 77
BUTTERFLY ........ 78
HONEYBEE ........ 80
GASTROPOD ........ 83
AMPHIBIANS ........ 84
FISH ........ 86
CRUSTACEAN ........ 90
MOLLUSC ........ 92
UNIVALVE SHELL ........ 94
BIVALVE SHELL ........ 95
REPTILE ........ 96
TYPES OF JAW ........ 98
PRINCIPAL TYPES OF HORN ........ 99
PRINCIPAL TYPES OF TUSK ........ 99
TYPES OF HOOF ........ 99
HORSE ........ 100
DEER FAMILY ........ 105
DOG ........ 106
CAT ........ 107
BIRD ........ 108
BAT ........ 112

# INSECTS AND SPIDERS
# INSECTES[M] ET ARAIGNÉE[F]
# INSEKTEN[N] UND SPINNE[F]
# INSECTOS[M] Y ARAÑA[F]

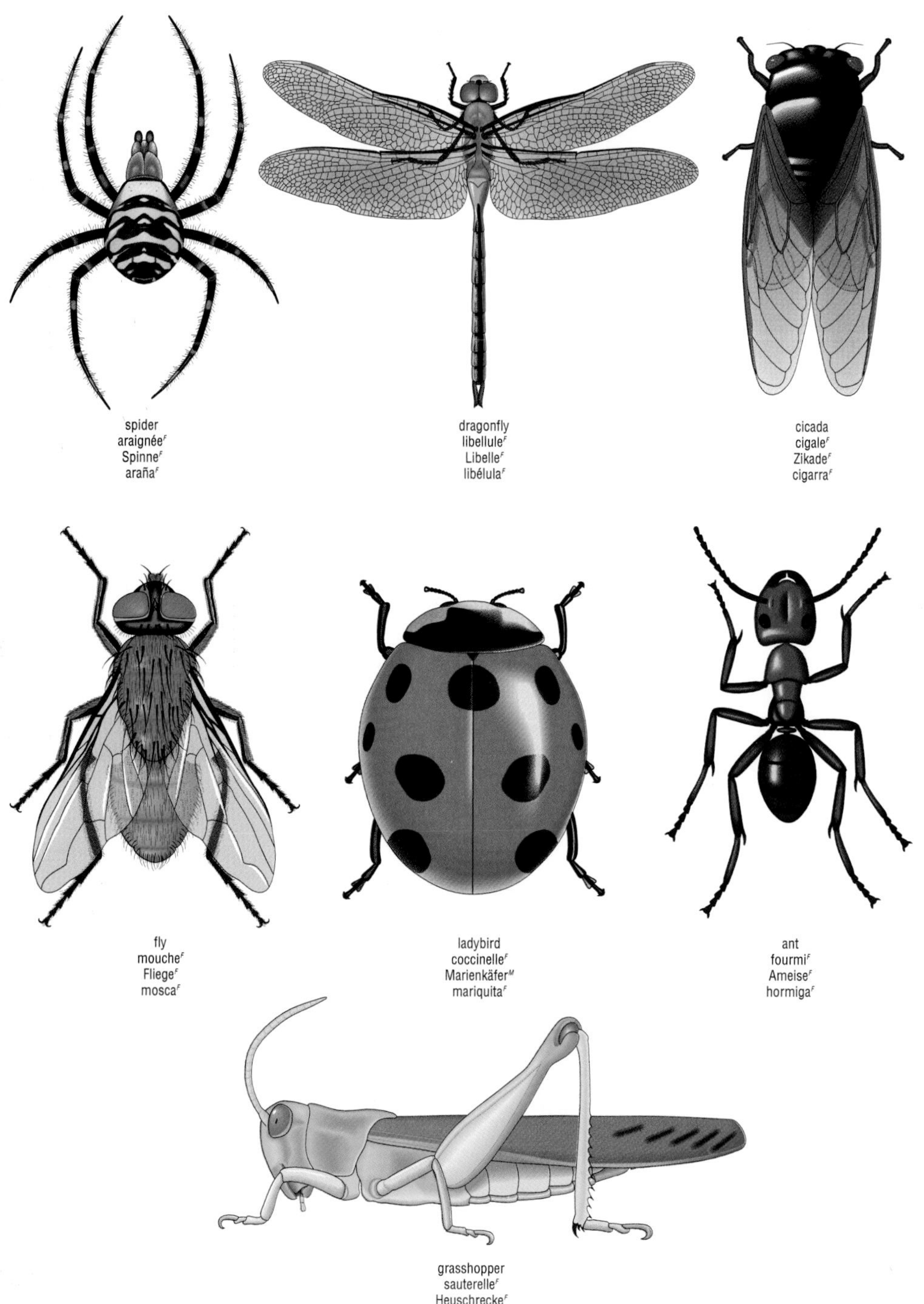

spider
araignée[F]
Spinne[F]
araña[F]

dragonfly
libellule[F]
Libelle[F]
libélula[F]

cicada
cigale[F]
Zikade[F]
cigarra[F]

fly
mouche[F]
Fliege[F]
mosca[F]

ladybird
coccinelle[F]
Marienkäfer[M]
mariquita[F]

ant
fourmi[F]
Ameise[F]
hormiga[F]

grasshopper
sauterelle[F]
Heuschrecke[F]
saltamontes[M]

# BUTTERFLY
# PAPILLON[M]
# SCHMETTERLING[M]
# MARIPOSA[F]

## CATERPILLAR
## CHENILLE[F]
## RAUPE[F]
## ORUGA[F]

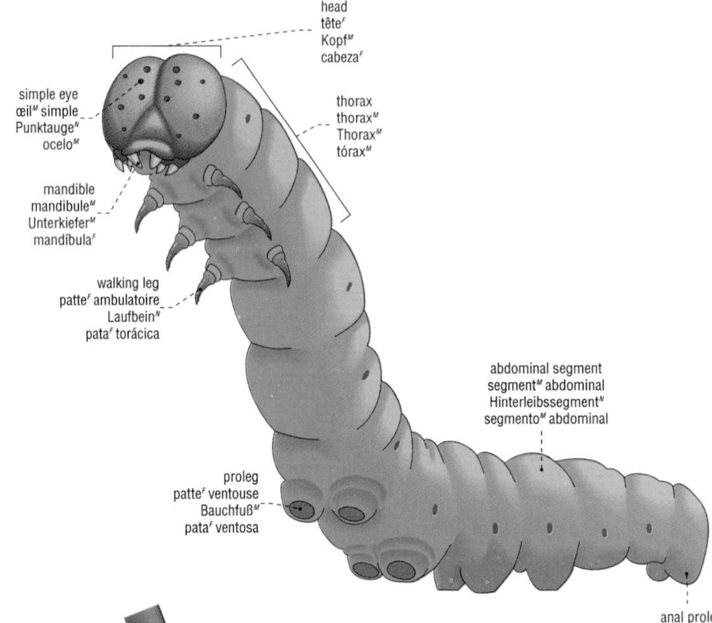

head
tête[F]
Kopf[M]
cabeza[F]
simple eye
œil[M] simple
Punktauge[N]
ocelo[M]
thorax
thorax[M]
Thorax[M]
tórax[M]
mandible
mandibule[M]
Unterkiefer[M]
mandíbula[F]
walking leg
patte[F] ambulatoire
Laufbein[N]
pata[F] torácica
abdominal segment
segment[M] abdominal
Hinterleibssegment[N]
segmento[M] abdominal
proleg
patte[F] ventouse
Bauchfuß[M]
pata[F] ventosa
anal proleg
patte[F] anale
Analfuß[M]
pata[F] anal

## CHRYSALIS
## CHRYSALIDE[F]
## PUPPE[F]
## CRISÁLIDA[F]

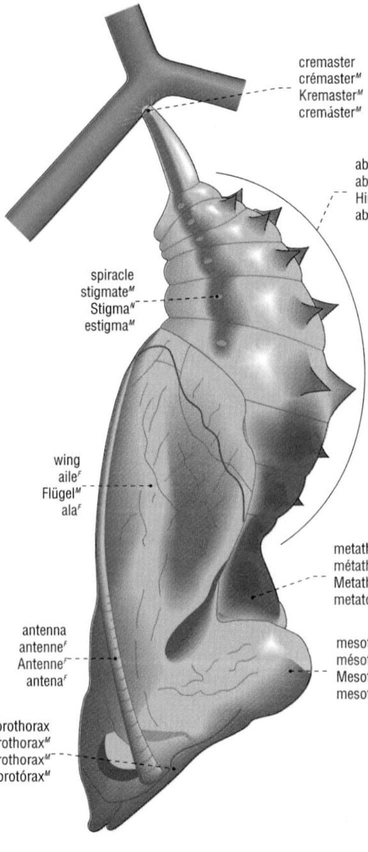

cremaster
crémaster[M]
Kremaster[M]
cremáster[M]
abdomen
abdomen[M]
Hinterleib[M]
abdomen[M]
spiracle
stigmate[M]
Stigma[N]
estigma[M]
wing
aile[F]
Flügel[M]
ala[F]
metathorax
métathorax[M]
Metathorax[M]
metatórax[M]
antenna
antenne[F]
Antenne[F]
antena[F]
mesothorax
mésothorax[M]
Mesothorax[M]
mesotórax[M]
prothorax
prothorax[M]
Prothorax[M]
protórax[M]

## HIND LEG
## PATTE[F] POSTÉRIEURE
## HINTERBEIN[N]
## PATA[F] POSTERIOR

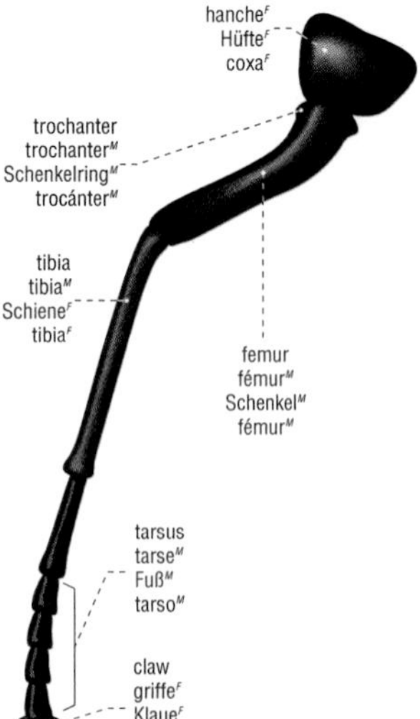

coxa
hanche[F]
Hüfte[F]
coxa[F]
trochanter
trochanter[M]
Schenkelring[M]
trocánter[M]
tibia
tibia[M]
Schiene[F]
tibia[F]
femur
fémur[M]
Schenkel[M]
fémur[M]
tarsus
tarse[M]
Fuß[M]
tarso[M]
claw
griffe[F]
Klaue[F]
tenacilla[F]

**BUTTERFLY**
**PAPILLON[M]**
**SCHMETTERLING[M]**
**MARIPOSA[F]**

# HONEYBEE
# ABEILLE[F]
# HONIGBIENE[F]
# ABEJA[F]

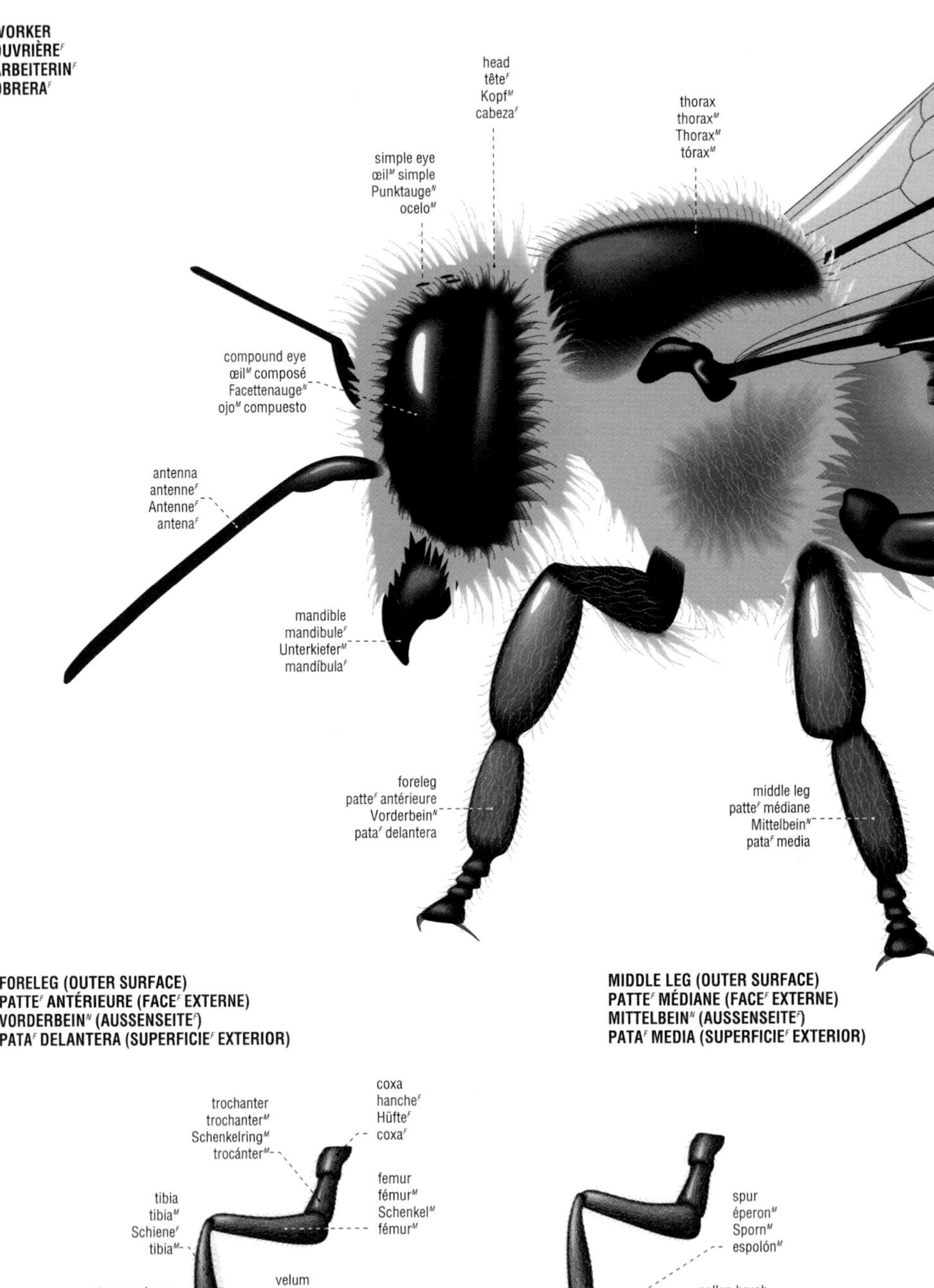

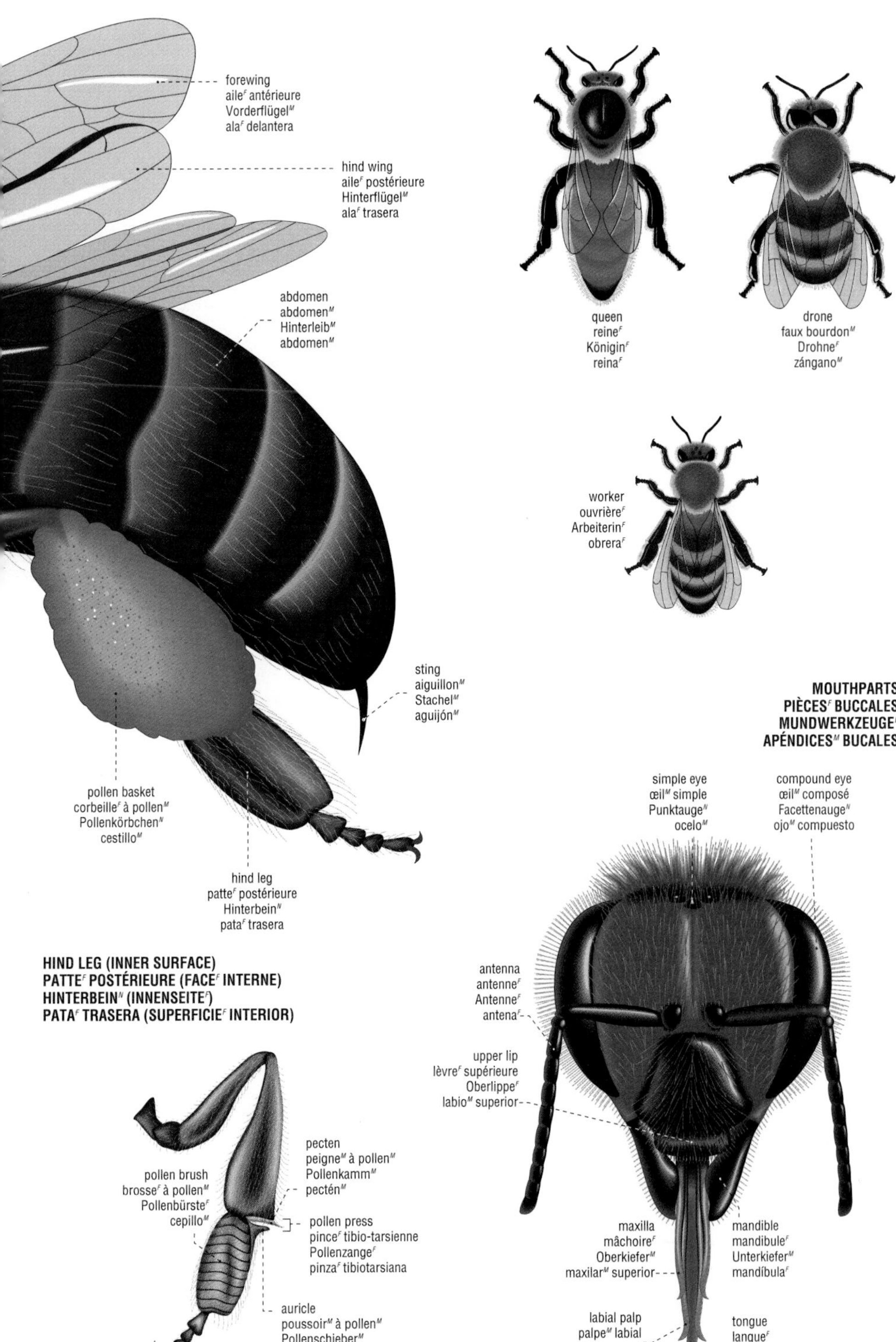
forewing
aile[F] antérieure
Vorderflügel[M]
ala[F] delantera
hind wing
aile[F] postérieure
Hinterflügel[M]
ala[F] trasera
abdomen
abdomen[M]
Hinterleib[M]
abdomen[M]
sting
aiguillon[M]
Stachel[M]
aguijón[M]
pollen basket
corbeille[F] à pollen[M]
Pollenkörbchen[N]
cestillo[M]
hind leg
patte[F] postérieure
Hinterbein[N]
pata[F] trasera
queen
reine[F]
Königin[F]
reina[F]
drone
faux bourdon[M]
Drohne[F]
zángano[M]
worker
ouvrière[F]
Arbeiterin[F]
obrera[F]
MOUTHPARTS
PIÈCES[F] BUCCALES
MUNDWERKZEUGE[N]
APÉNDICES[M] BUCALES
simple eye
œil[M] simple
Punktauge[N]
ocelo[M]
compound eye
œil[M] composé
Facettenauge[N]
ojo[M] compuesto
antenna
antenne[F]
Antenne[F]
antena[F]
upper lip
lèvre[F] supérieure
Oberlippe[F]
labio[M] superior
maxilla
mâchoire[F]
Oberkiefer[M]
maxilar[M] superior
mandible
mandibule[F]
Unterkiefer[M]
mandíbula[F]
labial palp
palpe[M] labial
Lippentaster[M]
palpo[M] labial
tongue
langue[F]
Zunge[F]
lengua[F]
HIND LEG (INNER SURFACE)
PATTE[F] POSTÉRIEURE (FACE[F] INTERNE)
HINTERBEIN[N] (INNENSEITE[F])
PATA[F] TRASERA (SUPERFICIE[F] INTERIOR)
pecten
peigne[M] à pollen[M]
Pollenkamm[M]
pectén[M]
pollen brush
brosse[F] à pollen[M]
Pollenbürste[F]
cepillo[M]
pollen press
pince[F] tibio-tarsienne
Pollenzange[F]
pinza[F] tibiotarsiana
auricle
poussoir[M] à pollen[M]
Pollenschieber[M]
aurícula[F]

# HONEYBEE
# ABEILLE[F]
# HONIGBIENE[F]
# ABEJA[F] DE COLMENA[F]

## HONEYCOMB SECTION
## COUPE[F] D'UN RAYON[M] DE MIEL[M]
## WABENAUSSCHNITT[M]
## CORTE[M] DE UN PANAL[M]

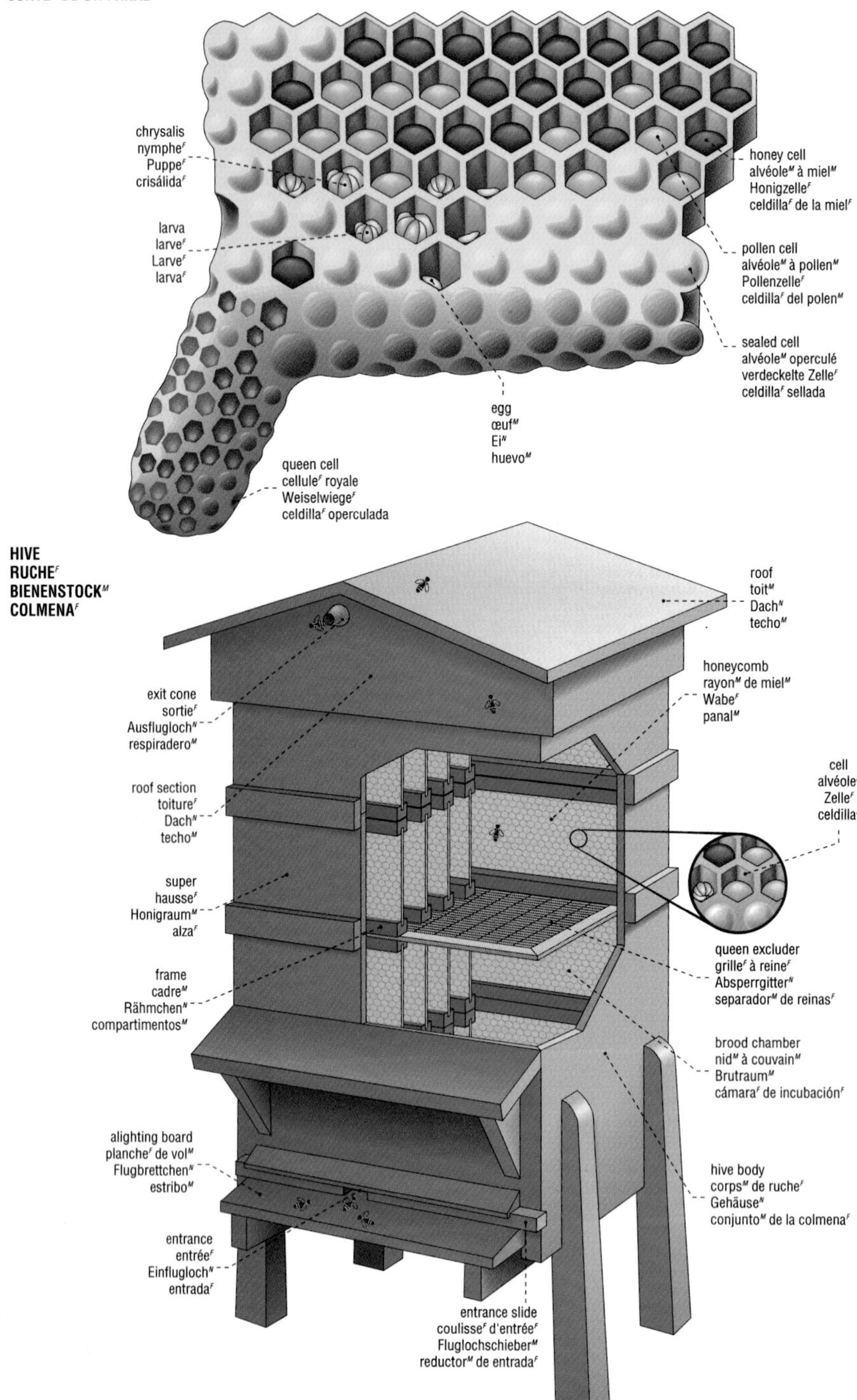

# GASTROPOD
# GASTÉROPODE[M]
# SCHNECKE[F]
# MOLUSCO[M] GASTERÓPODO

## SNAIL
## ESCARGOT[M]
## SCHNECKE[F]
## CARACOL[M] TERRESTRE

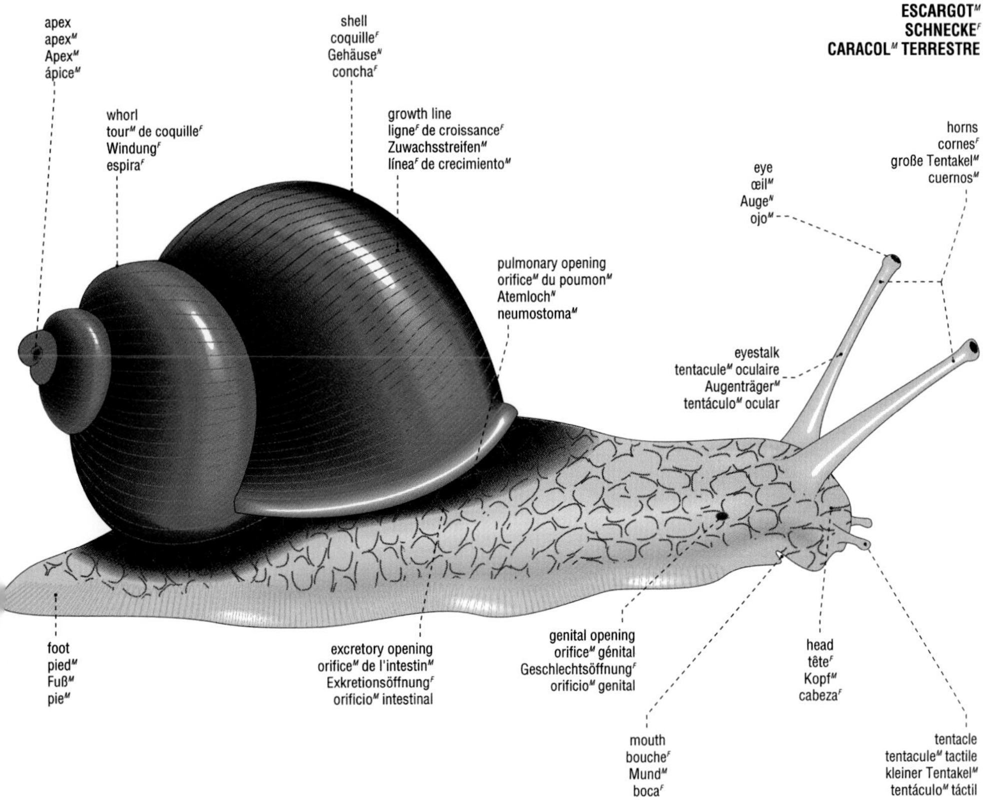

apex
apex[M]
Apex[M]
ápice[M]

shell
coquille[F]
Gehäuse[N]
concha[F]

whorl
tour[M] de coquille[F]
Windung[F]
espira[F]

growth line
ligne[F] de croissance[F]
Zuwachsstreifen[M]
línea[F] de crecimiento[M]

eye
œil[M]
Auge[N]
ojo[M]

horns
cornes[F]
große Tentakel[M]
cuernos[M]

pulmonary opening
orifice[M] du poumon[M]
Atemloch[N]
neumostoma[M]

eyestalk
tentacule[M] oculaire
Augenträger[M]
tentáculo[M] ocular

foot
pied[M]
Fuß[M]
pie[M]

excretory opening
orifice[M] de l'intestin[M]
Exkretionsöffnung[F]
orificio[M] intestinal

genital opening
orifice[M] génital
Geschlechtsöffnung[F]
orificio[M] genital

head
tête[F]
Kopf[M]
cabeza[F]

mouth
bouche[F]
Mund[M]
boca[F]

tentacle
tentacule[M] tactile
kleiner Tentakel[M]
tentáculo[M] táctil

## PRINCIPAL EDIBLE GASTROPODS
## PRINCIPAUX GASTÉROPODES[M] COMESTIBLES
## WICHTIGSTE ESSBARE SCHNECKEN[F]
## GASTERÓPODOS[M] COMESTIBLES

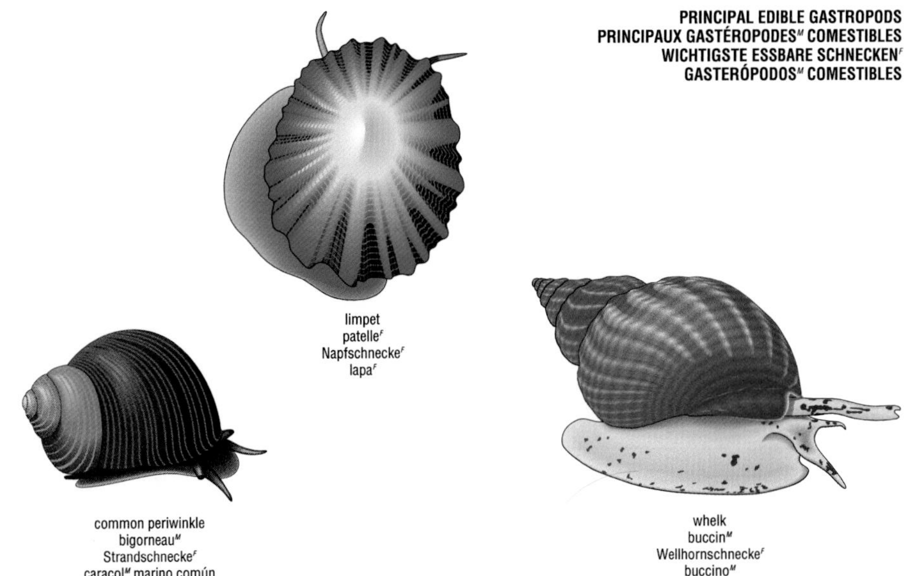

limpet
patelle[F]
Napfschnecke[F]
lapa[F]

common periwinkle
bigorneau[M]
Strandschnecke[F]
caracol[M] marino común

whelk
buccin[M]
Wellhornschnecke[F]
buccino[M]

# AMPHIBIANS
# AMPHIBIENS[M]
# AMPHIBIEN[F]
# ANFIBIOS[M]

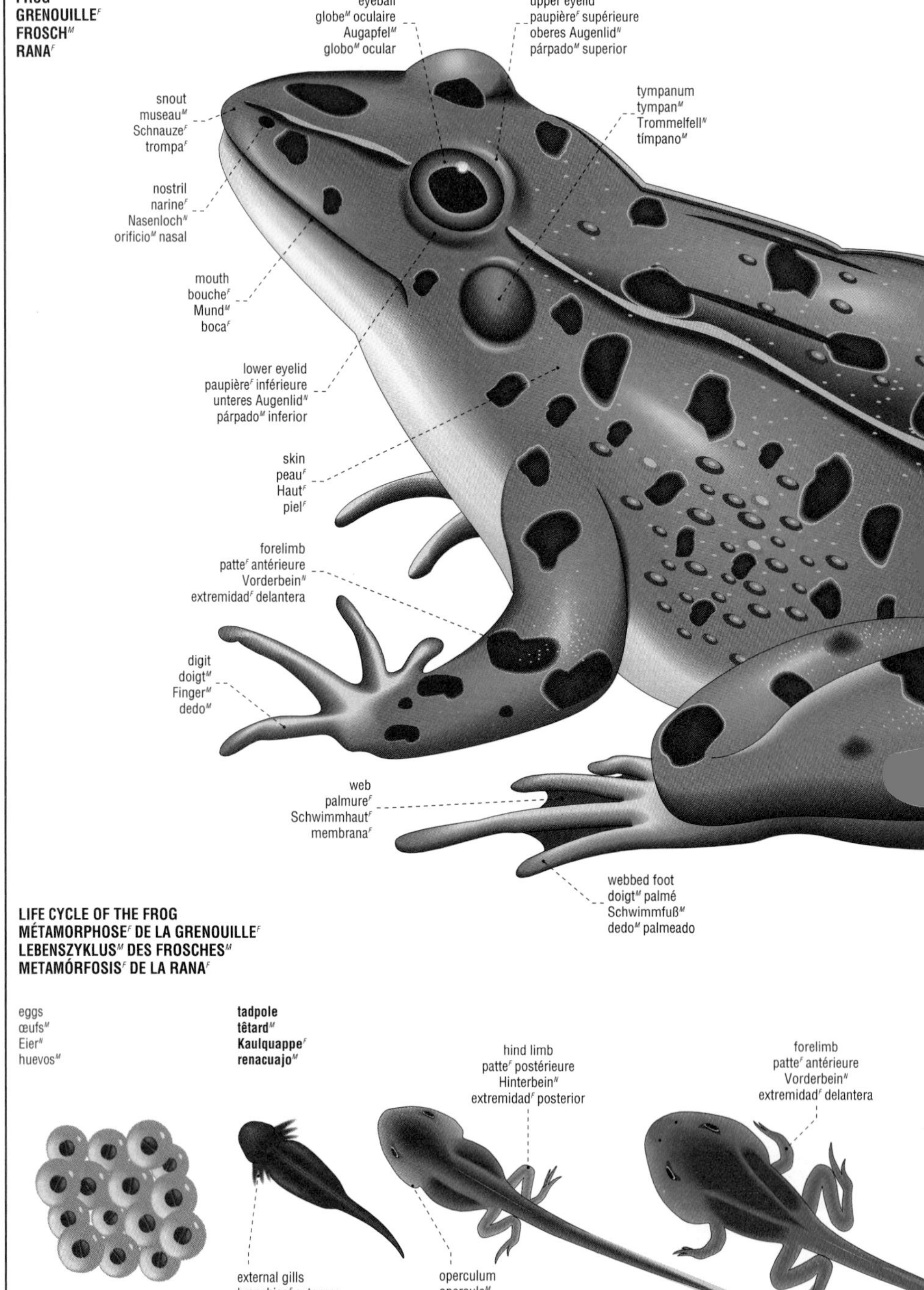

## PRINCIPAL AMPHIBIANS
## PRINCIPAUX AMPHIBIENS[M]
## WICHTIGSTE AMPHIBIEN[F]
## ANFIBIOS[M] COMUNES

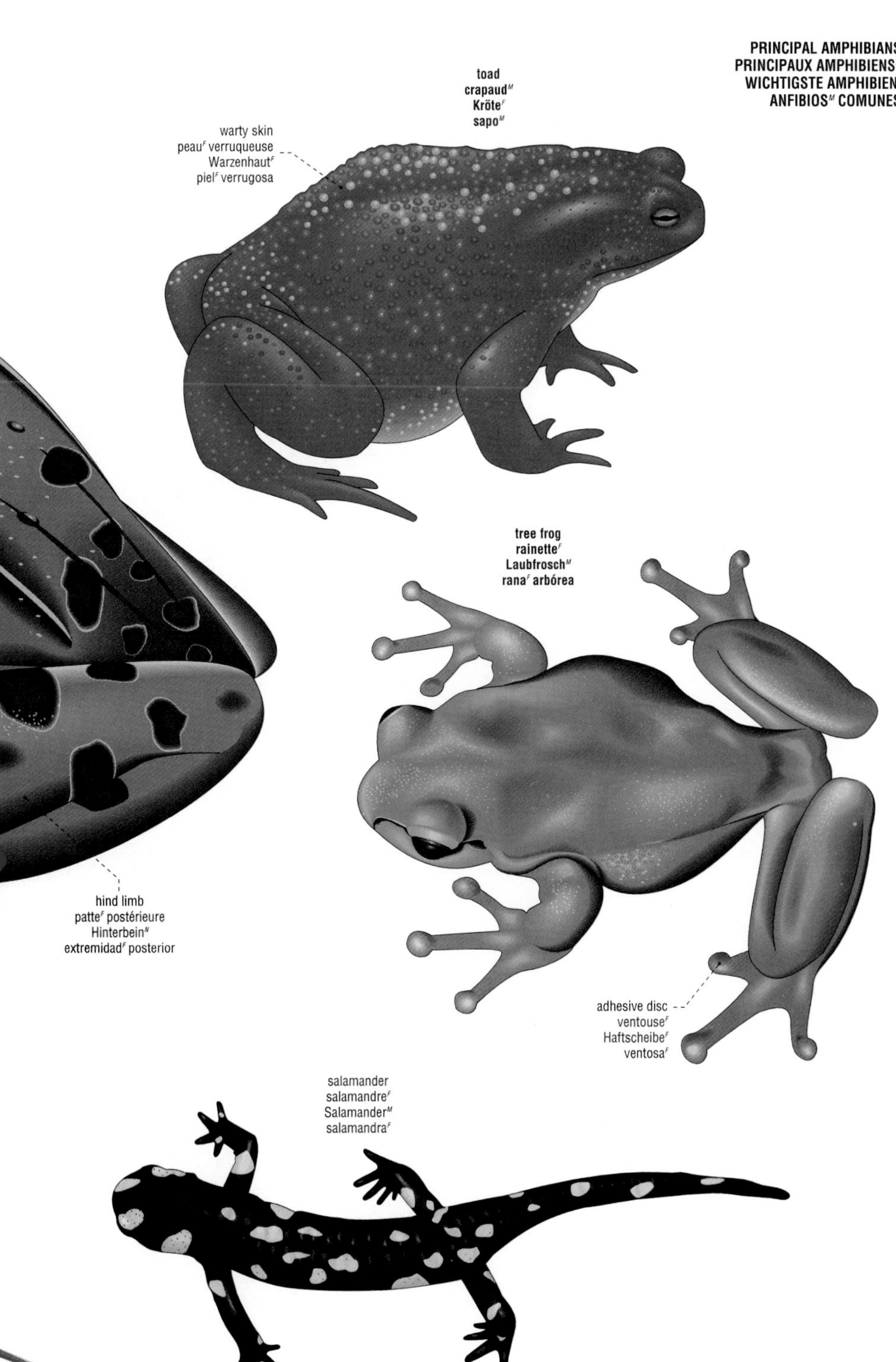

# FISH
# POISSON[M]
# FISCH[M]
# PEZ[M]

## MORPHOLOGY
## MORPHOLOGIE[F]
## MORPHOLOGIE[F]
## MORFOLOGÍA[F]

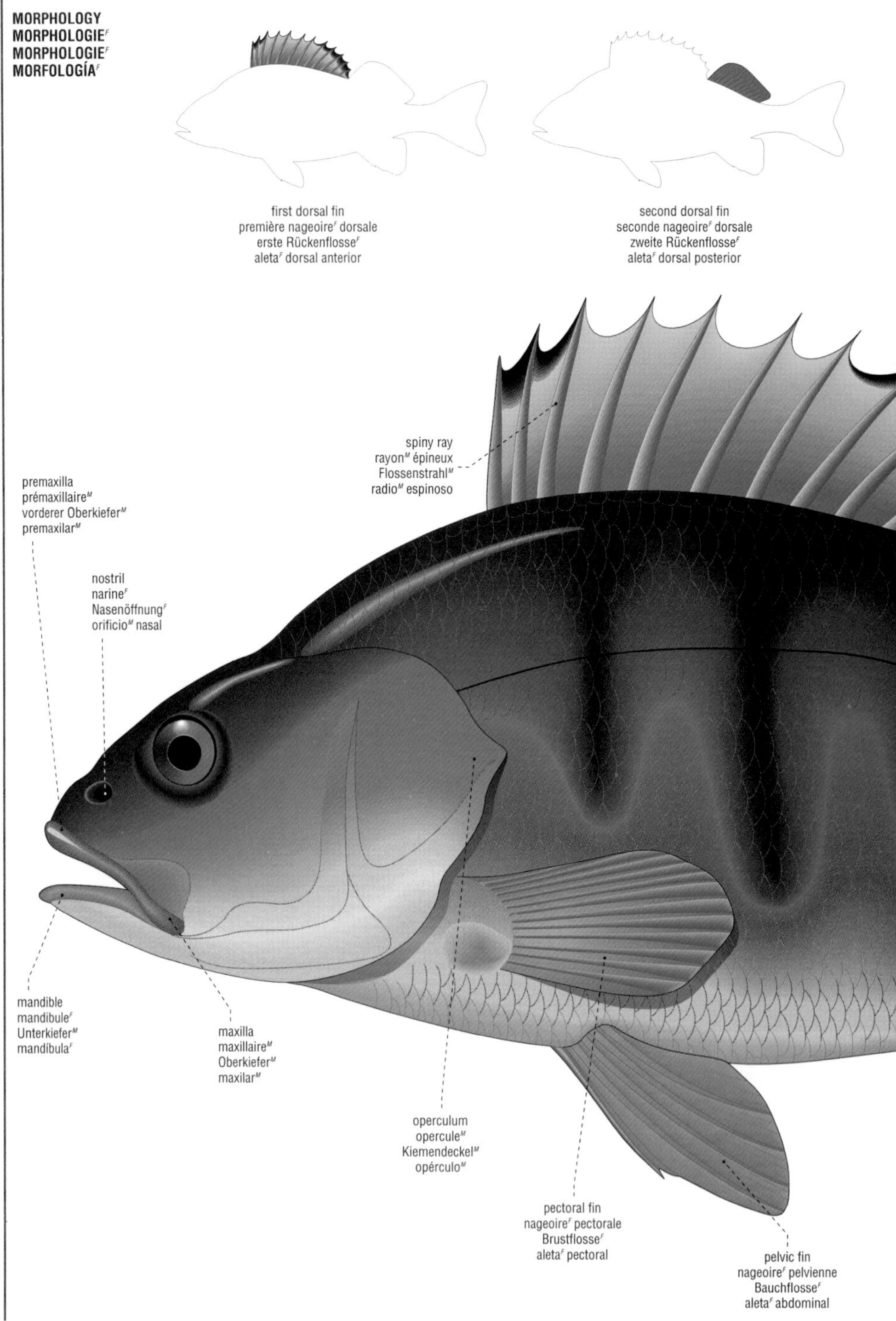

## GILLS
## BRANCHIES[F]
## KIEMEN[F]
## BRANQUIAS[F]

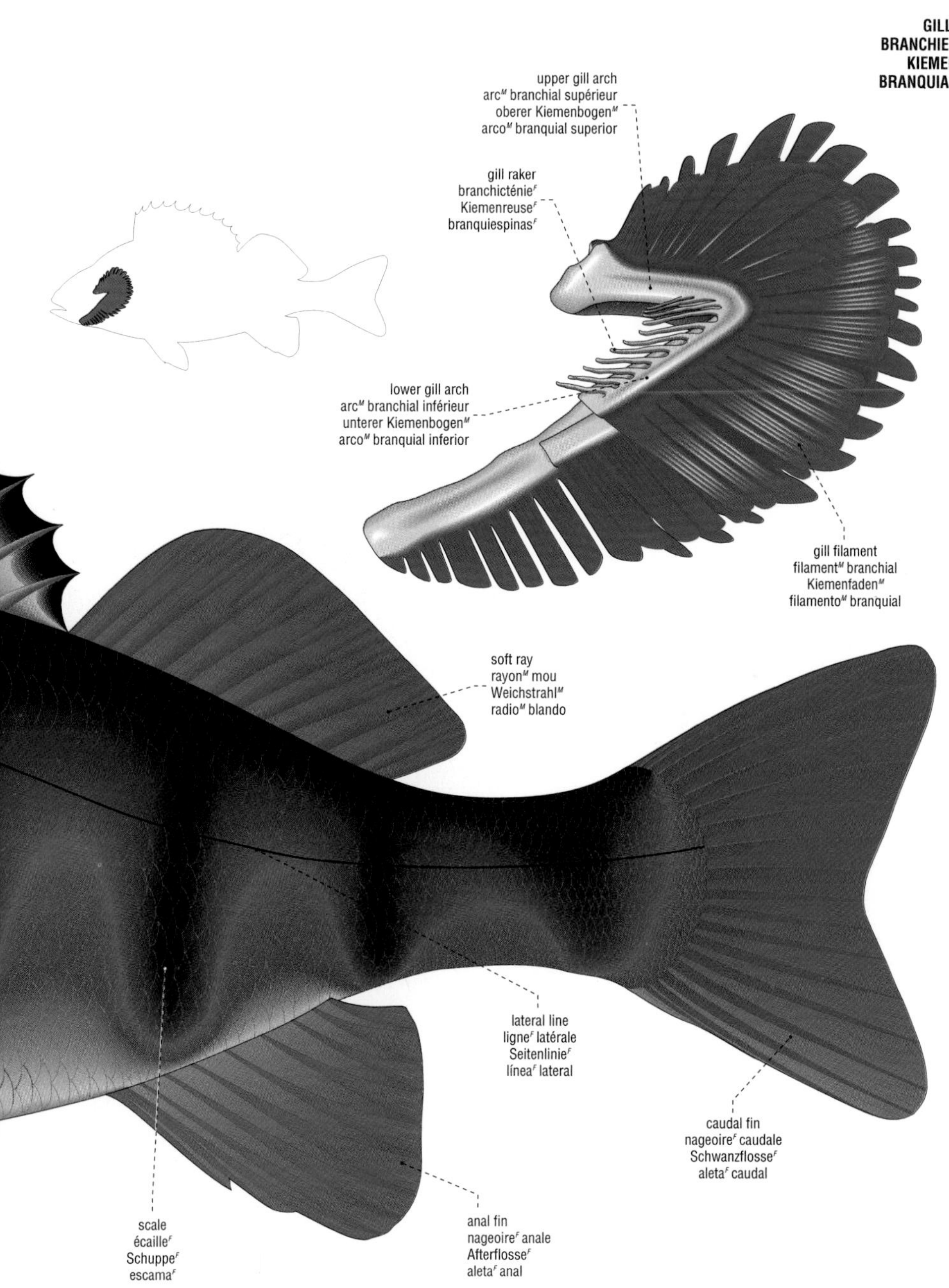

# FISH
# POISSON[M]
# FISCH[M]
# PEZ[M]

## ANATOMY
## ANATOMIE[F]
## ANATOMIE[F]
## ANATOMÍA[F]

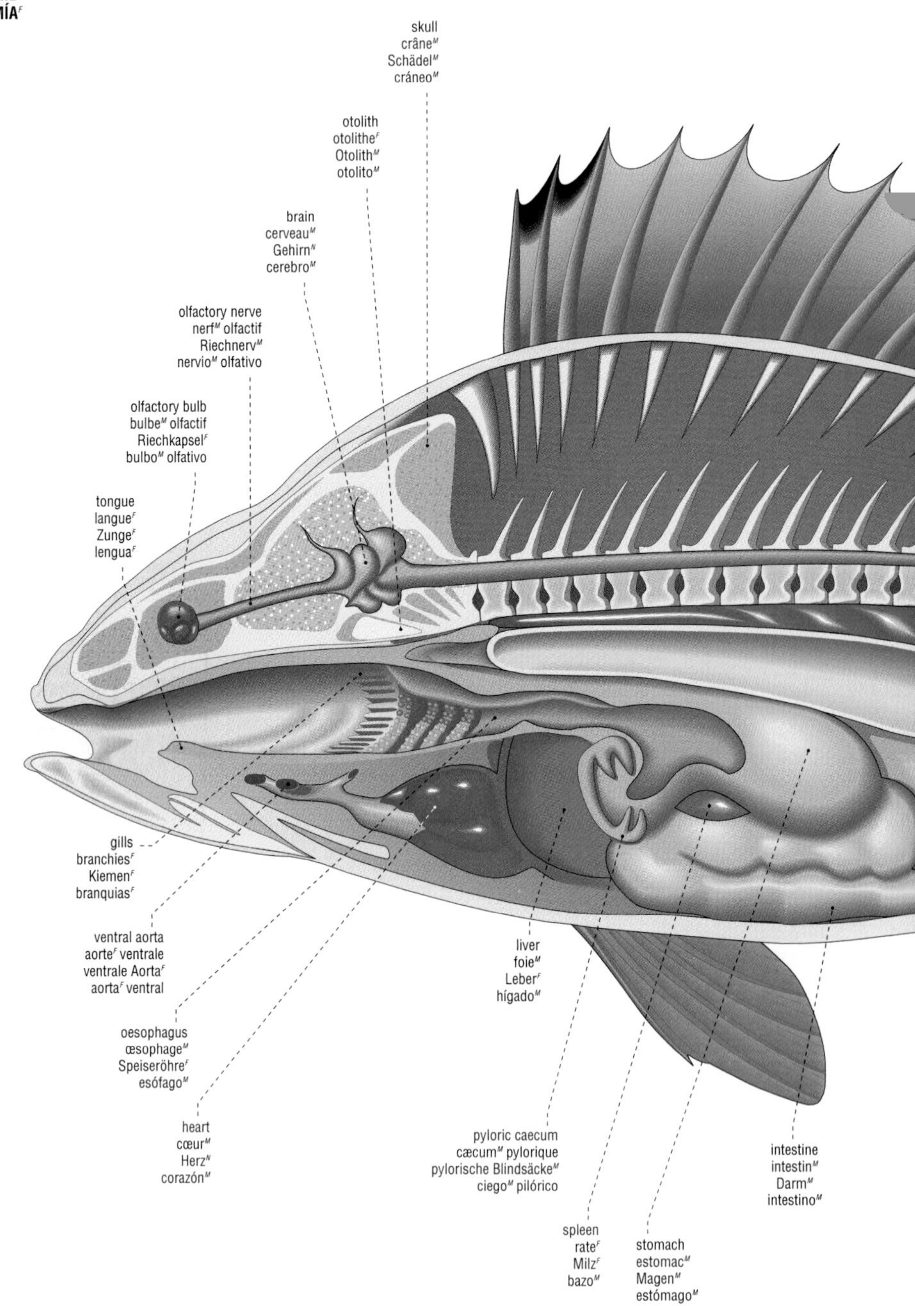

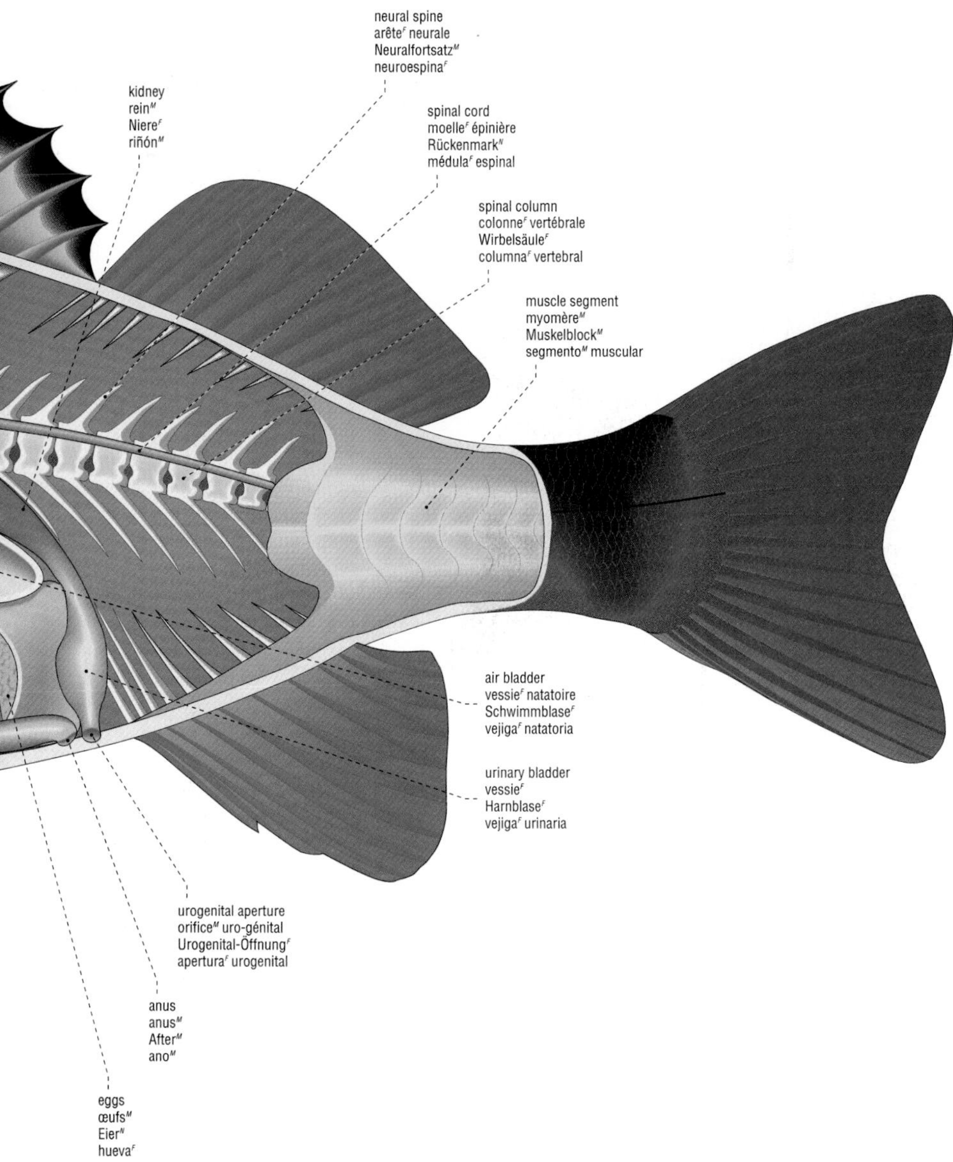
neural spine
arête$^{F}$ neurale
Neuralfortsatz$^{M}$
neuroespina$^{F}$
kidney
rein$^{M}$
Niere$^{F}$
riñón$^{M}$
spinal cord
moelle$^{F}$ épinière
Rückenmark$^{N}$
médula$^{F}$ espinal
spinal column
colonne$^{F}$ vertébrale
Wirbelsäule$^{F}$
columna$^{F}$ vertebral
muscle segment
myomère$^{M}$
Muskelblock$^{M}$
segmento$^{M}$ muscular
air bladder
vessie$^{F}$ natatoire
Schwimmblase$^{F}$
vejiga$^{F}$ natatoria
urinary bladder
vessie$^{F}$
Harnblase$^{F}$
vejiga$^{F}$ urinaria
urogenital aperture
orifice$^{M}$ uro-génital
Urogenital-Öffnung$^{F}$
apertura$^{F}$ urogenital
anus
anus$^{M}$
After$^{M}$
ano$^{M}$
eggs
œufs$^{M}$
Eier$^{N}$
hueva$^{F}$

# CRUSTACEAN
# CRUSTACÉ[M]
# KREBSTIERE[N]
# CRUSTÁCEO[M]

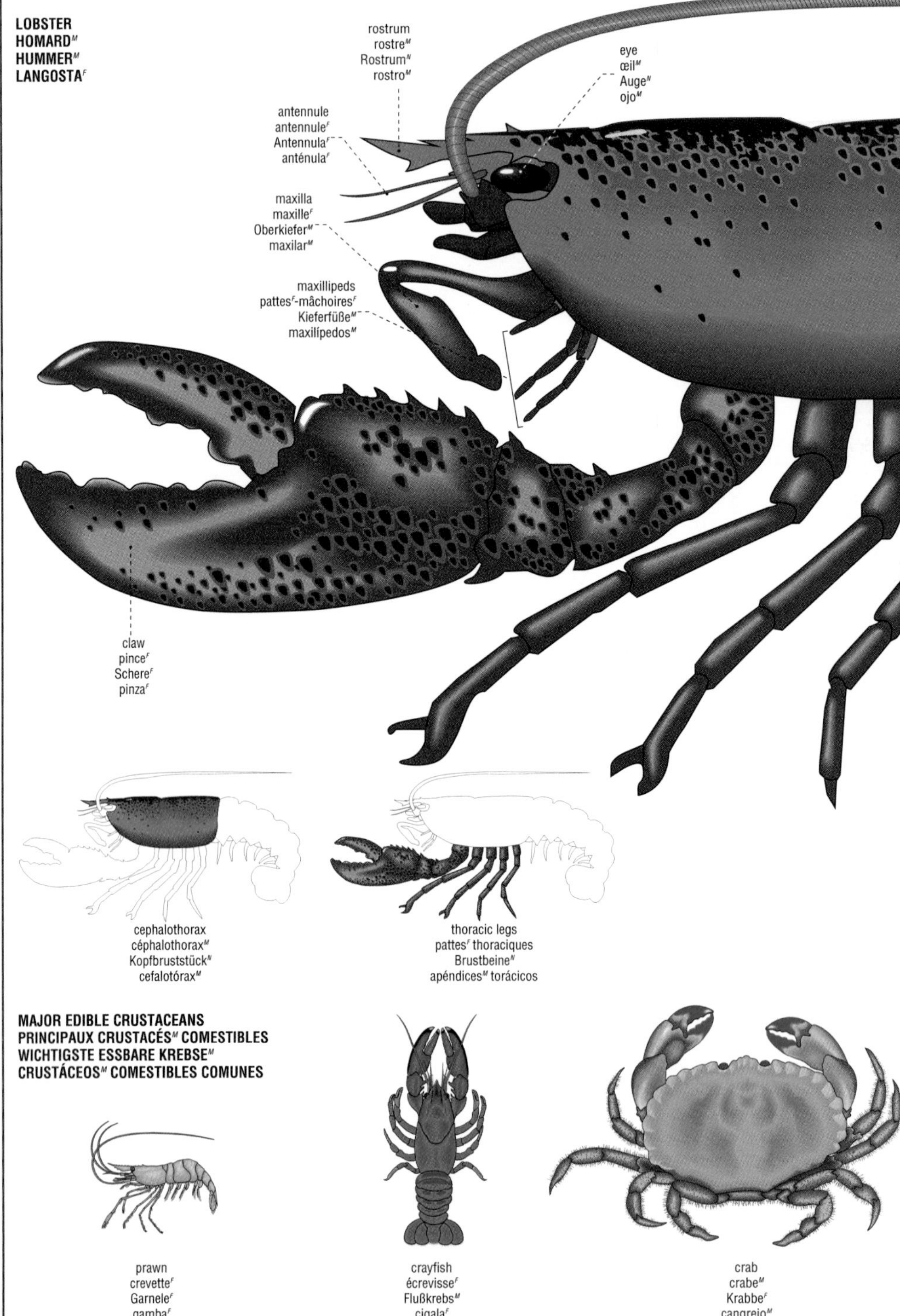

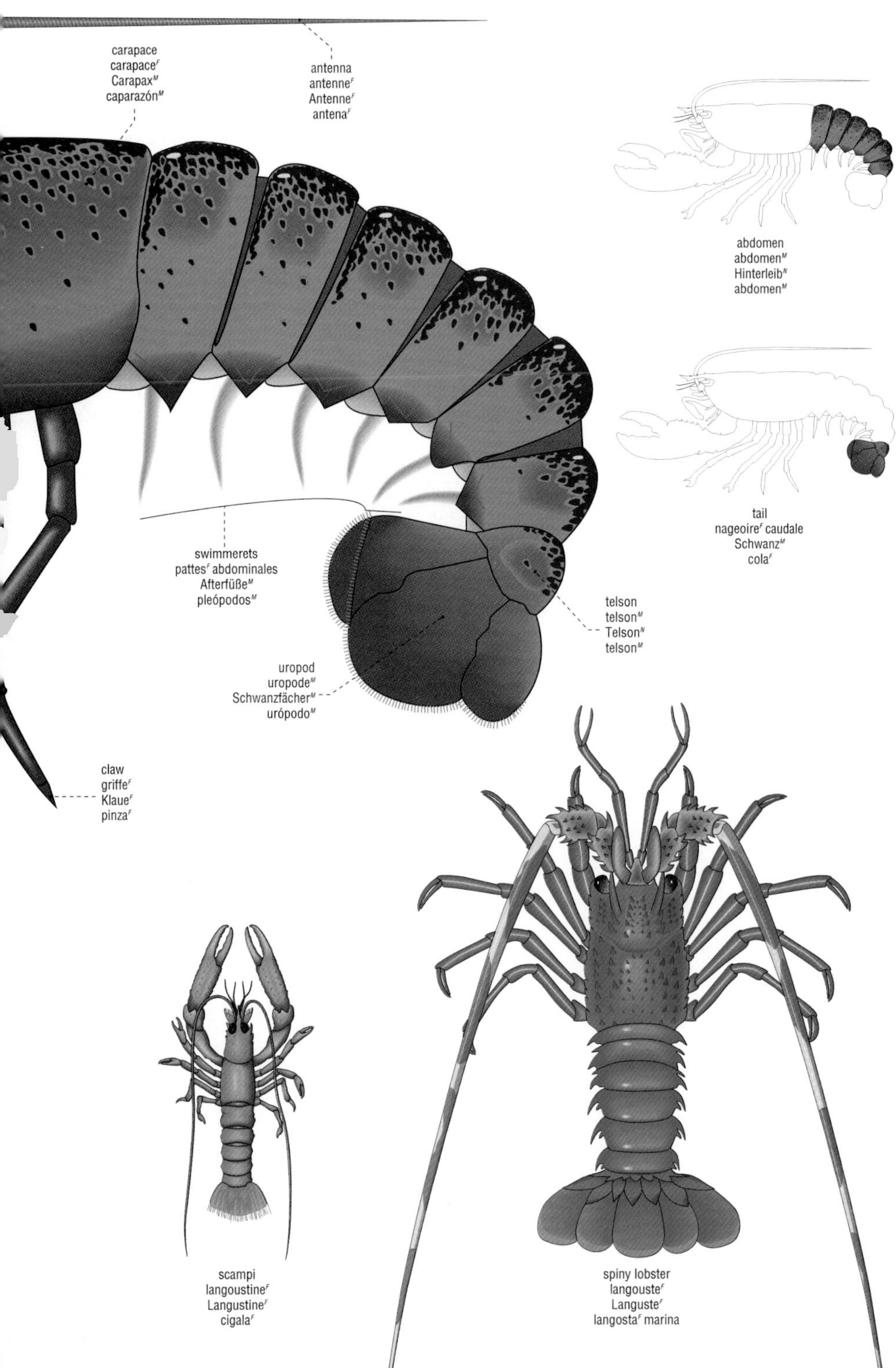
carapace
carapace^F
Carapax^M
caparazón^M
antenna
antenne^F
Antenne^F
antena^F
abdomen
abdomen^M
Hinterleib^N
abdomen^M
tail
nageoire^F caudale
Schwanz^M
cola^F
swimmerets
pattes^F abdominales
Afterfüße^M
pleópodos^M
telson
telson^M
Telson^N
telson^M
uropod
uropode^M
Schwanzfächer^M
urópodo^M
claw
griffe^F
Klaue^F
pinza^F
scampi
langoustine^F
Langustine^F
cigala^F
spiny lobster
langouste^F
Languste^F
langosta^F marina

# MOLLUSC
# MOLLUSQUE[M]
# WEICHTIER[N]
# MOLUSCO[M]

## OYSTER
## HUÎTRE[F]
## AUSTER[F]
## OSTRA[F]

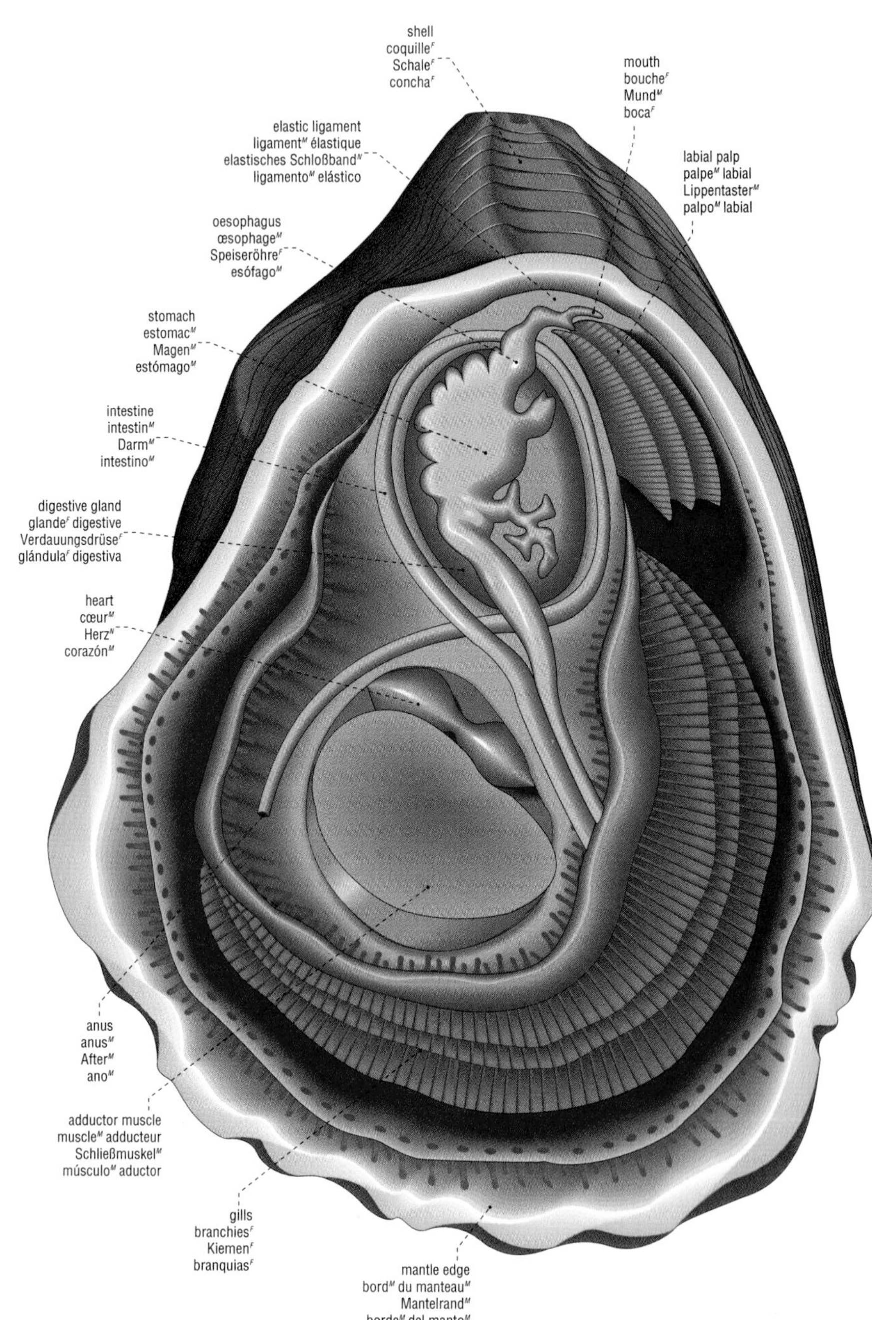

## PRINCIPAL EDIBLE MOLLUSCS
## PRINCIPAUX MOLLUSQUES[M] COMESTIBLES
## WICHTIGSTE ESSBARE WEICHTIERE[N]
## MOLUSCOS[M] COMESTIBLES

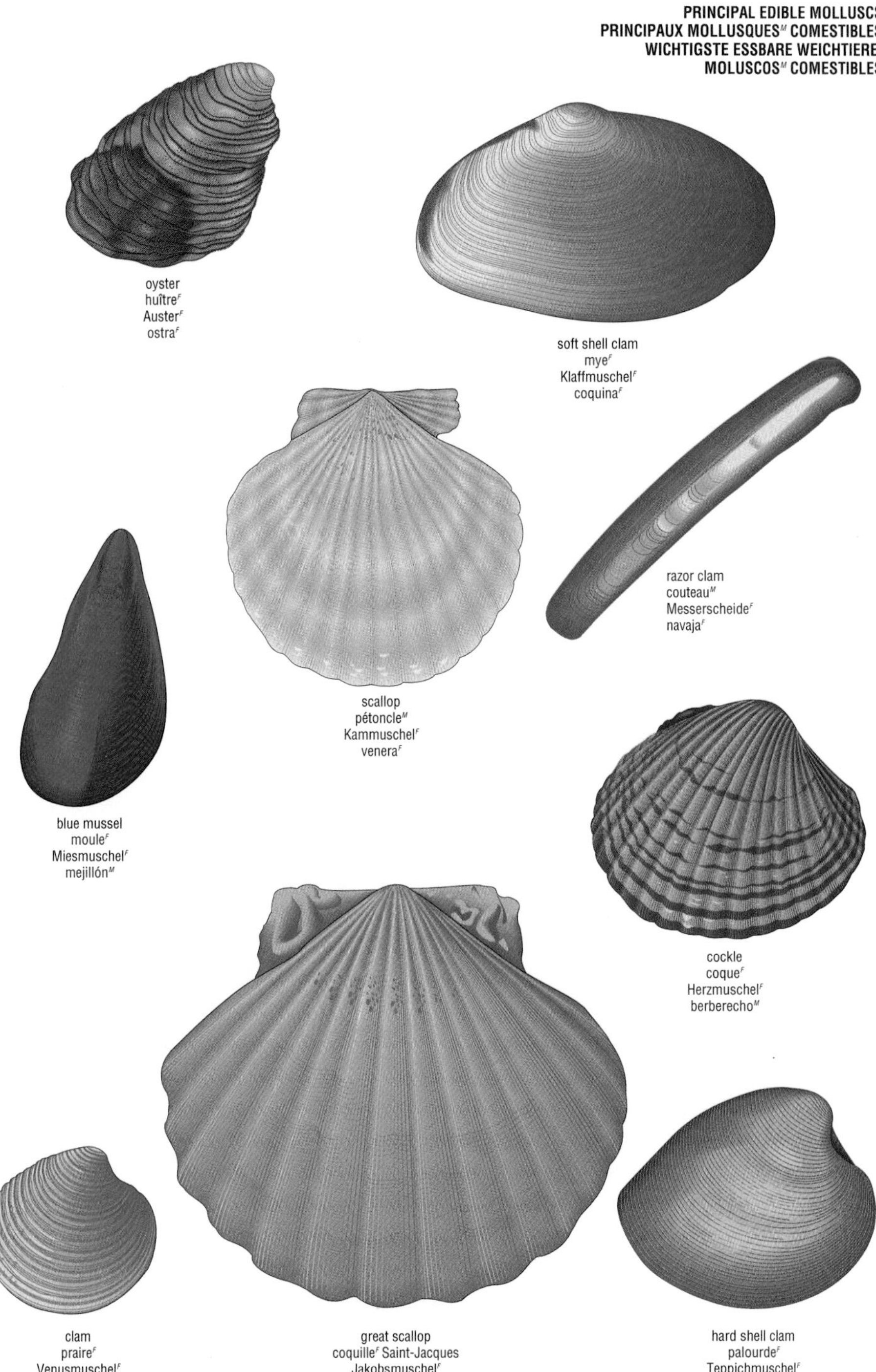

# UNIVALVE SHELL
# COQUILLE[F] UNIVALVE
# EINKLAPPIGE SCHALE[F]
# CONCHA[F] UNIVALVA

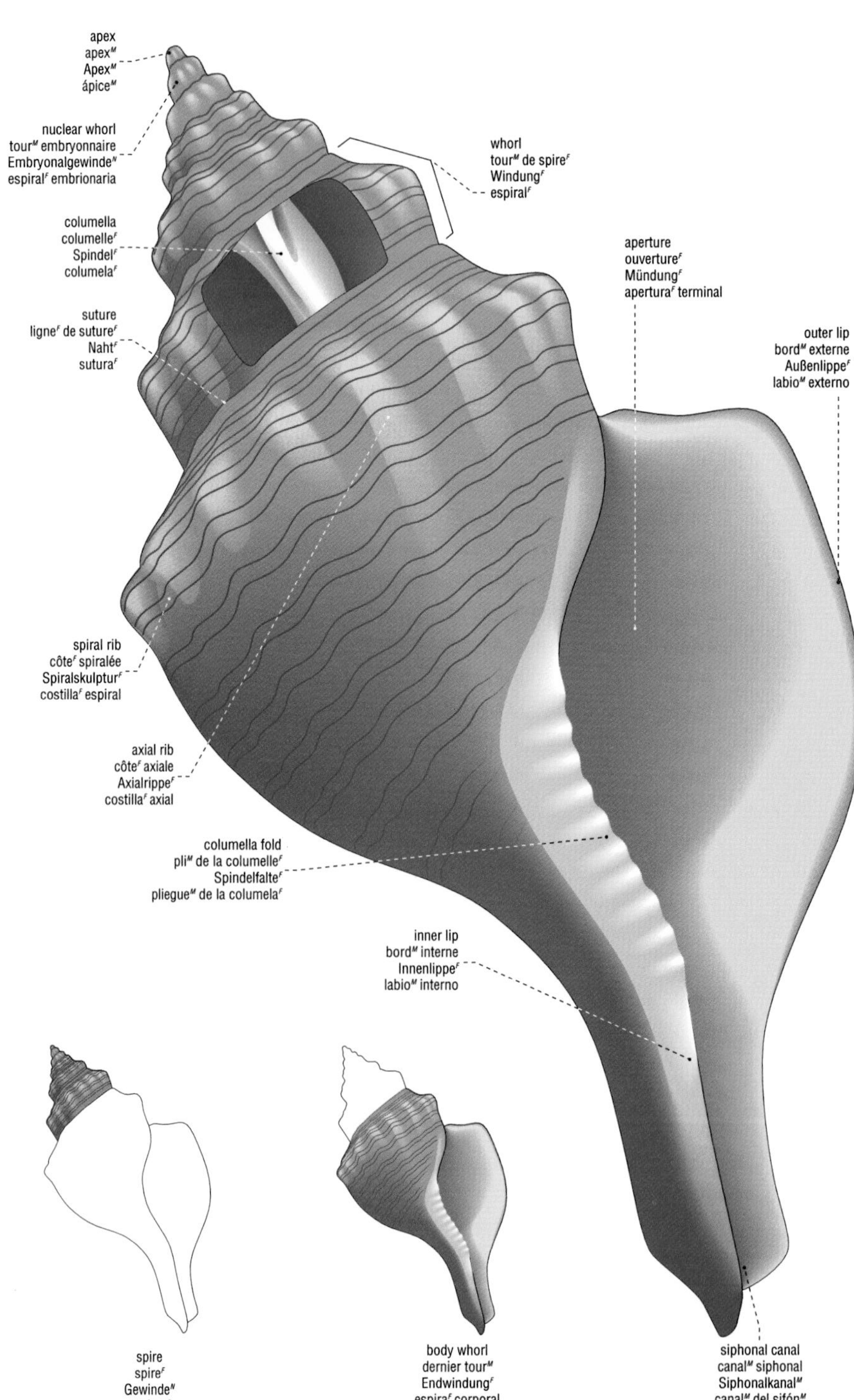

# BIVALVE SHELL
# COQUILLE^F BIVALVE
# ZWEIKLAPPIGE SCHALE^F
# CONCHA^F BIVALVA



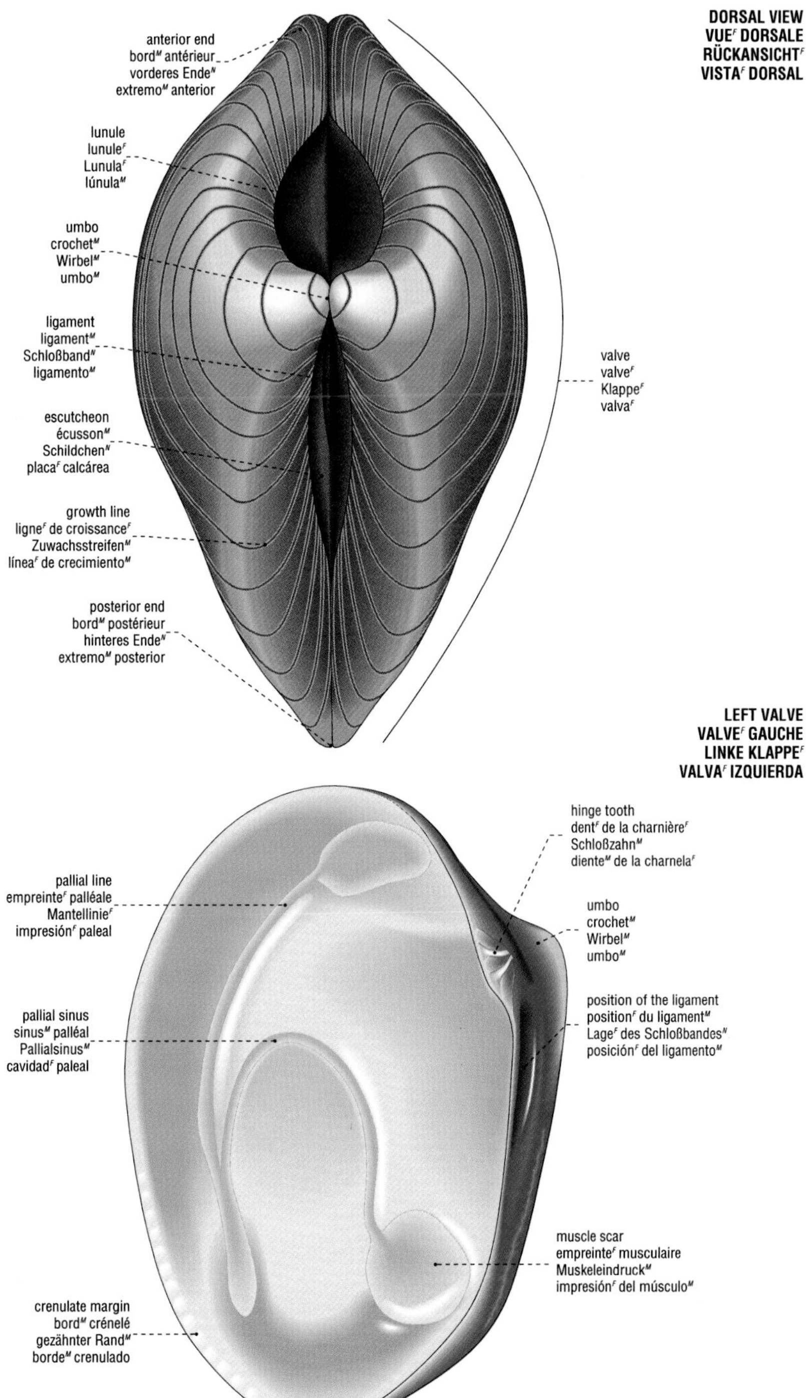

# REPTILE
# REPTILE[M]
# REPTIL[N]
# REPTIL[M]

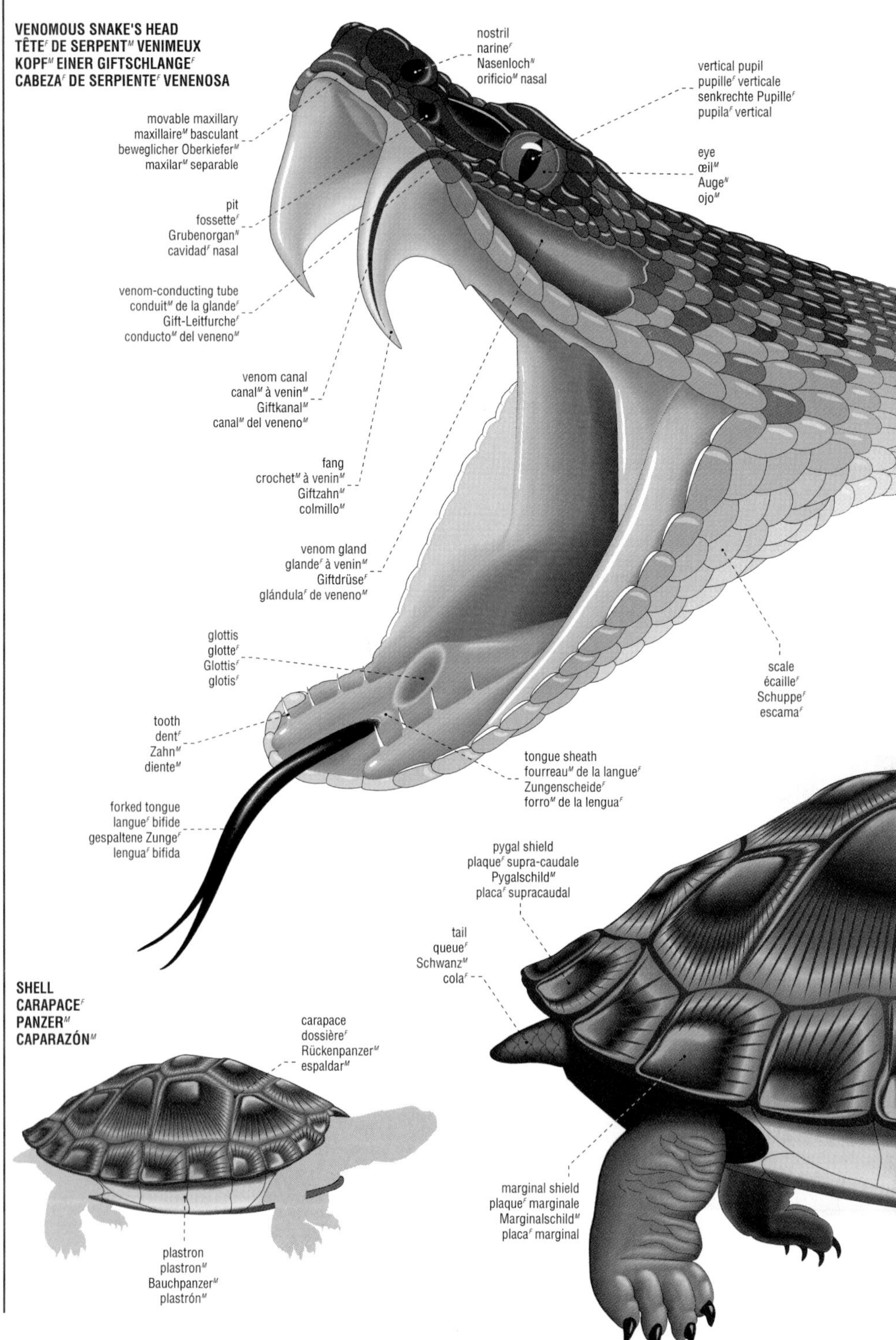

**RATTLESNAKE**
**SERPENT^M À SONNETTES^F**
**KLAPPERSCHLANGE^F**
**SERPIENTE^F DE CASCABEL^M**

**TURTLE**
**TORTUE^F**
**SCHILDKRÖTE^F**
**TORTUGA^F**

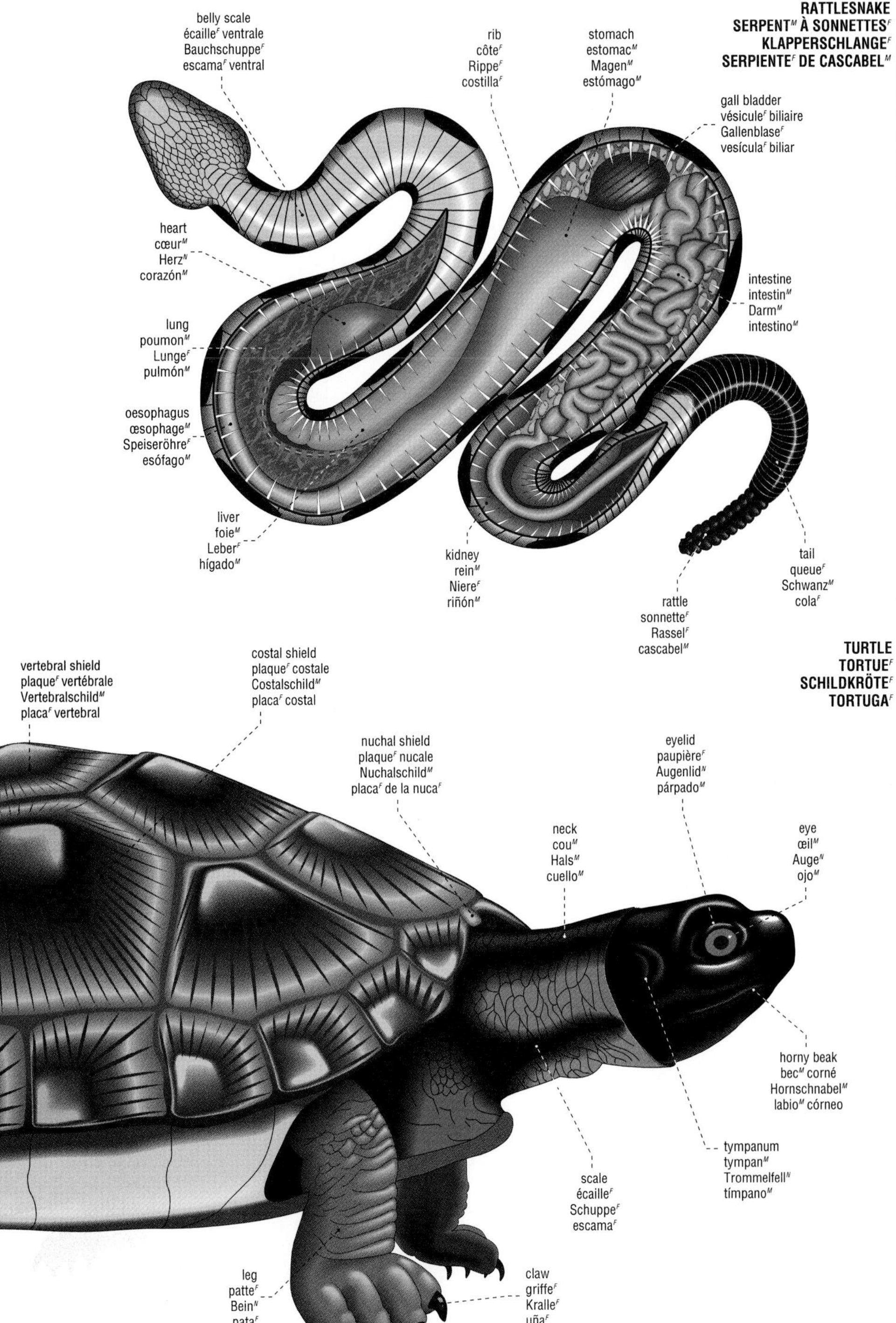

# TYPES OF JAW
# TYPES[M] DE MÂCHOIRES[F]
# GEBISSARTEN[F]
# TIPOS[M] DE MANDÍBULAS[F]

**BEAVER**
**CASTOR[M]**
**BIBER[M]**
**CASTOR[M]**

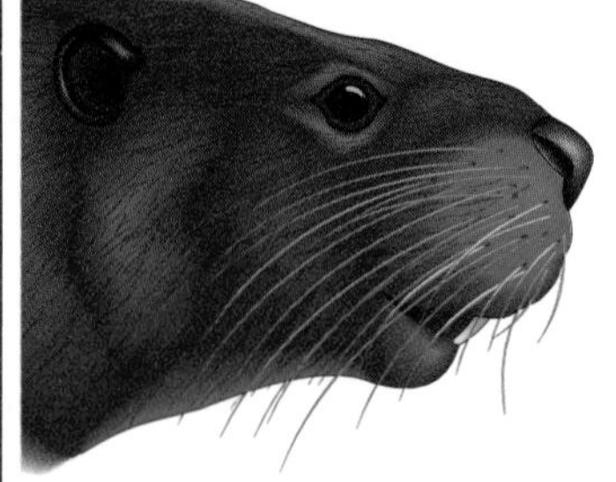

**RODENT'S JAW**
**MÂCHOIRE[F] DE RONGEUR[M]**
**NAGETIERGEBISS[N]**
**MANDÍBULA[F] DE ROEDOR[M]**

molar
molaire[F]
Molar[M]
molar[M]

premolar
prémolaire[F]
Prämolar[M]
premolar[M]

incisor
incisive[F]
Schneidezahn[M]
incisivo[M]

diastema
barre[F]
Laden[M]
diastema[F]

**LION**
**LION[M]**
**LÖWE[M]**
**LEÓN[M]**

**CARNIVORE'S JAW**
**MÂCHOIRE[F] DE CARNIVORE[M]**
**FLEISCHFRESSERGEBISS[N]**
**MANDÍBULA[F] DE CARNÍVORO[M]**

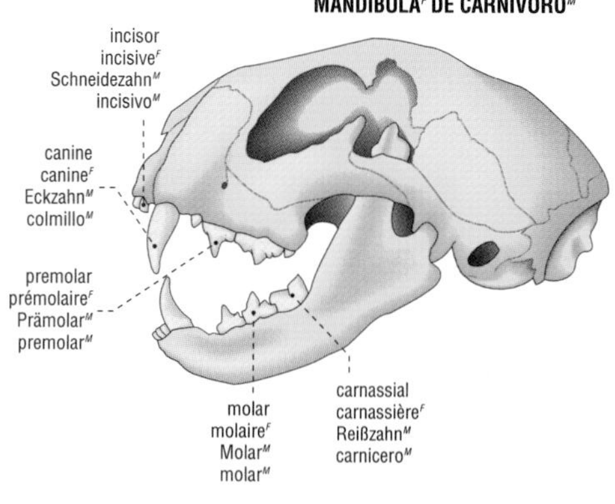


**HORSE**
**CHEVAL[M]**
**PFERD[N]**
**CABALLO[M]**

**HERBIVORE'S JAW**
**MÂCHOIRE[F] D'HERBIVORE[M]**
**PFLANZENFRESSERGEBISS[N]**
**MANDÍBULA[F] DE HERBÍVORO[M]**

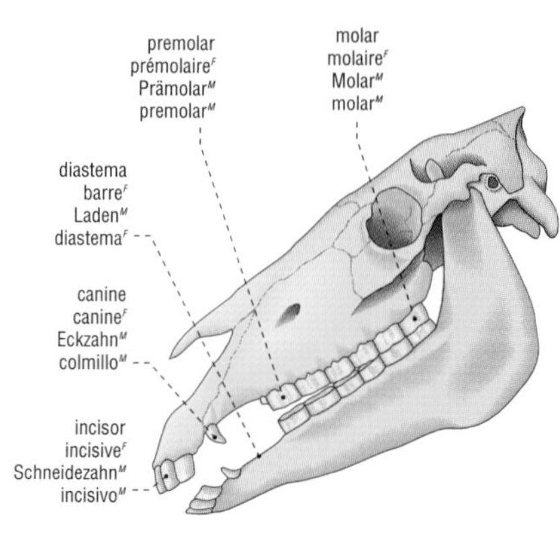

## PRINCIPAL TYPES OF HORN
## PRINCIPAUX TYPES[M] DE CORNES[F]
## WICHTIGSTE HORNARTEN[F]
## CUERNOS[M]: TIPOS[M] MÁS COMUNES

horns of a mouflon
cornes[F] de mouflon[M]
Hörner[N] eines Mufflons[M]
cuernos[M] de carnero[M]

horns of a giraffe
cornes[F] de girafe[F]
Hörner[N] einer Giraffe[F]
cuernos[M] de jirafa[F]

horns of a rhinoceros
cornes[F] de rhinocéros[M]
Hörner[N] eines Nashorns[N]
cuernos[M] de rinoceronte[M]

## PRINCIPAL TYPES OF TUSK
## PRINCIPAUX TYPES[M] DE DÉFENSES[F]
## WICHTIGSTE STOSSZÄHNE[M]
## COLMILOS[M]: TIPOS[M] MÁS COMUNES

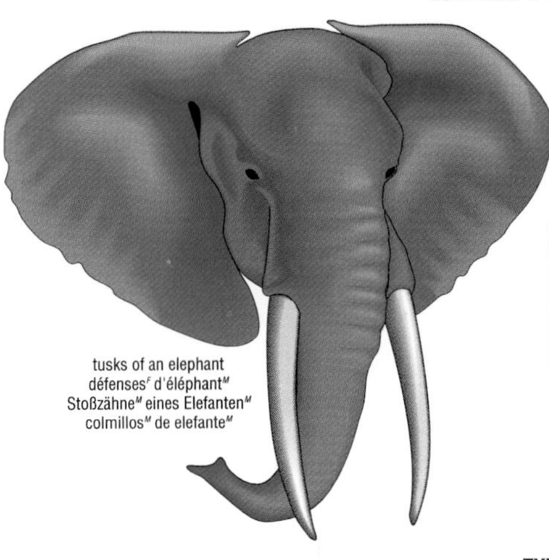

tusks of an elephant
défenses[F] d'éléphant[M]
Stoßzähne[M] eines Elefanten[M]
colmillos[M] de elefante[M]

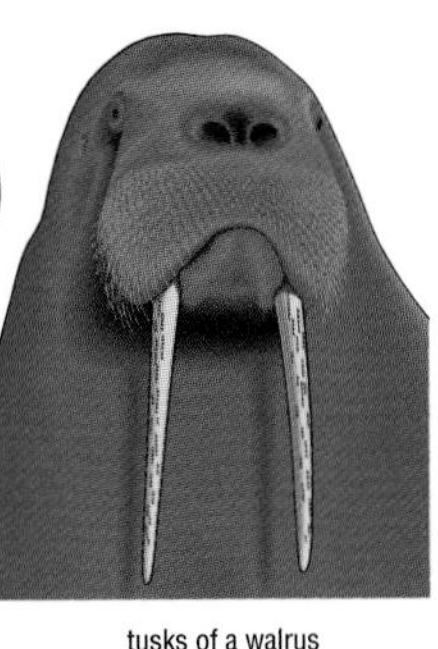

tusks of a walrus
défenses[F] de morse[M]
Eckzähne[M] eines Walrosses[N]
colmillos[M] de morsa[F]

tusks of a wart hog
défenses[F] de phacochère[M]
Hauer[M] eines Warzenschweins[N]
colmillos[M] de jabalí[M] verrugoso

## TYPES OF HOOF
## TYPES[M] DE SABOTS[M]
## HUFARTEN[F]
## PATAS[F] DE UNGULADOS[M]: TIPOS[M] MÁS COMUNES

one-toe hoof
sabot[M] à 1 doigt[M]
Ein-Zehenhuf[M]
de una pezuña[F]

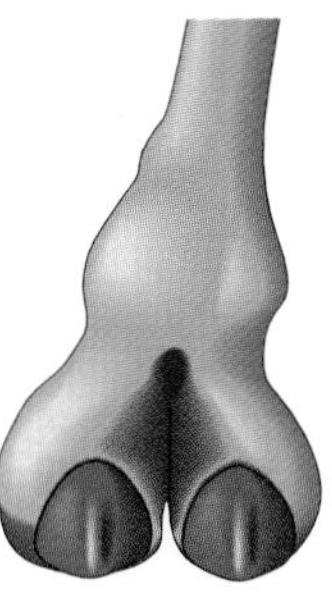

two-toed hoof
sabot[M] à 2 doigts[M]
Zwei-Zehenhuf[M]
de dos pezuñas[F]

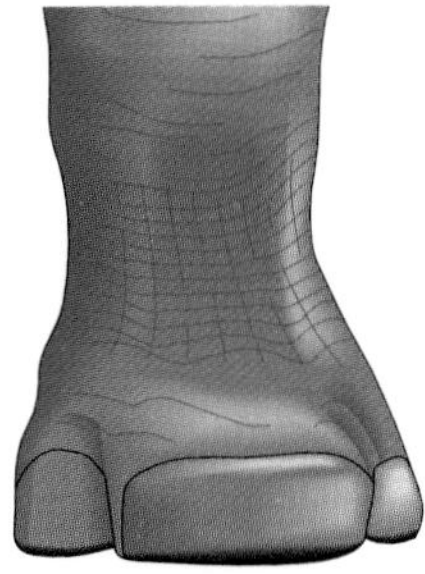

three-toed hoof
sabot[M] à 3 doigts[M]
Drei-Zehenhuf[M]
de tres pezuñas[F]

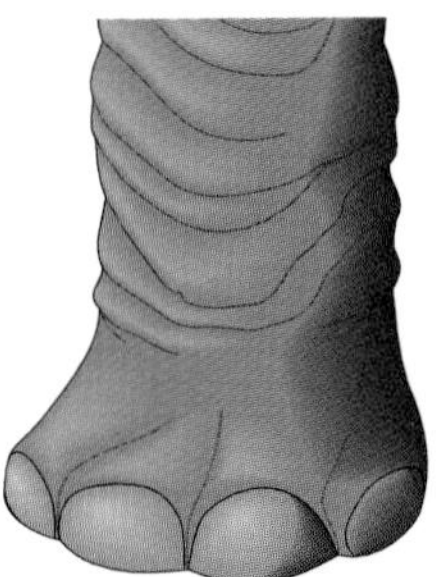

four-toed hoof
sabot[M] à 4 doigts[M]
Vier-Zehenhuf[M]
de cuatro pezuñas[F]

# HORSE
# CHEVAL[M]
# PFERD[N]
# CABALLO[M]

## MORPHOLOGY
## MORPHOLOGIE[F]
## MORPHOLOGIE[F]
## MORFOLOGÍA[F]

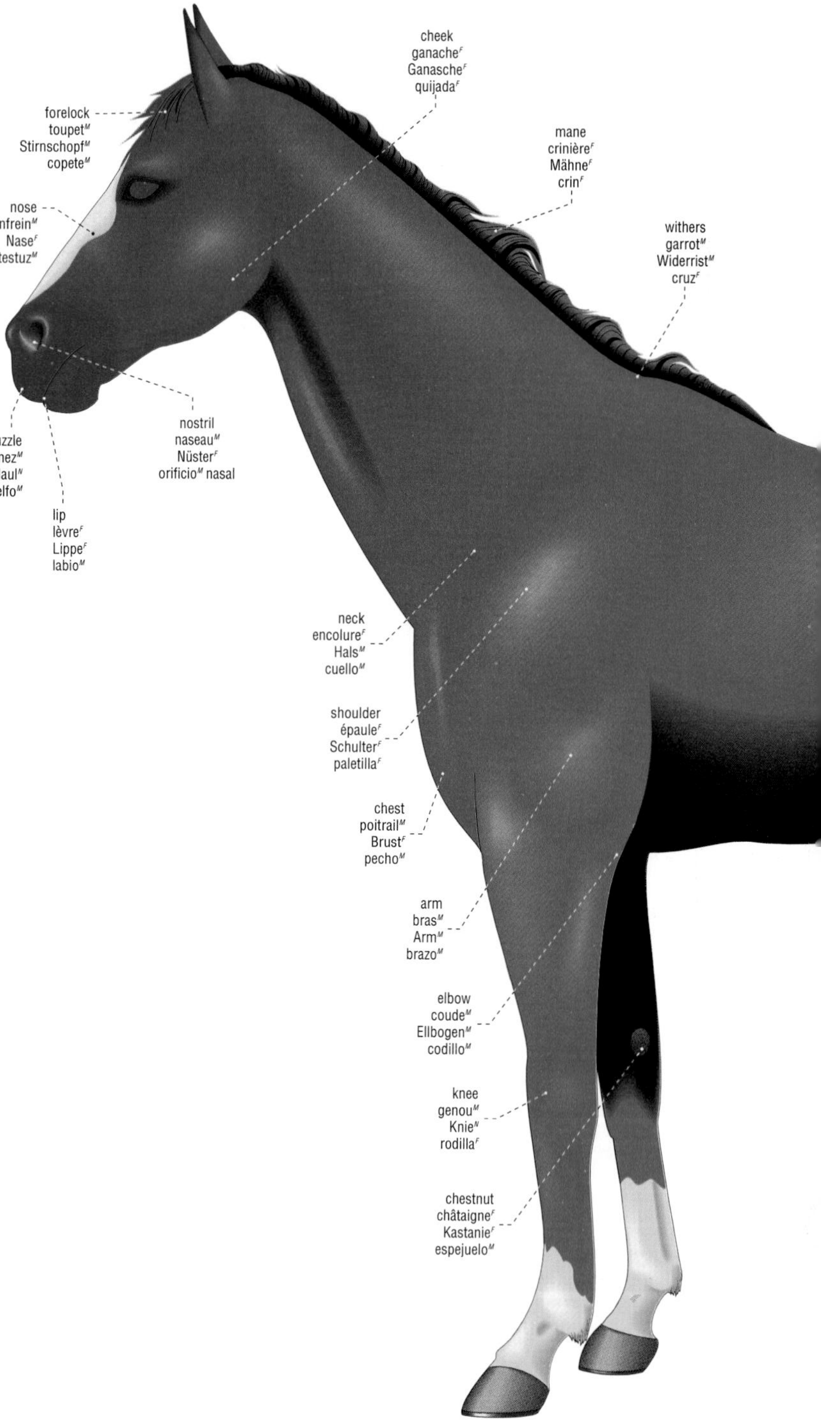

cheek
ganache[F]
Ganasche[F]
quijada[F]

forelock
toupet[M]
Stirnschopf[M]
copete[M]

mane
crinière[F]
Mähne[F]
crin[F]

nose
chanfrein[M]
Nase[F]
testuz[M]

withers
garrot[M]
Widerrist[M]
cruz[F]

muzzle
bout[M] du nez[M]
Maul[N]
belfo[M]

nostril
naseau[M]
Nüster[F]
orificio[M] nasal

lip
lèvre[F]
Lippe[F]
labio[M]

neck
encolure[F]
Hals[M]
cuello[M]

shoulder
épaule[F]
Schulter[F]
paletilla[F]

chest
poitrail[M]
Brust[F]
pecho[M]

arm
bras[M]
Arm[M]
brazo[M]

elbow
coude[M]
Ellbogen[M]
codillo[M]

knee
genou[M]
Knie[N]
rodilla[F]

chestnut
châtaigne[F]
Kastanie[F]
espejuelo[M]

## GAITS
## ALLURES[F]
## GANGARTEN[F]
## LOS PASOS[M]

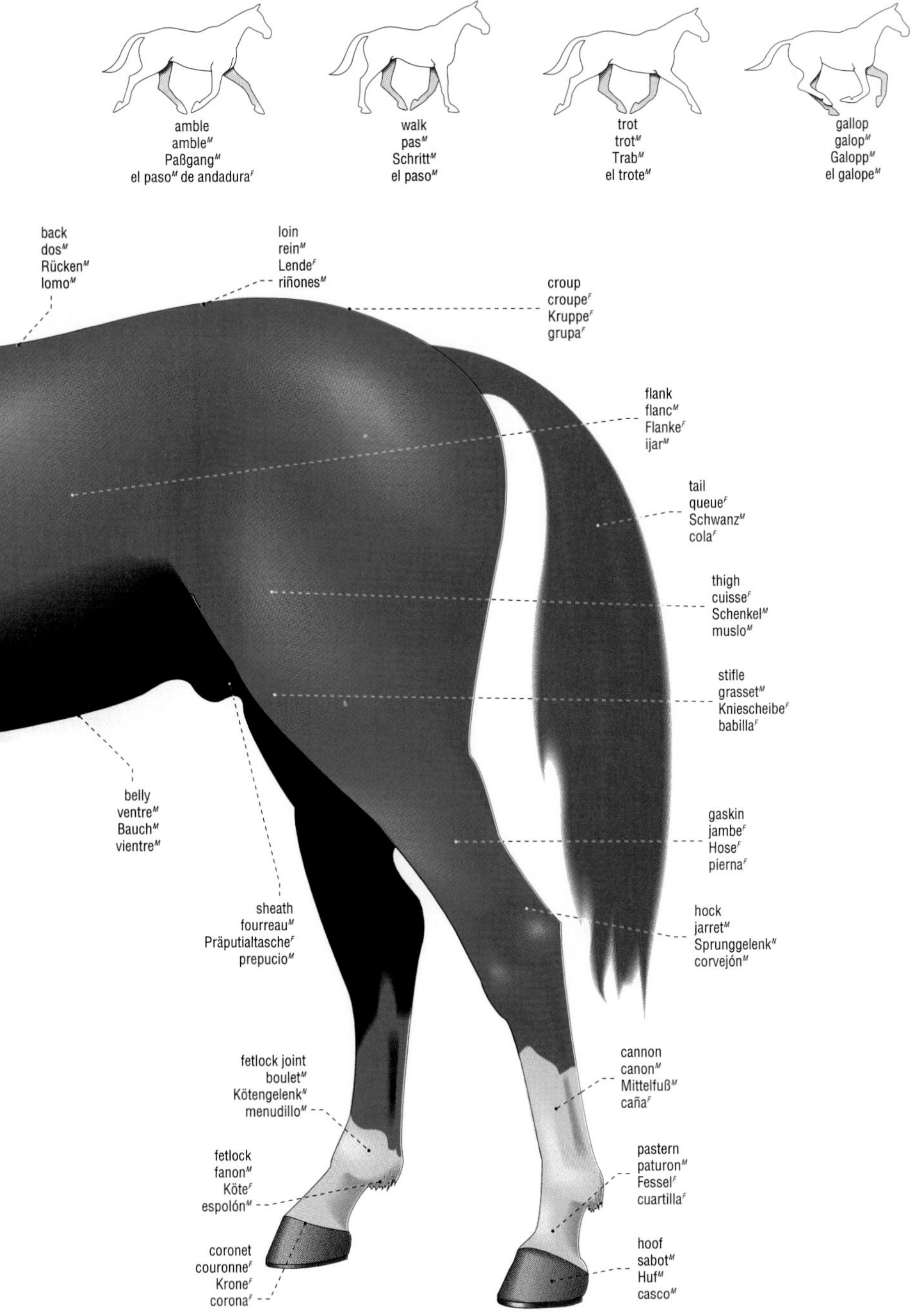

# HORSE
# CHEVAL[M]
# PFERD[N]
# CABALLO[M]



## SKELETON
## SQUELETTE[M]
## SKELETT[N]
## ESQUELETO[M]

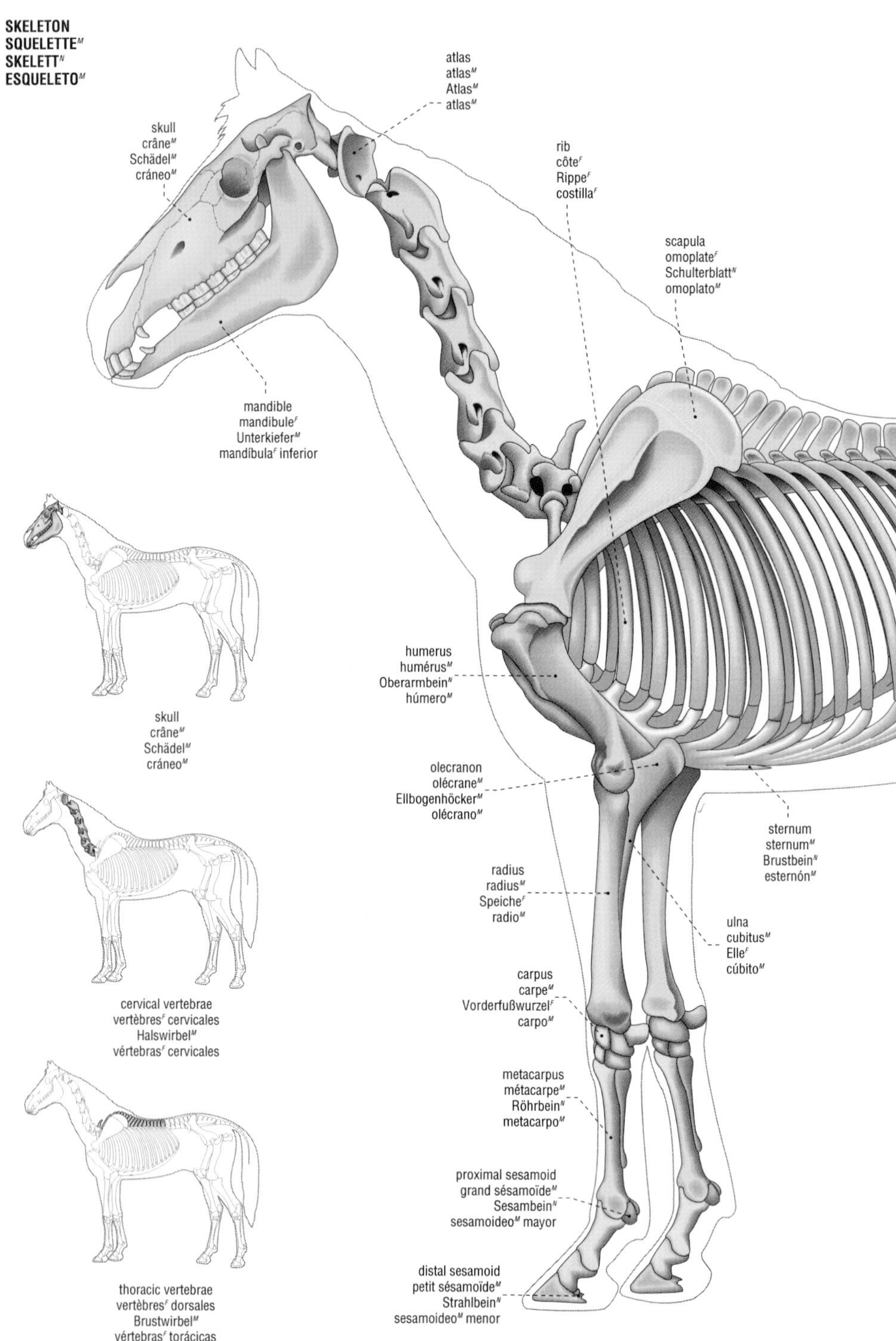

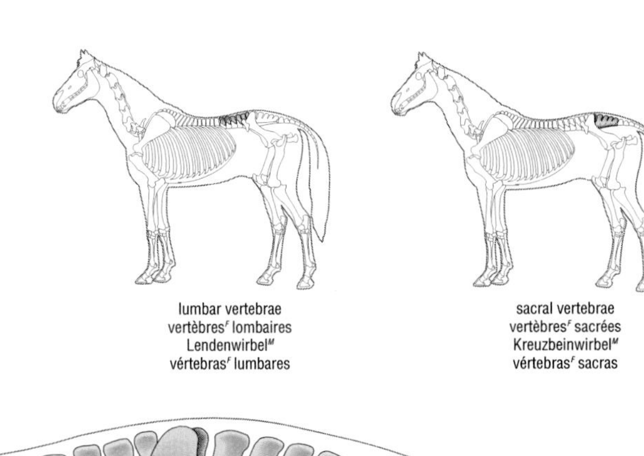

lumbar vertebrae
vertèbres[F] lombaires
Lendenwirbel[M]
vértebras[F] lumbares

sacral vertebrae
vertèbres[F] sacrées
Kreuzbeinwirbel[M]
vértebras[F] sacras

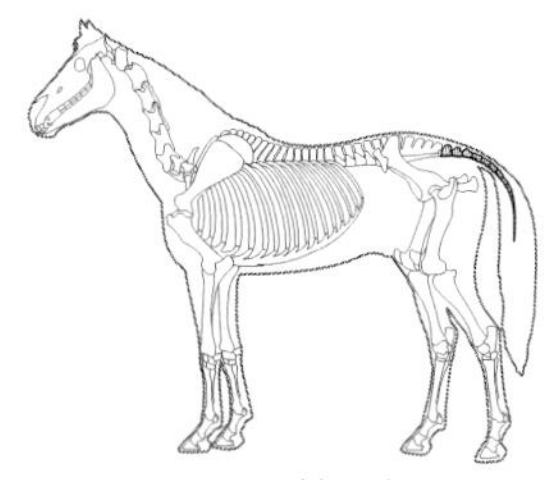

caudal vertebrae
vertèbres[F] coccygiennes
Schwanzwirbel[M]
vértebras[F] caudales

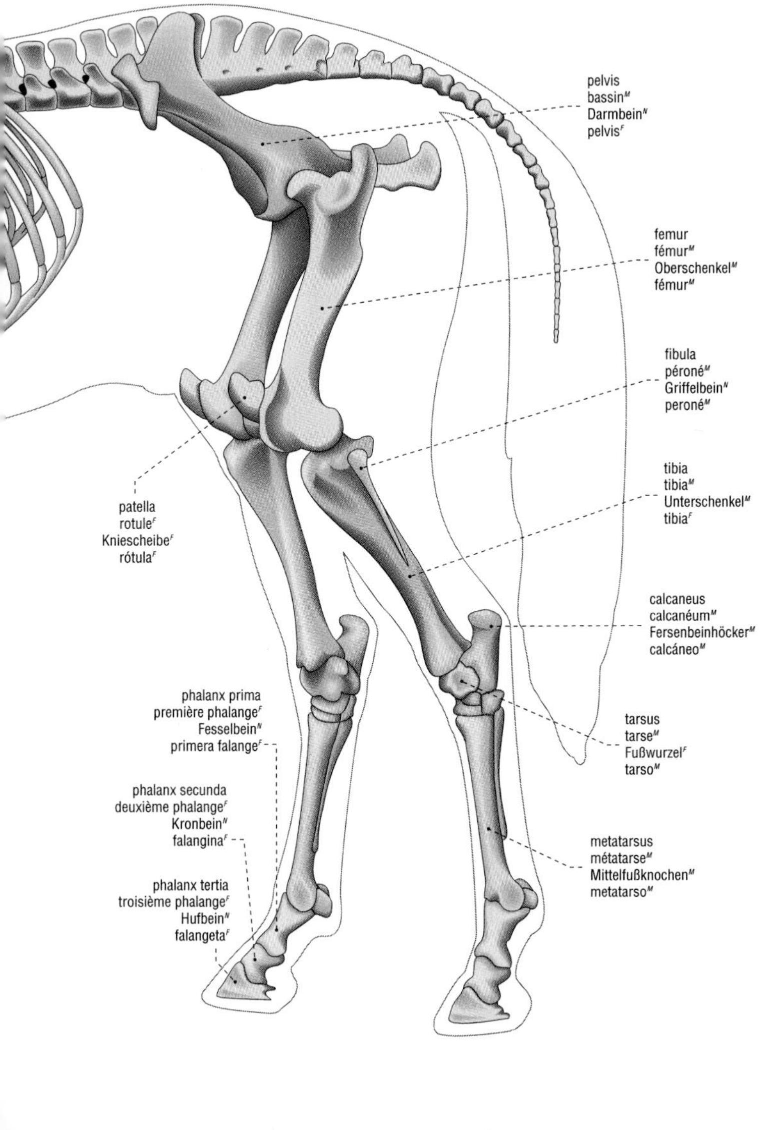

pelvis
bassin[M]
Darmbein[N]
pelvis[F]

femur
fémur[M]
Oberschenkel[M]
fémur[M]

fibula
péroné[M]
Griffelbein[N]
peroné[M]

patella
rotule[F]
Kniescheibe[F]
rótula[F]

tibia
tibia[M]
Unterschenkel[M]
tibia[F]

calcaneus
calcanéum[M]
Fersenbeinhöcker[M]
calcáneo[M]

phalanx prima
première phalange[F]
Fesselbein[N]
primera falange[F]

tarsus
tarse[M]
Fußwurzel[F]
tarso[M]

phalanx secunda
deuxième phalange[F]
Kronbein[N]
falangina[F]

metatarsus
métatarse[M]
Mittelfußknochen[M]
metatarso[M]

phalanx tertia
troisième phalange[F]
Hufbein[N]
falangeta[F]

# HORSE
# CHEVAL^M
# PFERD^N
# CABALLO^M

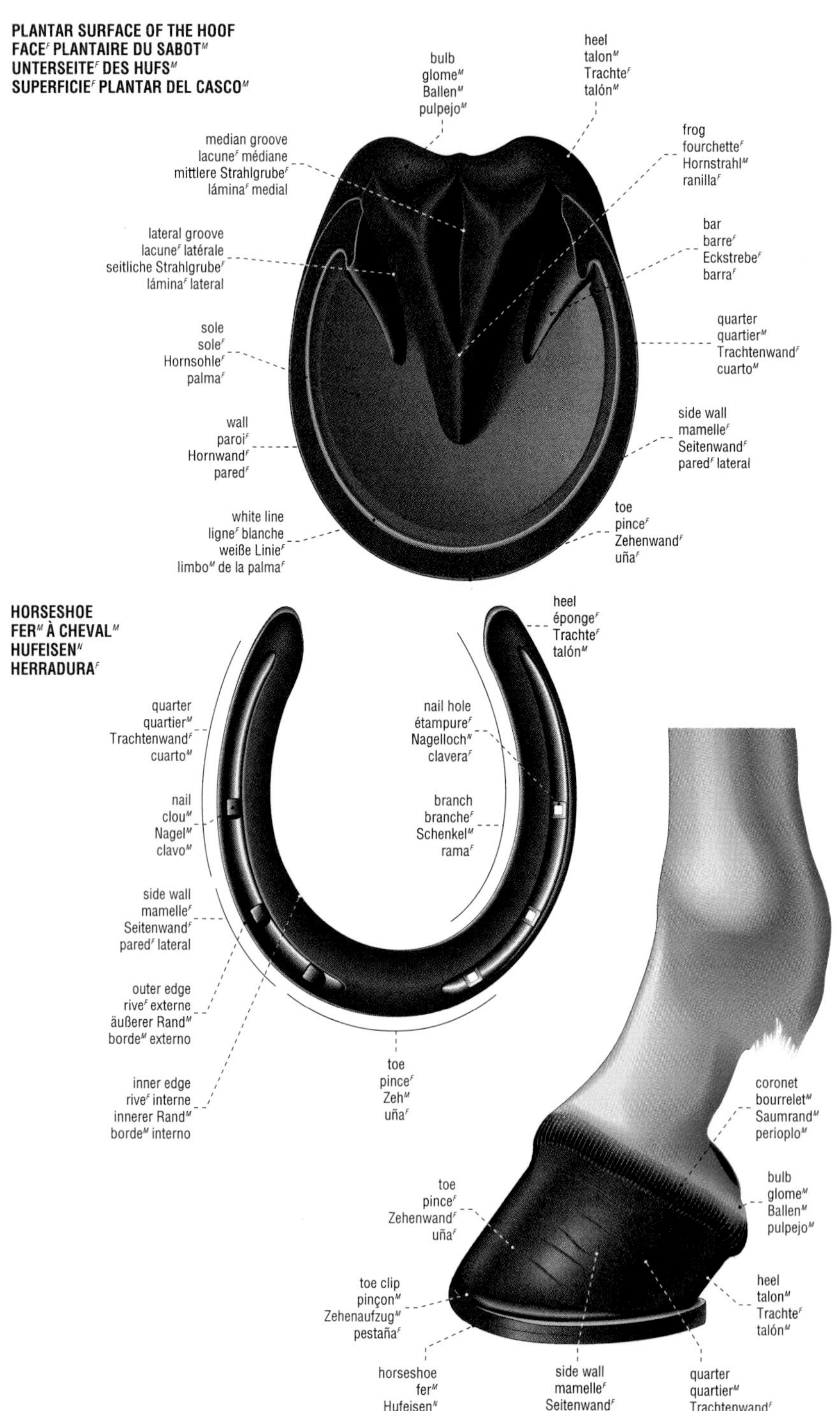

# DEER FAMILY
# CERVIDÉS[M]
# FAMILIE[F] DER HIRSCHE[M]
# CÉRVIDOS[M]

## DEER ANTLERS
## BOIS[M] DE CERF[M]
## HIRSCHGEWEIH[N]
## CORNAMENTA[F]

# DOG
# CHIEN[M]
# HUND[M]
# PERRO[M]

## MORPHOLOGY
## MORPHOLOGIE[F]
## MORPHOLOGIE[F]
## MORFOLOGÍA[F]

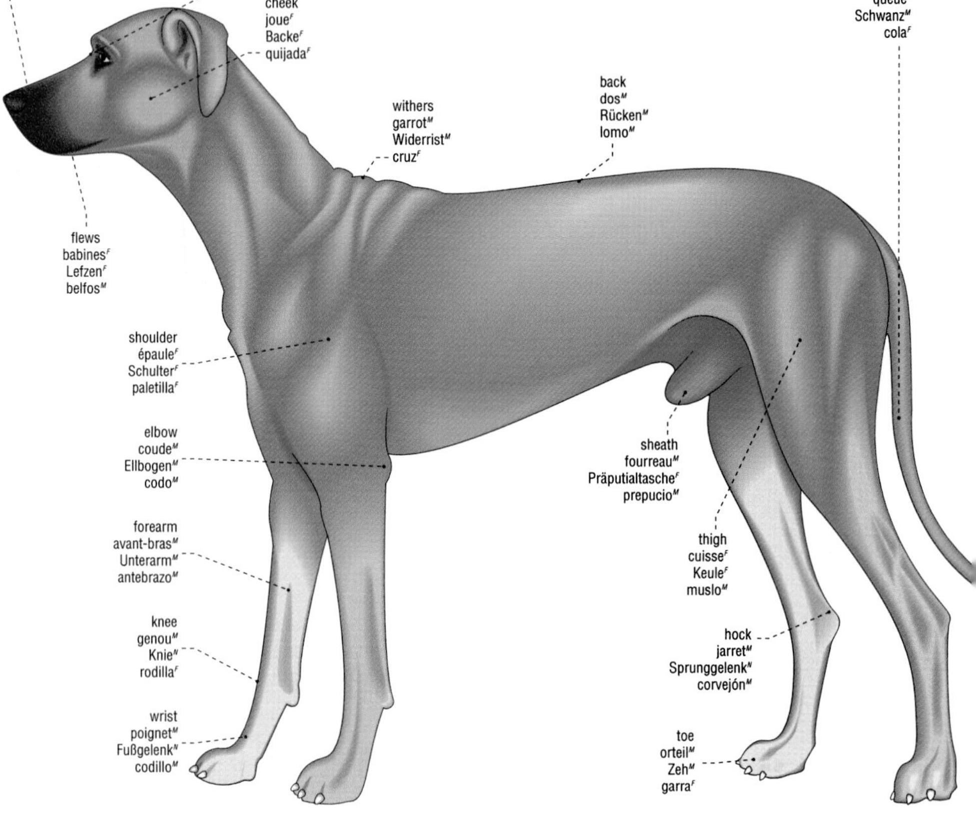

muzzle
museau[M]
Schnauze[F]
hocico[M]
stop
stop[M]
Stop[M]
entrecejo[M]
cheek
joue[F]
Backe[F]
quijada[F]
tail
queue[F]
Schwanz[M]
cola[F]
back
dos[M]
Rücken[M]
lomo[M]
withers
garrot[M]
Widerrist[M]
cruz[F]
flews
babines[F]
Lefzen[F]
belfos[M]
shoulder
épaule[F]
Schulter[F]
paletilla[F]
elbow
coude[M]
Ellbogen[M]
codo[M]
sheath
fourreau[M]
Präputialtasche[F]
prepucio[M]
forearm
avant-bras[M]
Unterarm[M]
antebrazo[M]
thigh
cuisse[F]
Keule[F]
muslo[M]
knee
genou[M]
Knie[N]
rodilla[F]
hock
jarret[M]
Sprunggelenk[N]
corvejón[M]
wrist
poignet[M]
Fußgelenk[N]
codillo[M]
toe
orteil[M]
Zeh[M]
garra[F]

## DOG'S FOREPAW
## PATTE[F] ANTÉRIEURE
## VORDERPFOTE[F] DES HUNDES[M]
## PATA[F] DELANTERA DEL PERRO[M]

palmar pad
coussinet[M] palmaire
Sohlenballen[M]
cojinete[M] palmar
carpal pad
coussinet[M] carpien
Karpalballen[M]
cojinete[M] carpal
digital pad
coussinet[M] digité
Zehenballen[M]
cojinete[M] digital
claw
griffe[F]
Kralle[F]
uña[F]
toe
orteil[M]
Zeh[M]
garra[F]
dew pad
coussinet[M] de l'ergot[M]
Afterkrallenballen[M]
cojinete[M]
dewclaw
ergot[M]
Afterkralle[F]
espolón[M]

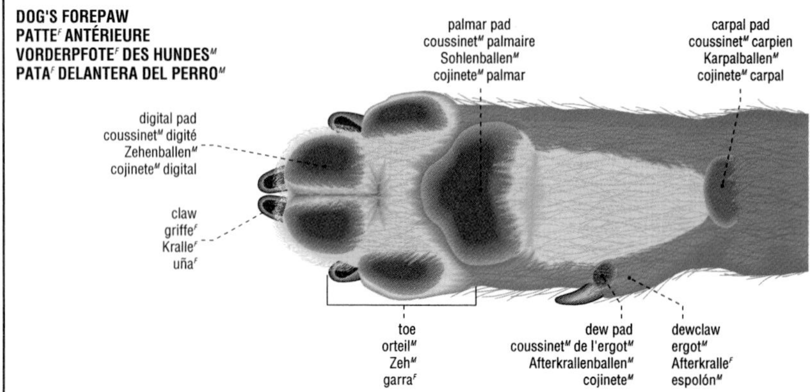

# CAT
# CHAT[M]
# KATZE[F]
# GATO[M] DOMÉSTICO

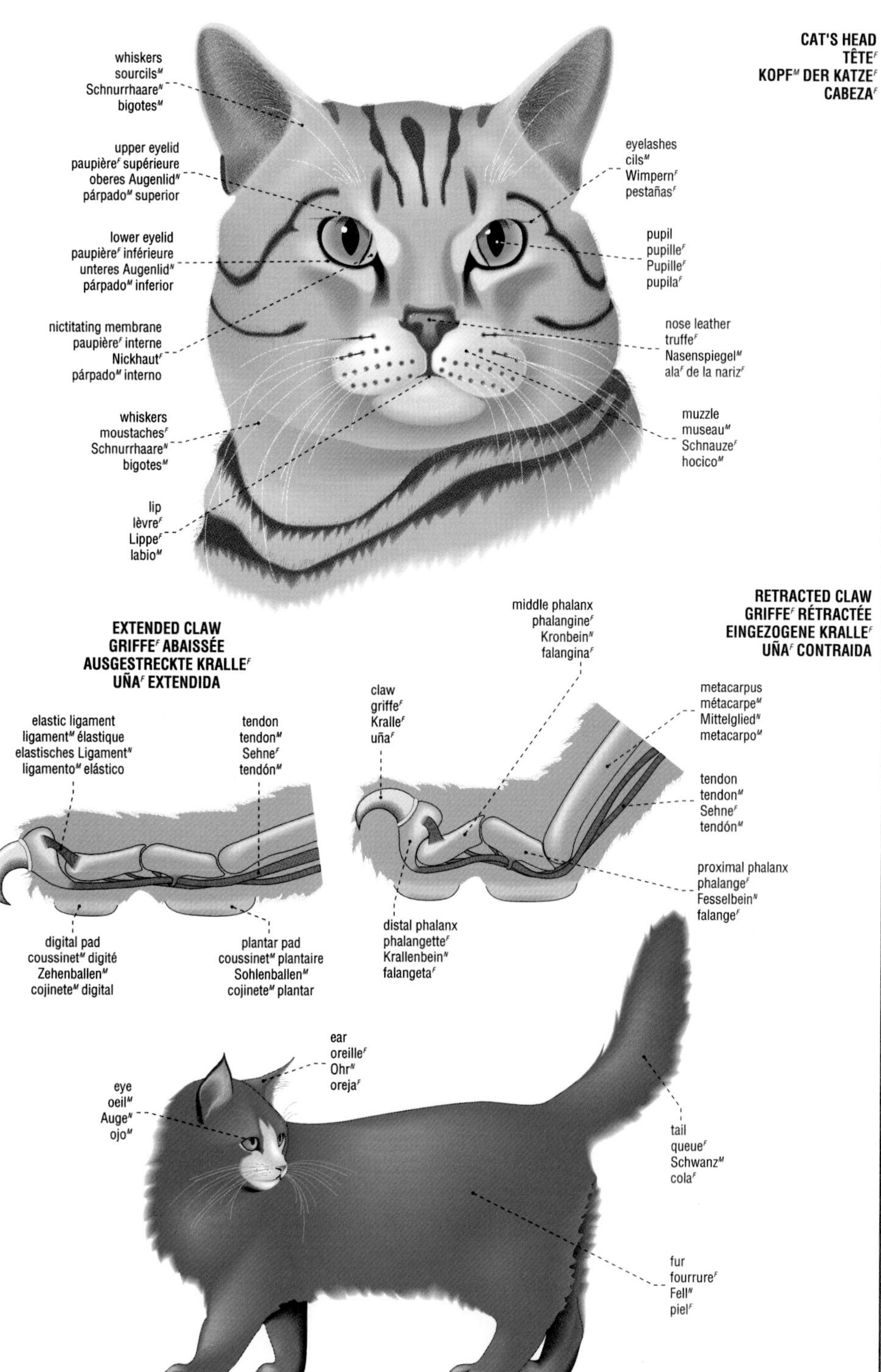

# BIRD
# OISEAU[M]
# VOGEL[M]
# AVE[F]

## MORPHOLOGY
## MORPHOLOGIE[F]
## MORPHOLOGIE[F]
## MORFOLOGÍA[F]

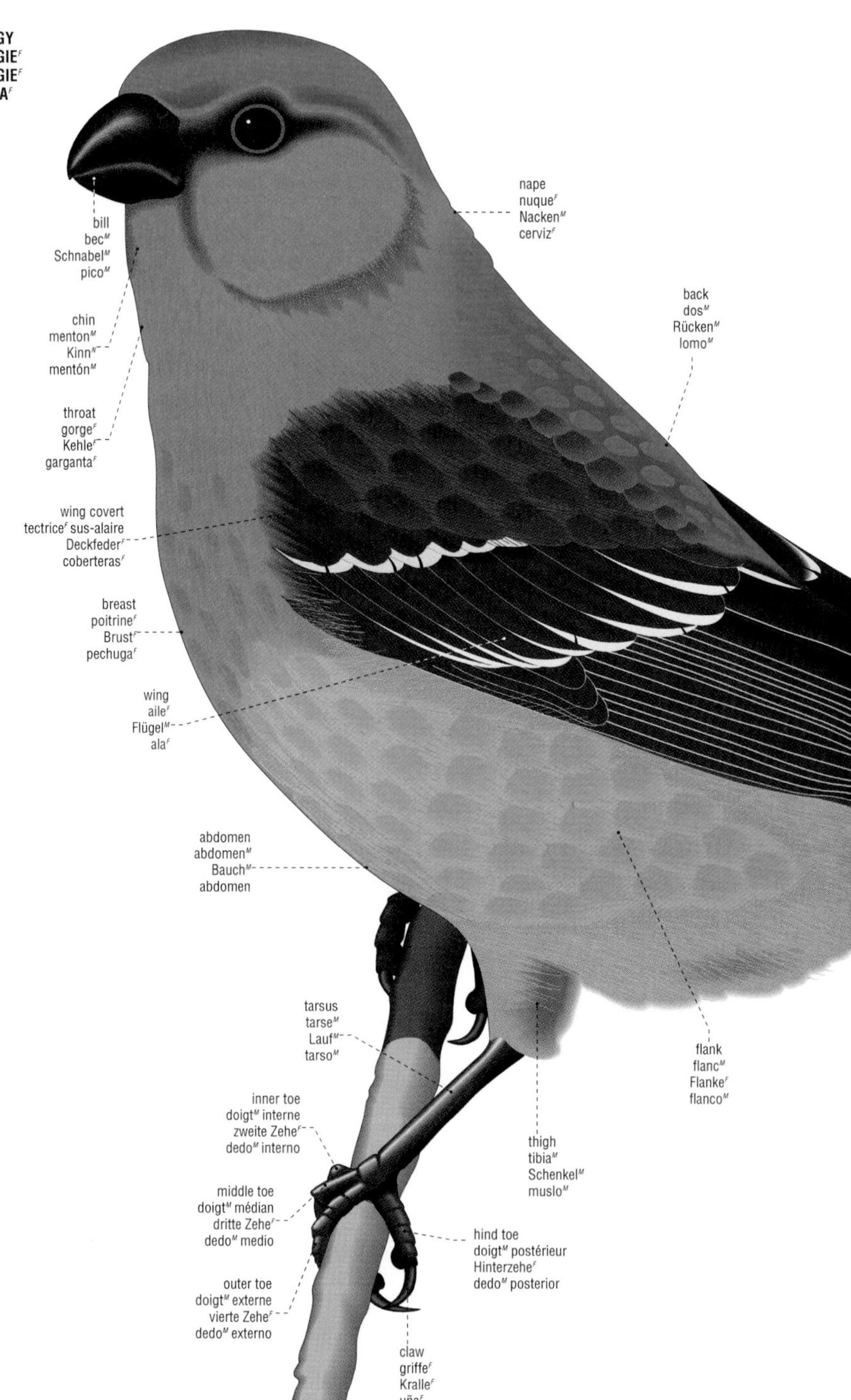

HEAD
TÊTE[F]
KOPF[M]
CABEZA[F]

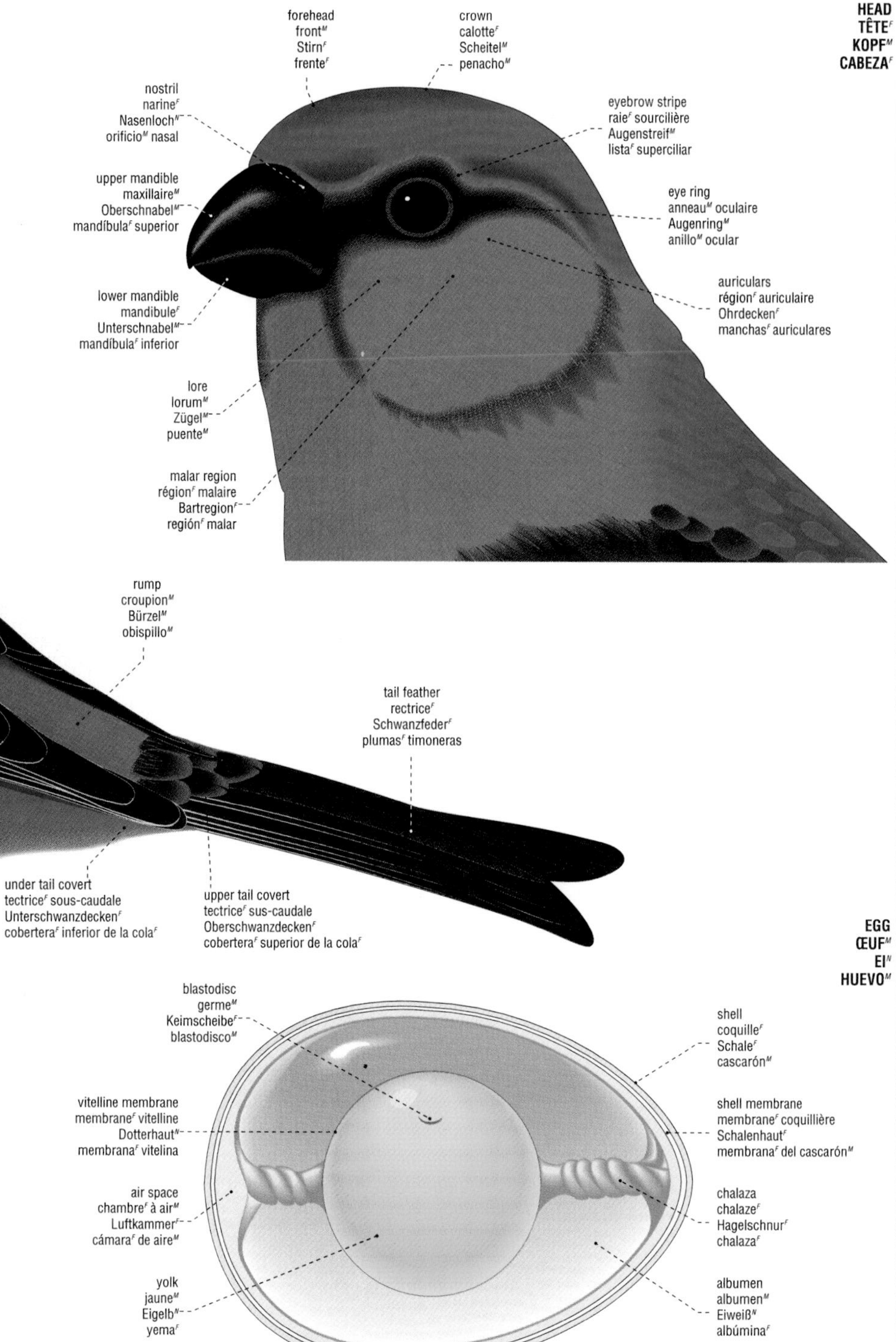

# BIRD
# OISEAU$^{M}$
# VOGEL$^{M}$
# AVE$^{F}$

**WING**
**AILE$^{F}$**
**FLÜGEL$^{M}$**
**ALA$^{F}$**

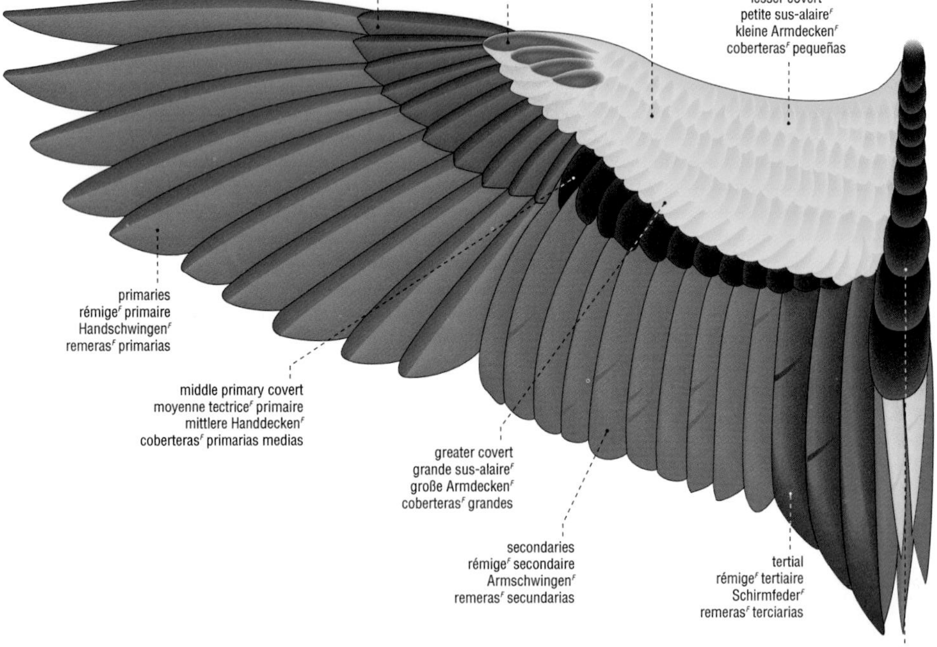

primary covert
tectrice$^{F}$ primaire
große Handdecken$^{F}$
coberteras$^{F}$ primarias
alula
alule$^{F}$
Daumenfittich$^{M}$
álula$^{F}$
middle covert
moyenne sus-alaire$^{F}$
mittlere Armdecken$^{F}$
coberteras$^{F}$ medias
lesser covert
petite sus-alaire$^{F}$
kleine Armdecken$^{F}$
coberteras$^{F}$ pequeñas
primaries
rémige$^{F}$ primaire
Handschwingen$^{F}$
remeras$^{F}$ primarias
middle primary covert
moyenne tectrice$^{F}$ primaire
mittlere Handdecken$^{F}$
coberteras$^{F}$ primarias medias
greater covert
grande sus-alaire$^{F}$
große Armdecken$^{F}$
coberteras$^{F}$ grandes
secondaries
rémige$^{F}$ secondaire
Armschwingen$^{F}$
remeras$^{F}$ secundarias
tertial
rémige$^{F}$ tertiaire
Schirmfeder$^{F}$
remeras$^{F}$ terciarias
scapular
scapulaire$^{F}$
Schulterfeder$^{F}$
escapulares$^{M}$

**CONTOUR FEATHER**
**PENNE$^{F}$**
**KONTURFEDER$^{F}$**
**PLUMA$^{F}$**

vane
vexille$^{M}$
Fahne$^{F}$
barbilla$^{F}$
afterfeather
duvet$^{M}$
Afterfeder$^{F}$
plumón$^{M}$
calamus
calamus$^{M}$
Spule$^{F}$
cañón$^{M}$
rachis
rachis$^{M}$
Schaft$^{M}$
raquis$^{M}$
barb
barbe$^{F}$
Ast$^{M}$
barba$^{F}$
inferior umbilicus
ombilic$^{M}$ inférieur
unterer Nabel$^{M}$
ombligo$^{M}$ inferior
superior umbilicus
ombilic$^{M}$ supérieur
oberer Nabel$^{M}$
ombligo$^{M}$ superior

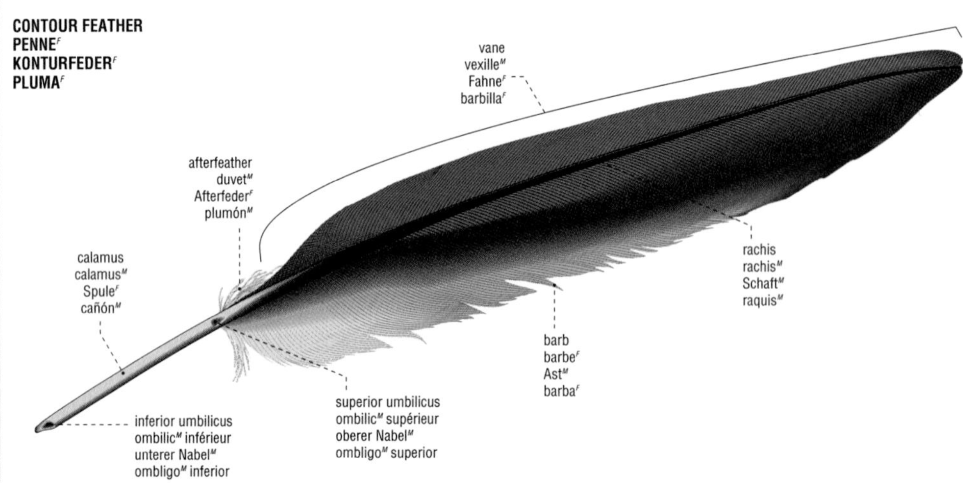

## PRINCIPAL TYPES OF BILL
## PRINCIPAUX TYPES$^{M}$ DE BECS$^{M}$
## WICHTIGSTE SCHNABELARTEN$^{F}$
## PRINCIPALES TIPOS$^{M}$ DE PICOS$^{M}$

bird of prey
oiseau$^{M}$ de proie$^{F}$
Raubvogel$^{M}$
ave$^{F}$ de rapiña

aquatic bird
oiseau$^{M}$ aquatique
Wasservogel$^{M}$
ave$^{F}$ acuática

wading bird
oiseau$^{M}$ échassier
Watvogel$^{M}$
ave$^{F}$ zancuda

granivorous bird
oiseau$^{M}$ granivore
Körnerfresser$^{M}$
ave$^{F}$ granívora

insectivorous bird
oiseau$^{M}$ insectivore
Insektenfresser$^{M}$
ave$^{F}$ insectívora

## PRINCIPAL TYPES OF FOOT
## PRINCIPAUX TYPES$^{M}$ DE PATTES$^{F}$
## WICHTIGSTE FUSSARTEN$^{F}$
## PRINCIPALES TIPOS$^{M}$ DE PATAS$^{F}$

**perching bird**
**oiseau$^{M}$ percheur**
**Baumvogel$^{M}$**
**aves$^{F}$ trepadoras**

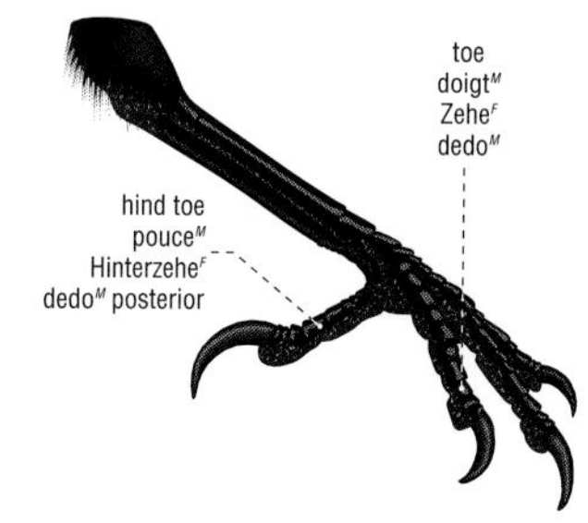


**bird of prey**
**oiseau$^{M}$ de proie$^{F}$**
**Raubvogel$^{M}$**
**aves$^{F}$ de rapiña**

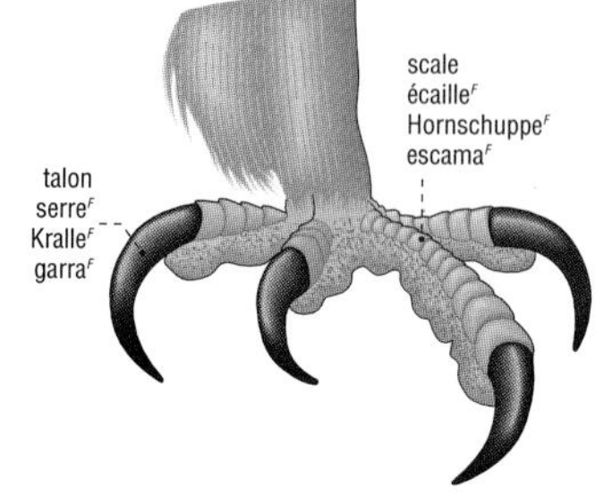


**aquatic bird**
**oiseau$^{M}$ aquatique**
**Wasservogel$^{M}$**
**aves$^{F}$ acuáticas**

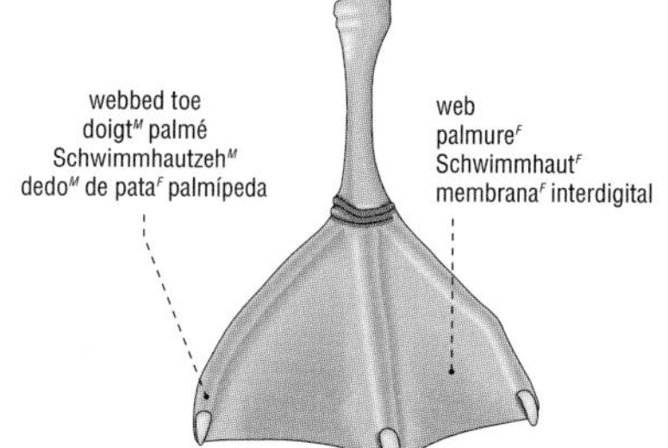


**aquatic bird**
**oiseau$^{M}$ aquatique**
**Wasservogel$^{M}$**
**aves$^{F}$ acuáticas**

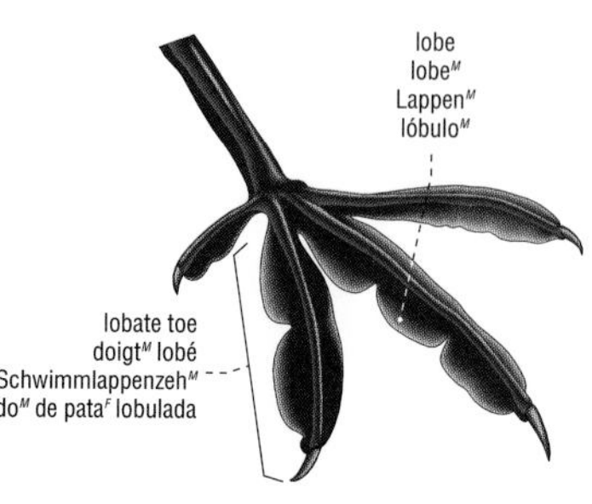

# BAT
# CHAUVE-SOURIS[F]
# FLEDERMAUS[F]
# MURCIÉLAGO[M]

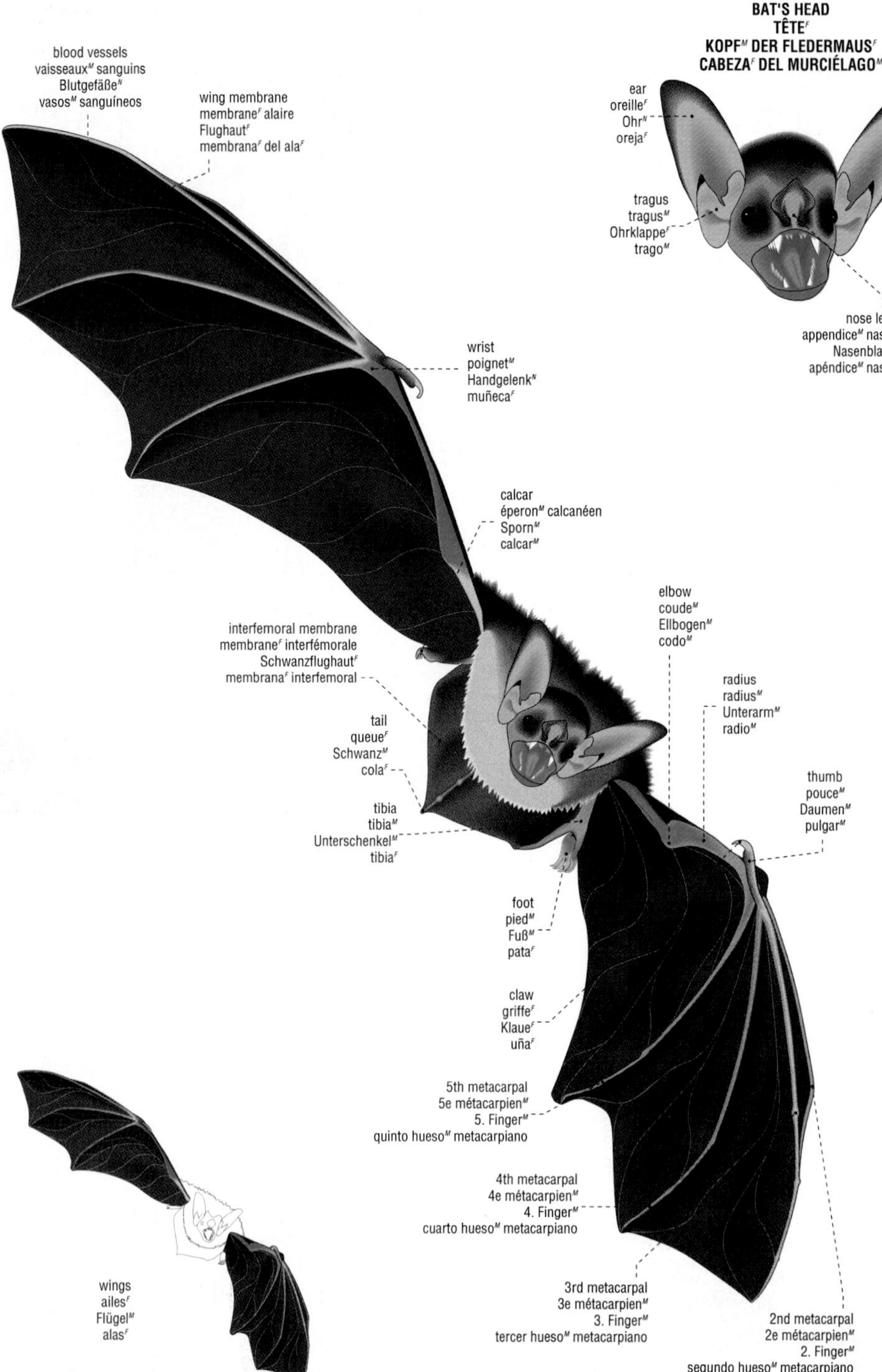

HUMAN BEING MENSCH
ÊTRE HUMAIN SER HUMANO

SUMMARY

PLANT CELL ... 115
ANIMAL CELL ... 115
HUMAN BODY ... 116
MUSCLES ... 120
SKELETON ... 122
BLOOD CIRCULATION ... 124
MALE GENITAL ORGANS ... 127
FEMALE GENITAL ORGANS ... 128
BREAST ... 129
RESPIRATORY SYSTEM ... 130
DIGESTIVE SYSTEM ... 131
URINARY SYSTEM ... 132
NERVOUS SYSTEM ... 133
SENSE ORGANS: TOUCH ... 136
SENSE ORGANS: HEARING ... 138
SENSE ORGANS: SIGHT ... 140
SENSE ORGANS: SMELL ... 141
SENSES OF SMELL AND TASTE ... 142
TEETH ... 144

## PLANT CELL
## CELLULE[F] VÉGÉTALE
## PFLANZENZELLE[F]
## CÉLULA[F] VEGETAL

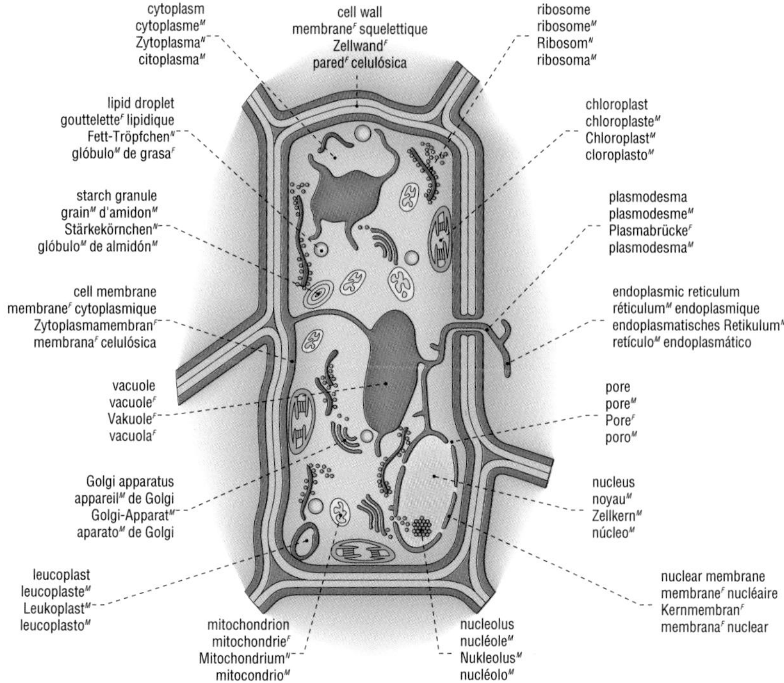


## ANIMAL CELL
## CELLULE[F] ANIMALE
## TIERISCHE ZELLE[F]
## CÉLULA[F] ANIMAL

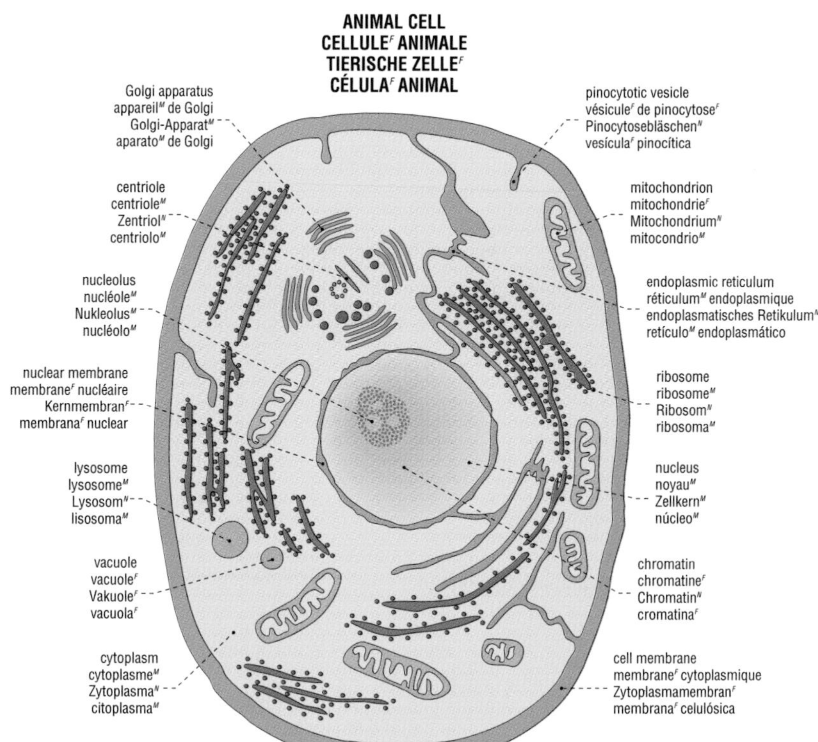

# HUMAN BODY
# CORPS[M] HUMAIN
# MENSCHLICHER KÖRPER[M]
# CUERPO[M] HUMANO

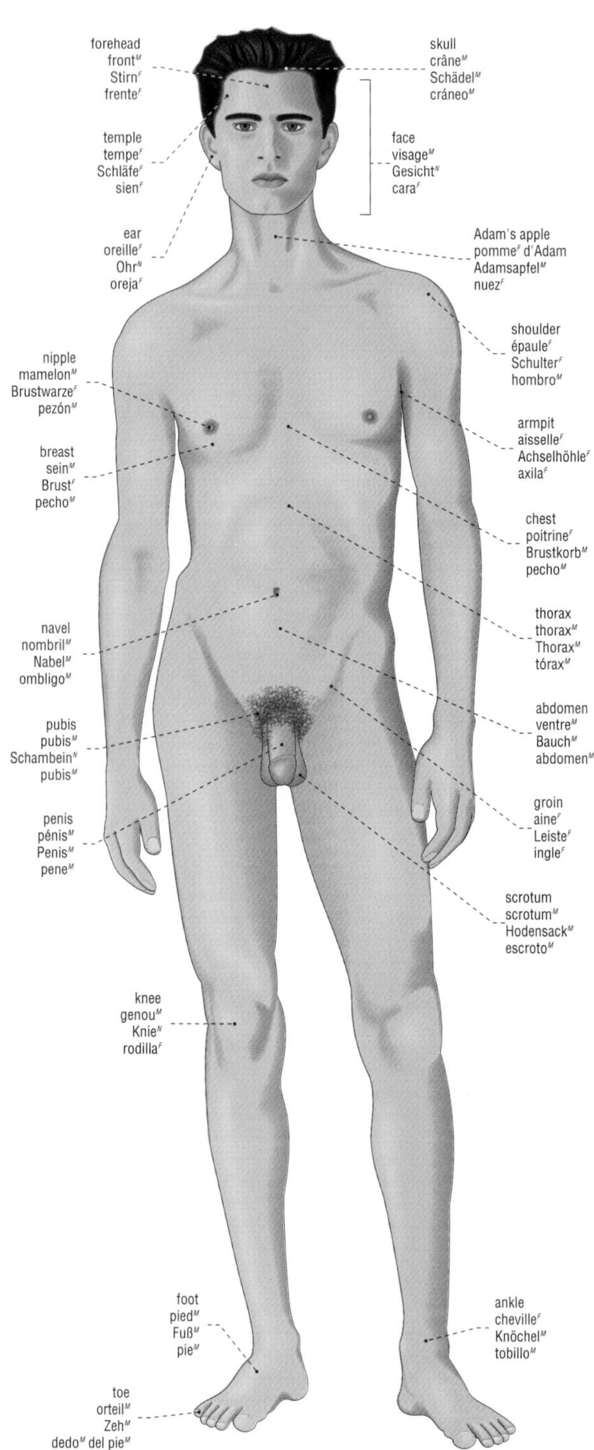

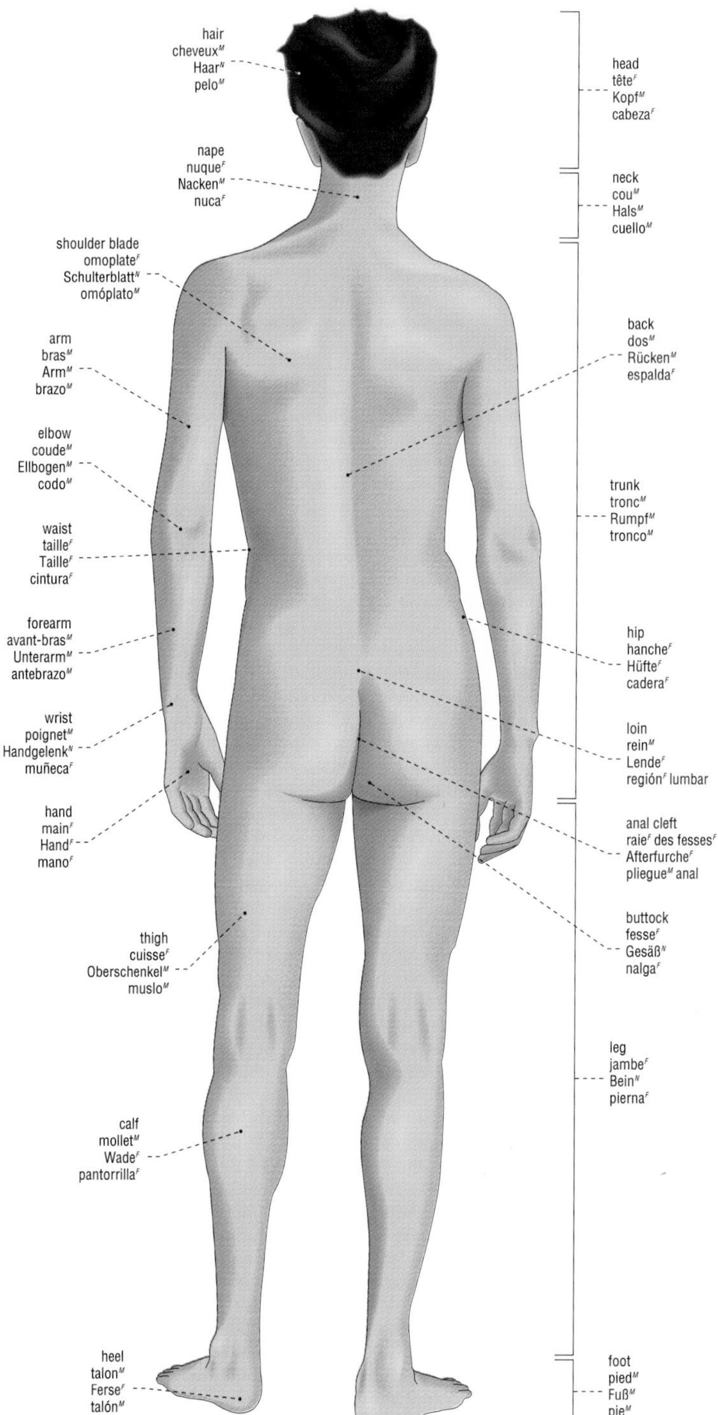
hair cheveux[M] Haar[N] pelo[M]
nape nuque[F] Nacken[M] nuca[F]
shoulder blade omoplate[F] Schulterblatt[N] omóplato[M]
arm bras[M] Arm[M] brazo[M]
elbow coude[M] Ellbogen[M] codo[M]
waist taille[F] Taille[F] cintura[F]
forearm avant-bras[M] Unterarm[M] antebrazo[M]
wrist poignet[M] Handgelenk[N] muñeca[F]
hand main[F] Hand[F] mano[F]
thigh cuisse[F] Oberschenkel[M] muslo[M]
calf mollet[M] Wade[F] pantorrilla[F]
heel talon[M] Ferse[F] talón[M]
head tête[F] Kopf[M] cabeza[F]
neck cou[M] Hals[M] cuello[M]
back dos[M] Rücken[M] espalda[F]
trunk tronc[M] Rumpf[M] tronco[M]
hip hanche[F] Hüfte[F] cadera[F]
loin rein[M] Lende[F] región[F] lumbar
anal cleft raie[F] des fesses[F] Afterfurche[F] pliegue[M] anal
buttock fesse[F] Gesäß[N] nalga[F]
leg jambe[F] Bein[N] pierna[F]
foot pied[M] Fuß[M] pie[M]

# HUMAN BODY
# CORPS[M] HUMAIN
# MENSCHLICHER KÖRPER[M]
# CUERPO[M] HUMANO

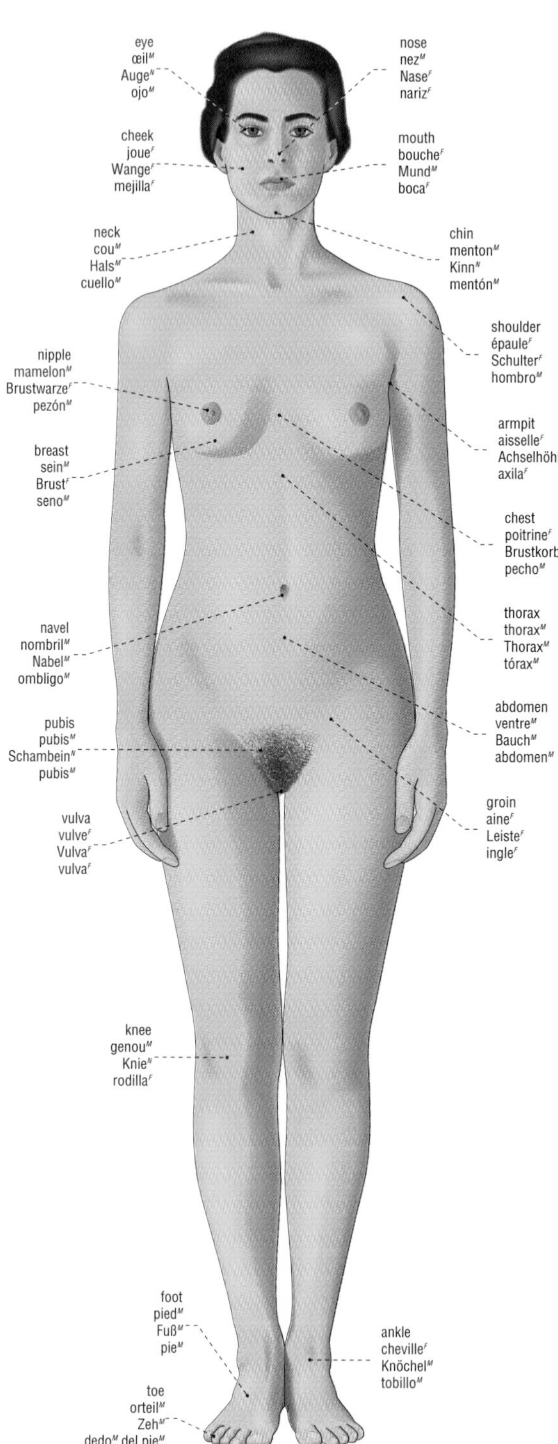

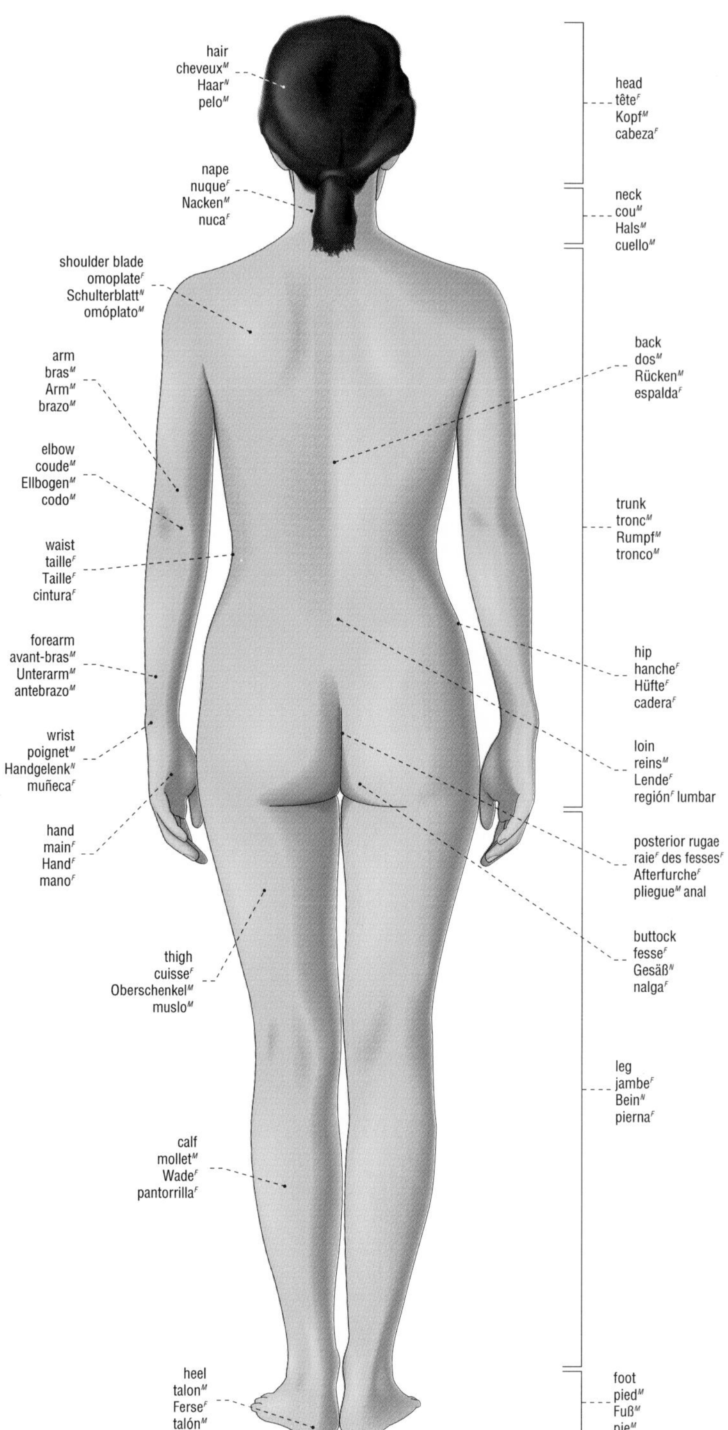
hair cheveux[M] Haar[N] pelo[M]
nape nuque[F] Nacken[M] nuca[F]
shoulder blade omoplate[F] Schulterblatt[N] omóplato[M]
arm bras[M] Arm[M] brazo[M]
elbow coude[M] Ellbogen[M] codo[M]
waist taille[F] Taille[F] cintura[F]
forearm avant-bras[M] Unterarm[M] antebrazo[M]
wrist poignet[M] Handgelenk[N] muñeca[F]
hand main[F] Hand[F] mano[F]
thigh cuisse[F] Oberschenkel[M] muslo[M]
calf mollet[M] Wade[F] pantorrilla[F]
heel talon[M] Ferse[F] talón[M]
head tête[F] Kopf[M] cabeza[F]
neck cou[M] Hals[M] cuello[M]
back dos[M] Rücken[M] espalda[F]
trunk tronc[M] Rumpf[M] tronco[M]
hip hanche[F] Hüfte[F] cadera[F]
loin reins[M] Lende[F] región[F] lumbar
posterior rugae raie[F] des fesses[F] Afterfurche[F] pliegue[M] anal
buttock fesse[F] Gesäß[N] nalga[F]
leg jambe[F] Bein[N] pierna[F]
foot pied[M] Fuß[M] pie[M]

# MUSCLES
# MUSCLES[M]
# MUSKELN[M]
# MÚSCULOS[M]

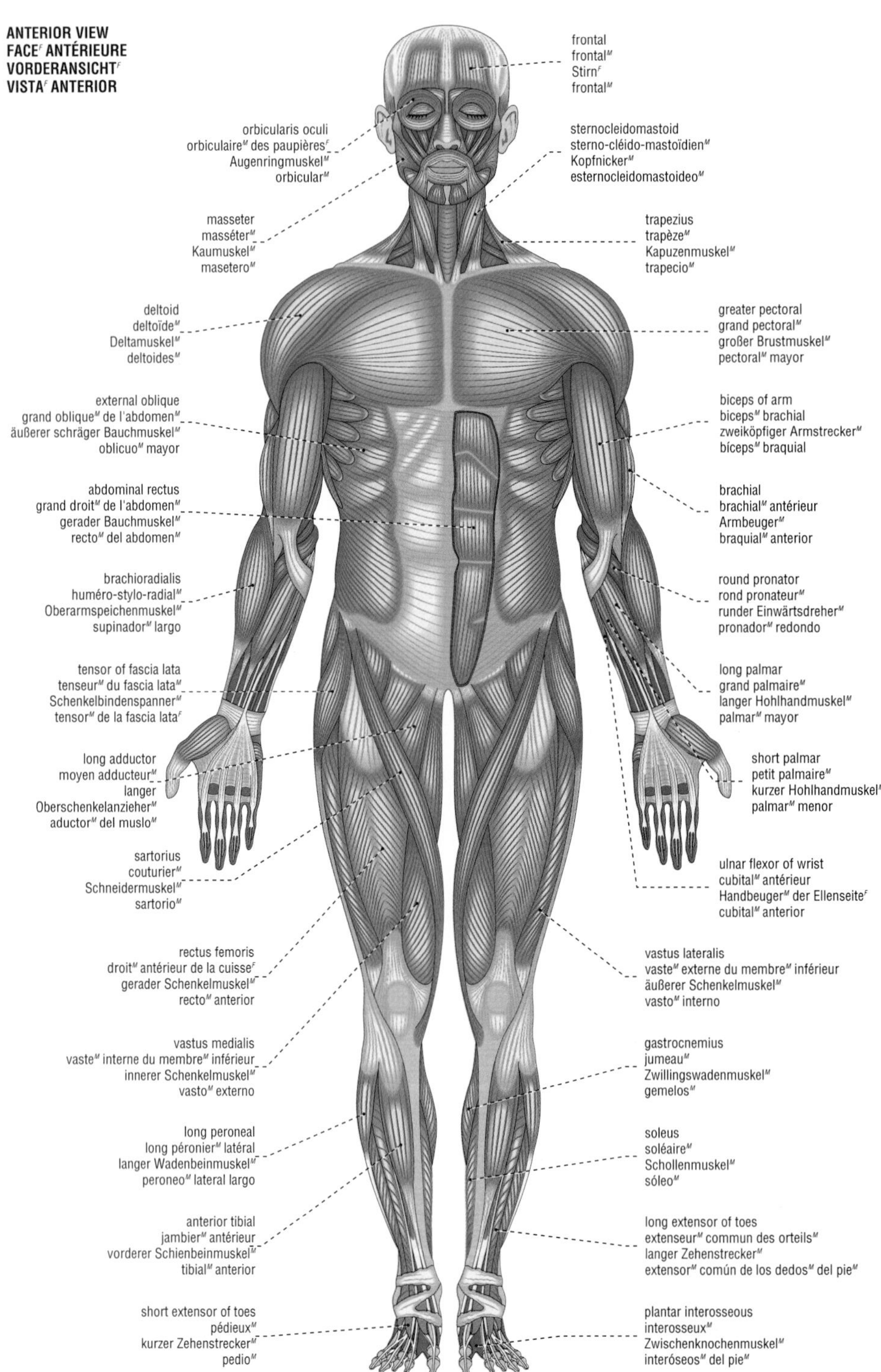

## POSTERIOR VIEW
## FACE[F] POSTÉRIEURE
## RÜCKANSICHT[F]
## VISTA[F] POSTERIOR

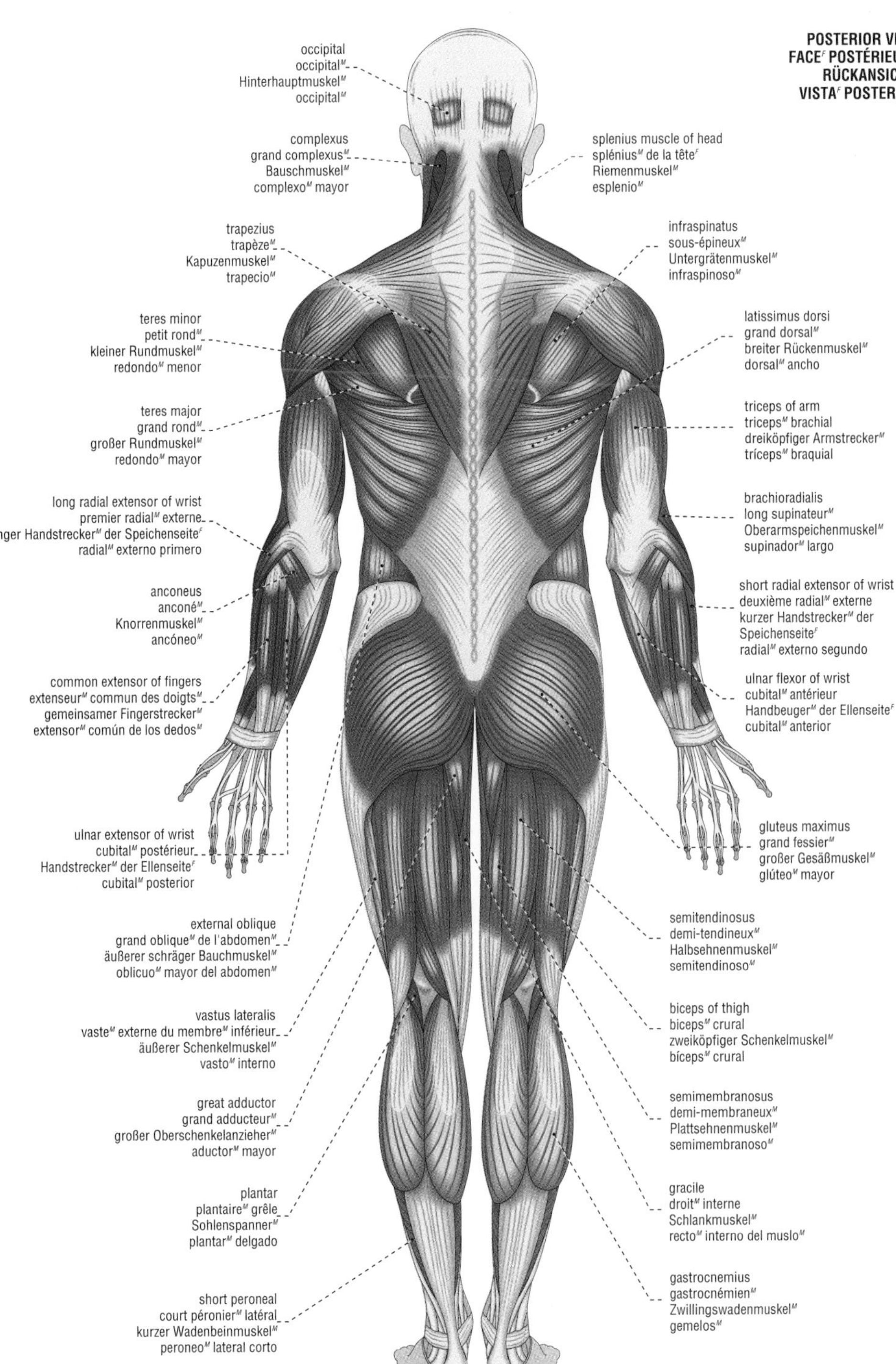

# SKELETON
# SQUELETTE[M]
# SKELETT[N]
# ESQUELETO[M]

**ANTERIOR VIEW**
**VUE[F] ANTÉRIEURE**
**VORDERANSICHT[F]**
**VISTA[F] ANTERIOR**

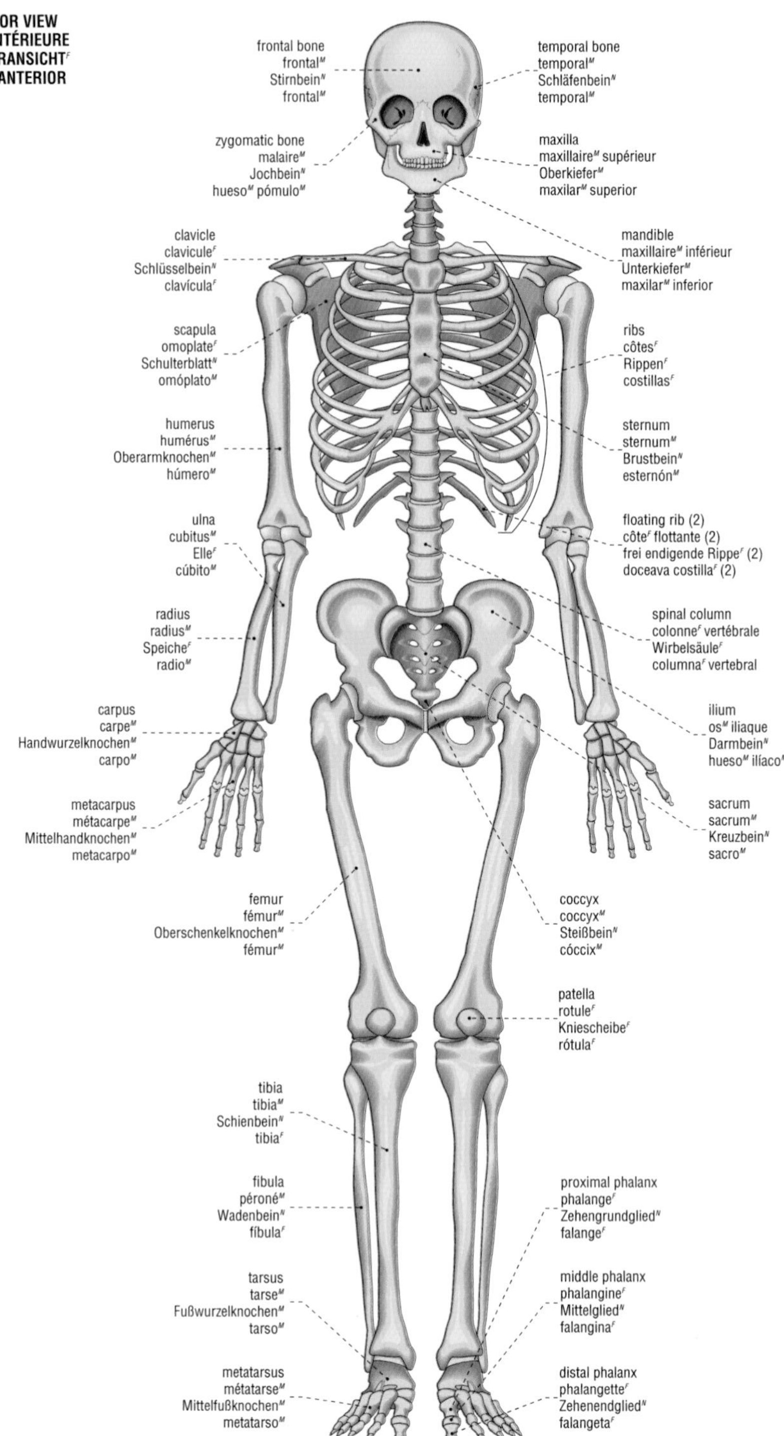

**POSTERIOR VIEW**
**VUE[F] POSTÉRIEURE**
**RÜCKANSICHT[F]**
**VISTA POSTERIOR**

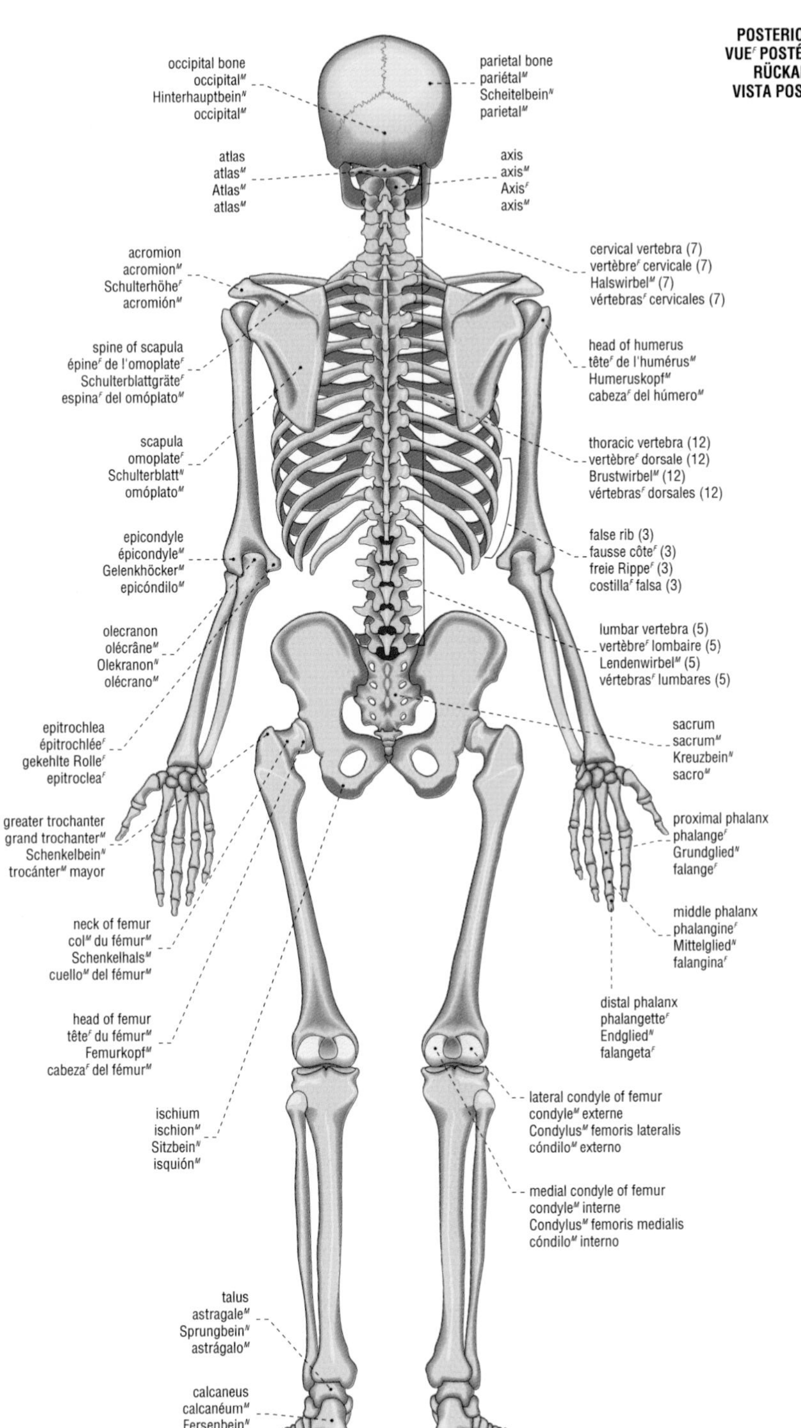

# BLOOD CIRCULATION
# CIRCULATION[F] SANGUINE
# BLUTKREISLAUF[M]
# CIRCULACIÓN[F] SANGUÍNEA

## CIRCULATION DIAGRAM
## SCHÉMA[M] DE LA CIRCULATION[F]
## SCHEMA[N] DES BLUTKREISLAUFS[M]
## DIAGRAMA[M] DE LA CIRCULACIÓN[F]

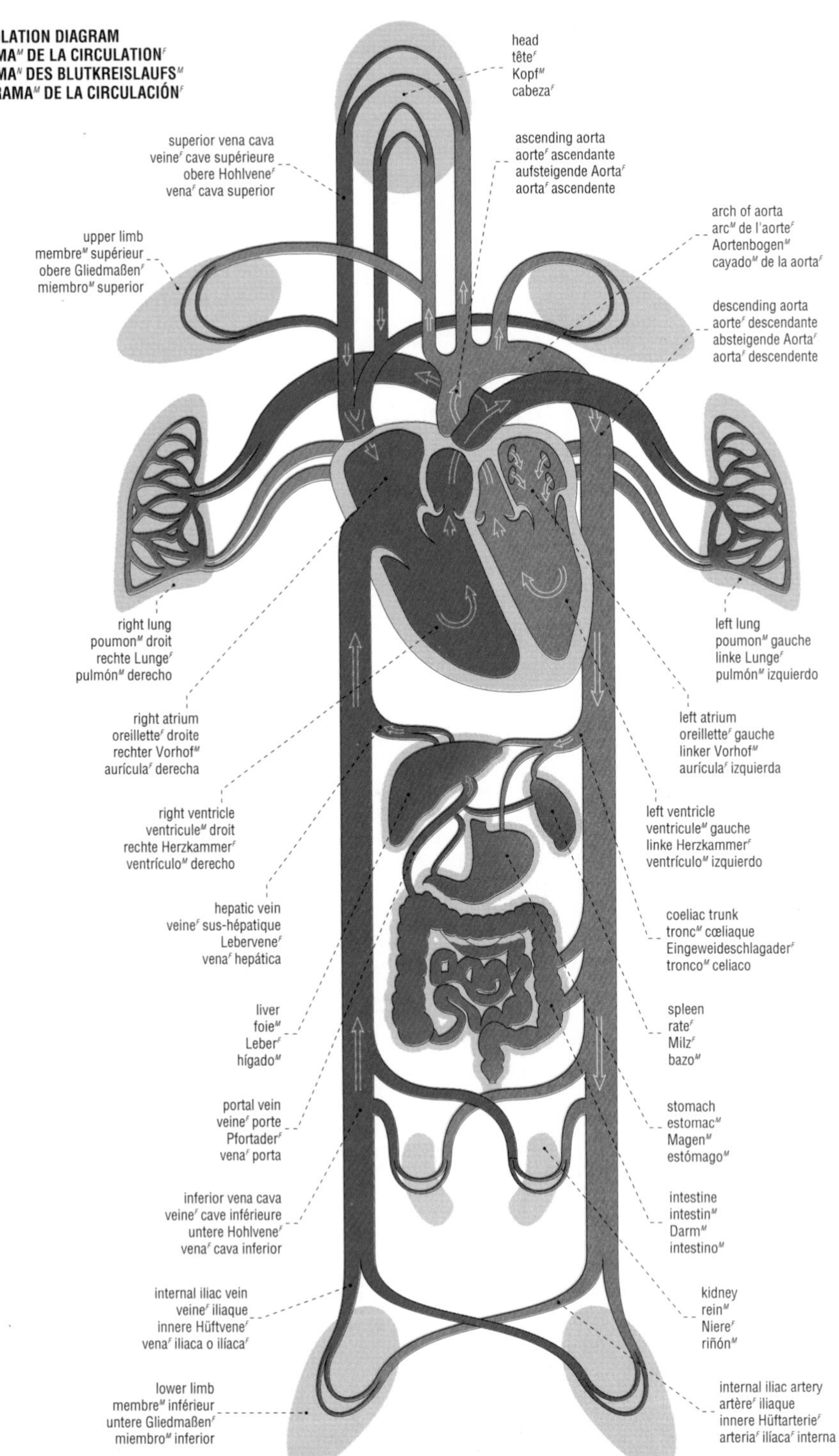

# HEART
# CŒUR[M]
# HERZ[N]
# CORAZÓN[M]

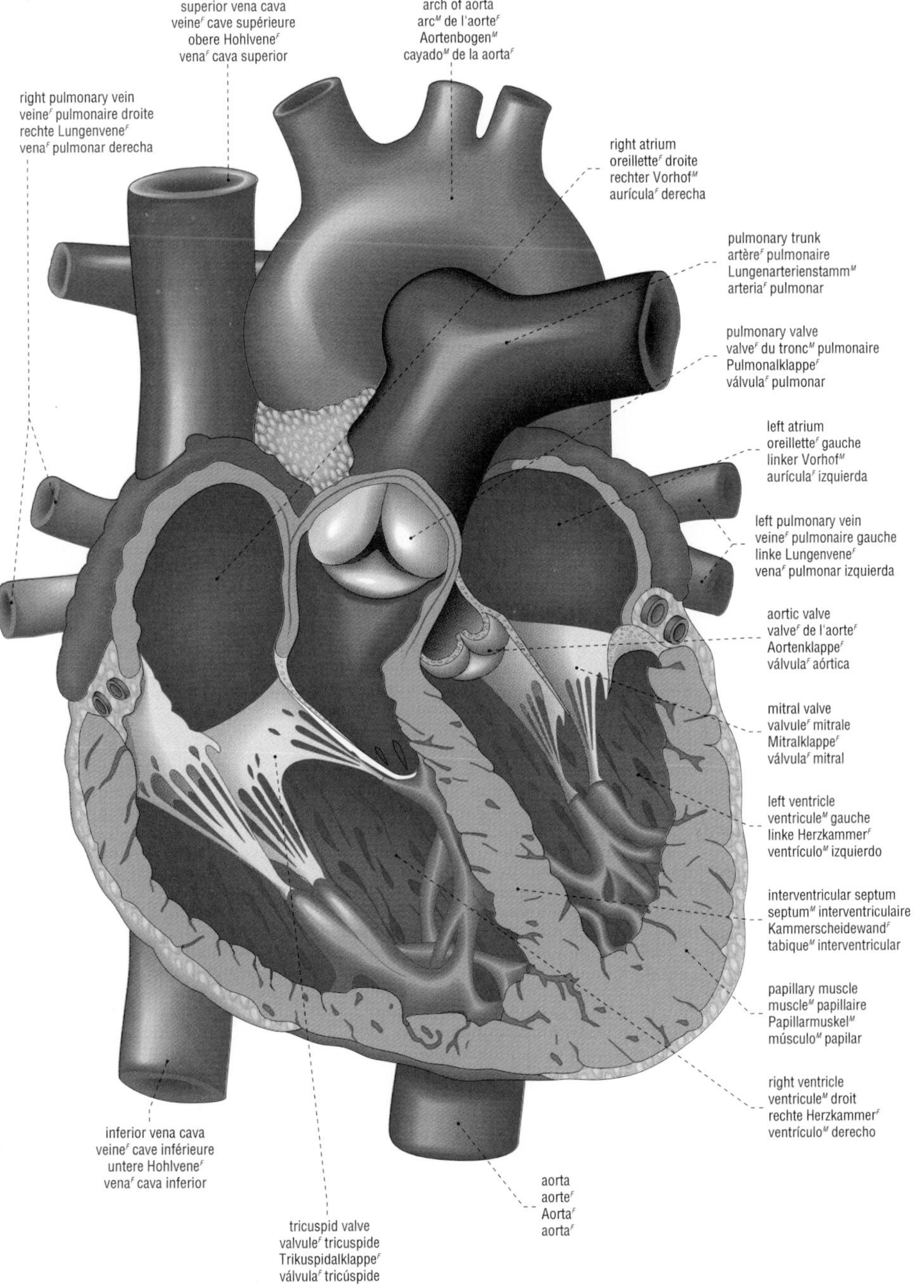

# BLOOD CIRCULATION
# CIRCULATION[F] SANGUINE
# BLUTKREISLAUF[M]
# CIRCULACIÓN[F] SANGUÍNEA

## PRINCIPAL VEINS AND ARTERIES
## PRINCIPALES VEINES[F] ET ARTÈRES[F]
## DIE WICHTIGSTEN VENEN[F] UND ARTERIEN[F]
## PRINCIPALES VENAS[F] Y ARTERIAS[F]

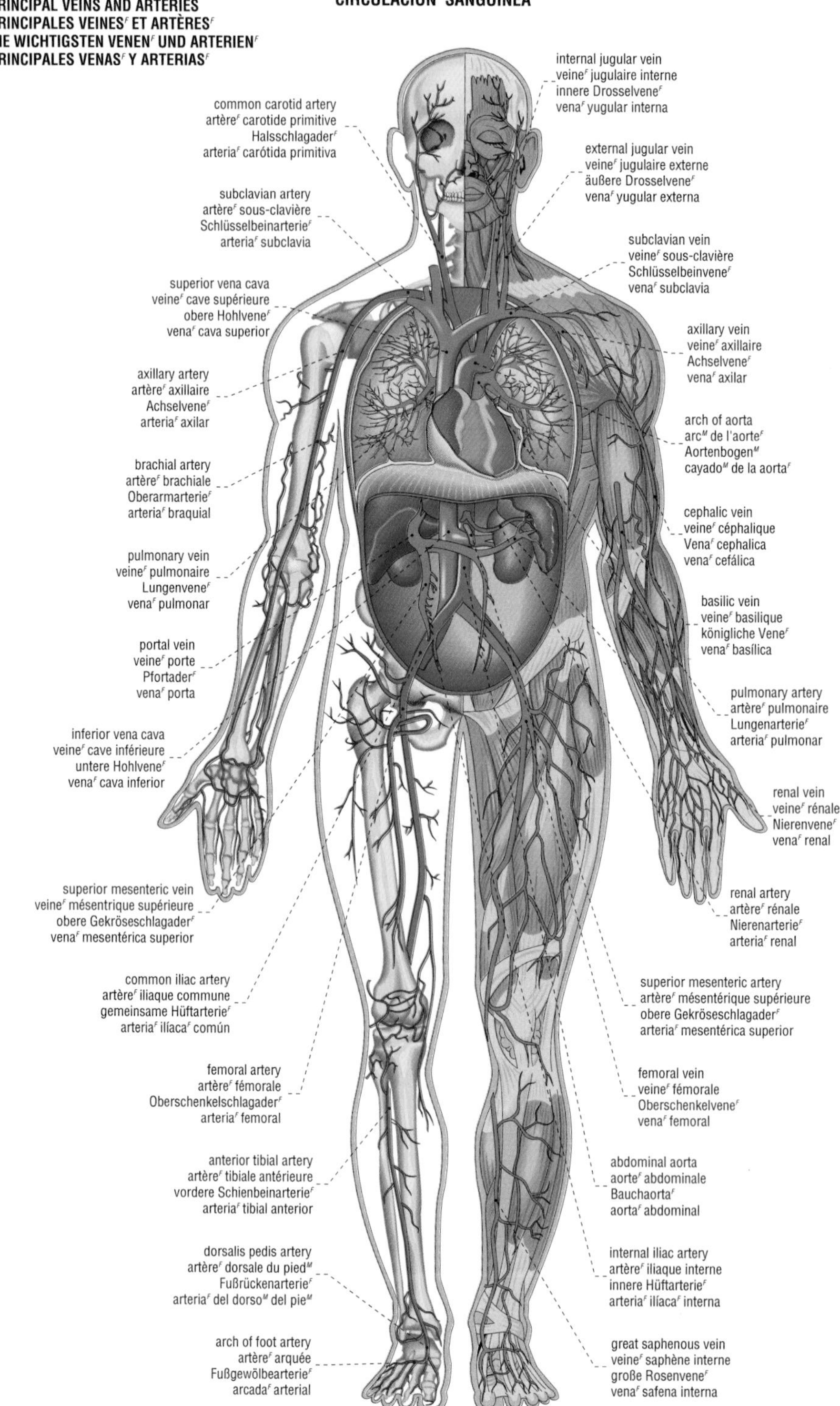

# MALE GENITAL ORGANS
# ORGANES[M] GÉNITAUX MASCULINS
# MÄNNLICHE GESCHLECHTSORGANE[N]
# ÓRGANOS[M] GENITALES MASCULINOS

## SAGITTAL SECTION
## COUPE[F] SAGITTALE
## SAGITTALSCHNITT[M]
## CORTE[M] SAGITAL

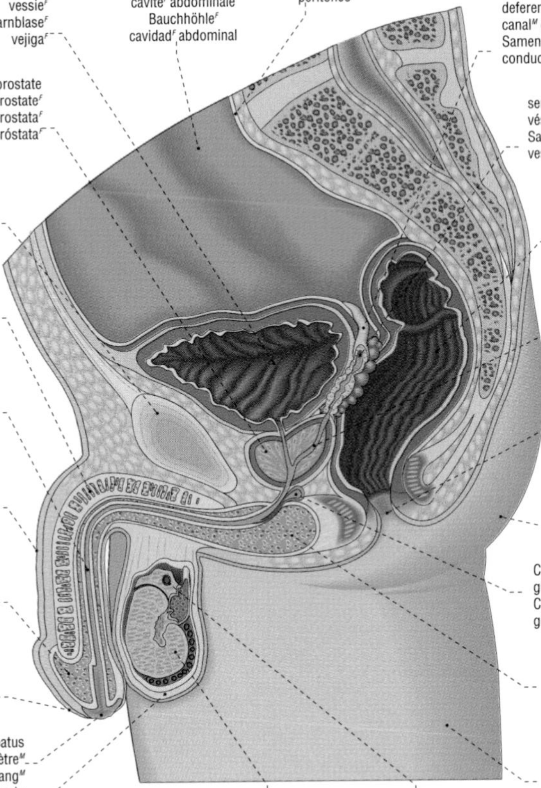

peritoneum
péritoine[M]
Bauchfell[N]
peritoneo[M]
urinary bladder
vessie[F]
Harnblase[F]
vejiga[F]
abdominal cavity
cavité[F] abdominale
Bauchhöhle[F]
cavidad[F] abdominal
deferent duct
canal[M] déférent
Samenleiter[M]
conducto[M] deferente
prostate
prostate[F]
Prostata[F]
próstata[F]
seminal vesicle
vésicule[F] séminale
Samenbläschen[N]
vesícula[F] seminal
symphysis pubis
symphyse[F] pubienne
Symphyse[F]
sínfisis[F] púbica
rectum
rectum[M]
Mastdarm[M]
recto[M]
corpus cavernosum
corps[M] caverneux
Rutenschwellkörper[M]
cuerpo[M] cavernoso
ejaculatory duct
canal[M] éjaculateur
Spritzkanälchen[N]
conducto[M] eyaculador
male urethra
urètre[M] pénien
Harnröhre[F]
uretra[F]
anus
anus[M]
After[M]
ano[M]
penis
verge[F]
Penis[M]
pene[M]
buttock
fesse[F]
Gesäß[N]
nalga[F]
glans penis
gland[M]
Eichel[F]
glande[M]
Cowper's gland
glande[F] de Cowper
Cowper-Drüse[F]
glándula[F] de Cowper
prepuce
prépuce[M]
Vorhaut[F]
prepucio[M]
bulbocavernous muscle
muscle[M] bulbo-caverneux
Musculus[M] bulbospongiosus
cuerpo[M] esponjoso de la uretra[F]
urinary meatus
méat[M] de l'urètre[M]
Harnröhrengang[M]
meato[M] urinario
thigh
cuisse[F]
Oberschenkel[M]
muslo[M]
testicle
testicule[M]
Hoden[M]
testículo[M]
spermatic cord
cordon[M] spermatique
Samenstrang[M]
cordón[M] espermático
scrotum
scrotum[M]
Hodensack[M]
escroto[M]

## SPERMATOZOON
## SPERMATOZOÏDE[M]
## SPERMA[N]
## ESPERMATOZOIDE[M]

tail
queue[F]
Schwanz[M]
aleta[F]
middle piece
pièce[F] intermédiaire
Mittelstück[N]
segmento[M] intermediario
head
tête[F]
Kopf[M]
cabeza[F]
neck
cou[M]
Hals[M]
cuello[M]
end piece
pièce[F] terminale
Endstück[N]
segmento[M] terminal

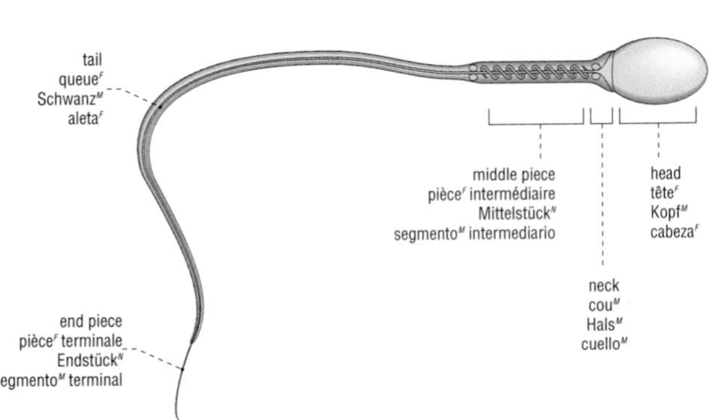

HUMAN BEING
ÊTRE HUMAIN

MENSCH
SER HUMANO

# FEMALE GENITAL ORGANS
# ORGANES$^{M}$ GÉNITAUX FÉMININS
# WEIBLICHE GESCHLECHTSORGANE$^{N}$
# ÓRGANOS$^{M}$ GENITALES FEMENINOS

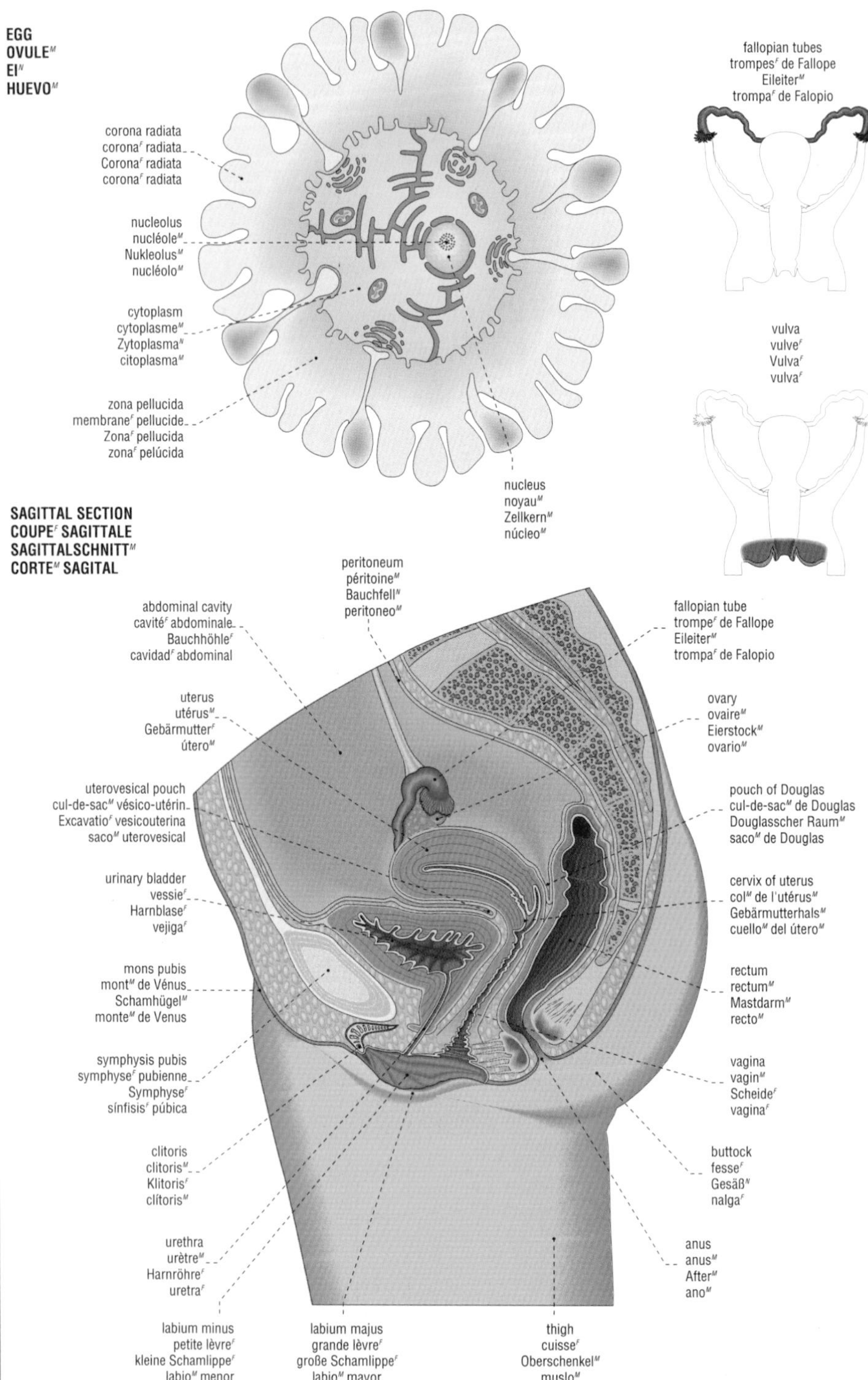

# FEMALE GENITAL ORGANS
# ORGANES[M] GÉNITAUX FÉMININS
# WEIBLICHE GESCHLECHTSORGANE[N]
# ÓRGANOS[M] GENITALES FEMENINOS

**POSTERIOR VIEW**
**VUE[F] POSTÉRIEURE**
**RÜCKANSICHT[F]**
**VISTA[F] POSTERIOR**

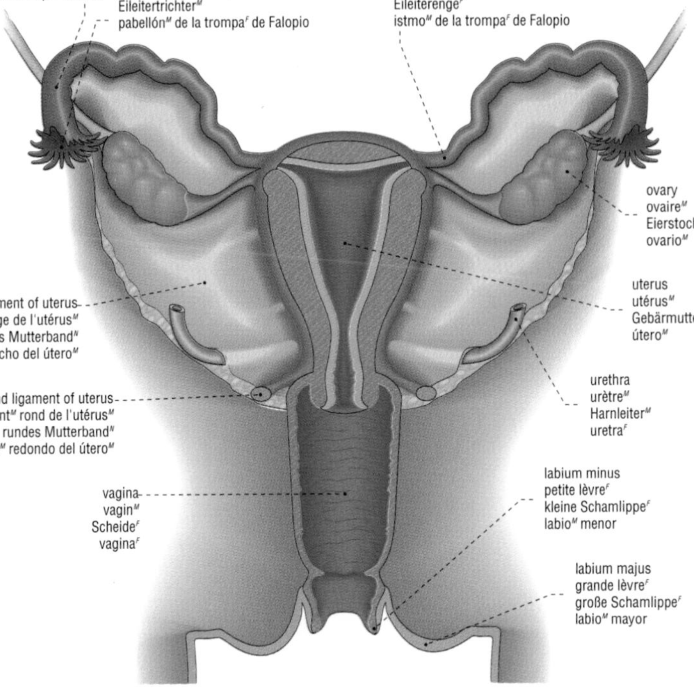

ampulla of fallopian tube
ampoule[F] de la trompe[F] utérine
Eileiterampulle[F]
ampolla[F] de la trompa[F] uterina
infundibulum of fallopian tube
pavillon[M] de la trompe[F] utérine
Eileitertrichter[M]
pabellón[M] de la trompa[F] de Falopio
isthmus of fallopian tube
isthme[M] de la trompe[F] utérine
Eileiterenge[F]
istmo[M] de la trompa[F] de Falopio
ovary
ovaire[M]
Eierstock[M]
ovario[M]
broad ligament of uterus
ligament[M] large de l'utérus[M]
breites Mutterband[N]
ligamento[M] ancho del útero[M]
uterus
utérus[M]
Gebärmutter[F]
útero[M]
round ligament of uterus
ligament[M] rond de l'utérus[M]
rundes Mutterband[N]
ligamento[M] redondo del útero[M]
urethra
urètre[M]
Harnleiter[M]
uretra[F]
vagina
vagin[M]
Scheide[F]
vagina[F]
labium minus
petite lèvre[F]
kleine Schamlippe[F]
labio[M] menor
labium majus
grande lèvre[F]
große Schamlippe[F]
labio[M] mayor

# BREAST
# SEIN[M]
# BRUST[F]
# SENO[M]

**SAGITTAL SECTION**
**COUPE[F] SAGITTALE**
**SAGITTALSCHNITT[M]**
**CORTE[M] SAGITAL**

rib
côte[F]
Rippe[F]
costilla[F]
adipose tissue
tissu[M] adipeux
Fettgewebe[N]
tejido[M] adiposo
mammary gland
glande[F] mammaire
Brustdrüse[F]
glándula[F] mamaria
areola
aréole[F]
Warzenhof[M]
areola[F]
nipple
mamelon[M]
Brustwarze[F]
pezón[M]
lactiferous duct
conduit[M] lactifère
Milchgang[M]
conducto[M] galactófero

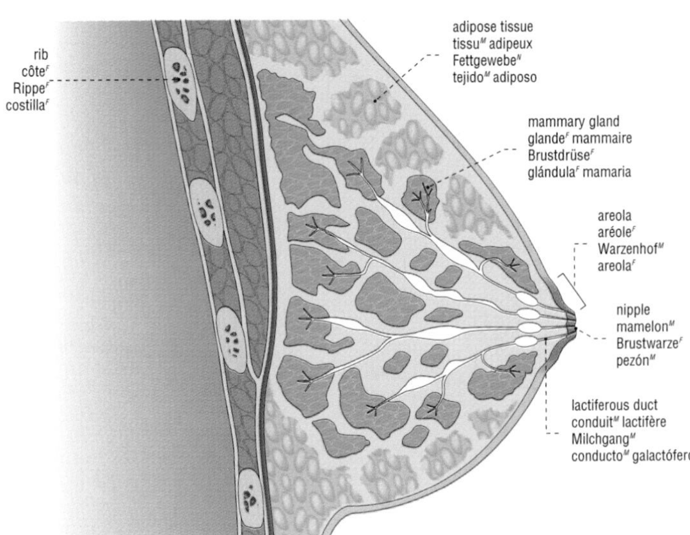

# RESPIRATORY SYSTEM
# APPAREIL[M] RESPIRATOIRE
# LUFTWEGE[M]
# APARATO[M] RESPIRATORIO

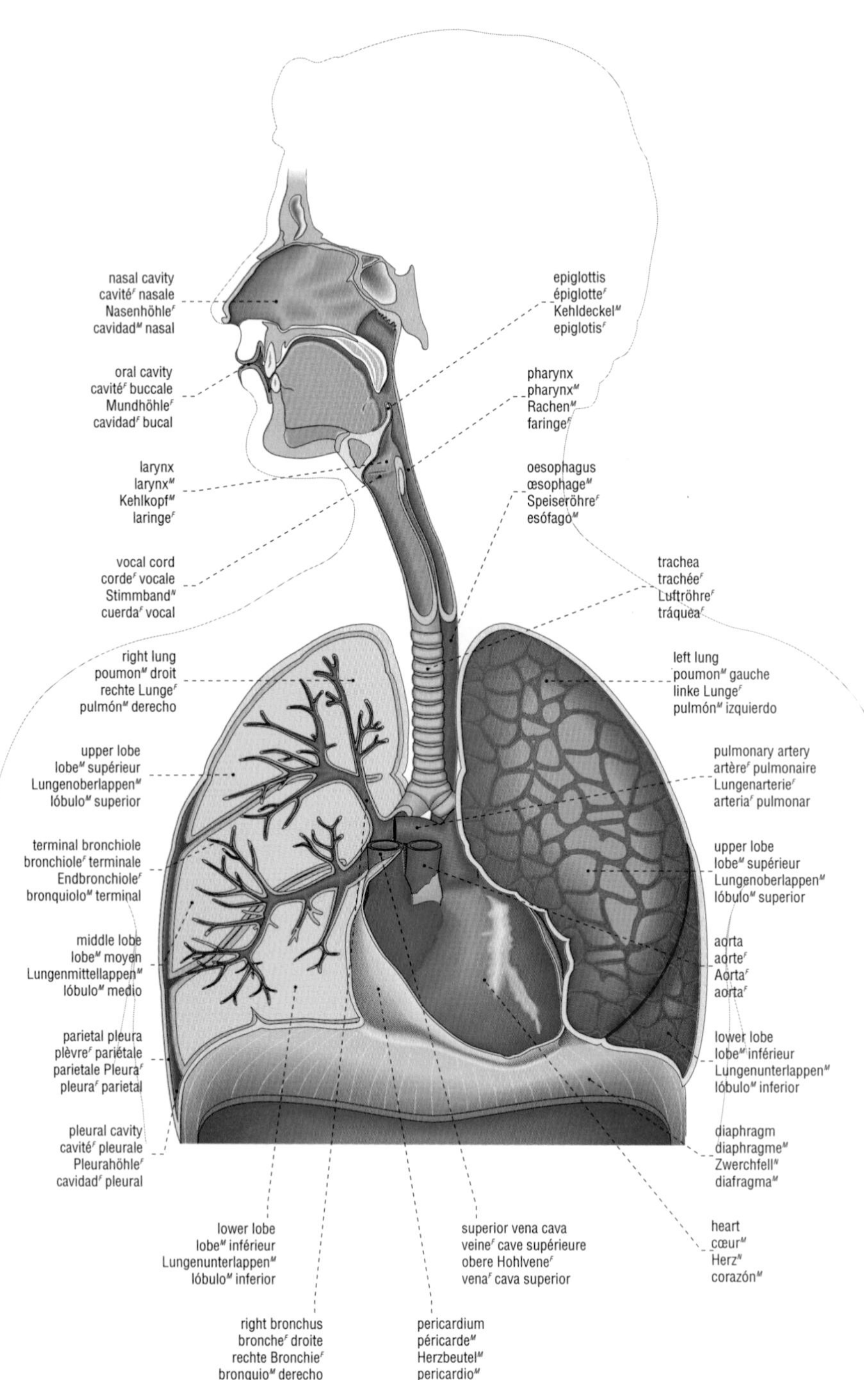

# DIGESTIVE SYSTEM
# APPAREIL[M] DIGESTIF
# VERDAUUNGSSYSTEM[N]
# APARATO[M] DIGESTIVO

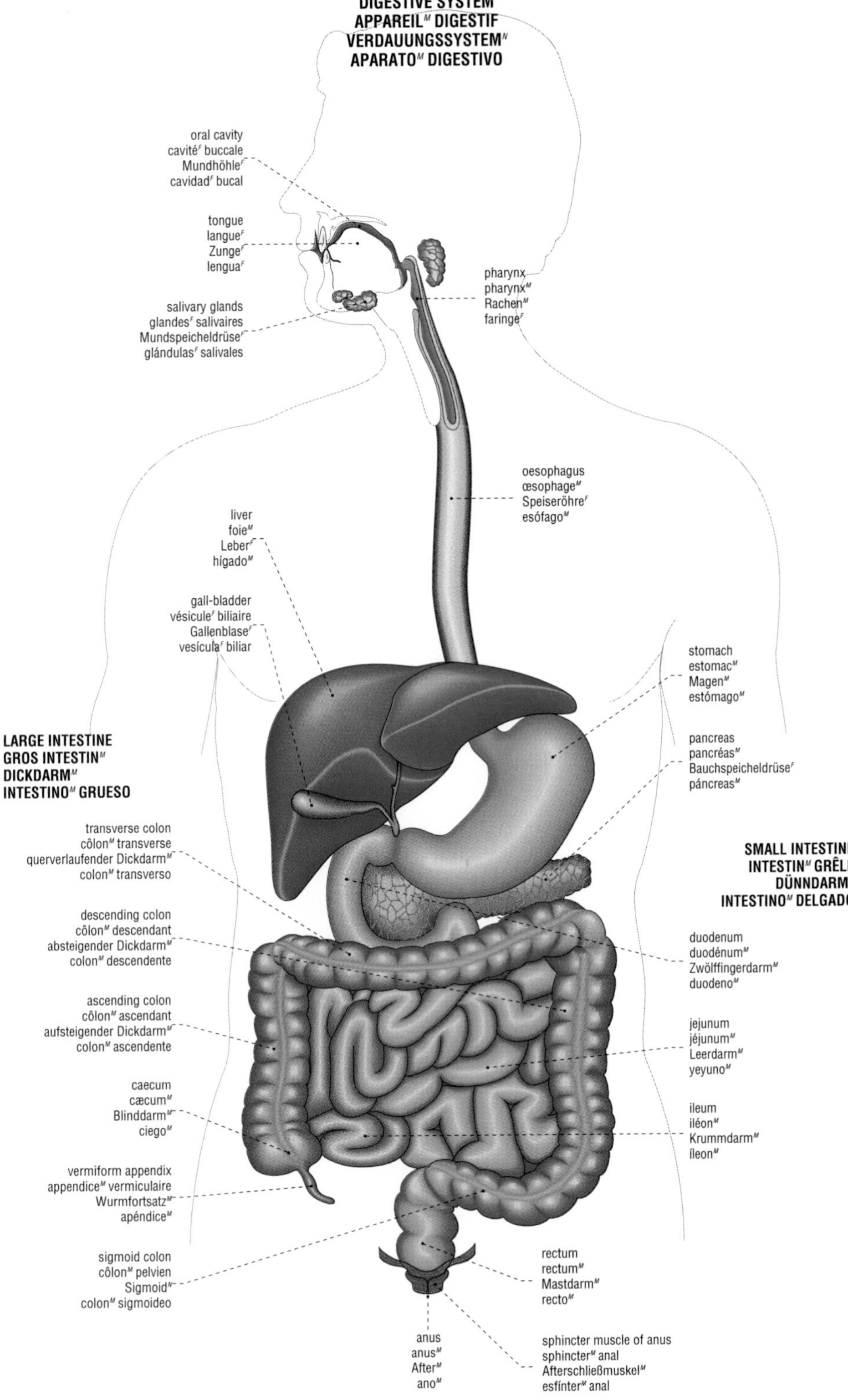

## URINARY SYSTEM
## APPAREIL[M] URINAIRE
## HARNSYSTEM[N]
## APARATO[M] URINARIO

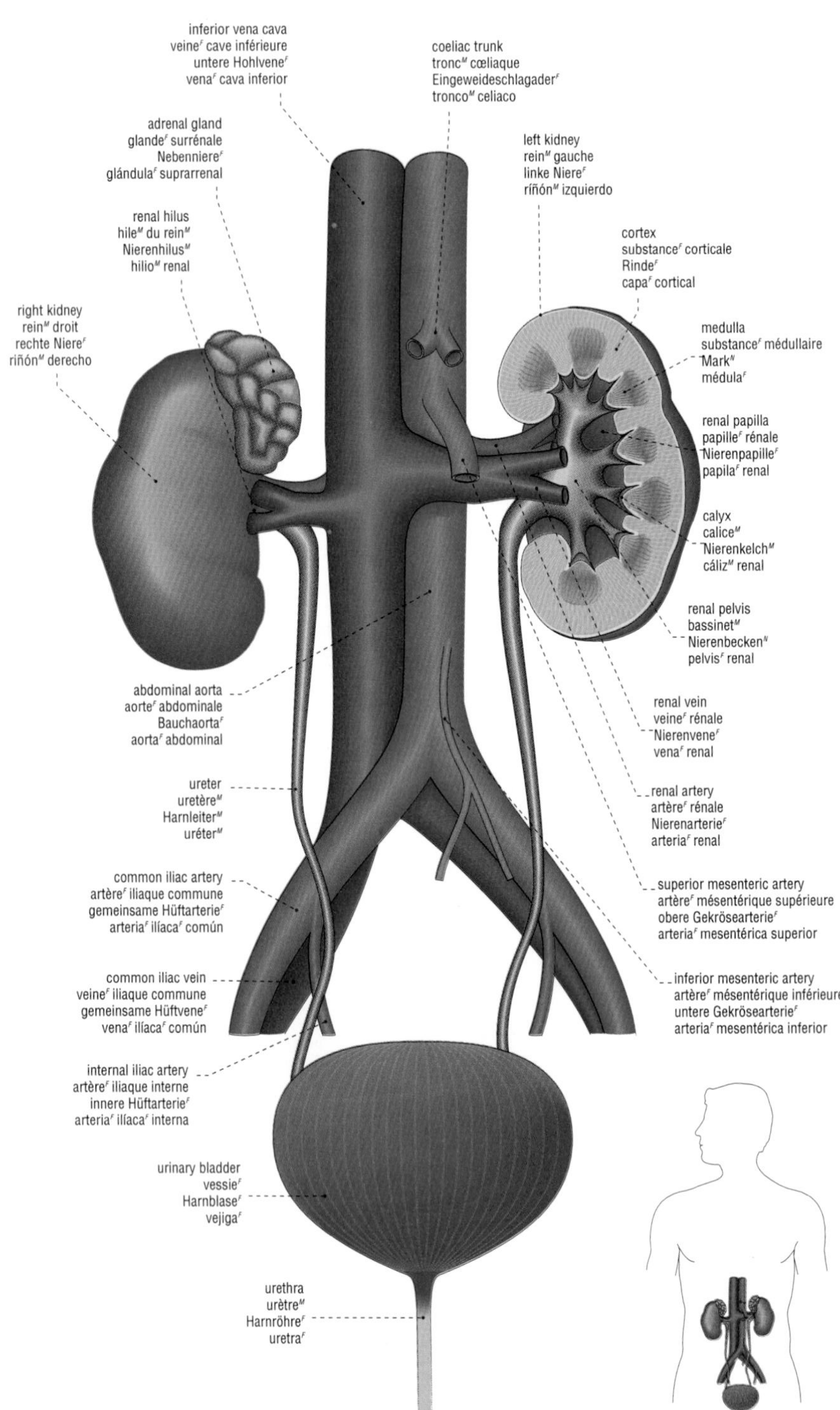

# NERVOUS SYSTEM
# SYSTÈME[M] NERVEUX
# NERVENSYSTEM[N]
# SISTEMA[M] NERVIOSO

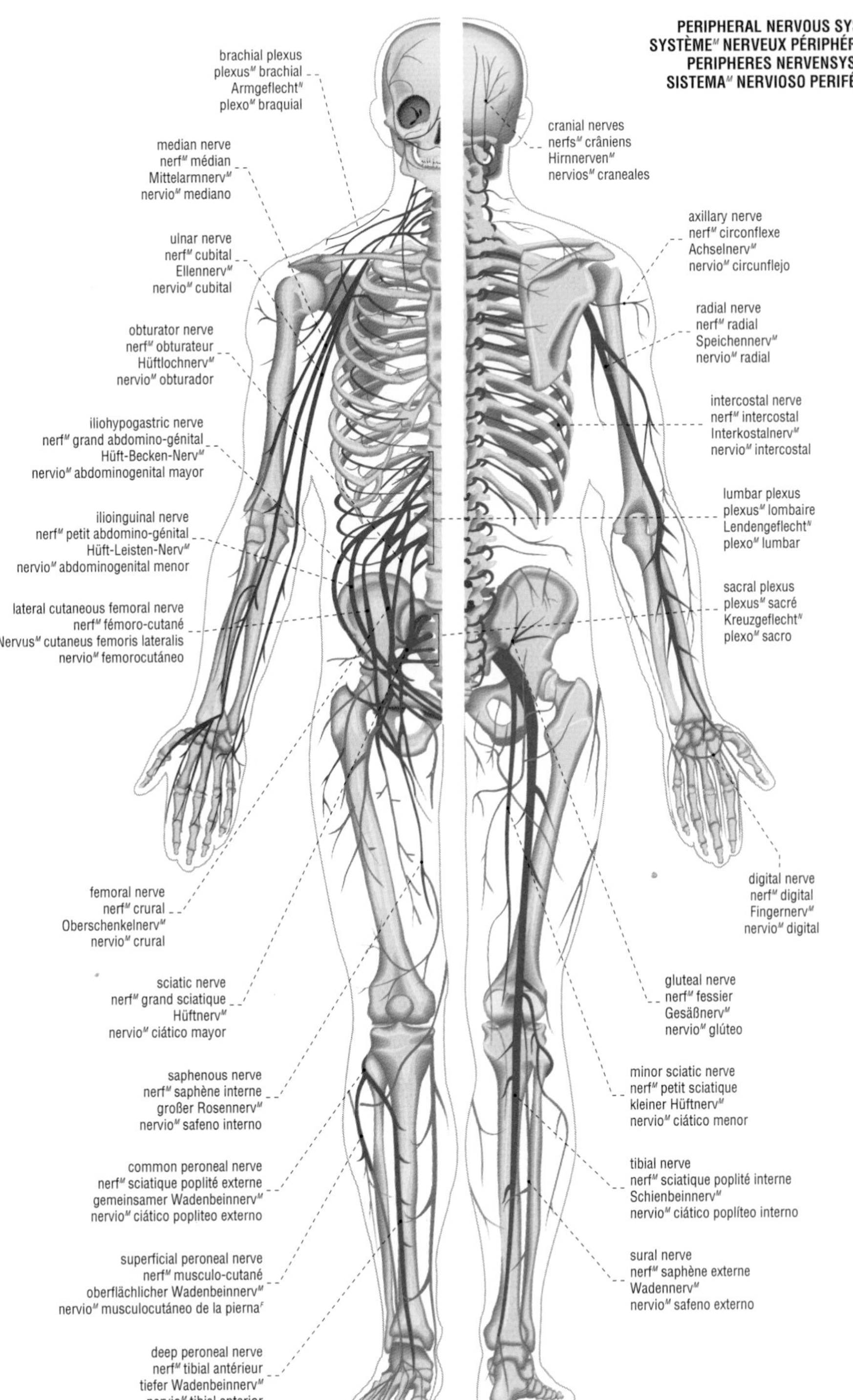

# NERVOUS SYSTEM
# SYSTÈME[M] NERVEUX
# NERVENSYSTEM[N]
# SISTEMA[M] NERVIOSO

## CENTRAL NERVOUS SYSTEM
## SYSTÈME[M] NERVEUX CENTRAL
## ZENTRALES NERVENSYSTEM[N]
## SISTEMA[M] NERVIOSO CENTRAL

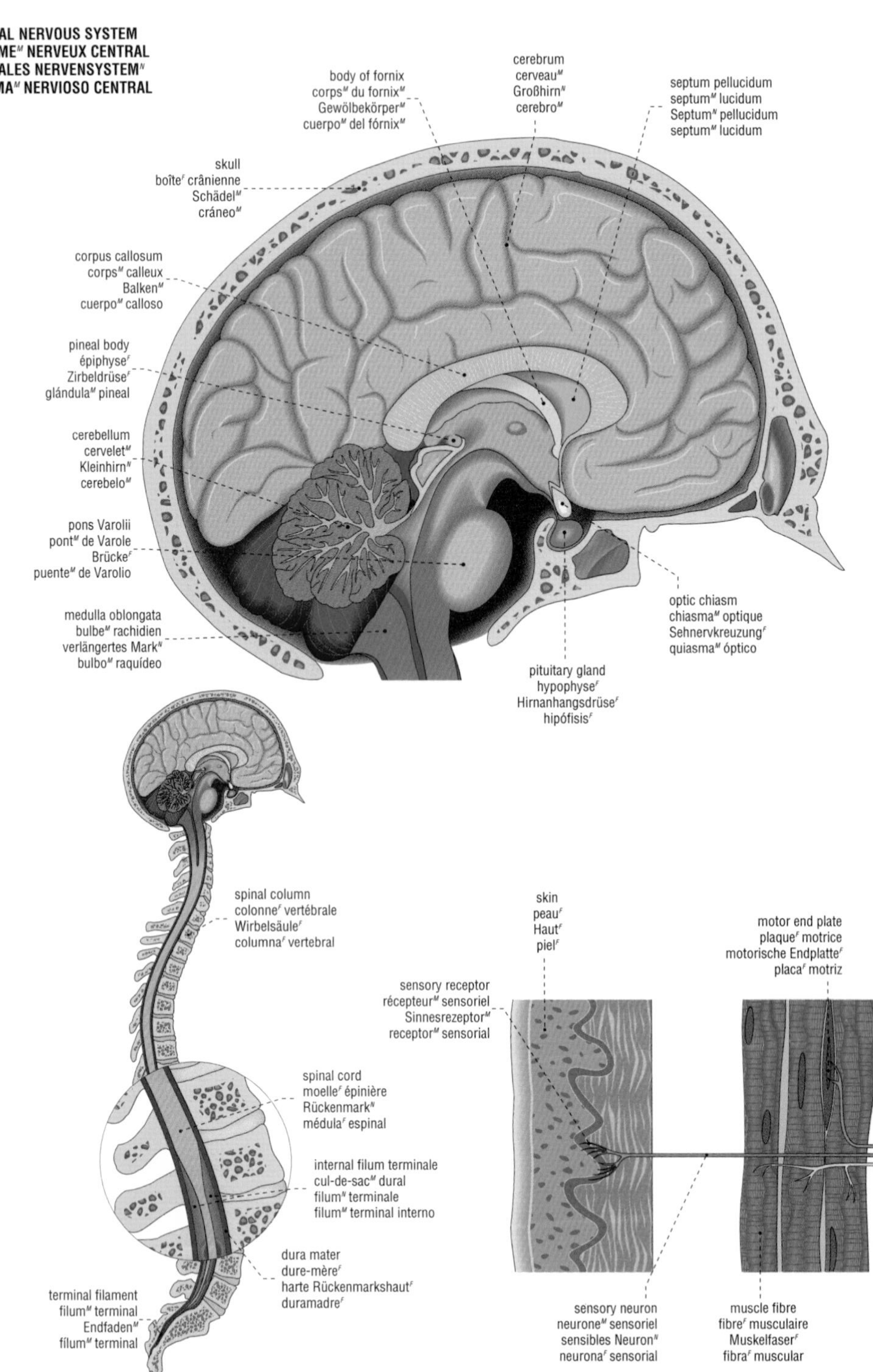

## LUMBAR VERTEBRA
## VERTÈBRE LOMBAIRE
## LENDENWIRBEL
## VÉRTEBRA LUMBAR

## CHAIN OF NEURONS
## CHAÎNE DE NEURONES
## NEURONENKETTE
## ENCADENAMIENTO DE NEURONAS

## SENSORY IMPULSE
## INFLUX NERVEUX
## SINNESIMPULS
## IMPULSO NERVIOSO

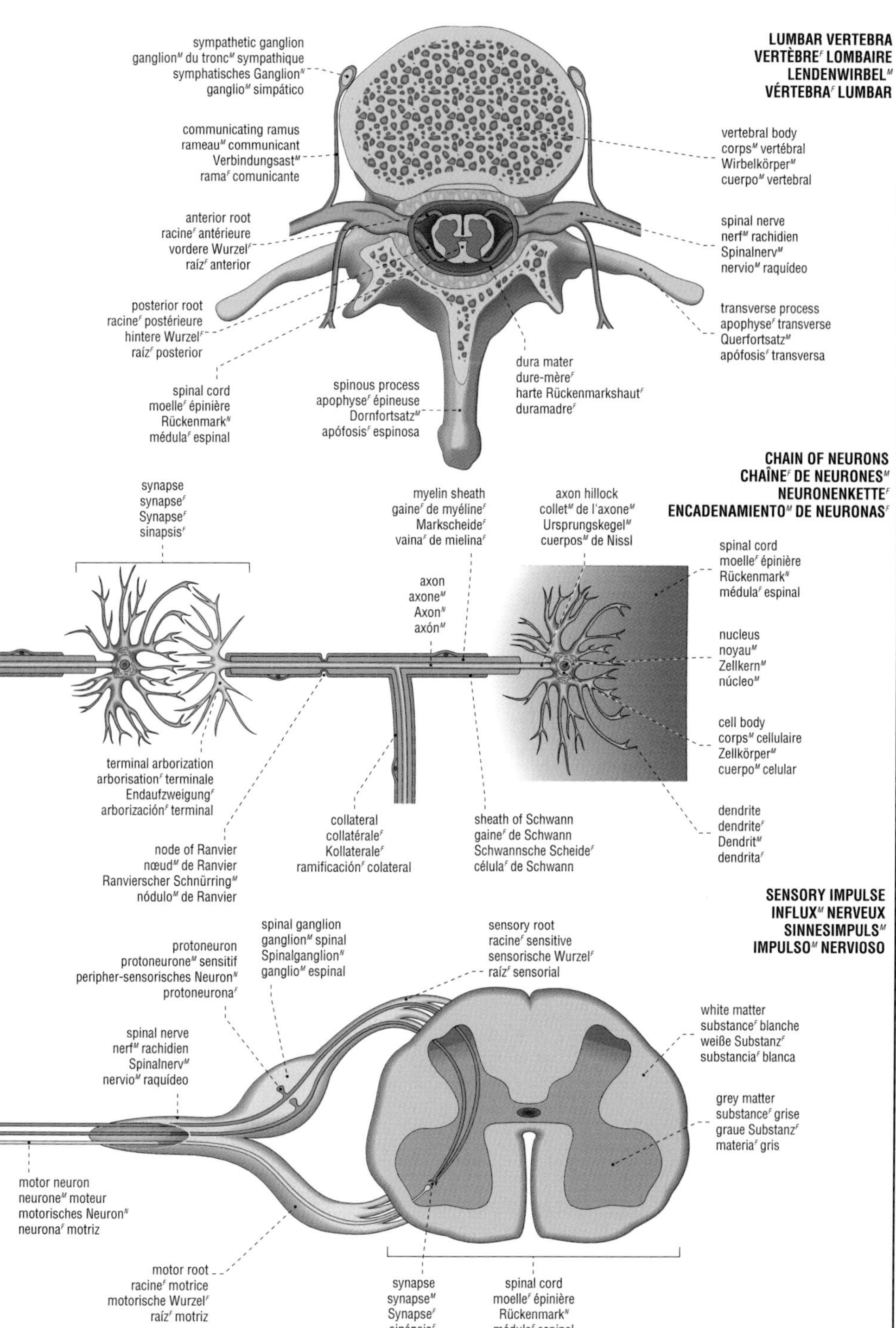

# SENSE ORGANS: TOUCH
# ORGANES[M] DES SENS[M]: TOUCHER[M]
# SINNESORGANE[N]: TASTSINN[M]
# TACTO[M]

SKIN
PEAU[F]
HAUT[F]
PIEL[F]

hair shaft
tige[F] du poil[M]
Haarschaft[M]
tallo[M]

hair
poil[M]
Haar[N]
pelo[M]

pore
pore[M] sudoripare
Pore[F]
poro[M]

stratum corneum
couche[F] cornée
Hornschicht[F]
capa[F] córnea

Ruffini's corpuscule
corpuscule[M] de Ruffini
Ruffinisches Körperchen[N]
corpúsculo[M] de Ruffini

Meissner's corpuscle
corpuscule[M] de Meissner
Meissnersches Tastkörperchen[N]
corpúsculo[M] de Meissner

stratum lucidum
couche[F] claire
Glanzschicht[F]
estrato[M] lúcido

stratum granulosum
couche[F] granuleuse
Körnerschicht[F]
capa[F] granular

stratum spinosum
couche[F] de Malpighi
Stachelzellenschicht[F]
estrato[M] de Malpighi

stratum basale
couche[F] basale
Basalschicht[F]
capa[F] basilar

nerve termination
terminaison[F] nerveuse
Nervenendigung[F]
terminación[F] nerviosa

arrector pili muscle
muscle[M] arrecteur
Haaraufrichter[M]
músculo[M] erector del pelo

sebaceous gland
glande[F] sébacée
Talgdrüse[F]
glándula[F] sebácea

hair follicle
follicule[M]
Haarbalg[M]
folículo[M] piloso

hair bulb
bulbe[M]
Haarzwiebel[F]
bulbo[M] piloso

nerve fibre
fibre[F] nerveuse
Nervenfaser[F]
fibra[F] nerviosa

papilla
papille[F]
Papille[F]
papila[F]

apocrine sweat gland
glande[F] sudoripare apocrine
apokrine Schweißdrüse[F]
glándula[F] sudoripara apocrina

nerve
nerf[M]
Nerv[M]
nervio[M]

sudoriferous duct
canal[M] sudoripare
Ausführungsgang[M] der Schweißdrüse[F]
conducto[M] sudorífero

Pacinian corpuscle
corpuscule[M] de Pacini
Vater-Pacinische Körperchen[N]
corpúscula[F] de Pacini

blood vessel
vaisseau[M] sanguin
Blutgefäß[N]
vaso[M] sanguíneo

eccrine sweat gland
glande[F] sudoripare eccrine
ekkrine Schweißdrüse[F]
glándula[F] sudorípara ecrina

adipose tissue
tissu[M] adipeux
Fettgewebe[N]
tejido[M] adiposo

FINGER
DOIGT[M]
FINGER[M]
DEDO[M]

HAND
MAIN[F]
HAND[F]
MANO[F]

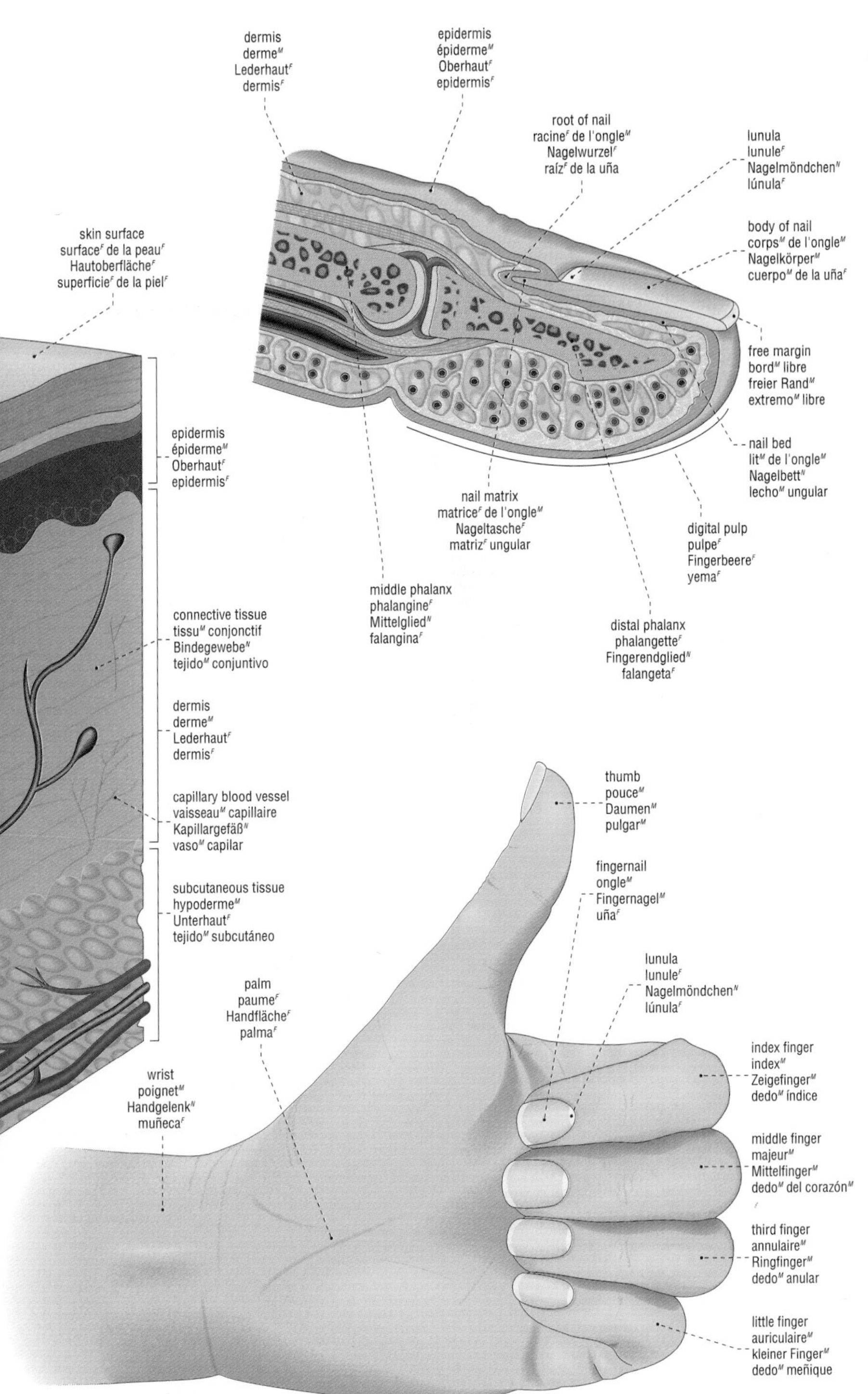

# SENSE ORGANS: HEARING
# ORGANES^M DES SENS^M: OUÏE^F
# SINNESORGANE^N: GEHÖR^N
# EL OÍDO^M

## PARTS OF THE EAR
## PARTIES^F DE L'OREILLE^F
## TEILE^N DES OHRS^N
## PARTES^F DEL OÍDO^M

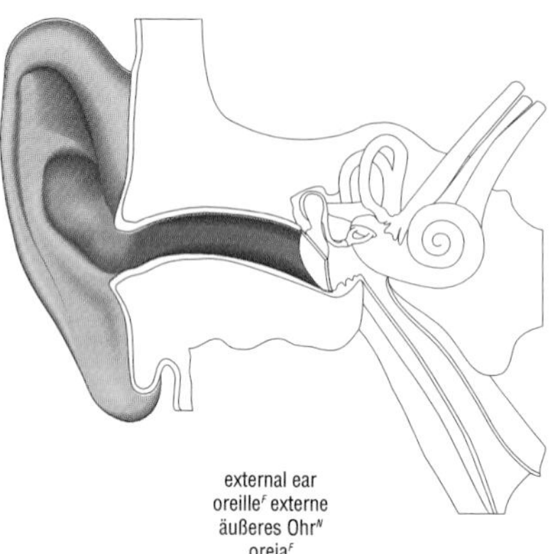

external ear
oreille^F externe
äußeres Ohr^N
oreja^F

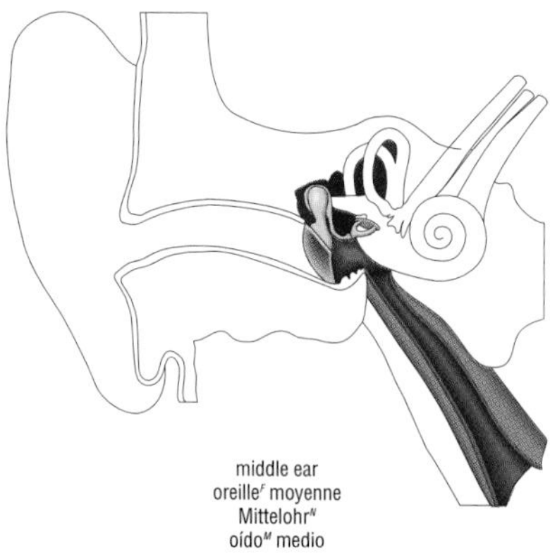

middle ear
oreille^F moyenne
Mittelohr^N
oído^M medio

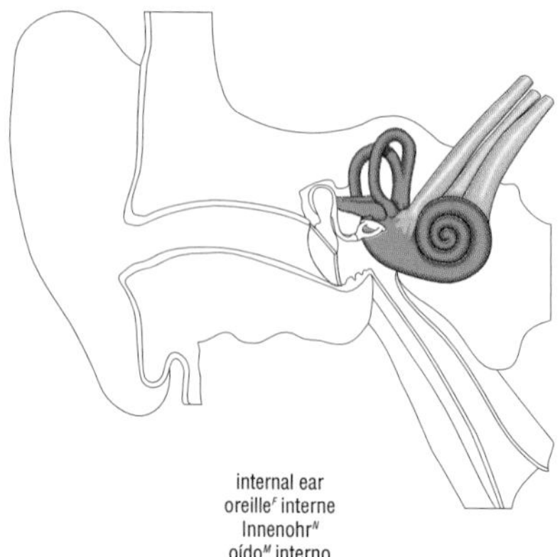

internal ear
oreille^F interne
Innenohr^N
oído^M interno

## AUDITORY OSSICLES
## OSSELETS^M
## GEHÖRKNÖCHELCHEN^N
## HUESECILLOS^M AUDITIVOS

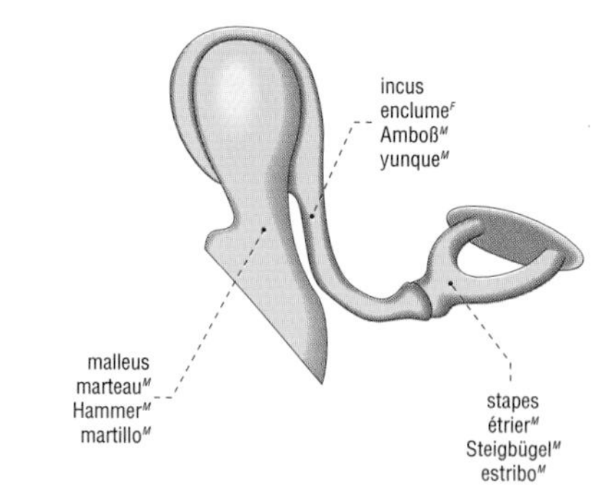


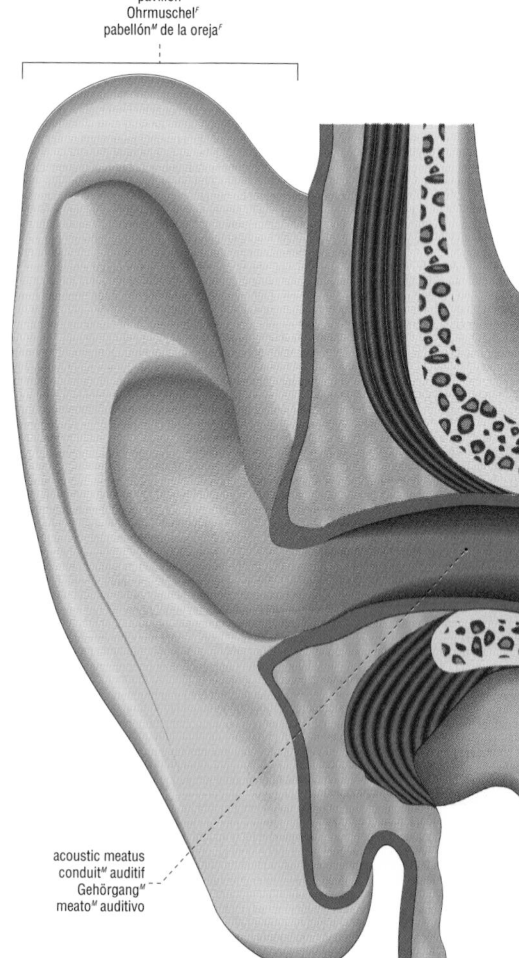


HUMAN BEING
ÊTRE HUMAIN
MENSCH
SER HUMANO

## AURICLE
## PAVILLON^M
## OHRMUSCHEL^F
## PABELLÓN^M DE LA OREJA^F

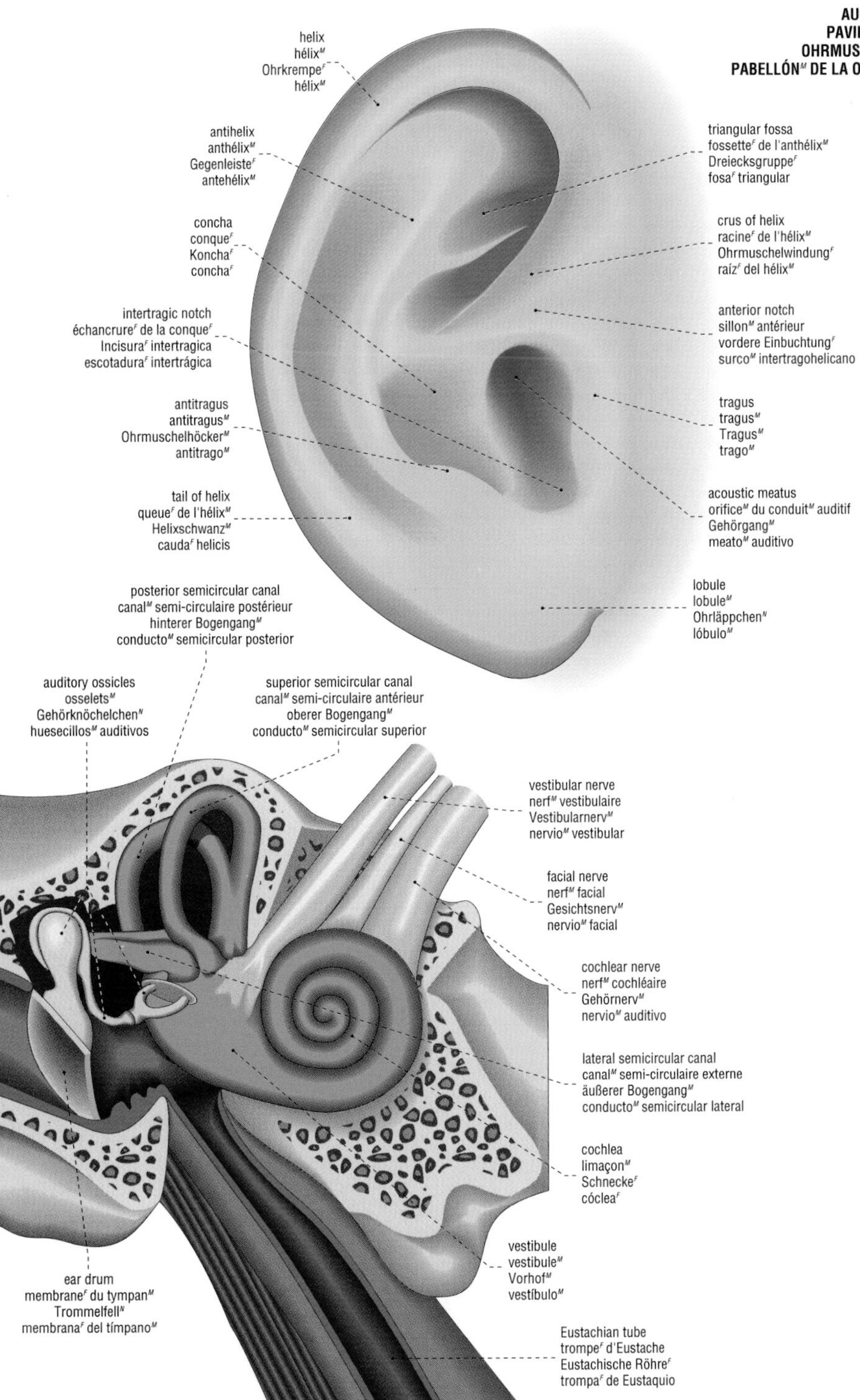

# SENSE ORGANS: SIGHT
# ORGANES[M] DES SENS[M]: VUE[F]
# SINNESORGANE[N]: SEHVERMÖGEN[N]
# LA VISTA[F]

## EYE
## ŒIL[M]
## AUGE[N]
## OJO[M]

eyebrow sourcil[M] Augenbraue[F] ceja[F]
upper eyelid paupière[F] supérieure Oberlid[N] párpado[M] superior
eyelash cil[M] Wimper[F] pestaña[F]
pupil pupille[F] Pupille[F] pupila[F]
lacrimal duct caroncule[F] lacrymale Tränenkanal[M] carúncula[F] lagrimal
sclera sclérotique[F] Sklera[F] esclerótica[F]
iris iris[M] Iris[F] iris[M]
lower eyelid paupière[F] inférieure Unterlid[N] párpado[M] inferior

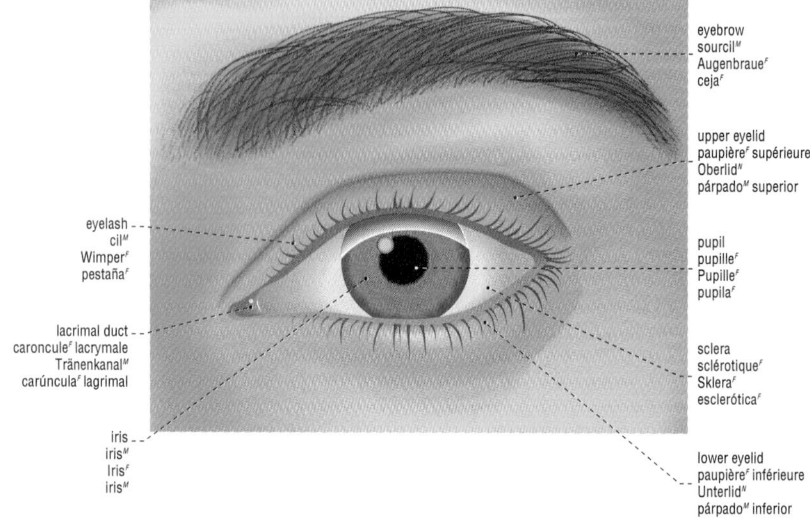

## EYEBALL
## GLOBE[M] OCULAIRE
## AUGAPFEL[M]
## GLOBO[M] OCULAR

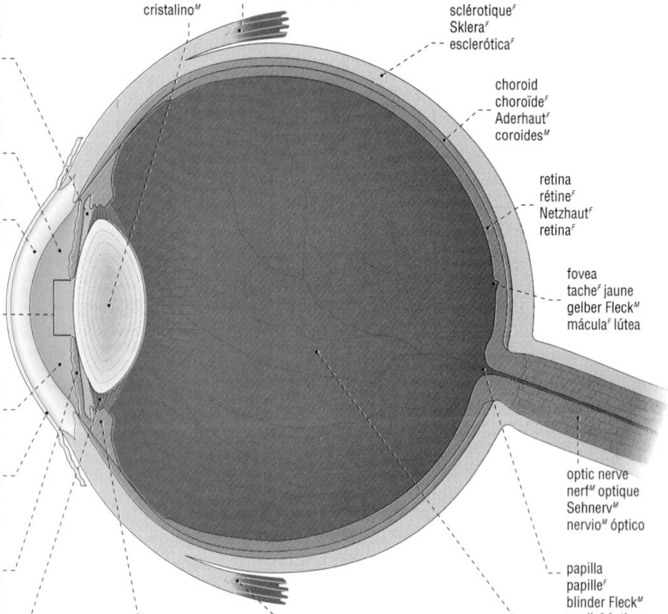

lens cristallin[M] Linse[F] cristalino[M]
lateral rectus muscle muscle[M] droit externe äußerer gerader Augenmuskel[M] músculo recto externo
posterior chamber chambre[F] postérieure hintere Augenkammer[F] cámara[F] posterior
sclera sclérotique[F] Sklera[F] esclerótica[F]
choroid choroïde[F] Aderhaut[F] coroides[M]
anterior chamber chambre[F] antérieure vordere Augenkammer[F] cámara[F] anterior
retina rétine[F] Netzhaut[F] retina[F]
cornea cornée[F] Hornhaut[F] córnea[F]
fovea tache[F] jaune gelber Fleck[M] mácula[F] lútea
pupil pupille[F] Pupille[F] pupila[F]
aqueous humour humeur[F] aqueuse Kammerwasser[N] humor[M] acuoso
conjunctiva conjonctive[F] Bindehaut[F] conjuntiva[F]
optic nerve nerf[M] optique Sehnerv[M] nervio[M] óptico
iris iris[M] Iris[F] iris[M]
papilla papille[F] blinder Fleck[M] papila[F] óptica
suspensory ligament ligament[M] suspenseur Aufhängeband[N] ligamento[M] suspensorio
ciliary body corps[M] ciliaire Ziliarkörper[M] procesos[M] ciliares
medial rectus muscle muscle[M] droit interne medialer gerader Augenmuskel[M] músculo recto interno
vitreous body corps[M] vitré Glaskörper[M] humor[M] vitreo

## SENSE ORGANS: SMELL
## ORGANES[M] DES SENS[M]: ODORAT[M]
## SINNESORGANE[N]: GERUCHSSINN[M]
## EL OLFATO[M]



### EXTERNAL NOSE
### PARTIES[F] EXTERNES DU NEZ[M]
### ÄUSSERE NASE[F]
### NARIZ[F]

bridge of nose
racine[F] du nez[M]
Nasenwurzel[F]
caballete[M]
dorsum of nose
dos[M] du nez[M]
Nasenrücken[M]
caballete[M]
septum
cloison[F]
Scheidewand[F]
septum[M]
philtrum
sillon[M] naso-labial
Philtrum[N]
surco[M] nasolabial
ala
aile[F] du nez[M]
Nasenflügel[M]
aleta[F] de la nariz[F]
naris
narine[F]
Naris[F]
ventana[F] de la nariz[F]
tip of nose
lobe[M] du nez[M]
Nasenspitze[F]
lóbulo[M]

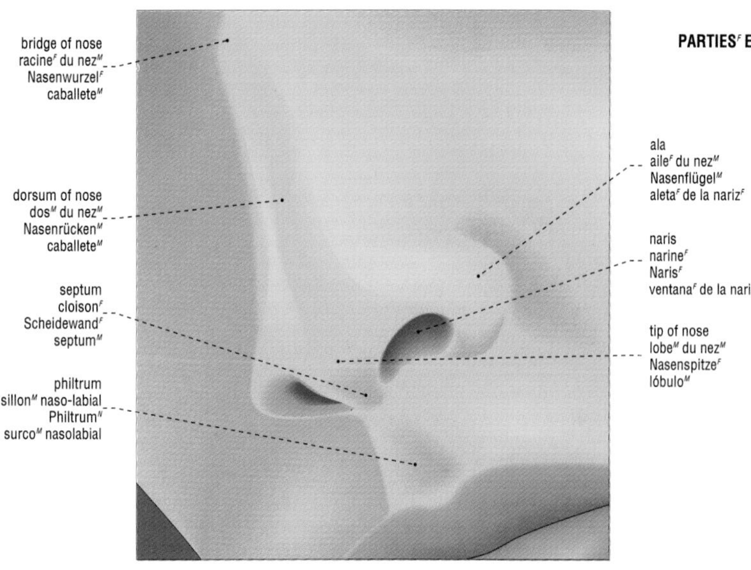

### NASAL FOSSAE
### FOSSES[F] NASALES
### NASENHÖHLE[F]
### FOSAS[F] NASALES

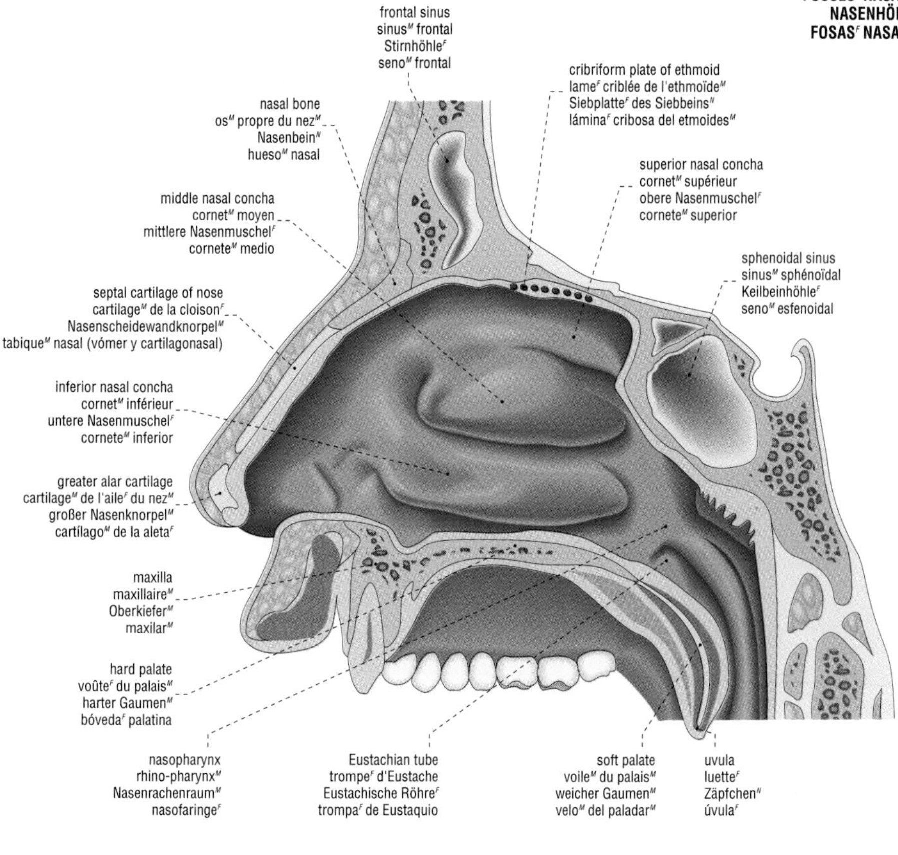

frontal sinus
sinus[M] frontal
Stirnhöhle[F]
seno[M] frontal
nasal bone
os[M] propre du nez[M]
Nasenbein[N]
hueso[M] nasal
cribriform plate of ethmoid
lame[F] criblée de l'ethmoïde[M]
Siebplatte[F] des Siebbeins[N]
lámina[F] cribosa del etmoides[M]
superior nasal concha
cornet[M] supérieur
obere Nasenmuschel[F]
cornete[M] superior
middle nasal concha
cornet[M] moyen
mittlere Nasenmuschel[F]
cornete[M] medio
sphenoidal sinus
sinus[M] sphénoïdal
Keilbeinhöhle[F]
seno[M] esfenoidal
septal cartilage of nose
cartilage[M] de la cloison[F]
Nasenscheidewandknorpel[M]
tabique[M] nasal (vómer y cartilagonasal)
inferior nasal concha
cornet[M] inférieur
untere Nasenmuschel[F]
cornete[M] inferior
greater alar cartilage
cartilage[M] de l'aile[F] du nez[M]
großer Nasenknorpel[M]
cartílago[M] de la aleta[F]
maxilla
maxillaire[M]
Oberkiefer[M]
maxilar[M]
hard palate
voûte[F] du palais[M]
harter Gaumen[M]
bóveda[F] palatina
nasopharynx
rhino-pharynx[M]
Nasenrachenraum[M]
nasofaringe[F]
Eustachian tube
trompe[F] d'Eustache
Eustachische Röhre[F]
trompa[F] de Eustaquio
soft palate
voile[M] du palais[M]
weicher Gaumen[M]
velo[M] del paladar[M]
uvula
luette[F]
Zäpfchen[N]
úvula[F]

# SENSES OF SMELL AND TASTE
# SENS^M DE L'ODORAT^M ET DU GOÛT^M
# GERUCHS- UND GESCHMACKSSINN^M
# EL OLFATO^M Y EL GUSTO^M



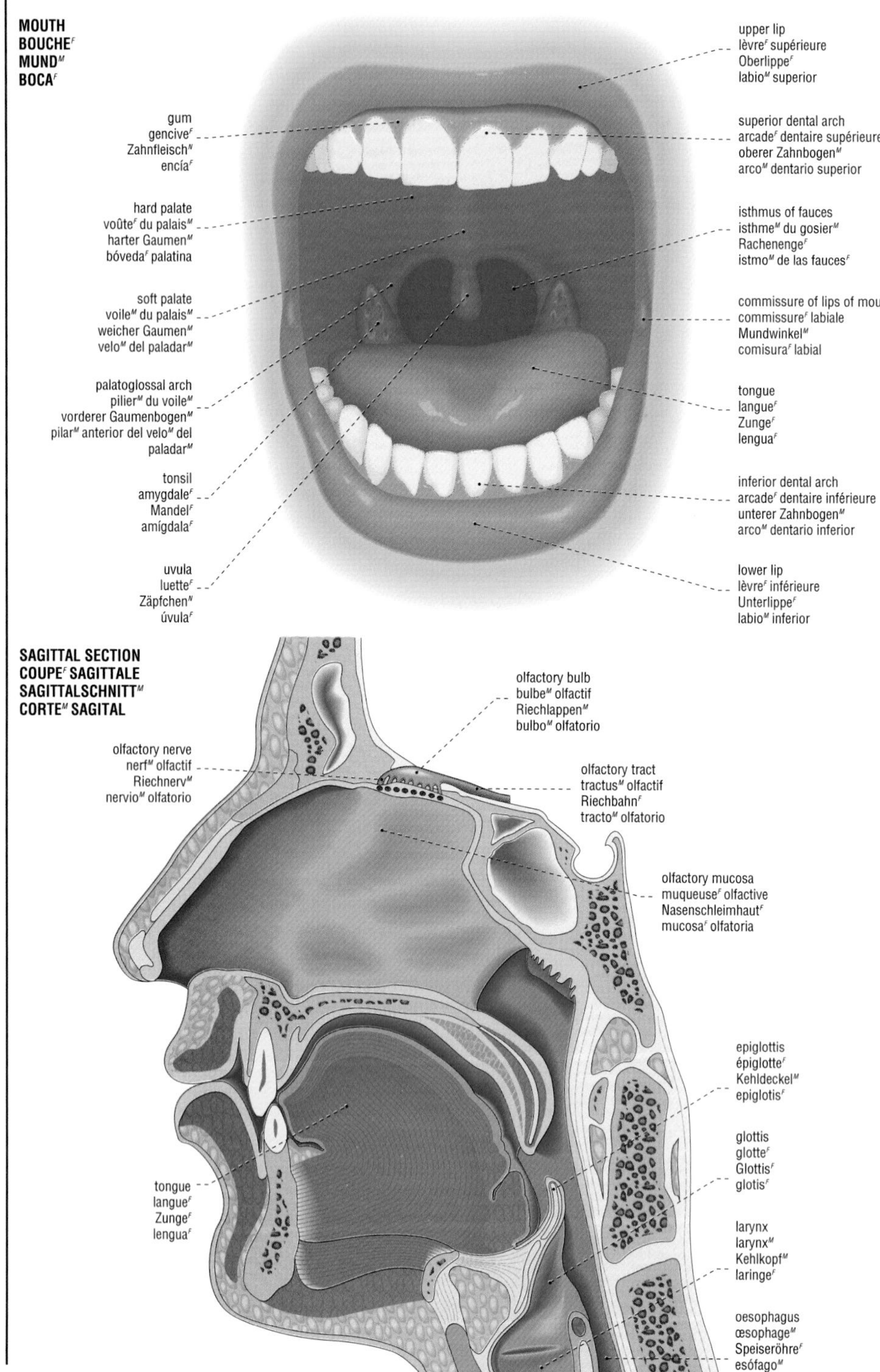

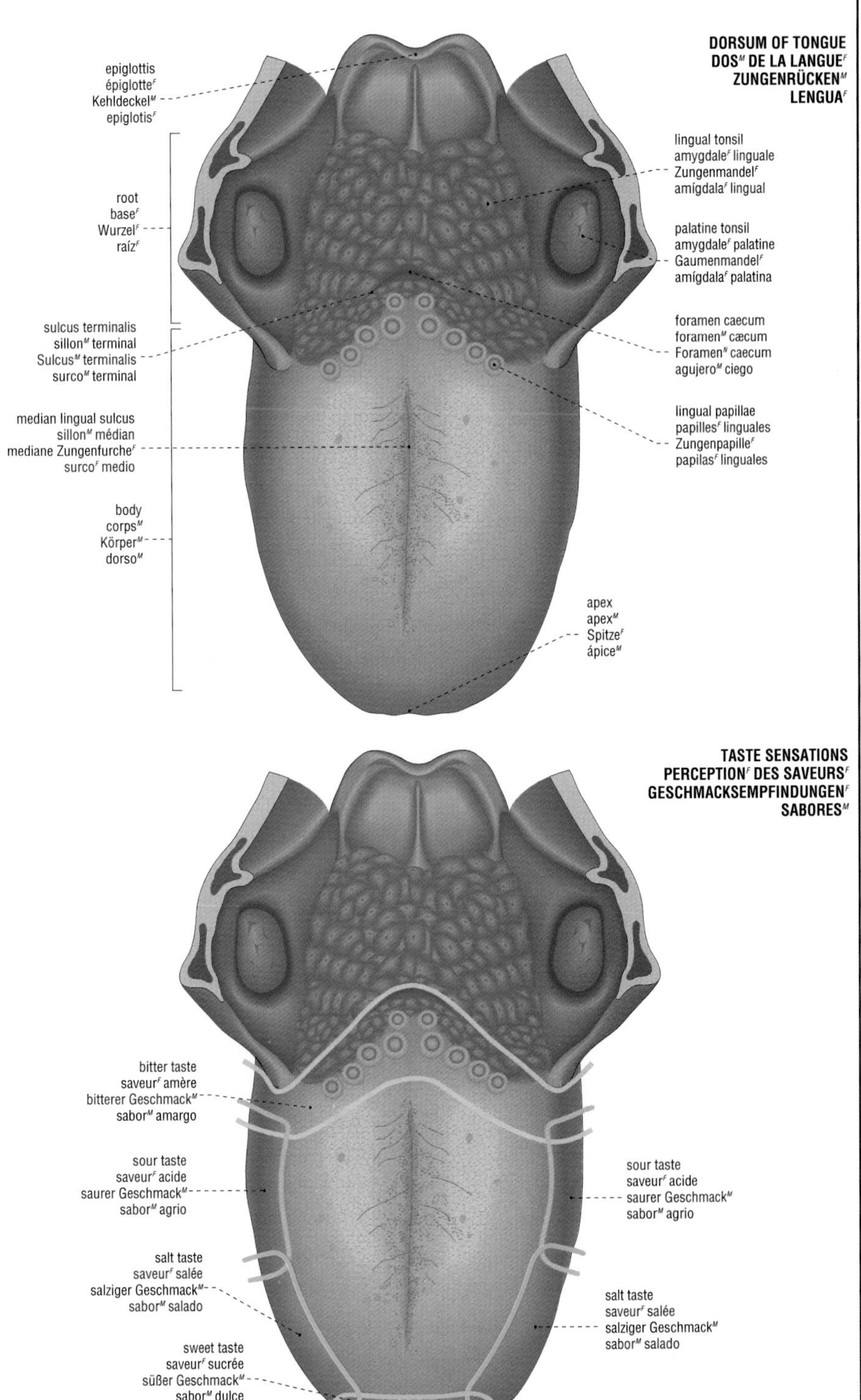
DORSUM OF TONGUE
DOS[M] DE LA LANGUE[F]
ZUNGENRÜCKEN[M]
LENGUA[F]
epiglottis
épiglotte[F]
Kehldeckel[M]
epiglotis[F]
lingual tonsil
amygdale[F] linguale
Zungenmandel[F]
amígdala[F] lingual
root
base[F]
Wurzel[F]
raíz[F]
palatine tonsil
amygdale[F] palatine
Gaumenmandel[F]
amígdala[F] palatina
foramen caecum
foramen[M] cæcum
Foramen[N] caecum
agujero[M] ciego
sulcus terminalis
sillon[M] terminal
Sulcus[M] terminalis
surco[M] terminal
lingual papillae
papilles[F] linguales
Zungenpapille[F]
papilas[F] linguales
median lingual sulcus
sillon[M] médian
mediane Zungenfurche[F]
surco[F] medio
body
corps[M]
Körper[M]
dorso[M]
apex
apex[M]
Spitze[F]
ápice[M]
TASTE SENSATIONS
PERCEPTION[F] DES SAVEURS[F]
GESCHMACKSEMPFINDUNGEN[F]
SABORES[M]
bitter taste
saveur[F] amère
bitterer Geschmack[M]
sabor[M] amargo
sour taste
saveur[F] acide
saurer Geschmack[M]
sabor[M] agrio
sour taste
saveur[F] acide
saurer Geschmack[M]
sabor[M] agrio
salt taste
saveur[F] salée
salziger Geschmack[M]
sabor[M] salado
salt taste
saveur[F] salée
salziger Geschmack[M]
sabor[M] salado
sweet taste
saveur[F] sucrée
süßer Geschmack[M]
sabor[M] dulce

# TEETH
# DENTS[F]
# ZÄHNE[M]
# DIENTES[M]

## HUMAN DENTURE
## DENTURE[F] HUMAINE
## MENSCHLICHES GEBISS[N]
## DENTADURA[F] HUMANA

incisors
incisives[F]
Schneidezähne[M]
incisivos[M]
premolars
prémolaires[F]
vordere Backenzähne[M]
premolares[M]
lateral incisor
incisive[F] latérale
äußerer Schneidezahn[M]
incisivo[M] lateral
molars
molaires[F]
Mahlzähne[M]
molares[M]
first premolar
première prémolaire[F]
erster vorderer Backenzahn[M]
primer premolar[M]
second molar
deuxième molaire[F]
zweiter Mahlzahn[M]
segundo molar[M]
second premolar
deuxième prémolaire[F]
zweiter vorderer Backenzahn[M]
segundo premolar[M]
wisdom tooth
dent[F] de sagesse[F]
Weisheitszahn[M]
muela[F] del juicio[M]
first molar
première molaire[F]
erster Mahlzahn[M]
primer molar[M]
canine
canine[F]
Eckzahn[M]
colmillo[M]
central incisor
incisive[F] centrale
mittlerer Schneidezahn[M]
incisivo[M] central

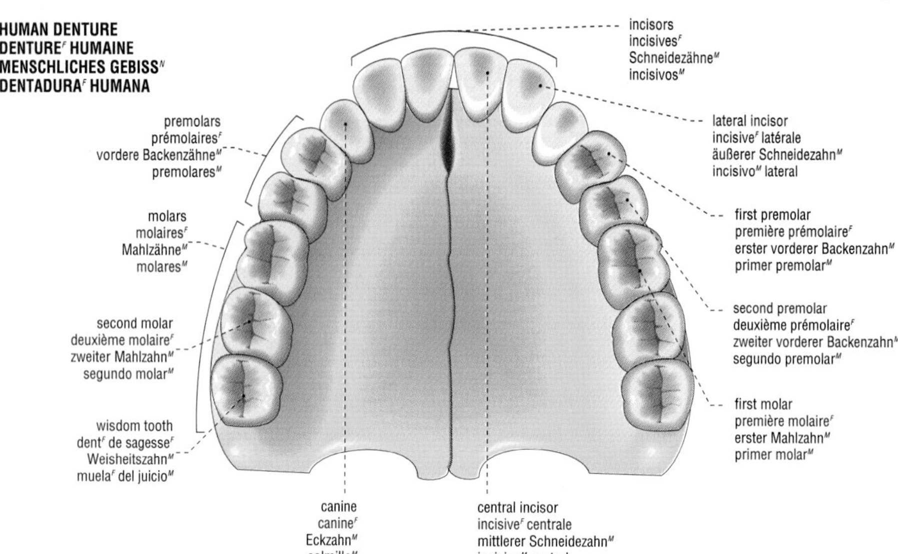

## CROSS SECTION OF A MOLAR
## COUPE[F] D'UNE MOLAIRE[F]
## LÄNGSSCHNITT[M] DURCH EINEN MAHLZAHN[M]
## CORTE[M] TRANSVERSAL DE UN MOLAR[M]

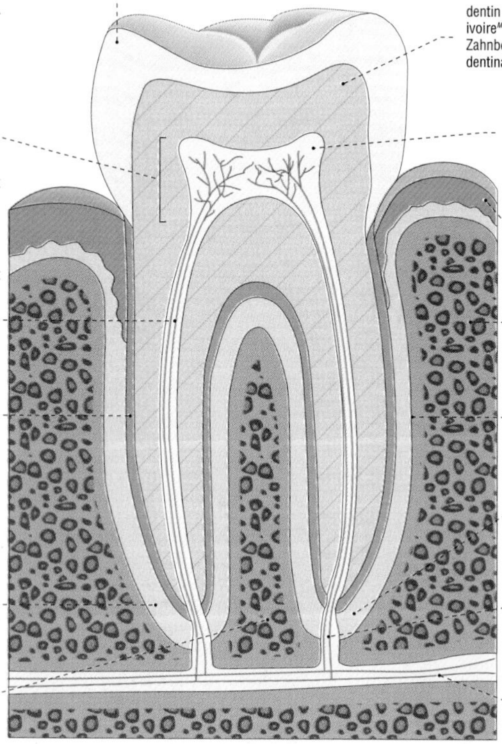

enamel
émail[M]
Schmelz[M]
esmalte[M]
crown
couronne[F]
Krone[F]
corona[F]
dentin
ivoire[M]
Zahnbein[N]
dentina[F]
pulp chamber
chambre[F] pulpaire
Pulpahöhle[F]
cámara[F] pulpar
pulp
pulpe[F]
Pulpa[F]
pulpa[F]
neck
collet[M]
Hals[M]
cuello[M]
gum
gencive[F]
Zahnfleisch[N]
encía[F]
root canal
canal[M] radiculaire
Wurzelkanal[M]
conducto[M] radicular
maxillary bone
os[M] maxillaire
Oberkieferknochen[M]
hueso[M] maxilar
cementum
cément[M]
Zement[M]
cemento[M]
periodontal ligament
ligament[M] alvéolo-dentaire
Wurzelhaut[F]
ligamento[M] alveolo-dentario
root
racine[F]
Wurzel[F]
raíz[F]
apex
apex[M]
Spitze[F]
ápice[M]
dental alveolus
alvéole[F] dentaire
Alveolenwand[F]
alvéolo[M] dental
apical foramen
foramen[M] apical
Zahnwurzelkanalöffnung[F]
agujero[M] apical
alveolar bone
os[M] alvéolaire
Alveolarknochen[M]
hueso[M] alveolar
plexus of nerves
réseau[M] nerveux
Nervengeflecht[N]
plexo[M] nervioso

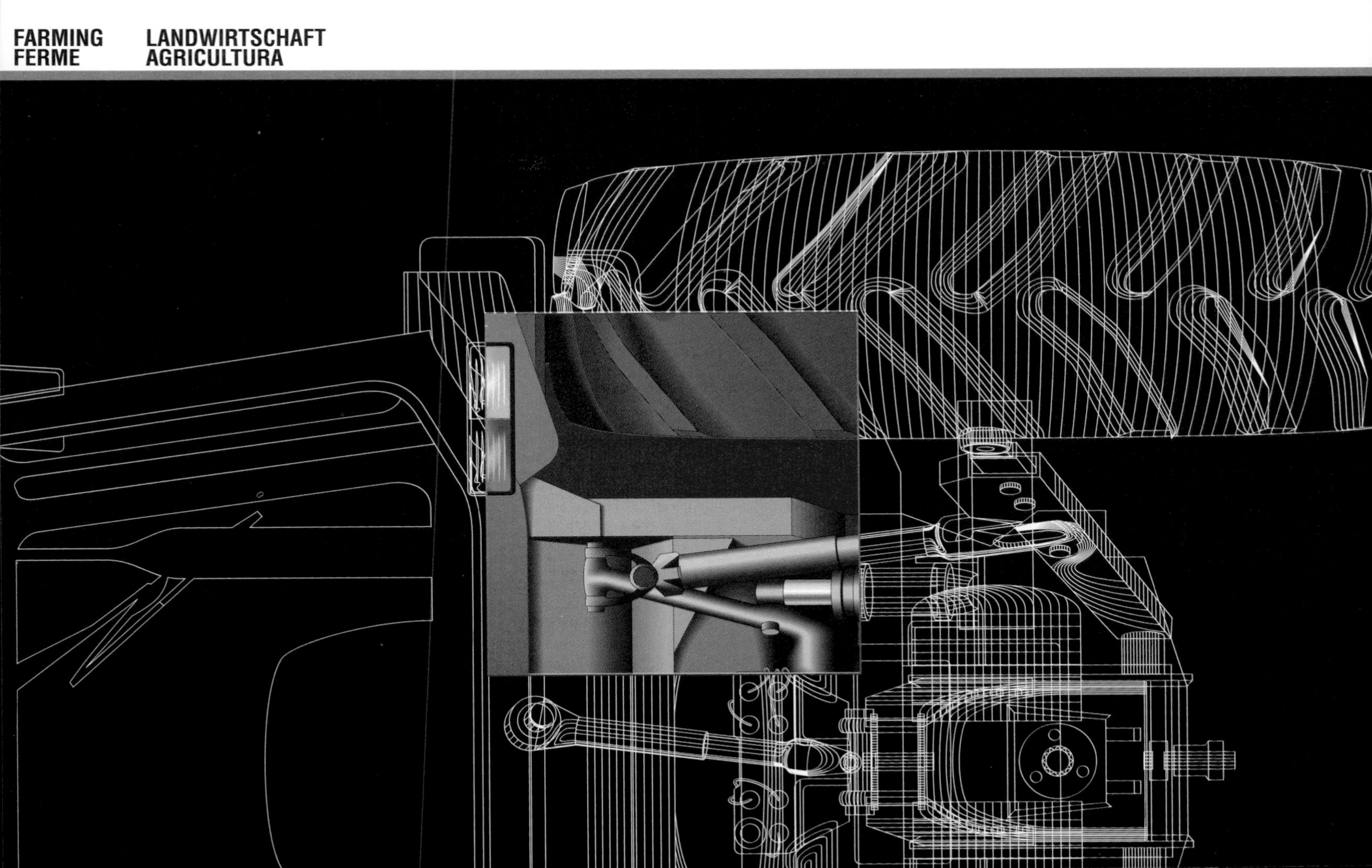
FARMING LANDWIRTSCHAFT
FERME AGRICULTURA

**SUMMARY**

TRACTOR ........ 147
FARMSTEAD ........ 148
FARM ANIMALS ........ 150
PRINCIPAL TYPES OF CEREAL ........ 152
BREAD ........ 153
STEPS IN SOIL CULTIVATION ........ 154
PLOUGHING ........ 156
FERTILIZING ........ 156
PULVERIZING ........ 157
PLANTING ........ 158
MOWING ........ 158
TEDDING ........ 159
HARVESTING ........ 159
ENSILING ........ 162

# TRACTOR
# TRACTEUR[M] AGRICOLE
# TRAKTOR[M]
# TRACTOR[M]

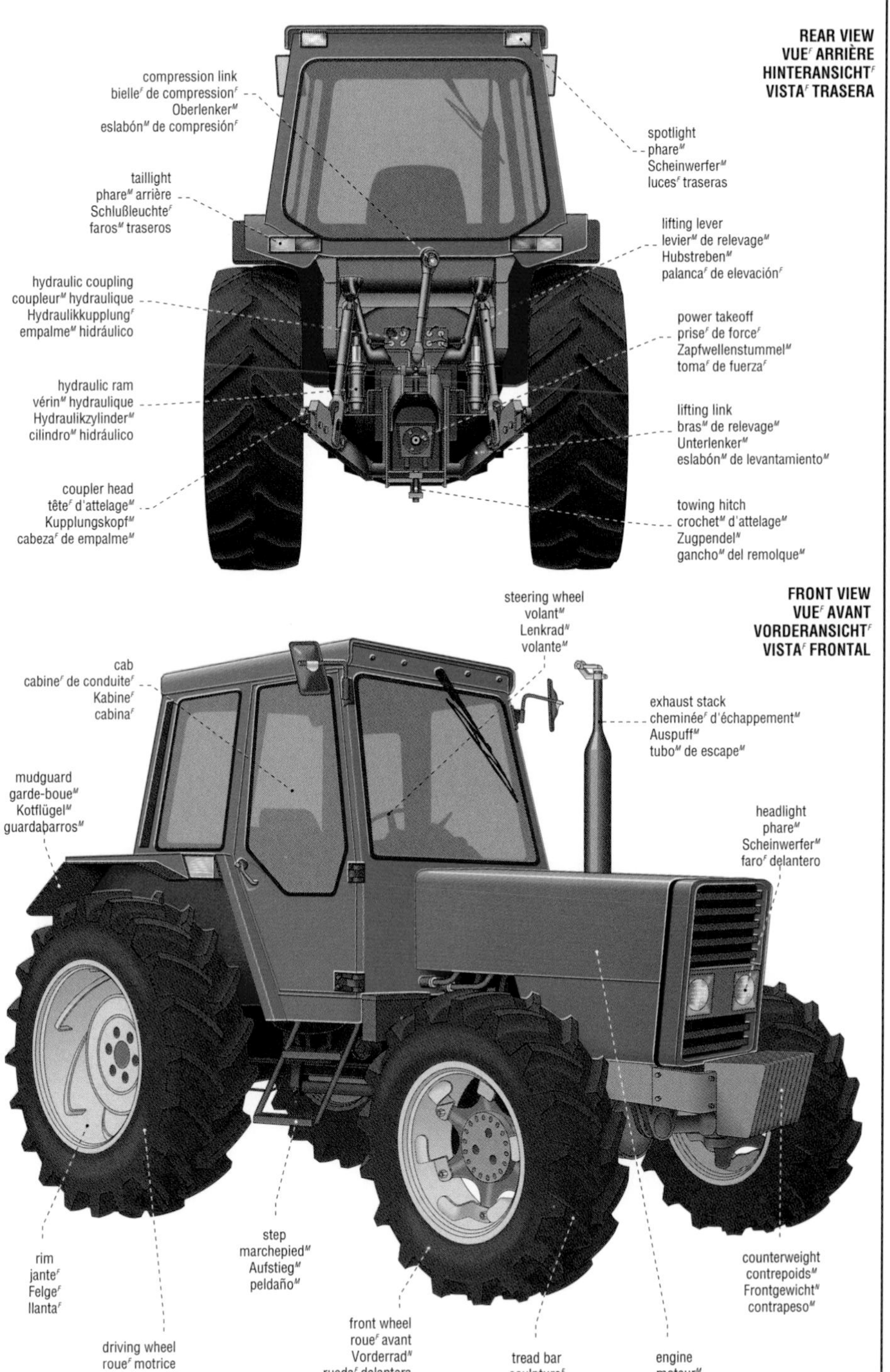

## FARMSTEAD
## FERME^F
## BAUERNHOF^M
## GRANJA^F

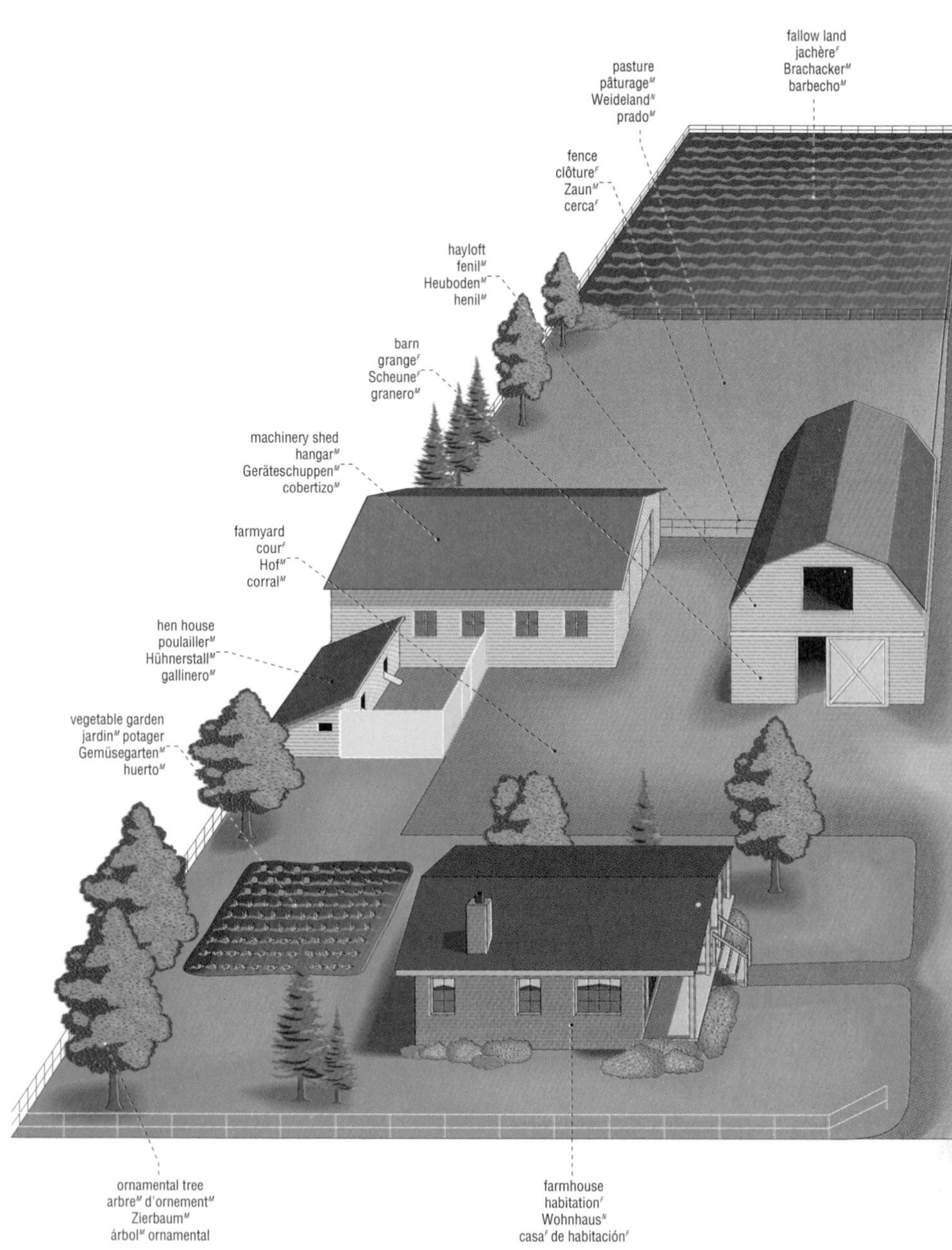

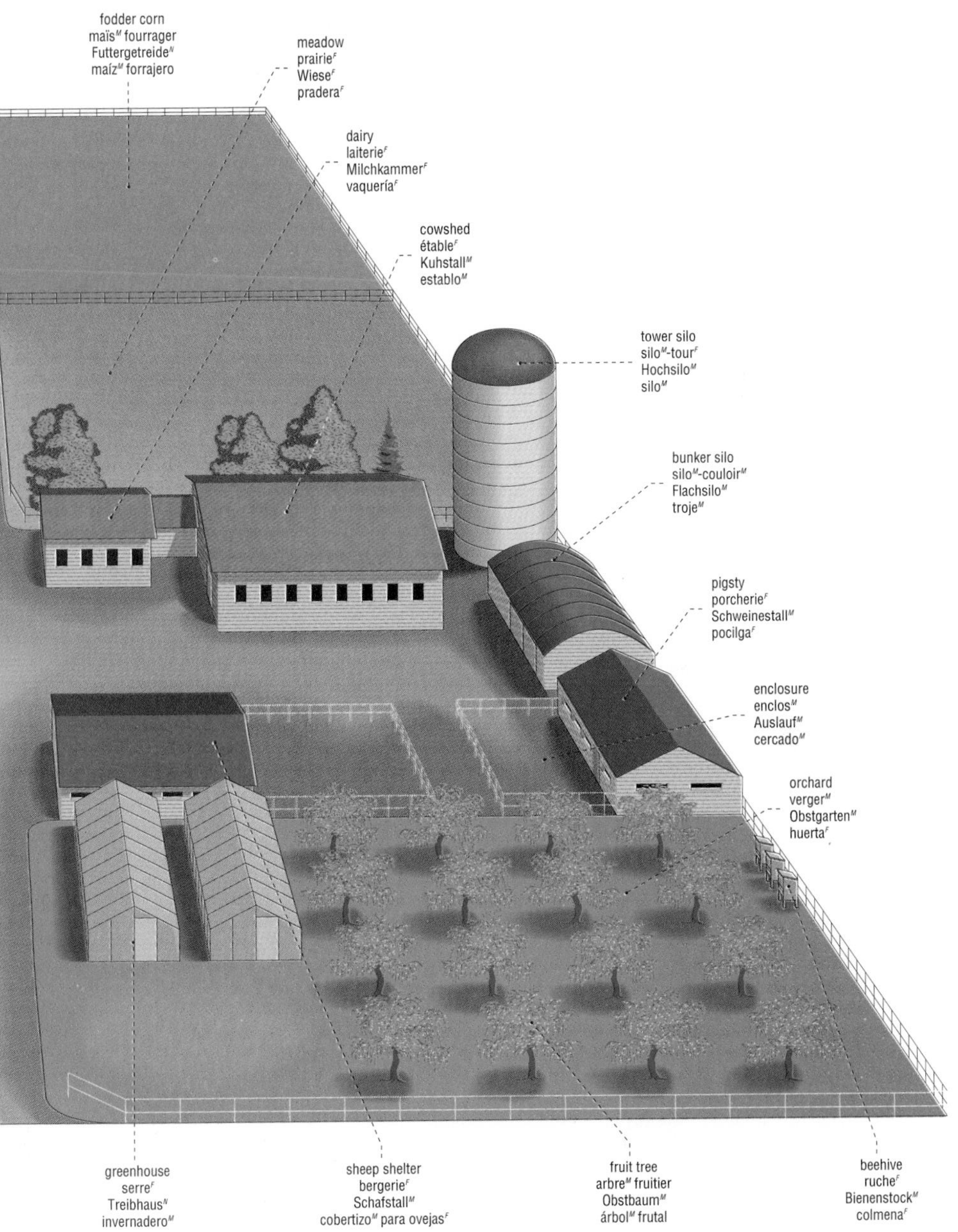
fodder corn
maïs[M] fourrager
Futtergetreide[N]
maíz[M] forrajero
meadow
prairie[F]
Wiese[F]
pradera[F]
dairy
laiterie[F]
Milchkammer[F]
vaquería[F]
cowshed
étable[F]
Kuhstall[M]
establo[M]
tower silo
silo[M]-tour[F]
Hochsilo[M]
silo[M]
bunker silo
silo[M]-couloir[M]
Flachsilo[M]
troje[M]
pigsty
porcherie[F]
Schweinestall[M]
pocilga[F]
enclosure
enclos[M]
Auslauf[M]
cercado[M]
orchard
verger[M]
Obstgarten[M]
huerta[F]
greenhouse
serre[F]
Treibhaus[N]
invernadero[M]
sheep shelter
bergerie[F]
Schafstall[M]
cobertizo[M] para ovejas[F]
fruit tree
arbre[M] fruitier
Obstbaum[M]
árbol[M] frutal
beehive
ruche[F]
Bienenstock[M]
colmena[F]

# FARM ANIMALS
# ANIMAUX[M] DE LA FERME[F]
# NUTZVIEH[N]
# ANIMALES[M] DE LA GRANJA[F]

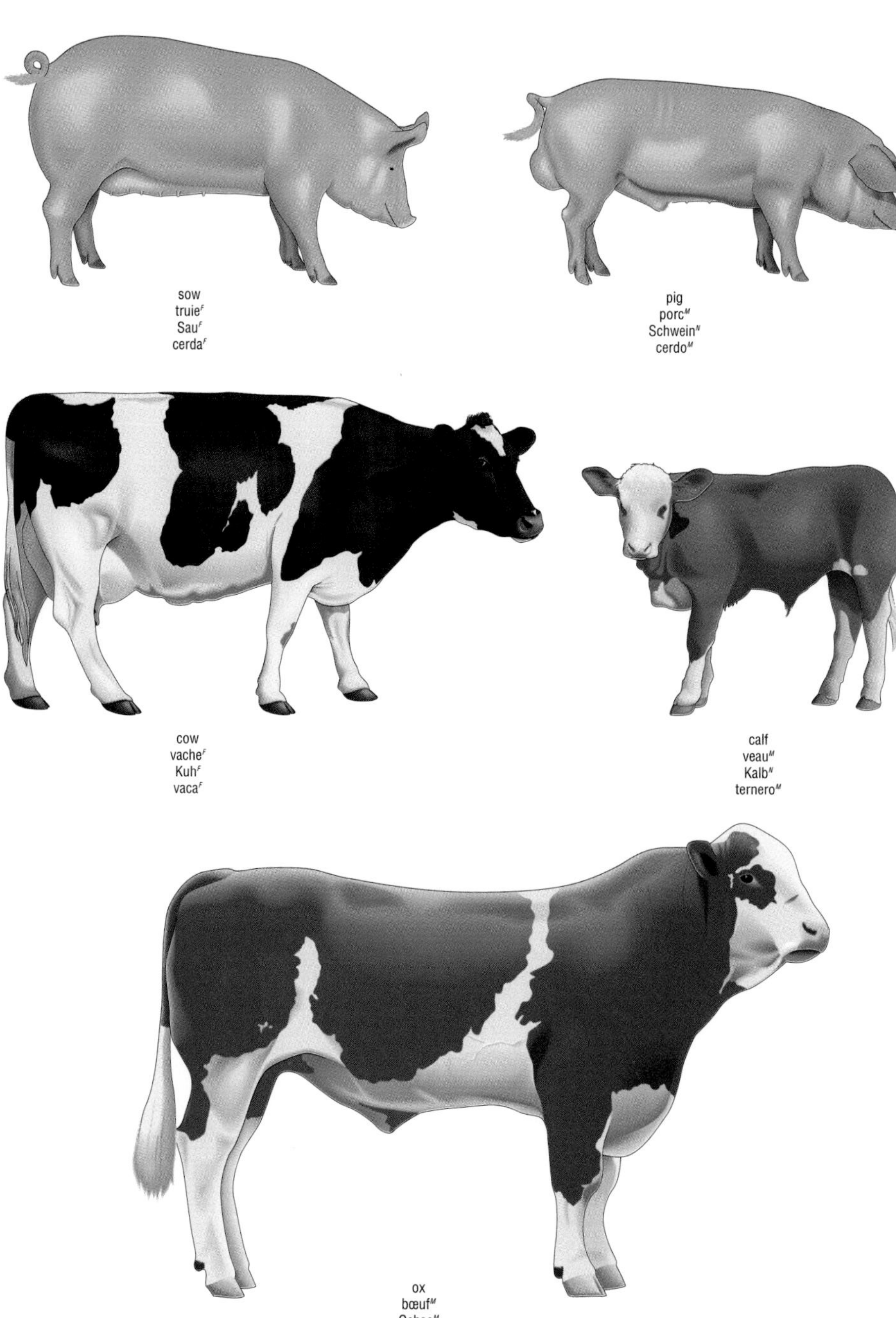
sow
truie^F
Sau^F
cerda^F
pig
porc^M
Schwein^N
cerdo^M
cow
vache^F
Kuh^F
vaca^F
calf
veau^M
Kalb^N
ternero^M
ox
bœuf^M
Ochse^M
buey^M

## PRINCIPAL TYPES OF CEREAL
## PRINCIPALES VARIÉTÉS[F] DE CÉRÉALES[F]
## DIE WICHTIGSTEN GETREIDESORTEN[F]
## PRINCIPALES TIPOS[M] DE CEREALES[M]

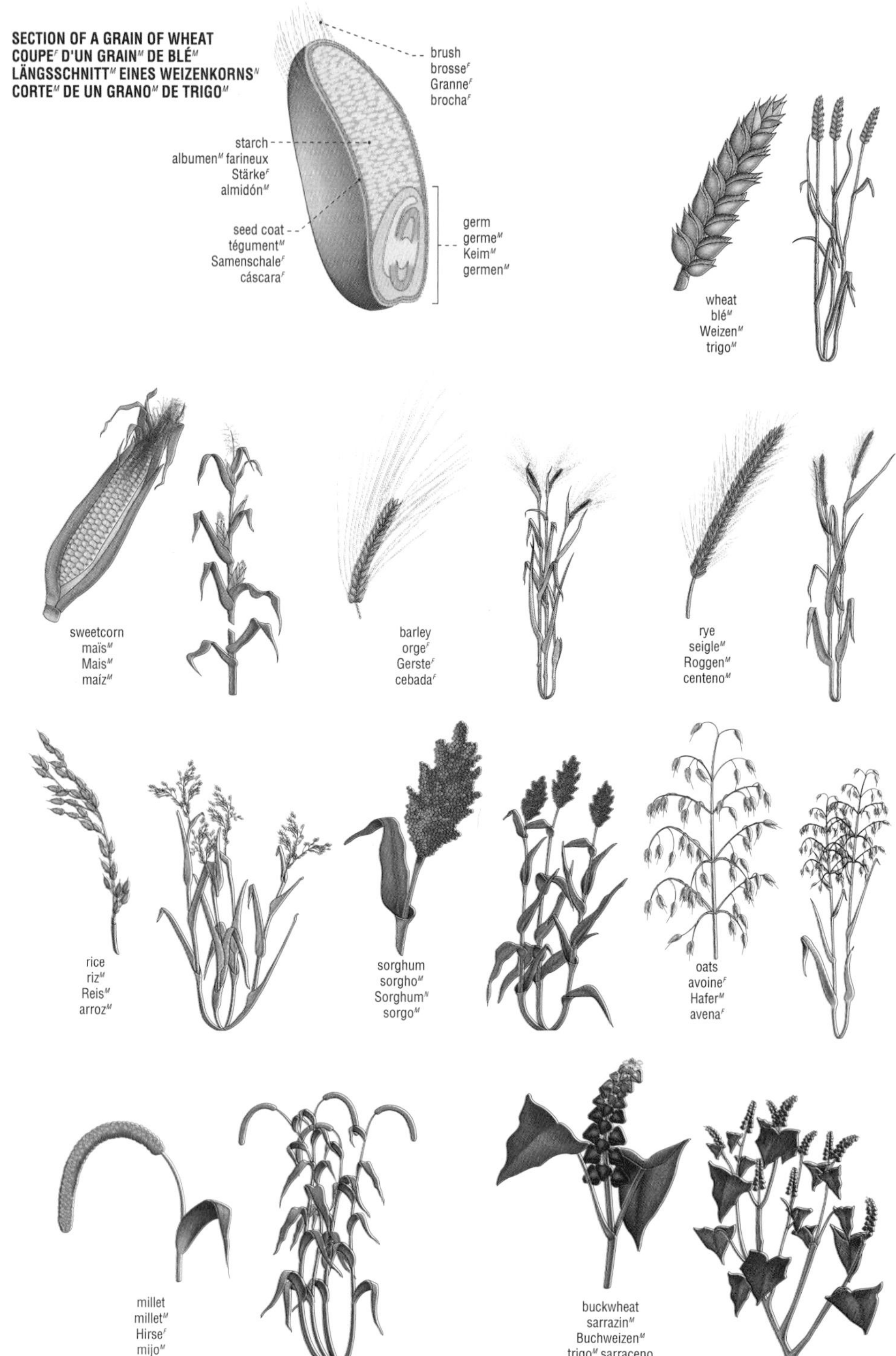

# BREAD
# PAIN^M
# BROT^N
# PAN^M

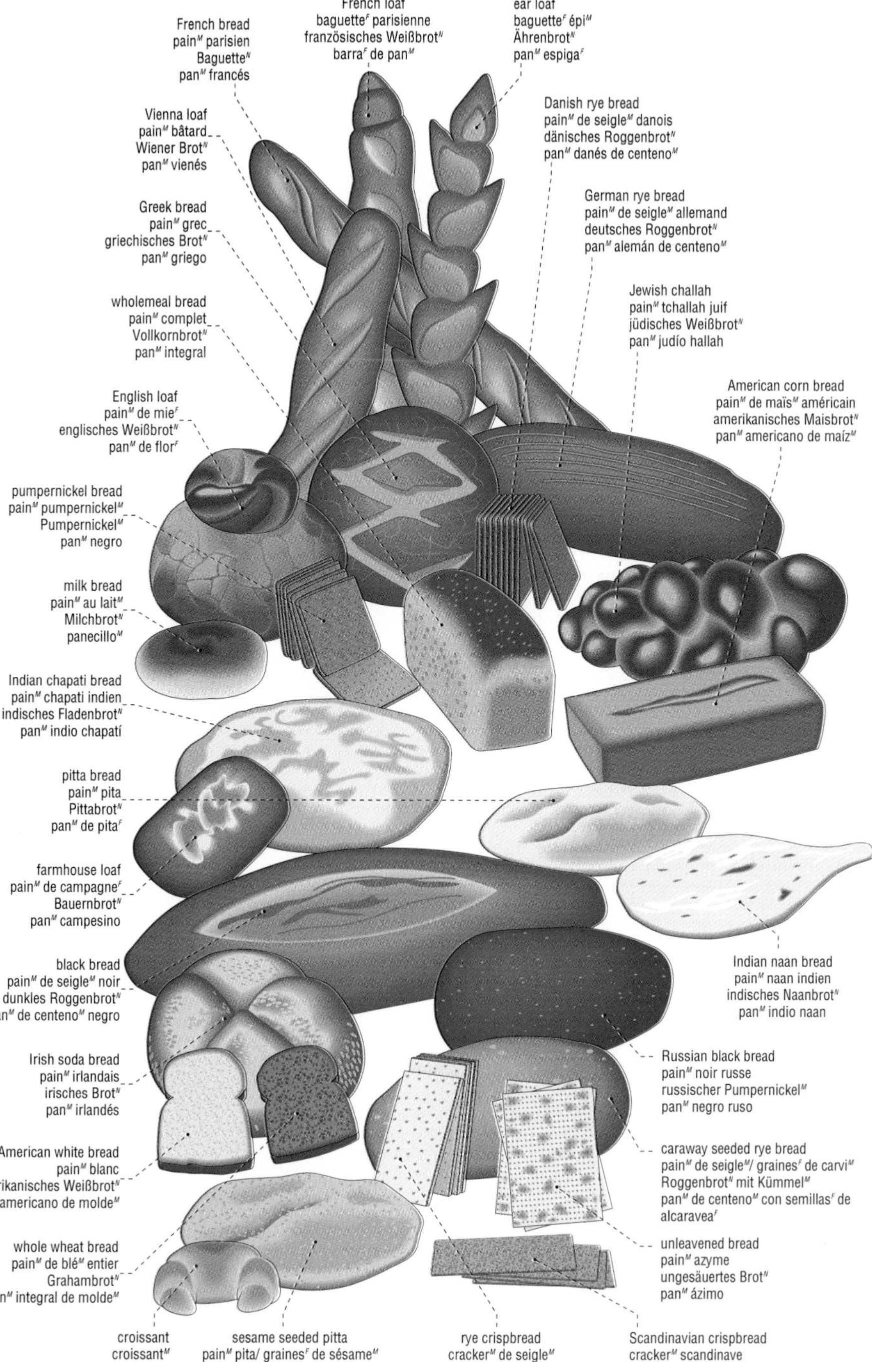

# STEPS IN SOIL CULTIVATION
# ÉTAPES$^{F}$ DE LA CULTURE$^{F}$ DU SOL$^{M}$
# ARBEITSVERFAHREN$^{N}$ DER BODENBEARBEITUNG$^{F}$
# PASOS$^{M}$ PARA EL CULTIVO$^{M}$ DEL SUELO$^{M}$

## PLOUGHING
## RETOURNER LA TERRE$^{F}$
## PFLÜGEN$^{N}$ DES BODENS$^{M}$
## ARADO$^{M}$

ribbing plough
charrue$^{F}$ à soc$^{M}$
Beetpflug$^{N}$
arado$^{M}$ de vertedera$^{F}$

## FERTILIZING
## FERTILISER LA TERRE$^{F}$
## DÜNGEN$^{N}$ DES BODENS$^{M}$
## ABONADO$^{M}$

manure spreader
épandeur$^{M}$ de fumier$^{M}$
Dungstreuer$^{M}$
esparcidora$^{F}$ de estiércol$^{M}$

## PULVERIZING
## AMEUBLIR LA TERRE$^{F}$
## EGGEN$^{N}$ DES BODENS$^{M}$
## PULVERIZACIÓN$^{F}$

tandem disc harrow
pulvérisateur$^{M}$ tandem$^{M}$
Scheibenegge$^{F}$
pulverizador$^{M}$ de discos$^{M}$

cultivator
cultivateur$^{M}$
Hackrahmen$^{M}$
cultivador$^{M}$

## PLANTING
## SEMER
## SÄEN$^{N}$
## SIEMBRA$^{F}$

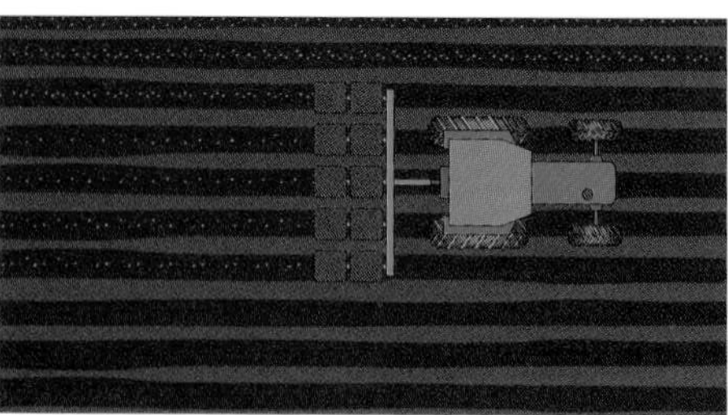

seed drill
semoir$^{M}$ en lignes$^{F}$
Drillmaschine$^{F}$
sembradora$^{F}$ a chorrillo$^{M}$

## MOWING
## FAUCHER
## MÄHEN$^{N}$
## SIEGA$^{F}$

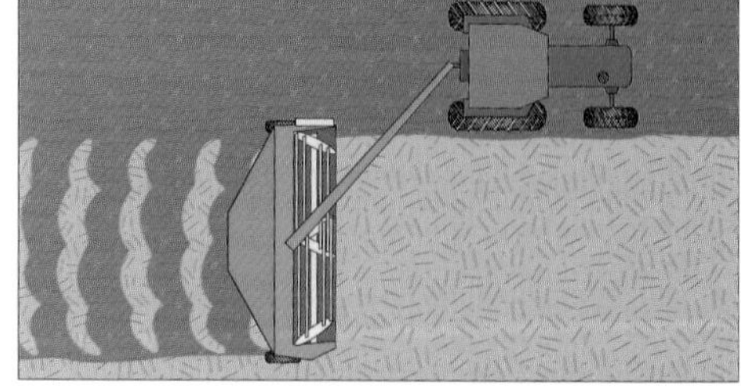

flail mower
faucheuse$^{F}$-conditionneuse$^{F}$
Anhängemähwerk$^{N}$
segadora$^{F}$

**TEDDING**
**FANER**
**ZETTEN[N] UND WENDEN[N]**
**HENIFICACIÓN[F]**

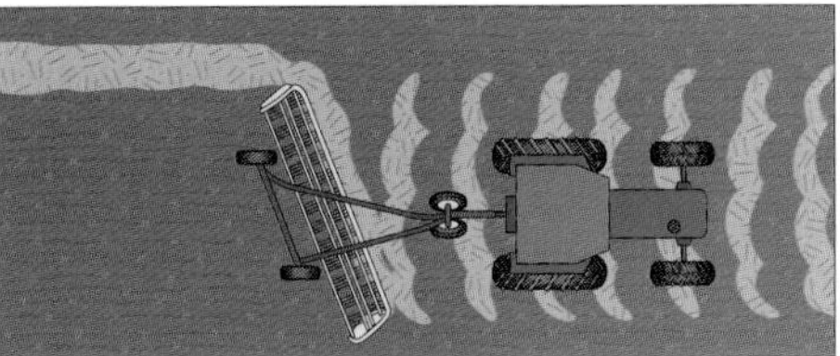

rake
râteau[M]
Schubrechwender[M]
rastrillo[M]

**HARVESTING**
**RÉCOLTER**
**ERNTEN[N]**
**COSECHA[F]**

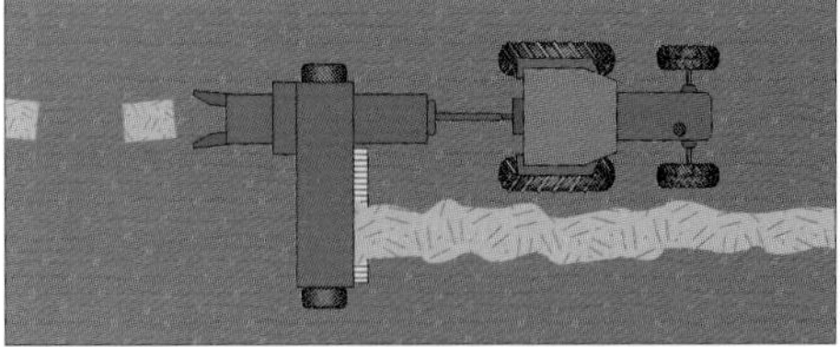

hay baler
ramasseuse[F]-presse[F]
Hochdruckpresse[F]
empacadora[F] de heno[M]

**HARVESTING**
**RÉCOLTER**
**ERNTEN[N]**
**COSECHA[F]**

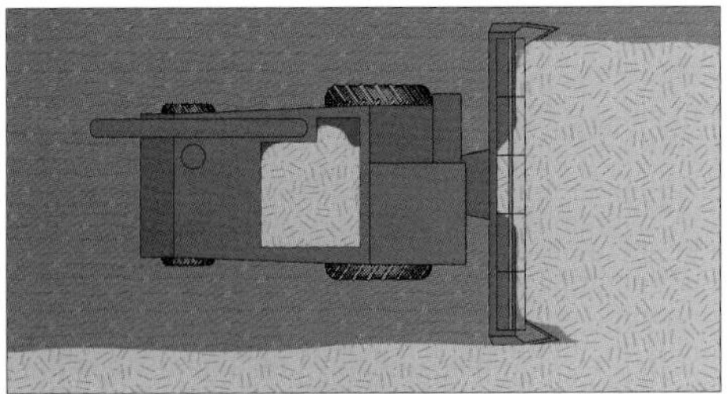

combine harvester
moissonneuse[F]-batteuse[F]
Mähdrescher[M]
cosechadora[F] trilladora[F]

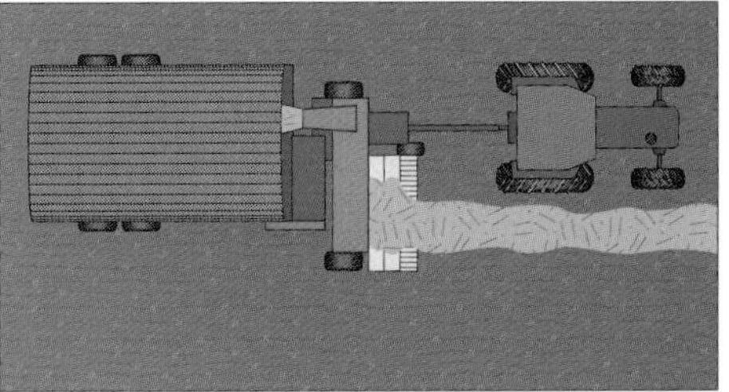

forage harvester
fourragère[F]
Feldhäckseler[M]
cosechadora[F] de forraje[M]

**ENSILING**
**ENSILER**
**SILIEREN[N]**
**ENSILAJE[M]**

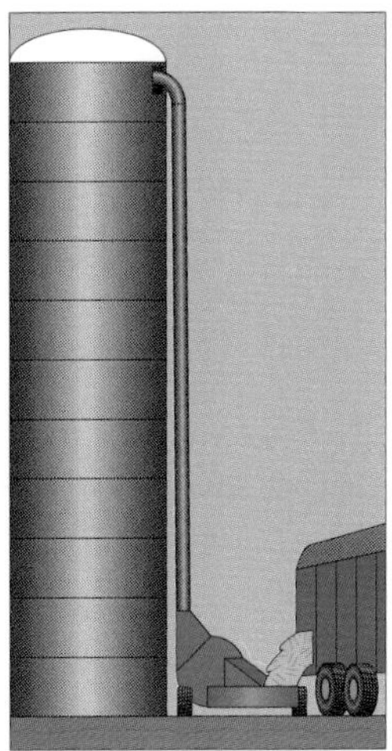

forage blower
souffleuse[F] de fourrage[M]
Abladegebläse[N]
aventador[M] de frorraje[M]

# PLOUGHING
# RETOURNER LA TERRE[F]
# PFLÜGEN[N]
# ARADO[M]

## RIBBING PLOUGH
## CHARRUE[F] À SOC[M]
## BEETPFLUG[N]
## ARADO[M] DE VERTEDERA[F]

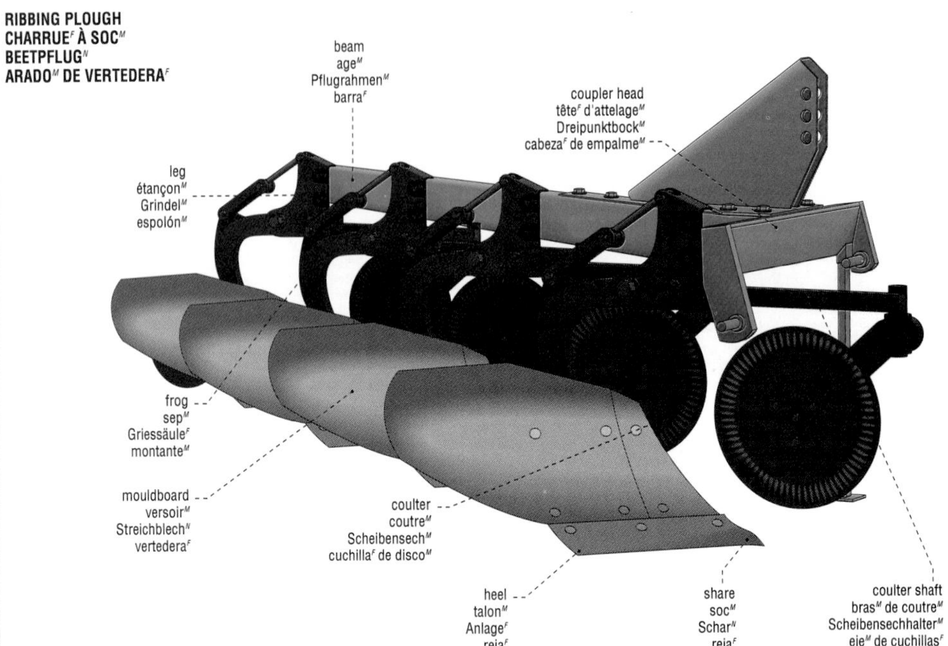


# FERTILIZING
# FERTILISER LA TERRE[F]
# DÜNGEN[N]
# ABONADO[M]

## MANURE SPREADER
## ÉPANDEUR[M] DE FUMIER[M]
## DUNGSTREUER[M]
## ESPARCIDORA[M] DE ESTIÉRCOL[M]

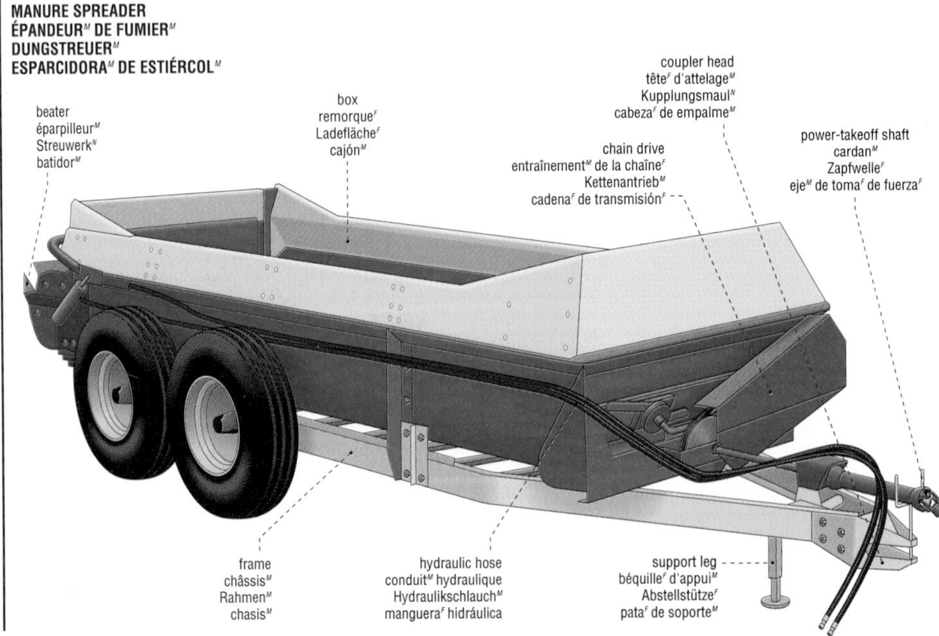

# PULVERIZING
# AMEUBLIR LA TERRE$^F$
# EGGEN$^N$ DES BODENS$^M$
# PULVERIZACIÓN$^F$

## TANDEM DISC HARROW
## PULVÉRISEUR$^M$ TANDEM$^M$
## SCHEIBENEGGE$^F$
## PULVERIZADOR$^M$ DE DISCOS$^M$

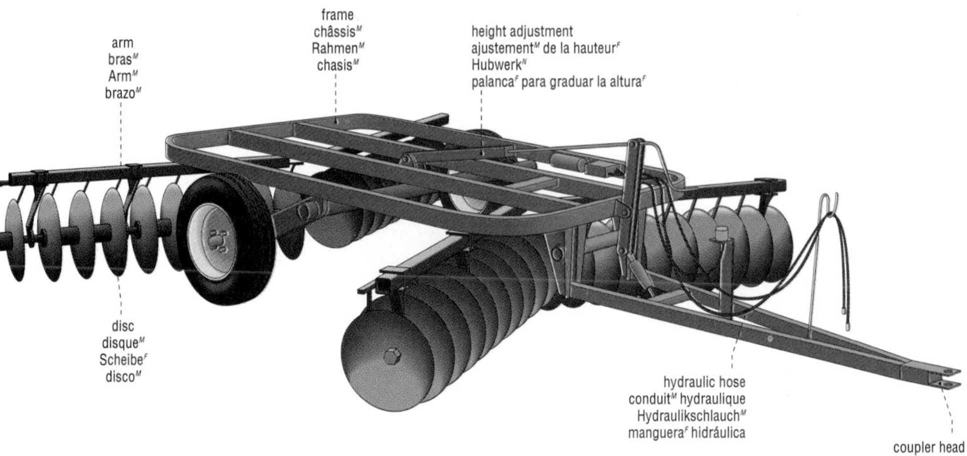


## CULTIVATOR
## CULTIVATEUR$^M$
## GRUBBER$^M$
## CULTIVADOR$^M$

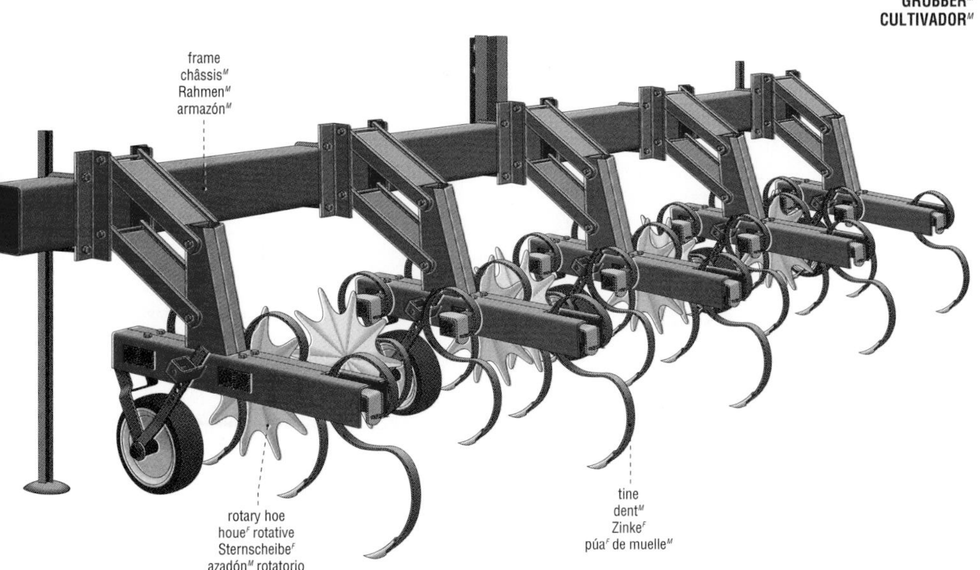

# PLANTING
# SEMER
# SÄEN[N]
# SIEMBRA[F]

## SEED DRILL
## SEMOIR[M] EN LIGNES[F]
## DRILLMASCHINE[F]
## SEMBRADORA[F] A CHORRILLO[M]

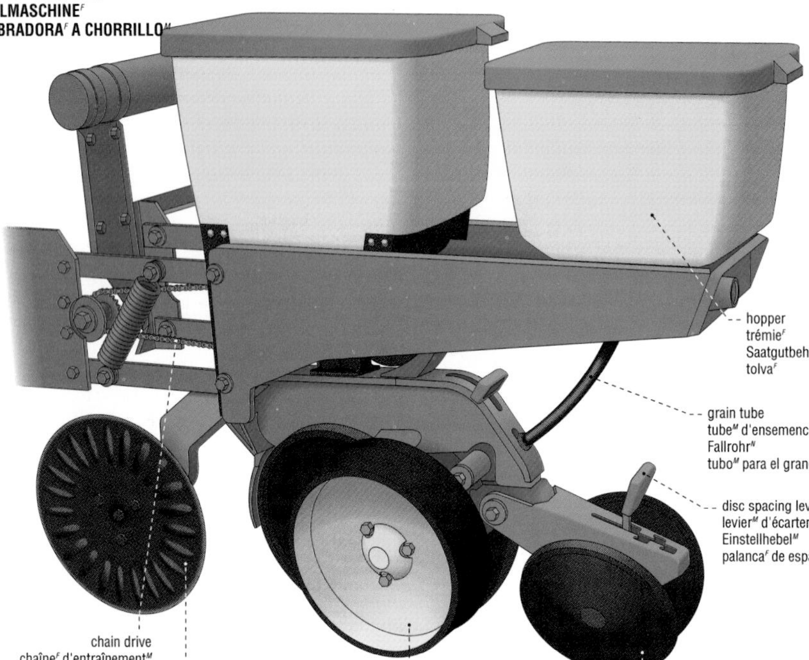

hopper
trémie[F]
Saatgutbehälter[M]
tolva[F]
grain tube
tube[M] d'ensemencement[M]
Fallrohr[N]
tubo[M] para el grano[M]
disc spacing lever
levier[M] d'écartement[M]
Einstellhebel[M]
palanca[F] de espaciamiento[M] de los discos
chain drive
chaîne[F] d'entraînement[M]
Antrieb[M]
cadena[F] de transmisión[F]
coulter
coutre[M]
Sech[M]
cuchilla[F]
press wheel
roue[F] de pression[F]
Druckrolle[F]
rueda[F] compresora
covering disc
disque[M] d'enterrage[M]
Zustreicher[M]
disco[M] tapador

# MOWING
# FAUCHER
# MÄHEN[N]
# SIEGA[F]

## FLAIL MOWER
## FAUCHEUSE[F]-CONDITIONNEUSE[F]
## ANHÄNGEMÄHWERK[N]
## SEGADORA[F]

crushing roll
rouleau[M] conditionneur
Konditionierer[M]
rodillo[M] triturador
pickup reel
rabatteur[M]
Haspel[F]
carrete[M] recogedor
tooth
dent[F]
Zinke[F]
diente[M]
tow bar
timon[M]
Zugrohr[N]
barra[F] de remolque[M]
hydraulic hose
conduit[M] hydraulique
Hydraulikanschluß[M]
manguera[F] hidráulica
cutter bar
barre[F] de coupe[F]
Messerbalken[M]
plataforma[F] de corte[M]
coupler head
tête[F] d'attelage[M]
Anhängemaul[N]
cabeza[F] de empalme[M]

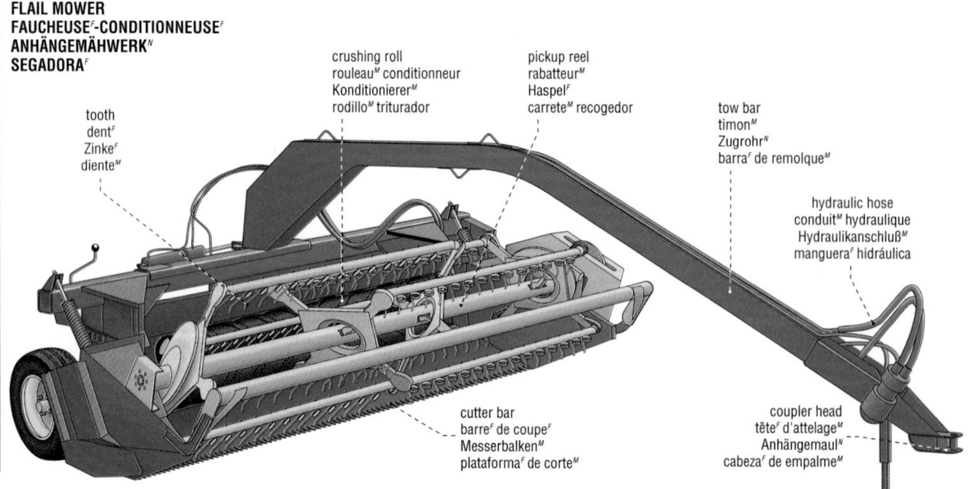

## TEDDING
## FANER
## ZETTEN[N] UND WENDEN[N]
## HENIFICACIÓN[M]

### RAKE
### RÂTEAU[M]
### SCHUBRECHWENDER[M]
### RASTRILLO[M]

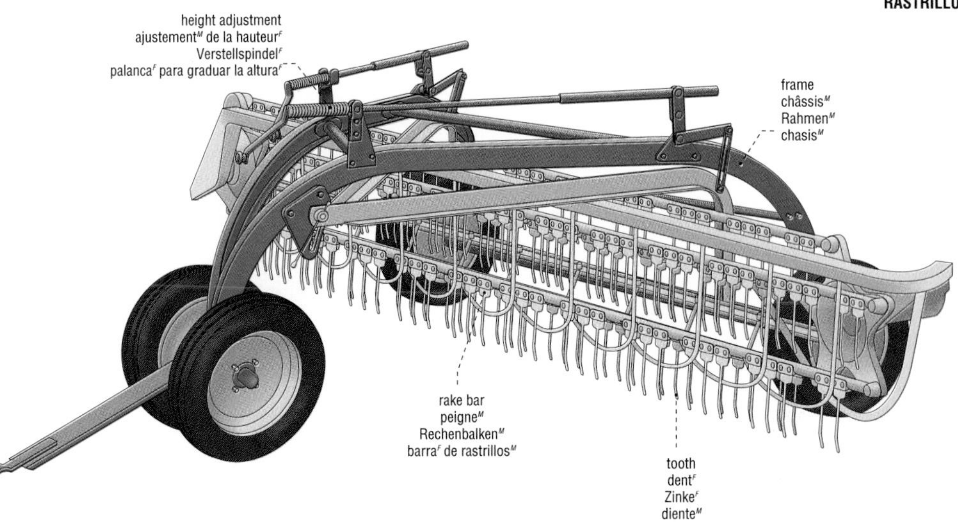


## HARVESTING
## RÉCOLTER
## ERNTEN[N]
## COSECHA[F]

### HAY BALER
### RAMASSEUSE[F]-PRESSE[F]
### HOCHDRUCKPRESSE[F]
### EMPACADORA[F] DE HENO[M]

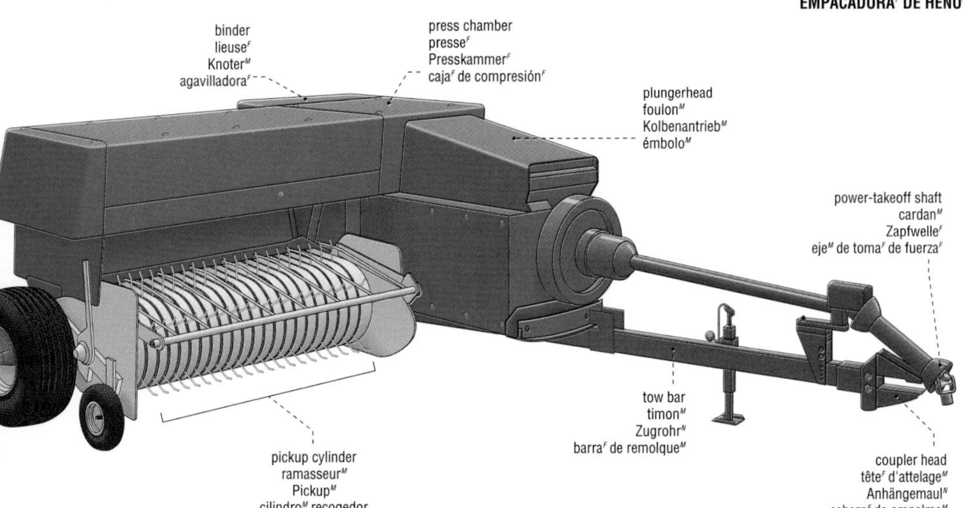

## HARVESTING
## RÉCOLTER
## ERNTEN[N]
## COSECHA[F]

### COMBINE HARVESTER
### MOISSONNEUSE[F]-BATTEUSE[F]
### MÄHDRESCHER[M]
### COSECHADORA[F] TRILLADORA[F]

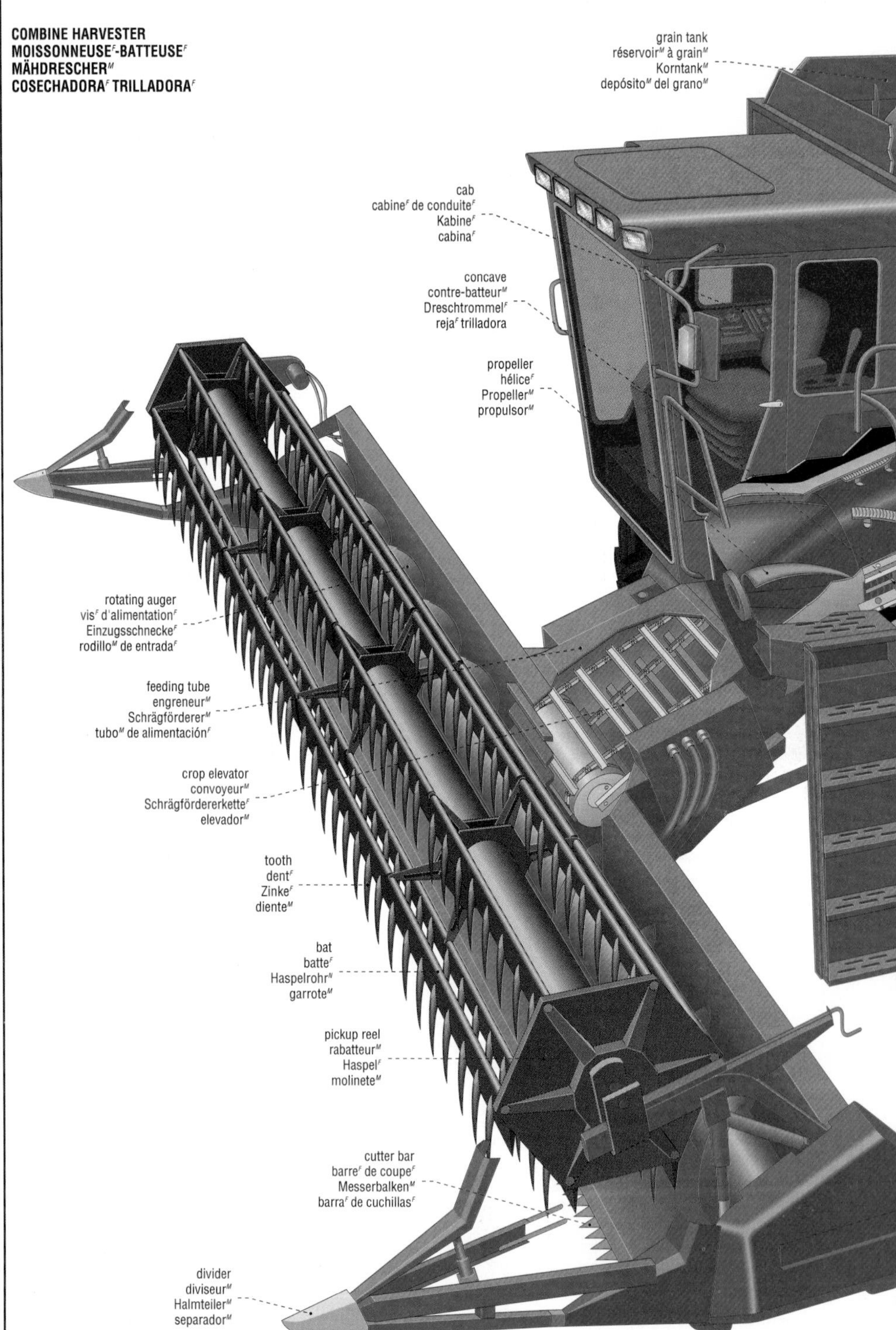

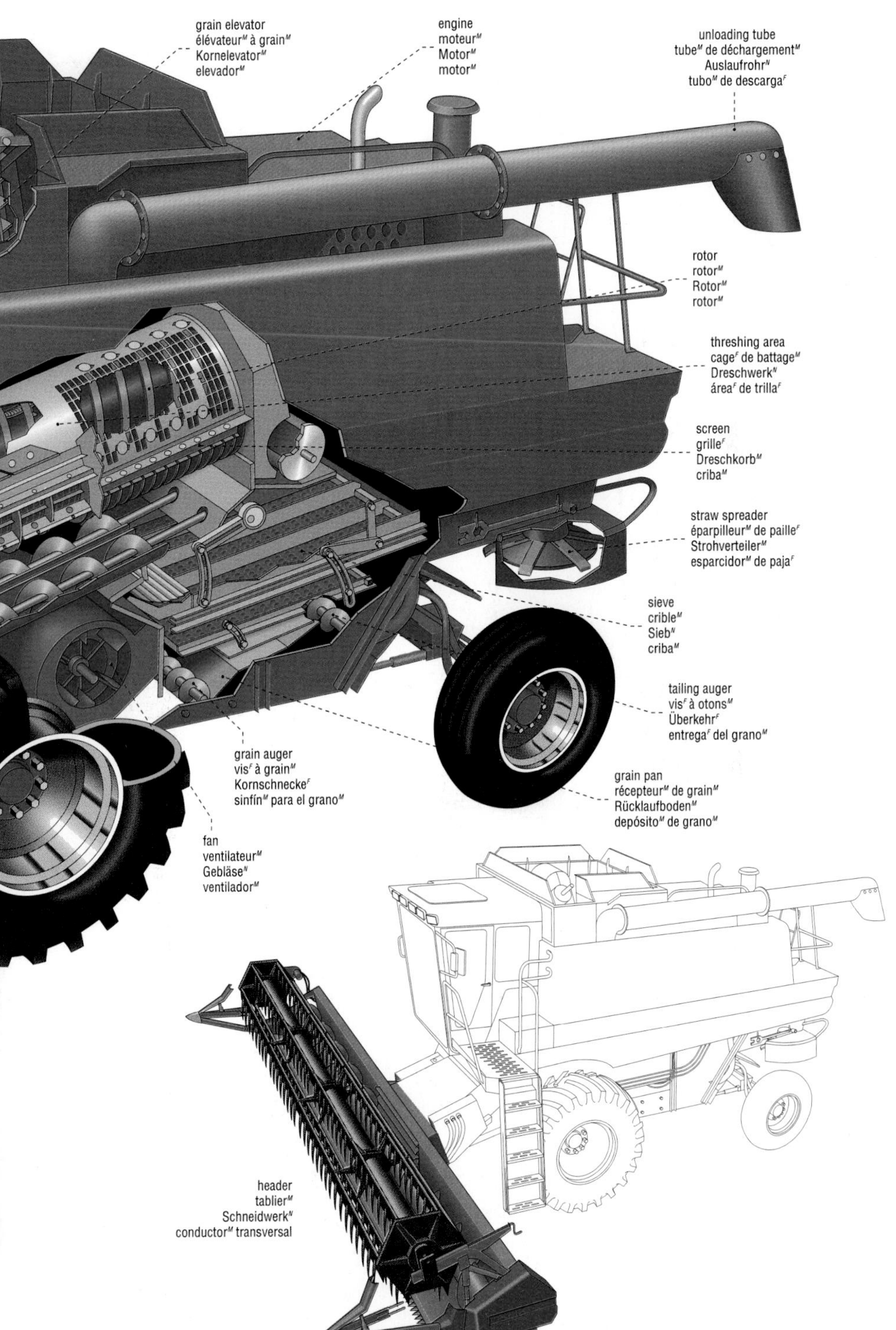
grain elevator
élévateur[M] à grain[M]
Kornelevator[M]
elevador[M]
engine
moteur[M]
Motor[M]
motor[M]
unloading tube
tube[M] de déchargement[M]
Auslaufrohr[N]
tubo[M] de descarga[F]
rotor
rotor[M]
Rotor[M]
rotor[M]
threshing area
cage[F] de battage[M]
Dreschwerk[N]
área[F] de trilla[F]
screen
grille[F]
Dreschkorb[M]
criba[M]
straw spreader
éparpilleur[M] de paille[F]
Strohverteiler[M]
esparcidor[M] de paja[F]
sieve
crible[M]
Sieb[N]
criba[M]
tailing auger
vis[F] à otons[M]
Überkehr[F]
entrega[F] del grano[M]
grain auger
vis[F] à grain[M]
Kornschnecke[F]
sinfín[M] para el grano[M]
grain pan
récepteur[M] de grain[M]
Rücklaufboden[M]
depósito[M] de grano[M]
fan
ventilateur[M]
Gebläse[N]
ventilador[M]
header
tablier[M]
Schneidwerk[N]
conductor[M] transversal

## HARVESTING
## RÉCOLTER
## ERNTEN[N]
## COSECHA[F]

### FORAGE HARVESTER
### FOURRAGÈRE[F]
### FELDHÄCKSELER[M]
### COSECHERA[F] DE FORRAJE[M]

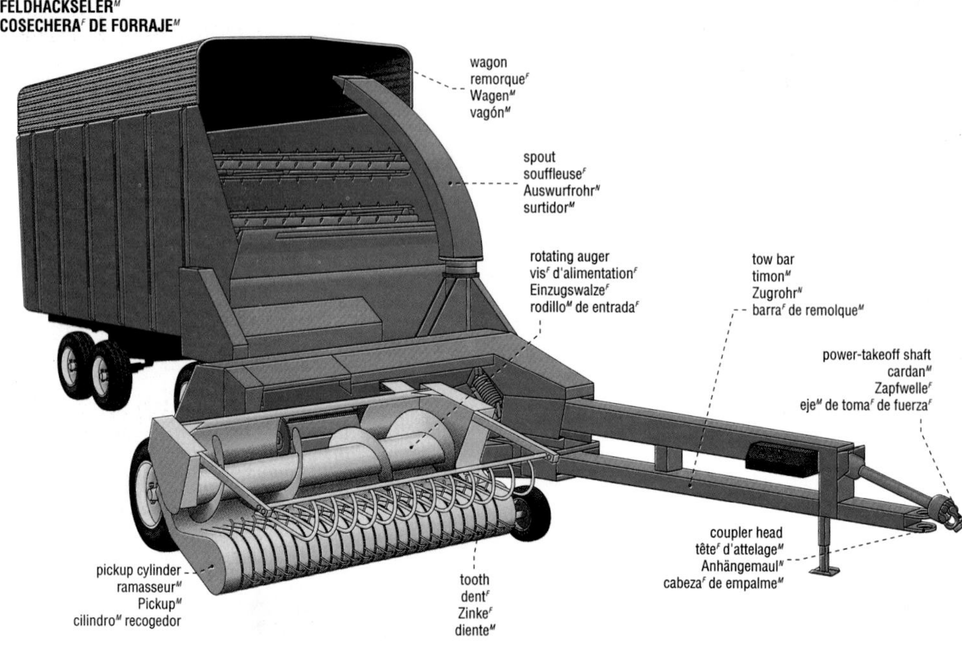


## ENSILING
## ENSILER
## SILIEREN[N]
## ENSILAJE[M]

### FORAGE BLOWER
### SOUFFLEUSE[F] DE FOURRAGE[M]
### ABLADEGEBLÄSE[N]
### AVENTADOR[M] DE FORRAJE[M]

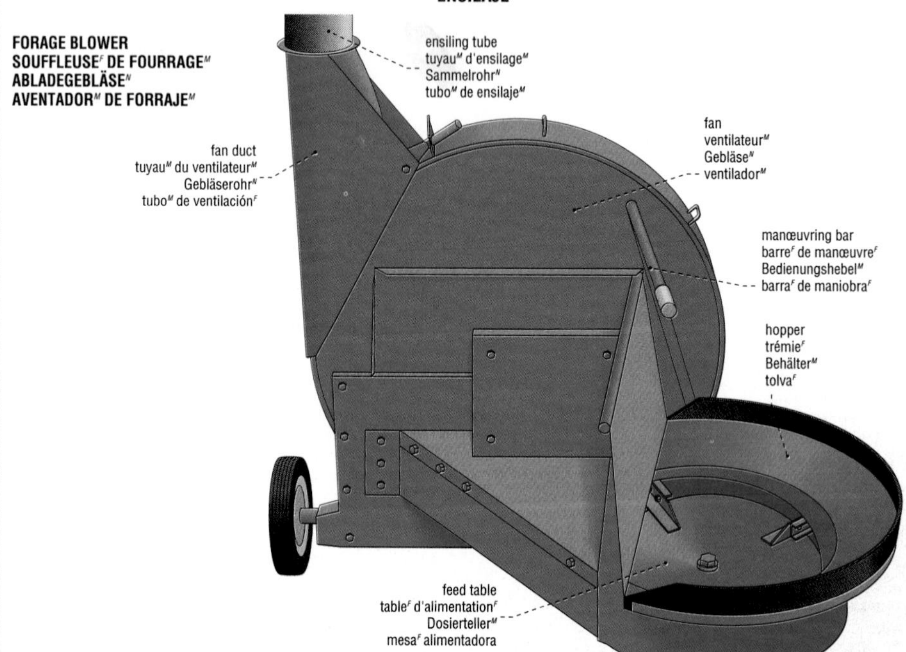

# ARCHITECTURE
# ARCHITECTURE
# ARCHITEKTUR
# ARQUITECTURA

**SUMMARY**

## TRADITIONAL DWELLINGS
## MAISONS[F] TRADITIONNELLES
## TRADITIONELLE WOHNHÄUSER[N]
## VIVIENDAS[F] TRADICIONALES

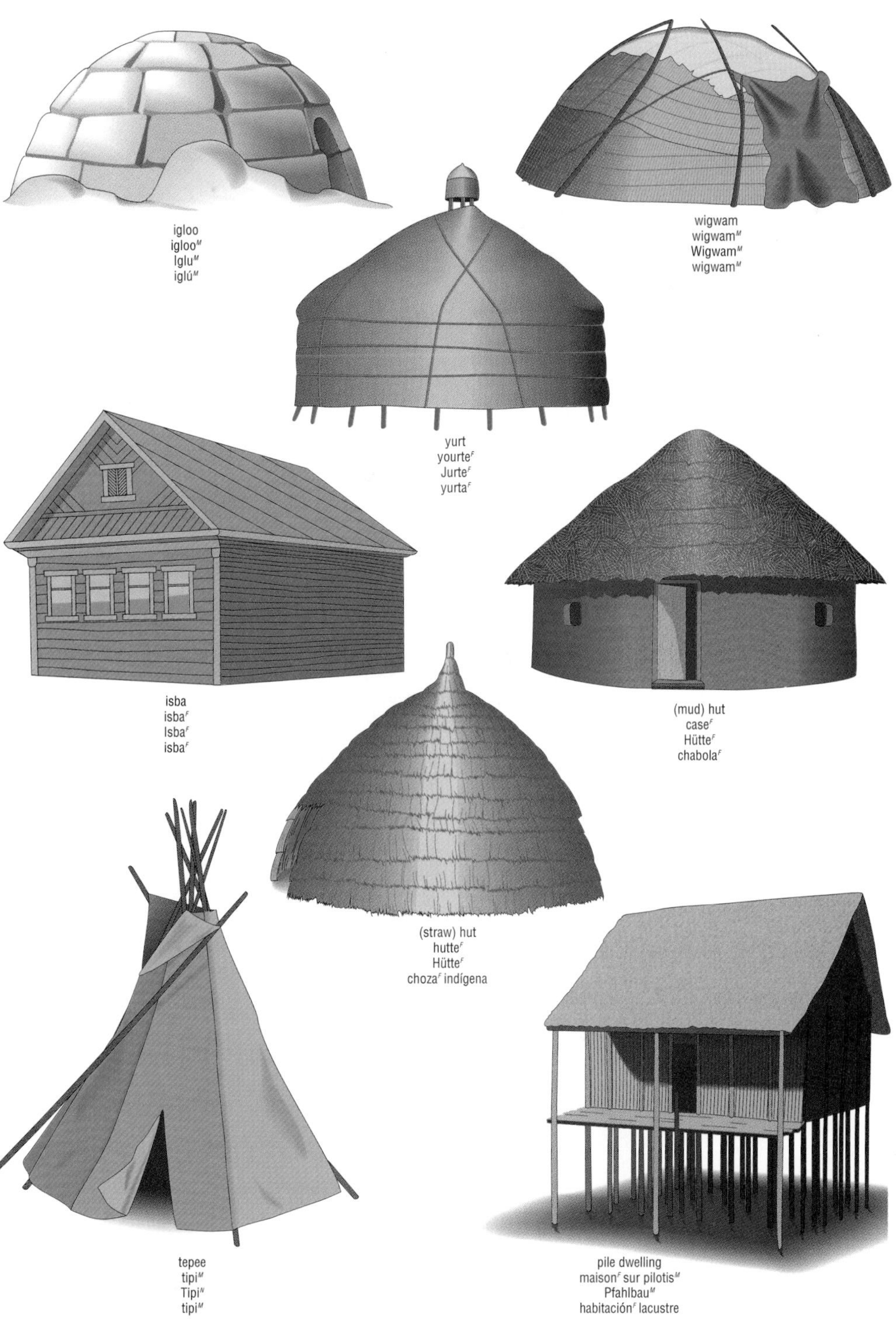

# ARCHITECTURAL STYLES
# STYLES[M] D'ARCHITECTURE[F]
# BAUSTILE[M]
# ESTILOS[M] ARQUITECTÓNICOS



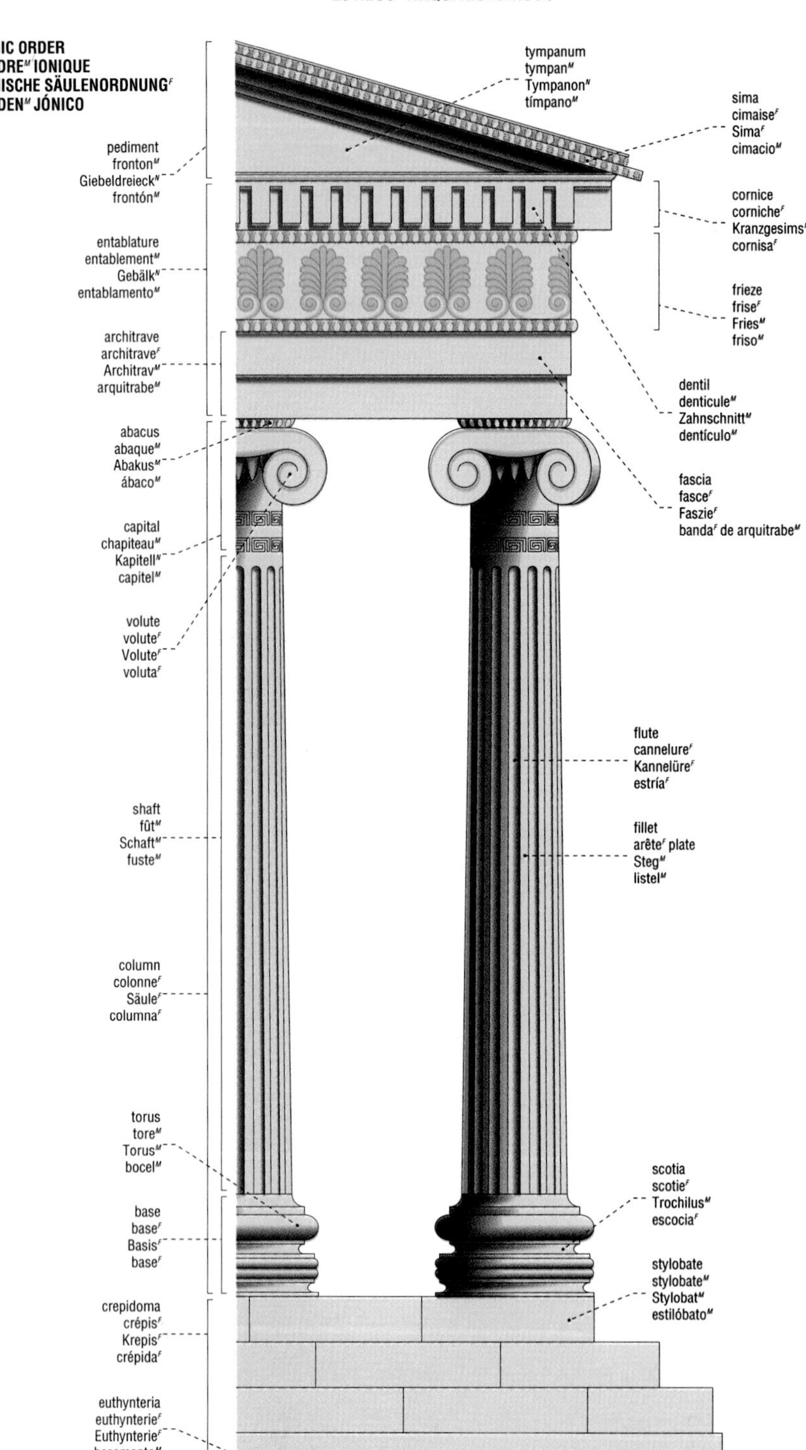

## DORIC ORDER
## ORDRE[M] DORIQUE
## DORISCHE SÄULENORDNUNG[F]
## ORDEN[M] DÓRICO

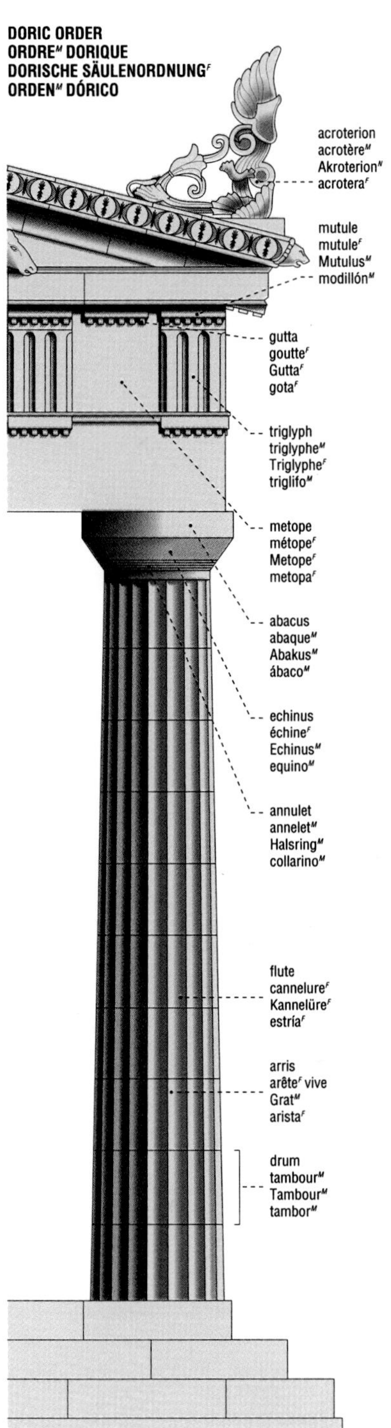


## CORINTHIAN ORDER
## ORDRE[M] CORINTHIEN
## KORINTHISCHE SÄULENORDNUNG[F]
## ORDEN[M] CORINTIO

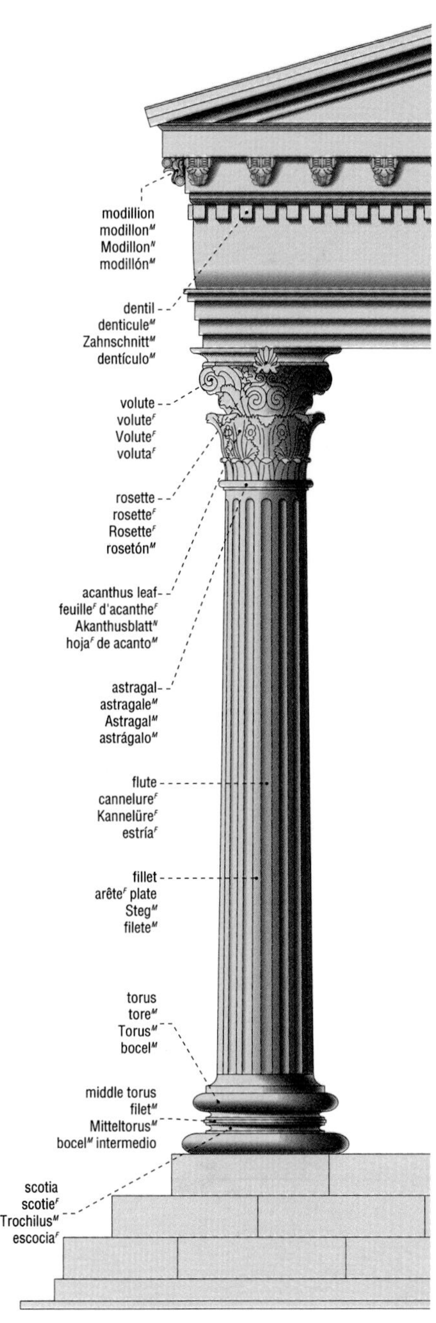

# GREEK TEMPLE
# TEMPLE$^{M}$ GREC
# GRIECHISCHER TEMPEL$^{M}$
# TEMPLO$^{M}$ GRIEGO

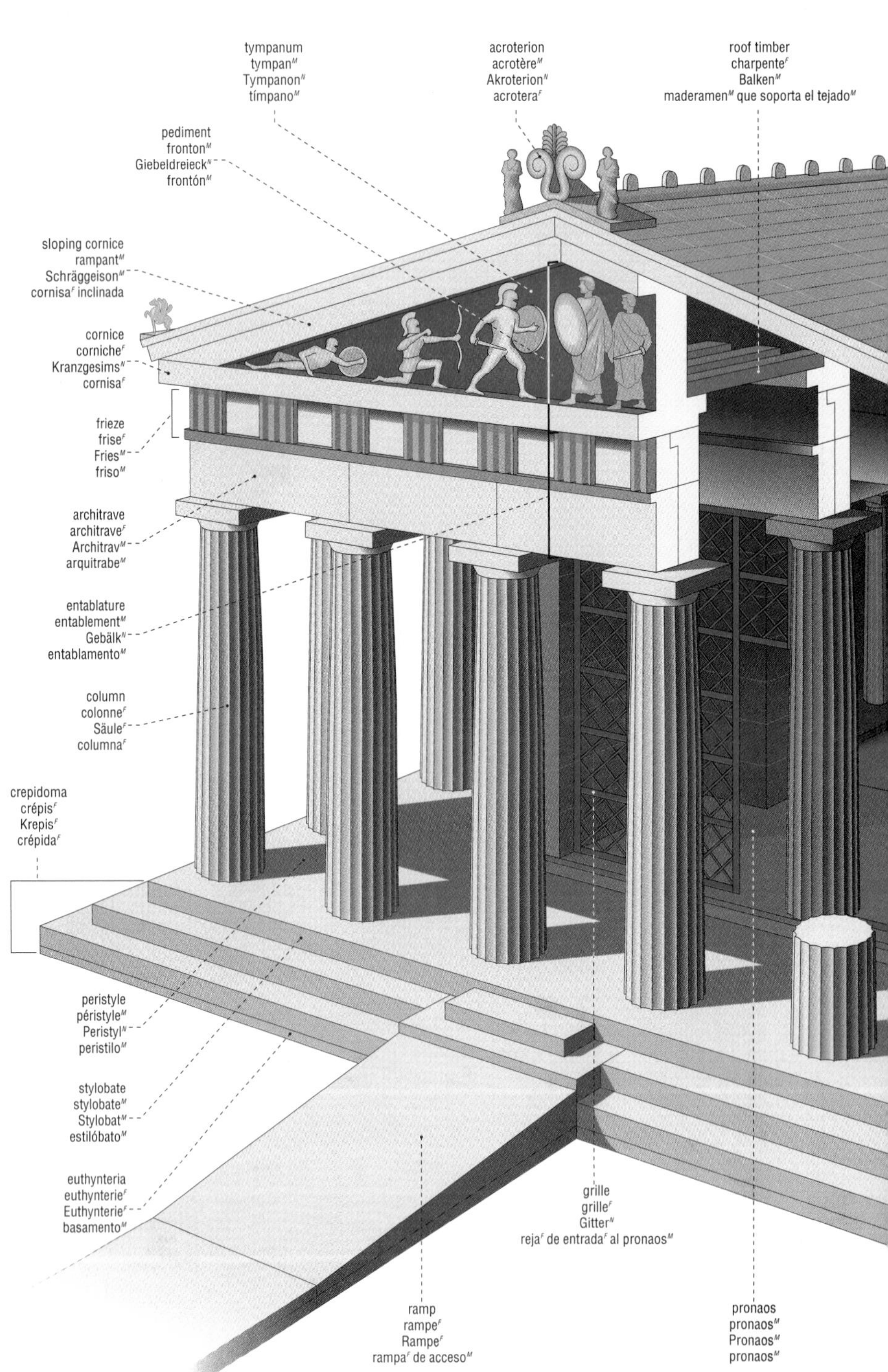

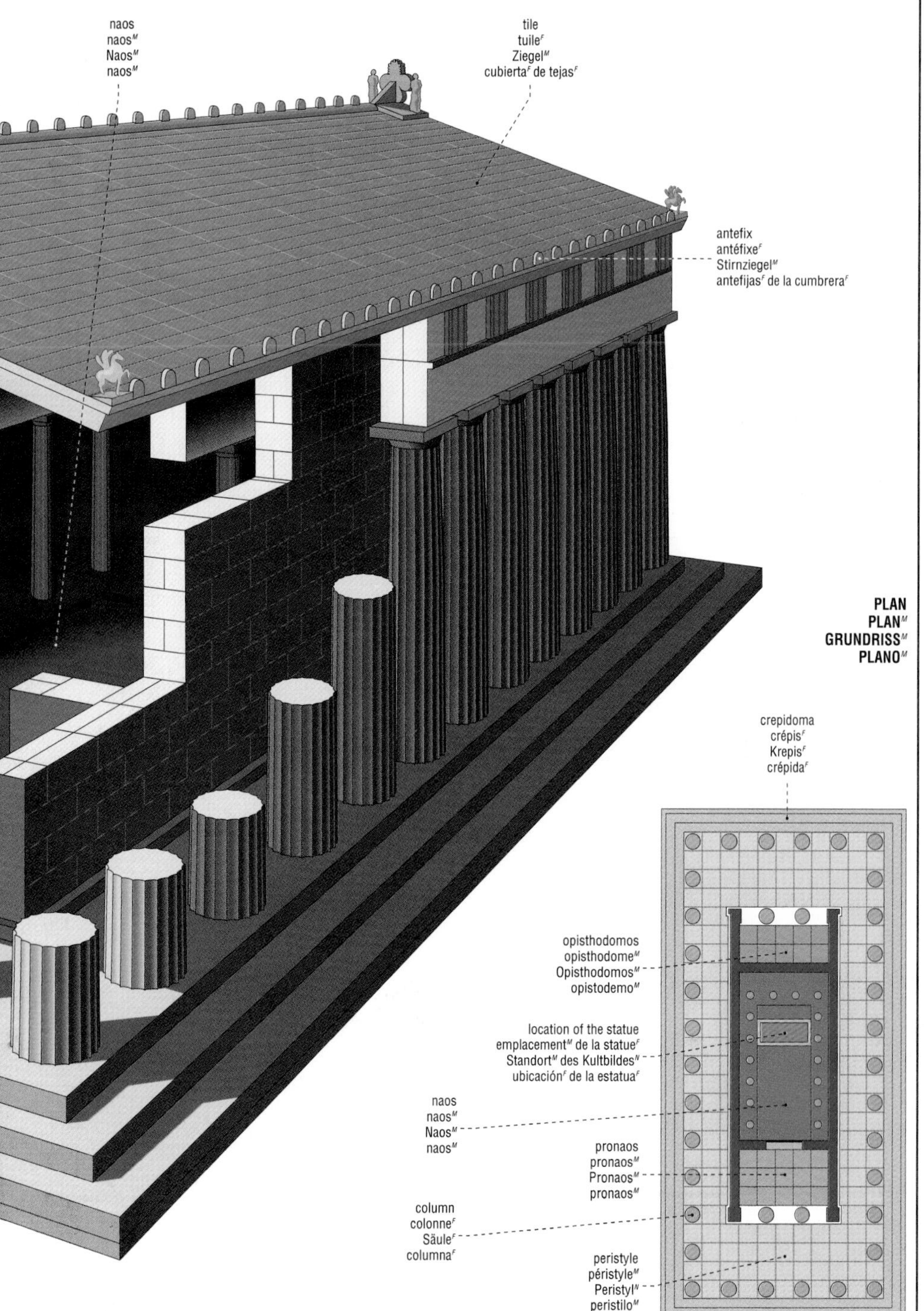
naos
naosᴹ
Naosᴹ
naosᴹ
tile
tuileᶠ
Ziegelᴹ
cubiertaᶠ de tejasᶠ
antefix
antéfixeᶠ
Stirnziegelᴹ
antefijasᶠ de la cumbreraᶠ
PLAN
PLANᴹ
GRUNDRISSᴹ
PLANOᴹ
crepidoma
crépisᶠ
Krepisᶠ
crépidaᶠ
opisthodomos
opisthodomeᴹ
Opisthodomosᴹ
opistodemoᴹ
location of the statue
emplacementᴹ de la statueᶠ
Standortᴹ des Kultbildesᴺ
ubicaciónᶠ de la estatuaᶠ
naos
naosᴹ
Naosᴹ
naosᴹ
pronaos
pronaosᴹ
Pronaosᴹ
pronaosᴹ
column
colonneᶠ
Säuleᶠ
columnaᶠ
peristyle
péristyleᴹ
Peristylᴺ
peristiloᴹ

# ROMAN HOUSE
# MAISON[F] ROMAINE
# RÖMISCHES WOHNHAUS[N]
# CASA[F] ROMANA



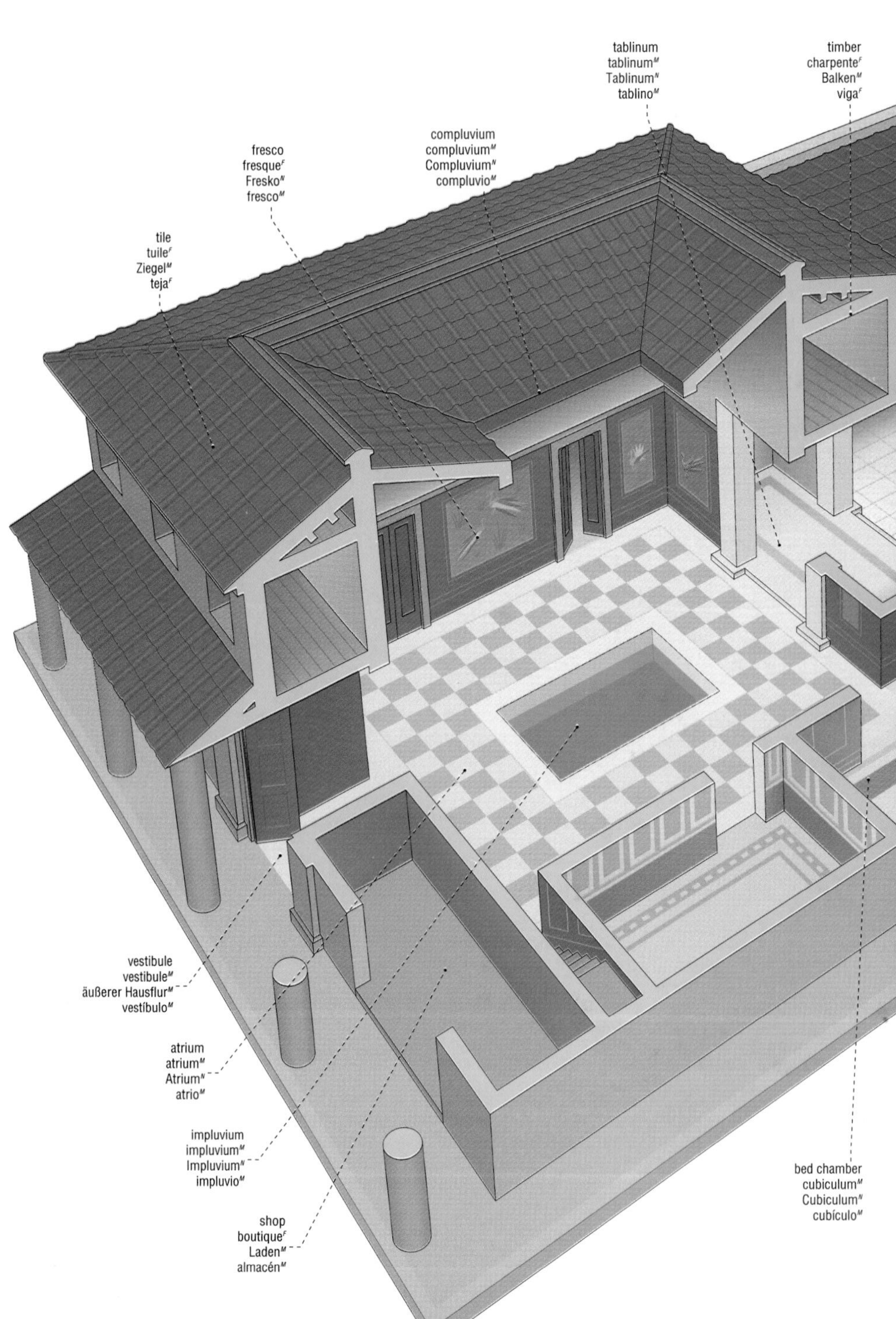

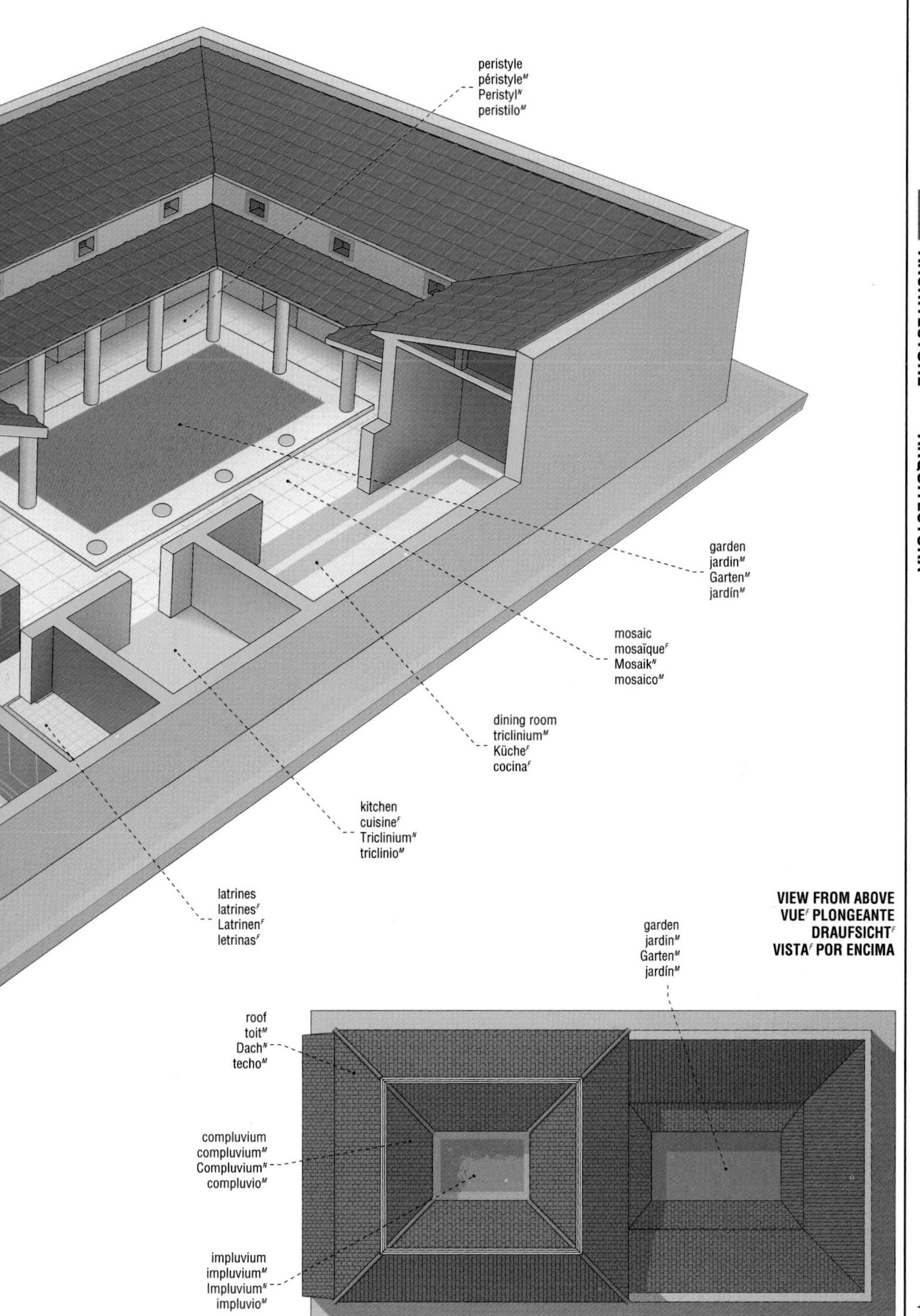
peristyle
péristyle[M]
Peristyl[N]
peristilo[M]
garden
jardin[M]
Garten[M]
jardín[M]
mosaic
mosaïque[F]
Mosaik[N]
mosaico[M]
dining room
triclinium[M]
Küche[F]
cocina[F]
kitchen
cuisine[F]
Triclinium[N]
triclinio[M]
latrines
latrines[F]
Latrinen[F]
letrinas[F]
VIEW FROM ABOVE
VUE[F] PLONGEANTE
DRAUFSICHT[F]
VISTA[F] POR ENCIMA
garden
jardin[M]
Garten[M]
jardín[M]
roof
toit[M]
Dach[N]
techo[M]
compluvium
compluvium[M]
Compluvium[N]
compluvio[M]
impluvium
impluvium[M]
Impluvium[N]
impluvio[M]

# MOSQUE
# MOSQUÉE^F
# MOSCHEE^F
# MEZQUITA^F

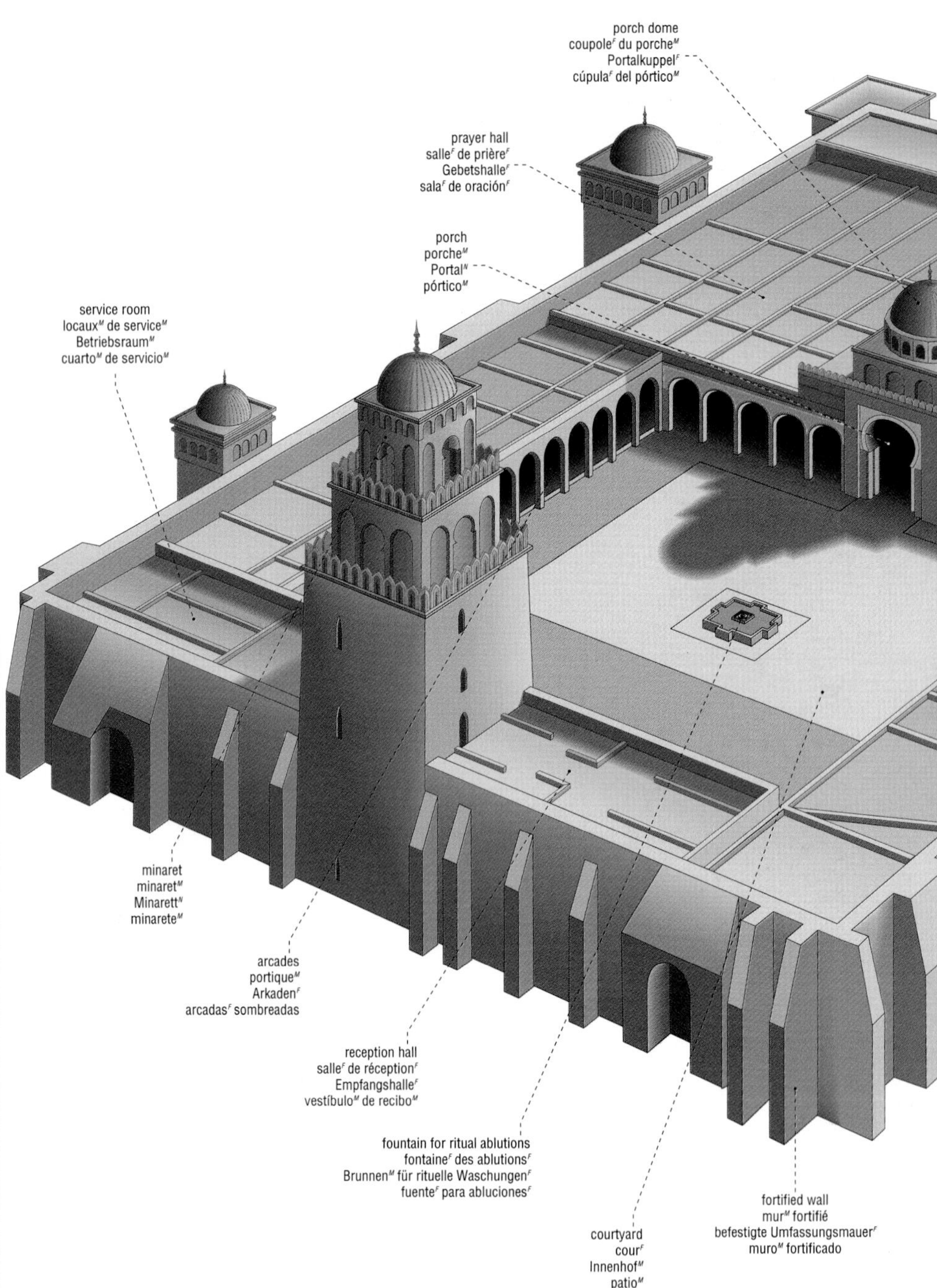

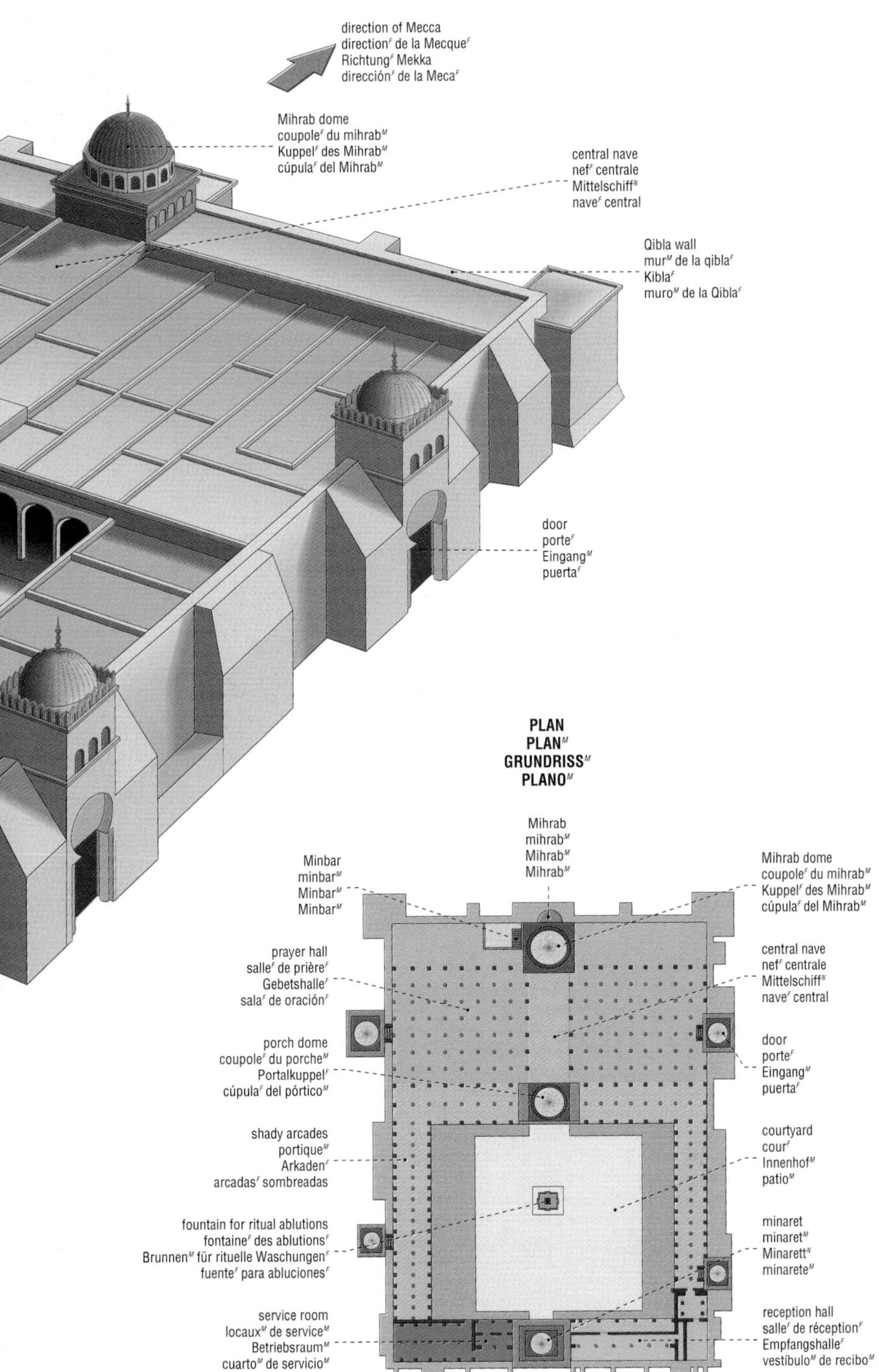
direction of Mecca
direction de la Mecque
Richtung Mekka
dirección de la Meca
Mihrab dome
coupole du mihrab
Kuppel des Mihrab
cúpula del Mihrab
central nave
nef centrale
Mittelschiff
nave central
Qibla wall
mur de la qibla
Kibla
muro de la Qibla
door
porte
Eingang
puerta
PLAN
PLAN
GRUNDRISS
PLANO
Mihrab
mihrab
Mihrab
Mihrab
Minbar
minbar
Minbar
Minbar
Mihrab dome
coupole du mihrab
Kuppel des Mihrab
cúpula del Mihrab
prayer hall
salle de prière
Gebetshalle
sala de oración
central nave
nef centrale
Mittelschiff
nave central
porch dome
coupole du porche
Portalkuppel
cúpula del pórtico
door
porte
Eingang
puerta
shady arcades
portique
Arkaden
arcadas sombreadas
courtyard
cour
Innenhof
patio
fountain for ritual ablutions
fontaine des ablutions
Brunnen für rituelle Waschungen
fuente para abluciones
minaret
minaret
Minarett
minarete
service room
locaux de service
Betriebsraum
cuarto de servicio
reception hall
salle de réception
Empfangshalle
vestíbulo de recibo

# TYPES OF ARCH
# ARC[M]
# BOGEN[M]
# ARCO[M]



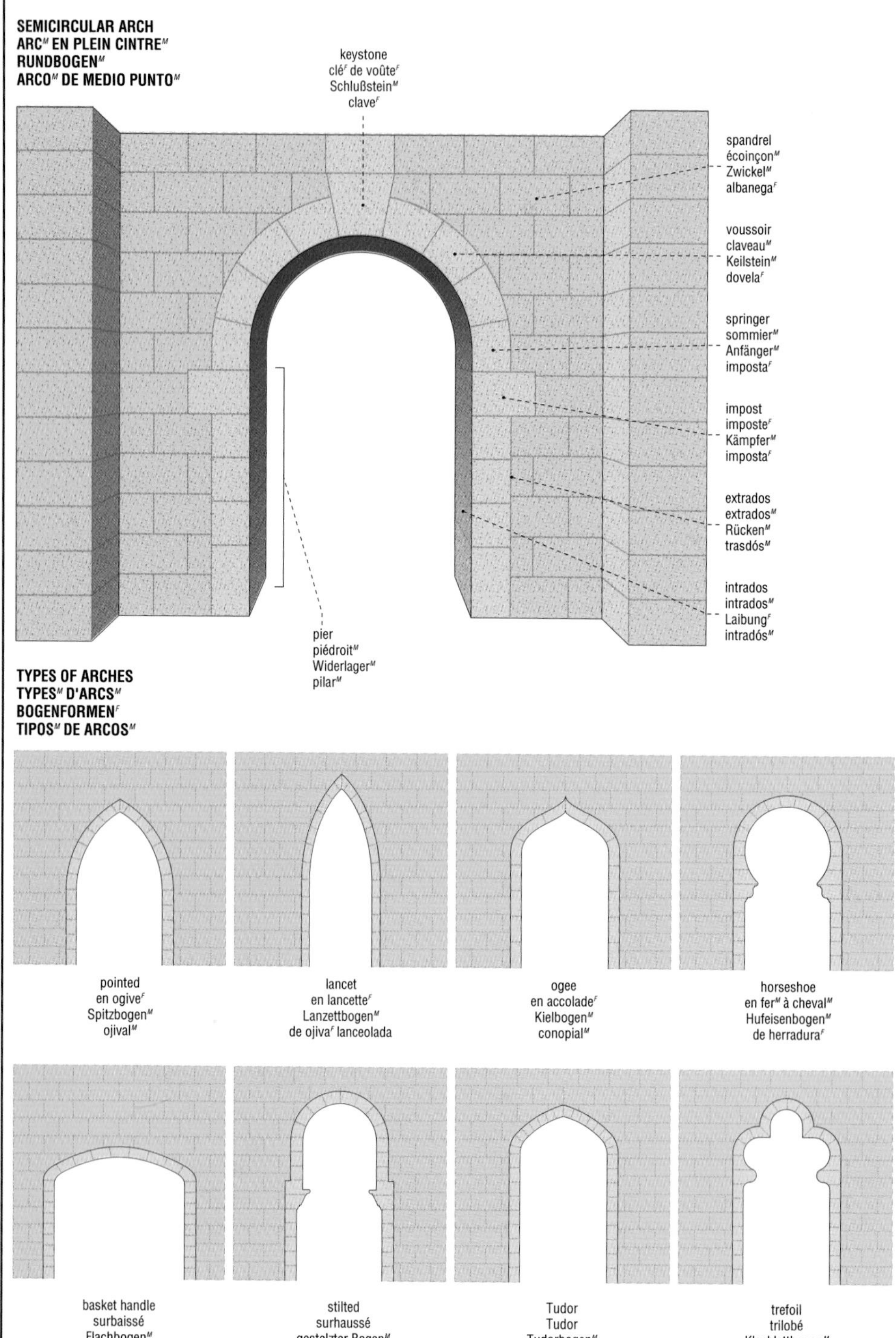

# GOTHIC CATHEDRAL
# CATHÉDRALE[F] GOTHIQUE
# GOTHISCHER DOM[M]
# CATEDRAL[F] GÓTICA



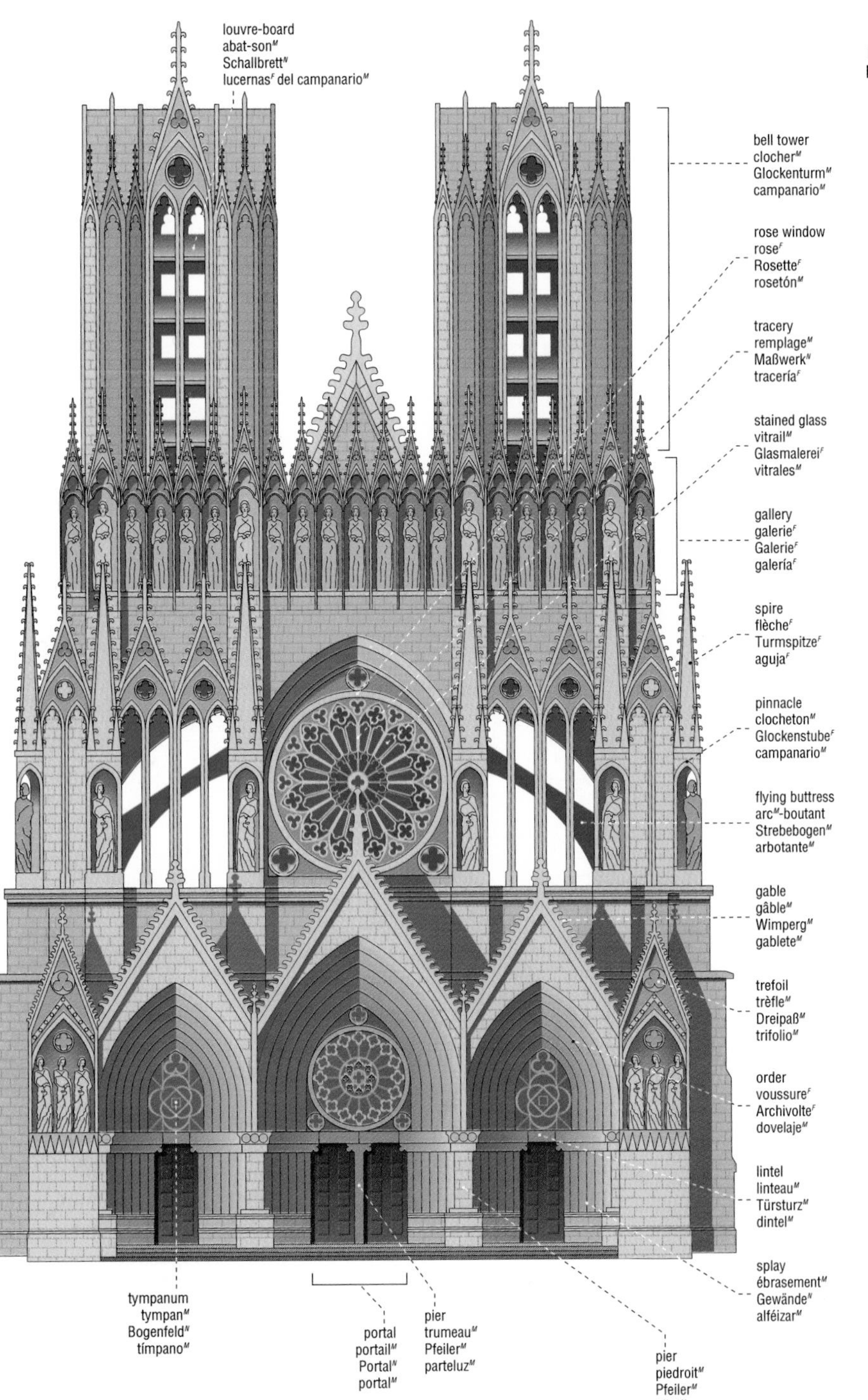

# GOTHIC CATHEDRAL
# CATHÉDRALE[F] GOTHIQUE
# GOTISCHER DOM[M]
# CATEDRAL[F] GÓTICA



**CATHEDRAL**
**CATHÉDRALE[F]**
**DOM[M]**
**CATEDRAL[F]**

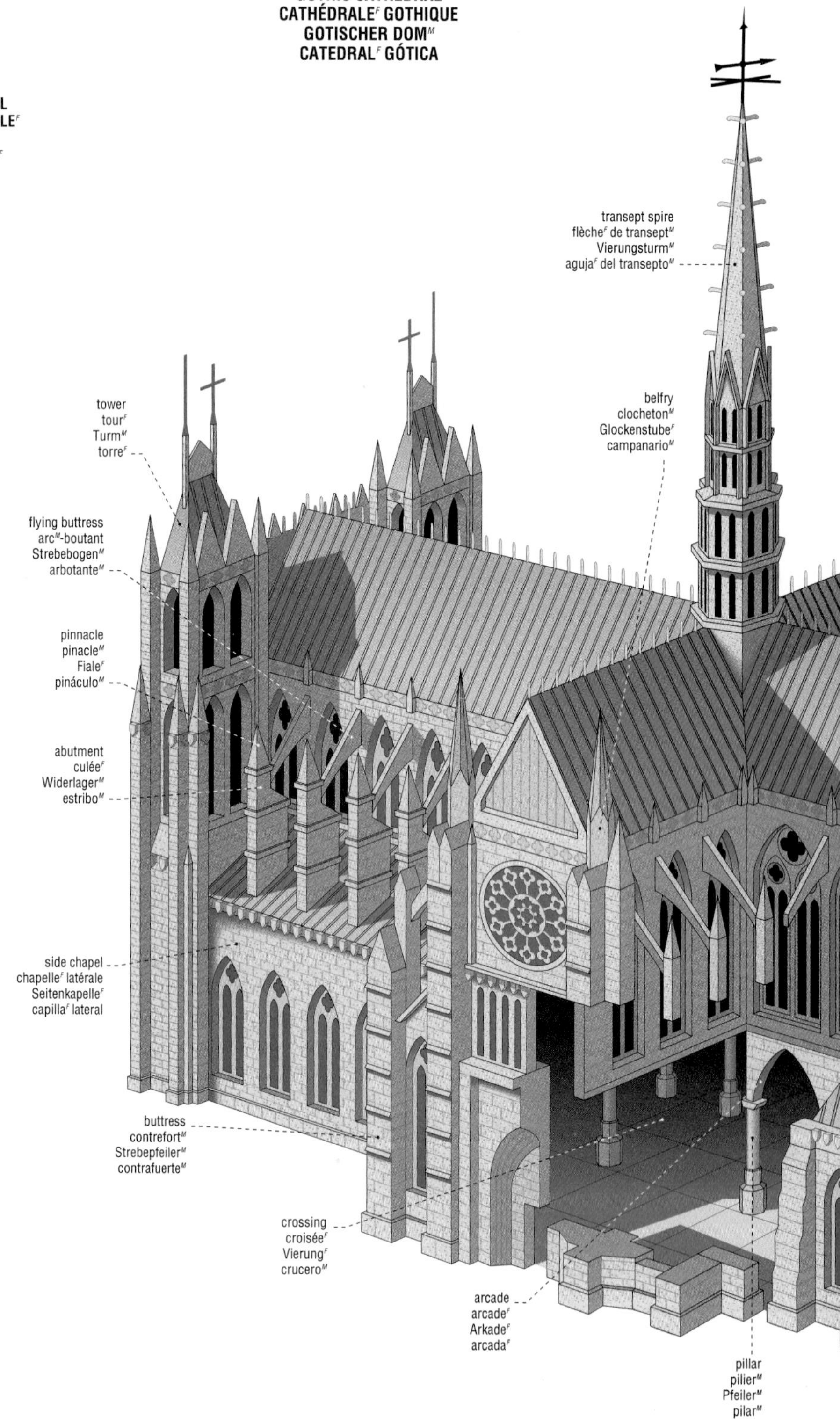

## PLAN
## PLAN[M]
## GRUNDRISS[M]
## PLANO[M]

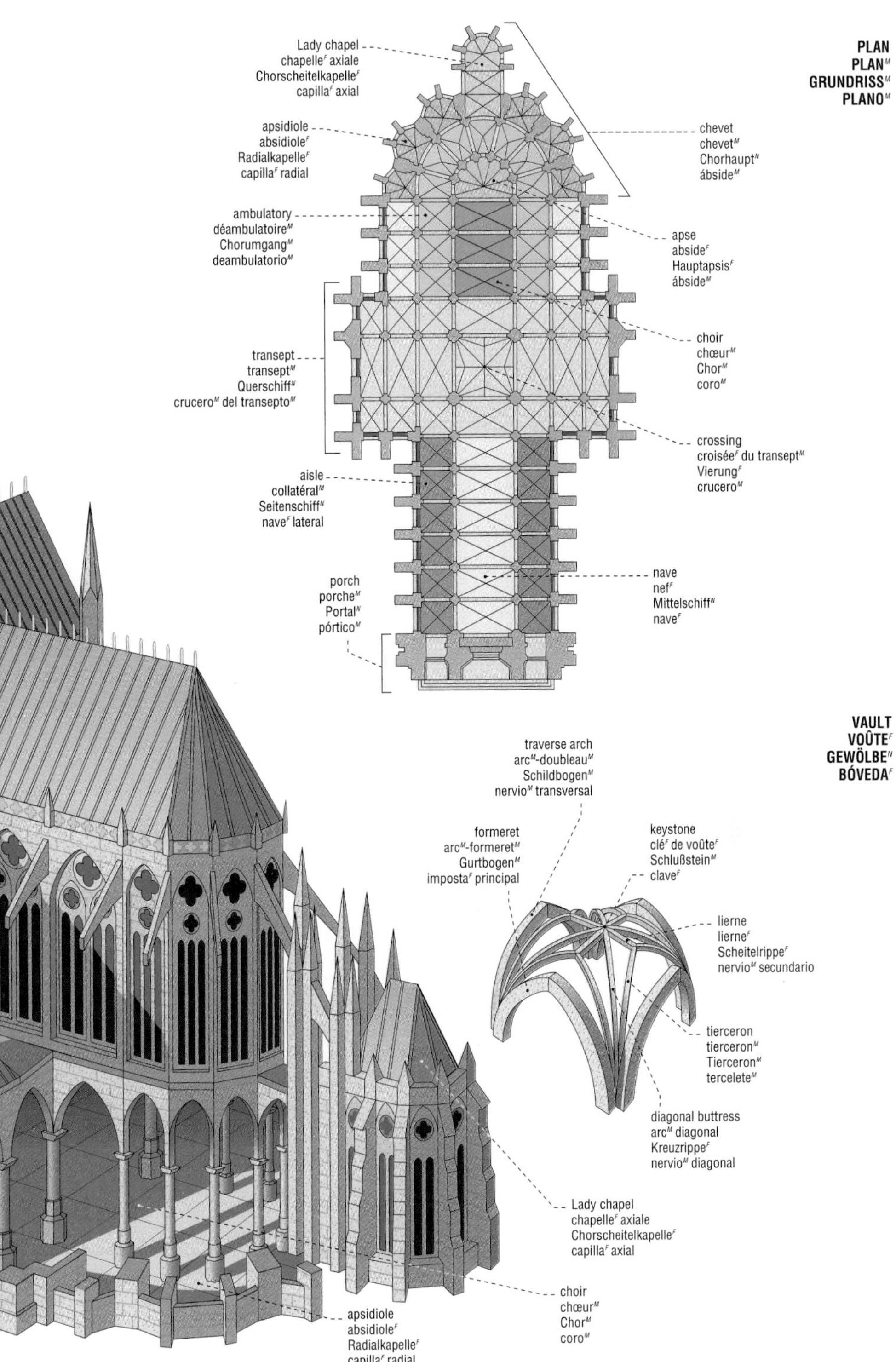

# VAUBAN FORTIFICATION
# FORTIFICATION^F À LA VAUBAN
# VAUBAN-FESTUNG^F
# FORTIFICACIÓN^F DE VAUBAN

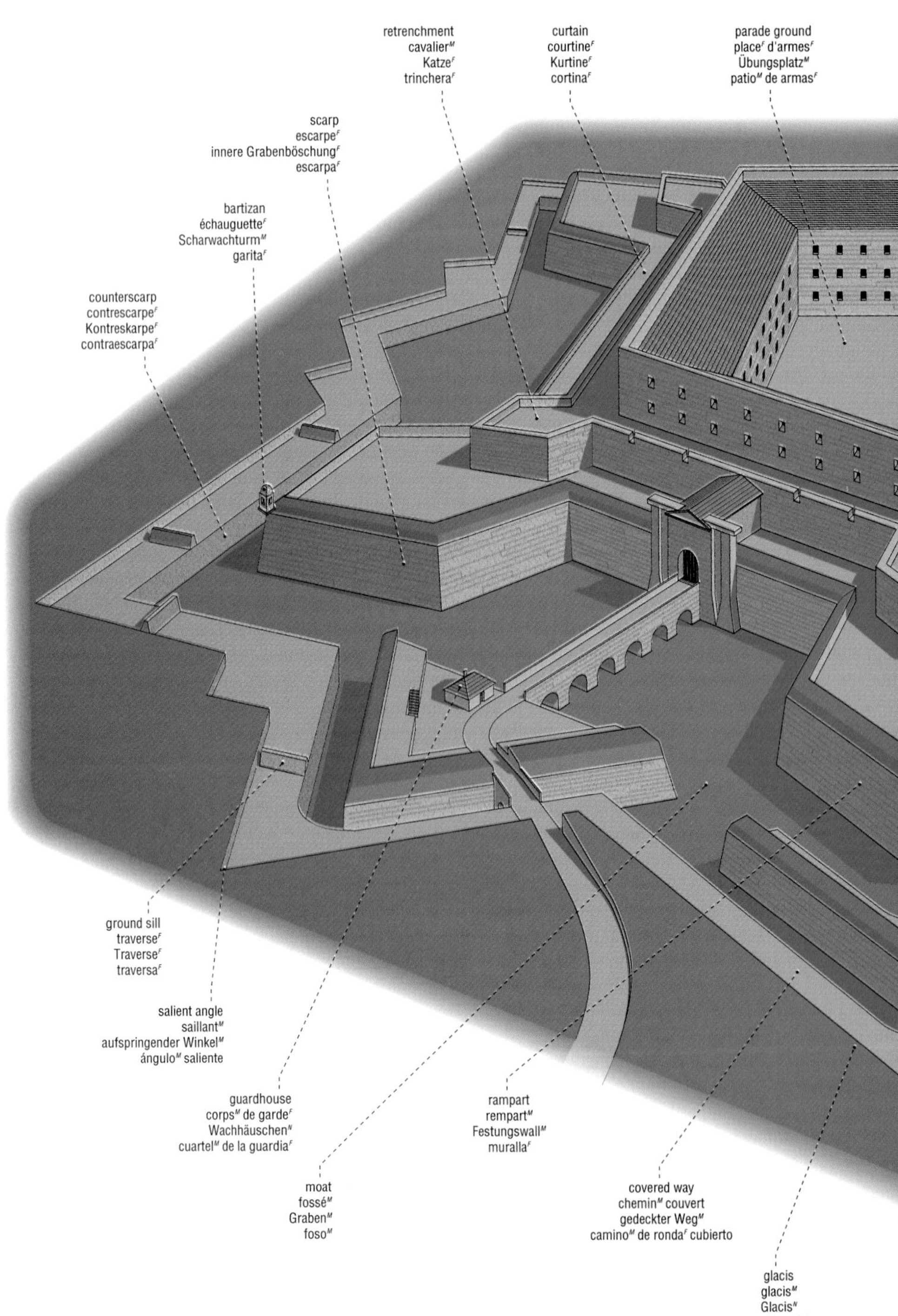

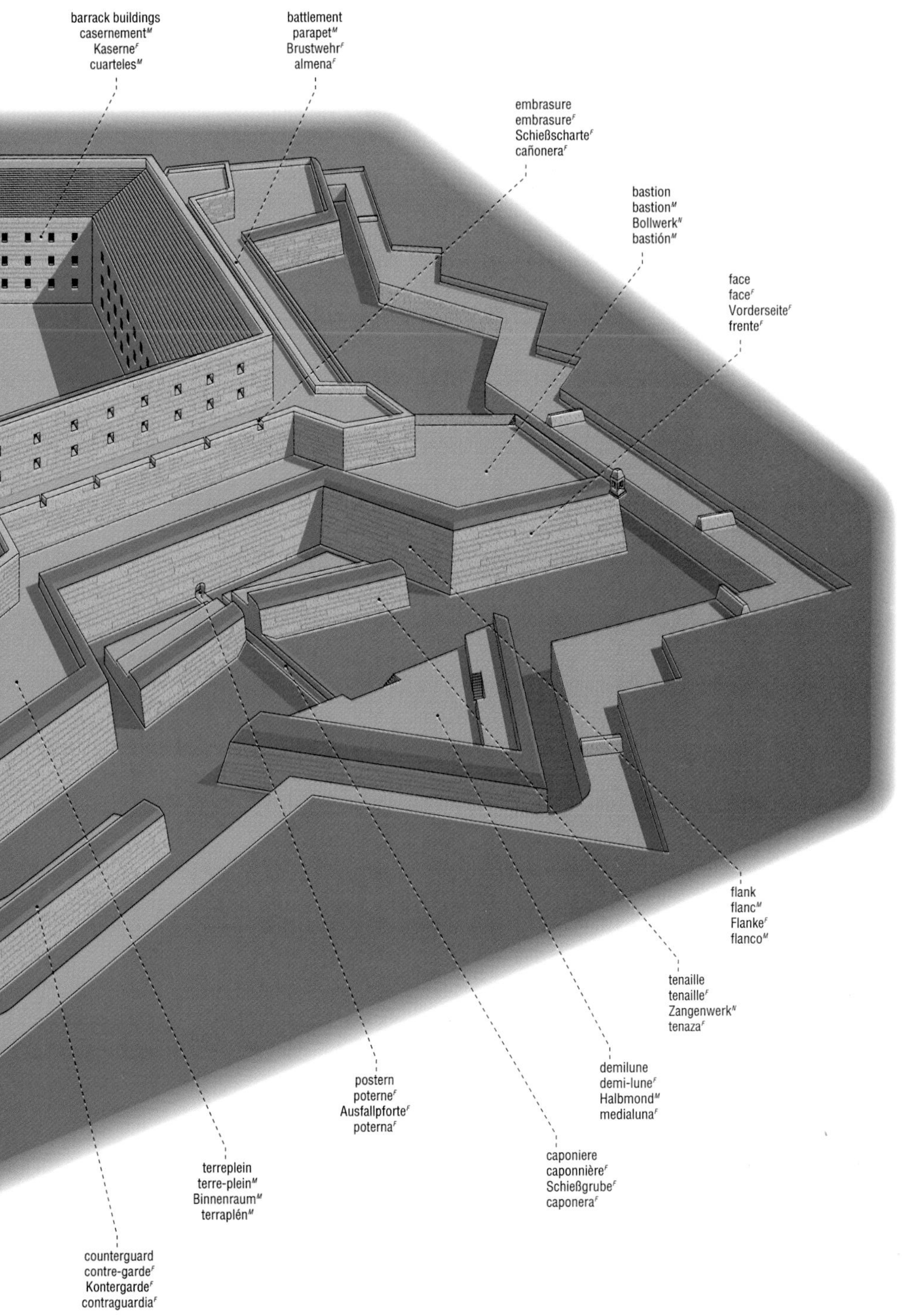
barrack buildings
casernement[M]
Kaserne[F]
cuarteles[M]
battlement
parapet[M]
Brustwehr[F]
almena[F]
embrasure
embrasure[F]
Schießscharte[F]
cañonera[F]
bastion
bastion[M]
Bollwerk[N]
bastión[M]
face
face[F]
Vorderseite[F]
frente[F]
flank
flanc[M]
Flanke[F]
flanco[M]
tenaille
tenaille[F]
Zangenwerk[N]
tenaza[F]
demilune
demi-lune[F]
Halbmond[M]
medialuna[F]
postern
poterne[F]
Ausfallpforte[F]
poterna[F]
caponiere
caponnière[F]
Schießgrube[F]
caponera[F]
terreplein
terre-plein[M]
Binnenraum[M]
terraplén[M]
counterguard
contre-garde[F]
Kontergarde[F]
contraguardia[F]

# CASTLE
# CHÂTEAU[M] FORT
# BURG[F]
# CASTILLO[M]

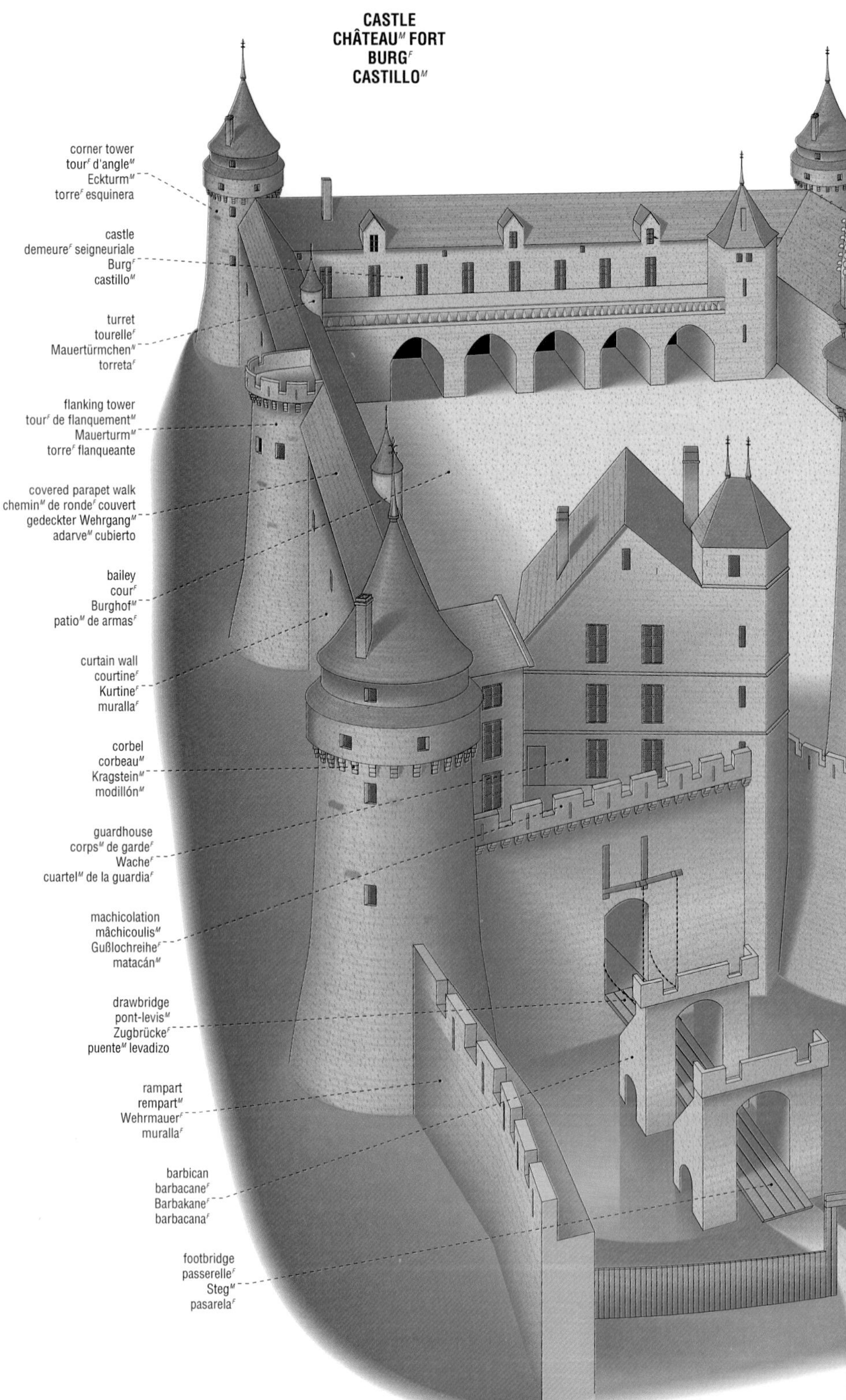

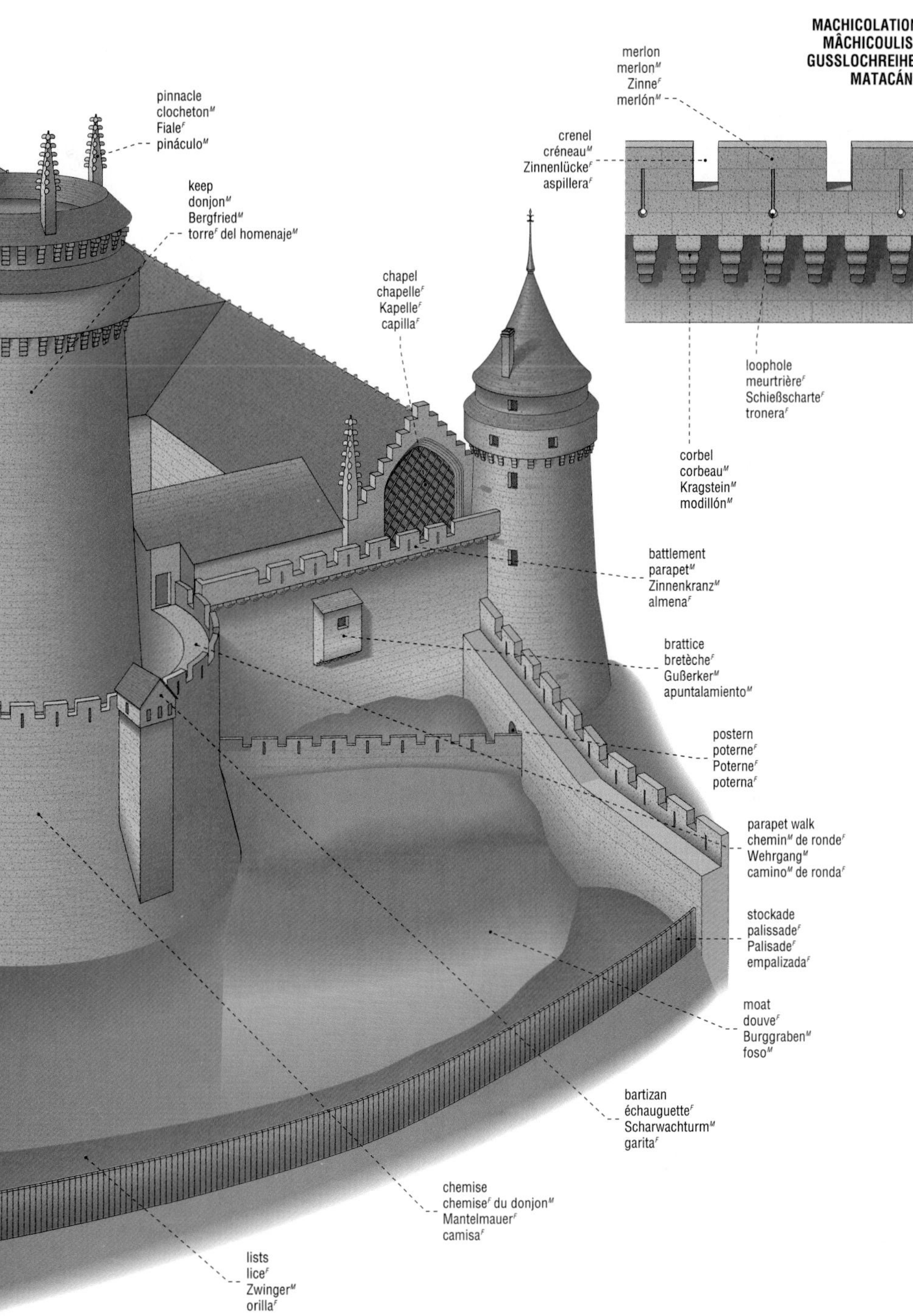
MACHICOLATION
MÂCHICOULIS[M]
GUSSLOCHREIHE[F]
MATACÁN[M]
merlon
merlon[M]
Zinne[F]
merlón[M]
crenel
créneau[M]
Zinnenlücke[F]
aspillera[F]
loophole
meurtrière[F]
Schießscharte[F]
tronera[F]
corbel
corbeau[M]
Kragstein[M]
modillón[M]
pinnacle
clocheton[M]
Fiale[F]
pináculo[M]
keep
donjon[M]
Bergfried[M]
torre[F] del homenaje[M]
chapel
chapelle[F]
Kapelle[F]
capilla[F]
battlement
parapet[M]
Zinnenkranz[M]
almena[F]
brattice
bretèche[F]
Gußerker[M]
apuntalamiento[M]
postern
poterne[F]
Poterne[F]
poterna[F]
parapet walk
chemin[M] de ronde[F]
Wehrgang[M]
camino[M] de ronda[F]
stockade
palissade[F]
Palisade[F]
empalizada[F]
moat
douve[F]
Burggraben[M]
foso[M]
bartizan
échauguette[F]
Scharwachturm[M]
garita[F]
chemise
chemise[F] du donjon[M]
Mantelmauer[F]
camisa[F]
lists
lice[F]
Zwinger[M]
orilla[F]

# ROOFS
# TOITS^M
# DÄCHER
# TECHOS^M



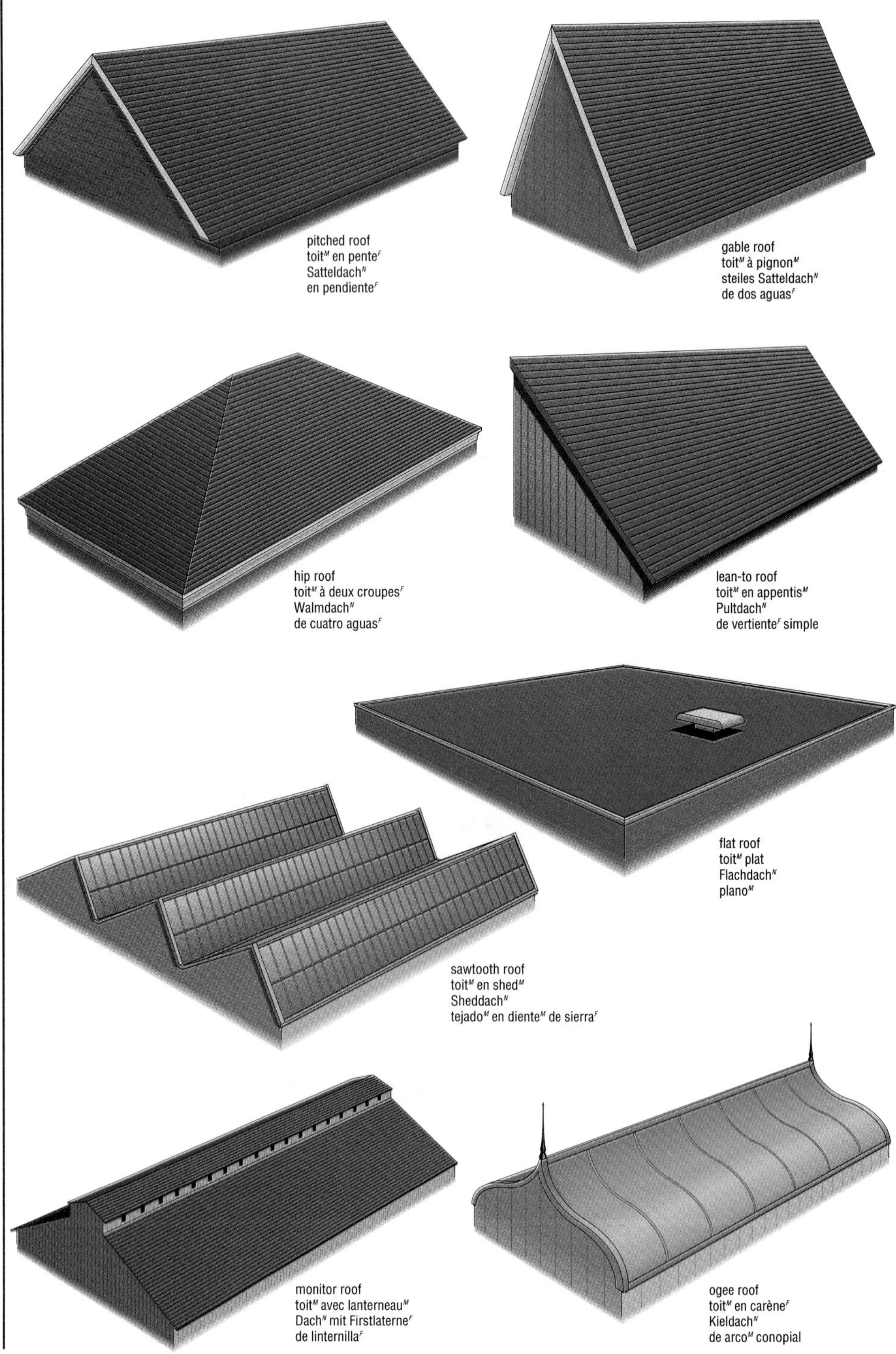

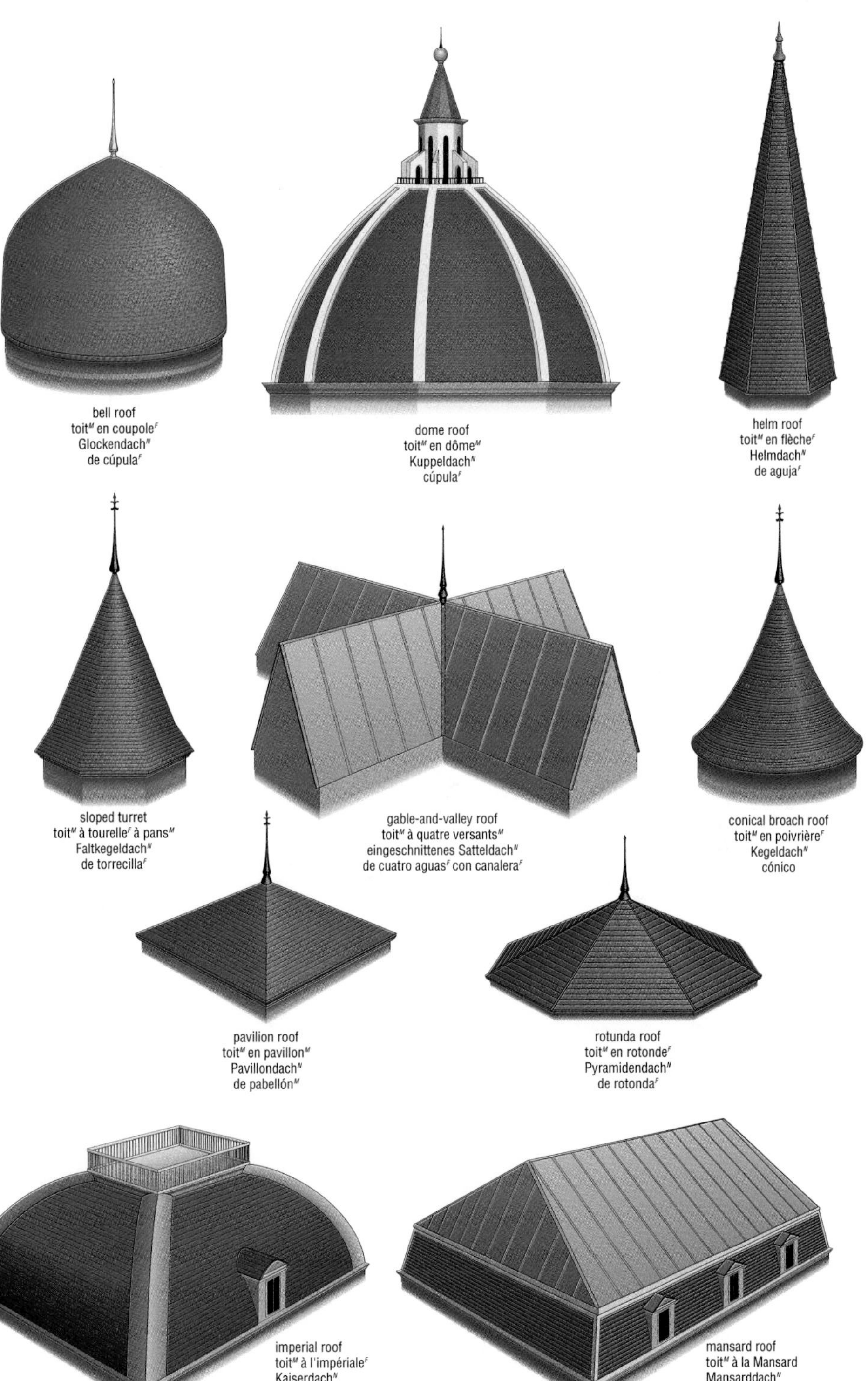
bell roof
toit[M] en coupole[F]
Glockendach[N]
de cúpula[F]
dome roof
toit[M] en dôme[M]
Kuppeldach[N]
cúpula[F]
helm roof
toit[M] en flèche[F]
Helmdach[N]
de aguja[F]
sloped turret
toit[M] à tourelle[F] à pans[M]
Faltkegeldach[N]
de torrecilla[F]
gable-and-valley roof
toit[M] à quatre versants[M]
eingeschnittenes Satteldach[N]
de cuatro aguas[F] con canalera[F]
conical broach roof
toit[M] en poivrière[F]
Kegeldach[N]
cónico
pavilion roof
toit[M] en pavillon[M]
Pavillondach[N]
de pabellón[M]
rotunda roof
toit[M] en rotonde[F]
Pyramidendach[N]
de rotonda[F]
imperial roof
toit[M] à l'impériale[F]
Kaiserdach[N]
imperial
mansard roof
toit[M] à la Mansard
Mansarddach[N]
abuhardillado

# CITY CENTRE
# CENTRE$^{M}$-VILLE$^{F}$
# CITY$^{F}$
# CENTRO$^{M}$ DE UNA CIUDAD$^{F}$

hotel
hôtel[M]
Hotel[N]
hotel[M]
skyscraper
gratte-ciel[M]
Wolkenkratzer[M]
rascacielos[M]
restaurant
restaurant[M]
Dachrestaurant[N]
restaurante[M]
church
église[F]
Kirche[F]
iglesia[F]
high-rise block
tour[F] d'habitation[F]
Hochhaus[N]
edificio[M] de apartamentos[M]
street light
lampadaire[M]
Straßenlaterne[F]
farol[M]
parking lot
aire[F] de stationnement[M]
Parkplatz[M]
estacionamiento[M]
commercial premises
immeuble[M] commercial
Geschäftshaus[N]
edificio[M] comercial
office building
immeuble[M] à bureaux[M]
Bürogebäude[N]
edificio[M] de oficinas[F]
museum
musée[M]
Museum[N]
museo[M]
stadium
stade[M]
Stadion[N]
estadio[M]

# CROSS SECTION OF A STREET
# COUPE^F D'UNE RUE^F
# QUERSCHNITT^M EINER STRASSE^F
# VISTA^F TRANSVERSAL DE UNA CALLE^F

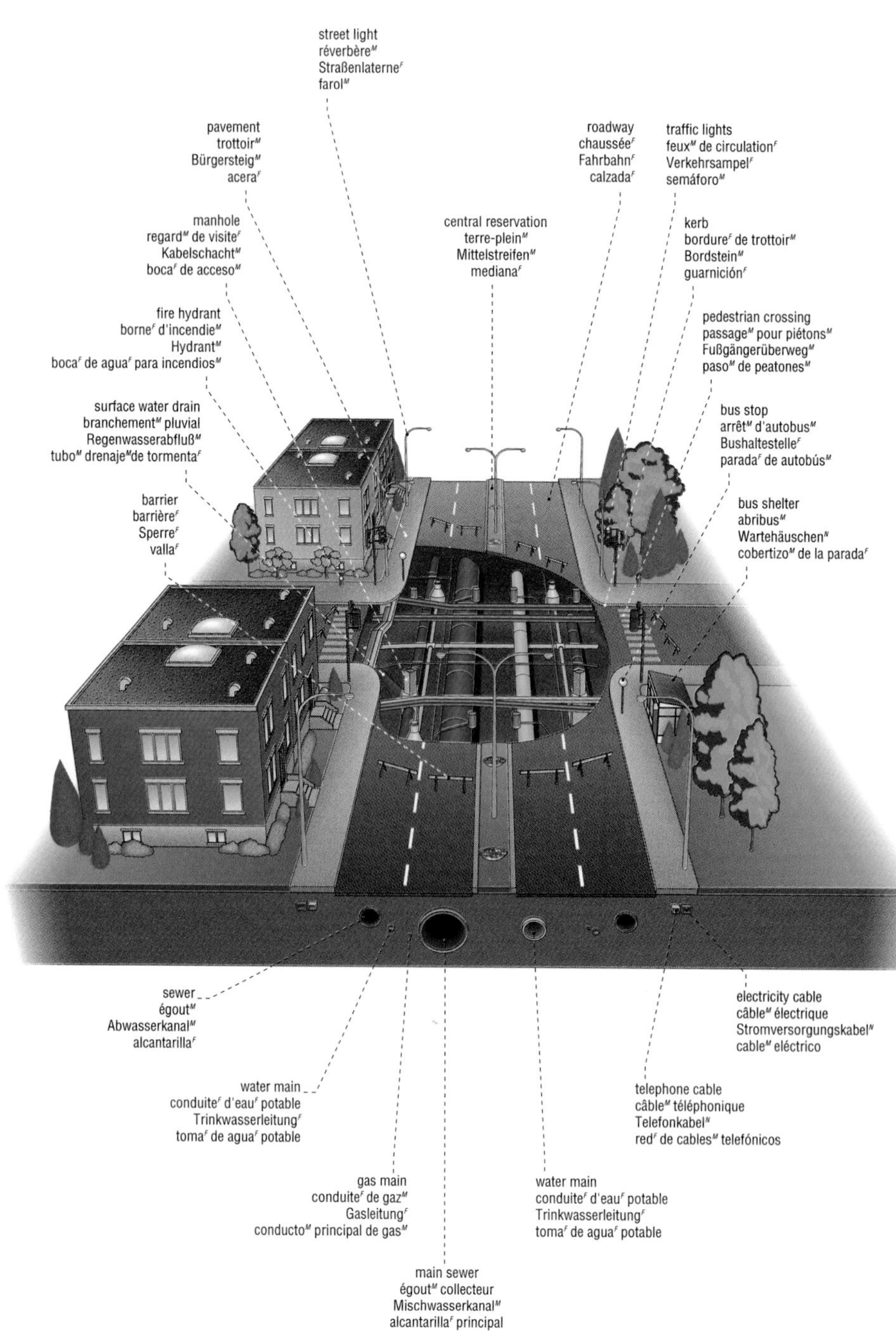

# TOWN HOUSES
# MAISONS[F] DE VILLE[F]
# HÄUSERFORMEN[F] IN DER STADT
# VIVIENDAS[F] URBANAS

small detached house
villa[F]
Cottage[N]
casa[F] de campo[M]

large detached house
maison[F] individuelle
Einfamilienhaus[N]
casas[F] independientes

freehold flats
appartements[M] en copropriété[F]
Eigentumswohnungen[F]
condominios[M]

semi-detached houses
maison[F] individuelle jumelée
Doppelhaus[N]
casas[F] gemelas

terraced houses
maisons[F] en rangée[F]
Reihenhaus[N]
casas[F] en serie[F]

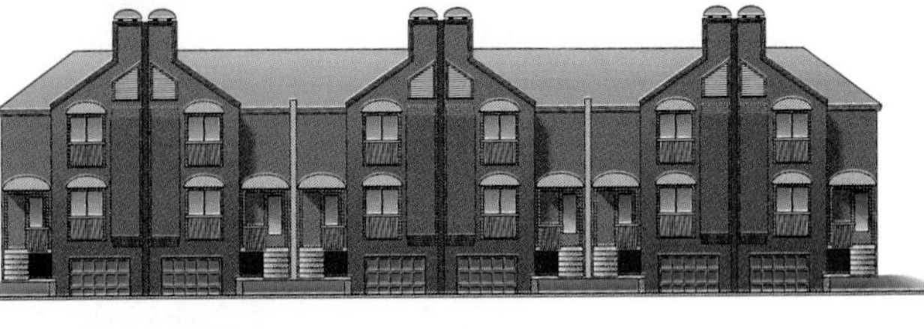

high-rise block
tour[F] d'habitation[F]
Wohnblock[N]
edificio[M] de apartamentos[M]

# THEATRE
# SALLE[F] DE SPECTACLE[M]
# THEATER[N]
# TEATRO[M]

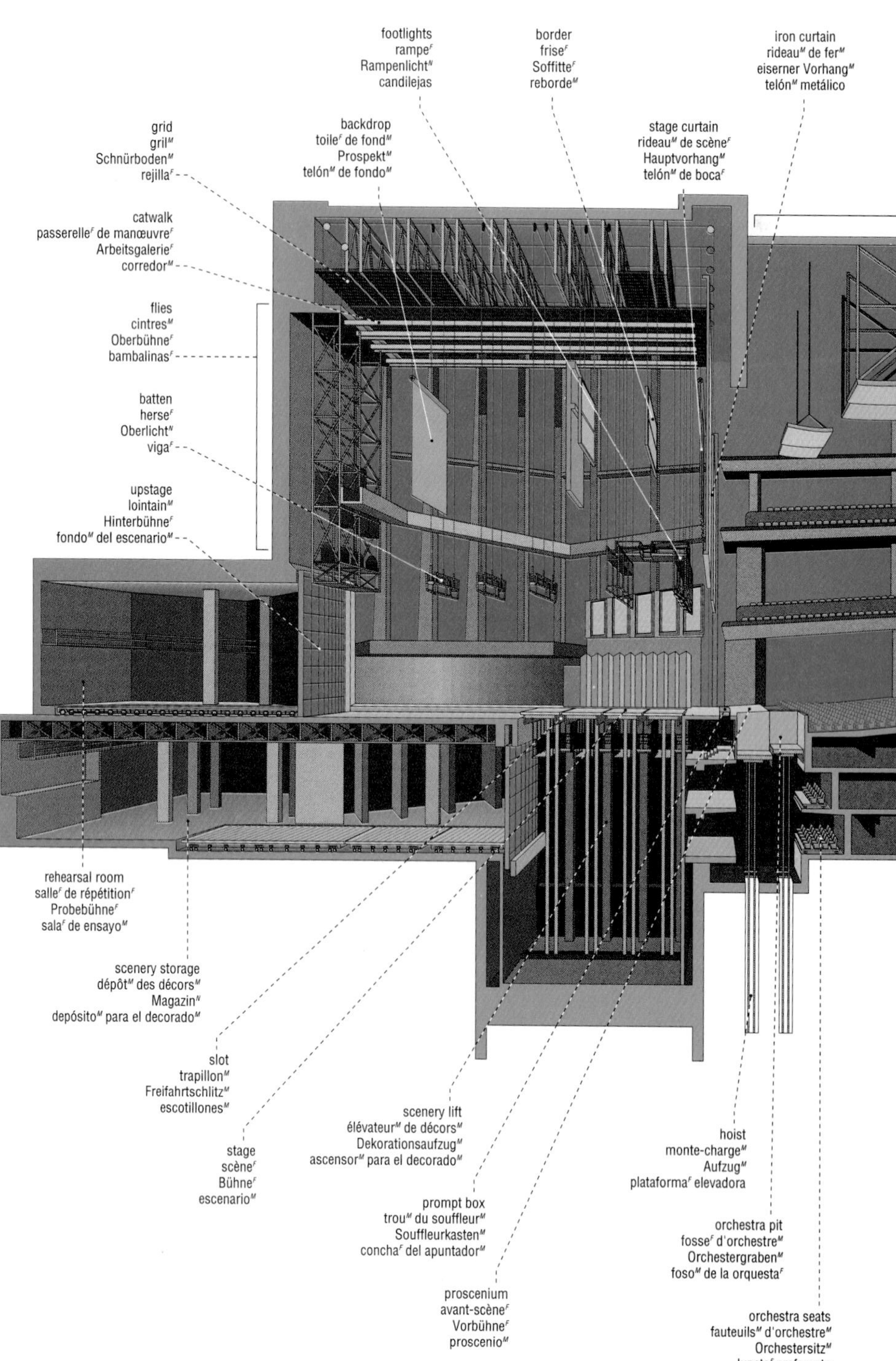

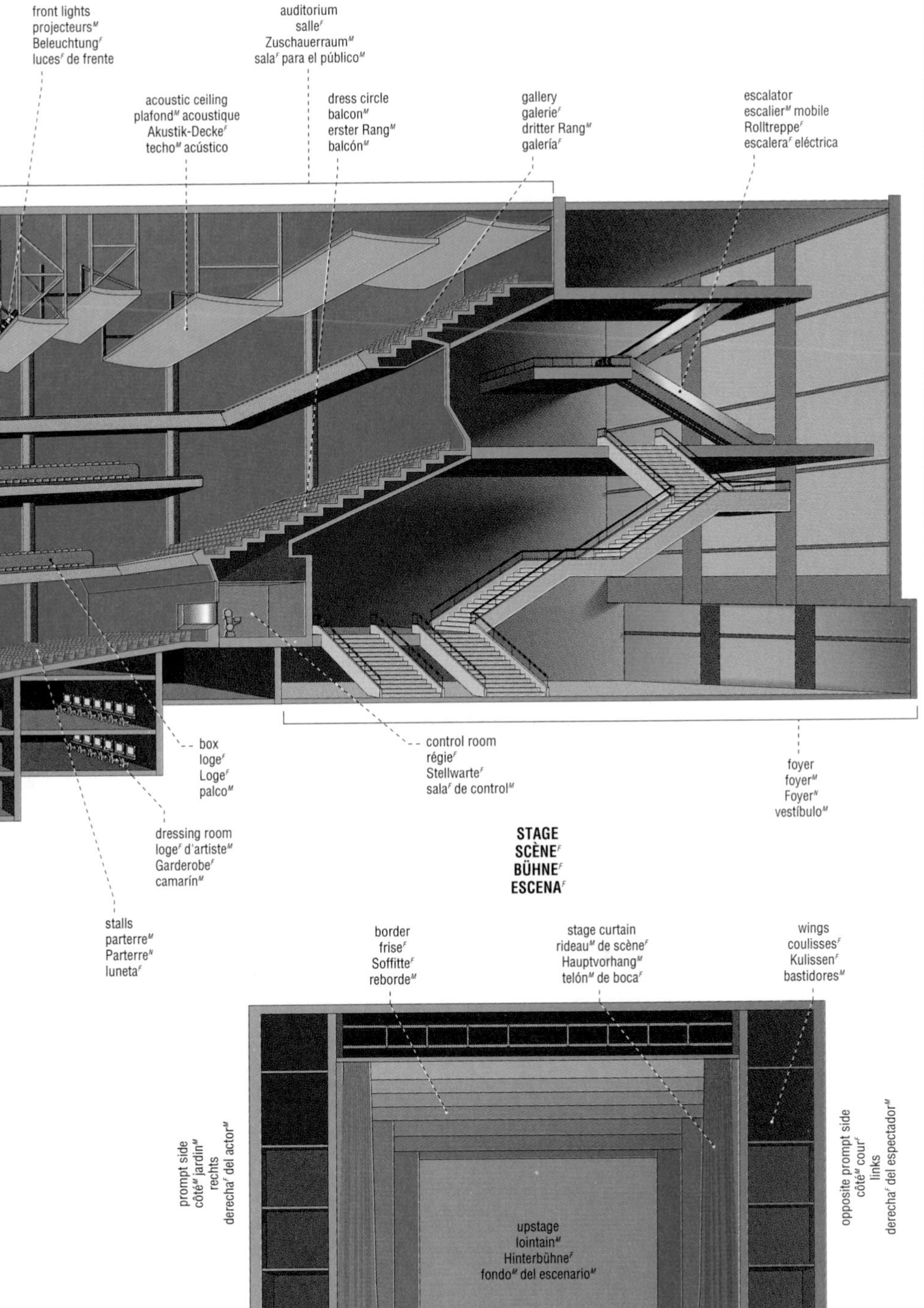


**STAGE**
**SCÈNE^F**
**BÜHNE^F**
**ESCENA^F**

# OFFICE BUILDING
# ÉDIFICE$^{M}$ À BUREAUX$^{M}$
# BÜROGEBÄUDE$^{N}$
# EDIFICIO$^{M}$ DE OFICINAS$^{F}$



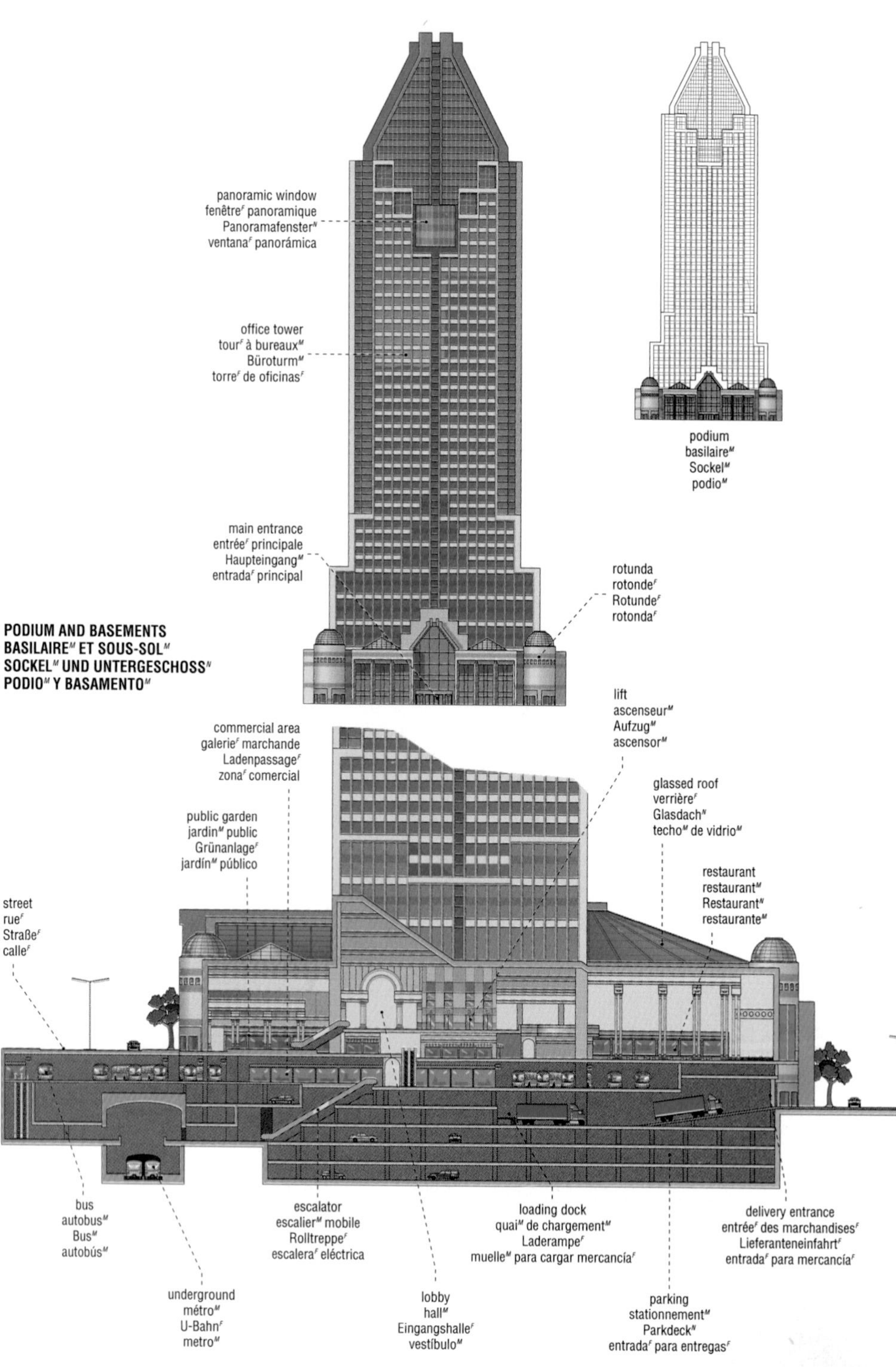

# HOUSE MAISON HAUS CASA

**SUMMARY**

READING PLANS ........ 193
EXTERIOR OF A HOUSE ........ 196
STRUCTURE OF A HOUSE ........ 198
WOOD FLOORING ........ 200
STAIRS ........ 201
DOOR ........ 202
WINDOW ........ 203
HEATING ........ 204
AIR CONDITIONING ........ 214
PLUMBING SYSTEM ........ 215
SEPTIC TANK ........ 216
PEDESTAL-TYPE CESSPIT PUMP ........ 216

# READING PLANS
# LECTURE[F] DE PLANS[M]
# GEBÄUDEPLANUNG[F]
# PLANO[M] DE UNA CASA

**ELEVATION**
**ÉLÉVATION[F]**
**ANSICHT[F]**
**ELEVACIÓN[F]**

**SITE PLAN**
**PLAN[M] DU TERRAIN[M]**
**LAGEPLAN[M]**
**PLANO[M] DEL TERRENO**

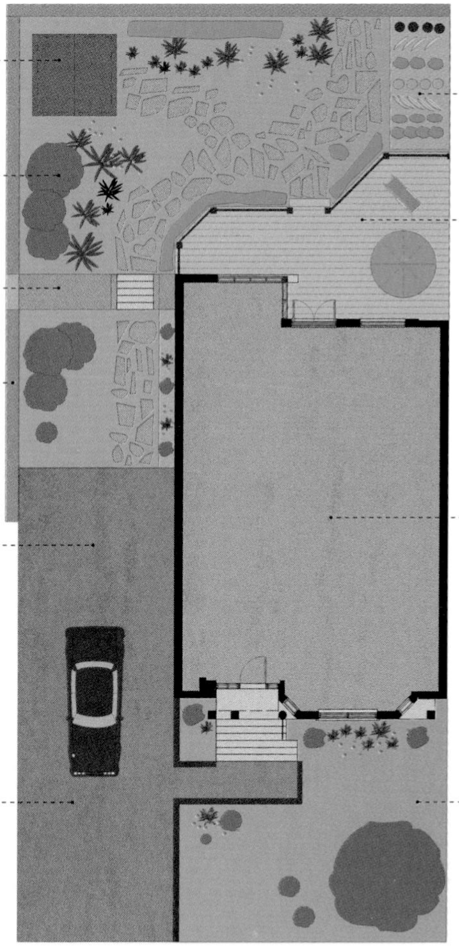

shed
remise[F]
Schuppen[M]
cobertizo[M]

vegetable garden
jardin[M] potager
Nutzgarten[M]
huerto[M]

ornamental garden
jardin[M] d'agrément[M]
Ziergarten[M]
jardín[M]

patio
terrasse[F]
Terrasse[F]
terraza[F]

bank
déclivité[F] du terrain[M]
Böschung[F]
desnivel[M]

property line
limite[F] du terrain[M]
Grundstücksgrenze[F]
lindero[M]

house
maison[F]
Haus[N]
casa[F]

parking
stationnement[M]
Abstellplatz[M]
estacionamiento[M]

driveway
allée[F]
Zufahrt[F]
entrada[F] del coche[M]

lawn
pelouse[F]
Rasen[M]
césped[M]

**MEZZANINE FLOOR**
**MEZZANINE[F]**
**HALBGESCHOSS[N]**
**ENTRESUELO[M]**

stairwell
cage[F] d'escalier[M]
Treppenhaus[N]
cubo[M] de la escalera[F]

master bedroom
chambre[F] principale
Elternschlafzimmer[N]
dormitorio[M]

window
fenêtre[F]
Fenster[N]
ventana[F]

**FIRST FLOOR**
**ÉTAGE[M]**
**ERSTER STOCK[M]**
**PLANTA[F] ALTA**

bedroom
chambre[F]
Schlafzimmer[N]
dormitorio[M]

folding door
porte[F] pliante
Falttür[F]
puerta[F] plegable

landing
palier[M]
Treppenabsatz[M]
rellano[M] de la escalera[F]

skylight
puits[M] de lumière[F]
Dachfenster[N]
tragaluz[M]

bathroom
salle[F] de bains[M]
Bad[N]
cuarto[M] de baño[M]

shower
douche[F]
Dusche[F]
ducha[F]

bath
baignoire[F]
Badewanne[F]
bañera[F]

master bedroom
chambre[F] principale
Elternschlafzimmer[N]
dormitorio[M] principal

**GROUND FLOOR**
**REZ-DE-CHAUSSÉE[M]**
**ERDGESCHOSS[N]**
**PLANTA[F] BAJA**

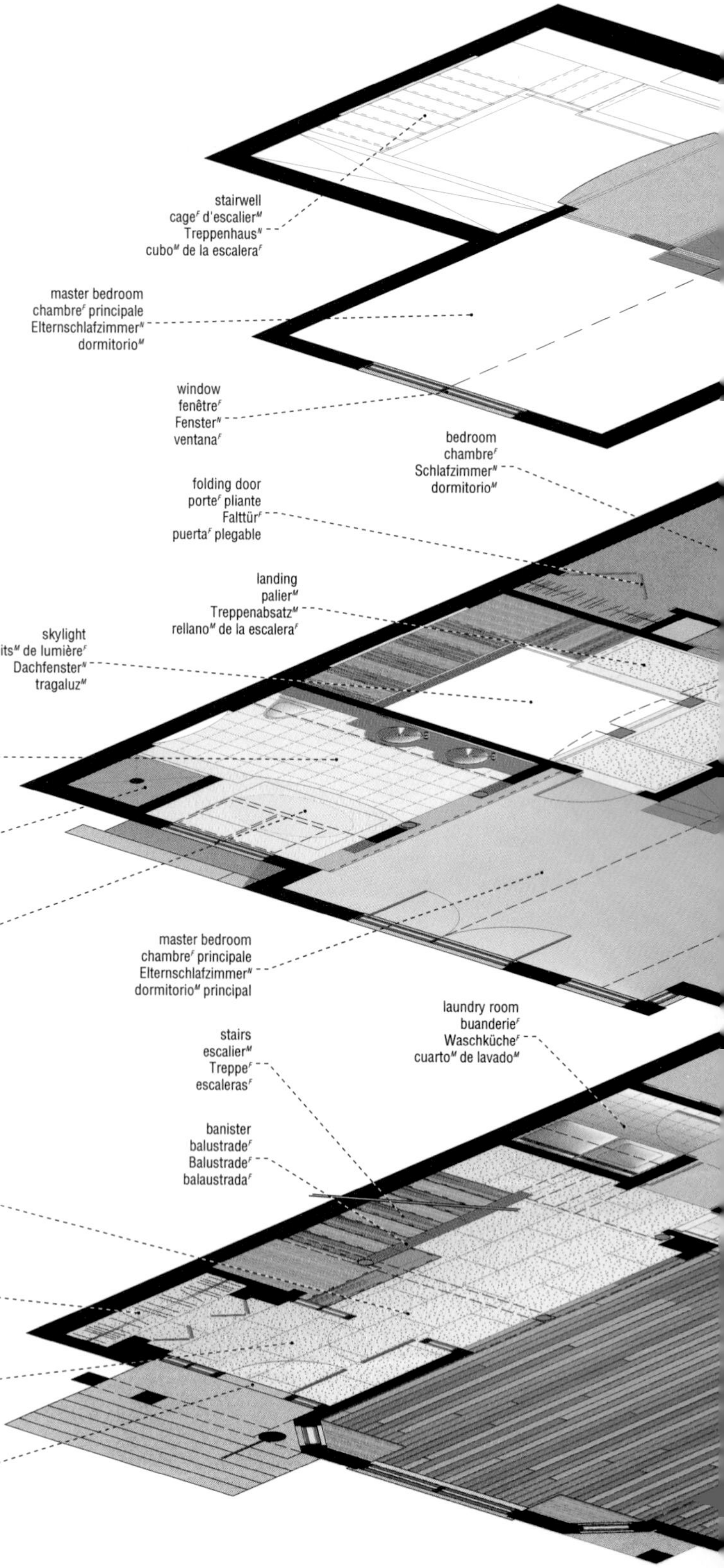

laundry room
buanderie[F]
Waschküche[F]
cuarto[M] de lavado[M]

stairs
escalier[M]
Treppe[F]
escaleras[F]

banister
balustrade[F]
Balustrade[F]
balaustrada[F]

hallway
couloir[M]
Flur[M]
pasillo[M]

hanging cupboard
vestiaire[M]
Garderobe[F]
armario[M] empotrado

hall
vestibule[M]
Diele[F]
vestíbulo[M]

main entrance
entrée[F] principale
Haupteingang[M]
entrada[F] principal

# READING PLANS
# LECTURE[F] DE PLANS[M]
# GEBÄUDEPLANUNG[F]
# ELEMENTOS[M] BÁSICOS DE UN PLANO[M]

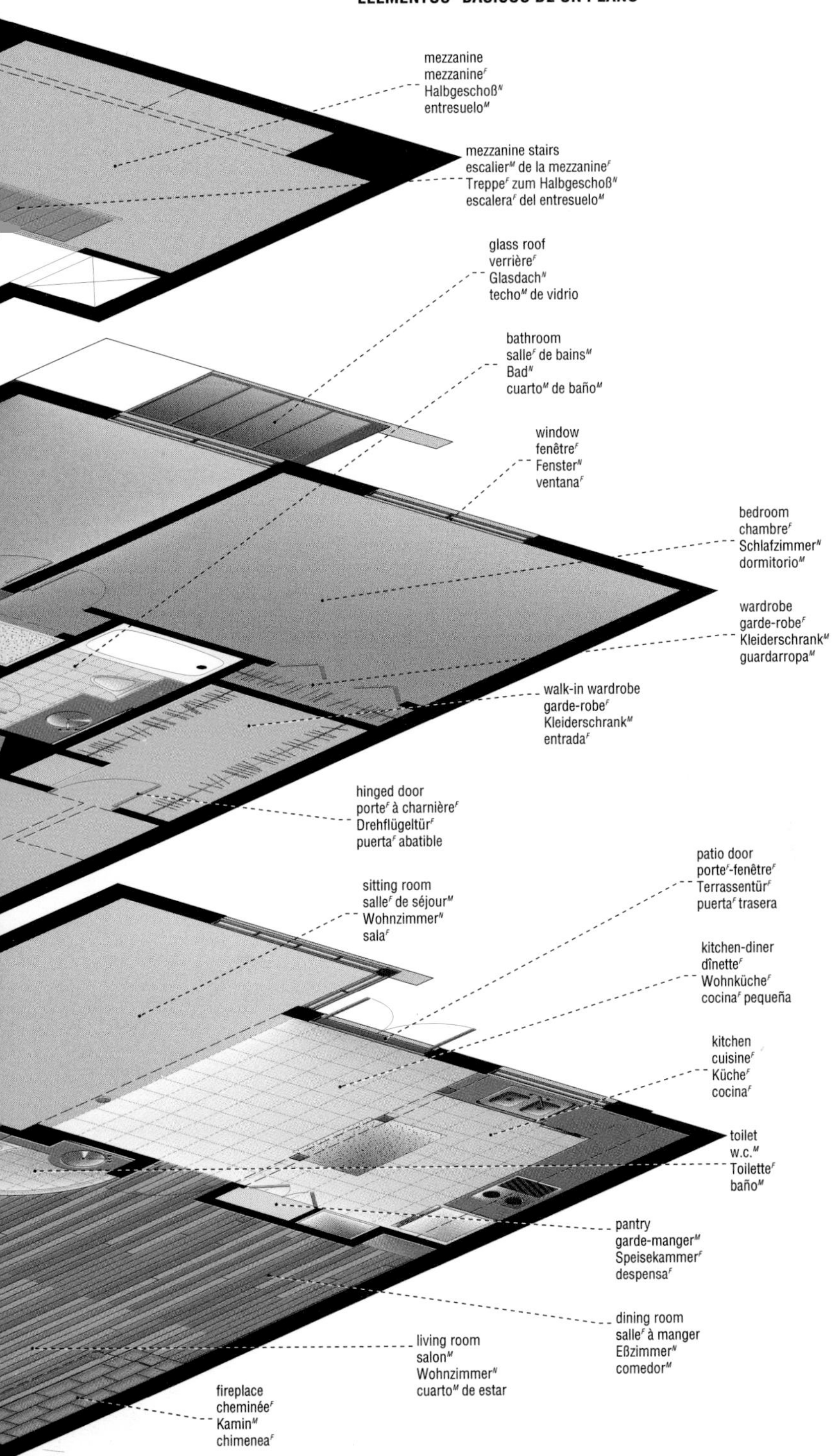

# EXTERIOR OF A HOUSE
# EXTÉRIEUR[M] D'UNE MAISON[F]
# AUSSENANSICHT[F] EINES HAUSES[N]
# EXTERIOR[M] DE UNA CASA[F]

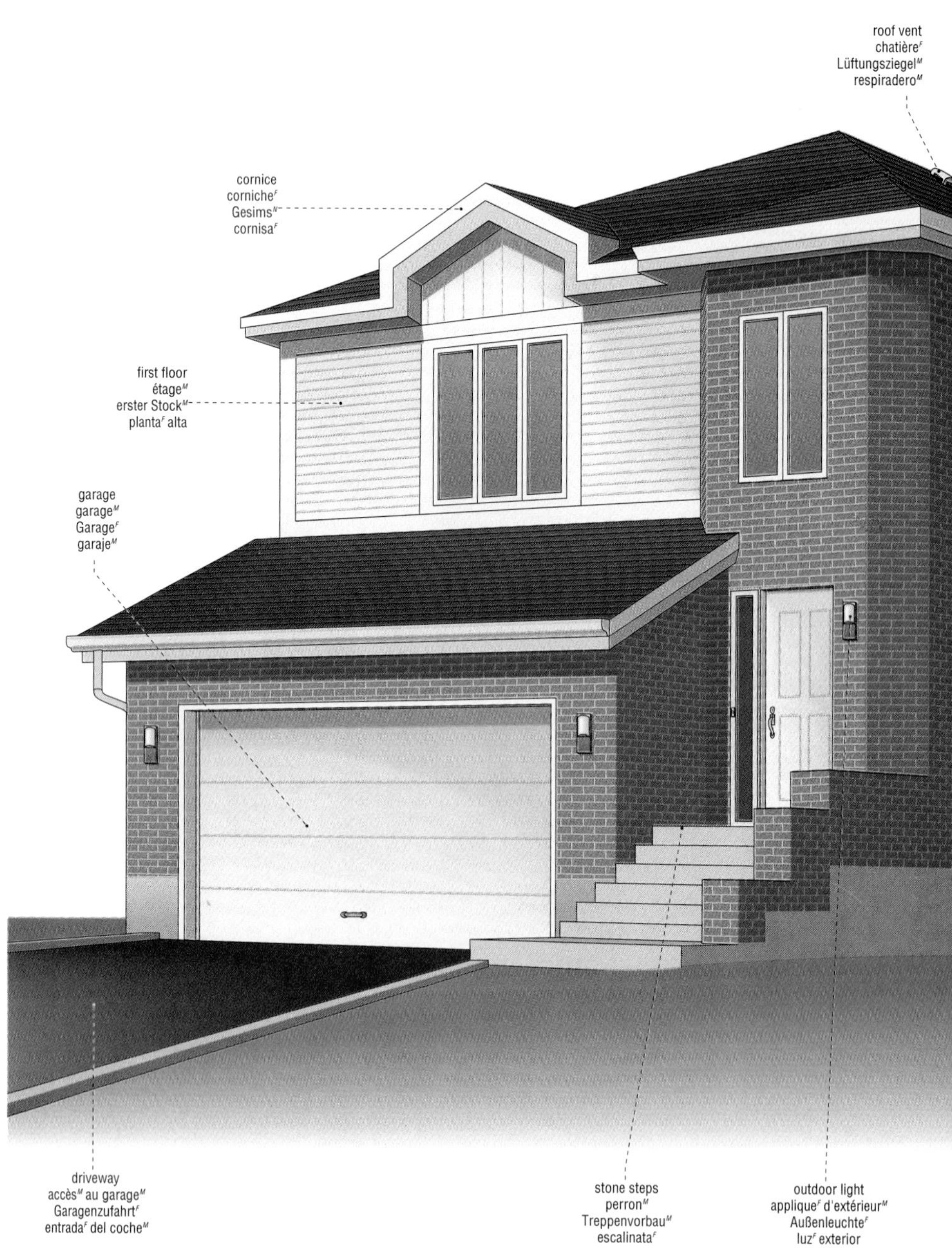

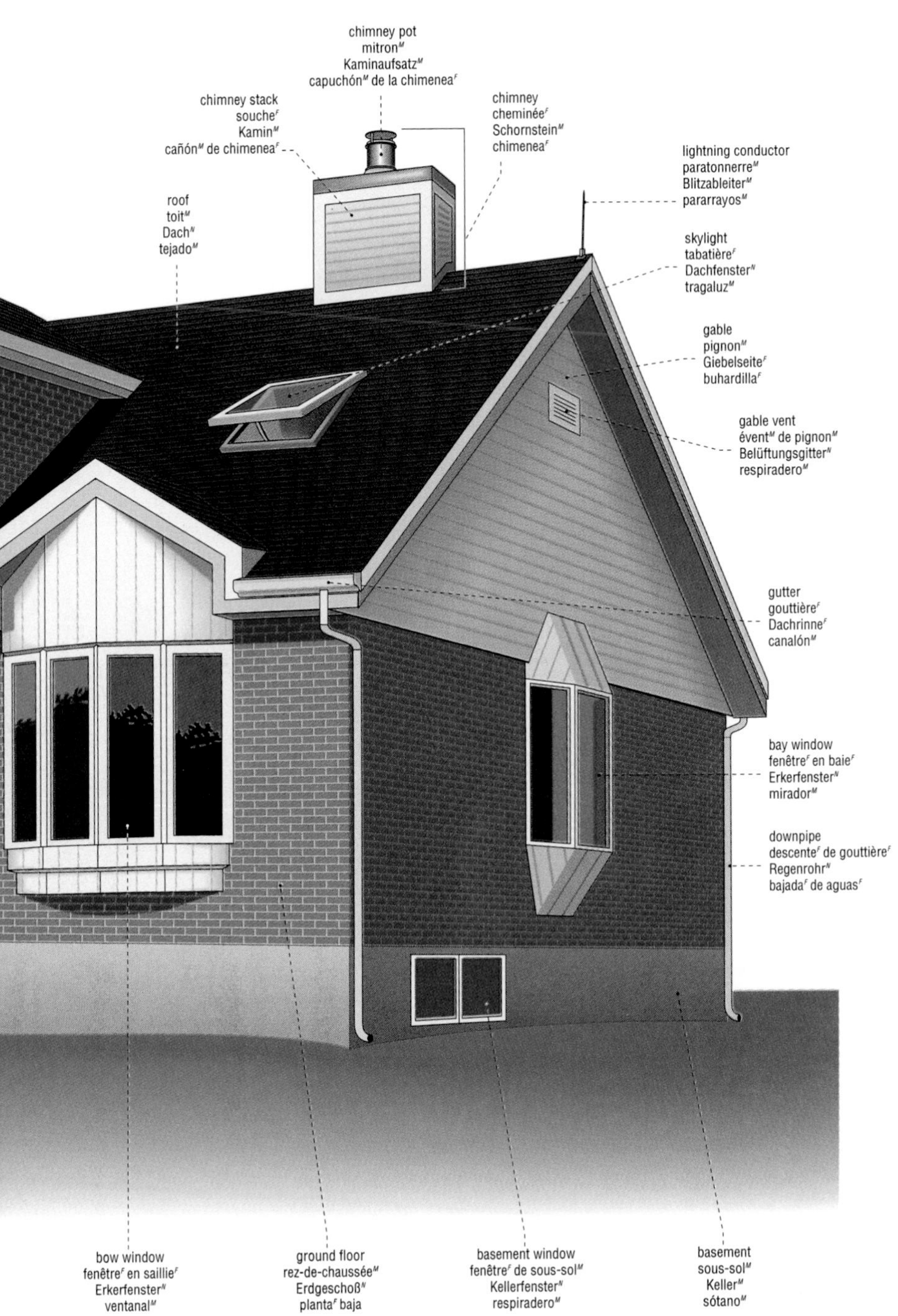
chimney pot
mitron[M]
Kaminaufsatz[M]
capuchón[M] de la chimenea[F]
chimney stack
souche[F]
Kamin[M]
cañón[M] de chimenea[F]
chimney
cheminée[F]
Schornstein[M]
chimenea[F]
lightning conductor
paratonnerre[M]
Blitzableiter[M]
pararrayos[M]
roof
toit[M]
Dach[N]
tejado[M]
skylight
tabatière[F]
Dachfenster[N]
tragaluz[M]
gable
pignon[M]
Giebelseite[F]
buhardilla[F]
gable vent
évent[M] de pignon[M]
Belüftungsgitter[N]
respiradero[M]
gutter
gouttière[F]
Dachrinne[F]
canalón[M]
bay window
fenêtre[F] en baie[F]
Erkerfenster[N]
mirador[M]
downpipe
descente[F] de gouttière[F]
Regenrohr[N]
bajada[F] de aguas[F]
bow window
fenêtre[F] en saillie[F]
Erkerfenster[N]
ventanal[M]
ground floor
rez-de-chaussée[M]
Erdgeschoß[N]
planta[F] baja
basement window
fenêtre[F] de sous-sol[M]
Kellerfenster[N]
respiradero[M]
basement
sous-sol[M]
Keller[M]
sótano[M]

# STRUCTURE OF A HOUSE
# STRUCTURE[F] D'UNE MAISON[F]
# KONSTRUKTION[F] EINES HAUSES[N]
# ESTRUCTURA[F] DE UNA CASA[F]

## TIMBER FRAME
## CHARPENTE[F]
## RAHMEN[M]
## ARMAZÓN[M]

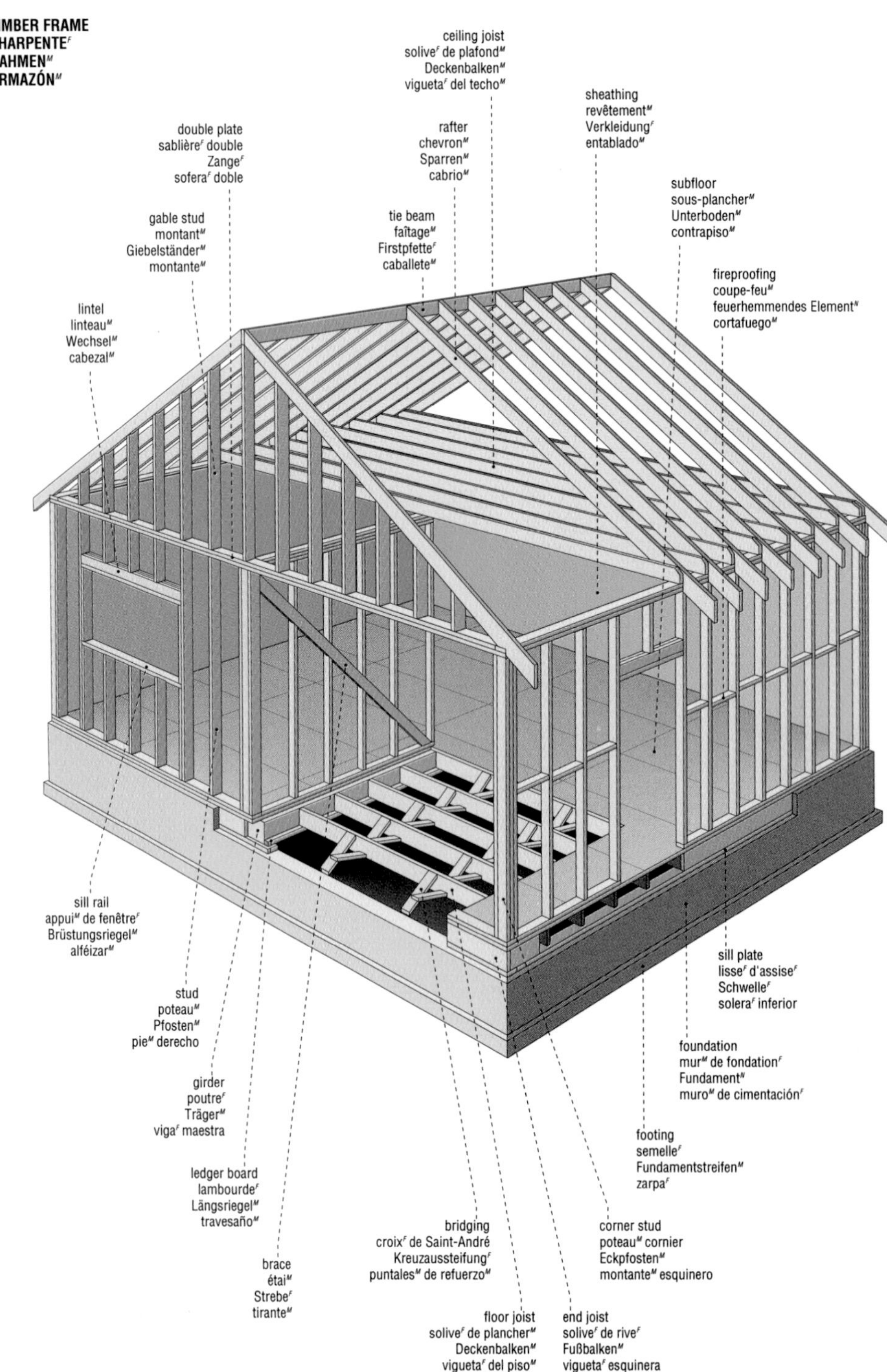

## ROOF TRUSS
## FERME[F] DE TOIT[M]
## DACHSTUHL[M]
## ARMADURA[F] DEL TECHO[M]

king post
poinçon[M]
Hängesäule[F]
pendolón[M]
side post
jambette[F]
Ständer[M]
virotillo[M]
principal rafter
arbalétrier[M]
Hauptsparren[M]
par[M]
tie beam
entrait[M]
Bundbalken[M]
tirante[M]
strut
contre-fiche[F]
Strebe[F]
puntal[M]

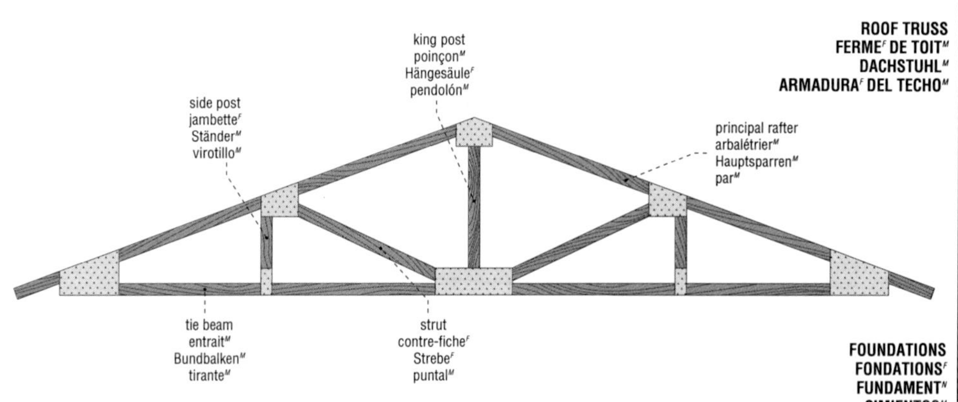

## FOUNDATIONS
## FONDATIONS[F]
## FUNDAMENT[N]
## CIMIENTOS[M]

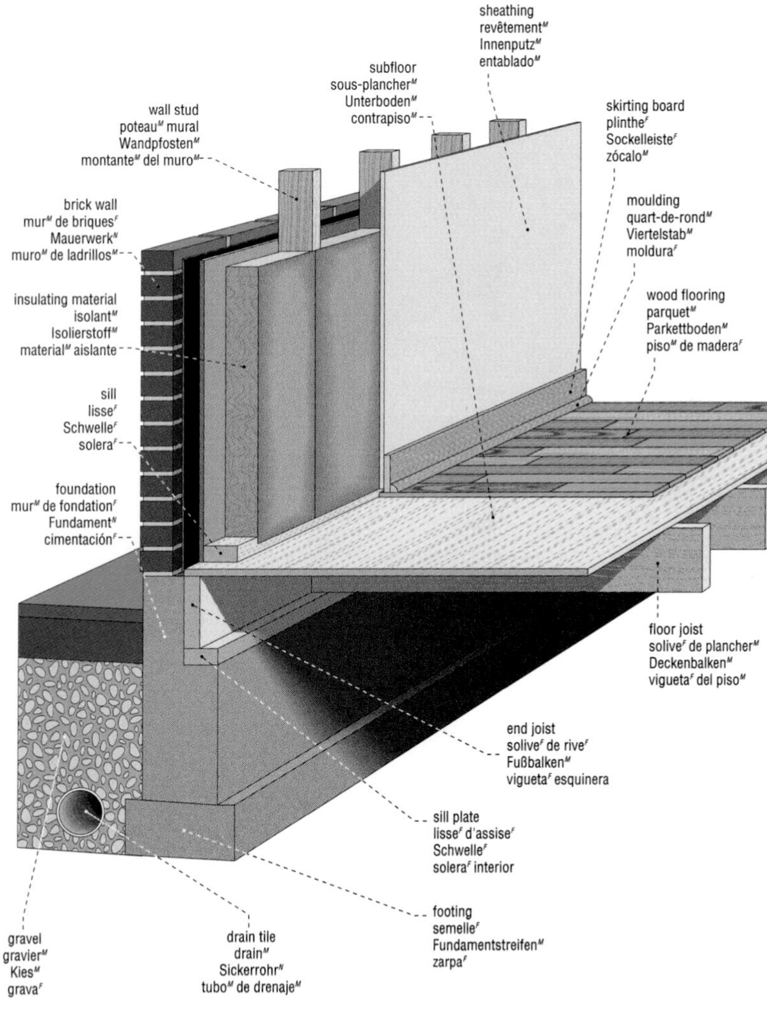

sheathing
revêtement[M]
Innenputz[M]
entablado[M]
subfloor
sous-plancher[M]
Unterboden[M]
contrapiso[M]
wall stud
poteau[M] mural
Wandpfosten[M]
montante[M] del muro[M]
skirting board
plinthe[F]
Sockelleiste[F]
zócalo[M]
brick wall
mur[M] de briques[F]
Mauerwerk[N]
muro[M] de ladrillos[M]
moulding
quart-de-rond[M]
Viertelstab[M]
moldura[F]
insulating material
isolant[M]
Isolierstoff[M]
material[M] aislante
wood flooring
parquet[M]
Parkettboden[M]
piso[M] de madera[F]
sill
lisse[F]
Schwelle[F]
solera[F]
foundation
mur[M] de fondation[F]
Fundament[N]
cimentación[F]
floor joist
solive[F] de plancher[M]
Deckenbalken[M]
vigueta[F] del piso[M]
end joist
solive[F] de rive[F]
Fußbalken[M]
vigueta[F] esquinera
sill plate
lisse[F] d'assise[F]
Schwelle[F]
solera[F] interior
footing
semelle[F]
Fundamentstreifen[M]
zarpa[F]
gravel
gravier[M]
Kies[M]
grava[F]
drain tile
drain[M]
Sickerrohr[N]
tubo[M] de drenaje[M]

# WOOD FLOORING
# PARQUET[M]
# PARKETTBODEN[M]
# PISOS[M] DE MADERA[F]

## WOOD FLOORING ON CEMENT SCREED
## PARQUET[M] SUR CHAPE[F] DE CIMENT[M]
## PARKETTBODEN[M] AUF ZEMENTESTRICH[M]
## PARQUÉ[M] SOBRE BASE[F] DE CEMENTO[M]

## WOOD FLOORING ON WOODEN BASE
## PARQUET[M] SUR OSSATURE[F] DE BOIS[M]
## PARKETTBODEN[M] AUF HOLZUNTERBAU[M]
## ENTARIMADO[M] SOBRE ESTRUCTURA[F] DE MADERA[F]

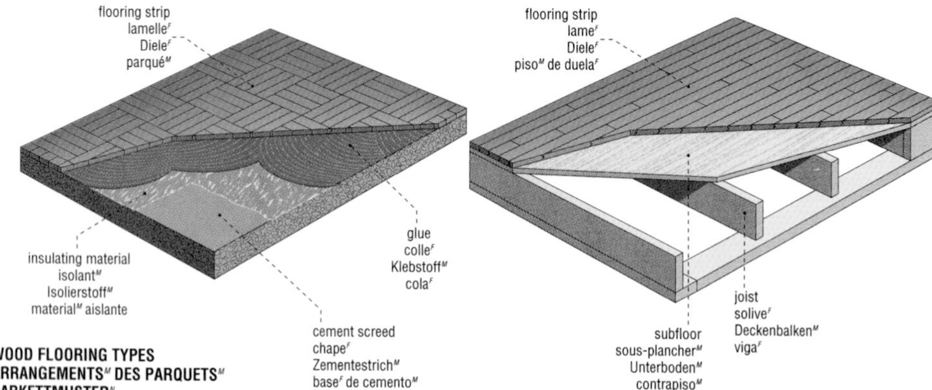


## WOOD FLOORING TYPES
## ARRANGEMENTS[M] DES PARQUETS[M]
## PARKETTMUSTER[N]
## TIPOS[M] DE PARQUÉ[M]

woodstrip flooring
parquet[M] à coupe[F] perdue
Stabparkett[N] im verlorenen Verband[M]
parqué[M] sobrepuesto

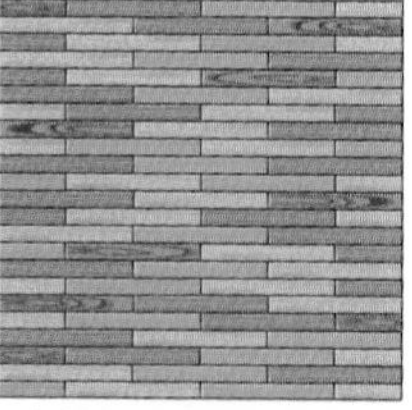
brick-bond woodstrip flooring
parquet[M] à coupe[F] de pierre[F]
Stabparkett[N]
parqué[M] alternado a la inglesa

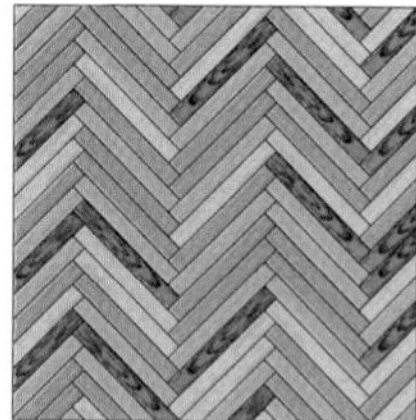
herringbone parquet
parquet[M] à bâtons[M] rompus
Fischgrätenparkett[N]
parqué[M] espinapez[M]

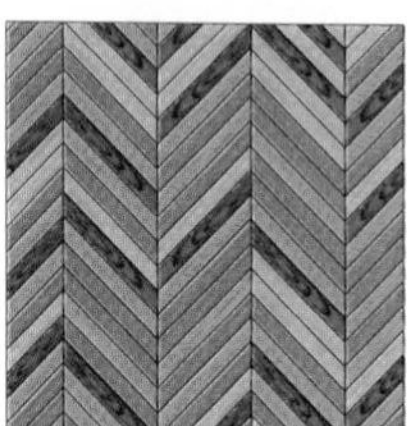
herringbone pattern
parquet[M] en chevrons[M]
Fischgrätenmuster[N]
espinapez[M]

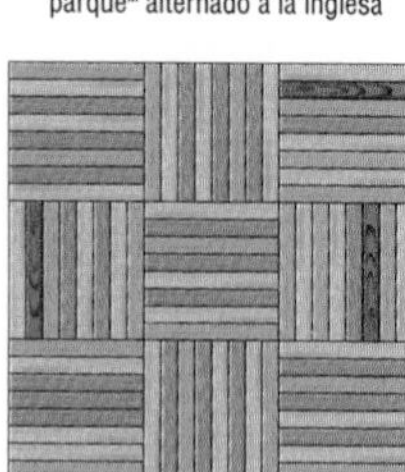
inlaid parquet
parquet[M] mosaïque[F]
Mosaikparkett[N]
parqué[M] entretejido

basket weave pattern
parquet[M] en vannerie[F]
Würfelmusterparkett[N]
parqué[M] de cestería[F]

Arenberg parquet
parquet[M] d'Arenberg
Arenberg-Parkett[N]
parqué[M] Arenberg

Chantilly parquet
parquet[M] Chantilly
Chantilly-Parkett[N]
parqué[M] Chantilly

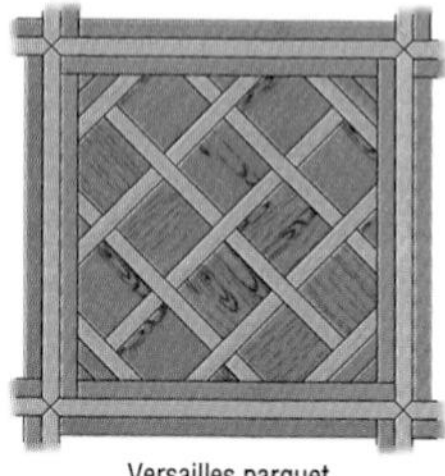
Versailles parquet
parquet[M] Versailles
Versailles-Parkett[N]
parqué[M] Versailles

# STAIRS
# ESCALIER^M
# TREPPE^F
# ESCALERA^F

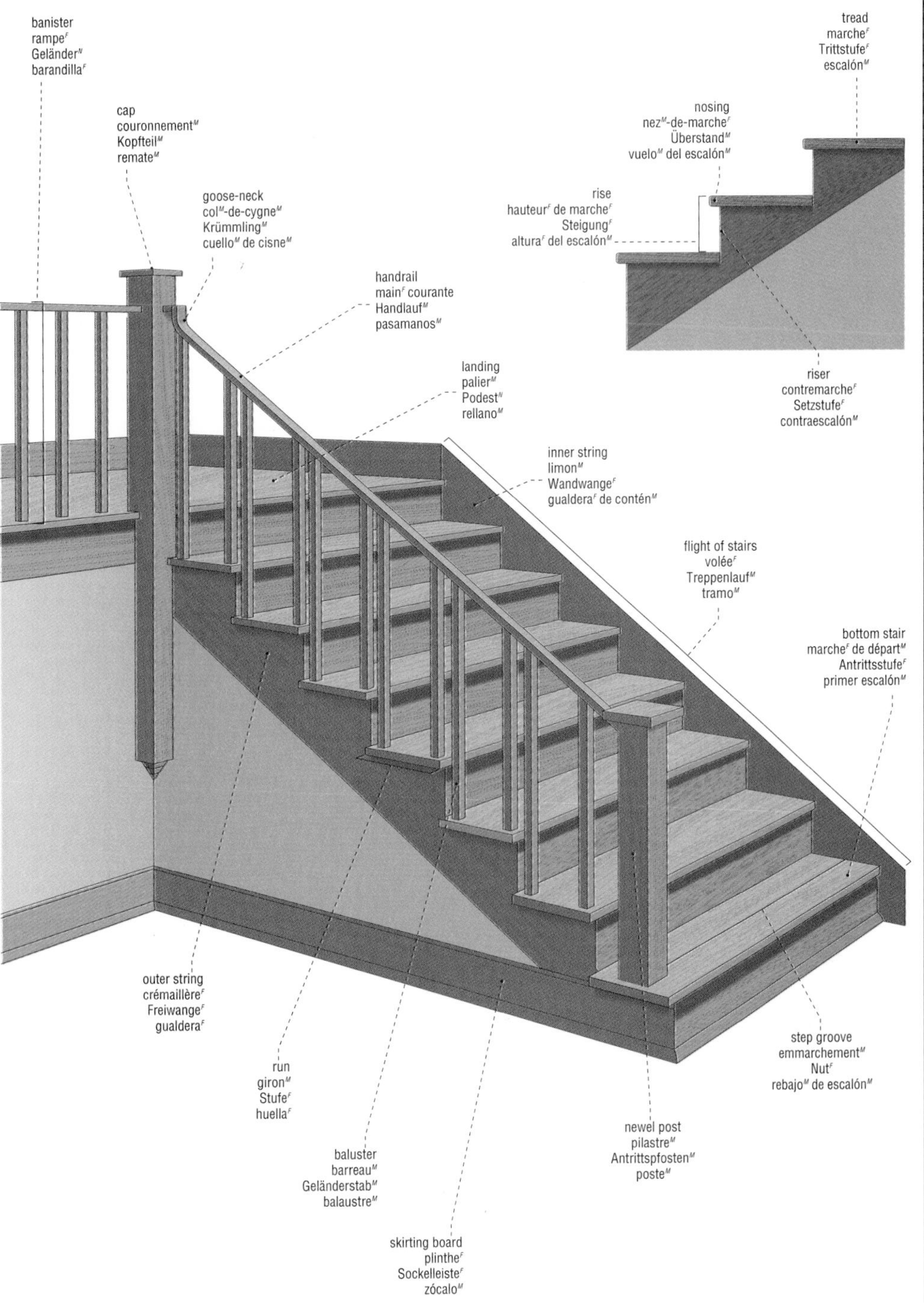

# DOOR
# PORTE^F
# TÜR^F
# PUERTA^F

## EXTERIOR DOOR
## PORTE^F EXTÉRIEURE
## HAUSTÜR^F
## PUERTA^F DE ENTRADA^F

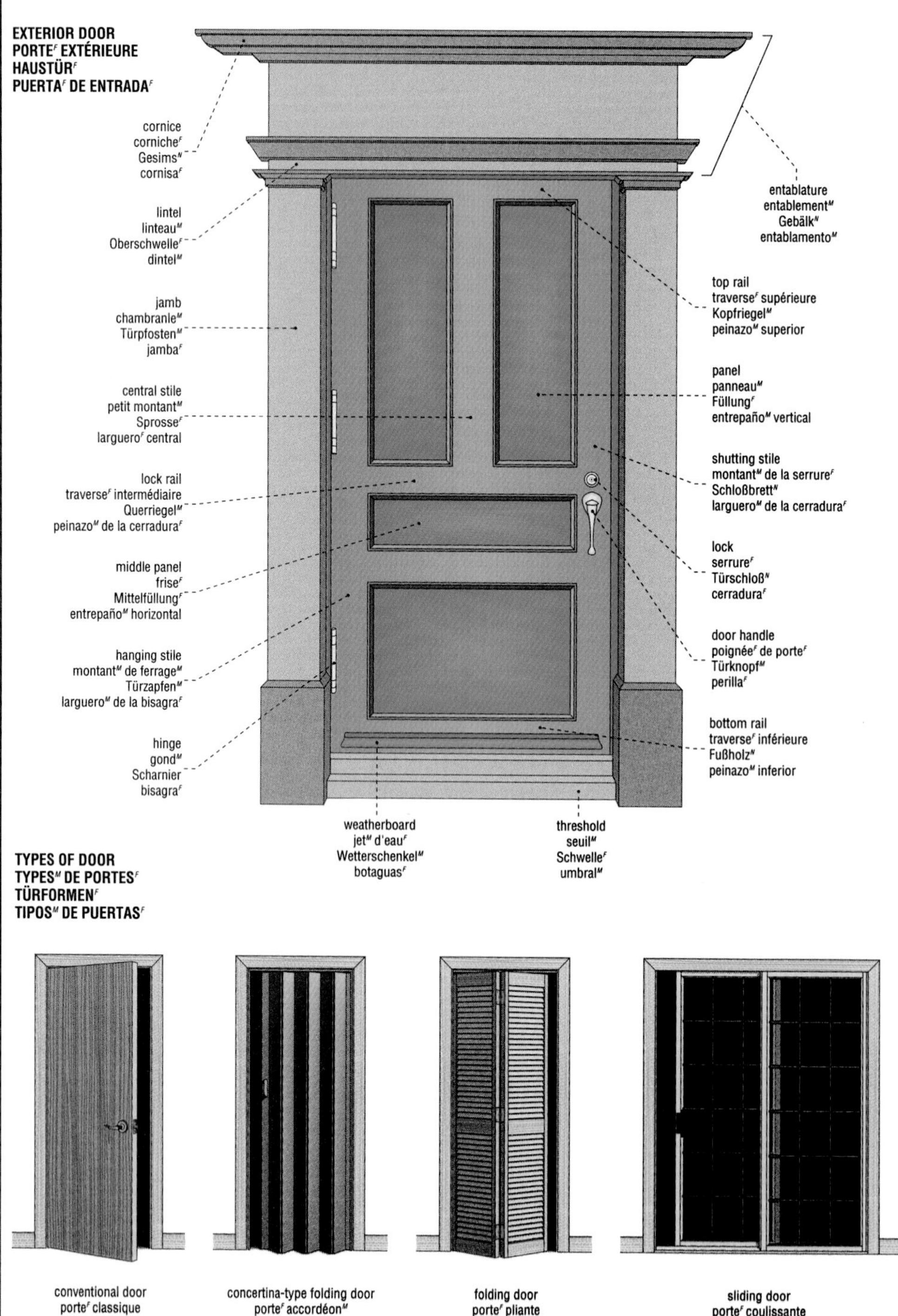

# WINDOW
# FENÊTRE[F]
# FENSTER[N]
# VENTANA[F]

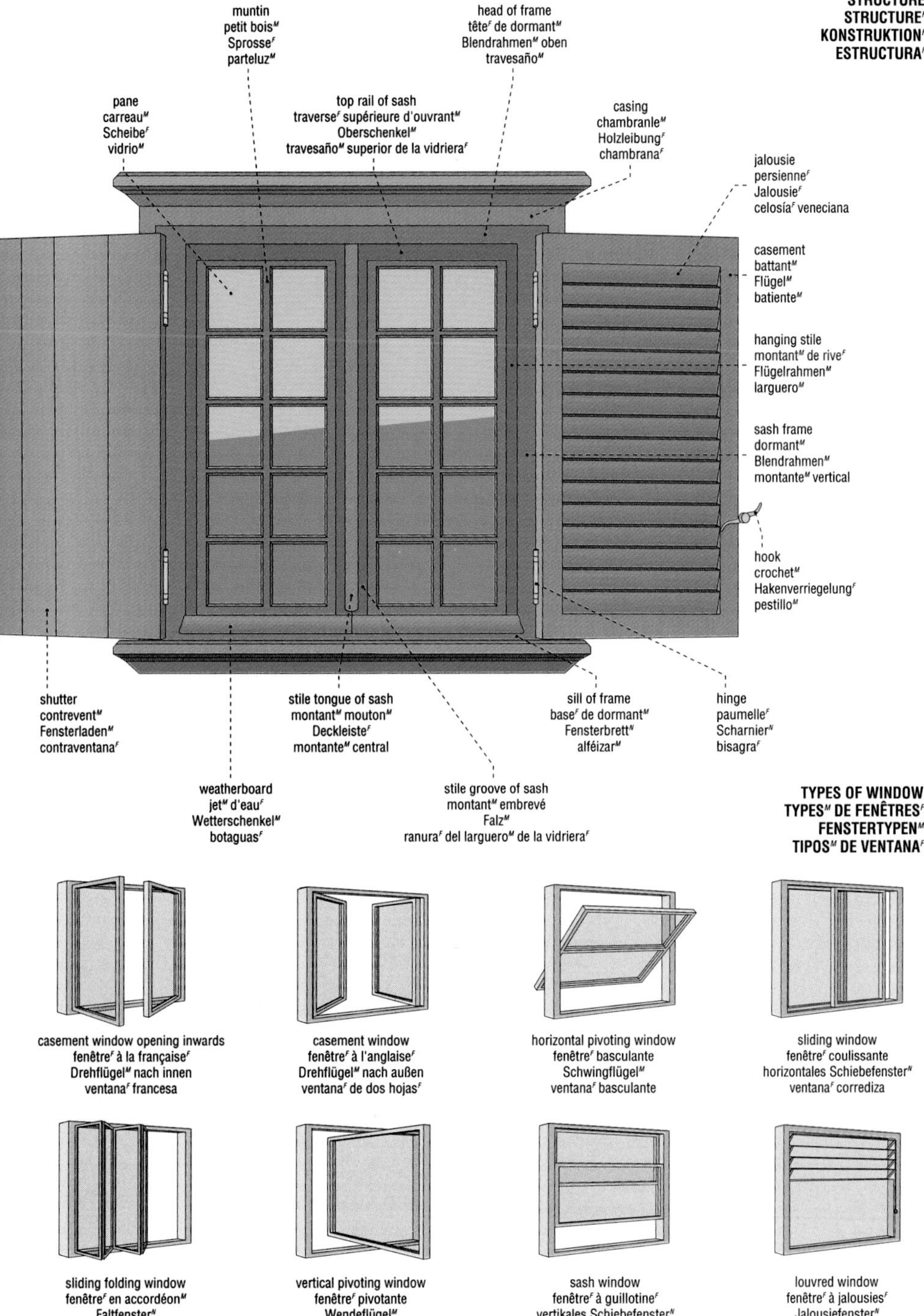

## HEATING
## CHAUFFAGEᴹ
## HEIZUNGᶠ
## CALEFACCIÓNᶠ

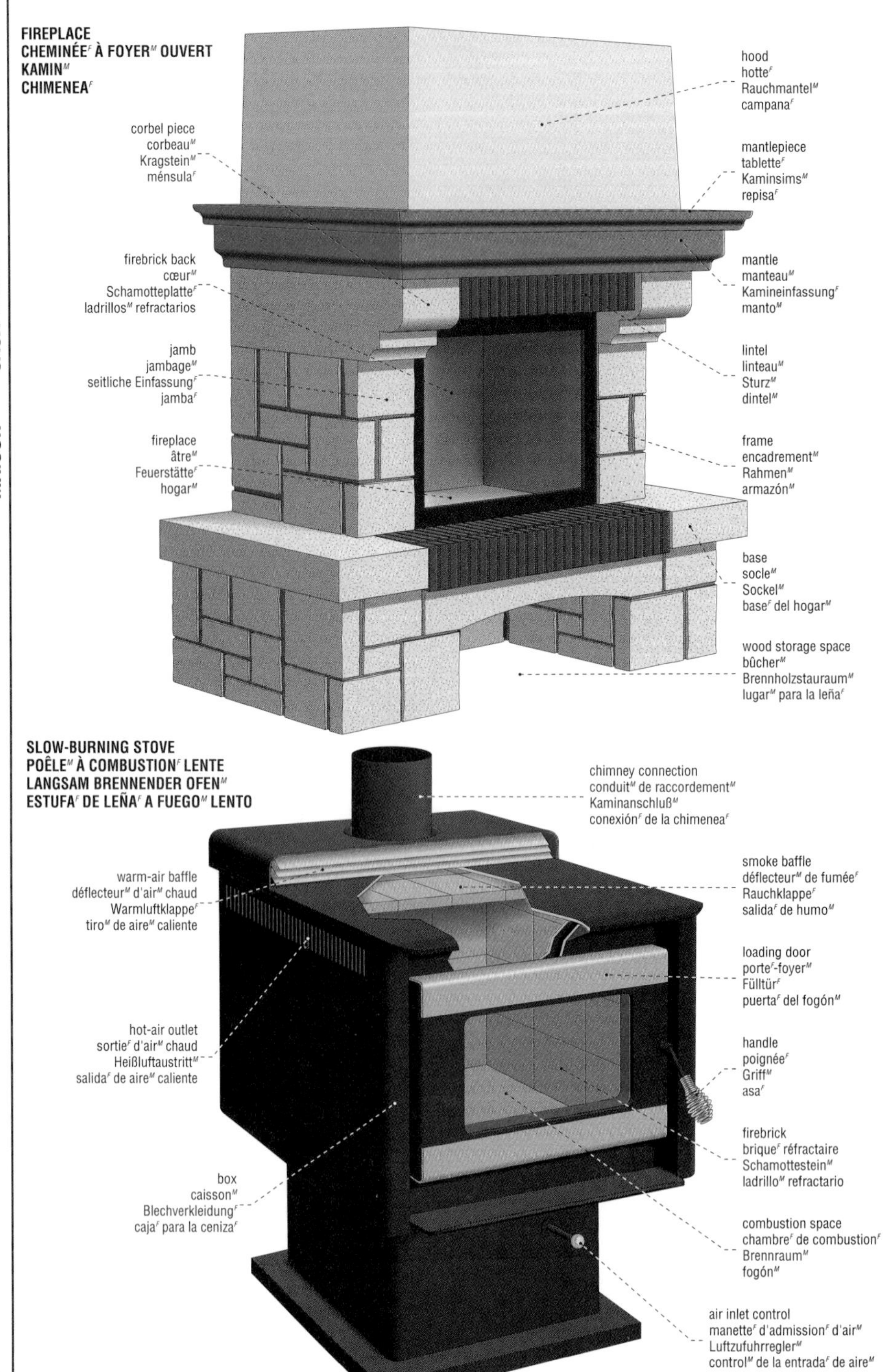


HOUSE MAISON HAUS CASA

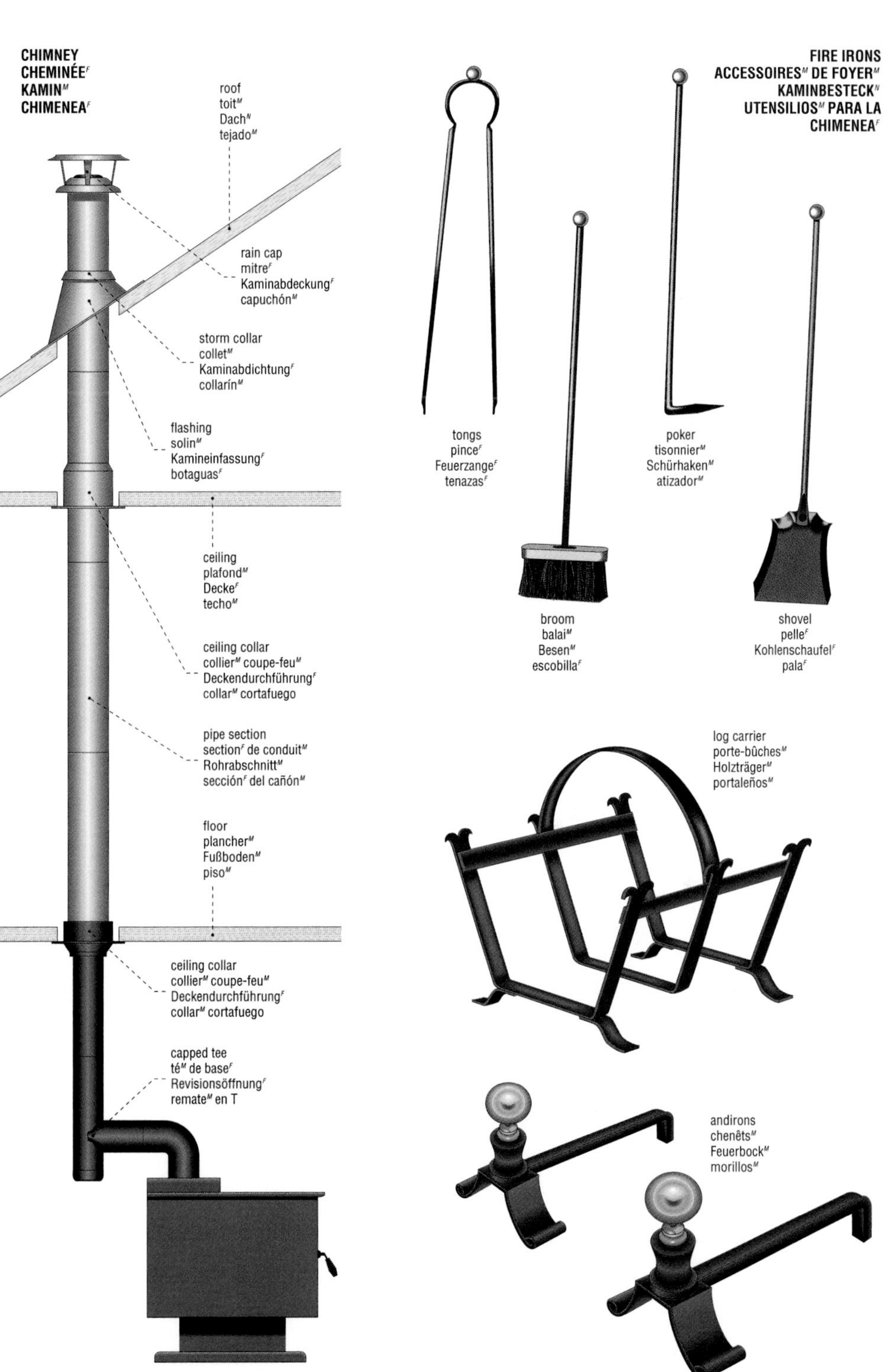


HOUSE MAISON HAUS CASA

# HEATING
# CHAUFFAGE[M]
# HEIZUNG[F]
# CALEFACCIÓN[F]

## FORCED WARM-AIR SYSTEM
## INSTALLATION[F] À AIR[M] CHAUD PULSÉ
## WARMLUFTSYSTEM[N] MIT ZWANGSUMLAUF[M]
## SISTEMA[M] DE AIRE[M] CALIENTE A PRESIÓN[F]

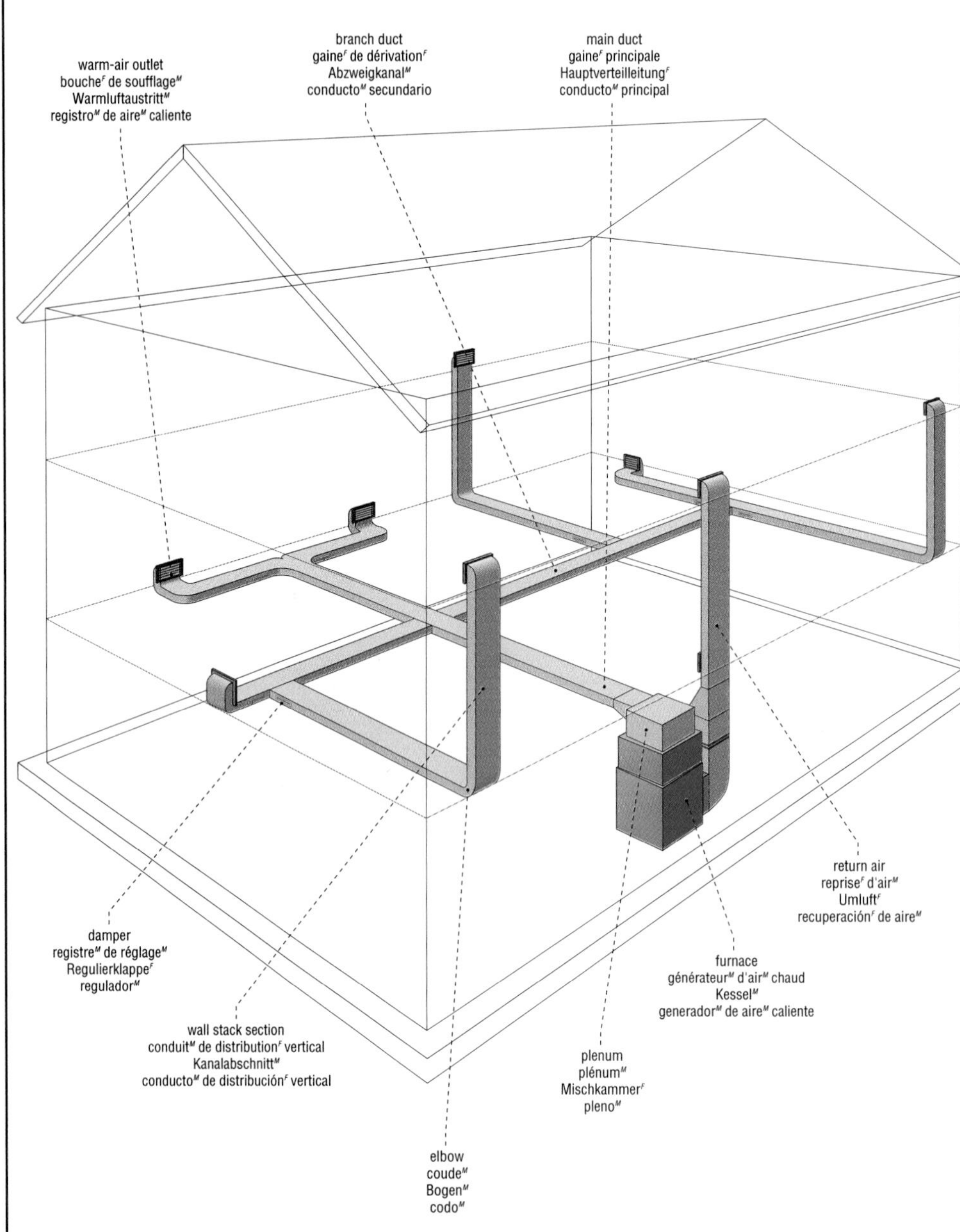

## ELECTRIC FURNACE
## GÉNÉRATEUR$^{M}$ D'AIR$^{M}$ CHAUD ÉLECTRIQUE
## ELEKTRISCHER KESSEL$^{M}$
## CALEFACCIÓN$^{F}$ ELÉCTRICA

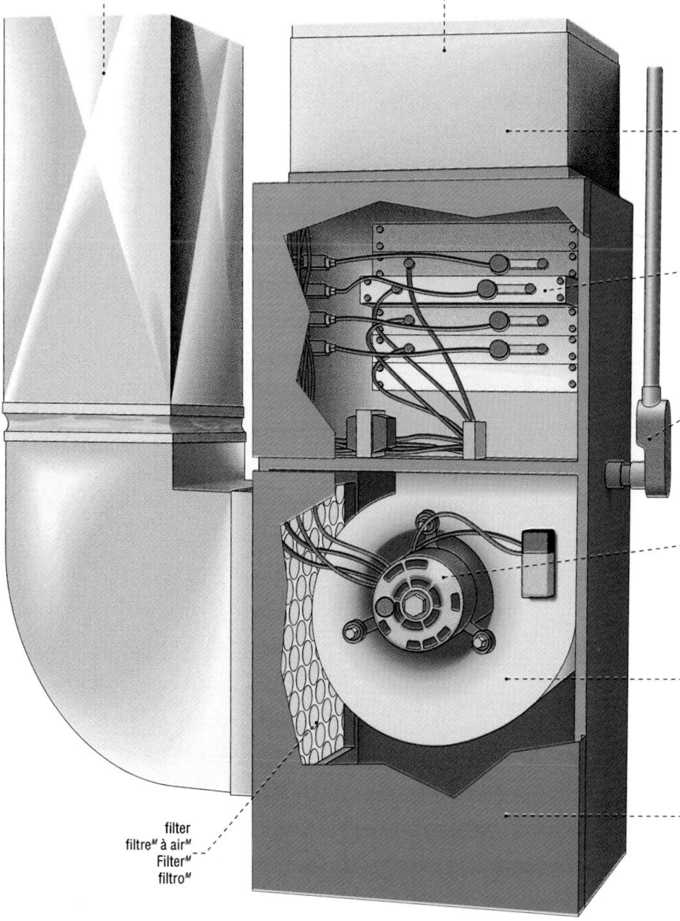

return air
reprise$^{F}$ d'air$^{M}$
Umluft$^{F}$
recuperación$^{F}$ de aire$^{M}$

warm-air outflow
sortie$^{F}$ d'air$^{M}$ chaud
Warmluftaustritt$^{M}$
salida$^{F}$ de aire$^{M}$ caliente

plenum
plénum$^{M}$
Mischkammer$^{F}$
pleno$^{M}$

heating element
élément$^{M}$ de chauffe$^{F}$
Heizelement$^{N}$
elemento$^{M}$ calorífero

mains connection
entrée$^{F}$ électrique
Stromanschluß$^{M}$
conexión$^{F}$ eléctrica

blower motor
moteur$^{M}$
Gebläsemotor$^{M}$
motor$^{M}$ del ventilador$^{M}$

blower
ventilateur$^{M}$
Gebläse$^{N}$
ventilador$^{M}$

access panel
panneau$^{M}$ d'accès$^{M}$
Revisionstür$^{F}$
panel$^{M}$ de acceso$^{M}$

filter
filtre$^{M}$ à air$^{M}$
Filter$^{M}$
filtro$^{M}$

## TYPES OF OUTLET
## TYPES$^{M}$ DE BOUCHES$^{F}$
## LUFTDURCHLÄSSE$^{M}$
## REJILLAS$^{F}$

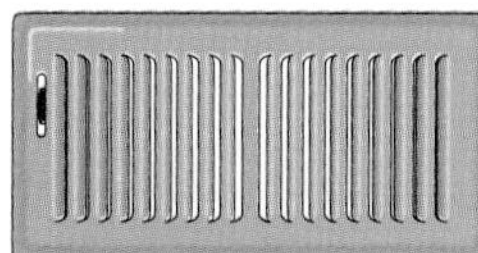

skirting outlet
bouche$^{F}$ de soufflage$^{M}$
Leistendurchlaß$^{M}$
rejilla$^{F}$ de piso$^{M}$

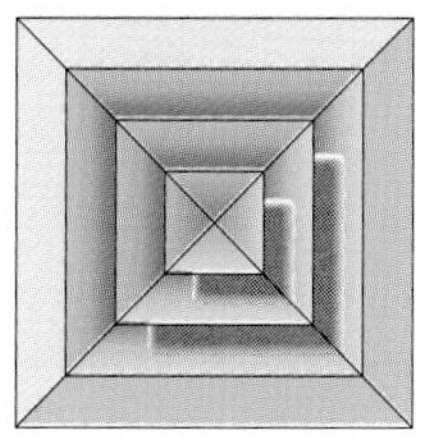

ceiling outlet
bouche$^{F}$ à induction$^{F}$
Deckendurchlaß$^{M}$
rejilla$^{F}$ de techo$^{M}$

wall grille
bouche$^{F}$ d'extraction$^{F}$
Wanddurchlaß$^{M}$
rejilla$^{F}$ de pared$^{F}$

# HEATING
# CHAUFFAGE$^{M}$
# HEIZUNG$^{F}$
# CALEFACCIÓN$^{F}$

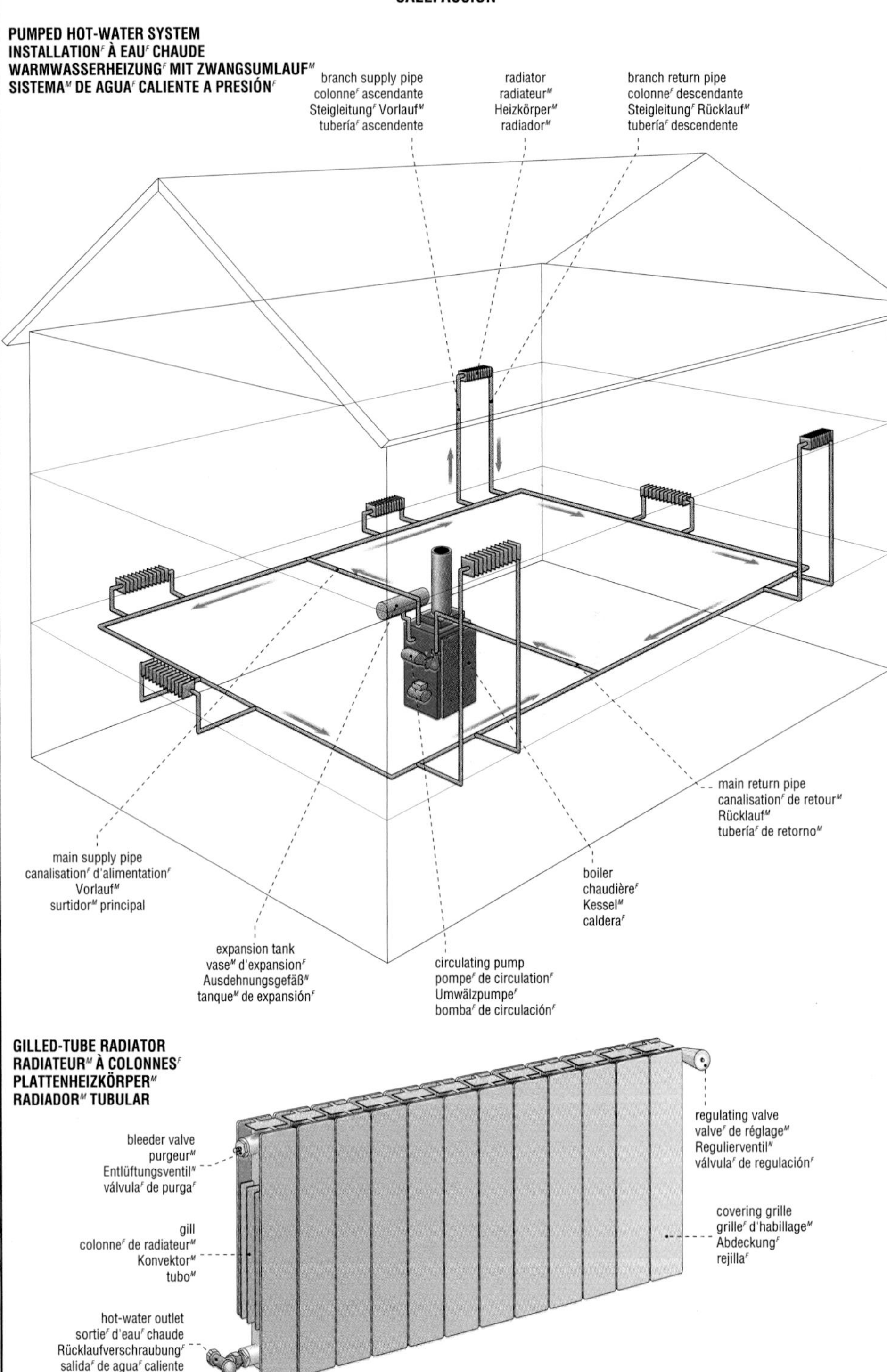

## BOILER
## CHAUDIÈRE[F]
## KESSEL[M]
## CALDERA[F]

## OIL BURNER
## BRÛLEUR[M] À MAZOUT[M]
## ÖLBRENNER[M]
## CALENTADOR[M] DE PETRÓLEO[M]

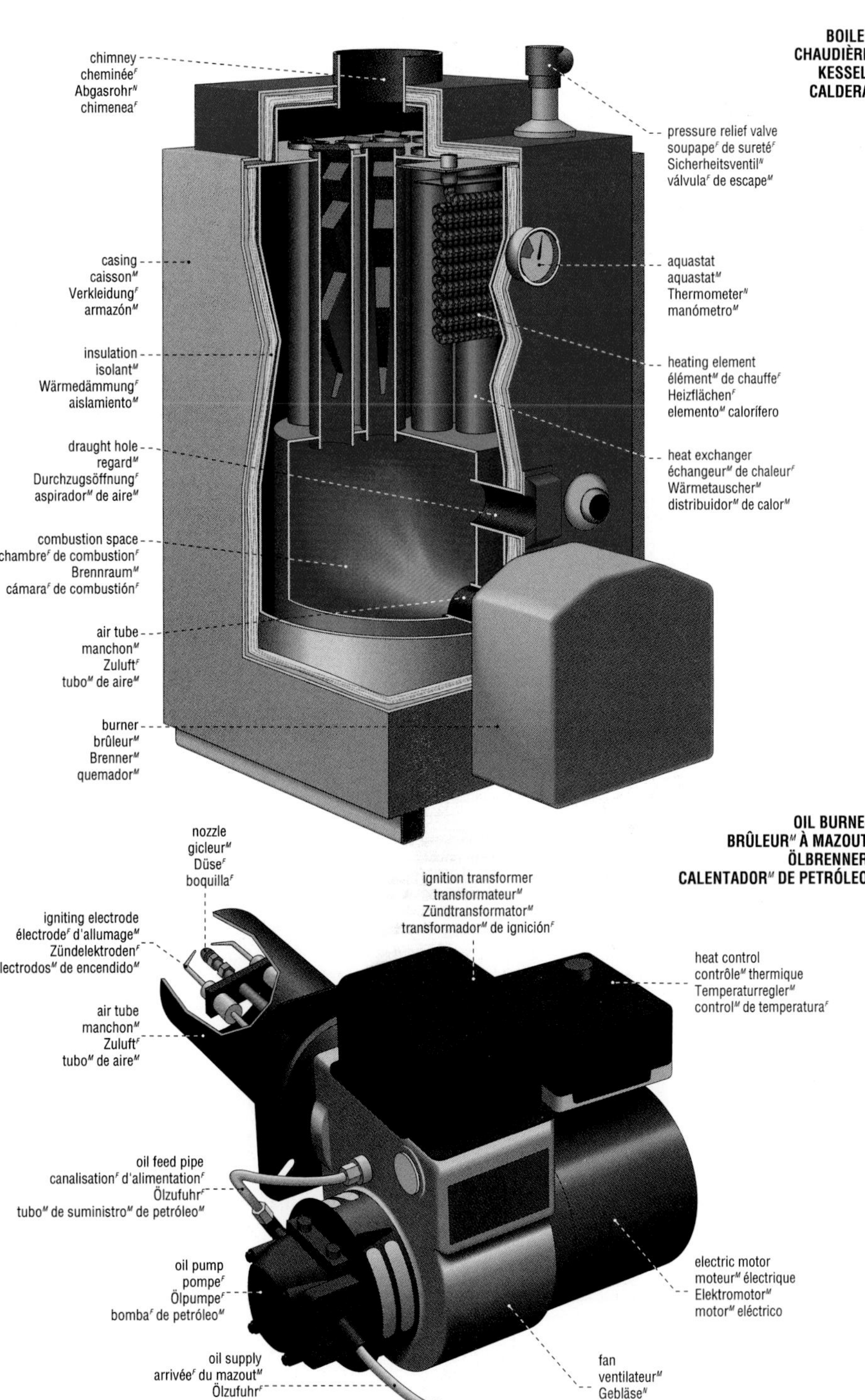

# HEATING
# CHAUFFAGE[M]
# HEIZUNG[F]
# CALEFACCIÓN[F]

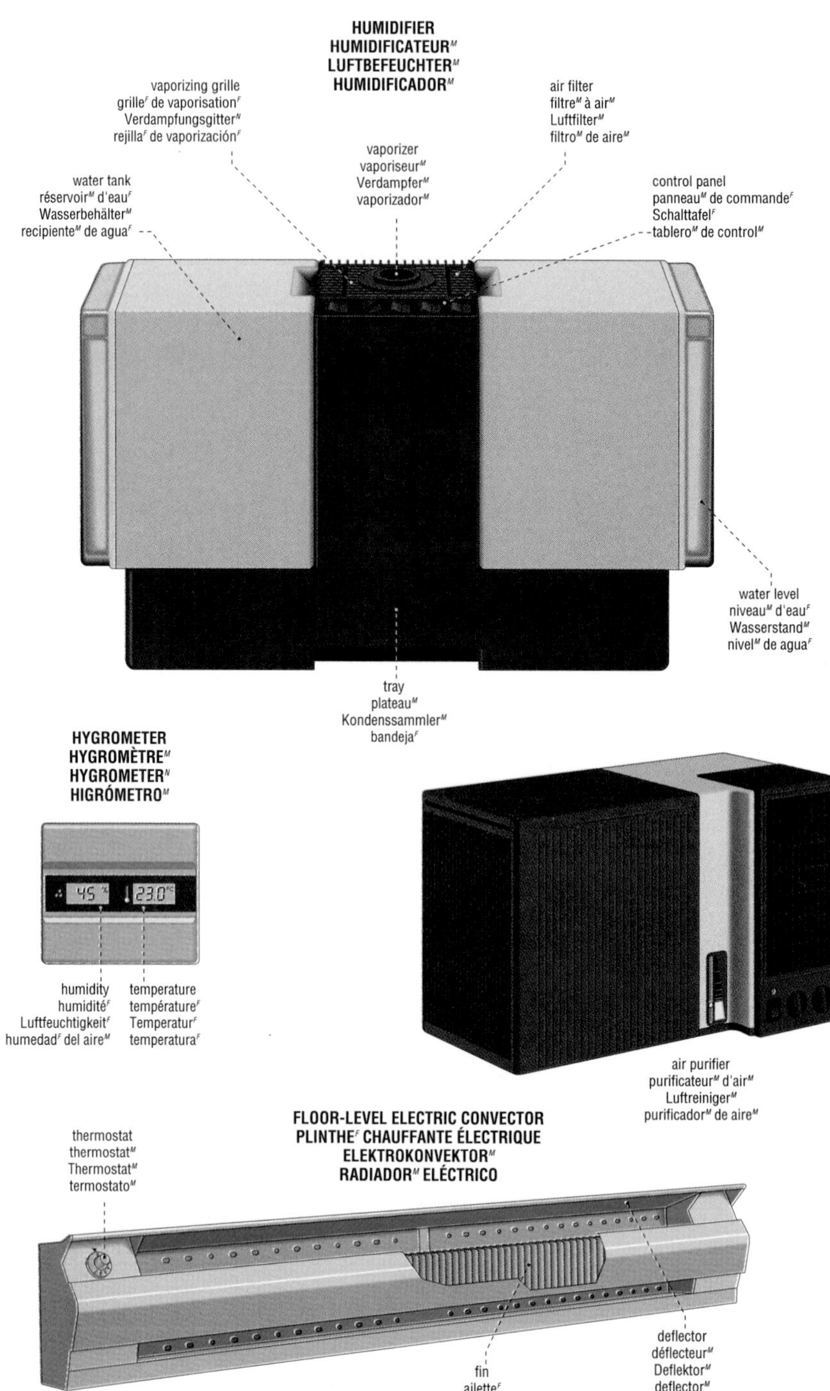

## CONVECTOR HEATER
## CONVECTEUR[M]
## KONVEKTOR[M]
## RADIADOR[M] DE CONVEXIÓN[F]

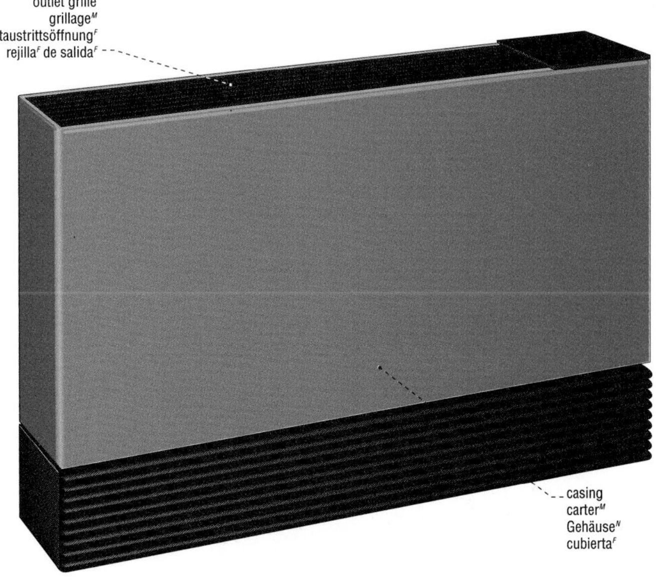


## AUXILIARY HEATING
## CHAUFFAGE[M] D'APPOINT[M]
## ZUSATZHEIZUNG[F]
## CALEFACCIÓN[F] AUXILIAR

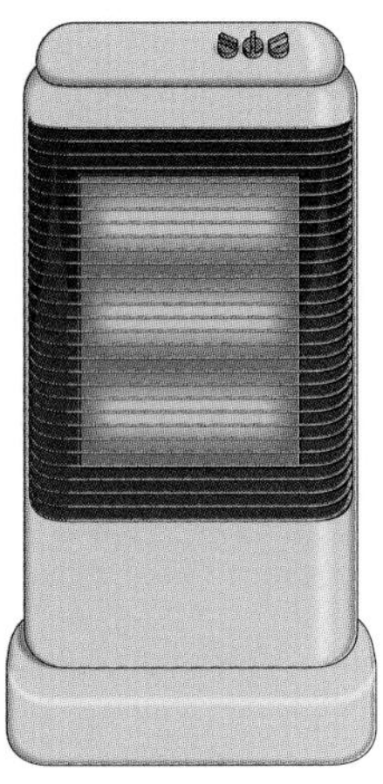

radiant heater
radiateur[M] rayonnant
Heizstrahler[M]
calentador[M] eléctrico

oil-filled radiator
radiateur[M] bain[M] d'huile[F]
ölgefüllter Heizkörper[M]
calentador[M] de aceite[M]

fan heater
radiateur[M] soufflant
Heizlüfter[M]
ventilador[M] de aire[M] caliente

## HEAT PUMP
## POMPE^F À CHALEUR^F
## WÄRMEPUMPE^F
## SISTEMA^M DE BOMBA^F DE CALOR^M

### OUTDOOR UNIT
### MODULE^M EXTÉRIEUR
### ANLAGE^F FÜR AUSSENAUFSTELLUNG^F
### UNIDAD^F EXTERIOR

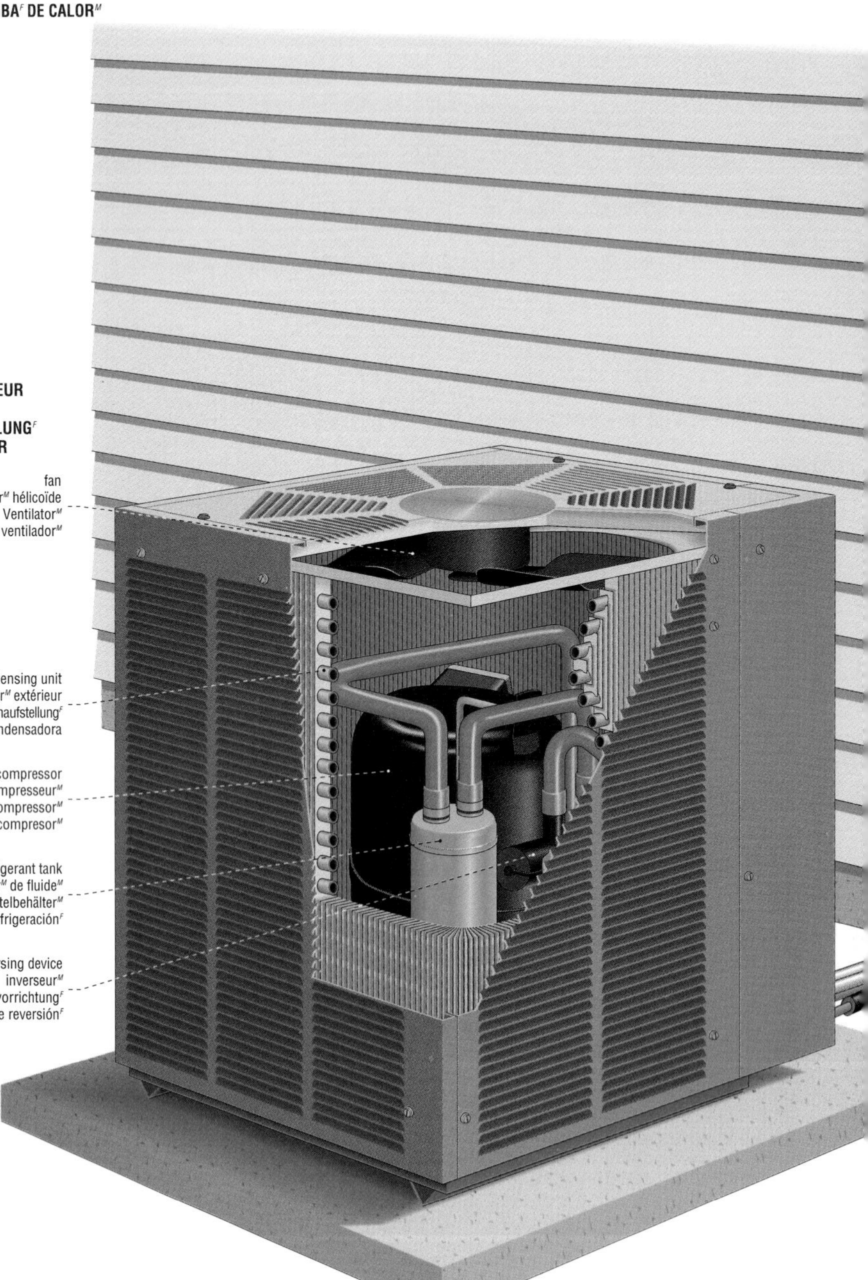

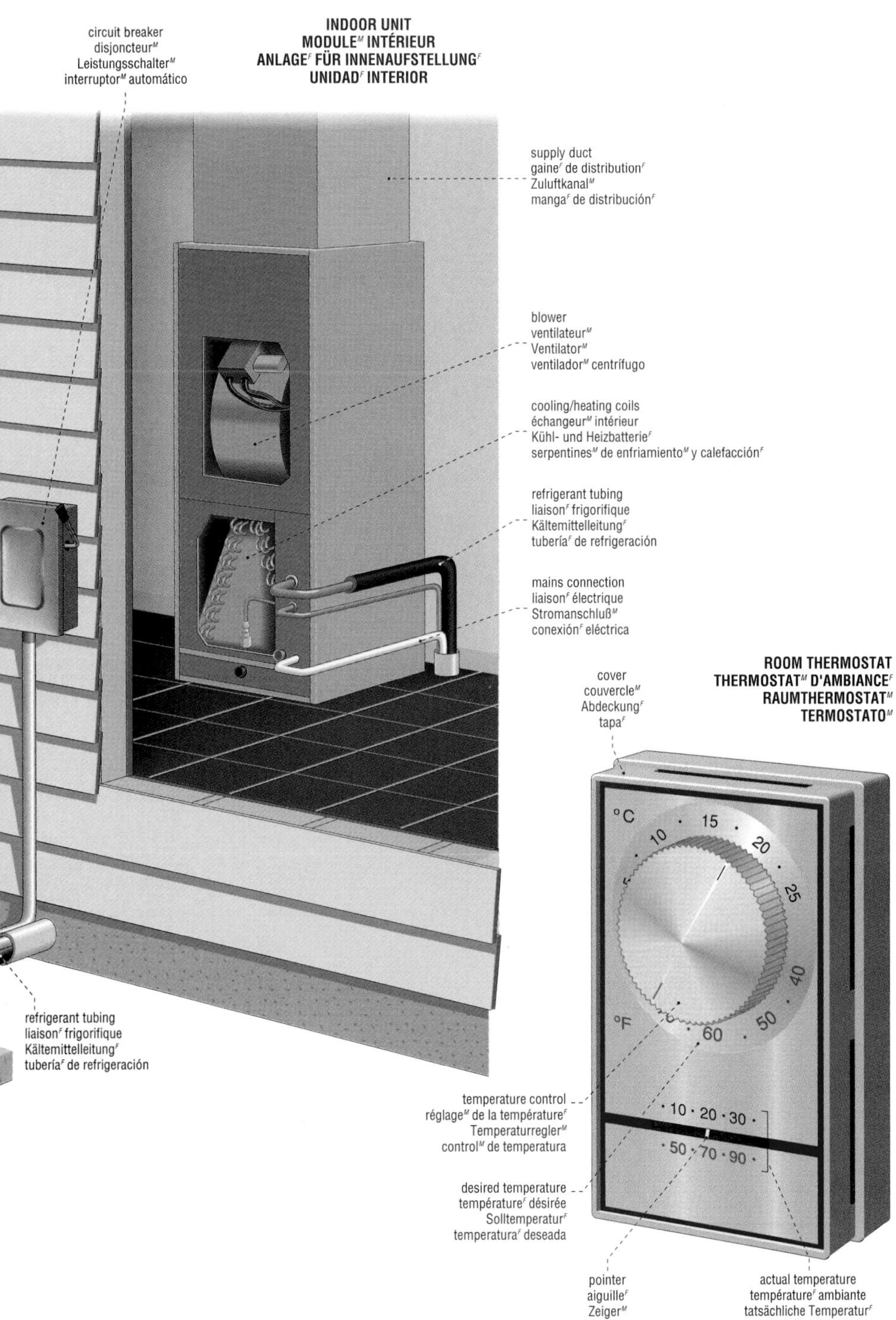

INDOOR UNIT
MODULE^M INTÉRIEUR
ANLAGE^F FÜR INNENAUFSTELLUNG^F
UNIDAD^F INTERIOR
circuit breaker
disjoncteur^M
Leistungsschalter^M
interruptor^M automático
supply duct
gaine^F de distribution^F
Zuluftkanal^M
manga^F de distribución^F
blower
ventilateur^M
Ventilator^M
ventilador^M centrífugo
cooling/heating coils
échangeur^M intérieur
Kühl- und Heizbatterie^F
serpentines^M de enfriamiento^M y calefacción^F
refrigerant tubing
liaison^F frigorifique
Kältemittelleitung^F
tubería^F de refrigeración
mains connection
liaison^F électrique
Stromanschluß^M
conexión^F eléctrica
refrigerant tubing
liaison^F frigorifique
Kältemittelleitung^F
tubería^F de refrigeración
ROOM THERMOSTAT
THERMOSTAT^M D'AMBIANCE^F
RAUMTHERMOSTAT^M
TERMOSTATO^M
cover
couvercle^M
Abdeckung^F
tapa^F
°C
10
15
20
25
°F
60
50
40
10 · 20 · 30
50 · 70 · 90
temperature control
réglage^M de la température^F
Temperaturregler^M
control^M de temperatura
desired temperature
température^F désirée
Solltemperatur^F
temperatura^F deseada
pointer
aiguille^F
Zeiger^M
aguja^F indicadora
actual temperature
température^F ambiante
tatsächliche Temperatur^F
temperatura^F real

# AIR CONDITIONING
# CLIMATISATION[F]
# KLIMAANLAGE[F]
# AIRE[M] ACONDICIONADO

## CEILING FAN
## VENTILATEUR[M] DE PLAFOND[M]
## DECKENVENTILATOR[M]
## VENTILADOR[M] DE TECHO[M]

rod
tige[F]
Stange[F]
flecha[F]

motor
moteur[M]
Motor[M]
motor[M]

blade
pale[F]
Blatt[N]
aspa[F]

## ROOM AIR CONDITIONER
## CLIMATISEUR[M] DE FENÊTRE[F]
## RAUMKLIMAANLAGE[F]
## ACONDICIONADOR[M] DE AIRE[M]

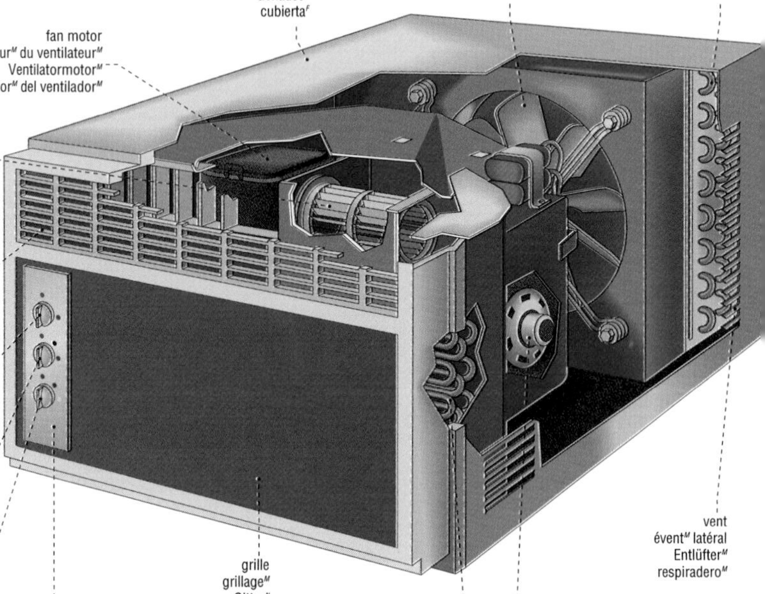

casing
boîtier[M]
Gehäuse[N]
cubierta[F]

condenser fan
ventilateur[M] du condenseur[M]
Ventilator[M]
ventilador[M] del condensador[M]

condenser coil
serpentin[M] du condenseur[M]
Wärmetauscher[M]
serpentín[M] del condensador[M]

fan motor
moteur[M] du ventilateur[M]
Ventilatormotor[M]
motor[M] del ventilador[M]

evaporator blower
ventilateur[M] de l'évaporateur[M]
Gebläse[N]
ventilador[M] del evaporador[M]

louvre
déflecteur[M]
Jalousie[F]
rejilla[F] de ventilación[F]

thermostat
thermostat[M]
Thermostat[M]
termostato[M]

fan control
commande[F] de ventilateur[M]
Ventilatorregler[M]
control[M] del ventilador[M]

function selector
sélecteur[M]
Funktionswähler[M]
selector[M]

vent
évent[M] latéral
Entlüfter[M]
respiradero[M]

grille
grillage[M]
Gitter[N]
rejilla[F]

control panel
tableau[M] de commande[F]
Schalttafel[F]
tablero[M] de control[M]

evaporator coils
serpentin[M] de l'évaporateur[M]
Verdampferschlangen[F]
serpentines[M] del evaporador[M]

blower motor
moteur[M] du ventilateur[M]
Ventilatormotor[M]
motor[M] del ventilador[M]

# PLUMBING SYSTEM
# CIRCUIT[M] DE PLOMBERIE[F]
# SANITÄRINSTALLATIONSSYSTEM[N]
# CAÑERÍAS[F]

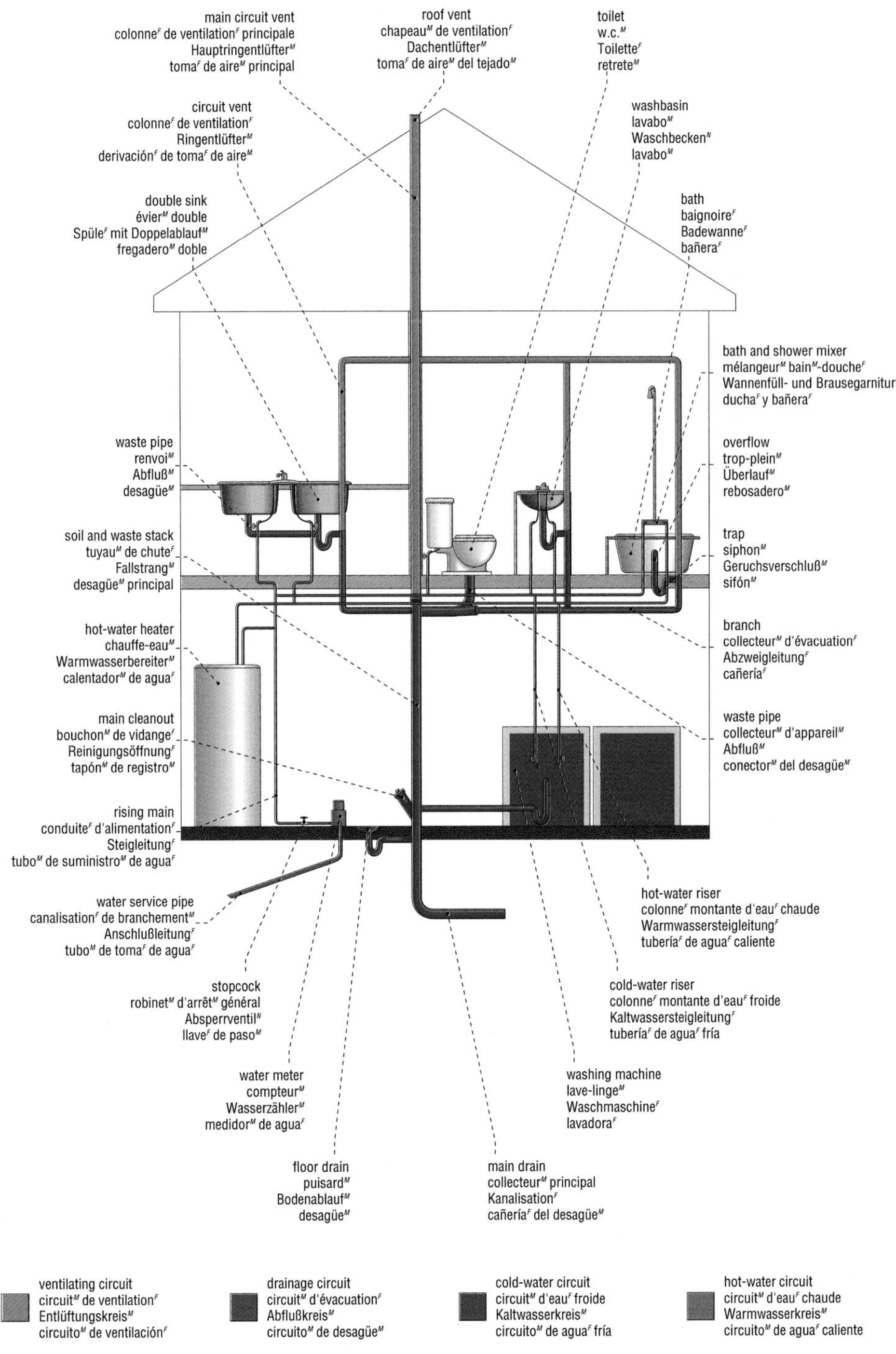

## PEDESTAL-TYPE CESSPIT PUMP
## POMPE[F] DE PUISARD[M]
## SCHMUTZWASSERHEBEANLAGE[F]
## BOMBA[F] TIPO[M] PEDESTAL[M] PARA SUMIDERO[M]

on-off switch
contacteur[M]
Ein-/Ausschalter[M]
interruptor[M] de arranque[M] automático
pump motor
moteur[M] électrique
Pumpenmotor[M]
motor[M] de la bomba[F]
check valve
clapet[M] de retenue[F]
Rückschlagventil[N]
válvula[F] de control[M]
waterproofed electricity supply
prise[F] avec borne[F] de terre[F]
wasserbeständiger Stromanschluß[M]
contacto[M] con conexión[F] a tierra[F]
discharge pipe
canalisation[F] de refoulement[M]
Auslaufleitung[F]
tubo[M] de salida[F]
float clamp
étrier[M] du flotteur[M]
Rohrschelle[F]
anillo[M] de retención[F]
float
flotteur[M]
Schwimmer[M]
flotador[M]
cesspit
puisard[M]
Pumpensumpf[M]
sumidero[M]
gravel
gravier[M]
Kies[M]
grava[F]
pump suction head
tête[F] d'aspiration[F]
Ansaugstutzen[M]
culata[F] de succión[F]

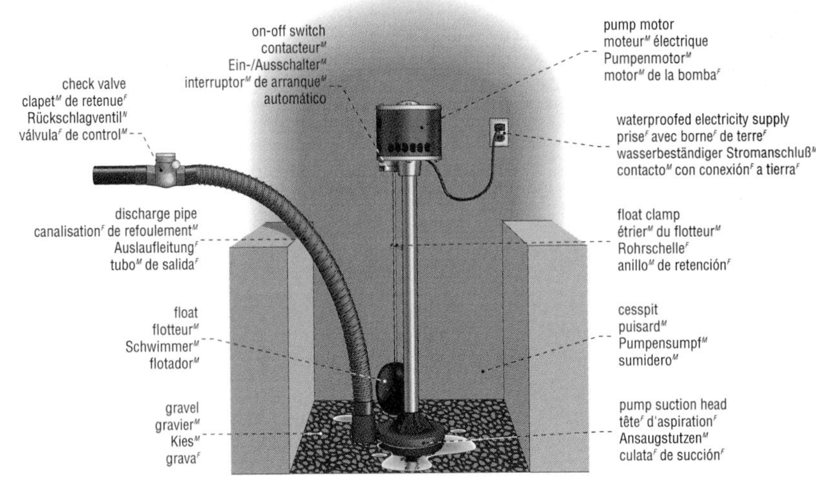

## SEPTIC TANK
## FOSSE[F] SEPTIQUE
## VERSITZGRUBE[F]
## FOSA[F] SÉPTICA

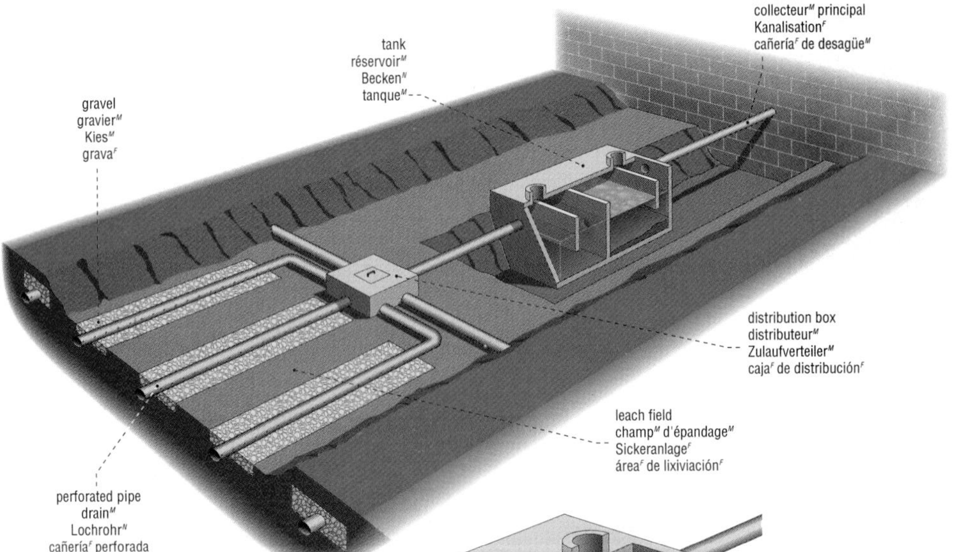

main drain
collecteur[M] principal
Kanalisation[F]
cañería[F] de desagüe[M]
tank
réservoir[M]
Becken[N]
tanque[M]
gravel
gravier[M]
Kies[M]
grava[F]
distribution box
distributeur[M]
Zulaufverteiler[M]
caja[F] de distribución[F]
leach field
champ[M] d'épandage[M]
Sickeranlage[F]
área[F] de lixiviación[F]
perforated pipe
drain[M]
Lochrohr[N]
cañería[F] perforada

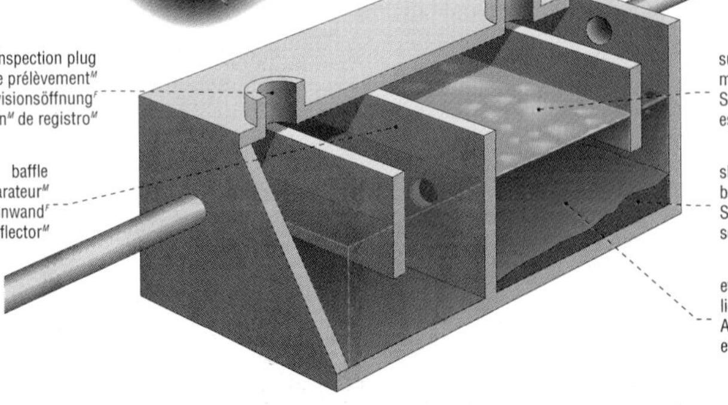

inspection plug
regard[M] de prélèvement[M]
Revisionsöffnung[F]
tapón[M] de registro[M]
surface scum
mousse[F] graisseuse
Schwimmschlamm[M]
espuma[F]
baffle
séparateur[M]
Trennwand[F]
deflector[M]
sludge
boue[F]
Sinkschlamm[M]
sedimento[M]
effluent
liquide[F]
Abwasser[N]
efluvio[M]

# HOUSE FURNITURE
# AMEUBLEMENT DE LA MAISON
# HAUSEINRICHTUNG
# ENSERES DOMÉSTICOS

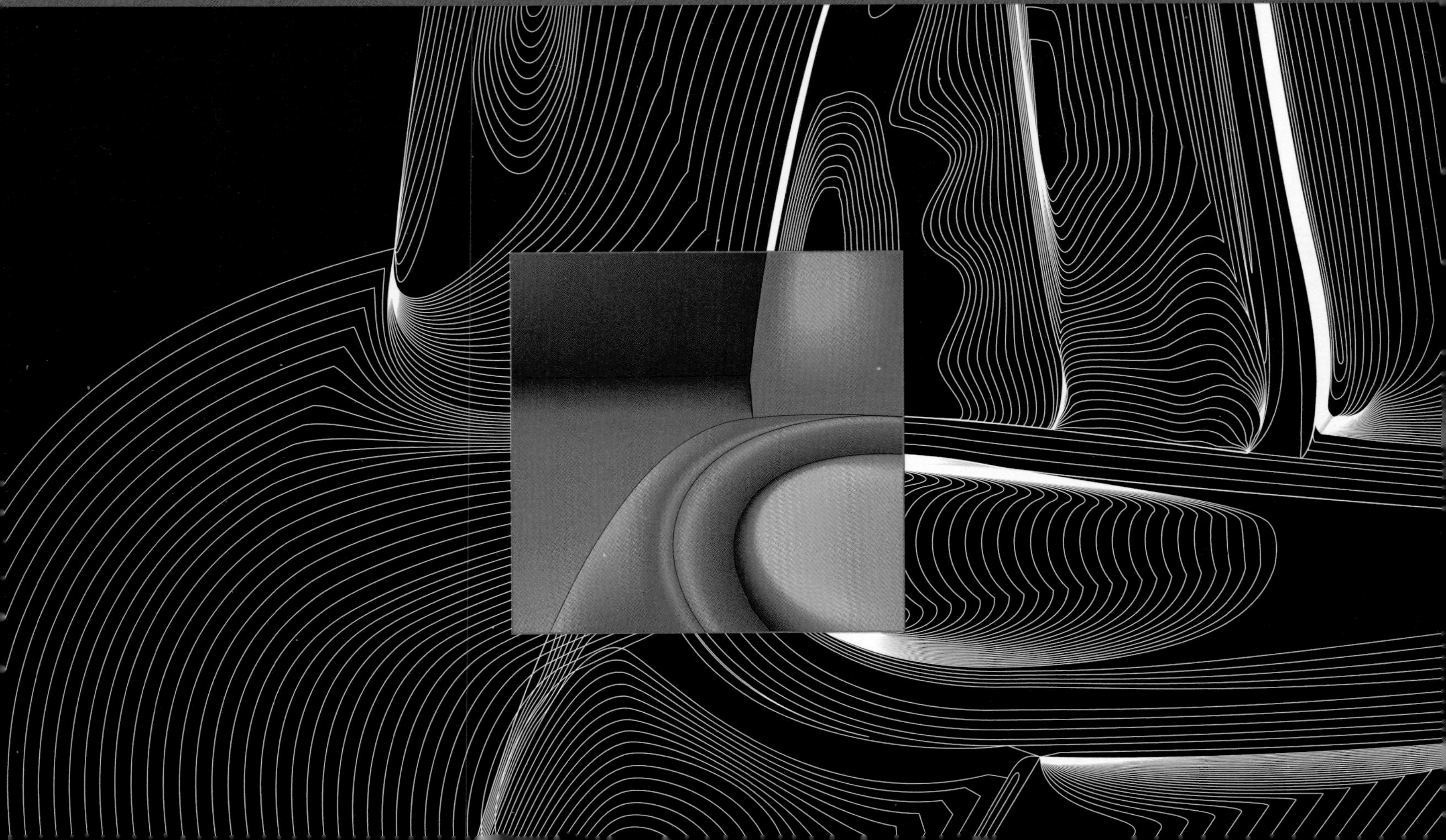

## SUMMARY

# TABLE
# TABLE^F
# TISCH^M
# MESA^F

## GATE-LEG TABLE
## TABLE^F À ABATTANTS^M
## KLAPPTISCH^M
## MESA^F DE HOJAS^F ABATIBLES

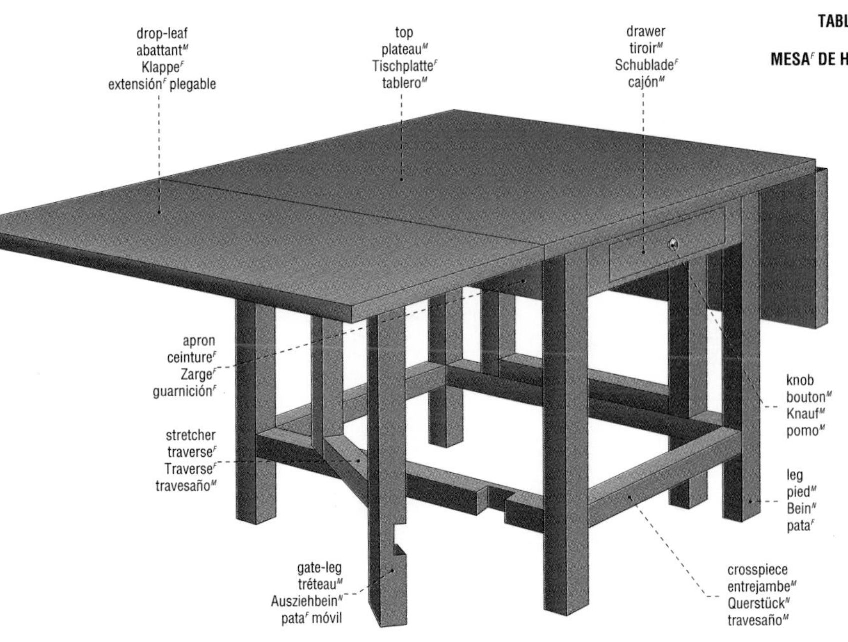


## PRINCIPAL TYPES OF TABLE
## PRINCIPAUX TYPES^M DE TABLES^F
## DIE WICHTIGSTEN TISCHTYPEN^M
## TIPOS^M DE MESAS^F

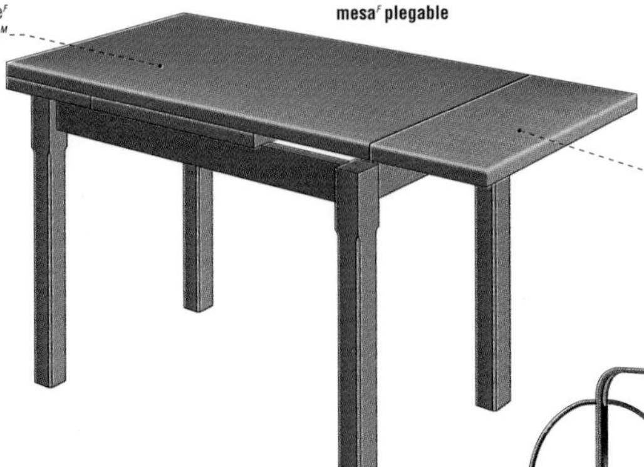

**extending table**
**table^F à rallonges^F**
**Ausziehtisch^M**
**mesa^F plegable**

top
plateau^M
Tischplatte^F
tablero^M

extension
rallonge^F
Auszug^M
extensión^F

serving trolley
desserte^F
Servierwagen^M
mesita^F de servicio^M

nest of tables
tables^F gigognes
Satztische^M
juego^M de mesas^F

# ARMCHAIR
# FAUTEUIL$^{M}$
# ARMLEHNSTUHL$^{M}$
# SILLA$^{F}$ DE BRAZOS$^{M}$

bergère
bergère$^{F}$
Bergère$^{F}$
silla$^{F}$ poltrona

cabriole chair
cabriolet$^{M}$
kleiner Lehnstuhl$^{M}$
silla$^{F}$ cabriolé

director's chair
fauteuil$^{M}$ metteur$^{M}$ en scène$^{F}$
Regiestuhl$^{M}$
silla$^{F}$ plegable de lona$^{F}$

sofa
canapé[M]
Sofa[N]
sofá[F]

two-seater settee
causeuse[F]
Zweisitzer[M]
confidente[M]

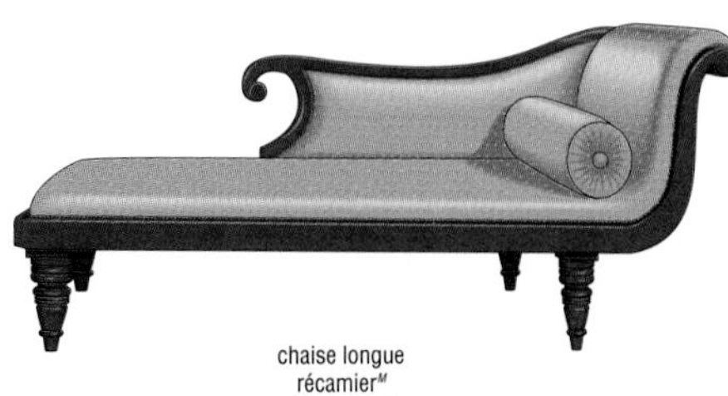

chaise longue
récamier[M]
Récamiere[F]
sofá[M] tipo[M] imperio

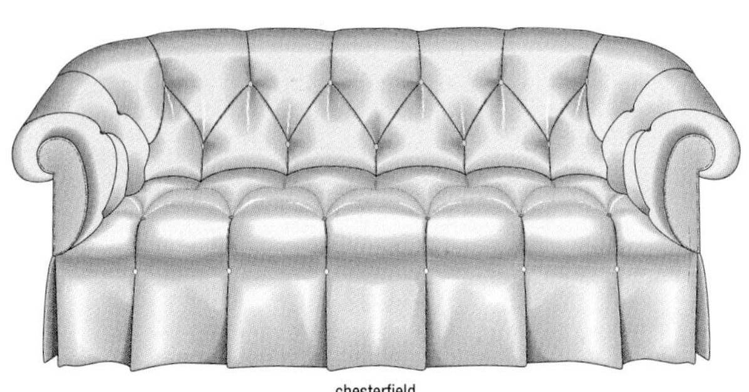

chesterfield
canapé[M] capitonné
Polstersofa[N]
chesterfield[M]

méridienne
méridienne[F]
Kanapee[N]
meridiana[F]

Wassily chair
fauteuil[M] Wassily
Wassily-Stuhl[M]
silla[F] Wassily

rocking chair
berceuse[F]
Schaukelstuhl[M]
mecedora[F]

club chair
fauteuil[M] club[M]
Clubsessel[M]
butaca[F]

# SEATS
# SIÈGES[M]
# SITZMÖBEL[N]
# ASIENTOS[M]

## SIDE CHAIR
## CHAISE[F]
## STUHL[M]
## SILLA[F] SIN BRAZOS[M]

recliner
chaise[F] longue
Liegestuhl[M]
tumbona[F]

stacking chairs
chaises[F] empilables
Stapelstühle[M]
sillas[F] apilables

rocking chair
chaise[F] berçante
Schaukelstuhl[M]
mecedora[F]

folding chair
chaise[F] pliante
Klappstuhl[M]
silla[F] plegable

# BED
# LIT$^{M}$
# BETT$^{N}$
# CAMA$^{F}$

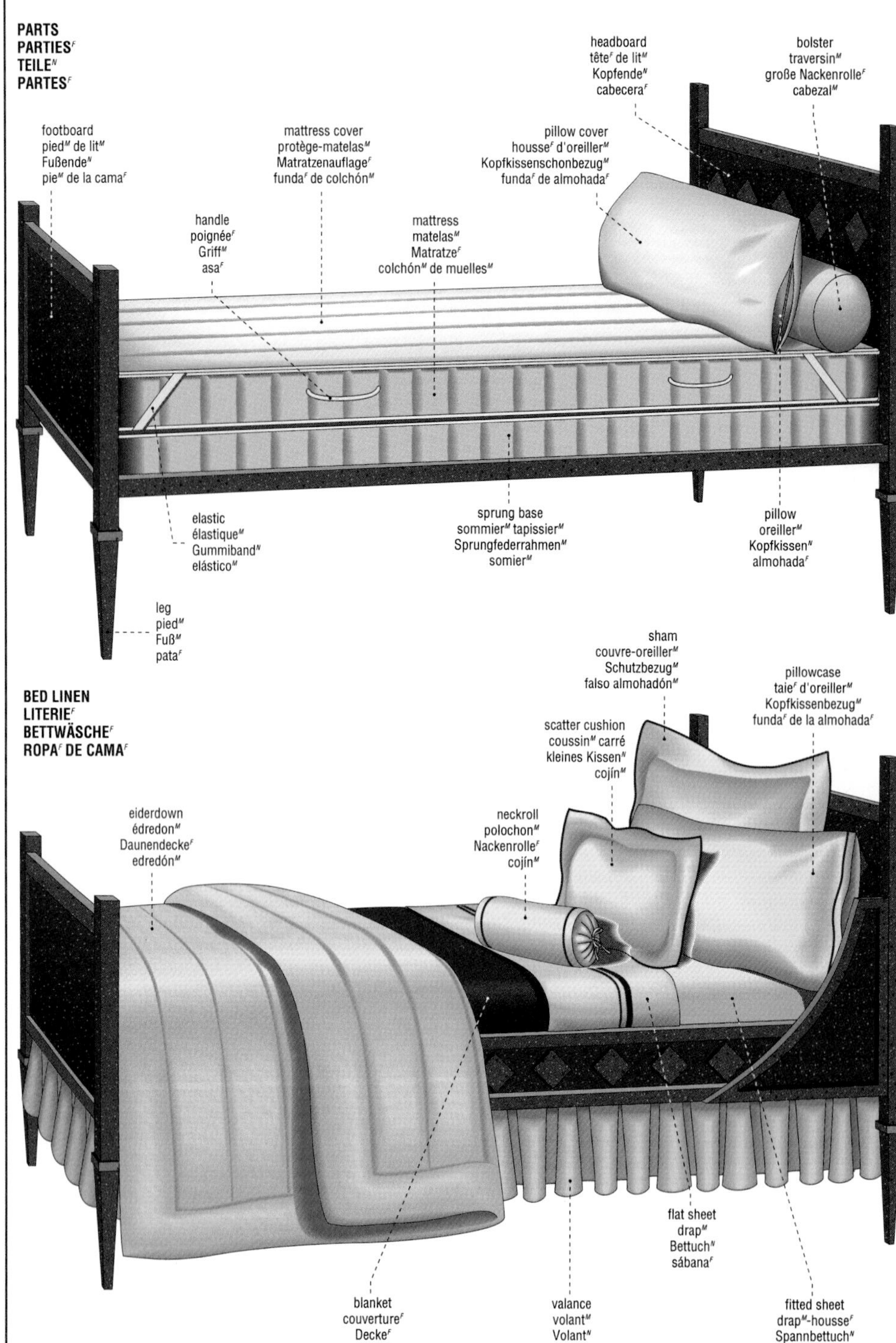

# STORAGE FURNITURE
# MEUBLES[M] DE RANGEMENT[M]
# AUFBEWAHRUNGSMÖBEL[N]
# ARMARIOS[M] Y GABINETES[M]

## ARMOIRE
## ARMOIRE[F]
## KLEIDERSCHRANK[M]
## ARMARIO[M]

# STORAGE FURNITURE
# MEUBLES[M] DE RANGEMENT[M]
# AUFBEWAHRUNGSMÖBEL[N]
# ARMARIOS[M] Y GABINETES[M]

linen chest
coffre[M]
Truhe[F]
baúl[M]

dressing table
commode[F]
Kommode[F]
tocador[M]

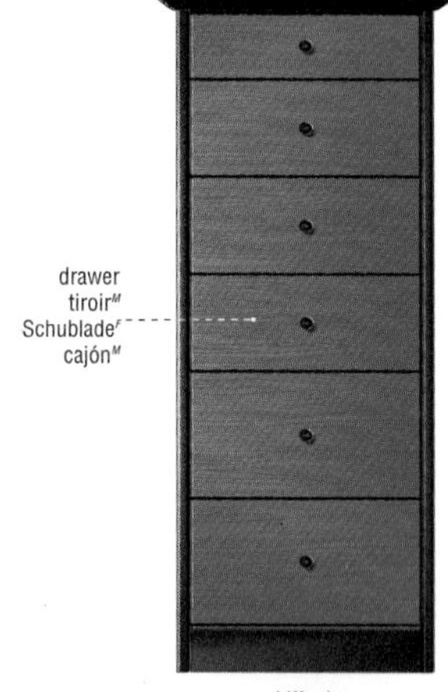


chiffonier
chiffonnier[M]
Chiffoniere[F]
chifonier[M]

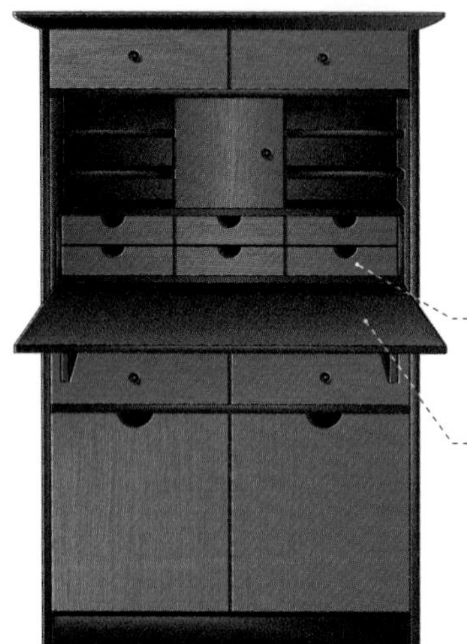


bureau
secrétaire[M]
Sekretär[M]
bufete[M]

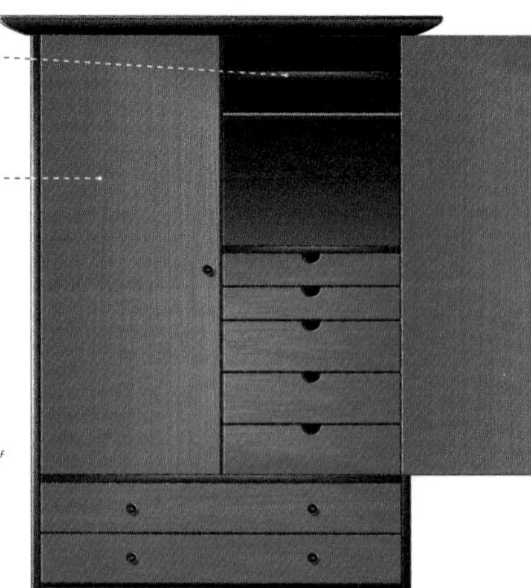


wardrobe
armoire[F]-penderie[F]
Kleiderschrank[M]
ropero[M]

cocktail cabinet
bar$^{M}$
Cocktailbar$^{F}$
mueble$^{M}$ bar$^{M}$

display cabinet
vitrine$^{F}$
Vitrine$^{F}$
vitrina$^{F}$

glass-fronted display cabinet
buffet$^{M}$-vaisselier$^{M}$
Vitrinenschrank$^{M}$
armario$^{M}$ de vajilla$^{F}$

corner cupboard
encoignure$^{F}$
Eckschrank$^{M}$
rinconera$^{F}$

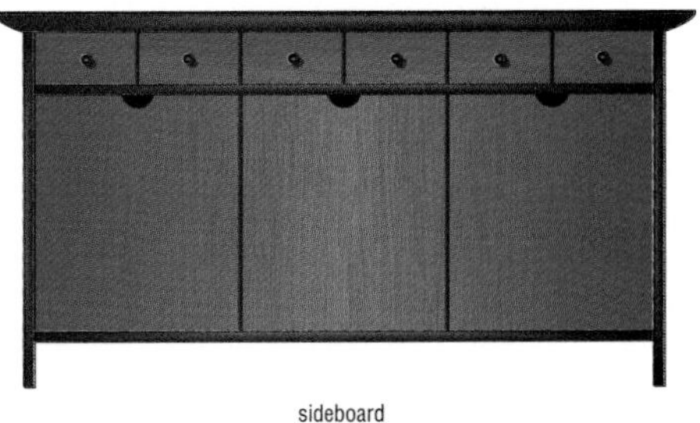

sideboard
buffet$^{M}$
Büfett$^{N}$
aparador$^{M}$

# WINDOW ACCESSORIES
# PARURES[F] DE FENÊTRE[F]
# DEKORATIONEN[F]
# ACCESORIOS[M] PARA LAS VENTANAS[F]

## TYPES OF CURTAIN
## TYPES[M] DE RIDEAUX[M]
## GARDINENTYPEN[M]
## TIPOS[M] DE CORTINAS[F]

### WINDOW CURTAIN
### RIDEAU[M] DE VITRAGE[M]
### SCHEIBENGARDINE[F]
### CORTINA[F] DE VENTANA[F]

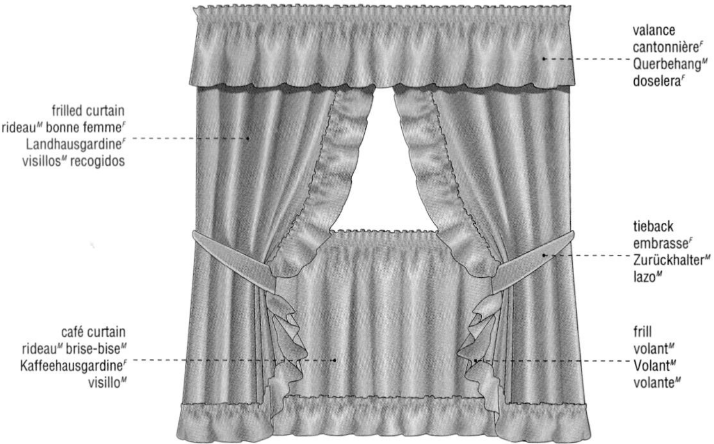


### ATTACHED CURTAIN
### RIDEAU[M] COULISSÉ
### SPANNER[M]
### CORTINA[F] SUJETA DE DOBLE BARRA[F]

### LOOSE CURTAIN
### RIDEAU[M] FLOTTANT
### LOSER VORHANG[M]
### CORTINA[F] SUELTA CORREDIZA

## TYPES OF PLEAT
## TYPES[M] DE PLIS[M]
## FALTENARTEN[F]
## TIPOS[M] DE CENEFAS[F]

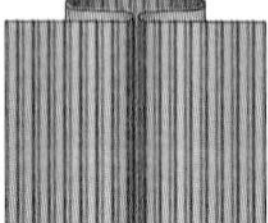

box pleat
pli[M] creux
Schachtelfalte[F]
pliegue[M] de cajón[M]

pinch pleat
pli[M] pincé
Kirsorfalte[F]
pliegue[M] de pinza[F]

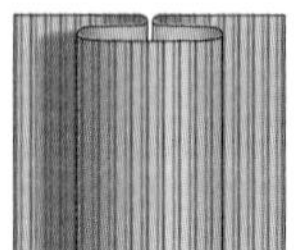

inverted pleat
pli[M] rond
eingelegte Falte[F]
pliegue[M] de cajón[M] invertido

## CURTAIN
## RIDEAU[M]
## VORHANG[M]
## CORTINA[F]

## BALLOON CURTAIN
## RIDEAU[M] BALLON[M]
## BALLONVORHANG[M]
## CORTINA[F] ABOMBADA

## CRISSCROSS CURTAINS
## RIDEAUX[M] CROISÉS
## RAFFGARDINE[F]
## CORTINAS[F] CRUZADAS

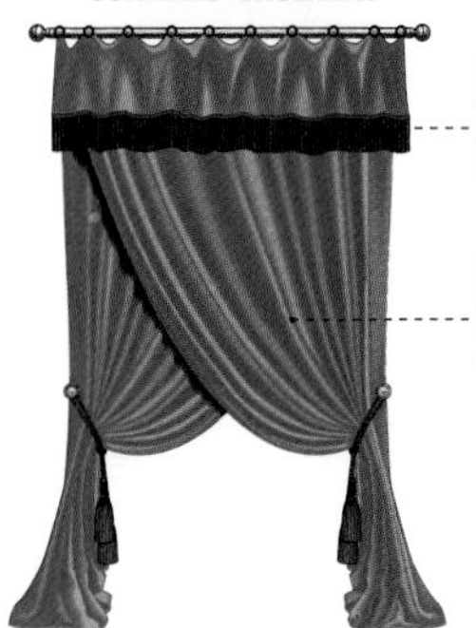


## TYPES OF HEADING
## TYPES[M] DE TÊTES[F]
## KÖPFCHENTYPEN[M]
## TIPOS[M] DE DOSELES[M]

draped swag
cantonnière[F] drapée
Freihand-Dekoration[F]
festón[M] colgado

pencil-pleated heading
fronçage[M] tuyauté
Bleistiftband[N]
dosel[M] plisado de canotillo[M]

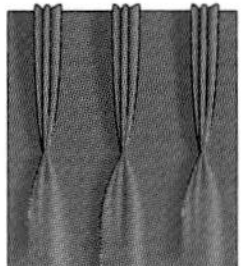

pinch-pleated heading
tête[F] plissée
Kirschband[N]
dosel[M] plisado

shirred heading
tête[F] froncée
Durchzug[M]
dosel[M] fruncido

# WINDOW ACCESSORIES
# PARURES^F DE FENÊTRE^F
# FENSTERZUBEHÖR^N
# ACCESORIOS^M PARA LAS VENTANAS^F

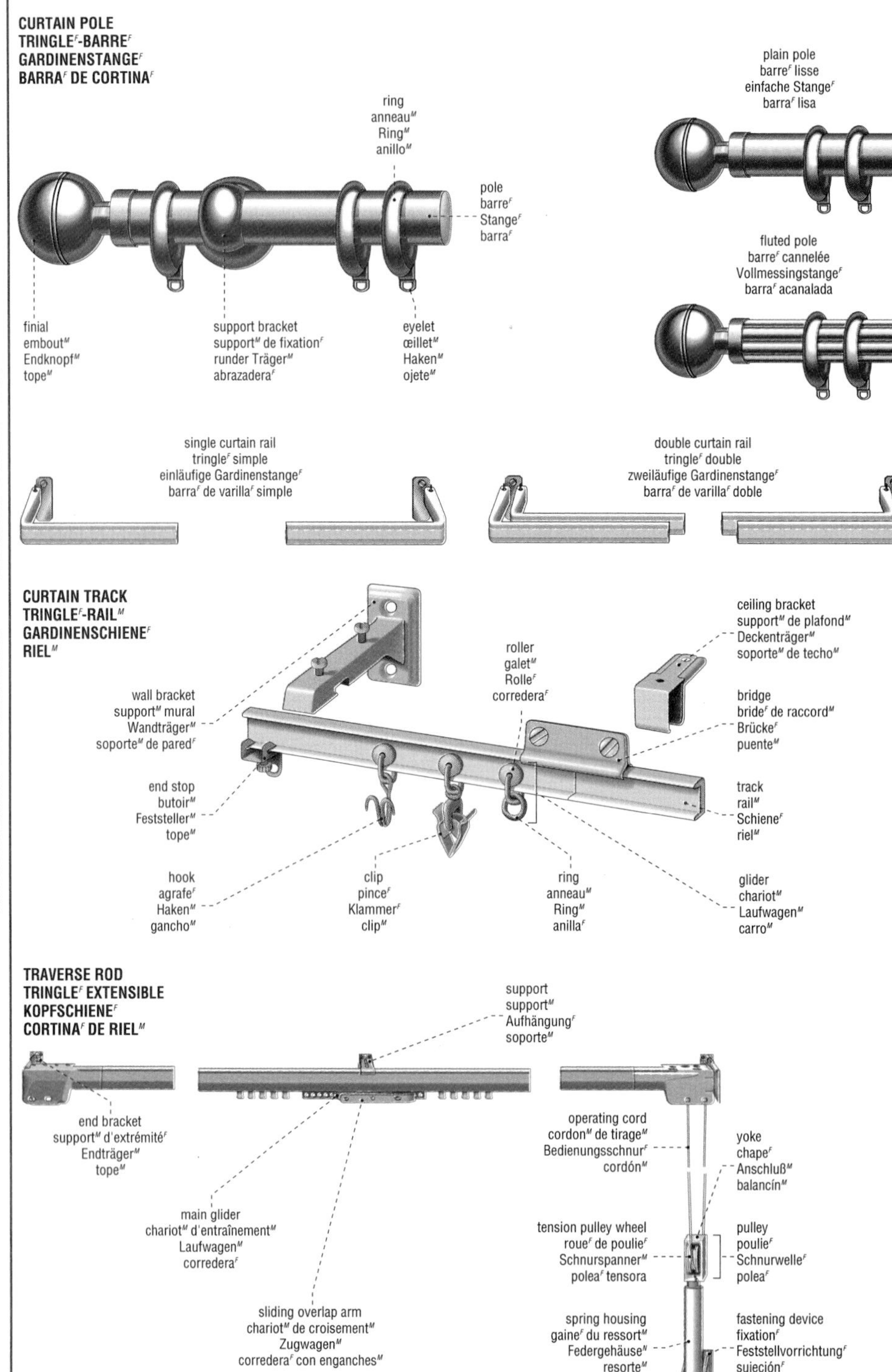

## ROLLER BLIND
## STORE$^{M}$ À ENROULEMENT$^{M}$ AUTOMATIQUE
## ROLLO$^{N}$
## PERSIANA$^{F}$ ENROLLABLE AUTOMÁTICA

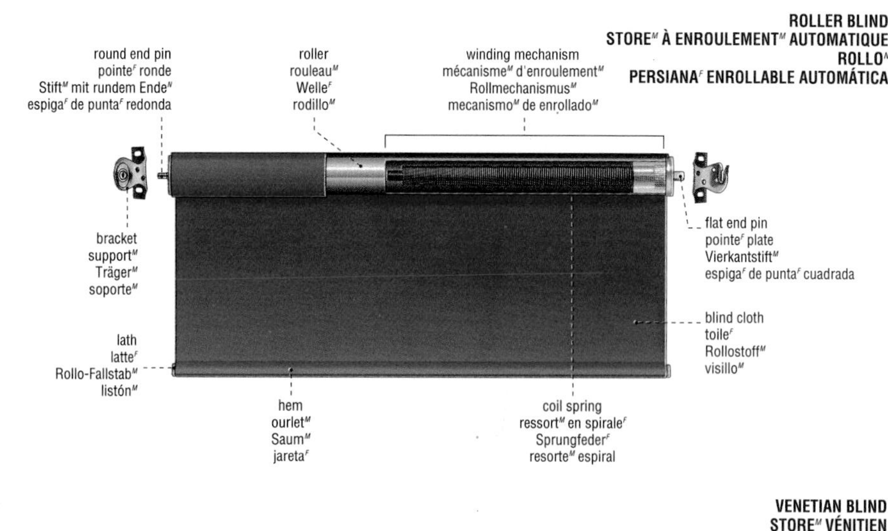


## VENETIAN BLIND
## STORE$^{M}$ VÉNITIEN
## JALOUSIE$^{F}$
## PERSIANA$^{F}$ VENECIANA

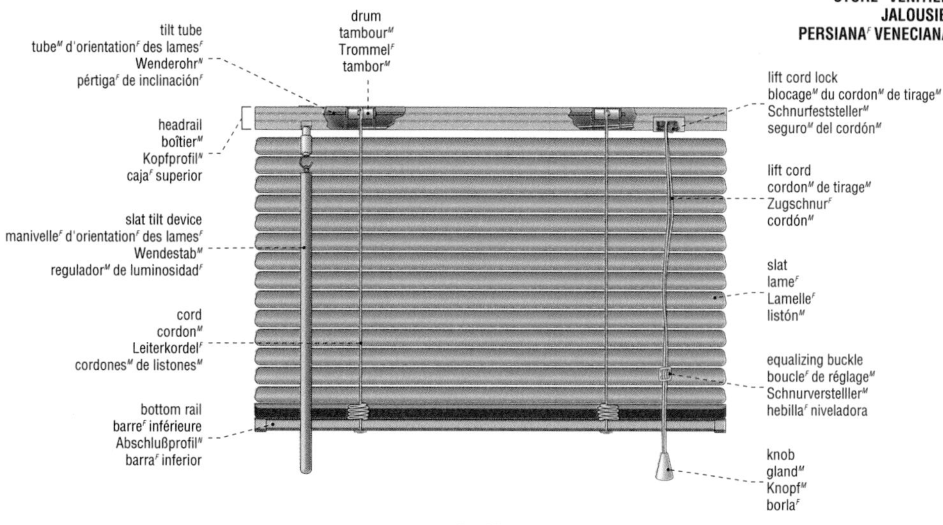


Roman blind
store$^{M}$ bateau$^{M}$
Raffrollo$^{N}$
persianas$^{F}$ romana

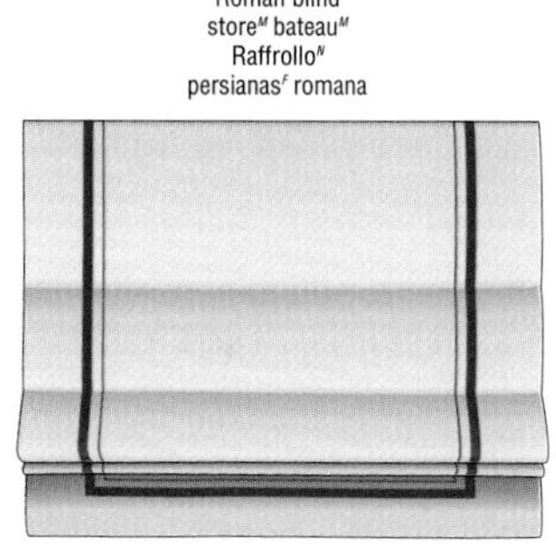

roll-up blind
store$^{M}$ à enroulement$^{M}$ manuel
Stäbchenrollo$^{N}$
persiana$^{F}$ enrollable

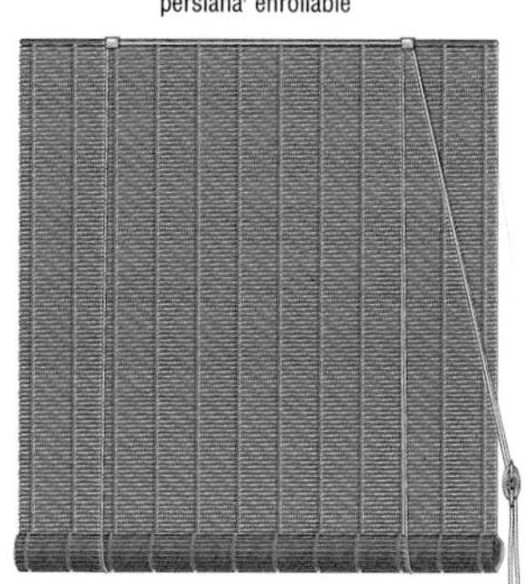

indoor shutters
volets$^{M}$ d'intérieur$^{M}$
Innenläden$^{M}$
postigos$^{M}$ interiores

# LIGHTS
# LUMINAIRES[M]
# LAMPEN[F]
# LÁMPARAS[F]

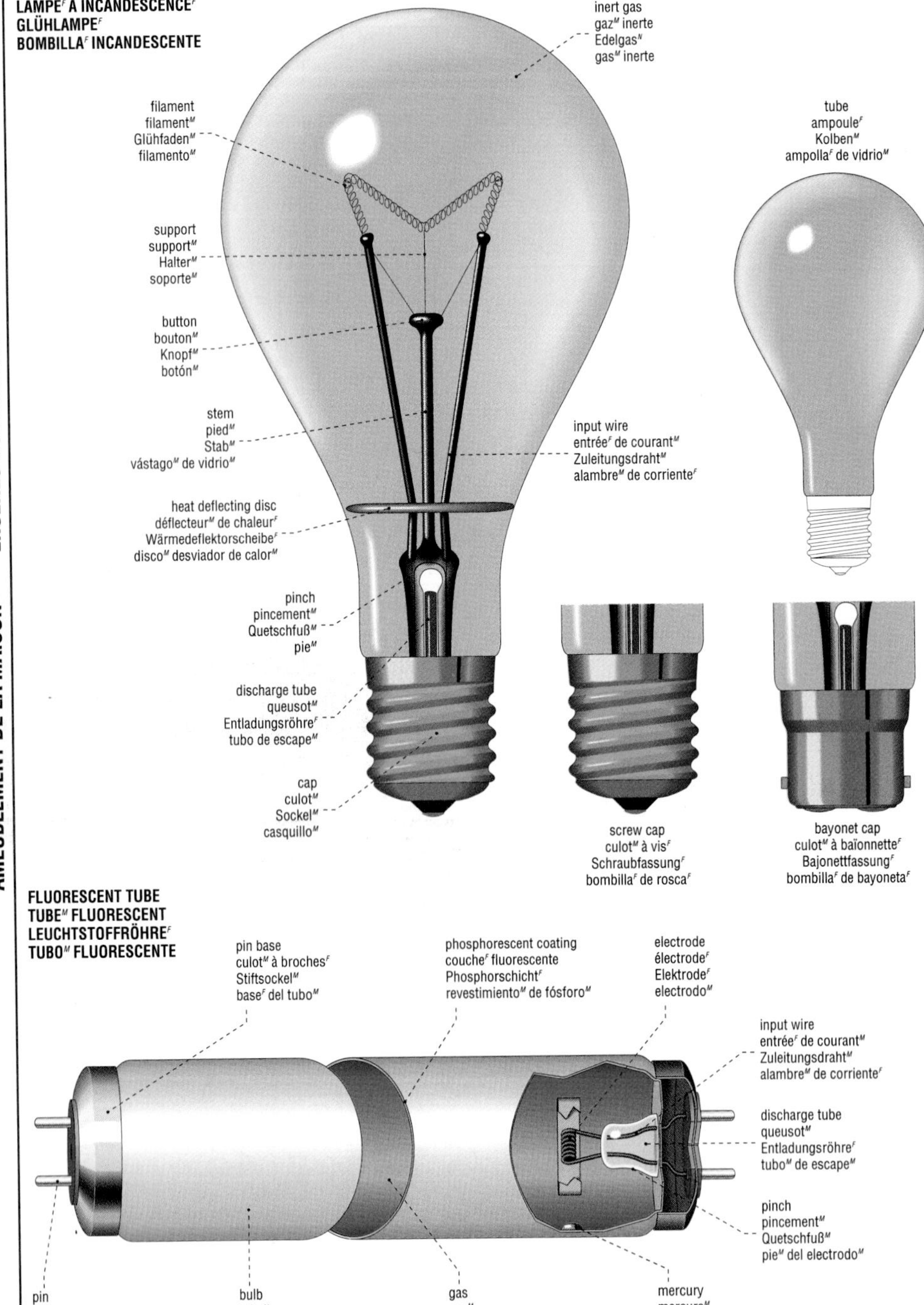

## TUNGSTEN-HALOGEN BULB
## LAMPE$^{F}$ À HALOGÈNE$^{M}$
## WOLFRAM-HALOGENLAMPE$^{F}$
## LÁMPARA$^{F}$ HALÓGENA

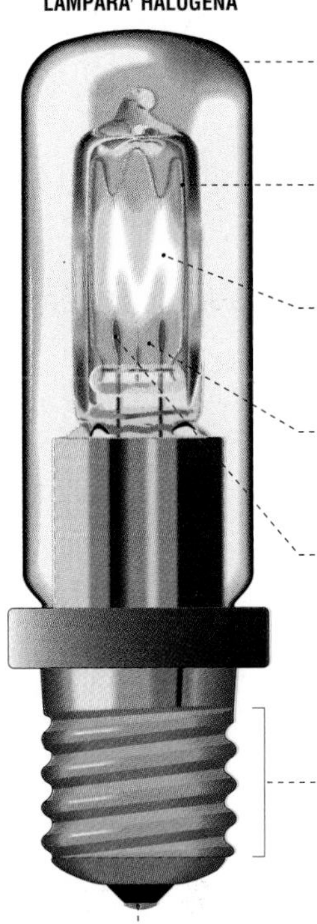


## TUNGSTEN-HALOGEN BULB
## LAMPE$^{F}$ À HALOGÈNE$^{M}$
## WOLFRAM-HALOGENLAMPE$^{F}$
## LÁMPARA$^{F}$ HALÓGENA

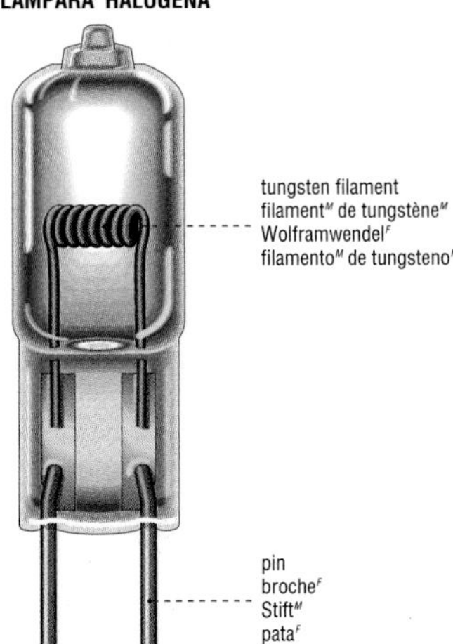


## ENERGY SAVING BULB
## LAMPE$^{F}$ À ÉCONOMIE$^{F}$ D'ÉNERGIE$^{F}$
## ENERGIESPARLAMPE$^{F}$
## BOMBILLA$^{F}$ ECONÓMICA

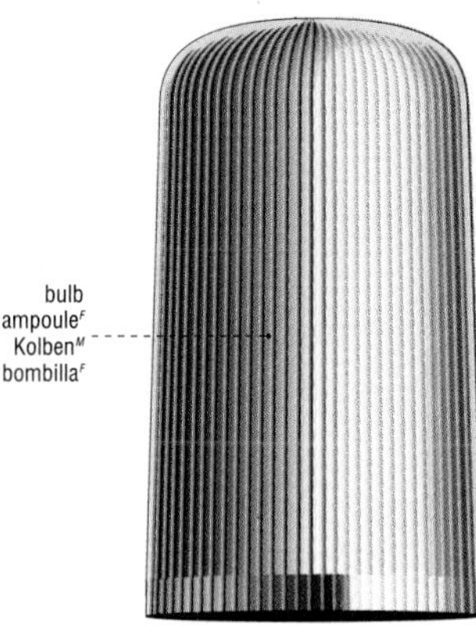


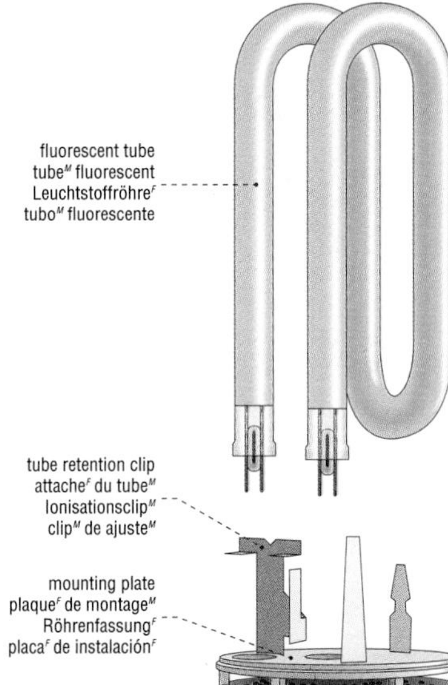


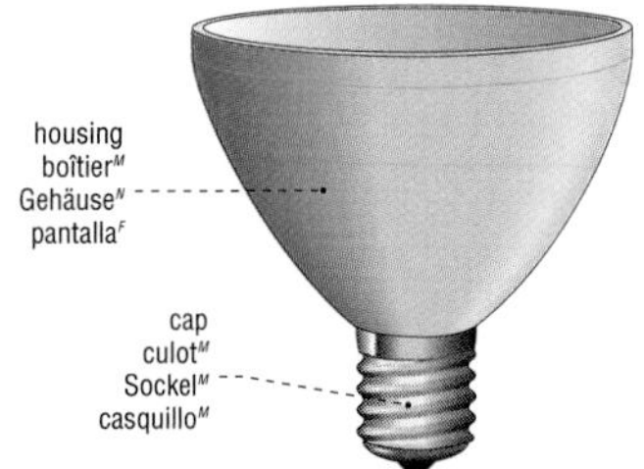

# LIGHTS
# LUMINAIRES[M]
# LAMPEN[F]
# LÁMPARAS[F]

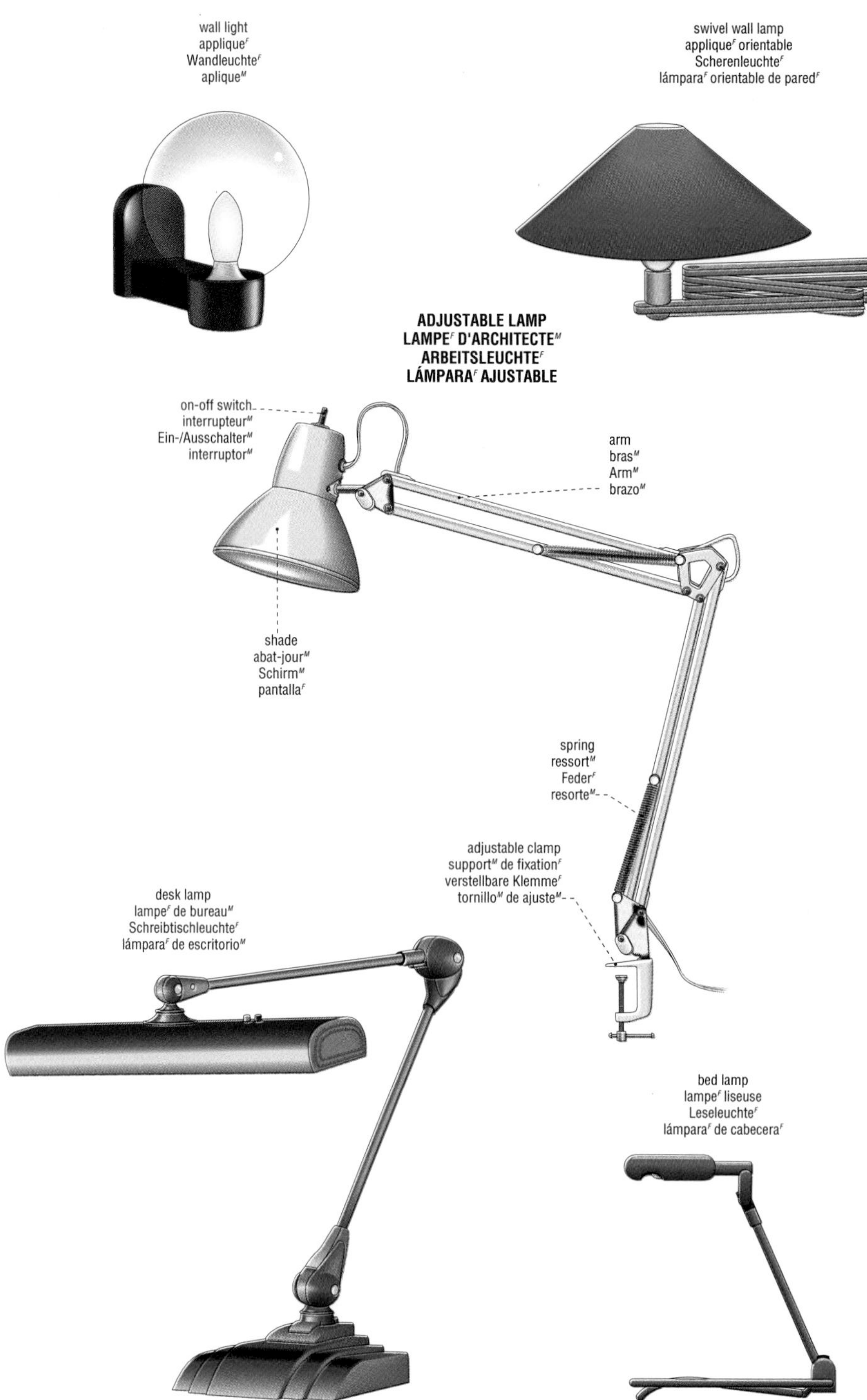

## TRACK LIGHTING
## RAIL^M D'ÉCLAIRAGE^M
## STROMSCHIENENLEUCHTE^F
## RIEL^M DE ILUMINACIÓN^F

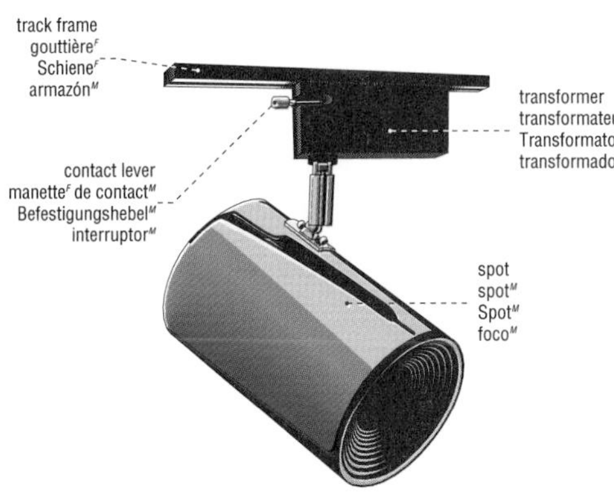


post lantern
lanterne^F de pied^M
Straßenlaterne^F
farola^F

clamp spotlight
spot^M à pince^F
Klemmspot^M
lámpara de pinza^F

wall lantern
lanterne^F murale
Wandlaterne^F
farol^M

multiple light fitting
rampe^F d'éclairage^M
Lampenreihe^F
lámparas^F en serie^F

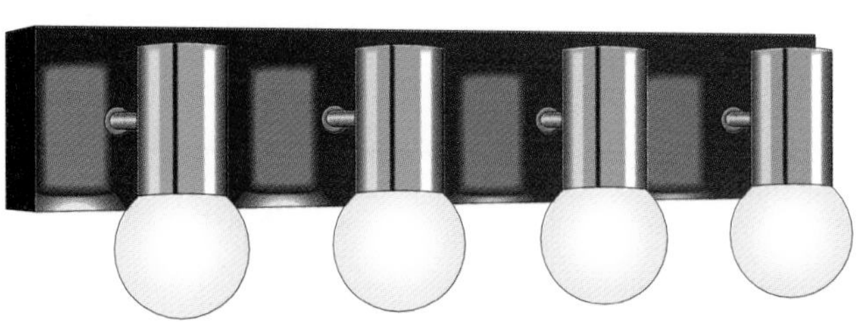

# LIGHTS
# LUMINAIRES^M
# LAMPEN^F
# LÁMPARAS^F

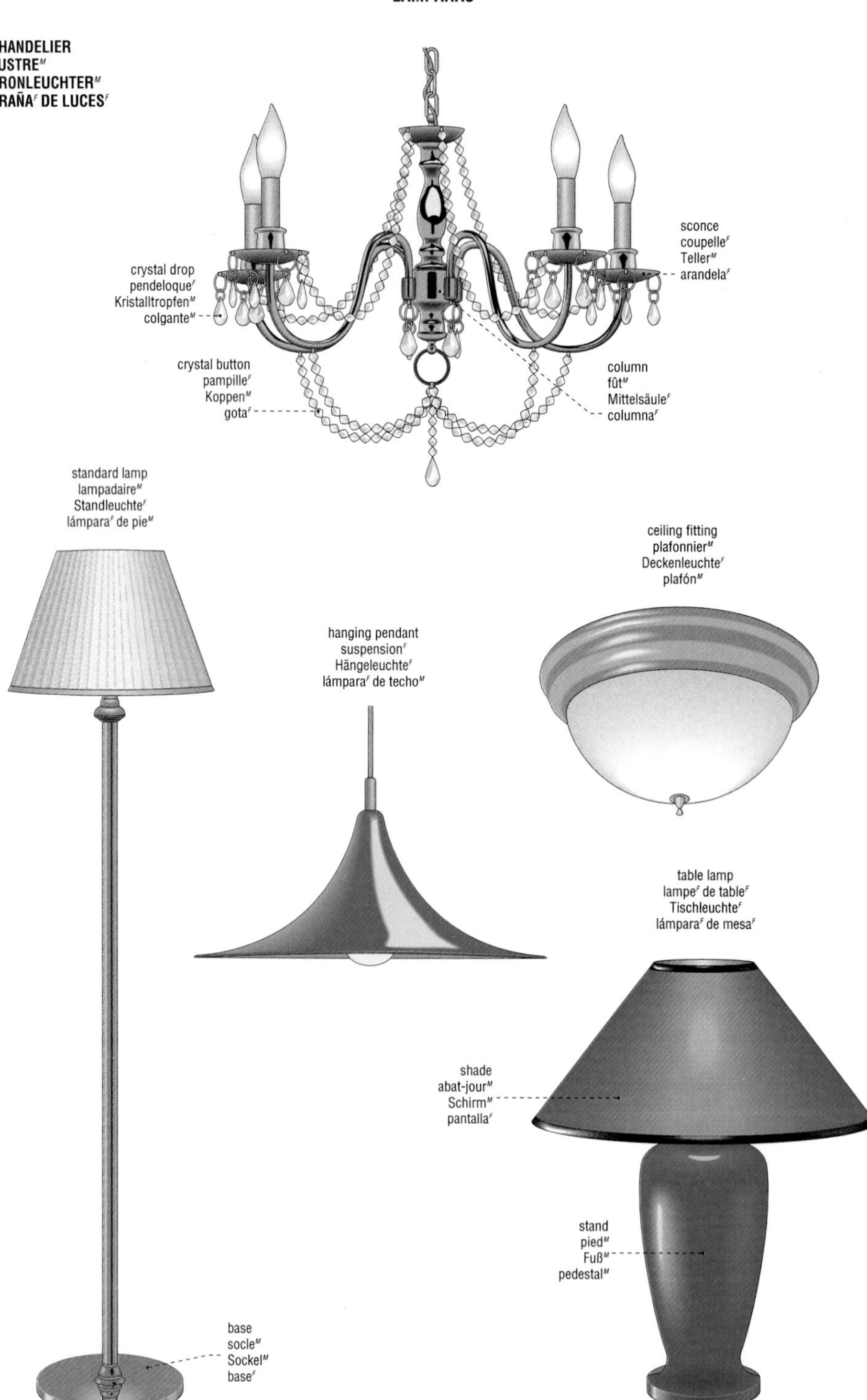

**GLASSWARE**
**VERRES^M**
**GLÄSER^N**
**CRISTALERÍA^F**

port glass
verre^M à porto^M
Süßweinglas^N
copa^F para oporto^M

champagne glass
coupe^F à mousseux^M
Sektschale^F
copa^F de cava^F

brandy glass
verre^M à cognac^M
Kognakschwenker^M
copa^F de coñac^M

liqueur glass
verre^M à liqueur^F
Likörglas^N
copa^F para licores^M

white wine glass
verre^M à vin^M blanc
Weißweinglas^N
copa^F de vino^M blanco

bordeaux glass
verre^M à bordeaux^M
Bordeauxglas^N
copa^F para vinos^M de Burdeos

burgundy glass
verre^M à bourgogne^M
Burgunderglas^N
copa^F para vinos^M de Borgoña

hock glass
verre^M à vin^M d'Alsace
Elsaßglas^N
copa^F para vino^M de Alsacia

whisky tumbler
verre^M à whisky^M
Whiskybecher^M
vaso^M corto

tall tumbler
verre^M à gin^M
Longdrinkglas^N
vaso^M largo

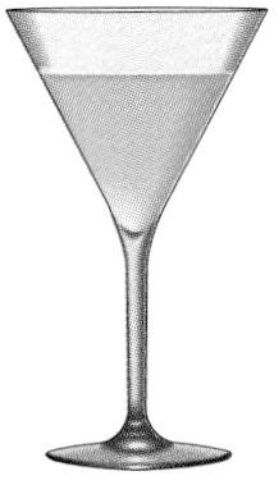
cocktail glass
verre^M à cocktail^M
Cocktailglas^N
copa^F de cóctel^M

water goblet
verre^M à eau^F
Wasserglas^N
copa^F para agua^F

decanter
carafe^F
Karaffe^F
garrafa^F

carafe
carafon^M
kleine Karaffe^F
garrafita^F

champagne flute
flûte^F à champagne^M
Sektkelch^M
copa^F de champaña^M

beer glass
chope^F à bière^F
Bierkrug^M
jarra^M para cerveza^F

# CROCKERY
# VAISSELLE[F]
# GESCHIRR[N]
# VAJILLA[F] Y SERVICIO[M] DE MESA[F]

demitasse
tasse[F] à café[M]
Mokkatasse[F]
tacita[F] de café[M]

tea cup
tasse[F] à thé[M]
Tasse[F]
taza[F]

coffee mug
chope[F] à café[M]
Becher[M]
jarra[F] para café[M]

cream jug
crémier[M]
Milchkännchen[N]
jarrita[F] de la leche[F]

sugar bowl
sucrier[M]
Zuckerdose[F]
azucarero[M]

pepperpot
poivrière[F]
Pfefferstreuer[M]
pimentera[F]

saltcellar
salière[F]
Salzstreuer[M]
salero[M]

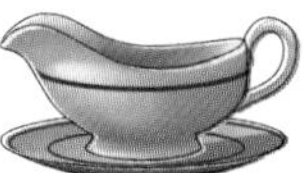

gravy boat
saucière[F]
Sauciere[F]
salsera[F]

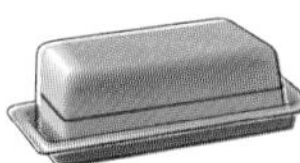

butter dish
beurrier[M]
Butterdose[F]
mantequera[F]

ramekin
ramequin[M]
Auflaufförmchen[N]
cuenco[M] de queso[M] blando

soup bowl
bol[M]
Suppenschale[F]
bol[M] para sopa[F]

rim soup bowl
assiette[F] creuse
Suppenteller[M]
plato[M] sopero

dinner plate
assiette[F] plate
flacher Teller[M]
plato[M] llano

salad plate
assiette[F] à salade[F]
Salatteller[M]
plato[M] para ensalada[F]

side plate
assiette[F] à dessert[M]
kleiner Teller[M]
plato[M] para pan[M] y mantequilla[F]

teapot
théière[F]
Teekanne[F]
tetera[F]

serving dish
plat[M] ovale
Platte[F]
fuente[F] de servir

vegetable dish
légumier[M]
Kartoffelschüssel[F]
fuente[F] de verdura[F]

fish dish
plat[M] à poisson[M]
Fischplatte[F]
fuente[F] para pescado[M]

hors d'oeuvre dish
ravier[M]
Horsd'oeuvre-Schale[F]
bandeja[F] para canapés[M]

water jug
pichet[M]
Wasserkrug[M]
jarra[F] para agua[F]

salad bowl
saladier[M]
Salatschüssel[F]
ensaladera[F]

salad dish
bol[M] à salade[F]
Salatschale[F]
bol[M] para ensalada[F]

soup tureen
soupière[F]
Suppenterrine[F]
sopera[F]

# CUTLERY
# COUVERT[M]
# SILBERBESTECK[N]
# CUBERTERÍA[F]

## KNIFE
## COUTEAU[M]
## MESSER[N]
## CUCHILLO[M]

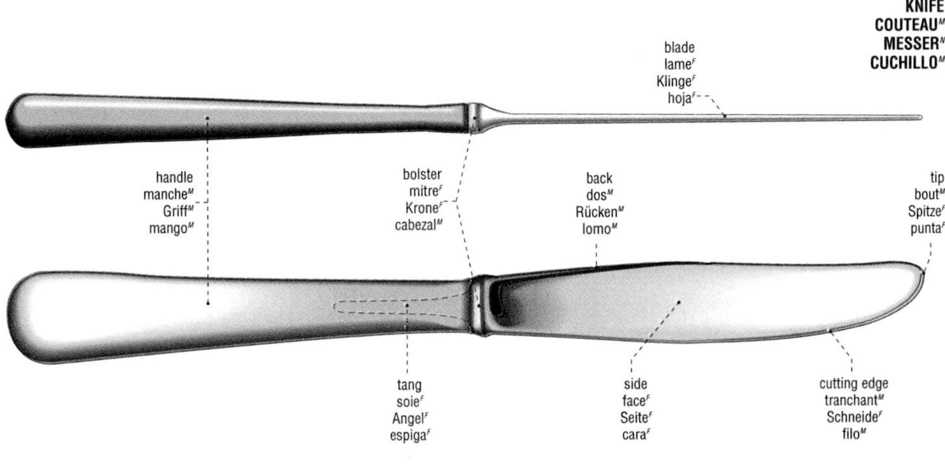


## PRINCIPAL TYPES OF KNIFE
## PRINCIPAUX TYPES[M] DE COUTEAUX[M]
## DIE WICHTIGSTEN MESSERTYPEN[M]
## TIPOS[M] DE CUCHILLOS[M]

butter knife
couteau[M] à beurre[M]
Buttermesser[N]
cuchillo[M] para mantequilla[F]

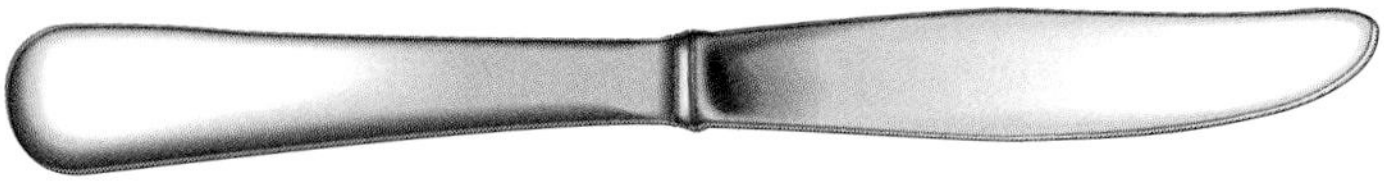

dessert knife
couteau[M] à dessert[M]
Dessertmesser[N]
cuchillo[M] para postre[M]

fish knife
couteau[M] à poisson[M]
Fischmesser[N]
cuchillo[M] para pescado[M]

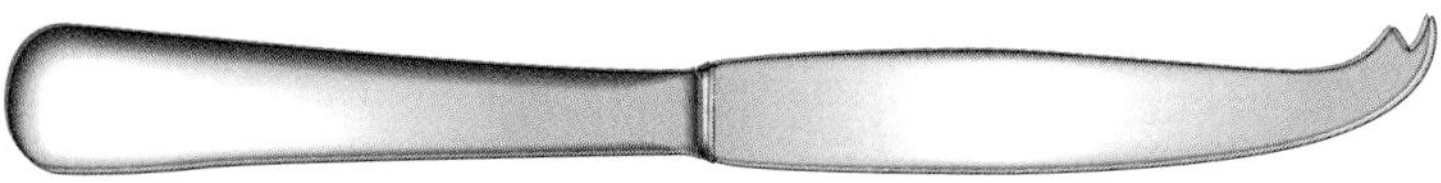

cheese knife
couteau[M] à fromage[M]
Käsemesser[N]
cuchillo[M] para queso[M]

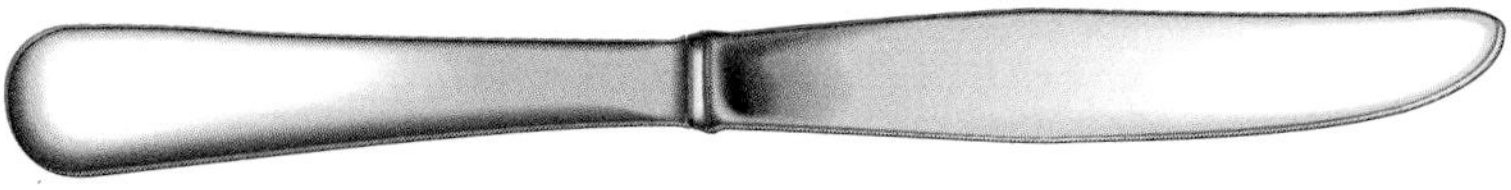

dinner knife
couteau[M] de table[F]
Menümesser[N]
cuchillo[M] de mesa[F]

steak knife
couteau[M] à bifteck[M]
Steakmesser[N]
cuchillo[M] para carne[F]

# CUTLERY
# COUVERT[M]
# SILBERBESTECK[N]
# CUBERTERÍA[F]

**FORK**
**FOURCHETTE[F]**
**GABEL[F]**
**TENEDOR[M]**

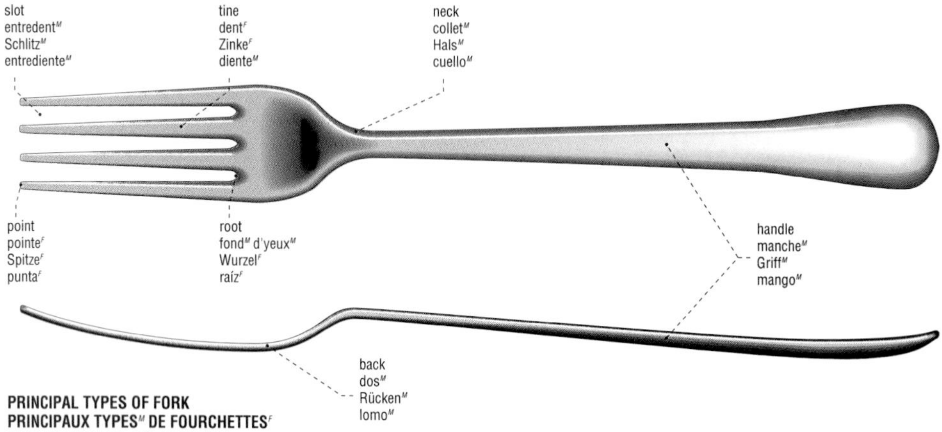

slot
entredent[M]
Schlitz[M]
entrediente[M]

tine
dent[F]
Zinke[F]
diente[M]

neck
collet[M]
Hals[M]
cuello[M]

point
pointe[F]
Spitze[F]
punta[F]

root
fond[M] d'yeux[M]
Wurzel[F]
raíz[F]

handle
manche[M]
Griff[M]
mango[M]

back
dos[M]
Rücken[M]
lomo[M]

**PRINCIPAL TYPES OF FORK**
**PRINCIPAUX TYPES[M] DE FOURCHETTES[F]**
**DIE WICHTIGSTEN GABELTYPEN[M]**
**TIPOS[M] DE TENEDORES[M]**

oyster fork
fourchette[F] à huîtres[F]
Austerngabel[F]
tenedor[M] para ostras[F]

dessert fork
fourchette[F] à dessert[M]
Dessertgabel[F]
tenedor[M] para postre[M]

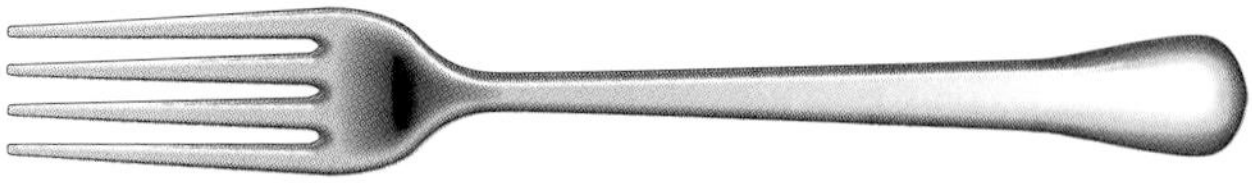

salad fork
fourchette[F] à salade[F]
Salatgabel[F]
tenedor[M] para ensalada[F]

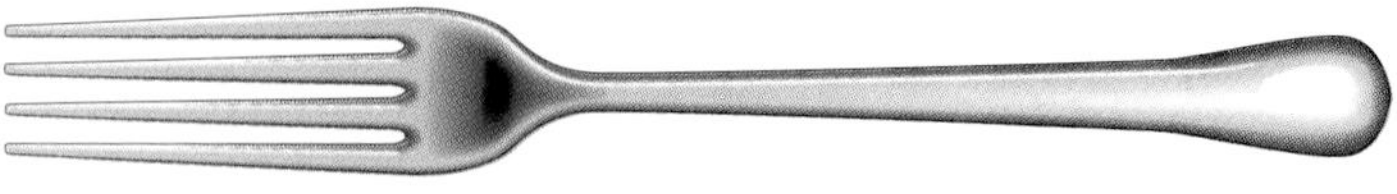

fish fork
fourchette[F] à poisson[M]
Fischgabel[F]
tenedor[M] para pescado[M]

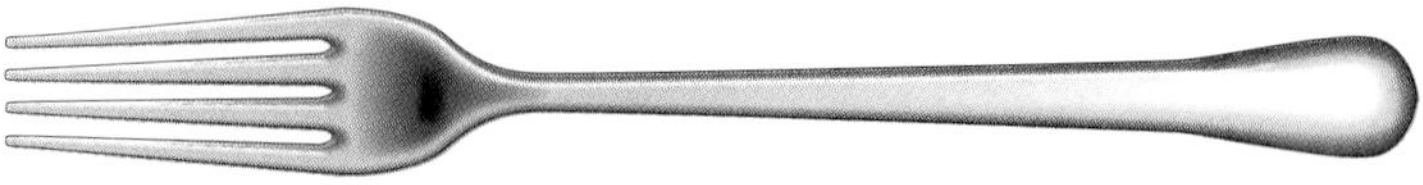

dinner fork
fourchette[F] de table[F]
Menügabel[F]
tenedor[M] de mesa[F]

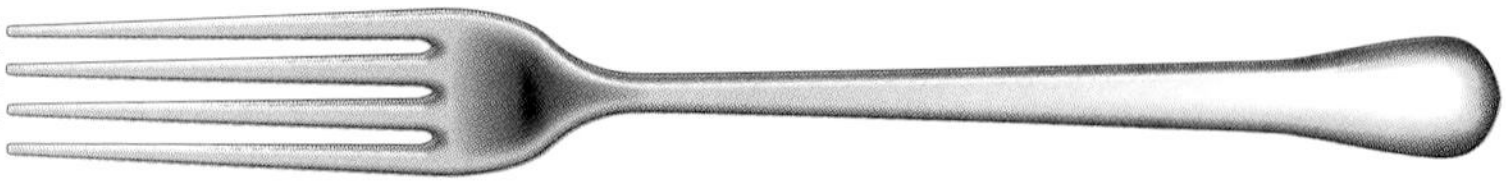

fondue fork
fourchette[F] à fondue[F]
Fonduegabel[F]
tenedor[M] para fondue[F]

## SPOON
## CUILLER[F]
## LÖFFEL[M]
## CUCHARA[F]

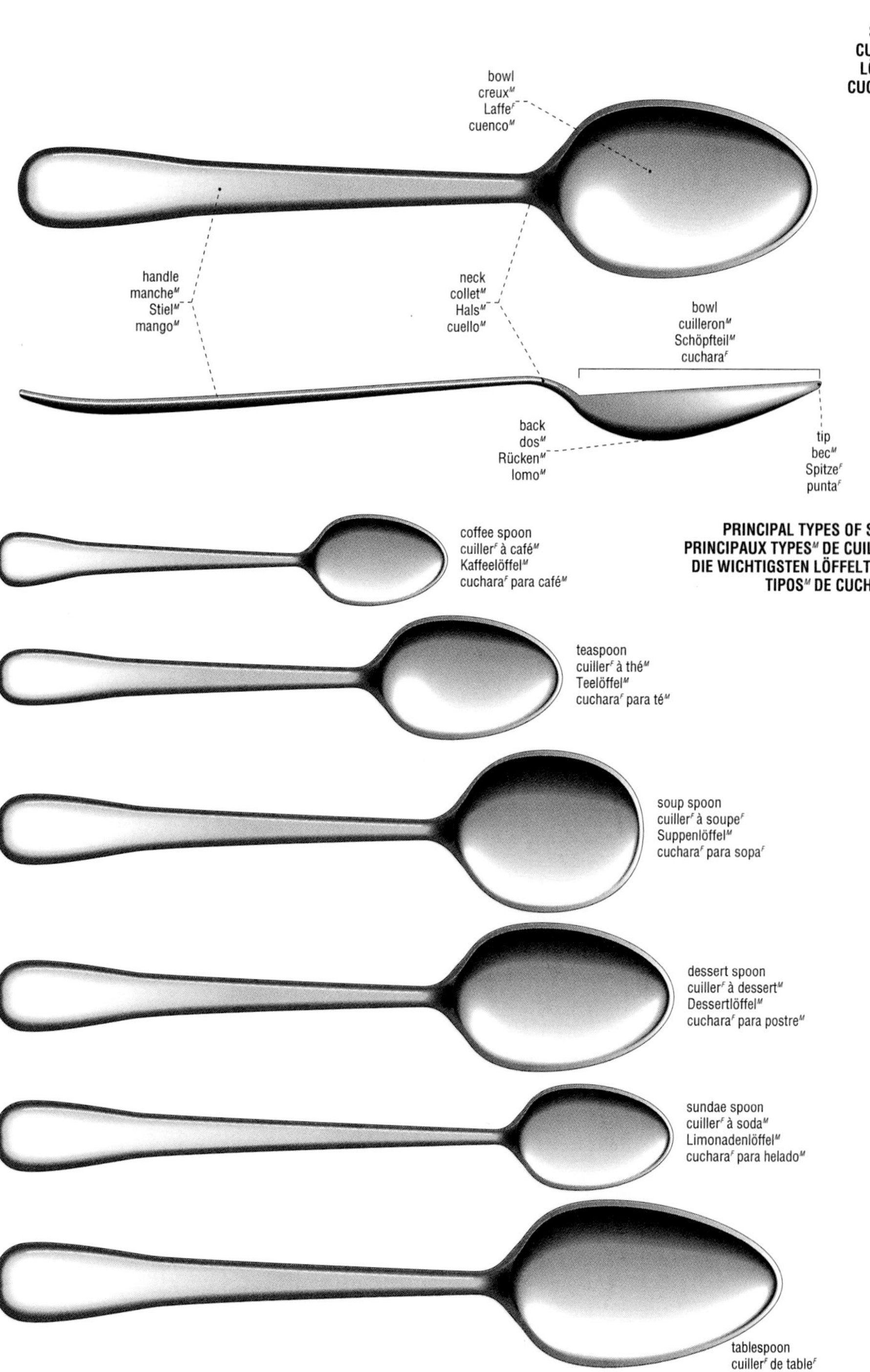


## PRINCIPAL TYPES OF SPOON
## PRINCIPAUX TYPES[M] DE CUILLERS[F]
## DIE WICHTIGSTEN LÖFFELTYPEN[M]
## TIPOS[M] DE CUCHARAS[F]

# KITCHEN UTENSILS
# USTENSILES[M] DE CUISINE[F]
# KÜCHENUTENSILIEN[N]
# UTENSILIOS[M] DE COCINA[F]

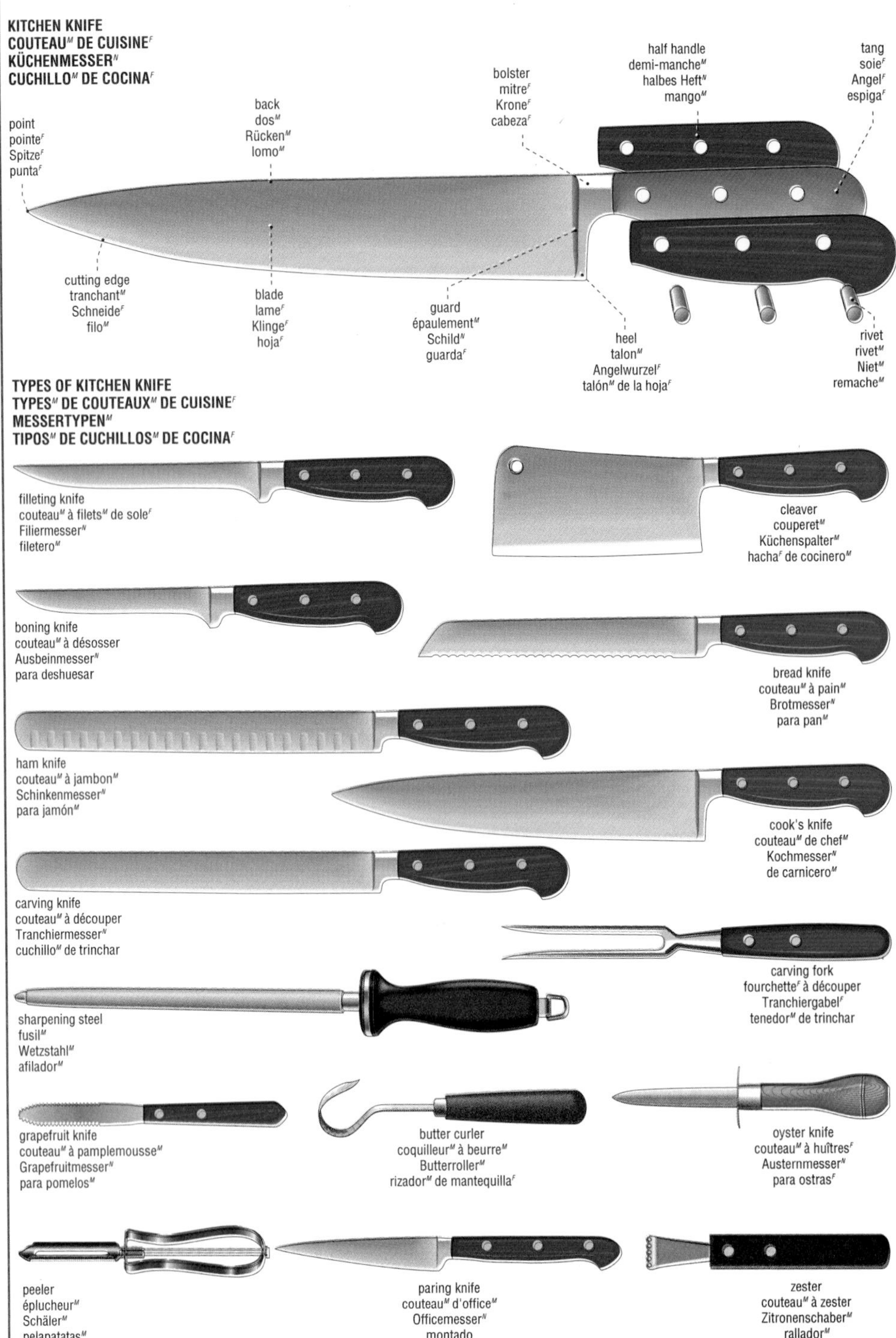

## FOR STRAINING AND DRAINING
## POUR PASSER ET ÉGOUTTER
## ZUM SIEBEN[N] UND TROCKNEN[N]
## COLADORES[M] Y ESCURRIDORES[M]

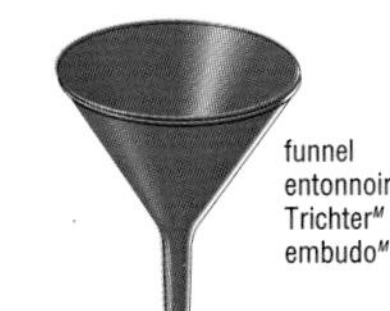

funnel
entonnoir[M]
Trichter[M]
embudo[M]

colander
passoire[F]
Durchschlag[M]
escurridor[M]

strainer
passoire[F]
Sieb[N]
cedazo[M]

salad spinner
essoreuse[F] à salade[F]
Salatschleuder[F]
secadora[F] de ensalada[F]

## FOR GRINDING AND GRATING
## POUR BROYER ET RÂPER
## ZUM ZERKLEINERN[N] UND ZERREIBEN[N]
## PARA MOLER Y RALLAR

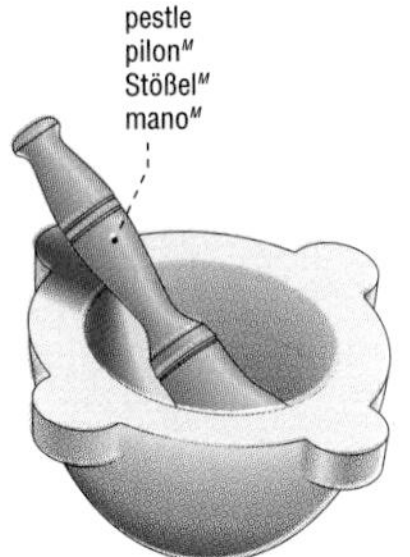


mortar
mortier[M]
Mörser[M]
mortero[M]

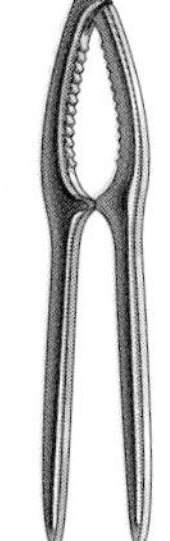

nutcracker
casse-noix[M]
Nußknacker[M]
cascanueces[M]

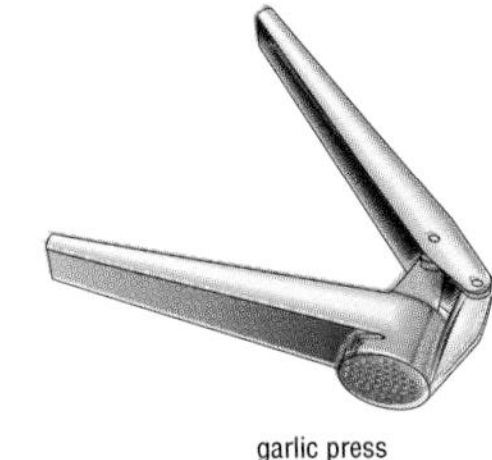

garlic press
presse-ail[M]
Knoblauchpresse[F]
triturador[M] de ajos[M]

lemon squeezer
presse-agrumes[M]
Zitronenpresse[F]
exprimelimones[M]

mincer
hachoir[M]
Fleischwolf[M]
máquina de picar carne[F]

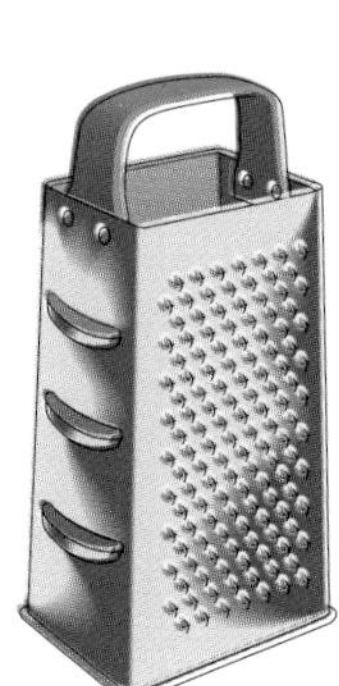

grater
râpe[F]
Reibe[F]
rallador[M]

pasta maker
machine[F] à faire les pâtes[F]
Nudelmaschine[F]
máquina[F] para hacer pasta[F] italiana

# KITCHEN UTENSILS
# USTENSILES[M] DE CUISINE[F]
# KÜCHENUTENSILIEN[N]
# UTENSILIOS[M] DE COCINA[F]

**SET OF UTENSILS**
**JEU[M] D'USTENSILES[M]**
**KÜCHENSET[N]**
**JUEGO[M] DE UTENSILIOS[M]**

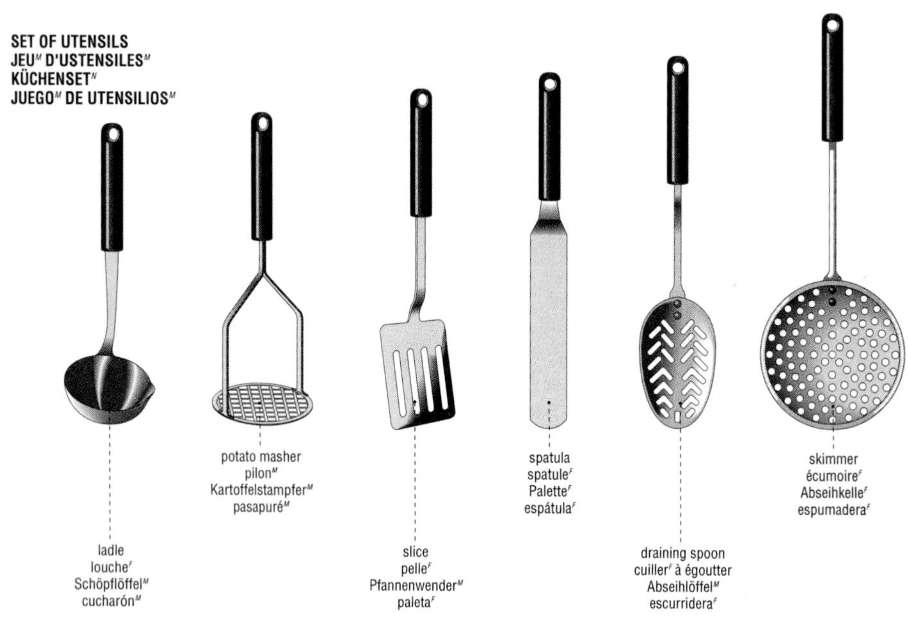

ladle
louche[F]
Schöpflöffel[M]
cucharón[M]

potato masher
pilon[M]
Kartoffelstampfer[M]
pasapuré[M]

slice
pelle[F]
Pfannenwender[M]
paleta[F]

spatula
spatule[F]
Palette[F]
espátula[F]

draining spoon
cuiller[F] à égoutter
Abseihlöffel[M]
escurridera[F]

skimmer
écumoire[F]
Abseihkelle[F]
espumadera[F]

**FOR OPENING**
**POUR OUVRIR**
**ZUM ÖFFNEN[N]**
**UTENSILIOS[M] PARA ABRIR Y DESCORCHAR**

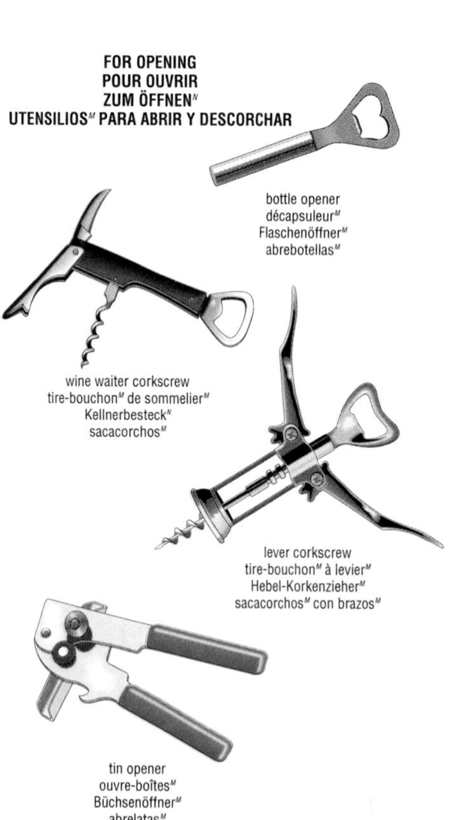

bottle opener
décapsuleur[M]
Flaschenöffner[M]
abrebotellas[M]

wine waiter corkscrew
tire-bouchon[M] de sommelier[M]
Kellnerbesteck[N]
sacacorchos[M]

lever corkscrew
tire-bouchon[M] à levier[M]
Hebel-Korkenzieher[M]
sacacorchos[M] con brazos[M]

tin opener
ouvre-boîtes[M]
Büchsenöffner[M]
abrelatas[M]

kitchen timer
minuteur[M]
Küchenuhr[F]
reloj[M] de cocina[F]

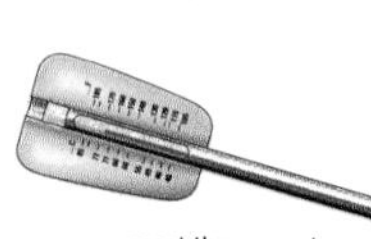

meat thermometer
thermomètre[M] à viande[F]
Fleischthermometer[N]
termómetro[M] para carne[F]

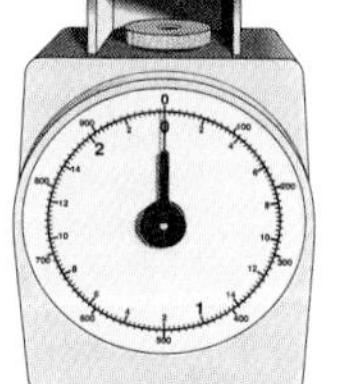

kitchen scale
balance[F] de cuisine[F]
Küchenwaage[F]
báscula[F] de cocina[F]

**FOR MEASURING**
**POUR MESURER**
**ZUM MESSEN[N]**
**UTENSILIOS[M] PARA MEDIR**

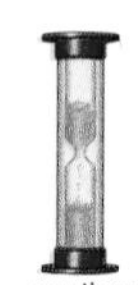

egg timer
sablier[M]
Eieruhr[F]
minutero[M] para huevos[M] pasados por agua[F]

measuring spoons
cuillers[F] doseuses
Meßlöffel[M]
cucharas[F] para medir

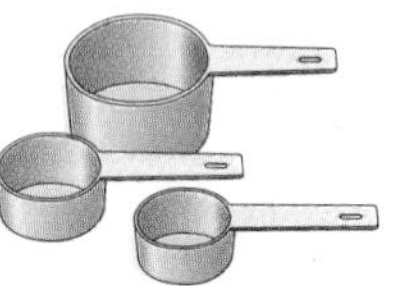

measuring cups
mesures[F]
Meßbecher[M]
tazas[F] para medir

## BAKING UTENSILS
## POUR LA PÂTISSERIE[F]
## BACKGERÄT[N]
## UTENSILIOS[M] PARA HORNEAR

pastry brush
pinceau[M] à pâtisserie[F]
Kuchenpinsel[M]
pincel[M] de repostería[F]

icing syringe
piston[M] à décorer
Garnierspritze[F]
tubito[M] de decoración[F]

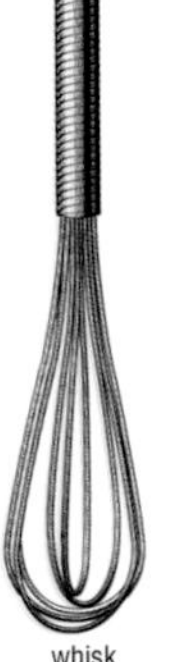
whisk
fouet[M]
Schneebesen[M]
batidor[M]

egg beater
batteur[M] à œufs[M]
Rad-Schneeschläger[M]
batidor[M] mecánico

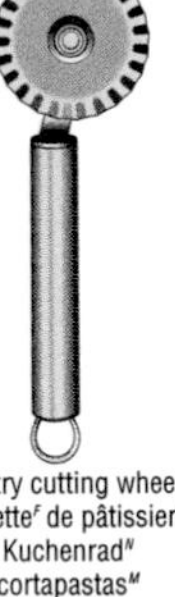
pastry cutting wheel
roulette[F] de pâtissier[M]
Kuchenrad[N]
cortapastas[M]

sifter
tamis[M] à farine[F]
Mehlsieb[N]
tamiz[M]

bun tin
moule[M] à muffins[M]
Mohrenkopfform[F]
molde[M] para magdalenas[F]

pastry bag and nozzles
poche[F] à douilles[F]
Spritzbeutel[M] mit Düsen[F]
manga[F] y boquillas[F]

biscuit sheet
plaque[F] à biscuits[M]
Backblech[N]
bandeja[F] para hornear galletas[F]

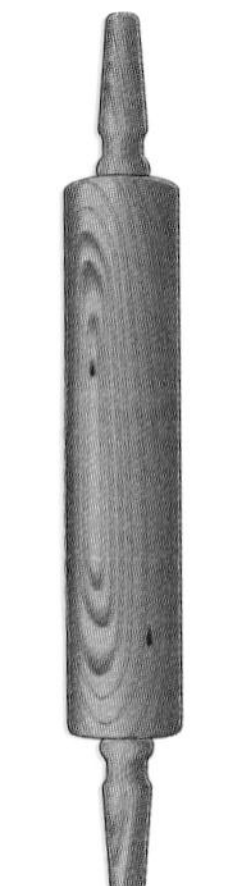

rolling pin
rouleau[M] à pâtisserie[F]
Nudelholz[N]
rodillo[M]

mixing bowls
bols[M] à mélanger
Rührschüsseln[F]
boles[M] para batir

biscuit cutters
emporte-pièces[M]
Ausstechformen[F]
moldes[M] de pastas[F]

removable-bottomed tin
moule[M] à fond[M] amovible
Springform[F]
molde[M] redondo con muelles[M]

pie tin
moule[M] à tarte[F]
flache Kuchenform[F]
molde[M] para tartas[F]

quiche tin
moule[M] à quiche[F]
Quicheform[F]
molde[M] acanalado

cake tin
moule[M] à gâteau[M]
Kuchenform[F]
molde[M] para bizcocho[M]

# KITCHEN UTENSILS
# USTENSILES[M] DE CUISINE[F]
# KÜCHENUTENSILIEN[N]
# UTENSILIOS[M] DE COCINA[F]

## MISCELLANEOUS UTENSILS
## USTENSILES[M] DIVERS
## VERSCHIEDENERLEI UTENSILIEN[N]
## UTENSILIOS[M] DIVERSOS

stoner
dénoyauteur[M]
Entsteiner[M]
deshuesador[M] de frutas[F]

ice cream scoop
cuiller[F] à glace[F]
Eisportionierer[M]
cuchara[F] para servir helado[M]

poultry shears
cisaille[F] à volaille[F]
Geflügelschere[F]
tijeras[F] para aves[F]

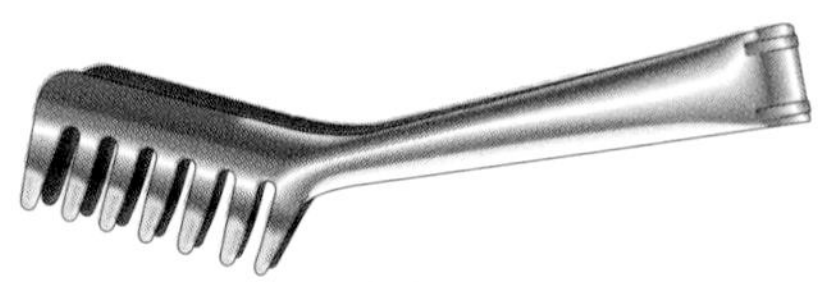

spaghetti tongs
pince[F] à spaghettis[M]
Spaghettizange[F]
tenacillas[F] para espagueti[M]

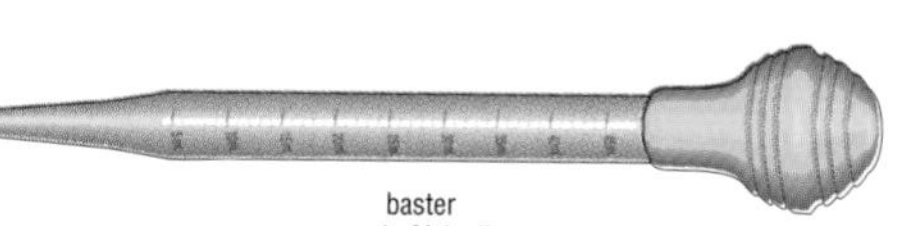

baster
poire[F] à jus[M]
Fettgießer[M]
engrasador[M]

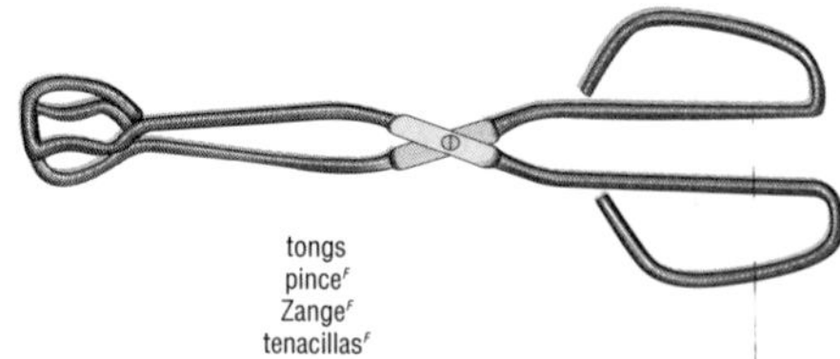

tongs
pince[F]
Zange[F]
tenacillas[F]

vegetable brush
brosse[F] à légumes[M]
Gemüsebürste[F]
cepillo[M] para verduras[F]

tea infuser
boule[F] à thé[M]
Tee-Ei[N]
esfera[F] de té[M]

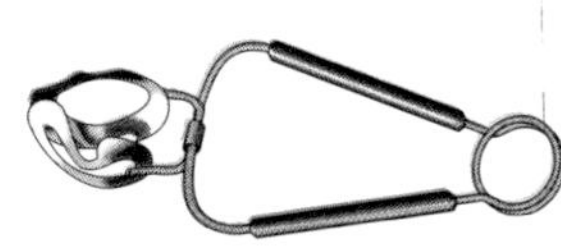

snail tongs
pince[F] à escargots[M]
Schneckenzange[F]
tenacillas[F] para caracoles[M]

dredger
saupoudreuse[F]
Streuer[M]
espolvoreador[M]

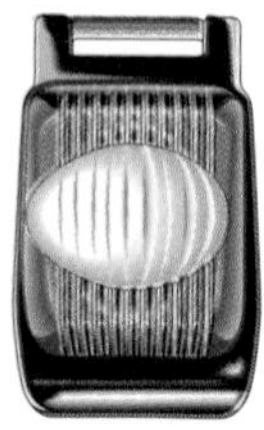

egg slicer
coupe-œuf[M]
Eierschneider[M]
cortador[M] de huevos[M] duros

snail dish
plat[M] à escargots[M]
Schneckenpfännchen[N]
plato[M] para caracoles[M]

# COFFEE MAKERS
# CAFETIÈRES[F]
# KAFFEEMASCHINEN[F]
# CAFETERAS[F]

# COOKING UTENSILS
# BATTERIE[F] DE CUISINE[F]
# KOCHGERÄTE[N]
# UTENSILIOS[M] DE COCINA[F]

## WOK SET
## WOK[M]
## WOK-SET[N]
## WOK[M]

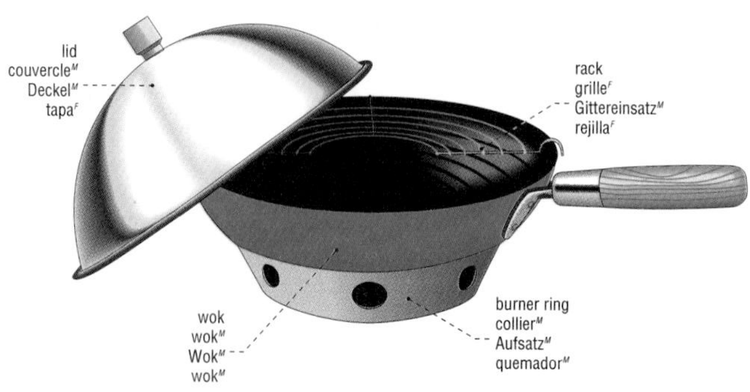


## FISH KETTLE
## POISSONNIÈRE[F]
## FISCHKOCHTOPF[M]
## BESUGUERA[F]

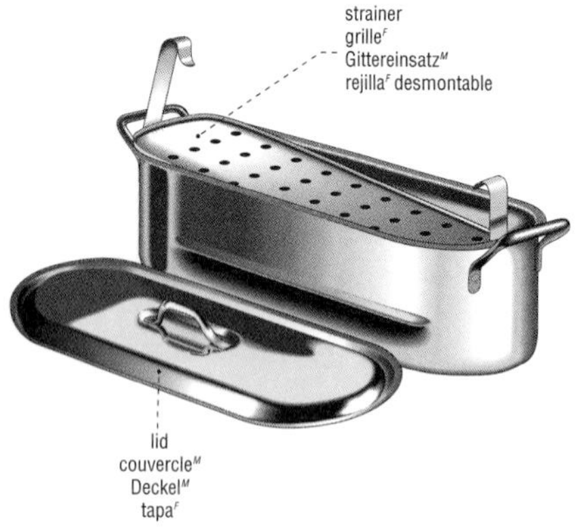

## FONDUE SET
## SERVICE[M] À FONDUE[F]
## FONDUE-SET[N]
## JUEGO[M] PARA FONDUE[F]

fondue pot
caquelon[M]
Fonduetopf[M]
cacerola[F] para fondue[F]

stand
support[M]
Ständer[M]
soporte[M]

burner
réchaud[M]
Brenner[M]
quemador[M]

## PRESSURE COOKER
## AUTOCUISEUR[M]
## DAMPFKOCHTOPF[M]
## OLLA[F] A PRESIÓN[F]

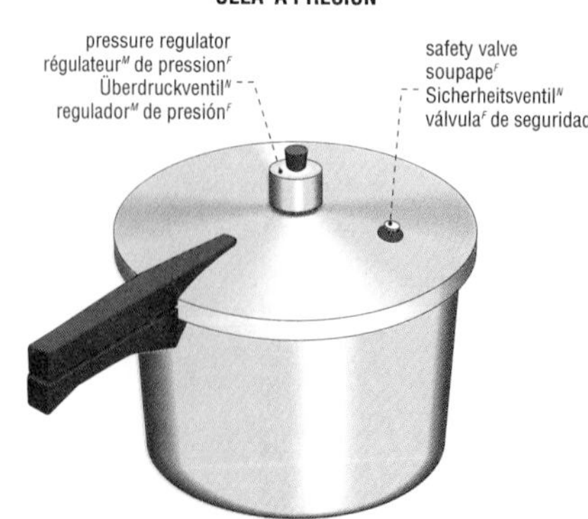


roasting pans
plats[M] à four[M]
Bräter[M]
asadores[M]

Dutch oven
faitout[M]
flacher Bratentopf[M]
cacerola[F] refractaria

stock pot
marmite[F]
Suppentopf[M]
olla[F]

frying pan
poêle[F] à frire
Bratpfanne[F]
sartén[F]

couscous kettle
couscoussier[M]
Kuskustopf[M]
olla[F] para alcuzcuz[M]

pancake pan
poêle[F] à crêpes[F]
Crêpe-Pfanne[F]
sartén[F] para crepes[F]

egg poacher
pocheuse[F]
Eipochierer[M]
escalfador[M] de huevos[M]

sauté pan
sauteuse[F]
Schmorpfanne[F]
sartén[F] honda

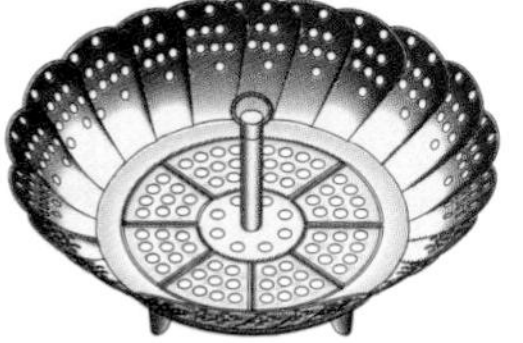

vegetable steamer
étuveuse[F]
Gemüsedünster[M]
alcachofa[F] para verduras[F]

double boiler
bain-marie[M]
Wasserbadtopf[M]
cacerola[F] para baño[M] de María

saucepan
casserole[F]
Stielkasserolle[F]
cacerola[F]

# DOMESTIC APPLIANCES
# APPAREILS$^{M}$ ÉLECTROMÉNAGERS
# HAUSHALTSGERÄTE$^{N}$
# APARATOS$^{M}$ ELECTRODOMÉSTICOS

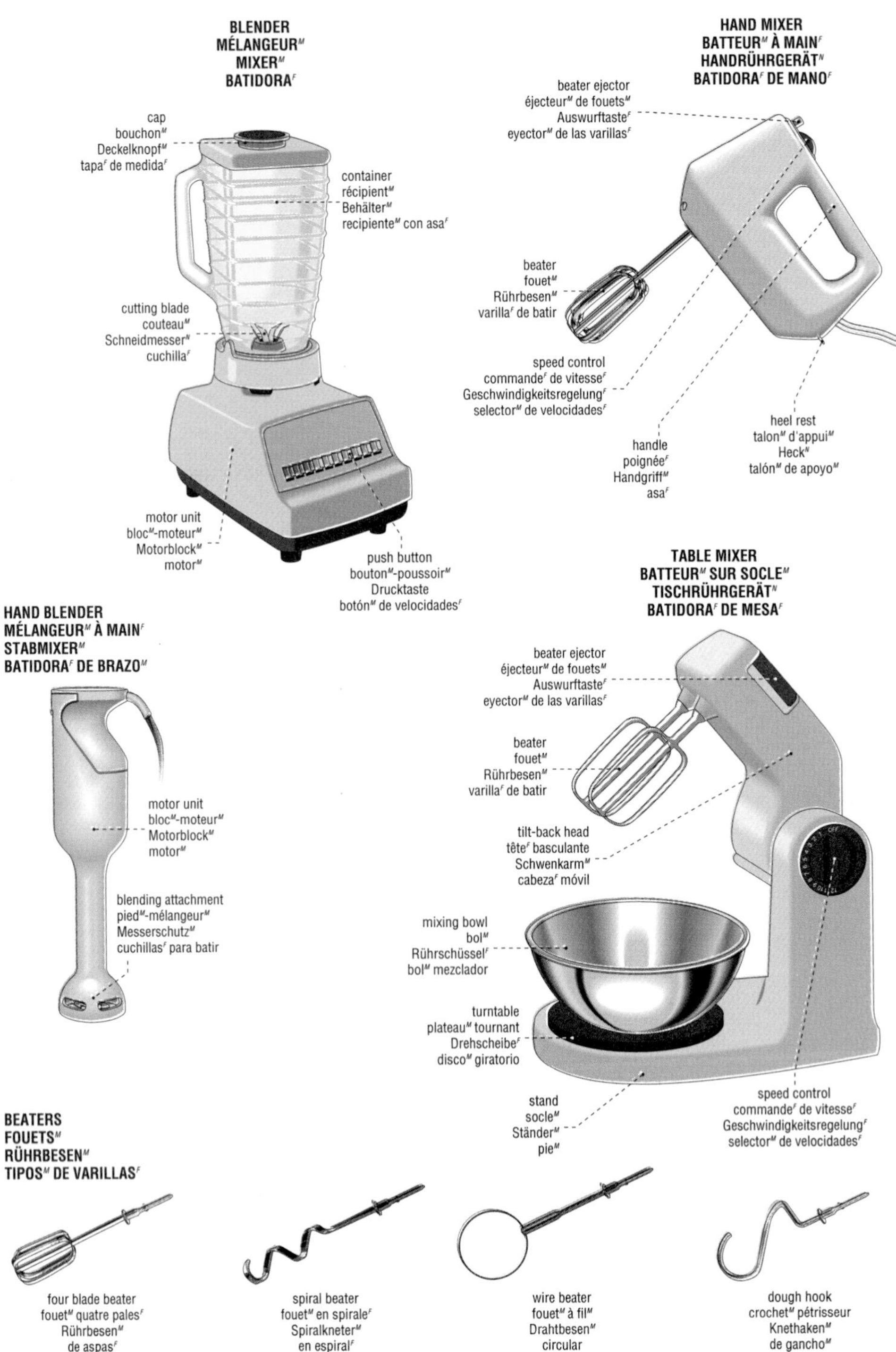

**FOOD PROCESSOR**
**ROBOT[M] DE CUISINE[F]**
**KÜCHENMASCHINE[F]**
**ROBOT[M] DE COCINA[F]**

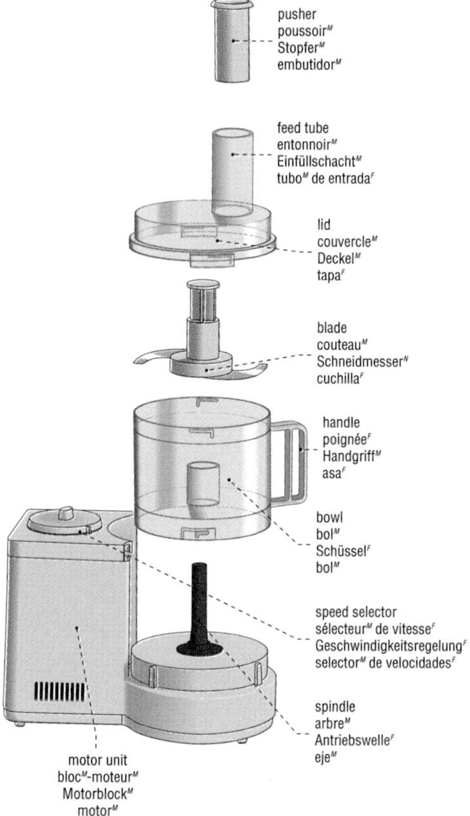


**ICE CREAM MAKER**
**SORBETIÈRE[F]**
**EISMASCHINE[F]**
**HELADERA[F]**

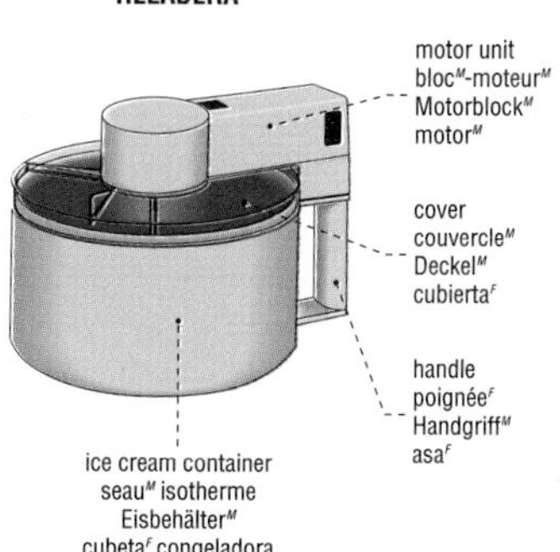

**DISCS**
**DISQUES[M]**
**SCHEIBEN[F]**
**DISCO[M]**

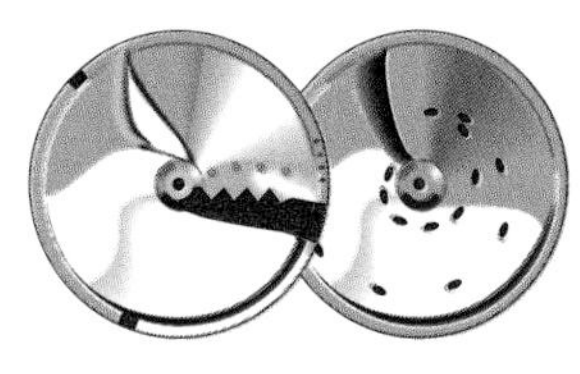

**LEMON SQUEEZER**
**PRESSE-AGRUMES[M]**
**ZITRUSPRESSE[F]**
**EXPRIMIDOR[M] DE CÍTRICOS[M]**

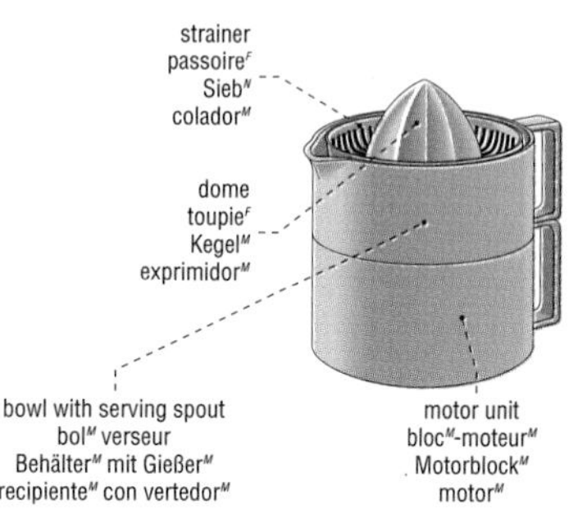


**JUICE EXTRACTOR**
**CENTRIFUGEUSE[F]**
**ENTSAFTER[M]**
**LICUADORA[F]**

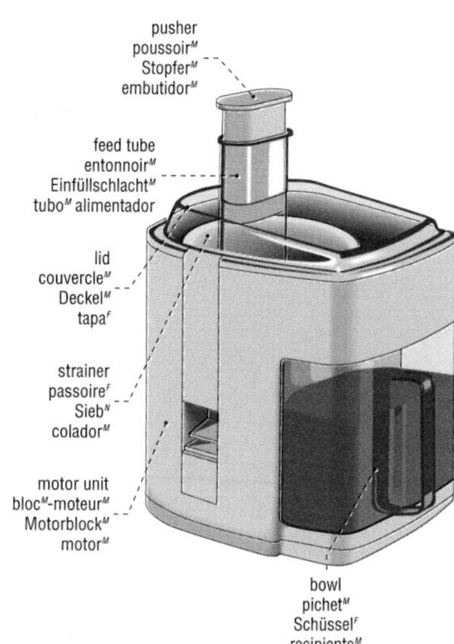

# DOMESTIC APPLIANCES
# APPAREILS[M] ÉLECTROMÉNAGERS
# HAUSHALTSGERÄTE[N]
# APARATOS[M] ELECTRODOMÉSTICOS

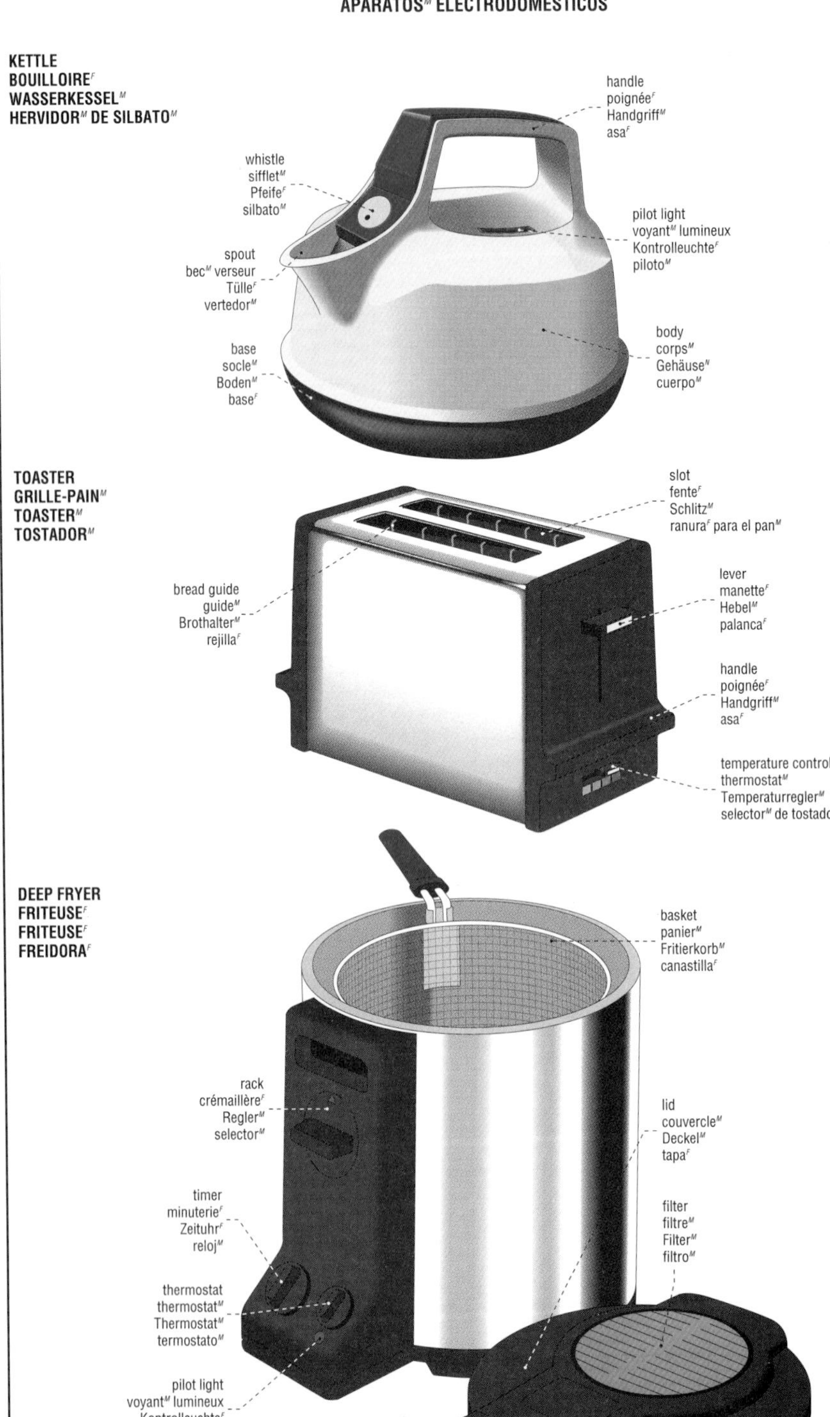

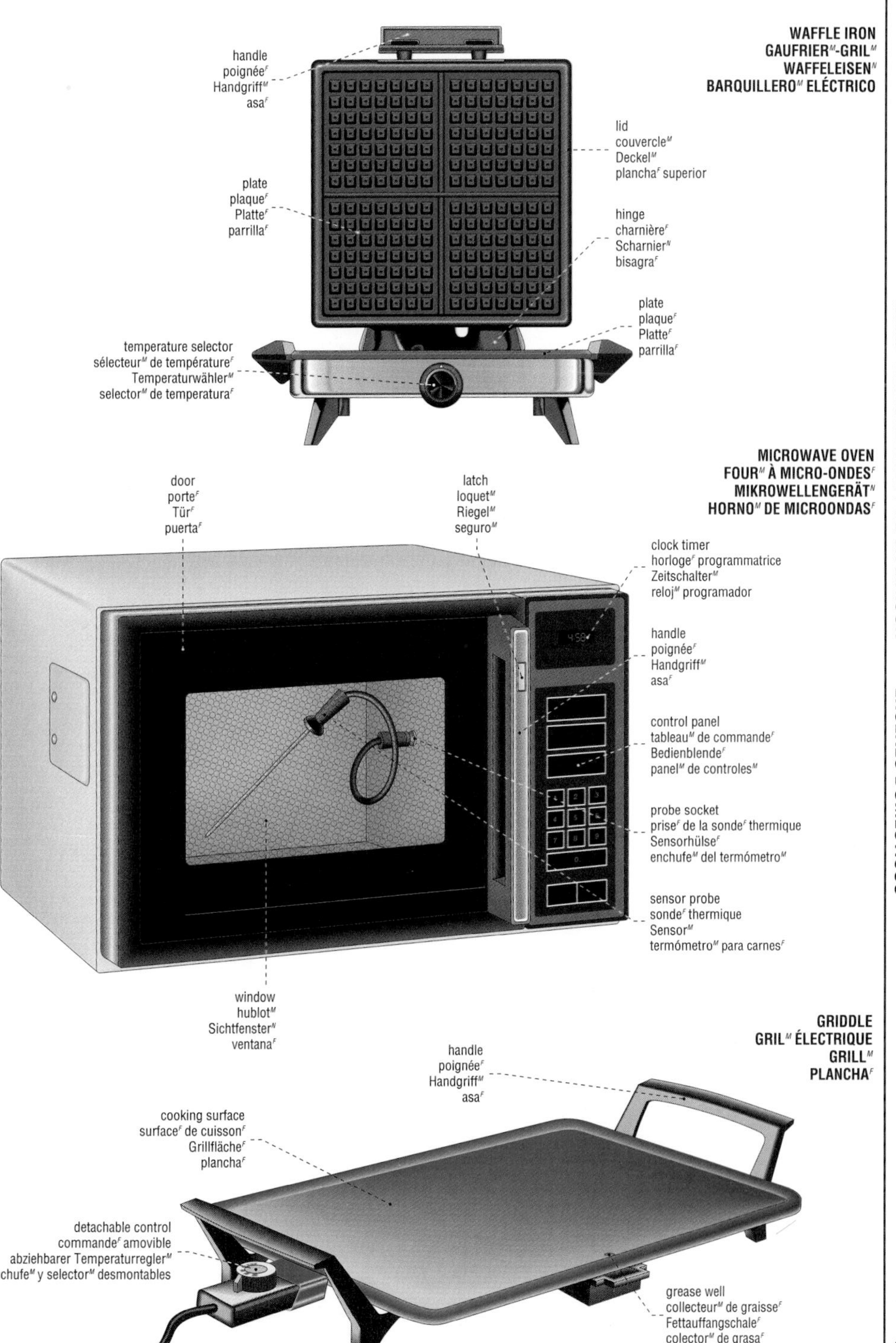
WAFFLE IRON
GAUFRIER[M]-GRIL[M]
WAFFELEISEN[N]
BARQUILLERO[M] ELÉCTRICO
handle
poignée[F]
Handgriff[M]
asa[F]
lid
couvercle[M]
Deckel[M]
plancha[F] superior
plate
plaque[F]
Platte[F]
parrilla[F]
hinge
charnière[F]
Scharnier[N]
bisagra[F]
plate
plaque[F]
Platte[F]
parrilla[F]
temperature selector
sélecteur[M] de température[F]
Temperaturwähler[M]
selector[M] de temperatura[F]
MICROWAVE OVEN
FOUR[M] À MICRO-ONDES[F]
MIKROWELLENGERÄT[N]
HORNO[M] DE MICROONDAS[F]
door
porte[F]
Tür[F]
puerta[F]
latch
loquet[M]
Riegel[M]
seguro[M]
clock timer
horloge[F] programmatrice
Zeitschalter[M]
reloj[M] programador
handle
poignée[F]
Handgriff[M]
asa[F]
control panel
tableau[M] de commande[F]
Bedienblende[F]
panel[M] de controles[M]
probe socket
prise[F] de la sonde[F] thermique
Sensorhülse[F]
enchufe[M] del termómetro[M]
sensor probe
sonde[F] thermique
Sensor[M]
termómetro[M] para carnes[F]
window
hublot[M]
Sichtfenster[N]
ventana[F]
GRIDDLE
GRIL[M] ÉLECTRIQUE
GRILL[M]
PLANCHA[F]
handle
poignée[F]
Handgriff[M]
asa[F]
cooking surface
surface[F] de cuisson[F]
Grillfläche[F]
plancha[F]
detachable control
commande[F] amovible
abziehbarer Temperaturregler[M]
enchufe[M] y selector[M] desmontables
grease well
collecteur[M] de graisse[F]
Fettauffangschale[F]
colector[M] de grasa[F]

## REFRIGERATOR
## RÉFRIGÉRATEUR^M
## KÜHLSCHRANK^M
## FRIGORÍFICO^M

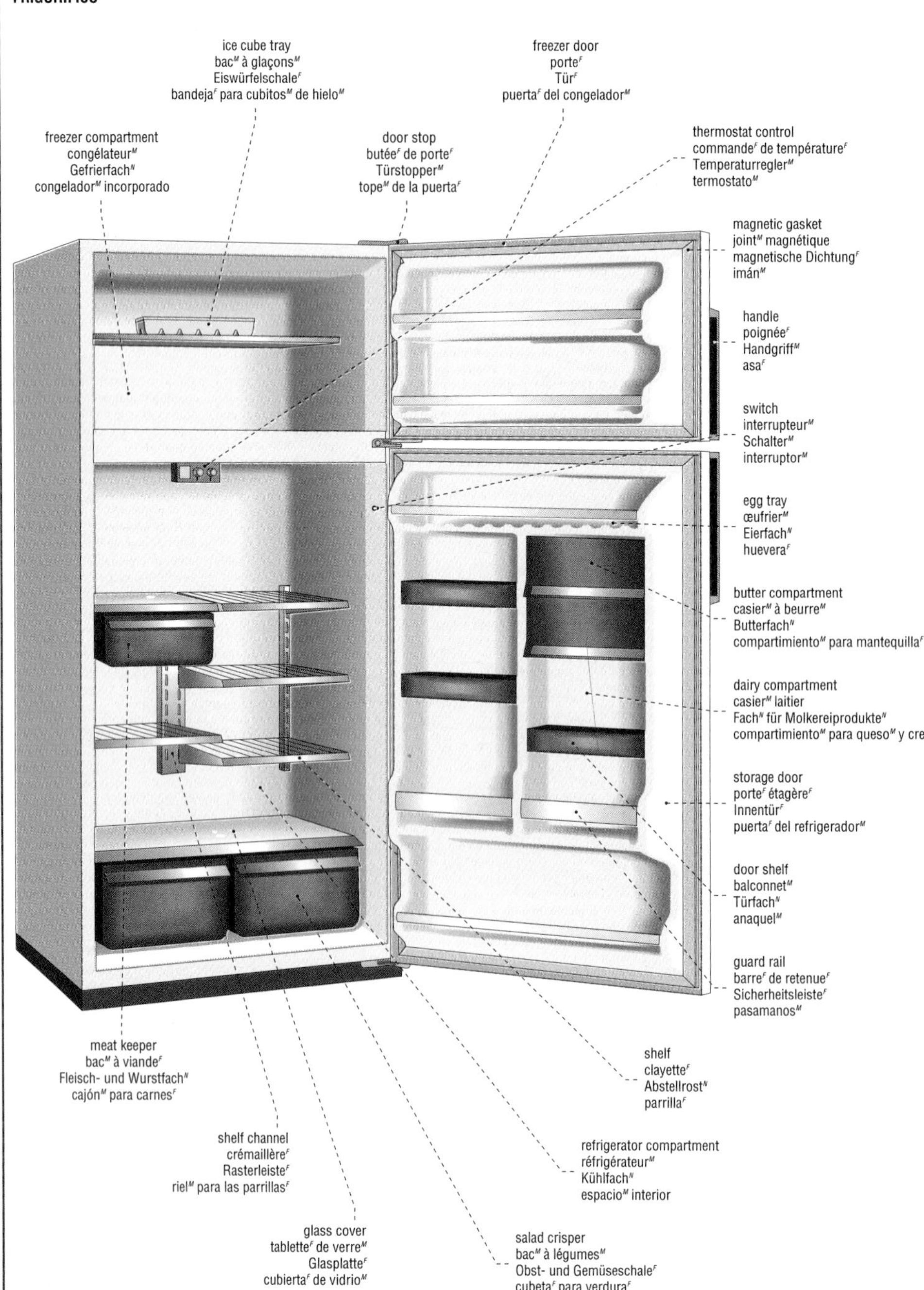

## EXTRACTOR HOOD
## HOTTE[F]
## DUNSTABZUGSHAUBE[F]
## CAMPANA[F]

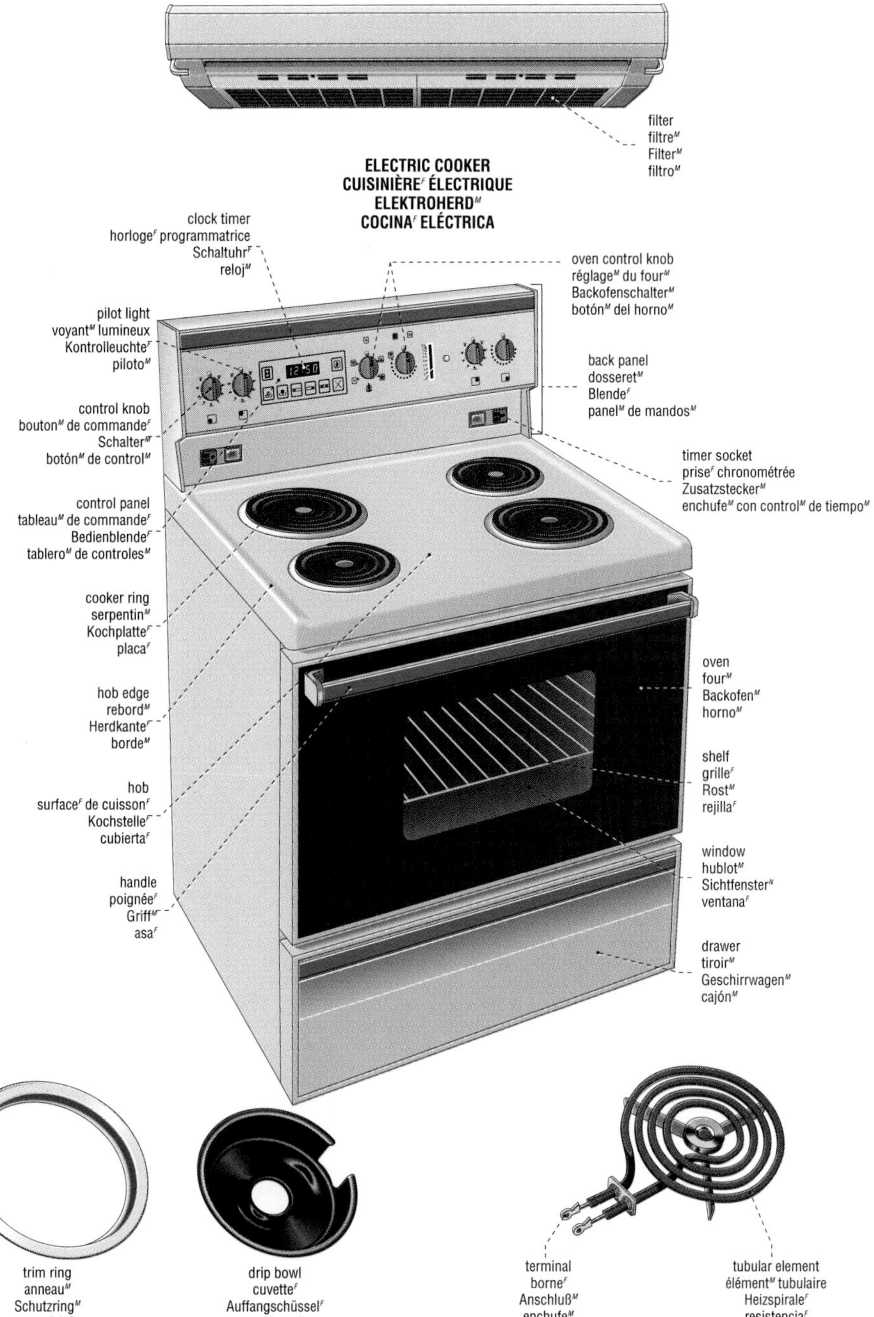

# DOMESTIC APPLIANCES
# APPAREILS[M] ÉLECTROMÉNAGERS
# HAUSHALTSGERÄTE[N]
# APARATOS[M] ELECTRODOMÉSTICOS

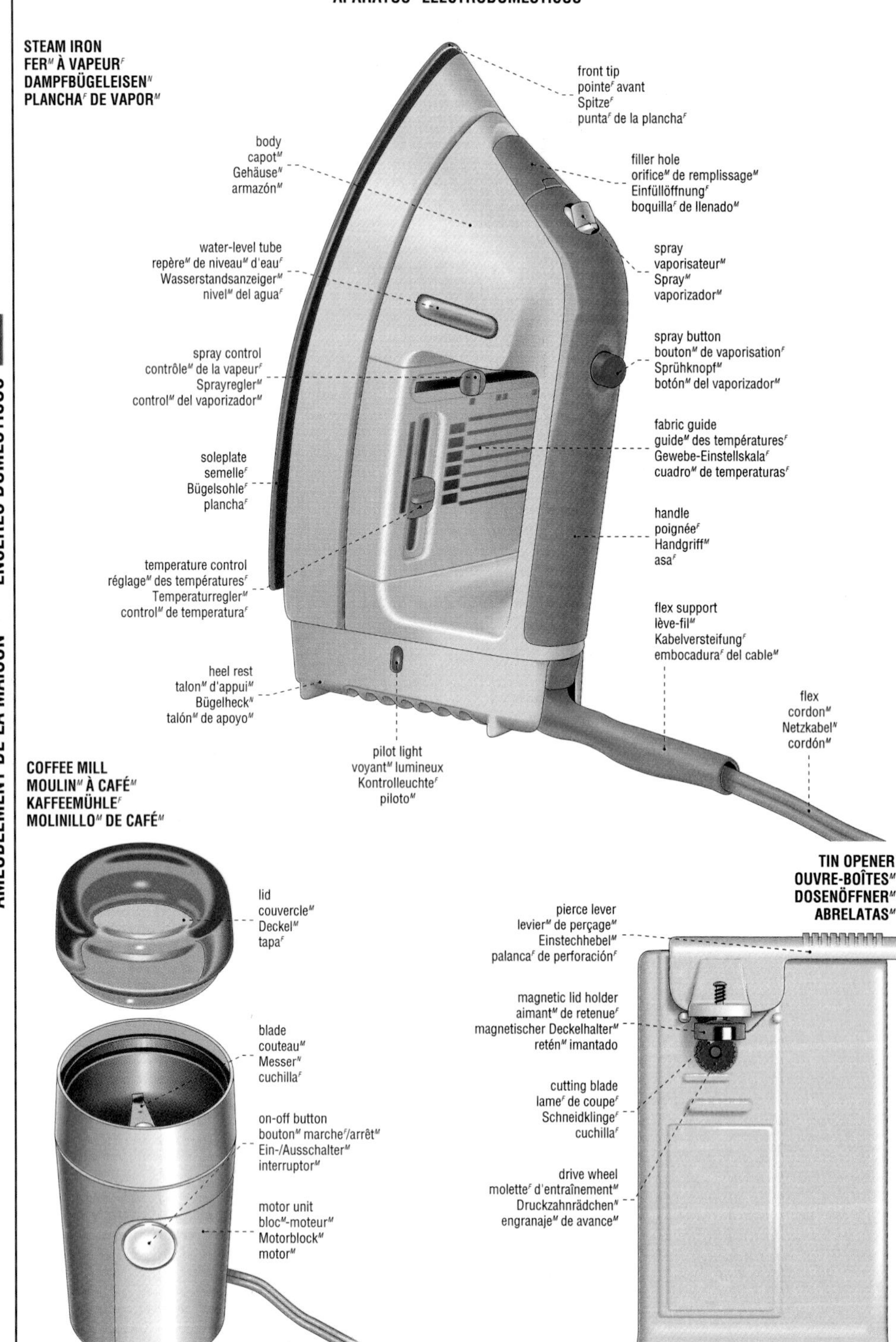

# DOMESTIC APPLIANCES
# APPAREILS[M] ÉLECTROMÉNAGERS
# HAUSHALTSGERÄTE[N]
# APARATOS[M] ELECTRODOMÉSTICOS

## CONTROL PANEL
## TABLEAU[M] DE COMMANDE[F]
## BEDIENBLENDE[F]
## PANEL[M] DE MANDOS[M]

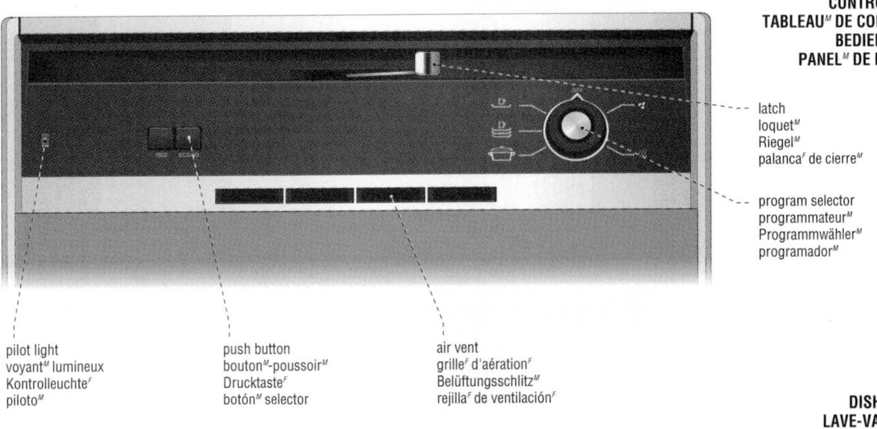

latch
loquet[M]
Riegel[M]
palanca[F] de cierre[M]

program selector
programmateur[M]
Programmwähler[M]
programador[M]

pilot light
voyant[M] lumineux
Kontrolleuchte[F]
piloto[M]

push button
bouton[M]-poussoir[M]
Drucktaste[F]
botón[M] selector

air vent
grille[F] d'aération[F]
Belüftungsschlitz[M]
rejilla[F] de ventilación[F]

## DISHWASHER
## LAVE-VAISSELLE[M]
## GESCHIRRSPÜLMASCHINE[F]
## LAVAVAJILLAS[M]

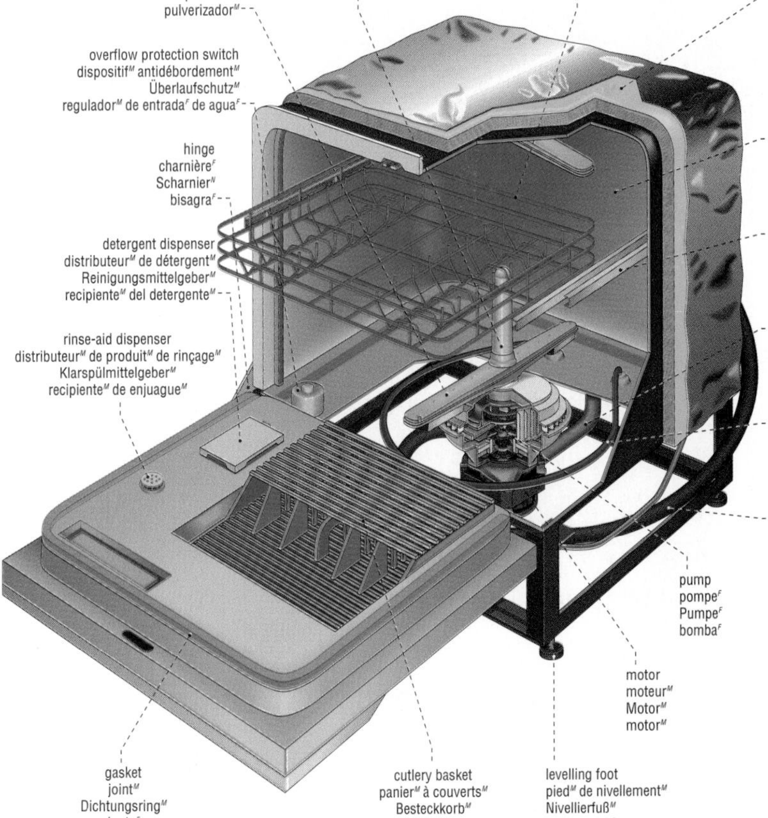

spray arm
bras[M] gicleur[M]
Sprüharm[M]
pulverizador[M]

wash tower
tourelle[F]
Wascherarm[M]
torrecilla[F] de lavado[M]

rack
panier[M]
Korb[M]
canastilla[F]

insulating material
isolant[M]
Isoliermaterial[N]
aislante[M]

overflow protection switch
dispositif[M] antidébordement[M]
Überlaufschutz[M]
regulador[M] de entrada[F] de agua[F]

hinge
charnière[F]
Scharnier[N]
bisagra[F]

tub
cuve[F]
Bottich[M]
cubeta[F] de lavado[M]

slide
glissière[F]
Schiene[F]
riel[M] corredizo

detergent dispenser
distributeur[M] de détergent[M]
Reinigungsmittelgeber[M]
recipiente[M] del detergente[M]

water hose
conduite[F] d'eau[F]
Wasserschlauch[M]
manguera[F] de alimentación[F]

rinse-aid dispenser
distributeur[M] de produit[M] de rinçage[M]
Klarspülmittelgeber[M]
recipiente[M] de enjuague[M]

heating element
élément[M] chauffant
Heizelement[N]
resistencia[F]

drain hose
tuyau[M] de vidange[F]
Ablaufschlauch[M]
manguera[F] de desagüe[M]

pump
pompe[F]
Pumpe[F]
bomba[F]

motor
moteur[M]
Motor[M]
motor[M]

gasket
joint[M]
Dichtungsring[M]
junta[F]

cutlery basket
panier[M] à couverts[M]
Besteckkorb[M]
canastilla[F] para cubiertos[M]

levelling foot
pied[M] de nivellement[M]
Nivellierfuß[M]
pie[M] ajustable

**WASHING MACHINE**
**LAVE-LINGE^M**
**WASCHMASCHINE^F**
**LAVADORA^F**

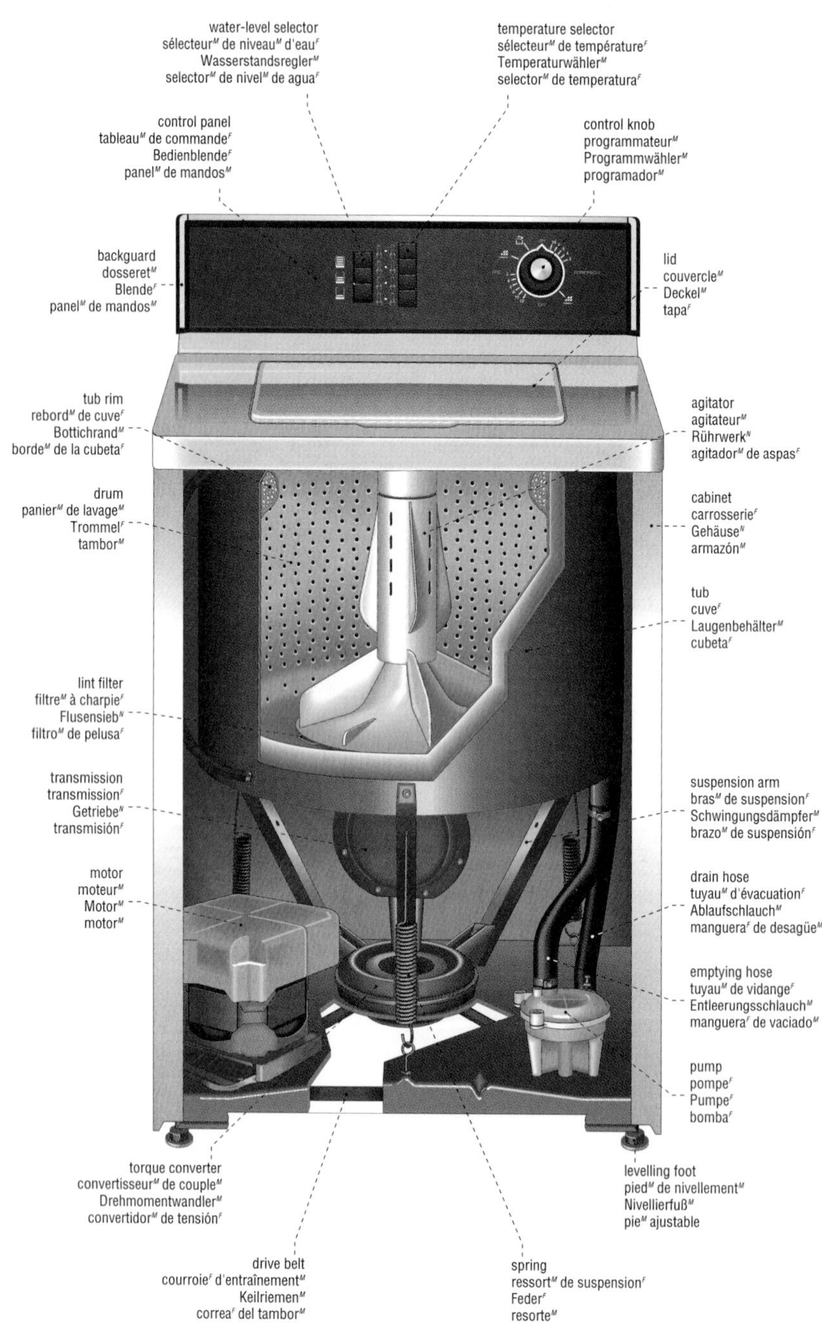

## ELECTRIC TUMBLE DRYER
## SÈCHE-LINGE[M] ÉLECTRIQUE
## WÄSCHETROCKNER[M]
## SECADORA[F] DE ROPA[F]

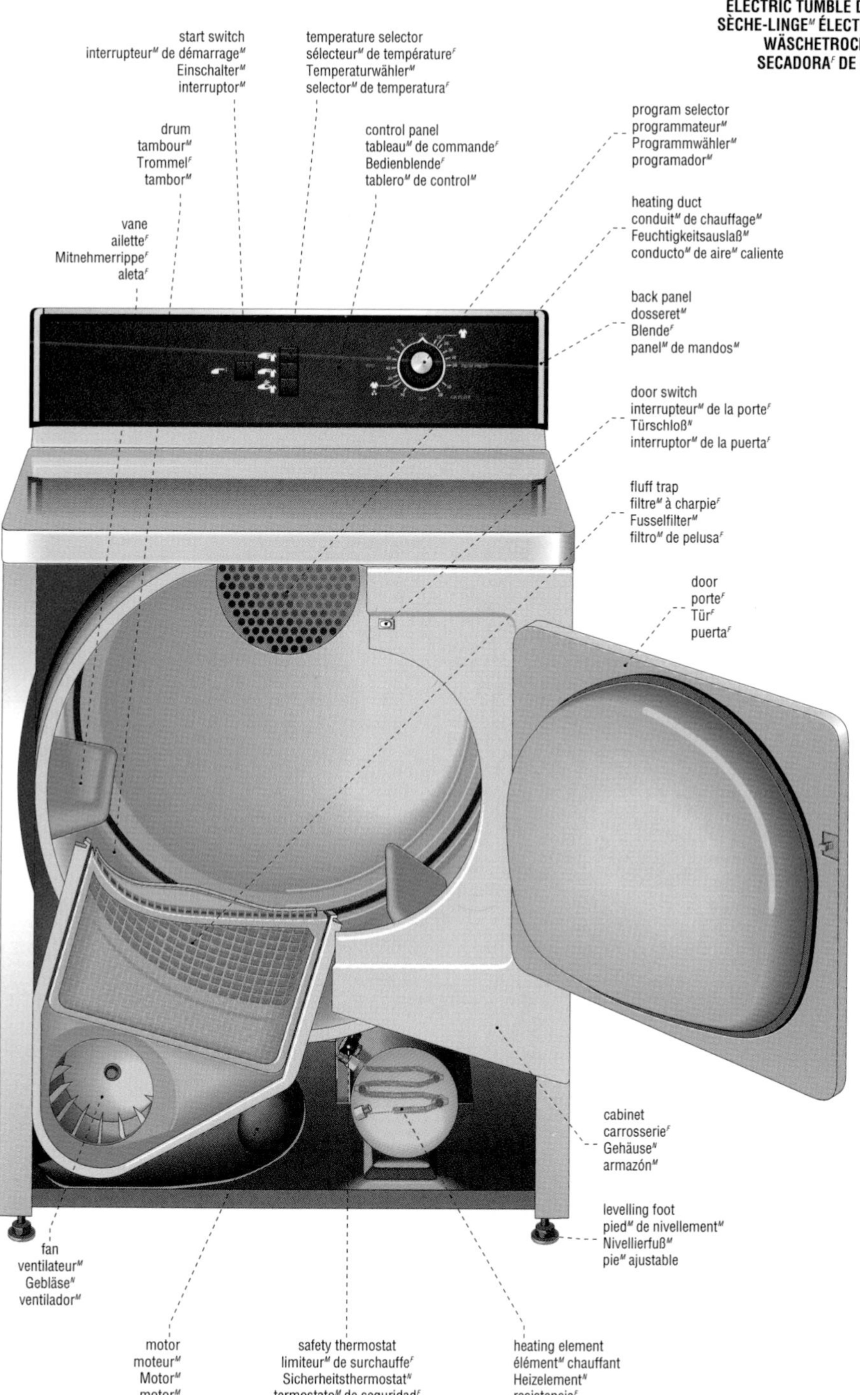

# DOMESTIC APPLIANCES
# APPAREILS[M] ÉLECTROMÉNAGERS
# HAUSHALTSGERÄTE[N]
# APARATOS[M] ELECTRODOMÉSTICOS

## HAND VACUUM CLEANER
## ASPIRATEUR[M] À MAIN[F]
## AKKU-MINI-STAUBSAUGER[M]
## ASPIRADOR[M] MANUAL

locking button
verrouillage[M]
Entriegelungstaste[F]
botón[M] de cierre[M]
dust receiver
godet[M] à poussière[M]
Staubbehälter[M]
depósito de polvo[M]
on-off switch
interrupteur[M]
Ein-/Ausschalter[M]
interruptor[M]
recharging base
socle[M]-chargeur[M]
Lade-Anschlußbuchse[F]
cargador[M]
motor unit
bloc[M]-moteur[M]
Motorblock[M]
motor[M]

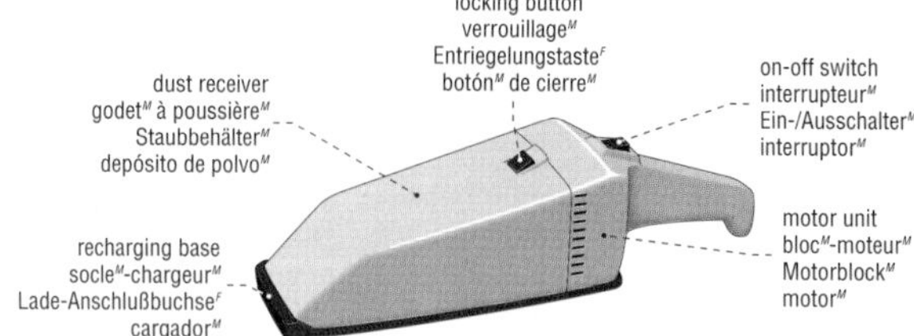

## CYLINDER VACUUM CLEANER
## ASPIRATEUR[M]-TRAÎNEAU[M]
## KESSELSTAUBSAUGER[M]
## ASPIRADOR[M]

locking device
système[M] de verrouillage[M]
Verschluß[M]
seguro[M]
on-off switch
interrupteur[M]
Ein-/Ausschalter[M]
interruptor[M]
rigid tube
tube[M] droit
Saugrohr[N]
tubo[M] rígido
hood
capot[M]
Haube[F]
tapa[F]
handle
poignée[F]
Handgriff[M]
asa[F]
ventilating grille
grille[F] de ventilation[F]
Luftaustrittsschlitz[M]
rejilla[F] del ventilador[M]
flexible hose
tuyau[M] flexible
beweglicher Schlauch[M]
manguera[F]
extension tube
rallonge[F]
Ansatzrohr[N]
tubo[M] de extensión[F]
bumper
pare-chocs[M]
Stoßleiste[F]
tope[M] amortiguador
flex
cordon[M]
Kabel[N]
cordón[M]
caster
roulette[F]
Lenkrolle[F]
ruedecilla[F]
carpet and floor brush
suceur[M] à tapis[M] et planchers[M]
Bodendüse[F]
boquilla[F] para pisos[M] y alfombras[F]

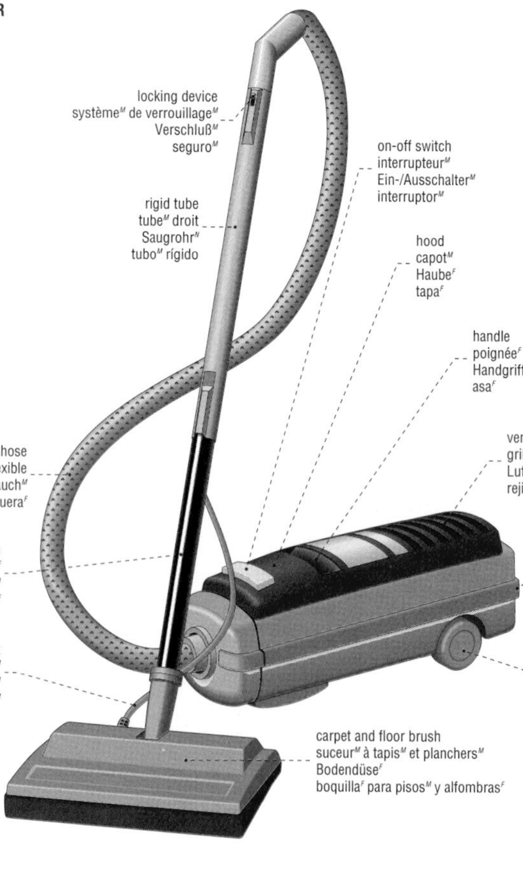

## CLEANING TOOLS
## ACCESSOIRES[M]
## SAUGZUBEHÖR[N]
## ACCESORIOS[M]

upholstery nozzle
suceur[M] triangulaire à tissus[M]
Polsterdüse[F]
boquilla[F] para tapicería[F]

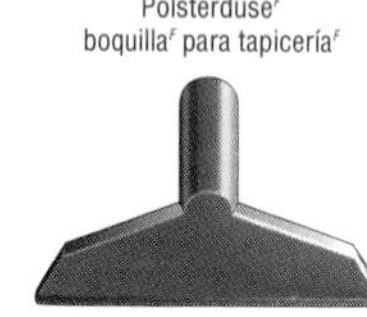

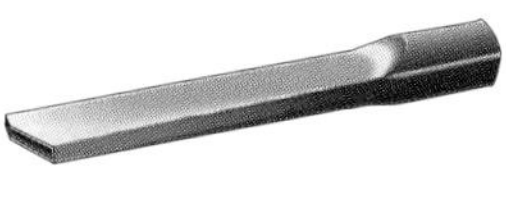

crevice tool
suceur[M] plat
Fugendüse[F]
boquilla[F] rinconera

floor brush
brosse[F] à planchers[M]
Bürste[F]
cepillo[M] para pisos[M]

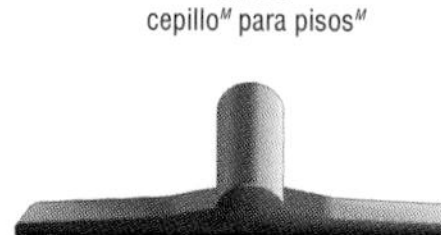

dusting brush
brosse[F] à épousseter
Saugpinsel[M]
cepillo[M]-plumero[M]

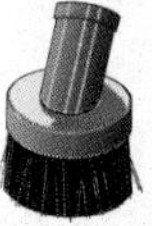

# GARDENING
# JARDINAGE
# GARTENARBEIT
# JARDINERIA

**SUMMARY**

# PLEASURE GARDEN
# JARDIN[M] D'AGRÉMENT[M]
# ZIERGARTEN[M]
# JARDÍN[M]

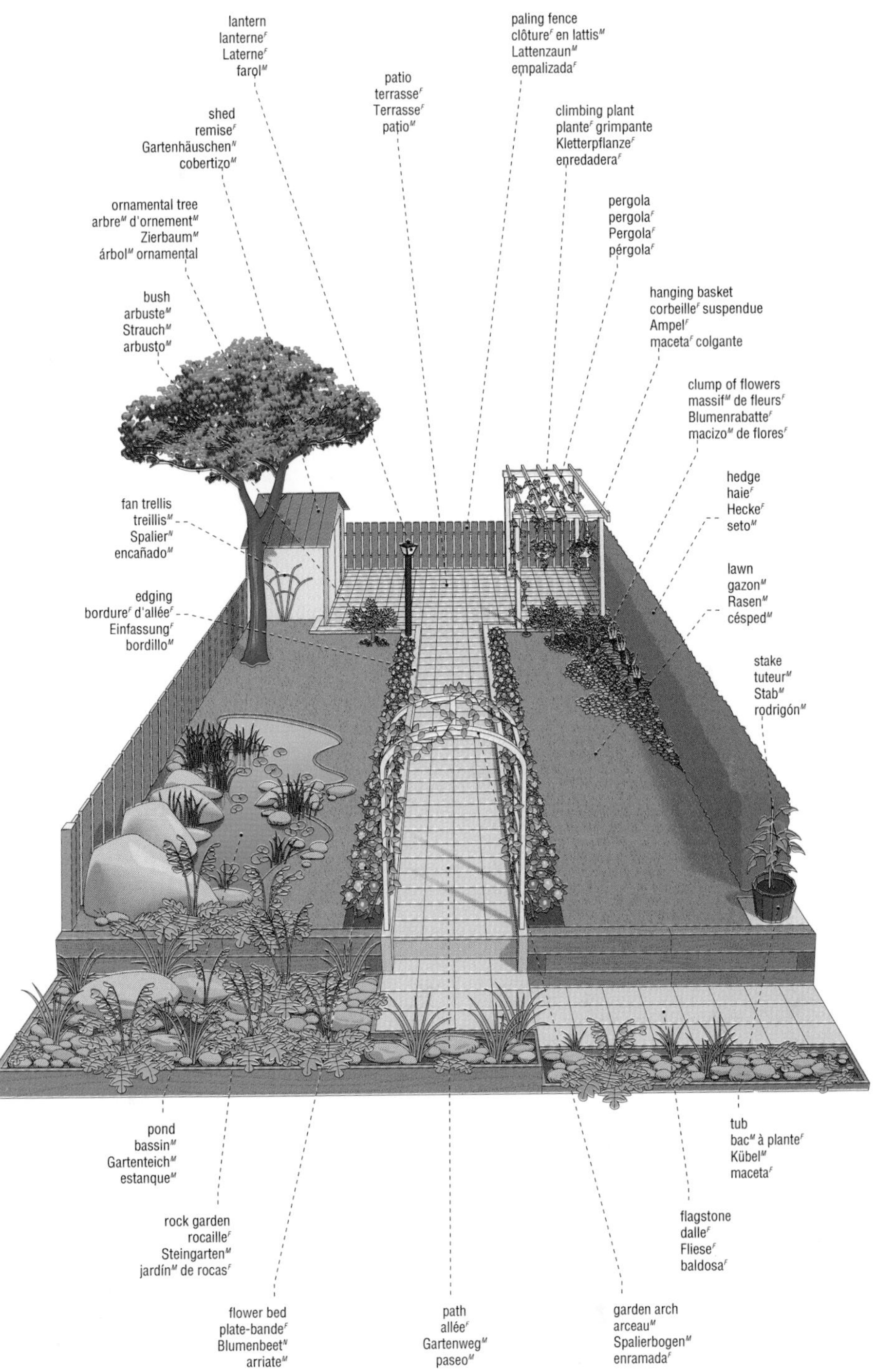

# TOOLS AND EQUIPMENT
# OUTILLAGE[M]
# GARTENGERÄT[N]
# HERRAMIENTAS[F] Y MÁQUINAS[F]

pistol nozzle
pistolet[M] d'arrosage[M]
Gießpistole[F]
pistola[F] pulverizadora

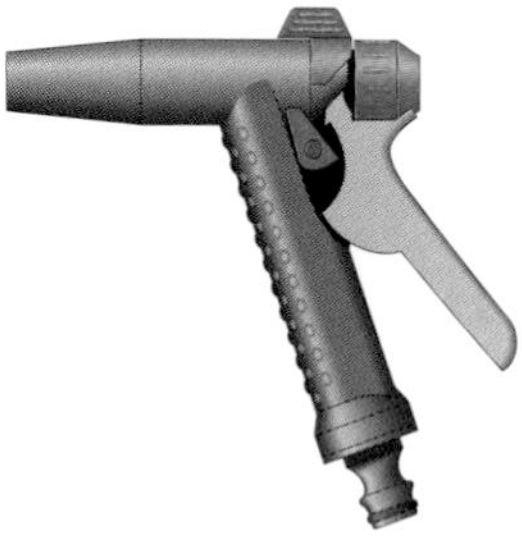

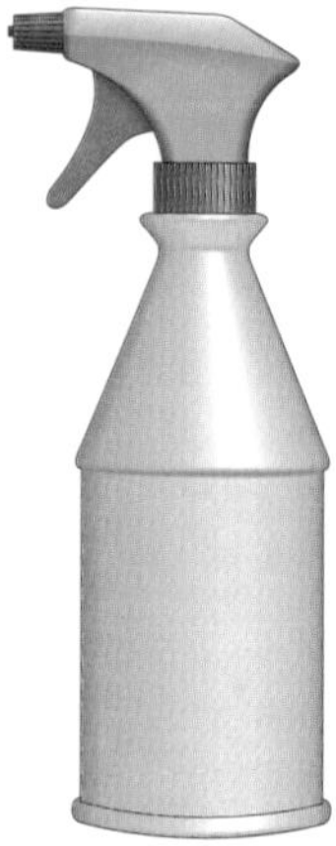

sprayer
vaporisateur[M]
Sprühflasche[F]
pulverizador[M]

spray nozzle
pistolet[M] arrosoir[M]
Gießbrause[F]
boquilla[F] pulverizadora

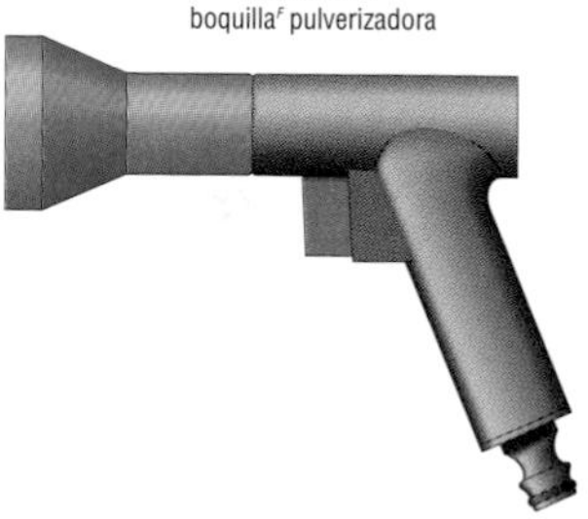

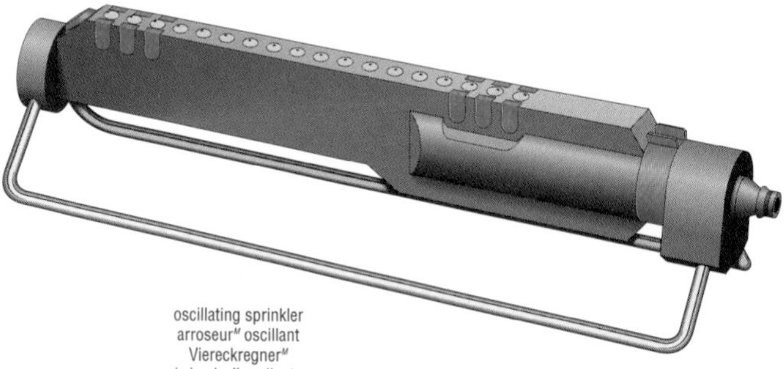

oscillating sprinkler
arroseur[M] oscillant
Viereckregner[M]
irrigador[M] oscilante

arm
bras[M]
Drehdüse[F]
brazo[M]

## REVOLVING SPRINKLER
## ARROSEUR[M] ROTATIF
## KREISREGNER[M]
## IRRIGADOR[M] GIRATORIO

## IMPULSE SPRINKLER
## ARROSEUR[M] CANON[M]
## IMPULSREGNER[M]
## IRRIGADOR[M] DE IMPULSO[M]

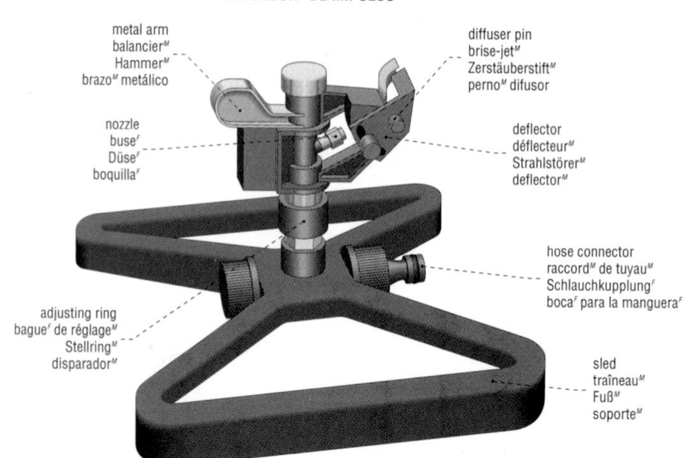

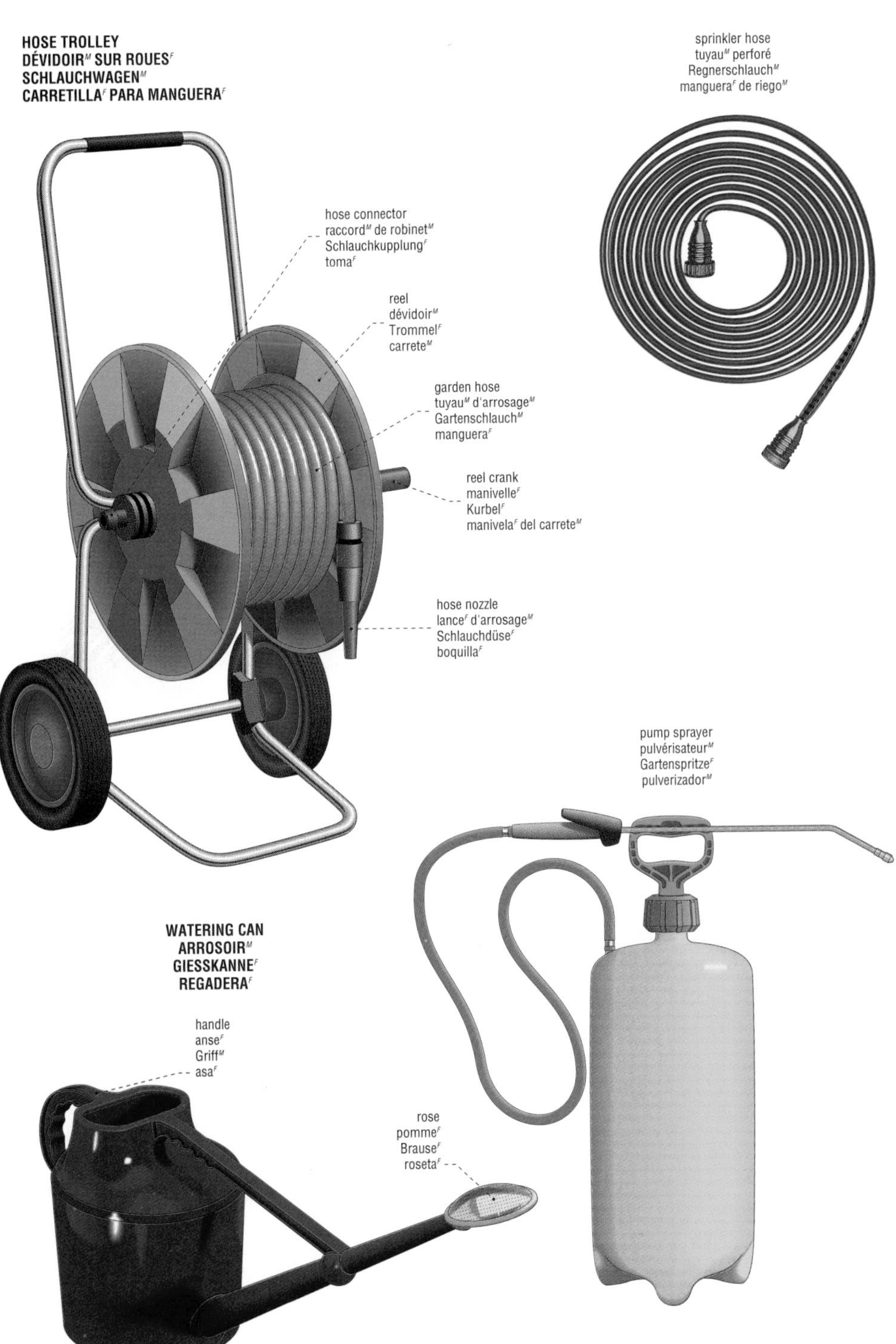
HOSE TROLLEY
DÉVIDOIR[M] SUR ROUES[F]
SCHLAUCHWAGEN[M]
CARRETILLA[F] PARA MANGUERA[F]
hose connector
raccord[M] de robinet[M]
Schlauchkupplung[F]
toma[F]
reel
dévidoir[M]
Trommel[F]
carrete[M]
garden hose
tuyau[M] d'arrosage[M]
Gartenschlauch[M]
manguera[F]
reel crank
manivelle[F]
Kurbel[F]
manivela[F] del carrete[M]
hose nozzle
lance[F] d'arrosage[M]
Schlauchdüse[F]
boquilla[F]
sprinkler hose
tuyau[M] perforé
Regnerschlauch[M]
manguera[F] de riego[M]
pump sprayer
pulvérisateur[M]
Gartenspritze[F]
pulverizador[M]
WATERING CAN
ARROSOIR[M]
GIESSKANNE[F]
REGADERA[F]
handle
anse[F]
Griff[M]
asa[F]
rose
pomme[F]
Brause[F]
roseta[F]

# TOOLS AND EQUIPMENT
# OUTILLAGE^M
# GARTENGERÄT^N
# HERRAMIENTAS^F Y MÁQUINAS^F

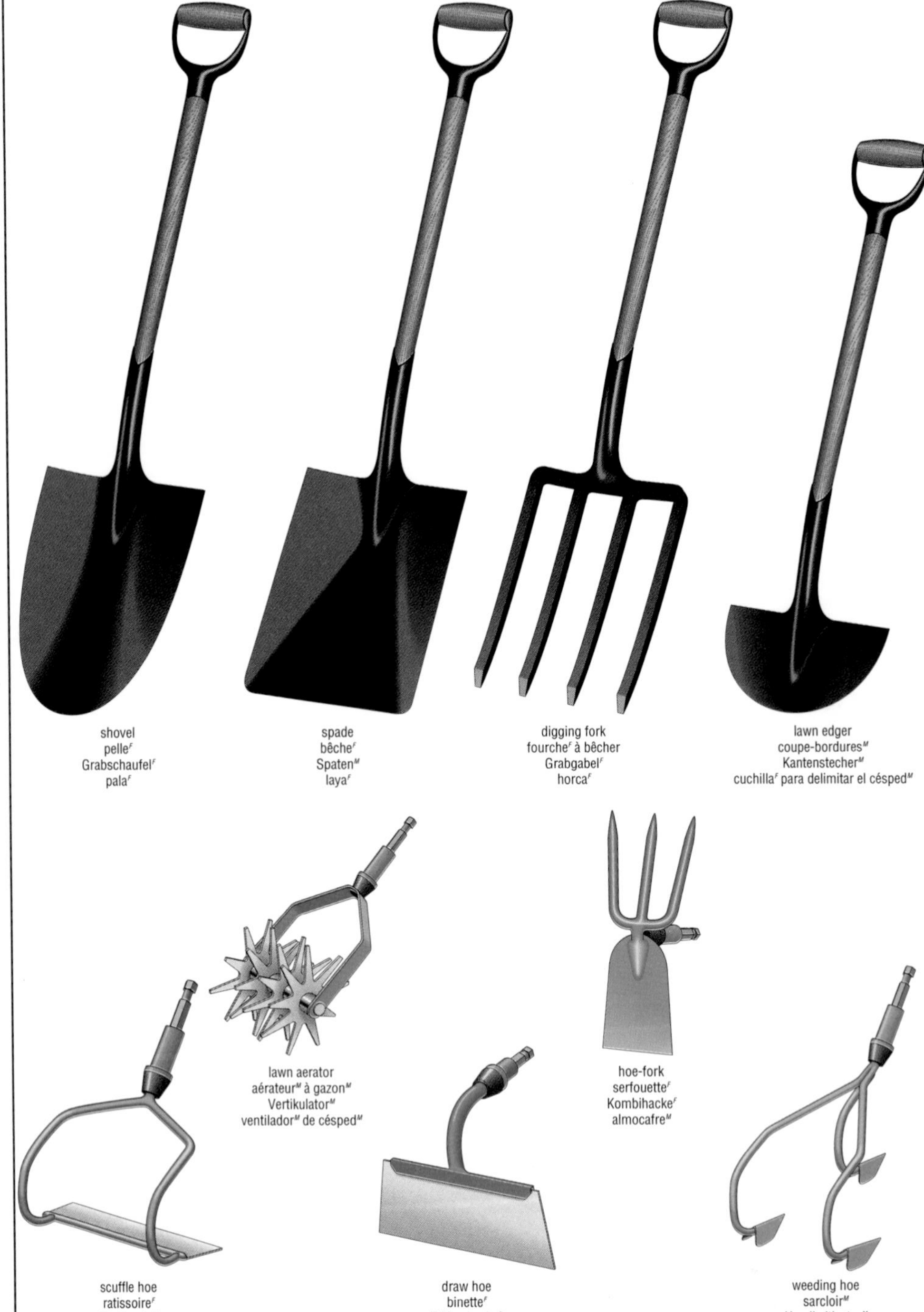

shovel
pelle^F
Grabschaufel^F
pala^F

spade
bêche^F
Spaten^M
laya^F

digging fork
fourche^F à bêcher
Grabgabel^F
horca^F

lawn edger
coupe-bordures^M
Kantenstecher^M
cuchilla^F para delimitar el césped^M

lawn aerator
aérateur^M à gazon^M
Vertikulator^M
ventilador^M de césped^M

hoe-fork
serfouette^F
Kombihacke^F
almocafre^M

scuffle hoe
ratissoire^F
Ziehhacke^F
azada^F de doble filo^M

draw hoe
binette^F
Rübenhacke^F
azada^F

weeding hoe
sarcloir^M
Handkultivator^M
escardillo^M

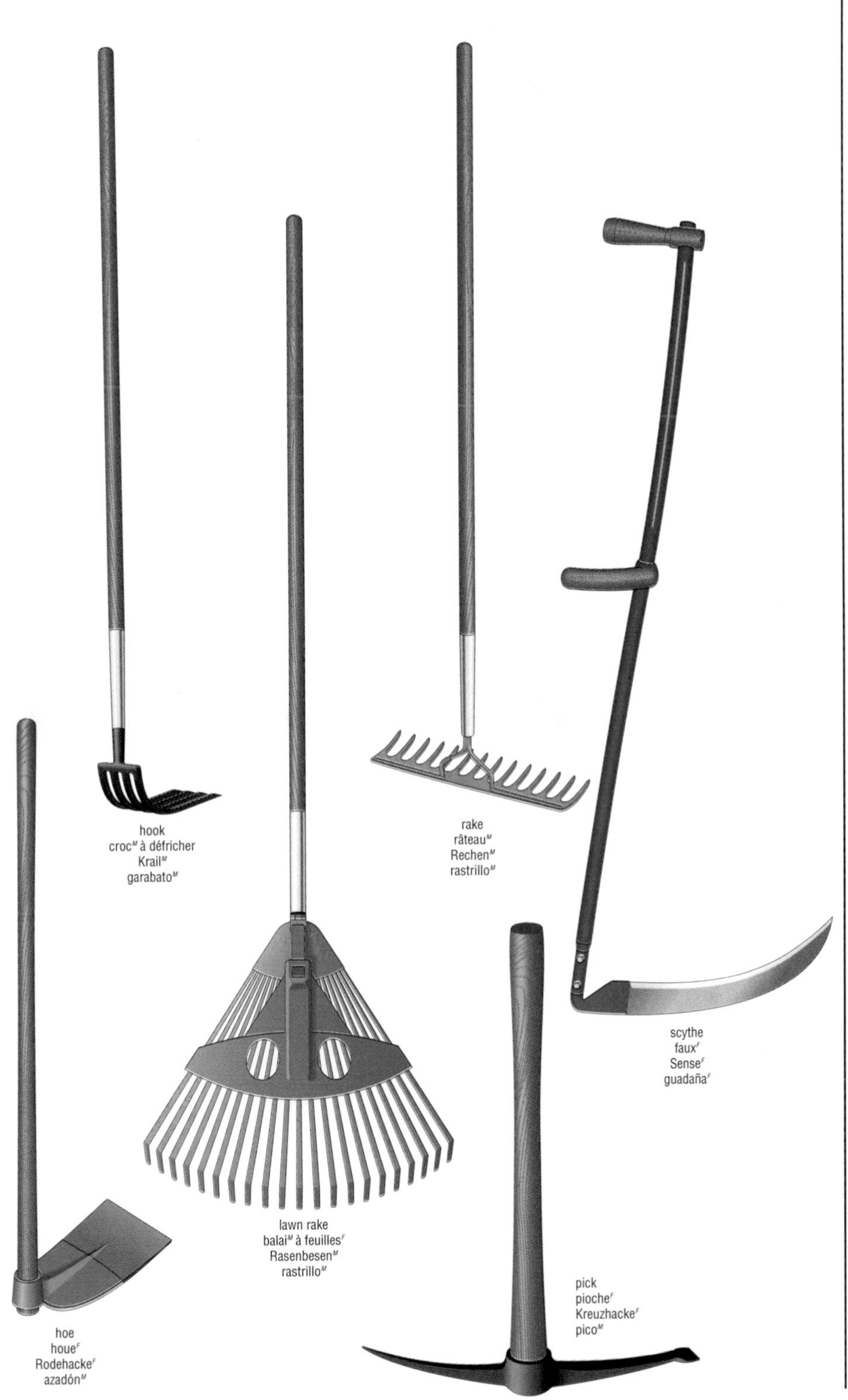
hook
croc^M à défricher
Krail^M
garabato^M
rake
râteau^M
Rechen^M
rastrillo^M
scythe
faux^F
Sense^F
guadaña^F
lawn rake
balai^M à feuilles^F
Rasenbesen^M
rastrillo^M
pick
pioche^F
Kreuzhacke^F
pico^M
hoe
houe^F
Rodehacke^F
azadón^M

## TOOLS AND EQUIPMENT
## OUTILLAGE[M]
## GARTENGERÄT[N]
## HERRAMIENTAS[F] Y MÁQUINAS[F]

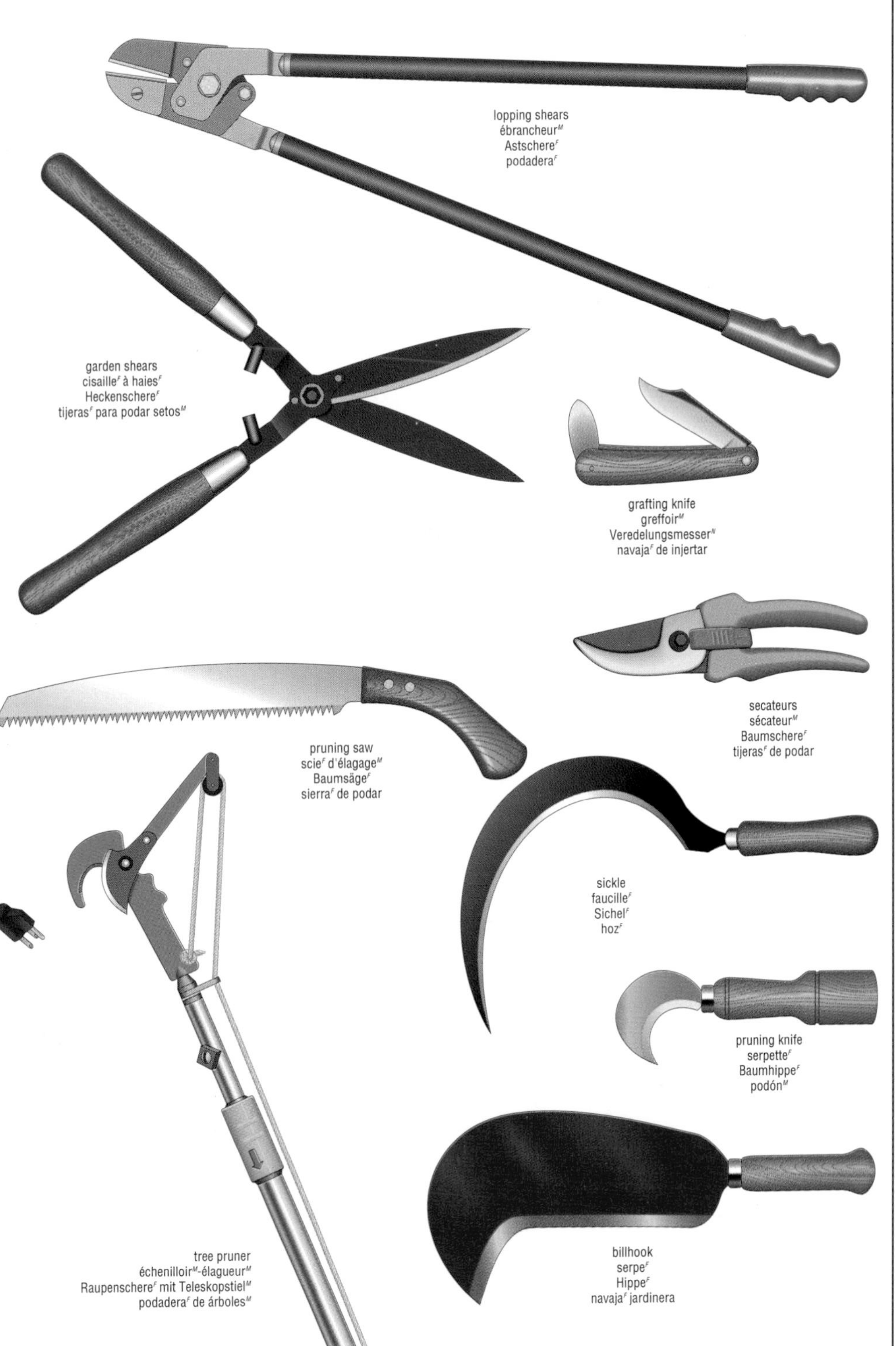
lopping shears
ébrancheur[M]
Astschere[F]
podadera[F]
garden shears
cisaille[F] à haies[F]
Heckenschere[F]
tijeras[F] para podar setos[M]
grafting knife
greffoir[M]
Veredelungsmesser[N]
navaja[F] de injertar
secateurs
sécateur[M]
Baumschere[F]
tijeras[F] de podar
pruning saw
scie[F] d'élagage[M]
Baumsäge[F]
sierra[F] de podar
sickle
faucille[F]
Sichel[F]
hoz[F]
pruning knife
serpette[F]
Baumhippe[F]
podón[M]
tree pruner
échenilloir[M]-élagueur[M]
Raupenschere[F] mit Teleskopstiel[M]
podadera[F] de árboles[M]
billhook
serpe[F]
Hippe[F]
navaja[F] jardinera

## TOOLS AND EQUIPMENT
## OUTILLAGE[M]
## GARTENGERÄT[N]
## HERRAMIENTAS[F] Y MÁQUINAS[F]

HAND MOWER
TONDEUSE^F MÉCANIQUE
HANDRASENMÄHER^M
CORTACÉSPED^M
blade
lame^F
Messer^N
cuchilla^F
cutting cylinder
cylindre^M de coupe^F
Schneidzylinder^M
cilindro^M de corte^M
TRIMMER
TAILLE-BORDURES^M
RASENTRIMMER^M
PODADORA^F DE BORDES^M
flex
cordon^M
Kabel^N
cable^M
electric motor
moteur^M électrique
Elektromotor^M
motor^M eléctrico
protective casing
carter^M de sécurité^F
Schutzgehäuse^N
cubierta^F de seguridad^F
nylon line
fil^M de nylon^M
Nylonschnur^F
hilo^M de nilón^M
POWER MOWER
TONDEUSE^F À MOTEUR^M
MOTORRASENMÄHER^M
CORTACÉSPED^M ELÉCTRICO
handle
guidon^M
Griff^M
barra^F
throttle
sélecteur^M de régime^M
Geschwindigkeitsregler^M
control^M de velocidad^F
safety handle
poignée^F de sécurité^F
Sicherheitsgriff^M
palanca^F de seguridad^F
ignition key
clé^F de contact^M
Zündschlüssel^M
encendido^M
grassbox
bac^M de ramassage^M
Grasfang^M
caja^F para el césped^M
motor
moteur^M
Motor^M
motor^M
starter
démarreur^M manuel
Anlasser^M
motor^M de arranque^M
throttle cable
câble^M d'accélération^F
Gaszug^M
cable^M del acelerador^M
filler cap
bouchon^M de remplissage^M
Einfüllstutzen^M
boca^F del tanque^M de combustible^M
sparking plug
bougie^F
Zündkerze^F
bujía^F
deflector
déflecteur^M
Leitblech^N
deflector^M
casing
carter^M
Gehäuse^N
caja^F

# TOOLS AND EQUIPMENT
# OUTILLAGE[M]
# GARTENGERÄT[N]
# HERRAMIENTAS[F] Y MÁQUINAS[F]

## CHAINSAW
## SCIE[F] À CHAÎNE[F]
## KETTENSÄGE[F]
## SIERRA[F] DE CADENA[F]

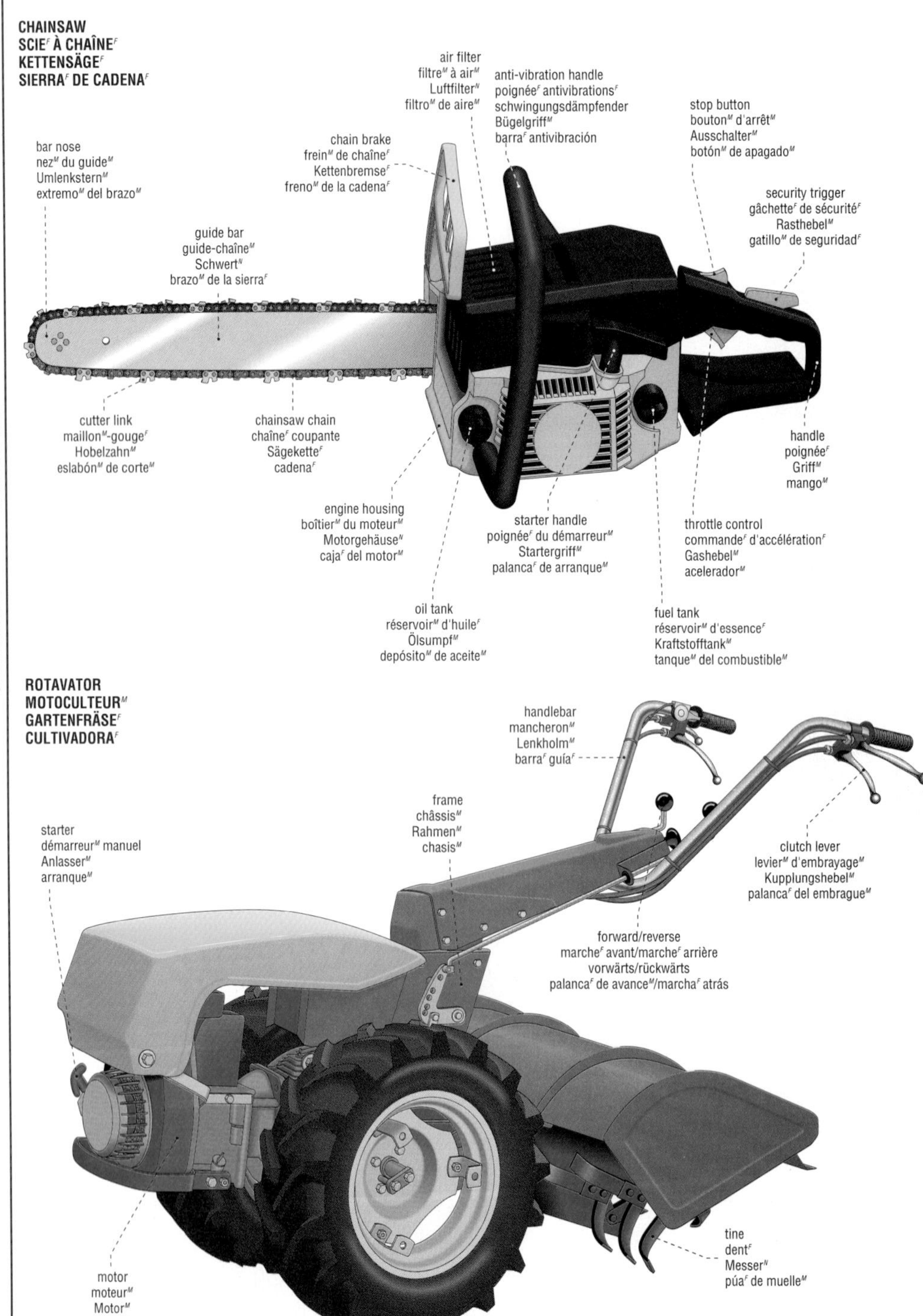

# DO-IT-YOURSELF
# BRICOLAGE

# DO-IT-YOURSELF
# REPARACIONES CASERAS

SUMMARY

## CARPENTRY: TOOLS
## MENUISERIE^F: OUTILS^M
## SCHREINEREI^F: WERKZEUGE^N
## CARPINTERÍA^F: HERRAMIENTAS^F

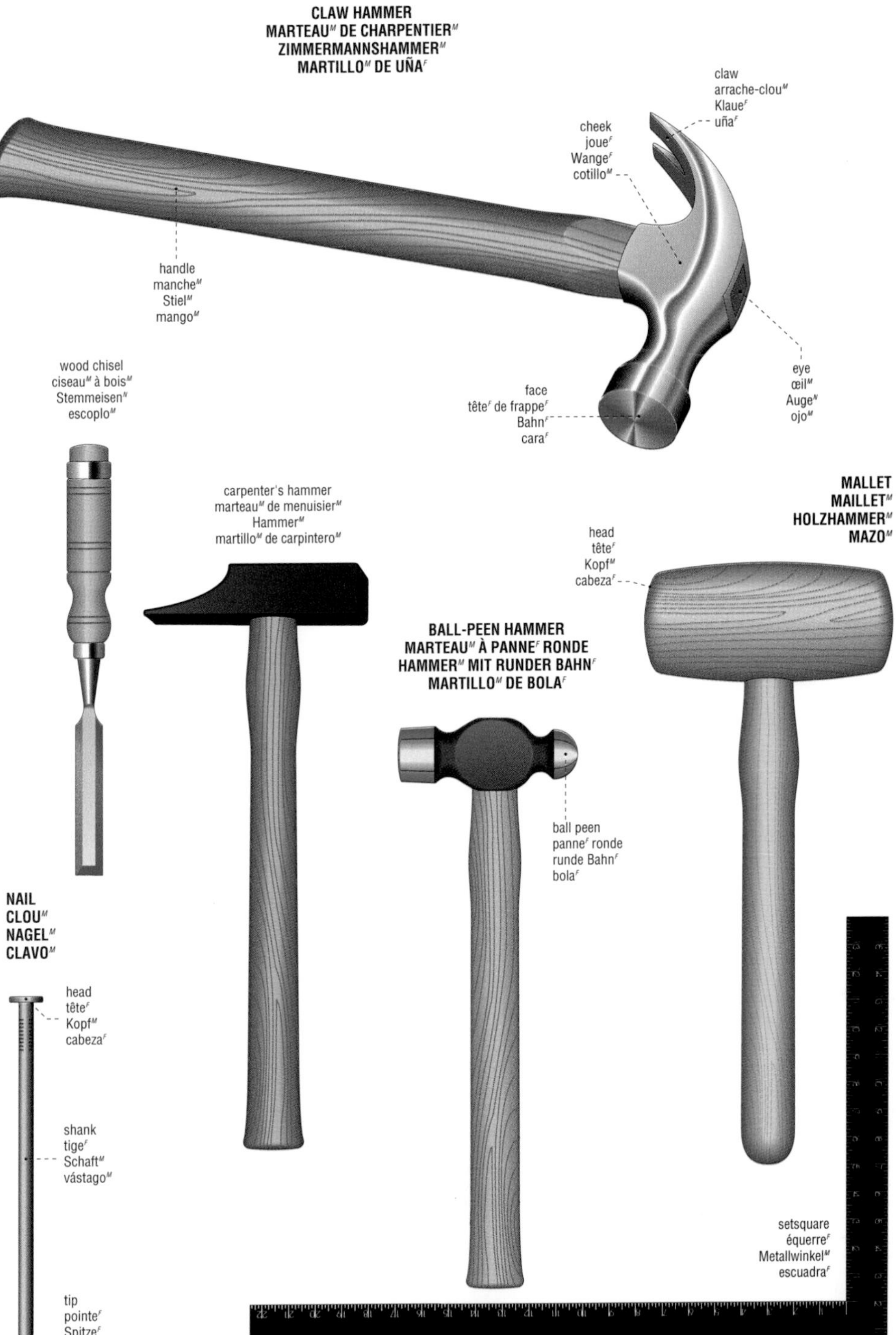

# CARPENTRY: TOOLS
# MENUISERIE[F]: OUTILS[M]
# SCHREINEREI[F]: WERKZEUGE[N]
# CARPINTERÍA[F]: HERRAMIENTAS[F]

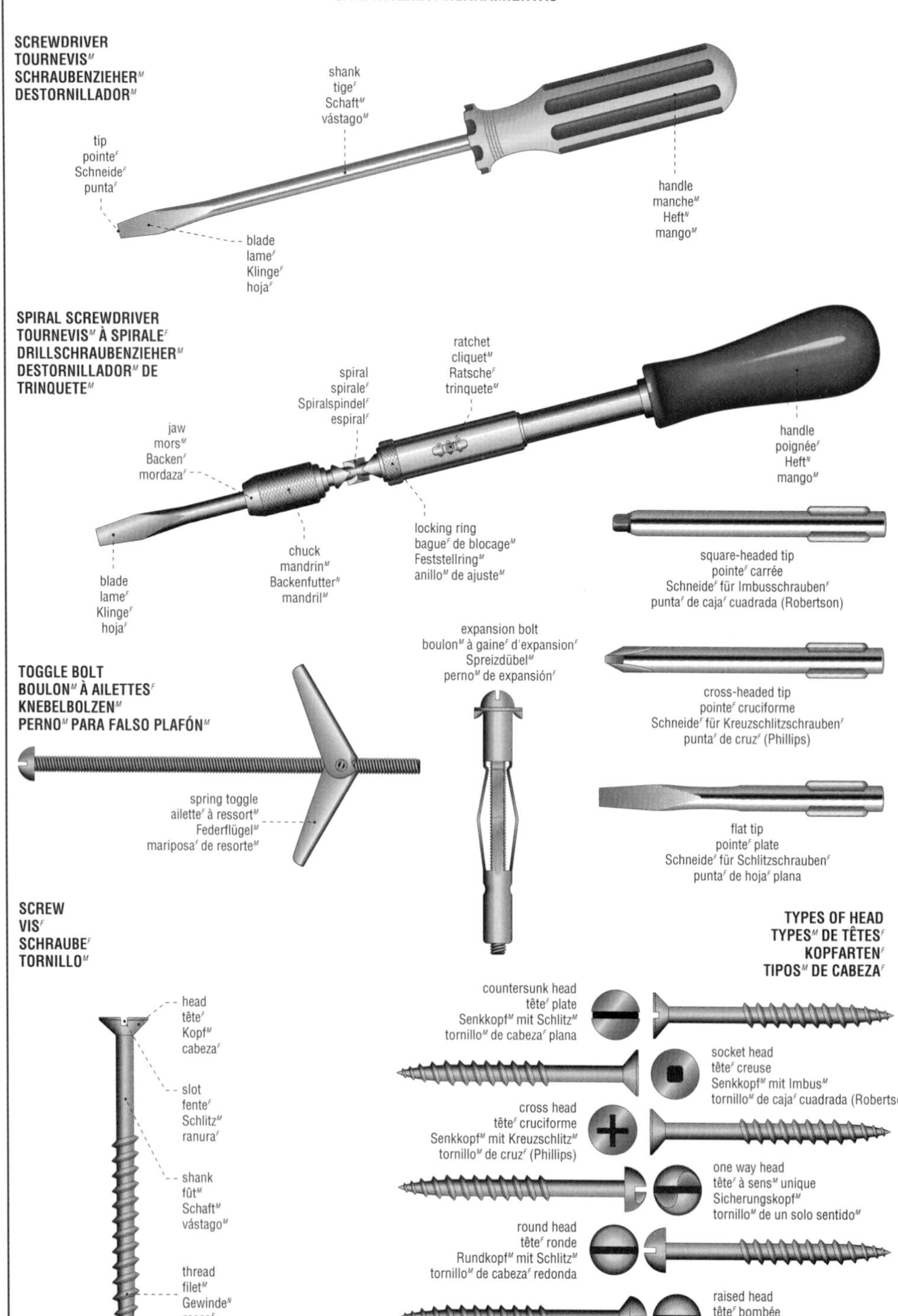

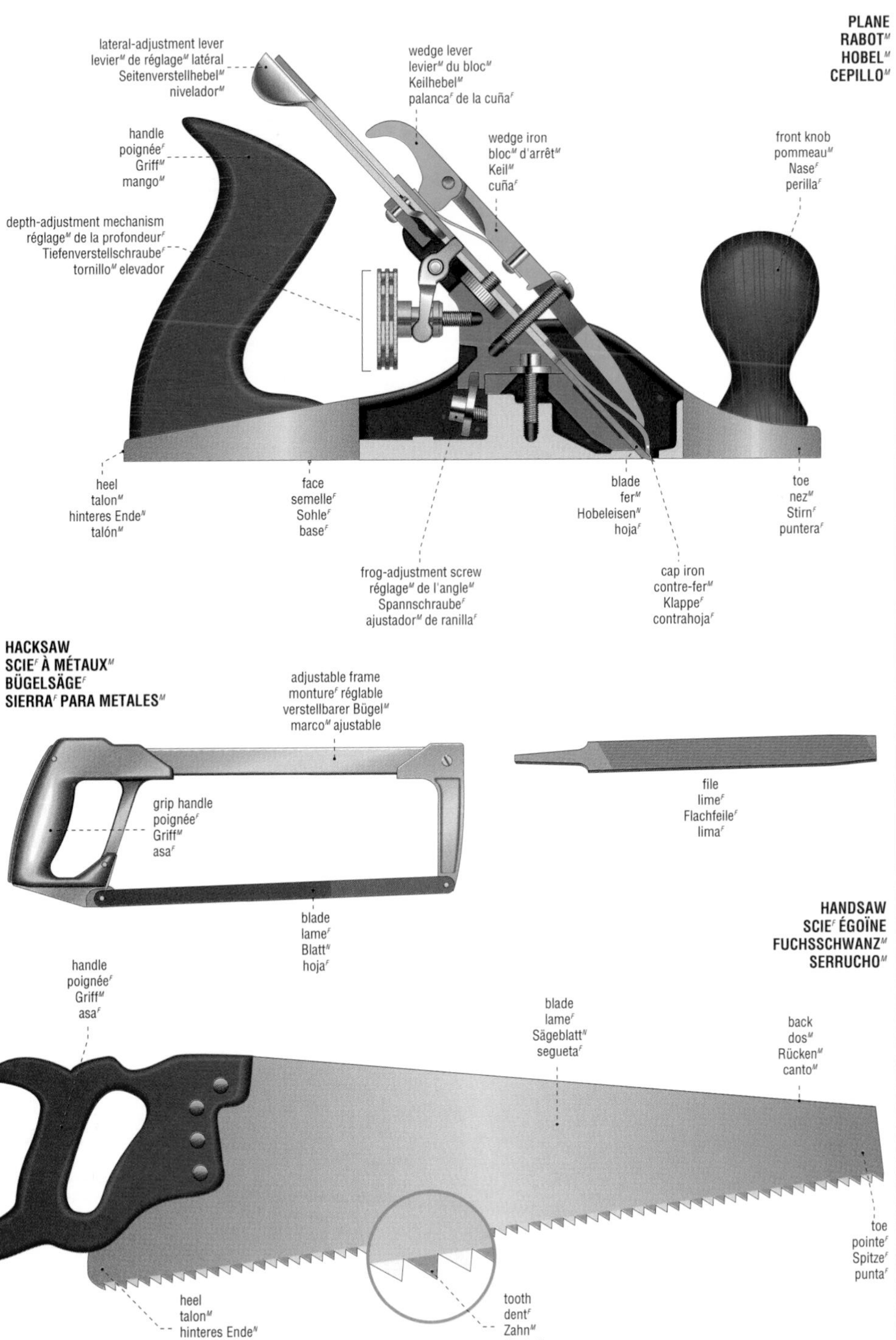
PLANE
RABOT[M]
HOBEL[M]
CEPILLO[M]
lateral-adjustment lever
levier[M] de réglage[M] latéral
Seitenverstellhebel[M]
nivelador[M]
wedge lever
levier[M] du bloc[M]
Keilhebel[M]
palanca[F] de la cuña[F]
handle
poignée[F]
Griff[M]
mango[M]
wedge iron
bloc[M] d'arrêt[M]
Keil[M]
cuña[F]
front knob
pommeau[M]
Nase[F]
perilla[F]
depth-adjustment mechanism
réglage[M] de la profondeur[F]
Tiefenverstellschraube[F]
tornillo[M] elevador
heel
talon[M]
hinteres Ende[N]
talón[M]
face
semelle[F]
Sohle[F]
base[F]
blade
fer[M]
Hobeleisen[N]
hoja[F]
toe
nez[M]
Stirn[F]
puntera[F]
frog-adjustment screw
réglage[M] de l'angle[M]
Spannschraube[F]
ajustador[M] de ranilla[F]
cap iron
contre-fer[M]
Klappe[F]
contrahoja[F]
HACKSAW
SCIE[F] À MÉTAUX[M]
BÜGELSÄGE[F]
SIERRA[F] PARA METALES[M]
adjustable frame
monture[F] réglable
verstellbarer Bügel[M]
marco[M] ajustable
grip handle
poignée[F]
Griff[M]
asa[F]
file
lime[F]
Flachfeile[F]
lima[F]
blade
lame[F]
Blatt[N]
hoja[F]
HANDSAW
SCIE[F] ÉGOÏNE
FUCHSSCHWANZ[M]
SERRUCHO[M]
handle
poignée[F]
Griff[M]
asa[F]
blade
lame[F]
Sägeblatt[N]
segueta[F]
back
dos[M]
Rücken[M]
canto[M]
toe
pointe[F]
Spitze[F]
punta[F]
heel
talon[M]
hinteres Ende[N]
talón[M]
tooth
dent[F]
Zahn[M]
diente[M]

# CARPENTRY: TOOLS
# MENUISERIE[F]: OUTILS[M]
# SCHREINEREI[F]: WERKZEUGE[N]
# CARPINTERÍA[F]: HERRAMIENTAS[F]

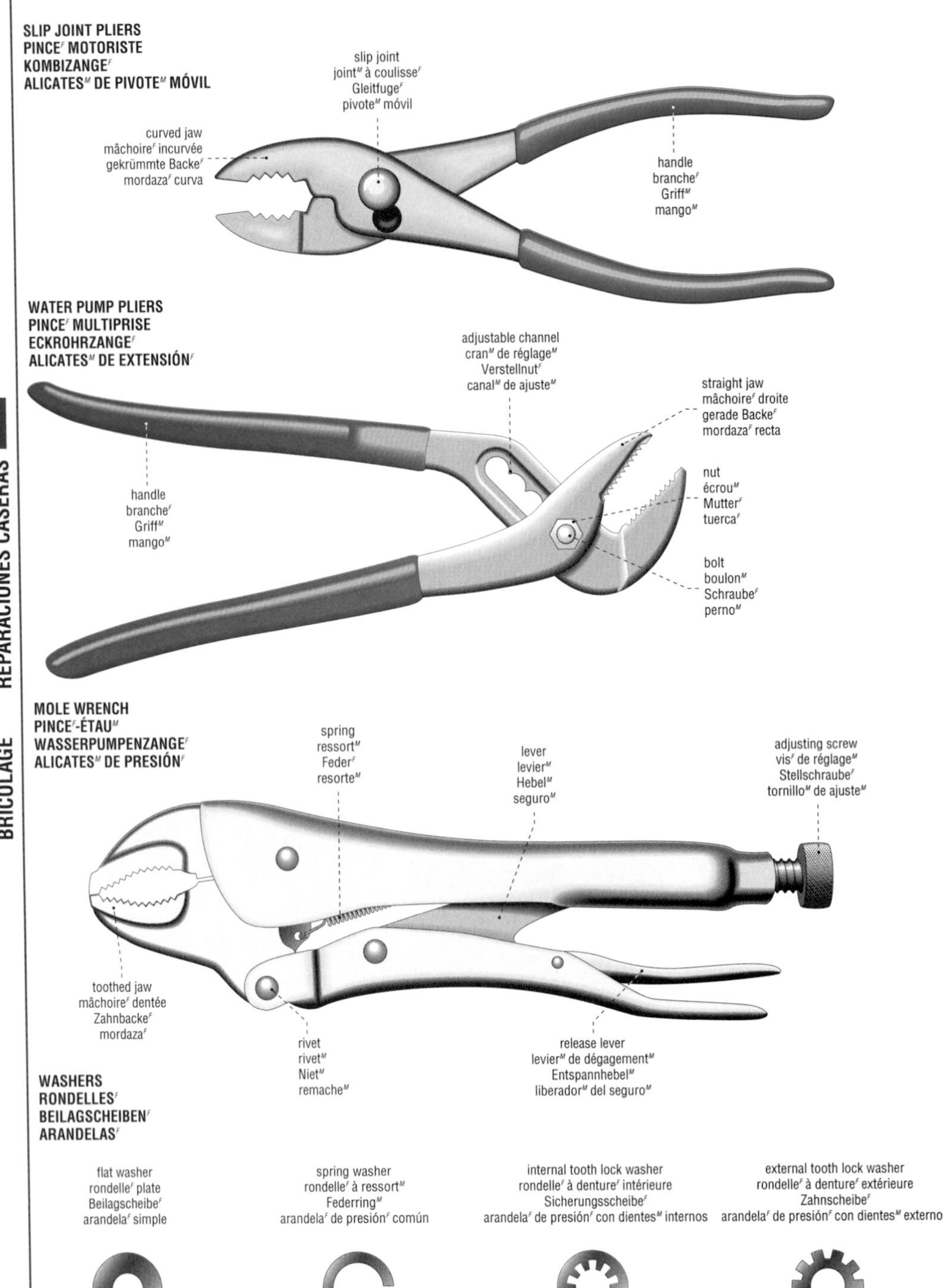

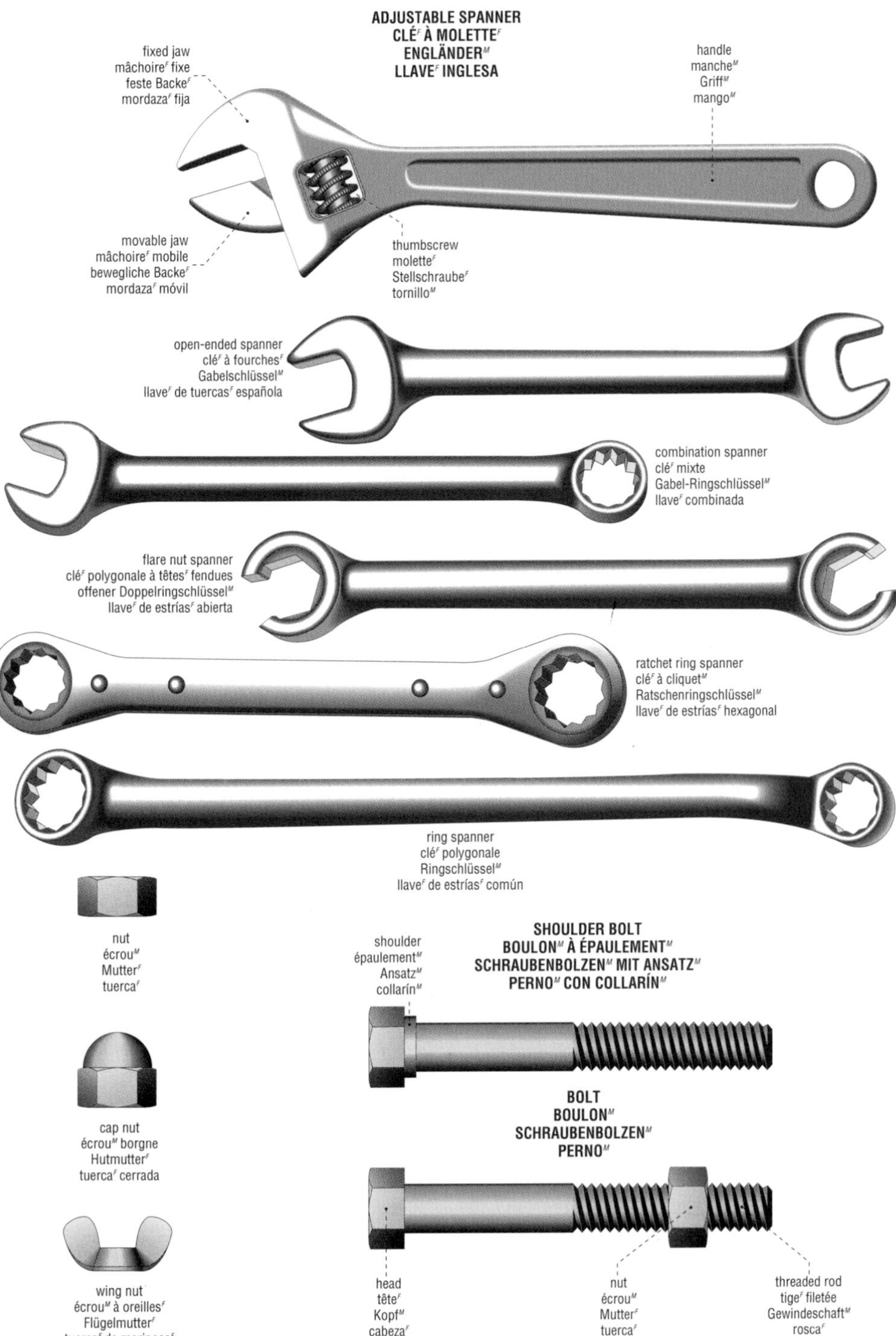
ADJUSTABLE SPANNER
CLÉ[F] À MOLETTE[F]
ENGLÄNDER[M]
LLAVE[F] INGLESA
fixed jaw
mâchoire[F] fixe
feste Backe[F]
mordaza[F] fija
handle
manche[M]
Griff[M]
mango[M]
movable jaw
mâchoire[F] mobile
bewegliche Backe[F]
mordaza[F] móvil
thumbscrew
molette[F]
Stellschraube[F]
tornillo[M]
open-ended spanner
clé[F] à fourches[F]
Gabelschlüssel[M]
llave[F] de tuercas[F] española
combination spanner
clé[F] mixte
Gabel-Ringschlüssel[M]
llave[F] combinada
flare nut spanner
clé[F] polygonale à têtes[F] fendues
offener Doppelringschlüssel[M]
llave[F] de estrías[F] abierta
ratchet ring spanner
clé[F] à cliquet[M]
Ratschenringschlüssel[M]
llave[F] de estrías[F] hexagonal
ring spanner
clé[F] polygonale
Ringschlüssel[M]
llave[F] de estrías[F] común
nut
écrou[M]
Mutter[F]
tuerca[F]
SHOULDER BOLT
BOULON[M] À ÉPAULEMENT[M]
SCHRAUBENBOLZEN[M] MIT ANSATZ[M]
PERNO[M] CON COLLARÍN[M]
shoulder
épaulement[M]
Ansatz[M]
collarín[M]
cap nut
écrou[M] borgne
Hutmutter[F]
tuerca[F] cerrada
BOLT
BOULON[M]
SCHRAUBENBOLZEN[M]
PERNO[M]
wing nut
écrou[M] à oreilles[F]
Flügelmutter[F]
tuerca[F] de mariposa[F]
head
tête[F]
Kopf[M]
cabeza[F]
nut
écrou[M]
Mutter[F]
tuerca[F]
threaded rod
tige[F] filetée
Gewindeschaft[M]
rosca[F]

ELECTRIC DRILL
PERCEUSE ÉLECTRIQUE
ELEKTRISCHE BOHRMASCHINE
TALADRO ELÉCTRICO
specification plate
plaque signalétique
Typenschild
placa de especificaciones
warning plate
plaque d'instructions
Sicherheitshinweisschild
placa de advertencias
housing
boîtier
Gehäuse
caja
switch lock
blocage de l'interrupteur
Feststellknopf
seguro del interruptor
switch
interrupteur
Schalter
interruptor
chuck
mandrin
Backenfutter
mandril
jaw
mors
Backen
mordaza
auxiliary handle
poignée auxiliaire
zusätzlicher Griff
mango auxiliar
pistol grip handle
poignée-pistolet
Pistolengriff
mango
cable sleeve
manchon de câble
Kabelmantel
protector del cable
cable
câble
Kabel
cable de corriente
plug
fiche
Stecker
enchufe
HAND DRILL
CHIGNOLE
HANDBOHRER
TALADRO DE MANO
turning handle
manivelle
Kurbel
manivela
side handle
poignée latérale
Seitengriff
perilla
main handle
poignée supérieure
Hauptgriff
mango
jaw
mors
Backe
mordaza
drive wheel
roue d'engrenage
Stirnzahnrad
cremallera
pinion
pignon
Kegelzahnrad
piñón
chuck
mandrin
Backenfutter
mandril
drill bit
foret
Bohrer
broca

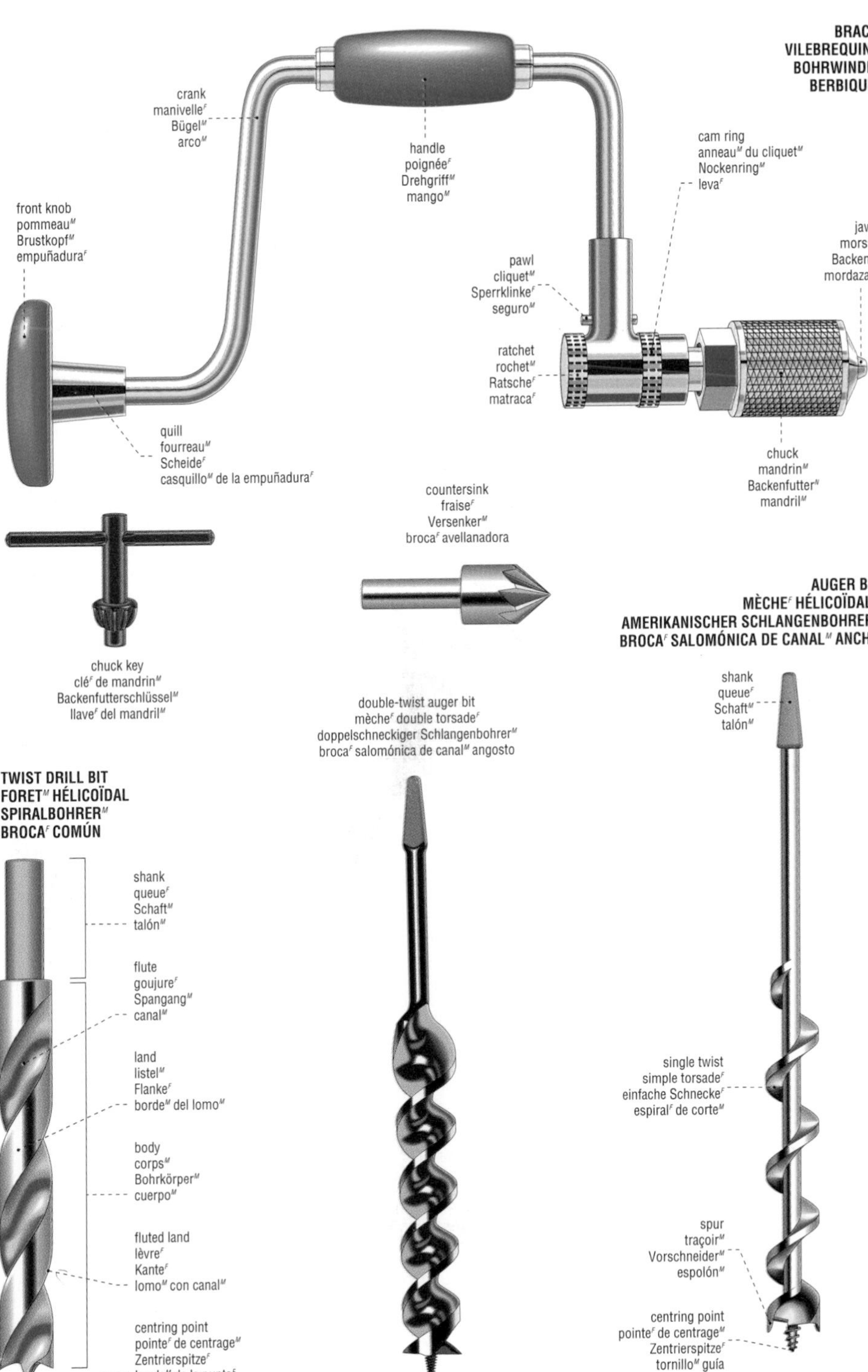
BRACE
VILEBREQUIN[M]
BOHRWINDE[F]
BERBIQUÍ[M]
crank
manivelle[F]
Bügel[M]
arco[M]
handle
poignée[F]
Drehgriff[M]
mango[M]
cam ring
anneau[M] du cliquet[M]
Nockenring[M]
leva[F]
front knob
pommeau[M]
Brustkopf[M]
empuñadura[F]
jaw
mors[M]
Backen[F]
mordaza[F]
pawl
cliquet[M]
Sperrklinke[F]
seguro[M]
ratchet
rochet[M]
Ratsche[F]
matraca[F]
quill
fourreau[M]
Scheide[F]
casquillo[M] de la empuñadura[F]
chuck
mandrin[M]
Backenfutter[N]
mandril[M]
countersink
fraise[F]
Versenker[M]
broca[F] avellanadora
AUGER BIT
MÈCHE[F] HÉLICOÏDALE
AMERIKANISCHER SCHLANGENBOHRER[M]
BROCA[F] SALOMÓNICA DE CANAL[M] ANCHO
chuck key
clé[F] de mandrin[M]
Backenfutterschlüssel[M]
llave[F] del mandril[M]
shank
queue[F]
Schaft[M]
talón[M]
double-twist auger bit
mèche[F] double torsade[F]
doppelschneckiger Schlangenbohrer[M]
broca[F] salomónica de canal[M] angosto
TWIST DRILL BIT
FORET[M] HÉLICOÏDAL
SPIRALBOHRER[M]
BROCA[F] COMÚN
shank
queue[F]
Schaft[M]
talón[M]
flute
goujure[F]
Spangang[M]
canal[M]
land
listel[M]
Flanke[F]
borde[M] del lomo[M]
single twist
simple torsade[F]
einfache Schnecke[F]
espiral[F] de corte[M]
body
corps[M]
Bohrkörper[M]
cuerpo[M]
fluted land
lèvre[F]
Kante[F]
lomo[M] con canal[M]
spur
traçoir[M]
Vorschneider[M]
espolón[M]
centring point
pointe[F] de centrage[M]
Zentrierspitze[F]
borde[M] de la punta[F]
centring point
pointe[F] de centrage[M]
Zentrierspitze[F]
tornillo[M] guía

# CARPENTRY: TOOLS
# MENUISERIE^F: OUTILS^M
# SCHREINEREI^F: WERKZEUGE^N
# CARPINTERÍA^F: HERRAMIENTAS^F

## G-CLAMP
## SERRE-JOINT^M
## ZWINGE^F
## PRENSA^F EN C

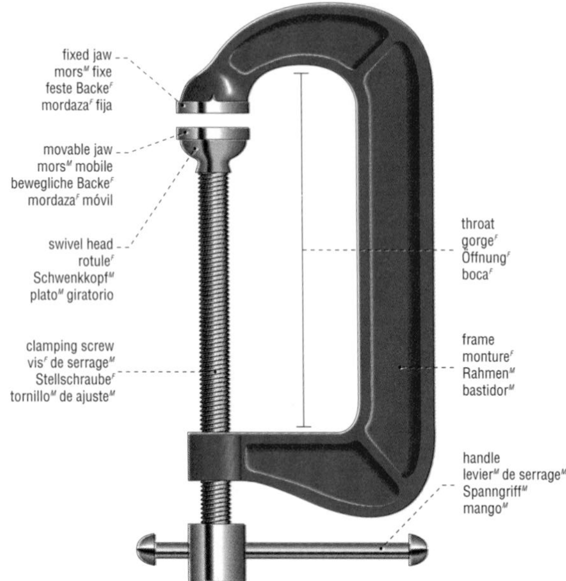


## VICE
## ÉTAU^M
## SCHRAUBSTOCK^M
## TORNO^M DE BANCO^M

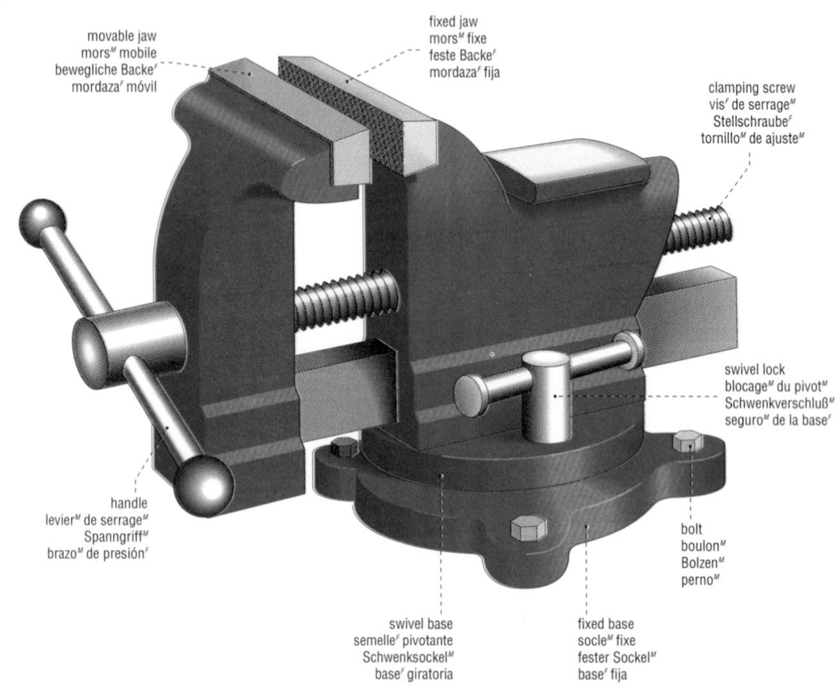

## ROUTER
## TOUPIE^F
## OBERFRÄSER^M
## ACANALADOR^M

head
tête^F
Kopf^M
parche^M
flex sleeve
manchon^M du cordon^M
Kabelmantel^M
protector^M del cable^M
guide handle
poignée^F de guidage^M
Führungsgriff^M
asa^F
collet
collet^M
Anlaufhülse^F
collarín^M
base
base^F
Fuß^M
base^F
motor
moteur^M
Motor^M
motor^M
switch
interrupteur^M
Schalter^M
interruptor^M
depth adjustment
réglage^M de profondeur^F
Tiefeneinstellung^F
ajuste^M de profundidad^F
tool holder
porte-outil^M
Werkzeugfutter^N
mordaza^F

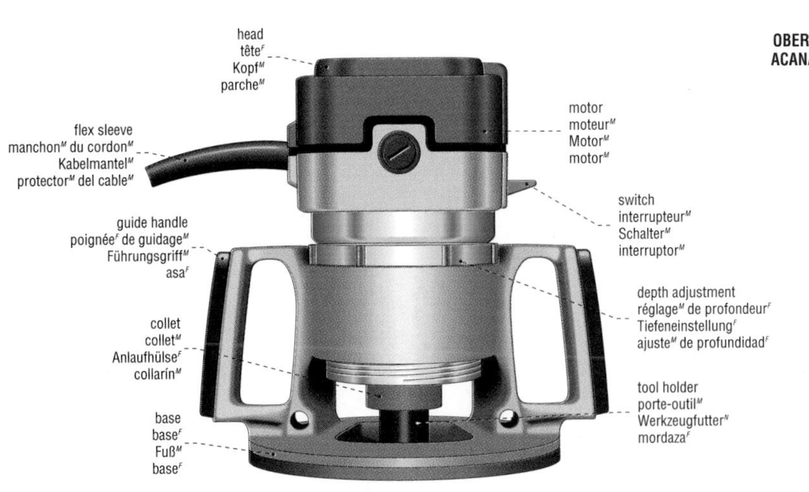

## PILLAR DRILL
## PERCEUSE^F À COLONNE^F
## STÄNDERBOHRMASCHINE^F
## TALADRO^M VERTICAL

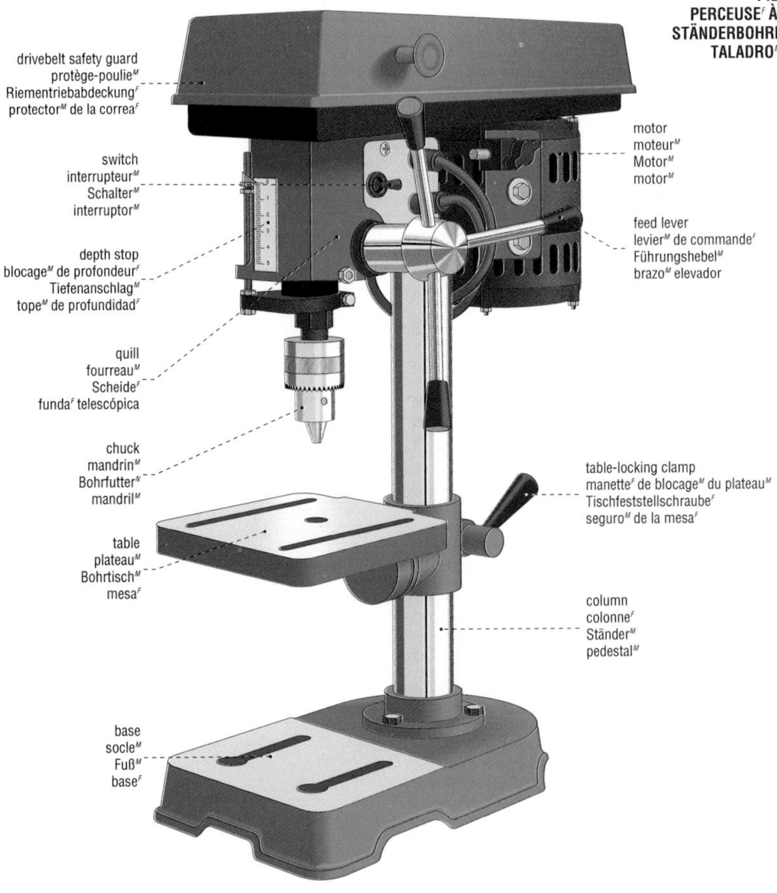

drivebelt safety guard
protège-poulie^M
Riementriebabdeckung^F
protector^M de la correa^F
switch
interrupteur^M
Schalter^M
interruptor^M
depth stop
blocage^M de profondeur^F
Tiefenanschlag^M
tope^M de profundidad^F
quill
fourreau^M
Scheide^F
funda^F telescópica
chuck
mandrin^M
Bohrfutter^N
mandril^M
table
plateau^M
Bohrtisch^M
mesa^F
base
socle^M
Fuß^M
base^F
motor
moteur^M
Motor^M
motor^M
feed lever
levier^M de commande^F
Führungshebel^M
brazo^M elevador
table-locking clamp
manette^F de blocage^M du plateau^M
Tischfeststellschraube^F
seguro^M de la mesa^F
column
colonne^F
Ständer^M
pedestal^M

# CARPENTRY: TOOLS
# MENUISERIE[F]: OUTILS[M]
# SCHREINEREI[F]: WERKZEUGE[N]
# CARPINTERÍA[F]: HERRAMIENTAS[F]

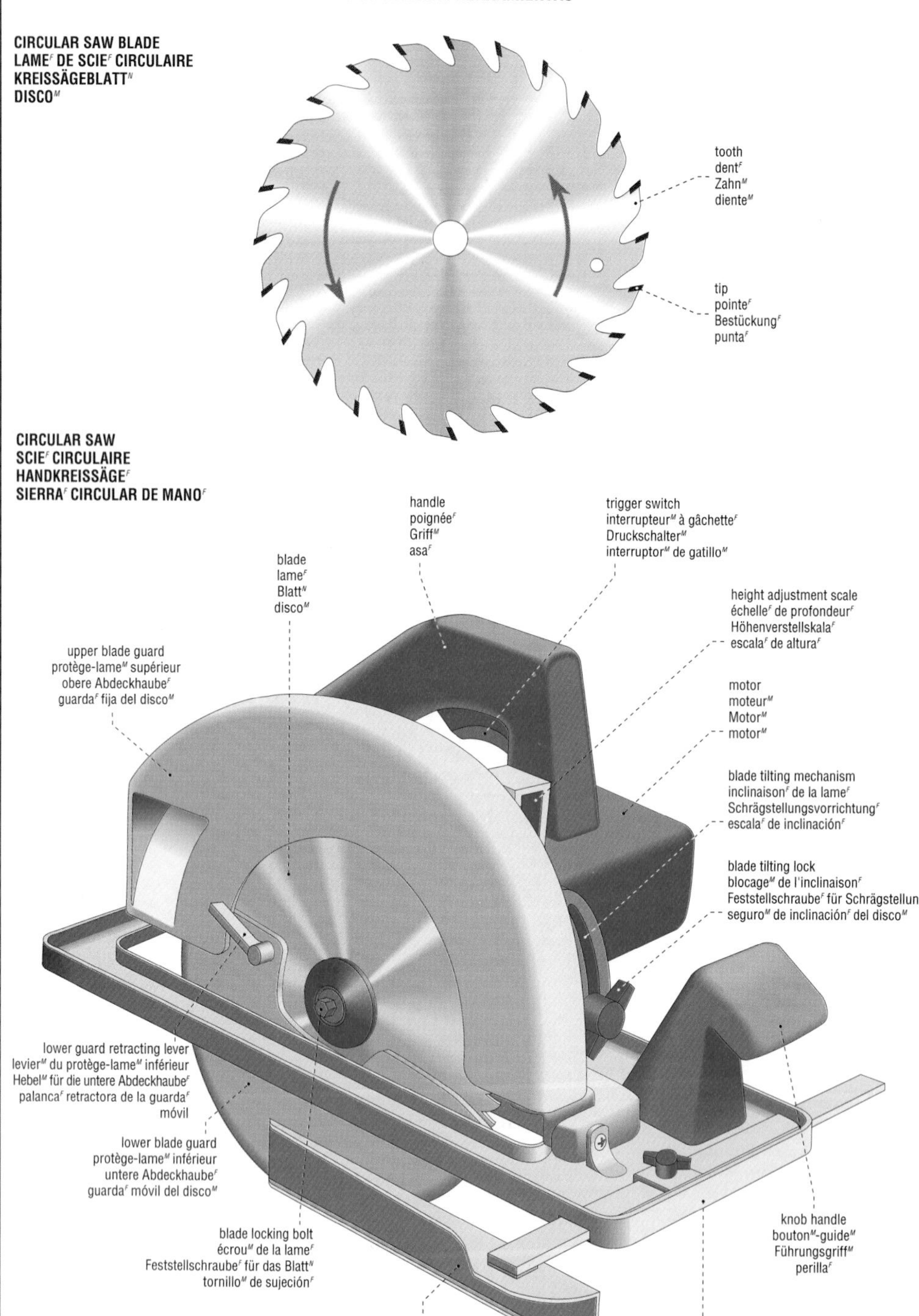

# TABLE SAW
# PLATEAU[M] DE SCIAGE[M]
# TISCHKREISSÄGE[F]
# SIERRA[F] CIRCULAR DE MESA[F]



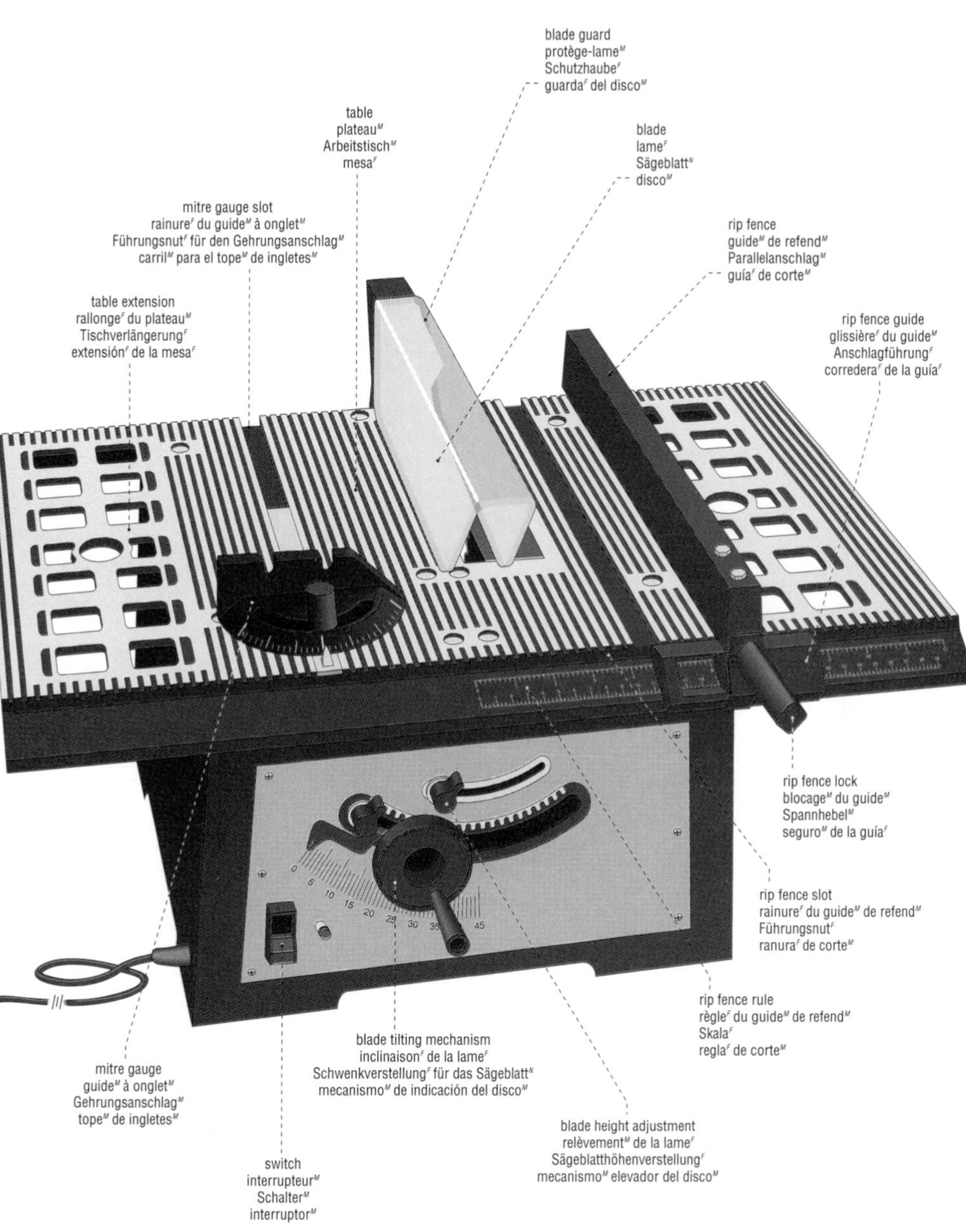

# BUILDING MATERIALS
# MATÉRIAUX[M] DE CONSTRUCTION[F]
# BAUMATERIALIEN[N]
# MATERIALES[M] DE CONSTRUCCIÓN[F]

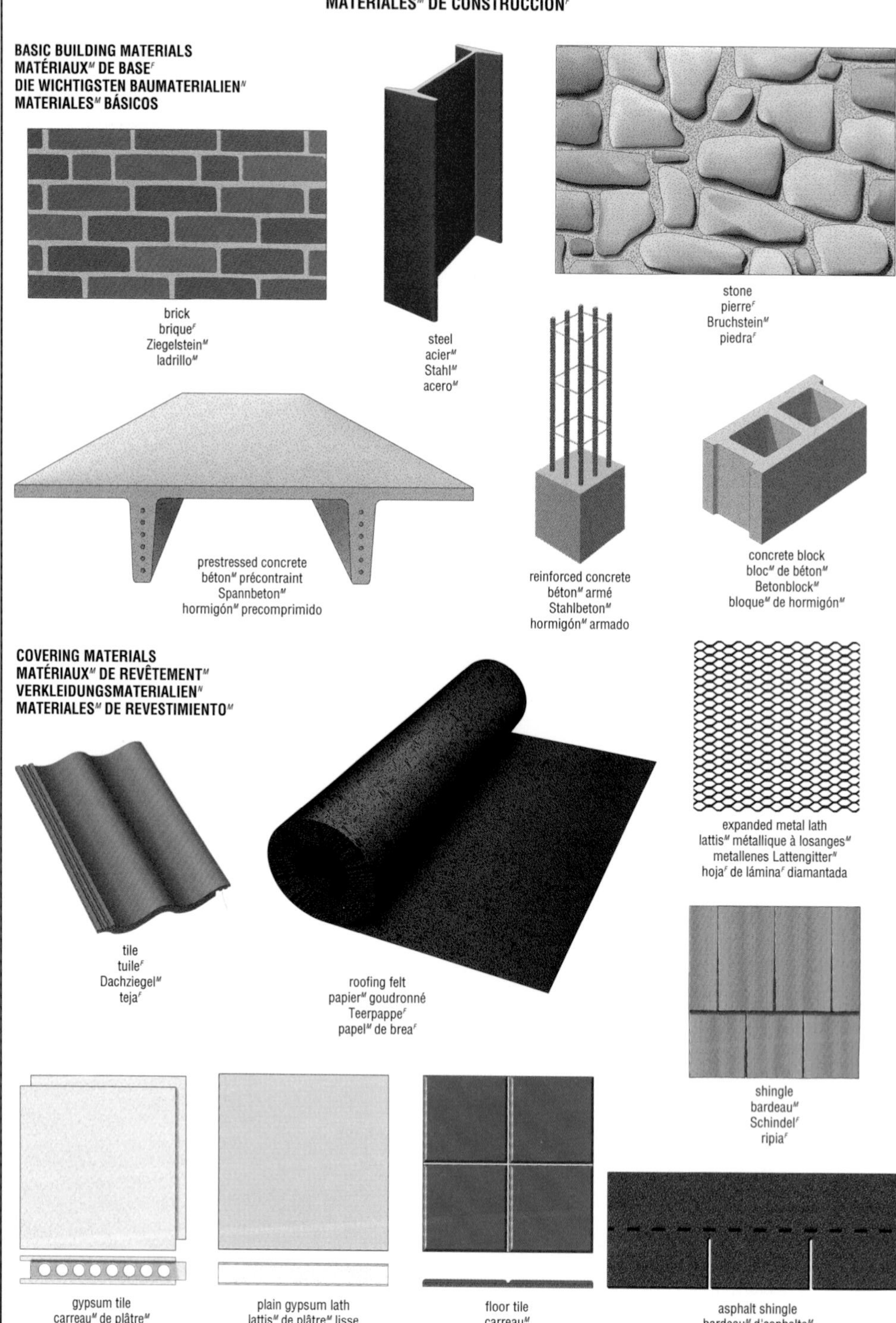

## INSULATING MATERIALS
## ISOLANTS[M]
## ISOLIERMATERIALIEN[N]
## MATERIALES[M] AISLANTES

sprung strip metal insulation
isolant[M] de ruban[M] métallique
Metallverbindung[F]
aislante[M] metálico

foam insulation
isolant[M] moussé
Bauschaumisolierung[F]
aislante[M] de espuma[F]

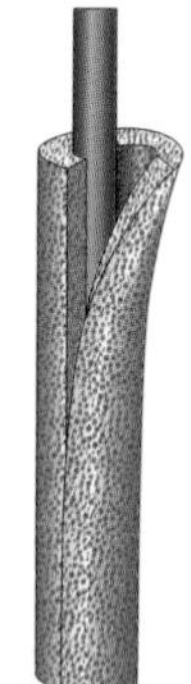

moulded insulation
isolant[M] en coquille[F]
geformte Rohrummantelung[F]
aislante[M] premoldeado

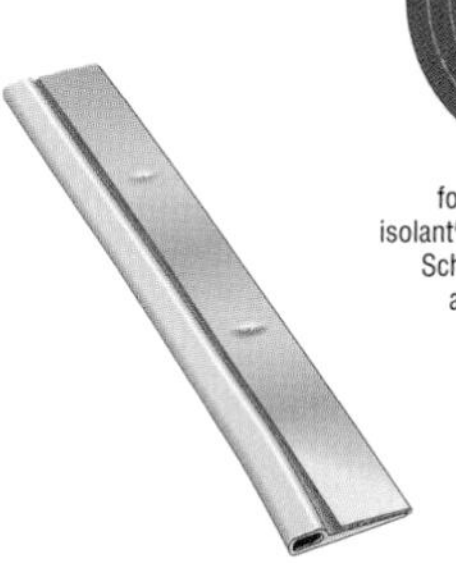

foam-rubber insulation
isolant[M] en caoutchouc[M]-mousse[F]
Schaumgummiisolierung[F]
aislante[M] de esponja[F]

vinyl insulation
isolant[M] en vinyle[M]
Vinylisolierung[F]
aislante[M] vinílico

board insulation
isolant[M] en panneau[M]
Plattenisolierung[F]
tablero[M] rígido aislante

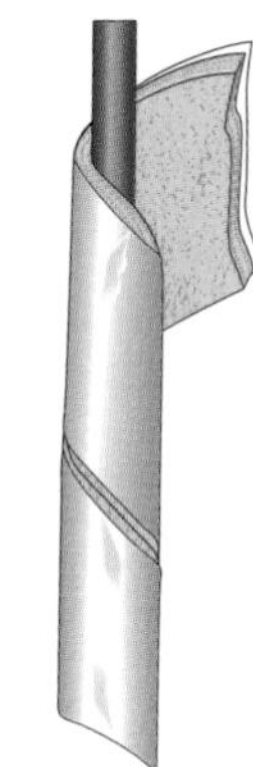

pipe-wrapping insulation
isolant[M] en ruban[M]
Rohrummantelung[F]
cinta[F] aislante para tubería[F]

loose fill insulation
isolant[M] en vrac[M]
Schüttungsisolierung[F]
aislante[M] a granel

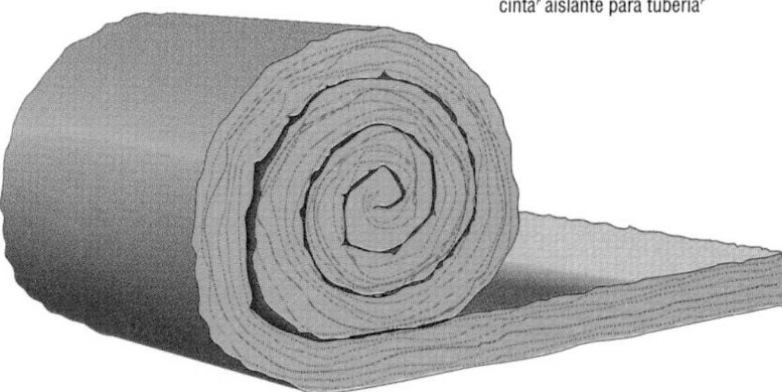

blanket insulation
isolant[M] en rouleau[M]
Mattenisolierung[F]
rollo[M] para recubrimiento[M] impermeabilizante

# BUILDING MATERIALS
# MATÉRIAUX^M DE CONSTRUCTION^F
# BAUMATERIALIEN^N
# MATERIALES^M DE CONSTRUCCIÓN^F

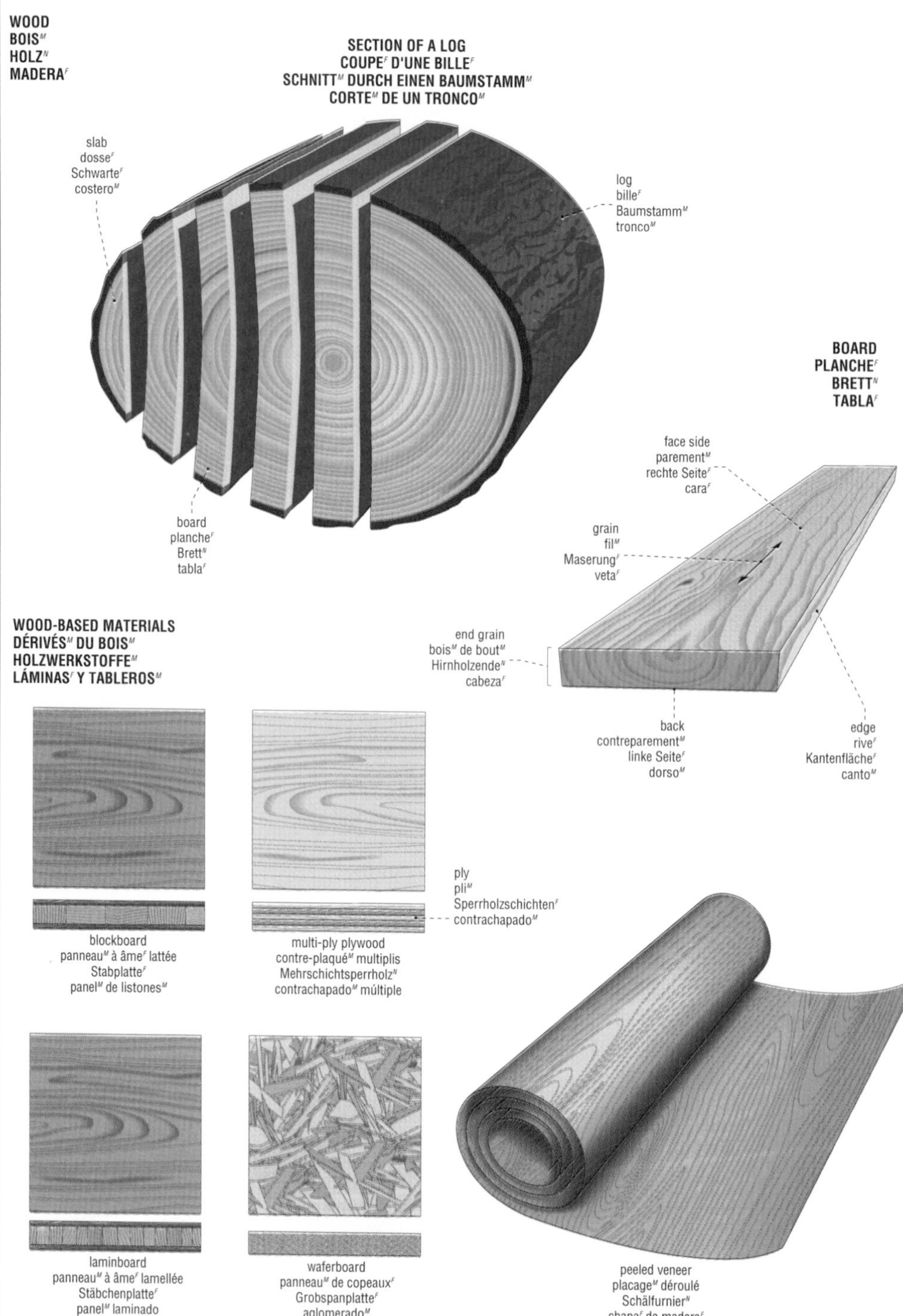

## WOOD-BASED MATERIALS
## DÉRIVÉS[M] DU BOIS[M]
## HOLZWERKSTOFFE[M]
## LÁMINAS[F] Y TABLEROS[M]

hardboard
panneau[M] de fibres[F]
Hartfaserplatte[F]
tablero[M] de fibra[F] de madera[F]

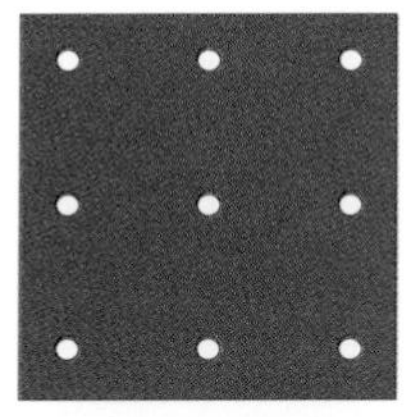

perforated hardboard
panneau[M] de fibres[F] perforé
gelochte Hartfaserplatte[F]
tablero[M] de fibra[F] de madera[F] perforada

plastic-coated chipboard
panneau[M] de particules[F] lamifié
kunststoffbeschichtete Hartfaserplatte[F]
tablero[M] de aglomerado[M] con laminado[M] de plástico[M]

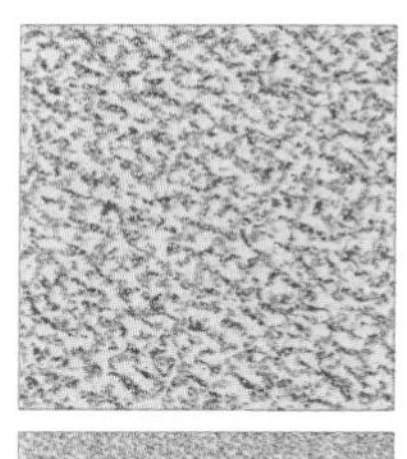

chipboard
panneau[M] de particules[F]
Spanplatte[F]
tablero[M] de aglomerado[M]

## LOCK
## SERRURE[F]
## SCHLOSS[N]
## CERRAJERÍA[F]

### GENERAL VIEW
### VUE[F] D'ENSEMBLE[M]
### ÜBERSICHT[F]
### VISTA[F] GENERAL

# LOCK
# SERRURE[F]
# SCHLOSS[N]
# CERRAJERÍA[F]

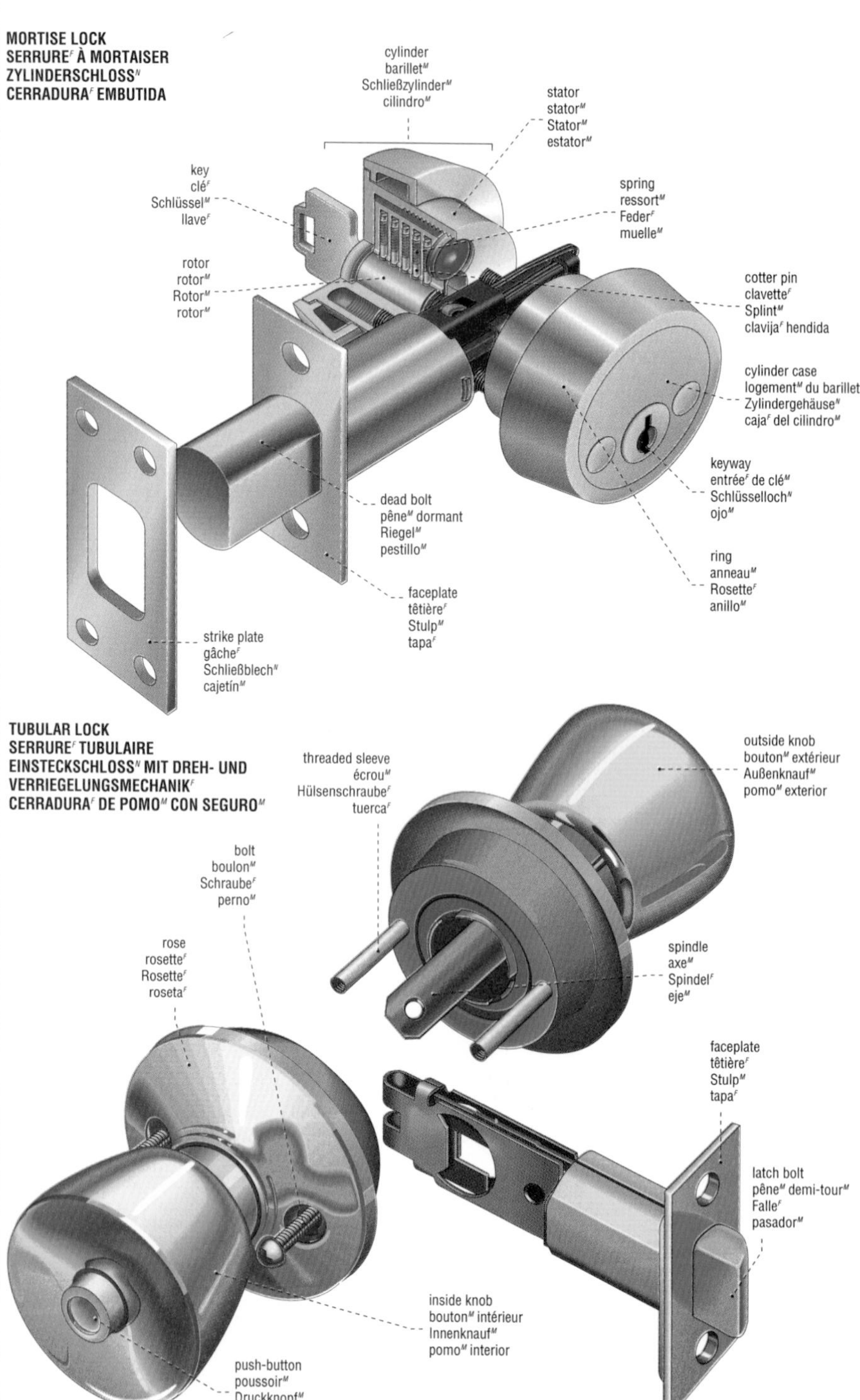

# MASONRY
# MAÇONNERIE$^{F}$
# MAUREREI$^{F}$
# HERRAMIENTAS$^{F}$ DE ALBAÑIL$^{M}$

## MASON'S TROWEL
## TRUELLE$^{F}$ DE MAÇON$^{M}$
## MAURERKELLE$^{F}$
## PALETA$^{F}$ DE ALBAÑIL$^{M}$

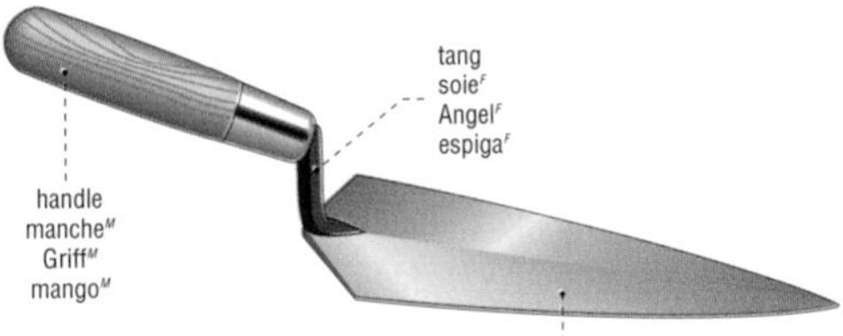

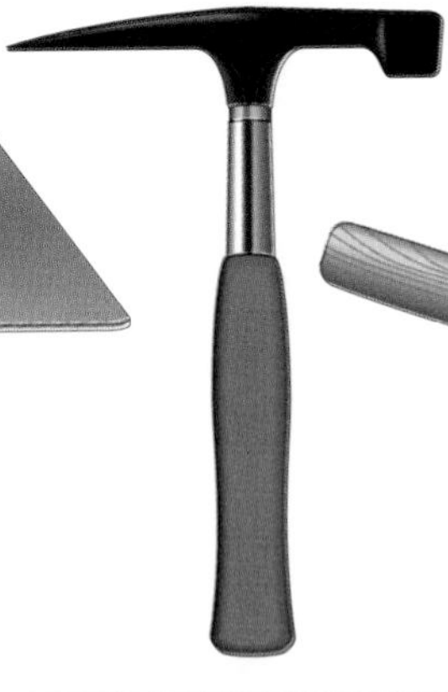

tang
soie$^{F}$
Angel$^{F}$
espiga$^{F}$
handle
manche$^{M}$
Griff$^{M}$
mango$^{M}$
blade
lame$^{F}$
Blatt$^{N}$
hoja$^{F}$


square trowel
truelle$^{F}$ de plâtrier$^{M}$
Putzkelle$^{F}$
llana$^{F}$


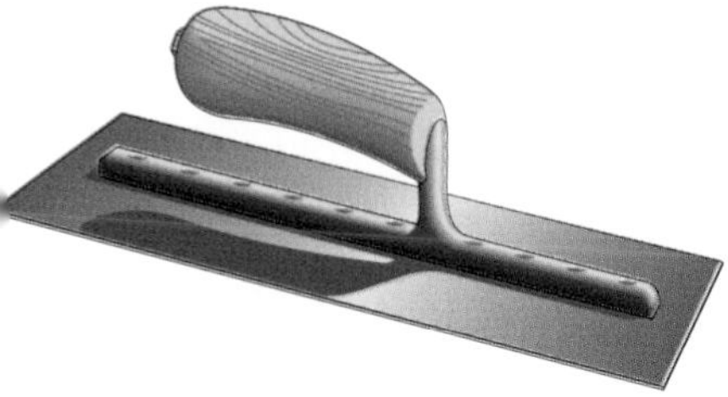

bricklayer's hammer
marteau$^{M}$ de maçon$^{M}$
Maurerhammer$^{M}$
martillo$^{M}$ de albañil$^{M}$


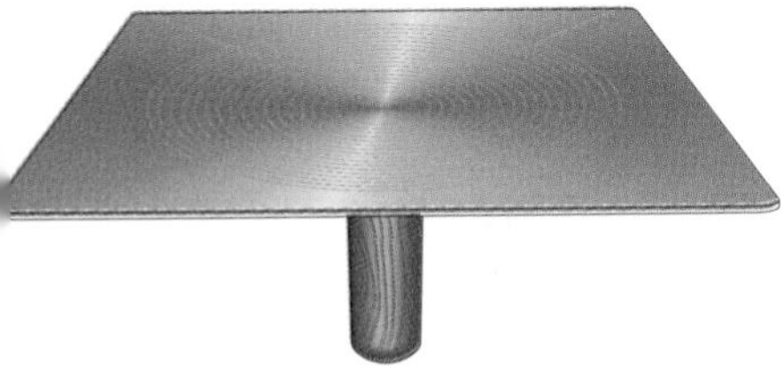

hawk
taloche$^{F}$
Reibebrett$^{F}$
esparavel$^{M}$


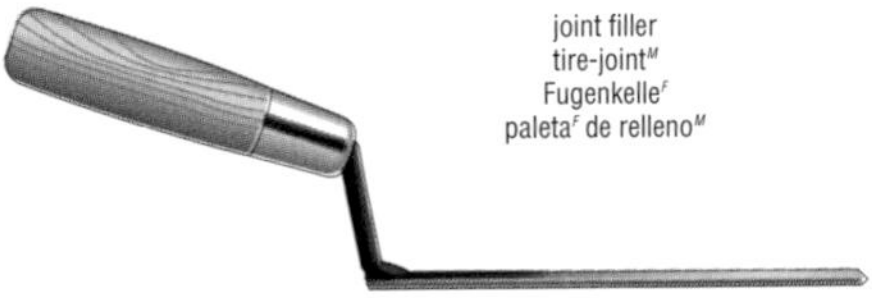

joint filler
tire-joint$^{M}$
Fugenkelle$^{F}$
paleta$^{F}$ de relleno$^{M}$


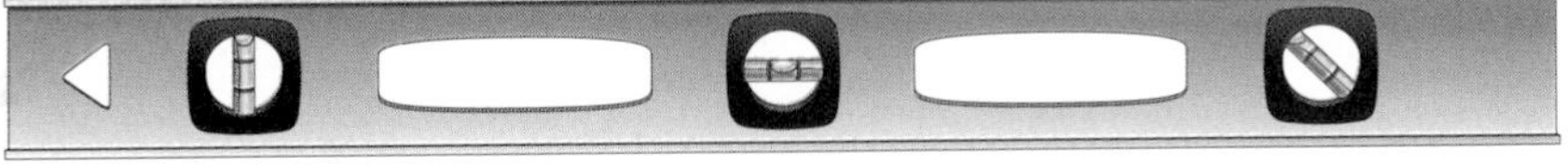

spirit level
niveau$^{M}$ à bulle$^{F}$
Wasserwaage$^{F}$
nivel$^{M}$ de aire$^{M}$


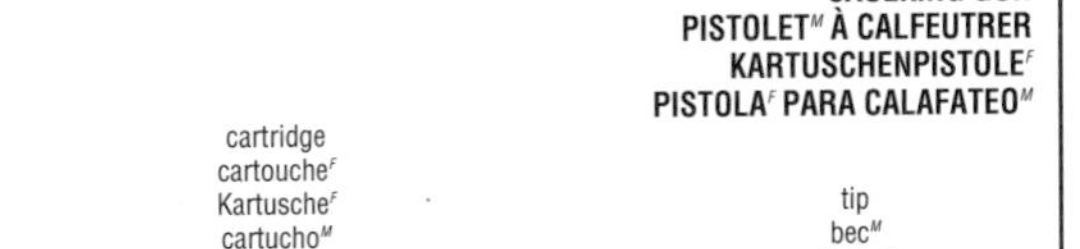

## CAULKING GUN
## PISTOLET$^{M}$ À CALFEUTRER
## KARTUSCHENPISTOLE$^{F}$
## PISTOLA$^{F}$ PARA CALAFATEO$^{M}$

piston release
dégagement$^{M}$ du piston$^{M}$
Druckstab$^{M}$
desenganchador$^{M}$
cartridge
cartouche$^{F}$
Kartusche$^{F}$
cartucho$^{M}$
tip
bec$^{M}$
Spitze$^{F}$
punta$^{F}$
piston lever
levier$^{M}$ du piston$^{M}$
Pumpengriff$^{M}$
gatillo$^{M}$
gun
pistolet$^{M}$
Zylinder$^{M}$
pistola$^{F}$
nozzle
buse$^{F}$
Düse$^{F}$
boquilla$^{F}$

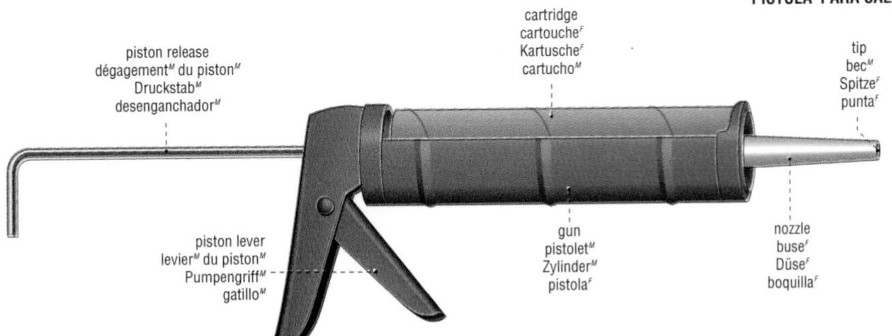

# PLUMBING: BATHROOM
# PLOMBERIE^F: SALLE^F DE BAINS^M
# SANITÄRINSTALLATION^F: BADEZIMMER^N
# FONTANERÍA: CUARTO^M DE BAÑO^M

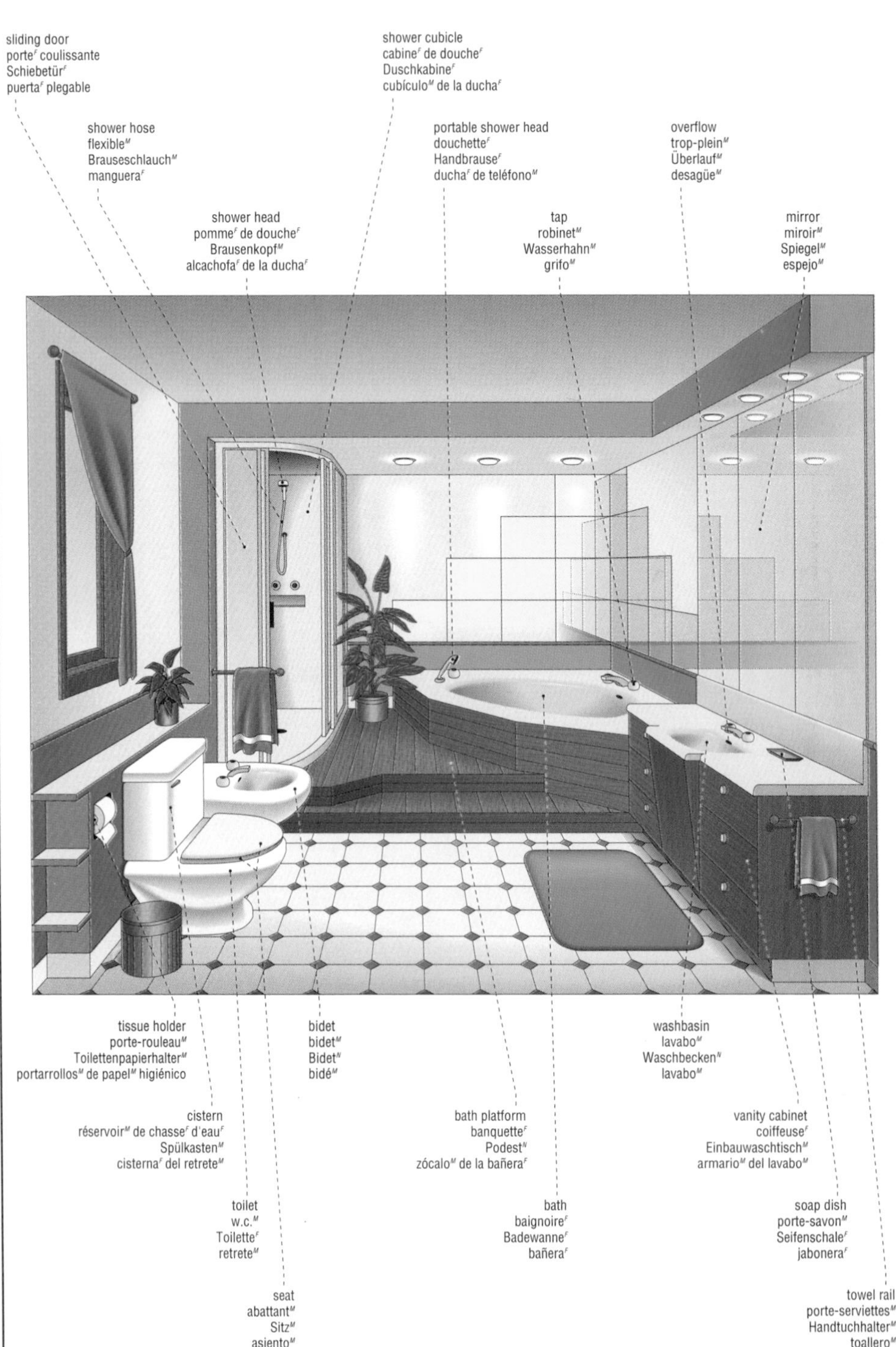

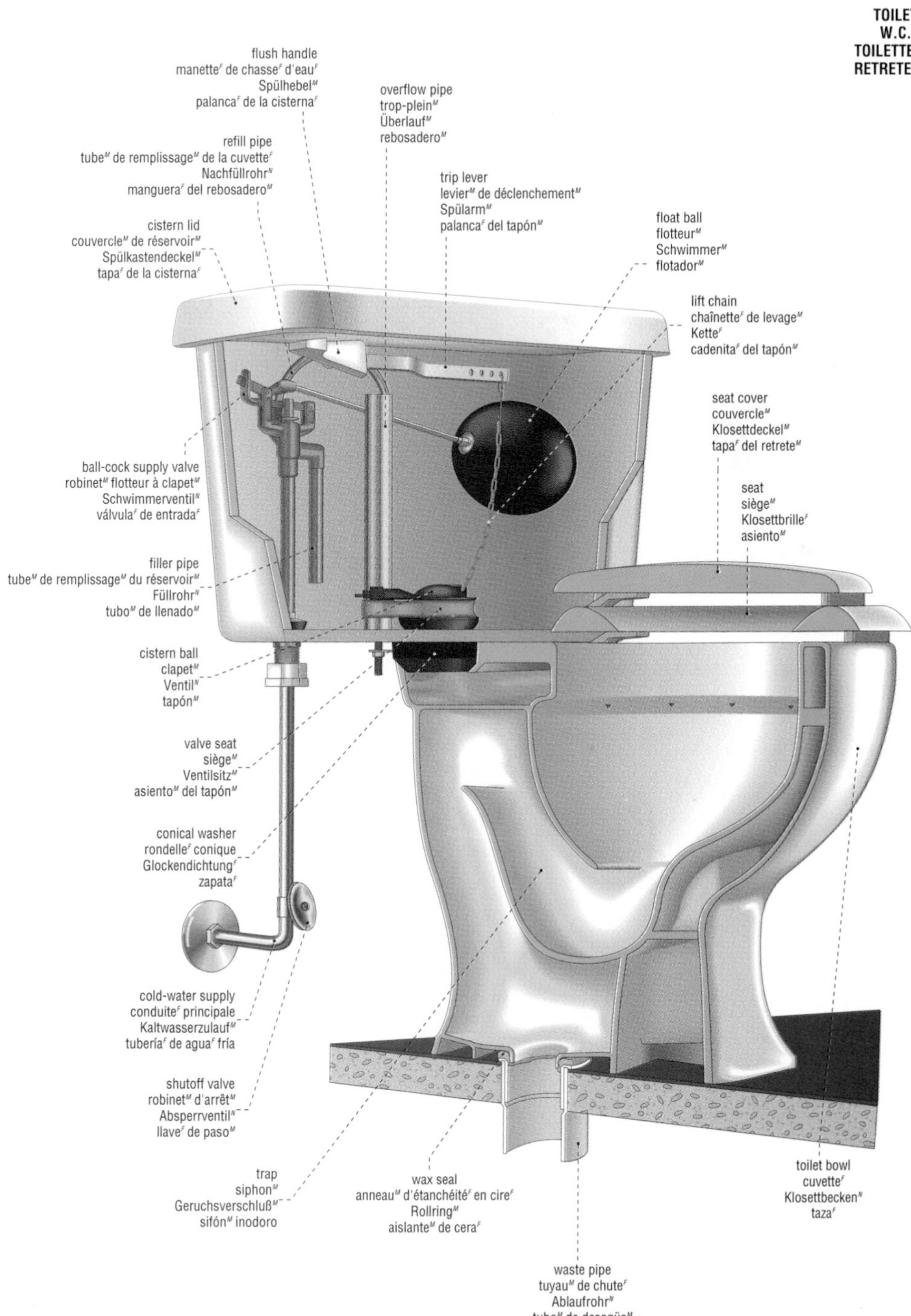
flush handle
manette^F de chasse^F d'eau^F
Spülhebel^M
palanca^F de la cisterna^F
overflow pipe
trop-plein^M
Überlauf^M
rebosadero^M
refill pipe
tube^M de remplissage^M de la cuvette^F
Nachfüllrohr^N
manguera^F del rebosadero^M
trip lever
levier^M de déclenchement^M
Spülarm^M
palanca^F del tapón^M
float ball
flotteur^M
Schwimmer^M
flotador^M
cistern lid
couvercle^M de réservoir^M
Spülkastendeckel^M
tapa^F de la cisterna^F
lift chain
chaînette^F de levage^M
Kette^F
cadenita^F del tapón^M
seat cover
couvercle^M
Klosettdeckel^M
tapa^F del retrete^M
ball-cock supply valve
robinet^M flotteur à clapet^M
Schwimmerventil^N
válvula^F de entrada^F
seat
siège^M
Klosettbrille^F
asiento^M
filler pipe
tube^M de remplissage^M du réservoir^M
Füllrohr^N
tubo^M de llenado^M
cistern ball
clapet^M
Ventil^N
tapón^M
valve seat
siège^M
Ventilsitz^M
asiento^M del tapón^M
conical washer
rondelle^F conique
Glockendichtung^F
zapata^F
cold-water supply
conduite^F principale
Kaltwasserzulauf^M
tubería^F de agua^F fría
shutoff valve
robinet^M d'arrêt^M
Absperrventil^N
llave^F de paso^M
trap
siphon^M
Geruchsverschluß^M
sifón^M inodoro
wax seal
anneau^M d'étanchéité^F en cire^F
Rollring^M
aislante^M de cera^F
toilet bowl
cuvette^F
Klosettbecken^N
taza^F
waste pipe
tuyau^M de chute^F
Ablaufrohr^N
tubo^M de desagüe^M

# PLUMBING
# PLOMBERIE[F]
# SANITÄRINSTALLATION[F]
# FONTANERÍA[F]

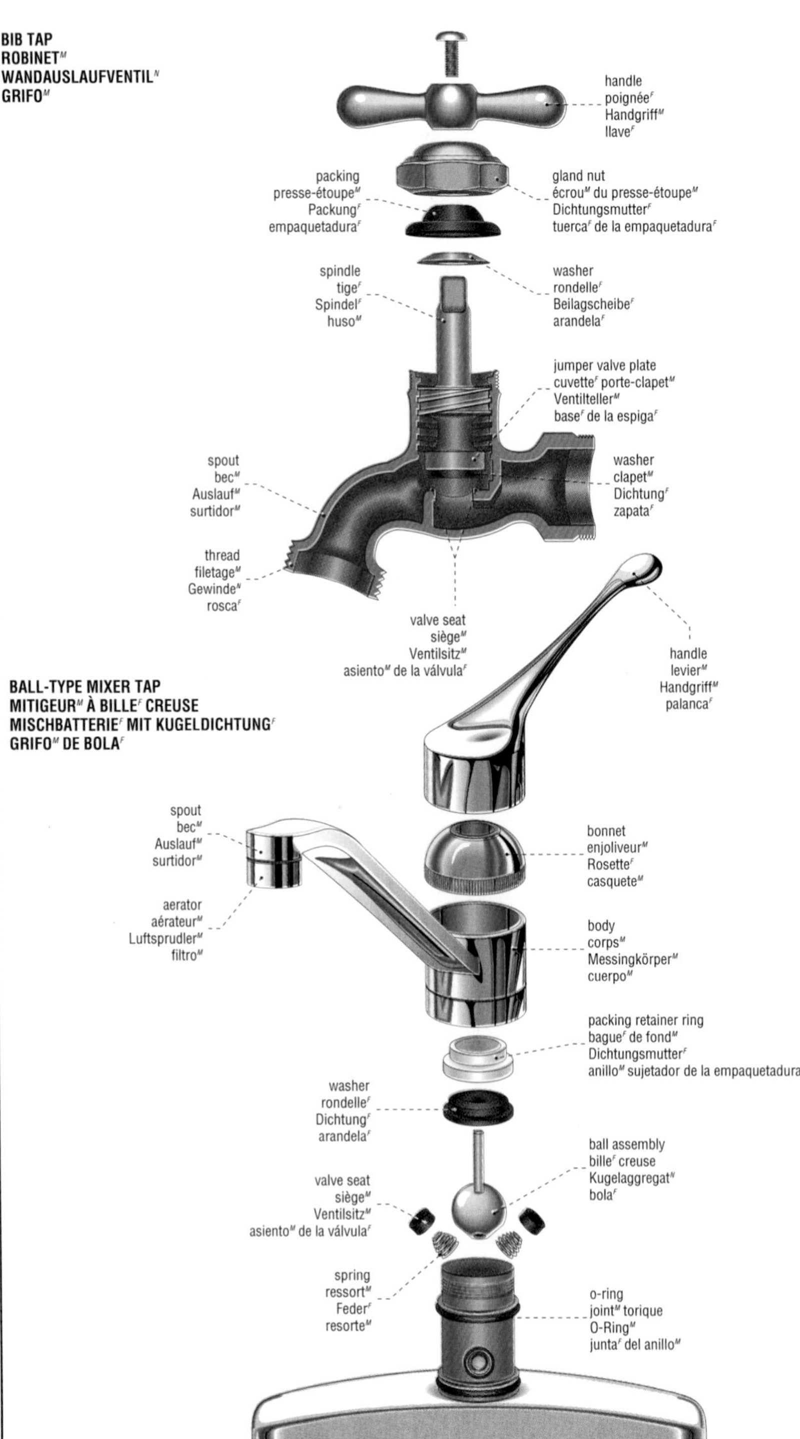

## DISC MIXER
## MITIGEUR[M] À DISQUE[M]
## MISCHBATTERIE[F] MIT KERAMIKDICHTUNG[F]
## GRIFO[M] DE DISCO[M]

handle
levier[M]
Handgriff[M]
palanca[F]
bonnet
enjoliveur[M]
Rosette[F]
casquete[M]
cylinder
cylindre[M]
Zylinder[M]
cilindro[M]
seal
anneau[M] d'étanchéité[F]
Dichtung[F]
zapata[F]
spout
bec[M]
Auslauf[M]
surtidor[M]
water inlet
entrée[F] d'eau[F]
Wasserzulauf[M]
entrada[F] de agua[F]
aerator
aérateur[M]
Luftsprudler[M]
filtro[M]
escutcheon
applique[F] du robinet[M]
Messingkörper[M]
placa[F]

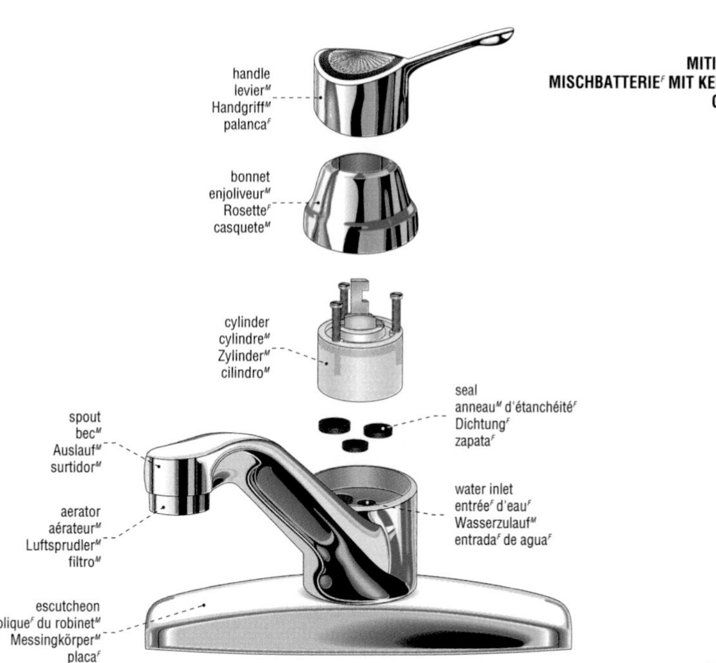

## CARTRIDGE MIXER
## MITIGEUR[M] À CARTOUCHE[F]
## MISCHBATTERIE[F] MIT KARTUSCHENDICHTUNG[F]
## GRIFO[M] DE CARTUCHO[M]

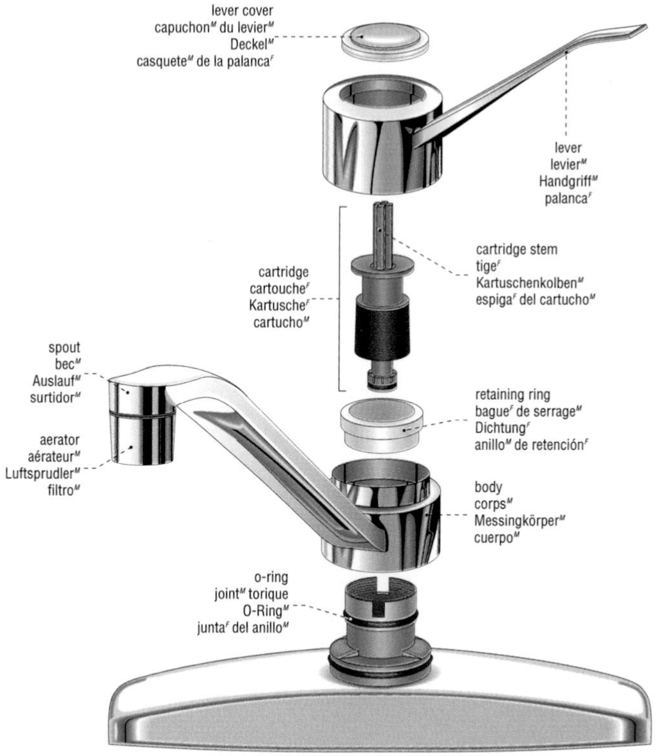

lever cover
capuchon[M] du levier[M]
Deckel[M]
casquete[M] de la palanca[F]
lever
levier[M]
Handgriff[M]
palanca[F]
cartridge stem
tige[F]
Kartuschenkolben[M]
espiga[F] del cartucho[M]
cartridge
cartouche[F]
Kartusche[F]
cartucho[M]
spout
bec[M]
Auslauf[M]
surtidor[M]
retaining ring
bague[F] de serrage[M]
Dichtung[F]
anillo[M] de retención[F]
aerator
aérateur[M]
Luftsprudler[M]
filtro[M]
body
corps[M]
Messingkörper[M]
cuerpo[M]
o-ring
joint[M] torique
O-Ring[M]
junta[F] del anillo[M]

# PLUMBING
# PLOMBERIE[F]
# SANITÄRINSTALLATION[F]
# FONTANERÍA[F]

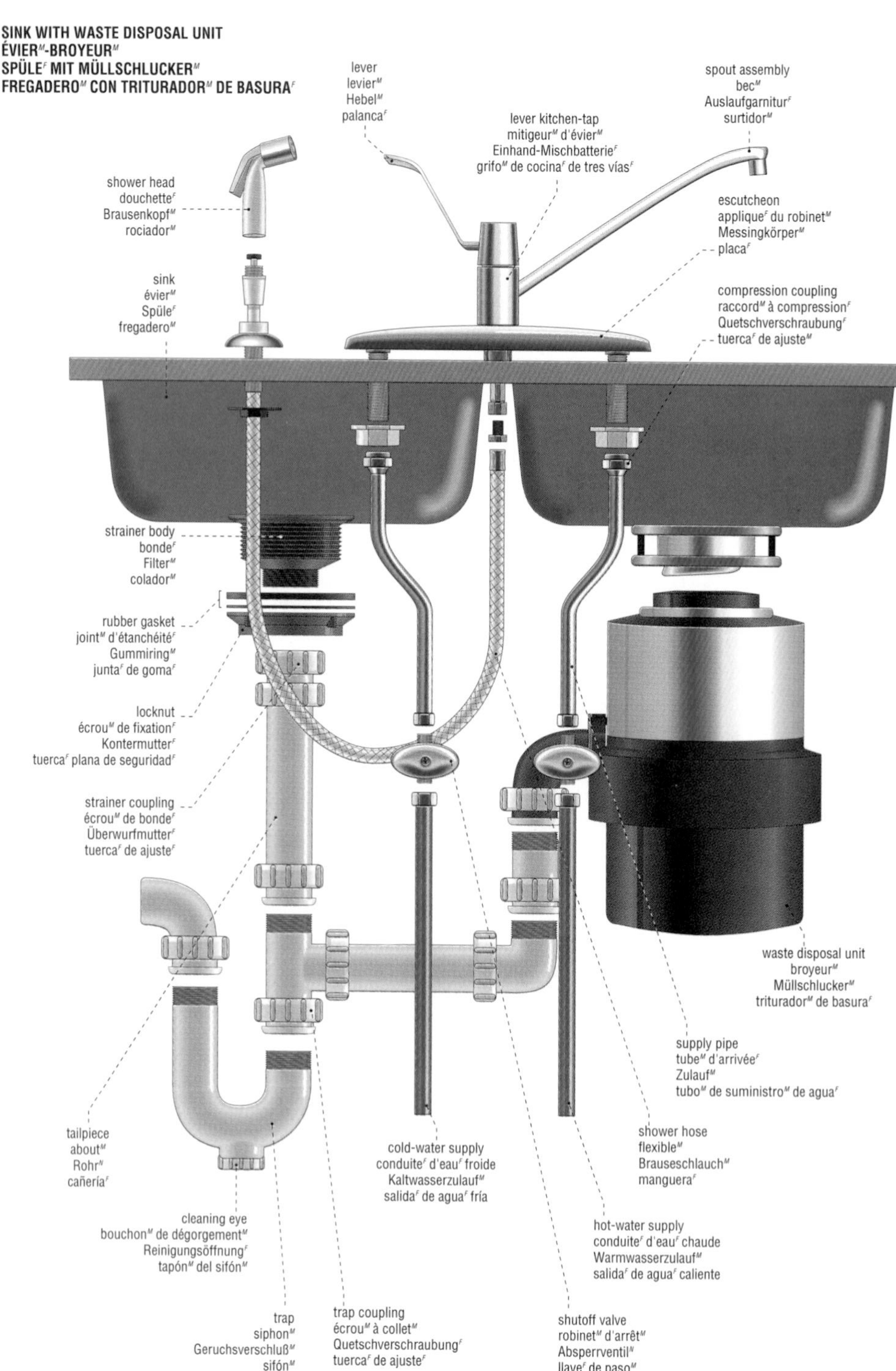

## GEYSER
## CHAUFFE-EAU[M] AU GAZ[M]
## GASWARMWASSERBEREITER[M]
## CALENTADOR[M] DE GAS[M]

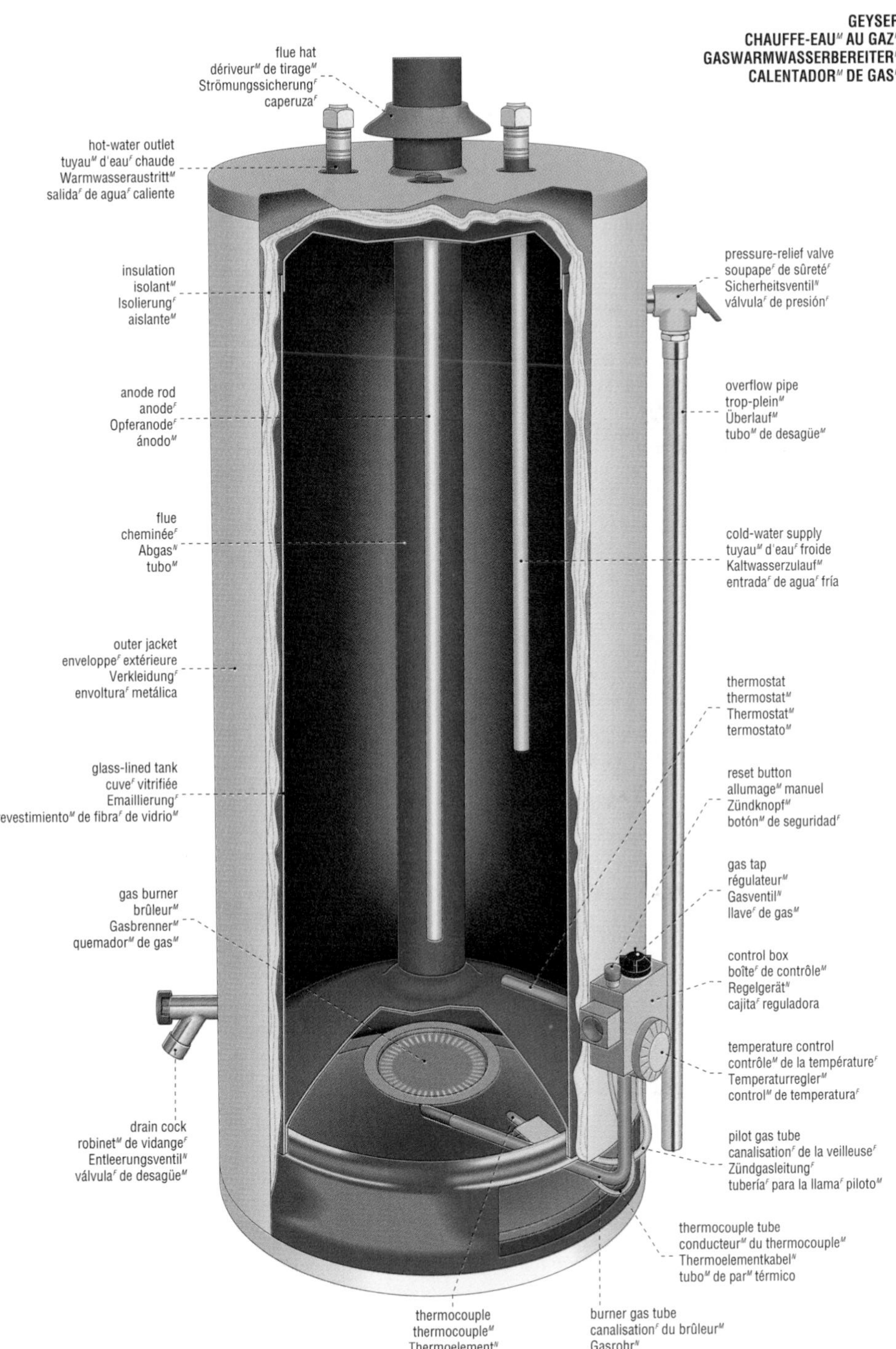

## PLUMBING: EXAMPLES OF BRANCHING
## PLOMBERIE[F]: EXEMPLES[M] DE BRANCHEMENT[M]
## SANITÄRINSTALLATION[F]: BEISPIELE[N] FÜR ABZWEIGUNGEN[F]
## FONTANERÍA[F]: CONEXIONES[F]

### WASHING MACHINE
### LAVE-LINGE[M]
### WASCHMASCHINE[F]
### LAVADORA[F]

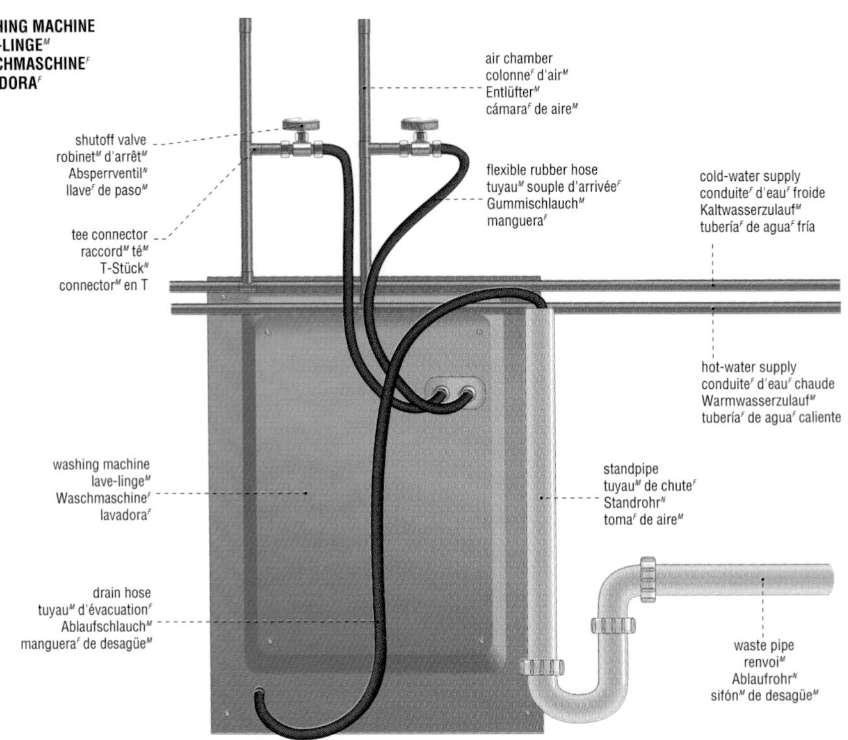


### DISHWASHER
### LAVE-VAISSELLE[M]
### GESCHIRRSPÜLMASCHINE[F]
### MÁQUINA[F] LAVAPLATOS[M]

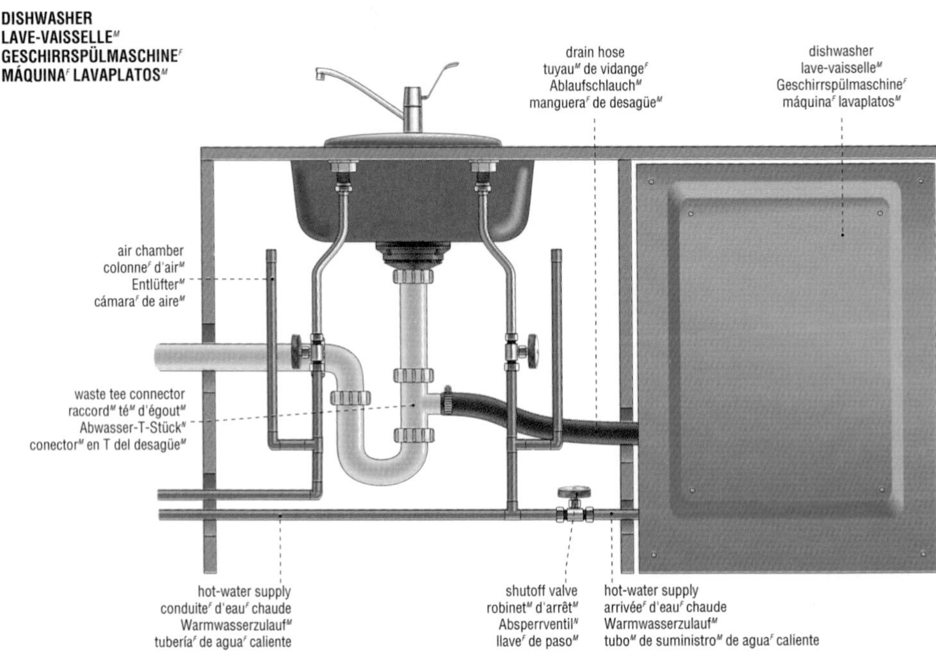

# PLUMBING
# PLOMBERIE[F]
# SANITÄRINSTALLATION[F]
# FONTANERÍA[F]

## PLUMBING TOOLS
## OUTILS[M] POUR PLOMBERIE[F]
## INSTALLATIONSWERKZEUGE[N]
## HERRAMIENTAS[F] DE FONTANERO[M]

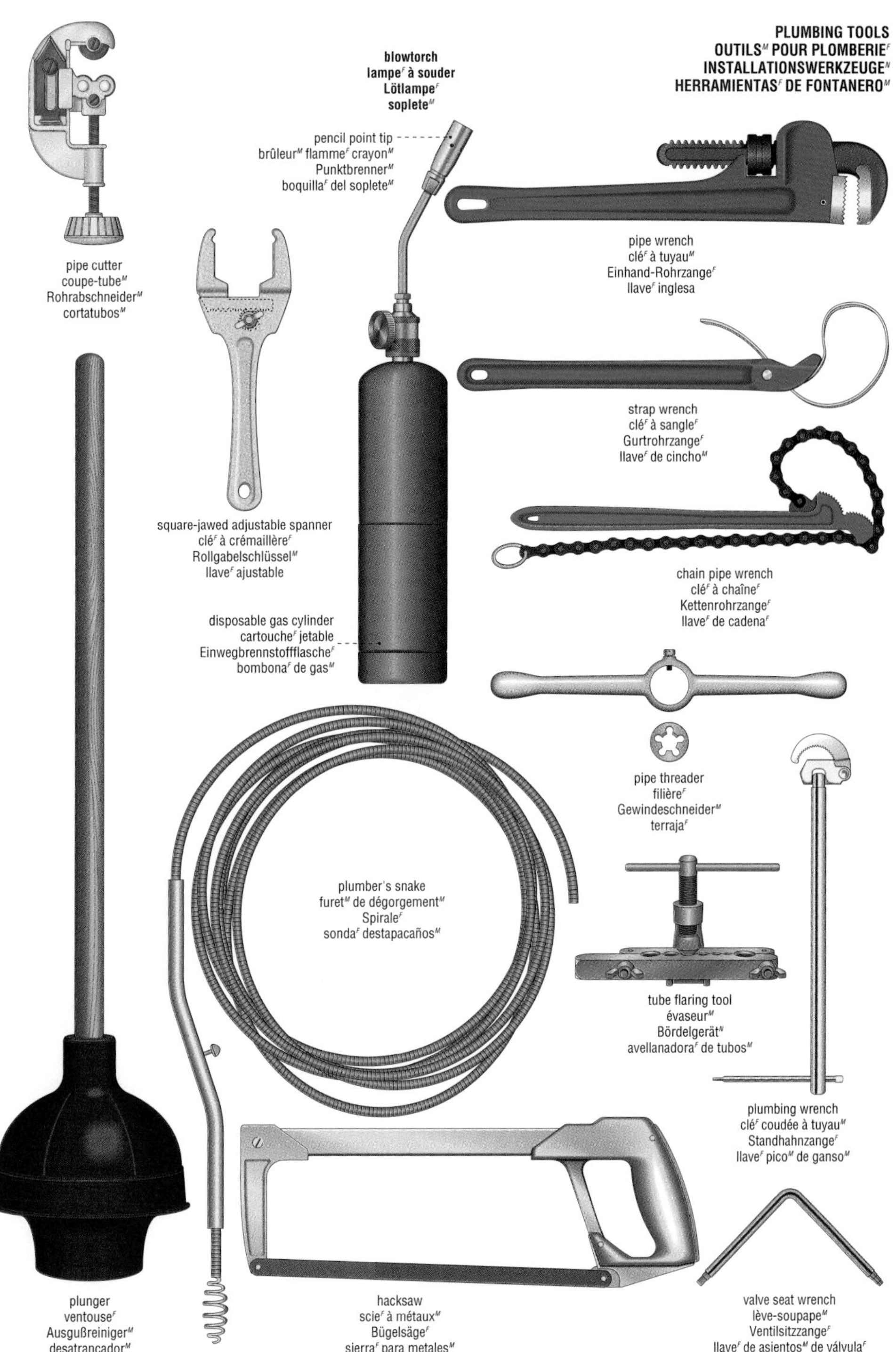

# PLUMBING
# PLOMBERIE^F
# SANITÄRINSTALLATION^F
# FONTANERÍA^F

## MECHANICAL CONNECTIONS
## RACCORDS^M MÉCANIQUES
## MECHANISCHE VERBINDUNGEN^F
## CONEXIONES^F MECÁNICAS

**compression fitting**
**raccord^M à compression^F**
**Quetschverschraubung^F**
**ensamblaje^M por compresión^F**

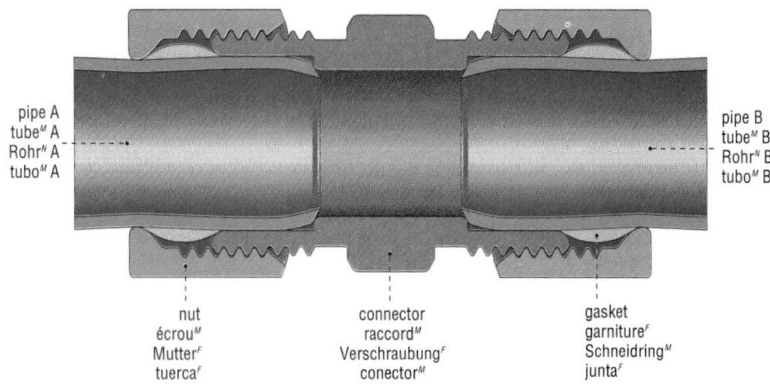


**flare joint**
**raccord^M à collet^M repoussé**
**Bördelverbindung^F**
**ensamblaje^M abocinado**

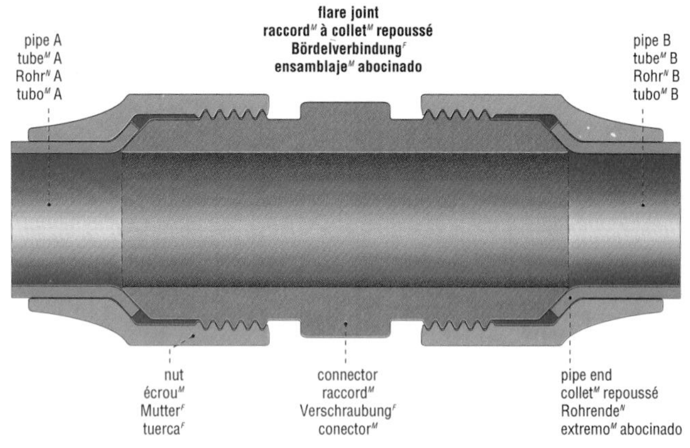


**union**
**raccord^M union^F**
**Verschraubung^F**
**unión^F**

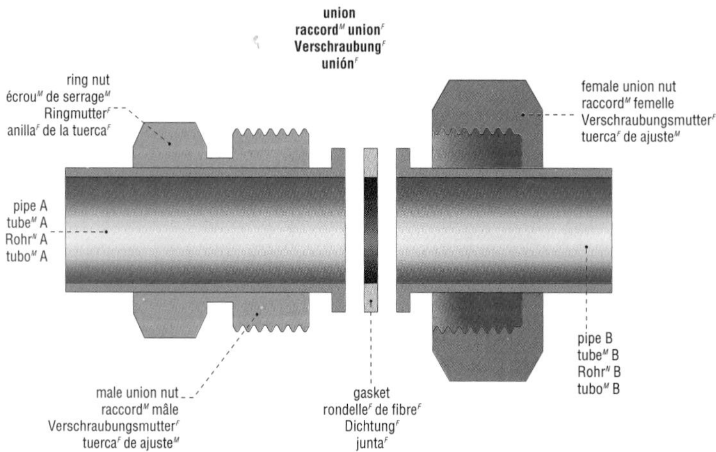

## TRANSITION FITTINGS
## ADAPTEURS[M]
## ÜBERGÄNGE[M]
## CONEXIONES[F] DE TRANSICIÓN[F]

steel to plastic
plastique[M] et acier[M]
Stahl[M] auf Kunststoff[M]
de acero[M] a plástico[M]

copper to plastic
plastique[M] et cuivre[M]
Kupfer[N] auf Kunststoff[M]
de cobre[M] a plástico[M]

copper to steel
cuivre[M] et acier[M]
Kupfer[N] auf Stahl[M]
de cobre[M] a acero[M]

## FITTINGS
## RACCORDS[M]
## FITTINGS[N]
## CONEXIONES[F]

45° elbow
coude[M] à 45°
Winkel[M] 45°
codo[M] de 45 grados[M]

elbow
coude[M]
Winkel[M]
codo[M] de 90 grados[M]

U-bend
coude[M] à 180°
Doppelbogen[M]
conexión[F] en U

tee connector
té[M]
Strömungs-T[N]
conexión[F] en T

Y-branch
culotte[F]
Abzweig[M] 45°
conexión[F] en Y

offset
coude[M] de renvoi[M]
Etagenbogen[M]
desviación[F]

trap
siphon[M]
Siphonwinkel[M]
sifón[M]

square head plug
bouchon[M] mâle sans bourrelet[M]
Vierkantstopfen[M]
tapón[M] macho[M]

cap
bouchon[M] femelle
Kappe[F]
tapón[M]

flush bushing
réduction[F] mâle-femelle
Muffe[F]
boquilla[F] de reducir

nipple
mamelon[M] double
Nippel[M]
boquilla[F]

reducing coupling
raccord[M] de réduction[F]
Reduziermuffenippel[M]
reductor[M] de calibre[M]

threaded cap
bouchon[M] femelle à visser
Gewindekappe[F]
tapón[M] hembra[F]

pipe coupling
manchon[M]
Rohrverschraubung[F]
unión[F]

hexagon bushing
réduction[F] mâle-femelle hexagonale
Sechskantstopfen[M]
boquilla[F] de reducir con cabeza[F] hexagonal

# LADDERS AND STEPLADDERS
# ÉCHELLES[F] ET ESCABEAUX[M]
# LEITERN[F] UND STEHLEITERN[F]
# ESCALERAS[F] DE MANO[F]

straight ladder
échelle droite
Anlegeleiter
escalera común
loft ladder
échelle escamotable
Dachbodenklappleiter
escalera de guardilla
hook ladder
échelle à crochets
Einhängeleiter
escalera de gancho
rope ladder
échelle de corde
Strickleiter
escalera de cuerda
multi-purpose ladder
échelle transformable
Mehrzweckleiter
escalera para usos múltiples
ladder scaffold
échelle d'échafaudage
Leitergerüst
andamio sobre ruedas
fruit-picking ladder
échelle fruitière
landwirtschaftliche Nutzleiter
escalera de recolección de fruta
rolling ladder
échelle roulante
Rollenleiter
escalera rodante

# PAINTING ACCESSORIES
# PEINTURE[F] D'ENTRETIEN[M]
# MALERBEDARF[M]
# HERRAMIENTAS[F] PARA PINTAR

## SOLDERING AND WELDING
## SOUDAGE[M]
## LÖTEN[N] UND SCHWEISSEN[N]
## SOLDADURA[F]

soldering iron
fer[M] à souder
Lötkolben[M]
hierro[M] para soldar

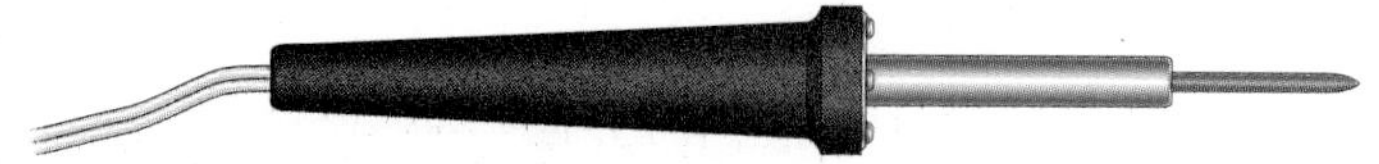

### SOLDERING GUN
### PISTOLET[M] À SOUDER
### LÖTPISTOLE[F]
### PISTOLA[F] PARA SOLDAR

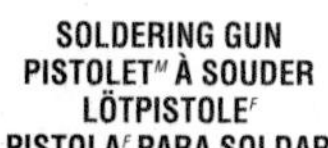

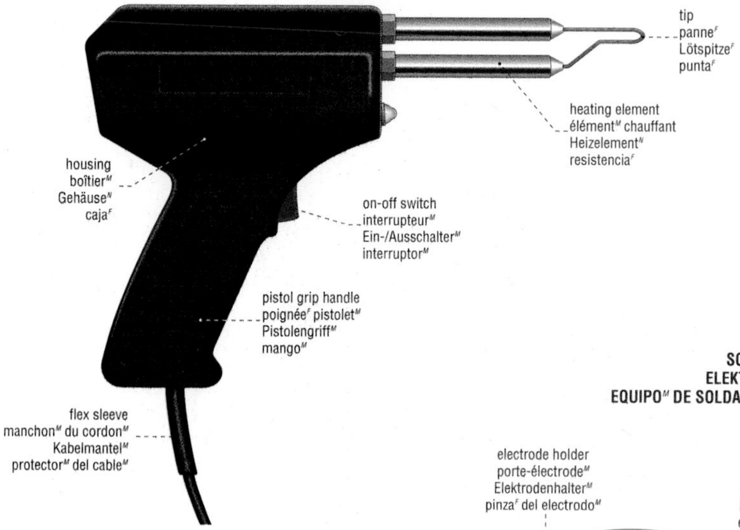

tip
panne[F]
Lötspitze[F]
punta[F]
heating element
élément[M] chauffant
Heizelement[N]
resistencia[F]
housing
boîtier[M]
Gehäuse[N]
caja[F]
on-off switch
interrupteur[M]
Ein-/Ausschalter[M]
interruptor[M]
pistol grip handle
poignée[F] pistolet[M]
Pistolengriff[M]
mango[M]
flex sleeve
manchon[M] du cordon[M]
Kabelmantel[M]
protector[M] del cable[M]

### ARC WELDING
### SOUDAGE[M] À L'ARC[M]
### ELEKTROSCHWEISSEN[N]
### EQUIPO[M] DE SOLDADURA[F] ELÉCTRICA

electrode holder
porte-électrode[M]
Elektrodenhalter[M]
pinza[F] del electrodo[M]
electrode
électrode[F]
Elektrode[F]
electrodo[M]
electrode lead
câble[M] d'alimentation[F] de l'électrode[F]
Elektrodenkabel[N]
cable[M] de corriente[F]
arc welder
poste[M] de soudage[M]
Schweißtransformator[M]
máquina[F] de soldar eléctrica
earth lead
câble[M] de masse[F]
Massekabel[N]
cable[M] de tierra[F]
earth clamp
prise[F] de masse[F]
Polzwinge[F]
pinza[F] de conexión[F] a tierra[F]

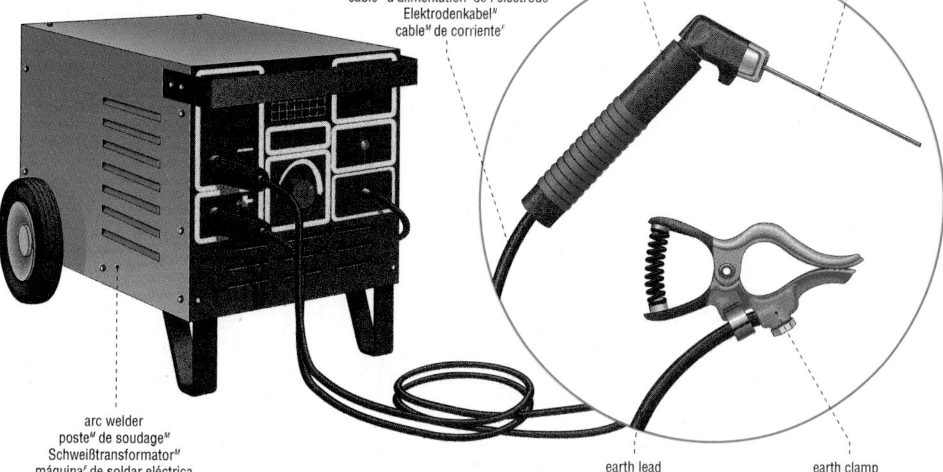

# SOLDERING AND WELDING
# SOUDAGE[M]
# LÖTEN[N] UND SCHWEISSEN[N]
# SOLDADURA[F]

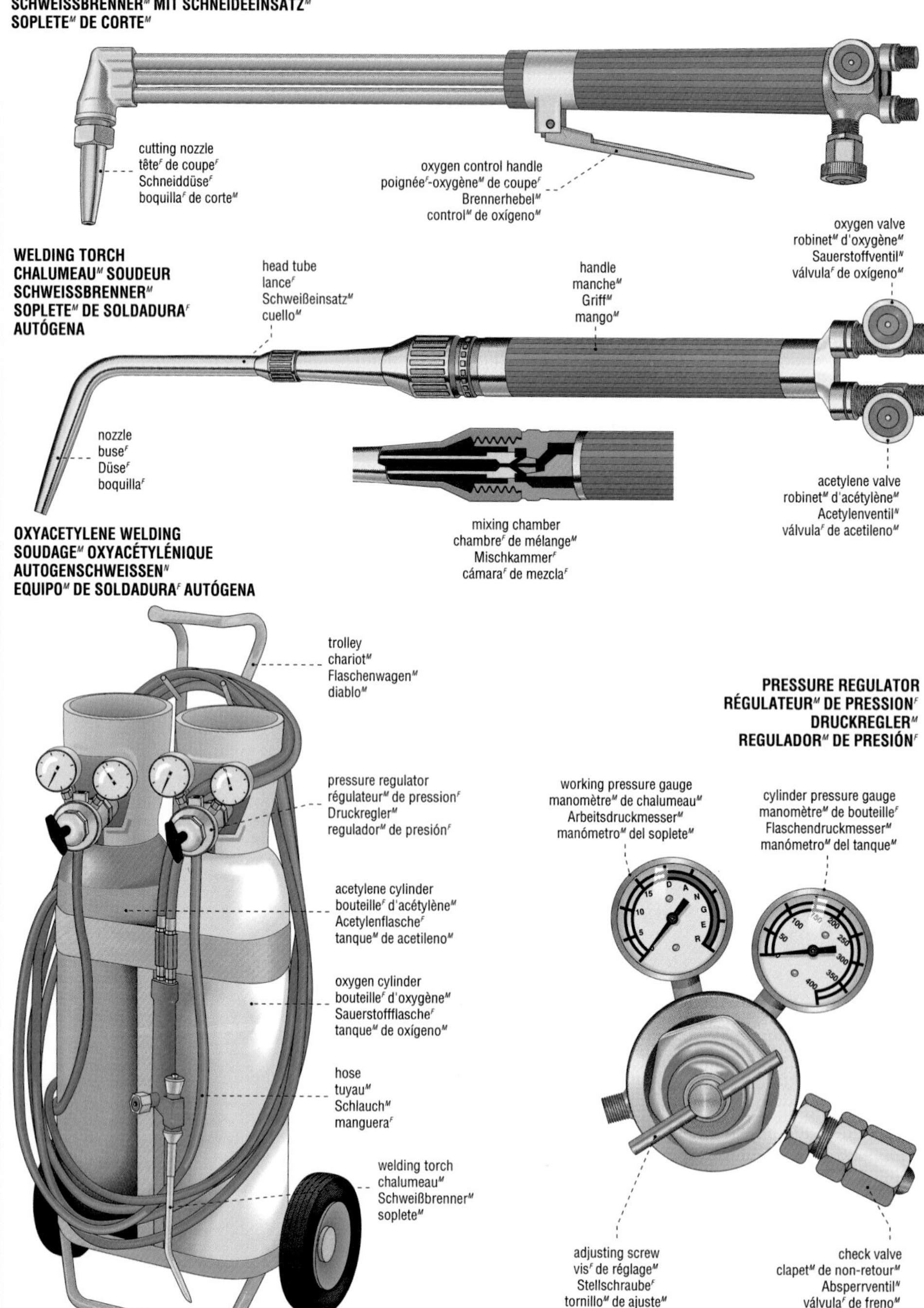

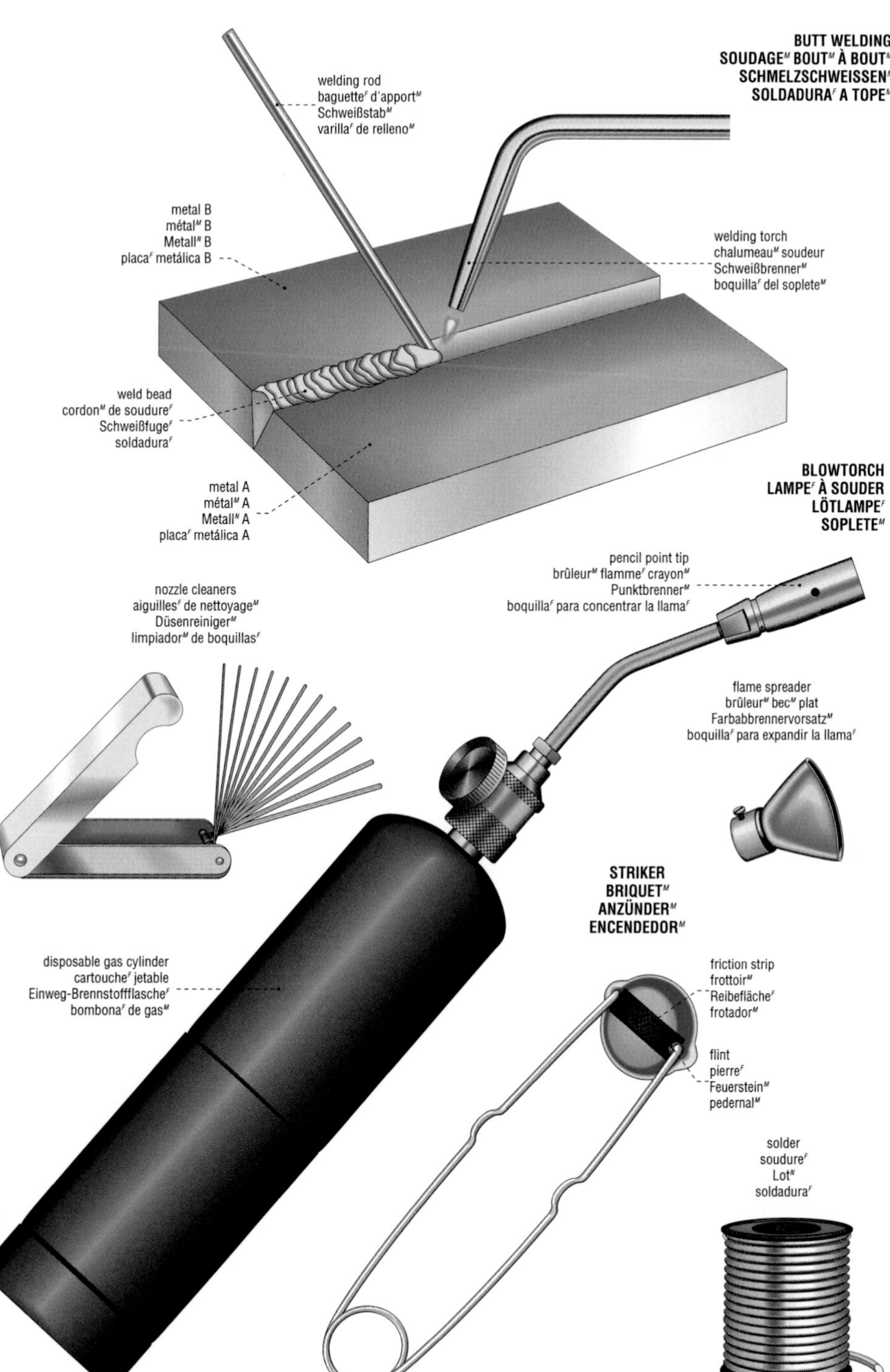
BUTT WELDING
SOUDAGE[M] BOUT[M] À BOUT[M]
SCHMELZSCHWEISSEN[N]
SOLDADURA[F] A TOPE[M]
welding rod
baguette[F] d'apport[M]
Schweißstab[M]
varilla[F] de relleno[M]
metal B
métal[M] B
Metall[N] B
placa[F] metálica B
welding torch
chalumeau[M] soudeur
Schweißbrenner[M]
boquilla[F] del soplete[M]
weld bead
cordon[M] de soudure[F]
Schweißfuge[F]
soldadura[F]
metal A
métal[M] A
Metall[N] A
placa[F] metálica A
BLOWTORCH
LAMPE[F] À SOUDER
LÖTLAMPE[F]
SOPLETE[M]
pencil point tip
brûleur[M] flamme[F] crayon[M]
Punktbrenner[M]
boquilla[F] para concentrar la llama[F]
nozzle cleaners
aiguilles[F] de nettoyage[M]
Düsenreiniger[M]
limpiador[M] de boquillas[F]
flame spreader
brûleur[M] bec[M] plat
Farbabbrennervorsatz[M]
boquilla[F] para expandir la llama[F]
STRIKER
BRIQUET[M]
ANZÜNDER[M]
ENCENDEDOR[M]
disposable gas cylinder
cartouche[F] jetable
Einweg-Brennstoffflasche[F]
bombona[F] de gas[M]
friction strip
frottoir[M]
Reibefläche[F]
frotador[M]
flint
pierre[F]
Feuerstein[M]
pedernal[M]
solder
soudure[F]
Lot[N]
soldadura[F]

# WELDING: PROTECTIVE EQUIPMENT
# SOUDAGE[M]: ÉQUIPEMENT[M] DE PROTECTION[F]
# LÖTEN[N] UND SCHWEISSEN[N]: SCHUTZKLEIDUNG[F]
# SOLDADURA[F]: ACCESORIOS[M] DE PROTECCIÓN[F]

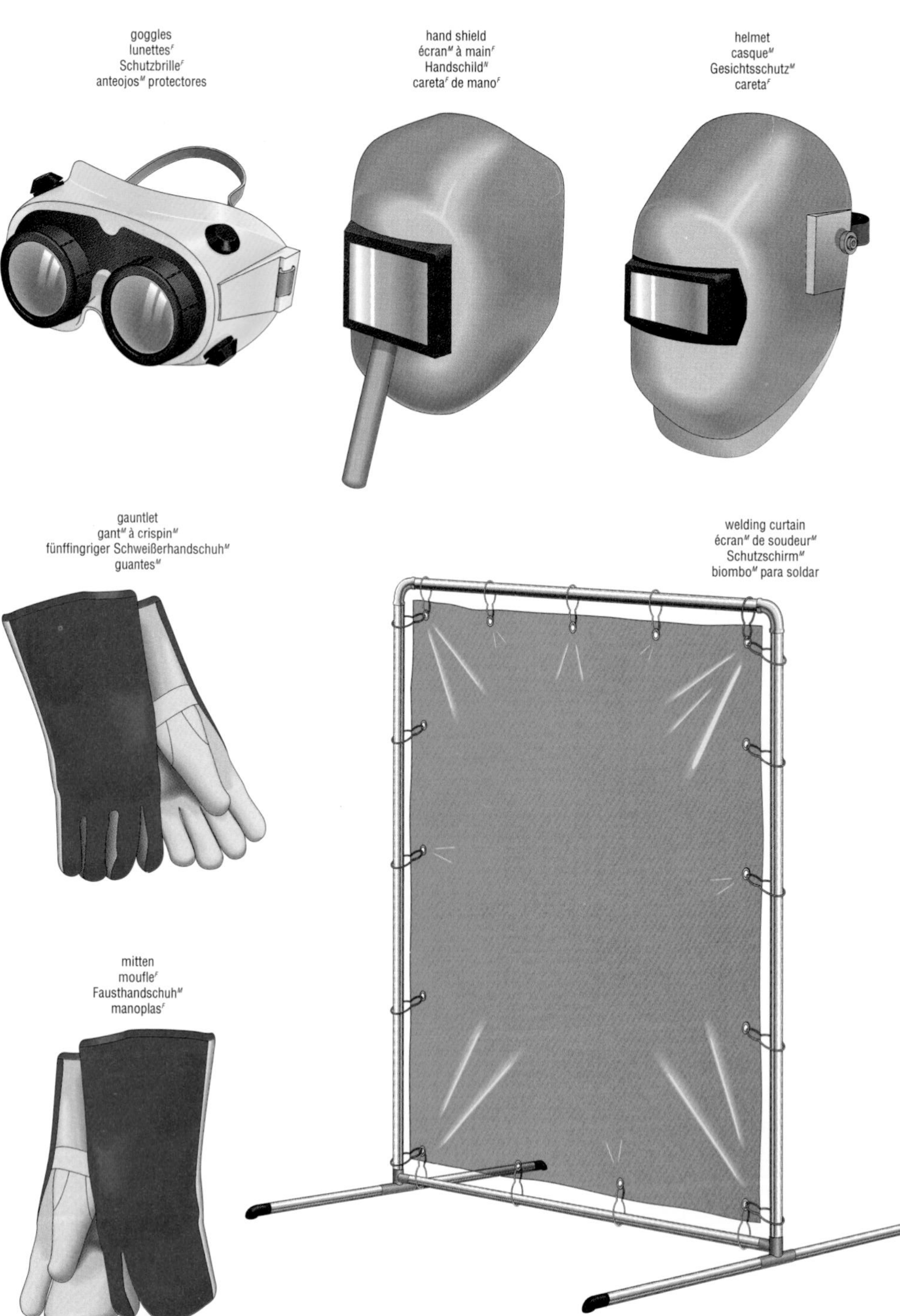

# ELECTRICITY
# ÉLECTRICITÉ[F]
# ELEKTRIZITÄT[F]
# ELECTRICIDAD[F]

dimmer switch
rhéostat[M]
Dimmerschalter[M]
conmutador[M] de intensidad[F]

escutcheon plate
plaque[F] de commutateur[M]
Schalterabdeckplatte[F]
placa[F] del interruptor[M]

## LAMPHOLDER
## DOUILLE[F] DE LAMPE[F]
## LAMPENFASSUNG[F]
## PORTALÁMPARAS[M]

cap
capuchon[M]
Kappe[F]
tapa[F]

socket
douille[F]
Fassung[F]
casquillo[M]

electrical box
boîte[F] électrique
Buchsenhalter[M]
caja[F] de conexiones[F]

switch
interrupteur[M]
Schalter[M]
interruptor[M]

three-pin socket
prise[F] de courant[M]
dreipolige Steckdose[F]
enchufe[M]

insulating sleeve
gaine[F] isolante
Isolierhülse[F]
manga[F] de aislamiento[M]

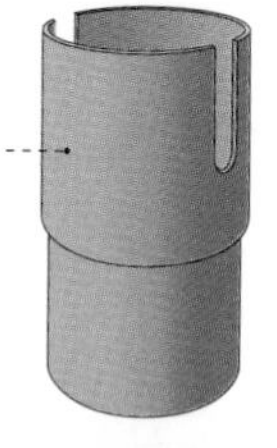

outer shell
enveloppe[F]
äußere Hülse[F]
cubierta[F]

## AMERICAN PLUG
## FICHE[F] AMÉRICAINE
## AMERIKANISCHER DREIPOLIGER STECKER[M]
## ENCHUFE[M] DE TIPO[M] AMERICANO

pin
lame[F]
Spannungsstift[M]
pata[F]

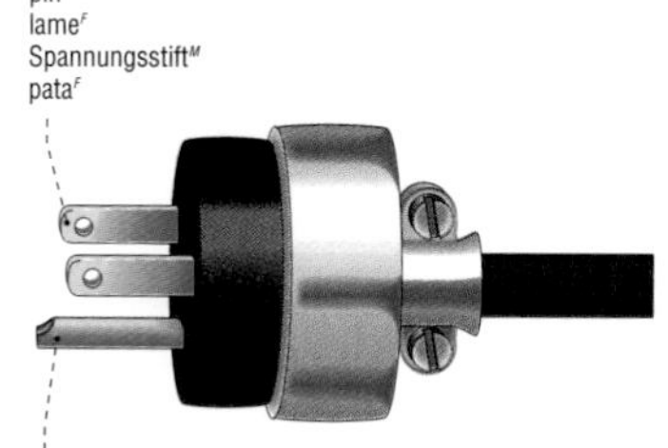

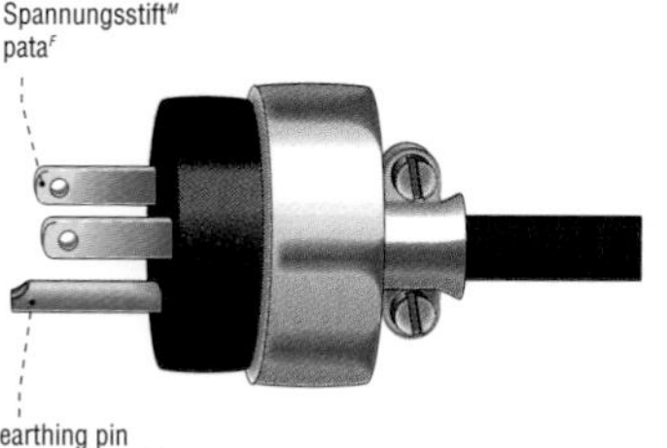

earthing pin
prise[F] de terre[F]
Erdungsstift[M]
pata[F] de conexión[F] a tierra[F]

## EUROPEAN PLUG
## FICHE[F] EUROPÉENNE
## STECKER[M]
## ENCHUFE[M] DE TIPO[M] EUROPEO

terminal
borne[F]
Anschlußklemme[F]
terminal[M]

earth terminal
prise[F] de terre[F]
Erdungsklemme[F]
terminal[M] de tierra[F]

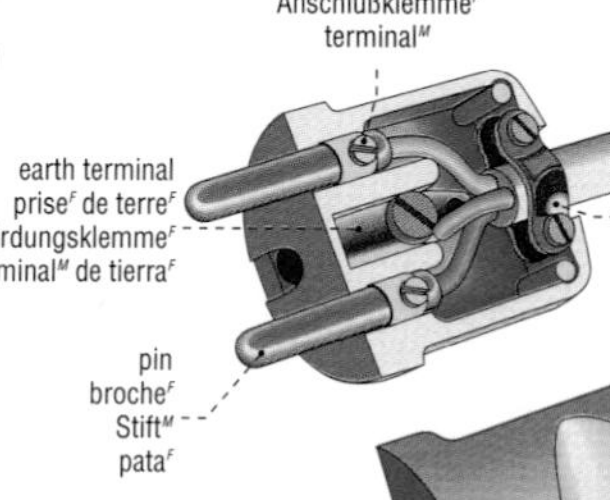

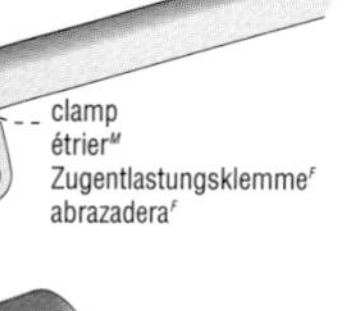

clamp
étrier[M]
Zugentlastungsklemme[F]
abrazadera[F]

pin
broche[F]
Stift[M]
pata[F]

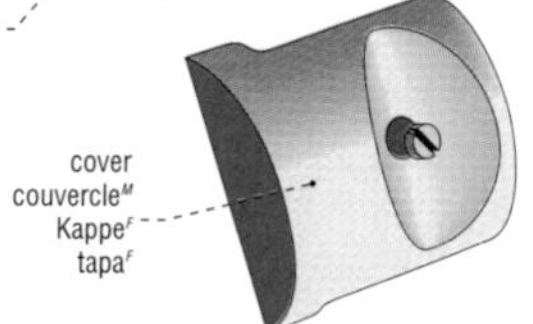

cover
couvercle[M]
Kappe[F]
tapa[F]

# ELECTRICITY
# ÉLECTRICITÉ[F]
# ELEKTRIZITÄT[F]
# ELECTRICIDAD[F]

## ELECTRICIAN'S TOOLS
## OUTILS[M] D'ÉLECTRICIEN[M]
## ELEKTROINSTALLATEURWERKZEUGE[N]
## HERRAMIENTAS[F] DE ELECTRICISTA[M]

**multimeter**
**multimètre[M]**
**Multimeter[N]**
**voltímetro[M]**

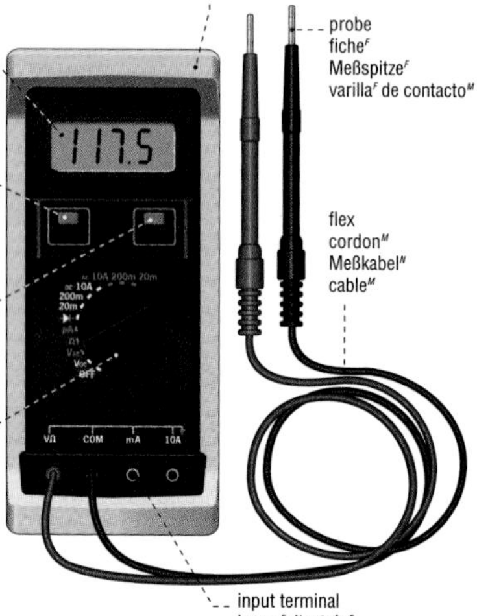

housing
boîtier[M]
Gehäuse[N]
caja[F]
probe
fiche[F]
Meßspitze[F]
varilla[F] de contacto[M]
digital display
afficheur[M] numérique
Digitalanzeige[F]
registro[M] digital
data hold
mémorisation[F] des données[F]
Meßspeicher[M]
retención[F] de datos[M]
flex
cordon[M]
Meßkabel[N]
cable[M]
auto/manual selector
lecture[F] automatique/manuelle
Auto-Manualumschalter[M]
selección auto/manual
function selection switch
commutateur[M]
Bereichsumschalter[M]
selector[M]
input terminal
borne[F] d'entrée[F]
Eingangsbuchse[F]
terminal[M] de entrada[F]
117.5
VΩ
COM
mA
10A

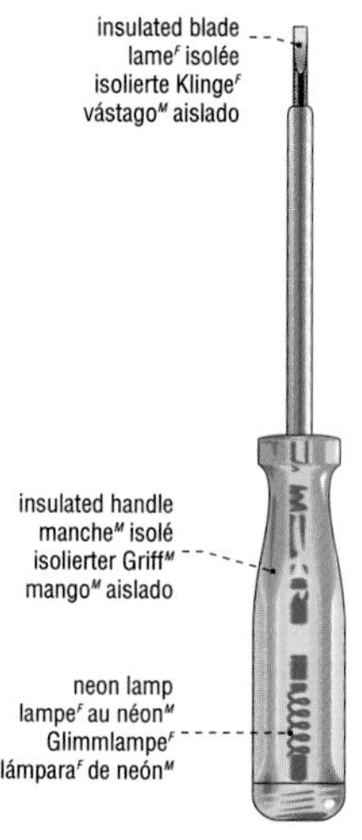

**tester screwdriver**
**vérificateur[M] de tension[F]**
**Spannungsprüfer[M]**
**detector[M] de tensión[F]**

insulated blade
lame[F] isolée
isolierte Klinge[F]
vástago[M] aislado
insulated handle
manche[M] isolé
isolierter Griff[M]
mango[M] aislado
neon lamp
lampe[F] au néon[M]
Glimmlampe[F]
lámpara[F] de neón[M]

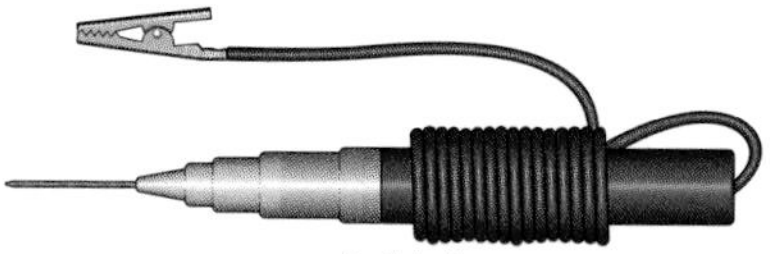

continuity tester
vérificateur[M] de continuité[F]
Durchgangsprüfer[M]
detector[M] de continuidad[F]

**inspection light**
**baladeuse[F]**
**Handlampe[F]**
**linterna[F] movible**

hook
crochet[M]
Haken[M]
gancho[M]
reflector
réflecteur[M]
Reflektor[M]
reflector[M]
bulb
lampe[F]
Glühbirne[F]
bombilla[F]
guard
grillage[M] de protection[F]
Schutzgitter[N]
reja[F]
convenience outlet
prise[F] de courant[M]
Zusatzsteckdose[F]
enchufe[M]
handle
manche[M]
Griff[M]
mango[M]
flex
cordon[M]
Kabel[N]
cable[M]

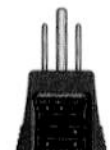

socket tester
vérificateur[M] de prise[F] de courant[M]
Steckdosenprüfer[M]
probador[M] de contactos[M] con tierra[F]

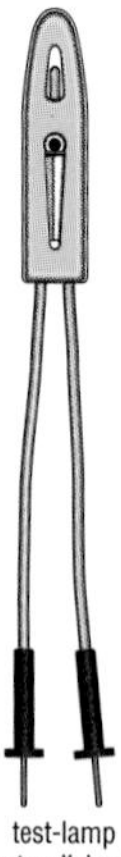

test-lamp
vérificateur[M] de circuit[M]
Prüflampe[F]
lámpara[F] de prueba[F] de neón[M]

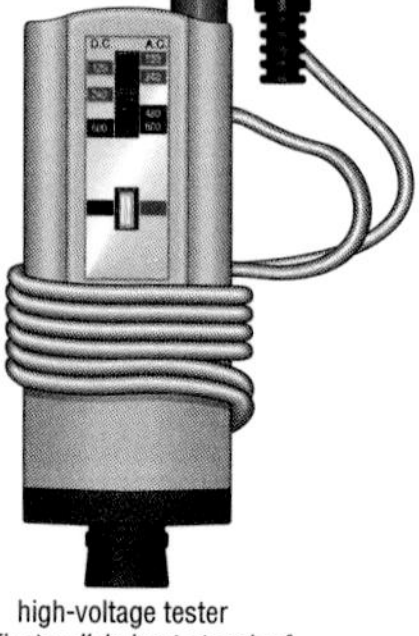

high-voltage tester
vérificateur[M] de haute tension[F]
Hochspannungsprüfer[M]
detector[M] de alta tensión[F]

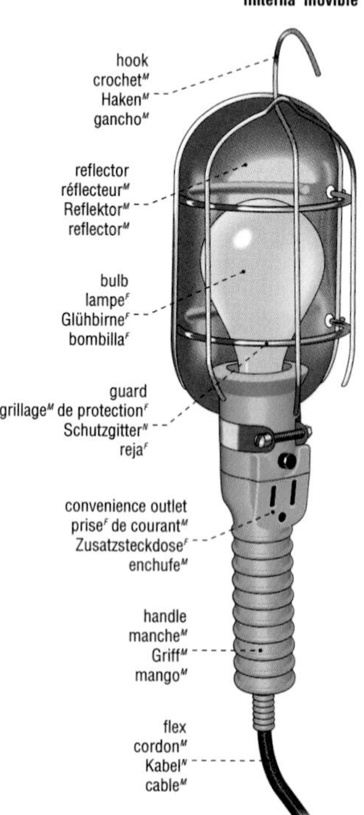

## ELECTRICIAN'S TOOLS
## OUTILS^M D'ÉLECTRICIEN^M
## ELEKTROINSTALLATEURWERKZEUGE^N
## HERRAMIENTAS^F DE ELECTRICISTA^M

**multipurpose tool**
**pince^F universelle**
**Mehrzweckzange^F**
**pinzas^F multiuso**

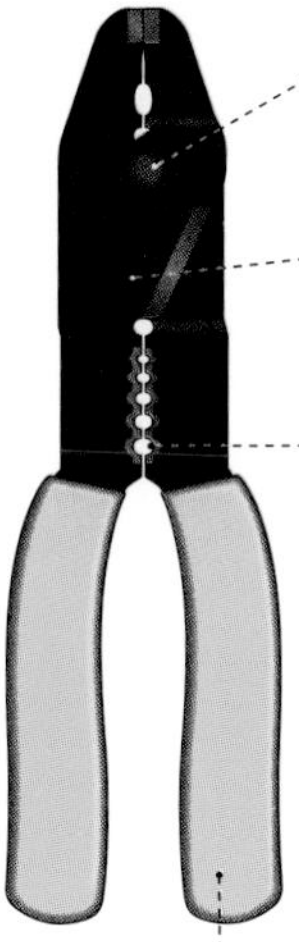

pivot
pivot^M
Drehzapfen^M
pivote^M

wire cutter
coupe-fil^M
Drahtschneider^M
cortador^M de alambre^M

wire stripper
dénude-fil^M
Abisolierer^M
pinzas^F pelacables

insulated handle
manche^M isolant
isolierter Griff^M
mango^M aislante

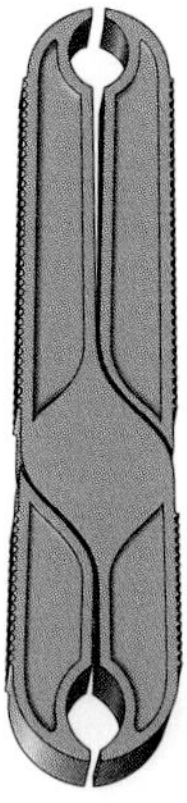

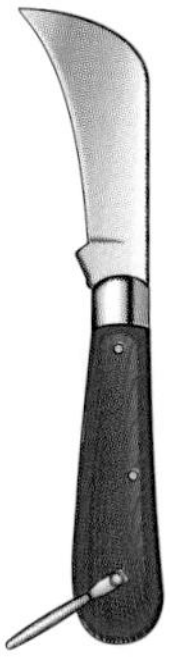

fuse puller
pince^F à fusible^M
Sicherungszieher^M
extractor^M de fusibles^M

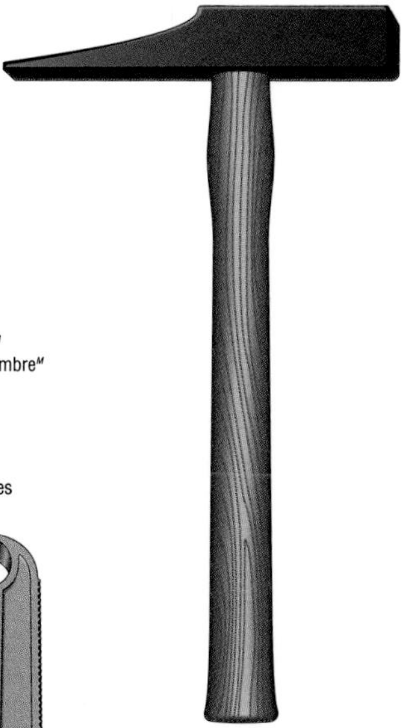

hammer
marteau^M d'électricien^M
Hammer^M
martillo^M

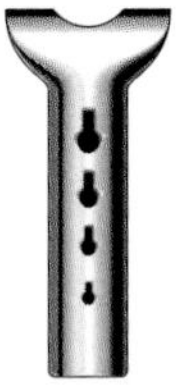

wire stripper
dénudeur^M de fil^M
Kabelabisolierer^M
pelacables^M

**combination pliers**
**pince^F d'électricien^M**
**Kombizange^F**
**alicates^M de electricista^M**

jaw
mâchoire^F
Backen^F
mordaza^F

wire cutter
coupe-fil^M
Drahtschneider^M
cortador^M de alambre^M

pivot
pivot^M
Drehzapfen^M
pivote^M

insulated handle
manche^M isolant
isolierter Griff^M
mango^M aislante

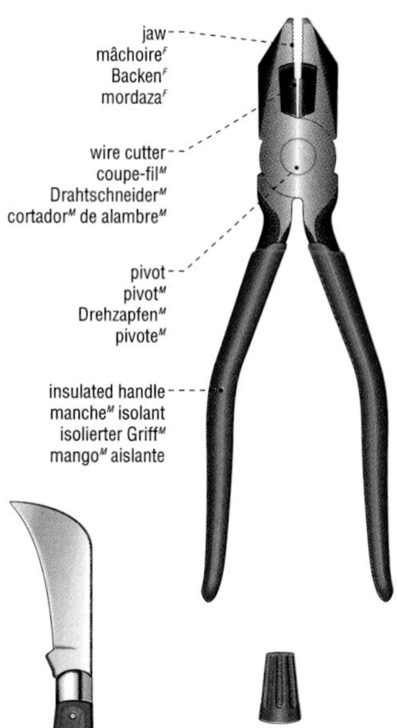

cutter
couteau^M d'électricien^M
Messer^N
cuchilla^F

wire nut
marette^F
Kabeltülle^F
capuchón^M de plástico^M

fish wire
câble^M de traction^F
Einziehdraht^M
alambre^M en tubo^M

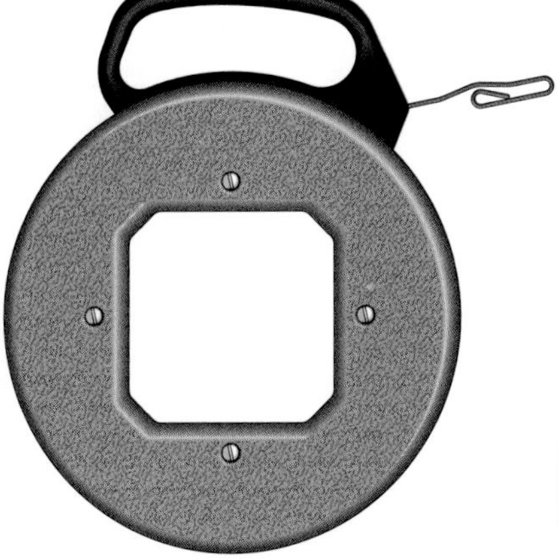

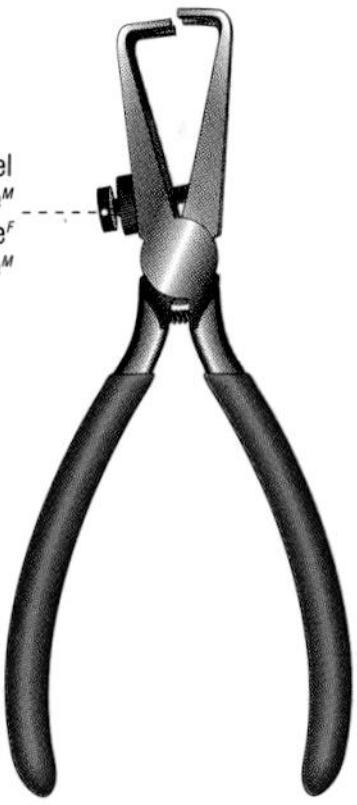

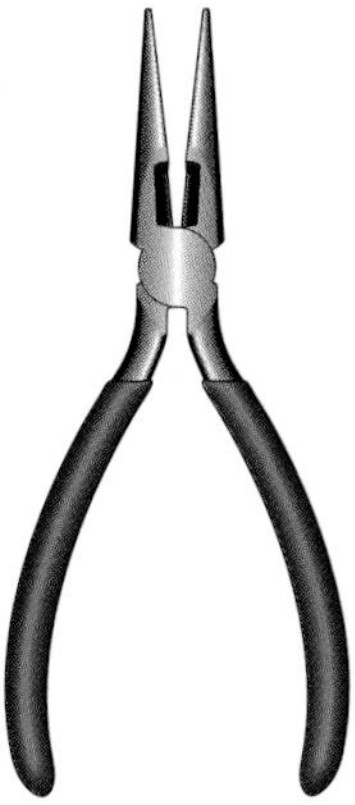

needle-nose pliers
pince^F à long bec^M
Spitzzange^F
alicates^M

adjustment wheel
molette^F de réglage^M
Stellschraube^F
tornillo^M de ajuste^M

**wire stripper**
**pince^F à dénuder**
**Abisolierzange^F**
**pinzas^F pelacables**

# ELECTRICITY
# ÉLECTRICITÉ[F]
# ELEKTRIZITÄT[F]
# ELECTRICIDAD[F]

## FUSE BOX
## TABLEAU[M] DE DISTRIBUTION[F]
## SICHERUNGSKASTEN[M]
## CAJETÍN[M] DE FUSIBLES[M]

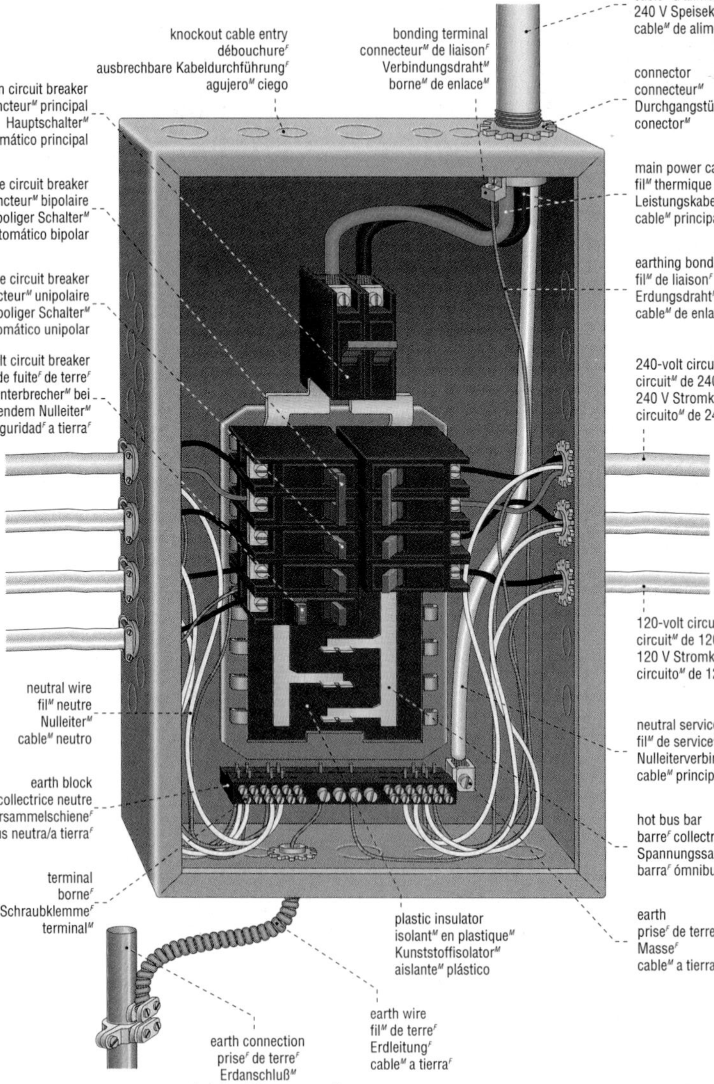

knockout cable entry
débouchure[F]
ausbrechbare Kabeldurchführung[F]
agujero[M] ciego

bonding terminal
connecteur[M] de liaison[F]
Verbindungsdraht[M]
borne[M] de enlace[M]

240-volt feeder cable
câble[M] d'alimentation[F] de 240 V
240 V Speisekabel[N]
cable[M] de alimentación[F] de 240 voltios

main circuit breaker
disjoncteur[M] principal
Hauptschalter[M]
interruptor[M] automático principal

connector
connecteur[M]
Durchgangstülle[F]
conector[M]

main power cable
fil[M] thermique
Leistungskabel[N]
cable[M] principal

double pole circuit breaker
disjoncteur[M] bipolaire
zweipoliger Schalter[M]
interruptor[M] automático bipolar

earthing bond
fil[M] de liaison[F]
Erdungsdraht[M]
cable[M] de enlace[M]

single pole circuit breaker
disjoncteur[M] unipolaire
einpoliger Schalter[M]
interruptor[M] automático unipolar

240-volt circuit
circuit[M] de 240 V
240 V Stromkreis[M]
circuito[M] de 240 voltios

earth fault circuit breaker
disjoncteur[M] de fuite[F] de terre[F]
Stromunterbrecher[M] bei spannungsführendem Nulleiter[M]
fusible[M] de seguridad[F] a tierra[F]

120-volt circuit
circuit[M] de 120 V
120 V Stromkreis[M]
circuito[M] de 120 voltios

neutral wire
fil[M] neutre
Nulleiter[M]
cable[M] neutro

neutral service wire
fil[M] de service[M] neutre
Nulleiterverbinder[M]
cable[M] principal neutro

earth block
barre[F] collectrice neutre
Nulleitersammelschiene[F]
barra[F] ómnibus neutra/a tierra[F]

hot bus bar
barre[F] collectrice thermique
Spannungssammelschiene[F]
barra[F] ómnibus de carga[F]

terminal
borne[F]
Schraubklemme[F]
terminal[M]

plastic insulator
isolant[M] en plastique[M]
Kunststoffisolator[M]
aislante[M] plástico

earth
prise[F] de terre[F]
Masse[F]
cable[M] a tierra[F]

earth wire
fil[M] de terre[F]
Erdleitung[F]
cable[M] a tierra[F]

earth connection
prise[F] de terre[F]
Erdanschluß[M]
cañería[F] metálica para agua[F]

## FUSES
## FUSIBLES[M]
## SICHERUNGEN[F]
## FUSIBLES[M]

cartridge fuse
fusible[M]-cartouche[F]
Patronensicherung[F]
fusible[M] de cartucho[M]

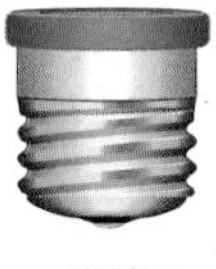

plug fuse
fusible[M] à culot[M]
Stöpselsicherung[F]
fusible[M] de rosca[F]

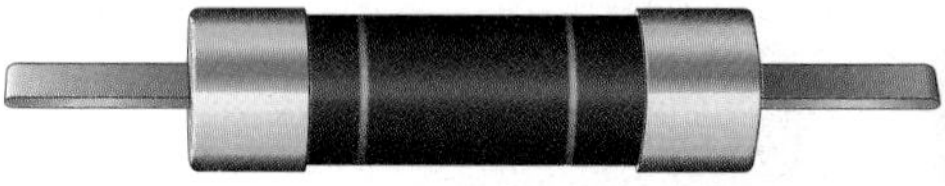

knife-blade cartridge fuse
fusible[M]-cartouche[F] à lames[F]
Hauptsicherung[F]
fusible[M] de bayoneta[F]

# CLOTHING KLEIDUNG
# VÊTEMENTS VESTIDO

SUMMARY

# FEATURES OF HISTORICAL COSTUME
# ÉLÉMENTS[M] DU COSTUME[M] ANCIEN
# ELEMENTE[N] HISTORISCHER KOSTÜME[N]
# VESTIDURAS[F] ANTIGUAS

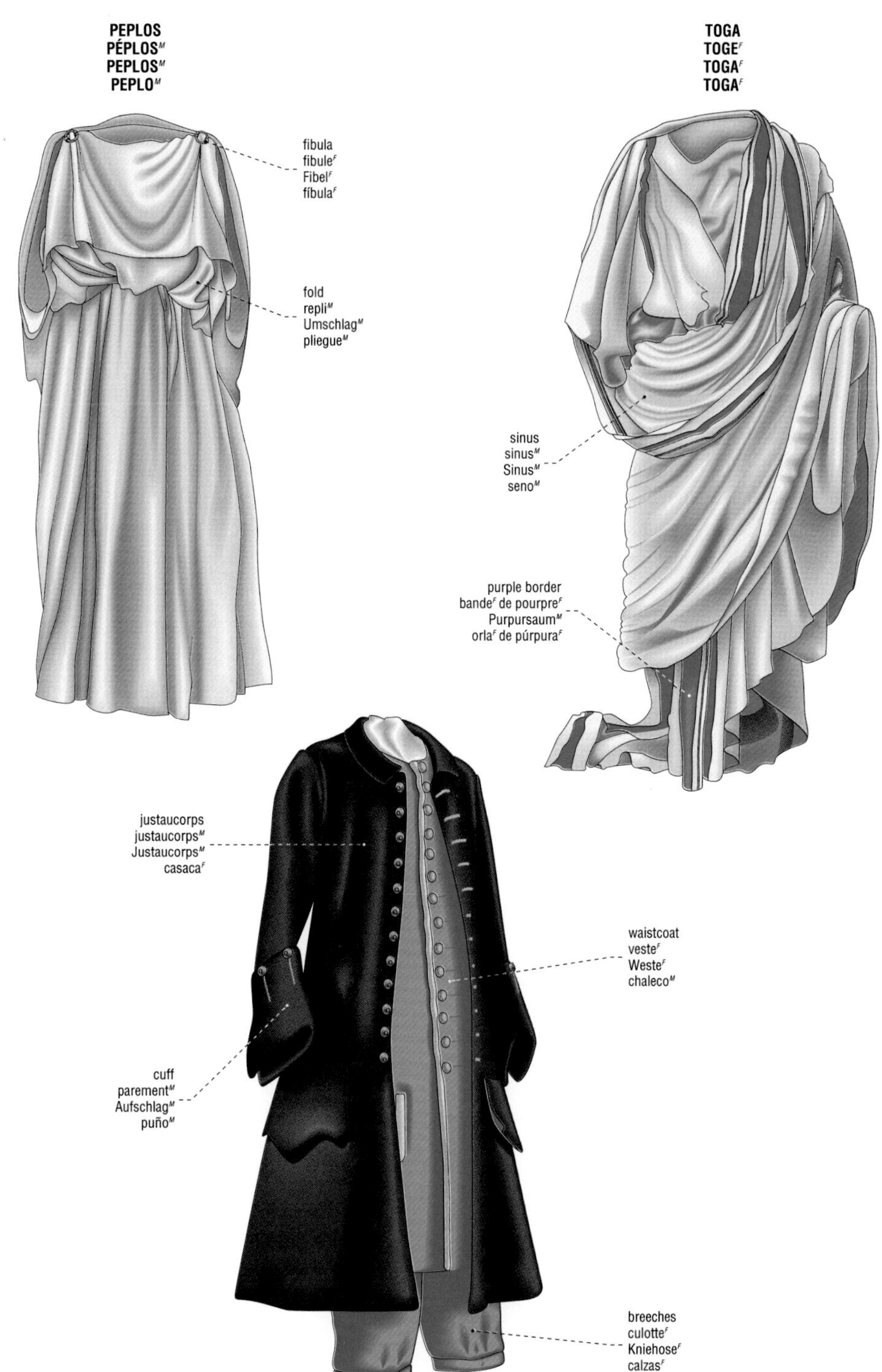


CLOTHING VÊTEMENTS KLEIDUNG VESTIDO

# FEATURES OF HISTORICAL COSTUME
# ÉLÉMENTS[M] DU COSTUME[M] ANCIEN
# ELEMENTE[N] HISTORISCHER KOSTÜME[N]
# VESTIDURAS[F] ANTIGUAS

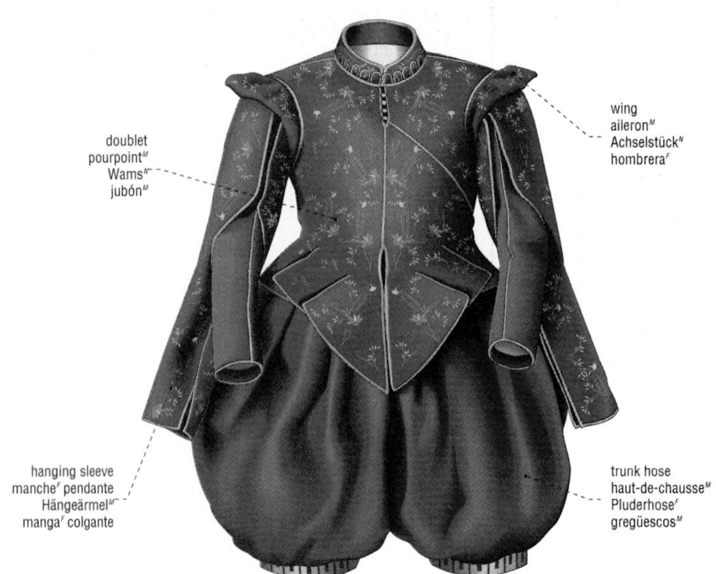


## COTEHARDIE
## COTARDIE[F]
## COTARDIE[F]
## TÚNICA[F] DE MANGA[F] LARGA

## DRESS WITH BUSTLE
## ROBE[F] À TOURNURE[F]
## KLEID[N] MIT TURNÜRE[F]
## VESTIDO[M] CON POLISÓN[M]

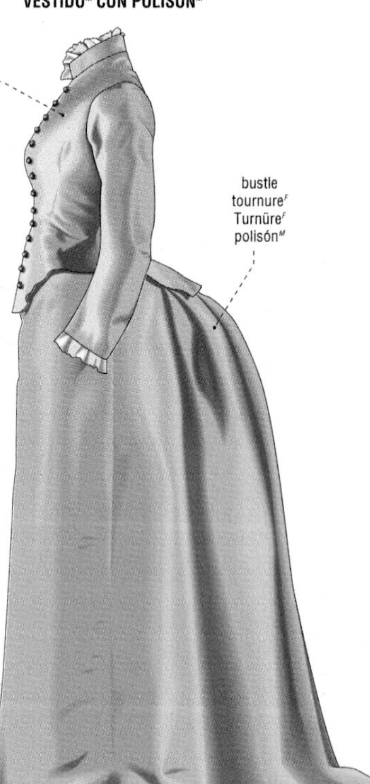

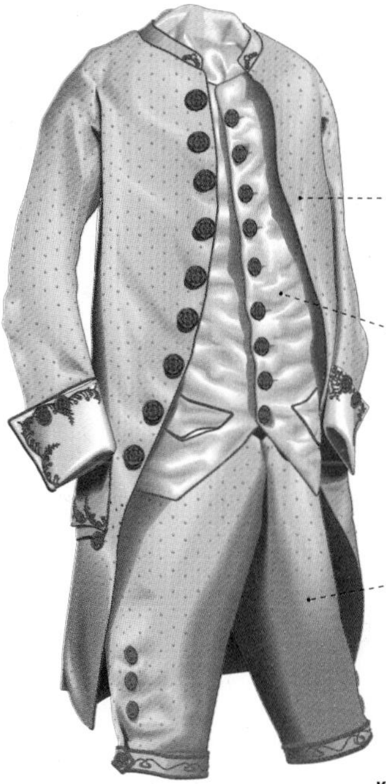

frock coat
frac$^{M}$
Schoßrock$^{M}$
levita$^{F}$

waistcoat
gilet$^{M}$
Weste$^{F}$
chaleco$^{M}$

breeches
culotte$^{F}$
Kniehose$^{F}$
calzas$^{F}$

**HOUPPELANDE**
**HOUPPELANDE$^{F}$**
**HOUPPELANDE$^{F}$**
**TOGA$^{F}$**

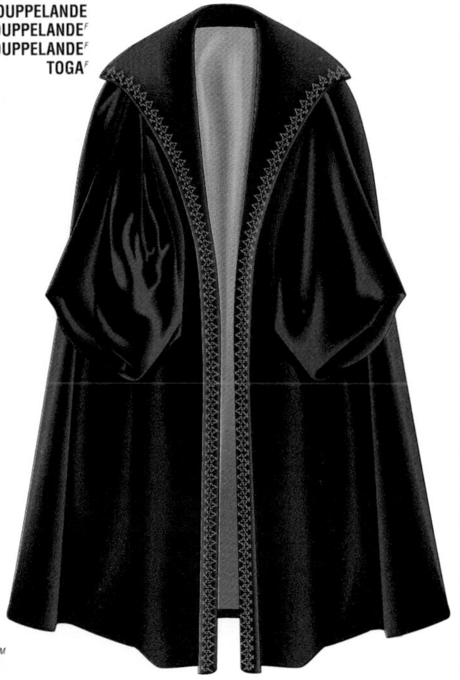

**DRESS WITH PANNIERS**
**ROBE$^{F}$ À PANIERS$^{M}$**
**KLEID$^{N}$ MIT FLACHEM REIFROCK$^{M}$**
**GUARDAINFANTE$^{M}$**

ruffle
engageante$^{F}$
Spitzenvolant$^{N}$
manga$^{F}$ de volante$^{M}$

stomacker
pièce$^{F}$ d'estomac$^{M}$
Mieder$^{N}$
peto$^{M}$

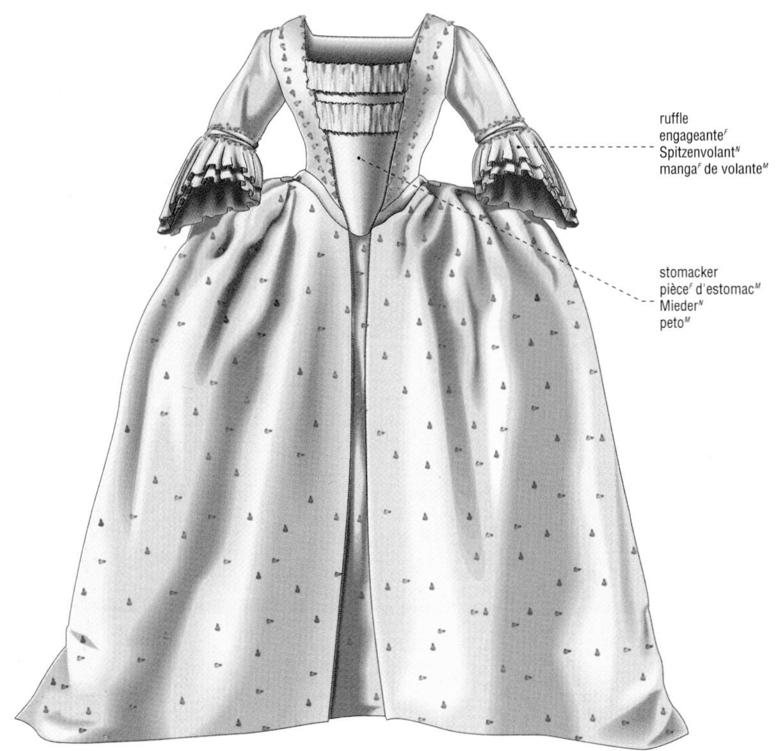

# FEATURES OF HISTORICAL COSTUME
# ÉLÉMENTS[M] DU COSTUME[M] ANCIEN
# ELEMENTE[N] HISTORISCHER KOSTÜME[N]
# VESTIDURAS[F] ANTIGUAS

## DRESS WITH CRINOLINE
## ROBE[F] À CRINOLINE[F]
## KLEID[N] MIT KRINOLINENROCK[M]
## VESTIDO[M] CON MIRIÑAQUE[M]

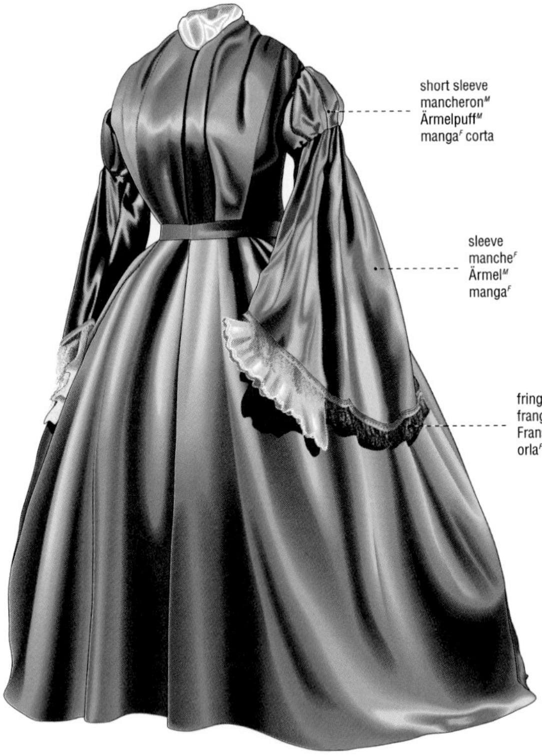

short sleeve
mancheron[M]
Ärmelpuff[M]
manga[F] corta

sleeve
manche[F]
Ärmel[M]
manga[F]

fringe
frange[F]
Franse[F]
orla[F]

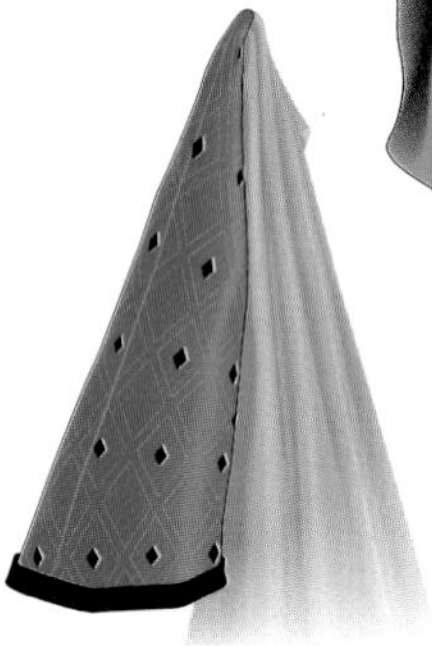

hennin
hennin[M]
Hennin[M]
cofia[F] cónica

bicorne
bicorne[M]
Zweispitz[M]
bicornio[M]

tricorne
tricorne[M]
Dreispitz[M]
tricornio[M]

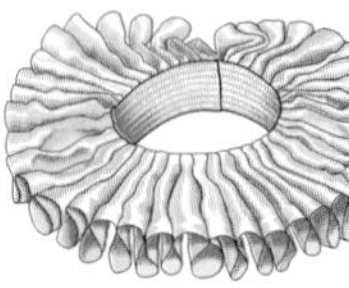

fraise
fraise[F]
Halskrause[F]
gorguera[F]

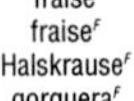

collaret
collerette[F]
kleiner Kragen[M]
cuello[M] de Holanda

heeled shoe
soulier[M] à talon[M]
Absatzschuh[M]
zapato[M] de tacón[M]

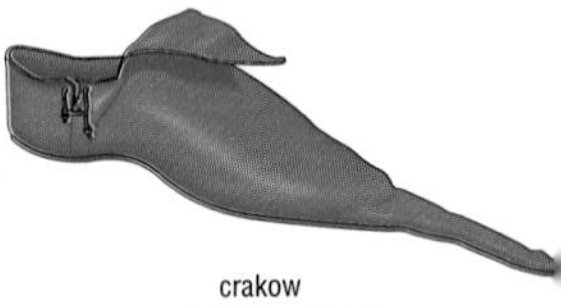

crakow
soulier[M] à la poulaine[F]
Schnabelschuh[M]
zapato[M] a la polaca

# MEN'S CLOTHING
# VÊTEMENTS[M] D'HOMME[M]
# HERRENKLEIDUNG[F]
# ROPA[F] DE HOMBRE[M]

## RAINCOAT
## IMPERMÉABLE[M]
## REGENMANTEL[M]
## IMPERMEABLE[M]

collar
col[M]
Kragen[M]
cuello[M]
raglan sleeve
manche[F] raglan
Raglanärmel[M]
manga[F] ranglán
notched lapel
revers[M] cranté
abfallendes Revers[N]
solapa[F] con ojal[M]
tab
patte[F]
Spange[F]
lengüeta[F]
broad welt side pocket
poche[F] raglan
Raglantasche[F]
bolsillo[M] de ribete[M] ancho
buttonhole
boutonnière[F]
Knopfloch[N]
ojal[M]
side panel
pan[M]
Seitenteil[N]
paño[M] lateral

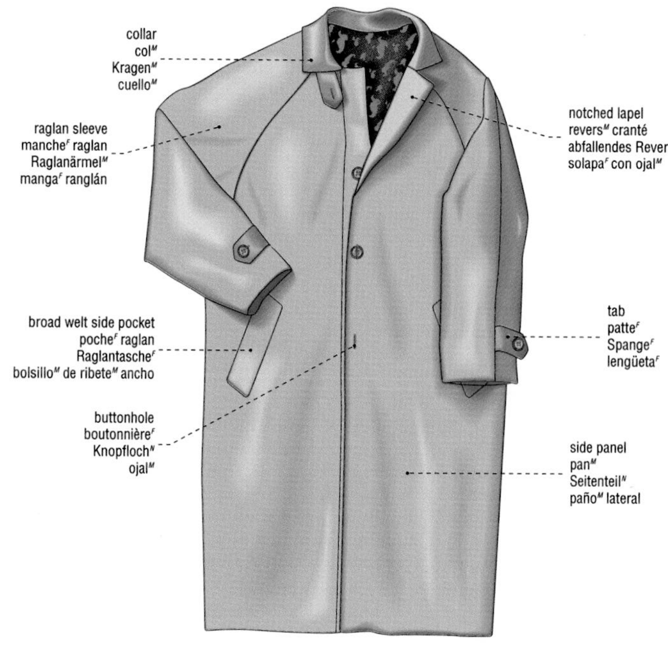

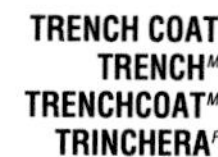

## TRENCH COAT
## TRENCH[M]
## TRENCHCOAT[M]
## TRINCHERA[F]

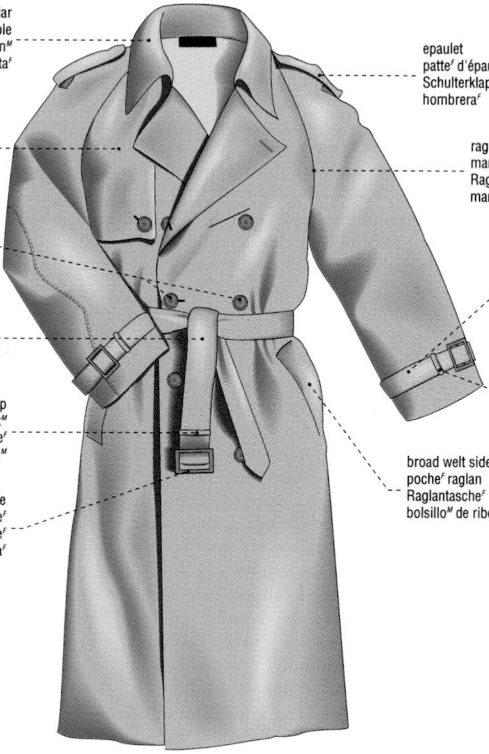

two-way collar
col[M] transformable
transformabler Kragen[M]
cuello[M] de doble vista[F]
epaulet
patte[F] d'épaule[F]
Schulterklappe[F]
hombrera[F]
gun flap
bavolet[M]
Koller[M]
protector[M]
raglan sleeve
manche[F] raglan
Raglanärmel[M]
manga[F] ranglán
double-breasted buttoning
double boutonnage[M]
zweireihig
botonadura[F] cruzada
sleeve strap
patte[F] de serrage[M]
Ärmellasche[F]
correa[F] de la manga[F]
belt
ceinture[F]
Gürtel[M]
cinturón[M]
sleeve strap loop
passant[M]
Riegel[M]
presilla[F] de la manga[F]
belt loop
passant[M]
Gürtelschlaufe[F]
presilla[F] del cinturón[M]
broad welt side pocket
poche[F] raglan
Raglantasche[F]
bolsillo[M] de ribete[M] ancho
buckle
boucle[F] de ceinture[F]
Schnalle[F]
hebilla[F]

# MEN'S CLOTHING
# VÊTEMENTS[M] D'HOMME[M]
# HERRENKLEIDUNG[F]
# ROPA[F] DE HOMBRE[M]

three-quarter coat
paletot[M]
dreiviertellanger Mantel[M]
abrigo[M] de tres cuartos

**PARKA**
**PARKA[F]**
**PARKA[M]**
**PARKA[M]**

zip fastener
fermeture[F] à glissière[F]
Reißverschluß[M]
cremallera[F]

snap-fastening tab
patte[F] à boutons[M]-pression[F]
Druckknopfleiste[F]
corchete[M] de presión[F]

**WINDCHEATER**
**BLOUSON[M] COURT**
**WINDJACKE[F]**
**CAZADORA[F]**

snap fastener
bouton[M]-pression[F]
Druckknopf[M]
broche[M] de presión[F]

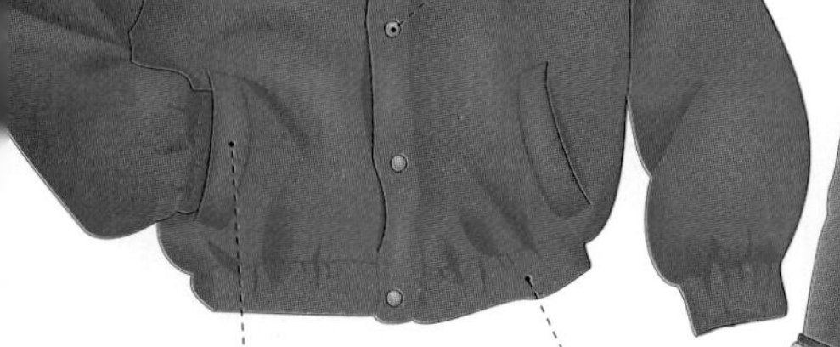

hand-warmer pocket
poche[F] repose-bras[M]
Mufftasche[F]
bolsillo[M] de ojal[M]

elastic waistband
ceinture[F] élastique
elastischer Bund[M]
pretina[F] elástica

sheepskin jacket
canadienne[F]
Lammfelljacke[F]
zamarra[F]

# MEN'S CLOTHING
# VÊTEMENTS[M] D'HOMME[M]
# HERRENKLEIDUNG[F]
# ROPA[F] DE HOMBRE[M]

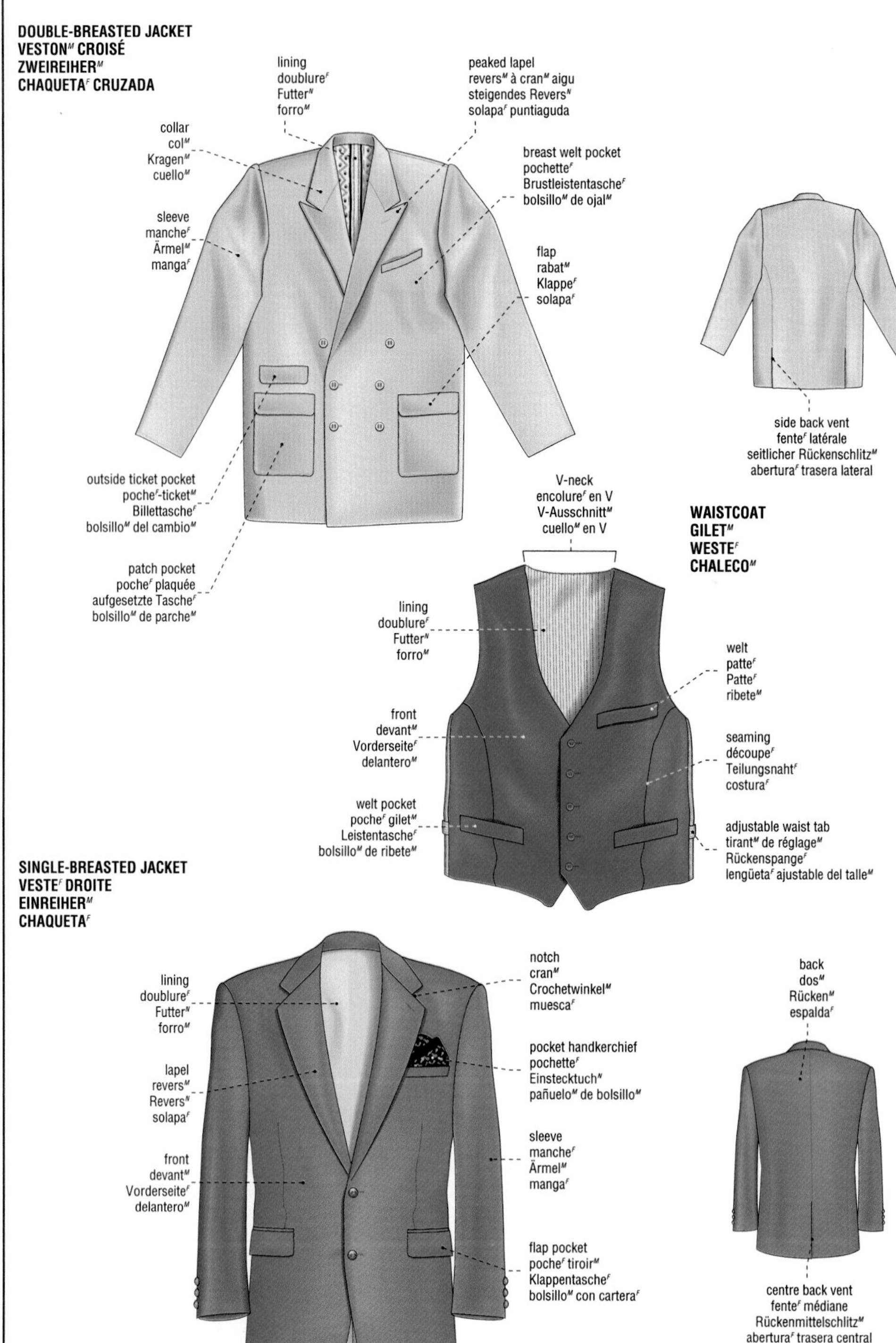

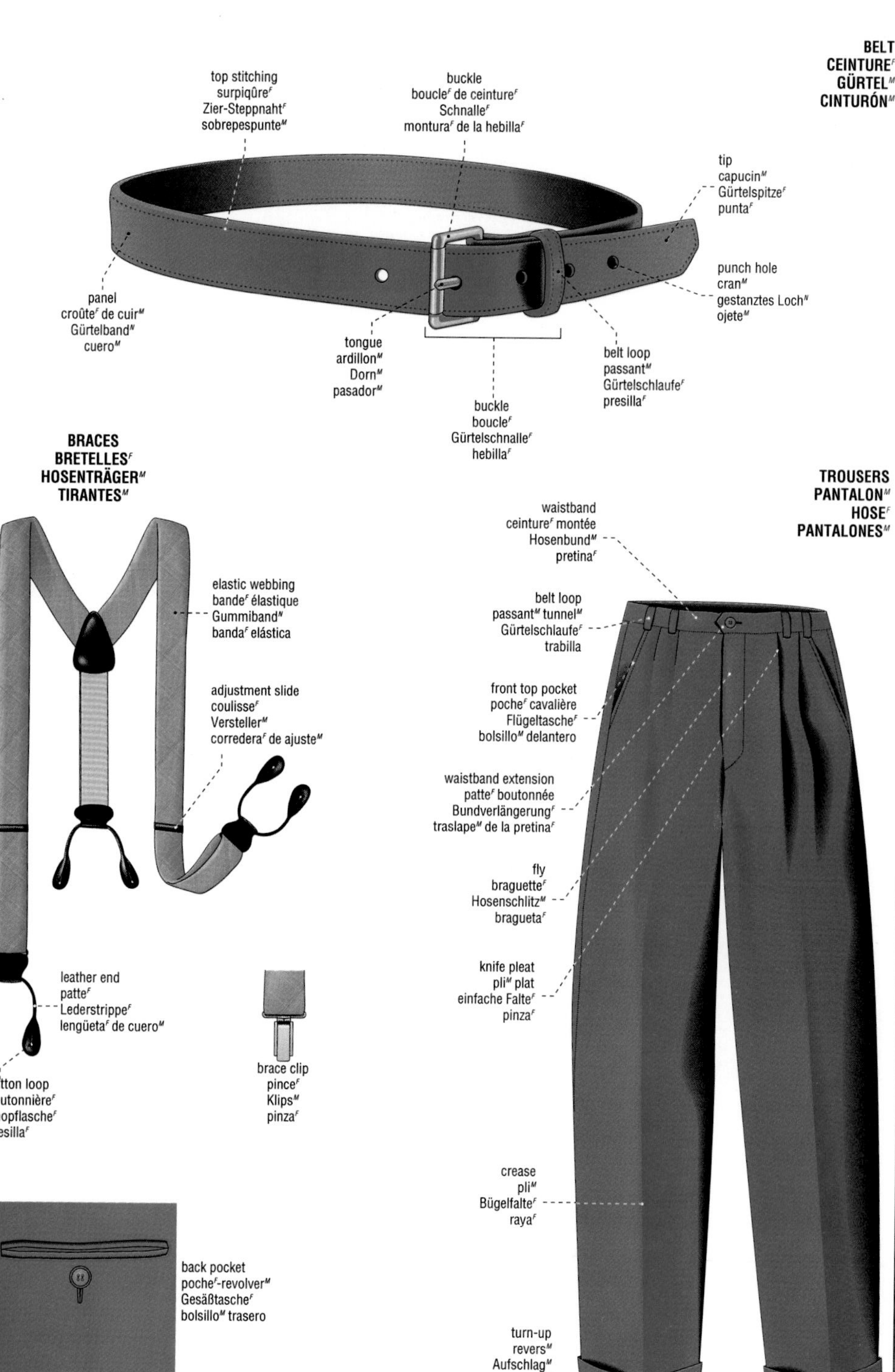
BELT
CEINTURE[F]
GÜRTEL[M]
CINTURÓN[M]
top stitching
surpiqûre[F]
Zier-Steppnaht[F]
sobrepespunte[M]
buckle
boucle[F] de ceinture[F]
Schnalle[F]
montura[F] de la hebilla[F]
tip
capucin[M]
Gürtelspitze[F]
punta[F]
punch hole
cran[M]
gestanztes Loch[N]
ojete[M]
panel
croûte[F] de cuir[M]
Gürtelband[N]
cuero[M]
tongue
ardillon[M]
Dorn[M]
pasador[M]
belt loop
passant[M]
Gürtelschlaufe[F]
presilla[F]
buckle
boucle[F]
Gürtelschnalle[F]
hebilla[F]
BRACES
BRETELLES[F]
HOSENTRÄGER[M]
TIRANTES[M]
elastic webbing
bande[F] élastique
Gummiband[N]
banda[F] elástica
adjustment slide
coulisse[F]
Versteller[M]
corredera[F] de ajuste[M]
leather end
patte[F]
Lederstrippe[F]
lengüeta[F] de cuero[M]
brace clip
pince[F]
Klips[M]
pinza[F]
button loop
boutonnière[F]
Knopflasche[F]
presilla[F]
back pocket
poche[F]-revolver[M]
Gesäßtasche[F]
bolsillo[M] trasero
TROUSERS
PANTALON[M]
HOSE[F]
PANTALONES[M]
waistband
ceinture[F] montée
Hosenbund[M]
pretina[F]
belt loop
passant[M] tunnel[M]
Gürtelschlaufe[F]
trabilla
front top pocket
poche[F] cavalière
Flügeltasche[F]
bolsillo[M] delantero
waistband extension
patte[F] boutonnée
Bundverlängerung[F]
traslape[M] de la pretina[F]
fly
braguette[F]
Hosenschlitz[M]
bragueta[F]
knife pleat
pli[M] plat
einfache Falte[F]
pinza[F]
crease
pli[M]
Bügelfalte[F]
raya[F]
turn-up
revers[M]
Aufschlag[M]
vuelta[F]

# MEN'S CLOTHING
# VÊTEMENTS[M] D'HOMME[M]
# HERRENKLEIDUNG[F]
# ROPA[F] DE HOMBRE[M]

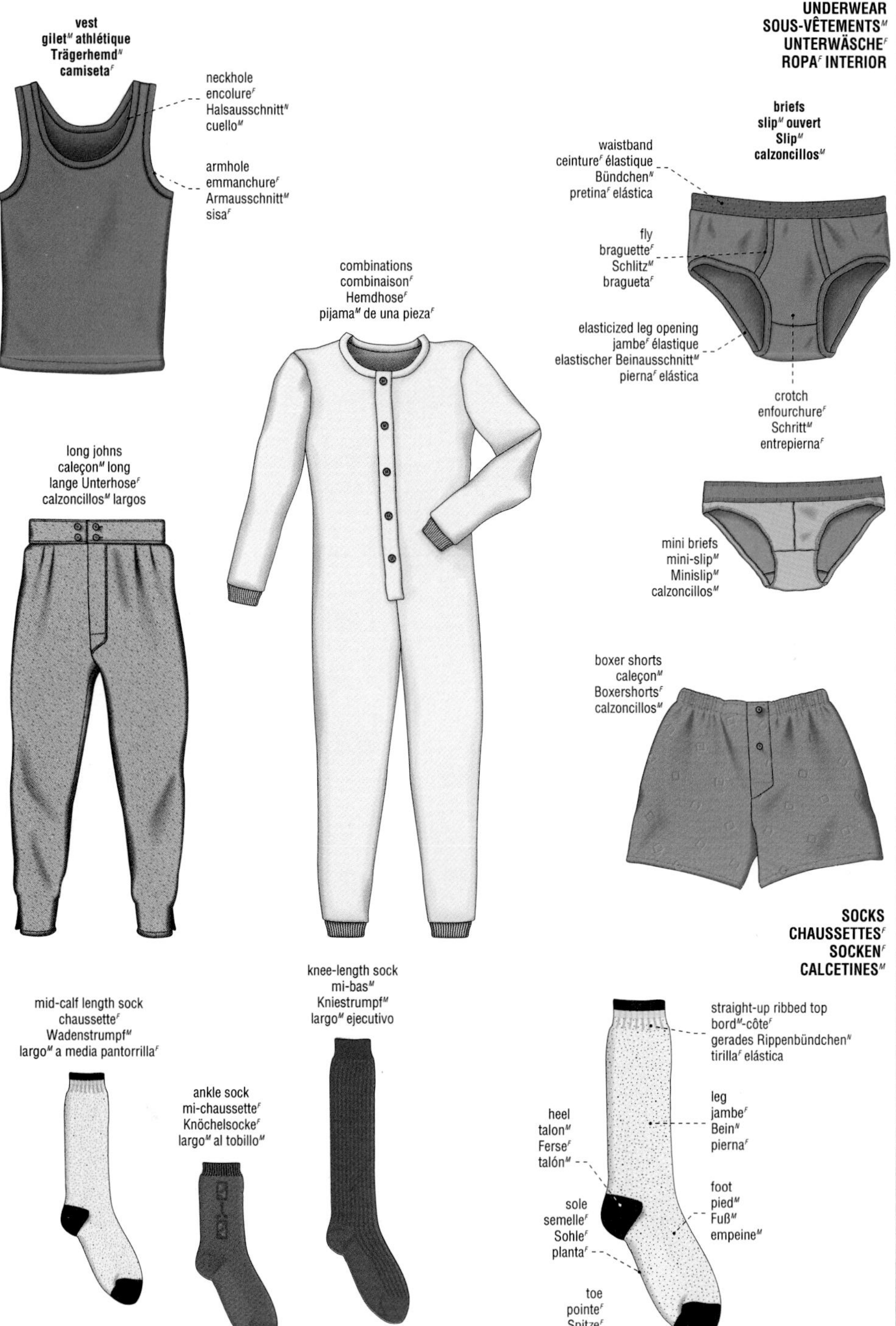

UNDERWEAR
SOUS-VÊTEMENTS[M]
UNTERWÄSCHE[F]
ROPA[F] INTERIOR
vest
gilet[M] athlétique
Trägerhemd[N]
camiseta[F]
neckhole
encolure[F]
Halsausschnitt[N]
cuello[M]
armhole
emmanchure[F]
Armausschnitt[M]
sisa[F]
briefs
slip[M] ouvert
Slip[M]
calzoncillos[M]
waistband
ceinture[F] élastique
Bündchen[N]
pretina[F] elástica
fly
braguette[F]
Schlitz[M]
bragueta[F]
elasticized leg opening
jambe[F] élastique
elastischer Beinausschnitt[M]
pierna[F] elástica
crotch
enfourchure[F]
Schritt[M]
entrepierna[F]
combinations
combinaison[F]
Hemdhose[F]
pijama[M] de una pieza[F]
long johns
caleçon[M] long
lange Unterhose[F]
calzoncillos[M] largos
mini briefs
mini-slip[M]
Minislip[M]
calzoncillos[M]
boxer shorts
caleçon[M]
Boxershorts[F]
calzoncillos[M]
SOCKS
CHAUSSETTES[F]
SOCKEN[F]
CALCETINES[M]
mid-calf length sock
chaussette[F]
Wadenstrumpf[M]
largo[M] a media pantorrilla[F]
ankle sock
mi-chaussette[F]
Knöchelsocke[F]
largo[M] al tobillo[M]
knee-length sock
mi-bas[M]
Kniestrumpf[M]
largo[M] ejecutivo
straight-up ribbed top
bord[M]-côte[F]
gerades Rippenbündchen[N]
tirilla[F] elástica
leg
jambe[F]
Bein[N]
pierna[F]
heel
talon[M]
Ferse[F]
talón[M]
foot
pied[M]
Fuß[M]
empeine[M]
sole
semelle[F]
Sohle[F]
planta[F]
toe
pointe[F]
Spitze[F]
punta[F]

# SWEATERS
# TRICOTS^M
# PULLOVER^M
# JERSEYS^M

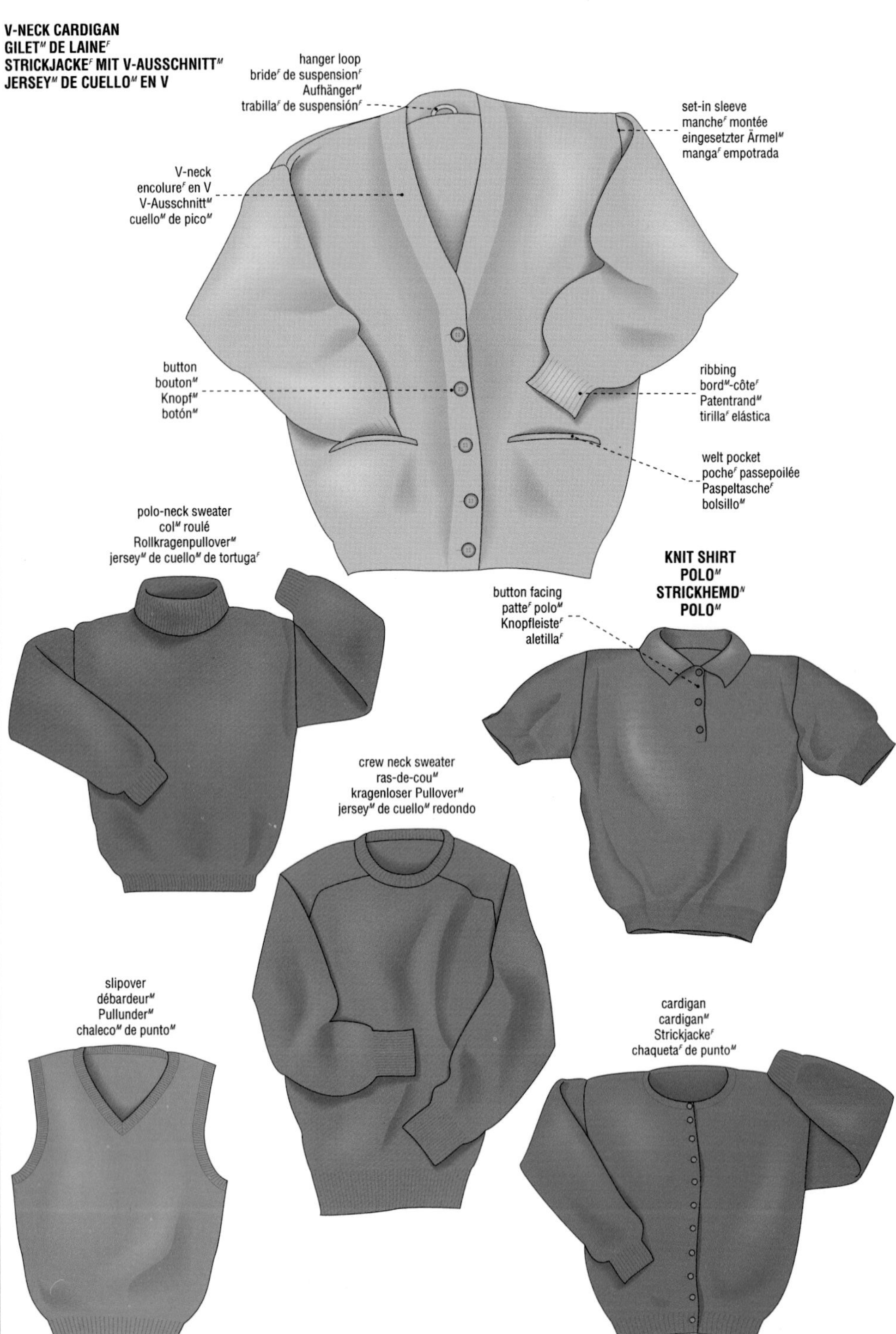

# GLOVES
# GANTS[M]
# HANDSCHUHE[M]
# GUANTES[M]

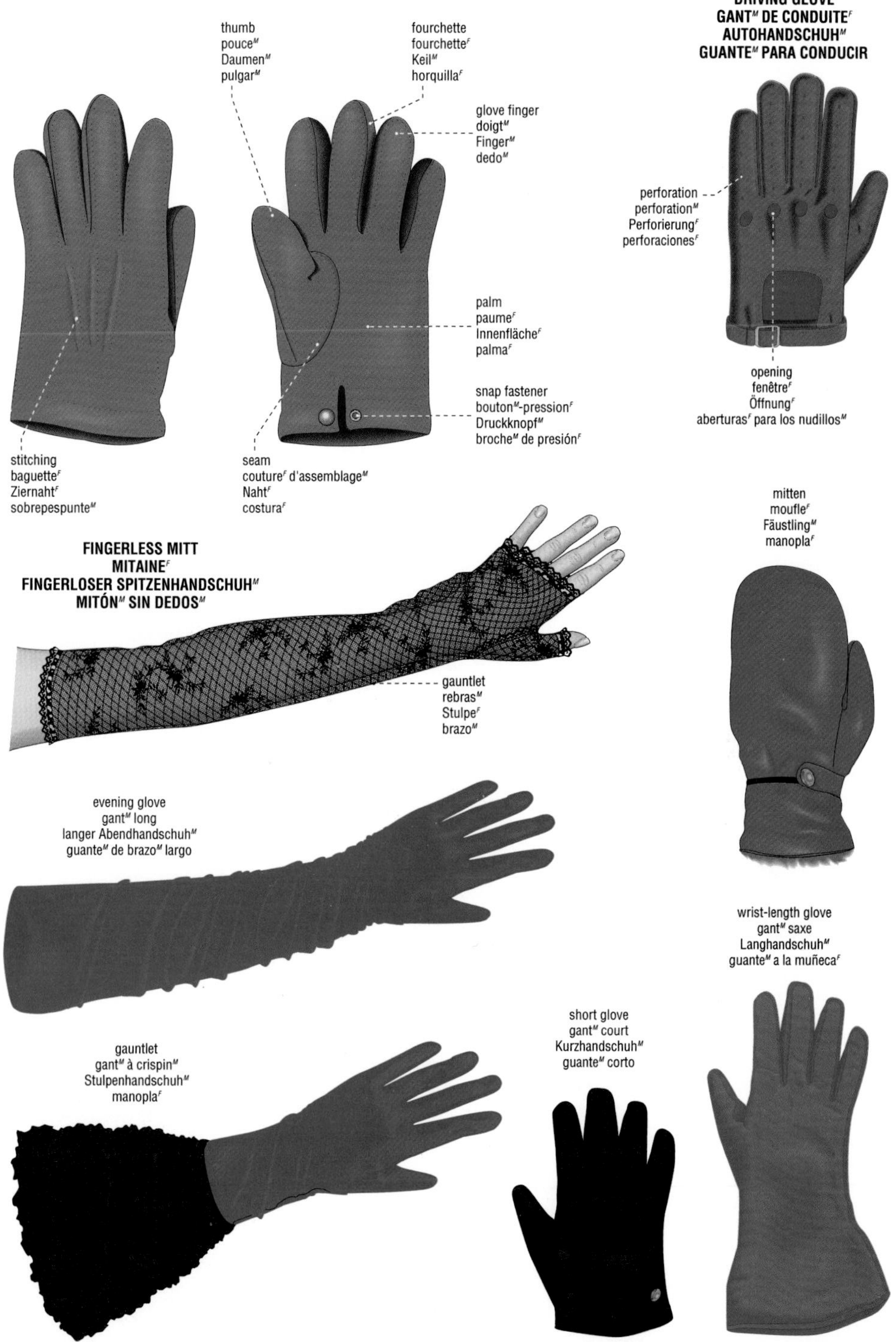

# HEADGEAR
# COIFFURE[F]
# KOPFBEDECKUNGEN[F]
# SOMBREROS[M]

toque
toque[F]
Toque[F]
toca[F]
pillbox hat
tambourin[M]
Pagenkäppi[N]
sombrero[M] sin alas[F]
beret
béret[M]
Baskenmütze[F]
boina[F]
turban
turban[M]
Turban[M]
turbante[M]
cloche
cloche[F]
Topfhut[M]
sombrero[M] de campana[F]
trilby
feutre[M]
Filzhut[M]
sombrero[M] de fieltro[M]
sou'wester
suroît[M]
Südwester[M]
sueste[M]
BALACLAVA
CAGOULE[F]
KAPUZENMÜTZE[F]
PASAMONTAÑAS[M]
peak
visière[F]
Mützenschirm[M]
visera[F]
bobble hat
bonnet[M] pompon[M]
Pudelmütze[F]
gorro[M] de punto[M]
knit cap
bonnet[M]
Strickmütze[F]
gorro[M] de punto[M]
RAIN HAT
BOB[M]
REGENHUT[M]
SOMBRERO[M] DE MARINERO[M]
crown
calotte[F]
Kopfteil[M]
copa[F]
cartwheel hat
capeline[F]
Wagenradhut[M]
pamela[F]
brim
bord[M]
Krempe[F]
ala[F]

TYPES OF COAT
TYPESM DE MANTEAUXM
MANTELARTENF
ABRIGOSM Y CHAQUETASF

**cape**
**cape[F]**
**Cape[N]**
**capa[F]**
overcoat
manteau[M]
Mantel[M]
abrigo[M]
riding coat
redingote[F]
Redingote[F]
abrigo[M] cruzado
arm slit
passe-bras[M]
Durchgrifftasche[F]
abertura[F] para el brazo[M]
poncho
poncho[M]
Poncho[M]
poncho[M]
**suit**
**tailleur[M]**
**Kostüm[N]**
**traje[M]**
jacket
veste[F]
Jacke[F]
chaqueta[F]
jacket
veste[F]
Blazer[M]
chaquetón[M]
skirt
jupe[F]
Rock[M]
falda[F]

# WOMEN'S CLOTHING
# VÊTEMENTS[M] DE FEMME[F]
# DAMENKLEIDUNG[F]
# ROPA[F] DE MUJER[F]

## TYPES OF DRESS
## TYPES[M] DE ROBES[F]
## KLEIDERARTEN[F]
## TIPOS[M] DE VESTIDO[M]

sheath dress
robe[F] fourreau[M]
Schlauchkleid[N]
recto entallado

princess dress
robe[F] princesse[F]
Prinzeßkleid[N]
corte[M] princesa[F]

coat dress
robe[F]-manteau[M]
Mantelkleid[N]
vestido[M] abrigo

drop waist dress
robe[F] taille[F] basse
Kleid[N] mit angesetztem Schoß[M]
de talle[M] largo

trapeze dress
robe[F] trapèze[M]
Trapez-Form[F]
de campana[F]

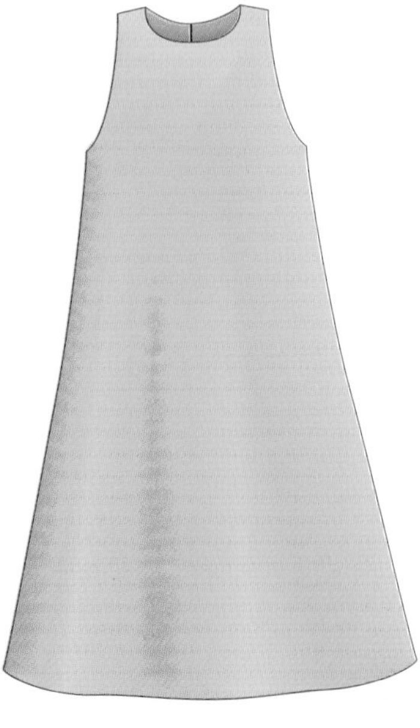

sundress
robe[F] bain[M]-de-soleil[M]
Trägerkleid[N]
de verano[M]

polo dress
robe$^{F}$-polo$^{M}$
Polokleid$^{N}$
de camiseta$^{F}$

house dress
robe$^{F}$ de maison$^{F}$
Hauskleid$^{N}$
casero

shirtwaist dress
robe$^{F}$ chemisier$^{M}$
Hemdblusenkleid$^{N}$
camisero$^{M}$

pinafore
chasuble$^{F}$
Kleiderrock$^{M}$
pichi$^{M}$

wrapover dress
robe$^{F}$ enveloppe$^{F}$
Wickelkleid$^{N}$
cruzado

tunic dress
robe$^{F}$ tunique$^{F}$
Tunikakleid$^{N}$
túnica$^{F}$

# WOMEN'S CLOTHING
# VÊTEMENTS[M] DE FEMME[F]
# DAMENKLEIDUNG[F]
# ROPA[F] DE MUJER[F]

kilt
kilt[M]
Schottenrock[M]
escocesa

gather skirt
jupe[F] froncée
Kräuselrock[M]
fruncida

**TYPES OF PLEAT**
**TYPES[M] DE PLIS[M]**
**FALTENARTEN[F]**
**TIPOS[M] DE PLIEGUE[M]**

inverted pleat
pli[M] creux
Kellerfalte[F]
tablón[M] delantero

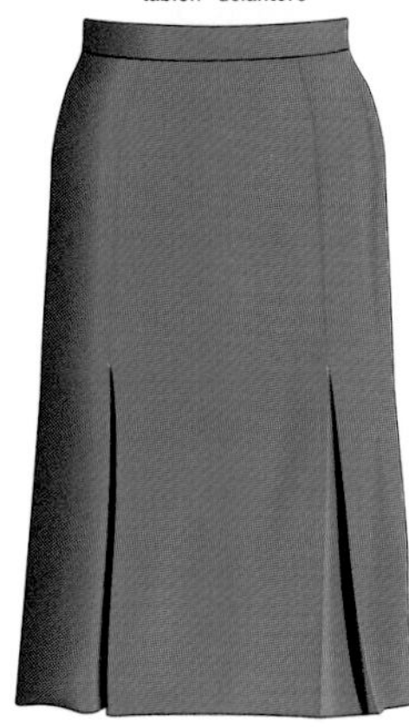

kick pleat
pli[M] d'aisance[F]
Gehfalte[F]
tabla[F] abierta

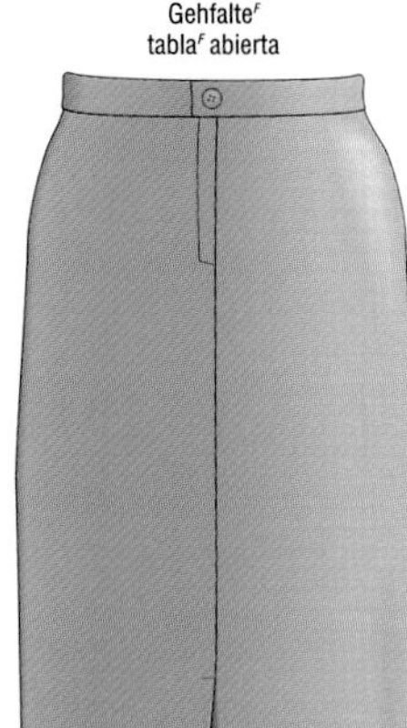

accordion pleat
plissé[M] accordéon[M]
Bahnenplissee[N]
plisada

knife pleat
pli[M] plat
einfache Falte[F]
tablas[F]

top stitched pleat
pli[M] surpiqué
abgesteppte Falte[F]
sobrepespunteada[F]

# WOMEN'S CLOTHING
# VÊTEMENTS^M DE FEMME^F
# DAMENKLEIDUNG^F
# ROPA^F DE MUJER^F

## TYPES OF BLOUSE
## TYPES[M] DE CHEMISIERS[M]
## BLUSENARTEN[F]
## BLUSAS[F]

## WOMEN'S CLOTHING
## VÊTEMENTS[M] DE FEMME[F]
## DAMENKLEIDUNG[F]
## ROPA[F] DE MUJER[F]

### WAISTCOATS AND JACKETS
### VESTES[F] ET PULLS[M]
### WESTEN[F] UND JACKEN[F]
### CHALECOS[M], JERSEYS[M] Y CHAQUETAS[F]

## TYPES OF POCKETS
## TYPES[M] DE POCHES[F]
## TASCHENARTEN[F]
## TIPOS[M] DE BOLSILLO[M]

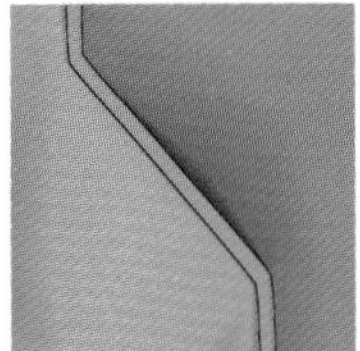
inset pocket
poche[F] prise dans une découpe[F]
eingesetzte Tasche[F]
simulado

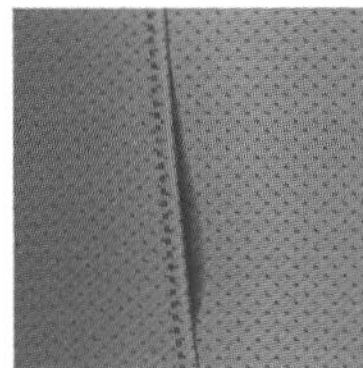
seam pocket
poche[F] prise dans une couture[F]
Nahttasche[F]
bolsillo[M] disimulado

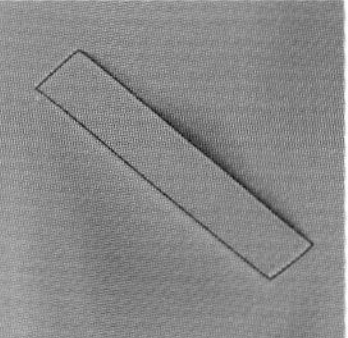
broad welt side pocket
poche[F] raglan
Raglantasche[F]
de ojal[M] con ribete[M]

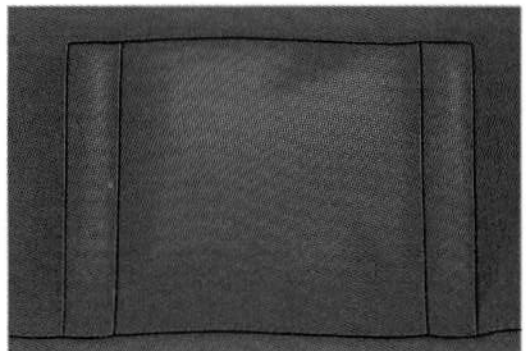
hand warmer pouch
poche[F] manchon[M]
Mufftasche[F]
de manguito[M]

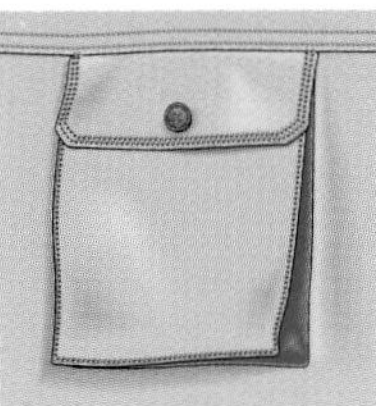
gusset pocket
poche[F] soufflet[M]
Blasebalgtasche[F]
de fuelle[M]

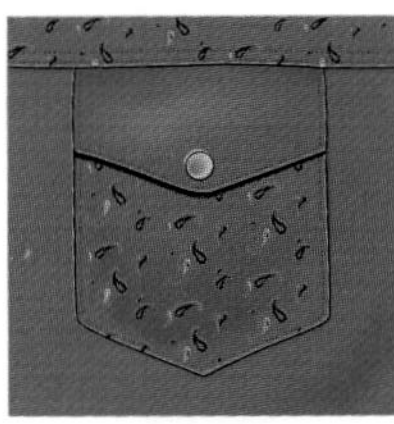
flap pocket
poche[F] à rabat[M]
Klappentasche[F]
bolsa[F] de parche[M] con cartera[F]

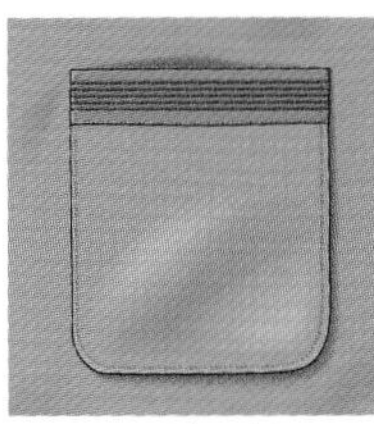
patch pocket
poche[F] plaquée
aufgesetzte Tasche[F]
de parche[M]

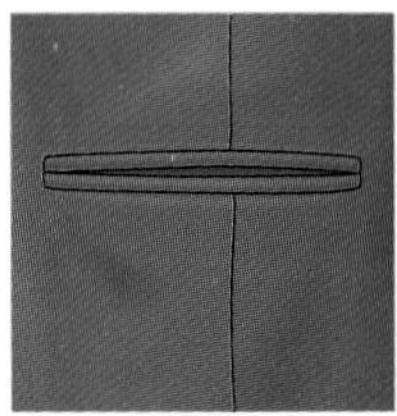
welt pocket
poche[F] passepoilée
Paspeltasche[F]
de ojal[M] de sastre[M]

## TYPES OF SLEEVES
## TYPES[M] DE MANCHES[F]
## ÄRMELARTEN[F]
## TIPOS[M] DE MANGA[F]

**French cuff**
**poignet[M] mousquetaire[M]**
**Doppelmanschette[F]**
**puño[M] para gemelos[M]**

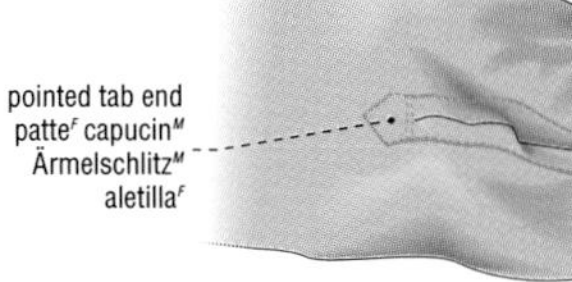


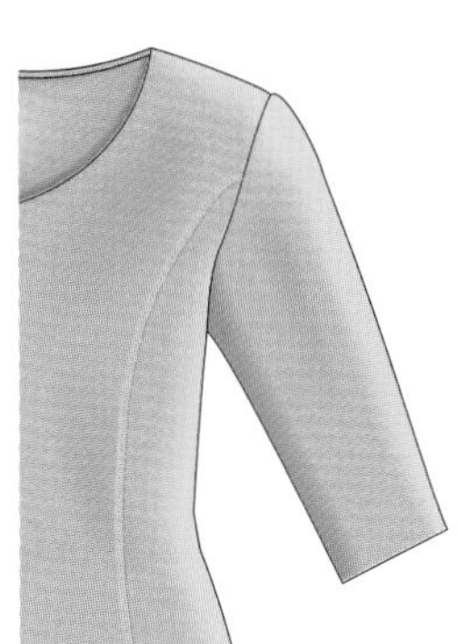
three-quarter sleeve
manche[F] trois-quarts
Dreiviertelarm[M]
recta de tres cuartos[M]

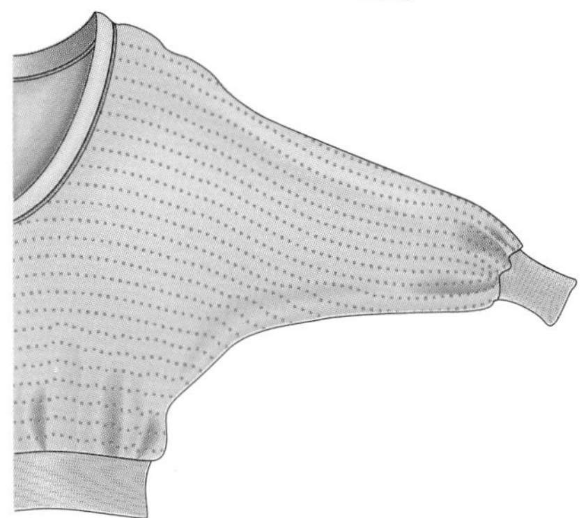
batwing sleeve
manche[F] chauve-souris[F]
Fledermausärmel[M]
de murciélago[M]

cap sleeve
mancheron[M]
angeschnittener Ärmel[M]
corta sencilla

# WOMEN'S CLOTHING
# VÊTEMENTS[M] DE FEMME[F]
# DAMENKLEIDUNG[F]
# ROPA[F] DE MUJER[F]

## TYPES OF SLEEVES
## TYPES[M] DE MANCHES[F]
## ÄRMELARTEN[F]
## TIPOS[M] DE MANGA[F]

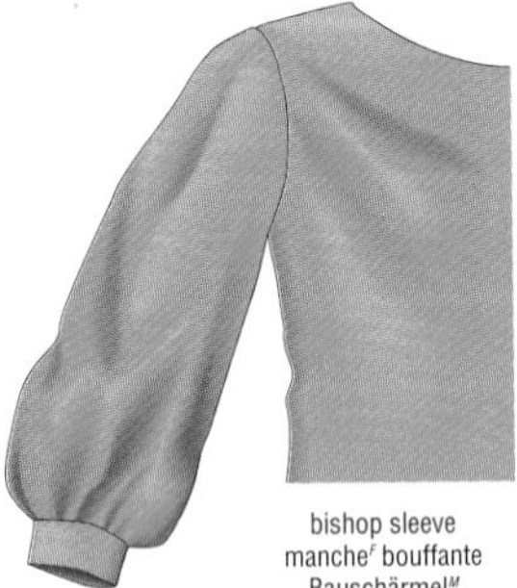

bishop sleeve
manche[F] bouffante
Bauschärmel[M]
común fruncida

leg-of-mutton sleeve
manche[F] gigot[M]
Keulenärmel[M]
de jamón[M]

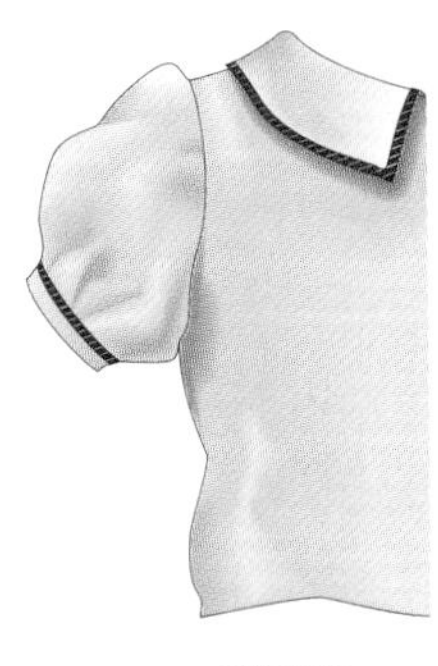

puff sleeve
manche[F] ballon[M]
Puffärmel[M]
de globo[M]

tailored sleeve
manche[F] tailleur[M]
Schneiderärmel[M]
hechura[F] sastre[M]

epaulet sleeve
manche[F] marteau[M]
Zungenraglan[M]
con hombrera[F]

kimono sleeve
manche[F] kimono[M]
Kimonoärmel[M]
kimono[M]

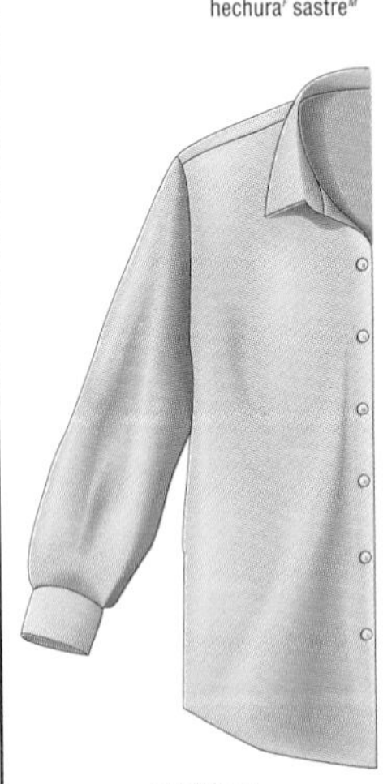

shirt sleeve
manche[F] chemisier[M]
Hemdblusenärmel[M]
camisera[F]

raglan sleeve
manche[F] raglan
Raglanärmel[M]
manga[F] ranglán

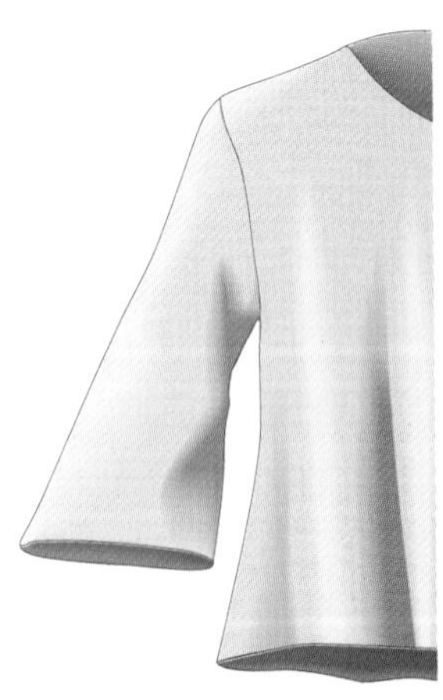

pagoda sleeve
manche[F] pagode[F]
Pagodenärmel[M]
de pagoda[F]

## COLLAR
## COL[M]
## KRAGEN[M]
## CUELLO[M]

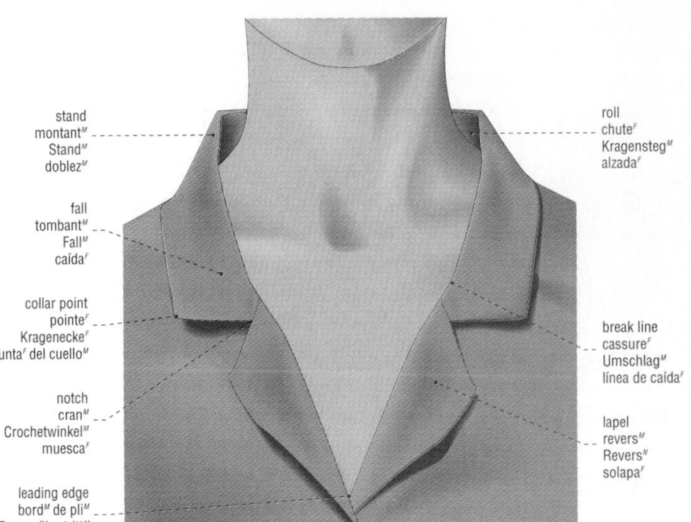

## TYPES OF COLLARS
## TYPES[M] DE COLS[M]
## KRAGENARTEN[F]
## CUELLOS[M]

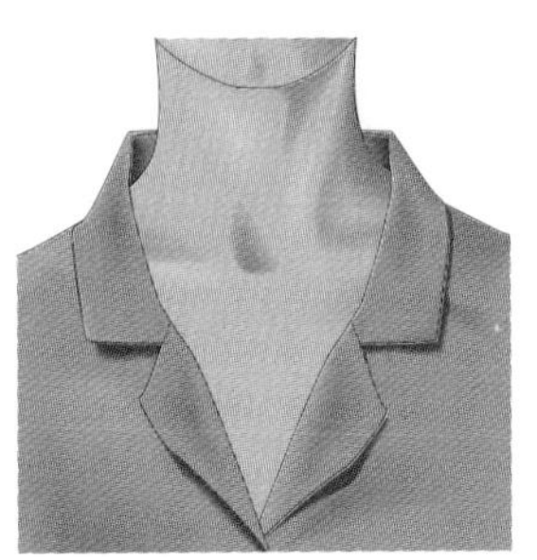

shirt collar
col[M] chemisier[M]
Hemdblusenkragen[M]
camisero

tailored collar
col[M] tailleur[M]
Schneiderkragen[M]
hechura[F] de sastre[M]

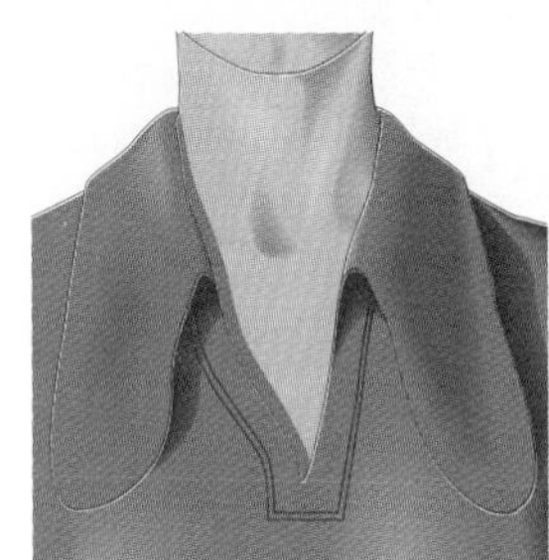

dog ear collar
col[M] banane[F]
Dackelohrkragen[M]
plano con orejas[F]

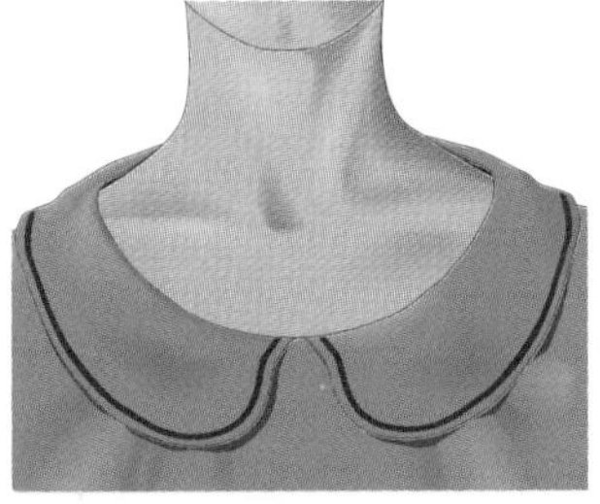

Peter Pan collar
col[M] Claudine
Bubikragen[M]
plano tipo[M] Peter Pan

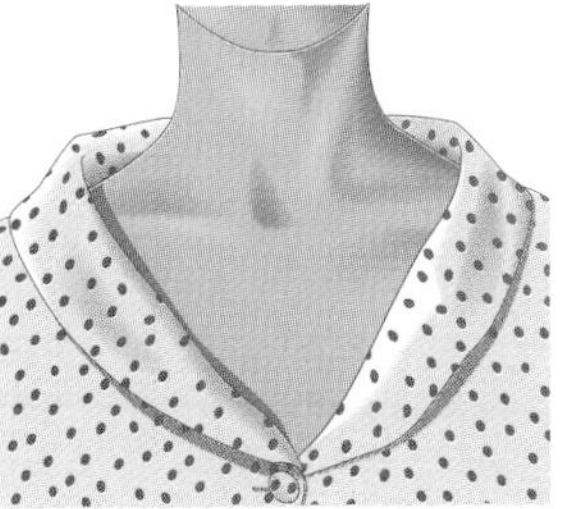

shawl collar
col[M] châle[M]
Schalkragen[M]
de chal[M]

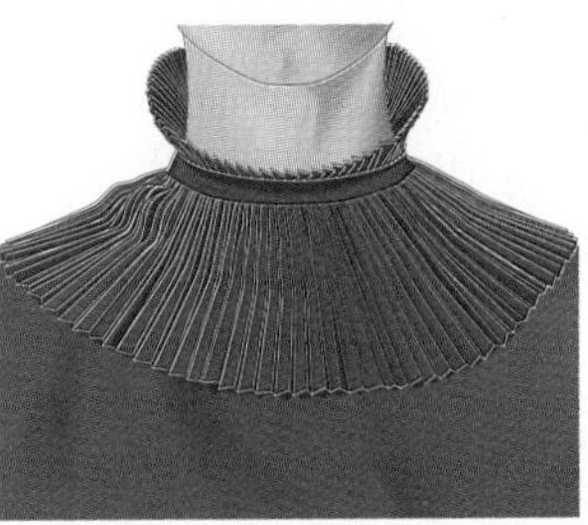

collaret
collerette[F]
Halskrause[F]
de volantes[M]

# WOMEN'S CLOTHING
# VÊTEMENTS[M] DE FEMME[F]
# DAMENKLEIDUNG[F]
# ROPA[F] DE MUJER[F]

## TYPES OF COLLARS
## TYPES[M] DE COLS[M]
## KRAGENARTEN[F]
## CUELLOS[M]

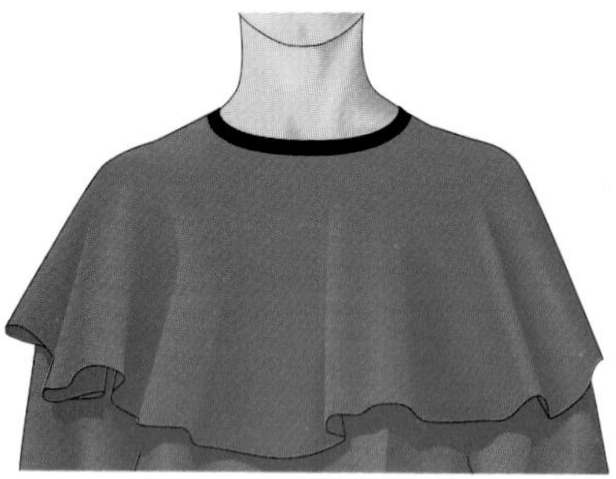

bertha collar
col[M] berthe[F]
Berthe[F]
Berta

bow collar
col[M] cravate[F]
Schleifenkragen[M]
de lazo[M]

sailor collar
col[M] marin[M]
Matrosenkragen[M]
marinero

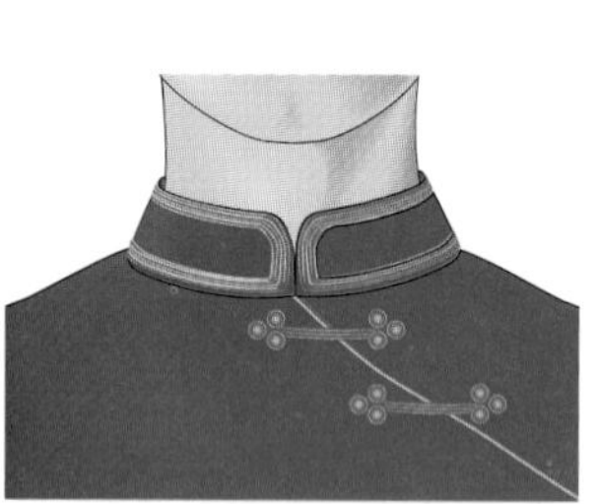

mandarin collar
col[M] chinois
Chinesenkragen[M]
chino

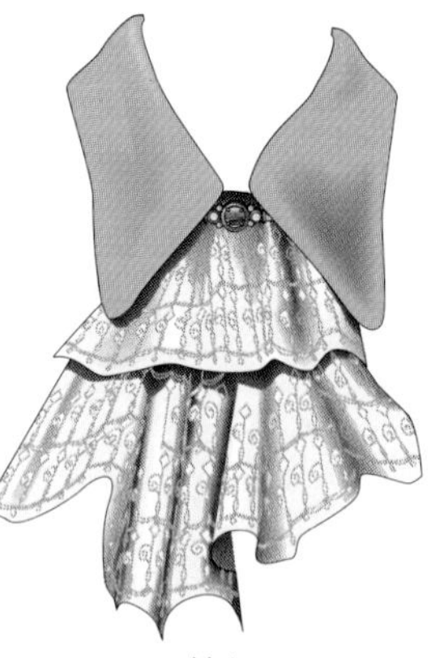

jabot
jabot[M]
Jabot[N]
con chorrera[F]

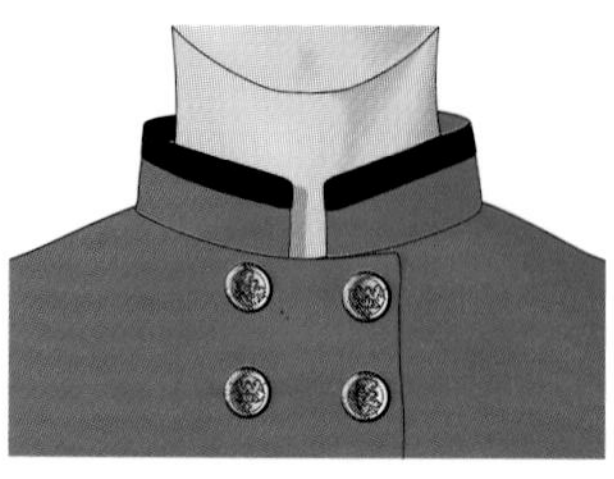

stand-up collar
col[M] officier[M]
Stehbordkragen[M]
Mao

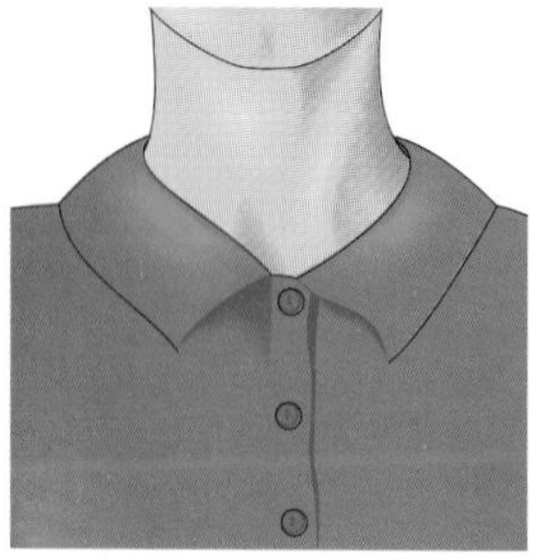

polo collar
col[M] polo[M]
Polokragen[M]
con aletilla[F]

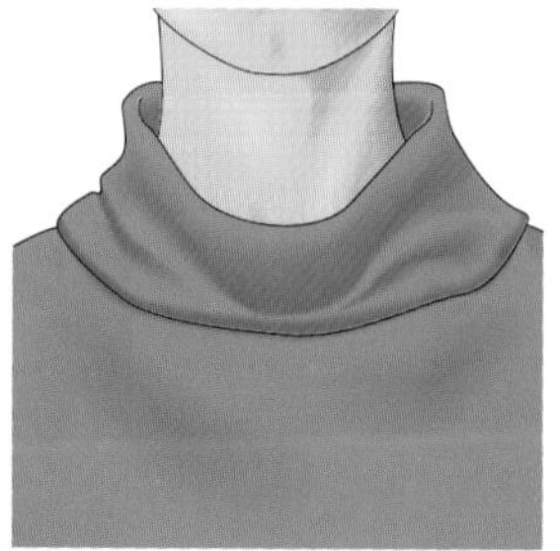

cowl neck
col[M] cagoule[F]
Kuttenkragen[M]
tipo[M] cogulla[F]

turtleneck
col[M] roulé
Rollkragen[M]
de tortuga[F]

## NECKLINES AND NECKS
## DÉCOLLETÉS[M] ET ENCOLURES[F]
## DEKOLLETÉS[N] UND AUSSCHNITTE[M]
## ESCOTES[M]

plunging neckline
décolleté[M] plongeant
spitzes Dekolleté[N]
bajo

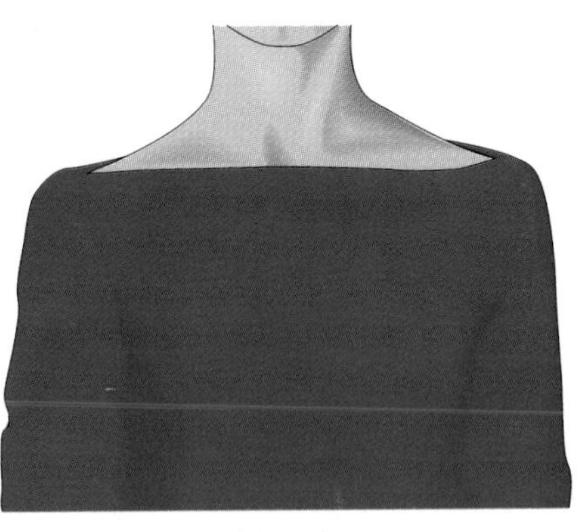

bateau neck
encolure[F] bateau[M]
Bateau-Kragen[M]
de ojal[M]

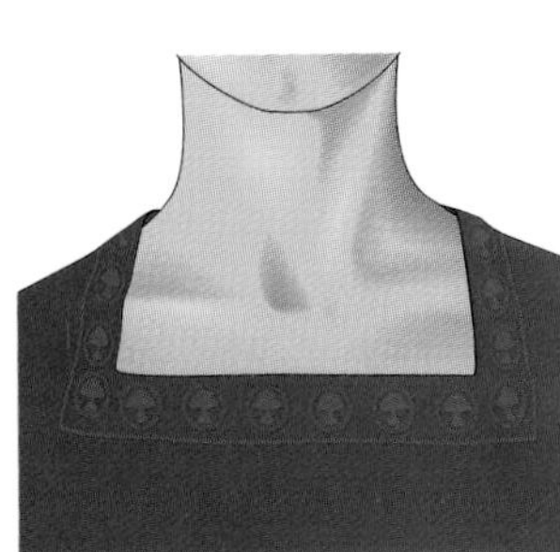

square neck
décolleté[M] carré
viereckiger Ausschnitt[M]
cuadrado

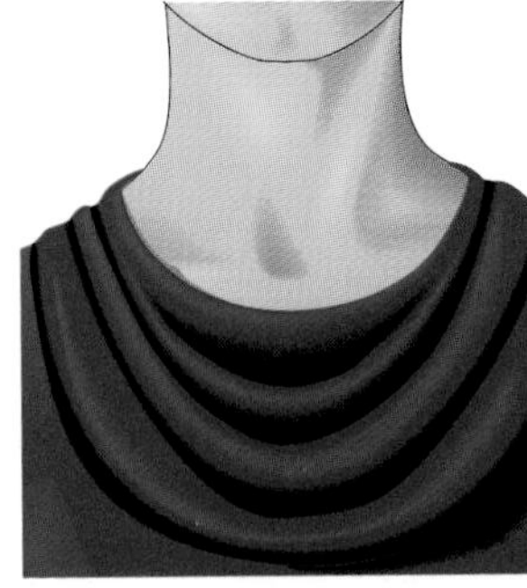

draped neck
encolure[F] drapée
drapierter Kragen[M]
drapeado

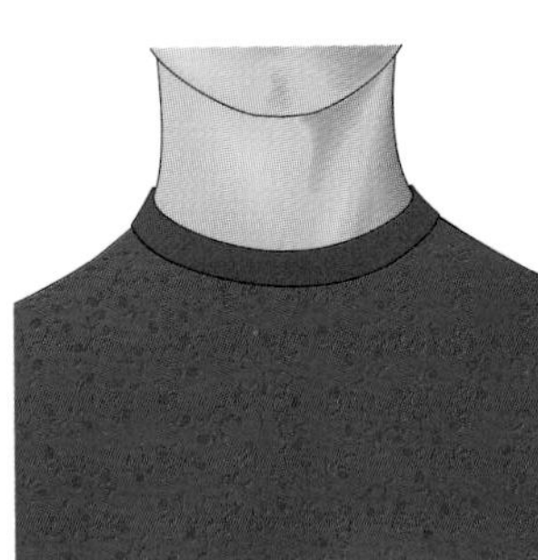

round neck
encolure[F] ras-de-cou[M]
runder Ausschnitt[M]
redondo

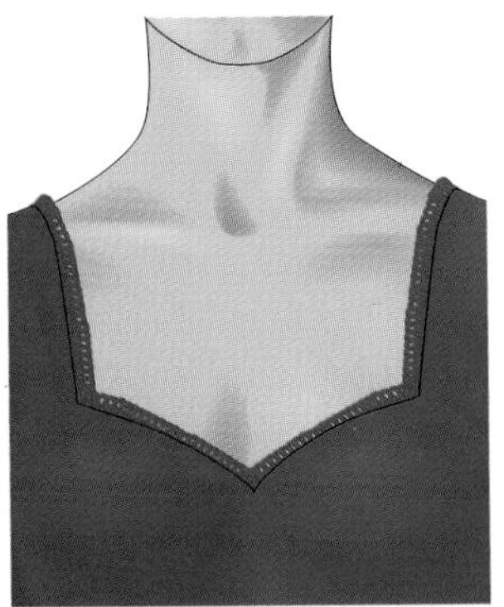

sweetheart neckline
décolleté[M] en cœur[M]
Coeur-Dekolleté[N]
de corazón[M]

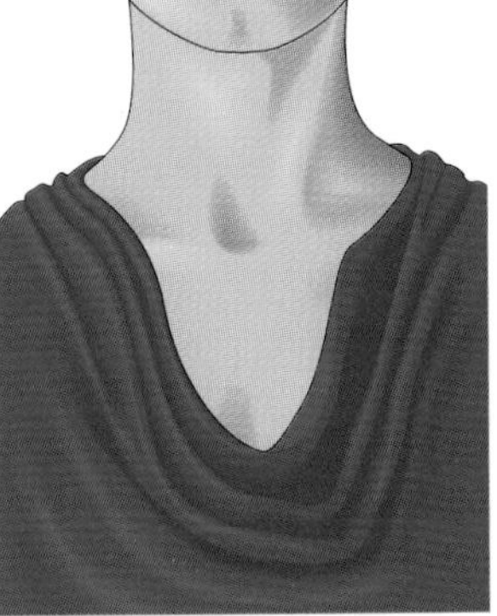

draped neckline
décolleté[M] drapé
drapierter Ausschnitt[M]
drapeado

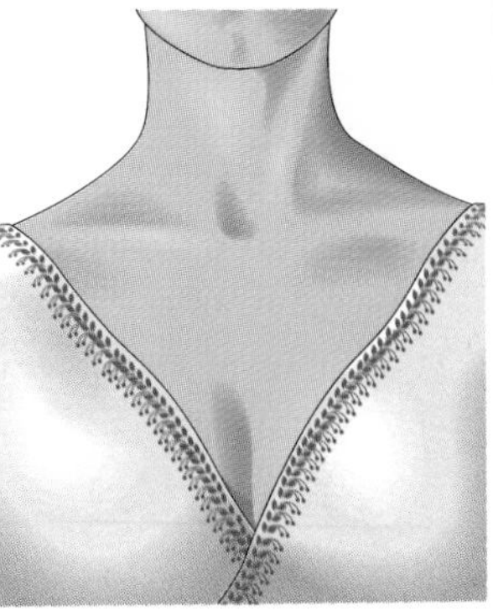

V-shaped neck
décolleté[M] en V
V-Ausschnitt[M]
de pico[M]

# WOMEN'S CLOTHING
# VÊTEMENTS[M] DE FEMME[F]
# DAMENKLEIDUNG[F]
# ROPA[F] DE MUJER[F]

## HOSE
## BAS[M]
## STRÜMPFE[M]
## MEDIAS[F]

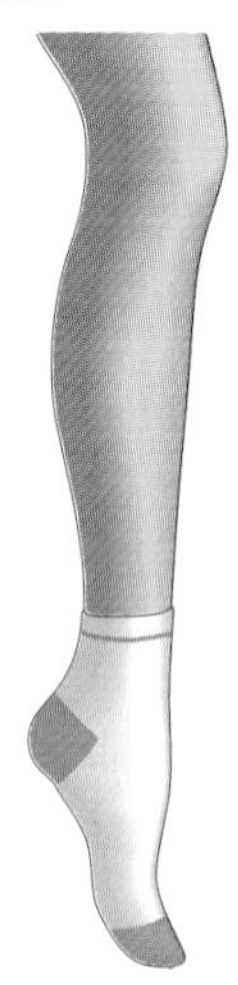

short sock
socquette[F]
Kurzsocke[F]
calcetín[M]

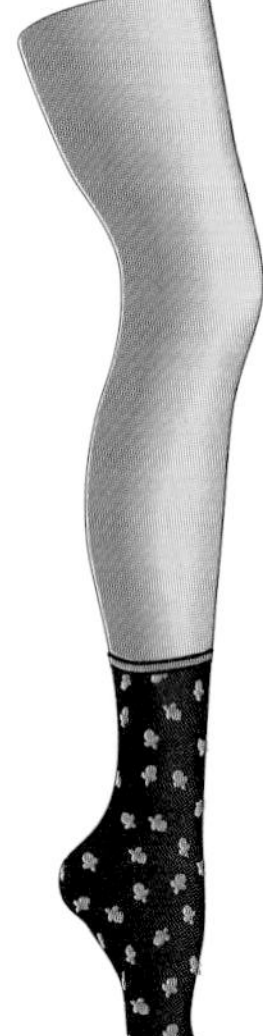

ankle sock
mi-chaussette[F]
Söckchen[N]
tobillera[F]

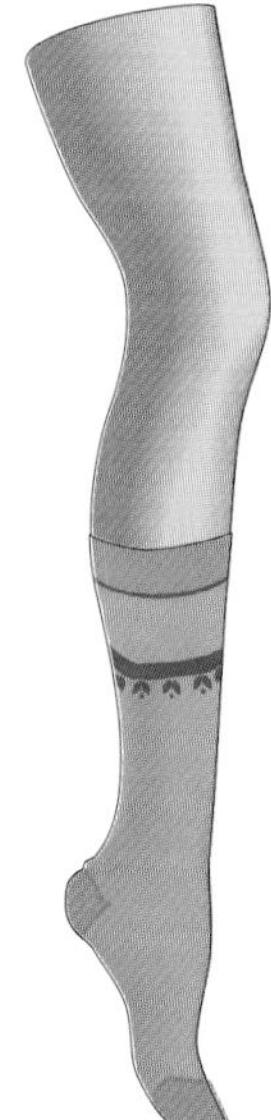

sock
chaussette[F]
Socke[F]
calcetín[M] largo

knee sock
mi-bas[M]
Kniestrumpf[M]
calceta[F]

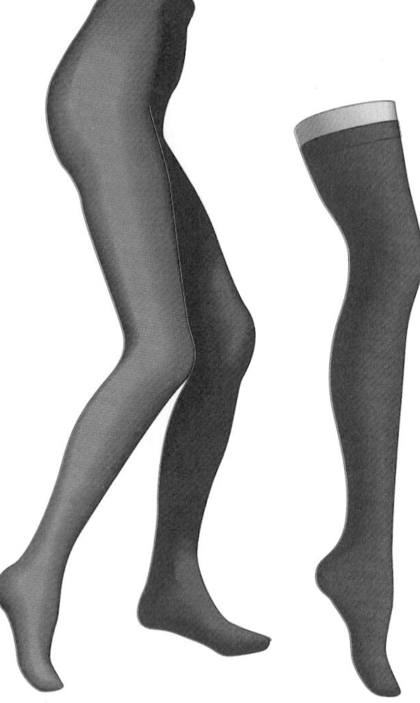

tights
collant[M]
Strumpfhose[F]
pantimedias[F]

stocking
bas[M]
Strumpf[M]
medias[F]

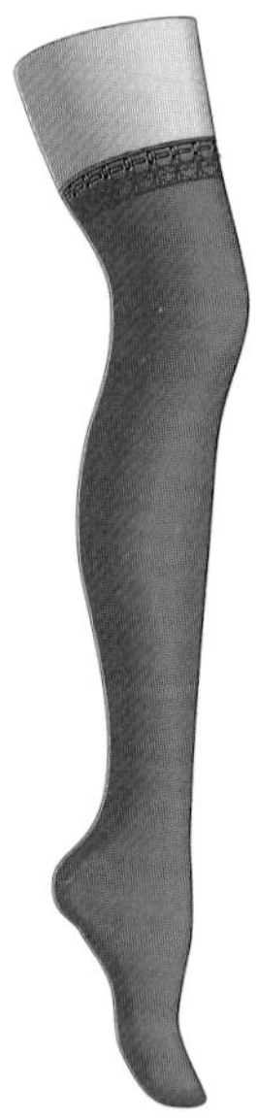

thigh stocking
bas[M]-cuissarde[F]
Overknee-Strumpf[M]
media[F] tres-cuartos

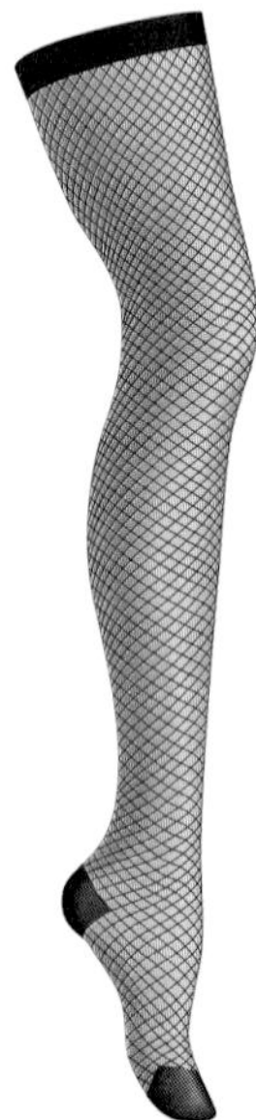

fishnet stocking
bas[M] résille[F]
Netzstrumpf[M]
medias[F] de malla[F]

## UNDERWEAR
## SOUS-VÊTEMENTS[M]
## UNTERWÄSCHE[F]
## ROPA[F] INTERIOR

# WOMEN'S CLOTHING
# VÊTEMENTS[M] DE FEMME[F]
# DAMENKLEIDUNG[F]
# ROPA[F] DE MUJER[F]



## UNDERWEAR
## SOUS-VÊTEMENTS[M]
## UNTERWÄSCHE[F]
## ROPA[F] INTERIOR

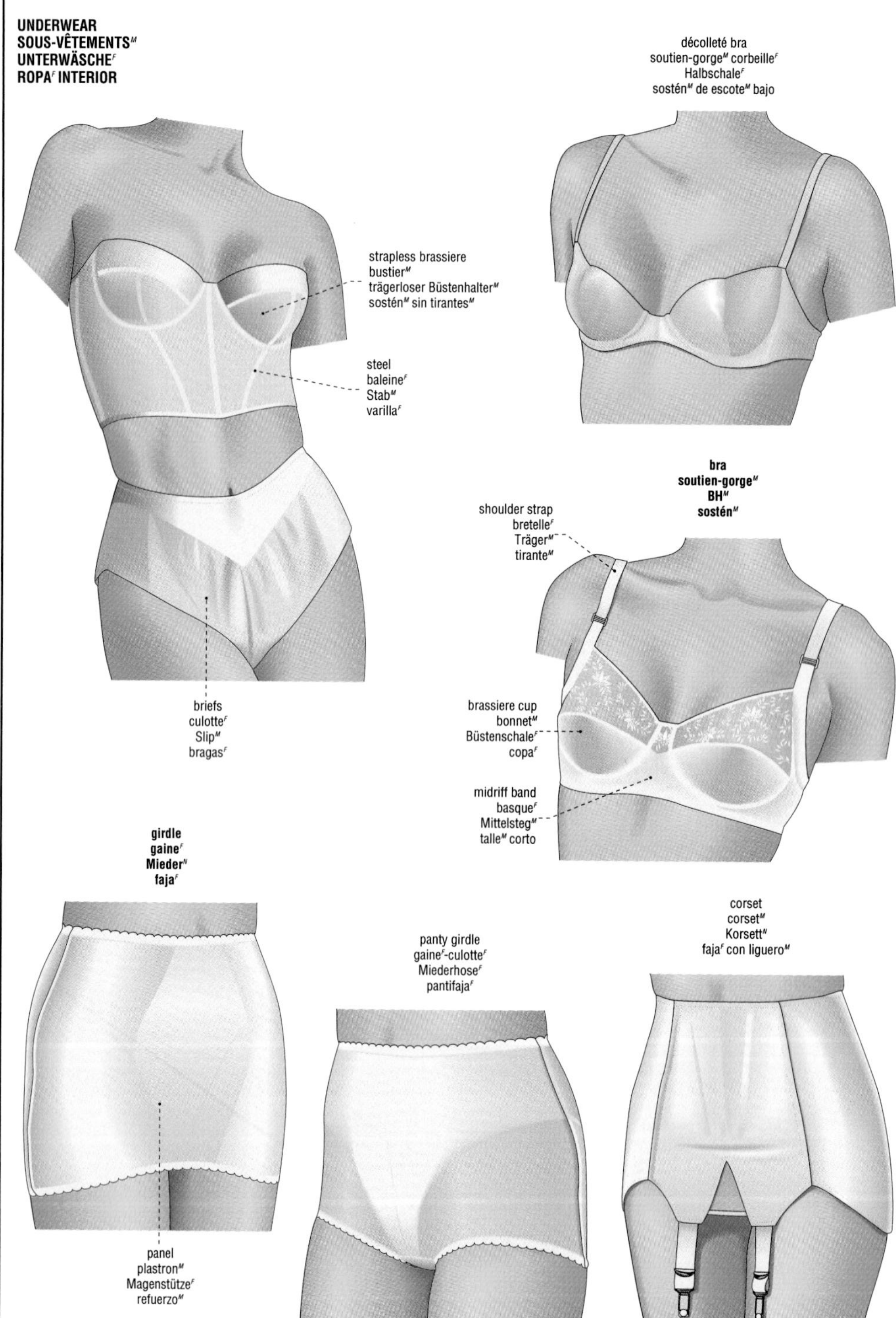

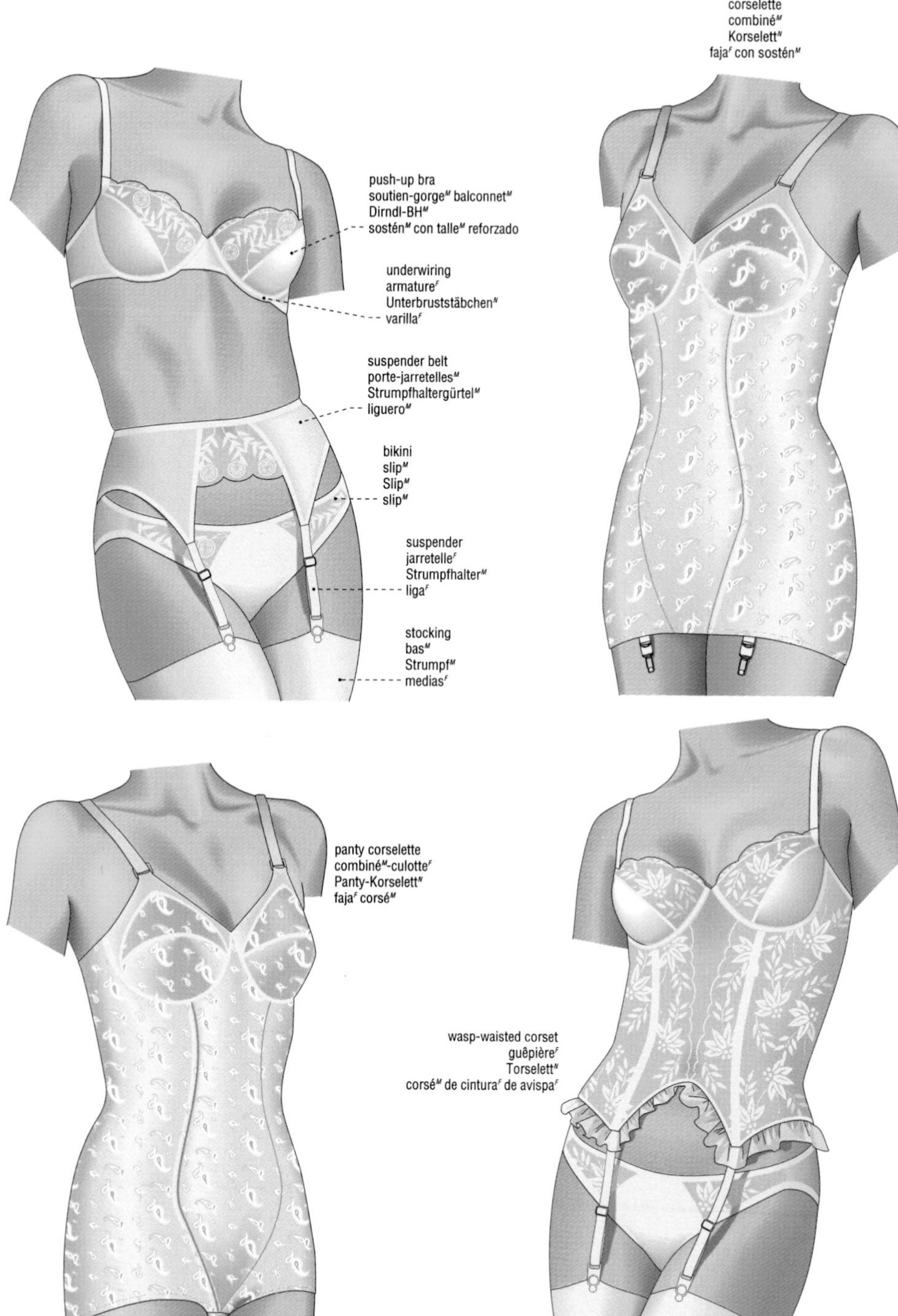
corselette
combiné
Korselett
faja con sostén
push-up bra
soutien-gorge balconnet
Dirndl-BH
sostén con talle reforzado
underwiring
armature
Unterbruststäbchen
varilla
suspender belt
porte-jarretelles
Strumpfhaltergürtel
liguero
bikini
slip
Slip
slip
suspender
jarretelle
Strumpfhalter
liga
stocking
bas
Strumpf
medias
panty corselette
combiné-culotte
Panty-Korselett
faja corsé
wasp-waisted corset
guêpière
Torselett
corsé de cintura de avispa

# WOMEN'S CLOTHING
# VÊTEMENTS[M] DE FEMME[F]
# DAMENKLEIDUNG[F]
# ROPA[F] DE MUJER[F]

## NIGHTWEAR
## VÊTEMENTS[M] DE NUIT[F]
## NACHTWÄSCHE[F]
## LENCERÍA[F]

# CHILDREN'S CLOTHING
# VÊTEMENTS[M] D'ENFANT[M]
# KINDERKLEIDUNG[F]
# ROPA[F] DE NIÑOS[M]

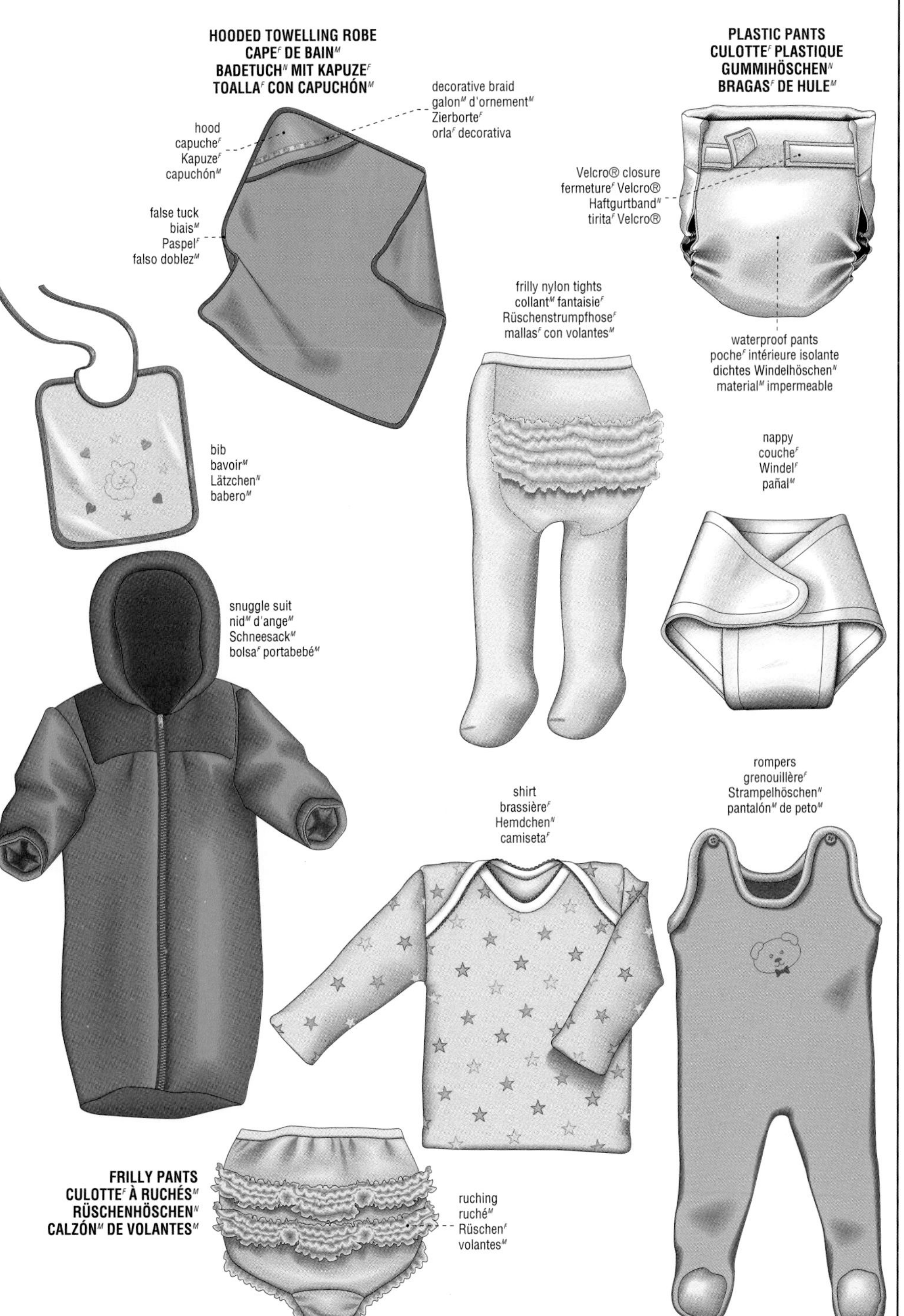

# CHILDREN'S CLOTHING
# VÊTEMENTS[M] D'ENFANT[M]
# KINDERKLEIDUNG[F]
# ROPA[F] DE NIÑOS[M]

TRAINING SET
TENUE[F] D'EXERCICE[M]
SPORTSET[N]
CONJUNTO[M] DEPORTIVO
tank top
débardeur[M]
Trägerhemdchen[N]
camiseta[F]
shorts
short[M]
kurze Hose[F]
pantalón[M] corto
DUNGAREES WITH CROSSOVER BACK STRAPS
SALOPETTE[F] À BRETELLES[F] CROISÉES
LATZHOSE[F] MIT GEKREUZTEN RÜCKENTRÄGERN[M]
MONO[M] DE TIRANTES CRUZADOS ATRÁS
button strap
bretelle[F] boutonnée
Träger[M] mit Knopf[M]
tirante[M] con botones[M]
bib
bavette[F]
Lätzchen[N]
peto[M]
slip-on pyjamas
polojama[M]
Schlafanzug[M] in Schlupfform[F]
pijama[M]
SNOWSUIT
ESQUIMAU[M]
SCHNEEANZUG[M]
TRAJE[M] DE INVIERNO[M] CON CAPUCHÓN[M]
drawstring hood
capuche[F] coulissée
Kapuze[F] mit Zugband[N]
capuchón[M] con cordón[M]
fly front closing
fermeture[F] sous patte[F]
Verschluß[M] mit verdeckter Knopfleiste[F]
cremallera[F]
rompers
barboteuse[F]
Spielanzug[M]
pelele[M]
jumpsuit
combinaison[F]
Overall[M]
traje[M] pantalón[M]
T-shirt dress
robe[F] tee-shirt[M]
T-Shirt Kleid[N]
camiseta[F] de cuerpo[M] entero

# SPORTSWEAR
# TENUE$^{F}$ D'EXERCICE$^{M}$
# SPORTKLEIDUNG$^{F}$
# ROPA$^{F}$ DEPORTIVA

## RUNNING SHOE
## CHAUSSURE$^{F}$ DE SPORT$^{M}$
## JOGGINGSCHUH$^{M}$
## ZAPATO$^{M}$ DEPORTIVO

tongue
languette$^{F}$
Zunge$^{F}$
lengüeta$^{F}$

nose of the quarter
aile$^{F}$ de quartier$^{M}$
Vorderteil$^{N}$
ala$^{F}$ del cuarto$^{M}$

collar
col$^{M}$
Fersenrand$^{M}$
ribete$^{M}$

lining
doublure$^{F}$
Futter$^{N}$
forro$^{M}$

counter
contrefort$^{M}$
Hinterkappe$^{F}$
contrafuerte$^{M}$

quarter
quartier$^{M}$
Quartier$^{N}$
cuarto$^{M}$

stitch
surpiqûre$^{F}$
Naht$^{F}$
pespunteado$^{M}$

heel
talon$^{M}$
Absatz$^{M}$
talón$^{M}$

middle sole
semelle$^{F}$ intercalaire
Zwischensohle$^{F}$
cambrillón$^{M}$

air cushion
coussin$^{M}$ d'air$^{M}$
Luftpolster$^{N}$
cámara$^{F}$ de aire$^{M}$

tag
ferret$^{M}$
Schnürsenkelende$^{N}$
herrete$^{M}$

shoelace
lacet$^{M}$
Schnürsenkel$^{M}$
cordón$^{M}$

## TRAINING SUIT
## SURVÊTEMENT$^{M}$
## TRAININGSANZUG$^{M}$
## TRAJE$^{M}$ DE ENTRENAMIENTO$^{M}$

hooded sweat shirt
pull$^{M}$ à capuche$^{F}$
Sweatshirt$^{N}$ mit Kapuze$^{F}$
camiseta$^{F}$ de chándal$^{M}$ con capucha$^{F}$

jogging pants
pantalon$^{M}$ molleton$^{M}$
Trainingshose$^{F}$
pantalones$^{M}$ de chándal$^{M}$

sweat shirt
pull$^{M}$ d'entraînement$^{M}$
Sweatshirt$^{N}$
camiseta$^{F}$ de chándal$^{M}$

## EXERCISE WEAR
## VÊTEMENT[M] D'EXERCICE[M]
## SPORTKLEIDUNG[F]
## ROPA[F] PARA EJERCICIO[M]

## SHOES
## CHAUSSURES^F
## SCHUHE^M
## ZAPATOS^M

CLOTHING VÊTEMENTS KLEIDUNG VESTIDO

## MAJOR TYPES OF SHOES
## PRINCIPAUX TYPES[M] DE CHAUSSURES[F]
## DIE WICHTIGSTEN SCHUHTYPEN[M]
## TIPOS[M] DE CALZADO[M]

# SHOES
# CHAUSSURES[F]
# SCHUHE[M]
# CALZADO[M]

## MAJOR TYPES OF SHOES
## PRINCIPAUX TYPES[M] DE CHAUSSURES[F]
## DIE WICHTIGSTEN SCHUHTYPEN[M]
## TIPOS[M] DE CALZADO[M]

toe-strap
nu-pied[M]
Sandale[F] mit Zehenriemchen[N]
sandalia[F]

flip-flop
tong[M]
Römerpantolette[F]
chancleta[F]

ankle boot
bottine[F]
knöchelhohe Stiefelette[F]
botín[M]

clog
socque[M]
Pantolette[F]
chanclo[M]

espadrille
espadrille[F]
Espadrille[F]
alpargata[F]

thigh-boot
cuissarde[F]
Schaftstiefel[M]
bota[F] de medio muslo[M]

sandal
sandalette[F]
Sandale[F]
sandalia[F]

# SHOES
# CHAUSSURES[F]
# SCHUHE[M]
# CALZADO[M]

## ACCESSORIES
## ACCESSOIRES[M]
## ZUBEHÖR[N]
## ACCESORIOS[M]

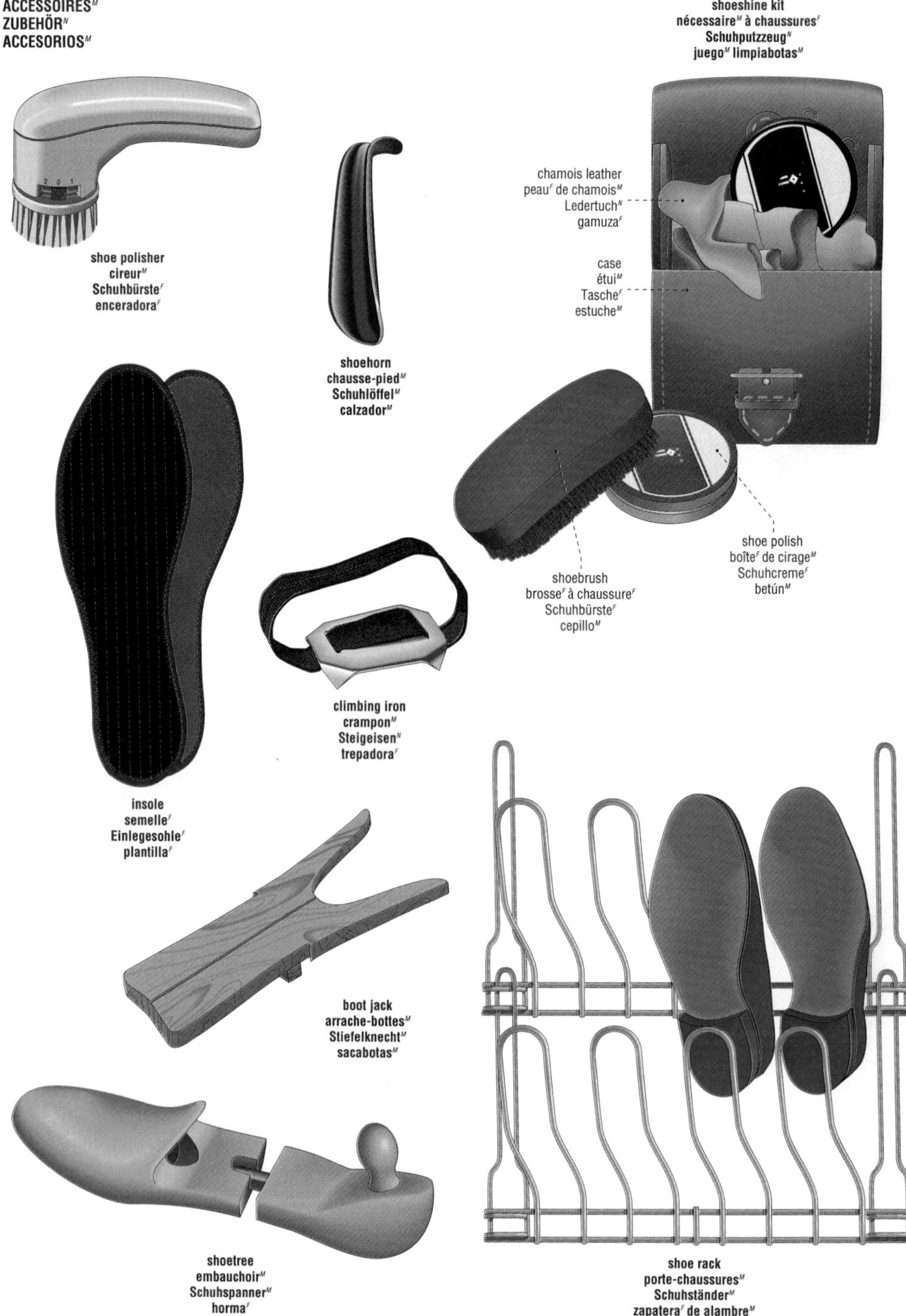

# PERSONAL ADORNMENT
# PARURE

# SCHMUCK UND SCHÖNHEITSPFLEGE
# ADORNOS PERSONALES

SUMMARY

# JEWELLERY
# BIJOUTERIE[F]
# SCHMUCK[M]
# JOYERÍA[F]

## EARRINGS
## BOUCLES[F] D'OREILLE[F]
## OHRRINGE[M]
## PENDIENTES[M]

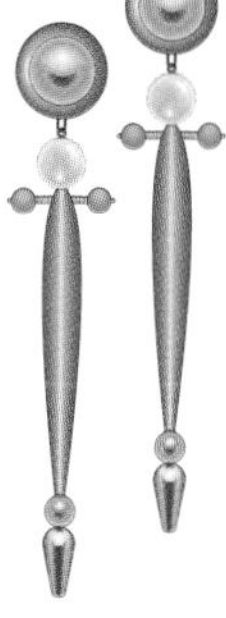

drop earrings
pendants[M] d'oreille[F]
Ohrgehänge[N]
pendientes[M]

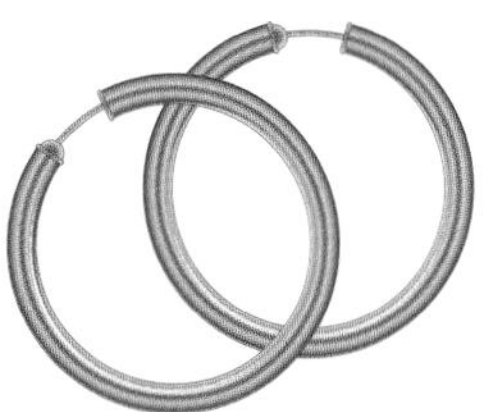

hoop earrings
anneaux[M]
Kreolen[F]
pendientes[M] de aro[M]

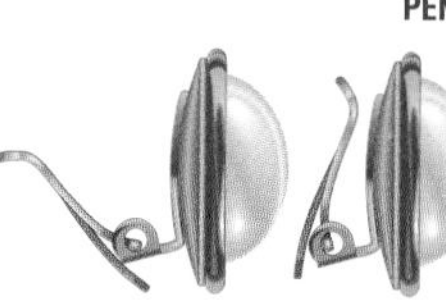

clip earrings
boucles[F] d'oreille[F] à pince[F]
Klips[M]
pendientes[M] de clip[M]

ear studs
boucles[F] d'oreille[F] à tige[F]
Ohrstecker[M]
pendientes[M] de espiga[F]

screw earrings
boucles[F] d'oreille[F] à vis[F]
Ohrringe[M] mit Schraubverschluß[M]
pendientes[M] de tornillo[M]

## NECKLACES
## COLLIERS[M]
## HALSKETTEN[F]
## COLLARES[M]

pendant
pendentif[M]
Anhänger[M]
pendiente[M]

locket
médaillon[M]
Medaillon[N]
relicario[M]

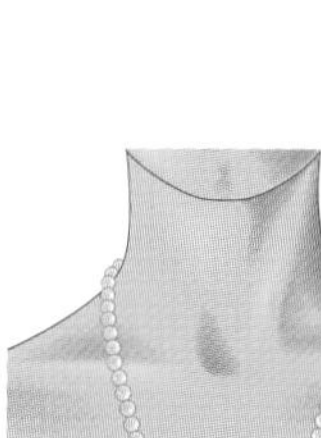

matinee-length necklace
collier[M] de perles[F], longueur[F] matinée[F]
Halskette[F] in Matineelänge[F]
collar[M] de una vuelta[F]

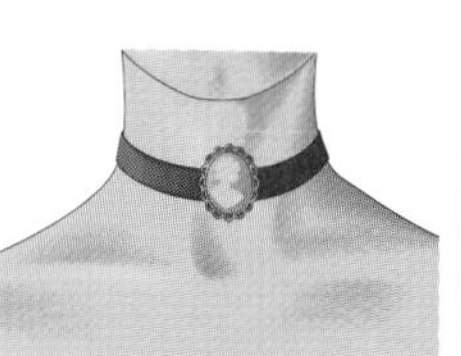

velvet-band choker
collier[M]-de-chien[M]
Samtkropfband[N]
garagantilla[F] de terciopelo[M]

opera-length necklace
sautoir[M], longueur[F] opéra[M]
Halskette[F] in Opernlänge[F]
collar[M] de una vuelta[F]

rope
sautoir[M]
Endlosperlenkette[F]
sarta[F]

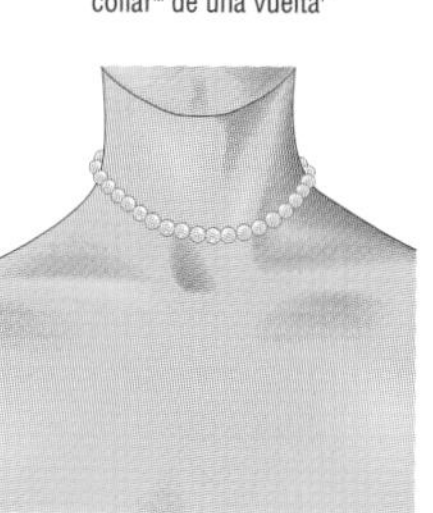

choker
ras-de-cou[M]
Chokerkette[F]
gargantilla[F]

bib necklace
collier[M] de soirée[F]
mehrreihige Halskette[F]
collar[M] de 5 hilos[M]

# JEWELLERY
# BIJOUTERIE[F]
# SCHMUCK[M]
# JOYERÍA[F]

## CUT FOR GEMSTONES
## TAILLE[F] DES PIERRES[F]
## SCHLIFFORMEN[F] FÜR EDELSTEINE[M]
## TALLAS[F] DE PIEDRAS[F] PRECIOSAS

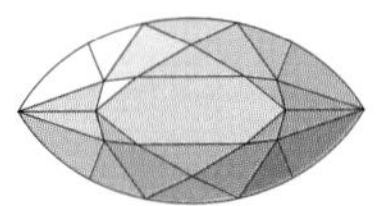
navette cut
taille[F] marquise[F]
Navette[F]
marquesa[F]

baguette cut
taille[F] baguette[F]
Baguetteform[F]
baguette[F]

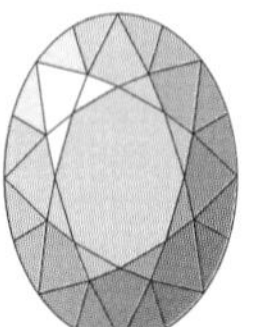
oval cut
taille[F] ovale
ovale Form[F]
oval

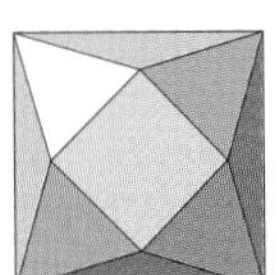
French cut
taille[F] française
French-cut[M]
francés

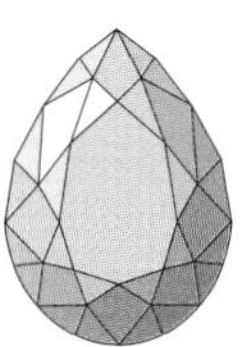
pear-shaped cut
taille[F] en poire[F]
Birnkernform[F]
pera[F]

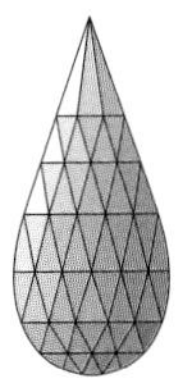
briolette cut
taille[F] en goutte[F]
Briolettform[F]
gota[F]

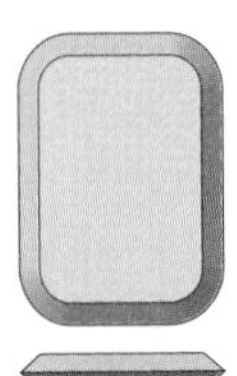
table cut
taille[F] en table[F]
Tafelschliff[M]
tabla[F]

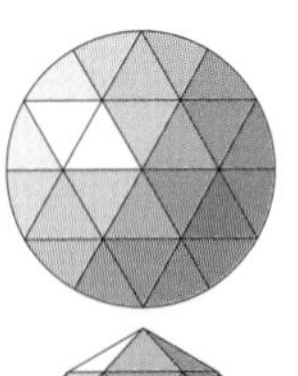
rose cut
taille[F] en rose[F]
Rosenschliff[M]
rosa[F] holandesa

cabochon cut
taille[F] cabochon[M]
Cabochonschliff[M]
cabujón[M]

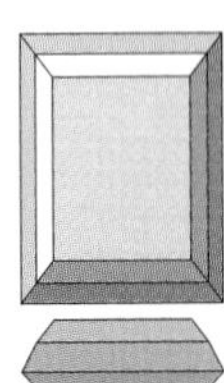
step cut
taille[F] en escalier[M]
Treppenschliff[M]
en escalera[F]

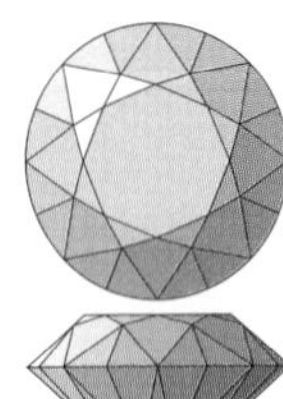
brilliant full cut
taille[F] brillant[M]
Vollbrillantschliff[M]
brillante[M]

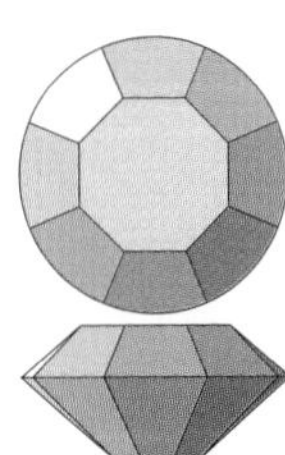
eight cut
taille[F] huit facettes[F]
Achtkant[M]
ocho facetas[F]

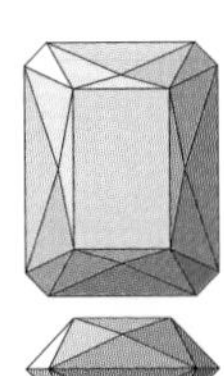
scissors cut
taille[F] en ciseaux[M]
Scherenschliff[M]
en tijera[F]

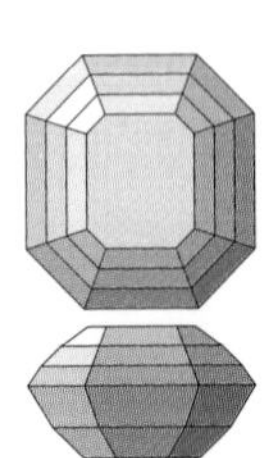
emerald cut
taille[F] émeraude[F]
Smaragdschliff[M]
esmeralda[F]

## BRILLIANT CUT FACETS
## TAILLE[F] D'UN DIAMANT[M]
## FACETTEN[F] DES BRILLANTSCHLIFFS[M]
## CORTE[M] DE UN DIAMANTE[M]

### BOTTOM FACE
### FACE[F] INFÉRIEURE
### RÜCKSEITE[F]
### CARA[F] INFERIOR

pavilion facet (8)
pavillon[M] (8)
Unterteilhauptfacette[F] (8)
faceta[F] de pabellón[M]

culet
colette[F]
Kulette[F]
culata[F]

lower girdle facet (16)
halefis[M] de culasse[F] (16)
untere Rondistenfacette[F] (16)
faceta[F] inferior del contorno[M]

### TOP FACE
### FACE[F] SUPÉRIEURE
### VORDERSEITE[F]
### CARA[F] SUPERIOR

star facet (8)
étoile[F] (8)
Tafelfacette[F] (8)
faceta[F] de estrella[F] (8)

table
table[F]
Tafel[F]
tabla[F]

bezel facet (8)
bezel[M] (8)
Oberteilhauptfacette[F] (8)
faceta[F] bisel (8)

upper girdle facet (16)
halefis[M] de table[F] (16)
obere Rondistenfacette[F] (16)
faceta[F] superior del contorno[M]

### SIDE FACE
### PROFIL[M]
### SEITENANSICHT[F]
### PERFIL[M]

table
table[F]
Tafel[F]
tabla[F]

girdle
rondiste[M]
Rondiste[F]
cinturón[M]

culet
colette[F]
Kulette[F]
culata[F]

crown
couronne[F] de table[F]
Krone[F]
corona[F]

pavilion
culasse[F]
Unterteil[N]
pabellón[M]

## PRECIOUS STONES
## PIERRES[F] PRÉCIEUSES
## EDELSTEINE[M]
## PIEDRAS[F] PRECIOSAS

emerald
émeraude[F]
Smaragd[M]
esmeralda[F]

ruby
rubis[M]
Rubin[M]
rubí[M]

sapphire
saphir[M]
Saphir[M]
zafiro[M]

diamond
diamant[M]
Diamant[M]
diamante[M]

## SEMIPRECIOUS STONES
## PIERRES[F] FINES
## HALBEDELSTEINE[M]
## PIEDRAS[F] SEMIPRECIOSAS

amethyst
améthyste[F]
Amethyst[M]
amatista[F]

garnet
grenat[M]
Granat[M]
granate[M]

topaz
topaze[F]
Topas[M]
topacio[M]

aquamarine
aigue-marine[F]
Aquamarin[M]
aguamarina[F]

tourmaline
tourmaline[F]
Turmalin[M]
turmalina[F]

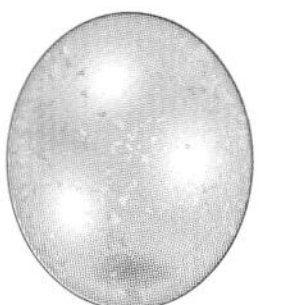

opal
opale[F]
Opal[M]
ópalo[M]

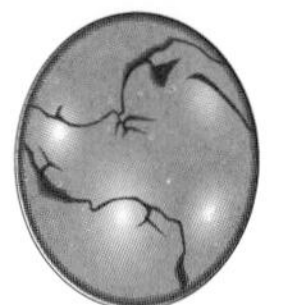

turquoise
turquoise[F]
Türkis[M]
turquesa[F]

lapis lazuli
lapis-lazuli[M]
Lapislazuli[M]
lapislázuli[M]

# JEWELLERY
# BIJOUTERIE[F]
# SCHMUCK[M]
# JOYERÍA[F]

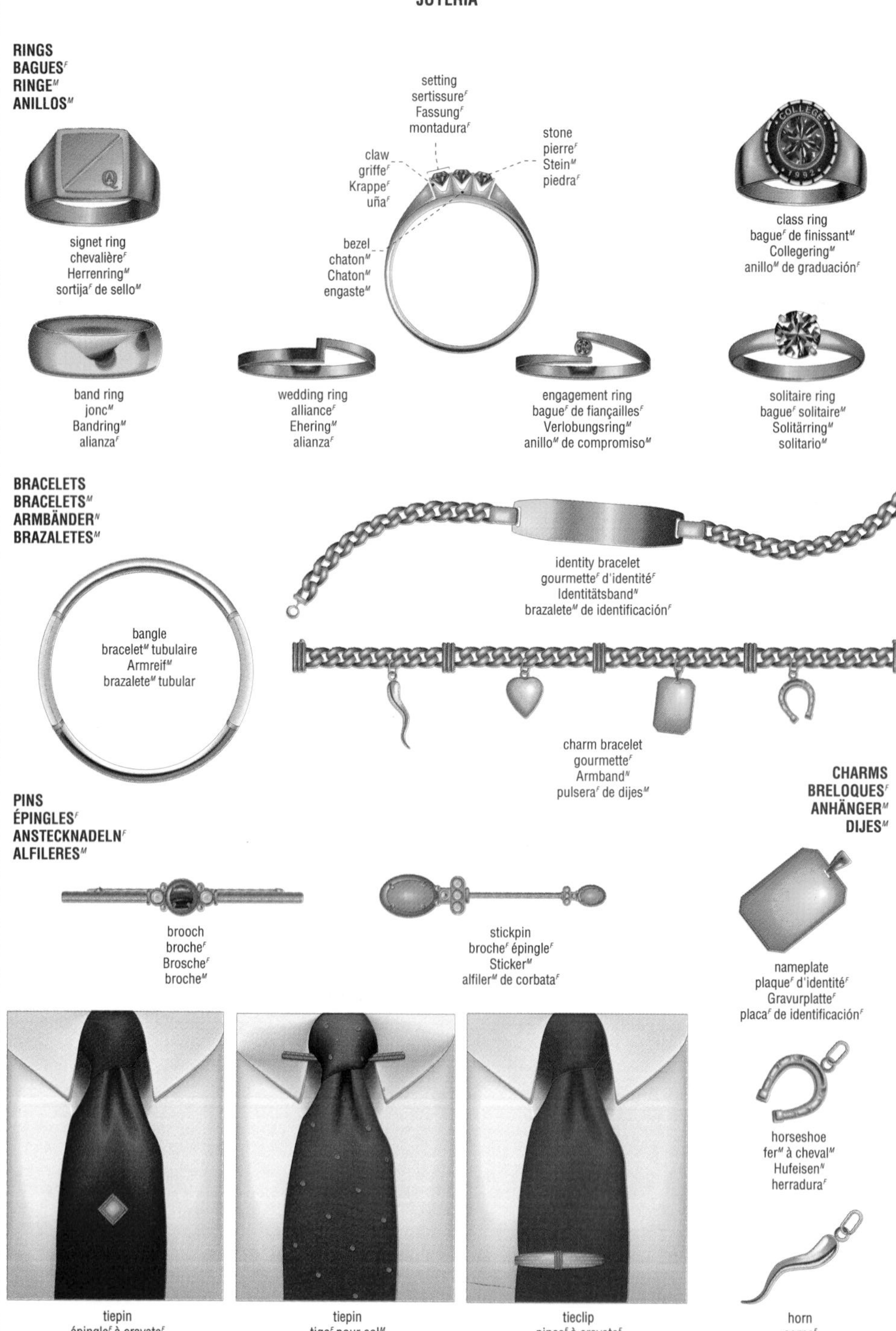

# MANICURE
# MANUCURE[F]
# MANIKÜRE[F]
# MANICURA[F]

## MANICURE SET
## TROUSSE[F] DE MANUCURE[F]
## NAGELNECESSAIRE[N]
## ESTUCHE[M] DE MANICURA[F]

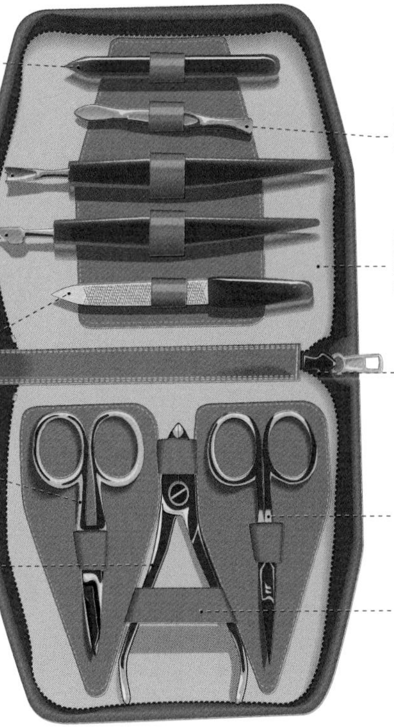

cuticle pusher
repousse-chair[M]
Nagelhautschieber[M]
empujacutículas[M]

cuticle trimmer
coupe-cuticules[M]
Nagelhautentferner[M]
desbastador[M] de cutícula[F]

nail shaper
gratte-ongles[M]
Nagelhautschaber[M]
cuchilla[F] para moldear

nail file
lime[F] à ongles[M]
Nagelfeile[F]
lima[F] de uñas[F]

nail scissors
ciseaux[M] à ongles[M]
Nagelschere[F]
tijeras[F]

cuticle nippers
pince[F] à cuticules[M]
Nagelzange[F]
alicates[M] para cutícula[F]

eyebrow tweezers
pince[F] à épiler
Augenbrauenpinzette[F]
pinzas[F] para depilar cejas[F]

case
étui[M]
Etui[N]
estuche[M]

zip
fermeture[F] à glissière[F]
Reißverschluß[M]
cremallera[F]

cuticle scissors
ciseaux[M] à cuticules[M]
Nagelhautschere[F]
tijeras[F] para cutícula[F]

strap
bride[F]
Schlaufe[F]
correa[F]

## NAIL CLIPPERS
## COUPE-ONGLES[M]
## NAGELKNIPSER[M]
## CORTAÚÑAS[M]

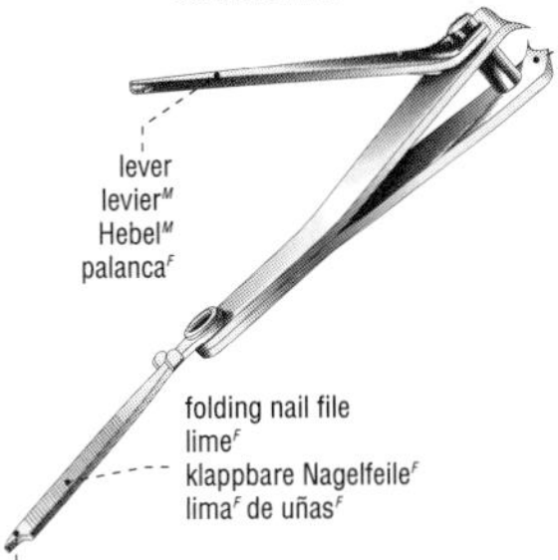

jaw
mors[M]
Klemmbacke[F]
mordaza[F]

lever
levier[M]
Hebel[M]
palanca[F]

folding nail file
lime[F]
klappbare Nagelfeile[F]
lima[F] de uñas[F]

nail cleaner
cure-ongles[M]
Nagelreiniger[M]
limpiador[M] de uñas[F]

## MANICURING IMPLEMENTS
## ACCESSOIRES[M] DE MANUCURE[F]
## NAGELPFLEGEZUBEHÖR[N]
## INSTRUMENTOS[M] DE MANICURA[F]

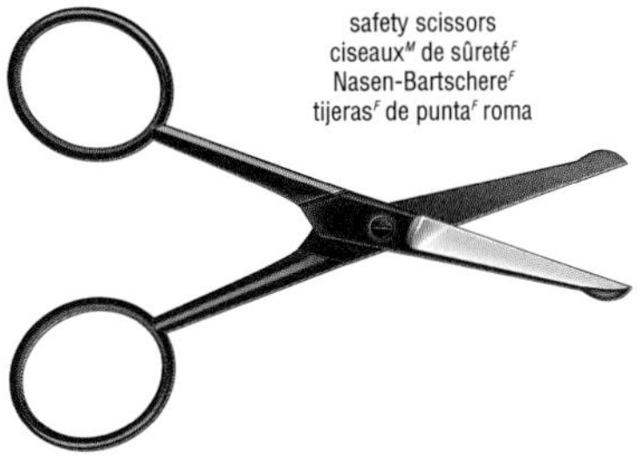

safety scissors
ciseaux[M] de sûreté[F]
Nasen-Bartschere[F]
tijeras[F] de punta[F] roma

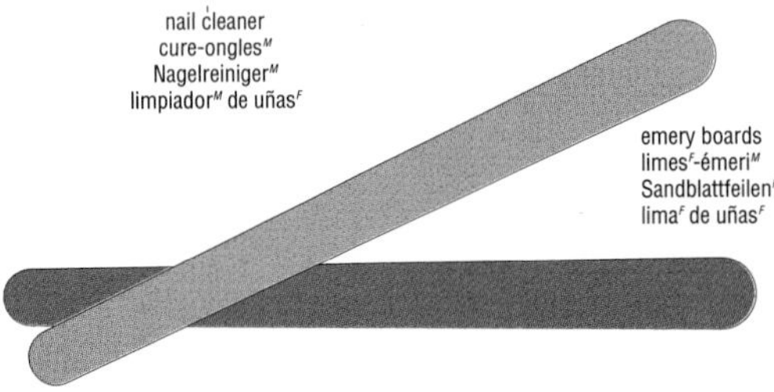

emery boards
limes[F]-émeri[M]
Sandblattfeilen[F]
lima[F] de uñas[F]

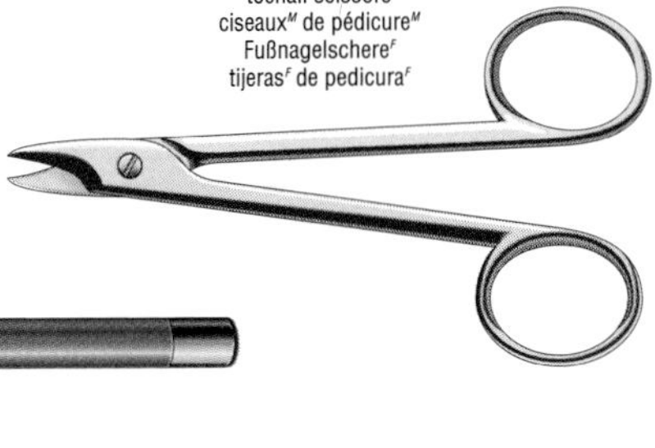

toenail scissors
ciseaux[M] de pédicure[M]
Fußnagelschere[F]
tijeras[F] de pedicura[F]

nail whitener pencil
crayon[M] blanchisseur d'ongles[M]
Nagelweißstift[M]
lápiz[M] blanco para uñas[F]

# MAKE-UP
# MAQUILLAGE[M]
# MAKE-UP[N]
# MAQUILLAJE[M]

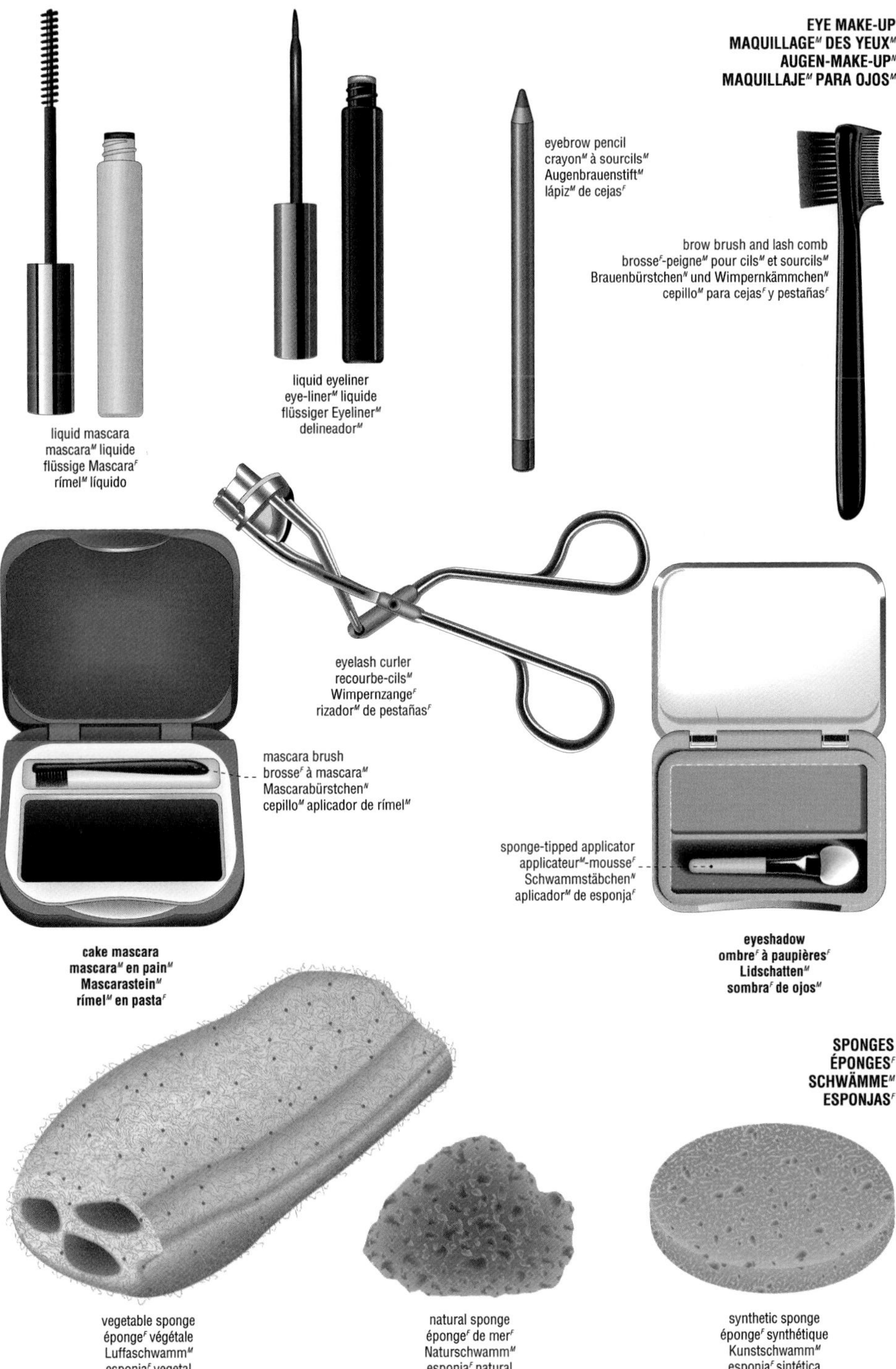
EYE MAKE-UP
MAQUILLAGE[M] DES YEUX[M]
AUGEN-MAKE-UP[N]
MAQUILLAJE[M] PARA OJOS[M]
eyebrow pencil
crayon[M] à sourcils[M]
Augenbrauenstift[M]
lápiz[M] de cejas[F]
brow brush and lash comb
brosse[F]-peigne[M] pour cils[M] et sourcils[M]
Brauenbürstchen[N] und Wimpernkämmchen[N]
cepillo[M] para cejas[F] y pestañas[F]
liquid eyeliner
eye-liner[M] liquide
flüssiger Eyeliner[M]
delineador[M]
liquid mascara
mascara[M] liquide
flüssige Mascara[F]
rímel[M] líquido
eyelash curler
recourbe-cils[M]
Wimpernzange[F]
rizador[M] de pestañas[F]
mascara brush
brosse[F] à mascara[M]
Mascarabürstchen[N]
cepillo[M] aplicador de rímel[M]
sponge-tipped applicator
applicateur[M]-mousse[F]
Schwammstäbchen[N]
aplicador[M] de esponja[F]
cake mascara
mascara[M] en pain[M]
Mascarastein[M]
rímel[M] en pasta[F]
eyeshadow
ombre[F] à paupières[F]
Lidschatten[M]
sombra[F] de ojos[M]
SPONGES
ÉPONGES[F]
SCHWÄMME[M]
ESPONJAS[F]
vegetable sponge
éponge[F] végétale
Luffaschwamm[M]
esponja[F] vegetal
natural sponge
éponge[F] de mer[F]
Naturschwamm[M]
esponja[F] natural
synthetic sponge
éponge[F] synthétique
Kunstschwamm[M]
esponja[F] sintética

# HAIRDRESSING
# COIFFURE[F]
# HAARPFLEGE[F]
# PEINADO[M]

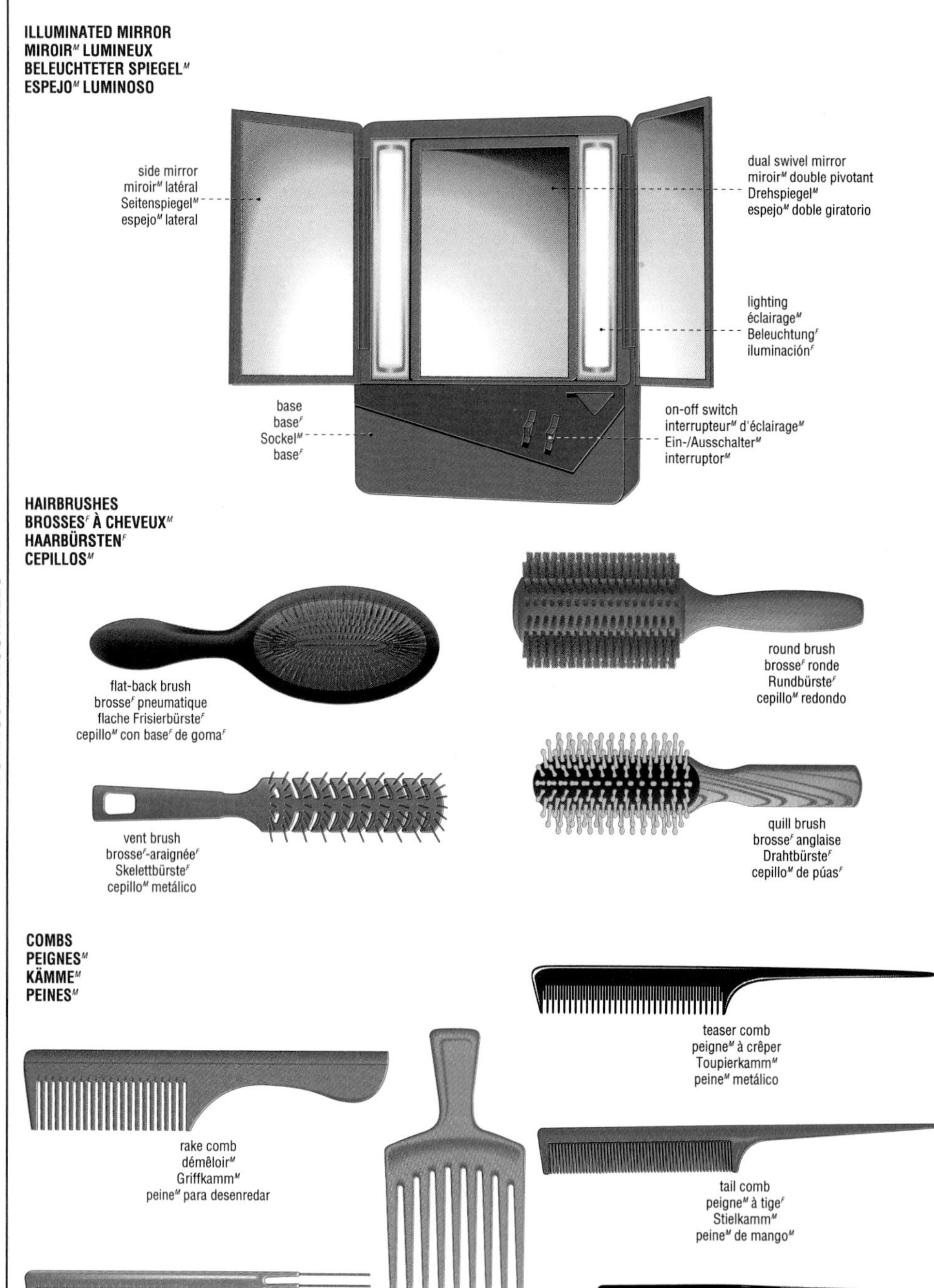

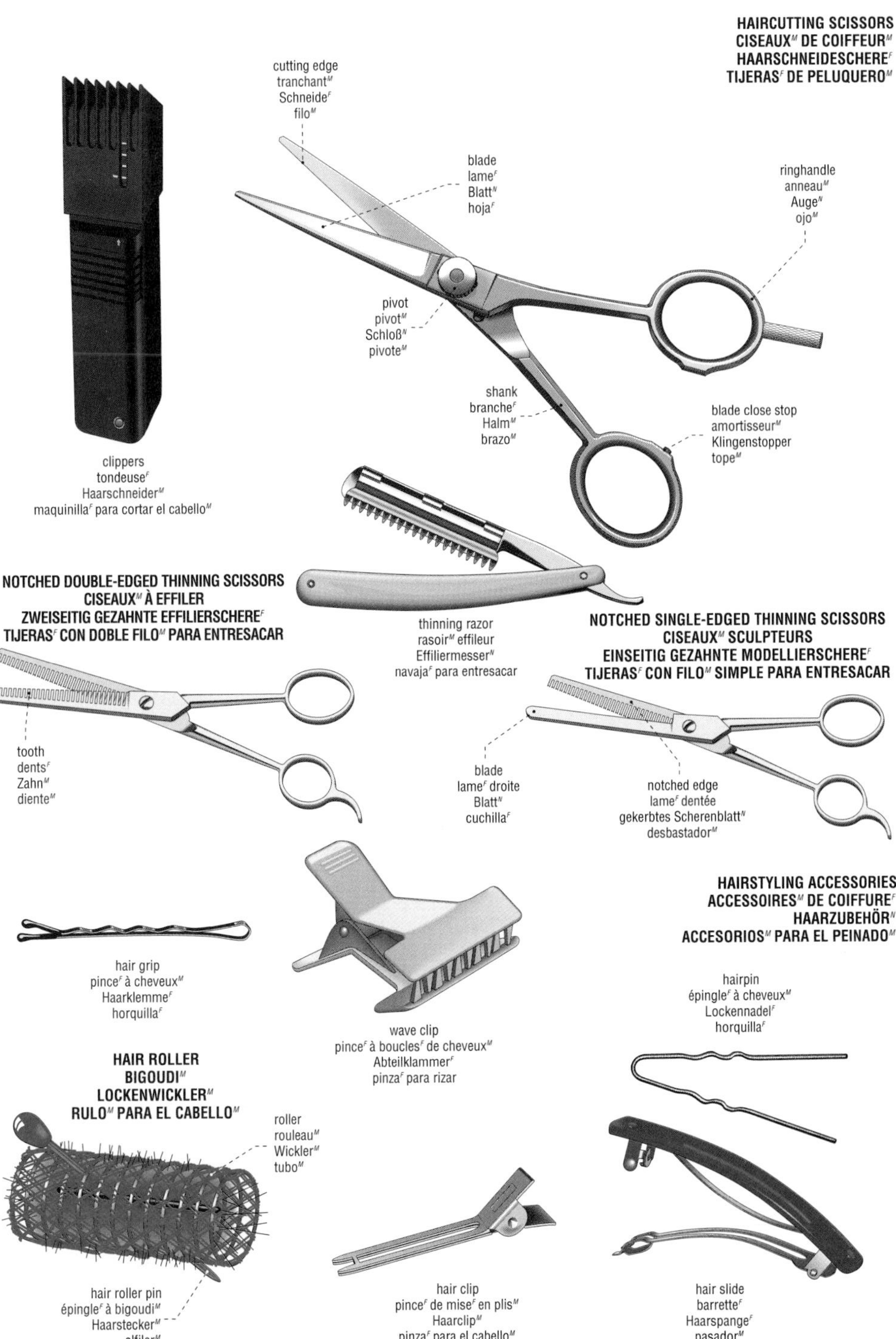

HAIRCUTTING SCISSORS
CISEAUX[M] DE COIFFEUR[M]
HAARSCHNEIDESCHERE[F]
TIJERAS[F] DE PELUQUERO[M]
cutting edge
tranchant[M]
Schneide[F]
filo[M]
blade
lame[F]
Blatt[N]
hoja[F]
ringhandle
anneau[M]
Auge[N]
ojo[M]
pivot
pivot[M]
Schloß[N]
pivote[M]
shank
branche[F]
Halm[M]
brazo[M]
blade close stop
amortisseur[M]
Klingenstopper
tope[M]
clippers
tondeuse[F]
Haarschneider[M]
maquinilla[F] para cortar el cabello[M]
NOTCHED DOUBLE-EDGED THINNING SCISSORS
CISEAUX[M] À EFFILER
ZWEISEITIG GEZAHNTE EFFILIERSCHERE[F]
TIJERAS[F] CON DOBLE FILO[M] PARA ENTRESACAR
thinning razor
rasoir[M] effileur
Effiliermesser[N]
navaja[F] para entresacar
NOTCHED SINGLE-EDGED THINNING SCISSORS
CISEAUX[M] SCULPTEURS
EINSEITIG GEZAHNTE MODELLIERSCHERE[F]
TIJERAS[F] CON FILO[M] SIMPLE PARA ENTRESACAR
tooth
dents[F]
Zahn[M]
diente[M]
blade
lame[F] droite
Blatt[N]
cuchilla[F]
notched edge
lame[F] dentée
gekerbtes Scherenblatt[N]
desbastador[M]
HAIRSTYLING ACCESSORIES
ACCESSOIRES[M] DE COIFFURE[F]
HAARZUBEHÖR[N]
ACCESORIOS[M] PARA EL PEINADO[M]
hair grip
pince[F] à cheveux[M]
Haarklemme[F]
horquilla[F]
wave clip
pince[F] à boucles[F] de cheveux[M]
Abteilklammer[F]
pinza[F] para rizar
hairpin
épingle[F] à cheveux[M]
Lockennadel[F]
horquilla[F]
HAIR ROLLER
BIGOUDI[M]
LOCKENWICKLER[M]
RULO[M] PARA EL CABELLO[M]
roller
rouleau[M]
Wickler[M]
tubo[M]
hair roller pin
épingle[F] à bigoudi[M]
Haarstecker[M]
alfiler[M]
hair clip
pince[F] de mise[F] en plis[M]
Haarclip[M]
pinza[F] para el cabello[M]
hair slide
barrette[F]
Haarspange[F]
pasador[M]

## HAIRDRESSING
## COIFFURE[F]
## HAARPFLEGE[F]
## PEINADO[M]

# PERSONAL ARTICLES
# OBJETS PERSONNELS

# PERSÖNLICHE ARTIKEL
# ARTÍCULOS PERSONALES

**SUMMARY**

**DENTAL CARE**
**HYGIÈNE[F] DENTAIRE**
**ZAHNPFLEGE[F]**
**HIGIENE[F] DENTAL**

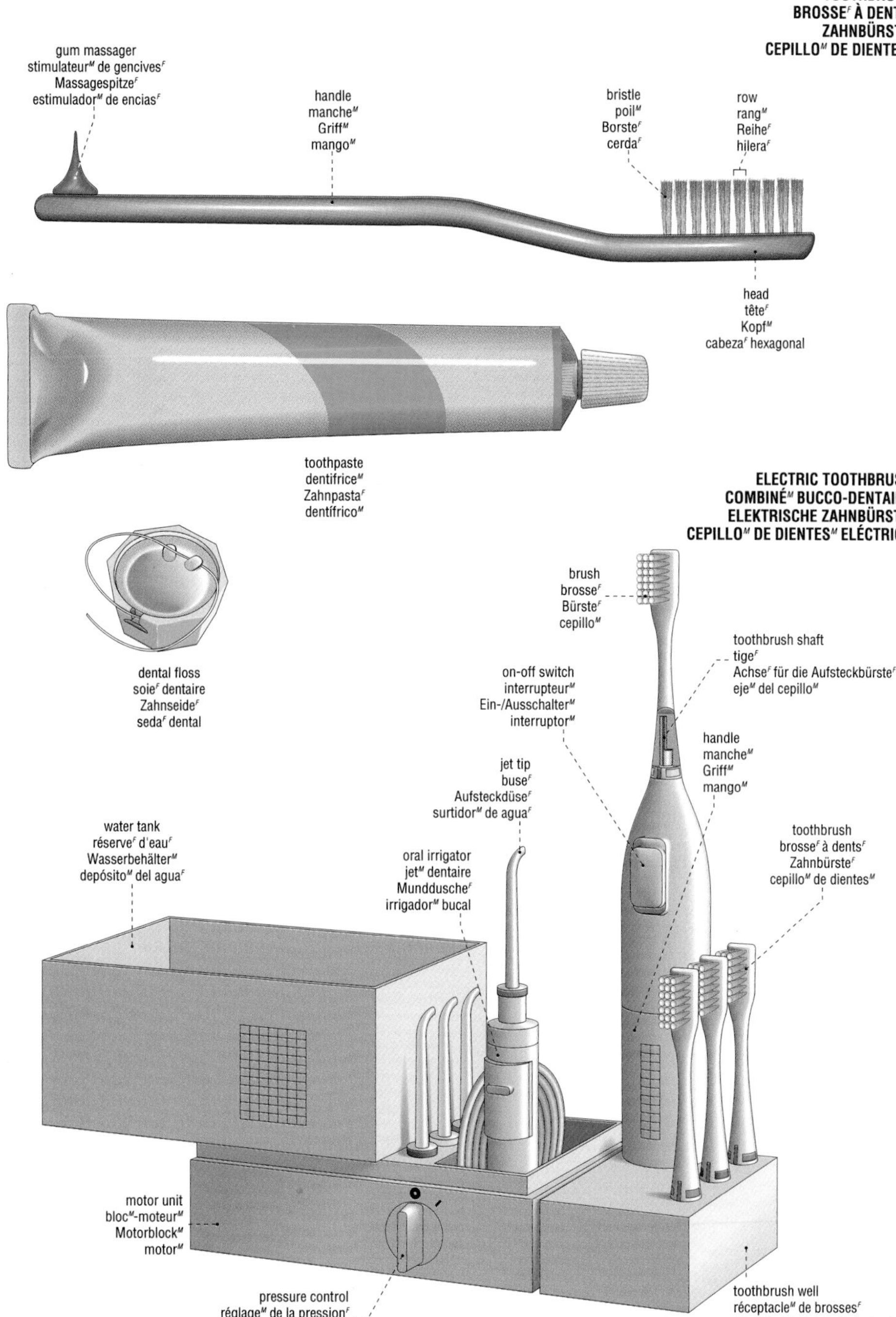

# RAZORS
# RASOIRS$^{M}$
# RASIERER$^{M}$
# RASURADORAS$^{F}$

## ELECTRIC RAZOR
## RASOIR$^{M}$ ÉLECTRIQUE
## ELEKTRORASIERER$^{M}$
## MAQUINILLA$^{F}$ DE AFEITAR ELÉCTRICA

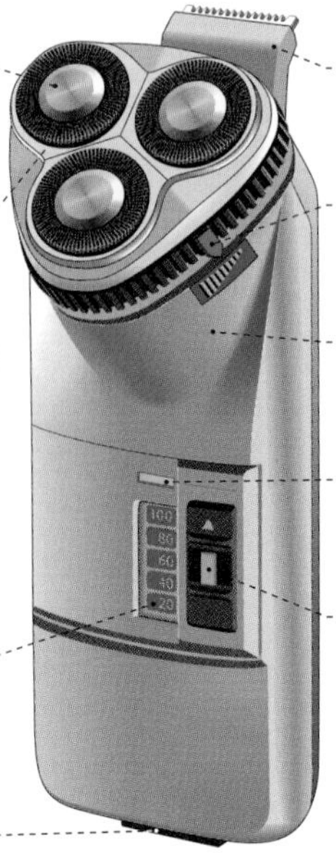

floating head
tête$^{F}$ flottante
Scherkopf$^{M}$
cabeza$^{F}$ flotante

screen
grille$^{F}$
Scherkopfhalter$^{M}$
peine$^{M}$ y cuchilla$^{F}$

trimmer
tondeuse$^{F}$
Langhaarschneider$^{M}$
recortador$^{M}$ de patillas$^{F}$

closeness setting
sélecteur$^{M}$ de coupe$^{F}$
Justierring$^{M}$
selector$^{M}$ de corte$^{M}$

housing
boîtier$^{M}$
Gehäuse$^{N}$
caja$^{F}$

charging light
voyant$^{M}$ de charge$^{F}$
Ladekontrollampe$^{F}$
luz$^{F}$ de encendido$^{M}$

on-off switch
interrupteur$^{M}$
Ein-/Ausschalter$^{M}$
interruptor$^{M}$

charge indicator
indicateur$^{M}$ de charge$^{F}$
Kapazitätsanzeige$^{F}$
indicador$^{M}$ de recarga$^{F}$

charging socket
prise$^{F}$ de charge$^{F}$
Geräteanschluß$^{M}$
enchufe$^{M}$ de recarga$^{F}$

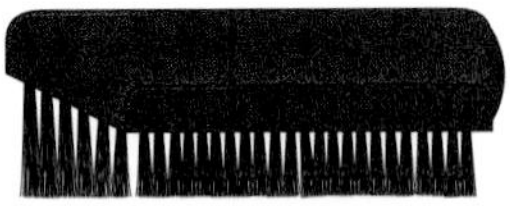

cleaning brush
brosse$^{F}$ de nettoyage$^{M}$
Reinigungsbürste$^{F}$
escobilla$^{F}$ limpiadora

flex
cordon$^{M}$ d'alimentation$^{F}$
Netzkabel$^{N}$
cable$^{M}$ de corriente$^{F}$

plug adapter
adaptateur$^{M}$ de fiche$^{F}$
Adapter$^{M}$
adaptador$^{M}$ de enchufes$^{M}$

## CUT-THROAT RAZOR
## RASOIR$^{M}$ À MANCHE$^{M}$
## RASIERMESSER$^{N}$
## NAVAJA$^{F}$ DE BARBERO$^{M}$

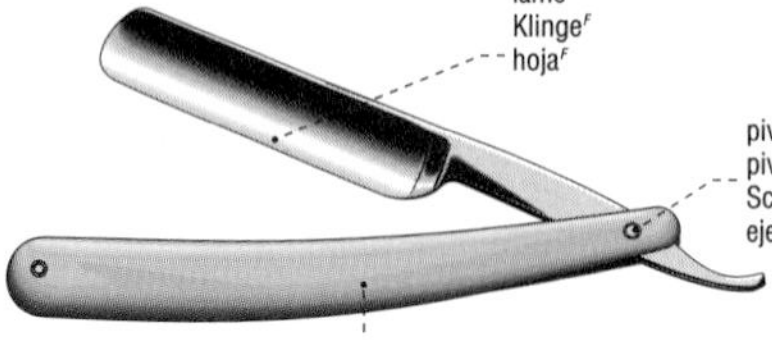

blade
lame$^{F}$
Klinge$^{F}$
hoja$^{F}$

pivot
pivot$^{M}$
Schloß$^{N}$
eje$^{M}$

handle
manche$^{M}$
Griff$^{M}$
mango$^{M}$

## DOUBLE-EDGED RAZOR
## RASOIR$^{M}$ À DOUBLE TRANCHANT$^{M}$
## ZWEISCHNEIDIGER RASIERER$^{M}$
## MAQUINILLA$^{F}$ DE AFEITAR

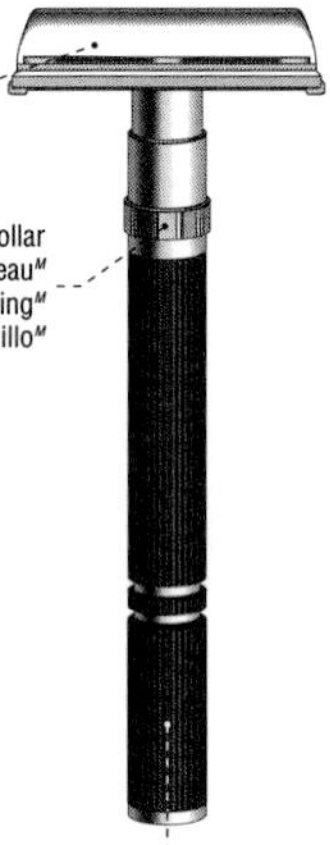

head
tête$^{F}$
Kopf$^{M}$
cabeza$^{F}$

collar
anneau$^{M}$
Ring$^{M}$
anillo$^{M}$

handle
manche$^{M}$
Griff$^{M}$
mango$^{M}$

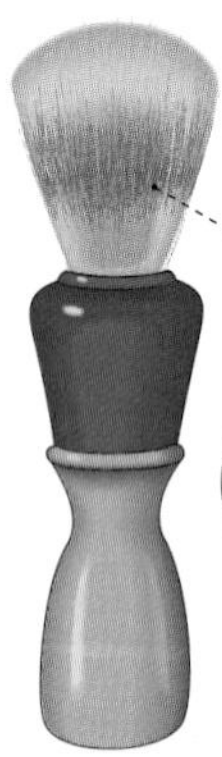

bristle
soie$^{F}$
Borste$^{F}$
cerdas$^{F}$

## SHAVING BRUSH
## BLAIREAU$^{M}$
## RASIERPINSEL$^{M}$
## BROCHA$^{F}$ DE AFEITAR

shaving mug
bol$^{M}$ à raser
Seifenbecher$^{M}$
jabonera$^{F}$

disposable razor
rasoir$^{M}$ jetable
Einwegrasierer$^{M}$
maquinilla$^{F}$ desechable

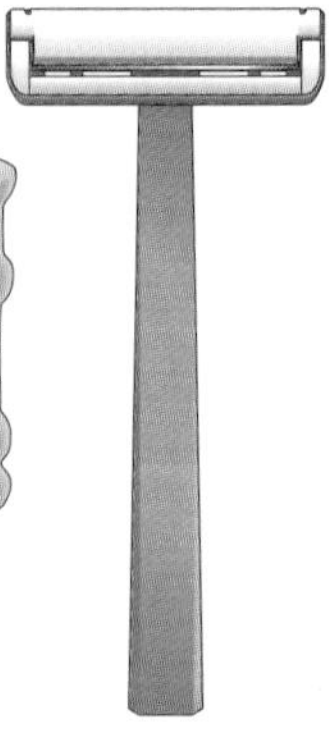

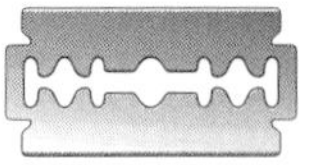

double-edged razor blade
lame$^{F}$ à double tranchant$^{M}$
zweischneidige Klinge$^{F}$
hoja$^{F}$ de afeitar

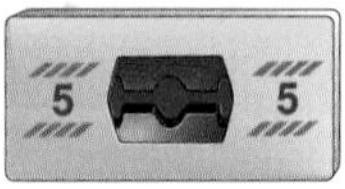

blade dispenser
distributeur$^{M}$ de lames$^{F}$
Klingenkassette$^{F}$
despachador$^{M}$ de hojas$^{F}$ de afeitar

# UMBRELLA AND STICK
# PARAPLUIE[M] ET CANNE[F]
# SCHIRM[M] UND STOCK[M]
# PARAGUAS[M] Y BASTONES[M]

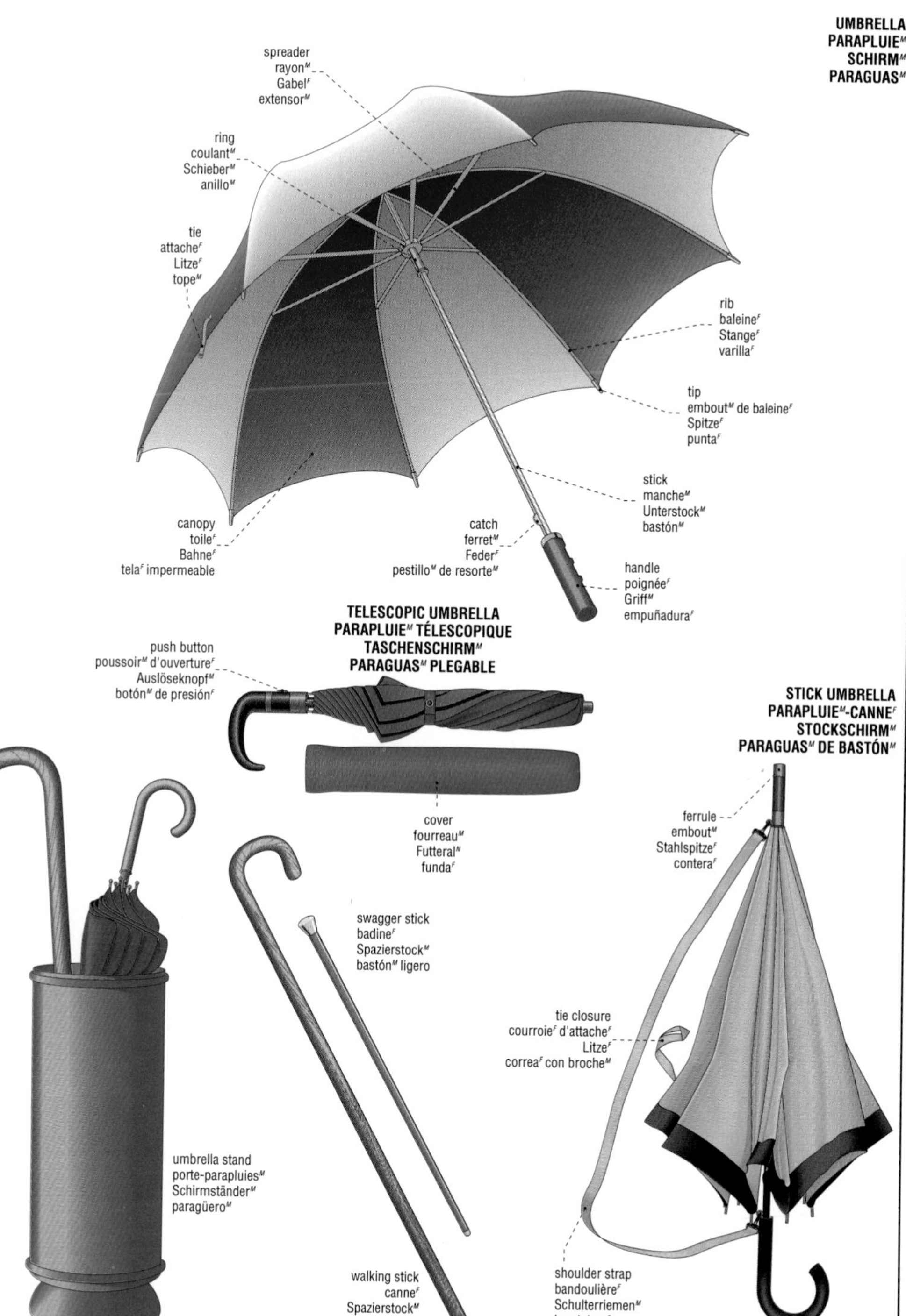

## SPECTACLES
## LUNETTES^F
## BRILLE^F
## GAFAS^F

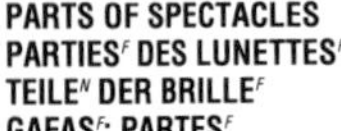

### PARTS OF SPECTACLES
### PARTIES^F DES LUNETTES^F
### TEILE^N DER BRILLE^F
### GAFAS^F: PARTES^F

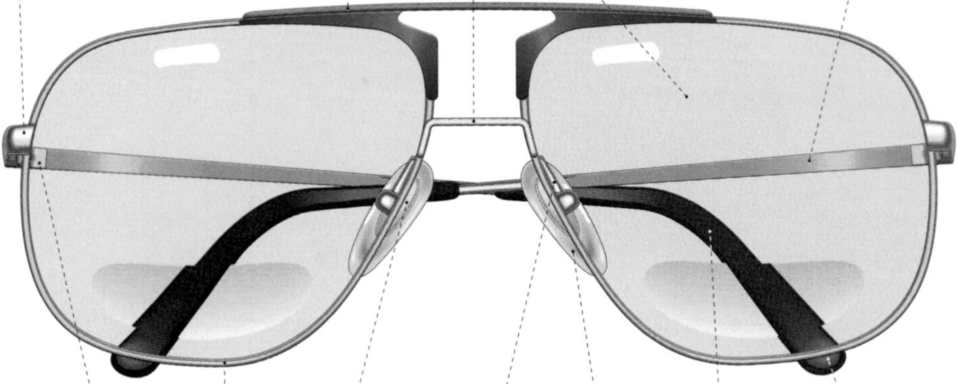

bridge pont^M Brücke^N puente^M
endpiece tenon^M Backe^F espiga^F
bar barre^F Steg^M barra^F
lens verre^M Glas^N lente^F
sidepiece branche^F Bügel^M patilla^F
butt-strap talon^M Bügelanschlag^M extremo^M
pad plate support^M de plaquette^F Stegplättchen^N placa^F del cojinete^M
nose pad plaquette^F Seitensteg^M cojinete^M
earpiece cambre^F Bügelende^N gafa^F
rim cercle^M Rand^M aro^M
pad arm bras^M de plaquette^F Stegstütze^F brazo^M del cojinete^M
bend coude^M Bügelbug^M codo^M

### BIFOCAL LENS
### VERRE^M BIFOCAL
### BIFOKALGLAS^N
### LENTE^F BIFOCAL

distance lens segment^M de loin Fernteil^N enfoque^M de lejos
rim cercle^M Rand^M aro^M
reading lens segment^M de près Nahteil^N enfoque^M de cerca

### FRAMES
### MONTURE^F
### FASSUNGEN^F
### MONTURA^F

PERSONAL ARTICLES
OBJETS PERSONNELS
PERSÖNLICHE ARTIKEL
ARTÍCULOS PERSONALES

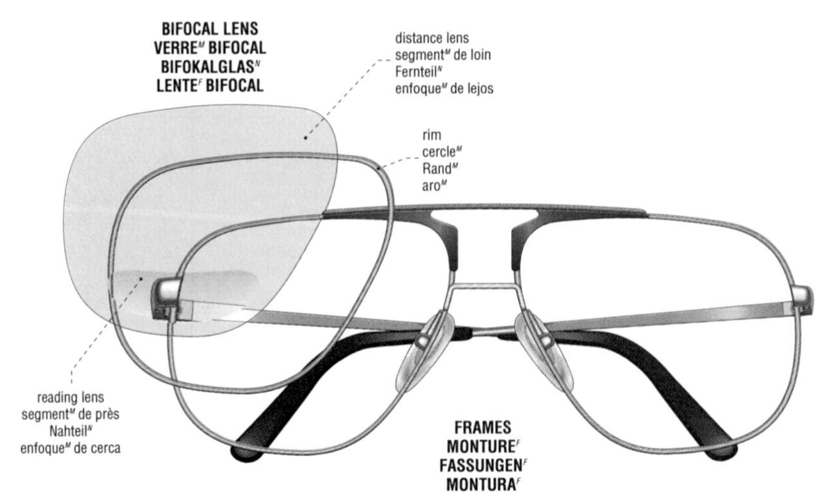

**PRINCIPAL TYPES OF SPECTACLES**
**PRINCIPAUX TYPES[M] DE LUNETTES[F]**
**DIE WICHTIGSTEN BRILLENARTEN[F]**
**PRINCIPALES TIPOS[M] DE LENTES[M]**

half-glasses
demi-lune[F]
Halbbrille[F]
media luna[F]

scissors-glasses
binocle[M]
Scherenbrille[F]
binóculos[M] de tijera[F]

sunglasses
lunettes[F] de soleil[M]
Sonnenbrille[F]
gafas[F] de sol[M]

pince-nez
bésicles[F] à pont[M] élastique
Kneifer[M]
quevedos[M]

lorgnette
face-à-main[M]
Lorgnette[F]
impertinentes[M]

monocle
monocle[M]
Monokel[N]
monóculo[M]

opera glasses
lorgnette[F]
Opernglas[N]
gemelos[M] de teatro[M]

# LEATHER GOODS
# ARTICLES$^{M}$ DE MAROQUINERIE$^{F}$
# LEDERWAREN$^{F}$
# ARTÍCULOS$^{M}$ DE PIEL$^{F}$

**ATTACHÉ CASE**
**MALLETTE$^{F}$ PORTE-DOCUMENTS$^{M}$**
**AKTENKOFFER$^{M}$**
**MALETÍN$^{M}$**

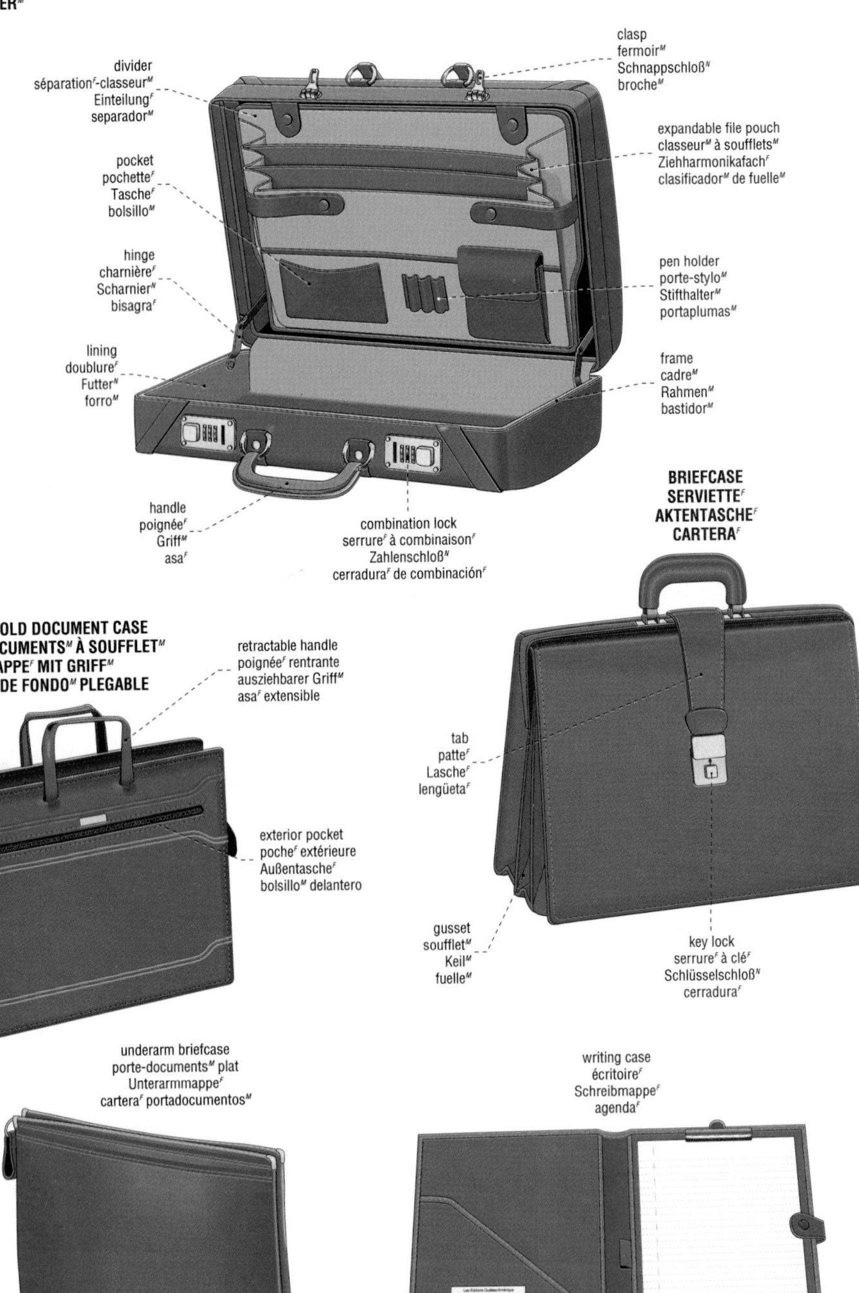

## CALCULATOR/CHEQUE BOOK HOLDER
## PORTEFEUILLE[M] CHÉQUIER[M]
## ETUI[N] FÜR RECHNER[M] UND SCHECKHEFT[N]
## PORTACHEQUERA[F] CON CALCULADORA[F]

spectacles case
étui[M] à lunettes[F]
Brillenetui[N]
funda[F] para gafas[F]

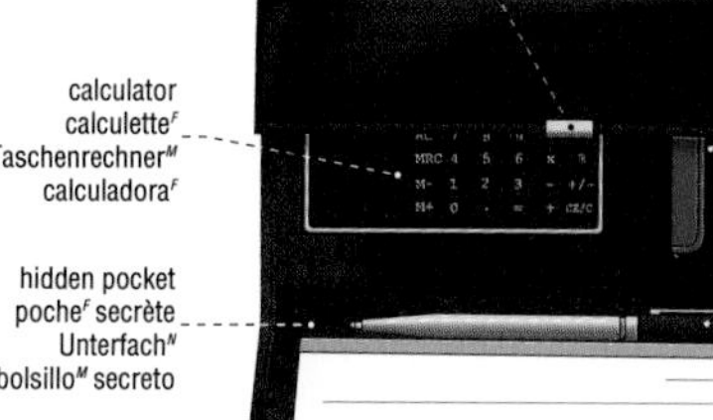

snap fastener
grébiche[F]
Druckverschluß[M]
broche[M] automático

calculator
calculette[F]
Taschenrechner[M]
calculadora[F]

hidden pocket
poche[F] secrète
Unterfach[N]
bolsillo[M] secreto

credit card wallet
porte-cartes[M]
Kreditkartenfach[N]
tarjetero[M]

pen holder
porte-stylo[M]
Stifthalter[M]
portaplumas[M]

cheque book
chéquier[M]
Scheckheft[N]
talonario[M] de cheques[M]

## CREDIT CARD WALLET
## PORTE-CARTES[M]
## KREDITKARTENETUI[N]
## TARJETERO[M]

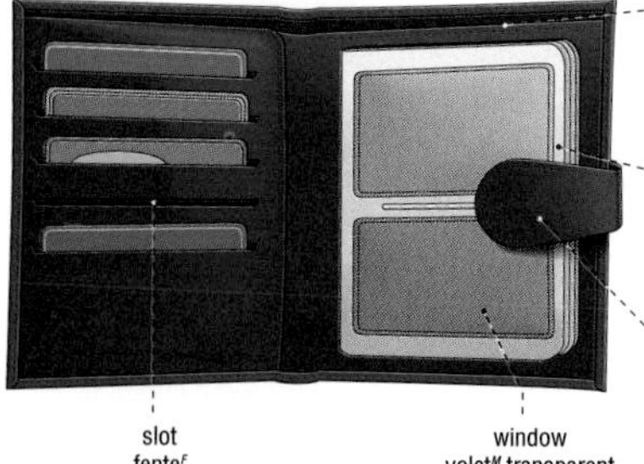

wallet section
poche[F] américaine
Scheinfach[N]
billetera[F]

transparent pockets
feuillets[M]
Klarsichtfenster[N]
plásticos[M] transparentes

tab
patte[F]
Lasche[F]
lengüeta[F]

slot
fente[F]
Fach[N]
ranura[F]

window
volet[M] transparent
Klarsichtfenster[N]
plástico[M] transparente

key case
porte-clés[M]
Schlüsseletui[N]
llavero[M]

wallet
porte-coupures[M]
Scheintasche[F]
billetera[F]

purse
bourse[F] à monnaie[F]
Knipsbörse[F]
monedero[M]

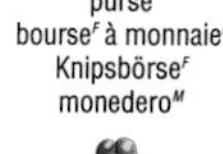

wallet
portefeuille[M]
Scheintasche[F]
billetera[F]

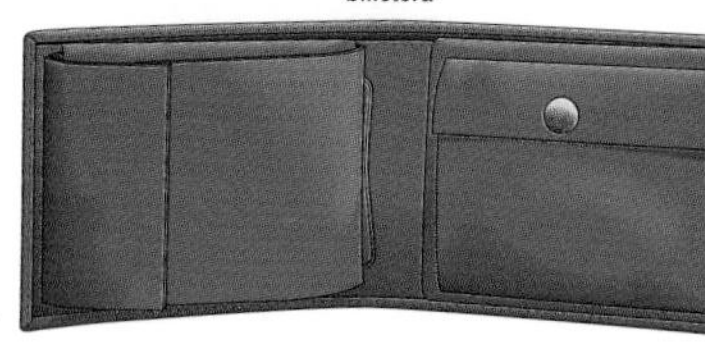

cheque book cover
porte-chéquier[M]
Scheckhülle[F]
talonario[M] de cheques[M]

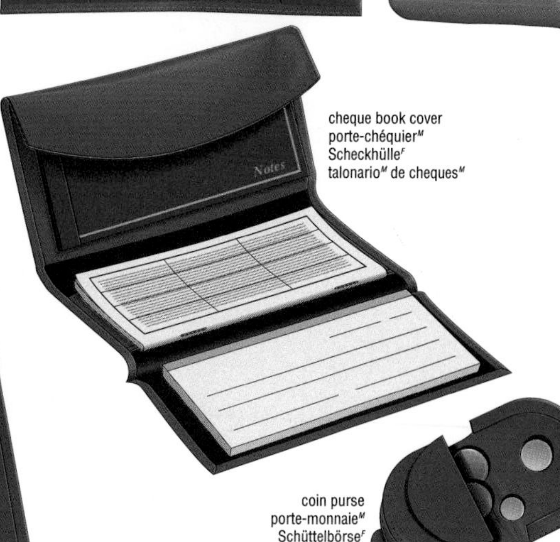


passport case
porte-passeport[M]
Brieftasche[F]
portapasaportes[M]

coin purse
porte-monnaie[M]
Schüttelbörse[F]
portamonedas[M]

## HANDBAGS
## SACS[M] À MAIN[F]
## HANDTASCHEN[F]
## BOLSAS[F] DE MANO[F]

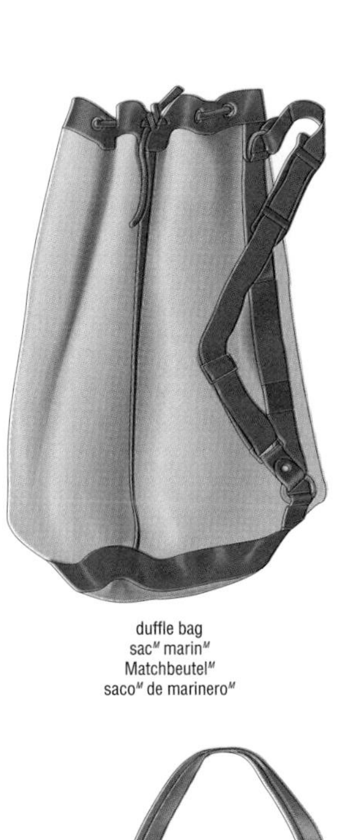

duffle bag
sac[M] marin[M]
Matchbeutel[M]
saco[M] de marinero[M]

box bag
sac[M] boîte[F]
Boxtasche[F]
bolso[M] de vestir

clutch bag
pochette[F]
Klemmtasche[F]
monedero[M]

holdall
sac[M] polochon[M]
Dreivierteltasche[F]
bolso[M] de viaje[M]

**DRAWSTRING BAG**
**SAC[M] SEAU[M]**
**BEUTELTASCHE[F]**
**BOLSA[F] DE CORDONES[M]**

muff
manchon[M]
Mufftasche[F]
bolso[M] manguito[M]

shopping bag
cabas[M]
Einkaufstasche[F]
bolso[M] de la compra[F]

shopping bag
sac[M] à provisions[F]
Tragetasche[F]
bolso[M] de la compra[F]

# LUGGAGE
# BAGAGES[M]
# GEPÄCK[N]
# EQUIPAJE[M]

## TRAVEL BAG
## SAC[M] DE VOL[M]
## REISETASCHE[F]
## BOLSO[M] DE VIAJE[M]

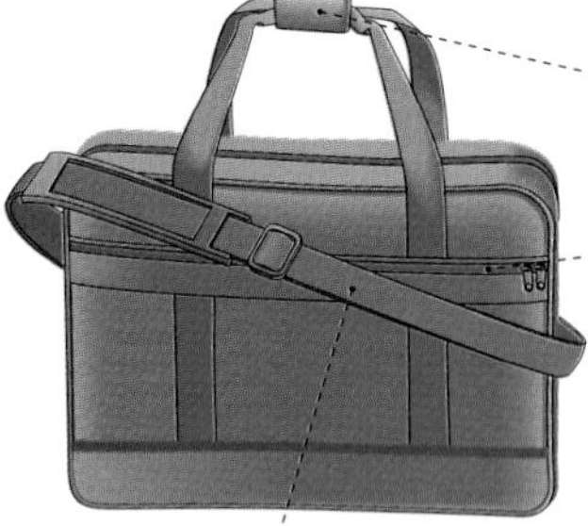

handle
poignée[F]
Griff[M]
asa[F]

exterior pocket
poche[F] extérieure
Außentasche[F]
bolsillo[M] exterior

shoulder strap
bandoulière[F]
Schulterriemen[M]
bandolera[F]

flight bag
sac[M] fourre-tout[M]
Flugtasche[F]
maletín[M]

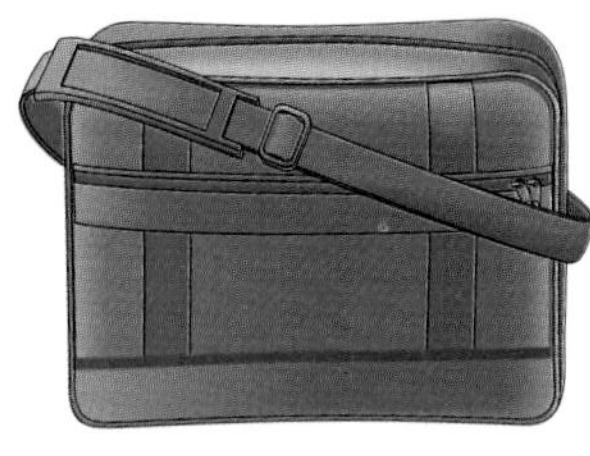

## VANITY CASE
## MALLETTE[F] DE TOILETTE[F]
## KOSMETIKKOFFER[M]
## NECESER[M]

mirror
miroir[M]
Spiegel[M]
espejo[M]

hinge
charnière[F]
Scharnier[N]
bisagra[F]

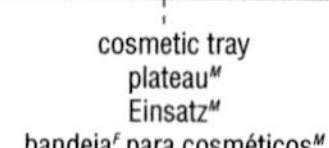

cosmetic tray
plateau[M]
Einsatz[M]
bandeja[F] para cosméticos[M]

toilet bag
trousse[F] de toilette[F]
Kulturbeutel[M]
estuche[M] de tocador[M]

## SUIT CARRIER
## HOUSSE[F] À VÊTEMENTS[M]
## KLEIDERSACK[M]
## BOLSA[F] PARA TRAJES[M]

zip
fermeture[F] à glissière[F]
Reißverschluß[M]
cremallera[F]

## LUGGAGE TROLLEY
## PORTE-BAGAGES[M]
## GEPÄCKROLLER[M]
## CARRITO[M] PORTAMALETAS[M]

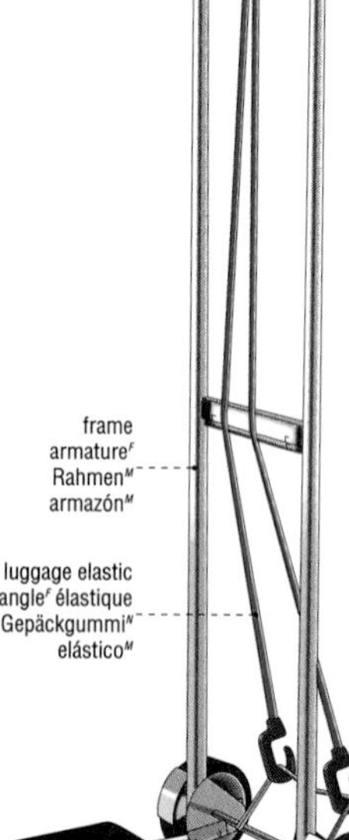

frame
armature[F]
Rahmen[M]
armazón[M]

luggage elastic
sangle[F] élastique
Gepäckgummi[N]
elástico[M]

stand
béquille[F]
Ständer[M]
soporte[M]

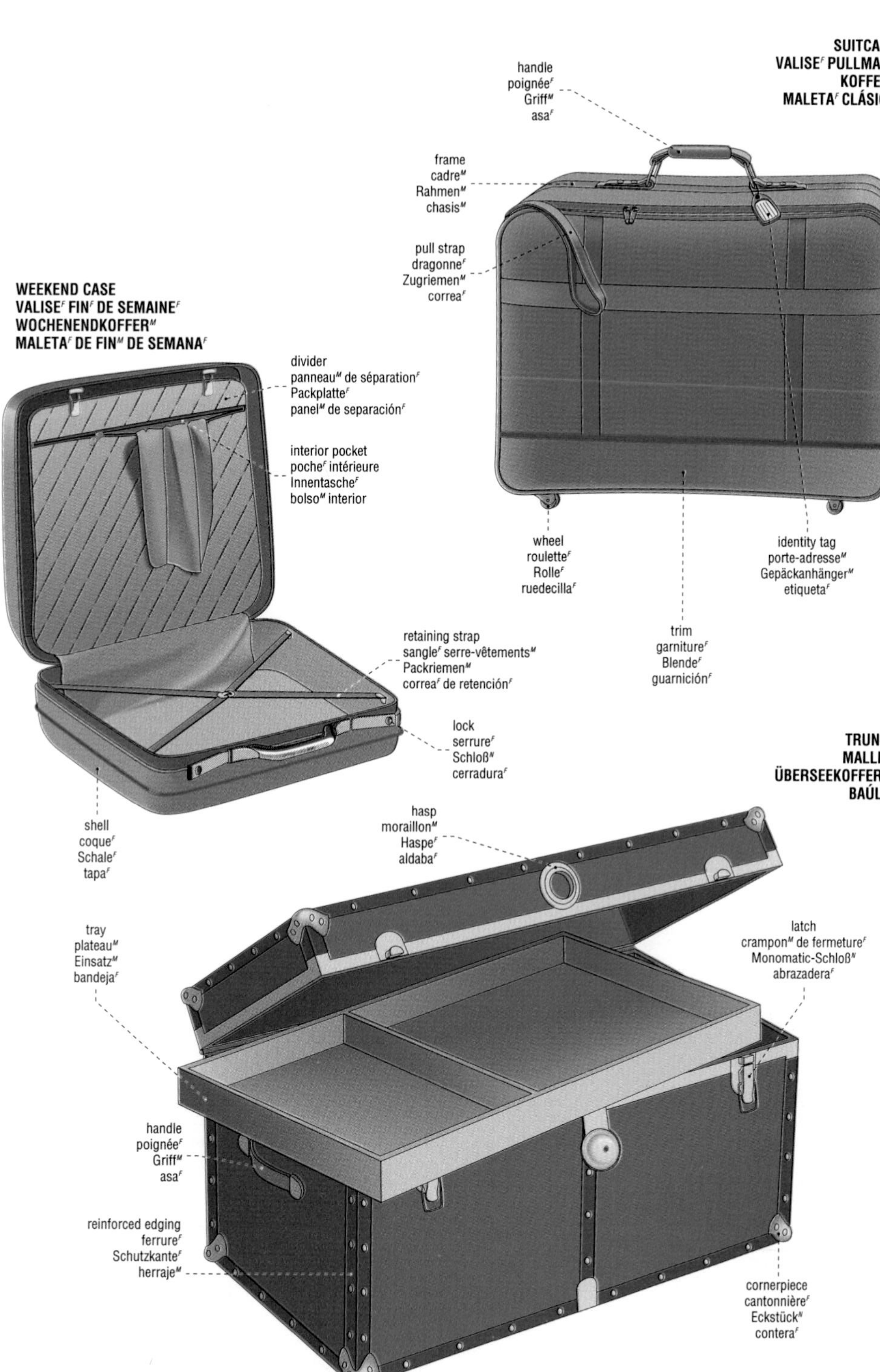
SUITCASE
VALISEF PULLMANM
KOFFERM
MALETAF CLÁSICA
handle
poignéeF
GriffM
asaF
frame
cadreM
RahmenM
chasisM
pull strap
dragonneF
ZugriemenM
correaF
wheel
rouletteF
RolleF
ruedecillaF
identity tag
porte-adresseM
GepäckanhängerM
etiquetaF
trim
garnitureF
BlendeF
guarniciónF
WEEKEND CASE
VALISEF FINF DE SEMAINEF
WOCHENENDKOFFERM
MALETAF DE FINM DE SEMANAF
divider
panneauM de séparationF
PackplatteF
panelM de separaciónF
interior pocket
pocheF intérieure
InnentascheF
bolsoM interior
retaining strap
sangleF serre-vêtementsM
PackriemenM
correaF de retenciónF
lock
serrureF
SchloßN
cerraduraF
shell
coqueF
SchaleF
tapaF
TRUNK
MALLEF
ÜBERSEEKOFFERM
BAÚLM
hasp
moraillonM
HaspeF
aldabaF
tray
plateauM
EinsatzM
bandejaF
latch
cramponM de fermetureF
Monomatic-SchloßN
abrazaderaF
handle
poignéeF
GriffM
asaF
reinforced edging
ferrureF
SchutzkanteF
herrajeM
cornerpiece
cantonnièreF
EckstückN
conteraF

# SMOKING ACCESSORIES
# ARTICLES[M] DE FUMEUR[M]
# RAUCHERBEDARF[M]
# ACCESORIOS[M] PARA FUMAR

## CIGAR
## CIGARE[M]
## ZIGARRE[F]
## PURO[M]

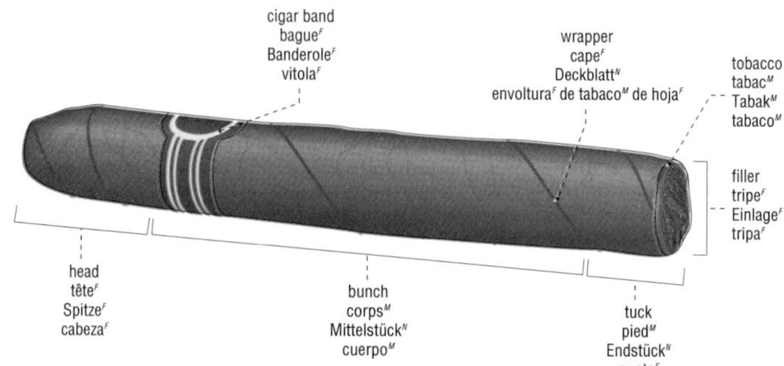


## CIGARETTE
## CIGARETTE[F]
## ZIGARETTE[F]
## CIGARRILLO[M]

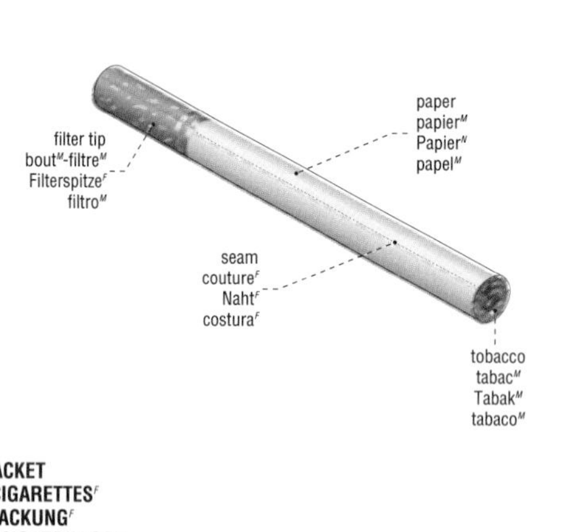


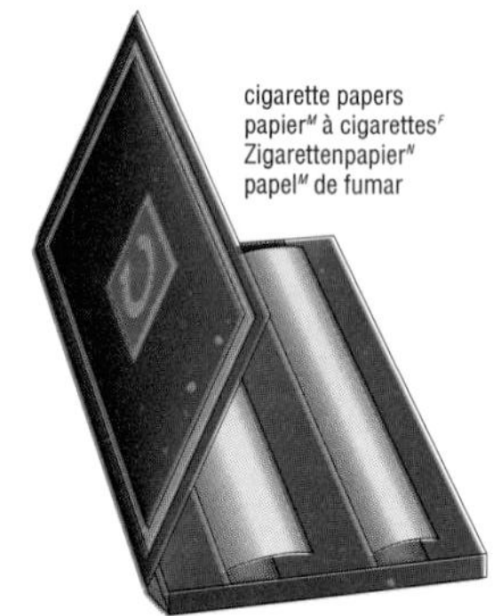


## CIGARETTE PACKET
## PAQUET[M] DE CIGARETTES[F]
## ZIGARETTENPACKUNG[F]
## PAQUETE[M] DE CIGARRILLOS[M]

## PIPE
## PIPE^F
## PFEIFE^F
## PIPA^F

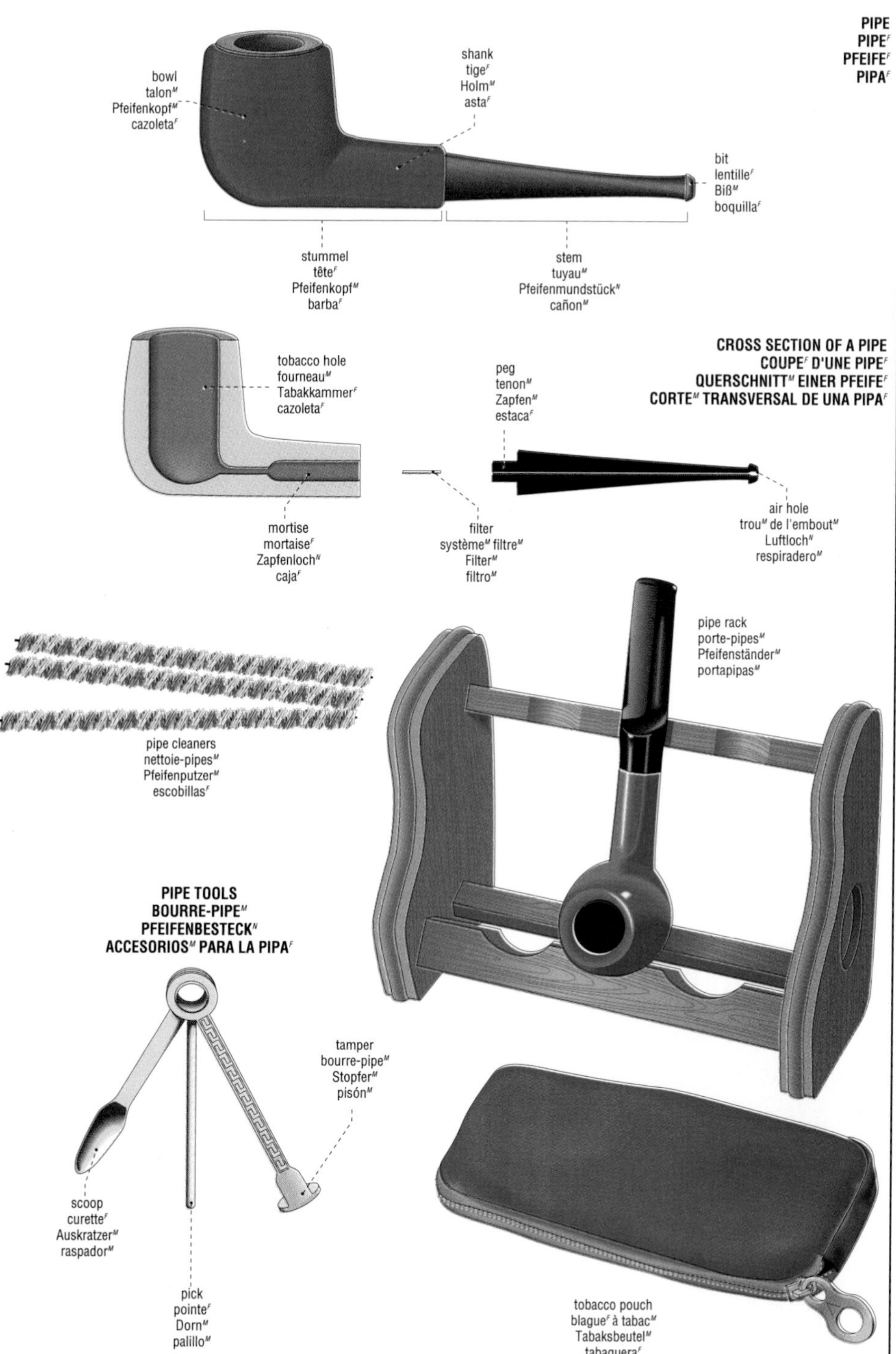

# SMOKING ACCESSORIES
# ARTICLES^M DE FUMEUR^M
# RAUCHERBEDARF^M
# ACCESORIOS^M PARA FUMAR

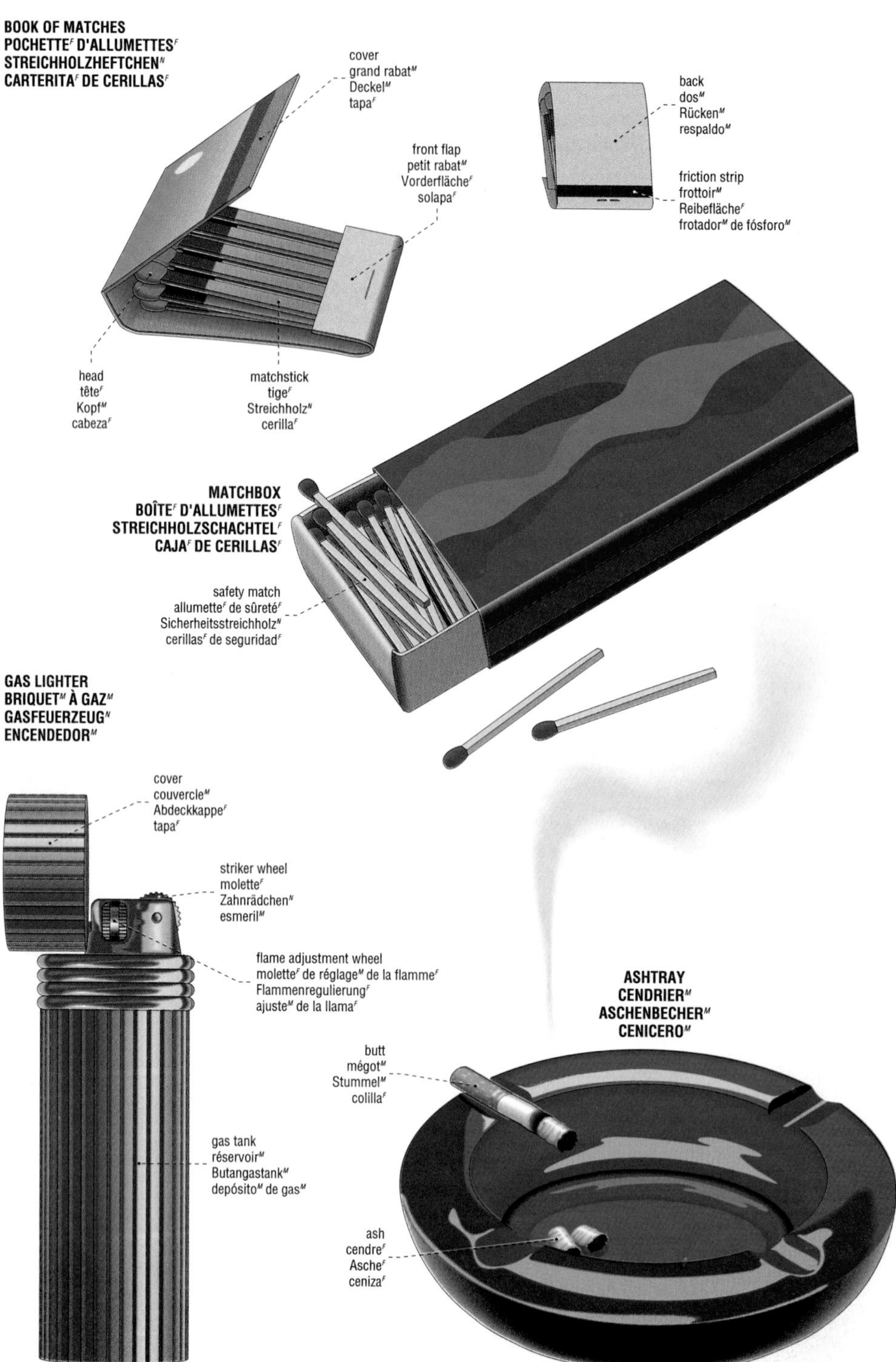

# COMMUNICATIONS
# COMMUNICATIONS
# KOMMUNIKATION
# COMUNICACIONES

## SUMMARY

# WRITING INSTRUMENTS
# INSTRUMENTS^M D'ÉCRITURE^F
# SCHREIBGERÄTE^N
# INSTRUMENTOS^M PARA ESCRIBIR

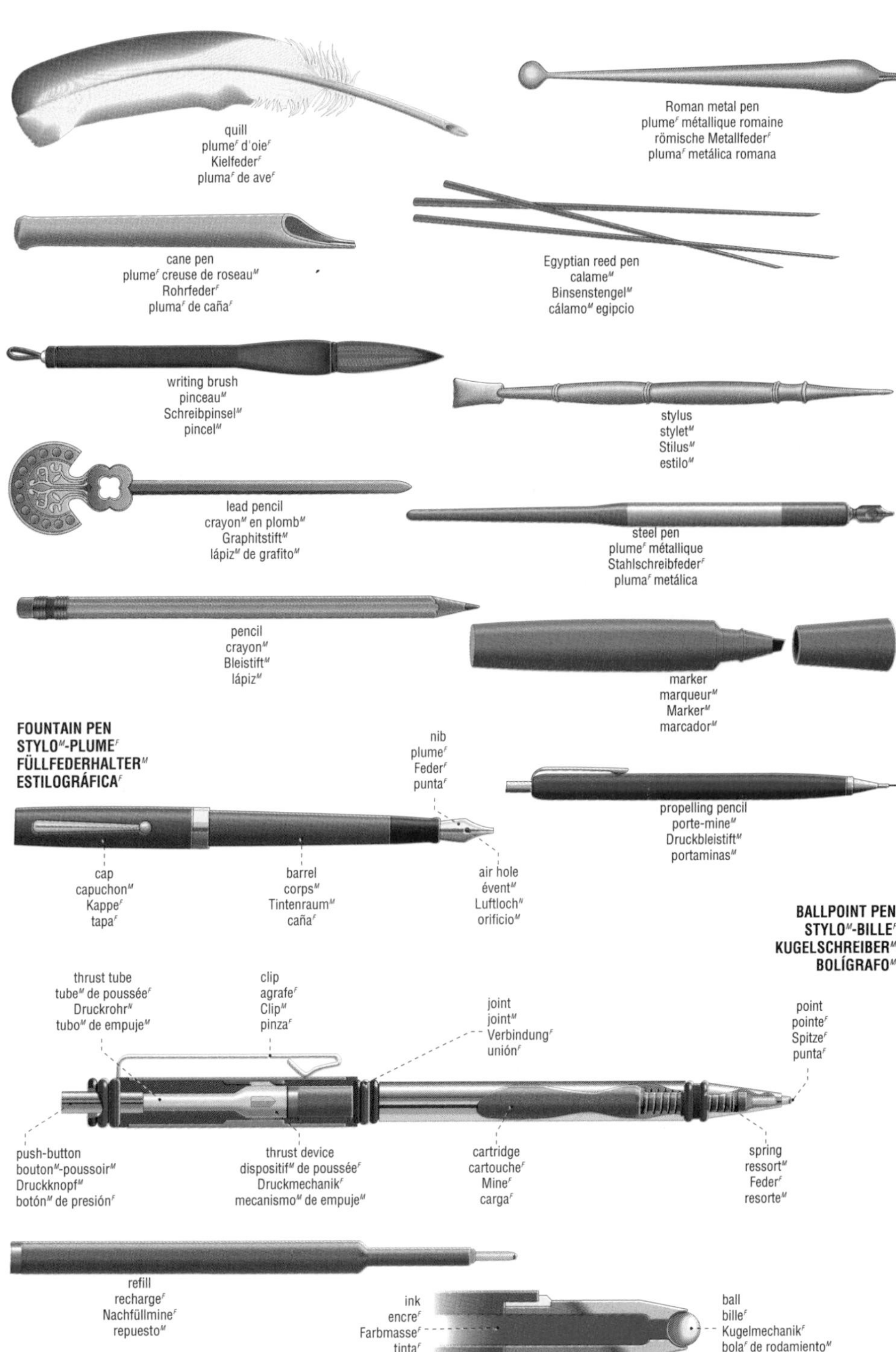

# PHOTOGRAPHY
# PHOTOGRAPHIE[F]
# FOTOGRAFIE[F]
# FOTOGRAFÍA[F]

## CROSS SECTION OF A REFLEX CAMERA
## COUPE[F] D'UN APPAREIL[M] REFLEX
## QUERSCHNITT[M] DURCH EINE SPIEGELREFLEXKAMERA[F]
## CORTE[M] TRANSVERSAL DE UNA CÁMARA[F] REFLEX

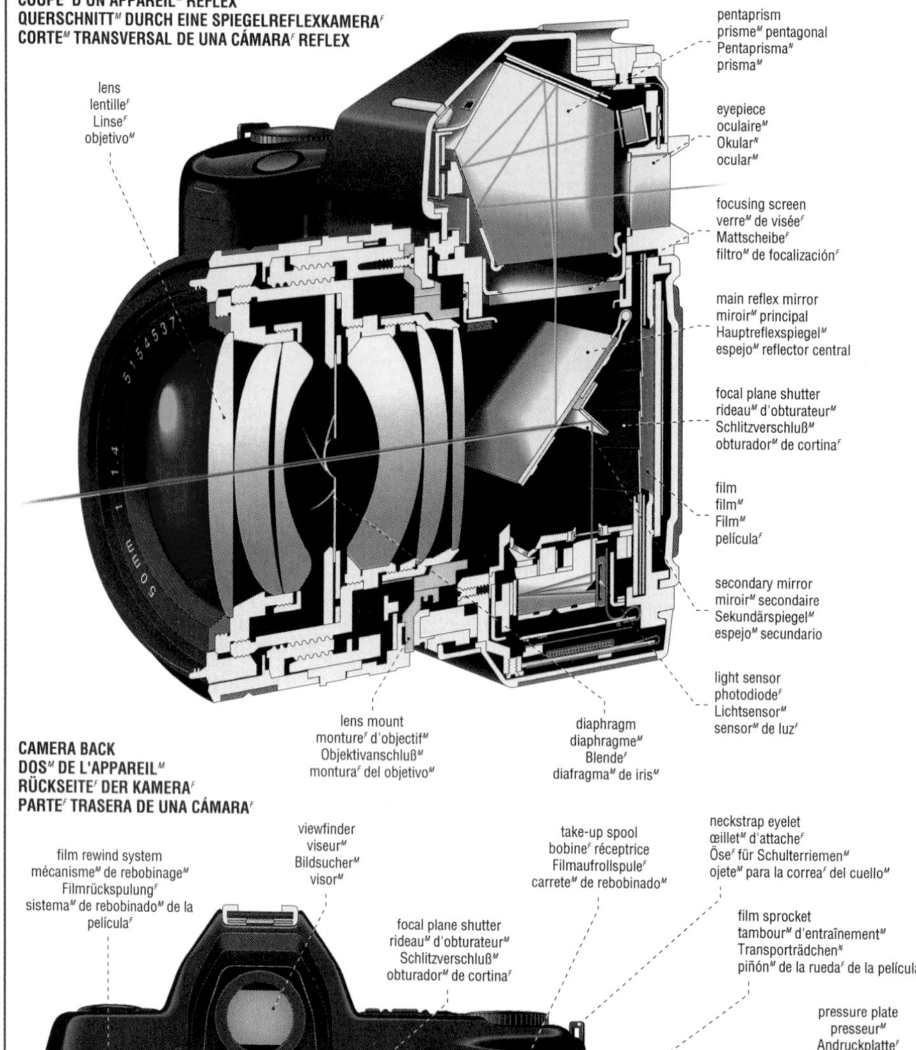


## CAMERA BACK
## DOS[M] DE L'APPAREIL[M]
## RÜCKSEITE[F] DER KAMERA[F]
## PARTE[F] TRASERA DE UNA CÁMARA[F]

film rewind system
mécanisme[M] de rebobinage[M]
Filmrückspulung[F]
sistema[M] de rebobinado[M] de la película[F]

viewfinder
viseur[M]
Bildsucher[M]
visor[M]

focal plane shutter
rideau[M] d'obturateur[M]
Schlitzverschluß[M]
obturador[M] de cortina[F]

take-up spool
bobine[F] réceptrice
Filmaufrollspule[F]
carrete[M] de rebobinado[M]

neckstrap eyelet
œillet[M] d'attache[F]
Öse[F] für Schulterriemen[M]
ojete[M] para la correa[F] del cuello[M]

film sprocket
tambour[M] d'entraînement[M]
Transporträdchen[N]
piñón[M] de la rueda[F] de la película[F]

pressure plate
presseur[M]
Andruckplatte[F]
lámina[F] de presión[F]

film cassette chamber
logement[M] de la bobine[F]
Patronenkammer[F]
cámara[F] para el cartucho[M] de la película[F]

film guide roller
cylindre[M] guide[M]-film[M]
Transportwalze[F]
rodillo[M] guía[F] de la película[F]

film guide rail
rail[M] guide[M]-film[M]
Transportschiene[F]
carril[M] guía[F] de la película[F]

film leader indicator
témoin[M] de l'amorce[F] du film[M]
Markierung[F] für Filmanfang[M]
indicador[M] principal de la película[F]

## SINGLE-LENS REFLEX (SLR) CAMERA
## APPAREIL[M] À VISÉE[F] REFLEX MONO-OBJECTIF[M]
## EINÄUGIGE SPIEGELREFLEXKAMERA[F]
## CÁMARA[F] RÉFLEX DE UN OBJETIVO[M]

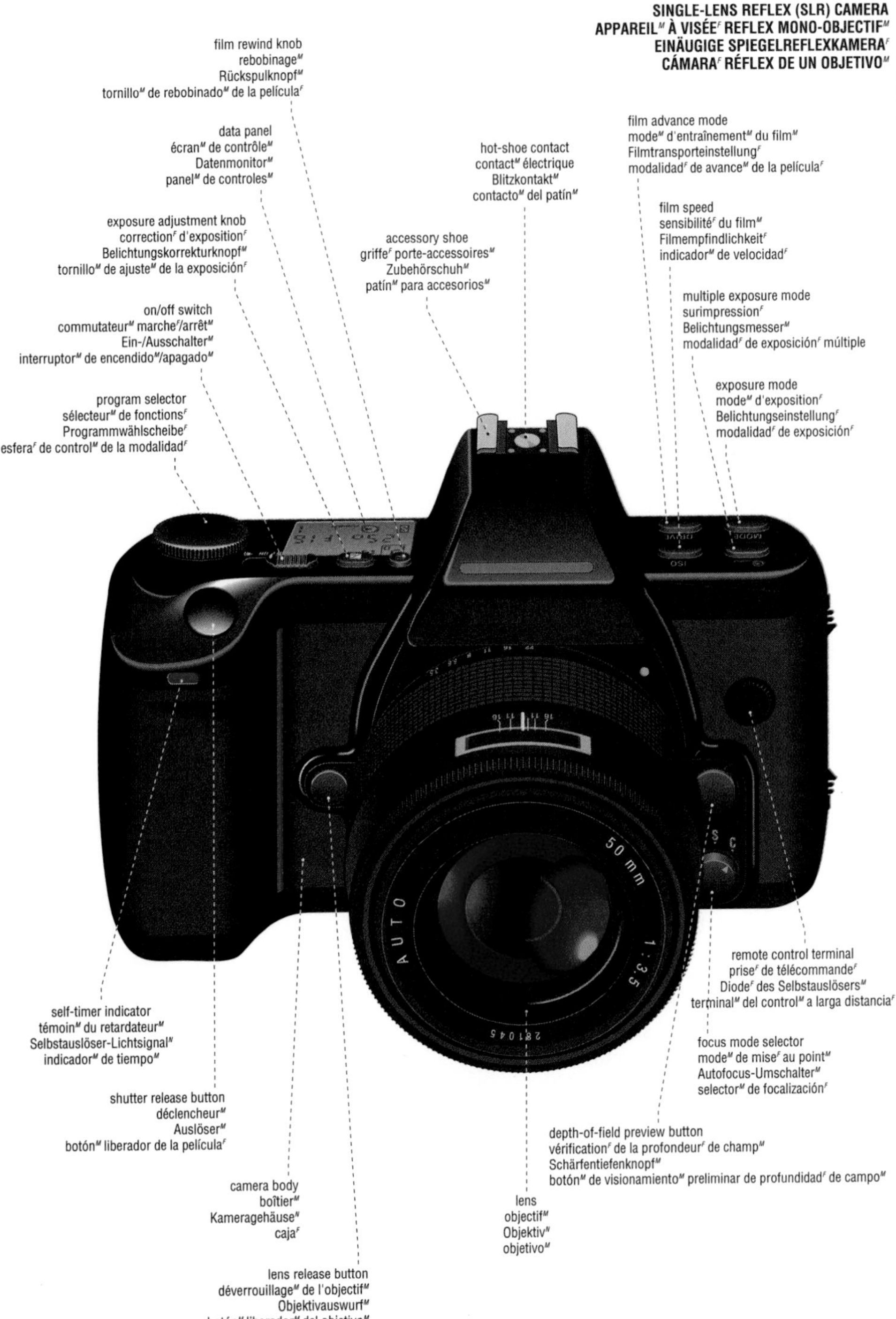

# PHOTOGRAPHY
# PHOTOGRAPHIE[F]
# FOTOGRAFIE[F]
# FOTOGRAFÍA[F]

## LENSES
## OBJECTIFS[M]
## OBJEKTIVE[N]
## OBJETIVOS[M]

**standard lens**
**objectif[M] normal**
**Standardobjektiv[N]**
**objetivo[M] normal**

lens
lentille[F]
Linse[F]
objetivo[M]

distance scale
échelle[F] des distances[F]
Entfernungsskala[F]
escala[F] de distancia[F]

focussing ring
bague[F] de mise[F] au point[M]
Blendenring[M]
anillo[M] de ajuste[M] del enfoque[M]

depth-of-field scale
échelle[F] de profondeur[F] de champ[M]
Schärfentiefenskala[F]
escala[F] de profundidad[F] de campo[M] de visión[F]

lens aperture scale
échelle[F] d'ouverture[F] de diaphragme[M]
Blendenskala[F]
escala[F] de abertura[F] del diafragma[M]

bayonet mount
monture[F] baïonnette[F]
Bayonettanschluß[M]
montura[F] de bayoneta[F]

wide-angle lens
objectif[M] grand-angulaire
Weitwinkelobjektiv[N]
gran angular[M]

zoom lens
objectif[M] zoom[M]
Zoomobjektiv[N]
zoom[M]

semi-fisheye lens
objectif[M] super-grand-angle[M]
Super-Weitwinkelobjektiv[N]
ojo[M] de pez[M]

telephoto lens
téléobjectif[M]
Teleobjektiv[N]
teleobjetivo[M]

fisheye lens
hypergone[M]
Fischaugenobjektiv[N]
lente[M] de 180 grados[M]

## LENS ACCESSORIES
## ACCESSOIRES[M] DE L'OBJECTIF[M]
## OBJEKTIVZUBEHÖR[N]
## OBJETIVOS[M] Y ACCESORIOS[M]

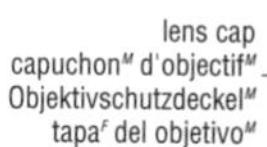

lens cap
capuchon[M] d'objectif[M]
Objektivschutzdeckel[M]
tapa[F] del objetivo[M]

lens hood
parasoleil[M]
Gegenlichtblende[F]
capuchón[M]

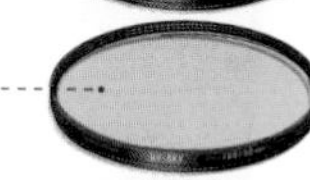

colour filter
filtre[M] de couleur[F]
Farbfilter[M]
filtro[M] de color[M]

close-up lens
lentille[F] de macrophotographie[F]
Nahlinse[F]
lente[M] de acercamiento[M]

polarizing filter
filtre[M] de polarisation[F]
Polarisationsfilter[M]
filtro[M] de polarización[F]

lens
objectif[M]
Objektiv[N]
objetivo[M] normal

tele-converter
multiplicateur[M] de focale[F]
Telekonverter[M]
teleconvertidor[M]

## PHOTOGRAPHIC ACCESSORIES
## ACCESSOIRES[M] PHOTOGRAPHIQUES
## FOTOGRAFISCHES ZUBEHÖR[N]
## ACCESORIOS[M] FOTOGRÁFICOS

**electronic flash**
**flash[M] électronique**
**Elektronenblitz[M]**
**flash[M] electrónico**

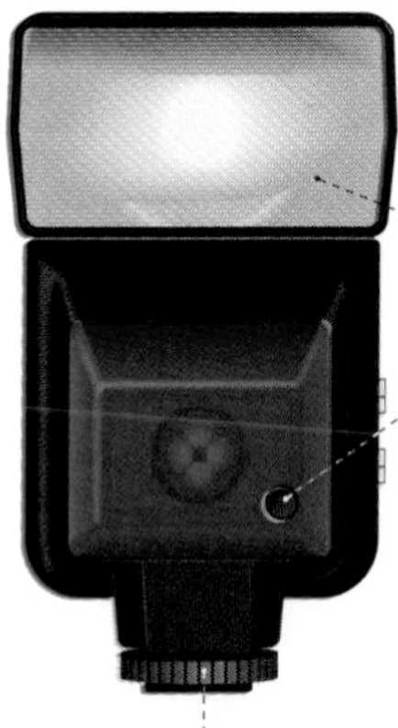


mounting foot
pied[M] de fixation[F]
Aufsteckschuh[M]
pie[M] de montura[F]

air bulb shutter release
déclencheur[M] pneumatique
pneumatischer Auslöser[M]
disparador[M] neumático

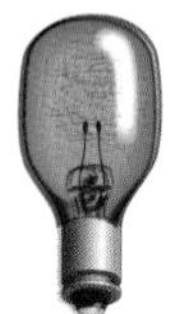

flash bulb
lampe[F]-éclair[M]
Blitzbirne[F]
bombilla[F] de flash[M]

flashcube
flash[M]-cube[M]
Blitzwürfel[M]
cubo[M] de flash[M]

battery
pile[F]
Batterie[F]
pila[F]

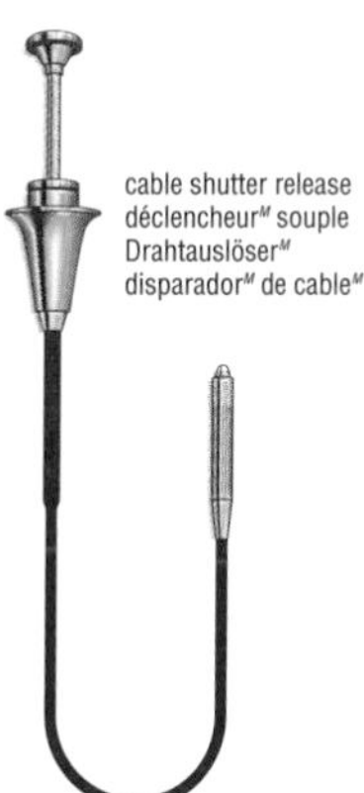

cable shutter release
déclencheur[M] souple
Drahtauslöser[M]
disparador[M] de cable[M]

## TRIPOD
## TRÉPIED[M]
## STATIV[N]
## TRÍPODE[M]

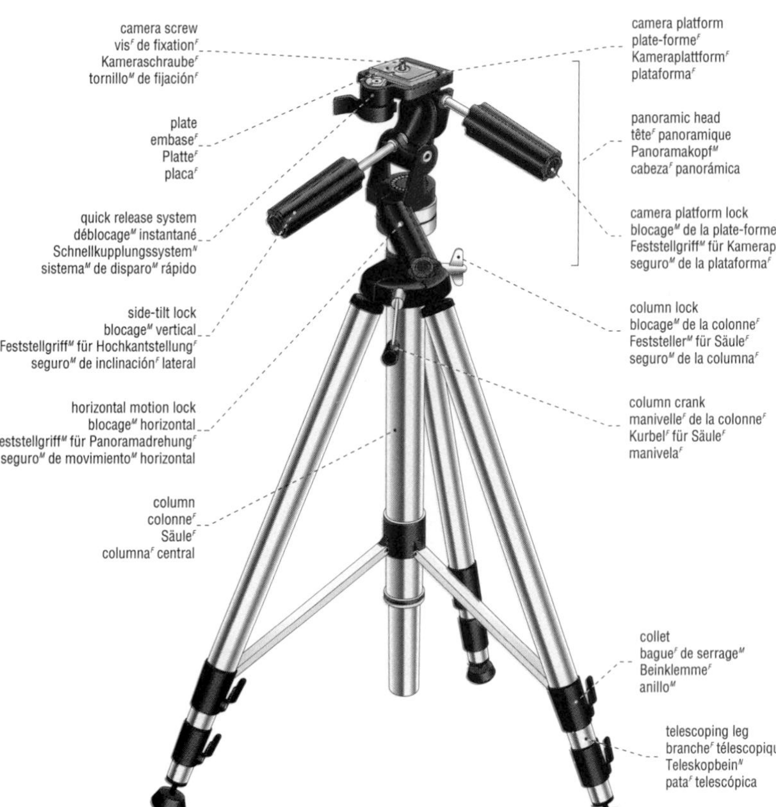

# PHOTOGRAPHY
# PHOTOGRAPHIE[F]
# FOTOGRAFIE[F]
# FOTOGRAFÍA[F]

## STILL CAMERAS
## APPAREILS[M] PHOTOGRAPHIQUES
## FOTOAPPARATE[M]
## CÁMARAS[M] FIJAS

rangefinder camera
appareil[M] à télémètre[M] couplé
Sucherkamera[F]
telémetro[M]

underwater camera
appareil[M] de plongée[F]
Unterwasserkamera[F]
cámara[F] submarina

Polaroid® Land camera
Polaroid®[M]
Sofortbildkamera[F]
cámara[F] Polaroid Land

single-lens reflex camera
appareil[M] à visée[F] reflex mono-objectif[M]
einäugige Spiegelreflexkamera[F]
cámara[F] reflex con objetivo[M] simple

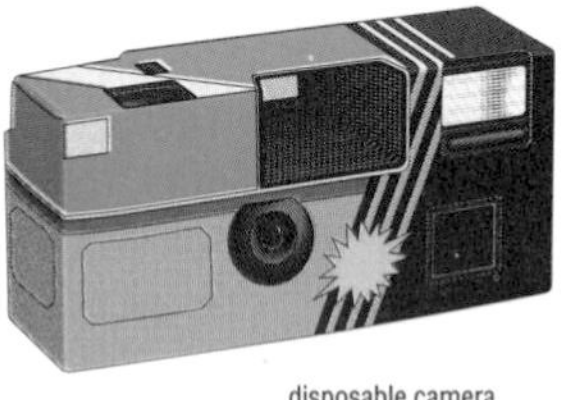

disposable camera
appareil[M] jetable
Einwegkamera[F]
cámara[F] desechable

twin-lens reflex camera
appareil[M] reflex à deux objectifs[M]
zweiäugige Spiegelreflexkamera[F]
cámara[F] tipo[M] réflex con dos objetivos[M]

view camera
chambre[F] photographique
Großformatkamera[F]
cámara[F] de enfoque[M]

## STILL CAMERAS
## APPAREILS^M PHOTOGRAPHIQUES
## FOTOAPPARATE^M
## DIFERENTES TIPOS^M DE CÁMARAS^F FOTOGRÁFICAS

pocket camera
appareil^M petit-format^M
Pocket-Instamatic Kamera^F
cámara^F de bolsillo^M

medium format SLR (6 x 6)
appareil^M reflex 6 X 6 mono-objectif^M
Mittelformatkamera^F SLR(6 x 6)
formato^M mediano SLR (6x6)

disc camera
appareil^M pour photodisque^M
Disc-Kamera^F
cámara^F de disco^M

stereoscopic camera
appareil^M stéréoscopique
Stereokamera^F
cámara^F estereofotogramétrica

still video camera
appareil^M de videophoto^F
Videokamera^F
cámara^F de video^M fijo

## FILMS
## PELLICULES^F
## FILME^M
## PELÍCULAS^F

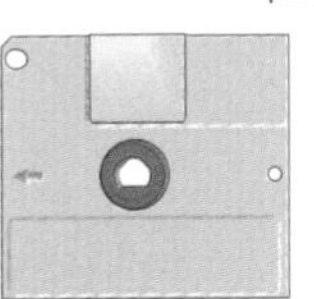

still video film disc
disque^M videophoto^F
Videofilmdiskette^F
película^F de disco^M para video^M fijo

film leader
amorce^F
Filmlasche^F
principio^M de la película^F

perforation
perforation^F
Perforierung^F
perforación^F

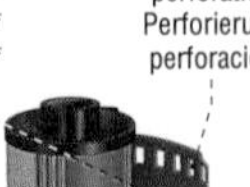

**cassette film**
**cartouche^F de pellicule^F**
**Patronenfilm^M**
**cartucho^M de la película^F**

film disc
film^M-disque^M
Filmdiskette^F
película^F de disco^M

cartridge film
cassette^F de pellicule^F
Kassettenfilm^M
cartucho^M de la película^F

sheet film
pellicule^F en feuille^F
Planfilm^M
hoja^F de la película^F

roll film
rouleau^M de pellicule^F
Rollfilm^M
rollo^M de la película^F

film pack
film^M-pack^M
Filmkassette^F
paquete^M de placas^F fotográficas

# PHOTOGRAPHY
# PHOTOGRAPHIE[F]
# FOTOGRAFIE[F]
# FOTOGRAFÍA[F]

## EXPOSURE METER
## POSEMÈTRE[M] PHOTO-ÉLECTRIQUE
## BELICHTUNGSMESSER[M]
## FOTÓMETRO[M]

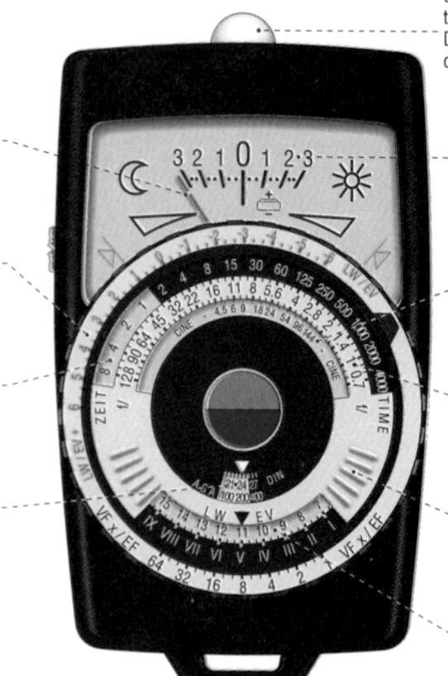


diffuser
tête[F] diffusante
Diffusionskalotte[F]
difusor[M]

indicator needle
aiguille[F]
Anzeigenadel[F]
aguja[F] indicadora

light-reading scale
échelle[F] de lecture[F] de la luminosité[F]
Lichtwertskala[F]
escala[F] de lectura[F]

exposure value
indice[F] d'exposition[F]
Belichtungswert[M]
índices[M] de exposición[F]

cine scale
cadence[F] images[F]/seconde[F]
Cine-Skala[F]
escala[F] de imágenes[F] por segundo[M]

exposure-time scale
échelle[F] des temps[M] d'exposition[F]
Belichtungszeitskala[F]
escala[F] de duración[F] de la exposición[F]

aperture scale
échelle[F] d'ouverture[F]
Blendenskala[F]
escala[F] de abertura[F]

film speed
sensibilité[F] du film[M]
Filmempfindlichkeit[F]
velocidad[F] de la película[F]

calculator dial
disque[M] de réglage[M]
Rechenscheibe[F]
cuadrante[M] calculador

transfer scale
report[M] de lecture[F]
Umrechnungsskala[F]
escala[F] de transferencia[F]

## SPOTMETER
## POSEMÈTRE[M] À VISÉE[F] REFLEX
## SPOTMETER[M]
## FOTÓMETRO[M] ELECTRÓNICO

average key
réglage[M] sur demi-teinte[F]
Taste[F] für Mittelwerte[M]
botón[M] de luminosidad[F] media

highlight key
réglage[M] sur haute lumière[F]
Hi.-Taste[F]
botón[M] de fuerte luminosidad[F]

shadow key
réglage[M] sur ombre[F]
Shadow-Taste[F]
botón[M] de sombra[F]

eyepiece
oculaire[M]
Okular[N]
ocular[M]

lock switch
fixe-lecture[M]
Ein-/Ausschalter[M]
seguro[M]

data display
écran[M] d'affichage[M]
Display[N]
visualización[F] de la información[F]

lens
objectif[M]
Objektiv[N]
objetivo[M]

memory cancel
effacement[M] de mémoire[F]
Speicherlöschtaste[F]
botón[M] para cancelar la memoria[F]

shutter speed setting
réglage[M] de la vitesse[F] d'obturation[F]
Tasten[F] für Erhöhen[N]/Absenken[N]
ajuste[M] de la velocidad[F] del obturador[M]

measuring button
bouton[M] de mise[F] en circuit[M]
Meßtaste[F]
botón[M] de medición[F]

aperture/exposure value display
affichage[M] ouverture[F]/temps[M] d'exposition[F]
Anzeige[F] für Blende[F]/Belichtungswert[M]
visualización[F] de valores[M] de abertura[F] y de exposición[F]

film speed
sensibilité[F] du film[M]
Filmempfindlichkeit[F]
sensibilidad[F] de la película[F]

memory recall key
rappel[M] de mémoire[F]
Rückruftaste[F]
botón[M] de llamado[M] de memoria[F]

data display illumination button
éclairage[M] de l'écran[M] d'affichage[M]
Displaybeleuchtungstaste[F]
botón[M] de iluminación[F] de la pantalla[F]

memory key
commande[F] de mémoire[F]
Speichertaste[F]
botón[M] de memoria[F]

## SLIDE PROJECTOR
## PROJECTEUR[M] DE DIAPOSITIVES[F]
## DIAPROJEKTOR[M]
## PROYECTOR[M] DE DIAPOSITIVAS[F]

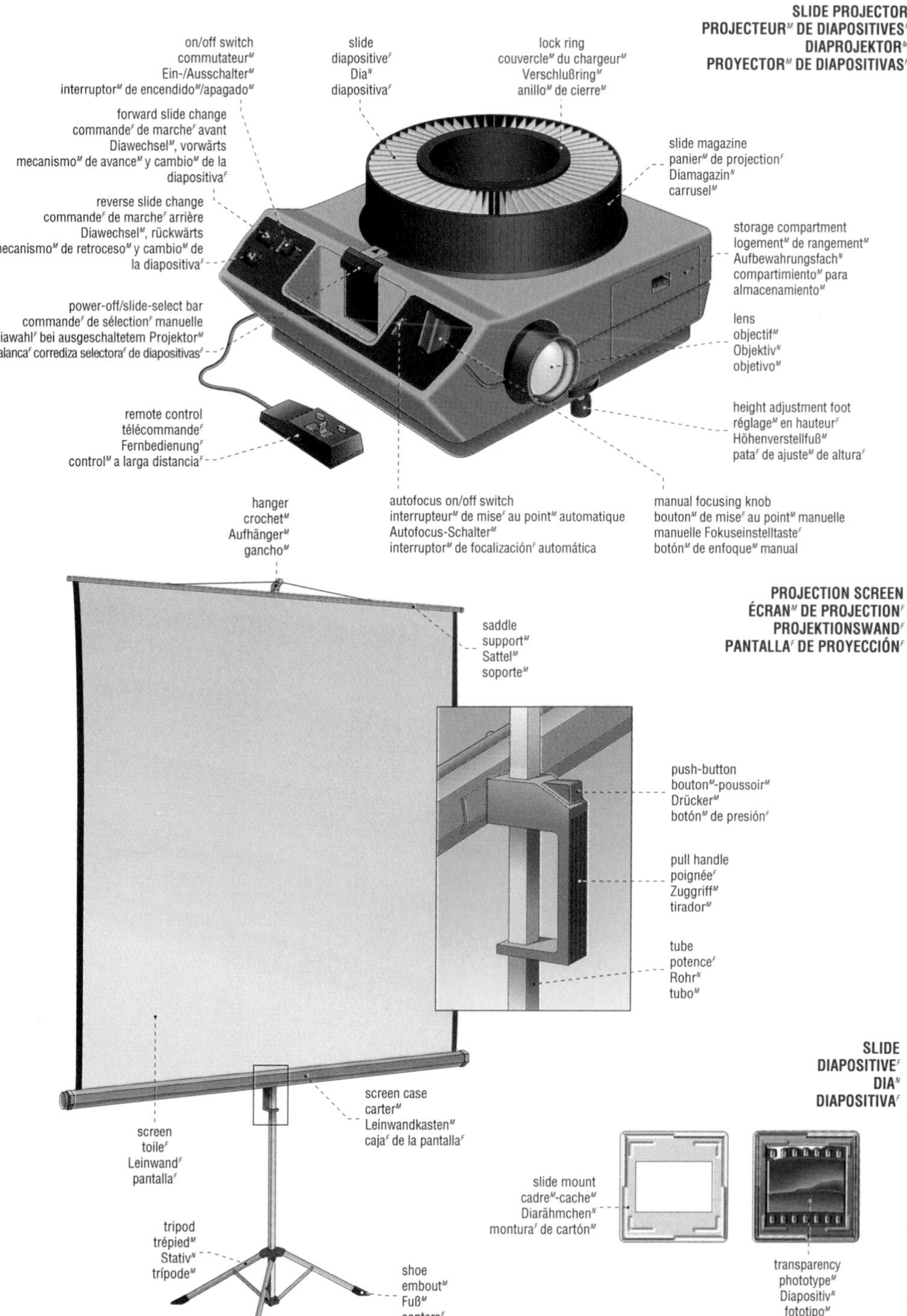


## PROJECTION SCREEN
## ÉCRAN[M] DE PROJECTION[F]
## PROJEKTIONSWAND[F]
## PANTALLA[F] DE PROYECCIÓN[F]

## SLIDE
## DIAPOSITIVE[F]
## DIA[N]
## DIAPOSITIVA[F]

# PHOTOGRAPHY
# PHOTOGRAPHIE[F]
# FOTOGRAFIE[F]
# FOTOGRAFÍA[F]

## NEGATIVE CARRIER
## PORTE-NÉGATIF[M]
## NEGATIVHALTER[M]
## PORTANEGATIVOS[M]

window
fenêtre[F]
Sichtfenster[N]
ventana[F]
negative
négatif[M]
Negativ[N]
negativo[M]

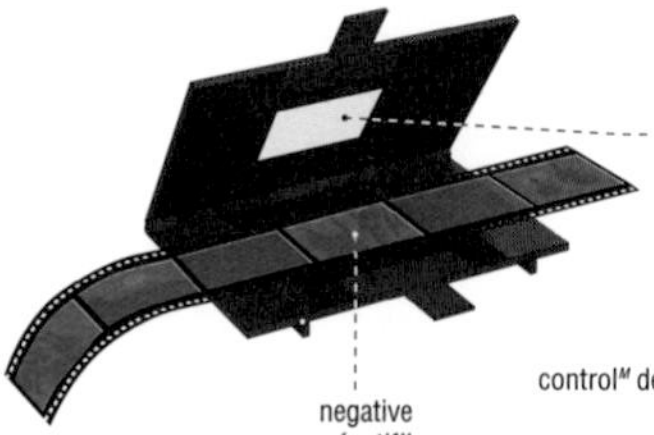

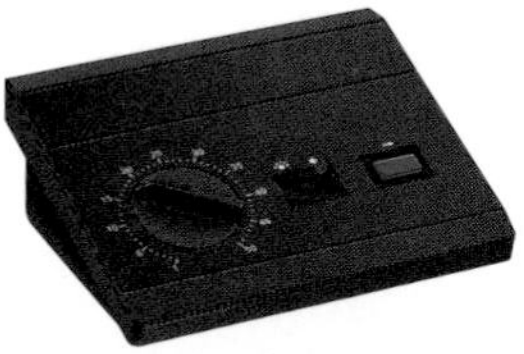

enlarger timer
compte-pose[M]
Belichtungs-Schaltuhr[F]
reloj[M] de la ampliadora[F]

## ENLARGER
## AGRANDISSEUR[M]
## VERGRÖSSERER[M]
## AMPLIADORA[F]

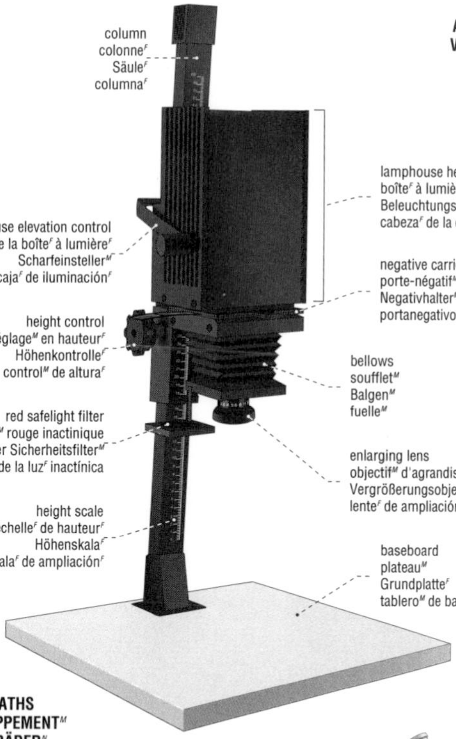

column
colonne[F]
Säule[F]
columna[F]
lamphouse elevation control
ouverture[F] de la boîte[F] à lumière[F]
Scharfeinsteller[M]
control[M] de elevación[F] de la caja[F] de iluminación[F]
height control
réglage[M] en hauteur[F]
Höhenkontrolle[F]
control[M] de altura[F]
red safelight filter
filtre[M] rouge inactinique
roter Sicherheitsfilter[M]
filtro[M] rojo[M] de la luz[F] inactínica
height scale
échelle[F] de hauteur[F]
Höhenskala[F]
escala[F] de ampliación[F]
lamphouse head
boîte[F] à lumière[F]
Beleuchtungskopf[M]
cabeza[F] de la caja[F] de iluminación[F]
negative carrier
porte-négatif[M]
Negativhalter[M]
portanegativos[M]
bellows
soufflet[M]
Balgen[M]
fuelle[M]
enlarging lens
objectif[M] d'agrandissement[M]
Vergrößerungsobjektiv[N]
lente[F] de ampliación[F]
baseboard
plateau[M]
Grundplatte[F]
tablero[M] de base[F]

## DEVELOPING BATHS
## BAINS[M] DE DÉVELOPPEMENT[M]
## ENTWICKLUNGSBÄDER[N]
## BAÑOS[M] DE REVELADO[M]

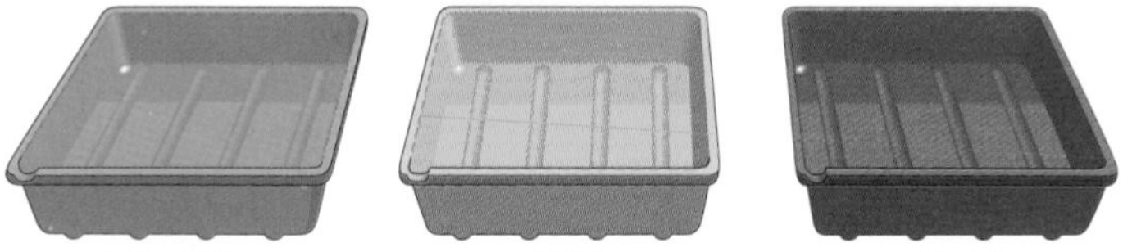

developer bath
bain[M] de révélateur[M]
Entwickler[M]
baño[M] de revelado[M]

stop bath
bain[M] d'arrêt[M]
Stoppbad[N]
baño[M] de pare[M]

fixing bath
bain[M] de fixation[F]
Fixierbad[N]
baño[M] de fijación[F]

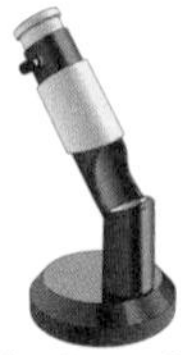

focusing magnifier
loupe[F] de mise[F] au point[M]
Scharfsteller[M]
lupa[F] de focalización[F]

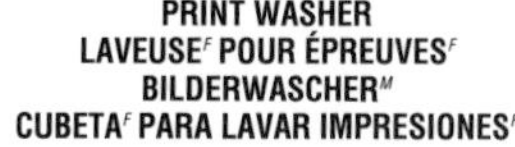

## PRINT WASHER
## LAVEUSE[F] POUR ÉPREUVES[F]
## BILDERWASCHER[M]
## CUBETA[F] PARA LAVAR IMPRESIONES[F]

tank
réservoir[M]
Wässerungswanne[F]
tanque[M]
cradle
cadre[M] porte-épreuves[M]
Fächerkorb[M]
soporte[M]
tap connector
raccord[M]
Adapter[M]
adaptador[M]
overflow tube
trop-plein[M]
Überlaufstutzen[M]
tubo[M] de drenaje[M]
inlet hose
flexible[M] de branchement[M]
Schlauch[M] für Wasserzufluß[M]
manguera[F] de llenado[M]
outlet hose
renvoi[M] d'eau[F]
Schlauch[M] für Wasserablauf[M]
manguera[F] de vaciado[M]

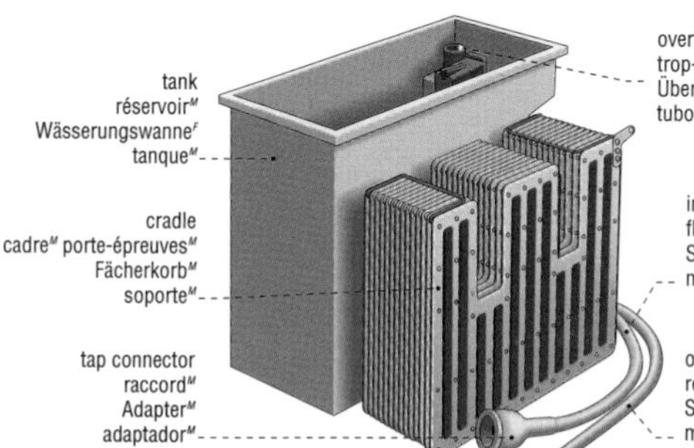

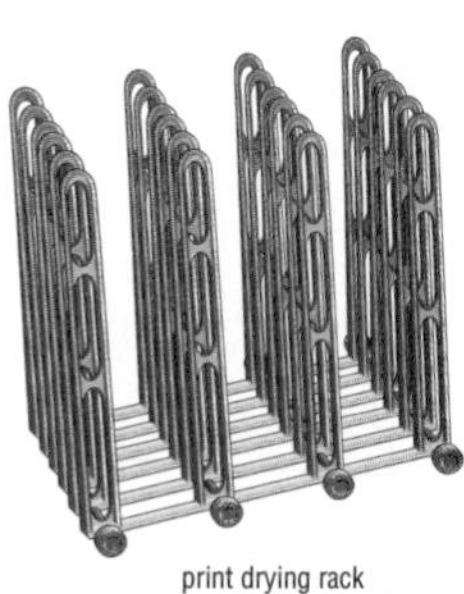

print drying rack
séchoir[M] d'épreuves[F]
Trockenständer[M]
secadora[F] de pruebas[F]

# STEREO SOUND SYSTEM
# CHAÎNE[F] STÉRÉO
# TONWIEDERGABESYSTEM[N]
# EQUIPO[M] ESTEREOFÓNICO

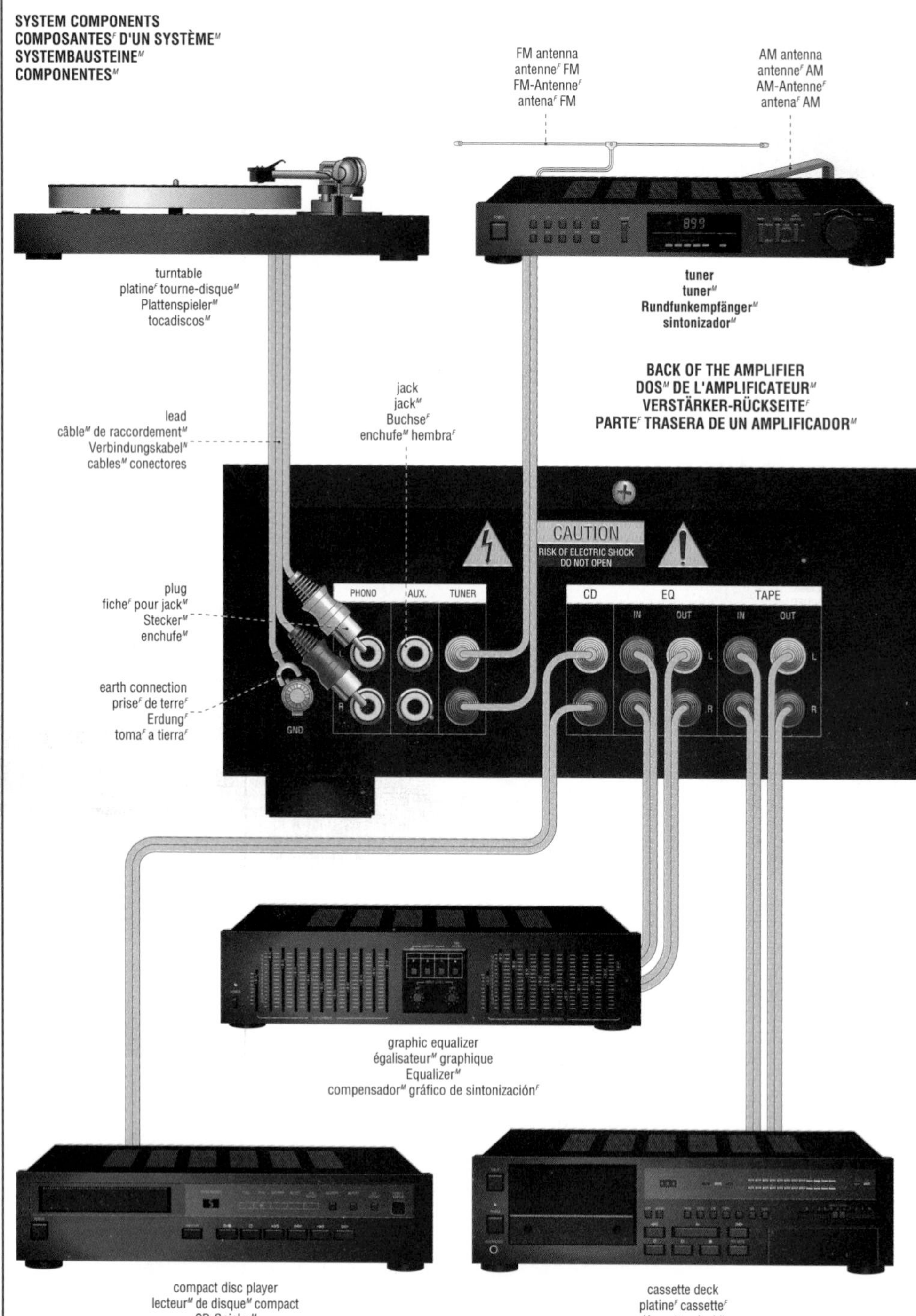

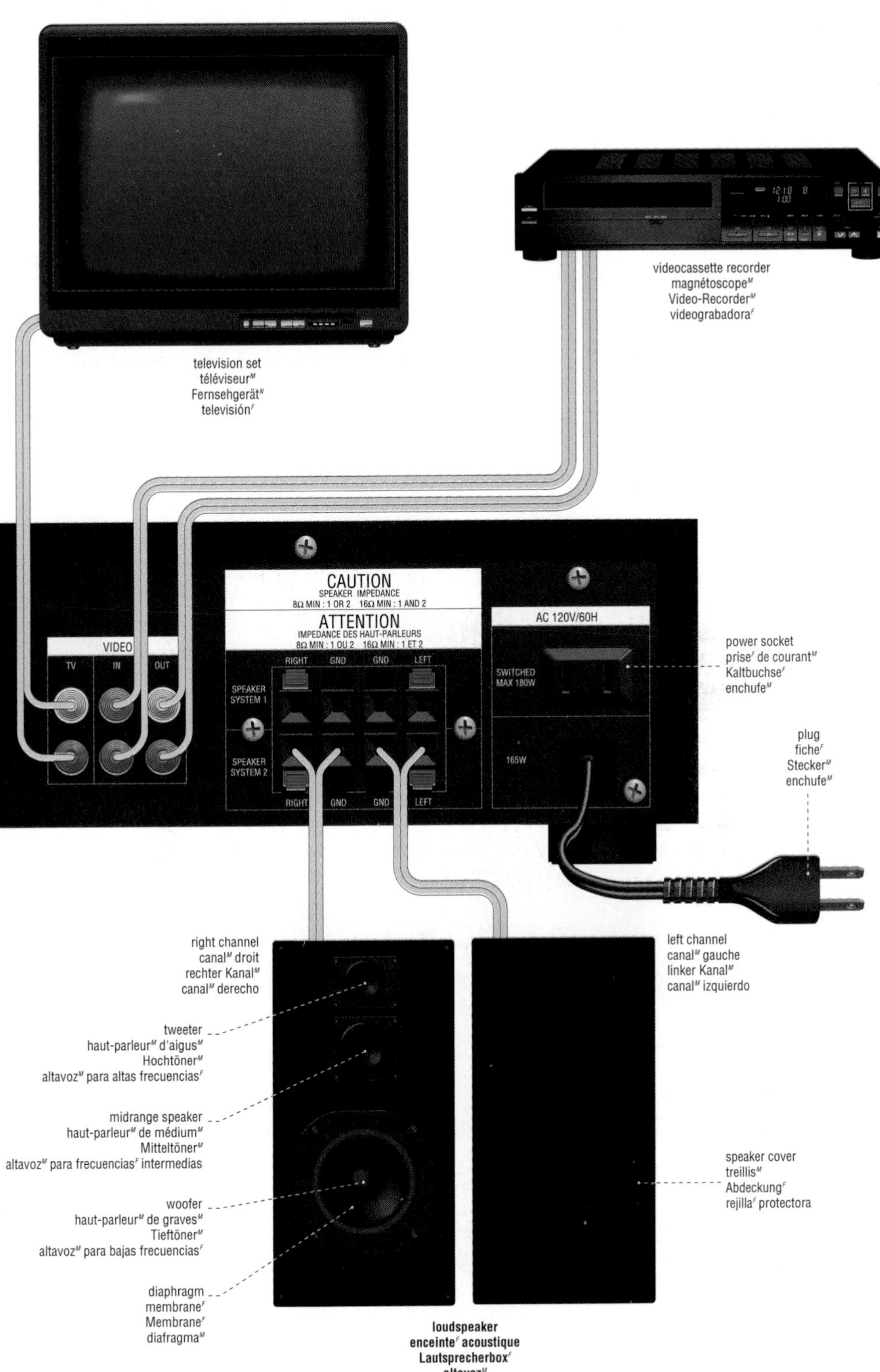


**loudspeaker**
**enceinte[F] acoustique**
**Lautsprecherbox[F]**
**altavoz[M]**

# STEREO SOUND SYSTEM
# CHAÎNE[F] STÉRÉO
# TONWIEDERGABESYSTEM[N]
# EQUIPO[M] ESTEREOFÓNICO

## TUNER
## TUNER[M]
## RUNDFUNKEMPFÄNGER[M]
## SINTONIZADOR[M]

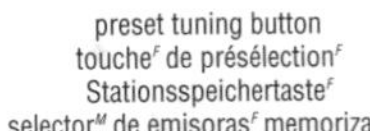

preset tuning button
touche[F] de présélection[F]
Stationsspeichertaste[F]
selector[M] de emisoras[F] memorizadas

memory button
touche[F] mémoire[F]
Speichertaste[F]
botón[M] de memoria[F]

mode selector
commutateur[M] mono[F]/stéréo[F]
Mono-Stereo-Taste[F]
selector[M] mono/estéreo

active tracking
balayage[M] automatique des stations[F]
automatischer Sendersuchlauf[M]
fonolocalización[F] activa

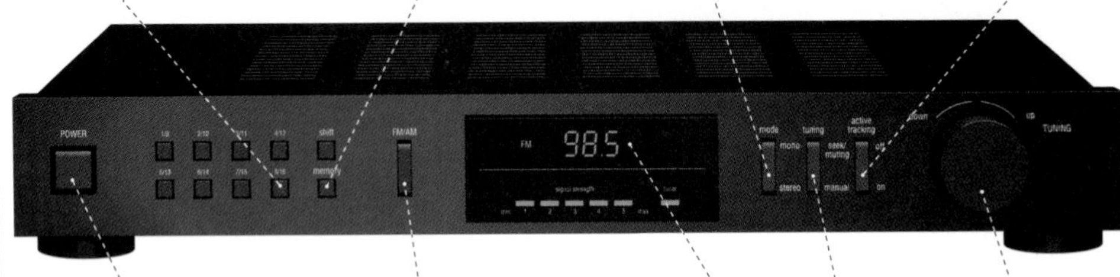


power button
interrupteur[M] d'alimentation[F]
Netzschalter[M]
botón[M] de encendido[M]

band selector
touche[F] de modulation[F]
Wellenbereichseinstellung[F]
selector[M] de banda[F]

digital frequency display
affichage[M] numérique des stations[F]
digitale Frequenzanzeige[F]
indicador[M] digital de frecuencia[F]

tuning control
sélecteur[M] de stations[F]
Sendereinstellung[F]
control[M] del sintetizador[M]

tuning mode
mode[M] de sélection[F] des stations[F]
Modus-Taste[F]
modalidad[F] sintetizador[M]

## AMPLIFIER
## AMPLIFICATEUR[M]
## VERSTÄRKER[M]
## AMPLIFICADOR[M]

power button
interrupteur[M] d'alimentation[F]
Netzschalter[M]
botón[M] de encendido[M]

speaker selector
sélecteur[M] d'enceintes[F]
Lautsprecherschalter[M]
selector[M] de altavoz[M]

balance control
équilibrage[M] des haut-parleurs[M]
Balanceregler[M]
control[M] de balance[M]

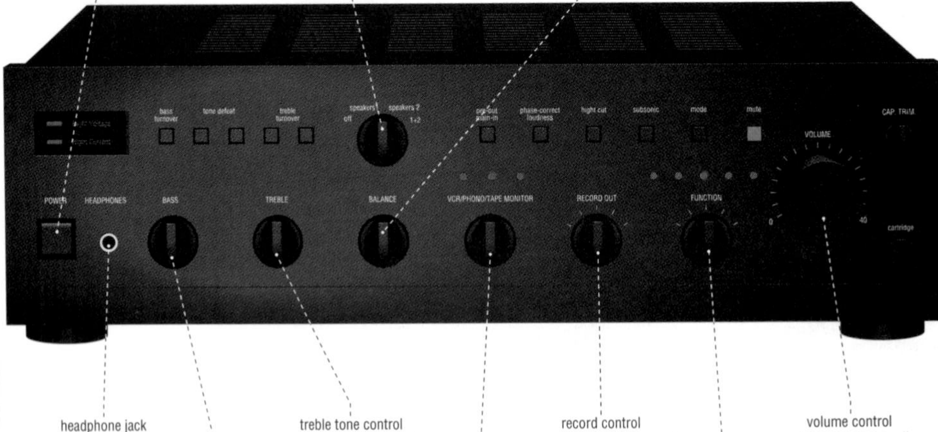


headphone jack
prise[F] casque[M]
Kopfhörerbuchse[F]
entrada[F] para audífonos[M]

treble tone control
contrôle[M] de tonalité[F] des aigus[M]
Höhenregler[M]
control[M] de agudos[M]

record control
contrôle[M] d'enregistrement[M]
Aufnahmeregler[M]
control[M] de grabación[F]

volume control
réglage[M] du volume[M]
Lautstärkeregler[M]
control[M] del volumen[M]

bass tone control
contrôle[M] de tonalité[F] des graves[M]
Baßregler[M]
control[M] de graves[M]

input selector
commutateur[M] d'entrée[F]
Eingangsschalter[M]
selector[M] de entrada[F]

function selector
commutateur[M] de fonctions[F]
Funktionsschalter[M]
selector[M] de función[F]

## CASSETTE
## CASSETTE[F]
## KASSETTE[F]
## CASETE[M]

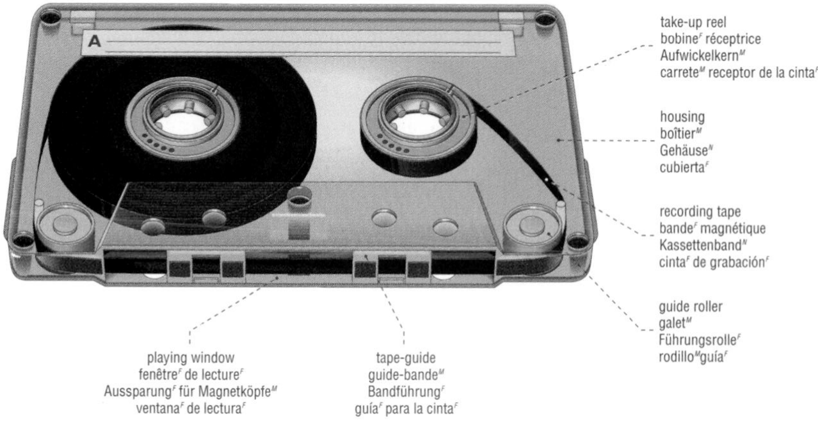

## CASSETTE TAPE DECK
## PLATINE[F] CASSETTE[F]
## KASSETTENDECK[N]
## GRABADORA[F] Y TOCACINTAS[M]

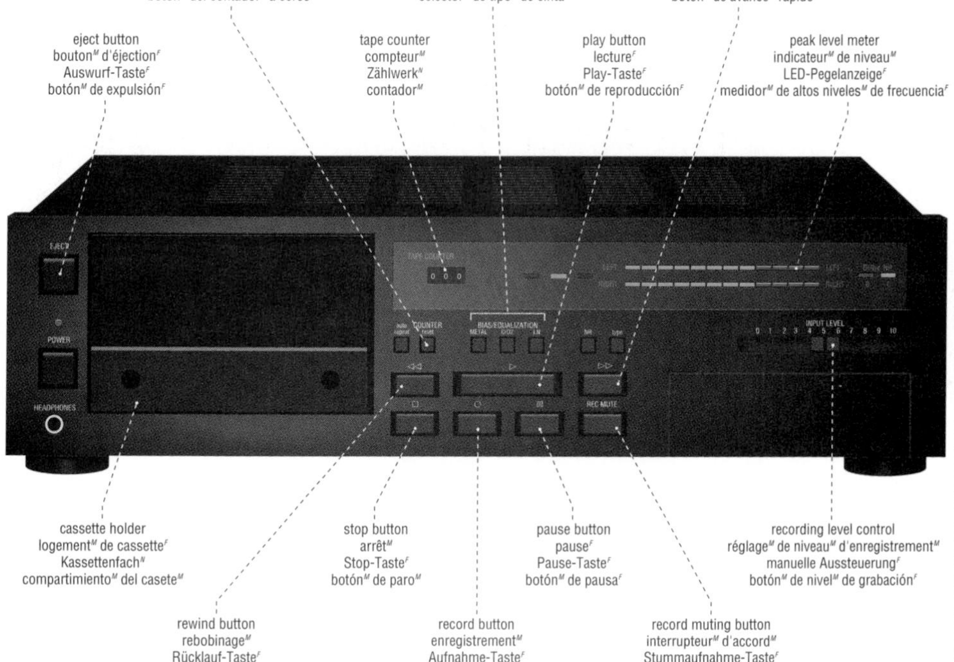

# STEREO SOUND SYSTEM
# CHAÎNE[F] STÉRÉO
# TONWIEDERGABESYSTEM[N]
# EQUIPO[M] ESTEREOFÓNICO

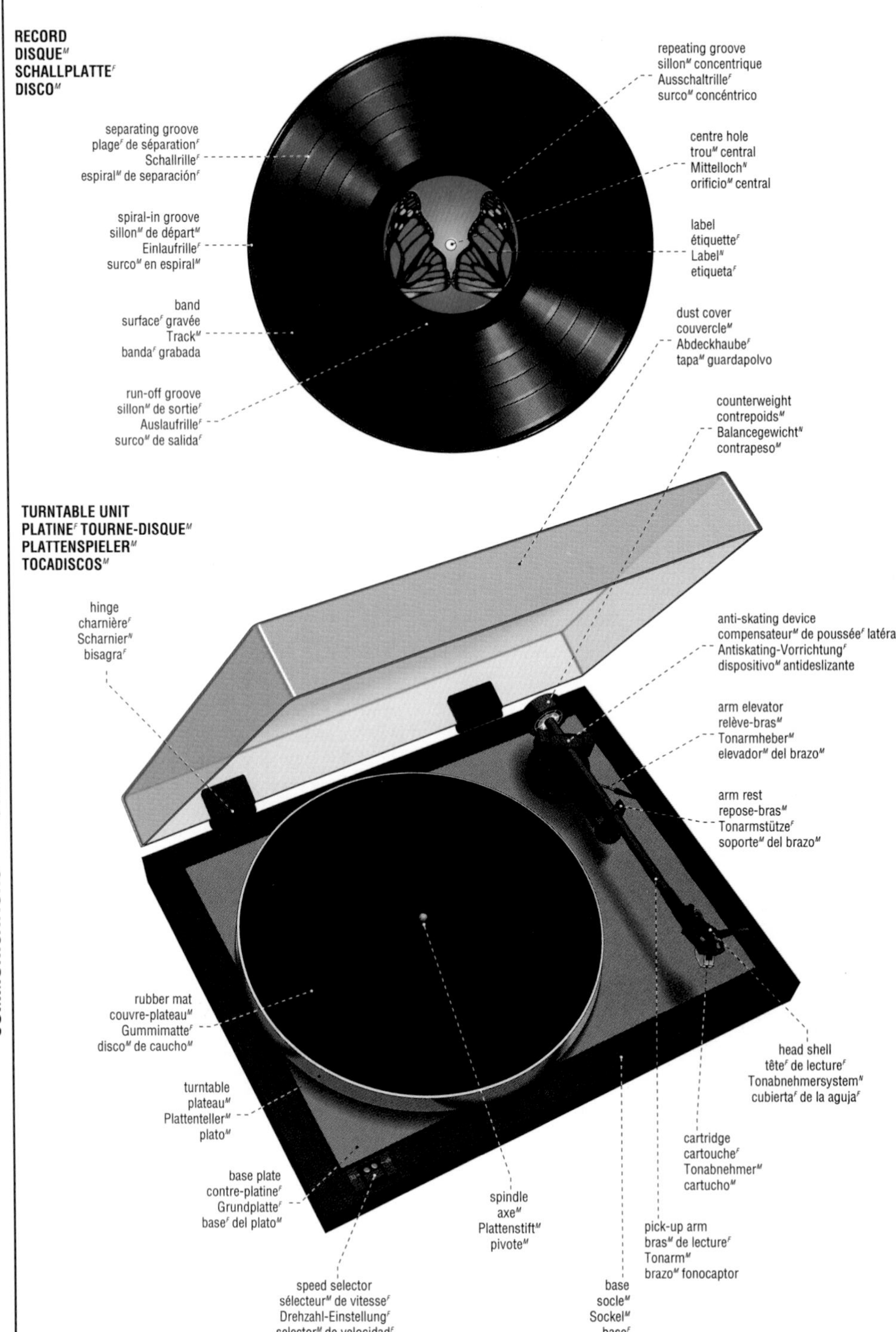

**COMPACT DISC**
**DISQUE[M] COMPACT**
**COMPACT DISC[F]**
**DISCO[M] COMPACTO**

**COMPACT DISC PLAYER**
**LECTEUR[M] DE DISQUE[M] COMPACT**
**CD-SPIELER[M]**
**LECTOR[M] DE DISCO[M] COMPACTO**

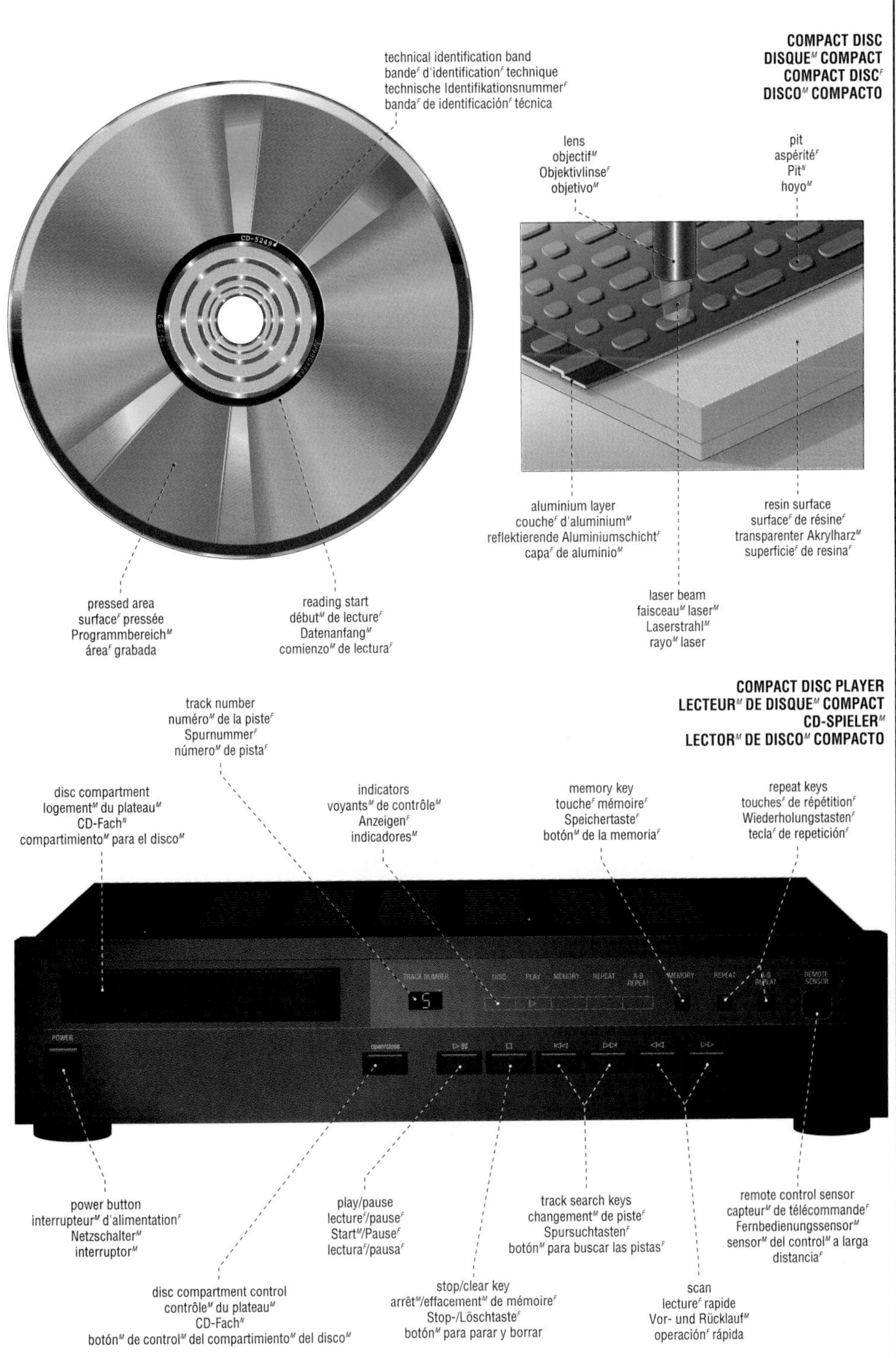

## DYNAMIC MICROPHONE
## MICROPHONE^M DYNAMIQUE
## ELEKTRODYNAMISCHES MIKROFON^N
## MICRÓFONO^M ELECTRODINÁMICO

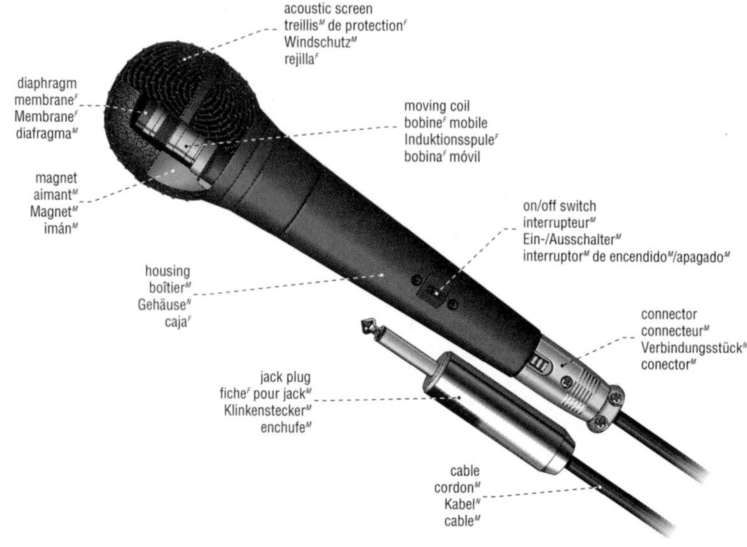


## HEADPHONES
## CASQUE^M D'ÉCOUTE^F
## KOPFHÖRER^M
## AURICULARES^M

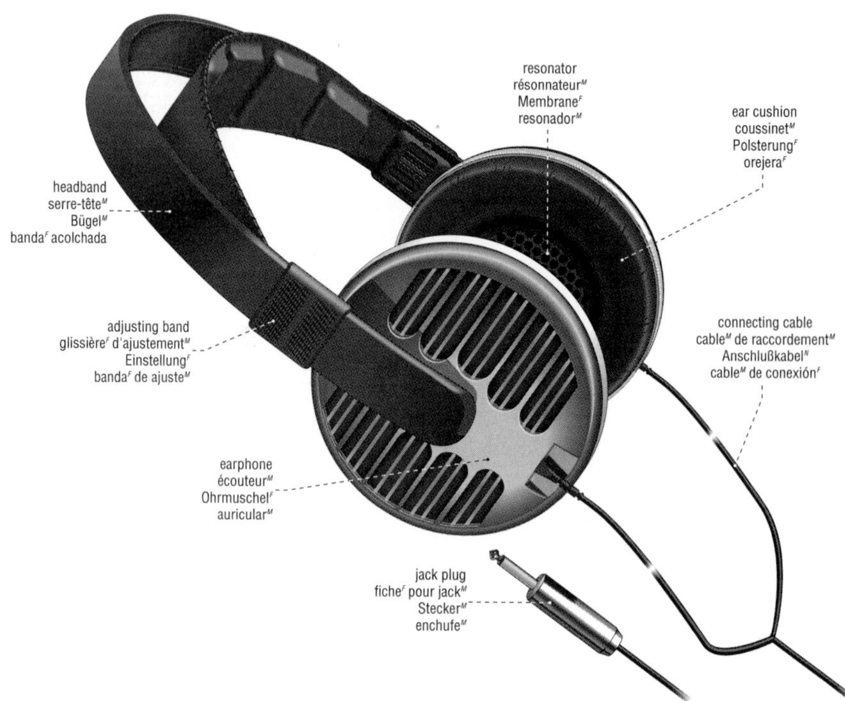

# RADIO: STUDIO AND CONTROL ROOM
# RADIO[F]: STUDIO[M] ET RÉGIE[F]
# RUNDFUNK[M]: SPRECHERRAUM[M] UND REGIERAUM[M]
# ESTUDIO[M] DE RADIO[M] Y SALA[F] DE CONTROL[M]

studio
studio[M]
Sprecherraum[M]
estudio[M]

microphone
microphone[M]
Mikrofon[N]
micrófono[M]

announcer console
consolette[F] de l'annonceur[M]
Sprecherpult[N]
torre[F] del locutor[M]

on-air warning light
voyant[M] de mise[F] en ondes[F]
Aufnahmelicht[N]
luz[F] de advertencia[F] de emisión[F]

tone leader generator
générateur[M] de tonalités[F] d'amorces[F]
Pegeltongenerator[M]
generador[M] principal de tono[M]

clock
horloge[F]
Uhr[F]
reloj[M]

VU meters
vumètres[M]
V.U.-Meter[N]
unidad[F] de medición[F] de volumen[M]

monitor speaker
haut-parleur[M] de contrôle[M]
Abhörlautsprecher[M]
monitor[M] de sonido[M]

cartridge tape recorder
magnétophone[M] à cartouches[F]
Magnetbandmaschine[F]
cartucho[M] de la cinta[F] grabadora[F]

digital audio tape recorder
magnétophone[M] à cassette[F] numérique
digitales Tonbandgerät[N]
cinta[F] digital grabadora[F]

compact disc player
lecteur[M] de disque[M] compact
CD-Spieler[M]
lector[M] de disco[M] compacto

cassette deck
platine[F] cassette[F]
Kassettendeck[N]
grabadora[F] y tocacintas[M]

stop watch
chronomètre[M]
Aufnahmezeitanzeige[F]
cronómetro[M]

producer console
consolette[F] du réalisateur[M]
Regiepult[N]
torre[F] del productor[M]

jack field
baie[F] de jacks[M]
Anschlußtafel[F]
entrada[F] de campo[M]

sound console
pupitre[M] de son[M]
Mischpult[N]
consola[F] de sonido[M]

bargraph type peak meter
crêtemètre[M] graphique
digitale Pegelanzeige[F]
gráfico[M] de lineas[F]

control room
régie[F]
Regieraum[M]
sala[F] de control[M]

turntable
platine[F] tourne-disque[M]
Plattenspieler[M]
tocadiscos[M]

# PORTABLE SOUND SYSTEMS
# APPAREILS[M] DE SON[M] PORTATIFS
# TRAGBARE TONWIEDERGABESYSTEME[N]
# SISTEMAS[M] DE SONIDO[M] PORTÁTILES

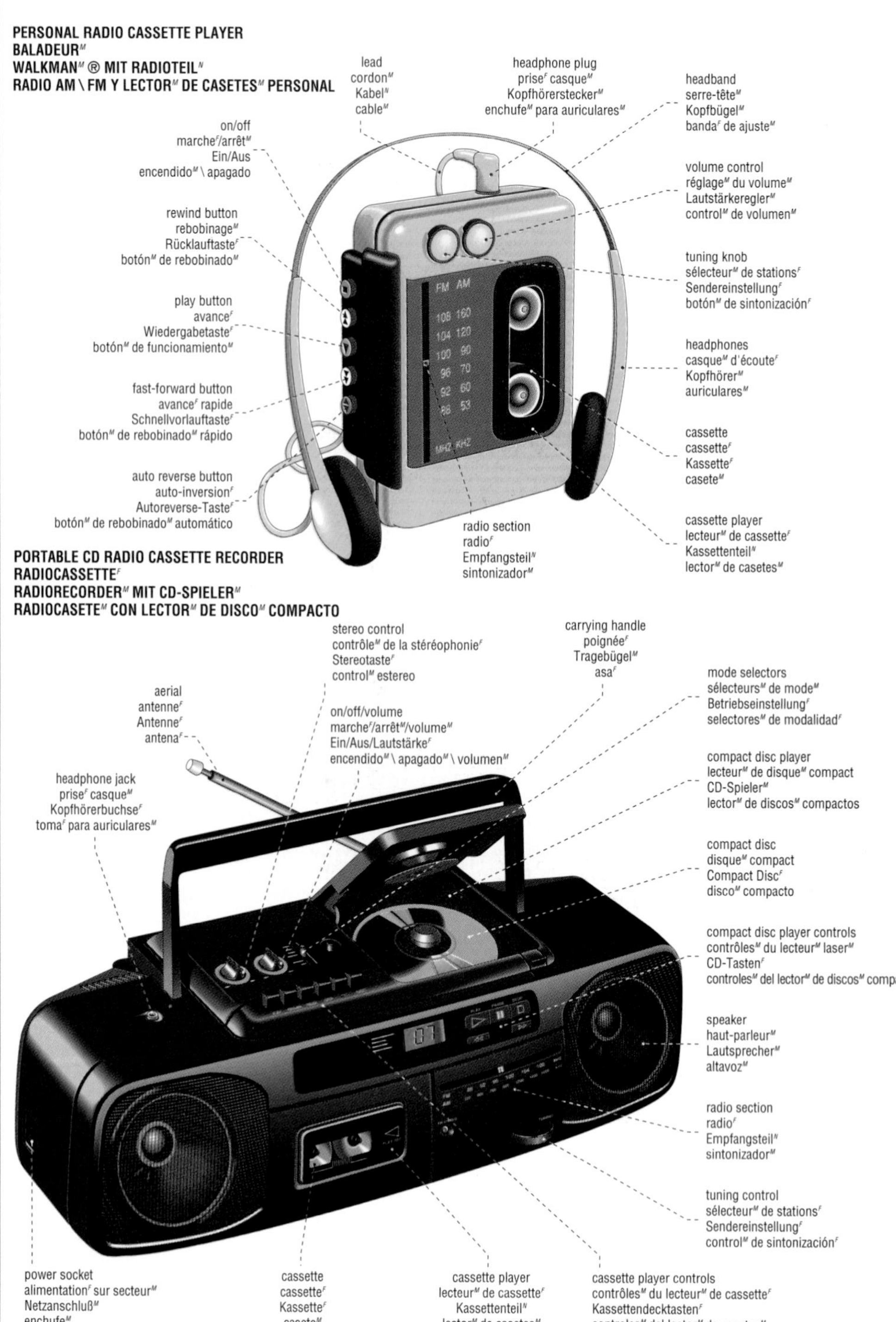

# VIDEO CAMERA
# CAMÉRA[M] VIDÉO
# VIDEOKAMERA[F]
# CÁMARA[F] DE VÍDEO[M]

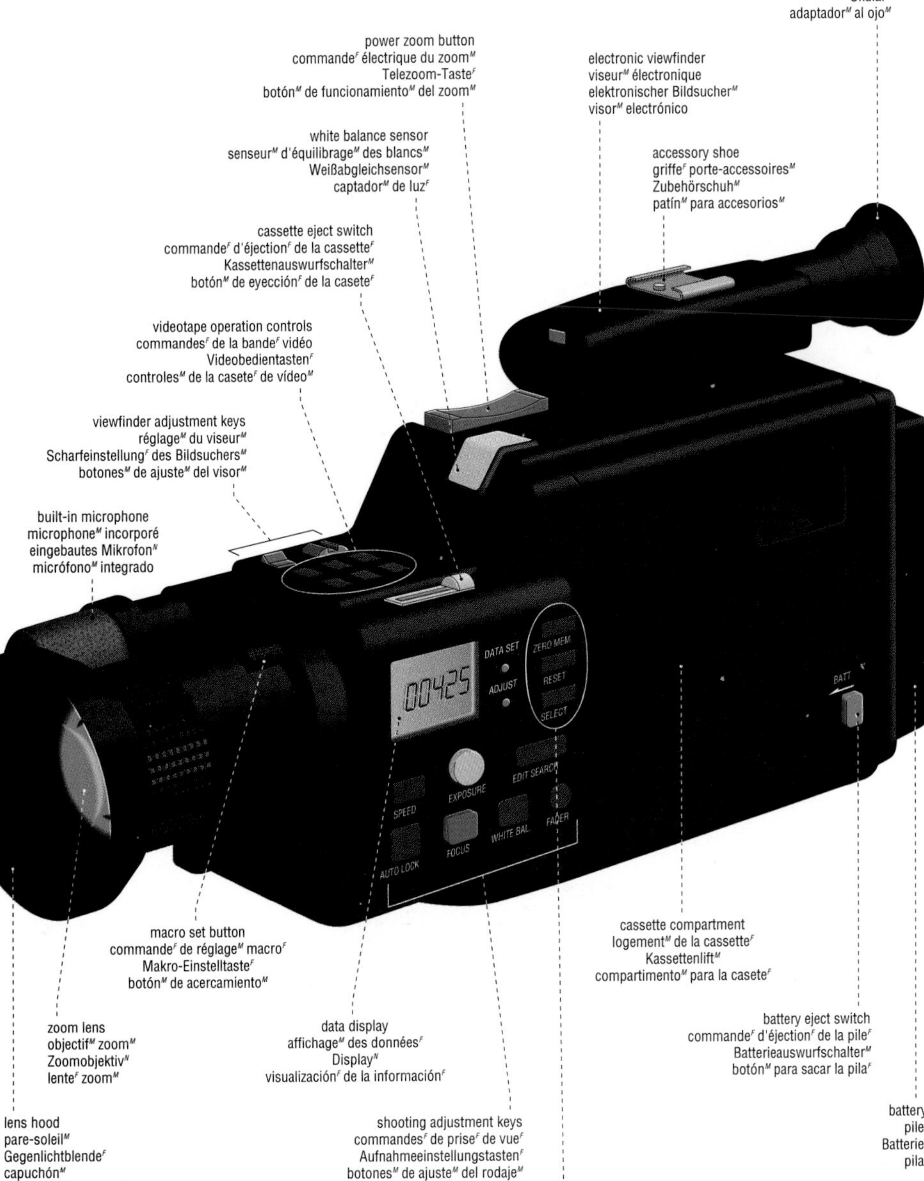

# TELEVISION
# TÉLÉVISION[F]
# FERNSEHEN[N]
# TELEVISIÓN[F]

## TELEVISION SET
## TÉLÉVISEUR[M]
## FERNSEHAPPARAT[M]
## TELEVISOR[M]

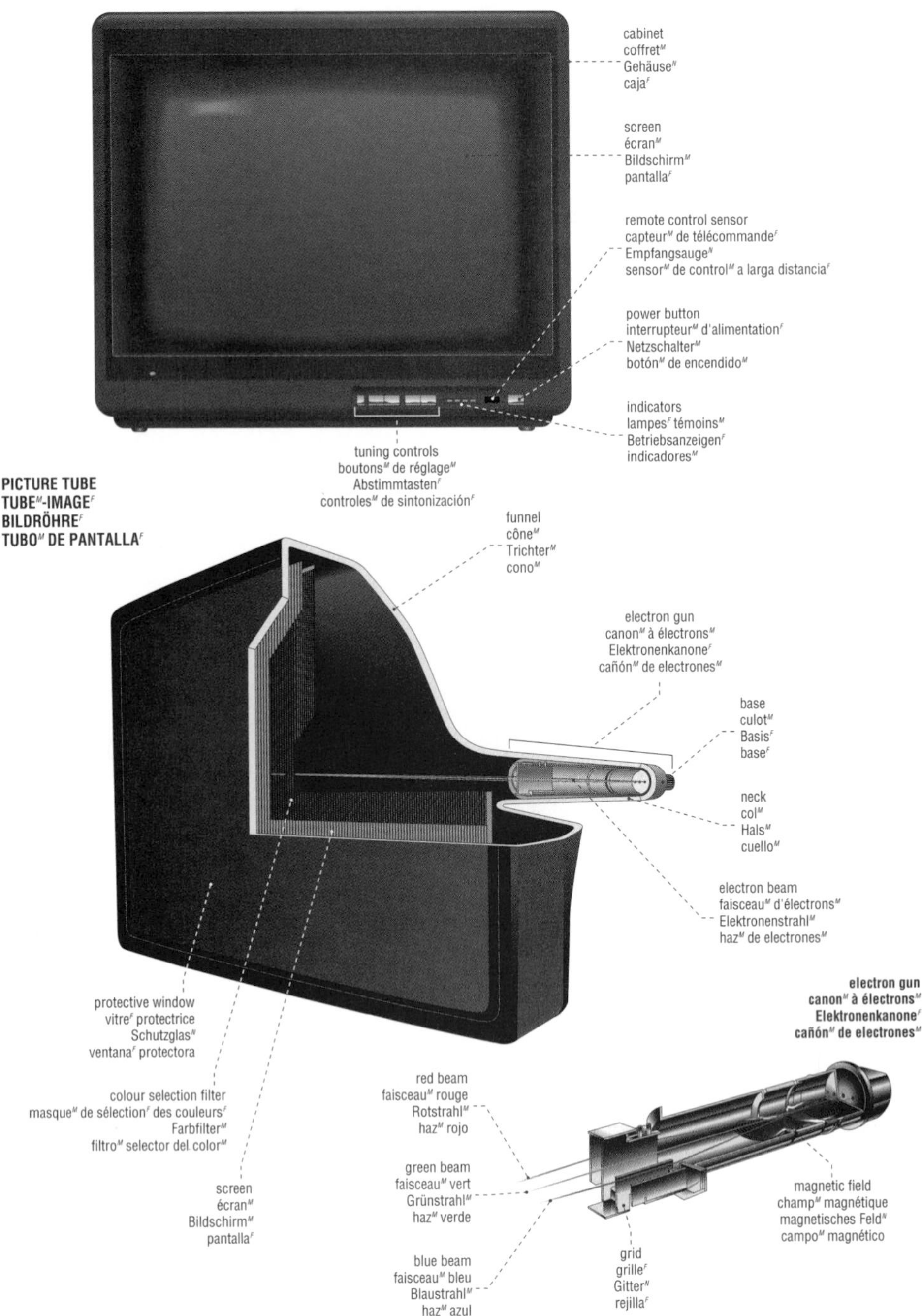

## REMOTE CONTROL
## TÉLÉCOMMANDE[F]
## FERNBEDIENUNG[F]
## CONTROL[M] A LARGA DISTANCIA[F]

## VIDEOCASSETTE RECORDER
## MAGNÉTOSCOPE[M]
## VIDEORECORDER[M]
## VIDEOGRABADORA[F]

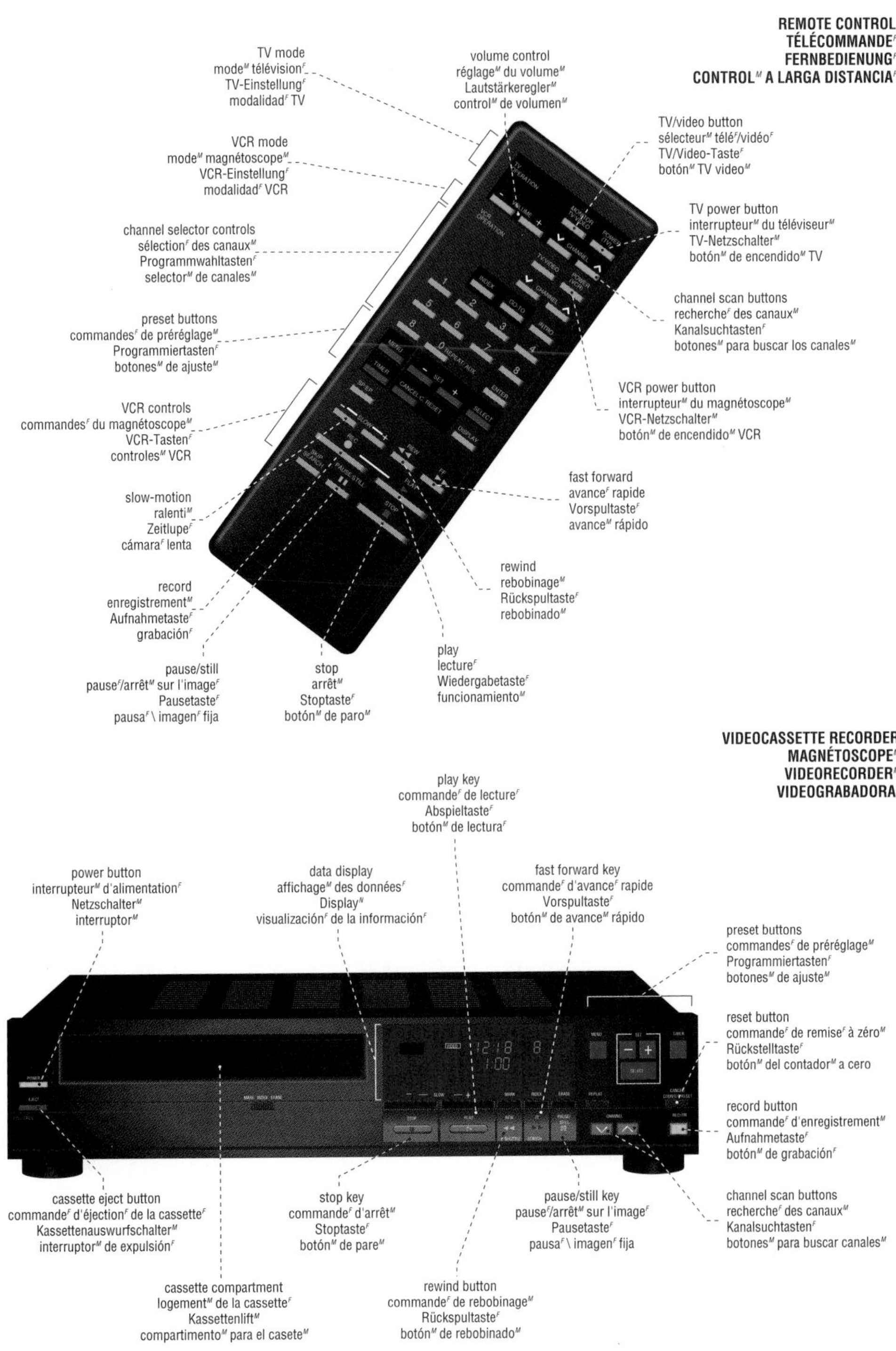

# TELEVISION
# TÉLÉVISION$^{F}$
# FERNSEHEN$^{N}$
# TELEVISIÓN$^{F}$

## STUDIO AND CONTROL ROOMS
## PLATEAU$^{M}$ ET RÉGIES$^{F}$
## SPRECHER- UND REGIERÄUME$^{M}$
## ESTUDIO$^{M}$ DE TELEVISIÓN$^{F}$ Y CABINAS$^{F}$ DE CONTROL$^{M}$

lighting grid access
accès$^{M}$ à la grille$^{F}$ d'éclairage$^{M}$
Zugang$^{M}$ zur Beleuchtungsanlage$^{F}$
puerta$^{F}$ de acceso$^{M}$ a la rejilla$^{F}$ de las luces$^{F}$

additional production personnel
personnel$^{M}$ additionnel de production$^{F}$
zusätzliches Studiopersonal$^{N}$
personal$^{M}$ suplementario de producción$^{F}$

lighting technician
éclairagiste$^{M}$
Beleuchter(in$^{F}$)$^{M}$
técnico$^{M}$ de luces$^{F}$

auxiliary facilities room
salle$^{F}$ polyvalente
allgemeiner Geräteraum$^{M}$
sala$^{F}$ de instalaciones$^{F}$ auxiliares

connection box
boîte$^{F}$ de raccordement$^{M}$
Kamera-Steckfeld$^{N}$
caja$^{F}$ de conexiones$^{F}$

dimmer room
salle$^{F}$ des gradateurs$^{M}$
abgedunkelter Raum$^{M}$
sala$^{F}$ de regulación$^{F}$ de luces

camera control unit
bloc$^{M}$ de commande$^{F}$ des caméras$^{F}$
Bildkontrolle$^{F}$
unidad$^{F}$ de control$^{M}$ de cámaras$^{F}$

camera
caméra$^{F}$
Kamera$^{F}$
cámara$^{F}$

lighting board operator
opérateur$^{M}$ de régie$^{F}$ d'éclairage$^{M}$
Oberbeleuchter(in$^{F}$)$^{M}$
tablero$^{M}$ de operación$^{F}$ de luces$^{F}$

camera control technician
contrôleur$^{M}$ d'images$^{F}$
Bildtechniker(in$^{F}$)$^{M}$
técnico$^{M}$ de control$^{M}$ de cámaras$^{F}$

microphone boom
perche$^{F}$
Mikrofonausleger$^{M}$
jirafa$^{F}$ del micrófono$^{M}$

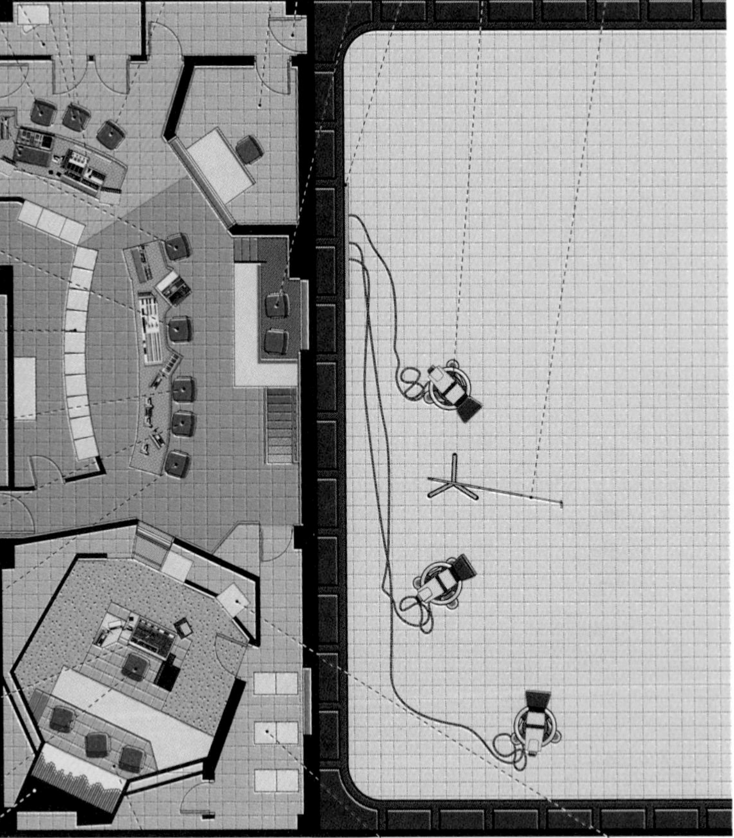

lighting board
pupitre$^{M}$ d'éclairage$^{M}$
Lichtregelanlage$^{F}$
tablero$^{M}$ de luces$^{F}$

technical producer
directeur$^{M}$ technique
Aufsichtsingenieur(in$^{F}$)$^{M}$
productor$^{M}$ técnico

video switcher technician
technicien$^{M}$ aiguilleur$^{M}$
Video-Switcher$^{M}$
operador$^{M}$ técnico de video$^{M}$

monitor wall
baie$^{F}$ de contrôle$^{M}$
Kontrollmonitore$^{M}$
panel$^{M}$ de monitores$^{M}$

producer
réalisateur$^{M}$
Sendeleiter(in$^{F}$)$^{M}$
productor$^{M}$

script assistant
assistant$^{M}$ à la réalisation$^{F}$
Skript-Assistent(in$^{F}$)$^{M}$
asistente$^{M}$ del guionista$^{M}$

production adviser
conseiller$^{M}$ de production$^{F}$
Regieassistent(in$^{F}$)$^{M}$
consejero$^{M}$ de producción$^{F}$

sound desk
pupitre$^{M}$ de son$^{M}$
Tonregiepult$^{N}$
consola$^{F}$ de sonido$^{M}$

sound technician
preneur$^{M}$ de son$^{M}$
Tontechniker(in$^{F}$)$^{M}$
técnico$^{M}$ de sonido$^{M}$

bass trap
trappe$^{F}$ acoustique
Baßfalle$^{F}$
panel$^{M}$ retenedor de frecuencias$^{F}$ bajas

musical advisers
conseillers$^{M}$ musicaux
Musikregie$^{F}$
consejeros$^{M}$ musicales

equipment rack
bâti$^{M}$ d'équipement$^{M}$
Ausrüstungsspind$^{M}$
soporte$^{M}$ para el equipo$^{M}$

sound monitor
haut-parleur$^{M}$ de contrôle$^{M}$
Lautsprecher$^{M}$
monitor$^{M}$ del sonido$^{M}$

studio floor
plateau$^{M}$
Studioebene$^{F}$
estudio$^{M}$

lighting/camera control area
régie$^{F}$ image$^{F}$/éclairage$^{M}$
Beleuchtung$^{F}$/Bildregie$^{F}$
sala$^{F}$ de control$^{M}$ de luces$^{F}$

sound control room
régie$^{F}$ du son$^{M}$
Tonregieraum$^{M}$
control$^{M}$ de sonido$^{M}$

production control room
régie$^{F}$ de production$^{F}$
Regieraum$^{M}$
sala$^{F}$ de producción$^{F}$ y control$^{M}$

## PRODUCTION CONTROL ROOM
## RÉGIE[F] DE PRODUCTION[F]
## REGIERAUM[M]
## SALA[F] DE CONTROL[M] DE PRODUCCIÓN[F]

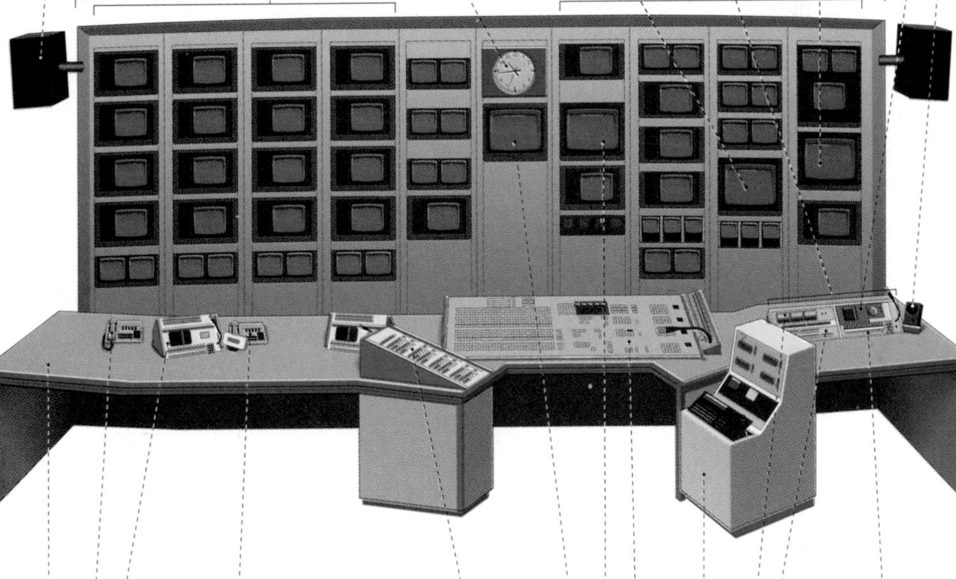

# TELEVISION
# TÉLÉVISION[F]
# FERNSEHEN[N]
# TELEVISIÓN[F]

## STUDIO FLOOR
## PLATEAU[M]
## STUDIOEBENE[F]
## ESTUDIO[M]

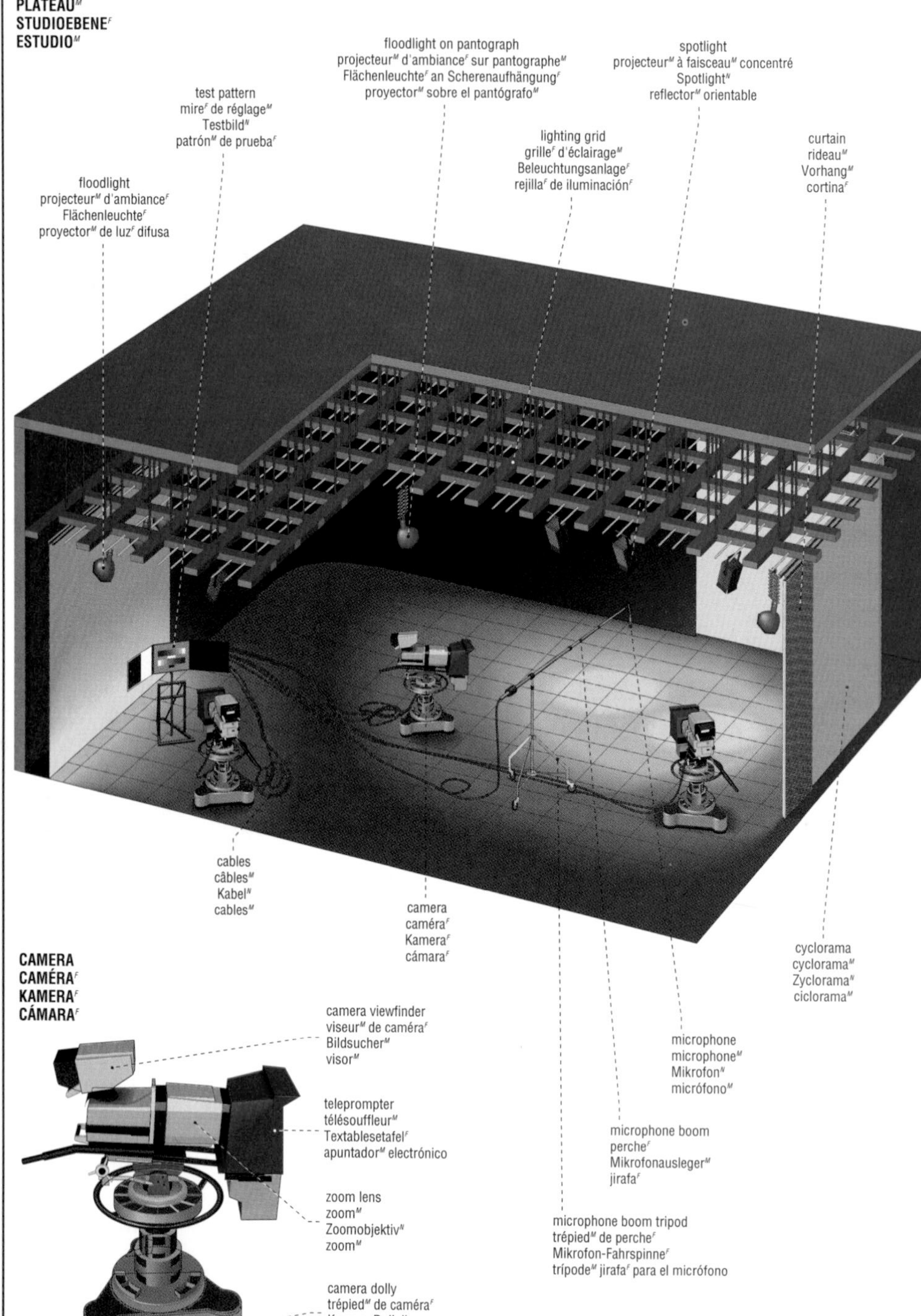

# MOBILE UNIT
# CAR[M] DE REPORTAGE[M]
# ÜBERTRAGUNGSWAGEN[M]
# UNIDAD[F] MÓBIL

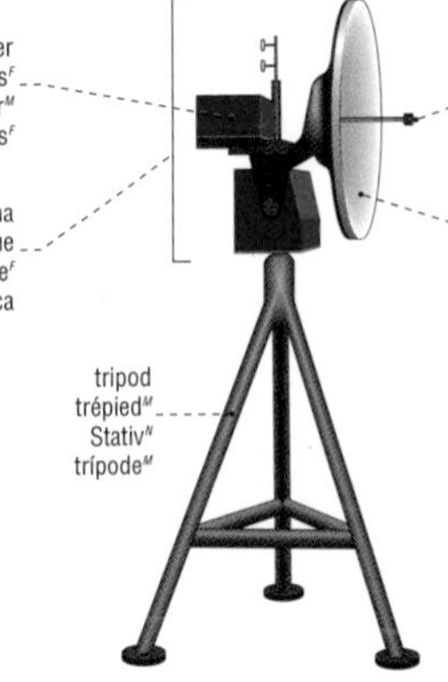

microwave transmitter
émetteur[M] micro-ondes[F]
Mikrowellensender[M]
transmisor[M] de microondas[F]

parabolic antenna
antenne[F] parabolique
Parabolantenne[F]
antena[F] parabólica

wave guide
guide[M] d'ondes[F]
Wellenleiter[M]
guía[F] de la onda[F]

microwave dish
réflecteur[M] parabolique
Mikrowellenschüssel[F]
disco[M] microondas[F]

tripod
trépied[M]
Stativ[N]
trípode[M]

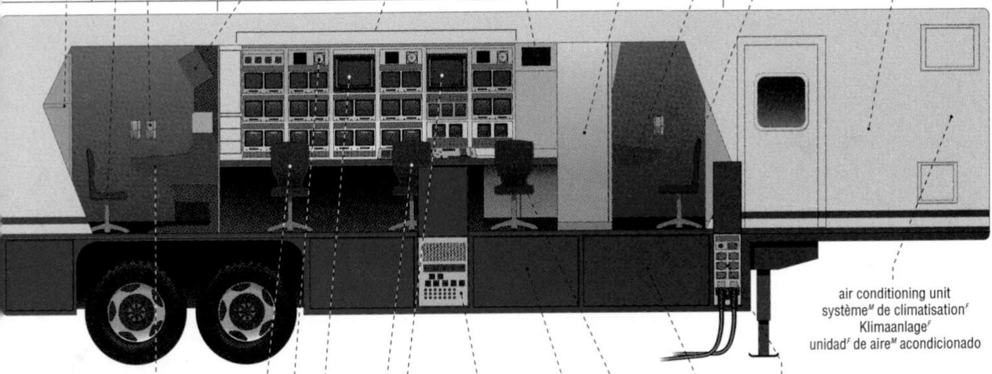

equipment rack
bâti[M] d'équipement[M]
Ausrüstungsspind[M]
equipo[M] de soporte[M]

sound control room
régie[F] du son[M]
Tonregieraum[M]
sala[F] de control[M] de sonido[M]

sound technician
preneur[M] de son[M]
Tontechniker(in[F])[M]
técnico[M] de sonido[M]

telephone set
poste[M] téléphonique
Telefonapparat[M]
teléfono[M]

sound monitor
haut-parleur[M] de contrôle[M]
Abhörlautsprecher[M]
monitor[M] de sonido[M]

production control room
régie[F] de production[F]
Regieraum[M]
sala[F] de control[M] de la producción[F]

monitor wall
baie[F] de contrôle[M]
Kontrollmonitore[M]
panel[M] de control[M]

sound monitor
haut-parleur[M] de contrôle[M]
Abhörlautsprecher[M]
monitor[M] de sonido[M]

equipment rack
bâti[M] d'équipement[M]
Ausrüstungsspind[M]
equipo[M] de soporte

camera control area
régie[F] image[F]
Bereich[M] der Bildkontrolle[F]
área[M] de control[M] de la cámara[F]

camera control unit
bloc[M] de commande[F] des caméras[F]
Bildkontrolle[F]
unidad[F] de control[M] de la cámara[F]

camera control technician
contrôleur[M] d'images[F]
Bildtechniker(in[F])[M]
técnico[M] de control[M] de la cámara[F]

maintenance area
secteur[M] maintenance[F]
Eingangsbereich[M]
área[M] de mantenimiento[M]

air conditioning unit
système[M] de climatisation[F]
Klimaanlage[F]
unidad[F] de aire[M] acondicionado

electrical connection panel
panneau[M] de raccordement[M] électrique
Stromverteiler[M]
panel[M] de conexiones[F] eléctricas

sound console
pupitre[M] de son[M]
Tonregiepult[N]
consola[F] de sonido[M]

producer
réalisateur[M]
Sendeleiter(in[F])[M]
productor[M]

clock
horloge[F]
Kontrolluhr[F]
reloj[M]

output monitor
écran[M] de sortie[F]
Ausgangsmonitor[M]
monitor[M] de producción[F]

video connection panel
panneau[M] de raccordement[M] vidéo
Videoschalttafel[F]
panel[M] de conexión[F] del video[M]

preview monitor
écran[M] de précontrôle[M]
Vorschaumonitor[M]
monitor[M] de visualización[F] previa

video switcher technician
technicien[M] aiguilleur[M]
Video-Switcher[M]
operador[M] técnico de video[M]

technical equipment compartment
soute[F] d'équipement[M] technique
Fach[N] für technische Ausrüstung[F]
compartimiento[M] del equipo[M] técnico

technical producer
directeur[M] technique
Aufsichtsingenieur(in[F])[M]
productor[M] técnico

cable drum compartment
soute[F] des bobines[F] de câbles[M]
Fach[N] für Kabeltrommel[F]
compartimiento[M] del cable[M] de la batería[F]

# SATELLITE BROADCASTING
# TÉLÉDIFFUSION[F] PAR SATELLITE[M]
# ÜBERTRAGUNGSSATELLITENTECHNIK[F]
# COMUNICACIÓN[F] POR SATÉLITE DE TRANSMISIÓN[F]

cable distributor
câblodistributeur[M]
Kabelverteiler[M]
cable[M] distribuidor

satellite
satellite[M]
Satellit[M]
satélite[M]

local station
station[F] locale
Ortsstation[F]
estación[F] local

private broadcasting network
réseau[M] privé
privates Rundfunknetz[N]
red[F] de transmisión[F] privada

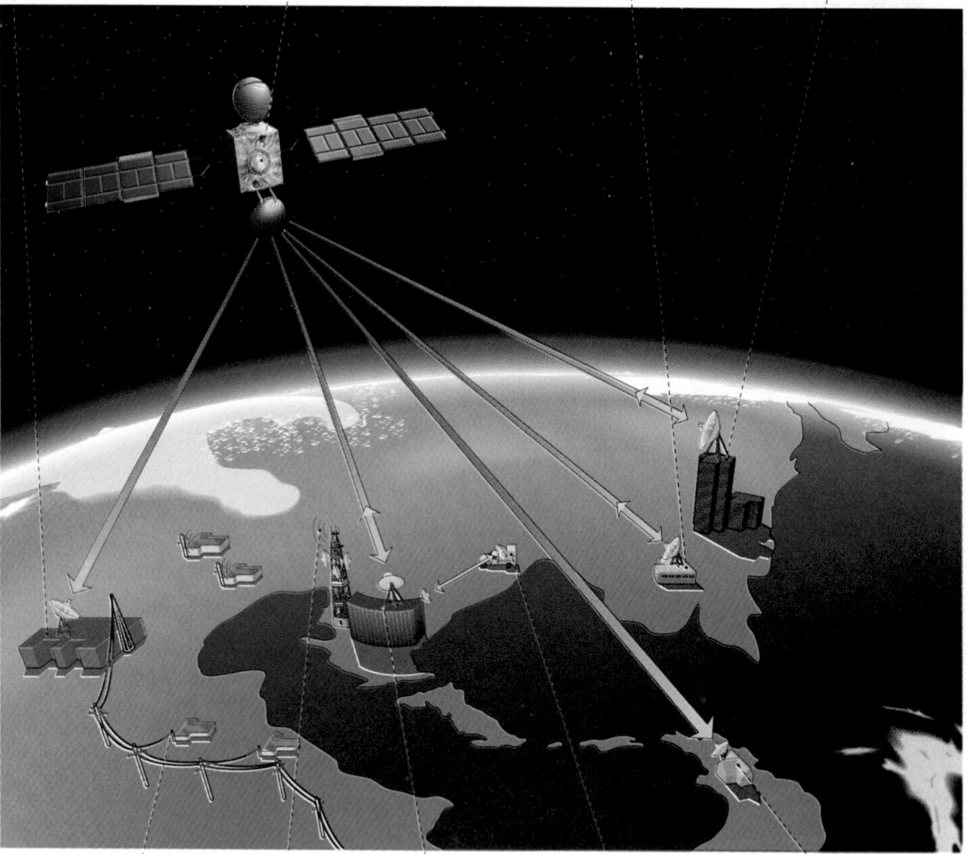

distribution by cable
transmission[F] par câble[M]
Verteilung[F] durch Kabelnetz[N]
distribución[F] por redes[F] de cable[M]

direct home reception
réception[F] directe
Satelliten-Direktempfang[M]
recepción[F] directa en la casa[F]

Hertzian wave transmission
transmission[F] hertzienne
Sendung[F] auf Hertz-Wellen[F]
transmisión[F] de ondas[F] Hertzianas

mobile unit
car[M] de reportage[M]
mobile Einheit[F]
unidad[F] móvil

national broadcasting network
réseau[M] national
öffentliches Übertragungsnetz[N]
red[F] nacional de transmisión[F]

# TELECOMMUNICATIONS BY SATELLITE
# TÉLÉCOMMUNICATIONS[F] PAR SATELLITE[M]
# TELEKOMMUNIKATION[F] ÜBER NACHRICHTENSATELLIT[M]
# TELECOMUNICACIONES[F] POR SATÉLITE[M]

industrial communications
communications[F] industrielles
industrielle Telekommunikation[F]
comunicaciones[F] industriales

teleport
téléport[M]
Teleport[M]
teleporte[M]

in-flight communications
communications[F] aériennes
Telekommunikation[F] für die Luftfahrt[F]
comunicaciones[F] aéreas

military communications
communications[F] militaires
militärische Telekommunikation[F]
comunicaciones[F] militares

maritime communications
communications[F] maritimes
maritime Telekommunikation[F]
comunicaciones[F] marítimas

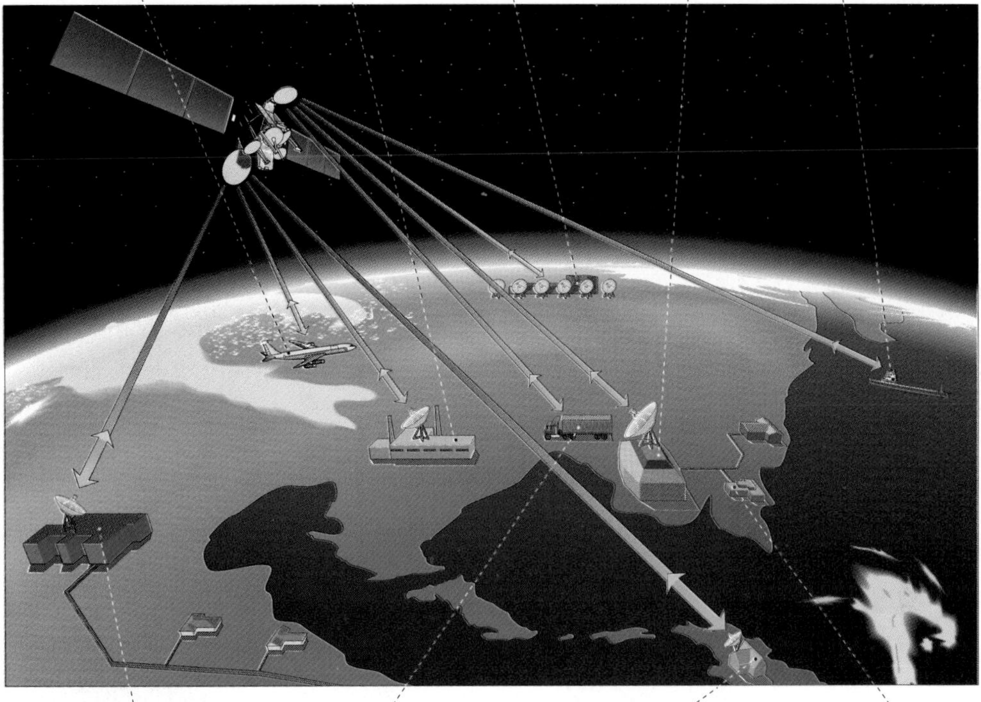

telephone network
réseau[M] téléphonique
Telefonnetz[N]
red[F] telefónica

road communications
communications[F] routières
Telekommunikation[F] für den Straßenverkehr[M]
comunicaciones[F] terrestres

personal communications
communications[F] individuelles
persönliche Telekommunikation[F]
comunicaciones[F] personales

consumer
client[M]
Konsument[M]
consumidor[M]

computer communication
téléinformatique[F]
Telekommunikation[F] über Computer[M]
comunicación[F] por computador[M]

facsimile machine
télécopieur[M]
Telefax-Gerät[N]
facsímil[M]

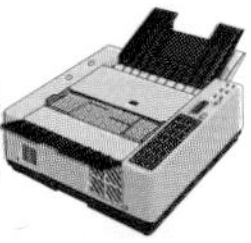

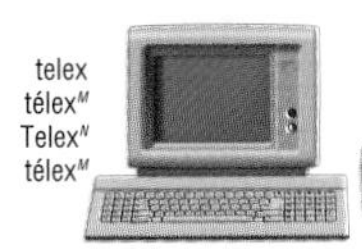

telex
télex[M]
Telex[N]
télex[M]

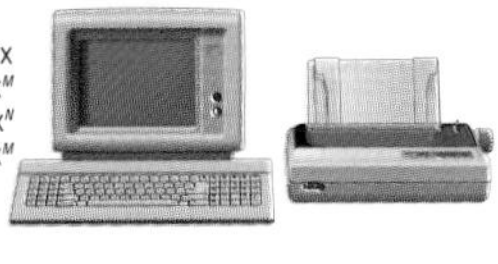

## TELECOMMUNICATIONS BY TELEPHONE NETWORK
## TÉLÉCOMMUNICATIONS[F] PAR LIGNE[F] TÉLÉPHONIQUE
## TELEKOMMUNIKATIONSTECHNIK[F] ÜBER DAS TELEFONNETZ[N]
## TELECOMUNICACIONES[F] POR RED[F] TELEFÓNICA

cellular telephone
téléphone[M] cellulaire
Zellfunktelefon[N]
teléfono[M] celular

telephone
poste[M] téléphonique
Telefonapparat[M]
teléfono[M]

# TELECOMMUNICATION SATELLITES
# SATELLITES[M] DE TÉLÉCOMMUNICATIONS[F]
# FERNMELDESATELLITEN[M]
# SATÉLITES[M] DE TELECOMUNICACIONES[F]

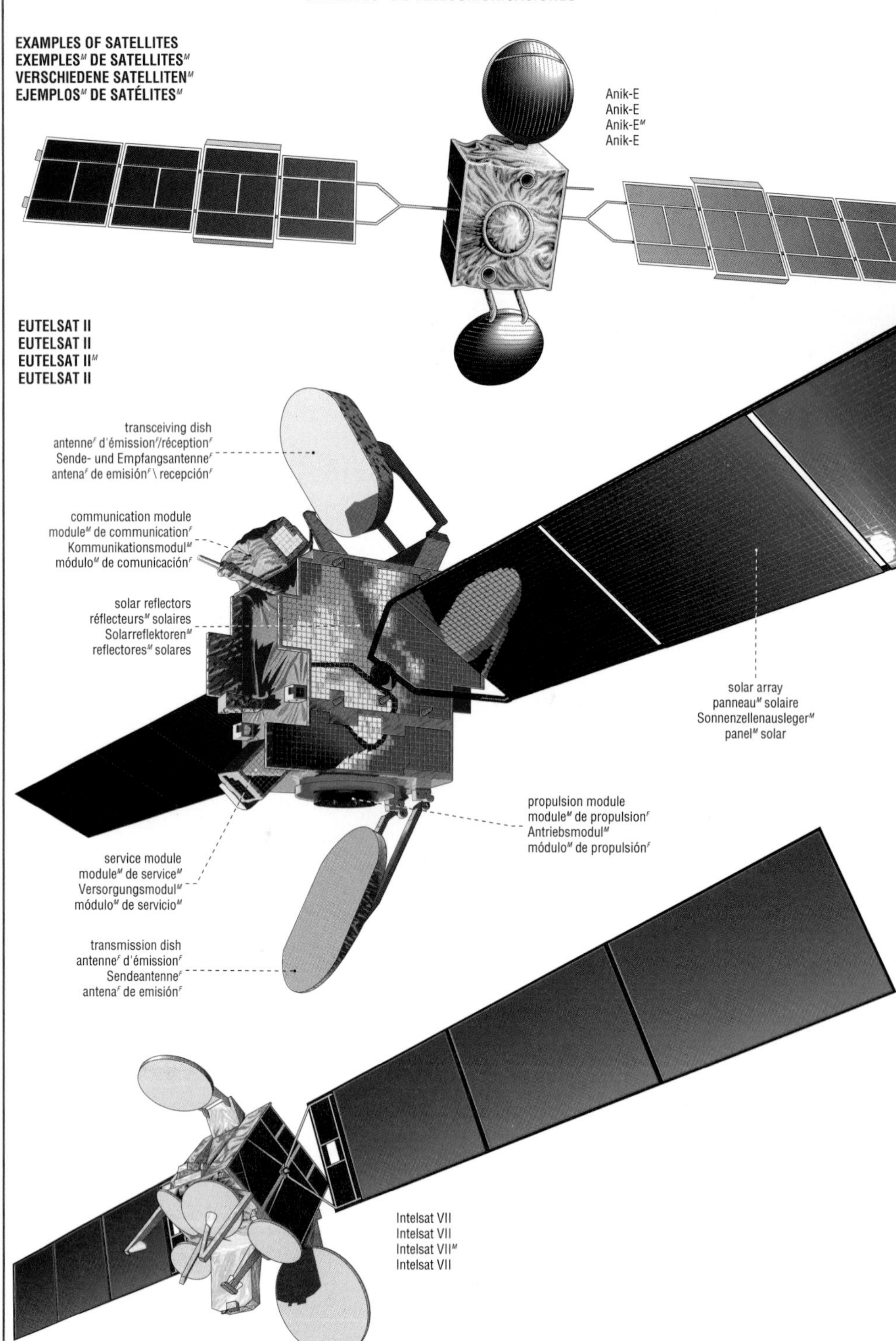

# LAUNCHING INTO ORBIT
# MISE[F] EN ORBITE[F]
# START[M] IN DIE UMLAUFBAHN[F]
# PUESTA[F] EN ÓRBITA[F]

# COMMUNICATION BY TELEPHONE
# COMMUNICATION$^{F}$ PAR TÉLÉPHONE$^{M}$
# TELEFONISCHE KOMMUNIKATION$^{F}$
# COMUNICACIONES$^{F}$ POR TELÉFONO$^{M}$



## TELEPHONE ANSWERING MACHINE
## RÉPONDEUR$^{M}$ TÉLÉPHONIQUE
## ANRUFBEANTWORTER$^{M}$
## CONTESTADORA$^{F}$ AUTOMÁTICA

incoming message cassette
cassette$^{F}$ messages$^{M}$
Aufzeichnungskassette$^{F}$
cassette$^{M}$ para grabar los mensajes$^{M}$

calls indicator
voyant$^{M}$ de réception$^{F}$ de messages$^{M}$
Nachrichtenanzeige$^{F}$
indicador$^{M}$ de llamadas$^{F}$

power-on light
voyant$^{M}$ de mise$^{F}$ en circuit$^{M}$
Netzkontrollampe$^{F}$
luz$^{F}$ de encendido$^{M}$

auto answer indicator
voyant$^{M}$ de réponse$^{F}$ automatique
Bereitschaftsanzeige$^{F}$
indicador$^{M}$ de respuesta$^{F}$ automática

outgoing announcement cassette
cassette$^{F}$ annonce$^{F}$
Ansagekassette$^{F}$
cassette$^{M}$ con saludo$^{M}$

listen button
écoute$^{F}$
Mithörtaste$^{F}$
botón$^{M}$ de reproducción$^{F}$

power-on button
bouton$^{M}$ de mise$^{F}$ en circuit$^{M}$
Netzschalter$^{M}$
botón$^{M}$ de encendido$^{M}$

fast-forward button
avance$^{F}$ rapide
Vorlauftaste$^{F}$
botón$^{M}$ de avance$^{M}$ rápido

speaker
haut-parleur$^{M}$
Lautsprecher$^{M}$
altavoz$^{M}$

microphone
microphone$^{M}$
Mikrofon$^{N}$
micrófono$^{M}$

record announcement button
enregistrement$^{M}$
Aufzeichnungstaste$^{F}$
botón$^{M}$ de grabación$^{F}$

stop button
arrêt$^{M}$
Stoptaste$^{F}$
botón$^{M}$ de paro$^{M}$

on/play button
mise$^{F}$ en marche$^{F}$
Einschalt-/Wiedergabetaste$^{F}$
botón$^{M}$ de encendido$^{M}$

rewind button
rebobinage$^{M}$
Rücklauftaste$^{F}$
botón$^{M}$ de rebobinado$^{M}$

volume control
commande$^{F}$ de volume$^{M}$
Lautstärkeregler$^{M}$
control$^{M}$ del volumen$^{M}$

erase button
effacement$^{M}$
Löschtaste$^{F}$
botón$^{M}$ para borrar

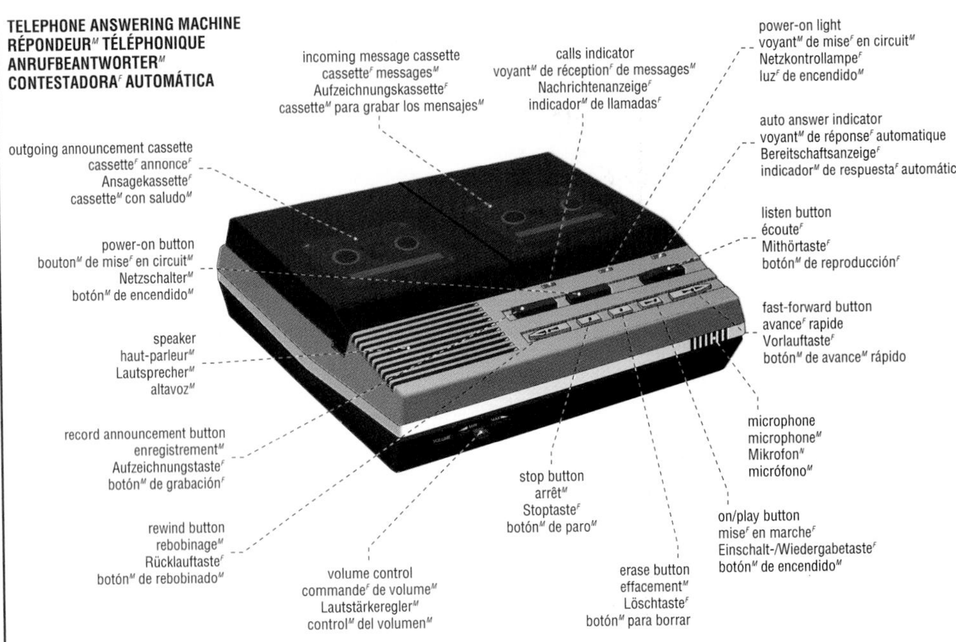

## TELEPHONE
## POSTE$^{M}$ TÉLÉPHONIQUE
## TELEFONAPPARAT$^{M}$
## TELÉFONO$^{M}$

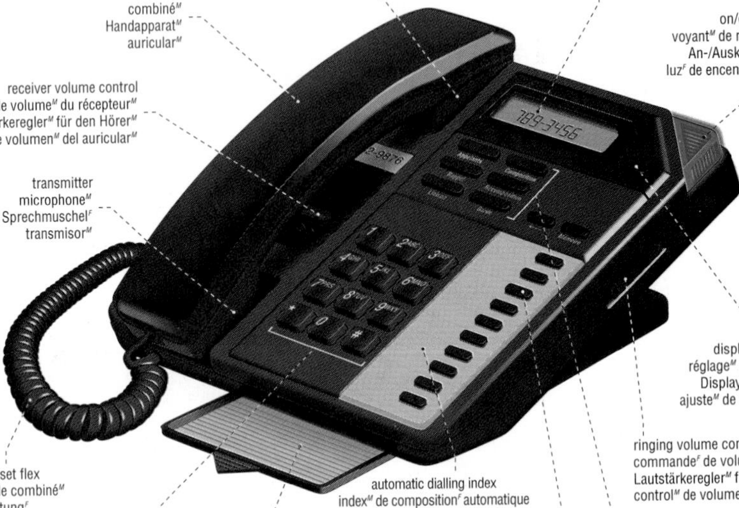

receiver
récepteur$^{M}$
Hörer$^{M}$
receptor$^{M}$

display
afficheur$^{M}$
Display$^{N}$
visualización$^{F}$

handset
combiné$^{M}$
Handapparat$^{M}$
auricular$^{M}$

on/off light
voyant$^{M}$ de mise$^{F}$ en circuit$^{M}$
An-/Auskontrollampe$^{F}$
luz$^{F}$ de encendido$^{M}$ \ apagado$^{M}$

receiver volume control
commande$^{F}$ de volume$^{M}$ du récepteur$^{M}$
Lautstärkeregler$^{M}$ für den Hörer$^{M}$
control$^{M}$ de volumen$^{M}$ del auricular$^{M}$

transmitter
microphone$^{M}$
Sprechmuschel$^{F}$
transmisor$^{M}$

display setting
réglage$^{M}$ de l'afficheur$^{M}$
Displayeinstellung$^{F}$
ajuste$^{M}$ de la visualización$^{F}$

ringing volume control
commande$^{F}$ de volume$^{M}$ de la sonnerie$^{F}$
Lautstärkeregler$^{M}$ für den Rufton$^{M}$
control$^{M}$ de volumen$^{M}$ de la campana$^{F}$

handset flex
cordon$^{M}$ de combiné$^{M}$
Leitung$^{F}$
cable$^{M}$ del auricular$^{M}$

automatic dialling index
index$^{M}$ de composition$^{F}$ automatique
Rufnummernregister$^{N}$ für automatische Wahl$^{F}$
marcador$^{M}$ automático

function selectors
sélecteurs$^{M}$ de fonctions$^{F}$
Funktionswähler$^{M}$
selectores$^{M}$ de funciones$^{F}$

push buttons
clavier$^{M}$
Tasten$^{F}$
teclado$^{M}$

telephone list
répertoire$^{M}$ téléphonique
Rufnummernregister$^{N}$
índice$^{M}$ de teléfonos$^{M}$

memory button
commande$^{F}$ mémoire$^{F}$
Speichertaste$^{F}$
botón$^{M}$ de memoria$^{F}$

## TELEX
## TÉLEX$^{M}$
## TELEX$^{N}$
## TÉLEX$^{M}$

**terminal**
**terminal$^{M}$**
**Terminal$^{N}$**
**terminal$^{M}$**

visual display unit
écran$^{M}$ d'affichage$^{M}$
Datensichtgerät$^{N}$
pantalla$^{F}$
transmission/reception of messages
expédition$^{F}$/réception$^{F}$ des messages$^{M}$
Senden/Empfangen$^{N}$ von Nachrichten$^{F}$
recepción$^{F}$ y transmisión de mensajes$^{M}$


**printer**
**imprimante$^{F}$**
**Drucker$^{M}$**
**impresora$^{F}$**

printing of messages
impression$^{F}$ des messages$^{M}$
Ausdrucken$^{N}$ von Nachrichten$^{F}$
impresión$^{F}$ de mensajes


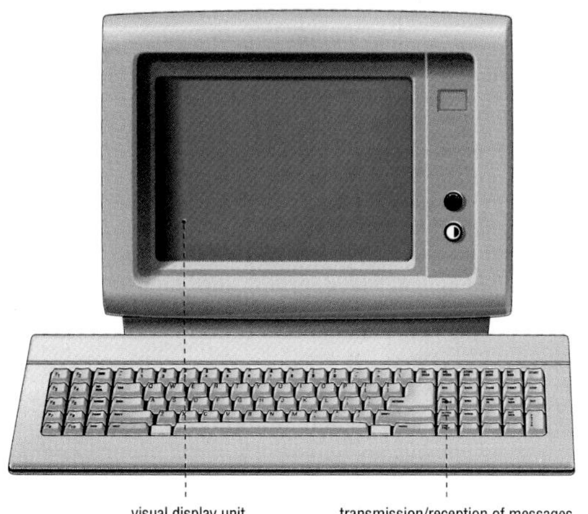

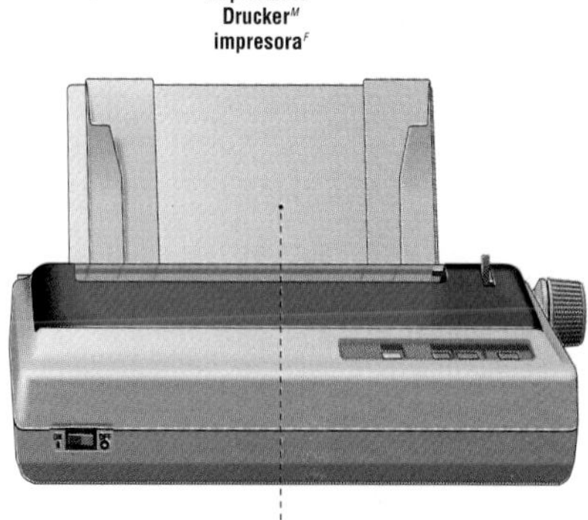

## FAX MACHINE
## TÉLÉCOPIEUR$^{M}$
## TELEFAXGERÄT$^{N}$
## FACSIMIL$^{M}$

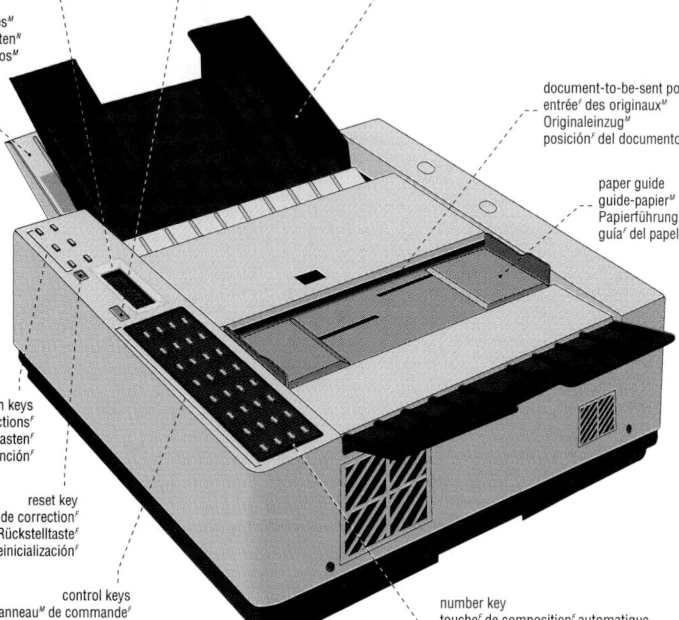

data display
écran$^{M}$ d'affichage$^{M}$
Datendisplay$^{N}$
visualización$^{F}$ de datos$^{M}$
start key
mise$^{F}$ en marche$^{F}$
Starttaste$^{F}$
tecla$^{F}$ de iniciación$^{M}$
sent document recovery
sortie$^{F}$ des originaux$^{M}$
Originalrückführung$^{F}$
recuperación$^{F}$ del documento$^{M}$ enviado
document receiving
réception$^{F}$ des messages$^{M}$
Empfang$^{M}$ von Dokumenten$^{N}$
recepción$^{F}$ de documentos$^{M}$
document-to-be-sent position
entrée$^{F}$ des originaux$^{M}$
Originaleinzug$^{M}$
posición$^{F}$ del documento$^{M}$ para enviar
paper guide
guide-papier$^{M}$
Papierführung$^{F}$
guía$^{F}$ del papel$^{M}$
function keys
panneau$^{M}$ de fonctions$^{F}$
Funktionstasten$^{F}$
teclas$^{F}$ de función$^{F}$
reset key
touche$^{F}$ de correction$^{F}$
Rückstelltaste$^{F}$
tecla$^{F}$ de reinicialización$^{F}$
control keys
panneau$^{M}$ de commande$^{F}$
Bedienungstasten$^{F}$
teclas$^{F}$ de control$^{M}$
number key
touche$^{F}$ de composition$^{F}$ automatique
Nummerntasten$^{F}$
teclas$^{F}$ de números$^{M}$

# COMMUNICATION BY TELEPHONE
# COMMUNICATION[F] PAR TÉLÉPHONE[M]
# TELEFONISCHE KOMMUNIKATION[F]
# COMUNICACIONES[F] POR TELÉFONO[M]

## TYPES OF TELEPHONE
## TYPES[M] DE POSTES[M] TÉLÉPHONIQUES
## TELEFONARTEN[F]
## TELÉFONOS[M]

### TELECOMMUNICATION TERMINAL
### TERMINAL[M] DE TÉLÉCOMMUNICATION[F]
### FERNMELDETERMINAL[N]
### TERMINAL[M] DE COMUNICACIONES[F]

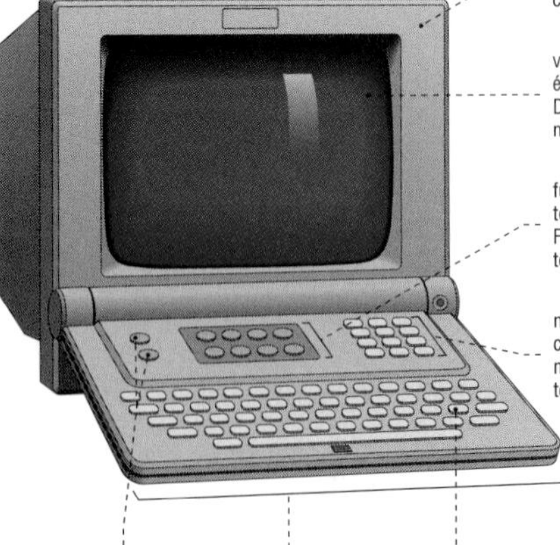


cordless telephone
poste[M] sans cordon[M]
drahtloses Telefon[N]
teléfono[M] sin cable[M]

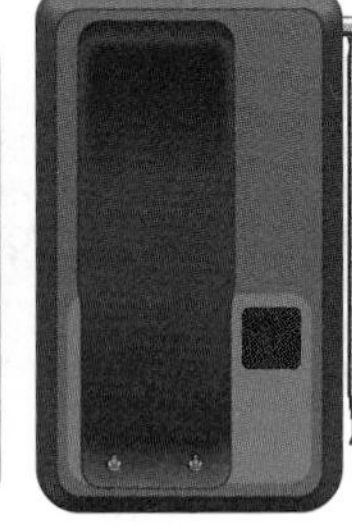

switchboard operator's set
pupitre[M] dirigeur
Abfrageapparat[M]
teléfono[M] para ejecutivo[M]

portable cellular telephone
téléphone[M] cellulaire portatif
mobiles Zellfunktelefon[N]
teléfono[M] celular portátil

push-button telephone
poste[M] à clavier[M]
Tastentelefon[N]
teléfono[M] de teclado[M]

### PAY PHONE
### TÉLÉPHONE[M] PUBLIC
### ÖFFENTLICHER FERNSPRECHER[M]
### TELÉFONO[M] PÚBLICO

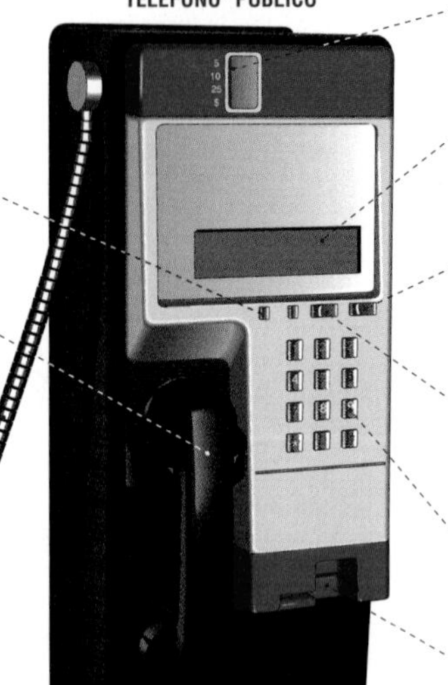

TRANSPORT FORTBEWEGUNG
TRANSPORT TRANSPORTE

SUMMARY

**ROAD TRANSPORT**

CAR ... 425
TRUCKING ... 440
MOTORCYCLE ... 442
SNOWMOBILE ... 445
BICYCLE ... 446
CARAVAN ... 449
ROAD SYSTEM ... 450
SERVICE STATION ... 453
FIXED BRIDGES ... 454
MOVABLE BRIDGES ... 457

**RAIL TRANSPORT**

HIGH-SPEED TRAIN ... 458
TYPES OF PASSENGER COACH ... 460
PASSENGER STATION ... 462
RAILWAY STATION ... 464
MARSHALLING YARD ... 465
RAILWAY TRACK ... 466
DIESEL-ELECTRIC LOCOMOTIVE ... 468
GOODS VAN ... 470
TYPES OF GOODS TRUCK ... 472

**UNDERGROUND TRANSPORT**

UNDERGROUND RAILWAY ... 474

**MARITIME TRANSPORT**

FOUR-MASTED BARK ... 478
TYPES OF SAIL ... 482
TYPES OF RIG ... 482
ANCHOR ... 483
NAVIGATION DEVICES ... 484
MARITIME SIGNALS ... 486
MARITIME BUOYAGE SYSTEM ... 488
HARBOUR ... 490
CANAL LOCK ... 492
HOVERCRAFT ... 492
FERRY ... 494
CONTAINER SHIP ... 494
HYDROFOIL BOAT ... 495
CRUISELINER ... 496

**AIR TRANSPORT**

LONG-RANGE JET AIRLINER ... 498
TYPES OF TAIL UNIT ... 498
TYPES OF WING ... 499
FLIGHT DECK ... 500
TURBOFAN ENGINE ... 501
AIRPORT ... 502
HELICOPTER ... 508

**SPACE TRANSPORT**

ROCKET ... 509
SPACE SHUTTLE ... 510
SPACESUIT ... 512

# CAR
# AUTOMOBILE[F]
# AUTO[N]
# AUTOMÓVIL[M]

## TYPES OF BODYWORK
## TYPES[M] DE CARROSSERIES[F]
## WAGENTYPEN[M]
## TIPOS[M] DE CARROCERÍAS[F]

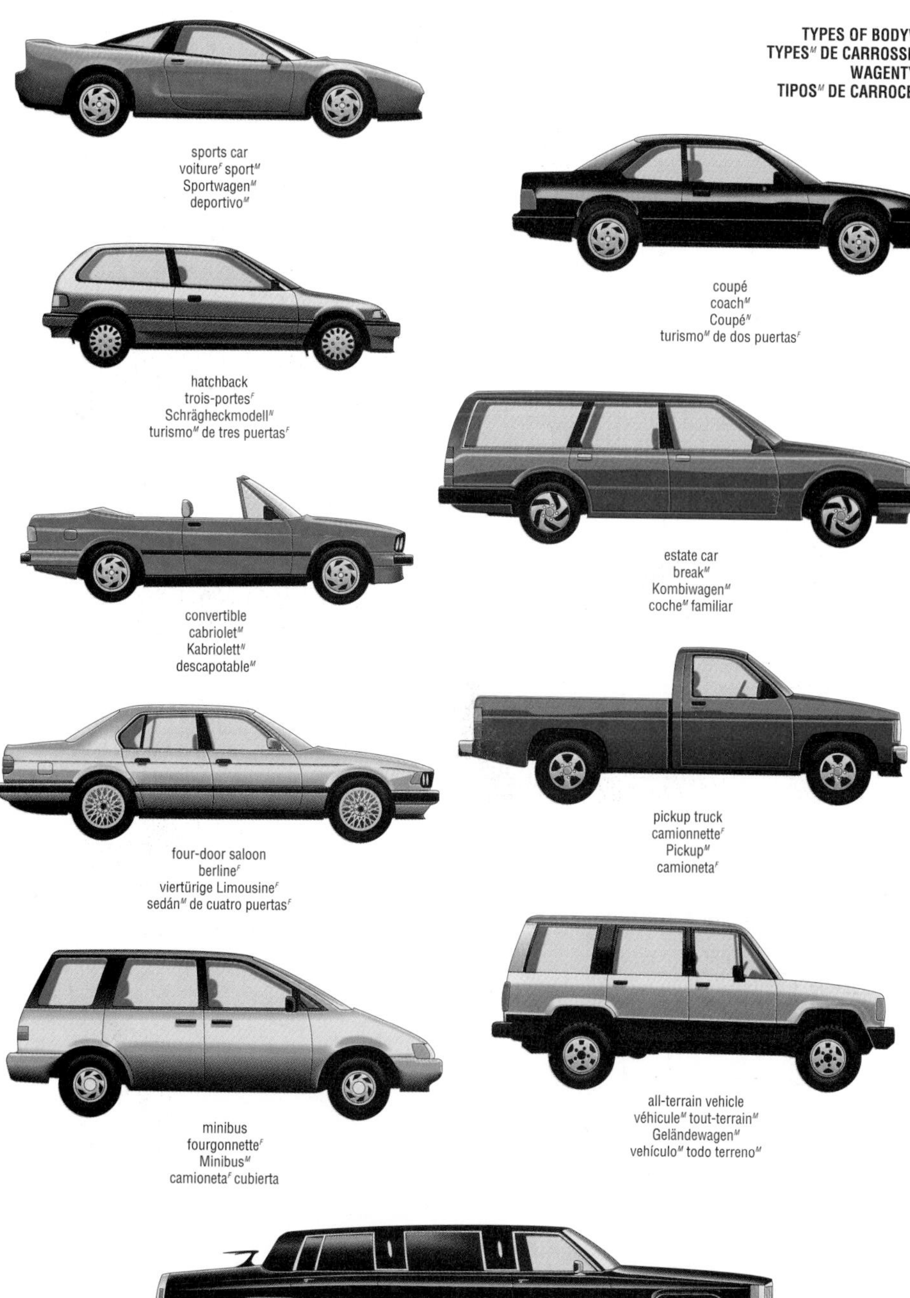

sports car
voiture[F] sport[M]
Sportwagen[M]
deportivo[M]

coupé
coach[M]
Coupé[N]
turismo[M] de dos puertas[F]

hatchback
trois-portes[F]
Schrägheckmodell[N]
turismo[M] de tres puertas[F]

estate car
break[M]
Kombiwagen[M]
coche[M] familiar

convertible
cabriolet[M]
Kabriolett[N]
descapotable[M]

pickup truck
camionnette[F]
Pickup[M]
camioneta[F]

four-door saloon
berline[F]
viertürige Limousine[F]
sedán[M] de cuatro puertas[F]

minibus
fourgonnette[F]
Minibus[M]
camioneta[F] cubierta

all-terrain vehicle
véhicule[M] tout-terrain[M]
Geländewagen[M]
vehículo[M] todo terreno[M]

stretch-limousine
limousine[F]
Pullman-Limousine[F]
pullman[M] de ocho plazas[F]

# CAR
# AUTOMOBILE^F
# AUTO^N
# AUTOMÓVIL^M

## BODY
## CARROSSERIE^F
## KAROSSERIE^F
## CARROCERÍA^F

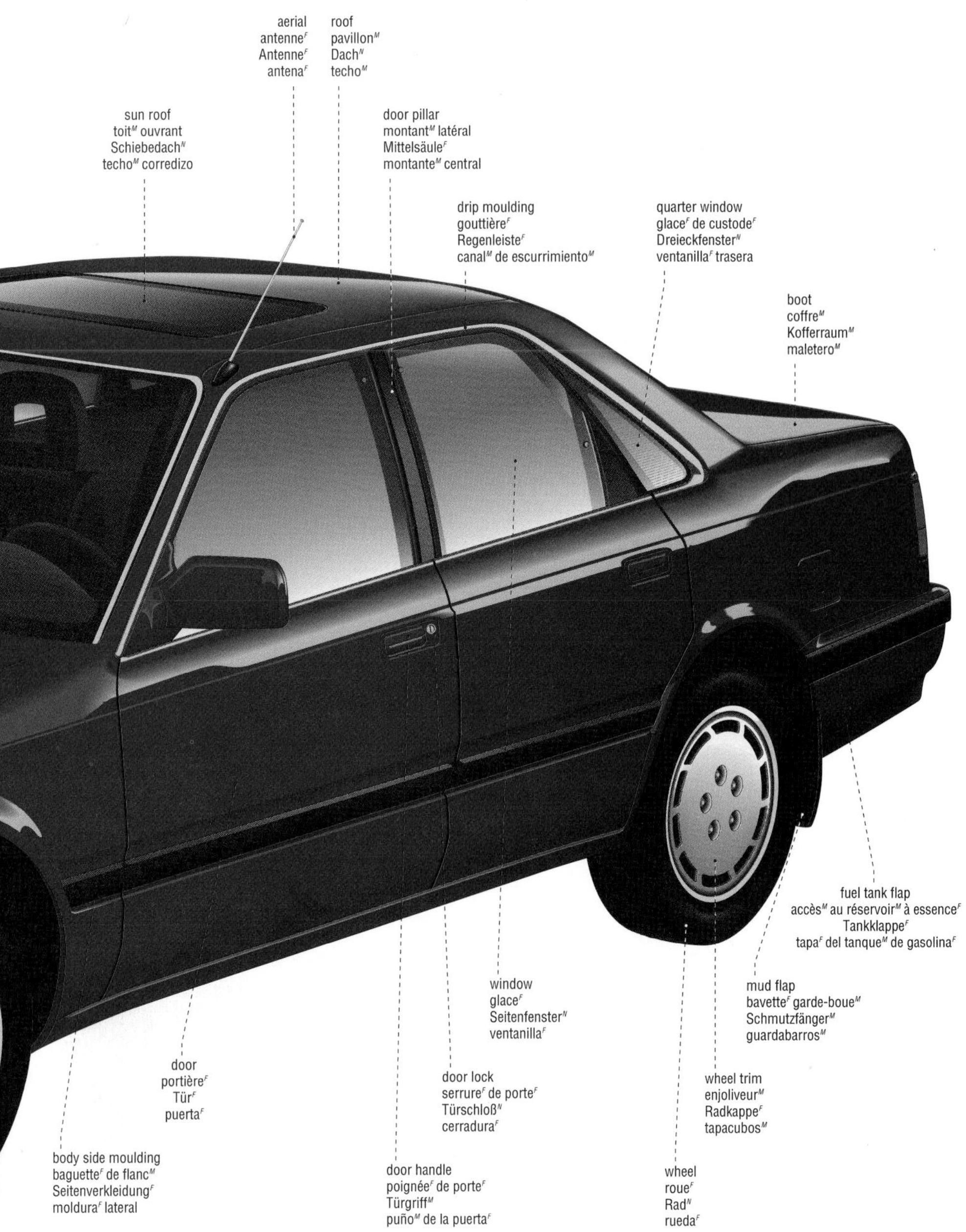
aerial
antenneF
AntenneF
antenaF
roof
pavillonM
DachN
techoM
sun roof
toitM ouvrant
SchiebedachN
techoM corredizo
door pillar
montantM latéral
MittelsäuleF
montanteM central
drip moulding
gouttièreF
RegenleisteF
canalM de escurrimientoM
quarter window
glaceF de custodeF
DreieckfensterN
ventanillaF trasera
boot
coffreM
KofferraumM
maleteroM
fuel tank flap
accèsM au réservoirM à essenceF
TankklappeF
tapaF del tanqueM de gasolinaF
window
glaceF
SeitenfensterN
ventanillaF
mud flap
bavetteF garde-boueM
SchmutzfängerM
guardabarrosM
door
portièreF
TürF
puertaF
door lock
serrureF de porteF
TürschloßN
cerraduraF
wheel trim
enjoliveurM
RadkappeF
tapacubosM
body side moulding
baguetteF de flancM
SeitenverkleidungF
molduraF lateral
door handle
poignéeF de porteF
TürgriffM
puñoM de la puertaF
wheel
roueF
RadN
ruedaF

# CAR
# AUTOMOBILE$^{F}$
# AUTO$^{N}$
# AUTOMÓVIL$^{M}$

## BUCKET SEAT
## SIÈGE$^{M}$-BAQUET$^{M}$
## SCHALENSITZ$^{M}$
## ASIENTO$^{M}$ RECLINABLE

headrest
appui-tête$^{M}$
Kopfstütze$^{F}$
soporte$^{M}$ para la cabeza$^{F}$
seat back
dossier$^{M}$
Rückenlehne$^{F}$
respaldo$^{M}$
seat belt
ceinture$^{F}$ de sécurité$^{F}$
Sicherheitsgurt$^{M}$
cinturón$^{M}$ de seguridad$^{F}$
seat
siège$^{M}$
Sitz$^{M}$
asiento$^{M}$
seat back adjustment knob
commande$^{F}$ de dossier$^{M}$
Einstellrad$^{N}$
rueda$^{F}$ para graduar el respaldo$^{M}$

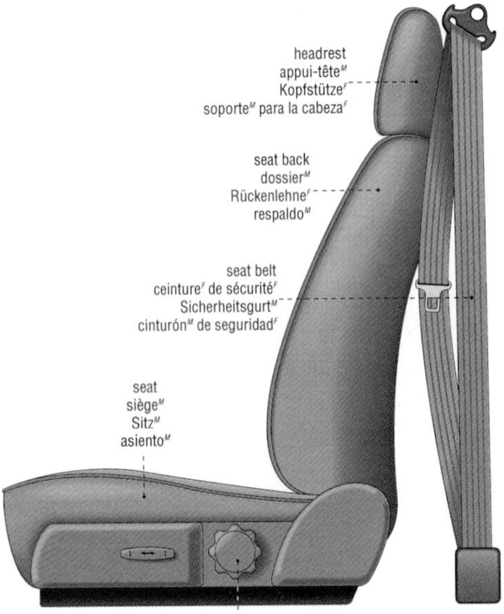

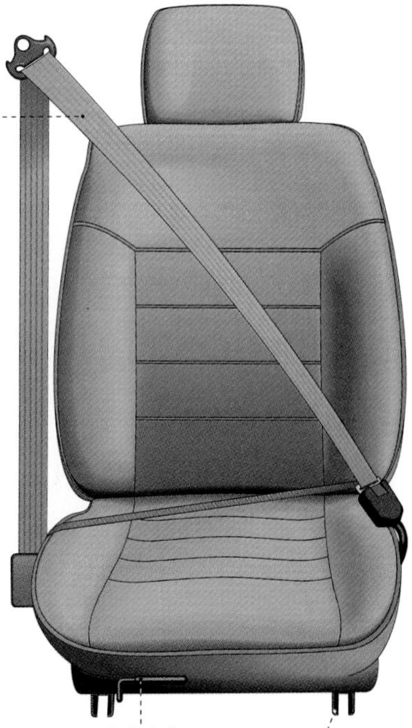

shoulder belt
baudrier$^{M}$
Schultergurt$^{M}$
cinturón$^{M}$ de hombros
seat adjuster lever
manette$^{F}$ de glissement$^{M}$
Entriegelungshebel$^{M}$
palanca$^{F}$ del deslizador$^{M}$
sliding rail
rail$^{M}$ de glissement$^{M}$
Führungsschiene$^{F}$
riel$^{M}$ deslizador

## REAR SEAT
## BANQUETTE$^{F}$ ARRIÈRE
## RÜCKSITZBANK$^{F}$
## ASIENTO$^{M}$ TRASERO

armrest
appui-bras$^{M}$
Armstütze$^{F}$
soporte$^{M}$ para el brazo$^{M}$
lap belt
sangle$^{F}$
Beckengurt$^{M}$
correa$^{F}$
buckle
boucle$^{F}$
Gurtschließe$^{F}$
hebilla$^{F}$
bench seat
banquette$^{F}$
Sitzbank$^{F}$
asiento$^{M}$

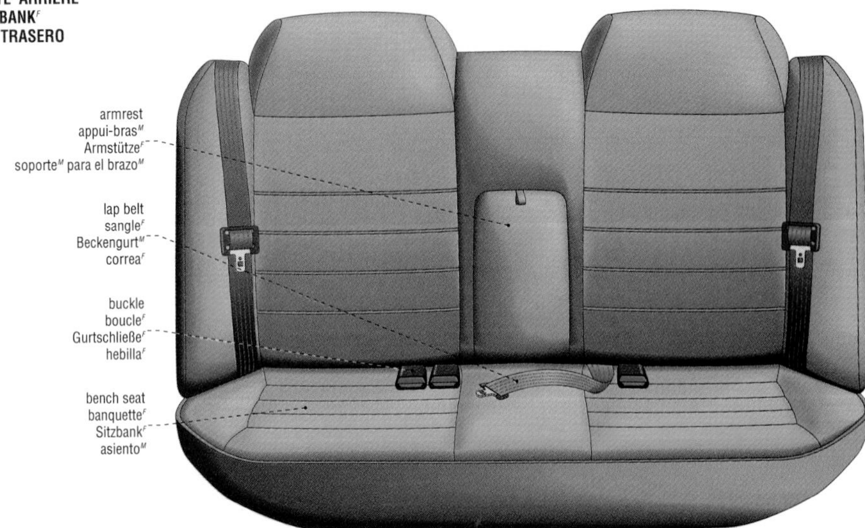

## DOOR
## PORTIÈRE[F]
## WAGENTÜR[F]
## PUERTA[F]

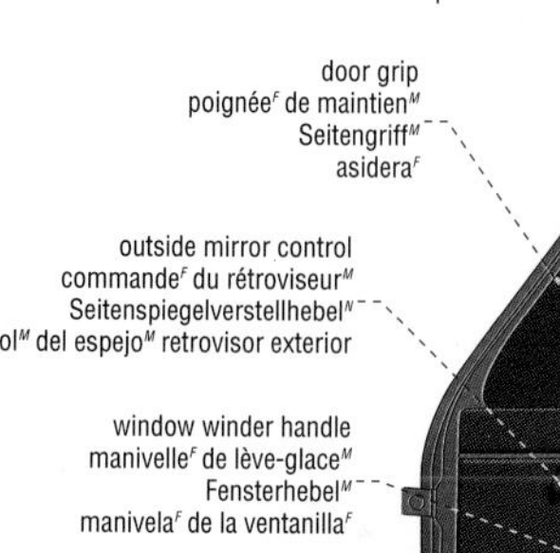


## LIGHTS
## FEUX[M]
## FAHRZEUGBELEUCHTUNG[F]
## FAROS[M]

**front lights**
**feux[M] avant**
**Bugleuchten[F]**
**faros[M] delanteros**

**rear lights**
**feux[M] arrière**
**Heckleuchten[F]**
**luces[F] traseras**

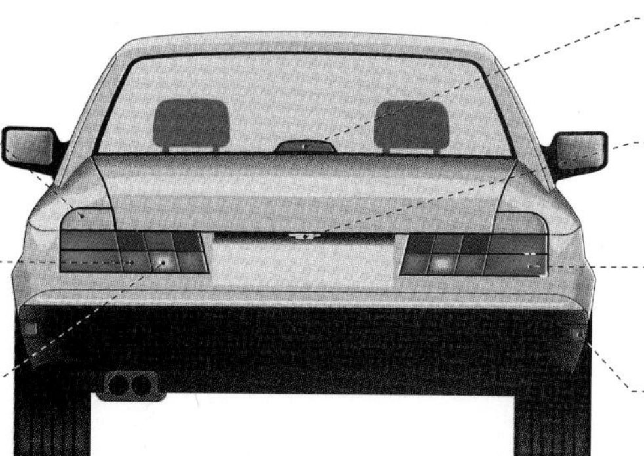

# CAR
# AUTOMOBILE[F]
# AUTO[N]
# AUTOMÓVIL[M]

## DASHBOARD
## TABLEAU[M] DE BORD[M]
## ARMATURENBRETT[N]
## SALPICADERO[M]

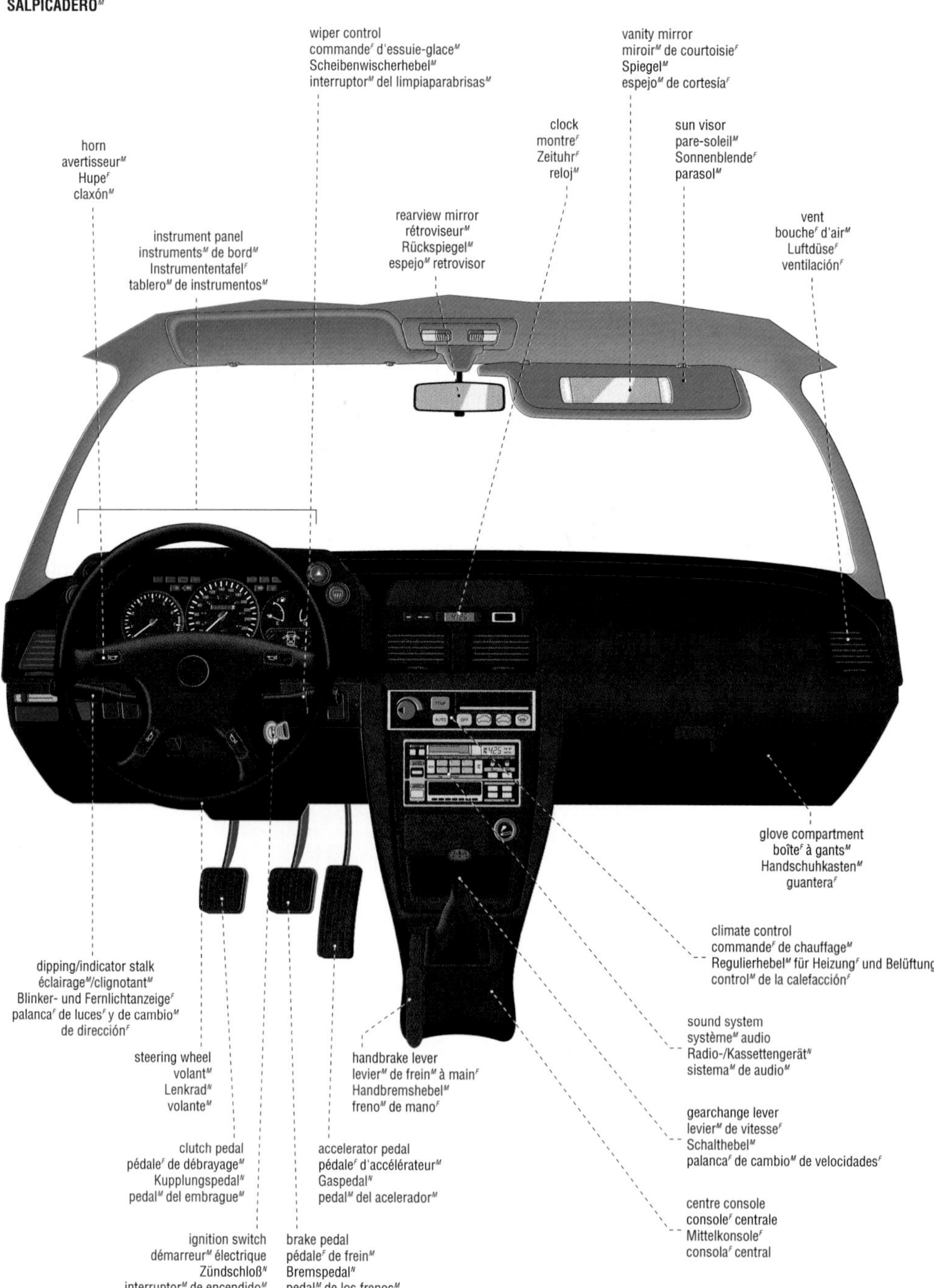

## INSTRUMENT PANEL
## INSTRUMENTS$^{M}$ DE BORD$^{M}$
## INSTRUMENTENTAFEL$^{F}$
## INSTRUMENTOS$^{M}$ DEL SALPICADERO$^{M}$

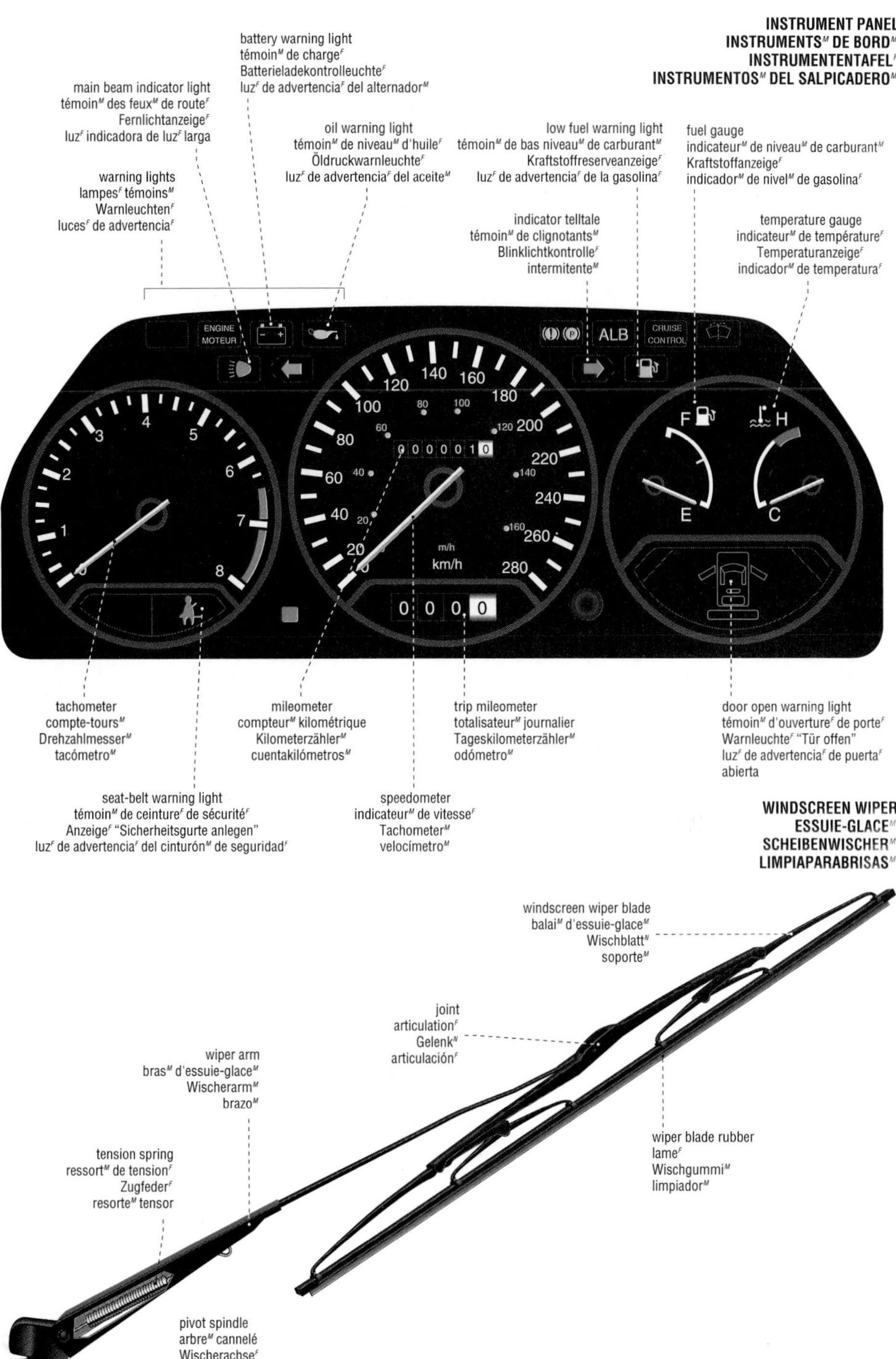

# CAR
# AUTOMOBILE[F]
# AUTO[N]
# AUTOMÓVIL[M]

## DISC BRAKE
## FREIN[M] À DISQUE[M]
## SCHEIBENBREMSE[F]
## FRENO[M] DE DISCO[M]

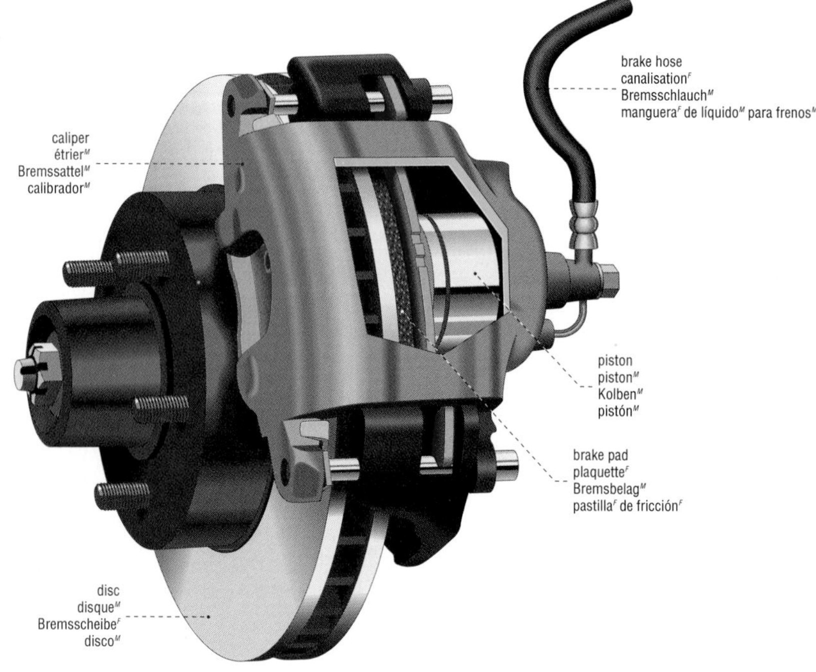


## DRUM BRAKE
## FREIN[M] À TAMBOUR[M]
## TROMMELBREMSE[F]
## FRENO[M] DE TAMBOR[M]

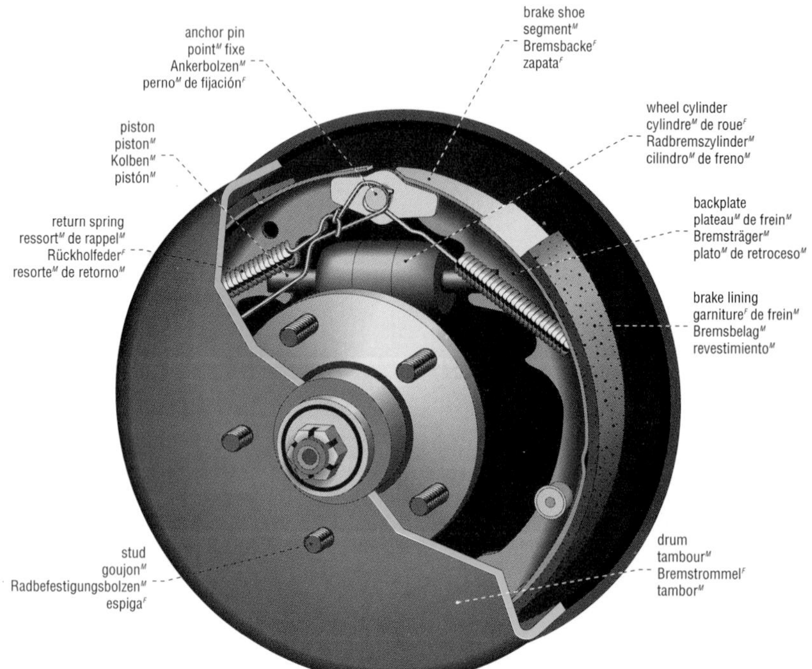

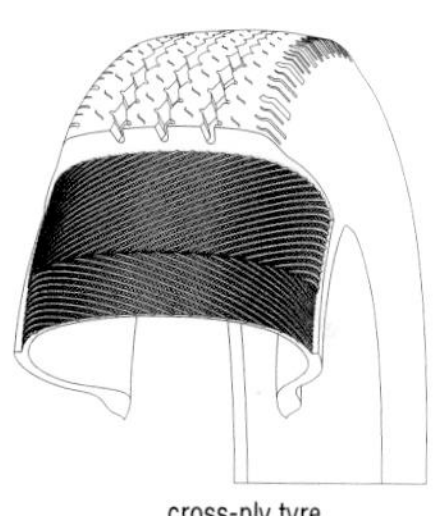
cross-ply tyre
pneu[M] à carcasse[F] diagonale
Diagonalreifen[M]
neumático[M] de capas[F] al sesgo[M]

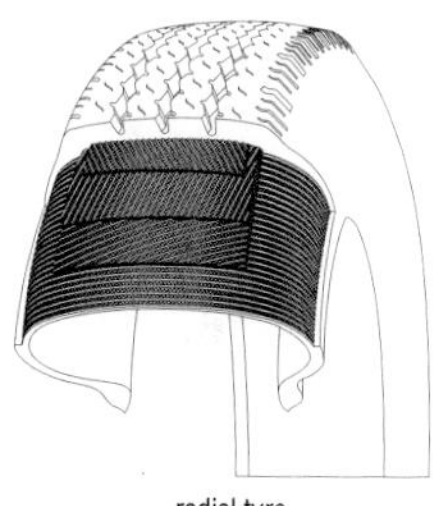
radial tyre
pneu[M] à carcasse[F] radiale
Radialreifen[M]
neumático[M] radial

## BELTED RADIAL TYRE
## PNEU[M] À CARCASSE[F] RADIALE CEINTURÉE
## RADIALGÜRTELREIFEN[M]
## NEUMÁTICO[M] RADIAL CON CINTURONES[M]

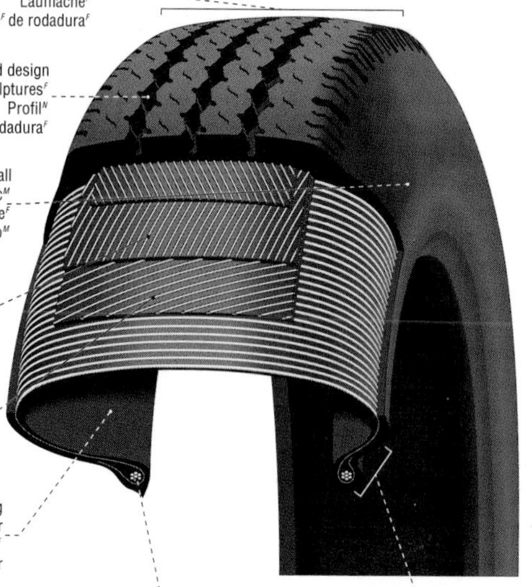

tread
bande[F] de roulement[M]
Lauffläche[F]
superficie[F] de rodadura[F]

tread design
sculptures[F]
Profil[N]
dibujo[M] de la superficie[F] de rodadura[F]

sidewall
flanc[M]
Reifenflanke[F]
costado[M]

belt
ceinture[F]
Gürtellage[F]
cinturón[M]

carcass ply
pli[M]
Radialkarkasse[F]
capa[F] del casco[M]

inner lining
revêtement[M] intérieur
Innendichtschicht[F]
revestimiento[M] interior

bead wire
tringle[F]
Wulstkern[M]
alambre[M] del reborde[M]

scuff rib
bourrelet[M]
Scheuerleiste[F]
banda[F] protectora

## TYRE
## PNEU[M]
## REIFEN[M]
## NEUMÁTICO[M]

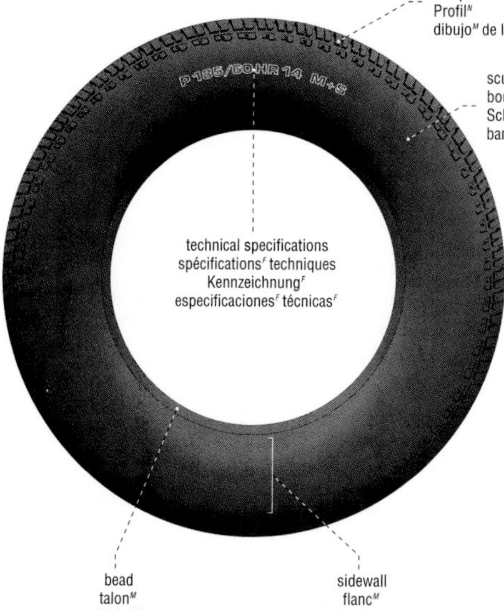

tread design
sculptures[F]
Profil[N]
dibujo[M] de la superficie[F] de rodadura[F]

P185/60HR14 M+S

scuff rib
bourrelet[M]
Scheuerleiste[F]
banda[F] protectora

technical specifications
spécifications[F] techniques
Kennzeichnung[F]
especificaciones[F] técnicas[F]

bead
talon[M]
Wulst[M]
moldura[F]

sidewall
flanc[M]
Reifenflanke[F]
costado[M]

## WHEEL
## ROUE[F]
## RAD[N]
## RUEDA[F]

disc
voile[M]
Radschüssel[F]
disco[M]

rim
jante[F]
Felge[F]
llanta[F]

rim flange
joue[F] de jante[F]
Felgenhorn[N]
pestaña[F] de la llanta[F]

# CAR
# AUTOMOBILE[F]
# AUTO[N]
# AUTOMÓVIL[M]

## PETROL ENGINE
## MOTEUR[M] À ESSENCE[F]
## OTTOMOTOR[M]
## MOTOR[M] DE GASOLINA[F]

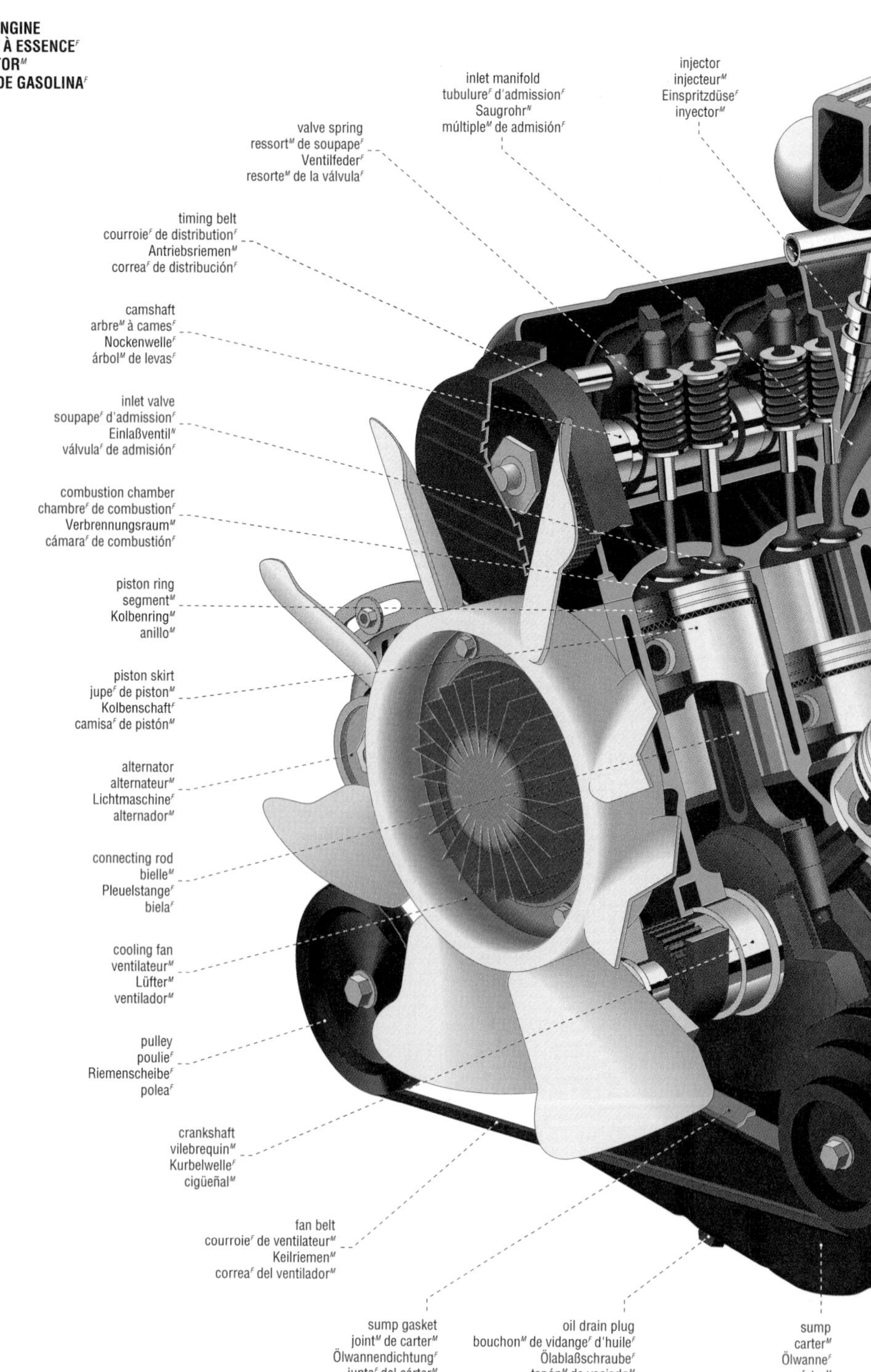

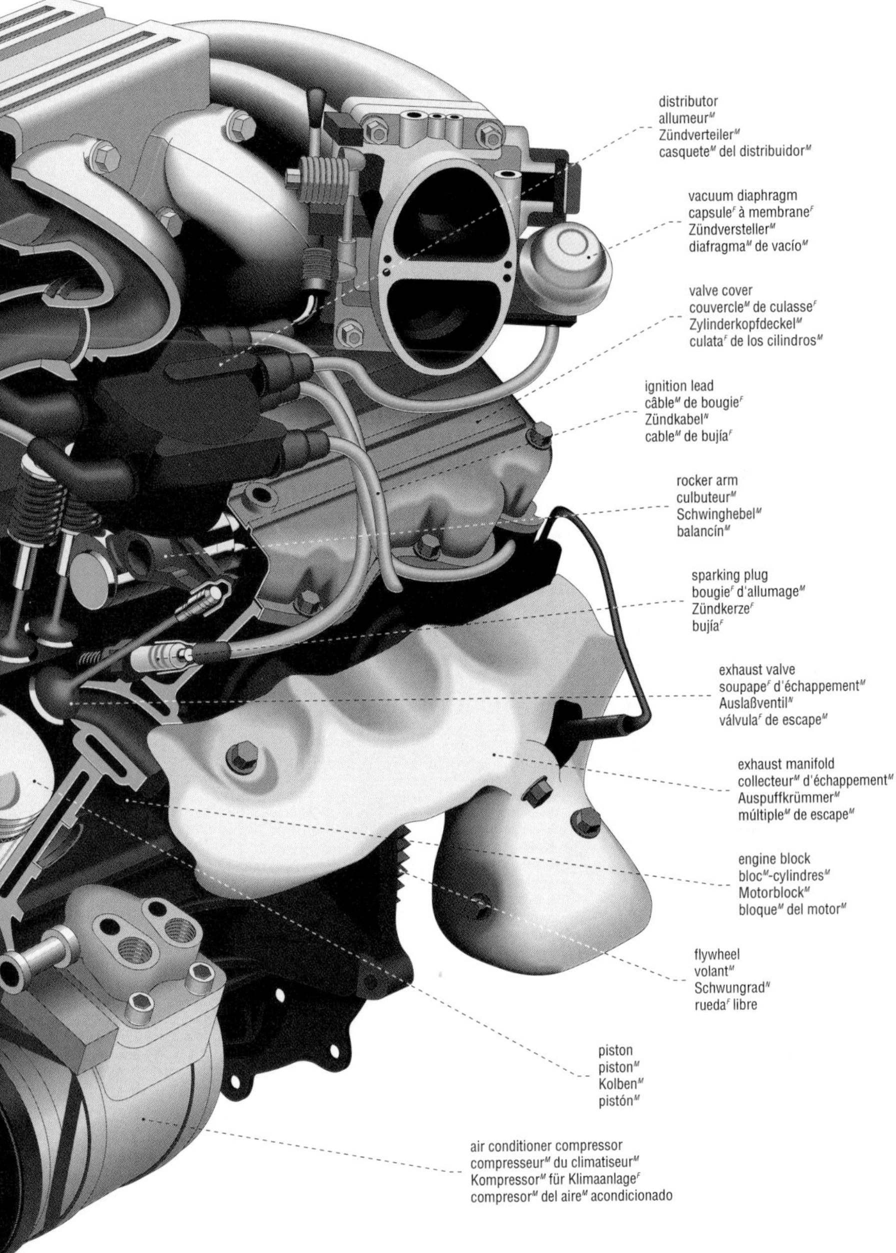
distributor
allumeur^M
Zündverteiler^M
casquete^M del distribuidor^M
vacuum diaphragm
capsule^F à membrane^F
Zündversteller^M
diafragma^M de vacío^M
valve cover
couvercle^M de culasse^F
Zylinderkopfdeckel^M
culata^F de los cilindros^M
ignition lead
câble^M de bougie^F
Zündkabel^N
cable^M de bujía^F
rocker arm
culbuteur^M
Schwinghebel^M
balancín^M
sparking plug
bougie^F d'allumage^M
Zündkerze^F
bujía^F
exhaust valve
soupape^F d'échappement^M
Auslaßventil^N
válvula^F de escape^M
exhaust manifold
collecteur^M d'échappement^M
Auspuffkrümmer^M
múltiple^M de escape^M
engine block
bloc^M-cylindres^M
Motorblock^M
bloque^M del motor^M
flywheel
volant^M
Schwungrad^N
rueda^F libre
piston
piston^M
Kolben^M
pistón^M
air conditioner compressor
compresseur^M du climatiseur^M
Kompressor^M für Klimaanlage^F
compresor^M del aire^M acondicionado

# TYPES OF ENGINE
# TYPES[M] DE MOTEURS[M]
# MOTORTYPEN[M]
# TIPOS[M] DE MOTORES[M]

## FOUR-STROKE ENGINE
## MOTEUR[M] À QUATRE TEMPS[M]
## VIERTAKTMOTOR[M]
## MOTOR[M] DE CUATRO TIEMPOS[M]

inlet valve
soupape[F] d'admission[F]
Einlaßventil[N]
válvula[F] de admisión[F]

air/fuel mixture
mélange[M] air[M]/carburant[M]
Kraftstoff-Luft-Gemisch[N]
mezcla[F] de aire[M] y combustible[M]

cylinder
cylindre[M]
Zylinder[M]
cilindro[M]

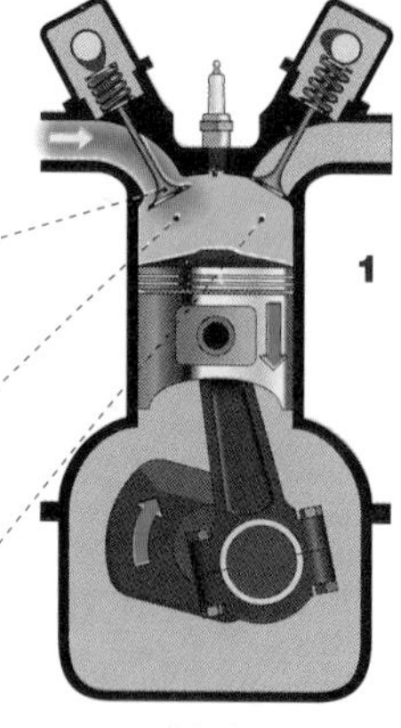


induction
admission[F]
Ansaugen[N]
admisión[F]

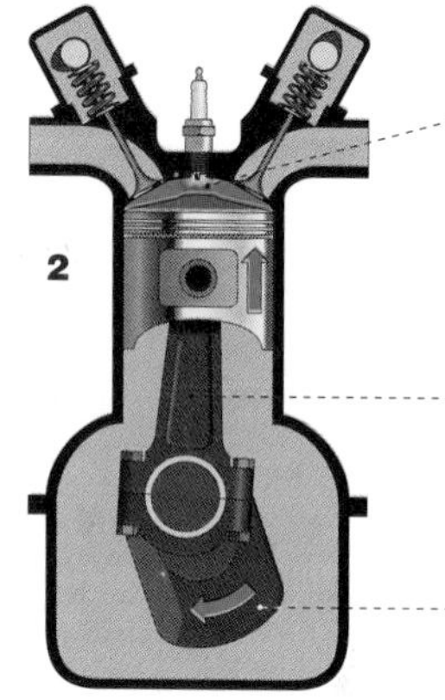
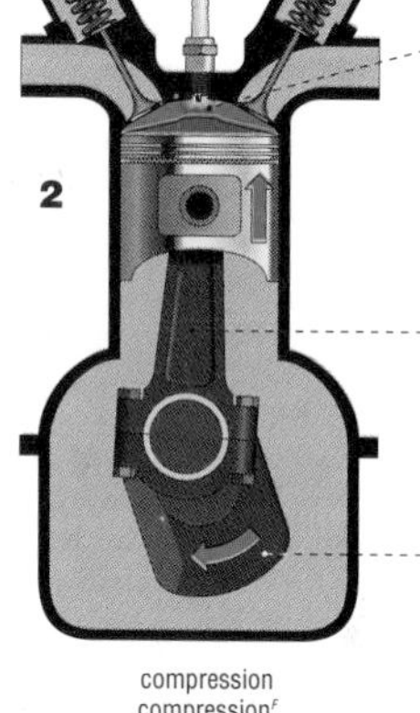


compression
compression[F]
Verdichten[N]
compresión[F]

spark
étincelle[F]
Funken[M]
chispa[F]

connecting rod
bielle[F]
Pleuelstange[F]
biela[F]

crankshaft
vilebrequin[M]
Kurbelwelle[F]
cigüeñal[M]

ignition
explosion[F]
Verbrennung[F]
explosión[F]

piston
piston[M]
Kolben[M]
pistón[M]

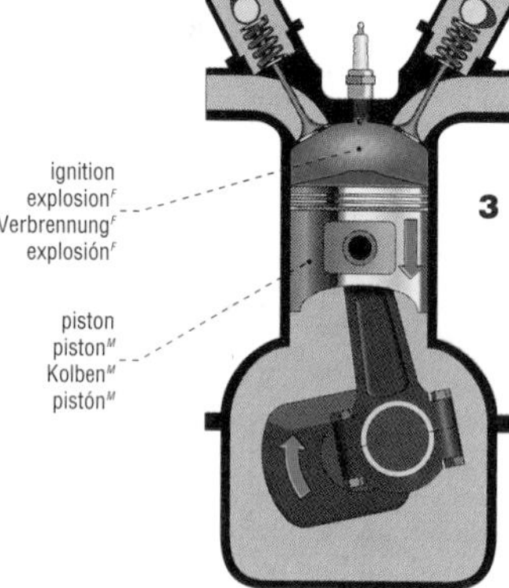


combustion
combustion[F]
Zünden[N]
combustión[F]

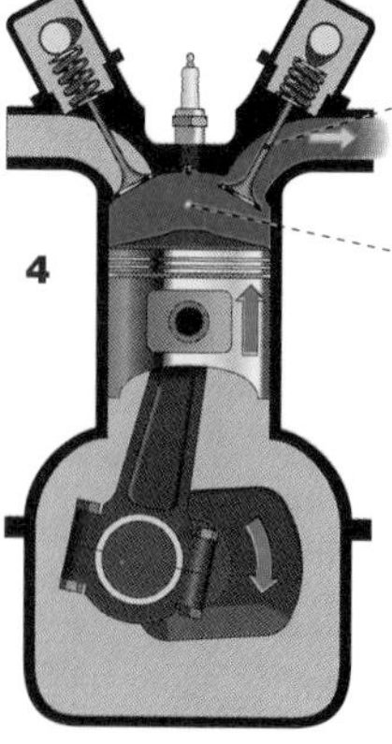


exhaust
échappement[M]
Ausstoßen[N]
escape[M]

exhaust valve
soupape[F] d'échappement[M]
Auslaßventil[N]
válvula[F] de escape[M]

burned gases
gaz[M] brûlés
Abgase[N]
gases[M] quemados

## TWO-STROKE ENGINE
## MOTEUR[M] À DEUX TEMPS[M]
## ZWEITAKTMOTOR[M]
## MOTOR[M] DE DOS TIEMPOS[M]

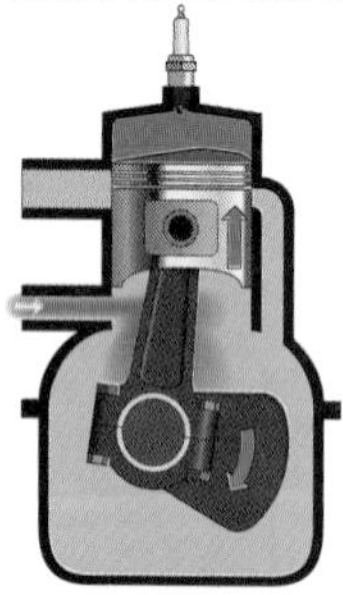

compression/induction
compression[F]/admission[F]
Verdichten[N]/Ansaugen[N]
compresión[F]/admisión[F]

exhaust port
canal[M] d'échappement[M]
Auspuffkanal[M]
lumbrera[F] de escape[M]

inlet port
canal[M] d'admission[F]
Ansaugkanal[M]
lumbrera[F] de admisión[F]

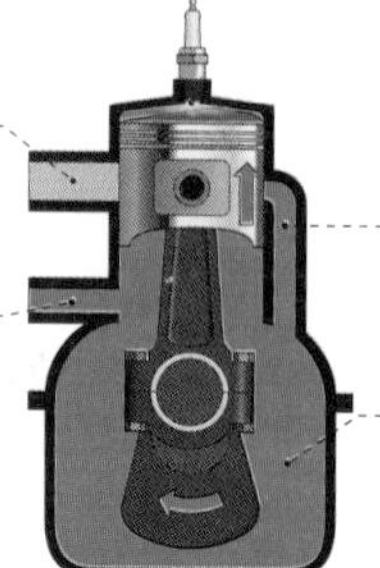

combustion
combustion[F]
Verbrennen[N]
combustión[F]

transfer port
canal[M] de transfert[M]
Überströmschlitz[M]
lumbrera[F] de transferencia[F]

crankcase
carter[M]
Kurbelgehäuse[N]
cárter[M]

exhaust
échappement[M]
Ausstoßen[N]
escape[M]

## DIESEL ENGINE
## MOTEUR[M] DIESEL
## DIESELMOTOR[M]
## MOTOR[M] DIÉSEL

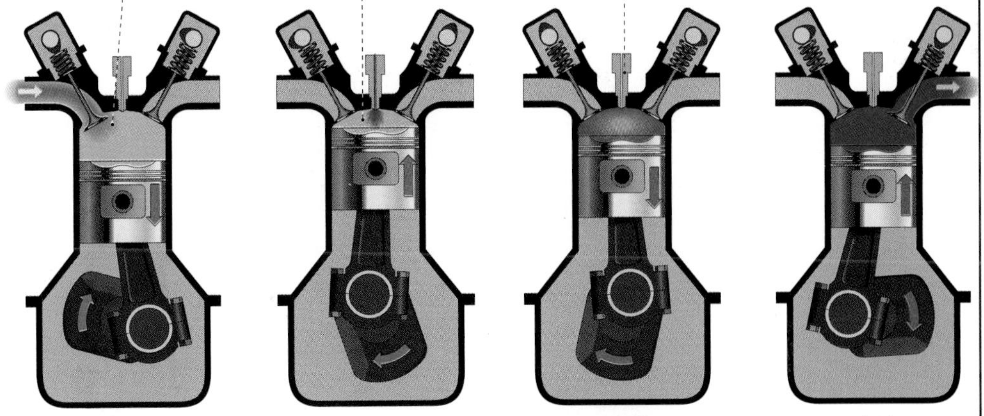

air
air[M]
Luft[F]
aire[M]

injection/ignition
injection[F]/explosion[F]
Einspritzung[F]/Verbrennung[F]
injección[F]/explosión[F]

fuel injector
injecteur[M]
Einspritzdüse[F]
injector[M] de combustible[M]

induction
admission[F]
Ansaugen[N]
admisión[F]

compression
compression[F]
Verdichten[N]
compresión[F]

combustion
combustion[F]
Zünden[N]
combustión[F]

exhaust
échappement[M]
Ausstoßen[N]
escape[M]

## ROTARY ENGINE
## MOTEUR[M] ROTATIF
## KREISKOLBENMOTOR[M]
## MOTOR[M] ROTATORIO

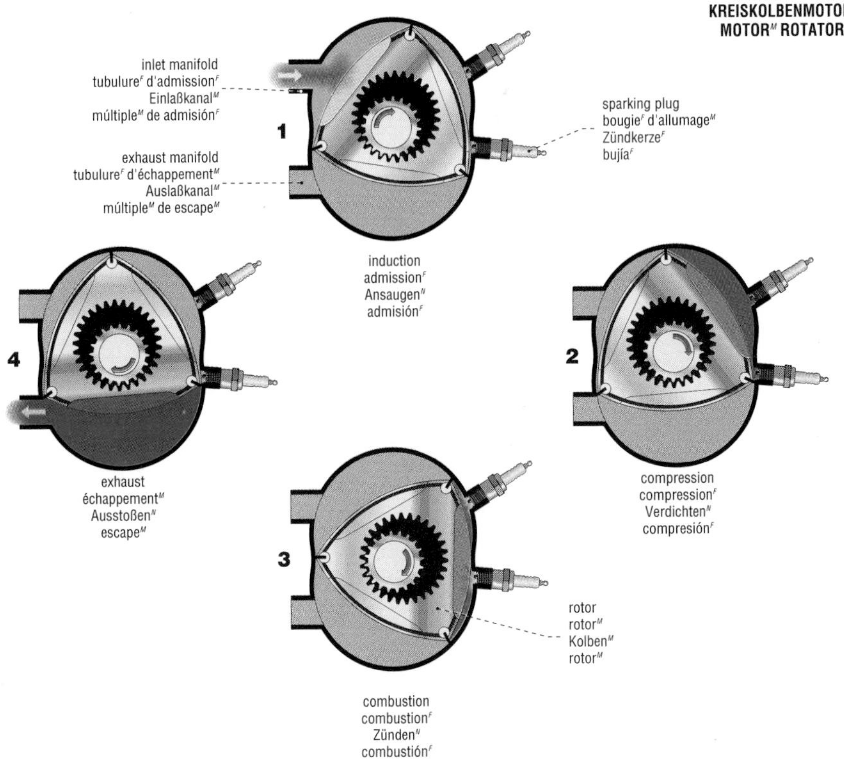

inlet manifold
tubulure[F] d'admission[F]
Einlaßkanal[M]
múltiple[M] de admisión[F]

1

sparking plug
bougie[F] d'allumage[M]
Zündkerze[F]
bujía[F]

exhaust manifold
tubulure[F] d'échappement[M]
Auslaßkanal[M]
múltiple[M] de escape[M]

induction
admission[F]
Ansaugen[N]
admisión[F]

4

2

exhaust
échappement[M]
Ausstoßen[N]
escape[M]

compression
compression[F]
Verdichten[N]
compresión[F]

3

rotor
rotor[M]
Kolben[M]
rotor[M]

combustion
combustion[F]
Zünden[N]
combustión[F]

# CAR
# AUTOMOBILE[F]
# AUTO[N]
# AUTOMÓVIL[M]

## RADIATOR
## RADIATEUR[M]
## KÜHLER[M]
## RADIADOR[M]

filler cap
bouchon[M] de remplissage[M]
Kühlerverschlußdeckel[M]
tapa[F]
radiator core
grille[F]
Kühlerblock[M]
rejilla[F]
cooling fan
ventilateur[M]
Lüfter[M]
ventilador[M]
electric motor
moteur[M] électrique
Elektromotor[M]
motor[M] eléctrico
fan thermostat
thermocontact[M]
Thermoschalter[M]
termostato[M] del ventilador[M]
radiator hose
durite[F] de radiateur[M]
Kühlwasserschlauch[M]
manguera[F]

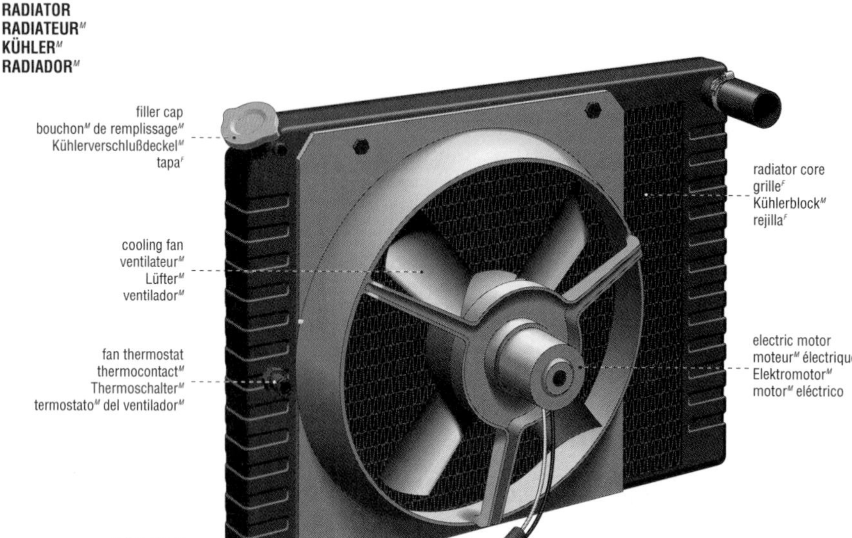

## TURBO-CHARGED ENGINE
## MOTEUR[M] À TURBOCOMPRESSION[F]
## MOTOR[M] MIT ABGASTURBOLADER[M]
## MOTOR[M] TURBO COMPRESOR

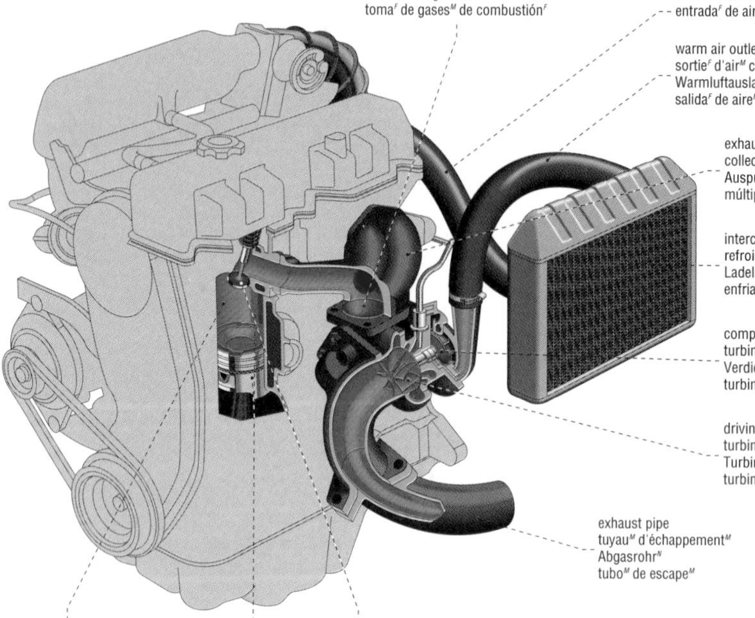

exhaust gas admission
entrée[F] des gaz[M] d'échappement[M]
Abgaseintritt[M]
toma[F] de gases[M] de combustión[F]
cold air inlet
admission[F] d'air[M] refroidi
Kaltluftzuleitung[F]
entrada[F] de aire[M] frío
warm air outlet
sortie[F] d'air[M] chaud
Warmluftauslaß[M]
salida[F] de aire[M] caliente
exhaust manifold
collecteur[M] d'échappement[M]
Auspuffkrümmer[M]
múltiple[M] de escape[M]
intercooler
refroidisseur[M] d'air[M]
Ladeluftkühler[M]
enfriador[M]
compressor turbine
turbine[F] du compresseur[M]
Verdichterrad[N]
turbina[F] del compresor[M]
driving turbine
turbine[F] d'entraînement[M]
Turbinenrad[N]
turbina[F] de transmisión[F]
exhaust pipe
tuyau[M] d'échappement[M]
Abgasrohr[N]
tubo[M] de escape[M]
combustion chamber
chambre[F] de combustion[F]
Verbrennungsraum[M]
cámara[F] de combustión[F]
piston
piston[M]
Kolben[M]
pistón[M]
exhaust valve
soupape[F] d'échappement[M]
Auslaßventil[N]
válvula[F] de escape[M]

## SPARKING PLUG
## BOUGIE[F] D'ALLUMAGE[M]
## ZÜNDKERZE[F]
## BUJÍA[F]

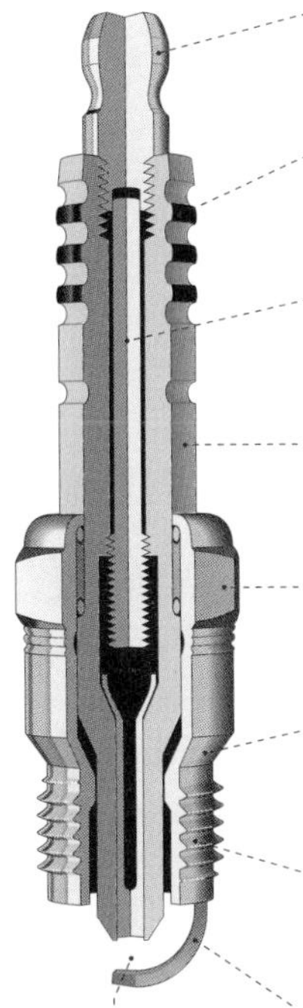

sparking plug
borne[F]
Anschlußbolzen[M]
borne[M]

groove
cannelure[F]
Kriechstrombarriere[F]
ranura[F]

centre electrode
électrode[F] centrale
Mittelelektrode[F]
electrodo[M] central

insulator
isolateur[M]
Isolator[M]
aislador[M]

hex nut
écrou[M] hexagonal
Sechskantmutter[F]
hexagonal[M]

sparking plug gasket
joint[M] de bougie[F]
Zündkerzendichtring[M]
junta[F]

sparking plug body
culot[M]
Zündkerzengehäuse[N]
cuerpo[M] metálico de la bujía[F]

side electrode
électrode[F] de masse[F]
Masseelektrode[F]
electrodo[M] de masa[F]

sparking plug gap
écartement[M] des électrodes[F]
Funkenstrecke[F]
espacio[M] para la chispa[F]

## EXHAUST SYSTEM
## SYSTÈME[M] D'ÉCHAPPEMENT[M]
## AUSPUFFANLAGE[F]
## SISTEMA[M] DE ESCAPE[M]

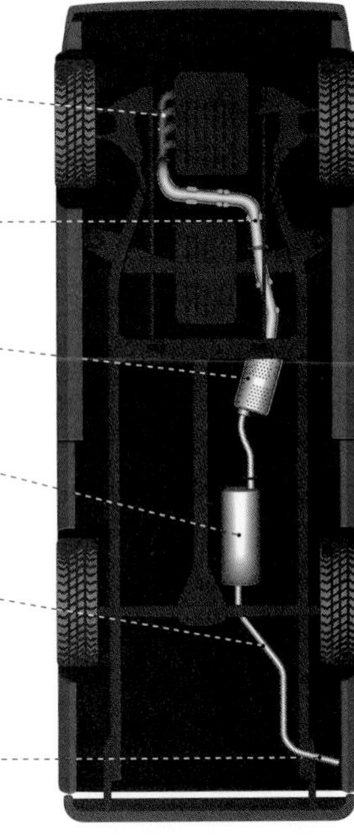

exhaust manifold
collecteur[M] d'échappement[M]
Auspuffkrümmer[M]
múltiple[M] de escape[M]

front pipe
tuyau[M] d'échappement[M]
vorderes Auspuffrohr[N]
tubo[M] de escape[M]

catalytic converter
convertisseur[M] catalytique
Katalysator[M]
convertidor[M] catalítico

silencer
pot[M] d'échappement[M]
Schalldämpfer[M]
silenciador[M]

tail pipe
tuyau[M] arrière
hinteres Auspuffrohr[N]
tubo[M] de cola[F]

tail pipe extension
embout[M]
Endrohr[N]
extensión[F]

## BATTERY
## BATTERIE[F] D'ACCUMULATEURS[M]
## BATTERIE[F]
## BATERÍA[F]

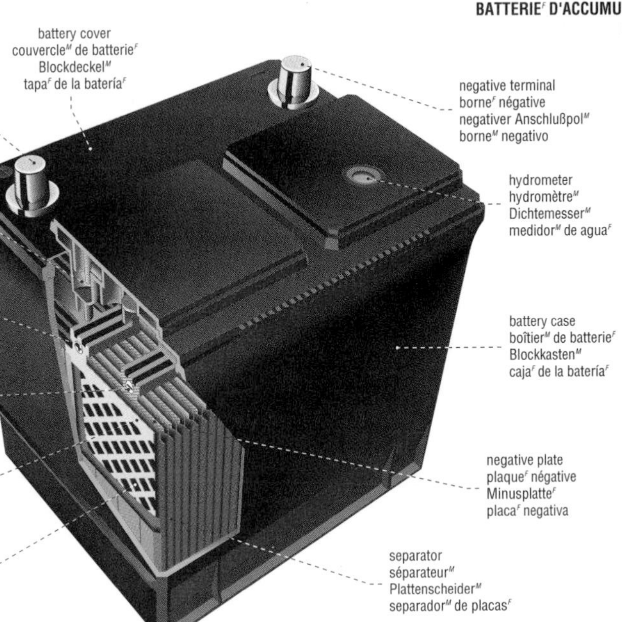

battery cover
couvercle[M] de batterie[F]
Blockdeckel[M]
tapa[F] de la batería[F]

positive terminal
borne[F] positive
positiver Anschlußpol[M]
borne[M] positivo

negative terminal
borne[F] négative
negativer Anschlußpol[M]
borne[M] negativo

liquid/gas separator
séparateur[M] liquide[M]/gaz[M]
Entgasungsbohrung[F]
separador[M] de gas[M] y líquido[M]

hydrometer
hydromètre[M]
Dichtemesser[M]
medidor[M] de agua[F]

positive plate strap
barrette[F] positive
Pluspolbrücke[F]
banda[F] de placa[F] positiva

battery case
boîtier[M] de batterie[F]
Blockkasten[M]
caja[F] de la batería[F]

negative plate strap
barrette[F] négative
Minuspolbrücke[F]
banda[F] de placa[F] negativa

positive plate
plaque[F] positive
Plusplatte[F]
placa[F] positiva

negative plate
plaque[F] négative
Minusplatte[F]
placa[F] negativa

plate grid
alvéole[F] de plaque[F]
Plattengitter[N]
rejilla[F]

separator
séparateur[M]
Plattenscheider[M]
separador[M] de placas[F]

# TRUCKING
# CAMIONNAGE[M]
# LASTKRAFTFAHRZEUGE[N]
# CAMIONES[M]

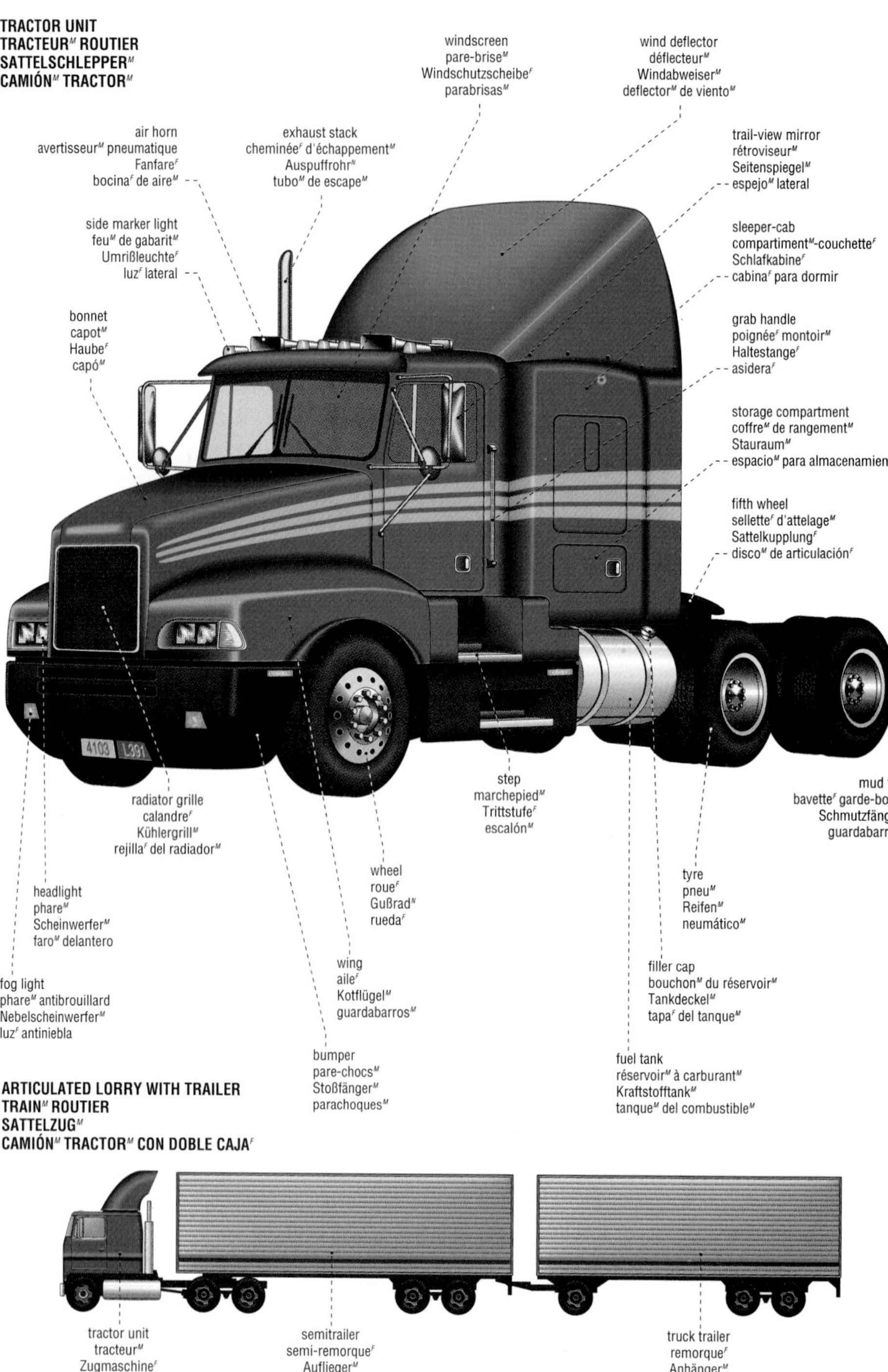

## SEMITRAILER
## SEMI-REMORQUE[F]
## AUFLIEGER[M]
## CAJA[F] TIPO[M] SEMIRREMOLQUE[M]

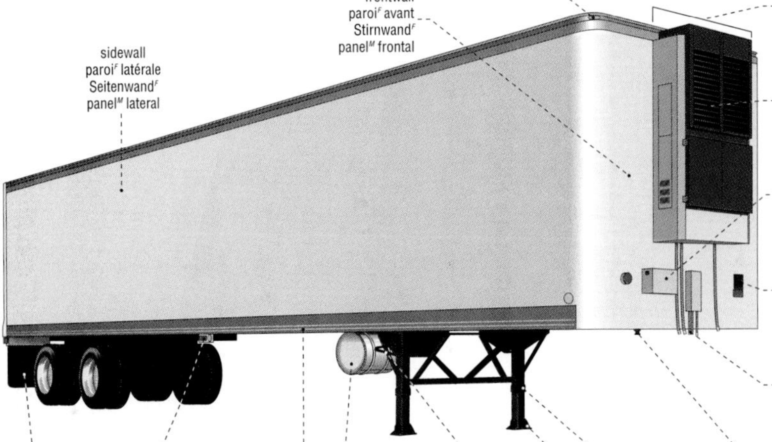

side marker light
feu[M] de gabarit[M]
Begrenzungsleuchte[F]
luz[F] lateral
frontwall
paroi[F] avant
Stirnwand[F]
panel[M] frontal
sidewall
paroi[F] latérale
Seitenwand[F]
panel[M] lateral
refrigeration unit
groupe[M] frigorifique
Kühlaggregat[N]
unidad[F] de refrigeración[F]
vent door
volet[M] d'air[M]
Luftklappe[F]
ventilador[M]
battery box
boîtier[M] de batterie[F]
Batteriekasten[M]
caja[F] del acumulador[M]
partlow chart
disque[M] de papier[M]-diagramme[M]
Partlow-Diagramm[N]
regulador[M] de temperatura[F]
electrical connection
accouplement[M] électrique
Stromanschluß[M]
conexiones[F]
kingpin
pivot[M] d'accouplement[M]
Zugsattelzapfen[M]
perno[M] maestro
support leg
béquille[F]
Standbein[N]
pata[F] soporte
sand shoe
sabot[M]
Stützfuß[M]
zapata[F]
support leg crank
manivelle[F]
Handkurbel[F]
manivela[F] de elevación[F] de patas[F]
reflector
réflecteur[M]
Rückstrahler[M]
reflector[M]
mud flap
bavette[F] garde-boue[M]
Schmutzfänger[M]
guardabarros[M]
auxiliary tank
réservoir[M] auxiliaire
Zusatztank[M]
tanque[M] auxiliar
side rail
longeron[M]
Wand-Untergurt[M]
banda[F] lateral protectora

## FLATBED
## SEMI-REMORQUE[F] PLATE-FORME[F]
## KOFFER-SATTELANHÄNGER[M]
## PLATAFORMA[F]

stake pocket
gaine[F] de rancher[M]
Rungentasche[F]
ranura[F] para toldo[M]
bulkhead
paroi[F] de bout[M]
Stirnwand[F]
mampara[F] de contención[F]
load platform
plate-forme[F]
Ladefläche[F]
plataforma[F]
rear light
feu[M] rouge arrière
Rücklicht[N]
luz[F] trasera
indicator
clignotant[M]
Richtungsanzeiger[M]
intermitente[M]
mud flap
bavette[F] garde-boue[M]
Spritzlappen[M]
guardabarros[M]
bumper
pare-chocs[M]
Unterfahrschutz[M]
parachoques[M]
rub rail
rail[M] de guidage[M]
Rammschutzleiste[F]
banda[F] protectora
support leg crank
manivelle[F]
Handkurbel[F]
manivela[F] de elevación[F] de patas[F]
side marker light
feu[M] de gabarit[M]
Begrenzungsleuchte[F]
luz[F] lateral

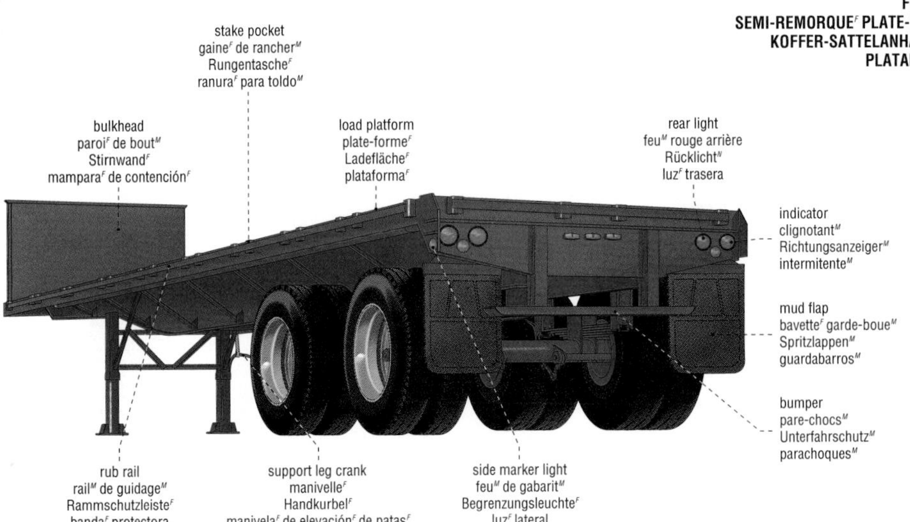

# MOTORCYCLE
# MOTO[F]
# MOTORRAD[N]
# MOTOCICLETA[F]

## SIDE VIEW
## VUE[F] LATÉRALE
## SEITENANSICHT[F]
## VISTA[F] LATERAL

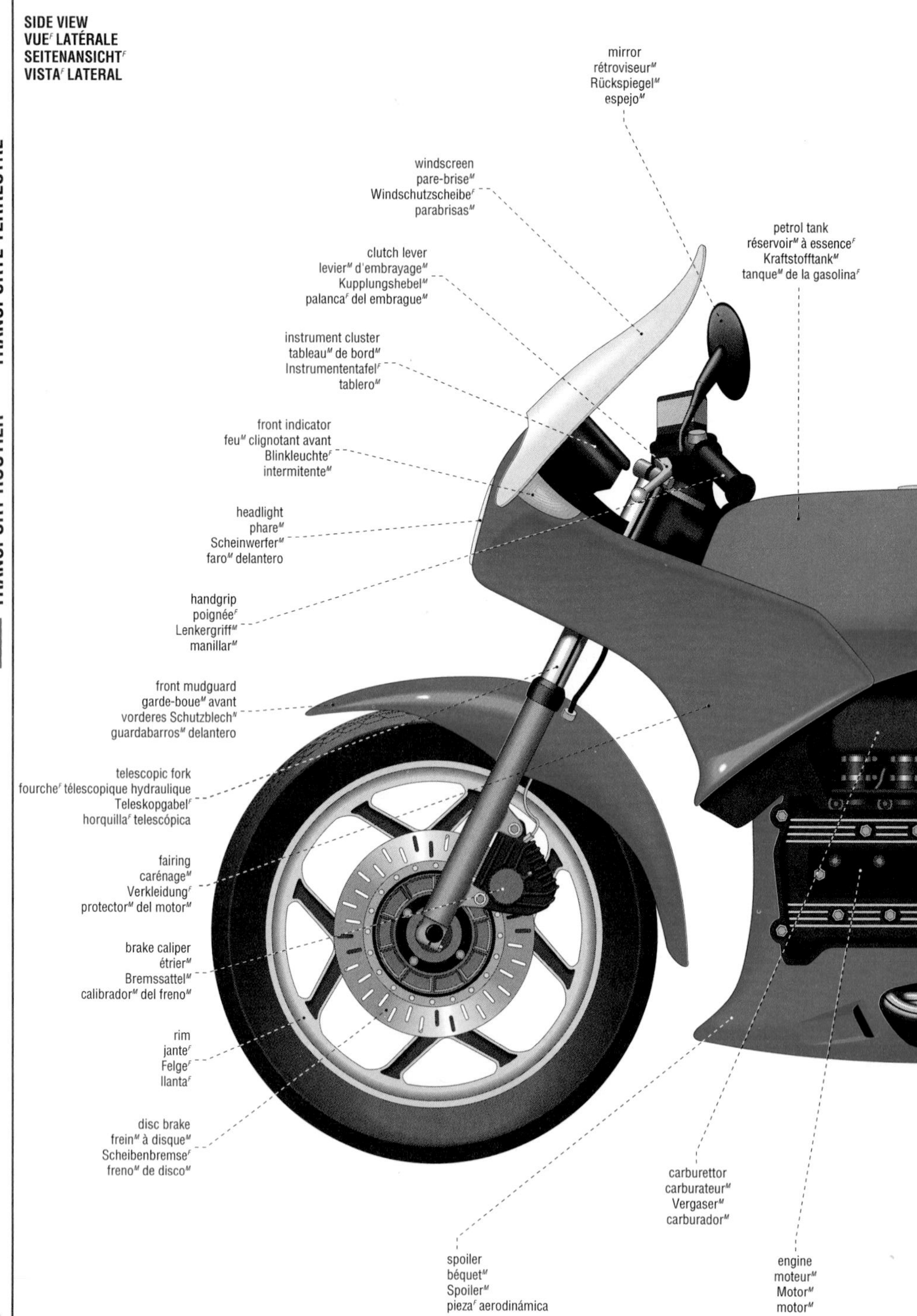

## CRASH HELMET
## CASQUE[M] DE PROTECTION[F]
## SCHUTZHELM[M]
## CASCO[M] PROTECTOR

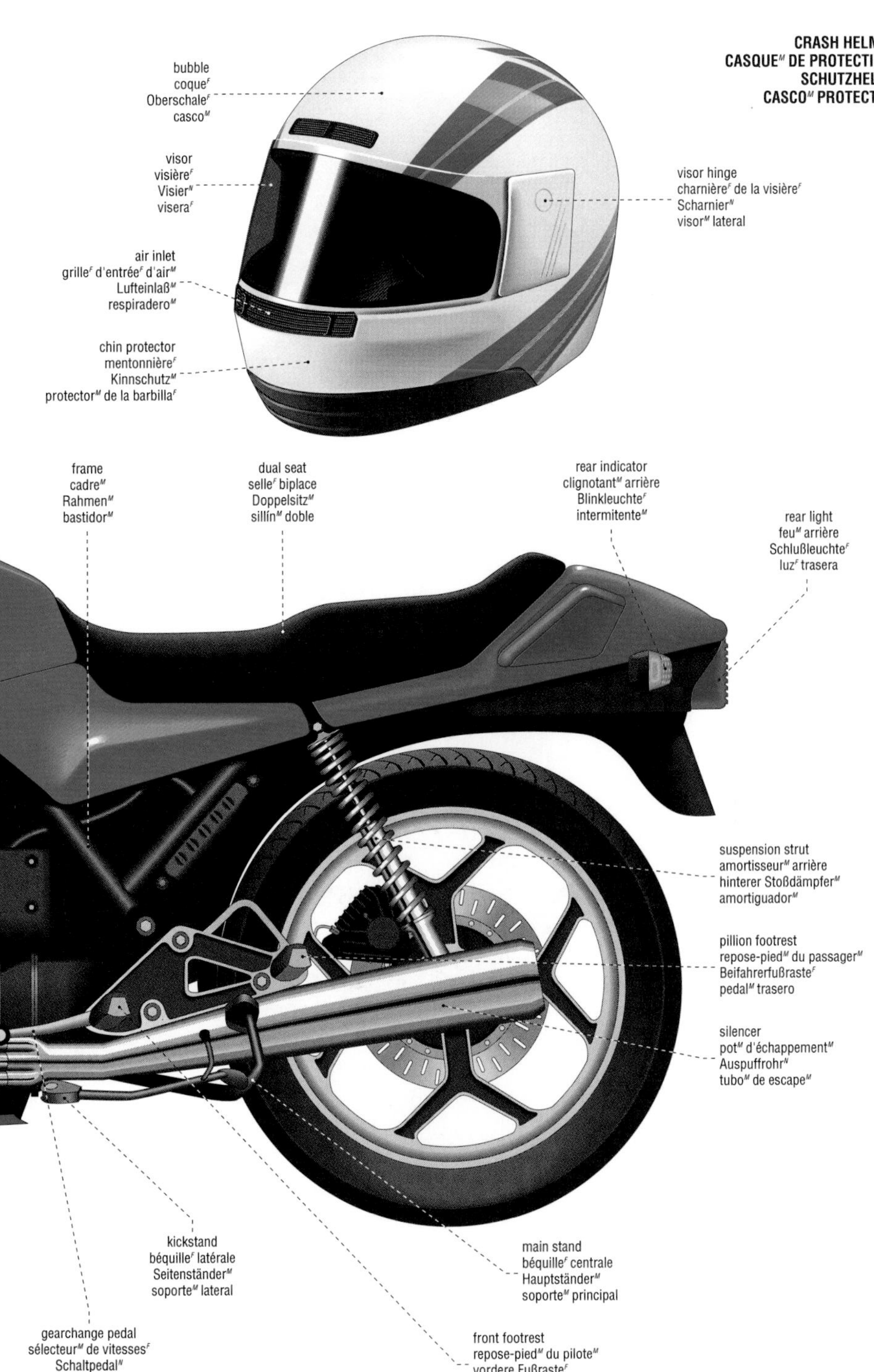

# MOTORCYCLE
# MOTO[F]
# MOTORRAD[N]
# MOTOCICLETA[F]

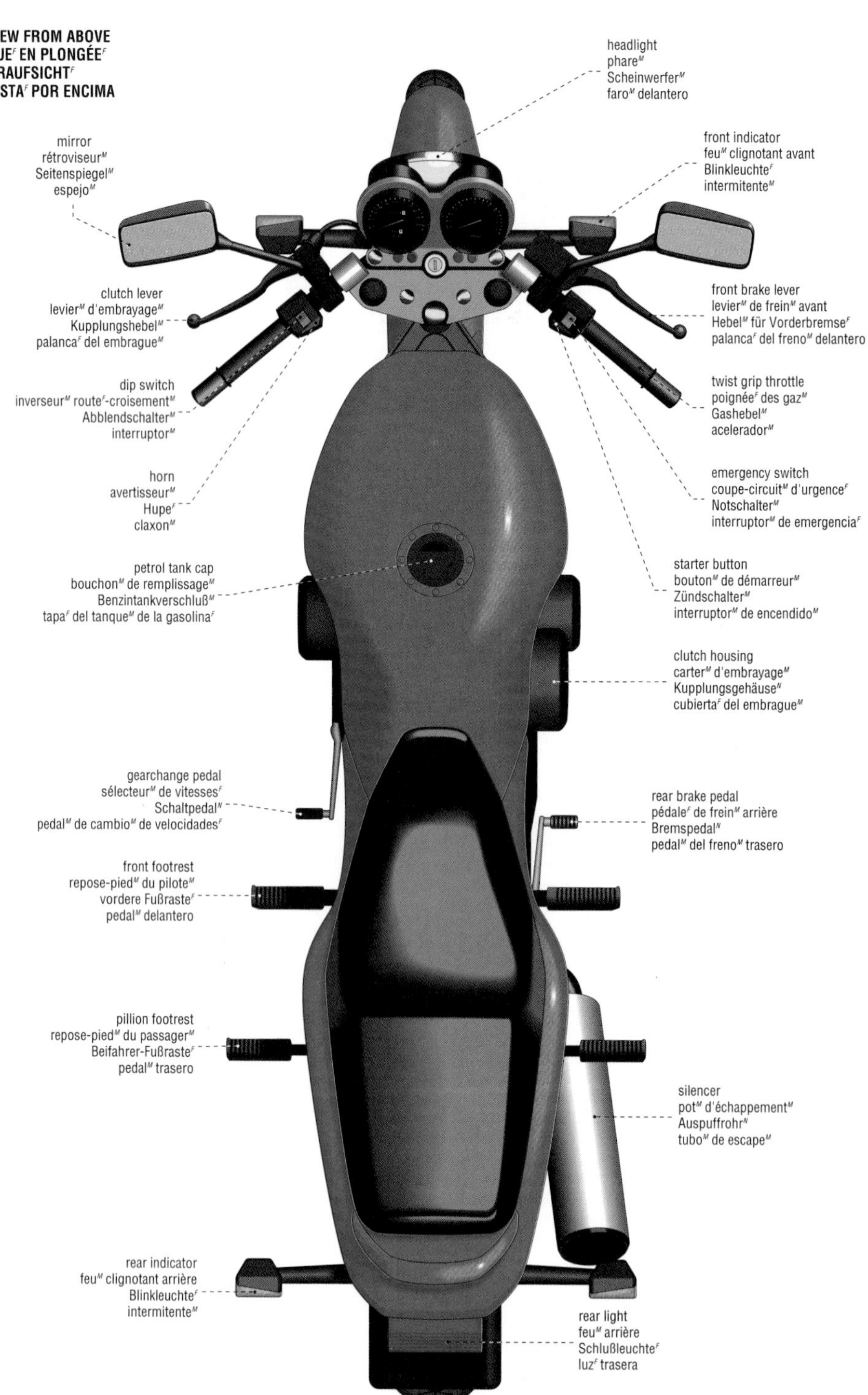

## INSTRUMENT CLUSTER
## TABLEAU$^{M}$ DE BORD$^{M}$
## INSTRUMENTENTAFEL$^{F}$
## TABLERO$^{M}$

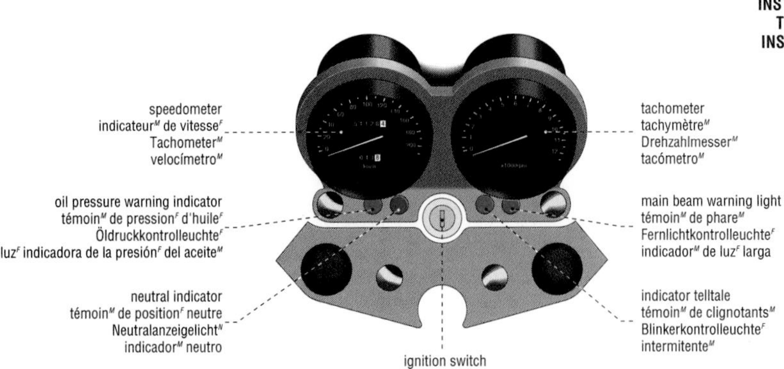


## SNOWMOBILE
## MOTONEIGE$^{F}$
## SCHNEEMOBIL$^{N}$
## TRINEO$^{M}$ MOTORIZADO

rear bumper
pare-chocs$^{M}$ arrière
Stoßstange$^{F}$
parachoques$^{M}$

luggage rack
support$^{M}$ à bagages$^{M}$
Gepäckträger$^{M}$
portaequipajes$^{M}$

backrest
dossier$^{M}$
Rückenlehne$^{F}$
respaldo$^{M}$

seat
selle$^{F}$
Sitzbank$^{F}$
asiento$^{M}$

brake handle
manette$^{F}$ du frein$^{M}$
Bremshebel$^{M}$
palanca$^{F}$ del freno$^{M}$

handlebars
guidon$^{M}$
Lenker$^{M}$
manillar$^{M}$

windscreen
pare-brise$^{M}$
Klarsichtscheibe$^{F}$
parabrisas$^{M}$

fairing
capot$^{M}$
Instrumente$^{N}$
cabina$^{F}$

headlight
phare$^{M}$
Scheinwerfer$^{M}$
faro$^{M}$ delantero

idler wheel
roue$^{F}$ de support$^{M}$
Zwischenrad$^{N}$
rueda$^{F}$ de transmisión$^{F}$

track
chenille$^{F}$
Kette$^{F}$
rueda$^{F}$ de cadena$^{F}$

reflector
catadioptre$^{M}$
Rückstrahler$^{M}$
reflector$^{M}$

body
coque$^{F}$
Rumpf$^{M}$
carrocería$^{F}$

sprocket
roue$^{F}$ dentée
Antriebsrad$^{N}$
diente$^{M}$

footboard
marchepied$^{M}$
Trittbrett$^{N}$
estribo$^{M}$

air scoop
prise$^{F}$ d'air$^{M}$
Lufteinlaß$^{M}$
entrada$^{F}$ de aire$^{M}$

snow guard
bavette$^{F}$ garde-neige$^{M}$
Schutzblech$^{N}$
guardanieve$^{M}$

shock absorber
amortisseur$^{M}$
Stoßdämpfer$^{M}$
amortiguador$^{M}$

ski
ski$^{M}$
Kufe$^{F}$
esquí$^{M}$

# BICYCLE
# BICYCLETTE[F]
# FAHRRAD[N]
# BICICLETA[F]

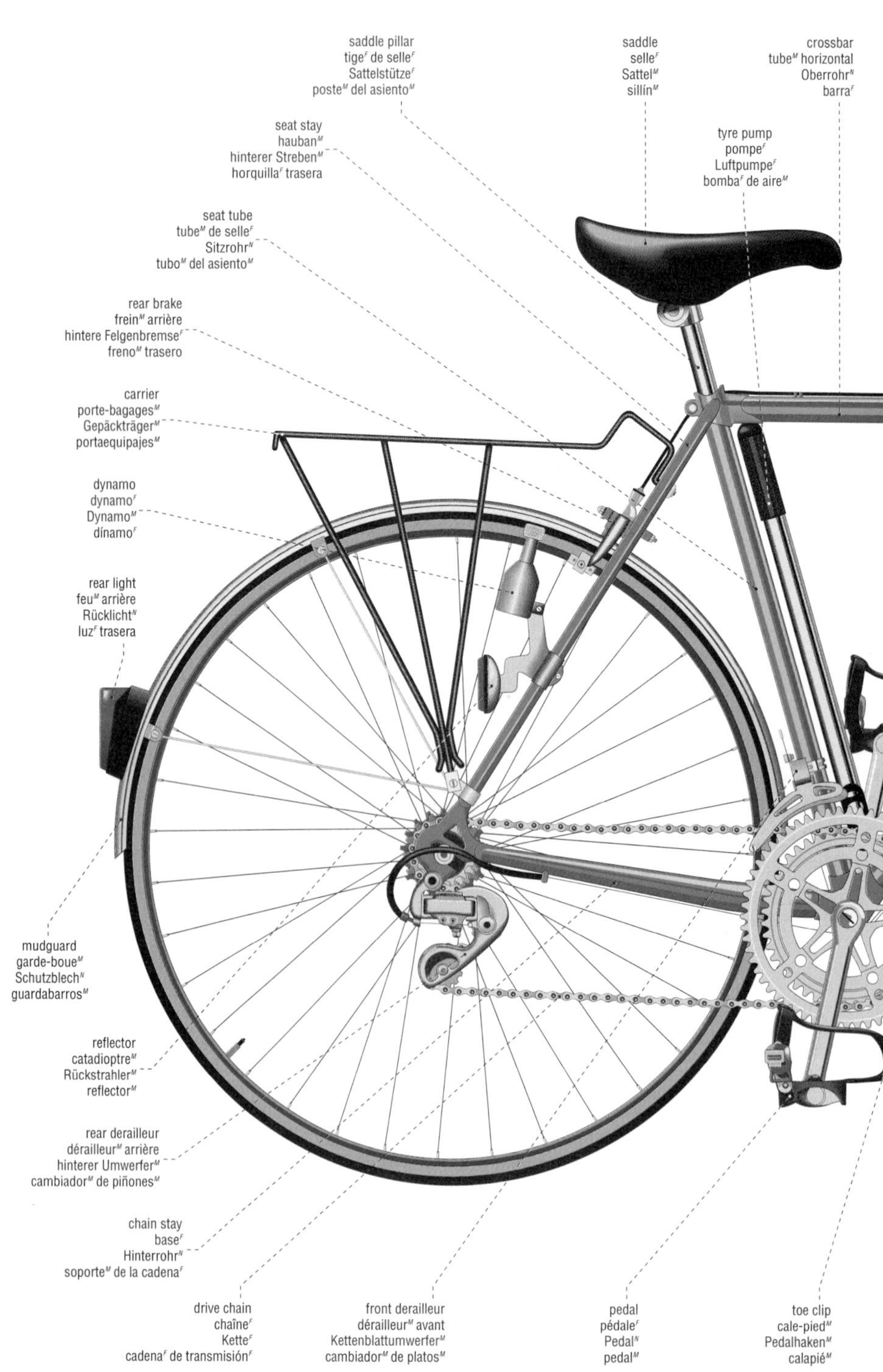

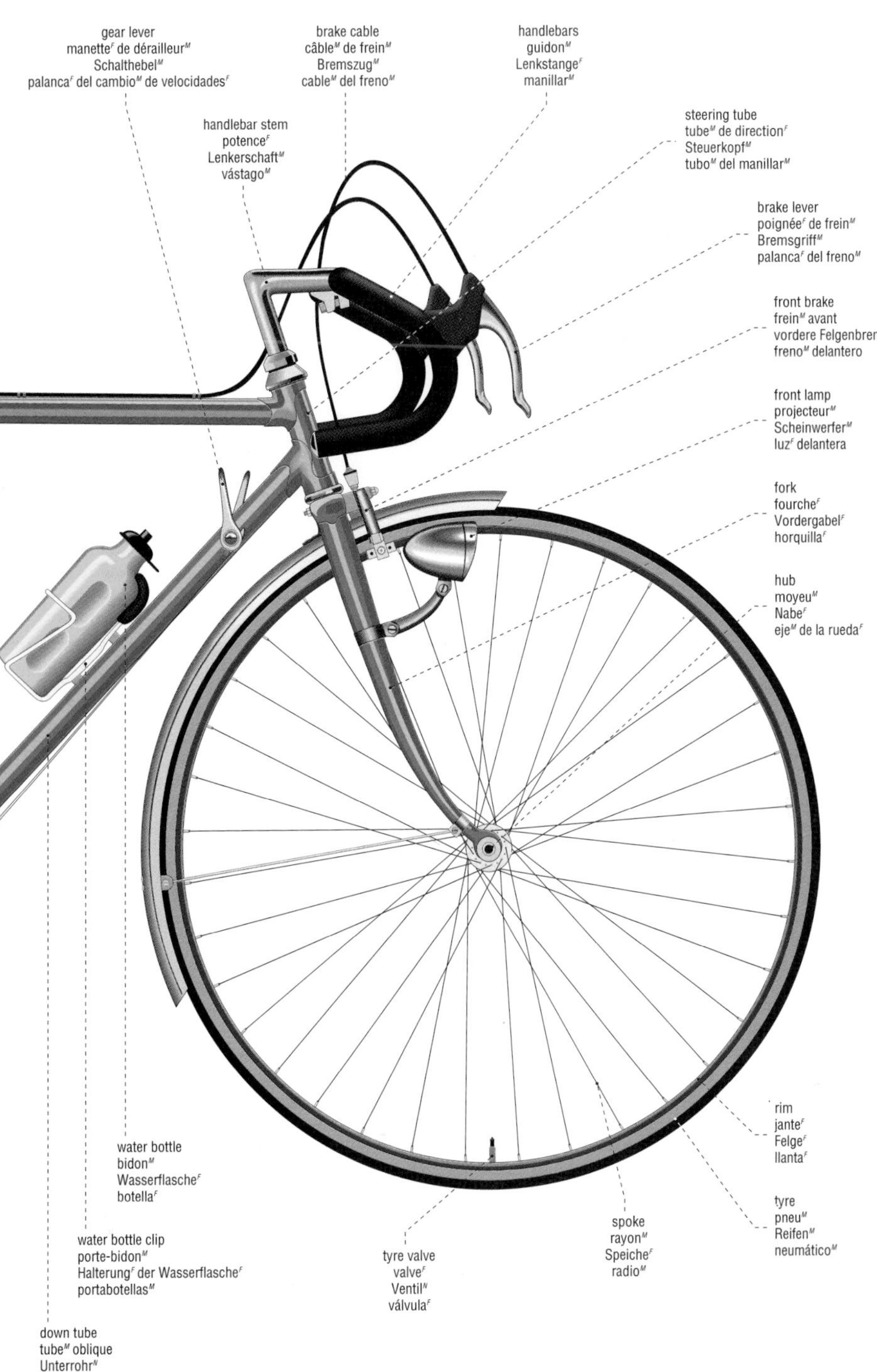
gear lever
manette[F] de dérailleur[M]
Schalthebel[M]
palanca[F] del cambio[M] de velocidades[F]
brake cable
câble[M] de frein[M]
Bremszug[M]
cable[M] del freno[M]
handlebars
guidon[M]
Lenkstange[F]
manillar[M]
handlebar stem
potence[F]
Lenkerschaft[M]
vástago[M]
steering tube
tube[M] de direction[F]
Steuerkopf[M]
tubo[M] del manillar[M]
brake lever
poignée[F] de frein[M]
Bremsgriff[M]
palanca[F] del freno[M]
front brake
frein[M] avant
vordere Felgenbremse[F]
freno[M] delantero
front lamp
projecteur[M]
Scheinwerfer[M]
luz[F] delantera
fork
fourche[F]
Vordergabel[F]
horquilla[F]
hub
moyeu[M]
Nabe[F]
eje[M] de la rueda[F]
rim
jante[F]
Felge[F]
llanta[F]
tyre
pneu[M]
Reifen[M]
neumático[M]
spoke
rayon[M]
Speiche[F]
radio[M]
tyre valve
valve[F]
Ventil[N]
válvula[F]
water bottle
bidon[M]
Wasserflasche[F]
botella[F]
water bottle clip
porte-bidon[M]
Halterung[F] der Wasserflasche[F]
portabotellas[M]
down tube
tube[M] oblique
Unterrohr[N]
tubo[M] inferior del cuadro[M]

# BICYCLE
# BICYCLETTE$^{F}$
# FAHRRAD$^{N}$
# BICICLETA$^{F}$

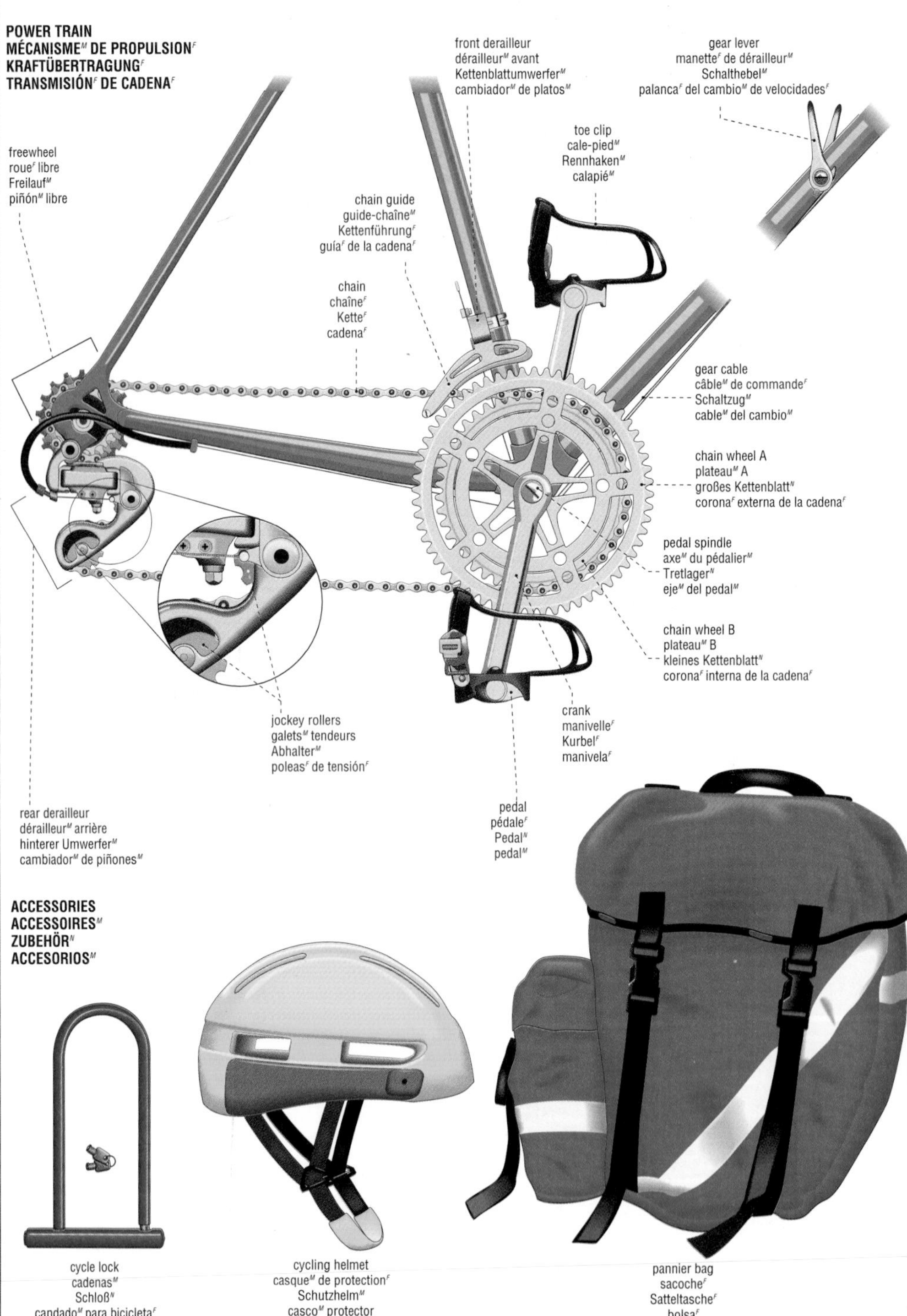

## CARAVAN
## CARAVANE[F]
## WOHNWAGEN[M]
## CARAVANA[F]

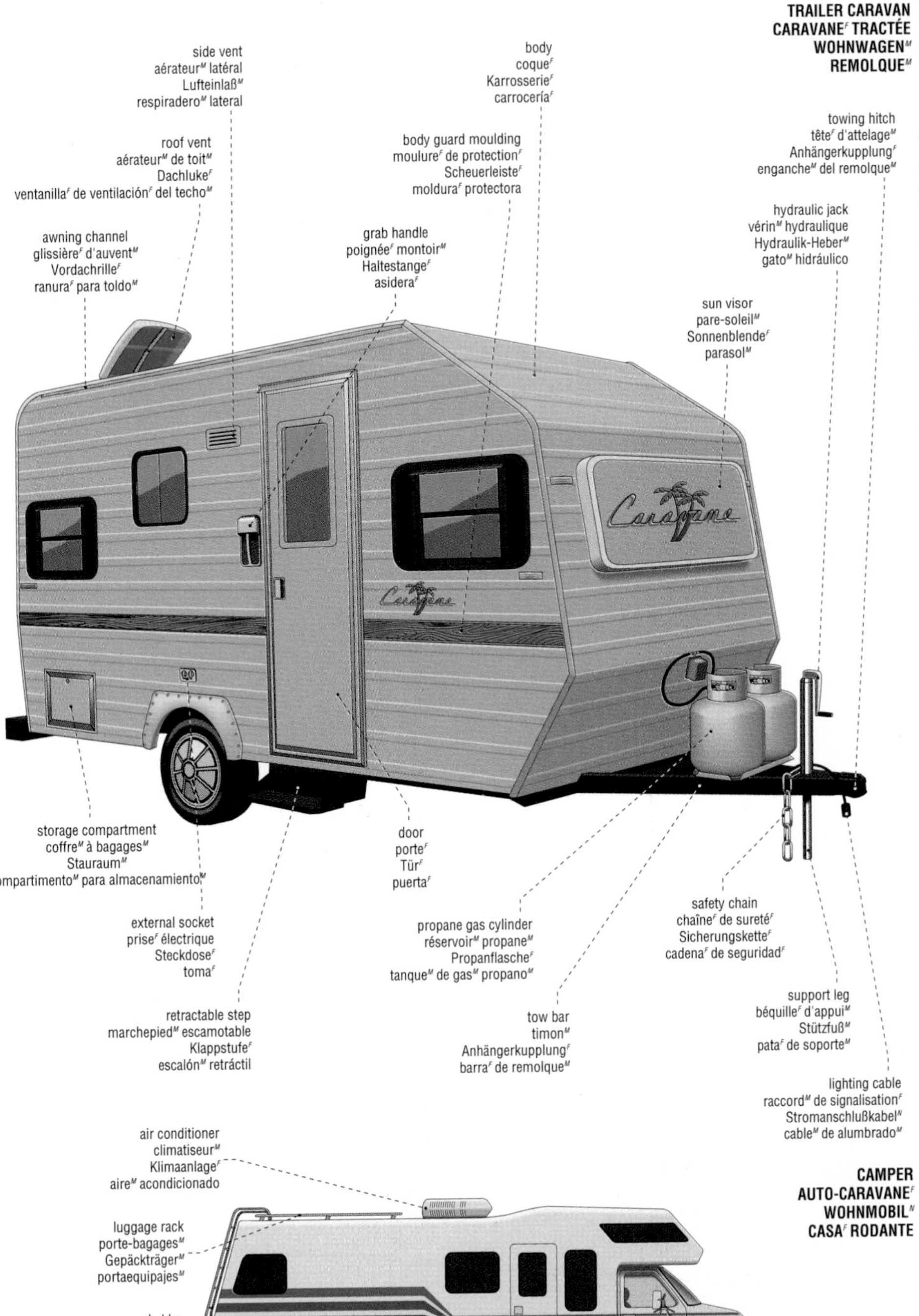

# ROAD SYSTEM
# SYSTÈME[M] ROUTIER
# STRASSENBAU[M]
# SISTEMA[M] DE CARRETERAS[F]

## CROSS SECTION OF A ROAD
## COUPE[F] D'UNE ROUTE[F]
## QUERSCHNITT[M] EINER STRASSE[F]
## VISTA[F] TRANSVERSAL DE UNA CARRETERA[F]

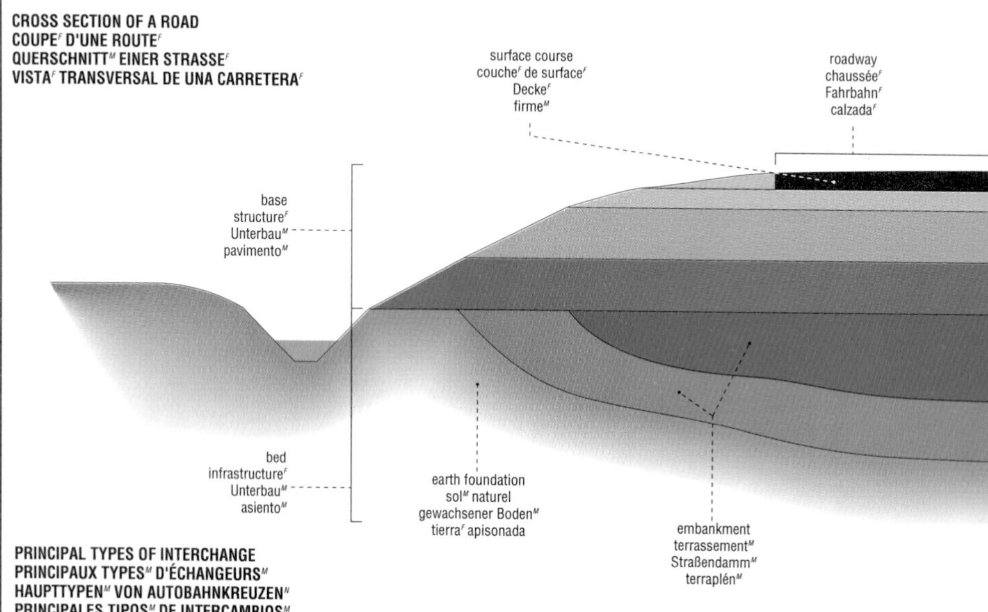


## PRINCIPAL TYPES OF INTERCHANGE
## PRINCIPAUX TYPES[M] D'ÉCHANGEURS[M]
## HAUPTTYPEN[M] VON AUTOBAHNKREUZEN[N]
## PRINCIPALES TIPOS[M] DE INTERCAMBIOS[M]

gyratory system
carrefour[M] giratoire
Verteiler[M]
glorieta[F]

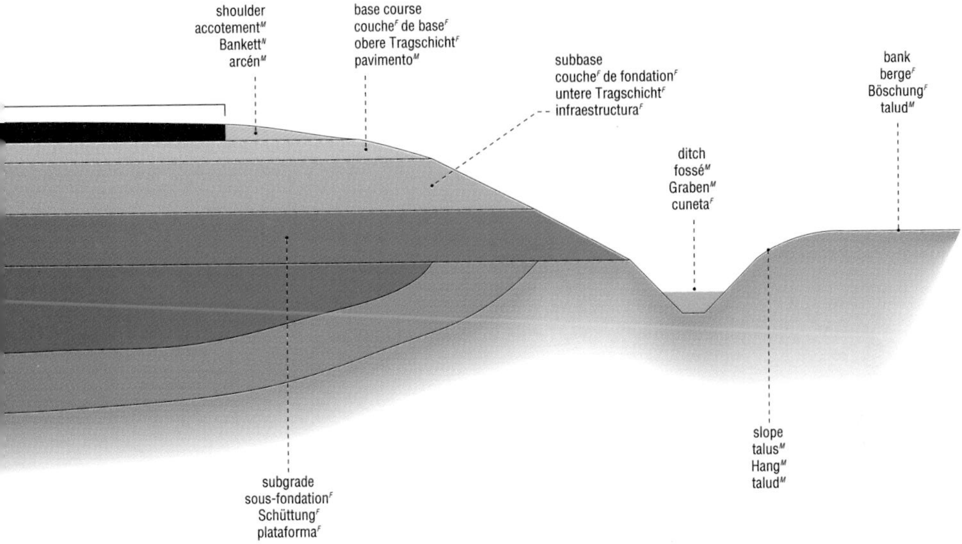

shoulder
accotement[M]
Bankett[N]
arcén[M]

base course
couche[F] de base[F]
obere Tragschicht[F]
pavimento[M]

subbase
couche[F] de fondation[F]
untere Tragschicht[F]
infraestructura[F]

bank
berge[F]
Böschung[F]
talud[M]

ditch
fossé[M]
Graben[M]
cuneta[F]

slope
talus[M]
Hang[M]
talud[M]

subgrade
sous-fondation[F]
Schüttung[F]
plataforma[F]

diamond interchange
échangeur[M] en losange[M]
Raute[F]
diamante[M]

trumpet interchange
échangeur[M] en trompette[F]
Trompete[F]
trompeta[F]

# ROAD SYSTEM
# SYSTÈME[M] ROUTIER
# AUTOBAHNKREUZ[N]
# SISTEMA[M] DE CARRETERAS[F]

**CLOVERLEAF**
**ÉCHANGEUR[M] EN TRÈFLE[M]**
**KLEEBLATT[N]**
**TRÉBOL[M]**

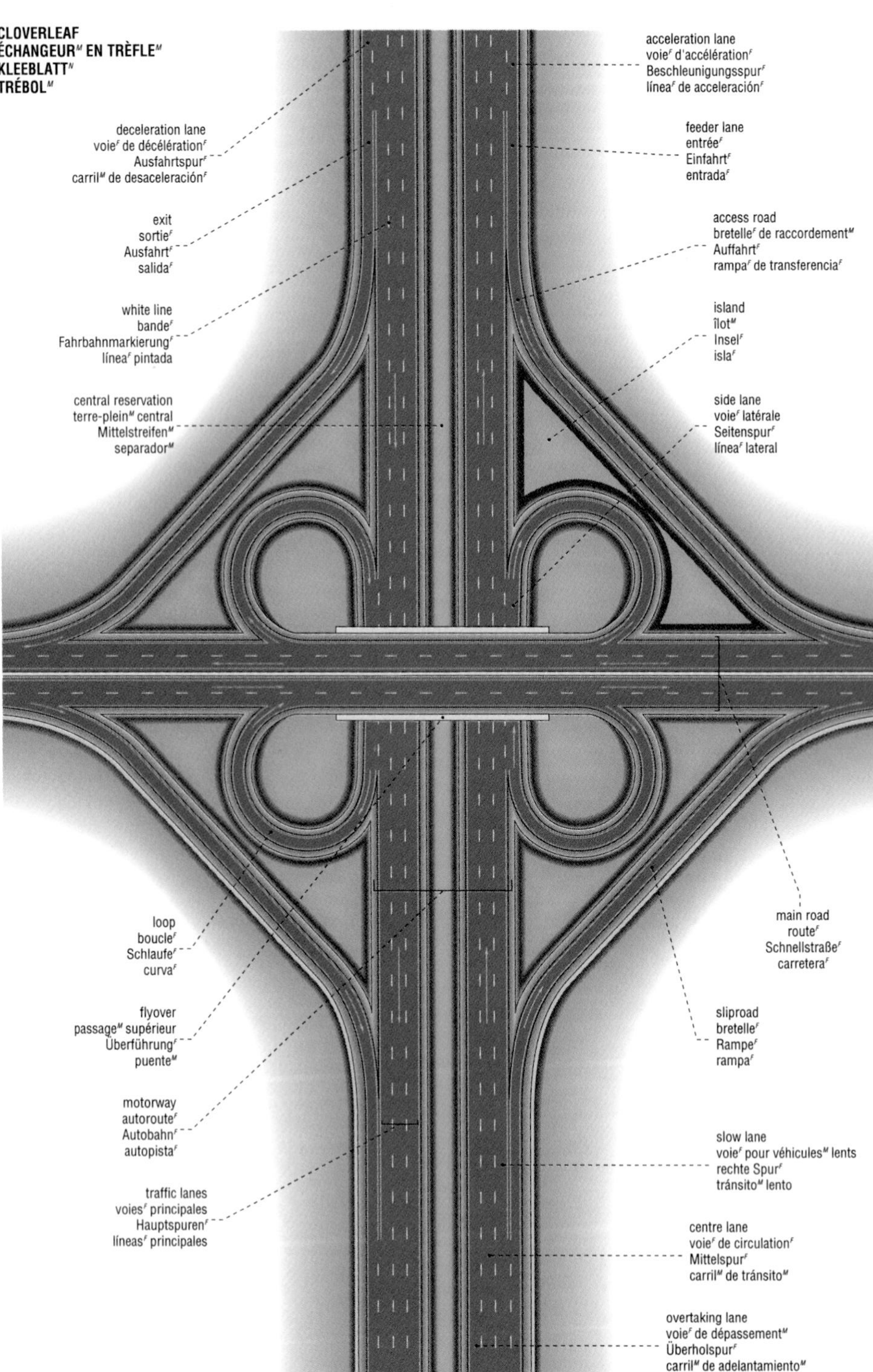

# SERVICE STATION
# STATION[F]-SERVICE[M]
# TANKSTELLE[F]
# ESTACIÓN[F] DE SERVICIO[M]

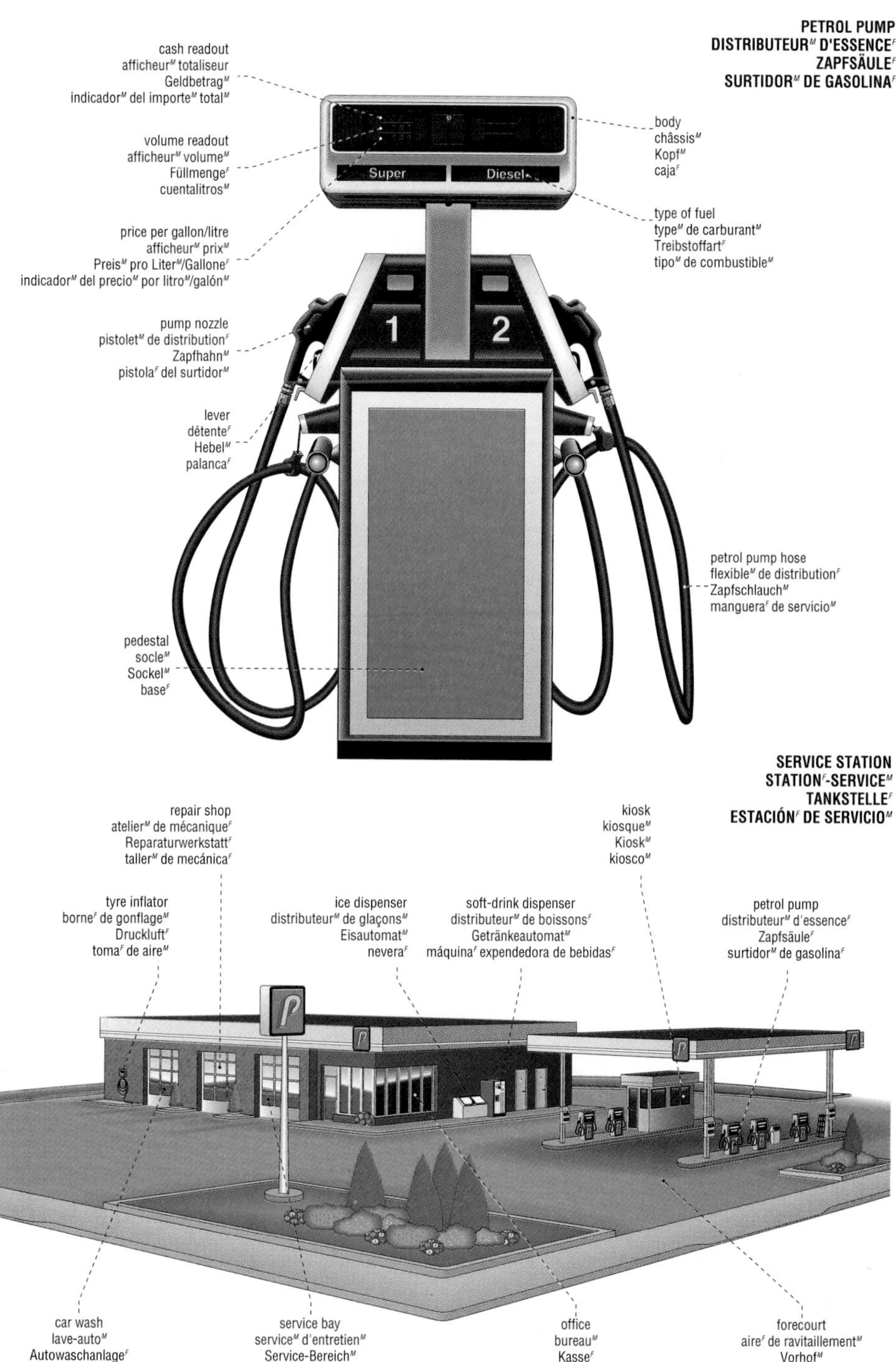

# FIXED BRIDGES
# PONTS[M] FIXES
# STARRE BRÜCKEN[F]
# PUENTES[M] FIJOS

## BEAM BRIDGE
## PONT[M] À POUTRE[F]
## BALKENBRÜCKE[F]
## PUENTE[M] DE VIGA[F]

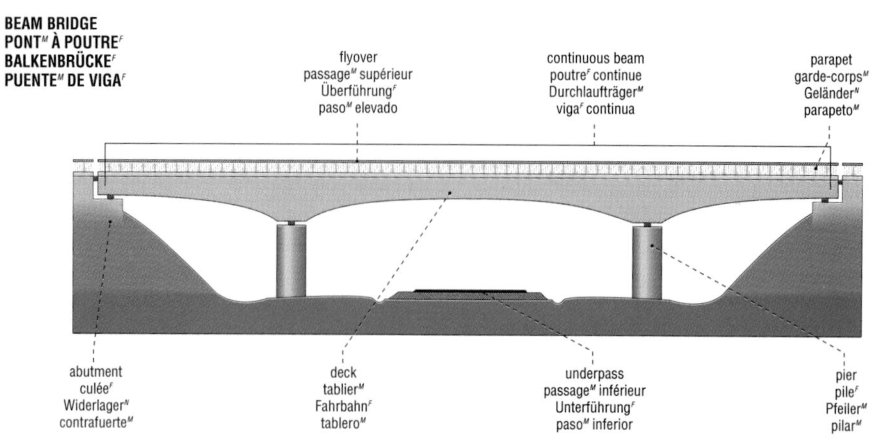


## TYPES OF BEAM BRIDGE
## TYPES[M] DE PONTS[M] À POUTRE[F]
## BALKENBRÜCKEN[F]
## TIPOS[M] DE PUENTES[M] DE VIGA[F]

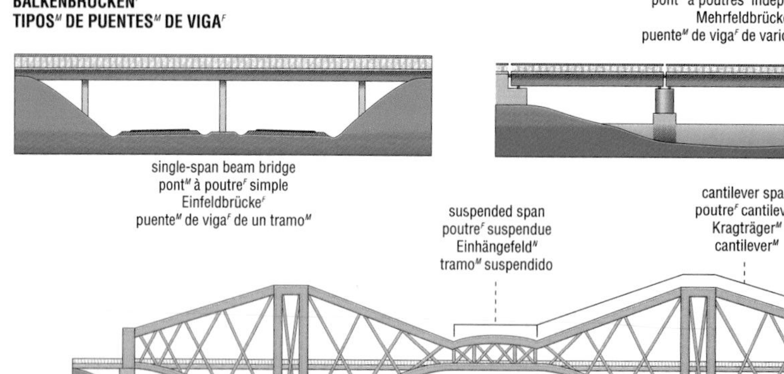

multiple-span beam bridge
pont[M] à poutres[F] indépendantes
Mehrfeldbrücke[F]
puente[M] de viga[F] de varios tramos[M]

single-span beam bridge
pont[M] à poutre[F] simple
Einfeldbrücke[F]
puente[M] de viga[F] de un tramo[M]

suspended span
poutre[F] suspendue
Einhängefeld[N]
tramo[M] suspendido

cantilever span
poutre[F] cantilever
Kragträger[M]
cantilever[M]

**cantilever bridge**
**pont[M] cantilever**
**Auslegerbrücke[F]**
**puente[M] voladizo**

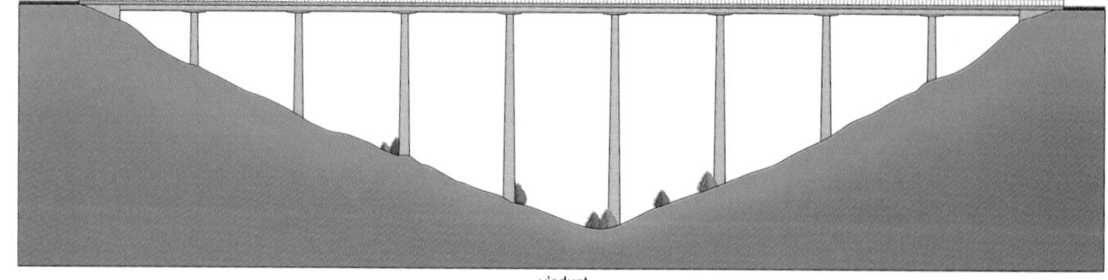

viaduct
viaduc[M]
Viadukt[M]
viaducto[M]

## ARCH BRIDGE
## PONT$^{M}$ EN ARC$^{M}$
## BOGENBRÜCKE$^{F}$
## PUENTE$^{M}$ DE ARCO$^{M}$

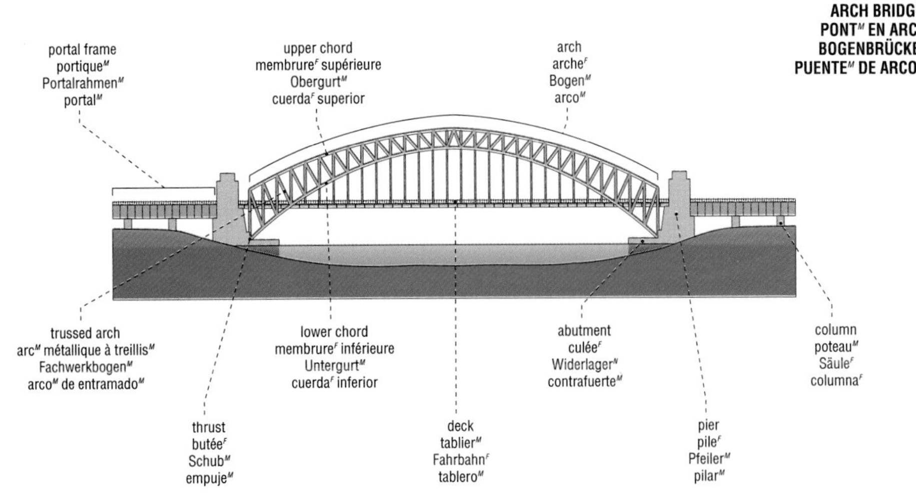


## TYPES OF ARCH BRIDGE
## TYPES$^{M}$ DE PONTS$^{M}$ EN ARC$^{M}$
## BOGENBRÜCKEN$^{F}$
## TIPOS$^{M}$ DE PUENTES$^{M}$ DE ARCO$^{M}$

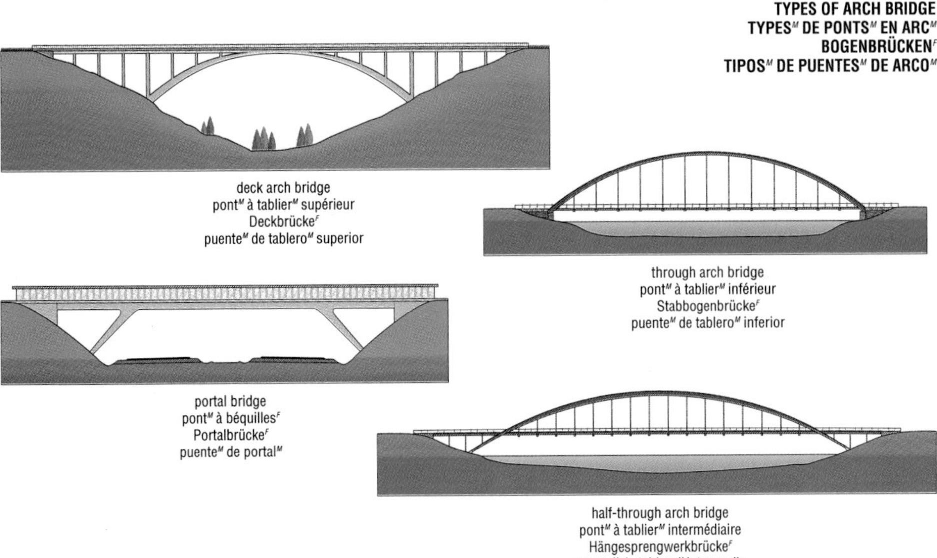

deck arch bridge
pont$^{M}$ à tablier$^{M}$ supérieur
Deckbrücke$^{F}$
puente$^{M}$ de tablero$^{M}$ superior

through arch bridge
pont$^{M}$ à tablier$^{M}$ inférieur
Stabbogenbrücke$^{F}$
puente$^{M}$ de tablero$^{M}$ inferior

portal bridge
pont$^{M}$ à béquilles$^{F}$
Portalbrücke$^{F}$
puente$^{M}$ de portal$^{M}$

half-through arch bridge
pont$^{M}$ à tablier$^{M}$ intermédiaire
Hängesprengwerkbrücke$^{F}$
puente$^{M}$ de tablero$^{M}$ intermedio

## TYPES OF ARCH
## TYPES$^{M}$ D'ARCS$^{M}$
## BOGENARTEN$^{F}$
## VARIEDADES$^{F}$ DE ARCOS$^{M}$

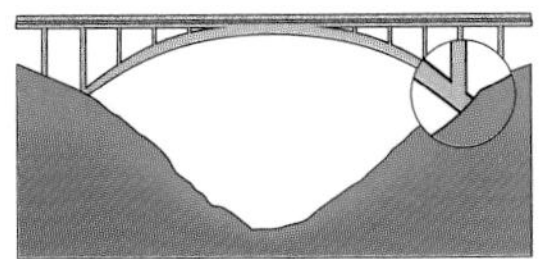

fixed arch
arc$^{M}$ encastré
gelenkloser Bogen$^{M}$
arco$^{M}$ fijo

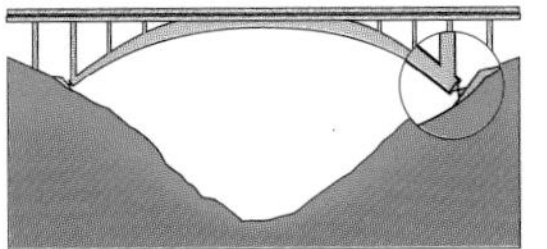

two-hinged arch
arc$^{M}$ à deux articulations$^{F}$
zweiteiliger Bogen$^{M}$
arco$^{M}$ de dos articulaciones$^{F}$

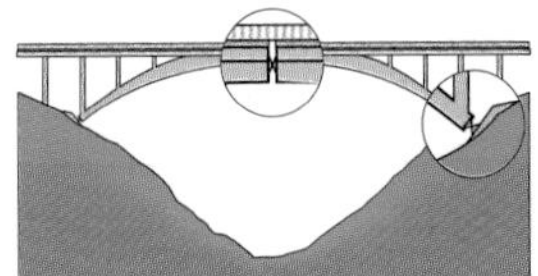

three-hinged arch
arc$^{M}$ à trois articulations$^{F}$
dreiteiliger Bogen$^{M}$
arco$^{M}$ de tres articulaciones$^{F}$

# FIXED BRIDGES
# PONTS[M] FIXES
# STARRE BRÜCKEN[F]
# PUENTES[M] FIJOS

## SUSPENSION BRIDGE
## PONT[M] SUSPENDU À CÂBLE[M] PORTEUR
## HÄNGEBRÜCKE[F]
## PUENTE[M] COLGANTE

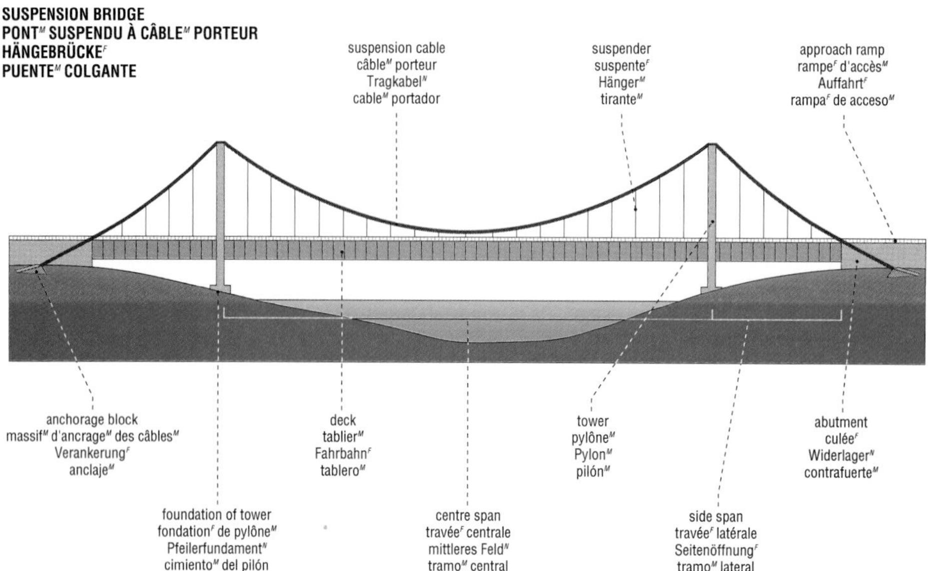


## CABLE-STAYED BRIDGES
## PONTS[M] SUSPENDUS À HAUBANS[M]
## SCHRÄGSEILBRÜCKE[F]
## PUENTES[M] DE TIRANTES[M]

**fan cable stays**
**haubans[M] en éventail[M]**
**Fächerschrägseile[N]**
**tirantes[M] en abanico[M]**

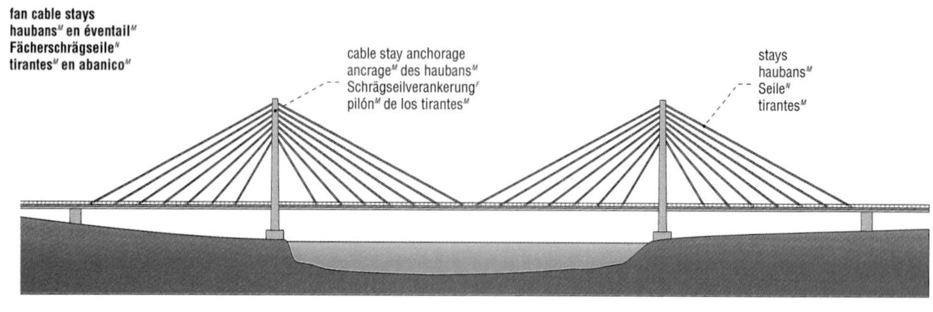


**harp cable stays**
**haubans[M] en harpe[F]**
**parallele Schrägseile[N]**
**tirantes[M] en forma[F] de arpa[F]**

## MOVABLE BRIDGES
## PONTS[M] MOBILES
## BEWEGLICHE BRÜCKEN[F]
## PUENTES[M] MOVIBLES

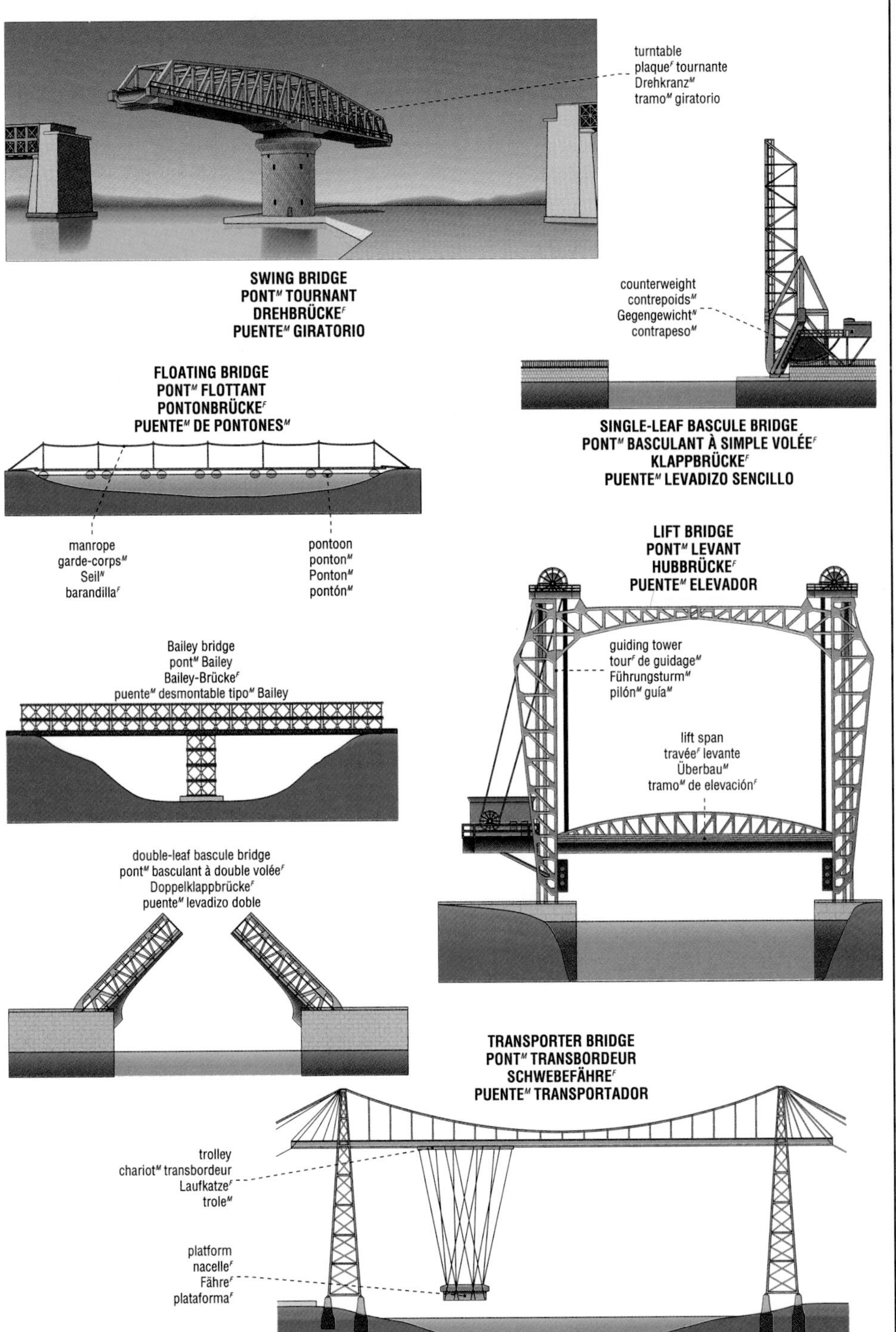

# HIGH-SPEED TRAIN
# TRAIN[M] À GRANDE VITESSE[F] (T.G.V.)
# HOCHGESCHWINDIGKEITSZUG[M]
# TREN[M] DE ALTA VELOCIDAD[F]

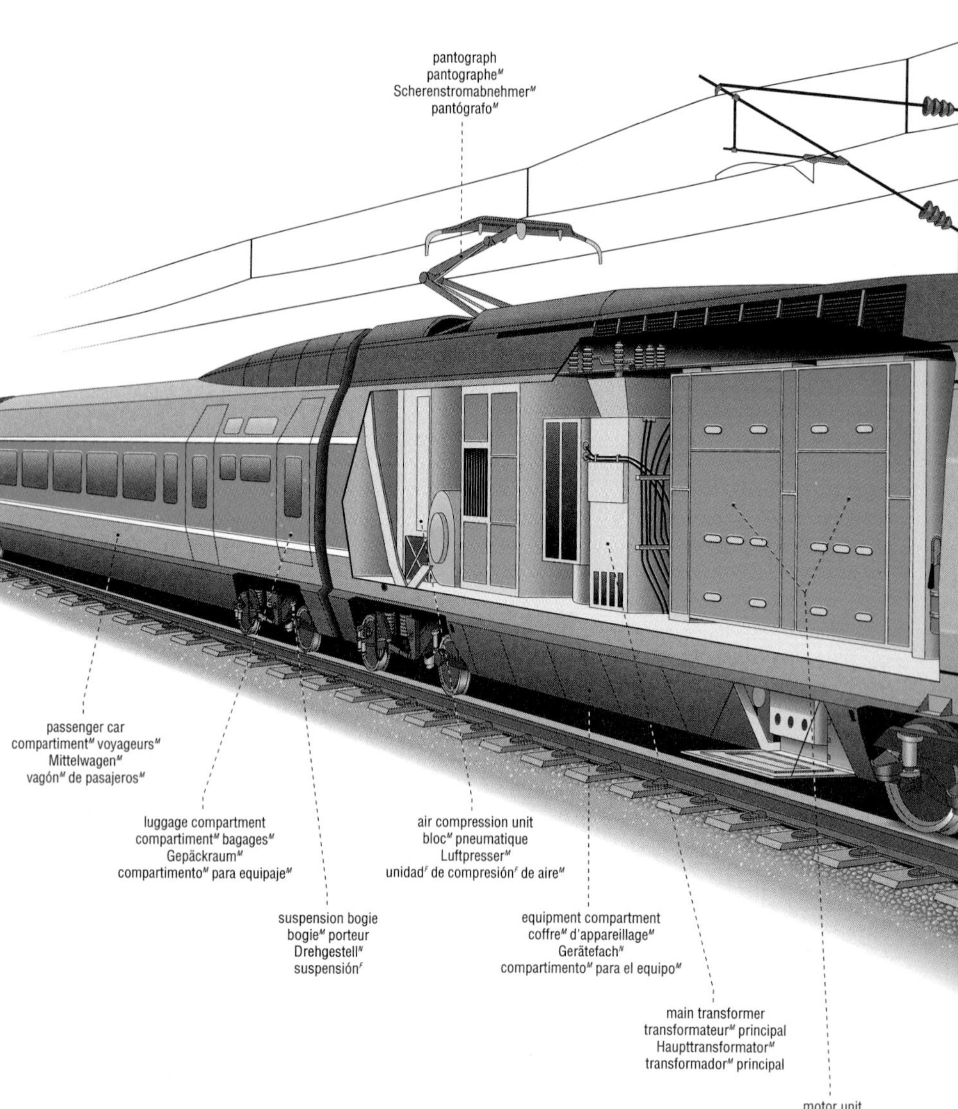

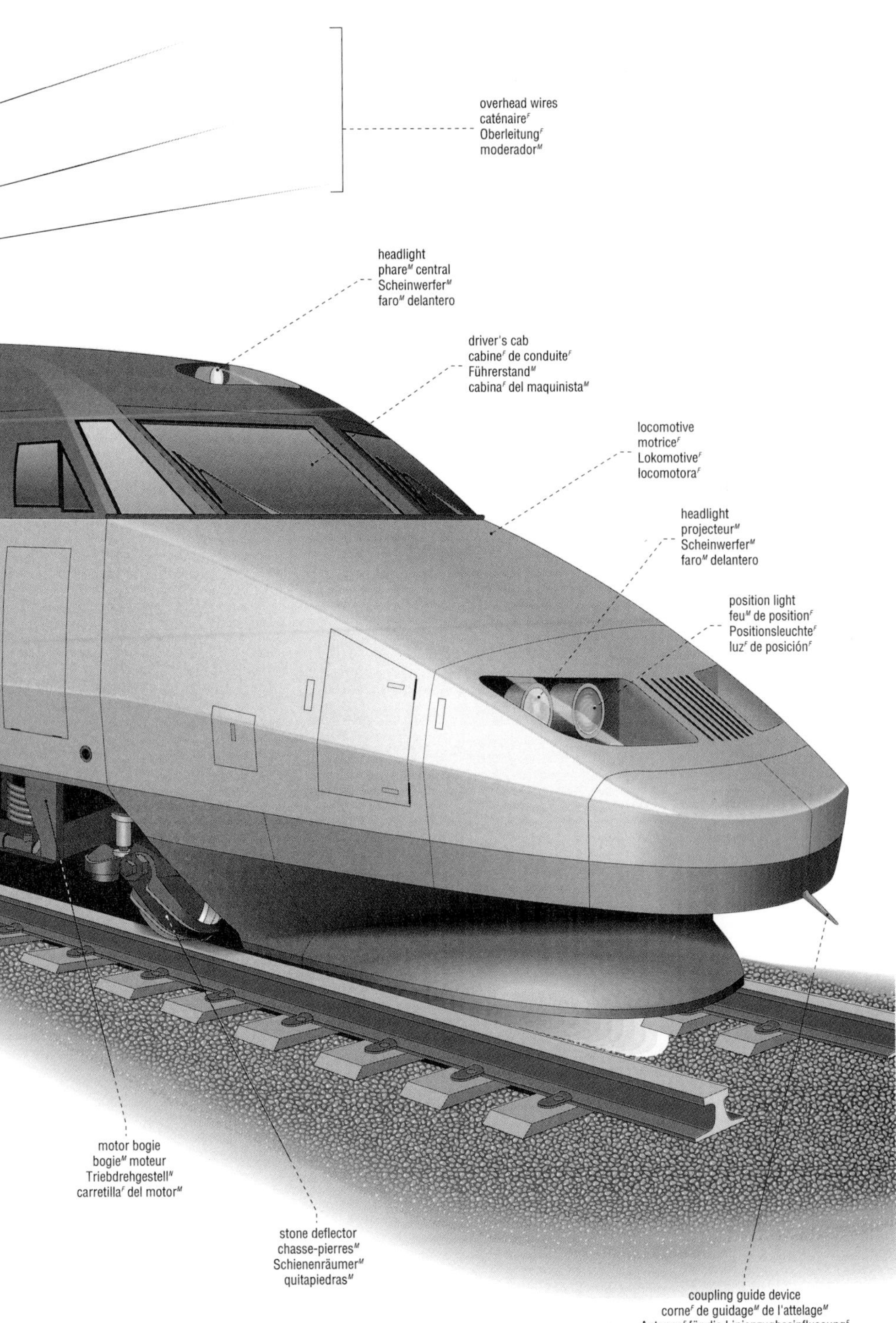
overhead wires
caténaire[F]
Oberleitung[F]
moderador[M]
headlight
phare[M] central
Scheinwerfer[M]
faro[M] delantero
driver's cab
cabine[F] de conduite[F]
Führerstand[M]
cabina[F] del maquinista[M]
locomotive
motrice[F]
Lokomotive[F]
locomotora[F]
headlight
projecteur[M]
Scheinwerfer[M]
faro[M] delantero
position light
feu[M] de position[F]
Positionsleuchte[F]
luz[F] de posición[F]
motor bogie
bogie[M] moteur
Triebdrehgestell[N]
carretilla[F] del motor[M]
stone deflector
chasse-pierres[M]
Schienenräumer[M]
quitapiedras[M]
coupling guide device
corne[F] de guidage[M] de l'attelage[M]
Antenne[F] für die Linienzugbeeinflussung[F]
guía[F] de enganche[M]

# TYPES OF PASSENGER COACH
# TYPES[M] DE VOITURES[F]
# PERSONENZÜGE[M]: WAGENTYPEN[M]
# VAGONES[M] DE PASAJEROS[M]

## OPEN-PLAN COACH
## VOITURE[F]-COACH[M]
## GROSSRAUMWAGEN[M]
## VAGÓN[M] DE PASAJEROS[M]

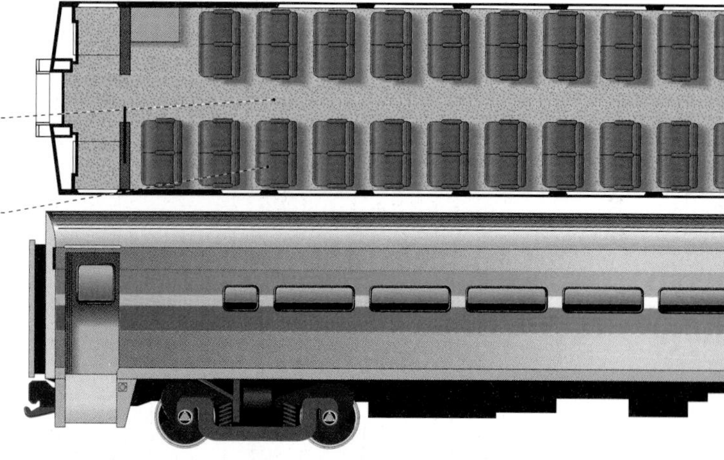


## SLEEPING CAR
## VOITURE[F]-LIT[M]
## SCHLAFWAGEN[M]
## COCHE[M] CAMA[F]

## RESTAURANT CAR
## VOITURE[F]-RESTAURANT[M]
## SPEISEWAGEN[M]
## VAGÓN[M] COMEDOR[M]

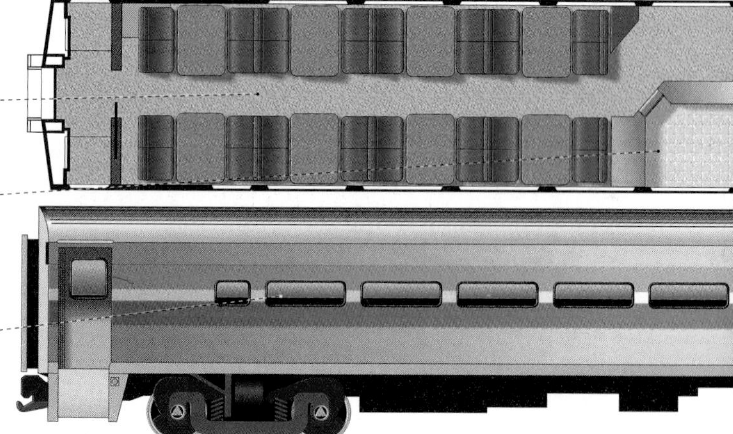

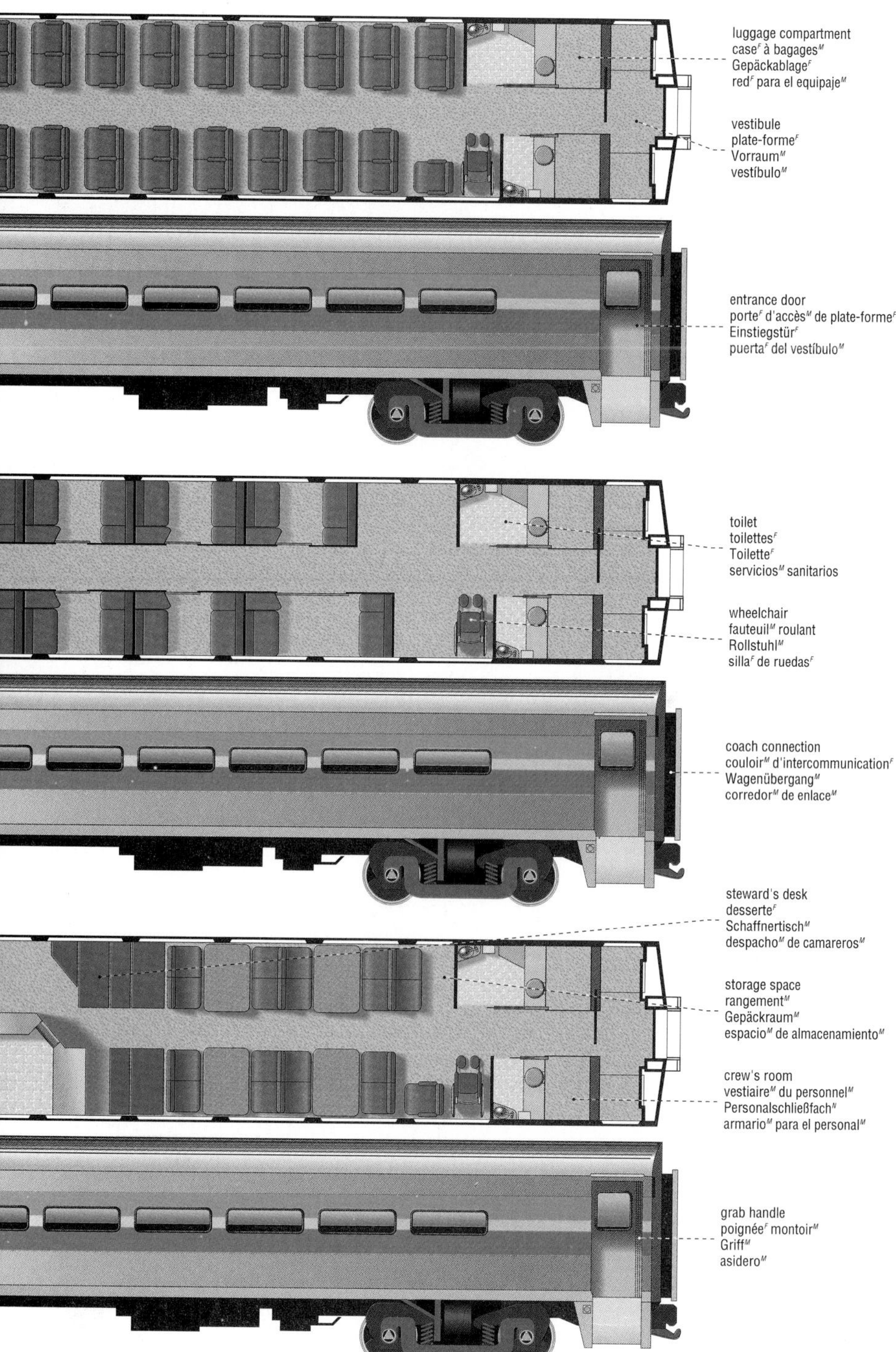
luggage compartment
case[F] à bagages[M]
Gepäckablage[F]
red[F] para el equipaje[M]
vestibule
plate-forme[F]
Vorraum[M]
vestíbulo[M]
entrance door
porte[F] d'accès[M] de plate-forme[F]
Einstiegstür[F]
puerta[F] del vestíbulo[M]
toilet
toilettes[F]
Toilette[F]
servicios[M] sanitarios
wheelchair
fauteuil[M] roulant
Rollstuhl[M]
silla[F] de ruedas[F]
coach connection
couloir[M] d'intercommunication[F]
Wagenübergang[M]
corredor[M] de enlace[M]
steward's desk
desserte[F]
Schaffnertisch[M]
despacho[M] de camareros[M]
storage space
rangement[M]
Gepäckraum[M]
espacio[M] de almacenamiento[M]
crew's room
vestiaire[M] du personnel[M]
Personalschließfach[N]
armario[M] para el personal[M]
grab handle
poignée[F] montoir[M]
Griff[M]
asidero[M]

# PASSENGER STATION
# GARE[F] DE VOYAGEURS[M]
# BAHNHOF[M]
# ESTACIÓN[F] DE FERROCARRIL[M]

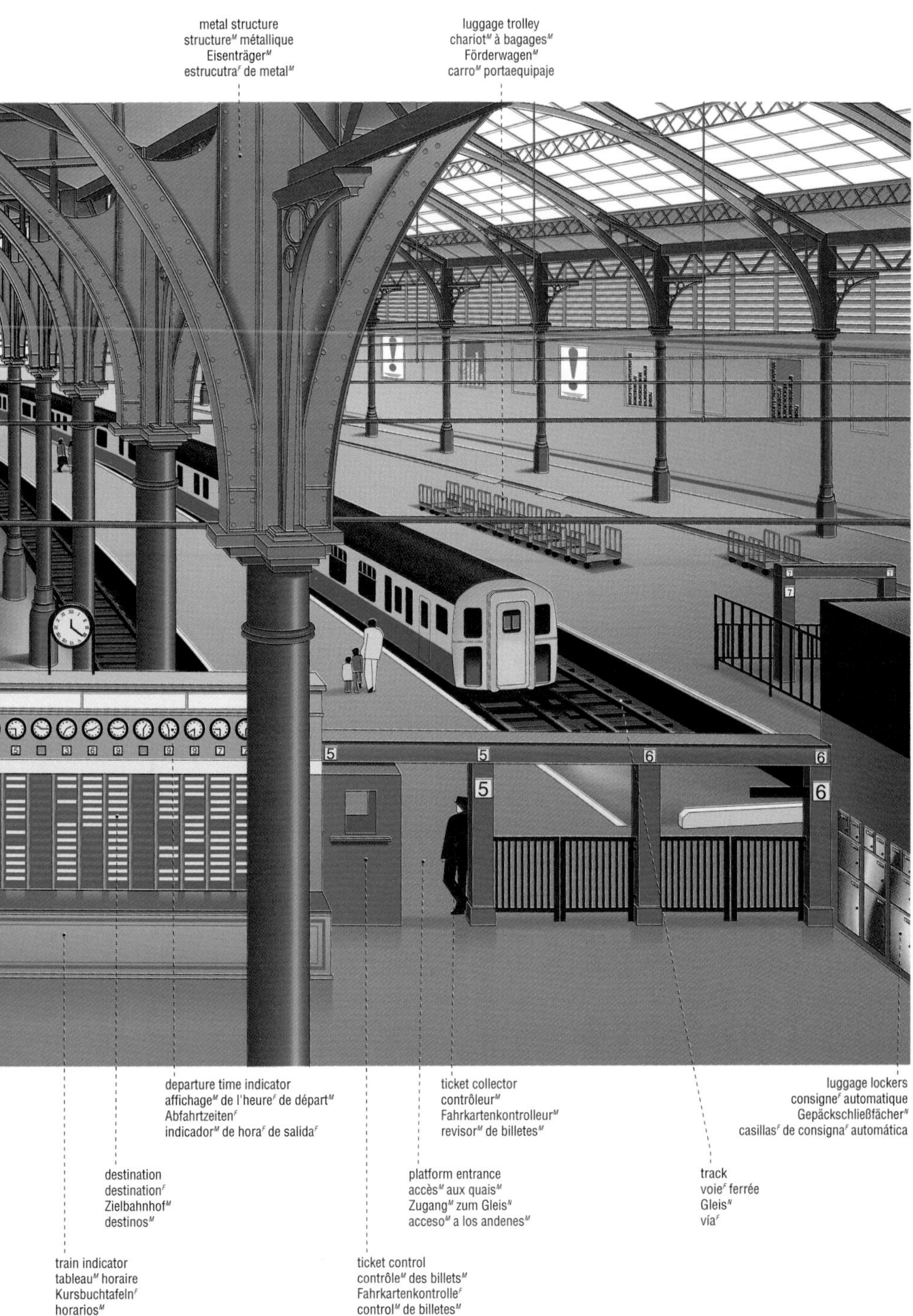
metal structure
structure[M] métallique
Eisenträger[M]
estrucutra[F] de metal[M]
luggage trolley
chariot[M] à bagages[M]
Förderwagen[M]
carro[M] portaequipaje
departure time indicator
affichage[M] de l'heure[F] de départ[M]
Abfahrtzeiten[F]
indicador[M] de hora[F] de salida[F]
ticket collector
contrôleur[M]
Fahrkartenkontrolleur[M]
revisor[M] de billetes[M]
luggage lockers
consigne[F] automatique
Gepäckschließfächer[N]
casillas[F] de consigna[F] automática
destination
destination[F]
Zielbahnhof[M]
destinos[M]
platform entrance
accès[M] aux quais[M]
Zugang[M] zum Gleis[N]
acceso[M] a los andenes[M]
track
voie[F] ferrée
Gleis[N]
vía[F]
train indicator
tableau[M] horaire
Kursbuchtafeln[F]
horarios[M]
ticket control
contrôle[M] des billets[M]
Fahrkartenkontrolle[F]
control[M] de billetes[M]

# RAILWAY STATION
# GARE$^{F}$
# BAHNHOF$^{M}$
# ESTACIÓN$^{F}$ DE FERROCARRIL$^{M}$

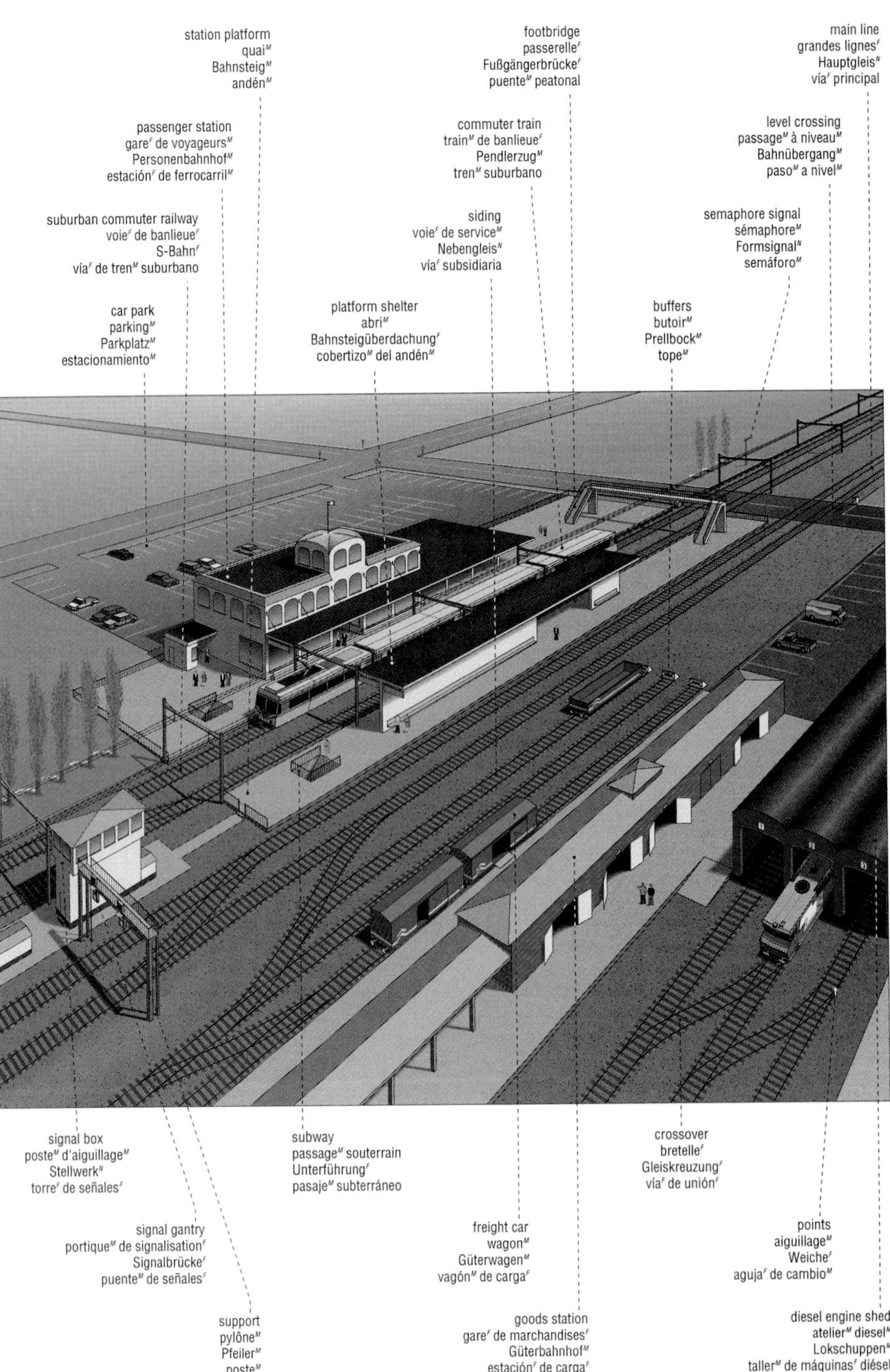

# MARSHALLING YARD
# GARE^F DE TRIAGE^M
# RANGIERBAHNHOF^M
# TALLERES^M DE FERROCARRIL^M

## RAILWAY TRACK
## VOIE[F] FERRÉE
## EISENBAHN-OBERBAU[M]
## VÍA[F] FÉRREA

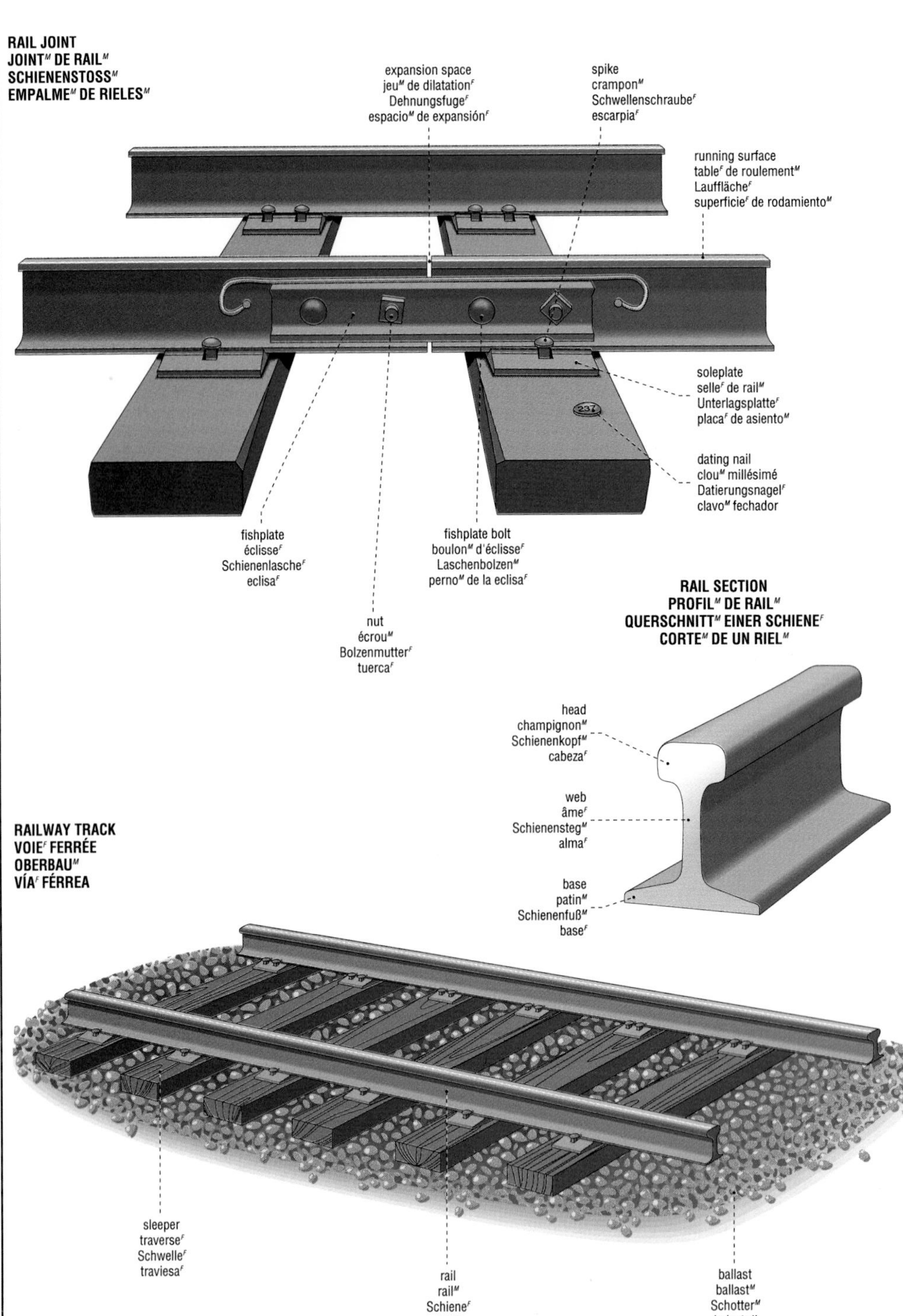

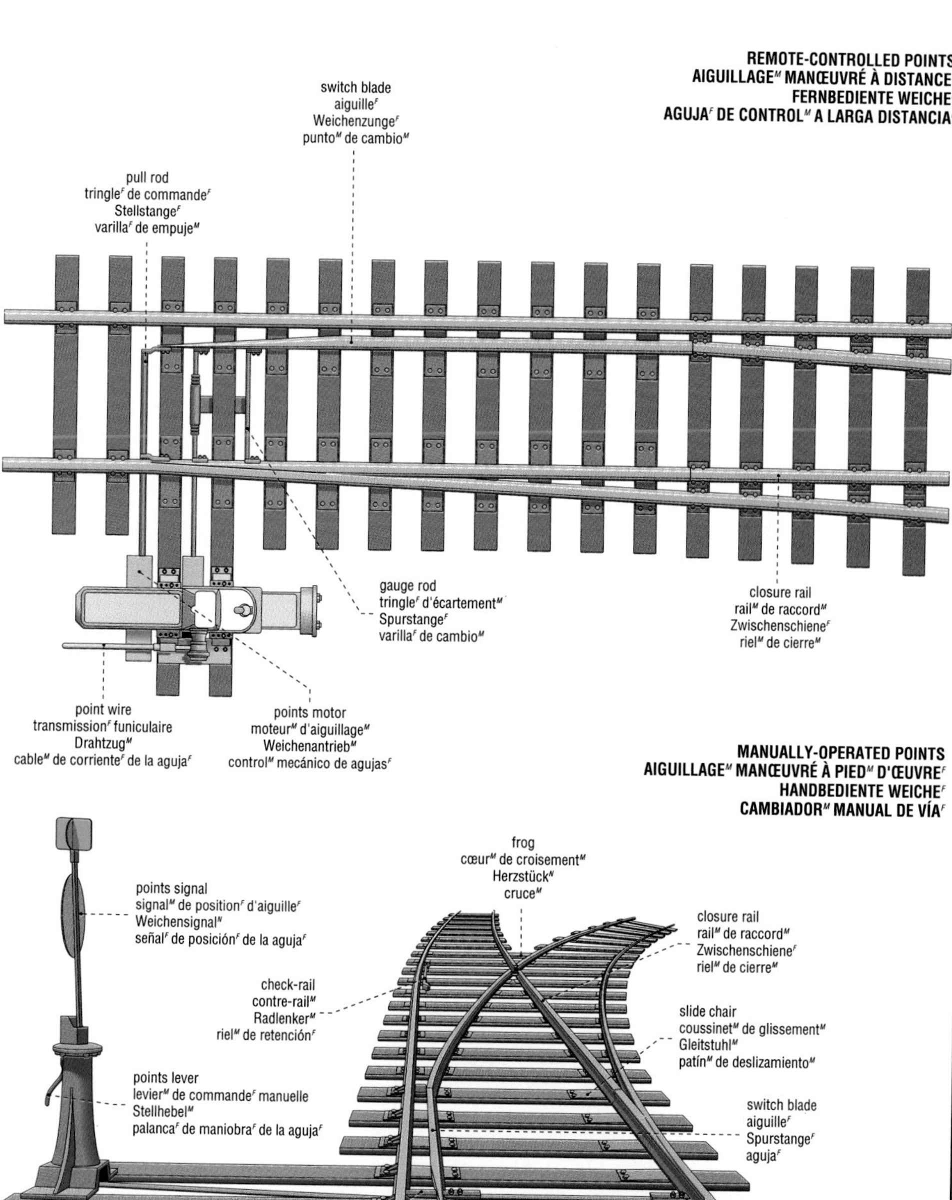
REMOTE-CONTROLLED POINTS
AIGUILLAGE[M] MANŒUVRÉ À DISTANCE[F]
FERNBEDIENTE WEICHE[F]
AGUJA[F] DE CONTROL[M] A LARGA DISTANCIA[F]
switch blade
aiguille[F]
Weichenzunge[F]
punto[M] de cambio[M]
pull rod
tringle[F] de commande[F]
Stellstange[F]
varilla[F] de empuje[M]
gauge rod
tringle[F] d'écartement[M]
Spurstange[F]
varilla[F] de cambio[M]
closure rail
rail[M] de raccord[M]
Zwischenschiene[F]
riel[M] de cierre[M]
point wire
transmission[F] funiculaire
Drahtzug[M]
cable[M] de corriente[F] de la aguja[F]
points motor
moteur[M] d'aiguillage[M]
Weichenantrieb[M]
control[M] mecánico de agujas[F]
MANUALLY-OPERATED POINTS
AIGUILLAGE[M] MANŒUVRÉ À PIED[M] D'ŒUVRE[F]
HANDBEDIENTE WEICHE[F]
CAMBIADOR[M] MANUAL DE VÍA[F]
frog
cœur[M] de croisement[M]
Herzstück[N]
cruce[M]
points signal
signal[M] de position[F] d'aiguille[F]
Weichensignal[N]
señal[F] de posición[F] de la aguja[F]
closure rail
rail[M] de raccord[M]
Zwischenschiene[F]
riel[M] de cierre[M]
check-rail
contre-rail[M]
Radlenker[M]
riel[M] de retención[F]
slide chair
coussinet[M] de glissement[M]
Gleitstuhl[M]
patín[M] de deslizamiento[M]
points lever
levier[M] de commande[F] manuelle
Stellhebel[M]
palanca[F] de maniobra[F] de la aguja[F]
switch blade
aiguille[F]
Spurstange[F]
aguja[F]
pull rod
tringle[F] de commande[F]
Stellstange[F]
varilla[F] de empuje[M]

# DIESEL-ELECTRIC LOCOMOTIVE
# LOCOMOTIVE[F] DIESEL-ÉLECTRIQUE
# DIESELELEKTRISCHE LOKOMOTIVE[F]
# LOCOMOTORA[F] DIÉSEL ELÉCTRICA

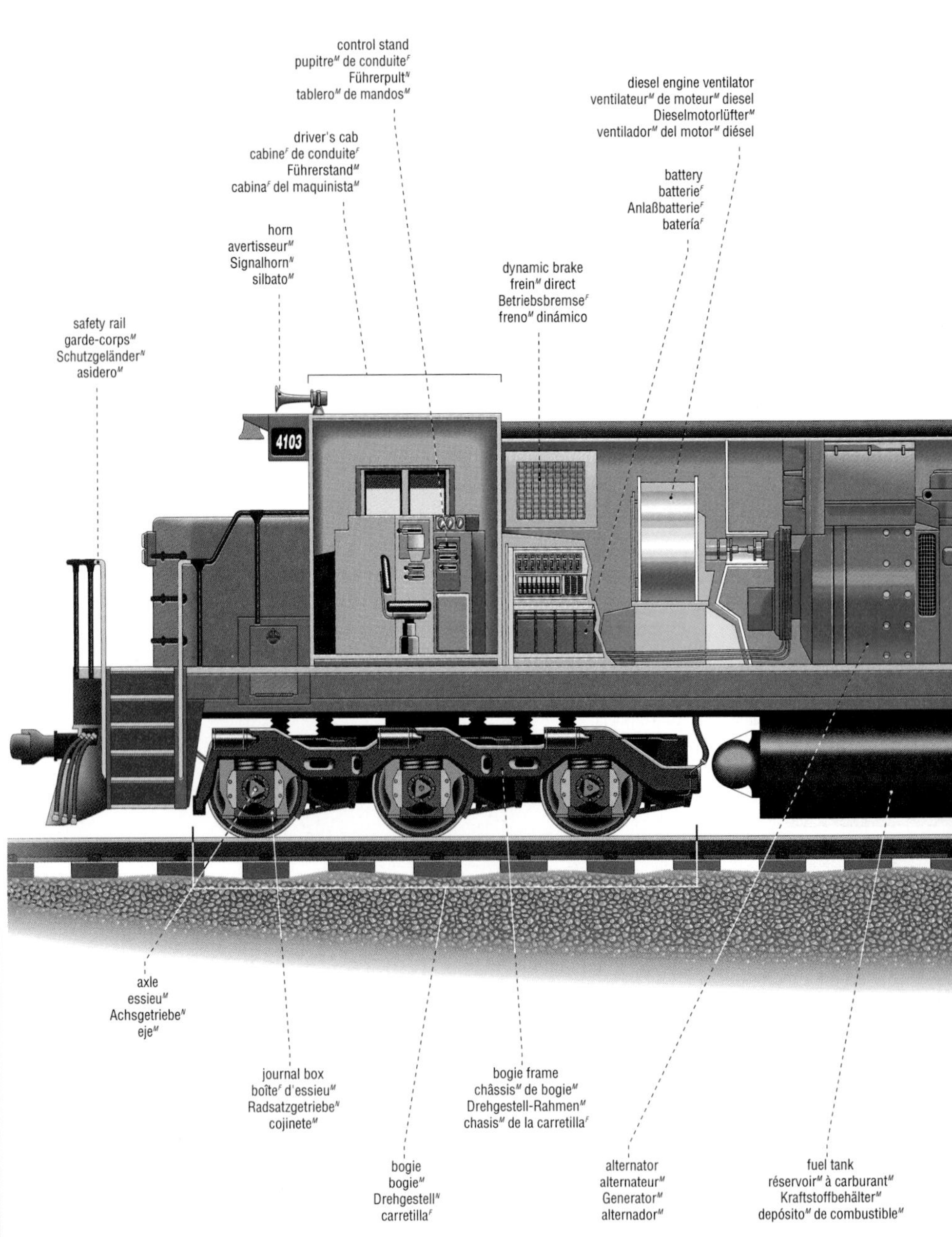

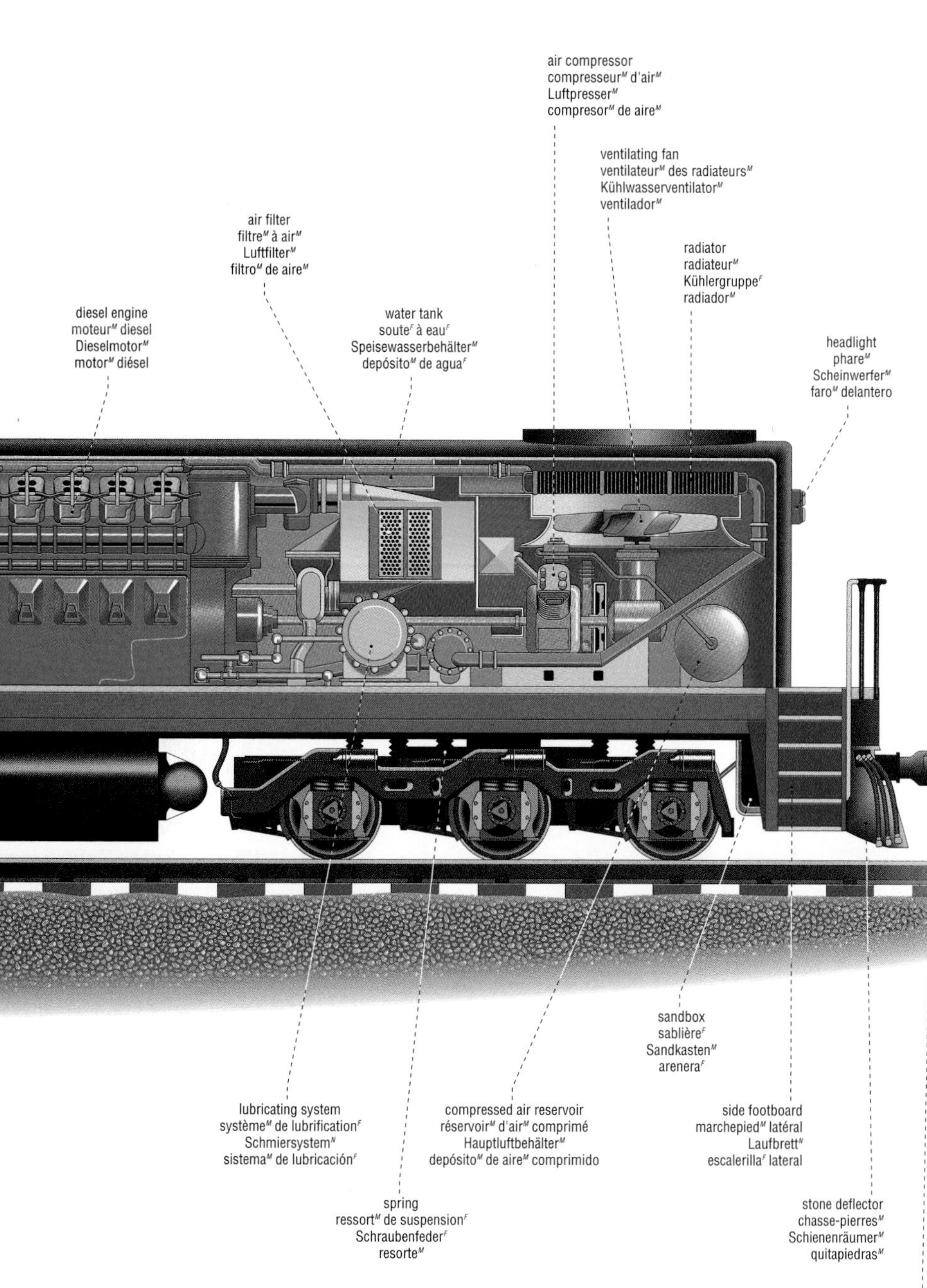
air compressor
compresseur[M] d'air[M]
Luftpresser[M]
compresor[M] de aire[M]
ventilating fan
ventilateur[M] des radiateurs[M]
Kühlwasserventilator[M]
ventilador[M]
air filter
filtre[M] à air[M]
Luftfilter[M]
filtro[M] de aire[M]
radiator
radiateur[M]
Kühlergruppe[F]
radiador[M]
diesel engine
moteur[M] diesel
Dieselmotor[M]
motor[M] diésel
water tank
soute[F] à eau[F]
Speisewasserbehälter[M]
depósito[M] de agua[F]
headlight
phare[M]
Scheinwerfer[M]
faro[M] delantero
sandbox
sablière[F]
Sandkasten[M]
arenera[F]
lubricating system
système[M] de lubrification[F]
Schmiersystem[N]
sistema[M] de lubricación[F]
compressed air reservoir
réservoir[M] d'air[M] comprimé
Hauptluftbehälter[M]
depósito[M] de aire[M] comprimido
side footboard
marchepied[M] latéral
Laufbrett[N]
escalerilla[F] lateral
spring
ressort[M] de suspension[F]
Schraubenfeder[F]
resorte[M]
stone deflector
chasse-pierres[M]
Schienenräumer[M]
quitapiedras[M]
coupling
tête[F] d'attelage[M]
Kupplungsbügel[M]
cabeza[F] de empalme[M]

## GOODS VAN
## WAGON[M]
## WAGEN[M]
## VAGÓN[M]

### BOGIE VAN
### WAGON[M] COUVERT
### DREHGESTELLKASTENWAGEN[M]
### FURGÓN[M]

corner cap
chapeau[M] d'angle[M]
Eckbeschlag[M]
esquinera[F]

horizontal end handhold
main[F] courante
Handstange[F]
asidero[M] horizontal

hand brake wheel
volant[M] de frein[M] à main[F]
Handbremsrad[N]
volante[M] del freno[M] manual

end ladder
échelle[F] de bout[M]
Stirnwandleiter[F]
escalerilla[F] de estribo[M]

hand brake gear housing
carter[M] d'engrenage[M] de frein[M] à main[F]
Schutzkasten[M] für Kegelräder[N]
cubierta[F] del mecanismo[M] del freno[M]

hand brake winding lever
levier[M] de frein[M] à main[F]
Handebremsehebel[M]
palanca[F] de enrrollado[M] del freno[M] de mano[F]

telescoping uncoupling rod
levier[M] télescopique de dételage[M]
Abkoppelvorrichtung[F]
varilla[F] telescópica de desenganche[M]

sill step
marchepied[M] en étrier[M]
Bügeltritt[M]
peldaño[M] inferior

side ladder
échelle[F] latérale
Seitensprossen[F]
escalerilla[F] lateral

sliding channel
glissière[F]
Türführungsschiene[F]
guía[F] corrediza

### CONTAINER
### CONTENEUR[M]
### CONTAINER[M]
### CONTENEDOR[M]

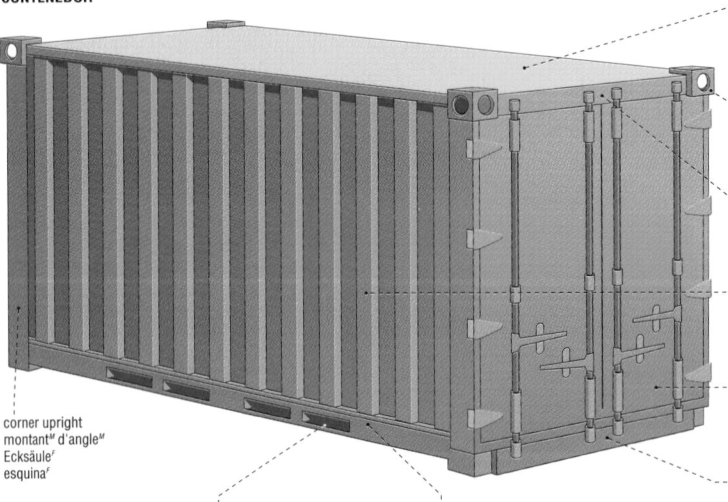

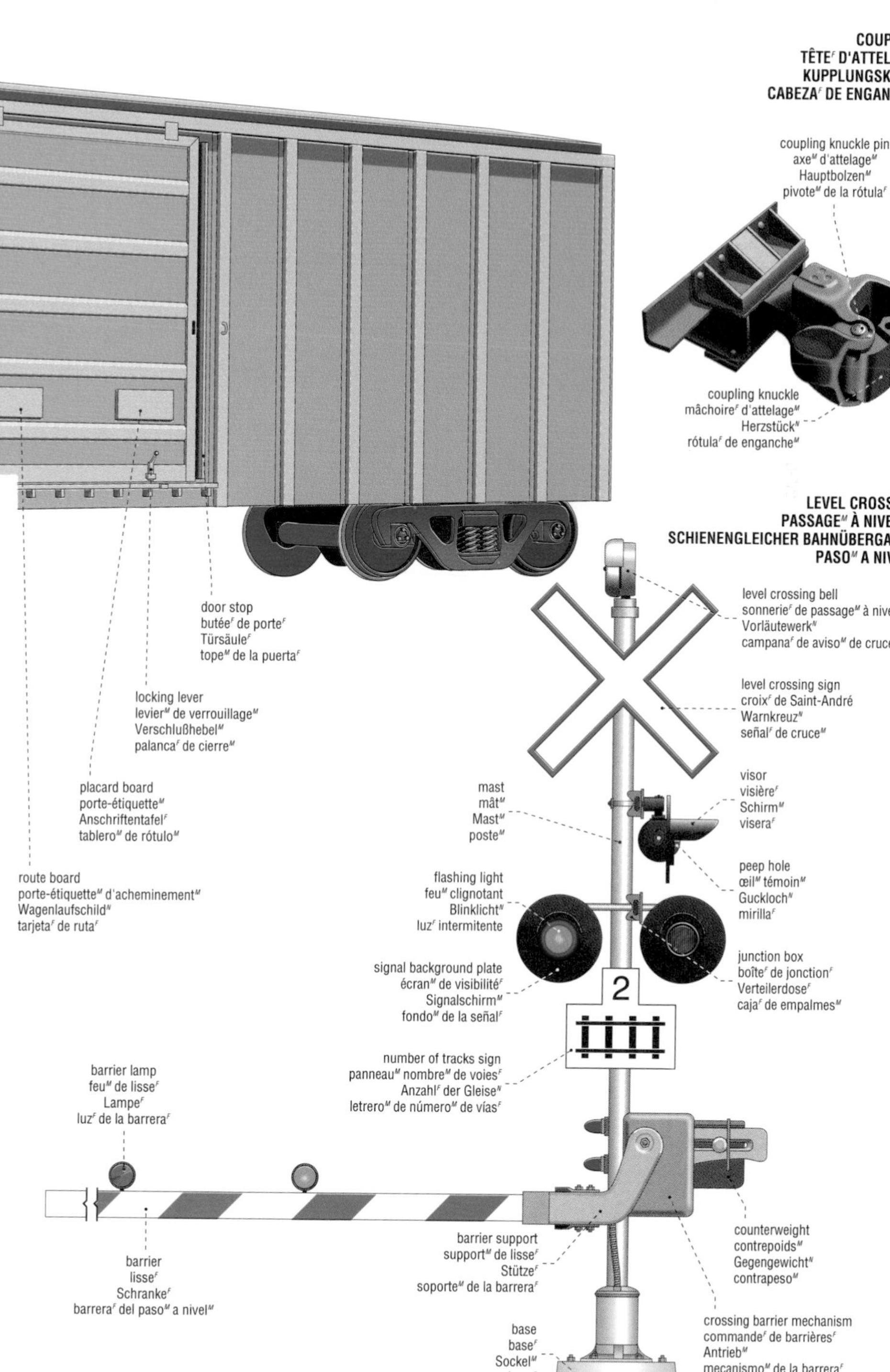
COUPLING
TÊTE[F] D'ATTELAGE[M]
KUPPLUNGSKOPF[M]
CABEZA[F] DE ENGANCHE[M]
coupling knuckle pin
axe[M] d'attelage[M]
Hauptbolzen[M]
pivote[M] de la rótula[F]
coupling knuckle
mâchoire[F] d'attelage[M]
Herzstück[N]
rótula[F] de enganche[M]
door stop
butée[F] de porte[F]
Türsäule[F]
tope[M] de la puerta[F]
locking lever
levier[M] de verrouillage[M]
Verschlußhebel[M]
palanca[F] de cierre[M]
placard board
porte-étiquette[M]
Anschriftentafel[F]
tablero[M] de rótulo[M]
route board
porte-étiquette[M] d'acheminement[M]
Wagenlaufschild[N]
tarjeta[F] de ruta[F]
LEVEL CROSSING
PASSAGE[M] À NIVEAU[M]
SCHIENENGLEICHER BAHNÜBERGANG[M]
PASO[M] A NIVEL[M]
level crossing bell
sonnerie[F] de passage[M] à niveau[M]
Vorläutewerk[N]
campana[F] de aviso[M] de cruce[M]
level crossing sign
croix[F] de Saint-André
Warnkreuz[N]
señal[F] de cruce[M]
visor
visière[F]
Schirm[M]
visera[F]
mast
mât[M]
Mast[M]
poste[M]
peep hole
œil[M] témoin[M]
Guckloch[N]
mirilla[F]
flashing light
feu[M] clignotant
Blinklicht[N]
luz[F] intermitente
junction box
boîte[F] de jonction[F]
Verteilerdose[F]
caja[F] de empalmes[M]
signal background plate
écran[M] de visibilité[F]
Signalschirm[M]
fondo[M] de la señal[F]
2
number of tracks sign
panneau[M] nombre[M] de voies[F]
Anzahl[F] der Gleise[N]
letrero[M] de número[M] de vías[F]
barrier lamp
feu[M] de lisse[F]
Lampe[F]
luz[F] de la barrera[F]
barrier
lisse[F]
Schranke[F]
barrera[F] del paso[M] a nivel[M]
barrier support
support[M] de lisse[F]
Stütze[F]
soporte[M] de la barrera[F]
counterweight
contrepoids[M]
Gegengewicht[N]
contrapeso[M]
crossing barrier mechanism
commande[F] de barrières[F]
Antrieb[M]
mecanismo[M] de la barrera[F]
base
base[F]
Sockel[M]
base[F]

# TYPES OF GOODS TRUCK
# TYPES[M] DE WAGONS[M]
# GÜTERWAGEN[M]
# TIPOS[M] DE VAGONES[M] DE CARGA[F]

bogie goods van
wagon[M] couvert
Drehgestellkastenwagen[M]
vagón[M] cerrado

bogie tank wagon
wagon[M]-citerne[F]
Kesselwagen[M]
vagón[M] cisterna[F]

wood chip wagon
wagon[M] à copeaux[M]
langer Kastenwagen[M]
vagón[M] para madera[F]

livestock van
wagon[M] à bestiaux[M]
Verschlagwagen[M]
vagón[M] para ganado[M]

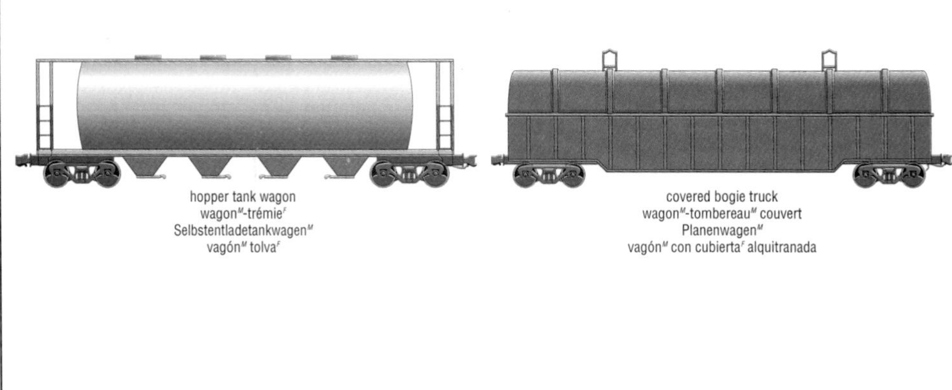

hopper tank wagon
wagon[M]-trémie[F]
Selbstentladetankwagen[M]
vagón[M] tolva[F]

covered bogie truck
wagon[M]-tombereau[M] couvert
Planenwagen[M]
vagón[M] con cubierta[F] alquitranada

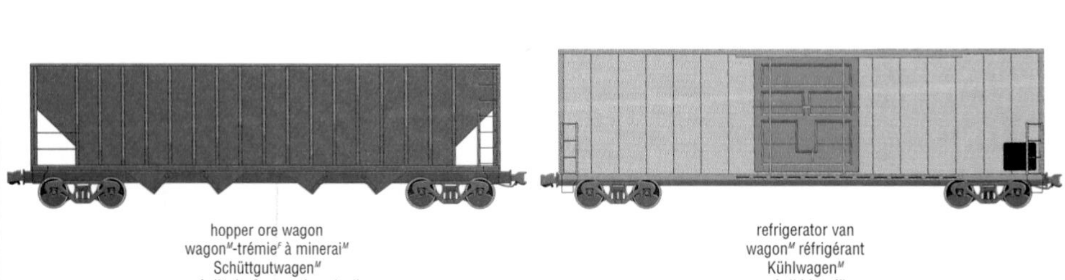

hopper ore wagon
wagon[M]-trémie[F] à minerai[M]
Schüttgutwagen[M]
vagón[M] tolva[F] para minerales[M]

refrigerator van
wagon[M] réfrigérant
Kühlwagen[M]
vagón[M] frigorífico

three-tier car carrier
wagon$^{M}$ porte-automobiles$^{M}$
Autotransportwagen$^{M}$
vagón$^{M}$ para automóviles$^{M}$

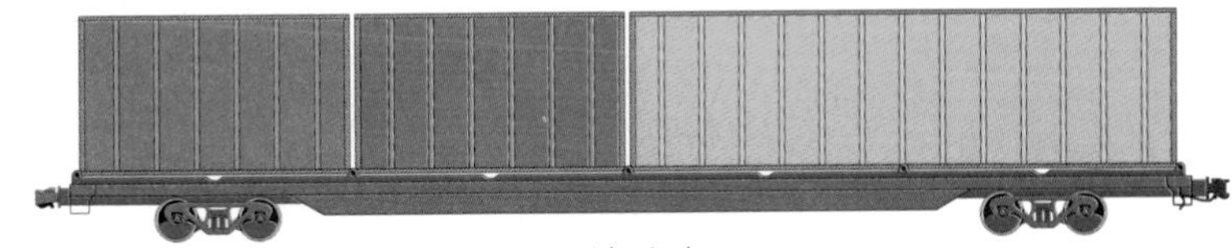

container truck
wagon$^{M}$ porte-conteneurs$^{M}$
Containerflachwagen$^{M}$
vagón$^{M}$ para contenedores$^{M}$

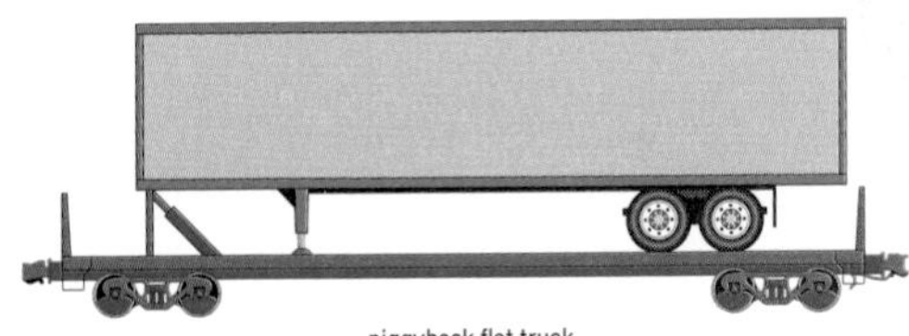

piggyback flat truck
wagon$^{M}$ rail$^{M}$-route$^{F}$
Spezialflachwagen$^{M}$ für den Transport$^{M}$ von Schwerfahrzeugen$^{N}$
plataforma$^{F}$ para transportar vagones$^{M}$

flat truck
wagon$^{M}$ plat
Drehgestellflachwagen$^{M}$
plataforma$^{F}$

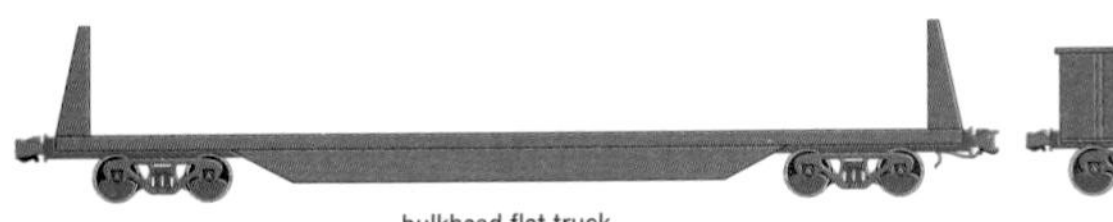

bulkhead flat truck
wagon$^{M}$ plat à parois$^{F}$ de bout$^{M}$
Stirnwandflachwagen$^{M}$
vagón$^{M}$ plano con retenedores$^{M}$

bogie goods truck
wagon$^{M}$-tombereau$^{M}$
offener Güterwagen$^{M}$
vagón$^{M}$ de mercancías$^{F}$

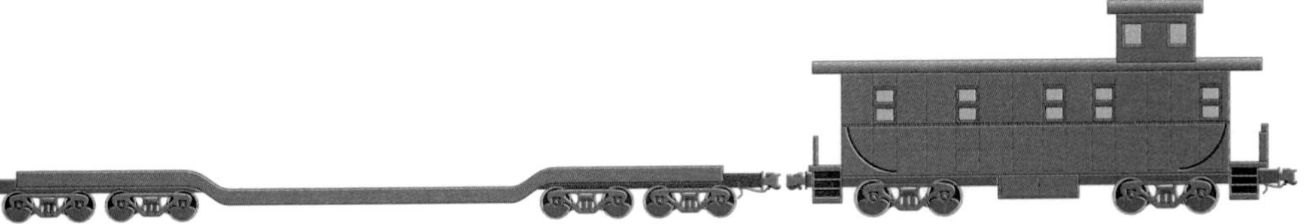

well wagon
wagon$^{M}$ plat surbaissé
Tiefladewagen$^{M}$
plataforma$^{F}$ de piso$^{M}$ bajo

brake van
wagon$^{M}$ de queue$^{F}$
Bremswagen$^{M}$
furgón$^{M}$ de cola$^{F}$

# UNDERGROUND RAILWAY
# CHEMIN[M] DE FER[M] MÉTROPOLITAIN
# U-BAHN[F]
# METRO[M]

## UNDERGROUND STATION
## STATION[F] DE MÉTRO[M]
## U-BAHN-STATION[F]
## ESTACIÓN[F] DE METRO[M]

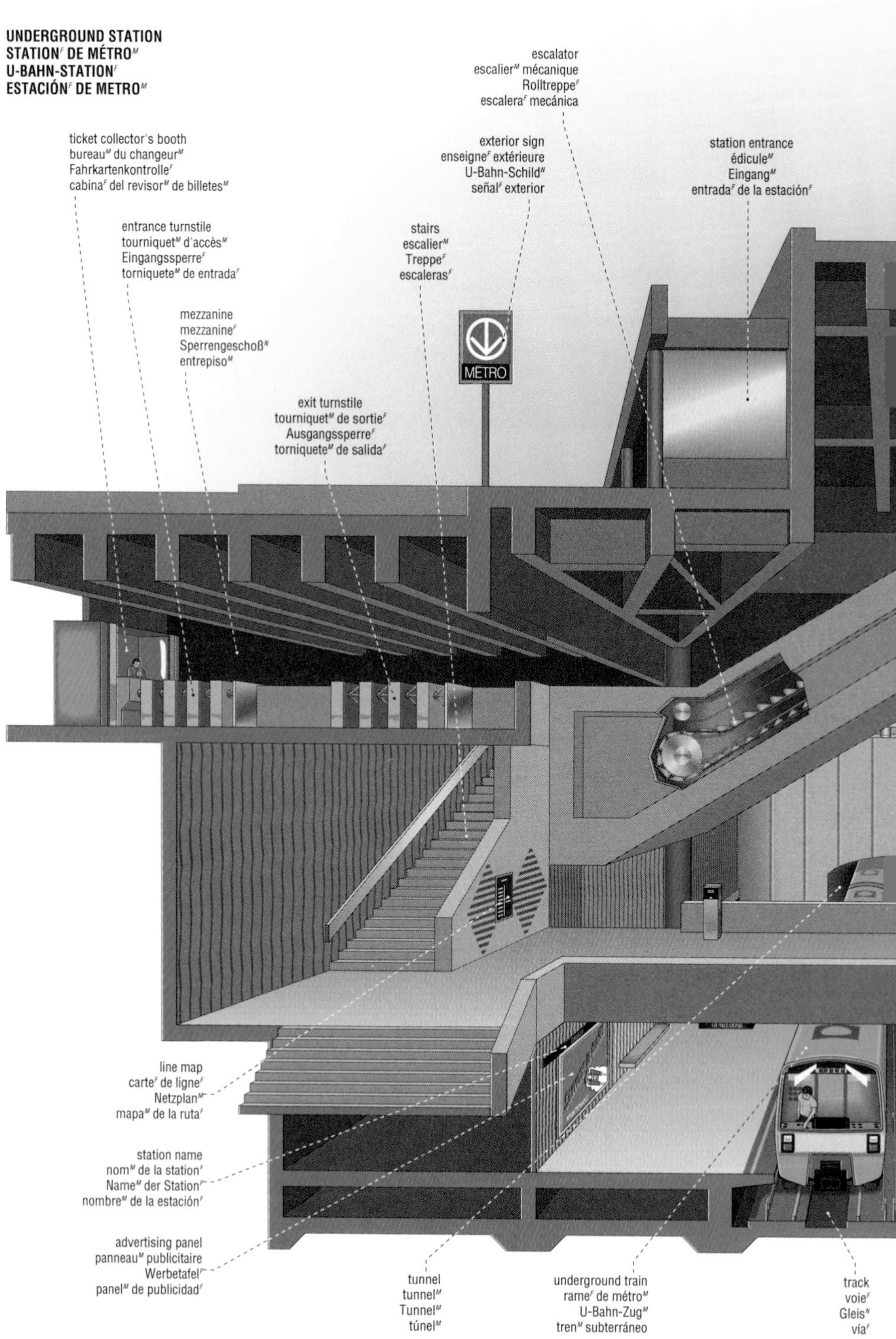

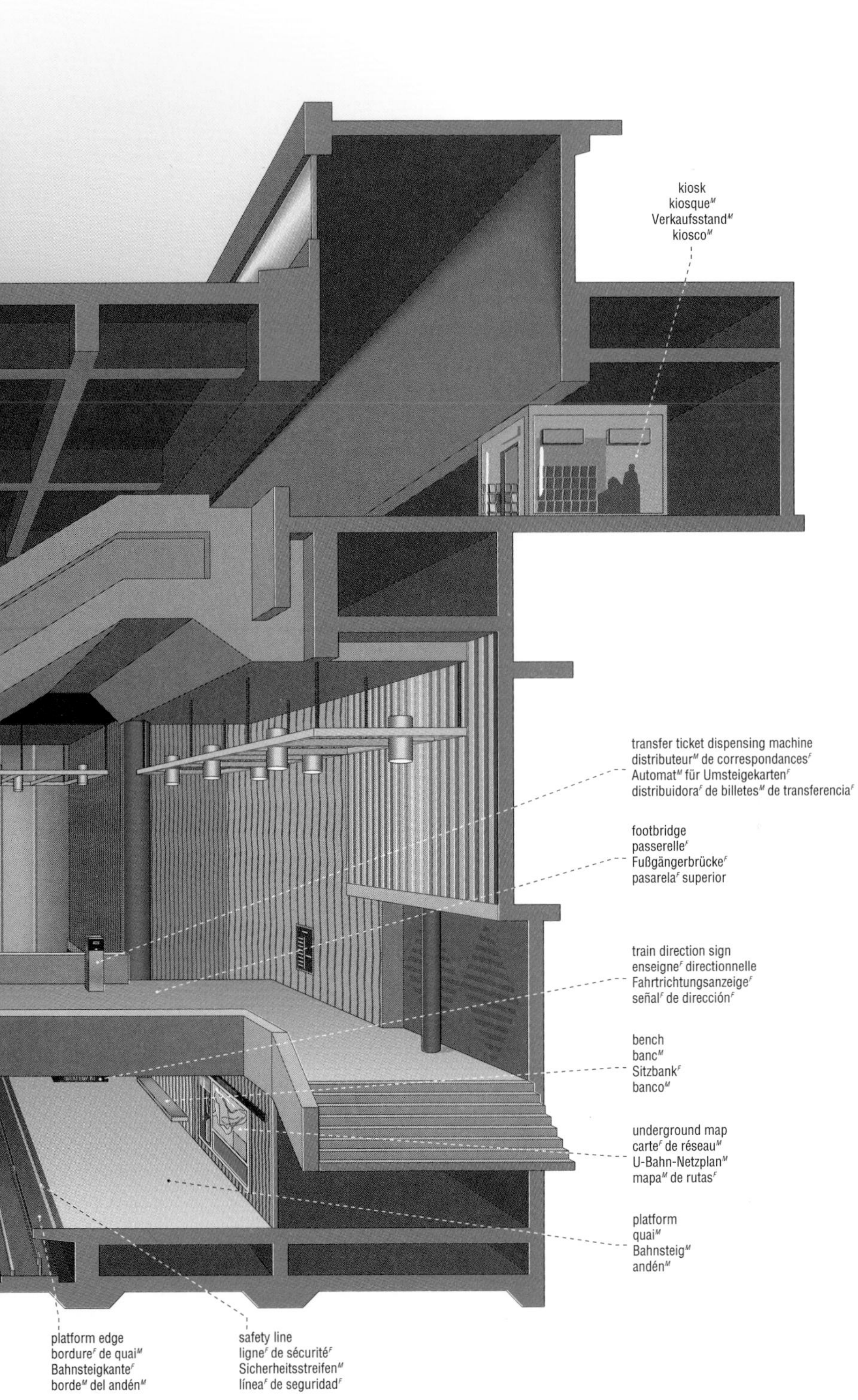
kiosk
kiosque[M]
Verkaufsstand[M]
kiosco[M]
transfer ticket dispensing machine
distributeur[M] de correspondances[F]
Automat[M] für Umsteigekarten[F]
distribuidora[F] de billetes[M] de transferencia[F]
footbridge
passerelle[F]
Fußgängerbrücke[F]
pasarela[F] superior
train direction sign
enseigne[F] directionnelle
Fahrtrichtungsanzeige[F]
señal[F] de dirección[F]
bench
banc[M]
Sitzbank[F]
banco[M]
underground map
carte[F] de réseau[M]
U-Bahn-Netzplan[M]
mapa[M] de rutas[F]
platform
quai[M]
Bahnsteig[M]
andén[M]
platform edge
bordure[F] de quai[M]
Bahnsteigkante[F]
borde[M] del andén[M]
safety line
ligne[F] de sécurité[F]
Sicherheitsstreifen[M]
línea[F] de seguridad[F]

# UNDERGROUND RAILWAY
# CHEMIN$^{M}$ DE FER$^{M}$ MÉTROPOLITAIN
# U-BAHN$^{F}$
# METRO$^{M}$

## BOGIE AND TRACK
## BOGIE$^{M}$ ET VOIE$^{F}$
## DREHGESTELL$^{N}$ UND GLEIS$^{N}$
## CARRETILLA$^{F}$ Y VÍA$^{F}$

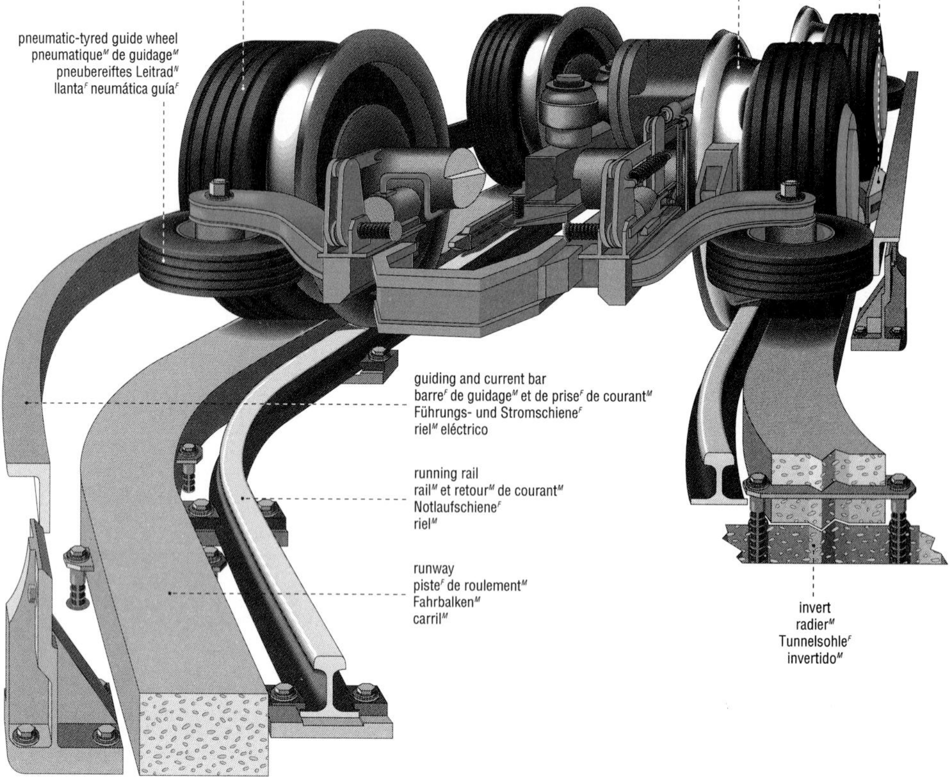

current-collecting shoe
frotteur$^{M}$
Stromabnehmer$^{M}$
bloque$^{M}$ corredizo

pneumatic-tyred running wheel
pneumatique$^{M}$ porteur
pneubereiftes Laufrad$^{N}$
llanta$^{F}$ neumática de tracción$^{F}$

steel safety wheel
roue$^{F}$ de sécurité$^{F}$
Spurkranzrad$^{N}$
rueda$^{F}$ metálica de seguridad$^{F}$

pneumatic-tyred guide wheel
pneumatique$^{M}$ de guidage$^{M}$
pneubereiftes Leitrad$^{N}$
llanta$^{F}$ neumática guía$^{F}$

guiding and current bar
barre$^{F}$ de guidage$^{M}$ et de prise$^{F}$ de courant$^{M}$
Führungs- und Stromschiene$^{F}$
riel$^{M}$ eléctrico

running rail
rail$^{M}$ et retour$^{M}$ de courant$^{M}$
Notlaufschiene$^{F}$
riel$^{M}$

runway
piste$^{F}$ de roulement$^{M}$
Fahrbalken$^{M}$
carril$^{M}$

invert
radier$^{M}$
Tunnelsohle$^{F}$
invertido$^{M}$

## UNDERGROUND TRAIN
## RAME$^{F}$ DE MÉTRO$^{M}$
## U-BAHN-ZUG$^{M}$
## TREN$^{M}$ SUBTERRÁNEO

motor car
motrice$^{F}$
Triebwagen$^{M}$
vagón$^{M}$ máquina$^{F}$

passenger car
remorque$^{F}$
Mittelwagen$^{M}$
vagón$^{M}$ de pasajeros$^{M}$

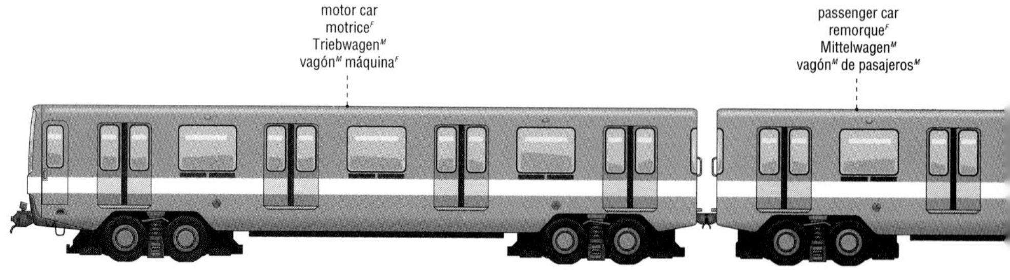

## PASSENGER CAR
## VOITURE[F]
## MITTELWAGEN[M]
## VAGÓN[M] DE PASAJEROS[M]

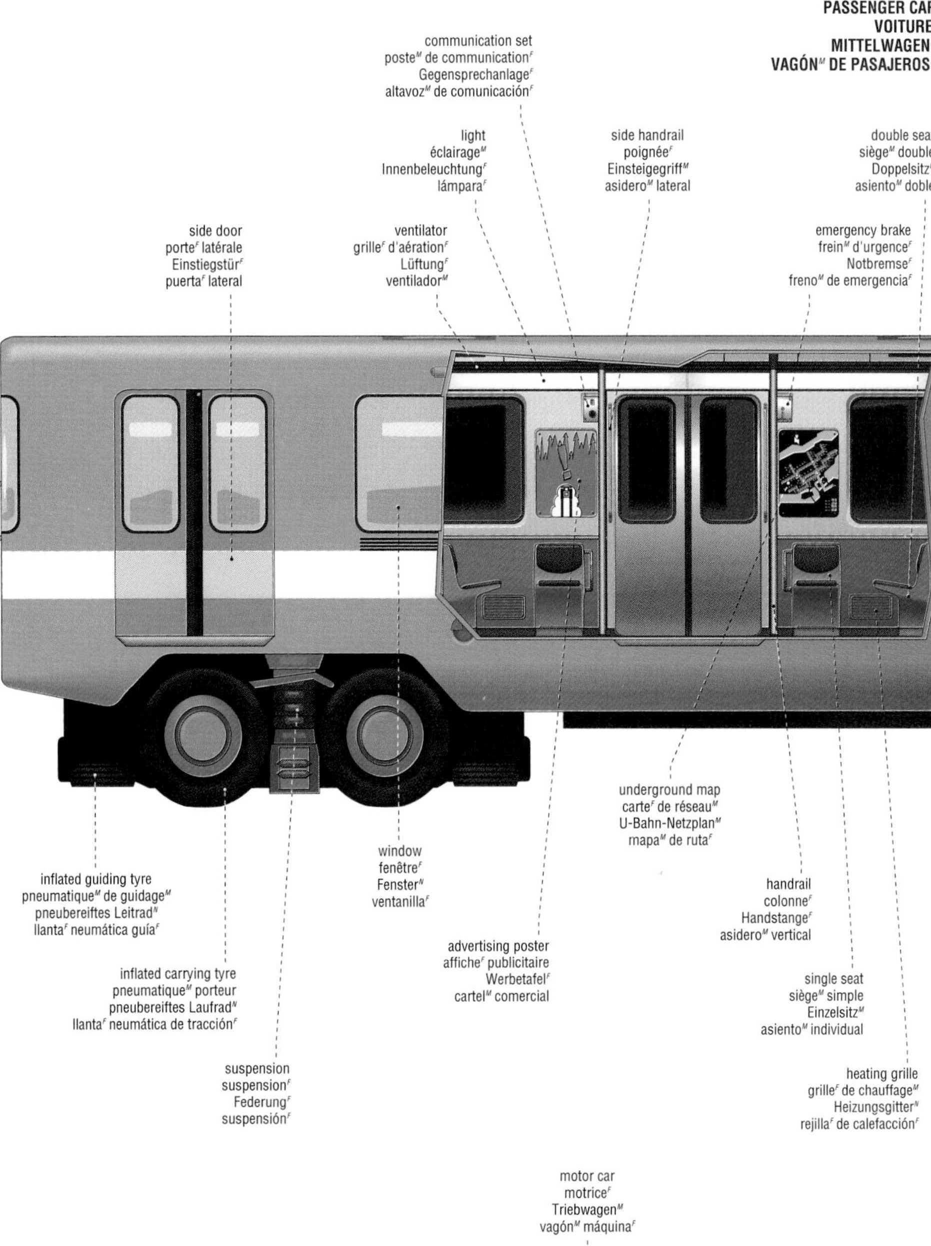

# FOUR-MASTED BARK
# QUATRE-MÂTS[M] BARQUE[F]
# VIERMASTBARK[F]
# BARCO[M] DE VELA[F] DE CUATRO PALOS[M]

## MASTS AND RIGGING
## MÂTURE[F] ET GRÉEMENT[M]
## TAKELAGE[F]
## ARBOLADURA[F] Y APAREJOS[M]

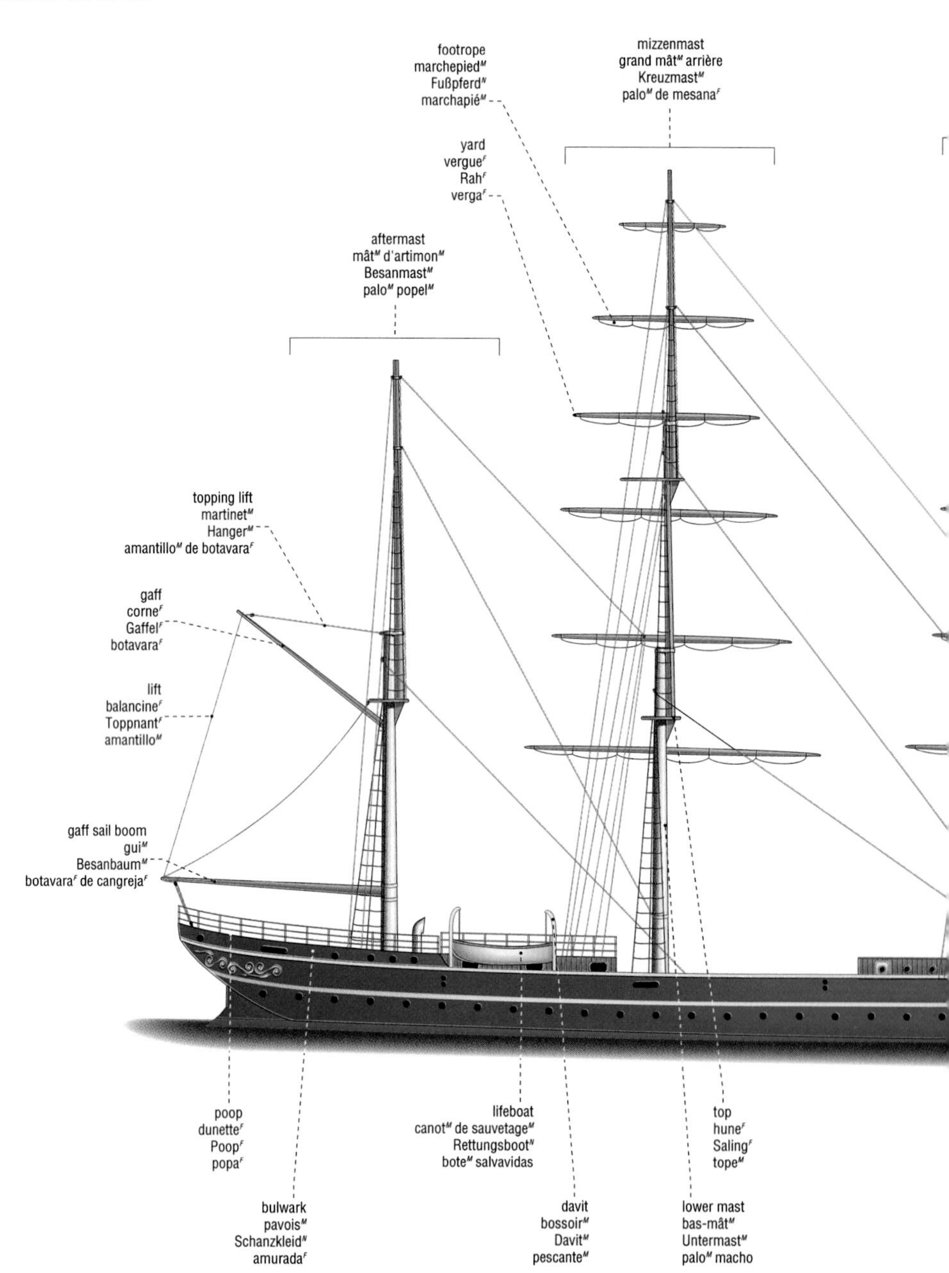

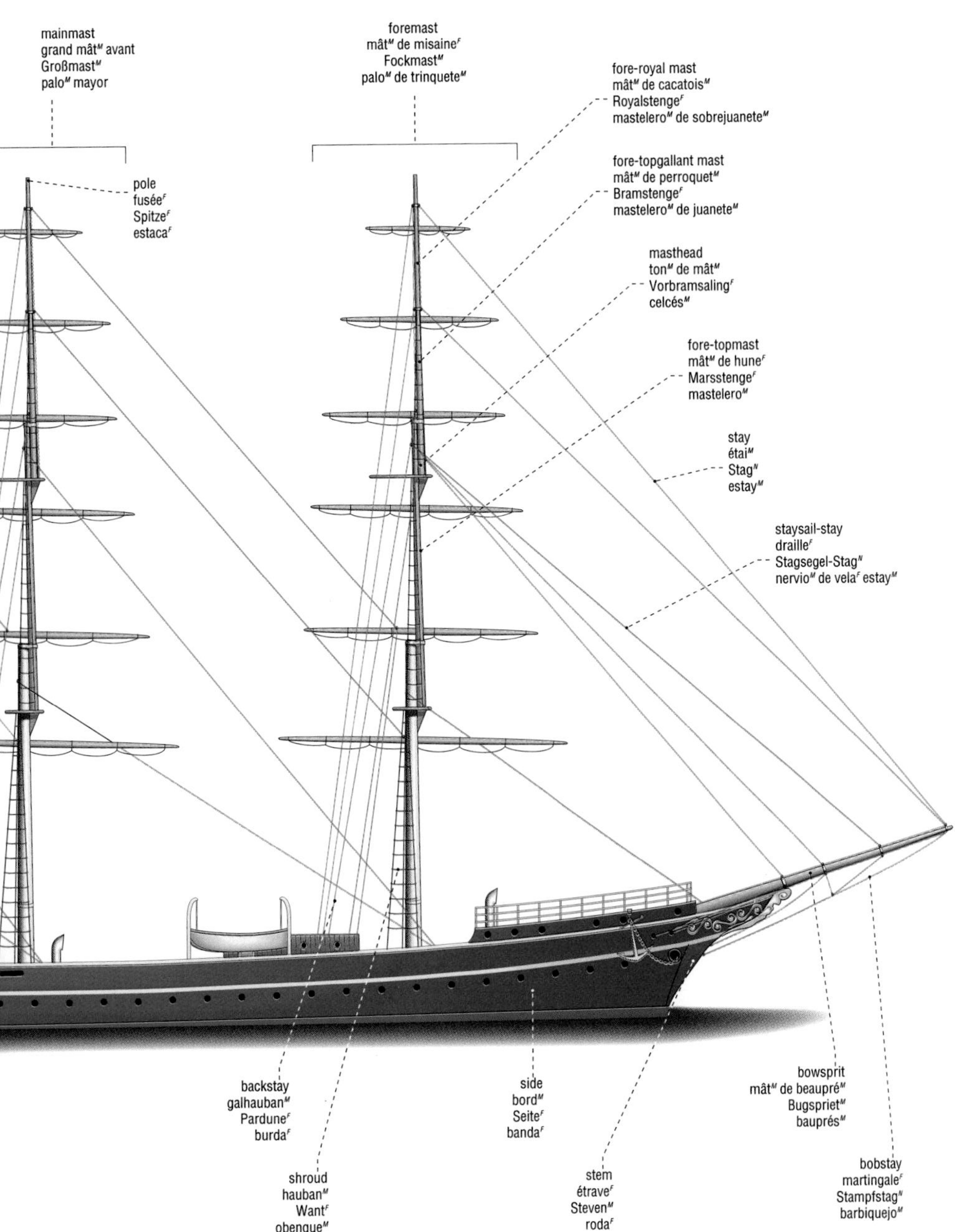
mainmast
grand mât[M] avant
Großmast[M]
palo[M] mayor
foremast
mât[M] de misaine[F]
Fockmast[M]
palo[M] de trinquete[M]
fore-royal mast
mât[M] de cacatois[M]
Royalstenge[F]
mastelero[M] de sobrejuanete[M]
pole
fusée[F]
Spitze[F]
estaca[F]
fore-topgallant mast
mât[M] de perroquet[M]
Bramstenge[F]
mastelero[M] de juanete[M]
masthead
ton[M] de mât[M]
Vorbramsaling[F]
celcés[M]
fore-topmast
mât[M] de hune[F]
Marsstenge[F]
mastelero[M]
stay
étai[M]
Stag[N]
estay[M]
staysail-stay
draille[F]
Stagsegel-Stag[N]
nervio[M] de vela[F] estay[M]
backstay
galhauban[M]
Pardune[F]
burda[F]
side
bord[M]
Seite[F]
banda[F]
bowsprit
mât[M] de beaupré[M]
Bugspriet[M]
bauprés[M]
shroud
hauban[M]
Want[F]
obenque[M]
stem
étrave[F]
Steven[M]
roda[F]
bobstay
martingale[F]
Stampfstag[N]
barbiquejo[M]

# FOUR-MASTED BARK
# QUATRE-MÂTS[M] BARQUE[F]
# VIERMASTBARK[F]
# BARCO[M] DE VELA[F] DE CUATRO PALOS[M]

**SAILS**
**VOILURE[F]**
**SEGEL[N]**
**VELAMEN[M]**

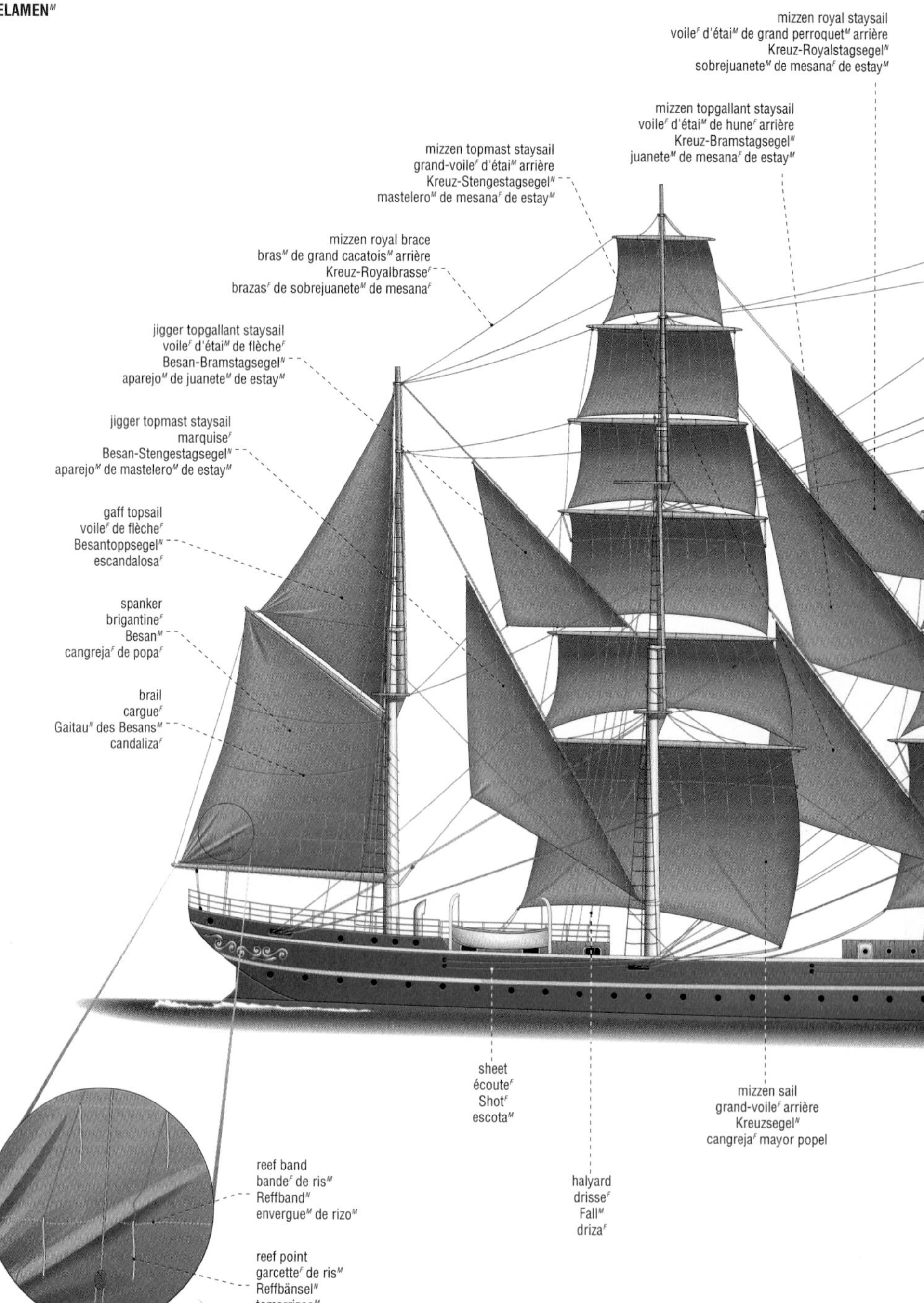

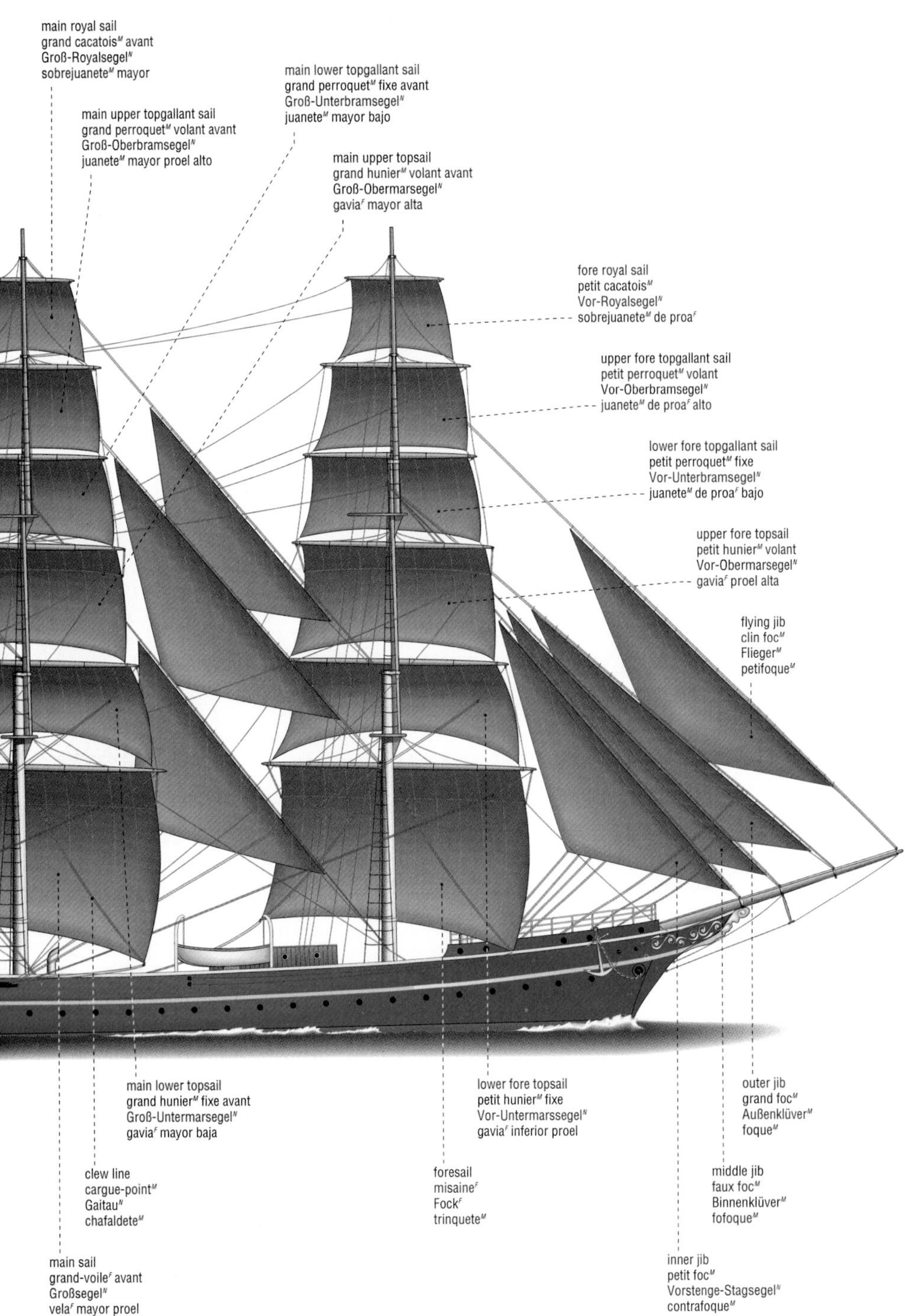
main royal sail
grand cacatois[M] avant
Groß-Royalsegel[N]
sobrejuanete[M] mayor
main upper topgallant sail
grand perroquet[M] volant avant
Groß-Oberbramsegel[N]
juanete[M] mayor proel alto
main lower topgallant sail
grand perroquet[M] fixe avant
Groß-Unterbramsegel[N]
juanete[M] mayor bajo
main upper topsail
grand hunier[M] volant avant
Groß-Obermarsegel[N]
gavia[F] mayor alta
fore royal sail
petit cacatois[M]
Vor-Royalsegel[N]
sobrejuanete[M] de proa[F]
upper fore topgallant sail
petit perroquet[M] volant
Vor-Oberbramsegel[N]
juanete[M] de proa[F] alto
lower fore topgallant sail
petit perroquet[M] fixe
Vor-Unterbramsegel[N]
juanete[M] de proa[F] bajo
upper fore topsail
petit hunier[M] volant
Vor-Obermarsegel[N]
gavia[F] proel alta
flying jib
clin foc[M]
Flieger[M]
petifoque[M]
main lower topsail
grand hunier[M] fixe avant
Groß-Untermarsegel[N]
gavia[F] mayor baja
lower fore topsail
petit hunier[M] fixe
Vor-Untermarssegel[N]
gavia[F] inferior proel
outer jib
grand foc[M]
Außenklüver[M]
foque[M]
clew line
cargue-point[M]
Gaitau[N]
chafaldete[M]
foresail
misaine[F]
Fock[F]
trinquete[M]
middle jib
faux foc[M]
Binnenklüver[M]
fofoque[M]
main sail
grand-voile[F] avant
Großsegel[N]
vela[F] mayor proel
inner jib
petit foc[M]
Vorstenge-Stagsegel[N]
contrafoque[M]

## TYPES OF SAIL
## TYPES[M] DE VOILES[F]
## SEGELTYPEN[M]
## TIPOS[M] DE VELAS[F]

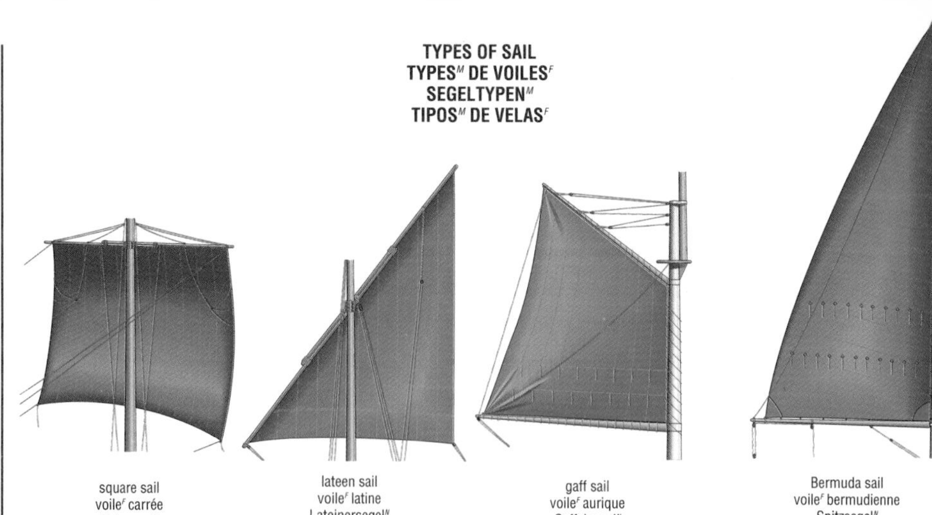

square sail
voile[F] carrée
Rahsegel[N]
vela[F] cuadrada

lateen sail
voile[F] latine
Lateinersegel[N]
vela[F] latina

gaff sail
voile[F] aurique
Gaffelsegel[N]
vela[F] cangreja

Bermuda sail
voile[F] bermudienne
Spitzsegel[N]
vela[F] Bermuda

## TYPES OF RIG
## TYPES[M] DE GRÉEMENTS[M]
## ARTEN[F] DER TAKELUNG[F]
## TIPOS[M] DE APAREJOS[M]

whale boat
baleinière[F]
Walboot[N]
ballenera[F]

brigantine
brigantin[M]
Brigantine[F]
bergantín[M] goleta[F]

ketch
ketch[M]
Ketsch[F]
queche[M]

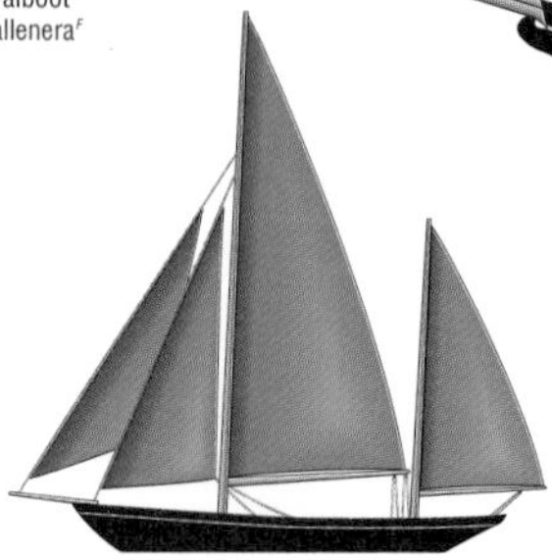

Marconi cutter
cotre[M] Marconi
Marconikutter[M]
cúter[M] Marconi

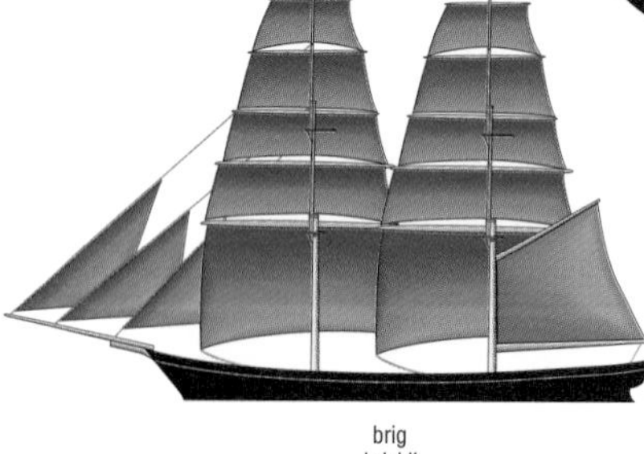

brig
brick[M]
Brigg[F]
bergantín[M]

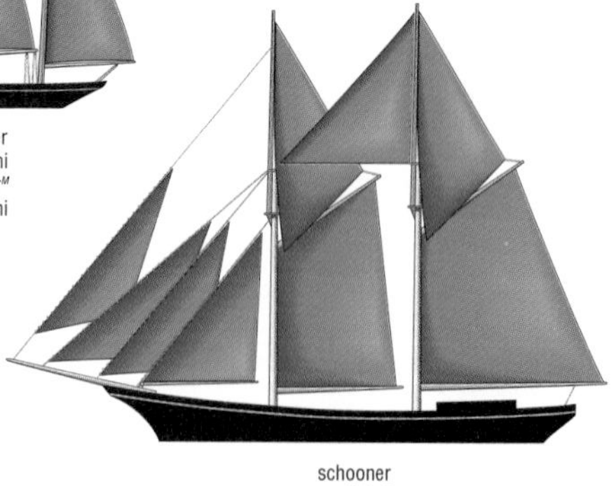

schooner
goélette[F]
Schoner[M]
goleta[F]

# ANCHOR
# ANCRE[F]
# ANKER[M]
# ANCLA[F]

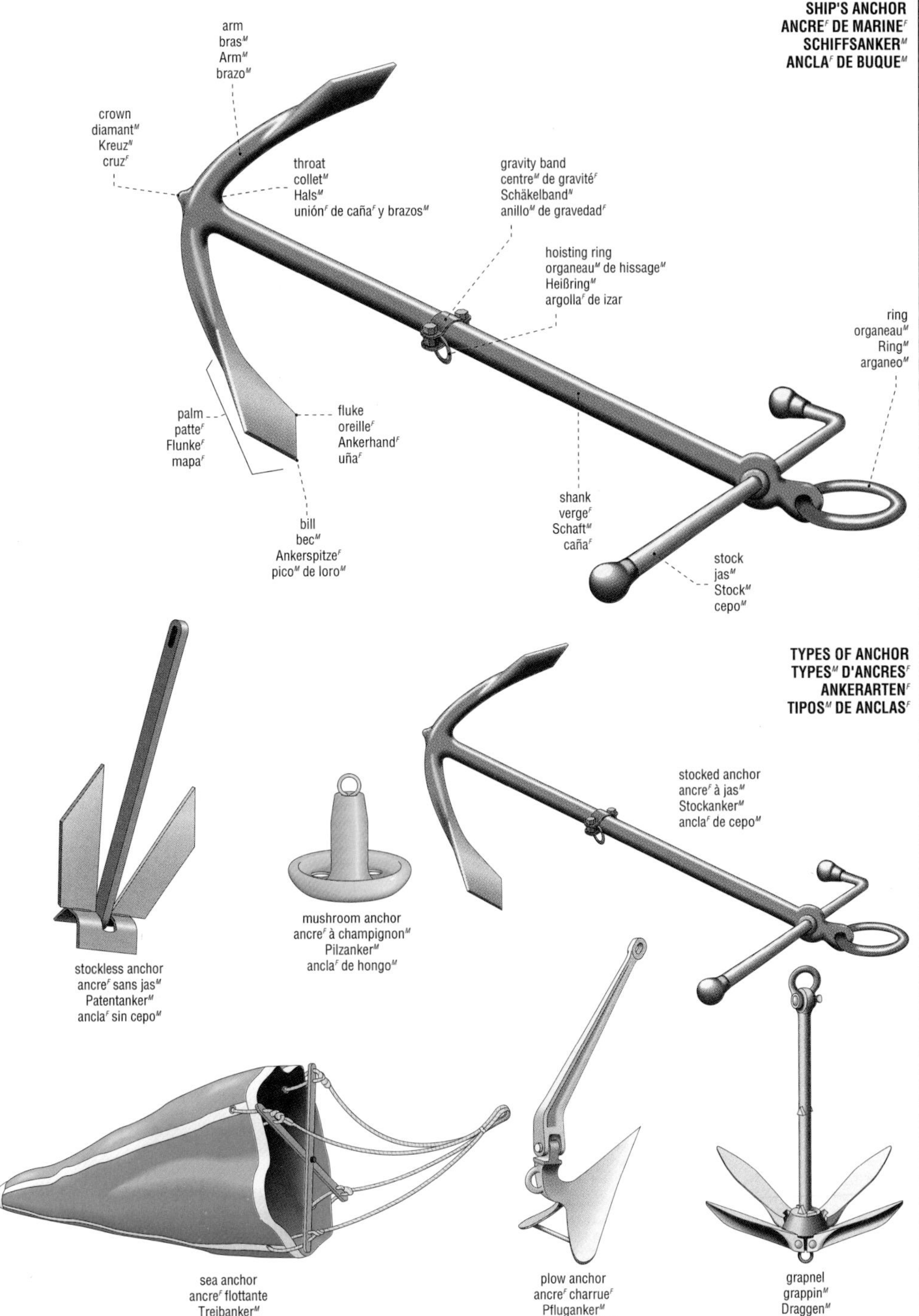

# NAVIGATION DEVICES
# APPAREILS[M] DE NAVIGATION[F]
# NAVIGATIONSINSTRUMENTE[N]
# APARATOS[M] DE NAVEGACIÓN[F]

## SEXTANT
## SEXTANT[M]
## SEXTANT[M]
## SEXTANTE[M]

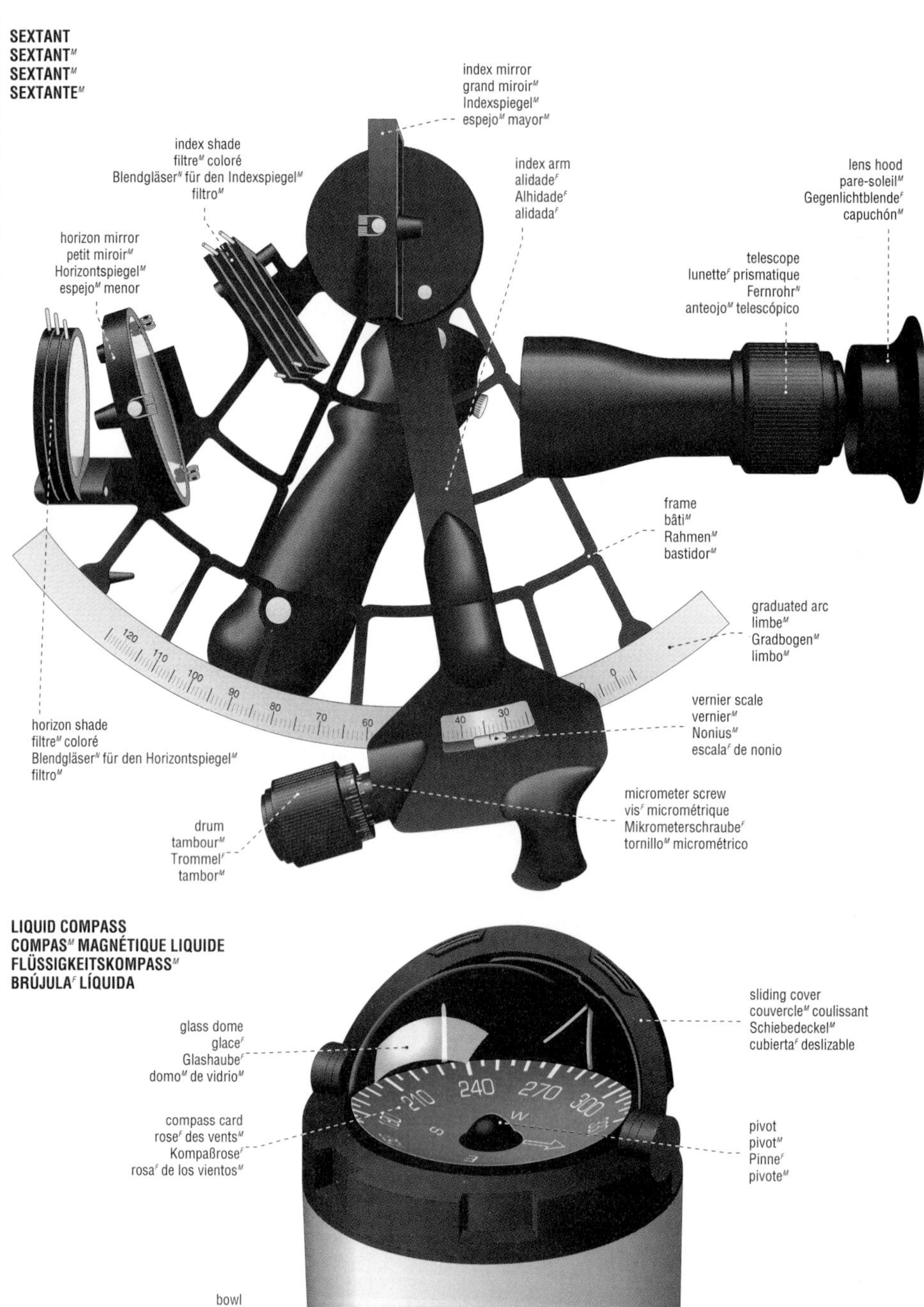

## ECHO SOUNDER
## SONDEURᴹ À ÉCLATSᴹ
## ECHOLOTᴺ
## SONARᴹ

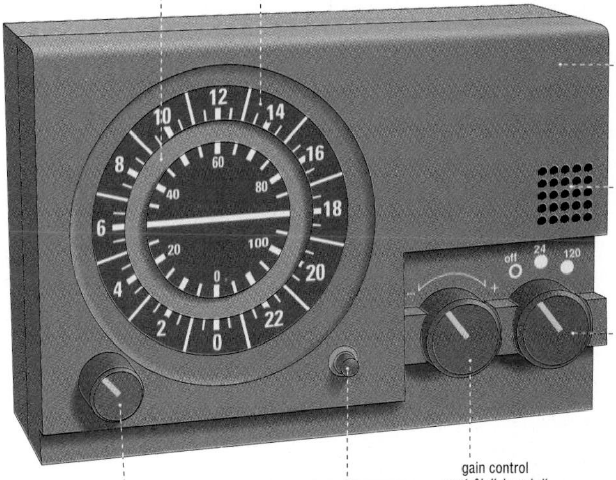

dial-type display
écranᴹ
Anzeigeskalaᶠ
indicadorᴹ del cuadranteᴹ

depth scale in metres
échelleᶠ de profondeurᶠ en m
Tiefenskalaᶠ in m
escalaᶠ de profundidadᶠ

housing
boîtierᴹ
Gehäuseᴺ
cajaᶠ

sound alarm
alarmeᶠ sonore
Lautsprecherᴹ
alarmaᶠ sonora

on-off switch
interrupteurᴹ
Ein-/Ausschalterᴹ
interruptorᴹ

gain control
contrôleᴹ du gainᴹ
Verstärkerreglerᴹ
controlᴹ de gananciaᶠ

alarm threshold display button
visualisationᶠ du seuilᴹ d'alarmeᶠ
Knopfᴹ für Alarmschwellenwert-Anzeigeᶠ
botónᴹ de visualizaciónᶠ del nivelᴹ de alarmaᶠ

alarm threshold setting
réglageᴹ du seuilᴹ d'alarmeᶠ
Alarmschwellenwert-Einstellungᶠ
controlᴹ del nivelᴹ de alarmaᶠ

## ECHO SOUNDER PROBE
## SONDEᶠ
## SCHWINGERᴹ
## SONDAᶠ

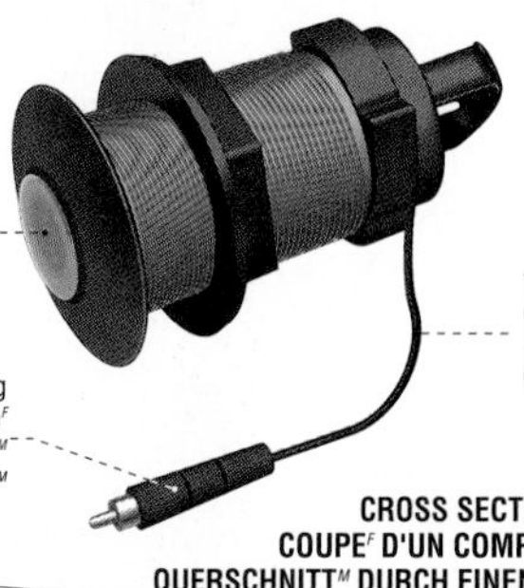

transducer
émetteurᴹ/récepteurᴹ
Überträgerᴹ
transductorᴹ

transmission cable
câbleᴹ de transmissionᶠ
Übertragungskabelᴺ
cableᴹ de transmisiónᶠ

plug
ficheᶠ
Steckerᴹ
enchufeᴹ

## CROSS SECTION OF A LIQUID COMPASS
## COUPEᶠ D'UN COMPASᴹ MAGNÉTIQUE LIQUIDE
## QUERSCHNITTᴹ DURCH EINEN FLÜSSIGKEITSKOMPASSᴹ
## CORTEᴹ TRANSVERSAL DE UNA BRÚJULAᶠ LÍQUIDA

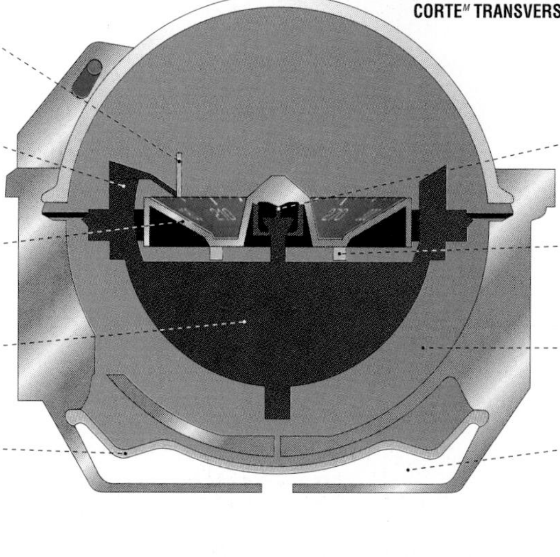

lubber's line
ligneᶠ de foiᶠ
Kursstrichᴹ
líneaᶠ de feᶠ

gimbal ring
suspensionᶠ à la Cardan
Kardanringᴹ
anilloᴹ balancín

pivot
pivotᴹ
Pinneᶠ
pivoteᴹ

jewel cap
chapeᶠ
Hütchenᴺ
cubiertaᶠ

magnet
aimantᴹ
Magnetᴹ
imánᴹ

float
flotteurᴹ
Schwimmerᴹ
flotadorᴹ

water/alcohol
eauᶠ/alcoolᴹ
Wasserᴺ/Alkoholᴹ
aguaᶠ/alcoholᴹ

expansion diaphragm
diaphragmeᴹ de dilatationᶠ
Ausdehnungsmembranᶠ
diafragmaᴹ de expansión

expansion chamber
chambreᶠ de dilatationᶠ
Ausdehnungskammerᶠ
estabilizadorᴹ

# MARITIME SIGNALS
# SIGNALISATION^F MARITIME
# SEEZEICHEN^N
# SEÑALES^F MARÍTIMAS

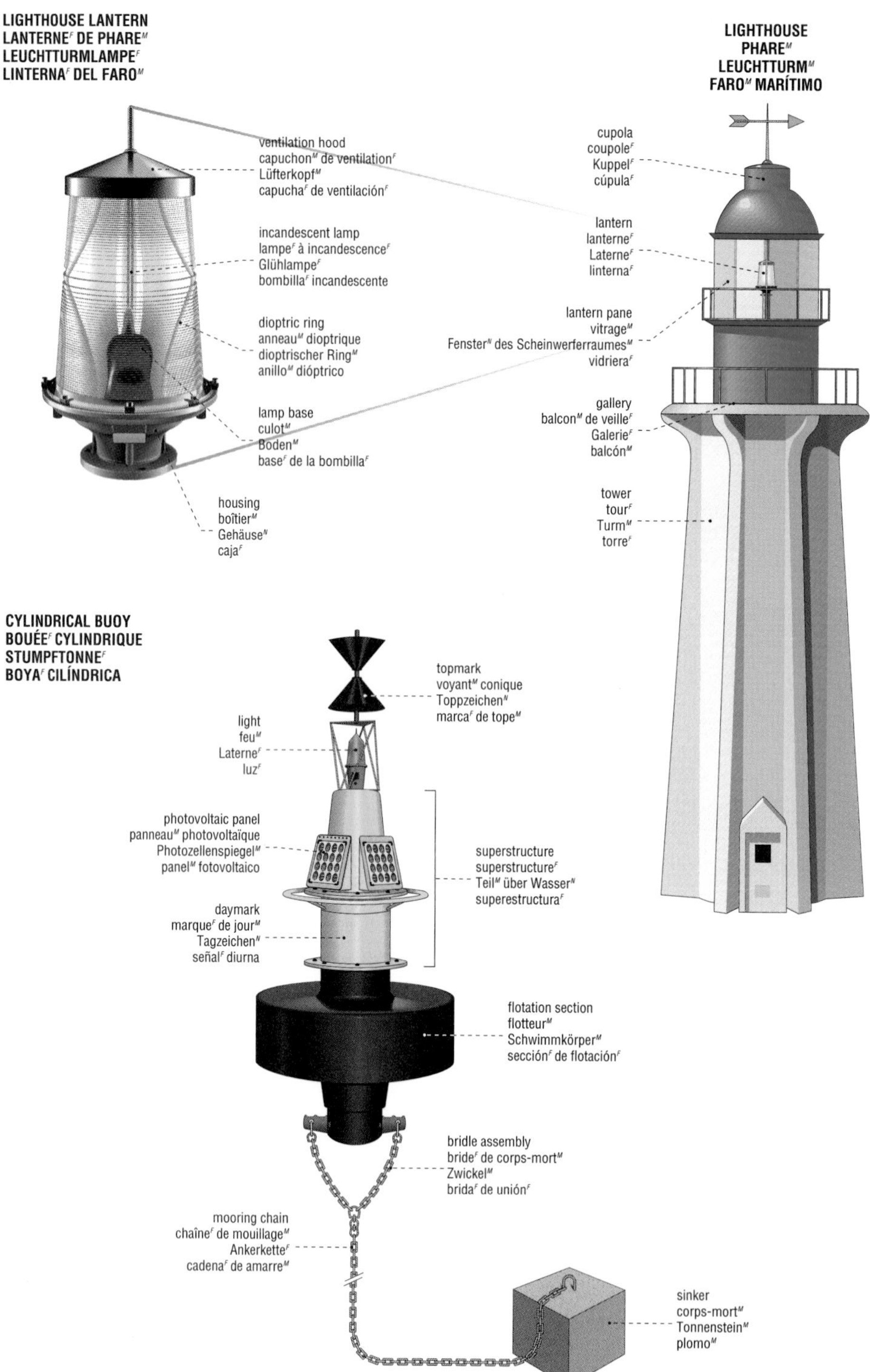

## HIGH FOCAL PLANE BUOY
## BOUÉE^F À PLAN^M FOCAL ÉLEVÉ
## GROSSTONNE^F
## BOYA^F DE PLANO^M FOCAL ELEVADO

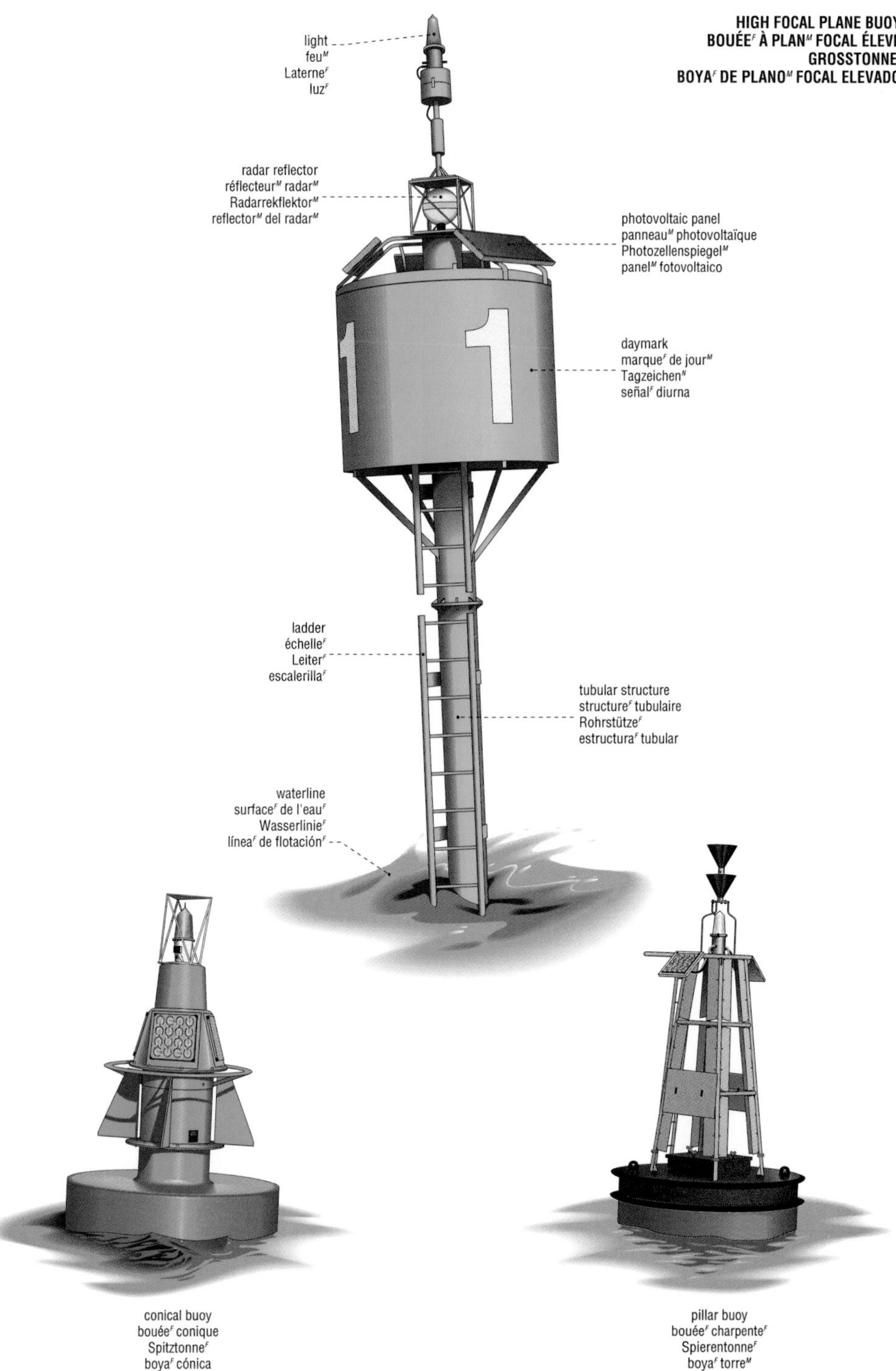


conical buoy
bouée^F conique
Spitztonne^F
boya^F cónica

pillar buoy
bouée^F charpente^F
Spierentonne^F
boya^F torre^M

# MARITIME BUOYAGE SYSTEM
# SYSTÈME[M] DE BALISAGE[M] MARITIME
# BETONNUNGSSYSTEM[N]
# SISTEMA[M] DE BOYAS[F] MARITIMAS

## CARDINAL MARKS
## MARQUES[F] CARDINALES
## KARDINALSEEZEICHEN[N]
## SEÑALES[F] DE LOS PUNTOS[M] CARDINALES

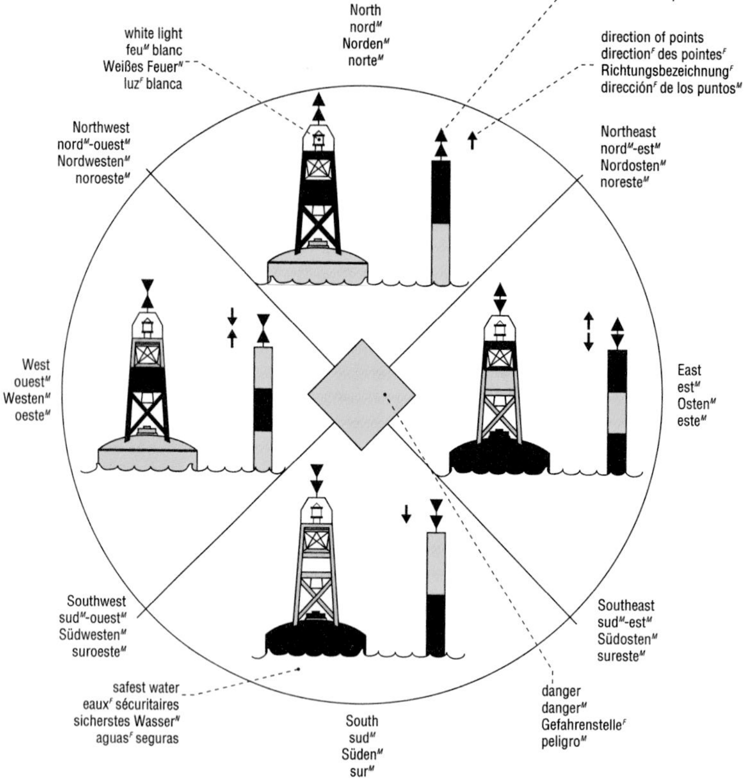

topmark
voyant[M] conique
Toppzeichen[N]
marca[F] de tope[M]

North
nord[M]
Norden[M]
norte[M]

white light
feu[M] blanc
Weißes Feuer[N]
luz[F] blanca

direction of points
direction[F] des pointes[F]
Richtungsbezeichnung[F]
dirección[F] de los puntos[M]

Northwest
nord[M]-ouest[M]
Nordwesten[M]
noroeste[M]

Northeast
nord[M]-est[M]
Nordosten[M]
noreste[M]

West
ouest[M]
Westen[M]
oeste[M]

East
est[M]
Osten[M]
este[M]

Southwest
sud[M]-ouest[M]
Südwesten[M]
suroeste[M]

Southeast
sud[M]-est[M]
Südosten[M]
sureste[M]

safest water
eaux[F] sécuritaires
sicherstes Wasser[N]
aguas[F] seguras

danger
danger[M]
Gefahrenstelle[F]
peligro[M]

South
sud[M]
Süden[M]
sur[M]

## BUOYAGE REGIONS
## RÉGIONS[F] DE BALISAGE[M]
## BETONNTE FAHRWASSER[N]
## REGIONES[F] DE BOYAS[F]

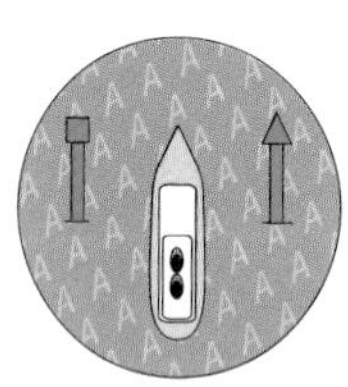

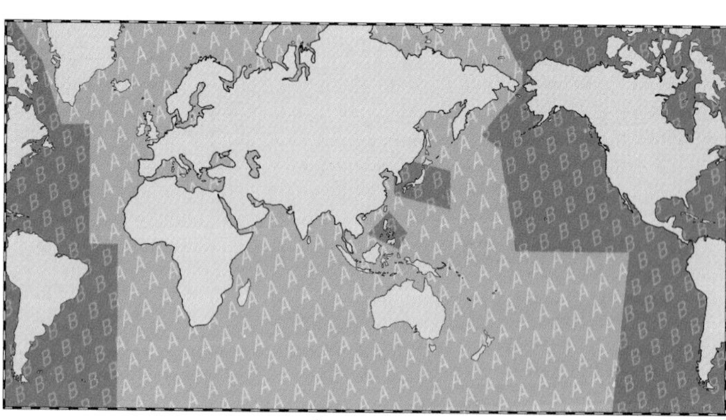

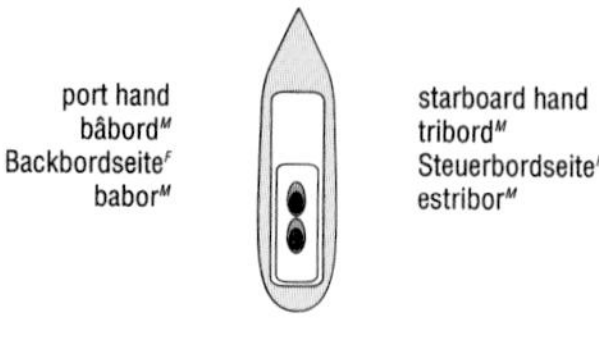

port hand
bâbord[M]
Backbordseite[F]
babor[M]

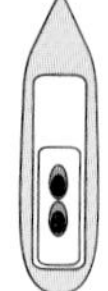

starboard hand
tribord[M]
Steuerbordseite[F]
estribor[M]

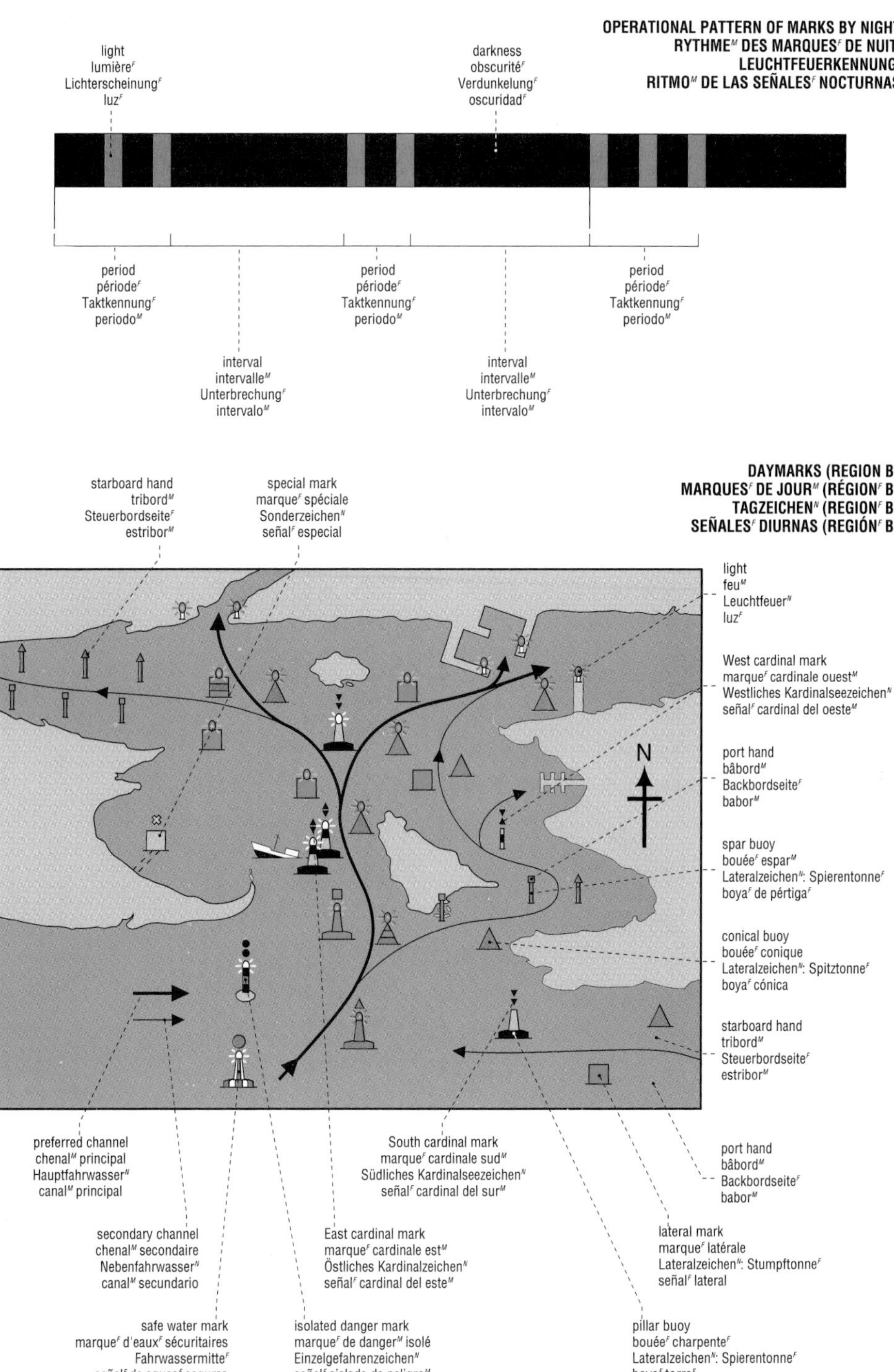
OPERATIONAL PATTERN OF MARKS BY NIGHT
RYTHME[M] DES MARQUES[F] DE NUIT[F]
LEUCHTFEUERKENNUNG[F]
RITMO[M] DE LAS SEÑALES[F] NOCTURNAS
light
lumière[F]
Lichterscheinung[F]
luz[F]
darkness
obscurité[F]
Verdunkelung[F]
oscuridad[F]
period
période[F]
Taktkennung[F]
periodo[M]
interval
intervalle[M]
Unterbrechung[F]
intervalo[M]
DAYMARKS (REGION B)
MARQUES[F] DE JOUR[M] (RÉGION[F] B)
TAGZEICHEN[N] (REGION[F] B)
SEÑALES[F] DIURNAS (REGIÓN[F] B)
starboard hand
tribord[M]
Steuerbordseite[F]
estribor[M]
special mark
marque[F] spéciale
Sonderzeichen[N]
señal[F] especial
light
feu[M]
Leuchtfeuer[N]
luz[F]
West cardinal mark
marque[F] cardinale ouest[M]
Westliches Kardinalseezeichen[N]
señal[F] cardinal del oeste[M]
port hand
bâbord[M]
Backbordseite[F]
babor[M]
N
spar buoy
bouée[F] espar[M]
Lateralzeichen[N]: Spierentonne[F]
boya[F] de pértiga[F]
conical buoy
bouée[F] conique
Lateralzeichen[N]: Spitztonne[F]
boya[F] cónica
starboard hand
tribord[M]
Steuerbordseite[F]
estribor[M]
port hand
bâbord[M]
Backbordseite[F]
babor[M]
preferred channel
chenal[M] principal
Hauptfahrwasser[N]
canal[M] principal
South cardinal mark
marque[F] cardinale sud[M]
Südliches Kardinalseezeichen[N]
señal[F] cardinal del sur[M]
secondary channel
chenal[M] secondaire
Nebenfahrwasser[N]
canal[M] secundario
East cardinal mark
marque[F] cardinale est[M]
Östliches Kardinalzeichen[N]
señal[F] cardinal del este[M]
lateral mark
marque[F] latérale
Lateralzeichen[N]: Stumpftonne[F]
señal[F] lateral
safe water mark
marque[F] d'eaux[F] sécuritaires
Fahrwassermitte[F]
señal[F] de aguas[F] seguras
isolated danger mark
marque[F] de danger[M] isolé
Einzelgefahrenzeichen[N]
señal[F] aislada de peligro[M]
pillar buoy
bouée[F] charpente[F]
Lateralzeichen[N]: Spierentonne[F]
boya[F] torre[F]

# HARBOUR
# PORT[M] MARITIME
# HAFEN[M]
# PUERTO[M]

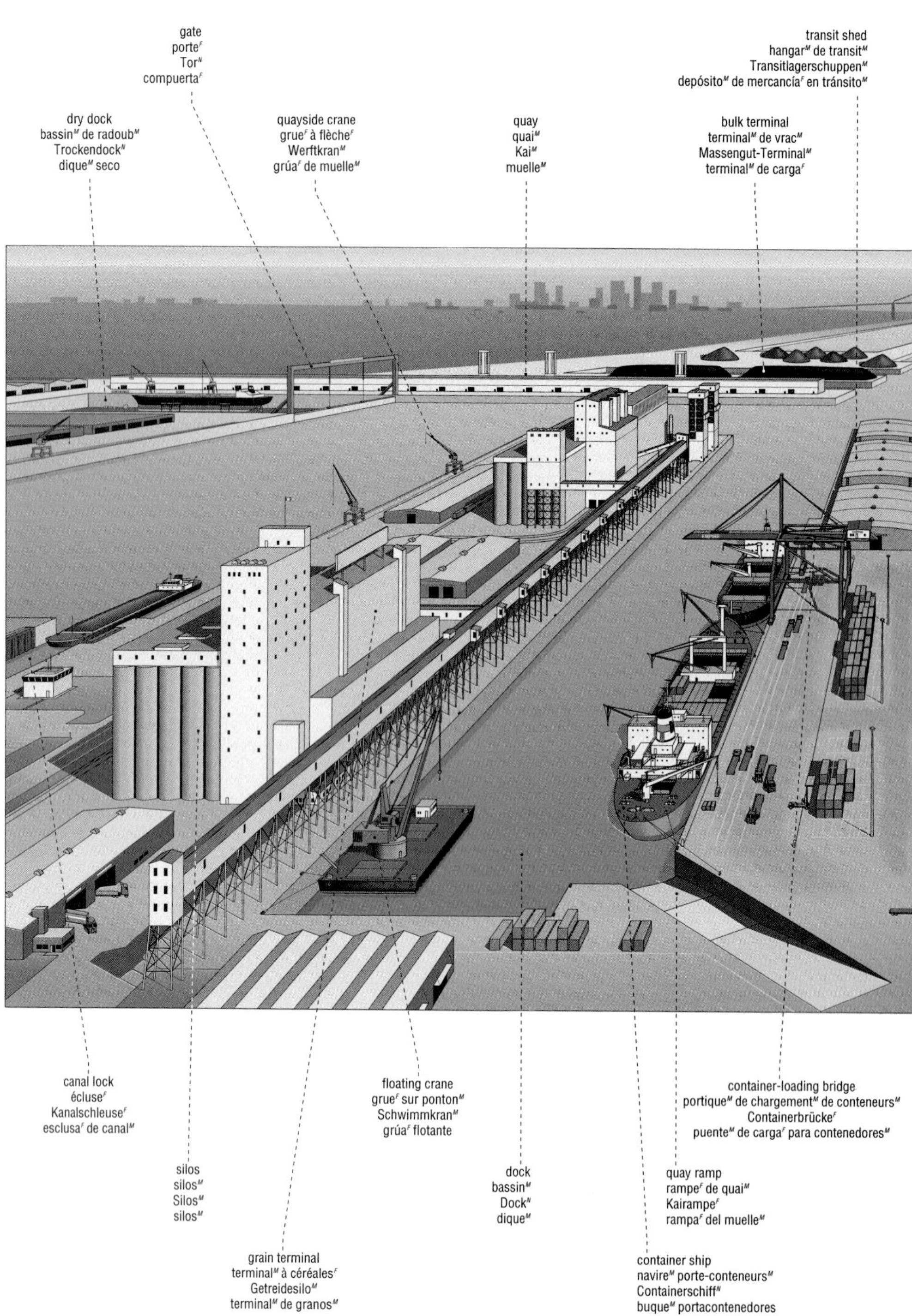

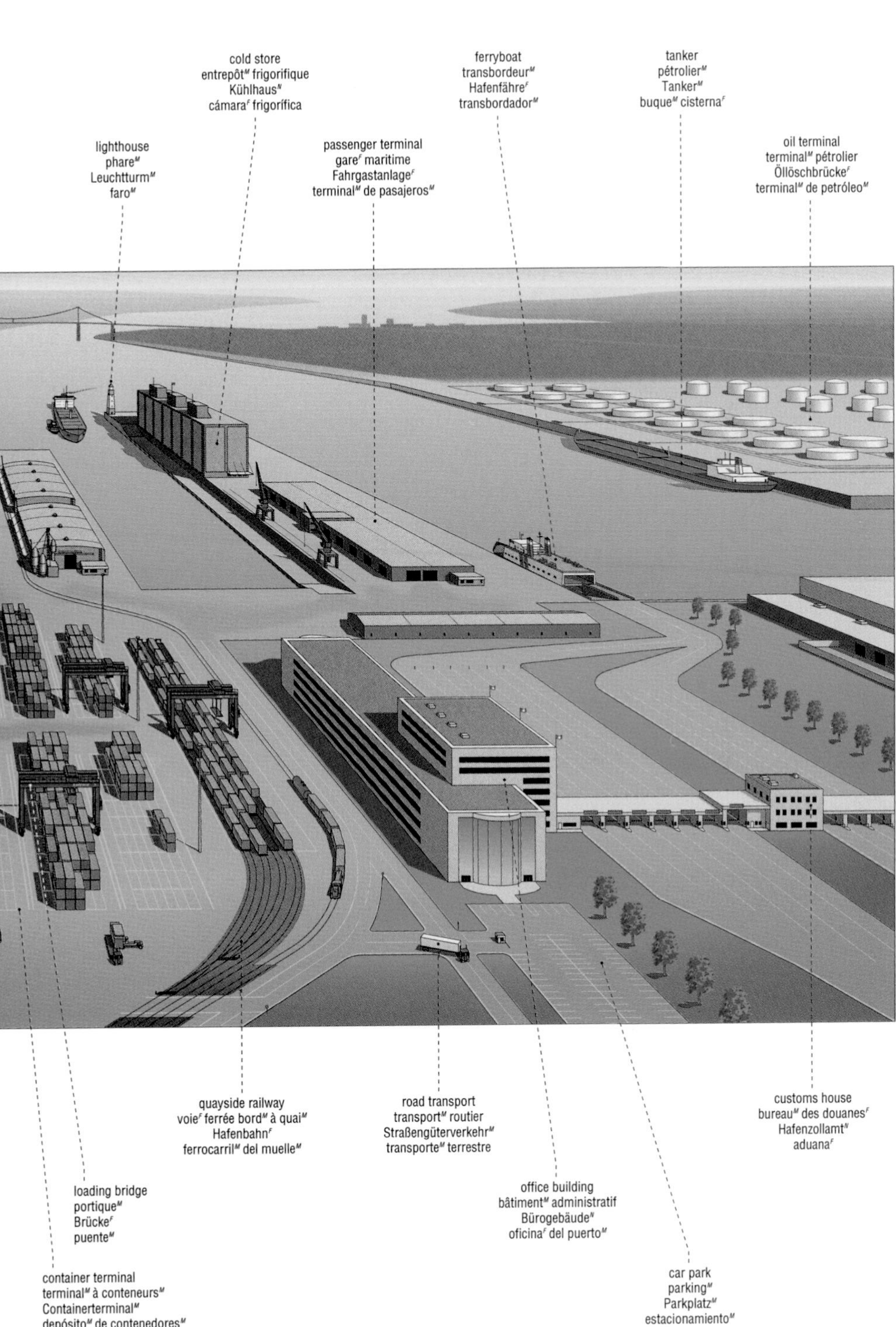
cold store
entrepôt[M] frigorifique
Kühlhaus[N]
cámara[F] frigorífica
ferryboat
transbordeur[M]
Hafenfähre[F]
transbordador[M]
tanker
pétrolier[M]
Tanker[M]
buque[M] cisterna[F]
lighthouse
phare[M]
Leuchtturm[M]
faro[M]
passenger terminal
gare[F] maritime
Fahrgastanlage[F]
terminal[M] de pasajeros[M]
oil terminal
terminal[M] pétrolier
Öllöschbrücke[F]
terminal[M] de petróleo[M]
quayside railway
voie[F] ferrée bord[M] à quai[M]
Hafenbahn[F]
ferrocarril[M] del muelle[M]
road transport
transport[M] routier
Straßengüterverkehr[M]
transporte[M] terrestre
customs house
bureau[M] des douanes[F]
Hafenzollamt[N]
aduana[F]
loading bridge
portique[M]
Brücke[F]
puente[M]
office building
bâtiment[M] administratif
Bürogebäude[N]
oficina[F] del puerto[M]
container terminal
terminal[M] à conteneurs[M]
Containerterminal[M]
depósito[M] de contenedores[M]
car park
parking[M]
Parkplatz[M]
estacionamiento[M]

## CANAL LOCK
## ÉCLUSE[F]
## KANALSCHLEUSE[F]
## ESCLUSA[F] DE CANAL[M]

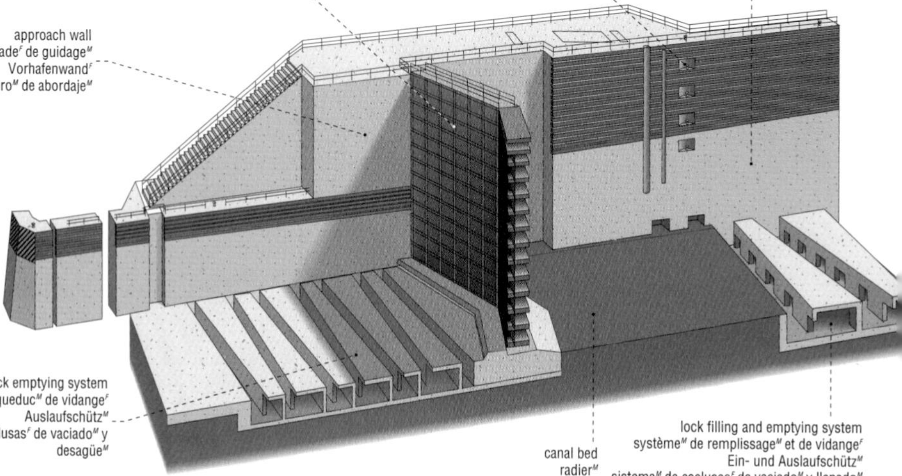

lower gate
porte[F] aval[M]
Untertor[N]
compuerta[F] inferior
bollard
taquet[M] d'amarrage[M]
Taubesfestigung[F]
gancho[M] para cuerda[F]
side wall
bajoyer[M]
Schleusenwand[F]
muro[M] lateral
approach wall
estacade[F] de guidage[M]
Vorhafenwand[F]
muro[M] de abordaje[M]
lock emptying system
aqueduc[M] de vidange[F]
Auslaufschütz[M]
sistema[M] de esclusas[F] de vaciado[M] y desagüe[M]
canal bed
radier[M]
Kanalsohle[F]
lecho[M]
lock filling and emptying system
système[M] de remplissage[M] et de vidange[F]
Ein- und Auslaufschütz[M]
sistema[M] de esclusas[F] de vaciado[M] y llenado[M]

## HOVERCRAFT
## AÉROGLISSEUR[M]
## LUFTKISSENFAHRZEUG[N]
## AERODESLIZADOR[M] (HOVERCRAFT[M])

driving propeller
hélice[F] de propulsion[F]
Luftpropeller[M]
hélice[F] propulsora
belt drive
courroie[F] de transmission[F]
Riemenantrieb[M]
correa[F] de transmisión[F]
blade lift fan
ventilateur[M] de sustentation[F]
Hubgebläse[N]
pala[F] del ventilador[M] de sustentación[F]
propeller duct
tuyère[F]
Propellerummantelung[F]
tubo[M] de la helice[F]
rudder
dérive[F] aérienne
Ruder[N]
timón[M]
drive shaft
arbre[M] de transmission[F]
Schraubenwelle[F]
eje[M] propulsor
diesel propulsion engine
moteur[M] diesel de propulsion[F]
Dieseltriebwerk[N]
motor[M] de propulsión[F] diésel
luggage racks
soute[F] à bagages[M]
Gepäckcontainer[M]
portaequipajes[M]
life raft
canot[M] pneumatique de sauvetage[M]
Rettungsfloß[M]
balsa[F] salvavidas

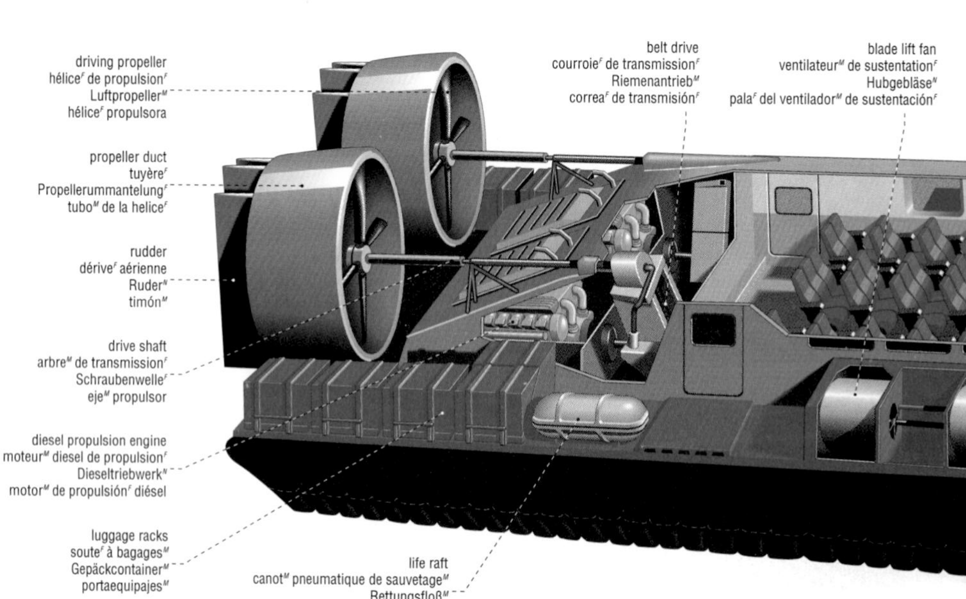

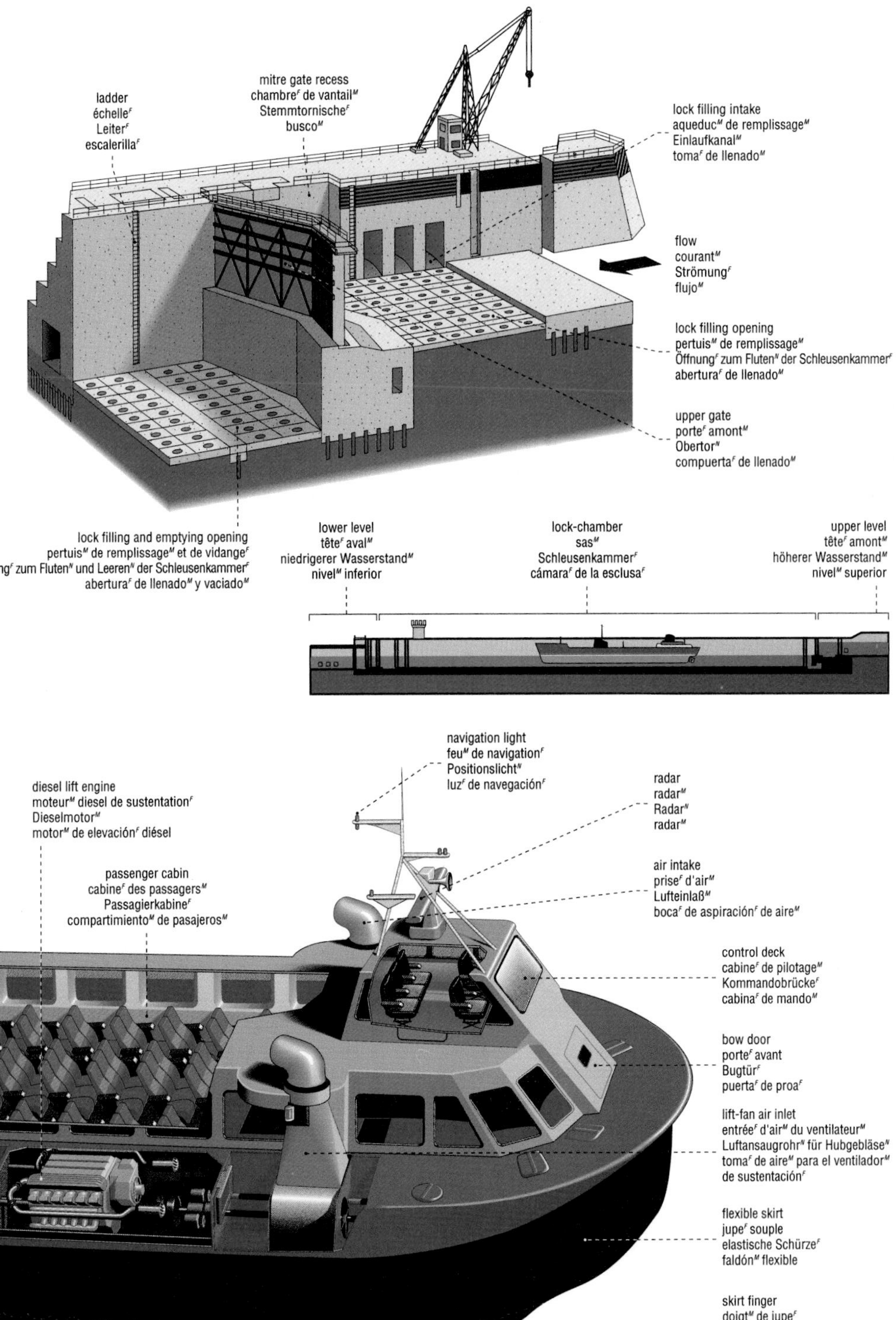
ladder
échelle[F]
Leiter[F]
escalerilla[F]
mitre gate recess
chambre[F] de vantail[M]
Stemmtornische[F]
busco[M]
lock filling intake
aqueduc[M] de remplissage[M]
Einlaufkanal[M]
toma[F] de llenado[M]
flow
courant[M]
Strömung[F]
flujo[M]
lock filling opening
pertuis[M] de remplissage[M]
Öffnung[F] zum Fluten[N] der Schleusenkammer[F]
abertura[F] de llenado[M]
upper gate
porte[F] amont[M]
Obertor[N]
compuerta[F] de llenado[M]
lock filling and emptying opening
pertuis[M] de remplissage[M] et de vidange[F]
nung[F] zum Fluten[N] und Leeren[N] der Schleusenkammer[F]
abertura[F] de llenado[M] y vaciado[M]
lower level
tête[F] aval[M]
niedrigerer Wasserstand[M]
nivel[M] inferior
lock-chamber
sas[M]
Schleusenkammer[F]
cámara[F] de la esclusa[F]
upper level
tête[F] amont[M]
höherer Wasserstand[M]
nivel[M] superior
navigation light
feu[M] de navigation[F]
Positionslicht[N]
luz[F] de navegación[F]
diesel lift engine
moteur[M] diesel de sustentation[F]
Dieselmotor[M]
motor[M] de elevación[F] diésel
radar
radar[M]
Radar[N]
radar[M]
air intake
prise[F] d'air[M]
Lufteinlaß[M]
boca[F] de aspiración[F] de aire[M]
passenger cabin
cabine[F] des passagers[M]
Passagierkabine[F]
compartimiento[M] de pasajeros[M]
control deck
cabine[F] de pilotage[M]
Kommandobrücke[F]
cabina[F] de mando[M]
bow door
porte[F] avant
Bugtür[F]
puerta[F] de proa[F]
lift-fan air inlet
entrée[F] d'air[M] du ventilateur[M]
Luftansaugrohr[N] für Hubgebläse[N]
toma[F] de aire[M] para el ventilador[M]
de sustentación[F]
flexible skirt
jupe[F] souple
elastische Schürze[F]
faldón[M] flexible
skirt finger
doigt[M] de jupe[F]
Schürzenfinger[M]
franja[F] del faldón[M]

## FERRY
## TRANSBORDEUR^M
## FÄHRE^F
## TRANSBORDADOR^M

telecommunication antenna
antenne^F de télécommunication^F
Fernmeldeantenne^F
antena^F de telecomunicaciones^F
radar
radar^M
Radar^N
radar^M
radio antenna
antenne^F radio^F
Funkantenne^F
antena^F de radio^M
compass bridge
passerelle^F de navigation^F
Peildeck^N
puente^M de mando^M
heating/air conditioning equipment
conditionnement^M d'air^M
Heizung^F/Klimaanlage^F
equipo^M de climatización^F
bow loading door
porte^F avant
Bugladeklappe^F
puerta^F de proa^F
restaurant
restaurant^M
Restaurant^N
restaurante^M
car deck
compartiment^M des voitures^F
Wagendeck^N
cubierta^F para automóviles^M
passenger cabin
cabine^F des passagers^M
Passagierkabine^F
cabina^F de pasajeros^M
folding ramp
rampe^F d'accès^M
klappbare Laderampe^F
rampa^F plegable

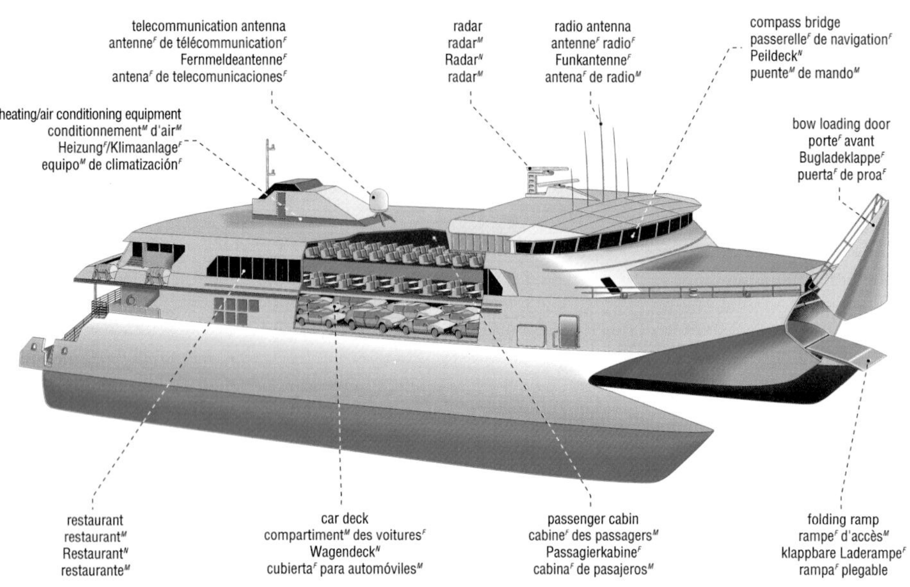

## CONTAINER SHIP
## CARGO^M PORTE-CONTENEURS^M
## CONTAINERSCHIFF^N
## CARGUERO^M PORTACONTENEDORES

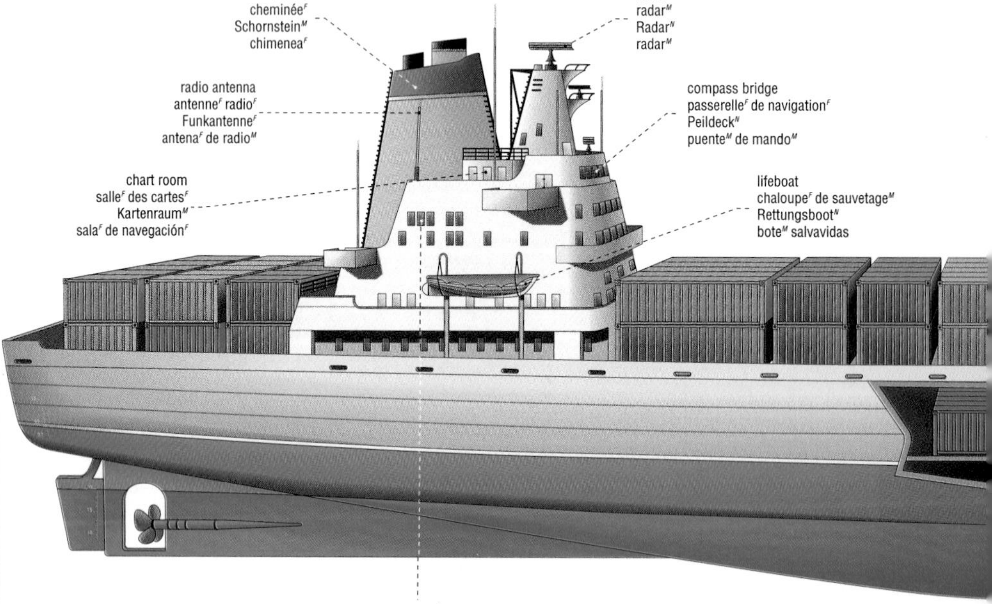

funnel
cheminée^F
Schornstein^M
chimenea^F
radar
radar^M
Radar^N
radar^M
radio antenna
antenne^F radio^F
Funkantenne^F
antena^F de radio^M
compass bridge
passerelle^F de navigation^F
Peildeck^N
puente^M de mando^M
chart room
salle^F des cartes^F
Kartenraum^M
sala^F de navegación^F
lifeboat
chaloupe^F de sauvetage^M
Rettungsboot^N
bote^M salvavidas
crew quarters
locaux^M du personnel^M
Besatzungsunterkünfte^F
camarotes^M de la tripulación^F

## HYDROFOIL BOAT
## HYDROPTÈRE[M]
## TRAGFLÜGELSCHIFF[N]
## AERODESLIZADOR[M]

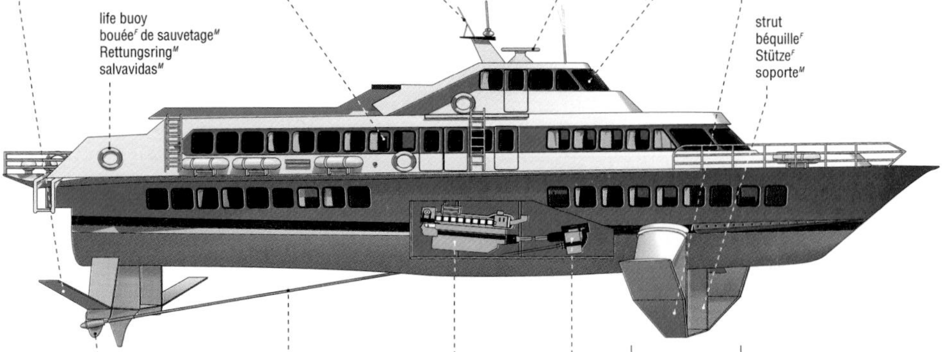

passenger cabin
cabine[F] des passagers[M]
Passagierkabine[F]
cabina[F] de pasajeros[M]

radio antenna
antenne[F] radio[F]
Funkantenne[F]
antena[F] de radio[M]

radar
radar[M]
Radar[N]
radar[M]

compass bridge
passerelle[F] de navigation[F]
Peildeck[N]
puente[M] de mando[M]

rear foil
aile[F] arrière
hinterer Tragflügel[M]
ala[F] de popa[F]

surface-piercing foils
ailes[F] en V
teilgetauchte Tragflügel[M]
aleta[F] de penetración[F] superficial

life buoy
bouée[F] de sauvetage[M]
Rettungsring[M]
salvavidas[M]

strut
béquille[F]
Stütze[F]
soporte[M]

propeller
hélice[F]
Schraube[F]
hélice[F]

diesel engine
moteur[M] diesel
Dieselmotor[M]
motor[M] diésel

front foil
aile[F] avant
vorderer Tragflügel[M]
aleta[F] de proa[F]

propeller shaft
arbre[M] de l'hélice[F]
Schraubenwelle[F]
árbol[M] de la hélice[F]

gearbox
boîte[F] de vitesses[F]
Getriebe[N]
caja[F] de engranajes[M]

# CRUISELINER
# PAQUEBOT^M
# PASSAGIERDAMPFER^M
# BUQUE^M TRASATLÁNTICO

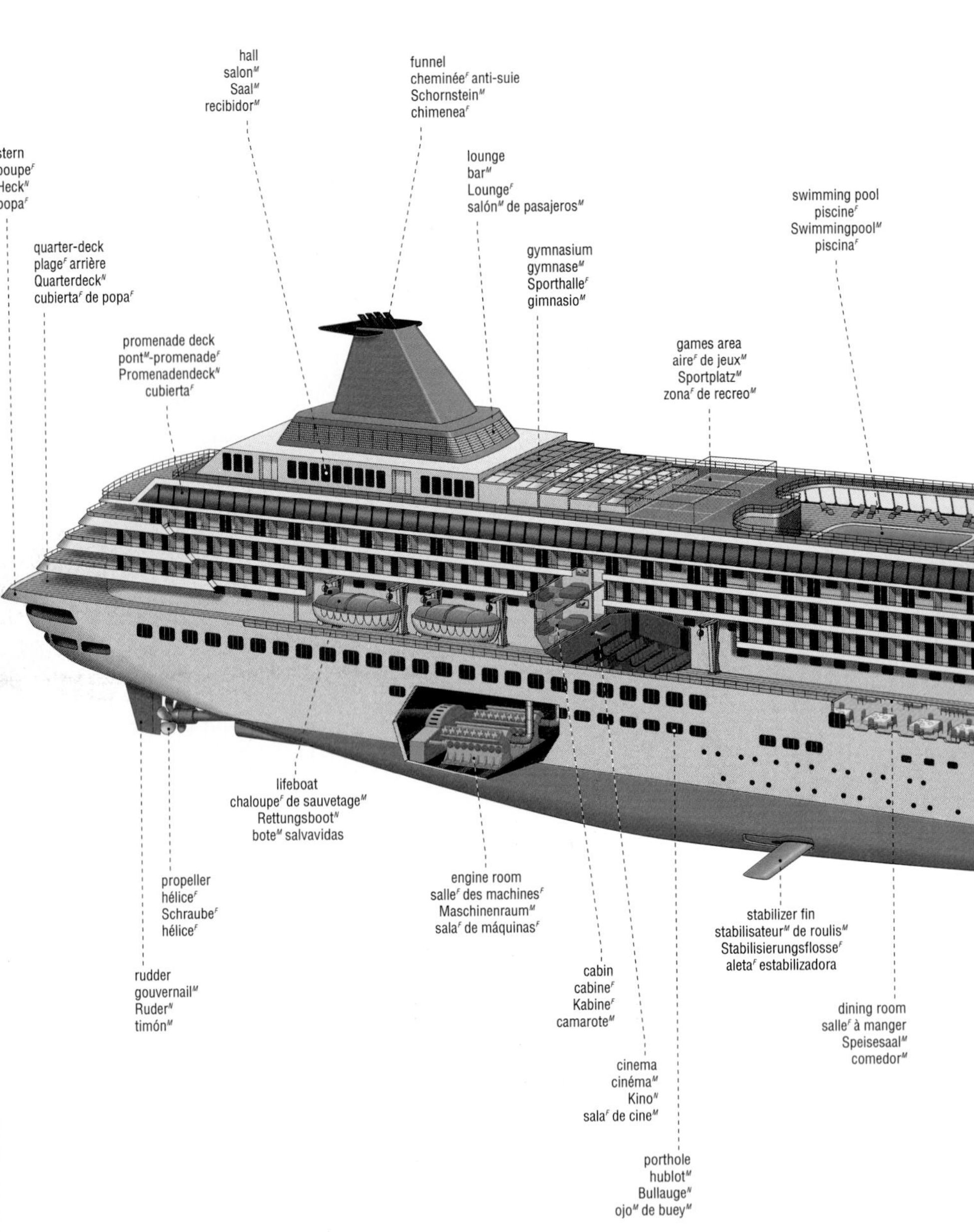

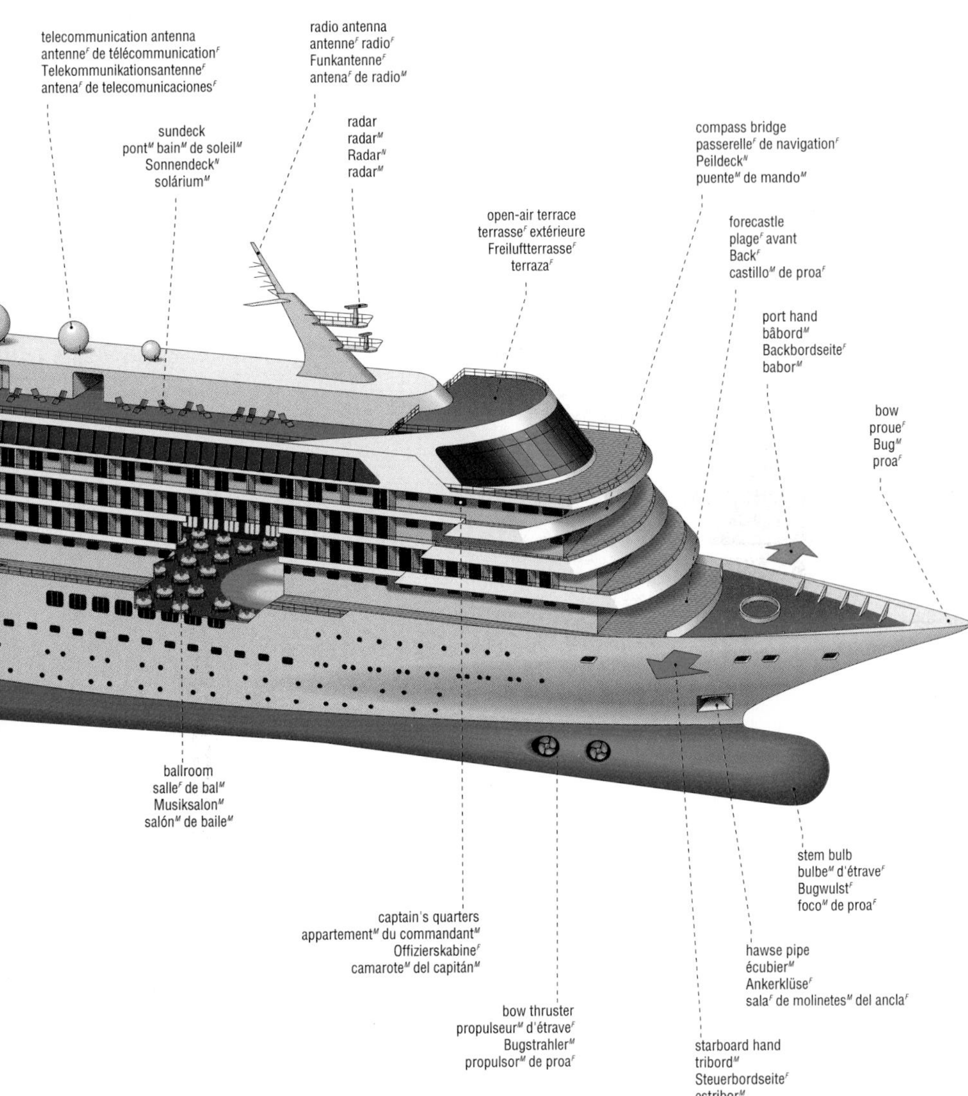
telecommunication antenna
antenne$^{F}$ de télécommunication$^{F}$
Telekommunikationsantenne$^{F}$
antena$^{F}$ de telecomunicaciones$^{F}$
radio antenna
antenne$^{F}$ radio$^{F}$
Funkantenne$^{F}$
antena$^{F}$ de radio$^{M}$
sundeck
pont$^{M}$ bain$^{M}$ de soleil$^{M}$
Sonnendeck$^{N}$
solárium$^{M}$
radar
radar$^{M}$
Radar$^{N}$
radar$^{M}$
compass bridge
passerelle$^{F}$ de navigation$^{F}$
Peildeck$^{N}$
puente$^{M}$ de mando$^{M}$
open-air terrace
terrasse$^{F}$ extérieure
Freiluftterrasse$^{F}$
terraza$^{F}$
forecastle
plage$^{F}$ avant
Back$^{F}$
castillo$^{M}$ de proa$^{F}$
port hand
bâbord$^{M}$
Backbordseite$^{F}$
babor$^{M}$
bow
proue$^{F}$
Bug$^{M}$
proa$^{F}$
ballroom
salle$^{F}$ de bal$^{M}$
Musiksalon$^{M}$
salón$^{M}$ de baile$^{M}$
stem bulb
bulbe$^{M}$ d'étrave$^{F}$
Bugwulst$^{F}$
foco$^{M}$ de proa$^{F}$
captain's quarters
appartement$^{M}$ du commandant$^{M}$
Offizierskabine$^{F}$
camarote$^{M}$ del capitán$^{M}$
hawse pipe
écubier$^{M}$
Ankerklüse$^{F}$
sala$^{F}$ de molinetes$^{M}$ del ancla$^{F}$
bow thruster
propulseur$^{M}$ d'étrave$^{F}$
Bugstrahler$^{M}$
propulsor$^{M}$ de proa$^{F}$
starboard hand
tribord$^{M}$
Steuerbordseite$^{F}$
estribor$^{M}$

# LONG-RANGE JET AIRLINER
# AVION[M] LONG-COURRIER[M]
# LANGSTRECKEN-DÜSENFLUGZEUG[N]
# AVIÓN[M] TURBORREACTOR DE PASAJEROS[M]

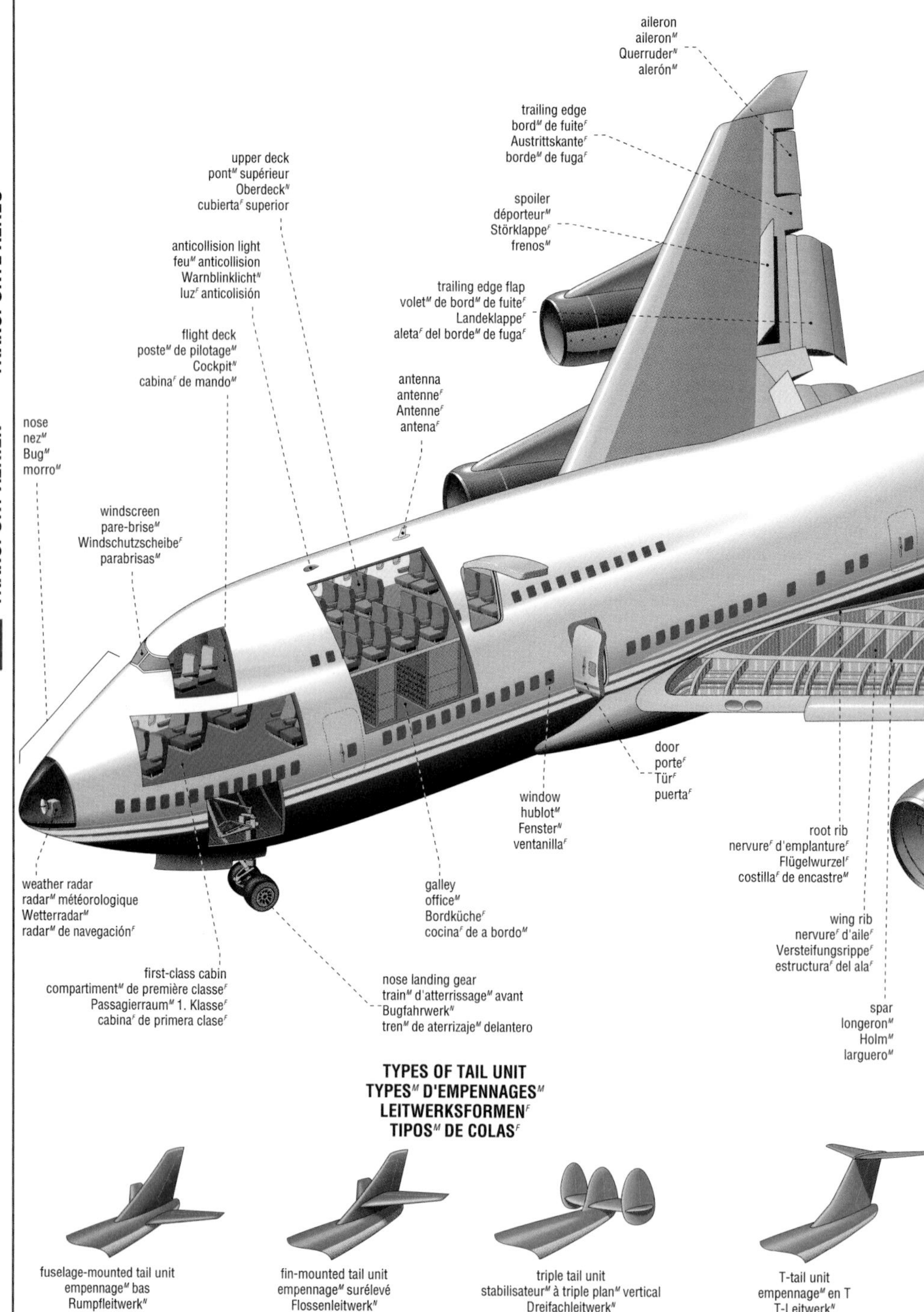

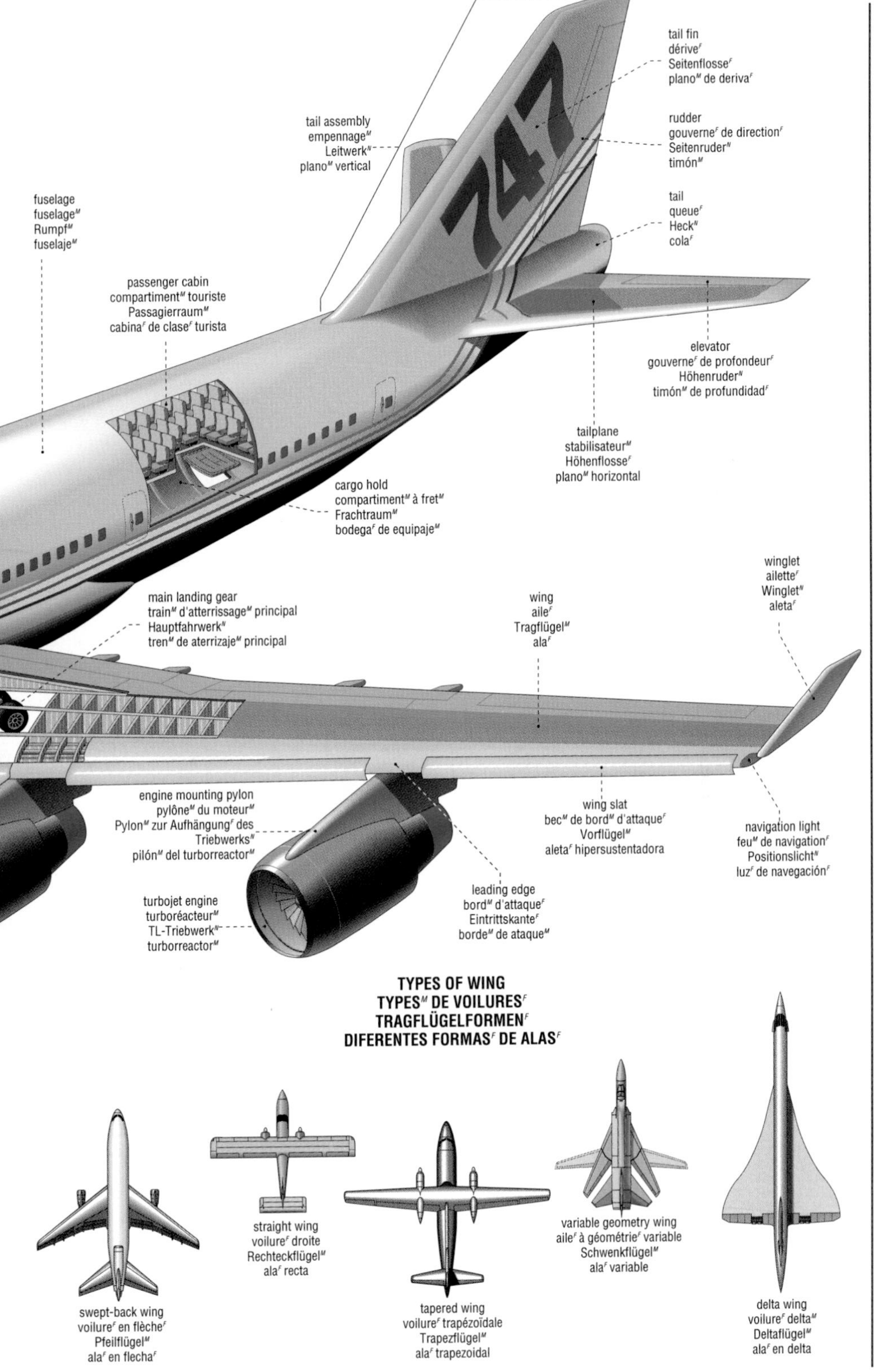
tail fin
dérive[F]
Seitenflosse[F]
plano[M] de deriva[F]
tail assembly
empennage[M]
Leitwerk[N]
plano[M] vertical
rudder
gouverne[F] de direction[F]
Seitenruder[N]
timón[M]
fuselage
fuselage[M]
Rumpf[M]
fuselaje[M]
tail
queue[F]
Heck[N]
cola[F]
passenger cabin
compartiment[M] touriste
Passagierraum[M]
cabina[F] de clase[F] turista
elevator
gouverne[F] de profondeur[F]
Höhenruder[N]
timón[M] de profundidad[F]
tailplane
stabilisateur[M]
Höhenflosse[F]
plano[M] horizontal
cargo hold
compartiment[M] à fret[M]
Frachtraum[M]
bodega[F] de equipaje[M]
winglet
ailette[F]
Winglet[N]
aleta[F]
main landing gear
train[M] d'atterrissage[M] principal
Hauptfahrwerk[N]
tren[M] de aterrizaje[M] principal
wing
aile[F]
Tragflügel[M]
ala[F]
engine mounting pylon
pylône[M] du moteur[M]
Pylon[M] zur Aufhängung[F] des Triebwerks[N]
pilón[M] del turborreactor[M]
wing slat
bec[M] de bord[M] d'attaque[F]
Vorflügel[M]
aleta[F] hipersustentadora
navigation light
feu[M] de navigation[F]
Positionslicht[N]
luz[F] de navegación[F]
leading edge
bord[M] d'attaque[F]
Eintrittskante[F]
borde[M] de ataque[M]
turbojet engine
turboréacteur[M]
TL-Triebwerk[N]
turborreactor[M]
TYPES OF WING
TYPES[M] DE VOILURES[F]
TRAGFLÜGELFORMEN[F]
DIFERENTES FORMAS[F] DE ALAS[F]
straight wing
voilure[F] droite
Rechteckflügel[M]
ala[F] recta
variable geometry wing
aile[F] à géométrie[F] variable
Schwenkflügel[M]
ala[F] variable
swept-back wing
voilure[F] en flèche[F]
Pfeilflügel[M]
ala[F] en flecha[F]
tapered wing
voilure[F] trapézoïdale
Trapezflügel[M]
ala[F] trapezoidal
delta wing
voilure[F] delta[M]
Deltaflügel[M]
ala[F] en delta

# FLIGHT DECK
# POSTE[M] DE PILOTAGE[M]
# COCKPIT[N]
# PUENTE[M] DE MANDO[M]

landing gear lever
levier[M] du train[M] d'atterrissage[M]
Fahrwerkhebel[M]
palanca[F] del tren[M] de aterrizaje delantero

speaker
haut-parleur[M]
Lautsprecher[M]
altavoz[M]

windscreen
pare-brise[M]
Windschutzscheibe[F]
parabrisas[M]

autopilot controls
commandes[F] du pilote[M] automatique
Selbststeueranlage[F]
controles[M] del piloto[M] automático

lighting
éclairage[M]
Beleuchtung[F]
luz[F]

standby attitude indicator
horizon[M] de secours[M]
Reserve-Fluglageanzeige[F]
indicador[M] de emergencia[F] de inclinación[F]

engine and crew alarm display
paramètres[M] moteurs[M]/alarmes[F]
Warnanzeige[F]- Besatzung[F] und Triebwerke[N]
pantalla[F] de alarma[F] de motor y tripulación[F]

overhead switch panel
panneau[M] de disjoncteurs[M]
Überkopfschaltbrett[N]
tablero[M] de conmutadores[M]

standby airspeed indicator
anémomètre[M] de secours[M]
Reserve-Fahrtmesser[M]
indicador[M] de emergencia[F] de velocidad[F]

standby altimeter
altimètre[M] de secours[M]
Reserve-Höhenmesser[M]
altímetro[M] de emergencia[F]

navigation display
informations[F]-navigation[F]
Navigationsanzeige[F]
pantalla[F] de navegación[F]

primary flight display
informations[F]-pilotage[M]
Hauptanzeige[F] der Flugdaten[N]
pantalla[F] principal de vuelo[M]

control column
manche[M] de commande[F]
Steuerknüppel[M]
columna[F] de control[M]

control wheel
volant[M] de manche[M]
Steuerrad[N]
timón[M] de control[M]

speedbrake lever
levier[M] des aérofreins[M]
Flugbremshebel[M]
palanca[F] de freno[M]

systems display
informations[F]-systèmes[M] de bord[M]
Displayanzeige[F]
pantalla[F] de los sistemas[M]

captain's seat
siège[M] du commandant[M]
Kapitänssitz[M]
asiento[M] del capitán[M]

throttles
manettes[F] de poussée[F]
Gashebel[M]
válvulas[F] de control[M] de combustible[M]

control console
pupitre[M] de commande[F]
Steuerpult[N]
consola[F] de control[M]

first officer's seat
siège[M] du copilote[M]
Kopilotensitz[M]
asiento[M] del copiloto[M]

communication panels
panneaux[M] de commandes[F] radio[F]
Fernmeldeschaltbrett[N]
paneles[M] de comunicación[F]

flap lever
levier[M] des volets[M]
Klappenhebel[M]
palanca[F] de los alerones[M] de hipersustentación[F]

flight management computer
ordinateur[M] de gestion[F] de vol[M]
Flugrechner[M]
computador[M] de gestión[F] de vuelo[M]

engine fuel valves
robinets[M] de carburant[M]
Brennstoffventile[N]
válvulas[F] de combustible[M] del motor[M]

air data computer
ordinateur[M] des données[F] aérodynamiques
Luftdatenrechner[M]
computador[M] de vuelo[M]

# TURBOFAN ENGINE
# TURBORÉACTEUR[M] À DOUBLE FLUX[M]
# ZWEISTROMTRIEBWERK[N]
# TURBOREACTOR[M]

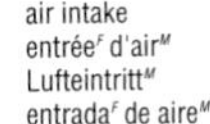

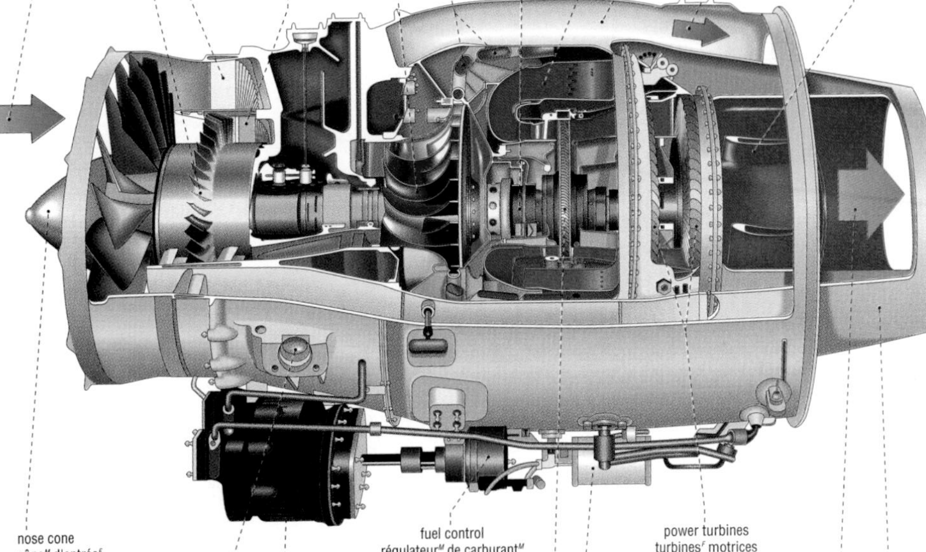


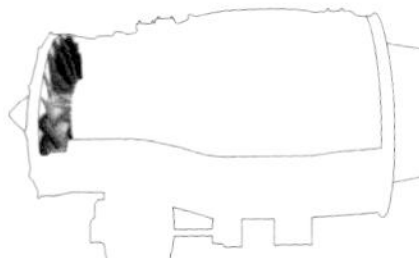

fan
soufflante[F]
Niederdruckverdichtung[F]
ventilador[M]

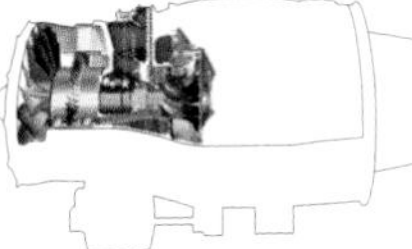

compression
compression[F]
Verdichtung[F]
compresión[F]

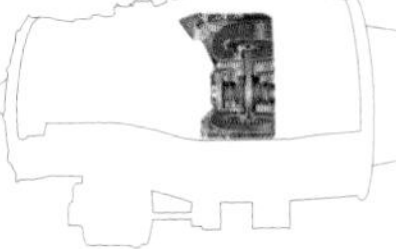

combustion
combustion[F]
Verbrennung[F]
combustión[F]

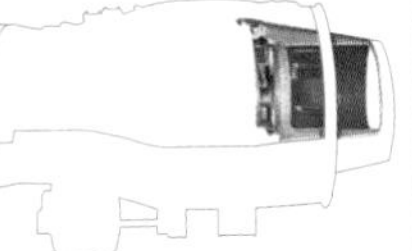

exhaust
échappement[M]
Abgas[N]
escape[M]

# AIRPORT
# AÉROPORT[M]
# FLUGHAFEN[M]
# AEROPUERTO[M]

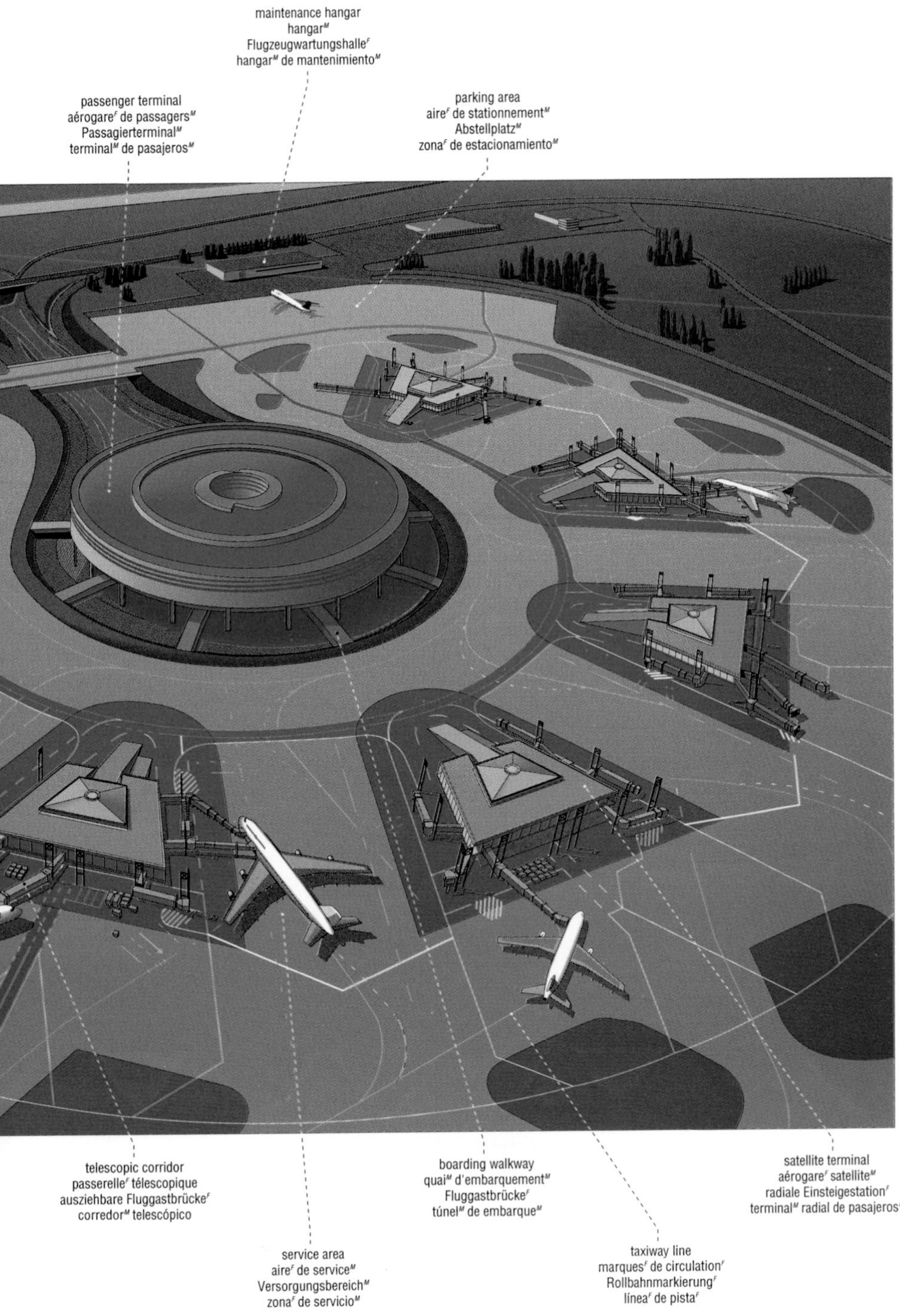
maintenance hangar
hangar^M
Flugzeugwartungshalle^F
hangar^M de mantenimiento^M
passenger terminal
aérogare^F de passagers^M
Passagierterminal^M
terminal^M de pasajeros^M
parking area
aire^F de stationnement^M
Abstellplatz^M
zona^F de estacionamiento^M
telescopic corridor
passerelle^F télescopique
ausziehbare Fluggastbrücke^F
corredor^M telescópico
boarding walkway
quai^M d'embarquement^M
Fluggastbrücke^F
túnel^M de embarque^M
satellite terminal
aérogare^F satellite^M
radiale Einsteigestation^F
terminal^M radial de pasajeros^M
service area
aire^F de service^M
Versorgungsbereich^M
zona^F de servicio^M
taxiway line
marques^F de circulation^F
Rollbahnmarkierung^F
línea^F de pista^F

# AIRPORT
# AÉROPORT[M]
# FLUGHAFEN[M]
# AEROPUERTO[M]

## PASSENGER TERMINAL
## AÉROGARE[F]
## PASSAGIERTERMINAL[M]
## TERMINAL[M] DE PASAJEROS[M]

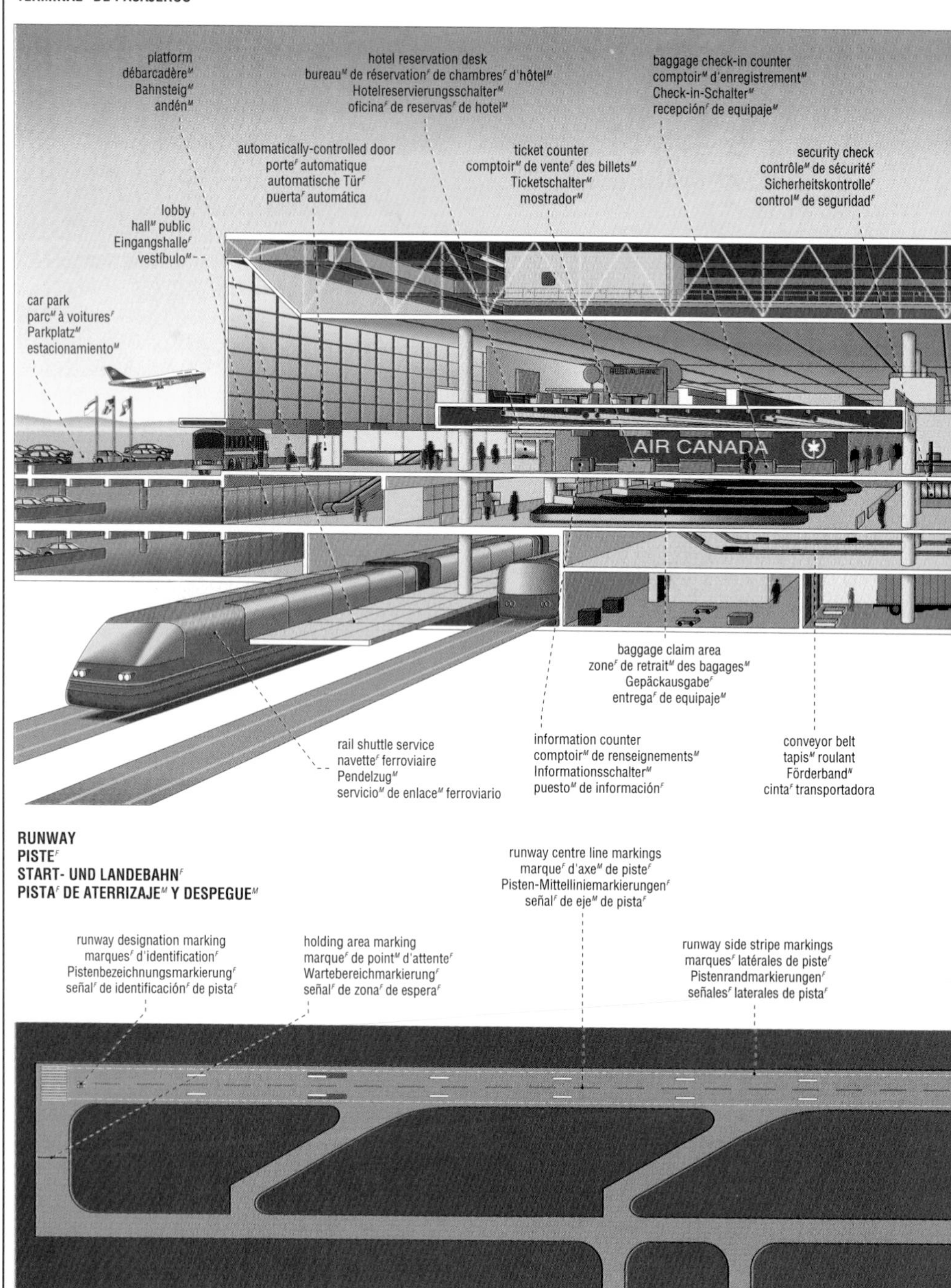

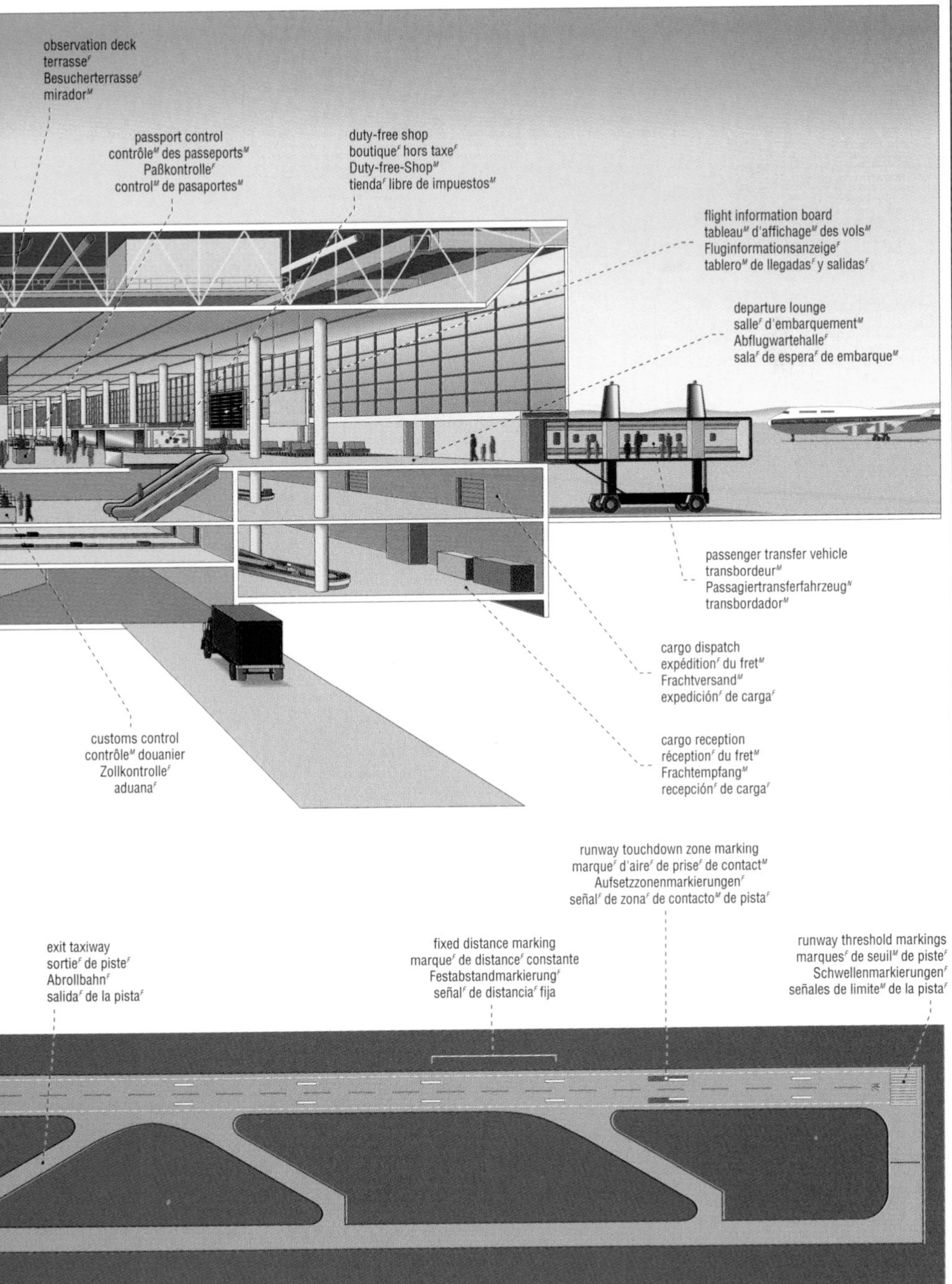
observation deck
terrasse^F
Besucherterrasse^F
mirador^M
passport control
contrôle^M des passeports^M
Paßkontrolle^F
control^M de pasaportes^M
duty-free shop
boutique^F hors taxe^F
Duty-free-Shop^M
tienda^F libre de impuestos^M
flight information board
tableau^M d'affichage^M des vols^M
Fluginformationsanzeige^F
tablero^M de llegadas^F y salidas^F
departure lounge
salle^F d'embarquement^M
Abflugwartehalle^F
sala^F de espera^F de embarque^M
passenger transfer vehicle
transbordeur^M
Passagiertransferfahrzeug^N
transbordador^M
cargo dispatch
expédition^F du fret^M
Frachtversand^M
expedición^F de carga^F
cargo reception
réception^F du fret^M
Frachtempfang^M
recepción^F de carga^F
customs control
contrôle^M douanier
Zollkontrolle^F
aduana^F
runway touchdown zone marking
marque^F d'aire^F de prise^F de contact^M
Aufsetzzonenmarkierungen^F
señal^F de zona^F de contacto^M de pista^F
exit taxiway
sortie^F de piste^F
Abrollbahn^F
salida^F de la pista^F
fixed distance marking
marque^F de distance^F constante
Festabstandmarkierung^F
señal^F de distancia^F fija
runway threshold markings
marques^F de seuil^M de piste^F
Schwellenmarkierungen^F
señales de limite^M de la pista^F

# AIRPORT
# AÉROPORT[M]
# FLUGHAFEN[M]
# AEROPUERTO[M]

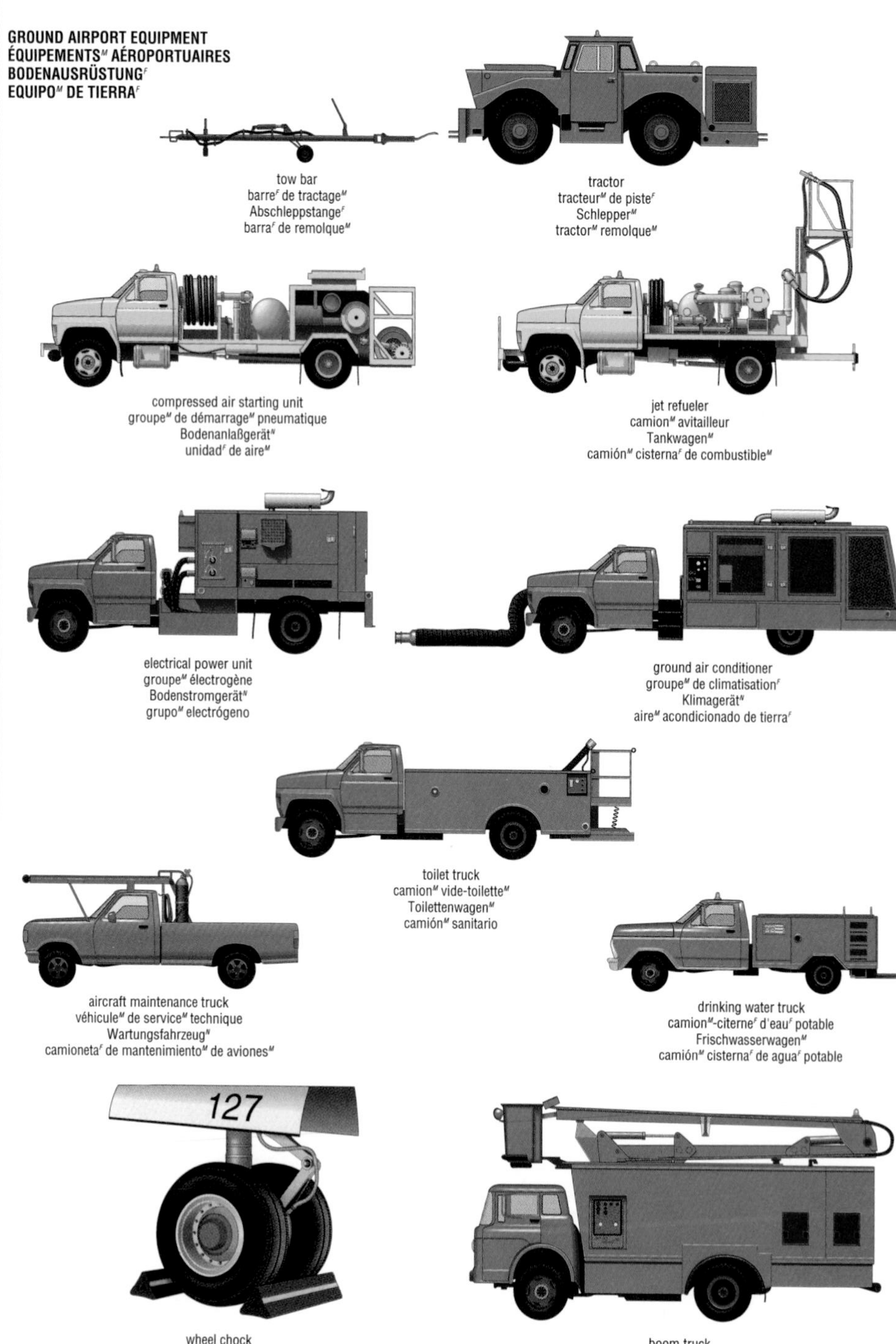

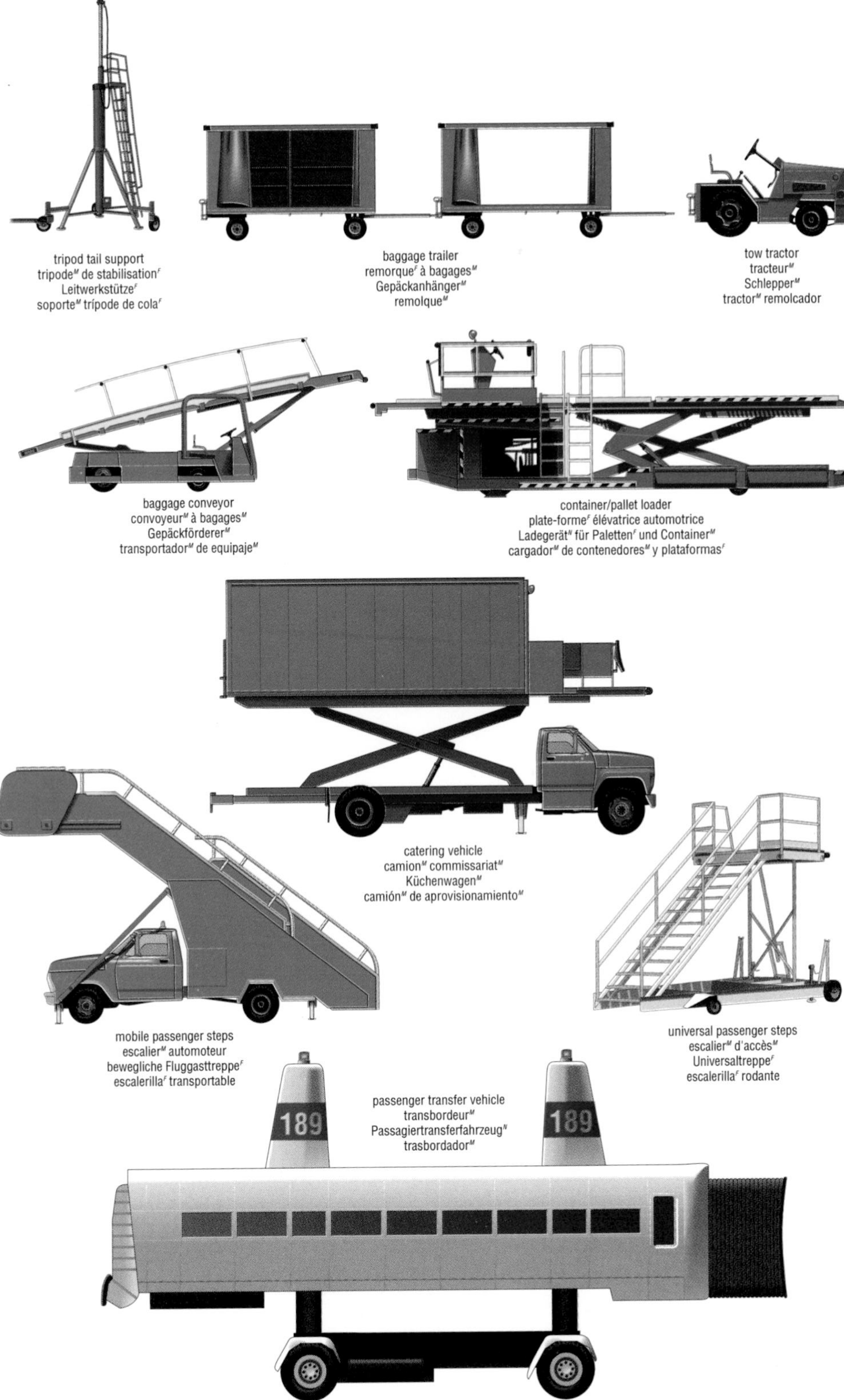
tripod tail support
tripode$^{M}$ de stabilisation$^{F}$
Leitwerkstütze$^{F}$
soporte$^{M}$ trípode de cola$^{F}$
baggage trailer
remorque$^{F}$ à bagages$^{M}$
Gepäckanhänger$^{M}$
remolque$^{M}$
tow tractor
tracteur$^{M}$
Schlepper$^{M}$
tractor$^{M}$ remolcador
baggage conveyor
convoyeur$^{M}$ à bagages$^{M}$
Gepäckförderer$^{M}$
transportador$^{M}$ de equipaje$^{M}$
container/pallet loader
plate-forme$^{F}$ élévatrice automotrice
Ladegerät$^{N}$ für Paletten$^{F}$ und Container$^{M}$
cargador$^{M}$ de contenedores$^{M}$ y plataformas$^{F}$
catering vehicle
camion$^{M}$ commissariat$^{M}$
Küchenwagen$^{M}$
camión$^{M}$ de aprovisionamiento$^{M}$
mobile passenger steps
escalier$^{M}$ automoteur
bewegliche Fluggasttreppe$^{F}$
escalerilla$^{F}$ transportable
universal passenger steps
escalier$^{M}$ d'accès$^{M}$
Universaltreppe$^{F}$
escalerilla$^{F}$ rodante
passenger transfer vehicle
transbordeur$^{M}$
Passagiertransferfahrzeug$^{N}$
trasbordador$^{M}$
189
189

# HELICOPTER
# HÉLICOPTÈRE^M
# HUBSCHRAUBER^M
# HELICÓPTERO^M

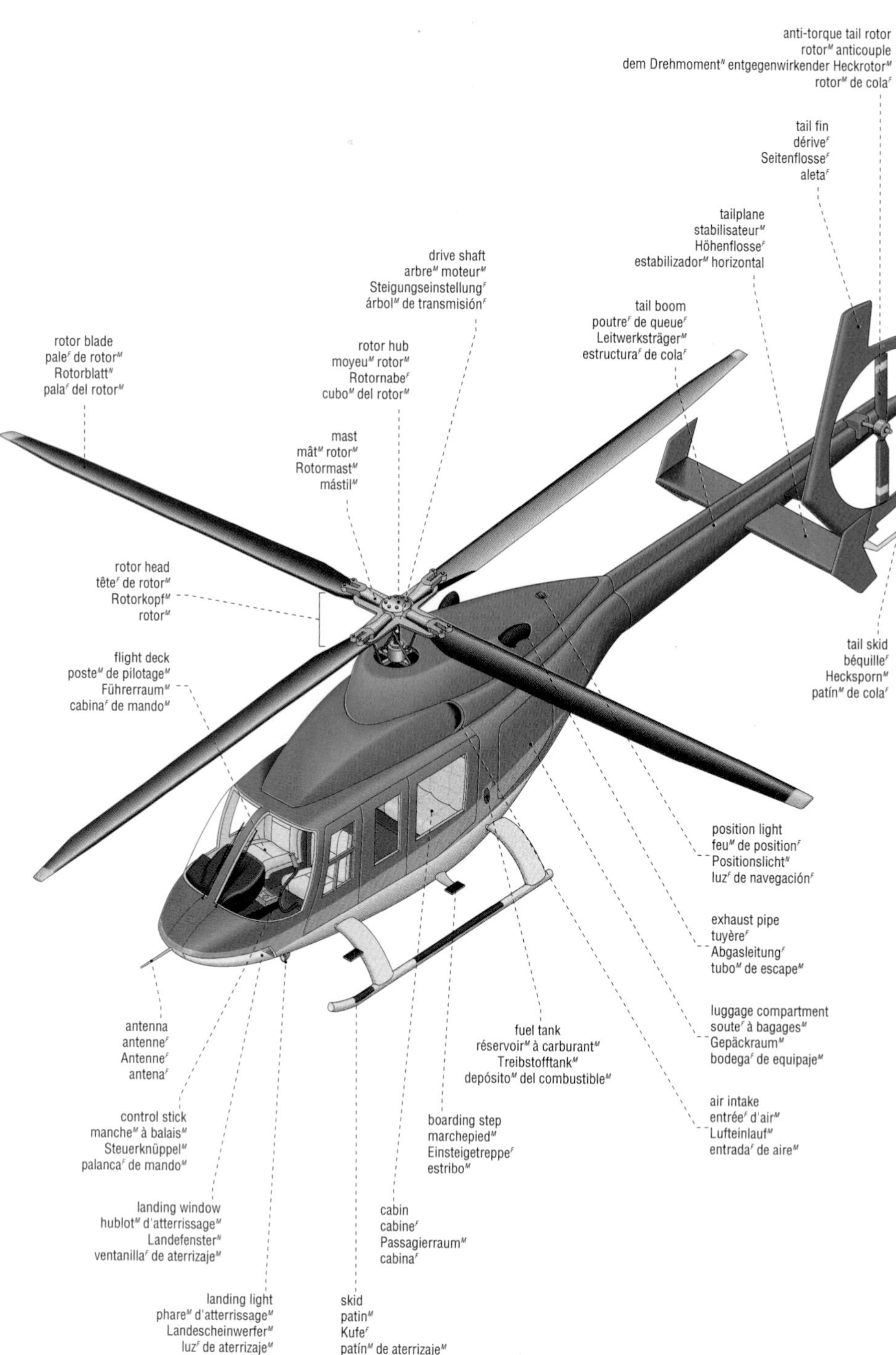

**ROCKET**
**FUSÉE[F]**
**RAKETE[F]**
**COHETE[M]**

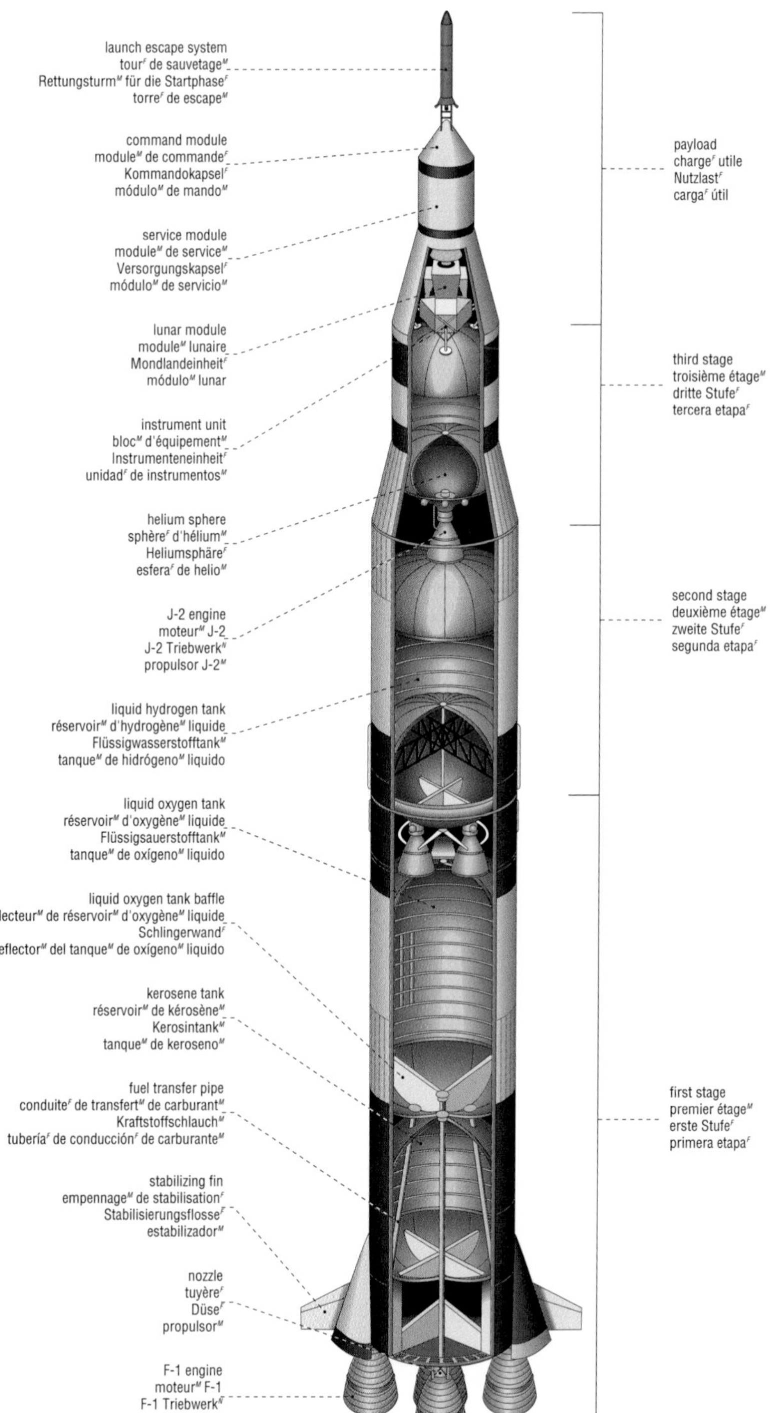

# SPACE SHUTTLE
# NAVETTE^F SPATIALE
# RAUMFÄHRE^F
# TRANSBORDADOR^M ESPACIAL

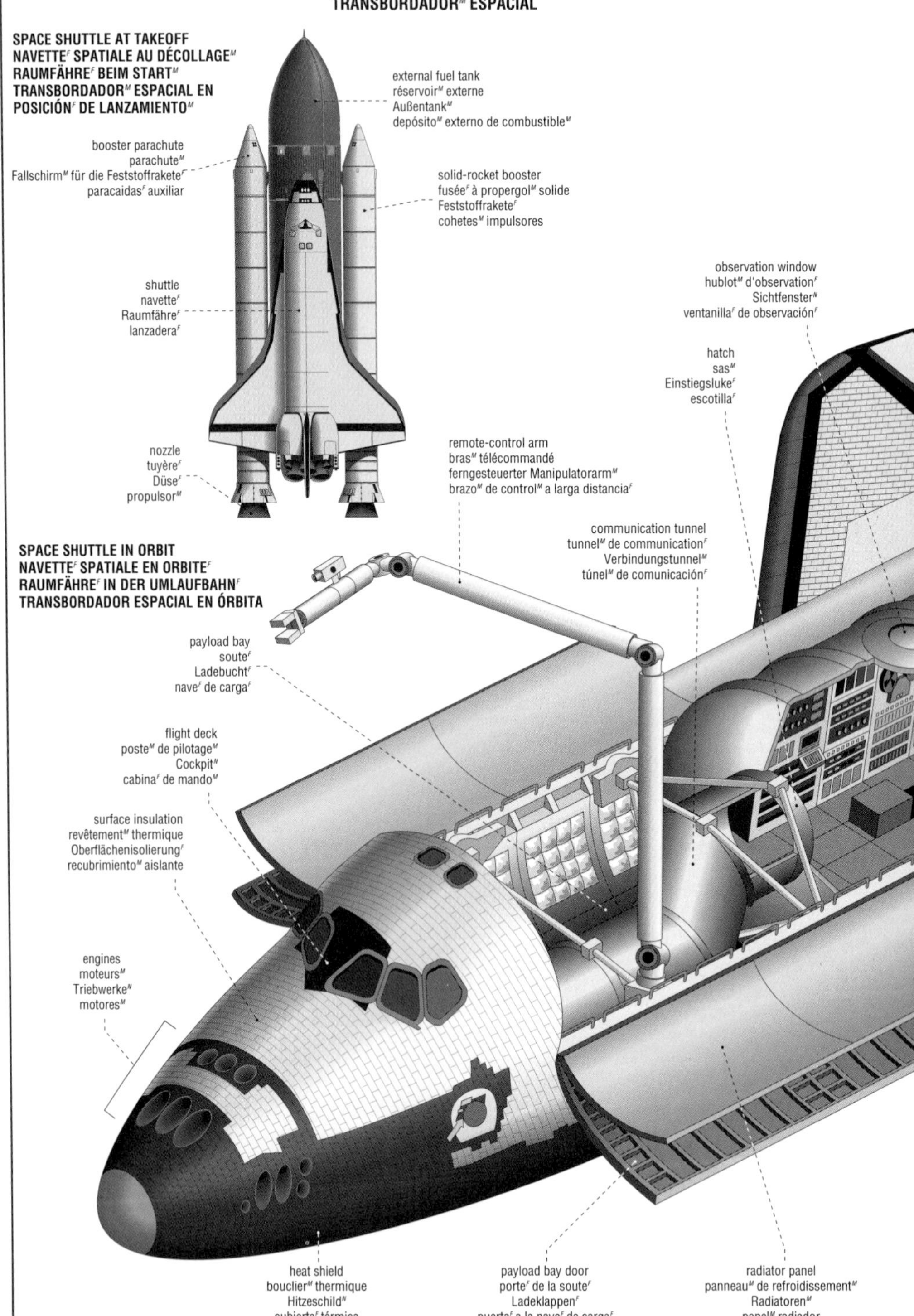

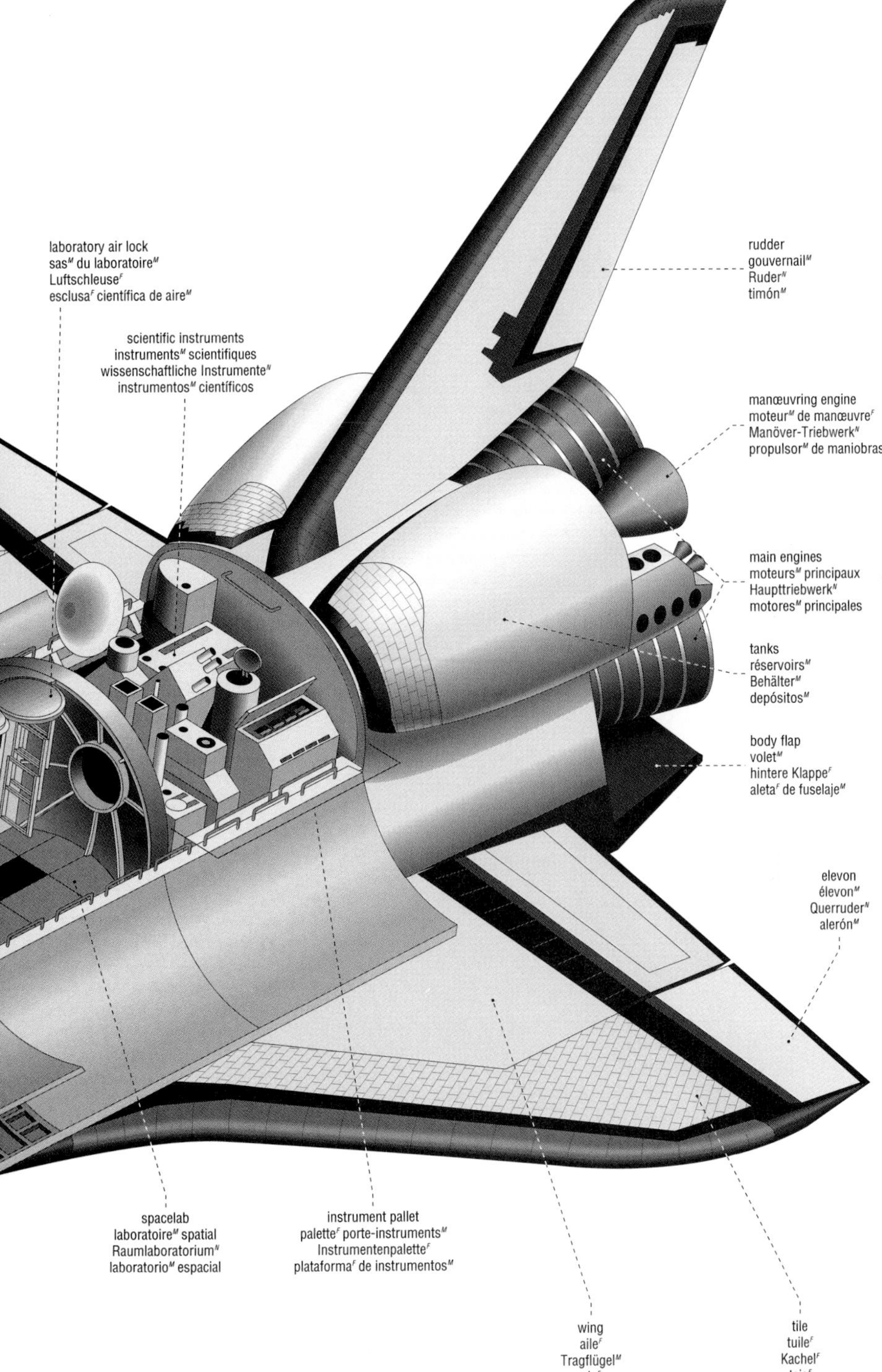
laboratory air lock
sas[M] du laboratoire[M]
Luftschleuse[F]
esclusa[F] científica de aire[M]
scientific instruments
instruments[M] scientifiques
wissenschaftliche Instrumente[N]
instrumentos[M] científicos
rudder
gouvernail[M]
Ruder[N]
timón[M]
manœuvring engine
moteur[M] de manœuvre[F]
Manöver-Triebwerk[N]
propulsor[M] de maniobras[F]
main engines
moteurs[M] principaux
Haupttriebwerk[N]
motores[M] principales
tanks
réservoirs[M]
Behälter[M]
depósitos[M]
body flap
volet[M]
hintere Klappe[F]
aleta[F] de fuselaje[M]
elevon
élevon[M]
Querruder[N]
alerón[M]
spacelab
laboratoire[M] spatial
Raumlaboratorium[N]
laboratorio[M] espacial
instrument pallet
palette[F] porte-instruments[M]
Instrumentenpalette[F]
plataforma[F] de instrumentos[M]
wing
aile[F]
Tragflügel[M]
ala[F]
tile
tuile[F]
Kachel[F]
teja[F]

# SPACESUIT
# SCAPHANDRE[M] SPATIAL
# RAUMANZUG[M]
# TRAJE[M] ESPACIAL

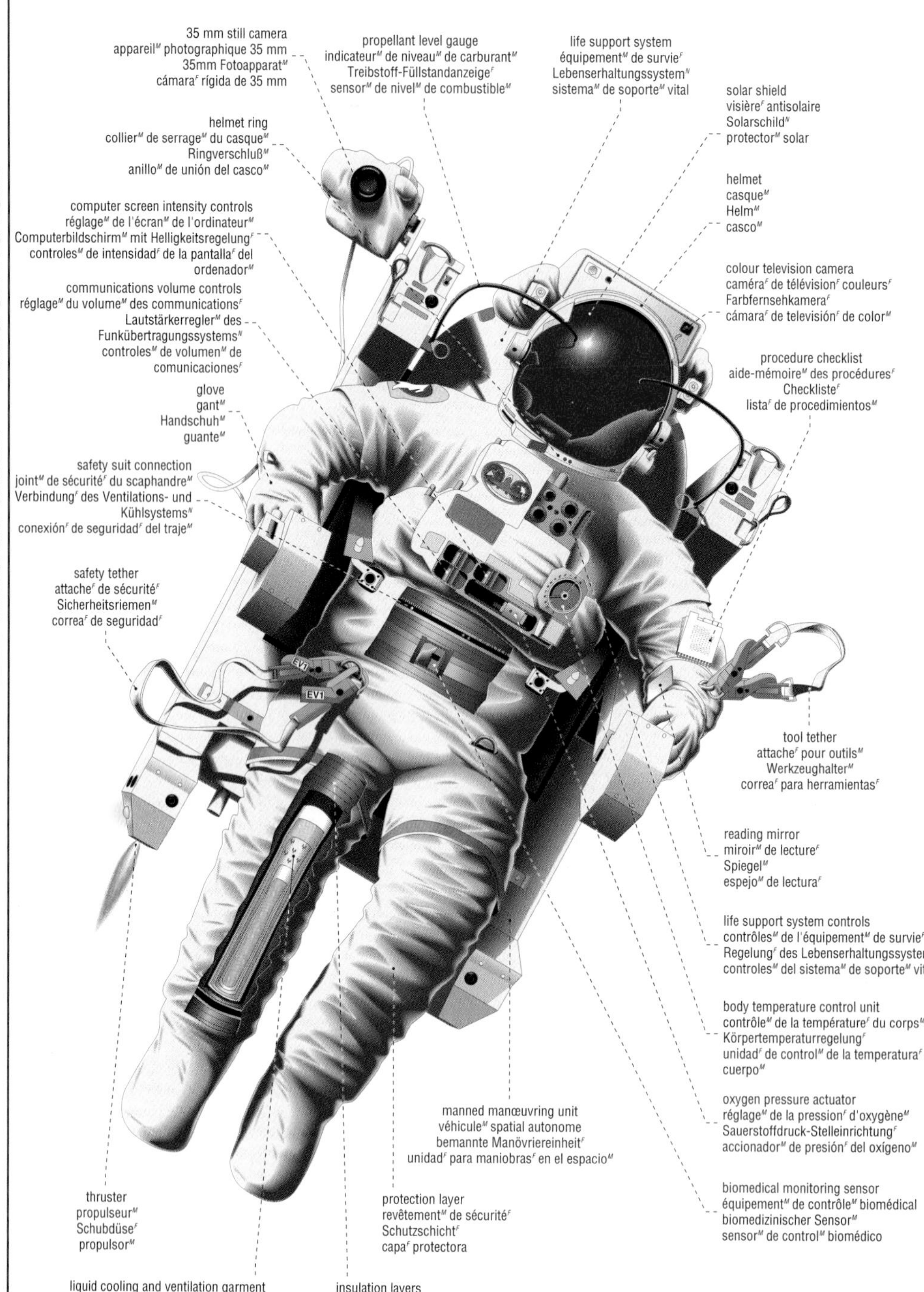

# OFFICE SUPPLIES
# FOURNITURES DE BUREAU
# BÜROBEDARF
# EQUIPO DE OFICINA

SUMMARY

**OFFICE SUPPLIES**



**OFFICE AUTOMATION**

# STATIONERY
# ARTICLES[M] DE BUREAU[M]
# SCHREIBWAREN[F]
# ARTÍCULOS[M] DE ESCRITORIO[M]

# STATIONERY
# ARTICLES[M] DE BUREAU[M]
# SCHREIBWAREN[F]
# ARTÍCULOS[M] DE ESCRITORIO[M]

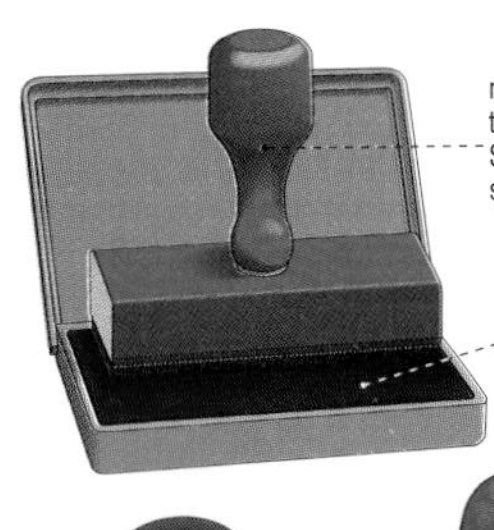

rubber stamp
timbre[M] caoutchouc[M]
Stempel[M]
sello[M] de goma[F]

stamp pad
tampon[M] encreur
Stempelkissen[N]
cojín[M] para sellos[M]

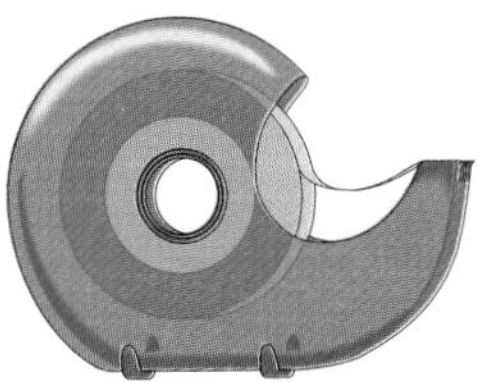

tape dispenser
dévidoir[M] de ruban[M] adhésif
Klebefilmspender[M]
carrete[M] de cinta[F] adhesiva

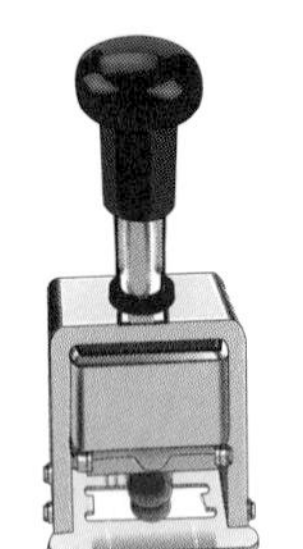

numbering stamp
numéroteur[M]
Numerierstempel[M]
foliador[M]

date stamp
timbre[M] dateur
Datumstempel[M]
fechador[M]

stamp rack
porte-timbres[M]
Stempelträger[M]
portasellos[M]

spike file
pique-notes[M]
Dornablage[F]
pinchador[M]

paper punch
perforatrice[F]
Locher[M]
perforadora[F]

label maker
pince[F] à étiqueter
Präger[M]
rotulador[M]

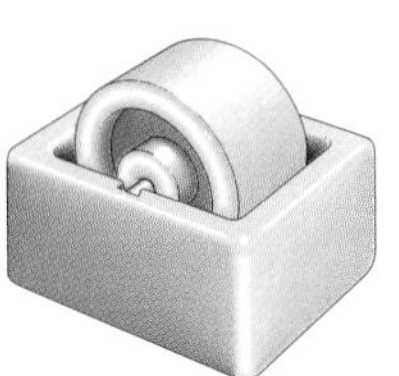

moistener
mouilleur[M]
Befeuchter[M]
rueda[F] humedecedora

rotary file
fichier[M] rotatif
Drehkartei[F]
fichero[M] giratorio

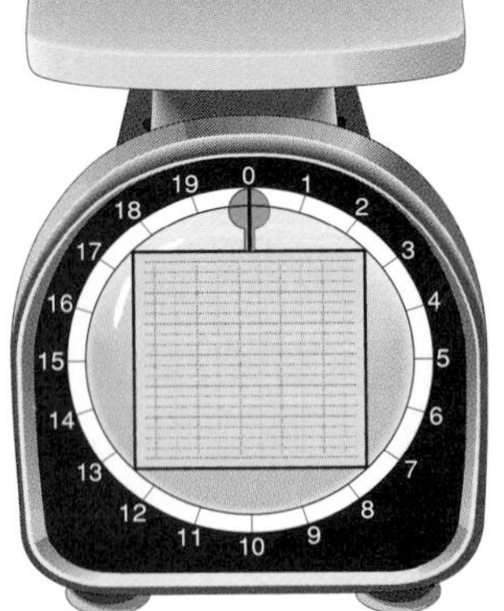


letter scale
pèse-lettres[M]
Briefwaage[F]
balanza[F] para cartas[F]

pencil sharpener
taille-crayon[M]
Bleistiftspitzer[M]
sacapuntas[M]

telephone index
répertoire[M] téléphonique
Telefonnummernverzeichnis[N]
directorio[M] telefónico

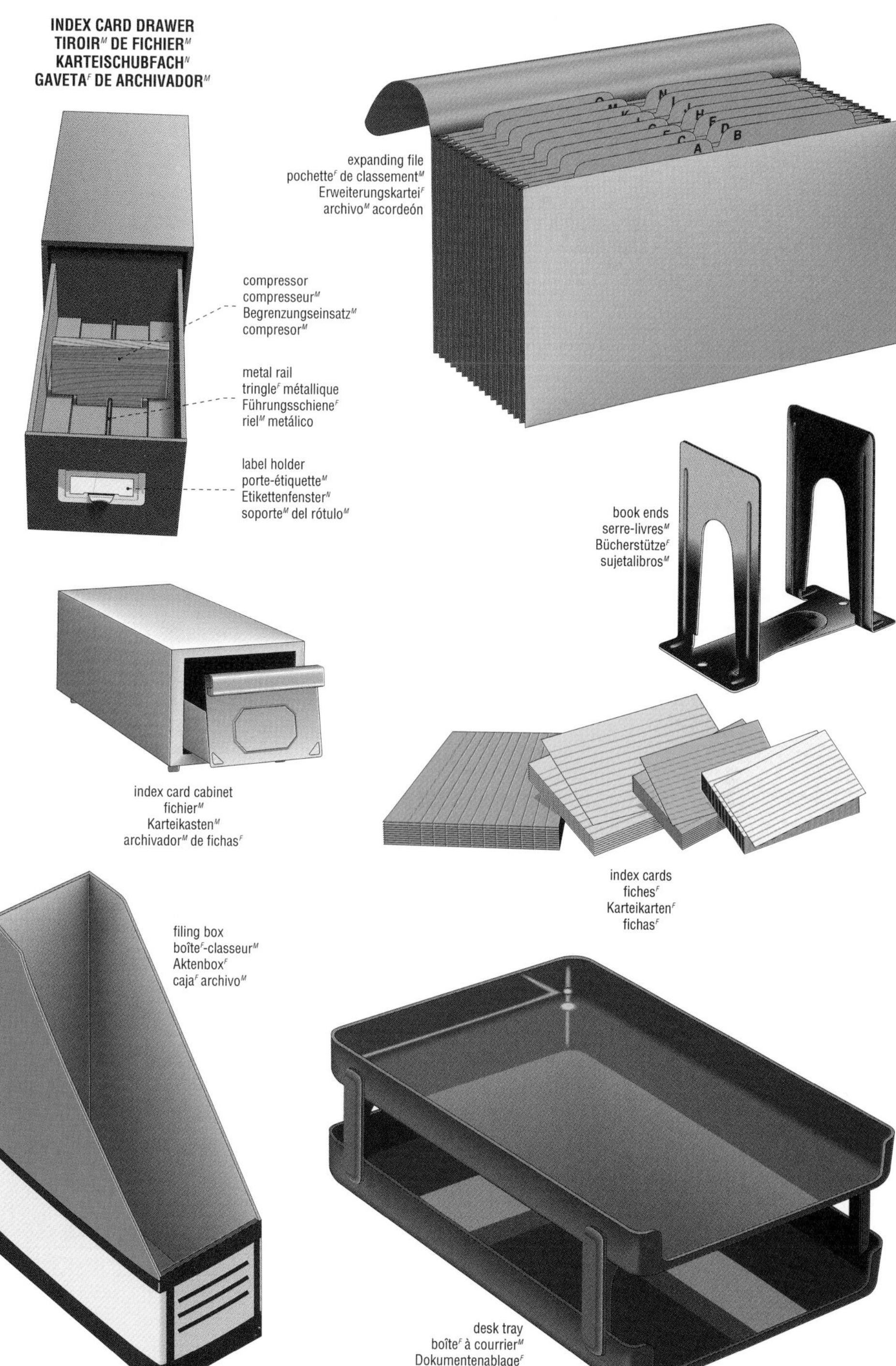
INDEX CARD DRAWER
TIROIR^M DE FICHIER^M
KARTEISCHUBFACH^N
GAVETA^F DE ARCHIVADOR^M
compressor
compresseur^M
Begrenzungseinsatz^M
compresor^M
metal rail
tringle^F métallique
Führungsschiene^F
riel^M metálico
label holder
porte-étiquette^M
Etikettenfenster^N
soporte^M del rótulo^M
expanding file
pochette^F de classement^M
Erweiterungskartei^F
archivo^M acordeón
book ends
serre-livres^M
Bücherstütze^F
sujetalibros^M
index card cabinet
fichier^M
Karteikasten^M
archivador^M de fichas^F
index cards
fiches^F
Karteikarten^F
fichas^F
filing box
boîte^F-classeur^M
Aktenbox^F
caja^F archivo^M
desk tray
boîte^F à courrier^M
Dokumentenablage^F
bandeja^F de correspondencia^F

# STATIONERY
# ARTICLES$^{M}$ DE BUREAU$^{M}$
# SCHREIBWAREN$^{F}$
# ARTÍCULOS$^{M}$ DE ESCRITORIO$^{M}$

tear-off calendar
calendrier$^{M}$-mémorandum$^{M}$
Abreißkalender$^{M}$
calendario$^{M}$ de pared$^{F}$

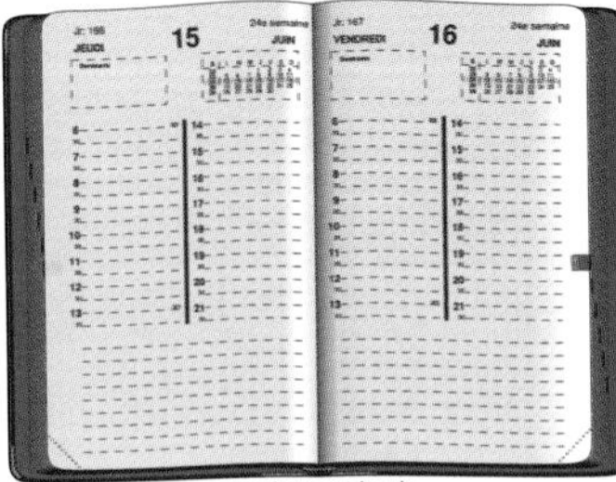

appointment book
agenda$^{M}$
Terminkalender$^{M}$
agenda$^{F}$

calendar pad
bloc$^{M}$-éphéméride$^{F}$
Ringbuchkalender$^{M}$
calendario$^{M}$ de escritorio$^{M}$

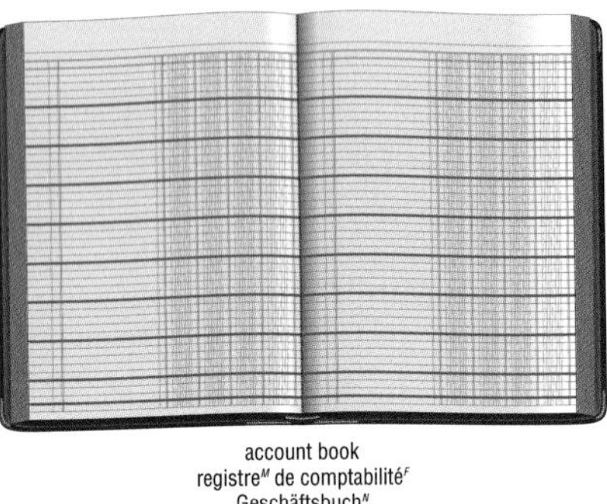

account book
registre$^{M}$ de comptabilité$^{F}$
Geschäftsbuch$^{N}$
agenda$^{F}$ de caja$^{F}$

memo pad
bloc$^{M}$-notes$^{F}$
Notizblock$^{M}$
libreta$^{F}$

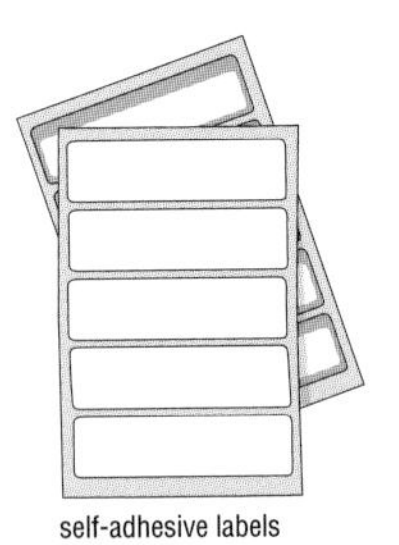

self-adhesive labels
étiquettes$^{F}$ autocollantes
Klebeetiketten$^{N}$
etiquetas$^{F}$ adhesivas

tab
onglet$^{M}$
Reiter$^{M}$
indicador$^{M}$

window tab
onglet$^{M}$ à fenêtre$^{F}$
durchsichtiger Reiter$^{M}$
indicador$^{M}$ transparente

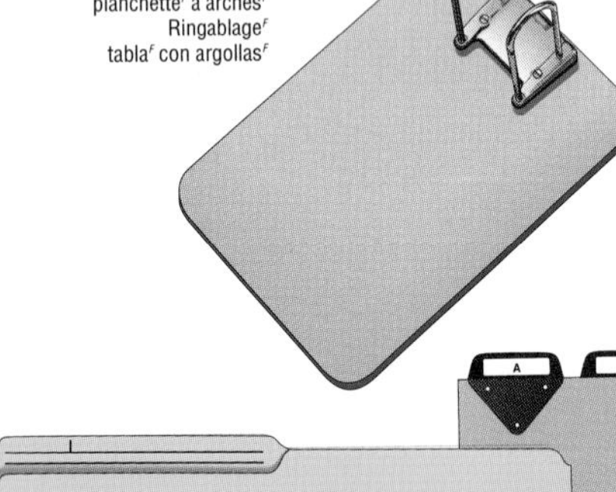

archboard
planchette$^{F}$ à arches$^{F}$
Ringablage$^{F}$
tabla$^{F}$ con argollas$^{F}$

suspension file
dossier$^{M}$ suspendu
Hängemappe$^{F}$
archivador$^{M}$ colgante

file guides
guides$^{M}$ de classement$^{M}$
Karteiregister$^{N}$
guías$^{F}$ de archivo$^{M}$

folder
chemise$^{F}$
Aktenmappe$^{F}$
carpeta$^{F}$ de archivo$^{M}$

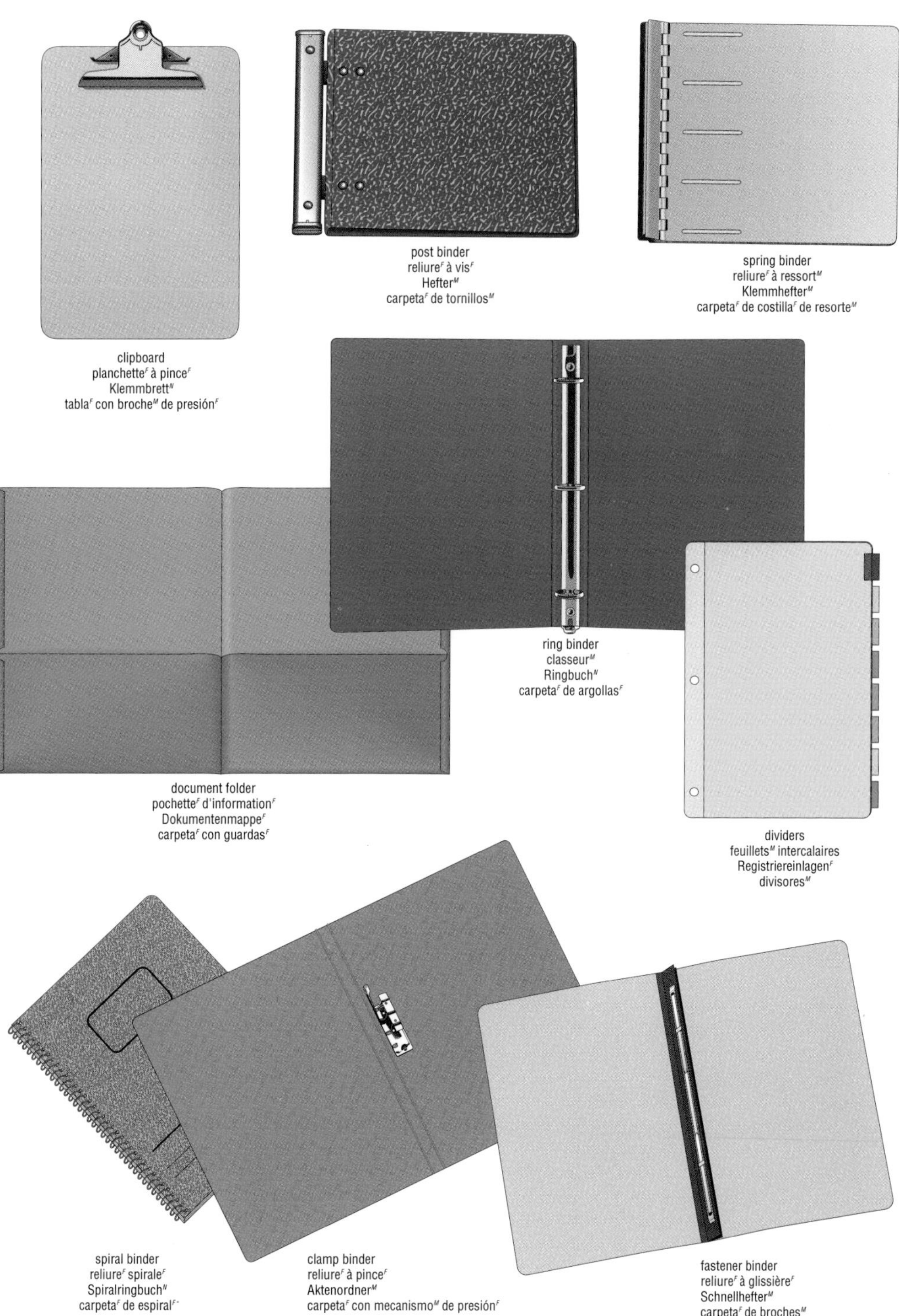

clipboard
planchette$^{F}$ à pince$^{F}$
Klemmbrett$^{N}$
tabla$^{F}$ con broche$^{M}$ de presión$^{F}$

post binder
reliure$^{F}$ à vis$^{F}$
Hefter$^{M}$
carpeta$^{F}$ de tornillos$^{M}$

spring binder
reliure$^{F}$ à ressort$^{M}$
Klemmhefter$^{M}$
carpeta$^{F}$ de costilla$^{F}$ de resorte$^{M}$

ring binder
classeur$^{M}$
Ringbuch$^{N}$
carpeta$^{F}$ de argollas$^{F}$

document folder
pochette$^{F}$ d'information$^{F}$
Dokumentenmappe$^{F}$
carpeta$^{F}$ con guardas$^{F}$

dividers
feuillets$^{M}$ intercalaires
Registriereinlagen$^{F}$
divisores$^{M}$

spiral binder
reliure$^{F}$ spirale$^{F}$
Spiralringbuch$^{N}$
carpeta$^{F}$ de espiral$^{F}$

clamp binder
reliure$^{F}$ à pince$^{F}$
Aktenordner$^{M}$
carpeta$^{F}$ con mecanismo$^{M}$ de presión$^{F}$

fastener binder
reliure$^{F}$ à glissière$^{F}$
Schnellhefter$^{M}$
carpeta$^{F}$ de broches$^{M}$

# OFFICE FURNITURE
# MOBILIER^M DE BUREAU^M
# BÜROMÖBEL^N
# MUEBLES^M DE OFICINA^F

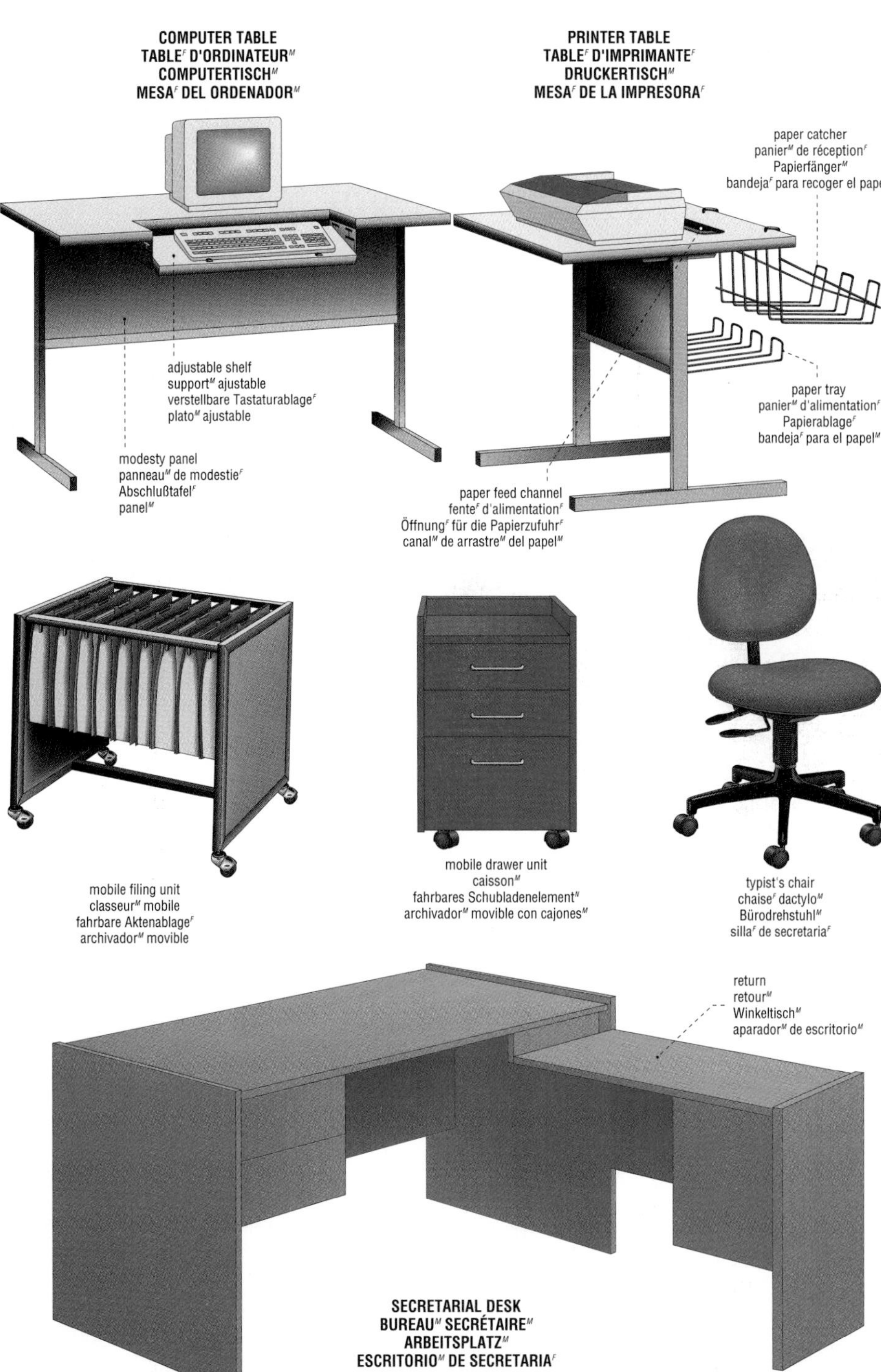
COMPUTER TABLE
TABLE^F D'ORDINATEUR^M
COMPUTERTISCH^M
MESA^F DEL ORDENADOR^M
adjustable shelf
support^M ajustable
verstellbare Tastaturablage^F
plato^M ajustable
modesty panel
panneau^M de modestie^F
Abschlußtafel^F
panel^M
PRINTER TABLE
TABLE^F D'IMPRIMANTE^F
DRUCKERTISCH^M
MESA^F DE LA IMPRESORA^F
paper catcher
panier^M de réception^F
Papierfänger^M
bandeja^F para recoger el papel^M
paper tray
panier^M d'alimentation^F
Papierablage^F
bandeja^F para el papel^M
paper feed channel
fente^F d'alimentation^F
Öffnung^F für die Papierzufuhr^F
canal^M de arrastre^M del papel^M
mobile filing unit
classeur^M mobile
fahrbare Aktenablage^F
archivador^M movible
mobile drawer unit
caisson^M
fahrbares Schubladenelement^N
archivador^M movible con cajones^M
typist's chair
chaise^F dactylo^M
Bürodrehstuhl^M
silla^F de secretaria^F
return
retour^M
Winkeltisch^M
aparador^M de escritorio^M
SECRETARIAL DESK
BUREAU^M SECRÉTAIRE^M
ARBEITSPLATZ^M
ESCRITORIO^M DE SECRETARIA^F

# OFFICE FURNITURE
# MOBILIER^M DE BUREAU^M
# BÜROMÖBEL^N
# MUEBLES^M DE OFICINA^F

# CALCULATOR
# CALCULATRICE[F]
# RECHNER[M]
# CALCULADORAS[F]

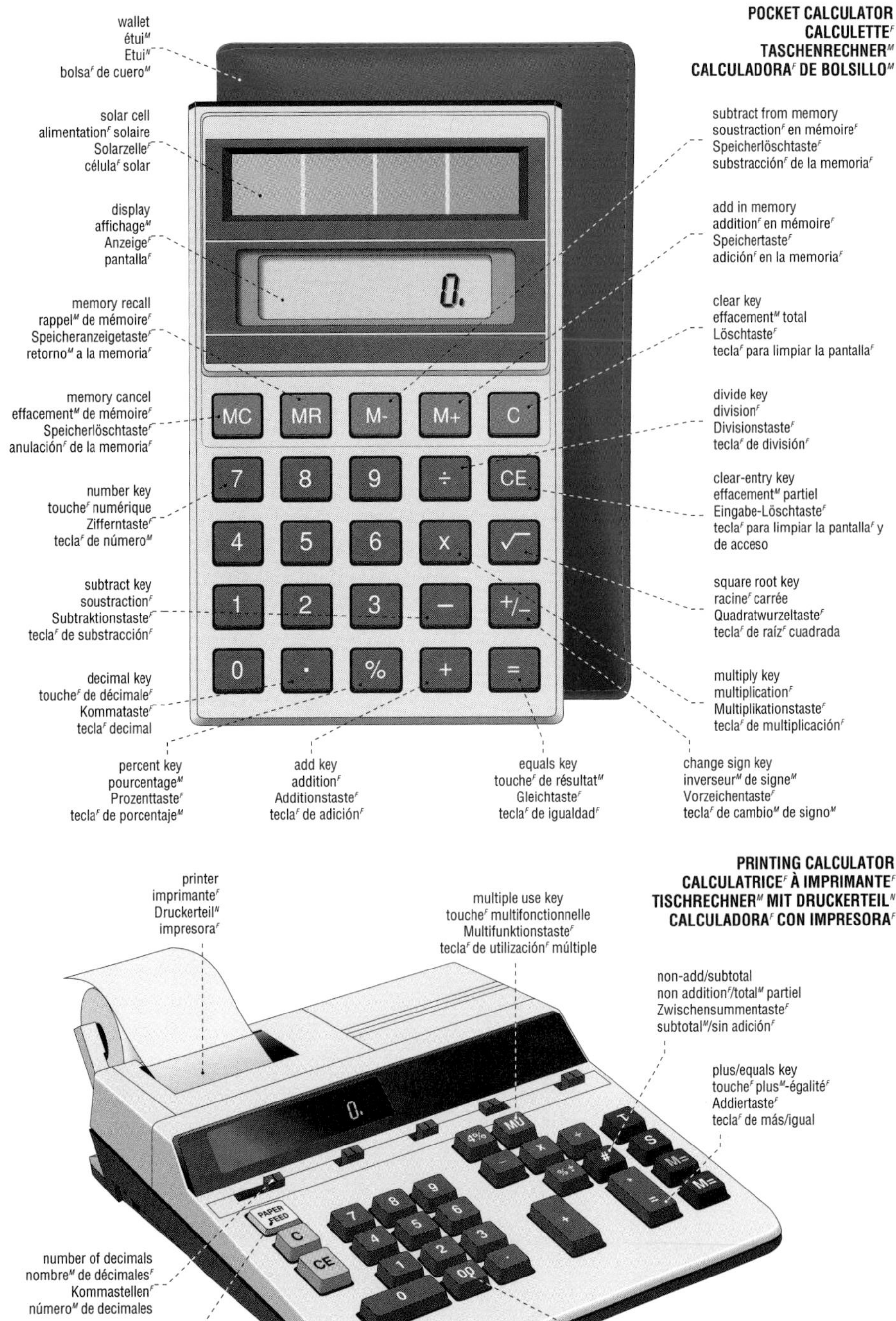

# ELECTRONIC TYPEWRITER
# MACHINE^F À ÉCRIRE ÉLECTRONIQUE
# ELEKTRISCHE SCHREIBMASCHINE^F
# MÁQUINA^F DE ESCRIBIR ELECTRÓNICA

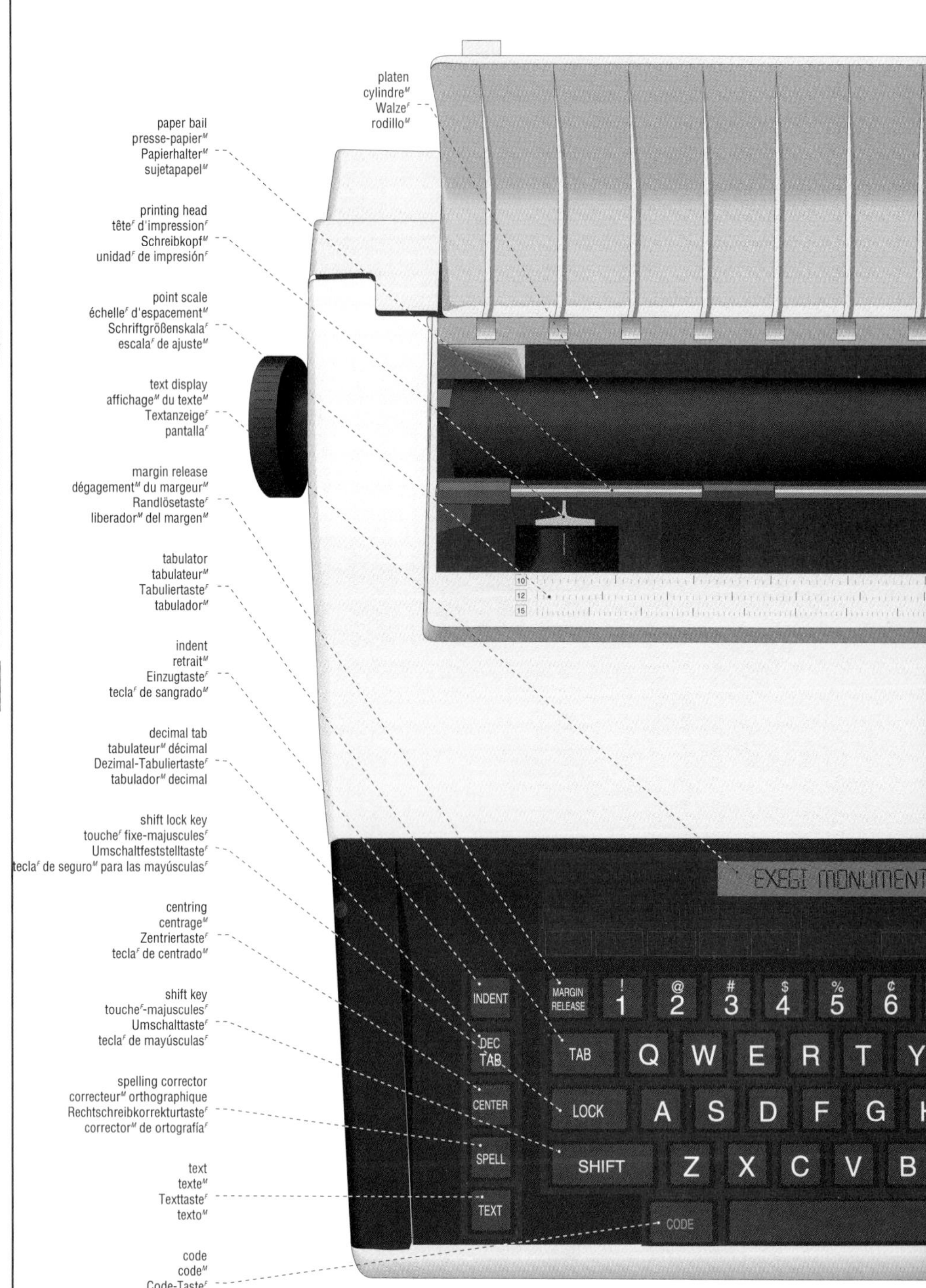

paper support
support-papier[M]
Papierstütze[F]
soporte[M] del papel[M]
paper release lever
levier[M] de dégagement[M] du papier[M]
Papierlösehebel[M]
palanca[F] de aflojar el papel[M]
paper bail release lever
levier[M] de dégagement[M] du presse-papier[M]
Papierfreigabehebel[M]
palanca[F] para liberar el sujetapapel[M]
platen knob
bouton[M] d'interligne[M] variable
Walzendrehknopf[M]
embrague[M] de espacios[M]
top plate
capot[M]
Gehäuseabdeckung[F]
lámina[F] superior
word correction
correction[F] de mots[M]
Wortkorrekturtaste[F]
corrección[F] de palabras[F]
character correction
correction[F] de caractères[M]
Zeichenkorrekturtaste[F]
corrección[F] de caracteres[M]
half indexing
positionnement[M] du papier[M]
Hoch-/Tiefstelltaste[F]
indicador[M] de la mitad[F]
carriage return
retour[M] de chariot[M]
Wagenrücklauftaste[F]
tecla[F] de regreso[M] del carro[M]
margin control
commande[F] de marge[F]
Randkontrolltaste[F]
control[M] del margen[M]
tab setting
contrôle[M] de tabulation[F]
Tabulatoreinstelltaste[F]
ajuste[M] del tabulador[M]
set
validation[F]
Tabulatorsetztaste[F]
ajuste[M]
relocation
repositionnement[M]
Fixiertaste[F]
otra posición[F]
mode
mode[M]
Mode-Taste[F]
modalidad[F]
space bar
barre[F] d'espacement[M]
Leertaste[F]
barra[F] espaciadora
ERE PERENNIUS
RELEASE
PHRASE
RETURN
SHIFT
MODE
RELOC
TAB
P MAR

# CONFIGURATION OF AN OFFICE AUTOMATION SYSTEM
# CONFIGURATION^F D'UN SYSTÈME^M BUREAUTIQUE
# ZUSAMMENSTELLUNG^F EINES AUTOMATISIERTEN BÜROS^N
# CONFIGURACIÓN^F DEL SISTEMA^M DE UNA OFICINA^F AUTOMATIZADA

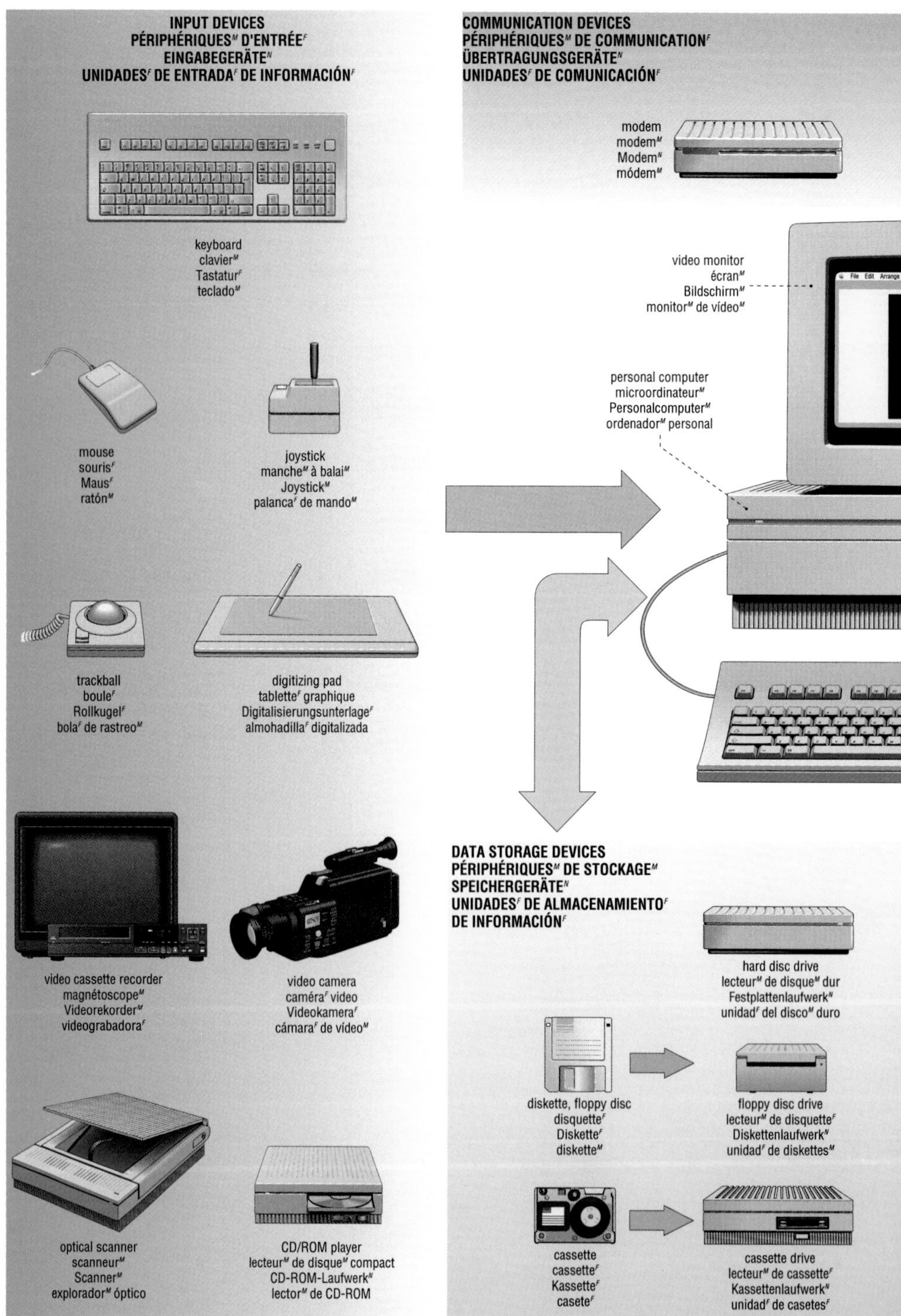

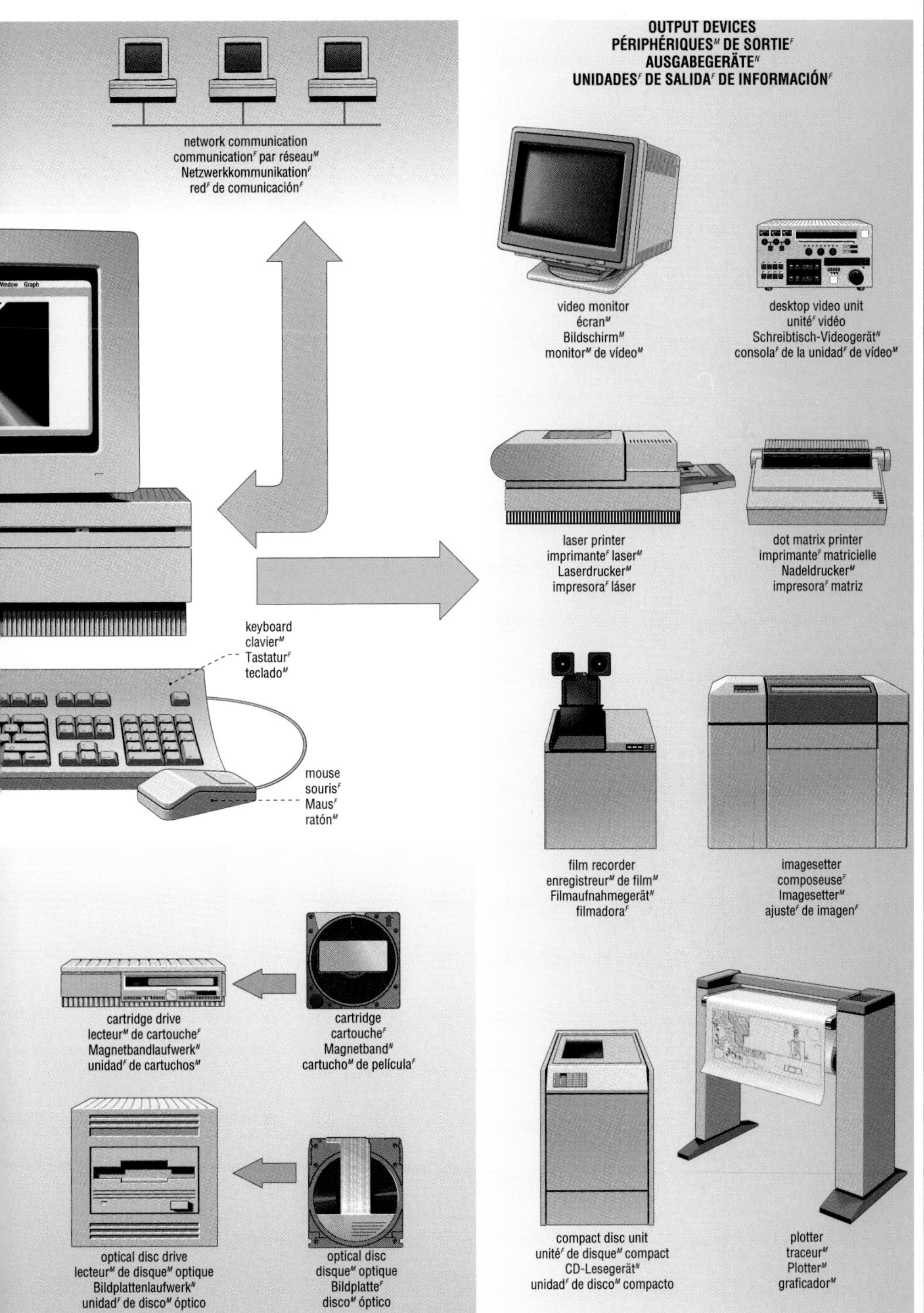


network communication
communication^F par réseau^M
Netzwerkkommunikation^F
red^F de comunicación^F

keyboard
clavier^M
Tastatur^F
teclado^M

mouse
souris^F
Maus^F
ratón^M

cartridge drive
lecteur^M de cartouche^F
Magnetbandlaufwerk^N
unidad^F de cartuchos^M

cartridge
cartouche^F
Magnetband^N
cartucho^M de película^F

optical disc drive
lecteur^M de disque^M optique
Bildplattenlaufwerk^N
unidad^F de disco^M óptico

optical disc
disque^M optique
Bildplatte^F
disco^M óptico

## OUTPUT DEVICES
## PÉRIPHÉRIQUES^M DE SORTIE^F
## AUSGABEGERÄTE^N
## UNIDADES^F DE SALIDA^F DE INFORMACIÓN^F

video monitor
écran^M
Bildschirm^M
monitor^M de vídeo^M

desktop video unit
unité^F vidéo
Schreibtisch-Videogerät^N
consola^F de la unidad^F de vídeo^M

laser printer
imprimante^F laser^M
Laserdrucker^M
impresora^F láser

dot matrix printer
imprimante^F matricielle
Nadeldrucker^M
impresora^F matriz

film recorder
enregistreur^M de film^M
Filmaufnahmegerät^N
filmadora^F

imagesetter
composeuse^F
Imagesetter^M
ajuste^F de imagen^F

compact disc unit
unité^F de disque^M compact
CD-Lesegerät^N
unidad^F de disco^M compacto

plotter
traceur^M
Plotter^M
graficador^M

# BASIC COMPONENTS
# SYSTÈME[M] DE BASE[F]
# GRUNDBAUTEILE[N]
# COMPONENTES[M] BÁSICOS

## PERSONAL COMPUTER (VIEW FROM ABOVE)
## MICRO-ORDINATEUR[M] (VUE[F] EN PLONGÉE[F])
## PERSONALCOMPUTER[M]
## VISTA[F] POR ENCIMA DE UN ORDENADOR[M] PERSONAL

expansion connector
connecteur[M] d'extension[F]
Speichererweiterungsanschluß[M]
conector[M] de expansión[F]

microprocessor
microprocesseur[M]
Mikroprozessor[M]
microprocesador[M]

random access memory (RAM) module
module[M] de mémoire[F] vive (RAM)
Arbeitsspeicher(RAM)-Modul[N]
módulo[M] de acceso[M] a la memoria[F] RAM

battery
pile[F]
Batterie[F]
batería[F]

connecting module
module[M] d'alimentation[F] électrique
Netzteil[N]
módulo[M] de conexión[F]

fan
ventilateur[M]
Kühlgebläse[N]
ventilador[M]

sound digitizing processor
processeur[M] de sons[M]
Klangprozessor[M]
procesador[M] digital de sonido[M]

coprocessor
coprocesseur[M]
Ko-Prozessor[M]
coprocesador[M]

read-only memory (ROM) module
module[M] de mémoire[F] morte (ROM)
ROM-Modul[N]
módulo[M] de lectura de memoria[F]
ROM unicamente

disc drive port
port[M] lecteur[M] de disque[M]
Anschluß[M] für Diskettenlaufwerk[N]
conexión[F] para unidad[F] de disco[M]

peripheral device port
port[M] périphérique[M]
Anschluß[M] für Peripheriegeräte[N]
conexión[F] para unidades[F] periféricas

video port
port[M] vidéo
Monitoranschluß[M]
conexión[F] para el vídeo[M]

network port
port[M] réseau[M]
Netzwerkanschluß[M]
conexión[F] para la red[F]

keyboard port
port[M] clavier[M]
Tastaturanschluß[M]
conexión[F] para el teclado[M]

modem port
port[M] modem[M]
Modemanschluß[M]
conexión[F] para el módem[M]

printer port
port[M] imprimante[F]
Druckeranschluß[M]
conexión[F] para la impresora[F]

insulating sheet
surface[F] isolante
Isolierabdeckung[F]
lámina[F] aislante

hard disc bus
bus[M] du disque[M] dur
Festplattenbus[M]
barra[F] colectora del disco[M] duro

printed circuit
circuit[M] imprimé
Platine[F]
circuito[M] impreso

floppy disc drive
lecteur[M] de disquette[F]
Diskettenlaufwerk[N]
unidad[F] del disco[M] flexible

hard disc drive
lecteur[M] de disque[M] dur
Festplattenlaufwerk[N]
unidad[F] del disco[M] duro

data bus
bus[M] de données[F]
Datenbus[M]
barra[F] colectora de información[F]

**VIDEO MONITOR**
**ÉCRAN[M]**
**BILDSCHIRMEINHEIT[F]**
**MONITOR[M] DEL VÍDEO[M]**

vertical control
réglage[M] vertical
vertikale Einstellung[F]
control[M] vertical
horizontal control
réglage[M] horizontal
horizontale Einstellung[F]
control[M] horizontal
centring control
réglage[M] de centrage[M]
Zentriereinstellung[F]
control[M] de centrado[M]
contrast control
réglage[M] du contraste[M]
Kontrastregler[M]
control[M] de contraste[M]
power indicator
témoin[M] d'alimentation[F]
Leuchtanzeige[F]
indicador[M] de encendido[M]
power switch
interrupteur[M]
Netzschalter[M]
interruptor[M]
brightness control
réglage[M] de la luminosité[F]
Helligkeitsregler[M]
control[M] de brillo[M]

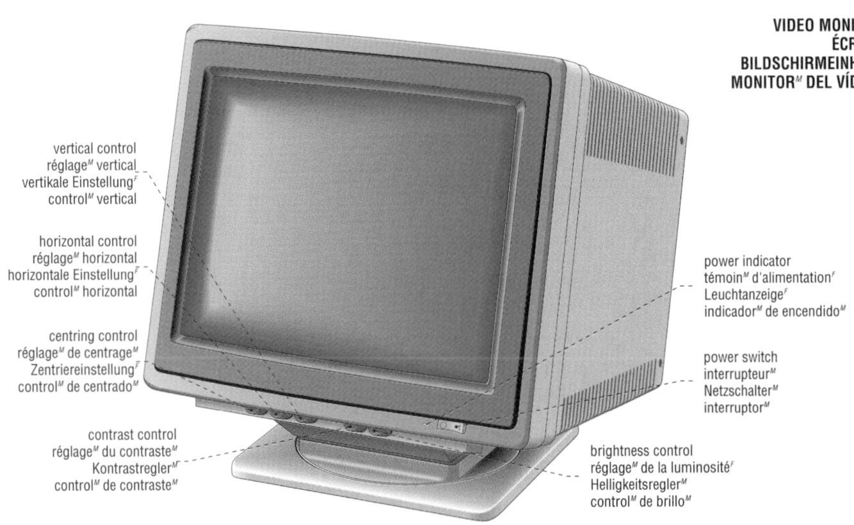

**FLOPPY DISC**
**DISQUETTE[F] SOUPLE**
**FLOPPY-DISK[F]**
**DISCO[M] FLEXIBLE**

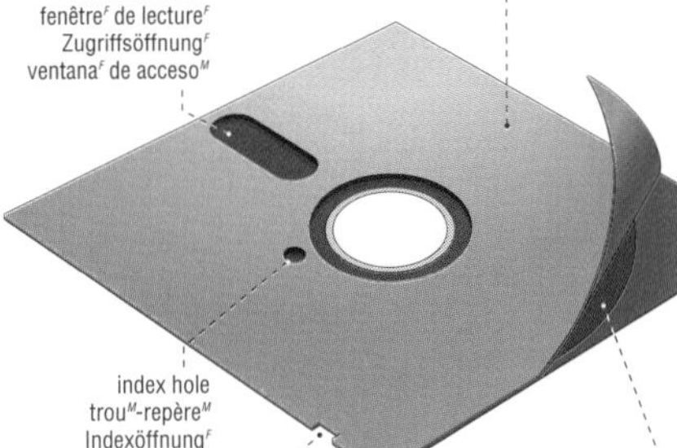

jacket
enveloppe[F]
Hülle[F]
cubierta[F]
access window
fenêtre[F] de lecture[F]
Zugriffsöffnung[F]
ventana[F] de acceso[M]
index hole
trou[M]-repère[M]
Indexöffnung[F]
índice[M]
write protect notch
encoche[F] de protection[F]
Schreibschutzöffnung[F]
muesca[F] de protección[F]
disc
disque[M]
Diskette[F]
disco[M]

**MINI-FLOPPY DISC**
**DISQUETTE[F] RIGIDE**
**MINI-DISKETTE[F]**
**DISCO[M] FLEXIBLE PEQUEÑO**

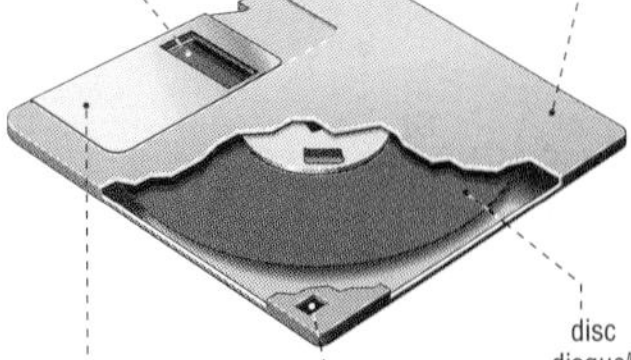

access window
fenêtre[F] de lecture[F]
Zugriffsöffnung[F]
ventana[F] de acceso[M]
jacket
enveloppe[F]
Hülle[F]
infraestructura[F]
shutter
volet[M]
Verschluß[M]
obturador[M]
disc
disque[M]
Platte[F]
disco[M]
protect tab
taquet[M] de verrouillage[M]
Schreibschutz[M]
lengüeta[F] protectora

**HARD DISC DRIVE**
**LECTEUR[M] DE DISQUE[M] DUR**
**FESTPLATTENLAUFWERK[N]**
**UNIDAD[F] DEL DISCO[M] DURO**

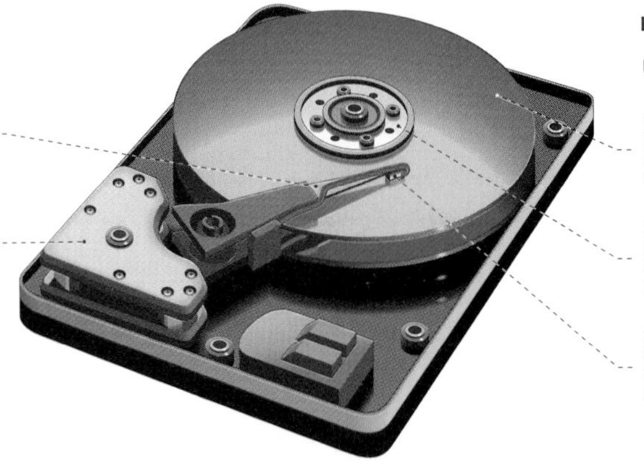

actuator arm
guide[M]
Sucharm[M]
brazo[M] actuador
actuator arm motor
moteur[M] de guides[M]
Führungsschienenantrieb[M]
motor[M] del brazo[M] actuador
disc
disque[M]
Platte[F]
disco[M]
disc motor
moteur[M] de disques[M]
Plattenantrieb[M]
motor[M] del disco[M]
read/write head
tête[F] de lecture[F]/écriture[F]
Schreib-/Lesekopf[M]
cabeza[F] de lectura[F] \ escritura[F]

# BASIC COMPONENTS
# SYSTÈME[M] DE BASE[F]
# GRUNDBAUTEILE[N]
# COMPONENTES[M] BÁSICOS

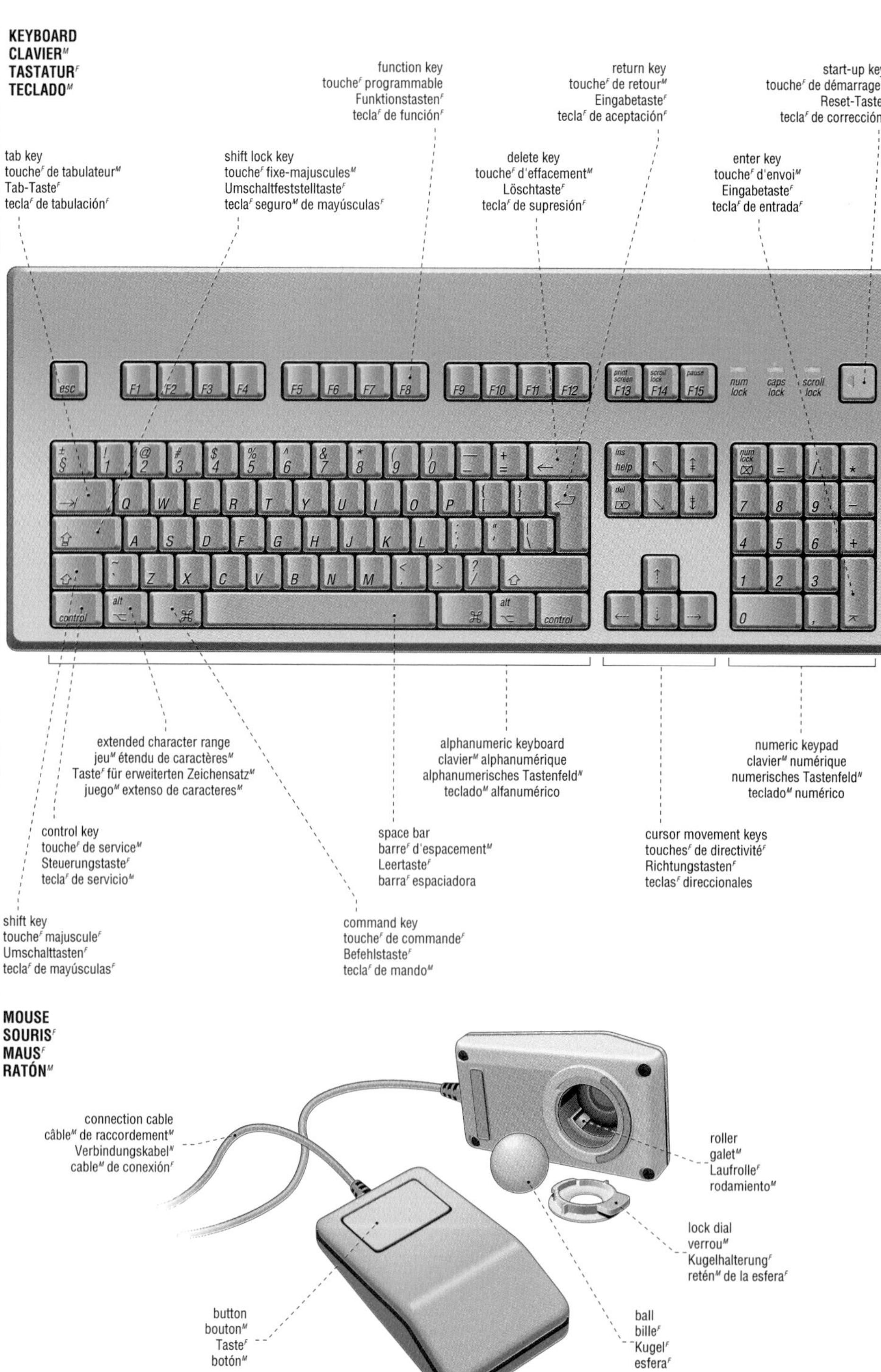

## DOT MATRIX PRINTER
## IMPRIMANTE[F] MATRICIELLE
## NADELDRUCKER[M]
## IMPRESORA[F] MATRIZ

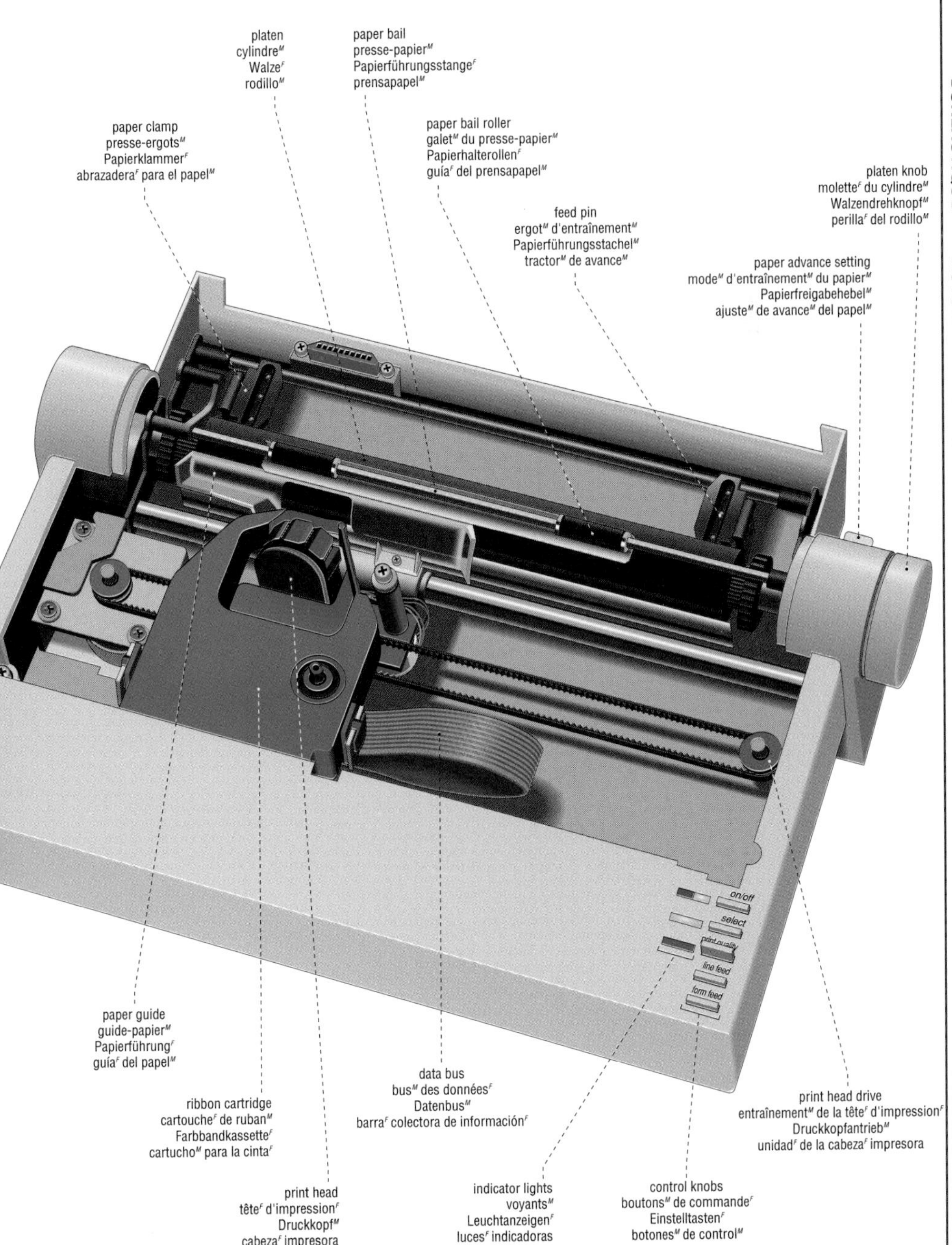

# PHOTOCOPIER
# PHOTOCOPIEUR[M]
# FOTOKOPIERER[M]
# FOTOCOPIADORA[F]

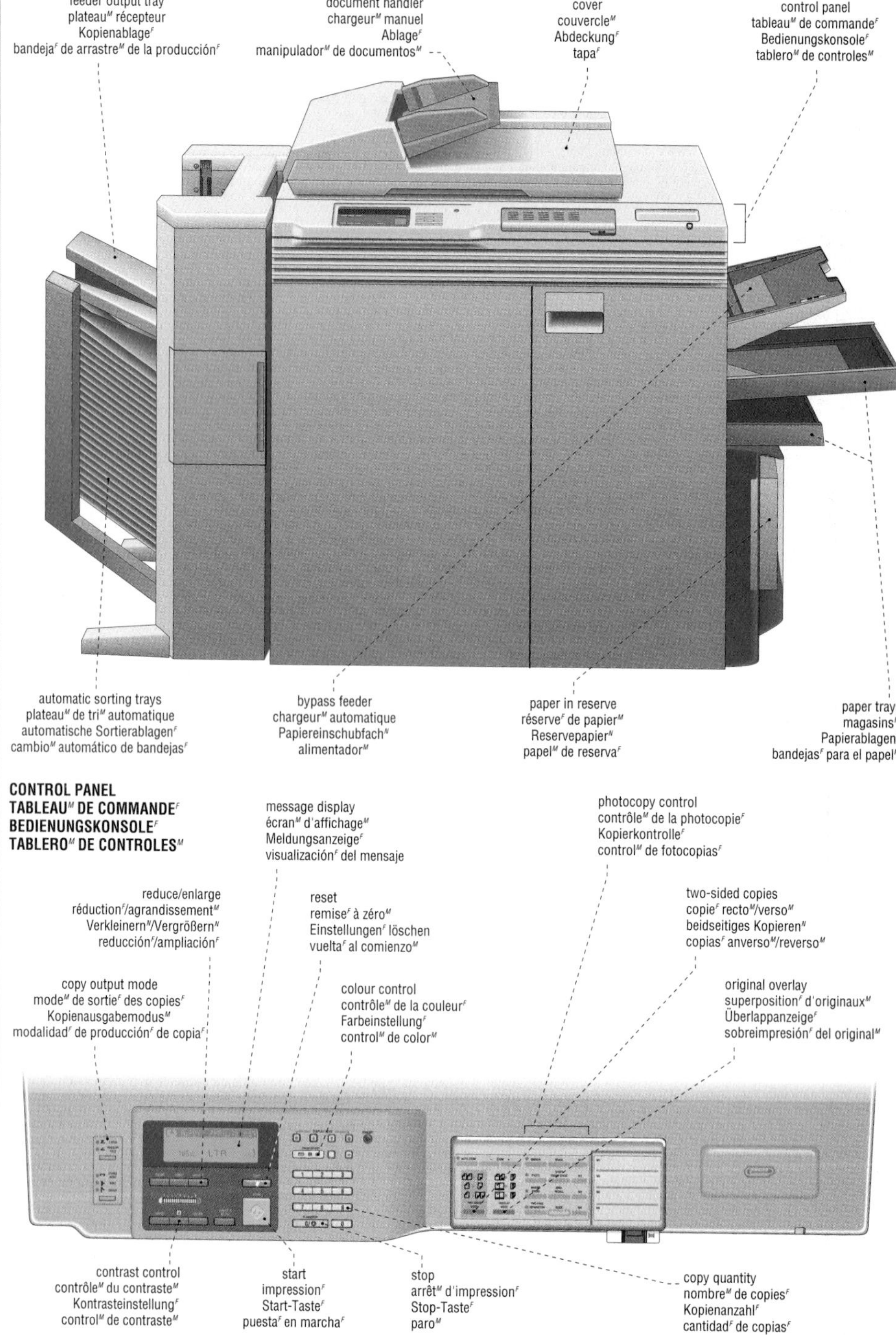

# MUSIC MUSIQUE MUSIK MUSICA

SUMMARY

TRADITIONAL MUSICAL INSTRUMENTS ..... 535
MUSICAL NOTATION ..... 537
MUSICAL ACCESSORIES ..... 539
KEYBOARD INSTRUMENTS ..... 540
ORGAN ..... 542
STRINGED INSTRUMENTS ..... 544
WIND INSTRUMENTS ..... 548
PERCUSSION INSTRUMENTS ..... 552
ELECTRONIC INSTRUMENTS ..... 555
SYMPHONY ORCHESTRA ..... 556
EXAMPLES OF INSTRUMENTAL GROUPS ..... 558

# TRADITIONAL MUSICAL INSTRUMENTS
# INSTRUMENTS^M TRADITIONNELS
# TRADITIONELLE MUSIKINSTRUMENTE^N
# INSTRUMENTOS^M MUSICALES TRADICIONALES

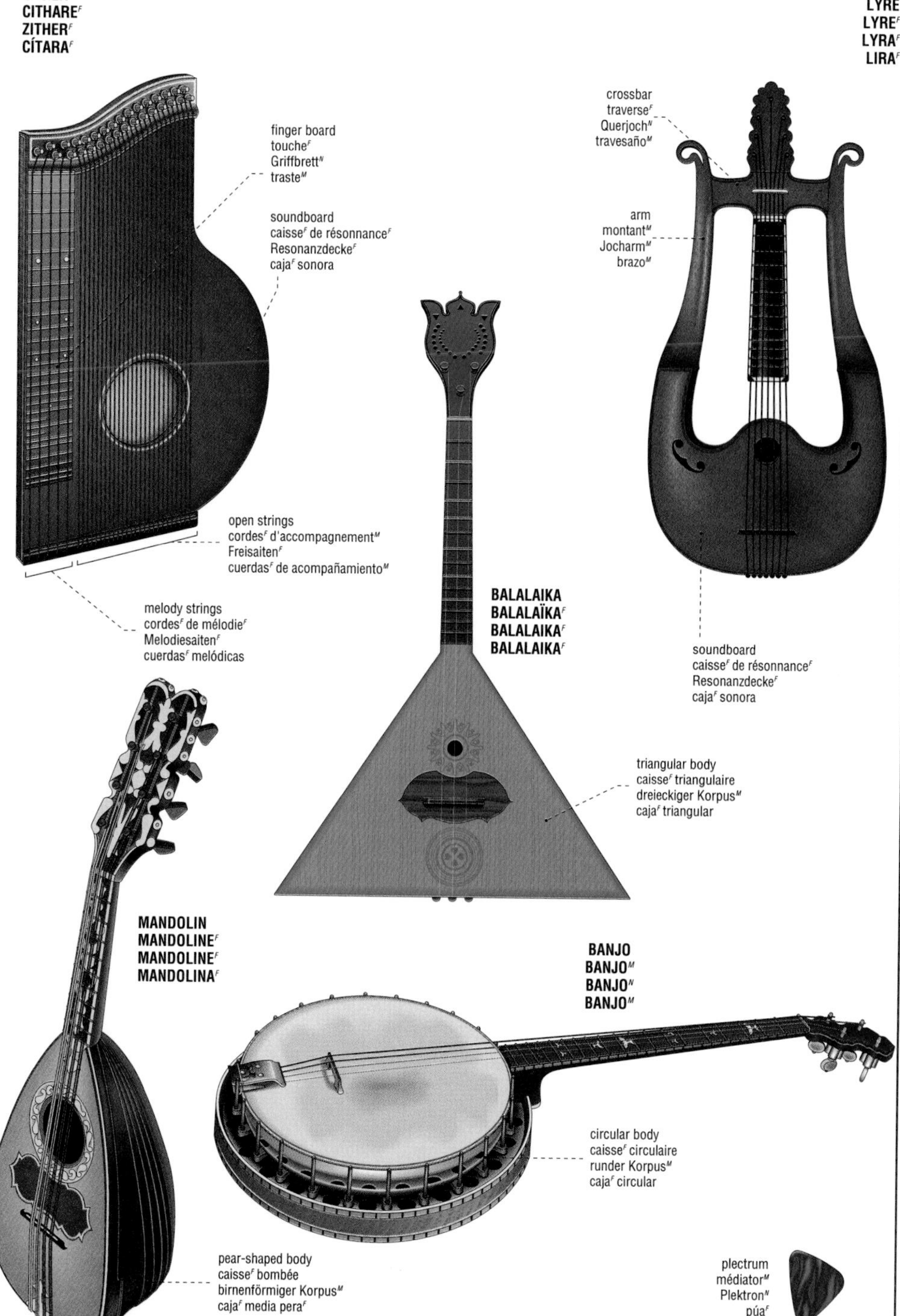

# TRADITIONAL MUSICAL INSTRUMENTS
# INSTRUMENTS^M TRADITIONNELS
# TRADITIONELLE MUSIKINSTRUMENTE^N
# INSTRUMENTOS^M MUSICALES TRADICIONALES

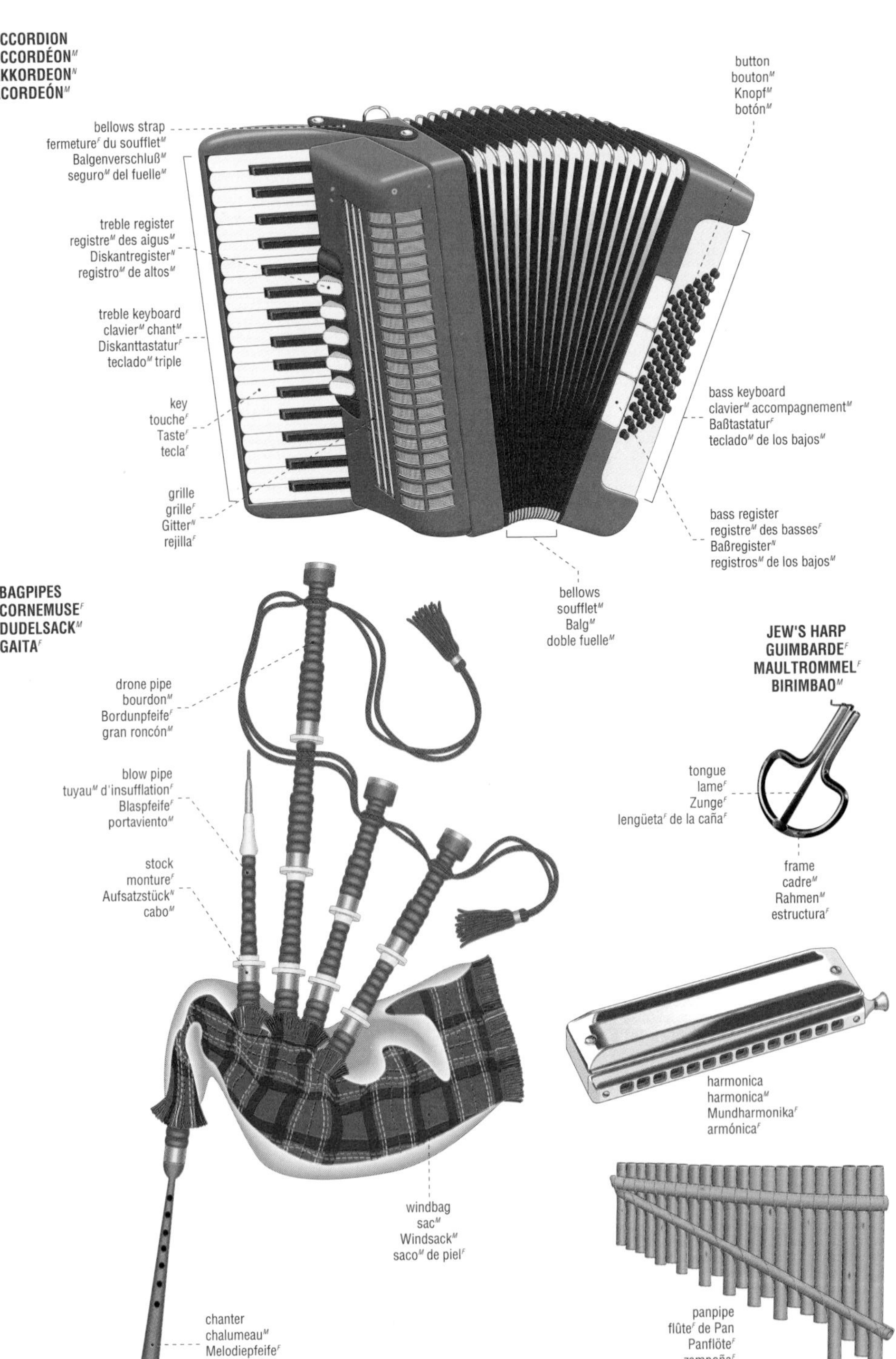

# MUSICAL NOTATION
# NOTATION[F] MUSICALE
# MUSIKNOTATION[F]
# NOTACIÓN[F] MUSICAL

MUSIC MUSIQUE MUSIK MÚSICA

# MUSICAL NOTATION
# NOTATION[F] MUSICALE
# MUSIKNOTATION[F]
# NOTACIÓN[F] MUSICAL[F]

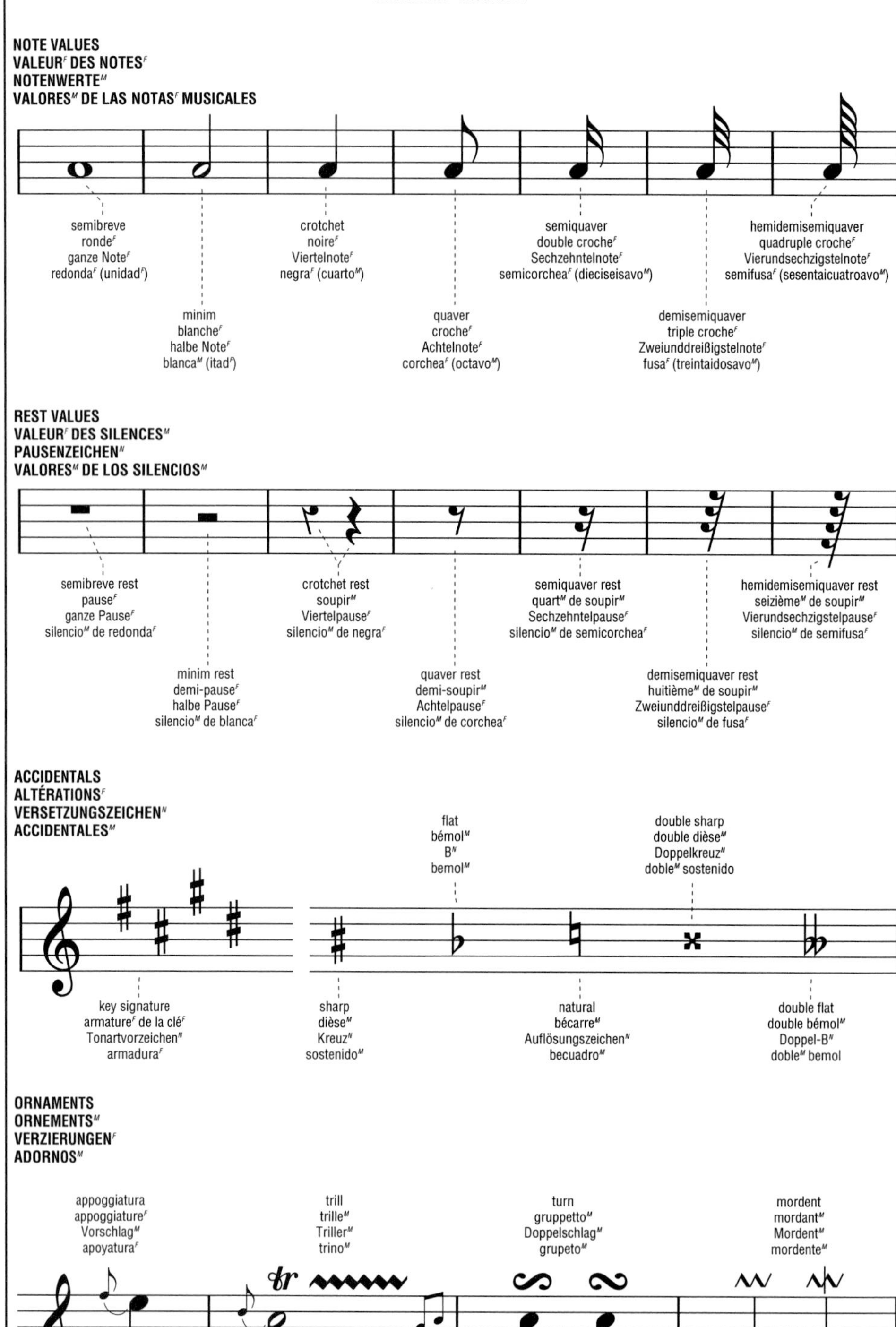

**CHORD**
**ACCORD[M]**
**AKKORD[M]**
**ACORDE[M]**

**OTHER SIGNS**
**AUTRES SIGNES[M]**
**ANDERE ZEICHEN[N]**
**OTROS SIGNOS[M]**

accent mark
accent[M]
Marcato-Zeichen[N]
acento[M]

arpeggio
arpège[M]
Arpeggio[N]
arpegio[M]

tie
liaison[F]
Bindebogen[M]
ligadura[F]

pause
point[M] d'orgue[M]
Pause[F]
calderón[M]

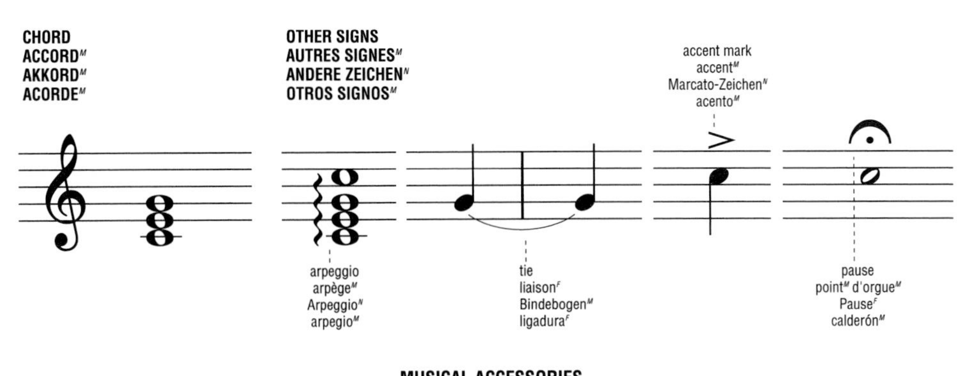

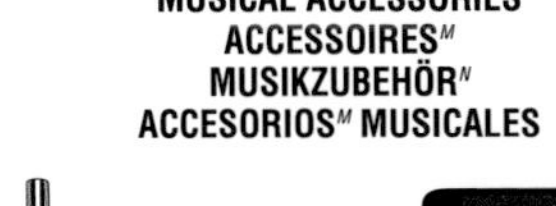

## MUSICAL ACCESSORIES
## ACCESSOIRES[M]
## MUSIKZUBEHÖR[N]
## ACCESORIOS[M] MUSICALES

**MUSIC STAND**
**PUPITRE[M] À MUSIQUE[F]**
**NOTENSTÄNDER[M]**
**ATRIL[M]**

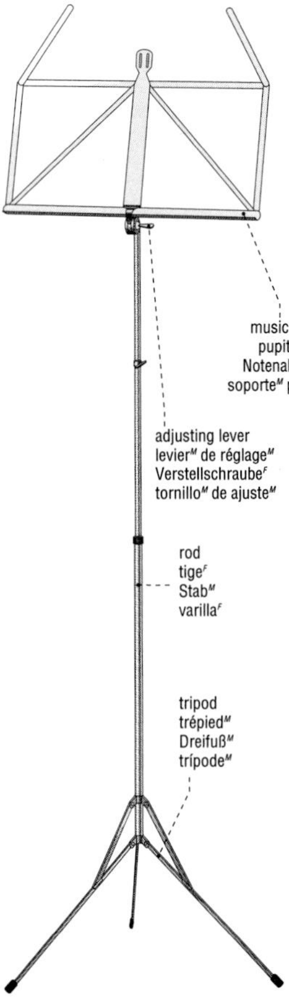

music rest
pupitre[M]
Notenablage[F]
soporte[M] plegable

adjusting lever
levier[M] de réglage[M]
Verstellschraube[F]
tornillo[M] de ajuste[M]

rod
tige[F]
Stab[M]
varilla[F]

tripod
trépied[M]
Dreifuß[M]
trípode[M]

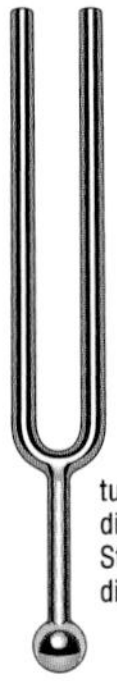

tuning fork
diapason[M]
Stimmgabel[F]
diapasón[M]

**QUARTZ METRONOME**
**MÉTRONOME[M] À QUARTZ[M]**
**QUARZMETRONOM[N]**
**METRÓNOMO[M] DE CUARZO[M]**

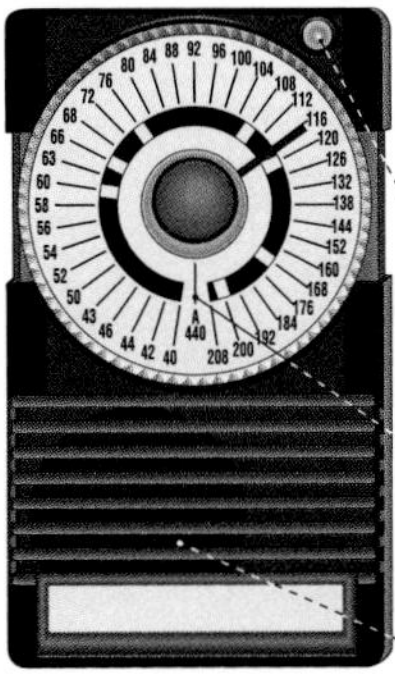

light signal
signal[M] lumineux
optisches Signal[N]
señal[F] luminosa

standard A
la[M] universel
Kammerton[M] A
pauta[F] A

sound signal
signal[M] sonore
akkustisches Signal[N]
señal[F] del sonido[M]

**METRONOME**
**MÉTRONOME[M] MÉCANIQUE**
**METRONOM[N]**
**METRÓNOMO[M]**

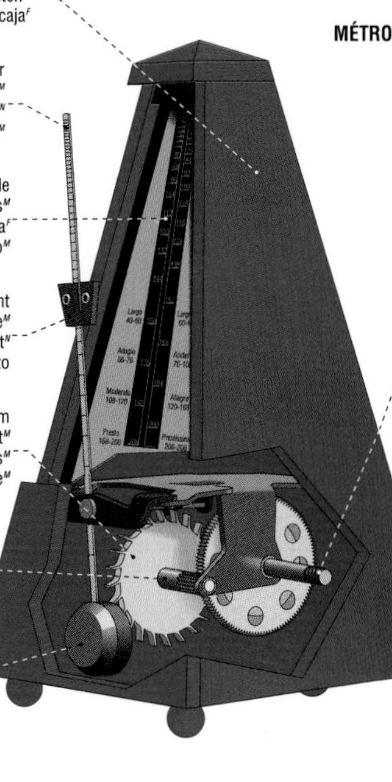

case
boîtier[M]
Kasten[M]
caja[F]

pendulum bar
tige[F] de pendule[M]
Pendel[N]
varilla[F] del péndulo[M]

tempo scale
échelle[F] des mouvements[M]
Temposkala[F]
escala[F] de tiempo[M]

sliding weight
massette[F] de réglage[M]
Laufgewicht[N]
peso[M] corredizo

escapement mechanism
mécanisme[M] à échappement[M]
Steigradmechanismus[M]
mecanismo[M] de escape[M]

pivot
pivot[M]
Pinne[F]
pivote[M]

fixed weight
masse[F] pendulaire
festehendes Gewicht[N]
péndulo[M]

key spindle
remontoir[M]
Schlüssel[M]
llave[F]

# KEYBOARD INSTRUMENTS
# INSTRUMENTS[M] À CLAVIER[M]
# TASTENINSTRUMENTE[N]
# INSTRUMENTOS[M] DE TECLADO[M]

## UPRIGHT PIANO
## PIANO[M] DROIT
## KLAVIER[N]
## PIANO[M] VERTICAL

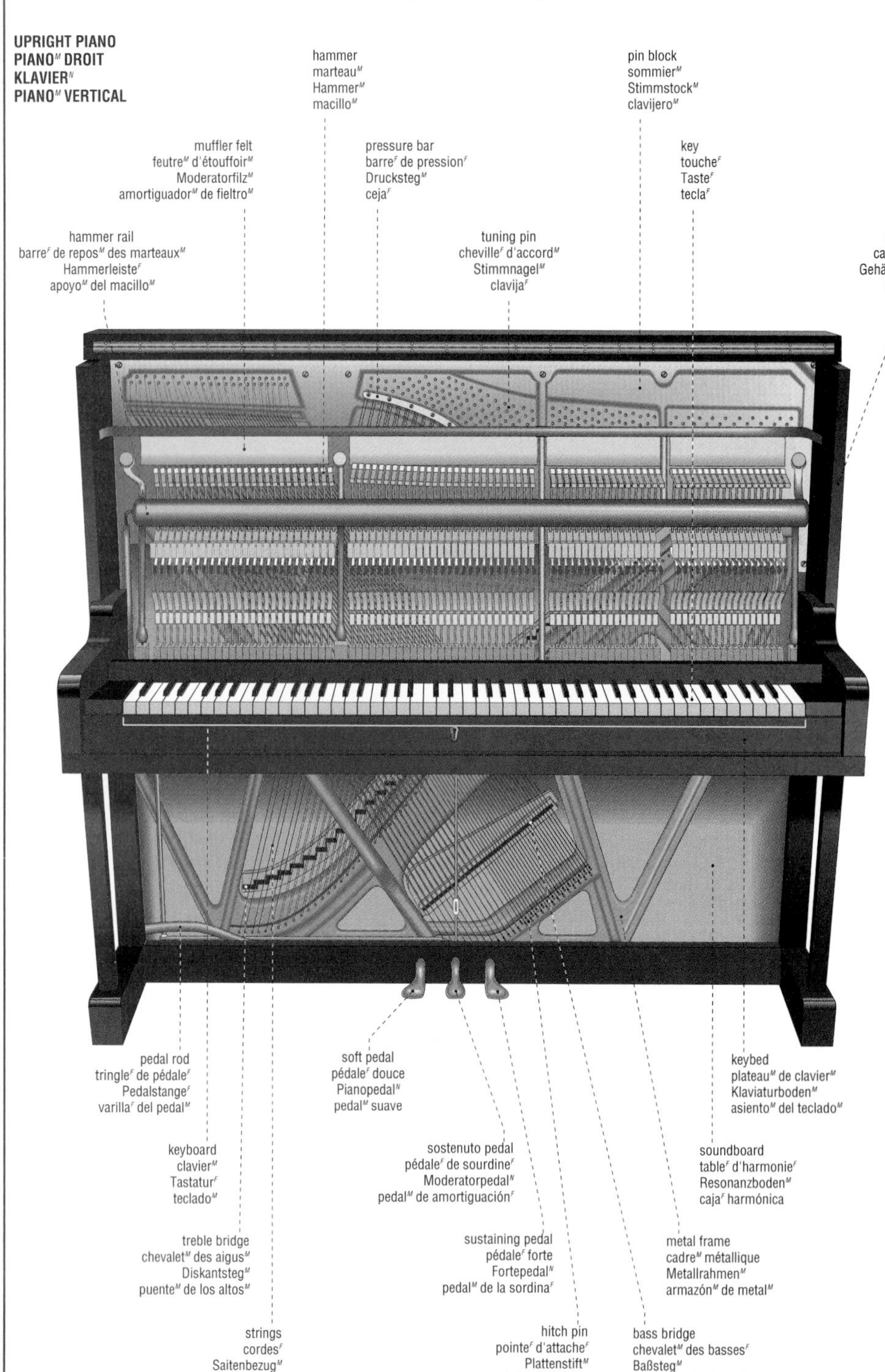

## UPRIGHT PIANO ACTION
## MÉCANIQUE[F] DU PIANO[M] DROIT
## KLAVIERMECHANIK[F]
## MECANISMO[M] DEL PIANO[M] VERTICAL

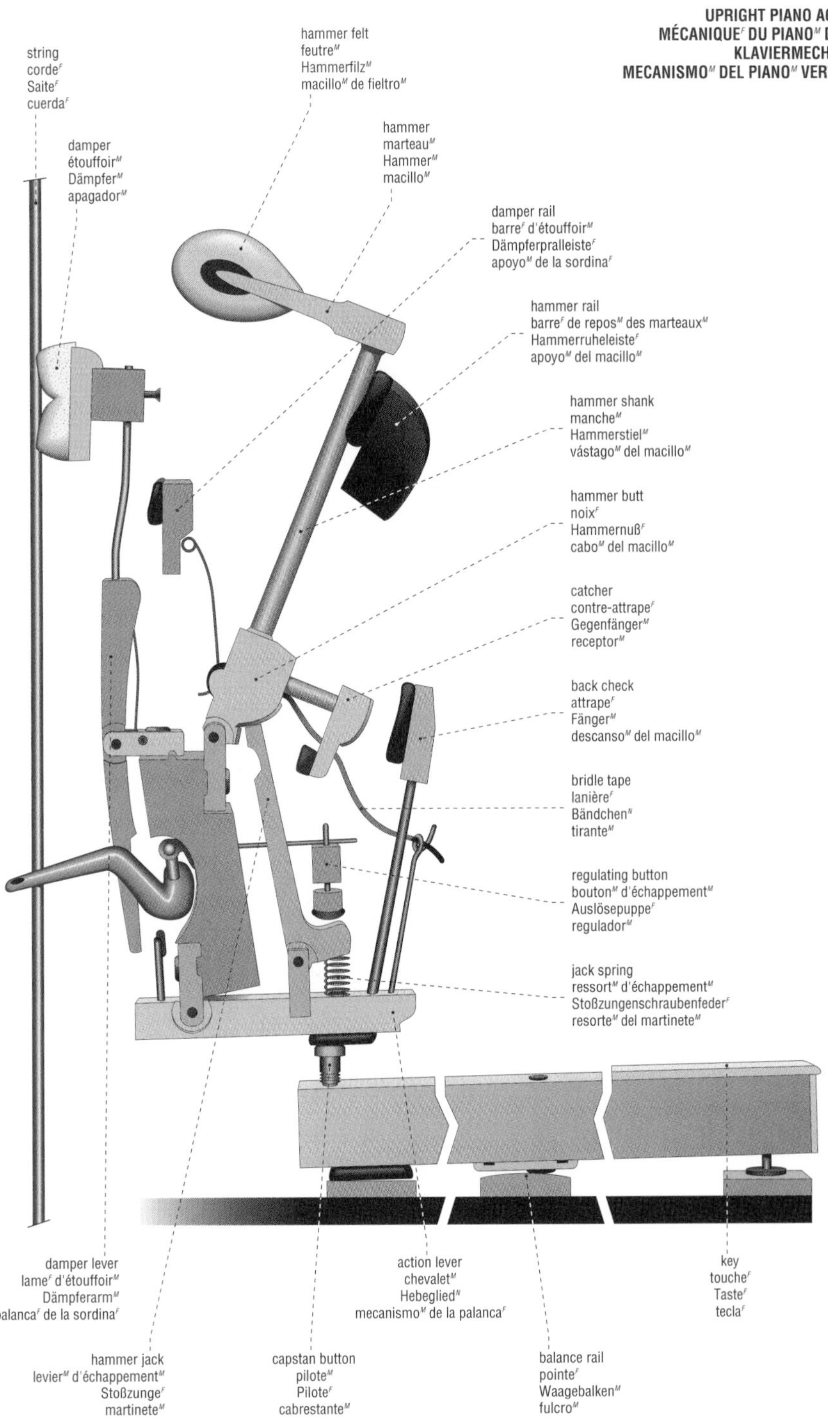

# ORGAN
# ORGUE[M]
# ORGEL[F]
# ÓRGANO[M] ELECTRONEUMÁTICO

## ORGAN CONSOLE
## CONSOLE[F] D'ORGUE[M]
## ORGELSPIELTISCH[M]
## CONSOLA[F]

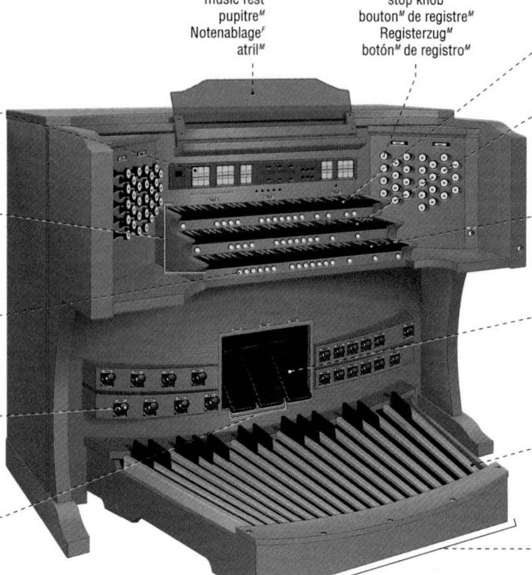


## FLUE PIPE
## TUYAU[M] À BOUCHE[F]
## LIPPENPFEIFE[F]
## CAÑO[M] DEL ÓRGANO[M]

## REED PIPE
## TUYAU[M] À ANCHE[F]
## ZUNGENPFEIFE[F]
## TUBO[M] DE LENGÜETA[F]

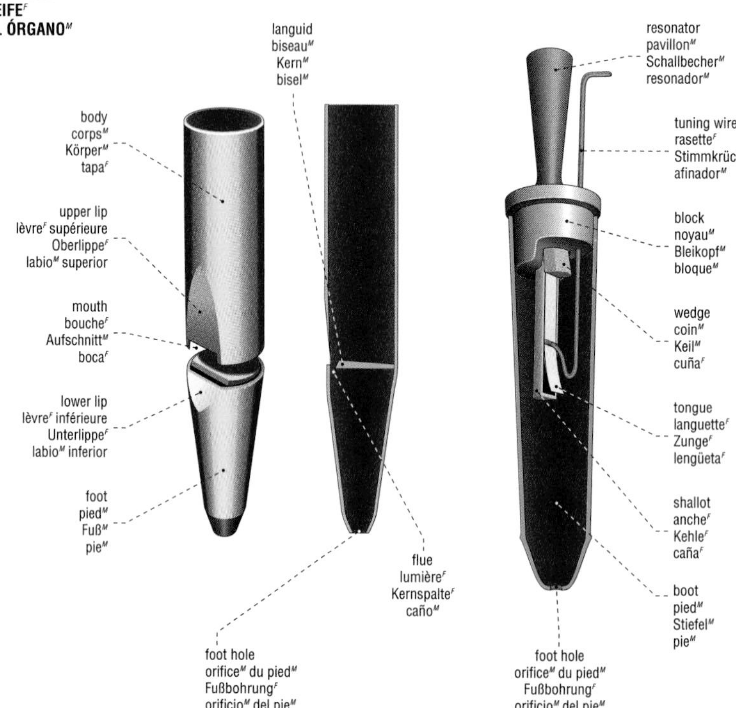

## MECHANISM OF THE ORGAN
## MÉCANISME DE L'ORGUE
## ORGELMECHANIK
## MECANISMO DEL ÓRGANO

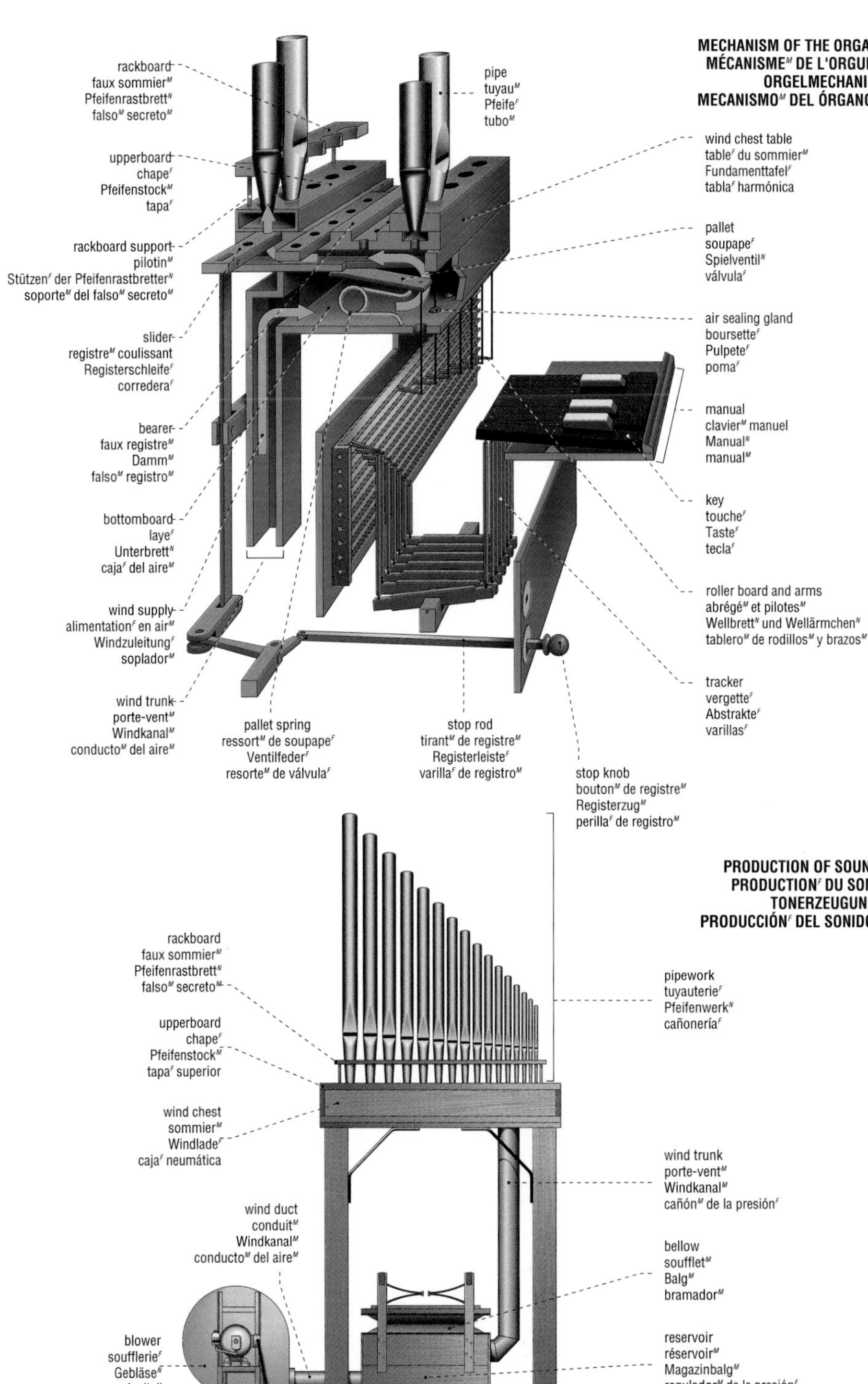

# STRINGED INSTRUMENTS
# INSTRUMENTS[M] À CORDES[F]
# SAITENINSTRUMENTE[N]
# INSTRUMENTOS[M] DE CUERDA[F]

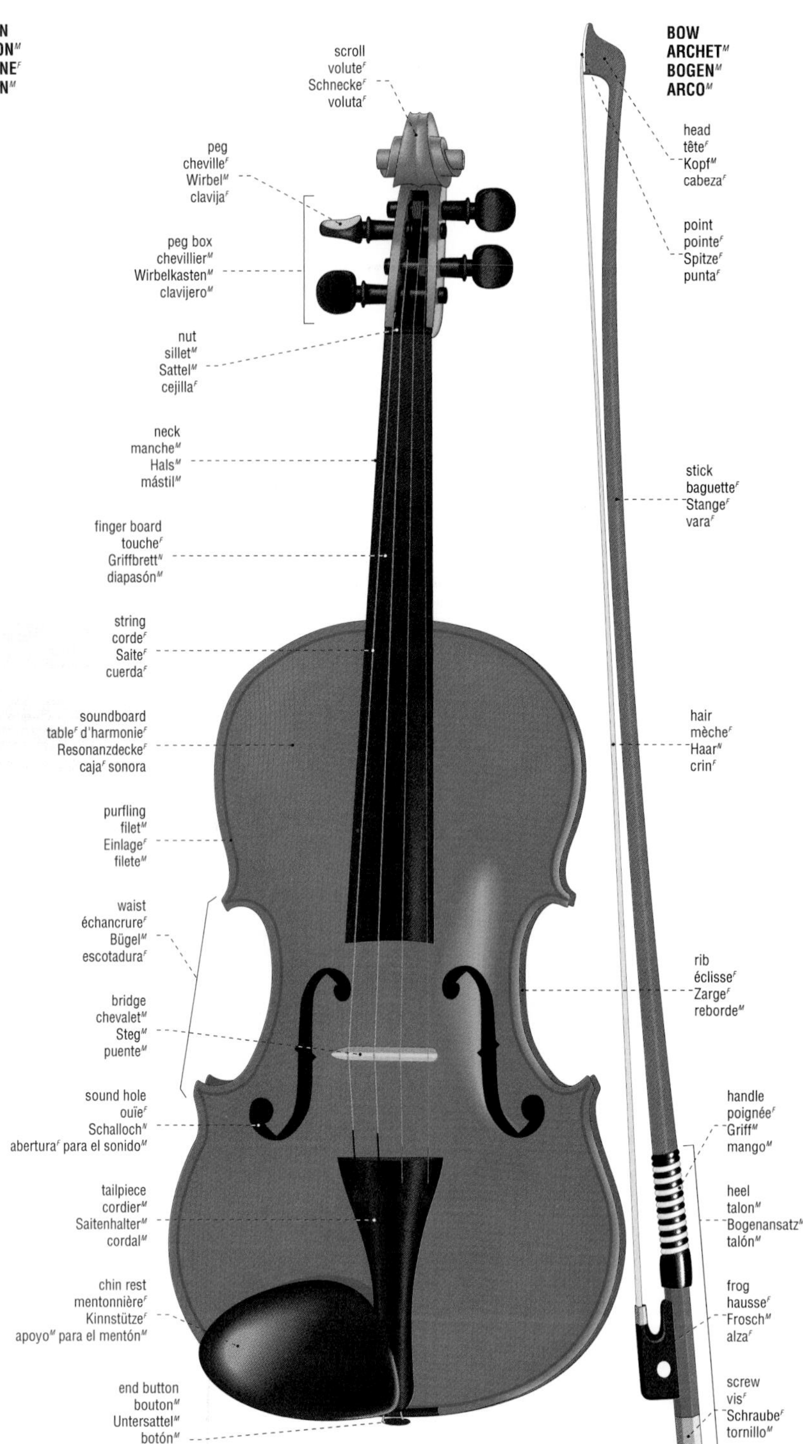

## VIOLIN FAMILY
## FAMILLE[F] DU VIOLON[M]
## GEIGENFAMILIE[F]
## FAMILIA[F] DE LOS VIOLINES[M]

## HARP
## HARPE[F]
## HARFE[F]
## ARPA[F]

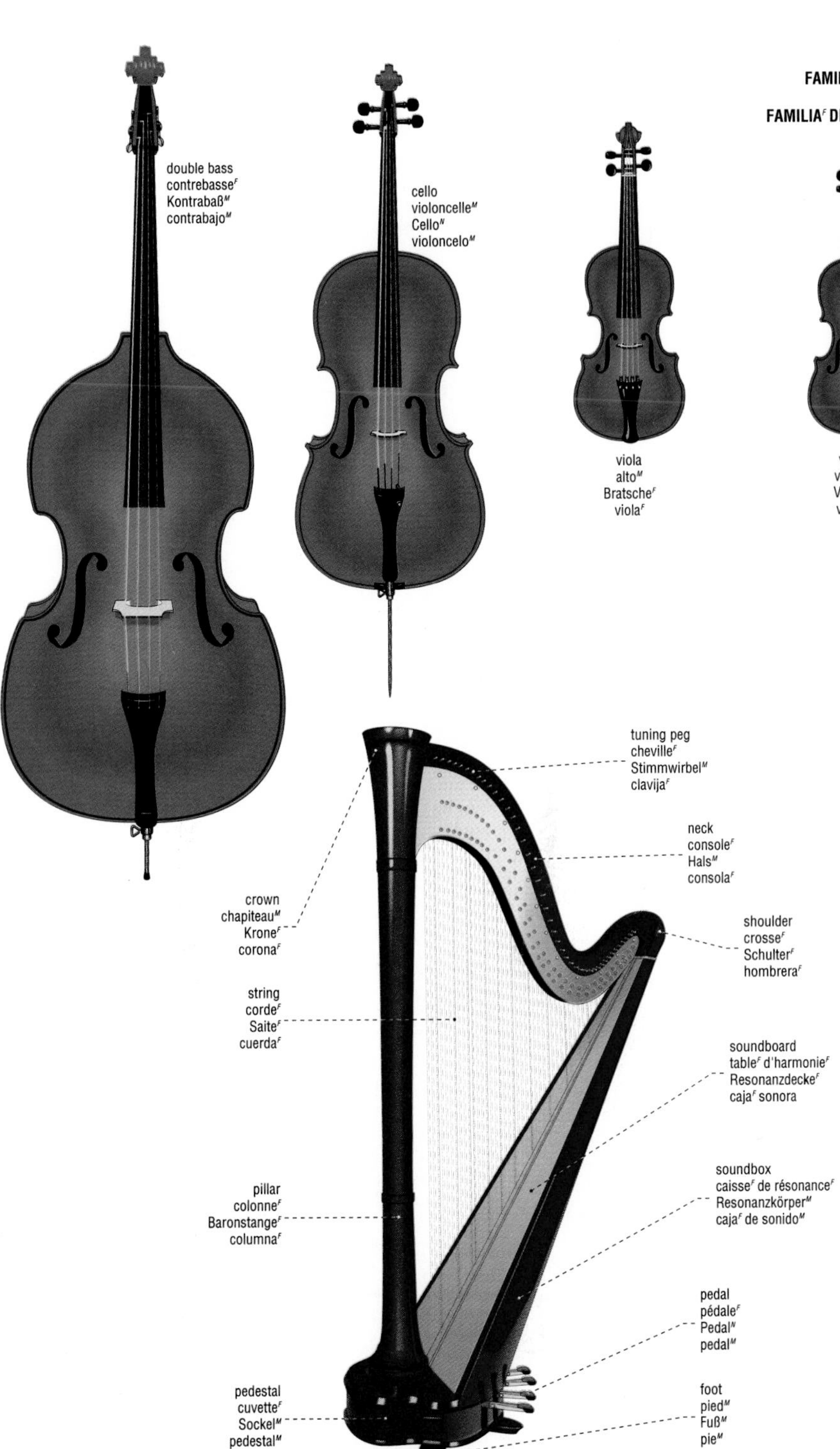

# STRINGED INSTRUMENTS
# INSTRUMENTS[M] À CORDES[F]
# SAITENINSTRUMENTE[N]
# INSTRUMENTOS[M] DE CUERDA[F]

## ACOUSTIC GUITAR
## GUITARE[F] ACOUSTIQUE
## AKUSTISCHE GITARRE[F]
## GUITARRA[F] CLÁSICA

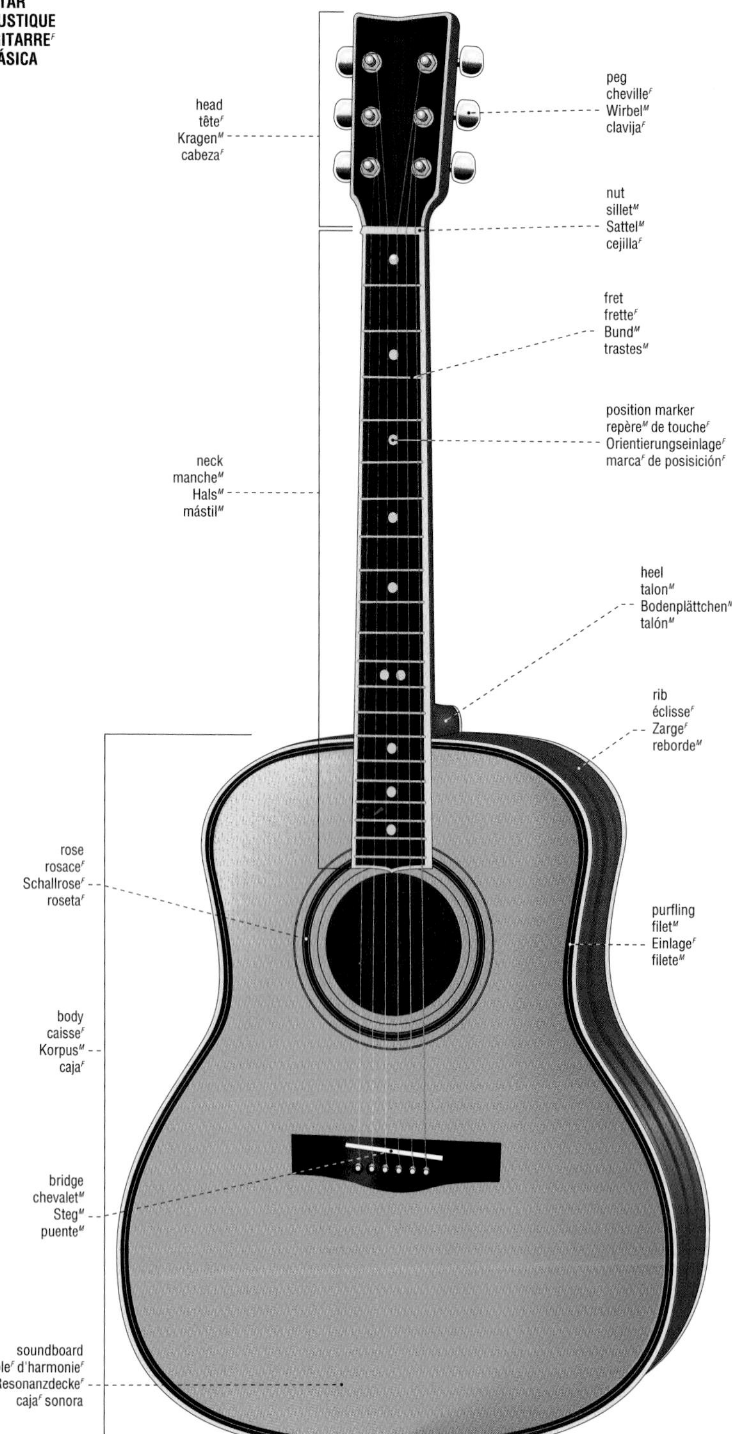

# ELECTRIC GUITAR
# GUITARE[F] ÉLECTRIQUE
# ELEKTRISCHE GITARRE[F]
# GUITARRA[F] ELÉCTRICA

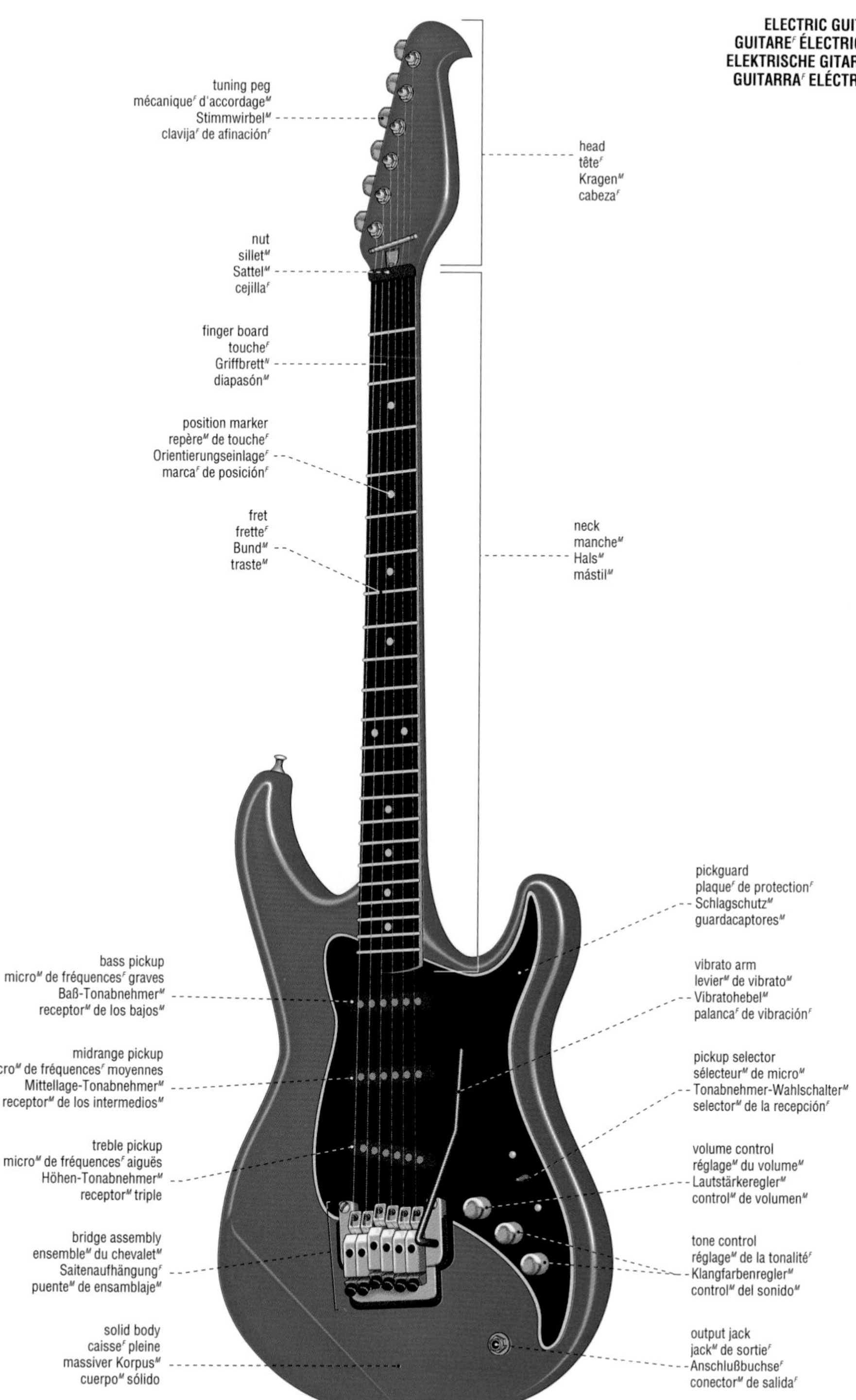

# WIND INSTRUMENTS
# INSTRUMENTS[M] À VENT[M]
# BLASINSTRUMENTE[N]
# INSTRUMENTOS[M] DE VIENTO[M]

## SAXOPHONE
## SAXOPHONE[M]
## SAXOPHON[N]
## SAXOFÓN[M]

## WOODWIND FAMILY
## FAMILLE[F] DES BOIS[M]
## FAMILIE[F] DER HOLZBLASINSTRUMENTE[N]
## FAMILIA[F] DE INSTRUMENTOS[M] DE MADERA[F]

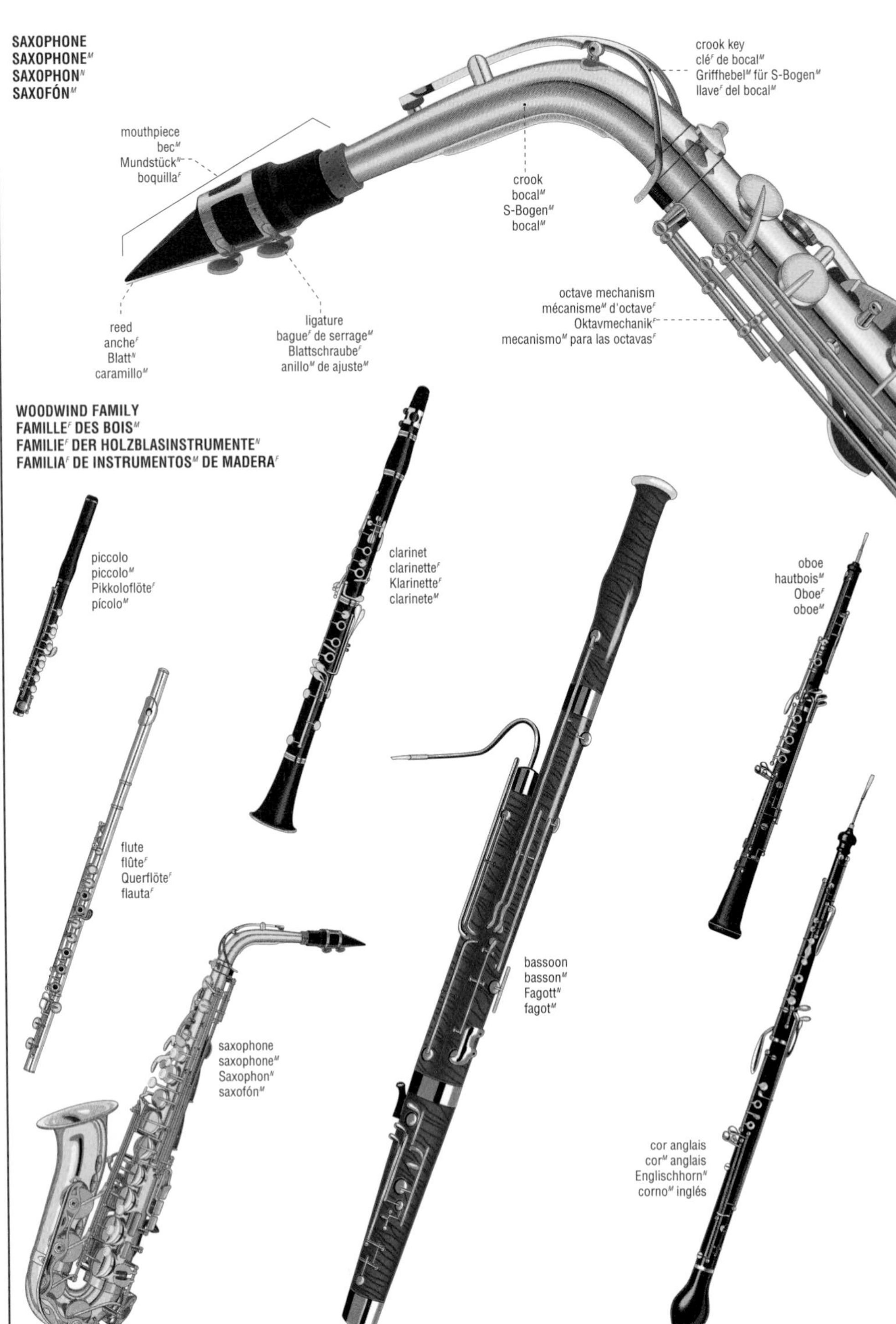

## REEDS
## ANCHES[F]
## BLÄTTER[N]
## CAÑAS[F]

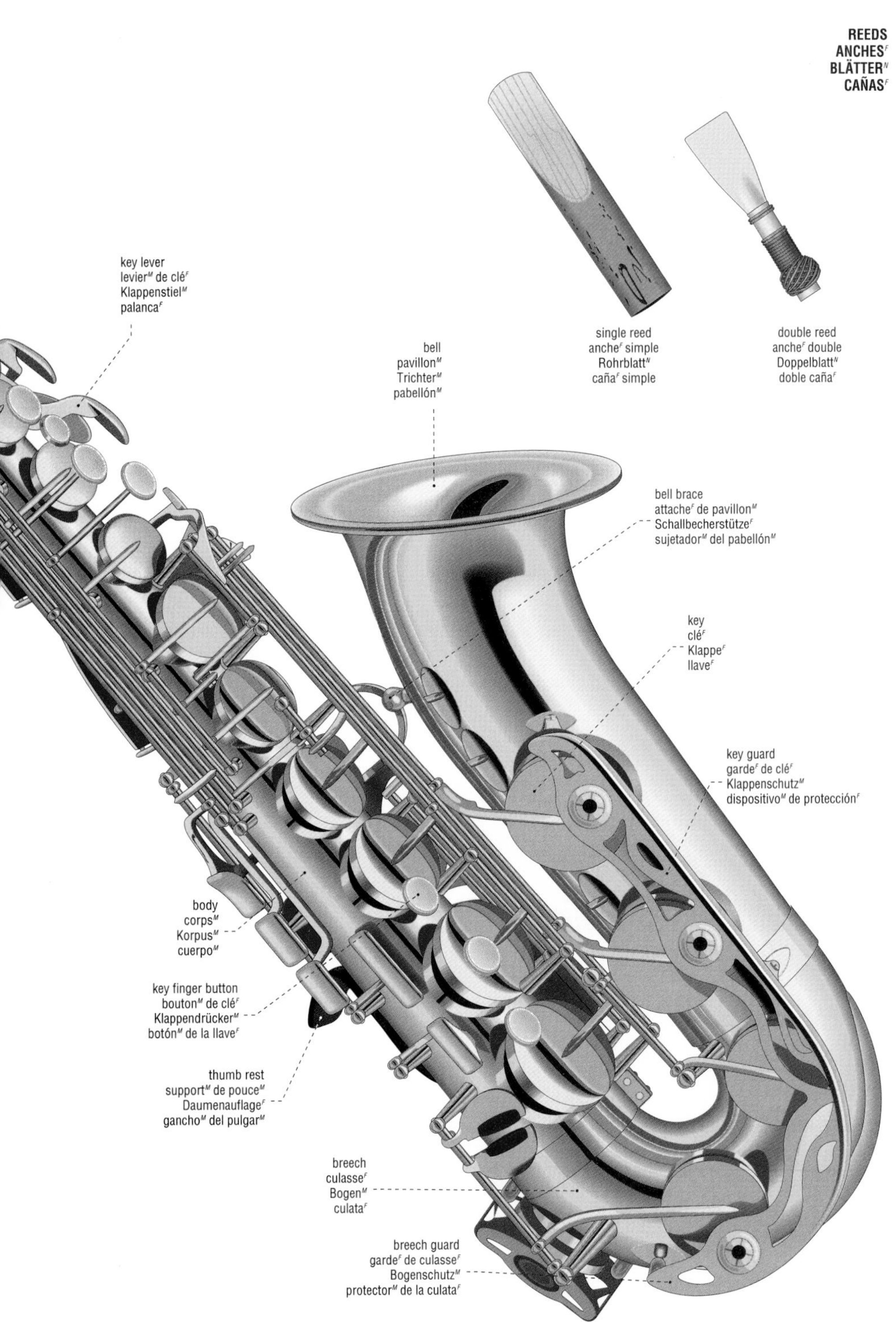

# WIND INSTRUMENTS
# INSTRUMENTS[M] À VENT[M]
# BLASINSTRUMENTE[N]
# INSTRUMENTOS[M] DE VIENTO[M]



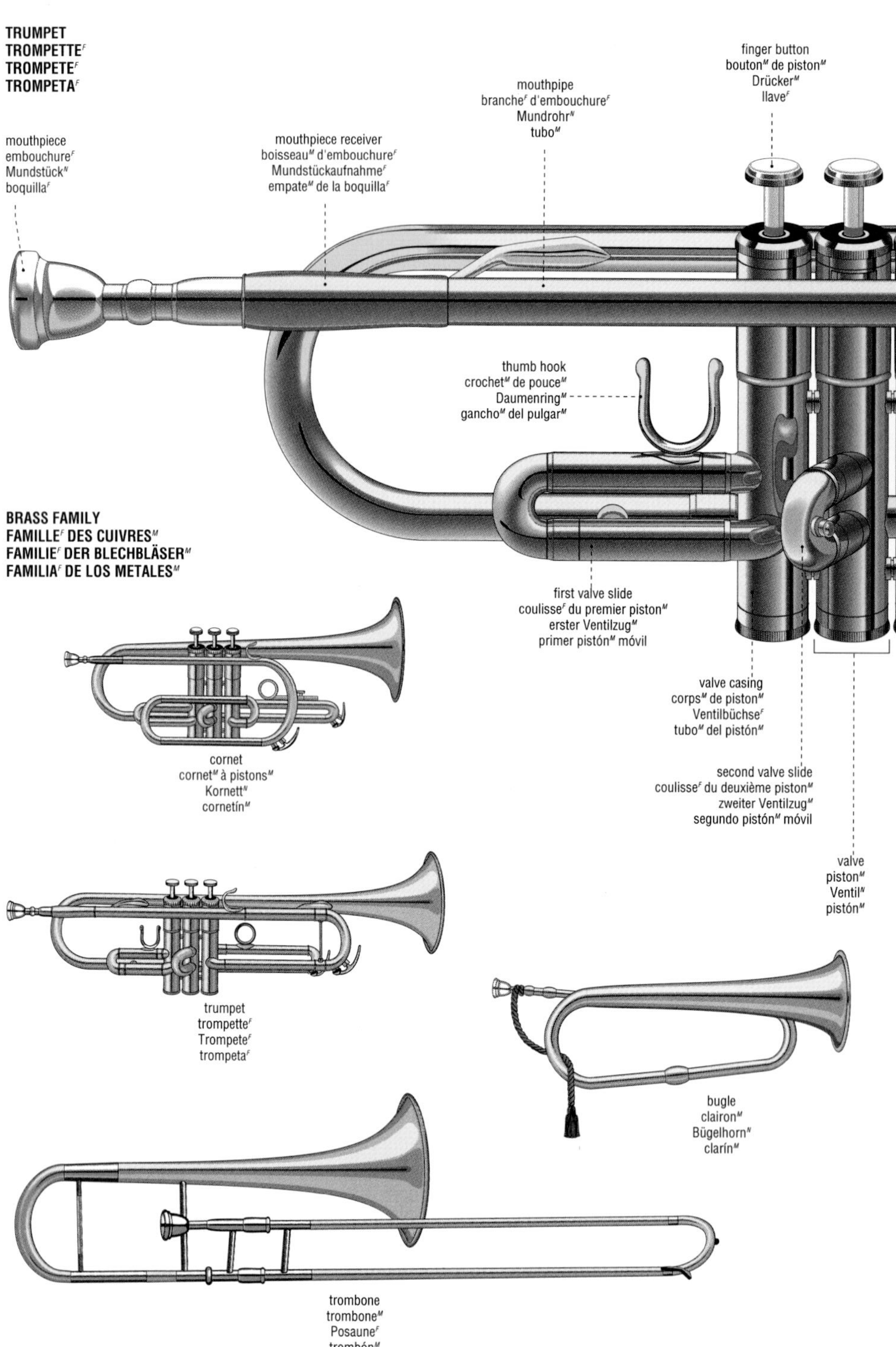

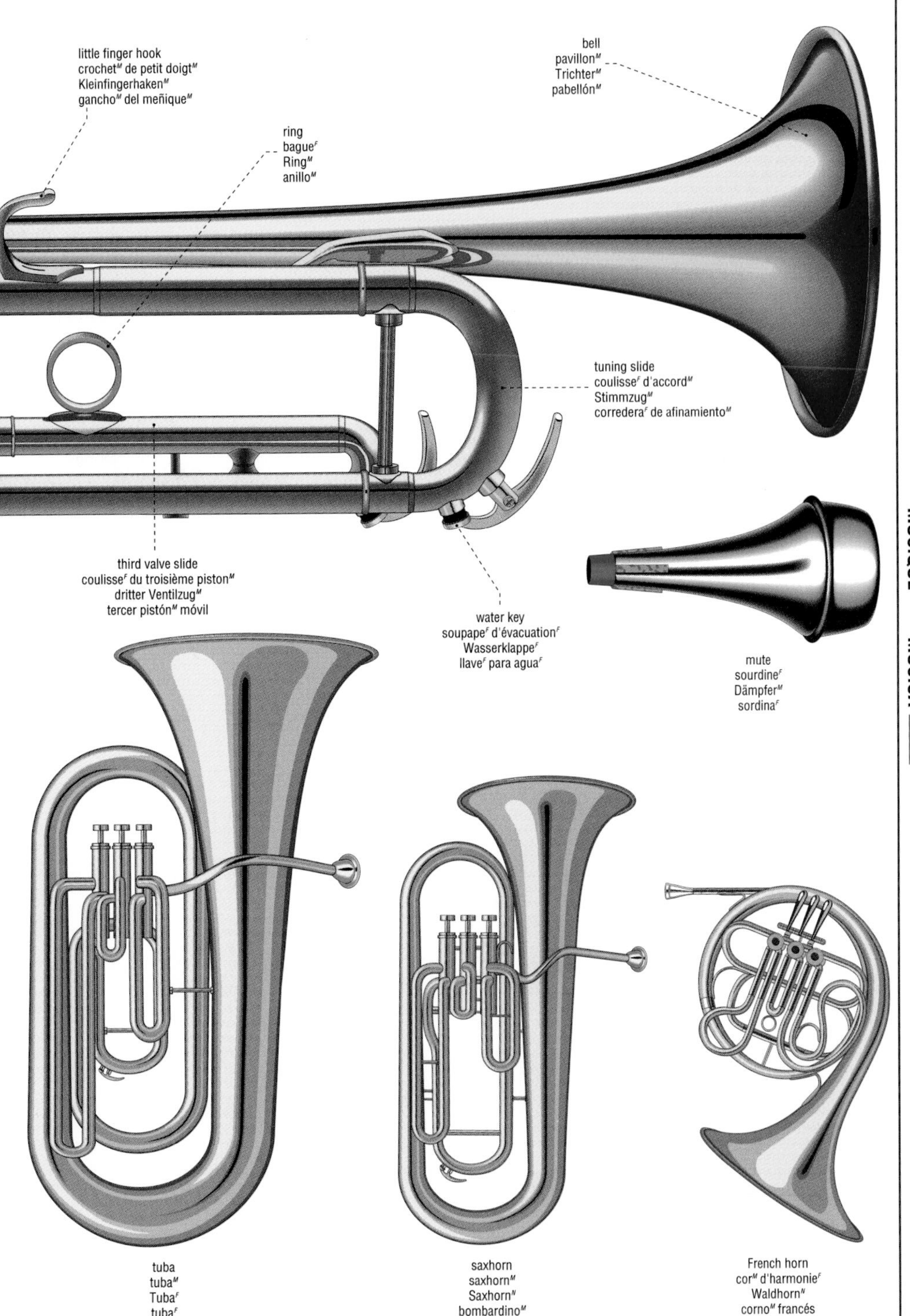

little finger hook
crochet de petit doigt
Kleinfingerhaken
gancho del meñique
ring
bague
Ring
anillo
bell
pavillon
Trichter
pabellón
tuning slide
coulisse d'accord
Stimmzug
corredera de afinamiento
third valve slide
coulisse du troisième piston
dritter Ventilzug
tercer pistón móvil
water key
soupape d'évacuation
Wasserklappe
llave para agua
mute
sourdine
Dämpfer
sordina
tuba
tuba
Tuba
tuba
saxhorn
saxhorn
Saxhorn
bombardino
French horn
cor d'harmonie
Waldhorn
corno francés

# PERCUSSION INSTRUMENTS
# INSTRUMENTS[M] À PERCUSSION[F]
# SCHLAGINSTRUMENTE[N]
# INSTRUMENTOS[M] DE PERCUSIÓN[F]

## DRUMS
## BATTERIE[F]
## TROMMELN[F]
## TAMBORES[M]

SNARE DRUM
CAISSE$^{F}$ CLAIRE
KLEINE TROMMEL$^{F}$
TAMBOR$^{M}$ DE TIRANTES$^{M}$
lug
attache$^{F}$
Böckchen$^{N}$
sujetador$^{M}$
tension rod
tringle$^{F}$ de tension$^{F}$
Stimmeinrichtung$^{F}$
varilla$^{F}$ de tensión$^{F}$
snare
cordes$^{F}$ de timbre$^{M}$
Schnarrsaite$^{F}$
cuerdas$^{F}$
snare strainer
tendeur$^{M}$ de timbre$^{M}$
Schnarrsaitenspanner$^{M}$
tensor$^{M}$ de las cuerdas$^{F}$
snare head
peau$^{F}$ de timbre$^{M}$
Resonanzfell$^{N}$
parche$^{M}$ inferior
sticks
baguettes$^{F}$
Stöcke$^{M}$
palillos$^{M}$
wire brush
balai$^{M}$ métallique
Jazzbesen$^{M}$
escobilla$^{F}$ metálica
mallets
mailloches$^{F}$
Schlegel$^{M}$
maza$^{F}$
tenor drum
caisse$^{F}$ roulante
Standtom$^{N}$
tamboril$^{M}$
KETTLEDRUM
TIMBALE$^{F}$
KESSELPAUKE$^{F}$
TIMBAL$^{M}$
drumhead
peau$^{F}$ de batterie$^{F}$
Schlagfell$^{N}$
parche$^{M}$ superior
tension screw
tirant$^{M}$
Spannschraube$^{F}$
barra$^{F}$ sujetadora
metal counterhoop
cercle$^{M}$ de serrage$^{M}$
Metallspannreifen$^{M}$
arco$^{M}$ tensor
tuning gauge
manomètre$^{M}$ d'accord$^{M}$
Stimmanzeiger$^{M}$
afinación$^{F}$
shell
fût$^{M}$
Kessel$^{M}$
concha$^{F}$
strut
châssis$^{M}$
Strebe$^{F}$
puntal$^{M}$
leg
pied$^{M}$
Bein$^{N}$
pata$^{F}$
tension rod
tringle$^{F}$ de tension$^{F}$
Stimmeinrichtung$^{F}$
varilla$^{F}$ de tensión$^{F}$
crown
couronne$^{F}$
Aufhängung$^{F}$
corona$^{F}$
caster
roulette$^{F}$
Rolle$^{F}$
ruedecilla$^{F}$
foot
pied$^{M}$
Bodenplatte$^{F}$
pata$^{F}$
pedal
pédale$^{F}$
Pedal$^{N}$
pedal$^{M}$

# PERCUSSION INSTRUMENTS
# INSTRUMENTS$^{M}$ À PERCUSSION$^{F}$
# SCHLAGINSTRUMENTE$^{N}$
# INSTRUMENTOS$^{M}$ DE PERCUSIÓN$^{F}$

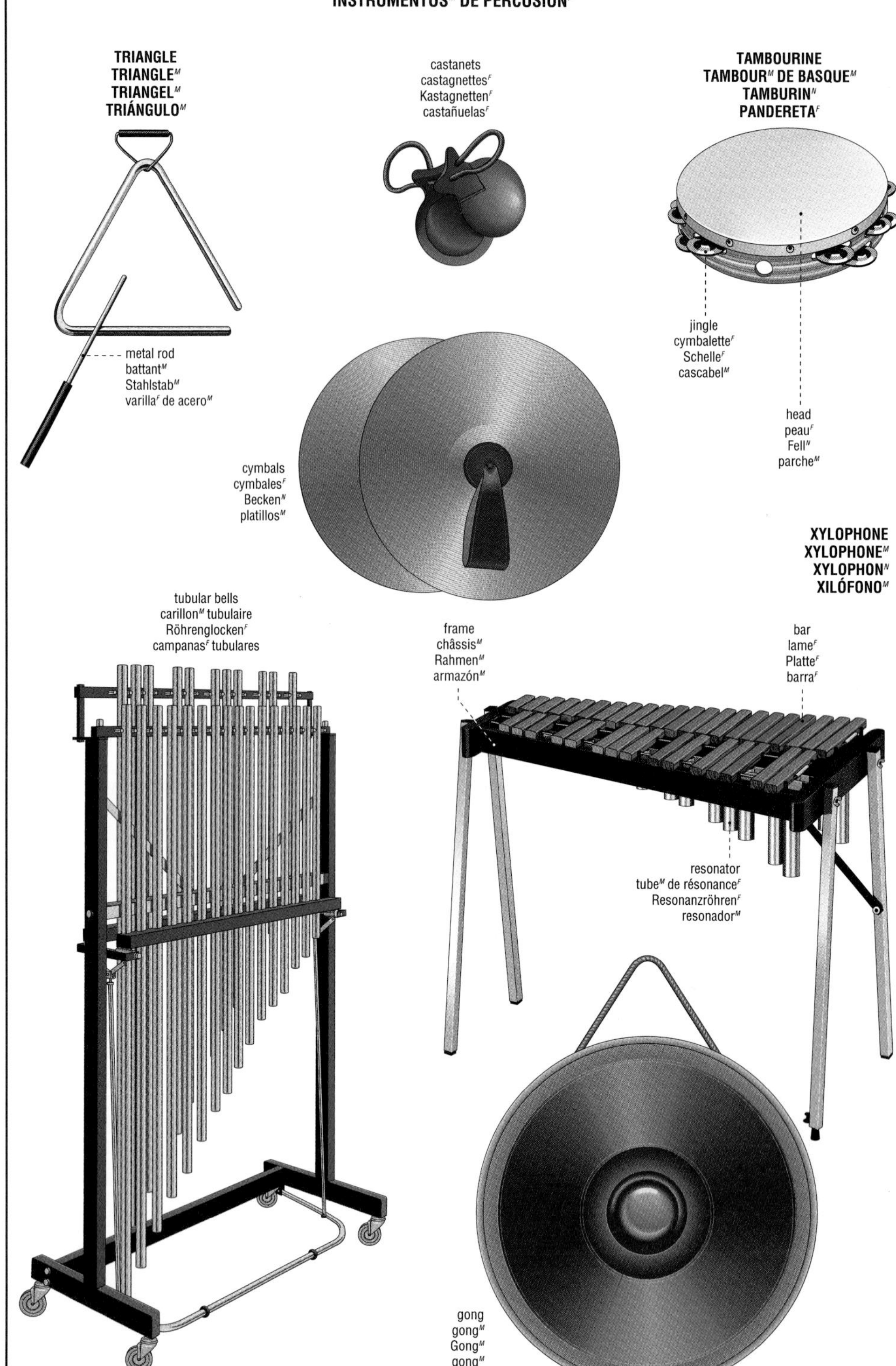

# ELECTRONIC INSTRUMENTS
# INSTRUMENTS$^{M}$ ÉLECTRONIQUES
# ELEKTRONISCHE INSTRUMENTE$^{N}$
# INSTRUMENTOS$^{M}$ ELECTRÓNICOS

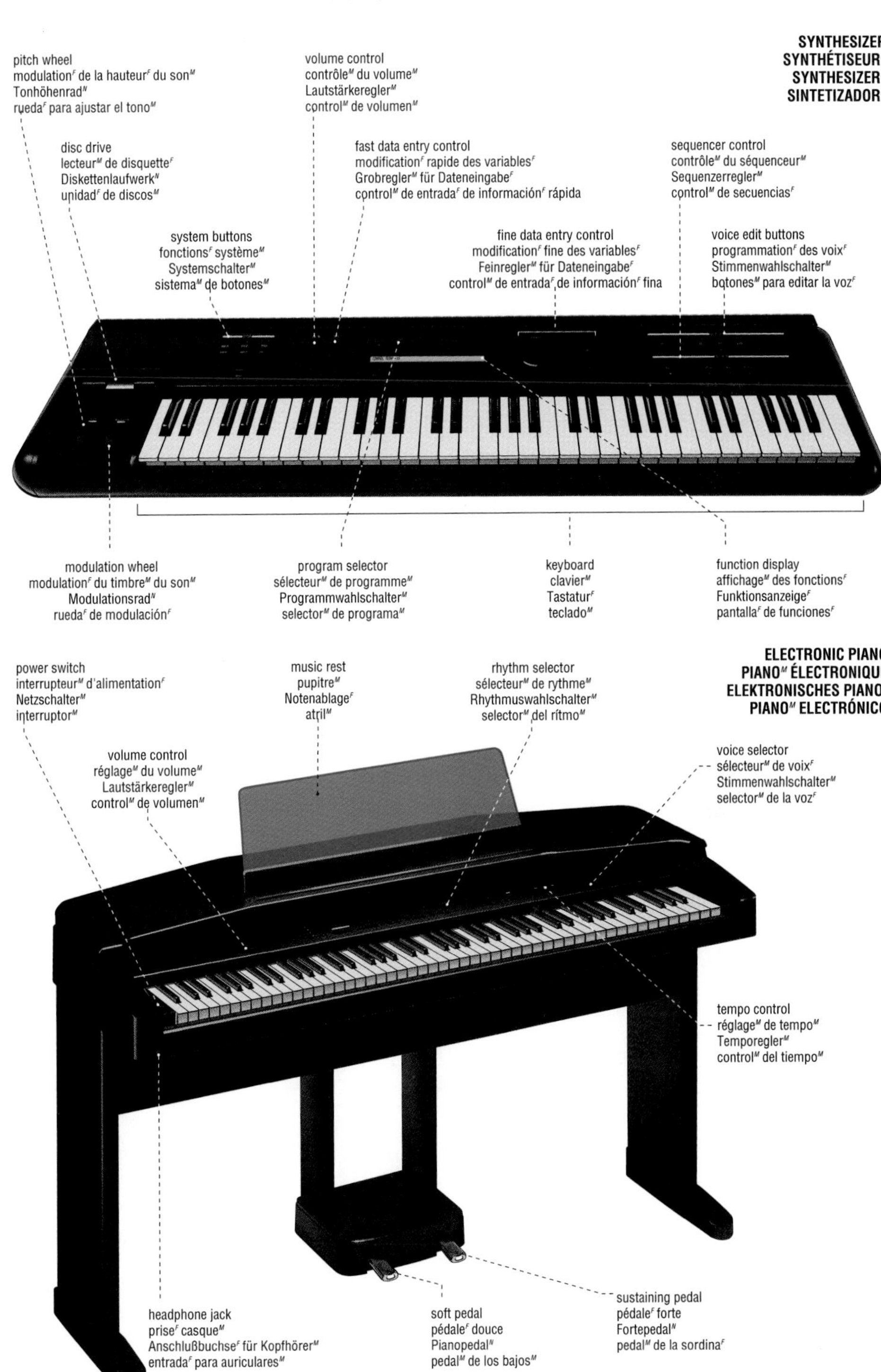

# SYMPHONY ORCHESTRA
# ORCHESTRE[M] SYMPHONIQUE
# SINFONIEORCHESTER[N]
# ORQUESTA[F] SINFÓNICA

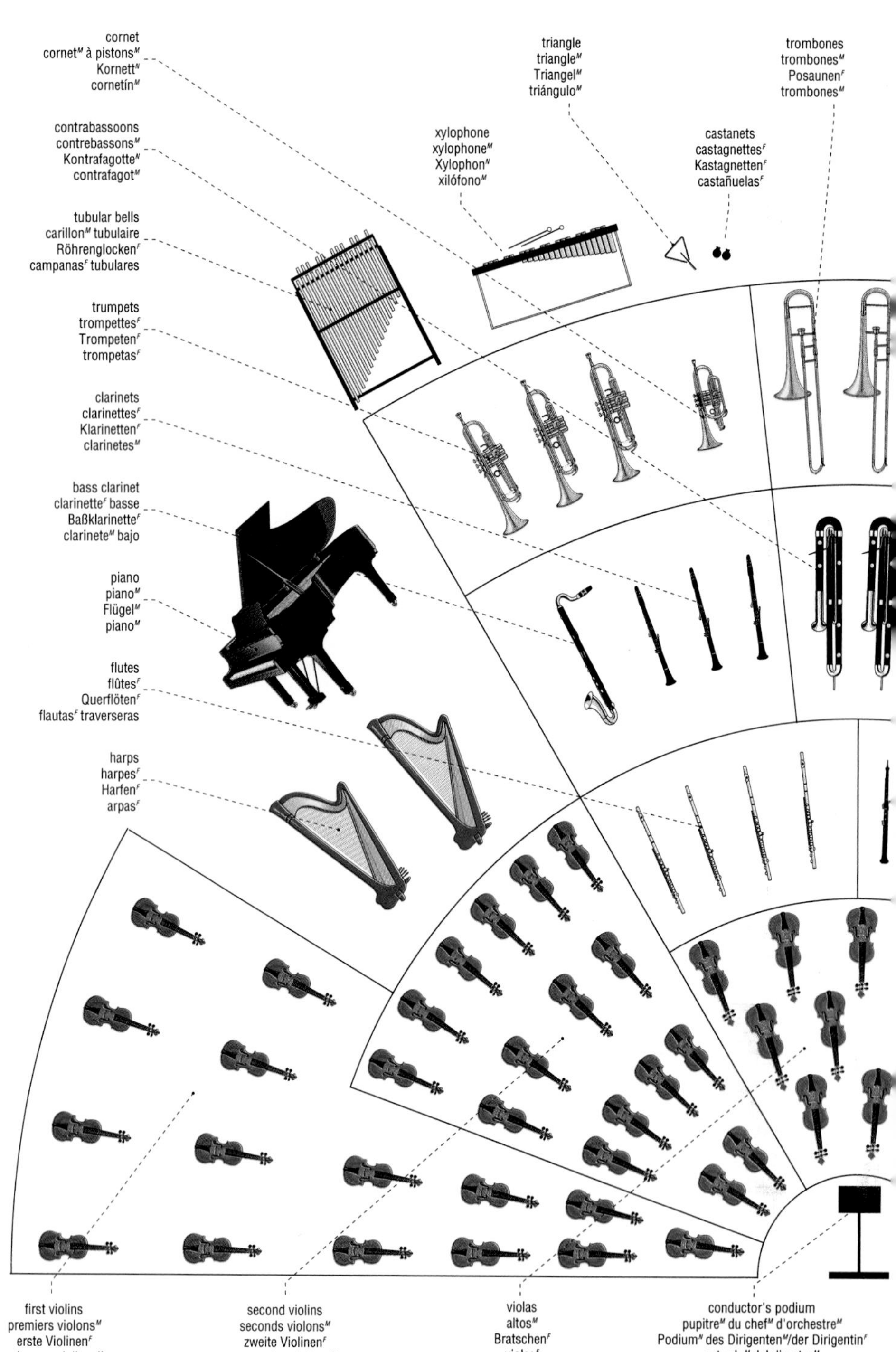

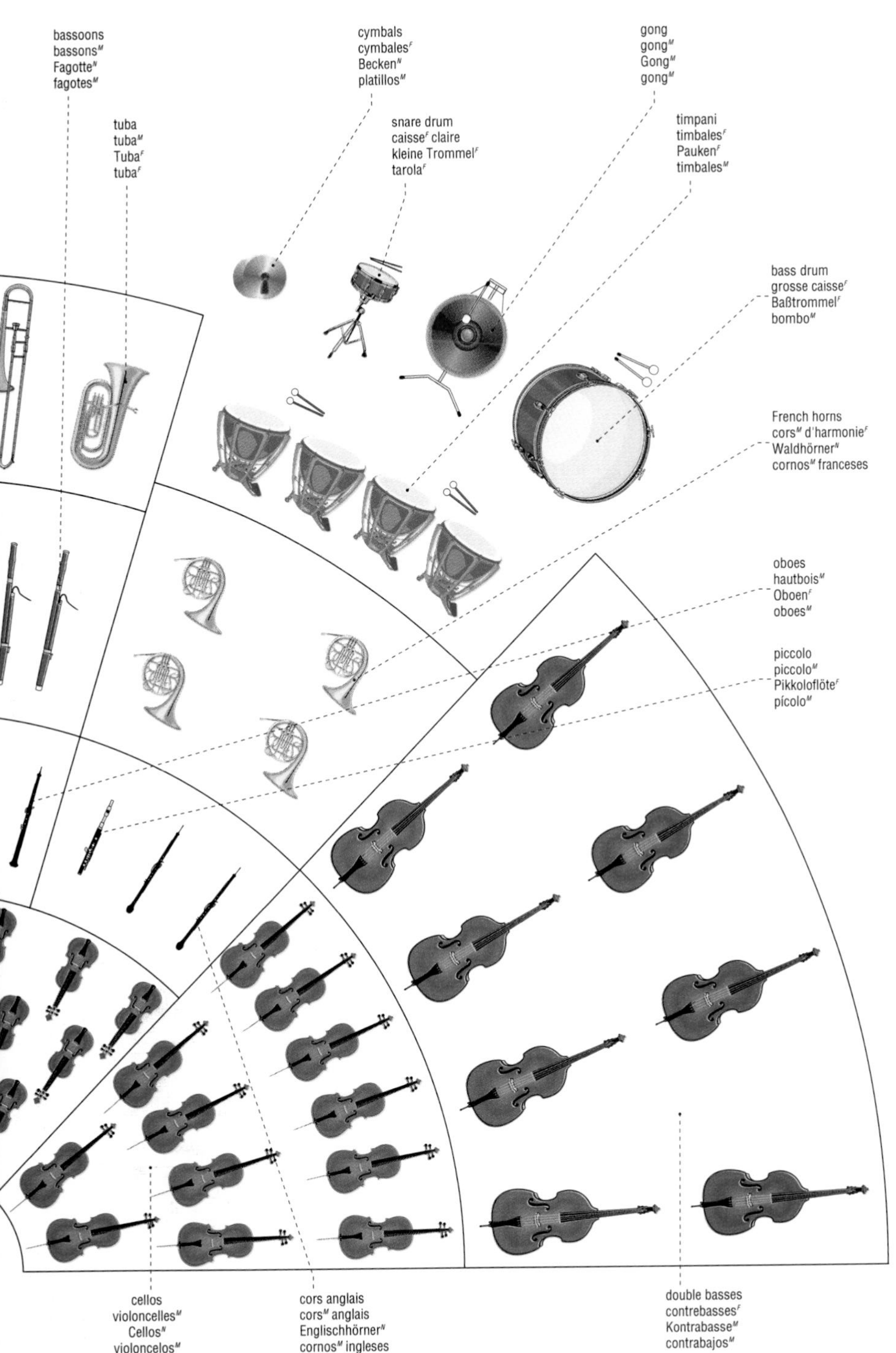
bassoons
bassons
Fagotte
fagotes
tuba
tuba
Tuba
tuba
cymbals
cymbales
Becken
platillos
snare drum
caisse claire
kleine Trommel
tarola
gong
gong
Gong
gong
timpani
timbales
Pauken
timbales
bass drum
grosse caisse
Baßtrommel
bombo
French horns
cors d'harmonie
Waldhörner
cornos franceses
oboes
hautbois
Oboen
oboes
piccolo
piccolo
Pikkoloflöte
pícolo
cellos
violoncelles
Cellos
violoncelos
cors anglais
cors anglais
Englischhörner
cornos ingleses
double basses
contrebasses
Kontrabasse
contrabajos

## EXAMPLES OF INSTRUMENTAL GROUPS
## EXEMPLES[M] DE GROUPES[M] INSTRUMENTAUX
## BEISPIELE[N] FÜR INSTRUMENTALGRUPPIERUNGEN[F]
## EJEMPLOS[M] DE CONJUNTOS[M] INSTRUMENTALES

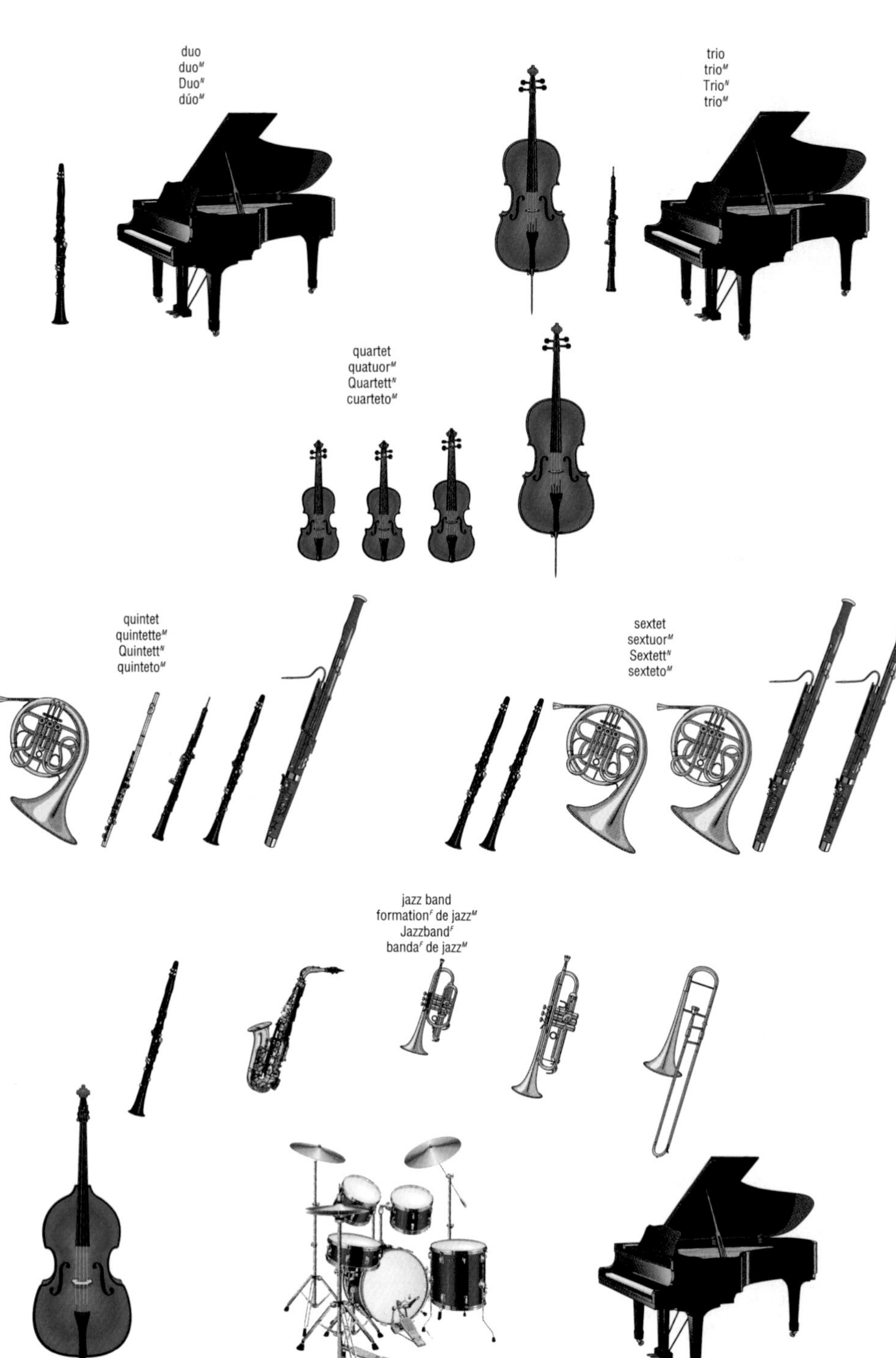

# CREATIVE LEISURE ACTIVITIES
# LOISIRS DE CRÉATION
# KREATIVE FREIZEITAKTIVITÄTEN
# TRABAJOS MANUALES

SUMMARY

# SEWING
# COUTURE[F]
# NÄHEN[N]
# COSTURA[F]

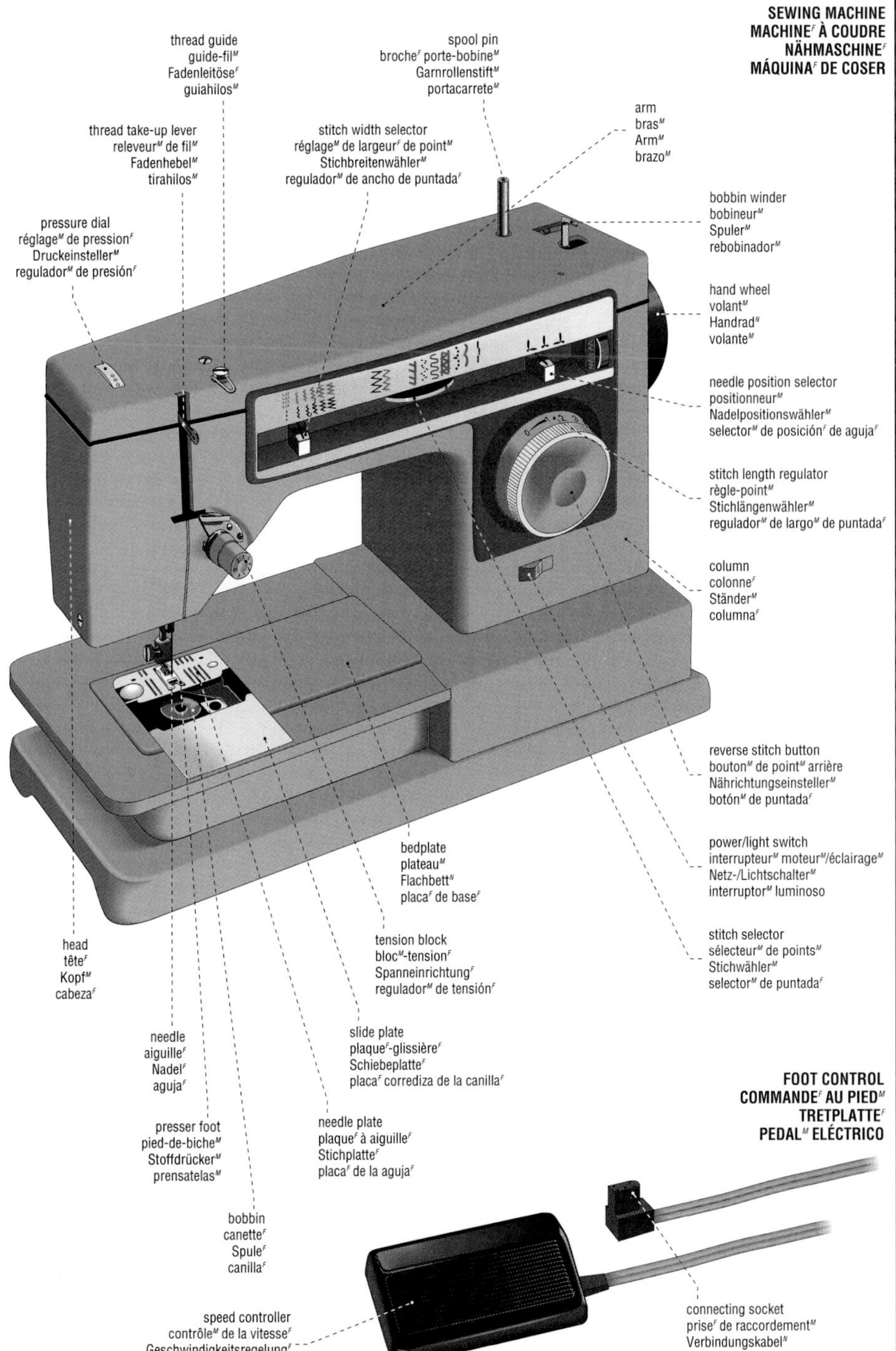

# SEWING
# COUTURE^F
# NÄHEN^N
# COSTURA^F



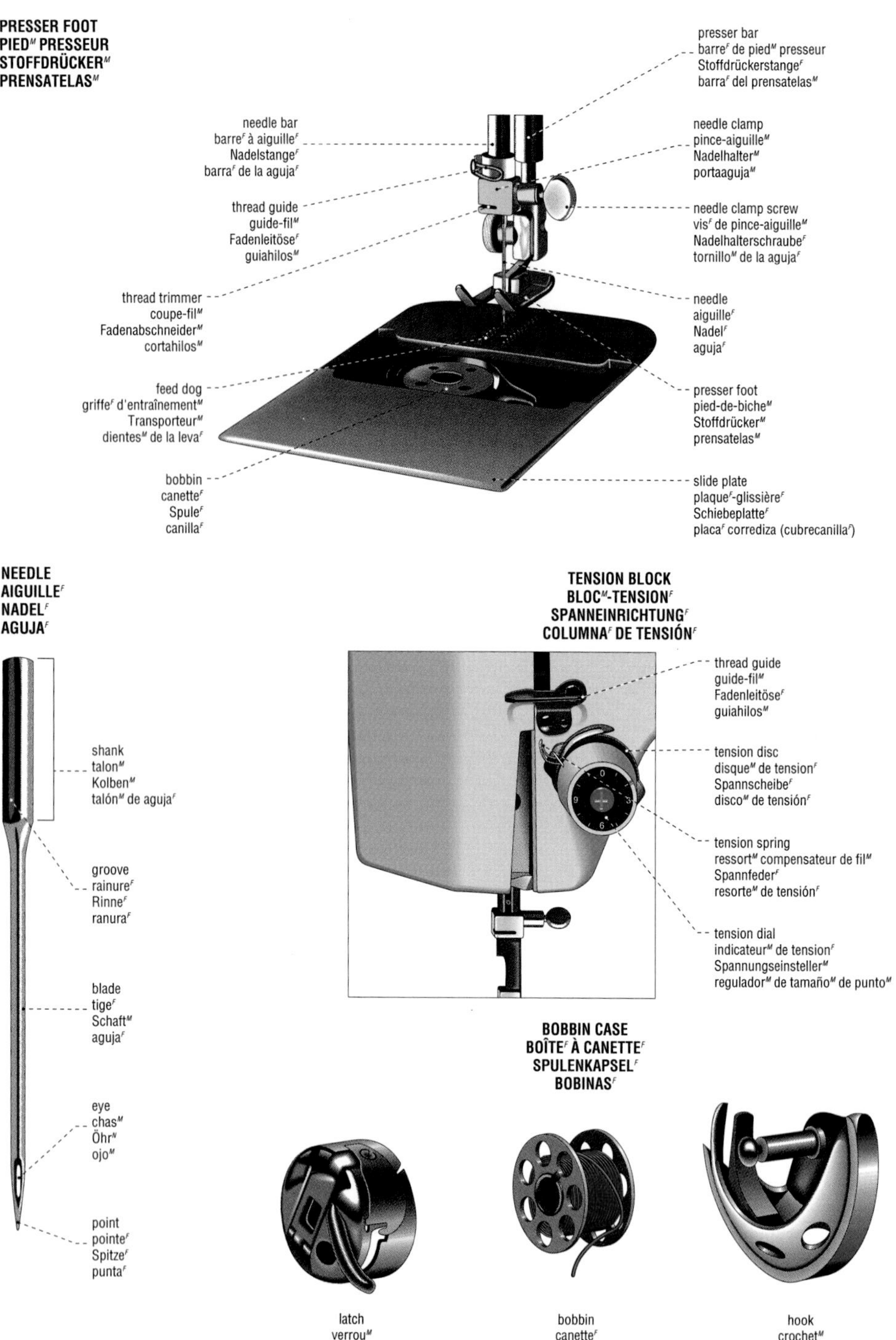

**ACCESSORIES**
**ACCESSOIRES[M]**
**ZUBEHÖR[N]**
**ACCESORIOS[M]**

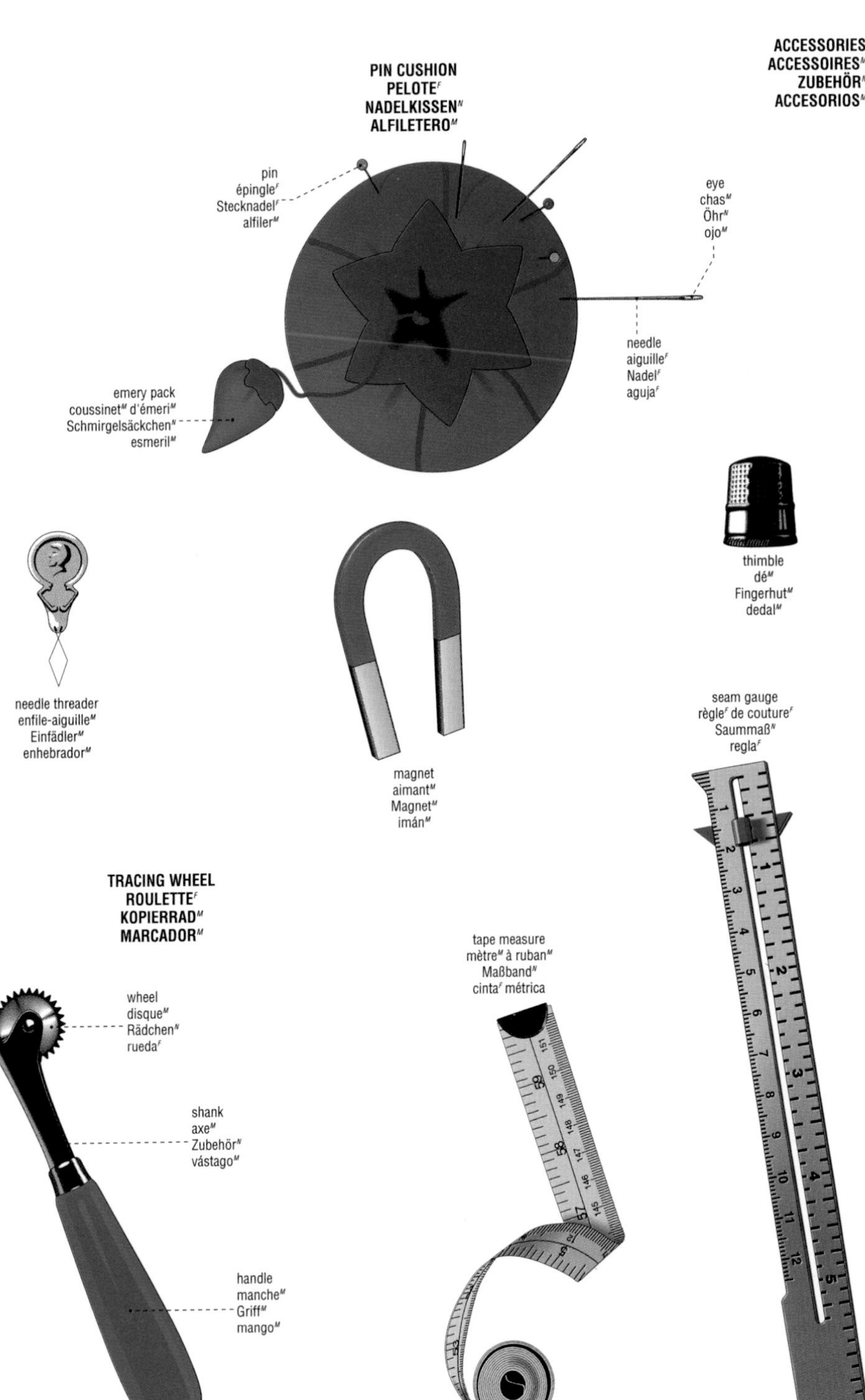

# SEWING
# COUTURE[F]
# NÄHEN[N]
# COSTURA[F]

## ACCESSORIES
## ACCESSOIRES[M]
## ZUBEHÖR[N]
## ACCESORIOS[M] DE COSTURA[F]

**scissors**
**ciseaux[M]**
**Schere[F]**
**tijeras[F] de modista[F]**

blade
lame[F]
Blatt[N]
hoja[F] de las tijeras[F]

pivot
entablure[F]
Schloß[N]
eje[M]

edge
tranchant[M]
Schneide[F]
filo[M]

shank
branche[F]
Halm[M]
mango[M]

handle
anneau[M]
Griff[M]
ojo[M]

dressmaker's model
mannequin[M]
Schneiderbüste[F]
maniquí[M]

pinking shears
ciseaux[M] à denteler
Zickzackschere[F]
tijeras[F] para rematar

skirt marker
arrondisseur[M]
Rockabrunder[M]
marcador[M] del dobladillo[M]

## LINING FABRICS
## TISSUS[M] DE SOUTIEN[M]
## FUTTERSTOFFE[M]
## FORRO[M] Y ENTRETELAS[F]

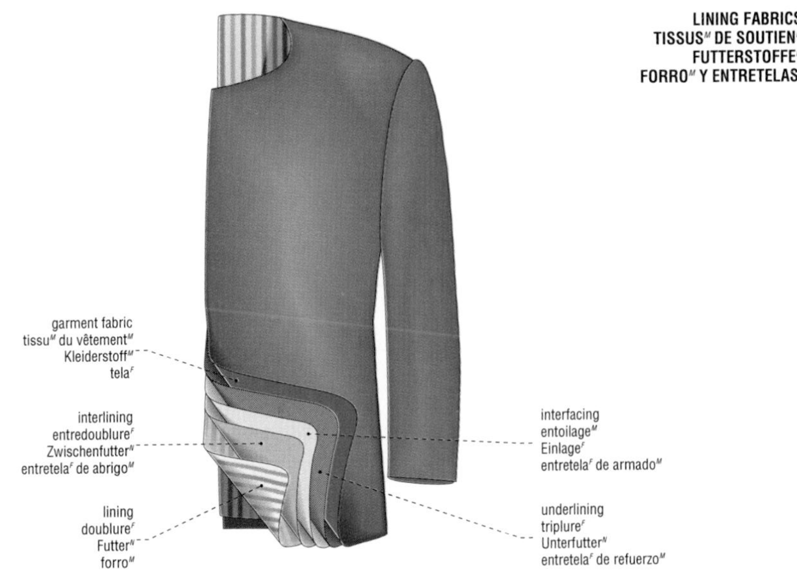


## PATTERN
## PATRON[M]
## SCHNITTMUSTER[N]
## PATRÓN[M]

cutting line
ligne[F] de coupe[F]
Schnittlinie[F]
línea[F] de corte[M]

seam line
ligne[F] de bâti[M]
Nahtlinie[F]
línea[F] de costura[F]

marking dot
point[M] de repère[M]
Markierungspunkt[M]
punto[M]

seam allowance
rentré[M]
Nahtzugabe[F]
pestaña[F]

alteration line
ligne[F] de modification[F]
Änderungslinie[F]
línea[F] para modificaciones[F]

dart
pince[F]
Abnäher[M]
pinzas[F]

notch
cran[M]
Ausschnitt[M]
pico[M] muesca[F]

fold line
pliure[F]
Stoffbruch[M]
doblez[M]

zip line
ligne[F] de piqûre[F] de la fermeture[F]
Reißverschlußlinie[F]
posición[F] de la cremallera[F]

lengthwise grain
droit fil[M]
Längsfaden[M]
pinzas[F] verticales

hemline
ligne[F] d'ourlet[M]
Saum[M]
línea[F] del dobladillo[M]

# SEWING
# COUTURE[F]
# NÄHEN[N]
# COSTURA[F]

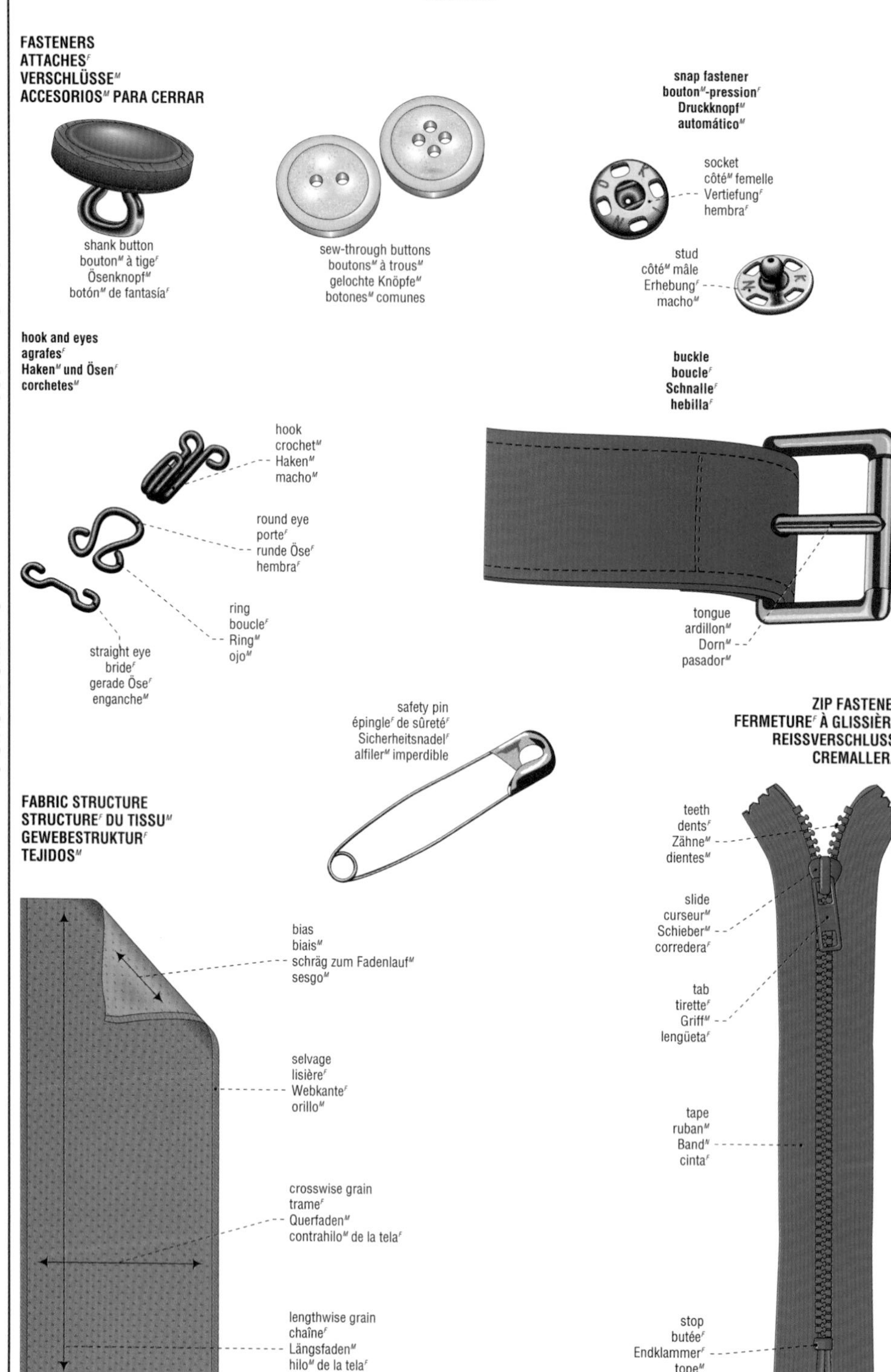

# KNITTING
# TRICOT[M]
# STRICKEN[N]
# TEJIDO[M] DE PUNTO[M]

## KNITTING NEEDLES
## AIGUILLES[F] À TRICOTER
## STRICKNADELN[F]
## AGUJAS[F] PARA TEJER

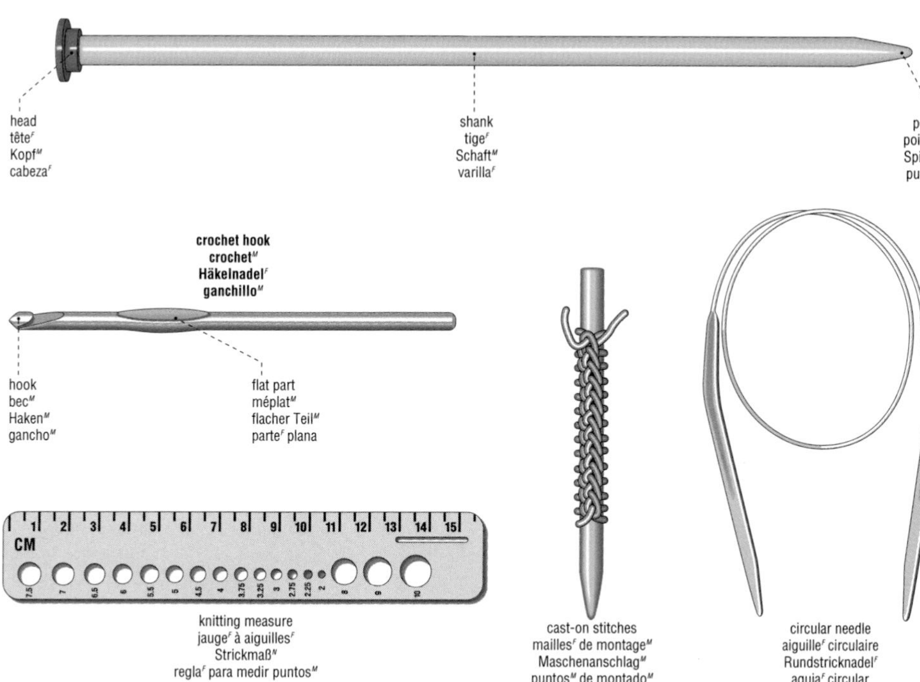


## STITCH PATTERNS
## POINTS[M] DE TRICOT[M]
## STRICKMUSTER[N]
## TIPOS[M] DE PUNTO[M]

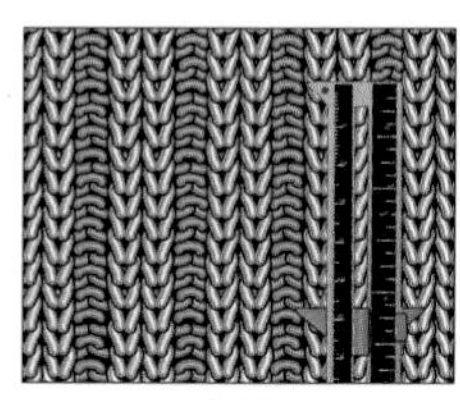

sample
échantillon[M]
Maschenprobe[F]
muestra[F]

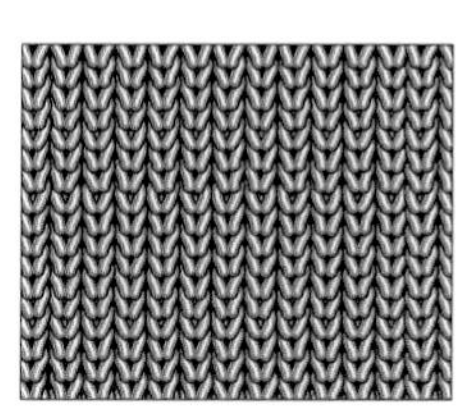

stocking stitch
point[M] de jersey[M]
Glattstrick[M]
derecho[M]

garter stitch
point[M] mousse[F]
Krausstrick[M]
revés[M]

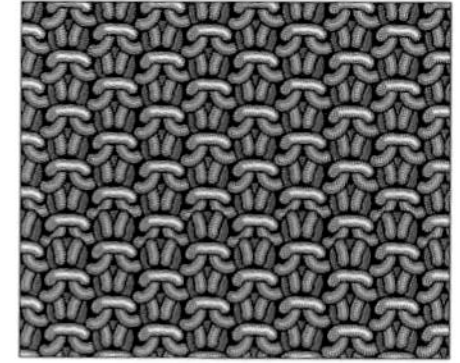

moss stitch
point[M] de riz[M]
Gerstenkornmuster[N]
punto[M] de musgo[M]

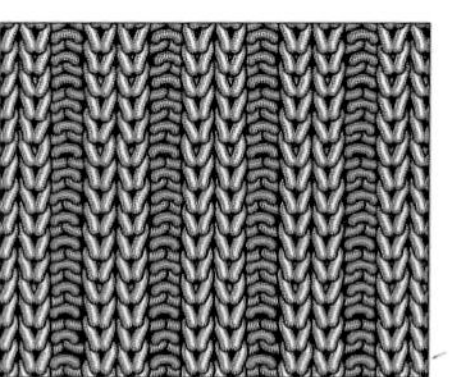

rib stitch
point[M] de côtes[F]
Perlrippen[F]
punto[M] de respiguilla[F]

basket stitch
point[M] de damier[M]
Korbstich[M]
punto[M] de malla[F]

cable stitch
point[M] de torsades[F]
Zopfmuster[N]
punto[M] de ochos[M]

# KNITTING MACHINE
# MACHINE^F À TRICOTER
# STRICKMASCHINE^F
# MÁQUINA DE TRICOTAR

## NEEDLE BED AND CARRIAGES
## FONTURE^F ET CHARIOTS^M
## NADELBETT^N UND SCHLITTEN^M
## TRICOTADORAS^F

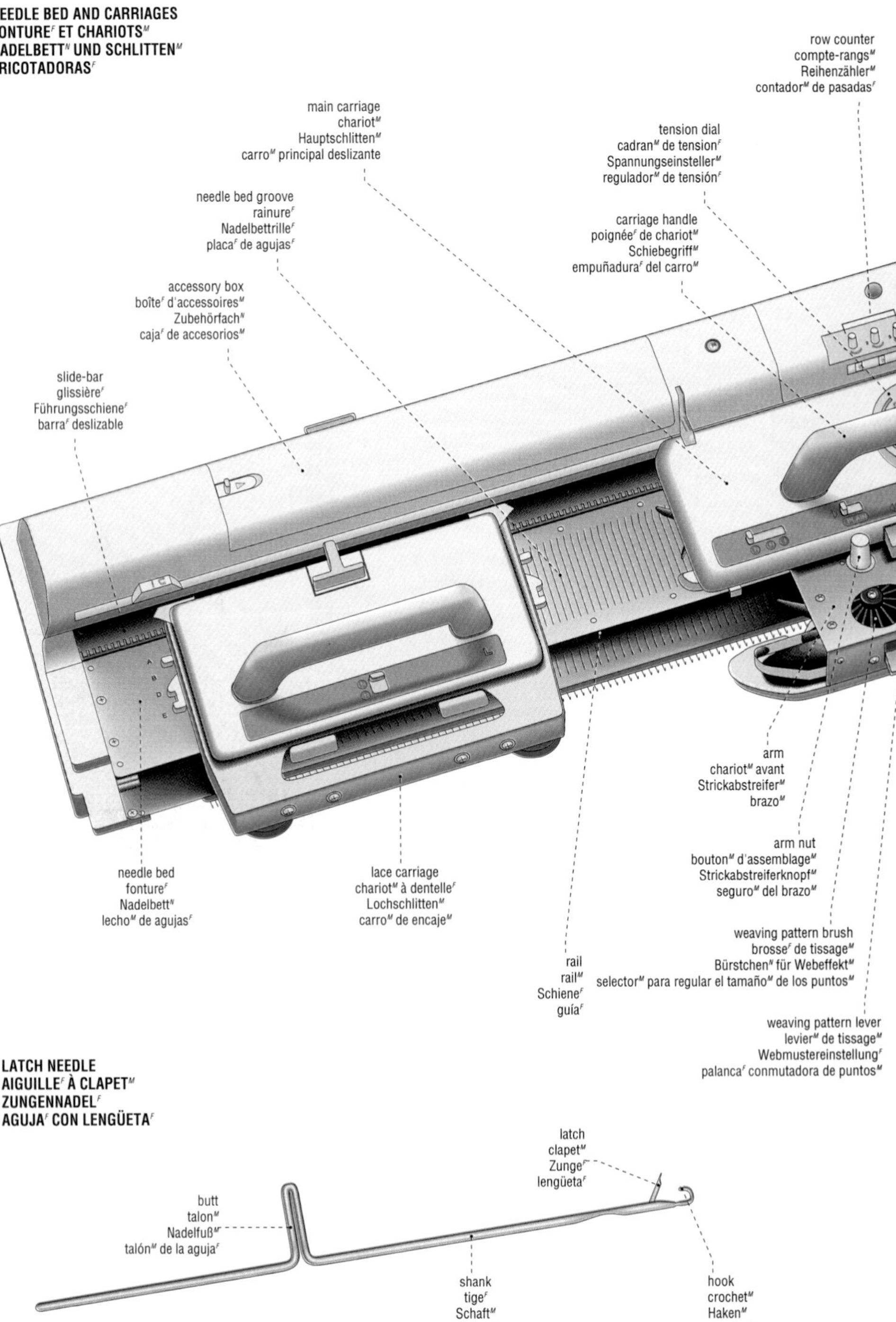


## LATCH NEEDLE
## AIGUILLE^F À CLAPET^M
## ZUNGENNADEL^F
## AGUJA^F CON LENGÜETA^F

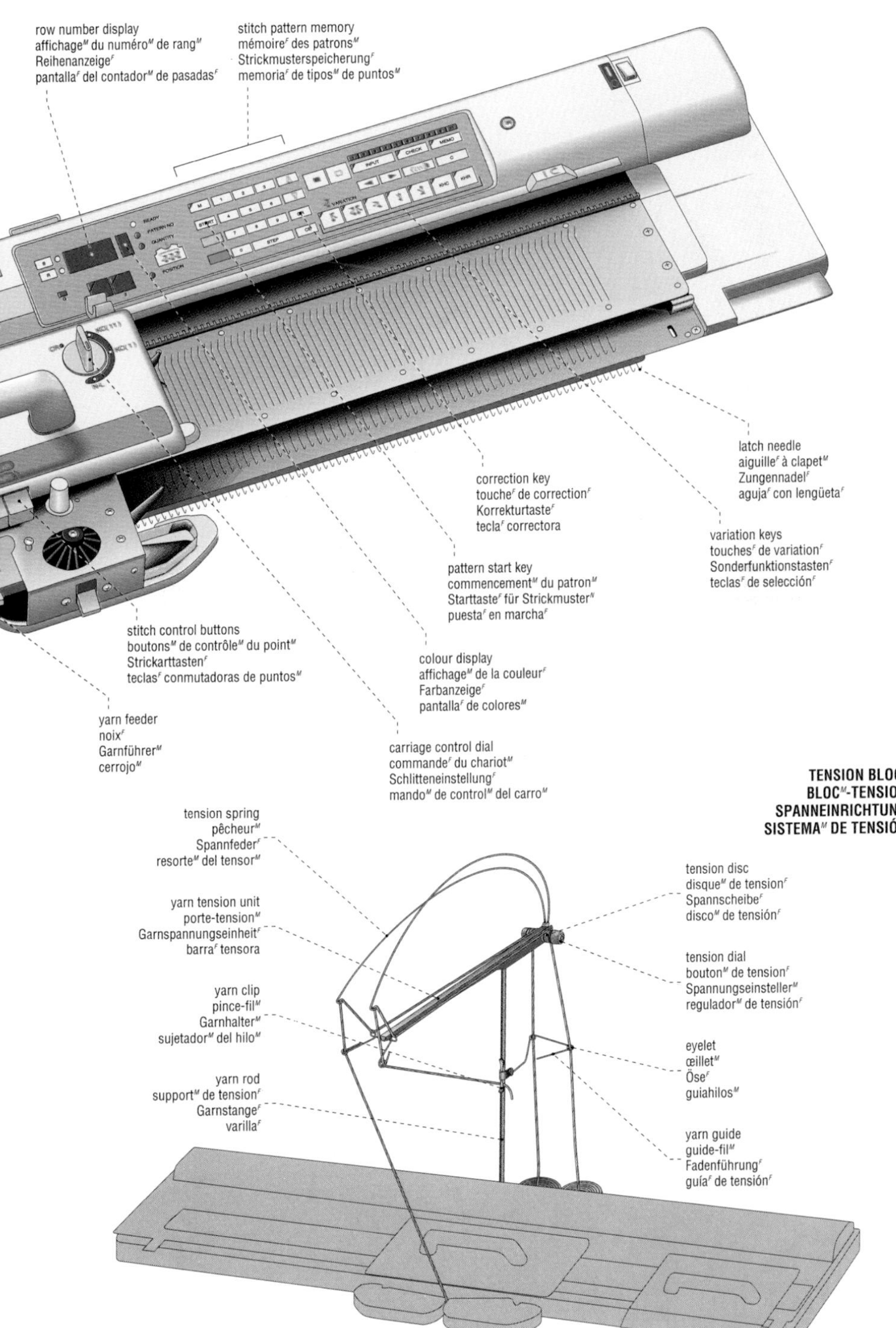
row number display
affichage[M] du numéro[M] de rang[M]
Reihenanzeige[F]
pantalla[F] del contador[M] de pasadas[F]
stitch pattern memory
mémoire[F] des patrons[M]
Strickmusterspeicherung[F]
memoria[F] de tipos[M] de puntos[M]
latch needle
aiguille[F] à clapet[M]
Zungennadel[F]
aguja[F] con lengüeta[F]
correction key
touche[F] de correction[F]
Korrekturtaste[F]
tecla[F] correctora
variation keys
touches[F] de variation[F]
Sonderfunktionstasten[F]
teclas[F] de selección[F]
pattern start key
commencement[M] du patron[M]
Starttaste[F] für Strickmuster[N]
puesta[F] en marcha[F]
stitch control buttons
boutons[M] de contrôle[M] du point[M]
Strickarttasten[F]
teclas[F] conmutadoras de puntos[M]
colour display
affichage[M] de la couleur[F]
Farbanzeige[F]
pantalla[F] de colores[M]
yarn feeder
noix[F]
Garnführer[M]
cerrojo[M]
carriage control dial
commande[F] du chariot[M]
Schlitteneinstellung[F]
mando[M] de control[M] del carro[M]
TENSION BLOCK
BLOC[M]-TENSION[F]
SPANNEINRICHTUNG[F]
SISTEMA[M] DE TENSIÓN[F]
tension spring
pêcheur[M]
Spannfeder[F]
resorte[M] del tensor[M]
tension disc
disque[M] de tension[F]
Spannscheibe[F]
disco[M] de tensión[F]
yarn tension unit
porte-tension[M]
Garnspannungseinheit[F]
barra[F] tensora
tension dial
bouton[M] de tension[F]
Spannungseinsteller[M]
regulador[M] de tensión[F]
yarn clip
pince-fil[M]
Garnhalter[M]
sujetador[M] del hilo[M]
eyelet
œillet[M]
Öse[F]
guiahilos[M]
yarn rod
support[M] de tension[F]
Garnstange[F]
varilla[F]
yarn guide
guide-fil[M]
Fadenführung[F]
guía[F] de tensión[F]

# BOBBIN LACE
# DENTELLE^F AUX FUSEAUX^M
# KLÖPPELSPITZE^F
# ENCAJE^M DE BOLILLOS^M

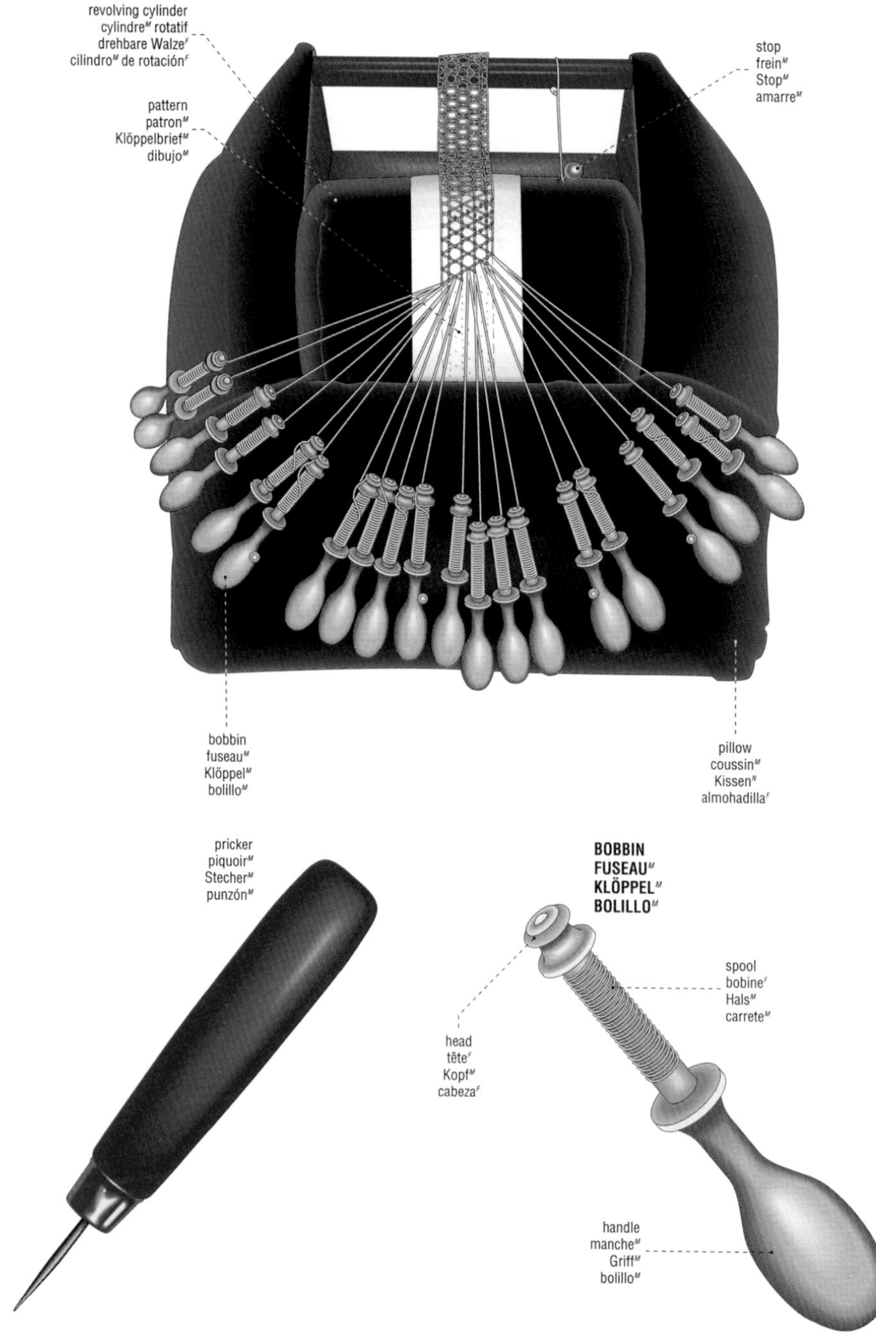

# EMBROIDERY
# BRODERIE[F]
# STICKEREI[F]
# BORDADO[M]



## FRAME
## MÉTIER[M] À BRODER
## RAHMEN[M]
## BASTIDOR[M]

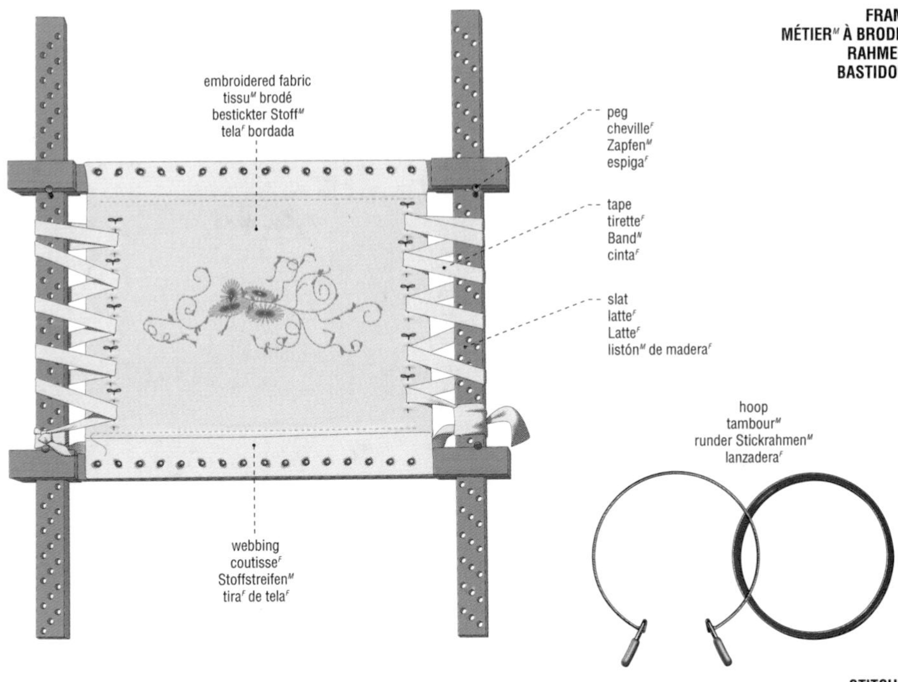


## STITCHES
## CATÉGORIES[F] DE POINTS[M]
## STICKSTICHE[M]
## TIPOS[M] DE PUNTOS[M]

**cross stitches**
**points[M] croisés**
**Kreuzstiche[M]**
**puntos[M] de cruz[F]**

chevron stitch
point[M] de chausson[M]
Smokstich[M]
punto[M] de escapulario[M]

herringbone stitch
point[M] de chevron[M]
Hexenstich[M]
punto[M] de cruz[F]

**flat stitches**
**points[M] plats**
**Plattstiche[M]**
**puntos[M] de relleno[M]**

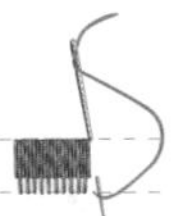

long and short stitch
point[M] passé empiétant
langer und kurzer Spannstich[M]
lanzado[M] desigual

fishbone stitch
point[M] d'arête[F]
Zopfstich[M]
punto[M] de espiga[F]

**couched stitches**
**points[M] couchés**
**Überfangstiche[M]**
**bordados[M] planos**

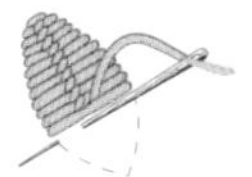

Romanian couching stitch
point[M] roumain
rumänischer Überfangstich[M]
bordado[M] plano

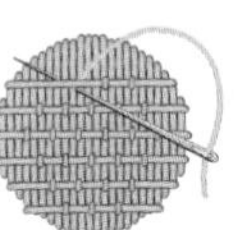

Oriental couching stitch
point[M] d'Orient[M]
orientalischer Überfangstich[M]
relleno[M] alternado

**knot stitches**
**points[M] noués**
**Knötchenstiche[M]**
**puntos[M] de relleno[M] sueltos**

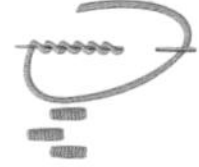

bullion stitch
point[M] de poste[F]
Tressenstich[M]
pespunte[M]

French knot stitch
point[M] de nœud[M]
französischer Knötchenstich[M]
punto[M] de nudos[M]

**loop stitches**
**points[M] bouclés**
**Schlingstiche[M]**
**puntos[M] de malla[F]**

chain stitch
point[M] de chaînette[F]
Kettenstich[M]
cadeneta[F]

feather stitch
point[M] d'épine[F]
Krähenfußstich[M]
pata[F] de gallo[M]

# WEAVING
# TISSAGE[M]
# WEBEN[N]
# TELAR[M]

## LOW WARP LOOM
## MÉTIER[M] DE BASSE LISSE[F]
## FLACHWEBSTUHL[M]
## TELAR[M] DE CUATRO MARCOS[M]

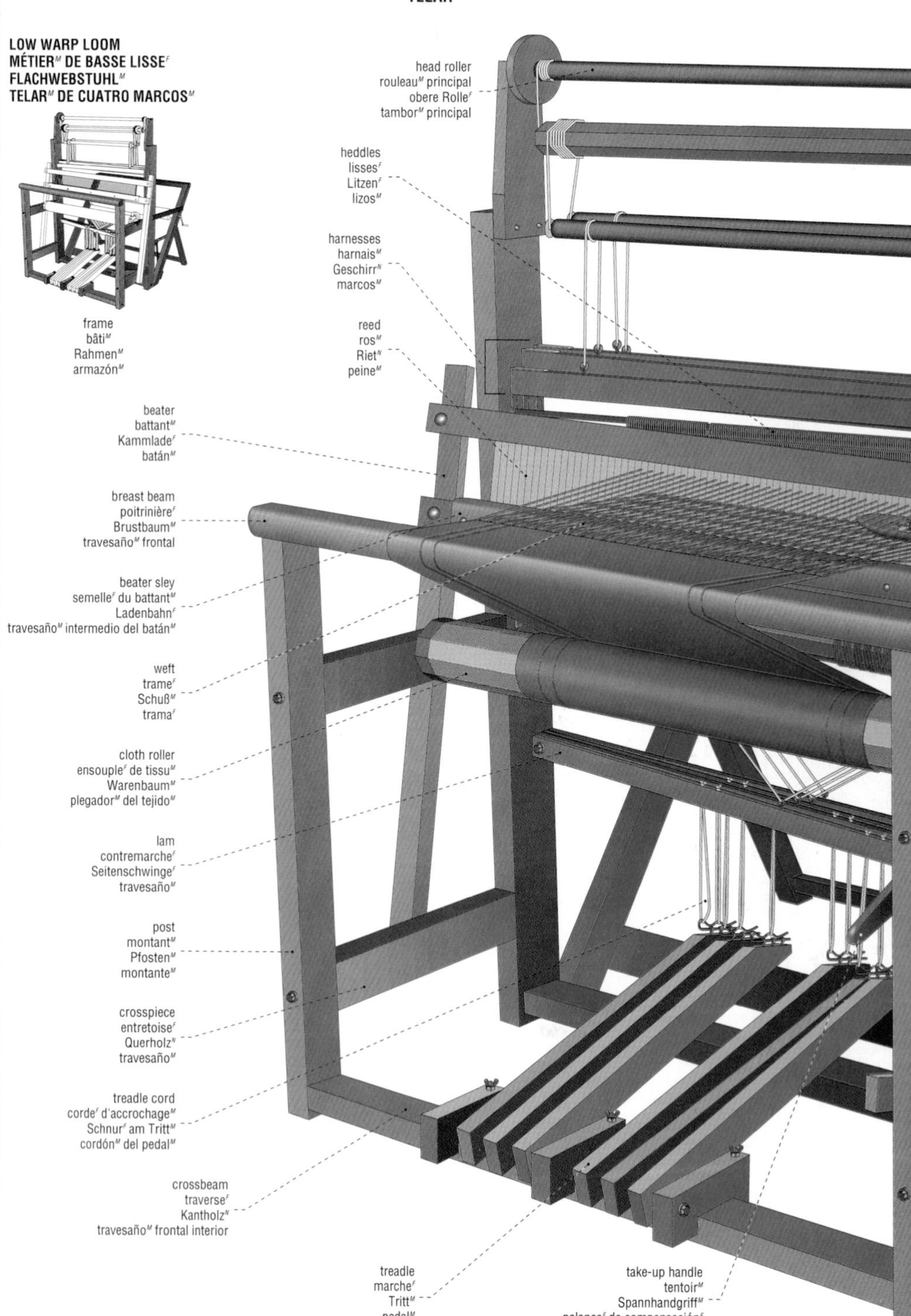

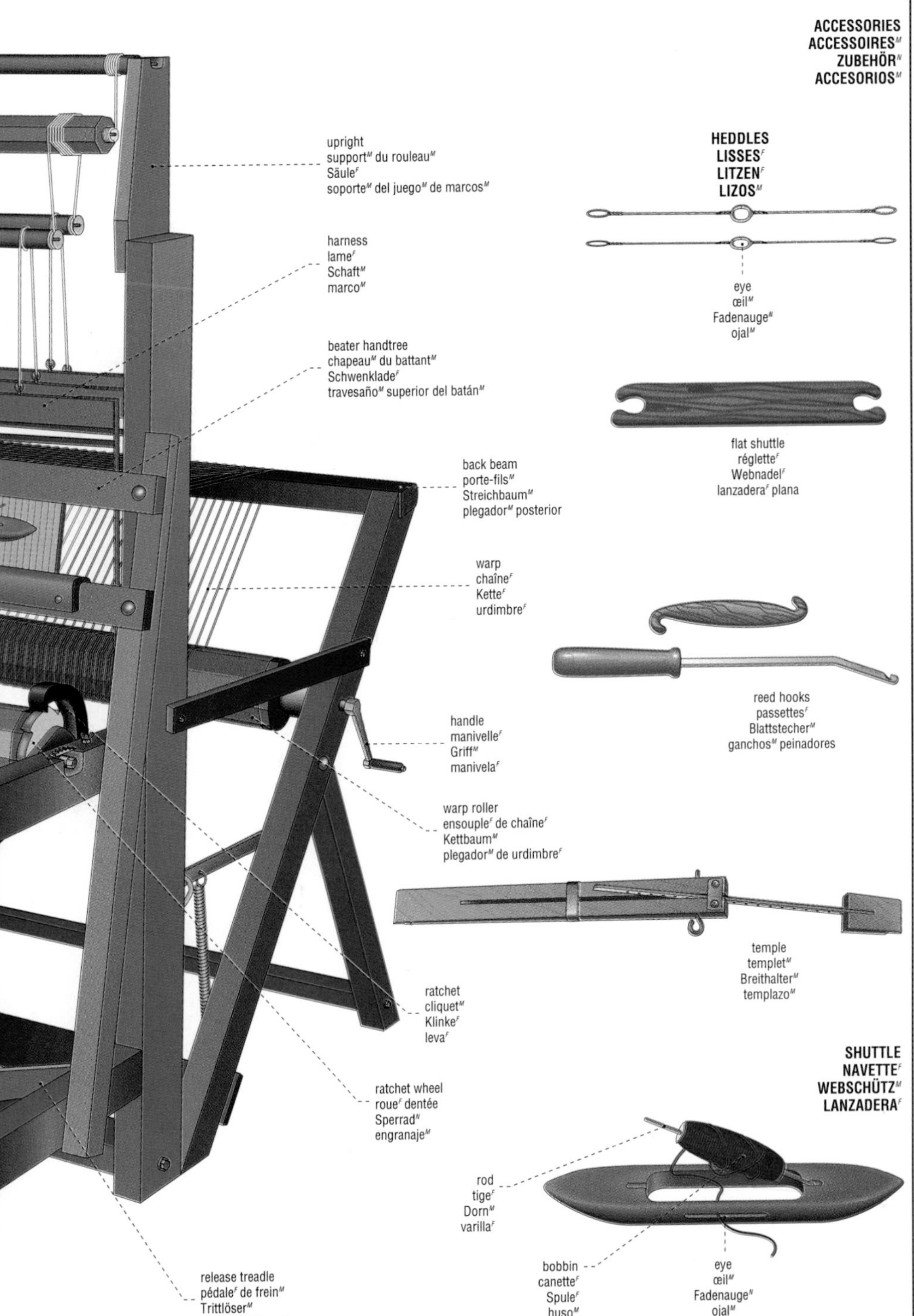
upright
support[M] du rouleau[M]
Säule[F]
soporte[M] del juego[M] de marcos[M]
harness
lame[F]
Schaft[M]
marco[M]
beater handtree
chapeau[M] du battant[M]
Schwenklade[F]
travesaño[M] superior del batán[M]
back beam
porte-fils[M]
Streichbaum[M]
plegador[M] posterior
warp
chaîne[F]
Kette[F]
urdimbre[F]
handle
manivelle[F]
Griff[M]
manivela[F]
warp roller
ensouple[F] de chaîne[F]
Kettbaum[M]
plegador[M] de urdimbre[F]
ratchet
cliquet[M]
Klinke[F]
leva[F]
ratchet wheel
roue[F] dentée
Sperrad[N]
engranaje[M]
release treadle
pédale[F] de frein[M]
Trittlöser[M]
pedal[M] del freno[M]
ACCESSORIES
ACCESSOIRES[M]
ZUBEHÖR[N]
ACCESORIOS[M]
HEDDLES
LISSES[F]
LITZEN[F]
LIZOS[M]
eye
œil[M]
Fadenauge[N]
ojal[M]
flat shuttle
réglette[F]
Webnadel[F]
lanzadera[F] plana
reed hooks
passettes[F]
Blattstecher[M]
ganchos[M] peinadores
temple
templet[M]
Breithalter[M]
templazo[M]
SHUTTLE
NAVETTE[F]
WEBSCHÜTZ[M]
LANZADERA[F]
rod
tige[F]
Dorn[M]
varilla[F]
bobbin
canette[F]
Spule[F]
huso[M]
eye
œil[M]
Fadenauge[N]
ojal[M]

# WEAVING
# TISSAGE[M]
# WEBEN[N]
# TEJIDO[M]

## HIGH WARP LOOM
## MÉTIER[M] DE HAUTE LISSE[F]
## HOCHWEBSTUHL[M]
## TELAR[M] DE TAPICERÍA[F]

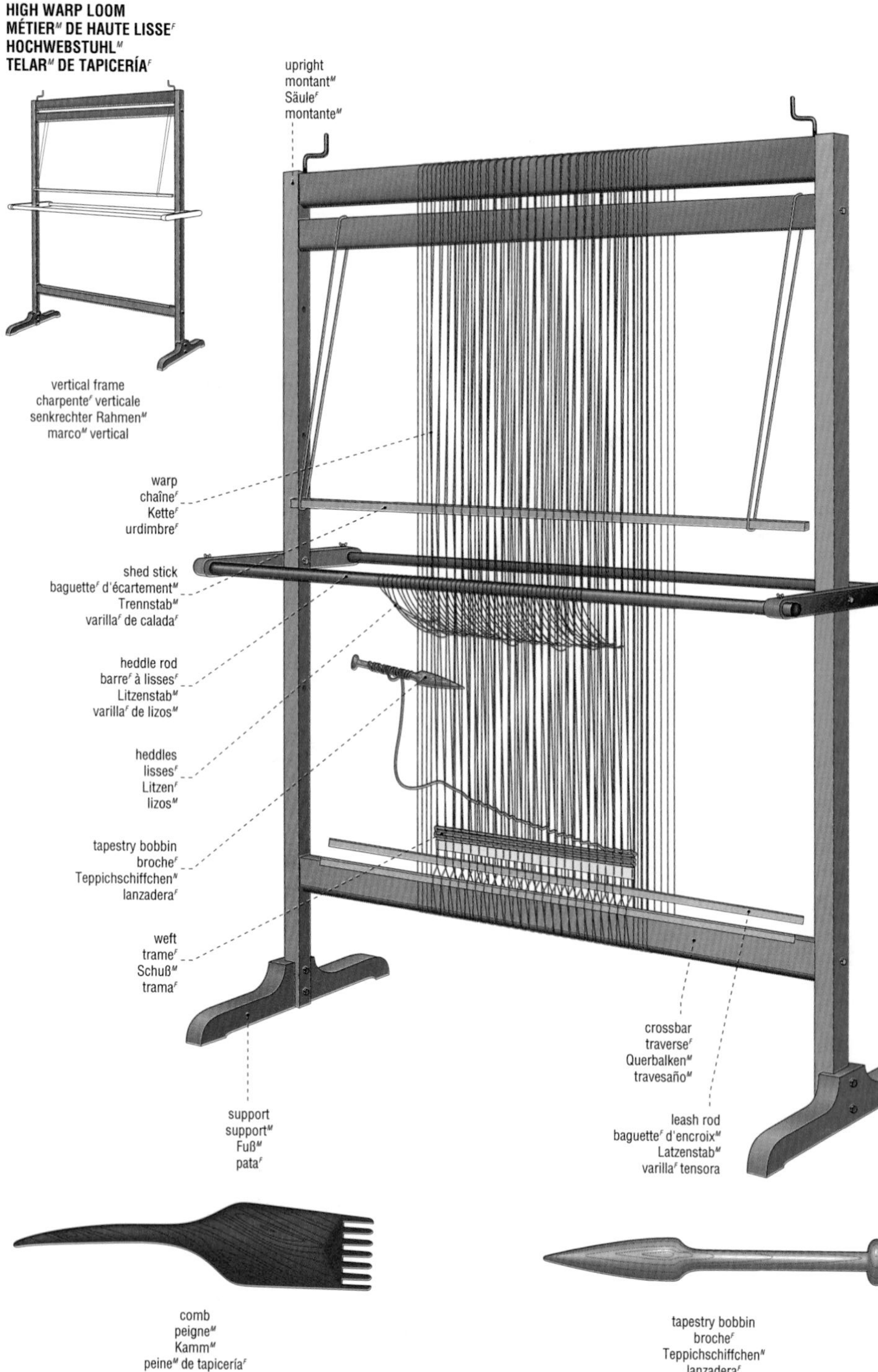

## ACCESSORIES
## ACCESSOIRES$^{M}$
## ZUBEHÖR$^{N}$
## ACCESORIOS$^{M}$

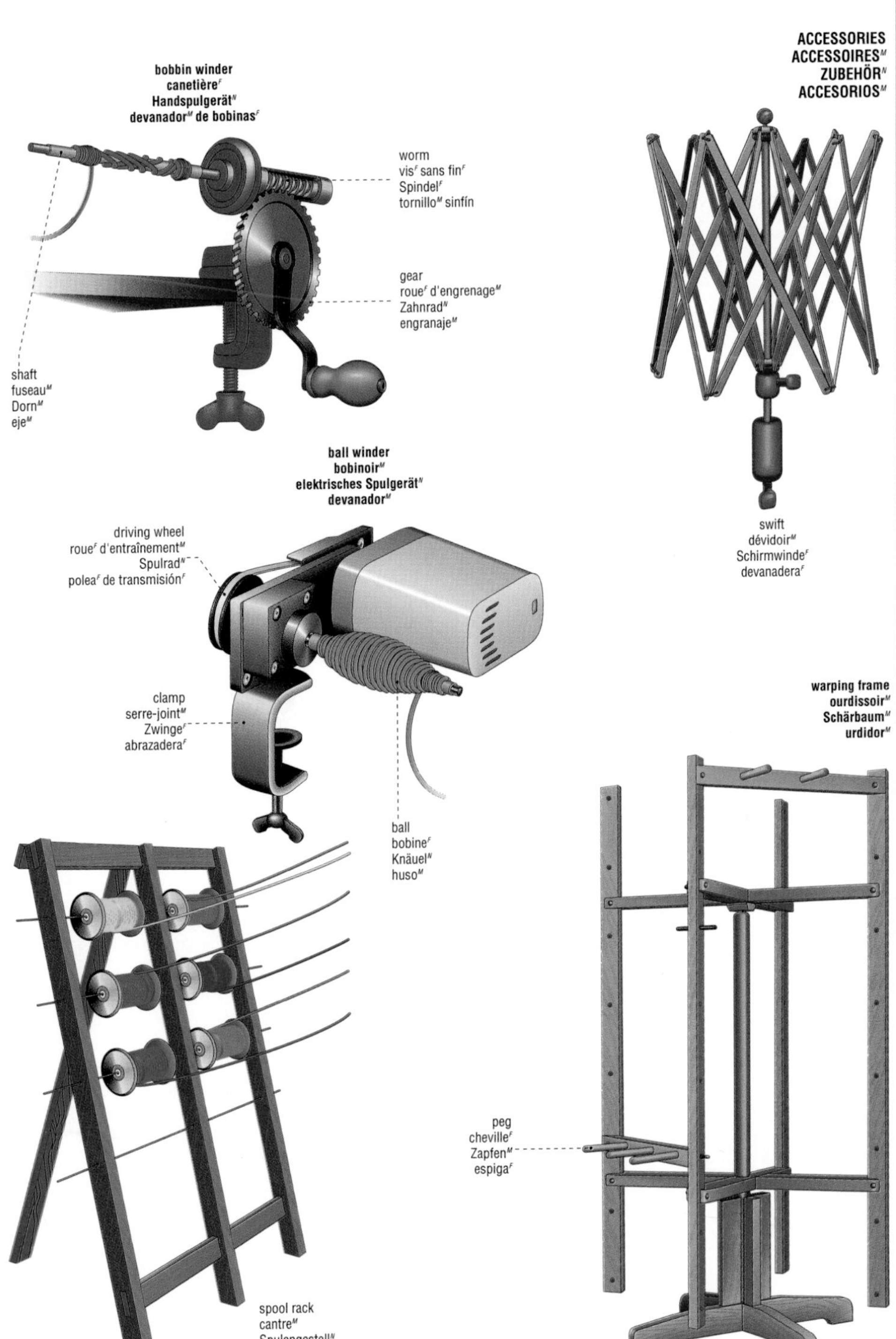

# WEAVING
# TISSAGE[M]
# WEBEN[N]
# TEJIDOS[M]

## DIAGRAM OF WEAVING PRINCIPLE
## SCHÉMA[M] DE PRINCIPE[M] DU TISSAGE[M]
## SCHAUBILD[N] FÜR DAS WEBPRINZIP[N]
## DIAGRAMAS[M] DE TEJIDOS[M]

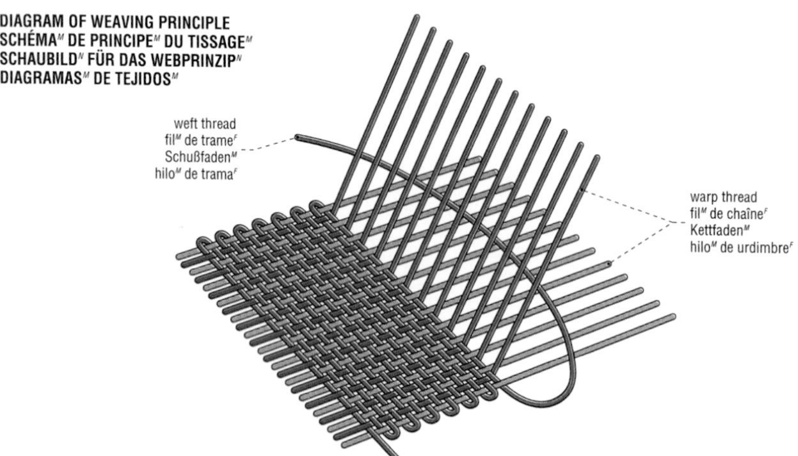


## BASIC WEAVES
## ARMURES[F] DE BASE[F]
## GRUNDBINDUNGEN[F]
## LIGAMENTOS[M] TEXTILES BÁSICOS

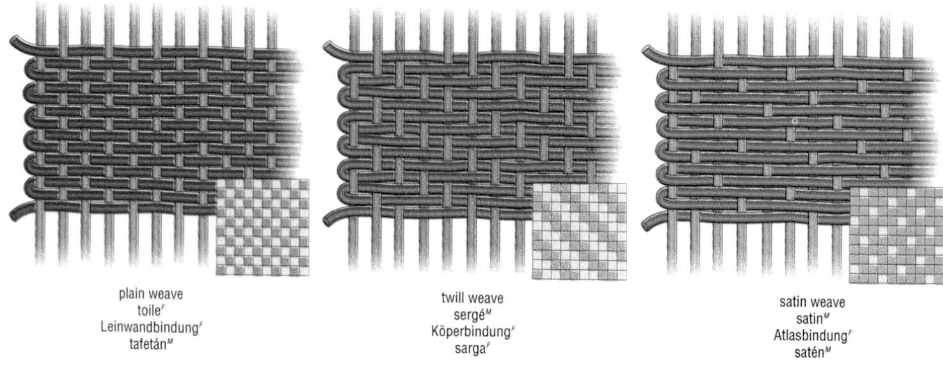

plain weave
toile[F]
Leinwandbindung[F]
tafetán[M]

twill weave
sergé[M]
Köperbindung[F]
sarga[F]

satin weave
satin[M]
Atlasbindung[F]
satén[M]

## OTHER TECHNIQUES
## AUTRES TECHNIQUES[F]
## ANDERE TECHNIKEN[F]
## OTROS LIGAMENTOS[M] TEXTILES

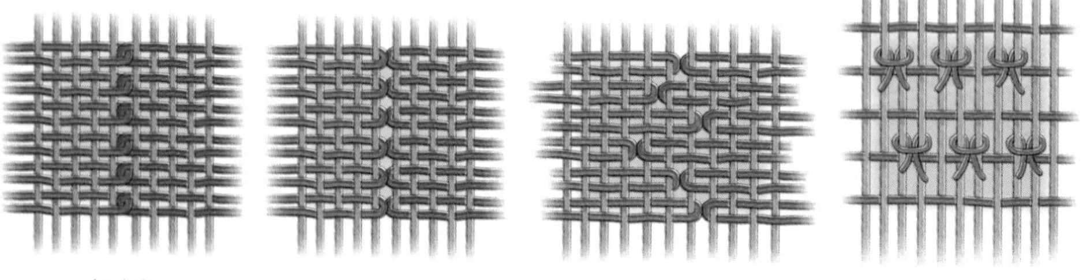

interlock
croisement[M]
Gobelinbindung[F]
ligamento[M] entrecruzado

slit
fente[F]
senkrechte Kelimbindung[F]
ligamento[M] vertical

hatching
hachure[F]
Kelimbindung[F] mit wechselnden Wenden[F]
ligamento[M] de rayas[F]

knot
nœud[M]
Knoten[M]
ligamento[M] de nudos[M]

# FINE BOOKBINDING
# RELIURE[F] D'ART[M]
# HANDBUCHBINDEREI[F]
# ENCUADERNACIÓN[F] ARTÍSTICA[F]



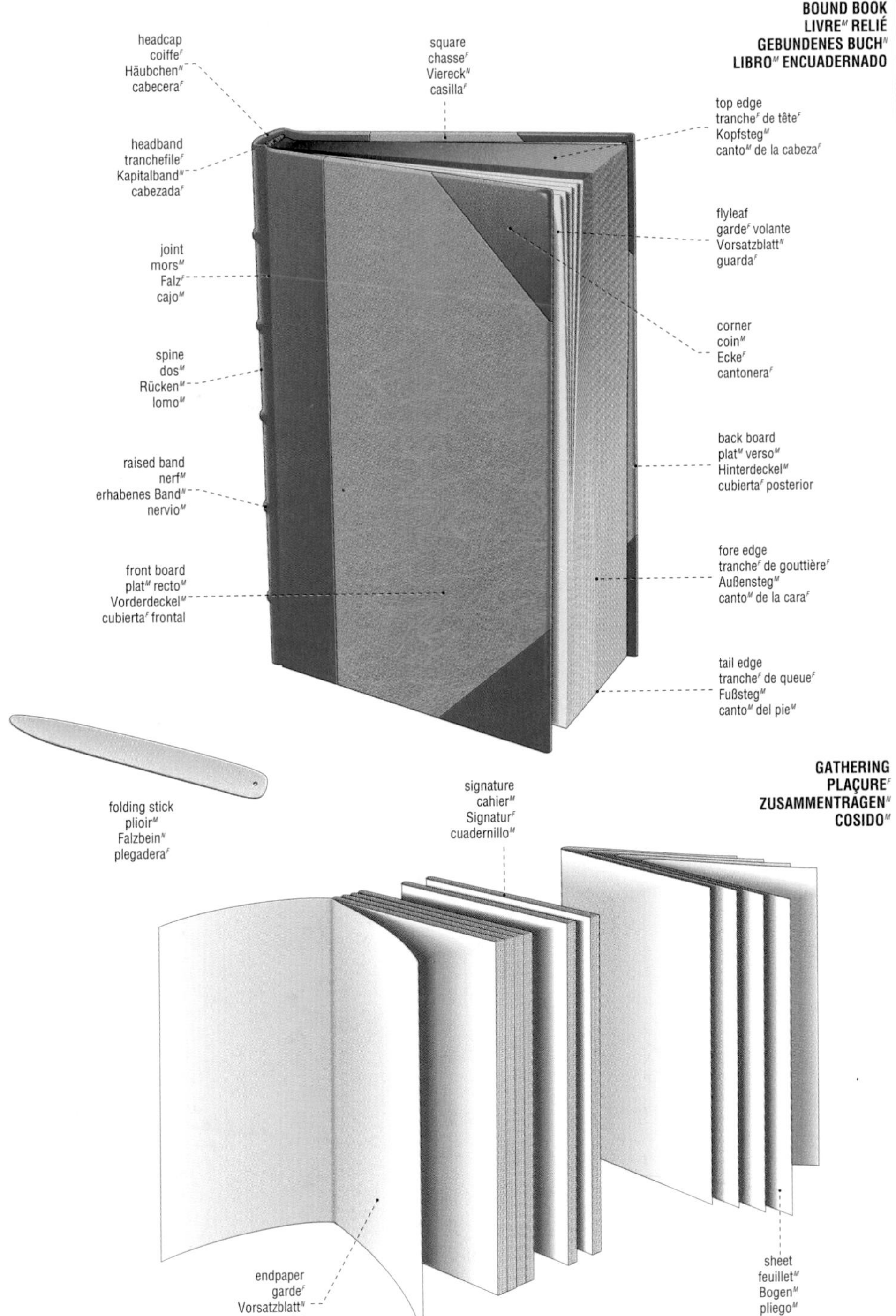

# FINE BOOKBINDING
# RELIURE^F D'ART^M
# HANDBUCHBINDEREI^F
# ENCUADERNACIÓN^F ARTÍSTICA

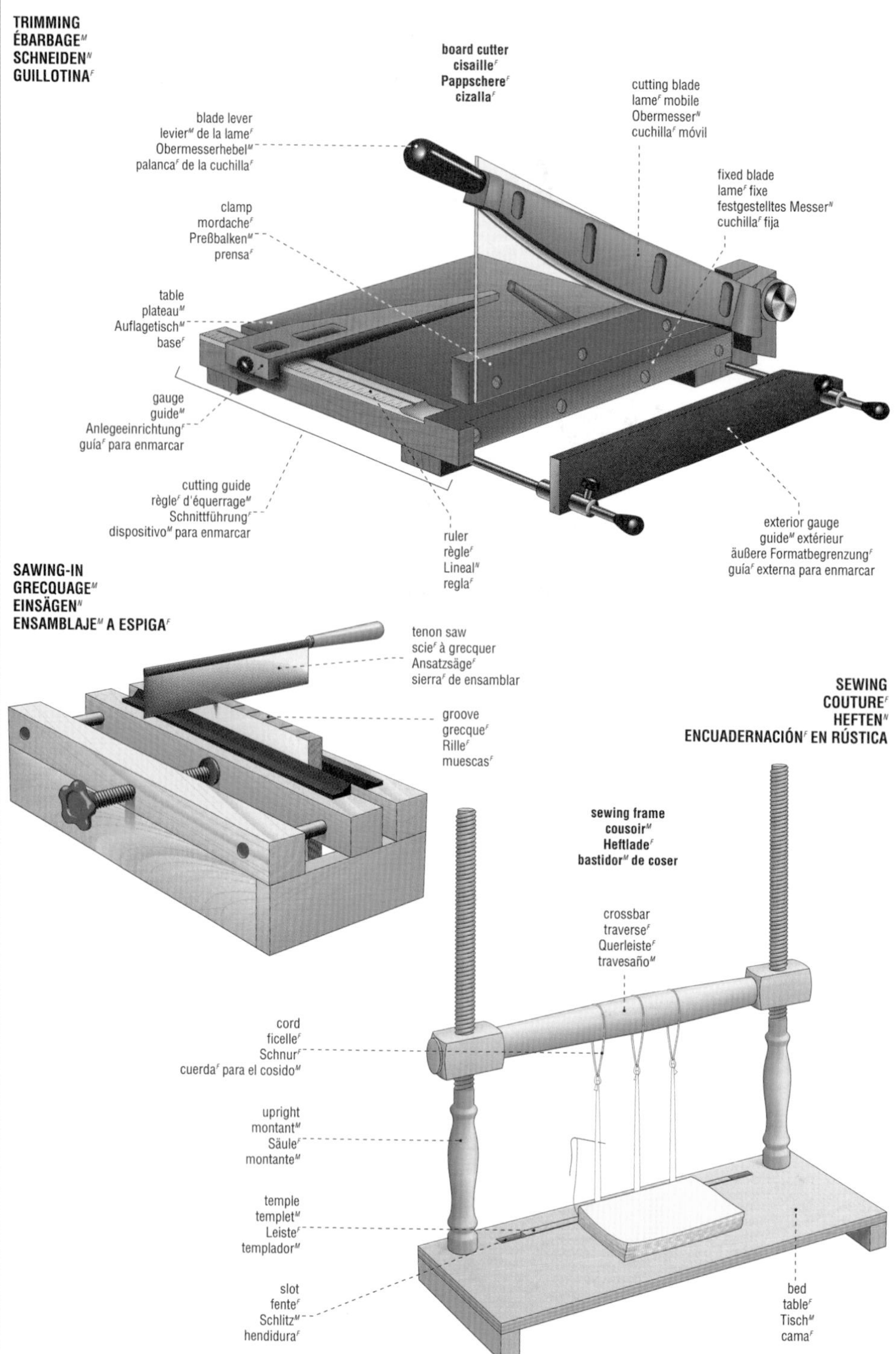

**BACKING**
**ENDOSSURE**[F]
**BUCHRÜCKENBEARBEITUNG**[F]
**REDONDEO**[M]

**PRESSING**
**MISE**[F] **EN PRESSE**[F]
**PRESSEN**[N]
**PRENSA**[F]

**BACKING PRESS**
**ÉTAU**[M] **À ENDOSSER**
**BUCHRÜCKENPRESSE**[F]
**PRENSA**[F] **DE CAJOS**[M]

**BACKING HAMMER**
**MARTEAU**[M] **À ENDOSSER**
**HAMMER**[M] **ZUM RUNDKLOPFEN**[N]
**MARTILLO**[M] **DE ENCUADERNADOR**[M]

**COVERING**
**COUVRURE**[F]
**EINBINDEN**[N]
**CUBIERTA**[F]

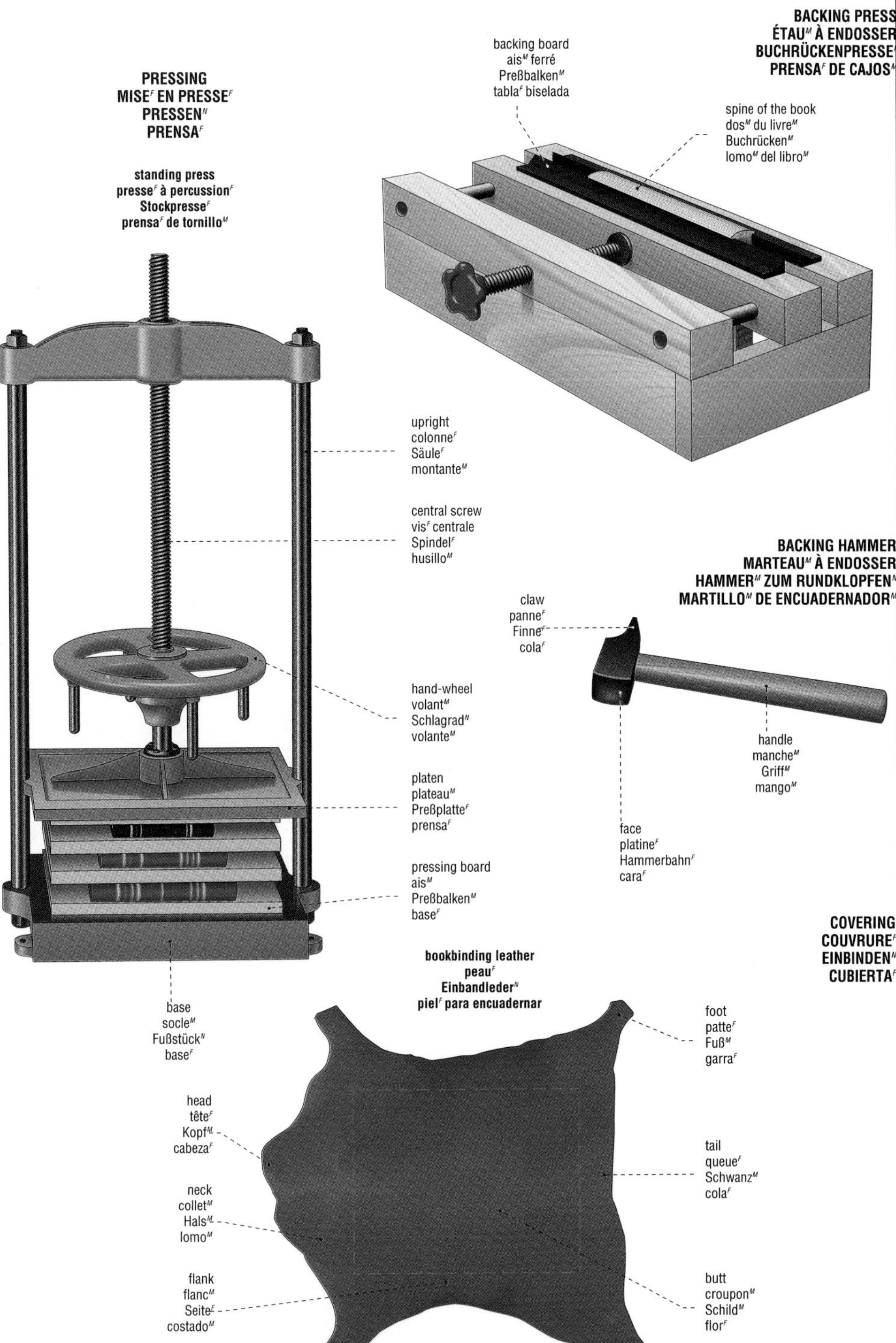

# PRINTING
# IMPRESSION[F]
# DRUCKEN[N]
# IMPRESIÓN[F]

## RELIEF PRINTING
## IMPRESSION[F] EN RELIEF[M]
## HOCHDRUCK[M]
## IMPRESIÓN[F] EN RELIEVE[M]

## INTAGLIO PRINTING
## IMPRESSION[F] EN CREUX[M]
## TIEFDRUCK[M]
## HUECOGRABADO[M]

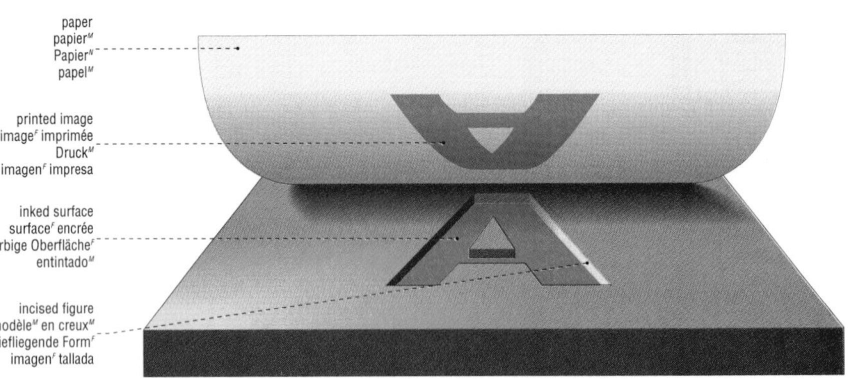


## LITHOGRAPHIC PRINTING
## IMPRESSION[F] À PLAT[M]
## LITHOGRAPHIE[F]
## IMPRESIÓN LITOGRÁFICA

printed image
image[F] imprimée
Druck[M]
imagen[F] impresa

paper
papier[M]
Papier[N]
papel[M]

moist surface
surface[F] mouillée
befeuchtete Oberfläche[F]
superficie[F] humedecida

inked surface
surface[F] encrée
farbige Oberfläche[F]
entintado[M]

plane figure
modèle[M] à plat[M]
Flachform[F]
figura[F] plana

## RELIEF PRINTING PROCESS
## GRAVURE^F EN RELIEF^M
## HOCHDRUCKVERFAHREN^N
## IMPRESIÓN^F EN RELIEVE^M

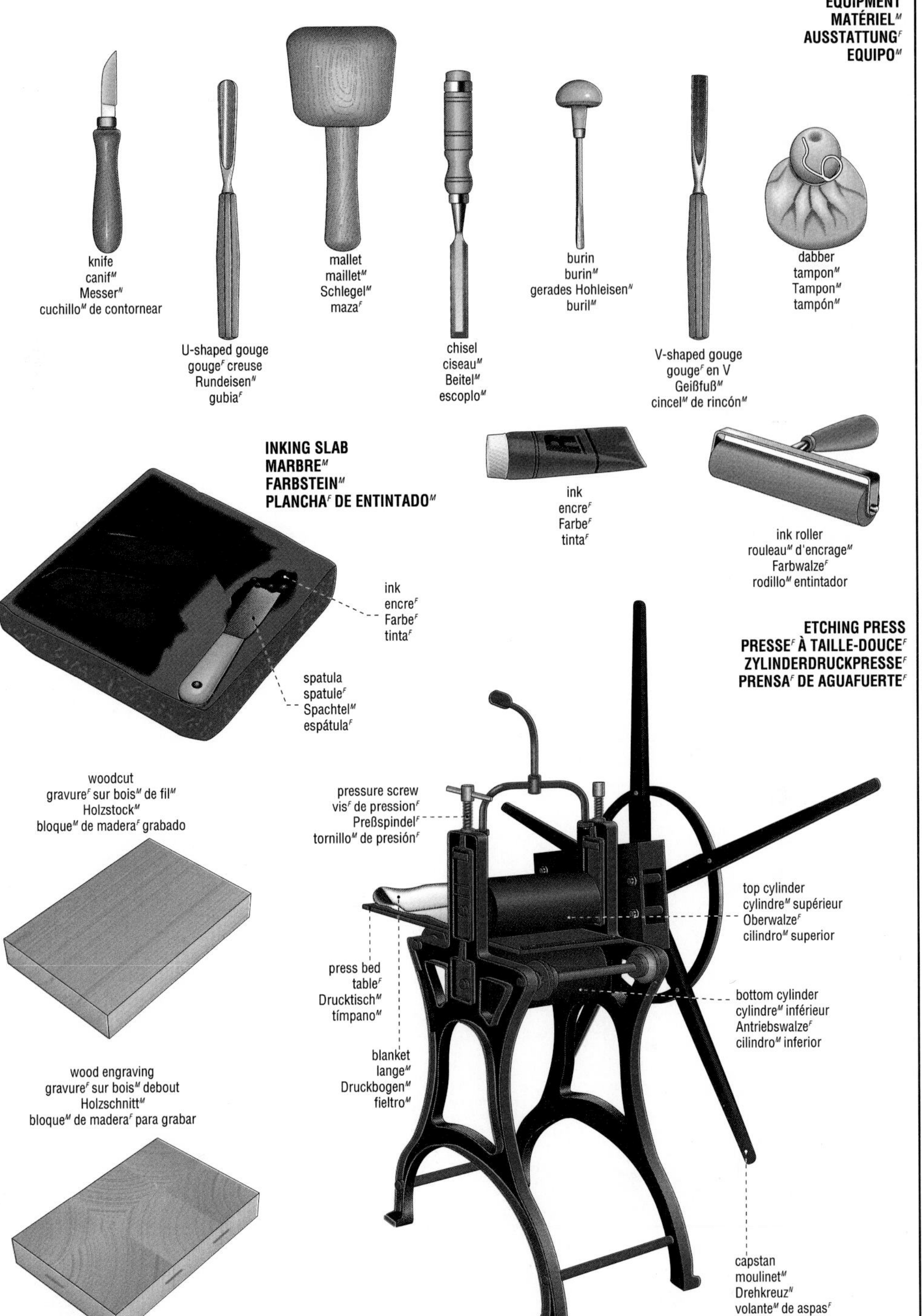

# INTAGLIO PRINTING PROCESS
# GRAVURE[F] EN CREUX[M]
# TIEFDRUCKVERFAHREN[N]
# IMPRESIÓN[F] EN HUECOGRABADO[M]

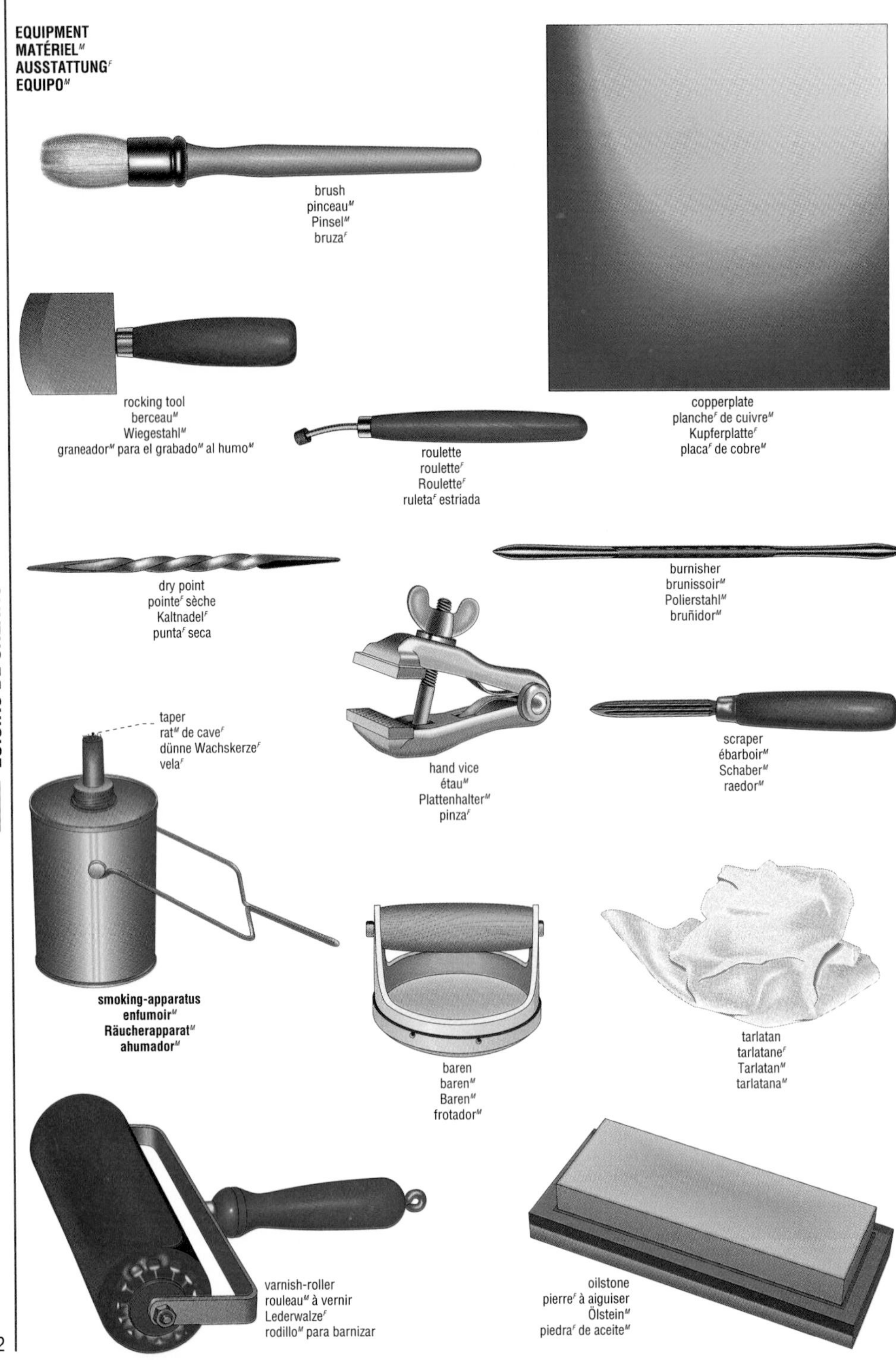

# LITHOGRAPHY
# LITHOGRAPHIE[F]
# LITHOGRAPHIE[F]
# LITOGRAFÍA[F]

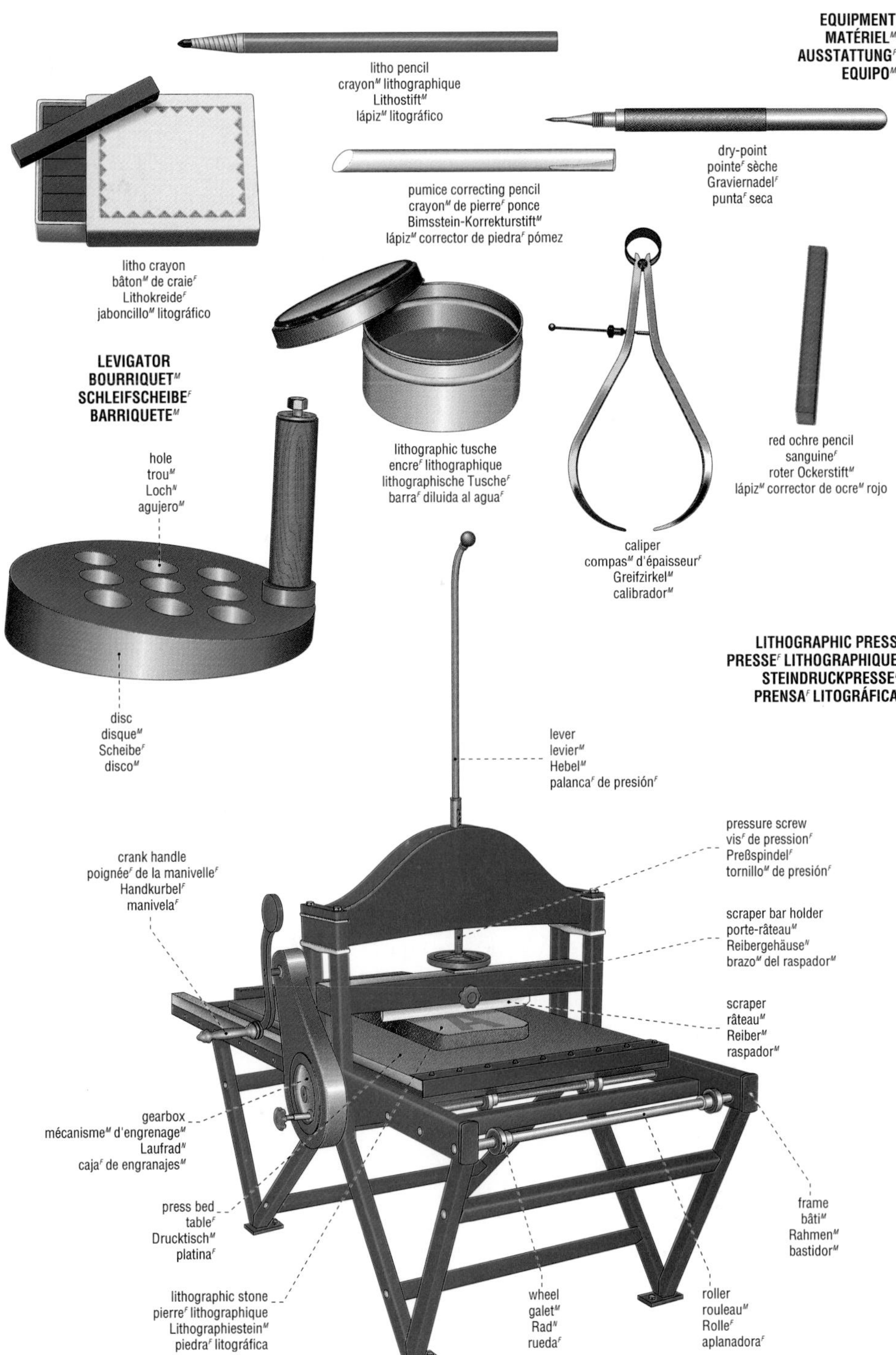

# POTTERY
# POTERIE$^{F}$
# TÖPFEREI$^{F}$
# CERÁMICA$^{F}$

## TURNING
## TOURNAGE$^{M}$
## DREHEN$^{N}$
## TORNO$^{M}$

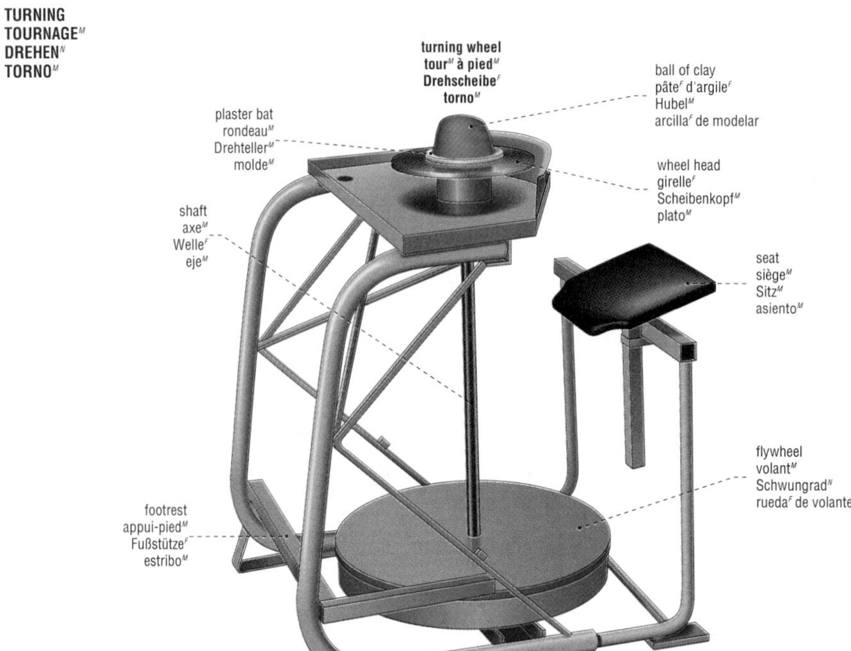


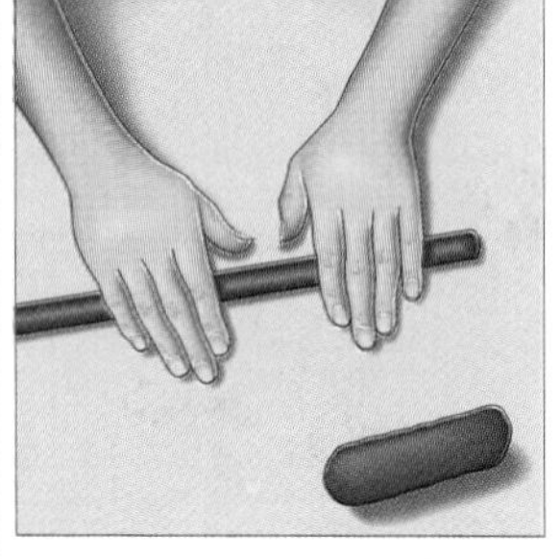

## COILING
## COLOMBIN$^{M}$
## SPIRALWÜLSTE$^{F}$ ROLLEN
## CORDÓN$^{M}$ PARA ESPIRALES$^{F}$

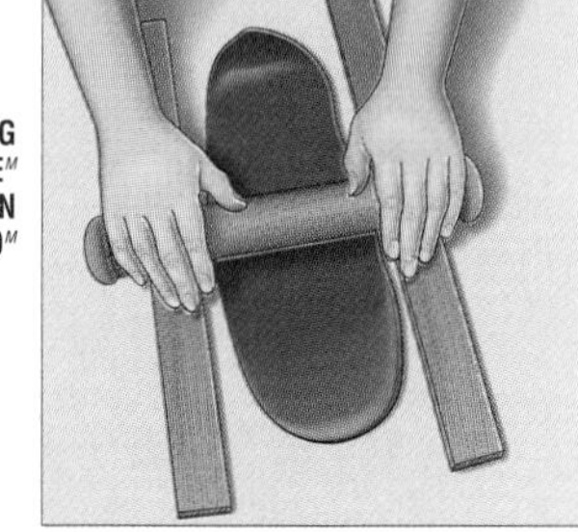

## SLAB BUILDING
## GALETTAGE$^{M}$
## PLATTEN$^{F}$ AUSROLLEN
## RODILLO$^{M}$

## TOOLS
## OUTILS$^{M}$
## WERKZEUG$^{N}$
## HERRAMIENTAS$^{F}$

ribs
esthèques$^{F}$
Drehschiene$^{F}$
costillar$^{M}$

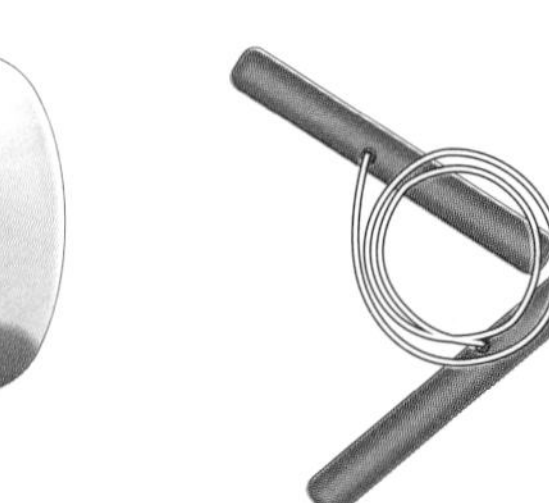

cutting wire
fil$^{M}$ à couper la pâte$^{F}$
Schneidedraht$^{M}$
alambre$^{M}$ para cortar

banding wheel
tournette$^{F}$
Modellierscheibe$^{F}$
torneta$^{F}$

TOOLS
OUTILS$^{M}$
WERKZEUG$^{N}$
HERRAMIENTAS$^{F}$

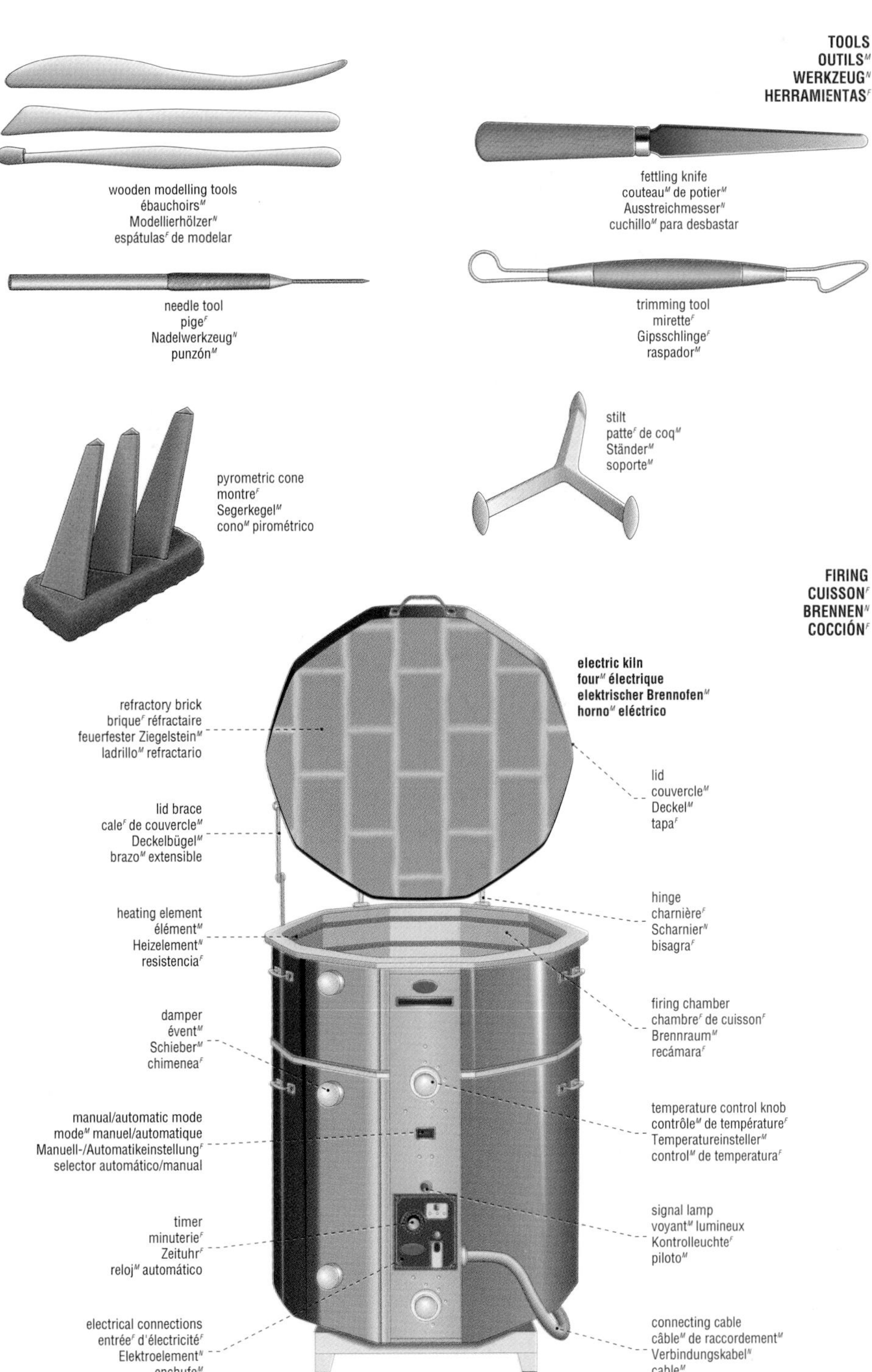

# WOOD CARVING
# SCULPTURE^F SUR BOIS^M
# HOLZSCHNITZEREI^F
# TALLA^F EN MADERA^F



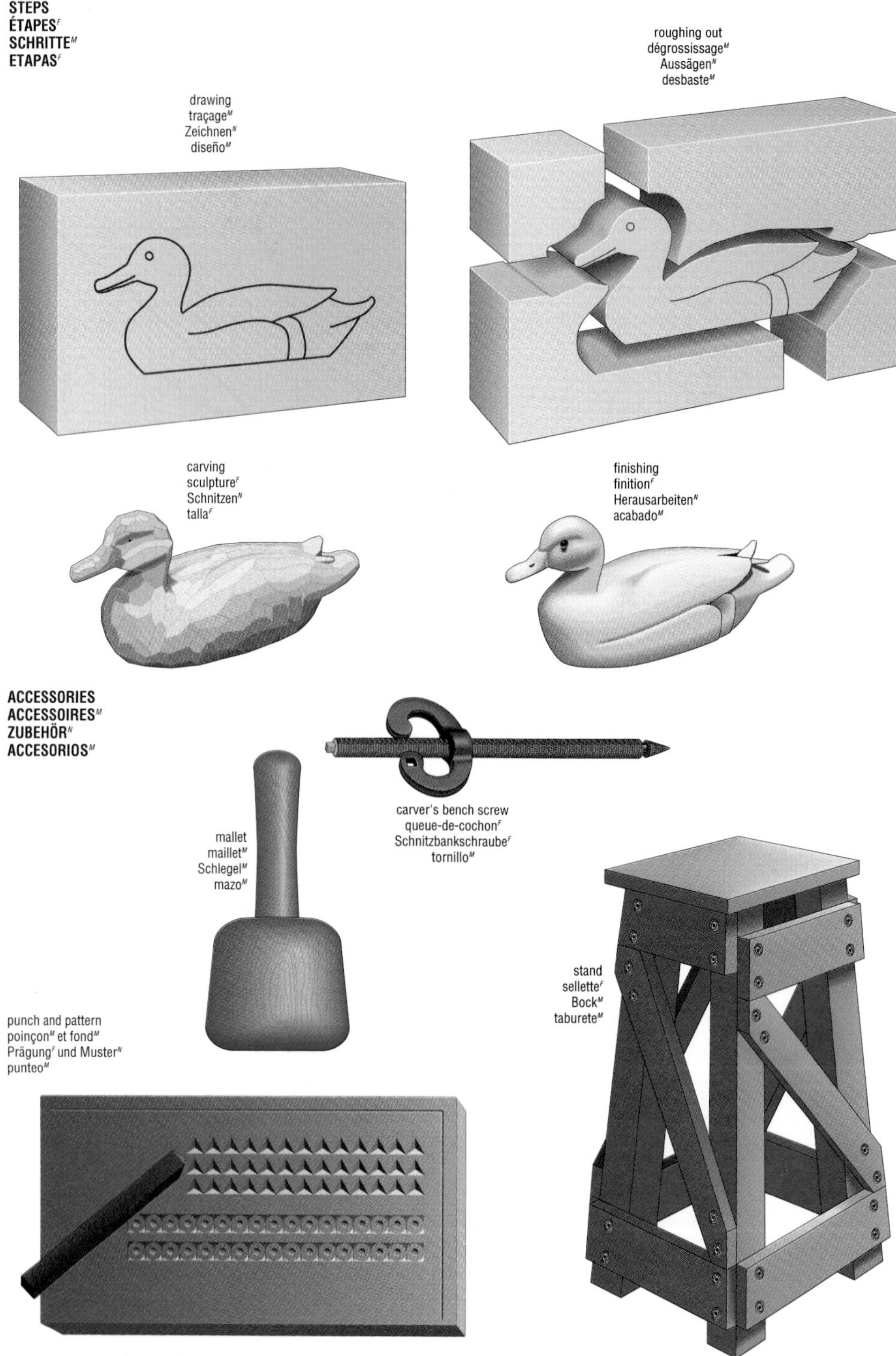

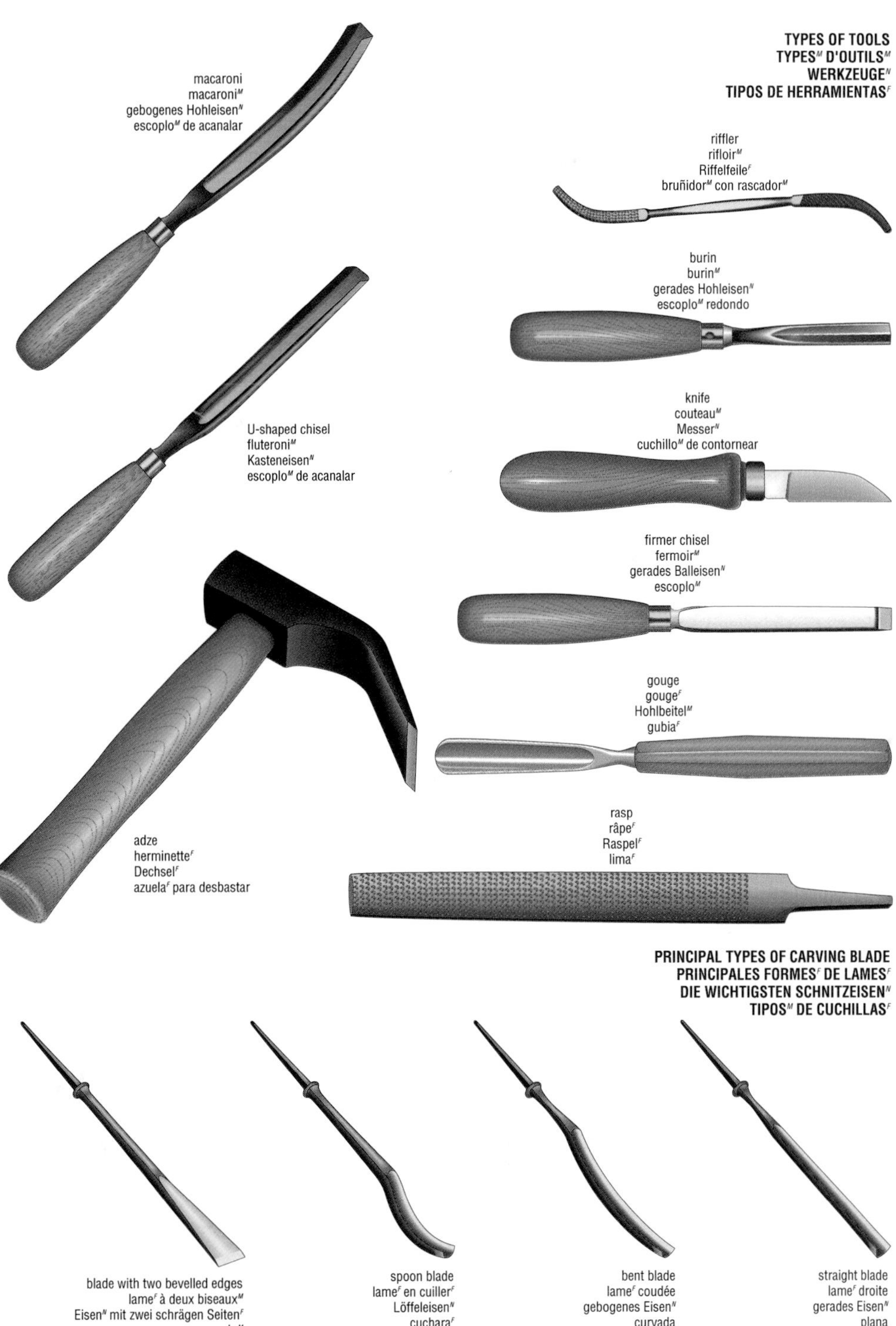
TYPES OF TOOLS
TYPES^M D'OUTILS^M
WERKZEUGE^N
TIPOS DE HERRAMIENTAS^F
macaroni
macaroni^M
gebogenes Hohleisen^N
escoplo^M de acanalar
riffler
rifloir^M
Riffelfeile^F
bruñidor^M con rascador^M
burin
burin^M
gerades Hohleisen^N
escoplo^M redondo
U-shaped chisel
fluteroni^M
Kasteneisen^N
escoplo^M de acanalar
knife
couteau^M
Messer^N
cuchillo^M de contornear
firmer chisel
fermoir^M
gerades Balleisen^N
escoplo^M
gouge
gouge^F
Hohlbeitel^M
gubia^F
rasp
râpe^F
Raspel^F
lima^F
adze
herminette^F
Dechsel^F
azuela^F para desbastar
PRINCIPAL TYPES OF CARVING BLADE
PRINCIPALES FORMES^F DE LAMES^F
DIE WICHTIGSTEN SCHNITZEISEN^N
TIPOS^M DE CUCHILLAS^F
blade with two bevelled edges
lame^F à deux biseaux^M
Eisen^N mit zwei schrägen Seiten^F
escoplo^M
spoon blade
lame^F en cuiller^F
Löffeleisen^N
cuchara^F
bent blade
lame^F coudée
gebogenes Eisen^N
curvada
straight blade
lame^F droite
gerades Eisen^N
plana

# PAINTING AND DRAWING
# PEINTURE[F] ET DESSIN[M]
# MALEN[N] UND ZEICHNEN[N]
# PINTURA[F] Y DIBUJO[M]

## PRINCIPAL TECHNIQUES
## PRINCIPALES TECHNIQUES[F]
## DIE WICHTIGSTEN TECHNIKEN[F]
## TÉCNICAS PRINCIPALES

## EQUIPMENT
## MATÉRIEL[M]
## AUSSTATTUNG[F]
## EQUIPO[M]

palette knife
spatule[F]
Palettmesser[N]
espátula[F]

painting knife
couteau[M] à peindre
Malspachtel[M]
cuchillo[M] paleta[F]

reservoir-nib pen
plume[F]
Graphosfeder[F]
plumafuente[F]

flat brush
brosse[F]
Flachpinsel[M]
pincel[M] plano

sumie
pinceau[M] à sumie[M]
Japanpinsel[M]
sumie[M]

fan brush
brosse[F] éventail[M]
Fächerpinsel[M]
brocha[F]

brush
pinceau[M]
Pinsel[M]
pincel[M]

## SUPPORTS
## SUPPORTS[M]
## BILDTRÄGER[M]
## LIENZOS[M]

paper
papier[M]
Papier[N]
papel[M]

cardboard
carton[M]
Malpappe[F]
cartón[M]

canvas
toile[F]
Leinwand[F]
lienzo[M]

panel
panneau[M]
Platte[F]
tabla[F]

# PAINTING AND DRAWING
# PEINTURE[F] ET DESSIN[M]
# MALEN[N] UND ZEICHNEN[N]
# PINTURA[F] Y DIBUJO[M]

## AIRBRUSH
## AÉROGRAPHE[M]
## SPRITZPISTOLE[F]
## PISTOLA[F] DE PINTAR

trigger
gâchette[F]
Hebel[M]
palanca[F] principal
cap
couvercle[M]
Deckel[M]
tapa[F]
paint cup
godet[M] à couleur[F]
Farbbehälter[M]
cazoleta[F]
air hose
flexible[M] d'air[M]
Luftschlauch[M]
conducto[M] de aire[M] comprimido
crown
couronne[F]
Düsenkappe[F]
corona[F]

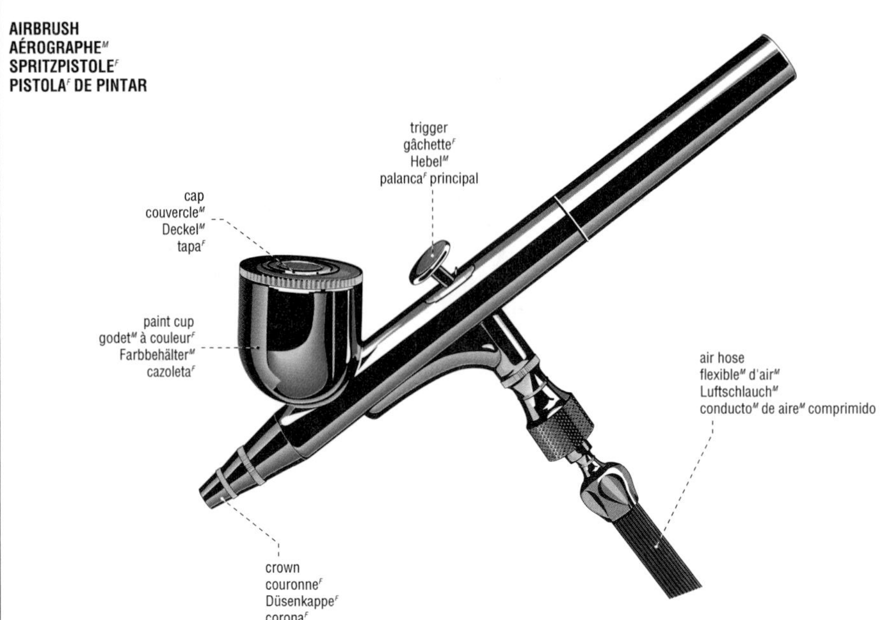

## CROSS SECTION OF AN AIRBRUSH
## COUPE[F] D'UN AÉROGRAPHE[M]
## QUERSCHNITT[M] DURCH EINE SPRITZPISTOLE[F]
## CORTE[M] TRANSVERSAL DE UNA PISTOLA[F] DE PINTAR

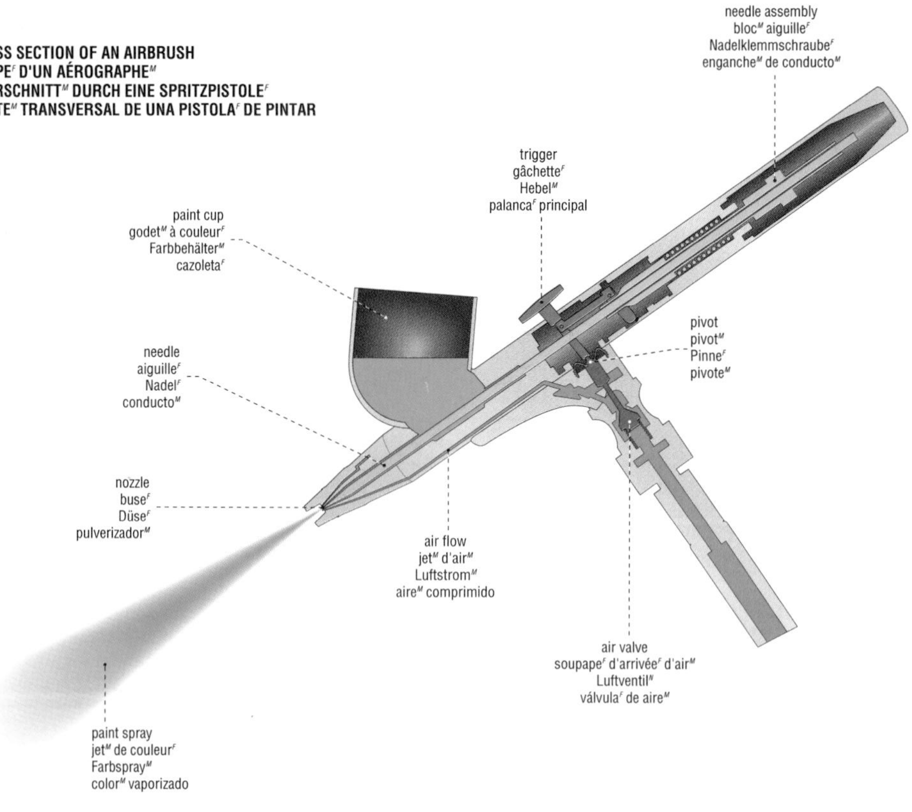

needle assembly
bloc[M] aiguille[F]
Nadelklemmschraube[F]
enganche[M] de conducto[M]
trigger
gâchette[F]
Hebel[M]
palanca[F] principal
paint cup
godet[M] à couleur[F]
Farbbehälter[M]
cazoleta[F]
pivot
pivot[M]
Pinne[F]
pivote[M]
needle
aiguille[F]
Nadel[F]
conducto[M]
nozzle
buse[F]
Düse[F]
pulverizador[M]
air flow
jet[M] d'air[M]
Luftstrom[M]
aire[M] comprimido
air valve
soupape[F] d'arrivée[F] d'air[M]
Luftventil[N]
válvula[F] de aire[M]
paint spray
jet[M] de couleur[F]
Farbspray[M]
color[M] vaporizado

ACCESSORIES
ACCESSOIRES[M]
ZUBEHÖR[N]
ACCESORIOS[M]

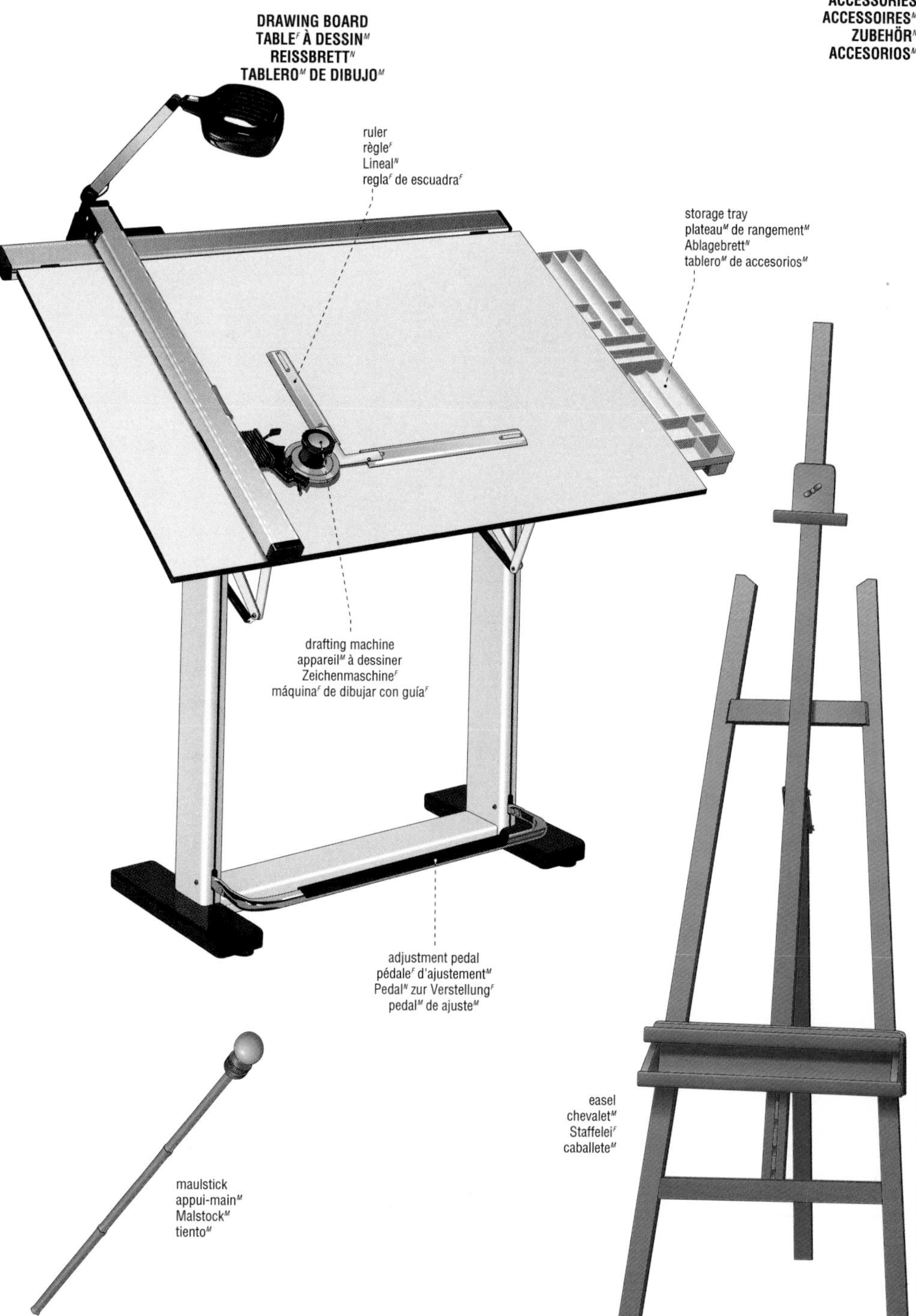

# PAINTING AND DRAWING
# PEINTURE[F] ET DESSIN[M]
# MALEN[N] UND ZEICHNEN[N]
# PINTURA[F] Y DIBUJO[M]

## ACCESSORIES
## ACCESSOIRES[M]
## ZUBEHÖR[N]
## ACCESORIOS[M]

colour chart
nuancier[M]
Farbtafel[F]
gama[F] de colores[M]

palette with hollows
palette[F] à alvéoles[F]
Palette[F] mit Vertiefungen[F]
paleta[F] con huecos[M] para pintura[F]

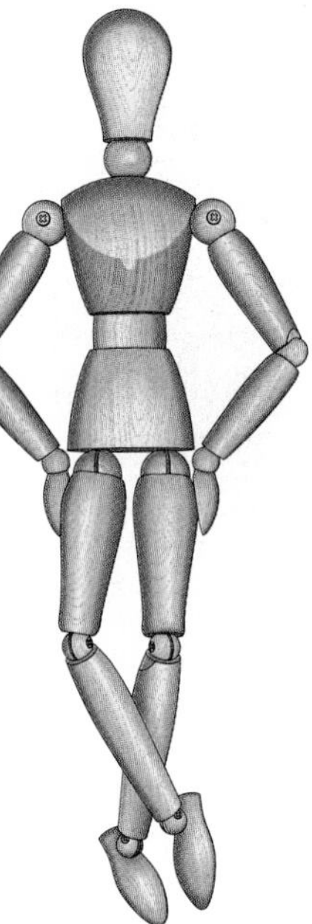

articulated mannequin
mannequin[M] articulé
Gliederpuppe[F]
maniquí[M]

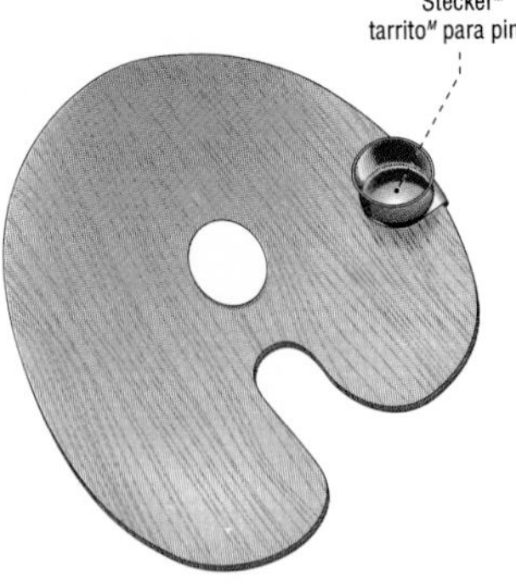


palette with dipper
palette[F] avec godet[M]
Palette[F] mit Stecker[M]
paleta[F] con tarrito[M]

## USEFUL LIQUIDS
## LIQUIDES[M] D'APPOINT[M]
## HILFSMITTEL[N]
## LÍQUIDOS[M] ACCESORIOS

varnish
vernis[M]
Firnis[M]
barniz[M]

linseed oil
huile[F] de lin[M]
Leinöl[N]
aceite[M] de linaza[F]

turpentine
térébenthine[F]
Terpentin[N]
aguarrás[M]

fixative
fixatif[M]
Fixativ[N]
fijador[M]

# SPORTS SPORTARTEN
# SPORTS DEPORTES

## SUMMARY

**TEAM GAMES**

BASEBALL ... 595
CRICKET ... 598
ASSOCIATION FOOTBALL ... 600
AMERICAN FOOTBALL ... 602
RUGBY ... 606
FIELD HOCKEY ... 607
ICE HOCKEY ... 608
BASKETBALL ... 610
NETBALL ... 611
HANDBALL ... 612
VOLLEYBALL ... 613
TENNIS ... 614
SQUASH ... 616
RACQUETBALL ... 617
BADMINTON ... 618
TABLE TENNIS ... 619
CURLING ... 620

**WATER SPORTS**

SWIMMING ... 621
DIVING ... 624
WATER POLO ... 626
SCUBA DIVING ... 627
SAILING ... 628
SAILBOARD ... 631
ROWING AND SCULLING ... 632
WATER SKIING ... 633

**AERIAL SPORTS**

BALLOONING ... 634
SKY DIVING ... 635
PARAGLIDING ... 636
HANG GLIDING ... 637
GLIDING ... 638

**WINTER SPORTS**

ALPINE SKIING ... 640
CROSS-COUNTRY SKIING ... 642
LUGE ... 643
BOBSLEIGH ... 643
SKATING ... 644
SNOWSHOE ... 645
ROLLER SKATE ... 645

**EQUESTRIAN SPORTS**

SHOW-JUMPING ... 646
TYPES OF BIT ... 650
HORSE RACING ... 651
HARNESS RACING ... 652

**ATHLETICS**

TRACK AND FIELD ATHLETICS ... 654
GYMNASTICS ... 659
WEIGHTLIFTING ... 662
FITNESS EQUIPMENT ... 663

**COMBAT SPORTS**

FENCING ... 666
JUDO ... 668
BOXING ... 669

**LEISURE SPORTS**

BILLIARDS ... 673
GOLF ... 676
MOUNTAINEERING ... 680
BOWLS AND PETANQUE ... 682
BOWLING ... 683
ARCHERY ... 684

**CAMPING**

CAMPING ... 685
KNOTS ... 691
CABLE ... 692

# BASEBALL
# BASEBALL$^{M}$
# BASEBALL$^{M}$
# BÉISBOL$^{M}$

# BASEBALL
# BASEBALL^M
# BASEBALL^M
# BÉISBOL^M

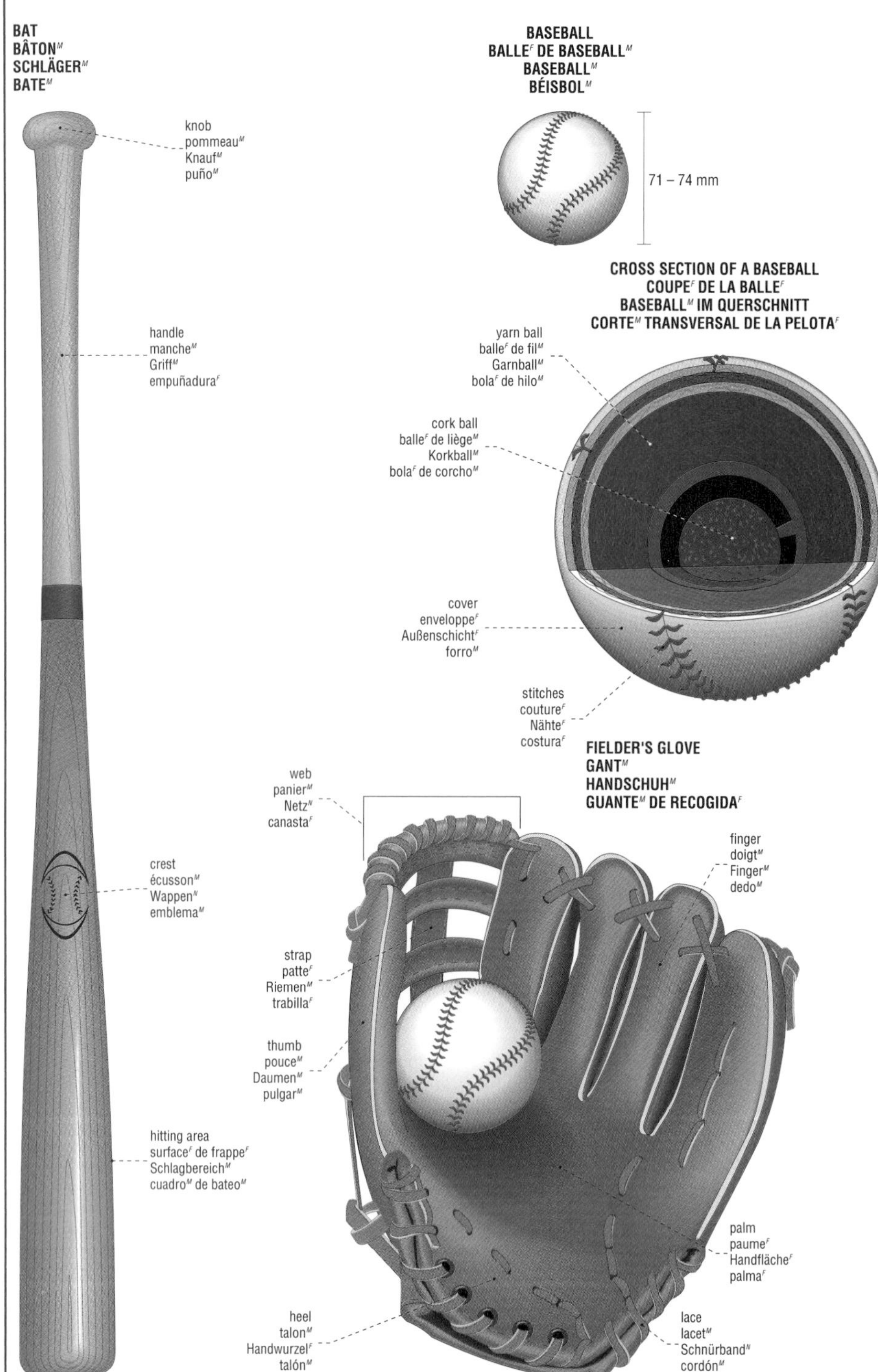

## FIELD
## TERRAIN[M]
## SPIELFELD[N]
## CAMPO[M]

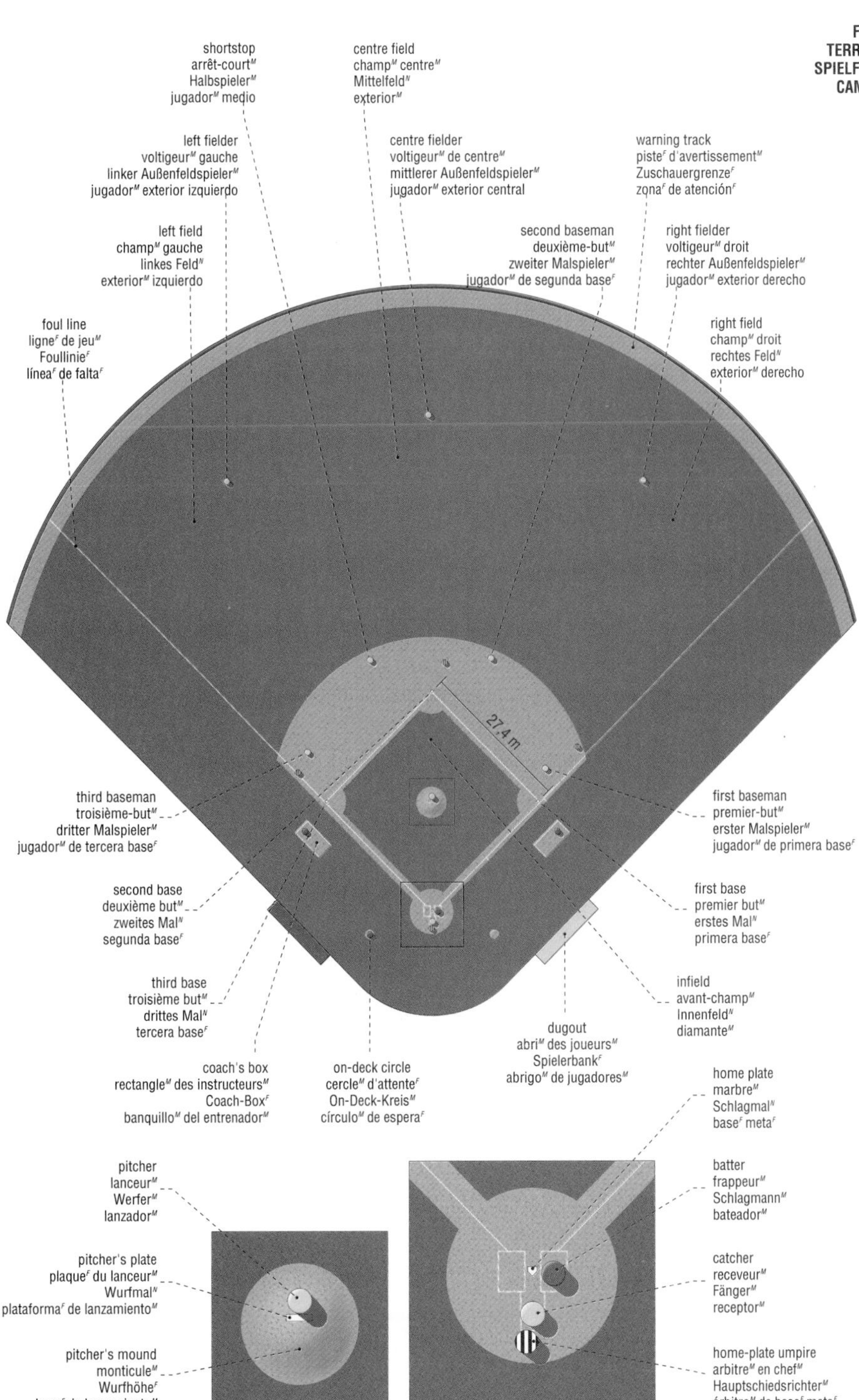

# CRICKET
# CRICKET[M]
# CRICKET[N]
# CRICKET[M]

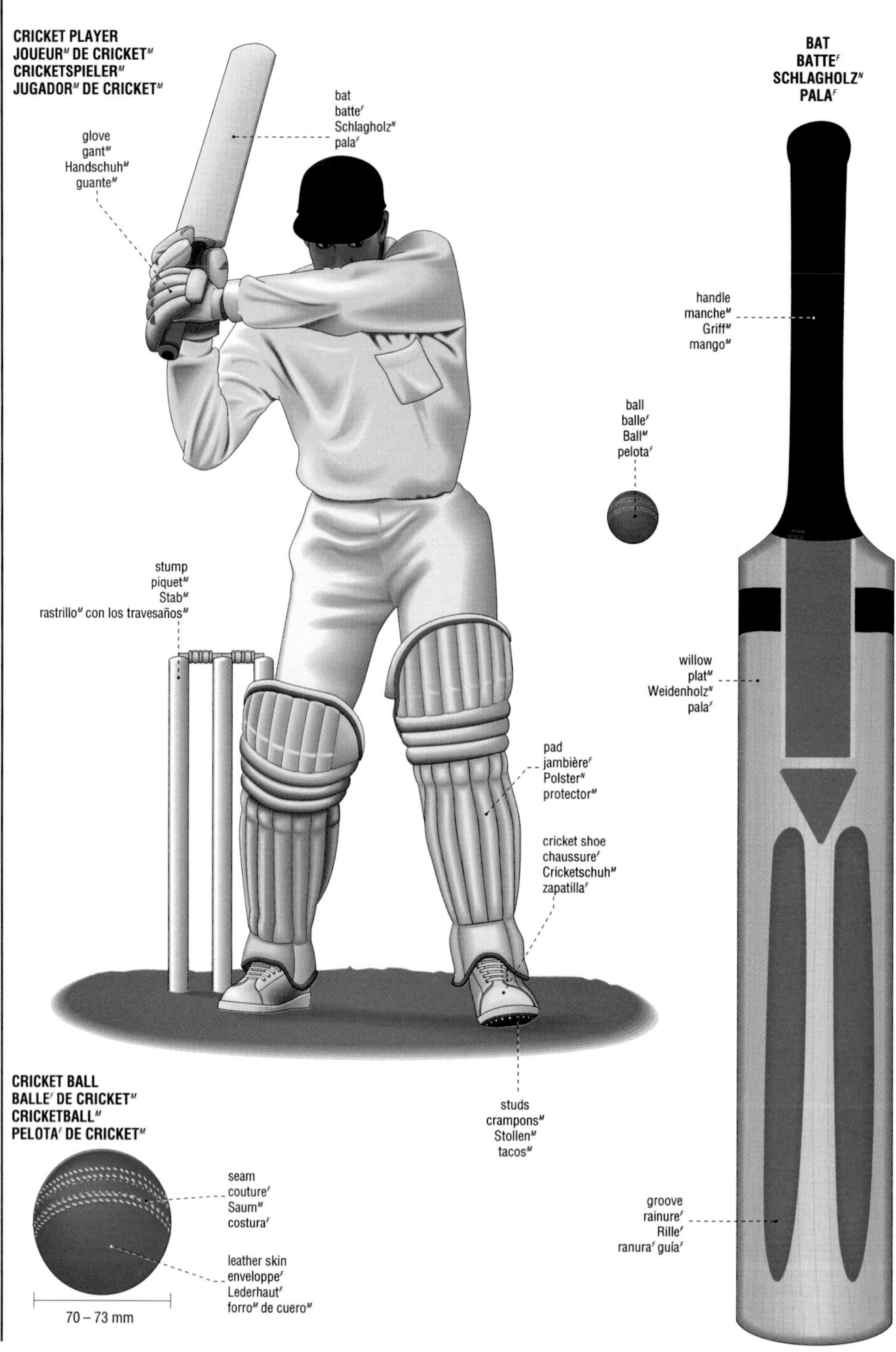

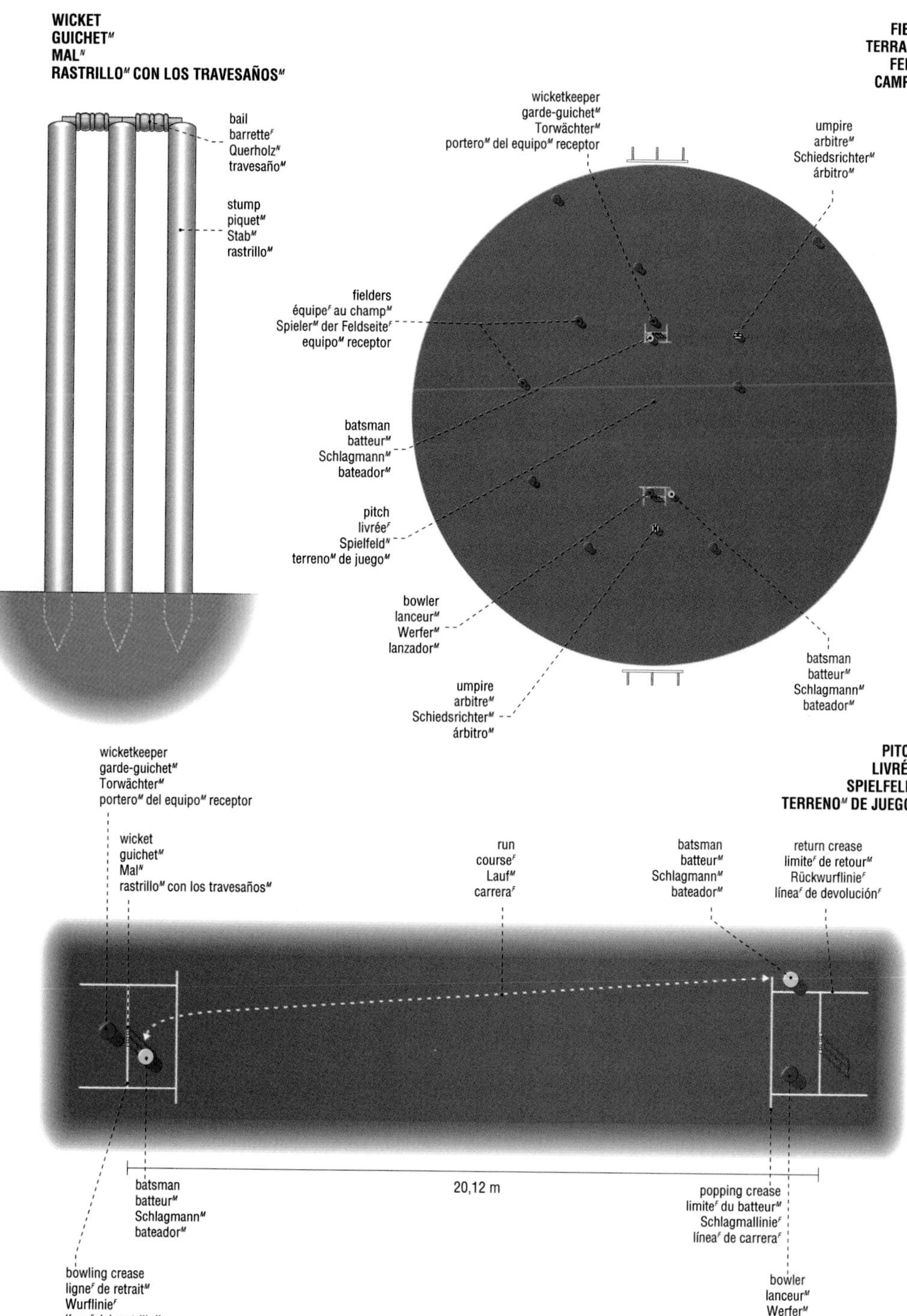
WICKET
GUICHET^M
MAL^N
RASTRILLO^M CON LOS TRAVESAÑOS^M
bail
barrette^F
Querholz^N
travesaño^M
stump
piquet^M
Stab^M
rastrillo^M
FIELD
TERRAIN^M
FELD^N
CAMPO^M
wicketkeeper
garde-guichet^M
Torwächter^M
portero^M del equipo^M receptor
umpire
arbitre^M
Schiedsrichter^M
árbitro^M
fielders
équipe^F au champ^M
Spieler^M der Feldseite^F
equipo^M receptor
batsman
batteur^M
Schlagmann^M
bateador^M
pitch
livrée^F
Spielfeld^N
terreno^M de juego^M
bowler
lanceur^M
Werfer^M
lanzador^M
umpire
arbitre^M
Schiedsrichter^M
árbitro^M
batsman
batteur^M
Schlagmann^M
bateador^M
PITCH
LIVRÉE^F
SPIELFELD^N
TERRENO^M DE JUEGO^M
wicketkeeper
garde-guichet^M
Torwächter^M
portero^M del equipo^M receptor
wicket
guichet^M
Mal^N
rastrillo^M con los travesaños^M
run
course^F
Lauf^M
carrera^F
batsman
batteur^M
Schlagmann^M
bateador^M
return crease
limite^F de retour^M
Rückwurflinie^F
línea^F de devolución^F
batsman
batteur^M
Schlagmann^M
bateador^M
20,12 m
popping crease
limite^F du batteur^M
Schlagmallinie^F
línea^F de carrera^F
bowling crease
ligne^F de retrait^M
Wurflinie^F
línea^F del rastrillo^M
bowler
lanceur^M
Werfer^M
lanzador^M

## ASSOCIATION FOOTBALL
## FOOTBALL^M
## FUSSBALL^M
## FÚTBOL^M

## PLAYING FIELD
## TERRAIN$^{M}$
## SPIELFELD$^{N}$
## CAMPO$^{M}$

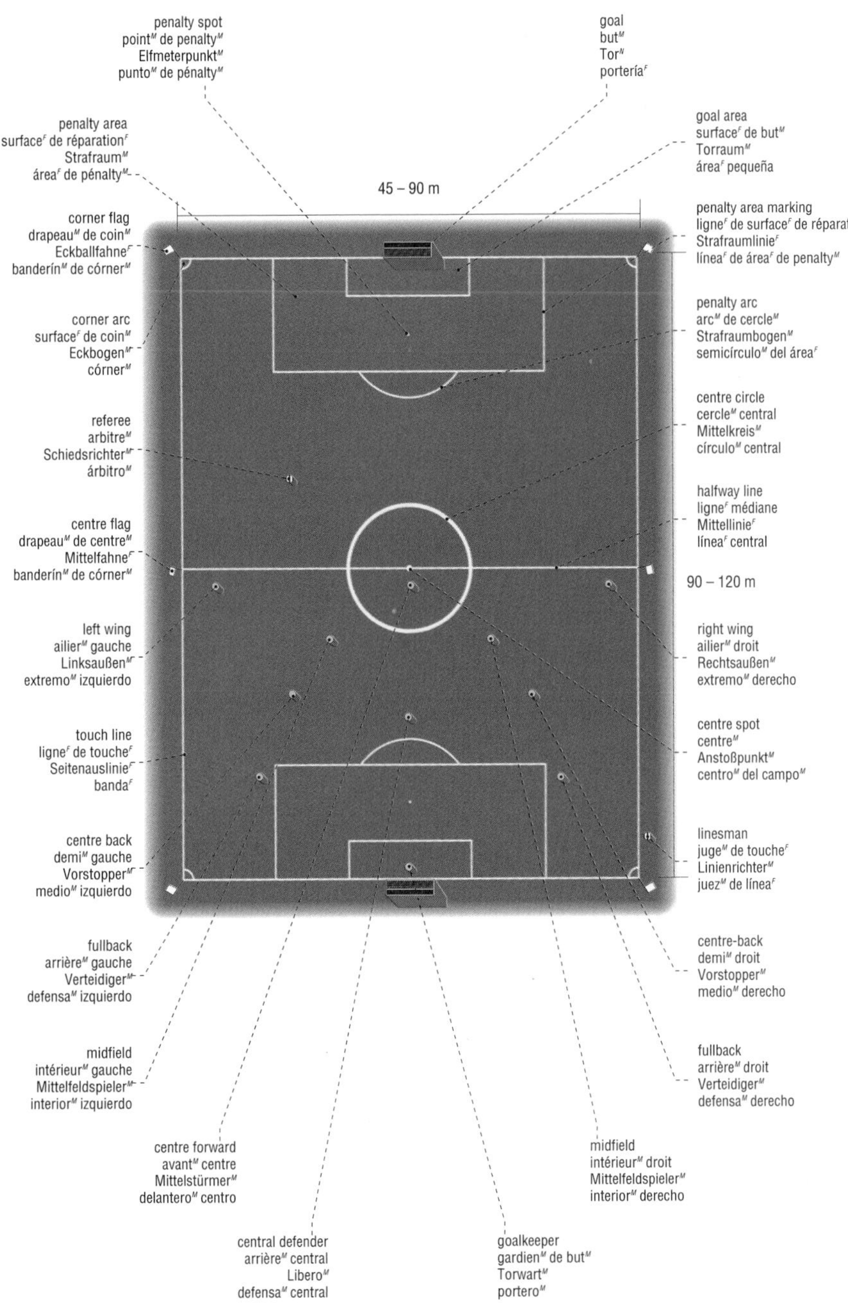

# AMERICAN FOOTBALL
# FOOTBALLᴹ AMÉRICAIN
# FOOTBALLᴺ
# FÚTBOLᴹ AMERICANO

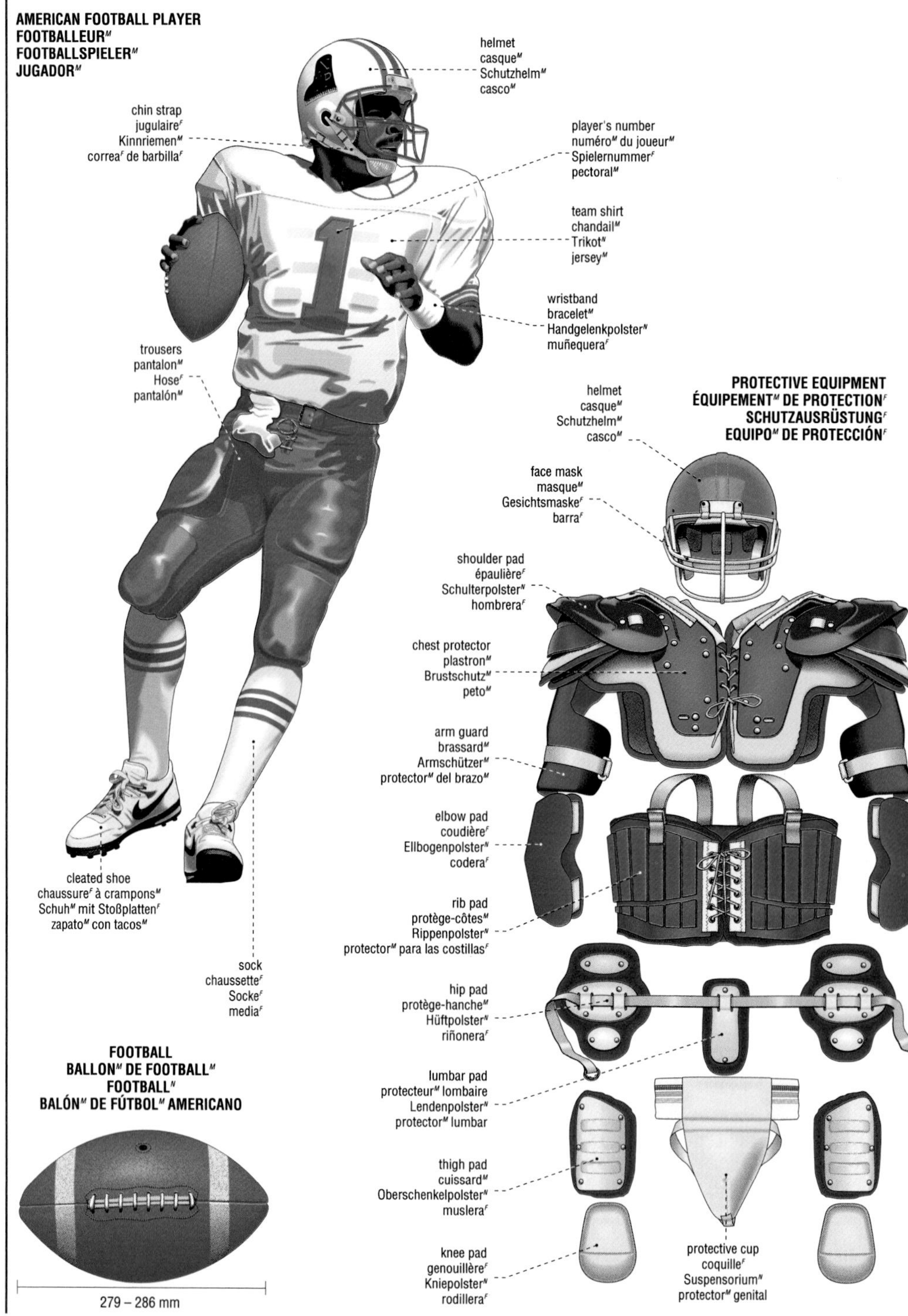

## SCRIMMAGE
## MÊLÉE$^{F}$
## SCRIMMAGE$^{N}$
## MELÉ$^{M}$

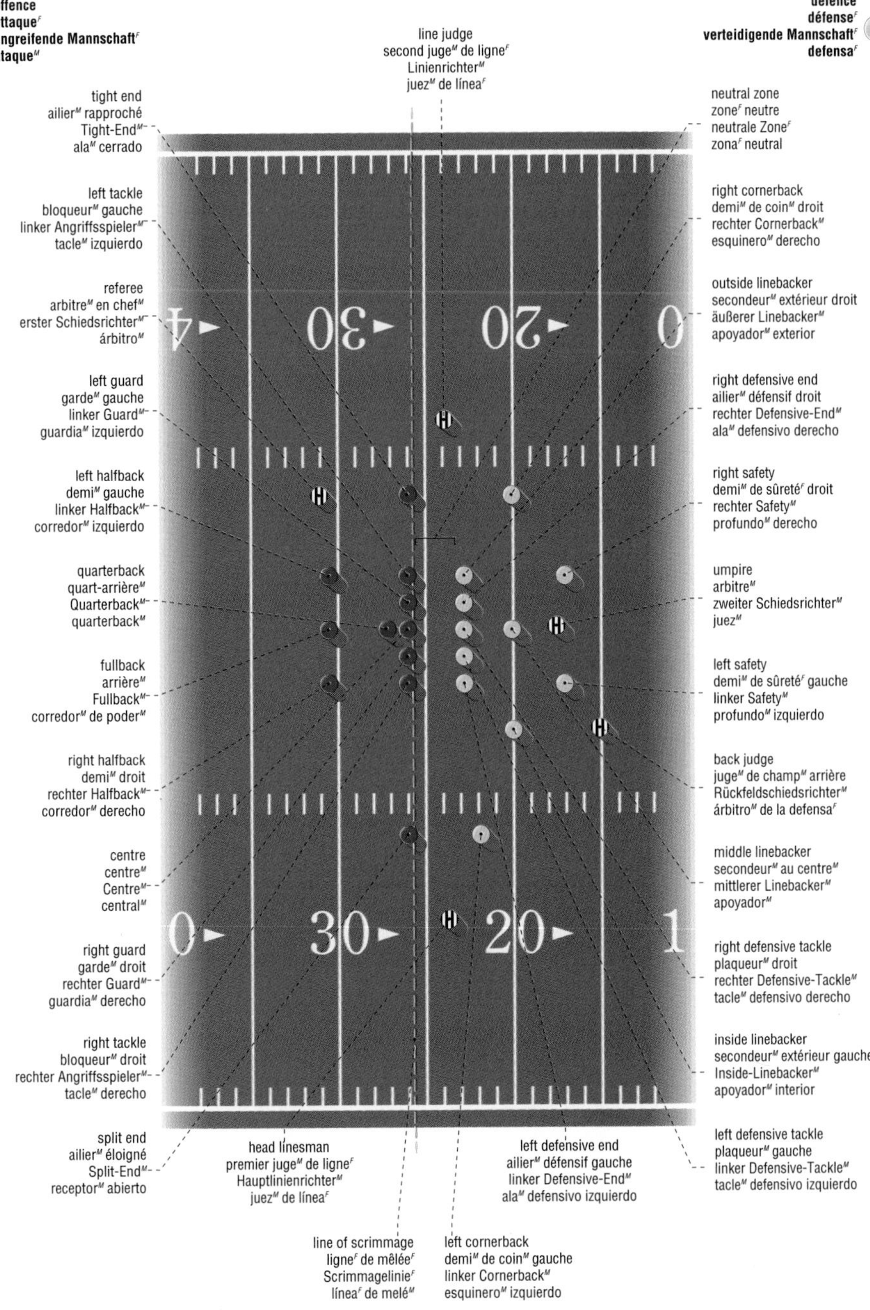

# AMERICAN/CANADIAN FOOTBALL
# FOOTBALL[M]
# FOOTBALL[N]
# FÚTBOL[M] AMERICANO

## PLAYING FIELD FOR AMERICAN FOOTBALL
## TERRAIN[M] DE FOOTBALL[M] AMÉRICAIN
## SPIELFELD[N] FÜR AMERIKANISCHES FOOTBALL[N]
## CAMPO[M] DE JUEGO[M] DE FÚTBOL[M] AMERICANO

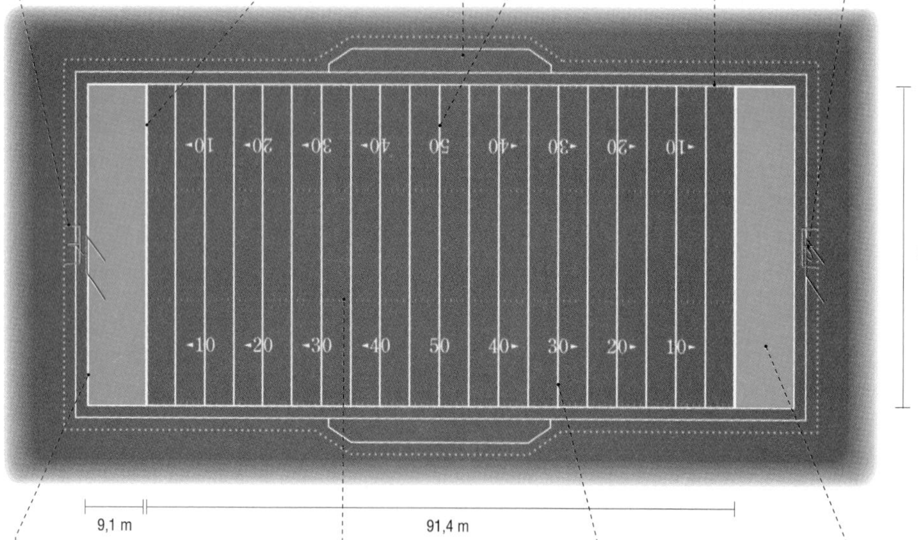

players' bench
banc[M] des joueurs[M]
Spielerbank[F]
banquillo[M] de jugadores[M]

sideline
ligne[F] de touche[F]
Seitenlinie[F]
banda[F]

goalpost
poteau[M] de but[M]
Torpfosten[M]
poste[M]

goal line
ligne[F] de but[M]
Torlinie[F]
línea[F] de gol[M]

centre line
ligne[F] de centre[M]
Mittellinie[F]
línea[F] media

goal
but[M]
Tor[N]
gol[M]

10 20 30 40 50 40 30 20 10

49 m

9,1 m

91,4 m

end line
ligne[F] de fond[M]
Endlinie[F]
línea[F] de fondo[M]

inbound line
trait[M] de mise[F] au jeu[M]
Inbound-Linie[F]
línea[F] límite[M] de inicio[M] de jugada[F]

yard line
ligne[F] des verges[F]
Yardlinie[F]
yardas[F]

end zone
zone[F] de but[M]
Endzone[F]
zona[F] de anotación[F]

## PLAYING FIELD FOR CANADIAN FOOTBALL
## TERRAIN[M] DE FOOTBALL[M] CANADIEN
## SPIELFELD[N] FÜR KANADISCHES FOOTBALL[N]
## CAMPO[M] DE JUEGO[M] DE FÚTBOL[M] CANADIENSE

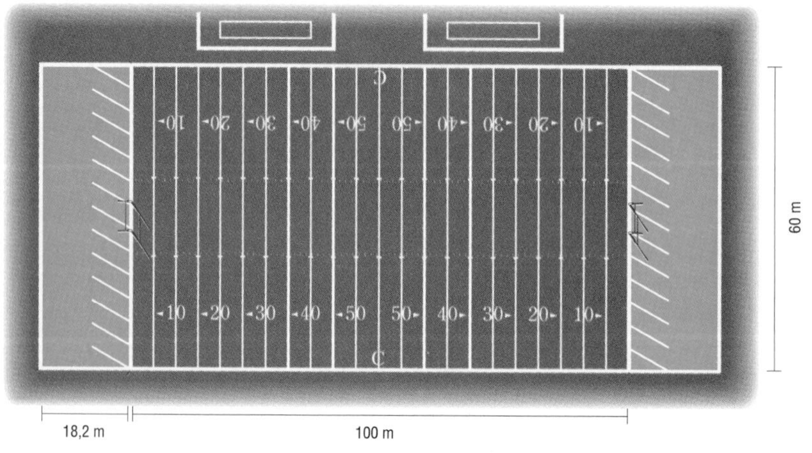

# SCRIMMAGE IN CANADIAN FOOTBALL
# MÊLÉE[F] AU FOOTBALL[M] CANADIEN
# SCRIMMAGE[N] IM KANADISCHEN FOOTBALL[M]
# MELÉ[M] EN EL FÚTBOL[M] CANADIENSE

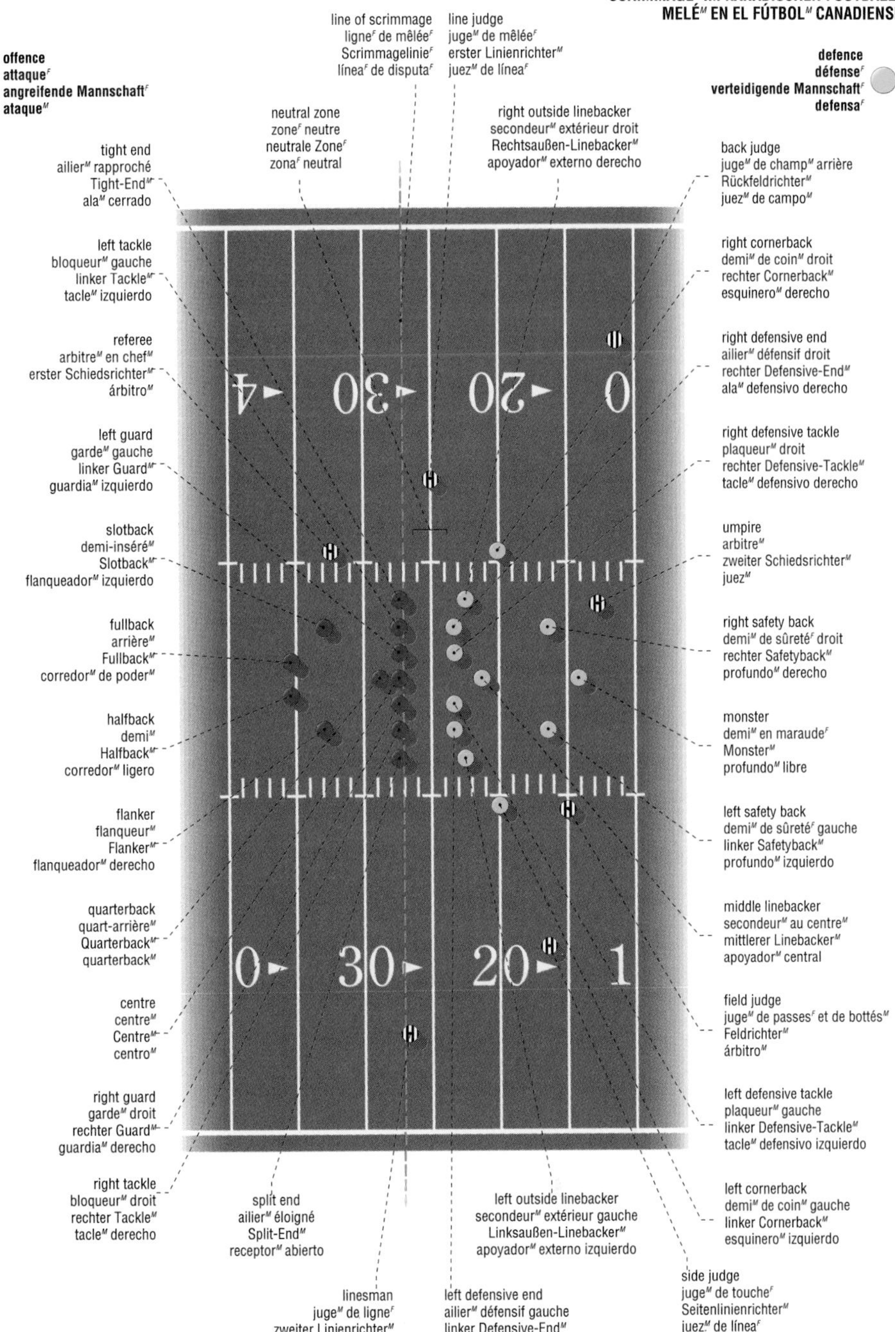

# RUGBY
# RUGBY$^{M}$
# RUGBY$^{N}$
# RUGBY$^{M}$

## FIELD
## TERRAIN$^{M}$
## SPIELFELD$^{N}$
## CAMPO$^{M}$ DE JUEGO$^{M}$

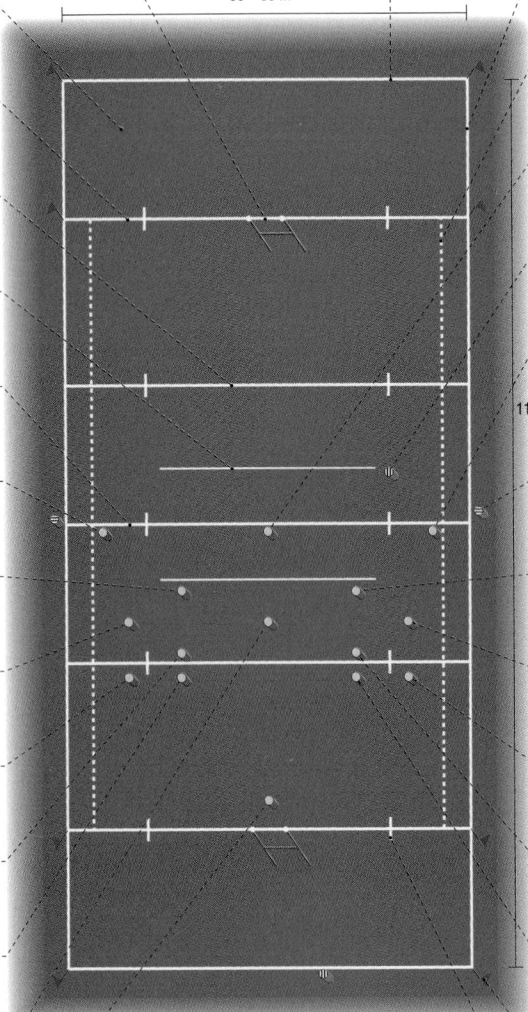

goal
but$^{M}$
Tor$^{N}$
gol$^{M}$

dead ball line
ligne$^{F}$ de ballon$^{M}$ mort
Auslinie$^{F}$
línea$^{F}$ de fondo$^{M}$

touchline
ligne$^{F}$ de touche$^{F}$
Seitenlinie$^{F}$
línea$^{F}$ de banda$^{F}$

66 – 69 m

in goal
en-but$^{M}$
Torbereich$^{M}$
zona$^{F}$ de gol$^{M}$

5 metre line
ligne$^{F}$ des 5 mètres$^{M}$
5-Meter-Linie$^{F}$
línea$^{F}$ de los 5 metros$^{M}$

goal line
ligne$^{F}$ de but$^{M}$
Torlinie$^{F}$
línea$^{F}$ de gol$^{M}$

hooker
talonneur$^{M}$
Hakler$^{M}$
taloneador$^{M}$

22 metre line
ligne$^{F}$ des 22 mètres$^{M}$
22-Meter-Linie$^{F}$
línea$^{F}$ de los 22 metros$^{M}$

referee
arbitre$^{M}$
Schiedsrichter$^{M}$
árbitro$^{M}$

10 metre line
ligne$^{F}$ des 10 mètres$^{M}$
10-Meter-Linie$^{F}$
línea$^{F}$ de los 10 metros$^{M}$

prop forward
pilier$^{M}$ droit
Prop-Forward$^{M}$
puntal$^{M}$ derecho

halfway line
ligne$^{F}$ médiane
Mittellinie$^{F}$
centro$^{M}$ del campo$^{M}$

119 – 144 m

prop forward
pilier$^{M}$ gauche
Prop-Forward$^{M}$
puntal$^{M}$ izquierdo

touch judge
juge$^{M}$ de touche$^{F}$
Linienrichter$^{M}$
juez$^{M}$ de línea$^{F}$

wing forward
avant$^{M}$ gauche
Wing-Forward$^{M}$
ala$^{M}$ delantero

wing forward
avant$^{M}$ droit
Wing-Forward$^{M}$
ala$^{M}$ delantero

lock forward
aile$^{F}$ gauche
Lock-Forward$^{M}$
delantero$^{M}$

lock forward
aile$^{F}$ droite
Lock-Forward$^{M}$
delantero$^{M}$

left wing
ailier$^{M}$ gauche
Left-Wing$^{M}$
extremo$^{M}$ izquierdo

right wing
ailier$^{M}$ droit
rechter Flügelspieler$^{M}$
extremo$^{M}$ derecho

fly half
demi$^{M}$ d'ouverture$^{F}$
Fly-Half$^{M}$
medio$^{M}$ alejado

scrum half
demi$^{M}$ de mêlée$^{F}$
Gedrängehalbspieler$^{M}$
medio de melé$^{M}$

left centre
centre$^{M}$ gauche
linker Centre$^{M}$
centro$^{M}$ izquierdo

right centre
centre$^{M}$ droit
rechter Centre$^{M}$
centro$^{M}$ derecho

no. 8 forward
centre$^{M}$
Nummer-8-Forward$^{M}$
delantero$^{M}$ número 8

flag
drapeau$^{M}$
Fahne$^{F}$
bandera$^{F}$

## RUGBY BALL
## BALLON$^{M}$ DE RUGBY$^{M}$
## RUGBYBALL$^{M}$
## BALÓN$^{M}$ DE RUGBY$^{M}$

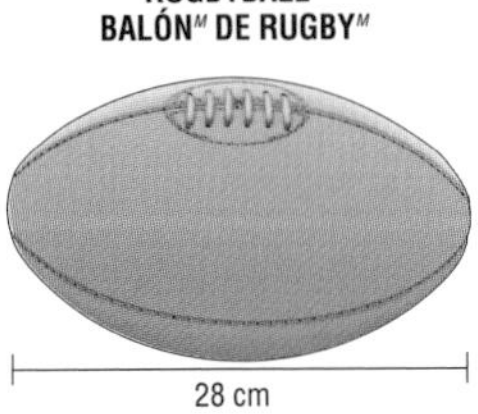

full back
arrière$^{M}$
Fullback$^{M}$
defensa$^{F}$ de cierre$^{M}$

15 metre line
ligne$^{F}$ des 15 mètres$^{M}$
15-Meter-Linie$^{F}$
línea$^{F}$ de los 15 metros$^{M}$

28 cm

# FIELD HOCKEY
# HOCKEY^M SUR GAZON^M
# HOCKEY^N
# HOCKEY^M SOBRE HIERBA^F

## PLAYING FIELD
## TERRAIN^M
## SPIELFELD^N
## CAMPO^M DE JUEGO^M

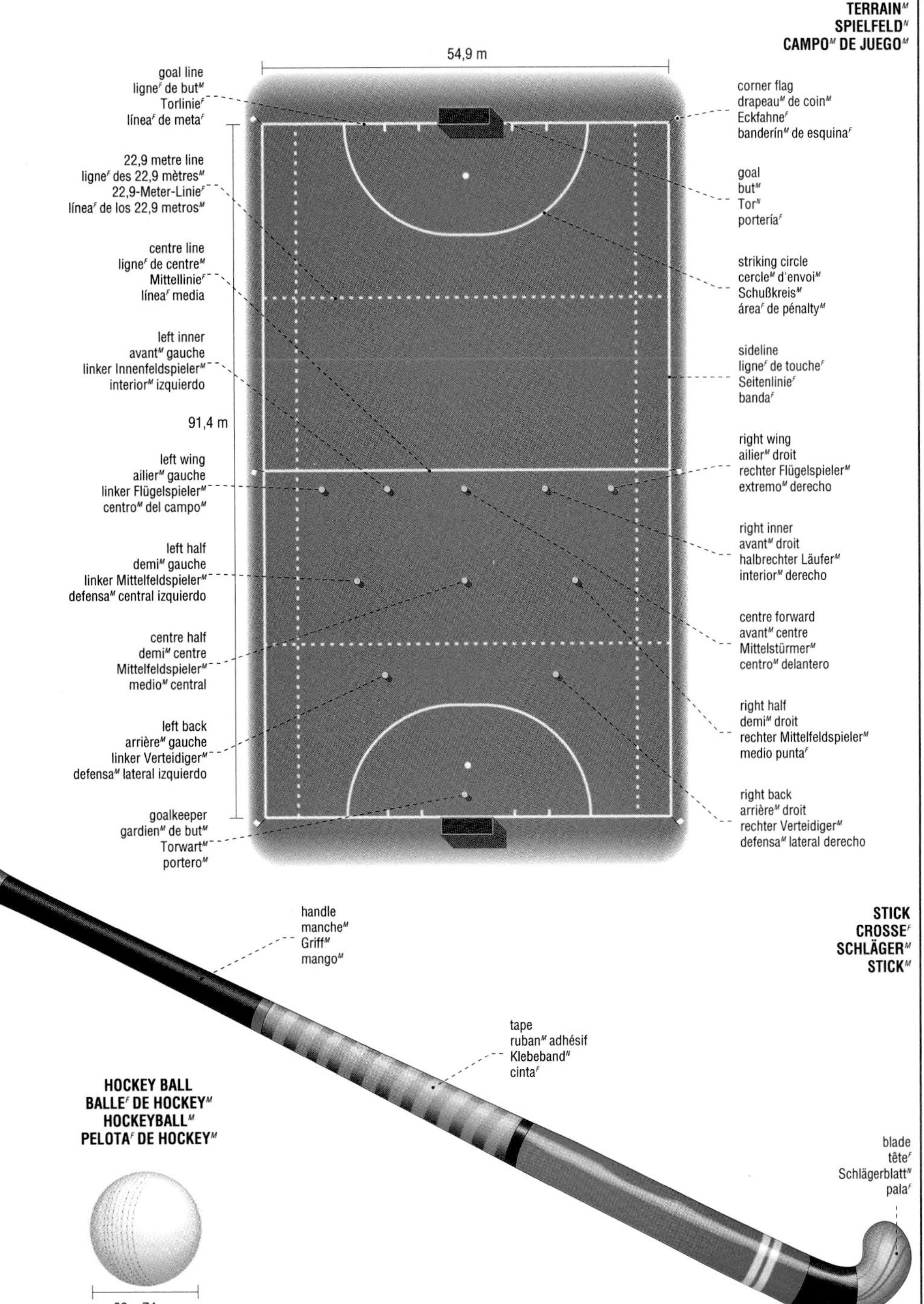


## STICK
## CROSSE^F
## SCHLÄGER^M
## STICK^M

## HOCKEY BALL
## BALLE^F DE HOCKEY^M
## HOCKEYBALL^M
## PELOTA^F DE HOCKEY^M

# ICE HOCKEY
# HOCKEY[M] SUR GLACE[F]
# EISHOCKEY[N]
# HOCKEY[M] SOBRE HIELO



## RINK
## PATINOIRE[F]
## EISFLÄCHE[F]
## PISTA[F]

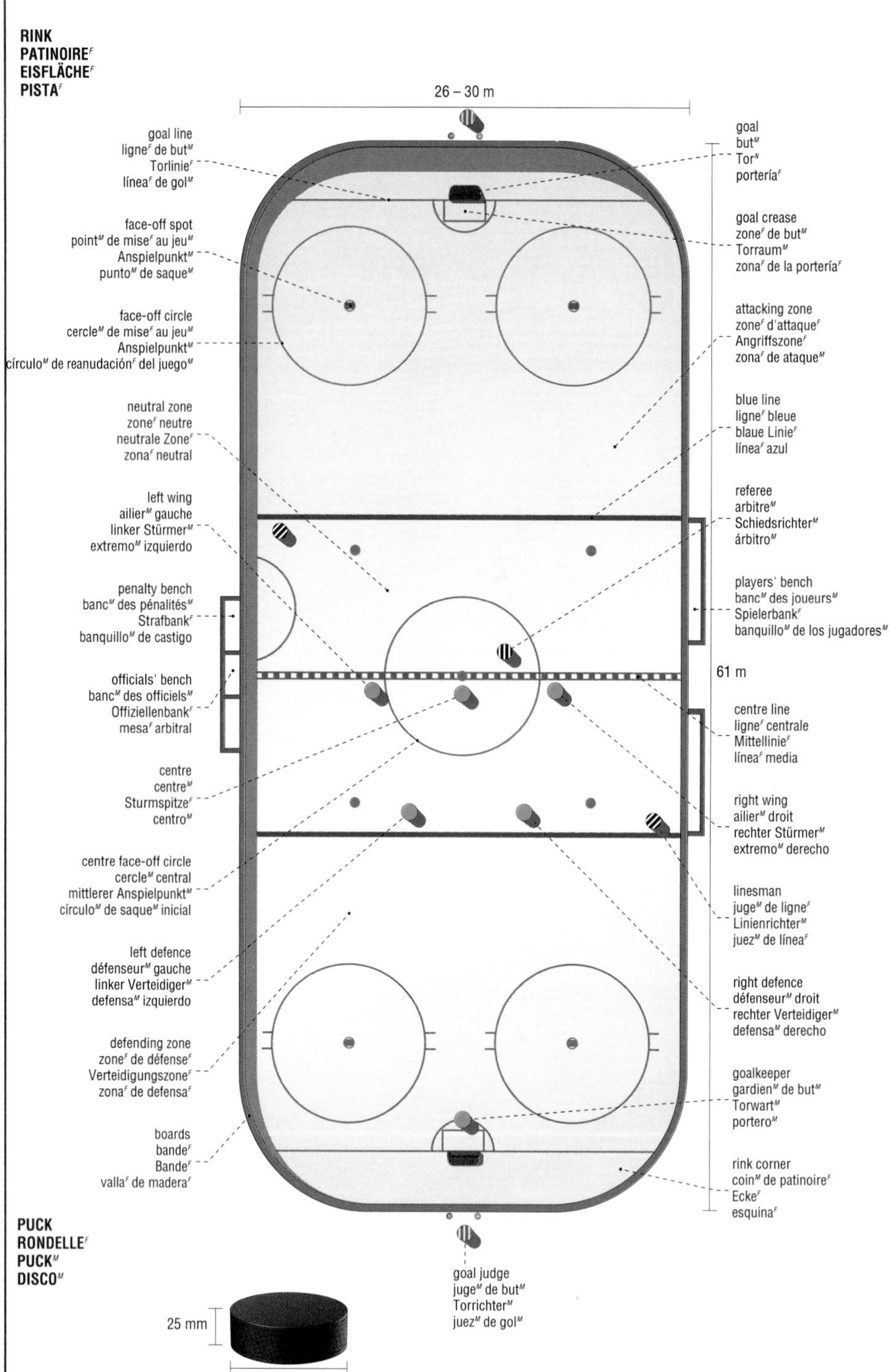


## PUCK
## RONDELLE[F]
## PUCK[M]
## DISCO[M]

25 mm

76 mm

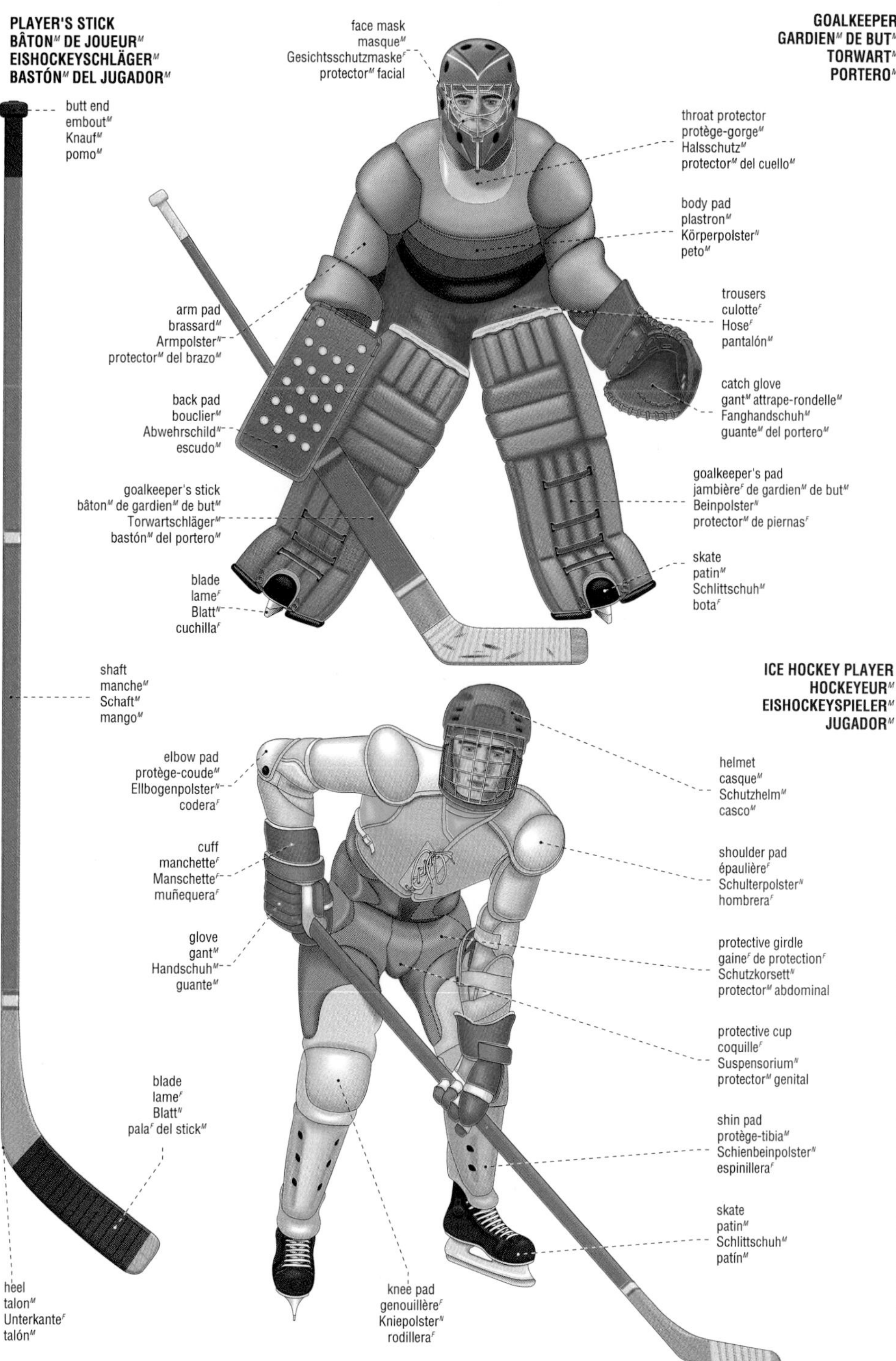
PLAYER'S STICK
BÂTON[M] DE JOUEUR[M]
EISHOCKEYSCHLÄGER[M]
BASTÓN[M] DEL JUGADOR[M]
butt end
embout[M]
Knauf[M]
pomo[M]
shaft
manche[M]
Schaft[M]
mango[M]
blade
lame[F]
Blatt[N]
pala[F] del stick[M]
heel
talon[M]
Unterkante[F]
talón[M]
face mask
masque[M]
Gesichtsschutzmaske[F]
protector[M] facial
GOALKEEPER
GARDIEN[M] DE BUT[M]
TORWART[M]
PORTERO[M]
throat protector
protège-gorge[M]
Halsschutz[M]
protector[M] del cuello[M]
body pad
plastron[M]
Körperpolster[N]
peto[M]
arm pad
brassard[M]
Armpolster[N]
protector[M] del brazo[M]
trousers
culotte[F]
Hose[F]
pantalón[M]
back pad
bouclier[M]
Abwehrschild[N]
escudo[M]
catch glove
gant[M] attrape-rondelle[M]
Fanghandschuh[M]
guante[M] del portero[M]
goalkeeper's stick
bâton[M] de gardien[M] de but[M]
Torwartschläger[M]
bastón[M] del portero[M]
goalkeeper's pad
jambière[F] de gardien[M] de but[M]
Beinpolster[N]
protector[M] de piernas[F]
blade
lame[F]
Blatt[N]
cuchilla[F]
skate
patin[M]
Schlittschuh[M]
bota[F]
ICE HOCKEY PLAYER
HOCKEYEUR[M]
EISHOCKEYSPIELER[M]
JUGADOR[M]
helmet
casque[M]
Schutzhelm[M]
casco[M]
elbow pad
protège-coude[M]
Ellbogenpolster[N]
codera[F]
shoulder pad
épaulière[F]
Schulterpolster[N]
hombrera[F]
cuff
manchette[F]
Manschette[F]
muñequera[F]
glove
gant[M]
Handschuh[M]
guante[M]
protective girdle
gaine[F] de protection[F]
Schutzkorsett[N]
protector[M] abdominal
protective cup
coquille[F]
Suspensorium[N]
protector[M] genital
shin pad
protège-tibia[M]
Schienbeinpolster[N]
espinillera[F]
skate
patin[M]
Schlittschuh[M]
patín[M]
knee pad
genouillère[F]
Kniepolster[N]
rodillera[F]

# BASKETBALL
# BASKETBALL[M]
# BASKETBALLSPIEL[N]
# BALONCESTO[M]

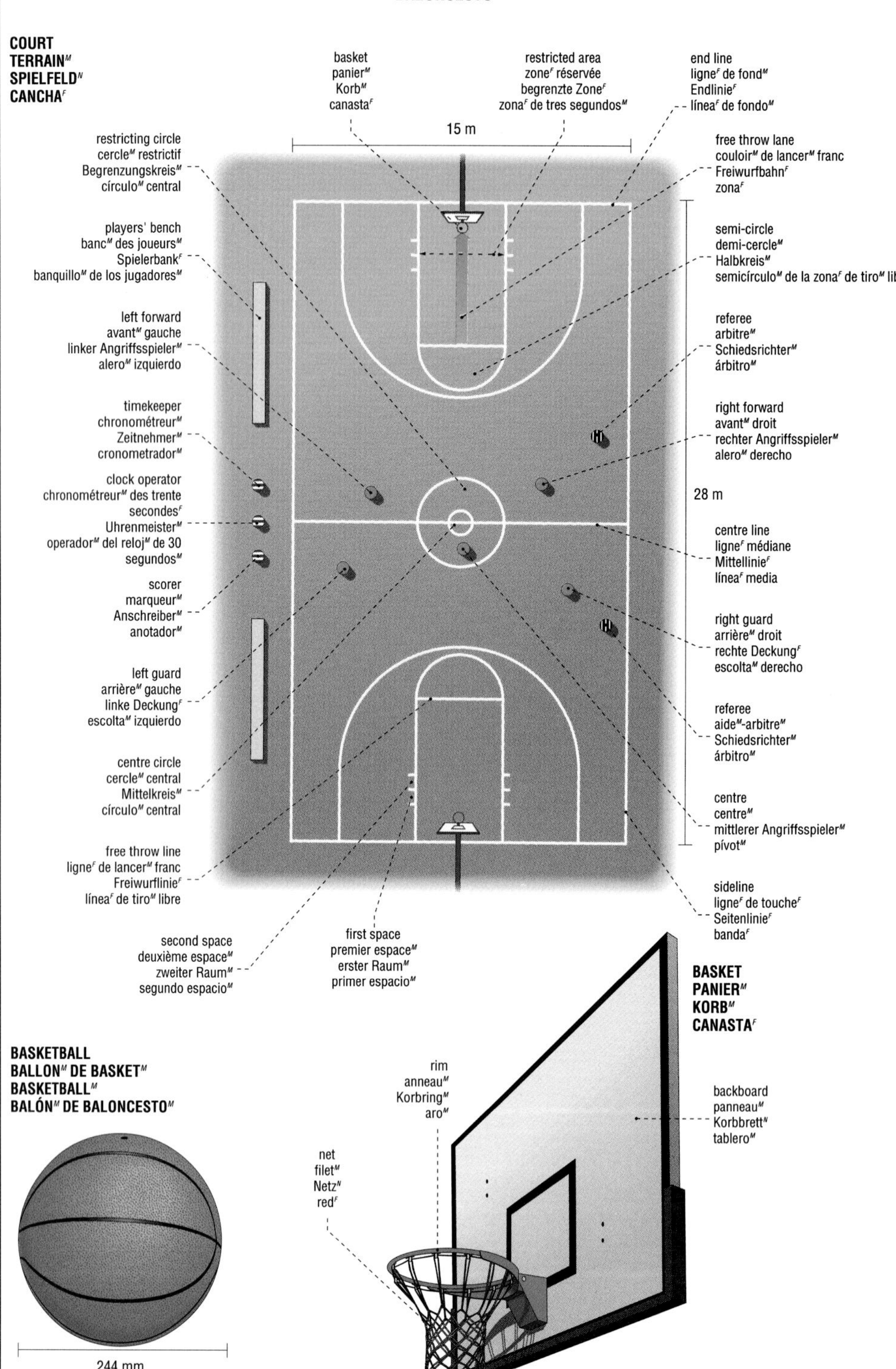

# NETBALL
# NETBALL$^{M}$
# NETZBALLSPIEL$^{N}$
# BALONCESTO$^{M}$ DE MUJERES$^{F}$



## COURT
## TERRAIN$^{M}$
## SPIELFELD$^{N}$
## CANCHA$^{F}$

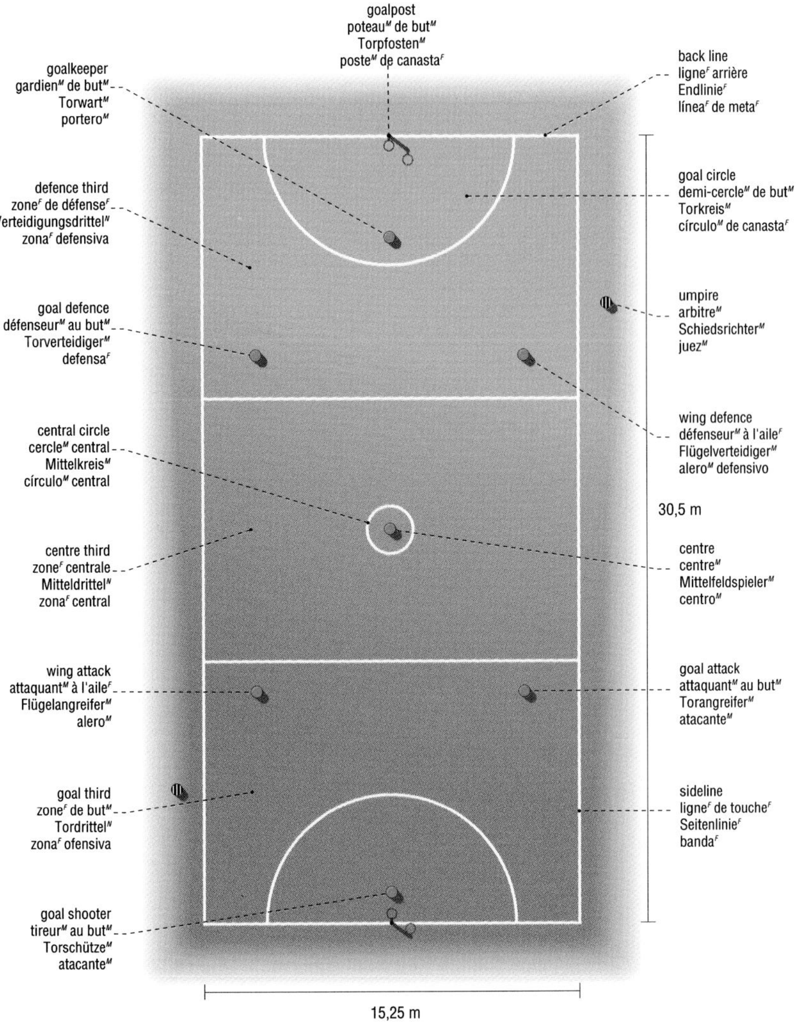

goalpost
poteau$^{M}$ de but$^{M}$
Torpfosten$^{M}$
poste$^{M}$ de canasta$^{F}$

goalkeeper
gardien$^{M}$ de but$^{M}$
Torwart$^{M}$
portero$^{M}$

back line
ligne$^{F}$ arrière
Endlinie$^{F}$
línea$^{F}$ de meta$^{F}$

goal circle
demi-cercle$^{M}$ de but$^{M}$
Torkreis$^{M}$
círculo$^{M}$ de canasta$^{F}$

defence third
zone$^{F}$ de défense$^{F}$
Verteidigungsdrittel$^{N}$
zona$^{F}$ defensiva

umpire
arbitre$^{M}$
Schiedsrichter$^{M}$
juez$^{M}$

goal defence
défenseur$^{M}$ au but$^{M}$
Torverteidiger$^{M}$
defensa$^{F}$

wing defence
défenseur$^{M}$ à l'aile$^{F}$
Flügelverteidiger$^{M}$
alero$^{M}$ defensivo

central circle
cercle$^{M}$ central
Mittelkreis$^{M}$
círculo$^{M}$ central

30,5 m

centre third
zone$^{F}$ centrale
Mitteldrittel$^{N}$
zona$^{F}$ central

centre
centre$^{M}$
Mittelfeldspieler$^{M}$
centro$^{M}$

wing attack
attaquant$^{M}$ à l'aile$^{F}$
Flügelangreifer$^{M}$
alero$^{M}$

goal attack
attaquant$^{M}$ au but$^{M}$
Torangreifer$^{M}$
atacante$^{M}$

goal third
zone$^{F}$ de but$^{M}$
Tordrittel$^{N}$
zona$^{F}$ ofensiva

sideline
ligne$^{F}$ de touche$^{F}$
Seitenlinie$^{F}$
banda$^{F}$

goal shooter
tireur$^{M}$ au but$^{M}$
Torschütze$^{M}$
atacante$^{M}$

15,25 m

## NETBALL
## BALLON$^{M}$ DE NETBALL$^{M}$
## NETZBALLSPIEL$^{N}$
## BALÓN$^{M}$

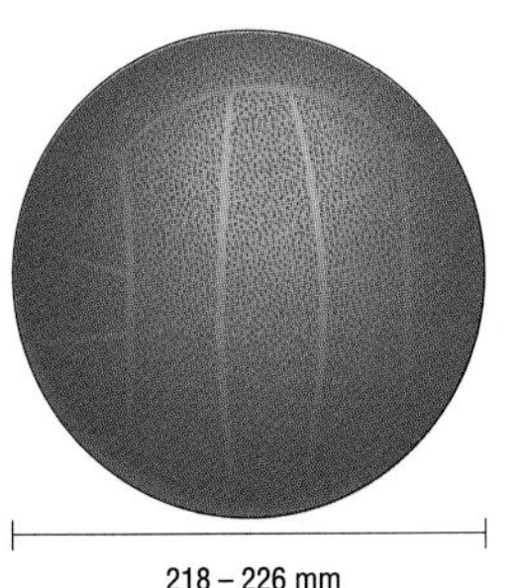

# HANDBALL
# HANDBALL[M]
# HANDBALL[M]
# BALONMANO[M]

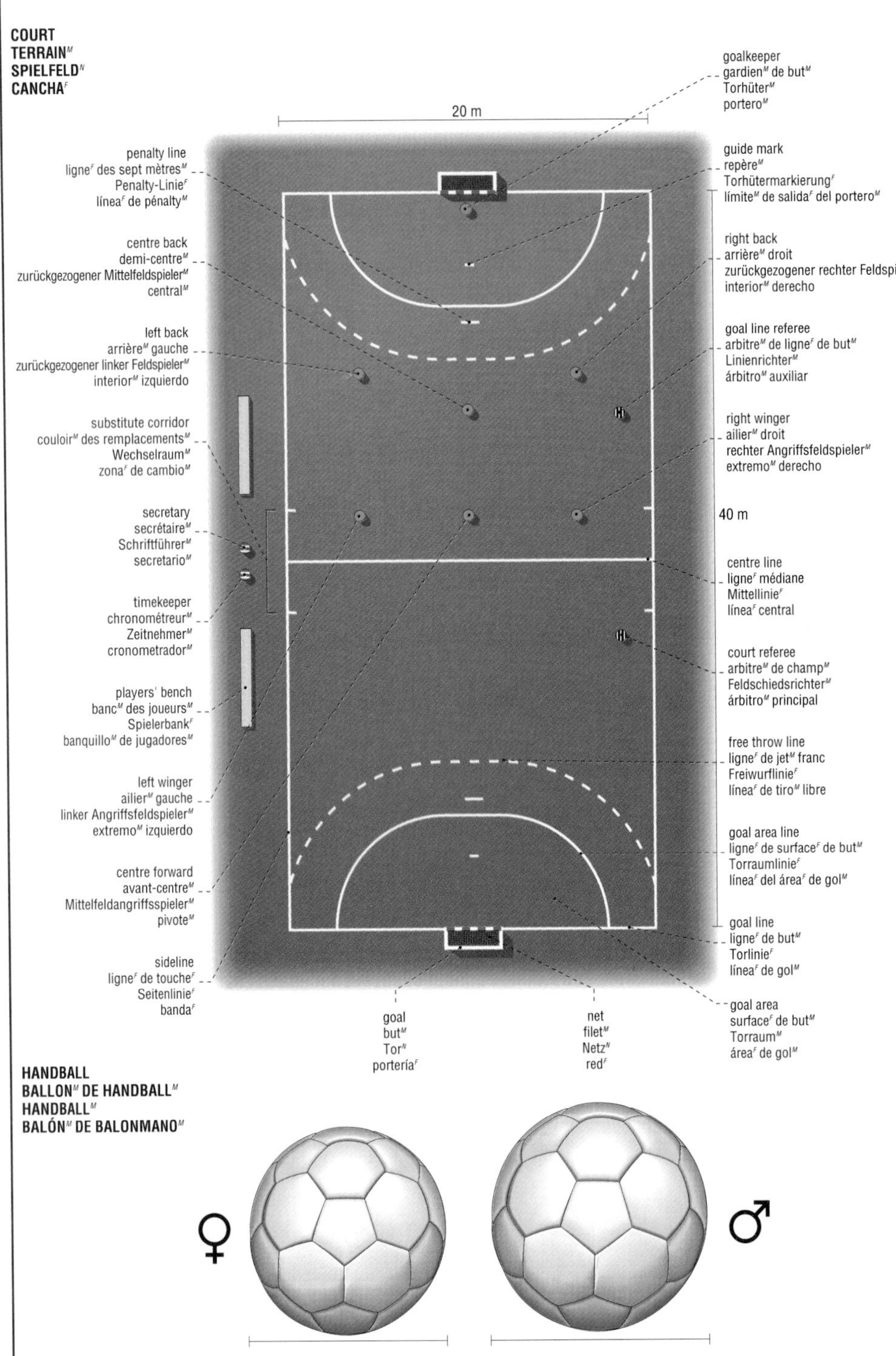

# VOLLEYBALL
# VOLLEYBALL[M]
# VOLLEYBALLSPIEL[N]
# BALÓN[M] VOLEA

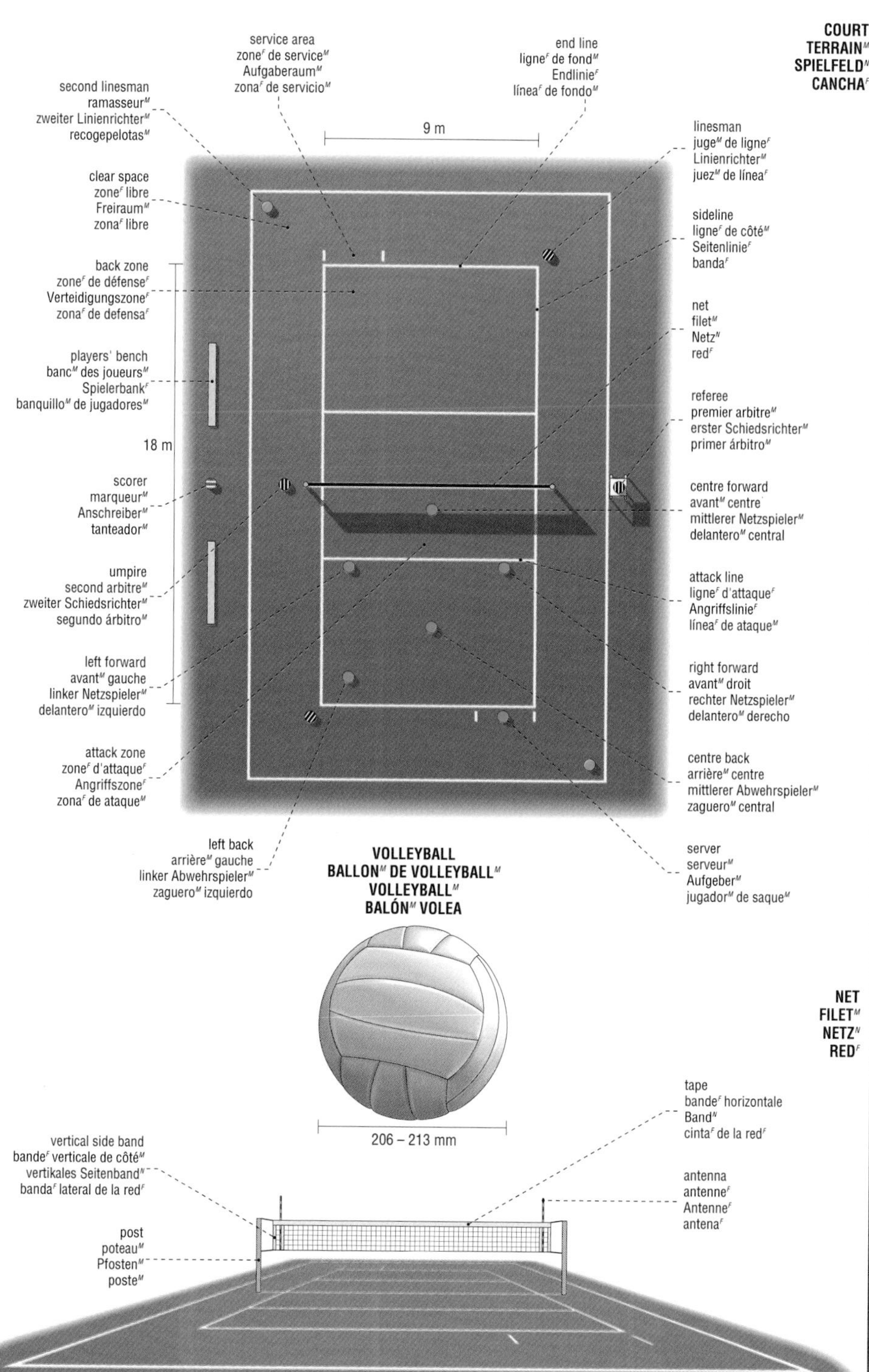

# TENNIS
# TENNIS[M]
# TENNIS[N]
# TENIS[M]

## COURT
## TERRAIN[M]
## TENNISPLATZ[M]
## CANCHA[F]

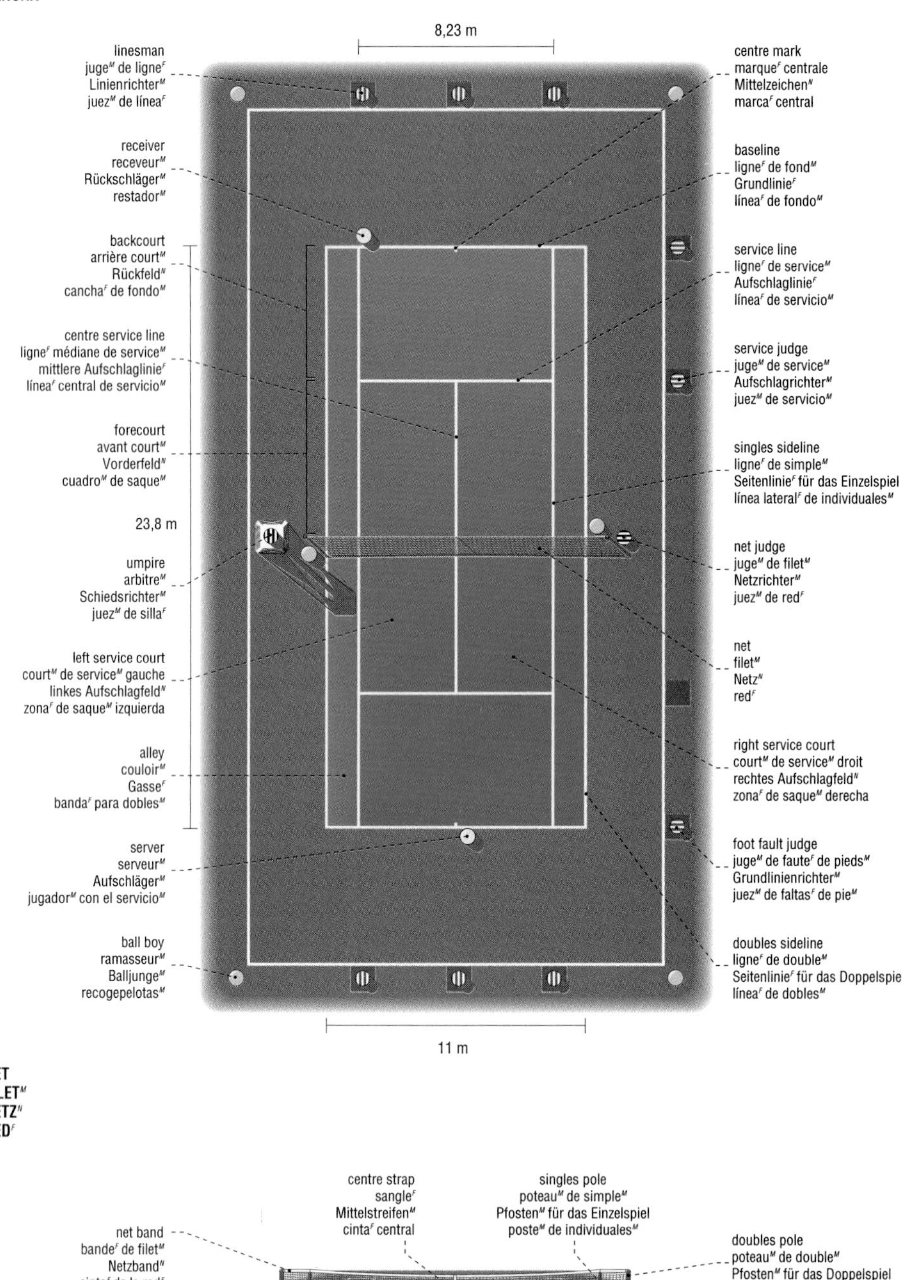


## NET
## FILET[M]
## NETZ[N]
## RED[F]

**TENNIS PLAYER**
**JOUEUSE[F] DE TENNIS[M]**
**TENNISSPIELERIN[F]**
**TENISTA[M/F]**

**TENNIS RACKET**
**RAQUETTE[F] DE TENNIS[M]**
**TENNISSCHLÄGER[M]**
**RAQUETA[F] DE TENIS[M]**

**TENNIS BALL**
**BALLE[F] DE TENNIS[M]**
**TENNISBALL[M]**
**PELOTA[F] DE TENIS[M]**

# SQUASH
# SQUASH[M]
# SQUASH[N]
# SQUASH[M]

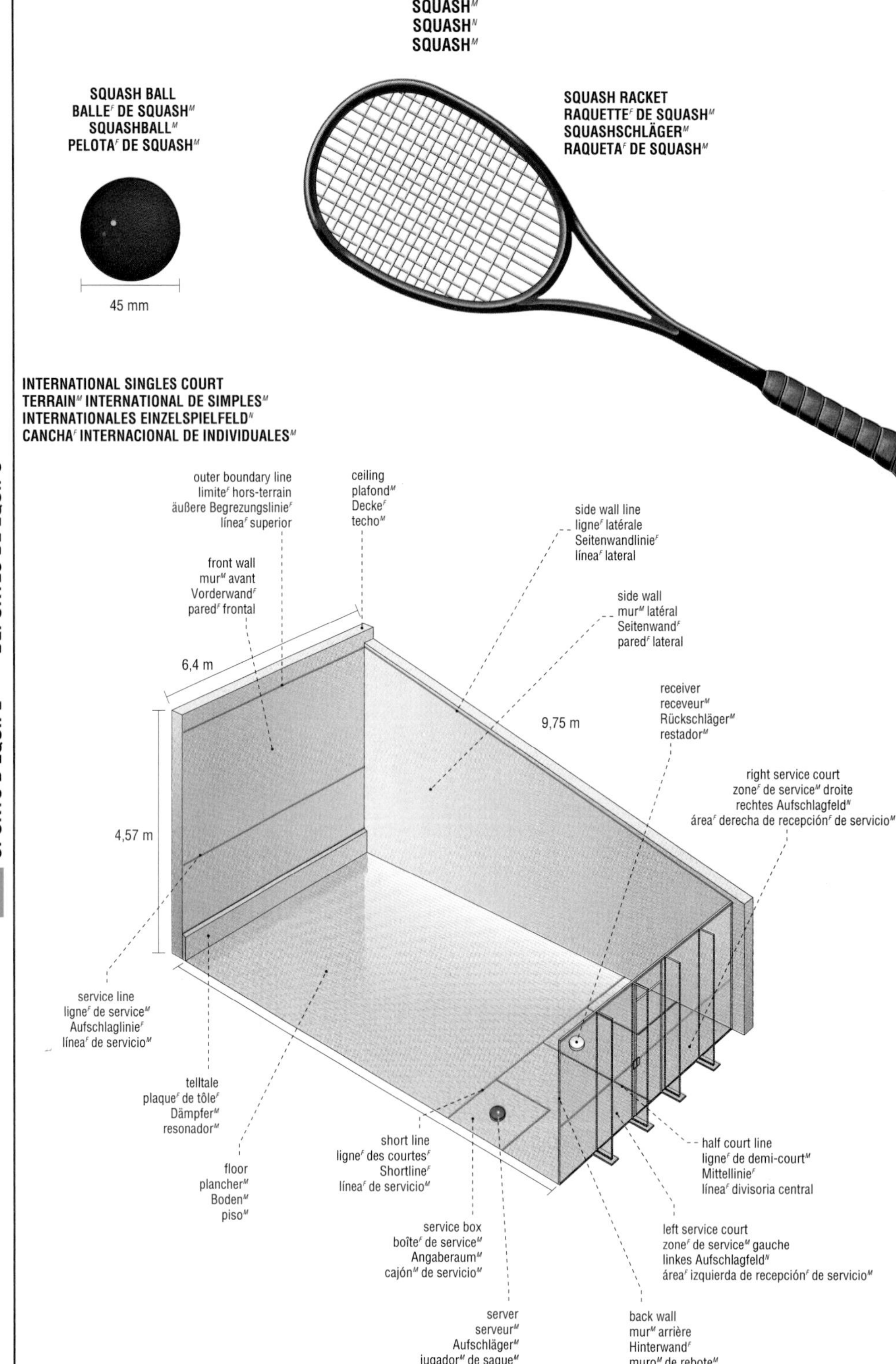

# RACQUETBALL
# RACQUETBALL[M]
# RACQUETBALLSPIEL[N]
# RAQUETBOL[M]

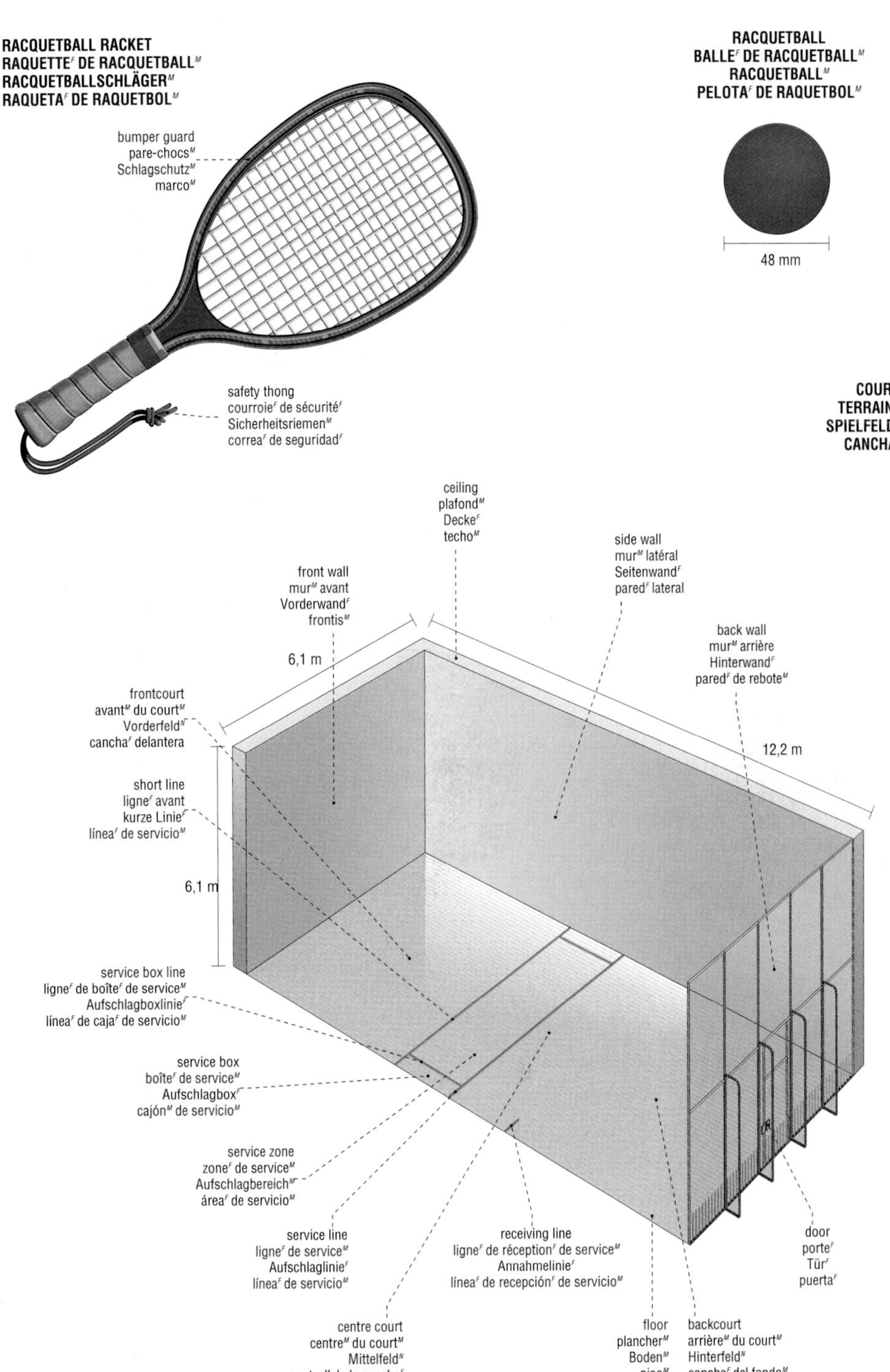

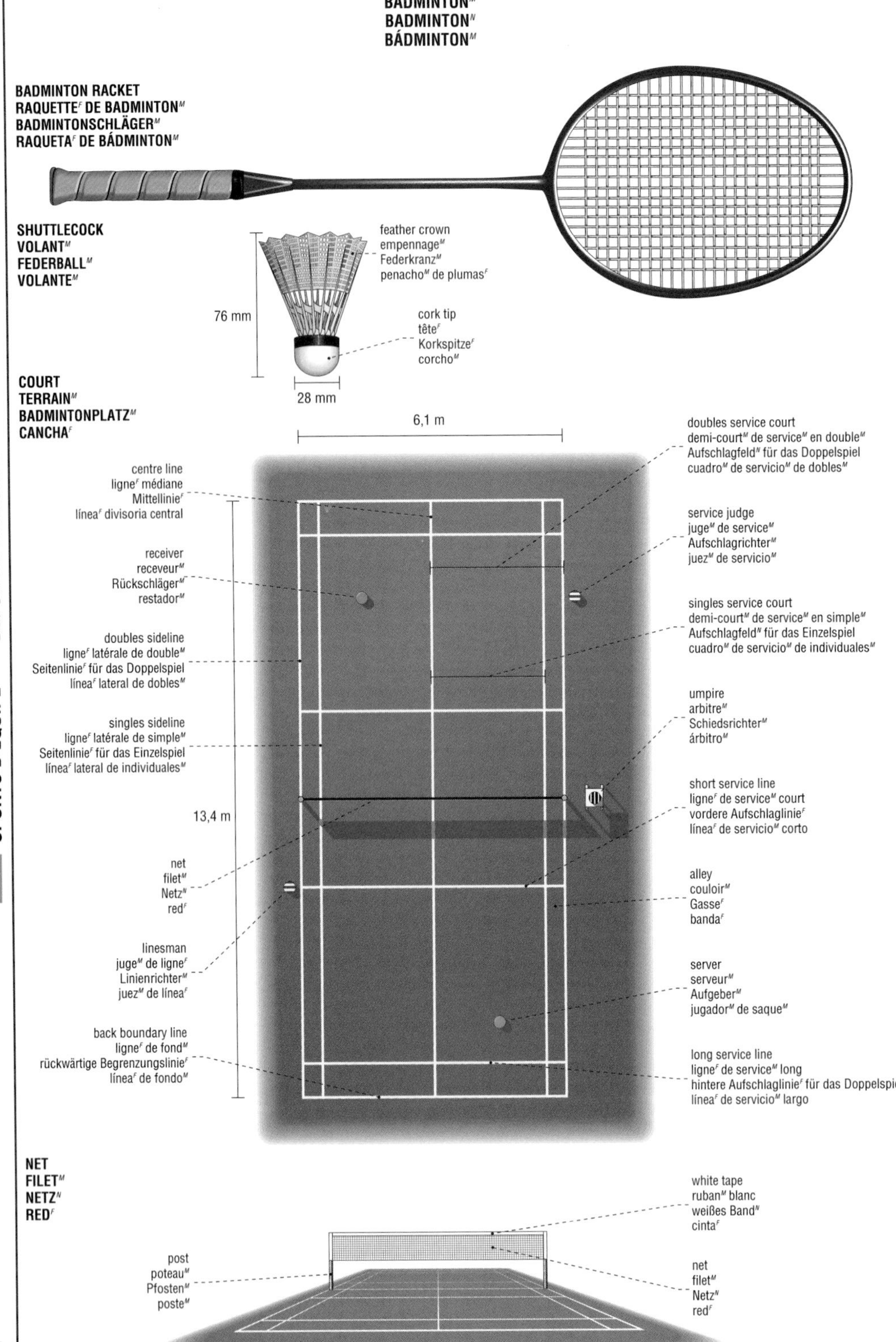
BADMINTON
BADMINTON[M]
BADMINTON[N]
BÁDMINTON[M]
BADMINTON RACKET
RAQUETTE[F] DE BADMINTON[M]
BADMINTONSCHLÄGER[M]
RAQUETA[F] DE BÁDMINTON[M]
SHUTTLECOCK
VOLANT[M]
FEDERBALL[M]
VOLANTE[M]
feather crown
empennage[M]
Federkranz[M]
penacho[M] de plumas[F]
76 mm
cork tip
tête[F]
Korkspitze[F]
corcho[M]
28 mm
COURT
TERRAIN[M]
BADMINTONPLATZ[M]
CANCHA[F]
6,1 m
doubles service court
demi-court[M] de service[M] en double[M]
Aufschlagfeld[N] für das Doppelspiel
cuadro[M] de servicio[M] de dobles[M]
centre line
ligne[F] médiane
Mittellinie[F]
línea[F] divisoria central
service judge
juge[M] de service[M]
Aufschlagrichter[M]
juez[M] de servicio[M]
receiver
receveur[M]
Rückschläger[M]
restador[M]
singles service court
demi-court[M] de service[M] en simple[M]
Aufschlagfeld[N] für das Einzelspiel
cuadro[M] de servicio[M] de individuales[M]
doubles sideline
ligne[F] latérale de double[M]
Seitenlinie[F] für das Doppelspiel
línea[F] lateral de dobles[M]
umpire
arbitre[M]
Schiedsrichter[M]
árbitro[M]
singles sideline
ligne[F] latérale de simple[M]
Seitenlinie[F] für das Einzelspiel
línea[F] lateral de individuales[M]
short service line
ligne[F] de service[M] court
vordere Aufschlaglinie[F]
línea[F] de servicio[M] corto
13,4 m
net
filet[M]
Netz[N]
red[F]
alley
couloir[M]
Gasse[F]
banda[F]
linesman
juge[M] de ligne[F]
Linienrichter[M]
juez[M] de línea[F]
server
serveur[M]
Aufgeber[M]
jugador[M] de saque[M]
back boundary line
ligne[F] de fond[M]
rückwärtige Begrenzungslinie[F]
línea[F] de fondo[M]
long service line
ligne[F] de service[M] long
hintere Aufschlaglinie[F] für das Doppelspiel[N]
línea[F] de servicio[M] largo
NET
FILET[M]
NETZ[N]
RED[F]
white tape
ruban[M] blanc
weißes Band[N]
cinta[F]
post
poteau[M]
Pfosten[M]
poste[M]
net
filet[M]
Netz[N]
red[F]

# TABLE TENNIS
# TENNIS[M] DE TABLE[F]
# TISCHTENNIS[N]
# PING PONG[M]

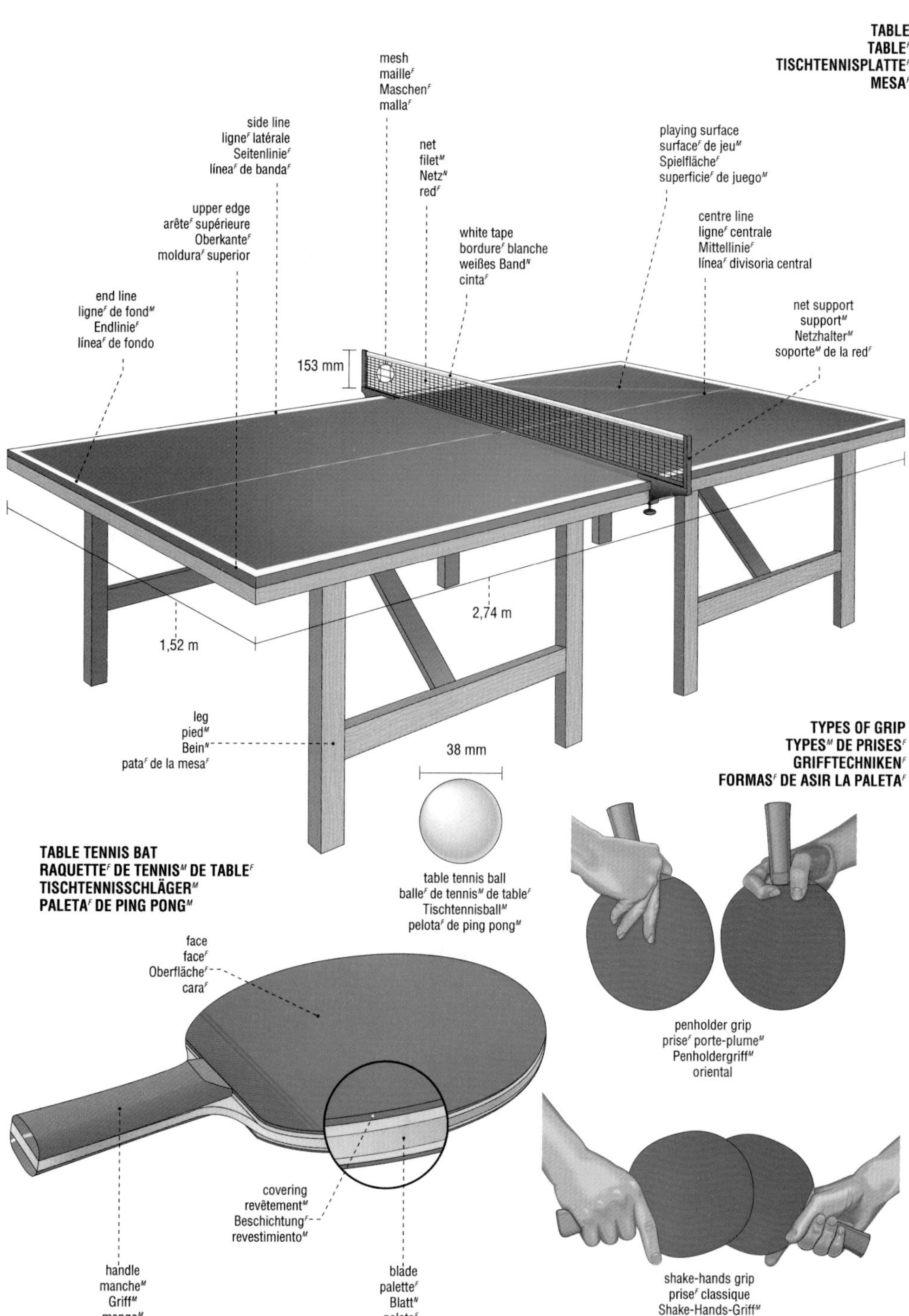

# CURLING
# CURLING^M
# CURLING^N
# CURLING^M

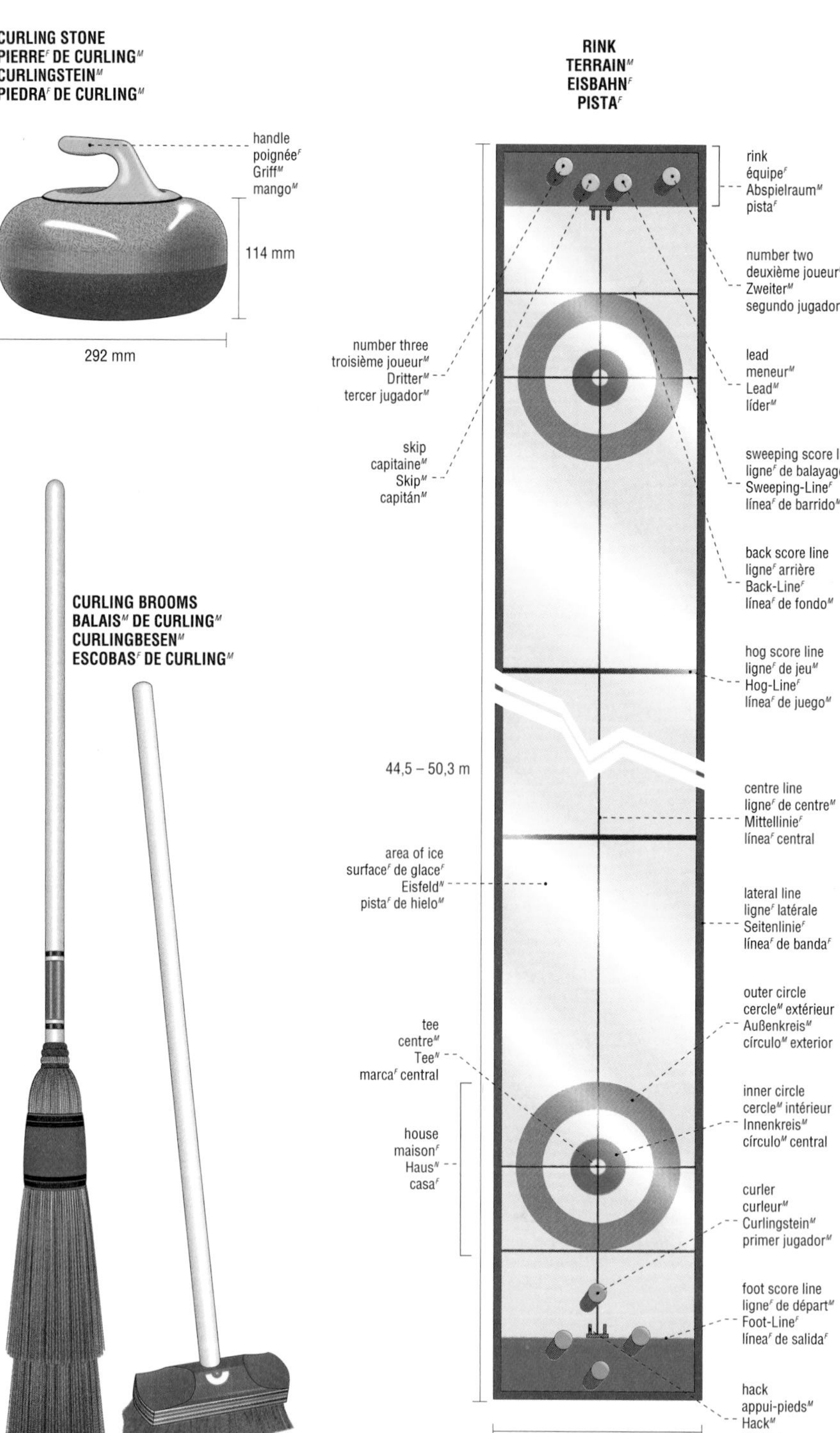

# SWIMMING
# NATATION$^{F}$
# SCHWIMMEN$^{N}$
# NATACIÓN$^{F}$

## COMPETITIVE COURSE
## BASSIN$^{M}$ DE COMPÉTITION$^{F}$
## WETTKAMPFBECKEN$^{N}$
## PISCINA$^{F}$ OLÍMPICA

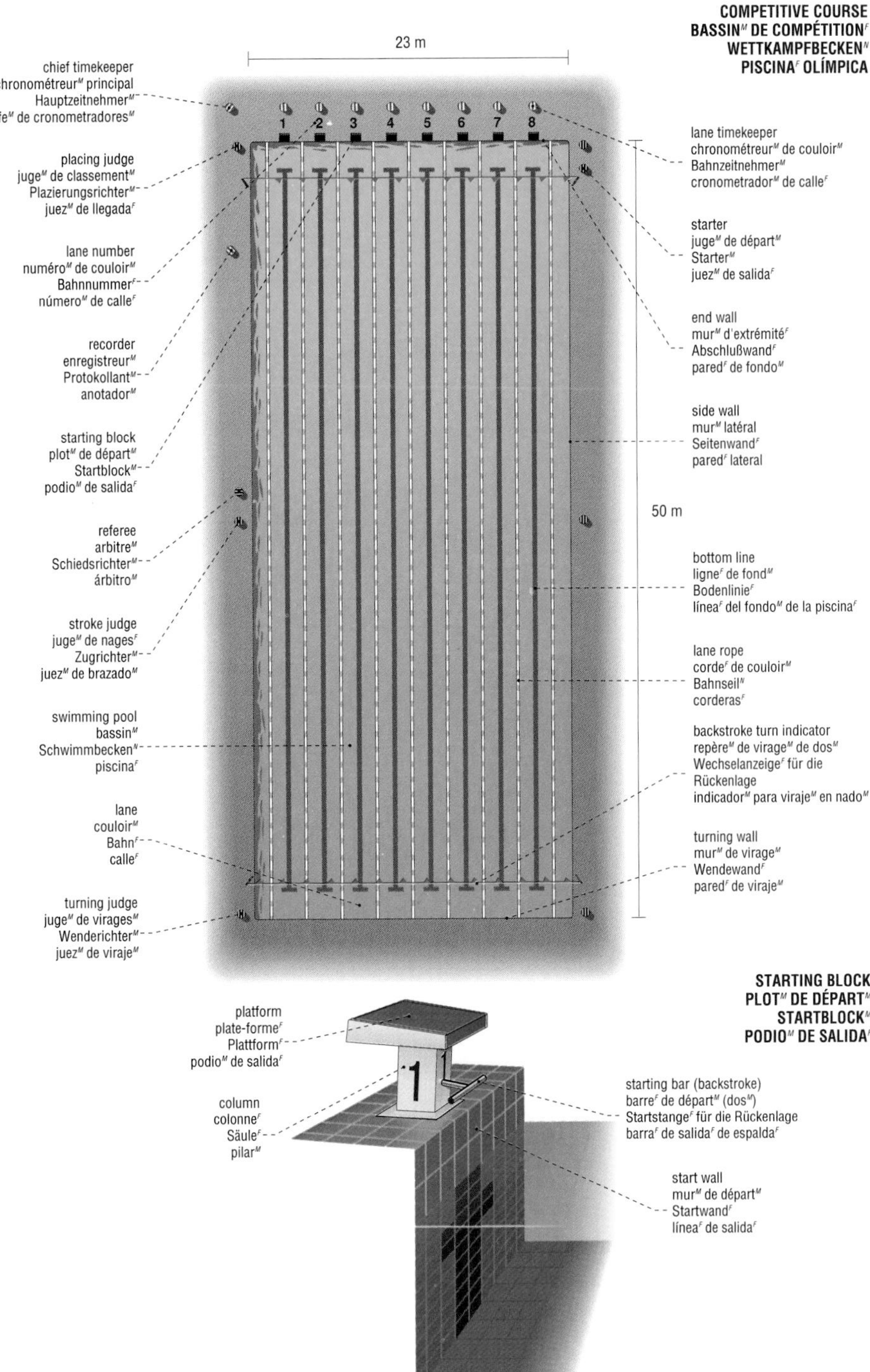

# SWIMMING
# NATATION[F]
# SCHWIMMEN[N]
# NATACIÓN[F]

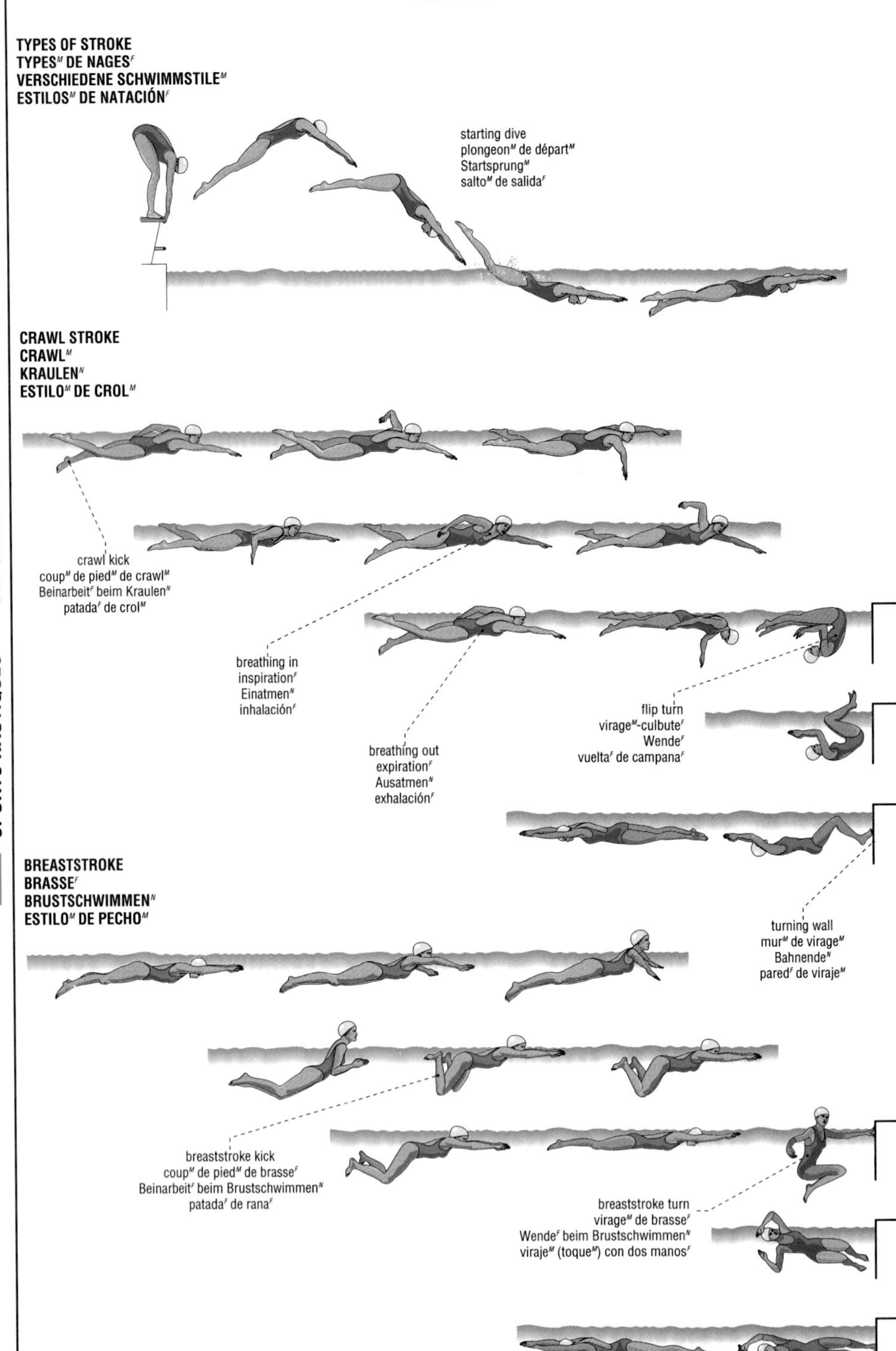

**BUTTERFLY STROKE**
**PAPILLON^M**
**BUTTERFLYSCHWIMMSTIL^M**
**ESTILO^M DE MARIPOSA^F**

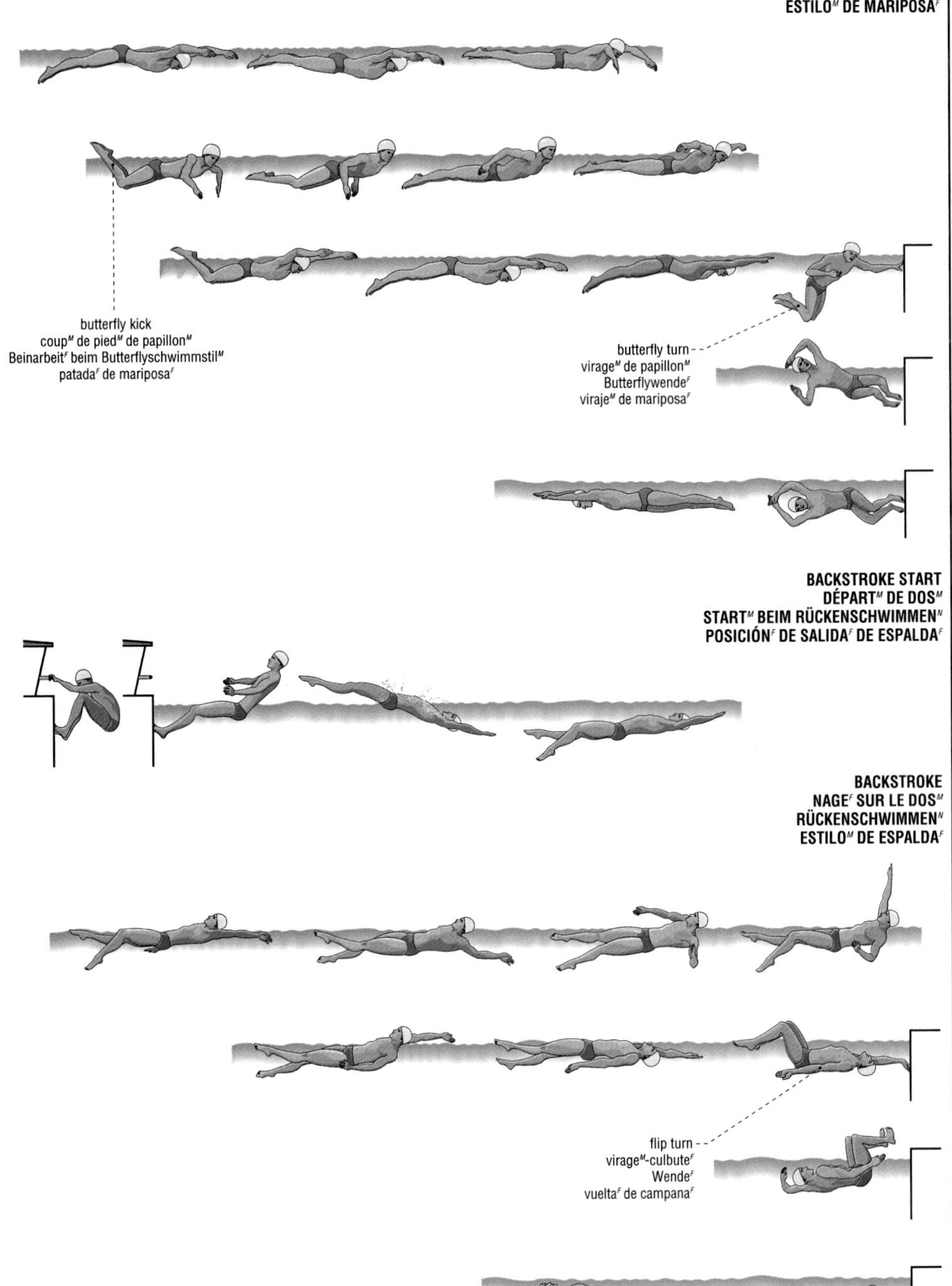

# DIVING
# PLONGEON[M]
# KUNSTSPRINGEN[N]
# SALTO[M]

## DIVING APPARATUS
## PLONGEOIR[M]
## SPRINGEINRICHTUNGEN[F]
## TORRE[F] DE SALTOS[M]

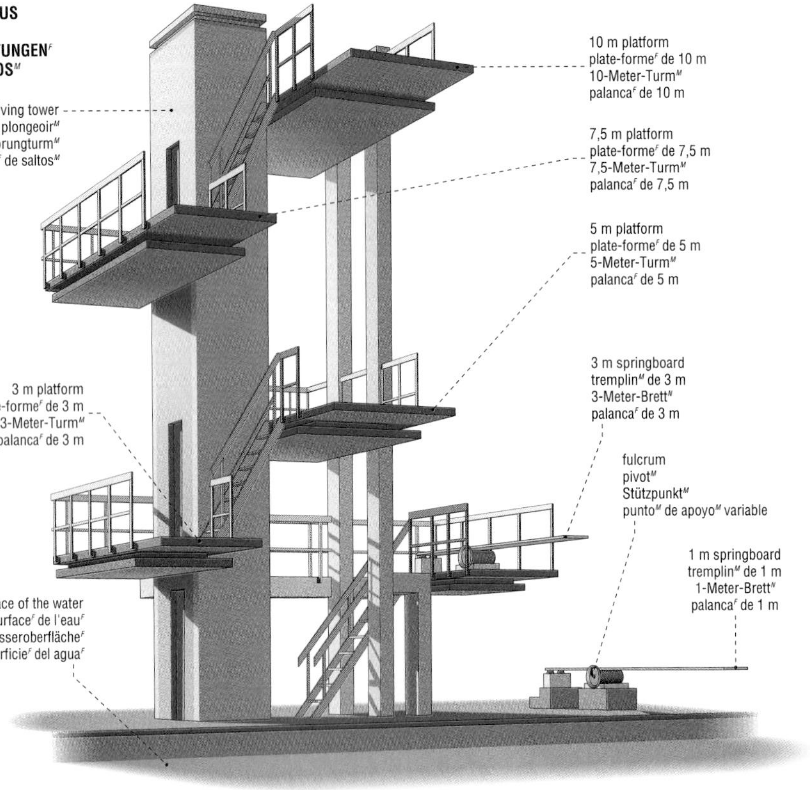

diving tower
tour[F] du plongeoir[M]
Sprungturm[M]
torre[F] de saltos[M]

10 m platform
plate-forme[F] de 10 m
10-Meter-Turm[M]
palanca[F] de 10 m

7,5 m platform
plate-forme[F] de 7,5 m
7,5-Meter-Turm[M]
palanca[F] de 7,5 m

5 m platform
plate-forme[F] de 5 m
5-Meter-Turm[M]
palanca[F] de 5 m

3 m springboard
tremplin[M] de 3 m
3-Meter-Brett[N]
palanca[F] de 3 m

3 m platform
plate-forme[F] de 3 m
3-Meter-Turm[M]
palanca[F] de 3 m

fulcrum
pivot[M]
Stützpunkt[M]
punto[M] de apoyo[M] variable

1 m springboard
tremplin[M] de 1 m
1-Meter-Brett[N]
palanca[F] de 1 m

surface of the water
surface[F] de l'eau[F]
Wasseroberfläche[F]
superficie[F] del agua[F]

## STARTING POSITIONS
## POSITIONS[F] DE DÉPART[M]
## STARTPOSITIONEN[F]
## POSICIONES[F] DE SALTO[M]

forward
avant
vorwärts
salto[M] al frente[M]

backward
arrière
rückwärts
salto[M] atrás

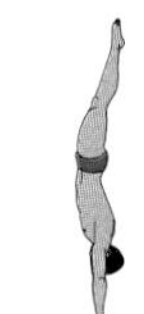

armstand
en équilibre[M]
Handstand[M]
equilibrio[M]

## FLIGHTS
## VOLS[M]
## SPRUNGFIGUREN[F]
## SALTOS[M]

pike position
position[F] carpée
Hechtsprungstellung[F]
posición[F] B - hacer la carpa[F]

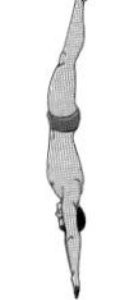

straight position
position[F] droite
Bohrerstellung[F]
posición[F] A - derecho

tuck position
position[F] groupée
Saltostellung[F]
posición[F] C - cuerpo[M] encogido

## ENTRIES
## ENTRÉES[F] DANS L'EAU[F]
## EINTAUCHSTELLUNGEN[F]
## ENTRADAS[F] AL AGUA[F]

head-first entry
entrée[F] tête[F] première
Kopf[M] voraus
entrada[F] de cabeza[F]

feet-first entry
entrée[F] pieds[M] premiers
Füße[M] voraus
entrada[F] de pie[M]

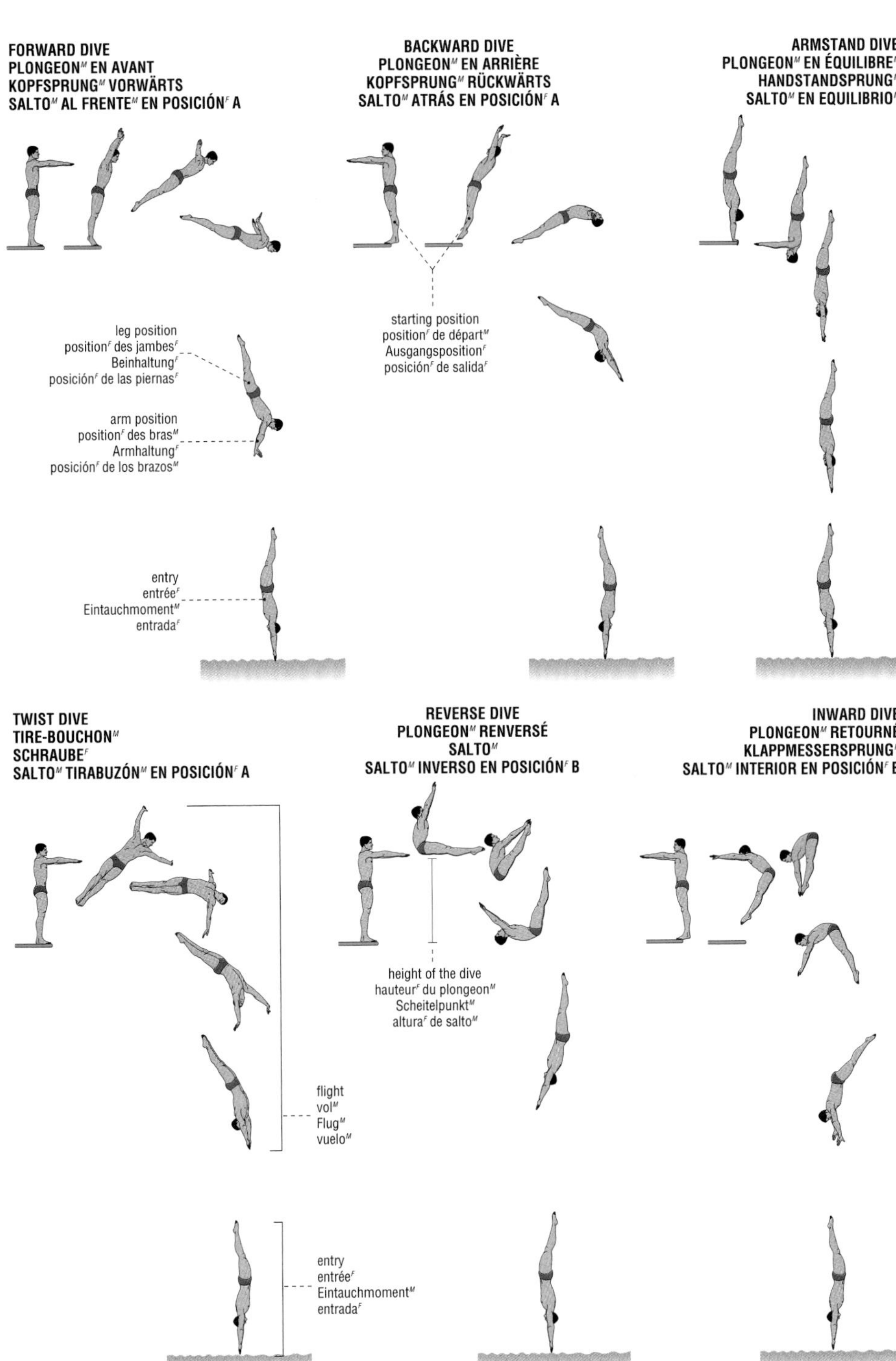
FORWARD DIVE
PLONGEON^M EN AVANT
KOPFSPRUNG^M VORWÄRTS
SALTO^M AL FRENTE^M EN POSICIÓN^F A
leg position
position^F des jambes^F
Beinhaltung^F
posición^F de las piernas^F
arm position
position^F des bras^M
Armhaltung^F
posición^F de los brazos^M
entry
entrée^F
Eintauchmoment^M
entrada^F
BACKWARD DIVE
PLONGEON^M EN ARRIÈRE
KOPFSPRUNG^M RÜCKWÄRTS
SALTO^M ATRÁS EN POSICIÓN^F A
starting position
position^F de départ^M
Ausgangsposition^F
posición^F de salida^F
ARMSTAND DIVE
PLONGEON^M EN ÉQUILIBRE^M
HANDSTANDSPRUNG^M
SALTO^M EN EQUILIBRIO^M
TWIST DIVE
TIRE-BOUCHON^M
SCHRAUBE^F
SALTO^M TIRABUZÓN^M EN POSICIÓN^F A
flight
vol^M
Flug^M
vuelo^M
entry
entrée^F
Eintauchmoment^M
entrada^F
REVERSE DIVE
PLONGEON^M RENVERSÉ
SALTO^M
SALTO^M INVERSO EN POSICIÓN^F B
height of the dive
hauteur^F du plongeon^M
Scheitelpunkt^M
altura^F de salto^M
INWARD DIVE
PLONGEON^M RETOURNÉ
KLAPPMESSERSPRUNG^M
SALTO^M INTERIOR EN POSICIÓN^F B

# WATER POLO
# WATER-POLO^M
# WASSERBALLSPIEL^N
# WATERPOLO^M

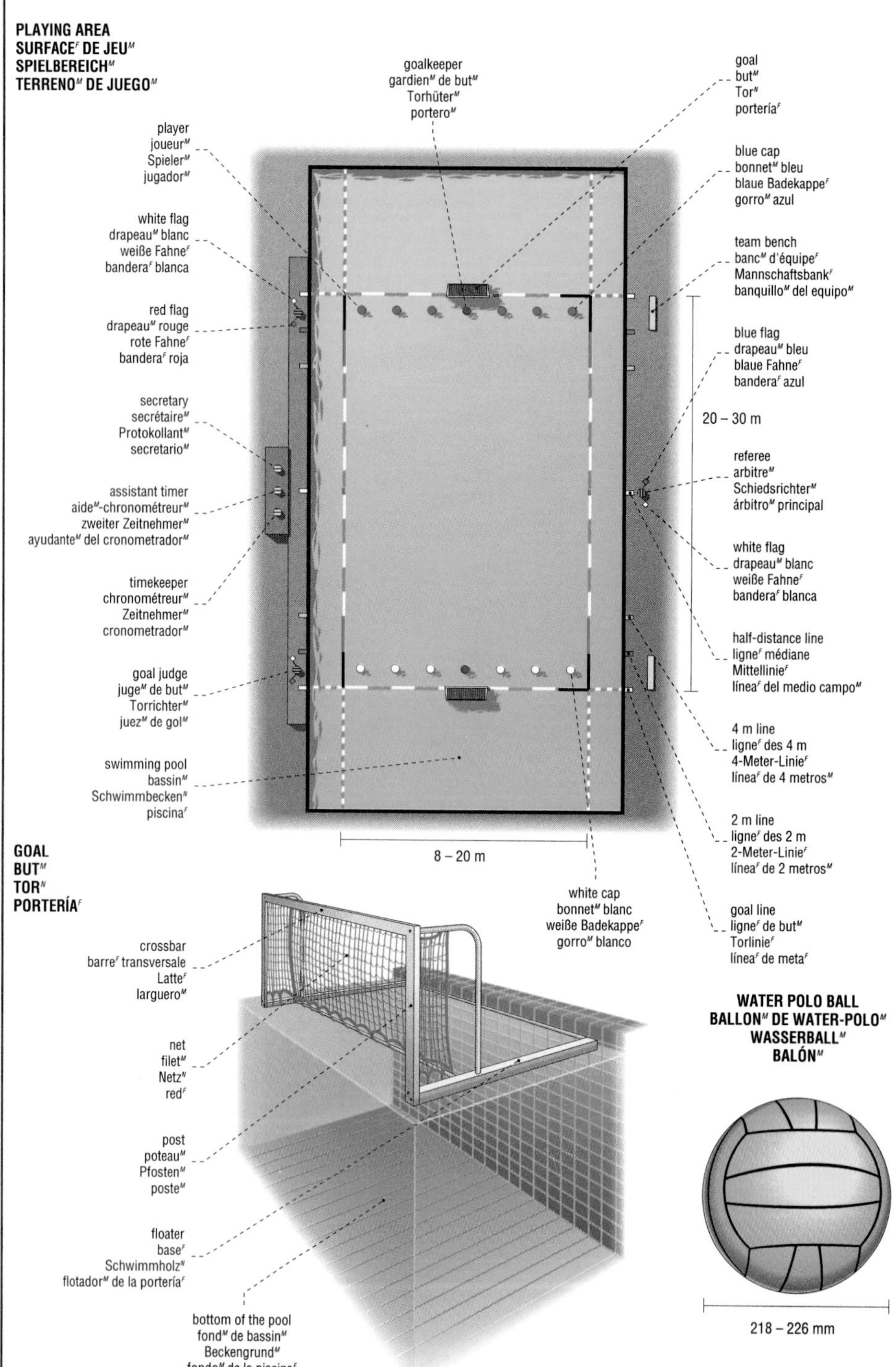

# SCUBA DIVING
# PLONGÉE[F] SOUS-MARINE
# TAUCHEN[N]
# BUCEO[M]

# SAILING
# VOILE[F]
# SEGELSPORT[M]
# VELA[F]

## SAILING BOAT
## DÉRIVEUR[M]
## SEGELBOOT[N]
## VELERO[M]

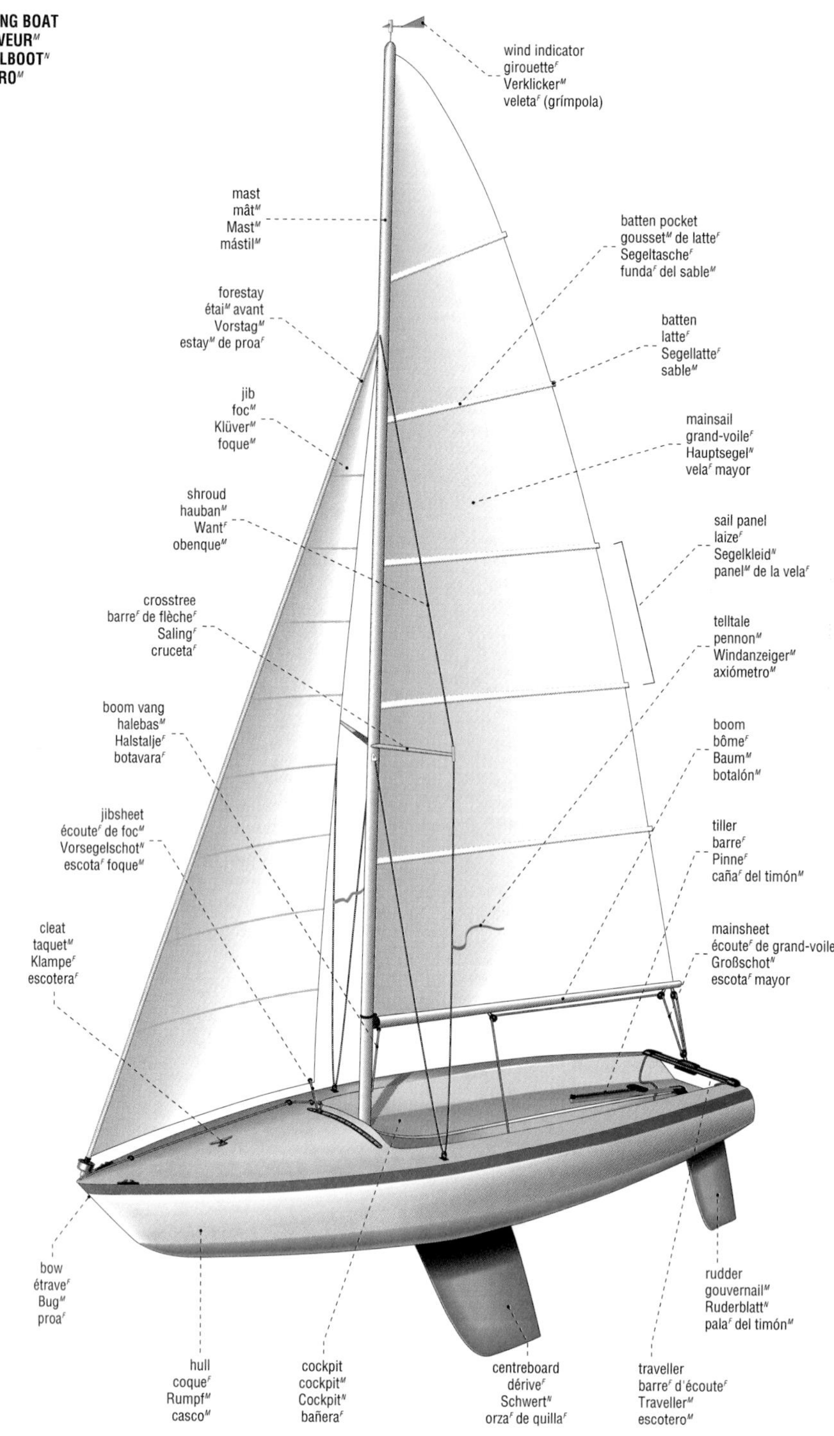

## POINTS OF SAILING
## ALLURES[F]
## KURSE[M]
## DISPOSICIONES[F] DE LAS VELAS[F]

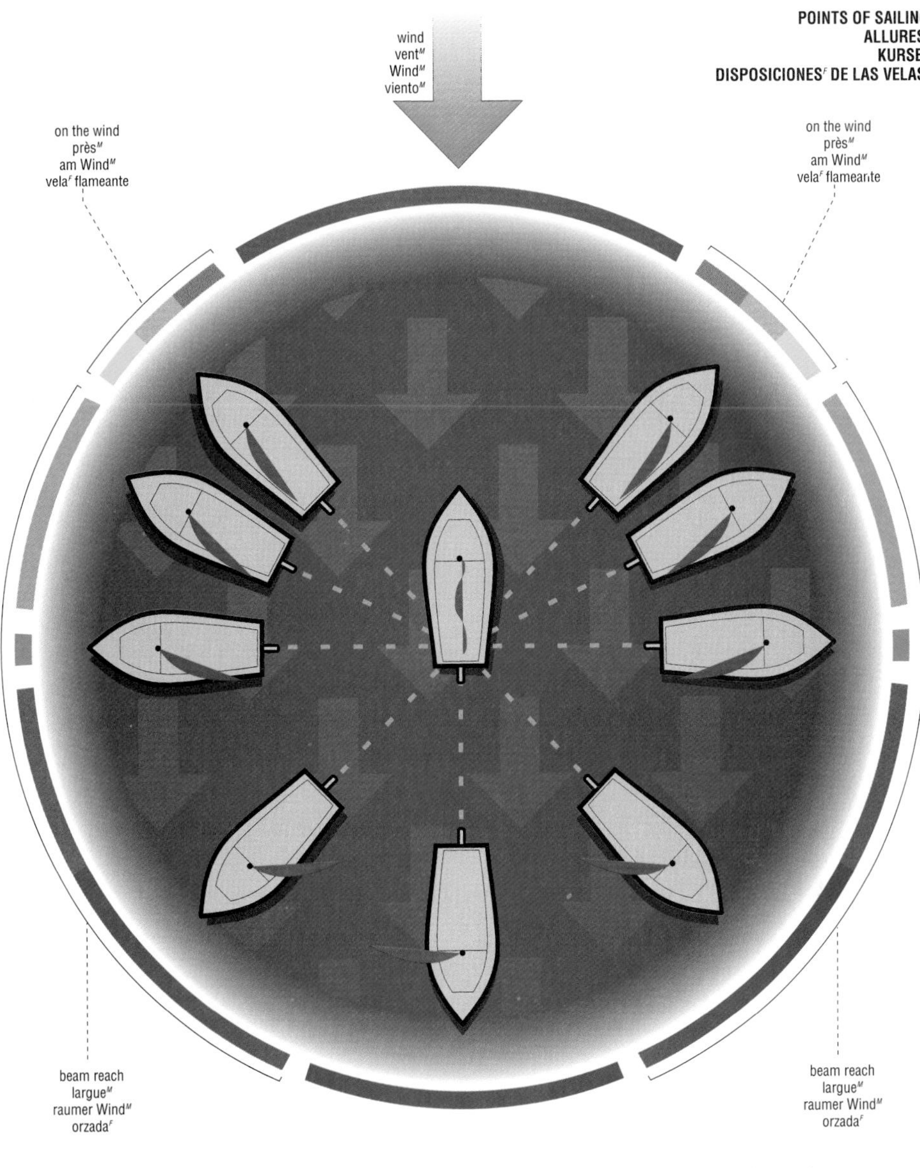


headwind
vent[M] debout
Boot[N] ohne Fahrt[F]
viento[M] en proa[F]

close hauled
près[M] serré
hart am Wind[M]
bolina[F]

on the wind
près[M]
am Wind[M]
viento[M] contrario

full and by
près[M] bon plein[M]
voll und bei
a buen viento[M]

close reach
petit largue[M]
Segeln[N] mit halbem Wind[M]
ciñendo el viento[M]

wind abeam
vent[M] de travers[M]
halber Wind[M]
viento[M] de través

beam reach
largue[M]
Wind[M] querab
por lo ancho[M]

broad reach
grand largue[M]
raumer Wind[M]
a un largo[M]

down wind
vent[M] arrière
mit dem Wind[M]
viento[M] en popa[F]

# SAILING
# VOILE[F]
# SEGELSPORT[M]
# VELA[F]

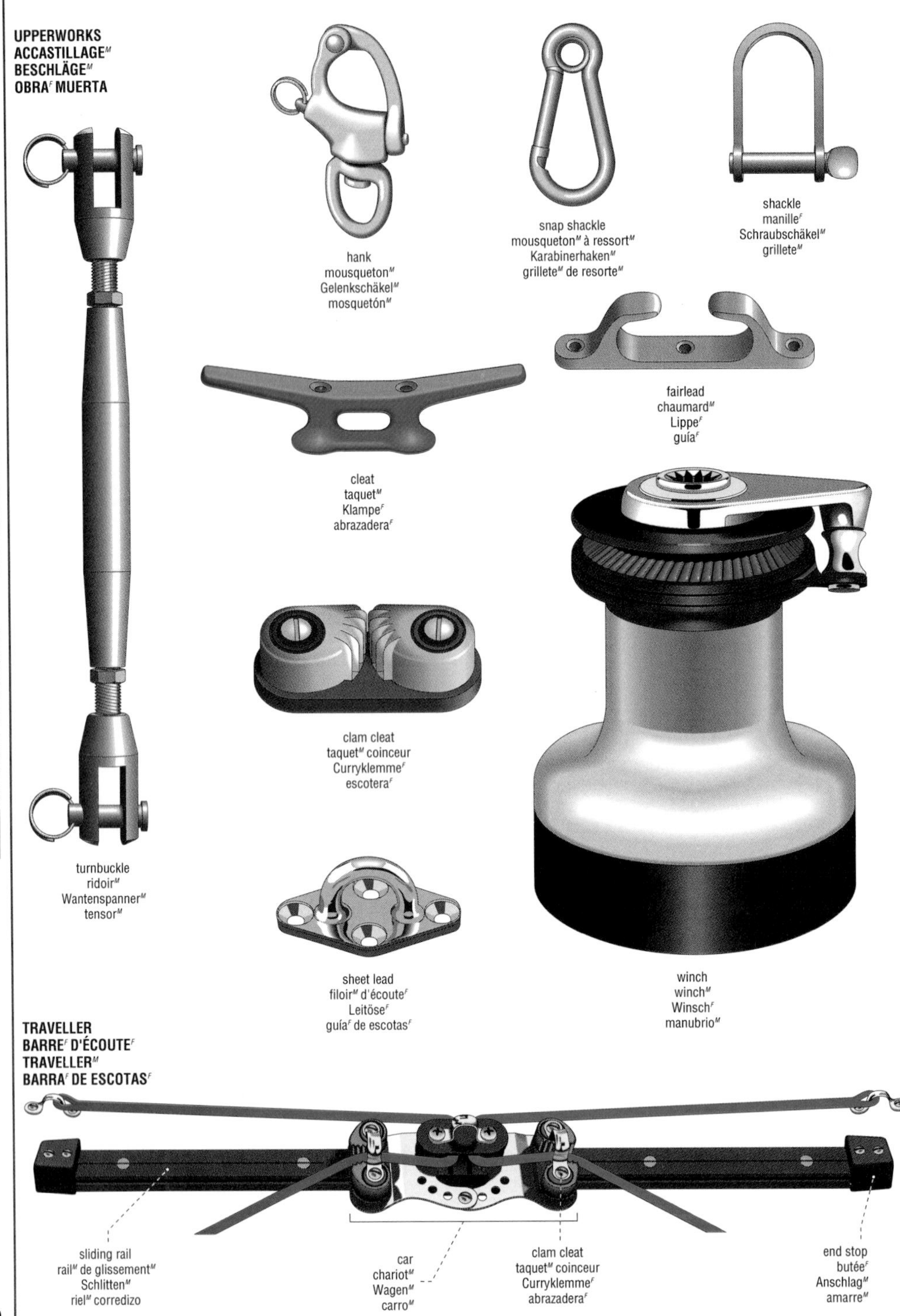

# SAILBOARD
# PLANCHE[F] À VOILE[M]
# SURFBRETT[N]
# PLANCHA[F] DE WINDSURF[M]

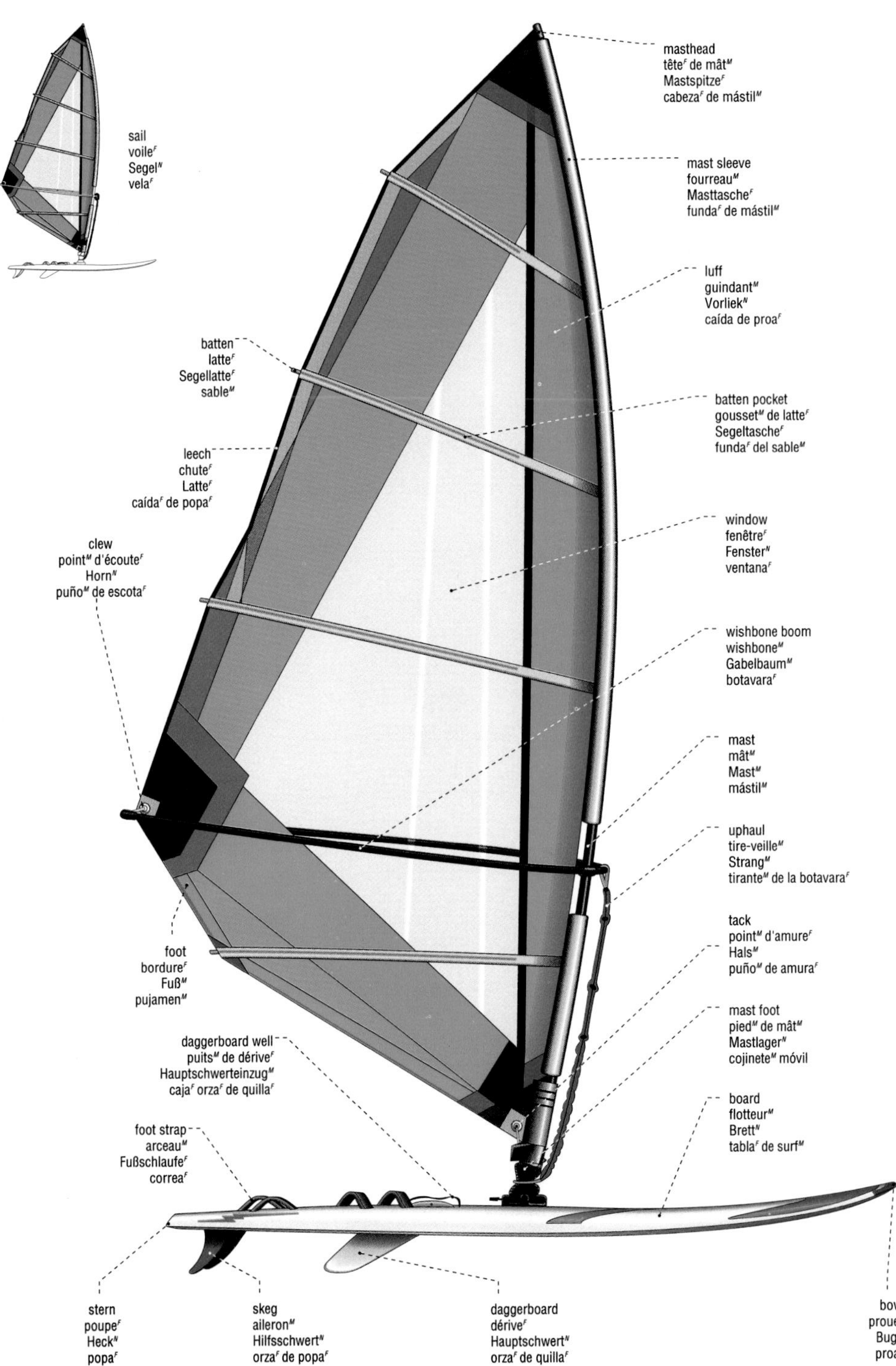

# ROWING AND SCULLING
# AVIRON[M]
# RUDERN[N] UND SKULLEN[N]
# REMO[M]

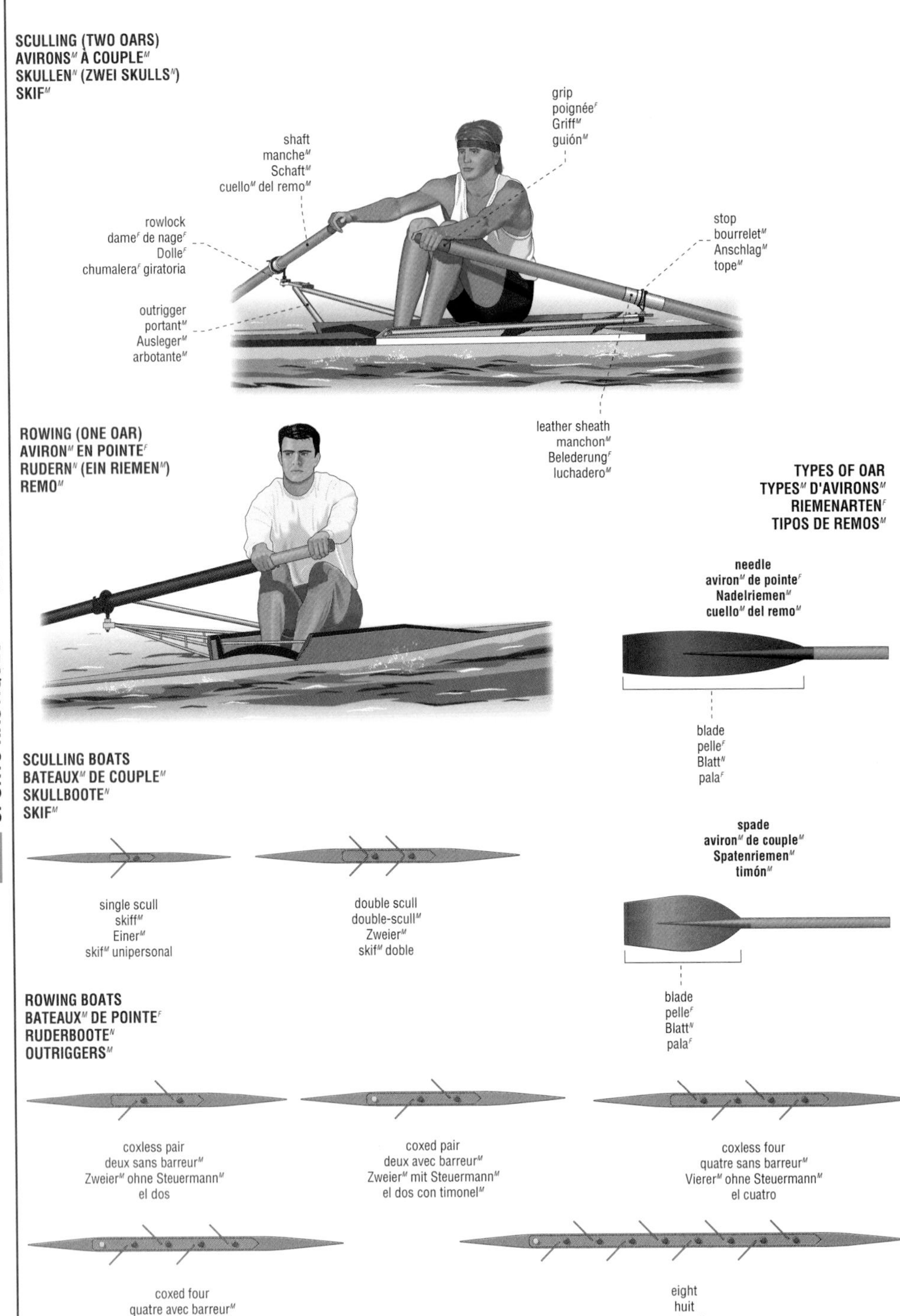

**WATER SKIING**
**SKI^M NAUTIQUE**
**WASSERSKI^N**
**ESQUÍ^M ACUÁTICO**

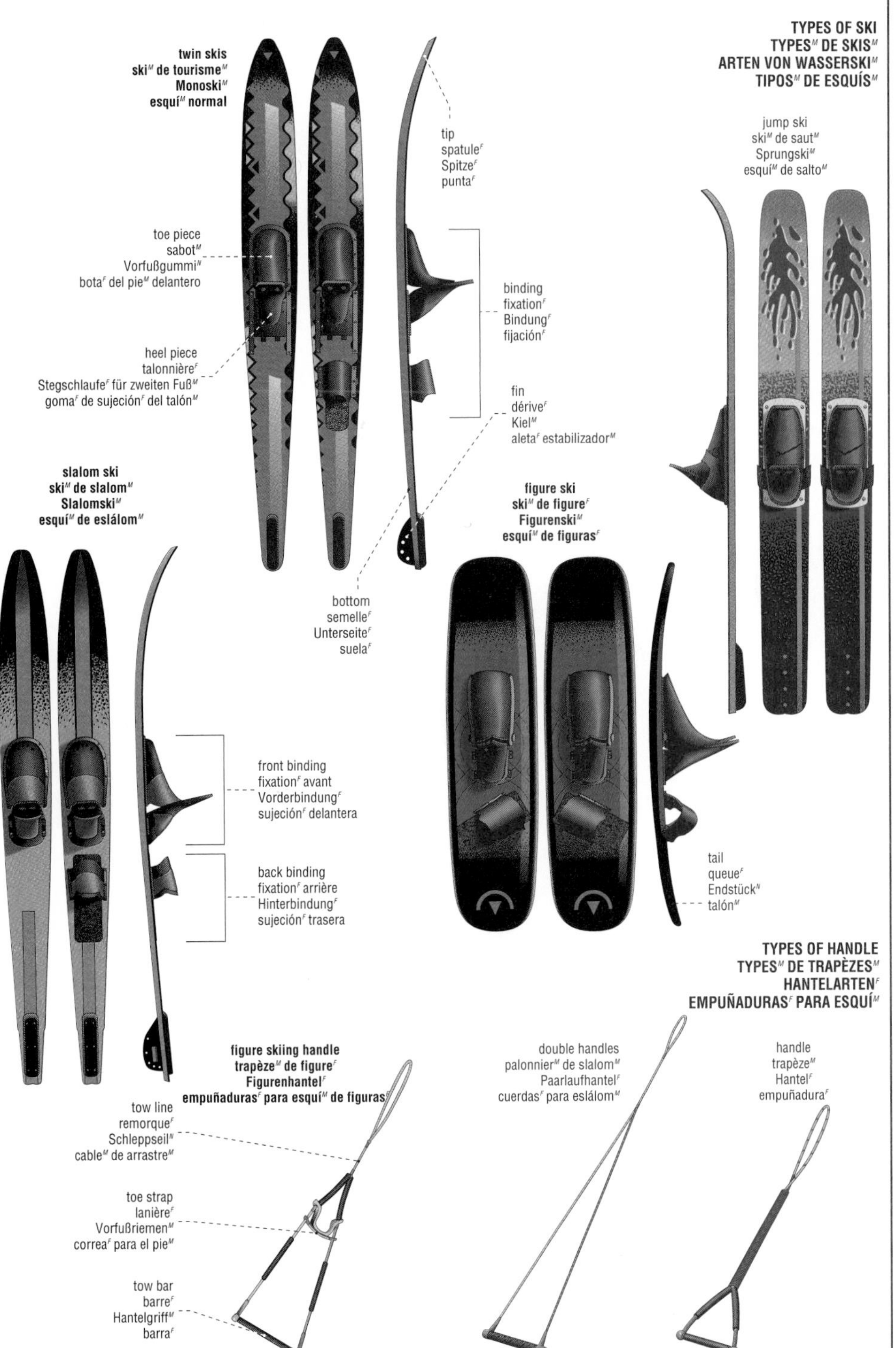

# BALLOONING
# MONTGOLFIÈRE[F]
# FREIBALLONSPORT[M]
# VUELO[M] EN GLOBO[M]



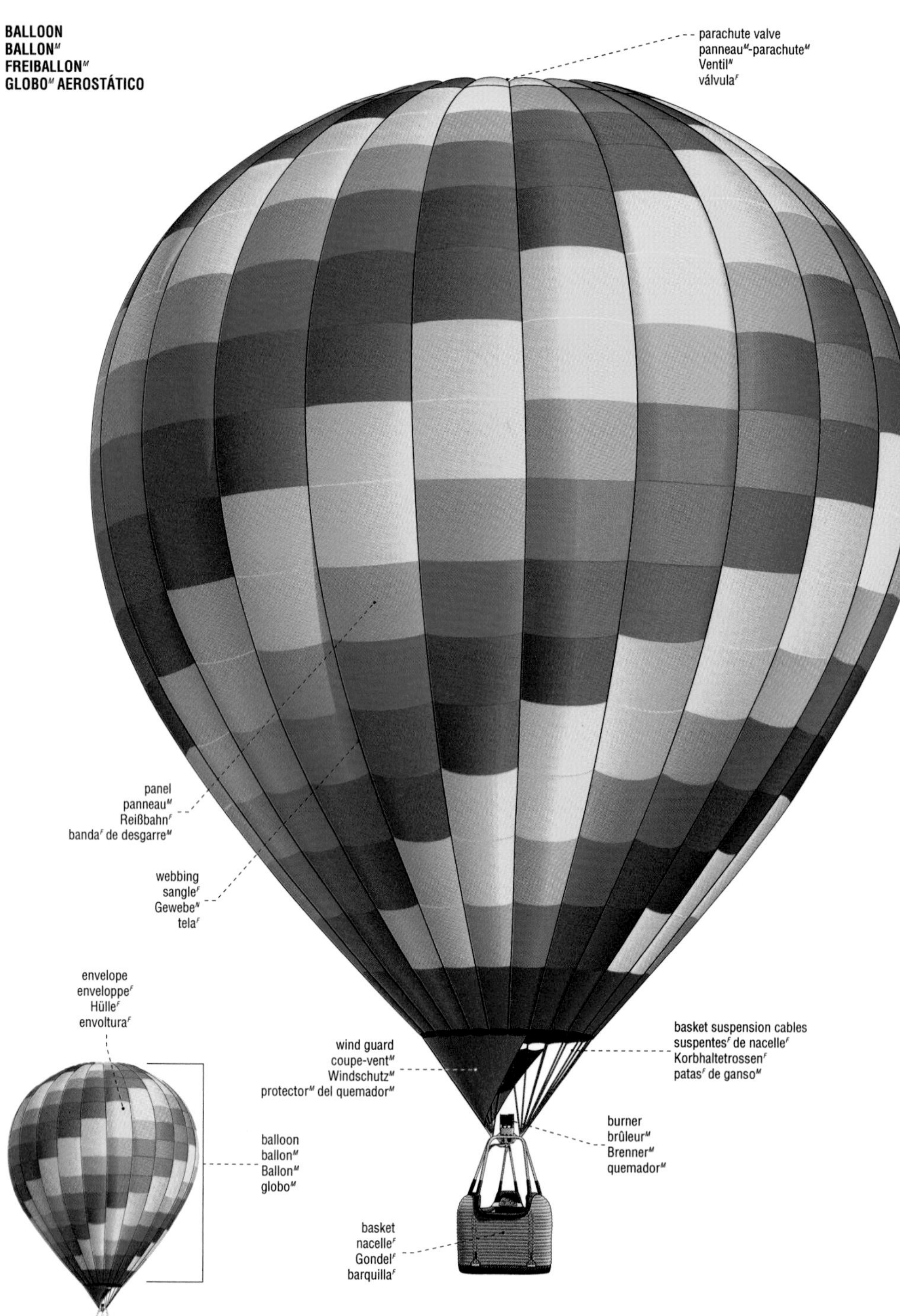

**BASKET**
**NACELLE[F]**
**GONDEL[F]**
**BARQUILLA[F]**

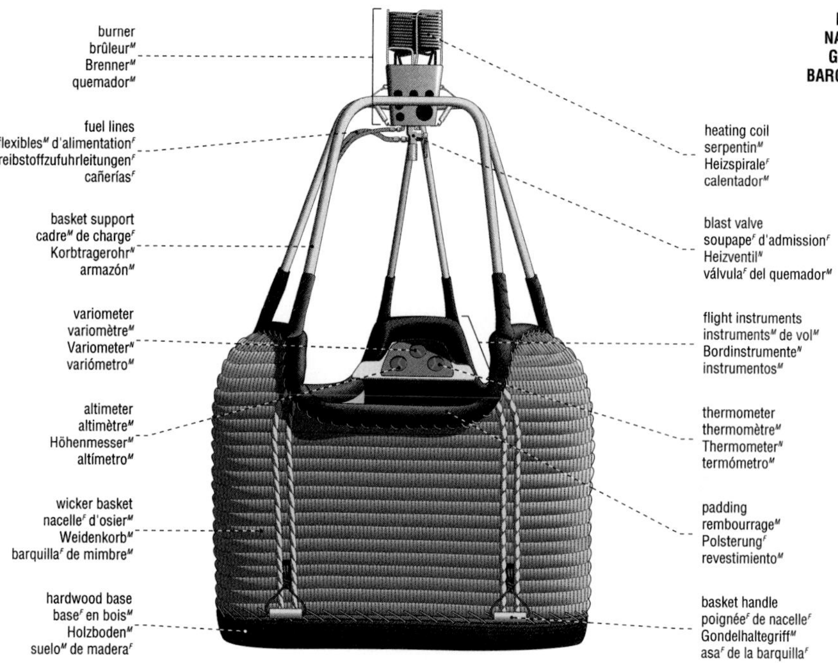


## SKY DIVING
## CHUTE[F] LIBRE
## FALLSCHIRMSPRINGEN[N]
## PARACAIDISMO[M]

**SKY DIVER**
**SAUTEUR[M]**
**FALLSCHIRMSPRINGER[M]**
**PARACAIDISTA[M/F]**

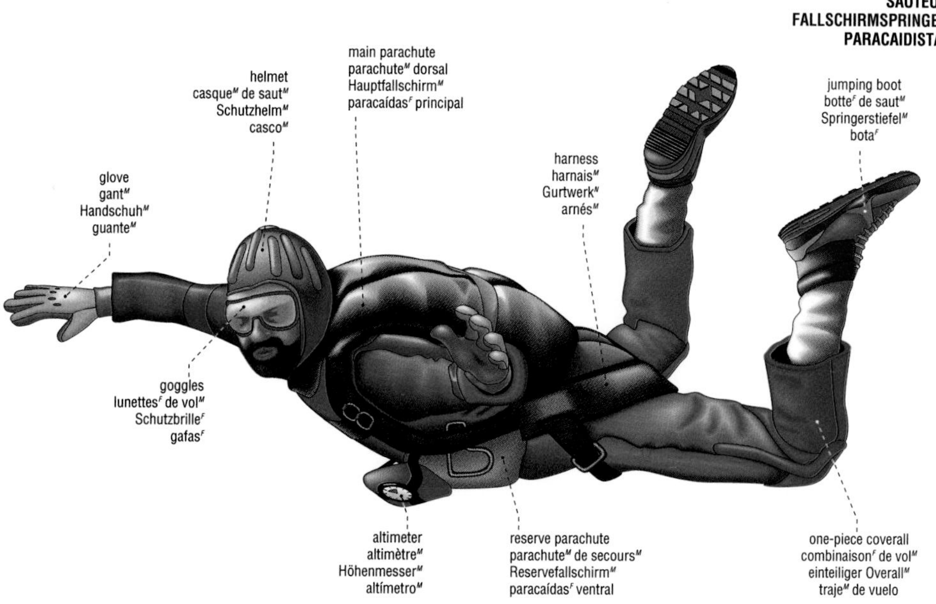

# PARAGLIDING
# PARAPENTE
# GLEITSCHIRMFLIEGEN
# PLANEADOR

CANOPY
AILE
GLEITSCHIRM
CASQUETE

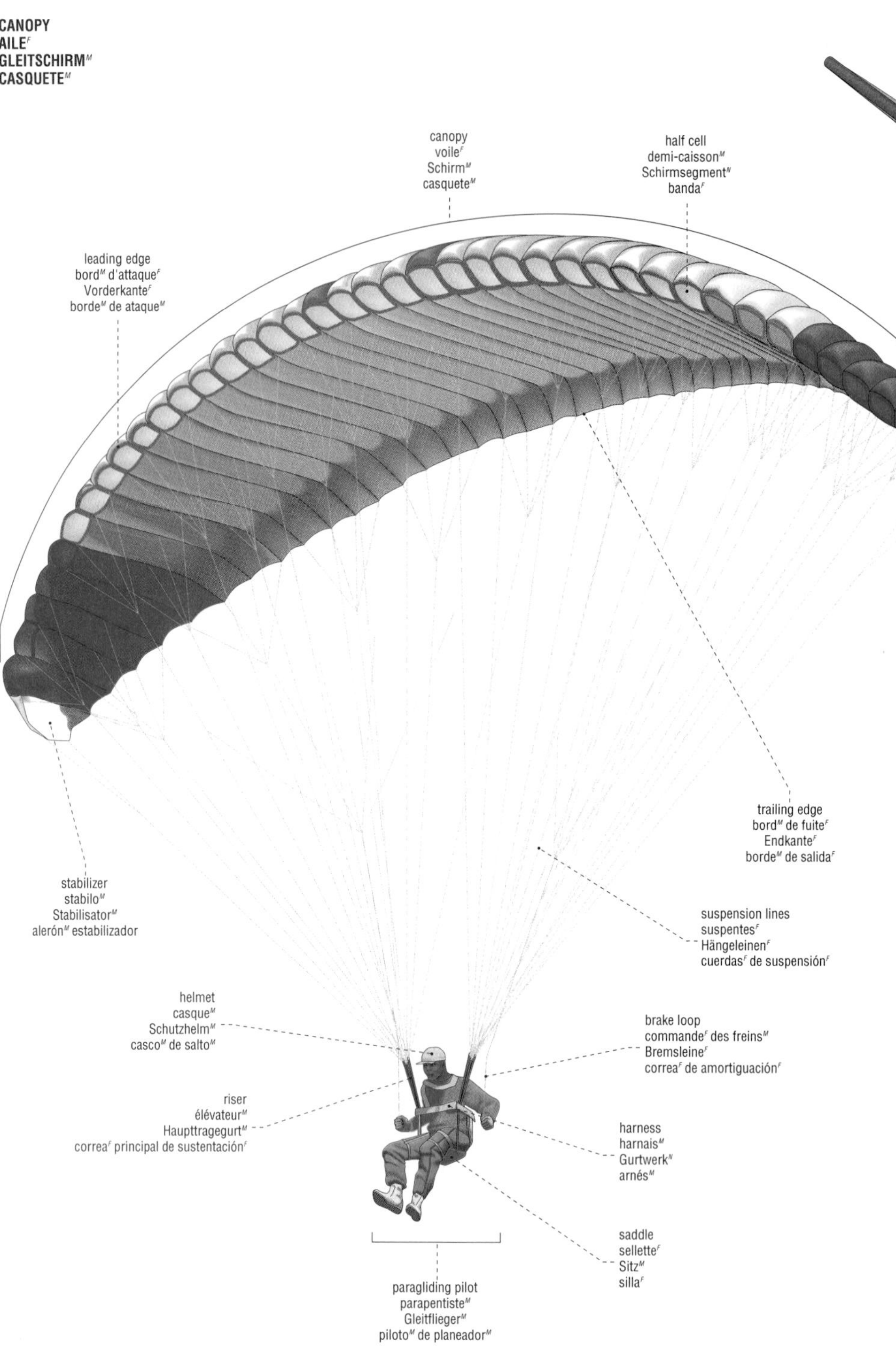

# HANG GLIDING
# VOL[M] LIBRE
# DRACHENFLIEGEN[N]
# VUELO[M] LIBRE

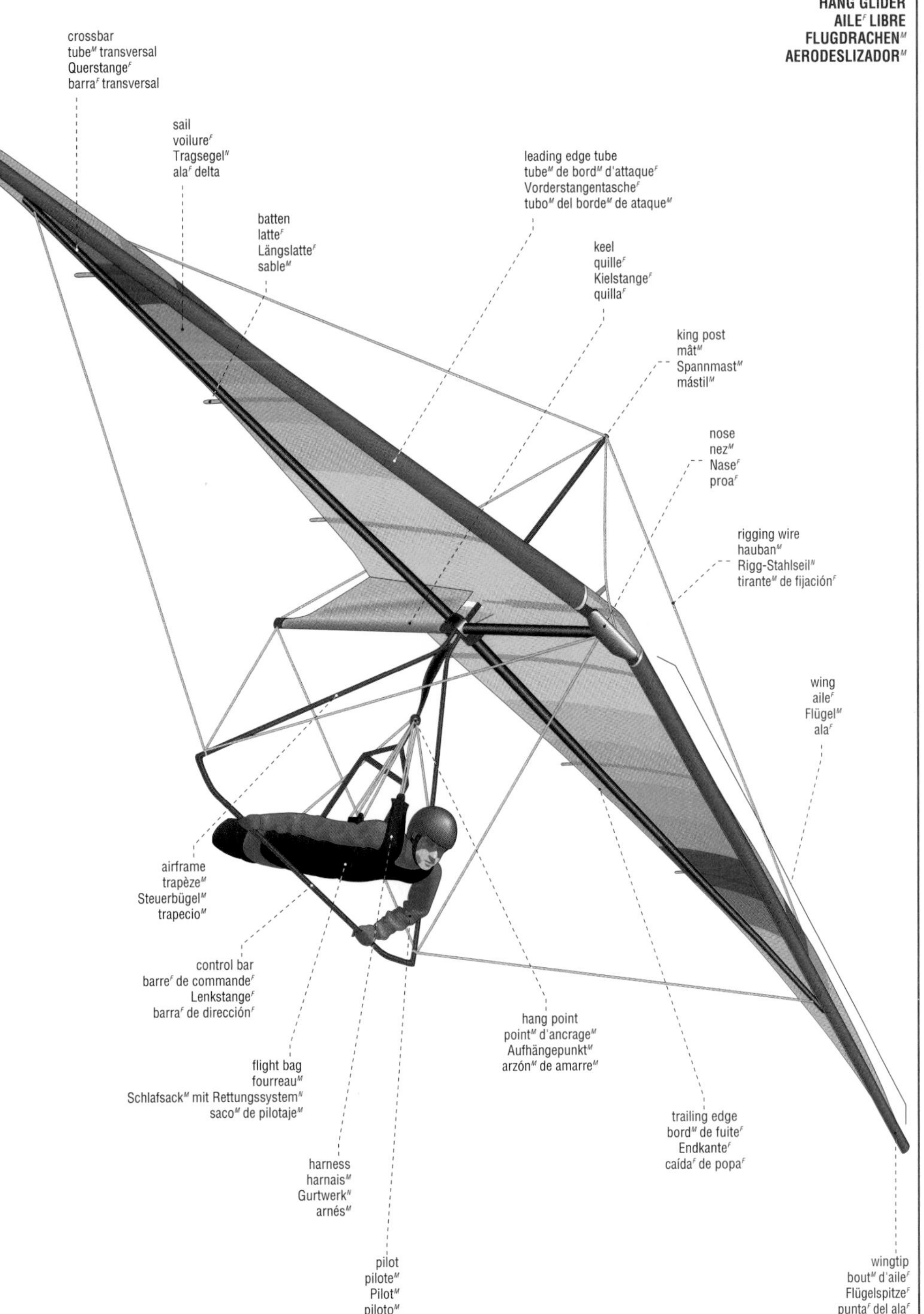

# GLIDING
# VOL^M À VOILE^F
# SEGELFLIEGEN^N
# VUELO^M SIN MOTOR^M



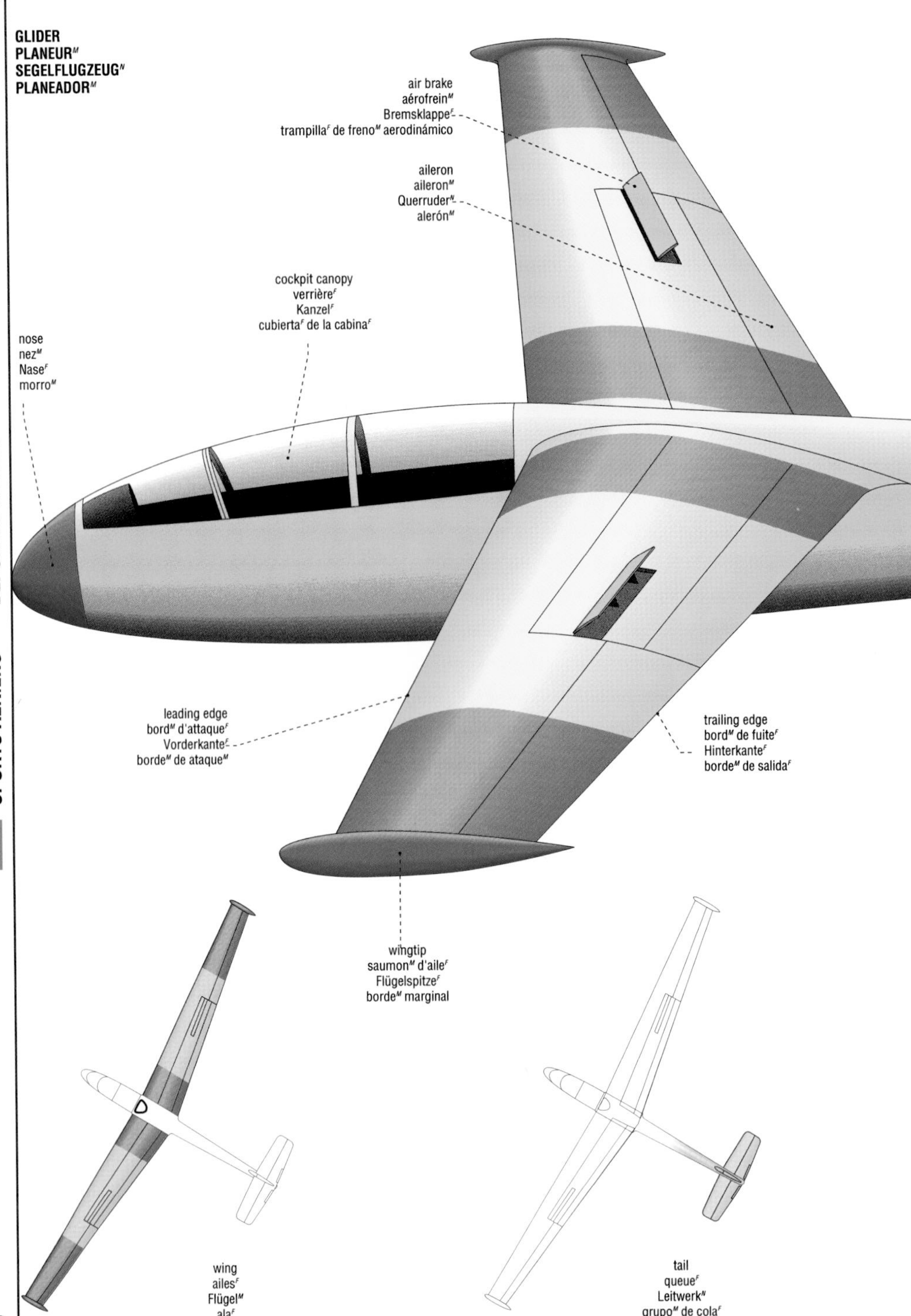

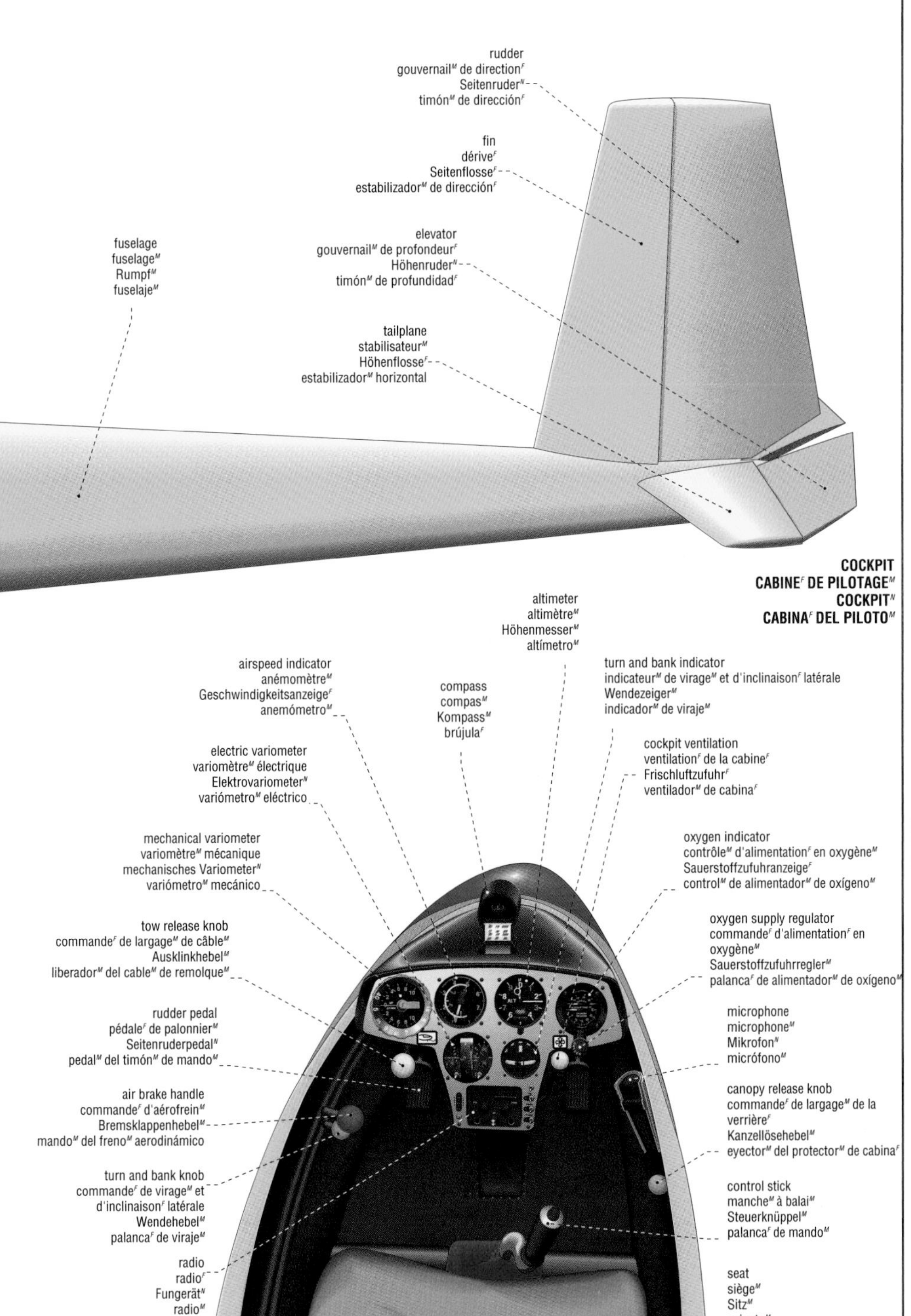
rudder
gouvernail[M] de direction[F]
Seitenruder[N]
timón[M] de dirección[F]
fin
dérive[F]
Seitenflosse[F]
estabilizador[M] de dirección[F]
fuselage
fuselage[M]
Rumpf[M]
fuselaje[M]
elevator
gouvernail[M] de profondeur[F]
Höhenruder[N]
timón[M] de profundidad[F]
tailplane
stabilisateur[M]
Höhenflosse[F]
estabilizador[M] horizontal
COCKPIT
CABINE[F] DE PILOTAGE[M]
COCKPIT[N]
CABINA[F] DEL PILOTO[M]
altimeter
altimètre[M]
Höhenmesser[M]
altímetro[M]
airspeed indicator
anémomètre[M]
Geschwindigkeitsanzeige[F]
anemómetro[M]
compass
compas[M]
Kompass[M]
brújula[F]
turn and bank indicator
indicateur[M] de virage[M] et d'inclinaison[F] latérale
Wendezeiger[M]
indicador[M] de viraje[M]
electric variometer
variomètre[M] électrique
Elektrovariometer[N]
variómetro[M] eléctrico
cockpit ventilation
ventilation[F] de la cabine[F]
Frischluftzufuhr[F]
ventilador[M] de cabina[F]
mechanical variometer
variomètre[M] mécanique
mechanisches Variometer[N]
variómetro[M] mecánico
oxygen indicator
contrôle[M] d'alimentation[F] en oxygène[M]
Sauerstoffzufuhranzeige[F]
control[M] de alimentador[M] de oxígeno[M]
tow release knob
commande[F] de largage[M] de câble[M]
Ausklinkhebel[M]
liberador[M] del cable[M] de remolque[M]
oxygen supply regulator
commande[F] d'alimentation[F] en oxygène[M]
Sauerstoffzufuhrregler[M]
palanca[F] de alimentador[M] de oxígeno[M]
rudder pedal
pédale[F] de palonnier[M]
Seitenruderpedal[N]
pedal[M] del timón[M] de mando[M]
microphone
microphone[M]
Mikrofon[N]
micrófono[M]
air brake handle
commande[F] d'aérofrein[M]
Bremsklappenhebel[M]
mando[M] del freno[M] aerodinámico
canopy release knob
commande[F] de largage[M] de la verrière[F]
Kanzellösehebel[M]
eyector[M] del protector[M] de cabina[F]
turn and bank knob
commande[F] de virage[M] et d'inclinaison[F] latérale
Wendehebel[M]
palanca[F] de viraje[M]
control stick
manche[M] à balai[M]
Steuerknüppel[M]
palanca[F] de mando[M]
radio
radio[F]
Fungerät[N]
radio[M]
seat
siège[M]
Sitz[M]
asiento[M]

# ALPINE SKIING
# SKI^M ALPIN
# ALPINES SKILAUFEN^N
# ESQUÍ^M ALPINO



## ALPINE SKIER
## SKIEUR^M ALPIN
## ALPINER SKILÄUFER^M
## ESQUIADOR^M ALPINO

## SAFETY BINDING
## FIXATION^F DE SÉCURITÉ^F
## SICHERHEITSBINDUNG^F
## FIJACIÓN^F DE SEGURIDAD^F DEL ESQUÍ^M

## SKI BOOT
## CHAUSSURE^F DE SKI^M
## SKISTIEFEL^M
## BOTAS^F PARA ESQUIAR

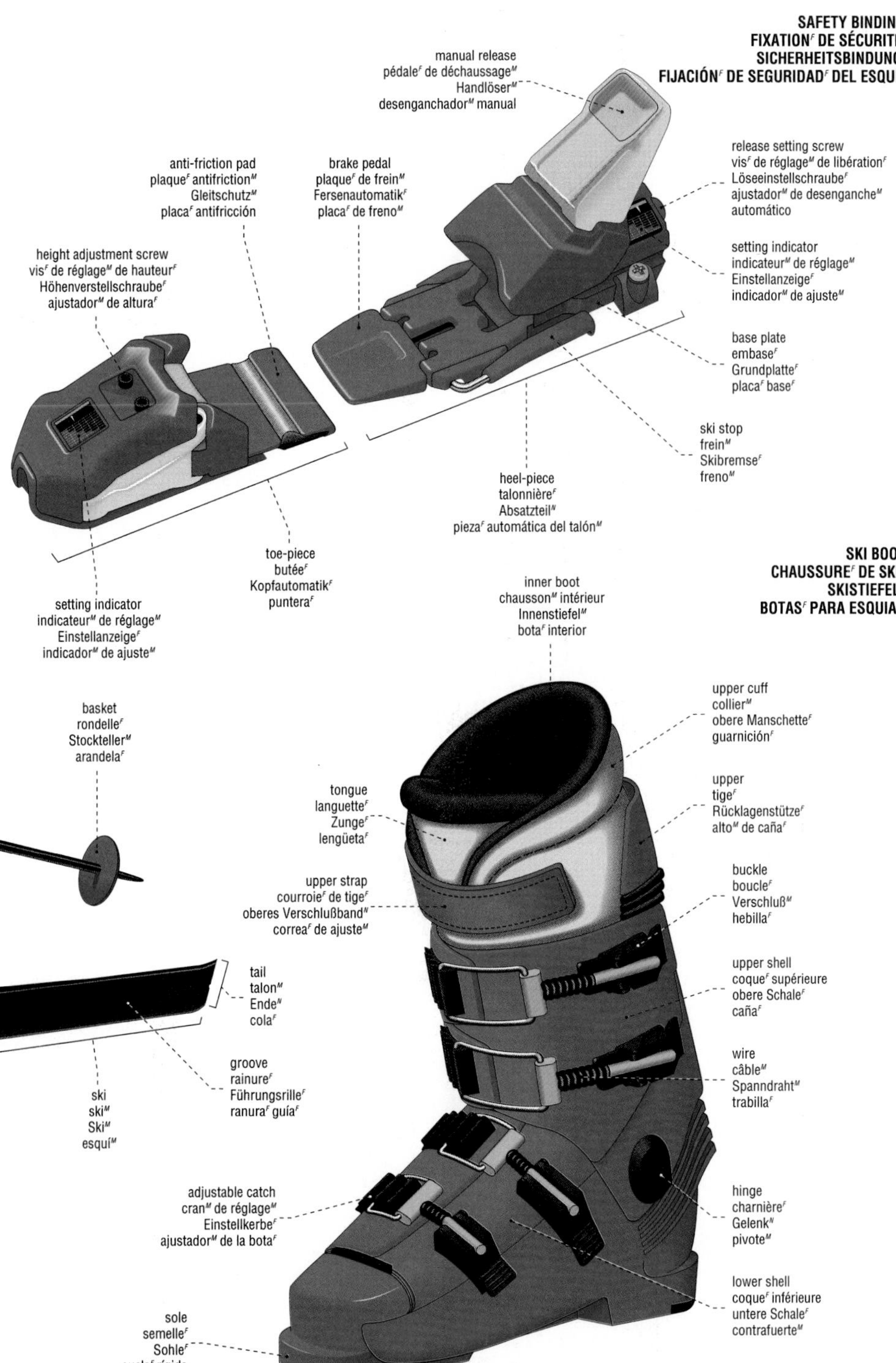

# CROSS-COUNTRY SKIING
# SKI[M] DE FOND[M]
# SKILANGLAUF[M]
# ESQUÍ[M] DE FONDO[M]

## CROSS-COUNTRY SKIER
## SKIEUSE[F] DE FOND[M]
## LANGLÄUFER (IN[F])[M]
## ESQUIADORA[F] DE CAMPO[M] TRAVIESA

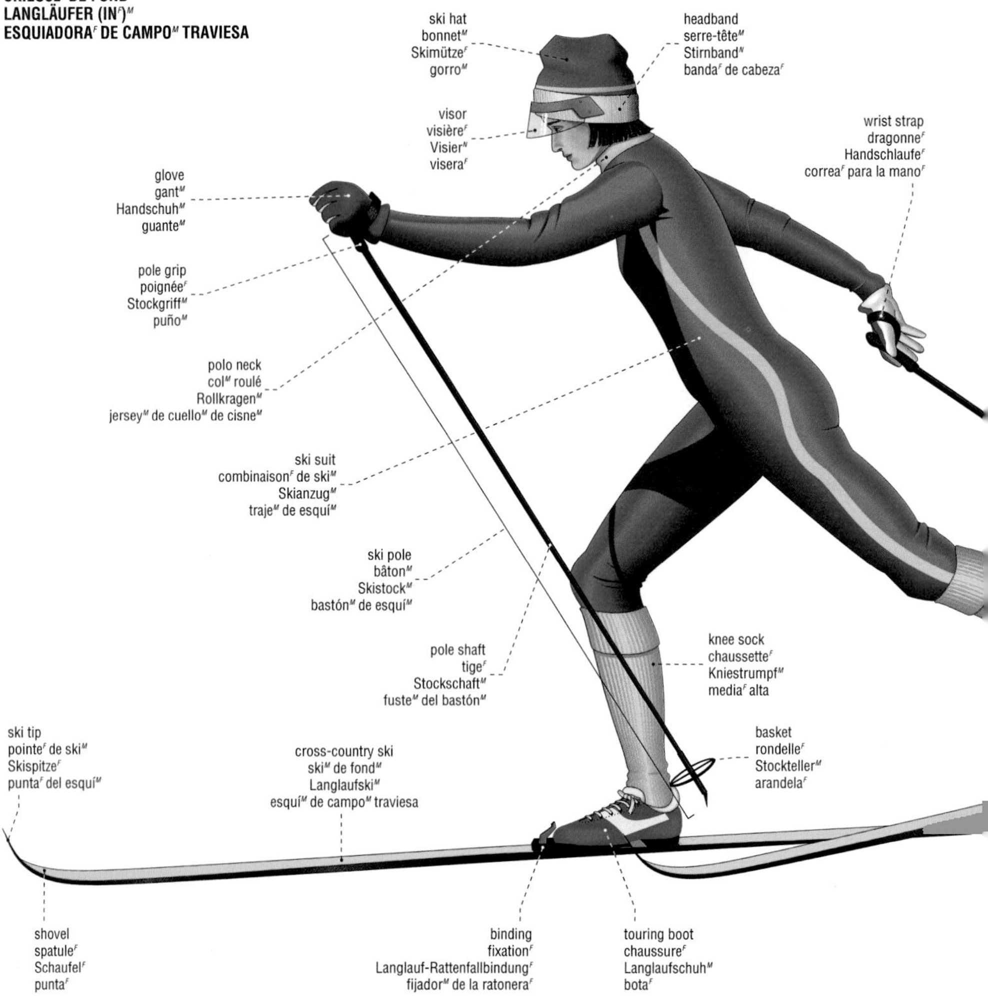

ski hat
bonnet[M]
Skimütze[F]
gorro[M]
headband
serre-tête[M]
Stirnband[N]
banda[F] de cabeza[F]
visor
visière[F]
Visier[N]
visera[F]
wrist strap
dragonne[F]
Handschlaufe[F]
correa[F] para la mano[F]
glove
gant[M]
Handschuh[M]
guante[M]
pole grip
poignée[F]
Stockgriff[M]
puño[M]
polo neck
col[M] roulé
Rollkragen[M]
jersey[M] de cuello[M] de cisne[M]
ski suit
combinaison[F] de ski[M]
Skianzug[M]
traje[M] de esquí[M]
ski pole
bâton[M]
Skistock[M]
bastón[M] de esquí[M]
pole shaft
tige[F]
Stockschaft[M]
fuste[M] del bastón[M]
knee sock
chaussette[F]
Kniestrumpf[M]
media[F] alta
ski tip
pointe[F] de ski[M]
Skispitze[F]
punta[F] del esquí[M]
cross-country ski
ski[M] de fond[M]
Langlaufski[M]
esquí[M] de campo[M] traviesa
basket
rondelle[F]
Stockteller[M]
arandela[F]
shovel
spatule[F]
Schaufel[F]
punta[F]
binding
fixation[F]
Langlauf-Rattenfallbindung[F]
fijador[M] de la ratonera[F]
touring boot
chaussure[F]
Langlaufschuh[M]
bota[F]

## CROSS-COUNTRY SKI
## SKI[M] DE FOND[M]
## LANGLAUFSKI[M]
## ESQUÍ[M] DE CAMPO[M] TRAVIESA

clamp
fourchette[F]
Backen[M]
ratonera[F]
toe binding
fixation[F] à butée[F] avant
Vorfußbindung[F]
fijación[F] para el pie[M]
shovel
spatule[F]
Schaufel[F]
punta[F]
toeplate
étrier[M]
Vorfußplatte[F]
apoyo[M] para el pie[M]
heelplate
talonnière[F]
Absatzplatte[F]
pieza[F] de talón[M]
tail
talon[M]
Ende[N]
cola[F]

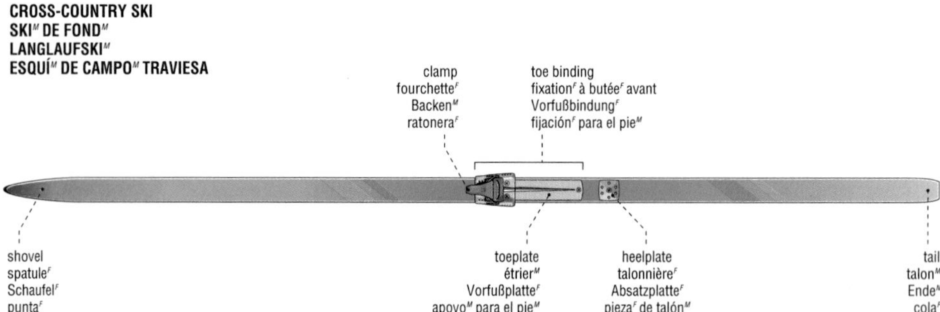

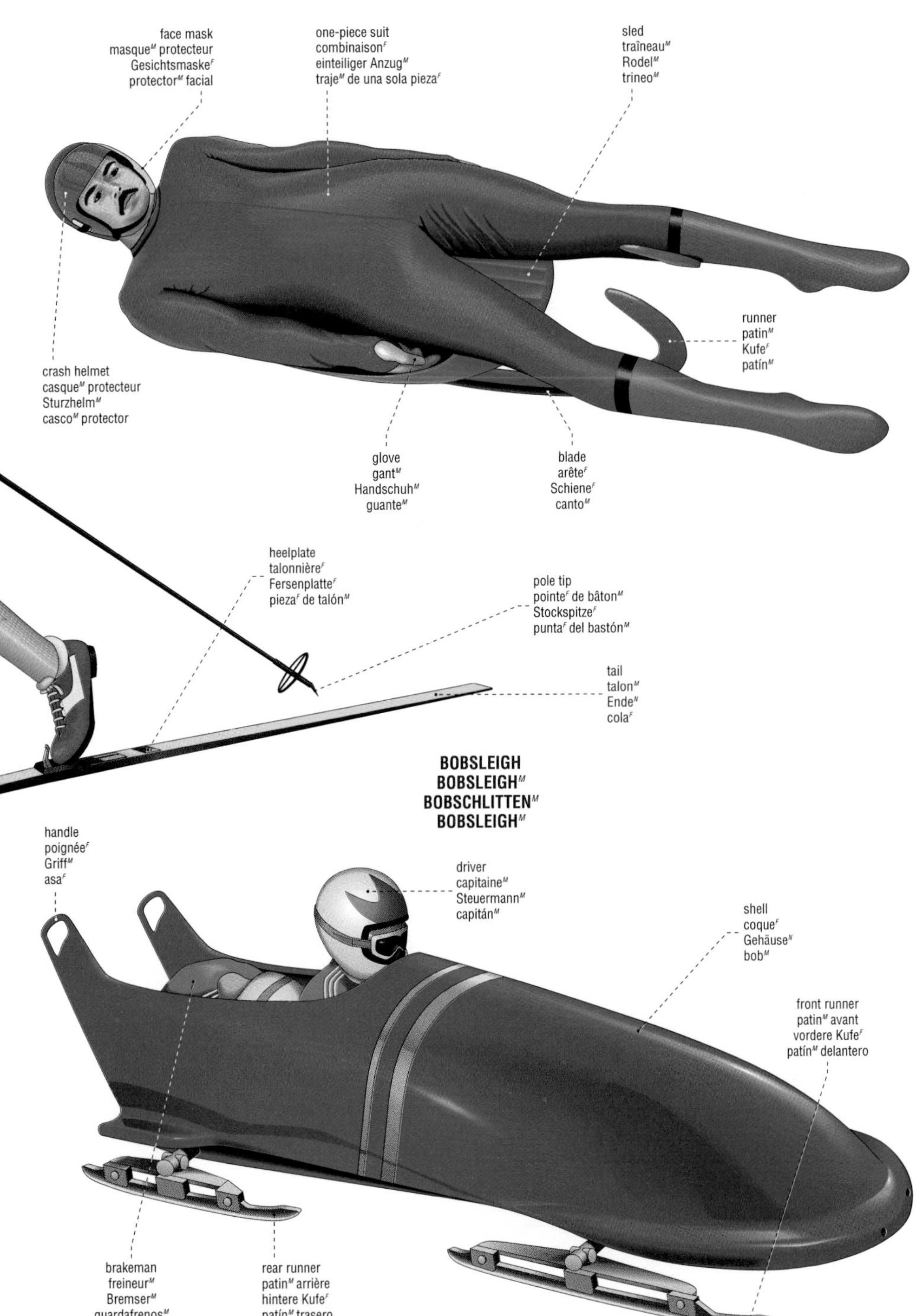
LUGE
LUGE
RENNRODEL
LUGE
face mask
masque protecteur
Gesichtsmaske
protector facial
one-piece suit
combinaison
einteiliger Anzug
traje de una sola pieza
sled
traîneau
Rodel
trineo
runner
patin
Kufe
patín
crash helmet
casque protecteur
Sturzhelm
casco protector
glove
gant
Handschuh
guante
blade
arête
Schiene
canto
heelplate
talonnière
Fersenplatte
pieza de talón
pole tip
pointe de bâton
Stockspitze
punta del bastón
tail
talon
Ende
cola
BOBSLEIGH
BOBSLEIGH
BOBSCHLITTEN
BOBSLEIGH
handle
poignée
Griff
asa
driver
capitaine
Steuermann
capitán
shell
coque
Gehäuse
bob
front runner
patin avant
vordere Kufe
patín delantero
brakeman
freineur
Bremser
guardafrenos
rear runner
patin arrière
hintere Kufe
patín trasero

# SKATING
# PATINAGE[M]
# EISLAUFEN[N]
# PATINAJE[M]



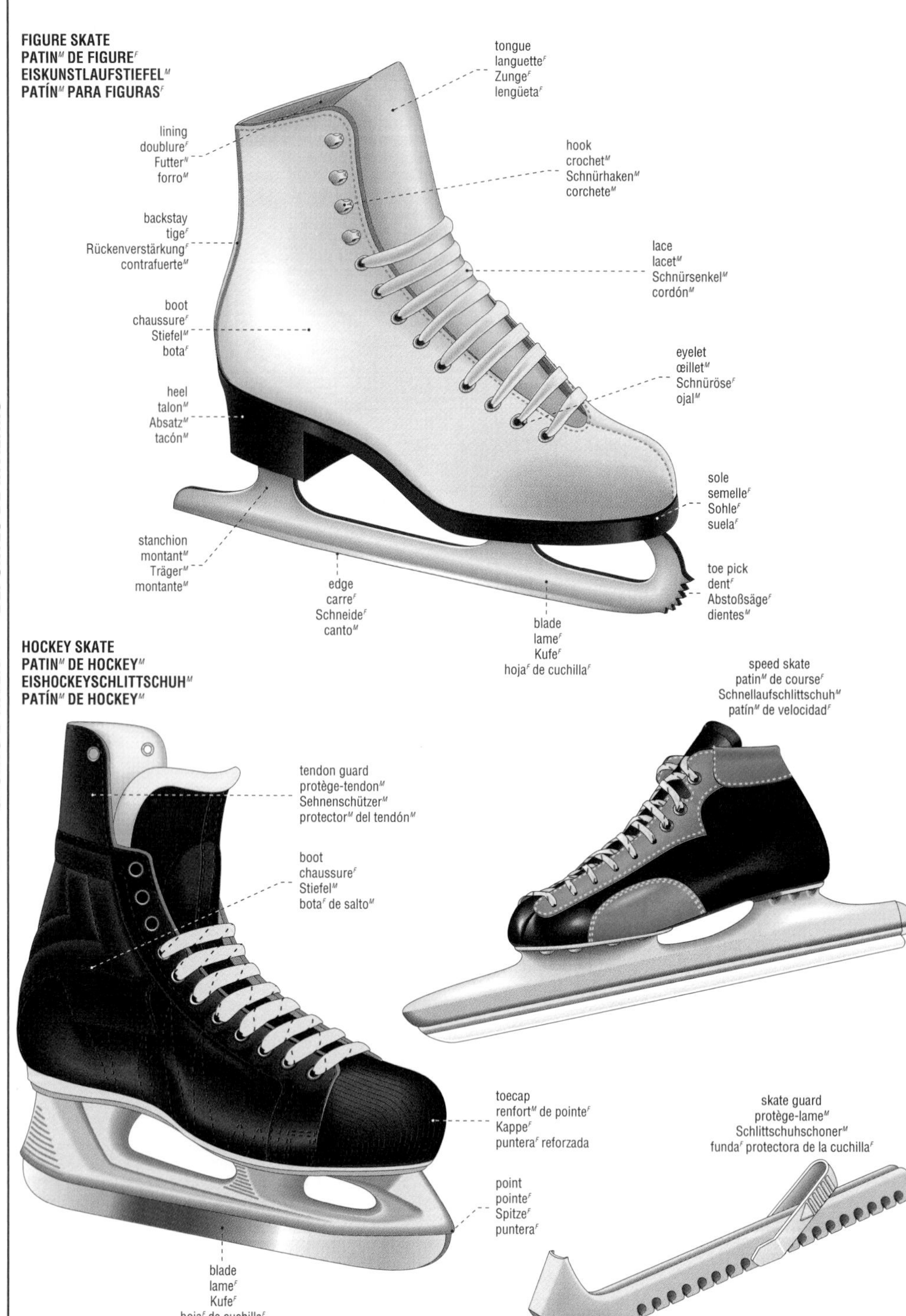

# SNOWSHOE
# RAQUETTE$^{F}$
# SCHNEESCHUH$^{M}$
# RAQUETA$^{F}$

## MICHIGAN SNOWSHOE
## RAQUETTE$^{F}$ ALGONQUINE
## MICHIGAN-SCHNEESCHUH$^{M}$
## TIPO$^{M}$ MICHIGAN

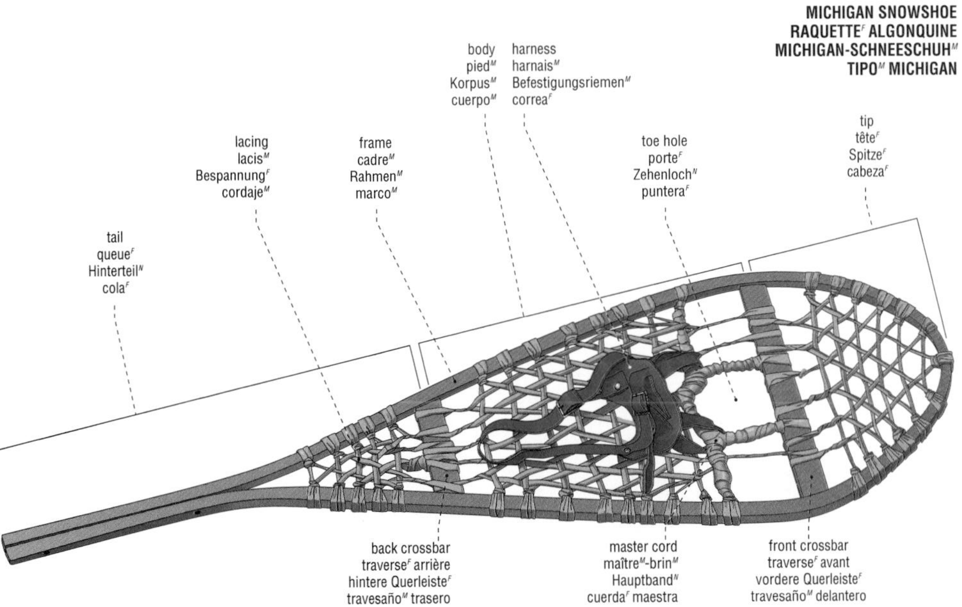

# ROLLER SKATE
# PATIN$^{M}$ À ROULETTES$^{F}$
# ROLLSCHUH$^{M}$
# PATÍN$^{M}$ DE RUEDAS$^{F}$

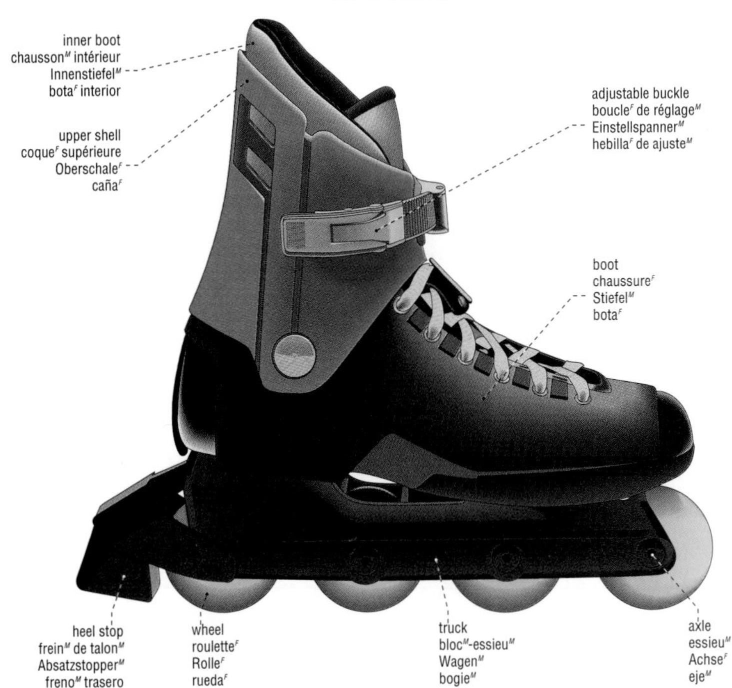

# SHOW-JUMPING
# ÉQUITATION[F]
# REITEN[N]
# EQUITACIÓN[F]: CONCURSO[M] DE SALTOS[M]

## SHOW-JUMPING COURSE
## PARCOURS[M] D'OBSTACLES[M]
## WETTKAMPFPARCOURS[M]
## PISTA[F] PARA PRUEBA[F] DE OBSTÁCULOS[M]

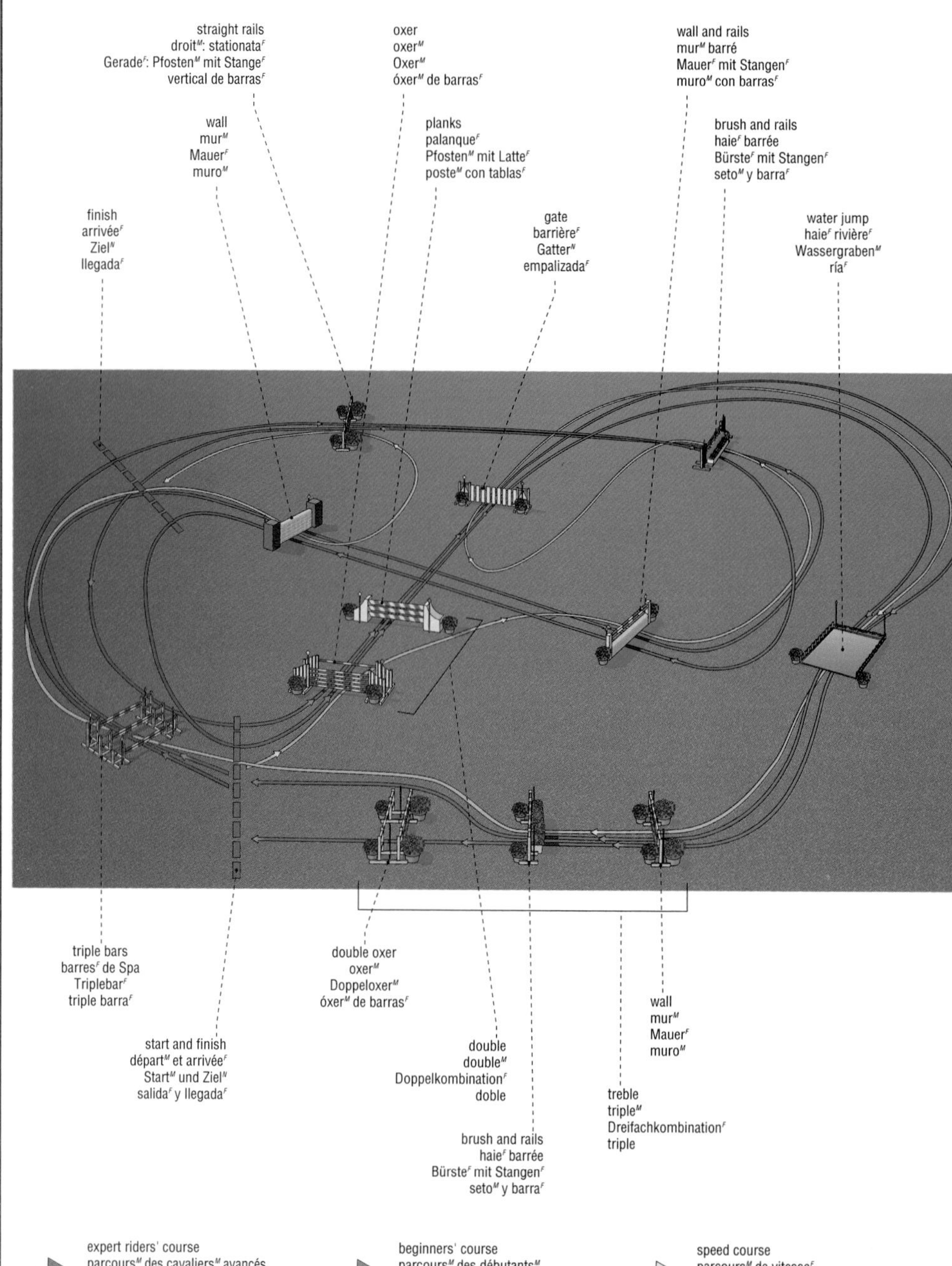


expert riders' course
parcours[M] des cavaliers[M] avancés
Fortgeschrittenenparcours[M]
concurso[M] profesional

beginners' course
parcours[M] des débutants[M]
Anfängerparcours[M]
carrera[F] de aprendices[M]

speed course
parcours[M] de vitesse[F]
Hochgeschwindigkeitsparcours[M]
concurso[M] de velocidad[F]

**OBSTACLES**
**OBSTACLES[M]**
**HÜRDEN[F]**
**OBSTÁCULOS[M]**

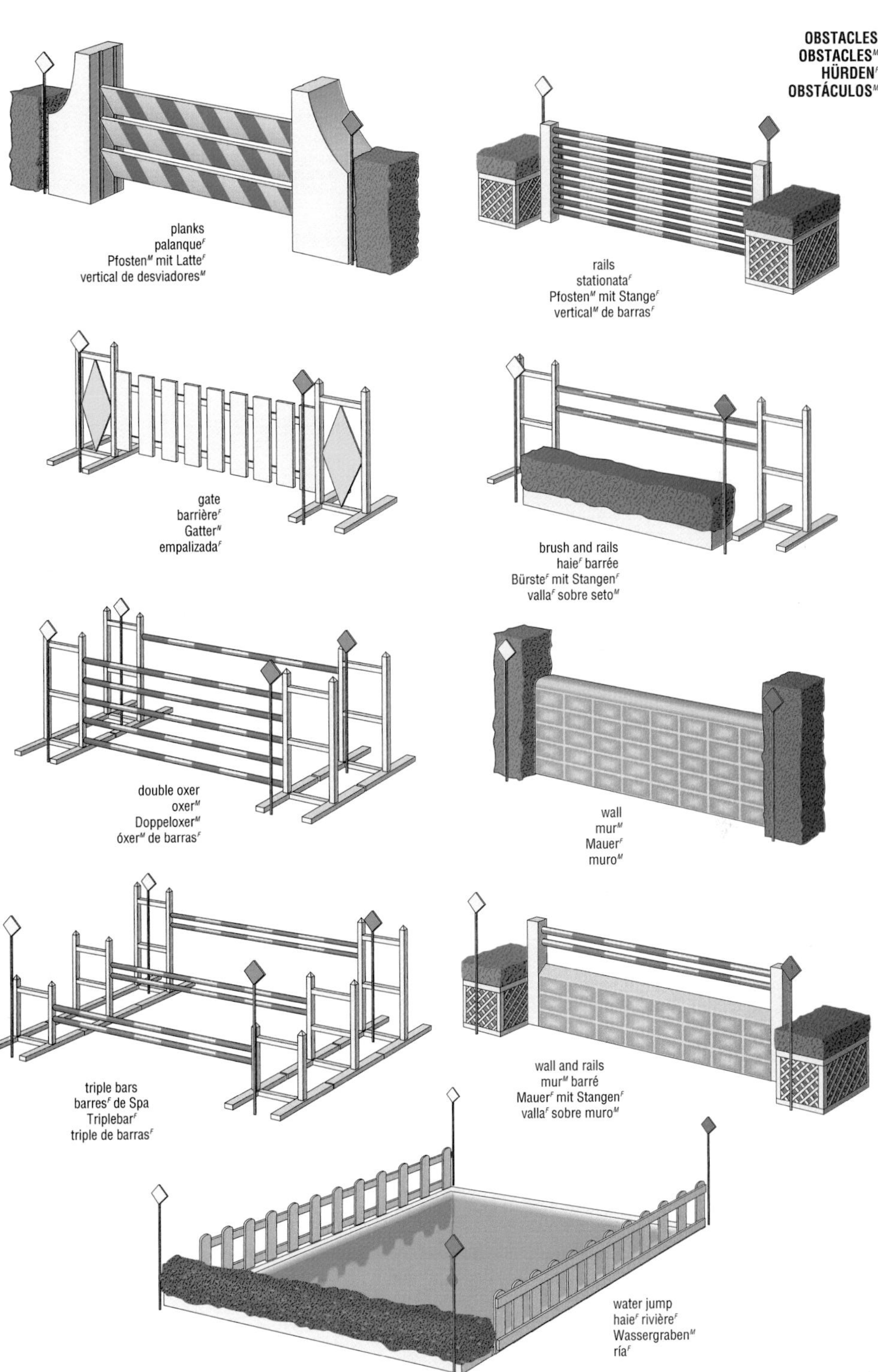

# RIDING
# ÉQUITATION^F
# REITEN^N
# EQUITACIÓN^F

## RIDER
## CAVALIER^M
## REITER^M
## JINETE^M

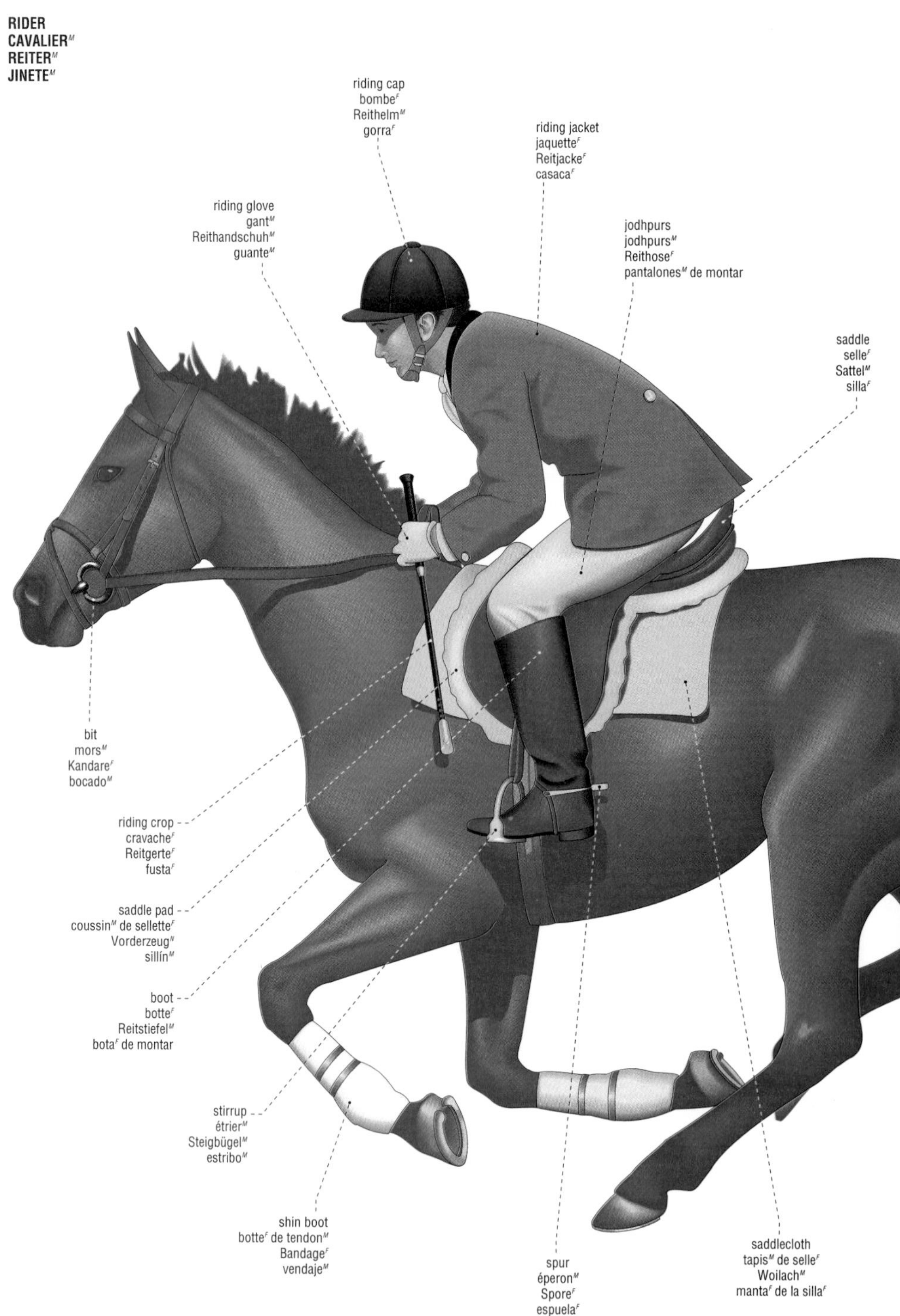

## SADDLE
## SELLE$^{F}$
## SATTEL$^{M}$
## SILLA$^{F}$ DE MONTAR

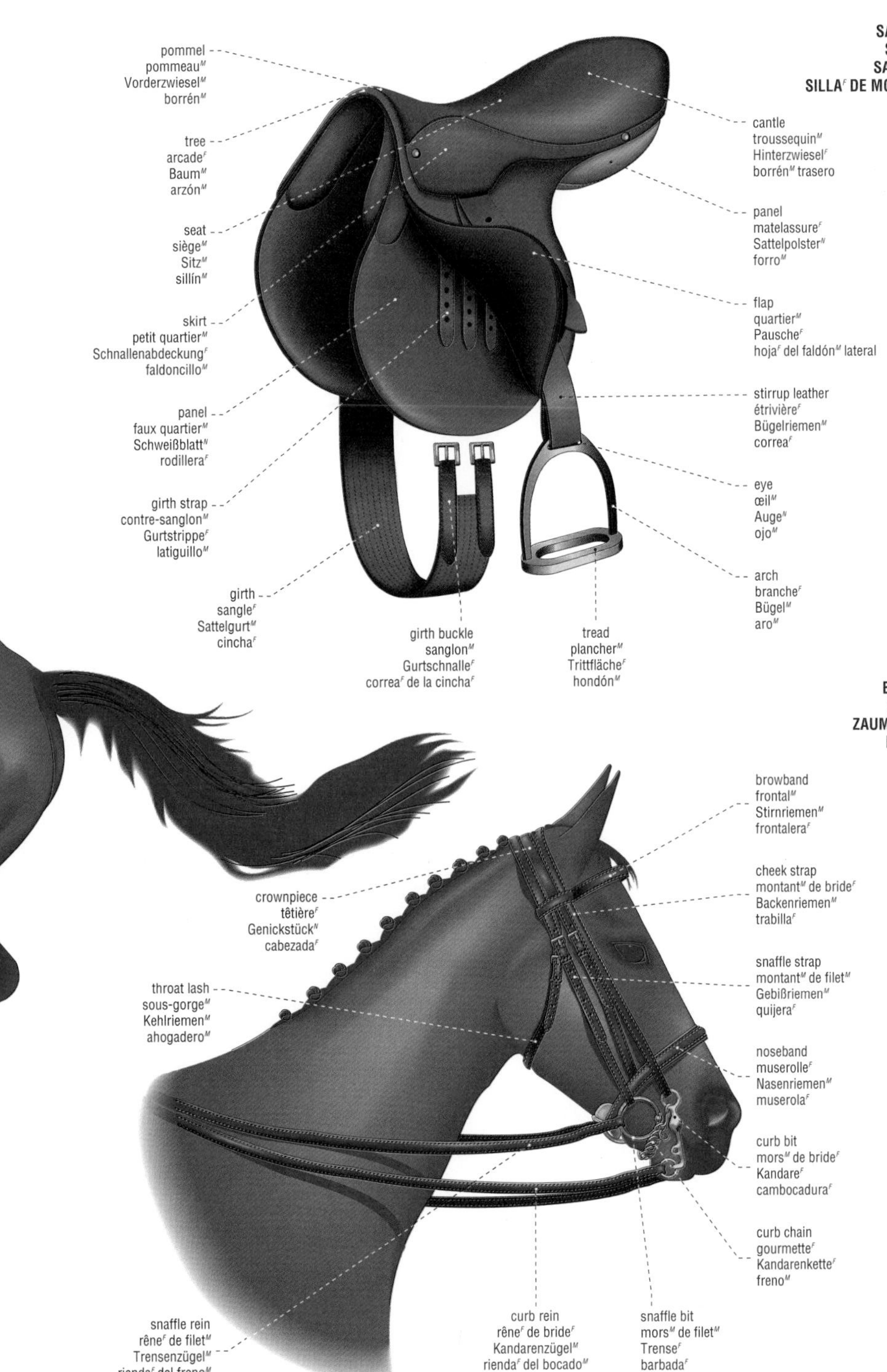

# TYPES OF BIT
# TYPES^M DE MORS^M
# GEBISSSTÜCKARTEN^F
# BOCADOS^M

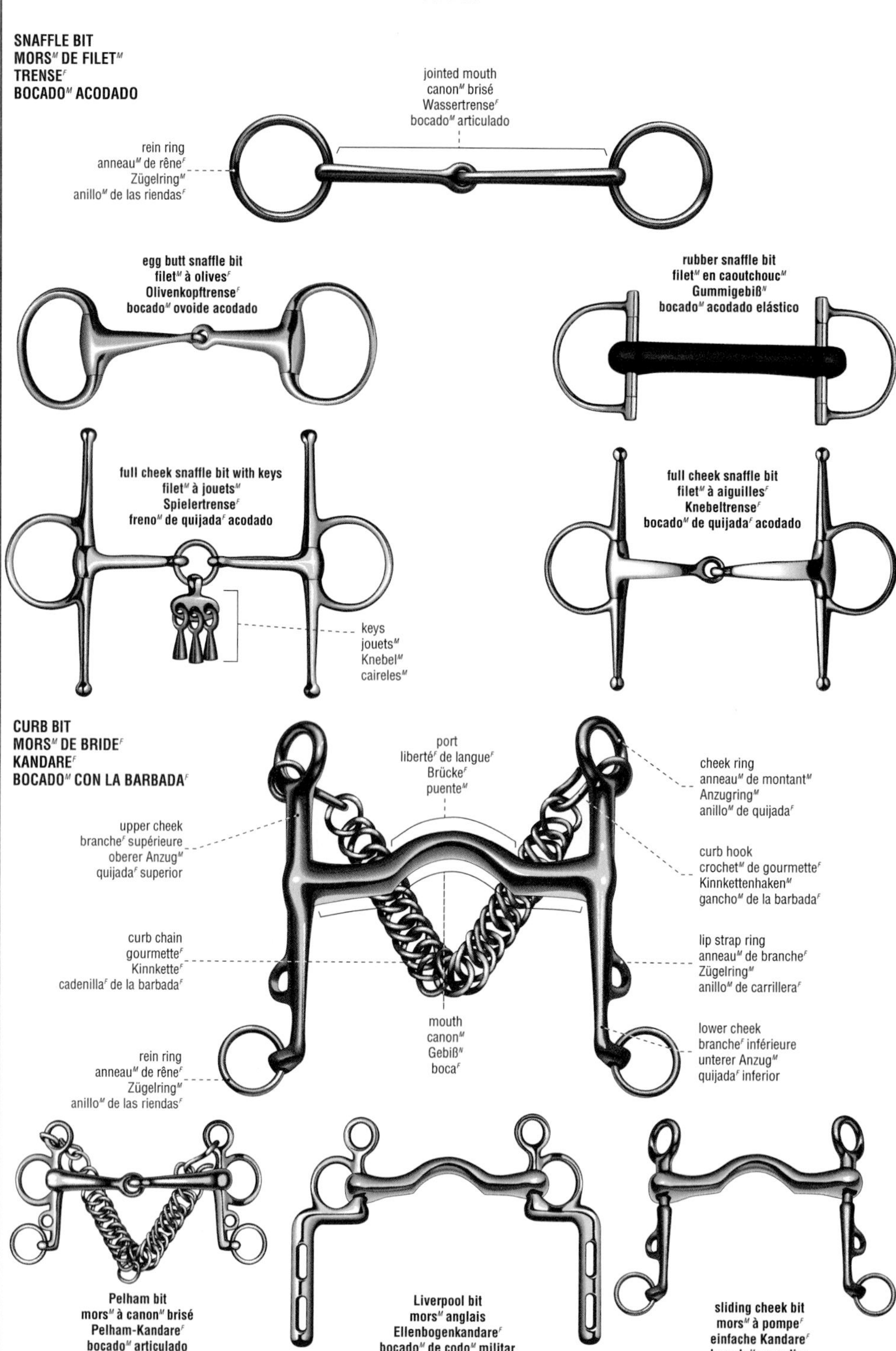

# HORSE RACING
# COURSE^F DE CHEVAUX^M
# GALOPPRENNEN^N
# CARRERA^F DE CABALLOS^M

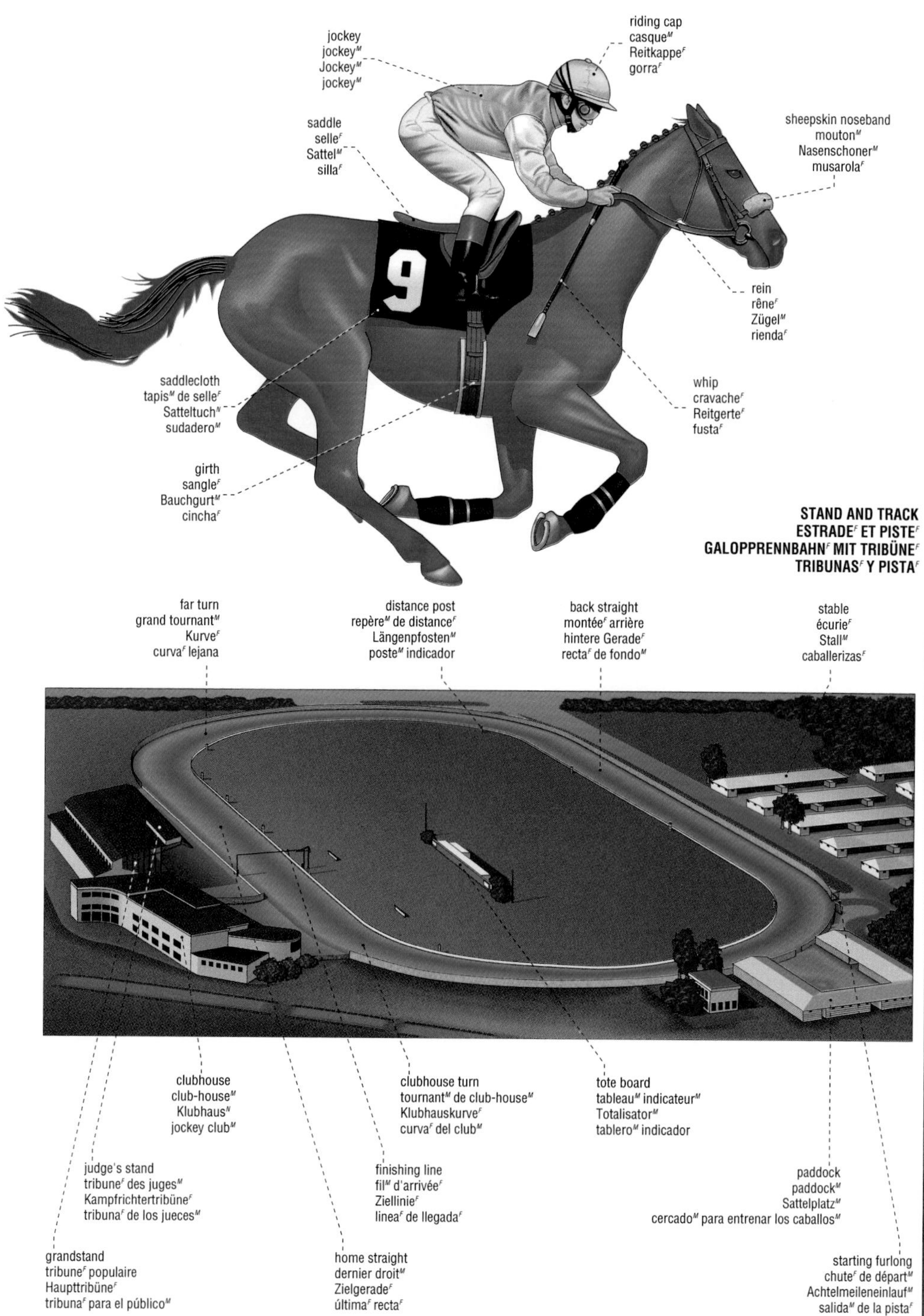

# HARNESS RACING
# COURSE SOUS HARNAIS
# TRABRENNSPORT
# CARRERAS DE TROTONES

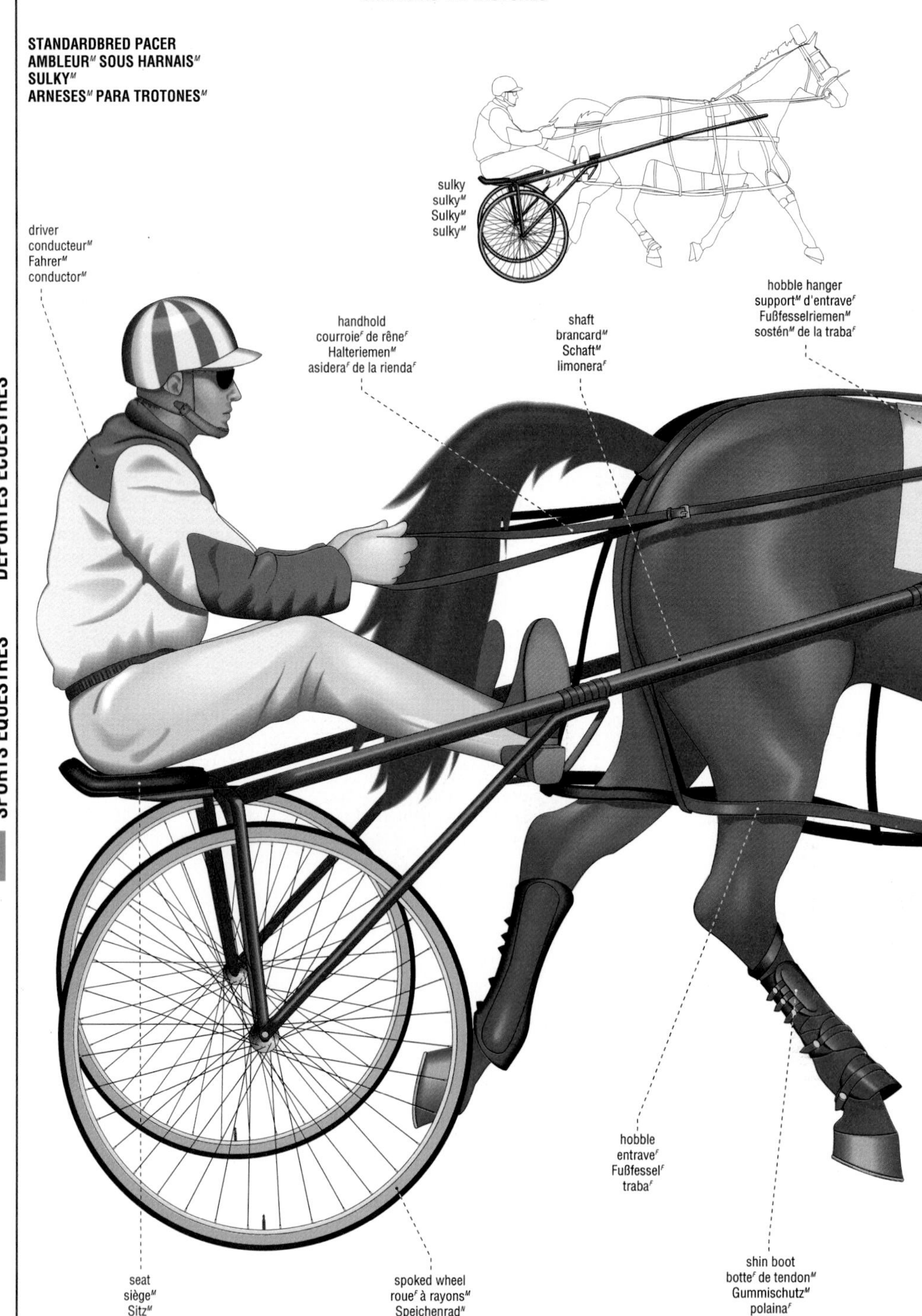

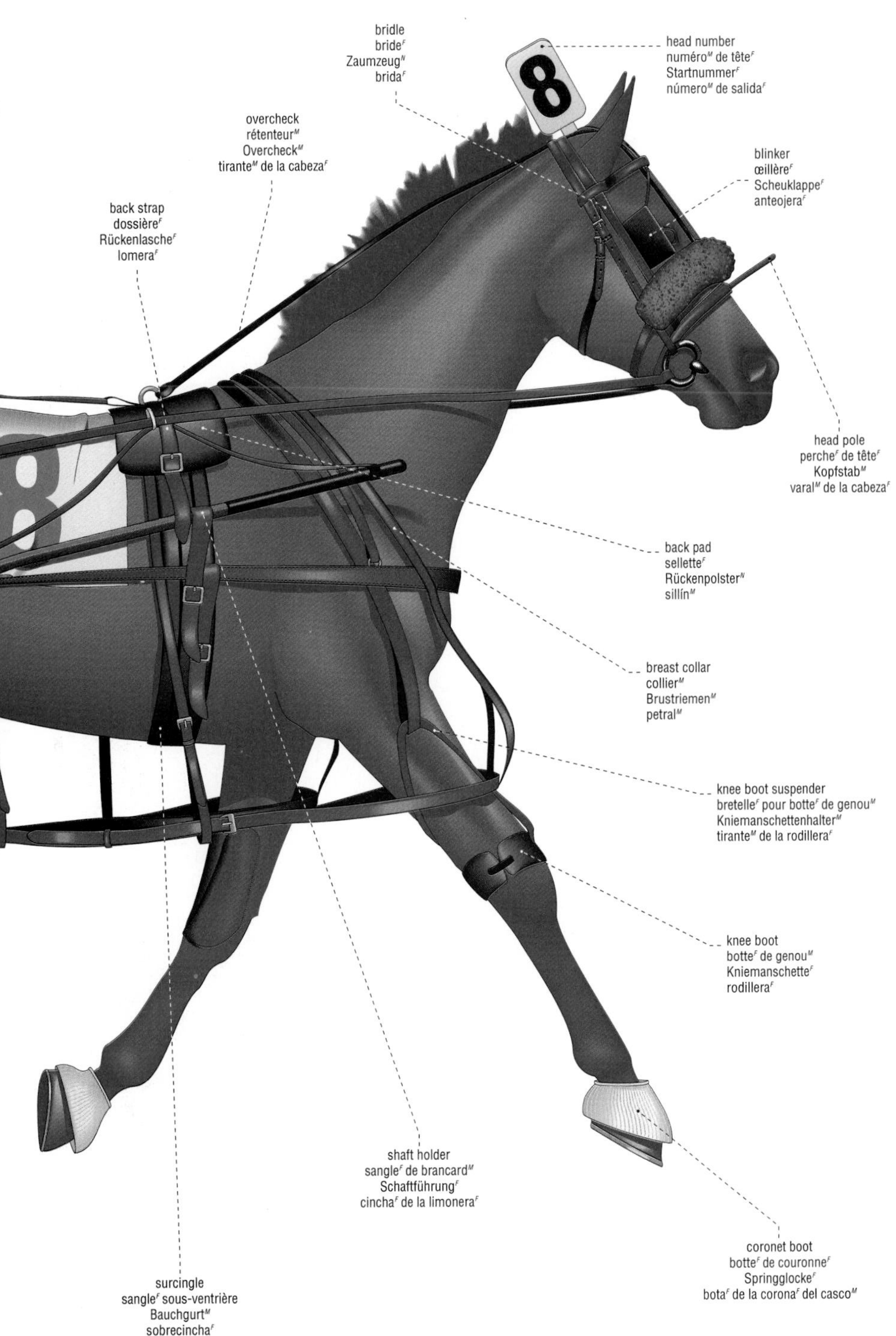

bridle
bride$^{F}$
Zaumzeug$^{N}$
brida$^{F}$
head number
numéro$^{M}$ de tête$^{F}$
Startnummer$^{F}$
número$^{M}$ de salida$^{F}$
8
overcheck
rétenteur$^{M}$
Overcheck$^{M}$
tirante$^{M}$ de la cabeza$^{F}$
blinker
œillère$^{F}$
Scheuklappe$^{F}$
anteojera$^{F}$
back strap
dossière$^{F}$
Rückenlasche$^{F}$
lomera$^{F}$
head pole
perche$^{F}$ de tête$^{F}$
Kopfstab$^{M}$
varal$^{M}$ de la cabeza$^{F}$
back pad
sellette$^{F}$
Rückenpolster$^{N}$
sillín$^{M}$
breast collar
collier$^{M}$
Brustriemen$^{M}$
petral$^{M}$
knee boot suspender
bretelle$^{F}$ pour botte$^{F}$ de genou$^{M}$
Kniemanschettenhalter$^{M}$
tirante$^{M}$ de la rodillera$^{F}$
knee boot
botte$^{F}$ de genou$^{M}$
Kniemanschette$^{F}$
rodillera$^{F}$
shaft holder
sangle$^{F}$ de brancard$^{M}$
Schaftführung$^{F}$
cincha$^{F}$ de la limonera$^{F}$
coronet boot
botte$^{F}$ de couronne$^{F}$
Springglocke$^{F}$
bota$^{F}$ de la corona$^{F}$ del casco$^{M}$
surcingle
sangle$^{F}$ sous-ventrière
Bauchgurt$^{M}$
sobrecincha$^{F}$

# TRACK AND FIELD ATHLETICS
# ATHLÉTISME^M
# LEICHTATHLETIK^F
# ATLETISMO^M DE CAMPO^M Y PISTA^F

## ARENA
## STADE^M
## STADION^N
## ESTADIO^M

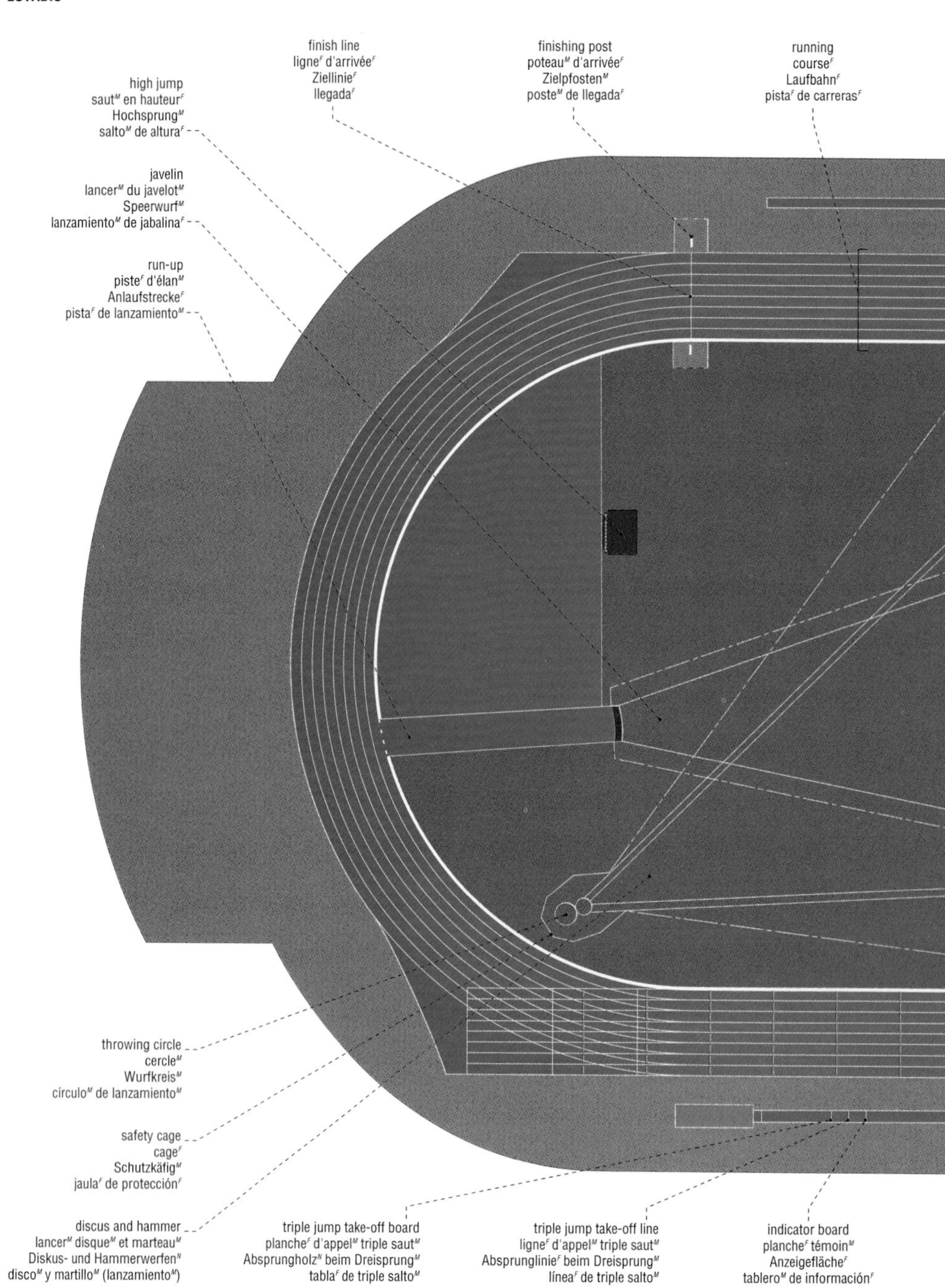

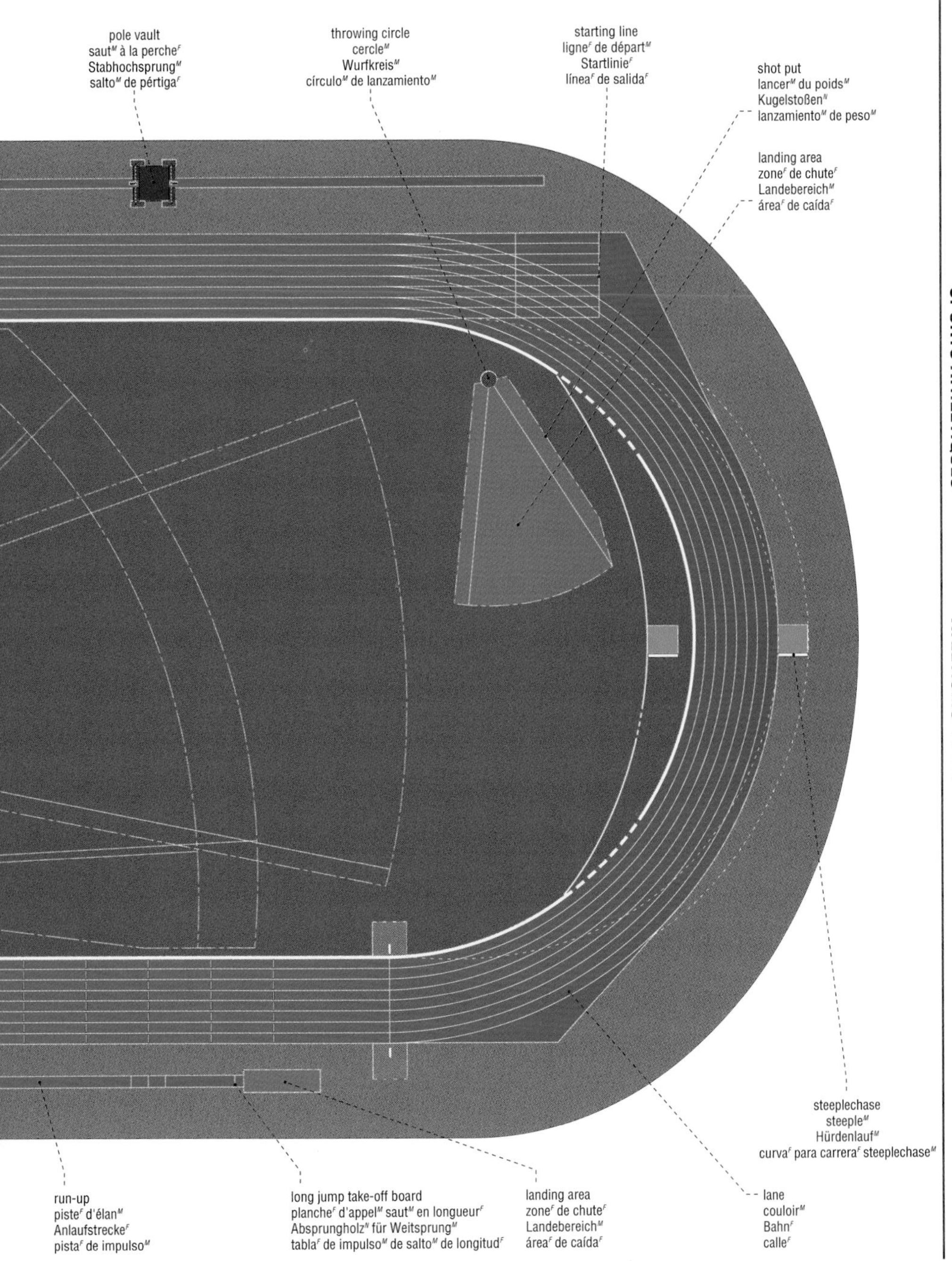
pole vault
saut[M] à la perche[F]
Stabhochsprung[M]
salto[M] de pértiga[F]
throwing circle
cercle[M]
Wurfkreis[M]
círculo[M] de lanzamiento[M]
starting line
ligne[F] de départ[M]
Startlinie[F]
línea[F] de salida[F]
shot put
lancer[M] du poids[M]
Kugelstoßen[N]
lanzamiento[M] de peso[M]
landing area
zone[F] de chute[F]
Landebereich[M]
área[F] de caída[F]
steeplechase
steeple[M]
Hürdenlauf[M]
curva[F] para carrera[F] steeplechase[M]
run-up
piste[F] d'élan[M]
Anlaufstrecke[F]
pista[F] de impulso[M]
long jump take-off board
planche[F] d'appel[M] saut[M] en longueur[F]
Absprungholz[N] für Weitsprung[M]
tabla[F] de impulso[M] de salto[M] de longitud[F]
landing area
zone[F] de chute[F]
Landebereich[M]
área[F] de caída[F]
lane
couloir[M]
Bahn[F]
calle[F]

# TRACK AND FIELD ATHLETICS
# ATHLÉTISME^M
# LEICHTATHLETIK^F
# ATLETISMO^M DE CAMPO^M Y PISTA^F

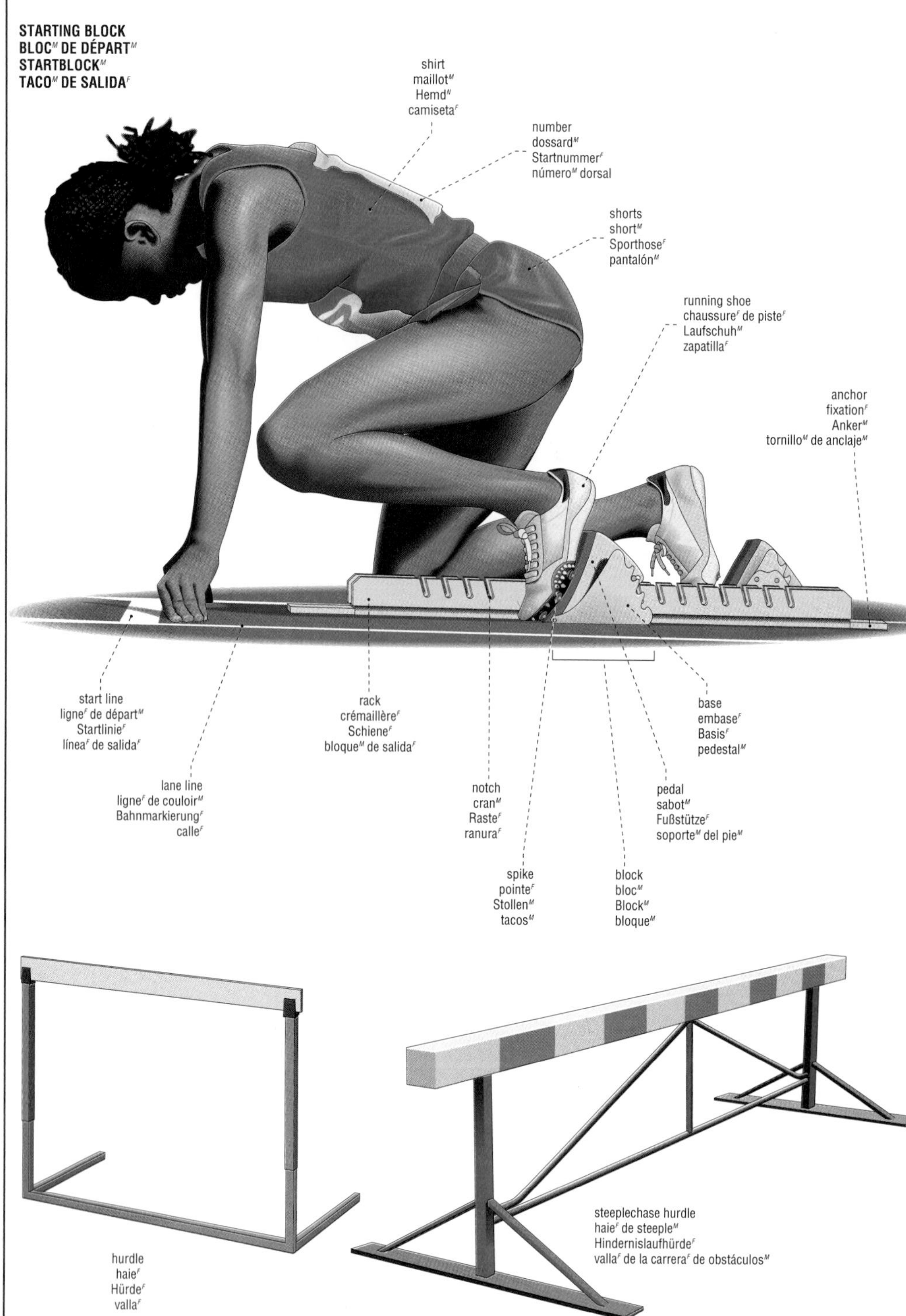

## HIGH JUMP
## SAUT[M] EN HAUTEUR[F]
## HOCHSPRUNG[M]
## SALTO[M] DE ALTURA[F]

## POLE VAULT
## SAUT[M] À LA PERCHE[F]
## STABHOCHSPRUNG[M]
## SALTO[M] DE PÉRTIGA[F]

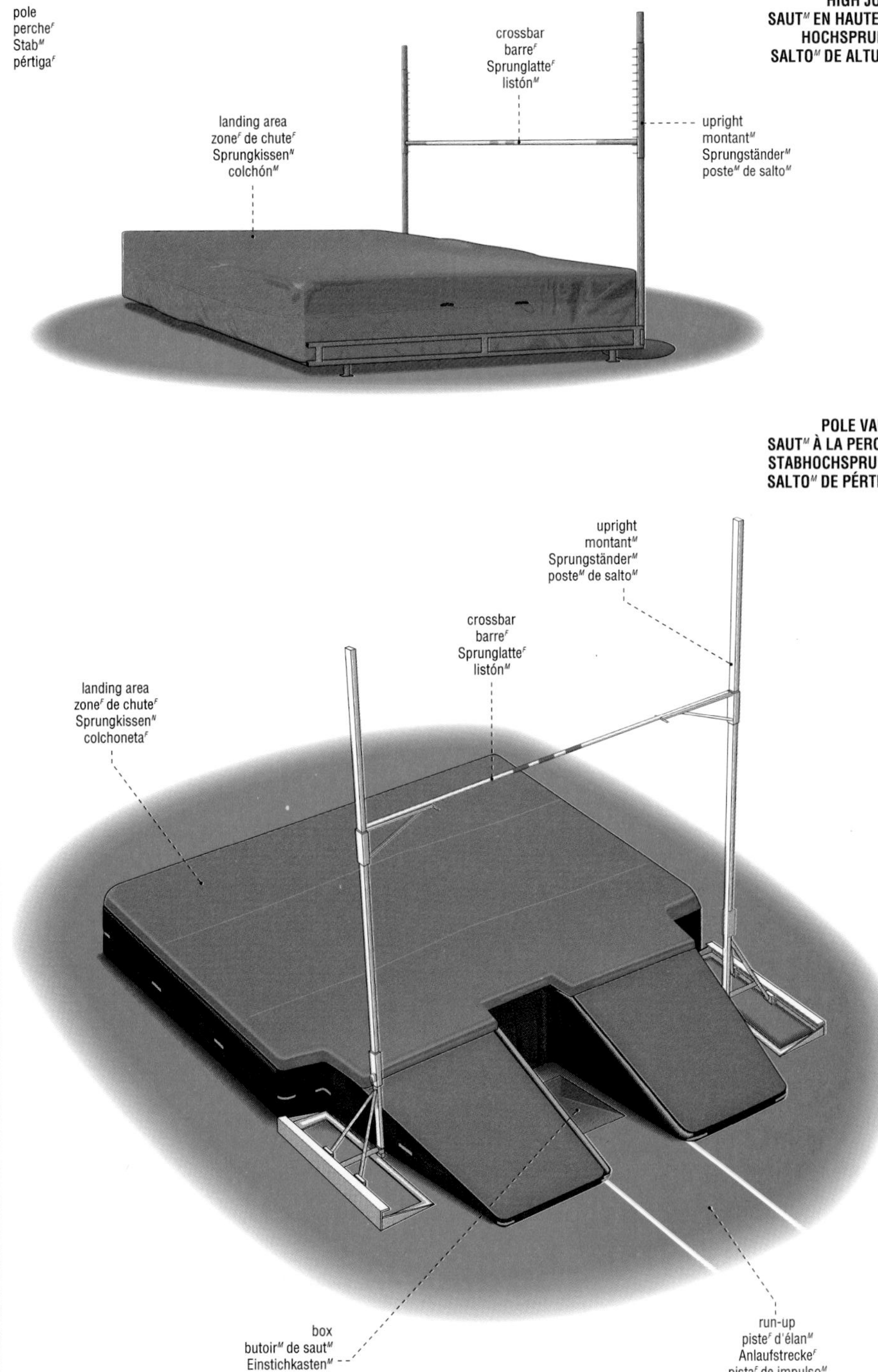

# TRACK AND FIELD ATHLETICS
# ATHLÉTISME^M
# LEICHTATHLETIK^F
# ATHLETISMO^M DE CAMPO^M Y PISTA^F

**THROWING APPARATUS**
**LANCERS^M**
**WURFGERÄTE^N**
**LANZAMIENTOS^M**

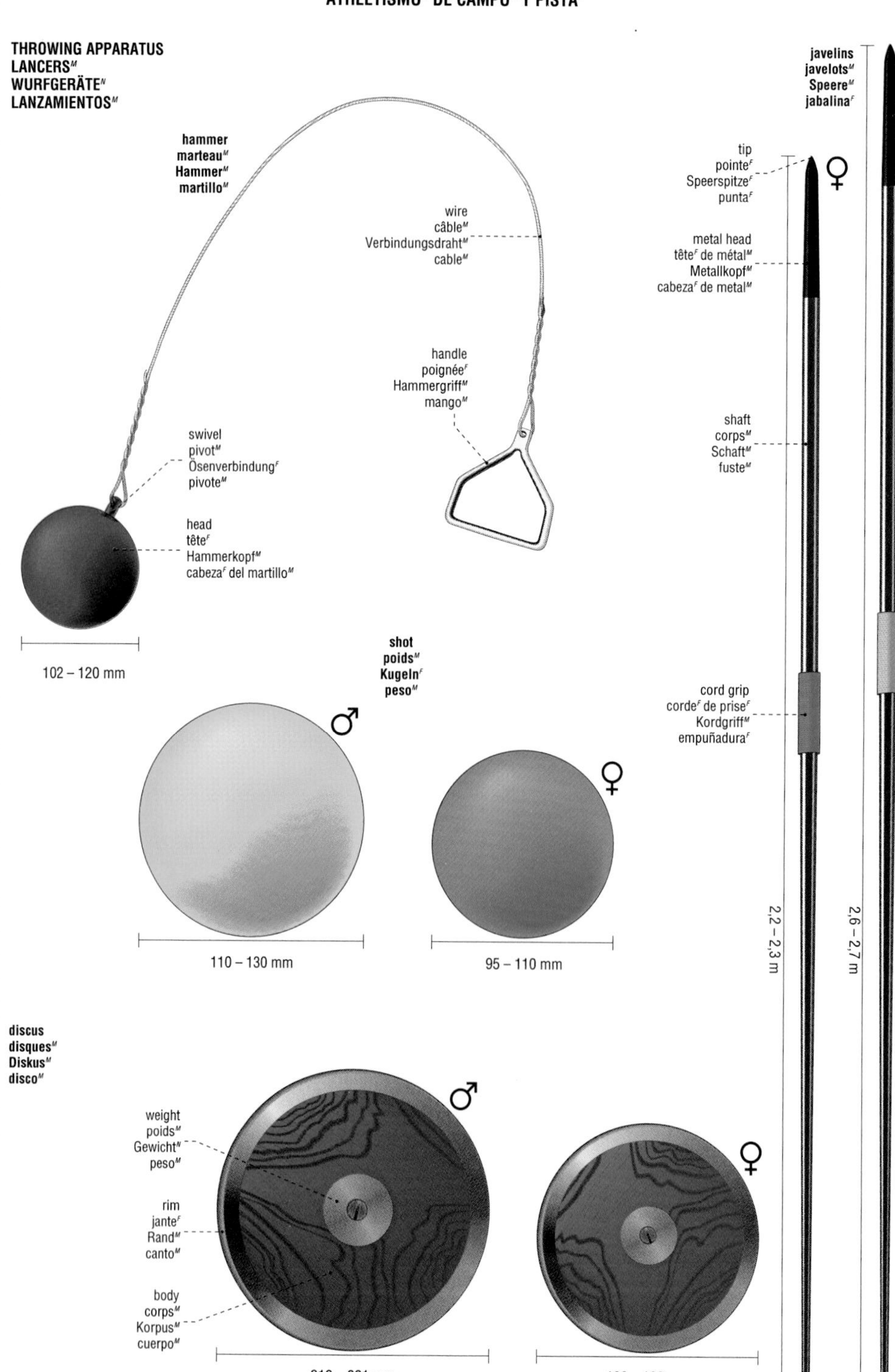

## GYMNASTICS
## GYMNASTIQUE[F]
## GERÄTETURNEN[N]
## GIMNASIA[F]

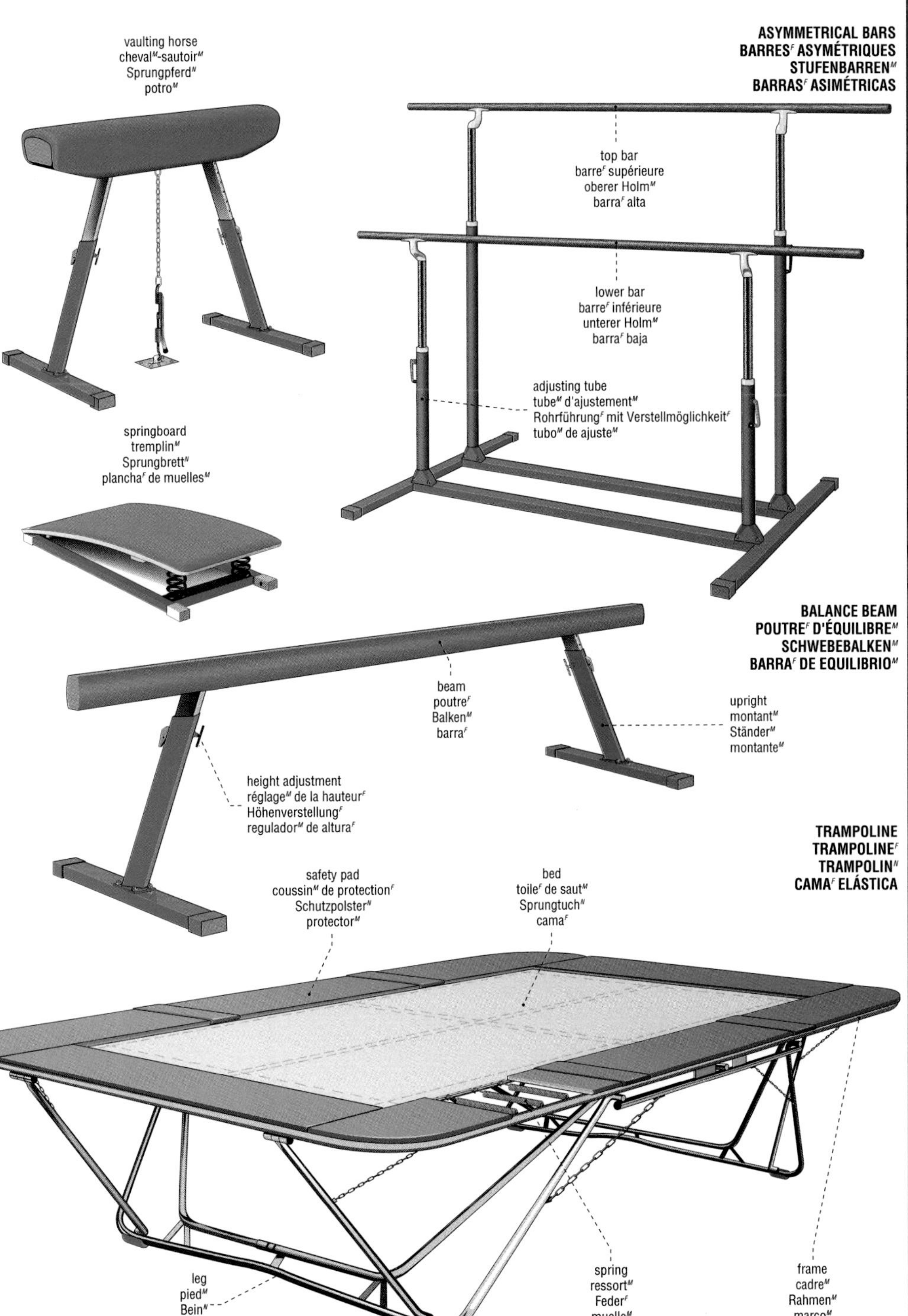

# GYMNASTICS
# GYMNASTIQUE[F]
# GERÄTETURNEN[N]
# GIMNASIA[F]

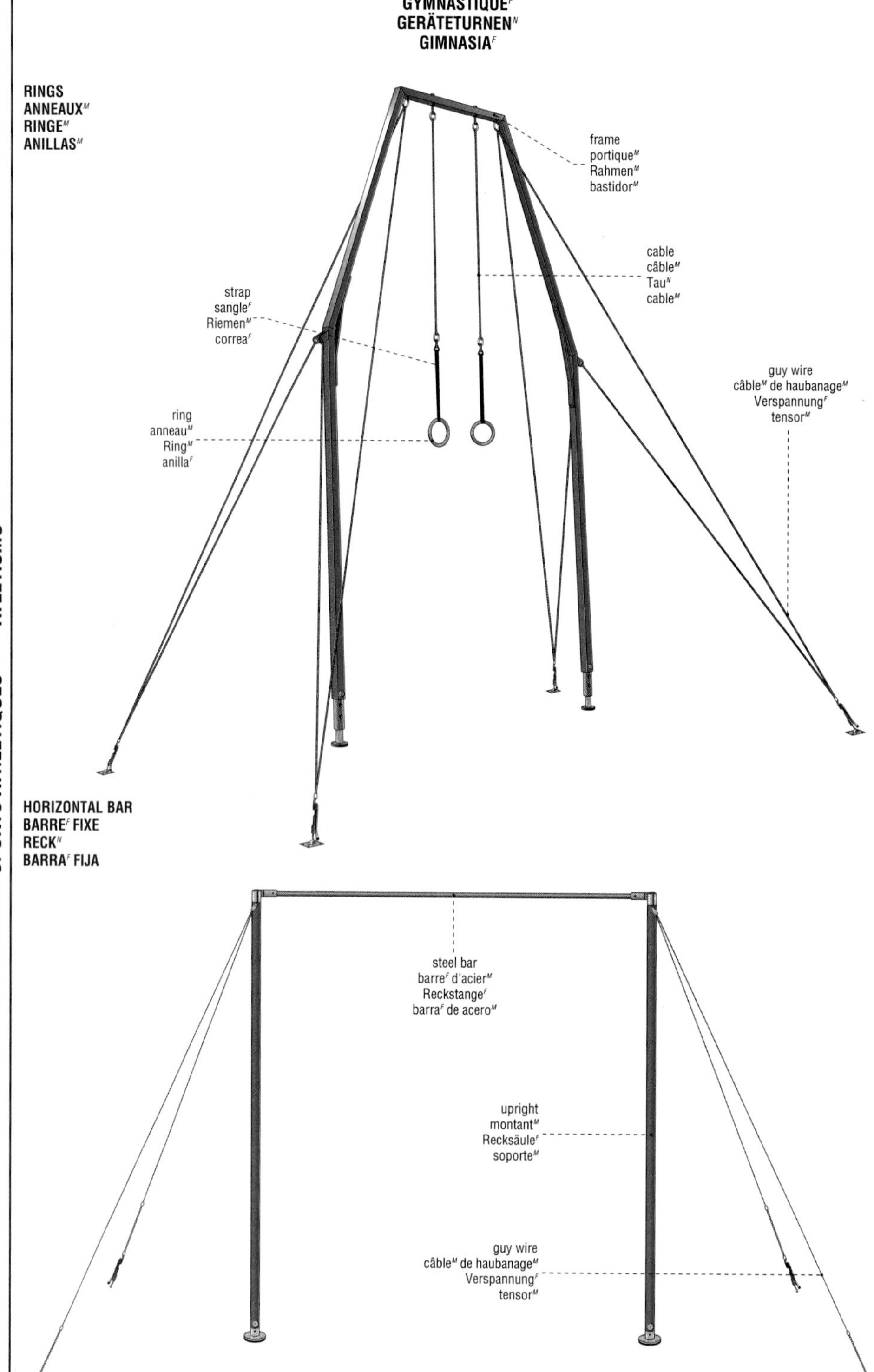

## POMMEL HORSE
## CHEVAL[M] D'ARÇONS[M]
## PAUSCHENPFERD[N]
## CABALLO[M] DE ARZÓN[M]

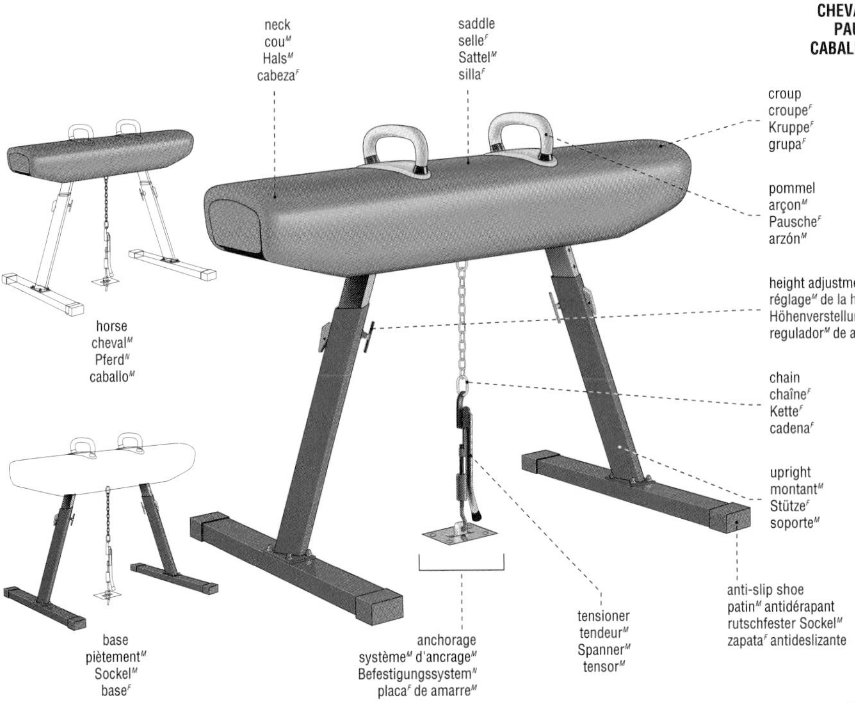

neck
cou[M]
Hals[M]
cabeza[F]
saddle
selle[F]
Sattel[M]
silla[F]
croup
croupe[F]
Kruppe[F]
grupa[F]
pommel
arçon[M]
Pausche[F]
arzón[M]
height adjustment
réglage[M] de la hauteur[F]
Höhenverstellung[F]
regulador[M] de altura[F]
horse
cheval[M]
Pferd[N]
caballo[M]
chain
chaîne[F]
Kette[F]
cadena[F]
upright
montant[M]
Stütze[F]
soporte[M]
anti-slip shoe
patin[M] antidérapant
rutschfester Sockel[M]
zapata[F] antideslizante
tensioner
tendeur[M]
Spanner[M]
tensor[M]
anchorage
système[M] d'ancrage[M]
Befestigungssystem[N]
placa[F] de amarre[M]
base
piètement[M]
Sockel[M]
base[F]

## PARALLEL BARS
## BARRES[F] PARALLÈLES
## PARALLELBARREN[M]
## BARRAS[F] PARALELAS

wooden bar
barre[F] de bois[M]
hölzerner Barrenholm[M]
barra[F] de madera[F]
adjustable support
tube[M] d'ajustement[M]
Rohrführung[F] mit Verstellmöglichkeit[F]
tubo[M] de ajuste[M]
base
base[F]
Sockel[M]
base[F]

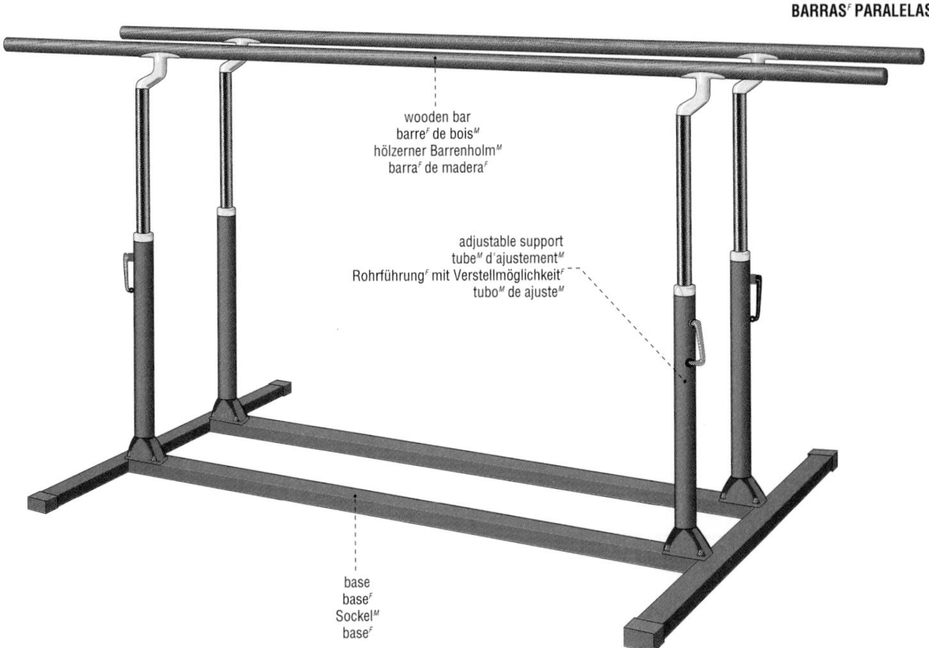

# WEIGHTLIFTING
# HALTÉROPHILIE[F]
# GEWICHTHEBEN[N]
# HALTEROFILIA[F]

## FITNESS EQUIPMENT
## APPAREILS^M DE CONDITIONNEMENT^M PHYSIQUE
## FITNESSGERÄTE^N
## APARATOS^M DE EJERCICIOS^M

### WEIGHT TRAINER
### BANC^M DE MUSCULATION^F
### MULTITRAINER^M
### UNIDAD^F DE PESAS^F

### BARBELL
### HALTÈRE^M LONG
### HANTEL^F
### HALTERA^F

# FITNESS EQUIPMENT
# APPAREILS^M DE CONDITIONNEMENT^M PHYSIQUE
# FITNESSGERÄTE^N
# APARATOS^M DE EJERCICIOS^M



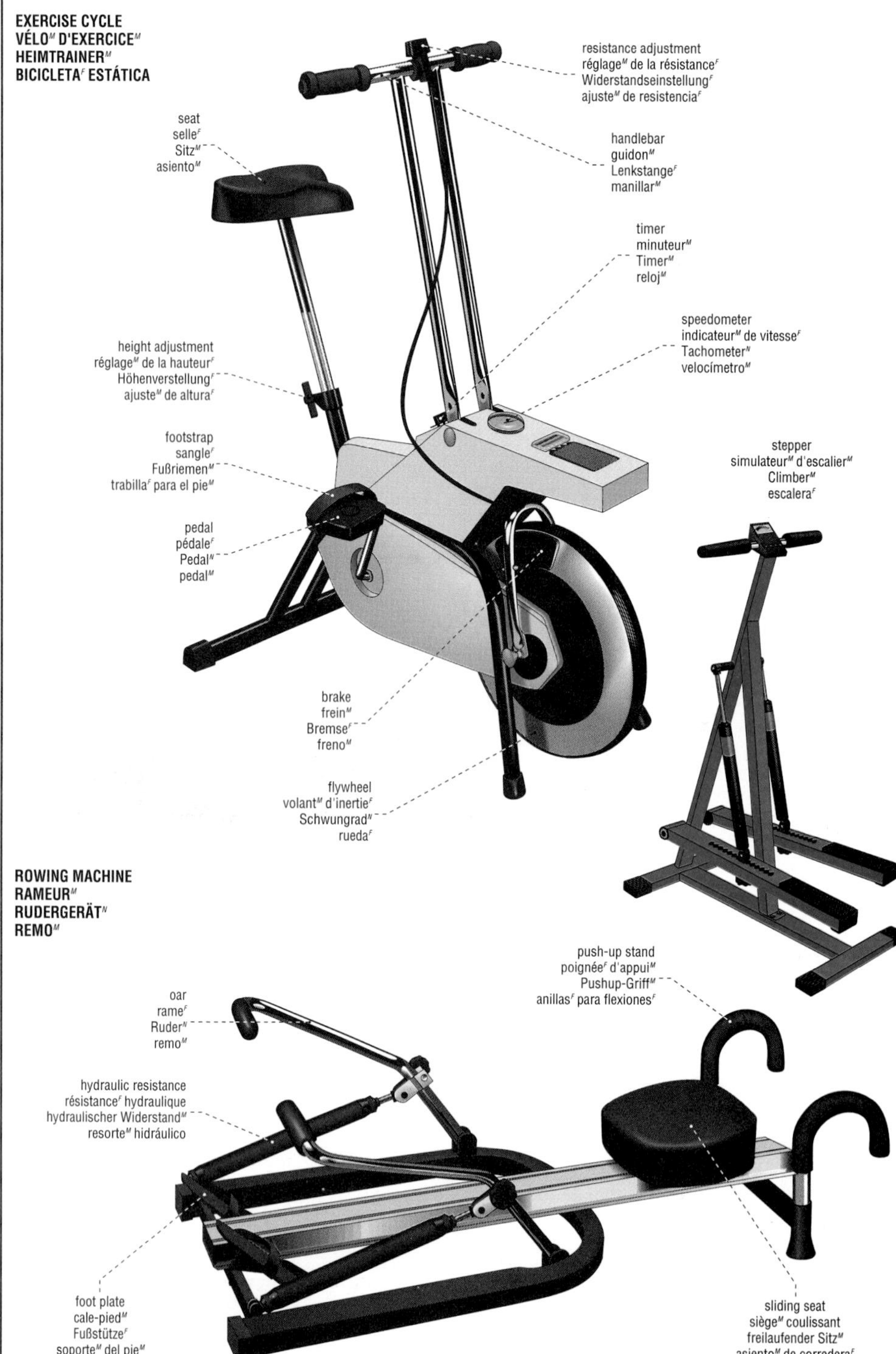

DUMBBELL
HALTÈRE[M] COURT
HANTEL[F]
PESAS[F]
weight
poids[M]
Gewicht[N]
pesas[F]
bar
barre[F]
Griff[M]
barra[F]
handgrips
poignée[F] à ressort[M]
Handmuskeltrainer[M]
empuñaderas[F]
ankle/wrist weight
bracelet[M] lesté
Fuß-/Handgelenksgewicht[N]
pesas[F] para muñecas[F] y tobillos[M]
skipping-rope
corde[F] à sauter
Springseil[N]
cuerda[F]
TWIST BAR
RESSORT[M] ATHLÉTIQUE
FEDERSTANGE[F]
BARRA[F] DE TORSIÓN[F]
grip
poignée[F]
Griff[M]
empuñadura[F]
tension spring
ressort[M] de tension[F]
Spannfeder[F]
resorte[M] de tensión[F]
chest expander
extenseur[M]
Expander[M]
tensores[M] pectorales

# FENCING
# ESCRIME[F]
# FECHTSPORT[M]
# ESGRIMA[F]

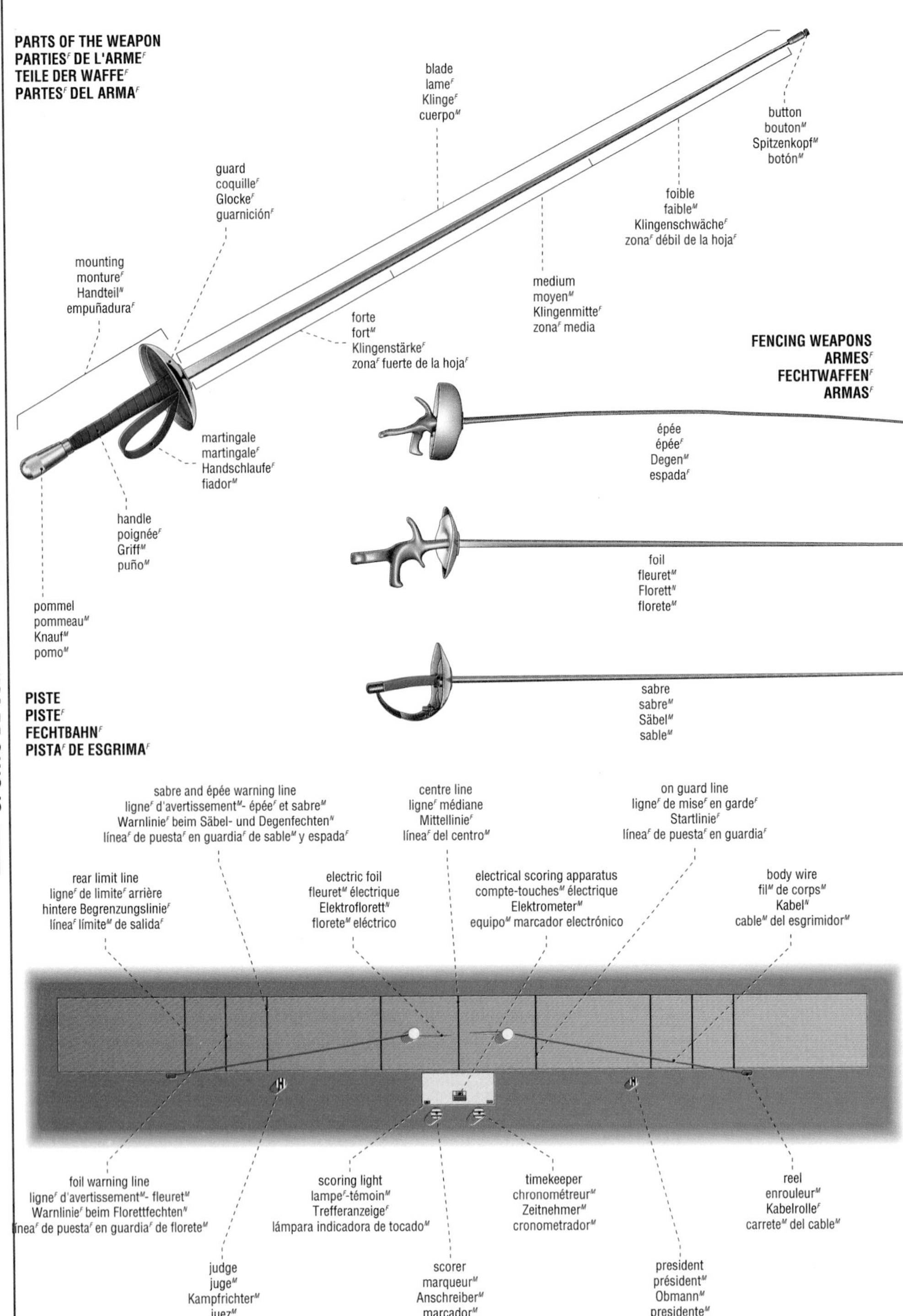

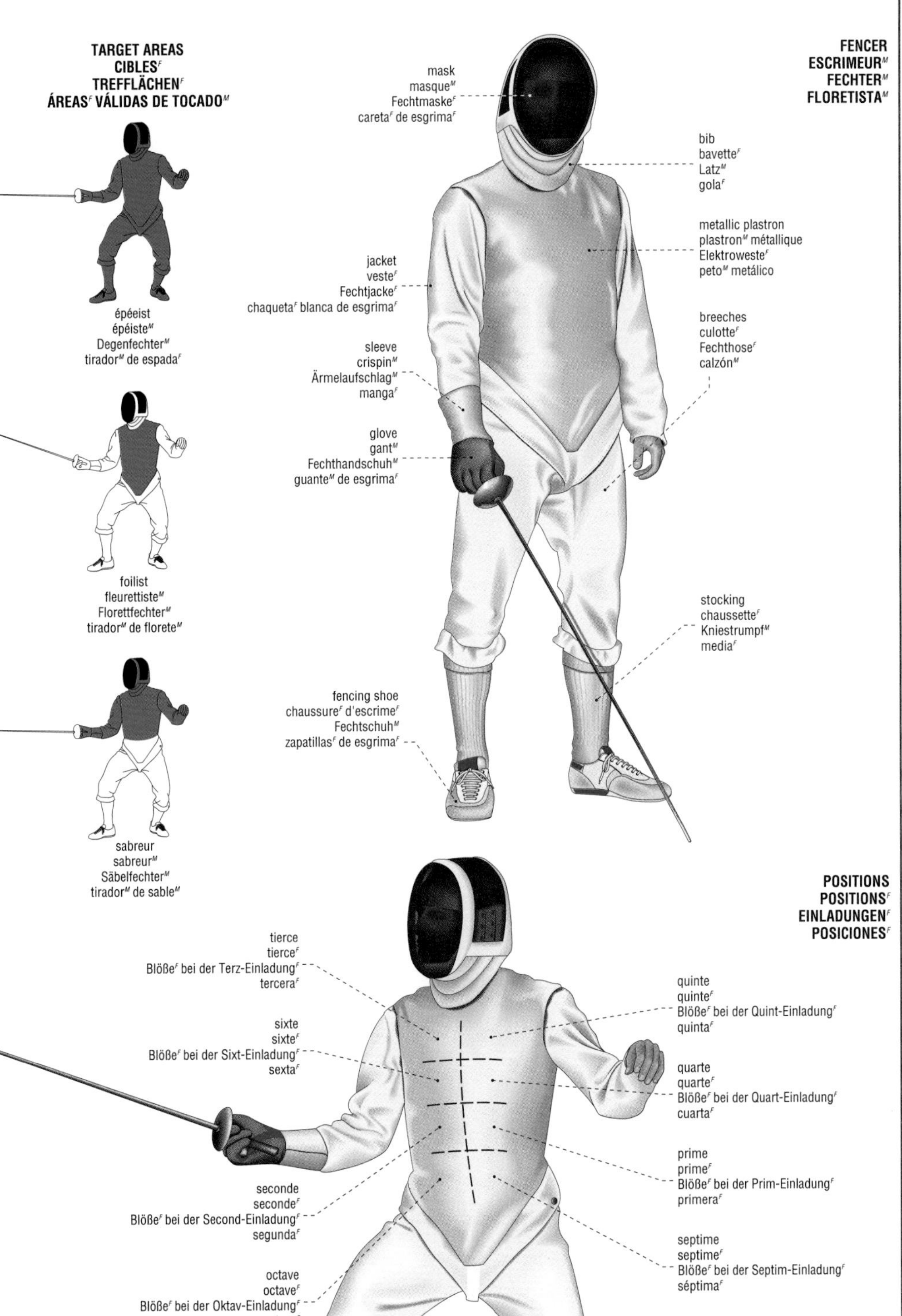
TARGET AREAS
CIBLES[F]
TREFFLÄCHEN[F]
ÁREAS[F] VÁLIDAS DE TOCADO[M]
épéeist
épéiste[M]
Degenfechter[M]
tirador[M] de espada[F]
foilist
fleurettiste[M]
Florettfechter[M]
tirador[M] de florete[M]
sabreur
sabreur[M]
Säbelfechter[M]
tirador[M] de sable[M]
FENCER
ESCRIMEUR[M]
FECHTER[M]
FLORETISTA[M]
mask
masque[M]
Fechtmaske[F]
careta[F] de esgrima[F]
bib
bavette[F]
Latz[M]
gola[F]
metallic plastron
plastron[M] métallique
Elektroweste[F]
peto[M] metálico
jacket
veste[F]
Fechtjacke[F]
chaqueta[F] blanca de esgrima[F]
breeches
culotte[F]
Fechthose[F]
calzón[M]
sleeve
crispin[M]
Ärmelaufschlag[M]
manga[F]
glove
gant[M]
Fechthandschuh[M]
guante[M] de esgrima[F]
stocking
chaussette[F]
Kniestrumpf[M]
media[F]
fencing shoe
chaussure[F] d'escrime[F]
Fechtschuh[M]
zapatillas[F] de esgrima[F]
POSITIONS
POSITIONS[F]
EINLADUNGEN[F]
POSICIONES[F]
tierce
tierce[F]
Blöße[F] bei der Terz-Einladung[F]
tercera[F]
quinte
quinte[F]
Blöße[F] bei der Quint-Einladung[F]
quinta[F]
sixte
sixte[F]
Blöße[F] bei der Sixt-Einladung[F]
sexta[F]
quarte
quarte[F]
Blöße[F] bei der Quart-Einladung[F]
cuarta[F]
prime
prime[F]
Blöße[F] bei der Prim-Einladung[F]
primera[F]
seconde
seconde[F]
Blöße[F] bei der Second-Einladung[F]
segunda[F]
septime
septime[F]
Blöße[F] bei der Septim-Einladung[F]
séptima[F]
octave
octave[F]
Blöße[F] bei der Oktav-Einladung[F]
octava[F]

# JUDO
# JUDO$^{M}$
# JUDO$^{N}$
# JUDO$^{M}$

## JUDO SUIT
## COSTUME$^{M}$ DE JUDO$^{M}$
## JUDOANZUG$^{M}$
## JUDOKA$^{M}$

## EXAMPLES OF HOLDS
## EXEMPLES$^{M}$ DE PRISES$^{F}$
## GRIFF- UND WURFBEISPIELE$^{N}$
## EJEMPLOS$^{M}$ DE LLAVES$^{F}$

arm lock
clé$^{F}$ de bras$^{M}$
Armhebel$^{M}$
presa$^{F}$ de brazo$^{M}$

holding
immobilisation$^{F}$
Haltegriffe$^{M}$
presa$^{F}$

major outer reaping throw
grand fauchage$^{M}$ extérieur
Große Außensichel$^{F}$
osoto-gari (gran siega$^{F}$) exterior

one-arm shoulder throw
projection$^{F}$ d'épaule$^{F}$ par un côté$^{M}$
einarmiger Schulterwurf$^{M}$
ippon-seoi-nage (proyección$^{F}$) por encima del hombro$^{M}$ con una mano$^{F}$

major inner reaping throw
grand fauchage$^{M}$ intérieur
Große Innensichel$^{F}$
o-uchi-gari (gran siega$^{F}$) interior

naked strangle
étranglement$^{M}$
Halsumklammerung$^{F}$
estrangulación$^{F}$

stomach throw
projection$^{F}$ en cercle$^{M}$
Kopfwurf$^{M}$
proyección$^{F}$ en círculo$^{M}$

sweeping hip throw
hanche$^{F}$ ailée
Hüftwurf$^{M}$
proyección$^{F}$ primera de cadera$^{F}$

## MAT
## TAPIS$^{M}$
## MATTE$^{F}$
## TATAMI$^{M}$

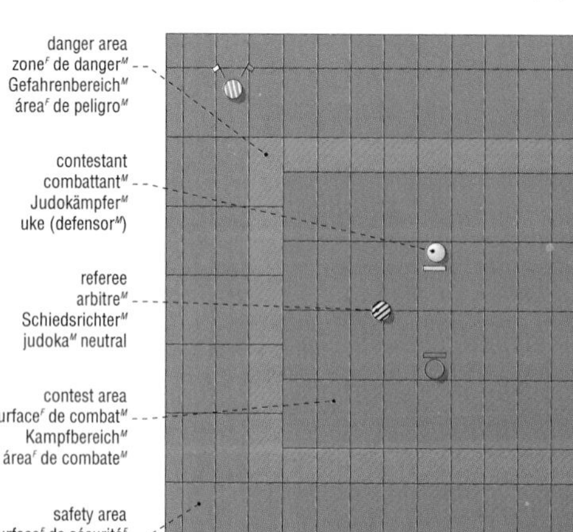

# BOXING
# BOXE$^F$
# BOXEN$^N$
# BOXEO$^M$

## RING
## RING$^M$
## RING$^M$
## RING$^M$ DE BOXEO$^M$

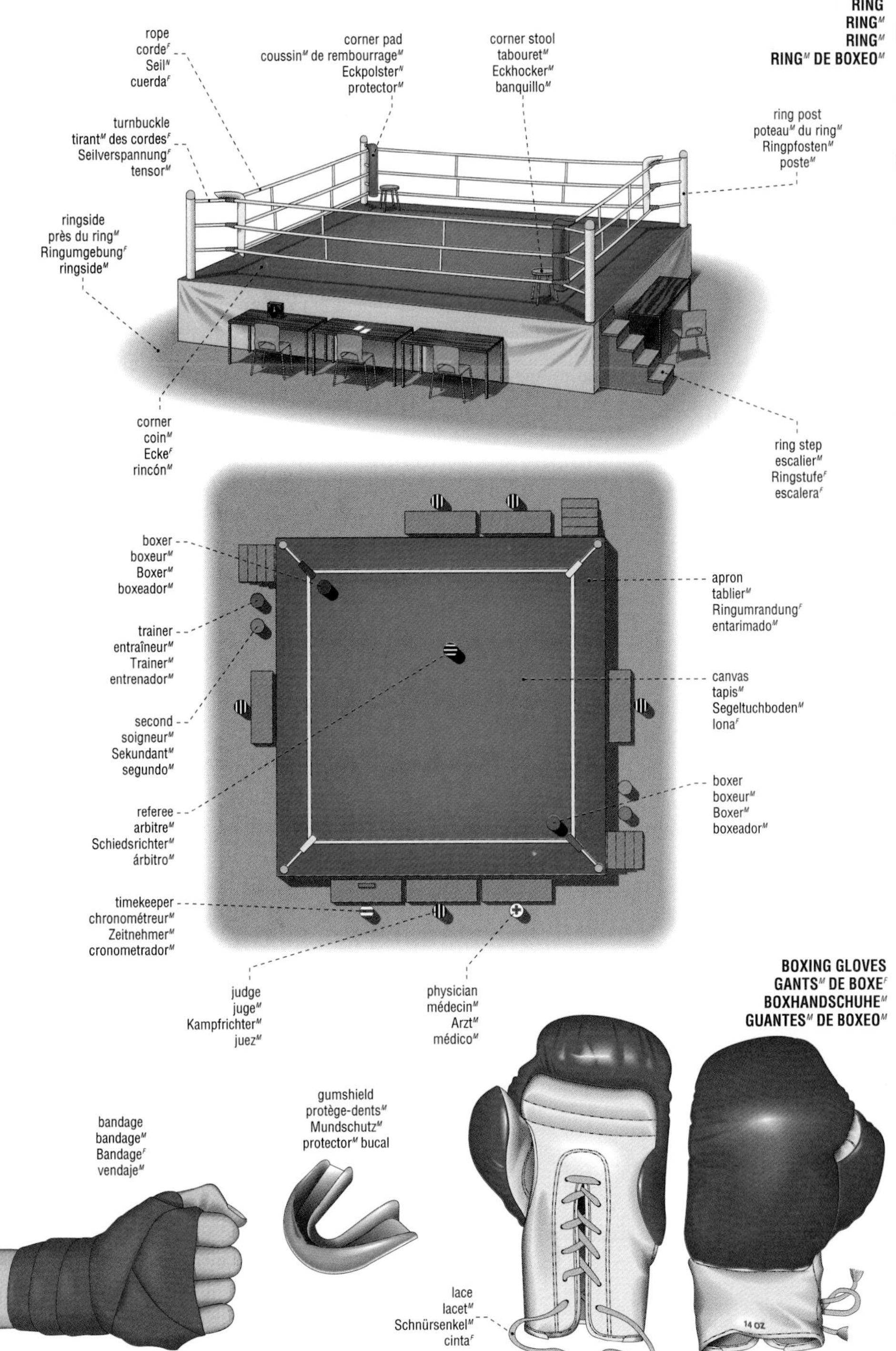

# FISHING
# PÊCHE$^{F}$
# SPORTFISCHEREI$^{F}$
# PESCA$^{F}$

## FLY ROD
## CANNE$^{F}$ À MOUCHE$^{F}$
## FLIEGENRUTE$^{F}$
## CAÑA$^{F}$ PARA MOSCA$^{F}$

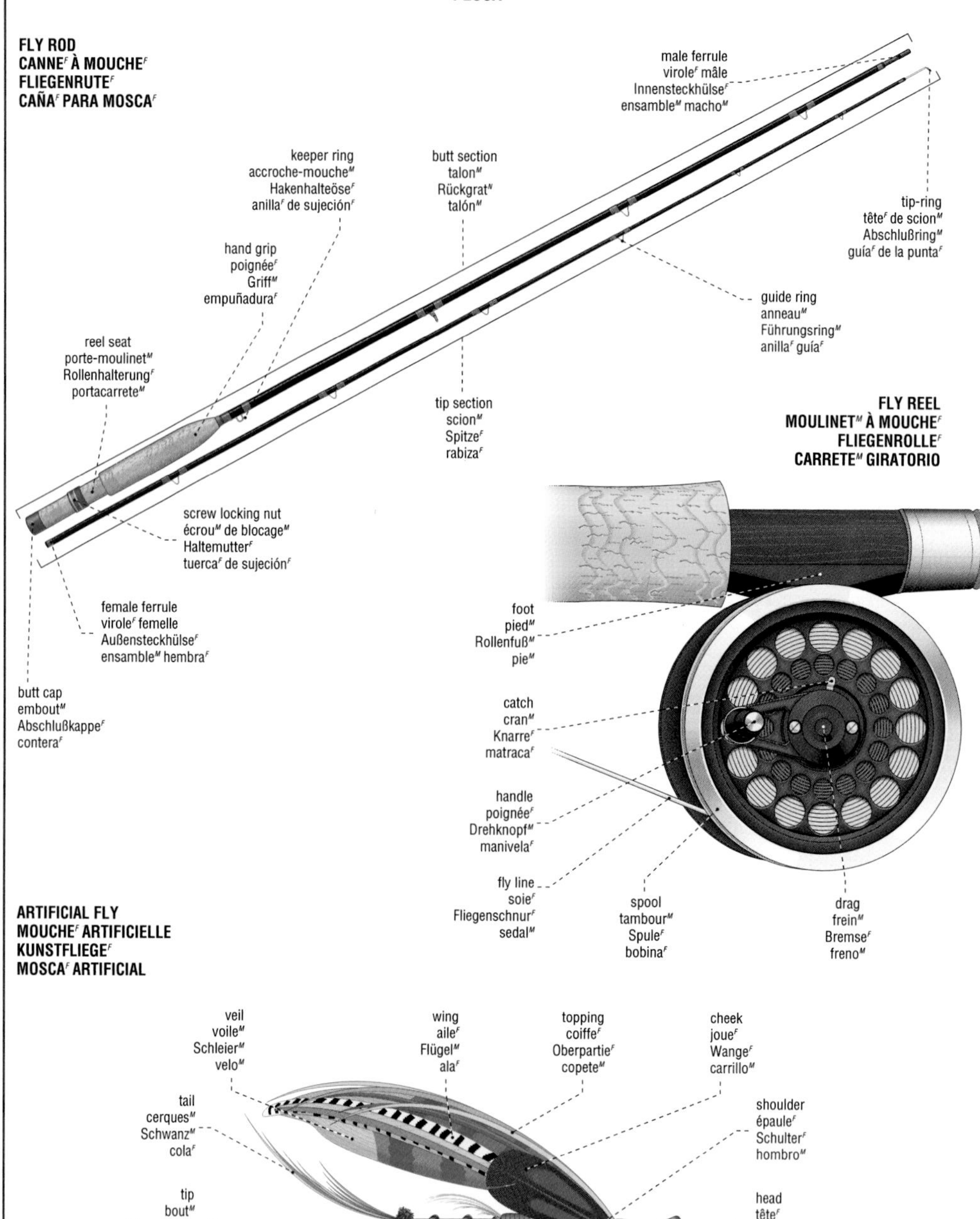


## ARTIFICIAL FLY
## MOUCHE$^{F}$ ARTIFICIELLE
## KUNSTFLIEGE$^{F}$
## MOSCA$^{F}$ ARTIFICIAL

veil
voile$^{M}$
Schleier$^{M}$
velo$^{M}$

wing
aile$^{F}$
Flügel$^{M}$
ala$^{F}$

topping
coiffe$^{F}$
Oberpartie$^{F}$
copete$^{M}$

cheek
joue$^{F}$
Wange$^{F}$
carrillo$^{M}$

tail
cerques$^{M}$
Schwanz$^{M}$
cola$^{F}$

shoulder
épaule$^{F}$
Schulter$^{F}$
hombro$^{M}$

tip
bout$^{M}$
Hinterpartie$^{F}$
cabo$^{M}$

head
tête$^{F}$
Kopf$^{M}$
cabeza$^{F}$

butt
talon$^{M}$
Stummel$^{M}$
talón$^{M}$

hackle
hackle$^{M}$
Nackenfeder$^{F}$
pelillo$^{M}$

fishhook
hameçon$^{M}$
Angelhaken$^{M}$
anzuelo$^{M}$

body
corps$^{M}$
Körper$^{M}$
cuerpo$^{M}$

ribbing
côte$^{F}$
Wicklung$^{F}$
costilla$^{F}$

joint
articulation$^{F}$
Spiralbindung$^{F}$
articulación$^{F}$

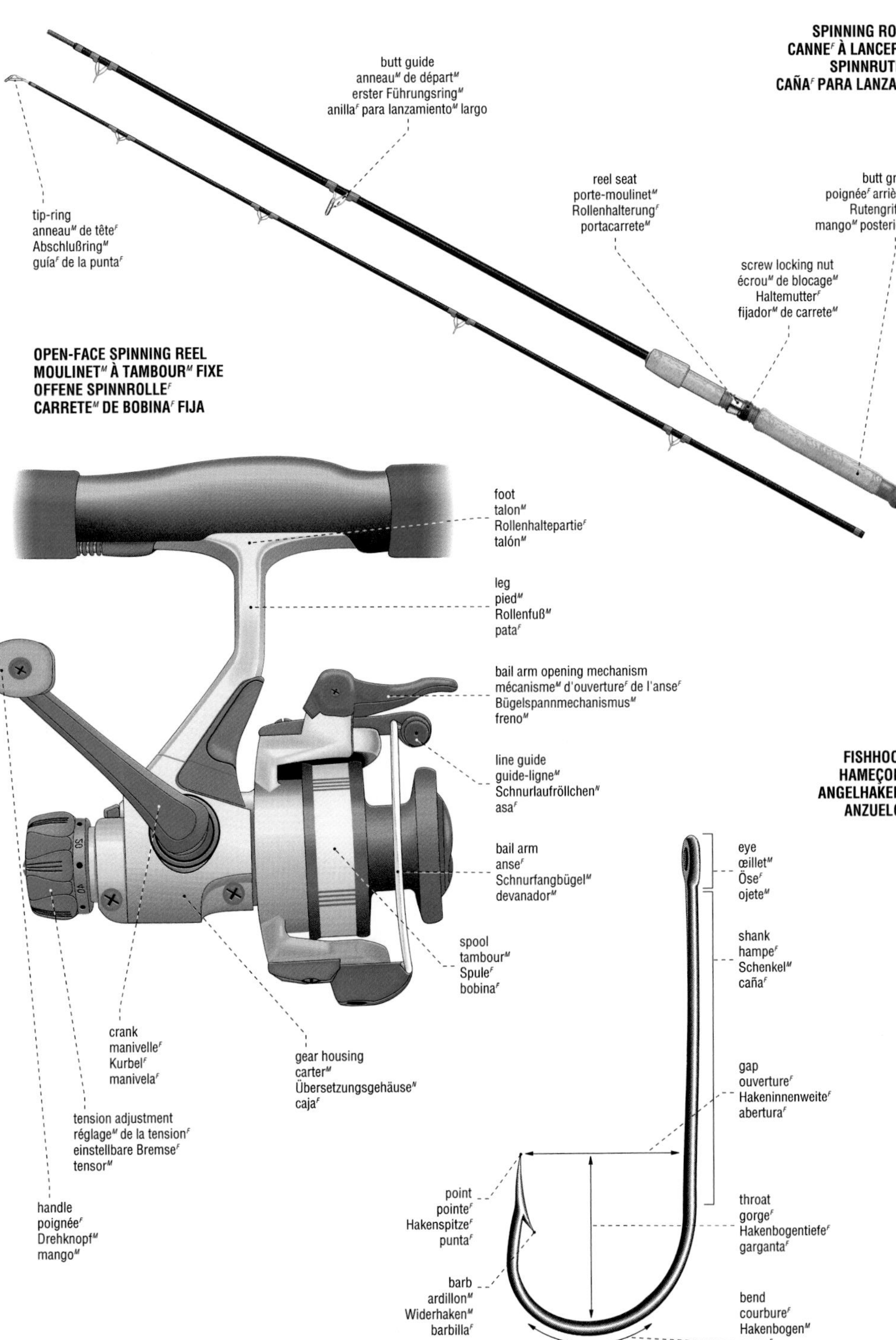
SPINNING ROD
CANNE[F] À LANCER[M]
SPINNRUTE[F]
CAÑA[F] PARA LANZAR
butt guide
anneau[M] de départ[M]
erster Führungsring[M]
anilla[F] para lanzamiento[M] largo
tip-ring
anneau[M] de tête[F]
Abschlußring[M]
guía[F] de la punta[F]
reel seat
porte-moulinet[M]
Rollenhalterung[F]
portacarrete[M]
butt grip
poignée[F] arrière
Rutengriff[M]
mango[M] posterior
screw locking nut
écrou[M] de blocage[M]
Haltemutter[F]
fijador[M] de carrete[M]
OPEN-FACE SPINNING REEL
MOULINET[M] À TAMBOUR[M] FIXE
OFFENE SPINNROLLE[F]
CARRETE[M] DE BOBINA[F] FIJA
foot
talon[M]
Rollenhaltepartie[F]
talón[M]
leg
pied[M]
Rollenfuß[M]
pata[F]
bail arm opening mechanism
mécanisme[M] d'ouverture[F] de l'anse[F]
Bügelspannmechanismus[M]
freno[M]
line guide
guide-ligne[M]
Schnurlaufröllchen[N]
asa[F]
bail arm
anse[F]
Schnurfangbügel[M]
devanador[M]
spool
tambour[M]
Spule[F]
bobina[F]
crank
manivelle[F]
Kurbel[F]
manivela[F]
gear housing
carter[M]
Übersetzungsgehäuse[N]
caja[F]
tension adjustment
réglage[M] de la tension[F]
einstellbare Bremse[F]
tensor[M]
handle
poignée[F]
Drehknopf[M]
mango[M]
FISHHOOK
HAMEÇON[M]
ANGELHAKEN[M]
ANZUELO[M]
eye
œillet[M]
Öse[F]
ojete[M]
shank
hampe[F]
Schenkel[M]
caña[F]
gap
ouverture[F]
Hakeninnenweite[F]
abertura[F]
point
pointe[F]
Hakenspitze[F]
punta[F]
throat
gorge[F]
Hakenbogentiefe[F]
garganta[F]
barb
ardillon[M]
Widerhaken[M]
barbilla[F]
bend
courbure[F]
Hakenbogen[M]
curva[F]

# FISHING
# PÊCHE[F]
# SPORTFISCHEREI[F]
# PESCA[F]

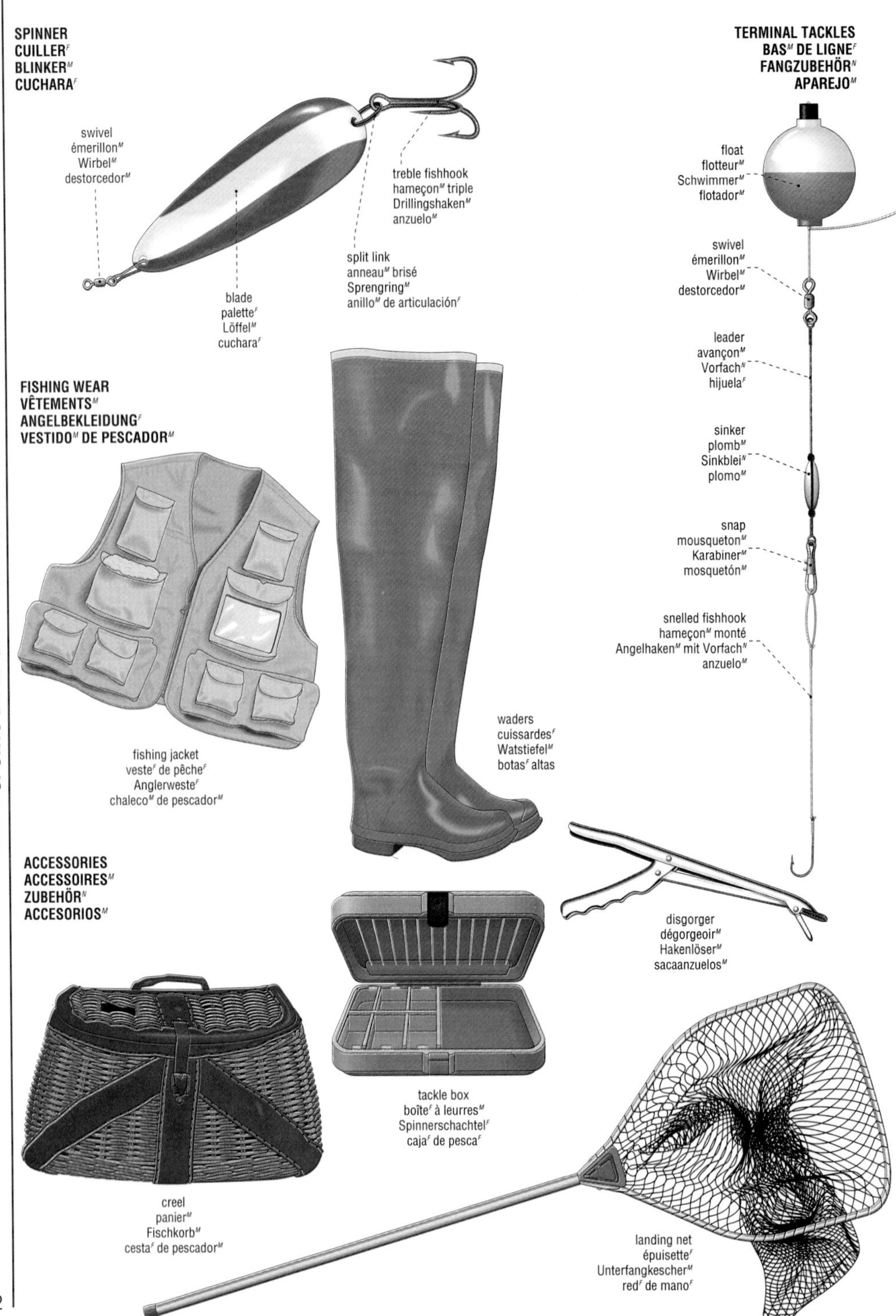

# BILLIARDS
# BILLARD$^{M}$
# BILLIARD$^{N}$
# BILLAR$^{M}$

## CAROM BILLIARDS
## BILLARD$^{M}$ FRANÇAIS
## KARAMBOLAGEBILLARD$^{N}$
## CARAMBOLA$^{F}$

cue ball
bille$^{F}$ de choc$^{M}$
Spielball$^{M}$
bola$^{F}$ blanca
red ball
bille$^{F}$ rouge
roter Stoßball$^{M}$
bola$^{F}$ roja
white spot ball
bille$^{F}$ de visée$^{F}$ blanche
weißer Punktball$^{M}$
bola$^{F}$ pinta
2,27 – 3 m
1,13 – 1,5 m

## POOL
## BILLARD$^{M}$ POOL
## POOL$^{N}$
## POOL$^{M}$

object balls
billes$^{F}$ numérotées
Zielbälle$^{M}$
bolas$^{F}$ numeradas
pocket
poche$^{F}$
Tasche$^{F}$
bolsillo$^{M}$
cue ball
bille$^{F}$ de choc$^{M}$
Spielball$^{M}$
bola$^{F}$ blanca
2,1 – 3 m
1,06 – 1,5 m

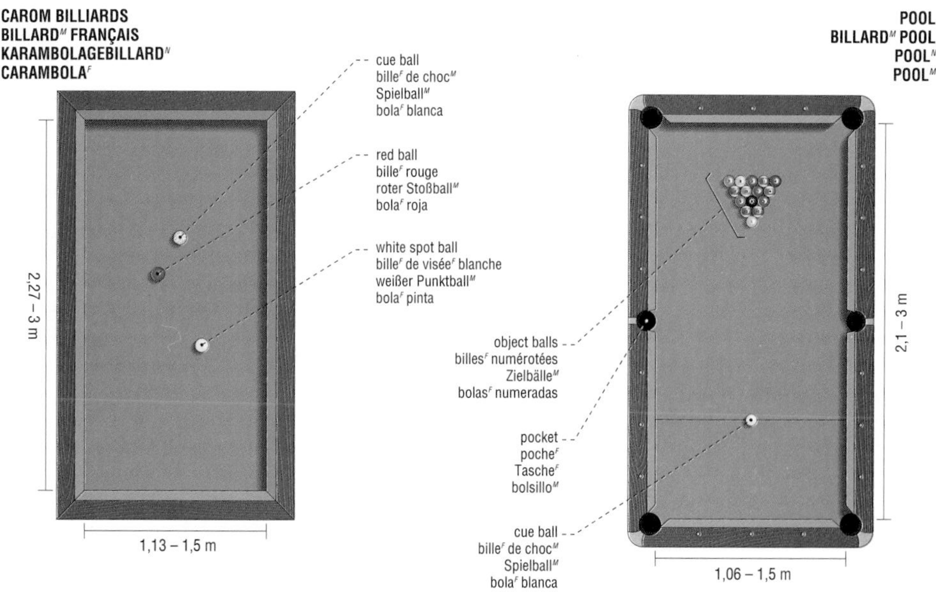

## ENGLISH BILLIARDS
## BILLARD$^{M}$ ANGLAIS
## LOCHBILLARD$^{N}$
## BILLAR$^{M}$ INGLÉS

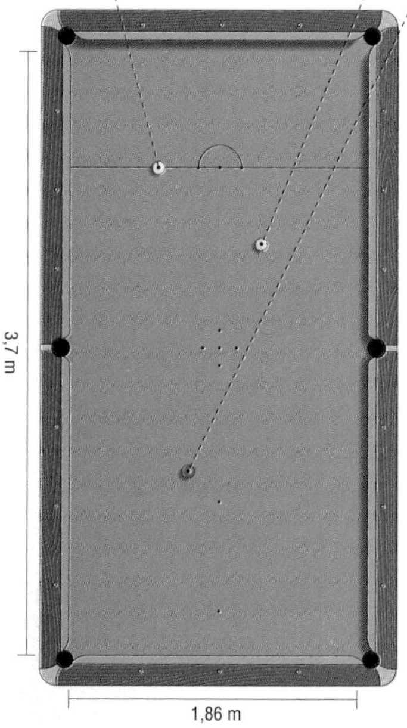

white cue ball
bille$^{F}$ blanche
weißer Spielball$^{M}$
bola$^{F}$ blanca
white spot ball
bille$^{F}$ blanche mouchetée
weißer Punktball$^{M}$
bola$^{F}$ pinta
red ball
bille$^{F}$ rouge
roter Ball$^{M}$
bola$^{F}$ roja
3,7 m
1,86 m

## SNOOKER
## SNOOKER$^{M}$
## SNOOKER$^{N}$
## SNOOKER$^{M}$

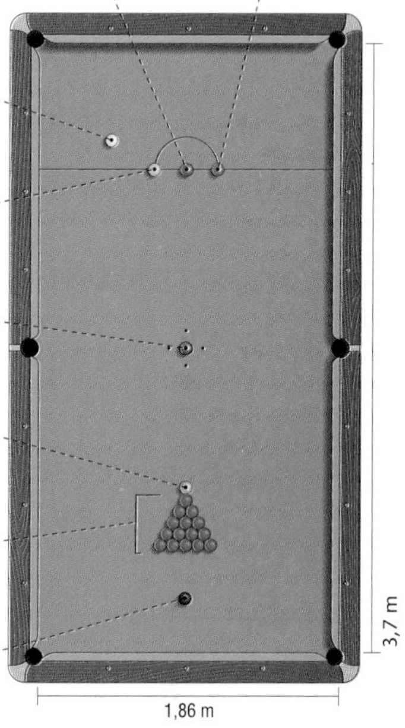

brown ball
bille$^{F}$ brune
brauner Ball$^{M}$
bola$^{F}$ café
green ball
bille$^{F}$ verte
grüner Ball$^{M}$
bola$^{F}$ verde
cue ball
bille$^{F}$ de choc$^{M}$
Spielball$^{M}$
bola$^{F}$ blanca
yellow ball
bille$^{F}$ jaune
gelber Ball$^{M}$
bola$^{F}$ amarilla
blue ball
bille$^{F}$ bleue
blauer Ball$^{M}$
bola$^{F}$ azul
pink ball
bille$^{F}$ rose
rosa Ball$^{M}$
bola$^{F}$ rosa
red balls
billes$^{F}$ rouges
rote Bälle$^{M}$
bolas$^{F}$ rojas
black ball
bille$^{F}$ noire
schwarzer Ball$^{M}$
bola$^{F}$ negra
3,7 m
1,86 m

# ENGLISH BILLIARDS AND SNOOKER
# BILLARD[M] ANGLAIS ET SNOOKER[M]
# LOCHBILLARD[N] UND SNOOKER[N]
# BILLAR[M] INGLÉS Y SNOOKER[M]

BILLIARD CUE
QUEUE[F] DE BILLARD[M]
BILLARDQUEUE[M]
TACO[M] DE BILLAR[M]
baize
tapis[M]
Bespannung[F]
tapete[M]
pyramid spot
mouche[F] supérieure
Aufstellpunkt[M]
mosca[F] superior
billiard spot
mouche[F]
Aufstellpunkt[M]
mosca[F]
top cushion
coussin[M] arrière
Stirnbande[F]
banda[F] de la cabecera[F]
top pocket
poche[F] supérieure
obere Tasche[F]
bolsillo[M]
tip
procédé[M]
Kuppe[F]
suela[F]
ferrule
virole[F]
Kuppenring[M]
casquillo[M]
shaft
flèche[F]
Schaft[M]
mango[M]
rail
bande[F]
Rahmen[M]
baranda[F]
joint
tourillon[M]
Gewinde[N]
articulación[F]
butt
talon[M]
Griffteil[N]
maza[F]
chalk
craie[F]
Kreide[F]
tiza[F]

# GOLF
# GOLF^M
# GOLFSPIEL^N
# ACCESORIOS^M DE GOLF^M

## COURSE
## PARCOURS^M
## GOLFPLATZ^M
## CAMPO^M DE GOLF^M

## CROSS SECTION OF A GOLF BALL
## COUPE$^F$ D'UNE BALLE$^F$ DE GOLF$^M$
## GOLFBALL$^M$ IM QUERSCHNITT
## CORTE$^M$ TRANSVERSAL DE UNA PELOTA$^F$ DE GOLF$^M$

## GOLF BALL
## BALLE$^F$ DE GOLF$^M$
## GOLFBALL$^M$
## PELOTA$^F$ DE GOLF$^M$

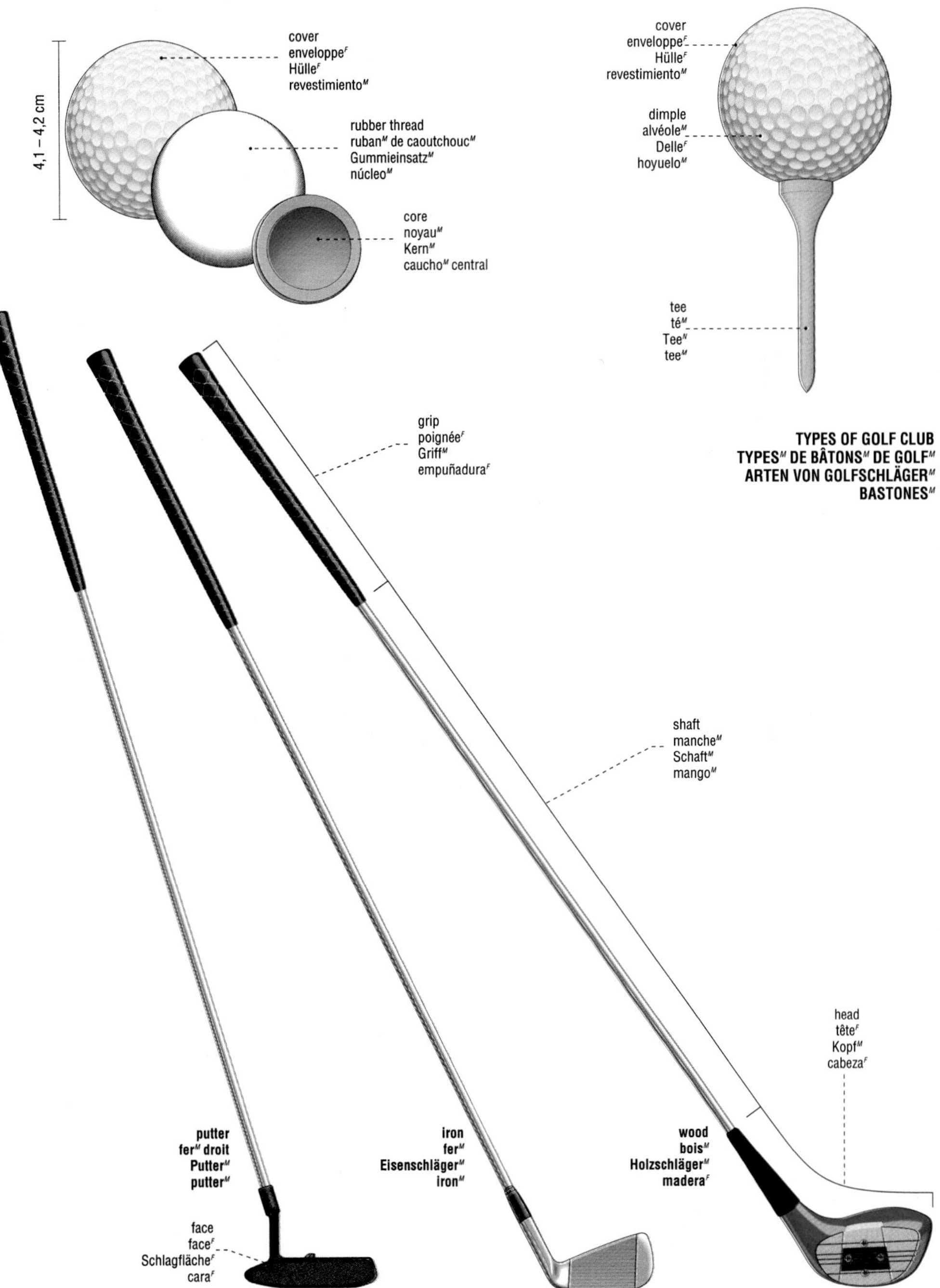

# GOLF
# GOLF^M
# GOLFSPIEL^N
# GOLF^M

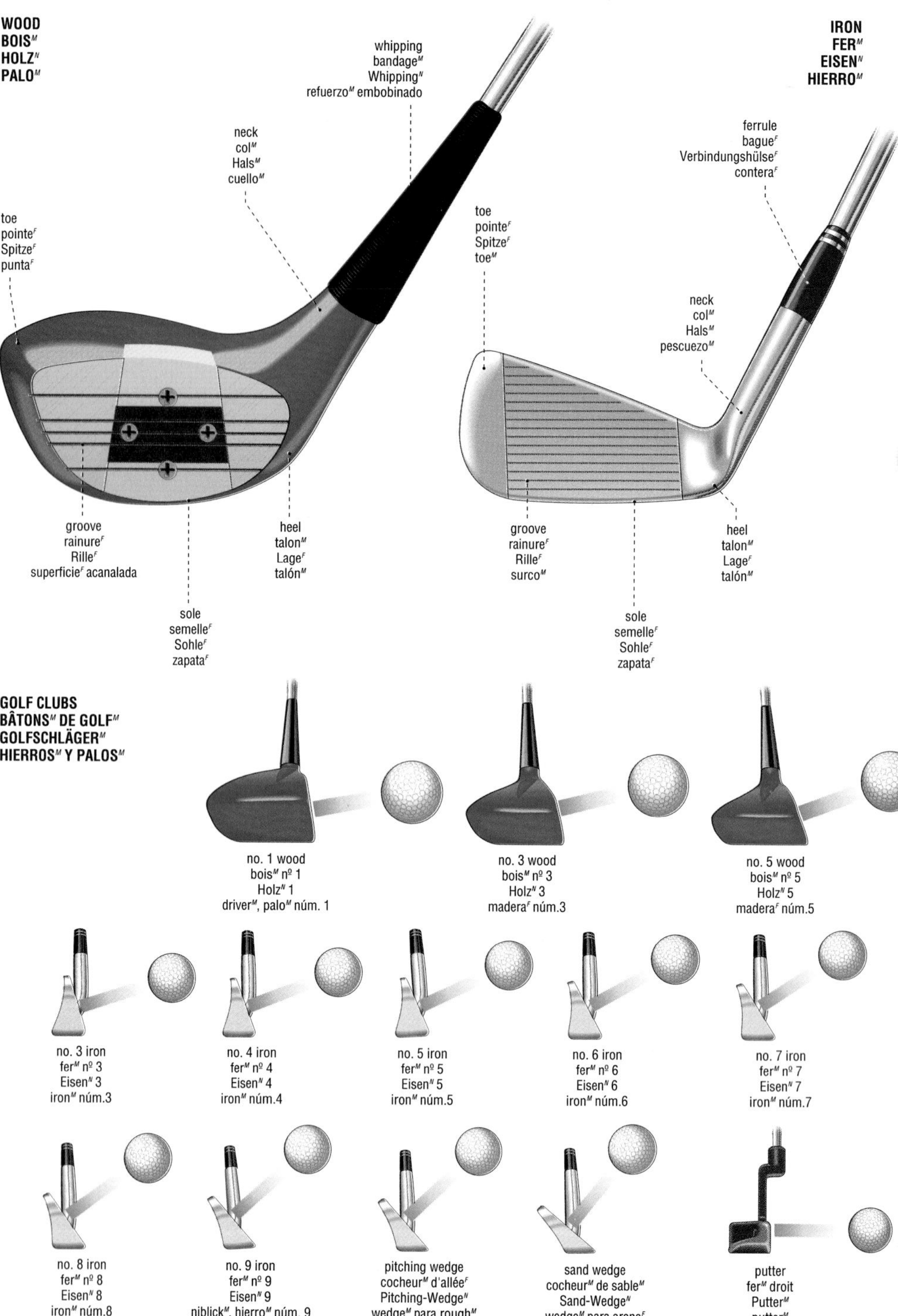

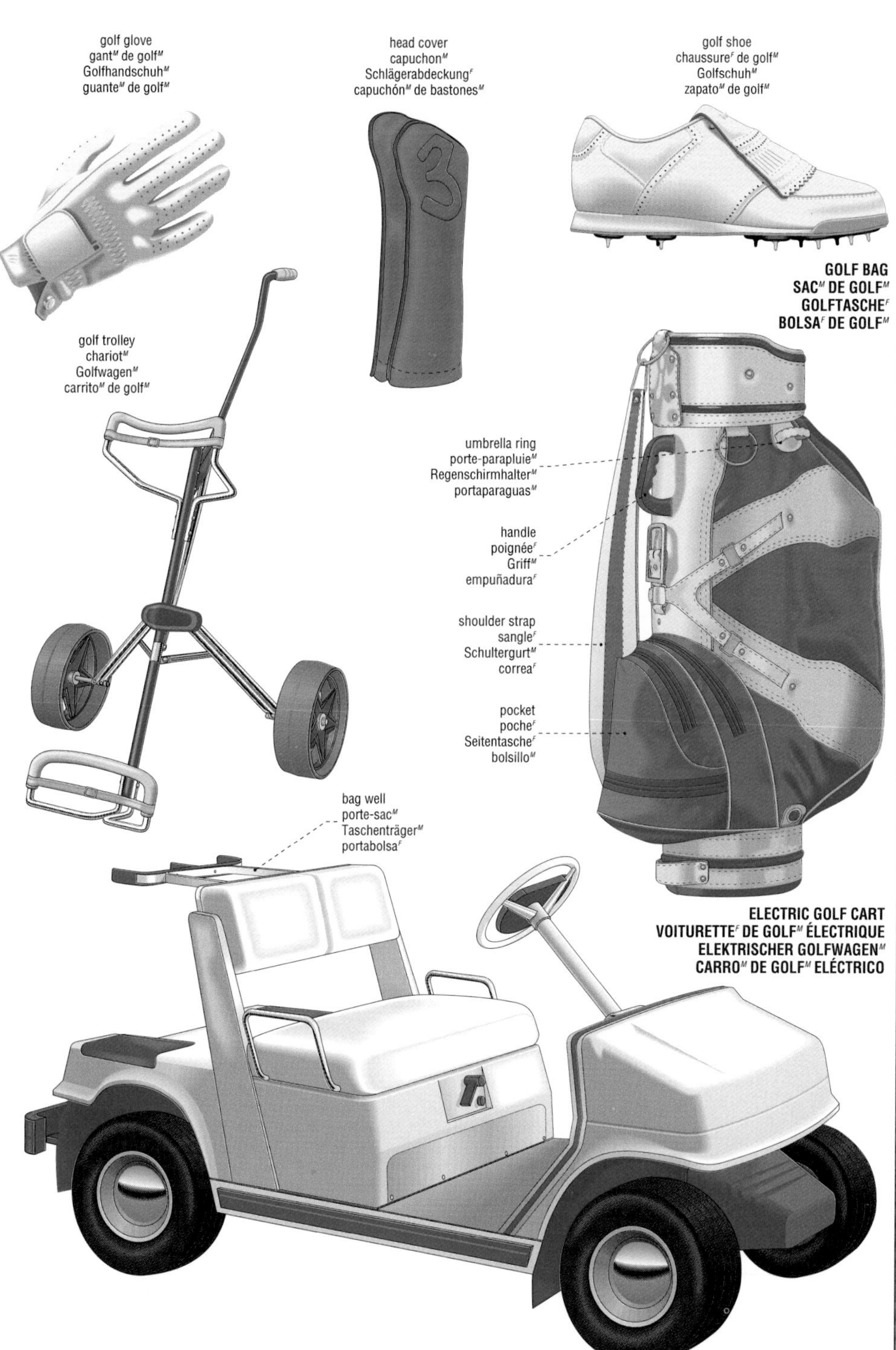
golf glove
gant^M de golf^M
Golfhandschuh^M
guante^M de golf^M
head cover
capuchon^M
Schlägerabdeckung^F
capuchón^M de bastones^M
golf shoe
chaussure^F de golf^M
Golfschuh^M
zapato^M de golf^M
GOLF BAG
SAC^M DE GOLF^M
GOLFTASCHE^F
BOLSA^F DE GOLF^M
golf trolley
chariot^M
Golfwagen^M
carrito^M de golf^M
umbrella ring
porte-parapluie^M
Regenschirmhalter^M
portaparaguas^M
handle
poignée^F
Griff^M
empuñadura^F
shoulder strap
sangle^F
Schultergurt^M
correa^F
pocket
poche^F
Seitentasche^F
bolsillo^M
bag well
porte-sac^M
Taschenträger^M
portabolsa^F
ELECTRIC GOLF CART
VOITURETTE^F DE GOLF^M ÉLECTRIQUE
ELEKTRISCHER GOLFWAGEN^M
CARRO^M DE GOLF^M ELÉCTRICO

# MOUNTAINEERING
# ALPINISME[M]
# BERGSTEIGEN[N]
# ALPINISMO[M]

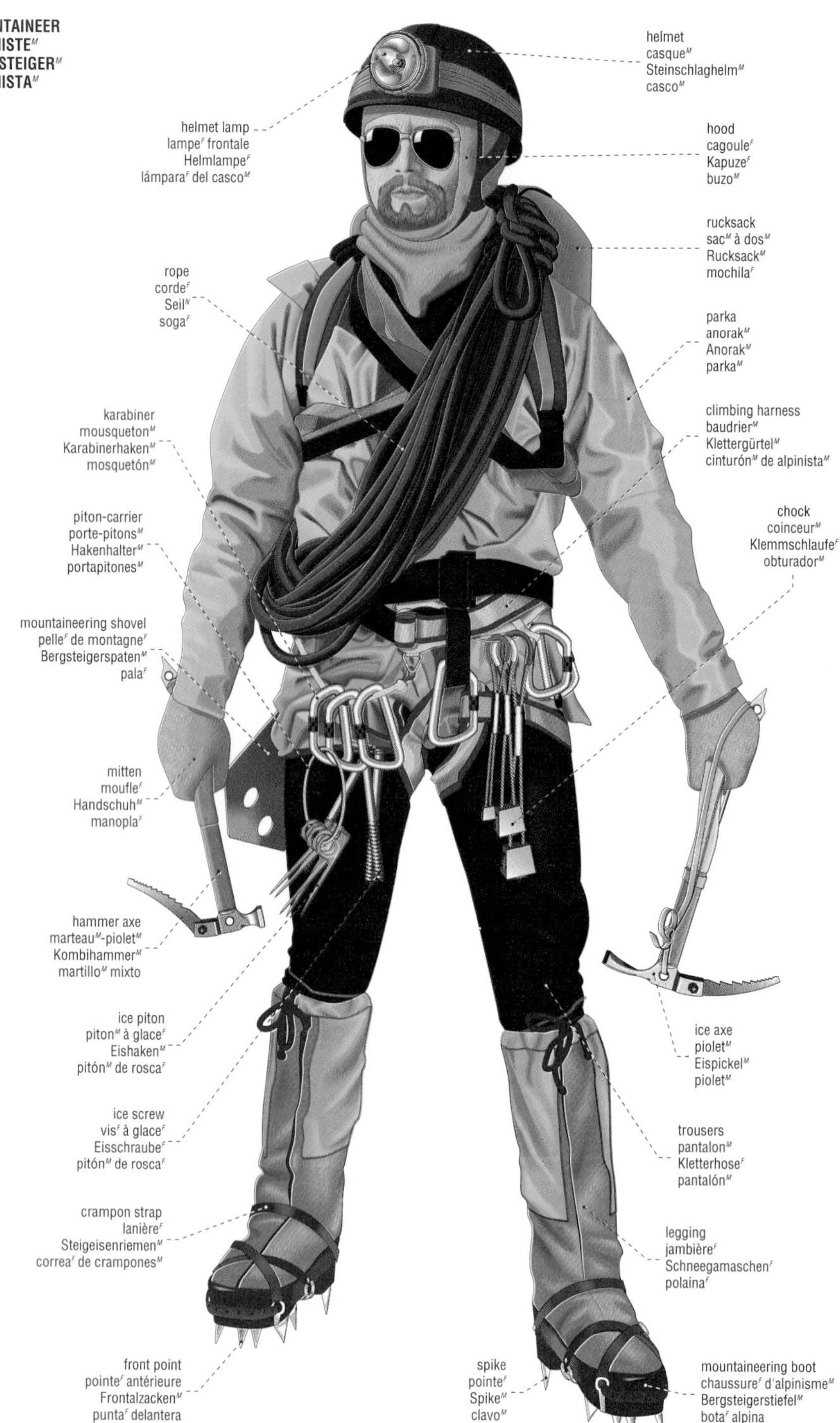

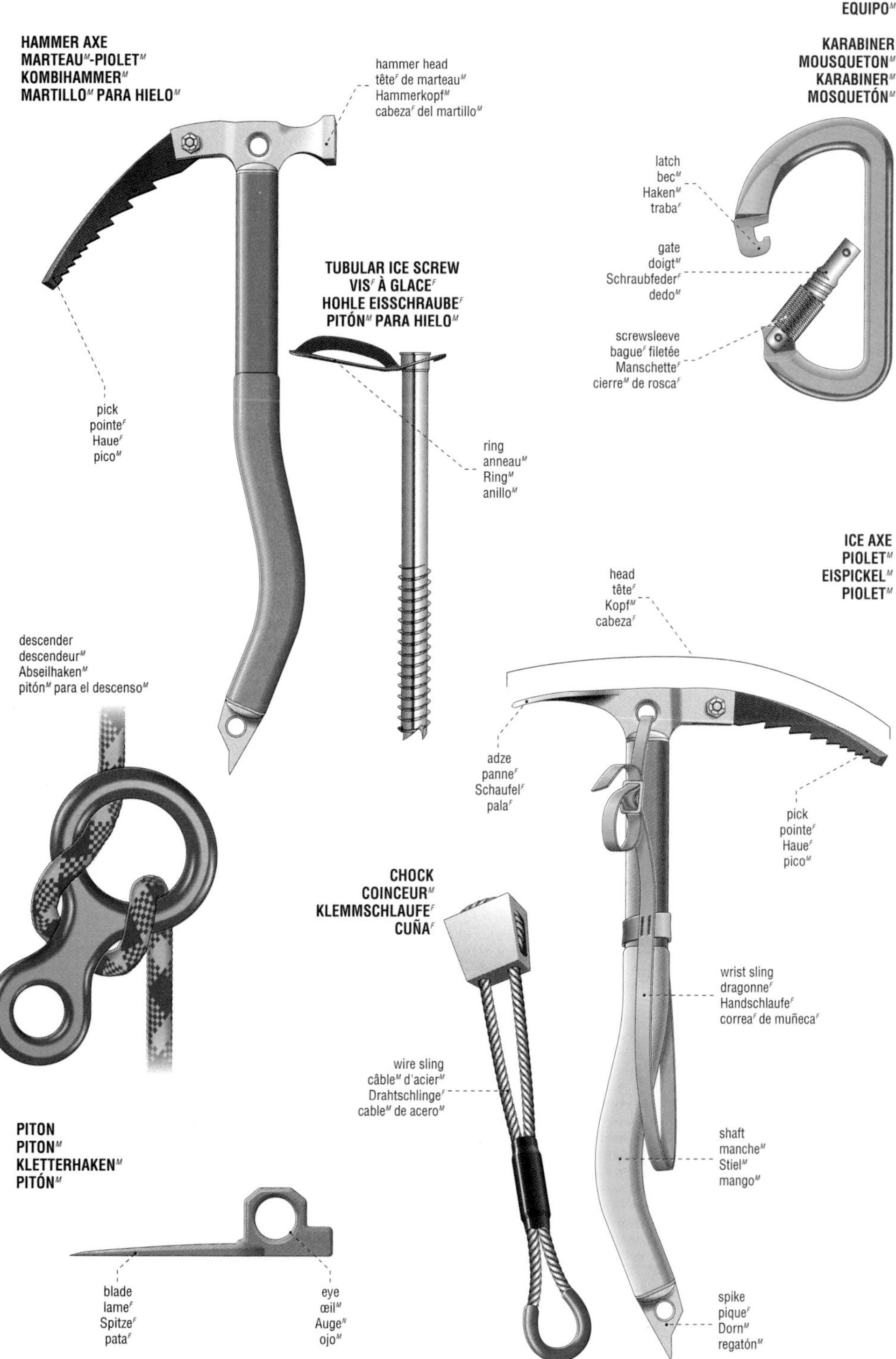
HAMMER AXE
MARTEAU[M]-PIOLET[M]
KOMBIHAMMER[M]
MARTILLO[M] PARA HIELO[M]
hammer head
tête[F] de marteau[M]
Hammerkopf[M]
cabeza[F] del martillo[M]
pick
pointe[F]
Haue[F]
pico[M]
TUBULAR ICE SCREW
VIS[F] À GLACE[F]
HOHLE EISSCHRAUBE[F]
PITÓN[M] PARA HIELO[M]
ring
anneau[M]
Ring[M]
anillo[M]
KARABINER
MOUSQUETON[M]
KARABINER[M]
MOSQUETÓN[M]
latch
bec[M]
Haken[M]
traba[F]
gate
doigt[M]
Schraubfeder[F]
dedo[M]
screwsleeve
bague[F] filetée
Manschette[F]
cierre[M] de rosca[F]
ICE AXE
PIOLET[M]
EISPICKEL[M]
PIOLET[M]
head
tête[F]
Kopf[M]
cabeza[F]
adze
panne[F]
Schaufel[F]
pala[F]
pick
pointe[F]
Haue[F]
pico[M]
wrist sling
dragonne[F]
Handschlaufe[F]
correa[F] de muñeca[F]
shaft
manche[M]
Stiel[M]
mango[M]
spike
pique[F]
Dorn[M]
regatón[M]
descender
descendeur[M]
Abseilhaken[M]
pitón[M] para el descenso[M]
CHOCK
COINCEUR[M]
KLEMMSCHLAUFE[F]
CUÑA[F]
wire sling
câble[M] d'acier[M]
Drahtschlinge[F]
cable[M] de acero[M]
PITON
PITON[M]
KLETTERHAKEN[M]
PITÓN[M]
blade
lame[F]
Spitze[F]
pata[F]
eye
œil[M]
Auge[N]
ojo[M]

# BOWLS AND PETANQUE
# BOULES ANGLAISES ET PÉTANQUE
# BOULE UND PETANQUE
# BOLOS Y PETANCA

## GREEN
## PELOUSE
## GRÜN
## BOLERA EN EL CÉSPED

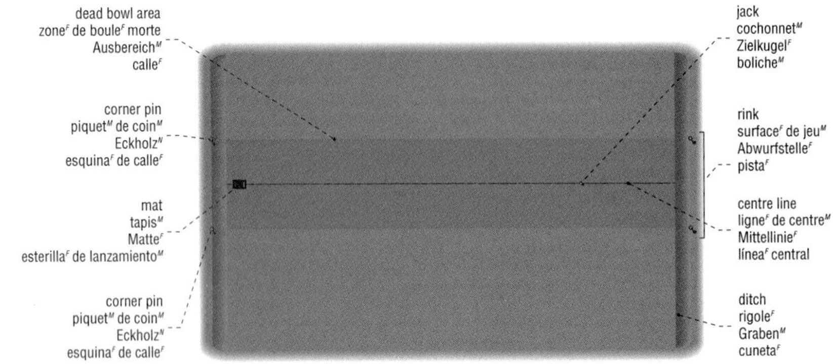


## DELIVERY
## LANCEMENT DE LA BOULE
## ABWURF
## LANZAMIENTO

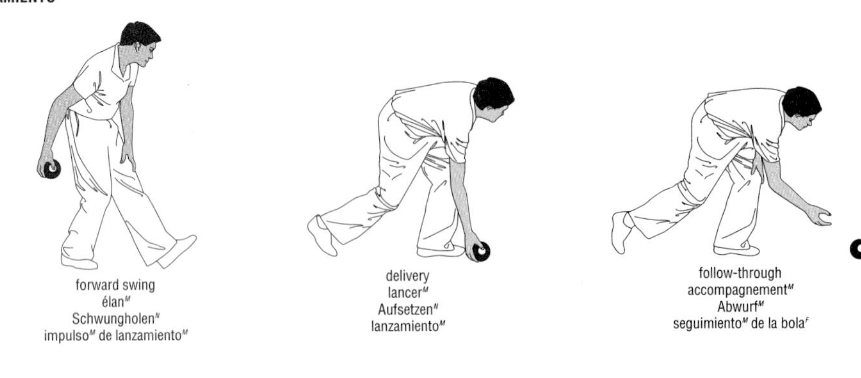

# BOWLING
# JEU$^{M}$ DE QUILLES$^{F}$
# BOWLING$^{N}$
# JUEGO$^{M}$ DE BOLOS$^{M}$

## BOWLING BALL
## BOULE$^{F}$ DE QUILLES$^{F}$
## BOWLINGKUGEL$^{F}$
## BOLA$^{F}$

tenpin
grosse quille$^{F}$
Zehnerpin$^{M}$
bolo$^{M}$

duckpin
Dauphine$^{F}$ américaine
Duckpin$^{M}$
bolo$^{M}$ chico

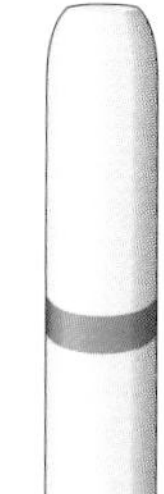

candlepin
quille$^{F}$ chandelle$^{F}$
Candlepin$^{M}$
bolo$^{M}$ cilíndrico

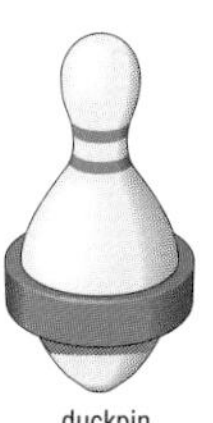

duckpin
Dauphine$^{F}$ canadienne
Duckpin$^{M}$
bolo$^{M}$ chico

## TYPES OF PINS
## TYPES$^{M}$ DE QUILLES$^{F}$
## VERSCHIEDENE PINS$^{M}$
## TIPOS$^{M}$ DE BOLOS$^{M}$

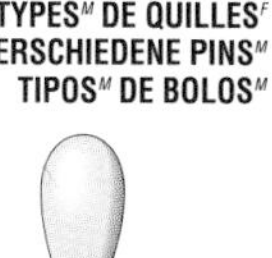

fivepin
petite quille$^{F}$
Fünferpin$^{M}$
bolo$^{M}$ pequeño

## SET-UP
## QUILLIER$^{M}$
## AUFSTELLUNG$^{F}$
## DISPOSICIÓN$^{F}$ DE LOS BOLOS$^{M}$

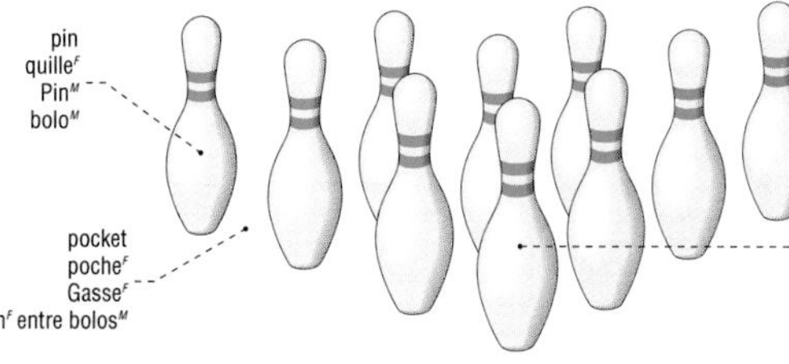

pin
quille$^{F}$
Pin$^{M}$
bolo$^{M}$

pocket
poche$^{F}$
Gasse$^{F}$
separación$^{F}$ entre bolos$^{M}$

headpin
quille$^{F}$-reine$^{F}$
Vordereckpin$^{M}$
bolo$^{M}$ delantero

## LANE
## PISTE$^{F}$
## BAHN$^{F}$
## PISTA$^{F}$

score-console
tableau$^{M}$ marqueur$^{M}$
Punktekonsole$^{F}$
marcador$^{M}$

ball return
monte-boules$^{M}$
Kugelrücklaufkasten$^{M}$
devolvedor$^{M}$

keyboard
clavier$^{M}$
Kontrollkonsole$^{F}$
teclado$^{M}$

ball stand
boulier$^{M}$
Kugelträger$^{M}$
stand$^{M}$ de bolos$^{M}$

set-up
quillier$^{M}$
Aufstellmaschine$^{F}$
disposición$^{F}$ de los bolos$^{M}$

pit
fosse$^{F}$ de réception$^{F}$
Grube$^{F}$
foso$^{M}$ de recepción$^{F}$

marker
point$^{M}$ de repère$^{M}$
Ziellinie$^{F}$
línea$^{F}$ de tiro$^{M}$

gutter
dalot$^{M}$
Rinne$^{F}$
canal$^{M}$

foul line
ligne$^{F}$ de jeu$^{M}$
Foullinie$^{F}$
línea$^{F}$ de lanzamiento$^{M}$

approach
piste$^{F}$ d'élan$^{M}$
Anlaufstrecke$^{F}$
antepista$^{F}$

ball
boule$^{F}$
Kugel$^{F}$
bola$^{F}$

# ARCHERY
# TIR[M] À L'ARC[M]
# BOGENSCHIESSEN[N]
# TIRO[M] AL ARCO[M]

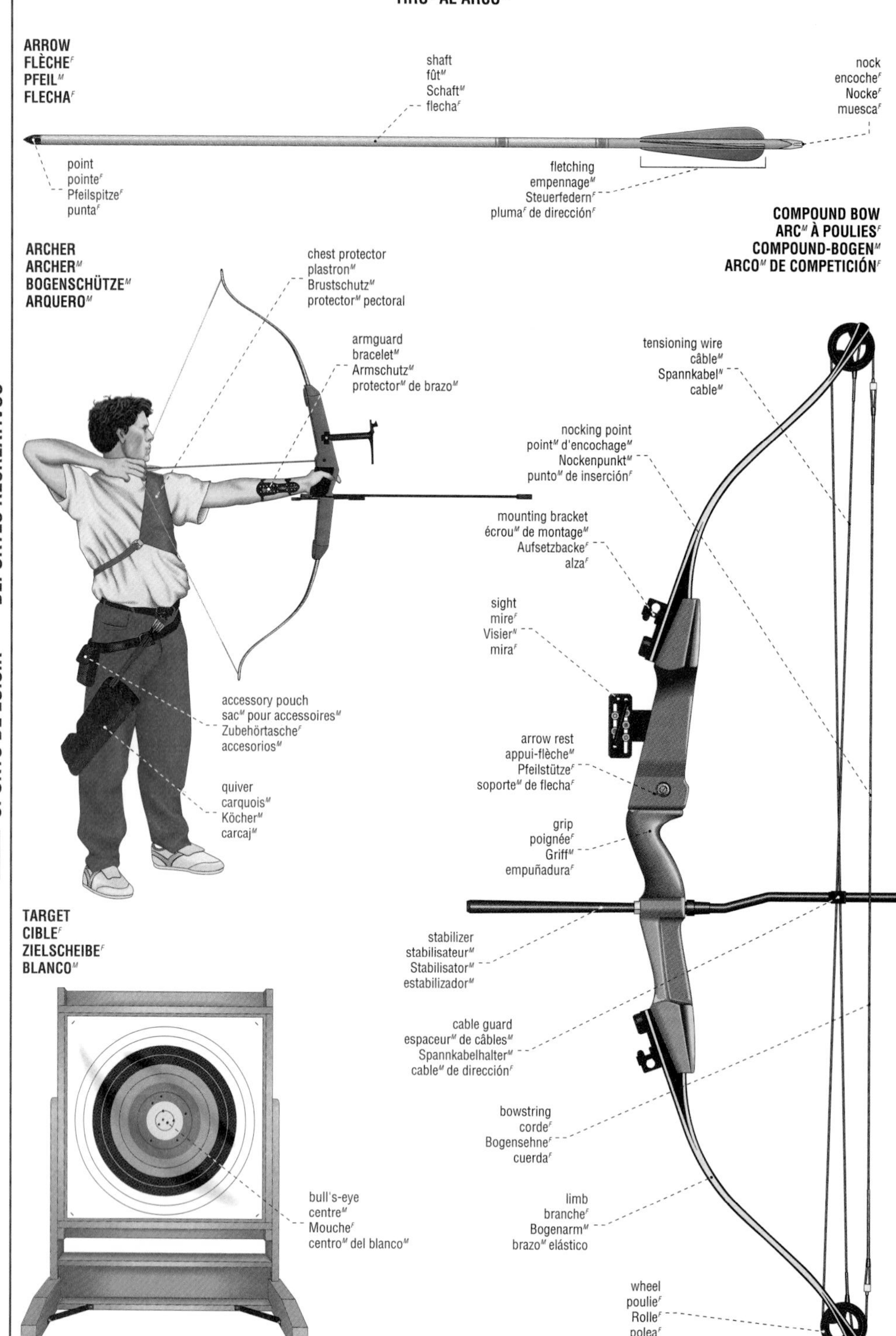

## TWO-PERSON TENT
## TENTE[F] DEUX PLACES[F]
## ZWEIPERSONENZELT[N]
## TIENDA[F] PARA DOS

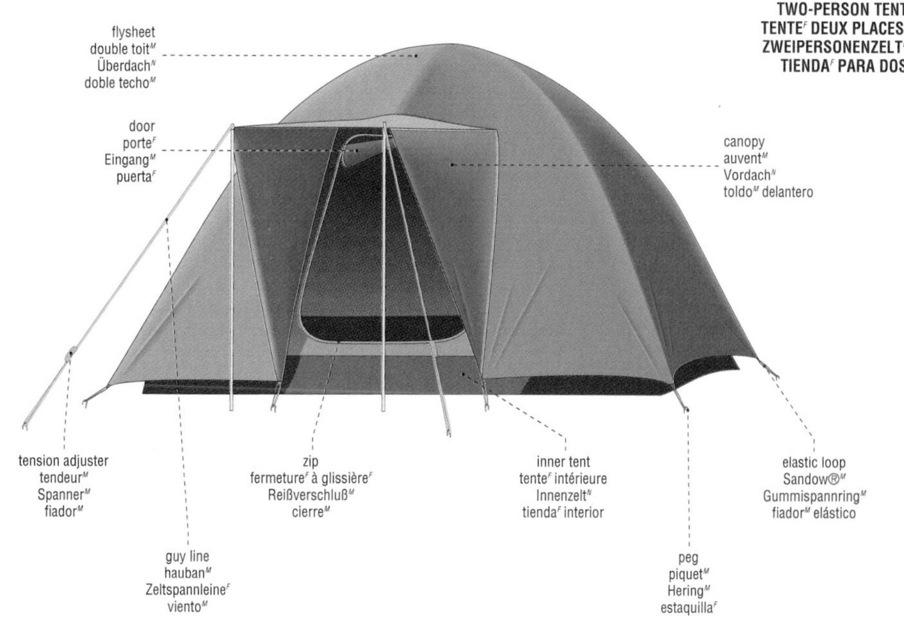


## FAMILY TENT
## TENTE[F] FAMILIALE
## FAMILIENZELT[N]
## TIENDA[F] DE CAMPAÑA[F] TAMAÑO[M] FAMILIAR

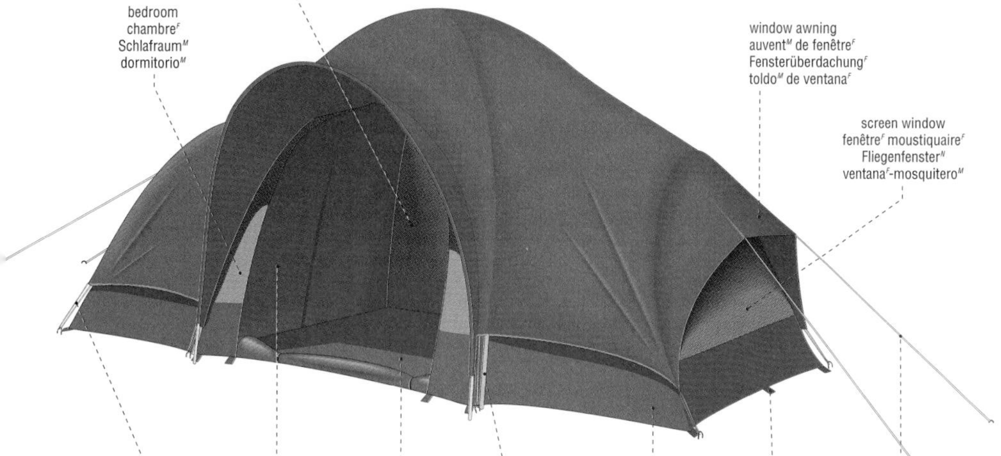

living room
séjour[M]
Wohnraum[M]
cuarto[M] de estar

bedroom
chambre[F]
Schlafraum[M]
dormitorio[M]

window awning
auvent[M] de fenêtre[F]
Fensterüberdachung[F]
toldo[M] de ventana[F]

screen window
fenêtre[F] moustiquaire[F]
Fliegenfenster[N]
ventana[F]-mosquitero[M]

elastic loop
Sandow®[M]
Gummispannring[M]
fiador[M] elástico

sewn-in groundsheet
tapis[M] de sol[M] cousu
eingenähter Boden[M]
piso[M] cosido

wall
mur[M]
Zeltwand[F]
muro[M]

guy line
hauban[M]
Zeltspannleine[F]
viento[M]

canvas divider
cloison[F]
Raumteiler[M]
lona[F] de separación[F]

frame
armature[F]
Gestänge[N]
armadura[F]

peg loop
boucle[F] de piquet[M]
Heringsschlaufe[F]
presilla[F] de estaquilla[F]

# CAMPING
# CAMPING[M]
# CAMPING[N]
# CAMPING[M]

## RIDGE TENT
## TENTE[F] CANADIENNE
## HAUSZELT[N]
## TIENDA[F] DE CAMPAÑA[F] CLÁSICA

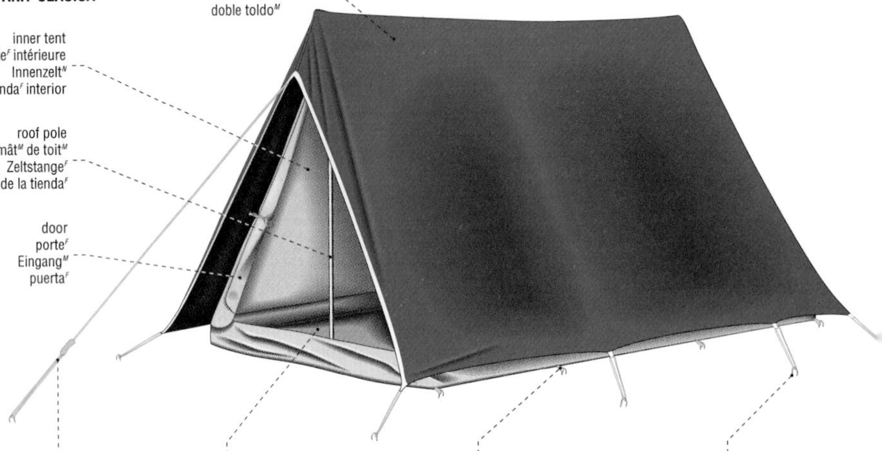

flysheet
double toit[M]
Überdach[N]
doble toldo[M]

inner tent
tente[F] intérieure
Innenzelt[N]
tienda[F] interior

roof pole
mât[M] de toit[M]
Zeltstange[F]
palo[M] de la tienda[F]

door
porte[F]
Eingang[M]
puerta[F]

elastic strainer
Sandow®[M]
Gummispannring[M]
fiador[M] elástico

sewn-in groundsheet
tapis[M] de sol[M] cousu
eingenähter Boden[M]
piso[M] cosido

peg loop
boucle[F] de piquet[M]
Heringsschlaufe[F]
presilla[F] de estaquilla[F]

peg
piquet[M]
Hering[M]
estaquilla[F]

## PRINCIPAL TYPES OF TENT
## PRINCIPAUX TYPES[M] DE TENTES[F]
## DIE WICHTIGSTEN ZELTARTEN[F]
## TIPOS[M] DE TIENDAS[F]

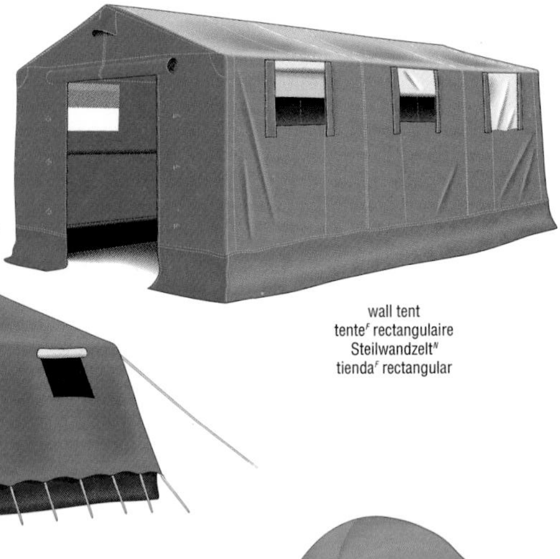

wagon tent
tente[F] grange[F]
Mannschaftszelt[N]
tienda[F] tipo[M] vagón[M]

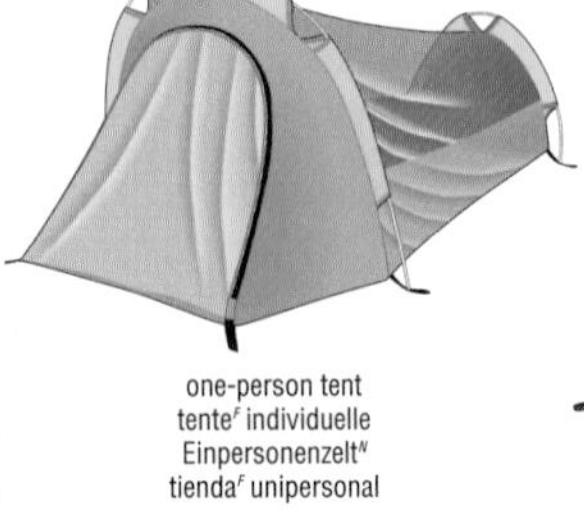

wall tent
tente[F] rectangulaire
Steilwandzelt[N]
tienda[F] rectangular

dome tent
tente[F] dôme[M]
Kuppelzelt[N]
tienda[F] tipo[M] domo[M]

one-person tent
tente[F] individuelle
Einpersonenzelt[N]
tienda[F] unipersonal

igloo tent
tente[F] igloo[M]
aufklappbares Igluzelt[N]
tienda[F] tipo[M] iglú[M]

**BED AND MATTRESS**
**LIT[M] ET MATELAS[M]**
**BETT[N] MIT MATRATZE[F]**
**CAMAS[F] Y COLCHONETAS[F]**

foam pad
matelas[M] mousse[F]
Schaumgummimatratze[F]
colchón[M] de espuma[F]

self-inflating mattress
matelas[M] autogonflant
Luftmatratze[F]
colchón[M] aislante

air mattress
matelas[M] pneumatique
Luftmatratze[F]
colchón[M] de aire[M]

inflator
gonfleur[M]
Blasebalg[M]
inflador[M]

inflator-deflator
gonfleur[M]-dégonfleur[M]
Kombipumpe[F]
muelle[M] para inflar y desinflar

camp bed
lit[M] de camp[M] pliant
Faltfeldbett[N]
catre[M] desmontable

**SLEEPING BAGS**
**SACS[M] DE COUCHAGE[M]**
**SCHLAFSÄCKE[M]**
**SACOS[M] DE DORMIR**

mummy
à cagoule[F]
Mumienschlafsack[M]
de momia[F]

semi-mummy
semi-rectangulaire
Halbmumienschlafsack[M]
saco[M] semirrectangular

rectangular
rectangulaire
Rechteckschlafsack[M]
saco[M] rectangular

# CAMPING EQUIPMENT
# MATÉRIEL[M] DE CAMPING[M]
# CAMPINGAUSRÜSTUNG[F]
# EQUIPO[M] PARA ACAMPAR

## PROPANE OR BUTANE APPLIANCES
## ACCESSOIRES[M] AU PROPANE[M] OU AU BUTANE[M]
## PROPAN-/BUTANGASBETRIEBENE GERÄTE[N]
## EQUIPO[M] DE GAS[M]

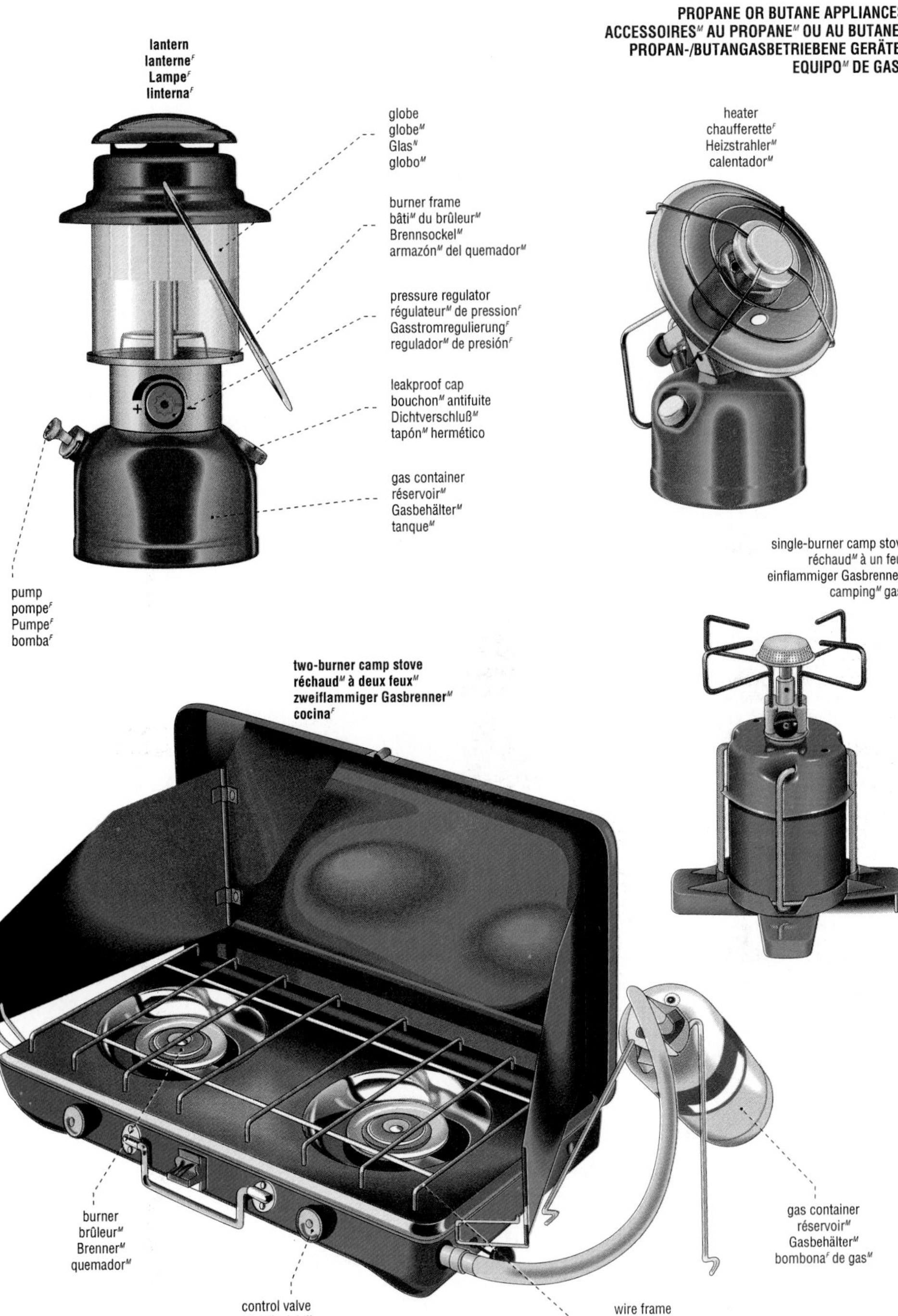

# CAMPING
# CAMPING[M]
# CAMPING[N]
# CAMPING[M]

## CAMPING EQUIPMENT
## MATÉRIEL[M] DE CAMPING[M]
## CAMPINGAUSRÜSTUNG[F]
## EQUIPO[M] PARA ACAMPAR

# KNOTS
# NŒUDS[M]
# KNOTEN[M]
# NUDOS[M]

reef knot
nœud[M] plat
Kreuzknoten[M]
nudo[M] de rizo[M]

overhand knot
nœud[M] simple
Hausfrauenknoten[M]
nudo[M] llano

granny knot
nœud[M] de vache[F]
Altweiberknoten[M]
nudo[M] de tejedor[M]

running bowline
nœud[M] coulant
laufender Pahlstek[M]
balso[M]

sheet bend
noeud[M] d'écoute[F] simple
einfacher Schotstek[M]
vuelta[F] de escota[F]

double sheet bend
noeud[M] d'écoute[F] double
doppelter Schotstek[M]
vuelta[F] de escota[F] doble

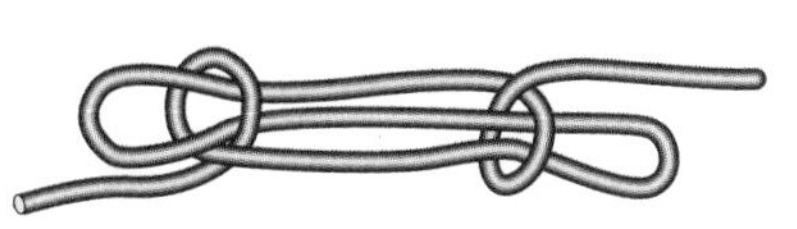

sheepshank
nœud[M] de jambe[F] de chien[M]
Verkürzungsstek[M]
margarita[F]

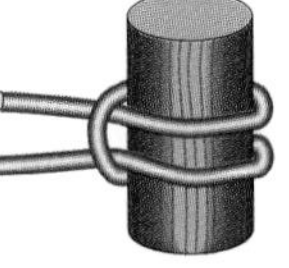

cow hitch
demi-clé[F] renversée
Kuhstek[M]
vuelta[F] de cabo[M]

heaving line knot
noeud[M] de Franciscain[M]
Wurflinienknoten[M]
nudo[M] de guía[M]

fisherman's knot
nœud[M] de pêcheur[M]
Fischerknoten[M]
nudo[M] de pescador[M]

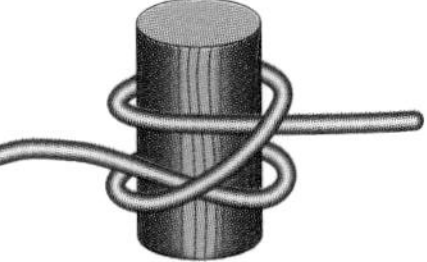

clove hitch
nœud[M] de cabestan[M]
Slipstek[M]
nudo[M] de dos cotes[M]

figure-eight knot
nœud[M] d'arrêt[M]
Achtknoten[M]
lasca[F] doble

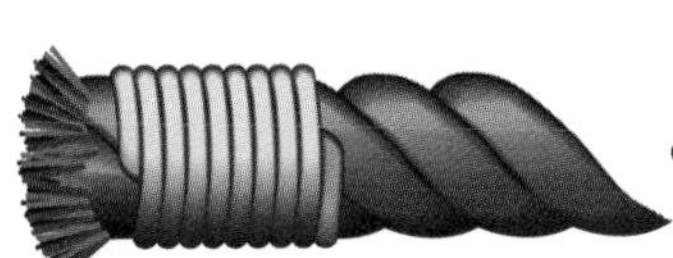

common whipping
surliure[F]
einfacher Takling[M]
sobrenudo[M]

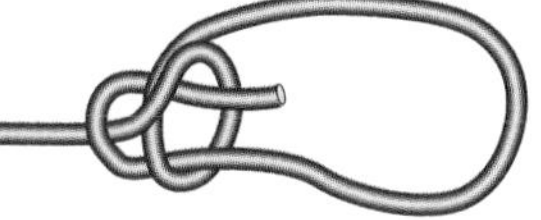

bowline
nœud[M] de chaise[F] simple
Pahlstek[M]
as[M] de guía[F]

bowline on a bight
nœud[M] de chaise[F] double
doppelter Pahlstek[M]
as[M] de guía[F] de eslinga[F] doble

# KNOTS
# NŒUDS[M]
# KNOTEN[M]
# NUDOS[M] NÁUTICOS

**SHORT SPLICE**
**ÉPISSURE[F] COURTE**
**SPLEISS[M]**
**EMPALMADURA[F]**

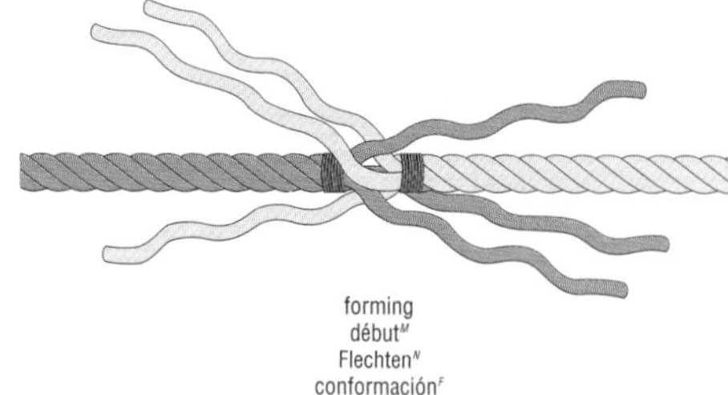


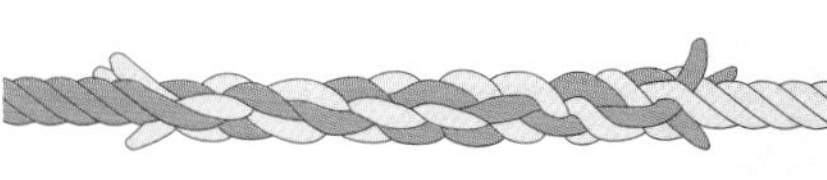


# CABLE
# CÂBLE[M]
# TAUWERK[N]
# CABLE[M]

**TWISTED ROPE**
**CORDAGE[M] COMMIS**
**GEDREHTES SEIL[N]**
**CABLE[M] TORCIDO**

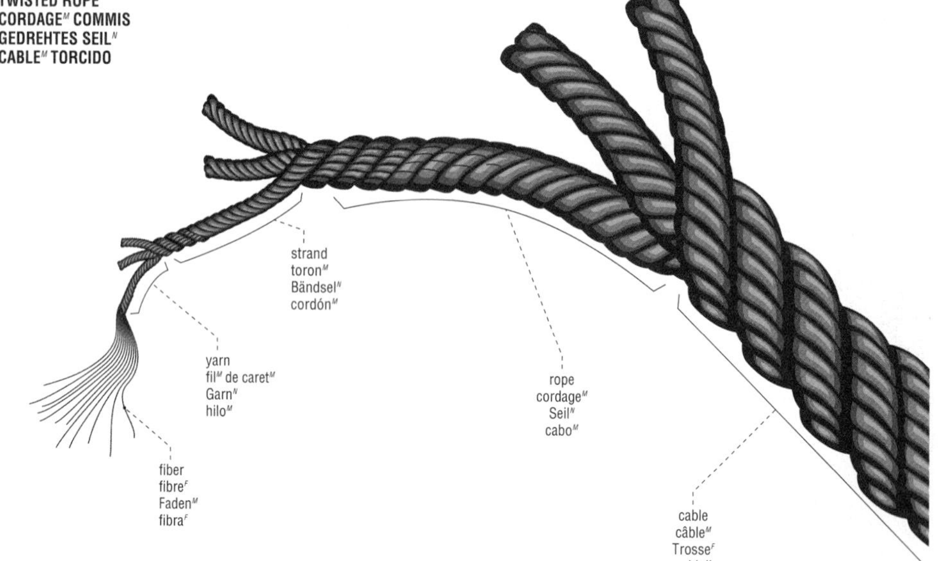


**BRAIDED ROPE**
**CORDAGE[M] TRESSÉ**
**GEFLOCHTENES SEIL[N]**
**CABLE[M] TRENZADO**

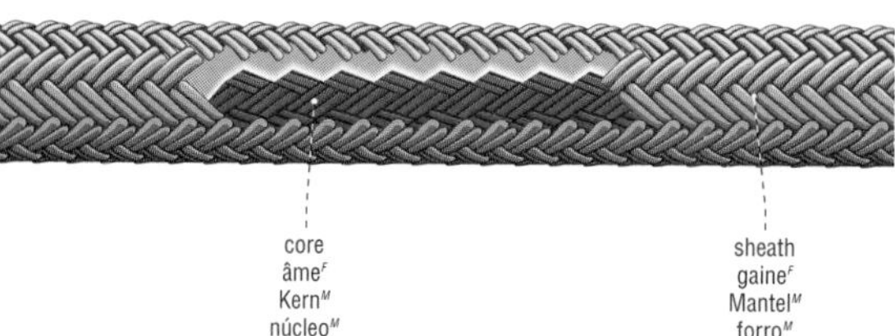

# INDOOR GAMES
# JEUX DE SOCIÉTÉ
# SPIELE
# JUEGOS DE INTERIOR

## SUMMARY

# CARD GAMES
# CARTES[F]
# KARTENSPIELE[N]
# BARAJA[F]

## SYMBOLS
## SYMBOLES[M]
## FARBEN[F]
## SÍMBOLOS[M]

heart
cœur[M]
Herz[N]
corazón[M]

diamond
carreau[M]
Karo[N]
diamante[M]

club
trèfle[M]
Kreuz[N]
trébol[M]

spade
pique[M]
Pik[N]
espada[F]

Joker
Joker[M]
Joker[M]
comodín[M]

Ace
As[M]
Ass[N]
as[M]

King
Roi[M]
König[M]
rey[M]

Queen
Dame[F]
Dame[F]
reina[F]

Jack
Valet[M]
Bube[M]
jota[F]

## STANDARD POKER HANDS
## COMBINAISONS[F] AU POKER[M]
## NORMALE POKERBLÄTTER[N]
## MANOS[F] DE PÓQUER[M]

royal flush
quinte[F] royale
Royal Flush[M]
escalera[F] real

straight flush
quinte[F]
Straight Flush[M]
escalera[F] de color[M]

four-of-a-kind
carré[M]
Vierling[M]
póquer[M]

full house
main[F] pleine
Full House[N]
full

flush
couleur[F]
Flush[M]
color[M]

straight
séquence[F]
Straße[F]
escalera[F]

three-of-a-kind
brelan[M]
Drilling[M]
trío[M]

two pairs
double paire[F]
zwei Pärchen[N]
dos pares[M]

one pair
paire[F]
ein Pärchen[N]
un par[M]

high card
carte[F] isolée
höchste Karte[F]
cartas[F] altas

# DOMINOES
# DOMINOS[M]
# DOMINO[N]
# DOMINÓ[M]

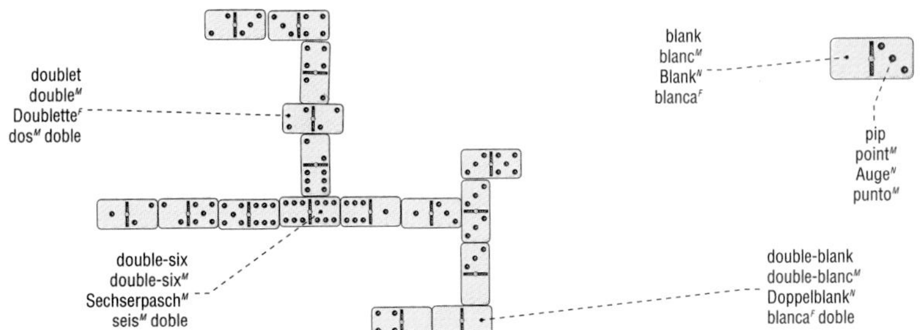

blank
blanc[M]
Blank[N]
blanca[F]

doublet
double[M]
Doublette[F]
dos[M] doble

pip
point[M]
Auge[N]
punto[M]

double-six
double-six[M]
Sechserpasch[M]
seis[M] doble

double-blank
double-blanc[M]
Doppelblank[N]
blanca[F] doble

# CHESS
# ÉCHECS[M]
# SCHACH[N]
# AJEDREZ[M]

## CHESSBOARD
## ÉCHIQUIER[M]
## SCHACHBRETT[N]
## TABLERO[M] DE AJEDREZ[M]

## TYPES OF MOVE
## TYPES[M] DE DÉPLACEMENTS[M]
## GANGARTEN[F]
## TIPOS[M] DE MOVIMIENTOS[M]

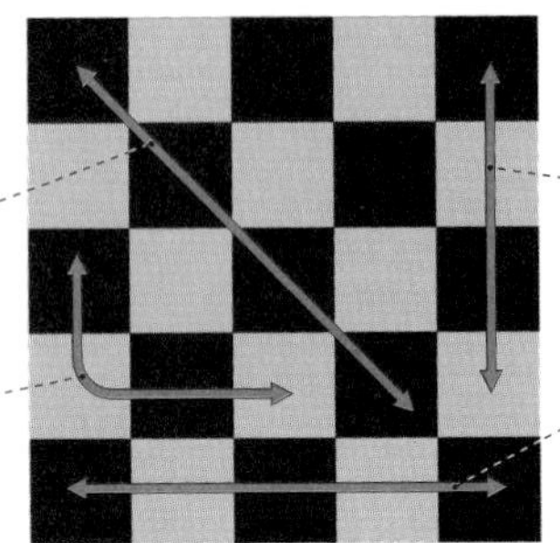


## MEN
## PIÈCES[F]
## FIGUREN[F]
## PIEZAS[F]

Pawn
Pion[M]
Bauer[M]
peón[M]

Castle
Tour[F]
Turm[M]
torre[F]

King
Roi[M]
König[M]
rey[M]

Queen
Dame[F]
Dame[F]
reina[F]

Bishop
Fou[M]
Läufer[M]
alfil[M]

Knight
Cavalier[M]
Pferd[N]
caballo[M]

## BACKGAMMON
## JACQUET[M]
## BACKGAMMON[N]
## BACKGAMMON[M]

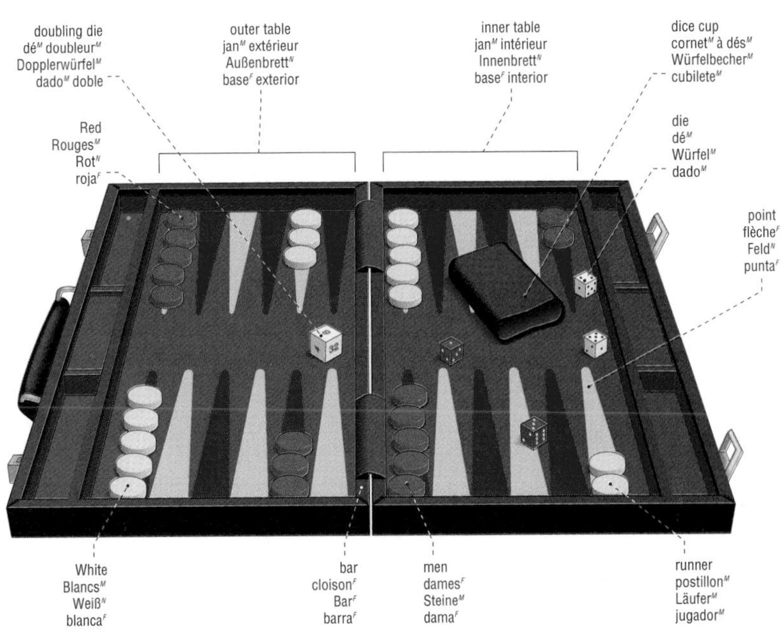

## GO
## GO[M]
## GO[N]
## GO(SUN-TSE)

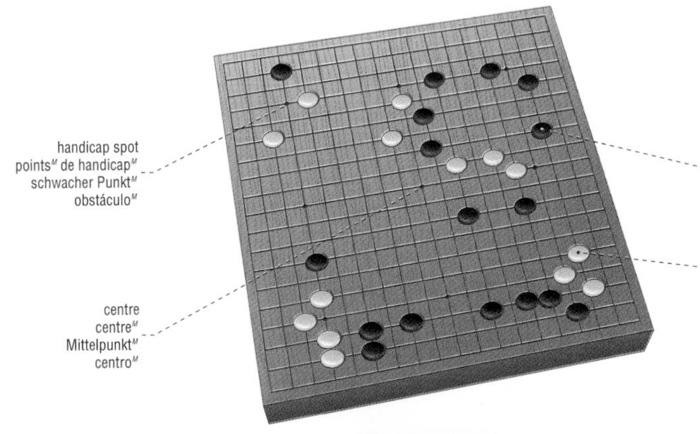


### MAJOR MOTIONS
### PRINCIPAUX MOUVEMENTS[M]
### HAUPTSPIELZÜGE[M]
### MOVIMIENTOS[M] PRINCIPALES

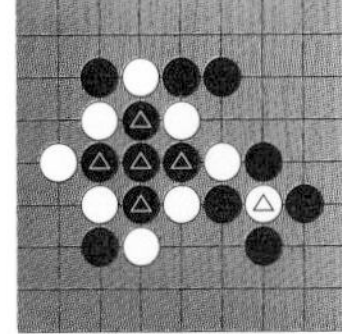

capture
capture[F]
Fangen[N]
captura[F]

contact
contact[M]
Berührung[F]
contacto[M]

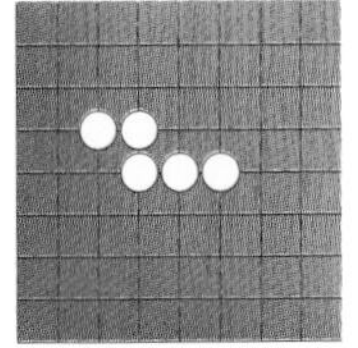

connection
connexion[F]
Verbindung[F]
conexión[F]

GAME OF DARTS
JEU[M] DE FLÉCHETTES[F]
DARTSPIEL[N]
JUEGO[M] DE DARDOS[M]

## VIDEO ENTERTAINMENT SYSTEM
## SYSTÈME[M] DE JEUX[M] VIDÉO
## VIDEOSPIELSYSTEM[N]
## SISTEMA[M] DE JUEGOS[M] DE VÍDEO[M]

visual display
écran[M]
Monitor[M]
pantalla[F]

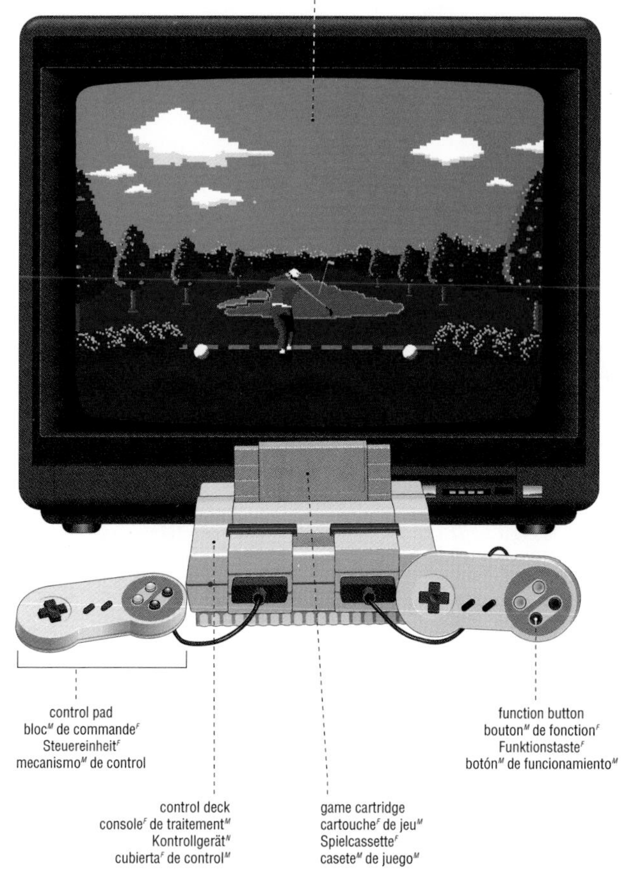

control pad
bloc[M] de commande[F]
Steuereinheit[F]
mecanismo[M] de control

function button
bouton[M] de fonction[F]
Funktionstaste[F]
botón[M] de funcionamiento[M]

control deck
console[F] de traitement[M]
Kontrollgerät[N]
cubierta[F] de control[M]

game cartridge
cartouche[F] de jeu[M]
Spielcassette[F]
casete[M] de juego[M]

## DICE
## DÉS[M]
## WÜRFEL[M]
## DADOS[M]

poker die
dé[M] à poker[M]
Pokerwürfel[M]
dado[M] de póquer[M]

ordinary die
dé[M] régulier
gewöhnlicher Würfel[M]
dado[M] común

## ROULETTE TABLE
## TABLE[F] DE ROULETTE
## ROULETTESPIELTISCH[M]
## MESA[F] DE LA RULETA[F]

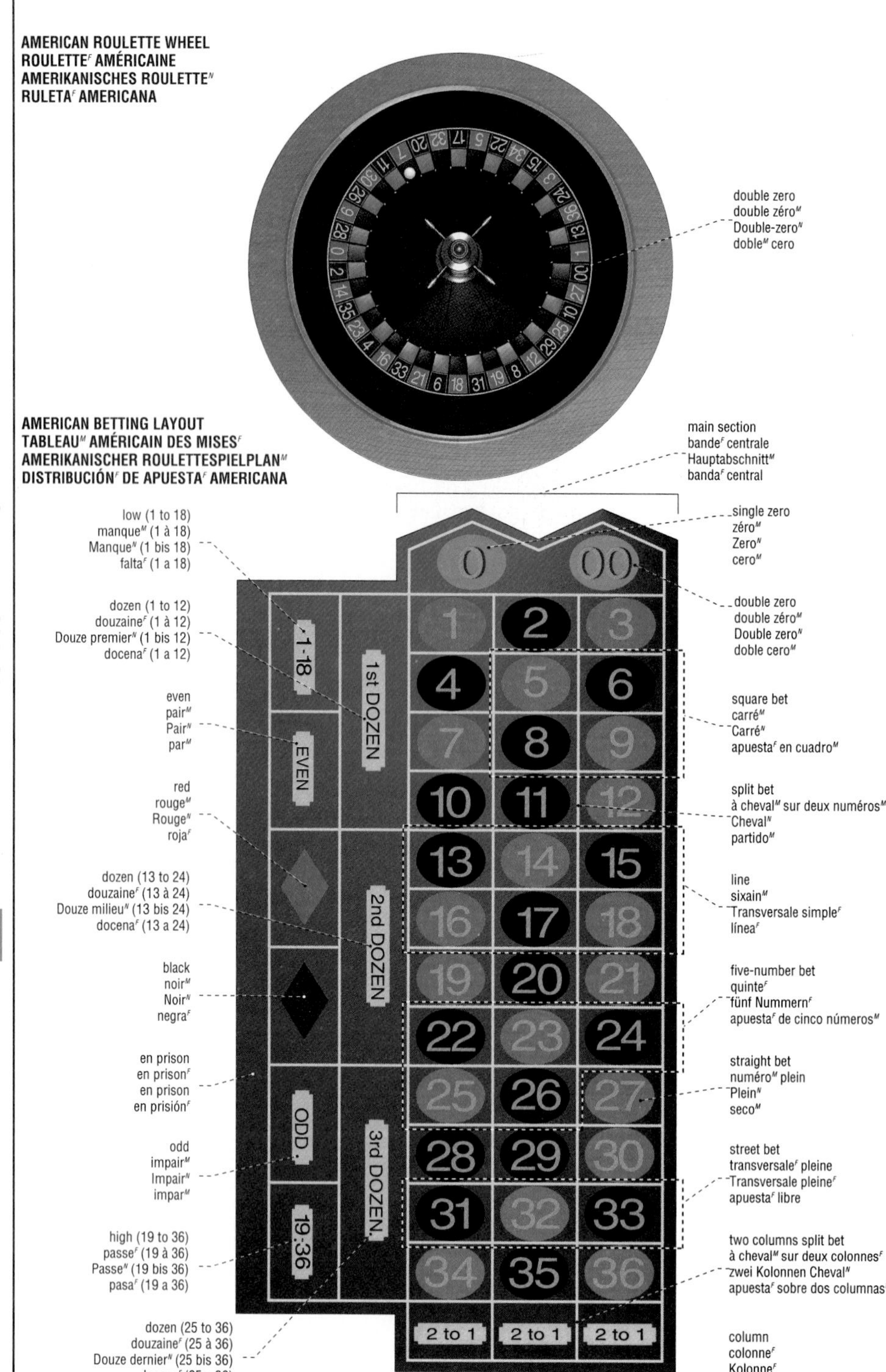

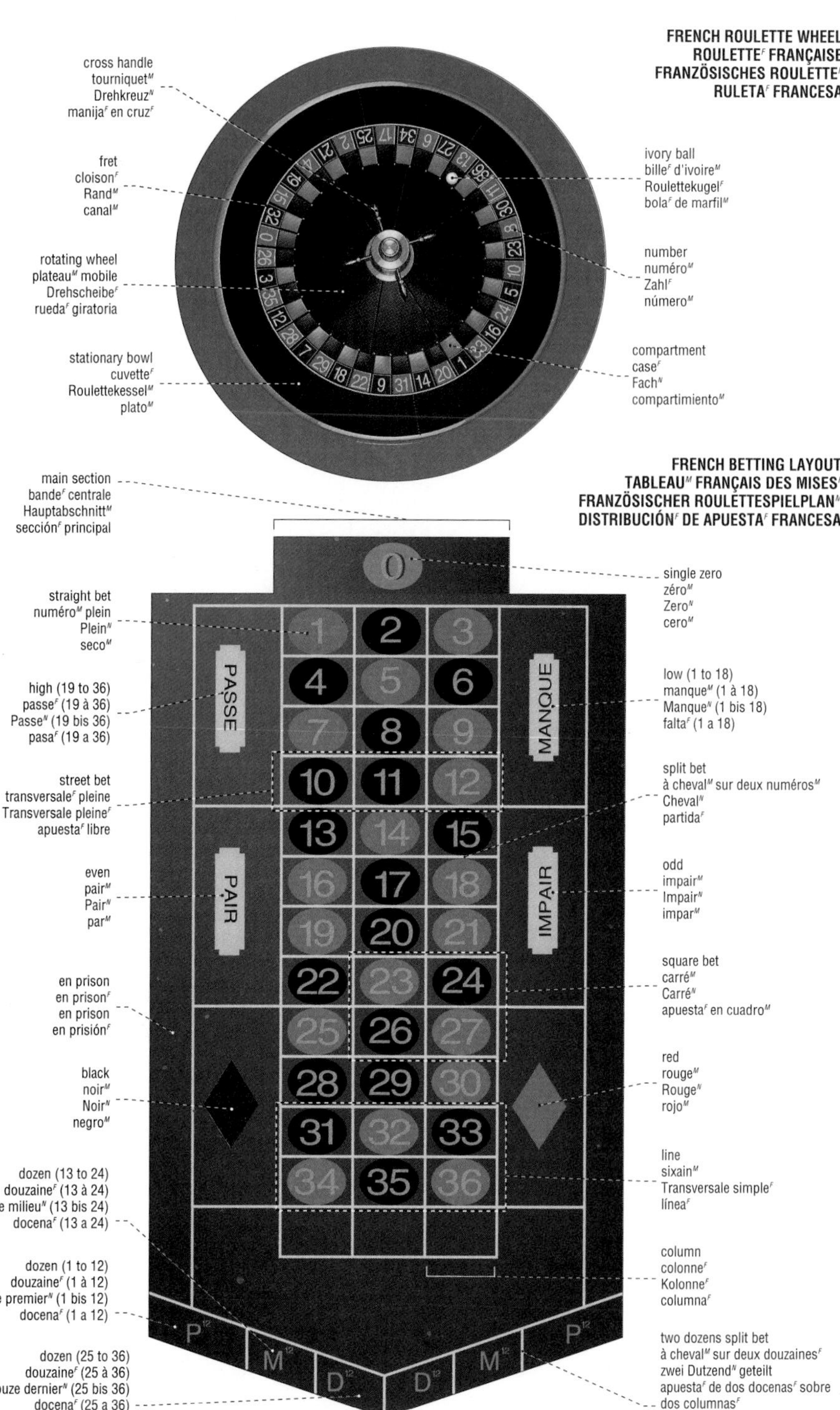
FRENCH ROULETTE WHEEL
ROULETTE[F] FRANÇAISE
FRANZÖSISCHES ROULETTE[N]
RULETA[F] FRANCESA
cross handle
tourniquet[M]
Drehkreuz[N]
manija[F] en cruz[F]
fret
cloison[F]
Rand[M]
canal[M]
rotating wheel
plateau[M] mobile
Drehscheibe[F]
rueda[F] giratoria
stationary bowl
cuvette[F]
Roulettekessel[M]
plato[M]
ivory ball
bille[F] d'ivoire[M]
Roulettekugel[F]
bola[F] de marfil[M]
number
numéro[M]
Zahl[F]
número[M]
compartment
case[F]
Fach[N]
compartimiento[M]
FRENCH BETTING LAYOUT
TABLEAU[M] FRANÇAIS DES MISES[F]
FRANZÖSISCHER ROULETTESPIELPLAN[M]
DISTRIBUCIÓN[F] DE APUESTA[F] FRANCESA
main section
bande[F] centrale
Hauptabschnitt[M]
sección[F] principal
straight bet
numéro[M] plein
Plein[N]
seco[M]
high (19 to 36)
passe[F] (19 à 36)
Passe[N] (19 bis 36)
pasa[F] (19 a 36)
street bet
transversale[F] pleine
Transversale pleine[F]
apuesta[F] libre
even
pair[M]
Pair[N]
par[M]
en prison
en prison[F]
en prison
en prisión[F]
black
noir[M]
Noir[N]
negro[M]
dozen (13 to 24)
douzaine[F] (13 à 24)
Douze milieu[N] (13 bis 24)
docena[F] (13 a 24)
dozen (1 to 12)
douzaine[F] (1 à 12)
Douze premier[N] (1 bis 12)
docena[F] (1 a 12)
dozen (25 to 36)
douzaine[F] (25 à 36)
Douze dernier[N] (25 bis 36)
docena[F] (25 a 36)
single zero
zéro[M]
Zero[N]
cero[M]
low (1 to 18)
manque[M] (1 à 18)
Manque[N] (1 bis 18)
falta[F] (1 a 18)
split bet
à cheval[M] sur deux numéros[M]
Cheval[N]
partida[F]
odd
impair[M]
Impair[N]
impar[M]
square bet
carré[M]
Carré[N]
apuesta[F] en cuadro[M]
red
rouge[M]
Rouge[N]
rojo[M]
line
sixain[M]
Transversale simple[F]
línea[F]
column
colonne[F]
Kolonne[F]
columna[F]
two dozens split bet
à cheval[M] sur deux douzaines[F]
zwei Dutzend[N] geteilt
apuesta[F] de dos docenas[F] sobre
dos columnas[F]
PASSE
MANQUE
PAIR
IMPAIR

# FRUIT MACHINE
# MACHINE[F] À SOUS[M]
# EINARMIGER BANDIT[M]
# TRAGAPERRAS[M]

## CROSS SECTION
## COUPE[F]
## QUERSCHNITT
## CORTE[M] TRANSVERSAL

# MEASURING DEVICES
# APPAREILS DE MESURE
# MESSINSTRUMENTE
# APARATOS DE MEDICIÓN

SUMMARY

MEASURE OF TEMPERATURE .......... 705
MEASURE OF TIME .......... 706
MEASUREMENT OF WEIGHT .......... 708
MEASUREMENT OF PRESSURE .......... 710
MEASUREMENT OF LENGTH .......... 711
MEASUREMENT OF DISTANCE .......... 711
MEASUREMENT OF THICKNESS .......... 711
WATT-HOUR METER .......... 712
MEASURE OF ANGLES .......... 713
MEASUREMENT OF SEISMIC WAVES .......... 714

# MEASURE OF TEMPERATURE
# MESURE[F] DE LA TEMPÉRATURE[F]
# TEMPERATURMESSUNG[F]
# MEDICIÓN[F] DE LA TEMPERATURA[F]

## THERMOMETER
## THERMOMÈTRE[M]
## THERMOMETER[N]
## TERMÓMETRO[M]

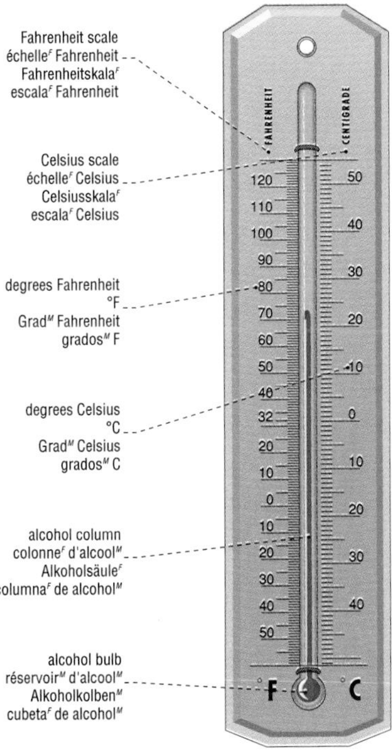

## CLINICAL THERMOMETER
## THERMOMÈTRE[M] MÉDICAL
## FIEBERTHERMOMETER[N]
## TERMÓMETRO[M] CLÍNICO

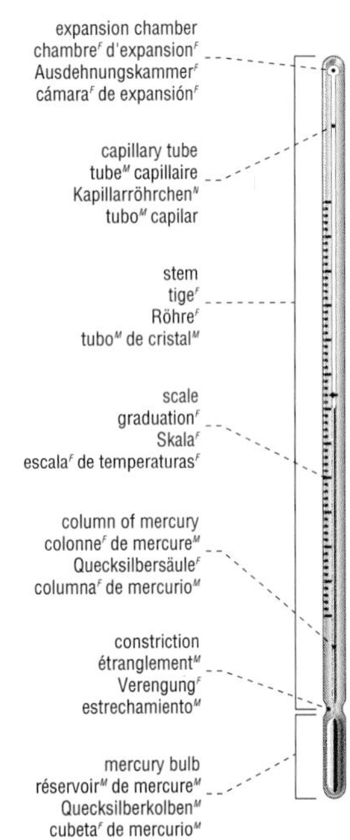


## BIMETALLIC THERMOMETER
## THERMOMÈTRE[M] BIMÉTALLIQUE
## BIMETALL-THERMOMETER[N]
## TERMÓMETRO[M] BIMETÁLICO

pointer
aiguille[F]
Zeiger[M]
aguja[F]

case
boîtier[M]
Gehäuse[N]
caja[F]

dial
cadran[M]
Anzeigeskala[F]
cuadrante[M]

shaft
arbre[M]
Welle[F]
barra[F]

bimetallic helix
élément[M] bimétallique hélicoïdal
Bimetallfeder[F]
hélice[F] bimetálica

## ROOM THERMOSTAT
## THERMOSTAT[M] D'AMBIANCE[F]
## RAUMTHERMOSTAT[M]
## TERMOSTATO[M] AMBIENTAL

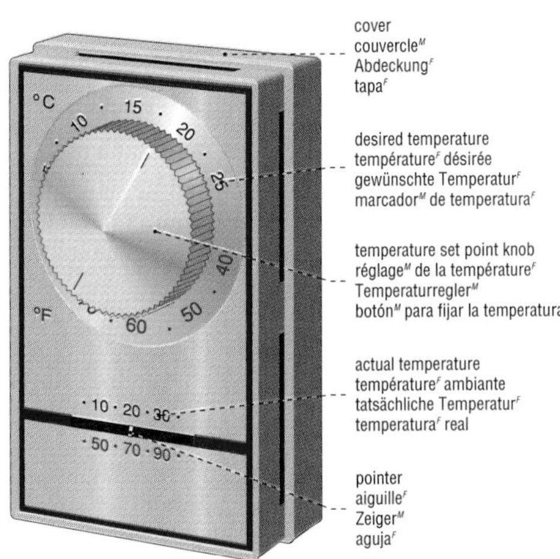

# MEASURE OF TIME
# MESURE[F] DU TEMPS[M]
# ZEITMESSUNG[F]
# MEDICIÓN[F] DEL TIEMPO[M]

## STOPWATCH
## CHRONOMÈTRE[M]
## STOPPUHR[F]
## CRONÓMETRO[M]

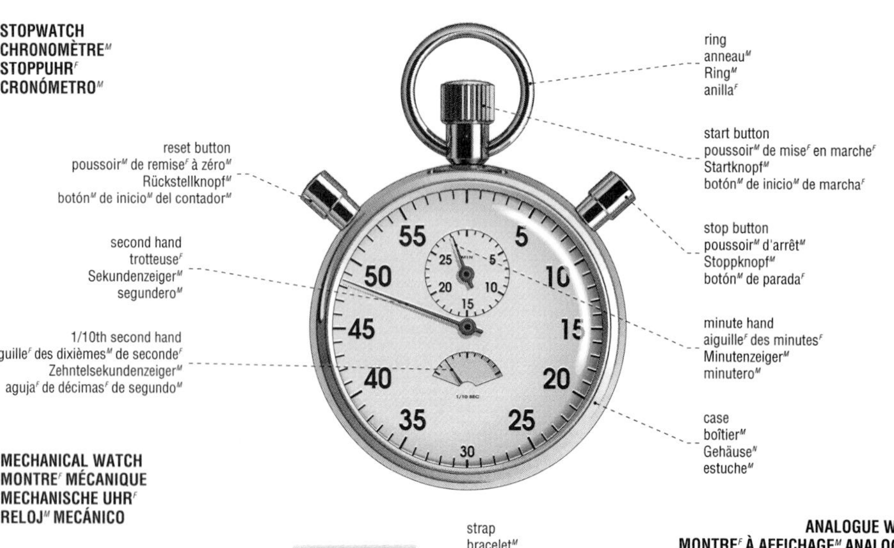

ring
anneau[M]
Ring[M]
anilla[F]

start button
poussoir[M] de mise[F] en marche[F]
Startknopf[M]
botón[M] de inicio[M] de marcha[F]

reset button
poussoir[M] de remise[F] à zéro[M]
Rückstellknopf[M]
botón[M] de inicio[M] del contador[M]

stop button
poussoir[M] d'arrêt[M]
Stoppknopf[M]
botón[M] de parada[F]

second hand
trotteuse[F]
Sekundenzeiger[M]
segundero[M]

minute hand
aiguille[F] des minutes[F]
Minutenzeiger[M]
minutero[M]

1/10th second hand
aiguille[F] des dixièmes[M] de seconde[F]
Zehntelsekundenzeiger[M]
aguja[F] de décimas[F] de segundo[M]

case
boîtier[M]
Gehäuse[N]
estuche[M]

## MECHANICAL WATCH
## MONTRE[F] MÉCANIQUE
## MECHANISCHE UHR[F]
## RELOJ[M] MECÁNICO

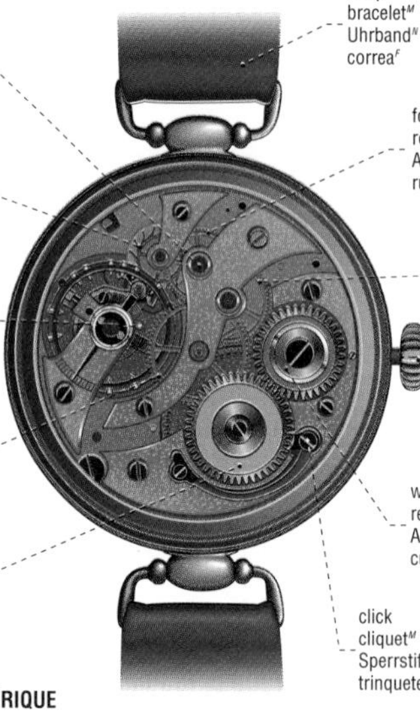

strap
bracelet[M]
Uhrband[N]
correa[F]

jewel
rubis[M]
Stein[M]
rubí[M]

fourth wheel
roue[F] de champ[M]
Ankerrad[N]
rueda[F] de los segundos[M]

escape wheel
roue[F] d'échappement[M]
Hemmrad[N]
rueda[F] de escape[M]

third wheel
roue[F] petite moyenne
Antriebswerk[N]
rueda[F] media

hairspring
spiral[M]
Spiralfeder[F]
espiral[M]

crown
couronne[F]
Krone[F]
corona[F]

centre wheel
roue[F] de centre[M]
Spannrad[N]
rueda[F] central

winder
remontoir[M]
Aufzugsrad[N]
cuerda[F]

barrel
rochet[M]
Federhaus[N]
rueda[F] de trinquete[M]

click
cliquet[M]
Sperrstift[M]
trinquete[M]

## ANALOGUE WATCH
## MONTRE[F] À AFFICHAGE[M] ANALOGIQUE
## ANALOGUHR[F]
## RELOJ[M] DE PULSERA[F]

dial
cadran[M]
Ziffernblatt[N]
cuadrante[M]

## DIGITAL WATCH
## MONTRE[F] À AFFICHAGE[M] NUMÉRIQUE
## DIGITALUHR[F]
## RELOJ[M] DIGITAL

## SUNDIAL
## CADRAN[M] SOLAIRE
## SONNENUHR[F]
## RELOJ[M] DE SOL[M]

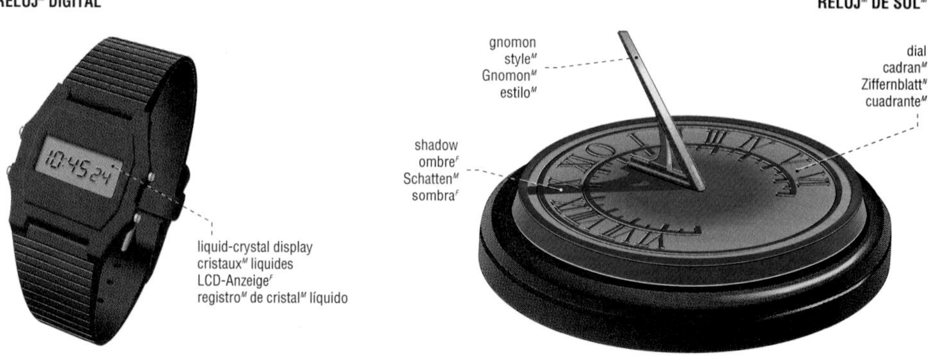

gnomon
style[M]
Gnomon[M]
estilo[M]

dial
cadran[M]
Ziffernblatt[N]
cuadrante[M]

shadow
ombre[F]
Schatten[M]
sombra[F]

liquid-crystal display
cristaux[M] liquides
LCD-Anzeige[F]
registro[M] de cristal[M] líquido

## GRANDFATHER CLOCK
## HORLOGE[F] DE PARQUET[M]
## STANDUHR[F]
## RELOJ[M] DE PÉNDULO[M]

pediment
corniche[F]
Giebeldreieck[N]
frontón[M]
body
caisse[F]
Gehäuse[N]
caja[F]
hour hand
aiguille[F] des heures[F]
Sekundenzeiger[M]
manecilla[F] de las horas[F]
dial
cadran[M]
Ziffernblatt[N]
esfera[F]
plinth
socle[M]
Plinthe[F]
zócalo[M]
moon dial
cadran[M] des phases[F] de la Lune[F]
Mondphasenzeiger[M]
esfera[F] lunar
minute hand
aiguille[F] des minutes[F]
Minutenzeiger[M]
minutero[M]
weight
poids[M]
Gewicht[N]
pesa[F]
pendulum
pendule[M]
Pendel[N]
péndulo[M]
chain
chaîne[F]
Kette[F]
cadena[F]


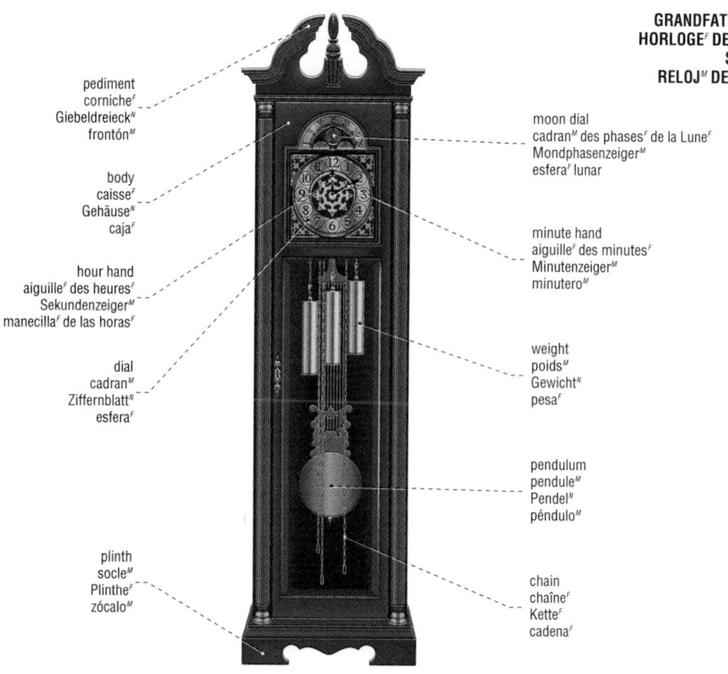

## WEIGHT-DRIVEN CLOCK MECHANISM
## MÉCANISME[M] DE L'HORLOGE[F] À POIDS[M]
## ZUGGETRIEBENES UHRWERK[N]
## MECANISMO[M] DEL RELOJ[M] DE PESAS[F]

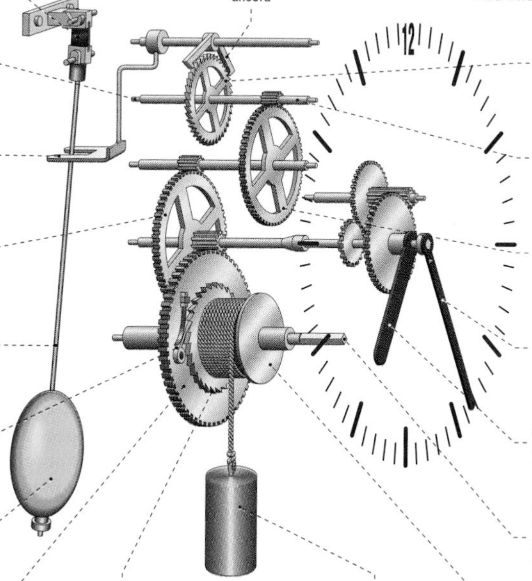

suspension spring
lame[F] de suspension[F]
Aufhängefeder[F]
resorte[M] de suspensión[F]
pinion
pignon[M]
Ritzel[N]
piñón[M]
fork
fourchette[F]
Gabel[F]
diapasón[M]
centre wheel
roue[F] de centre[M]
Spannrad[N]
rueda[F] central
pendulum rod
tige[F]
Pendelstab[M]
varilla[F] del péndulo[M]
click
cliquet[M]
Sperrstift[M]
trinquete[M]
pendulum
lentille[F]
Pendel[N]
péndulo[M]
main wheel
roue[F] motrice
Hauptrad[N]
rueda[F] motriz
pallet
ancre[F]
Hemmungslappen[M]
áncora[F]
ratchet wheel
rochet[M]
Sperrad[N]
rueda[F] de trinquete[M]
weight
poids[M]
Gewicht[N]
pesa[F]
escape wheel
roue[F] d'échappement[M]
Hemmrad[N]
rueda[F] de escape[M]
spindle
arbre[M]
Spindel[F]
eje[M]
third wheel
roue[F] petite moyenne
Antriebswerk[N]
rueda[F] de corona[F]
minute hand
aiguille[F] des minutes[F]
Minutenzeiger[M]
minutero[M]
hour hand
aiguille[F] des heures[F]
Stundenzeiger[M]
manecilla[F] de las horas[F]
winding mechanism
remontoir[M]
Aufzugsmechanismus[M]
mecanismo[M] de cuerda[F]
drum
tambour[M]
Trommel[F]
cilindro[M]

# MEASUREMENT OF WEIGHT
# MESURE^F DE LA MASSE^F
# WIEGEN^N
# MEDICIÓN^F DEL PESO^M

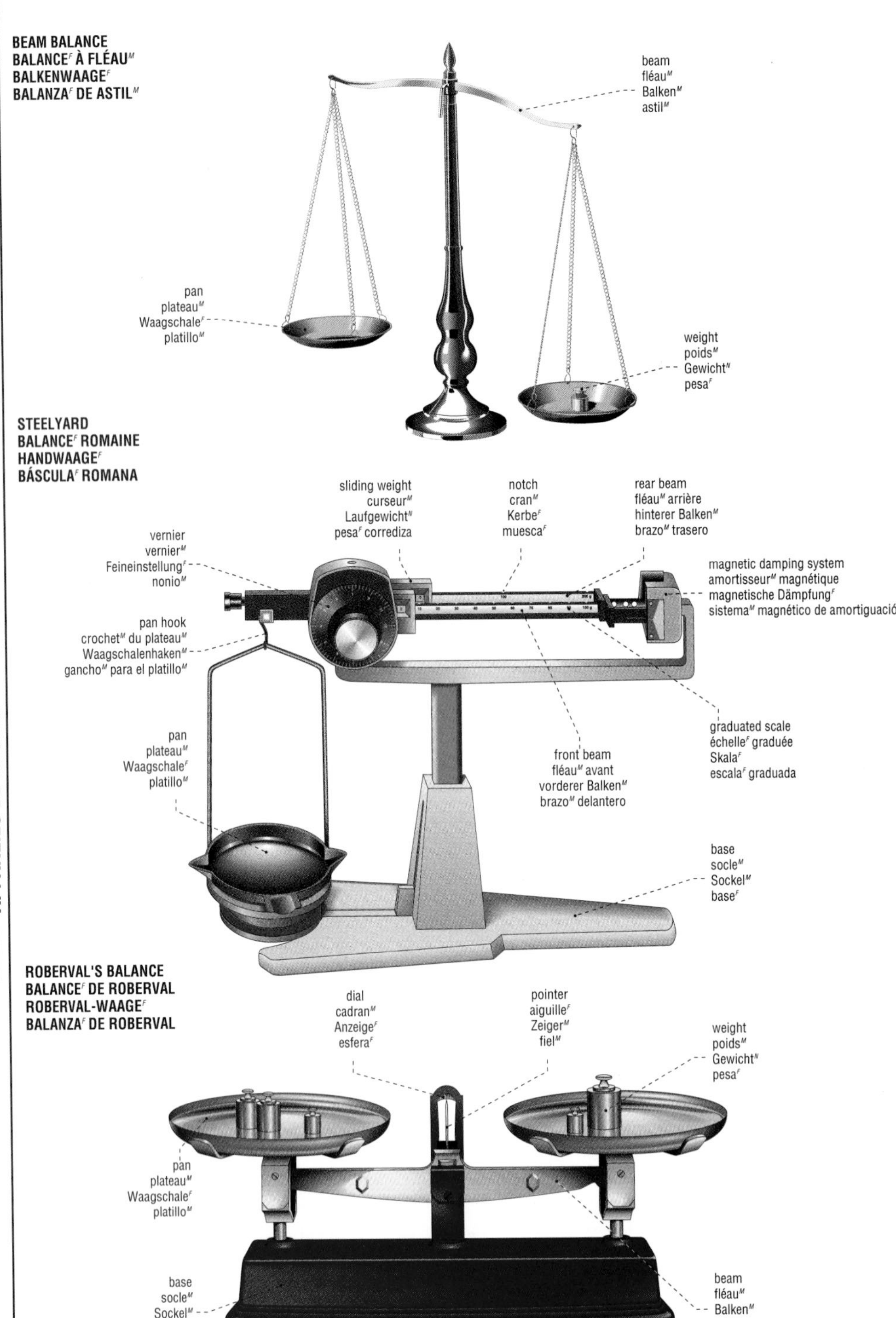

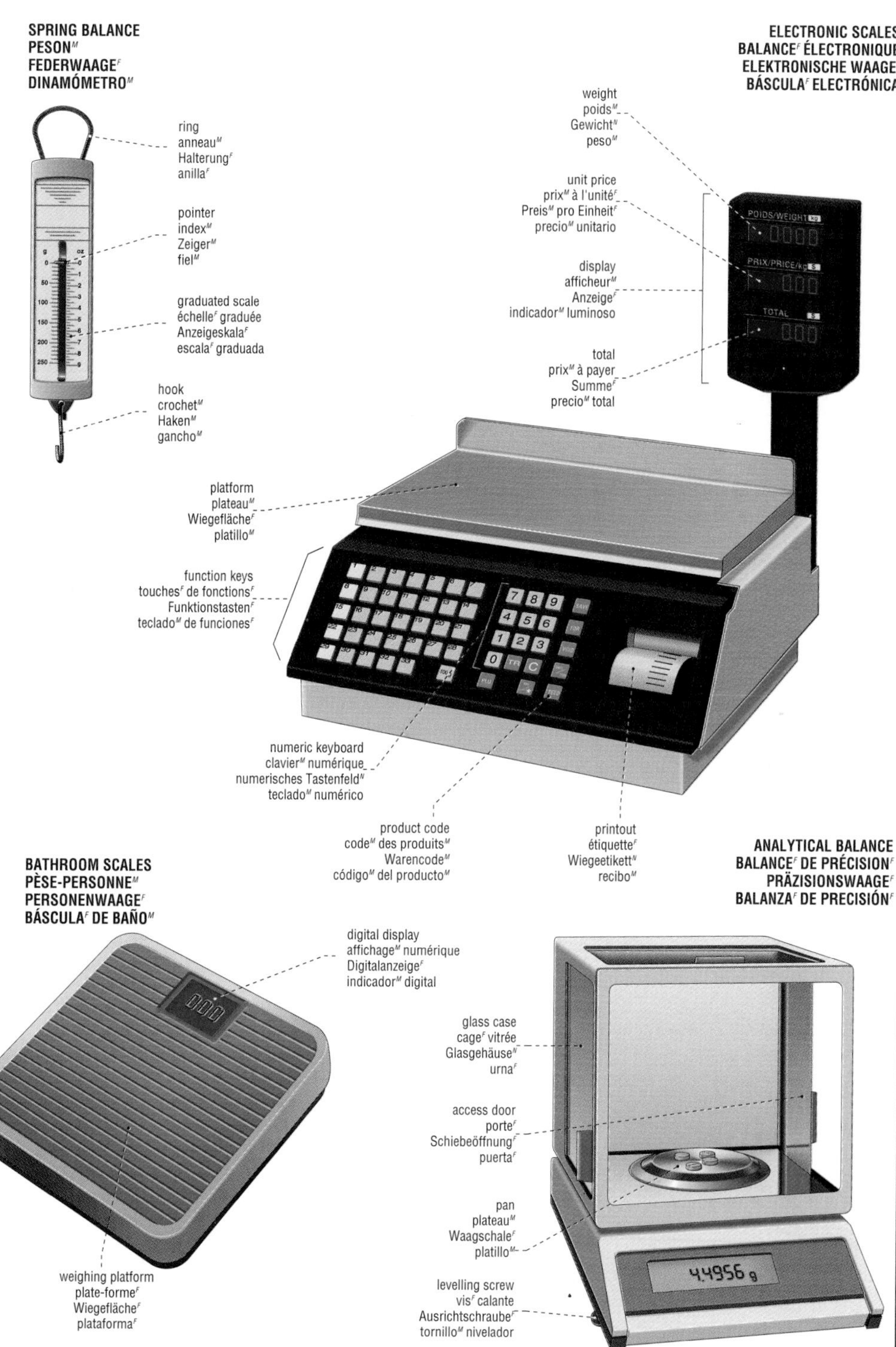
SPRING BALANCE
PESON[M]
FEDERWAAGE[F]
DINAMÓMETRO[M]
ring
anneau[M]
Halterung[F]
anilla[F]
pointer
index[M]
Zeiger[M]
fiel[M]
graduated scale
échelle[F] graduée
Anzeigeskala[F]
escala[F] graduada
hook
crochet[M]
Haken[M]
gancho[M]
ELECTRONIC SCALES
BALANCE[F] ÉLECTRONIQUE
ELEKTRONISCHE WAAGE[F]
BÁSCULA[F] ELECTRÓNICA
weight
poids[M]
Gewicht[N]
peso[M]
unit price
prix[M] à l'unité[F]
Preis[M] pro Einheit[F]
precio[M] unitario
display
afficheur[M]
Anzeige[F]
indicador[M] luminoso
total
prix[M] à payer
Summe[F]
precio[M] total
platform
plateau[M]
Wiegefläche[F]
platillo[M]
function keys
touches[F] de fonctions[F]
Funktionstasten[F]
teclado[M] de funciones[F]
numeric keyboard
clavier[M] numérique
numerisches Tastenfeld[N]
teclado[M] numérico
product code
code[M] des produits[M]
Warencode[M]
código[M] del producto[M]
printout
étiquette[F]
Wiegeetikett[N]
recibo[M]
BATHROOM SCALES
PÈSE-PERSONNE[M]
PERSONENWAAGE[F]
BÁSCULA[F] DE BAÑO[M]
digital display
affichage[M] numérique
Digitalanzeige[F]
indicador[M] digital
weighing platform
plate-forme[F]
Wiegefläche[F]
plataforma[F]
ANALYTICAL BALANCE
BALANCE[F] DE PRÉCISION[F]
PRÄZISIONSWAAGE[F]
BALANZA[F] DE PRECISIÓN[F]
glass case
cage[F] vitrée
Glasgehäuse[N]
urna[F]
access door
porte[F]
Schiebeöffnung[F]
puerta[F]
pan
plateau[M]
Waagschale[F]
platillo[M]
levelling screw
vis[F] calante
Ausrichtschraube[F]
tornillo[M] nivelador
POIDS/WEIGHT kg
PRIX/PRICE/kg $
TOTAL $
4.4956 g

# MEASUREMENT OF PRESSURE
# MESURE[F] DE LA PRESSION[F]
# DRUCKMESSUNG[F]
# MEDICIÓN[F] DE LA PRESIÓN[F]

## BAROMETER/THERMOMETER
## BAROMÈTRE[M]/THERMOMÈTRE[M]
## BAROMETER[N]/THERMOMETER[N]
## BARÓMETRO[M]/TERMÓMETRO[M]

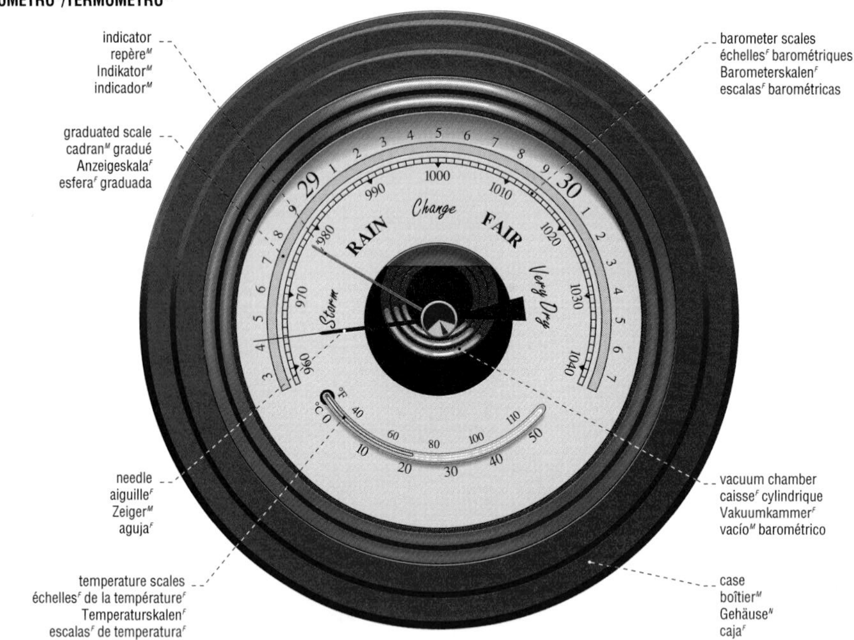


## SPHYGMOMANOMETER
## TENSIOMÈTRE[M]
## BLUTDRUCKMESSGERÄT[N]
## TENSIÓMETRO[M]

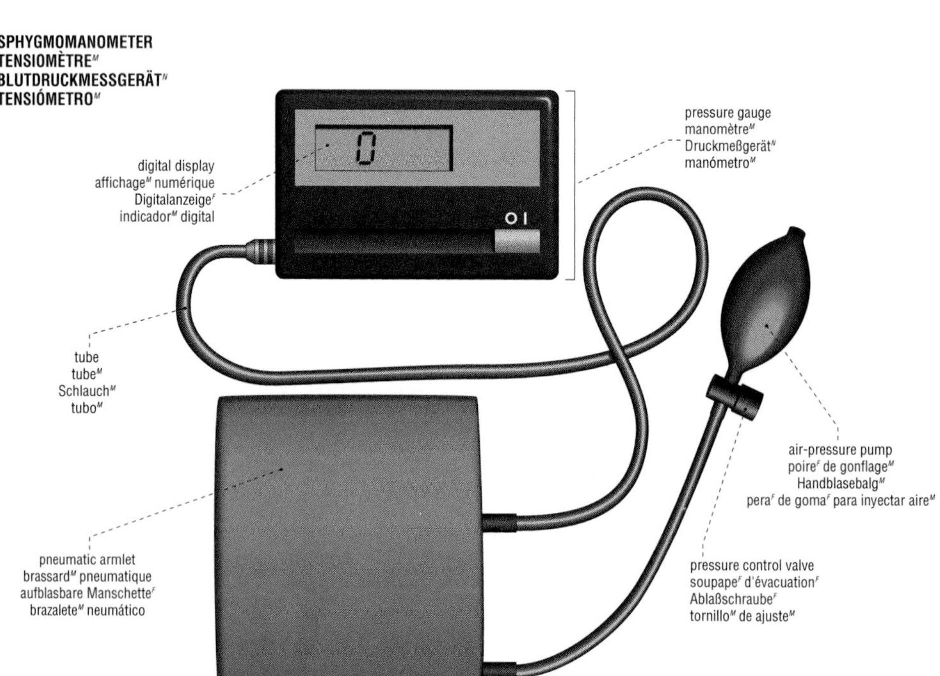

## MEASUREMENT OF LENGTH
## MESURE[F] DE LA LONGUEUR[F]
## LÄNGENMESSUNG[F]
## MEDICIÓN[F] DE LA LONGITUD[F]

**TAPE MEASURE**
**MÈTRE[M] À RUBAN[M]**
**MESSBAND[N]**
**CINTA[F] MÉTRICA**

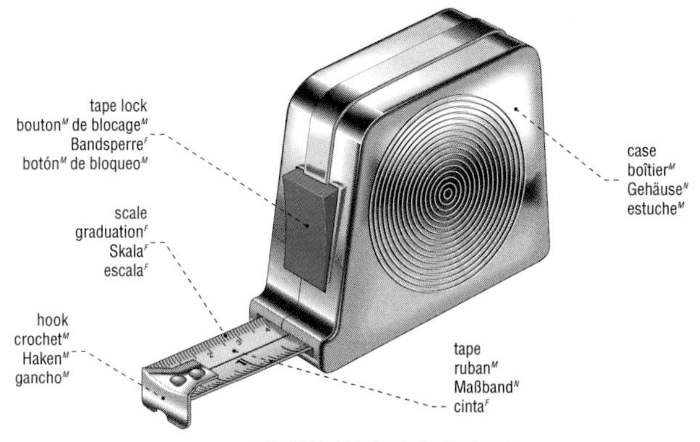


## MEASUREMENT OF DISTANCE
## MESURE[F] DE LA DISTANCE[F]
## ENTFERNUNGSMESSUNG[F]
## MEDICIÓN[F] DE LA DISTANCIA[F]

**PEDOMETER**
**PODOMÈTRE[M]**
**PEDOMETER[N]**
**ODÓMETRO[M]**

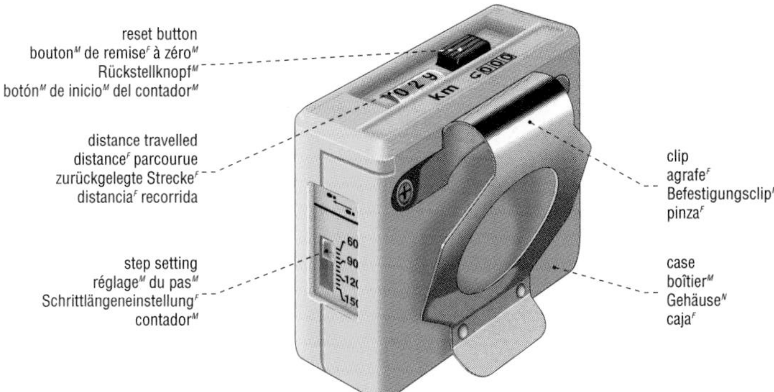


## MEASUREMENT OF THICKNESS
## MESURE[F] DE L'ÉPAISSEUR[F]
## DICKEMESSUNG[F]
## MEDICIÓN[F] DEL ESPESOR[M]

**MICROMETER CALIPER**
**MICROMÈTRE[M] PALMER[M]**
**MIKROMETERSCHRAUBE[F]**
**MICRÓMETRO[M]**

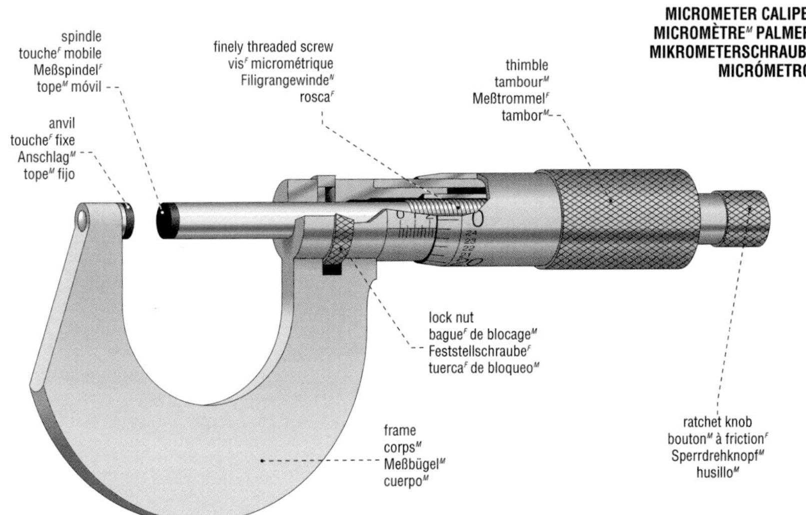

# WATT-HOUR METER
# WATTHEUREMÈTRE[M]
# STROMZÄHLER[M]
# VATÍMETRO[M]

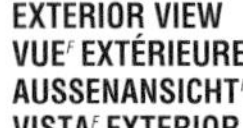

## EXTERIOR VIEW
## VUE[F] EXTÉRIEURE
## AUSSENANSICHT[F]
## VISTA[F] EXTERIOR

cover
couvercle[M]
Abdeckung[F]
tapa[F]
full-load adjustment screw
vis[F] de réglage[M] de grand débit[M]
Vollbelastungseinstellschraube[F]
tornillo[M] de regulación[F] para carga[F] completa
kWh
register
minuterie[F]
Registriereinheit[F]
registro[M]
dial
cadran[M]
Ziffernblatt[N]
cuadrante[M]
MULT. X 10
Rr 138 8/9
TYPE I-70 S Kh 7.2
392 J 3185467
4 185 577
2.0- 200 AMP. 240 VOLTS. 1 PH. 3 FILS WIRE. 60 Hz.
name plate
plaque[F] signalétique
Kennplakette[F]
placa[F] indicadora
disc
disque[M]
Drehscheibe[F]
disco[M]
light-load adjustment screw
vis[F] de réglage[M] de petit débit[M]
Leichtbelastungseinstellschraube[F]
tornillo[M] de regulación[F] para carga[F] ligera
consumer number
numéro[M] de l'abonné[M]
Stromverbrauchernummer[F]
número[M] del consumidor[M]

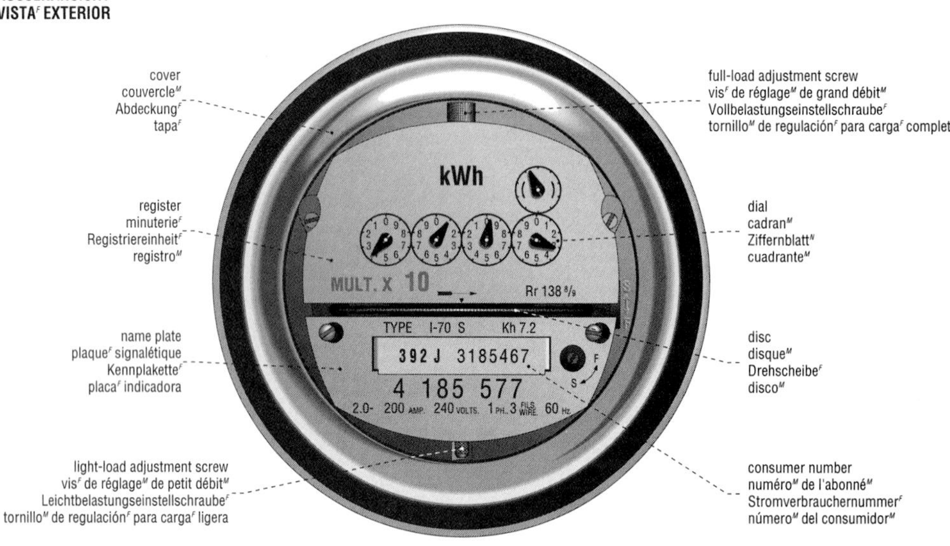

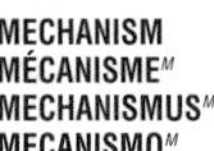

## MECHANISM
## MÉCANISME[M]
## MECHANISMUS[M]
## MECANISMO[M]

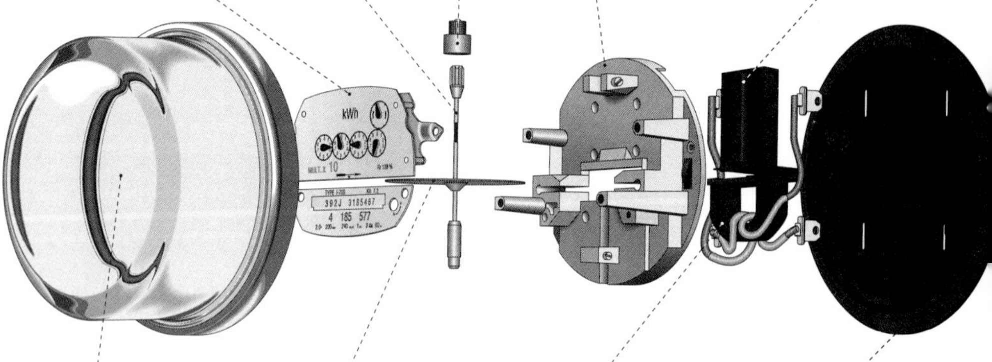

magnetic suspension
palier[M] magnétique
Magnetaufhängung[F]
suspensión[F] magnética
register
minuterie[F]
Registriereinheit[F]
registro[M]
spindle
arbre[M]
Spindel[F]
árbol[M]
retarding magnet
aimant[M]-frein[M]
Retardiermagnet[M]
imán[M] frenador
potential coil
bobine[F] de tension[F]
Potentialspule[F]
bobina[F] de tensión[F]
cover
couvercle[M]
Abdeckung[F]
tapa[F]
disc
disque[M]
Drehscheibe[F]
disco[M]
current coil
bobine[F] de courant[M]
Stromspule[F]
bobina[F] de corriente[F]
base
socle[M]
Grundplatte[F]
base[F]

# MEASURE OF ANGLES
# MESURE[F] DES ANGLES[M]
# WINKELMESSUNG[F]
# MEDICIÓN[F] DE ÁNGULOS[M]

## THEODOLITE
## THÉODOLITE[M]
## THEODOLIT[M]
## TEODOLITO[M]

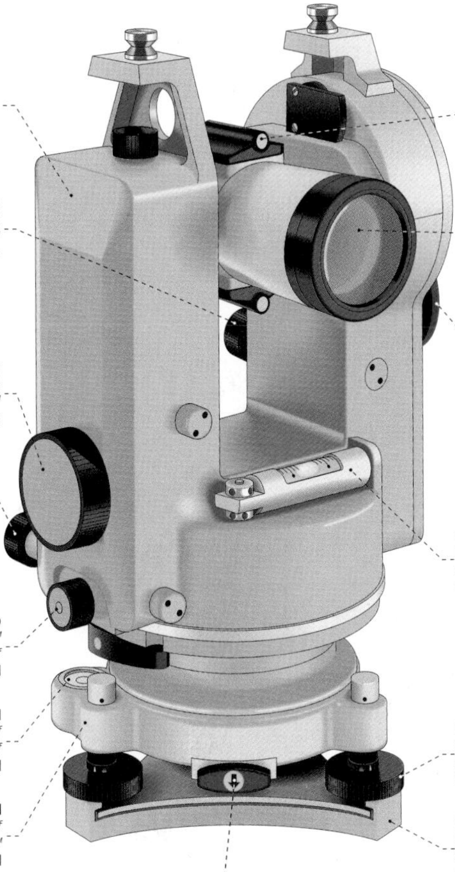

alidade
alidade[F]
Alhidade[F]
alidada[F] móvil

adjustment for vertical-circle image
ajustement[M] de l'image[F] du cercle[M] vertical
Höhenfeintrieb[M]
botón[M] para ajustar la imágen[F] verticalmente

micrometer screw
bouton[M] de réglage[M] du micromètre[M] optique
Mikrometerknopf[M]
tornillo[M] micrométrico

adjustment for horizontal-circle image
ajustement[M] de l'image[F] du cercle[M] horizontal
Seitenfeintrieb[M]
botón[M] para ajustar la imágen[F] horizontalmente

horizontal clamp
blocage[M] du pivotement[M]
Seitenklemme[F]
tornillo[M] de fijación[F] horizontal

levelling head level
nivelle[F] d'embase[F]
Ausrichtkopfebene[F]
nivelador[M] principal

levelling head
embase[F]
Ausrichtknopf[M]
nivelación[F] principal

optical sight
viseur[M]
Mikroskopokular[N]
visor[M]

telescope
lunette[F]
Fernrohr[N]
telescopio[M]

illumination mirror
miroir[M] d'éclairage[M]
Beleuchtungsspiegel[M]
espejo[M] iluminador

alidade level
nivelle[F] d'alidade[F]
Alhidadenebene[F]
nivelador[M] de la alidada[F]

levelling screw
vis[F] calante
Ausrichtschraube[F]
tornillo[M] nivelador

base plate
plaque[F] de fixation[F]
Sockelplatte[F]
placa[F] de fijación[F]

levelling head locking knob
bouton[M] de verrouillage[M] de l'embase[F]
Ausrichtkopfblockierung[F]
botón[M] de fijación[F] del nivel[M] principal

bevel square
fausse-équerre[F]
Schrägmaß[N]
falsa escuadra[F]

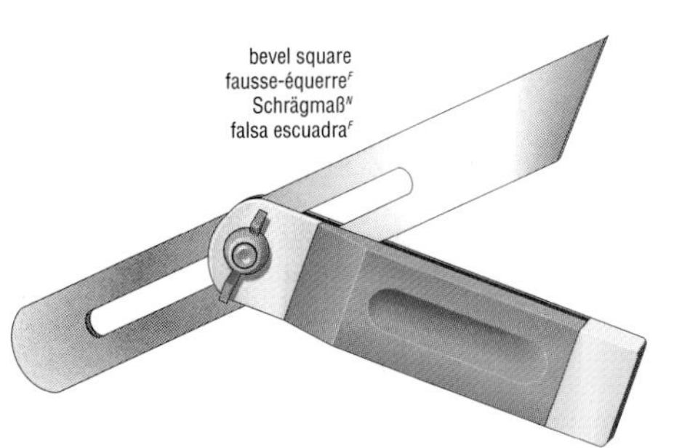

protractor
rapporteur[M] d'angle[M]
Winkelmesser[M]
transportador[M]

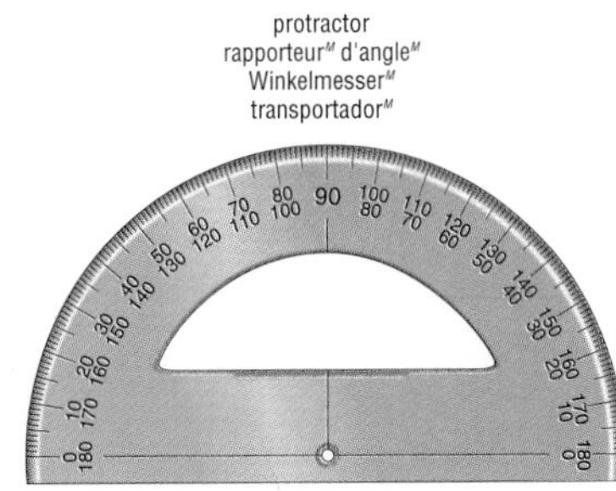

# MEASUREMENT OF SEISMIC WAVES
# MESURE[F] DES ONDES[F] SISMIQUES
# MESSUNG[F] SEISMISCHER WELLEN[F]
# MEDICIÓN[F] DE ONDAS[F] SÍSMICAS

## DETECTION OF SEISMIC WAVES
## DÉTECTION[F] DES ONDES[F] SISMIQUES
## REGISTRIERUNG[F] SEISMISCHER WELLEN[F]
## DETECCIÓN[F] DE ONDAS[F] SÍSMICAS

horizontal seismograph
sismographe[M] horizontal
Horizontalseismograph[M]
sismógrafo[M] horizontal
concrete base
base[F] de béton[M]
Betonsockel[M]
base[F] de cemento[M]
bedrock
roc[M]
Grundgestein[N]
roca[F] firme

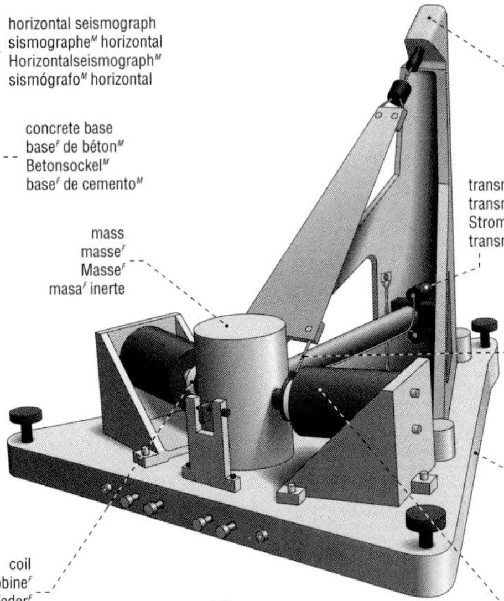

pillar
pilier[M]
Pendelaufhängung[F]
pilar[M]
transmission of the electric current
transmission[F] du courant[M] induit
Stromweiterleitung[F]
transmisión[F] de la corriente[F] eléctrica
mass
masse[F]
Masse[F]
masa[F] inerte
wire
fil[M]
Draht[M]
alambre[M]
stand
socle[M]
Standsockel[M]
plataforma[F]
coil
bobine[F]
Feder[F]
bobina[F]
magnet
aimant[M]
Magnet[M]
imán[M]

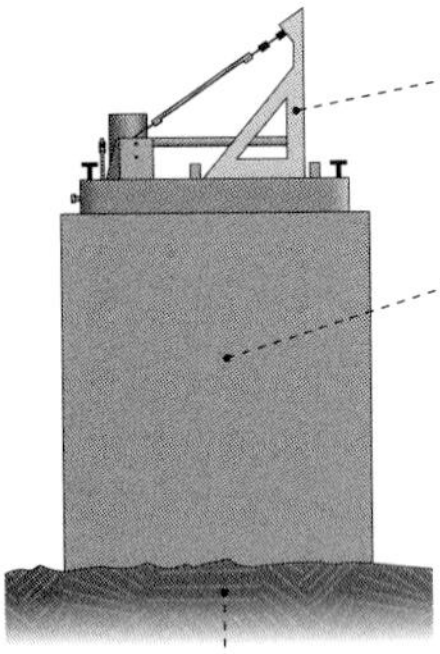

## AMPLIFICATION OF SEISMIC WAVES
## AMPLIFICATION[F] DES ONDES[F] SISMIQUES
## VERSTÄRKUNG[F] SEISMISCHER WELLEN[F]
## AMPLIFICACIÓN[F] DE ONDAS[F] SÍSMICAS

amplifier
amplificateur[M]
Verstärker[M]
amplificador[M]

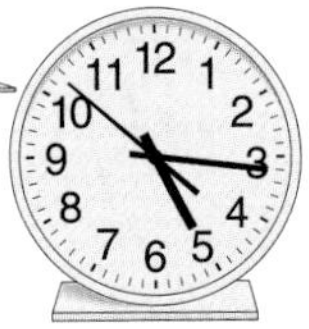

clock
horloge[F]
Uhr[F]
reloj[M]

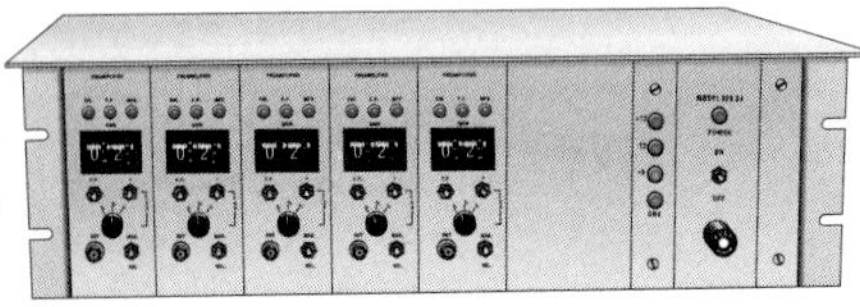

## TRANSCRIPTION OF SEISMIC WAVES
## TRANSCRIPTION[F] DES ONDES[F] SISMIQUES
## AUFZEICHNUNG[F] SEISMISCHER WELLEN[F]
## TRANSCRIPCIÓN[F] DE ONDAS[F] SÍSMICAS

**rotating drum**
**cylindre[M] enregistreur**
**Drehwalze[F]**
**tambor[M] rotativo**

pen
plume[F]
Schreibspitze[F]
punta grabadora[F]
drum
tambour[M]
Walze[F]
tambor[M]
sheet of paper
feuille[F] de papier[M]
Registrierpapier[N]
papel[M]

**visualization of seismic waves**
**visualisation[F] des ondes[F] sismiques**
**Sichtbarmachung[F] seismischer Wellen[F]**
**visualización[F] de las ondas[F] sísmicas**

seismogram
sismogramme[M]
Seismogramm[N]
sismograma[M]

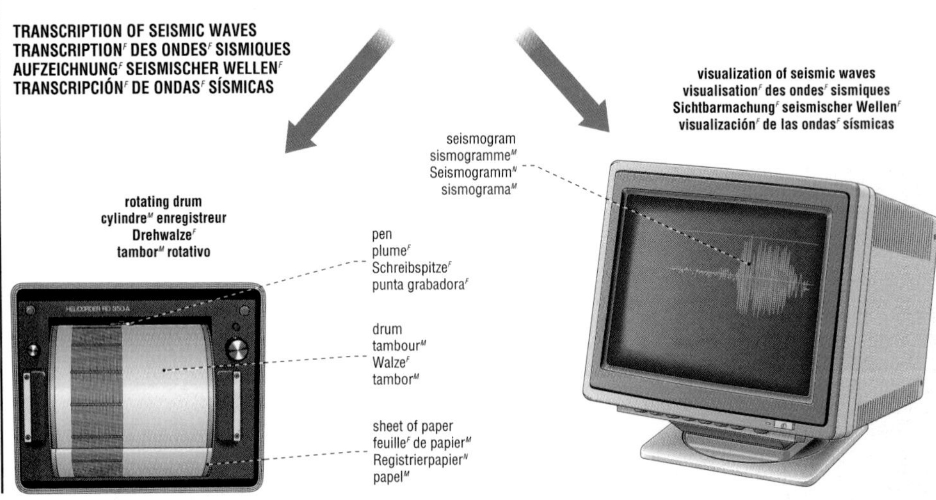

# OPTICAL INSTRUMENTS
# APPAREILS DE VISION
# OPTISCHE INSTRUMENTE
# INSTRUMENTOS ÓPTICOS

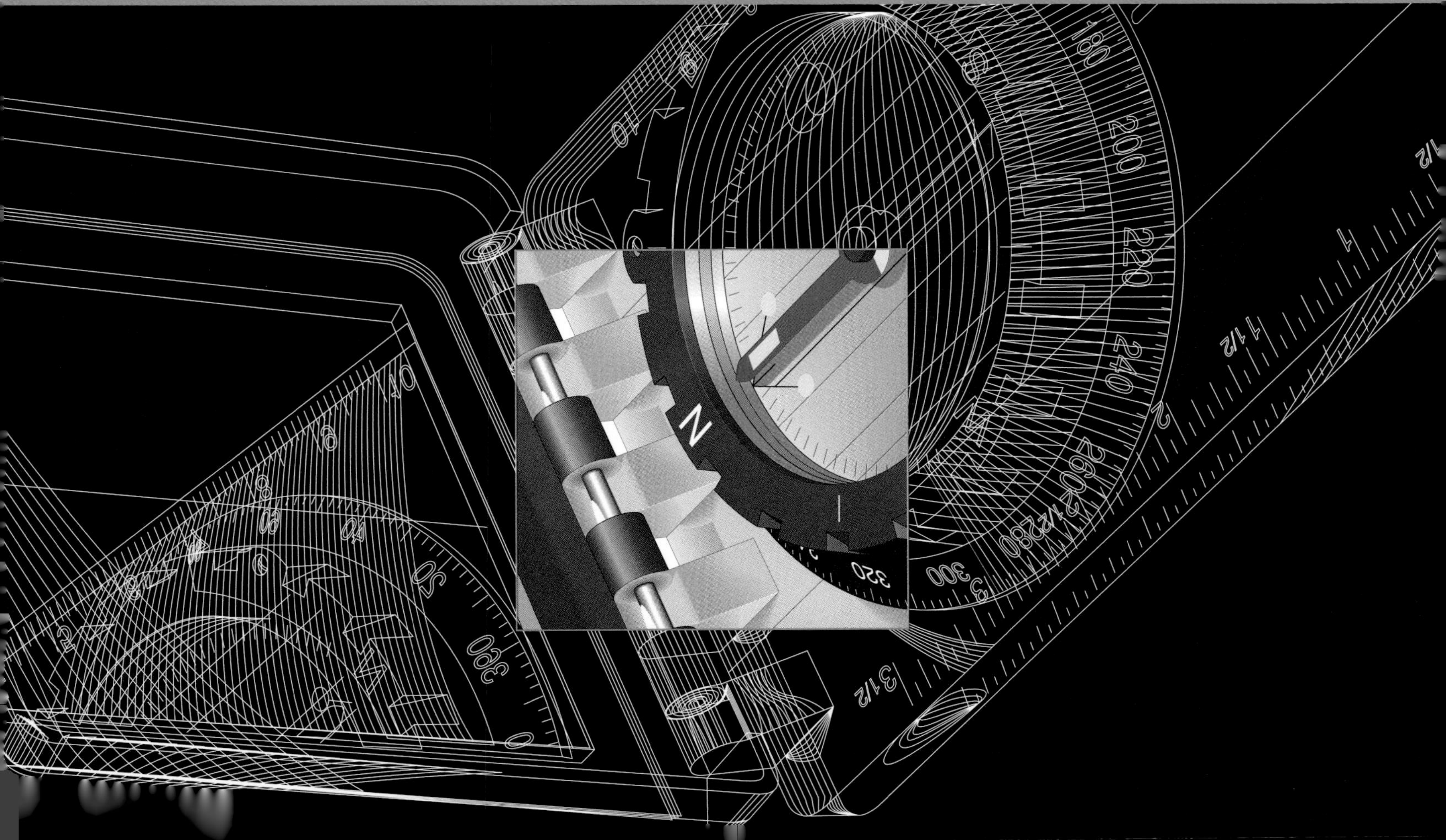

## SUMMARY

# ELECTRON MICROSCOPE
# MICROSCOPE[M] ÉLECTRONIQUE
# ELEKTRONENMIKROSKOP[N]
# MICROSCOPIO[M] DE ELECTRONES

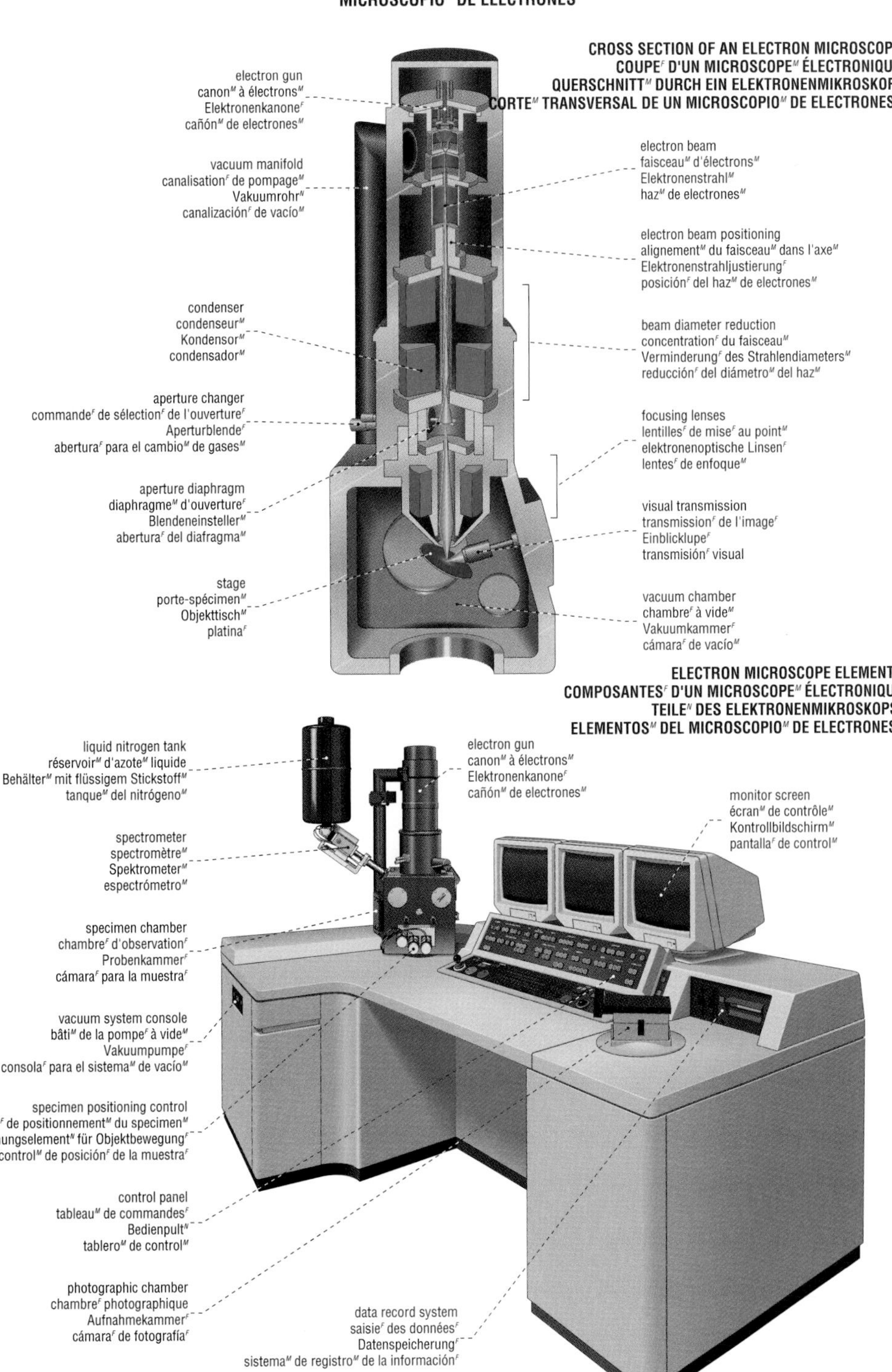

## BINOCULAR MICROSCOPE
## MICROSCOPE[M] BINOCULAIRE
## BINOKULARMIKROSKOP[N]
## MICROSCOPIO[M] BINOCULAR

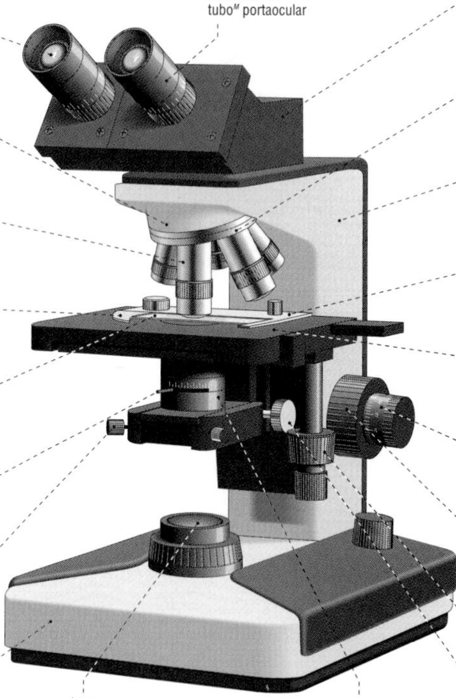

eyepiece
oculaire[M]
Okular[N]
ocular[M]
limb top
porte-tube[M]
Tubusträger[M]
portatubo[M]
objective
objectif[M]
Objektiv[N]
objetivo[M]
stage clip
valet[M]
Objektklammer[F]
sujetador[M]
glass slide
lame[F] porte-objet[M]
Glasscheibe[F]
portaobjetos[M]
field lens adjustment
réglage[M] du diaphragme[M]
Feldlinseneinstellung[F]
ajuste[M] de la lente[M] de campo[M]
condenser adjustment knob
vis[F] de réglage[M] du condenseur[M]
Kondensoreinstellung[F]
tornillo[M] de ajuste[M] del condensador[M]
base
pied[M]
Fuß[M]
pie[M]
lamp
lampe[F]
Lampe[F]
lámpara[F]
draw tube
tube[M] porte-oculaire[M]
Okulartubus[M]
tubo[M] portaocular
condenser
condenseur[M]
Kondensor[M]
condensador[M]
body tube
corps[M]
Tubus[M]
tubo[M] binocular
revolving nosepiece
tourelle[F] porte-objectifs[M]
Objektivrevolver[M]
portaobjetivo[M] rotatorio
arm
potence[F]
Stativ[N]
brazo[M]
mechanical stage
chariot[M]
Kreuztisch[M]
platina[F] mecánica
stage
platine[F]
Objekttisch[M]
platina[F]
fine adjustment knob
vis[F] micrométrique
Feintrieb[M]
botón[M] de ajuste[M] fino
coarse adjustment knob
vis[F] macrométrique
Grobtrieb[M]
botón[M] de ajuste[M] grueso
mechanical stage control
commande[F] du chariot[M]
Kreuztischeinstellung[F]
control[M] de la plataforma[F] corrediza
condenser height adjustment
réglage[M] en hauteur[F] du condenseur[M]
Kondensorhöhenverstellung[F]
ajuste[M] de la altura[F] del condensador[M]

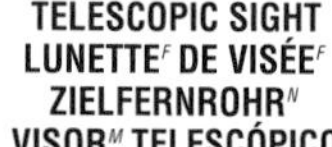

## TELESCOPIC SIGHT
## LUNETTE[F] DE VISÉE[F]
## ZIELFERNROHR[N]
## VISOR[M] TELESCÓPICO

reticle
réticule[M]
Fadenkreuz[N]
retícula[F]
erecting lenses
lentilles[F] de redressement[M]
Umkehrsystem[N]
lentes[F] de imágen[F] recta
elevation adjustment
réglage[M] de hausse[F]
Höheneinstellung[F]
ajuste[M] de elevación[F]
main scope tube
tube[M]
Tubus[M]
tubo[M] principal de observación[F]
objective lens
lentille[F] objectif[M]
Objektiv[N]
objetivo[M]
eyepiece
oculaire[M]
Okular[N]
ocular[M]
field lens
lentille[F] de champ[M]
Feldlinse[F]
lente[F] de campo[M]
dovetail
glissière[F] de fixation[F]
Befestigungsschiene[F]
cremallera[F] de fijación[F]
turret cap
capuchon[M] de protection[F]
Schutzkappe[F]
capuchón[M] de protección[F]
winding adjustment
réglage[M] latéral
Spielraumeinstellung[F]
huelgo[M] de ajuste[M]

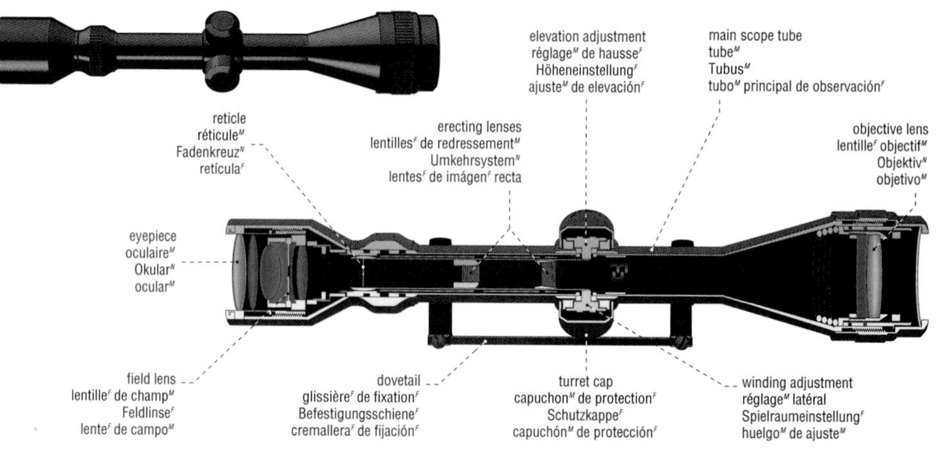

## PRISM BINOCULARS
## JUMELLES[F] À PRISMES[M]
## PRISMENFERNGLAS[N]
## PRISMÁTICOS[M] BINOCULARES

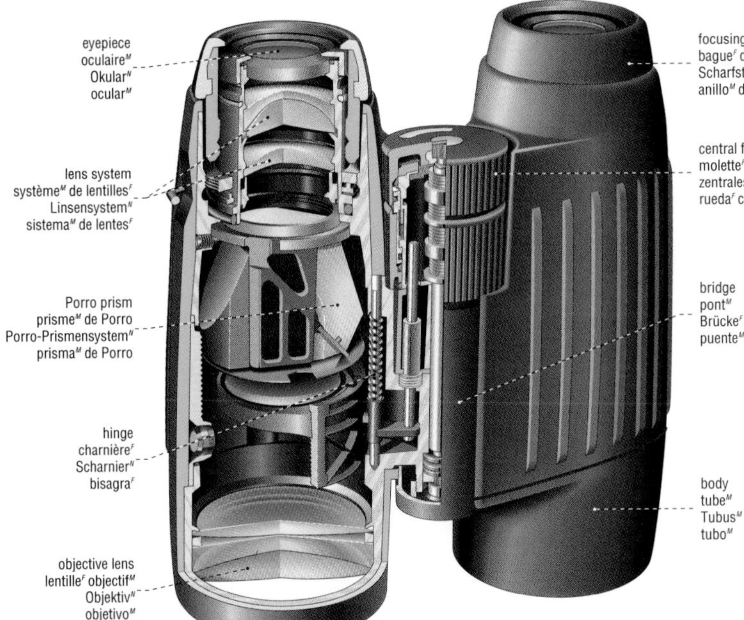


## MAGNETIC COMPASS
## BOUSSOLE[F] MAGNÉTIQUE
## MAGNETKOMPASS[M]
## BRÚJULA[F] MAGNÉTICA

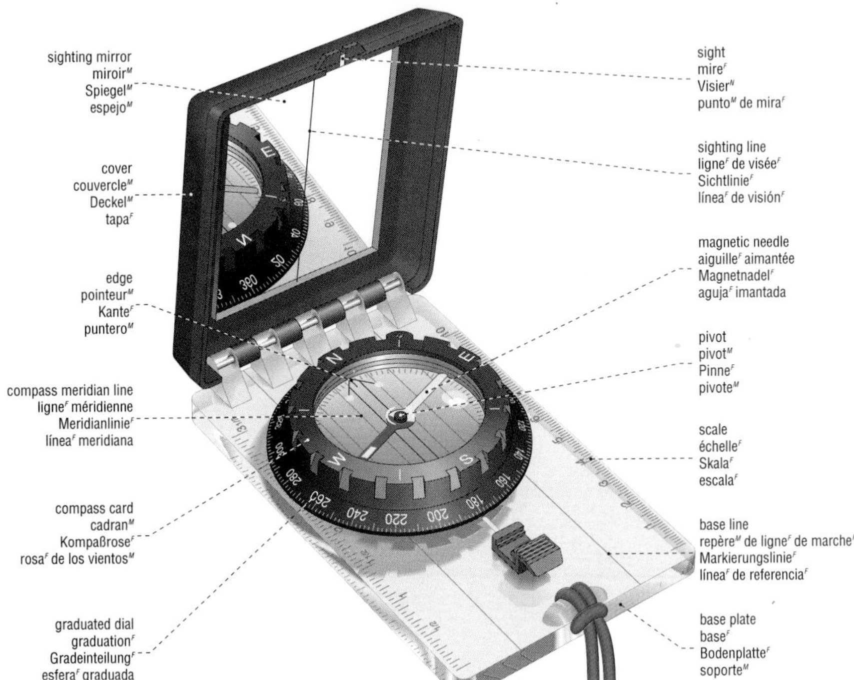

# REFLECTING TELESCOPE
# TÉLESCOPE[M]
# SPIEGELTELESKOP[N]
# TELESCOPIO[M] REFLECTOR

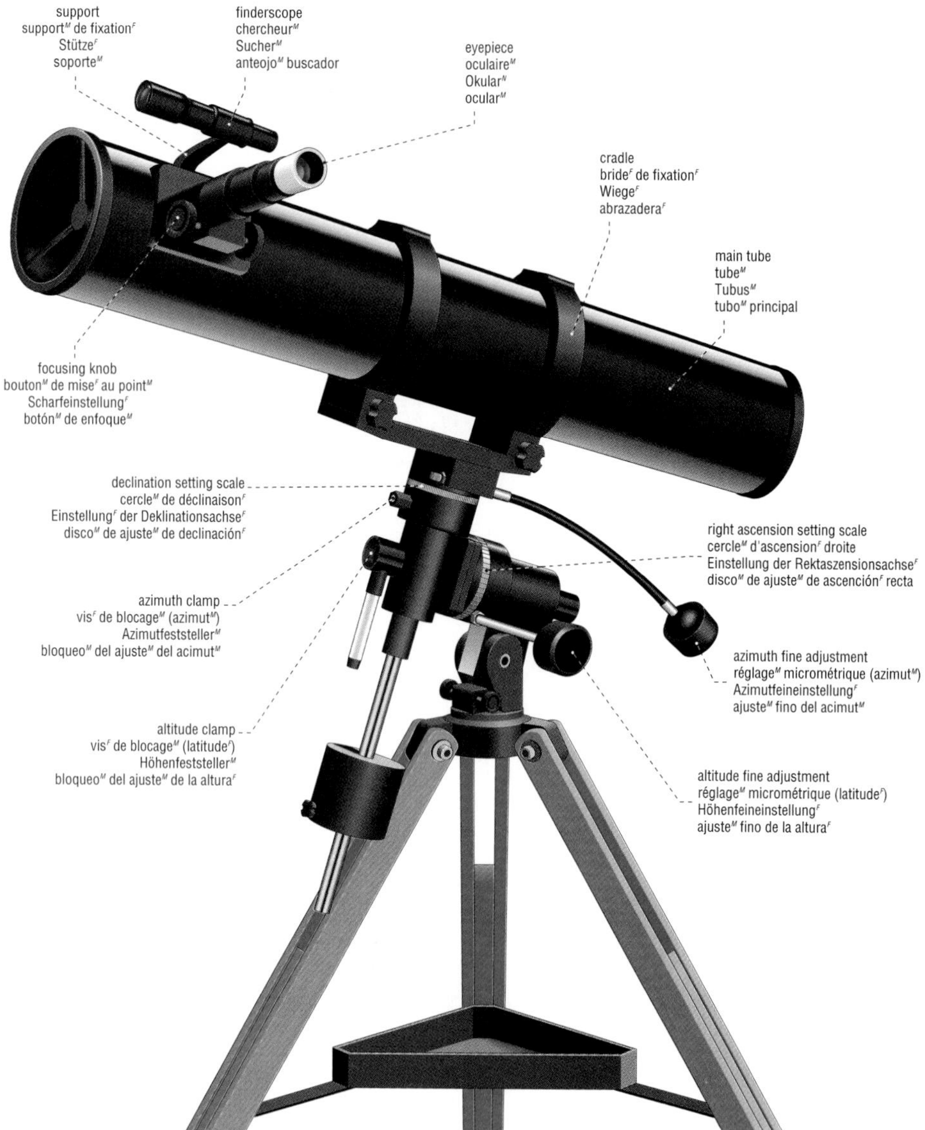

support
support[M] de fixation[F]
Stütze[F]
soporte[M]
finderscope
chercheur[M]
Sucher[M]
anteojo[M] buscador
eyepiece
oculaire[M]
Okular[N]
ocular[M]
cradle
bride[F] de fixation[F]
Wiege[F]
abrazadera[F]
main tube
tube[M]
Tubus[M]
tubo[M] principal
focusing knob
bouton[M] de mise[F] au point[M]
Scharfeinstellung[F]
botón[M] de enfoque[M]
declination setting scale
cercle[M] de déclinaison[F]
Einstellung[F] der Deklinationsachse[F]
disco[M] de ajuste[M] de declinación[F]
right ascension setting scale
cercle[M] d'ascension[F] droite
Einstellung der Rektaszensionsachse[F]
disco[M] de ajuste[M] de ascención[F] recta
azimuth clamp
vis[F] de blocage[M] (azimut[M])
Azimutfeststeller[M]
bloqueo[M] del ajuste[M] del acimut[M]
azimuth fine adjustment
réglage[M] micrométrique (azimut[M])
Azimutfeineinstellung[F]
ajuste[M] fino del acimut[M]
altitude clamp
vis[F] de blocage[M] (latitude[F])
Höhenfeststeller[M]
bloqueo[M] del ajuste[M] de la altura[F]
altitude fine adjustment
réglage[M] micrométrique (latitude[F])
Höhenfeineinstellung[F]
ajuste[M] fino de la altura[F]

## CROSS SECTION OF A REFLECTING TELESCOPE
## COUPE[F] D'UN TÉLESCOPE[M]
## QUERSCHNITT[M] DURCH EIN SPIEGELTELESKOP[N]
## CORTE[M] TRANSVERSAL DE UN TELECOPIO[M] REFLECTOR

main tube
tube[M]
Tubus[M]
tubo[M] principal
eyepiece
oculaire[M]
Okular[N]
ocular[M]
light
lumière[F]
Licht[N]
luz[F]
flat mirror
miroir[M] plan[M]
Umlenkspiegel[M]
espejo[M] plano
main mirror
miroir[M] primaire parabolique
Hauptspiegel[M]
espejo[M] principal

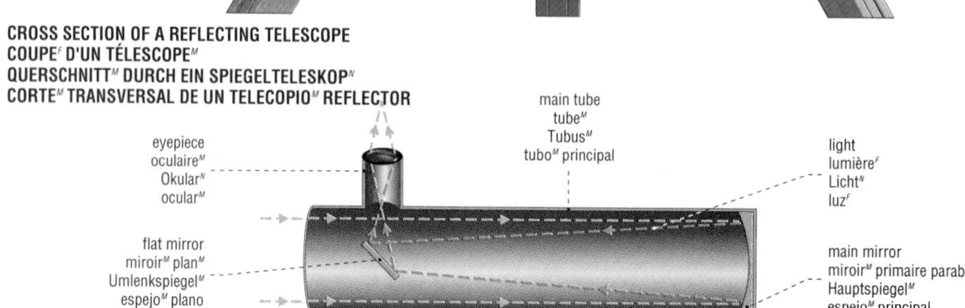

## REFRACTING TELESCOPE
## LUNETTE[F] ASTRONOMIQUE
## LINSENFERNROHR[N]
## TELESCOPIO[M] REFRACTOR

cradle
bride[F] de fixation[F]
Wiege[F]
abrazadera[F]
lens hood
pare-soleil[M]
Sonnenblende[F]
protección[F] contra el vaho[M]
objective lens
lentille[F] objectif[M]
Objektiv[N]
objetivo[M]
finderscope
chercheur[M]
Sucher[M]
anteojo[M] buscador
main tube
tube[M]
Tubus[M]
tubo[M] principal
eyepiece
oculaire[M]
Okular[N]
ocular[M]
eyepiece holder
tube[M] porte-oculaire[M]
Okularträger[M]
portaocular[M]
declination setting scale
cercle[M] de déclinaison[F]
Einstellung[F] der Deklinationsachse[F]
disco[M] de ajuste[M] de declinación[F]
star diagonal
oculaire[M] coudé
Coudé-Okular[N]
ocular[M] acodado
azimuth clamp
vis[F] de blocage[M] (azimut[M])
Azimutfesteller[M]
bloqueo[M] del ajuste[M] del acimut[M]
focusing knob
bouton[M] de mise[F] au point[M]
Scharfeinstellung[F]
botón[M] de enfoque[M]
altitude clamp
vis[F] de blocage[M] (latitude[F])
Höhenfeststeller[M]
bloqueo[M] del ajuste[M] de la altura[F]
azimuth fine adjustment
réglage[M] micrométrique (azimut[M])
Azimutfeineinstellung[F]
ajuste[M] fino del acimut[M]
right ascension setting scale
cercle[M] d'ascension[F] droite
Einstellung[F] der Rektaszensionsachse[F]
disco[M] de ajuste[M] de ascención[F] recta
altitude fine adjustment
réglage[M] micrométrique (latitude[F])
Höhenfeineinstellung[F]
ajuste[M] fino de la altura[F]
counterweight
contrepoids[M]
Massestück[N]
contrapeso[M]
fork
fourche[F]
Gabel[F]
horquilla[F]
tripod
trépied[M]
Stativ[N]
trípode[M]
tripod accessories shelf
plateau[M] pour accessoires[M]
Stativablage[F]
repisa[F] para accesorios[M]


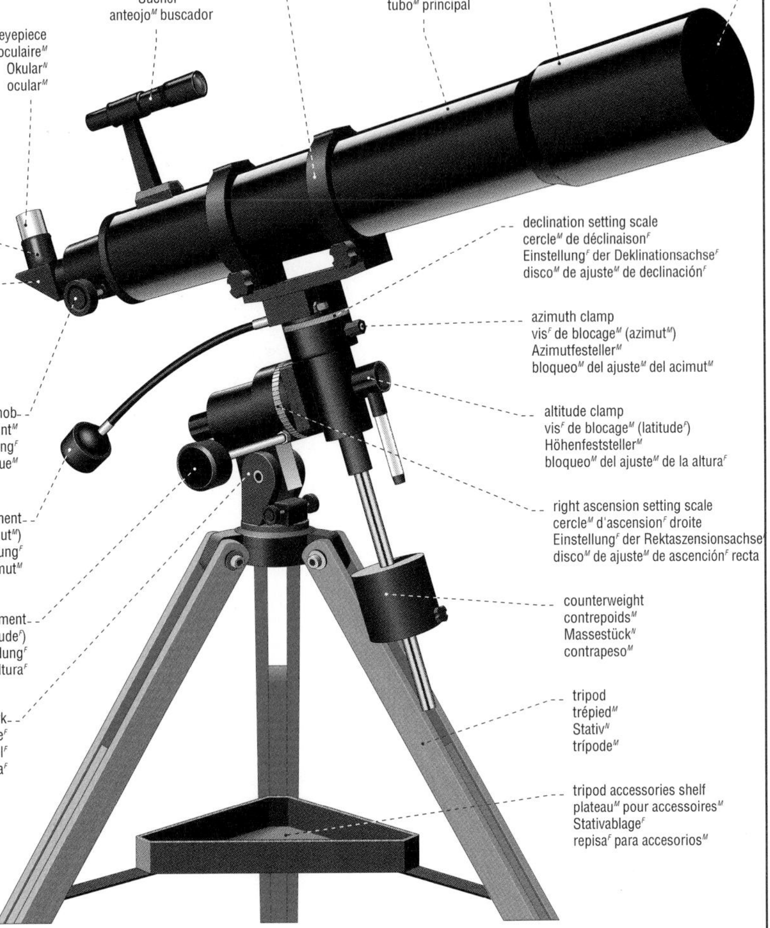

## CROSS SECTION OF A REFRACTING TELESCOPE
## COUPE[F] D'UNE LUNETTE[F] ASTRONOMIQUE
## QUERSCHNITT[M] DURCH EIN LINSENFERNROHR[N]
## CORTE[M] TRANSVERSAL DE UN TELESCOPIO[M] REFRACTOR

eyepiece
oculaire[M]
Okular[N]
ocular[M]
light
lumière[F]
Licht[N]
luz[F]
objective lens
lentille[F] objectif[M]
Objektiv[N]
objetivo[M]
main tube
tube[M]
Tubus[M]
tubo[M] principal

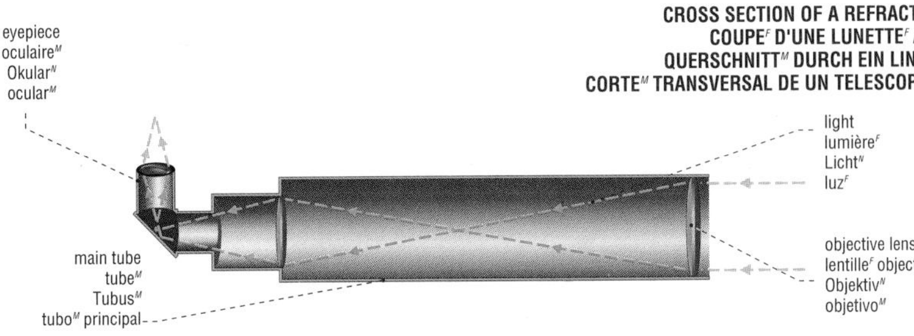

## LENSES
## LENTILLES^F
## LINSEN^F
## LENTES^F

### CONVERGING LENSES
### LENTILLES^F CONVERGENTES
### SAMMELLINSEN^F
### LENTES^F CONVERGENTES

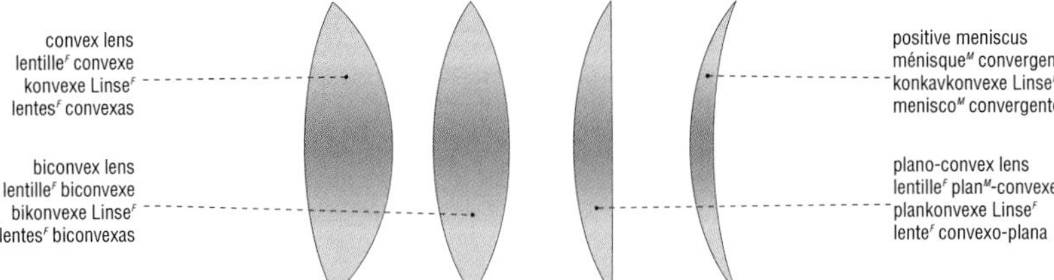


### DIVERGING LENSES
### LENTILLES^F DIVERGENTES
### ZERSTREUUNGSLINSEN^F
### LENTES^F DIVERGENTES

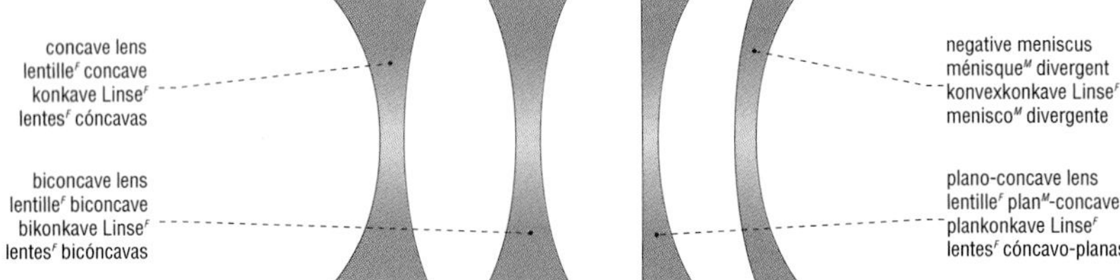


## RADAR
## RADAR^M
## RADAR^N
## RADAR^M

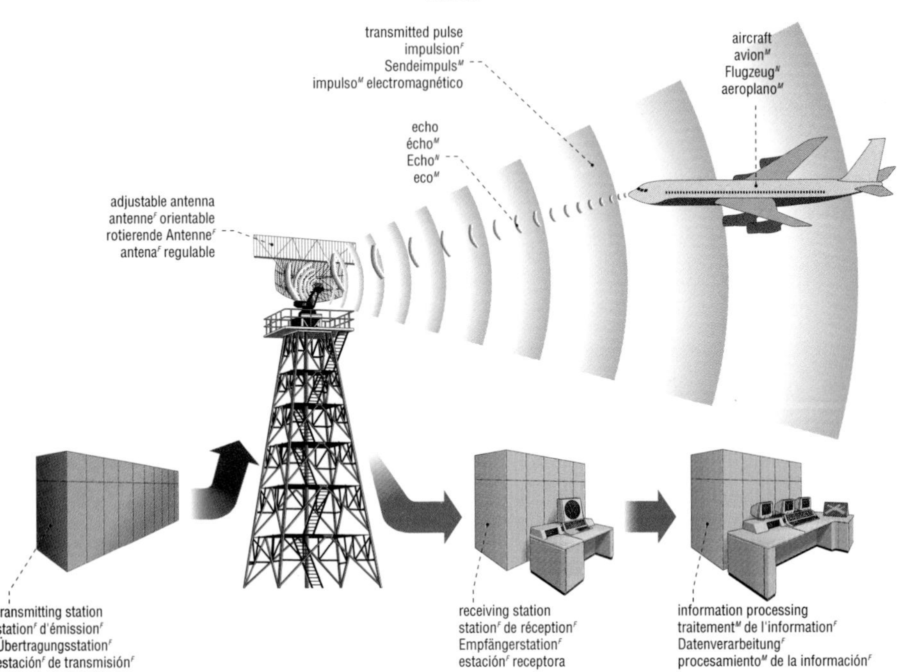

# HEALTH AND SAFETY
# SANTÉ ET SÉCURITÉ
# GESUNDHEIT UND UNFALLSCHUTZ
# SALUD Y SEGURIDAD

## SUMMARY

# FIRST AID KIT
# TROUSSE[F] DE SECOURS[M]
# ERSTE-HILFE-KASTEN[M]
# BOTIQUÍN[M] DE PRIMEROS AUXILIOS[M]

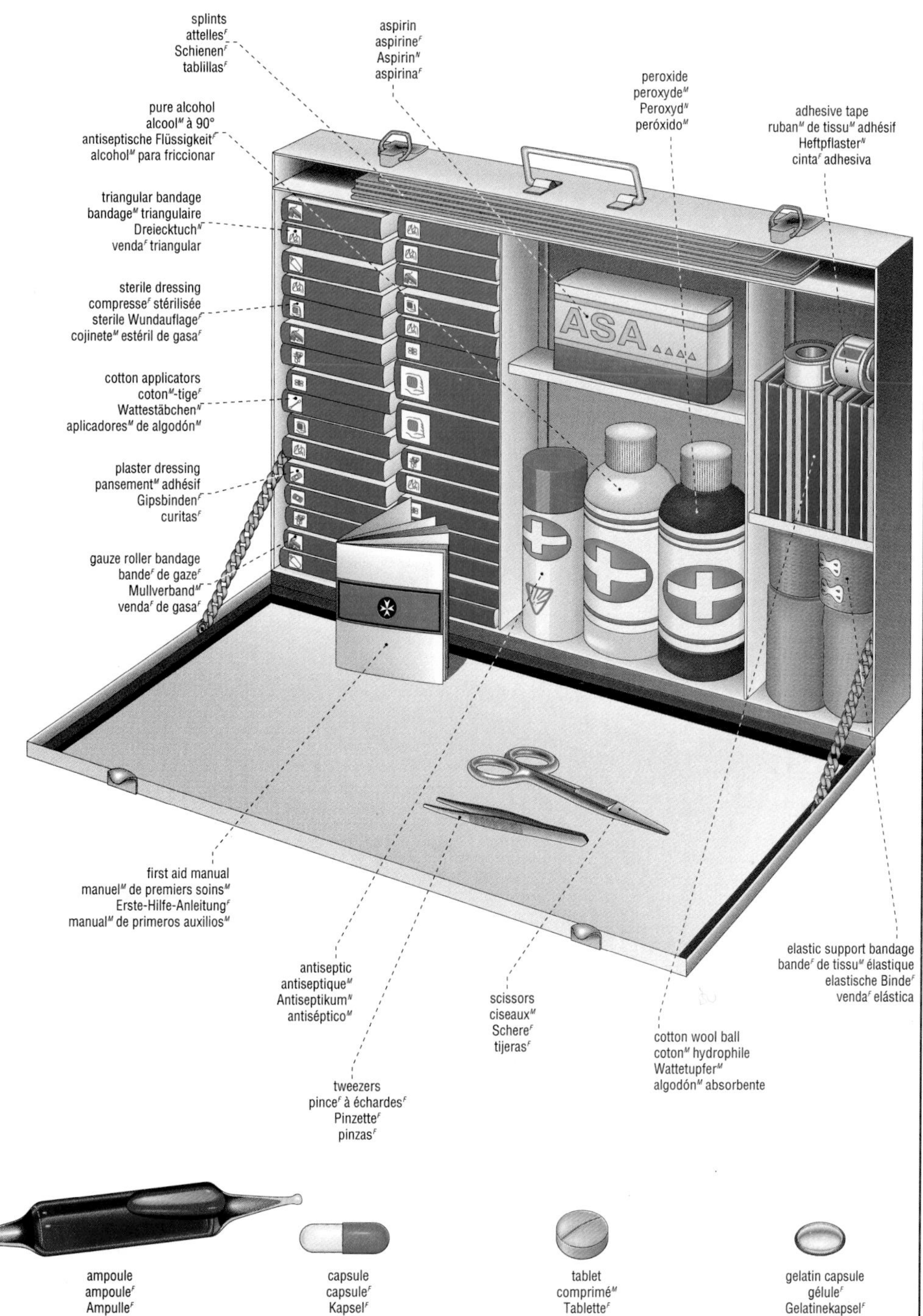

# FIRST AID EQUIPMENT
# MATÉRIEL[M] DE SECOURS[M]
# NOTFALLAUSRÜSTUNG[F]
# EQUIPO[M] DE PRIMEROS AUXILIOS[M]

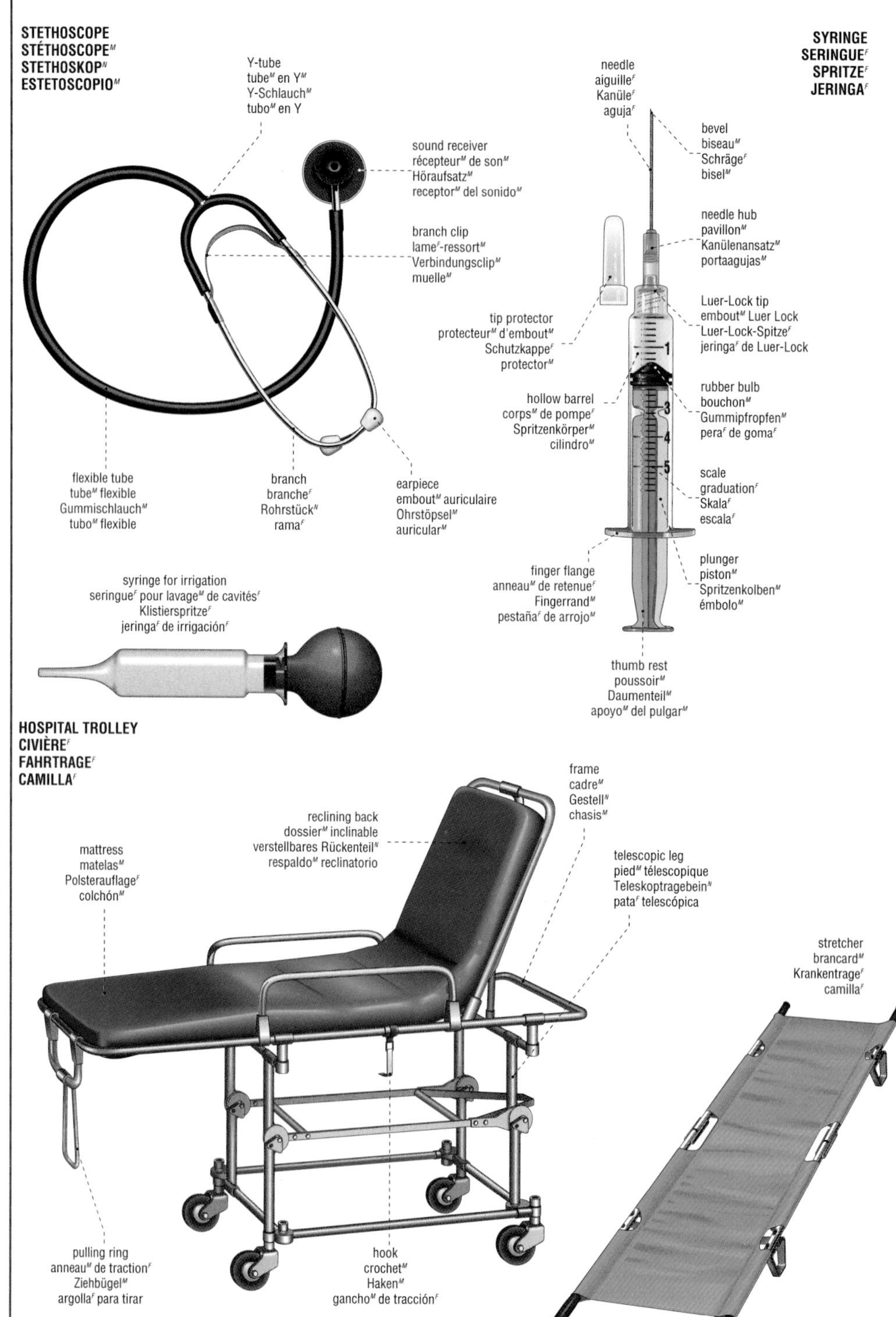

## WHEELCHAIR
## FAUTEUIL[M] ROULANT
## ROLLSTUHL[M]
## SILLA[F] DE RUEDAS[F]

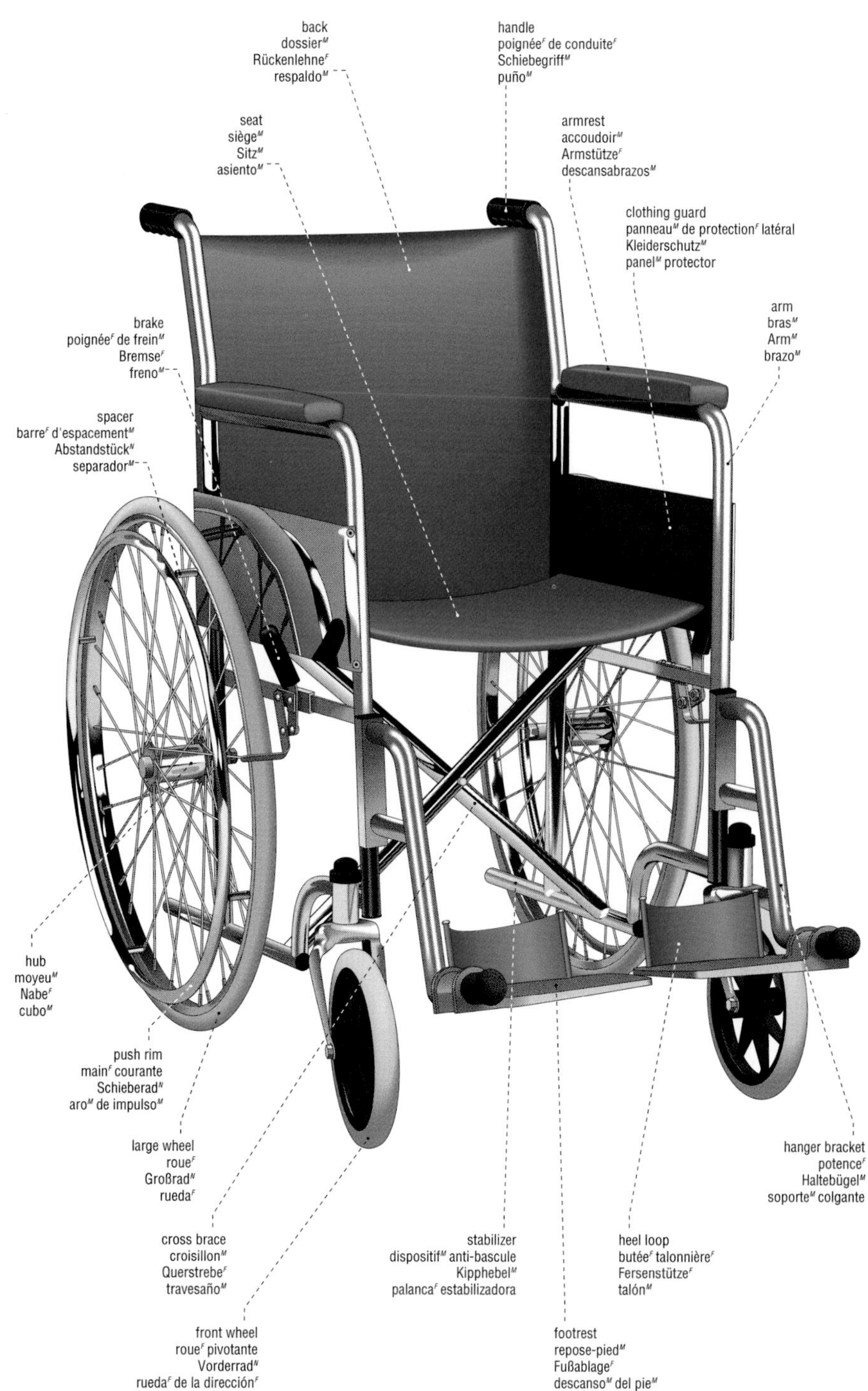

# WALKING AIDS
# AIDES$^{F}$ À LA MARCHE$^{F}$
# GEHHILFEN$^{F}$
# AUXILIARES$^{M}$ ORTOPÉDICOS PARA CAMINAR

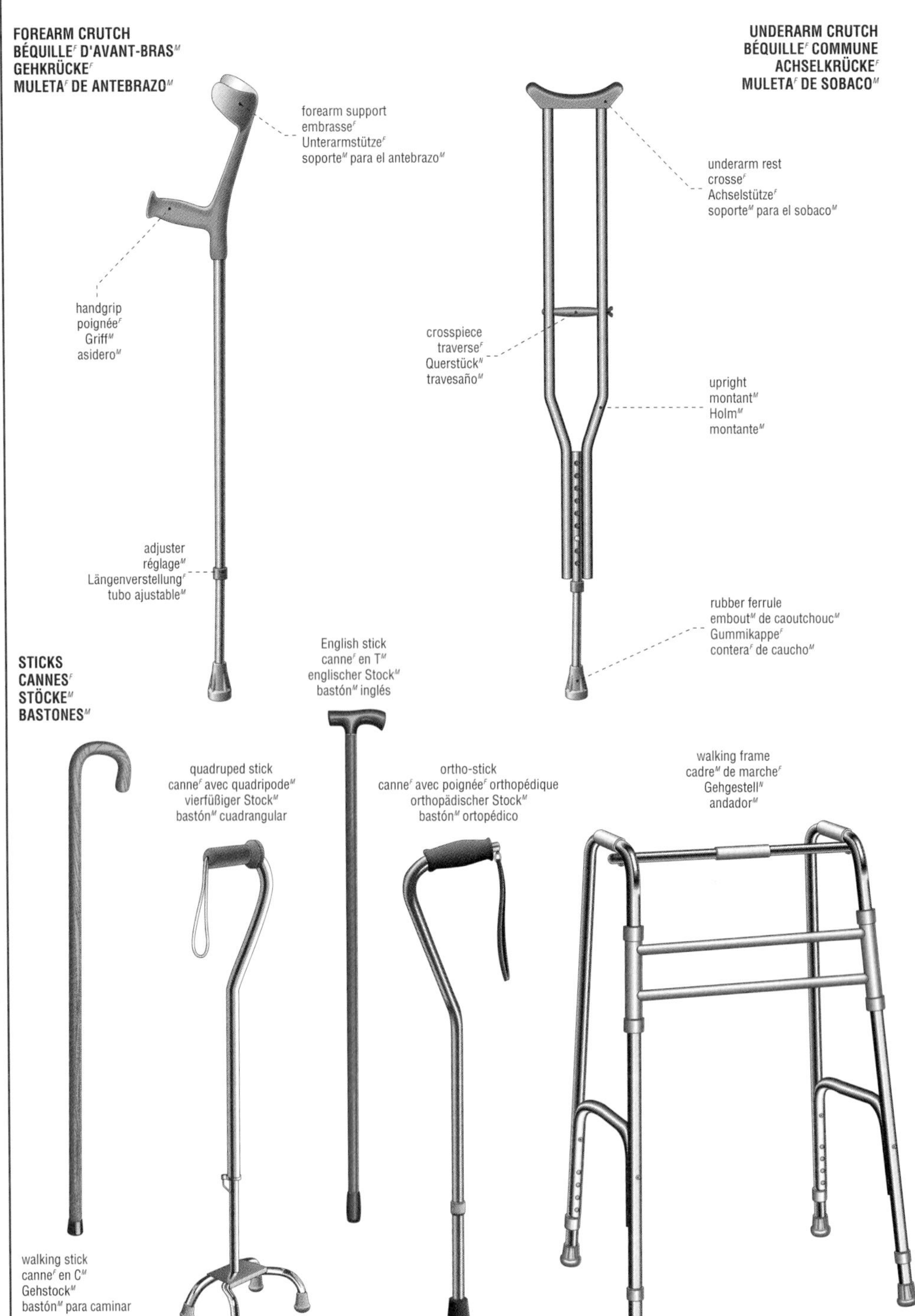

## EAR PROTECTION
## PROTECTION^F DE L'OUÏE^F
## GEHÖRSCHUTZ^M
## PROTECCIÓN^F PARA LOS OÍDOS^M

## EYE PROTECTION
## PROTECTION^F DES YEUX^M
## AUGENSCHUTZ^M
## PROTECCIÓN^F PARA LOS OJOS^M

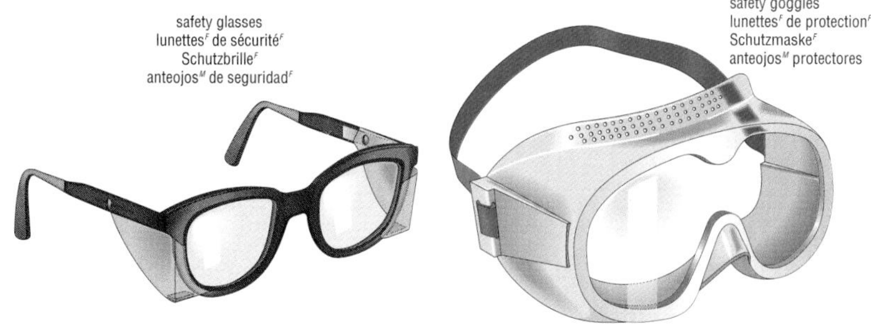


## HEAD PROTECTION
## PROTECTION^F DE LA TÊTE^F
## KOPFSCHUTZ^M
## PROTECCIÓN^F PARA LA CABEZA^F

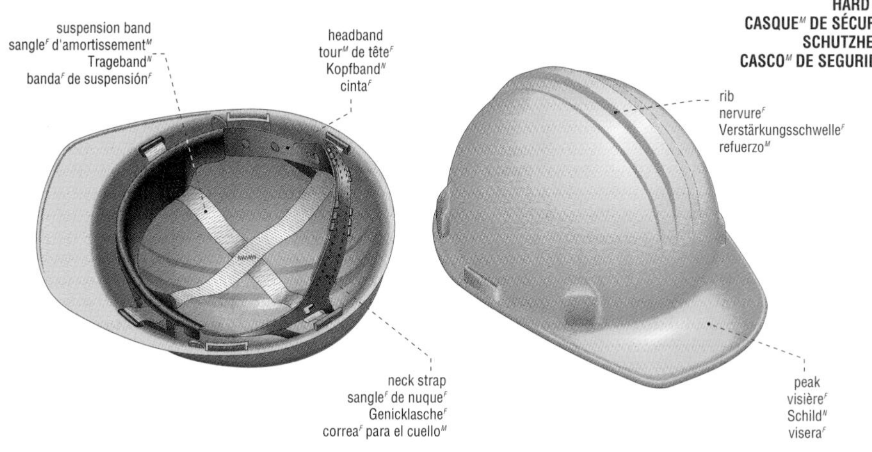

## RESPIRATORY SYSTEM PROTECTION
## PROTECTION[F] DES VOIES[F] RESPIRATOIRES
## ATEMSCHUTZ[M]
## PROTECCIÓN[F] PARA EL SISTEMA[M] RESPIRATORIO[M]

**RESPIRATOR**
**MASQUE[M] RESPIRATOIRE**
**GASMASKE[F]**
**MÁSCARA[F] DE GAS[M]**

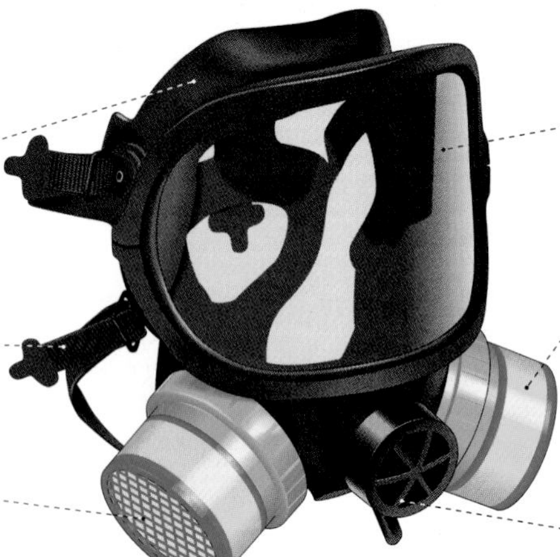

facepiece
jupe[F] de masque[M]
Gesichtsstück[N]
sección[F] frontal
head harness
jeu[M] de brides[F]
Trageriemen[M]
correas[F]
filter cover
couvre-filtre[M]
Filterabdeckung[F]
tapa[F] del filtro[M]
visor
oculaire[M]
Visier[N]
careta[F]
cartridge
cartouche[F]
Kartusche[F]
cartucho[M]
inhalation valve
soupape[F] inspiratoire
Einatemventil[N]
válvula[F] de inhalación[F]
exhalation valve
soupape[F] expiratoire
Ausatemventil[N]
válvula[F] de exhalación[F]

**HALF-MASK RESPIRATOR**
**MASQUE[M] BUCCO-NASAL**
**LEICHTE ATEMSCHUTZMASKE[F]**
**MÁSCARA[F] PARA EL POLVO[M]**

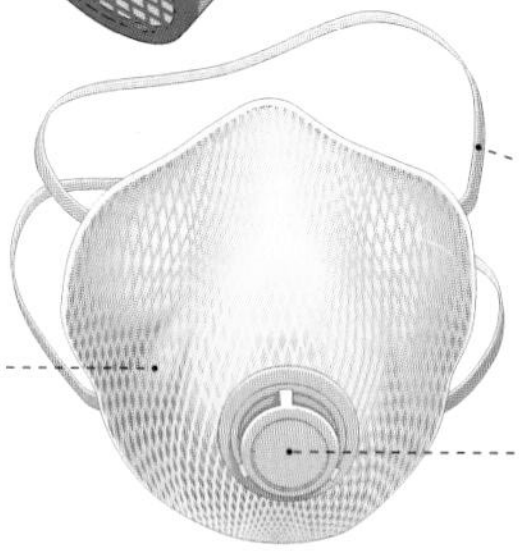

headband
serre-tête[M]
Kopfband[N]
cinta[F]
cup gasket
coupelle[F] d'étanchéité[F]
Maskendichtung[F]
mascarilla[F]
exhalation valve
soupape[F] expiratoire
Ausatemventil[N]
válvula[F] de exhalación[F]

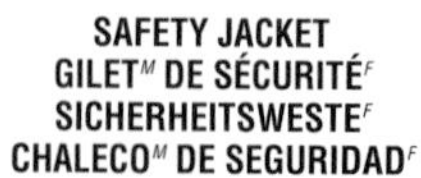

## SAFETY JACKET
## GILET[M] DE SÉCURITÉ[F]
## SICHERHEITSWESTE[F]
## CHALECO[M] DE SEGURIDAD[F]

reflective stripe
bande[F] réfléchissante
Leuchtstreifen[M]
banda[F] reflectora

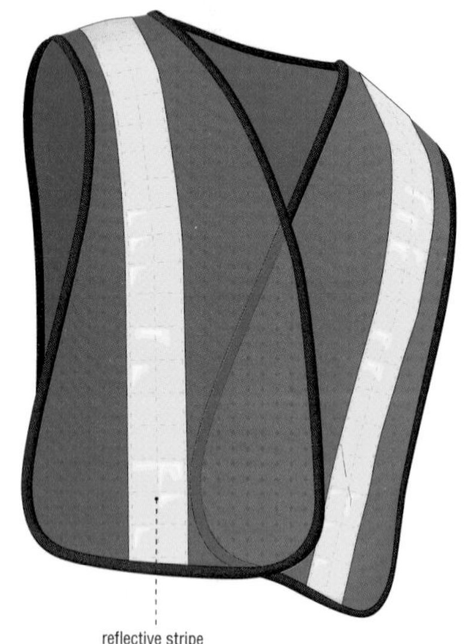

## FEET PROTECTION
## PROTECTION[F] DES PIEDS[M]
## FUSSSCHUTZ[M]
## PROTECCIÓN[F] PARA LOS PIES[M]

toe guard
protège-orteils[M]
Zehenschützer[M]
puntera[F] protectora

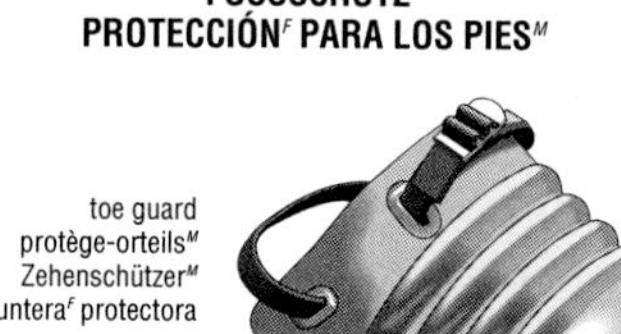

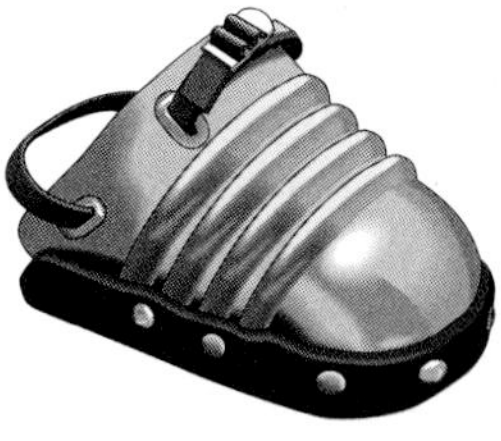

**SAFETY BOOT**
**BRODEQUIN[M] DE SÉCURITÉ[F]**
**SICHERHEITSSCHUH[M]**
**BOTA[F] DE SEGURIDAD[F]**

reinforced toe
embout[M] de protection[F]
Stahlkappe[F]
tope[M]

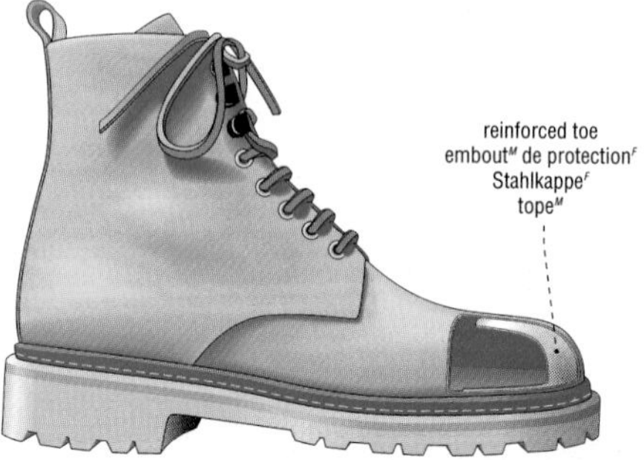

ENERGY ÉNERGIES ENERGIE ENERGÍA

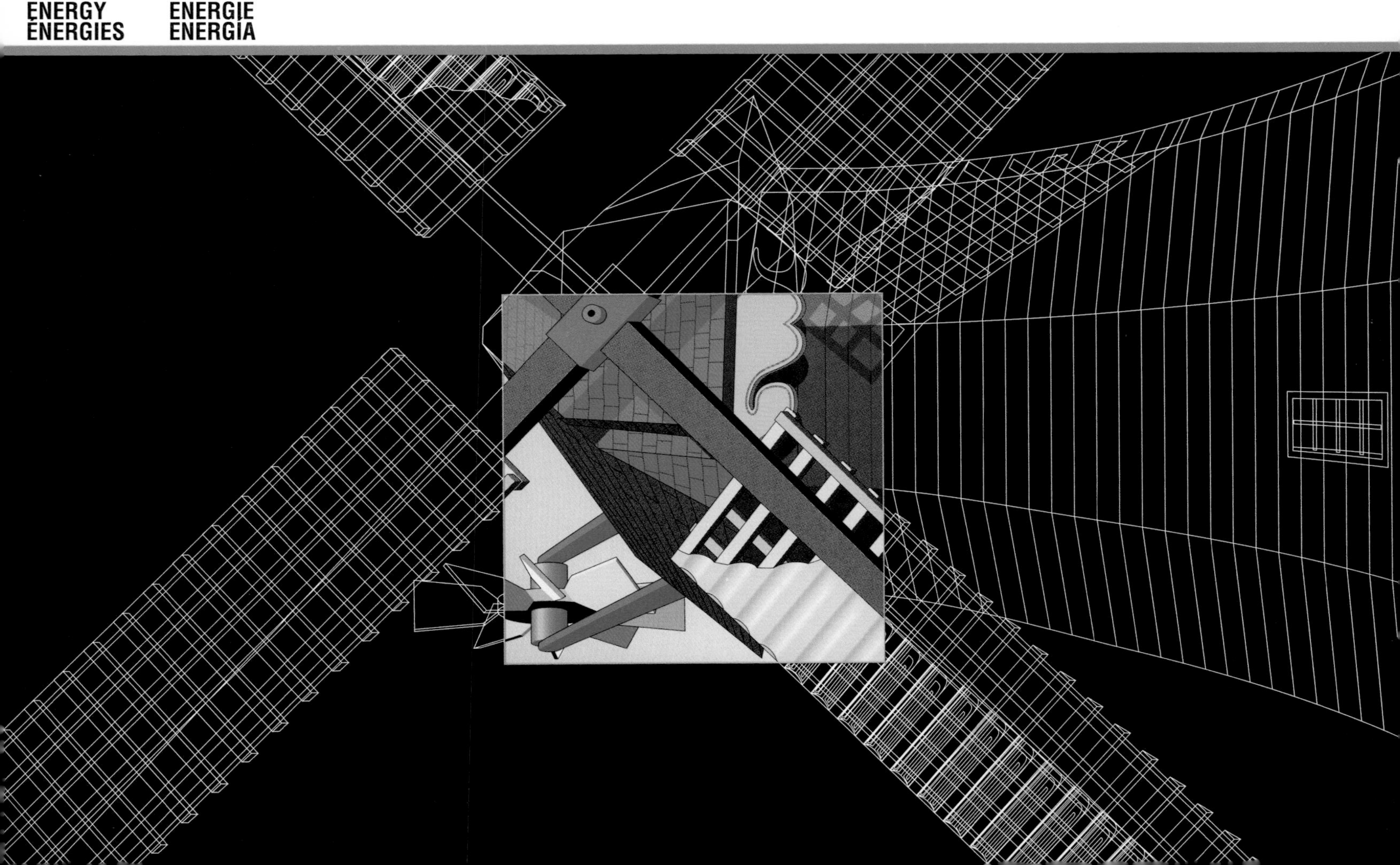

**SUMMARY**

# COAL MINE
# MINE[F] DE CHARBON[M]
# KOHLEBERGWERK[N]
# MINAS[F] DE CARBÓN[M]

## OPEN-PIT MINE
## CARRIÈRE[F] EN ENTONNOIR[M]
## OFFENE GRUBE[F]
## MINA[F] A CIELO[M] ABIERTO

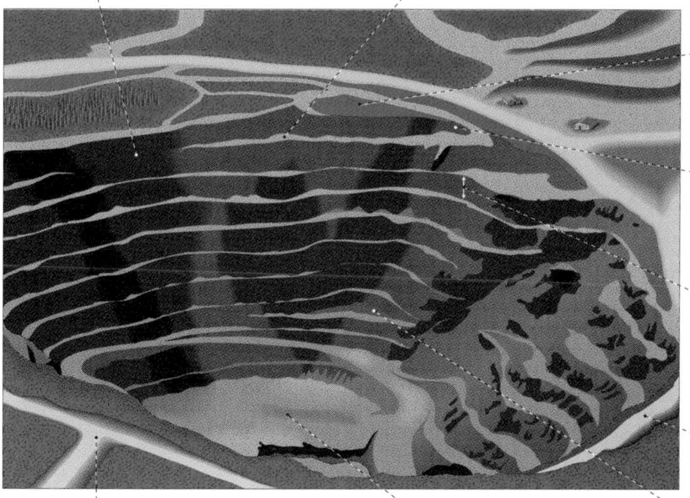

face
front[M] de taille[F]
Streb[M]
frente[M] de corte[M]
bench
gradin[M]
Bank[F]
antepecho[M]
ground surface
terrain[M] naturel
Erdoberfläche[F]
superficie[F] del terreno[M]
overburden
morts-terrains[M]
Obergestein[N]
relleno[M] exterior
bench height
hauteur[F] du gradin[M]
Bankhöhe[F]
altura[F] del antepecho[M]
ramp
rampe[F]
Rampe[F]
talud[M]
haulage road
voie[F] de transport[M]
Straße[F] für den Abtransport[M]
camino[M] de arrastrre[M]
crater
cratère[M]
Krater[M]
cráter[M]
ore
minerai[M]
Erz[N]
mineral[M]

## OPENCAST STRIP MINE
## CARRIÈRE[F] EXPLOITÉE EN CHASSANT
## ÜBERTAGEABBAU[M]
## EXCAVACIÓN[F] A CIELO[M] ABIERTO

dump
terril[M]
Bergehalde[F]
basurero[M]
conveyor
convoyeur[M]
Förderband[N]
banda[F] transportadora
mechanical shovel
pelle[F] mécanique
Standbagger[M]
pala[F] mecánica
bucket wheel excavator
excavatrice[F] à roue[F]
Schaufelradbagger[M]
excavadora[F] de rueda[F] de cangilones[M]
belt loader
sauterelle[F]
Ladeband[N]
banda[F] de carga[F]
overburden
morts-terrains[M]
Obergestein[N]
relleno exterior[M]
roof
toit[M] de la couche[F]
Dach[N]
terreno[M] de recubrimiento
trench
tranchée[F]
Graben[M]
zanja[F]
bulldozer
bouteur[M]
Bulldozer[M]
tractor[M] nivelador
face
front[M]
Streb[M]
frente[M] de corte[M]

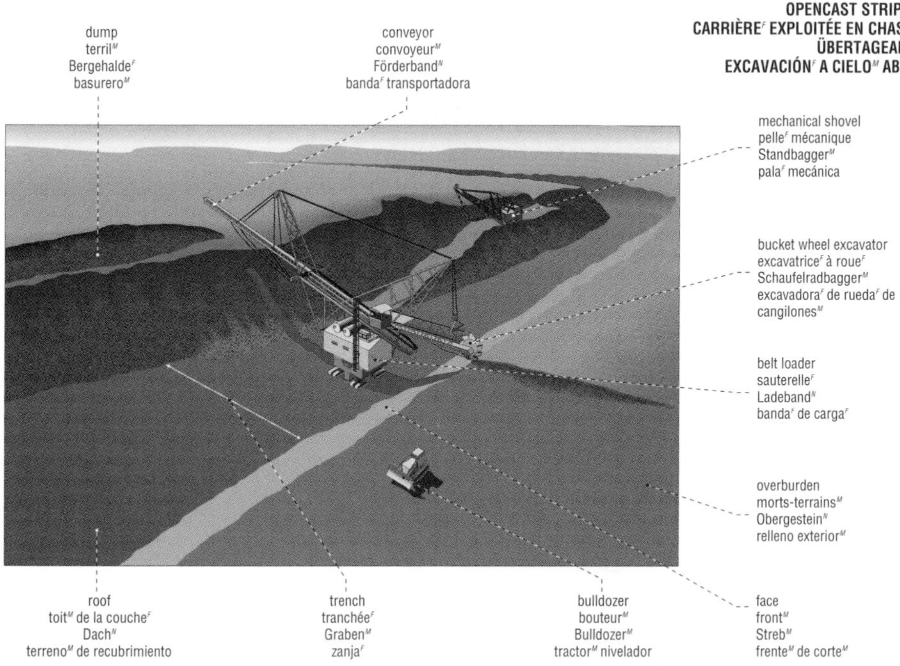

## COAL MINE
## MINE<sup>F</sup> DE CHARBON<sup>M</sup>
## KOHLEBERGWERK<sup>N</sup>
## MINA<sup>F</sup> DE CARBÓN<sup>M</sup> SUBTERRÁNEA

### JACKLEG DRILL
### MARTEAU<sup>M</sup> PERFORATEUR À POUSSOIR<sup>M</sup> PNEUMATIQUE
### BOHRHAMMER<sup>M</sup>
### TALADRO<sup>M</sup> DE POSTE<sup>M</sup> EXTENSIBLE

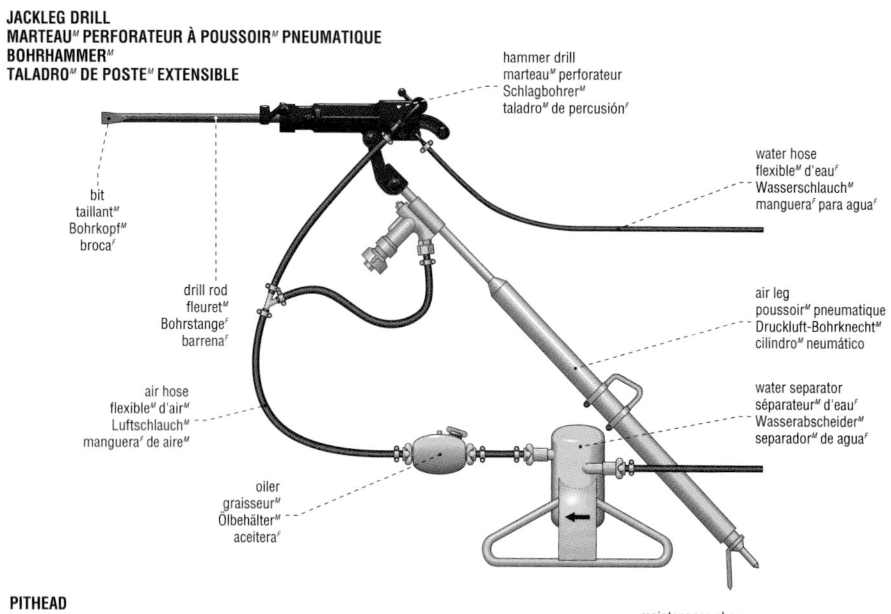


### PITHEAD
### CARREAU[M] DE MINE[F]
### ÜBERTAGEANLAGEN[F]
### PLANTA[F] EXTERIOR

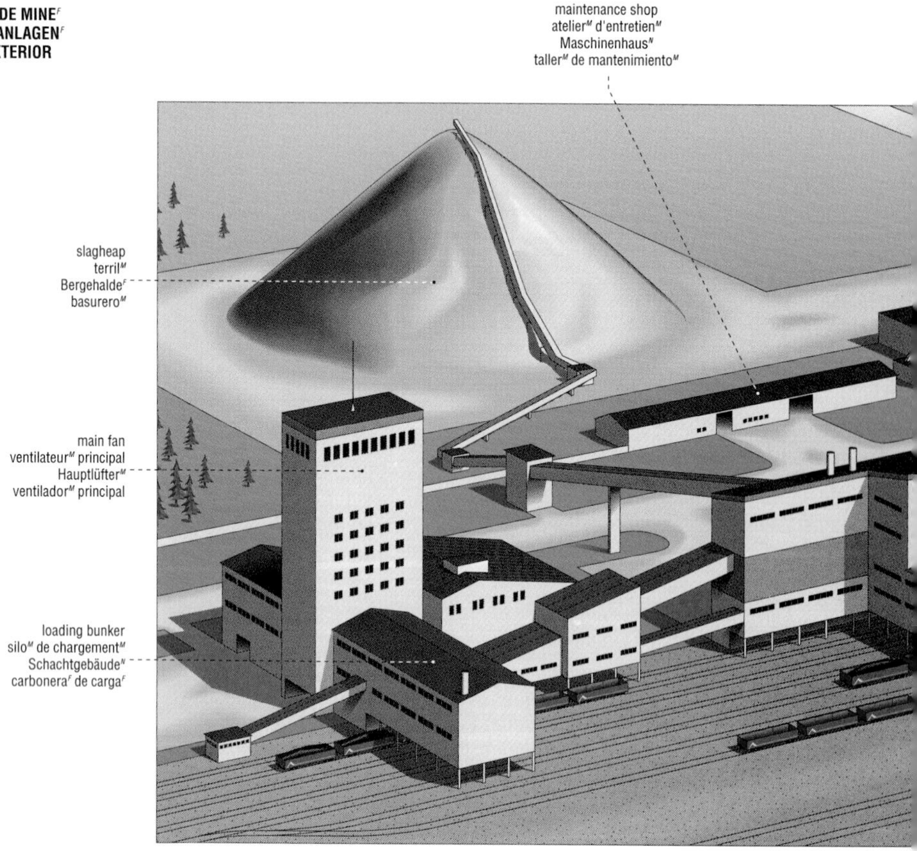

maintenance shop
atelier[M] d'entretien[M]
Maschinenhaus[N]
taller[M] de mantenimiento[M]

slagheap
terril[M]
Bergehalde[F]
basurero[M]

main fan
ventilateur[M] principal
Hauptlüfter[M]
ventilador[M] principal

loading bunker
silo[M] de chargement[M]
Schachtgebäude[N]
carbonera[F] de carga[F]

## PNEUMATIC DRILL
## MARTEAU[M] PNEUMATIQUE
## PRESSLUFTBOHRER[M]
## MARTILLO[M] NEUMÁTICO

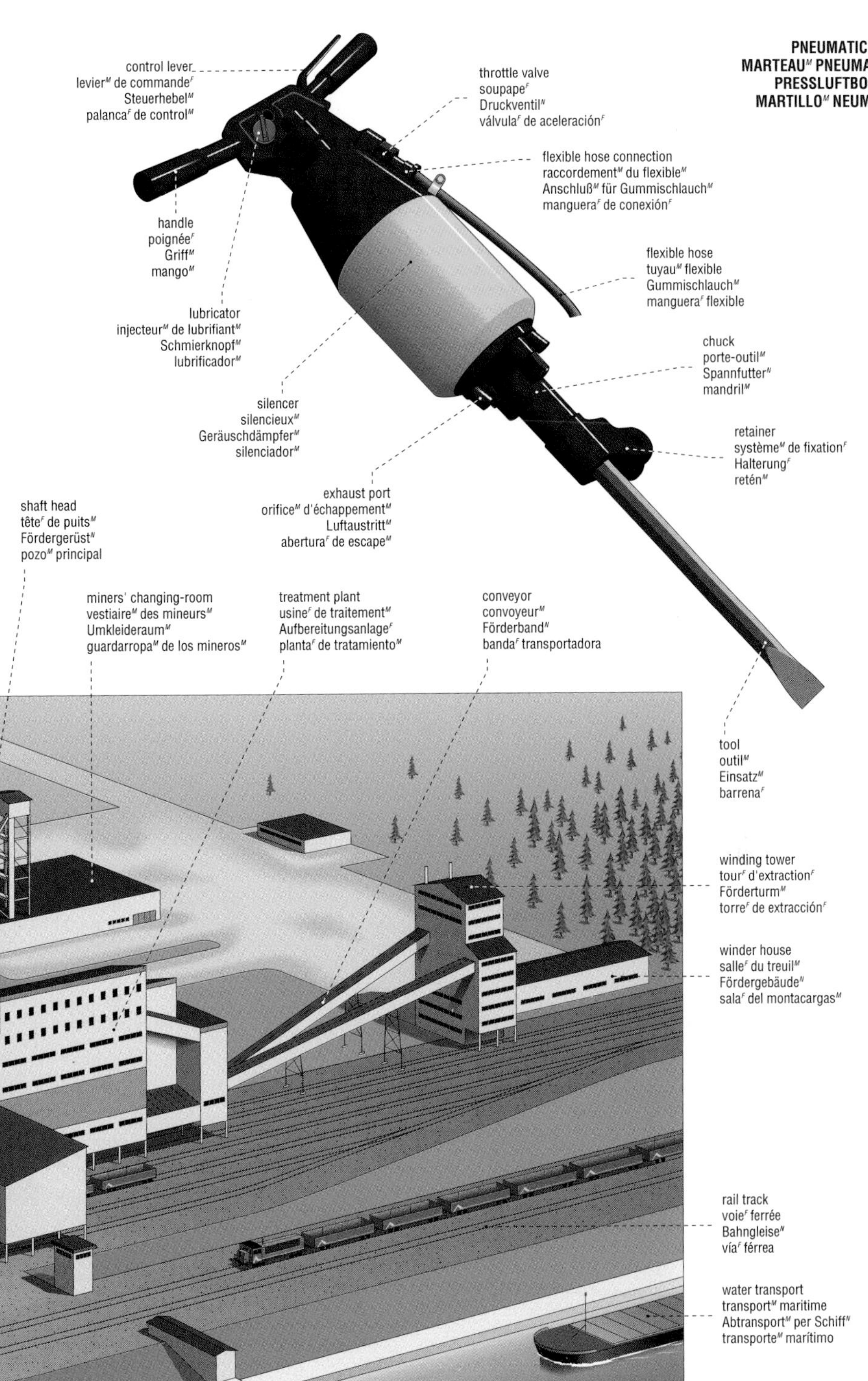

# COAL MINE
# MINE[F] DE CHARBON[M]
# KOHLEBERGWERK[N]
# MINA[F] DE CARBÓN[M]

## UNDERGROUND MINE
## MINE[F] SOUTERRAINE
## GRUBE[F]
## MINA[F] SUBTERRÁNEA

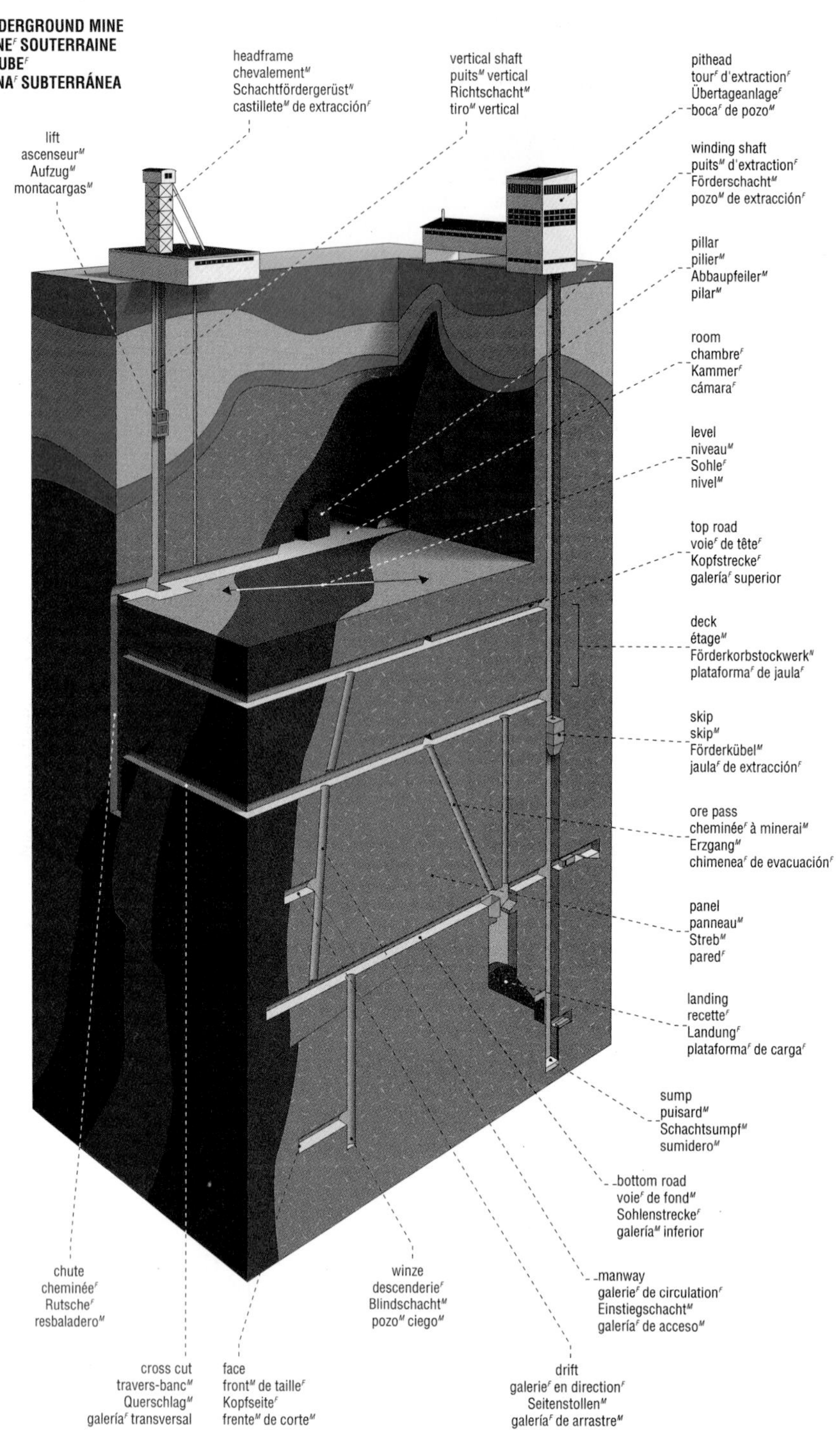

## OIL
## PÉTROLE$^{M}$
## ERDÖL$^{N}$
## PETRÓLEO$^{M}$

### DRILLING RIG
### APPAREIL$^{M}$ DE FORAGE$^{M}$
### BOHRANLAGE$^{F}$
### TORRE$^{F}$ DE PERFORACIÓN$^{F}$

### ROTARY SYSTEM
### SYSTÈME$^{M}$ ROTARY
### DREHBOHRVERFAHREN$^{F}$
### SISTEMA$^{M}$ ROTATIVO

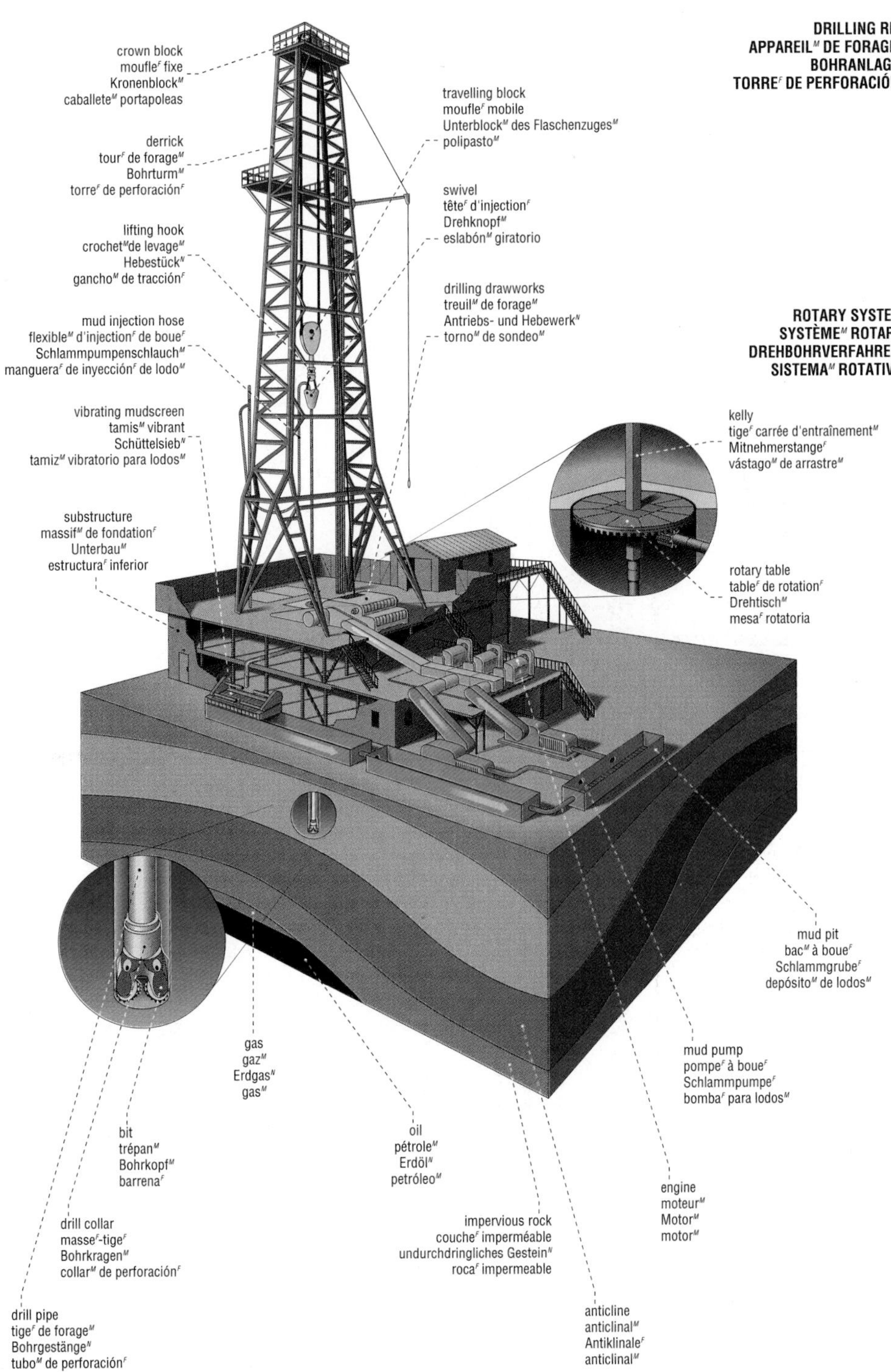

# OIL
# PÉTROLE[M]
# ERDÖL[N]
# PETRÓLEO[M]

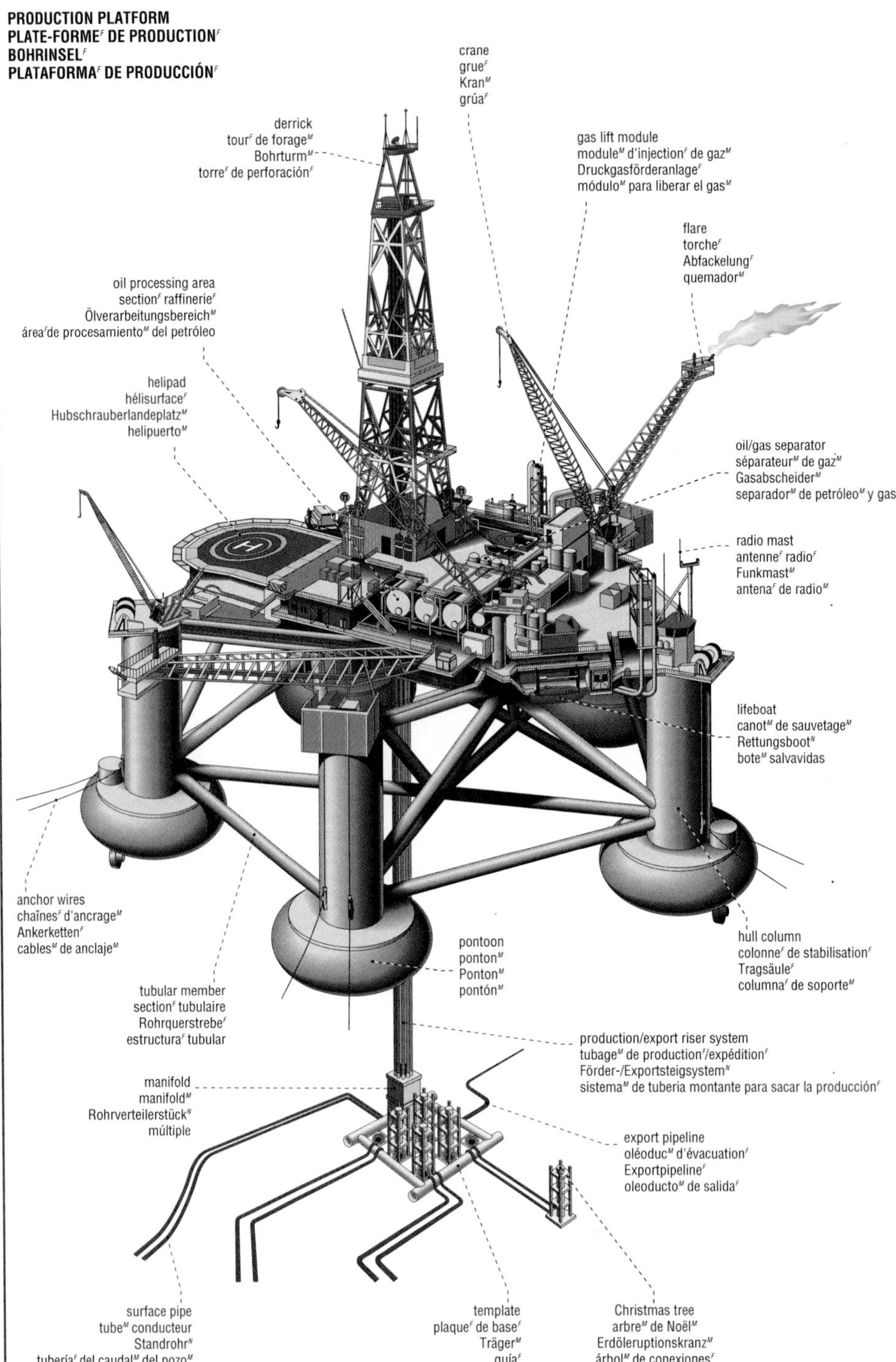

# OFFSHORE DRILLING
# FORAGE^M EN MER^F
# BOHREN^N VOR DER MEERESKÜSTE^F
# PERFORACIÓN^F MARINA

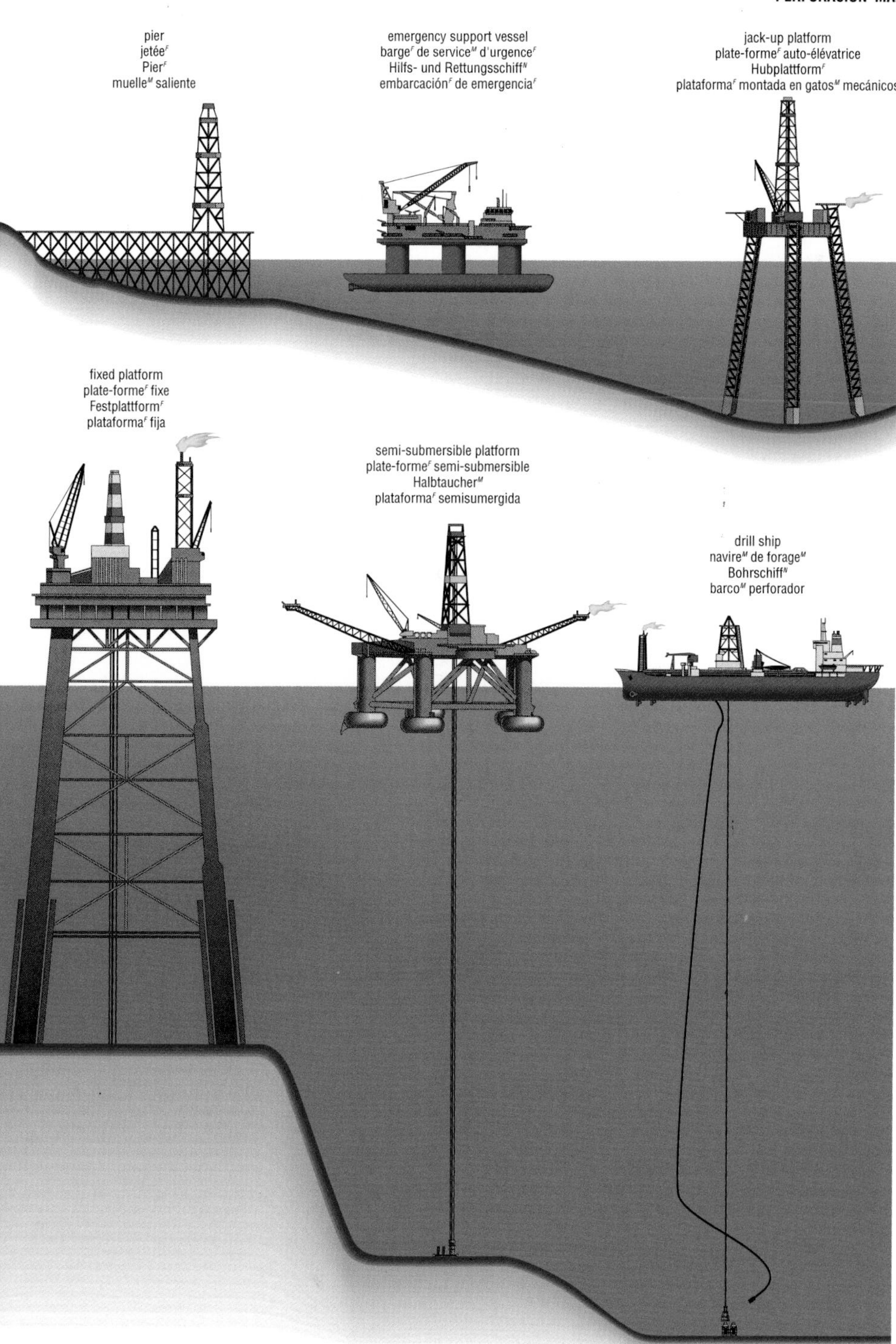

# OIL
# PÉTROLE[M]
# ERDÖL[N]
# PETRÓLEO[M]

## CHRISTMAS TREE
## ARBRE[M] DE NOËL[M]
## ERDÖLERUPTIONSKRANZ[M]
## ÁRBOL[M] DE CONEXIONES[F]

pressure gauge
manomètre[M]
Druckmesser[M]
manómetro[M]

flow bean
duse[F]
Eruptionsdüse[F]
reductor[M] de flujo[M]

master gate valve
vanne[F] maîtresse
Hauptschieber[M]
válvula[F] maestra

pipeline
oléoduc[M]
Pipeline[F]
oleoducto[M]

tubing head
tête[F] de puits[M]
Steigrohrkopf[M]
cabeza[F] de la tubería[F]

tubing valve
vanne[F] de production[F]
Steigrohrventil[N]
válvula[F] de la tubería[F]

tubing
colonne[F] de production[F]
Steigrohr[N]
tubería[F]

casing first string
tubage[M] de surface[F]
Rohrfahrteingang[M]
recubrimiento[M] de la primera tubería[F]

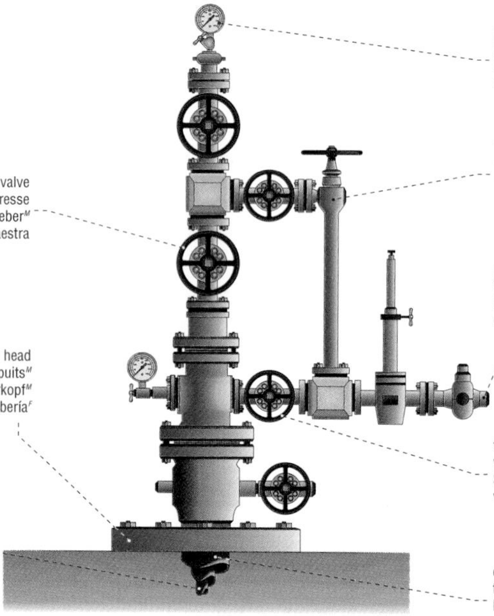

## CRUDE-OIL PIPELINE
## RÉSEAU[M] D'OLÉODUCS[M]
## ROHÖLPIPELINE[F]
## OLEODUCTO[M] PARA PETRÓLEO[M] CRUDO

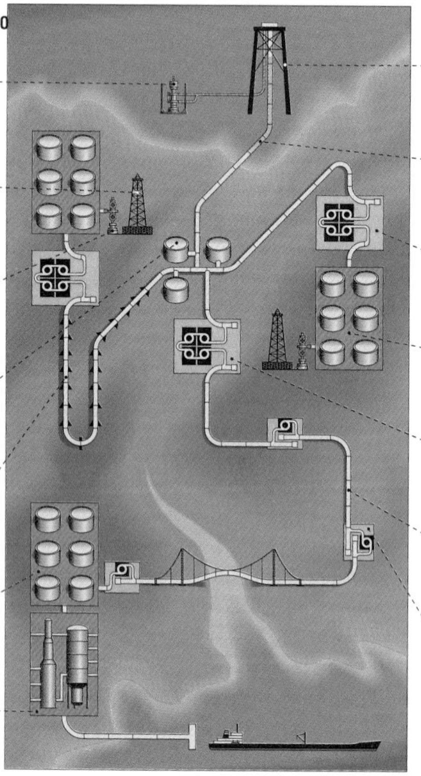

offshore well
puits[M] sous-marin
Bohranlage[F] vor der Meeresküste[F]
pozo[M] marino

production platform
plate-forme[F] de production[F]
Förderplattform[F]
plataforma[F] de producción[F]

derrick
tour[F] de forage[M]
Bohrturm[M]
torre[F] de perforación[F]

submarine pipeline
oléoduc[M] sous-marin
Unterwasserpipeline[F]
oleoducto[M] submarino

pumping station
station[F] de pompage[M]
Pumpstation[F]
planta[F] de bombeo[M]

Christmas tree
arbre[M] de Noël[M]
Erdöleruptionskranz[M]
árbol[M] de conexiones[F]

tank farm
parc[M] de stockage[M]
Tankanlage[F]
patio[M] de tanques[M]

buffer tank
réservoir[M] tampon[M]
Puffertank[M]
tanque[M] de regulación[F] de presión[F]

central pumping station
station[F] de pompage[M] principale
zentrale Pumpstation[F]
estación[F] central de bombeo[M]

aboveground pipeline
oléoduc[M] surélevé
überirdische Pipeline[F]
oleoducto[M] de superficie[F]

pipeline
oléoduc[M]
Pipeline[F]
oleoducto[M]

terminal
parc[M] de stockage[M] terminal
Erdölterminal[N]
terminal[M]

intermediate booster station
station[F] de pompage[M] intermédiaire
Druckverstärkerpumpanlage[F]
planta[F] intermedia de refuerzo[M]

refinery
raffinerie[F]
Raffinerie[F]
refinería[F]

## FIXED-ROOF TANK
## RÉSERVOIR^M À TOIT^M FIXE
## FESTDACHTANK^M
## TANQUE^M DE TECHO^M FIJO

## FLOATING-ROOF TANK
## RÉSERVOIR^M À TOIT^M FLOTTANT
## SCHWIMMDACHTANK^M
## TANQUE^M DE TECHO^M PONTÓN

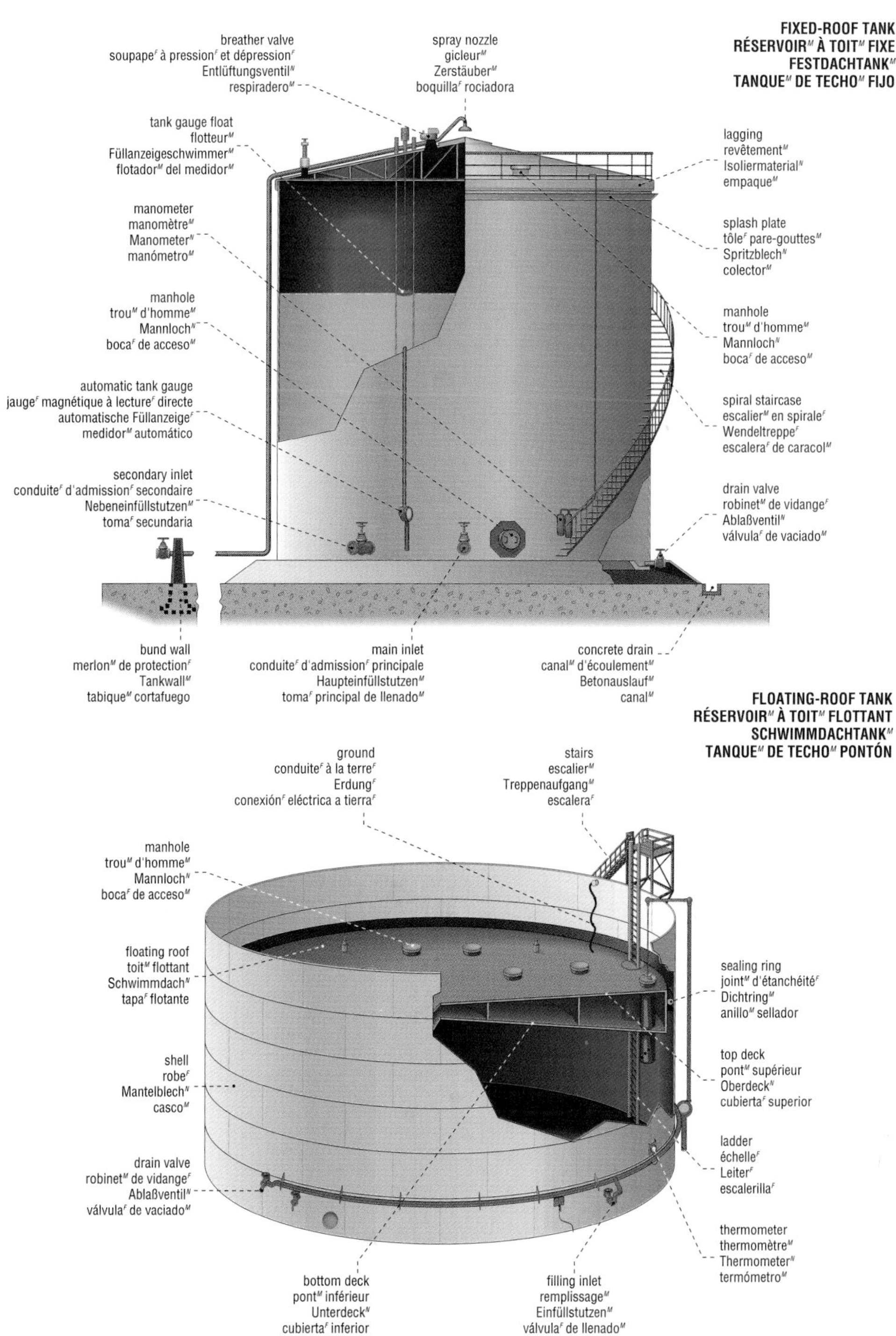

# OIL
# PÉTROLE^M
# ERDÖL^N
# PETRÓLEO^M

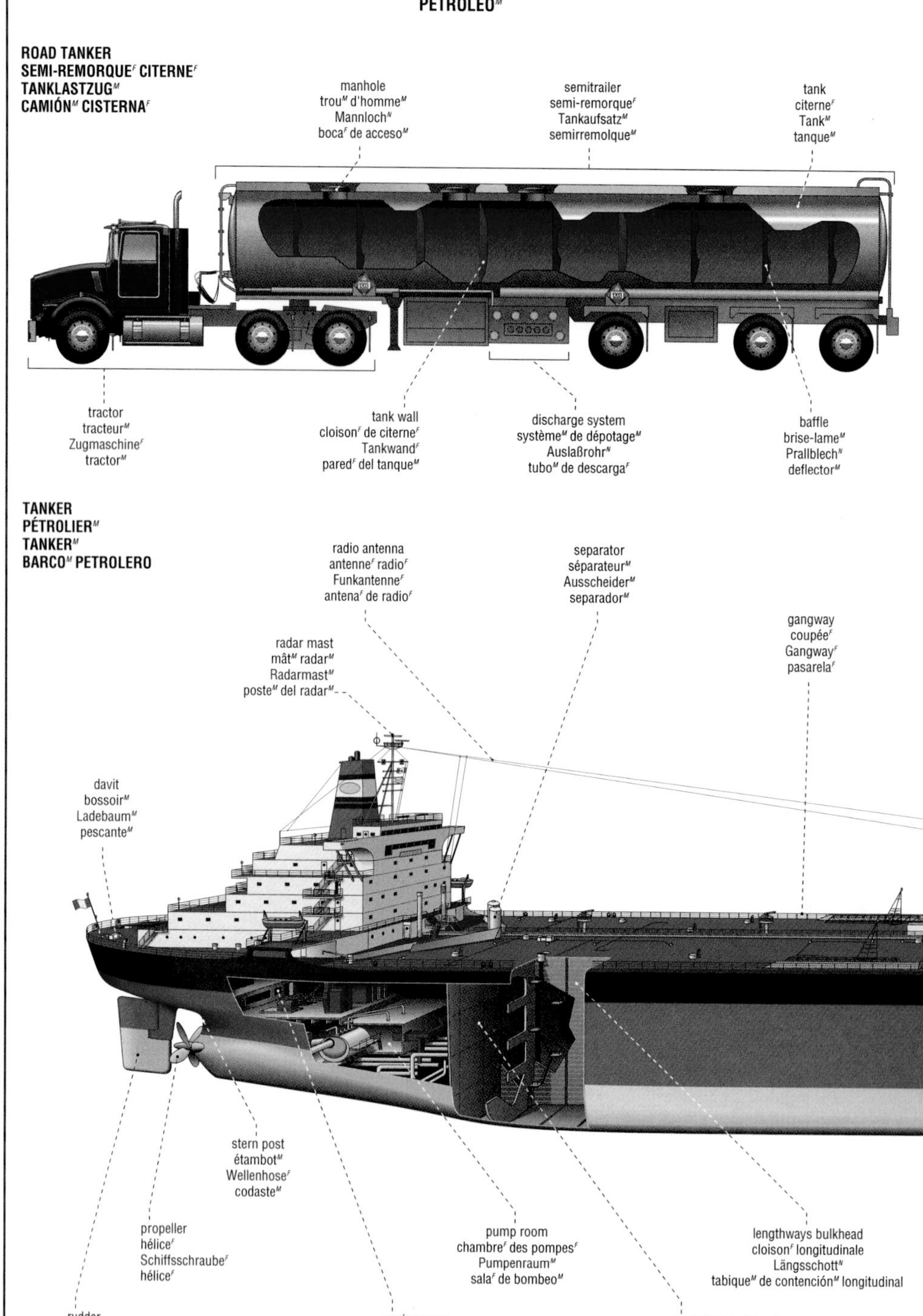

## TANK WAGON
## WAGON^M-CITERNE^F
## TANKANHÄNGER^M
## VAGÓN^M CISTERNA^F

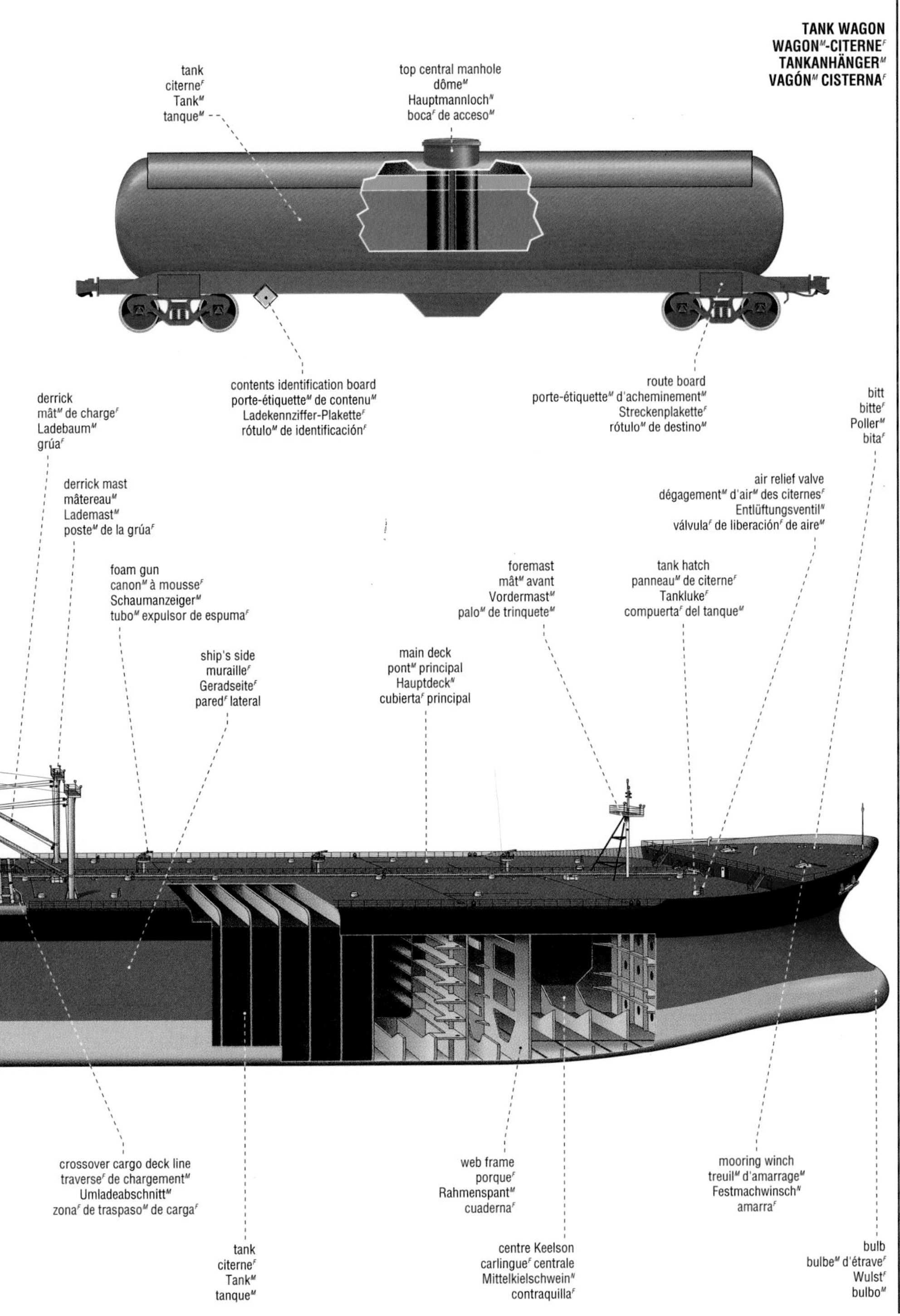

## REFINERY PRODUCTS
## PRODUITS[M] DE LA RAFFINERIE[F]
## RAFFINERIEERZEUGNISSE[N]
## PRODUCTOS[M] DEL REFINADO[M]

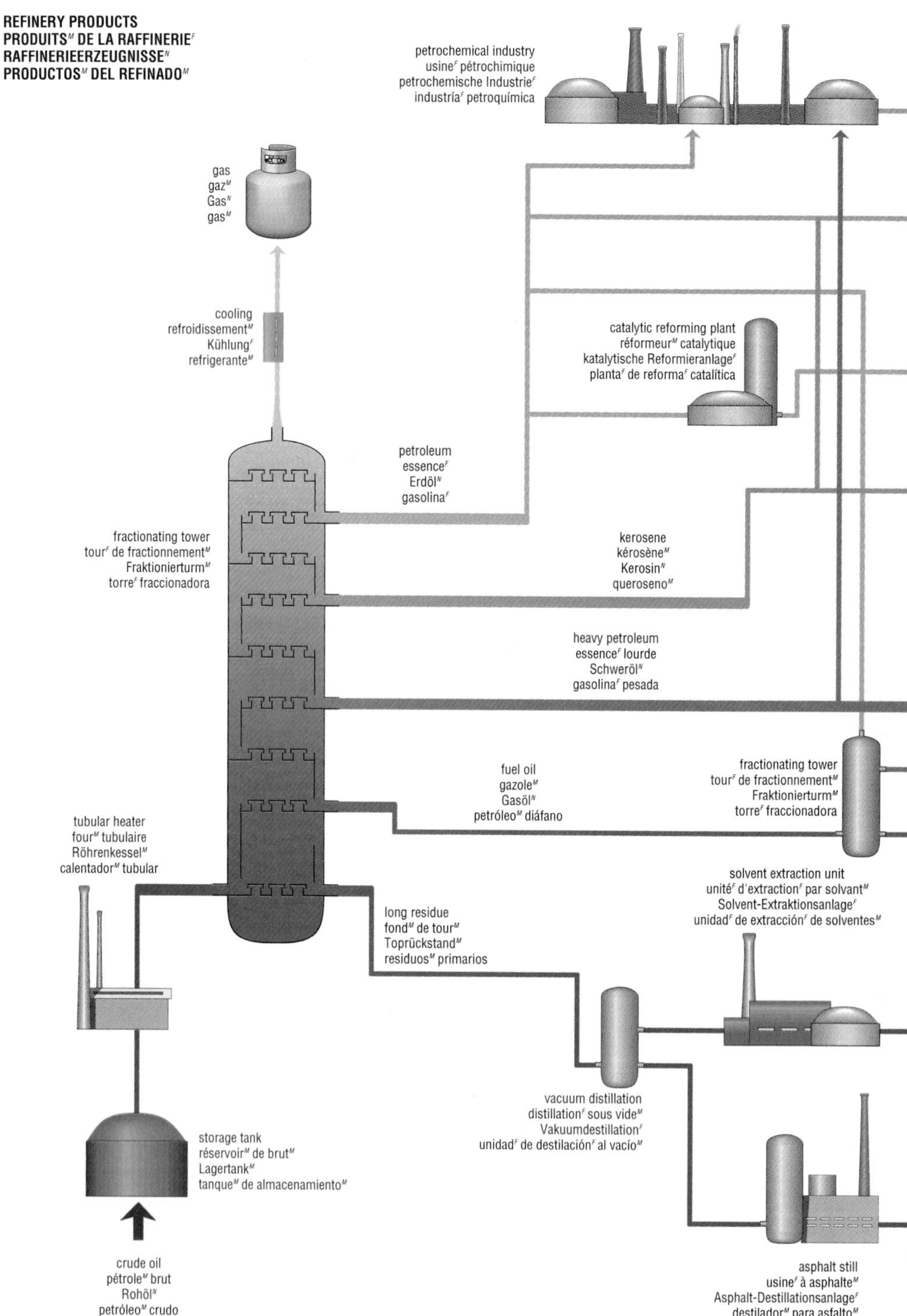

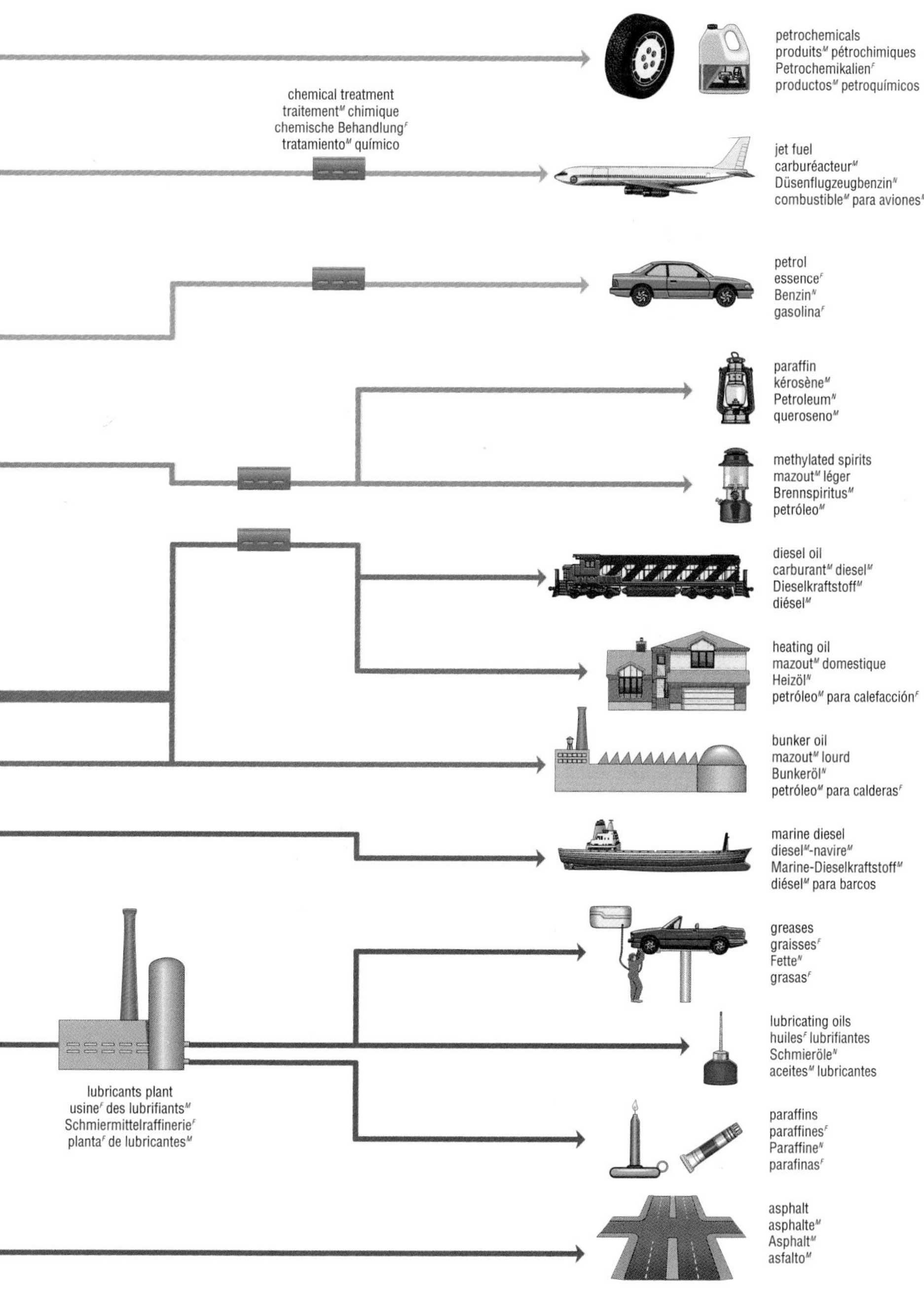


petrochemicals
produits[M] pétrochimiques
Petrochemikalien[F]
productos[M] petroquímicos

jet fuel
carburéacteur[M]
Düsenflugzeugbenzin[N]
combustible[M] para aviones[M]

petrol
essence[F]
Benzin[N]
gasolina[F]

paraffin
kérosène[M]
Petroleum[N]
queroseno[M]

methylated spirits
mazout[M] léger
Brennspiritus[M]
petróleo[M]

diesel oil
carburant[M] diesel[M]
Dieselkraftstoff[M]
diésel[M]

heating oil
mazout[M] domestique
Heizöl[N]
petróleo[M] para calefacción[F]

bunker oil
mazout[M] lourd
Bunkeröl[N]
petróleo[M] para calderas[F]

marine diesel
diesel[M]-navire[M]
Marine-Dieselkraftstoff[M]
diésel[M] para barcos

greases
graisses[F]
Fette[N]
grasas[F]

lubricating oils
huiles[F] lubrifiantes
Schmieröle[N]
aceites[M] lubricantes

paraffins
paraffines[F]
Paraffine[N]
parafinas[F]

asphalt
asphalte[M]
Asphalt[M]
asfalto[M]

## HYDROELECTRIC COMPLEX
## COMPLEXE[M] HYDROÉLECTRIQUE
## WASSERKRAFTWERK[N]
## COMPLEJO[M] HIDROELÉCTRICO

# CROSS SECTION OF A HYDROELECTRIC POWER STATION
# COUPE[F] D'UNE CENTRALE[F] HYDROÉLECTRIQUE
# WASSERKRAFTWERK[N] IM QUERSCHNITT[M]
# CORTE[M] TRANSVERSAL DE UNA CENTRAL[F] HIDROELÉCTRICA

gate
vanne[F]
Schieber[M]
compuerta[F]

gantry crane
portique[M]
Bockkran[M]
grúa[F] de caballete[M]

circuit breaker
disjoncteur[M]
Abschalter[M]
interruptor[M] automático

bushing
traversée[F] de transformateur[M]
Stromführung[F]
boquilla[F] reducidora

transformer
transformateur[M]
Transformator[M]
transformador[M]

lightning conductor
parafoudre[M]
Blitzableiter[M]
pararrayos[M]

travelling crane
pont[M] roulant
Laufkran[M]
grúa[F] de puente[M]

machine hall
salle[F] des machines[F]
Maschinenhalle[F]
sala[F] de máquinas[F]

access gallery
galerie[F] de visite[F]
Zugang[M]
galería[F] de acceso[M]

gantry crane
portique[M]
Bockkran[M]
grúa[F] de caballete[M]

scroll case
bâche[F] spirale
Umlaufgehäuse[N]
caja[F] de caracol[M]

gate
vanne[F]
Rechen[M]
compuerta[F]

afterbay
bief[M] d'aval[M]
Unterwasser[N]
cámara[F] de salida[F]

tailrace
canal[M] de fuite[F]
Auslaufrohr[N]
canal[M] de descarga[F]

generator unit
groupe[M] turbo-alternateur[M]
Generatoreinheit[F]
turbinas[F]

water intake
prise[F] d'eau[F]
Wassereinlaß[M]
entrada[F] de agua[F]

draught tube
aspirateur[M]
Saugrohr[N]
tubo[M] de aspiración[F]

screen
grille[F]
Rechen[M]
enrejado[M]

busbar
barre[F] blindée
Sammelschiene[F]
barra[F] colectora

reservoir
réservoir[M]
Stausee[M]
embalse[M] de la presa[F]

penstock
conduite[F] forcée
Falleitung[F]
tubería[F] de carga[F]

## EMBANKMENT DAM
## BARRAGE$^{M}$ EN REMBLAI$^{M}$
## UFERDAMM$^{M}$
## DIQUE$^{M}$ DE TERRAPLÉN$^{M}$

## CROSS SECTION OF AN EMBANKMENT DAM
## COUPE$^{F}$ D'UN BARRAGE$^{M}$ EN REMBLAI$^{M}$
## UFERDAMM$^{M}$ IM QUERSCHNITT$^{M}$
## CORTE$^{M}$ TRANSVERSAL DE UN DIQUE$^{M}$ DE TERRAPLÉN$^{M}$

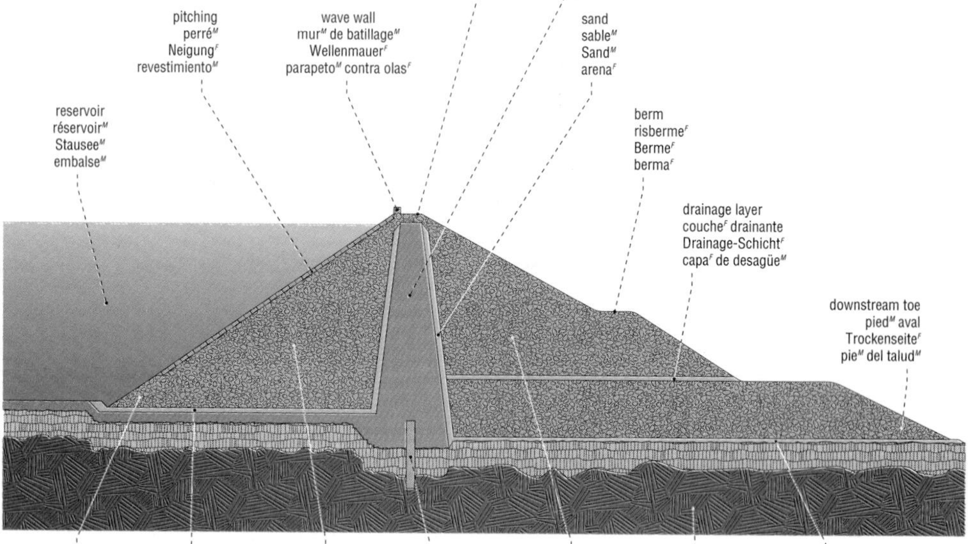

top of dam
crête$^{F}$
Dammkrone$^{F}$
tope$^{M}$ del dique$^{M}$

clay core
noyau$^{M}$ d'argile$^{F}$
Lehmkern$^{M}$
núcleo$^{M}$ de greda$^{F}$

pitching
perré$^{M}$
Neigung$^{F}$
revestimiento$^{M}$

wave wall
mur$^{M}$ de batillage$^{M}$
Wellenmauer$^{F}$
parapeto$^{M}$ contra olas$^{F}$

sand
sable$^{M}$
Sand$^{M}$
arena$^{F}$

reservoir
réservoir$^{M}$
Stausee$^{M}$
embalse$^{M}$

berm
risberme$^{F}$
Berme$^{F}$
berma$^{F}$

drainage layer
couche$^{F}$ drainante
Drainage-Schicht$^{F}$
capa$^{F}$ de desagüe$^{M}$

downstream toe
pied$^{M}$ aval
Trockenseite$^{F}$
pie$^{M}$ del talud$^{M}$

upstream toe
pied$^{M}$ amont
Dammbrust$^{F}$
pie$^{M}$ del talud$^{M}$

upstream shoulder
recharge$^{F}$ amont
Oberstützmauer$^{F}$
talud$^{M}$ de aguas$^{F}$ contenidas

downstream shoulder
recharge$^{F}$ aval
Unterstützmauer$^{F}$
talud$^{M}$ de aguas$^{F}$ abajo

drainage blanket
tapis$^{M}$ drainant
Drainage-Decke$^{F}$
plantilla$^{F}$ de desagüe$^{M}$

upstream blanket
tapis$^{M}$ amont
Oberwasserdecke$^{F}$
plantilla$^{F}$ de arcilla$^{F}$

cut-off trench
parafouille$^{M}$
Dichtungsschleier$^{M}$
cortina$^{F}$ de inyecciones$^{F}$

dam foundation
terrain$^{M}$ de fondation$^{F}$
Dammsockel$^{M}$
cimientos$^{M}$ del dique$^{M}$

## GRAVITY DAM
## BARRAGE[M]-POIDS[M]
## GEWICHTSSTAUDAMM[M]
## PRESA[F]

## CROSS SECTION OF A GRAVITY DAM
## COUPE[F] D'UN BARRAGE[M]-POIDS[M]
## GEWICHTSSTAUDAMM[M] IM QUERSCHNITT[M]
## CORTE[M] TRANSVERSAL DE UNA PRESA[F]

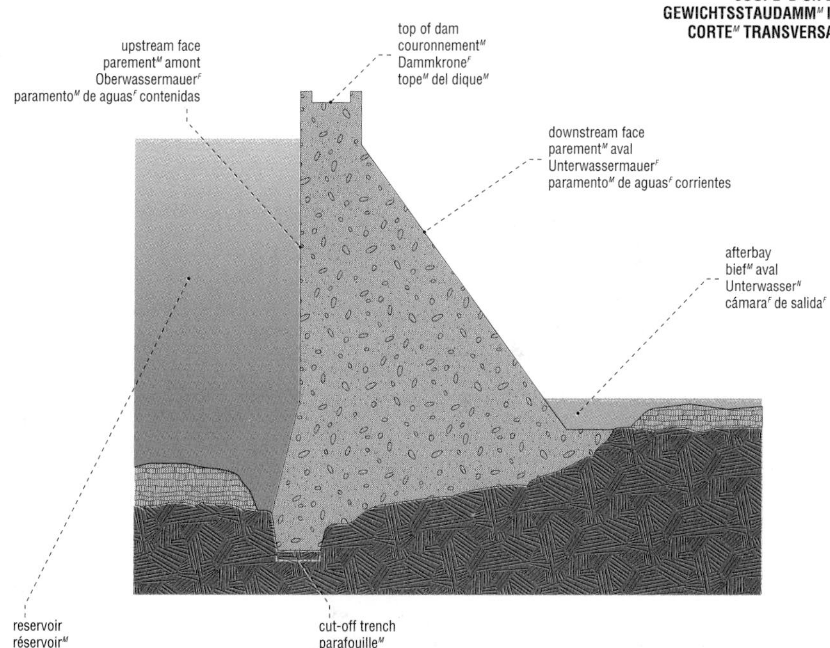

# ELECTRICITY
# ÉLECTRICITÉ$^{F}$
# ELEKTRIZITÄT$^{F}$
# ELECTRICIDAD$^{F}$

## ARCH DAM
## BARRAGE$^{M}$-VOÛTE$^{F}$
## BOGENSTAUDAMM$^{M}$
## PRESA$^{F}$ DE ARCO$^{M}$

## CROSS SECTION OF AN ARCH DAM
## COUPE$^{F}$ D'UN BARRAGE$^{M}$-VOÛTE$^{F}$
## BOGENSTAUDAMM$^{M}$ IM QUERSCHNITT$^{M}$
## CORTE$^{M}$ TRANSVERSAL DE UNA PRESA$^{F}$ DE ARCO$^{M}$

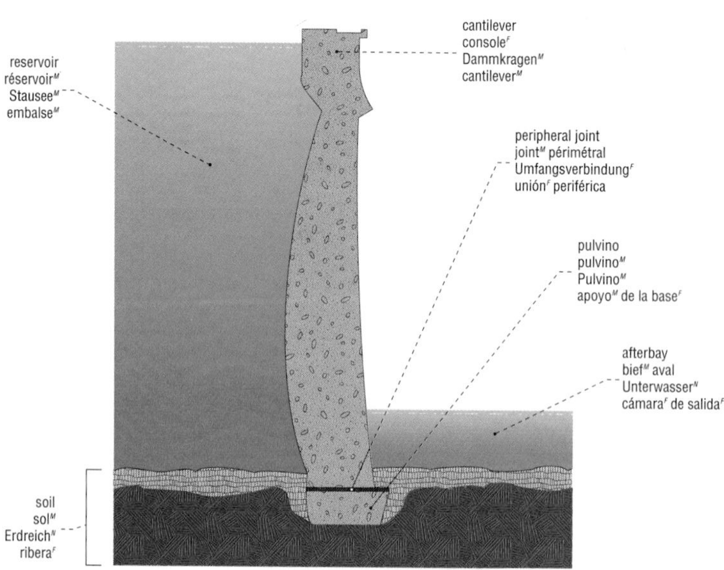

## BUTTRESS DAM
## BARRAGE[M] À CONTREFORTS[M]
## STÜTZPFEILERSTAUDAMM[M]
## DIQUE[M] DE MACHONES[M]

## CROSS SECTION OF A BUTTRESS DAM
## COUPE[F] D'UN BARRAGE[M] À CONTREFORTS[M]
## STÜTZPFEILERSTAUDAMM[M] IM QUERSCHNITT[M]
## CORTE[M] TRANSVERSAL DE UN DIQUE[M] DE MACHONES[M]

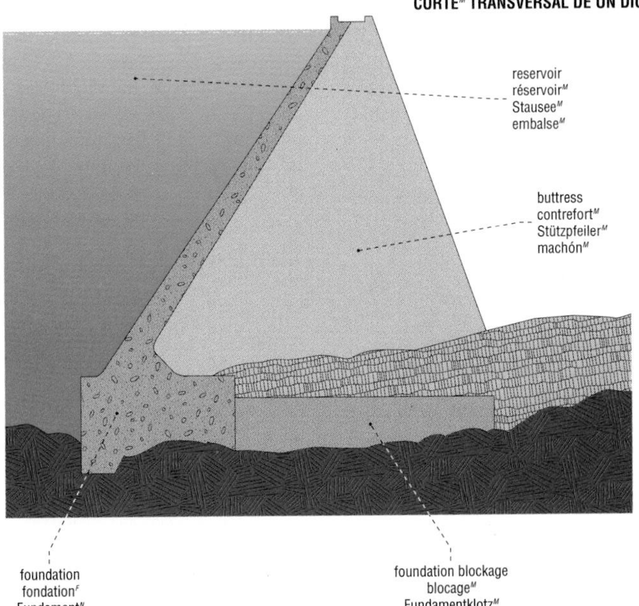


ENERGY
ÉNERGIES
ENERGIE
ENERGÍA

# ELECTRICITY
# ÉLECTRICITÉ[F]
# ELEKTRIZITÄT[F]
# ELECTRICIDAD[F]

## TIDAL POWER PLANT
## USINE[F] MARÉMOTRICE
## GEZEITENKRAFTWERK[N]
## CENTRAL[F] MAREMOTRIZ

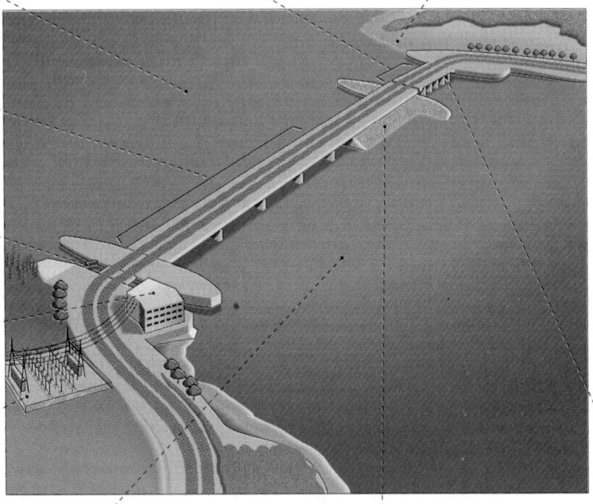

operating dam
barrage[M] mobile
Stromerzeugungsabschnitt[M]
dique[M] de operación[F]
bank
rive[F]
Ufer[N]
orilla[F]
sea
mer[F]
Meer[N]
mar[M] abierto
power station
usine[F]
Kraftwerk[N]
planta[F] maremotriz
lock
écluse[F]
Schleuse[F]
esclusa[F]
administrative building
bâtiment[M] administratif
Verwaltungsgebäude[N]
edificio[M] de la administración[F]
substation
poste[M]
Umspannwerk[N]
subestación[F]
basin
bassin[M]
Becken[N]
embalse[M]
inactive dyke
digue[F] morte
unbewegter Deich[M]
dique[M] inerte
gate
vanne[F]
Rechen[M]
compuerta[F]


## CROSS SECTION OF A POWER PLANT
## COUPE[F] DE L'USINE[F]
## KRAFTWERK[N] IM QUERSCHNITT[M]
## CORTE[M] TRANSVERSAL DE UNA PLANTA[F] MAREMOTRIZ

top of dam
couronnement[M] du barrage[M]
Deichkrone[F]
tope[M] del dique[M]
operating floor
étage[M] d'exploitation[F]
Betriebsebene[F]
piso[M] de operaciones[F]
sea side
côté[M] mer[F]
Meeresseite[F]
lado[M] del mar[M]
access shaft
puits[M] d'accès[M]
Zugangschacht[M]
pozo[M] de acceso[M]
bulb unit
groupe[M] bulbe[M]
Rohrturbine[F]
bulbo[M]
runner blade
pale[F]
Laufblatt[N]
paleta[F] del rotor[M]
turbine runner
roue[F] de turbine[F]
Turbinenläufer[M]
rotor[M] de la turbina[F]
penstock
conduite[F] forcée
Falleitung[F]
canal[M] de carga[F]
basin side
côté[M] bassin[M]
Beckenseite[F]
lado[M] hacia el embalse[M]

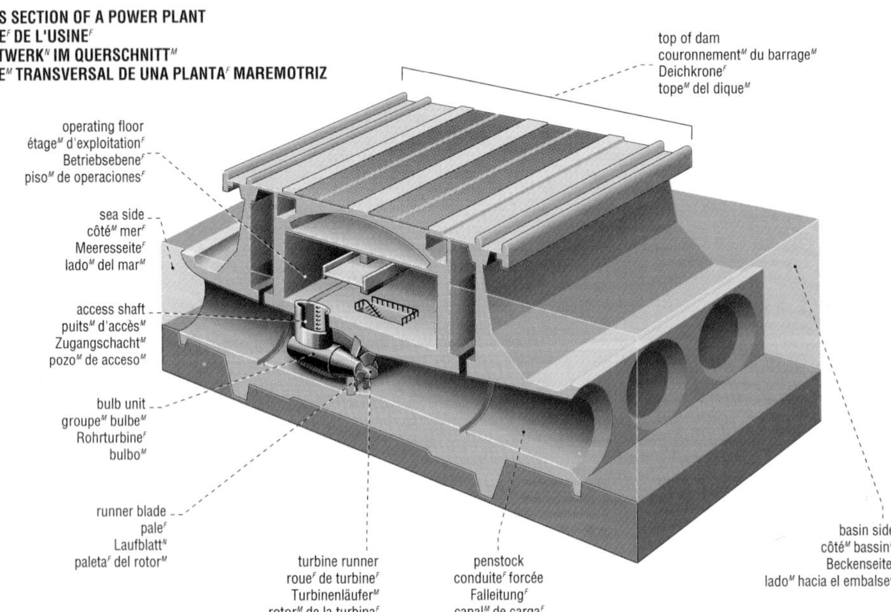

# GENERATOR UNIT
# GROUPE[M] TURBO-ALTERNATEUR[M]
# STROMGENERATOR[M]
# UNIDAD[F] GENERADORA

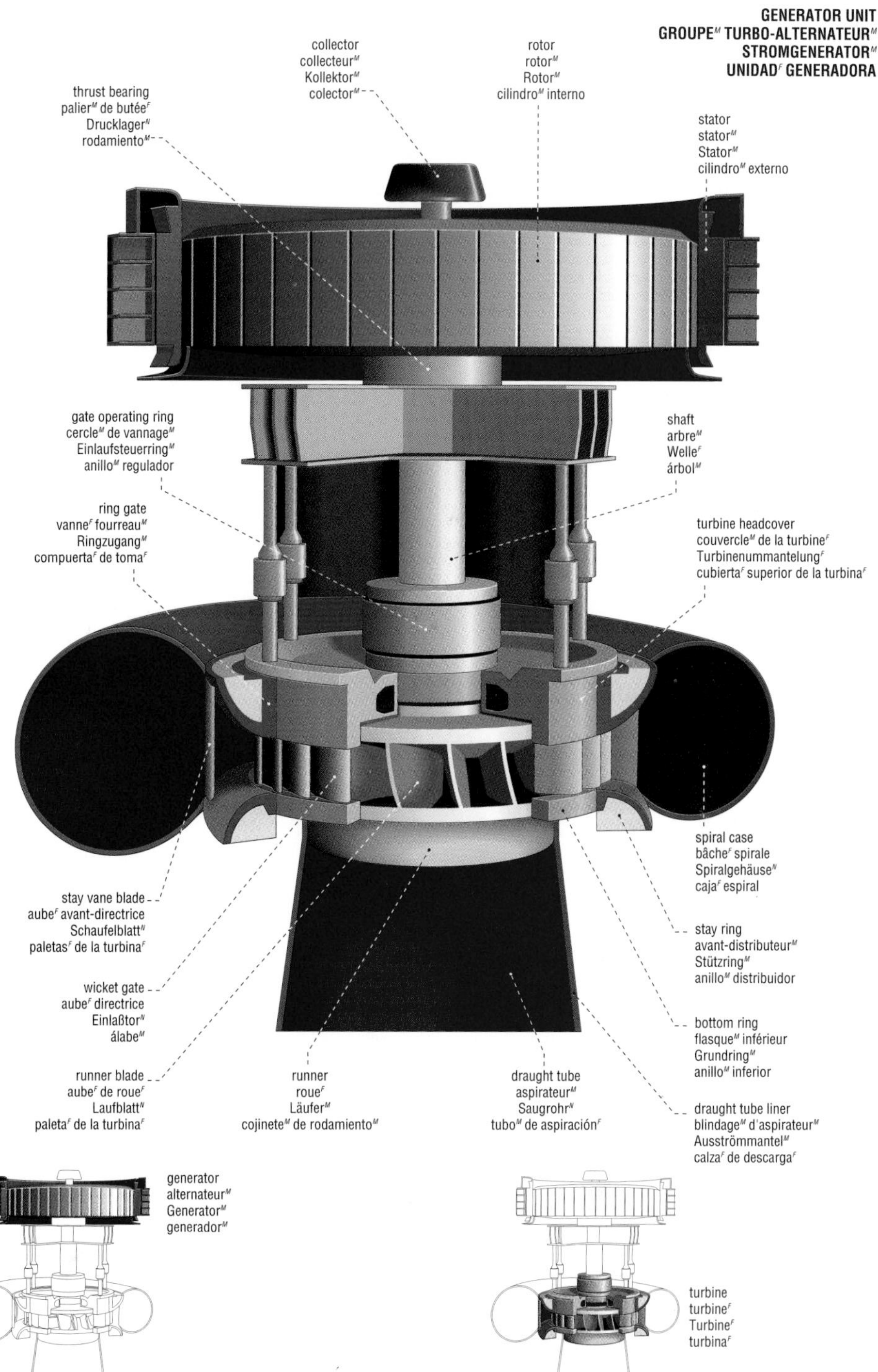

# ELECTRICITY
# ÉLECTRICITÉ[F]
# ELEKTRIZITÄT[F]
# ELECTRICIDAD[F]

**FRANCIS RUNNER**
**ROUE[F] FRANCIS**
**FRANCISTURBINE[F]**
**TURBINA[F] FRANCIS**

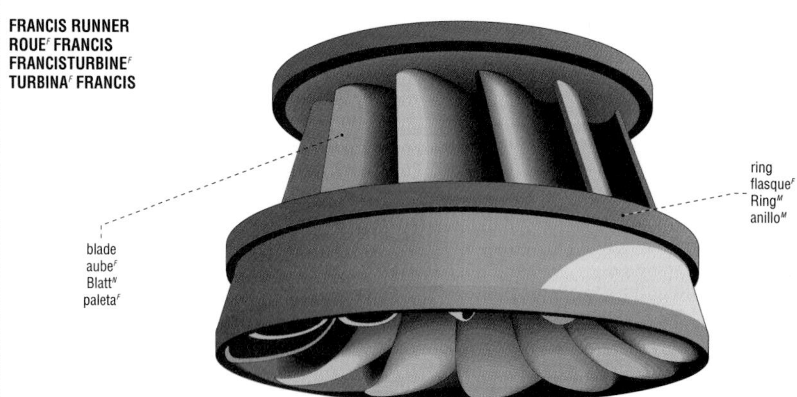


**KAPLAN RUNNER**
**ROUE[F] KAPLAN**
**KAPLANTURBINE[F]**
**TURBINA[F] KAPLAN**

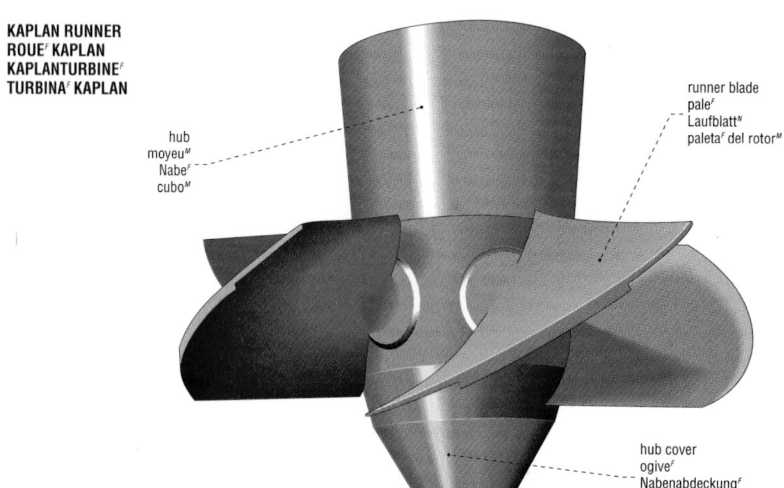


**PELTON RUNNER**
**ROUE[F] PELTON**
**PELTONTURBINE[F]**
**TURBINA[F] PELTON**

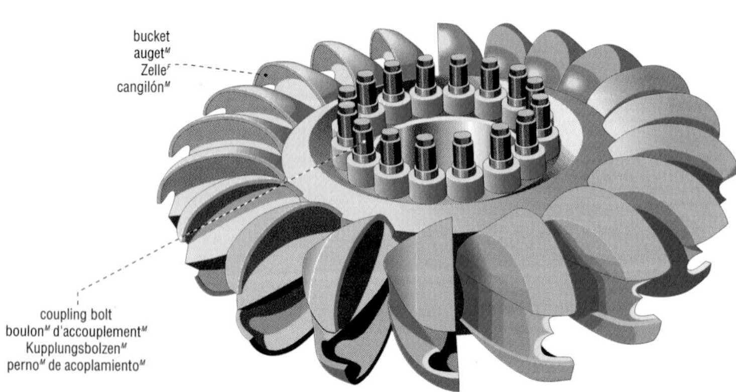

## STEPS IN THE PRODUCTION OF ELECTRICITY
## ÉTAPES[F] DE PRODUCTION[F] DE L'ÉLECTRICITÉ[F]
## EINZELSCHRITTE[M] BEI DER STROMERZEUGUNG[F]
## ETAPAS[F] DE LA PRODUCCIÓN[F] DE ELECTRICIDAD

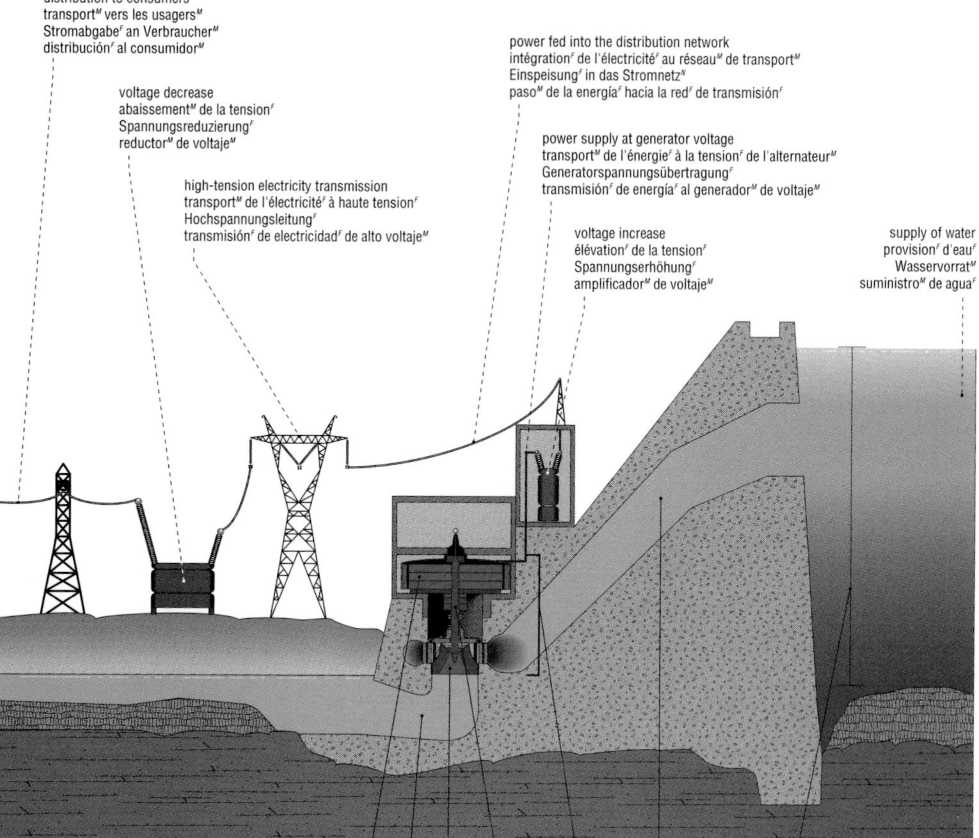

# ELECTRICITY
# ÉLECTRICITÉ[F]
# ELEKTRIZITÄT[F]
# ELECTRICIDAD[F]

## PYLON
## PYLÔNE[M]
## HOCHSPANNUNGSMAST[M]
## TORRE[F] DE ALTA TENSIÓN[F]

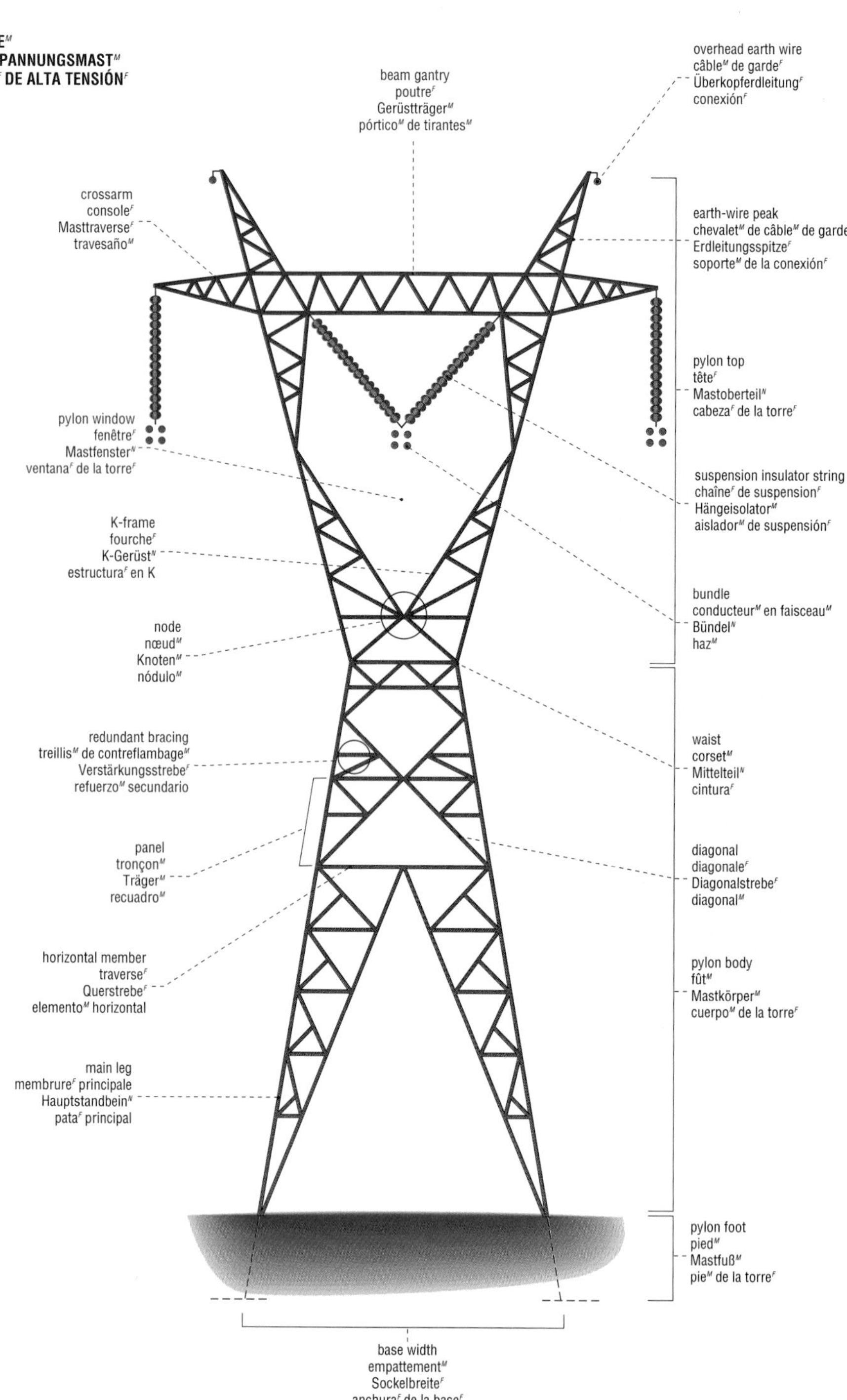

## ELECTRICITY DISTRIBUTION
## TRANSPORT[M] DE L'ÉLECTRICITÉ[F]
## STROMTRANSPORT[M]
## TRANSMISIÓN[F] DE ELECTRICIDAD[F]

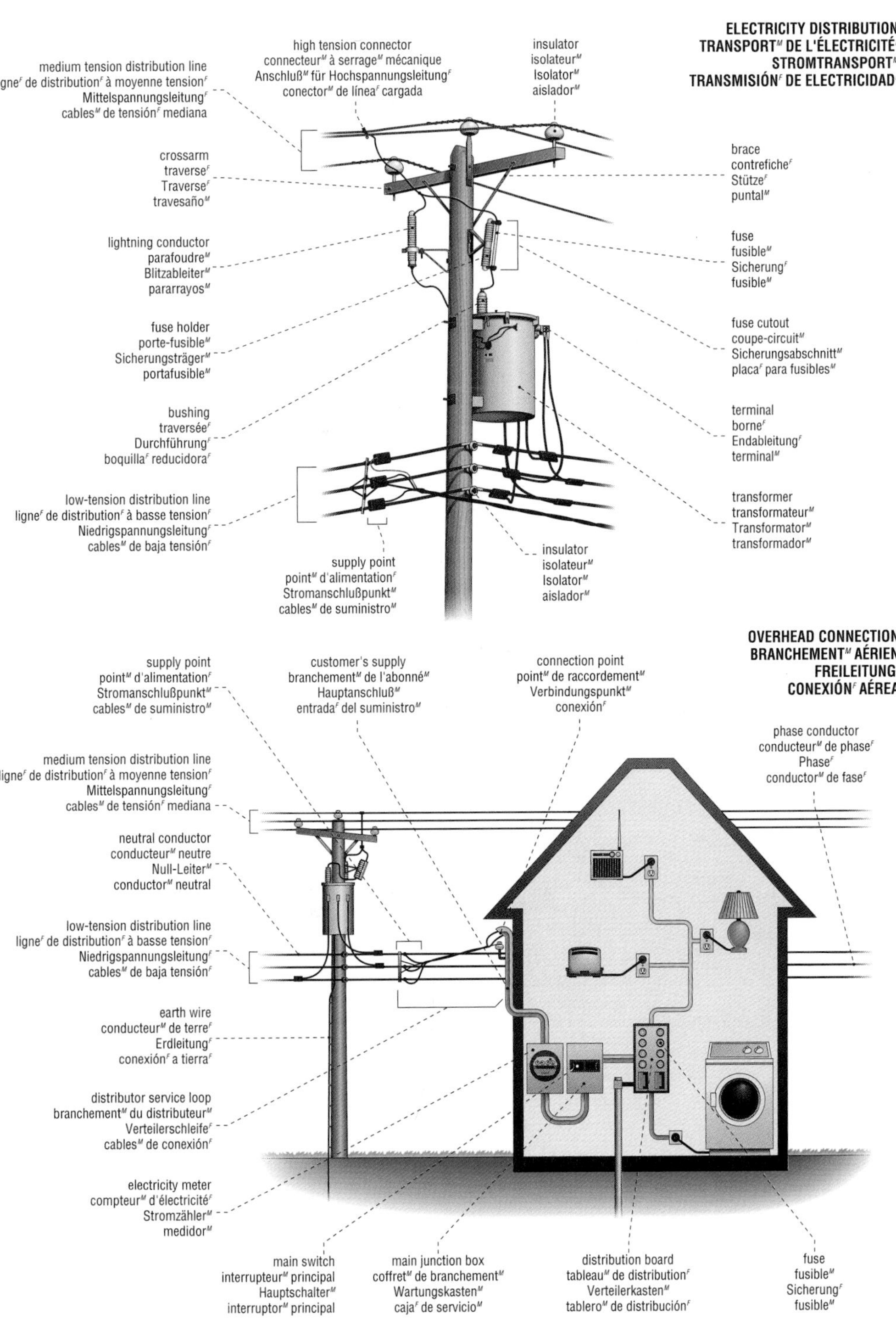

# NUCLEAR ENERGY
# ÉNERGIE[F] NUCLÉAIRE
# KERNENERGIE[F]
# ENERGÍA[F] NUCLEAR

## NUCLEAR POWER STATION
## CENTRALE[F] NUCLÉAIRE
## KERNKRAFTWERK[N]
## CENTRAL[F] NUCLEAR

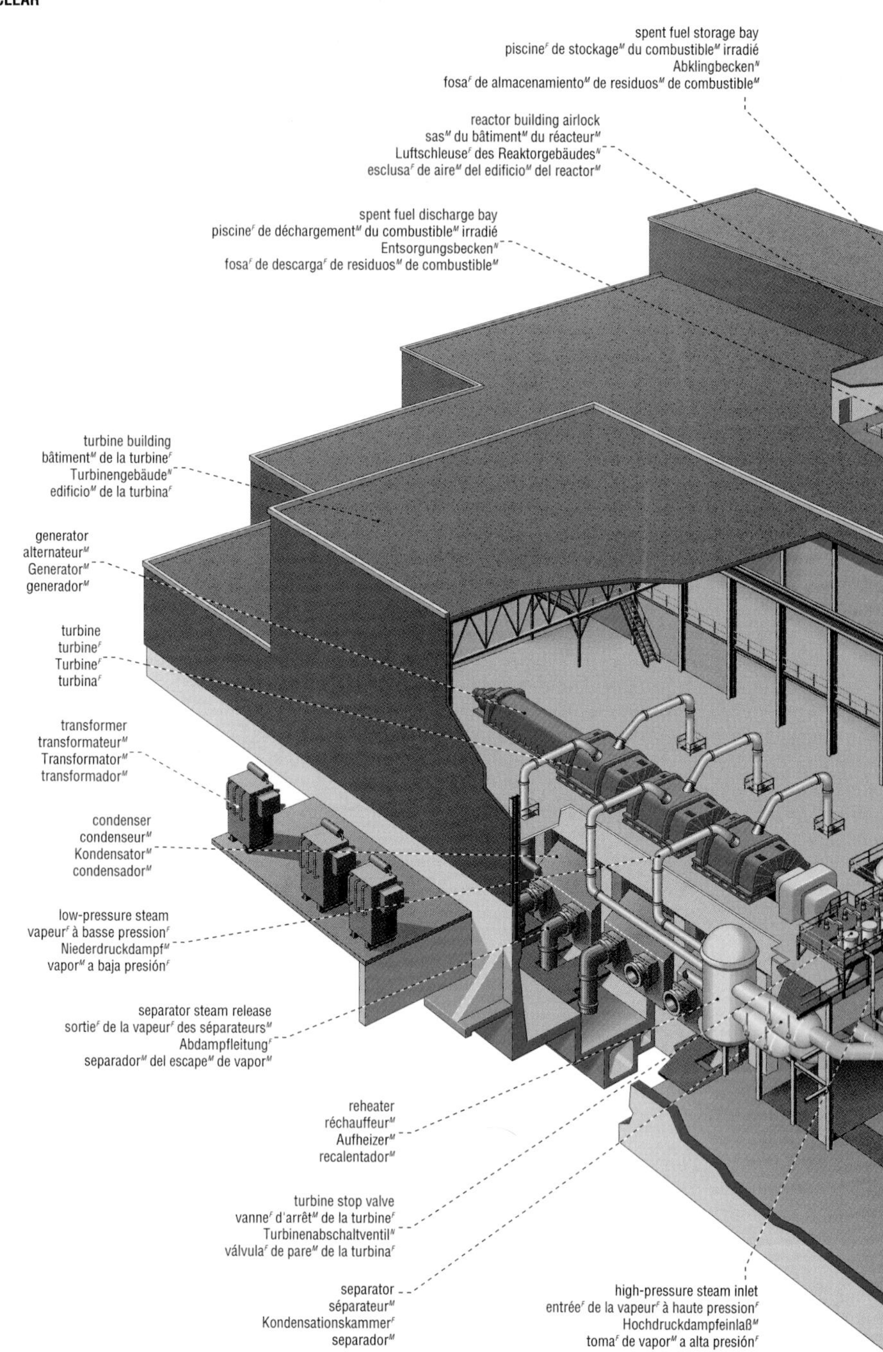

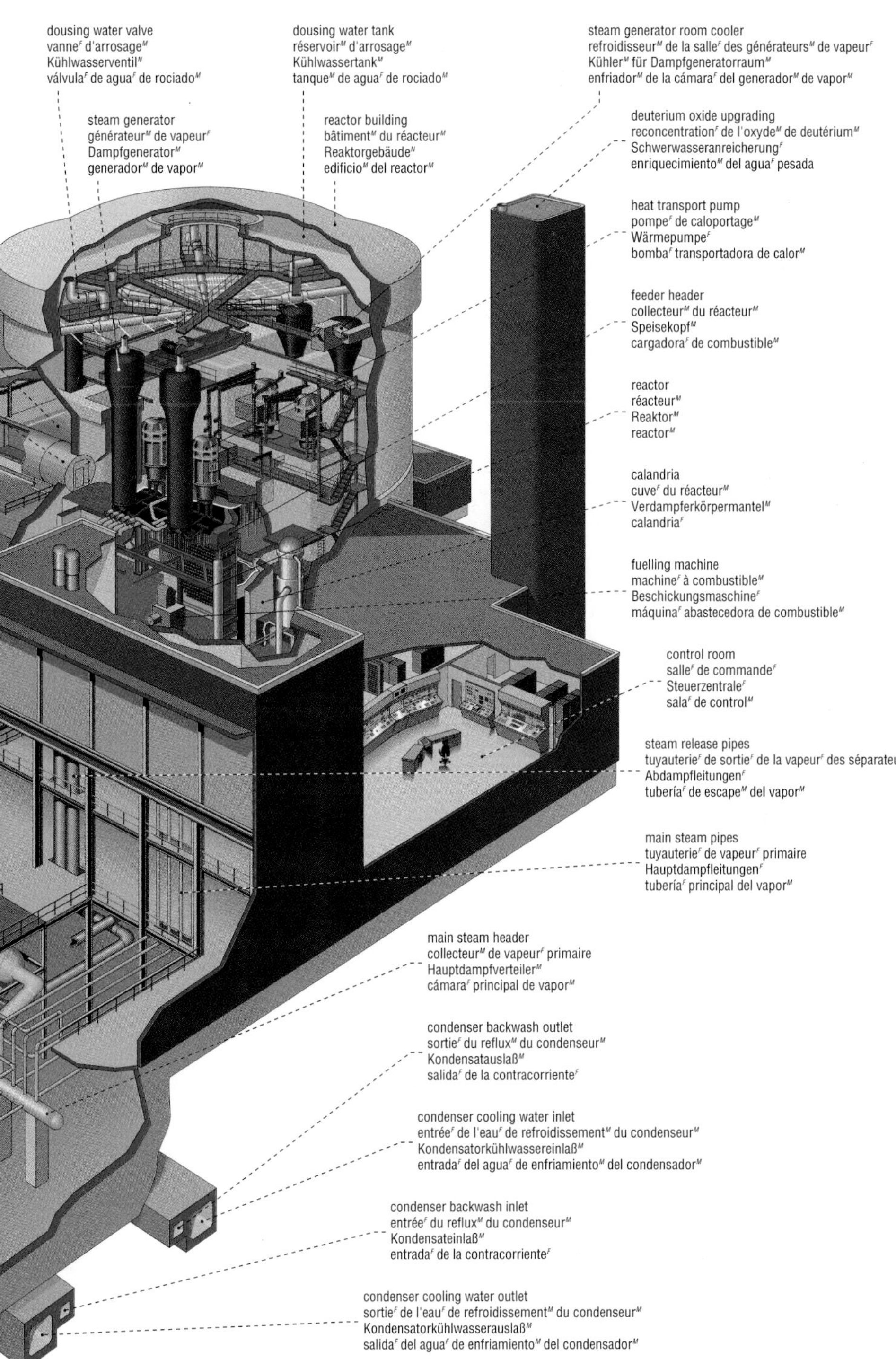

dousing water valve
vanne[F] d'arrosage[M]
Kühlwasserventil[N]
válvula[F] de agua[F] de rociado[M]
steam generator
générateur[M] de vapeur[F]
Dampfgenerator[M]
generador[M] de vapor[M]
dousing water tank
réservoir[M] d'arrosage[M]
Kühlwassertank[M]
tanque[M] de agua[F] de rociado[M]
reactor building
bâtiment[M] du réacteur[M]
Reaktorgebäude[N]
edificio[M] del reactor[M]
steam generator room cooler
refroidisseur[M] de la salle[F] des générateurs[M] de vapeur[F]
Kühler[M] für Dampfgeneratorraum[M]
enfriador[M] de la cámara[F] del generador[M] de vapor[M]
deuterium oxide upgrading
reconcentration[F] de l'oxyde[M] de deutérium[M]
Schwerwasseranreicherung[F]
enriquecimiento[M] del agua[F] pesada
heat transport pump
pompe[F] de caloportage[M]
Wärmepumpe[F]
bomba[F] transportadora de calor[M]
feeder header
collecteur[M] du réacteur[M]
Speisekopf[M]
cargadora[F] de combustible[M]
reactor
réacteur[M]
Reaktor[M]
reactor[M]
calandria
cuve[F] du réacteur[M]
Verdampferkörpermantel[M]
calandria[F]
fuelling machine
machine[F] à combustible[M]
Beschickungsmaschine[F]
máquina[F] abastecedora de combustible[M]
control room
salle[F] de commande[F]
Steuerzentrale[F]
sala[F] de control[M]
steam release pipes
tuyauterie[F] de sortie[F] de la vapeur[F] des séparateurs[M]
Abdampfleitungen[F]
tubería[F] de escape[M] del vapor[M]
main steam pipes
tuyauterie[F] de vapeur[F] primaire
Hauptdampfleitungen[F]
tubería[F] principal del vapor[M]
main steam header
collecteur[M] de vapeur[F] primaire
Hauptdampfverteiler[M]
cámara[F] principal de vapor[M]
condenser backwash outlet
sortie[F] du reflux[M] du condenseur[M]
Kondensatauslaß[M]
salida[F] de la contracorriente[F]
condenser cooling water inlet
entrée[F] de l'eau[F] de refroidissement[M] du condenseur[M]
Kondensatorkühlwassereinlaß[M]
entrada[F] del agua[F] de enfriamiento[M] del condensador[M]
condenser backwash inlet
entrée[F] du reflux[M] du condenseur[M]
Kondensateinlaß[M]
entrada[F] de la contracorriente[F]
condenser cooling water outlet
sortie[F] de l'eau[F] de refroidissement[M] du condenseur[M]
Kondensatorkühlwasserauslaß[M]
salida[F] del agua[F] de enfriamiento[M] del condensador[M]

# NUCLEAR ENERGY
# ÉNERGIE[F] NUCLÉAIRE
# KERNENERGIE[F]
# ENERGÍA[F] NUCLEAR

## GAS-COOLED REACTOR
## RÉACTEUR[M] AU GAZ[M] CARBONIQUE
## KOHLENDIOXIDREAKTOR[M]
## REACTOR[M] DE BIÓXIDO[M] DE CARBONO[M]

fuelling machine
machine[F] de chargement[M]
Beschickungsmaschine[F]
mecanismo[M] de carga[F] del combustible[M]

concrete shielding
enceinte[F] en béton[M]
Betonmantel[M]
resguardo[M] de hormigón[M]

control rod
barre[F] de contrôle[M]
Steuerstab[M]
varilla[F] de control[M]

carbon dioxide gas coolant
gaz[M] carbonique de refroidissement[M]
Kohlendioxidkühlgas[N]
gas refrigerante de bióxido de carbono

reactor core
cœur[M] du réacteur[M]
Reaktorkern[M]
núcleo[M] del reactor[M]

heat exchanger
échangeur[M] de chaleur[F]
Wärmetauscher[M]
intercambiador[M] de calor[M]

blower
soufflante[F]
Gebläse[N]
ventilador[M] del evaporador[M]

steam outlet
sortie[F] de la vapeur[F]
Dampfauslaß[M]
salida[F] de vapor[M]

feedwater
alimentation[F] en eau[F]
Speisewasser[N]
alimentación[F] de agua[F]

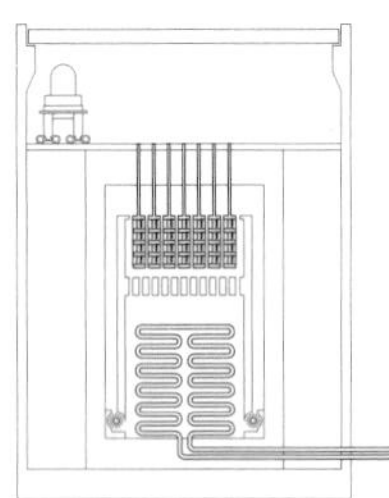

fuel: natural uranium
combustible[M]: uranium[M] naturel
Brennstoff[M]: nichtangereichertes Uran[N]
combustible[M]: uranio[M] natural

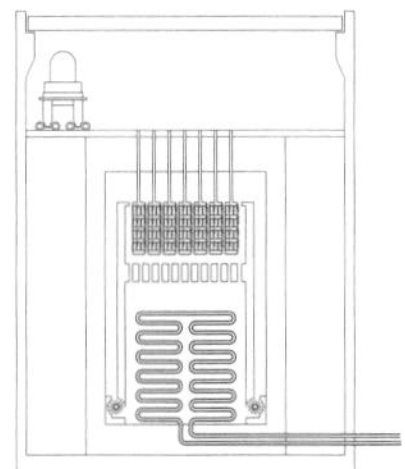

moderator: graphite
modérateur[M]: graphite[M]
Moderator[M]: Graphit[M]
moderador[M]: grafito[M]

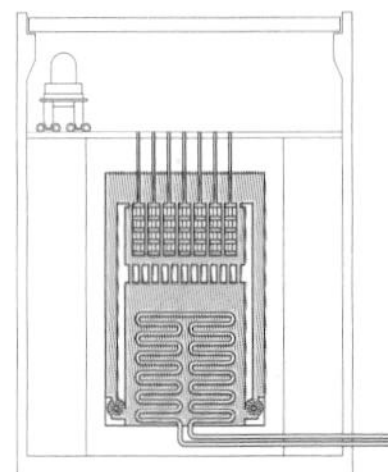

coolant: carbon dioxide
caloporteur[M]: gaz[M] carbonique
Kühlmittel[N]: Kohlendioxid[N]
refrigerante[M]: bióxido[M] de carbono[M]

# HEAVY-WATER REACTOR
# RÉACTEUR[M] À EAU[F] LOURDE
# SCHWERWASSERREAKTOR[M]
# REACTOR[M] DE AGUA[F] PESADA

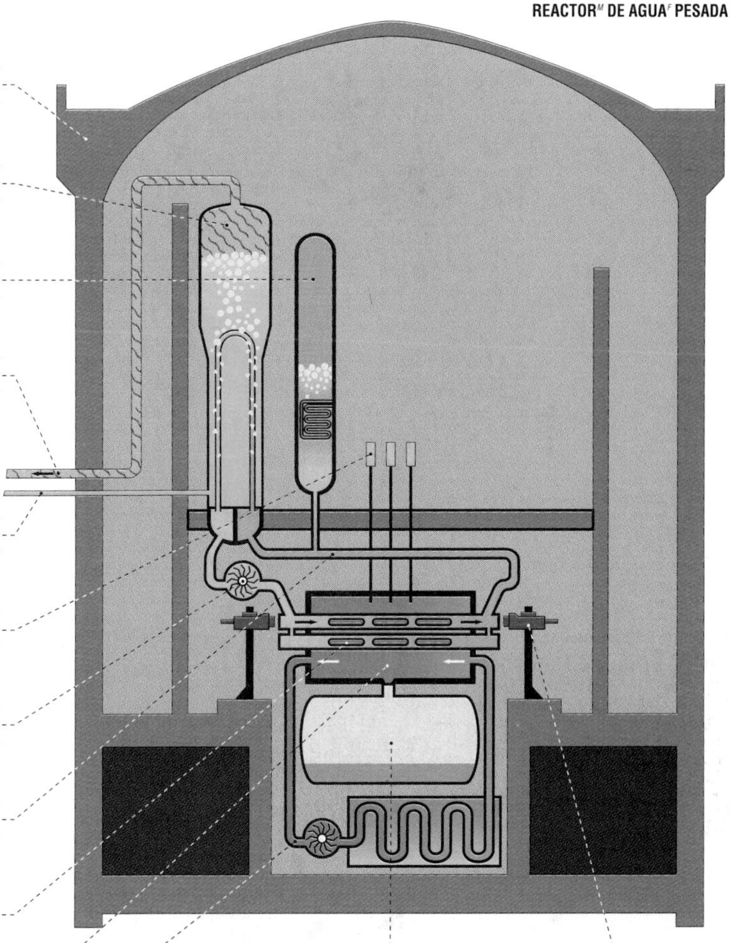

concrete shielding
enceinte[F] en béton[M]
Betonmantel[M]
resguardo[M] de hormigón[M]

steam generator
générateur[M] de vapeur[F]
Dampfgenerator[M]
generador[M] de vapor[M]

pressurizer
pressuriseur[M]
Druckerzeuger[M]
compresor[M]

steam outlet
sortie[F] de la vapeur[F]
Dampfauslaß[M]
salida[F] de vapor[M]

feedwater
alimentation[F] en eau[F]
Speisewasser[N]
alimentación[F] de agua[F]

control rod
barre[F] de contrôle[M]
Steuerstab[M]
varilla[F] de control[M]

pump
pompe[F]
Pumpe[F]
bomba[F]

pressurized heavy water
eau[F] lourde sous pression[F]
Schwerwasser[N] unter Druck[M]
agua[F] pesada a presión[F]

fuel
combustible[M]
Brennelement[N]
combustible[M]

moderator tank
cuve[F] du modérateur[M]
Moderatortank[M]
tanque[M] moderador

cold heavy water
eau[F] lourde froide
kaltes Schwerwasser[N]
agua[F] pesada de enfriamiento[M]

safety tank
réservoir[M] de sécurité[F]
Sicherheitstank[M]
tanque[M] de seguridad[F]

fuelling machine
machine[F] de chargement[M]
Beschickungsmaschine[F]
máquina[F] cargadora de combustible[M]

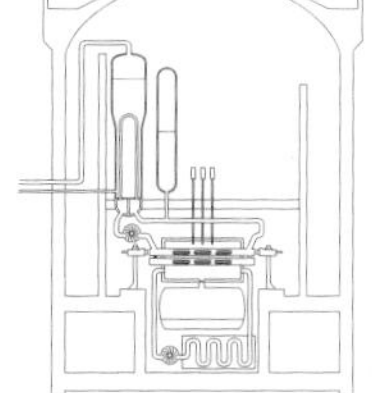

fuel: natural uranium
combustible[M]: uranium[M] naturel
Brennstoff[M]: nichtangereichertes Uran[N]
combustible[M]: uranio[M] natural

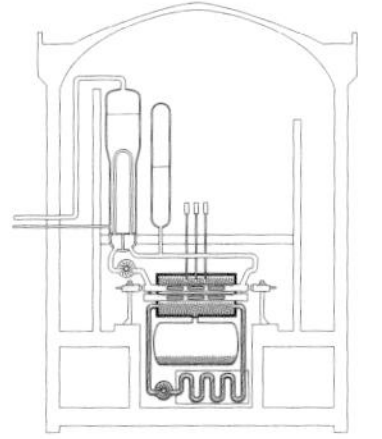

moderator: heavy water
modérateur[M]: eau[F] lourde
Moderator[M]: schweres Wasser[N]
moderador[M]: agua[F] pesada

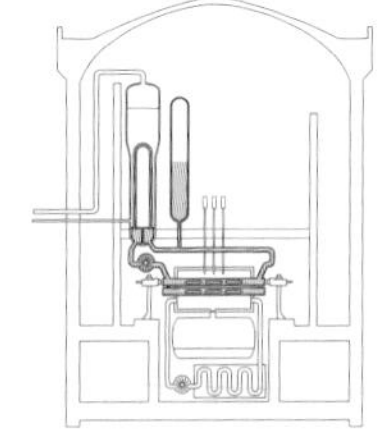

coolant: pressurized heavy water
caloporteur[M]: eau[F] lourde sous pression[F]
Kühlmittel[N]: Druckwasser[N]
refrigerante[M]: agua[F] pesada a presión[F]

# NUCLEAR ENERGY
# ÉNERGIE^F NUCLÉAIRE
# KERNENERGIE^F
# ENERGÍA^F NUCLEAR

## PRESSURIZED-WATER REACTOR
## RÉACTEUR^M À EAU^F SOUS PRESSION^F
## DRUCKWASSERREAKTOR^M
## REACTOR^M DE AGUA^F A PRESIÓN^F

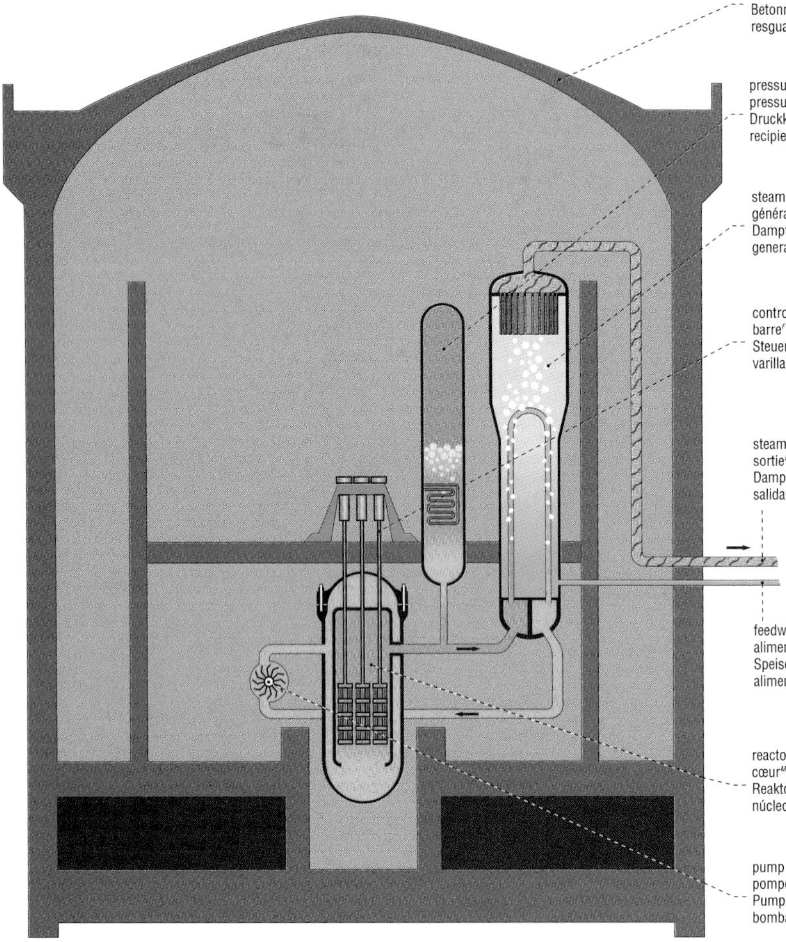

concrete shielding
enceinte^F en béton^M
Betonmantel^M
resguardo^M de hormigón^M

pressure vessel
pressuriseur^M
Druckkessel^M
recipiente^M de presión^F

steam generator
générateur^M de vapeur^F
Dampfgenerator^M
generador^M de vapor^M

control rod
barre^F de contrôle^M
Steuerstab^M
varilla^F de control^M

steam outlet
sortie^F de la vapeur^F
Dampfauslaß^M
salida^F de vapor^M

feedwater
alimentation^F en eau^F
Speisewasser^N
alimentación^F de agua^F

reactor core
cœur^M du réacteur^M
Reaktorkern^M
núcleo^M del reactor^M

pump
pompe^F
Pumpe^F
bomba^F

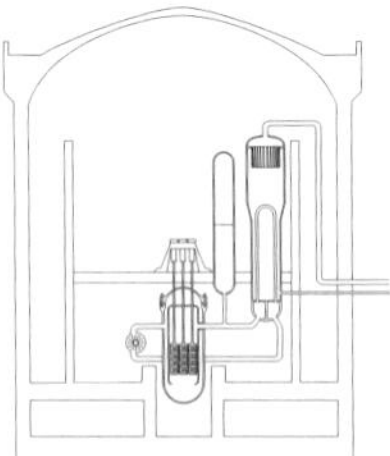

fuel: enriched uranium
combustible^M: uranium^M enrichi
Brennstoff^M: angereichertes Uran^N
combustible^M: uranio^M enriquecido

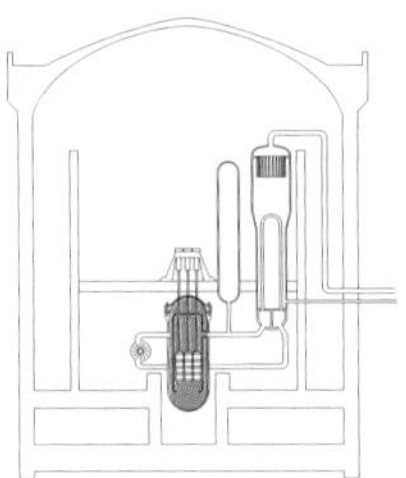

moderator: natural water
modérateur^M: eau^F naturelle
Moderator^M: Wasser^N
moderador^M: agua^F natural

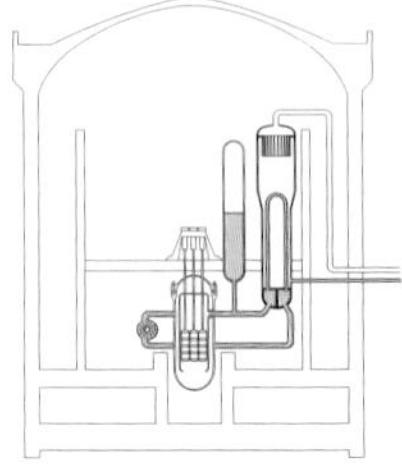

coolant: pressurized water
caloporteur^M: eau^F sous pression^F
Kühlmittel^N: Druckwasser^N
refrigerante^M: agua^F a presión^F

## BOILING-WATER REACTOR
## RÉACTEUR[M] À EAU[F] BOUILLANTE
## SIEDEWASSERREAKTOR[M]
## REACTOR[M] DE AGUA[F] HIRVIENTE

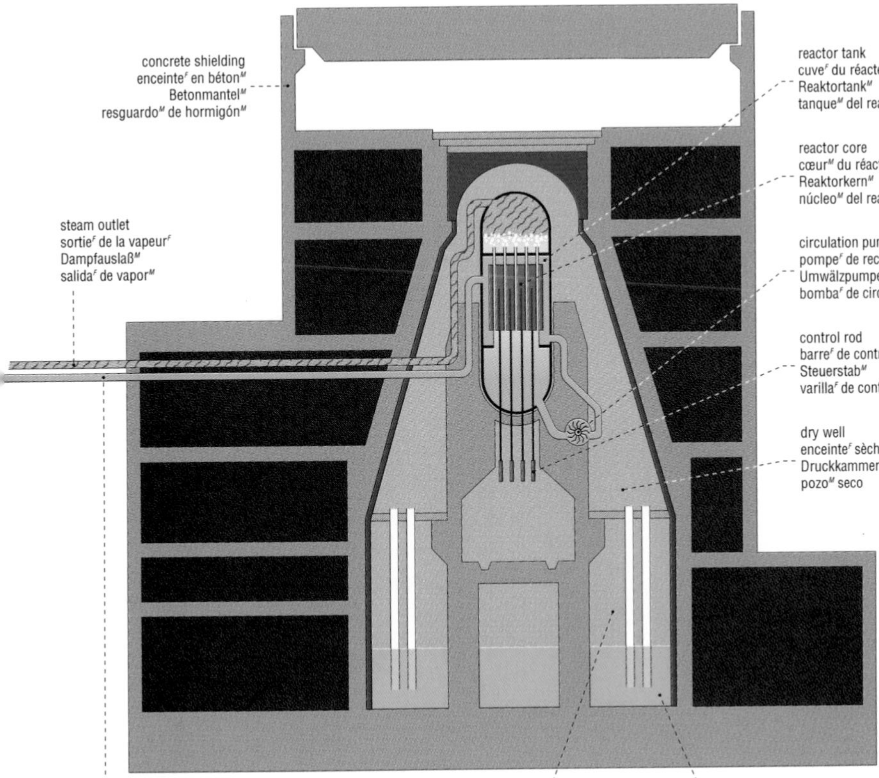

concrete shielding
enceinte[F] en béton[M]
Betonmantel[M]
resguardo[M] de hormigón[M]

reactor tank
cuve[F] du réacteur[M]
Reaktortank[M]
tanque[M] del reactor[M]

reactor core
cœur[M] du réacteur[M]
Reaktorkern[M]
núcleo[M] del reactor[M]

steam outlet
sortie[F] de la vapeur[F]
Dampfauslaß[M]
salida[F] de vapor[M]

circulation pump
pompe[F] de recirculation[F]
Umwälzpumpe[F]
bomba[F] de circulación[F]

control rod
barre[F] de contrôle[M]
Steuerstab[M]
varilla[F] de control[M]

dry well
enceinte[F] sèche
Druckkammer[F]
pozo[M] seco

feedwater
alimentation[F] en eau[F]
Speisewasser[N]
agua[F] de alimentación[F]

wet well
enceinte[F] humide
Naßkammer[F]
pozo[M]

condensation pool
piscine[F] de condensation[F]
Kondensatorkühlwasserbecken[N]
piscina[F] para enfriamiento[M] del condensador[M]



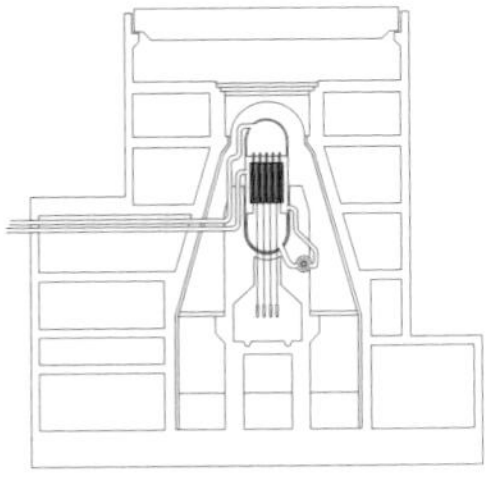

fuel: enriched uranium
combustible[M]: uranium[M] enrichi
Brennstoff[M]: angereichertes Uran[N]
combustible[M]: uranio[M] enriquecido

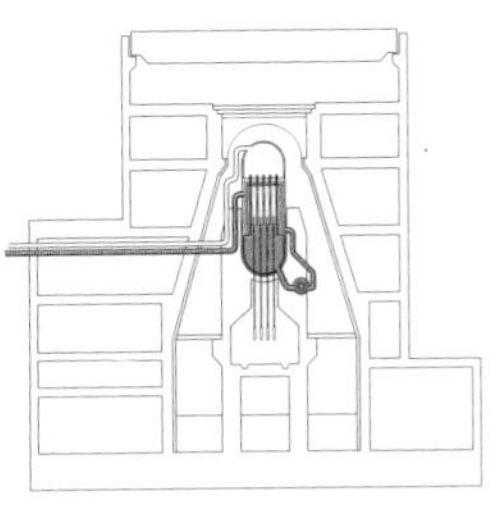

moderator: natural water
modérateur[M]: eau[F] naturelle
Moderator[M]: Wasser[N]
moderador[M]: agua[F] natural

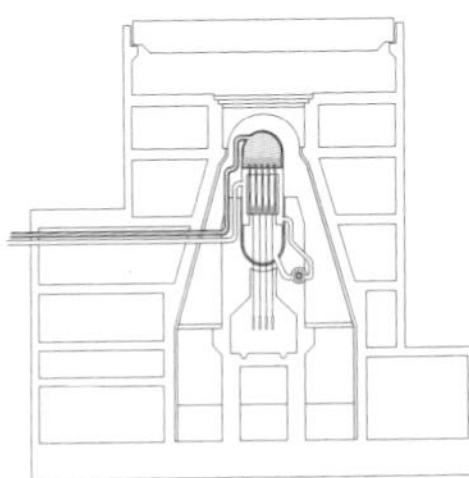

coolant: boiling water
caloporteur[M]: eau[F] bouillante
Kühlmittel[N]: Siedewasser[N]
refrigerante[M]: agua[F] hirviente

# NUCLEAR ENERGY
# ÉNERGIE^F NUCLÉAIRE
# KERNENERGIE^F
# ENERGÍA^F NUCLEAR

## FUEL HANDLING SEQUENCE
## SÉQUENCE^F DE MANIPULATION^F DU COMBUSTIBLE^M
## BRENNELEMENTEBESCHICKUNG^F
## SECUENCIA^F EN EL MANEJO^M DE COMBUSTIBLE^M

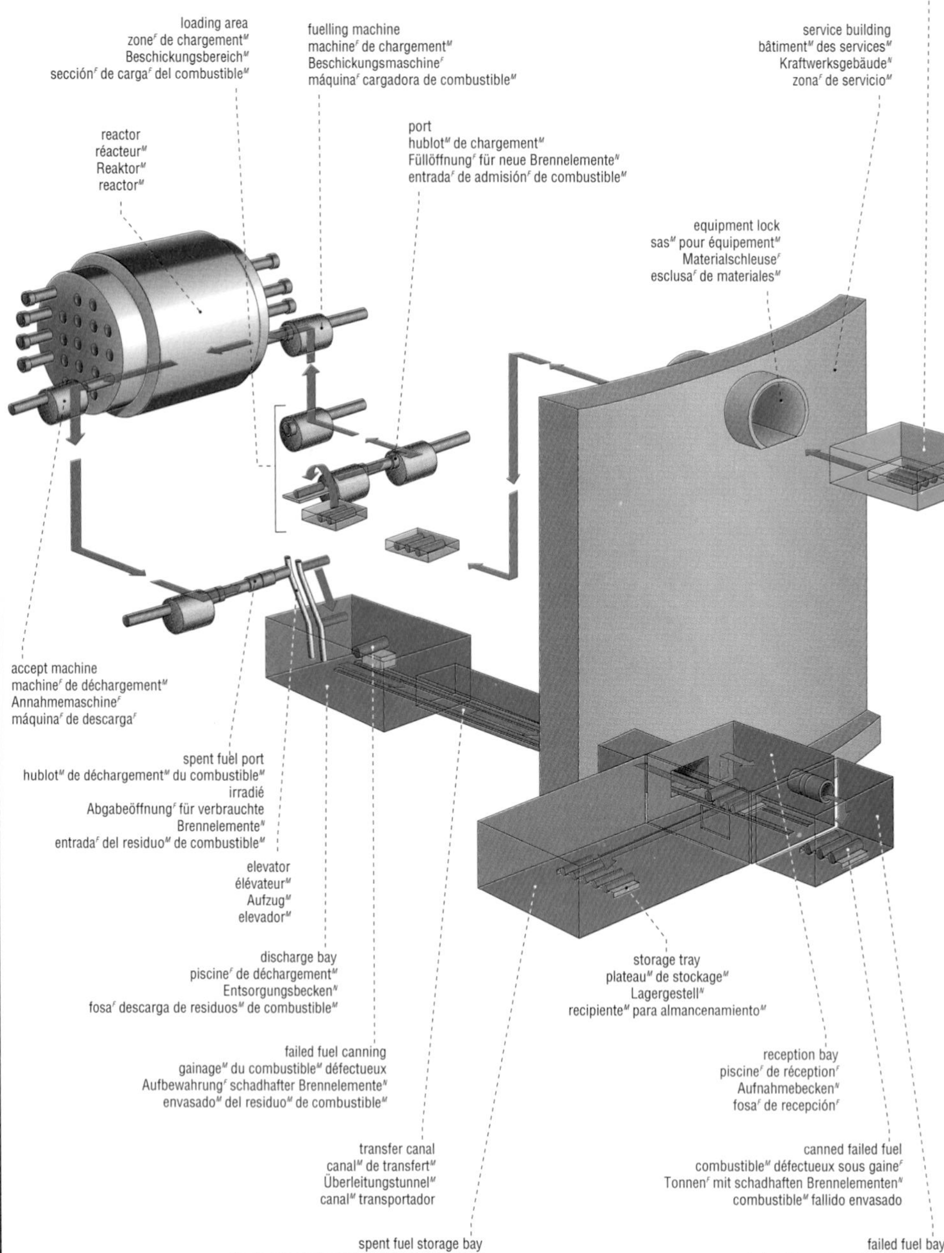

## FUEL BUNDLE
## GRAPPE[F] DE COMBUSTIBLE[M]
## BRENNELEMENT[N]
## ELEMENTO[M] CARGADOR DE COMBUSTIBLE[M]

## NUCLEAR REACTOR
## RÉACTEUR[M] NUCLÉAIRE
## KERNREAKTOR[M]
## CARGA[F] DEL REACTOR[M] NUCLEAR

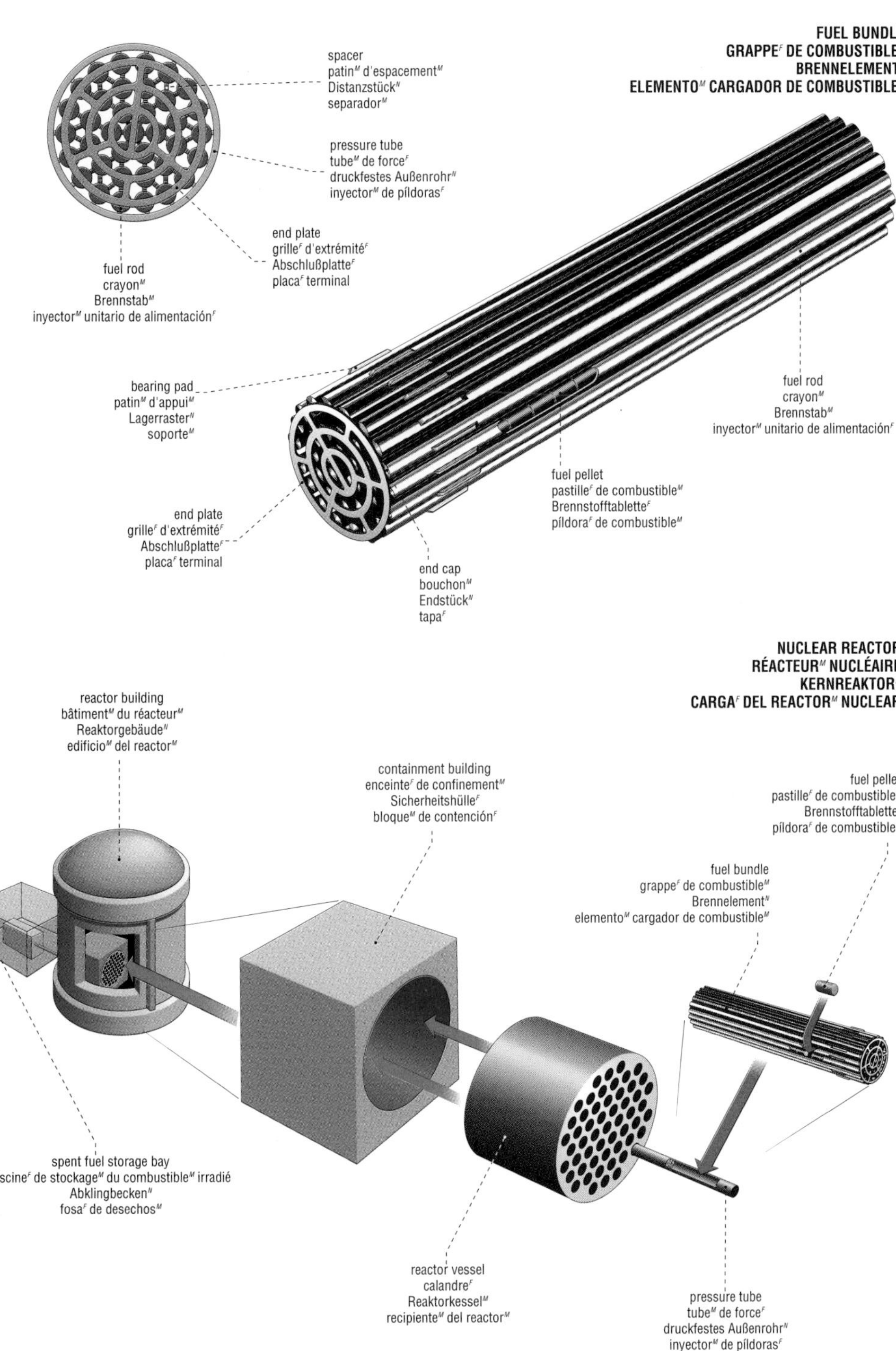

# NUCLEAR ENERGY
# ÉNERGIE[F] NUCLÉAIRE
# KERNENERGIE[F]
# ENERGÍA[F] NUCLEAR

## PRODUCTION OF ELECTRICITY FROM NUCLEAR ENERGY
## PRODUCTION[F] D'ÉLECTRICITÉ[F] PAR ÉNERGIE[F] NUCLÉAIRE
## STROMERZEUGUNG[F] AUS KERNENERGIE[F]
## PRODUCCIÓN[F] DE ELECTRICIDAD[F] POR MEDIO DE ENERGÍA[F] NUCLEAR

water turns into steam
transformation[F] de l'eau[F] en vapeur[F]
Wasser[N] verdampft
conversión[F] del agua[F] en vapor[M]

containment building
enceinte[F] de confinement[M]
Sicherheitshülle[F]
edificio[M]

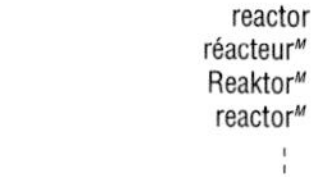

reactor
réacteur[M]
Reaktor[M]
reactor[M]

dousing water tank
réservoir[M] d'arrosage[M]
Kühlwassertank[M]
tanque[M] de agua[F] de rociado[M]

transfer of heat to water
transmission[F] de la chaleur[F] à l'eau[F]
Wärmeabgabe[F] an Wasser[N]
transferencia[F] de calor[M] al agua[F]

sprinklers
gicleurs[M]
Sprinkler[M]
rociadores[M]

safety valve
soupape[F] de sûreté[F]
Sicherheitsventil[N]
válvula[F] de seguridad[F]

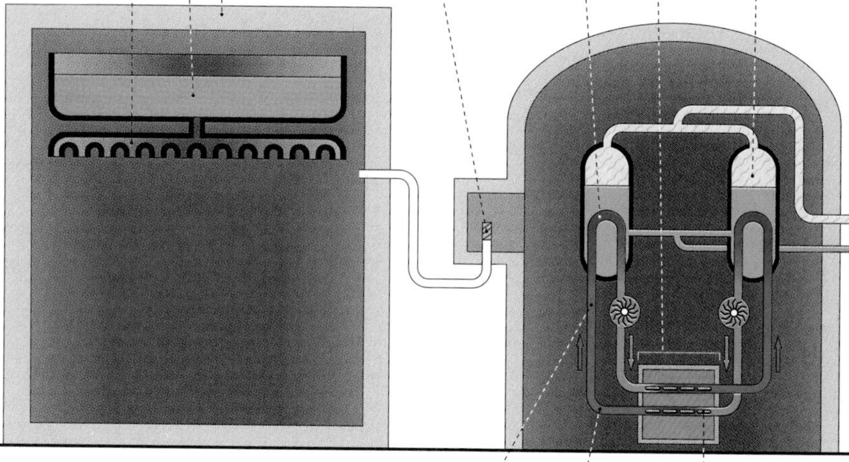

coolant transfers the heat to the steam generator
acheminement[M] de la chaleur[F] au générateur[M] de vapeur[F] par le caloporteur[M]
Kühlmittel[N] überträgt Wärme[F] an Dampfgenerator[M]
el refrigerante[M] transfiere el calor[M] al generador[M] de vapor[M]

heat production
production[F] de chaleur[F]
Wärmeerzeugung[F]
producción[F] de calor[M]

fission of uranium fuel
fission[F] de l'uranium[M]
Spaltung[F] des Uranbrennstoffs[M]
uranio[M] en fisión[F]

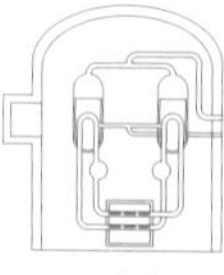

fuel
combustible[M]
Brennstoff[M]
combustible[M]

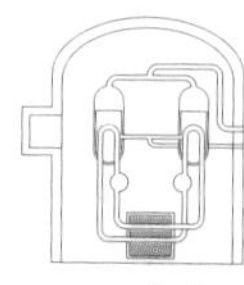

moderator
modérateur[M]
Moderator[M]
moderador[M]

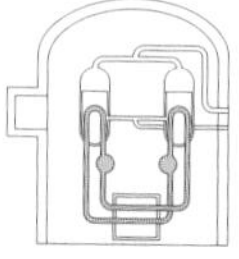

coolant
caloporteur[M]
Kühlmittel[N]
refrigerante[M]

steam pressure drives turbine
entraînement[M] de la turbine[F] par la vapeur[F]
Dampfdruck[M] treibt Turbine[F] an
la presión[F] del vapor[M] impulsa las turbinas[F]

electricity transmission
transport[M] de l'électricité[F]
Stromfortleitung[F]
transmisión[F] de electricidad[F]

voltage increase
élévation[F] de la tension[F]
Spannungserhöhung[F]
ampliación[F] del voltaje[M]

turbine shaft turns generator
entraînement[M] du rotor[M] de l'alternateur[M]
Turbinenwelle[F] treibt Generator[M] an
la flecha[F] de la turbina[F] hace girar el generador[M]

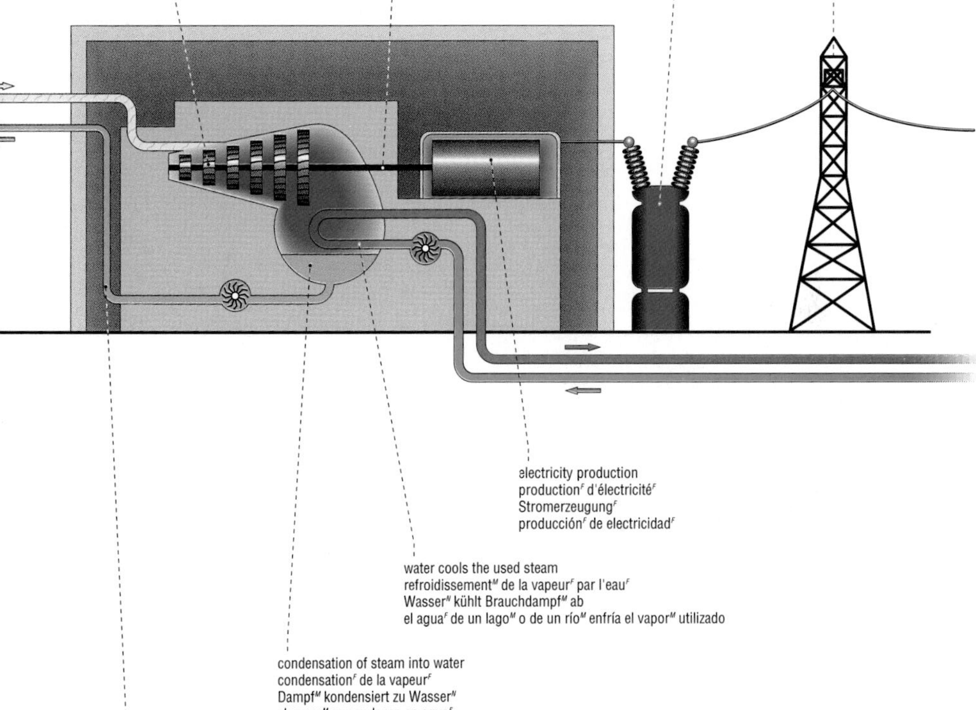


water is pumped back into the steam generator
retour[M] de l'eau[F] au générateur[M] de vapeur[F]
Wasser[N] wird zum Dampfgenerator[M] zurückgepumpt
el agua[F] regresa al generador[M] de vapor[M]

# SOLAR ENERGY
# ÉNERGIE[F] SOLAIRE
# SONNENENERGIE[F]
# ENERGÍA[F] SOLAR

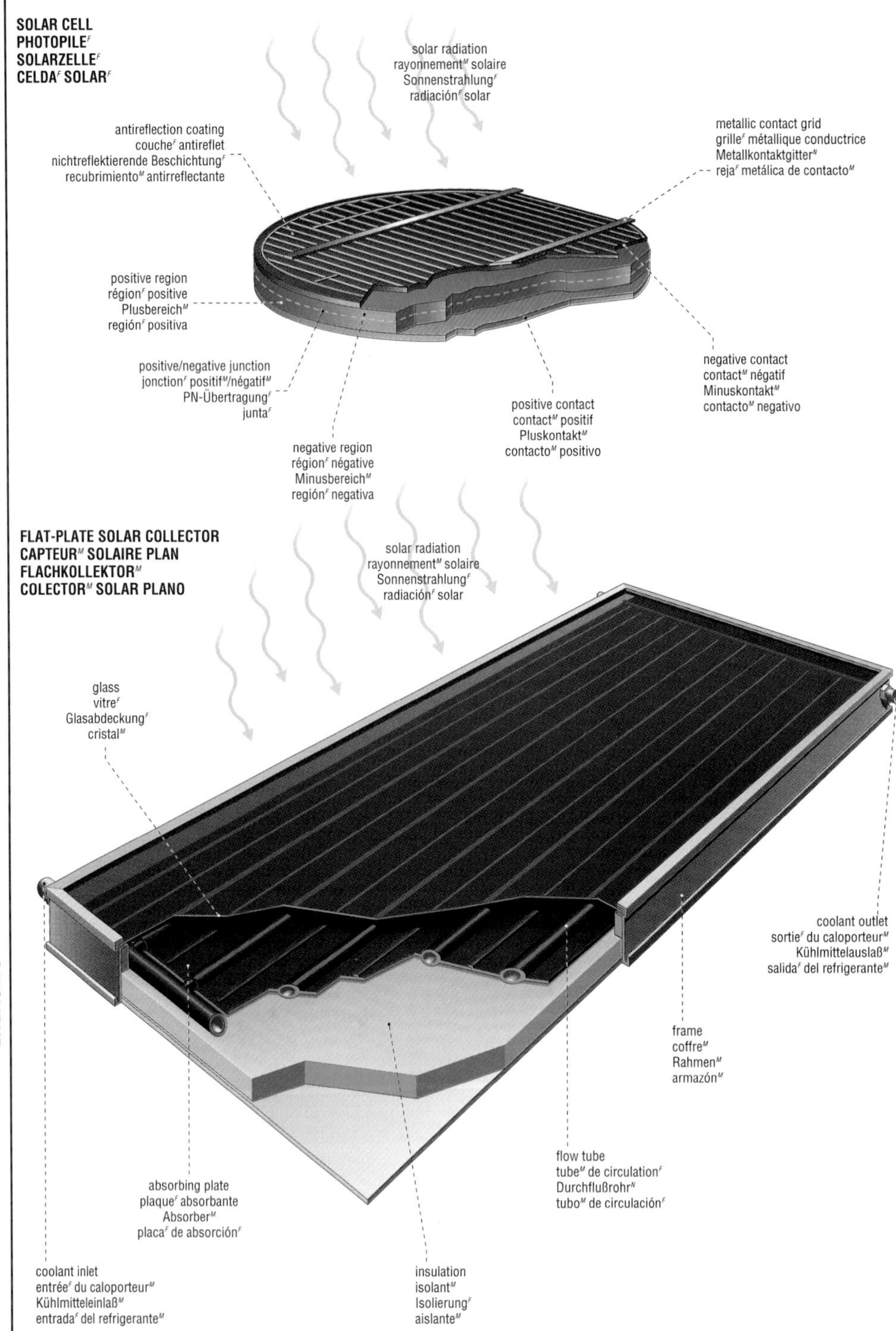

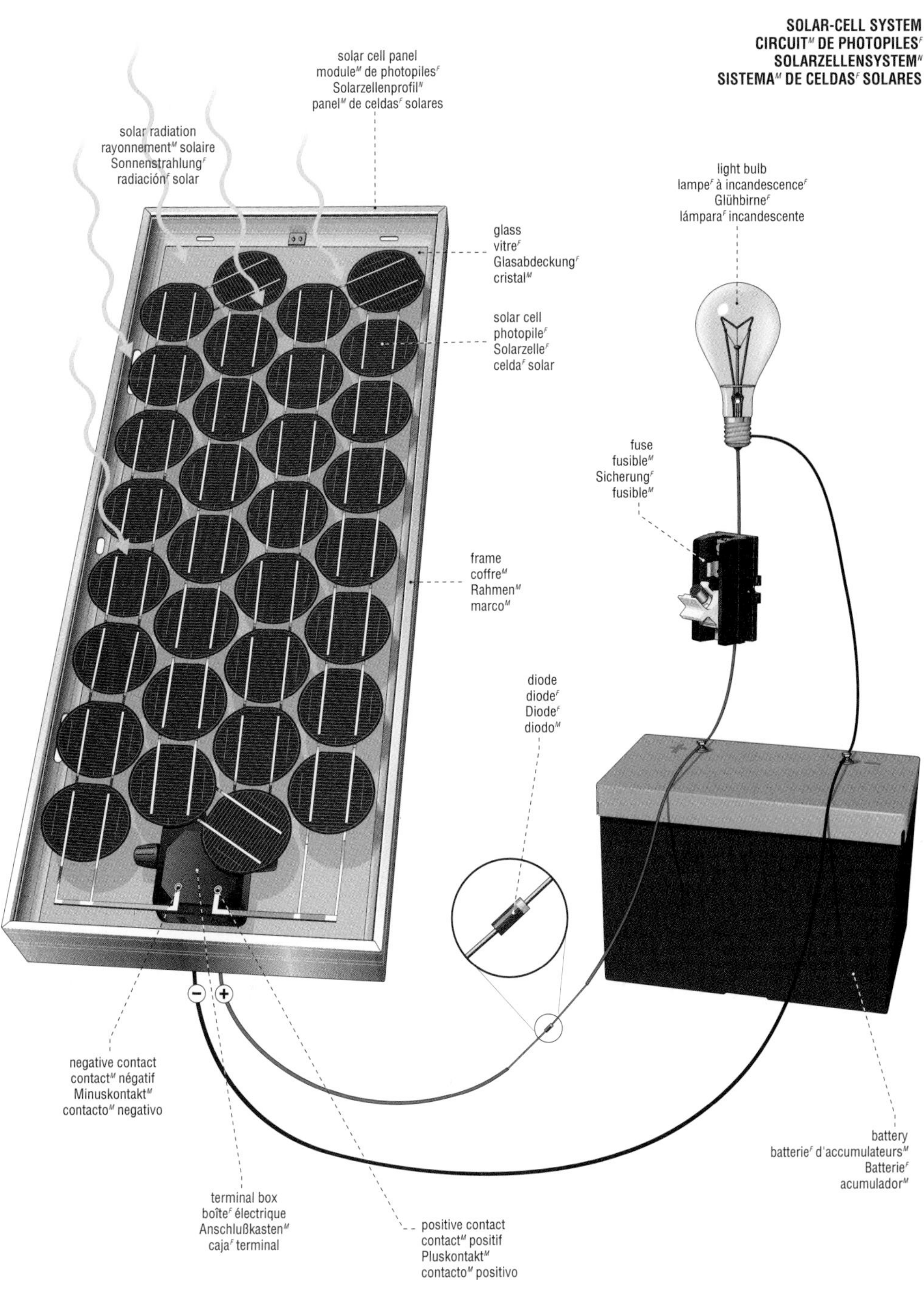
solar cell panel
module$^{M}$ de photopiles$^{F}$
Solarzellenprofil$^{N}$
panel$^{M}$ de celdas$^{F}$ solares
solar radiation
rayonnement$^{M}$ solaire
Sonnenstrahlung$^{F}$
radiación$^{F}$ solar
light bulb
lampe$^{F}$ à incandescence$^{F}$
Glühbirne$^{F}$
lámpara$^{F}$ incandescente
glass
vitre$^{F}$
Glasabdeckung$^{F}$
cristal$^{M}$
solar cell
photopile$^{F}$
Solarzelle$^{F}$
celda$^{F}$ solar
fuse
fusible$^{M}$
Sicherung$^{F}$
fusible$^{M}$
frame
coffre$^{M}$
Rahmen$^{M}$
marco$^{M}$
diode
diode$^{F}$
Diode$^{F}$
diodo$^{M}$
negative contact
contact$^{M}$ négatif
Minuskontakt$^{M}$
contacto$^{M}$ negativo
battery
batterie$^{F}$ d'accumulateurs$^{M}$
Batterie$^{F}$
acumulador$^{M}$
terminal box
boîte$^{F}$ électrique
Anschlußkasten$^{M}$
caja$^{F}$ terminal
positive contact
contact$^{M}$ positif
Pluskontakt$^{M}$
contacto$^{M}$ positivo

## SOLAR ENERGY
## ÉNERGIE^F SOLAIRE
## SONNENENERGIE^F
## ENERGÍA^F SOLAR

### SOLAR FURNACE
### FOUR^M SOLAIRE
### SONNENOFEN^M
### HORNO^M SOLAR

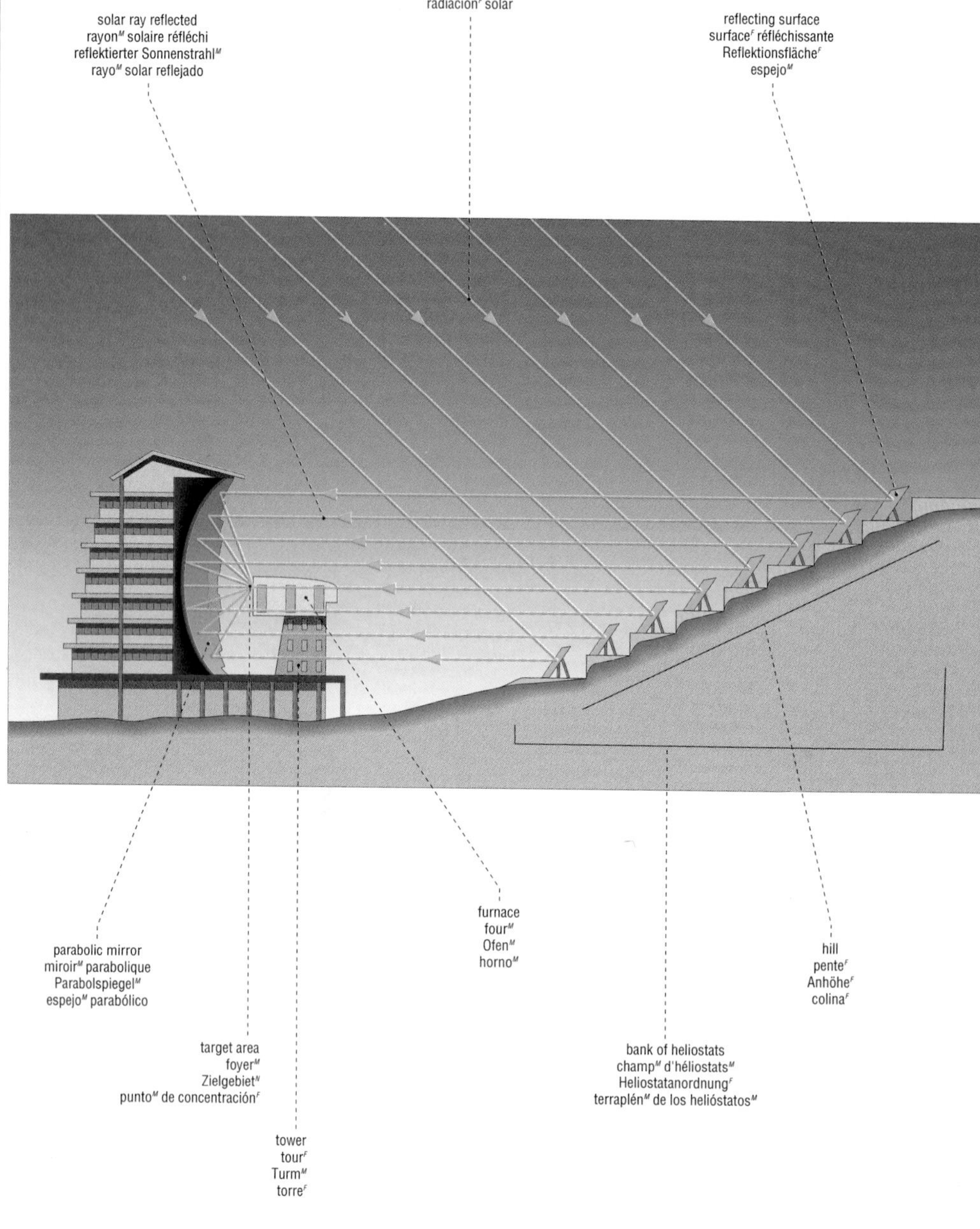

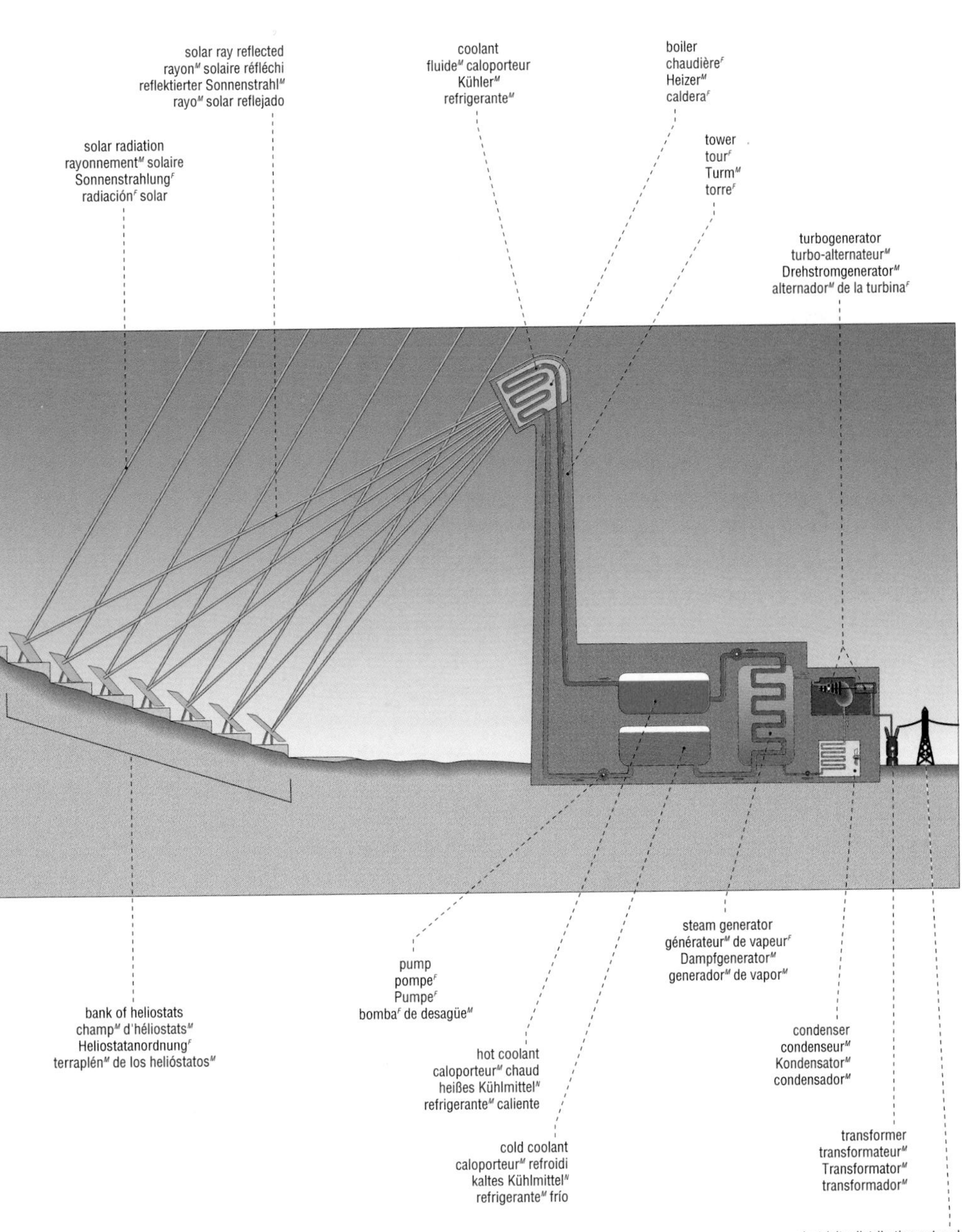
solar ray reflected
rayon[M] solaire réfléchi
reflektierter Sonnenstrahl[M]
rayo[M] solar reflejado
coolant
fluide[M] caloporteur
Kühler[M]
refrigerante[M]
boiler
chaudière[F]
Heizer[M]
caldera[F]
solar radiation
rayonnement[M] solaire
Sonnenstrahlung[F]
radiación[F] solar
tower
tour[F]
Turm[M]
torre[F]
turbogenerator
turbo-alternateur[M]
Drehstromgenerator[M]
alternador[M] de la turbina[F]
steam generator
générateur[M] de vapeur[F]
Dampfgenerator[M]
generador[M] de vapor[M]
pump
pompe[F]
Pumpe[F]
bomba[F] de desagüe[M]
bank of heliostats
champ[M] d'héliostats[M]
Heliostatanordnung[F]
terraplén[M] de los helióstatos[M]
condenser
condenseur[M]
Kondensator[M]
condensador[M]
hot coolant
caloporteur[M] chaud
heißes Kühlmittel[N]
refrigerante[M] caliente
transformer
transformateur[M]
Transformator[M]
transformador[M]
cold coolant
caloporteur[M] refroidi
kaltes Kühlmittel[N]
refrigerante[M] frío
electricity distribution network
réseau[M] de transport[M] d'électricité[F]
Stromnetz[N]
red[F] de transmisión[F] de electricidad[F]

# SOLAR ENERGY
# ÉNERGIE^F SOLAIRE
# SONNENENERGIE^F
# ENERGÍA^F SOLAR

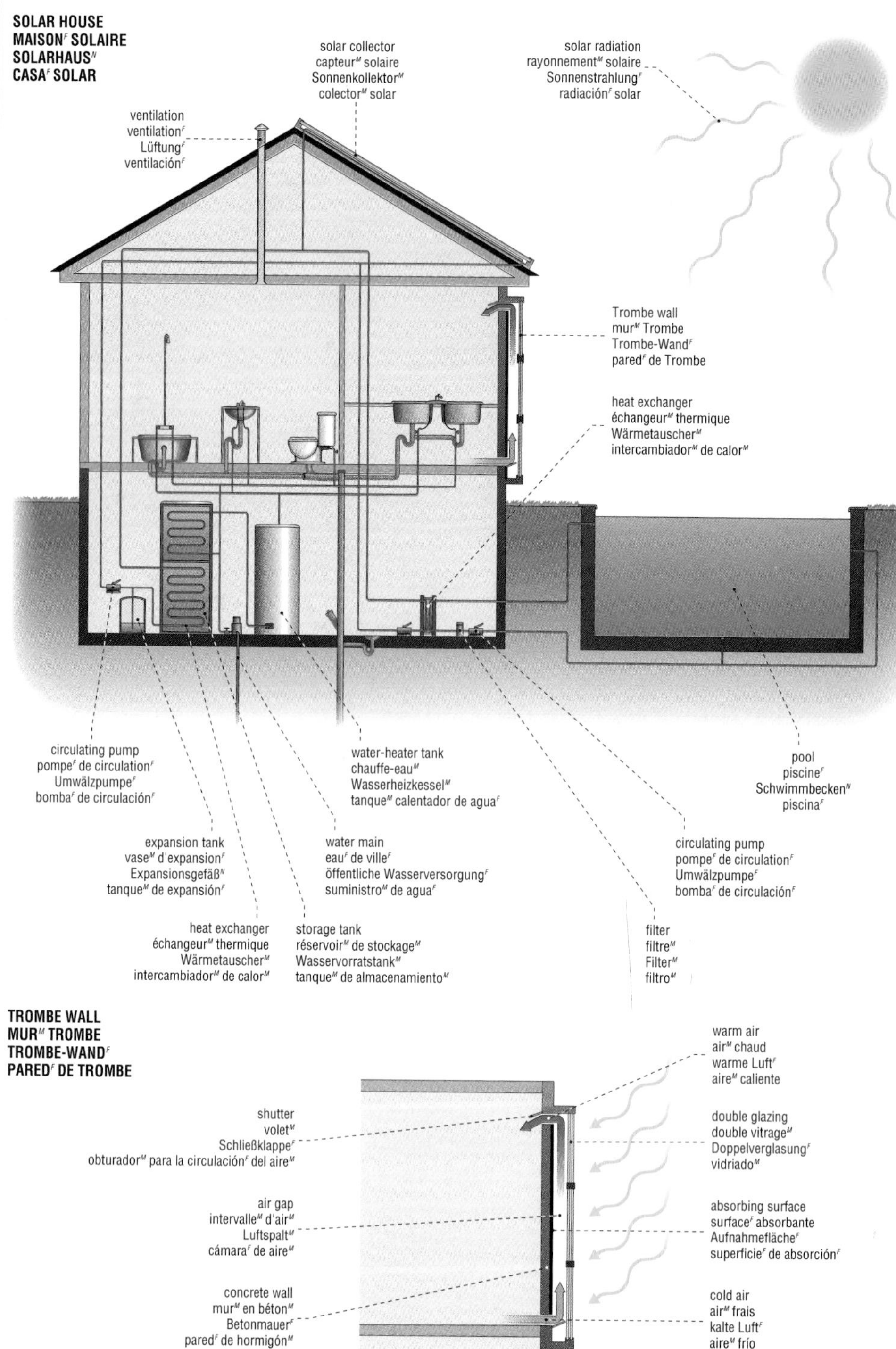

# WIND ENERGY
# ÉNERGIE[F] ÉOLIENNE
# WINDENERGIE[F]
# ENERGÍA[F] EÓLICA

## WINDMILL
## MOULIN[M] À VENT[M]
## WINDMÜHLE[F]
## MOLINO[M] DE VIENTO[M]

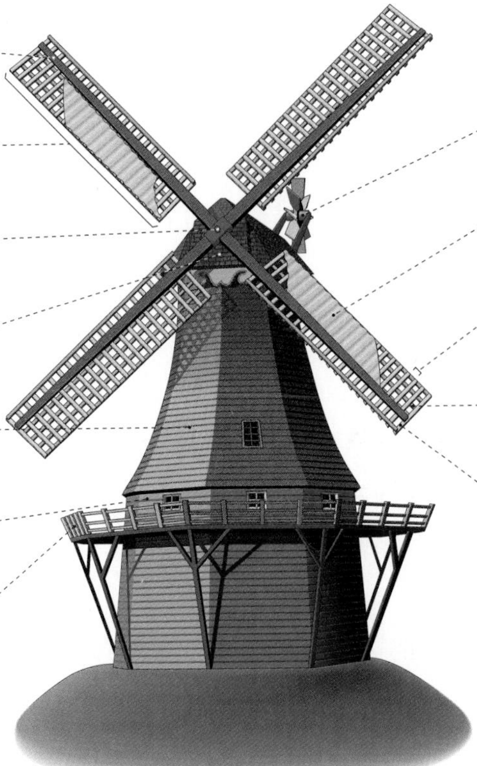

stock
bras[M]
Schaft[M]
larguero[M]
sail
aile[F]
Flügel[M]
aspa[F]
windshaft
arbre[M]
Welle[F]
eje[M] de las aspas[F]
cap
calotte[F]
Windmühlenkappe[F]
capucha[F] giratoria
tower
tour[F]
Turm[M]
torre[F]
floor
étage[M]
Stockwerk[N]
piso[M]
gallery
galerie[F]
Galerie[F]
pasillo[M]
fantail
gouvernail[M]
Fächergerüst[N]
molinete[M]
sail cloth
voile[F]
Segeltuchbespannung[F]
lona[F]
hemlath
cotret[M]
Stabwerk[N]
lama[F]
sailbar
latte[F]
Segelstange[F]
travesaño[M]
frame
cadre[M]
Stabwerk[N]
armazón[M]

## POST MILL
## MOULIN[M] PIVOT[M]
## BOCKMÜHLE[F]
## MOLINO[M] DE PLATAFORMA[F] GIRATORIA

rotor
rotor[M]
Rotor[M]
rotor[M]
steps
escalier[M]
Treppe[F]
escalera[F]
tail pole
queue[F]
Stert[M]
puntal[M] trasero
post
pivot[M]
Hausbaum[M]
soporte[M] de la plataforma[F]

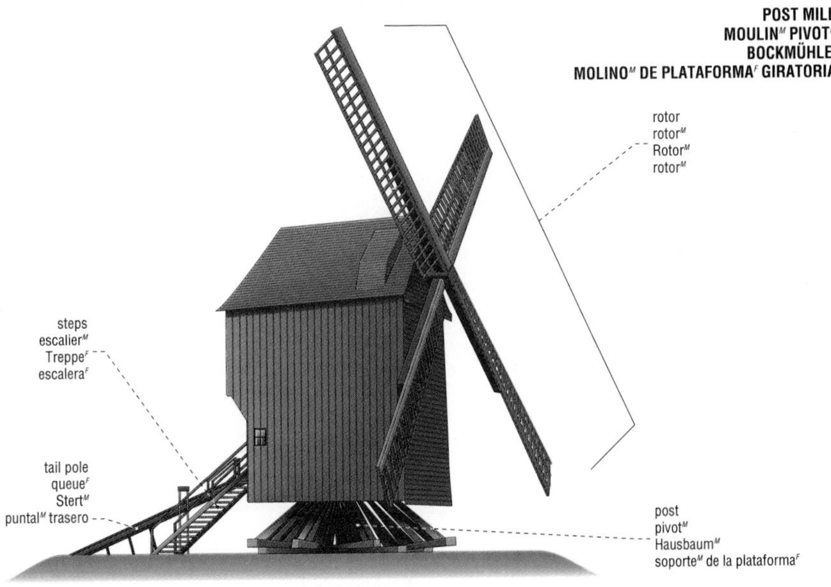

# WIND ENERGY
# ÉNERGIE[F] ÉOLIENNE
# WINDENERGIE[F]
# ENERGÍA[F] EÓLICA

## HORIZONTAL-AXIS WIND TURBINE
## ÉOLIENNE[F] À AXE[M] HORIZONTAL
## LÄNGSACHSENWINDTURBINE[F]
## TURBINA[F] DE VIENTO[M] DE EJE[M] HORIZONTAL

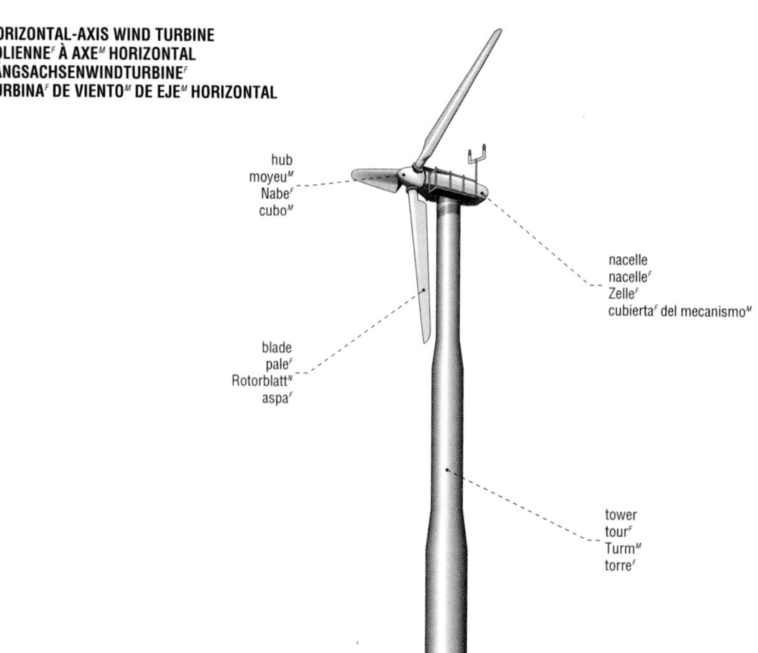


## VERTICAL-AXIS WIND TURBINE
## ÉOLIENNE[F] À AXE[M] VERTICAL
## VERTIKALACHSENWINDTURBINE[F]
## TURBINA[F] DE VIENTO[M] DE EJE[M] VERTICAL

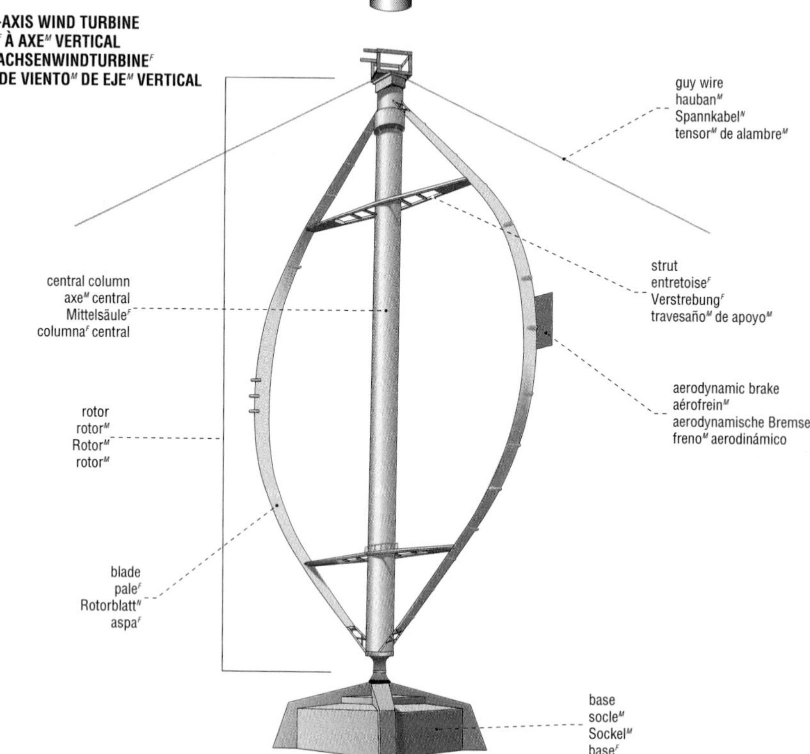

# HEAVY MACHINERY
# ENGINS ET MACHINES
# SCHWERMASCHINEN
# MAQUINARIA PESADA

## SUMMARY

# FIRE PREVENTION
# PRÉVENTION^F DES INCENDIES^M
# BRANDBEKÄMPFUNG^F
# PREVENCIÓN^F DE INCENDIOS^M

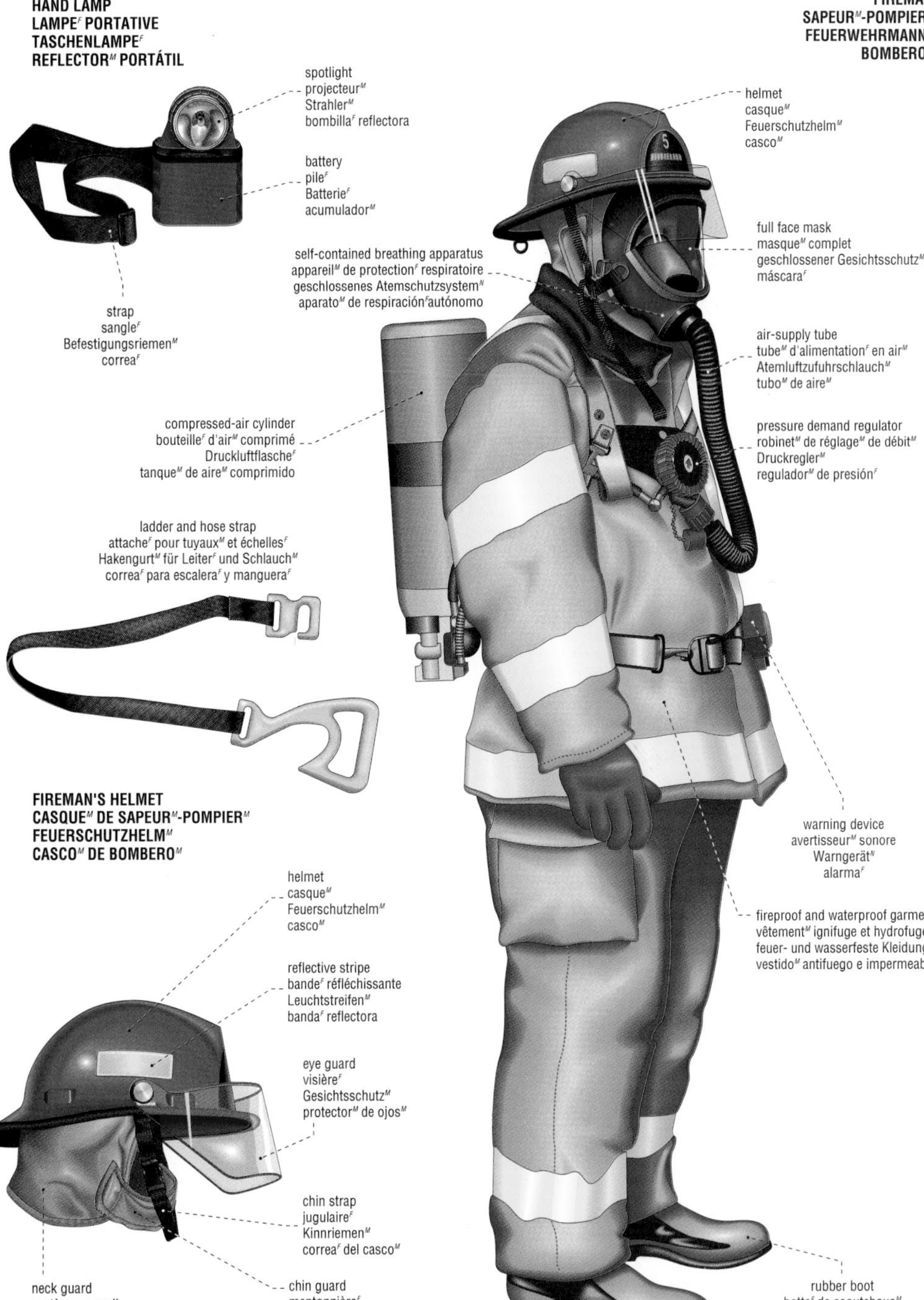

FIRE ENGINE
VÉHICULES[M] D'INCENDIE[M]
FEUERWEHRAUTO[N]
COCHE[M] DE BOMBEROS[M]

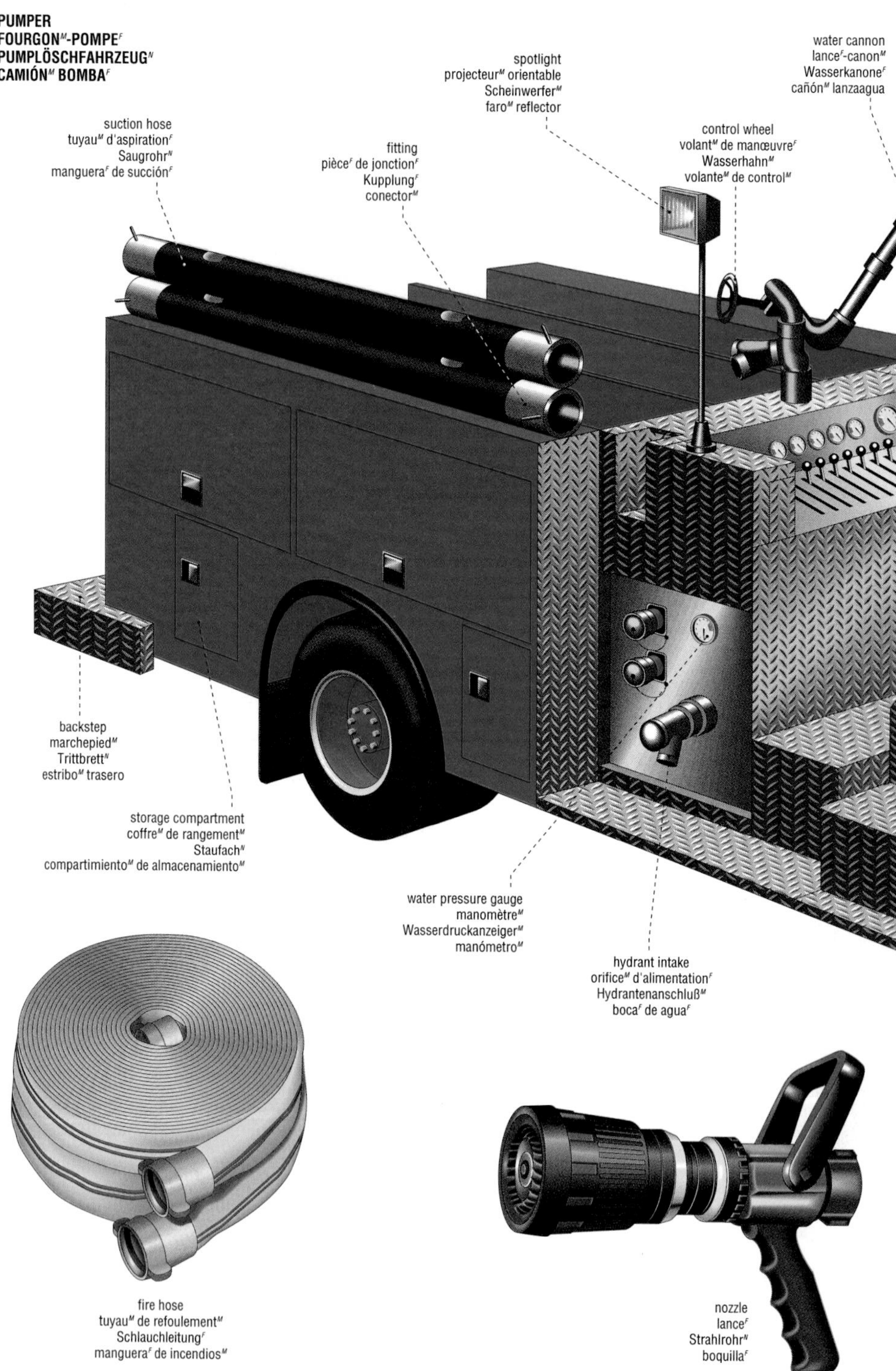

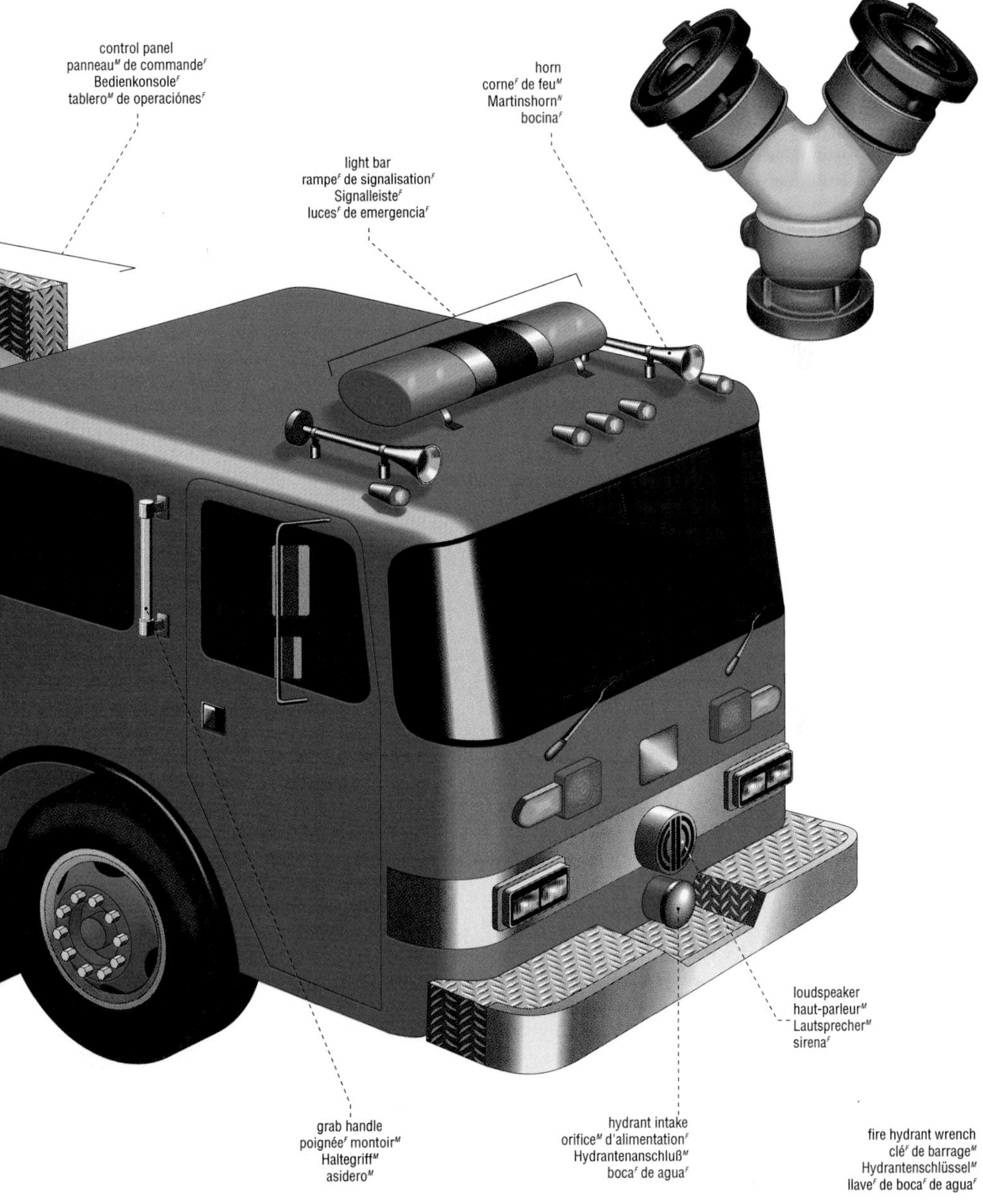

dividing connector
pièce[F] d'embranchement[M]
Y-Verbindungsstück[N]
separador[M] de boca[F] de agua[F]
control panel
panneau[M] de commande[F]
Bedienkonsole[F]
tablero[M] de operaciónes[F]
horn
corne[F] de feu[M]
Martinshorn[N]
bocina[F]
light bar
rampe[F] de signalisation[F]
Signalleiste[F]
luces[F] de emergencia[F]
loudspeaker
haut-parleur[M]
Lautsprecher[M]
sirena[F]
grab handle
poignée[F] montoir[M]
Haltegriff[M]
asidero[M]
hydrant intake
orifice[M] d'alimentation[F]
Hydrantenanschluß[M]
boca[F] de agua[F]
fire hydrant wrench
clé[F] de barrage[M]
Hydrantenschlüssel[M]
llave[F] de boca[F] de agua[F]

# FIRE ENGINE
# VÉHICULES[M] D'INCENDIE[M]
# FEUERWEHRAUTO[N]
# COCHE[M] DE BOMBEROS[M]

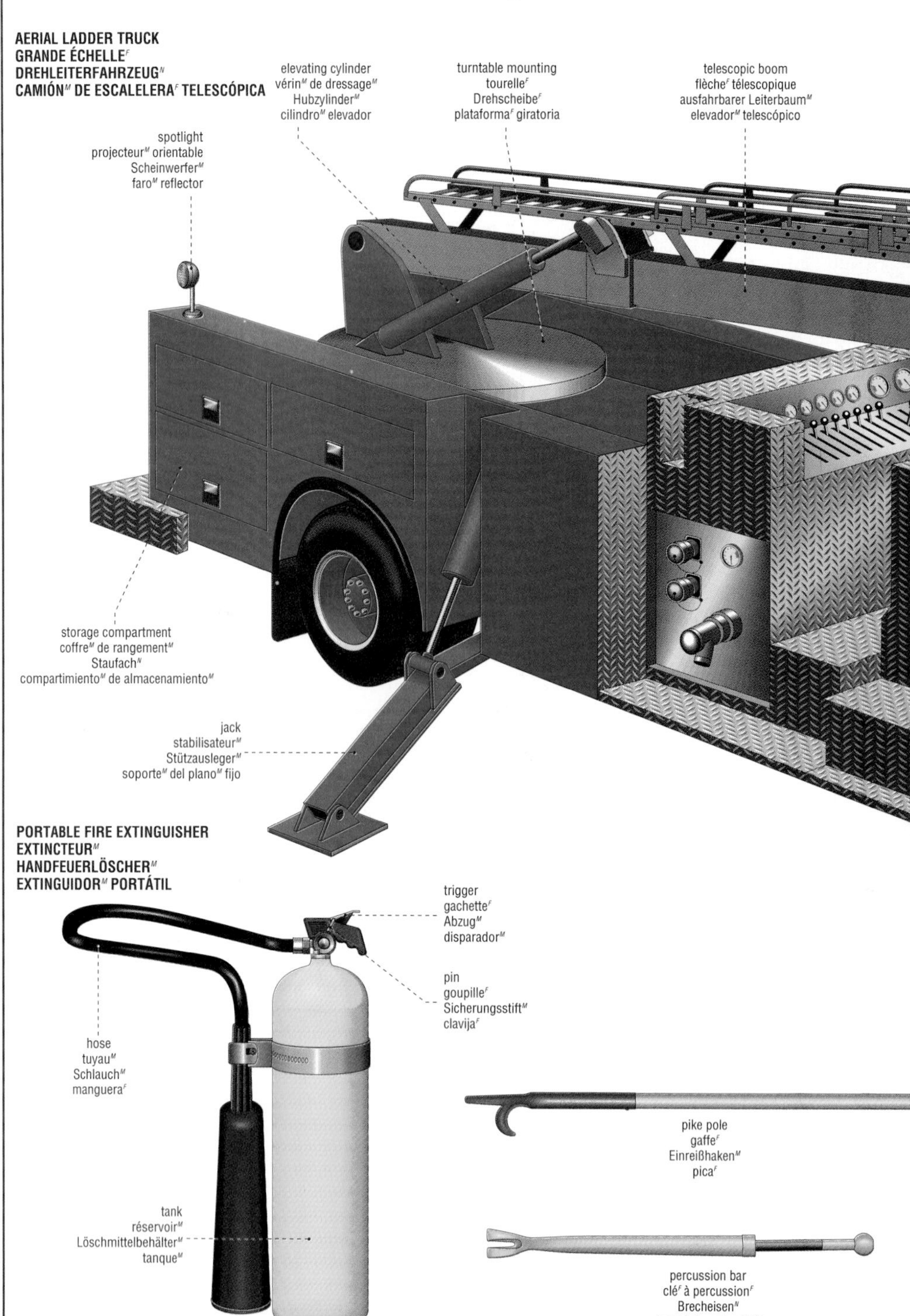

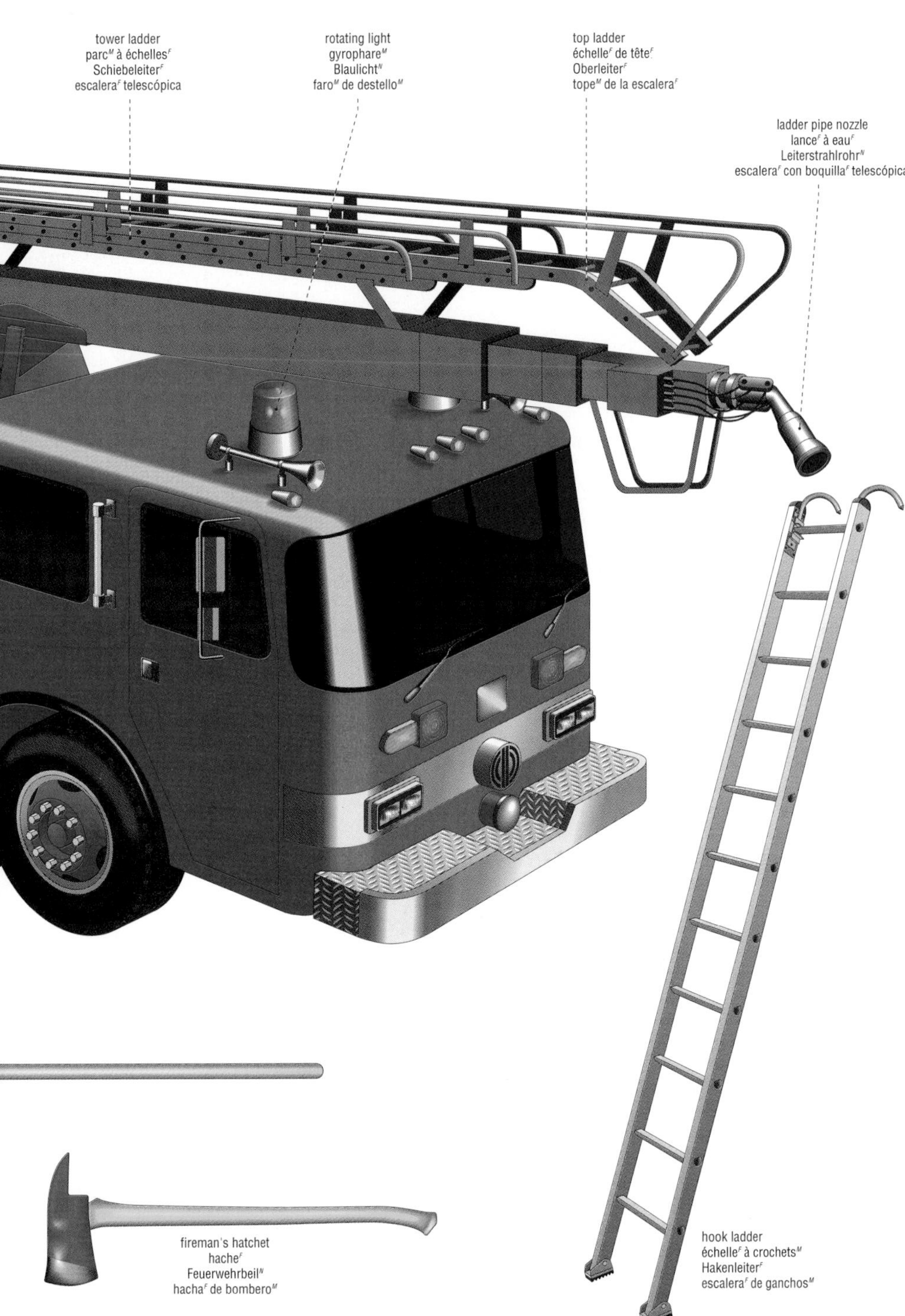
tower ladder
parc^M à échelles^F
Schiebeleiter^F
escalera^F telescópica
rotating light
gyrophare^M
Blaulicht^N
faro^M de destello^M
top ladder
échelle^F de tête^F
Oberleiter^F
tope^M de la escalera^F
ladder pipe nozzle
lance^F à eau^F
Leiterstrahlrohr^N
escalera^F con boquilla^F telescópica
fireman's hatchet
hache^F
Feuerwehrbeil^N
hacha^F de bombero^M
hook ladder
échelle^F à crochets^M
Hakenleiter^F
escalera^F de ganchos^M

# HEAVY VEHICLES
# MACHINERIE[F] LOURDE
# SCHWERFAHRZEUGE[N]
# VEHÍCULOS[M] PESADOS

## BACKHOE LOADER
## CHARGEUSE[F]-PELLETEUSE[F]
## RADLADER[M]
## RETROEXCAVADORA[F] CARGADORA[F]

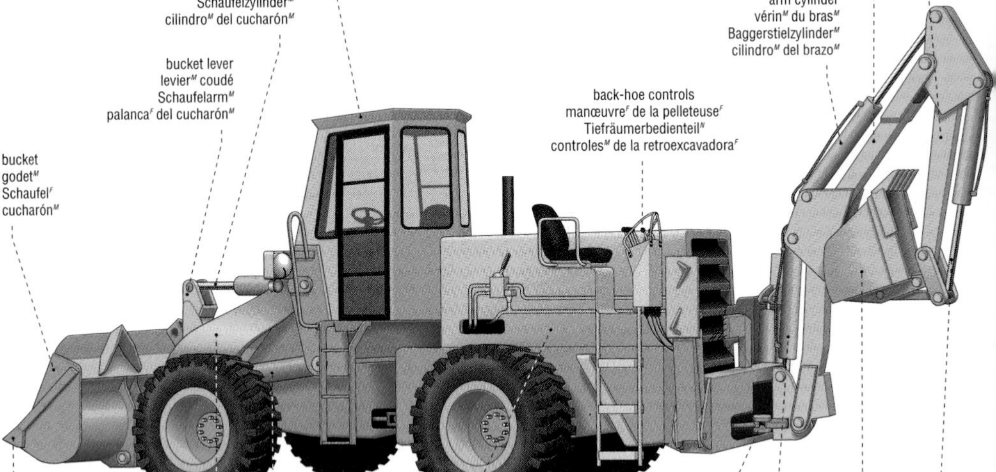

arm
bras[M]
Baggerstiel[M]
brazo[M]

cab
cabine[F]
Führerkabine[F]
cabina[F]

boom
flèche[F]
Ausleger[M]
elevador[M]

bucket cylinder
vérin[M] du godet[M]
Schaufelzylinder[M]
cilindro[M] del cucharón[M]

arm cylinder
vérin[M] du bras[M]
Baggerstielzylinder[M]
cilindro[M] del brazo[M]

bucket lever
levier[M] coudé
Schaufelarm[M]
palanca[F] del cucharón[M]

back-hoe controls
manœuvre[F] de la pelleteuse[F]
Tiefräumerbedienteil[N]
controles[M] de la retroexcavadora[F]

bucket
godet[M]
Schaufel[F]
cucharón[M]

bucket hinge pin
articulation[F] de la pelleteuse[F]
Schaufelbolzengelenk[N]
perno[M] de articulación[F] del cucharón[M]

bucket tooth
dent[F] de godet[M]
Schaufelzahn[M]
diente[M] de cucharón[M]

diesel engine
moteur[M] diesel
Dieselmotor[M]
motor[M] diésel

boom cylinder
vérin[M] de la flèche[F]
Auslegerzylinder[M]
cilindro[M] del elevador[M]

lift arm
bras[M] de levage[M]
Hubarm[M]
brazo[M] levantador

backward bucket
godet[M] rétro
hintere Schaufel[F]
cangilón[M] trasero

lift-arm cylinder
vérin[M] du bras[M] de levage[M]
Hubarmzylinder[M]
cilindro[M] del brazo[M] levantador

backward bucket cylinder
vérin[M] du godet[M] rétro
hinterer Schaufelzylinder[M]
cilindro[M] del cangilón[M] trasero

front-end loader
chargeuse[F] frontale
Schaufellader[M]
cargador[M] delantero

wheel tractor
tracteur[M]
Radtraktor[M]
tractor[M] de ruedas[F]

backhoe
pelleteuse[F]
Tiefräumer[M]
retroexcavadora[F]

## BULLDOZER
## BOUTEUR[M]
## PLANIERRAUPE[F]
## BULLDOZER[M]

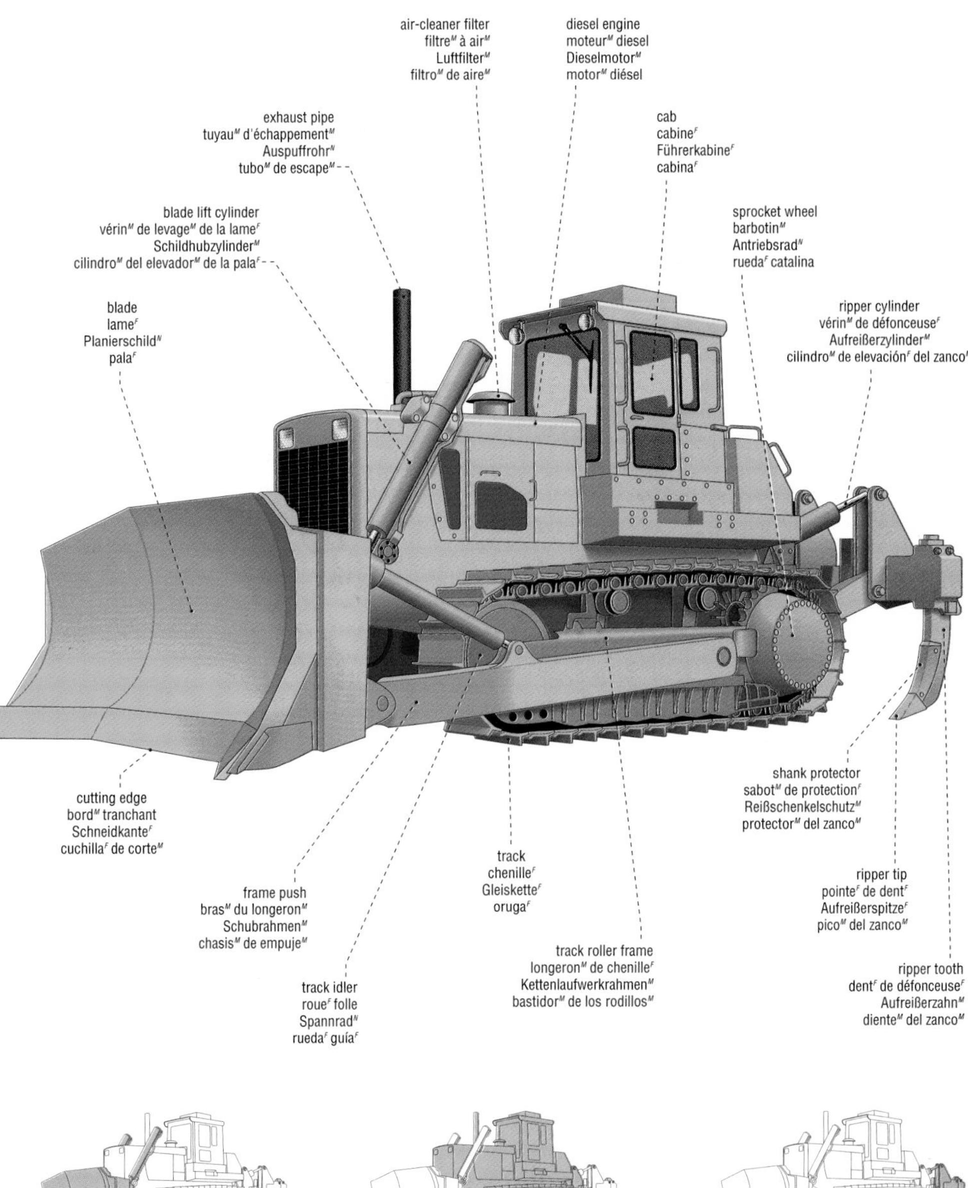


blade
lame[F]
Planierschaufel[F]
pala[F]

tracklaying tractor
tracteur[M] à chenilles[F]
Gleiskettenschlepper[M]
tractor[M] de orugas[F]

ripper
défonceuse[F]
Aufreißer[M]
zanco[M]

# HEAVY VEHICLES
# MACHINERIE^F LOURDE
# SCHWERFAHRZEUGE^N
# VEHÍCULOS^M PESADOS

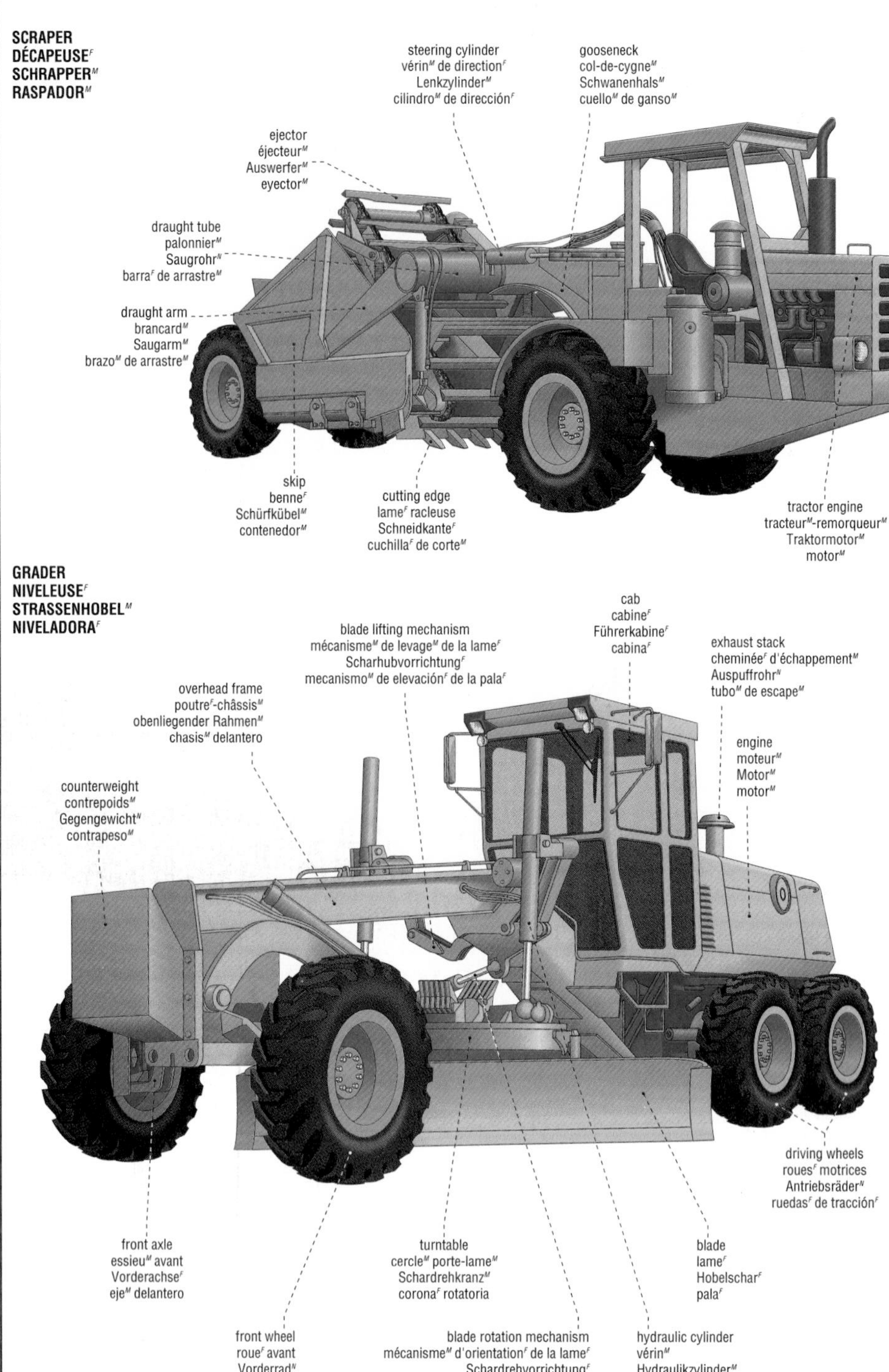

## HEAVY MACHINERY
## MACHINERIE[F] LOURDE
## SCHWERMASCHINEN[F]
## MAQUINARIA[F] PESADA

### TIPPER TRUCK
### CAMION[M]-BENNE[F]
### HINTERKIPPER[M]
### CAMIÓN[M] BASCULANTE

cab
cabine[F]
Führerhaus[N]
cabina[F]
tipper body
benne[F] basculante
Kippermulde[F]
caja[F] basculante
canopy
auvent[M]
Stirnwand[F]
cubierta[F] protectora
diesel engine
moteur[M] diesel
Dieselmotor[M]
motor[M] diésel
ladder
échelle[F]
Leiter[F]
escalerilla[F]
rib
nervure[F]
Verstärkungsrippe[F]
cuaderna[F]
frame
châssis[M]
Rahmen[M]
chasis[M]

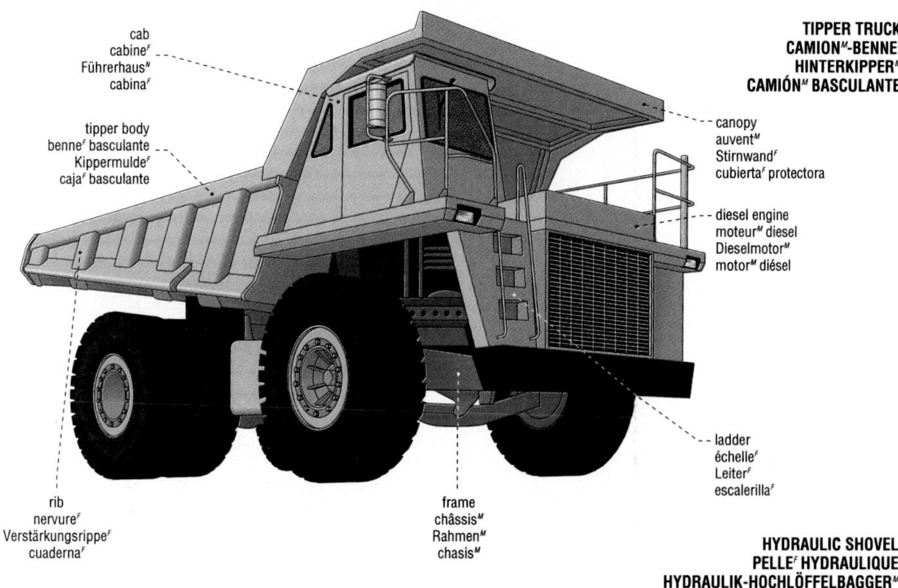

### HYDRAULIC SHOVEL
### PELLE[F] HYDRAULIQUE
### HYDRAULIK-HOCHLÖFFELBAGGER[M]
### PALA[F] HIDRÁULICA

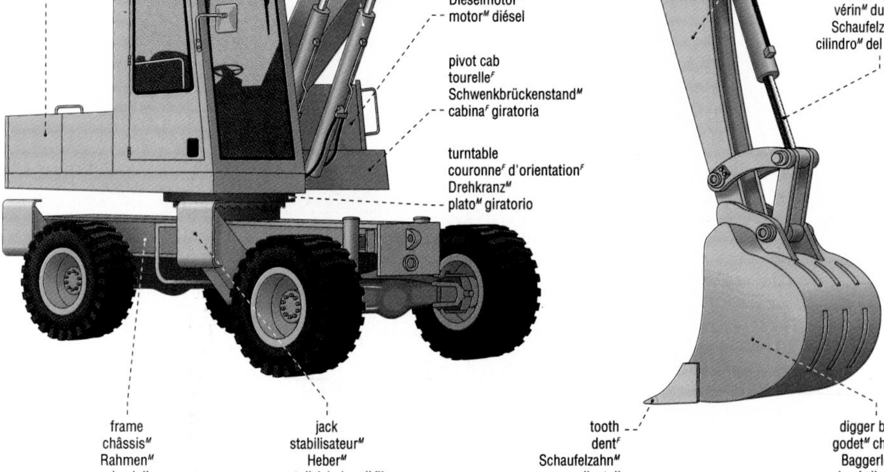

boom cylinder
vérin[M] de la flèche[F]
Auslegerzylinder[M]
cilindro[M] del elevador[M]
boom
flèche[F]
Ausleger[M]
pluma[F]
arm cylinder
vérin[M] du bras[M]
Baggerstielzylinder[M]
cilindro[M] del brazo[M]
cab
cabine[F]
Führerkabine[F]
cabina[F]
hinge pin
point[M] d'articulation[F]
Gelenk[N]
perno[M] de la bisagra[F]
counterweight
contrepoids[M]
Gegengewicht[N]
contrapeso[M]
arm
bras[M]
Baggerstiel[M]
brazo[M]
diesel engine
moteur[M] diesel
Dieselmotor[M]
motor[M] diésel
bucket cylinder
vérin[M] du godet[M]
Schaufelzylinder[M]
cilindro[M] del cucharón[M]
pivot cab
tourelle[F]
Schwenkbrückenstand[M]
cabina[F] giratoria
turntable
couronne[F] d'orientation[F]
Drehkranz[M]
plato[M] giratorio
frame
châssis[M]
Rahmen[M]
chasis[M]
jack
stabilisateur[M]
Heber[M]
soporte[M] del plano[M] fijo
tooth
dent[F]
Schaufelzahn[M]
diente[M]
digger bucket
godet[M] chargeur
Baggerlöffel[M]
cucharón[M] excavador

# MATERIAL HANDLING
# MANUTENTION[F]
# LASTENFORTBEWEGUNG[F]
# MANEJO[M] DE MATERIALES[M]

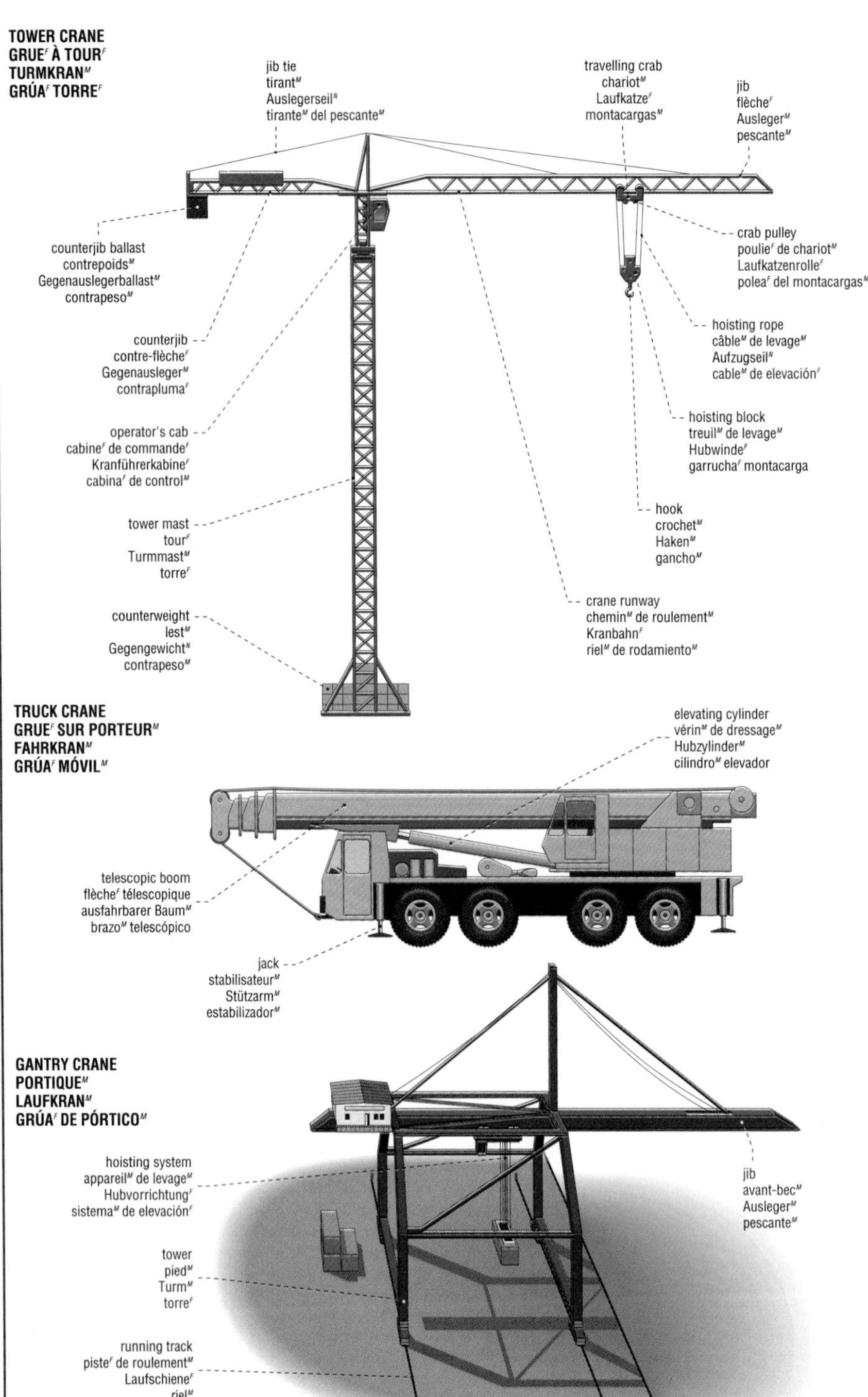

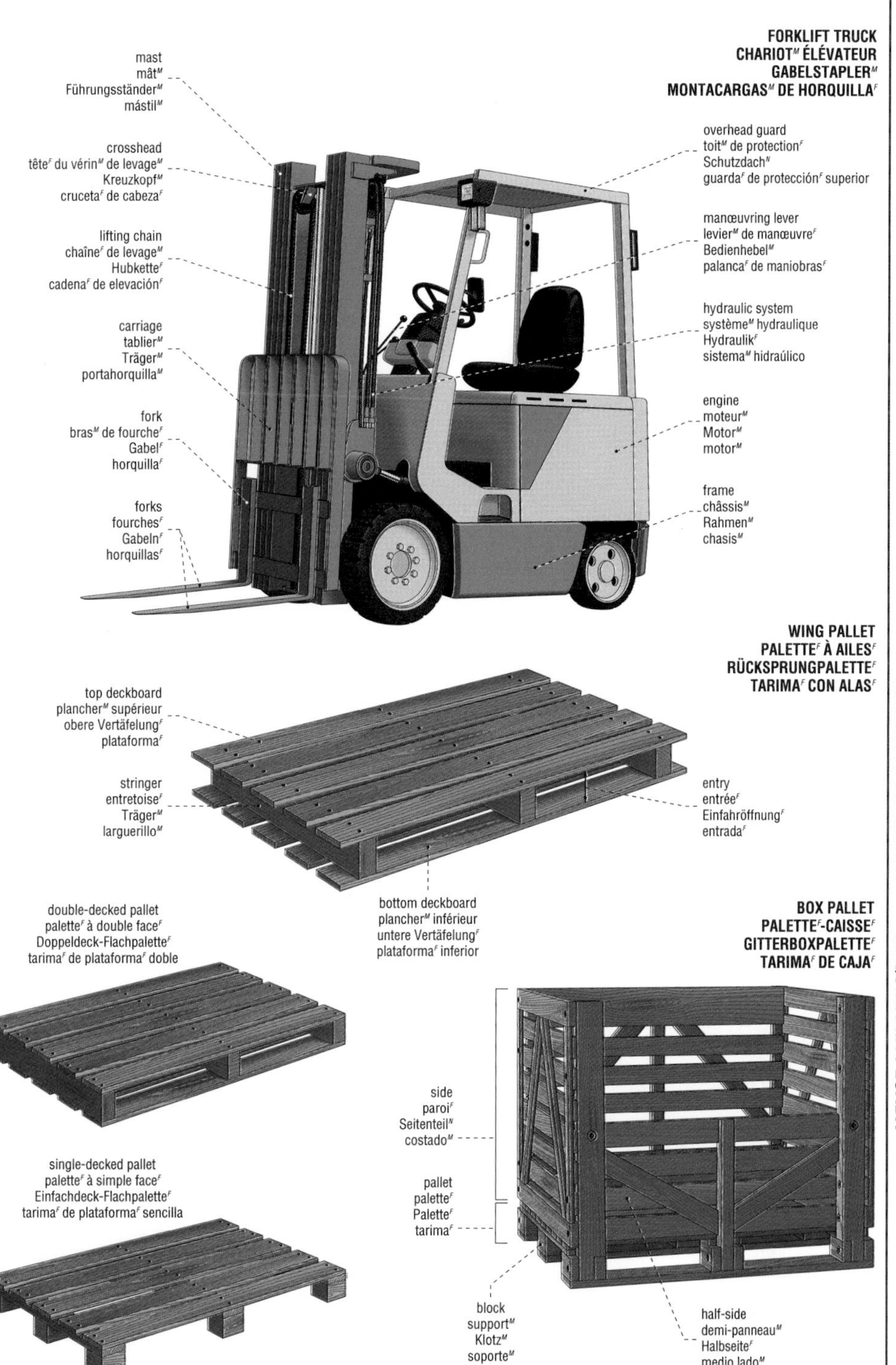
FORKLIFT TRUCK
CHARIOT[M] ÉLÉVATEUR
GABELSTAPLER[M]
MONTACARGAS[M] DE HORQUILLA[F]
mast
mât[M]
Führungsständer[M]
mástil[M]
crosshead
tête[F] du vérin[M] de levage[M]
Kreuzkopf[M]
cruceta[F] de cabeza[F]
lifting chain
chaîne[F] de levage[M]
Hubkette[F]
cadena[F] de elevación[F]
carriage
tablier[M]
Träger[M]
portahorquilla[M]
fork
bras[M] de fourche[F]
Gabel[F]
horquilla[F]
forks
fourches[F]
Gabeln[F]
horquillas[F]
overhead guard
toit[M] de protection[F]
Schutzdach[N]
guarda[F] de protección[F] superior
manœuvring lever
levier[M] de manœuvre[F]
Bedienhebel[M]
palanca[F] de maniobras[F]
hydraulic system
système[M] hydraulique
Hydraulik[F]
sistema[M] hidraúlico
engine
moteur[M]
Motor[M]
motor[M]
frame
châssis[M]
Rahmen[M]
chasis[M]
WING PALLET
PALETTE[F] À AILES[F]
RÜCKSPRUNGPALETTE[F]
TARIMA[F] CON ALAS[F]
top deckboard
plancher[M] supérieur
obere Vertäfelung[F]
plataforma[F]
stringer
entretoise[F]
Träger[M]
larguerillo[M]
entry
entrée[F]
Einfahröffnung[F]
entrada[F]
bottom deckboard
plancher[M] inférieur
untere Vertäfelung[F]
plataforma[F] inferior
double-decked pallet
palette[F] à double face[F]
Doppeldeck-Flachpalette[F]
tarima[F] de plataforma[F] doble
single-decked pallet
palette[F] à simple face[F]
Einfachdeck-Flachpalette[F]
tarima[F] de plataforma[F] sencilla
BOX PALLET
PALETTE[F]-CAISSE[F]
GITTERBOXPALETTE[F]
TARIMA[F] DE CAJA[F]
side
paroi[F]
Seitenteil[N]
costado[M]
pallet
palette[F]
Palette[F]
tarima[F]
block
support[M]
Klotz[M]
soporte[M]
half-side
demi-panneau[M]
Halbseite[F]
medio lado[M]

MATERIAL HANDLING
MANUTENTION[F]
LASTENFORTBEWEGUNG[F]
MANEJO[M] DE MATERIALES[M]
HYDRAULIC PALLET TRUCK
GERBEUR[M]
HYDRAULISCHER PALETTENHUBWAGEN[M]
MONTACARGAS[M] HIDRÁULICO DE TARIMA[F]
pallet truck
transpalette[F] manuel
Palettenhubwagen[M]
carretilla[F] hidráulica
manœuvring lever
levier[M] de manœuvre[F]
Bedienhebel[M]
palanca[F] de maniobras[F]
mast
mât[M]
Führungsständer[M]
mástil[M]
steering lever
levier[M] de conduite[F]
Lenkhebel[M]
palanca[F] de dirección[F]
hydraulic cylinder
vérin[M] hydraulique
Hydraulikzylinder[M]
cilindro[M] hidráulico
barrow
diable[M]
Sackkarren[M]
carretilla[F]
forks
fourches[F]
Gabeln[F]
horquillas[F]
solid rubber tyre
bandage[M] de roue[F] caoutchoutée
Vollgummirad[N]
llanta[F] maciza
stabilizing leg
longeron[M] stabilisateur
Stabilisator[M]
barra[F] estabilizadora
steering axle
essieu[M] directeur
Lenkachse[F]
eje[M] de dirección[F]
frame
châssis[M]
Rahmen[M]
chasis[M]
roller
roulette[F]
Rolle[F]
rueda[F]
platform pallet truck
chariot[M] à palette[F]
Flachpalettenwagen[M]
plataforma[F] hidráulica
platform trolley
chariot[M] à plateau[M]
Handwagen[M]
plataforma[F] móvil

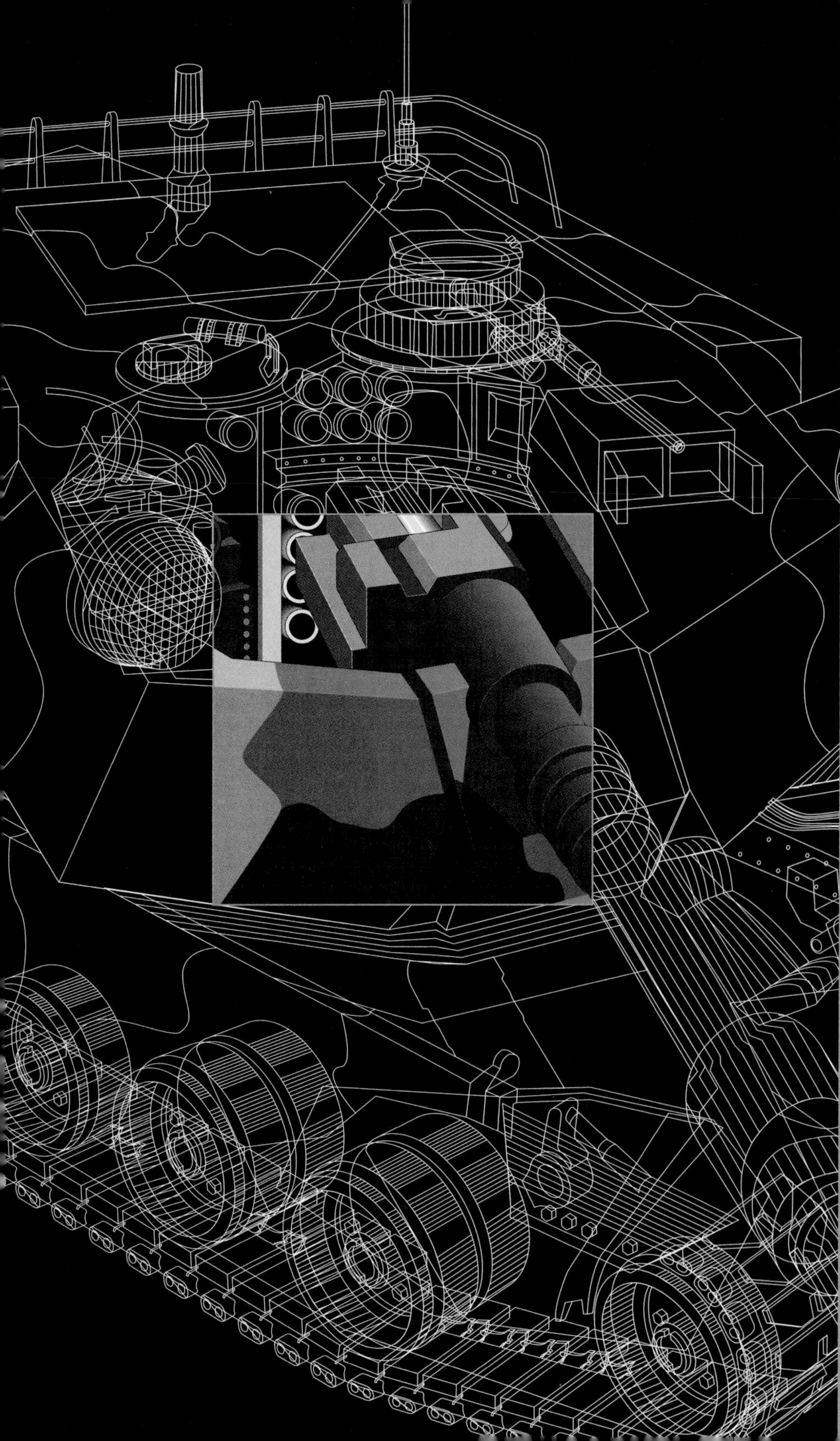

**SUMMARY**

STONE AGE WEAPONS ... 791
WEAPONS IN THE AGE OF THE ROMANS ... 791
ARMOUR ... 792
BOWS AND CROSSBOW ... 793
THRUSTING AND CUTTING WEAPONS ... 794
ARQUEBUS ... 795
SUBMACHINE GUN ... 795
AUTOMATIC RIFLE ... 796
LIGHT MACHINE GUN ... 796
REVOLVER ... 797
PISTOL ... 797
HUNTING WEAPONS ... 798
SEVENTEENTH-CENTURY CANNON ... 800
MODERN HOWITZER ... 802
MORTAR ... 803
HAND GRENADE ... 804
BAZOOKA ... 804
RECOILLESS RIFLE ... 804
TANK ... 805
SUBMARINE ... 806
FRIGATE ... 808
AIRCRAFT CARRIER ... 810
COMBAT AIRCRAFT ... 812
MISSILES ... 814

# STONE AGE WEAPONS
# ARMES[F] DE L'ÂGE[M] DE PIERRE[F]
# WAFFEN[F] IN DER STEINZEIT[F]
# ARMAS[F] DE LA EDAD[F] DE PIEDRA[F]

polished stone hand axe
hache[F] en pierre[F] polie
polierter Steinfaustkeil[M]
hacha[F] de piedra[F] pulida

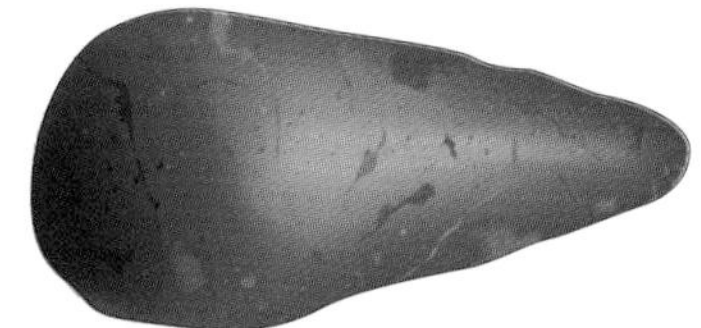

flint arrowhead
pointe[F] de flèche[F] en silex[M]
Pfeilspitze[F] aus Feuerstein[M]
punta[F] de flecha[F] de pedernal[M]

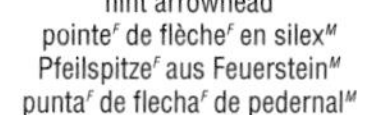

flint knife
couteau[M] en silex[M]
Messer[N] aus Feuerstein[M]
cuchillo[M] de pedernal[M]

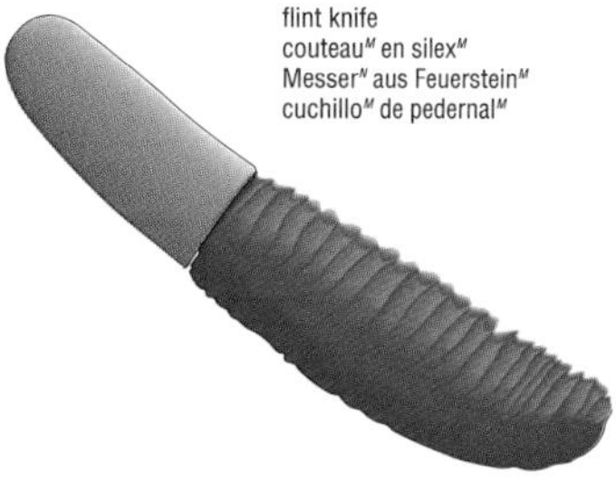

# WEAPONS IN THE AGE OF THE ROMANS
# ARMES[F] DE L'ÉPOQUE[F] ROMAINE
# WAFFEN[F] IN DER RÖMERZEIT[F]
# ARMAS[F] DEL IMPERIO[M] ROMANO

## GALLIC WARRIOR
## GUERRIER[M] GAULOIS
## GALLISCHER KRIEGER[M]
## GUERRERO[M] GALO

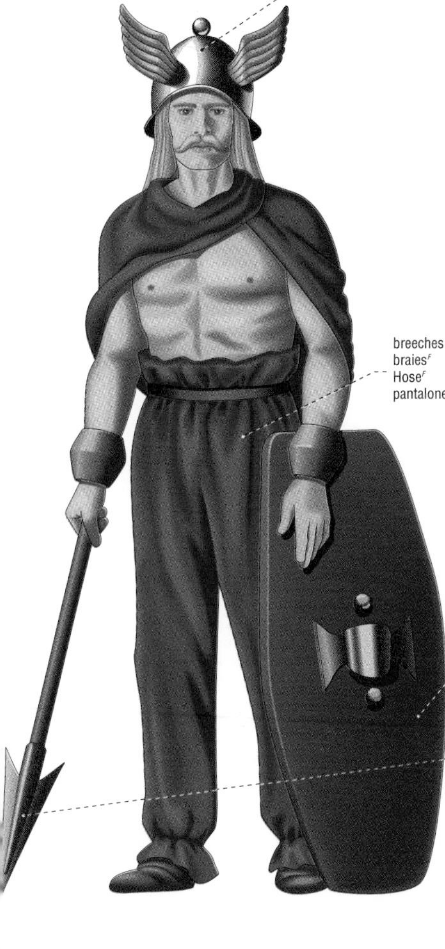

helmet
casque[M]
Helm[M]
casco[M]

breeches
braies[F]
Hose[F]
pantalones[M]

shield
bouclier[M]
Schild[M]
escudo[M]

spear
lance[F]
Speer[M]
lanza[F]

## ROMAN LEGIONARY
## LÉGIONNAIRE[M] ROMAIN
## RÖMISCHER LEGIONÄR[M]
## LEGIONARIO[M] ROMANO

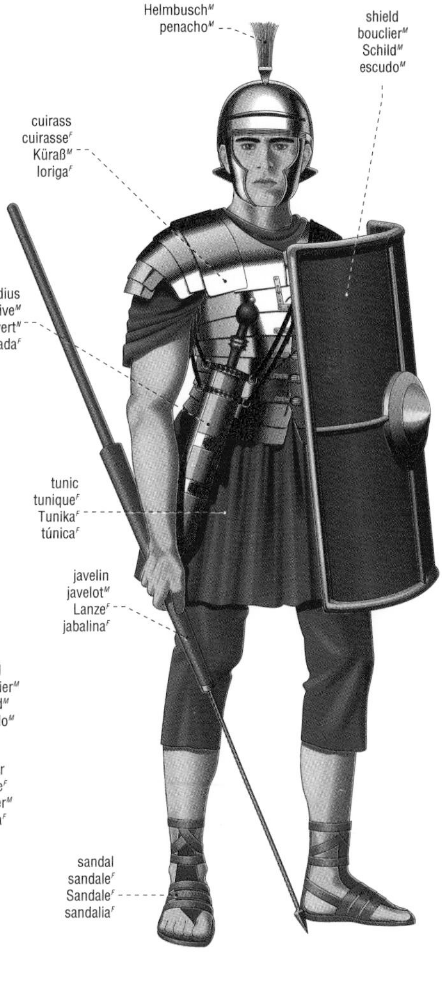

crest
cimier[M]
Helmbusch[M]
penacho[M]

shield
bouclier[M]
Schild[M]
escudo[M]

cuirass
cuirasse[F]
Küraß[M]
loriga[F]

gladius
glaive[M]
Kurzschwert[N]
espada[F]

tunic
tunique[F]
Tunika[F]
túnica[F]

javelin
javelot[M]
Lanze[F]
jabalina[F]

sandal
sandale[F]
Sandale[F]
sandalia[F]

# ARMOUR
# ARMURE^F
# RÜSTUNG^F
# ARMADURA^F

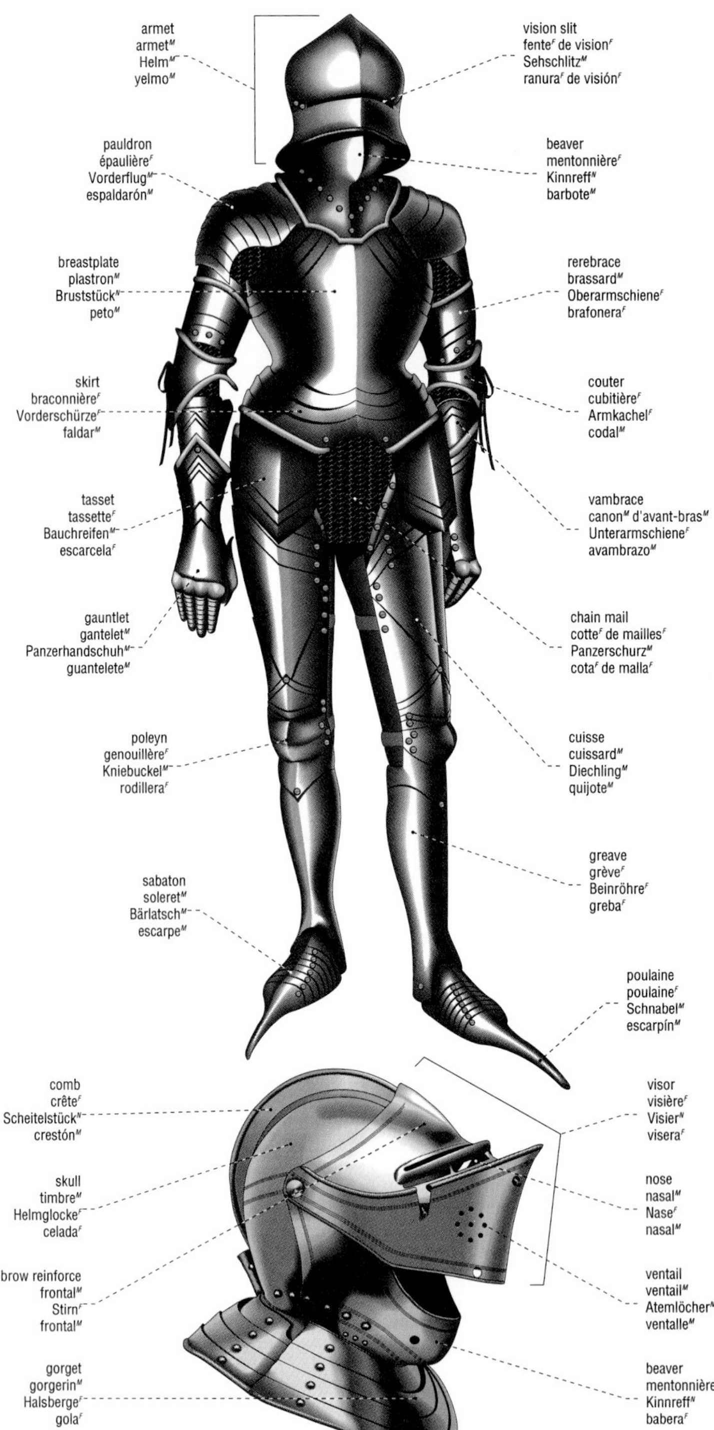

# BOWS AND CROSSBOW
# ARCS[M] ET ARBALÈTE[F]
# BOGEN[M] UND ARMBRUST[F]
# ARCOS[M] Y BALLESTA[F]

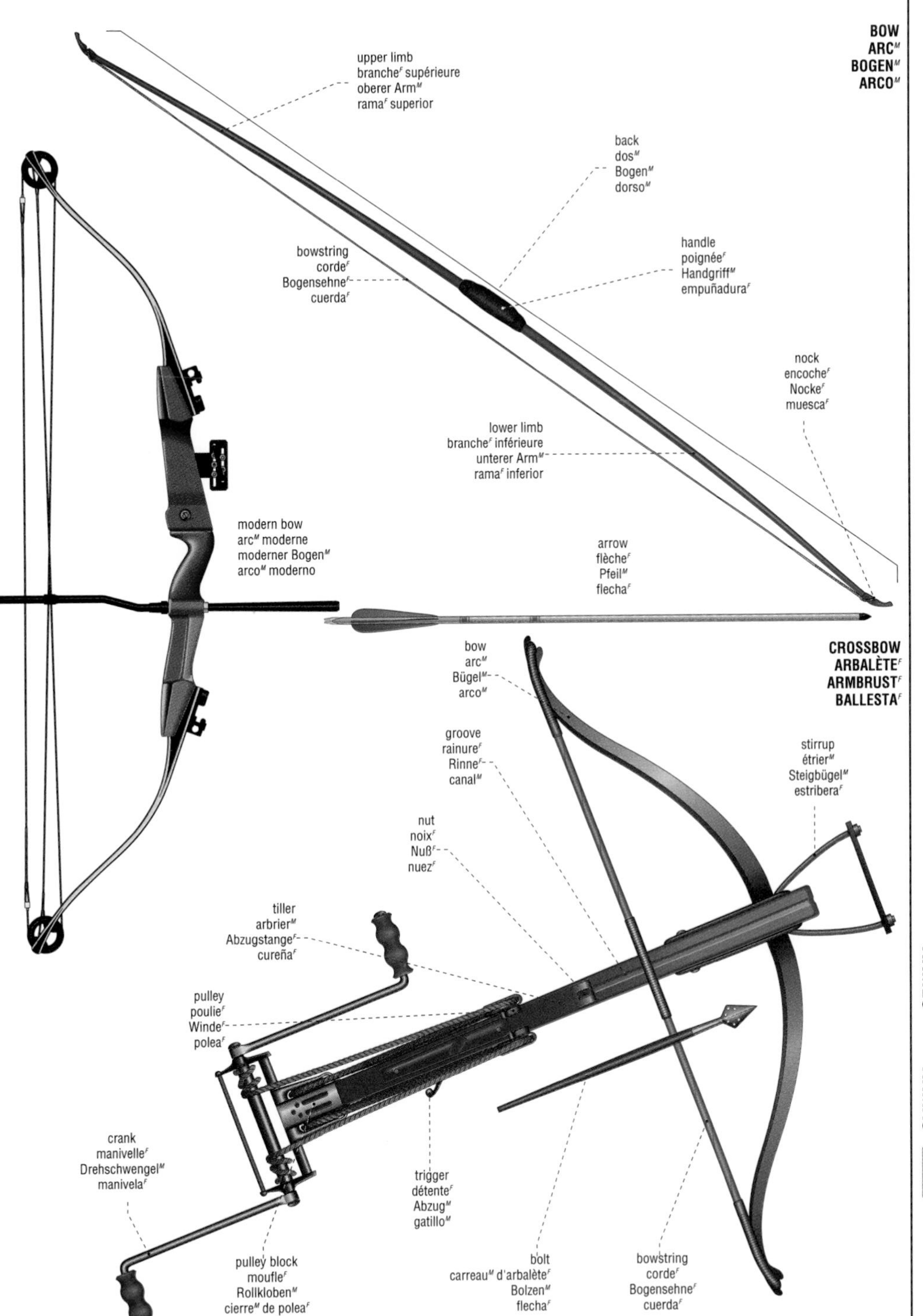

# THRUSTING AND CUTTING WEAPONS
# ARMES[F] BLANCHES
# HIEB- UND STICHWAFFEN[F]
# ARMAS[F] CORTANTES Y DE ESTOCADA[F]

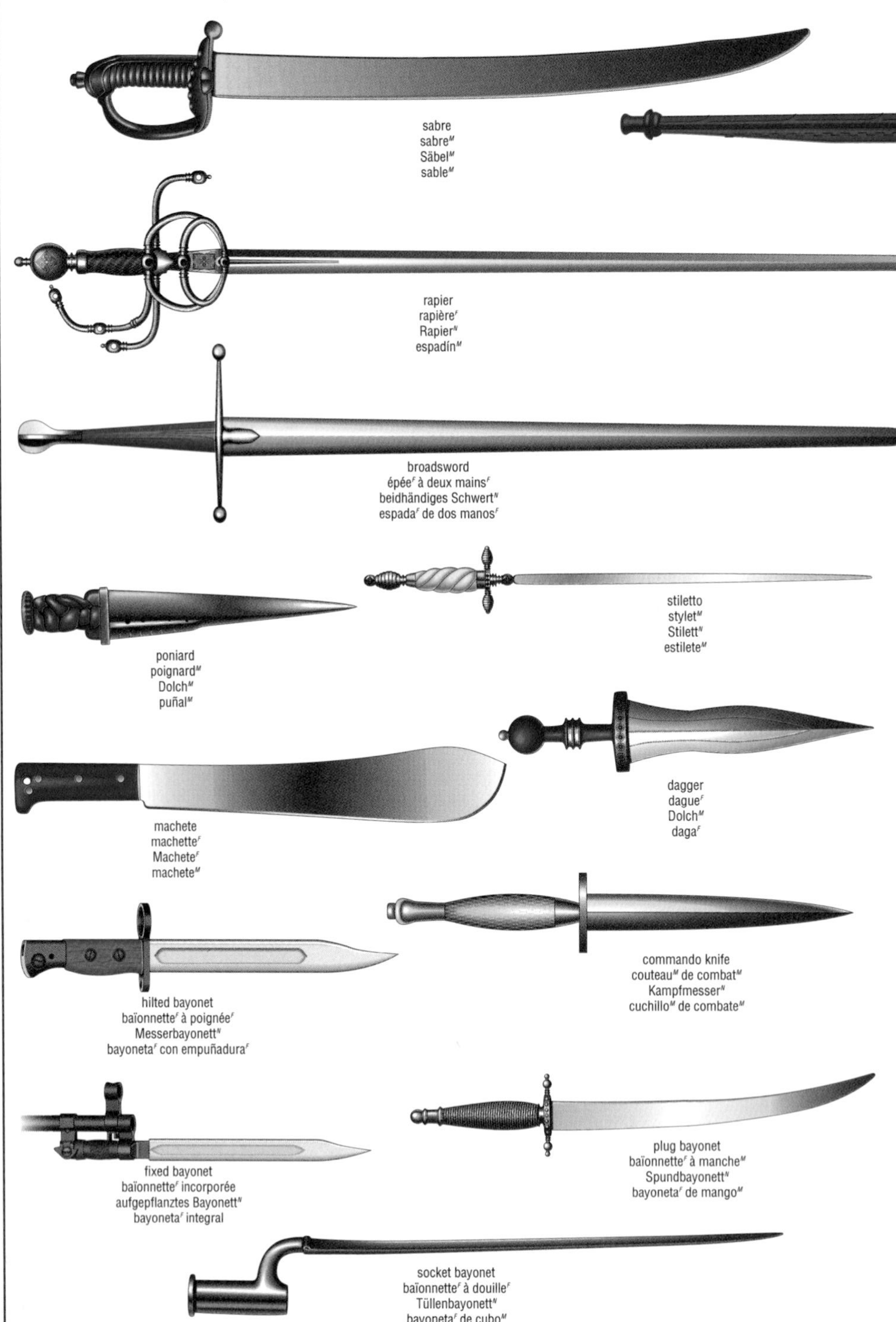

## ARQUEBUS
## ARQUEBUSE[F]
## ARKEBUSE[F]
## ARCABUZ[M]

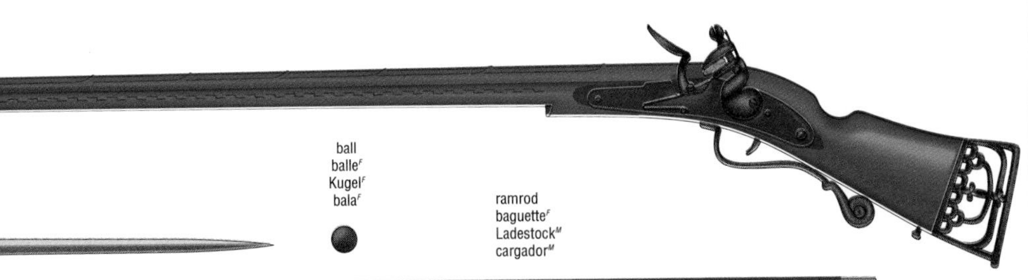


## FLINTLOCK
## PLATINE[F] À SILEX[M]
## STEINSCHLOSS[N]
## PEDERNAL[M]

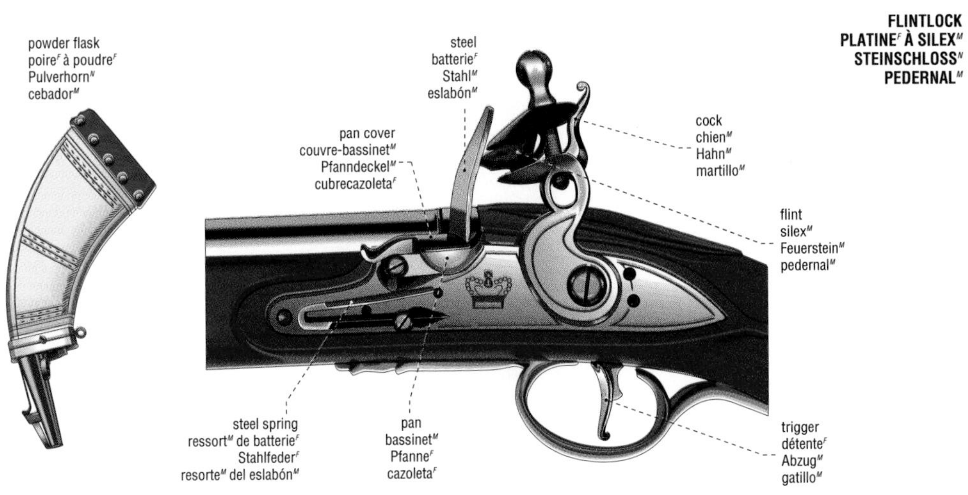


## SUBMACHINE GUN
## PISTOLET[M] MITRAILLEUR[M]
## MASCHINENPISTOLE[F]
## METRALLETA[F]

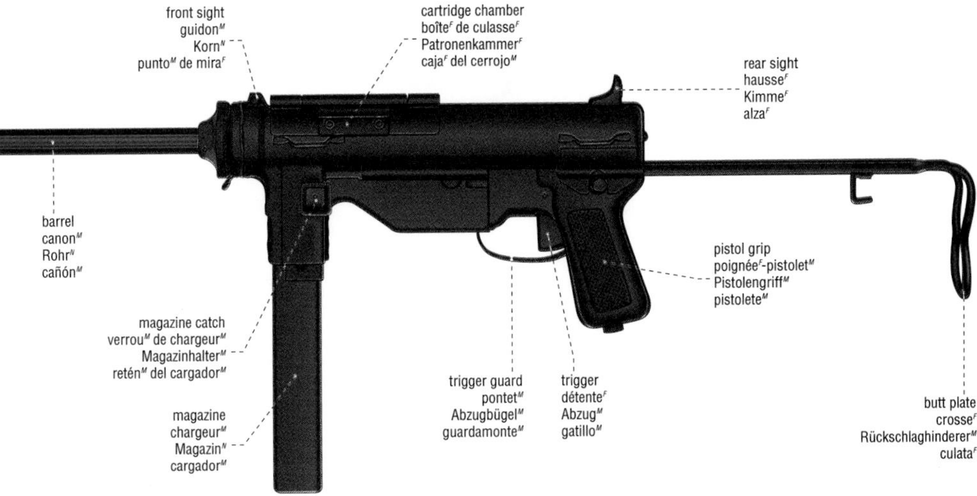

# AUTOMATIC RIFLE
# FUSIL$^{M}$ AUTOMATIQUE
# AUTOMATISCHES GEWEHR$^{N}$
# FUSIL$^{M}$ AUTOMÁTICO

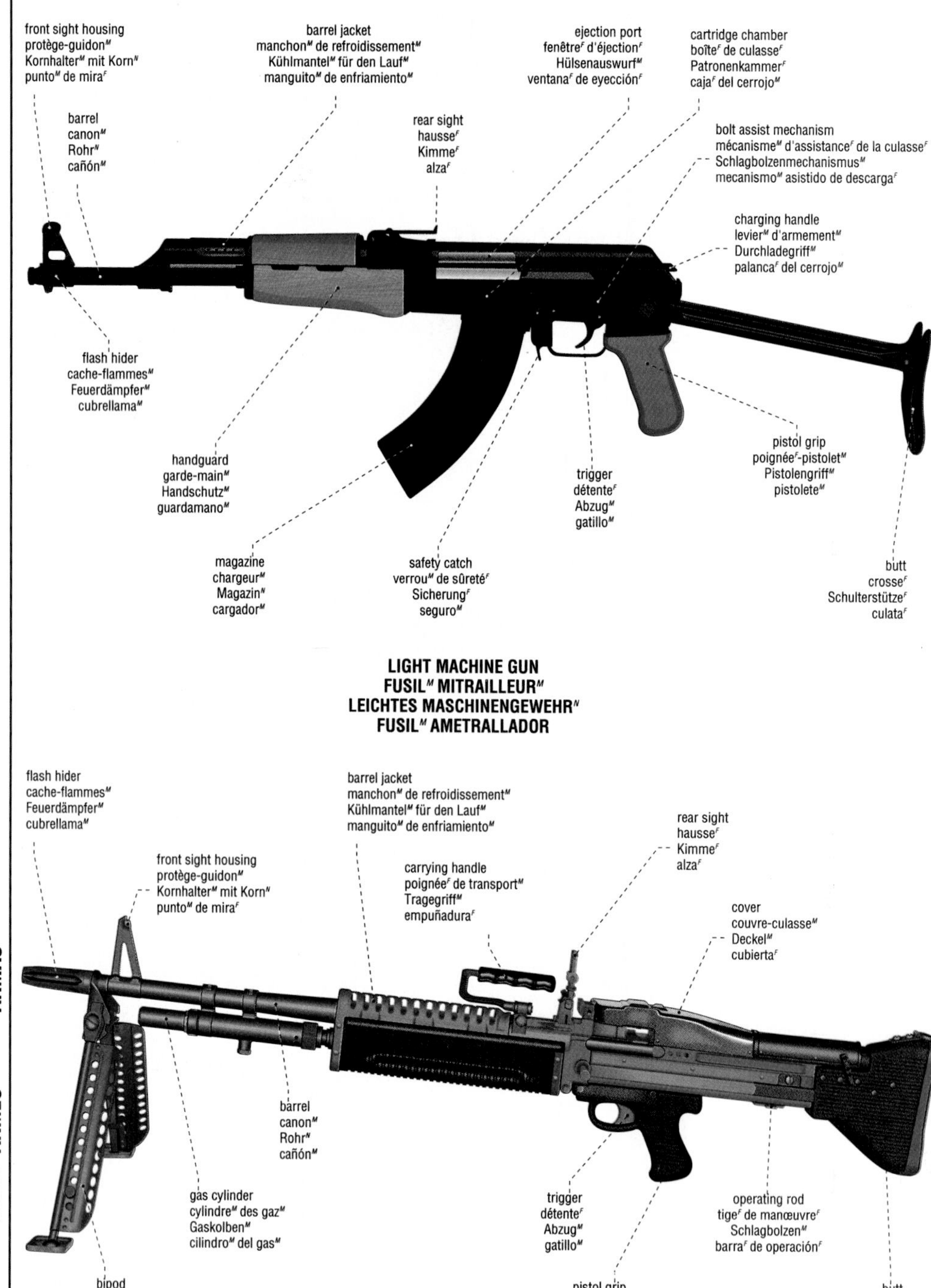


# LIGHT MACHINE GUN
# FUSIL$^{M}$ MITRAILLEUR$^{M}$
# LEICHTES MASCHINENGEWEHR$^{N}$
# FUSIL$^{M}$ AMETRALLADOR

## REVOLVER
## REVOLVER[M]
## REVOLVER[M]
## REVÓLVER[M]

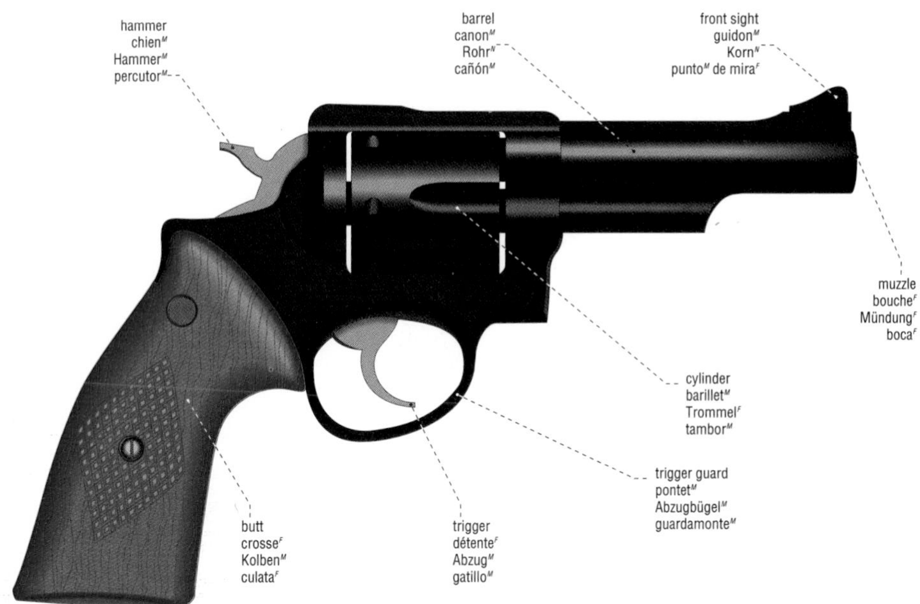


## PISTOL
## PISTOLET[M]
## PISTOLE[F]
## PISTOLA[F]

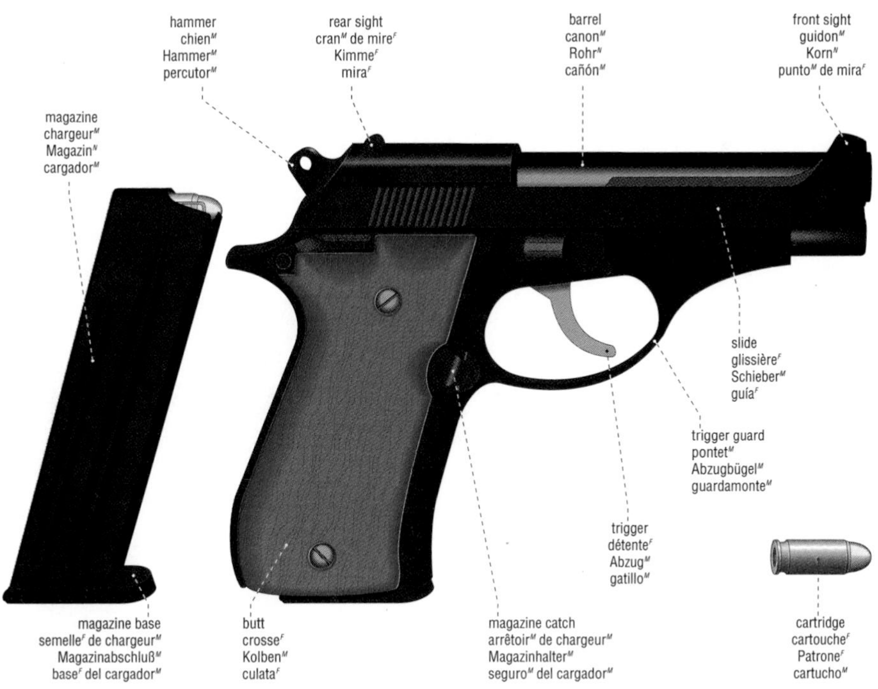

# HUNTING WEAPONS
# ARMES[F] DE CHASSE[F]
# JAGDWAFFEN[F]
# ARMAS[F] DE CAZA[F]

**CARTRIDGE (RIFLE)**
**CARTOUCHE[F] (CARABINE[F])**
**PATRONE[F] (GEWEHR[N])**
**CARTUCHO[M] DE RIFLE[M]**

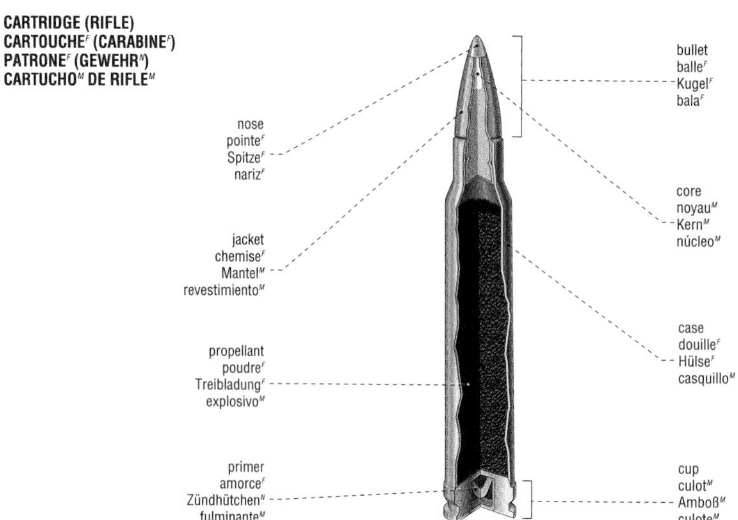


**RIFLE (RIFLED BORE)**
**CARABINE[F] (CANON[M] RAYÉ)**
**GEWEHR[N] (GEZOGENER LAUF[M])**
**RIFLE[M]**

front sight
guidon[M]
Korn[N]
punto[M] de mira[F]

muzzle
bouche[F]
Mündung[F]
boca[F]

ventilated rib
bande[F] ventilée
Laufschiene[F]
banda[F] de ventilación[F]

barrel
canon[M]
Rohr[N]
cañón[M]

forearm
fût[M]
Vorderschaft[M]
caña[F]

**CARTRIDGE (SHOTGUN)**
**CARTOUCHE[F] (FUSIL[M])**
**PATRONE[F] (SCHROTFLINTE[F])**
**CARTUCHO[M] DE ESCOPETA[F]**

**SHOTGUN (SMOOTH-BORE)**
**FUSIL[M] (CANON[M] LISSE)**
**SCHROTFLINTE[F] (GLATTER LAUF[M])**
**ESCOPETA[F]**

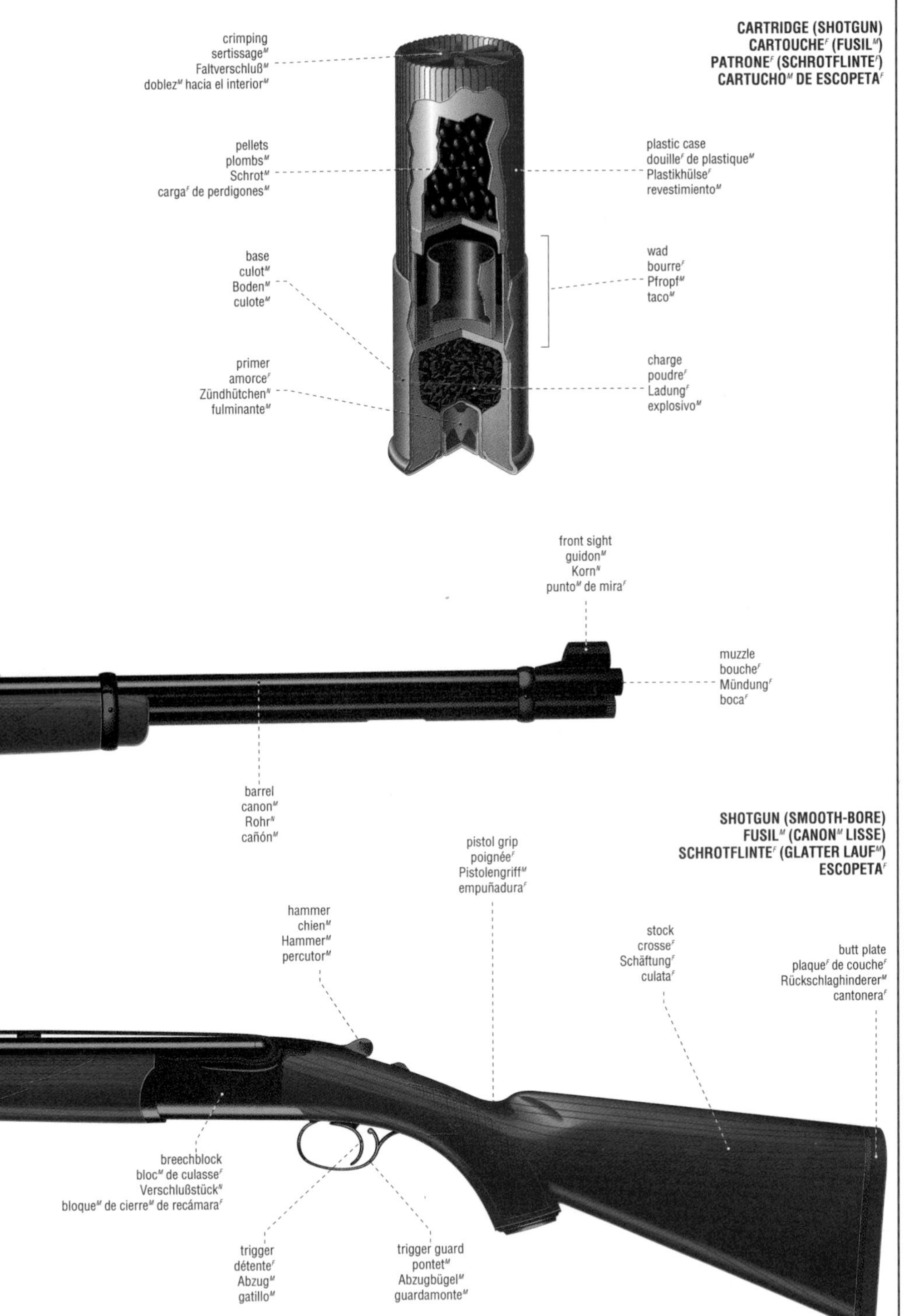

# SEVENTEENTH-CENTURY CANNON
# CANON$^{M}$ DU XVII$^{e}$ SIÈCLE$^{M}$
# KANONE$^{F}$ AUS DEM 17. JAHRHUNDERT$^{N}$
# CAÑÓN$^{M}$ DEL SIGLO$^{M}$ XVII

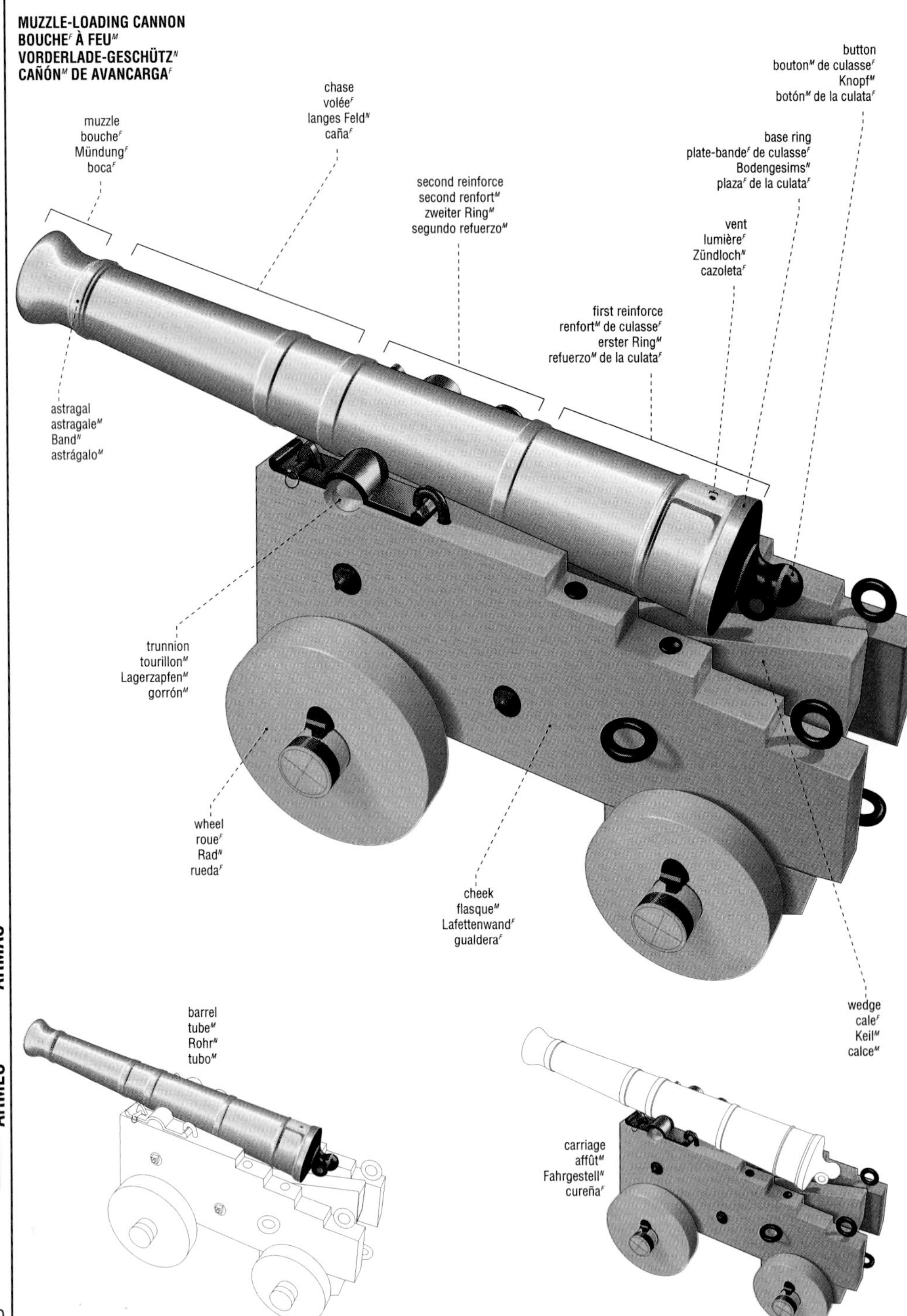

## CROSS SECTION OF A MUZZLE-LOADING CANNON
## COUPE[F] D'UNE BOUCHE[F] À FEU[M]
## QUERSCHNITT[M] EINER VORDERLADUNG[F]
## CORTE[M] TRANSVERSAL DE UN CAÑÓN[M] DE AVANCARGA[F]

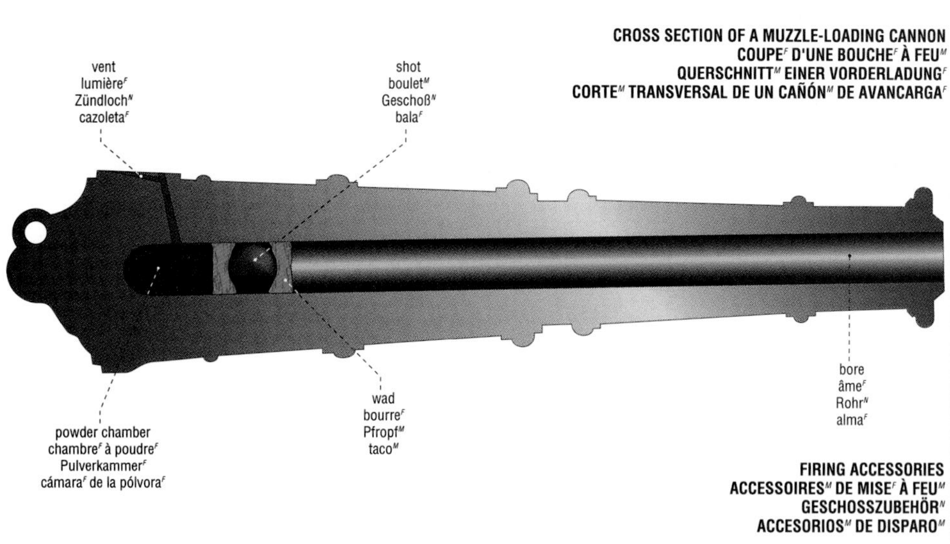


## FIRING ACCESSORIES
## ACCESSOIRES[M] DE MISE[F] À FEU[M]
## GESCHOSSZUBEHÖR[N]
## ACCESORIOS[M] DE DISPARO[M]

rammer
refouloir[M]
Ladestock[M]
atacador[M]

linstock
boutefeu[M]
Luntenstock[M]
botafuego[M]

worm
tire-bourre[M]
Spirale[F]
sacatrapos[M]

ladle
lanterne[F]
Ladeschaufel[F]
cucharón[M]

sponge
écouvillon[M]
Schwamm[M]
escobillón[M]

## PROJECTILES
## PROJECTILES[M]
## PROJEKTILE[N]
## PROYECTILES[M]

bar shot
boulet[M] ramé
Stangenkugel[F]
bala[F] de barra[F]

grapeshot
grappe[F] de raisin[M]
Kartätsche[F]
metralla[F]

solid shot
boulet[M]
Vollgeschoß[N]
bala[F] sólida

hollow shot
boulet[M] creux
Hohlladungsgeschoß[N]
bala[F] con perdigones[M]

# MODERN HOWITZER
# OBUSIER^M MODERNE
# MODERNE HAUBITZE^F
# OBÚS^M MODERNO

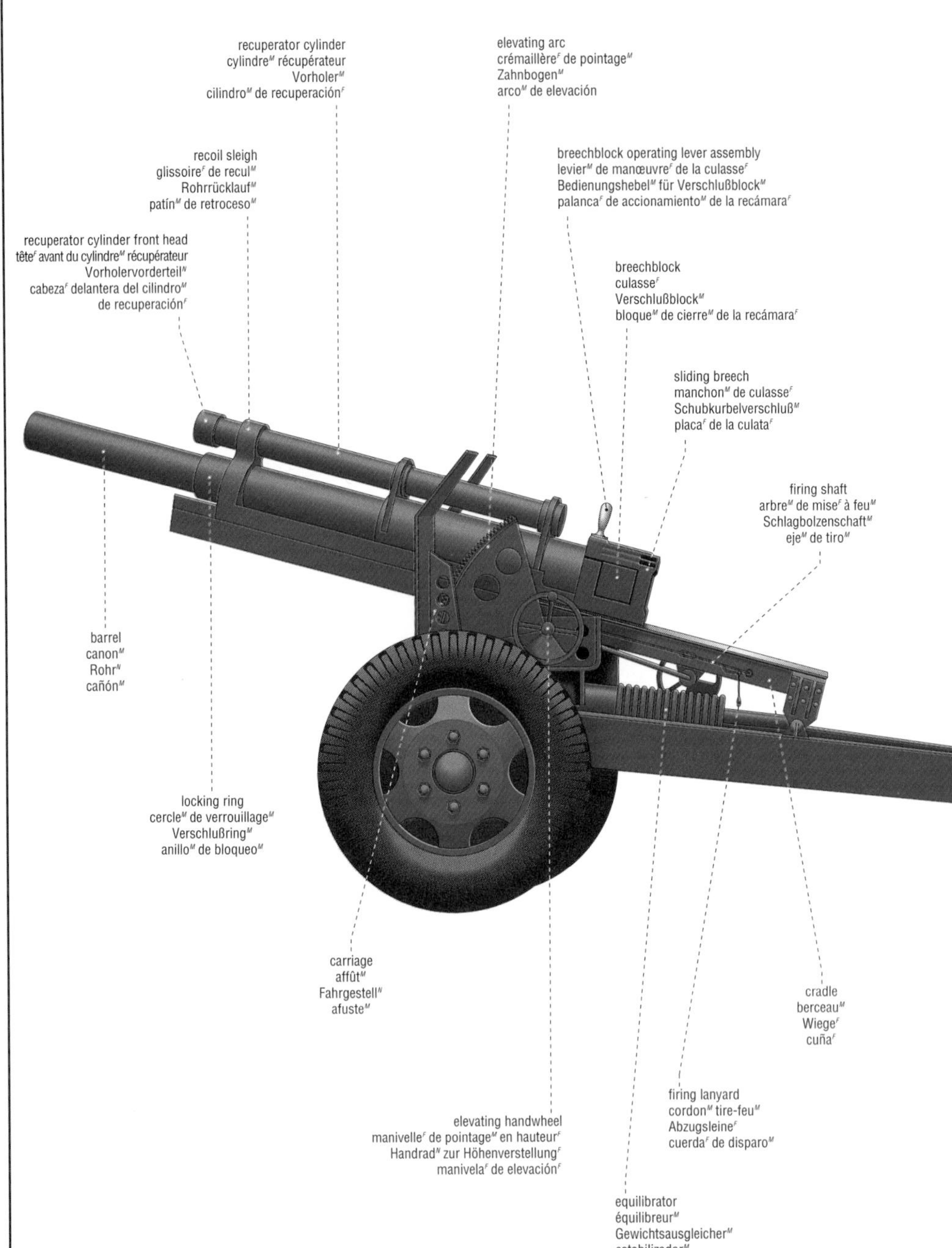

# MORTAR
# MORTIER^M
# MÖRSER^M
# MORTEROS^M

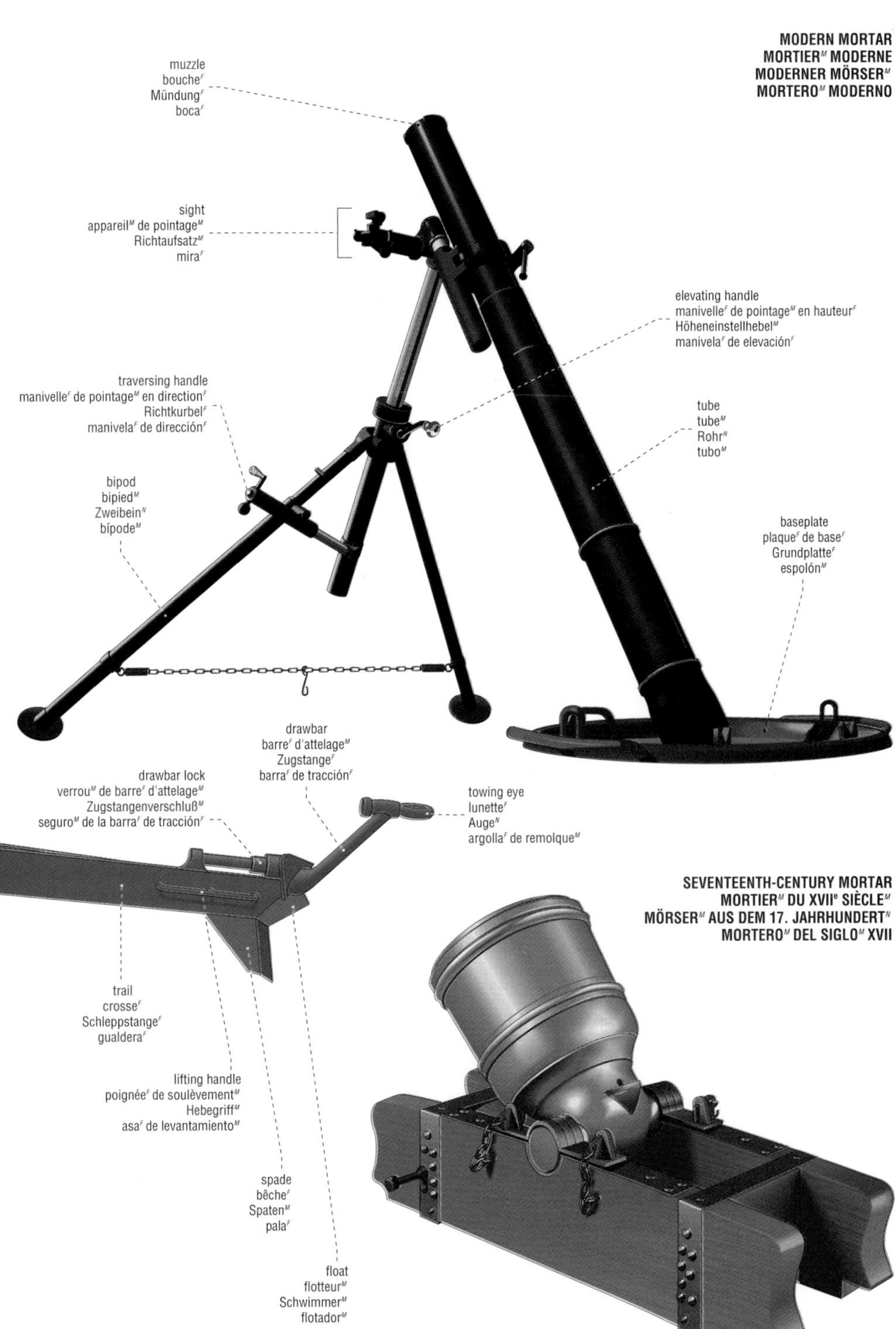

## HAND GRENADE
## GRENADE^F À MAIN^F
## HANDGRANATE^F
## GRANADA^F DE MANO^F

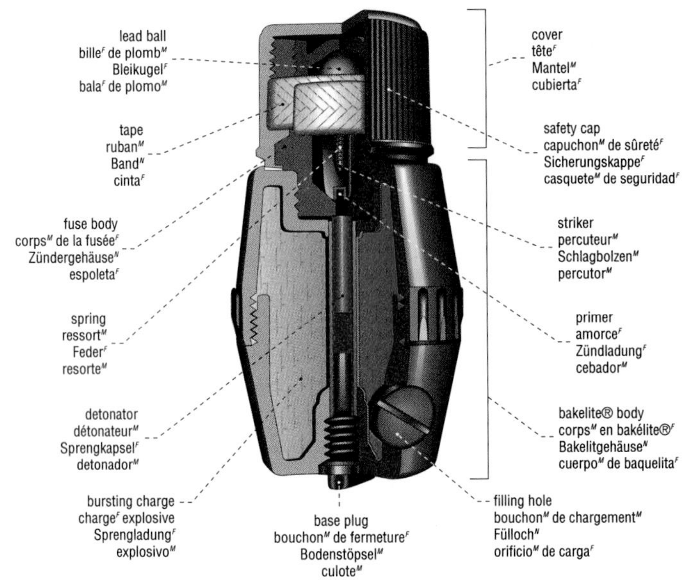


## BAZOOKA
## BAZOOKA^M
## PANZERFAUST^F
## BAZUCA^F

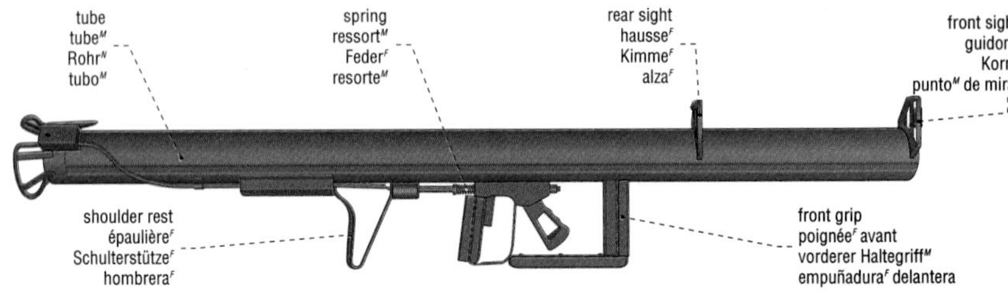


## RECOILLESS RIFLE
## CANON^M SANS RECUL^M
## RÜCKSTOSSFREIES GESCHÜTZ^N
## FUSIL^M SIN RETROCESO

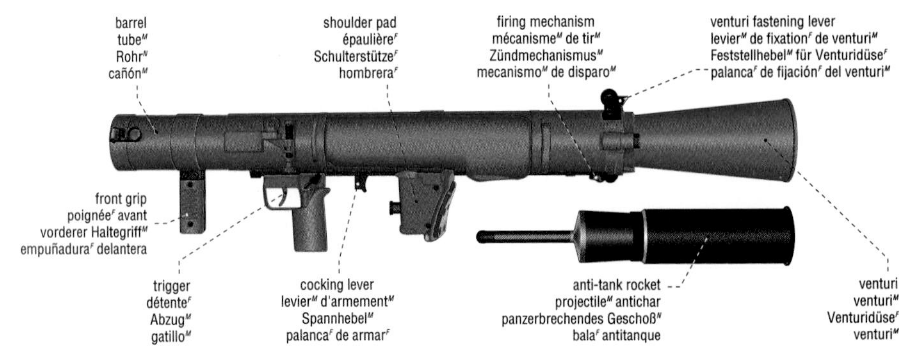

# TANK
# CHAR[M] D'ASSAUT[M]
# PANZER[M]
# TANQUE[M]

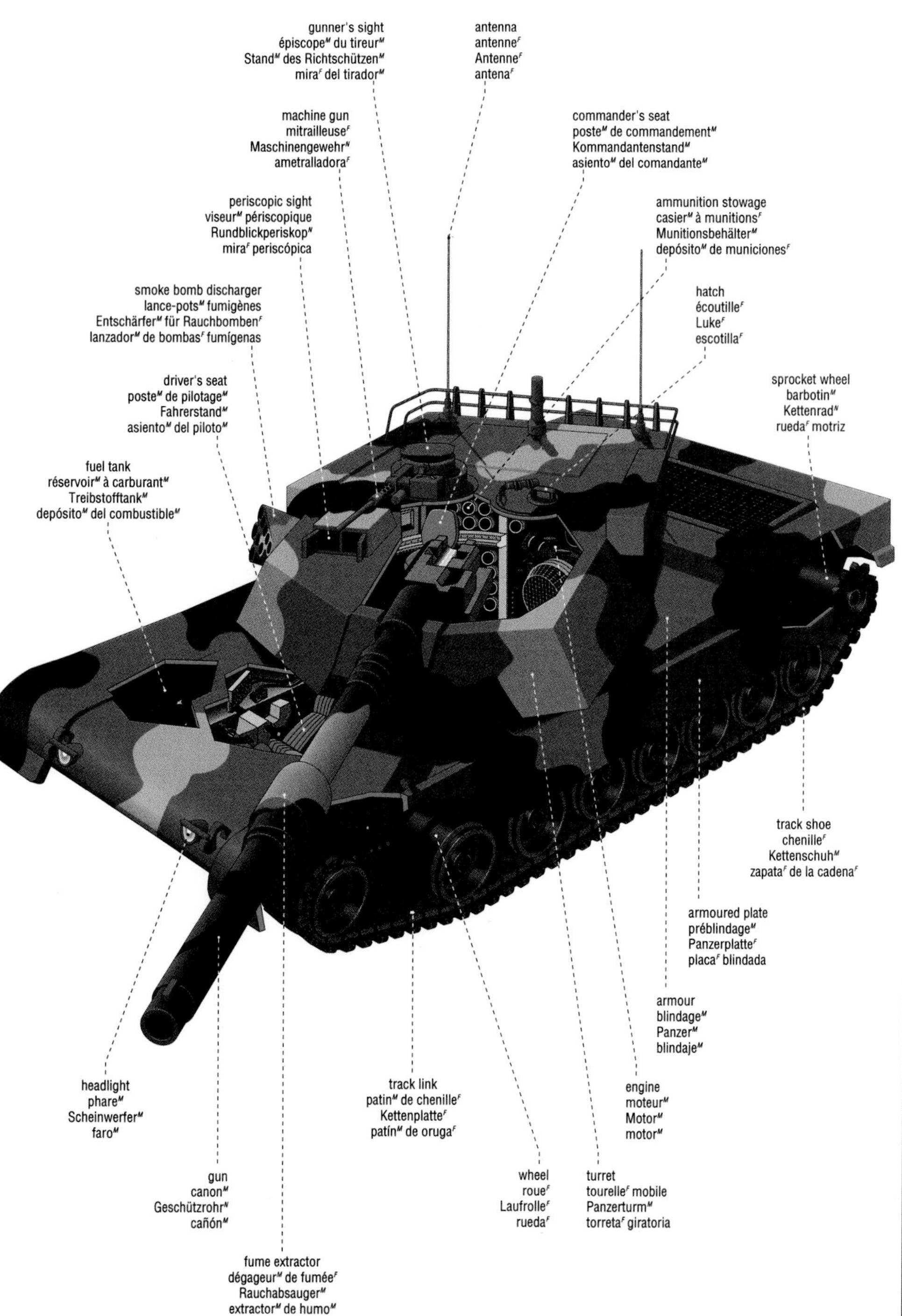

# SUBMARINE
# SOUS-MARIN$^{M}$
# UNTERSEEBOOT$^{N}$
# SUBMARINO$^{M}$

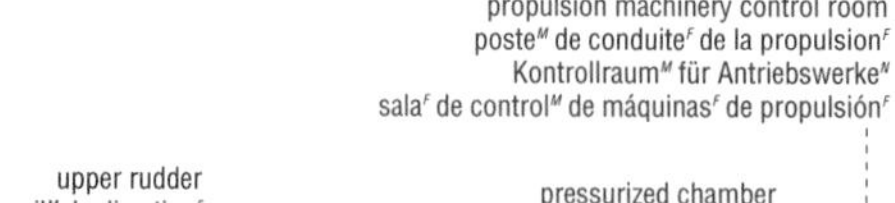


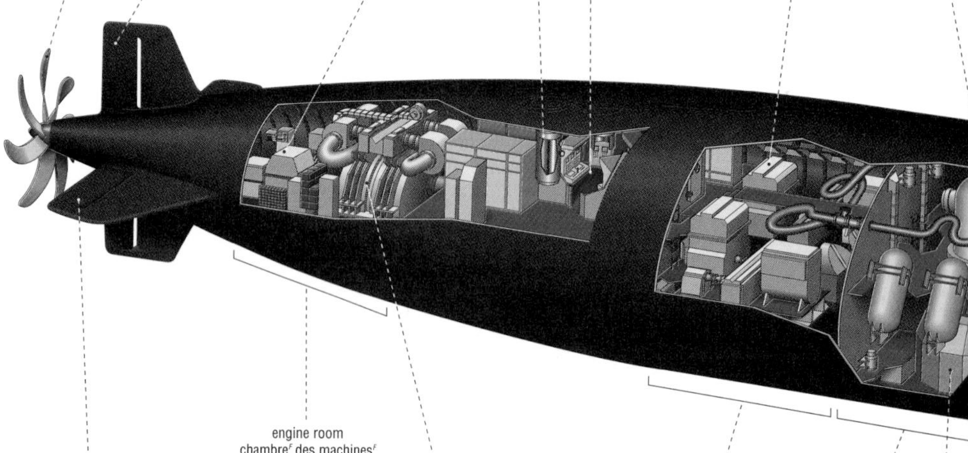

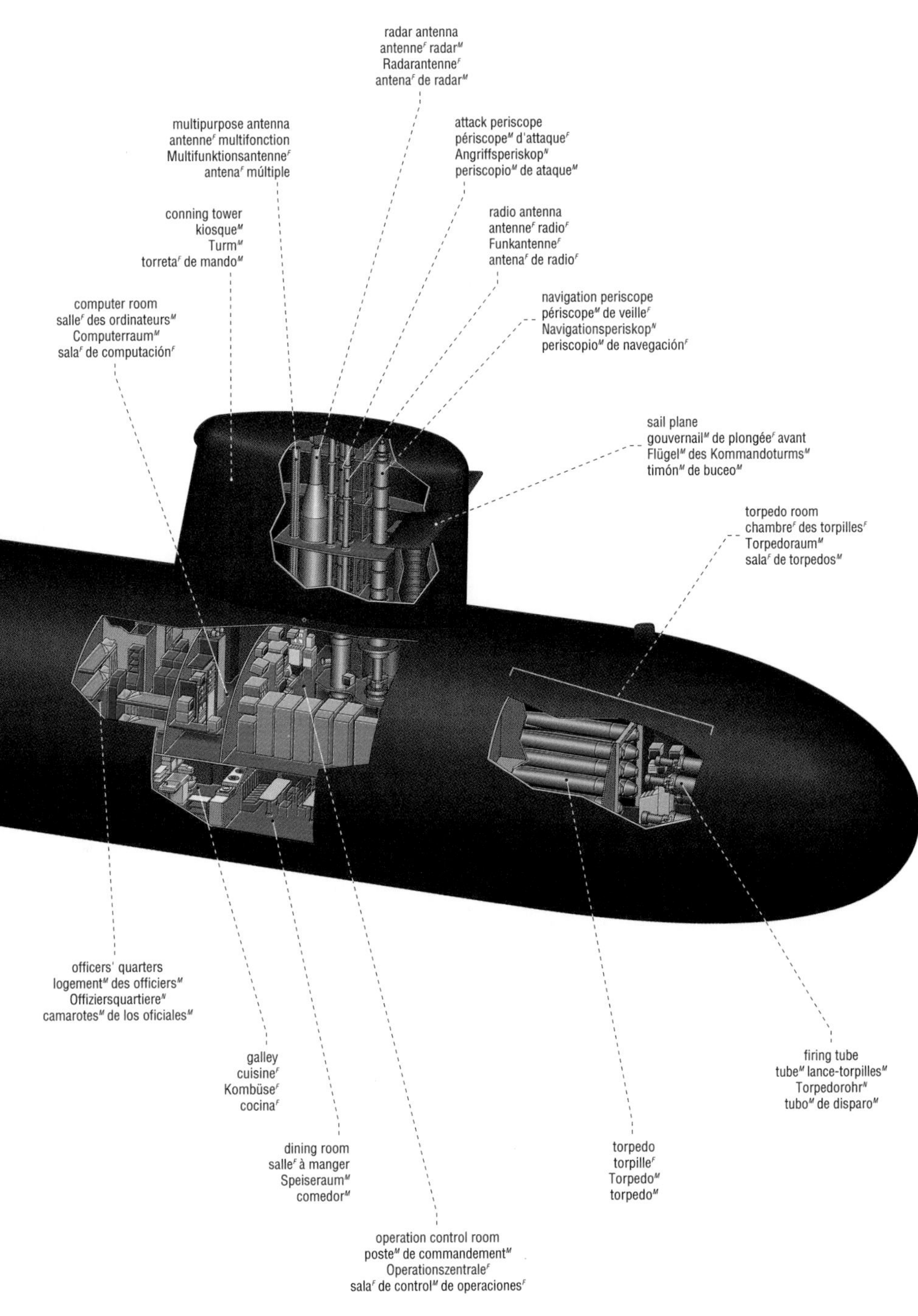


WEAPONS
ARMES
WAFFEN
ARMAS

# FRIGATE
# FRÉGATE^F
# FREGATTE^F
# FRAGATA^F

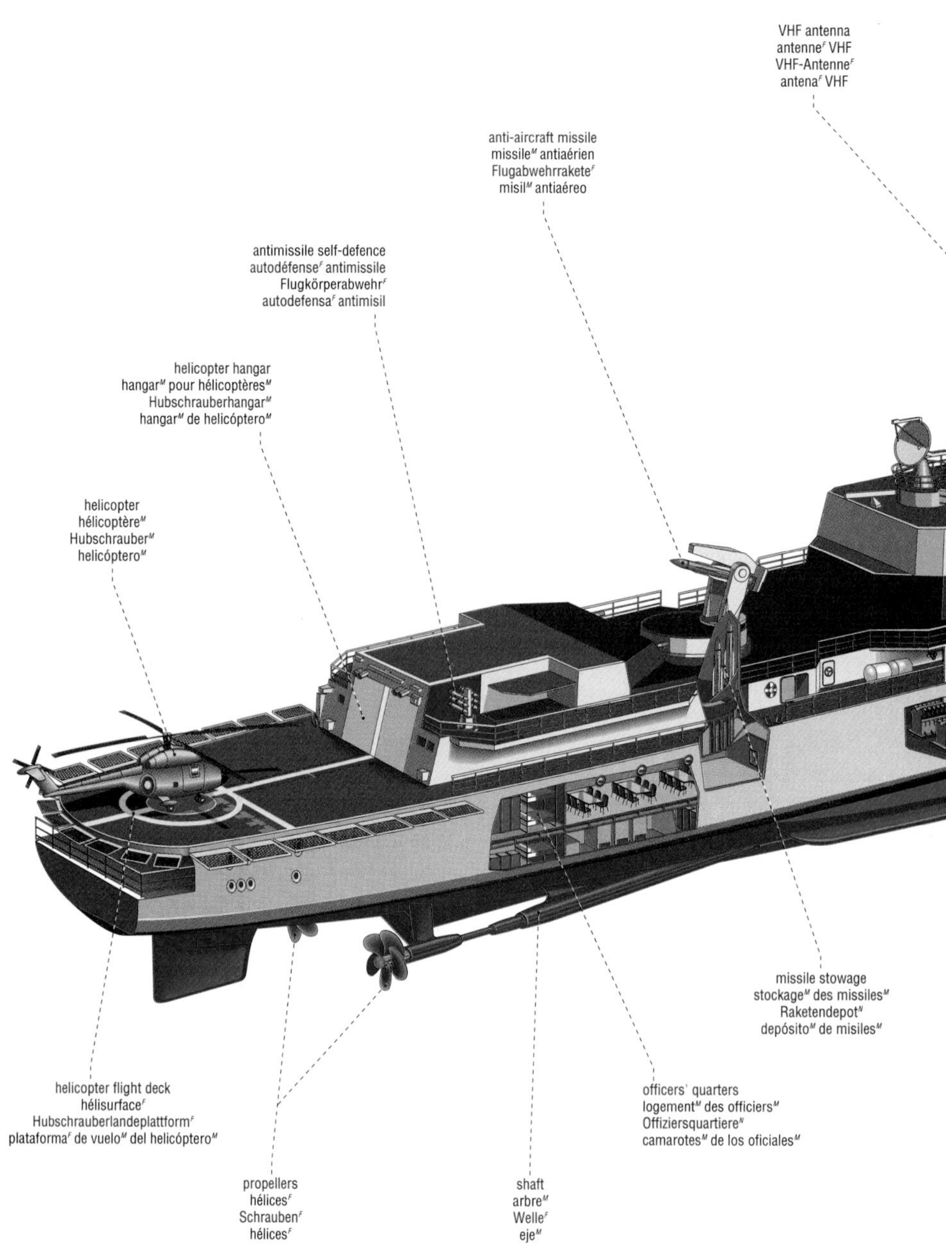

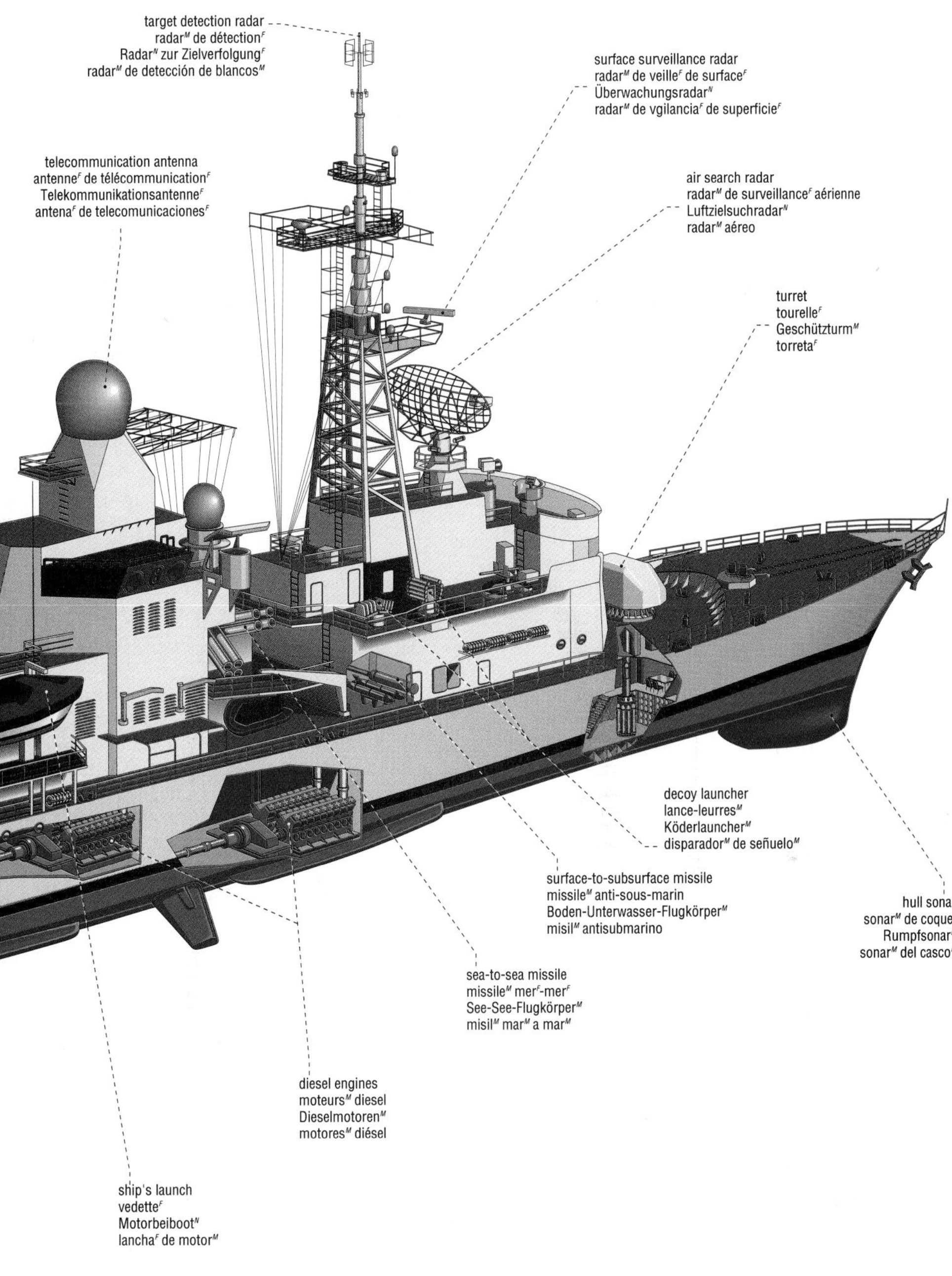
target detection radar
radar[M] de détection[F]
Radar[N] zur Zielverfolgung[F]
radar[M] de detección de blancos[M]
surface surveillance radar
radar[M] de veille[F] de surface[F]
Überwachungsradar[N]
radar[M] de vgilancia[F] de superficie[F]
telecommunication antenna
antenne[F] de télécommunication[F]
Telekommunikationsantenne[F]
antena[F] de telecomunicaciones[F]
air search radar
radar[M] de surveillance[F] aérienne
Luftzielsuchradar[N]
radar[M] aéreo
turret
tourelle[F]
Geschützturm[M]
torreta[F]
decoy launcher
lance-leurres[M]
Köderlauncher[M]
disparador[M] de señuelo[M]
surface-to-subsurface missile
missile[M] anti-sous-marin
Boden-Unterwasser-Flugkörper[M]
misil[M] antisubmarino
hull sonar
sonar[M] de coque[F]
Rumpfsonar[M]
sonar[M] del casco[M]
sea-to-sea missile
missile[M] mer[F]-mer[F]
See-See-Flugkörper[M]
misil[M] mar[M] a mar[M]
diesel engines
moteurs[M] diesel
Dieselmotoren[M]
motores[M] diésel
ship's launch
vedette[F]
Motorbeiboot[N]
lancha[F] de motor[M]

# AIRCRAFT CARRIER
# PORTE-AVIONS M
# FLUGZEUGTRÄGER M
# PORTAAVIONES M

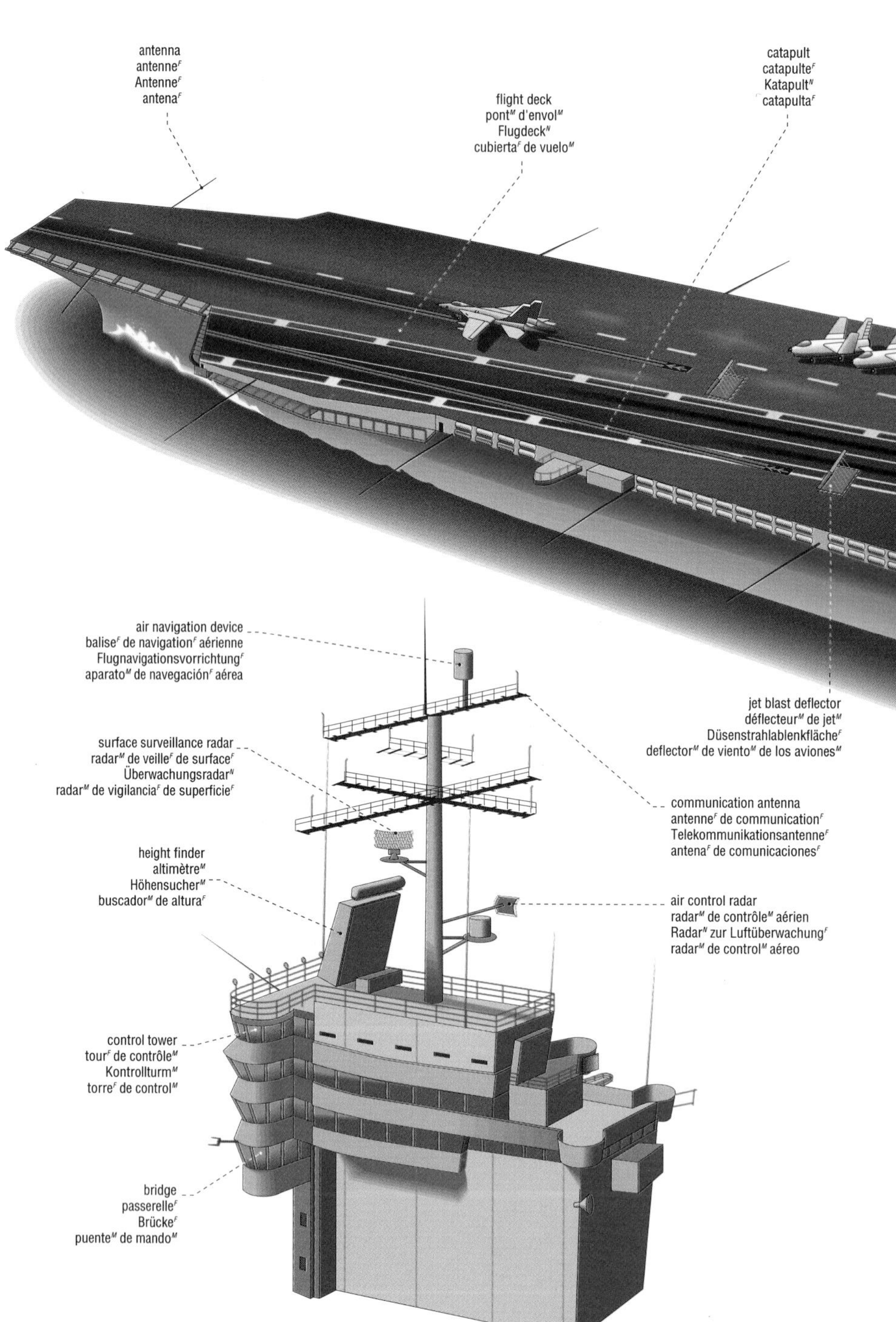

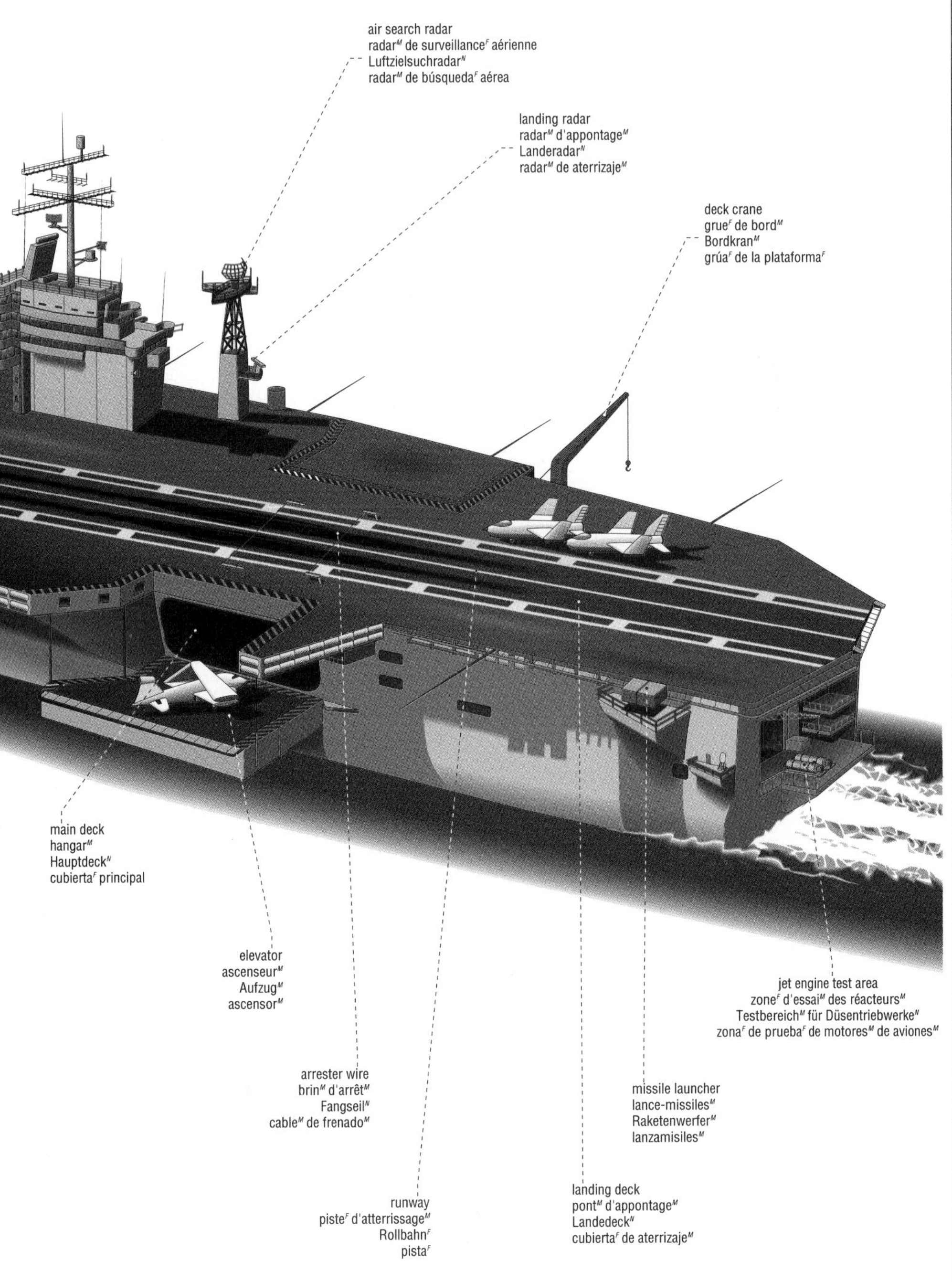
air search radar
radar de surveillance aérienne
Luftzielsuchradar
radar de búsqueda aérea
landing radar
radar d'appontage
Landeradar
radar de aterrizaje
deck crane
grue de bord
Bordkran
grúa de la plataforma
main deck
hangar
Hauptdeck
cubierta principal
elevator
ascenseur
Aufzug
ascensor
jet engine test area
zone d'essai des réacteurs
Testbereich für Düsentriebwerke
zona de prueba de motores de aviones
arrester wire
brin d'arrêt
Fangseil
cable de frenado
missile launcher
lance-missiles
Raketenwerfer
lanzamisiles
runway
piste d'atterrissage
Rollbahn
pista
landing deck
pont d'appontage
Landedeck
cubierta de aterrizaje

# COMBAT AIRCRAFT
# AVION[M] DE COMBAT[M]
# KAMPFFLUGZEUG[N]
# AVIÓN[M] DE COMBATE[M]

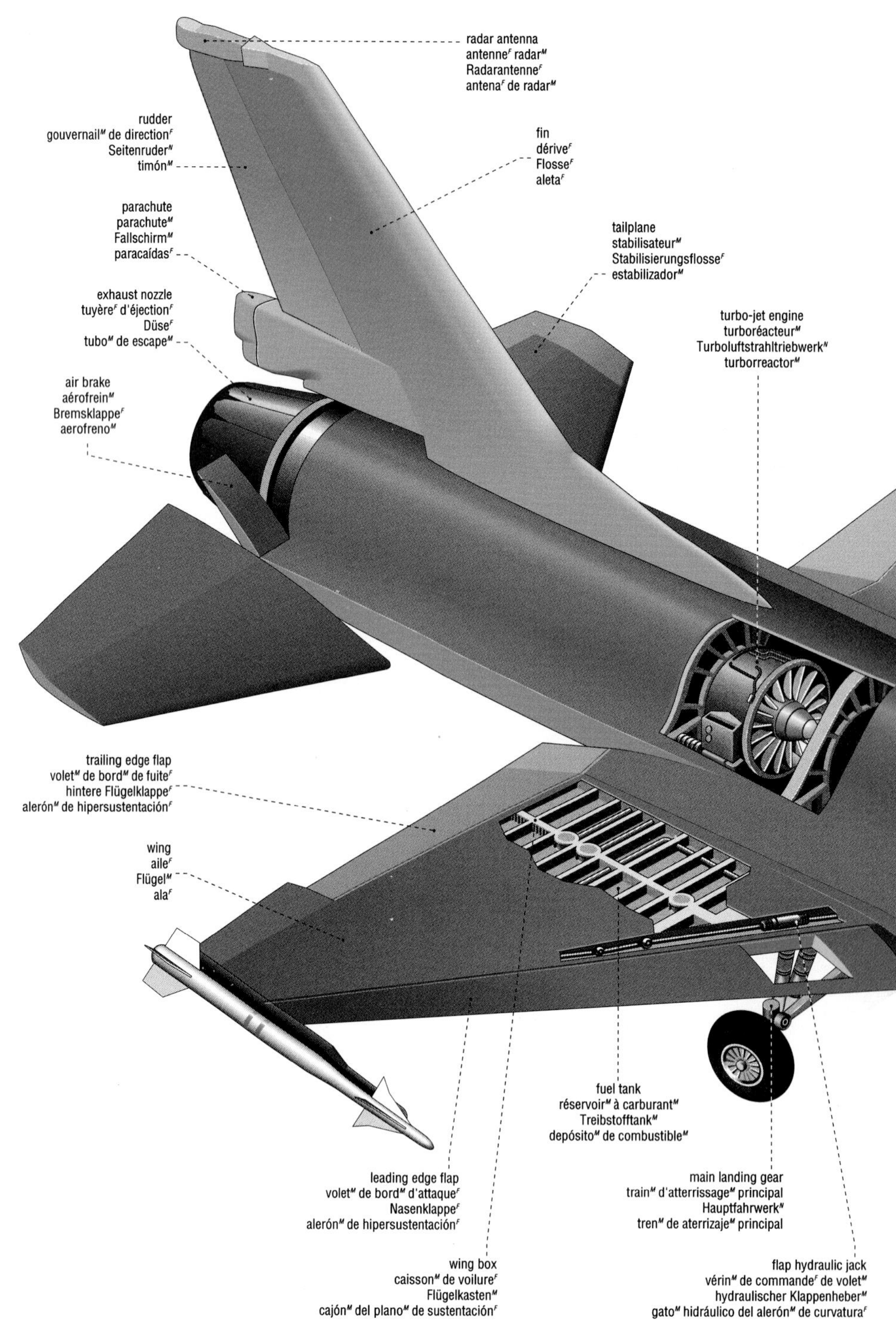

## IN-FLIGHT REFUELLING
## RAVITAILLEMENT[M] EN VOL[M]
## LUFTBETANKUNG[F]
## REAPROVISIONAMIENTO[M] DE COMBUSTIBLE[M] EN VUELO[M]

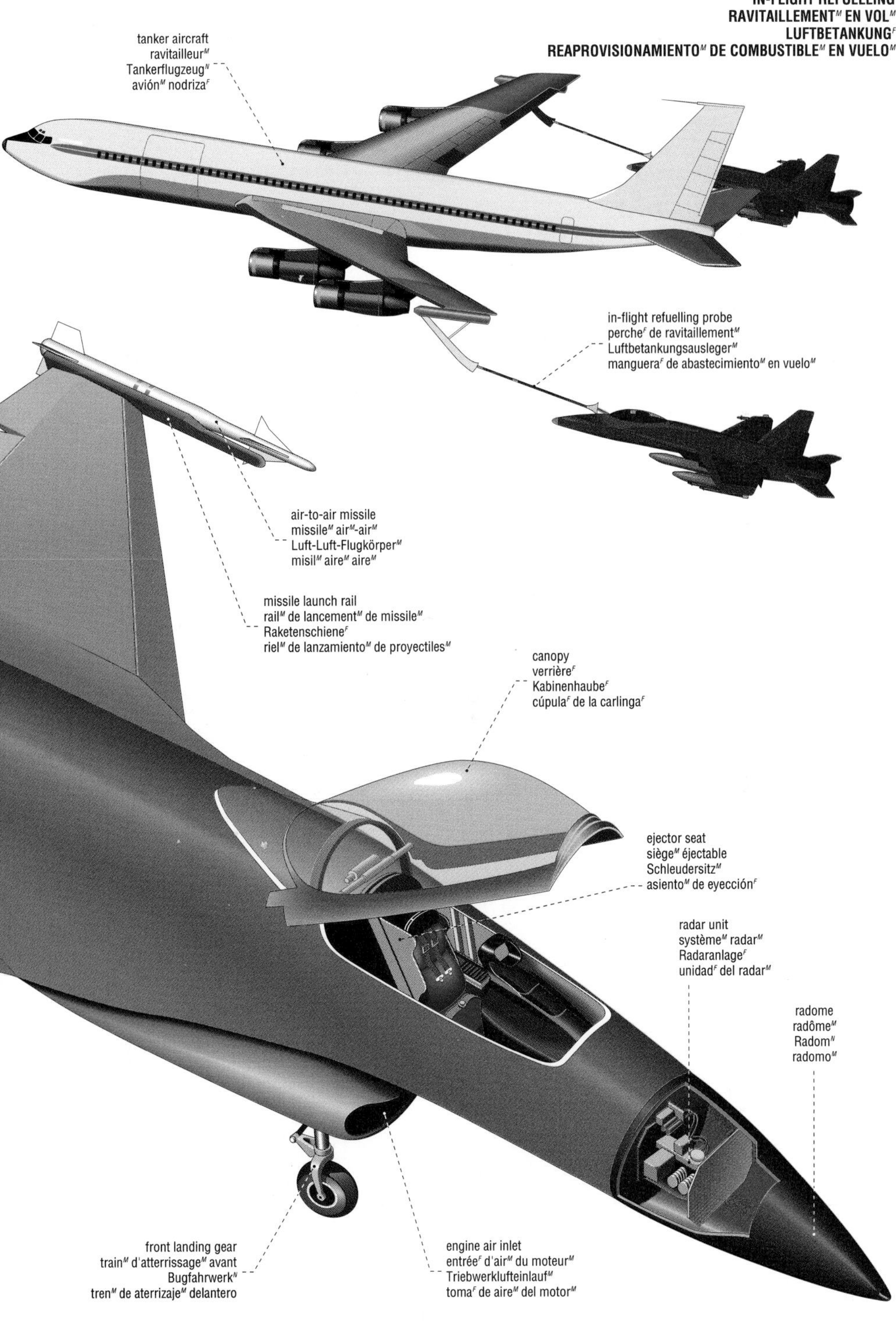

# MISSILES
# MISSILES[M]
# FLUGKÖRPER[M]
# PROYECTILES[M]

## STRUCTURE OF A MISSILE
## STRUCTURE[F] D'UN MISSILE[M]
## AUFBAU[M] EINES FLUGKÖRPERS[M]
## ESTRUCTURA[F] DE UN MISIL[M]

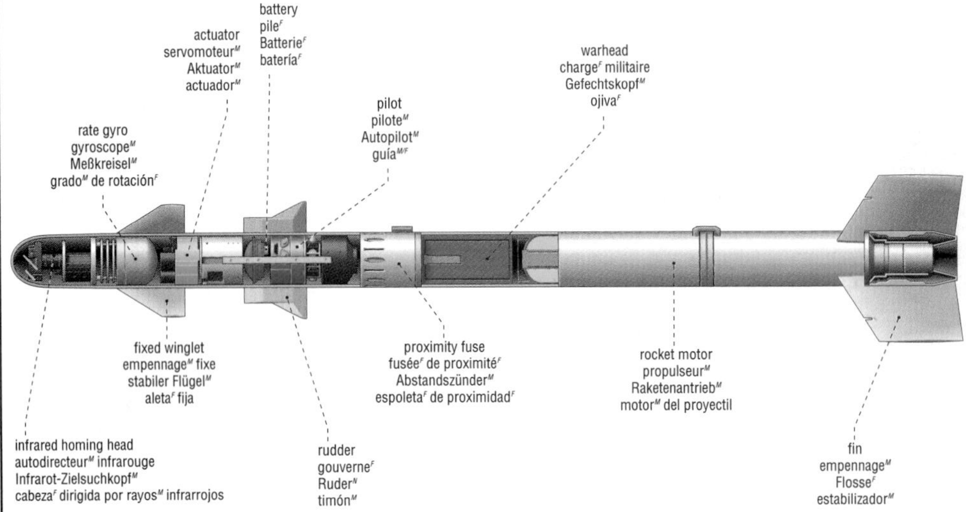


## PRINCIPAL TYPES OF MISSILE
## PRINCIPAUX TYPES[M] DE MISSILES[M]
## DIE WICHTIGSTEN FLUGKÖRPER[M]
## PRINCIPALES TIPOS[M] DE MISILES[M]

surface-to-air missile
missile[M] sol[M]-air[M]
Boden-Luft-Flugkörper[M]
misil[M] tierra[F] aire[M]

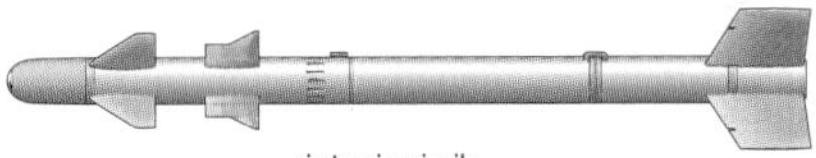

air-to-air missile
missile[M] air[M]-air[M]
Luft-Luft-Flugkörper[M]
misil[M] aire[M] aire[M]

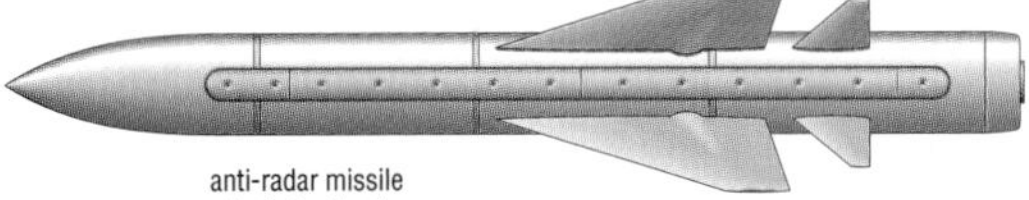

anti-radar missile
missile[M] antiradar
Radarabwehrflugkörper[M]
misil[M] antiradar

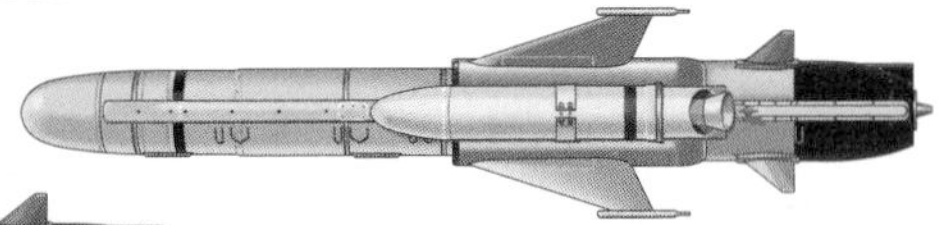

anti-ship missile
missile[M] antinavire
Seezielflugkörper[M]
misil[M] antibuques

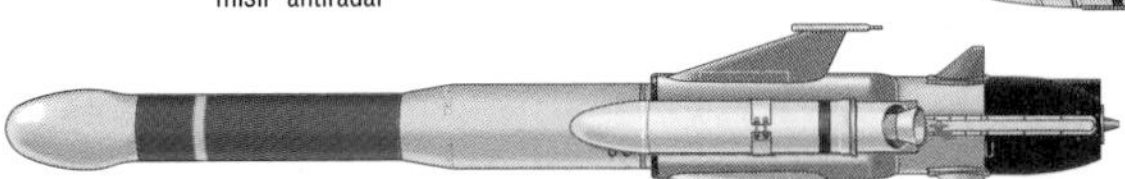

surface-to-subsurface missile
missile[M] anti-sous-marin
Boden-Unterwasser-Flugkörper[M]
misil[M] antisubmarino

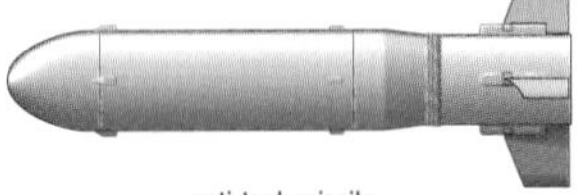

anti-tank missile
missile[M] antichar
Panzerabwehrflugkörper[M]
misil[M] antitanque

air-to-surface missile
missile[M] air[M]-sol[M]
Luft-Boden-Flugkörper[M]
misil[M] aire[M] tierra[F]

SYMBOLS
SYMBOLES

SYMBOLE
SÍMBOLOS

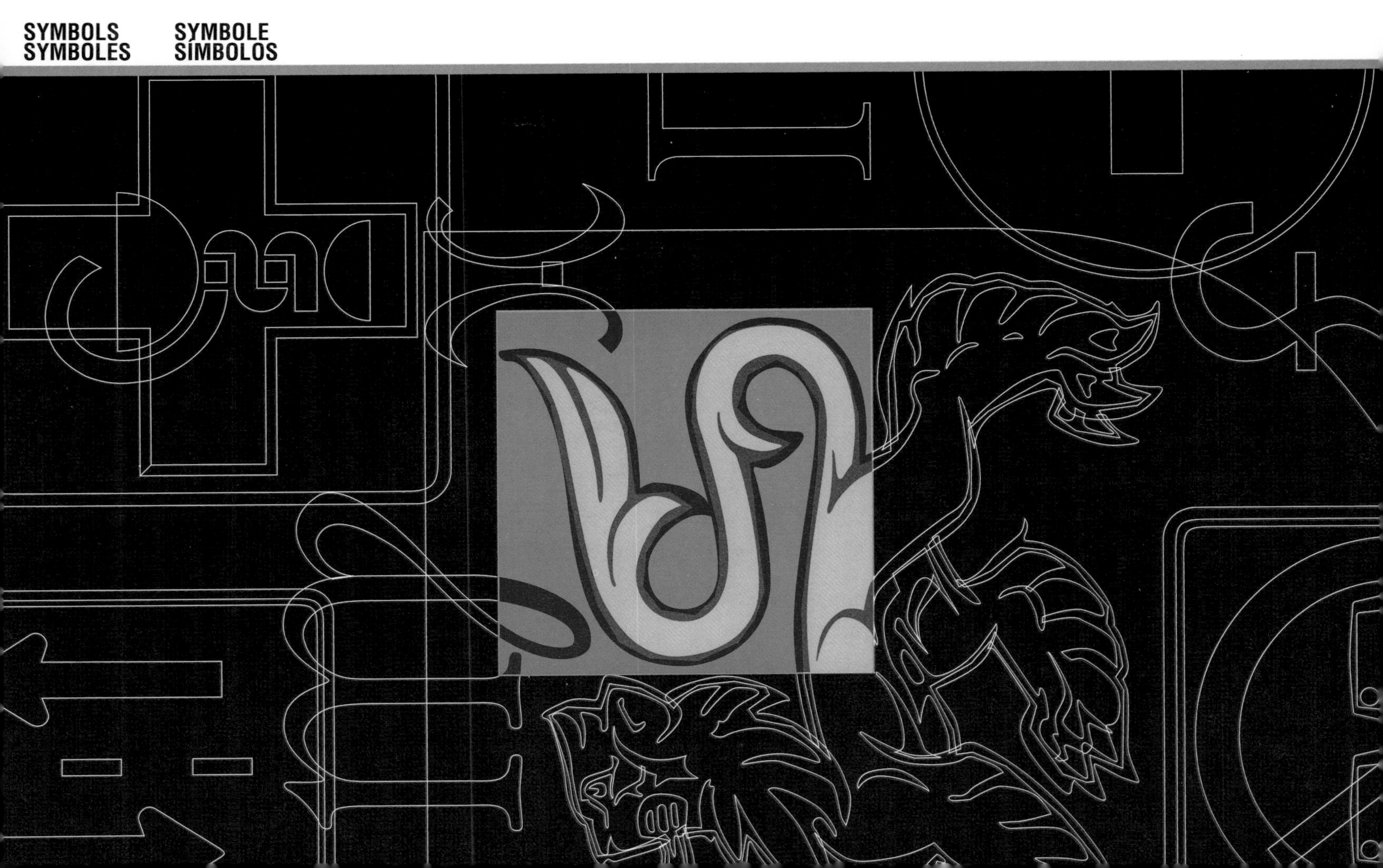

SUMMARY

# HERALDRY
# HÉRALDIQUE[F]
# HERALDIK[F]
# HERÁLDICA[F]

## PARTS OF A FLAG
## ÉLÉMENTS[M] D'UN DRAPEAU[M]
## TEILE[N] DER FAHNE[F]
## PARTES[F] DE UNA BANDERA[F]

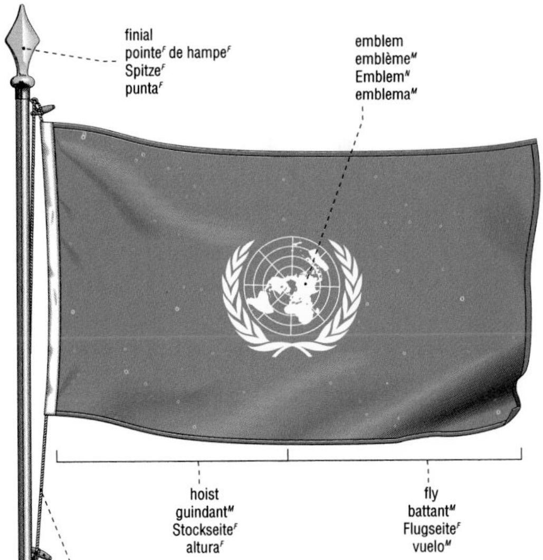

finial
pointe[F] de hampe[F]
Spitze[F]
punta[F]

emblem
emblème[M]
Emblem[N]
emblema[M]

hoist
guindant[M]
Stockseite[F]
altura[F]

fly
battant[M]
Flugseite[F]
vuelo[M]

halyard
drisse[F]
Leine[F]
driza[F]

toggle
cabillot[M]
Knebel[M]
cazonete[M]

staff
hampe[F]
Stange[F]
asta[F]

base
base[F]
Fuß[M]
base[F]

## FLAG SHAPES
## FORMES[F] DE DRAPEAUX[M]
## FAHNENFORMEN[F]
## FORMAS[F] DE BANDERAS[F]

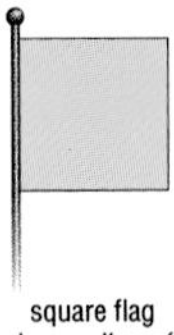

square flag
drapeau[M] carré
viereckige Fahne[F]
bandera[F] cuadrada

rectangular flag
drapeau[M] rectangulaire
rechteckige Fahne[F]
bandera[F] rectangular

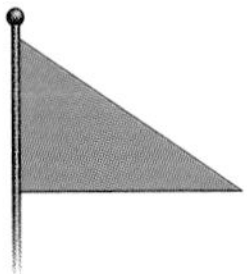

pennant
pennon[M]
Wimpel[M]
pendón[M]

double pennant
pennon[M] double
Doppelwimpel[M]
banderín[M] doble

swallowtail
pavillon[M] à deux pointes[F]
Doppelstander[M]
bandera[F] de dos puntas[F]

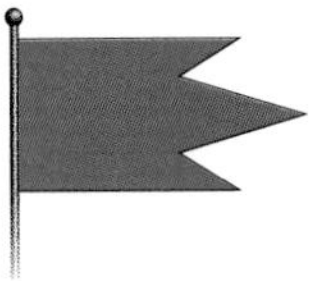

swallowtail and tongue
pavillon[M] à deux pointes[F] et langue[F]
Doppelstander[M] mit Zunge[F]
bandera[F] de dos puntas[F] y lengua[F]

burgee
guidon[M]
Guidon[M]
corneta[F]

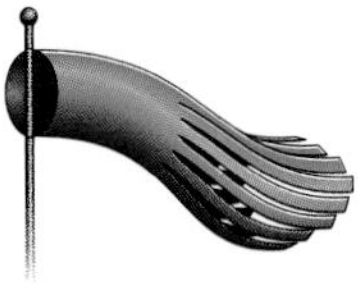

wind sock
manche[F] à air[M]
Windsack[M]
manga[F]

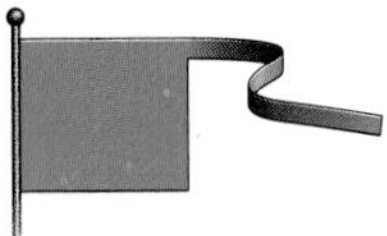

flag with Schwenkel
drapeau[M] à Schwenkel
Fahne[F] mit Schwenkel[M]
bandera[F] con Schwenkel

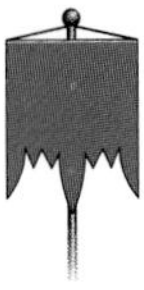

gonfalon
gonfalon[M]
Gonfalon[M]
gonfalón[M]

oriflamme
oriflamme[F]
Oriflamme[F]
oriflama[F]

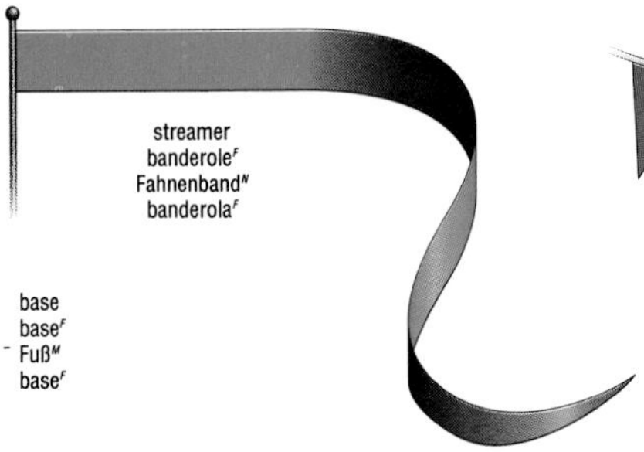

streamer
banderole[F]
Fahnenband[N]
banderola[F]

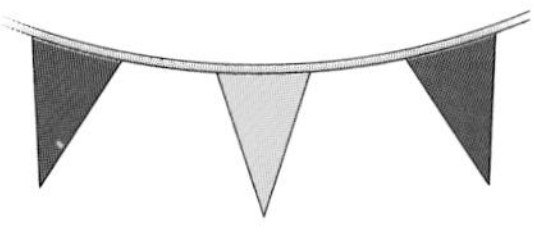

bunting
pavois[M]
Bunting[N]
lanilla[F]

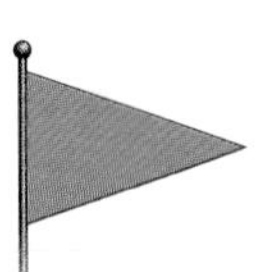

fanion
fanion[M]
Fanion[M]
banderín[M]

# HERALDRY
# HÉRALDIQUE[F]
# HERALDIK[F]
# HERÁLDICA[F]

## SHIELD DIVISIONS
## DIVISIONS[F] DE L'ÉCU[M]
## SCHILDPLÄTZE[M]
## DIVISIONES[F] DE LOS ESCUDOS[M]

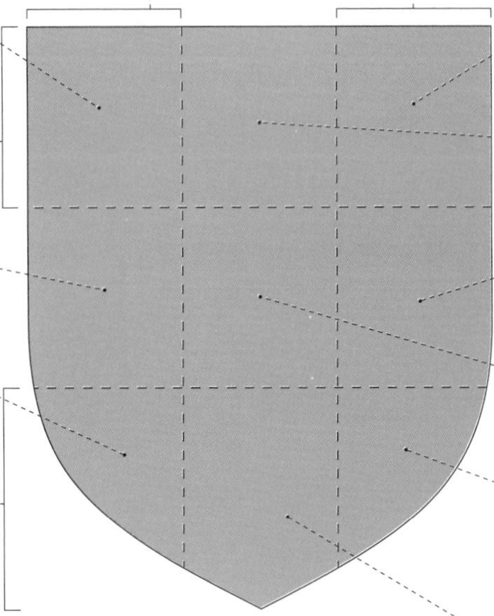

dexter
dextre[F]
rechte Flanke[F]
tercio[M] diestro

sinister
senestre[F]
linke Flanke[F]
tercio[M] siniestro

dexter chief
canton[M] dextre du chef[M]
rechtes Obereck[N]
cantón[M] diestro del jefe[M]

sinister chief
canton[M] senestre du chef[M]
linkes Obereck[N]
cantón[M] siniestro del jefe[M]

chief
chef[M]
Schildhaupt[N]
jefe[M]

centre chief
point[M] du chef[M]
Ort[N]
centro[M] del jefe[M]

dexter flank
flanc[M] dextre
rechte Hüftstelle[F]
flanco[M] diestro

sinister flank
flanc[M] senestre
linke Hüftstelle[F]
flanco[M] siniestro

centre point
centre[M]
Herzstelle[F]
corazón[M]

dexter base
canton[M] dextre de la pointe[F]
rechtes Untereck[N]
cantón[M] diestro de la punta[F]

base
pointe[F]
Fußrand[M]
punta

sinister base
canton[M] senestre de la pointe[F]
linkes Untereck[N]
cantón[M] siniestro de la punta[F]

centre base
pointe[F]
Fußstelle[F]
centro[M] de la punta[F]

## EXAMPLES OF PARTITIONS
## EXEMPLES[M] DE PARTITIONS[F]
## TEILUNGSBEISPIELE[N]
## EJEMPLOS[M] DE PARTICIONES[F]

per fess
coupé
geteilt
escudo[M] cortado

per pale
parti
gespalten
escudo[M] partido

per bend
tranché
schrägrechts geteilt
escudo[M] tronchado

quarterly
écartelé
geviert
escudo[M] acuartelado

## EXAMPLES OF ORDINARIES
## EXEMPLES[M] DE PIÈCES[F] HONORABLES
## BEISPIELE[N] FÜR HEROLDSBILDER[N]
## EJEMPLOS[M] DE PIEZAS[F] HONORABLES

chief
chef[M]
Hauptrand[M]
jefe[M]

chevron
chevron[M]
Sparren[M]
cheurón[M]

pale
pal[M]
Pfahl[M]
palo[M]

cross
croix[F]
Kreuz[N]
cruz[F]

**EXAMPLES OF CHARGES**
**EXEMPLES[M] DE MEUBLES[M]**
**BEISPIELE[N] FÜR WAPPENZEICHEN[N]**
**EJEMPLOS[M] DE CARGAS[F]**

fleur-de-lis
fleur[F] de lis[M]
Lilie[F]
flor[F] de lis[F]

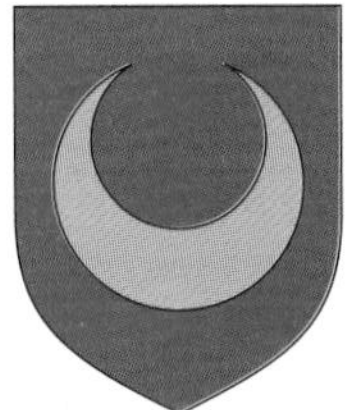

crescent
croissant[M]
Mond[M]
creciente[M]

lion passant
lion[M] passant
schreitender Löwe[M]
león[M] rampante

eagle
aigle[M]
Adler[M]
aguila[F]

mullet
étoile[F]
Stern[M]
estrella[F]

**EXAMPLES OF METALS**
**EXEMPLES[M] DE MÉTAUX[M]**
**BEISPIELE[N] FÜR METALL[N]**
**EJEMPLOS[M] DE METALES[M]**

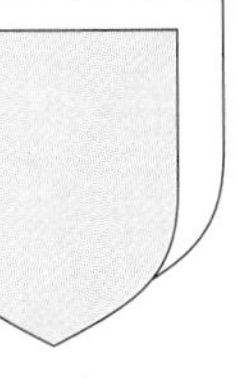

argent
argent[M]
Silber[N]
plata[F]

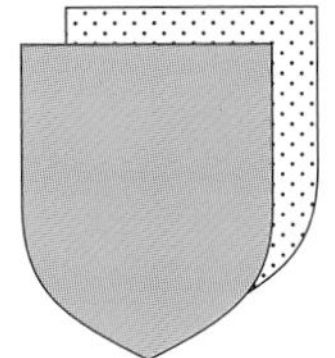

or
or[M]
Gold[N]
oro[M]

**EXAMPLES OF FURS**
**EXEMPLES[M] DE FOURRURES[F]**
**BEISPIELE[N] FÜR PELZWERK[N]**
**EJEMPLOS[M] DE FORROS[M]**

ermine
hermine[F]
Hermelin[M]
armiño[M]

vair
vair[M]
Eishutfeh[N]
cerros[M]

**EXAMPLES OF COLOURS**
**EXEMPLES[M] DE COULEURS[F]**
**FARBBEISPIELE[N]**
**EJEMPLOS[M] DE COLORES[M]**

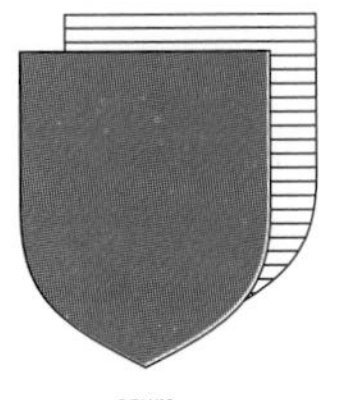

azure
azur[M]
blau
azur[M]

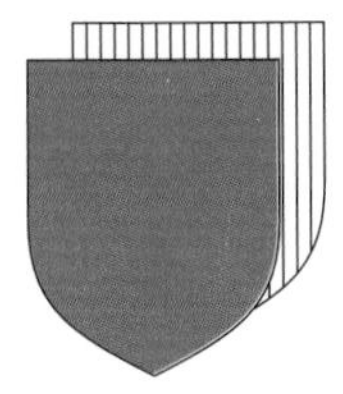

gules
gueules[M]
rot
gules[M]

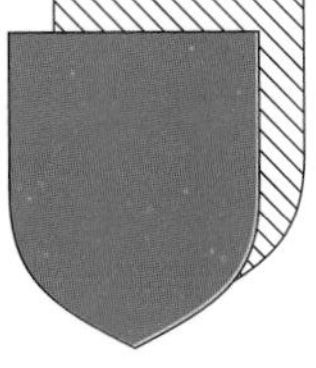

vert
sinople[M]
grün
sinople[M]

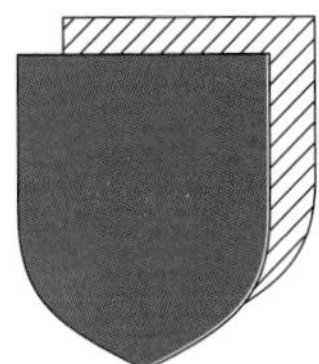

purpure
pourpre[M]
purpur
púrpura[M]

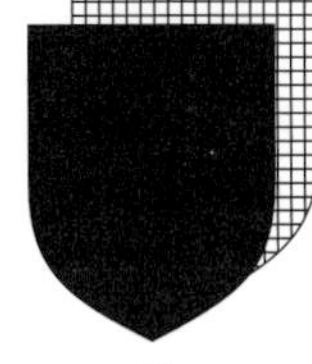

sable
sable[M]
schwarz
sable[M]

# SIGNS OF THE ZODIAC
# SIGNES^M DU ZODIAQUE^M
# TIERKREISZEICHEN^N
# SIGNOS^M DEL ZODÍACO^M

## FIRE SIGNS
## SIGNES^M DE FEU^M
## FEUERZEICHEN^N
## SIGNOS^M DE FUEGO^M

Aries the Ram (March 21)
Bélier^M (21 mars)
Widder^M, Aries (21. März)
Aries, el Carnero (21 de marzo)

Leo the Lion (July 23)
Lion^M (23 juillet)
Löwe^M, Leo (23. Juli)
Leo, el León (23 de julio)

Sagittarius the Archer (November 22)
Sagittaire^M (22 novembre)
Schütze^M, Sagittarius (22. November)
Sagitario, el Arquero (22 de noviembre)

## EARTH SIGNS
## SIGNES^M DE TERRE^F
## ERDZEICHEN
## SIGNOS^M DE TIERRA^F

Taurus the Bull (April 20)
Taureau^M (20 avril)
Stier^M, Taurus (20. April)
Tauro, el Toro (20 de abril)

Virgo the Virgin (August 23)
Vierge^F (23 août)
Jungfrau^F, Virgo (23. August)
Virgo, la Virgen (23 de agosto)

Capricorn the Goat (December 22)
Capricorne^M (22 décembre)
Steinbock^M, Capricornus (22. Dezember)
Capricornio, la Cabra (22 de diciembre)

## AIR SIGNS
## SIGNES^M D'AIR^M
## LUFTZEICHEN^N
## SIGNOS^M DE AIRE^M

Libra the Balance (September 23)
Balance^F (23 septembre)
Waage^F, Libra (23. September)
Libra, la Balanza (23 de septiembre)

Aquarius the Water Bearer (January 20)
Verseau^M (20 janvier)
Wassermann^M, Aquarius (20. Januar)
Acuario, el Aguador (20 de enero)

Gemini the Twins (May 21)
Gémeaux^M (21 mai)
Zwillinge^M, Gemini (21. Mai)
Géminis, los Gemelos (21 de mayo)

## WATER SIGNS
## SIGNES^M D'EAU^F
## WASSERZEICHEN^N
## SIGNOS^M DE AGUA^F

Cancer the Crab (June 22)
Cancer^M (22 juin)
Krebs^M, Cancer (22. Juni)
Cáncer, el Cangrejo (22 de junio)

Scorpio the Scorpion (October 24)
Scorpion^M (24 octobre)
Skorpion^M, Scorpius (24. Oktober)
Escorpio, el Escorpión (24 de octubre)

Pisces the Fishes (February 19)
Poissons^M (19 février)
Fische^M, Pisces (19. Februar)
Piscis, los peces (19 de febrero)

# SAFETY SYMBOLS
# SYMBOLES$^{M}$ DE SÉCURITÉ$^{F}$
# WARN- UND GEBOTSZEICHEN$^{N}$
# SÍMBOLOS$^{M}$ DE SEGURIDAD$^{F}$

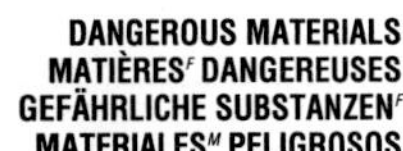

## DANGEROUS MATERIALS
## MATIÈRES$^{F}$ DANGEREUSES
## GEFÄHRLICHE SUBSTANZEN$^{F}$
## MATERIALES$^{M}$ PELIGROSOS

corrosive
matières$^{F}$ corrosives
ätzend
corrosivo

electrical hazard
danger$^{M}$ électrique
elektrische Spannung$^{F}$
alto voltaje$^{M}$

explosive
matières$^{F}$ explosives
explosionsgefährlich
explosivo

flammable
matières$^{F}$ inflammables
leicht entzündlich
inflamable

radioactive
matières$^{F}$ radioactives
radioaktiv
radioactivo

poison
matières$^{F}$ toxiques
Gift$^{N}$
veneno$^{M}$

## PROTECTION
## PROTECTION$^{F}$
## SCHUTZMASSNAHMEN$^{F}$
## PROTECCIÓN$^{F}$

eye protection
protection$^{F}$ obligatoire de la vue$^{F}$
Augenschutz$^{M}$ tragen
protección$^{F}$ de los ojos$^{M}$

ear protection
protection$^{F}$ obligatoire de l'ouïe$^{F}$
Gehörschutz$^{M}$ tragen
protección$^{F}$ de los oidos$^{M}$

head protection
protection$^{F}$ obligatoire de la tête$^{F}$
Schutzhelm$^{M}$ tragen
protección$^{F}$ de la cabeza$^{F}$

hand protection
protection$^{F}$ obligatoire des mains$^{F}$
Schutzhandschuhe$^{M}$ tragen
protección$^{F}$ de las manos$^{F}$

feet protection
protection$^{F}$ obligatoire des pieds$^{M}$
Schutzschuhe$^{M}$ tragen
protección$^{F}$ de los pies$^{M}$

respiratory system protection
protection$^{F}$ obligatoire des voies$^{F}$ respiratoires
Atemschutz$^{M}$ tragen
protección del sistema$^{M}$ respiratorio

## COMMON SYMBOLS
## SYMBOLES^M D'USAGE^M COURANT
## ALLGEMEINE ZEICHEN^N
## SÍMBOLOS^M DE USO^M COMÚN

buffet
casse-croûte^M
Cafeteria^F
cafetería^F

telephone
téléphone^M
Telefon^N
teléfono^M

restaurant
restaurant^M
Restaurant^N
restaurante^M

men's toilet
toilettes^F pour hommes^M
Toiletten^F (Herren^M)
Servicios^M (Caballeros^M)

women's toilet
toilettes^F pour dames^F
Toiletten^F (Damen^F)
Servicios^M (Señoras^F)

access for physically handicapped
accès^M pour handicapés^M physiques
für Schwerbehinderte^M
acceso^M para minusválidos^M

chemist's shop
pharmacie^F
Apotheke^F
farmacia^F

no access for wheelchairs
ne pas utiliser avec une chaise^F roulante
nicht für Rollstuhlfahrer^M
prohibido usar silla^F de ruedas^F

first aid
premiers soins^M
Erste Hilfe^F
puesto^M de socorro^M

hospital
hôpital^M
Krankenhaus^N
hospital^M

police
police^F
Polizei^F
policía^F

taxi rank
transport^M par taxi^M
Taxi^N
servicio^M de taxis^M

camping (tent)
camping[M]
Zeltplatz[M]
zona[F] para acampar

camping prohibited
camping[M] interdit
Zelten[N] verboten
prohibido acampar

camping (caravan)
caravaning[M]
Platz[M] für Wohnwagen[M]
zona[F] para caravanas[F]

camping (caravan and tent)
camping[M] et caravaning[M]
Platz[M] für Zelte[N] und Wohnwagen[M]
zona[F] para acampar y para caravanas[F]

picnics prohibited
pique-nique[M] interdit
Picknick[N] verboten
prohibido hacer comidas[F] campestres

picnic area
pique-nique[M]
Rastplatz[M]
zona[F] de comidas[F] campestres

petrol station
poste[M] de carburant[M]
Tankstelle[F]
gasolinera[F]

information
renseignements[M]
Information[F]
información[F]

information
renseignements[M]
Information[F]
información[F]

currency exchange
change[M]
Geldwechsel[M]
casa[F] de cambio[M]

lost property
articles[M] perdus et retrouvés
Fundbüro[N]
oficina[F] de objetos[M] perdidos

fire extinguisher
extincteur[M] d'incendie[M]
Feuerlöscher[M]
extintor[M] de incendios[M]

# ROAD SIGNS
# SIGNALISATION[F] ROUTIÈRE
# VERKEHRSZEICHEN[N]
# SEÑALES[F] DE CIRCULACIÓN[F]

## MAJOR NORTH AMERICAN ROAD SIGNS
## PRINCIPAUX PANNEAUX[M] NORD-AMÉRICAINS
## DIE WICHTIGSTEN NORDAMERIKANISCHEN VERKEHRSZEICHEN[N]
## PRINCIPALES SEÑALES[F] DE CIRCULACIÓN[F] NORTEAMERICANAS

stop at intersection
arrêt[M] à l'intersection[F]
Halt! Vorfahrt[F] gewähren
alto

no entry
accès[M] interdit
Verbot[N] der Einfahrt[F]
prohibido el paso[M]

give way
cédez le passage[M]
Vorfahrt[F] gewähren
ceda el paso[M]

one-way traffic
voie[F] à sens[M] unique
Einbahnstraße[F]
una vía[F]

direction to be followed
direction[F] obligatoire
vorgeschriebene Fahrtrichtung[F]
dirección[F] obligatoria

direction to be followed
direction[F] obligatoire
vorgeschriebene Fahrtrichtung[F]
dirección[F] obligatoria

direction to be followed
direction[F] obligatoire
vorgeschriebene Fahrtrichtung[F]
dirección[F] obligatoria

direction to be followed
direction[F] obligatoire
vorgeschriebene Fahrtrichtung[F]
dirección[F] obligatoria

no U-turn
interdiction[F] de faire demi-tour[M]
Wenden[N] verboten
prohibido dar vuelta[F] en U

passing prohibited
interdiction[F] de dépasser
Überholverbot[N]
prohibido adelantar

two-way traffic
circulation[F] dans les deux sens[M]
Gegenverkehr[M]
doble vía[F]

merging traffic
intersection[F] avec priorité[F]
Vorfahrt[F] an nächster Einmündung[F]
señal[F] de unión[M]

## MAJOR INTERNATIONAL ROAD SIGNS
## PRINCIPAUX PANNEAUX[M] INTERNATIONAUX
## DIE WICHTIGSTEN INTERNATIONALEN VERKEHRSZEICHEN[N]
## PRINCIPALES SEÑALES[F] DE CIRCULACIÓN[F] NORTEAMERICANAS

stop at intersection
arrêt[M] à l'intersection[F]
Halt! Vorfahrt[F] gewähren
alto

no entry
accès[M] interdit
Verbot[N] der Einfahrt[F]
prohibido el paso

give way
cédez le passage[M]
Vorfahrt[F] gewähren
ceda el paso[M]

one-way traffic
voie[F] à sens[M] unique
Einbahnstraße[F]
una vía[F]

direction to be followed
direction[F] obligatoire
vorgeschriebene Fahrtrichtung[F]
dirección[F] obligatoria

direction to be followed
direction[F] obligatoire
vorgeschriebene Fahrtrichtung[F]
dirección[F] obligatoria

direction to be followed
direction[F] obligatoire
vorgeschriebene Fahrtrichtung[F]
dirección[F] obligatoria

direction to be followed
direction[F] obligatoire
vorgeschriebene Fahrtrichtung[F]
dirección[F] obligatoria

no U-turn
interdiction[F] de faire demi-tour[M]
Wenden[N] verboten
prohibido dar vuelta[F] en U

passing prohibited
interdiction[F] de dépasser
Überholen[N] verboten
prohibido adelantar

two-way traffic
circulation[F] dans les deux sens[M]
Gegenverkehr[M]
doble vía[F]

priority intersection
intersection[F] avec priorité[F]
Vorfahrt[F] an nächster Einmündung[F]
cruce[M] con preferencia[F]

# ROAD SIGNS
# SIGNALISATION^F ROUTIÈRE
# VERKEHRSZEICHEN^N
# SEÑALES^F DE CIRCULACIÓN^F

## MAJOR NORTH AMERICAN ROAD SIGNS
## PRINCIPAUX PANNEAUX^M NORD-AMÉRICAINS
## DIE WICHTIGSTEN NORDAMERIKANISCHEN VERKEHRSZEICHEN^N
## PRINCIPALES SEÑALES^F DE CIRCULACIÓN^F NORTEAMERICANAS

bend to right
virage^M à droite^F
Rechtskurve^F
curva^F a la derecha^F

double bend
double virage^M
Doppelkurve^F
curva^F doble

roadway narrows
chaussée^F rétrécie
verengte Fahrbahn^F
estrechamiento^M del camino^M

slippery road
chaussée^F glissante
Schleudergefahr^F
camino^M resbaladizo

uneven surface
chaussée^F cahoteuse
unebene Fahrbahn^F
superficie^F irregular

steep hill
descente^F dangereuse
Gefälle^N
bajada^F pronunciada

falling rocks
chutes^F de pierres^F
Steinschlag^M
zona^F de derrumbes^M

no vehicles over height shown
limitation^F de hauteur^F
Verbot^N für Fahrzeuge^N über angegebene Höhe^F
altura^F máxima

signal ahead
signalisation^F lumineuse
Lichtzeichenanlage^F
semáforo^M

school zone
zone^F scolaire
Schule^F
zona^F escolar

pedestrian crossing
passage^M pour piétons^M
Fußgängerüberweg^M
paso^M de peatones^M

road works ahead
travaux^M
Baustelle^F
obras^F

## MAJOR INTERNATIONAL ROAD SIGNS
## PRINCIPAUX PANNEAUX$^{M}$ INTERNATIONAUX
## DIE WICHTIGSTEN INTERNATIONALEN VERKEHRSZEICHEN$^{N}$
## PRINCIPALES SEÑALES$^{F}$ DE CIRCULACIÓN$^{F}$ INTERNACIONALES

bend to right
virage$^{M}$ à droite$^{F}$
Rechtskurve$^{F}$
curva$^{F}$ a la derecha$^{F}$

double bend
double virage$^{M}$
Doppelkurve$^{F}$
curva$^{F}$ doble

road narrows
chaussée$^{F}$ rétrécie
verengte Fahrbahn$^{F}$
estrechamiento$^{M}$ del camino$^{M}$

slippery road
chaussée$^{F}$ glissante
Schleudergefahr$^{F}$
camino$^{M}$ resbaladizo

bumps
chaussée$^{F}$ cahoteuse
unebene Fahrbahn$^{F}$
badén$^{M}$

steep hill
descente$^{F}$ dangereuse
Gefälle$^{N}$
bajada$^{F}$ pronunciada

falling rocks
chutes$^{F}$ de pierres$^{F}$
Steinschlag$^{M}$
zona$^{F}$ de derrumbes$^{M}$

no vehicles over height shown
limitation$^{F}$ de hauteur$^{F}$
Verbot$^{N}$ für Fahrzeuge$^{N}$ über angegebene Höhe$^{F}$
altura$^{F}$ máxima

traffic signals ahead
signalisation$^{F}$ lumineuse
Lichtzeichenanlage$^{F}$
semáforo$^{M}$

school
zone$^{F}$ scolaire
Schule$^{F}$
zona$^{F}$ escolar

pedestrian crossing
passage$^{M}$ pour piétons$^{M}$
Fußgängerüberweg$^{M}$
paso$^{M}$ de peatones$^{M}$

road works ahead
travaux$^{M}$
Baustelle$^{F}$
obras$^{F}$

# ROAD SIGNS
# SIGNALISATION[F] ROUTIÈRE
# VERKEHRSZEICHEN[N]
# SEÑALES[F] DE CIRCULACIÓN[F]

## MAJOR NORTH AMERICAN ROAD SIGNS
## PRINCIPAUX PANNEAUX[M] NORD-AMÉRICAINS
## DIE WICHTIGSTEN NORDAMERIKANISCHEN VERKEHRSZEICHEN[N]
## PRINCIPALES SEÑALES[F] DE CIRCULACIÓN[F] NORTEAMERICANAS

level crossing
passage[M] à niveau[M]
Bahnübergang[M]
paso[M] a nivel[M]

wild animals
passage[M] d'animaux[M] sauvages
Wildwechsel[M]
cruce[M] de animales[M] salvajes

closed to pedestrians
accès[M] interdit aux piétons[M]
gesperrt für Fußgänger[M]
prohibido el paso[M] de peatones[M]

closed to bicycles
accès[M] interdit aux bicyclettes[F]
gesperrt für Radfahrer[M]
prohibido el paso[M] de bicicletas[F]

closed to motorcycles
accès[M] interdit aux motocycles[M]
gesperrt für Krafträder[N]
prohibido el paso[M] de motocicletas[F]

closed to trucks
accès[M] interdit aux camions[M]
gesperrt für Kfz[N] über 2,8t
prohibido el paso[M] de camiones[M]

## MAJOR INTERNATIONAL ROAD SIGNS
## PRINCIPAUX PANNEAUX[M] INTERNATIONAUX
## DIE WICHTIGSTEN INTERNATIONALEN VERKEHRSZEICHEN[N]
## PRINCIPALES SEÑALES[F] DE CIRCULACIÓN[F] INTERNACIONALES

level crossing
passage[M] à niveau[M]
Bahnübergang[M]
paso[M] a nivel[M]

wild animals
passage[M] d'animaux[M] sauvages
Wildwechsel[M]
cruce[M] de animales[M] salvajes

closed to pedestrians
accès[M] interdit aux piétons[M]
gesperrt für Fußgänger[M]
prohibido el paso[M] de peatones[M]

closed to bicycles
accès[M] interdit aux bicyclettes[F]
gesperrt für Radfahrer[M]
prohibido el paso[M] de bicicletas[F]

closed to motorcycles
accès[M] interdit aux motocycles[M]
gesperrt für Krafträder[N]
prohibido el paso[M] de motocicletas[F]

closed to trucks
accès[M] interdit aux camions[M]
gesperrt für Kfz[N] über 2,8t
prohibido el paso[M] de camiones[M]

# FABRIC CARE
# ENTRETIEN[M] DES TISSUS[M]
# TEXTILPFLEGE[F]
# CUIDADO[M] DE TELAS[F]

## WASHING
## LAVAGE[M]
## WASCHEN[N]
## LAVADO[M]

do not wash
ne pas laver
nicht waschen
no se lave

hand wash in lukewarm water
laver à la main[F] à l'eau[F] tiède
Handwäsche[F] in handwarmem Wasser[N]
lávese a mano[F] con agua[F] tibia

machine wash in lukewarm water at a gentle setting/reduced agitation
laver à la machine[F] à l'eau[F] tiède avec agitation[F] réduite
Hand- und Maschinenwäsche[F], Schonwaschgang[M]
lávese en lavadora[F] con agua[F] tibia en el ciclo[M] para ropa[F] delicada

machine wash in warm water at a gentle setting/reduced agitation
laver à la machine[F] à l'eau[F] chaude avec agitation[F] réduite
Hand- und Maschinenwäsche[F], Schonwaschgang[M]
lávese en lavadora[F] con agua[F] caliente en el ciclo[M] para ropa[F] delicada

machine wash in warm water at a normal setting
laver à la machine[F] à l'eau[F] chaude avec agitation[F] normale
Hand- und Maschinenwäsche[F], Normalwaschgang[M]
lávese en lavadora[F] con agua[F] caliente, en el ciclo[M] normal

machine wash in hot water at a normal setting
laver à la machine[F] à l'eau[F] très chaude avec agitation[F] normale
Hand- und Maschinenwäsche[F], Normalwaschgang[M]
lávese en lavadora[F] con agua[F] muy caliente, en el ciclo[M] normal

do not use chlorine bleach
ne pas utiliser de chlorure[M] décolorant
nicht chloren
no use lejía[F] de cloro[M]

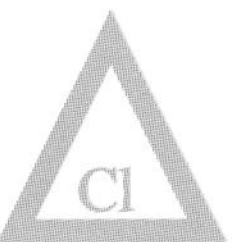


use chlorine bleach as directed
utiliser un chlorure[M] décolorant suivant les indications[F]
chloren möglich
use lejía[F] de cloro[M] siguiendo las indicaciones[F]

## DRYING
## SÉCHAGE[M]
## TROCKNEN[N]
## SECADO[M]

hang to dry
suspendre pour sécher
zum Trocknen[N] hängen
cuelgue al aire[M] libre después de escurrir

dry flat
sécher à plat
zum Trocknen[N] legen
seque extendido sobre una toalla[F] después de escurrir

tumble dry at medium to high temperature
sécher par culbutage[M] à moyenne ou haute température[F]
Wäschetrockner[M] mit mittlerer bis hoher Temperatur[F]
seque en secadora[F] a temperatura[F] de mediana a alta

tumble dry at low temperature
sécher par culbutage[M] à basse température[F]
Wäschetrockner[M] mit niedriger Temperatur[F]
seque en secadora[F] a temperatura[F] baja

drip dry
suspendre pour sécher sans essorer
tropfnaß hängen
cuelgue sin exprimir, dando forma[F] a mano[F]

## IRONING
## REPASSAGE[M]
## BÜGELN[N]
## PLANCHADO[M]

do not iron
ne pas repasser
nicht bügeln
no use plancha[F]

iron at low setting
repasser à basse température[F]
bügeln bei niedriger Einstellung[F]
use plancha[F] tibia

iron at medium setting
repasser à moyenne température[F]
bügeln bei mittlerer Einstellung[F]
use plancha[F] caliente

iron at high setting
repasser à haute température[F]
bügeln bei hoher Einstellung[F]
use plancha[F] muy caliente

# COMMON SCIENTIFIC SYMBOLS
# SYMBOLES[M] SCIENTIFIQUES USUELS
# ALLGEMEINE SYMBOLE[N] IN DEN WISSENSCHAFTEN[F]
# SÍMBOLOS[M] CIENTÍFICOS COMUNES

## MATHEMATICS
## MATHÉMATIQUES[F]
## MATHEMATIK[F]
## MATEMÁTICAS[F]

−

subtraction
soustraction[F]
Subtraktion[F]
menos[M]

+

addition
addition[F]
Addition[F]
más[M]

multiplication
multiplication[F]
Multiplikation[F]
por[M]

division
division[F]
Division[F]
entre[M]

=

is equal to
égale
ist gleich
igual a

is not equal to
n'égale pas
ist ungleich
desigual a

is approximately equal to
égale à peu près
ist annähernd gleich
casi igual a

is equivalent to
équivaut à
ist äquivalent mit
equivalente a

is identical with
est identique à
ist identisch mit
idéntico a

is not identical with
n'est pas identique à
ist nicht identisch mit
no es idéntico a

plus or minus
plus ou moins
plus oder minus
más[M] o menos[M]

empty set
ensemble[M] vide
Leermenge[F]
conjunto[M] vacío

>

is greater than
plus grand que
ist größer als
mayor que

is equal to or greater than
égal ou plus grand que
ist gleich oder größer als
igual o mayor que

is less than
plus petit que
ist kleiner als
menor que

is equal to or less than
égal ou plus petit que
ist gleich oder kleiner als
igual o menor que

∪

union
réunion[F]
Vereinigung[F]
unión[F]

intersection
intersection[F]
Durchschnitt[M]
intersección[F]

is contained in
inclusion[F]
echte Teilmenge[F] von
contenido en

%

percent
pourcentage[M]
Prozent[N]
porcentaje[M]

∈

belongs to
appartenance[F]
Element[N] von
pertenece a

does not belong to
non-appartenance[F]
nicht Element[N] von
no pertenece a

square root of
racine[F] carrée de
Quadratwurzel[F] aus
raíz[F] cuadrada de

sum
sommation[F]
Summe[F]
suma[F]

∞

infinity
infini[M]
unendlich
infinito[M]

integral
intégrale[F]
Integral[N]
integral

!

factorial
factorielle[F]
Fakultät[F]
factorial

## GEOMETRY
## GÉOMÉTRIE[F]
## GEOMETRIE[F]
## GEOMETRÍA[F]

°

degree
degré[M]
Grad[M]
grado[M]

′

minute
minute[F]
Minute[F]
minuto[M]

″

second
seconde[F]
Sekunde[F]
segundo[M]

π

pi
pi[M]
Pi[N]
pi

⊥

perpendicular
perpendiculaire[F]
Senkrechte[F]
perpendicular

∠

acute angle
angle[M] aigu
spitzer Winkel[M]
ángulo[M] agudo

∟

right angle
angle[M] droit
rechter Winkel[M]
ángulo[M] recto

obtuse angle
angle[M] obtu
stumpfer Winkel[M]
ángulo[M] obtuso

is parallel to
parallèle
ist parallel zu
es paralelo a

is not parallel to
non-parallèle
ist nicht parallel zu
no es paralelo a

## BIOLOGY
## BIOLOGIE[F]
## BIOLOGIE[F]
## BIOLOGÍA[F]

♂

male
mâle[M]
männlich
masculino[M]

female
femelle[F]
weiblich
femenino[M]

born
naissance[F]
geboren
nacimiento[M]

Rh+

blood factor positive
facteur[M] Rhésus positif
Rhesusfaktor[M] positiv
factor[M] RH positivo

Rh-

blood factor negative
facteur[M] Rhésus négatif
Rhesusfaktor[M] negativ
factor[M] RH negativo

died
mort[F]
gestorben
muerte[F]

## CHEMISTRY
## CHIMIE[F]
## CHEMIE[F]
## QUÍMICA[F]

—

negative charge
négatif[M]
negativ geladen
elemento[M] negativo

positive charge
positif[M]
positiv geladen
elemento[M] positivo

reversible reaction
réaction[F] réversible
reversible Reaktion[F]
reacción[F]

reaction direction
direction[F] d'une réaction[F]
Reaktionsrichtung[F]
dirección[F]

## MISCELLANEOUS
## SYMBOLES[M] DIVERS[M]
## WEITERE SYMBOLE[N]
## VARIOS

recycled
recyclé
wiederverwertet
recuperado

recyclable
recyclable
wiederverwertbar
recuperable

ampersand
esperluette[F]
Et-Zeichen[N]
y

registered trademark
marque[F] déposée
eingetragenes Warenzeichen[N]
marca[F] registrada

copyright
copyright[M]
Copyright[N]
copyright (derechos[M] de autor[M])

prescription
ordonnance[F]
verschreibungspflichtig
receta[F] médica

pause/still
pause[F]/arrêt[M] sur l'image[F]
Pause[F]
pausa[F]

stop
arrêt[M]
Stop[M]
paro[M]

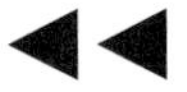

rewind
rebobinage[M]
Rücklauf[M]
rebobinado[M]

play
lecture[F]
Spiel[N]
reproducción[F]

fast forward
avance[F] rapide
Vorlauf[M]
avance rápido

## DIACRITIC SYMBOLS
## SIGNES$^{M}$ DIACRITIQUES
## DIAKRITISCHE ZEICHEN$^{N}$
## SIGNOS$^{M}$ DIACRÍTICOS

acute accent
accent$^{M}$ aigu
Accent$^{M}$ aigu
acento$^{M}$ agudo

umlaut
tréma$^{M}$
Umlaut$^{M}$
diéresis$^{F}$

grave accent
accent$^{M}$ grave
Accent$^{M}$ grave
acento$^{M}$ grave

circumflex accent
accent$^{M}$ circonflexe
Accent$^{M}$ circonflexe
acento$^{M}$ circunflejo

cedilla
cédille$^{F}$
Cedille$^{F}$
cedilla$^{F}$

tilde
tilde$^{M}$
Tilde$^{F}$
tilde$^{F}$

## PUNCTUATION MARKS
## SIGNES$^{M}$ DE PONCTUATION$^{F}$
## SATZZEICHEN$^{N}$
## SIGNOS$^{M}$ DE PUNTUACIÓN$^{F}$

semicolon
point$^{M}$-virgule$^{F}$
Semikolon$^{N}$
punto$^{M}$ y coma$^{F}$

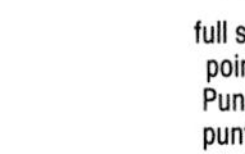
full stop
point$^{M}$
Punkt$^{M}$
punto$^{M}$

comma
virgule$^{F}$
Komma$^{N}$
coma$^{F}$

ellipsis
points$^{M}$ de suspension$^{F}$
Fortführungspunkte$^{M}$
puntos$^{M}$ suspensivos

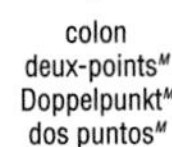
colon
deux-points$^{M}$
Doppelpunkt$^{M}$
dos puntos$^{M}$

asterisk
astérisque$^{M}$
Sternchen$^{N}$
asterisco$^{M}$

quotation marks (French)
guillemets$^{M}$
Anführungszeichenn (französische)
comillas$^{F}$

single quotation marks
guillemets$^{M}$
halbe Anführungszeichen$^{N}$
comillas$^{F}$ sencillas

quotation marks
guillemets$^{M}$
Anführungszeichen$^{N}$
comillas$^{F}$

dash
tiret$^{M}$
Gedankenstrich$^{M}$
guión$^{M}$ largo

parentheses
parenthèses$^{F}$
runde Klammern$^{F}$
paréntesis$^{M}$

slash
barre$^{F}$ oblique
Querstrich$^{M}$
diagonal$^{F}$

exclamation mark
point$^{M}$ d'exclamation$^{F}$
Ausrufezeichen$^{N}$
admiración$^{F}$

question mark
point$^{M}$ d'interrogation$^{F}$
Fragezeichen$^{N}$
interrogación$^{F}$

square brackets
crochets$^{M}$
eckige Klammern$^{F}$
corchetes$^{M}$

## EXAMPLES OF CURRENCY ABBREVIATIONS
## EXEMPLES$^{M}$ D'UNITÉS$^{F}$ MONÉTAIRES
## BEISPIELE$^{N}$ FÜR WÄHRUNGSABKÜRZUNGEN$^{F}$
## EJEMPLOS$^{M}$ DE ABREVIACIONES$^{F}$ DE MONEDAS$^{F}$

dollar
dollar$^{M}$
Dollar$^{M}$
dólar$^{M}$

cent
cent$^{M}$
Cent$^{M}$
centavo$^{M}$

pound
livre$^{F}$
Pfund$^{N}$
libra$^{F}$

yen
yen$^{M}$
Yen$^{M}$
yen$^{M}$

**F**
franc
franc$^{M}$
Franc$^{M}$
franco$^{M}$

**DM**
Deutsche Mark
mark$^{M}$
Deutsche Mark$^{F}$
marco$^{M}$

**Dr**
drachma
drachme$^{M}$
Drachme$^{F}$
dracma$^{M}$

**L**
lira
lire$^{F}$
Lira$^{F}$
lira$^{F}$

**Kr**
krone
couronne$^{F}$
Krone$^{F}$
corona$^{F}$

**IS**
shekel
shekel$^{M}$
Schekel$^{M}$
shekel$^{M}$

**ECU**
European Currency Unit
écu$^{M}$
Europäische Verrechnungseinheit$^{F}$
moneda$^{F}$ de la Comunidad$^{F}$ Europea

**Esc**
escudo
escudo$^{M}$
Escudo$^{M}$
escudo$^{M}$

**Pta**
peseta
peseta$^{F}$
Peseta$^{F}$
peseta$^{F}$

florin
florin$^{M}$
Florin$^{M}$
florín$^{M}$

# ENGLISH INDEX

# A

a 537.
abacus 166, 167.
abdomen 78, 79, 81, 91, 108, 116, 118.
abdominal aorta 126, 132.
abdominal cavity 127, 128.
abdominal rectus 120.
abdominal segment 78.
aboveground pipeline 740.
absorbing plate 768.
absorbing surface 772.
abutment 176, 454, 455, 456.
abyssal hill 29.
**abyssal plain 29.**
abyssal plain 29.
acanthus leaf 167, 220.
acceleration lane 452.
accelerator pedal 430.
accent mark 539.
accept machine 764.
access door 709.
access for physically handicapped 822.
access gallery 747.
access panel 207.
access road 452, 502.
access shaft 752.
access window 529.
**accessories 586, 672.**
accessory box 568.
accessory gear box 501.
accessory pouch 684.
accessory shoe 391, 409.
**accidentals 538.**
**accordion 536.**
**accordion bag 380.**
accordion pleat 335.
account book 518.
Ace 695.
acetylene cylinder 306.
acetylene valve 306.
achene 62, 66.
acid precipitation 32, 33, 35.
acoustic ceiling 189.
**acoustic guitar 546.**
acoustic meatus 138, 139.
acoustic screen 406.
acromion 123.
acroterion 167, 168.
action lever 541.
action of wind 35.
active tracking 402.
actual temperature 213, 705.
actuator 814.
actuator arm 529.
actuator arm motor 529.
acute accent 832.
acute angle 830.
Adam's apple 116.
add in memory 523.
add key 523.
addition 830.
additional production personnel 412.
adductor muscle 92.
adhesive disc 85.
adhesive tape 725.
adipose tissue 129, 136.
adjustable antenna 722.
adjustable buckle 645.
adjustable catch 641.
adjustable channel 278.
adjustable clamp 234.
adjustable frame 277.
**adjustable lamp 234.**
adjustable seat 460.
adjustable shelf 521.
**adjustable spanner 279.**
adjustable strap 350.
adjustable support 661.
adjustable waist tab 322.
adjuster 728.
adjusting band 406.
adjusting lever 539.
adjusting ring 264.
adjusting screw 278, 306.
adjusting tube 659.
adjustment for horizontal-circle image 713.
adjustment for vertical-circle image 713.
adjustment pedal 591.
adjustment slide 323.
adjustment wheel 311.
administrative building 752.
adrenal gland 132.
advertising panel 474.
advertising poster 477.
adze 587, 681.
aerator 294, 295.
aerial 408, 427.
**aerial ladder truck 780.**
aerodynamic brake 774.
Africa 21.
Afro pick 368.
aft shroud 16.
afterbay 746, 747, 749, 750.
afterfeather 110.
aftermast 478.
agitator 258.
agricultural pollution 32.
aileron 498, 638.
air 437.
air bladder 89.
air brake 638, 812.
air brake handle 639.
air bulb shutter release 393.
air cap 304.
air chamber 298.
air compression unit 458.
air compressor 469.
air concentrator 370.
air conditioner 449.
air conditioner compressor 435.
AIR CONDITIONING 214.
air conditioning unit 415.
air control radar 810.
air cushion 352.
air data computer 500.
air filter 210, 272, 469.
air flow 590.
air gap 772.
air hole 385, 389.
air horn 440.
air hose 590, 627, 734.
air hose connection 304.
air inlet 443.
air inlet control 204.
air intake 14, 493, 501, 508.
air leg 734.
air mattress 687.
air navigation device 810.
air purifier 210.
air relief valve 743.
air scoop 445.
air sealing gland 543.
air search radar 809, 811.
**air signs 820.**
air space 14, 109.
air temperature 38.
air tube 209.
air valve 304, 590.
air vent 257.
air-cleaner filter 783.
air-inlet grille 370.
air-outlet grille 370.
air-pressure pump 710.
air-supply tube 777.
air-to-air missile 813, 814.
air-to-surface missile 814.
air/fuel mixture 436.
**airbrush 590.**
**airbrush, cross section 590.**
aircraft 722.
AIRCRAFT CARRIER 810.
aircraft maintenance truck 506.
airframe 637.
airlock 14.
AIRPORT 502, 504, 506.
airport 52.
airspeed indicator 639.
aisle 177.
ala 141.
alarm threshold display button 485.
alarm threshold setting 485.
albumen 109.
alcohol bulb 705.
alcohol column 705.
alidade 41, 713.
alidade level 713.
alighting board 82.
all-terrain vehicle 425.
alley 614, 618.
almond 63, 66.
alphanumeric keyboard 422, 530.
**alpine skier 640.**
ALPINE SKIING 640.
Altar 13.
**altazimuth mounting 15.**
alteration line 565.
alternator 434, 468.
altimeter 635, 639.
altitude clamp 720, 721.
altitude fine adjustment 720, 721.
altitude scale 19.
alto clef 537.
altocumulus 44.
altostratus 44.
alula 110.
aluminium layer 405.
alveolar bone 144.
AM antenna 400.
amble 101.
ambulatory 177.
**American betting layout 700.**
American corn bread 153.
AMERICAN FOOTBALL 602.
**american football player 602.**
**American football, playing field 604.**
**american plug 309.**
**American roulette wheel 700.**
American white bread 153.
AMERICAN/CANADIAN FOOTBALL 604.
amethyst 363.
ammunition stowage 805.
ampersand 831.
AMPHIBIANS 84.
**amplification of seismic waves 714.**
**amplifier 402.**
amplifier 714.
ampoule 725.
ampulla of fallopian tube 129.
anal cleft 117.
anal fin 87.
anal proleg 78.
**analogue watch 706.**
**analytical balance 709.**
ANCHOR 483.
anchor 656.
anchor pin 432.
anchor wires 738.
anchorage 661.
anchorage block 456.
anconeus 121.
andirons 205.
Andromeda 11.
anemometer 41.
Anik-E 418.
ANIMAL CELL 115.
ankle 116, 118.
ankle boot 357.
ankle sock 325, 344.
ankle-strap 356.
ankle/wrist weight 665.
announcer console 407.
annual ring 59.
annular combustion chamber 501.
annular eclipse 8.
annulet 167.
anode rod 297.
anorak 353.
ant 77.
Antarctic Circle 3.
Antarctica 20.
antefix 169.
antenna 16, 43, 78, 79, 80, 81, 91, 498, 508, 613, 805, 810.
antennae cleaner 80.
antennule 90.
anterior chamber 140.
anterior end 95.
anterior notch 139.
anterior root 135.
anterior tibial 120.
anterior tibial artery 126.
**anterior view 120, 122.**
anther 60.
anti-aircraft missile 808.
anti-friction pad 641.
anti-radar missile 814.
anti-ship missile 814.
anti-skating device 404.
anti-slip foot 302.
anti-slip shoe 661.
anti-tank missile 814.
anti-tank rocket 804.
anti-torque tail rotor 508.
anti-vibration handle 272.
anticline 737.
anticollision light 498.
anticyclone 38.
antihelix 139.
antimissile self-defence 808.
antireflection coating 768.
antiseptic 725.
antitragus 139.
anus 89, 92, 127, 128, 131.
anvil 711.
aorta 125, 130.
aortic valve 125.
aperture 94.
aperture changer 717.
aperture diaphragm 717.
aperture door 16.
aperture scale 396.
aperture/exposure value display 396.
apex 83, 94, 143, 144.
apical foramen 144.
apocrine sweat gland 136.
apogee motor firing 419.
apogee passage 419.
**apple 64.**
apple 64.
appoggiatura 538.
appointment book 518.
approach 683.
approach ramp 456.
approach wall 492.
apricot 63.
apron 219, 220, 223, 502, 669.
apse 177.
apsidiole 177.
aquamarine 363.
Aquarius the Water Bearer (January 20) 820.
aquastat 209.
**aquatic bird 111.**
aquatic bird 111.
aqueous humour 140.
arc welder 305.
**arc welding 305.**
arcade 176.
arcades 172.
arch 14, 455, 649.
**arch bridge 455.**
**arch dam 750.**
**arch dam, cross section 750.**
arch of aorta 124, 125, 126.
arch of foot artery 126.
archboard 518.
**archer 684.**
Archer 13.
ARCHERY 684.
**arches, types 174.**
archipelago 51.
ARCHITECTURAL STYLES 166.
architrave 166, 168.
Arctic 20.
Arctic Circle 3, 47.
Arctic Ocean 21.
area of ice 620.
**arena 654.**
Arenberg parquet 200.
areola 129.
argent 819.
Aries the Ram (March 21) 820.
arm 100, 117, 119, 157, 220, 234, 264, 483, 535, 561, 568, 718, 727, 782, 785.
arm cylinder 782, 785.
arm elevator 404.
arm guard 602.
arm lock 668.
arm nut 568.
arm pad 609.
arm position 625.
arm rest 404.
arm slit 331.
arm stump 220.
ARMCHAIR 220.
**armet 792.**
armet 792.
armguard 684.
armhole 325.
**armoire 225.**
ARMOUR 792.
armour 805.
armoured flex 422.
armoured plate 805.
armpit 116, 118.
armrest 428, 429, 727.
armstand 624.
**armstand dive 625.**
arpeggio 539.
ARQUEBUS 795.
arrector pili muscle 136.
arrester wire 811.
arris 167.
**arrow 684.**
Arrow 11.
arrow 793.
arrow rest 684.
**arteries 126.**
artichoke 69.
**articulated lorry with trailer 440.**
articulated mannequin 592.
**artificial fly 670.**
artificial satellite 19.
ascending aorta 124.
ascending colon 131.
ash 386.
ash layer 25.
**ashtray 386.**
Asia 21.
**asparagus 72.**
asphalt 745.

The terms in **bold type** correspond to an illustration; those in CAPITALS indicate a title.

asphalt shingle 286.
asphalt still 745.
aspirin 725.
assistant timer 626.
ASSOCIATION FOOTBALL 600.
asterisk 832.
asteroid belt 4.
asthenosphere 22.
astragal 167, 800.
astrakhan cap 328.
ASTRONOMICAL OBSERVATORY 14.
**asymmetrical bars 659.**
Atlantic Ocean 20.
atlas 102, 123.
atmosphere 22, 31.
atoll 28.
atrium 170.
**attaché case 378.**
**attached curtain 228.**
attack line 613.
attack on humans 35.
attack on nature 35.
attack periscope 807.
attack zone 613.
attacking zone 608.
aubergine 69.
auditorium 16, 189.
**auditory ossicles 138.**
auditory ossicles 139.
**auger bit 281.**
auger bit 270.
auricle 81, 138.
**auricle, ear 139.**
auriculars 109.
Australia 21.
auto answer indicator 420.
auto reverse button 408.
auto/manual selector 310.
autofocus on/off switch 397.
automatic dialling index 420.
**automatic filter coffee maker 247.**
AUTOMATIC RIFLE 796.
automatic sorting trays 532.
automatic tank gauge 741.
automatically-controlled door 504.
autopilot controls 500.
autumn 8.
autumn squash 69.
autumnal equinox 8.
auxiliary facilities room 412.
auxiliary handle 280.
**auxiliary heating 211.**
auxiliary projector 16.
auxiliary tank 441.
auxiliary video switcher 413.
avenue 52.
average key 396.
avocado 68.
awl 688.
awning channel 449.
axial compressor blade 501.
axial rib 94.
axillary artery 126.
axillary bud 57.
axillary nerve 133.
axillary vein 126.
axis 123.
axle 468, 645.
axon 135.
axon hillock 135.
azimuth clamp 720, 721.
azimuth fine adjustment 720, 721.
azure 819.

## B

b 537.
baby doll 348.
**babygro 350.**
back 101, 106, 108, 117, 119, 223, 239, 240, 241, 242, 277, 288, 322, 386, 727, 793.
back beam 573.
back belt 330.
back binding 633.
back board 577.
back boundary line 618.
back check 541.
back crossbar 645.
back judge 603, 605.
back line 611.
**back of the amplifier 400.**
back pad 609, 653.
back panel 255, 259.
back pocket 323.
back score line 620.
back straight 651.
back strap 653.
back wall 616, 617.
back zone 613.
back-hoe controls 782.
backboard 610.
backcourt 614, 617.
backdrop 188.
BACKGAMMON 697.
backguard 258.
backhoe 782.
**backhoe loader 782.**
**backing 579.**
backing board 579.
**backing hammer 579.**
**backing press 579.**
backplate 432.
backrest 445.
backstay 479, 644.
backstep 778.
**backstroke 623.**
**backstroke start 623.**
backstroke turn indicator 621.
backward 624.
backward bucket 782.
backward bucket cylinder 782.
**backward dive 625.**
BADMINTON 618.
**badminton racket 618.**
**badminton, court 618.**
**badminton, net 618.**
baffle 216, 742.
bag well 679.
baggage check-in counter 504.
baggage claim area 504.
baggage conveyor 507.
baggage trailer 507.
**bagpipes 536.**
baguette cut 362.
bail 599.
bail arm 671.
bail arm opening mechanism 671.
bailey 180.
Bailey bridge 457.
baize 675.
bakelite® body 804.
**baking utensils 245.**
**balaclava 329.**
**balalaika 535.**
Balance 13.
**balance beam 659.**
balance control 402.
balance rail 541.
ball 389, 530, 575, 598, 683, 795.
ball assembly 294.
ball boy 614.
ball of clay 584.
ball peen 275.
ball return 683.
ball stand 683.
**ball winder 575.**
ball-cock supply valve 293.
**ball-peen hammer 275.**
**ball-type mixer tap 294.**
ballast 466.
**balloon 634.**
balloon 634.
**balloon curtain 229.**
BALLOONING 634.
**ballpoint pen 389.**
ballpoint pen 515.
ballroom 497.
baluster 201.
banana 68.
band 404.
band ring 364.
band selector 402.
bandage 669.
banding wheel 584.
bangle 364.
banister 194, 201.
**banjo 535.**
bank 193, 451, 752.
bank of heliostats 770, 771.
banquette 222.
bar 104, 376, 554, 662, 663, 665, 697.
bar line 537.
bar nose 272.
bar shot 801.
bar stool 222.
barb 38, 110, 671.
**barbell 663.**
barber comb 368.
barbican 180.
baren 582.
bargraph type peak meter 407.
bark 59.
barley 152.
barn 148.
barograph 41.
barometer scales 710.
**barometer/thermometer 710.**
barometric pressure 38.
barometric tendency 38.
barrack buildings 179.
barred spiral galaxy 9.
barrel 370, 389, 698, 706, 795, 796, 797, 798, 799, 800, 802, 804.
barrel jacket 796.
barrier 186, 471.
barrier lamp 471.
barrier support 471.
barrow 788.
bartizan 178, 181.
basaltic layer 22.
base 166, 204, 236, 252, 283, 368, 404, 410, 450, 466, 471, 579, 656, 661, 708, 712, 718, 774, 799, 817, 818.
base course 451.
base line 719.
base of splat 220.
base plate 40, 284, 404, 641, 713, 719.
base plug 804.
base ring 800.
base width 756.
BASEBALL 595, 596.
**baseball 596.**
**baseball, cross section of a 596.**
**baseball, field 597.**
baseboard 399.
baseline 614.
basement 197.
basement window 197.
baseplate 803.
**basic building materials 286.**
BASIC COMPONENTS 528, 530.
basic source of food 31.
**basic weaves 576.**
basil 74.
basilic vein 126.
basin 752.
basin side 752.
**basket 610, 635.**
basket 252, 610, 634, 641, 642.
basket handle 174, 635.
basket stitch 567.
basket support 635.
basket suspension cables 634.
basket weave pattern 200.
BASKETBALL 610.
**basketball 610.**
**basketball, court 610.**
bass bridge 540.
bass clarinet 556.
bass clef 537.
bass drum 552, 557.
bass keyboard 536.
bass loudspeaker 16.
bass pickup 547.
bass register 536.
bass tone control 402.
bass trap 412.
bassoon 548.
bassoons 557.
baster 246.
bastion 179.
BAT 112.
**bat 596, 598.**
bat 160, 595, 598.
bateau neck 343.
bath 194, 215, 292.
bath and shower mixer 215.
bath platform 292.
bathrobe 348.
BATHROOM 292.
bathroom 194, 195.
**bathroom scales 709.**
batsman 599.
batten 188, 628, 631, 637.
batten pocket 628, 631.
**batter 595.**
batter 597.
batter's helmet 595.
**battery 439.**
battery 393, 409, 468, 528, 769, 777, 814.
battery box 441.
battery case 439.
battery cover 439.
battery eject switch 409.
battery modules 43.
battery radiator 49.
battery warning light 431.
batting glove 595.
battlement 179, 181.
batwing sleeve 339.
baulk 674.
baulk line 674.
baulk line spot 674.
bay 7, 51, 74.
bay antler 105.
bay window 197.
bayonet cap 232.
bayonet mount 392.
BAZOOKA 804.
beach 23, 30.
bead 433.
bead wire 433.
beam 105, 156, 659, 708.
**beam balance 708.**
**beam bridge 454.**
beam diameter reduction 717.
beam gantry 756.
beam reach 629.
bean bag chair 222.
bean sprouts 72.
bearer 543.
bearing pad 765.
beater 156, 250, 572.
beater ejector 250.
beater handtree 573.
beater sley 572.
**beaters 250.**
**beaver 98.**
beaver 792.
BED 224.
**bed 687.**
bed 450, 578, 659.
bed chamber 170.
bed lamp 234.
**bed linen 224.**
bedplate 561.
bedrock 714.
bedroom 194, 195, 685.
beehive 149.
beer glass 237.
beetroot 71.
beginners' course 646.
belfry 176.
bell 549, 551.
bell bottoms 336.
bell brace 549.
bell roof 183.
bell tower 175.
bellow 543.
bellows 399, 536.
bellows strap 536.
belly 101.
belly scale 97.
belongs to 830.
**belt 323.**
belt 319, 433, 668.
belt drive 492.
belt loader 733.
belt loop 319, 323, 688.
**belted radial tyre 433.**
bench 222, 475, 663, 733.
bench height 733.
bench seat 428.
bend 376, 671.
bend to right 826, 827.
bent blade 587.
Berenice's Hair 11.
beret 329.
bergère 220.
bergschrund 26.
Bering Sea 21.
berm 748.
Bermuda sail 482.
Bermuda shorts 336.
BERRY FRUITS 62.
**berry, section 62.**
berth 460.
bertha collar 342.
bevel 726.
bevel square 713.
bezel 364.
bezel facet (8) 363.
bias 566.
bib 349, 350, 351, 667.
bib necklace 361.
**bib tap 294.**
biceps of arm 120.
biceps of thigh 121.
biconcave lens 722.
biconvex lens 722.
bicorne 318.
BICYCLE 446, 448.
**bicycle, accessories 448.**
bidet 292.
**bifocal lens 376.**
Big Dog 13.
bikini 347.
bill 108, 483.
billhook 269.
**billiard cue 675.**
billiard spot 675.

The terms in **bold type** correspond to an illustration; those in CAPITALS indicate a title.

BILLIARDS 673.
bimetallic helix 705.
**bimetallic thermometer 705.**
binder 159.
binding 328, 633, 642.
BINOCULAR MICROSCOPE 718.
**biology 831.**
biomedical monitoring sensor 512.
**biosphere, structure 31.**
biparous cyme 60.
bipod 796, 803.
BIRD 108, 110.
Bird of Paradise 13.
**bird of prey 111.**
bird of prey 111.
**bird, morphology 108.**
biscuit cutters 245.
biscuit sheet 245.
Bishop 696.
bishop sleeve 340.
bit 385, 648, 734, 737.
bitt 743.
bitter taste 143.
BIVALVE SHELL 95.
Black 696.
black 700, 701.
black ball 673.
black bread 153.
black salsify 71.
Black Sea 21.
black square 696.
black stone 697.
blackcurrant 62.
blade 57, 214, 239, 242, 251, 256, 268, 271, 276, 277, 284, 285, 291, 304, 369, 374, 562, 564, 607, 609, 619, 627, 632, 643, 644, 666, 672, 681, 754, 774, 783, 784.
blade close stop 369.
blade dispenser 374.
blade guard 285.
blade height adjustment 285.
blade lever 578.
blade lift cylinder 783.
blade lift fan 492.
blade lifting mechanism 784.
blade locking bolt 284.
blade rotation mechanism 784.
blade tilting lock 284.
blade tilting mechanism 284, 285.
blade with two bevelled edges 587.
blank 695.
blanket 224, 581.
blanket insulation 287.
**blanket sleepsuit 350.**
blast valve 635.
blastodisc 109.
blazer 338.
bleeder valve 208.
**blender 250.**
blending attachment 250.
blind cloth 231.
blinker 653.
block 542, 656, 787.
blockboard 288.
BLOOD CIRCULATION 124, 126.
blood factor negative 831.
blood factor positive 831.
blood vessel 136.
blood vessels 112.
blow pipe 536.
blower 207, 213, 543, 760.
blower motor 207, 214.
**blowtorch 299, 307.**
blue ball 673.
blue beam 410.
blue cap 626.
blue flag 626.
blue line 608.
blue mussel 93.
blueberry 62.
blusher brush 366.
**board 288.**
board 288, 631.
**board cutter 578.**
board insulation 287.
boarding step 508.
boarding walkway 503.
boards 608.
boater 328.
**bobbin 570.**
bobbin 561, 562, 570, 573.
**bobbin case 562.**
BOBBIN LACE 570.
**bobbin winder 575.**
bobbin winder 561.
bobble hat 329.
BOBSLEIGH 643.
bobstay 479.
**body 426.**
body 143, 252, 256, 281, 294, 295, 445, 449, 453, 542, 546, 549, 645, 658, 670, 707, 719.
body flap 511.
body guard moulding 449.
body of fornix 134.
body of nail 137.
body pad 609.
**body shirt 337.**
body side moulding 427.
body suit 345.
body temperature control unit 512.
body tube 718.
body whorl 94.
body wire 666.
**bogie 476.**
bogie 468.
bogie frame 468.
bogie goods truck 473.
bogie goods van 472.
bogie tank wagon 472.
**bogie van 470.**
**boiler 209.**
boiler 208, 771.
**boiling-water reactor 763.**
bole 59.
bolero 338.
boletus 55.
bollard 492.
bolster 224, 239, 242.
**bolt 279.**
bolt 278, 282, 290, 793.
bolt assist mechanism 796.
bonding terminal 312.
boning knife 242.
bonnet 294, 295, 426, 440.
book ends 517.
**book of matches 386.**
**bookbinding leather 579.**
boom 628, 782, 785.
boom cylinder 782, 785.
boom truck 506.
boom vang 628.
booster parachute 510.
boot 356, 427, 542, 627, 644, 645, 648.
**boot jack 358.**
bootee 354.
borage 74.
bordeaux glass 237.
border 188, 189.
bore 801.
born 831.
bottle opener 244, 688.
bottom 633.
bottom cross-member 470.
bottom cushion 674.
bottom cylinder 581.
bottom deck 741.
bottom deckboard 787.
**bottom face 363.**
bottom face 640.
bottom line 621.
bottom of the pool 626.
bottom pocket 674.
bottom rail 202, 225, 231.
bottom ring 753.
bottom road 736.
bottom side rail 470.
bottom stair 201.
**bottom-fold document case 378.**
bottomboard 543.
boulevard 52, 184.
**bound book 577.**
**bow 544, 793.**
bow 328, 497, 628, 631, 793.
bow collar 342.
bow door 493.
bow loading door 494.
bow saw 690.
bow thruster 497.
bow tie 324.
bow window 197.
bowl 241, 251, 385, 484, 682.
bowl with serving spout 251.
bowler 328, 599.
bowline 691.
bowline on a bight 691.
BOWLING 683.
**bowling ball 683.**
bowling crease 599.
**bowling lane 683.**
BOWLS AND PETANQUE 682.
BOWS 793.
bowsprit 479.
bowstring 684, 793.
box 156, 189, 204, 657.
box bag 381.
**box pallet 787.**
box pleat 228.
boxer 669.
boxer shorts 325, 353.
BOXING 669.
**boxing gloves 669.**
**bra 346.**
**brace 281.**
brace 198, 302, 757.
brace clip 323.
**bracelets 364.**
**braces 323.**
brachial 120.
brachial artery 126.
brachial plexus 133.
brachioradialis 120, 121.
bracket 231.
bracket base 225.
bract 66.
**braided rope 692.**
brail 480.
brain 88.
brake 664, 727.
brake cable 447.
brake caliper 442.
brake handle 445.
brake hose 432.
brake lever 447.
brake light 429.
brake lining 432.
brake loop 636.
brake pad 432.
brake pedal 430, 641.
brake shoe 432.
brake van 473.
brakeman 643.
**branch 58.**
branch 59, 61, 72, 104, 215, 726.
branch clip 726.
branch duct 206.
branch return pipe 208.
branch supply pipe 208.
branches 59.
BRANCHING, PLUMBING 298.
brandy glass 237.
**brass family 550.**
brassiere cup 346.
brattice 181.
Brazil nut 66.
BREAD 153.
bread guide 252.
bread knife 242.
break line 341.
breaker 30.
BREAST 129.
breast 108, 116, 118.
breast beam 572.
breast collar 653.
breast dart 320.
breast pocket 320, 324.
breast welt pocket 322.
breastplate 792.
**breaststroke 622.**
breaststroke kick 622.
breaststroke turn 622.
breather valve 741.
breathing in 622.
breathing out 622.
breech 549.
breech guard 549.
breechblock 798, 799, 802.
breechblock operating lever assembly 802.
breeches 315, 317, 667, 791.
brick 286.
brick wall 199.
brick-bond woodstrip flooring 200.
bricklayer's hammer 291.
**bridge 674.**
bridge 52, 230, 376, 544, 546, 719, 810.
bridge assembly 547.
bridge of nose 141.
bridging 198.
**bridle 649.**
bridle 653.
bridle assembly 486.
bridle tape 541.
**briefcase 378.**
**briefs 325.**
briefs 346.
brig 482.
brigantine 482.
brightness control 529.
**brilliant cut facets 363.**
brilliant full cut 362.
brim 328, 329.
briolette cut 362.
bristle 373, 374.
bristles 304.
broad beans 72.
broad ligament of uterus 129.
broad reach 629.
broad welt side pocket 319, 330, 339.
broad-leaved endive 73.
broadsword 794.
broccoli 69.
brooch 364.
brood chamber 82.
broom 205.
brow brush and lash comb 367.
brow reinforce 792.
brow tine 105.
browband 649.
brown ball 673.
brush 152, 373, 582, 589.
brush and rails 646, 647.
Brussels sprouts 73.
bubble 443.
bucket 754, 782.
bucket cylinder 782, 785.
bucket hinge pin 782.
bucket lever 782.
bucket ring 754.
**bucket seat 428.**
bucket tooth 782.
bucket wheel excavator 733.
**buckle 566.**
buckle 319, 323, 380, 428, 641.
buckwheat 152.
bud 70.
buffer tank 740.
buffers 464.
buffet 822.
bugle 550.
BUILDING MATERIALS 286, 288.
built-in microphone 409.
bulb 72, 104, 232, 233, 310, 743.
bulb dibber 268.
bulb unit 752.
**bulb vegetables 70.**
bulbil 70.
bulbocavernous muscle 127.
bulk terminal 490.
bulkhead 441.
bulkhead flat truck 473.
Bull 11.
bull's-eye 684, 698.
**bulldozer 783.**
bulldozer 733.
bullet 798.
bullion stitch 571.
bulwark 478.
bumper 260, 426, 440, 441.
bumper guard 617.
bumper moulding 426.
bumps 827.
bun tin 245.
bunch 384.
**bunch of grapes 61.**
bund wall 741.
bundle 72, 756.
bunker 676.
bunker oil 745.
bunker silo 149.
bunting 817.
**buoyage regions 488.**
buoyancy compensator 627.
bureau 226.
burgee 817.
burgundy glass 237.
burin 581, 587.
burned gases 436.
burner 209, 248, 634, 635, 689.
burner frame 689.
burner gas tube 297.
burner ring 248.
burnisher 582.
burr 105.
bursting charge 804.
bus 190.
bus module 49.
bus shelter 186.
bus stop 186.
busbar 747.
bush 263.
bushing 746, 747, 757.
bustle 316.
butt 386, 568, 579, 615, 670, 675, 796, 797.
butt cap 670.
butt end 609.
butt grip 671.
butt guide 671.
butt plate 795, 798, 799.
butt section 670.
**butt welding 307.**
butt-strap 376.
butte 46.
butter compartment 254.
butter curler 242.
butter dish 238.

The terms in **bold type** correspond to an illustration; those in CAPITALS indicate a title.

butter knife 239.
BUTTERFLY 78.
**butterfly 79.**
butterfly kick 623.
**butterfly stroke 623.**
butterfly turn 623.
**butterfly, hind leg 78.**
buttock 117, 119, 127, 128.
button 232, 324, 326, 530, 536, 666, 800.
button facing 324, 326.
button loop 323.
button strap 351.
**button-through smock 337.**
buttondown collar 324.
buttonhole 319.
buttress 176, 751.
**buttress dam 751.**
**buttress dam, cross section 751.**
by-pass taxiway 502.
bypass duct 501.
bypass feeder 532.

## C

c 537.
cab 147, 160, 782, 783, 784, 785.
cabbage lettuce 73.
cabin 496, 508.
cabinet 258, 259, 410.
CABLE 692.
cable 280, 406, 660, 692.
cable distributor 416.
cable drum compartment 415.
cable guard 684.
cable shutter release 393.
cable sleeve 280.
cable stay anchorage 456.
cable stitch 567.
**cable-stayed bridges 456.**
cables 414.
cabochon cut 362.
cabriole chair 220.
cabriole leg 220.
caecum 131.
café curtain 228.
**cafetière with plunger 247.**
**cake mascara 367.**
cake tin 245.
cakes 588.
calamus 110.
calandria 759.
calcaneus 103, 123.
calcar 112.
CALCULATOR 523.
calculator 379.
calculator dial 396.
**calculator/cheque book holder 379.**
calendar pad 518.
calf 117, 119, 151.
caliper 432, 583.
Callisto 4.
calls indicator 420.
calm 38.
calyx 60, 62, 67, 132.
cam ring 281.
cambium 59.
**camera 414.**
camera 16, 412, 414.
**camera back 390.**
camera body 391.
camera control area 415.
camera control technician 412, 415.
camera control unit 412, 415.
camera dolly 414.
camera platform 393.
camera platform lock 393.
camera screw 393.
camera viewfinder 414.
camisole 345.
camp bed 687.
**camper 449.**
CAMPING 685, 686, 690.
camping (caravan and tent) 823.
camping (caravan) 823.
camping (tent) 823.
CAMPING EQUIPMENT 688.
**camping equipment 690.**
camping prohibited 823.
**camping tools 690.**
camshaft 434.
Canadian elk 105.
**Canadian football, playing field 604.**
canal bed 492.
CANAL LOCK 492.
canal lock 490.
Cancer the Crab (June 22) 820.
candlepin 683.
cane pen 389.
canine 98, 144.
canned failed fuel 764.
cannon 101.
**canopy 636.**
canopy 375, 636, 685, 785, 813.
canopy release knob 639.
cantaloupe 69.
canteen 690.
cantilever 750.
**cantilever bridge 454.**
cantilever span 454.
cantle 649.
canvas 589, 669.
canvas divider 685.
**cap 328.**
cap 55, 201, 232, 233, 250, 301, 309, 389, 398, 590, 773.
cap iron 277.
cap nut 279.
cap sleeve 339.
**cape 331.**
cape 51.
capillary blood vessel 137.
capillary tube 705.
capital 51, 166.
capitulum 60.
caponiere 179.
capped column 37.
capped tee 205.
Capricorn the Goat (December 22) 820.
capstan 581.
capstan button 541.
capsule 725.
**capsule, section 67.**
captain's quarters 497.
captain's seat 500.
capture 697.
CAR 425, 426, 428, 430, 432, 434, 438.
car 630.
car coat 330.
car deck 494.
car park 464, 491, 504.
car wash 453.
caraco jacket 316.
carafe 237.
carapace 91, 96.
CARAVAN 449.
caraway seeded rye bread 153.
carbon dioxide gas coolant 760.
carburettor 442.
carcass ply 433.
CARD GAMES 695.
**card games, symbols 695.**
card reader 422.
card support 40.
cardboard 589.
cardigan 326.
**cardinal marks 488.**
cardoon 72.
cargo dispatch 505.
cargo hold 499.
cargo reception 505.
Caribbean Sea 20.
carnassial 98.
**carnivore's jaw 98.**
carnivores 31, 33.
**carom billiards 673.**
carpal pad 106.
carpenter's hammer 275.
CARPENTRY: TOOLS 275, 276, 278, 280, 282, 284.
carpet and floor brush 260.
carpus 102, 122.
carriage 787, 800, 802.
carriage control dial 569.
carriage handle 568.
carriage return 525.
**carriages 568.**
carrier 446.
carrot 71.
carrying handle 408, 796.
CARTOGRAPHY 47, 50, 52.
carton 384.
cartridge 291, 295, 389, 404, 527, 730, 797.
**cartridge (rifle) 798.**
**cartridge (shotgun) 799.**
cartridge chamber 795, 796.
cartridge drive 527.
cartridge film 395.
cartridge fuse 312.
**cartridge mixer 295.**
cartridge stem 295.
cartridge tape recorder 407.
cartwheel hat 329.
carver's bench screw 586.
carving 586.
carving fork 242.
carving knife 242.
case 358, 365, 539, 540, 705, 706, 710, 711, 798.
casement 203.
casement window 203.
casement window opening inwards 203.
cash readout 453.
cashew 66.
casing 203, 209, 211, 214, 271, 702.
casing first string 740.
Caspian Sea 21.
**cassette 403.**
cassette 408, 526.
cassette compartment 409, 411.
cassette deck 400, 407.
cassette drive 526.
cassette eject button 411.
cassette eject switch 409.
**cassette film 395.**
cassette holder 403.
cassette player 408.
cassette player controls 408.
**cassette tape deck 403.**
Cassiopeia 11.
cast-on stitches 567.
castanets 554, 556.
caster 260, 553.
CASTLE 180.
castle 180.
Castle 696.
casual shoe 356.
CAT 107.
**cat's head 107.**
catalytic converter 439.
catalytic reforming plant 744.
catapult 810.
catch 375, 670.
catch glove 609.
**catcher 595.**
catcher 541, 597.
catcher's glove 595.
catering vehicle 507.
**caterpillar 78.**
**cathedral 176.**
cathedral 184.
**cathedral, plan 177.**
catwalk 188.
caudal fin 87.
caudal vertebrae 103.
cauliflower 69.
**caulking gun 291.**
CAVE 24.
cave 30.
CD/ROM player 526.
cedilla 832.
ceiling 205, 616, 617.
ceiling bracket 230.
ceiling collar 205.
**ceiling fan 214.**
ceiling fitting 236.
ceiling joist 198.
ceiling outlet 207.
ceiling projector 41.
celeriac 71.
**celery 72.**
CELESTIAL COORDINATE SYSTEM 3.
celestial equator 3.
celestial meridian 3.
celestial sphere 3.
cell 79, 82.
cell body 135.
cell membrane 115.
cell wall 115.
cello 545.
cellos 557.
cellular telephone 417.
Celsius scale 705.
cement screed 200.
cementum 144.
cemetery 52.
cent 832.
Centaur 13.
Central America 20.
central circle 611.
central column 774.
central defender 601.
central focusing wheel 719.
central incisor 144.
central nave 173.
**central nervous system 134.**
central pumping station 740.
central reservation 184, 186, 452.
central screw 579.
central stile 202.
centre 603, 605, 608, 610, 611, 697.
centre back 601, 612, 613.
centre back vent 322.
centre base 818.
centre chief 818.
centre circle 601, 610.
centre console 430.
centre court 617.
centre electrode 439.
centre face-off circle 608.
centre field 597.
centre fielder 597.
centre flag 601.
centre forward 601, 607, 612, 613.
centre half 607.
centre hole 404.
centre Keelson 743.
centre lane 452.
centre line 604, 607, 608, 610, 612, 618, 619, 620, 666, 682.
centre mark 614.
centre pocket 674.
centre point 818.
centre post 225.
centre service line 614.
centre span 456.
centre spot 601, 674.
centre strap 614.
centre third 611.
centre wheel 706, 707.
centre-aisle 460.
centre-back 601.
centreboard 628.
centrifugal compressor 501.
centring 524.
centring control 529.
centring point 281.
centriole 115.
cephalic vein 126.
cephalothorax 90.
Cepheus 11.
cerebellum 134.
cerebrum 134.
cervical vertebra (7) 123.
cervical vertebrae 102.
cervix of uterus 128.
cesspit 216.
chain 448, 661, 707.
chain brake 272.
chain drive 156, 158.
chain guide 448.
chain mail 792.
chain of dunes 46.
**chain of neurons 135.**
chain pipe wrench 299.
chain stay 446.
chain stitch 571.
chain wheel A 448.
chain wheel B 448.
**chainsaw 272.**
chainsaw chain 272.
chaise longue 221.
chalaza 109.
chalk 675.
Chameleon 13.
chamois leather 358.
champagne flute 237.
champagne glass 237.
**chandelier 236.**
change sign key 523.
channel scan buttons 411.
channel selector controls 411.
chanter 536.
chanterelle 55.
Chantilly parquet 200.
chapel 181.
character correction 525.
charcoal 588.
charge 799.
charge indicator 374.
**charges, examples 819.**
charging handle 796.
charging light 374.
charging socket 374.
Charioteer 11.
Charleston cymbal 552.
charm bracelet 364.
**charms 364.**
Charon 5.
chart room 494.
chase 800.
check nut 40.
check valve 216, 306.
check-rail 467.
cheek 100, 106, 118, 275, 670, 800.
cheek ring 650.
cheek strap 649.
cheese knife 239.
chemical treatment 745.
chemise 181.
chemist's shop 822.
**chemistry 831.**
cheque book 379.

cheque book cover 379.
cherimoya 68.
cherry 63.
chervil 74.
CHESS 696.
chess notation 696.
**chess, men 696.**
**chessboard 696.**
chest 100, 116, 118.
chest expander 665.
chest protector 595, 602, 684.
chesterfield 221.
chestnut 66, 100.
chevet 177.
chevron 818.
chevron stitch 571.
chick 150.
chick peas 72.
chicory 73.
chief 818.
chief timekeeper 621.
chiffonier 226.
CHILDREN'S CLOTHING 349, 350.
chilli 69.
**chimney 205.**
chimney 197, 209.
chimney connection 204.
chimney pot 197.
chimney stack 197.
chin 108, 118.
chin guard 777.
chin protector 443.
chin rest 544.
chin strap 602, 777.
China Sea 21.
Chinese cabbage 73.
chipboard 289.
Chisel 13.
chisel 581.
chive 70.
chloroplast 115.
**chock 681.**
chock 680.
choir 177.
choir organ manual 542.
choker 361.
**chord 539.**
choroid 140.
**Christmas tree 740.**
Christmas tree 738, 740.
chromatin 115.
chromosphere 6.
**chrysalis 78.**
chrysalis 82.
chuck 276, 280, 281, 283, 735.
chuck key 281.
chukka 354.
church 185.
chute 736.
cicada 77.
**cigar 384.**
cigar band 384.
**cigarette 384.**
cigarette holder 384.
**cigarette packet 384.**
cigarette papers 384.
ciliary body 140.
ciliate 56.
cine scale 396.
cinema 496.
circuit breaker 212, 747.
circuit vent 215.
circular body 535.
circular needle 567.
**circular saw 284.**
**circular saw blade 284.**
circulating pump 208, 772.
**circulation diagram 124.**
circulation pump 763.
circumflex accent 832.
cirque 7.
cirrocumulus 44.
cirrostratus 44.
cirrus 44.
cistern 292.
cistern ball 293.
cistern lid 293.
**citrus fruit, section 65.**
CITRUS FRUITS 65.
city 51.
city boundary 52.
CITY CENTRE 184.
clam 93.
clam cleat 630.
clamp 309, 370, 575, 578, 642.
clamp binder 519.
clamp lever 370.
clamp spotlight 235.
clamping screw 282.
clarinet 548.
clarinets 556.
clasp 378, 380.
class ring 364.
classic blouse 337.
clavicle 122.
claw 78, 80, 90, 91, 97, 106, 107, 108, 112, 275, 364, 579.
**claw hammer 275.**
**claw, extended 107.**
**claw, retracted 107.**
clay core 748.
cleaning brush 374.
cleaning eye 296.
**cleaning tools 260.**
clear key 523.
clear sky 39.
clear space 613.
clear-entry key 523.
cleat 628, 630.
cleated shoe 602.
cleaver 242.
**clefs 537.**
clew 631.
clew line 481.
click 706, 707.
cliff 7, 23, 27, 30.
climate control 430.
CLIMATES OF THE WORLD 45.
climbing harness 680.
**climbing iron 358.**
climbing plant 263.
**clinical thermometer 705.**
clip 230, 389, 515, 711.
clip earrings 361.
clipboard 519.
clippers 369.
clitoris 128.
cloche 329.
clock 407, 413, 415, 430, 714.
clock operator 610.
clock timer 253, 255.
clog 357.
close hauled 629.
close reach 629.
close-up lens 392.
closed to bicycles 828.
closed to motorcycles 828.
closed to pedestrians 828.
closed to trucks 828.
closeness setting 374.
closure rail 467.
cloth roller 572.
clothing guard 727.
cloud 36.
**cloud amount 39.**
cloud of volcanic ash 25.
CLOUDS 44.
CLOUDS SYMBOLS 44.
**clouds with vertical development 44.**
cloudy sky 39.
clove hitch 691.
**cloverleaf 452.**
cloverleaf 450.
club 695.
club chair 221.
clubhouse 651, 676.
clubhouse turn 651.
**clubs, golf 678.**
clump of flowers 263.
clutch bag 381.
clutch housing 444.
clutch lever 272, 442, 444.
clutch pedal 430.
coach connection 461.
coach's box 597.
COAL MINE 733, 734, 736.
coarse adjustment knob 718.
COASTAL FEATURES 30.
coat dress 332.
coat hook 522.
coat rack 522.
cob 72.
coccyx 122.
cochlea 139.
cochlear nerve 139.
cock 795.
cocking lever 804.
cockle 93.
cockleshell 220.
**cockpit 639.**
cockpit 628.
cockpit canopy 638.
cockpit ventilation 639.
cocktail cabinet 227.
cocktail glass 237.
coconut 66.
code 524.
coeliac trunk 124, 132.
COFFEE MAKERS 247.
**coffee mill 256.**
coffee mug 238.
coffee pot 688.
coffee spoon 241.
coil 714.
coil spring 231.
**coiling 584.**
coin chute 702.
coin purse 379.
coin reject slot 702.
coin return bucket 422.
coin slot 422, 702.
colander 243.
cold air 501, 772.
cold air inlet 438.
cold coolant 771.
cold heavy water 761.
cold store 491.
cold-water circuit 215.
cold-water riser 215.
cold-water supply 293, 296, 297, 298.
**collar 341.**
collar 57, 319, 322, 324, 352, 374, 663.
collar point 324, 341.
collar stiffener 324.
collaret 318, 341.
**collars, types 341, 342.**
collateral 135.
collecting funnel 40.
collecting vessel 40.
collector 753.
collet 283, 393.
colon 832.
colour chart 592.
colour control 532.
colour display 569.
colour filter 392.
colour selection filter 410.
colour television camera 512.
colouring pencils 588.
**colours, examples 819.**
columella 94.
columella fold 94.
column 24, 36, 166, 168, 169, 236, 283, 393, 399, 455, 561, 621, 700, 701.
column crank 393.
column lock 393.
column of mercury 705.
coma 9.
comb 574, 792.
COMBAT AIRCRAFT 812.
combination lock 378.
**combination pliers 311.**
combination spanner 279.
combinations 325.
**combine harvester 160.**
combine harvester 155.
**combs 368.**
combustion 436, 437, 501.
combustion chamber 434, 438.
combustion space 204, 209.
COMET 9.
comma 832.
command key 530.
command module 509.
commander's seat 805.
commando knife 794.
commercial area 190.
commercial premises 185.
commissure of lips of mouth 142.
common carotid artery 126.
common extensor of fingers 121.
common iliac artery 126, 132.
common iliac vein 132.
common periwinkle 83.
common peroneal nerve 133.
COMMON SCIENTIFIC SYMBOLS 830.
COMMON SYMBOLS 822.
common whipping 691.
communicating ramus 135.
communication antenna 810.
**communication devices 526.**
communication module 418.
communication panels 500.
communication set 477.
communication tunnel 510.
communications volume controls 512.
commuter train 464.
compact 366.
**compact disc 405.**
compact disc 408.
**compact disc player 405.**
compact disc player 400, 407, 408.
compact disc player controls 408.
compact disc unit 527.
compartment 701.
Compass 13.
compass 639.
compass bridge 494, 495, 497.
compass card 484, 719.
compass meridian line 719.
**competitive course 621.**
completion 692.
complex dune 46.
complexus 121.
compluvium 170, 171.
**compound bow 684.**
compound eye 79, 80, 81.
**compound leaves 56.**
compressed air reservoir 469.
compressed air starting unit 506.
compressed-air cylinder 627, 777.
compression 436, 437, 501.
compression coupling 296.
**compression fitting 300.**
compression link 147.
compression/induction 436.
compressor 212, 517.
compressor turbine 438, 501.
computer communication 417.
computer room 807.
computer screen intensity controls 512.
**computer table 521.**
concave 160.
concave lens 722.
concertina-type folding door 202.
concha 139.
Concorde 19.
concrete base 714.
concrete block 286.
concrete drain 741.
concrete shielding 760, 761, 762, 763.
concrete wall 772.
condensation 35.
condensation of steam into water 767.
condensation pool 763.
condenser 717, 718, 758, 771.
condenser adjustment knob 718.
condenser backwash inlet 759.
condenser backwash outlet 759.
condenser coil 214.
condenser cooling water inlet 759.
condenser cooling water outlet 759.
condenser fan 214.
condenser height adjustment 718.
conductor's podium 556.
cone 24, 58.
conference centre 184.
CONFIGURATION OF AN OFFICE AUTOMATION SYSTEM 526.
conic projection 50.
conical broach roof 183.
conical buoy 487, 489.
conical washer 293.
CONIFER 58.
conjunctiva 140.
connecting cable 406, 585.
connecting module 528.
connecting rod 434, 436.
connecting socket 561.
connection 697.
connection box 412.
connection cable 530.
connection point 757.
connective tissue 137.
connector 300, 312, 406.
conning tower 807.
CONSTELLATIONS OF THE NORTHERN HEMISPHERE 10.
CONSTELLATIONS OF THE SOUTHERN HEMISPHERE 12.
constriction 705.
consumer 417.
consumer number 712.
contact 233, 697.
contact lever 235.
contact printer 398.
**container 470.**
container 40, 250, 270, 304, 495.
container hold 495.
CONTAINER SHIP 494.
container ship 490.
container terminal 491.
container truck 473.
container-loading bridge 490.
container/pallet loader 507.
containment building 765, 766.
contents identification board 743.
contest area 668.
contestant 668.
continent 29.
**continental climates 45.**
**continental margin 29.**
continental rise 29.
continental shelf 22, 29.
continental slope 22, 29.
CONTINENTS, CONFIGURATION 20.
continuity tester 310.

The terms in **bold type** correspond to an illustration; those in CAPITALS indicate a title.

continuous beam 454.
continuous drizzle 39.
continuous rain 39.
continuous snow 39.
**contour feather 110.**
contrabassoons 556.
contrast control 529, 532.
control bar 637.
control box 297.
control cable 270.
control column 500.
control console 16, 500.
control deck 493, 699.
control key 530.
control keys 421.
control knob 255, 258.
control knobs 531.
control lever 735.
control pad 699.
**control panel 257, 532.**
control panel 210, 214, 253, 255, 258, 259, 532, 717, 779.
control rod 760, 761, 762, 763.
control room 14, 15, 16, 189, 407, 746, 759.
CONTROL ROOM, RADIO 407.
**control rooms, television 412.**
control stand 468.
control stick 508, 639.
control tower 502, 810.
control valve 689.
control wheel 500, 778.
convection zone 6.
**convector heater 211.**
convenience outlet 310.
conventional door 202.
**converging lenses 722.**
convertible 425.
convex lens 722.
conveyor 733, 735.
conveyor belt 504.
cook's knife 242.
cooker ring 255.
**cooking set 688.**
cooking surface 253.
COOKING UTENSILS 248.
cool tip 370.
coolant 766, 771.
coolant inlet 768.
coolant outlet 768.
coolant transfers the heat to the steam generator 766.
coolant: boiling water 763.
coolant: carbon dioxide 760.
coolant: pressurized heavy water 761.
coolant: pressurized water 762.
cooler 690.
cooling 744.
cooling fan 434, 438.
cooling/heating coils 213.
copper to plastic 301.
copper to steel 301.
copperplate 582.
coprocessor 528.
copy output mode 532.
copy quantity 532.
copyright 831.
cor anglais 548.
corbel 180, 181.
corbel piece 204.
cord 231, 578.
cord grip 658.
cord tieback 229.
cordate 56.
cordless telephone 422.
core 6, 64, 677, 692, 798.
coriander 74.
**corinthian order 167.**
cork ball 596.
cork tip 618.
corkscrew 688.
corn salad 73.
cornea 140.
corner 577, 669.
corner arc 601.
corner cap 470.
corner cupboard 227.
corner fitting 470.
corner flag 601, 607.
corner pad 669.
corner pin 682.
corner stool 669.
corner stud 198.
corner tower 180.
corner upright 470.
cornerpiece 383.
cornet 550, 556.
cornice 166, 168, 196, 202, 225.
corolla 60.
corona 6.
corona radiata 128.
coronet 101, 104.
coronet boot 653.
corpus callosum 134.
corpus cavernosum 127.
correction fluid 515.
correction key 569.
correction paper 515.
corrosive 821.
cors anglais 557.
corselette 347.
corset 346.
cortex 132.
corymb 60.
cos lettuce 73.
cosmetic tray 382.
costal shield 97.
**cotehardie 316.**
cotter pin 290.
cotton applicators 725.
cotton wool ball 725.
cotyledon 57.
**couched stitches 571.**
coulter 156, 158.
coulter shaft 156.
counter 352.
counter reset button 403.
counterguard 179.
counterjib 786.
counterjib ballast 786.
counterscarp 178.
countersink 281.
countersunk head 276.
counterweight 15, 147, 404, 457, 471, 721, 784, 785, 786.
country 51.
coupé 425.
coupler head 147, 156, 157, 158, 159, 162.
coupler-tilt tablet 542.
**coupling 471.**
coupling 469.
coupling bolt 754.
coupling guide device 459.
coupling knuckle 471.
coupling knuckle pin 471.
courgette 69.
**course, golf 676.**
court 356.
court referee 612.
courtyard 172, 173.
couscous kettle 249.
couter 792.
cover 213, 251, 309, 375, 386, 532, 596, 677, 705, 712, 719, 796, 804.
covered bogie truck 472.
covered parapet walk 180.
covered way 178.
**covering 579.**
covering 619.
covering disc 158.
covering grille 208.
**covering materials 286.**
cow 151.
cow hitch 691.
cowl neck 342.
Cowper's gland 127.
cowshed 149.
coxa 78, 80.
coxed four 632.
coxed pair 632.
coxless four 632.
coxless pair 632.
Crab 11.
crab 90.
crab pulley 786.
cradle 399, 720, 721, 802.
crakow 318.
crampon strap 680.
cranberry 62.
Crane 13.
crane 14, 738.
crane runway 786.
cranial nerves 133.
crank 281, 448, 671, 793.
crank handle 583.
crankcase 436.
crankshaft 434, 436.
**crash helmet 443.**
crash helmet 643.
crater 7, 25, 733.
cravat 324.
crawl kick 622.
**crawl stroke 622.**
crayfish 90.
cream jug 238.
crease 323.
credenza 520.
**credit card wallet 379.**
credit card wallet 379.
creel 672.
cremaster 78.
crenate 56.
crenel 181.
crenulate margin 95.
crepidoma 166, 168, 169.
crescendo pedal 542.
crescent 819.
crescentic dune 46.
crest 27, 30, 596, 791.
crest of spillway 746.
crevasse 26.
crevice tool 260.
crew neck 350.
crew neck sweater 326.
crew quarters 494.
crew's room 461.
cribriform plate of ethmoid 141.
CRICKET 598.
**cricket ball 598.**
**cricket player 598.**
cricket shoe 598.
**cricquet, field 599.**
crimping 799.
**crisscross curtains 229.**
**crochet hook 567.**
CROCKERY 238.
croissant 153.
crook 548.
crook key 548.
crop elevator 160.
cross 818.
cross brace 727.
cross cut 736.
cross handle 701.
cross head 276.
cross rail 223.
**cross section 702.**
**cross section of a hydroelectric power station 747.**
**cross section of a muzzle-loading cannon 801.**
**cross section of a power plant 752.**
**cross section of an electron microscope 717.**
**cross stitches 571.**
**cross-country ski 642.**
cross-country ski 642.
**cross-country skier 642.**
CROSS-COUNTRY SKIING 642.
cross-headed tip 276.
cross-ply tyre 433.
cross-tip screwdriver 688.
crossarm 756, 757.
crossbar 446, 535, 574, 578, 626, 637, 657.
crossbeam 572.
CROSSBOW 793.
**crossbow 793.**
crosshead 787.
crossing 176, 177.
crossing barrier mechanism 471.
crossover 464.
crossover cargo deck line 743.
crosspiece 219, 572, 728.
crosstree 628.
crosswise grain 566.
crotch 325.
crotch piece 337.
crotchet 538.
crotchet rest 538.
croup 101, 661.
Crow 13.
crown 59, 109, 144, 328, 329, 363, 483, 545, 553, 590, 706.
crown block 737.
crown tine 105.
crownpiece 649.
crude oil 744.
**crude-oil pipeline 740.**
CRUISELINER 496.
crus of helix 139.
crushing roll 158.
CRUSTACEAN 90.
crystal button 236.
crystal drop 236.
cucumber 69.
cue ball 673.
cuff 315, 324, 354, 609.
cuff link 339.
cuirass 791.
cuisse 792.
culet 363.
culottes 334.
cultivated mushroom 55.
**cultivator 157.**
cultivator 154.
cumulonimbus 44.
cumulus 44.
Cup 13.
cup 688, 798.
cup gasket 730.
cupola 486.
cupule 66.
**curb bit 650.**
curb bit 649.
curb chain 649, 650.
curb hook 650.
curb rein 649.
curler 620.
CURLING 620.
**curling brooms 620.**
curling brush 370.
**curling iron 370.**
**curling stone 620.**
**curling, rink 620.**
curly endive 73.
curly kale 73.
CURRENCY ABBREVIATIONS, EXAMPLES 832.
currency exchange 823.
current coil 712.
current-collecting shoe 476.
cursor movement keys 530.
**curtain 229.**
curtain 178, 414.
**curtain pole 230.**
**curtain track 230.**
curtain wall 180.
curved jaw 278.
customer's supply 757.
customs control 505.
customs house 491.
**cut for gemstones 362.**
cut-off trench 748, 749.
**cut-throat razor 374.**
cuticle nippers 365.
cuticle pusher 365.
cuticle scissors 365.
cuticle trimmer 365.
CUTLERY 239, 240.
cutlery basket 257.
**cutlery set 688.**
cutter 311.
cutter bar 158, 160.
cutter link 272.
cutting blade 250, 256, 578.
cutting cylinder 271.
cutting edge 239, 242, 369, 783, 784.
cutting guide 578.
cutting line 565.
cutting nozzle 306.
**cutting torch 306.**
cutting wire 584.
cycle lock 448.
cycling helmet 448.
cyclorama 414.
cylinder 290, 295, 436, 797.
cylinder case 290.
cylinder pressure gauge 306.
**cylinder vacuum cleaner 260.**
**cylindrical buoy 486.**
cylindrical projection 50.
cymbal 552.
cymbals 554, 557.
cytoplasm 115, 128.

## D

D 674.
d 537.
dabber 581.
dagger 794.
daggerboard 631.
daggerboard well 631.
dairy 149.
dairy compartment 254.
dairy products 33.
dam 746.
dam foundation 748.
damper 206, 541, 585.
damper lever 541.
damper rail 541.
dandelion 73.
danger 488.
danger area 668.
Danish rye bread 153.
darkness 489.
**dart 698.**
dart 565.
**dart, playing area 698.**
**dartboard 698.**
dash 832.
**dashboard 430.**
data bus 528, 531.
data display 396, 409, 411, 421.
data display illumination button 396.
data hold 310.

The terms in **bold type** correspond to an illustration; those in CAPITALS indicate a title.

data panel 391.
data record system 717.
**data storage devices 526.**
date 63.
date stamp 516.
dating nail 466.
davit 478, 742.
daymark 486, 487.
**daymarks (region B) 489.**
dead ball line 606.
dead bolt 289, 290.
dead bowl area 682.
**deadly poisonous mushroom 55.**
decanter 237.
deceleration lane 452.
decimal key 523.
decimal tab 524.
deck 454, 455, 456, 736.
deck arch bridge 455.
deck crane 811.
declination 3.
declination axis 14.
declination setting scale 720, 721.
décolleté bra 346.
decorative braid 349.
decoy launcher 809.
**deep fryer 252.**
deep peroneal nerve 133.
deep-sea floor 22.
**deer antlers 105.**
DEER FAMILY 105.
**defence 603, 605.**
defence third 611.
defending zone 608.
deferent duct 127.
deflector 210, 264, 271.
degree 830.
degrees Celsius 705.
degrees Fahrenheit 705.
Deimos 4.
delete key 530.
delicious lactarius 55.
**delivery 682.**
delivery 682.
delivery entrance 190.
delivery ramp 184.
delta wing 499.
deltoid 120.
demilune 179.
demisemiquaver 538.
demisemiquaver rest 538.
demitasse 238.
dendrite 135.
dental alveolus 144.
DENTAL CARE 373.
dental floss 373.
dentil 166, 167.
dentin 144.
departure lounge 505.
departure time indicator 463.
deployment mechanism 49.
depression 38.
depth adjustment 283.
depth gauge 627.
depth of focus 23.
depth scale in metres 485.
depth stop 283.
depth-adjustment mechanism 277.
depth-of-field preview button 391.
depth-of-field scale 392.
dermis 137.
derrick 737, 738, 740, 743.
derrick mast 743.
descender 681.
descending aorta 124.
descending colon 131.
DESERT 46.
desert 45.
designated orbit 48.
desired temperature 213, 705.
desk lamp 234.
desk pad 520.
desk tray 517.
desktop video unit 527.
despun section 42.
dessert fork 240.
dessert knife 239.
dessert spoon 241.
destination 463.
destroying angel 55.
detachable control 253.
**detection of seismic waves 714.**
detergent dispenser 257.
detonator 804.
deuterium oxide upgrading 759.
Deutsche Mark 832.
developer bath 399.
**developing baths 399.**
**developing tank 398.**
dew 37.
dew pad 106.
dewclaw 106.
dexter 818.
dexter base 818.
dexter chief 818.
dexter flank 818.
DIACRITIC SYMBOLS 832.
diagonal 756.
diagonal buttress 177.
diagonal move 696.
**diagram of weaving, diagram of principle 576.**
dial 705, 706, 707, 708, 712.
dial-type display 485.
diamond 363, 695.
diamond interchange 451.
diamond point 225.
diaphragm 130, 390, 401, 406.
diastema 98.
dibber 268.
DICE 699.
dice cup 697.
die 697.
died 831.
**diesel engine 437.**
diesel engine 469, 495, 782, 783, 785.
diesel engine shed 464.
diesel engine ventilator 468.
diesel engines 809.
diesel lift engine 493.
diesel oil 745.
diesel propulsion engine 492.
DIESEL-ELECTRIC LOCOMOTIVE 468.
diffuser 396.
diffuser pin 264.
digestive gland 92.
DIGESTIVE SYSTEM 131.
digger bucket 785.
digging fork 266.
digit 84.
digital audio tape recorder 407.
digital display 310, 709, 710.
digital frequency display 402.
digital nerve 133.
digital pad 106, 107.
digital pulp 137.
digital video effects monitor 413.
digital video special effects 413.
**digital watch 706.**
digitizing pad 526.
dike 25.
dill 74.
dimmer room 412.
dimmer switch 309.
dimple 677.
dining room 171, 195, 496, 807.
dining section 460.
dinner fork 240.
dinner knife 239.
dinner plate 238.
diode 769.
dioptric ring 486.
dioxide 33.
dip switch 444.
dipped beam headlight 429.
dipper 592.
dipping/indicator stalk 430.
direct home reception 416.
**direct-reading rain gauge 40.**
direction of Mecca 173.
direction of points 488.
direction to be followed 824, 825.
director's chair 220.
disc 157, 432, 433, 529, 583, 663, 712.
**disc brake 432.**
disc brake 442.
disc camera 395.
disc compartment 405.
disc compartment control 405.
disc drive 555.
disc drive port 528.
**disc mixer 295.**
disc motor 529.
disc spacing lever 158.
discharge bay 764.
discharge pipe 216.
discharge system 742.
discharge tube 232.
**discs 251.**
**discus 658.**
discus and hammer 654.
disgorger 672.
**dishwasher 257, 298.**
dishwasher 298.
diskette, floppy disc 526.
display 420, 422, 523, 709.
display cabinet 227, 522.
display setting 420.
disposable camera 394.
disposable gas cylinder 299, 307.
disposable razor 374.
distal phalanx 107, 122, 123, 137.
distal sesamoid 102.
distance lens 376.
distance post 651.
distance scale 392.
distance travelled 711.
distribution board 757.
distribution box 216.
distribution by cable 416.
distribution to consumers 755.
distributor 435.
distributor service loop 757.
district 52.
district boundary 52.
ditch 451, 682.
**diverging lenses 722.**
diversion channel 746.
divide key 523.
divider 160, 378, 383.
dividers 519.
dividing connector 779.
DIVING 624.
**diving apparatus 624.**
diving glove 627.
diving plane 806.
diving tower 624.
**diving, entries 624.**
**diving, flights 624.**
**diving, starting positions 624.**
division 830.
do not iron 829.
do not use chlorine bleach 829.
do not wash 829.
dock 490.
document folder 519.
document handler 532.
document receiving 421.
document-to-be-sent position 421.
does not belong to 830.
DOG 106.
dog ear collar 341.
**dog's forepaw 106.**
**dog, morphology 106.**
dolina 24.
dollar 832.
Dolphin 11.
dome 251.
dome roof 183.
dome shutter 14.
dome tent 686.
DOMESTIC APPLIANCES 250, 252, 254, 256, 257, 258, 260.
DOMINOES 695.
DOOR 202.
**door 429.**
door 173, 225, 253, 259, 427, 449, 498, 617, 685, 686.
door grip 429.
door handle 202, 289, 427.
door lock 427.
door open warning light 431.
door panel 225.
door pillar 427.
door pocket 429.
door shelf 254.
door stop 254, 471.
door switch 259.
**doric order 167.**
dormant volcano 24.
**dorsal view 95.**
dorsalis pedis artery 126.
dorsum of nose 141.
**dot matrix printer 531.**
dot matrix printer 527.
double 646.
double bass 545.
double basses 557.
double bend 826, 827.
double boiler 249.
double curtain rail 230.
double flat 538.
double glazing 772.
double handles 633.
double oxer 646, 647.
double pennant 817.
double plate 198.
double pole circuit breaker 312.
double reed 549.
double ring 698.
double scull 632.
double seat 477.
double sharp 538.
double sheet bend 691.
double sink 215.
double zero 700.
double zero key 523.
double-blank 695.
double-breasted buttoning 319.
**double-breasted jacket 322.**
double-decked pallet 787.
**double-edged razor 374.**
double-edged razor blade 374.
double-leaf bascule bridge 457.
double-six 695.
double-twist auger bit 281.
doubles pole 614.
doubles service court 618.
doubles sideline 614, 618.
doublet 316, 695.
doubling die 697.
doubly toothed 56.
dough hook 250.
dousing water tank 759, 766.
dousing water valve 759.
Dove 13.
dovetail 718.
down tube 447.
down wind 629.
downpipe 197.
downstream face 749.
downstream shoulder 748.
downstream toe 748.
dozen (1 to 12) 700, 701.
dozen (13 to 24) 700, 701.
dozen (25 to 36) 700, 701.
drachma 832.
drafting machine 591.
drag 670.
Dragon 11.
dragonfly 77.
drain cock 297.
drain hose 257, 258, 298.
drain tile 199.
drain valve 741.
drainage blanket 748.
drainage circuit 215.
drainage layer 748.
draining spoon 244.
draped neck 343.
draped neckline 343.
draped swag 229.
draught arm 784.
draught hole 209.
draught tube 747, 753, 784.
draught tube liner 753.
draw curtain 229.
draw hoe 266.
draw tube 718.
drawbar 803.
drawbar lock 803.
drawbridge 180.
drawer 219, 226, 255.
DRAWING 588, 590, 592.
drawing 586.
**drawing board 591.**
drawing pins 515.
**drawing, accessories 591, 592.**
**drawing, equipment 589.**
drawstring 320, 381.
**drawstring bag 381.**
drawstring hood 351.
dredger 246.
dress circle 189.
**dress with bustle 316.**
**dress with crinoline 318.**
**dress with panniers 317.**
dressing room 189.
dressing table 226.
dressmaker's model 564.
drift 736.
drill bit 280.
drill collar 737.
drill pipe 737.
drill rod 734.
drill ship 739.
drilling drawworks 737.
**drilling rig 737.**
drinking water truck 506.
drip bowl 255.
drip dry 829.
drip moulding 427.
drive belt 258.
drive chain 446.
drive shaft 492, 508.
drive wheel 256, 280.
drivebelt safety guard 283.
driver 643, 652.
driver's cab 459, 468.
driver's seat 805.
driveway 193, 196.
**driving glove 327.**
driving propeller 492.
driving turbine 438.
driving wheel 147, 575.
driving wheels 784.
drone 81.
drone pipe 536.
drop earrings 361.

The terms in **bold type** correspond to an illustration; those in CAPITALS indicate a title.

drop waist dress 332.
drop-leaf 219.
drum 167, 231, 258, 259, 432, 484, 707, 714.
**drum brake 432.**
drumhead 552, 553.
**drums 552.**
drupelet 62.
dry continental - arid 45.
dry continental - semiarid 45.
dry dock 490.
dry flat 829.
DRY FRUITS 66.
dry gallery 24.
dry point 582.
dry subtropical 45.
dry well 763.
dry-point 583.
**drying 829.**
dual seat 443.
dual swivel mirror 368.
duck 150.
duckpin 683.
duffle bag 381.
**duffle coat 320.**
dugout 597.
**dumbbell 665.**
dump 733.
dune 30.
dungarees 336.
**dungarees with crossover back straps 351.**
duo 558.
duodenum 131.
dura mater 134, 135.
dust 34, 35.
dust cover 404.
dust receiver 260.
dust tail 9.
dusting brush 260.
Dutch oven 249.
duty-free shop 505.
dynamic brake 468.
DYNAMIC MICROPHONE 406.
dynamo 446.

## E

e 537.
Eagle 11.
eagle 819.
ear 107, 112, 116, 223.
ear cushion 406.
ear drum 139.
ear flap 328.
ear loaf 153.
ear plugs 729.
EAR PROTECTION 729.
ear protection 821.
ear studs 361.
**ear, auricle 139.**
**ear, parts 138.**
earphone 406.
earpiece 376, 726.
**earrings 361.**
Earth 4, 8.
earth 312.
earth block 312.
earth clamp 305.
earth connection 312, 400.
EARTH COORDINATE SYSTEM 3.
earth fault circuit breaker 312.
earth foundation 450.
earth lead 305.
earth radiation scanner 43.
earth radiation sensor 43.
earth sensor 42, 43.
Earth sensor 49.
**earth signs 820.**
earth terminal 309.
earth wire 312, 757.
EARTH'S ATMOSPHERE, PROFILE 19.
Earth's crust 22, 23.
EARTH'S CRUST, SECTION 22.
EARTH, STRUCTURE 22.
earth-wire peak 756.
earthing bond 312.
earthing pin 309.
EARTHQUAKE 23.
easel 591.
East 488.
East cardinal mark 489.
East reflector deployment 419.
Eastern hemisphere 47.
Eastern meridian 47.
eccrine sweat gland 136.
echinus 167.
echo 722.
**echo sounder 485.**
**echo sounder probe 485.**
**eclipses, types 8.**
ecliptic 3.
ECOLOGY 31, 32, 34.
edge 288, 564, 640, 644, 719.
edging 263.
**edible crustaceans 90.**
**edible molluscs, principal 93.**
**edible mushrooms 55.**
edit/search buttons 409.
effluent 216.
**egg 109, 128.**
egg 82.
egg beater 245.
**egg butt snaffle bit 650.**
egg poacher 249.
egg slicer 246.
egg timer 244.
egg tray 254.
eggs 84, 89.
Egyptian reed pen 389.
eiderdown 224.
eight 632.
eight cut 362.
ejaculatory duct 127.
eject button 403.
ejection port 796.
ejector 784.
ejector seat 813.
elastic 224.
elastic ligament 92, 107.
elastic loop 685.
elastic strainer 686.
elastic support bandage 725.
elastic waistband 321.
elastic webbing 323.
elasticized leg opening 325.
elbow 100, 106, 112, 117, 119, 206, 301.
elbow pad 602, 609.
elbow, 45° 301.
electric circuit 233.
**electric cooker 255.**
**electric drill 280.**
electric foil 666.
**electric furnace 207.**
**electric golf cart 679.**
**electric guitar 547.**
**electric kiln 585.**
electric motor 209, 268, 271, 438.
**electric razor 374.**
**electric toothbrush 373.**
**electric tumble dryer 259.**
electric variometer 639.
electrical box 309.
electrical connection 441.
electrical connection panel 415.
electrical connections 585.
electrical hazard 821.
electrical payout linkage 702.
electrical power unit 506.
electrical scoring apparatus 666.
**electrician's tools 311.**
ELECTRICITY 309, 310, 312, 746, 748, 750, 752, 754, 756.
electricity cable 186.
**electricity distribution 757.**
electricity distribution network 771.
electricity generating room 806.
electricity meter 757.
electricity production 767.
electricity transmission 767.
**electricity, tools 310.**
electricity, tools 311.
electrode 232, 305.
electrode holder 305.
electrode lead 305.
electron beam 410, 717.
electron beam positioning 717.
**electron gun 410.**
electron gun 410, 717.
ELECTRON MICROSCOPE 717.
**electron microscope elements 717.**
electronic ballast 233.
**electronic flash 393.**
ELECTRONIC INSTRUMENTS 555.
**electronic piano 555.**
**electronic scales 709.**
ELECTRONIC TYPEWRITER 524.
electronic viewfinder 409.
elevating arc 802.
elevating cylinder 780, 786.
elevating handle 803.
elevating handwheel 802.
**elevation 193.**
elevation adjustment 718.
elevator 499, 639, 764, 811.
elevon 511.
elk 105.
ellipsis 832.
elliptical galaxy 9.
embankment 450.
**embankment dam 748.**
**embankment dam, cross section 748.**
emblem 817.
embrasure 179.
embroidered fabric 571.
EMBROIDERY 571.
emerald 363.
emerald cut 362.
emergency brake 477.
emergency electric motor 806.
emergency regulator 627.
emergency support vessel 739.
emergency switch 444.
emery boards 365.
emery pack 563.
empty set 830.
emptying hose 258.
en prison 700, 701.
enamel 144.
enclosure 149.
end bracket 230.
end button 544.
end cap 765.
end door 470.
end grain 288.
end joist 198, 199.
end ladder 470.
end line 604, 610, 613, 619.
end piece 127.
end plate 765.
end stop 230, 630.
end wall 621.
end zone 604.
end-piece 674.
endocarp 63, 64.
endoplasmic reticulum 115.
endpaper 577.
endpiece 376.
**energy saving bulb 233.**
engagement ring 364.
engine 147, 161, 442, 737, 784, 787, 805.
engine air inlet 813.
engine and crew alarm display 500.
engine block 435.
engine fuel valves 500.
engine housing 272.
engine mounting pylon 499.
engine room 496, 742, 806.
engines 510.
**English billiards 673.**
ENGLISH BILLIARDS AND SNOOKER 674.
English loaf 153.
English stick 728.
**enlarger 399.**
enlarger timer 399.
enlarging easel 398.
enlarging lens 399.
ENSILING 162.
**ensiling 155.**
ensiling tube 162.
entablature 166, 168, 202.
enter key 530.
entire 56.
entrance 82.
entrance door 461.
entrance slide 82.
entrance turnstile 474.
**entries 624.**
entry 625, 787.
envelope 634.
epaulet 319.
epaulet sleeve 340.
épée 666.
épéeist 667.
epicalyx 62.
epicentre 23.
epicondyle 123.
epidermis 137.
epiglottis 130, 142, 143.
epitrochlea 123.
equalizing buckle 231.
equals key 523.
equator 3, 47.
equilibrator 802.
equipment compartment 458.
equipment lock 764.
equipment rack 412, 415.
equipment section 16.
erase button 420.
eraser 515.
eraser holder 515.
erecting lenses 718.
ermine 819.
escalator 189, 190, 474.
escape wheel 706, 707.
escapement mechanism 539.
escudo 832.
escutcheon 95, 289, 295, 296.
escutcheon plate 309.
espadrille 357.
**espresso coffee maker 247.**
estate car 425.
estuary 30, 51.
**etching press 581.**
Eurasia 21.
Europa 4.
Europe 21.
European Currency Unit 832.
**European plug 309.**
Eustachian tube 139, 141.
**Eutelsat II 418.**
euthynteria 166, 168.
evaporation 34, 35.
evaporator blower 214.
evaporator coils 214.
even 700, 701.
evening glove 327.
EXAMPLES OF INSTRUMENTAL GROUPS 558.
exclamation mark 832.
excretory opening 83.
executive desk 520.
**exercise cycle 664.**
**exercise wear 353.**
exhalation valve 730.
exhaust 436, 437, 501.
exhaust duct 501.
exhaust gas admission 438.
exhaust guide vanes 501.
exhaust manifold 435, 437, 438, 439.
exhaust nozzle 812.
exhaust pipe 438, 508, 783.
exhaust port 436, 735.
exhaust stack 147, 440, 784.
**exhaust system 439.**
exhaust valve 435, 436, 438.
exit 452.
exit cone 82.
exit taxiway 505.
exit track 465.
exit turnstile 474.
exocarp 62, 63, 64.
exosphere 19.
expandable file pouch 378.
expanded metal lath 286.
expanding file 517.
expansion bolt 276.
expansion chamber 485, 705.
expansion connector 528.
expansion diaphragm 485.
expansion space 466.
expansion tank 208, 772.
expert riders' course 646.
explosive 821.
export pipeline 738.
exposure adjustment knob 391.
**exposure meter 396.**
exposure mode 391.
exposure value 396.
exposure-time scale 396.
extended character range 530.
**extended claw 107.**
**extending table 219.**
extension 219.
**extension ladder 302.**
extension tube 260.
exterior dome shell 14.
**exterior door 202.**
exterior gauge 578.
EXTERIOR OF A HOUSE 196.
exterior pocket 378, 382.
exterior sign 474.
**exterior view 712.**
external ear 138.
external fuel tank 510.
external gills 84.
external jugular vein 126.
external oblique 120, 121.
external socket 449.
external tooth lock washer 278.
**extractor hood 255.**
extrados 174.
**eye 140.**
eye 83, 90, 96, 97, 107, 118, 275, 562, 563, 573, 649, 671, 681.
eye guard 777.
**eye make-up 367.**
EYE PROTECTION 729.
eye protection 821.
eye ring 109.
**eyeball 140.**
eyeball 84.
eyebrow 140.
eyebrow pencil 367.

The terms in **bold type** correspond to an illustration; those in CAPITALS indicate a title.

eyebrow stripe 109.
eyebrow tweezers 365.
eyelash 140.
eyelash curler 367.
eyelashes 107.
eyelet 230, 353, 354, 381, 569, 644.
eyelet tab 354.
eyelid 97.
eyepiece 390, 396, 409, 718, 719, 720, 721.
eyepiece holder 721.
**eyeshadow 367.**
eyestalk 83.

## F

f 537.
F-1 engine 509.
FABRIC CARE 829.
fabric guide 256.
**fabric structure 566.**
**façade 175.**
face 116, 179, 275, 277, 579, 619, 677, 733, 736.
face mask 602, 609, 643.
face side 288.
face-off circle 608.
face-off spot 608.
facepiece 730.
faceplate 289, 290.
facial nerve 139.
facsimile machine 417.
factorial 830.
faculae 6.
Fahrenheit scale 705.
failed fuel bay 764.
failed fuel canning 764.
fairing 442, 445.
fairlead 630.
fairway 676.
fall 341.
fall front 226.
falling rocks 826, 827.
fallopian tube 128.
fallopian tubes 128.
fallout 35.
fallow land 148.
false rib (3) 123.
false tuck 349.
**family tent 685.**
fan 161, 162, 209, 212, 259, 501, 528.
fan belt 434.
fan brush 366, 589.
**fan cable stays 456.**
fan control 214.
fan duct 162.
fan heater 211.
fan housing 370.
fan motor 214.
fan thermostat 438.
fan trellis 263.
fang 96.
fanion 817.
fantail 773.
far turn 651.
FARM ANIMALS 150.
farmhouse 148.
farmhouse loaf 153.
FARMSTEAD 148.
farmyard 148.
fascia 166.
fast data entry control 555.
fast forward 411, 831.
fast forward key 411.
fast-forward button 403, 408, 420.
fastener binder 519.
**fasteners 566.**
fastening device 230.
fault 23.
**fax machine 421.**
feather crown 618.
feather stitch 571.
FEATURES OF HISTORICAL COSTUME 315, 316, 318.
feed dog 562.
feed lever 283.
feed pin 531.
feed table 162.
feed tube 251.
feeder header 759.
feeder lane 452.
feeder output tray 532.
feeding tube 160.
feedwater 760, 761, 762, 763.
FEET PROTECTION 730.
feet protection 821.
feet-first entry 624.
felt tip pen 588.
female 831.
female cone 58.
female ferrule 670.
FEMALE GENITAL ORGANS 128, 129.
female union nut 300.
femoral artery 126.
femoral nerve 133.
femoral vein 126.
femur 78, 80, 103, 122.
fence 148.
**fencer 667.**
FENCING 666.
fencing shoe 667.
**fencing weapons 666.**
**fencing, parts of the weapon 666.**
**fencing, piste 666.**
**fencing, positions 667.**
**fencing, target areas 667.**
**fennel 72.**
ferrule 304, 375, 675, 678.
FERRY 494.
ferryboat 491.
fertilizers 32.
FERTILIZING 156.
**fertilizing 154.**
fetlock 101.
fetlock joint 101.
fettling knife 585.
fiber 692.
fibula 102, 122, 315.
FIELD HOCKEY 607.
field judge 605.
field lens 718.
field lens adjustment 718.
**fielder's glove 596.**
fielders 599.
fifth 537.
fifth wheel 440.
**figure skate 644.**
**figure ski 633.**
**figure skiing handle 633.**
figure-eight knot 691.
filament 6, 60, 232.
filament support 233.
file 277, 688.
file guides 518.
filing box 517.
filler 384.
filler cap 271, 438, 440.
filler hole 256.
filler pipe 293.
fillet 166, 167.
filleting knife 242.
filling hole 804.
filling inlet 741.
film 390.
film advance mode 391.
film cassette chamber 390.
film disc 395.
film drying cabinet 398.
film guide rail 390.
film guide roller 390.
film leader 395.
film leader indicator 390.
film pack 395.
film recorder 527.
film rewind knob 391.
film rewind system 390.
film speed 391, 396.
film sprocket 390.
**films 395.**
filter 207, 247, 252, 255, 385, 772.
filter cover 730.
filter tip 384.
fin 210, 627, 633, 639, 812, 814.
fin-mounted tail unit 498.
finderscope 720, 721.
fine adjustment knob 718.
FINE BOOKBINDING 577, 578.
fine data entry control 555.
fine guidance system 16.
finely threaded screw 711.
**finger 137.**
finger 596.
finger board 535, 544, 547.
finger button 550.
finger flange 726.
**fingerless mitt 327.**
fingernail 137.
finial 230, 817.
finish 646.
finish line 654.
finishing 586.
finishing line 651.
finishing post 654.
fir needles 58.
FIRE ENGINE 778, 780.
fire extinguisher 823.
fire hose 778.
fire hydrant 186.
fire hydrant wrench 779.
**fire irons 205.**
FIRE PREVENTION 777.
**fire signs 820.**
firebrick 204.
firebrick back 204.
**fireman 777.**
fireman's hatchet 781.
**fireman's helmet 777.**
**fireplace 204.**
fireplace 195, 204.
fireproof and waterproof garment 777.
fireproofing 198.
**firing 585.**
**firing accessories 801.**
firing chamber 585.
firing lanyard 802.
firing mechanism 804.
firing shaft 802.
firing tube 807.
firmer chisel 587.
first aid 822.
FIRST AID EQUIPMENT 726.
FIRST AID KIT 725.
first aid manual 725.
first base 597.
first baseman 597.
first dorsal fin 86.
**first floor 194.**
first floor 196.
first focal room 15.
first molar 144.
first officer's seat 500.
first premolar 144.
first quarter 6.
first reinforce 800.
first space 610.
first stage 509.
first valve slide 550.
first violins 556.
first-class cabin 498.
FISH 86, 88.
fish dish 238.
fish fork 240.
**fish kettle 248.**
fish knife 239.
fish scaler 688.
fish wire 311.
**fish, anatomy 88.**
**fish, morphology 86.**
fishbone stitch 571.
fisherman's knot 691.
Fishes 11.
fisheye lens 392.
**fishhook 671.**
fishhook 670.
FISHING 670, 672.
fishing jacket 672.
**fishing wear 672.**
fishnet stocking 344.
fishplate 466.
fishplate bolt 466.
fission of uranium fuel 766.
FITNESS EQUIPMENT 663, 664.
fitted sheet 224.
fitting 778.
**fittings 301.**
five-number bet 700.
fivepin 683.
fixative 592.
fixed arch 455.
fixed base 282.
fixed bayonet 794.
fixed blade 578.
FIXED BRIDGES 454, 456.
fixed distance marking 505.
fixed jaw 279, 282.
fixed platform 739.
fixed weight 539.
fixed winglet 814.
**fixed-roof tank 741.**
fixing bath 399.
flag 606.
**flag shapes 817.**
flag with Schwenkel 817.
**flag, parts 817.**
flagstone 263.
**flail mower 158.**
flail mower 154.
flame adjustment wheel 386.
flame spreader 307.
flammable 821.
flank 101, 108, 179, 579.
flanker 605.
flanking tower 180.
flap 322, 380, 649.
flap hydraulic jack 812.
flap lever 500.
flap pocket 320, 322, 339.
flare 6, 738.
**flare joint 300.**
flare nut spanner 279.
flash bulb 393.
flash hider 796.
flashcube 393.
flashing 205.
flashing light 471.
flashtube 393.
flat 538.
flat brush 589.
flat end pin 231.
flat mirror 14, 720.
flat part 567.
flat roof 182.
flat sheet 224.
flat shuttle 573.
**flat stitches 571.**
flat tip 276.
flat truck 473.
flat washer 278.
flat-back brush 368.
**flat-plate solar collector 768.**
**flatbed 441.**
flesh 62, 63, 64.
FLESHY FRUITS 62, 65.
fleshy leaf 70.
FLESHY POMES 64.
FLESHY STONE FRUITS 63.
fletching 684.
fleur-de-lis 819.
flews 106.
flex 256, 260, 268, 271, 310, 370, 374.
flex sleeve 283, 305.
flex support 256.
flexible hose 260, 735.
flexible hose connection 735.
flexible rubber hose 298.
flexible skirt 493.
flexible tube 726.
flies 188.
flight 625, 698.
flight bag 382, 637.
FLIGHT DECK 500.
flight deck 498, 508, 510, 810.
flight information board 505.
flight instruments 635.
flight management computer 500.
flight of stairs 201.
**flights 624.**
flint 307, 795.
flint arrowhead 791.
flint knife 791.
**flintlock 795.**
flip turn 622, 623.
flip-flop 357.
float 216, 485, 672, 803.
float ball 293.
float clamp 216.
floater 626.
**floating bridge 457.**
floating crane 490.
floating head 374.
floating rib 122.
floating roof 741.
floating sleeve 316.
**floating-roof tank 741.**
floodlight 414.
floodlight on pantograph 414.
floor 205, 616, 617, 773.
floor brush 260.
floor drain 215.
floor joist 198, 199.
floor tile 286.
**floor-level electric convector 210.**
flooring strip 200.
**floppy disc 529.**
floppy disc drive 526, 528.
florin 832.
flotation section 486.
flow 493.
flow bean 740.
flow tube 768.
flower 57.
flower bed 263.
flower bud 57.
FLOWER, STRUCTURE 60.
flowering 61.
flue 297, 542.
flue hat 297.
**flue pipe 542.**
fluff trap 259.
fluid adjustment screw 304.
fluke 483.
**fluorescent tube 232.**
fluorescent tube 233.
flush 695.

The terms in **bold type** correspond to an illustration; those in CAPITALS indicate a title.

flush bushing 301.
flush handle 293.
flute 166, 167, 281, 548.
fluted land 281.
fluted pole 230.
flutes 556.
Fly 13.
fly 77, 323, 325, 350, 817.
fly agaric 55.
fly front closing 330, 351.
fly half 606.
fly line 670.
**fly reel 670.**
**fly rod 670.**
flying buttress 175, 176.
Flying Fish 13.
flying jib 481.
flyleaf 577.
flyover 452, 454.
flysheet 685, 686.
flywheel 435, 584, 664.
FM antenna 400.
foam 30.
foam cushion 729.
foam gun 743.
foam insulation 287.
foam pad 687.
foam-rubber insulation 287.
focal plane shutter 390.
focus 23.
focus mode selector 391.
focusing knob 720, 721.
focusing lenses 717.
focusing magnifier 399.
focusing ring 719.
focusing screen 390.
focussing ring 392.
fodder corn 149.
fog 37, 39.
fog lamp 429.
fog light 440.
foible 666.
foil 666.
foil warning line 666.
foilist 667.
fold 315.
fold line 565.
folder 518.
folding chair 223.
folding door 194, 202.
folding grill 690.
folding nail file 365.
folding ramp 494.
folding shovel 690.
folding stick 577.
foliage 59.
follicle 67.
**follicle, section 67.**
follow-through 682.
fondue fork 240.
fondue pot 248.
**fondue set 248.**
**food chain 31.**
**food pollution 32.**
**food processor 251.**
foot 83, 112, 116, 117, 118, 119, 225, 325, 350, 542, 545, 553, 579, 631, 670, 671.
**foot control 561.**
foot fault judge 614.
foot hole 542.
foot plate 664.
foot pocket 627.
foot score line 620.
foot strap 631.
**football 600, 602.**
football boot 600.
**footballer 600.**
footboard 224, 445.
footbridge 180, 464, 475.
footing 198, 199.
footless tights 353.
footlights 188.
footrest 584, 727.
footrope 478.
footstool 222.
footstrap 336, 664.
**forage blower 162.**
forage blower 155.
**forage harvester 162.**
forage harvester 155.
foramen caecum 143.
**forced warm-air system 206.**
fore edge 577.
fore royal sail 481.
fore-royal mast 479.
fore-topgallant mast 479.
fore-topmast 479.
forearm 106, 117, 119, 798.
**forearm crutch 728.**
forearm support 728.
forecastle 495, 497.
forecourt 453, 614.
forehead 109, 116.
foreleg 79, 80.
**foreleg, honeybee 80.**
forelimb 84.
forelock 100.
foremast 479, 743.
foresail 481.
forest 27.
forestay 628.
forewing 79, 81.
**fork 240.**
fork 105, 447, 688, 707, 721, 787.
fork pocket 470.
forked tongue 96.
**forklift truck 787.**
forks 787, 788.
formeret 177.
forming 692.
forte 666.
fortified wall 172.
forward 624.
**forward dive 625.**
forward slide change 397.
forward swing 682.
forward/reverse 272.
foul line 597, 683.
foundation 198, 199, 751.
foundation blockage 751.
foundation of tower 456.
**foundation slip 345.**
**foundations 199.**
fountain for ritual ablutions 172, 173.
**fountain pen 389.**
fountain pen 515.
four blade beater 250.
four-door saloon 425.
four-four time 537.
FOUR-MASTED BARK 478, 480.
four-of-a-kind 695.
**four-stroke engine 436.**
four-toed hoof 99.
fourchette 327.
fourth 537.
fourth wheel 706.
fovea 140.
foyer 189.
fractionating tower 744.
fraise 318.
frame 82, 156, 157, 159, 204, 225, 272, 282, 302, 378, 382, 383, 443, 484, 536, 554, 572, 583, 595, 615, 645, 659, 660, 685, 711, 726, 768, 769, 773, 785, 787, 788.
frame push 783.
frame stile 225.
**frame, embroidery 571.**
**frames 376.**
franc 832.
**Francis runner 754.**
free margin 137.
free throw lane 610.
free throw line 610, 612.
freehold flats 187.
freewheel 448.
freezer compartment 254.
freezer door 254.
freezing rain 39.
freight car 464.
**French betting layout 701.**
French bread 153.
**French cuff 339.**
French cut 362.
French horn 551.
French horns 557.
French knot stitch 571.
French loaf 153.
**French roulette wheel 701.**
fresco 170.
fret 546, 547, 701.
friction strip 307, 386.
frieze 166, 168, 225.
FRIGATE 808.
frill 228.
frilled curtain 228.
frilly nylon tights 349.
**frilly pants 349.**
fringe 318.
fringe trimming 229.
frock coat 317.
**frog 84.**
frog 104, 156, 320, 467, 544.
**frog, life cycle 84.**
frog-adjustment screw 277.
front 322, 324.
front apron 324.
front axle 784.
front beam 708.
front binding 633.
front board 577.
front brake 447.
front brake lever 444.
front crossbar 645.
front derailleur 446, 448.
front flap 386.
front foil 495.
front footrest 443, 444.
front grip 804.
front indicator 442, 444.
front knob 277, 281.
front lamp 447.
front landing gear 813.
front leg 223.
**front lights 429.**
front lights 189.
front mudguard 442.
front pipe 439.
front pocket 381.
front point 680.
front runner 643.
front sight 795, 797, 798, 799, 804.
front sight housing 796.
front tip 256.
front top pocket 323.
**front view 147.**
front wall 616, 617.
front wheel 147, 727, 784.
front-end loader 782.
frontal 120.
frontal bone 122.
frontal sinus 141.
frontcourt 617.
frontier 51.
**fronts 39.**
frontwall 441.
fruit branch 61.
FRUIT MACHINE 702.
fruit tree 149.
**fruit vegetables 69.**
fruit-picking ladder 303.
fruiting 61.
**frying pan 688.**
frying pan 249.
fuel 761, 766.
**fuel bundle 765.**
fuel bundle 765.
fuel control 501.
fuel gauge 431.
**fuel handling sequence 764.**
fuel injector 437.
fuel lines 635.
fuel oil 744.
fuel pellet 765.
fuel rod 765.
fuel tank 272, 440, 468, 508, 805, 812.
fuel tank flap 427.
fuel transfer pipe 509.
fuel: enriched uranium 762, 763.
fuel: natural uranium 760, 761.
fuelling machine 759, 760, 761, 764.
fulcrum 624.
full and by 629.
full back 606.
**full cheek snaffle bit 650.**
**full cheek snaffle bit with keys 650.**
full deployment 419.
full face mask 777.
full house 695.
full moon 7.
full stop 832.
full-load adjustment screw 712.
fullback 601, 603, 605.
fumarole 24.
fume extractor 805.
function button 699.
function display 555.
function key 530.
function keys 421, 422, 709.
function selection switch 310.
function selector 214, 402.
function selectors 420.
funiculus 62, 67.
funnel 243, 410, 494, 496.
fur 107.
Furnace 13.
furnace 206, 770.
**furs, examples 819.**
fuse 757, 769.
fuse body 804.
**fuse box 312.**
fuse cutout 757.
fuse holder 757.
fuse puller 311.
fuselage 499, 639.
fuselage-mounted tail unit 498.
**fuses 312.**

## G

g 537.
**G-clamp 282.**
gable 175, 197.
gable roof 182.
gable stud 198.
gable vent 197.
gable-and-valley roof 183.
gaff 478.
gaff sail 482.
gaff sail boom 478.
gaff topsail 480.
gain control 485.
**gaits, horse 101.**
GALAXY 9.
**galaxy, classification 9.**
gall bladder 97.
gall-bladder 131.
gallery 175, 189, 486, 773.
galley 498, 807.
**Gallic warrior 791.**
gallop 101.
galosh 355.
game cartridge 699.
GAME OF DARTS 698.
games area 496.
gangway 742.
**gantry crane 786.**
gantry crane 746, 747.
Ganymede 4.
gap 671.
garage 196.
garden 171.
garden arch 263.
garden hose 265.
garden line 268.
garden shears 269.
garden sorrel 73.
GARDENING EQUIPMENT 264, 266, 268, 270, 272.
GARDENING TOOLS 264, 266, 268, 270, 272.
garlic 70.
garlic press 243.
garment fabric 565.
garnet 363.
garter stitch 567.
gas 34, 35, 232, 737, 744.
gas burner 297.
gas container 689.
gas cylinder 796.
gas lift module 738.
**gas lighter 386.**
gas main 186.
gas tail 9.
gas tank 386.
gas tap 297.
**gas-cooled reactor 760.**
gasket 257, 300.
gaskin 101.
gastrocnemius 120, 121.
GASTROPOD 83.
gate 462, 490, 646, 647, 681, 747, 752.
gate operating ring 753.
gate-leg 219.
**gate-leg table 219.**
gather 337.
gather skirt 335.
**gathering 577.**
gauge 578.
gauge rod 467.
gauntlet 308, 327, 792.
gauze bandage 662.
gauze roller bandage 725.
gear 575.
gear cable 448.
gear housing 671.
gear lever 447, 448.
gearbox 495, 583.
gearchange lever 430.
gearchange pedal 443, 444.
gelatin capsule 725.
Gemini the Twins (May 21) 820.
General Index 833.
**general view 289.**
generator 753, 758.
**generator unit 753.**
generator unit 747.
genital opening 83.
**geometry 830.**
geostationary orbit 43.
**geostationary satellite 42.**
germ 152.
German rye bread 153.
**geyser 297.**
geyser 25.
gill 55, 208.

The terms in **bold type** correspond to an illustration; those in CAPITALS indicate a title.

gill filament 87.
gill raker 87.
**gilled-tube radiator 208.**
**gills 87.**
gills 88, 92.
gimbal ring 485.
Giraffe 11.
girder 14, 198.
**girdle 346.**
girdle 363.
girth 649, 651.
girth buckle 649.
girth strap 649.
give way 824, 825.
glacial cirque 26.
GLACIER 26.
glacier tongue 26.
glacis 178.
gladius 791.
gland nut 294.
glans penis 127.
glass 768, 769.
glass case 709.
glass cover 254.
glass dome 484.
glass roof 195, 462.
glass slide 718.
glass sphere 40.
glass-fronted display cabinet 227.
glass-lined tank 297.
glassed roof 190.
GLASSWARE 237.
glazed frost 37.
**glider 638.**
glider 230.
GLIDING 638.
globe 689.
glottis 96, 142.
glove 512, 598, 609, 635, 642, 643, 667.
glove compartment 430.
glove finger 327.
GLOVES 327.
glue 200.
glue stick 515.
gluteal nerve 133.
gluteus maximus 121.
gnomon 706.
GO 697.
**go, board 697.**
goal 601, 604, 606, 607, 608, 612, 626.
goal area 601, 612.
goal area line 612.
goal attack 611.
goal circle 611.
goal crease 608.
goal defence 611.
goal judge 608, 626.
goal line 604, 606, 607, 608, 612, 626.
goal line referee 612.
goal shooter 611.
goal third 611.
**goalkeeper 609.**
goalkeeper 601, 607, 608, 611, 612, 626.
goalkeeper's pad 609.
goalkeeper's stick 609.
goalpost 604, 611.
goat 150.
goggles 308, 635.
GOLF 676, 678.
**golf bag 679.**
**golf ball 677.**
**golf ball, cross-section 677.**
**golf clubs 678.**
**golf course 676.**
golf glove 679.
golf shoe 679.
golf trolley 679.
**golf, iron 678.**
**golf, wood 678.**
Golgi apparatus 115.
gonfalon 817.
gong 554, 557.
goods station 464.
GOODS VAN 470.
goose 150.
goose-neck 201.
gooseberry 62.
gooseneck 784.
gored skirt 334.
gorge 24.
gorget 792.
GOTHIC CATHEDRAL 175, 176.
gouge 587.
gour 24.
grab handle 440, 449, 461, 779.
gracile 121.
**grader 784.**
graduated arc 484.
graduated dial 719.
graduated scale 708, 709, 710.
grafting knife 269.
grain 288.
grain auger 161.
grain elevator 161.
**grain of wheat, section 152.**
grain pan 161.
grain tank 160.
grain terminal 490.
grain tube 158.
**grandfather clock 707.**
grandstand 651.
granitic layer 22.
granivorous bird 111.
granny knot 691.
granulation 6.
GRAPE 61.
**grape 62.**
grape 61, 62.
grapefruit 65.
grapefruit knife 242.
grapeshot 801.
graphic equalizer 400.
grapnel 483.
grassbox 271.
grasshopper 77.
grater 243.
**grating, utensils for 243.**
grave accent 832.
gravel 199, 216.
gravity band 483.
**gravity dam 749.**
**gravity dam, cross section 749.**
gravy boat 238.
grease well 253.
greases 745.
great adductor 121.
Great Bear 11.
great organ manual 542.
great saphenous vein 126.
great scallop 93.
greater alar cartilage 141.
greater covert 110.
greater pectoral 120.
greater trochanter 123.
greave 792.
Greek bread 153.
GREEK TEMPLE 168.
**Greek temple, plan 169.**
**green 682.**
green 676.
green ball 673.
green beam 410.
green bean 69.
green cabbage 73.
green peas 72.
green russula 55.
green space 184.
green walnut 66.
greenhouse 149.
Greenland Sea 20.
grey matter 135.
grid 188, 410.
**grid system 47.**
**griddle 253.**
grike 24.
grille 168, 214, 426, 536.
**grinding, utensils for 243.**
grip 632, 665, 677, 684.
grip handle 277.
groin 116, 118.
groove 439, 562, 578, 598, 641, 678, 793.
ground 741.
ground air conditioner 506.
**ground airport equipment 506.**
**ground floor 194.**
ground floor 197.
ground moraine 26.
ground sill 178.
ground surface 733.
growth line 83, 95.
guard 242, 310, 666.
guard rail 254.
guardhouse 178, 180.
guava 68.
guide bar 272.
guide handle 283.
guide mark 612.
guide ring 670.
guide roller 403.
guiding and current bar 476.
guiding tower 457.
guillotine 398.
gules 819.
gulf 51.
gum 142, 144.
gum massager 373.
gumshield 669.
gun 291, 805.
gun flap 319.
gun handle 304.
gunner's sight 805.
gusset 378, 380.
gusset pocket 338, 339.
Gutenberg discontinuity 22.
gutta 167.
gutter 105, 197, 683.
guy line 685.
guy wire 660, 774.
guyot 28.
gymnasium 496.
GYMNASTICS 659, 660.
gypsum tile 286.
gyratory system 450.

## H

hack 620.
hackle 670.
**hacksaw 277.**
hacksaw 299.
hail 37.
hail shower 39.
hair 117, 119, 136, 544.
hair bulb 136.
hair clip 369.
**hair dryer 370.**
hair follicle 136.
hair grip 369.
**hair roller 369.**
hair roller pin 369.
hair shaft 136.
hair slide 369.
**hairbrushes 368.**
**haircutting scissors 369.**
HAIRDRESSING 368, 370.
hairpin 369.
hairspring 706.
**hairstyling accessories 369.**
half barb 38.
half cell 636.
half court line 616.
half handle 242.
half indexing 525.
half-distance line 626.
half-glasses 377.
**half-mask respirator 730.**
half-side 787.
half-slip 345.
half-through arch bridge 455.
halfback 605.
halfway line 601, 606.
hall 194, 496.
hallway 194.
halyard 480, 817.
ham knife 242.
**hammer 658.**
hammer 311, 540, 541, 797, 798, 799.
**hammer axe 681.**
hammer axe 680.
hammer butt 541.
hammer drill 734.
hammer felt 541.
hammer head 681.
hammer jack 541.
hammer rail 540, 541.
hammer shank 541.
**hand 137.**
hand 117, 119.
**hand blender 250.**
hand brake gear housing 470.
hand brake wheel 470.
hand brake winding lever 470.
**hand drill 280.**
hand fork 268.
HAND GRENADE 804.
hand grip 670.
**hand lamp 777.**
**hand mixer 250.**
**hand mower 271.**
hand protection 821.
hand protector 268.
hand shield 308.
**hand vacuum cleaner 260.**
hand vice 582.
hand warmer pocket 330.
hand warmer pouch 339.
hand wash in lukewarm water 829.
hand wheel 561.
hand-warmer pocket 321.
hand-wheel 579.
HANDBAGS 380.
HANDBALL 612.
**handball 612.**
**handball, court 612.**
handbrake lever 430.
handgrip 442, 728.
handgrips 665.
handguard 796.
handhold 652.
handicap spot 697.
handle 204, 224, 239, 240, 241, 250, 251, 252, 253, 254, 255, 256, 260, 265, 270, 271, 272, 275, 276, 277, 278, 279, 281, 282, 284, 291, 294, 295, 304, 306, 310, 370, 373, 374, 375, 378, 380, 382, 383, 544, 563, 564, 570, 573, 579, 596, 598, 607, 615, 619, 620, 640, 643, 658, 666, 670, 671, 679, 688, 727, 735, 793.
handlebar 272, 664.
handlebar stem 447.
handlebars 445, 447.
handrail 201, 477.
**handsaw 277.**
handset 420, 422.
handset flex 420.
**hang glider 637.**
HANG GLIDING 637.
hang point 637.
hang to dry 829.
hang-up ring 370.
hanger 397.
hanger bracket 727.
hanger loop 326.
hanging basket 263.
hanging cupboard 194, 226.
hanging glacier 26.
hanging pendant 236.
hanging sleeve 316.
hanging stile 202, 203, 225.
hank 630.
HARBOUR 490.
hard disc bus 528.
**hard disc drive 529.**
hard disc drive 526, 528.
**hard hat 729.**
hard palate 141, 142.
hard shell clam 93.
hardboard 289.
hardwood base 635.
Hare 13.
harmonica 536.
harness 573, 627, 635, 636, 637, 645.
HARNESS RACING 652.
harnesses 572.
**harp 545.**
Harp 11.
**harp cable stays 456.**
harpoon gun 627.
harps 556.
HARVESTING 159, 160, 162.
**harvesting 155.**
hasp 383.
hastate 56.
hat stand 522.
hatband 328.
hatch 510, 805.
hatchback 425.
hatchet 690.
hatching 576.
haulage road 733.
hawk 291.
hawse pipe 495, 497.
**hay baler 159.**
hay baler 155.
hayloft 148.
hazelnut 66.
**hazelnut, section 66.**
**head 112.**
head 9, 72, 78, 79, 80, 83, 117, 119, 124, 127, 275, 276, 279, 283, 373, 374, 384, 386, 466, 544, 546, 547, 554, 561, 567, 570, 579, 615, 658, 670, 677, 681.
head cover 679.
head harness 730.
head linesman 603.
head number 653.
head of femur 123.
head of frame 203.
head of humerus 123.
head of water 755.
head pole 653.
HEAD PROTECTION 729.
head protection 821.
head roller 572.
head shell 404.
head tube 306.
**head, bat 112.**
**head, bird 109.**
head-first entry 624.
headband 406, 408, 577, 615, 642, 729, 730.
headbay 746.
headboard 224.

The terms in **bold type** correspond to an illustration; those in CAPITALS indicate a title.

headcap 577.
header 161.
headframe 736.
HEADGEAR 328.
headland 30.
headlight 147, 426, 440, 442, 444, 445, 459, 469, 805.
headphone jack 402, 408, 555.
headphone plug 408.
HEADPHONES 406.
headphones 408.
headpin 683.
headrail 231.
headrest 428.
headwind 629.
HEARING 138.
**heart 125.**
heart 88, 92, 97, 130, 695.
heartwood 59.
heat control 209.
heat deflecting disc 232.
heat exchanger 209, 760, 772.
heat production 766.
**heat pump 212.**
heat ready indicator 370.
heat selector switch 370.
heat shield 510.
heat transport pump 759.
heater 689.
HEATING 204, 206, 208, 210, 212.
heating coil 635.
heating duct 259.
heating element 207, 209, 257, 259, 305, 585.
heating grille 477.
heating oil 745.
**heating, forced warm-air system 206.**
heating/air conditioning equipment 494.
heaving line knot 691.
heavy drifting snow at ground level 39.
heavy duty boot 355.
HEAVY MACHINERY 785.
heavy petroleum 744.
heavy thunderstorm 39.
HEAVY VEHICLES 782, 784.
**heavy-water reactor 761.**
heddle rod 574.
**heddles 573.**
heddles 572, 574.
hedge 263.
**hedge trimmer 268.**
heel 104, 117, 119, 156, 242, 277, 325, 352, 354, 544, 546, 596, 609, 644, 678.
heel grip 354.
heel loop 727.
heel piece 633, 640.
heel rest 250, 256.
heel stop 645.
heel-piece 641.
heeled shoe 318.
heelplate 642, 643.
height adjustment 157, 159, 659, 661, 664.
height adjustment foot 397.
height adjustment scale 284.
height adjustment screw 641.
height control 399.
height finder 810.
height of the dive 625.
height scale 399.
HELICOPTER 508.
helicopter 808.
helicopter flight deck 808.
helicopter hangar 808.
helipad 738.
helium sphere 509.
helix 139.
helm roof 183.
helmet 308, 512, 602, 609, 635, 636, 680, 777, 791.
helmet lamp 680.
helmet ring 512.
hem 231.
hemidemisemiquaver 538.
hemidemisemiquaver rest 538.
**hemispheres 47.**
hemlath 773.
hemline 565.
hen 150.
hen house 148.
hennin 318.
hepad 42.
hepatic vein 124.
HERALDRY 817, 818.
**herbivore's jaw 98.**
herbivores 31, 33.
HERBS 74.
Hercules 11.
Herdsman 11.
herringbone parquet 200.
herringbone pattern 200.
herringbone stitch 571.
Hertzian wave transmission 416.
hex nut 439.
hexagon bushing 301.
hidden pocket 379.
high (19 to 36) 700, 701.
high card 695.
**high clouds 44.**
**high focal plane buoy 487.**
**high jump 657.**
high jump 654.
high tension connector 757.
**high warp loom 574.**
**high-back dungarees 350.**
high-pressure steam inlet 758.
high-rise block 185, 187.
high-speed exit taxiway 502.
HIGH-SPEED TRAIN 458.
high-tension electricity transmission 755.
high-voltage tester 310.
**highland climates 45.**
highland climates 45.
highlight key 396.
highlighter pen 515.
hill 27, 770.
hilted bayonet 794.
hind leg 79, 81.
**hind leg, butterfly 78.**
**hind leg, honeybee 81.**
hind limb 84, 85.
hind toe 108, 111.
hind wing 79, 81.
hinge 202, 203, 225, 253, 257, 378, 382, 404, 429, 585, 641, 719.
hinge pin 785.
hinge tooth 95.
hinged door 195.
hip 117, 119.
hip pad 602.
hip roof 182.
hitch pin 540.
hitting area 596.
**hive 82.**
hive body 82.
hob 255.
hob edge 255.
hobble 652.
hobble hanger 652.
hock 101, 106.
hock glass 237.
**hockey ball 607.**
**hockey skate 644.**
**hockey, playing field 607.**
hoe 267.
hoe-fork 266.
hog score line 620.
hoist 188, 817.
hoisting block 786.
hoisting ring 483.
hoisting rope 302, 786.
hoisting system 786.
holdall 381.
holding 668.
holding area marking 504.
holding timekeeper 668.
**holds, judo 668.**
hole 583, 676.
hollow barrel 726.
hollow shot 801.
home plate 597.
home straight 651.
home-plate umpire 597.
honey cell 82.
HONEYBEE 80, 82.
**honeybee, foreleg 80.**
**honeybee, hind leg 81.**
**honeybee, middle leg 80.**
honeycomb 82.
**honeycomb section 82.**
hood 204, 260, 320, 349, 627, 680.
hooded sweat shirt 352.
**hooded towelling robe 349.**
**hoof 104.**
hoof 101.
**hoof, plantar surface 104.**
hook 203, 230, 267, 310, 562, 566, 567, 568, 644, 674, 709, 711, 726, 786.
**hook and eyes 566.**
hook ladder 303, 781.
hooker 606.
hoop 571.
hoop earrings 361.
hopper 158, 162.
hopper ore wagon 472.
hopper tank wagon 472.
horizon mirror 484.
horizon shade 484.
**horizontal bar 660.**
horizontal clamp 713.
horizontal control 529.
horizontal end handhold 470.
horizontal member 756.
horizontal motion lock 393.
horizontal move 696.
horizontal pivoting window 203.
horizontal seismograph 714.
**horizontal-axis wind turbine 774.**
horn 364, 430, 444, 468, 779.
horns 83.
horns of a giraffe 99.
horns of a mouflon 99.
horns of a rhinoceros 99.
horny beak 97.
hors d'oeuvre dish 238.
HORSE 100, 102, 104.
**horse 98.**
horse 661.
HORSE RACING 651.
**horse, gaits 101.**
**horse, morphology 100.**
**horse, skeleton 102.**
horseradish 71.
**horseshoe 104.**
horseshoe 104, 174, 364.
horseshoe mount 14.
**hose 344.**
hose 306, 780.
hose connector 264, 265.
hose nozzle 265.
**hose trolley 265.**
hospital 822.
**hospital trolley 726.**
hot air 501.
hot bus bar 312.
hot coolant 771.
hot-air outlet 204.
hot-shoe contact 391.
hot-water circuit 215.
hot-water heater 215.
hot-water outlet 208, 297.
hot-water riser 215.
hot-water supply 296, 298.
hotel 185.
hotel reservation desk 504.
**houppelande 317.**
hour angle gear 14.
hour hand 707.
house 193, 620.
house dress 333.
HOUSE, EXTERIOR 196.
**house, foundations 199.**
HOUSE, STRUCTURE 198.
housing 233, 280, 305, 310, 374, 403, 406, 422, 485, 486.
HOVERCRAFT 492.
hub 447, 727, 754, 774.
hub cover 754.
HUBBLE SPACE TELESCOPE 16.
**Hubble's classification 9.**
huckleberry 62.
hull 67, 628.
hull column 738.
hull sonar 809.
HUMAN BODY 116, 118.
**human denture 144.**
humerus 102, 122.
humid - long summer 45.
humid - short summer 45.
humid subtropical 45.
**humidifier 210.**
humidity 210.
hump 465.
hump approach 465.
hump control 465.
**hunting cap 328.**
Hunting Dogs 11.
HUNTING WEAPONS 798.
hurdle 656.
hurricane 39.
hurricane lamp 690.
**husk 66.**
husk 72.
hut(mud) 165.
hut(straw) 165.
hydrant intake 778, 779.
hydraulic coupling 147.
hydraulic cylinder 784, 788.
hydraulic hose 156, 157, 158.
hydraulic jack 449.
**hydraulic pallet truck 788.**
hydraulic ram 147.
hydraulic resistance 664.
**hydraulic shovel 785.**
hydraulic system 787.
**hydroelectric complex 746.**
HYDROFOIL BOAT 495.
**hydrologic cycle 34.**
hydrometer 439.
hydrosphere 31.
hydrostatic pad 14.
hygrograph 41.
**hygrometer 210.**
hypha 55.
hyssop 74.

# I

ice 34.
**ice axe 681.**
ice axe 680.
ice cream container 251.
**ice cream maker 251.**
ice cream scoop 246.
ice cube tray 254.
ice dispenser 453.
ICE HOCKEY 608.
**ice hockey player 609.**
**ice hockey, rink 608.**
ice piton 680.
ice screw 680.
icing syringe 245.
identity bracelet 364.
identity tag 383.
idler wheel 445.
igloo 165.
igloo tent 686.
igneous rocks 23.
igniting electrode 209.
ignition 436.
ignition box 501.
ignition key 271.
ignition lead 435.
ignition switch 430, 445.
ignition transformer 209.
ileum 131.
iliohypogastric nerve 133.
ilioinguinal nerve 133.
ilium 122.
**illuminated mirror 368.**
illumination mirror 713.
imagesetter 527.
imperial roof 183.
impervious rock 737.
impluvium 170, 171.
impost 174.
**impulse sprinkler 264.**
in goal 606.
in-flight communications 417.
**in-flight refuelling 813.**
in-flight refuelling probe 813.
inactive dyke 752.
inbound line 604.
incandescent lamp 486.
**incandescent light bulb 232.**
incised figure 580.
incisor 98.
incisors 144.
incoming message cassette 420.
incus 138.
indent 524.
index arm 484.
index card cabinet 517.
**index card drawer 517.**
index cards 517.
index finger 137.
index hole 529.
index mirror 484.
index shade 484.
Indian 13.
Indian chapati bread 153.
Indian fig 68.
Indian naan bread 153.
Indian Ocean 21.
indicator 429, 441, 710.
indicator board 654.
indicator lights 531.
indicator needle 396.
indicator telltale 431, 445.
indicators 405, 410.
indoor shutters 231.
**indoor unit 213.**
induction 436, 437.
industrial communications 417.
industrial pollution 32, 33.
inert gas 232, 233.
inferior cymbal 552.
inferior dental arch 142.
inferior mesenteric artery 132.
inferior nasal concha 141.
inferior umbilicus 110.
inferior vena cava 124, 125, 126, 132.
infield 597.

The terms in **bold type** correspond to an illustration; those in CAPITALS indicate a title.

infiltration 34.
infinity 830.
inflated carrying tyre 477.
inflated guiding tyre 477.
inflator 627, 687.
inflator valve 627.
inflator-deflator 687.
**inflorescent vegetables 69.**
information 823.
information console 627.
information counter 504.
information processing 722.
infrared homing head 814.
infrared sounder 43.
infraspinatus 121.
infundibulum of fallopian tube 129.
inhalation valve 730.
injection/ignition 437.
injector 434.
ink 389, 581, 588.
ink roller 581.
inked surface 580.
**inking slab 581.**
inlaid parquet 200.
inlet hose 399.
inlet manifold 434, 437.
inlet port 436.
inlet valve 434, 436.
inner boot 641, 645.
inner circle 620.
inner core 22.
inner door shell 429.
inner edge 104.
inner jib 481.
inner lining 433.
inner lip 94.
inner stators 501.
inner string 201.
inner table 697.
inner tent 685, 686.
inner toe 108.
**input devices 526.**
input monitors 413.
input selector 402.
input terminal 310.
input wire 232.
insectivores 31.
insectivorous bird 111.
INSECTS AND SPIDERS 77.
inset pocket 339.
inside knob 290.
inside linebacker 603.
inside-leg snap-fastening 350.
**insole 358.**
**inspection light 310.**
inspection plug 216.
**instrument cluster 445.**
instrument cluster 442.
instrument pallet 511.
**instrument panel 431.**
instrument panel 430.
instrument platform 43.
**instrument shelter 41.**
instrument unit 509.
insulated blade 310.
insulated handle 310, 311.
insulating material 199, 200, 257.
**insulating materials 287.**
insulating sheet 528.
insulating sleeve 309.
insulation 209, 297, 768.
insulation layers 512.
insulator 439, 757.
**intaglio printing 580.**
INTAGLIO PRINTING PROCESS 582.
**intaglio printing process, equipment 582.**
integral 830.
Intelsat VII 418.
interchangeable end assembly 14.
intercom microphone 413.
intercom station 413.
intercooler 438.
intercostal nerve 133.
interfacing 565.
interfemoral membrane 112.
interior dome shell 14.
interior door handle 429.
interior door lock button 429.
interior pocket 383.
interlining 565.
interlock 576.
intermediate booster station 740.
intermittent drizzle 39.
intermittent rain 39.
intermittent snow 39.
internal boundary 51.
internal ear 138.
internal filum terminale 134.
internal iliac artery 124, 126, 132.
internal iliac vein 124.
internal jugular vein 126.
internal tooth lock washer 278.
**international road signs 825, 827, 828.**
INTERNATIONAL WEATHER SYMBOLS 39.
internode 57.
interrupted projection 50.
intersection 830.
intertragic notch 139.
interval 489.
**intervals 537.**
interventricular septum 125.
intestine 88, 92, 97, 124.
intrados 174.
intrusive rocks 23.
invert 476.
inverted pleat 228, 335.
**inward dive 625.**
Io 4.
**Ionic order 166.**
iris 140.
Irish soda bread 153.
**iron 677.**
iron at high setting 829.
iron at low setting 829.
iron at medium setting 829.
iron curtain 188.
**iron, golf 678.**
**ironing 829.**
irregular crystal 37.
irregular galaxy 9.
is approximately equal to 830.
is contained in 830.
is equal to 830.
is equal to or greater than 830.
is equal to or less than 830.
is equivalent to 830.
is greater than 830.
is identical with 830.
is less than 830.
is not equal to 830.
is not identical with 830.
is not parallel to 830.
is parallel to 830.
isba 165.
ischium 123.
island 51, 452.
isobar 38.
isolated danger mark 489.
isoseismal line 23.
isthmus 51.
isthmus of fallopian tube 129.
isthmus of fauces 142.
ivory ball 701.

## J

J-2 engine 509.
jabot 342.
jack 400, 682, 780, 785, 786.
Jack 695.
jack field 407.
jack plug 406.
jack spring 541.
jack-up platform 739.
jacket 331, 529, 667, 668, 798.
**jackleg drill 734.**
jackpot box 702.
jackpot feed 702.
jalousie 203.
jamb 202, 204.
Japanese persimmon 68.
javelin 654, 791.
**javelins 658.**
jaw 276, 280, 281, 311, 365.
**jaw, carnivore's 98.**
**jaw, herbivore's 98.**
**jaw, rodent's 98.**
jazz band 558.
jeans 336.
jejunum 131.
Jerusalem artichoke 71.
jet blast deflector 810.
jet engine test area 811.
jet fuel 745.
jet refueler 506.
jet tip 373.
**Jew's harp 536.**
jewel 706.
jewel cap 485.
JEWELLERY 361, 362, 364.
Jewish challah 153.
jib 628, 786.
jib tie 786.
jibsheet 628.
jigger topgallant staysail 480.
jigger topmast staysail 480.
jingle 554.
jockey 651.
jockey rollers 448.
jodhpurs 648.
jogging pants 352.
joint 389, 431, 577, 670, 675.
joint filler 291.
jointed mouth 650.
joist 200.
Joker 695.
journal box 468.
joystick 526.
judge 666, 668, 669.
judge's stand 651.
JUDO 668.
**judo suit 668.**
jug 247.
**juice extractor 251.**
juice sac 65.
jump ski 633.
jumper valve plate 294.
jumping boot 635.
jumpsuit 336, 351.
junction box 471.
Jupiter 4.
justaucorps 315.

## K

K-frame 756.
**Kaplan runner 754.**
**karabiner 681.**
karabiner 680.
keel 637.
keep 181.
keeper ring 670.
kelly 737.
kerb 186.
kernel 72.
kerosene 744.
kerosene tank 509.
ketch 482.
**kettle 252.**
**kettledrum 553.**
key 290, 536, 540, 541, 543, 549.
key case 379.
key finger button 549.
key guard 549.
key lever 549.
key lock 378.
key signature 538.
key spindle 539.
keybed 540.
**keyboard 530.**
keyboard 422, 526, 527, 540, 555, 683.
KEYBOARD INSTRUMENTS 540.
keyboard port 528.
keys 650.
keystone 174, 177.
keyway 290.
kick pleat 335.
kickstand 443.
kidney 89, 97, 124.
kilt 335.
kimono 348.
kimono sleeve 340.
King 695, 696.
king post 199, 637.
King's side 696.
kingpin 441.
kiosk 453, 475.
kitchen 171, 195, 460.
**kitchen knife 242.**
kitchen scale 244.
kitchen timer 244.
KITCHEN UTENSILS 242, 244, 246.
kitchen-diner 195.
kiwi 68.
knee 100, 106, 116, 118.
knee boot 653.
knee boot suspender 653.
knee pad 595, 602, 609.
knee sock 344, 642.
knee-length sock 325.
knickerbockers 336.
**knife 239.**
knife 581, 587, 688, 690.
knife pleat 323, 335.
knife-blade cartridge fuse 312.
Knight 696.
knit cap 329.
**knit shirt 326.**
KNITTING 567.
KNITTING MACHINE 568.
knitting measure 567.
**knitting needles 567.**
knob 219, 231, 596.
knob handle 284.
knockout cable entry 312.
knot 576.
**knot stitches 571.**
KNOTS 691, 692.
knurled bolt 304.
kohlrabi 71.
krone 832.
kumquat 65.

## L

label 404.
label holder 517.
label maker 516.
labial palp 79, 81, 92.
labium majus 128, 129.
labium minus 128, 129.
laboratory 15.
laboratory air lock 511.
laccolith 25.
lace 596, 644, 669.
lace carriage 568.
lace-up 355.
lacing 645.
lacrimal duct 140.
lactiferous duct 129.
ladder 449, 487, 493, 741, 785.
ladder and hose strap 777.
ladder pipe nozzle 781.
ladder scaffold 303.
LADDERS 302.
ladle 244, 801.
Lady chapel 177.
ladybird 77.
lagging 741.
lagoon 30.
lake 7, 27, 51.
lam 572.
lamb 150.
laminboard 288.
lamp 718.
lamp base 486.
**lampholder 309.**
lamphouse elevation control 399.
lamphouse head 399.
lanceolate 56.
lancet 174.
land 281.
landing 194, 201, 736.
landing area 655, 657.
landing deck 811.
landing gear lever 500.
landing light 508.
landing net 672.
landing radar 811.
landing window 508.
**lane 683.**
lane 621, 655.
lane line 656.
lane number 621.
lane rope 621.
lane timekeeper 621.
language display button 422.
languid 542.
**lantern 689.**
lantern 263, 486.
lantern pane 486.
lap belt 428.
lapel 322, 341.
lapis lazuli 363.
larch 58.
large blade 688.
large detached house 187.
**large intestine 131.**
large wheel 727.
larva 82.
larynx 130, 142.
laser beam 405.
laser printer 527.
last quarter 7.
latch 253, 257, 383, 562, 568, 681.
latch bolt 289, 290.
**latch needle 568.**
latch needle 569.
lateen sail 482.
lateral bar 663.
lateral condyle of femur 123.
lateral cutaneous femoral nerve 133.
lateral filing cabinet 520.
lateral groove 104.
lateral incisor 144.
lateral line 87, 620.
lateral mark 489.
lateral moraine 27.
lateral rectus muscle 140.
lateral semicircular canal 139.
lateral-adjustment lever 277.
lath 231.
latissimus dorsi 121.

The terms in **bold type** correspond to an illustration; those in CAPITALS indicate a title.

latitude 3.
latitude scale 40.
latrines 171.
launch escape system 509.
launcher/satellite separation 419.
**launching into orbit 419.**
launching orbit 48.
laundry room 194.
lava flow 25.
lava layer 25.
lawn 193, 263.
lawn aerator 266.
lawn edger 266.
lawn rake 267.
leach field 216.
lead 400, 408, 620.
lead ball 804.
lead pencil 389.
leader 672.
leading edge 341, 499, 636, 638.
leading edge flap 812.
leading edge tube 637.
**leaf 56.**
leaf 57, 72.
leaf axil 56.
**leaf margin 56.**
leaf node 57.
**leaf vegetables 73.**
leakproof cap 689.
lean-to roof 182.
leash rod 574.
leather end 323.
LEATHER GOODS 378.
leather sheath 632, 690.
leather skin 598.
**leaves, types of 58.**
ledger board 198.
ledger line 537.
leech 631.
leek 70.
left atrium 124, 125.
left back 607, 612, 613.
left centre 606.
left channel 401.
left cornerback 603, 605.
left defence 608.
left defensive end 603, 605.
left defensive tackle 603, 605.
left field 597.
left fielder 597.
left forward 610, 613.
left guard 603, 605, 610.
left half 607.
left halfback 603.
left inner 607.
left kidney 132.
left lung 124, 130.
left outside linebacker 605.
left pulmonary vein 125.
left safety 603.
left safety back 605.
left service court 614, 616.
left tackle 603, 605.
**left valve, shell 95.**
left ventricle 124, 125.
left wing 601, 606, 607, 608.
left winger 612.
left-luggage office 462.
leg 97, 117, 119, 156, 219, 224, 270, 325, 553, 619, 659, 671.
leg curl bar 663.
leg extension bar 663.
leg position 625.
leg-of-mutton sleeve 340.
leg-warmer 353.
legging 680.
**legume, section 67.**
lemon 65.
**lemon squeezer 251.**
lemon squeezer 243.
lengthways bulkhead 742.
lengthwise grain 565, 566.
lens 140, 376, 390, 391, 392, 396, 397, 405.
**lens accessories 392.**
lens aperture scale 392.
lens cap 392.
lens hood 392, 409, 484, 721.
lens mount 390.
lens release button 391.
lens system 719.
LENSES 722.
**lenses 392.**
lenticular galaxy 9.
lentils 72.
Leo the Lion (July 23) 820.
leotard 353.
lesser covert 110.
letter opener 515.
letter scale 516.
leucoplast 115.
level 736.
**level crossing 471.**
level crossing 464, 828.
level crossing bell 471.
level crossing sign 471.
levelling foot 257, 258, 259.
levelling head 713.
levelling head level 713.
levelling head locking knob 713.
levelling screw 40, 709, 713.
lever 252, 278, 295, 296, 365, 453, 583, 702, 798.
lever corkscrew 244.
lever cover 295.
lever kitchen-tap 296.
**levigator 583.**
Libra the Balance (September 23) 820.
lid 247, 248, 251, 252, 253, 256, 258, 398, 585.
lid brace 585.
lierne 177.
life buoy 495.
life raft 492.
life support system 512.
life support system controls 512.
lifeboat 478, 494, 496, 738.
lift 15, 190, 478, 736.
lift arm 782.
**lift bridge 457.**
lift chain 293.
lift cord 231.
lift cord lock 231.
lift span 457.
lift-arm cylinder 782.
lift-fan air inlet 493.
lifting chain 787.
lifting handle 803.
lifting hook 737.
lifting lever 147.
lifting link 147.
ligament 95.
ligature 548.
light 477, 486, 487, 489, 720, 721.
light bar 779.
light bulb 769.
LIGHT MACHINE GUN 796.
light sensor 390.
light shield 16.
light signal 539.
light-load adjustment screw 712.
light-reading scale 396.
lightbox 398.
**lighthouse 486.**
lighthouse 491.
**lighthouse lantern 486.**
lighting 368, 500.
lighting board 412.
lighting board operator 412.
lighting cable 449.
lighting grid 414.
lighting grid access 412.
lighting technician 412.
lighting/camera control area 412.
lightning 36.
lightning conductor 197, 747, 757.
LIGHTS 232, 234, 236.
**lights 429.**
limb 59, 684.
limb top 718.
limpet 83.
line 537, 700, 701.
line guide 671.
line judge 603, 605.
line map 474.
line of scrimmage 603, 605.
linear 56.
linen 460.
linen chest 226.
**lines of latitude 47.**
**lines of longitude 47.**
linesman 601, 605, 608, 613, 614, 618.
lingual papillae 143.
lingual tonsil 143.
lining 322, 324, 352, 354, 378, 565, 644.
**lining fabrics 565.**
linseed oil 592.
linstock 801.
lint filter 258.
lintel 175, 198, 202, 204.
**lion 98.**
Lion 11.
lion passant 819.
lip 100, 107.
**lip make-up 366.**
lip strap ring 650.
lipbrush 366.
lipid droplet 115.
lipliner 366.
lipstick 366.
liqueur glass 237.
**liquid compass 484.**
**liquid compass, cross section 485.**
liquid cooling and ventilation garment 512.
liquid eyeliner 367.
liquid foundation 366.
liquid hydrogen tank 509.
liquid mascara 367.
liquid nitrogen tank 717.
liquid oxygen tank 509.
liquid oxygen tank baffle 509.
liquid-crystal display 706.
liquid/gas separator 439.
lira 832.
listen button 420.
lists 181.
litchi 68.
litho crayon 583.
litho pencil 583.
**lithographic press 583.**
**lithographic printing 580.**
lithographic stone 583.
lithographic tusche 583.
LITHOGRAPHY 583.
**lithography, equipment 583.**
lithosphere 31.
Little Bear 11.
Little Dog 11.
little finger 137.
little finger hook 551.
Little Horse 11.
Little Lion 11.
liver 88, 97, 124, 131.
**Liverpool bit 650.**
livestock van 472.
living room 195, 685.
Lizard 11.
load platform 441.
loading area 764.
loading bridge 491.
loading bunker 734.
loading dock 190.
loading door 204.
lobate 56.
lobate toe 111.
lobby 190, 504.
lobe 111.
**lobster 90.**
lobule 139.
local station 416.
location of the statue 169.
LOCK 289, 290.
lock 202, 225, 289, 380, 383, 429, 752.
lock dial 530.
lock emptying system 492.
lock filling and emptying opening 493.
lock filling and emptying system 492.
lock filling intake 493.
lock filling opening 493.
lock forward 606.
lock nut 40, 711.
lock rail 202.
lock ring 397.
lock switch 396.
lock-chamber 493.
locker 522.
locket 361.
locking button 260.
locking device 260, 302.
locking lever 471.
locking ring 276, 802.
locknut 296.
locomotive 459.
locomotive track 465.
loculus 64.
loft ladder 303.
log 288.
log carrier 205.
log chute 746.
**log, section 288.**
loin 101, 117, 119.
long adductor 120.
long and short stitch 571.
long extensor of toes 120.
long johns 325.
long jump take-off board 655.
long palmar 120.
long peroneal 120.
long radial extensor of wrist 121.
long residue 744.
long service line 618.
LONG-RANGE JET AIRLINER 498.
longitude 3.
longitudinal dunes 46.
loop 324, 452.
**loop stitches 571.**
loophole 181.
**loose curtain 228.**
loose fill insulation 287.
loose powder 366.
loose powder brush 366.
lopping shears 269.
lore 109.
lorgnette 377.
lost property 823.
**loudspeaker 401.**
loudspeaker 779.
lounge 496.
louvre 214.
louvre-board 175.
louvred window 203.
lovage 74.
low (1 to 18) 700, 701.
**low clouds 44.**
low fuel warning light 431.
**low warp loom 572.**
low-pressure steam 758.
low-tension distribution line 757.
lower bar 659.
lower blade guard 284.
lower bowl 247.
lower cheek 650.
lower chord 455.
lower eyelid 84, 107, 140.
lower fore topgallant sail 481.
lower fore topsail 481.
lower gate 492.
lower gill arch 87.
lower girdle facet (16) 363.
lower guard retracting lever 284.
lower lateral lobe 61.
lower lateral sinus 61.
lower level 493.
lower limb 124, 793.
lower lip 142, 542.
lower lobe 130.
lower mandible 109.
lower mantle 22.
lower mast 478.
lower shell 641.
lower sphere clamp 40.
lower support screw 40.
lubber's line 485.
lubricants plant 745.
lubricating oils 745.
lubricating system 469.
lubricator 735.
Luer-Lock tip 726.
luff 631.
lug 553.
LUGE 643.
LUGGAGE 382.
luggage compartment 458, 461, 508.
luggage elastic 382.
luggage lockers 463.
luggage rack 445, 449.
luggage racks 492.
**luggage trolley 382.**
luggage trolley 463.
lumbar pad 602.
lumbar plexus 133.
**lumbar vertebra 135.**
lumbar vertebra (5) 123.
lumbar vertebrae 103.
LUNAR ECLIPSE 8.
**lunar features 7.**
lunar module 509.
lung 97.
lunula 137.
lunule 95.
lychee 68.
Lynx 11.
**lyre 535.**
lysosome 115.

## M

macaroni 587.
machete 794.
**machicolation 181.**
machicolation 180.
machine gun 805.
machine hall 746, 747.
machine wash in hot water at a normal setting 829.
machine wash in lukewarm water at a gentle setting/reduced agitation 829.
machine wash in warm water at a gentle setting/reduced agitation 829.
machine wash in warm water at a normal setting 829.
machinery shed 148.

The terms in **bold type** correspond to an illustration; those in CAPITALS indicate a title.

macro set button 409.
magazine 795, 796, 797.
magazine base 797.
magazine catch 795, 797.
magma 25, 28.
magma chamber 25.
magnet 406, 485, 563, 714.
MAGNETIC COMPASS 719.
magnetic damping system 708.
magnetic field 410.
magnetic gasket 254.
magnetic lid holder 256.
magnetic needle 719.
magnetic suspension 712.
magnetometer 42.
magnifier 688.
main beam headlight 429.
main beam indicator light 431.
main beam warning light 445.
main carriage 568.
main circuit breaker 312.
main circuit vent 215.
main cleanout 215.
main deck 743, 811.
main drain 215, 216.
main duct 206.
main electric motor 806.
main engines 511.
main entrance 190, 194.
main fan 734.
main glider 230.
main handle 280.
main inlet 741.
main junction box 757.
main landing gear 499, 812.
main leg 756.
main line 464.
main lower topgallant sail 481.
main lower topsail 481.
main mirror 720.
main parachute 635.
main power cable 312.
main preview monitor 413.
main reflex mirror 390.
main return pipe 208.
main road 452.
main royal sail 481.
main sail 481.
main scope tube 718.
main section 700, 701.
main sewer 186.
main stalk 61.
main stand 443.
main steam header 759.
main steam pipes 759.
main supply pipe 208.
main switch 757.
main transformer 458.
main tube 720, 721.
main upper topgallant sail 481.
main upper topsail 481.
main vent 25.
main wheel 707.
mainmast 479.
mains connection 207, 213.
mainsail 628.
mainsheet 628.
maintenance area 415.
maintenance hangar 503.
maintenance shop 734.
major inner reaping throw 668.
**major motions 697.**
major outer reaping throw 668.
MAKE-UP 366.
**make-up 366.**
malar region 109.
male 831.
male cone 58.
male ferrule 670.
MALE GENITAL ORGANS 127.
male union nut 300.
male urethra 127.
**mallet 275.**
mallet 552, 581, 586.
mallets 553.
malleus 138.
mammary gland 129.
mandarin 65.
mandarin collar 342.
mandible 78, 80, 81, 86, 102, 122.
**mandolin 535.**
mane 100.
mangetout 72.
mango 63.
manhole 186, 741, 742.
MANICURE 365.
**manicure set 365.**
**manicuring implements 365.**
manifold 738.
manned manœuvring unit 512.
manœuvring bar 162.
manœuvring engine 511.
manœuvring lever 787, 788.
manometer 741.
manrope 457.
mansard roof 183.
mantle 204.
mantle edge 92.
mantlepiece 204.
manual 543.
manual focusing knob 397.
manual release 641.
manual/automatic mode 585.
**manually-operated points 467.**
manuals 542.
**manure spreader 156.**
manure spreader 154.
manway 736.
**map projections 50.**
Marconi cutter 482.
margin 57.
margin control 525.
margin release 524.
marginal shield 96.
marine 45.
marine diesel 745.
MARITIME BUOYAGE SYSTEM 488.
maritime communications 417.
MARITIME SIGNALS 486.
marker 389, 683.
marker pen 515, 588.
marking dot 565.
marrow 69.
Mars 4.
MARSHALLING YARD 465.
marshalling yard 465.
martingale 666.
mascara brush 367.
mask 595, 627, 667.
**mason's trowel 291.**
MASONRY 291.
mass 714.
masseter 120.
massif 51.
mast 471, 508, 628, 631, 787, 788.
mast foot 631.
mast sleeve 631.
master bedroom 194.
master cord 645.
master gate valve 740.
masthead 479, 631.
masthead light 495.
**masts 478.**
**mat 668.**
mat 682.
**matchbox 386.**
matchstick 386.
MATERIAL HANDLING 786, 788.
**mathematics 830.**
matinee-length necklace 361.
**mattress 687.**
mattress 224, 726.
mattress cover 224.
maulstick 591.
maxilla 81, 86, 90, 122, 141.
maxillary bone 144.
maxillipeds 90.
maximum thermometer 41.
meadow 149.
MEASURE OF ANGLES 713.
MEASURE OF TEMPERATURE 705.
MEASURE OF TIME 706.
**measurement of air pressure 41.**
**measurement of cloud ceiling 41.**
MEASUREMENT OF DISTANCE 711.
**measurement of humidity 41.**
MEASUREMENT OF LENGTH 711.
MEASUREMENT OF PRESSURE 710.
**measurement of rainfall 40.**
MEASUREMENT OF SEISMIC WAVES 714.
**measurement of snowfall 41.**
**measurement of sunshine 40.**
**measurement of temperature 41.**
MEASUREMENT OF THICKNESS 711.
MEASUREMENT OF WEIGHT 708.
**measurement of wind direction 41.**
**measurement of wind strength 41.**
measuring button 396.
measuring cups 244.
measuring spoons 244.
measuring tube 40.
**measuring, utensils 244.**
meat 33.
meat keeper 254.
meat thermometer 244.
**mechanical connections 300.**
mechanical pencil 515.
mechanical shovel 733.
mechanical stage 718.
mechanical stage control 718.
mechanical variometer 639.
**mechanical watch 706.**
medial condyle of femur 123.
medial moraine 26.
medial rectus muscle 140.
median groove 104.
median lingual sulcus 143.
median nerve 133.
Mediterranean Sea 21.
Mediterranean subtropical 45.
medium 666.
medium format SLR (6 x 6) 395.
medium tension distribution line 757.
medlar 64.
medulla 132.
medulla oblongata 134.
medullary ray 59.
Meissner's corpuscle 136.
melody strings 535.
meltwater 27.
memo pad 518.
memory button 402, 420.
memory cancel 396, 523.
memory key 396, 405.
memory recall 523.
memory recall key 396.
men 697.
men's bag 380.
MEN'S CLOTHING 319, 320, 322, 324.
men's toilet 822.
Mercury 4.
mercury 232.
mercury barometer 41.
mercury bulb 705.
merging traffic 824.
méridienne 221.
merlon 181.
mesa 46.
mesh 619.
mesocarp 62, 63, 64, 65.
mesosphere 19.
mesothorax 78.
message display 532.
metacarpus 102, 107, 122.
metal A 307.
metal arm 264.
metal B 307.
metal counterhoop 553.
metal frame 540.
metal head 658.
metal rail 517.
metal rod 554.
metal structure 463.
metallic contact grid 768.
metallic plastron 667.
metals 33.
**metals, examples 819.**
metamorphic rocks 23.
metatarsus 80, 103, 122.
metathorax 78.
METEOROLOGY 38.
METEOROLOGY, MEASURING INSTRUMENTS 40.
**meteorology, station model 38.**
methylated spirits 745.
metope 167.
**metronome 539.**
mezzanine 195, 474.
**mezzanine floor 194.**
mezzanine stairs 195.
**Michigan snowshoe 645.**
**micrometer caliper 711.**
micrometer screw 484, 713.
microphone 407, 414, 420, 639.
microphone boom 412, 414.
microphone boom tripod 414.
microprocessor 528.
microwave dish 415.
**microwave oven 253.**
microwave scanner 43.
microwave transmitter 415.
mid-calf length sock 325.
**mid-ocean ridge 28.**
**middle clouds 44.**
middle covert 110.
middle ear 138.
middle finger 137.
middle jib 481.
middle leg 79, 80.
**middle leg, honeybee 80.**
middle linebacker 603, 605.
middle lobe 130.
middle nasal concha 141.
middle panel 202.
middle phalanx 107, 122, 123, 137.
middle piece 127.
middle primary covert 110.
middle sole 352.
middle toe 108.
middle torus 167.
midfield 601.
midrange loudspeaker 16.
midrange pickup 547.
midrange speaker 401.
midrib 56, 67.
midriff band 346.
Mihrab 173.
Mihrab dome 173.
mileometer 431.
military communications 417.
milk bread 153.
Milky Way 11.
millet 152.
minaret 172, 173.
Minbar 173.
mincer 243.
miners' changing-room 735.
mini briefs 325.
**mini-floppy disc 529.**
minibus 425.
minim 538.
minim rest 538.
minimum thermometer 41.
minor sciatic nerve 133.
mint 74.
minute 830.
minute hand 706, 707.
mirror 292, 382, 442, 444.
**miscellaneous 831.**
**miscellaneous utensils 246.**
missile launch rail 813.
missile launcher 811.
missile stowage 808.
**missile, structure 814.**
MISSILES 814.
mist 37, 39.
mitochondrion 115.
mitral valve 125.
mitre gate recess 493.
mitre gauge 285.
mitre gauge slot 285.
mitten 308, 327, 680.
mixing bowl 250.
mixing bowls 245.
mixing chamber 306.
mizzen royal brace 480.
mizzen royal staysail 480.
mizzen sail 480.
mizzen topgallant staysail 480.
mizzen topmast staysail 480.
mizzenmast 478.
moat 178, 181.
mobile drawer unit 521.
mobile filing unit 521.
mobile passenger steps 507.
MOBILE UNIT 415.
mobile unit 416.
moccasin 355.
mock pocket 330.
mode 525.
mode selector 402.
mode selectors 408.
modem 526.
modem port 528.
moderator 766.
moderator tank 761.
moderator: graphite 760.
moderator: heavy water 761.
moderator: natural water 762, 763.
modern bow 793.
MODERN HOWITZER 802.
**modern mortar 803.**
modesty panel 521.
modillion 167.
modulation wheel 555.
Mohorovicic discontinuity 22.
moist surface 580.
moistener 516.
moisture in the air 34.
molar 98.
**molar, cross section 144.**
molars 144.
**mole wrench 278.**
MOLLUSC 92.
monitor roof 182.
monitor screen 717.
monitor speaker 407.
monitor wall 412, 413, 415.
monocle 377.
mons pubis 128.
monster 605.
monument 52.
MOON 7.
Moon 4, 8.
moon dial 707.
Moon's orbit 8.
MOON, PHASES 6.
**moons 4.**
mooring chain 486.

The terms in **bold type** correspond to an illustration; those in CAPITALS indicate a title.

mooring winch 743.
mordent 538.
morel 55.
MORTAR 803.
mortar 243.
mortise 385.
**mortise lock 290.**
mosaic 171.
MOSQUE 172.
**mosque, plan 173.**
moss stitch 567.
motor 214, 257, 258, 259, 270, 271, 272, 283, 284.
motor bogie 459.
motor car 476, 477.
motor end plate 134.
motor neuron 135.
motor root 135.
motor unit 250, 251, 256, 260, 373, 458.
MOTORCYCLE 442, 444.
**motorized ground auger 270.**
motorway 52, 184, 452.
motorway number 52.
mouldboard 156.
moulded insulation 287.
moulding 199.
MOUNTAIN 27.
mountain range 7, 23, 51.
mountain slope 27.
mountain torrent 27.
**mountaineer 680.**
MOUNTAINEERING 680.
mountaineering boot 680.
mountaineering shovel 680.
**mountaineering, equipment 681.**
mounting 666.
mounting bracket 684.
mounting foot 393.
mounting plate 233.
mounting point 501.
**mouse 530.**
mouse 526, 527.
**mouth 142.**
mouth 83, 84, 92, 118, 542, 650.
**mouthparts 81.**
mouthpiece 548, 550, 627.
mouthpiece receiver 550.
mouthpipe 550.
MOVABLE BRIDGES 457.
movable jaw 279, 282.
movable maxillary 96.
moving coil 406.
MOWING 158.
**mowing 154.**
Mt Everest 19.
mud flap 427, 440, 441.
mud injection hose 737.
mud pit 737.
mud pump 737.
mudguard 147, 446.
muff 381.
muffler felt 540.
mule 355.
mullet 819.
multi-ply plywood 288.
multi-purpose ladder 303.
**multimeter 310.**
multiple exposure mode 391.
multiple light fitting 235.
multiple use key 523.
multiple-span beam bridge 454.
multiplication 830.
multiply key 523.
multipurpose antenna 807.
**multipurpose tool 311.**
mummy 687.
muntin 203.
muscle fibre 134.
muscle scar 95.
muscle segment 89.
MUSCLES 120.
museum 185.
MUSHROOM 55.
mushroom anchor 483.
**mushroom, structure 55.**
music rest 539, 542, 555.
**music stand 539.**
MUSICAL ACCESSORIES 539.
musical advisers 412.
MUSICAL NOTATION 537, 538.
muskmelon 69.
**mustard 67.**
mute 551.
mutule 167.
muzzle 100, 106, 107, 797, 798, 799, 800, 803.
**muzzle-loading cannon 800.**
mycelium 55.
myelin sheath 135.

## N

nacelle 774.
nacreous cloud 19.
**nail 275.**
nail 104.
nail bed 137.
nail cleaner 365.
**nail clippers 365.**
nail file 365.
nail groove 688.
nail hole 104.
nail matrix 137.
nail scissors 365.
nail shaper 365.
nail whitener pencil 365.
naked strangle 668.
name plate 712.
nameplate 364.
naos 169.
nape 108, 117, 119.
nappy 349.
naris 141.
nasal bone 141.
nasal cavity 130.
**nasal fossae 141.**
nasopharynx 141.
national broadcasting network 416.
national park 52.
natural 538.
natural arch 30.
natural sponge 367.
nave 177.
navel 116, 118.
navette cut 362.
NAVIGATION DEVICES 484.
navigation display 500.
navigation light 493, 499.
navigation periscope 807.
**Neapolitan coffee maker 247.**
neck 97, 100, 117, 118, 119, 127, 144, 240, 241, 410, 544, 545, 546, 547, 579, 661, 678.
neck end 324.
neck guard 777.
neck of femur 123.
neck strap 729.
neckhole 325.
**necklaces 361.**
**necklines 343.**
neckroll 224.
**necks 343.**
neckstrap eyelet 390.
**necktie 324.**
nectarine 63.
**needle 562, 632.**
needle 36, 561, 562, 563, 590, 710, 726.
needle assembly 590.
needle bar 562.
**needle bed 568.**
needle bed 568.
needle bed groove 568.
needle clamp 562.
needle clamp screw 562.
needle hub 726.
needle plate 561.
needle position selector 561.
needle threader 563.
needle tool 585.
needle-nose pliers 311.
negative 399.
**negative carrier 399.**
negative carrier 399.
negative charge 831.
negative contact 768, 769.
negative meniscus 722.
negative plate 439.
negative plate strap 439.
negative region 768.
negative terminal 439.
negligee 348.
neon lamp 310.
Neptune 5.
nerve 136.
nerve fibre 136.
nerve termination 136.
nerve, olfactory 142.
NERVOUS SYSTEM 133, 134.
nest of tables 219.
**net 613, 614, 618.**
Net 13.
net 610, 612, 613, 614, 618, 619, 626.
net band 614.
net judge 614.
net support 619.
NETBALL 611.
**netball 611.**
**netball, court 611.**
network communication 527.
network port 528.
neural spine 89.
**neurons 135.**
neutral conductor 757.
neutral indicator 445.
neutral service wire 312.
neutral wire 312.
neutral zone 603, 605, 608.
névé 26.
new crescent 6.
new fuel storage room 764.
new moon 6.
newel post 201.
next call 422.
nib 389.
nictitating membrane 107.
nightgown 348.
**nightwear 348.**
nimbostratus 44.
nipple 116, 118, 129, 301.
no access for wheelchairs 822.
no entry 824, 825.
no U-turn 824, 825.
no vehicles over height shown 826, 827.
no. 1 wood 678.
no. 3 iron 678.
no. 3 wood 678.
no. 4 iron 678.
no. 5 iron 678.
no. 5 wood 678.
no. 6 iron 678.
no. 7 iron 678.
no. 8 forward 606.
no. 8 iron 678.
no. 9 iron 678.
nock 684, 793.
nocking point 684.
noctilucent cloud 19.
node 756.
node of Ranvier 135.
non-add/subtotal 523.
North 488.
North America 20.
**North American road signs 824, 826, 828.**
North celestial pole 3.
North Pole 3.
North Sea 21.
Northeast 488.
Northern Crown 11.
Northern hemisphere 3, 47.
Northwest 488.
**nose 141.**
nose 100, 118, 498, 637, 638, 792, 798.
nose cone 501.
nose landing gear 498.
nose leaf 112.
nose leather 107.
nose of the quarter 352, 354.
nose pad 376.
noseband 649.
nosing 201.
nostril 84, 86, 96, 100, 109.
notch 322, 341, 565, 656, 674, 708.
**notched double-edged thinning scissors 369.**
notched edge 369.
notched lapel 319, 320.
**notched single-edged thinning scissors 369.**
**note values 538.**
nozzle 209, 264, 291, 304, 306, 509, 510, 590, 778.
nozzle cleaners 307.
nuchal shield 97.
nuclear boiler room 806.
NUCLEAR ENERGY 758, 760, 762, 764, 766.
**nuclear fuel handling sequence 764.**
nuclear membrane 115.
**nuclear power station 758.**
**nuclear reactor 765.**
nuclear whorl 94.
nucleolus 115, 128.
nucleus 9, 115, 128, 135.
number 656, 701.
number key 421, 523.
number of decimals 523.
number of tracks sign 471.
number plate light 429.
number three 620.
number two 620.
numbering stamp 516.
numeric keyboard 422, 709.
numeric keypad 530.
nut 278, 279, 300, 466, 544, 546, 547, 793.
nutcracker 243.
NUTS 66.
nylon line 271.

## O

o-ring 294, 295.
oar 664.
oasis 46.
oats 152.
object balls 673.
objective 718.
objective lens 718, 719, 721.
oboe 548.
oboes 557.
obscured sky 39.
observation deck 505.
observation window 510.
**observatory 14.**
**obstacles 647.**
obturator nerve 133.
obtuse angle 830.
occipital 121.
occipital bone 123.
occluded front 39.
ocean 7, 35, 51.
OCEAN FLOOR 28.
**ocean, topography 28.**
Oceania 21.
oche 698.
octave 537, 667.
octave mechanism 548.
odd 700, 701.
odd pinnate 56.
oesophagus 88, 92, 97, 130, 131, 142.
**offence 603, 605.**
office 453, 462.
OFFICE BUILDING 190.
office building 185, 491.
OFFICE FURNITURE 520, 522.
office tower 184, 190.
officers' quarters 807, 808.
officials' bench 608.
offset 301.
**offshore drilling 739.**
offshore well 740.
ogee 174.
ogee roof 182.
OIL 737, 738, 740, 742, 744.
oil 737.
**oil burner 209.**
oil drain plug 434.
oil feed pipe 209.
oil paint 588.
oil pastel 588.
oil pressure warning indicator 445.
oil processing area 738.
oil pump 209.
oil supply 209.
oil tank 272.
oil terminal 491.
oil warning light 431.
oil-filled radiator 211.
oil/gas separator 738.
oiler 734.
oilstone 582.
okra 69.
old crescent 7.
olecranon 102, 123.
olfactory bulb 88, 142.
olfactory mucosa 142.
olfactory nerve 88, 142.
olfactory tract 142.
olive 63.
on guard line 666.
on the wind 629.
on-air warning light 407.
on-deck circle 597.
on-off button 256.
on-off indicator 370.
on-off switch 216, 234, 247, 260, 305, 368, 370, 373, 374, 485.
on/off 408.
on/off light 420.
on/off switch 391, 397, 406.
on/off/volume 408.
on/play button 420.
one pair 695.
one way head 276.
one-arm shoulder throw 668.
one-bar shoe 356.
one-person tent 686.
one-piece coverall 635.
one-piece suit 643.
one-toe hoof 99.
one-way traffic 824, 825.

The terms in **bold type** correspond to an illustration; those in CAPITALS indicate a title.

opal 363.
open strings 535.
open-air terrace 497.
open-ended spanner 279.
**open-face spinning reel 671.**
**open-pit mine 733.**
**open-plan coach 460.**
**opencast strip mine 733.**
opening 327.
**opening, utensils 244.**
opera glasses 377.
opera-length necklace 361.
operating cord 230.
operating dam 752.
operating floor 752.
operating rod 796.
operation control room 807.
operation keys 422.
**operational pattern of marks by night 489.**
operator's cab 786.
operculum 84, 86.
opisthodomos 169.
opposite prompt side 189.
optic chiasm 134.
optic nerve 140.
optical disc 527.
optical disc drive 527.
optical scanner 526.
optical sight 713.
or 819.
oral cavity 130, 131.
oral irrigator 373.
**orange 65.**
orange 65.
orbicularis oculi 120.
orbiculate 56.
**orbit of the satellites 43.**
**orbits of the planets 4.**
orchard 149.
orchestra pit 188.
orchestra seats 188.
order 175.
**ordinaries, examples 818.**
ordinary die 699.
ore 733.
ore pass 736.
oregano 74.
ORGAN 542.
**organ console 542.**
**organ, mechanism 543.**
**organ, production of sound 543.**
Oriental couching stitch 571.
oriflamme 817.
original overlay 532.
Orion 11, 13.
ornamental garden 193.
ornamental tree 148, 263.
**ornaments 538.**
ortho-stick 728.
oscillating sprinkler 264.
**other signs 539.**
**other techniques 576.**
otolith 88.
ottoman 222.
outdoor condensing unit 212.
outdoor light 196.
**outdoor unit 212.**
outer boundary line 616.
outer circle 620.
outer core 22.
outer edge 104.
outer jacket 297.
outer jib 481.
outer lip 94.
outer shell 309.
outer stators 501.
outer string 201.
outer table 697.
outer toe 108.
outgoing announcement cassette 420.
outlet grille 211.
outlet hose 399.
**output devices 527.**
output jack 547.
output monitor 413, 415.
outrigger 632.
outside counter 354.
outside knob 290.
outside linebacker 603.
outside mirror 426.
outside mirror control 429.
outside ticket pocket 322.
outsole 353, 355.
outwash plain 27.
oval cut 362.
ovary 60, 128, 129.
ovate 56.
oven 255.
oven control knob 255.
over curtain 229.
overburden 733.
overcast sky 39.
overcheck 653.
**overcoat 320.**
overcoat 331.
overflow 215, 292.
overflow pipe 293, 297.
overflow protection switch 257.
overflow tube 399.
overhand knot 691.
**overhead connection 757.**
overhead earth wire 756.
overhead frame 784.
overhead guard 787.
overhead switch panel 500.
overhead wires 459.
**overshirt 337.**
overtaking lane 452.
ovule 60.
ox 151.
oxer 646.
oxford shoe 354.
**oxyacetylene welding 306.**
oxygen control handle 306.
oxygen cylinder 306.
oxygen indicator 639.
oxygen pressure actuator 512.
oxygen supply regulator 639.
oxygen valve 306.
**oyster 92.**
oyster 93.
oyster fork 240.
oyster knife 242.
oyster mushroom 55.
ozone 19.

# P

Pacific Ocean 20.
Pacinian corpuscle 136.
packing 294.
packing retainer ring 294.
pad 598.
pad arm 376.
pad plate 376.
padding 635.
paddock 651.
pagoda sleeve 340.
paint cup 590.
**paint roller 304.**
paint spray 590.
**paintbrush 304.**
Painter's Easel 13.
PAINTING 588, 590, 592.
PAINTING ACCESSORIES 304.
painting knife 589.
**painting, accessories 591, 592.**
**painting, equipment 589.**
palatine tonsil 143.
palatoglossal arch 142.
pale 818.
palette knife 589.
palette with dipper 592.
palette with hollows 592.
paling fence 263.
pallet 543, 707, 787.
pallet spring 543.
pallet truck 788.
pallial line 95.
pallial sinus 95.
palm 105, 137, 327, 483, 596.
palm grove 46.
palmar pad 106.
palmate 56.
palmette 220.
pan 708, 709, 795.
pan cover 795.
pan hook 708.
panama 328.
pancake pan 249.
pancreas 131.
pane 203.
panel 202, 229, 323, 346, 589, 634, 649, 736, 756.
pannier bag 448.
panoramic head 393.
panoramic window 190, 460.
panpipe 536.
pantograph 458.
pantry 195.
panty corselette 347.
panty girdle 346.
papaya 68.
paper 384, 580, 589.
paper advance setting 531.
paper bail 524, 531.
paper bail release lever 525.
paper bail roller 531.
paper catcher 521.
paper clamp 531.
paper clips 515.
paper fasteners 515.
paper feed channel 521.
paper feed key 523.
paper guide 421, 531.
paper in reserve 532.
paper punch 516.
paper release lever 525.
paper support 525.
paper tray 521.
paper trays 532.
papilla 136, 140.
papillary muscle 125.
parabolic antenna 415.
parabolic dune 46.
parabolic mirror 770.
parabolic reflector 15.
parachute 812.
parachute valve 634.
parade ground 178.
paraffin 745.
paraffins 745.
PARAGLIDING 636.
paragliding pilot 636.
parallel 47.
**parallel bars 661.**
parapet 454.
parapet walk 181.
parcels office 462.
parentheses 832.
parietal bone 123.
parietal pleura 130.
paring knife 242.
paripinnate 56.
park 52, 184.
**parka 321.**
parka 680.
parking 190, 193.
parking area 503.
parking lot 185.
parsley 74.
parsnip 71.
partial eclipse 8.
partition 66, 520.
**partitions, examples 818.**
partlow chart 441.
**parts 220, 223, 224.**
**parts of spectacles 376.**
pass 27.
passenger cabin 493, 494, 495, 499.
**passenger car 477.**
passenger car 458, 476.
passenger platform 462.
PASSENGER STATION 462.
passenger station 464.
**passenger terminal 504.**
passenger terminal 491, 503.
passenger train 462.
passenger transfer vehicle 505, 507.
passing prohibited 824, 825.
passing through the eclipse 419.
passport case 379.
passport control 505.
pasta maker 243.
pastern 101.
pastry bag and nozzles 245.
pastry brush 245.
pastry cutting wheel 245.
pasture 148.
patch pocket 320, 322, 339, 350.
patella 103, 122.
patera 220.
path 263, 676.
patio 193, 263.
patio door 195.
**pattern 565.**
pattern 570, 586.
pattern start key 569.
pauldron 792.
pause 539.
pause button 403.
pause/still 411, 831.
pause/still key 411.
pavement 186.
pavilion 363.
pavilion facet (8) 363.
pavilion roof 183.
pawl 281.
Pawn 696.
**pay phone 422.**
payload 509.
payload bay 510.
payload bay door 510.
payload module 49.
payout tray 702.
payout trigger 702.
**pea 67.**
pea 67.
**pea jacket 330.**
**peach 63.**
peach 63.
Peacock 13.
peak 27, 328, 329, 729.
peak level meter 403.
peaked lapel 322.
peanut 66.
pear 64.
pear-shaped body 535.
pear-shaped cut 362.
pearl 105.
pearls 105.
pecan nut 66.
pecten 81.
pectoral deck 663.
pectoral fin 86.
pedal 446, 448, 545, 552, 553, 656, 664.
pedal key 542.
pedal keyboard 542.
**pedal pushers 336.**
pedal rod 540.
pedal spindle 448.
pedestal 453, 545.
PEDESTAL-TYPE CESSPIT PUMP 216.
pedestrian crossing 186, 826, 827.
pedicle 105.
pediment 166, 168, 707.
**pedometer 711.**
peduncle 60, 61, 62, 63, 64.
peel 65.
peeled veneer 288.
peeler 242.
peep hole 471.
peg 225, 385, 544, 546, 571, 575, 685, 686.
peg box 544.
peg loop 685, 686.
Pegasus 11.
**pelerine 330.**
pelerine 330.
**Pelham bit 650.**
pellets 799.
pelmet 229.
peltate 56.
**Pelton runner 754.**
pelvic fin 86.
pelvis 103.
pen 714.
pen holder 378, 379.
penalty arc 601.
penalty area 601.
penalty area marking 601.
penalty bench 608.
penalty line 612.
penalty spot 601.
pencil 389, 515.
pencil point tip 299, 307.
pencil sharpener 515, 516.
pencil-pleated heading 229.
pendant 361.
pendulum 707.
pendulum bar 539.
pendulum rod 707.
penholder grip 619.
peninsula 51.
penis 116, 127.
pennant 38, 817.
penstock 746, 747, 752.
pentaprism 390.
penumbra 8.
**peplos 315.**
pepperpot 238.
per bend 818.
per fess 818.
per pale 818.
percent 830.
percent key 523.
**perching bird 111.**
**percolator 247.**
percussion bar 780.
PERCUSSION INSTRUMENTS 552, 554.
perforated hardboard 289.
perforated pipe 216.
perforated toe cap 355.
perforation 327, 395.
pergola 263.
pericardium 130.
pericarp 65, 66.
period 489.
periodontal ligament 144.
peripheral device port 528.
peripheral joint 750.
**peripheral nervous system 133.**
periscopic sight 805.
peristyle 168, 169, 171.
peritoneum 127, 128.
peroxide 725.
perpendicular 830.

The terms in **bold type** correspond to an illustration; those in CAPITALS indicate a title.

perpetual snows 27.
Perseus 11.
personal communications 417.
personal computer 526.
**personal computer (view from above) 528.**
**personal radio cassette player 408.**
peseta 832.
pesticides 32.
pestle 243.
petal 60.
petanque bowl 682.
Peter Pan collar 341.
petiolar sinus 61.
petiole 56.
petrochemical industry 744.
petrochemicals 745.
petrol 745.
**petrol engine 434.**
**petrol pump 453.**
petrol pump 453.
petrol pump hose 453.
petrol station 823.
petrol tank 442.
petrol tank cap 444.
petroleum 744.
phalanx prima 103.
phalanx secunda 103.
phalanx tertia 103.
pharynx 130, 131.
phase conductor 757.
PHASES OF THE MOON 6.
philtrum 141.
phloem 59.
Phobos 4.
Phoenix 13.
phosphorescent coating 232.
PHOTOCOPIER 532.
photocopy control 532.
photoelectric cell 393.
**photographic accessories 393.**
photographic chamber 717.
PHOTOGRAPHY 390, 392, 394, 396, 398.
photosphere 6.
photovoltaic panel 486, 487.
**physical map 51.**
physician 669.
pi 830.
piano 556.
piccolo 548, 557.
pick 267, 385, 681.
pick-up arm 404.
pickguard 547.
pickling onion 70.
pickup cylinder 159, 162.
pickup reel 158, 160.
pickup selector 547.
pickup truck 425.
picnic area 823.
picnics prohibited 823.
**picture tube 410.**
pie tin 245.
piedmont glacier 27.
pier 174, 175, 454, 455, 739.
pierce lever 256.
pig 151.
piggyback flat truck 473.
pigsty 149.
pike pole 780.
pike position 624.
pile dwelling 165.
pillar 176, 545, 714, 736.
pillar buoy 487, 489.
**pillar drill 283.**
pillbox hat 329.
pillion footrest 443, 444.
**pillow 570.**
pillow 224, 570.
pillow cover 224.
pillowcase 224.
pilot 637, 814.
pilot gas tube 297.
pilot light 247, 252, 255, 256, 257.
pin 232, 233, 309, 563, 683, 780.
pin base 232.
pin block 540.
**pin cushion 563.**
pinafore 333.
pince-nez 377.
pinch 232.
pinch pleat 228.
pinch-pleated heading 229.
pine needles 58.
pine nut 66.
pine seed 58.
pineal body 134.
pineapple 68.
pinion 280, 707.
pink ball 673.
pinking shears 564.
pinnacle 175, 176, 181.
pinnatifid 56.
pinocytotic vesicle 115.
**pins 364.**
**pins, types 683.**
pip 62, 64, 65, 695.
**pipe 385.**
pipe 543.
pipe A 300.
pipe B 300.
pipe cleaners 385.
pipe coupling 301.
pipe cutter 299.
pipe diffusers 501.
pipe end 300.
pipe rack 385.
pipe section 205.
pipe threader 299.
**pipe tools 385.**
pipe wrench 299.
**pipe, cross section 385.**
pipe-wrapping insulation 287.
pipeline 740.
pipework 543.
Pisces the Fishes (February 19) 820.
pistachio nut 66.
**piste 666.**
pistil 60.
PISTOL 797.
pistol grip 795, 796, 798, 799.
pistol grip handle 280, 305.
pistol nozzle 264.
piston 432, 435, 436, 438.
piston lever 291.
piston release 291.
piston ring 434.
piston skirt 434.
pit 96, 405, 683.
**pitch 599.**
pitch 599.
pitch wheel 555.
pitched roof 182.
pitcher 597.
pitcher's mound 597.
pitcher's plate 597.
pitchfork comb 368.
pitching 748.
pitching wedge 678.
pith 59.
**pithead 734.**
pithead 736.
**piton 681.**
piton-carrier 680.
pitta bread 153.
pituitary gland 134.
pivot 311, 369, 374, 484, 485, 539, 564, 590, 719.
pivot cab 785.
pivot spindle 431.
placard board 471.
placing judge 621.
plain 51.
plain gypsum lath 286.
plain pole 230.
plain weave 576.
**plan reading, elevation 193.**
**plane 277.**
plane figure 580.
plane projection 50.
PLANETARIUM 16.
planetarium 184.
planetarium projector 16.
**planets 4.**
**planets, orbits 4.**
planks 646, 647.
plano-concave lens 722.
plano-convex lens 722.
PLANT CELL 115.
PLANT, STRUCTURE 57.
plantar 121.
plantar interosseous 120.
plantar pad 107.
**plantar surface of the hoof 104.**
PLANTING 158.
**planting 154.**
plasmodesma 115.
plaster bat 584.
plaster dressing 725.
plastic case 799.
plastic insulator 312.
**plastic pants 349.**
plastic-coated chipboard 289.
plastron 96.
plate 253, 393, 688.
plate crystal 36.
plate grid 439.
plateau 27, 51.
platen 524, 531, 579.
platen knob 525, 531.
platform 302, 457, 475, 504, 621, 709.
platform edge 462, 475.
platform entrance 463.
**platform ladder 302.**
platform number 462.
platform pallet truck 788.
platform shelter 464.
platform trolley 788.
play 411, 831.
play button 403, 408.
play key 411.
play/pause 405.
player 626.
player's number 602.
**player's stick 609.**
players' bench 604, 608, 610, 612, 613.
playing surface 619.
playing window 403.
PLEASURE GARDEN 263.
plectrum 535.
plenum 206, 207.
pleural cavity 130.
plexus of nerves 144.
plimsoll 355.
plinth 707.
plotter 527.
PLOUGHING 156.
**ploughing 154.**
plow anchor 483.
plug 280, 400, 401, 485.
plug adapter 374.
plug bayonet 794.
plug fuse 312.
plum 63.
plumber's snake 299.
PLUMBING 292, 294, 296, 298, 299, 300.
PLUMBING SYSTEM 215.
**plumbing tools 299.**
plumbing wrench 299.
plunger 299, 726.
plungerhead 159.
plunging neckline 343.
plus or minus 830.
plus/equals key 523.
Pluto 5.
ply 288.
pneumatic armlet 710.
**pneumatic drill 735.**
pneumatic-tyred guide wheel 476.
pneumatic-tyred running wheel 476.
pocket 378, 673, 679, 683.
**pocket calculator 523.**
pocket camera 395.
pocket handkerchief 322.
**pockets, types 339.**
podium 190.
**podium and basements 190.**
point 240, 242, 389, 544, 562, 567, 644, 671, 684, 697, 698.
point of interest 52.
point scale 524.
point wire 467.
pointed 174.
pointed tab end 324, 339.
pointer 213, 705, 708, 709.
points 464.
points lever 467.
points motor 467.
points signal 467.
poison 821.
**poisonous mushroom 55.**
poker 205.
poker die 699.
**poker, standard hands 695.**
polar axis 14.
**polar climates 45.**
polar ice cap 45.
polar lights 19.
polar orbit 43.
polar tundra 45.
**polar-orbiting satellite 43.**
polarizing filter 392.
Polaroid® Land camera 394.
pole 230, 479, 657.
pole grip 642.
pole shaft 642.
Pole Star 11.
pole tip 643.
**pole vault 657.**
pole vault 655.
poleyn 792.
police 822.
polished stone hand axe 791.
**political map 51.**
pollen basket 81.
pollen brush 80, 81.
pollen cell 82.
pollen press 81.
**pollution of food on and in the ground 32.**
**pollution, atmospheric 34.**
**pollution, food 32.**
polo collar 342.
polo dress 333.
polo neck 338, 642.
polo shirt 337, 615.
polo-neck sweater 326.
pomegranate 68.
pommel 649, 661, 666.
**pommel horse 661.**
poncho 331.
pond 263.
poniard 794.
pons Varolii 134.
pontoon 457, 738.
**pool 673.**
pool 772.
poop 478.
popping crease 599.
**poppy 67.**
**popular terms 62, 64, 65.**
porch 172, 177.
porch dome 172, 173.
pore 67, 115, 136.
Porro prism 719.
port 650, 764.
port glass 237.
port hand 488, 489, 497.
**portable CD radio cassette recorder 408.**
portable cellular telephone 422.
**portable fire extinguisher 780.**
portable shower head 292.
PORTABLE SOUND SYSTEMS 408.
portal 175.
portal bridge 455.
portal frame 455.
portal vein 124, 126.
porthole 496.
position light 459, 508.
position marker 546, 547.
position of the ligament 95.
positive charge 831.
positive contact 768, 769.
positive meniscus 722.
positive plate 439.
positive plate strap 439.
positive region 768.
positive terminal 439.
positive/negative junction 768.
post 572, 613, 618, 626, 773.
post binder 519.
post lantern 235.
**post mill 773.**
posterior chamber 140.
posterior end 95.
posterior root 135.
posterior rugae 119.
posterior semicircular canal 139.
**posterior view 121, 123, 129.**
postern 179, 181.
potato 71.
potato masher 244.
potential coil 712.
pothole 24.
POTTERY 584.
**pottery, tools 584, 585.**
pouch 380, 688.
pouch of Douglas 128.
poulaine 792.
poultry shears 246.
pound 832.
**powder blusher 366.**
powder chamber 801.
powder flask 795.
powder puff 366.
power button 402, 405, 410, 411.
power fed into the distribution network 755.
power indicator 529.
**power mower 271.**
power socket 401, 408.
power station 752.
power supply at generator voltage 755.
power switch 529, 555.
power takeoff 147.
**power train 448.**
power turbines 501.
power zoom button 409.
power-off/slide-select bar 397.
power-on button 420.
power-on light 420.
power-takeoff shaft 156, 159, 162.
power/light switch 561.
powerhouse 746.

The terms in **bold type** correspond to an illustration; those in CAPITALS indicate a title.

practice green 676.
prairie 51.
prawn 90.
prayer hall 172, 173.
**precious stones 363.**
precipitation 34, 35.
precipitation area 38.
PRECIPITATIONS 36.
preferred channel 489.
premaxilla 86.
premolar 98.
premolars 144.
preparation for the eclipse 419.
prepuce 127.
prescription 831.
present state of weather 38.
**present weather 39.**
preset buttons 411.
preset tuning button 402.
president 666.
press bar 663.
press bed 581, 583.
press chamber 159.
press wheel 158.
pressed area 405.
**pressed powder 366.**
presser bar 562.
**presser foot 562.**
presser foot 561, 562.
**pressing 579.**
pressing board 579.
pressure bar 540.
pressure change 38.
pressure control 373.
pressure control valve 710.
**pressure cooker 248.**
pressure demand regulator 777.
pressure dial 561.
pressure gauge 627, 710, 740.
pressure plate 390.
**pressure regulator 306.**
pressure regulator 248, 306, 689.
pressure relief valve 209.
pressure screw 581, 583.
pressure tube 765.
pressure vessel 762.
pressure-relief valve 297.
pressurized chamber 806.
pressurized heavy water 761.
**pressurized-water reactor 762.**
pressurizer 761.
prestressed concrete 286.
preview monitor 415.
preview monitors 413.
price per gallon/litre 453.
pricker 570.
primaries 110.
**primary consumers 31.**
primary covert 110.
primary flight display 500.
primary marshalling track 465.
primary mirror 14, 16.
primary root 57.
prime 667.
prime focus 14.
prime focus observing capsule 14.
prime meridian 47.
primer 798, 799, 804.
princess dress 332.
princess seaming 345.
**principal amphibians 85.**
**principal edible gastropods 83.**
**principal kinds of deer 105.**
principal rafter 199.
**principal techniques 588.**
**principal types of armchair 220.**
**principal types of berry 62.**
**principal types of bill 111.**
**principal types of carving blade 587.**
PRINCIPAL TYPES OF CEREAL 152.
**principal types of citrus fruit 65.**
**principal types of foot 111.**
**principal types of fork 240.**
PRINCIPAL TYPES OF HORN 99.
**principal types of interchange 450.**
**principal types of knife 239.**
**principal types of missile 814.**
**principal types of nut 66.**
**principal types of pome 64.**
**principal types of shoe 354.**
**principal types of spectacles 377.**
**principal types of spoon 241.**
**principal types of stone fruit 63.**
**principal types of table 219.**
**principal types of tent 686.**
**principal types of tropical fruit 68.**
PRINCIPAL TYPES OF TUSK 99.
print drying rack 399.
print head 531.
print head drive 531.
**print washer 399.**
printed circuit 528.
printed image 580.
**printer 421.**
printer 523.
printer port 528.
**printer table 521.**
PRINTING 580.
**printing calculator 523.**
printing head 524.
printing of messages 421.
printout 709.
priority intersection 825.
PRISM BINOCULARS 719.
private broadcasting network 416.
probe 310.
probe socket 253.
proboscis 79.
procedure checklist 512.
producer 412, 415.
producer console 407.
product code 709.
production adviser 412.
**production control room 413.**
production control room 412, 415.
production desk 413.
production of electricity by the generator 755.
**production of electricity from nuclear energy 766.**
**production of electricity from solar energy 771.**
**production platform 738.**
production platform 740.
production video switcher 413.
production/export riser system 738.
program selector 257, 259, 391, 555.
progressive wave 30.
**projectiles 801.**
projection dome 16.
**projection screen 397.**
proleg 78.
promenade deck 496.
prominence 6.
prompt box 188.
prompt side 189.
pronaos 168, 169.
prop forward 606.
propane gas cylinder 449.
**propane or butane appliances 689.**
propellant 798.
propellant level gauge 512.
propeller 160, 495, 496, 742, 806.
propeller duct 492.
propeller shaft 495.
propellers 808.
propelling pencil 389.
property line 193.
propulsion machinery control room 806.
propulsion module 418.
proscenium 188.
prostate 127.
protect tab 529.
protection layer 512.
protective casing 271.
protective cup 602, 609.
**protective equipment 602.**
protective girdle 609.
protective surround 698.
protective window 410.
prothorax 78.
protoneuron 135.
protractor 713.
province 51.
proximal phalanx 107, 122, 123.
proximal sesamoid 102.
proximity fuse 814.
pruning knife 269.
pruning saw 269.
psychrometer 41.
pubis 116, 118.
public building 52.
public garden 190.
**puck 608.**
puff sleeve 340.
pull handle 397.
pull rod 467.
pull strap 383.
pulley 230, 302, 434, 793.
pulley block 793.
pulling ring 726.
pulmonary artery 126, 130.
pulmonary opening 83.
pulmonary trunk 125.
pulmonary valve 125.
pulmonary vein 126.
pulp 65, 144.
pulp chamber 144.
**pulses 72.**
PULVERIZING 157.
**pulverizing 154.**
pulvino 750.
pumice correcting pencil 583.
pump 257, 258, 356, 689, 761, 762, 771.
pump motor 216.
pump nozzle 453.
pump room 742.
pump sprayer 265.
pump suction head 216.
**pumped hot-water system 208.**
**pumper 778.**
pumpernickel bread 153.
pumping station 740.
pumpkin 69.
punch 586.
punch hole 323, 353, 355.
PUNCTUATION MARKS 832.
pupil 107, 140.
pure alcohol 725.
purfling 544, 546.
purge valve 627.
purple border 315.
purpure 819.
purse 379.
push button 250, 257, 375.
push buttons 420, 422.
push rim 727.
push-button 290, 389, 397.
push-button telephone 422.
push-up bra 347.
push-up stand 664.
pusher 251.
**putter 677.**
putter 678.
pygal shield 96.
pyjamas 348.
**pylon 756.**
pylon body 756.
pylon foot 756.
pylon top 756.
pylon window 756.
pyloric caecum 88.
pyramid spot 675.
pyrometric cone 585.

## Q

Qibla wall 173.
quadruped stick 728.
quarte 667.
quarter 104, 352, 354.
quarter window 427.
quarter-deck 496.
quarterback 603, 605.
quarterly 818.
quartet 558.
**quartz metronome 539.**
quaver 538.
quaver rest 538.
quay 490.
quay ramp 490.
quayside crane 490.
quayside railway 491.
Queen 695, 696.
queen cell 82.
queen excluder 82.
Queen's side 696.
queen, honeybee 81.
question mark 832.
quiche tin 245.
quick release system 393.
quill 281, 283, 389.
quill brush 368.
quince 64.
quinte 667.
quintet 558.
quiver 684.
quotation marks 832.
quotation marks (French) 832.

## R

raceme 60.
rachis 110.
rack 248, 252, 257, 656, 674.
rackboard 543.
rackboard support 543.
RACQUETBALL 617.
**racquetball 617.**
**racquetball racket 617.**
**racquetball, court 617.**
RADAR 722.
radar 493, 494, 495, 497.
radar antenna 48, 807, 812.
radar antenna deployment 49.
radar mast 742.
radar reflector 487.
radar unit 813.
**Radarsat satellite 49.**
radial nerve 133.
radial thruster 42.
radial tyre 433.
radiant heater 211.
radiation zone 6.
**radiator 438.**
radiator 16, 208, 469.
radiator core 438.
radiator grille 440.
radiator hose 438.
radiator panel 510.
radicle 57, 59.
radio 639.
radio antenna 494, 495, 497, 742, 807.
radio mast 738.
radio section 408.
RADIO TELESCOPE 15.
radio wave 15.
radioactive 821.
radiometer 42, 43.
radish 71.
radius 102, 112, 122.
radome 813.
rafter 198.
**raglan 330.**
raglan sleeve 319, 330, 340, 350.
rail 225, 466, 568, 627, 675.
**rail joint 466.**
**rail section 466.**
rail shuttle service 504.
rail track 735.
rails 647.
railway 52, 184.
RAILWAY STATION 464.
railway station 52.
RAILWAY TRACK 466.
**railway track 466.**
rain 36.
rain cap 205.
**rain gauge recorder 40.**
**rain hat 329.**
rain shower 39.
rainbow 36.
**raincoat 319.**
raindrop 36.
**raining, utensils for 243.**
raised band 577.
raised figure 580.
raised head 276.
**rake 159.**
rake 155, 267.
rake bar 159.
rake comb 368.
Ram 11.
ramekin 238.
rammer 801.
ramp 168, 733.
rampart 178, 180.
ramrod 795.
random access memory (RAM) module 528.
rangefinder camera 394.
rapier 794.
rasp 587.
**raspberry, section 62.**
ratchet 276, 281, 573.
ratchet knob 711.
ratchet ring spanner 279.
ratchet wheel 573, 707.
rate gyro 814.
rattle 97.
**rattlesnake 97.**
razor clam 93.
RAZORS 374.
reaction direction 831.
reaction engine 43.
reactor 759, 764, 766, 806.
reactor building 759, 765.
reactor building airlock 758.
reactor core 760, 762, 763.
reactor tank 763.
reactor vessel 765.
read-only memory (ROM) module 528.
read/write head 529.
reading lens 376.
reading mirror 512.
READING PLANS 193, 195.
reading start 405.
rear apron 324.
rear beam 708.
rear brake 446.
rear brake pedal 444.

The terms in **bold type** correspond to an illustration; those in CAPITALS indicate a title.

rear bumper 445.
rear derailleur 446, 448.
rear foil 495.
rear indicator 443, 444.
rear leg 223.
rear light 429, 441, 443, 444, 446.
**rear lights 429.**
rear limit line 666.
rear runner 643.
**rear seat 428.**
rear sight 795, 796, 797, 798, 804.
**rear view 147.**
rearview mirror 430.
receiver 15, 420, 614, 616, 618.
receiver volume control 420.
receiving line 617.
receiving station 722.
receiving yard 465.
receptacle 60, 62.
reception bay 764.
reception hall 172, 173.
recharging base 260.
recliner 223.
reclining back 726.
recoil sleigh 802.
RECOILLESS RIFLE 804.
**record 404.**
record 411.
record announcement button 420.
record button 403, 411.
record control 402.
record muting button 403.
recorder 621.
recording level control 403.
recording tape 403.
recording unit 40.
rectangular 687.
rectangular flag 817.
rectum 127, 128, 131.
rectus femoris 120.
recuperator cylinder 802.
recuperator cylinder front head 802.
recyclable 831.
recycled 831.
Red 697.
red 700, 701.
red ball 673.
red balls 673.
red beam 410.
red flag 626, 668.
red ochre pencil 583.
red safelight filter 399.
Red Sea 21.
redcurrant 62.
reduce/enlarge 532.
reducing coupling 301.
redundant bracing 756.
reed 548, 572.
reed hooks 573.
**reed pipe 542.**
**reeds 549.**
reef band 480.
reef knot 691.
reef point 480.
reel 265, 398, 666, 702.
reel crank 265.
reel plate 702.
reel seat 670, 671.
referee 601, 603, 605, 606, 608, 610, 613, 621, 626, 668, 669.
refill 389.
refill pipe 293.
refinery 740.
**refinery products 744.**
reflecting surface 770.
REFLECTING TELESCOPE 720.
**reflecting telescope, cross section 720.**
reflective stripe 730, 777.
reflector 310, 441, 445, 446.
**reflex camera, cross section 390.**
REFRACTING TELESCOPE 721.
**refracting telescope, cross section 721.**
refractory brick 585.
refrigerant tank 212.
refrigerant tubing 213.
refrigeration unit 441.
**refrigerator 254.**
refrigerator compartment 254.
refrigerator van 472.
register 712.
registered trademark 831.
regulating button 541.
regulating valve 208.
regulator first stage 627.
regulator second stage 627.
rehearsal room 188.
reheater 758.
rein 651.
rein ring 650.
reindeer 105.
reinforced concrete 286.
reinforced edging 383.
reinforced toe 730.
release lever 278.
release setting screw 641.
release treadle 573.
**relief printing 580.**
RELIEF PRINTING PROCESS 581.
**relief printing process, equipment 581.**
relocation 525.
remote command antenna 49.
**remote control 411.**
remote control 397.
remote control sensor 405, 410.
remote control terminal 391.
REMOTE DETECTION SATELLITE 48.
remote-control arm 510.
**remote-controlled points 467.**
removable-bottomed tin 245.
renal artery 126, 132.
renal hilus 132.
renal papilla 132.
renal pelvis 132.
renal vein 126, 132.
reniform 56.
repair shop 453.
repeat keys 405.
repeat mark 537.
repeating groove 404.
REPTILE 96.
rerebrace 792.
reserve parachute 635.
reservoir 247, 543, 746, 747, 748, 749, 750, 751.
reservoir-nib pen 589.
reset 532.
reset button 297, 411, 706, 711.
reset key 421.
resin surface 405.
resistance adjustment 664.
resonator 406, 542, 554.
**respirator 730.**
RESPIRATORY SYSTEM 130.
RESPIRATORY SYSTEM PROTECTION 730.
respiratory system protection 821.
rest area 52.
**rest values 538.**
restaurant 185, 190, 494, 822.
**restaurant car 460.**
restricted area 610.
restricting circle 610.
retainer 735.
retaining ring 295.
retaining strap 383.
retarding magnet 712.
reticle 718.
retina 140.
retractable handle 378.
retractable step 449.
**retracted claw 107.**
retrenchment 178.
return 521.
return air 206, 207.
return crease 599.
return key 530.
return spring 432.
**reverse dive 625.**
reverse slide change 397.
reverse stitch button 561.
reversible reaction 831.
reversing device 212.
reversing light 429.
REVOLVER 797.
revolving cylinder 570.
revolving nosepiece 718.
**revolving sprinkler 264.**
rewind 411, 831.
rewind button 403, 408, 411, 420.
rhubarb 72.
rhythm selector 555.
rib 72, 97, 102, 129, 375, 544, 546, 729, 785.
rib pad 602.
rib stitch 567.
ribbing 326, 350, 670.
**ribbing plough 156.**
ribbing plough 154.
ribbon cartridge 531.
ribosome 115.
ribs 122, 584.
rice 152.
**rider 648.**
ridge 27.
**ridge tent 686.**
RIDING 648.
riding cap 648, 651.
riding coat 331.
riding crop 648.
riding glove 648.
riding jacket 648.
riffler 587.
**rifle (rifled bore) 798.**
rift 28.
**rigging 478.**
rigging wire 637.
right angle 830.
right ascension 3.
right ascension setting scale 720, 721.
right atrium 124, 125.
right back 607, 612.
right bronchus 130.
right centre 606.
right channel 401.
right cornerback 603, 605.
right defence 608.
right defensive end 603, 605.
right defensive tackle 603, 605.
right field 597.
right fielder 597.
right forward 610, 613.
right guard 603, 605, 610.
right half 607.
right halfback 603.
right inner 607.
right kidney 132.
right lung 124, 130.
right outside linebacker 605.
right pulmonary vein 125.
right safety 603.
right safety back 605.
right service court 614, 616.
right tackle 603, 605.
right ventricle 124, 125.
right wing 601, 606, 607, 608.
right winger 612.
rigid tube 260.
rim 147, 376, 433, 442, 447, 610, 658.
rim flange 433.
rim soup bowl 238.
rinceau 220.
rind 65.
**ring 669.**
ring 55, 230, 290, 375, 483, 551, 566, 660, 681, 706, 709, 754.
ring binder 519.
ring gate 753.
ring motorway 52.
ring nut 300.
ring post 669.
ring road 52.
ring spanner 279.
ring step 669.
ringhandle 369.
ringing volume control 420.
**rings 364, 660.**
ringside 669.
**rink 608, 620.**
rink 620, 682.
rink corner 608.
rinse-aid dispenser 257.
rip fence 284, 285.
rip fence guide 285.
rip fence lock 285.
rip fence rule 285.
rip fence slot 285.
ripeness 61.
ripening 61.
ripper 783.
ripper cylinder 783.
ripper tip 783.
ripper tooth 783.
rise 201.
riser 201, 636.
rising main 215.
river 51, 52.
River Eridanus 13.
rivet 242, 278.
road 52.
road communications 417.
**road map 52.**
road narrows 827.
road number 52.
ROAD SIGNS 824, 826, 828.
ROAD SYSTEM 450, 452.
**road tanker 742.**
road transport 491.
road works ahead 826, 827.
**road, cross section 450.**
roadway 186, 450.
roadway narrows 826.
roasting pans 248.
**Roberval's balance 708.**
rock 30.
rock basin 26.
rock garden 263.
rock step 26.
rocker arm 435.
ROCKET 509.
rocket motor 814.
rocking chair 221, 223.
rocking tool 582.
rocky desert 46.
rod 214, 539, 573.
**rodent's jaw 98.**
roll 341.
roll film 395.
roll-up blind 231.
roller 230, 231, 270, 369, 530, 583, 788.
**roller blind 231.**
roller board and arms 543.
roller frame 304.
ROLLER SKATE 645.
roller sleeve 304.
rolling ladder 303.
rolling pin 245.
rolling stock cleaning yard 465.
rolling stock repair shop 465.
Roman blind 231.
ROMAN HOUSE 170.
**Roman legionary 791.**
Roman metal pen 389.
Romanian couching stitch 571.
rompers 349, 351.
roof 82, 171, 197, 205, 427, 470, 733.
roof pole 686.
roof section 82.
roof timber 168.
**roof truss 199.**
roof vent 196, 215, 449.
roofing felt 286.
ROOFS 182.
room 736.
**room air conditioner 214.**
**room thermostat 213, 705.**
rooster 150.
root 70, 143, 144, 240.
root canal 144.
root cap 57.
root hairs 57.
root of nail 137.
root rib 498.
root system 57, 61.
**root vegetables 71.**
root-hair zone 59.
rope 361, 669, 680, 692.
rope ladder 303.
rope, skipping- 665.
rose 265, 289, 290, 546.
rose cut 362.
rose window 175.
rosemary 74.
rosette 167.
rostrum 90.
**rotary engine 437.**
rotary file 516.
rotary hoe 157.
**rotary system 737.**
rotary table 737.
rotating auger 160, 162.
rotating dome 14.
rotating dome truck 14.
**rotating drum 714.**
rotating light 781.
rotating track 15.
rotating wheel 701.
rotation of the turbine 755.
**Rotavator 272.**
rotor 161, 290, 437, 753, 773, 774.
rotor blade 508.
rotor head 508.
rotor hub 508.
rotunda 190.
rotunda roof 183.
rough 676.
roughing out 586.
roulette 582.
ROULETTE TABLE 700.
round brush 368.
round end pin 231.
round eye 566.
round head 276.
round ligament of uterus 129.
round neck 343.
round pronator 120.
roundabout 52.
route board 471, 743.
**router 283.**
row 373.
row counter 568.
row number display 569.
**rowing (one oar) 632.**
ROWING AND SCULLING 632.
**rowing boats 632.**

The terms in **bold type** correspond to an illustration; those in CAPITALS indicate a title.

**rowing machine 664.**
rowlock 632.
royal agaric 55.
royal antler 105.
royal flush 695.
rub rail 441.
rubber boot 777.
rubber bulb 726.
rubber ferrule 728.
rubber gasket 296.
rubber mat 404.
**rubber snaffle bit 650.**
rubber stamp 516.
rubber stopper 302.
rubber thread 677.
ruby 363.
ruching 349.
rucksack 680.
rudder 492, 496, 499, 511, 628, 639, 742, 812, 814.
rudder pedal 639.
Ruffini's corpuscule 136.
ruffle 317.
ruffled skirt 334.
RUGBY 606.
**rugby ball 606.**
**rugby, field 606.**
ruler 578, 591, 688.
rump 109.
run 201, 599.
run-off groove 404.
run-up 654, 655, 657.
rung 302.
runner 643, 697, 753.
runner blade 752, 753, 754.
running 654.
running bowline 691.
running rail 476.
**running shoe 352.**
running shoe 656.
running surface 466.
running track 786.
**runway 504.**
runway 476, 811.
runway centre line markings 504.
runway designation marking 504.
runway side stripe markings 504.
runway threshold markings 505.
runway touchdown zone marking 505.
Russian black bread 153.
rye 152.
rye crispbread 153.

## S

S-band antenna 43.
S-band high gain antenna 42.
S-band omnidirectional antenna 42.
sabaton 792.
sable 819.
sabre 666, 794.
sabre and épée warning line 666.
sabreur 667.
sacral plexus 133.
sacral vertebrae 103.
sacrum 122, 123.
**saddle 649.**
saddle 397, 446, 636, 648, 651, 661.
saddle pad 648.
saddle pillar 446.
saddlecloth 648, 651.
**safari jacket 338.**
safe water mark 489.
safelight 398.
safest water 488.
safety area 668.
**safety binding 641.**
**safety boot 730.**
safety cage 654.
safety cap 804.
safety catch 796.
safety chain 449.
**safety earmuff 729.**
safety glasses 729.
safety goggles 729.
safety handle 271.
SAFETY JACKET 730.
safety line 475.
safety match 386.
safety pad 659.
safety pin 566.
safety rail 302, 468.
safety scissors 365.
safety suit connection 512.
SAFETY SYMBOLS 821.
safety tank 761.
safety tether 512.
safety thermostat 259.
safety thong 617.
safety valve 248, 766.
sage 74.
**sagittal section 127, 128, 129, 142.**
Sagittarius the Archer (November 22) 820.
sail 631, 637, 773.
sail cloth 773.
sail panel 628.
sail plane 807.
sailbar 773.
SAILBOARD 631.
SAILING 628, 630.
**sailing boat 628.**
**sailing, points 629.**
sailor collar 342.
sailor tunic 337.
**sails 480.**
salad bowl 238.
salad crisper 254.
salad dish 238.
salad fork 240.
salad plate 238.
salad spinner 243.
salamander 85.
salient angle 178.
salivary glands 131.
salsify 71.
salt lake 46.
salt marsh 30.
salt taste 143.
saltcellar 238.
sample 567.
sand 748.
sand island 30.
sand shoe 441.
sand wedge 678.
sandal 357, 791.
sandbank 30.
sandbox 469.
sandstorm or dust storm 39.
sandy desert 46.
saphenous nerve 133.
sapphire 363.
sapwood 59.
sarong 334.
sartorius 120.
sash frame 203.
sash window 203.
**satchel bag 380.**
satellite 416.
SATELLITE BROADCASTING 416.
satellite terminal 503.
satin weave 576.
Saturn 5.
saucepan 249, 688.
sauté pan 249.
savory 74.
**sawing-in 578.**
sawtooth roof 182.
saxhorn 551.
**saxophone 548.**
saxophone 548.
**scale 537.**
scale 87, 96, 97, 111, 705, 711, 719, 726.
scale leaf 70.
scalelike leaves of the cypress 58.
scallop 93.
scampi 91.
scan 405.
Scandinavian crispbread 153.
scapula 102, 122, 123.
scapular 110.
scarp 178.
scatter cushion 224.
scattered cloud 39.
scenery lift 188.
scenery storage 188.
scenic route 52.
school 827.
school zone 826.
schooner 482.
sciatic nerve 133.
scientific instruments 16, 511.
**scientific terms 62, 64, 65.**
**scissors 564.**
scissors 688, 725.
scissors cut 362.
scissors-glasses 377.
sclera 140.
sconce 236.
scoop 385.
score-console 683.
scoreboard 698.
scorer 610, 613, 666, 668.
scoring light 666.
Scorpio the Scorpion (October 24) 820.
Scorpion 13.
scotia 166, 167.
**scraper 304, 784.**
scraper 582, 583.
scraper bar holder 583.
screen 161, 374, 397, 410, 747.
screen case 397.
screen print 350.
screen window 685.
**screw 276.**
screw 544.
screw cap 232.
screw earrings 361.
screw locking nut 670, 671.
screw-in studs 600.
**screwdriver 276.**
screwdriver 688.
screwsleeve 681.
**scrimmage 603.**
**scrimmage in Canadian football 605.**
script assistant 412.
scroll 544.
scroll case 747.
scroll foot 220.
scrotum 116, 127.
scrum half 606.
**scuba diver 627.**
SCUBA DIVING 627.
scuff rib 433.
scuffle hoe 266.
**sculling (two oars) 632.**
**sculling boats 632.**
scuttle panel 426.
scythe 267.
sea 7, 51, 752.
sea anchor 483.
Sea Goat 13.
sea level 22, 28.
Sea Serpent 13.
sea side 752.
sea-level pressure 38.
sea-to-sea missile 809.
seal 295.
sealed cell 82.
sealing ring 741.
seam 327, 384, 598.
seam allowance 565.
seam gauge 563.
seam line 565.
seam pocket 330, 339.
seaming 322.
seamount 29.
search-and-rescue antennas 43.
SEASONS OF THE YEAR 8.
seat 220, 223, 292, 293, 428, 445, 584, 639, 649, 652, 664, 727.
seat adjuster lever 428.
seat back 428.
seat back adjustment knob 428.
seat belt 428.
seat cover 293.
seat stay 446.
seat tube 446.
seat-belt warning light 431.
SEATS 222.
sebaceous gland 136.
secateurs 269.
second 537, 669, 830.
second base 597.
second baseman 597.
second dorsal fin 86.
second focal room 15.
second hand 706.
second linesman 613.
second molar 144.
second premolar 144.
second reinforce 800.
second space 610.
second stage 509.
second valve slide 550.
second violins 556.
secondaries 110.
secondary channel 489.
**secondary consumers 31.**
secondary inlet 741.
secondary marshalling track 465.
secondary mirror 16, 390.
secondary reflector 15.
secondary road 52.
secondary root 57.
seconde 667.
**secretarial desk 521.**
secretary 612, 626.
**section of a bulb 70.**
**section of a pome 64.**
security check 504.
security trigger 272.
sedimentary rocks 23.
seed 62, 63, 64, 65, 66, 67.
seed coat 63, 152.
**seed drill 158.**
seed drill 154.
seeder 268.
segment 65.
segment score number 698.
seismic wave 23.
seismogram 714.
self-adhesive labels 518.
self-contained breathing apparatus 777.
self-inflating mattress 687.
self-timer indicator 391.
selvage 566.
semaphore signal 464.
semi-circle 610.
semi-detached houses 187.
semi-fisheye lens 392.
semi-mummy 687.
semi-submersible platform 739.
semibreve 538.
semibreve rest 538.
**semicircular arch 174.**
semicolon 832.
semimembranosus 121.
seminal vesicle 127.
**semiprecious stones 363.**
semiquaver 538.
semiquaver rest 538.
semitendinosus 121.
**semitrailer 441.**
semitrailer 440, 742.
SENSE ORGANS 136, 138, 140, 141.
SENSES OF SMELL 142.
SENSES OF TASTE 142.
sensor probe 253.
**sensory impulse 135.**
sensory neuron 134.
sensory receptor 134.
sensory root 135.
sent document recovery 421.
sepal 60, 62, 64.
separating groove 404.
separator 439, 742, 758.
separator steam release 758.
septal cartilage of nose 141.
SEPTIC TANK 216.
septime 667.
septum 67, 141.
septum pellucidum 134.
sequencer control 555.
serac 26.
Serpent 11, 13.
Serpent Bearer 11, 13.
serrate 56.
server 613, 614, 616, 618.
service area 52, 503, 613.
service bay 453.
service box 616, 617.
service box line 617.
service building 764.
service judge 614, 618.
service line 614, 616, 617.
service module 418, 509.
service road 502.
service room 172, 173.
SERVICE STATION 453.
**service station 453.**
service zone 617.
serving dish 238.
serving trolley 219.
sesame seeded pitta 153.
set 525.
**set of utensils 244.**
set-in sleeve 324, 326.
**set-up 683.**
set-up 683.
setsquare 275.
setting 364.
setting indicator 641.
SEVENTEENTH-CENTURY CANNON 800.
**seventeenth-century mortar 803.**
seventh 537.
sew-through buttons 566.
sewer 186.
SEWING 561, 562, 564, 566.
**sewing 578.**
**sewing frame 578.**
**sewing machine 561.**
**sewing, accessories 563, 564.**
sewn-in groundsheet 685, 686.
**sextant 484.**
Sextant 13.
sextet 558.
shackle 630.
shade 234, 236.
shadow 706.
shadow key 396.
shady arcades 173.

The terms in **bold type** correspond to an illustration; those in CAPITALS indicate a title.

shaft 38, 166, 575, 584, 609, 615, 632, 652, 658, 674, 675, 677, 681, 684, 698, 705, 753, 808.
shaft head 734.
shaft holder 653.
shake-hands grip 619.
shallot 70, 542.
shallow root 59.
sham 224.
shank 275, 276, 281, 369, 385, 483, 562, 563, 564, 567, 568, 671.
shank button 566.
shank protector 783.
shaped handle 370.
shapka 328.
share 156.
sharp 538.
sharpening steel 242.
**shaving brush 374.**
shaving mug 374.
shawl collar 341.
sheath 56, 101, 106, 690, 692.
sheath dress 332.
sheath of Schwann 135.
sheath skirt 334.
sheathing 198, 199.
shed 193, 263.
shed stick 574.
sheep 150.
sheep shelter 149.
sheepshank 691.
sheepskin jacket 321.
sheepskin noseband 651.
sheer curtain 229.
sheet 480, 577.
sheet bend 691.
sheet film 395.
sheet lead 630.
sheet of paper 714.
shekel 832.
shelf 226, 254, 255, 302.
shelf channel 254.
**shell 96.**
shell 66, 83, 92, 109, 383, 553, 643, 741.
shell membrane 109.
**shell, valve 95.**
shield 791.
**shield divisions 818.**
shift key 524, 530.
shift lock key 524, 530.
shin boot 648, 652.
shin guard 595, 600.
shin pad 609.
shingle 286.
**ship's anchor 483.**
Ship's Keel 13.
ship's launch 809.
Ship's Sails 13.
ship's side 743.
Ship's Stern 13.
shirred heading 229.
**shirt 324.**
shirt 349, 656.
shirt collar 341.
shirt sleeve 340.
shirttail 324, 337.
shirtwaist dress 333.
shock absorber 445.
shoe 397.
shoe polish 358.
**shoe polisher 358.**
**shoe rack 358.**
**shoe, parts 354.**
shoebrush 358.
**shoehorn 358.**
shoelace 352, 354.
SHOES 354, 356, 358.
**shoes, accessories 358.**
**shoes, major types 355, 356.**
**shoeshine kit 358.**
**shoetree 358.**
shoot 57, 59.
shooting adjustment keys 409.
shooting star 19.
shop 170.
shopping bag 381.
shore 30.
short extensor of toes 120.
short glove 327.
short line 616, 617.
short palmar 120.
short peroneal 121.
short radial extensor of wrist 121.
short service line 618.
short sleeve 318.
short sock 344.
**short splice 692.**
shorts 336, 351, 600, 656, 662.
shortstop 597.
**shot 658.**
shot 801.
shot put 655.
**shotgun (smooth-bore) 799.**
shoulder 100, 106, 116, 118, 279, 451, 545, 615, 670.
**shoulder bag 380.**
shoulder bag with zip 380.
shoulder belt 428.
shoulder blade 117, 119.
**shoulder bolt 279.**
shoulder pad 602, 609, 804.
shoulder rest 804.
shoulder strap 346, 375, 380, 382, 679.
shovel 205, 266, 640, 642.
SHOW-JUMPING 646.
**show-jumping course 646.**
shower 194.
shower cubicle 292.
shower head 292, 296.
shower hose 292, 296.
shroud 479, 628.
shutoff valve 293, 296, 298.
shutter 203, 529, 772.
shutter release button 391.
shutter speed setting 396.
shutting stile 202.
**shuttle 573.**
shuttle 510.
**shuttlecock 618.**
sickle 269.
side 239, 479, 787.
side back vent 322.
SIDE CHAIR 223.
side chapel 176.
side door 477.
side electrode 439.
**side face 363.**
side footboard 469.
side handle 280.
side handrail 477.
side judge 605.
side ladder 470.
side lane 452.
side line 619.
side marker light 429, 440, 441.
side mirror 368.
side panel 319.
side plate 238.
side post 199.
side rail 302, 441.
side span 456.
side vent 25, 449.
**side view 442.**
side wall 104, 470, 492, 616, 617, 621.
side wall line 616.
side-tilt lock 393.
sideboard 227.
sideline 604, 607, 610, 611, 612, 613.
sidepiece 376.
sideshoot 57.
sidewall 433, 441.
siding 464.
sieve 161.
sifter 245.
SIGHT 140.
sight 684, 719, 803.
sighting line 719.
sighting mirror 719.
sigmoid colon 131.
signal ahead 826.
signal background plate 471.
signal box 464.
signal gantry 464.
signal lamp 585.
signature 577.
signet ring 364.
SIGNS OF THE ZODIAC 820.
silencer 439, 443, 444, 735.
**silique, section 67.**
silk 72.
sill 24, 199.
sill of frame 203.
sill plate 198, 199.
sill rail 198.
sill step 470.
silos 490.
sima 166.
simple eye 78, 80, 81.
**simple leaves 56.**
single curtain rail 230.
single pole circuit breaker 312.
single quotation marks 832.
single reed 549.
single scull 632.
single seat 477.
single twist 281.
single zero 700, 701.
**single-breasted jacket 322.**
single-burner camp stove 689.
single-decked pallet 787.
**single-leaf bascule bridge 457.**
**single-lens reflex (SLR) camera 391.**
single-lens reflex camera 394.
single-span beam bridge 454.
singles pole 614.
singles service court 618.
singles sideline 614, 618.
singlet 662.
sinister 818.
sinister base 818.
sinister chief 818.
sinister flank 818.
sink 296.
**sink with waste disposal unit 296.**
sinker 486, 672.
sinus 315.
siphon 24.
siphonal canal 94.
**site plan 193.**
sitting room 195.
sixte 667.
sixth 537.
skate 609.
skate guard 644.
SKATING 644.
skeg 631.
SKELETON 122.
**skeleton, horse 102.**
ski 445, 641.
**ski boot 641.**
ski boot 640.
ski glove 640.
ski goggles 640.
ski hat 640, 642.
**ski pants 336.**
ski pole 640, 642.
ski stop 640, 641.
ski suit 640, 642.
ski tip 642.
skid 508.
skimmer 244.
**skin 136.**
skin 62, 63, 64, 84, 134.
skin surface 137.
skip 620, 736, 784.
skipping-rope 665.
skirt 331, 615, 649, 792.
skirt finger 493.
skirt marker 564.
skirting board 199, 201.
skirting outlet 207.
skull 88, 102, 116, 134, 792.
skullcap 328.
**sky diver 635.**
SKY DIVING 635.
skylight 194, 197.
skyscraper 185.
slab 288.
**slab building 584.**
slagheap 734.
**slalom ski 633.**
slash 832.
slat 231, 571.
slat tilt device 231.
sled 264, 643.
sleeper 466.
sleeper-cab 440.
**sleeping bags 687.**
**sleeping car 460.**
sleeping compartment 460.
**sleepsuit 350.**
sleet 37, 39.
sleeve 318, 322, 663, 667.
sleeve strap 319.
sleeve strap loop 319.
**sleeves, types 339, 340.**
slice 244.
**slide 397.**
slide 257, 397, 566, 797.
slide chair 467.
slide magazine 397.
slide mount 397.
slide plate 561, 562.
**slide projector 397.**
slide-bar 568.
slider 543.
sliding breech 802.
sliding channel 470.
**sliding cheek bit 650.**
sliding cover 484.
sliding door 202, 292.
sliding folding window 203.
sliding overlap arm 230.
sliding rail 428, 630.
sliding seat 664.
sliding weight 539, 708.
sliding window 203.
slight drifting snow at ground level 39.
slightly covered sky 39.
sling back shoe 356.
slip 345.
slip joint 278.
**slip joint pliers 278.**
slip-on 355.
slip-on pyjamas 351.
slip-stitched seam 324.
slipover 326.
slippery road 826, 827.
sliproad 452.
slit 576.
slope 451.
sloped turret 183.
sloping cornice 168.
slot 188, 240, 252, 276, 379, 578.
slotback 605.
slow lane 452.
**slow-burning stove 204.**
slow-motion 411.
sludge 216.
small blade 688.
small detached house 187.
small drawstring bag 380.
small hand cultivator 268.
**small intestine 131.**
SMELL 141.
smock 337.
smoke 39.
smoke baffle 204.
smoke bomb discharger 805.
SMOKING ACCESSORIES 384, 386.
**smoking-apparatus 582.**
**snaffle bit 650.**
snaffle bit 649.
snaffle rein 649.
snaffle strap 649.
**snail 83.**
snail dish 246.
snail tongs 246.
snap 672.
**snap fastener 566.**
snap fastener 321, 327, 379.
snap shackle 630.
snap-fastening front 350.
snap-fastening tab 321.
snap-fastening waist 350.
snare 553.
**snare drum 553.**
snare drum 552, 557.
snare head 553.
snare strainer 553.
snelled fishhook 672.
**snooker 673.**
snorkel 627.
snout 84.
snow 34.
**snow crystals, classification 36.**
snow gauge 41.
snow guard 445.
snow pellet 37.
snow shower 39.
**snowmobile 445.**
SNOWSHOE 645.
**snowsuit 351.**
snuggle suit 349.
soap dish 292.
**soccer, playing field 601.**
sock 344, 602, 615.
socket 309, 566.
socket bayonet 794.
socket head 276.
socket tester 310.
**socks 325.**
sofa 221.
soft palate 141, 142.
soft pastel 588.
soft pedal 540, 555.
soft ray 87.
soft shell clam 93.
soft-drink dispenser 453.
soil 750.
soil and waste stack 215.
solar array 42, 48, 418.
solar array deployment 48, 419.
solar array drive 42.
solar array extended 48.
**solar cell 768.**
solar cell 523, 769.
solar cell panel 769.
solar cells 42.
solar collector 772.
SOLAR ECLIPSE 8.
SOLAR ENERGY 768, 770, 772.
**solar furnace 770.**
**solar house 772.**
solar panel 16.

ENGLISH INDEX

The terms in **bold type** correspond to an illustration; those in CAPITALS indicate a title.

solar radiation 768, 769, 770, 771, 772.
solar ray reflected 770, 771.
solar reflectors 418.
solar shield 512.
SOLAR SYSTEM 4.
**solar-cell system 769.**
solder 307.
SOLDERING 305, 306.
**soldering gun 305.**
soldering iron 305.
sole 104, 325, 641, 644, 678.
soleplate 256, 466.
soleus 120.
solid body 547.
solid rubber tyre 788.
solid shot 801.
solid-rocket booster 510.
solitaire ring 364.
solvent extraction unit 744.
sorghum 152.
sostenuto pedal 540.
sou'wester 329.
sound alarm 485.
sound console 407, 415.
sound control room 412, 415.
sound desk 412.
sound digitizing processor 528.
sound hole 544.
sound monitor 412, 413, 415.
sound monitoring selector 413.
sound receiver 726.
**sound reproducing system, components 400.**
sound signal 539.
sound system 430.
sound technician 412, 415.
sound/video preview unit 413.
soundboard 535, 540, 544, 545, 546.
soundbox 545.
soup bowl 238.
soup spoon 241.
soup tureen 238.
sour taste 143.
sources of pollution 34.
South 488.
South America 20.
South cardinal mark 489.
South celestial pole 3.
South Pole 3.
Southeast 488.
Southern Cross 13.
Southern Crown 13.
Southern Fish 13.
Southern hemisphere 3, 47.
Southern Triangle 13.
Southwest 488.
sow 151.
soybeans 72.
space 537.
space bar 525, 530.
space probe 19.
SPACE SHUTTLE 510.
**space shuttle at takeoff 510.**
**space shuttle in orbit 510.**
spacelab 511.
spacer 727, 765.
SPACESUIT 512.
**spade 632.**
spade 266, 695, 803.
spadix 60.
spaghetti tongs 246.
spandrel 174.
spanker 480.
spar 498.
spar buoy 489.
spark 436.
**sparking plug 439.**
sparking plug 271, 435, 437, 439.
sparking plug body 439.
sparking plug gap 439.
sparking plug gasket 439.
spatial dendrite 36.
spatula 244, 581.
spatulate 56.
speaker 408, 420, 500.
speaker cover 401.
speaker selector 402.
spear 72, 791.
special mark 489.
specification plate 280.
specimen chamber 717.
specimen positioning control 717.
SPECTACLES 376.
spectacles case 379.
spectrometer 717.
speed control 250.
speed controller 561.
speed course 646.
speed selector 251, 404.
speed selector switch 370.
speed skate 644.
speedbrake lever 500.
speedometer 431, 445, 664.
spelling corrector 524.
spencer 338.
spent fuel discharge bay 758.
spent fuel port 764.
spent fuel storage bay 758, 764, 765.
spermatic cord 127.
**spermatozoon 127.**
sphenoidal sinus 141.
sphere support 40.
sphincter muscle of anus 131.
**sphygmomanometer 710.**
spicules 6.
spider 77.
spike 60, 466, 656, 680, 681.
spike file 516.
spiked shoe 595.
spillway 746.
spillway chute 746.
spillway gate 746.
spinach 73.
spinal column 89, 122, 134.
spinal cord 89, 134, 135.
spinal ganglion 135.
spinal nerve 135.
spindle 223, 251, 290, 294, 404, 707, 711, 712.
spine 577.
spine of scapula 123.
spine of the book 579.
**spinner 672.**
**spinning rod 671.**
spinous process 135.
spiny lobster 91.
spiny ray 86.
spiracle 78, 79.
spiral 276.
spiral arm 9.
spiral beater 250.
spiral binder 519.
spiral case 753.
spiral galaxy 9.
spiral rib 94.
**spiral screwdriver 276.**
spiral staircase 741.
spiral-in groove 404.
spire 94, 175.
spirit level 291.
spit 30.
splash plate 741.
splat 220.
splay 175.
spleen 88, 124.
splenius muscle of head 121.
splints 725.
split bet 700, 701.
split end 603, 605.
split link 672.
spoiler 442, 498.
spoke 447.
spoked wheel 652.
sponge 801.
sponge-tipped applicator 367.
**sponges 367.**
spool 570, 670, 671.
spool pin 561.
spool rack 575.
**spoon 241.**
spoon 688.
spoon blade 587.
spores 55.
sports car 425.
SPORTSWEAR 352.
spot 235.
spotlight 147, 414, 777, 778, 780.
**spotmeter 396.**
spout 162, 247, 252, 294, 295.
spout assembly 296.
spray 256.
spray arm 257.
spray button 256.
spray control 256.
**spray gun 304.**
spray nozzle 264, 741.
sprayer 264.
**spread collar 324.**
spreader 270, 375.
spreader adjustment screw 304.
spring 8, 234, 258, 278, 290, 294, 389, 469, 659, 804.
**spring balance 709.**
spring binder 519.
spring housing 230.
spring linkage 702.
spring onion 70.
spring toggle 276.
spring washer 278.
springboard 659.
springer 174.
sprinkler hose 265.
sprinklers 766.
sprocket 445.
sprocket wheel 783, 805.
sprung base 224.
sprung strip metal insulation 287.
spur 27, 80, 281, 552, 648.
squall 39.
square 577.
square bet 700, 701.
square brackets 832.
square flag 817.
square head plug 301.
square move 696.
square neck 343.
square root key 523.
square root of 830.
square sail 482.
square trowel 291.
square-headed tip 276.
square-jawed adjustable spanner 299.
SQUASH 616.
**squash ball 616.**
**squash racket 616.**
**squash, court 616.**
stabilizer 636, 684, 727.
stabilizer fin 496.
stabilizing fin 509.
stabilizing leg 788.
stable 651.
stack 30.
stacking chairs 223.
stadium 185.
**staff 537.**
staff 817.
**stage 189.**
stage 188, 717, 718.
stage clip 718.
stage curtain 188, 189.
stained glass 175.
STAIRS 201.
stairs 194, 474, 741.
stairwell 194.
stake 263.
stake pocket 441.
stalactite 24.
stalagmite 24.
stalk 62, 63, 64, 72.
**stalk vegetables 72.**
stalls 189.
stamen 60, 64.
stamp 384.
stamp pad 516.
stamp rack 516.
stanchion 644.
**stand 651.**
stand 236, 248, 250, 341, 370, 382, 552, 586, 714.
stand-up collar 342.
standard A 539.
standard lamp 236.
**standard lens 392.**
**standardbred pacer 652.**
standby airspeed indicator 500.
standby altimeter 500.
standby attitude indicator 500.
**standing press 579.**
standpipe 298.
stapes 138.
staple remover 515.
stapler 515.
staples 515.
**star anise 67.**
star diagonal 721.
star facet (8) 363.
star tracker 16.
starboard hand 488, 489, 497.
starch 152.
starch granule 115.
start 532.
start and finish 646.
start button 706.
start key 421.
start line 656.
start switch 259.
start wall 621.
start-up key 530.
starter 271, 272, 621.
starter button 444.
starter handle 272.
starting bar (backstroke) 621.
**starting block 621, 656.**
starting block 621.
starting cable 270.
starting dive 622.
starting furlong 651.
starting line 655.
starting position 625.
state 51.
station circle 38.
station concourse 462.
station entrance 474.
station name 474.
station platform 464.
stationary bowl 701.
stationary front 39.
STATIONERY 515, 516, 518.
stationery cabinet 522.
stator 290, 753.
stay 479.
stay ring 753.
stay vane blade 753.
stays 456.
staysail-stay 479.
steak knife 239.
steam generator 759, 761, 762, 771, 806.
steam generator room cooler 759.
**steam iron 256.**
steam outlet 760, 761, 762, 763.
steam pressure drives turbine 767.
steam release pipes 759.
steel 286, 346, 795.
steel bar 660.
steel pen 389.
steel safety wheel 476.
steel spring 795.
steel to plastic 301.
**steelyard 708.**
steep hill 826, 827.
steeplechase 655.
steeplechase hurdle 656.
steering axle 788.
steering cylinder 784.
steering lever 788.
steering tube 447.
steering wheel 147, 430.
stellar crystal 36.
stem 55, 57, 70, 232, 247, 385, 479, 705.
stem bulb 497.
step 147, 302, 440.
step chair 222.
step cut 362.
step groove 201.
step setting 711.
step stool 302.
**stepladder 302.**
STEPLADDERS 302.
steppe 45.
stepper 664.
**steps 586.**
steps 773.
STEPS IN SOIL CULTIVATION 154.
**steps in the production of electricity 755.**
**steps to ripeness 61.**
stereo control 408.
stereo phase monitor 413.
STEREO SOUND SYSTEM 400, 402, 404.
stereoscopic camera 395.
sterile dressing 725.
stern 496, 631.
stern post 742.
sternocleidomastoid 120.
sternum 102, 122.
**stethoscope 726.**
steward's desk 461.
STICK 375.
**stick 607.**
stick 375, 544.
stick eraser 515.
**stick umbrella 375.**
stickpin 364.
**sticks 728.**
sticks 553.
stifle 101.
stigma 60, 66.
stile 223.
stile groove of sash 203.
stile tongue of sash 203.
stiletto 794.
**still cameras 394, 395.**
still video camera 395.
still video film disc 395.
still water level 30.
stilt 585.
stilted 174.
sting 81.
stipule 56.
stirrup 648, 793.
stirrup leather 649.
stirrup sock 595.
stitch 352, 355.
stitch control buttons 569.
stitch length regulator 561.
stitch pattern memory 569.

The terms in **bold type** correspond to an illustration; those in CAPITALS indicate a title.

**stitch patterns 567.**
stitch selector 561.
stitch width selector 561.
stitches 596.
**stitches, embroidery 571.**
stitching 327.
stock 483, 536, 773, 798, 799.
stock pot 249.
stockade 181.
stocked anchor 483.
stocking 344, 347, 667.
stocking stitch 567.
stockless anchor 483.
stomach 88, 92, 97, 124, 131.
stomach throw 668.
stomacker 317.
stone 63, 286, 364.
STONE AGE WEAPONS 791.
stone deflector 459, 469.
**stone fruit, section 63.**
stone steps 196.
stoner 246.
stop 106, 411, 532, 566, 570, 632, 831.
stop at intersection 824, 825.
stop bath 399.
stop button 272, 403, 420, 706.
stop key 411.
stop knob 542, 543.
stop rod 543.
stop watch 407.
stop/clear key 405.
stopcock 215.
**stopwatch 706.**
storage compartment 397, 440, 449, 778, 780.
storage door 254.
STORAGE FURNITURE 225, 226.
storage space 461.
storage tank 744, 772.
storage tray 591, 764.
storm collar 205.
**stormy sky 36.**
stowed configuration 48.
straight 695.
straight bet 700, 701.
straight blade 587.
straight eye 566.
straight flush 695.
straight jaw 278.
straight ladder 303.
straight position 624.
straight rails 646.
straight skirt 334.
straight wing 499.
straight-up ribbed top 325.
strainer 243, 248, 251.
strainer body 296.
strainer coupling 296.
**straining, utensils for 243.**
strait 51.
strand 692.
strap 365, 596, 660, 662, 706, 777.
strap wrench 299.
strapless brassiere 346.
stratocumulus 44.
stratosphere 19.
stratum basale 136.
stratum corneum 136.
stratum granulosum 136.
stratum lucidum 136.
stratum spinosum 136.
stratus 44.
straw spreader 161.
**strawberry, section 62.**
stream 676.
streamer 817.
street 52, 184, 190.
street bet 700, 701.
street light 185, 186.
STREET, CROSS SECTION 186.
stretch-limousine 425.
stretcher 219, 726.
strike plate 290.
**striker 307.**
striker 804.
striker wheel 386.
striking circle 607.
string 541, 544, 545.
STRINGED INSTRUMENTS 544, 546.
stringer 787.
stringing 615.
strings 540.
stroke judge 621.
strongbox 702.
**structure 203.**
**structure of the Sun 6.**
strut 199, 495, 553, 774.
stud 198, 353, 432, 566.
studio 407.
studio floor 412.
STUDIO, RADIO 407.
**studio, television 412, 414.**
studs 598.
stummel 385.
**stump 59.**
stump 598, 599.
style 60, 62, 63, 64, 67.
**styling brush 370.**
stylobate 166, 168.
stylus 389.
sub-base 40.
**subarctic climates 45.**
subarctic climates 45.
subbase 451.
subclavian artery 126.
subclavian vein 126.
subcutaneous tissue 137.
subfloor 198, 199, 200.
subgrade 451.
sublimation 34.
SUBMACHINE GUN 795.
SUBMARINE 806.
submarine canyon 29.
submarine pipeline 740.
substation 752.
substitute corridor 612.
substructure 737.
subterranean stream 24.
subtract from memory 523.
subtract key 523.
subtraction 830.
**subtropical climates 45.**
suburban commuter railway 464.
suburbs 52.
subway 464.
sucker 61.
suction hose 778.
sudoriferous duct 136.
sugar bowl 238.
**suit 331.**
**suit carrier 382.**
**suitcase 383.**
sulcus terminalis 143.
sulky 652.
sum 830.
sumie 589.
summer 8.
summer solstice 8.
summit 27.
sump 434, 736.
sump gasket 434.
SUN 6.
Sun 4, 8.
Sun mode position 419.
sun roof 427.
sun sensor 42, 43.
Sun sensor 49.
sun visor 430, 449.
**Sun, structure 6.**
sundae spoon 241.
sundeck 497.
**sundial 706.**
sundress 332.
sunglasses 377.
sunshade 42.
**sunshine recorder 40.**
sunspot 6.
super 82.
superficial peroneal nerve 133.
superior cymbal 552.
superior dental arch 142.
superior mesenteric artery 126, 132.
superior mesenteric vein 126.
superior nasal concha 141.
superior semicircular canal 139.
superior umbilicus 110.
superior vena cava 124, 125, 126, 130.
superstructure 486.
supply duct 213.
supply of water 755.
supply pipe 296.
supply point 757.
support 40, 223, 230, 232, 464, 574, 720.
support bracket 230.
support leg 156, 441, 449.
support leg crank 441.
support structure 15, 48.
**supports 589.**
sural nerve 133.
surcingle 653.
surface cold front 39.
surface course 450.
surface insulation 510.
surface of the water 624.
surface pipe 738.
surface runoff 32, 34.
surface scum 216.
surface surveillance radar 809, 810.
surface warm front 39.
surface water drain 186.
surface-piercing foils 495.
surface-to-air missile 814.
surface-to-subsurface missile 809, 814.
surroyal antler 105.
suspended span 454.
suspender 347, 456.
suspender belt 347.
suspension 477.
suspension arm 258.
suspension band 729.
suspension bogie 458.
**suspension bridge 456.**
suspension cable 456.
suspension file 518.
suspension insulator string 756.
suspension lines 636.
suspension spring 707.
suspension strut 443.
suspensory ligament 140.
sustaining pedal 540, 555.
suture 67, 94.
swagger stick 375.
swallow hole 24.
swallowtail 817.
swallowtail and tongue 817.
Swan 11.
sweat shirt 352.
SWEATERS 326.
**sweaters 338.**
swede 71.
sweeping hip throw 668.
sweeping score line 620.
sweet pepper 69.
sweet potato 71.
sweet taste 143.
**sweetcorn 72.**
sweetcorn 152.
sweetheart neckline 343.
swell organ manual 542.
swell pedals 542.
swept-back wing 499.
swift 575.
swimmerets 91.
SWIMMING 621, 622.
swimming pool 496, 621, 626.
swimming trunks 353.
swimsuit 353.
**swing bridge 457.**
**Swiss army knife 688.**
**Swiss chard 72.**
switch 254, 280, 283, 285, 309.
switch blade 467.
switch lock 280.
switchboard operator's set 422.
swivel 658, 672, 737.
swivel base 282.
swivel flex 370.
swivel head 282.
swivel lock 282.
swivel wall lamp 234.
swivel-tilter armchair 520.
Swordfish 13.
symbol 702.
**symbols, dangerous materials 821.**
**symbols, protection 821.**
sympathetic ganglion 135.
SYMPHONY ORCHESTRA 556.
symphysis pubis 127, 128.
synapse 135.
**synthesizer 555.**
synthetic sponge 367.
**syringe 726.**
syringe for irrigation 726.
system buttons 555.
systems display 500.

## T

T-shirt dress 351.
T-strap shoe 356.
T-tail unit 498.
tab 319, 378, 379, 518, 566.
tab key 530.
tab setting 525.
TABLE 219.
**table 674.**
table 283, 285, 363, 578.
table cut 362.
table extension 285.
table lamp 236.
**table mixer 250.**
**table saw 285.**
TABLE TENNIS 619.
table tennis ball 619.
**table tennis bat 619.**
**table, tennis 619.**
table-locking clamp 283.
tablespoon 241.
tablet 725.
tablinum 170.
tabulator 524.
tachometer 431, 445.
tack 631.
tackle box 672.
**tadpole 84.**
tag 352, 354.
tail 91, 96, 97, 101, 106, 107, 112, 127, 499, 579, 633, 638, 641, 642, 643, 645, 670.
tail assembly 499.
tail boom 508.
tail comb 368.
tail edge 577.
tail feather 109.
tail fin 499, 508.
tail of helix 139.
tail pipe 439.
tail pipe extension 439.
tail pole 773.
tail skid 508.
tailing auger 161.
taillight 147.
tailored collar 330, 341.
tailored sleeve 340.
tailpiece 296, 544.
tailplane 499, 508, 639, 812.
tailrace 747.
take-up handle 572.
take-up reel 403.
take-up spool 390.
tall tumbler 237.
talon 111.
talus 123.
**tambourine 554.**
tamper 385.
**tandem disc harrow 157.**
tandem disc harrow 154.
tang 239, 242, 291.
TANK 805.
tank 216, 398, 399, 742, 743, 780.
tank farm 740.
tank gauge float 741.
tank hatch 743.
tank top 351, 353.
**tank wagon 743.**
tank wall 742.
**tanker 742.**
tanker 491.
tanker aircraft 813.
tanks 511.
tap 292.
tap connector 399.
tape 566, 571, 607, 613, 711, 804.
tape counter 403.
tape dispenser 516.
tape lock 711.
**tape measure 711.**
tape measure 563.
tape selector 403.
tape-guide 403.
taper 582.
tapered wing 499.
tapestry bobbin 574.
taproot 59.
**target 684.**
target area 770.
**target areas 667.**
target detection radar 809.
tarlatan 582.
tarragon 74.
tarsus 78, 80, 103, 108, 122.
tassel 229.
tasset 792.
**taste sensations 143.**
Taurus the Bull (April 20) 820.
taxi rank 822.
taxiway 502.
taxiway line 503.
tea cup 238.
tea infuser 246.
team bench 626.
team shirt 595, 600, 602.
teapot 238.
tear tape 384.
tear-off calendar 518.
teaser comb 368.
teaspoon 241.
technical equipment compartment 415.
technical identification band 405.
technical producer 412, 415.
technical producer monitor 413.
technical specifications 433.
**technical terms 63.**
TEDDING 159.

The terms in **bold type** correspond to an illustration; those in CAPITALS indicate a title.

**tedding 155.**
teddy 345.
tee 620, 677.
tee connector 298, 301.
teeing ground 676.
TEETH 144.
teeth 566.
tele-converter 392.
telecommunication antenna 494, 497, 809.
TELECOMMUNICATION SATELLITES 418.
**telecommunication satellites, examples 418.**
**telecommunication terminal 422.**
TELECOMMUNICATIONS BY SATELLITE 417.
**telecommunications by telephone network 417.**
**telephone 420.**
telephone 413, 417, 822.
**telephone answering machine 420.**
telephone cable 186.
telephone index 516.
telephone list 420.
telephone network 417.
telephone set 415.
TELEPHONE, COMMUNICATION 420, 422.
telephoto lens 392.
teleport 417.
teleprompter 414.
**telescope 14.**
telescope 14, 42, 484, 713.
telescope base 14.
telescopic boom 780, 786.
telescopic corridor 503.
telescopic fork 442.
telescopic leg 726.
TELESCOPIC SIGHT 718.
telescopic sight 798.
**telescopic umbrella 375.**
telescoping leg 393.
telescoping uncoupling rod 470.
TELEVISION 410, 412, 414.
**television set 410.**
television set 401.
**telex 421.**
telex 417.
telltale 616, 628.
telson 91.
**temperate climates 45.**
temperature 210.
temperature control 213, 252, 256, 297.
temperature control knob 585.
temperature gauge 431.
temperature of dew point 38.
temperature scale 19.
temperature scales 710.
temperature selector 253, 258, 259.
temperature set point knob 705.
template 738.
temple 116, 573, 578.
tempo control 555.
tempo scale 539.
temporal bone 122.
tenaille 179.
tendon 107.
tendon guard 644.
tendril 61.
TENNIS 614.
**tennis ball 615.**
**tennis player 615.**
**tennis racket 615.**
tennis shoe 615.
**tennis, court 614.**
**tennis, net 614.**
tenon saw 578.
tenor drum 553.
tenpin 683.
tension adjuster 685.
tension adjustment 671.
**tension block 562, 569.**
tension block 561.
tension dial 562, 568, 569.
tension disc 562, 569.
tension pulley wheel 230.
tension rod 553.
tension screw 552, 553.
tension spring 431, 562, 569, 665.
tensioner 661.
tensioning wire 684.
tensor of fascia lata 120.
tentacle 83.
tepee 165.
teres major 121.
teres minor 121.
**terminal 421.**
terminal 255, 309, 312, 740, 757.
terminal arborization 135.
terminal box 769.
terminal bronchiole 130.
terminal bud 57.
terminal filament 134.
terminal lobe 61.
terminal moraine 27.
**terminal tackles 672.**
terraced houses 187.
terreplein 179.
terrestrial globe 3.
tertial 110.
**tertiary consumers 31.**
test pattern 414.
test-lamp 310.
**tester screwdriver 310.**
testicle 127.
text 524.
text display 524.
THEATRE 188.
**theodolite 713.**
theodolite 41.
thermal barrier 42.
thermal louvre 43.
thermocouple 297.
thermocouple tube 297.
**thermometer 705.**
thermometer 627, 635, 741.
thermosphere 19.
thermostat 210, 214, 252, 297.
thermostat control 254.
thigh 101, 106, 108, 117, 119, 127, 128.
thigh pad 602.
thigh stocking 344.
thigh-boot 357.
thimble 563, 711.
thinning razor 369.
third 537.
third base 597.
third baseman 597.
third finger 137.
third stage 509.
third valve slide 551.
third wheel 706, 707.
thoracic legs 90.
thoracic vertebra (12) 123.
thoracic vertebrae 102.
thorax 78, 79, 80, 116, 118.
thread 276, 294.
thread guide 561, 562.
thread take-up lever 561.
thread trimmer 562.
threaded cap 301.
threaded rod 279.
threaded sleeve 290.
three-four time 537.
three-hinged arch 455.
three-of-a-kind 695.
three-pin socket 309.
three-quarter coat 321.
three-quarter sleeve 339.
three-tier car carrier 473.
three-toed hoof 99.
threshing area 161.
threshold 202.
throat 108, 282, 483, 615, 671.
throat lash 649.
throat protector 595, 609.
throttle 271.
throttle cable 271.
throttle control 272.
throttle valve 735.
throttles 500.
through arch bridge 455.
**throwing apparatus 658.**
throwing circle 654, 655.
thrust 455.
thrust bearing 753.
thrust device 389.
thrust tube 389.
thruster 49, 512.
THRUSTING AND CUTTING WEAPONS 794.
thumb 112, 137, 327, 596.
thumb hook 550.
thumb piston 542.
thumb rest 549, 726.
thumbscrew 279.
thunderstorm 39.
thyme 74.
tibia 78, 80, 103, 112, 122.
tibial nerve 133.
ticket collector 463.
ticket collector's booth 474.
ticket control 463.
ticket counter 504.
**tidal power plant 752.**
tie 375, 539.
tie beam 198, 199.
tie closure 375.
tieback 228.
tieback knob 229.
tieclip 364.
tiepin 364.
tierce 667.
tierceron 177.
tight end 603, 605.
tightening band 40.
tights 344.
tilde 832.
tile 169, 170, 286, 511.
tiller 628, 793.
tilt tube 231.
tilt-back head 250.
timber 170.
**timber frame 198.**
**time signatures 537.**
timekeeper 610, 612, 626, 666, 668, 669.
timer 252, 398, 585, 664.
timer socket 255.
timetable 462.
timing belt 434.
timpani 557.
**tin opener 256.**
tin opener 244, 688.
tine 157, 240, 272.
tip 57, 72, 239, 241, 275, 276, 284, 291, 305, 323, 375, 633, 640, 645, 658, 670, 675.
tip of nose 141.
tip protector 726.
tip section 670.
tip-ring 670, 671.
tipper body 785.
**tipper truck 785.**
tissue holder 292.
Titan 5.
**toad 85.**
**toaster 252.**
tobacco 384.
tobacco hole 385.
tobacco pouch 385.
toe 104, 106, 111, 116, 118, 277, 325, 678.
toe binding 642.
toe clip 104, 446, 448.
toe guard 595, 730.
toe hole 645.
toe pick 644.
toe piece 633, 640.
toe piston 542.
toe strap 633.
toe-piece 641.
toe-strap 357.
toecap 644.
toenail scissors 365.
toeplate 642.
**toga 315.**
toggle 320, 817.
**toggle bolt 276.**
**toilet 293.**
toilet 195, 215, 292, 461.
toilet bag 382.
toilet bowl 293.
toilet truck 506.
tom-tom 552.
tomato 69.
tombolo 30.
tone control 547.
tone leader generator 407.
tongs 205, 246.
tongue 81, 88, 131, 142, 323, 352, 354, 536, 542, 566, 641, 644.
tongue sheath 96.
**tongue, dorsum 143.**
tonsil 142.
tool 735.
tool holder 283.
tool shelf 302.
tool tether 512.
TOOLS, CARPENTRY 275, 276, 278, 280, 282, 284.
**tools, electricity 310.**
tools, electricity 311.
**tools, plumbing 299.**
**tools, wood carving 587.**
tooth 96, 158, 159, 160, 162, 268, 277, 284, 369, 785.
**toothbrush 373.**
toothbrush 373.
toothbrush shaft 373.
toothbrush well 373.
toothed jaw 278.
toothpaste 373.
top 59, 219, 302, 478.
top bar 659.
top central manhole 743.
top cross-member 470.
top cushion 675.
top cylinder 581.
top deck 741.
top deckboard 787.
top edge 577.
**top face 363.**
top hat 328.
top ladder 781.
top lift 354.
top of dam 746, 748, 749, 752.
top plate 525.
top pocket 675.
top rail 202, 223, 225.
top rail of sash 203.
top road 736.
top stitched pleat 335.
top stitching 323, 350.
topaz 363.
topmark 486, 488.
topping 670.
topping lift 478.
toque 329.
torpedo 807.
torpedo room 807.
torque converter 258.
torus 166, 167.
total 709.
total eclipse 8.
tote bag 380.
tote board 651.
Toucan 13.
TOUCH 136.
touch judge 606.
touch line 601.
touchline 606.
touring boot 642.
tourmaline 363.
tow bar 158, 159, 162, 449, 506, 633.
tow line 633.
tow release knob 639.
tow tractor 507.
towel rail 292.
tower 176, 456, 486, 770, 771, 773, 774, 786.
tower control room 502.
**tower crane 786.**
tower ladder 781.
tower mast 786.
tower silo 149.
towing eye 803.
towing hitch 147, 449.
TOWN HOUSES 187.
tracery 175.
trachea 130.
**tracing wheel 563.**
**track 651.**
track 230, 445, 463, 474, 783.
TRACK AND FIELD ATHLETICS 654, 656, 658.
track frame 235.
track idler 783.
**track lighting 235.**
track link 805.
track number 405.
track roller frame 783.
track search keys 405.
track shoe 805.
trackball 526.
tracker 543.
tracklaying tractor 783.
TRACTOR 147.
tractor 506, 742.
tractor engine 784.
**tractor unit 440.**
tractor unit 440.
trade name 384.
TRADITIONAL DWELLINGS 165.
TRADITIONAL MUSICAL INSTRUMENTS 535, 536.
traffic island 184.
traffic lanes 452.
traffic lights 186.
traffic signals ahead 827.
tragus 112, 139.
trail 803.
trail-view mirror 440.
**trailer caravan 449.**
trailing edge 498, 636, 637, 638.
trailing edge flap 498, 812.
train direction sign 475.
train indicator 463.
train station 184.
trainer 669.
**training set 351.**
**training suit 352.**
training wall 746.
**trampoline 659.**
transceiving dish 418.

The terms in **bold type** correspond to an illustration; those in CAPITALS indicate a title.

**transcription of seismic waves 714.**
transducer 485.
transept 177.
transept spire 176.
transfer canal 764.
transfer of heat to water 766.
transfer port 436.
transfer scale 396.
transfer ticket dispensing machine 475.
transform fault 28.
transformation of mechanical work into electricity 755.
transformer 235, 747, 757, 758, 771.
transit shed 490.
**transition fittings 301.**
translation wave 30.
transmission 258.
transmission cable 485.
transmission dish 418.
transmission of the electric current 714.
transmission of the rotary motion to the rotor 755.
transmission/reception of messages 421.
transmitted pulse 722.
transmitter 420.
transmitting station 722.
transparency 397.
transparent pockets 379.
transpiration 35.
**transporter bridge 457.**
transverse bulkhead 742.
transverse colon 131.
transverse dunes 46.
transverse process 135.
trap 215, 293, 296, 301.
trap coupling 296.
trapeze dress 332.
trapezius 120, 121.
**travel bag 382.**
**traveller 630.**
traveller 628.
travelling block 737.
travelling crab 786.
travelling crane 747.
traverse arch 177.
**traverse rod 230.**
traversing handle 803.
tray 210, 226, 304, 383.
tread 201, 433, 649.
tread bar 147.
tread design 433.
treadle 572.
treadle cord 572.
treatment plant 735.
treble 646.
treble bridge 540.
treble clef 537.
treble fishhook 672.
treble keyboard 536.
treble loudspeaker 16.
treble pickup 547.
treble register 536.
treble ring 698.
treble tone control 402.
**tree 59.**
tree 649.
**tree frog 85.**
tree pruner 269.
TREE, STRUCTURE 59.
**tree, trunk 59.**
trees 676.
trefoil 174, 175.
trench 28, 733.
**trench coat 319.**
**triangle 554.**
Triangle 11.
triangle 556.
triangular bandage 725.
triangular body 535.
triangular fossa 139.
triceps bar 663.
triceps of arm 121.
tricorne 318.
tricuspid valve 125.
trifoliate 56.
trigger 268, 304, 590, 780, 793, 795, 796, 797, 798, 799, 804.
trigger guard 795, 797, 798, 799.
trigger switch 284.
triglyph 167.
**trilby 328.**
trilby 329.
trill 538.
trim 383.
trim panel 429.
trim ring 255.
**trimmer 271.**
trimmer 374.
**trimming 578.**
trimming tool 585.
trio 558.
trip lever 293.
trip mileometer 431.
triple bars 646, 647.
triple jump take-off board 654.
triple jump take-off line 654.
triple tail unit 498.
**tripod 393.**
tripod 397, 415, 539, 721.
tripod accessories shelf 721.
tripod stand 552.
tripod tail support 507.
Triton 5.
trochanter 78, 80.
trolley 306, 457.
**Trombe wall 772.**
Trombe wall 772.
trombone 550.
trombones 556.
tropic of Cancer 3, 47.
tropic of Capricorn 3, 47.
**tropical climates 45.**
TROPICAL FRUITS 68.
tropical rain forest 45.
tropical savanna 45.
tropical storm 39.
troposphere 19.
trot 101.
trough 30, 38.
**trousers 323.**
trousers 353, 595, 602, 609, 668, 680.
**trousers, types 336.**
trowel 268.
truck 645.
**truck crane 786.**
truck trailer 440.
TRUCKING 440.
truffle 55.
**trumpet 550.**
trumpet 550.
trumpet interchange 451.
trumpets 556.
**trunk 383.**
trunk 59, 61, 117, 119.
trunk hose 316.
**trunk, cross section 59.**
trunnion 800.
trussed arch 455.
tub 257, 258, 263.
tub rim 258.
tuba 551, 557.
tube 232, 397, 588, 710, 803, 804.
tube flaring tool 299.
tube retention clip 233.
**tuber vegetables 71.**
tubing 740.
tubing head 740.
tubing valve 740.
tubular bells 554, 556.
tubular element 255.
tubular heater 744.
**tubular ice screw 681.**
**tubular lock 290.**
tubular member 738.
tubular structure 487.
tuck 384.
tuck position 624.
Tudor 174.
tumble dry at low temperature 829.
tumble dry at medium to high temperature 829.
**tuner 400, 402.**
tungsten filament 233.
**tungsten-halogen bulb 233.**
tunic 337, 791.
tunic dress 333.
tuning control 402, 408.
tuning controls 410.
tuning fork 539.
tuning gauge 553.
tuning knob 408.
tuning mode 402.
tuning peg 545, 547.
tuning pin 540.
tuning slide 551.
tuning wire 542.
tunnel 474.
turban 329.
turbine 753, 758.
turbine building 758.
turbine headcover 753.
turbine runner 752.
turbine shaft turns generator 767.
turbine stop valve 758.
turbine-compressor shaft 501.
turbined water draining 755.
**turbo-charged engine 438.**
turbo-jet engine 812.
TURBOFAN ENGINE 501.
turbogenerator 771, 806.
turbojet engine 499.
turkey 150.
turn 538.
turn and bank indicator 639.
turn and bank knob 639.
turn-up 323.
turnbuckle 630, 669.
**turning 584.**
turning handle 280.
turning judge 621.
turning wall 621, 622.
**turning wheel 584.**
turnip 71.
turntable 250, 400, 404, 407, 457, 784, 785.
turntable mounting 780.
**turntable unit 404.**
turpentine 592.
turquoise 363.
turret 180, 805, 809.
turret cap 718.
**turtle 97.**
turtleneck 342.
tusks of a walrus 99.
tusks of a wart hog 99.
tusks of an elephant 99.
TV mode 411.
TV power button 411.
TV/video button 411.
tweeter 401.
tweezers 725.
twig 59.
twill weave 576.
**twin skis 633.**
twin-lens reflex camera 394.
**twin-set 338.**
Twins 11.
**twist bar 665.**
**twist dive 625.**
**twist drill bit 281.**
twist grip throttle 444.
**twisted rope 692.**
two columns split bet 700.
two dozens split bet 701.
two pairs 695.
**two-burner camp stove 689.**
**two-hand clean and jerk 662.**
**two-hand snatch 662.**
two-hinged arch 455.
**two-person tent 685.**
two-seater settee 221.
two-sided copies 532.
**two-stroke engine 436.**
two-toed hoof 99.
two-two time 537.
two-way collar 319.
two-way traffic 824, 825.
tympanum 84, 97, 166, 168, 175.
type of air mass 38.
type of fuel 453.
type of high cloud 38.
type of low cloud 38.
type of middle cloud 38.
**types of anchor 483.**
TYPES OF ARCH 174.
**types of arch 455.**
**types of arch bridge 455.**
**types of beam bridge 454.**
TYPES OF BIT 650.
**types of blouse 337.**
**types of bodywork 425.**
**types of chair 223.**
**types of coat 330.**
**types of curtain 228.**
**types of door 202.**
**types of dress 332.**
TYPES OF ENGINE 436.
**types of golf club 677.**
TYPES OF GOODS TRUCK 472.
**types of grip 619.**
**types of handle 633.**
**types of head 276.**
**types of heading 229.**
TYPES OF HOOF 99.
**types of inflorescence 60.**
TYPES OF JAW 98.
**types of kitchen knife 242.**
TYPES OF LEAF 56.
**types of move 696.**
**types of oar 632.**
**types of outlet 207.**
TYPES OF PASSENGER COACH 460.
**types of pleat 228, 335.**
TYPES OF RIG 482.
TYPES OF SAIL 482.
**types of ski 633.**
**types of skirt 334.**
**types of stroke 622.**
TYPES OF TAIL UNIT 498.
**types of telephone 422.**
**types of window 203.**
TYPES OF WING 499.
typist's chair 521.
**tyre 433.**
tyre 440, 447.
tyre inflator 453.
tyre pump 446.
tyre valve 447.

## U

U-bend 301.
U-shaped chisel 587.
U-shaped gouge 581.
UHF antenna 42.
ulna 102, 122.
ulnar extensor of wrist 121.
ulnar flexor of wrist 120, 121.
ulnar nerve 133.
ultraviolet spectrometer 43.
umbel 60.
umbo 95.
umbra 8.
UMBRELLA 375.
**umbrella 375.**
umbrella pine 58.
umbrella ring 679.
umbrella stand 375.
umlaut 832.
umpire 599, 603, 605, 611, 613, 614, 618.
under tail covert 109.
underarm briefcase 378.
**underarm crutch 728.**
underarm rest 728.
underground 190.
underground flow 32, 35.
underground map 475, 477.
**underground mine 736.**
UNDERGROUND RAILWAY 474, 476.
**underground station 474.**
underground stem 70.
**underground train 476.**
underground train 474.
underlining 565.
underpass 454.
undershirt 595.
underwater camera 394.
**underwear 325, 345, 346.**
underwiring 347.
uneven surface 826.
**union 300.**
union 830.
uniparous cyme 60.
unison 537.
unit price 709.
UNIVALVE SHELL 94.
universal passenger steps 507.
unleavened bread 153.
unloading tube 161.
uphaul 631.
upholstery nozzle 260.
upper 641.
upper blade guard 284.
upper bowl 247.
upper cheek 650.
upper chord 455.
upper cold front 39.
upper cuff 641.
upper deck 498.
upper edge 619.
upper eyelid 84, 107, 140.
upper fore topgallant sail 481.
upper fore topsail 481.
upper gate 493.
upper gill arch 87.
upper girdle facet (16) 363.
upper laboratory 15.
upper lateral lobe 61.
upper lateral sinus 61.
upper level 493.
upper limb 124, 793.
upper lip 81, 142, 542.
upper lobe 130.
upper mandible 109.
upper mantle 22.
upper rudder 806.
upper shell 641, 645.
upper sphere clamp 40.
upper strap 641.
upper support screw 40.
upper tail covert 109.
upper warm front 39.
upperboard 543.

The terms in **bold type** correspond to an illustration; those in CAPITALS indicate a title.

**upperworks 630.**
upright 573, 574, 578, 579, 657, 659, 660, 661, 728.
**upright piano 540.**
**upright piano action 541.**
upstage 188, 189.
upstream blanket 748.
upstream face 749.
upstream shoulder 748.
upstream toe 748.
Uranus 5.
**urban map 52.**
ureter 132.
urethra 128, 129, 132.
urinary bladder 89, 127, 128, 132.
urinary meatus 127.
URINARY SYSTEM 132.
urogenital aperture 89.
uropod 91.
use chlorine bleach as directed 829.
**useful liquids 592.**
**usual terms 63.**
**utensils, set 244.**
uterovesical pouch 128.
uterus 128, 129.
uvula 141, 142.

## V

V-neck 322, 326.
**V-neck cardigan 326.**
V-neck cardigan 338.
V-shaped gouge 581.
V-shaped neck 343.
vacuole 115.
vacuum chamber 710, 717.
**vacuum coffee maker 247.**
vacuum diaphragm 435.
vacuum distillation 744.
vacuum flask 690.
vacuum manifold 717.
vacuum system console 717.
vagina 128, 129.
vair 819.
valance 224, 228.
valley 27.
valve 67, 95, 550.
valve casing 550.
valve cover 435.
valve seat 293, 294.
valve seat wrench 299.
valve spring 434.
vambrace 792.
vamp 353, 355.
vane 110, 259.
vanity cabinet 292.
**vanity case 382.**
vanity mirror 430.
vaporizer 210.
vaporizing grille 210.
variable geometry wing 499.
variation keys 569.
variometer 635.
VARIOUS DRY FRUITS 67.
varnish 592.
varnish-roller 582.
vastus lateralis 120, 121.
vastus medialis 120.
VAUBAN FORTIFICATION 178.
**vault 177.**
vaulting horse 659.
VCR controls 411.
VCR mode 411.
VCR power button 411.
vector/waveform monitor 413.
vegetable brush 246.
vegetable dish 238.
vegetable garden 148, 193.
vegetable sponge 367.
vegetable steamer 249.
VEGETABLES 69, 70, 71, 72, 73.
vegetables 33.
veil 670.
vein 56.
**veins 126.**
Velcro® closure 349.
velum 80.
velvet-band choker 361.
**Venetian blind 231.**
venom canal 96.
venom gland 96.
venom-conducting tube 96.
**venomous snake's head 96.**
vent 214, 430, 800, 801.
vent brush 368.
vent door 441.
vent hole 304.
ventail 792.
ventilated rib 798.
ventilating circuit 215.
ventilating fan 469.
ventilating grille 260.
ventilation 772.
ventilation hood 486.
ventilator 477.
ventral aorta 88.
venturi 804.
venturi fastening lever 804.
Venus 4.
vermiform appendix 131.
vernal equinox 3, 8.
vernier 708.
vernier scale 484.
Versailles parquet 200.
vert 819.
vertebral body 135.
vertebral shield 97.
vertical control 529.
vertical frame 574.
vertical move 696.
vertical pivoting window 203.
vertical pocket 316.
vertical pupil 96.
vertical shaft 736.
vertical side band 613.
**vertical-axis wind turbine 774.**
very cloudy sky 39.
**vest 325.**
vestibular nerve 139.
vestibule 139, 170, 461.
VHF antenna 808.
viaduct 454.
vibrating mudscreen 737.
vibrato arm 547.
**vice 282.**
VIDEO CAMERA 409.
video camera 526.
video cassette recorder 526.
video connection panel 415.
VIDEO ENTERTAINMENT SYSTEM 699.
**video monitor 529.**
video monitor 526, 527.
video monitoring selector 413.
video port 528.
video switcher technician 412, 415.
**videocassette recorder 411.**
videocassette recorder 401.
videotape operation controls 409.
Vienna loaf 153.
view camera 394.
**view from above 171, 444.**
viewfinder 390.
viewfinder adjustment keys 409.
**vine leaf 61.**
vine leaf 73.
vine shoot 61.
**vine stock 61.**
vinyl grip sole 350.
vinyl insulation 287.
viola 545.
violas 556.
**violin 544.**
violin 545.
**violin family 545.**
Virgin 11, 13.
Virgo the Virgin (August 23) 820.
vision slit 792.
visor 443, 471, 642, 730, 792.
visor hinge 443.
visual display 699.
visual display unit 421, 422.
visual transmission 717.
**visualization of seismic waves 714.**
vitelline membrane 109.
vitreous body 140.
vocal cord 130.
voice edit buttons 555.
voice selector 555.
volcanic bombs 25.
volcanic island 28.
VOLCANO 25.
volcano 23.
**volcano during eruption 25.**
VOLLEYBALL 613.
**volleyball 613.**
**volleyball, court 613.**
**volleyball, net 613.**
voltage decrease 755.
voltage increase 755, 767.
volume control 402, 408, 411, 420, 422, 547, 555.
volume readout 453.
volute 166, 167, 220.
volva 55.
voussoir 174.
VU meters 407, 413.
vulva 118, 128.

## W

wad 799, 801.
waders 672.
wading bird 111.
waferboard 288.
**waffle iron 253.**
wagon 162.
wagon tent 686.
waist 117, 119, 354, 544, 756.
waistband 320, 323, 325.
waistband extension 323.
**waistcoat 322.**
waistcoat 315, 317, 338.
**waistcoats and jackets 338.**
walk 101.
walk-in wardrobe 195.
WALKING AIDS 728.
walking frame 728.
walking leg 78.
walking stick 375, 728.
wall 7, 65, 104, 646, 647, 685.
wall and rails 646, 647.
wall bracket 230.
wall grille 207.
wall lantern 235.
wall light 234.
wall stack section 206.
wall stud 199.
wall tent 686.
wallet 379, 523.
wallet section 379.
walnut 66.
**walnut, section 66.**
waning gibbous 7.
wardrobe 195, 226.
warhead 814.
warm air 772.
warm air outlet 438.
warm-air baffle 204.
warm-air outflow 207.
warm-air outlet 206.
warming plate 247.
warning device 777.
warning lights 431.
warning plate 280.
warning track 597.
warp 573, 574.
warp roller 573.
warp thread 576.
**warping frame 575.**
warty skin 85.
wash tower 257.
washbasin 215, 292.
washer 294.
washer nozzle 426.
**washers 278.**
**washing 829.**
**washing machine 258, 298.**
washing machine 215, 298.
wasp-waisted corset 347.
Wassily chair 221.
waste disposal unit 296.
waste pipe 215, 293, 298.
waste tee connector 298.
Water Bearer 13.
water bottle 447.
water bottle clip 447.
water cannon 778.
water carrier 690.
water cools the used steam 767.
water goblet 237.
water hazard 676.
water hose 257, 734.
water inlet 295.
water intake 747.
water is pumped back into the steam generator 767.
water jug 238.
water jump 646, 647.
water key 551.
water level 210, 247.
water main 186, 772.
water meter 215.
Water Monster 11, 13.
WATER POLO 626.
**water polo ball 626.**
**water polo, goal 626.**
**water polo, playing area 626.**
water pressure gauge 778.
**water pump pliers 278.**
water separator 734.
water service pipe 215.
**water signs 820.**
WATER SKIING 633.
water table 24.
water tank 210, 373, 469.
water tower 465.
water transport 735.
water turns into steam 766.
water under pressure 755.
water-heater tank 772.
water-level selector 258.
water-level tube 256.
water/alcohol 485.
**watercolour and gouache 588.**
watercress 73.
waterfall 27.
**watering can 265.**
waterline 487.
watermelon 69.
waterproof pants 349.
waterproofed electricity supply 216.
WATT-HOUR METER 712.
**watt-hour meter, mechanism 712.**
WAVE 30.
wave base 30.
wave clip 369.
wave guide 415.
wave height 30.
wave length 30.
wave wall 748.
wax seal 293.
waxing gibbous 6.
WEAPONS IN THE AGE OF THE ROMANS 791.
**weather map 38.**
weather radar 498.
WEATHER SATELLITE 42.
weatherboard 202, 203.
WEAVING 572, 574, 576.
weaving pattern brush 568.
weaving pattern lever 568.
**weaving, accessories 573, 575.**
web 84, 111, 466, 596.
web frame 743.
webbed foot 84.
webbed toe 111.
webbing 571, 634.
wedding ring 364.
wedge 542, 800.
wedge iron 277.
wedge lever 277.
weeder 268.
weeding hoe 266.
**weekend case 383.**
weft 572, 574.
weft thread 576.
weighing platform 709.
weight 658, 665, 707, 708, 709.
weight belt 627.
**weight trainer 663.**
**weight-driven clock mechanism 707.**
**weightlifter 662.**
WEIGHTLIFTING 662.
weightlifting belt 662.
weightlifting shoe 662.
weights 663.
weld bead 307.
WELDING 305, 306.
welding curtain 308.
welding rod 307.
**welding torch 306.**
welding torch 306, 307.
WELDING: PROTECTIVE EQUIPMENT 308.
well wagon 473.
welt 322, 355.
welt pocket 322, 326, 339.
West 488.
West cardinal mark 489.
Western hemisphere 47.
Western meridian 47.
wet suit 627.
wet well 763.
Whale 11, 13.
whale boat 482.
wheat 152.
**wheat, grain 152.**
**wheel 433.**
wheel 270, 383, 427, 440, 563, 583, 645, 684, 800, 805.
wheel chock 506.
wheel cylinder 432.
wheel head 584.
wheel tractor 782.
wheel trim 427.
**wheelbarrow 270.**
WHEELCHAIR 727.
wheelchair 461.
whelk 83.
whip 651.
whipping 678.
whisk 245.
whiskers 107.
whisky tumbler 237.
whistle 252.
White 696, 697.

The terms in **bold type** correspond to an illustration; those in CAPITALS indicate a title.

white balance sensor 409.
white cabbage 73.
white cap 626.
white cue ball 673.
white flag 626.
white light 488.
white line 104, 452.
white matter 135.
white spot ball 673.
white square 696.
white stone 697.
white tape 618, 619.
white wine glass 237.
white-tailed deer 105.
whole wheat bread 153.
wholemeal bread 153.
whorl 83, 94.
wicker basket 635.
**wicket 599.**
wicket 599.
wicket gate 753.
wicketkeeper 599.
wide-angle lens 392.
wigwam 165.
wild animals 828.
willow 598.
winch 630.
**wind 38.**
wind 629.
wind abeam 629.
wind arrow 38.
wind chest 543.
wind chest table 543.
wind deflector 440.
wind direction 38.
wind direction and speed 38.
wind duct 543.
WIND ENERGY 773, 774.
wind guard 634.
wind indicator 628.
WIND INSTRUMENTS 548, 550.
wind sock 817.
wind speed 38.
wind supply 543.
wind trunk 543.
wind vane 41.
windbag 536.
**windcheater 320, 321.**
winder 706.
winder house 735.
winding adjustment 718.
winding mechanism 231, 707.
winding shaft 736.
winding tower 735.
**windmill 773.**
WINDOW 203.
window 194, 195, 253, 255, 379, 399, 427, 429, 477, 498, 631.
WINDOW ACCESSORIES 228, 230.
window awning 685.
**window curtain 228.**
window tab 518.
window winder handle 429.
windscreen 14, 426, 440, 442, 445, 498, 500.
**windscreen wiper 431.**
windscreen wiper 426.
windscreen wiper blade 431.
windshaft 773.
wine waiter corkscrew 244.
wing 78, 108, 316, 426, 440, 499, 511, 637, 638, 670, 812.
wing attack 611.
wing box 812.
wing covert 108.
wing defence 611.
wing forward 606.
wing membrane 112.
wing nut 279.
**wing pallet 787.**
wing rib 498.
wing slat 499.
wing vein 79.
**wing, bird 110.**
winglet 499.
wings 112, 189.
wings, bat 112.
wingtip 637, 638.
winning line 702.
winter 8.
winter solstice 8.
winze 736.
wiper arm 431.
wiper blade rubber 431.
wiper control 430.
wire 641, 658, 663, 714.
wire beater 250.
wire brush 553.
wire cutter 311.
wire frame 689.
wire sling 681.
**wire stripper 311.**
wire stripper 311.
wisdom tooth 144.
wishbone boom 631.
withers 100, 106.
wok 248.
**wok set 248.**
WOMEN'S CLOTHING 330, 332, 334, 336, 338, 340, 342, 344, 346, 348.
women's toilet 822.
**wood 288, 677.**
WOOD CARVING 586.
wood chip wagon 472.
wood chisel 275.
wood engraving 581.
WOOD FLOORING 200.
wood flooring 199.
**wood flooring on cement screed 200.**
**wood flooring on wooden base 200.**
**wood flooring types 200.**
wood storage space 204.
**wood, golf 678.**
**wood-based materials 288, 289.**
woodcut 581.
wooden bar 661.
wooden modelling tools 585.
woods 52.
woodstrip flooring 200.
**woodwind family 548.**
woofer 401.
word correction 525.
**worker, honeybee 80.**
worker, honeybee 81.
working area 16.
working pressure gauge 306.
worm 575, 801.
wrapover dress 333.
wrapover skirt 334.
wrapover top 337.
wrapper 384.
wrist 106, 112, 117, 119, 137.
wrist sling 681.
wrist strap 640, 642.
wrist-length glove 327.
wristband 602, 615.
write protect notch 529.
writing brush 389.
writing case 378.
WRITING INSTRUMENTS 389.

## X

X-band antenna 49.
**xylophone 554.**
xylophone 556.

## Y

Y-branch 301.
Y-tube 726.
yard 478.
yard line 604.
yarn 692.
yarn ball 596.
yarn clip 569.
yarn feeder 569.
yarn guide 569.
yarn rod 569.
yarn tension unit 569.
yellow ball 673.
yellow onion 70.
yen 832.
yoke 230, 320, 324, 337.
yoke skirt 334.
yolk 109.
yurt 165.

## Z

zenith 16.
zenith S-band antenna 49.
zester 242.
zip 350, 365, 382, 685.
**zip fastener 566.**
zip fastener 321.
zip line 565.
**zither 535.**
zona pellucida 128.
zoom lens 392, 409, 414.
zygomatic bone 122.

The terms in **bold type** correspond to an illustration; those in CAPITALS indicate a title.

# FRENCH INDEX

## A

à cagoule(f) 687.
à cheval(m) sur deux colonnes(f) 700.
à cheval(m) sur deux douzaines(f) 701.
à cheval(m) sur deux numéros(m) 700, 701.
abaissement(m) de la tension(f) 755.
abaque(m) 166, 167.
abat-jour(m) 234, 236.
abat-son(m) 175.
abattant(m) 219, 226, 292.
abdomen(m) 78, 79, 81, 91, 108.
ABEILLE(F) 80, 82.
**abeille(f), ouvrière(f) 80.**
**abeille(f), patte(f) antérieure 80.**
**abeille(f), patte(f) médiane 80.**
**abeille(f), patte(f) postérieure 81.**
about(m) 296.
abrégé(m) et pilotes(m) 543.
abri(m) 464.
abri(m) des joueurs(m) 597.
**abri(m) météorologique 41.**
abribus(m) 186.
abricot(m) 63.
abside(f) 177.
absidiole(f) 177.
**accastillage(m) 630.**
accent(m) 539.
accent(m) aigu 832.
accent(m) circonflexe 832.
accent(m) grave 832.
accès(m) à la grille(f) d'éclairage(m) 412.
accès(m) au garage(m) 196.
accès(m) au réservoir(m) à essence(f) 427.
accès(m) aux quais(m) 463.
accès(m) interdit 824, 825.
accès(m) interdit aux bicyclettes(f) 828.
accès(m) interdit aux camions(m) 828.
accès(m) interdit aux motocycles(m) 828.
accès(m) interdit aux piétons(m) 828.
accès(m) pour handicapés(m) physiques 822.
**accessoires(m) 586, 672.**
**accessoires(m) de coiffure(f) 369.**
**accessoires(m) de manucure(f) 365.**
**accessoires(m) photographiques 393.**
**accessoires(m), aspirateur(m) 260.**
accompagnement(m) 682.
**accord(m) 539.**
**accordéon(m) 536.**
accotement(m) 451.
accotoir(m) 220.
accoudoir(m) 727.
accouplement(m) électrique 441.
accroche-mouche(m) 670.
acheminement(m) de la chaleur(f) au générateur(m) de vapeur(f) par le caloporteu 766.
acier(m) 286.
acromion(m) 123.
acrotère(m) 167, 168.
action(f) du vent(m) 35.
adaptateur(m) de fiche(f) 374.
**adapteurs(m) 301.**
addition(f) 523, 830.
addition(f) en mémoire(f) 523.
admission(f) 436, 437.
admission(f) d'air(m) refroidi 438.
aérateur(m) 294, 295.
aérateur(m) à gazon(m) 266.
aérateur(m) de toit(m) 449.
aérateur(m) latéral 449.
aérofrein(m) 638, 774, 812.
**aérogare(f) 504.**
aérogare(f) de passagers(m) 503.
aérogare(f) satellite(m) 503.
AÉROGLISSEUR(M) 492.
**aérographe(m) 590.**
**aérographe(m), coupe(f) 590.**
AÉROPORT(M) 502, 504, 506.
aéroport(m) 52.
affichage(m) 523.
affichage(m) de l'heure(f) de départ(m) 463.
affichage(m) de la couleur(f) 569.
affichage(m) des données(f) 409, 411.
affichage(m) des fonctions(f) 555.
affichage(m) du numéro(m) de rang(m) 569.
affichage(m) du texte(m) 524.
affichage(m) numérique 709, 710.
affichage(m) numérique des stations(f) 402.
affichage(m) ouverture(f)/temps(m) d'exposition(f) 396.
affiche(f) publicitaire 477.
afficheur(m) 420, 709.
afficheur(m) numérique 310.
afficheur(m) prix(m) 453.
afficheur(m) totaliseur 453.
afficheur(m) volume(m) 453.
affût(m) 800, 802.
Afrique(f) 21.
age(m) 156.
agenda(m) 518.
agitateur(m) 258.
agneau(m) 150.
agrafe(f) 230, 389, 711.
**agrafes(f) 566.**
agrafes(f) 515.
agrafeuse(f) 515.
**agrandisseur(m) 399.**
**agrume(m), coupe(f) 65.**
AGRUMES(M) 65.
**agrumes(m), principales variétés(f) 65.**
aide(m)-arbitre(m) 610.
aide(m)-chronométreur(m) 626.
aide-mémoire(m) des procédures(f) 512.
AIDES(F) À LA MARCHE(F) 728.
Aigle(m) 11.
aigle(m) 819.
aigue-marine(f) 363.
aiguillage(m) 464.
**aiguillage(m) manœuvré à distance(f) 467.**
**aiguillage(m) manœuvré à pied(m) d'œuvre(f) 467.**
**aiguille(f) 562.**
aiguille(f) 30, 36, 213, 396, 467, 561, 562, 563, 590, 705, 708, 710, 726.
**aiguille(f) à clapet(m) 568.**
aiguille(f) à clapet(m) 569.
aiguille(f) aimantée 719.
aiguille(f) circulaire 567.
aiguille(f) des dixièmes(m) de seconde(f) 706.
aiguille(f) des heures(f) 707.
aiguille(f) des minutes(f) 706, 707.
**aiguilles(f) à tricoter 567.**
aiguilles(f) de nettoyage(m) 307.
aiguilles(f) de pin(m) 58.
aiguilles(f) de sapin(m) 58.
aiguilleur(m) vidéo de production(f) 413.
aiguillon(m) 81.
ail(m) 70.
**aile(f) 636.**
aile(f) 78, 108, 426, 440, 499, 511, 637, 670, 773, 812.
aile(f) à géométrie(f) variable 499.
aile(f) antérieure 79, 81.
aile(f) arrière 495.
aile(f) avant 495.
aile(f) Dame(f) 696.
aile(f) de quartier(m) 352, 354.
aile(f) droite 606.
aile(f) du nez(m) 141.
aile(f) gauche 606.
**aile(f) libre 637.**
aile(f) postérieure 79, 81.
aile(f) Roi(m) 696.
**aile(f), oiseau(m) 110.**
aileron(m) 316, 498, 631, 638.
ailes(f) 112, 638.
ailes(f) en V 495.
ailes(f), chauve-souris(f) 112.
ailette(f) 210, 259, 499.
ailette(f) à ressort(m) 276.
ailier(m) défensif droit 603, 605.
ailier(m) défensif gauche 603, 605.
ailier(m) droit 601, 606, 607, 608, 612.
ailier(m) éloigné 603, 605.
ailier(m) gauche 601, 606, 607, 608, 612.
ailier(m) rapproché 603, 605.
aimant(m) 406, 485, 563, 714.
aimant(m) de retenue(f) 256.
aimant(m)-frein(m) 712.
aine(f) 116, 118.
air(m) 437.
air(m) calme 38.
air(m) chaud 501, 772.
air(m) frais 772.
air(m) froid 501.
**air(m), pollution(f) 34.**
aire(f) de jeux(m) 496.
aire(f) de manœuvre(f) 502.
aire(f) de ravitaillement(m) 453.
aire(f) de repos(m) 52.
aire(f) de service(m) 52, 503.
aire(f) de stationnement(m) 185, 503.
aire(f) de trafic(m) 502.
airelle(f) 62.
ais(m) 579.
ais(m) ferré 579.
aisselle(f) 116, 118.
ajustement(m) de l'image(f) du cercle(m) horizontal 713.
ajustement(m) de l'image(f) du cercle(m) vertical 713.
ajustement(m) de la hauteur(f) 157, 159.
akène(m) 62, 66.
alarme(f) sonore 485.
albumen(m) 109.
albumen(m) farineux 152.
alcool(m) à 90° 725.
alidade(f) 41, 484, 713.
alignement(m) du faisceau(m) dans l'axe(m) 717.
alimentation(f) en air(m) 543.
alimentation(f) en eau(f) 760, 761, 762, 763.
alimentation(f) jackpot(m) 702.
alimentation(f) solaire 523.
alimentation(f) sur secteur(m) 408.
**aliments(m), pollution(f) 32.**
allée(f) 193, 263, 676.
alliance(f) 364.
allumage(m) manuel 297.
allumette(f) de sûreté(f) 386.
allumeur(m) 435.
**allures(f), cheval(m) 101.**
**allures(f), voile(f) 629.**
ALPINISME(M) 680.
**alpinisme(m), équipement(m) 681.**
**alpinisme(m), matériel(m) 681.**
**alpiniste(m) 680.**
**altérations(f) 538.**
alternateur(m) 434, 468, 753, 758.
altimètre(m) 635, 639, 810.
altimètre(m) de secours(m) 500.
alto(m) 545.
alto-cumulus(m) 44.
alto-stratus(m) 44.
altos(m) 556.
alule(f) 110.
alvéole(f) 82.
alvéole(f) de plaque(f) 439.
alvéole(f) dentaire 144.
alvéole(m) 677.
alvéole(m) à miel(m) 82.
alvéole(m) à pollen(m) 82.
alvéole(m) operculé 82.
amande(f) 63, 66.
amanite(f) vireuse 55.
amble(m) 101.
**ambleur(m) sous harnais(m) 652.**
âme(f) 466, 692, 801.
Amérique(f) centrale 20.
Amérique(f) du Nord(m) 20.
Amérique(f) du Sud(m) 20.
améthyste(f) 363.
AMEUBLIR LA TERRE(F) 157.
**ameublir la terre(f) 154.**
amorce(f) 395, 798, 799, 804.
amortisseur(m) 369, 445.
amortisseur(m) arrière 443.
amortisseur(m) magnétique 708.
AMPHIBIENS(M) 84.
**amplificateur(m) 402.**
amplificateur(m) 714.
**amplification(f) des ondes(f) sismiques 714.**
ampoule(f) 232, 233, 725.
ampoule(f) de la trompe(f) utérine 129.
amygdale(f) 142.
amygdale(f) linguale 143.
amygdale(f) palatine 143.
ananas(m) 68.
anche(f) 542, 548.
anche(f) double 549.
anche(f) simple 549.
**anches(f) 549.**
anconé(m) 121.
ancrage(m) des haubans(m) 456.
ANCRE(F) 483.
ancre(f) 707.
ancre(f) à champignon(m) 483.
ancre(f) à jas(m) 483.
ancre(f) charrue(f) 483.
**ancre(f) de marine(f) 483.**
ancre(f) flottante 483.
ancre(f) sans jas(m) 483.
**ancres(f), types(m) 483.**
andouiller(m) de massacre(m) 105.
Andromède 11.
anémomètre(m) 41, 639.
anémomètre(m) de secours(m) 500.
aneth(m) 74.
angle(m) aigu 830.
angle(m) droit 830.
angle(m) obtu 830.
Anik-E 418.
ANIMAUX(M) DE LA FERME(F) 150.
**anis(m) étoilé 67.**
anneau(m) 55, 230, 255, 290, 369, 374, 564, 610, 660, 670, 681, 706, 709.
anneau(m) brisé 672.
anneau(m) d'étanchéité(f) 295.
anneau(m) d'étanchéité(f) en cire(f) 293.
anneau(m) de branche(f) 650.
anneau(m) de départ(m) 671.
anneau(m) de montant(m) 650.
anneau(m) de rêne(f) 650.
anneau(m) de retenue(f) 726.
anneau(m) de suspension(f) 370.
anneau(m) de tête(f) 671.
anneau(m) de tête(f) amovible 14.
anneau(m) de traction(f) 726.
anneau(m) dioptrique 486.
anneau(m) du cliquet(m) 281.
anneau(m) oculaire 109.
**anneaux(m) 660.**
anneaux(m) 361.
annelet(m) 167.
annulaire(m) 137.
anode(f) 297.
anorak(m) 353, 680.
anse(f) 265, 671.
Antarctique(f) 20.
antéfixe(f) 169.
antenne(f) 16, 43, 78, 79, 80, 81, 91, 408, 427, 498, 508, 613, 805, 810.
antenne(f) AM 400.
antenne(f) d'émission(f) 43, 418.
antenne(f) d'émission(f) à haut gain(m) 42.
antenne(f) d'émission(f) équidirective 42.
antenne(f) d'émission(f)/réception(f) 418.
antenne(f) de bande(f) S au zénith(m) 49.
antenne(f) de communication(f) 810.
antenne(f) de télécommande(f) 49.
antenne(f) de télécommunication(f) 494, 497, 809.
antenne(f) en bande(f) X 49.
antenne(f) FM 400.
antenne(f) multifonction 807.
antenne(f) orientable 722.
antenne(f) parabolique 415.
antenne(f) radar(m) 48, 807, 812.
antenne(f) radio(f) 494, 495, 497, 738, 742, 807.
antenne(f) UHF 42.
antenne(f) VHF 808.
antennule(f) 90.
anthélix(m) 139.
anthère(f) 60.
anticlinal(m) 737.
anticyclone(m) 38.
antiseptique(m) 725.
antitragus(m) 139.
anus(m) 89, 92, 127, 128, 131.
aorte(f) 125, 130.
aorte(f) abdominale 126, 132.
aorte(f) ascendante 124.
aorte(f) descendante 124.
aorte(f) ventrale 88.
apex(m) 83, 94, 143, 144.
apophyse(f) épineuse 135.
apophyse(f) transverse 135.
appareil(m) à dessiner 591.
appareil(m) à télémètre(m) couplé 394.
**appareil(m) à visée(f) reflex mono-objectif(m) 391.**
appareil(m) à visée(f) reflex mono-objectif(m) 394.
**appareil(m) de forage(m) 737.**
appareil(m) de Golgi 115.
appareil(m) de levage(m) 786.
appareil(m) de plongée(f) 394.
appareil(m) de pointage(m) 803.
appareil(m) de protection(f) respiratoire 777.
appareil(m) de videophoto(f) 395.
APPAREIL(M) DIGESTIF 131.
appareil(m) enregistreur 40.
appareil(m) jetable 394.
appareil(m) petit-format(m) 395.
appareil(m) photographique 35 mm 512.
appareil(m) pour photodisque(m) 395.

Les termes en **caractères gras** renvoient à une illustration, ceux en CAPITALES indiquent un titre.

appareil(m) reflex 6 X 6 mono-objectif(m) 395.
appareil(m) reflex à deux objectifs(m) 394.
**appareil(m) reflex, coupe(f) 390.**
APPAREIL(M) RESPIRATOIRE 130.
appareil(m) stéréoscopique 395.
APPAREIL(M) URINAIRE 132.
APPAREILS(M) DE CONDITIONNEMENT(M) PHYSIQUE 663, 664.
APPAREILS(M) DE NAVIGATION(F) 484.
APPAREILS(M) DE SON(M) PORTATIFS 408.
APPAREILS(M) ÉLECTROMÉNAGERS 250, 252, 254, 256, 257, 258, 260.
**appareils(m) photographiques 394, 395.**
appareils(m) scientifiques 16.
appartement(m) du commandant(m) 497.
appartements(m) en copropriété(f) 187.
appartenance(f) 830.
appel(m) suivant 422.
appendice(m) nasal 112.
appendice(m) vermiculaire 131.
applicateur(m)-mousse(f) 367.
applique(f) 234.
applique(f) d'extérieur(m) 196.
applique(f) du robinet(m) 295, 296.
applique(f) orientable 234.
appoggiature(f) 538.
appui(m) de fenêtre(f) 198.
appui-bras(m) 428, 429.
appui-flèche(m) 684.
appui-main(m) 591.
appui-pied(m) 584.
appui-pieds(m) 620.
appui-tête(m) 428.
**aquarelle(f) et gouache(f) 588.**
aquastat(m) 209.
aqueduc(m) de remplissage(m) 493.
aqueduc(m) de vidange(f) 492.
arachide(f) 66.
ARAIGNÉE(F) 77.
araignée(f) 77.
ARBALÈTE(F) 793.
**arbalète(f) 793.**
arbalétrier(m) 199.
arbitre(m) 599, 601, 603, 605, 606, 608, 610, 611, 614, 618, 621, 626, 668, 669.
arbitre(m) de champ(m) 612.
arbitre(m) de ligne(f) de but(m) 612.
arbitre(m) en chef(m) 597, 603, 605.
arborisation(f) terminale 135.
**arbre(m) 59.**
arbre(m) 251, 705, 707, 712, 753, 773, 808.
arbre(m) à cames(f) 434.
arbre(m) cannelé 431.
arbre(m) d'ornement(m) 148, 263.
arbre(m) de l'hélice(f) 495.
arbre(m) de mise(f) à feu(m) 802.
**arbre(m) de Noël(m) 740.**
arbre(m) de Noël(m) 738, 740.
arbre(m) de transmission(f) 492.
arbre(m) fruitier 149.
arbre(m) moteur(m) 508.
arbre(m) turbine(f)-compresseur(m) 501.
ARBRE(M), STRUCTURE(F) 59.
**arbre(m), tronc(m) 59.**
arbres(m) 676.
arbrier(m) 793.
arbuste(m) 263.
ARC(M) 174.
**arc(m) 793.**
arc(m) 793.
arc(m) à deux articulations(f) 455.
**arc(m) à poulies(f) 684.**
arc(m) à trois articulations(f) 455.
arc(m) branchial inférieur 87.
arc(m) branchial supérieur 87.
arc(m) de cercle(m) 601.
arc(m) de l'aorte(f) 124, 125, 126.
arc(m) diagonal 177.
**arc(m) en plein cintre(m) 174.**
arc(m) encastré 455.
arc(m) métallique à treillis(m) 455.
arc(m) moderne 793.
arc(m)-boutant 175, 176.
arc(m)-doubleau(m) 177.
arc(m)-formeret(m) 177.
arc-en-ciel(m) 36.
arcade(f) 176, 649.
arcade(f) dentaire inférieure 142.
arcade(f) dentaire supérieure 142.
arceau(m) 263, 631.
arche(f) 14, 455.
arche(f) naturelle 30.
**archer(m) 684.**
**archet(m) 544.**
archipel(m) 51.
ARCHITECTURE(F), STYLES(M) 166.
architrave(f) 166, 168.
arçon(m) 661.
ARCS(M) 793.
**arcs(m), types(m) 174, 455.**
Arctique(f) 20.
ardillon(m) 323, 566, 671.
aréole(f) 129.
arête(f) 27, 643.
arête(f) neurale 89.
arête(f) plate 166, 167.
arête(f) supérieure 619.
arête(f) vive 167.
argent(m) 819.
armature(f) 304, 347, 382, 685.
armature(f) de la clé(f) 538.
**armes(f) 666.**
ARMES(F) BLANCHES 794.
ARMES(F) DE CHASSE(F) 798.
ARMES(F) DE L'ÂGE(M) DE PIERRE(F) 791.
ARMES(F) DE L'ÉPOQUE(F) ROMAINE 791.
**armet(m) 792.**
armet(m) 792.
**armoire(f) 225.**
armoire(f) à papeterie(f) 522.
armoire(f) de séchage(m) 398.
armoire(f)-penderie(f) 226.
armoire(f)-vestiaire(m) 522.
ARMURE(F) 792.
**armures(f) de base(f) 576.**
arpège(m) 539.
ARQUEBUSE(F) 795.
**arraché(m) à deux bras(m) 662.**
**arrache-bottes(m) 358.**
arrache-clou(m) 275.
arrêt(m) 403, 411, 420, 831.
arrêt(m) à l'intersection(f) 824, 825.
arrêt(m) d'autobus(m) 186.
arrêt(m) d'impression(f) 532.
arrêt(m)/effacement(m) de mémoire(f) 405.
arrêt-court(m) 597.
arrêtoir(m) de chargeur(m) 797.
arrière 624.
arrière court(m) 614.
arrière(m) 603, 605, 606.
arrière(m) central 601.
arrière(m) centre 613.
arrière(m) droit 601, 607, 610, 612.
arrière(m) du court(m) 617.
arrière(m) gauche 601, 607, 610, 612, 613.
arrivée(f) 646.
arrivée(f) d'eau(f) chaude 298.
arrivée(f) du mazout(m) 209.
arrondie 56.
arrondissement(m) 52.
arrondisseur(m) 564.
**arroseur(m) canon(m) 264.**
arroseur(m) oscillant 264.
**arroseur(m) rotatif 264.**
**arrosoir(m) 265.**
artère(f) arquée 126.
artère(f) axillaire 126.
artère(f) brachiale 126.
artère(f) carotide primitive 126.
artère(f) dorsale du pied(m) 126.
artère(f) fémorale 126.
artère(f) iliaque 124.
artère(f) iliaque commune 126, 132.
artère(f) iliaque interne 126, 132.
artère(f) mésentérique inférieure 132.
artère(f) mésentérique supérieure 126, 132.
artère(f) pulmonaire 125, 126, 130.
artère(f) rénale 126, 132.
artère(f) sous-clavière 126.
artère(f) tibiale antérieure 126.
**artères(f) 126.**
artichaut(m) 69.
ARTICLES(M) DE BUREAU(M) 515, 516, 518.
ARTICLES(M) DE FUMEUR(M) 384, 386.
ARTICLES(M) DE MAROQUINERIE(F) 378.
articles(m) perdus et retrouvés 823.
articulation(f) 431, 670.
articulation(f) de la pelleteuse(f) 782.
As(m) 695.
ascenseur(m) 15, 190, 736, 811.
ascension(f) droite 3.
Asie(f) 21.
**asperge(f) 72.**
aspérité(f) 405.
asphalte(m) 745.
aspirateur(m) 747, 753.
**aspirateur(m) à main(f) 260.**
**aspirateur(m)-traîneau(m) 260.**
aspirine(f) 725.
assiette(f) à dessert(m) 238.
assiette(f) à salade(f) 238.
assiette(f) creuse 238.
assiette(f) plate 238, 688.
assistant(m) à la réalisation(f) 412.
astérisque(m) 832.
astéroïdes(m) 4.
asthénosphère(f) 22.
astragale(m) 123, 167, 800.
atelier(m) d'entretien(m) 734.
atelier(m) de mécanique(f) 453.
atelier(m) de réparation(f) des wagons(m) 465.
atelier(m) diesel(m) 464.
ATHLÉTISME(M) 654, 656, 658.
atlas(m) 102, 123.
atmosphère(f) 22, 31.
ATMOSPHÈRE(F) TERRESTRE, COUPE(F) 19.
atoll(m) 28.
âtre(m) 204.
atrium(m) 170.
attache(f) 375, 553.
attache(f) de pavillon(m) 549.
attache(f) de sécurité(f) 512.
attache(f) du tube(m) 233.
attache(f) pour outils(m) 512.
attache(f) pour tuyaux(m) et échelles(f) 777.
**attaches(f) 566.**
attaches(f) parisiennes 515.
attaquant(m) à l'aile(f) 611.
attaquant(m) au but(m) 611.
**attaque(f) 603, 605.**
atteinte(f) à la nature(f) 35.
atteinte(f) à la personne(f) 35.
attelles(f) 725.
attrape(f) 541.
aubage(m) directeur de sortie(f) 501.
aube(f) 754.
aube(f) avant-directrice 753.
aube(f) de roue(f) 753.
aube(f) directrice 753.
aube(f) du compresseur(m) axial 501.
aubergine(f) 69.
aubier(m) 59.
auget(m) 754.
aumonière(f) 380.
auriculaire(m) 137.
aurore(f) polaire 19.
Australie(f) 21.
Autel(m) 13.
**auto-caravane(f) 449.**
auto-inversion(f) 408.
autobus(m) 190.
**autocuiseur(m) 248.**
autodéfense(f) antimissile 808.
autodirecteur(m) infrarouge 814.
automne(m) 8.
AUTOMOBILE(F) 425, 426, 428, 430, 432, 434, 438.
autoroute(f) 52, 184, 452.
autoroute(f) de ceinture(f) 52.
**autres signes(m) 539.**
**autres techniques(f) 576.**
auvent(m) 426, 685, 785.
auvent(m) de fenêtre(f) 685.
avance(f) 408.
avance(f) rapide 403, 408, 411, 420, 831.
avançon(m) 672.
avant 624.
avant court(m) 614.
avant(m) centre 601, 607, 613.
avant(m) droit 606, 607, 610, 613.
avant(m) du court(m) 617.
avant(m) gauche 606, 607, 610, 613.
avant-bec(m) 786.
avant-bras(m) 106, 117, 119.
avant-centre(m) 612.
avant-champ(m) 597.
avant-distributeur(m) 753.
avant-scène(f) 188.
aven(m) 24.
avenue(f) 52.
averse(f) de grêle(f) 39.
averse(f) de neige(f) 39.
averse(f) de pluie(f) 39.
avertisseur(m) 430, 444, 468.
avertisseur(m) pneumatique 440.
avertisseur(m) sonore 777.
avion(m) 722.
AVION(M) DE COMBAT(M) 812.
AVION(M) LONG-COURRIER(M) 498.
AVIRON(M) 632.
**aviron(m) de couple(m) 632.**
**aviron(m) de pointe(f) 632.**
**aviron(m) en pointe(f) 632.**
**avirons(m) à couple(m) 632.**
**avirons(m), types(m) 632.**
avocat(m) 68.
avoine(f) 152.
axe(m) 290, 404, 563, 584.
axe(m) central 774.
axe(m) d'attelage(m) 471.
axe(m) de déclinaison(f) 14.
axe(m) du pédalier(m) 448.
axe(m) horaire 14.
axe(m) principal 61.
axis(m) 123.
axone(m) 135.
azur(m) 819.

**B**

babines(f) 106.
bâbord(m) 488, 489, 497.
bac(m) 304.
bac(m) à boue(f) 737.
bac(m) à glaçons(m) 254.
bac(m) à légumes(m) 254.
bac(m) à plante(f) 263.
bac(m) à viande(f) 254.
bac(m) de ramassage(m) 271.
bâche(f) spirale 747, 753.
badine(f) 375.
BADMINTON(M) 618.
**badminton(m), filet(m) 618.**
**badminton(m), raquette(f) 618.**
**badminton(m), terrain(m) 618.**
BAGAGES(M) 382.
bague(f) 384, 551, 678.
bague(f) de blocage(m) 276, 711.
bague(f) de correction(f) dioptrique 719.
bague(f) de fiançailles(f) 364.
bague(f) de finissant(m) 364.
bague(f) de fond(m) 294.
bague(f) de mise(f) au point(m) 392.
bague(f) de réglage(m) 264.
bague(f) de serrage(m) 295, 393, 548.
bague(f) filetée 681.
bague(f) inférieure de blocage(m) de la sphère(f) 40.
bague(f) solitaire(m) 364.
bague(f) supérieure de blocage(m) de la sphère(f) 40.
**bagues(f) 364.**
baguette(f) 327, 544, 795.
baguette(f) d'apport(m) 307.
baguette(f) d'écartement(m) 574.
baguette(f) d'encroix(m) 574.
baguette(f) de flanc(m) 427.
baguette(f) épi(m) 153.
baguette(f) parisienne 153.
baguettes(f) 553.
bahut(m) 520.
baie(f) 7, 51.
baie(f) de contrôle(m) 412, 413, 415.
baie(f) de jacks(m) 407.
**baie(f), coupe(f) 62.**
BAIES(F) 62.
**baies(f), principales variétés(f) 62.**
baignoire(f) 194, 215, 292.
bain(m) d'arrêt(m) 399.
bain(m) de fixation(f) 399.
bain(m) de révélateur(m) 399.
bain-marie(m) 249.
**bains(m) de développement(m) 399.**
baïonnette(f) à douille(f) 794.
baïonnette(f) à manche(m) 794.
baïonnette(f) à poignée(f) 794.
baïonnette(f) incorporée 794.
bajoyer(m) 492.
**baladeur(m) 408.**
**baladeuse(f) 310.**
balai(m) 205.
balai(m) à feuilles(f) 267.
balai(m) d'essuie-glace(m) 431.
balai(m) métallique 553.
**balais(m) de curling(m) 620.**
**balalaïka(f) 535.**
Balance(f) 13.
Balance(f) (23 septembre) 820.
**balance(f) à fléau(m) 708.**
balance(f) de cuisine(f) 244.
**balance(f) de précision(f) 709.**
**balance(f) de Roberval 708.**
**balance(f) électronique 709.**

FRENCH INDEX

Les termes en **caractères gras** renvoient à une illustration, ceux en CAPITALES indiquent un titre.

**balance(f) romaine 708.**
balancier(m) 264.
balancier(m) d'extension(f) 663.
balancier(m) de traction(f) 663.
balancine(f) 478.
balayage(m) automatique des stations(f) 402.
balcon(m) 189.
balcon(m) de veille(f) 486.
balconnet(m) 254.
Baleine(f) 11, 13.
baleine(f) 346, 375.
baleine(f) de col(m) 324.
baleinière(f) 482.
BALISAGE(M) MARITIME, SYSTÈME(M) 488.
balise(f) de navigation(f) aérienne 810.
ballast(m) 466.
ballast(m) électronique 233.
balle(f) 598, 795, 798.
**balle(f) de baseball(m) 596.**
**balle(f) de baseball(m), coupe(f) 596.**
balle(f) de fil(m) 596.
**balle(f) de golf(m) 677.**
**balle(f) de golf(m), coupe(f) 677.**
**balle(f) de hockey(m) 607.**
balle(f) de liège(m) 596.
**balle(f) de racquetball(m) 617.**
**balle(f) de squash(m) 616.**
**balle(f) de tennis(m) 615.**
balle(f) de tennis(m) de table(f) 619.
ballerine(f) 356.
**ballon(m) 634.**
ballon(m) 247, 634.
**ballon(m) de basket(m) 610.**
**ballon(m) de football(m) 600, 602.**
**ballon(m) de handball(m) 612.**
**ballon(m) de netball(m) 611.**
**ballon(m) de rugby(m) 606.**
**ballon(m) de volleyball(m) 613.**
**ballon(m) de water-polo(m) 626.**
balluchon(m) 380.
balustrade(f) 194.
banane(f) 68.
banc(m) 222, 475.
banc(m) d'équipe(f) 626.
**banc(m) de musculation(f) 663.**
banc(m) de sable(m) 30.
banc(m) des joueurs(m) 604, 608, 610, 612, 613.
banc(m) des officiels(m) 608.
banc(m) des pénalités(m) 608.
bandage(m) 669, 678.
bandage(m) de gaze(f) 662.
bandage(m) de roue(f) caoutchoutée 788.
bandage(m) triangulaire 725.
bande(f) 452, 608, 675.
bande(f) centrale 700, 701.
bande(f) d'identification(f) technique 405.
bande(f) de filet(m) 614.
bande(f) de gaze(f) 725.
bande(f) de pourpre(f) 315.
bande(f) de ris(m) 480.
bande(f) de roulement(m) 433.
bande(f) de tissu(m) élastique 725.
bande(f) élastique 323.
bande(f) horizontale 613.
bande(f) magnétique 403.
bande(f) réfléchissante 730, 777.
bande(f) ventilée 798.
bande(f) verticale de côté(m) 613.
bandeau(m) 229.
bandelette(f) d'arrachage(m) 384.
banderole(f) 817.
bandoulière(f) 375, 380, 382.
**banjo(m) 535.**
banlieue(f) 52.
banquette(f) 222, 292, 428.
**banquette(f) arrière 428.**
bar(m) 227, 496.
barbacane(f) 180.
barbe(f) 72, 110.
barboteuse(f) 351.
barbotin(m) 783, 805.
barbule(f) 38.
bardeau(m) 286.
bardeau(m) d'asphalte(m) 286.
baren(m) 582.
barge(f) de service(m) d'urgence(f) 739.
barillet(m) 290, 797.
baromètre(m) à mercure(m) 41.
baromètre(m) enregistreur 41.
**baromètre(m)/thermomètre(m) 710.**
barrage(m) 746.
**barrage(m) à contreforts(m) 751.**
**barrage(m) à contreforts(m), coupe(f) 751.**
**barrage(m) en remblai(m) 748.**
**barrage(m) en remblai(m), coupe(f) 748.**
barrage(m) mobile 752.
**barrage(m)-poids(m) 749.**
**barrage(m)-poids(m), coupe(f) 749.**
**barrage(m)-voûte(f) 750.**
**barrage(m)-voûte(f), coupe(f) 750.**
barre(f) 98, 104, 230, 376, 628, 633, 657, 663, 665.
barre(f) à aiguille(f) 562.
barre(f) à dorsaux(m) 663.
barre(f) à lisses(f) 574.
barre(f) à pectoraux(m) 663.
barre(f) à triceps(m) 663.
barre(f) blindée 747.
barre(f) cannelée 230.
barre(f) collectrice neutre 312.
barre(f) collectrice thermique 312.
barre(f) d'acier(m) 660.
barre(f) d'attelage(m) 803.
**barre(f) d'écoute(f) 630.**
barre(f) d'écoute(f) 628.
barre(f) d'espacement(m) 525, 530, 727.
barre(f) d'étouffoir(m) 541.
barre(f) de bois(m) 661.
barre(f) de commande(f) 637.
barre(f) de contrôle(m) 760, 761, 762, 763.
barre(f) de coupe(f) 158, 160.
barre(f) de départ(m) (dos(m)) 621.
barre(f) de flèche(f) 628.
barre(f) de guidage(m) et de prise(f) de courant(m) 476.
barre(f) de manœuvre(f) 162.
barre(f) de mesure(f) 537.
barre(f) de pied(m) presseur 562.
barre(f) de plongée(f) 806.
barre(f) de pression(f) 540.
barre(f) de repos(m) des marteaux(m) 540, 541.
barre(f) de reprise(f) 537.
barre(f) de retenue(f) 254.
barre(f) de tractage(m) 506.
**barre(f) fixe 660.**
barre(f) inférieure 231, 659.
barre(f) lisse 230.
barre(f) oblique 832.
barre(f) supérieure 659.
barre(f) transversale 626.
barreau(m) 201, 223.
**barres(f) asymétriques 659.**
barres(f) de Spa 646, 647.
**barres(f) parallèles 661.**
barrette(f) 369, 599.
barrette(f) négative 439.
barrette(f) positive 439.
barrière(f) 186, 462, 646, 647.
barrière(f) thermique 42.
**bas(m) 344.**
bas(m) 344, 347.
**bas(m) de ligne(f) 672.**
bas(m) résille(f) 344.
bas(m)-cuissarde(f) 344.
bas-mât(m) 478.
base(f) 14, 40, 143, 166, 283, 368, 446, 471, 626, 661, 719, 817.
base(f) de béton(m) 714.
base(f) de dormant(m) 203.
base(f) de la vague(f) 30.
base(f) en bois(m) 635.
BASEBALL(M) 595, 596.
**baseball(m), balle(f) 596.**
**baseball(m), terrain(m) 597.**
**basilaire(m) 190.**
basilaire(m) 190.
basilic(m) 74.
**basket(m), ballon(m) 610.**
BASKETBALL(M) 610.
**basketball(m), terrain(m) 610.**
basque(f) 346.
bassin(m) 103, 263, 490, 621, 626, 752.
**bassin(m) de compétition(f) 621.**
bassin(m) de radoub(m) 490.
bassinet(m) 132, 795.
basson(m) 548.
bassons(m) 557.
bastion(m) 179.
**bateaux(m) de couple(m) 632.**
**bateaux(m) de pointe(f) 632.**
bâti(m) 225, 484, 572, 583.
bâti(m) d'équipement(m) 412, 415.
bâti(m) de la pompe(f) à vide(m) 717.
bâti(m) du brûleur(m) 689.
bâtiment(m) administratif 491, 752.
bâtiment(m) de la turbine(f) 758.
bâtiment(m) des services(m) 764.
bâtiment(m) du réacteur(m) 759, 765.
**bâton(m) 596.**
bâton(m) 595, 642.
bâton(m) de craie(f) 583.
bâton(m) de gardien(m) de but(m) 609.
**bâton(m) de joueur(m) 609.**
bâton(m) de ski(m) 640.
bâtonnet(m) de colle(f) 515.
**bâtons(m) de golf(m) 678.**
**bâtons(m) de golf(m), types(m) 677.**
battant(m) 203, 554, 572, 817.
**batte(f) 598.**
batte(f) 160, 598.
**batterie(f) 552.**
batterie(f) 468, 795.
**batterie(f) d'accumulateurs(m) 439.**
batterie(f) d'accumulateurs(m) 769.
BATTERIE(F) DE CUISINE(F) 248.
batteries 43.
batteur(m) 599.
**batteur(m) à main(f) 250.**
batteur(m) à œufs(m) 245.
**batteur(m) sur socle(m) 250.**
baudrier(m) 428, 680.
bavette(f) 350, 351, 667.
bavette(f) garde-boue(m) 427, 440, 441.
bavette(f) garde-neige(m) 445.
bavoir(m) 349.
bavolet(m) 319.
BAZOOKA(M) 804.
bec(m) 108, 241, 291, 294, 295, 296, 483, 548, 567, 681.
bec(m) corné 97.
bec(m) de bord(m) d'attaque(f) 499.
bec(m) verseur 252.
bec(m) verseur(m) 247.
bec-de-cane(m) 289.
bécarre(m) 538.
bêche(f) 266, 803.
**becs(m), principaux types(m) 111.**
Bélier(m) 11.
Bélier(m) (21 mars) 820.
bémol(m) 538.
benne(f) 784.
benne(f) basculante 785.
béquet(m) 442.
béquille(f) 382, 441, 495, 508.
béquille(f) centrale 443.
**béquille(f) commune 728.**
béquille(f) d'appui(m) 156, 449.
**béquille(f) d'avant-bras(m) 728.**
béquille(f) latérale 443.
berceau(m) 582, 802.
berceuse(f) 221.
béret(m) 329.
berge(f) 451.
bergère(f) 220.
bergerie(f) 149.
berline(f) 425.
bermuda(m) 336.
bésicles(f) à pont(m) élastique 377.
béton(m) armé 286.
béton(m) précontraint 286.
**bette(f) à carde(f) 72.**
betterave(f) 71.
beurrier(m) 238.
bezel(m) (8) 363.
biais(m) 349, 566.
biceps(m) brachial 120.
biceps(m) crural 121.
bicorne(m) 318.
BICYCLETTE(F) 446, 448.
**bicyclette(f), accessoires(m) 448.**
bidet(m) 292.
bidon(m) 447.
bief(m) aval 749, 750.
bief(m) d'amont(m) 746.
bief(m) d'aval(m) 746, 747.
bielle(f) 436.
bielle(f) de compression(f) 147.
bielle(m) 434.
bigorneau(m) 83.
**bigoudi(m) 369.**
BIJOUTERIE(F) 361, 362, 364.
BILLARD(M) 673.
**billard(m) anglais 673.**
BILLARD(M) ANGLAIS ET SNOOKER(M) 674.
**billard(m) français 673.**
**billard(m) pool 673.**
bille(f) 288, 389, 530.
bille(f) blanche 673.
bille(f) blanche mouchetée 673.
bille(f) bleue 673.
bille(f) brune 673.
bille(f) creuse 294.
bille(f) d'ivoire(m) 701.
bille(f) de choc(m) 673.
bille(f) de plomb(m) 804.
bille(f) de visée(f) blanche 673.
bille(f) jaune 673.
bille(f) noire 673.
bille(f) rose 673.
bille(f) rouge 673.
bille(f) verte 673.
**bille(f), coupe(f) 288.**
billes(f) numérotées 673.
billes(f) rouges 673.
binette(f) 266.
binocle(m) 377.
**biologie(f) 831.**
**biosphère(f), structure(f) 31.**
bipied(m) 796, 803.
biseau(m) 542, 726.
bitte(f) 743.
blague(f) à tabac(m) 385.
**blaireau(m) 374.**
blanc(m) 695.
blanche(f) 538.
Blancs(m) 696, 697.
blazer(m) 338.
blé(m) 152.
**blé(m), grain(m) 152.**
blindage(m) 805.
blindage(m) d'aspirateur(m) 753.
bloc(m) 656.
bloc(m) aiguille(f) 590.
bloc(m) d'arrêt(m) 277.
bloc(m) d'équipement(m) 509.
bloc(m) de béton(m) 286.
bloc(m) de commande(f) 699.
bloc(m) de commande(f) des caméras(f) 412, 415.
bloc(m) de culasse(f) 798, 799.
**bloc(m) de départ(m) 656.**
bloc(m) pneumatique 458.
bloc(m)-cylindres(m) 435.
bloc(m)-éphéméride(f) 518.
bloc(m)-essieu(m) 645.
bloc(m)-moteur(m) 250, 251, 256, 260, 373, 458.
bloc(m)-notes(f) 518.
**bloc(m)-tension(f) 562, 569.**
bloc(m)-tension(f) 561.
blocage(m) 751.
blocage(m) de l'inclinaison(f) 284.
blocage(m) de l'interrupteur(m) 280.
blocage(m) de la colonne(f) 393.
blocage(m) de la plate-forme(f) 393.
blocage(m) de profondeur(f) 283.
blocage(m) du cordon(m) de tirage(m) 231.
blocage(m) du guide(m) 285.
blocage(m) du pivot(m) 282.
blocage(m) du pivotement(m) 713.
blocage(m) horizontal 393.
blocage(m) vertical 393.
bloqueur(m) droit 603, 605.
bloqueur(m) gauche 603, 605.
**blouson(m) court 321.**
**blouson(m) long 320.**
**bob(m) 329.**
bobine(f) 570, 575, 714.
bobine(f) de courant(m) 712.
bobine(f) de tension(f) 712.
bobine(f) mobile 406.
bobine(f) réceptrice 390, 403.
bobineur(m) 561.
**bobinoir(m) 575.**
BOBSLEIGH(M) 643.
bocal(m) 548.
body(m) 345.
bœuf(m) 151.
boggie(m) 14.
**bogie(m) 476.**
bogie(m) 468.
bogie(m) moteur 459.
bogie(m) porteur 458.
**bois(m) 288, 677.**
bois(m) 52.
bois(m) de bout(m) 288.
**bois(m) de cerf(m) 105.**
bois(m) de cœur(m) 59.
bois(m) nº 1 678.
bois(m) nº 3 678.
bois(m) nº 5 678.
**bois(m), dérivés(m) 288, 289.**
**bois(m), famille(f) 548.**
**bois(m), golf(m) 678.**

Les termes en **caractères gras** renvoient à une illustration, ceux en CAPITALES indiquent un titre.

boisseau(m) d'embouchure(f) 550.
**boîte(f) à canette(f) 562.**
boîte(f) à courrier(m) 517.
boîte(f) à gants(m) 430.
boîte(f) à leurres(m) 672.
boîte(f) à lumière(f) 399.
boîte(f) à lumière(f), ouverture(f) de la 399.
boîte(f) crânienne 134.
boîte(f) d'accessoires(m) 568.
boîte(f) d'allumage(m) 501.
**boîte(f) d'allumettes(f) 386.**
boîte(f) d'essieu(m) 468.
boîte(f) de cirage(m) 358.
boîte(f) de contrôle(m) 297.
boîte(f) de culasse(f) 795, 796.
boîte(f) de jonction(f) 471.
boîte(f) de raccordement(m) 412.
boîte(f) de service(m) 616, 617.
boîte(f) de vitesses(f) 495.
boîte(f) électrique 309, 769.
boîte(f) jackpot(m) 702.
boîte(f)-classeur(m) 517.
boîtier(m) 214, 231, 233, 280, 305, 310, 374, 391, 403, 406, 422, 485, 486, 539, 702, 705, 706, 710, 711.
boîtier(m) de batterie(f) 439, 441.
boîtier(m) du moteur(m) 272.
boîtier(m) du ventilateur(m) 370.
bol(m) 238, 250, 251.
bol(m) à raser 374.
bol(m) à salade(f) 238.
bol(m) verseur 251.
boléro(m) 338.
bols(m) à mélanger 245.
bombe(f) 648.
bombe(f) volcanique 25.
bôme(f) 628.
bonbout(m) 354.
bonde(f) 296.
bonnet(m) 329, 346, 640, 642.
bonnet(m) blanc 626.
bonnet(m) bleu 626.
bonnet(m) pompon(m) 329.
bord(m) 57, 328, 329, 479.
bord(m) antérieur 95.
bord(m) crénelé 95.
bord(m) d'attaque(f) 499, 636, 638.
**bord(m) d'une feuille(f) 56.**
bord(m) de fuite(f) 498, 636, 637, 638.
bord(m) de pli(m) 341.
bord(m) du manteau(m) 92.
bord(m) externe 94.
bord(m) interne 94.
bord(m) libre 137.
bord(m) postérieur 95.
bord(m) tranchant 783.
bord(m)-côte(f) 325, 326, 350.
bordure(f) 631.
bordure(f) blanche 619.
bordure(f) d'allée(f) 263.
bordure(f) de quai(m) 462, 475.
bordure(f) de trottoir(m) 186.
borne(f) 255, 309, 312, 439, 757.
borne(f) d'entrée(f) 310.
borne(f) d'incendie(m) 186.
borne(f) de gonflage(m) 453.
borne(f) négative 439.
borne(f) positive 439.
bossoir(m) 478, 742.
botte(f) 72, 356, 648.
botte(f) de caoutchouc(m) 777.
botte(f) de couronne(f) 653.
botte(f) de genou(m) 653.
botte(f) de saut(m) 635.
botte(f) de tendon(m) 648, 652.
bottillon(m) 354, 627.
bottine(f) 357.
**bouche(f) 142.**
bouche(f) 83, 84, 92, 118, 542, 797, 798, 799, 800, 803.
**bouche(f) à feu(m) 800.**
**bouche(f) à feu(m), coupe(f) 801.**
bouche(f) à induction(f) 207.
bouche(f) d'air(m) 430.
bouche(f) d'extraction(f) 207.
bouche(f) de soufflage(m) 206, 207.
**bouches(f), types(m) 207.**
bouchon(m) 250, 726, 765.
bouchon(m) antifuite 689.
bouchon(m) d'air(m) 304.
bouchon(m) de chargement(m) 804.
bouchon(m) de dégorgement(m) 296.
bouchon(m) de fermeture(f) 804.
bouchon(m) de remplissage(m) 271, 438, 444.
bouchon(m) de vidange(f) 215.
bouchon(m) de vidange(f) d'huile(f) 434.
bouchon(m) du réservoir(m) 440.
bouchon(m) femelle 301.
bouchon(m) femelle à visser 301.
bouchon(m) mâle sans bourrelet(m) 301.
**boucle(f) 566.**
boucle(f) 323, 380, 428, 452, 566, 641.
boucle(f) de ceinture(f) 319, 323.
boucle(f) de piquet(m) 685, 686.
boucle(f) de réglage(m) 231, 645.
**boucles(f) d'oreille(f) 361.**
boucles(f) d'oreille(f) à pince(f) 361.
boucles(f) d'oreille(f) à tige(f) 361.
boucles(f) d'oreille(f) à vis(f) 361.
bouclier(m) 268, 426, 609, 791.
bouclier(m) annulaire 15.
bouclier(m) arrière 16.
bouclier(m) thermique 510.
boue(f) 216.
**bouée(f) à plan(m) focal élevé 487.**
bouée(f) charpente(f) 487, 489.
bouée(f) conique 487, 489.
**bouée(f) cylindrique 486.**
bouée(f) de sauvetage(m) 495.
bouée(f) espar(m) 489.
bougie(f) 271.
**bougie(f) d'allumage(m) 439.**
bougie(f) d'allumage(m) 435, 437.
**bouilloire(f) 252.**
boule(f) 526, 683.
boule(f) à thé(m) 246.
boule(f) anglaise 682.
boule(f) de pétanque(f) 682.
**boule(f) de quilles(f) 683.**
BOULES(F) ANGLAISES ET PÉTANQUE(F) 682.
boulet(m) 101, 801.
boulet(m) creux 801.
boulet(m) ramé 801.
boulevard(m) 52, 184.
boulevard(m) périphérique 52.
boulier(m) 683.
**boulon(m) 279.**
boulon(m) 278, 282, 290.
**boulon(m) à ailettes(f) 276.**
**boulon(m) à épaulement(m) 279.**
boulon(m) à gaine(f) d'expansion(f) 276.
boulon(m) d'accouplement(m) 754.
boulon(m) d'éclisse(f) 466.
bourdalou(m) 328.
bourdon(m) 536.
bourgeon(m) 70.
bourgeon(m) axillaire 57.
bourgeon(m) terminal 57.
bourrache(f) 74.
bourre(f) 799, 801.
**bourre-pipe(m) 385.**
bourre-pipe(m) 385.
bourrelet(m) 104, 433, 632.
**bourriquet(m) 583.**
bourse(f) à monnaie(f) 379.
boursette(f) 543.
Boussole(f) 13.
BOUSSOLE(F) MAGNÉTIQUE 719.
bout(m) 239, 670.
bout(m) d'aile(f) 637.
bout(m) du nez(m) 100.
bout(m) fleuri 355.
bout(m)-filtre(m) 384.
boutefeu(m) 801.
bouteille(f) d'acétylène(m) 306.
bouteille(f) d'air(m) comprimé 627, 777.
bouteille(f) d'oxygène(m) 306.
bouteille(f) isolante 690.
**bouteur(m) 783.**
bouteur(m) 733.
boutique(f) 170.
boutique(f) hors taxe(f) 505.
bouton(m) 219, 232, 324, 326, 530, 536, 544, 666.
bouton(m) à friction(f) 711.
bouton(m) à tige(f) 566.
bouton(m) d'arrêt(m) 272.
bouton(m) d'assemblage(m) 568.
bouton(m) d'échappement(m) 541.
bouton(m) d'éjection(f) 403.
bouton(m) d'interligne(m) variable 525.
bouton(m) de blocage(m) 711.
bouton(m) de clé(f) 549.
bouton(m) de combinaisons(f) 542.
bouton(m) de commande(f) 255.
bouton(m) de culasse(f) 800.
bouton(m) de démarreur(m) 444.
bouton(m) de fonction(f) 699.
bouton(m) de manchette(f) 339.
bouton(m) de mise(f) au point(m) 720, 721.
bouton(m) de mise(f) au point(m) manuelle 397.
bouton(m) de mise(f) en circuit(m) 396, 420.
bouton(m) de piston(m) 550.
bouton(m) de point(m) arrière 561.
bouton(m) de registre(m) 542, 543.
bouton(m) de réglage(m) du micromètre(m) optique 713.
bouton(m) de remise(f) à zéro(m) 403, 711.
bouton(m) de tension(f) 569.
bouton(m) de vaporisation(f) 256.
bouton(m) de verrouillage(m) 429.
bouton(m) de verrouillage(m) de l'embase(f) 713.
bouton(m) extérieur 290.
bouton(m) floral 57.
bouton(m) intérieur 290.
bouton(m) marche(f)/arrêt(m) 256.
bouton(m) moleté 304.
bouton(m)-guide(m) 284.
bouton(m)-poussoir(m) 250, 257, 389, 397.
**bouton(m)-pression(f) 566.**
bouton(m)-pression(f) 321, 327.
boutonnage(m) sous patte(f) 330.
boutonnière(f) 319, 323.
boutons(m) à trous(m) 566.
boutons(m) de commande(f) 531.
boutons(m) de contrôle(m) du point(m) 569.
boutons(m) de réglage(m) 410.
Bouvier(m) 11.
BOXE(F) 669.
boxeur(m) 669.
bracelet(m) 602, 684, 706.
bracelet(m) lesté 665.
bracelet(m) tubulaire 364.
**bracelets(m) 364.**
brachial(m) antérieur 120.
braconnière(f) 792.
bractée(f) 66.
braguette(f) 323, 325, 350.
braies(f) 791.
brancard(m) 270, 652, 726, 784.
branche(f) 72, 104, 278, 369, 376, 564, 649, 684, 726.
branche(f) à fruits(m) 61.
branche(f) d'embouchure(f) 550.
branche(f) inférieure 650, 793.
branche(f) maîtresse 59.
branche(f) supérieure 650, 793.
branche(f) télescopique 393.
**branchement(m) aérien 757.**
branchement(m) de l'abonné(m) 757.
branchement(m) du distributeur(m) 757.
branchement(m) pluvial 186.
BRANCHEMENT(M), PLOMBERIE(F) 298.
branchicténie(f) 87.
**branchies(f) 87.**
branchies(f) 88, 92.
branchies(f) externes 84.
brandebourg(m) 320.
bras(m) 100, 117, 119, 157, 234, 264, 483, 561, 702, 727, 773, 782, 785.
bras(m) d'essuie-glace(m) 431.
bras(m) de coutre(m) 156.
bras(m) de fourche(f) 787.
bras(m) de grand cacatois(m) arrière 480.
bras(m) de lecture(f) 404.
bras(m) de levage(m) 782.
bras(m) de plaquette(f) 376.
bras(m) de relevage(m) 147.
bras(m) de suspension(f) 258.
bras(m) du longeron(m) 783.
bras(m) gicleur(m) 257.
bras(m) spiral 9.
bras(m) télécommandé 510.
brassard(m) 602, 609, 792.
brassard(m) pneumatique 710.
**brasse(f) 622.**
brassière(f) 349.
break(m) 425.
brelan(m) 695.
**breloques(f) 364.**
bretèche(f) 181.
bretelle(f) 346, 452, 464, 502.
bretelle(f) boutonnée 351.
bretelle(f) de raccordement(m) 452.
bretelle(f) pour botte(f) de genou(m) 653.
bretelle(f) réglable 350.
**bretelles(f) 323.**
brick(m) 482.
**bride(f) 649.**
bride(f) 365, 566, 653.
bride(f) de corps-mort(m) 486.
bride(f) de fixation(f) 720, 721.
bride(f) de raccord(m) 230.
bride(f) de suspension(f) 326.
brigantin(m) 482.
brigantine(f) 480.
brin(m) d'arrêt(m) 811.
brique(f) 286.
brique(f) réfractaire 204, 585.
**briquet(m) 307.**
**briquet(m) à gaz(m) 386.**
brise-jet(m) 264.
brise-lame(m) 742.
broche(f) 232, 233, 309, 364, 574.
broche(f) épingle(f) 364.
broche(f) porte-bobine(m) 561.
brocoli(m) 69.
brodequin(m) 355.
**brodequin(m) de sécurité(f) 730.**
BRODERIE(F) 571.
bronche(f) droite 130.
bronchiole(f) terminale 130.
brosse(f) 152, 373, 589.
brosse(f) à chaussure(f) 358.
**brosse(f) à coiffer 370.**
**brosse(f) à dents(f) 373.**
brosse(f) à dents(f) 373.
brosse(f) à épousseter 260.
brosse(f) à légumes(m) 246.
brosse(f) à mascara(m) 367.
brosse(f) à peignes(m) 370.
brosse(f) à planchers(m) 260.
brosse(f) à pollen(m) 80, 81.
brosse(f) anglaise 368.
brosse(f) d'antennes(f) 80.
brosse(f) de nettoyage(m) 374.
brosse(f) de tissage(m) 568.
brosse(f) éventail(m) 589.
brosse(f) pneumatique 368.
brosse(f) ronde 368.
brosse(f)-araignée(f) 368.
brosse(f)-peigne(m) pour cils(m) et sourcils(m) 367.
**brosses(f) à cheveux(m) 368.**
**brou(m) 66.**
**brouette(f) 270.**
brouillard(m) 37, 39.
**broyer, ustensils(m) pour 243.**
broyeur(m) 296.
bruine(f) continue 39.
bruine(f) intermittente 39.
brûleur(m) 209, 297, 634, 635, 689.
**brûleur(m) à mazout(m) 209.**
brûleur(m) bec(m) plat 307.
brûleur(m) flamme(f) crayon(m) 299, 307.
brume(f) 37, 39.
brunissoir(m) 582.
buanderie(f) 194.
buccin(m) 83.
bûcher(m) 204.
bûchette(f) 320.
buffet(m) 227.
buffet(m)-vaisselier(m) 227.
bulbe(m) 72, 136.
bulbe(m) d'étrave(f) 497, 743.
bulbe(m) olfactif 88, 142.
bulbe(m) rachidien 134.
**bulbe(m), coupe(f) 70.**
bureau(m) 453.
bureau(m) de direction(f) 520.
bureau(m) de réservation(f) de chambres(f) d'hôtel(m) 504.
bureau(m) des douanes(f) 491.
bureau(m) du changeur(m) 474.
**bureau(m) secrétaire(m) 521.**
Burin(m) 13.
burin(m) 581, 587.
bus(m) de données(f) 528.
bus(m) des données(f) 531.
bus(m) du disque(m) dur 528.
buse(f) 264, 291, 306, 370, 373, 590.
buse(f) à fluide(m) 304.
bustier(m) 346.
but(m) 601, 604, 606, 607, 608, 612, 626.
butée(f) 455, 566, 630, 640, 641.
butée(f) de porte(f) 254, 471.
butée(f) talonnière(f) 727.
butoir(m) 230, 464.
butoir(m) de saut(m) 657.
butte(f) 46.
butte(f) de débranchement(m) 465.

Les termes en **caractères gras** renvoient à une illustration, ceux en CAPITALES indiquent un titre.

# C

**caban(m) 330.**
cabas(m) 381.
cabillot(m) 817.
cabine(f) 496, 508, 782, 783, 784, 785.
cabine(f) de commande(f) 786.
cabine(f) de commandes(f) 15.
cabine(f) de conduite(f) 147, 160, 459, 468.
cabine(f) de douche(f) 292.
**cabine(f) de pilotage(m) 639.**
cabine(f) de pilotage(m) 493.
cabine(f) des passagers(m) 493, 494, 495.
CÂBLE(M) 692.
câble(m) 280, 641, 658, 660, 663, 684, 692.
câble(m) d'accélération(f) 271.
câble(m) d'acier(m) 681.
câble(m) d'alimentation(f) de 240 V 312.
câble(m) d'alimentation(f) de l'électrode(f) 305.
câble(m) de bougie(f) 435.
câble(m) de commande(f) 270, 448.
câble(m) de frein(m) 447.
câble(m) de garde(f) 756.
câble(m) de haubanage(m) 660.
câble(m) de levage(m) 786.
câble(m) de masse(f) 305.
cable(m) de raccordement(m) 406.
câble(m) de raccordement(m) 400, 530, 585.
câble(m) de traction(f) 311.
câble(m) de transmission(f) 485.
câble(m) du démarreur(m) 270.
câble(m) électrique 186.
câble(m) porteur 456.
câble(m) téléphonique 186.
câbles(m) 414.
câblodistributeur(m) 416.
cabriolet(m) 220, 425.
cache-cœur(m) 337.
cache-flammes(m) 796.
cache-oreilles(m) abattant 328.
cadenas(m) 448.
cadence(f) images(f)/seconde(f) 396.
cadran(m) 705, 706, 707, 708, 712, 719.
cadran(m) de tension(f) 568.
cadran(m) des phases(f) de la Lune(f) 707.
cadran(m) gradué 710.
**cadran(m) solaire 706.**
cadre(m) 82, 378, 383, 443, 536, 615, 645, 659, 674, 726, 773.
cadre(m) de charge(f) 635.
cadre(m) de marche(f) 728.
cadre(m) métallique 540.
cadre(m) porte-épreuves(m) 399.
cadre(m)-cache(m) 397.
cæcum(m) 131.
cæcum(m) pylorique 88.
cafetière(f) 688.
**cafetière(f) à infusion(f) 247.**
**cafetière(f) à piston(m) 247.**
**cafetière(f) espresso(m) 247.**
**cafetière(f) filtre(m) 247.**
**cafetière(f) napolitaine 247.**
CAFETIÈRES(F) 247.
cage(f) 654.
cage(f) d'escalier(m) 194.
cage(f) de battage(m) 161.
cage(f) vitrée 709.
**cagoule(f) 329.**
cagoule(f) 627, 680.
cahier(m) 577.
caïeu(m) 70.
caisse(f) 270, 540, 546, 707.
caisse(f) blindée 702.
caisse(f) bombée 535.
caisse(f) circulaire 535.
**caisse(f) claire 553.**
caisse(f) claire 552, 557.
caisse(f) cylindrique 710.
caisse(f) de résonance(f) 545.
caisse(f) de résonnance(f) 535.
caisse(f) pleine 547.
caisse(f) roulante 553.
caisse(f) triangulaire 535.
caisson(m) 204, 209, 521.
caisson(m) de porte(f) 429.
caisson(m) de voilure(f) 812.
calame(m) 389.
calamus(m) 110.
calandre(f) 426, 440, 765.
calcanéum(m) 103, 123.
CALCULATRICE(F) 523.
**calculatrice(f) à imprimante(f) 523.**
**calculette(f) 523.**
calculette(f) 379.
cale(f) 506, 800.
cale(f) à conteneurs(m) 495.
cale(f) de couvercle(m) 585.
cale-pied(m) 446, 448, 664.
caleçon(m) 325.
caleçon(m) long 325.
calendrier(m)-mémorandum(m) 518.
calice(m) 60, 62, 67, 132.
calicule(m) 62.
Callisto 4.
caloporteur(m) 766.
caloporteur(m) chaud 771.
caloporteur(m) refroidi 771.
caloporteur(m): eau(f) bouillante 763.
caloporteur(m): eau(f) lourde sous pression(f) 761.
caloporteur(m): eau(f) sous pression(f) 762.
caloporteur(m): gaz(m) carbonique 760.
calot(m) 328.
calotte(f) 109, 328, 329, 773.
calotte(f) glaciaire 45.
cambium (m) 59.
cambre(f) 376.
cambrure(f) 354.
Caméléon(m) 13.
**caméra(f) 414.**
caméra(f) 16, 412, 414.
caméra(f) de télévision(f) couleurs(f) 512.
caméra(f) video 526.
CAMÉRA(M) VIDÉO 409.
camion(m) avitailleur 506.
camion(m) commissariat(m) 507.
camion(m) vide-toilette(m) 506.
**camion(m)-benne(f) 785.**
camion(m)-citerne(f) d'eau(f) potable 506.
CAMIONNAGE(M) 440.
camionnette(f) 425.
CAMPING(M) 685, 686, 690.
camping(m) 823.
camping(m) et caravaning(m) 823.
camping(m) interdit 823.
**camping(m), accessoires(m) 689.**
**camping(m), matériel(m) 690.**
**camping(m), outils(m) 690.**
canadienne(f) 321.
canal(m) à venin(m) 96.
canal(m) d'admission(f) 436.
canal(m) d'échappement(m) 436.
canal(m) d'écoulement(m) 741.
canal(m) de dérivation(f) 501, 746.
canal(m) de fuite(f) 747.
canal(m) de transfert(m) 436, 764.
canal(m) déférent 127.
canal(m) droit 401.
canal(m) éjaculateur 127.
canal(m) gauche 401.
canal(m) radiculaire 144.
canal(m) semi-circulaire antérieur 139.
canal(m) semi-circulaire externe 139.
canal(m) semi-circulaire postérieur 139.
canal(m) siphonal 94.
canal(m) sudoripare 136.
canalisation(f) 432.
canalisation(f) d'alimentation(f) 208, 209.
canalisation(f) de branchement(m) 215.
canalisation(f) de la veilleuse(f) 297.
canalisation(f) de pompage(m) 717.
canalisation(f) de refoulement(m) 216.
canalisation(f) de retour(m) 208.
canalisation(f) du brûleur(m) 297.
canapé(m) 221.
canapé(m) capitonné 221.
canard(m) 150.
Cancer(m) 11.
Cancer(m) (22 juin) 820.
**canetière(f) 575.**
canette(f) 561, 562, 573.
canif(m) 581.
canine(f) 98, 144.
CANNE(F) 375.
canne(f) 375.
**canne(f) à lancer(m) 671.**
**canne(f) à mouche(f) 670.**
canne(f) avec poignée(f) orthopédique 728.
canne(f) avec quadripode(m) 728.
canne(f) en C(m) 728.
canne(f) en T(m) 728.
canneberge(f) 62.
cannelure(f) 166, 167, 439.
**cannes(f) 728.**
canon(m) 101, 650, 795, 796, 797, 798, 799, 802, 805.
**canon(m) à électrons(m) 410.**
canon(m) à électrons(m) 410, 717.
canon(m) à mousse(f) 743.
canon(m) brisé 650.
canon(m) d'avant-bras(m) 792.
CANON(M) DU XVII{E} SIÈCLE(M) 800.
CANON(M) SANS RECUL(M) 804.
canot(m) de sauvetage(m) 478, 738.
canot(m) pneumatique de sauvetage(m) 492.
canotier(m) 328.
cantaloup(m) 69.
canton(m) dextre de la pointe(f) 818.
canton(m) dextre du chef(m) 818.
canton(m) senestre de la pointe(f) 818.
canton(m) senestre du chef(m) 818.
cantonnière(f) 228, 383.
cantonnière(f) drapée 229.
cantre(m) 575.
canyon(m) sous-marin 29.
cap(m) 51.
**cape(f) 331.**
cape(f) 384.
**cape(f) de bain(m) 349.**
capeline(f) 329.
capitaine(m) 620, 643.
capitale(f) 51.
capitule(m) 60.
caponnière(f) 179.
capot(m) 256, 260, 426, 440, 445, 525.
Capricorne(m) 13.
Capricorne(m) (22 décembre) 820.
capsule(f) 725.
capsule(f) à membrane(f) 435.
**capsule(f), coupe(f) 67.**
capteur(m) de radiations(f) terrestres 43.
capteur(m) de signaux(m) de détresse(f) 43.
capteur(m) de télécommande(f) 405, 410.
capteur(m) solaire 772.
**capteur(m) solaire plan 768.**
capture(f) 697.
capuche(f) 349.
capuche(f) coulissée 351.
capuchon(m) 309, 320, 389, 398, 679.
capuchon(m) d'objectif(m) 392.
capuchon(m) de protection(f) 718.
capuchon(m) de sûreté(f) 804.
capuchon(m) de ventilation(f) 486.
capuchon(m) du levier(m) 295.
capucin(m) 323.
caquelon(m) 248.
CAR(M) DE REPORTAGE(M) 415.
car(m) de reportage(m) 416.
**carabine(f) (canon(m) rayé) 798.**
caraco(m) 316, 345.
carafe(f) 237.
carafon(m) 237.
**carapace(f) 96.**
carapace(f) 91.
CARAVANE(F) 449.
**caravane(f) tractée 449.**
caravaning(m) 823.
carburant(m) diesel(m) 745.
carburateur(m) 442.
carburéacteur(m) 745.
cardan(m) 156, 159, 162.
carde(f) 72.
cardigan(m) 326.
cardon(m) 72.
carénage(m) 442.
Carène(f) 13.
CARGO(M) PORTE-CONTENEURS(M) 494.
cargue(f) 480.
cargue-point(m) 481.
carillon(m) tubulaire 554, 556.
carlingue(f) centrale 743.
carnassière(f) 98.
**carnivore(m), mâchoire(f) 98.**
carnivores(m) 31, 33.
caroncule(f) lacrymale 140.
carotte(f) 71.
carpe(m) 102, 122.
carquois(m) 684.
carre(f) 640, 644.
carré(m) 695, 700, 701.
**carreau(m) 570.**
carreau(m) 203, 286, 695.
carreau(m) d'arbalète(f) 793.
**carreau(m) de mine(f) 734.**
carreau(m) de plâtre(m) 286.
carrefour(m) giratoire 450.
**carrière(f) en entonnoir(m) 733.**
**carrière(f) exploitée en chassant 733.**
**carrosserie(f) 426.**
carrosserie(f) 258, 259.
**carrosseries(f), types(m) 425.**
carte(f) de ligne(f) 474.
carte(f) de réseau(m) 475, 477.
carte(f) isolée 695.
**carte(f) météorologique 38.**
**carte(f) physique 51.**
**carte(f) politique 51.**
**carte(f) routière 52.**
carter(m) 211, 271, 397, 434, 436, 671.
carter(m) d'embrayage(m) 444.
carter(m) d'engrenage(m) de frein(m) à main(f) 470.
carter(m) de sécurité(f) 271.
CARTES(F) 695.
**cartes(f), symboles(m) 695.**
cartilage(m) de l'aile(f) du nez(m) 141.
cartilage(m) de la cloison(f) 141.
CARTOGRAPHIE(F) 47, 50, 52.
carton(m) 589.
cartouche(f) 291, 295, 384, 389, 404, 527, 730, 797.
**cartouche(f) (carabine(f)) 798.**
**cartouche(f) (fusil(m)) 799.**
cartouche(f) de jeu(m) 699.
**cartouche(f) de pellicule(f) 395.**
cartouche(f) de ruban(m) 531.
cartouche(f) jetable 299, 307.
casaque(f) 337.
case(f) 165, 701.
case(f) à bagages(m) 461.
case(f) blanche 696.
case(f) d'équipement(m) 16.
case(f) noire 696.
casernement(m) 179.
casier(m) 226.
casier(m) à beurre(m) 254.
casier(m) à munitions(f) 805.
casier(m) laitier 254.
casque(m) 308, 512, 602, 609, 636, 651, 680, 777, 791.
CASQUE(M) D'ÉCOUTE(F) 406.
casque(m) d'écoute(f) 408.
casque(m) de frappeur(m) 595.
**casque(m) de protection(f) 443.**
casque(m) de protection(f) 448.
**casque(m) de sapeur(m)-pompier(m) 777.**
casque(m) de saut(m) 635.
**casque(m) de sécurité(f) 729.**
casque(m) protecteur 643.
**casquette(f) 328.**
**casquette(f) norvégienne 328.**
casse-croûte(m) 822.
casse-noix(m) 243.
casserole(f) 249.
**cassette(f) 403.**
cassette(f) 408, 526.
cassette(f) annonce(f) 420.
cassette(f) de pellicule(f) 395.
cassette(f) messages(m) 420.
Cassiopée 11.
cassis(m) 62.
cassure(f) 341.
castagnettes(f) 554, 556.
**castor(m) 98.**
catadioptre(m) 445, 446.
catapulte(f) 810.
caténaire(f) 459.
**cathédrale(f) 176.**
cathédrale(f) 184.
CATHÉDRALE(F) GOTHIQUE 175, 176.
**cathédrale(f), plan(m) 177.**
causeuse(f) 221.
**cavalier(m) 648.**
cavalier(m) 178.
Cavalier(m) 696.
cavité(f) abdominale 127, 128.
cavité(f) buccale 130, 131.
cavité(f) nasale 130.
cavité(f) pleurale 130.
cédez le passage(m) 824, 825.
cédille(f) 832.
**ceinture(f) 323.**
ceinture(f) 219, 220, 223, 319, 433, 668.
ceinture(f) d'haltérophilie(f) 662.
ceinture(f) de sécurité(f) 428.
ceinture(f) élastique 321, 325.
ceinture(f) lestée 627.
ceinture(f) montée 320, 323.
**céleri(m) 72.**
céleri(m)-rave(f) 71.

Les termes en **caractères gras** renvoient à une illustration, ceux en CAPITALES indiquent un titre.

cellule(f) 79.
CELLULE(F) ANIMALE 115.
cellule(f) photoélectrique 393.
cellule(f) royale 82.
CELLULE(F) VÉGÉTALE 115.
cellules(f) solaires 42.
cément(m) 144.
cendre(f) 386.
**cendrier(m) 386.**
cent(m) 832.
Centaure(m) 13.
centrage(m) 524.
centrale(f) 746.
**centrale(f) hydroélectrique, coupe(f) 747.**
**centrale(f) nucléaire 758.**
centre(m) 601, 603, 605, 606, 608, 610, 611, 620, 684, 697, 818.
centre(m) de gravité(f) 483.
centre(m) droit 606.
centre(m) du court(m) 617.
centre(m) gauche 606.
CENTRE(M)-VILLE(F) 184.
**centrifugeuse(f) 251.**
centriole(m) 115.
**cep(m) de vigne(f) 61.**
cèpe(m) 55.
céphalothorax(m) 90.
Céphée 11.
cercle(m) 376, 654, 655.
cercle(m) central 601, 608, 610, 611.
cercle(m) d'ascension(f) droite 720, 721.
cercle(m) d'attente(f) 597.
cercle(m) d'envoi(m) 607.
cercle(m) de déclinaison(f) 720, 721.
cercle(m) de la station(f) 38.
cercle(m) de mise(f) au jeu(m) 608.
cercle(m) de serrage(m) 553.
cercle(m) de vannage(m) 753.
cercle(m) de verrouillage(m) 802.
cercle(m) extérieur 620.
cercle(m) intérieur 620.
cercle(m) polaire antarctique 3.
cercle(m) polaire arctique 3, 47.
cercle(m) porte-lame(m) 784.
cercle(m) restrictif 610.
CÉRÉALES(F), PRINCIPALES VARIÉTÉS(F) 152.
cerf(m) de Virginie 105.
cerf(m) du Canada 105.
**cerf(m), bois(m) 105.**
cerfeuil(m) 74.
cerise(f) 63.
cerne(m) annuel 59.
cerneau(m) 66.
cerques(m) 670.
cerveau(m) 88, 134.
cervelet(m) 134.
CERVIDÉS(M) 105.
**cervidés(m), principaux 105.**
chaîne(f) 446, 448, 566, 573, 574, 661, 707.
**chaîne(f) alimentaire 31.**
chaîne(f) coupante 272.
chaîne(f) d'entraînement(m) 158.
chaîne(f) de levage(m) 787.
chaîne(f) de montagnes(f) 7, 23, 51.
chaîne(f) de mouillage(m) 486.
**chaîne(f) de neurones(m) 135.**
chaîne(f) de sureté(f) 449.
chaîne(f) de suspension(f) 756.
CHAÎNE(F) STÉRÉO 400, 402, 404.
**chaîne(f) stéréo, composantes(f) 400.**
chaînes(f) d'ancrage(m) 738.
chaînette(f) de levage(m) 293.
CHAISE(F) 223.
chaise(f) berçante 223.
chaise(f) dactylo(m) 521.
chaise(f) longue 223.
chaise(f) pliante 223.
chaise(f)-escabeau(m) 222.
chaises(f) empilables 223.
**chaises(f), types(m) 223.**
chalaze(f) 109.
chalet(m) 676.
chaloupe(f) de sauvetage(m) 494, 496.
chalumeau(m) 306, 536.
**chalumeau(m) coupeur 306.**
**chalumeau(m) soudeur 306.**
chalumeau(m) soudeur 307.
chambranle(m) 202, 203.
chambre(f) 194, 195, 460, 685, 736.
chambre(f) à air(m) 109.
chambre(f) à poudre(f) 801.
chambre(f) à vide(m) 717.
chambre(f) antérieure 140.
chambre(f) d'expansion(f) 705.
chambre(f) d'observation(f) 717.
chambre(f) de combustion(f) 204, 209, 434, 438.
chambre(f) de combustion(f) annulaire 501.
chambre(f) de cuisson(f) 585.
chambre(f) de dilatation(f) 485.
chambre(f) de mélange(m) 306.
chambre(f) de vantail(m) 493.
chambre(f) des machines(f) 806.
chambre(f) des pompes(f) 742.
chambre(f) des torpilles(f) 807.
chambre(f) photographique 394, 717.
chambre(f) postérieure 140.
chambre(f) principale 194.
chambre(f) pulpaire 144.
champ(m) centre(m) 597.
champ(m) d'épandage(m) 216.
champ(m) d'héliostats(m) 770, 771.
champ(m) droit 597.
champ(m) gauche 597.
champ(m) magnétique 410.
CHAMPIGNON(M) 55.
champignon(m) 466.
champignon(m) de couche(f) 55.
**champignon(m) mortel 55.**
**champignon(m) vénéneux 55.**
**champignon(m), structure(f) 55.**
**champignons(m) comestibles 55.**
chandail(m) 602.
chandail(m) d'équipe(f) 595, 600.
chandail(m) de dessous(m) 595.
chanfrein(m) 100.
change(m) 823.
changement(m) de piste(f) 405.
chanterelle(f) commune 55.
chape(f) 200, 230, 485, 543.
chapeau(m) 55.
chapeau(m) d'angle(m) 470.
**chapeau(m) de feutre(m) 328.**
chapeau(m) de ventilation(f) 215.
chapeau(m) du battant(m) 573.
chapelle(f) 181.
chapelle(f) axiale 177.
chapelle(f) latérale 176.
chapiteau(m) 166, 545.
chapka(m) 328.
CHAR(M) D'ASSAUT(M) 805.
charge(f) explosive 804.
charge(f) militaire 814.
charge(f) utile 509.
chargeur(m) 795, 796, 797.
chargeur(m) automatique 532.
chargeur(m) manuel 532.
chargeuse(f) frontale 782.
**chargeuse(f)-pelleteuse(f) 782.**
chariot(m) 230, 306, 568, 630, 679, 718, 786.
chariot(m) à bagages(m) 463.
chariot(m) à dentelle(f) 568.
chariot(m) à palette(f) 788.
chariot(m) à plateau(m) 788.
chariot(m) avant 568.
chariot(m) d'entraînement(m) 230.
chariot(m) de croisement(m) 230.
**chariot(m) élévateur 787.**
chariot(m) transbordeur 457.
**chariots(m) 568.**
Charles IX(m) 356.
charnière(f) 253, 257, 378, 382, 404, 429, 585, 641, 719.
charnière(f) de la visière(f) 443.
Charon 5.
**charpente(f) 198.**
charpente(f) 168, 170.
charpente(f) verticale 574.
**charrue(f) à soc(m) 156.**
charrue(f) à soc(m) 154.
chas(m) 562, 563.
chasse(f) 577.
chasse-neige(f) faible basse 39.
chasse-neige(f) forte basse 39.
chasse-pierres(m) 459, 469.
châssis(m) 156, 157, 159, 272, 453, 553, 554, 785, 787, 788.
châssis(m) de bogie(m) 468.
châssis(m)-presse(f) 398.
chasuble(f) 333.
CHAT(M) 107.
**chat(m), tête(f) 107.**
châtaigne(f) 100.
château(m) d'eau(f) 465.
CHÂTEAU(M) FORT 180.
chatière(f) 196.
chaton(m) 364.
**chaudière(f) 209.**
chaudière(f) 208, 771.
CHAUFFAGE(M) 204, 206, 208, 210, 212.
**chauffage(m) à air(m) chaud pulsé 206.**
**chauffage(m) à eau(f) chaude 208.**
**chauffage(m) d'appoint(m) 211.**
**chauffage(m), bouches(f) 207.**
chauffe-eau(m) 215, 772.
**chauffe-eau(m) au gaz(m) 297.**
chaufferette(f) 689.
chaumard(m) 630.
**chausse-pied(m) 358.**
chaussée(f) 186, 450.
chaussée(f) cahoteuse 826, 827.
chaussée(f) glissante 826, 827.
chaussée(f) rétrécie 826, 827.
chaussette(f) 325, 344, 602, 615, 642, 667.
chaussette(f)-étrier(m) 595.
**chaussettes(f) 325.**
chausson(m) 627.
chausson(m) intérieur 641, 645.
chaussure(f) 598, 642, 644, 645.
chaussure(f) à crampons(m) 595, 602.
chaussure(f) d'alpinisme(m) 680.
chaussure(f) d'escrime(f) 667.
chaussure(f) d'haltérophilie(f) 662.
chaussure(f) de football(m) 600.
chaussure(f) de golf(m) 679.
chaussure(f) de piste(f) 656.
**chaussure(f) de ski(m) 641.**
chaussure(f) de ski(m) 640.
**chaussure(f) de sport(m) 352.**
chaussure(f) de tennis(m) 615.
**chaussure(f), parties(f) 354.**
CHAUSSURES(F) 354, 356, 358.
**chaussures(f), principaux types(m) 354, 355, 356.**
**chaussures, accessoires(m) 358.**
CHAUVE-SOURIS(F) 112.
chef(m) 818.
chemin(m) 676.
chemin(m) couvert 178.
chemin(m) de fer(m) 52.
CHEMIN(M) DE FER(M) MÉTROPOLITAIN 474, 476.
chemin(m) de ronde(f) 181.
chemin(m) de ronde(f) couvert 180.
chemin(m) de roulement(m) 786.
**cheminée(f) 205.**
cheminée(f) 25, 195, 197, 209, 297, 494, 736.
**cheminée(f) à foyer(m) ouvert 204.**
cheminée(f) à minerai(m) 736.
cheminée(f) anti-suie 496.
cheminée(f) d'échappement(m) 147, 440, 784.
**chemise(f) 324.**
chemise(f) 518, 798.
chemise(f) de nuit(f) 348.
chemise(f) du donjon(m) 181.
chemisier(m) classique 337.
**chemisiers(m), types(m) 337.**
chenal(m) principal 489.
chenal(m) secondaire 489.
chenêts(m) 205.
**chenille(f) 78.**
chenille(f) 445, 783, 805.
chéquier(m) 379.
chercheur(m) 720, 721.
chérimole(f) 68.
CHEVAL(M) 100, 102, 104.
**cheval(m) 98.**
cheval(m) 661.
**cheval(m) d'arçons(m) 661.**
**cheval(m), allures(f) 101.**
**cheval(m), morphologie(f) 100.**
**cheval(m), squelette(m) 102.**
cheval(m)-sautoir(m) 659.
chevalement(m) 736.
chevalet(m) 541, 544, 546, 591.
chevalet(m) de câble(m) de garde(f) 756.
chevalet(m) des aigus(m) 540.
chevalet(m) des basses(f) 540.
Chevalet(m) du Peintre(m) 13.
chevalière(f) 364.
chevelu(m) 59.
chevelure(f) 9.
Chevelure(f) de Bérénice 11.
chevet(m) 177.
cheveux(m) 117, 119.
cheville(f) 116, 118, 225, 544, 545, 546, 571, 575.
cheville(f) d'accord(m) 540.
chevillier(m) 544.
chevillure(f) 105.
chèvre(f) 150.
chevron(m) 198, 818.
chiasma(m) optique 134.
chicorée(f) 73.
CHIEN(M) 106.
chien(m) 795, 797, 798, 799.
**chien(m), morphologie(f) 106.**
Chiens(m) de chasse(f) 11.
chiffonnier(m) 226.
**chignole(f) 280.**
**chimie(f) 831.**
chloroplaste(m) 115.
chœur(m) 177.
choix(m) de la langue(f) d'affichage(m) 422.
chope(f) à bière(f) 237.
chope(f) à café(m) 238.
choroïde(f) 140.
chou(m) chinois 73.
chou(m) frisé 73.
chou(m) pommé blanc 73.
chou(m) pommé vert 73.
chou(m)-fleur(f) 69.
chou(m)-rave(f) 71.
choux(m) de Bruxelles 73.
chromatine(f) 115.
chromosphère(f) 6.
**chronomètre(m) 706.**
chronomètre(m) 407.
chronométreur(m) 610, 612, 626, 666, 668, 669.
chronométreur(m) de couloir(m) 621.
chronométreur(m) des immobilisations(f) 668.
chronométreur(m) des trente secondes(f) 610.
chronométreur(m) principal 621.
**chrysalide(f) 78.**
chukka(m) 354.
chute(f) 27, 341, 631.
chute(f) de départ(m) 651.
CHUTE(F) LIBRE 635.
chutes(f) de pierres(f) 826, 827.
**cible(f) 684, 698.**
**cibles(f) 667.**
ciboulette(f) 70.
ciel(m) à nébulosité(f) dispersée 39.
ciel(m) clair 39.
ciel(m) couvert 39.
**ciel(m) d'orage(m) 36.**
ciel(m) noir 39.
ciel(m) nuageux 39.
ciel(m) peu nuageux 39.
ciel(m) très nuageux 39.
cigale(f) 77.
**cigare(m) 384.**
**cigarette(f) 384.**
cil(m) 140.
cilié 56.
cils(m) 107.
cimaise(f) 166.
cime(f) 59.
cimetière(m) 52.
cimier(m) 791.
cimier(m) mobile 14.
cinéma(m) 496.
cintres(m) 188.
circuit(m) d'eau(f) chaude 215.
circuit(m) d'eau(f) froide 215.
circuit(m) d'évacuation(f) 215.
circuit(m) de 120 V 312.
circuit(m) de 240 V 312.
**circuit(m) de photopiles(f) 769.**
CIRCUIT(M) DE PLOMBERIE(F) 215.
circuit(m) de ventilation(f) 215.
circuit(m) électrique 233.
circuit(m) imprimé 528.
circulation(f) dans les deux sens(m) 824, 825.
CIRCULATION(F) SANGUINE 124, 126.
**circulation(f) sanguine, schéma(m) 124.**
**cireur(m) 358.**
cirque(m) 7.
cirque(m) glaciaire 26.
cirro-cumulus(m) 44.
cirro-stratus(m) 44.
cirrus(m) 44.
**cisaille(f) 578.**
cisaille(f) 398.
cisaille(f) à haies(f) 269.
cisaille(f) à volaille(f) 246.
ciseau(m) 581.
ciseau(m) à bois(m) 275.
**ciseaux(m) 564.**
ciseaux(m) 688, 725.
ciseaux(m) à cuticules(m) 365.
ciseaux(m) à denteler 564.
**ciseaux(m) à effiler 369.**
ciseaux(m) à ongles(m) 365.
**ciseaux(m) de coiffeur(m) 369.**
ciseaux(m) de pédicure(m) 365.

ciseaux(m) de sûreté(f) 365.
**ciseaux(m) sculpteurs 369.**
citerne(f) 742, 743.
**cithare(f) 535.**
citron(m) 65.
citrouille(f) 69.
**civière(f) 726.**
clairon(m) 550.
clapet(m) 293, 294, 568.
clapet(m) de non-retour(m) 306.
clapet(m) de retenue(f) 216.
claque(f) 353, 355.
clarinette(f) 548.
clarinette(f) basse 556.
clarinettes(f) 556.
classeur(m) 519.
classeur(m) à clapets(m) 520.
classeur(m) à soufflets(m) 378.
classeur(m) mobile 521.
**classification(f) de Hubble 9.**
claveau(m) 174.
clavette(f) 290.
clavicule(f) 122.
**clavier(m) 530.**
clavier(m) 420, 422, 526, 527, 540, 555, 683.
clavier(m) à pédales(f) 542.
clavier(m) accompagnement(m) 536.
clavier(m) alphanumérique 422, 530.
clavier(m) chant(m) 536.
clavier(m) de grand orgue(m) 542.
clavier(m) de positif(m) 542.
clavier(m) de récit(m) 542.
clavier(m) manuel 543.
clavier(m) numérique 422, 530, 709.
claviers(m) manuels 542.
clayette(f) 254.
clé(f) 290, 549.
clé(f) à chaîne(f) 299.
clé(f) à cliquet(m) 279.
clé(f) à crémaillère(f) 299.
clé(f) à fourches(f) 279.
**clé(f) à molette(f) 279.**
clé(f) à percussion(f) 780.
clé(f) à sangle(f) 299.
clé(f) à tuyau(m) 299.
clé(f) coudée à tuyau(m) 299.
clé(f) d'ut(m) 537.
clé(f) de barrage(m) 779.
clé(f) de bocal(m) 548.
clé(f) de bras(m) 668.
clé(f) de contact(m) 271.
clé(f) de fa(m) 537.
clé(f) de mandrin(m) 281.
clé(f) de sol(m) 537.
clé(f) de voûte(f) 174, 177.
clé(f) mixte 279.
clé(f) polygonale 279.
clé(f) polygonale à têtes(f) fendues 279.
**clés(f) 537.**
client(m) 417.
clignotant(m) 441.
clignotant(m) arrière 443.
CLIMATISATION(F) 214.
climatiseur(m) 449.
**climatiseur(m) de fenêtre(f) 214.**
**climats(m) continentaux 45.**
**climats(m) de montagne(f) 45.**
climats(m) de montagne(f) 45.
CLIMATS(M) DU MONDE(M) 45.
**climats(m) polaires 45.**
**climats(m) subarctiques 45.**
climats(m) subarctiques 45.
**climats(m) subtropicaux 45.**
**climats(m) tempérés 45.**
**climats(m) tropicaux 45.**
clin foc(m) 481.
cliquet(m) 276, 281, 573, 706, 707.
clitoris(m) 128.
cloche(f) 329.
clocher(m) 175.
clocheton(m) 175, 176, 181.
cloison(f) 65, 141, 685, 697, 701.
cloison(f) amovible 520.
cloison(f) de citerne(f) 742.
cloison(f) longitudinale 742.
cloison(f) transversale 742.
clôture(f) 148.
clôture(f) en lattis(m) 263.
**clou(m) 275.**
clou(m) 104.
clou(m) millésimé 466.
club-house(m) 651.
coach(m) 425.
coccinelle(f) 77.
coccyx(m) 122.
Cocher(m) 11.
cocheur(m) d'allée(f) 678.
cocheur(m) de sable(m) 678.
cochonnet(m) 682.
cockpit(m) 628.
code(m) 524.
code(m) des produits(m) 709.
**cœur(m) 125.**
cœur(m) 64, 88, 92, 97, 130, 204, 615, 695.
cœur(m) de croisement(m) 467.
cœur(m) du réacteur(m) 760, 762, 763.
coffre(m) 226, 427, 768, 769.
coffre(m) à bagages(m) 449.
coffre(m) d'appareillage(m) 458.
coffre(m) de rangement(m) 440, 778, 780.
coffret(m) 410.
coffret(m) de branchement(m) 757.
coiffe(f) 57, 577, 670.
coiffeuse(f) 292.
COIFFURE(F) 328, 368, 370.
**coiffure(f), accessoires(m) 369.**
coin(m) 542, 577, 669.
coin(m) de patinoire(f) 608.
**coinceur(m) 681.**
coinceur(m) 680.
coing(m) 64.
**col(m) 341.**
col(m) 27, 319, 322, 324, 352, 410, 678.
col(m) banane(f) 341.
col(m) berthe(f) 342.
col(m) cagoule(f) 342.
col(m) châle(m) 341.
col(m) chemisier(m) 341.
col(m) chinois 342.
col(m) Claudine 341.
col(m) cravate(f) 342.
col(m) de l'utérus(m) 128.
col(m) du fémur(m) 123.
**col(m) italien 324.**
col(m) marin(m) 342.
col(m) officier(m) 342.
col(m) pointes(f) boutonnées 324.
col(m) polo(m) 342.
col(m) roulé 326, 338, 342, 642.
col(m) tailleur(m) 330, 341.
col(m) transformable 319.
col(m)-de-cygne(m) 201.
col-de-cygne(m) 784.
colette(f) 363.
collant(m) 344.
collant(m) fantaisie(f) 349.
collant(m) sans pied(m) 353.
collatéral(m) 177.
collatérale(f) 135.
colle(f) 200.
collecteur(m) 753.
collecteur(m) d'appareil(m) 215.
collecteur(m) d'échappement(m) 435, 438, 439.
collecteur(m) d'évacuation(f) 215.
collecteur(m) de graisse(f) 253.
collecteur(m) de vapeur(f) primaire 759.
collecteur(m) du réacteur(m) 759.
collecteur(m) principal 215, 216.
collerette(f) 318, 341.
collet(m) 57, 144, 205, 240, 241, 283, 483, 579.
collet(m) de l'axone(m) 135.
collet(m) repoussé 300.
collier(m) 248, 641, 653.
collier(m) coupe-feu(m) 205.
collier(m) de perles(f), longueur(f) matinée(f) 361.
collier(m) de serrage(m) 40, 663.
collier(m) de serrage(m) du casque(m) 512.
collier(m) de soirée(f) 361.
collier(m)-de-chien(m) 361.
**colliers(m) 361.**
colline(f) 27.
colline(f) abyssale 29.
Colombe(f) 13.
**colombin(m) 584.**
côlon(m) ascendant 131.
côlon(m) descendant 131.
côlon(m) pelvien 131.
côlon(m) transverse 131.
colonne(f) 24, 36, 166, 168, 169, 283, 393, 399, 477, 545, 561, 579, 621, 700, 701.
colonne(f) ascendante 208.
colonne(f) avec capuchon(m) 37.
colonne(f) d'air(m) 298.
colonne(f) d'alcool(m) 705.
colonne(f) de mercure(m) 705.
colonne(f) de production(f) 740.
colonne(f) de radiateur(m) 208.
colonne(f) de stabilisation(f) 738.
colonne(f) de ventilation(f) 215.
colonne(f) de ventilation(f) principale 215.
colonne(f) descendante 208.
colonne(f) montante d'eau(f) chaude 215.
colonne(f) montante d'eau(f) froide 215.
colonne(f) vertébrale 89, 122, 134.
**cols(m), types(m) 341, 342.**
columelle(f) 94.
combattant(m) 668.
combinaison(f) 325, 351, 643.
**combinaison(f) de nuit(f) 350.**
combinaison(f) de ski(m) 640, 642.
combinaison(f) de vol(m) 635.
combinaison(f) gagnante 702.
combinaison(f)-jupon(m) 345.
combinaison(f)-pantalon(m) 336.
combiné(m) 347, 420, 422.
combiné(m) 2 dans 1 368.
**combiné(m) bucco-dentaire 373.**
combiné(m)-culotte(f) 347.
combustible(m) 761, 766.
combustible(m) défectueux sous gaine(f) 764.
**combustible(m) nucléaire, manipulation(f) 764.**
combustible(m): uranium(m) enrichi 762, 763.
combustible(m): uranium(m) naturel 760, 761.
combustion(f) 436, 437, 501.
COMÈTE(F) 9.
commande(f) amovible 253.
**commande(f) au pied(m) 561.**
commande(f) d'accélération(f) 272.
commande(f) d'aérofrein(m) 639.
commande(f) d'alimentation(f) en oxygène(m) 639.
commande(f) d'arrêt(m) 411.
commande(f) d'avance(f) rapide 411.
commande(f) d'éjection(f) de la cassette(f) 409, 411.
commande(f) d'éjection(f) de la pile(f) 409.
commande(f) d'enregistrement(m) 411.
commande(f) d'essuie-glace(m) 430.
commande(f) d'insertion(f) du papier(m) 523.
commande(f) de barrières(f) 471.
commande(f) de chauffage(m) 430.
commande(f) de dossier(m) 428.
commande(f) de largage(m) de câble(m) 639.
commande(f) de largage(m) de la verrière(f) 639.
commande(f) de lecture(f) 411.
commande(f) de marche(f) arrière 397.
commande(f) de marche(f) avant 397.
commande(f) de marge(f) 525.
commande(f) de mémoire(f) 396.
commande(f) de panneau(m) solaire 42.
commande(f) de positionnement(m) du specimen(m) 717.
commande(f) de rebobinage(m) 411.
commande(f) de réglage(m) macro(f) 409.
commande(f) de remise(f) à zéro(m) 411.
commande(f) de sélection(f) de l'ouverture(f) 717.
commande(f) de sélection(f) manuelle 397.
commande(f) de température(f) 254.
commande(f) de ventilateur(m) 214.
commande(f) de virage(m) et d'inclinaison(f) latérale 639.
commande(f) de vitesse(f) 250.
commande(f) de volume(m) 420.
commande(f) de volume(m) de la sonnerie(f) 420.
commande(f) de volume(m) du récepteur(m) 420.
commande(f) des freins(m) 636.
commande(f) du chariot(m) 569, 718.
commande(f) du rétroviseur(m) 429.
commande(f) électrique de paiement(m) 702.
commande(f) électrique du zoom(m) 409.
commande(f) mémoire(f) 420.
commandes(f) de la bande(f) vidéo 409.
commandes(f) de montage(m) 409.
commandes(f) de préréglage(m) 411.
commandes(f) de prise(f) de vue(f) 409.
commandes(f) du magnétoscope(m) 411.
commandes(f) du pilote(m) automatique 500.
commencement(m) du patron(m) 569.
commissure(f) labiale 142.
commode(f) 226.
communication(f) par réseau(m) 527.
communications(f) aériennes 417.
communications(f) individuelles 417.
communications(f) industrielles 417.
communications(f) maritimes 417.
communications(f) militaires 417.
communications(f) routières 417.
commutateur(m) 310, 397.
commutateur(m) d'entrée(f) 402.
commutateur(m) de fonctions(f) 402.
commutateur(m) marche(f)/arrêt(m) 391.
commutateur(m) mono(f)/stéréo(f) 402.
compartiment(m) à fret(m) 499.
compartiment(m) bagages(m) 458.
compartiment(m) de la production(f) d'électricité(f) 806.
compartiment(m) de première classe(f) 498.
compartiment(m) des instruments(m) 43.
compartiment(m) des voitures(f) 494.
compartiment(m) du réacteur(m) 806.
compartiment(m) touriste 499.
compartiment(m) voyageurs(m) 458.
compartiment(m)-couchette(f) 440.
compas(m) 639.
compas(m) d'épaisseur(f) 583.
**compas(m) magnétique liquide 484.**
**compas(m) magnétique liquide, coupe(f) 485.**
compensateur(m) de poussée(f) latérale 404.
**complexe(m) hydroélectrique 746.**
compluvium(m) 170, 171.
composeuse(f) 527.
compresse(f) stérilisée 725.
compresseur(m) 212, 517.
compresseur(m) centrifuge 501.
compresseur(m) d'air(m) 469.
compresseur(m) du climatiseur(m) 435.
compression(f) 436, 437, 501.
compression(f)/admission(f) 436.
comprimé(m) 725.
compte-pose(m) 399.
compte-rangs(m) 568.
compte-touches(m) électrique 666.
compte-tours(m) 431.
compteur(m) 215, 403.
compteur(m) d'électricité(f) 757.
compteur(m) kilométrique 431.
comptoir(m) d'enregistrement(m) 504.
comptoir(m) de renseignements(m) 504.
comptoir(m) de vente(f) des billets(m) 504.
concentration(f) du faisceau(m) 717.
concombre(m) 69.
Concorde(m) 19.
condensation(f) 35.
condensation(f) de la vapeur(f) 767.
condenseur(m) 717, 718, 758, 771.
conditionnement(m) d'air(m) 494.
CONDITIONNEMENT(M) PHYSIQUE, APPAREILS(M) 664.
conducteur(m) 652.
conducteur(m) de phase(f) 757.
conducteur(m) de terre(f) 757.
conducteur(m) du thermocouple(m) 297.
conducteur(m) en faisceau(m) 756.
conducteur(m) neutre 757.
conduit(m) 543.
conduit(m) auditif 138.
conduit(m) de chauffage(m) 259.
conduit(m) de distribution(f) vertical 206.
conduit(m) de la glande(f) 96.
conduit(m) de raccordement(m) 204.
conduit(m) hydraulique 156, 157, 158.
conduit(m) lactifère 129.
conduite(f) à la terre(f) 741.
conduite(f) d'admission(f) principale 741.
conduite(f) d'admission(f) secondaire 741.
conduite(f) d'alimentation(f) 215.

Les termes en **caractères gras** renvoient à une illustration, ceux en CAPITALES indiquent un titre.

conduite(f) d'eau(f) 257.
conduite(f) d'eau(f) chaude 296, 298.
conduite(f) d'eau(f) froide 296, 298.
conduite(f) d'eau(f) potable 186.
conduite(f) de gaz(m) 186.
conduite(f) de transfert(m) de carburant(m) 509.
conduite(f) des pièces(f) 702.
conduite(f) forcée 746, 747, 752.
conduite(f) principale 293.
condyle(m) externe 123.
condyle(m) interne 123.
cône(m) 24, 58, 410.
cône(m) adventif 25.
cône(m) d'entrée(f) 501.
cône(m) d'ombre(f) 8.
cône(m) de pénombre(f) 8.
cône(m) femelle 58.
cône(m) mâle 58.
CONFIGURATION(F) D'UN SYSTÈME(M) BUREAUTIQUE 526.
congélateur(m) 254.
CONIFÈRE(M) 58.
conjonctive(f) 140.
connecteur(m) 312, 406.
connecteur(m) à serrage(m) mécanique 757.
connecteur(m) d'extension(f) 528.
connecteur(m) de liaison(f) 312.
connexion(f) 697.
conque(f) 139.
conseiller(m) de production(f) 412.
conseillers(m) musicaux 412.
consigne(f) automatique 463.
console(f) 545, 750, 756.
console(f) centrale 430.
console(f) d'accotoir(m) 220.
console(f) d'instruments(m) 627.
**console(f) d'orgue(m) 542.**
console(f) de traitement(m) 699.
consolette(f) de l'annonceur(m) 407.
consolette(f) du réalisateur(m) 407.
**consommateurs(m) primaires 31.**
**consommateurs(m) secondaires 31.**
**consommateurs(m) tertiaires 31.**
CONSTELLATIONS(F) DE L'HÉMISPHÈRE(M) AUSTRAL 12.
CONSTELLATIONS(F) DE L'HÉMISPHÈRE(M) BORÉAL 10.
CONSTRUCTION(F), MATÉRIAUX(M) 286, 288.
contact(m) 697.
contact(m) électrique 391.
contact(m) négatif 768, 769.
contact(m) positif 768, 769.
contacteur(m) 216.
**conteneur(m) 470.**
conteneur(m) 495.
continent(m) 29.
continental aride 45.
continental semi-aride 45.
CONTINENTS(M), CONFIGURATION(F) 20.
contre-attrape(f) 541.
contre-batteur(m) 160.
contre-fer(m) 277.
contre-fiche(f) 199.
contre-flèche(f) 786.
contre-garde(f) 179.
contre-plaqué(m) multiplis 288.
contre-platine(f) 404.
contre-rail(m) 467.
contre-sanglon(m) 649.
contrebasse(f) 545.
contrebasses(f) 557.
contrebassons(m) 556.
contrefiche(f) 757.
contrefort(m) 27, 176, 352, 751.
contremarche(f) 201, 572.
contreparement(m) 288.
contrepoids(m) 15, 147, 404, 457, 471, 721, 784, 785, 786.
contrescarpe(f) 178.
contrevent(m) 203.
contrôle(m) d'alimentation(f) en oxygène(m) 639.
contrôle(m) d'enregistrement(m) 402.
contrôle(m) de la couleur(f) 532.
contrôle(m) de la photocopie(f) 532.
contrôle(m) de la stéréophonie(f) 408.
contrôle(m) de la température(f) 297.
contrôle(m) de la température(f) du corps(m) 512.
contrôle(m) de la vapeur(f) 256.
contrôle(m) de la vitesse(f) 561.
contrôle(m) de sécurité(f) 504.
contrôle(m) de tabulation(f) 525.
contrôle(m) de température(f) 585.
contrôle(m) de tonalité(f) des aigus(m) 402.
contrôle(m) de tonalité(f) des graves(m) 402.
contrôle(m) des billets(m) 463.
contrôle(m) des passeports(m) 505.
contrôle(m) douanier 505.
contrôle(m) du contraste(m) 532.
contrôle(m) du gain(m) 485.
contrôle(m) du plateau(m) 405.
contrôle(m) du séquenceur(m) 555.
contrôle(m) du volume(m) 422, 555.
contrôle(m) thermique 209.
contrôles(m) de l'équipement(m) de survie(f) 512.
contrôles(m) du lecteur(m) de cassette(f) 408.
contrôles(m) du lecteur(m) laser(m) 408.
contrôleur(m) 463.
contrôleur(m) d'images(f) 412, 415.
**convecteur(m) 211.**
conversion(f) du travail(m) mécanique en électricité(f) 755.
convertisseur(m) catalytique 439.
convertisseur(m) de couple(m) 258.
convoyeur(m) 160, 733, 735.
convoyeur(m) à bagages(m) 507.
COORDONNÉES(F) CÉLESTES 3.
COORDONNÉES(F) TERRESTRES 3.
copie(f) recto(m)/verso(m) 532.
coprocesseur(m) 528.
copyright(m) 831.
coq(m) 150.
coque(f) 66, 93, 383, 443, 445, 449, 628, 643.
coque(f) inférieure 641.
coque(f) supérieure 641, 645.
coquille(f) 83, 92, 109, 220, 602, 609, 666.
COQUILLE(F) BIVALVE 95.
coquille(f) Saint-Jacques 93.
COQUILLE(F) UNIVALVE 94.
**coquille(f), valve 95.**
coquilleur(m) à beurre(m) 242.
cor(m) anglais 548.
cor(m) d'harmonie(f) 551.
Corbeau(m) 13.
corbeau(m) 180, 181, 204.
corbeille(f) à pollen(m) 81.
corbeille(f) suspendue 263.
cordage(m) 692.
**cordage(m) commis 692.**
**cordage(m) tressé 692.**
corde(f) 541, 544, 545, 669, 680, 684, 793.
corde(f) à sauter 665.
corde(f) d'accrochage(m) 572.
corde(f) de couloir(m) 621.
corde(f) de prise(f) 658.
corde(f) de tirage(m) 302.
corde(f) vocale 130.
cordeau(m) 268.
cordée 56.
cordelière(f) 229.
cordes(f) 540.
cordes(f) d'accompagnement(m) 535.
cordes(f) de mélodie(f) 535.
cordes(f) de timbre(m) 553.
cordier(m) 544.
cordon(m) 231, 256, 260, 268, 271, 310, 406, 408.
cordon(m) à gaine(f) métallique 422.
cordon(m) coulissant 320.
cordon(m) d'alimentation(f) 370, 374.
cordon(m) d'alimentation(f) pivotant 370.
cordon(m) de combiné(m) 420.
cordon(m) de dunes(f) 46.
cordon(m) de soudure(f) 307.
cordon(m) de tirage(m) 230, 231.
cordon(m) spermatique 127.
cordon(m) tire-feu(m) 802.
coriandre(f) 74.
corne(f) 364, 478.
corne(f) de feu(m) 779.
corne(f) de guidage(m) de l'attelage(m) 459.
cornée(f) 140.
**cornemuse(f) 536.**
cornes(f) 83.
cornes(f) de girafe(f) 99.
cornes(f) de mouflon(m) 99.
cornes(f) de rhinocéros(m) 99.
CORNES(F), PRINCIPAUX TYPES(M) 99.
cornet(m) à dés(m) 697.
cornet(m) à pistons(m) 550, 556.
cornet(m) inférieur 141.
cornet(m) moyen 141.
cornet(m) supérieur 141.
corniche(f) 166, 168, 196, 202, 225, 707.
corolle(f) 60.
corona(f) radiata 128.
corps(m) 143, 252, 281, 294, 295, 370, 384, 389, 542, 549, 658, 670, 698, 711, 718.
corps(m) calleux 134.
corps(m) caverneux 127.
corps(m) cellulaire 135.
corps(m) ciliaire 140.
corps(m) de garde(f) 178, 180.
corps(m) de l'ongle(m) 137.
corps(m) de la fusée(f) 804.
corps(m) de piston(m) 550.
corps(m) de pompe(f) 726.
corps(m) de ruche(f) 82.
corps(m) du fornix(m) 134.
corps(m) du pistolet(m) 304.
corps(m) en bakélite®(f) 804.
CORPS(M) HUMAIN 116, 118.
corps(m) vertébral 135.
corps(m) vitré 140.
corps-mort(m) 486.
corpuscule(m) de Meissner 136.
corpuscule(m) de Pacini 136.
corpuscule(m) de Ruffini 136.
correcteur(m) liquide 515.
correcteur(m) orthographique 524.
correction(f) d'exposition(f) 391.
correction(f) de caractères(m) 525.
correction(f) de mots(m) 525.
cors(m) anglais 557.
cors(m) d'harmonie(f) 557.
**corsage(m)-culotte(f) 337.**
**corsaire(m) 336.**
corset(m) 346, 756.
corymbe(m) 60.
cosse(f) 67.
COSTUME(M) ANCIEN, ÉLÉMENTS(M) 315, 316, 318.
**costume(m) de judo(m) 668.**
**cotardie(f) 316.**
côte(f) 30, 97, 102, 129, 670.
côte(f) axiale 94.
côte(f) flottante (2) 122.
côte(f) spiralée 94.
côté(m) bassin(m) 752.
côté(m) cour(f) 189.
côté(m) femelle 566.
côté(m) jardin(m) 189.
côté(m) mâle 566.
côté(m) mer(f) 752.
côtes(f) 122.
coton(m) hydrophile 725.
coton(m)-tige(f) 725.
cotre(m) Marconi 482.
cotret(m) 773.
cotte(f) de mailles(f) 792.
cotylédon(m) 57.
cou(m) 97, 117, 118, 119, 127, 661.
couche(f) 349.
couche(f) antireflet 768.
couche(f) basale 136.
couche(f) claire 136.
couche(f) cornée 136.
couche(f) d'aluminium(m) 405.
couche(f) de base(f) 451.
couche(f) de cendres(f) 25.
couche(f) de fondation(f) 451.
couche(f) de laves(f) 25.
couche(f) de Malpighi 136.
couche(f) de surface(f) 450.
couche(f) drainante 748.
couche(f) fluorescente 232.
couche(f) granuleuse 136.
couche(f) imperméable 737.
couchette(f) 460.
coude(m) 100, 106, 112, 117, 119, 206, 301, 376.
coude(m) à 180° 301.
coude(m) à 45° 301.
coude(m) de renvoi(m) 301.
coudière(f) 602.
coulant(m) 375.
coulée(f) de laves(f) 25.
couleur(f) 695.
couleur(f) à l'huile(f) 588.
**couleurs(f), exemples(m) 819.**
coulisse(f) 323.
coulisse(f) d'accord(m) 551.
coulisse(f) d'entrée(f) 82.
coulisse(f) du deuxième piston(m) 550.
coulisse(f) du premier piston(m) 550.
coulisse(f) du troisième piston(m) 551.
coulisses(f) 189.
couloir(m) 194, 614, 618, 621, 655.
couloir(m) central 460.
couloir(m) d'intercommunication(f) 461.
couloir(m) de lancer(m) franc 610.
couloir(m) des remplacements(m) 612.
coup(m) de pied(m) de brasse(f) 622.
coup(m) de pied(m) de crawl(m) 622.
coup(m) de pied(m) de papillon(m) 623.
coupé 818.
**coupe(f) 702.**
Coupe(f) 13.
coupe(f) à mousseux(m) 237.
**coupe(f) d'un microscope(m) électronique 717.**
**coupe(f) d'une noisette(f) 66.**
**coupe(f) sagittale 127, 128, 129, 142.**
coupe-bordures(m) 266.
coupe-circuit(m) 757.
coupe-circuit(m) d'urgence(f) 444.
coupe-cuticules(m) 365.
coupe-feu(m) 198.
coupe-fil(m) 311, 562.
coupe-œuf(m) 246.
**coupe-ongles(m) 365.**
coupe-papier(m) 515.
coupe-tube(m) 299.
coupe-vent(m) 634.
coupée(f) 742.
coupelle(f) 236.
coupelle(f) d'étanchéité(f) 730.
couperet(m) 242.
coupleur(m) hydraulique 147.
coupole(f) 486.
coupole(f) du mihrab(m) 173.
coupole(f) du porche(m) 172, 173.
coupole(f) rotative 14.
cour(f) 148, 172, 173, 180.
courant(m) 493.
courbure(f) 671.
courge(f) 69.
courgette(f) 69.
couronne(f) 6, 101, 144, 553, 590, 706, 832.
Couronne(f) australe 13.
Couronne(f) boréale 11.
couronne(f) d'aubage(m) 754.
couronne(f) d'orientation(f) 785.
couronne(f) de base(f) 14.
couronne(f) de table(f) 363.
couronnement(m) 201, 749.
couronnement(m) du barrage(m) 752.
courroie(f) d'attache(f) 375.
courroie(f) d'entraînement(m) 258.
courroie(f) de distribution(f) 434.
courroie(f) de rêne(f) 652.
courroie(f) de sécurité(f) 617.
courroie(f) de tige(f) 641.
courroie(f) de transmission(f) 492.
courroie(f) de ventilateur(m) 434.
course(f) 599, 654.
COURSE(F) DE CHEVAUX(M) 651.
COURSE(F) SOUS HARNAIS(M) 652.
coursier(m) d'évacuateur(m) 746.
court péronier(m) latéral 121.
court(m) de service(m) droit 614.
court(m) de service(m) gauche 614.
courtine(f) 178, 180.
couscoussier(m) 249.
**cousoir(m) 578.**
coussin(m) 570.
coussin(m) arrière 675.
coussin(m) carré 224.
coussin(m) d'air(m) 352.
coussin(m) de protection(f) 659.
coussin(m) de rembourrage(m) 669.
coussin(m) de sellette(f) 648.
coussin(m) de tête(f) 674.
coussinet(m) 406.
coussinet(m) carpien 106.
coussinet(m) d'émeri(m) 563.
coussinet(m) de glissement(m) 467.
coussinet(m) de l'ergot(m) 106.
coussinet(m) digité 106, 107.
coussinet(m) en mousse(f) 729.
coussinet(m) palmaire 106.
coussinet(m) plantaire 107.
**couteau(m) 239.**
couteau(m) 93, 250, 251, 256, 587, 688, 690.
couteau(m) à beurre(m) 239.
couteau(m) à bifteck(m) 239.
couteau(m) à découper 242.
couteau(m) à désosser 242.
couteau(m) à dessert(m) 239.
couteau(m) à filets(m) de sole(f) 242.
couteau(m) à fromage(m) 239.
couteau(m) à huîtres(f) 242.

Les termes en **caractères gras** renvoient à une illustration, ceux en CAPITALES indiquent un titre.

couteau(m) à jambon(m) 242.
couteau(m) à pain(m) 242.
couteau(m) à pamplemousse(m) 242.
couteau(m) à peindre 589.
couteau(m) à poisson(m) 239.
couteau(m) à zester 242.
couteau(m) d'électricien(m) 311.
couteau(m) d'office(m) 242.
couteau(m) de chef(m) 242.
couteau(m) de combat(m) 794.
**couteau(m) de cuisine(f) 242.**
couteau(m) de potier(m) 585.
couteau(m) de table(f) 239.
couteau(m) en silex(m) 791.
**couteau(m) suisse 688.**
**couteaux(m) de cuisine(f), types(m) 242.**
**couteaux(m), principaux types(m) 239.**
coutisse(f) 571.
coutre(m) 156, 158.
COUTURE(F) 561, 562, 564, 566.
**couture(f) 578.**
couture(f) 384, 596, 598.
couture(f) d'assemblage(m) 327.
couture(f) médiane 324.
**couture(f), accessoires(m) 563, 564.**
couturier(m) 120.
couvercle(m) 16, 213, 247, 248, 251, 252, 253, 256, 258, 293, 309, 386, 398, 404, 532, 585, 590, 705, 712, 719.
couvercle(m) coulissant 484.
couvercle(m) de batterie(f) 439.
couvercle(m) de culasse(f) 435.
couvercle(m) de la turbine(f) 753.
couvercle(m) de réservoir(m) 293.
couvercle(m) du chargeur(m) 397.
COUVERT(M) 239, 240.
couverture(f) 224.
couvre-bassinet(m) 795.
couvre-culasse(m) 796.
couvre-filtre(m) 730.
couvre-oreiller(m) 224.
couvre-plateau(m) 404.
**couvrure(f) 579.**
crabe(m) 90.
cracker(m) de seigle(m) 153.
cracker(m) scandinave 153.
craie(f) 675.
**crampon(m) 358.**
crampon(m) 353, 466.
crampon(m) de fermeture(f) 383.
crampons(m) 598.
crampons(m) interchangeables 600.
cran(m) 322, 323, 341, 565, 656, 670, 708.
cran(m) de mire(f) 797.
cran(m) de réglage(m) 278, 641.
crâne(m) 88, 102, 116.
**crapaud(m) 85.**
cratère(m) 7, 25, 733.
cravache(f) 648, 651.
**cravate(f) 324.**
**crawl(m) 622.**
crayon(m) 389, 515, 765.
crayon(m) à sourcils(m) 367.
crayon(m) blanchisseur d'ongles(m) 365.
crayon(m) contour(m) des lèvres(f) 366.
crayon(m) de pierre(f) ponce 583.
crayon(m) en plomb(m) 389.
crayon(m) gomme(f) 515.
crayon(m) lithographique 583.
crayons(m) de couleur(f) 588.
crémaillère(f) 201, 252, 254, 656.
crémaillère(f) de pointage(m) 802.
crémaster(m) 78.
crémier(m) 238.
créneau(m) 181.
crénelé 56.
crépis(f) 166, 168, 169.
cresson(m) de fontaine(f) 73.
crête(f) 27, 30, 746, 748, 792.
crêtemètre(m) graphique 407.
creux(m) 30, 241.
creux(m) barométrique 38.
crevasse(f) 26.
crevette(f) 90.
crible(m) 161.
CRICKET(M) 598.
**cricket(m), balle(f) 598.**
cricket(m), balle(f) 598.
**cricquet(m), terrain(m) 599.**
crinière(f) 100.
crispin(m) 667.
cristallin(m) 140.
**cristaux(m) de neige(f), classification(f) 36.**
cristaux(m) irréguliers 37.
cristaux(m) liquides 706.
croc(m) à défricher 267.
croche(f) 538.
**crochet(m) 567.**
crochet(m) 95, 203, 310, 397, 562, 566, 568, 644, 674, 709, 711, 726, 786.
crochet(m) à venin(m) 96.
crochet(m) d'attelage(m) 147.
crochet(m) de gourmette(f) 650.
crochet(m) de petit doigt(m) 551.
crochet(m) de pouce(m) 550.
crochet(m) du plateau(m) 708.
crochet(m) pétrisseur 250.
crochet(m)de levage(m) 737.
crochets(m) 832.
croisée(f) 176.
croisée(f) du transept(m) 177.
croisement(m) 576.
croisillon(m) 727.
croissant(m) 153, 819.
croix(f) 818.
croix(f) de Saint-André 198, 471.
Croix(f) du Sud(m) 13.
**crosse(f) 607.**
crosse(f) 545, 728, 795, 796, 797, 798, 799, 803.
croupe(f) 101, 661.
croupion(m) 109.
croupon(m) 579.
croûte(f) basaltique 22.
croûte(f) de cuir(m) 323.
croûte(f) granitique 22.
croûte(f) terrestre 22, 23.
CROÛTE(F) TERRESTRE, COUPE(F) 22.
cruche(f) 690.
CRUSTACÉ(M) 90.
**crustacés(m) comestibles 90.**
cubiculum(m) 170.
cubital(m) antérieur 120, 121.
cubital(m) postérieur 121.
cubitière(f) 792.
cubitus(m) 102, 122.
**cuiller(f) 241, 672.**
cuiller(f) 688.
cuiller(f) à café(m) 241.
cuiller(f) à dessert(m) 241.
cuiller(f) à égoutter 244.
cuiller(f) à glace(f) 246.
cuiller(f) à soda(m) 241.
cuiller(f) à soupe(f) 241.
cuiller(f) à thé(m) 241.
cuiller(f) de table(f) 241.
cuilleron(m) 241.
cuillers(f) doseuses 244.
**cuillers(f), principaux types(m) 241.**
cuirasse(f) 791.
cuisine(f) 171, 195, 460, 807.
**cuisinière(f) électrique 255.**
cuissard(m) 602, 792.
cuissarde(f) 357.
cuissardes(f) 672.
cuisse(f) 101, 106, 117, 119, 127, 128.
**cuisson(f) 585.**
cuivre(m) et acier(m) 301.
**cuivres(m), famille(f) 550.**
cul-de-sac(m) de Douglas 128.
cul-de-sac(m) dural 134.
cul-de-sac(m) vésico-utérin 128.
culasse(f) 363, 549, 802.
culbuteur(m) 435.
culée(f) 176, 454, 455, 456.
culot(m) 232, 233, 410, 439, 486, 798, 799.
culot(m) à baïonnette(f) 232.
culot(m) à broches(f) 232.
culot(m) à vis(f) 232.
culotte(f) 301, 315, 317, 346, 609, 662, 667.
**culotte(f) à ruchés(m) 349.**
**culotte(f) plastique 349.**
**cultivateur(m) 157.**
cultivateur(m) 154.
CULTURE(F) DU SOL(M), ÉTAPES(F) 154.
cumulo-nimbus(m) 44.
cumulus(m) 44.
cupule(f) 66.
cure-ongles(m) 365.
curette(f) 385.
curiosité(f) 52.
curleur(m) 620.
CURLING(M) 620.
**curling(m), balais(m) 620.**
**curling(m), pierre(f) 620.**
**curling(m), terrain(m) 620.**
curseur(m) 566, 708.
cuve(f) 257, 258, 398.
**cuve(f) de développement(m) 398.**
cuve(f) du modérateur(m) 761.
cuve(f) du réacteur(m) 759, 763.
cuve(f) vitrifiée 297.
cuvette(f) 255, 293, 484, 545, 701.
cuvette(f) porte-clapet(m) 294.
**cycle(m) de l'eau(f) 34.**
CYCLE(M) DES SAISONS(F) 8.
cyclorama(m) 414.
Cygne(m) 11.
cylindre(m) 295, 436, 524, 531.
cylindre(m) de coupe(f) 271.
cylindre(m) de roue(f) 432.
cylindre(m) des gaz(m) 796.
**cylindre(m) enregistreur 714.**
cylindre(m) guide(m)-film(m) 390.
cylindre(m) inférieur 581.
cylindre(m) récupérateur 802.
cylindre(m) rotatif 570.
cylindre(m) supérieur 581.
cymbale(f) charleston 552.
cymbale(f) inférieure 552.
cymbale(f) supérieure 552.
cymbale(f) suspendue 552.
cymbales(f) 554, 557.
cymbalette(f) 554.
cyme(f) bipare 60.
cyme(f) unipare 60.
cytoplasme(m) 115, 128.

# D

dague(f) 794.
dalle(f) 263.
dalot(m) 683.
Dame(f) 695, 696.
dame(f) de nage(f) 632.
dames(f) 697.
danger(m) 488.
danger(m) électrique 821.
datte(f) 63.
Dauphin(m) 11.
Dauphine(f) américaine 683.
Dauphine(f) canadienne 683.
dé(m) 563, 697.
dé(m) à poker(m) 699.
dé(m) doubleur(m) 697.
dé(m) régulier 699.
déambulatoire(m) 177.
débarcadère(m) 504.
débardeur(m) 326, 351, 353.
déblocage(m) instantané 393.
débouchure(f) 312.
début(m) 692.
début(m) de lecture(f) 405.
**décapeuse(f) 784.**
décapsuleur(m) 244, 688.
déclencheur(m) 391.
déclencheur(m) de paiement(m) 702.
déclencheur(m) pneumatique 393.
déclencheur(m) souple 393.
déclinaison(f) 3.
déclivité(f) du terrain(m) 193.
décolleté(m) carré 343.
décolleté(m) drapé 343.
décolleté(m) en cœur(m) 343.
décolleté(m) en V 343.
décolleté(m) plongeant 343.
**décolletés(m) 343.**
découpe(f) 322.
découpe(f) princesse(f) 345.
**défense(f) 603, 605.**
défenses(f) d'éléphant(m) 99.
défenses(f) de morse(m) 99.
défenses(f) de phacochère(m) 99.
DÉFENSES(F), PRINCIPAUX TYPES(M) 99.
défenseur(m) à l'aile(f) 611.
défenseur(m) au but(m) 611.
défenseur(m) droit 608.
défenseur(m) gauche 608.
déflecteur(m) 210, 214, 264, 271, 440.
déflecteur(m) d'air(m) chaud 204.
déflecteur(m) de chaleur(f) 232.
déflecteur(m) de fumée(f) 204.
déflecteur(m) de jet(m) 810.
déflecteur(m) de réservoir(m) d'oxygène(m) liquide 509.
défonceuse(f) 783.
dégagement(m) d'air(m) des citernes(f) 743.
dégagement(m) du margeur(m) 524.
dégagement(m) du piston(m) 291.
dégageur(m) de fumée(f) 805.
dégorgeoir(m) 672.
dégrafeuse(f) 515.
degré(m) 830.
dégrossissage(m) 586.
Deimos 4.
deltoïde(m) 120.
démarreur(m) électrique 430, 445.
démarreur(m) manuel 271, 272.
démêloir(m) 368.
demeure(f) seigneuriale 180.
demi(m) 605.
demi(m) centre 607.
demi(m) d'ouverture(f) 606.
demi(m) de coin(m) droit 603, 605.
demi(m) de coin(m) gauche 603, 605.
demi(m) de mêlée(f) 606.
demi(m) de sûreté(f) droit 603, 605.
demi(m) de sûreté(f) gauche 603, 605.
demi(m) droit 601, 603, 607.
demi(m) en maraude(f) 605.
demi(m) gauche 601, 603, 607.
demi-barbule(f) 38.
demi-caisson(m) 636.
demi-centre(m) 612.
demi-cercle(m) 610.
demi-cercle(m) de but(m) 611.
demi-clé(f) renversée 691.
demi-court(m) de service(m) en double(m) 618.
demi-court(m) de service(m) en simple(m) 618.
demi-inséré(m) 605.
demi-lune(f) 179, 377.
demi-manche(m) 242.
demi-membraneux(m) 121.
demi-panneau(m) 787.
demi-pause(f) 538.
demi-soupir(m) 538.
demi-tendineux(m) 121.
dendrite(f) 135.
dendrite(f) spatiale 36.
dénoyauteur(m) 246.
dent(f) 96, 158, 159, 160, 162, 240, 268, 272, 277, 284, 644, 674, 785.
dent(f) de défonceuse(f) 783.
dent(f) de godet(m) 782.
dent(f) de la charnière(f) 95.
dent(f) de sagesse(f) 144.
dent(m) 157.
denté 56.
DENTELLE(F) AUX FUSEAUX(M) 570.
denticule(m) 166, 167.
dentifrice(m) 373.
DENTS(F) 144.
dents(f) 369, 566.
**denture(f) humaine 144.**
dénude-fil(m) 311.
dénudeur(m) de fil(m) 311.
départ(m) 676.
**départ(m) de dos(m) 623.**
départ(m) et arrivée(f) 646.
déplacement(m) diagonal 696.
déplacement(m) en équerre(f) 696.
déplacement(m) horizontal 696.
déplacement(m) vertical 696.
déploiement(m) de l'antenne(f) radar(m) 49.
déploiement(m) des panneaux(m) solaires 48.
déploiement(m) du panneau(m) solaire 419.
déploiement(m) du réflecteur(m) est 419.
déporteur(m) 498.
dépôt(m) des décors(m) 188.
dépression(f) 38.
dérailleur(m) arrière 446, 448.
dérailleur(m) avant 446, 448.
derby(m) 355.
dérive(f) 499, 508, 628, 631, 633, 639, 812.
dérive(f) aérienne 492.
**dérivés(m) du bois(m) 288, 289.**
**dériveur(m) 628.**
dériveur(m) de tirage(m) 297.
derme(m) 137.
dernier croissant(m) 7.
dernier droit(m) 651.
dernier quartier(m) 7.
dernier tour(m) 94.
DÉS(M) 699.
descenderie(f) 736.
descendeur(m) 681.
descente(f) dangereuse 826, 827.
descente(f) de gouttière(f) 197.
DÉSERT(M) 46.
désert(m) 45.
désert(m) de pierres(f) 46.
désert(m) de sable(m) 46.
déshabillé(m) 348.
desserte(f) 219, 461.
DESSIN(M) 588, 590, 592.

Les termes en **caractères gras** renvoient à une illustration, ceux en CAPITALES indiquent un titre.

**dessin(m), accessoires(m) 591, 592.**
**dessin(m), matériel(m) 589.**
destination(f) 463.
détecteur(m) à infrarouge(m) 43.
détecteur(m) d'horizon(m) terrestre 49.
détecteur(m) de particules(f) 42.
détecteur(m) solaire 42, 43, 49.
détecteur(m) terrestre 42, 43.
**détection(f) des ondes(f) sismiques 714.**
détendeur(m) de secours(m) 627.
détendeur(m) premier étage(m) 627.
détendeur(m) second étage(m) 627.
détente(f) 453, 793, 795, 796, 797, 798, 799, 804.
détonateur(m) 804.
détroit(m) 51.
deux avec barreur(m) 632.
deux sans barreur(m) 632.
deux-points(m) 832.
deuxième but(m) 597.
deuxième cabine(f) focale 15.
deuxième espace(m) 610.
deuxième étage(m) 509.
deuxième joueur(m) 620.
deuxième molaire(f) 144.
deuxième phalange(f) 103.
deuxième prémolaire(f) 144.
deuxième radial(m) externe 121.
deuxième-but(m) 597.
devant(m) 322, 324.
déverrouillage(m) de l'objectif(m) 391.
déversoir(m) 746.
dévidoir(m) 265, 575.
dévidoir(m) de ruban(m) adhésif 516.
**dévidoir(m) sur roues(f) 265.**
dextre(f) 818.
diable(m) 788.
diagonale(f) 756.
diamant(m) 363, 483.
diapason(m) 539.
diaphragme(m) 130, 390.
diaphragme(m) d'ouverture(f) 717.
diaphragme(m) de dilatation(f) 485.
**diapositive(f) 397.**
diapositive(f) 397.
dièse(m) 538.
diesel(m)-navire(m) 745.
diffuseurs(m) tubulaires 501.
digue(f) morte 752.
dindon(m) 150.
dînette(f) 195.
diode(f) 769.
dioxyde(m) 33.
directeur(m) technique 412, 415.
direction(f) d'une réaction(f) 831.
direction(f) de la Mecque(f) 173.
direction(f) des pointes(f) 488.
direction(f) du vent(m) 38.
direction(f) et force(f) du vent(m) 38.
direction(f) obligatoire 824, 825.
discontinuité(f) de Gutenberg 22.
discontinuité(f) de Mohorovicic 22.
disjoncteur(m) 212, 747.
disjoncteur(m) bipolaire 312.
disjoncteur(m) de fuite(f) de terre(f) 312.
disjoncteur(m) principal 312.
disjoncteur(m) unipolaire 312.
dispositif(m) anti-bascule 727.
dispositif(m) antidébordement(m) 257.
dispositif(m) contrarotatif 42.
dispositif(m) de blocage(m) 302.
dispositif(m) de poussée(f) 389.
**disque(m) 404.**
disque(m) 157, 432, 529, 563, 583, 663, 712.
**disque(m) compact 405.**
disque(m) compact 408.
disque(m) d'enterrage(m) 158.
disque(m) de papier(m)-diagramme(m) 441.
disque(m) de réglage(m) 396.
disque(m) de tension(f) 562, 569.
disque(m) optique 527.
disque(m) videophoto(f) 395.
**disques(m) 251, 658.**
disquette(f) 526.
**disquette(f) rigide 529.**
**disquette(f) souple 529.**
distance(f) parcourue 711.
distillation(f) sous vide(m) 744.
distributeur(m) 216.
**distributeur(m) d'essence(f) 453.**
distributeur(m) d'essence(f) 453.
distributeur(m) de boissons(f) 453.
distributeur(m) de correspondances(f) 475.
distributeur(m) de détergent(m) 257.
distributeur(m) de glaçons(m) 453.
distributeur(m) de lames(f) 374.
distributeur(m) de produit(m) de rinçage(m) 257.
diviseur(m) 160.
division(f) 523, 830.
division(f) territoriale 51.
**divisions(f) cartographiques 47.**
**divisions(f) de l'écu(m) 818.**
do(m) 537.
**doigt(m) 137.**
doigt(m) 84, 111, 327, 596, 681.
doigt(m) de jupe(f) 493.
doigt(m) externe 108.
doigt(m) interne 108.
doigt(m) lobé 111.
doigt(m) médian 108.
doigt(m) palmé 84, 111.
doigt(m) postérieur 108.
doline(f) 24.
dollar(m) 832.
dôme(m) 743.
domino(m) d'accouplement(m) 542.
DOMINOS(M) 695.
donjon(m) 181.
Dorade(f) 13.
dormant(m) 203, 225.
**dormeuse(f) de croissance(f) 350.**
**dormeuse(f)-couverture(f) 350.**
dos(m) 101, 106, 108, 117, 119, 239, 240, 241, 242, 277, 322, 386, 577, 793.
**dos(m) de l'amplificateur(m) 400.**
**dos(m) de l'appareil(m) 390.**
dos(m) du livre(m) 579.
dos(m) du nez(m) 141.
dossard(m) 656.
dosse(f) 288.
dosseret(m) 255, 258, 259.
dossier(m) 223, 428, 445, 727.
dossier(m) inclinable 726.
dossier(m) suspendu 518.
dossière(f) 96, 653.
double bémol(m) 538.
double boutonnage(m) 319.
double croche(f) 538.
double dièse(m) 538.
double paire(f) 695.
double rideau(m) 229.
double toit(m) 685, 686.
double virage(m) 826, 827.
double vitrage(m) 772.
double zéro(m) 700.
double(m) 646, 695.
double-blanc(m) 695.
double-scull(m) 632.
double-six(m) 695.
doublement denté 56.
doublure(f) 322, 324, 352, 354, 378, 565, 644.
douche(f) 194.
douchette(f) 292, 296.
douille(f) 309, 798.
**douille(f) de lampe(f) 309.**
douille(f) de plastique(m) 799.
douve(f) 181.
douzaine(f) (1 à 12) 700, 701.
douzaine(f) (13 à 24) 700, 701.
douzaine(f) (25 à 36) 700, 701.
drachme(m) 832.
Dragon(m) 11.
dragonne(f) 383, 640, 642, 681.
draille(f) 479.
drain(m) 199, 216.
drap(m) 224.
drap(m)-housse(f) 224.
drapeau(m) 606.
drapeau(m) à Schwenkel 817.
drapeau(m) blanc 626.
drapeau(m) bleu 626.
drapeau(m) carré 817.
drapeau(m) de centre(m) 601.
drapeau(m) de coin(m) 601, 607.
drapeau(m) rectangulaire 817.
drapeau(m) rouge 626, 668.
**drapeau(m), éléments(m) 817.**
**drapeaux(m), formes(f) 817.**
drisse(f) 480, 817.
droit fil(m) 565.
droit(m) antérieur de la cuisse(f) 120.
droit(m) interne 121.
droit(m): stationata(f) 646.
drupéole(f) 62.
**duffle-coat(m) 320.**
dune(f) 30.
dune(f) complexe 46.
dune(f) en croissant(m) 46.
dune(f) parabolique 46.
dunes(f) longitudinales 46.
dunes(f) transversales 46.
dunette(f) 478.
duo(m) 558.
duodénum(m) 131.
dure-mère(f) 134, 135.
durite(f) de radiateur(m) 438.
duse(f) 740.
duvet(m) 110.
dyke(m) 25.
dynamo(f) 446.

## E

eau(f) de fonte(f) 27.
eau(f) de ville(f) 772.
eau(f) lourde froide 761.
eau(f) lourde sous pression(f) 761.
eau(f) sous pression(f) 755.
**eau(f), cycle(m) 34.**
eau(f)/alcool(m) 485.
eaux(f) sécuritaires 488.
**ébarbage(m) 578.**
ébarboir(m) 582.
ébauchoirs(m) 585.
ébrancheur(m) 269.
ébrasement(m) 175.
écaille(f) 70, 87, 96, 97, 111.
écaille(f) ventrale 97.
écailles(f) de cyprès(m) 58.
écailleur(m) 688.
écartelé 818.
écartement(m) des électrodes(f) 439.
échalote(f) 70.
échalote(f) nouvelle 70.
échancrure(f) 544.
échancrure(f) de la conque(f) 139.
échangeur(m) de chaleur(f) 209, 760.
échangeur(m) en losange(m) 451.
**échangeur(m) en trèfle(m) 452.**
échangeur(m) en trèfle(m) 450.
échangeur(m) en trompette(f) 451.
échangeur(m) extérieur 212.
échangeur(m) intérieur 213.
échangeur(m) thermique 772.
**échangeurs(m), principaux types(m) 450.**
échantillon(m) 567.
échappement(m) 436, 437, 501.
échauguette(f) 178, 181.
ÉCHECS(M) 696.
**échecs(m), déplacements(m) 696.**
**échecsm, pièces(f) 696.**
échelle(f) 449, 487, 493, 719, 741, 785.
échelle(f) à crochets(m) 303, 781.
échelle(f) Celsius 705.
**échelle(f) coulissante 302.**
échelle(f) d'échafaudage(m) 303.
échelle(f) d'espacement(m) 524.
échelle(f) d'ouverture(f) 396.
échelle(f) d'ouverture(f) de diaphragme(m) 392.
échelle(f) de bout(m) 470.
échelle(f) de corde(f) 303.
échelle(f) de hauteur(f) 399.
échelle(f) de latitude(f) 40.
échelle(f) de lecture(f) de la luminosité(f) 396.
échelle(f) de profondeur(f) 284.
échelle(f) de profondeur(f) de champ(m) 392.
échelle(f) de profondeur(f) en m 485.
échelle(f) de tête(f) 781.
échelle(f) des altitudes(f) 19.
échelle(f) des distances(f) 392.
échelle(f) des mouvements(m) 539.
échelle(f) des températures(f) 19.
échelle(f) des temps(m) d'exposition(f) 396.
échelle(f) droite 303.
échelle(f) escamotable 303.
échelle(f) Fahrenheit 705.
échelle(f) fruitière 303.
échelle(f) graduée 708, 709.
échelle(f) latérale 470.
échelle(f) roulante 303.
échelle(f) transformable 303.
ÉCHELLES(F) 302.
échelles(f) barométriques 710.
échelles(f) de la température(f) 710.
échelon(m) 302.
échenilloir(m)-élagueur(m) 269.
échine(f) 167.
**échiquier(m) 696.**
écho(m) 722.
éclair(m) 36.
éclairage(m) 368, 477, 500.
éclairage(m) de l'écran(m) d'affichage(m) 396.
éclairage(m) inactinique 398.
éclairage(m)/clignotant(m) 430.
éclairagiste(m) 412.
éclipse(f) annulaire 8.
ÉCLIPSE(F) DE LUNE(F) 8.
ÉCLIPSE(F) DE SOLEIL(M) 8.
éclipse(f) partielle 8.
éclipse(f) totale 8.
**éclipses(f), types 8.**
**éclipses(f), types(m) 8.**
écliptique(m) 3.
éclisse(f) 466, 544, 546.
ÉCLUSE(F) 492.
écluse(f) 490, 752.
écoinçon(m) 174.
ÉCOLOGIE(F) 31, 32, 34.
écorce(f) 59, 65.
écoulement(m) souterrain 32, 35.
écoute(f) 420, 480.
écoute(f) de foc(m) 628.
écoute(f) de grand-voile(f) 628.
écouteur(m) 406.
écoutille(f) 805.
écouvillon(m) 801.
**écran(m) 529.**
écran(m) 410, 422, 485, 526, 527, 699.
écran(m) à main(f) 308.
écran(m) d'affichage(m) 396, 421, 532.
écran(m) de contrôle(m) 391, 717.
écran(m) de précontrôle(m) 415.
**écran(m) de projection(f) 397.**
écran(m) de sortie(f) 413, 415.
écran(m) de soudeur(m) 308.
écran(m) de visibilité(f) 471.
écran(m) du directeur(m) technique 413.
écran(m) du truqueur(m) numérique 413.
écran(m) principal de précontrôle(m) 413.
écran(m) protecteur 16.
écrans(m) d'entrée(f) 413.
écrans(m) de précontrôle(m) 413.
écrevisse(f) 90.
écritoire(f) 378.
ÉCRITURE(F), INSTRUMENTS(M) 389.
écrou(m) 278, 279, 290, 300, 466.
écrou(m) à cabestan(m) 40.
écrou(m) à collet(m) 296.
écrou(m) à oreilles(f) 279.
écrou(m) borgne 279.
écrou(m) de blocage(m) 670, 671.
écrou(m) de bonde(f) 296.
écrou(m) de contrôle(m) 40.
écrou(m) de fixation(f) 296.
écrou(m) de la lame(f) 284.
écrou(m) de montage(m) 684.
écrou(m) de serrage(m) 300.
écrou(m) du presse-étoupe(m) 294.
écrou(m) hexagonal 439.
écu(m) 832.
**écu(m), divisions(f) 818.**
écubier(m) 495, 497.
écume(f) 30.
écumoire(f) 244.
écurie(f) 651.
écusson(m) 95, 289, 596.
édicule(m) 474.
ÉDIFICE(M) À BUREAUX(M) 190.
édifice(m) public 52.
édredon(m) 224.
effacement(m) 420.
effacement(m) de mémoire(f) 396, 523.
effacement(m) partiel 523.
effacement(m) total 523.
égal ou plus grand que 830.
égal ou plus petit que 830.
égale 830.
égale à peu près 830.
égalisateur(m) graphique 400.
église(f) 185.
égout(m) 186.
égout(m) collecteur 186.
**égoutter, ustensils(m) pour 243.**
éjecteur(m) 784.
éjecteur(m) de fouets(m) 250.
élan(m) 105, 682.
élastique(m) 224.
ÉLECTRICITÉ(F) 309, 310, 312, 746, 748, 750, 752, 754, 756.
**électricité(f), outils(m) 310, 311.**
électrode(f) 232, 305.
électrode(f) centrale 439.
électrode(f) d'allumage(m) 209.

Les termes en **caractères gras** renvoient à une illustration, ceux en CAPITALES indiquent un titre.

électrode(f) de masse(f) 439.
élément(m) 585.
élément(m) bimétallique hélicoïdal 705.
élément(m) chauffant 257, 259, 305.
élément(m) de chauffe(f) 207, 209.
élément(m) tubulaire 255.
élévateur(m) 636, 764.
élévateur(m) à grain(m) 161.
élévateur(m) de décors(m) 188.
**élévation(f) 193.**
élévation(f) de la tension(f) 755, 767.
élevon(m) 511.
émail(m) 144.
embase(f) 393, 641, 656, 713.
embase(f) de plat(m) de dos(m) 220.
**embauchoir(m) 358.**
emblème(m) 817.
embouchure(f) 550.
embout(m) 230, 302, 375, 397, 439, 609, 627, 670.
embout(m) auriculaire 726.
embout(m) de baleine(f) 375.
embout(m) de caoutchouc(m) 728.
embout(m) de protection(f) 730.
embout(m) isolant 370.
embout(m) Luer Lock 726.
embrasse(f) 228, 728.
embrasure(f) 179.
émeraude(f) 363.
émerillon(m) 672.
émetteur(m) micro-ondes(f) 415.
émetteur(m)/récepteur(m) 485.
emmanchure(f) 325.
emmarchement(m) 201.
empattement(m) 756.
empaumure(f) 105.
empennage(m) 499, 618, 684, 698, 814.
empennage(m) bas 498.
empennage(m) de stabilisation(f) 509.
empennage(m) en T 498.
empennage(m) fixe 814.
empennage(m) surélevé 498.
EMPENNAGES(M), TYPES(M) 498.
empiècement(m) 320, 324, 337.
emplacement(m) de la statue(f) 169.
emporte-pièces(m) 245.
empreinte(f) musculaire 95.
empreinte(f) palléale 95.
en accolade(f) 174.
en équilibre(m) 624.
en fer(m) à cheval(m) 174.
en lancette(f) 174.
en ogive(f) 174.
en prison(f) 700, 701.
en-but(m) 606.
encadrement(m) 204.
**enceinte(f) acoustique 401.**
enceinte(f) de confinement(m) 765, 766.
enceinte(f) en béton(m) 760, 761, 762, 763.
enceinte(f) humide 763.
enceinte(f) sèche 763.
enclos(m) 149.
enclume(f) 138.
encoche(f) 684, 793.
encoche(f) de protection(f) 529.
encoignure(f) 227.
encolure(f) 100, 325.
encolure(f) bateau(m) 343.
encolure(f) drapée 343.
encolure(f) en V 322, 326.
encolure(f) ras-de-cou(m) 343, 350.
**encolures(f) 343.**
encre(f) 389, 581, 588.
encre(f) lithographique 583.
endive(f) 73.
endocarpe(m) 63, 64.
**endossure(f) 579.**
ÉNERGIE(F) ÉOLIENNE 773, 774.
ÉNERGIE(F) NUCLÉAIRE 758, 760, 762, 764, 766.
ÉNERGIE(F) SOLAIRE 768, 770, 772.
**énergie(f) solaire, production(f) d'électricité(f) 771.**
enfile-aiguille(m) 563.
enfourchure(f) 105, 325.
**enfumoir(m) 582.**
engageante(f) 317.
engrenage(m) horaire 14.
engreneur(m) 160.
enjoliveur(m) 294, 295, 427.
enregistrement(m) 403, 411, 420.
enregistrement(m) des bagages(m) 462.
enregistreur(m) 621.
enregistreur(m) de film(m) 527.
enrouleur(m) 666.
enseigne(f) directionnelle 475.
enseigne(f) extérieure 474.
ensemble(m) du chevalet(m) 547.
ensemble(m) vide 830.
ENSILER 162.
**ensiler 155.**
**ensoleillement(m), mesure(f) 40.**
ensouple(f) de chaîne(f) 573.
ensouple(f) de tissu(m) 572.
entablement(m) 166, 168, 202.
entablure(f) 564.
entier 56.
entoilage(m) 565.
entonnoir(m) 243, 251.
entonnoir(m) collecteur 40.
entraînement(m) de la chaîne(f) 156.
entraînement(m) de la tête(f) d'impression(f) 531.
entraînement(m) de la turbine(f) par la vapeur(f) 767.
entraînement(m) du rotor(m) de l'alternateur(m) 767.
entraîneur(m) 669.
entrait(m) 199.
entrave(f) 652.
entre-nœud(m) 57.
entredent(m) 240.
entredoublure(f) 565.
entrée(f) 82, 452, 625, 787.
entrée(f) d'air(m) 501, 508.
entrée(f) d'air(m) du moteur(m) 813.
entrée(f) d'air(m) du ventilateur(m) 493.
entrée(f) d'eau(f) 295.
entrée(f) d'électricité(f) 585.
entrée(f) de clé(m) 290.
entrée(f) de courant(m) 232.
entrée(f) de l'eau(f) de refroidissement(m) du condenseur(m) 759.
entrée(f) de la vapeur(f) à haute pression(f) 758.
entrée(f) des gaz(m) d'échappement(m) 438.
entrée(f) des marchandises(f) 190.
entrée(f) des originaux(m) 421.
entrée(f) du caloporteur(m) 768.
entrée(f) du reflux(m) du condenseur(m) 759.
entrée(f) électrique 207.
entrée(f) pieds(m) premiers 624.
entrée(f) principale 190, 194.
entrée(f) tête(f) première 624.
**entrées(f) dans l'eau(f) 624.**
entrejambe(m) 219.
entrejambe(m) pressionné 350.
entrepôt(m) frigorifique 491.
ENTRETIEN(M) DES TISSUS(M) 829.
entretoise(f) 302, 572, 774, 787.
enveloppe(f) 309, 529, 596, 598, 634, 677.
enveloppe(f) extérieure 14, 297.
enveloppe(f) intérieure 14.
**éolienne(f) à axe(m) horizontal 774.**
**éolienne(f) à axe(m) vertical 774.**
épandeur(m) 270.
**épandeur(m) de fumier(m) 156.**
épandeur(m) de fumier(m) 154.
éparpilleur(m) 156.
éparpilleur(m) de paille(f) 161.
épaule(f) 100, 106, 116, 118, 615, 670.
**épaulé(m)-jeté(m) à deux bras(m) 662.**
épaulement(m) 242, 279.
épaulière(f) 602, 609, 792, 804.
épée(f) 666.
épée(f) à deux mains(f) 794.
épéiste(m) 667.
éperon(m) 80, 552, 648.
éperon(m) calcanéen 112.
épi(m) 60, 72.
épicarpe(m) 62, 63, 64.
épicentre(m) 23.
épicondyle(m) 123.
épiderme(m) 137.
épiglotte(f) 130, 142, 143.
épinard(m) 73.
épine(f) de l'omoplate(f) 123.
épingle(f) 563.
épingle(f) à bigoudi(m) 369.
épingle(f) à cheveux(m) 369.
épingle(f) à cravate(f) 364.
épingle(f) de sûreté(f) 566.
**épingles(f) 364.**
épiphyse(f) 134.
épiscope(m) du tireur(m) 805.
**épissure(f) courte 692.**
épitrochlée(f) 123.
éplucheur(m) 242.
époi(m) 105.
éponge(f) 104.
éponge(f) de mer(f) 367.
éponge(f) synthétique 367.
éponge(f) végétale 367.
**éponges(f) 367.**
éprouvette(f) graduée 40.
épuisette(f) 672.
équateur(m) 3, 47.
équateur(m) céleste 3.
équerre(f) 275.
équilibrage(m) des haut-parleurs(m) 402.
équilibreur(m) 802.
équinoxe(m) d'automne(m) 8.
équinoxe(m) de printemps(m) 8.
équipe(f) 620.
équipe(f) au champ(m) 599.
équipement(m) de contrôle(m) biomédical 512.
**équipement(m) de protection(f) 602.**
ÉQUIPEMENT(M) DE PROTECTION(F), SOUDAGE(M) 308.
équipement(m) de survie(f) 512.
**équipements(m) aéroportuaires 506.**
ÉQUITATION(F) 646, 648.
équivaut à 830.
ergot(m) 106.
ergot(m) d'entraînement(m) 531.
Éridan 13.
éruption(f) 6.
**escabeau(m) 302.**
ESCABEAUX(M) 302.
ESCALIER(M) 201.
escalier(m) 194, 474, 669, 741, 773.
escalier(m) automoteur 507.
escalier(m) d'accès(m) 507.
escalier(m) de la mezzanine(f) 195.
escalier(m) en spirale(f) 741.
escalier(m) mécanique 474.
escalier(m) mobile 189, 190.
**escargot(m) 83.**
escarpe(f) 178.
escarpin(m) 356.
escarpin(m)-sandale(f) 356.
ESCRIME(F) 666.
**escrime(f) piste(f) 666.**
**escrime(f), cibles(f) 667.**
**escrime(f), parties(f) de l'arme(f), 666.**
**escrime(f), positions(f) 667.**
**escrime(f)armes(f) 666.**
**escrimeur(m) 667.**
escudo(m) 832.
espace(m) vert 184.
espaceur(m) de câbles(m) 684.
espadrille(f) 357.
esperluette(f) 831.
**esquimau(m) 351.**
essence(f) 744, 745.
essence(f) lourde 744.
essieu(m) 468, 645.
essieu(m) avant 784.
essieu(m) directeur 788.
essoreuse(f) à salade(f) 243.
**essuie-glace(m) 431.**
essuie-glace(m) 426.
est identique à 830.
est(m) 488.
estacade(f) de guidage(m) 492.
esthèques(f) 584.
estomac(m) 88, 92, 97, 124, 131.
**estrade(f) 651.**
estragon(m) 74.
estuaire(m) 30, 51.
étable(f) 149.
**étage(m) 194.**
étage(m) 196, 736, 773.
étage(m) d'exploitation(f) 752.
étai(m) 198, 479.
étai(m) avant 628.
étambot(m) 742.
étamine(f) 60, 64.
étampure(f) 104.
étançon(m) 156.
**étapes(f) 586.**
état(m) 51.
état(m) présent du temps(m) 38.
**étau(m) 282.**
étau(m) 582.
**étau(m) à endosser 579.**
été(m) 8.
étincelle(f) 436.
étiquette(f) 404, 709.
étiquettes(f) autocollantes 518.
étoile(f) 36, 819.
étoile(f) (8) 363.
étoile(f) filante 19.
étoile(f) Polaire 11.
étouffoir(m) 541.
étranglement(m) 668, 705.
étrave(f) 479, 628.
étrier(m) 138, 309, 432, 442, 642, 648, 793.
étrier(m) du flotteur(m) 216.
étrivière(f) 649.
étui(m) 358, 365, 523, 688.
étui(m) à lunettes(f) 379.
étui(m) de cuir(m) 690.
étuveuse(f) 249.
Eurasie(f) 21.
Europe 4.
Europe(f) 21.
**Eutelsat II 418.**
euthynterie(f) 166, 168.
évacuation(f) de l'eau(f) turbinée 755.
évaporation(f) 34, 35.
évaseur(m) 299.
évent(m) 389, 585.
évent(m) de pignon(m) 197.
évent(m) latéral 214.
évier(m) 296.
évier(m) double 215.
**évier(m)-broyeur(m) 296.**
évolution(f) de la pression(f) 38.
excavatrice(f) à roue(f) 733.
EXEMPLES(M) DE GROUPES(M) INSTRUMENTAUX 558.
exosphère(f) 19.
expédition(f) du fret(m) 505.
expédition(f)/réception(f) des messages(m) 421.
expiration(f) 622.
explosion(f) 436.
extenseur(m) 665.
extenseur(m) commun des doigts(m) 121.
extenseur(m) commun des orteils(m) 120.
EXTÉRIEUR(M) D'UNE MAISON(F) 196.
**extincteur(m) 780.**
extincteur(m) d'incendie(m) 823.
extrados(m) 174.
eye-liner(m) liquide 367.

## F

fa(m) 537.
**façade(f) 175.**
face(f) 179, 239, 619, 677.
**face(f) antérieure 120.**
**face(f) inférieure 363.**
**face(f) plantaire du sabot(m) 104.**
**face(f) postérieure 121.**
**face(f) supérieure 363.**
face-à-main(m) 377.
facteur(m) Rhésus négatif 831.
facteur(m) Rhésus positif 831.
factorielle(f) 830.
facule(f) 6.
faible(m) 666.
faille(f) 23.
faille(f) transformante 28.
faisceau(m) bleu 410.
faisceau(m) d'électrons(m) 410, 717.
faisceau(m) laser(m) 405.
faisceau(m) rouge 410.
faisceau(m) vert 410.
faîtage(m) 198.
faitout(m) 249, 688.
falaise(f) 7, 23, 27, 30.
FANER 159.
**faner 155.**
fanion(m) 38, 817.
fanon(m) 101.
**fard(m) à joues(f) en poudre(f) 366.**
fasce(f) 166.
FAUCHER 158.
**faucher 154.**
**faucheuse(f)-conditionneuse(f) 158.**
faucheuse(f)-conditionneuse(f) 154.
faucille(f) 269.
fausse côte(f) (3) 123.
fausse oronge(f) 55.
fausse poche(f) 330.
fausse-équerre(f) 713.
FAUTEUIL(M) 220.
fauteuil(m) club(m) 221.
fauteuil(m) metteur(m) en scène(f) 220.
fauteuil(m) pivotant à bascule(f) 520.
FAUTEUIL(M) ROULANT 727.
fauteuil(m) roulant 461.
fauteuil(m) Wassily 221.

Les termes en **caractères gras** renvoient à une illustration, ceux en CAPITALES indiquent un titre.

fauteuil(m)-sac(m) 222.
fauteuils(m) d'orchestre(m) 188.
**fauteuils(m), principaux types(m) 220.**
faux bourdon(m) 81.
faux foc(m) 481.
faux quartier(m) 649.
faux registre(m) 543.
faux sommier(m) 543.
faux(f) 267.
femelle(f) 831.
fémur(m) 78, 80, 103, 122.
FENÊTRE(F) 203.
fenêtre(f) 194, 195, 327, 399, 477, 631, 756.
fenêtre(f) à guillotine(f) 203.
fenêtre(f) à jalousies(f) 203.
fenêtre(f) à l'anglaise(f) 203.
fenêtre(f) à la française(f) 203.
fenêtre(f) basculante 203.
fenêtre(f) coulissante 203.
fenêtre(f) d'éjection(f) 796.
fenêtre(f) de lecture(f) 403, 529.
fenêtre(f) de sous-sol(m) 197.
fenêtre(f) en accordéon(m) 203.
fenêtre(f) en baie(f) 197.
fenêtre(f) en saillie(f) 197.
fenêtre(f) moustiquaire(f) 685.
fenêtre(f) panoramique 190, 460.
fenêtre(f) pivotante 203.
**fenêtres(f), types(m) 203.**
fenil(m) 148.
**fenouil(m) 72.**
fente(f) 252, 276, 379, 576, 578.
fente(f) à monnaie(f) 422, 702.
fente(f) d'alimentation(f) 521.
fente(f) de vision(f) 792.
fente(f) latérale 322.
fente(f) médiane 322.
**fer(m) 677.**
fer(m) 104, 277.
**fer(m) à cheval(m) 104.**
fer(m) à cheval(m) 364.
**fer(m) à friser 370.**
fer(m) à souder 305.
**fer(m) à vapeur(f) 256.**
**fer(m) droit 677.**
fer(m) droit 678.
fer(m) nº 3 678.
fer(m) nº 4 678.
fer(m) nº 5 678.
fer(m) nº 6 678.
fer(m) nº 7 678.
fer(m) nº 8 678.
fer(m) nº 9 678.
**fer(m), golf(m) 678.**
FERME(F) 148.
**ferme(f) de toit(m) 199.**
FERME(F), ANIMAUX(M) 150.
**fermeture(f) à glissière(f) 566.**
fermeture(f) à glissière(f) 321, 350, 365, 382, 685.
fermeture(f) du soufflet(m) 536.
fermeture(f) sous patte(f) 351.
fermeture(f) Velcro® 349.
fermoir(m) 378, 380, 587.
ferret(m) 352, 354, 375.
ferrure(f) 383.
fertilisants(m) 32.
FERTILISER LA TERRE(F) 156.
**fertiliser la terre(f) 154.**
fesse(f) 117, 119, 127, 128.
feu(m) 486, 487, 489.
feu(m) anticollision 498.
feu(m) arrière 443, 444, 446.
feu(m) blanc 488.
feu(m) clignotant 471.
feu(m) clignotant arrière 444.
feu(m) clignotant avant 442, 444.
feu(m) de gabarit(m) 440, 441.
feu(m) de lisse(f) 471.
feu(m) de navigation(f) 493, 499.
feu(m) de plaque(f) 429.
feu(m) de position(f) 459, 508.
feu(m) de tête(f) de mât(m) 495.
feu(m) rouge arrière 441.
feu(m) stop(m) 429.
feuillage(m) 59.
**feuille(f) 56.**
feuille(f) 57, 72.
feuille(f) d'acanthe(f) 167, 220.
feuille(f) de papier(m) 714.
**feuille(f) de vigne(f) 61.**
feuille(f) de vigne(f) 73.
**feuille(f), bord(m) 56.**
**feuilles(f) composées 56.**
**feuilles(f) simples 56.**
FEUILLES(F), TYPES(M) 56.
**feuilles(f), types(m) 58.**
feuillet(m) 577.
feuillets(m) 379.
feuillets(m) intercalaires 519.
feutre(m) 329, 541, 588.
feutre(m) d'étouffoir(m) 540.
**feux(m) 429.**
**feux(m) arrière 429.**
**feux(m) avant 429.**
feux(m) clignotants 429.
feux(m) de brouillard(m) 429.
feux(m) de circulation(f) 186.
feux(m) de croisement(m) 429.
feux(m) de gabarit(m) 429.
feux(m) de recul(m) 429.
feux(m) de route(f) 429.
feux(m) rouges arrière 429.
feux(m) stop(m) 429.
fèves(f) 72.
fibre(f) 692.
fibre(f) musculaire 134.
fibre(f) nerveuse 136.
fibule(f) 315.
ficelle(f) 578.
fiche(f) 280, 310, 401, 485.
**fiche(f) américaine 309.**
**fiche(f) européenne 309.**
fiche(f) pour jack(m) 400, 406.
fiches(f) 517.
fichier(m) 517.
fichier(m) rotatif 516.
figue(f) de Barbarie 68.
fil(m) 288, 714.
fil(m) à couper la pâte(f) 584.
fil(m) d'arrivée(f) 651.
fil(m) de caret(m) 692.
fil(m) de chaîne(f) 576.
fil(m) de corps(m) 666.
fil(m) de liaison(f) 312.
fil(m) de nylon(m) 271.
fil(m) de service(m) neutre 312.
fil(m) de terre(f) 312.
fil(m) de trame(f) 576.
fil(m) neutre 312.
fil(m) thermique 312.
filament(m) 6, 232.
filament(m) branchial 87.
filament(m) de tungstène(m) 233.
**filet(m) 613, 614, 618.**
filet(m) 60, 167, 276, 544, 546, 610, 612, 613, 614, 618, 619, 626.
**filet(m) à aiguilles(f) 650.**
**filet(m) à jouets(m) 650.**
**filet(m) à olives(f) 650.**
**filet(m) en caoutchouc(m) 650.**
filetage(m) 294.
filière(f) 299.
film(m) 390.
film(m)-disque(m) 395.
film(m)-pack(m) 395.
filoir(m) d'écoute(f) 630.
filtre(m) 252, 255, 772.
filtre(m) à air(m) 207, 210, 272, 469, 783.
filtre(m) à charpie(f) 258, 259.
filtre(m) coloré 484.
filtre(m) de couleur(f) 392.
filtre(m) de polarisation(f) 392.
filtre(m) rouge inactinique 399.
filum(m) terminal 134.
fin(f) 692.
FINES HERBES(F) 74.
finition(f) 586.
fission(f) de l'uranium(m) 766.
fixatif(m) 592.
fixation(f) 230, 633, 642, 656.
fixation(f) à butée(f) avant 642.
fixation(f) arrière 633.
fixation(f) avant 633.
**fixation(f) de sécurité(f) 641.**
fixe-lecture(m) 396.
flanc(m) 101, 108, 179, 433, 579.
flanc(m) dextre 818.
flanc(m) senestre 818.
flanqueur(m) 605.
**flash(m) électronique 393.**
flash(m)-cube(m) 393.
flasque(f) 754.
flasque(m) 800.
flasque(m) inférieur 753.
fléau(m) 708.
fléau(m) arrière 708.
fléau(m) avant 708.
**flèche(f) 684.**
Flèche(f) 11.
flèche(f) 175, 675, 697, 782, 785, 786, 793.
flèche(f) de transept(m) 176.
flèche(f) du vent(m) 38.
flèche(f) littorale 30.
flèche(f) télescopique 780, 786.
**fléchette(f) 698.**
**fléchette(f), aire(f) de jeu(m) 698.**
fleur(f) 57.
fleur(f) de lis(m) 819.
**fleur(f), inflorescence(f), 60.**
FLEUR(F), STRUCTURE(F) 60.
fleuret(m) 666, 734.
fleuret(m) électrique 666.
fleurettiste(m) 667.
fleuve(m) 51, 52.
flexible(m) 292, 296.
flexible(m) d'air(m) 590, 734.
flexible(m) d'eau(f) 734.
flexible(m) d'injection(f) de boue(f) 737.
flexible(m) de branchement(m) 399.
flexible(m) de distribution(f) 453.
flexibles(m) d'alimentation(f) 635.
floraison(f) 61.
florin(m) 832.
flotteur(m) 216, 293, 485, 486, 631, 672, 741, 803.
fluide(m) caloporteur 771.
flûte(f) 548.
flûte(f) à champagne(m) 237.
flûte(f) de Pan 536.
fluteroni(m) 587.
flûtes(f) 556.
foc(m) 628.
foie(m) 88, 97, 124, 131.
follicule(m) 67, 136.
**follicule(m), coupe(f) 67.**
fonctions(f) système(m) 555.
fond(m) 586.
fond(m) d'yeux(m) 240.
fond(m) de bassin(m) 626.
FOND(M) DE L'OCÉAN(M) 28.
fond(m) de l'océan(m) 22.
fond(m) de protection(f) 698.
**fond(m) de robe(f) 345.**
fond(m) de teint(m) liquide 366.
fond(m) de tour(m) 744.
fondation(f) 751.
fondation(f) de pylône(m) 456.
**fondations(f) 199.**
fontaine(f) des ablutions(f) 172, 173.
**fonture(f) 568.**
fonture(f) 568.
FOOTBALL(M) 600, 604.
FOOTBALL(M) AMÉRICAIN 602.
**football(m) américain, terrain(m) 604.**
**football(m) canadien, terrain(m) 604.**
**football(m), ballon(m) 600, 602.**
**football(m), terrain(m) 601.**
**footballeur(m) 600, 602.**
**forage(m) en mer(f) 739.**
foramen(m) apical 144.
foramen(m) cæcum 143.
force(f) du vent(m) 38.
forêt(f) 27.
forêt(f) tropicale 45.
foret(m) 280.
**foret(m) hélicoïdal 281.**
formation(f) de jazz(m) 558.
fort(m) 666.
FORTIFICATION(F) À LA VAUBAN 178.
fosse(f) abyssale 28.
fosse(f) d'orchestre(m) 188.
fosse(f) de réception(f) 683.
fosse(f) de sable(m) 676.
FOSSE(F) SEPTIQUE 216.
fossé(m) 178, 451.
**fosses(f) nasales 141.**
fossette(f) 96.
fossette(f) de l'anthélix(m) 139.
Fou(m) 696.
fouet(m) 245, 250.
fouet(m) à fil(m) 250.
fouet(m) en spirale(f) 250.
fouet(m) quatre pales(f) 250.
**fouets(m) 250.**
foulon(m) 159.
four(m) 255, 770.
**four(m) à micro-ondes(f) 253.**
**four(m) électrique 585.**
**four(m) solaire 770.**
four(m) tubulaire 744.
fourche(f) 447, 721, 756.
fourche(f) à bêcher 266.
fourche(f) à fleurs(f) 268.
fourche(f) télescopique hydraulique 442.
fourches(f) 787, 788.
**fourchette(f) 240.**
fourchette(f) 104, 327, 642, 688, 707.
fourchette(f) à découper 242.
fourchette(f) à dessert(m) 240.
fourchette(f) à fondue(f) 240.
fourchette(f) à huîtres(f) 240.
fourchette(f) à poisson(m) 240.
fourchette(f) à salade(f) 240.
fourchette(f) de table(f) 240.
**fourchettes(f), principaux types(m) 240.**
**fourgon(m)-pompe(f) 778.**
fourgonnette(f) 425.
fourmi(f) 77.
Fourneau(m) 13.
fourneau(m) 385.
**fourragère(f) 162.**
fourragère(f) 155.
fourreau(m) 101, 106, 281, 283, 375, 631, 637.
fourreau(m) de la langue(f) 96.
fourrure(f) 107.
**fourrures(f), exemples(m) 819.**
foyer(m) 23, 189, 770.
foyer(m) primaire 14.
**foyer(m), accessoires(m) 205.**
frac(m) 317.
fraise(f) 281, 318.
**fraise(f), coupe(f) 62.**
**framboise(f), coupe(f) 62.**
franc(m) 832.
frange(f) 318.
frange(f) de passementerie(f) 229.
**frappeur(m) 595.**
frappeur(m) 597.
FRÉGATE(F) 808.
frein(m) 570, 640, 641, 664, 670.
**frein(m) à disque(m) 432.**
frein(m) à disque(m) 442.
**frein(m) à tambour(m) 432.**
frein(m) arrière 446.
frein(m) avant 447.
frein(m) d'urgence(f) 477.
frein(m) de chaîne(f) 272.
frein(m) de talon(m) 645.
frein(m) direct 468.
freineur(m) 643.
fresque(f) 170.
frette(f) 546, 547.
frise(f) 166, 168, 188, 189, 202, 225.
**friteuse(f) 252.**
fronçage(m) tuyauté 229.
fronce(f) 337.
front(m) 109, 116, 733.
front(m) chaud en altitude(f) 39.
front(m) chaud en surface(f) 39.
front(m) de taille(f) 733, 736.
front(m) froid en altitude(f) 39.
front(m) froid en surface(f) 39.
front(m) occlus 39.
front(m) stationnaire 39.
frontal(m) 120, 122, 649, 792.
frontière(f) 51.
fronton(m) 166, 168.
**fronts(m) 39.**
frotteur(m) 476.
frottoir(m) 307, 386.
**fruit(m) à noyau(m), coupe(f) 63.**
**fruit(m) à pépins(m), coupe(f) 64.**
**fruits(m) à noyau(m), principales variétés(f) 63.**
**fruits(m) à pépins(m), principales variétés(f) 64.**
FRUITS(M) CHARNUS 62, 65.
FRUITS(M) CHARNUS À NOYAU(M) 63.
FRUITS(M) CHARNUS À PÉPINS(M) 64.
FRUITS(M) SECS 66.
FRUITS(M) SECS DIVERS 67.
FRUITS(M) TROPICAUX 68.
**fruits(m) tropicaux, principaux 68.**
fume-cigarettes(m) 384.
fumée(f) 39.
fumerolle(f) 24.
funicule(m) 62, 67.
furet(m) de dégorgement(m) 299.
fusain(m) 588.
**fuseau(m) 336, 570.**
fuseau(m) 570, 575.
FUSÉE(F) 509.
fusée(f) 479.
fusée(f) à propergol(m) solide 510.
fusée(f) de proximité(f) 814.
fuselage(m) 499, 639.
fusible(m) 757, 769.
fusible(m) à culot(m) 312.
fusible(m)-cartouche(f) 312.
fusible(m)-cartouche(f) à lames(f) 312.
**fusibles(m) 312.**
fusil(m) 242.
**fusil(m) (canon(m) lisse) 799.**

Les termes en **caractères gras** renvoient à une illustration, ceux en CAPITALES indiquent un titre.

fusil(m) à air(m) comprimé 627.
FUSIL(M) AUTOMATIQUE 796.
FUSIL(M) MITRAILLEUR(M) 796.
fût(m) 59, 166, 236, 276, 553, 684, 698, 756, 798.

## G

gâble(m) 175.
gâche(f) 290.
gachette(f) 780.
gâchette(f) 268, 304, 590.
gâchette(f) de sécurité(f) 272.
gaffe(f) 780.
gainage(m) du combustible(m) défectueux 764.
**gaine(f) 346.**
gaine(f) 56, 690, 692.
gaine(f) de dérivation(f) 206.
gaine(f) de distribution(f) 213.
gaine(f) de myéline(f) 135.
gaine(f) de protection(f) 609.
gaine(f) de rancher(m) 441.
gaine(f) de Schwann 135.
gaine(f) du ressort(m) 230.
gaine(f) isolante 309.
gaine(f) principale 206.
gaine(f)-culotte(f) 346.
GALAXIE(F) 9.
galaxie(f) elliptique 9.
galaxie(f) irrégulière 9.
galaxie(f) lenticulaire 9.
galaxie(f) spirale 9.
galaxie(f) spirale barrée 9.
**galaxie(f), classification(f) 9.**
galerie(f) 175, 189, 773.
galerie(f) de circulation(f) 736.
galerie(f) de visite(f) 747.
galerie(f) en direction(f) 736.
galerie(f) marchande 190.
galerie(f) sèche 24.
galet(m) 230, 403, 530, 583.
galet(m) du presse-papier(m) 531.
galets(m) tendeurs 448.
**galettage(m) 584.**
galhauban(m) 479.
galon(m) 328.
galon(m) d'ornement(m) 349.
galop(m) 101.
**gamme(f) 537.**
ganache(f) 100.
ganglion(m) du tronc(m) sympathique 135.
ganglion(m) spinal 135.
ganse(f) 688.
**gant(m) 596.**
gant(m) 512, 598, 609, 635, 642, 643, 648, 667.
gant(m) à crispin(m) 308, 327.
gant(m) attrape-rondelle(m) 609.
gant(m) court 327.
**gant(m) de conduite(f) 327.**
gant(m) de frappeur(m) 595.
gant(m) de golf(m) 679.
gant(m) de plongée(f) 627.
gant(m) de receveur(m) 595.
gant(m) de ski(m) 640.
gant(m) long 327.
gant(m) saxe 327.
gantelet(m) 792.
GANTS(M) 327.
**gants(m) de boxe(f) 669.**
Ganymède 4.
garage(m) 196.
garant(m) 354.
garcette(f) de ris(m) 480.
garde(f) 577.
garde(f) de clé(f) 549.
garde(f) de culasse(f) 549.
garde(f) volante 577.
garde(m) droit 603, 605.
garde(m) gauche 603, 605.
garde-boue(m) 147, 446.
garde-boue(m) avant 442.
garde-corps(m) 302, 454, 457, 468.
garde-guichet(m) 599.
garde-main(m) 796.
garde-manger(m) 195.
garde-robe(f) 195.
**gardien(m) de but(m) 609.**
gardien(m) de but(m) 601, 607, 608, 611, 612, 626.
GARE(F) 464.
gare(f) 52, 184.
gare(f) de marchandises(f) 464.
GARE(F) DE TRIAGE(M) 465.
GARE(F) DE VOYAGEURS(M) 462.
gare(f) de voyageurs(m) 464.
gare(f) maritime 491.
garniture(f) 300, 383.
garniture(f) de frein(m) 432.
garrot(m) 100, 106.
GASTÉROPODE(M) 83.
**gastéropodes(m) comestibles 83.**
gastrocnémien(m) 121.
**gaufrier(m)-gril(m) 253.**
gaz(m) 34, 35, 232, 737, 744.
gaz(m) brûlés 436.
gaz(m) carbonique de refroidissement(m) 760.
gaz(m) inerte 232, 233.
gazole(m) 744.
gazon(m) 263.
gélule(f) 725.
Gémeaux(m) 11.
Gémeaux(m) (21 mai) 820.
gencive(f) 142, 144.
générateur(m) d'air(m) chaud 206.
**générateur(m) d'air(m) chaud électrique 207.**
générateur(m) de tonalités(f) d'amorces(f) 407.
générateur(m) de vapeur(f) 759, 761, 762, 771, 806.
genou(m) 100, 106, 116, 118.
genouillère(f) 595, 602, 609, 792.
**géométrie(f) 830.**
**gerbeur(m) 788.**
germe(m) 109, 152.
germes(m) de soja(m) 72.
geyser(m) 25.
gibbeuse(f) croissante 6.
gibbeuse(f) décroissante 7.
gicleur(m) 209, 741.
gicleur(m) de lave-glace(m) 426.
gicleurs(m) 766.
**gilet(m) 322.**
gilet(m) 317, 338.
**gilet(m) athlétique 325.**
**gilet(m) de laine(f) 326.**
gilet(m) de laine(f) 338.
GILET(M) DE SÉCURITÉ(F) 730.
gilet(m) de stabilisation(f) 627.
Girafe(f) 11.
girelle(f) 584.
giron(m) 201.
girouette(f) 41, 628.
glace(f) 34, 427, 429, 484.
glace(f) de custode(f) 427.
GLACIER(M) 26.
glacier(m) de piémont(m) 27.
glacier(m) suspendu 26.
glacière(f) 690.
glacis(m) 178.
glaive(m) 791.
gland(m) 127, 229, 231.
glande(f) à venin(m) 96.
glande(f) de Cowper 127.
glande(f) digestive 92.
glande(f) mammaire 129.
glande(f) sébacée 136.
glande(f) sudoripare apocrine 136.
glande(f) sudoripare eccrine 136.
glande(f) surrénale 132.
glandes(f) salivaires 131.
glissière(f) 257, 470, 568, 797.
glissière(f) d'ajustement(m) 406.
glissière(f) d'auvent(m) 449.
glissière(f) de fixation(f) 718.
glissière(f) du guide(m) 285.
glissoir(m) 354.
glissoire(f) de recul(m) 802.
globe(m) 689.
**globe(m) oculaire 140.**
globe(m) oculaire 84.
glome(m) 104.
glotte(f) 96, 142.
GO(M) 697.
**go(m), terrain(m) 697.**
godet(m) 304, 592, 782.
godet(m) à couleur(f) 590.
godet(m) à poussière(m) 260.
godet(m) chargeur 785.
godet(m) rétro 782.
goélette(f) 482.
GOLF(M) 676, 678.
**golf(m), bâtons(m) 678.**
**golf(m), bois(m) 678.**
**golf(m), fer(m) 678.**
**golf(m), parcours(m) 676.**
golfe(m) 51.
gombo(m) 69.
gomme(f) 515.
gond(m) 202, 225.
gonfalon(m) 817.
gonfleur(m) 627, 687.
gonfleur(m)-dégonfleur(m) 687.
gong(m) 554, 557.
gorge(f) 24, 108, 282, 671.
gorgerin(m) 792.
gouffre(m) 24.
gouge(f) 587.
gouge(f) creuse 581.
gouge(f) en V 581.
goujon(m) 432.
goujure(f) 281.
goupille(f) 780.
gour(m) 24.
gourde(f) 690.
gourmand(m) 61.
gourmette(f) 364, 649, 650.
gourmette(f) d'identité(f) 364.
**gousse(f), coupe(f) 67.**
gousset(m) de latte(f) 628, 631.
goutte(f) 167.
goutte(f) de pluie(f) 36.
gouttelette(f) lipidique 115.
gouttière(f) 105, 197, 235, 427.
gouvernail(m) 496, 511, 628, 742, 773.
gouvernail(m) de direction(f) 639, 806, 812.
gouvernail(m) de plongée(f) avant 807.
gouvernail(m) de profondeur(f) 639.
gouverne(f) 814.
gouverne(f) de direction(f) 499.
gouverne(f) de profondeur(f) 499.
goyave(f) 68.
gradin(m) 733.
graduation(f) 705, 711, 719, 726.
grain(m) 39, 72.
grain(m) d'amidon(m) 115.
**grain(m) de blé(m), coupe(f) 152.**
graine(f) 62, 63, 64, 65, 66, 67.
graines(f) de soja(m) 72.
graisses(f) 745.
graisseur(m) 734.
grand adducteur(m) 121.
grand cacatois(m) avant 481.
Grand Chien(m) 13.
grand complexus(m) 121.
grand dorsal(m) 121.
grand droit(m) de l'abdomen(m) 120.
grand fauchage(m) extérieur 668.
grand fauchage(m) intérieur 668.
grand fessier(m) 121.
grand foc(m) 481.
grand hunier(m) fixe avant 481.
grand hunier(m) volant avant 481.
grand largue(m) 629.
grand mât(m) arrière 478.
grand mât(m) avant 479.
grand miroir(m) 484.
grand oblique(m) de l'abdomen(m) 120, 121.
grand palmaire(m) 120.
grand pectoral(m) 120.
grand perroquet(m) fixe avant 481.
grand perroquet(m) volant avant 481.
grand rabat(m) 386.
grand rond(m) 121.
grand sésamoïde(m) 102.
grand tournant(m) 651.
grand trochanter(m) 123.
grand-voile(f) 628.
grand-voile(f) arrière 480.
grand-voile(f) avant 481.
grand-voile(f) d'étai(m) arrière 480.
**grande échelle(f) 780.**
grande lame(f) 688.
grande lèvre(f) 128, 129.
Grande Ourse(f) 11.
grande sus-alaire(f) 110.
grande ville(f) 51.
grandes lignes(f) 464.
grange(f) 148.
granulation(f) 6.
grappe(f) 60.
**grappe(f) de combustible(m) 765.**
grappe(f) de combustible(m) 765.
grappe(f) de raisin(m) 801.
**grappe(f) de raisins(m) 61.**
grappin(m) 483.
grasset(m) 101.
gratte-ciel(m) 185.
gratte-ongles(m) 365.
**grattoir(m) 304.**
gravier(m) 199, 216.
GRAVURE(F) EN CREUX(M) 582.
**gravure(f) en creux(m), matériel(m) 582.**
GRAVURE(F) EN RELIEF(M) 581.
**gravure(f) en relief(m), matériel(m) 581.**
gravure(f) sur bois(m) de fil(m) 581.
gravure(f) sur bois(m) debout 581.
grébiche(f) 379.
**grecquage(m) 578.**
grecque(f) 578.
**gréement(m) 478.**
GRÉEMENTS(M), TYPES(M) 482.
greffoir(m) 269.
grêlon(m) 37.
grenade(f) 68.
GRENADE(F) À MAIN(F) 804.
grenat(m) 363.
**grenouille(f) 84.**
**grenouille(f), métamorphose(f) 84.**
grenouillère(f) 349.
grésil(m) 37, 39.
grève(f) 792.
griffe(f) 78, 80, 91, 97, 106, 107, 108, 112, 364.
griffe(f) à fleurs(f) 268.
**griffe(f) abaissée, chat(m) 107.**
griffe(f) d'entraînement(m) 562.
griffe(f) porte-accessoires(m) 391, 409.
**griffe(f) rétractée, chat(m) 107.**
gril(m) 188.
**gril(m) électrique 253.**
gril(m) pliant 690.
grillage(m) 211, 214.
grillage(m) de protection(f) 310.
grille(f) 161, 168, 248, 255, 374, 410, 438, 536, 595, 747.
grille(f) à reine(f) 82.
grille(f) d'aération(f) 257, 477.
grille(f) d'aspiration(f) 370.
grille(f) d'éclairage(m) 414.
grille(f) d'entrée(f) d'air(m) 443.
grille(f) d'extrémité(f) 765.
grille(f) d'habillage(m) 208.
grille(f) de chauffage(m) 477.
grille(f) de sortie(f) d'air(m) 370.
grille(f) de vaporisation(f) 210.
grille(f) de ventilation(f) 260.
grille(f) métallique conductrice 768.
grille(f) stabilisatrice 689.
**grille-pain(m) 252.**
**gros intestin(m) 131.**
groseille(f) à grappes(f) 62.
groseille(f) à maquereau(m) 62.
grosse caisse(f) 552, 557.
grosse quille(f) 683.
GROTTE(F) 24.
grotte(f) 30.
groupe(m) bulbe(m) 752.
groupe(m) de climatisation(f) 506.
groupe(m) de démarrage(m) pneumatique 506.
groupe(m) électrogène 506.
groupe(m) frigorifique 441.
**groupe(m) turbo-alternateur(m) 753.**
groupe(m) turbo-alternateur(m) 747.
Grue(f) 13.
grue(f) 738.
grue(f) à flèche(f) 490.
**grue(f) à tour(f) 786.**
grue(f) de bord(m) 811.
grue(f) sur ponton(m) 490.
**grue(f) sur porteur(m) 786.**
gruppetto(m) 538.
guêpière(f) 347.
**guerrier(m) gaulois 791.**
gueules(m) 819.
gui(m) 478.
**guichet(m) 599.**
guichet(m) 599.
guide(m) 252, 529, 578.
guide(m) à onglet(m) 285.
guide(m) d'ondes(f) 415.
guide(m) de refend(m) 284, 285.
guide(m) des températures(f) 256.
guide(m) extérieur 578.
guide-bande(m) 403.
guide-chaîne(m) 272, 448.
guide-fil(m) 561, 562, 569.
guide-ligne(m) 671.
guide-papier(m) 421, 531.
guides(m) de classement(m) 518.
guidon(m) 271, 445, 447, 664, 795, 797, 798, 799, 804, 817.
guillemets(m) 832.
**guimbarde(f) 536.**
guindant(m) 631, 817.
**guitare(f) acoustique 546.**
**guitare(f) électrique 547.**
guyot(m) 28.
gymnase(m) 496.
GYMNASTIQUE(F) 659, 660.
gyrophare(m) 781.
gyroscope(m) 814.

Les termes en **caractères gras** renvoient à une illustration, ceux en CAPITALES indiquent un titre.

## H

habitation(f) 148.
hache(f) 781.
hache(f) en pierre(f) polie 791.
hachette(f) 690.
hachoir(m) 243.
hachure(f) 576.
hackle(m) 670.
haie(f) 263, 656.
haie(f) barrée 646, 647.
haie(f) de steeple(m) 656.
haie(f) rivière(f) 646, 647.
halebas(m) 628.
halefis(m) de culasse(f) (16) 363.
halefis(m) de table(f) (16) 363.
hall(m) 190.
hall(m) public 504.
**haltère(m) court 665.**
**haltère(m) long 663.**
**haltérophile(m) 662.**
HALTÉROPHILIE(F) 662.
**hameçon(m) 671.**
hameçon(m) 670.
hameçon(m) monté 672.
hameçon(m) triple 672.
hampe(f) 38, 671, 817.
hanche(f) 78, 80, 117, 119.
hanche(f) ailée 668.
HANDBALL(M) 612.
**handball(m), ballon(m) 612.**
**handball(m), terrain(m) 612.**
hangar(m) 148, 503, 811.
hangar(m) de transit(m) 490.
hangar(m) pour hélicoptères(m) 808.
haricot(m) vert 69.
harmonica(m) 536.
harnais(m) 572, 627, 635, 636, 637, 645.
**harpe(f) 545.**
harpes(f) 556.
hastée 56.
hauban(m) 446, 479, 628, 637, 685, 774.
haubans(m) 456.
**haubans(m) en éventail(m) 456.**
**haubans(m) en harpe(f) 456.**
hausse(f) 82, 544, 795, 796, 798, 804.
haut-de-chausse(m) 316.
haut-de-forme(m) 328.
haut-parleur(m) 408, 420, 500, 779.
haut-parleur(m) d'aigus(m) 16, 401.
haut-parleur(m) de contrôle(m) 407, 412, 413, 415.
haut-parleur(m) de graves(m) 16, 401.
haut-parleur(m) de médium(m) 401.
haut-parleur(m) de médiums(m) 16.
hautbois(m) 548, 557.
hauteur(f) de chute(f) 755.
hauteur(f) de la vague(f) 30.
hauteur(f) de marche(f) 201.
hauteur(f) du gradin(m) 733.
hauteur(f) du plongeon(m) 625.
hélice(f) 160, 495, 496, 742, 806.
hélice(f) de propulsion(f) 492.
hélices(f) 808.
HÉLICOPTÈRE(M) 508.
hélicoptère(m) 808.
**héliographe(m) 40.**
hélisurface(f) 738, 808.
hélix(m) 139.
hémisphère(m) austral 3.
hémisphère(m) boréal 3.
hémisphère(m) Est 47.
hémisphère(m) Nord 47.
hémisphère(m) Ouest 47.
hémisphère(m) Sud 47.
**hémisphères(m) 47.**
hennin(m) 318.
HÉRALDIQUE(F) 817, 818.
**herbivore(m), mâchoire(f) 98.**
herbivores(m) 31, 33.
Hercule 11.
hermine(f) 819.
herminette(f) 587.
herse(f) 188.
hile(m) du rein(m) 132.
hiver(m) 8.
HOCKEY(M) SUR GAZON(M) 607.
**hockey(m) sur gazon(m), terrain(m) 607.**
HOCKEY(M) SUR GLACE(F) 608.
**hockey(m), balle(f) 607.**
**hockeyeur(m) 609.**
**homard(m) 90.**
hôpital(m) 822.
horizon(m) de secours(m) 500.
horloge(f) 407, 413, 415, 714.
**horloge(f) de parquet(m) 707.**
horloge(f) programmatrice 253, 255.
hôtel(m) 185.
**hotte(f) 255.**
hotte(f) 204.
houe(f) 267.
houe(f) rotative 157.
houpette(f) 366.
**houppelande(f) 317.**
houppier(m) 59.
**housse(f) à vêtements(m) 382.**
housse(f) d'oreiller(m) 224.
hublot(m) 253, 255, 496, 498.
hublot(m) d'atterrissage(m) 508.
hublot(m) d'observation(f) 510.
hublot(m) de chargement(m) 764.
hublot(m) de déchargement(m) du combustible(m) irradié 764.
huile(f) de lin(m) 592.
huiles(f) lubrifiantes 745.
huit 632.
huitième(m) de soupir(m) 538.
**huître(f) 92.**
huître(f) 93.
huméro-stylo-radial(m) 120.
humérus(m) 102, 122.
humeur(f) aqueuse 140.
humide, à été(m) court 45.
humide, à été(m) long 45.
**humidificateur(m) 210.**
humidité(f) 210.
humidité(f) de l'air(m) 34.
**humidité(f), mesure(f) 41.**
hune(f) 478.
hutte(f) 165.
Hydre(f) femelle 11, 13.
Hydre(f) mâle 13.
hydromètre(m) 439.
HYDROPTÈRE(M) 495.
hydrosphère(f) 31.
HYGIÈNE(F) DENTAIRE 373.
**hygromètre(m) 210.**
hygromètre(m) enregistreur 41.
hypergone(m) 392.
hyphe(m) 55.
hypoderme(m) 137.
hypophyse(f) 134.
hysope(f) 74.

## I

igloo(m) 165.
île(f) 51.
île(f) de sable(m) 30.
île(f) volcanique 28.
iléon(m) 131.
îlot(m) 452.
îlot(m) refuge(m) 184.
îlot(m) rocheux 30.
image(f) imprimée 580.
immeuble(m) à bureaux(m) 185.
immeuble(m) commercial 185.
immobilisation(f) 668.
impair(m) 700, 701.
imparipennée 56.
**imperméable(m) 319.**
impluvium(m) 170, 171.
imposte(f) 174.
IMPRESSION(F) 580.
impression(f) 532.
**impression(f) à plat(m) 580.**
impression(f) des messages(m) 421.
**impression(f) en creux(m) 580.**
**impression(f) en relief(m) 580.**
**imprimante(f) 421.**
imprimante(f) 523.
imprimante(f) laser(m) 527.
**imprimante(f) matricielle 531.**
imprimante(f) matricielle 527.
impulsion(f) 722.
incisive(f) 98.
incisive(f) centrale 144.
incisive(f) latérale 144.
incisives(f) 144.
inclinaison(f) de la lame(f) 284, 285.
inclusion(f) 830.
index(m) de composition(f) automatique 420.
indicateur(m) de charge(f) 374.
indicateur(m) de niveau(m) 403.
indicateur(m) de niveau(m) de carburant(m) 431, 512.
indicateur(m) de réglage(m) 641.
indicateur(m) de température(f) 431.
indicateur(m) de tension(f) 562.
indicateur(m) de virage(m) et d'inclinaison(f) latérale 639.
indicateur(m) de vitesse(f) 431, 445, 664.
indice(f) d'exposition(f) 396.
Indien(m) 13.
infiltration(f) 34.
infini(m) 830.
**inflorescence(f), modes(m) 60.**
**influx(m) nerveux 135.**
informations(f)-navigation(f) 500.
informations(f)-pilotage(m) 500.
informations(f)-systèmes(m) de bord(m) 500.
infrastructure(f) 450.
injecteur(m) 434, 437.
injecteur(m) de lubrifiant(m) 735.
injection(f)/explosion(f) 437.
INSECTES(M) 77.
insectivores(m) 31.
inspiration(f) 622.
**installation(f) à air(m) chaud pulsé 206.**
**installation(f) à eau(f) chaude 208.**
INSTRUMENTS(M) À CLAVIER(M) 540.
INSTRUMENTS(M) À CORDES(F) 544, 546.
INSTRUMENTS(M) À PERCUSSION(F) 552, 554.
INSTRUMENTS(M) À VENT(M) 548, 550.
INSTRUMENTS(M) D'ÉCRITURE(F) 389.
**instruments(m) de bord(m) 431.**
instruments(m) de bord(m) 430.
instruments(m) de vol(m) 635.
INSTRUMENTS(M) ÉLECTRONIQUES 555.
instruments(m) scientifiques 511.
INSTRUMENTS(M) TRADITIONNELS 535, 536.
intégrale(f) 830.
intégration(f) de l'électricité(f) au réseau(m) de transport(m) 755.
Intelsat VII 418.
interdiction(f) de dépasser 824, 825.
interdiction(f) de faire demi-tour(m) 824, 825.
intérieur(m) droit 601.
intérieur(m) gauche 601.
interligne(m) 537.
interosseux(m) 120.
interphone(m) 413.
interrupteur(m) 234, 247, 254, 260, 280, 283, 285, 305, 309, 370, 373, 374, 406, 485, 529.
interrupteur(m) à gâchette(f) 284.
interrupteur(m) d'accord(m) 403.
interrupteur(m) d'alimentation(f) 402, 405, 410, 411, 555.
interrupteur(m) d'éclairage(m) 368.
interrupteur(m) de démarrage(m) 259.
interrupteur(m) de la porte(f) 259.
interrupteur(m) de mise(f) au point(m) automatique 397.
interrupteur(m) du magnétoscope(m) 411.
interrupteur(m) du téléviseur(m) 411.
interrupteur(m) moteur(m)/éclairage(m) 561.
interrupteur(m) principal 757.
intersection(f) 830.
intersection(f) avec priorité(f) 824, 825.
intervalle(m) 489.
intervalle(m) d'air(m) 772.
**intervalles(m) 537.**
intestin(m) 88, 92, 97, 124.
**intestin(m) grêle 131.**
intrados(m) 174.
inverseur(m) 212.
inverseur(m) de signe(m) 523.
inverseur(m) route(f)-croisement(m) 444.
Io 4.
iris(m) 140.
isba(f) 165.
ischion(m) 123.
isobare(f) 38.
isolant(m) 199, 200, 209, 257, 297, 768.
isolant(m) de ruban(m) métallique 287.
isolant(m) en caoutchouc(m)-mousse(f) 287.
isolant(m) en coquille(f) 287.
isolant(m) en panneau(m) 287.
isolant(m) en plastique(m) 312.
isolant(m) en rouleau(m) 287.
isolant(m) en ruban(m) 287.
isolant(m) en vinyle(m) 287.
isolant(m) en vrac(m) 287.
isolant(m) moussé 287.
**isolants(m) 287.**
isolateur(m) 439, 757.
isthme(m) 51.
isthme(m) de la trompe(f) utérine 129.
isthme(m) du gosier(m) 142.
ivoire(m) 144.

## J

jabot(m) 342.
jachère(f) 148.
jack(m) 400.
jack(m) de sortie(f) 547.
JACQUET(M) 697.
jambage(m) 204.
jambe(f) 101, 117, 119, 325.
jambe(f) élastique 325.
jambette(f) 199.
jambier(m) antérieur 120.
jambière(f) 353, 598, 680.
jambière(f) de gardien(m) de but(m) 609.
jan(m) extérieur 697.
jan(m) intérieur 697.
jante(f) 147, 433, 442, 447, 658.
jaquette(f) 648.
jardin(m) 171.
JARDIN(M) D'AGRÉMENT(M) 263.
jardin(m) d'agrément(m) 193.
jardin(m) potager 148, 193.
jardin(m) public 190.
JARDIN(M), OUTILLAGE(M) 264, 266, 268, 270, 272.
jarret(m) 101, 106.
jarretelle(f) 347.
jas(m) 483.
jauge(f) à aiguilles(f) 567.
jauge(f) magnétique à lecture(f) directe 741.
jaune(m) 109.
javelot(m) 791.
**javelots(m) 658.**
jean(m) 336.
jéjunum(m) 131.
jet(m) d'air(m) 590.
jet(m) d'eau(f) 202, 203.
jet(m) de couleur(f) 590.
jet(m) dentaire 373.
jetée(f) 739.
**jeu(m) d'ustensiles(m) 244.**
jeu(m) de brides(f) 730.
jeu(m) de dilatation(f) 466.
JEU(M) DE FLÉCHETTES(F) 698.
JEU(M) DE QUILLES(F) 683.
jeu(m) étendu de caractères(m) 530.
JEUX(M) VIDÉO, SYSTÈME(M) 699.
jockey(m) 651.
jodhpurs(m) 648.
joint(m) 257, 389.
joint(m) à coulisse(f) 278.
joint(m) d'étanchéité(f) 296, 741.
joint(m) de bougie(f) 439.
joint(m) de carter(m) 434.
joint(m) de sécurité(f) du scaphandre(m) 512.
joint(m) magnétique 254.
joint(m) périmétral 750.
joint(m) torique 294, 295.
Joker(m) 695.
jonc(m) 364.
jonction(f) positif(m)/négatif(m) 768.
joue(f) 106, 118, 275, 670.
joue(f) de jante(f) 433.
jouets(m) 650.
joueur(m) 626.
**joueur(m) de cricket(m) 598.**
**joueuse(f) de tennis(m) 615.**
JUDO(M) 668.
juge(m) 666, 668, 669.
juge(m) de but(m) 608, 626.
juge(m) de champ(m) arrière 603, 605.
juge(m) de classement(m) 621.
juge(m) de départ(m) 621.
juge(m) de faute(f) de pieds(m) 614.
juge(m) de filet(m) 614.
juge(m) de ligne(f) 605, 608, 613, 614, 618.
juge(m) de mêlée(f) 605.
juge(m) de nages(f) 621.
juge(m) de passes(f) et de bottés(m) 605.
juge(m) de service(m) 614, 618.
juge(m) de touche(f) 601, 605, 606.
juge(m) de virages(m) 621.
jugulaire(f) 602, 777.
jumeau(m) 120.
JUMELLES(F) À PRISMES(M) 719.
jupe(f) 331.

Les termes en **caractères gras** renvoient à une illustration, ceux en CAPITALES indiquent un titre.

jupe(f) à empiècement(m) 334.
jupe(f) à lés(m) 334.
jupe(f) à volants(m) étagés 334.
jupe(f) de masque(m) 730.
jupe(f) de piston(m) 434.
jupe(f) droite 334.
jupe(f) fourreau(m) 334.
jupe(f) froncée 335.
jupe(f) portefeuille(m) 334.
jupe(f) souple 493.
jupe(f)-culotte(f) 334.
**jupes(f), types(m) 334.**
jupette(f) 615.
Jupiter 4.
jupon(m) 345.
justaucorps(m) 315, 353.

## K

kaki(m) 68.
kérosène(m) 744, 745.
ketch(m) 482.
kilt(m) 335.
kimono(m) 348.
kiosque(m) 453, 475, 807.
kiwi(m) 68.
knicker(m) 336.
kumquat(m) 65.

## L

la(m) 537.
la(m) universel 539.
laboratoire(m) 15.
laboratoire(m) spatial 511.
laboratoire(m) supérieur 15.
lac(m) 7, 27, 51.
lac(m) salé 46.
laccolite(f) 25.
lacet(m) 352, 354, 596, 644, 669.
lacet(m) de serrage(m) 381.
lacis(m) 645.
lactaire(m) délicieux 55.
lacune(f) latérale 104.
lacune(f) médiane 104.
lagune(f) 30.
laiterie(f) 149.
laitue(f) pommée 73.
laize(f) 628.
lambourde(f) 198.
lame(f) 200, 231, 239, 242, 268, 271, 276, 277, 284, 285, 291, 304, 309, 369, 374, 431, 536, 554, 564, 573, 609, 644, 666, 681, 783, 784.
lame(f) à deux biseaux(m) 587.
lame(f) à double tranchant(m) 374.
lame(f) coudée 587.
lame(f) criblée de l'ethmoïde(m) 141.
lame(f) d'étouffoir(m) 541.
lame(f) de coupe(f) 256.
**lame(f) de scie(f) circulaire 284.**
lame(f) de suspension(f) 707.
lame(f) dentée 369.
lame(f) droite 369, 587.
lame(f) en cuiller(f) 587.
lame(f) fixe 578.
lame(f) isolée 310.
lame(f) mobile 578.
lame(f) porte-objet(m) 718.
lame(f) racleuse 784.
lame(f)-ressort(m) 726.
lamelle(f) 55, 200.
**lames(f), principales formes(f) 587.**
lampadaire(m) 185, 236.
lampe(f) 310, 718.
**lampe(f) à économie(f) d'énergie(f) 233.**
**lampe(f) à halogène(m) 233.**
**lampe(f) à incandescence(f) 232.**
lampe(f) à incandescence(f) 486, 769.
**lampe(f) à souder 299, 307.**
lampe(f) au néon(m) 310.
**lampe(f) d'architecte(m) 234.**
lampe(f) de bureau(m) 234.
lampe(f) de table(f) 236.
lampe(f) frontale 680.
lampe(f) liseuse 234.
**lampe(f) portative 777.**
lampe(f)-éclair(m) 393.
lampe(f)-témoin(m) 666.
lampe(f)-tempête(f) 690.
lampes(f) témoins(m) 410, 431.
lance(f) 306, 778, 791.
lance(f) à eau(f) 781.
lance(f) d'arrosage(m) 265.
lance(f)-canon(m) 778.
lance-leurres(m) 809.
lance-missiles(m) 811.
lance-pots(m) fumigènes 805.
**lancement(m) de la boule(f) 682.**
lancéolée 56.
lancer(m) 682.
lancer(m) disque(m) et marteau(m) 654.
lancer(m) du javelot(m) 654.
lancer(m) du poids(m) 655.
**lancers(m) 658.**
lanceur(m) 597, 599.
lange(m) 581.
langouste(f) 91.
langoustine(f) 91.
langue(f) 81, 88, 131, 142.
langue(f) bifide 96.
langue(f) glaciaire 26.
**langue(f), dos(m) 143.**
languette(f) 352, 354, 542, 641, 644.
lanière(f) 541, 633, 662, 680.
**lanterne(f) 689.**
lanterne(f) 263, 486, 801.
**lanterne(f) de phare(m) 486.**
lanterne(f) de pied(m) 235.
lanterne(f) murale 235.
lapiaz(m) 24.
lapis-lazuli(m) 363.
largue(m) 629.
larve(f) 82.
larynx(m) 130, 142.
**latitude(f) 47.**
latitude(f) 3.
latrines(f) 171.
latte(f) 231, 571, 628, 631, 637, 773.
lattis(m) de plâtre(m) lisse 286.
lattis(m) métallique à losanges(m) 286.
laurier(m) 74.
lavabo(m) 215, 292.
**lavage(m) 829.**
lavallière(f) 324.
lave-auto(m) 453.
**lave-linge(m) 258, 298.**
lave-linge(m) 215, 298.
**lave-vaisselle(m) 257, 298.**
lave-vaisselle(m) 298.
laver à la machine(f) à l'eau(f) chaude avec agitation(f) normale 829.
laver à la machine(f) à l'eau(f) chaude avec agitation(f) réduite 829.
laver à la machine(f) à l'eau(f) tiède avec agitation(f) réduite 829.
laver à la machine(f) à l'eau(f) très chaude avec agitation(f) normale 829.
laver à la main(f) à l'eau(f) tiède 829.
**laveuse(f) pour épreuves(f) 399.**
laye(f) 543.
lecteur(m) de carte(f) 422.
lecteur(m) de cartouche(f) 527.
lecteur(m) de cassette(f) 408, 526.
**lecteur(m) de disque(m) compact 405.**
lecteur(m) de disque(m) compact 400, 407, 408, 526.
**lecteur(m) de disque(m) dur 529.**
lecteur(m) de disque(m) dur 526, 528.
lecteur(m) de disque(m) optique 527.
lecteur(m) de disquette(f) 526, 528, 555.
lecture(f) 403, 411, 831.
lecture(f) automatique/manuelle 310.
LECTURE(F) DE PLANS(M) 193, 195.
lecture(f) rapide 405.
lecture(f)/pause(f) 405.
**légionnaire(m) romain 791.**
LÉGUMES(M) 69, 70, 71, 72, 73.
légumes(m) 33.
**légumes(m) bulbes(m) 70.**
**légumes(m) feuilles(f) 73.**
**légumes(m) fleurs(f) 69.**
**légumes(m) fruits(m) 69.**
**légumes(m) graines(f) 72.**
**légumes(m) racines(f) 71.**
**légumes(m) tiges(f) 72.**
**légumes(m) tubercules(m) 71.**
légumier(m) 238.
lentille(f) 385, 390, 392, 707.
lentille(f) biconcave 722.
lentille(f) biconvexe 722.
lentille(f) concave 722.
lentille(f) convexe 722.
lentille(f) de champ(m) 718.
lentille(f) de macrophotographie(f) 392.
lentille(f) objectif(m) 718, 719, 721.
lentille(f) plan(m)-concave 722.
lentille(f) plan(m)-convexe 722.
LENTILLES(F) 722.
lentilles(f) 72.
**lentilles(f) convergentes 722.**
lentilles(f) de mise(f) au point(m) 717.
lentilles(f) de redressement(m) 718.
**lentilles(f) divergentes 722.**
lest(m) 786.
leucoplaste(m) 115.
lève-fil(m) 256.
lève-soupape(m) 299.
levier(m) 278, 294, 295, 296, 365, 370, 583, 798.
levier(m) à ressort(m) 702.
levier(m) coudé 782.
levier(m) d'armement(m) 796, 804.
levier(m) d'écartement(m) 158.
levier(m) d'échappement(m) 541.
levier(m) d'embrayage(m) 272, 442, 444.
levier(m) de clé(f) 549.
levier(m) de commande(f) 283, 735.
levier(m) de commande(f) manuelle 467.
levier(m) de conduite(f) 788.
levier(m) de déclenchement(m) 293.
levier(m) de dégagement(m) 278.
levier(m) de dégagement(m) du papier(m) 525.
levier(m) de dégagement(m) du presse-papier(m) 525.
levier(m) de fixation(f) de venturi(m) 804.
levier(m) de frein(m) à main(f) 430, 470.
levier(m) de frein(m) avant 444.
levier(m) de la lame(f) 578.
levier(m) de manœuvre(f) 787, 788.
levier(m) de manœuvre(f) de la culasse(f) 802.
levier(m) de perçage(m) 256.
levier(m) de réglage(m) 539.
levier(m) de réglage(m) latéral 277.
levier(m) de relevage(m) 147.
levier(m) de serrage(m) 282.
levier(m) de tissage(m) 568.
levier(m) de verrouillage(m) 471.
levier(m) de vibrato(m) 547.
levier(m) de vitesse(f) 430.
levier(m) des aérofreins(m) 500.
levier(m) des volets(m) 500.
levier(m) du bloc(m) 277.
levier(m) du piston(m) 291.
levier(m) du protège-lame(m) inférieur 284.
levier(m) du train(m) d'atterrissage(m) 500.
levier(m) télescopique de dételage(m) 470.
lèvre(f) 100, 107, 281.
lèvre(f) inférieure 142, 542.
lèvre(f) supérieure 81, 142, 542.
Lézard(m) 11.
liaison(f) 539.
liaison(f) électrique 213.
liaison(f) frigorifique 213.
libellule(f) 77.
liber(m) 59.
liberté(f) de langue(f) 650.
lice(f) 181.
lierne(f) 177.
lieuse(f) 159.
Lièvre(m) 13.
ligament(m) 95.
ligament(m) alvéolo-dentaire 144.
ligament(m) élastique 92, 107.
ligament(m) large de l'utérus(m) 129.
ligament(m) rond de l'utérus(m) 129.
ligament(m) suspenseur 140.
ligne(f) 537.
ligne(f) arrière 611, 620.
ligne(f) avant 617.
ligne(f) blanche 104.
ligne(f) bleue 608.
ligne(f) centrale 608, 619.
ligne(f) d'appel(m) triple saut(m) 654.
ligne(f) d'arrivée(f) 654.
ligne(f) d'attaque(f) 613.
ligne(f) d'avertissement(m)- épée(f) et sabre(m) 666.
ligne(f) d'avertissement(m)- fleuret(m) 666.
ligne(f) d'ourlet(m) 565.
ligne(f) de balayage(m) 620.
ligne(f) de ballon(m) mort 606.
ligne(f) de bâti(m) 565.
ligne(f) de boîte(f) de service(m) 617.
ligne(f) de but(m) 604, 606, 607, 608, 612, 626.
ligne(f) de cadre(m) 674.
ligne(f) de centre(m) 604, 607, 620, 682.
ligne(f) de côté(m) 613.
ligne(f) de couloir(m) 656.
ligne(f) de coupe(f) 565.
ligne(f) de croissance(f) 83, 95.
ligne(f) de demi-court(m) 616.
ligne(f) de départ(m) 620, 655, 656.
ligne(f) de distribution(f) à basse tension(f) 757.
ligne(f) de distribution(f) à moyenne tension(f) 757.
ligne(f) de double(m) 614.
ligne(f) de foi(f) 485.
ligne(f) de fond(m) 604, 610, 613, 614, 618, 619, 621.
ligne(f) de jet(m) franc 612.
ligne(f) de jeu(m) 597, 620, 683, 698.
ligne(f) de lancer(m) franc 610.
ligne(f) de limite(f) arrière 666.
ligne(f) de mêlée(f) 603, 605.
ligne(f) de mise(f) en garde(f) 666.
ligne(f) de modification(f) 565.
ligne(f) de piqûre(f) de la fermeture(f) 565.
ligne(f) de réception(f) de service(m) 617.
ligne(f) de retrait(m) 599.
ligne(f) de sécurité(f) 475.
ligne(f) de service(m) 614, 616, 617.
ligne(f) de service(m) court 618.
ligne(f) de service(m) long 618.
ligne(f) de simple(m) 614.
ligne(f) de surface(f) de but(m) 612.
ligne(f) de surface(f) de réparation(f) 601.
ligne(f) de suture(f) 94.
ligne(f) de touche(f) 601, 604, 606, 607, 610, 611, 612.
ligne(f) de visée(f) 719.
ligne(f) des 10 mètres(m) 606.
ligne(f) des 15 mètres(m) 606.
ligne(f) des 2 m 626.
ligne(f) des 22 mètres(m) 606.
ligne(f) des 22,9 mètres(m) 607.
ligne(f) des 4 m 626.
ligne(f) des 5 mètres(m) 606.
ligne(f) des courtes(f) 616.
ligne(f) des sept mètres(m) 612.
ligne(f) des verges(f) 604.
ligne(f) isosiste 23.
ligne(f) latérale 87, 616, 619, 620.
ligne(f) latérale de double(m) 618.
ligne(f) latérale de simple(m) 618.
ligne(f) médiane 601, 606, 610, 612, 618, 626, 666.
ligne(f) médiane de service(m) 614.
ligne(f) méridienne 719.
ligne(f) supplémentaire 537.
limaçon(m) 139.
limbe(m) 57, 484.
lime(f) 277, 365, 688.
lime(f) à ongles(m) 365.
limes(f)-émeri(m) 365.
limitation(f) de hauteur(f) 826, 827.
limite(f) d'arrondissement(m) 52.
limite(f) de la ville(f) 52.
limite(f) de retour(m) 599.
limite(f) du batteur(m) 599.
limite(f) du terrain(m) 193.
limite(f) hors-terrain 616.
limiteur(m) de surchauffe(f) 259.
limon(m) 201.
limousine(f) 425.
linéaire 56.
lingerie(f) 460.
linteau(m) 175, 198, 202, 204.
**lion(m) 98.**
Lion(m) 11.
Lion(m) (23 juillet) 820.
lion(m) passant 819.
**liquette(f) 337.**
liquide(f) 216.
**liquides(m) d'appoint(m) 592.**
lire(f) 832.
lisière(f) 566.
lisse(f) 199, 471.
lisse(f) d'assise(f) 198, 199.
**lisses(f) 573.**
lisses(f) 572, 574.
listel(m) 281.
LIT(M) 224.
**lit(m) 687.**
lit(m) de camp(m) pliant 687.
lit(m) de l'ongle(m) 137.
litchi(m) 68.
**literie(f) 224.**
LITHOGRAPHIE(F) 583.
**lithographie(f), matériel(m) 583.**
lithosphère(f) 31.

Les termes en **caractères gras** renvoient à une illustration, ceux en CAPITALES indiquent un titre.

LITTORAL(M), CONFIGURATION(F) 30.
livèche(f) 74.
livre(f) 832.
**livre(m) relié 577.**
**livrée(f) 599.**
livrée(f) 599.
loafer(m) 355.
lobé 56.
lobe(m) 111.
lobe(m) du nez(m) 141.
lobe(m) inférieur 130.
lobe(m) latéral inférieur 61.
lobe(m) latéral supérieur 61.
lobe(m) moyen 130.
lobe(m) supérieur 130.
lobe(m) terminal 61.
lobule(m) 139.
locaux(m) administratifs 462.
locaux(m) de service(m) 172, 173.
locaux(m) du personnel(m) 494.
LOCOMOTIVE(F) DIESEL-ÉLECTRIQUE 468.
loge(f) 64, 65, 189.
loge(f) d'artiste(m) 189.
logement(m) de cassette(f) 403.
logement(m) de la bobine(f) 390.
logement(m) de la cassette(f) 409, 411.
logement(m) de rangement(m) 397.
logement(m) des officiers(m) 807, 808.
logement(m) du barillet(m) 290.
logement(m) du plateau(m) 405.
lointain(m) 188, 189.
long péronier(m) latéral 120.
long supinateur(m) 121.
longeron(m) 441, 498.
longeron(m) de chenille(f) 783.
longeron(m) latéral inférieur 470.
longeron(m) stabilisateur 788.
**longitude(f) 47.**
longitude(f) 3.
longueur(f) de la vague(f) 30.
loquet(m) 253, 257.
lorgnette(f) 377.
lorum(m) 109.
louche(f) 244.
loupe(f) 688.
loupe(f) de mise(f) au point(m) 399.
luette(f) 141, 142.
LUGE(F) 643.
lumière(f) 489, 542, 720, 721, 800, 801.
LUMINAIRES(M) 232, 234, 236.
LUNE(F) 7.
Lune(f) 4, 8.
LUNE(F), ÉCLIPSE(F) 8.
LUNE(F), PHASES(F) 6.
lunette(f) 713, 803.
LUNETTE(F) ASTRONOMIQUE 721.
**lunette(f) astronomique, coupe(f) 721.**
LUNETTE(F) DE VISÉE(F) 718.
lunette(f) de visée(f) 798.
lunette(f) prismatique 484.
LUNETTES(F) 376.
lunettes(f) 308.
lunettes(f) de protection(f) 729.
lunettes(f) de sécurité(f) 729.
lunettes(f) de ski(m) 640.
lunettes(f) de soleil(m) 377.
lunettes(f) de vol(m) 635.
**lunettes(f), parties(f) 376.**
**lunettes(f), principaux types(m) 377.**
lunule(f) 95, 137.
**lustre(m) 236.**
Lynx(m) 11.
**lyre(f) 535.**
Lyre(f) 11.
lysosome(m) 115.

## M

macaroni(m) 587.
mâche(f) 73.
machette(f) 794.
**mâchicoulis(m) 181.**
mâchicoulis(m) 180.
machine(f) à combustible(m) 759.
**machine(f) à coudre 561.**
MACHINE(F) À ÉCRIRE ÉLECTRONIQUE 524.
machine(f) à faire les pâtes(f) 243.
MACHINE(F) À SOUS(M) 702.
MACHINE(F) À TRICOTER 568.
machine(f) de chargement(m) 760, 761, 764.
machine(f) de déchargement(m) 764.
MACHINERIE(F) LOURDE 782, 784, 785.
mâchoire(f) 81, 311.
mâchoire(f) d'attelage(m) 471.
**mâchoire(f) d'herbivore(m) 98.**
**mâchoire(f) de carnivore(m) 98.**
**mâchoire(f) de rongeur(m) 98.**
mâchoire(f) dentée 278.
mâchoire(f) droite 278.
mâchoire(f) fixe 279.
mâchoire(f) incurvée 278.
mâchoire(f) mobile 279.
MÂCHOIRES(F), TYPES(M) 98.
MAÇONNERIE(F) 291.
magasins(m) 532.
magma(m) 25, 28.
magnétomètre(m) 42.
magnétophone(m) à cartouches(f) 407.
magnétophone(m) à cassette(f) numérique 407.
**magnétoscope(m) 411.**
magnétoscope(m) 401, 526.
maille(f) 619.
mailles(f) de montage(m) 567.
**maillet(m) 275.**
maillet(m) 581, 586.
mailloche(f) 552.
mailloches(f) 553.
maillon(m)-gouge(f) 272.
maillot(m) 656.
maillot(m) de bain(m) 353.
maillot(m) de corps(m) 662.
**main(f) 137.**
main(f) 117, 119.
main(f) courante 201, 470, 727.
main(f) pleine 695.
**maïs(m) 72.**
maïs(m) 152.
maïs(m) fourrager 149.
maison(f) 193, 620.
maison(f) individuelle 187.
maison(f) individuelle jumelée 187.
MAISON(F) ROMAINE 170.
**maison(f) solaire 772.**
maison(f) sur pilotis(m) 165.
**maison(f), charpente(f) 198.**
MAISON(F), EXTÉRIEUR(M) 196.
**maison(f), fondations(f) 199.**
MAISON(F), STRUCTURE(F) 198.
MAISONS(F) DE VILLE(F) 187.
maisons(f) en rangée(f) 187.
MAISONS(F) TRADITIONNELLES 165.
maître(m)-brin(m) 645.
majeur(m) 137.
malaire(m) 122.
mâle(m) 831.
**malle(f) 383.**
**mallette(f) de toilette(f) 382.**
**mallette(f) porte-documents(m) 378.**
mamelle(f) 104.
mamelon(m) 116, 118, 129.
mamelon(m) double 301.
manche(f) 318, 322.
manche(f) à air(m) 817.
manche(f) ballon(m) 340.
manche(f) bouffante 340.
manche(f) chauve-souris(f) 339.
manche(f) chemisier(m) 340.
manche(f) flottante 316.
manche(f) gigot(m) 340.
manche(f) kimono(m) 340.
manche(f) marteau(m) 340.
manche(f) montée 324, 326.
manche(f) pagode(f) 340.
manche(f) pendante 316.
manche(f) raglan 319, 330, 340, 350.
manche(f) tailleur(m) 340.
manche(f) trois-quarts 339.
manche(m) 239, 240, 241, 275, 276, 279, 291, 304, 306, 310, 373, 374, 375, 541, 544, 546, 547, 563, 570, 579, 596, 598, 607, 609, 615, 619, 632, 674, 677, 681.
manche(m) à balai(m) 526, 639.
manche(m) à balais(m) 508.
manche(m) de commande(f) 500.
manche(m) isolant 311.
manche(m) isolé 310.
mancheron(m) 270, 272, 318, 339.
**manches(f), types(m) 339, 340.**
manchette(f) 609.
manchon(m) 209, 301, 304, 381, 632, 662, 663.
manchon(m) de câble(m) 280.
manchon(m) de culasse(f) 802.
manchon(m) de refroidissement(m) 796.
manchon(m) du cordon(m) 283, 305.
mandarine(f) 65.
mandibule(f) 80, 81, 86, 102, 109.
mandibule(m) 78.
**mandoline(f) 535.**
mandrin(m) 276, 280, 281, 283.
manette(f) 252.
manette(f) d'admission(f) d'air(m) 204.
manette(f) de blocage(m) du plateau(m) 283.
manette(f) de chasse(f) d'eau(f) 293.
manette(f) de contact(m) 235.
manette(f) de dérailleur(m) 447, 448.
manette(f) de glissement(m) 428.
manette(f) du frein(m) 445.
manettes(f) de poussée(f) 500.
mangue(f) 63.
manifold(m) 738.
manille(f) 630.
manivelle(f) 265, 280, 281, 441, 448, 573, 671, 793.
manivelle(f) d'orientation(f) des lames(f) 231.
manivelle(f) de la colonne(f) 393.
manivelle(f) de lève-glace(m) 429.
manivelle(f) de pointage(m) en direction(f) 803.
manivelle(f) de pointage(m) en hauteur(f) 802, 803.
mannequin(m) 564.
mannequin(m) articulé 592.
manœuvre(f) de la pelleteuse(f) 782.
manœuvres(f) d'apogée(m) 419.
manomètre(m) 627, 710, 740, 741, 778.
manomètre(m) d'accord(m) 553.
manomètre(m) de bouteille(f) 306.
manomètre(m) de chalumeau(m) 306.
manque(m) (1 à 18) 700, 701.
manteau(m) 204, 331.
manteau(m) inférieur 22.
manteau(m) supérieur 22.
**manteaux(m), types(m) 330.**
MANUCURE(F) 365.
**manucure(f), accessoires(m) 365.**
manuel(m) de premiers soins(m) 725.
MANUTENTION(F) 786, 788.
MAQUILLAGE(M) 366.
**maquillage(m) 366.**
**maquillage(m) des lèvres(f) 366.**
**maquillage(m) des yeux(m) 367.**
marais(m) salant 30.
**marbre(m) 581.**
marbre(m) 597.
marche(f) 201, 302, 572.
marche(f) avant/marche(f) arrière 272.
marche(f) de départ(m) 201.
marche(f)/arrêt(m) 408.
marche(f)/arrêt(m)/volume(m) 408.
**marchepied(m) 302.**
marchepied(m) 147, 440, 445, 478, 508, 778.
marchepied(m) en étrier(m) 470.
marchepied(m) escamotable 449.
marchepied(m) latéral 469.
marette(f) 311.
**marge(f) continentale 29.**
margeur(m) 398.
marinière(f) 337.
mark(m) 832.
marmite(f) 249.
marque(f) cardinale est(m) 489.
marque(f) cardinale ouest(m) 489.
marque(f) cardinale sud(m) 489.
marque(f) centrale 614.
marque(f) d'aire(f) de prise(f) de contact(m) 505.
marque(f) d'axe(m) de piste(f) 504.
marque(f) d'eaux(f) sécuritaires 489.
marque(f) de danger(m) isolé 489.
marque(f) de distance(f) constante 505.
marque(f) de jour(m) 486, 487.
marque(f) de point(m) d'attente(f) 504.
marque(f) déposée 384, 831.
marque(f) latérale 489.
marque(f) spéciale 489.
**marques(f) cardinales 488.**
marques(f) d'identification(f) 504.
marques(f) de circulation(f) 503.
**marques(f) de jour(m) (région(f) B) 489.**
**marques(f) de nuit(f), rythme(m) 489.**
marques(f) de seuil(m) de piste(f) 505.
marques(f) latérales de piste(f) 504.
marqueur(m) 389, 515, 588, 610, 613, 666, 668.
marquise(f) 480.
marron(m) 66.
Mars 4.
**marteau(m) 658.**
marteau(m) 138, 540, 541.
**marteau(m) à endosser 579.**
**marteau(m) à panne(f) ronde 275.**
marteau(m) d'électricien(m) 311.
**marteau(m) de charpentier(m) 275.**
marteau(m) de maçon(m) 291.
marteau(m) de menuisier(m) 275.
marteau(m) perforateur 734.
**marteau(m) perforateur à poussoir(m) pneumatique 734.**
**marteau(m) pneumatique 735.**
**marteau(m)-piolet(m) 681.**
marteau(m)-piolet(m) 680.
martinet(m) 478.
martingale(f) 330, 479, 666.
**mascara(m) en pain(m) 367.**
mascara(m) liquide 367.
masque(m) 595, 602, 609, 627, 667.
**masque(m) bucco-nasal 730.**
masque(m) complet 777.
masque(m) de sélection(f) des couleurs(f) 410.
masque(m) protecteur 643.
**masque(m) respiratoire 730.**
masse(f) 714.
masse(f) pendulaire 539.
masse(f)-tige(f) 737.
masséter(m) 120.
massette(f) de réglage(m) 539.
massif(m) d'ancrage(m) des câbles(m) 456.
massif(m) de fleurs(f) 263.
massif(m) de fondation(f) 737.
massif(m) montagneux 51.
mât(m) 471, 628, 631, 637, 787, 788.
mât(m) avant 743.
mât(m) d'artimon(m) 478.
mât(m) de beaupré(m) 479.
mât(m) de cacatois(m) 479.
mât(m) de charge(f) 743.
mât(m) de hune(f) 479.
mât(m) de misaine(f) 479.
mât(m) de perroquet(m) 479.
mât(m) de toit(m) 686.
mât(m) radar(m) 742.
mât(m) rotor(m) 508.
**matelas(m) 687.**
matelas(m) 224, 726.
matelas(m) autogonflant 687.
matelas(m) mousse(f) 687.
matelas(m) pneumatique 687.
matelassure(f) 649.
mâtereau(m) 743.
**matériaux(m) de base(f) 286.**
MATÉRIAUX(M) DE CONSTRUCTION(F) 286, 288.
**matériaux(m) de revêtement(m) 286.**
MATÉRIEL(M) DE CAMPING(M) 688.
MATÉRIEL(M) DE SECOURS(M) 726.
**mathématiques(f) 830.**
matières(f) corrosives 821.
matières(f) explosives 821.
matières(f) inflammables 821.
matières(f) radioactives 821.
matières(f) toxiques 821.
matrice(f) de l'ongle(m) 137.
**maturation(f), vigne(f) 61.**
**mâture(f) 478.**
maturité(f) 61.
maxillaire(m) 86, 109, 141.
maxillaire(m) basculant 96.
maxillaire(m) inférieur 122.
maxillaire(m) supérieur 122.
maxille(f) 90.
mazout(m) domestique 745.
mazout(m) léger 745.
mazout(m) lourd 745.
méat(m) de l'urètre(m) 127.
mécanique(f) d'accordage(m) 547.
mécanisme(m) à échappement(m) 539.
mécanisme(m) d'assistance(f) de la culasse(f) 796.
mécanisme(m) d'engrenage(m) 583.
mécanisme(m) d'enroulement(m) 231.
mécanisme(m) d'octave(f) 548.
mécanisme(m) d'orientation(f) de la lame(f) 784.
mécanisme(m) d'ouverture(f) de l'anse(f) 671.
mécanisme(m) de déploiement(m) 49.
**mécanisme(m) de l'horloge(f) à poids(m) 707.**
mécanisme(m) de levage(m) de la lame(f) 784.
**mécanisme(m) de propulsion(f) 448.**
mécanisme(m) de rebobinage(m) 390.

Les termes en **caractères gras** renvoient à une illustration, ceux en CAPITALES indiquent un titre.

mécanisme(m) de tir(m) 804.
mèche(f) 544.
mèche(f) de tarière(f) 270.
mèche(f) double torsade(f) 281.
**mèche(f) hélicoïdale 281.**
médaillon(m) 361.
médecin(m) 669.
médiator(m) 535.
méditerranéen 45.
mégot(m) 386.
mélange(m) air(m)/carburant(m) 436.
**mélangeur(m) 250.**
**mélangeur(m) à main(f) 250.**
mélangeur(m) bain(m)-douche(f) 215.
**mêlée(f) 603.**
**mêlée(f) au football(m) canadien 605.**
mélèze(m) 58.
melon(m) 328.
melon(m) brodé 69.
membrane(f) 401, 406.
membrane(f) alaire 112.
membrane(f) coquillière 109.
membrane(f) cytoplasmique 115.
membrane(f) du tympan(m) 139.
membrane(f) interfémorale 112.
membrane(f) médiane 67.
membrane(f) nucléaire 115.
membrane(f) pellucide 128.
membrane(f) squelettique 115.
membrane(f) vitelline 109.
membre(m) inférieur 124.
membre(m) supérieur 124.
membrure(f) inférieure 455.
membrure(f) principale 756.
membrure(f) supérieure 455.
mémoire(f) des patrons(m) 569.
mémorisation(f) des données(f) 310.
meneur(m) 620.
ménisque(m) convergent 722.
ménisque(m) divergent 722.
menthe(f) 74.
menton(m) 108, 118.
mentonnière(f) 443, 544, 777, 792.
MENUISERIE(F): OUTILS(M) 275, 276, 278, 280, 282, 284.
méplat(m) 567.
mer(f) 7, 51, 752.
mer(f) Caspienne 21.
mer(f) de Béring 21.
mer(f) de Chine(f) 21.
mer(f) des Antilles(f) 20.
mer(f) du Groenland(m) 20.
mer(f) du Nord(m) 21.
mer(f) Méditerranée(f) 21.
mer(f) Noire 21.
mer(f) Rouge 21.
Mercure 4.
mercure(m) 232.
méridien(m) céleste 3.
méridien(m) de Greenwich 47.
méridien(m) est 47.
méridien(m) ouest 47.
méridienne(f) 221.
merlon(m) 181.
merlon(m) de protection(f) 741.
merrain(m) 105.
mésa(f) 46.
mésocarpe(m) 62, 63, 64, 65.
mésosphère(f) 19.
mésothorax(m) 78.
mesure(f) à deux temps(m) 537.
mesure(f) à quatre temps(m) 537.
mesure(f) à trois temps(m) 537.
**mesure(f) de l'ensoleillement(m) 40.**
MESURE(F) DE L'ÉPAISSEUR(F) 711.
**mesure(f) de l'humidité(f) 41.**
**mesure(f) de la direction(f) du vent(m) 41.**
MESURE(F) DE LA DISTANCE(F) 711.
**mesure(f) de la hauteur(f) des nuages(m) 41.**
MESURE(F) DE LA LONGUEUR(F) 711.
MESURE(F) DE LA MASSE(F) 708.
**mesure(f) de la neige(f) 41.**
**mesure(f) de la pluviosité(f) 40.**
MESURE(F) DE LA PRESSION(F) 710.
**mesure(f) de la pression(f) 41.**
MESURE(F) DE LA TEMPÉRATURE(F) 705.
**mesure(f) de la température(f) 41.**
**mesure(f) de la vitesse(f) du vent(m) 41.**
MESURE(F) DES ANGLES(M) 713.
MESURE(F) DES ONDES(F) SISMIQUES 714.
MESURE(F) DU TEMPS(M) 706.
MESURE(F) MÉTÉOROLOGIQUE 40.
**mesurer, ustensilsm 244.**
**mesures(f) 537.**
mesures(f) 244.
métacarpe(m) 102, 107, 122.
métal(m) A 307.
métal(m) B 307.
métatarse(m) 80, 103, 122.
métathorax(m) 78.
métaux(m) 33.
**métaux(m), exemples(m) 819.**
**météores(m) 39.**
MÉTÉOROLOGIE(F) 38.
MÉTÉOROLOGIE(F), INSTRUMENTS(M) DE MESURE(F) 40.
**météorologie(f), station(f) 38.**
**métier(m) à broder 571.**
**métier(m) de basse lisse(f) 572.**
**métier(m) de haute lisse(f) 574.**
métope(f) 167.
**mètre(m) à ruban(m) 711.**
mètre(m) à ruban(m) 563.
métro(m) 190.
**métronome(m) à quartz(m) 539.**
**métronome(m) mécanique 539.**
MEUBLES(M) DE RANGEMENT(M) 225, 226.
**meubles(m), exemples(m) 819.**
meule(f) 105.
meurtrière(f) 181.
**mezzanine(f) 194.**
mezzanine(f) 195, 474.
mi(m) 537.
mi-bas(m) 325, 344.
mi-chaussette(f) 325, 344.
micro(m) de fréquences(f) aiguës 547.
micro(m) de fréquences(f) graves 547.
micro(m) de fréquences(f) moyennes 547.
**micro-ordinateur(m) (vue(f) en plongée(f)) 528.**
**micromètre(m) palmer(m) 711.**
microordinateur(m) 526.
microphone(m) 407, 414, 420, 639.
microphone(m) d'interphone(m) 413.
MICROPHONE(M) DYNAMIQUE 406.
microphone(m) incorporé 409.
microprocesseur(m) 528.
MICROSCOPE(M) BINOCULAIRE 718.
MICROSCOPE(M) ÉLECTRONIQUE 717.
**microscope(m) électronique, composantes(f) 717.**
mihrab(m) 173.
millet(m) 152.
minaret(m) 172, 173.
minbar(m) 173.
MINE(F) DE CHARBON(M) 733, 734, 736.
**mine(f) souterraine 736.**
minerai(m) 733.
mini-slip(m) 325.
minute(f) 830.
minuterie(f) 252, 398, 585, 712.
minuteur(m) 244, 664.
mire(f) 684, 719.
mire(f) de réglage(m) 414.
mirette(f) 585.
miroir(m) 292, 382, 719.
miroir(m) d'éclairage(m) 713.
miroir(m) de courtoisie(f) 430.
miroir(m) de lecture(f) 512.
miroir(m) double pivotant 368.
miroir(m) latéral 368.
**miroir(m) lumineux 368.**
miroir(m) parabolique 770.
miroir(m) plan rétractable 14.
miroir(m) plan(m) 720.
miroir(m) primaire 16.
miroir(m) primaire concave 14.
miroir(m) primaire parabolique 720.
miroir(m) principal 390.
miroir(m) secondaire 16, 390.
misaine(f) 481.
**mise(f) à feu(m), accessoires(m) 801.**
mise(f) en marche(f) 420, 421.
**mise(f) en orbite(f) 419.**
**mise(f) en presse(f) 579.**
missile(m) air(m)-air(m) 813, 814.
missile(m) air(m)-sol(m) 814.
missile(m) anti-sous-marin 809, 814.
missile(m) antiaérien 808.
missile(m) antichar 814.
missile(m) antinavire 814.
missile(m) antiradar 814.
missile(m) mer(f)-mer(f) 809.
missile(m) sol(m)-air(m) 814.
**missile(m), structure(f) 814.**
MISSILES(M) 814.
**missiles(m), principaux types(m) 814.**
**mitaine(f) 327.**
**mitigeur(m) à bille(f) creuse 294.**
**mitigeur(m) à cartouche(f) 295.**
**mitigeur(m) à disque(m) 295.**
mitigeur(m) d'évier(m) 296.
mitochondrie(f) 115.
mitrailleuse(f) 805.
mitre(f) 205, 239, 242.
mitron(m) 197.
MOBILIER(M) DE BUREAU(M) 520, 522.
mocassin(m) 355.
mode(m) 525.
mode(m) d'entraînement(m) du film(m) 391.
mode(m) d'entraînement(m) du papier(m) 531.
mode(m) d'exposition(f) 391.
mode(m) de mise(f) au point(m) 391.
mode(m) de sélection(f) des stations(f) 402.
mode(m) de sortie(f) des copies(f) 532.
mode(m) magnétoscope(m) 411.
mode(m) manuel/automatique 585.
mode(m) télévision(f) 411.
modèle(m) à plat(m) 580.
modèle(m) en creux(m) 580.
modèle(m) en relief(m) 580.
modem(m) 526.
modérateur(m) 766.
modérateur(m): eau(f) lourde 761.
modérateur(m): eau(f) naturelle 762, 763.
modérateur(m): graphite(m) 760.
modification(f) fine des variables(f) 555.
modification(f) rapide des variables(f) 555.
modillon(m) 167.
modulation(f) de la hauteur(f) du son(m) 555.
modulation(f) du timbre(m) du son(m) 555.
module(m) d'alimentation(f) électrique 528.
module(m) d'injection(f) de gaz(m) 738.
module(m) de charge(f) utile 49.
module(m) de commande(f) 509.
module(m) de communication(f) 418.
module(m) de mémoire(f) morte (ROM) 528.
module(m) de mémoire(f) vive (RAM) 528.
module(m) de photopiles(f) 769.
module(m) de propulsion(f) 418.
module(m) de service(m) 418, 509.
**module(m) extérieur 212.**
**module(m) intérieur 213.**
module(m) lunaire 509.
moelle(f) 59.
moelle(f) épinière 89, 134, 135.
**moissonneuse(f)-batteuse(f) 160.**
moissonneuse(f)-batteuse(f) 155.
molaire(f) 98.
**molaire(f), coupe(f) 144.**
molaires(f) 144.
molette(f) 279, 386.
molette(f) d'entraînement(m) 256.
molette(f) de mise(f) au point(m) 719.
molette(f) de réglage(m) 311.
molette(f) de réglage(m) de la flamme(f) 386.
molette(f) du cylindre(m) 531.
mollet(m) 117, 119.
MOLLUSQUE(M) 92.
**mollusques(m) comestibles 93.**
monocle(m) 377.
mont(m) de Vénus 128.
MONTAGNE(F) 27.
montant(m) 198, 223, 302, 341, 535, 572, 574, 578, 644, 657, 659, 660, 661, 728.
montant(m) d'angle(m) 470.
montant(m) de bâti(m) 225.
montant(m) de bride(f) 649.
montant(m) de ferrage(m) 202, 225.
montant(m) de filet(m) 649.
montant(m) de la serrure(f) 202.
montant(m) de rive(f) 203.
montant(m) embrevé 203.
montant(m) latéral 427.
montant(m) mouton(m) 203.
monte-boules(m) 683.
monte-charge(m) 188.
montée(f) arrière 651.
MONTGOLFIÈRE(F) 634.
monticule(m) 597.
montre(f) 430, 585.
**montre(f) à affichage(m) analogique 706.**
**montre(f) à affichage(m) numérique 706.**
**montre(f) mécanique 706.**
**monture(f) 376.**
monture(f) 282, 536, 666.
**monture(f) altazimutale 15.**
monture(f) baïonnette(f) 392.
monture(f) d'objectif(m) 390.
monture(f) en fer(m) à cheval(m) 14.
monture(f) réglable 277.
monument(m) 52.
moraillon(m) 383.
moraine(f) de fond(m) 26.
moraine(f) frontale 27.
moraine(f) latérale 27.
moraine(f) médiane 26.
mordache(f) 578.
mordant(m) 538.
morille(f) 55.
mors(m) 276, 280, 281, 365, 577, 648.
**mors(m) à canon(m) brisé 650.**
**mors(m) à pompe(f) 650.**
**mors(m) anglais 650.**
**mors(m) de bride(f) 650.**
mors(m) de bride(f) 649.
**mors(m) de filet(m) 650.**
mors(m) de filet(m) 649.
mors(m) fixe 282.
mors(m) mobile 282.
MORS(M), TYPES(M) 650.
mort(f) 831.
mortaise(f) 385.
MORTIER(M) 803.
mortier(m) 243.
**mortier(m) du XVII{e} siècle(m) 803.**
**mortier(m) moderne 803.**
morts-terrains(m) 733.
mosaïque(f) 171.
MOSQUÉE(F) 172.
**mosquée(f), plan(m) 173.**
moteur(m) 147, 161, 207, 214, 257, 258, 259, 270, 271, 272, 283, 284, 442, 737, 784, 787, 805.
**moteur(m) à deux temps(m) 436.**
**moteur(m) à essence(f) 434.**
**moteur(m) à quatre temps(m) 436.**
**moteur(m) à turbocompression(f) 438.**
moteur(m) d'aiguillage(m) 467.
moteur(m) de disques(m) 529.
moteur(m) de guides(m) 529.
moteur(m) de manœuvre(f) 511.
**moteur(m) diesel 437.**
moteur(m) diesel 469, 495, 782, 783, 785.
moteur(m) diesel de propulsion(f) 492.
moteur(m) diesel de sustentation(f) 493.
moteur(m) du ventilateur(m) 214.
moteur(m) électrique 209, 216, 268, 271, 438.
moteur(m) électrique auxiliaire 806.
moteur(m) électrique principal 806.
moteur(m) F-1 509.
moteur(m) J-2 509.
**moteur(m) rotatif 437.**
moteur(m)-fusée(f) 43.
moteurs(m) 510.
moteurs(m) diesel 809.
moteurs(m) principaux 511.
MOTEURS(M), TYPES(M) 436.
motif(m) 350.
MOTO(F) 442, 444.
**moto(m), tableau(m) de bord(m) 445.**
**motoculteur(m) 272.**
**motoneige(f) 445.**
motrice(f) 459, 476, 477.
Mouche(f) 13.
mouche(f) 77, 675.
**mouche(f) artificielle 670.**
mouche(f) centrale 674.
mouche(f) de ligne(f) de cadre(m) 674.
mouche(f) supérieure 675.
moufle(f) 308, 327, 680, 793.
moufle(f) fixe 737.
moufle(f) mobile 737.
mouilleur(m) 516.
moule(f) 93.
moule(m) à fond(m) amovible 245.
moule(m) à gâteau(m) 245.
moule(m) à muffins(m) 245.
moule(m) à quiche(f) 245.

Les termes en **caractères gras** renvoient à une illustration, ceux en CAPITALES indiquent un titre.

moule(m) à tarte(f) 245.
**moulin(m) à café(m) 256.**
**moulin(m) à vent(m) 773.**
**moulin(m) pivot(m) 773.**
moulinet(m) 581.
**moulinet(m) à mouche(f) 670.**
**moulinet(m) à tambour(m) fixe 671.**
moulure(f) de protection(f) 449.
**mousqueton(m) 681.**
mousqueton(m) 630, 672, 680.
mousqueton(m) à ressort(m) 630.
mousse(f) graisseuse 216.
moustaches(f) 107.
**moutarde(f) 67.**
mouton(m) 150, 651.
mouvement(m) rotatif de la turbine(f) 755.
moyen adducteur(m) 120.
moyen(m) 666.
moyenne sus-alaire(f) 110.
moyenne tectrice(f) primaire 110.
moyeu(m) 447, 727, 754, 774.
moyeu(m) rotor(m) 508.
Mt Everest(m) 19.
mule(f) 355.
**multimètre(m) 310.**
multiplicateur(m) de focale(f) 392.
multiplication(f) 523, 830.
muqueuse(f) olfactive 142.
mur(m) 646, 647, 685.
mur(m) arrière 616, 617.
mur(m) avant 616, 617.
mur(m) bajoyer(m) 746.
mur(m) barré 646, 647.
mur(m) d'extrémité(f) 621.
mur(m) de batillage(m) 748.
mur(m) de briques(f) 199.
mur(m) de départ(m) 621.
mur(m) de fondation(f) 198, 199.
mur(m) de la qibla(f) 173.
mur(m) de virage(m) 621, 622.
mur(m) en béton(m) 772.
mur(m) fortifié 172.
mur(m) latéral 616, 617, 621.
**mur(m) Trombe 772.**
mur(m) Trombe 772.
muraille(f) 743.
muscle(m) adducteur 92.
muscle(m) arrecteur 136.
muscle(m) bulbo-caverneux 127.
muscle(m) droit externe 140.
muscle(m) droit interne 140.
muscle(m) papillaire 125.
MUSCLES(M) 120.
museau(m) 84, 106, 107.
musée(m) 185.
muserolle(f) 649.
MUSIQUE(F), ACCESSOIRES(M) 539.
mutule(f) 167.
mycélium(m) 55.
mye(f) 93.
myomère(m) 89.
myrtille(f) 62.

## N

n'égale pas 830.
n'est pas identique à 830.
**nacelle(f) 635.**
nacelle(f) 457, 634, 774.
nacelle(f) d'observation(f) 14.
nacelle(f) d'osier(m) 635.
nacelle(f) élévatrice 506.
**nage(f) sur le dos(m) 623.**
nageoire(f) anale 87.
nageoire(f) caudale 87, 91.
nageoire(f) pectorale 86.
nageoire(f) pelvienne 86.
**nages(f), types(m) 622.**
naissance(f) 831.
naos(m) 169.
nappe(f) phréatique 24.
narine(f) 84, 86, 96, 109, 141.
nasal(m) 792.
naseau(m) 100.
NATATION(F) 621, 622.
navet(m) 71.
**navette(f) 573.**
navette(f) 510.
navette(f) ferroviaire 504.
NAVETTE(F) SPATIALE 510.
**navette(f) spatiale au décollage(m) 510.**
**navette(f) spatiale en orbite(f) 510.**
NAVIGATION(F), APPAREILS(M) 484.
navire(m) de forage(m) 739.
navire(m) porte-conteneurs(m) 490.
ne pas laver 829.
ne pas repasser 829.
ne pas utiliser avec une chaise(f) roulante 822.
ne pas utiliser de chlorure(m) décolorant 829.
**nébulosité(f) 39.**
**nécessaire(m) à chaussures(f) 358.**
nectarine(f) 63.
nef(f) 177.
nef(f) centrale 173.
nèfle(f) du Japon(m) 64.
négatif(m) 399, 831.
négatoscope(m) 398.
neige(f) 34.
neige(f) continue 39.
neige(f) intermittente 39.
neige(f) roulée 37.
**neige(f), classification(f) des cristaux(m) 36.**
**neige(f), mesure(f) 41.**
neiges(f) éternelles 27.
Neptune 5.
nerf(m) 136, 577.
nerf(m) circonflexe 133.
nerf(m) cochléaire 139.
nerf(m) crural 133.
nerf(m) cubital 133.
nerf(m) digital 133.
nerf(m) facial 139.
nerf(m) fémoro-cutané 133.
nerf(m) fessier 133.
nerf(m) grand abdomino-génital 133.
nerf(m) grand sciatique 133.
nerf(m) intercostal 133.
nerf(m) médian 133.
nerf(m) musculo-cutané 133.
nerf(m) obturateur 133.
nerf(m) olfactif 88, 142.
nerf(m) optique 140.
nerf(m) petit abdomino-génital 133.
nerf(m) petit sciatique 133.
nerf(m) rachidien 135.
nerf(m) radial 133.
nerf(m) saphène externe 133.
nerf(m) saphène interne 133.
nerf(m) sciatique poplité externe 133.
nerf(m) sciatique poplité interne 133.
nerf(m) tibial antérieur 133.
nerf(m) vestibulaire 139.
nerfs(m) crâniens 133.
nervure(f) 79, 627, 729, 785.
nervure(f) d'aile(f) 498.
nervure(f) d'emplanture(f) 498.
nervure(f) principale 56, 67.
nervure(f) secondaire 56.
NETBALL(M) 611.
**netball(m), ballon(m) 611.**
**netball(m), terrain(m) 611.**
nettoie-pipes(m) 385.
neurone(m) moteur 135.
neurone(m) sensoriel 134.
**neurones(m) 135.**
névé(m) 26.
nez(m) 118, 277, 498, 637, 638.
nez(m) du guide(m) 272.
**nez(m), parties(f) externes 141.**
nez(m)-de-marche(f) 201.
nid(m) à couvain(m) 82.
nid(m) d'ange(m) 349.
nimbo-stratus(m) 44.
niveau(m) 736.
niveau(m) à bulle(f) 291.
niveau(m) d'eau(f) 210, 247.
niveau(m) d'équilibre(m) 30.
niveau(m) de la mer(f) 22, 28.
**niveleuse(f) 784.**
nivelle(f) d'alidade(f) 713.
nivelle(f) d'embase(f) 713.
nivomètre(m) 41.
nœud(m) 57, 576, 756.
nœud(m) coulant 691.
nœud(m) d'arrêt(m) 691.
noeud(m) d'écoute(f) double 691.
noeud(m) d'écoute(f) simple 691.
nœud(m) de cabestan(m) 691.
nœud(m) de chaise(f) double 691.
nœud(m) de chaise(f) simple 691.
noeud(m) de Franciscain(m) 691.
nœud(m) de jambe(f) de chien(m) 691.
nœud(m) de pêcheur(m) 691.
nœud(m) de Ranvier 135.
nœud(m) de vache(f) 691.
nœud(m) papillon(m) 324.
nœud(m) plat 328, 691.
nœud(m) simple 691.
NŒUDS(M) 691, 692.
noir(m) 700, 701.
noire(f) 538.
Noirs(m) 696.
noisette(f) 66.
NOIX(F) 66.
noix(f) 66, 541, 569, 793.
noix(f) de cajou(m) 66.
noix(f) de coco(m) 66.
noix(f) de pacane(f) 66.
noix(f) du Brésil(m) 66.
**noix(f), coupe(f) 66.**
**noix(f), principales variétés(f) 66.**
nom(m) de la station(f) 474.
nombre(m) de copies(f) 532.
nombre(m) de décimales(f) 523.
nombril(m) 116, 118.
non addition(f)/total(m) partiel 523.
non-appartenance(f) 830.
non-parallèle 830.
nord(m) 488.
nord(m)-est(m) 488.
nord(m)-ouest(m) 488.
notation(f) algébrique 696.
NOTATION(F) MUSICALE 537, 538.
nouaison(f) 61.
nouvelle Lune(f) 6.
noyau(m) 6, 9, 63, 115, 128, 135, 542, 677, 798.
noyau(m) d'argile(f) 748.
noyau(m) externe 22.
noyau(m) galactique 9.
noyau(m) interne 22.
nu-pied(m) 357.
nuage(m) 36.
nuage(m) de cendres(f) 25.
nuage(m) nacré 19.
nuage(m) nocturne lumineux 19.
NUAGES(M) 44.
**nuages(m) à développement(m) vertical 44.**
**nuages(m) de basse altitude(f) 44.**
**nuages(m) de haute altitude(f) 44.**
**nuages(m) de moyenne altitude(f) 44.**
**nuages(m), mesure(f) de la hauteur(f) 41.**
nuancier(m) 592.
nucléole(m) 115, 128.
nuisette(f) 348.
numéro(m) 701.
numéro(m) d'autoroute(f) 52.
numéro(m) de couloir(m) 621.
numéro(m) de l'abonné(m) 712.
numéro(m) de la piste(f) 405.
numéro(m) de quai(m) 462.
numéro(m) de route(f) 52.
numéro(m) de tête(f) 653.
numéro(m) du joueur(m) 602.
numéro(m) plein 700, 701.
numéroteur(m) 516.
nuque(f) 108, 117, 119.
nymphe(f) 82.

## O

oasis(f) 46.
objectif(m) 391, 392, 396, 397, 405, 718.
objectif(m) d'agrandissement(m) 399.
objectif(m) grand-angulaire 392.
**objectif(m) normal 392.**
objectif(m) super-grand-angle(m) 392.
objectif(m) zoom(m) 392, 409.
**objectif(m), accessoires(m) 392.**
**objectifs(m) 392.**
obscurité(f) 489.
**observatoire(m) 14.**
OBSERVATOIRE(M) ASTRONOMIQUE 14.
obstacle(m) d'eau(f) 676.
**obstacles(m) 647.**
OBUSIER(M) MODERNE 802.
occipital(m) 121, 123.
océan(m) 7, 35, 51.
océan(m) Arctique 21.
océan(m) Atlantique 20.
océan(m) Indien 21.
océan(m) Pacifique 20.
**océan(m), dorsale(f) 28.**
OCÉAN(M), FOND(M) 28.
**océan(m), topographie 28.**
Océanie(f) 21.
océanique 45.
octave(f) 537, 667.
oculaire(m) 390, 396, 409, 718, 719, 720, 721, 730.
oculaire(m) coudé 721.
ODORAT(M) 141.
oeil(m) 107.
**œil(m) 140.**
œil(m) 83, 90, 96, 97, 118, 275, 573, 649, 681.
œil(m) composé 79, 80, 81.
œil(m) simple 78, 80, 81.
œil(m) témoin(m) 471.
œillère(f) 653.
œillet(m) 230, 353, 354, 381, 569, 644, 671.
œillet(m) d'attache(f) 390.
œsophage(m) 88, 92, 97, 130, 131, 142.
**œuf(m) 109.**
œuf(m) 82.
œufrier(m) 254.
œufs(m) 84, 89.
office(m) 498.
ogive(f) 754.
oie(f) 150.
oignon(m) 70.
oignon(m) jaune 70.
OISEAU(M) 108, 110.
**oiseau(m) aquatique 111.**
oiseau(m) aquatique 111.
Oiseau(m) de Paradis(m) 13.
**oiseau(m) de proie(f) 111.**
oiseau(m) de proie(f) 111.
oiseau(m) échassier 111.
oiseau(m) granivore 111.
oiseau(m) insectivore 111.
**oiseau(m) percheur 111.**
**oiseau(m), morphologie(f) 108.**
olécrane(m) 102.
olécrâne(m) 123.
oléoduc(m) 740.
oléoduc(m) d'évacuation(f) 738.
oléoduc(m) sous-marin 740.
oléoduc(m) surélevé 740.
olive(f) 63.
ombelle(f) 60.
ombilic(m) 26.
ombilic(m) inférieur 110.
ombilic(m) supérieur 110.
ombre(f) 706.
**ombre(f) à paupières(f) 367.**
omoplate(f) 102, 117, 119, 122, 123.
onde(f) radio 15.
onde(f) sismique 23.
ongle(m) 137.
onglet(m) 518, 688.
onglet(m) à fenêtre(f) 518.
opale(f) 363.
opérateur(m) de régie(f) d'éclairage(m) 412.
opercule(m) 84, 86.
Ophiucus 11, 13.
opisthodome(m) 169.
or(m) 819.
orage(m) 39.
orage(m) violent 39.
**orange(f) 65.**
orange(f) 65.
orbiculaire(m) des paupières(f) 120.
orbite(f) de lancement(m) 48.
**orbite(f) des satellites(m) 43.**
orbite(f) géostationnaire 43.
orbite(f) lunaire 8.
orbite(f) polaire 43.
orbite(f) présélectionnée 48.
**orbites(f) des planètes(f) 4.**
ORCHESTRE(M) SYMPHONIQUE 556.
ordinateur(m) de gestion(f) de vol(m) 500.
ordinateur(m) des données(f) aérodynamiques 500.
ordonnance(f) 831.
**ordre(m) corinthien 167.**
**ordre(m) dorique 167.**
**ordre(m) ionique 166.**
oreille(f) 107, 112, 116, 223, 483.
oreille(f) externe 138.
oreille(f) interne 138.
oreille(f) moyenne 138.
**oreille(f), parties(f) 138.**
**oreille(f), pavillon(m) 139.**
oreiller(m) 224.
oreillette(f) droite 124, 125.
oreillette(f) gauche 124, 125.
organeau(m) 483.
organeau(m) de hissage(m) 483.
ORGANES(M) DES SENS(M) 136, 138, 140, 141.
ORGANES(M) GÉNITAUX FÉMININS 128, 129.
ORGANES(M) GÉNITAUX MASCULINS 127.
orge(f) 152.
ORGUE(M) 542.

Les termes en **caractères gras** renvoient à une illustration, ceux en CAPITALES indiquent un titre.

**orgue(m), mécanisme(m) 543.**
**orgue(m), production(f) du son(m) 543.**
orifice(m) d'aération(f) 304.
orifice(m) d'alimentation(f) 778, 779.
orifice(m) d'échappement(m) 735.
orifice(m) de l'intestin(m) 83.
orifice(m) de remplissage(m) 256.
orifice(m) du conduit(m) auditif 139.
orifice(m) du pied(m) 542.
orifice(m) du poumon(m) 83.
orifice(m) génital 83.
orifice(m) uro-génital 89.
oriflamme(f) 817.
origan(m) 74.
Orion 11, 13.
**ornements(m) 538.**
oronge(f) vraie 55.
orteil(m) 106, 116, 118.
os(m) alvéolaire 144.
os(m) iliaque 122.
os(m) maxillaire 144.
os(m) propre du nez(m) 141.
oscilloscope(m) de phase(f) audio 413.
oscilloscope(m)/vectoscope(m) 413.
oseille(f) 73.
**osselets(m) 138.**
osselets(m) 139.
otolithe(f) 88.
ouest(m) 488.
OUÏE(F) 138.
ouïe(f) 544.
ouragan(m) 39.
**ourdissoir(m) 575.**
ourlet(m) 231.
outil(m) 735.
OUTILLAGE(M) DE JARDIN(M) 264, 266, 268, 270, 272.
**outils(m), électricité(f) 310, 311.**
OUTILS(M), MENUISERIE(F) 275, 276, 278, 280, 282, 284.
**outils(m), plomberie(f) 299.**
**outils(m), sculpture(f) 587.**
ouverture(f) 94, 671.
**ouvre-boîtes(m) 256.**
ouvre-boîtes(m) 244, 688.
**ouvrière(f), abeille(f) 80.**
ouvrière(f), abeille(f) 81.
**ouvrir, ustensils(m) 244.**
ovaire(m) 60, 128, 129.
ovoïde 56.
**ovule(m) 128.**
ovule(m) 60.
oxer(m) 646, 647.
ozone(m) 19.

## P

paddock(m) 651.
PAIN(M) 153.
pain(m) au lait(m) 153.
pain(m) azyme 153.
pain(m) bâtard 153.
pain(m) blanc 153.
pain(m) chapati indien 153.
pain(m) complet 153.
pain(m) de blé(m) entier 153.
pain(m) de campagne(f) 153.
pain(m) de maïs(m) américain 153.
pain(m) de mie(f) 153.
pain(m) de seigle(m) allemand 153.
pain(m) de seigle(m) danois 153.
pain(m) de seigle(m) noir 153.
pain(m) de seigle(m)/ graines(f) de carvi(m) 153.
pain(m) grec 153.
pain(m) irlandais 153.
pain(m) naan indien 153.
pain(m) noir russe 153.
pain(m) parisien 153.
pain(m) pita 153.
pain(m) pita/ graines(f) de sésame(m) 153.
pain(m) pumpernickel(m) 153.
pain(m) tchallah juif 153.
pair(m) 700, 701.
paire(f) 695.
pal(m) 818.
palais(m) des congrès(m) 184.
palanque(f) 646, 647.
pale(f) 214, 752, 754, 774.
pale(f) de rotor(m) 508.
paletot(m) 321, 330.
palette(f) 619, 672, 787.
**palette(f) à ailes(f) 787.**
palette(f) à alvéoles(f) 592.
palette(f) à double face(f) 787.
palette(f) à simple face(f) 787.
palette(f) avec godet(m) 592.
palette(f) porte-instruments(m) 511.
**palette(f)-caisse(f) 787.**
palier(m) 194, 201.
palier(m) de butée(f) 753.
palier(m) magnétique 712.
palissade(f) 181.
palme(f) 627.
palmée 56.
palmeraie(f) 46.
palmette(f) 220.
palmure(f) 84, 111.
palonnier(m) 784.
palonnier(m) de slalom(m) 633.
palourde(f) 93.
palpe(m) labial 79, 81, 92.
pampille(f) 236.
pamplemousse(m) 65.
pan(m) 319, 324, 337.
pan(m) arrière 324.
pan(m) avant 324.
panais(m) 71.
panama(m) 328.
pancréas(m) 131.
**panier(m) 610.**
panier(m) 247, 252, 257, 596, 610, 672.
panier(m) à couverts(m) 257.
panier(m) d'alimentation(f) 521.
panier(m) de lavage(m) 258.
panier(m) de projection(f) 397.
panier(m) de réception(f) 521.
panne(f) 305, 579, 681.
panne(f) ronde 275.
panneau(m) 202, 229, 589, 610, 634, 736.
panneau(m) à âme(f) lamellée 288.
panneau(m) à âme(f) lattée 288.
panneau(m) d'accès(m) 207.
panneau(m) de citerne(f) 743.
panneau(m) de commande(f) 210, 421, 779.
panneau(m) de copeaux(f) 288.
panneau(m) de disjoncteurs(m) 500.
panneau(m) de fibres(f) 289.
panneau(m) de fibres(f) perforé 289.
panneau(m) de fonctions(f) 421.
panneau(m) de garnissage(m) 429.
panneau(m) de modestie(f) 521.
panneau(m) de particules(f) 289.
panneau(m) de particules(f) lamifié 289.
panneau(m) de protection(f) latéral 727.
panneau(m) de raccordement(m) électrique 415.
panneau(m) de raccordement(m) vidéo 415.
panneau(m) de refroidissement(m) 510.
panneau(m) de séparation(f) 383.
panneau(m) de vantail(m) 225.
panneau(m) indicateur 462.
panneau(m) nombre(m) de voies(f) 471.
panneau(m) photovoltaïque 486, 487.
panneau(m) publicitaire 474.
panneau(m) solaire 16, 42, 48, 418.
panneau(m)-parachute(m) 634.
panneaux(m) de commandes(f) radio(f) 500.
**panneaux(m) internationaux 825, 827, 828.**
**panneaux(m) nord-américains 824, 826, 828.**
panneaux(m) solaires déployés 48.
pansement(m) adhésif 725.
**pantalon(m) 323.**
pantalon(m) 353, 595, 602, 668, 680.
pantalon(m) molleton(m) 352.
pantalon(m) pattes(f) d'éléphant(m) 336.
**pantalons(m), types(m) 336.**
pantographe(m) 458.
Paon(m) 13.
papaye(f) 68.
papier(m) 384, 580, 589.
papier(m) à cigarettes(f) 384.
papier(m) goudronné 286.
papille(f) 136, 140.
papille(f) rénale 132.
papilles(f) linguales 143.
PAPILLON(M) 78.
**papillon(m) 79, 623.**
**papillon(m), patte(f) postérieure 78.**
PAQUEBOT(M) 496.
**paquet(m) de cigarettes(f) 384.**
parachute(m) 510, 812.
parachute(m) de secours(m) 635.
parachute(m) dorsal 635.
paraffines(f) 745.
parafoudre(m) 747, 757.
parafouille(m) 748, 749.
parallèle 830.
parallèle(f) 47.
paramètres(m) moteurs(m)/alarmes(f) 500.
PARAPENTE(M) 636.
parapentiste(m) 636.
parapet(m) 179, 181.
PARAPLUIE(M) 375.
**parapluie(m) 375.**
**parapluie(m) télescopique 375.**
**parapluie(m)-canne(f) 375.**
parasoleil(m) 392.
paratonnerre(m) 197.
parc(m) 52, 184.
parc(m) à échelles(f) 781.
parc(m) à voitures(f) 504.
parc(m) de stockage(m) 740.
parc(m) de stockage(m) terminal 740.
parc(m) national 52.
**parcours(m) d'obstacles(m) 646.**
**parcours(m) de golf(m) 676.**
parcours(m) de vitesse(f) 646.
parcours(m) des cavaliers(m) avancés 646.
parcours(m) des débutants(m) 646.
parcours(m) pittoresque 52.
**pardessus(m) 320.**
pare-brise(m) 426, 440, 442, 445, 498, 500.
pare-chocs(m) 260, 426, 440, 441, 617.
pare-chocs(m) arrière 445.
pare-soleil(m) 42, 409, 430, 449, 484, 721.
parement(m) 288, 315.
parement(m) amont 749.
parement(m) aval 749.
parenthèses(f) 832.
paréo(m) 334.
pariétal(m) 123.
paripennée 56.
**parka(f) 321.**
parking(m) 464, 491.
paroi(f) 104, 787.
paroi(f) avant 441.
paroi(f) de bout(m) 441.
paroi(f) latérale 441, 470.
PARQUET(M) 200.
parquet(m) 199.
parquet(m) à bâtons(m) rompus 200.
parquet(m) à coupe(f) de pierre(f) 200.
parquet(m) à coupe(f) perdue 200.
parquet(m) Chantilly 200.
parquet(m) d'Arenberg 200.
parquet(m) en chevrons(m) 200.
parquet(m) en vannerie(f) 200.
parquet(m) mosaïque(f) 200.
**parquet(m) sur chape(f) de ciment(m) 200.**
**parquet(m) sur ossature(f) de bois(m) 200.**
parquet(m) Versailles 200.
**parquets(m), arrangements(m) 200.**
parterre(m) 189.
parti 818.
**parties(f) 220, 223, 224.**
**partitions(f), exemples(m) 818.**
PARURES(F) DE FENÊTRE(F) 228, 230.
pas(m) 101.
**passage(m) à niveau(m) 471.**
passage(m) à niveau(m) 464, 828.
passage(m) d'animaux(m) sauvages 828.
passage(m) de fourche(f) 470.
passage(m) en apogée(m) 419.
passage(m) en éclipse(f) 419.
passage(m) inférieur 454.
passage(m) pour piétons(m) 186, 826, 827.
passage(m) souterrain 464.
passage(m) supérieur 452, 454.
passant(m) 319, 323, 324.
passant(m) tunnel(m) 323.
passe(f) (19 à 36) 700, 701.
passe(f) à billes(f) 746.
passe-bras(m) 331.
**passer, ustensils(m) pour 243.**
passerelle(f) 180, 464, 475, 810.
passerelle(f) de manœuvre(f) 188.
passerelle(f) de navigation(f) 494, 495, 497.
passerelle(f) télescopique 503.
passettes(f) 573.
passoire(f) 243, 251.
pastel(m) gras 588.
pastel(m) sec 588.
pastèque(f) 69.
pastille(f) de combustible(m) 765.
pastilles(f) 588.
patate(f) 71.
pâte(f) d'argile(f) 584.
patelle(f) 83.
patère(f) 220, 522.
patère(f) à embrasse(f) 229.
patin(m) 466, 508, 609, 643.
PATIN(M) À ROULETTES(F) 645.
patin(m) antidérapant 302, 661.
patin(m) arrière 643.
patin(m) avant 643.
patin(m) d'appui(m) 765.
patin(m) d'espacement(m) 765.
patin(m) de chenille(f) 805.
patin(m) de course(f) 644.
**patin(m) de figure(f) 644.**
**patin(m) de hockey(m) 644.**
patin(m) hydrostatique 14.
PATINAGE(M) 644.
**patinoire(f) 608.**
**pâtisserie(f), ustensils(m) 245.**
**patron(m) 565.**
patron(m) 570.
patte(f) 97, 319, 322, 323, 378, 379, 483, 579, 596.
patte(f) à boutons(m)-pression(f) 321.
patte(f) ambulatoire 78.
patte(f) anale 78.
patte(f) antérieure 79, 80, 84.
**patte(f) antérieure, abeille(f) 80.**
**patte(f) antérieure, chien(m) 106.**
patte(f) boutonnée 323.
patte(f) capucin(m) 324, 339.
patte(f) d'entrejambe(m) 337.
patte(f) d'épaule(f) 319.
patte(f) de boutonnage(m) 324.
patte(f) de coq(m) 585.
patte(f) de serrage(m) 319.
patte(f) médiane 79, 80.
**patte(f) médiane, abeille(f) 80.**
patte(f) polo(m) 326.
patte(f) postérieure 79, 81, 84, 85.
**patte(f) postérieure, abeille(f) 81.**
**patte(f) postérieure, papillon(m) 78.**
patte(f) ventouse 78.
pattes(f) abdominales 91.
pattes(f) thoraciques 90.
**pattes(f), principaux types(m) 111.**
pattes(f)-mâchoires(f) 90.
pâturage(m) 148.
paturon(m) 101.
paume(f) 137, 327, 596.
paumelle(f) 203.
paupière(f) 97.
paupière(f) inférieure 84, 107, 140.
paupière(f) interne 107.
paupière(f) supérieure 84, 107, 140.
pause(f) 403, 538.
pause(f)/arrêt(m) sur l'image(f) 411, 831.
pavillon(m) 138, 427, 542, 549, 551, 726.
pavillon(m) (8) 363.
pavillon(m) à deux pointes(f) 817.
pavillon(m) à deux pointes(f) et langue(f) 817.
pavillon(m) de la trompe(f) utérine 129.
**pavillon(m), oreille(f) 139.**
pavois(m) 478, 817.
**pavot(m) 67.**
pays(m) 51.
**peau(f) 136, 579.**
peau(f) 62, 63, 64, 84, 134, 554.
peau(f) de batterie(f) 552, 553.
peau(f) de chamois(m) 358.
peau(f) de timbre(m) 553.
peau(f) verruqueuse 85.
PÊCHE(F) 670, 672.
**pêche(f) 63.**
pêche(f) 63.
**pêche(f), vêtements(m) 672.**
pêcheur(m) 569.
pédale(f) 446, 448, 545, 552, 553, 664.
pédale(f) crescendo(m) 542.
pédale(f) d'accélérateur(m) 430.
pédale(f) d'ajustement(m) 591.
pédale(f) de combinaisons(f) 542.
pédale(f) de débrayage(m) 430.
pédale(f) de déchaussage(m) 641.
pédale(f) de frein(m) 430, 573.

pédale(f) de frein(m) arrière 444.
pédale(f) de palonnier(m) 639.
pédale(f) de sourdine(f) 540.
pédale(f) douce 540, 555.
pédale(f) forte 540, 555.
pédales(f) d'expression(f) 542.
pédieux(m) 120.
pédoncule(m) 60, 61, 62, 63, 64.
Pégase(m) 11.
peigne(m) 159, 574.
peigne(m) à crêper 368.
peigne(m) à pollen(m) 81.
peigne(m) à tige(f) 368.
peigne(m) afro 368.
peigne(m) de coiffeur(m) 368.
**peignes(m) 368.**
peignoir(m) 348.
PEINTURE(F) 588, 590, 592.
PEINTURE(F) D'ENTRETIEN(M) 304.
**peinture(f), accessoires(m) 591, 592.**
**peinture(f), matériel(m) 589.**
**pèlerine(f) 330.**
pèlerine(f) 330.
pelle(f) 205, 244, 266, 632.
pelle(f) de montagne(f) 680.
**pelle(f) hydraulique 785.**
pelle(f) mécanique 733.
pelle(f)-pioche(f) pliante 690.
pelleteuse(f) 782.
pellicule(f) en feuille(f) 395.
**pellicules(f) 395.**
**pelote(f) 563.**
**pelouse(f) 682.**
pelouse(f) 193.
peltée 56.
pendants(m) d'oreille(f) 361.
pendeloque(f) 236.
pendentif(m) 361.
penderie(f) 226.
pendule(m) 707.
pêne(m) demi-tour(m) 289, 290.
pêne(m) dormant 289, 290.
péninsule(f) 51.
pénis(m) 116.
**penne(f) 110.**
pennée 56.
pennon(m) 628, 817.
pennon(m) double 817.
pente(f) 770.
pépin(m) 62, 64, 65.
**péplos(m) 315.**
**perception(f) des saveurs(f) 143.**
**perceuse(f) à colonne(f) 283.**
**perceuse(f) électrique 280.**
perche(f) 412, 414, 657.
perche(f) de ravitaillement(m) 813.
perche(f) de tête(f) 653.
**percolateur(m) 247.**
percuteur(m) 804.
perforation(f) 353, 355, 395.
perforation(m) 327.
perforatrice(f) 516.
pergola(f) 263.
péricarde(m) 130.
péricarpe(m) 65, 66.
période(f) 489.
**périphériques(m) d'entrée(f) 526.**
**périphériques(m) de communication(f) 526.**
**périphériques(m) de sortie(f) 527.**
**périphériques(m) de stockage(m) 526.**
périscope(m) d'attaque(f) 807.
périscope(m) de veille(f) 807.
péristyle(m) 168, 169, 171.
péritoine(m) 127, 128.
perlure(f) 105.
péroné(m) 102, 122.
peroxyde(m) 725.
perpendiculaire(f) 830.
perré(m) 748.
perron(m) 196.
Persée 11.
persienne(f) 203.
persil(m) 74.
personnel(m) additionnel de production(f) 412.
pertuis(m) de remplissage(m) 493.
pertuis(m) de remplissage(m) et de vidange(f) 493.
pèse-lettres(m) 516.
**pèse-personne(m) 709.**
peseta(f) 832.
**peson(m) 709.**
pesticides(m) 32.
pétale(m) 60.
pétiole(m) 56.
petit bois(m) 203.
petit cacatois(m) 481.
Petit Cheval(m) 11.
Petit Chien(m) 11.
petit foc(m) 481.
petit hunier(m) fixe 481.
petit hunier(m) volant 481.
petit largue(m) 629.
Petit Lion(m) 11.
petit miroir(m) 484.
petit montant(m) 202.
petit palmaire(m) 120.
petit perroquet(m) fixe 481.
petit perroquet(m) volant 481.
petit quartier(m) 649.
petit rabat(m) 386.
petit rond(m) 121.
petit sésamoïde(m) 102.
petite lame(f) 688.
petite lèvre(f) 128, 129.
Petite Ourse(f) 11.
petite quille(f) 683.
petite sus-alaire(f) 110.
petits pois(m) 72.
pétoncle(m) 93.
PÉTROLE(M) 737, 738, 740, 742, 744.
pétrole(m) 737.
pétrole(m) brut 744.
**pétrolier(m) 742.**
pétrolier(m) 491.
phalange(f) 107, 122, 123.
phalangette(f) 107, 122, 123, 137.
phalangine(f) 107, 122, 123, 137.
**phare(m) 486.**
phare(m) 147, 426, 440, 442, 444, 445, 469, 491, 805.
phare(m) antibrouillard 440.
phare(m) arrière 147.
phare(m) central 459.
phare(m) d'atterrissage(m) 508.
pharmacie(f) 822.
pharynx(m) 130, 131.
PHASES(F) DE LA LUNE(F) 6.
Phénix(m) 13.
Phobos 4.
PHOTOCOPIEUR(M) 532.
photodiode(f) 390.
PHOTOGRAPHIE(F) 390, 392, 394, 396, 398.
**photopile(f) 768.**
photopile(f) 769.
**photopiles(f), circuit(m) 769.**
photosphère(f) 6.
phototype(m) 397.
pi(m) 830.
piano(m) 556.
**piano(m) droit 540.**
**piano(m) droit, mécanique(f) 541.**
**piano(m) électronique 555.**
pic(m) 27.
piccolo(m) 548, 557.
pichet(m) 238, 251.
pièce(f) d'embranchement(m) 779.
pièce(f) d'estomac(m) 317.
pièce(f) de coin(m) 470.
pièce(f) de jonction(f) 778.
pièce(f) intermédiaire 127.
pièce(f) terminale 127.
**pièces(f) buccales 81.**
**pièces(f) honorables, exemples(m) 818.**
pied(m) 55, 72, 83, 112, 116, 117, 118, 119, 219, 224, 225, 232, 236, 270, 325, 350, 384, 542, 545, 553, 619, 645, 659, 670, 671, 718, 756, 786.
pied(m) amont 748.
pied(m) arrière 223.
pied(m) aval 748.
pied(m) avant 223.
pied(m) cambré 220.
pied(m) de fixation(f) 393.
pied(m) de lit(m) 224.
pied(m) de mât(m) 631.
pied(m) de nivellement(m) 257, 258, 259.
**pied(m) presseur 562.**
pied(m) télescopique 726.
pied(m)-mélangeur(m) 250.
pied-de-biche(m) 561, 562.
piedroit(m) 175.
piédroit(m) 174.
pierre(f) 286, 307, 364.
pierre(f) à aiguiser 582.
pierre(f) blanche 697.
**pierre(f) de curling(m) 620.**
pierre(f) lithographique 583.
pierre(f) noire 697.
**pierres(f) fines 363.**
**pierres(f) précieuses 363.**
pierrures(f) 105.
piètement(m) 223, 302, 661.
pige(f) 585.
pignon(m) 58, 66, 197, 280, 707.
pilastre(m) 201.
pile(f) 393, 409, 454, 455, 528, 777, 814.
pilier(m) 176, 714, 736.
pilier(m) droit 606.
pilier(m) du voile(m) 142.
pilier(m) gauche 606.
pilon(m) 243, 244.
pilote(m) 541, 637, 814.
pilotin(m) 543.
piment(m) 69.
pin(m) parasol(m) 58.
pinacle(m) 176.
pince(f) 90, 104, 205, 230, 246, 323, 370, 565.
pince(f) à boucles(f) de cheveux(m) 369.
pince(f) à cheveux(m) 369.
pince(f) à cravate(f) 364.
pince(f) à cuticules(m) 365.
**pince(f) à dénuder 311.**
pince(f) à échardes(f) 725.
pince(f) à épiler 365.
pince(f) à escargots(m) 246.
pince(f) à étiqueter 516.
pince(f) à fusible(m) 311.
pince(f) à long bec(m) 311.
pince(f) à spaghettis(m) 246.
**pince(f) d'électricien(m) 311.**
pince(f) de mise(f) en plis(m) 369.
pince(f) de taille(f) 320.
**pince(f) motoriste 278.**
**pince(f) multiprise 278.**
pince(f) tibio-tarsienne 81.
**pince(f) universelle 311.**
**pince(f)-étau(m) 278.**
pince-aiguille(m) 562.
pince-fil(m) 569.
pince-notes(m) 515.
**pinceau(m) 304.**
pinceau(m) 389, 582, 589.
pinceau(m) à lèvres(f) 366.
pinceau(m) à pâtisserie(f) 245.
pinceau(m) à sumie(m) 589.
pinceau(m) éventail(m) 366.
pinceau(m) pour fard(m) à joues(f) 366.
pinceau(m) pour poudre(f) libre 366.
pincement(m) 232.
pinçon(m) 104.
pioche(f) 267.
**piolet(m) 681.**
piolet(m) 680.
Pion(m) 696.
**pipe(f) 385.**
**pipe(f), coupe(f) 385.**
pique(f) 681.
pique(m) 695.
pique-nique(m) 823.
pique-nique(m) interdit 823.
pique-notes(m) 516.
piquet(m) 598, 599, 685, 686.
piquet(m) de coin(m) 682.
piquoir(m) 570.
piscine(f) 496, 772.
piscine(f) de condensation(f) 763.
piscine(f) de déchargement(m) 764.
piscine(f) de déchargement(m) du combustible(m) irradié 758.
piscine(f) de réception(f) 764.
piscine(f) de stockage(m) du combustible(m) irradié 758, 764, 765.
piscine(f) du combustible(m) défectueux 764.
pissenlit(m) 73.
pistache(f) 66.
**piste(f) 504, 651, 666, 683.**
piste(f) d'atterrissage(m) 811.
piste(f) d'avertissement(m) 597.
piste(f) d'élan(m) 654, 655, 657, 683.
piste(f) de roulement(m) 476, 786.
pistil(m) 60.
PISTOLET(M) 797.
pistolet(m) 291.
**pistolet(m) à calfeutrer 291.**
**pistolet(m) à peinture(f) 304.**
**pistolet(m) à souder 305.**
pistolet(m) arrosoir(m) 264.
pistolet(m) d'arrosage(m) 264.
pistolet(m) de distribution(f) 453.
PISTOLET(M) MITRAILLEUR(M) 795.
piston(m) 432, 435, 436, 438, 550, 726.
piston(m) à décorer 245.
**piton(m) 681.**
piton(m) à glace(f) 680.
piton(m) sous-marin 29.
pivot(m) 105, 311, 369, 374, 484, 485, 539, 590, 624, 658, 719, 773.
pivot(m) d'accouplement(m) 441.
placage(m) déroulé 288.
place(f) d'armes(f) 178.
**plaçure(f) 577.**
plafond(m) 205, 616, 617.
plafond(m) acoustique 189.
plafonnier(m) 236.
plage(f) 23, 30.
plage(f) arrière 496.
plage(f) avant 495, 497.
plage(f) de séparation(f) 404.
plaine(f) 51.
**plaine(f) abyssale 29.**
plaine(f) abyssale 29.
plaine(f) fluvio-glaciaire 27.
**plan(m) du terrain(m) 193.**
**plan(m) urbain 52.**
**plan(m), élévation(f) 193.**
**planche(f) 288.**
planche(f) 288, 663.
PLANCHE(F) À VOILE(M) 631.
planche(f) d'appel(m) saut(m) en longueur(f) 655.
planche(f) d'appel(m) triple saut(m) 654.
planche(f) de cuivre(m) 582.
planche(f) de vol(m) 82.
planche(f) témoin(m) 654.
plancher(m) 205, 616, 617, 649.
plancher(m) inférieur 787.
plancher(m) supérieur 787.
planchette(f) à arches(f) 518.
planchette(f) à pince(f) 519.
planétaire(m) 16.
PLANÉTARIUM(M) 16.
planétarium(m) 184.
**planètes(f) 4.**
**planètes(f), orbites(f) 4.**
**planeur(m) 638.**
PLANS(M), LECTURE(F) 193, 195.
plantaire(m) grêle 121.
plante(f) grimpante 263.
PLANTE(F), STRUCTURE(F) 57.
plantoir(m) 268.
plantoir(m) à bulbes(m) 268.
plaque(f) 253.
plaque(f) à aiguille(f) 561.
plaque(f) à biscuits(m) 245.
plaque(f) absorbante 768.
plaque(f) antifriction(m) 641.
plaque(f) chauffante 247.
plaque(f) costale 97.
plaque(f) d'identité(f) 364.
plaque(f) d'instructions(f) 280.
plaque(f) de base(f) 803.
plaque(f) de base(f) 738.
plaque(f) de commutateur(m) 309.
plaque(f) de couche(f) 798, 799.
plaque(f) de fixation(f) 713.
plaque(f) de frein(m) 641.
plaque(f) de montage(m) 233.
plaque(f) de protection(f) 547.
plaque(f) de rouleau(m) 702.
plaque(f) de tôle(f) 616.
plaque(f) du lanceur(m) 597.
plaque(f) marginale 96.
plaque(f) motrice 134.
plaque(f) négative 439.
plaque(f) nucale 97.
plaque(f) positive 439.
plaque(f) signalétique 280, 712.
plaque(f) supra-caudale 96.
plaque(f) tournante 457.
plaque(f) vertébrale 97.
plaque(f)-glissière(f) 561, 562.
plaquette(f) 36, 376, 432.
plaqueur(m) droit 603, 605.
plaqueur(m) gauche 603, 605.
plasmodesme(m) 115.
plastique(m) et acier(m) 301.
plastique(m) et cuivre(m) 301.
plastron(m) 96, 346, 602, 609, 684, 792.
plastron(m) métallique 667.
plat(m) 598.

Les termes en **caractères gras** renvoient à une illustration, ceux en CAPITALES indiquent un titre.

plat(m) à escargots(m) 246.
plat(m) à poisson(m) 238.
plat(m) de dos(m) 220.
plat(m) ovale 238.
plat(m) recto(m) 577.
plat(m) verso(m) 577.
plate-bande(f) 263.
plate-bande(f) de culasse(f) 800.
plate-forme(f) 49, 302, 393, 441, 461, 621, 709.
plate-forme(f) auto-élévatrice 739.
plate-forme(f) de 10 m 624.
plate-forme(f) de 3 m 624.
plate-forme(f) de 5 m 624.
plate-forme(f) de 7,5 m 624.
**plate-forme(f) de production(f) 738.**
plate-forme(f) de production(f) 740.
plate-forme(f) élévatrice automotrice 507.
plate-forme(f) fixe 739.
plate-forme(f) semi-submersible 739.
plateau(m) 27, 51, 70, 210, 219, 283, 285, 302, 382, 383, 399, 404, 412, 561, 578, 579, 708, 709.
plateau(m) A 448.
plateau(m) B 448.
plateau(m) continental 22, 29.
plateau(m) de clavier(m) 540.
plateau(m) de frein(m) 432.
plateau(m) de rangement(m) 591.
**plateau(m) de sciage(m) 285.**
plateau(m) de stockage(m) 764.
plateau(m) de tri(m) automatique 532.
plateau(m) mobile 701.
plateau(m) pour accessoires(m) 721.
plateau(m) réceptacle(m) de paiement(m) 702.
plateau(m) récepteur 532.
plateau(m) tournant 250.
**plateau(m), télévision(f) 412, 414.**
platine(f) 579, 718.
**platine(f) à silex(m) 795.**
**platine(f) cassette(f) 403.**
platine(f) cassette(f) 400, 407.
**platine(f) tourne-disque(m) 404.**
platine(f) tourne-disque(m) 400, 407.
plats(m) à four(m) 248.
pleine Lune(f) 7.
plénum(m) 206, 207.
pleurote(m) en huître(f) 55.
plèvre(f) pariétale 130.
plexus(m) brachial 133.
plexus(m) lombaire 133.
plexus(m) sacré 133.
pli(m) 288, 323, 433.
pli(m) creux 228, 335.
pli(m) d'aisance(f) 335.
pli(m) de la columelle(f) 94.
pli(m) pincé 228.
pli(m) plat 323, 335.
pli(m) rond 228.
pli(m) surpiqué 335.
plinthe(f) 199, 201.
**plinthe(f) chauffante électrique 210.**
plioir(m) 577.
**plis(m), types(m) 228, 335.**
plissé(m) accordéon(m) 335.
pliure(f) 565.
plomb(m) 672.
PLOMBERIE(F) 292, 294, 296, 298, 299, 300.
PLOMBERIE(F), CIRCUIT(M) 215.
**plomberie(f), outils(m) 299.**
plombs(m) 799.
PLONGÉE(F) SOUS-MARINE 627.
**plongeoir(m) 624.**
PLONGEON(M) 624.
plongeon(m) de départ(m) 622.
**plongeon(m) en arrière 625.**
**plongeon(m) en avant 625.**
**plongeon(m) en équilibre(m) 625.**
**plongeon(m) renversé 625.**
**plongeon(m) retourné 625.**
**plongeon(m), départ(m) 624.**
**plongeon(m), entrées(f) 624.**
**plongeon(m), vols(m) 624.**
**plongeur(m) 627.**
plot(m) 233.
**plot(m) de départ(m) 621.**
plot(m) de départ(m) 621.
pluie(f) 36.
pluie(f) acide 32, 33, 35.
pluie(f) continue 39.
pluie(f) intermittente 39.
pluie(f) verglaçante 39.
plume(f) 389, 589, 714.
plume(f) creuse de roseau(m) 389.
plume(f) d'oie(f) 389.
plume(f) métallique 389.
plume(f) métallique romaine 389.
plus grand que 830.
plus ou moins 830.
plus petit que 830.
Pluton 5.
**pluviomètre(m) à lecture(f) directe 40.**
**pluviomètre(m) enregistreur 40.**
**pluviosité(f), mesure(f) 40.**
**pneu(m) 433.**
pneu(m) 440, 447.
pneu(m) à carcasse(f) diagonale 433.
pneu(m) à carcasse(f) radiale 433.
**pneu(m) à carcasse(f) radiale ceinturée 433.**
pneumatique(m) de guidage(m) 476, 477.
pneumatique(m) porteur 476, 477.
poche(f) 673, 679, 683.
poche(f) à douilles(f) 245.
poche(f) à rabat(m) 320, 339.
poche(f) américaine 379.
poche(f) cavalière 323.
poche(f) centrale 674.
poche(f) extérieure 378, 382.
poche(f) frontale 381.
poche(f) gilet(m) 322.
poche(f) inférieure 674.
poche(f) intérieure 383.
poche(f) intérieure isolante 349.
poche(f) manchon(m) 339.
poche(f) passepoilée 326, 339.
poche(f) plaquée 320, 322, 339, 350.
poche(f) poitrine(f) 320, 324.
poche(f) prise dans une couture(f) 330, 339.
poche(f) prise dans une découpe(f) 339.
poche(f) raglan 319, 330, 339.
poche(f) repose-bras(m) 321, 330.
poche(f) secrète 379.
poche(f) soufflet(m) 338, 339.
poche(f) supérieure 675.
poche(f) tiroir(m) 322.
poche(f) verticale 316.
poche(f)-revolver(m) 323.
poche(f)-ticket(m) 322.
**poches(f), types(m) 339.**
pochette(f) 322, 378, 381.
**pochette(f) d'allumettes(f) 386.**
pochette(f) d'homme(m) 380.
pochette(f) d'information(f) 519.
pochette(f) de classement(m) 517.
pocheuse(f) 249.
**podomètre(m) 711.**
**poêle(f) 688.**
poêle(f) à crêpes(f) 249.
poêle(f) à frire 249.
**poêle(m) à combustion(f) lente 204.**
**poids(m) 658.**
poids(m) 658, 663, 665, 707, 708, 709.
poignard(m) 794.
poignée(f) 204, 224, 250, 251, 252, 253, 254, 255, 256, 260, 272, 276, 277, 281, 284, 294, 304, 370, 375, 378, 380, 382, 383, 397, 408, 442, 477, 544, 615, 620, 632, 640, 642, 643, 658, 665, 666, 670, 671, 677, 679, 684, 728, 735, 793, 798, 799.
poignée(f) à ressort(m) 665.
poignée(f) antivibrations(f) 272.
poignée(f) arrière 671.
poignée(f) auxiliaire 280.
poignée(f) avant 804.
poignée(f) d'appui(m) 664.
poignée(f) de chariot(m) 568.
poignée(f) de conduite(f) 727.
poignée(f) de frein(m) 447, 727.
poignée(f) de guidage(m) 283.
poignée(f) de la manivelle(f) 583.
poignée(f) de maintien(m) 429.
poignée(f) de nacelle(f) 635.
poignée(f) de porte(f) 202, 427.
poignée(f) de sécurité(f) 271.
poignée(f) de soulèvement(m) 803.
poignée(f) de transport(m) 796.
poignée(f) des gaz(m) 444.
poignée(f) du démarreur(m) 272.
poignée(f) intérieure 429.
poignée(f) latérale 280.
poignée(f) montoir(m) 440, 449, 461, 779.
poignée(f) pistolet(m) 305.
poignée(f) profilée 370.
poignée(f) rentrante 378.
poignée(f) supérieure 280.
poignée(f)-oxygène(m) de coupe(f) 306.
poignée(f)-pistolet(m) 280, 795, 796.
poignet(m) 106, 112, 117, 119, 137, 324.
**poignet(m) mousquetaire(m) 339.**
poil(m) 136, 373.
poils(m) absorbants 57.
poinçon(m) 199, 586, 688.
point(m) 695, 832.
point(m) d'alimentation(f) 757.
point(m) d'amure(f) 631.
point(m) d'ancrage(m) 637.
point(m) d'arête(f) 571.
point(m) d'articulation(f) 785.
point(m) d'attache(f) 56, 501.
point(m) d'écoute(f) 631.
point(m) d'encochage(m) 684.
point(m) d'épine(f) 571.
point(m) d'exclamation(f) 832.
point(m) d'interrogation(f) 832.
point(m) d'orgue(m) 539.
point(m) d'Orient(m) 571.
point(m) de chaînette(f) 571.
point(m) de chausson(m) 571.
point(m) de chevron(m) 571.
point(m) de côtes(f) 567.
point(m) de damier(m) 567.
point(m) de jersey(m) 567.
point(m) de mise(f) au jeu(m) 608.
point(m) de nœud(m) 571.
point(m) de penalty(m) 601.
point(m) de poste(f) 571.
point(m) de raccordement(m) 757.
point(m) de repère(m) 565, 683.
point(m) de riz(m) 567.
point(m) de torsades(f) 567.
point(m) du chef(m) 818.
point(m) fixe 432.
point(m) indicateur(m) de température(f) 370.
point(m) mousse(f) 567.
point(m) passé empiétant 571.
point(m) roumain 571.
point(m) vernal 3.
point(m)-virgule(f) 832.
pointe(f) 30, 57, 72, 240, 242, 275, 276, 277, 284, 325, 341, 385, 389, 541, 544, 562, 567, 640, 644, 656, 658, 671, 678, 680, 681, 684, 698, 798, 818.
pointe(f) antérieure 680.
pointe(f) avant 256.
pointe(f) carrée 276.
pointe(f) cruciforme 276.
pointe(f) d'attache(f) 540.
pointe(f) de bâton(m) 643.
pointe(f) de centrage(m) 281.
pointe(f) de col(m) 324.
pointe(f) de dent(f) 783.
pointe(f) de diamant(m) 225.
pointe(f) de flèche(f) en silex(m) 791.
pointe(f) de hampe(f) 817.
pointe(f) de ski(m) 642.
pointe(f) plate 231, 276.
pointe(f) ronde 231.
pointe(f) sèche 582, 583.
pointeur(m) 719.
**points(m) bouclés 571.**
**points(m) couchés 571.**
**points(m) croisés 571.**
points(m) de handicap(m) 697.
points(m) de suspension(f) 832.
**points(m) de tricot(m) 567.**
**points(m) noués 571.**
**points(m) plats 571.**
**points(m), broderie(f) 571.**
poire(f) 64.
poire(f) à jus(m) 246.
poire(f) à poudre(f) 795.
poire(f) de gonflage(m) 710.
poireau(m) 70.
**pois(m) 67.**
pois(m) 67.
pois(m) chiches 72.
pois(m) mange-tout(m) 72.
POISSON(M) 86, 88.
Poisson(m) austral 13.
Poisson(m) volant 13.
**poisson(m), anatomie(f) 88.**
**poisson(m), morphologie(f) 86.**
**poissonnière(f) 248.**
Poissons(m) 11.
Poissons(m) (19 février) 820.
poitrail(m) 100.
poitrine(f) 108, 116, 118.
poitrinière(f) 572.
poivrière(f) 238.
poivron(m) 69.
**poker(m), combinaisons(f) 695.**
Polaroid®(m) 394.
pôle(m) Nord 3.
pôle(m) Nord céleste 3.
pôle(m) Sud 3.
pôle(m) Sud céleste 3.
police(f) 822.
pollution(f) agricole 32.
**pollution(f) de l'air(m) 34.**
**pollution(f) des aliments(m) 32.**
pollution(f) industrielle 32, 33.
**polo(m) 326.**
polo(m) 337, 615.
polochon(m) 224.
polojama(m) 351.
**pomme(f) 64.**
pomme(f) 64, 265.
pomme(f) d'Adam 116.
pomme(f) de douche(f) 292.
pomme(f) de terre(f) 71.
pommeau(m) 277, 281, 596, 649, 666.
pompe(f) 209, 257, 258, 446, 689, 761, 762, 771.
pompe(f) à boue(f) 737.
**pompe(f) à chaleur(f) 212.**
pompe(f) de caloportage(m) 759.
pompe(f) de circulation(f) 208, 772.
POMPE(F) DE PUISARD(M) 216.
pompe(f) de recirculation(f) 763.
poncho(m) 331.
pont(m) 52, 376, 719.
pont(m) à béquilles(f) 455.
**pont(m) à poutre(f) 454.**
pont(m) à poutre(f) simple 454.
pont(m) à poutres(f) indépendantes 454.
pont(m) à tablier(m) inférieur 455.
pont(m) à tablier(m) intermédiaire 455.
pont(m) à tablier(m) supérieur 455.
pont(m) Bailey 457.
pont(m) bain(m) de soleil(m) 497.
pont(m) basculant à double volée(f) 457.
**pont(m) basculant à simple volée(f) 457.**
**pont(m) cantilever 454.**
pont(m) d'appontage(m) 811.
pont(m) d'envol(m) 810.
pont(m) de Varole 134.
**pont(m) en arc(m) 455.**
**pont(m) flottant 457.**
pont(m) inférieur 741.
**pont(m) levant 457.**
pont(m) principal 743.
pont(m) roulant 747.
pont(m) supérieur 498, 741.
**pont(m) suspendu à câble(m) porteur 456.**
**pont(m) tournant 457.**
**pont(m) transbordeur 457.**
pont(m)-promenade(f) 496.
pont-levis(m) 180.
pontet(m) 795, 797, 798, 799.
ponton(m) 457, 738.
**ponts(m) à poutre(f), types(m) 454.**
**ponts(m) en arc(m), types(m) 455.**
PONTS(M) FIXES 454, 456.
PONTS(M) MOBILES 457.
**ponts(m) suspendus à haubans(m) 456.**
**popote(f) 688.**
porc(m) 151.
porche(m) 172, 177.
porcherie(f) 149.
pore(m) 67, 115.
pore(m) sudoripare 136.
porque(f) 743.
port(m) clavier(m) 528.
port(m) imprimante(f) 528.
port(m) lecteur(m) de disque(m) 528.
PORT(M) MARITIME 490.
port(m) modem(m) 528.
port(m) périphérique(m) 528.
port(m) réseau(m) 528.
port(m) vidéo 528.
portail(m) 175.
portant(m) 632.
PORTE(F) 202.
porte(f) 173, 253, 254, 259, 449, 490, 498, 566, 617, 645, 685, 686, 709.
porte(f) à charnière(f) 195.

Les termes en **caractères gras** renvoient à une illustration, ceux en CAPITALES indiquent un titre.

porte(f) accordéon(m) 202.
porte(f) amont(m) 493.
porte(f) automatique 504.
porte(f) aval(m) 492.
porte(f) avant 493, 494.
porte(f) classique 202.
porte(f) coulissante 202, 292.
porte(f) d'accès(m) de plate-forme(f) 461.
porte(f) d'extrémité(f) 470.
porte(f) de la soute(f) 510.
porte(f) étagère(f) 254.
**porte(f) extérieure 202.**
porte(f) latérale 477.
porte(f) pliante 194, 202.
porte(f)-fenêtre(f) 195.
porte(f)-foyer(m) 204.
porte-adresse(m) 383.
PORTE-AVIONS(M) 810.
**porte-bagages(m) 382.**
porte-bagages(m) 446, 449.
porte-bidon(m) 447.
porte-bûches(m) 205.
**porte-cartes(m) 379.**
porte-cartes(m) 40, 379.
**porte-chaussures(m) 358.**
porte-chéquier(m) 379.
porte-clés(m) 379.
porte-coupures(m) 379.
**porte-documents(m) à soufflet(m) 378.**
porte-documents(m) plat 378.
porte-électrode(m) 305.
porte-étiquette(m) 471, 517.
porte-étiquette(m) d'acheminement(m) 471, 743.
porte-étiquette(m) de contenu(m) 743.
porte-fils(m) 573.
porte-fusible(m) 757.
porte-gomme(m) 515.
porte-jarretelles(m) 347.
porte-manteau(m) 522.
porte-mine(m) 389, 515.
porte-monnaie(m) 379.
porte-moulinet(m) 670, 671.
**porte-négatif(m) 399.**
porte-négatif(m) 399.
porte-outil(m) 283, 735.
porte-parapluie(m) 679.
porte-parapluies(m) 375.
porte-passeport(m) 379.
porte-pipes(m) 385.
porte-pitons(m) 680.
porte-râteau(m) 583.
porte-rouleau(m) 292.
porte-sac(m) 679.
porte-savon(m) 292.
porte-serviettes(m) 292.
porte-spécimen(m) 717.
porte-stylo(m) 378, 379.
porte-tension(m) 569.
porte-timbres(m) 516.
porte-tube(m) 718.
porte-vent(m) 543.
**portée(f) 537.**
portefeuille(m) 379.
**portefeuille(m) chéquier(m) 379.**
**portes(f), types(m) 202.**
**portière(f) 429.**
portière(f) 427.
**portique(m) 786.**
portique(m) 172, 173, 455, 491, 660, 746, 747.
portique(m) de chargement(m) de conteneurs(m) 490.
portique(m) de signalisation(f) 464.
**posemètre(m) à visée(f) reflex 396.**
**posemètre(m) photo-électrique 396.**
positif(m) 831.
position(f) carpée 624.
position(f) de départ(m) 625.
position(f) des bras(m) 625.
position(f) des jambes(f) 625.
position(f) droite 624.
position(f) du ligament(m) 95.
position(f) en mode(m) solaire 419.
position(f) groupée 624.
position(f) repliée 48.
positionnement(m) du papier(m) 525.
positionneur(m) 561.
poste(m) 752.
poste(m) à clavier(m) 422.
poste(m) d'aiguillage(m) 464.
poste(m) de carburant(m) 823.
poste(m) de commandement(m) 805, 807.
poste(m) de communication(f) 477.
poste(m) de conduite(f) de la propulsion(f) 806.
poste(m) de contrôle(m) audio/vidéo 413.
poste(m) de débranchement(m) 465.
POSTE(M) DE PILOTAGE(M) 500.
poste(m) de pilotage(m) 498, 508, 510, 805.
poste(m) de soudage(m) 305.
poste(m) sans cordon(m) 422.
**poste(m) téléphonique 420.**
poste(m) téléphonique 413, 415, 417.
**postes(m) téléphoniques, types(m) 422.**
postillon(m) 697.
pot(m) d'échappement(m) 439, 443, 444.
poteau(m) 198, 455, 613, 618, 626.
poteau(m) cornier 198.
poteau(m) d'arrivée(f) 654.
poteau(m) de but(m) 604, 611.
poteau(m) de double(m) 614.
poteau(m) de simple(m) 614.
poteau(m) du ring(m) 669.
poteau(m) mural 199.
potence(f) 397, 447, 718, 727.
POTERIE(F) 584.
**poterie(f), outils(m) 584, 585.**
poterne(f) 179, 181.
potiron(m) 69.
pouce(m) 111, 112, 137, 327, 596.
poudre(f) 798, 799.
poudre(f) libre 366.
**poudre(f) pressée 366.**
poudrier(m) 366.
pouf(m) 222.
poulailler(m) 148.
poulaine(f) 792.
poule(f) 150.
poulie(f) 230, 302, 434, 684, 793.
poulie(f) de chariot(m) 786.
poumon(m) 97.
poumon(m) droit 124, 130.
poumon(m) gauche 124, 130.
Poupe(f) 13.
poupe(f) 496, 631.
pourcentage(m) 523, 830.
pourpoint(m) 316.
pourpre(m) 819.
pousse(f) 57.
poussière(f) 34, 35.
poussin(m) 150.
poussoir(m) 251, 290, 726.
poussoir(m) à pollen(m) 81.
poussoir(m) d'arrêt(m) 706.
poussoir(m) d'ouverture(f) 375.
poussoir(m) de mise(f) en marche(f) 706.
poussoir(m) de remise(f) à zéro(m) 706.
poussoir(m) pneumatique 734.
poutre(f) 198, 659, 756.
poutre(f) cantilever 454.
poutre(f) continue 454.
**poutre(f) d'équilibre(m) 659.**
poutre(f) de queue(f) 508.
poutre(f) suspendue 454.
poutre(f)-châssis(m) 784.
praire(f) 93.
prairie(f) 51, 149.
préblindage(m) 805.
précipitation(f) 34, 35.
PRÉCIPITATIONS(F) 36.
prémaxillaire(m) 86.
premier arbitre(m) 613.
premier but(m) 597.
premier croissant(m) 6.
premier espace(m) 610.
premier étage(m) 509.
premier juge(m) de ligne(f) 603.
premier quartier(m) 6.
premier radial(m) externe 121.
premier-but(m) 597.
première cabine(f) focale 15.
première molaire(f) 144.
première nageoire(f) dorsale 86.
première phalange(f) 103.
première prémolaire(f) 144.
premiers soins(m) 822.
premiers violons(m) 556.
prémolaire(f) 98.
prémolaires(f) 144.
preneur(m) de son(m) 412, 415.
préparation(f) avant éclipse(f) 419.
prépuce(m) 127.
près du ring(m) 669.
près(m) 629.
près(m) bon plein(m) 629.
près(m) serré 629.
présentoir(m) à revues(f) 522.
président(m) 666.
presse(f) 159.
presse(f) à pectoraux(m) 663.
**presse(f) à percussion(f) 579.**
**presse(f) à taille-douce(f) 581.**
**presse(f) lithographique 583.**
**presse-agrumes(m) 251.**
presse-agrumes(m) 243.
presse-ail(m) 243.
presse-ergots(m) 531.
presse-étoupe(m) 294.
presse-papier(m) 524, 531.
presseur(m) 390.
pression(f) à la taille(f) 350.
pression(f) au niveau(m) de la mer(f) 38.
pression(f) barométrique 38.
pression(f) devant 350.
**pression(f), mesure(f) 41.**
pressuriseur(m) 761, 762.
PRÉVENTION(F) DES INCENDIES(M) 777.
prime(f) 667.
**principales techniques(f) 588.**
**principaux amphibiens(m) 85.**
**principaux mouvements(m) 697.**
printemps(m) 8.
prise(f) avec borne(f) de terre(f) 216.
prise(f) casque(m) 402, 408, 555.
prise(f) chronométrée 255.
prise(f) classique 619.
prise(f) d'air(m) 445, 493.
prise(f) d'air(m) de ventilation(f) 14.
prise(f) d'eau(f) 747.
prise(f) de charge(f) 374.
prise(f) de courant(m) 309, 310, 401.
prise(f) de force(f) 147.
prise(f) de la sonde(f) thermique 253.
prise(f) de masse(f) 305.
prise(f) de raccordement(m) 561.
prise(f) de télécommande(f) 391.
prise(f) de terre(f) 309, 312, 400.
prise(f) électrique 449.
prise(f) porte-plume(m) 619.
**prises(f), judo(m) 668.**
**prises(f), tennis(m) sur table(f) 619.**
**prises(f), types(m) 619.**
prisme(m) de Porro 719.
prisme(m) pentagonal 390.
prix(m) à l'unité(f) 709.
prix(m) à payer 709.
procédé(m) 675.
processeur(m) de sons(m) 528.
production(f) d'électricité(f) 767.
**production(f) d'électricité(f) par énergie(f) nucléaire 766.**
**production(f) d'électricité(f) par énergie(f) solaire 771.**
production(f) d'électricité(f) par l'alternateur(m) 755.
production(f) de chaleur(f) 766.
**production(f) de l'électricité(f), étapes(f) 755.**
**produits(m) de la raffinerie(f) 744.**
produits(m) laitiers 33.
produits(m) pétrochimiques 745.
**profil(m) 363.**
profondeur(f) du foyer(m) 23.
profondimètre(m) 627.
programmateur(m) 257, 258, 259.
programmation(f) des voix(f) 555.
projecteur(m) 447, 459, 777.
projecteur(m) à faisceau(m) concentré 414.
projecteur(m) auxiliaire 16.
projecteur(m) d'ambiance(f) 414.
projecteur(m) d'ambiance(f) sur pantographe(m) 414.
**projecteur(m) de diapositives(f) 397.**
projecteur(m) de plafond(m) 41.
projecteur(m) orientable 778, 780.
projecteurs(m) 189.
projectile(m) antichar 804.
**projectiles(m) 801.**
projection(f) conique 50.
projection(f) cylindrique 50.
projection(f) d'épaule(f) par un côté(m) 668.
projection(f) en cercle(m) 668.
projection(f) horizontale 50.
projection(f) interrompue 50.
**projections(f) cartographiques 50.**
pronaos(m) 168, 169.
propulseur(m) 49, 512, 814.
propulseur(m) d'étrave(f) 497.
propulseur(m) radial 42.
prostate(f) 127.
protecteur(m) d'embout(m) 726.
protecteur(m) de poitrine(f) 595.
protecteur(m) lombaire 602.
PROTECTION(F) DE L'OUÏE(F) 729.
PROTECTION(F) DE LA TÊTE(F) 729.
PROTECTION(F) DES PIEDS(M) 730.
PROTECTION(F) DES VOIES(F) RESPIRATOIRES 730.
PROTECTION(F) DES YEUX(M) 729.
protection(f) obligatoire de l'ouïe(f) 821.
protection(f) obligatoire de la tête(f) 821.
protection(f) obligatoire de la vue(f) 821.
protection(f) obligatoire des mains(f) 821.
protection(f) obligatoire des pieds(m) 821.
protection(f) obligatoire des voies(f) respiratoires 821.
protège-côtes(m) 602.
protège-coude(m) 609.
protège-dents(m) 669.
protège-gorge(m) 595, 609.
protège-guidon(m) 796.
protège-hanche(m) 602.
protège-lame(m) 285, 644.
protège-lame(m) inférieur 284.
protège-lame(m) supérieur 284.
protège-matelas(m) 224.
protège-nuque(m) 777.
protège-orteils(m) 595, 730.
protège-poulie(m) 283.
protège-tendon(m) 644.
protège-tibia(m) 595, 600, 609.
protège-tympan(m) 729.
prothorax(m) 78.
protoneurone(m) sensitif 135.
protubérance(f) 6.
proue(f) 497, 631.
province(f) 51.
provision(f) d'eau(f) 755.
prune(f) 63.
psychromètre(m) 41.
pubis(m) 116, 118.
puisard(m) 215, 216, 736.
puits(m) d'accès(m) 752.
puits(m) d'extraction(f) 736.
puits(m) de dérive(f) 631.
puits(m) de lumière(f) 194.
puits(m) sous-marin 740.
puits(m) vertical 736.
pull(m) à capuche(f) 352.
pull(m) d'entraînement(m) 352.
**pulls(m) 338.**
pulpe(f) 62, 63, 64, 65, 137, 144.
pulvérisateur(m) 265.
pulvérisateur(m) tandem(m) 154.
**pulvériseur(m) tandem(m) 157.**
pulvino(m) 750.
punaises(f) 515.
pupille(f) 107, 140.
pupille(f) verticale 96.
pupitre(m) 539, 542, 555.
**pupitre(m) à musique(f) 539.**
pupitre(m) d'éclairage(m) 412.
pupitre(m) de commande(f) 500.
pupitre(m) de commandes(f) 16.
pupitre(m) de conduite(f) 468.
pupitre(m) de son(m) 407, 412, 415.
pupitre(m) dirigeur 422.
pupitre(m) du chef(m) d'orchestre(m) 556.
purgeur(m) 208.
purificateur(m) d'air(m) 210.
pyjama(m) 348.
**pylône(m) 756.**
pylône(m) 456, 464.
pylône(m) du moteur(m) 499.

## Q

quadruple croche(f) 538.
quai(m) 464, 475, 490.
quai(m) d'embarquement(m) 503.
quai(m) de chargement(m) 190.
quai(m) de gare(f) 462.
quart(m) de soupir(m) 538.
quart-arrière(m) 603, 605.
quart-de-rond(m) 199.
quarte(f) 537, 667.
quartier(m) 65, 104, 352, 354, 649.
quatre avec barreur(m) 632.
quatre sans barreur(m) 632.
QUATRE-MÂTS(M) BARQUE(F) 478, 480.
quatuor(m) 558.

Les termes en **caractères gras** renvoient à une illustration, ceux en CAPITALES indiquent un titre.

queue(f) 62, 63, 64, 96, 97, 101, 106, 107, 112, 127, 281, 499, 579, 633, 638, 645, 688, 773.
**queue(f) de billard(m) 675.**
queue(f) de gaz(m) 9.
queue(f) de l'hélix(m) 139.
queue(f) de poussières(f) 9.
queue-de-cochon(f) 586.
queusot(m) 232.
quille(f) 637, 683.
quille(f) chandelle(f) 683.
quille(f)-reine(f) 683.
**quilles(f), piste(f) 683.**
**quilles(f), types(m) 683.**
**quillier(m) 683.**
quillier(m) 683.
quinte(f) 537, 667, 695, 700.
quinte(f) royale 695.
quintette(m) 558.

## R

rabat(m) 322, 380.
rabatteur(m) 158, 160.
**rabot(m) 277.**
raccord(m) 300, 399.
**raccord(m) à collet(m) repoussé 300.**
**raccord(m) à compression(f) 300.**
raccord(m) à compression(f) 296.
raccord(m) d'arrivée(f) d'air(m) 304.
raccord(m) de réduction(f) 301.
raccord(m) de robinet(m) 265.
raccord(m) de signalisation(f) 449.
raccord(m) de tuyau(m) 264.
raccord(m) femelle 300.
raccord(m) mâle 300.
raccord(m) té(m) 298.
raccord(m) té(m) d'égout(m) 298.
**raccord(m) union(f) 300.**
raccordement(m) du flexible(m) 735.
**raccords(m) 301.**
**raccords(m) mécaniques 300.**
rachis(m) 110.
racine(f) 70, 144.
racine(f) antérieure 135.
racine(f) carrée 523.
racine(f) carrée de 830.
racine(f) de l'hélix(m) 139.
racine(f) de l'ongle(m) 137.
racine(f) du nez(m) 141.
racine(f) motrice 135.
racine(f) pivotante 59.
racine(f) postérieure 135.
racine(f) principale 57.
racine(f) secondaire 57.
racine(f) sensitive 135.
racine(f) traçante 59.
RACQUETBALL(M) 617.
**racquetball(m), balle(f) 617.**
**racquetball(m), raquette(f) 617.**
**racquetball(m), terrain(m) 617.**
RADAR(M) 722.
radar(m) 493, 494, 495, 497.
radar(m) d'appontage(m) 811.
radar(m) de contrôle(m) aérien 810.
radar(m) de détection(f) 809.
radar(m) de surveillance(f) aérienne 809, 811.
radar(m) de veille(f) de surface(f) 809, 810.
radar(m) météorologique 498.
**radiateur(m) 438.**
radiateur(m) 16, 208, 469.
**radiateur(m) à colonnes(f) 208.**
radiateur(m) bain(m) d'huile(f) 211.
radiateur(m) de batterie(f) 49.
radiateur(m) rayonnant 211.
radiateur(m) soufflant 211.
radicelle(f) 57, 59.
radier(m) 476, 492.
radio(f) 408, 639.
**radiocassette(f) 408.**
radiomètre(m) 42, 43.
RADIOTÉLESCOPE(M) 15.
radis(m) 71.
radius(m) 102, 112, 122.
radôme(m) 813.
raffinerie(f) 740.
**raffinerie(f), produits(m) 744.**
**raglan(m) 330.**
raie(f) des fesses(f) 117, 119.
raie(f) sourcilière 109.
raifort(m) 71.
rail(m) 230, 466, 568.
**rail(m) d'éclairage(m) 235.**
rail(m) de glissement(m) 428, 630.
rail(m) de guidage(m) 15, 441.
rail(m) de lancement(m) de missile(m) 813.
rail(m) de raccord(m) 467.
rail(m) et retour(m) de courant(m) 476.
rail(m) guide(m)-film(m) 390.
**rail(m), joint(m) 466.**
**rail(m), profil(m) 466.**
**rainette(f) 85.**
rainure(f) 562, 568, 598, 641, 678, 793.
rainure(f) du guide(m) à onglet(m) 285.
rainure(f) du guide(m) de refend(m) 285.
**raisin(m) 62.**
raisin(m) 61, 62.
ralenti(m) 411.
rallonge(f) 219, 260.
rallonge(f) du plateau(m) 285.
ramasseur(m) 159, 162, 613, 614.
**ramasseuse(f)-presse(f) 159.**
ramasseuse(f)-presse(f) 155.
rame(f) 664.
**rame(f) de métro(m) 476.**
rame(f) de métro(m) 474.
**rameau(m) 58.**
rameau(m) 57, 59, 61.
rameau(m) communicant 135.
ramequin(m) 238.
**rameur(m) 664.**
ramille(f) 59.
rampant(m) 168.
rampe(f) 168, 188, 201, 733.
rampe(f) d'accès(m) 456, 494.
rampe(f) d'éclairage(m) 235.
rampe(f) de livraison(f) 184.
rampe(f) de quai(m) 490.
rampe(f) de signalisation(f) 779.
ramure(f) 59.
rang(m) 373.
rangement(m) 461.
râpe(f) 243, 587.
**râper, ustensils(m) pour 243.**
rapière(f) 794.
rappel(m) de mémoire(f) 396, 523.
rapporteur(m) d'angle(m) 713.
RAQUETTE(F) 645.
**raquette(f) algonquine 645.**
**raquette(f) de badminton(m) 618.**
**raquette(f) de racquetball(m) 617.**
**raquette(f) de squash(m) 616.**
**raquette(f) de tennis(m) 615.**
**raquette(f) de tennis(m) de table(f) 619.**
ras-de-cou(m) 326, 361.
rasette(f) 542.
**rasoir(m) à double tranchant(m) 374.**
**rasoir(m) à manche(m) 374.**
rasoir(m) effileur 369.
**rasoir(m) électrique 374.**
rasoir(m) jetable 374.
RASOIRS(M) 374.
rat(m) de cave(f) 582.
rate(f) 88, 124.
**râteau(m) 159, 674.**
râteau(m) 155, 267, 583.
ratissoire(f) 266.
ravier(m) 238.
**ravitaillement(m) en vol(m) 813.**
ravitailleur(m) 813.
rayon(m) 375, 447.
rayon(m) de miel(m) 82.
**rayon(m) de miel(m), coupe(f) 82.**
rayon(m) épineux 86.
rayon(m) médullaire 59.
rayon(m) mou 87.
rayon(m) solaire réfléchi 770, 771.
rayonnement(m) solaire 768, 769, 770, 771, 772.
ré(m) 537.
réacteur(m) 759, 764, 766, 806.
**réacteur(m) à eau(f) bouillante 763.**
**réacteur(m) à eau(f) lourde 761.**
**réacteur(m) à eau(f) sous pression(f) 762.**
**réacteur(m) au gaz(m) carbonique 760.**
**réacteur(m) nucléaire 765.**
réaction(f) réversible 831.
réalisateur(m) 412, 415.
rebobinage(m) 391, 403, 408, 411, 420, 831.
rebord(m) 255.
rebord(m) de cuve(f) 258.
rebras(m) 327.
récamier(m) 221.
réceptacle(m) 60, 62.
réceptacle(m) de brosses(f) 373.
réceptacle(m) pour les pièces(f) refusées 702.
récepteur(m) 15, 420.
récepteur(m) de grain(m) 161.
récepteur(m) de son(m) 726.
récepteur(m) sensoriel 134.
réception(f) des messages(m) 421.
réception(f) directe 416.
réception(f) du fret(m) 505.
recette(f) 736.
**receveur(m) 595.**
receveur(m) 597, 614, 616, 618.
recharge(f) 389.
recharge(f) amont 748.
recharge(f) aval 748.
réchaud(m) 248.
**réchaud(m) à deux feux(m) 689.**
réchaud(m) à un feu(m) 689.
réchauffeur(m) 758.
recherche(f) des canaux(m) 411.
récipient(m) 40, 250.
récipient(m) collecteur 40.
RÉCOLTER 159, 160, 162.
**récolter 155.**
reconcentration(f) de l'oxyde(m) de deutérium(m) 759.
recourbe-cils(m) 367.
rectangle(m) des instructeurs(m) 597.
rectangulaire 687.
rectrice(f) 109.
rectum(m) 127, 128, 131.
recyclable 831.
recyclé 831.
redingote(f) 331.
réduction(f) mâle-femelle 301.
réduction(f) mâle-femelle hexagonale 301.
réduction(f)/agrandissement(m) 532.
réflecteur(m) 310, 393, 441.
réflecteur(m) parabolique 15, 415.
réflecteur(m) radar(m) 487.
réflecteur(m) secondaire 15.
réflecteurs(m) solaires 418.
réformeur(m) catalytique 744.
refouloir(m) 801.
**réfrigérateur(m) 254.**
réfrigérateur(m) 254.
refroidissement(m) 744.
refroidissement(m) de la vapeur(f) par l'eau(f) 767.
refroidisseur(m) d'air(m) 438.
refroidisseur(m) de la salle(f) des générateurs(m) de vapeur(f) 759.
regard(m) 209.
regard(m) de prélèvement(m) 216.
regard(m) de visite(f) 186.
régie(f) 189, 407.
**régie(f) de production(f) 413.**
régie(f) de production(f) 412, 415.
régie(f) du son(m) 412, 415.
régie(f) image(f) 415.
régie(f) image(f)/éclairage(m) 412.
RÉGIE(F), RADIO(F) 407.
**régies(f), télévision(f) 412.**
région(f) auriculaire 109.
région(f) malaire 109.
région(f) négative 768.
région(f) positive 768.
**régions(f) de balisage(m) 488.**
registre(m) coulissant 543.
registre(m) de comptabilité(f) 518.
registre(m) de réglage(m) 206.
registre(m) des aigus(m) 536.
registre(m) des basses(f) 536.
réglage(m) 728.
réglage(m) de centrage(m) 529.
réglage(m) de hausse(f) 718.
réglage(m) de l'afficheur(m) 420.
réglage(m) de l'angle(m) 277.
réglage(m) de l'écran(m) de l'ordinateur(m) 512.
réglage(m) de la hauteur(f) 659, 661, 664.
réglage(m) de la luminosité(f) 529.
réglage(m) de la pression(f) 373.
réglage(m) de la pression(f) d'oxygène(m) 512.
réglage(m) de la profondeur(f) 277.
réglage(m) de la résistance(f) 664.
réglage(m) de la température(f) 213, 705.
réglage(m) de la tension(f) 671.
réglage(m) de la tonalité(f) 547.
réglage(m) de la vitesse(f) d'obturation(f) 396.
réglage(m) de largeur(f) de point(m) 561.
réglage(m) de niveau(m) d'enregistrement(m) 403.
réglage(m) de pression(f) 561.
réglage(m) de profondeur(f) 283.
réglage(m) de tempo(m) 555.
réglage(m) des températures(f) 256.
réglage(m) du contraste(m) 529.
réglage(m) du diaphragme(m) 718.
réglage(m) du four(m) 255.
réglage(m) du pas(m) 711.
réglage(m) du pointeau(m) du fluide(m) 304.
réglage(m) du seuil(m) d'alarme(f) 485.
réglage(m) du viseur(m) 409.
réglage(m) du volume(m) 402, 408, 411, 547, 555.
réglage(m) du volume(m) des communications(f) 512.
réglage(m) en hauteur(f) 397, 399.
réglage(m) en hauteur(f) du condenseur(m) 718.
réglage(m) horizontal 529.
réglage(m) latéral 718.
réglage(m) micrométrique (azimut(m)) 720, 721.
réglage(m) micrométrique (latitude(f)) 720, 721.
réglage(m) sur demi-teinte(f) 396.
réglage(m) sur haute lumière(f) 396.
réglage(m) sur ombre(f) 396.
réglage(m) vertical 529.
règle(f) 578, 591.
règle(f) d'équerrage(m) 578.
règle(f) de couture(f) 563.
règle(f) du guide(m) de refend(m) 285.
règle(f) graduée 688.
règle-point(m) 561.
réglette(f) 573.
régulateur(m) 297.
régulateur(m) de carburant(m) 501.
**régulateur(m) de pression(f) 306.**
régulateur(m) de pression(f) 248, 306, 689.
rein(m) 89, 97, 101, 117, 124.
rein(m) droit 132.
rein(m) gauche 132.
reine(f), abeille(f) 81.
reins(m) 119.
rejet(m) 59.
relais(m) d'accessoires(m) 501.
relève-bras(m) 404.
relèvement(m) de la lame(f) 285.
releveur(m) de fil(m) 561.
**relief(m) lunaire 7.**
reliure(f) à glissière(f) 519.
reliure(f) à pince(f) 519.
reliure(f) à ressort(m) 519.
reliure(f) à vis(f) 519.
RELIURE(F) D'ART(M) 577, 578.
reliure(f) spirale(f) 519.
rembourrage(m) 635.
rémige(f) primaire 110.
rémige(f) secondaire 110.
rémige(f) tertiaire 110.
remise(f) 193, 263.
remise(f) à zéro(m) 532.
remontée(f) continentale 29.
remontoir(m) 539, 706, 707.
remorque(f) 156, 162, 440, 476, 633.
remorque(f) à bagages(m) 507.
rempart(m) 7, 178, 180.
remplage(m) 175.
remplissage(m) 741.
rêne(f) 651.
rêne(f) de bride(f) 649.
rêne(f) de filet(m) 649.
renfort(m) de culasse(f) 800.
renfort(m) de pointe(f) 644.
réniforme 56.
renne(m) 105.
renseignements(m) 823.
rentré(m) 565.
renvoi(m) 215, 298.
renvoi(m) d'eau(f) 399.
**repassage(m) 829.**
repasser à basse température(f) 829.
repasser à haute température(f) 829.
repasser à moyenne température(f) 829.
repère(m) 612, 710.
repère(m) de distance(f) 651.
repère(m) de ligne(f) de marche(f) 719.
repère(m) de niveau(m) d'eau(f) 256.
repère(m) de touche(f) 546, 547.
repère(m) de virage(m) de dos(m) 621.
répertoire(m) téléphonique 420, 516.
repli(m) 315.
**répondeur(m) téléphonique 420.**
report(m) de lecture(f) 396.

Les termes en **caractères gras** renvoient à une illustration, ceux en CAPITALES indiquent un titre.

repose-bras(m) 404.
repose-pied(m) 727.
repose-pied(m) du passager(m) 443, 444.
repose-pied(m) du pilote(m) 443, 444.
repositionnement(m) 525.
repousse-chair(m) 365.
reprise(f) d'air(m) 206, 207.
REPTILE(M) 96.
**réseau(m) d'oléoducs(m) 740.**
réseau(m) de transport(m) d'électricité(f) 771.
réseau(m) national 416.
réseau(m) nerveux 144.
réseau(m) privé 416.
réseau(m) téléphonique 417.
réserve(f) d'eau(f) 373.
réserve(f) de papier(m) 532.
réservoir(m) 216, 247, 386, 399, 543, 689, 746, 747, 748, 749, 750, 751, 780.
réservoir(m) à carburant(m) 440, 468, 508, 805, 812.
réservoir(m) à essence(f) 442.
réservoir(m) à grain(m) 160.
**réservoir(m) à toit(m) fixe 741.**
**réservoir(m) à toit(m) flottant 741.**
réservoir(m) auxiliaire 441.
réservoir(m) d'air(m) comprimé 469.
réservoir(m) d'alcool(m) 705.
réservoir(m) d'arrosage(m) 759, 766.
réservoir(m) d'azote(m) liquide 717.
réservoir(m) d'eau(f) 210.
réservoir(m) d'essence(f) 272.
réservoir(m) d'huile(f) 272.
réservoir(m) d'hydrogène(m) liquide 509.
réservoir(m) d'oxygène(m) liquide 509.
réservoir(m) de brut(m) 744.
réservoir(m) de chasse(f) d'eau(f) 292.
réservoir(m) de fluide(m) 212.
réservoir(m) de kérosène(m) 509.
réservoir(m) de mercure(m) 705.
réservoir(m) de sécurité(f) 761.
réservoir(m) de stockage(m) 772.
réservoir(m) externe 510.
réservoir(m) magmatique 25.
réservoir(m) propane(m) 449.
réservoir(m) tampon(m) 740.
réservoirs(m) 511.
résistance(f) hydraulique 664.
résonnateur(m) 406.
ressort(m) 234, 278, 290, 294, 389, 659, 804.
**ressort(m) athlétique 665.**
ressort(m) compensateur de fil(m) 562.
ressort(m) d'échappement(m) 541.
ressort(m) de batterie(f) 795.
ressort(m) de rappel(m) 432.
ressort(m) de soupape(f) 434, 543.
ressort(m) de suspension(f) 258, 469.
ressort(m) de tension(f) 431, 665.
ressort(m) en spirale(f) 231.
restaurant(m) 185, 190, 494, 822.
rétenteur(m) 653.
Réticule(f) 13.
réticule(m) 718.
réticulum(m) endoplasmique 115.
rétine(f) 140.
retombées(f) 35.
retour(m) 521.
retour(m) de chariot(m) 525.
retour(m) de l'eau(f) au générateur(m) de vapeur(f) 767.
RETOURNER LA TERRE(F) 156.
**retourner la terre(f) 154.**
retrait(m) 524.
rétroviseur(m) 430, 440, 442, 444.
rétroviseur(m) extérieur 426.
réunion(f) 830.
réverbère(m) 186.
revers(m) 322, 323, 341, 354.
revers(m) à cran(m) aigu 322.
revers(m) cranté 319, 320.
revêtement(m) 198, 199, 619, 741.
revêtement(m) de sécurité(f) 512.
revêtement(m) intérieur 433.
revêtement(m) thermique 510.
**revêtement(m), matériaux(m) 286.**
REVOLVER(M) 797.
**rez-de-chaussée(m) 194.**
rez-de-chaussée(m) 197.
rhéostat(m) 309.
rhino-pharynx(m) 141.
rhubarbe(f) 72.
ribosome(m) 115.
richelieu(m) 354.
**rideau(m) 229.**
rideau(m) 229, 414.
**rideau(m) ballon(m) 229.**
rideau(m) bonne femme(f) 228.
rideau(m) brise-bise(m) 228.
**rideau(m) coulissé 228.**
rideau(m) d'obturateur(m) 390.
rideau(m) de fer(m) 188.
rideau(m) de scène(f) 188, 189.
**rideau(m) de vitrage(m) 228.**
**rideau(m) flottant 228.**
rideau(m) pare-vent(m) 14.
**rideaux(m) croisés 229.**
**rideaux(m), types(m) 228.**
ridoir(m) 630.
rifloir(m) 587.
rift(f) 28.
rigole(f) 682.
rimaye(f) 26.
rinceau(m) 220.
**ring(m) 669.**
risberme(f) 748.
rive(f) 288, 752.
rive(f) externe 104.
rive(f) interne 104.
rivet(m) 242, 278.
rivière(f) 51.
rivière(f) souterraine 24.
riz(m) 152.
robe(f) 741.
**robe(f) à crinoline(f) 318.**
**robe(f) à paniers(m) 317.**
**robe(f) à tournure(f) 316.**
robe(f) bain(m)-de-soleil(m) 332.
robe(f) chemisier(m) 333.
robe(f) de maison(f) 333.
robe(f) enveloppe(f) 333.
robe(f) fourreau(m) 332.
robe(f) princesse(f) 332.
robe(f) taille(f) basse 332.
robe(f) tee-shirt(m) 351.
robe(f) trapèze(m) 332.
robe(f) tunique(f) 333.
robe(f)-manteau(m) 332.
robe(f)-polo(m) 333.
**robes(f), types(m) 332.**
**robinet(m) 294.**
robinet(m) 292.
robinet(m) d'acétylène(m) 306.
robinet(m) d'arrêt(m) 293, 296, 298.
robinet(m) d'arrêt(m) général 215.
robinet(m) d'oxygène(m) 306.
robinet(m) de réglage(m) de débit(m) 777.
robinet(m) de vidange(f) 297, 741.
robinet(m) flotteur à clapet(m) 293.
robinet(m) relais(m) 689.
robinets(m) de carburant(m) 500.
**robot(m) de cuisine(f) 251.**
roc(m) 714.
rocaille(f) 263.
roches(f) d'intrusion(f) 23.
roches(f) ignées 23.
roches(f) métamorphiques 23.
roches(f) sédimentaires 23.
rochet(m) 281, 706, 707.
Roi(m) 695, 696.
romaine(f) 73.
romarin(m) 74.
rond pronateur(m) 120.
rond-point(m) 52.
ronde(f) 538.
rondeau(m) 584.
**rondelle(f) 608.**
rondelle(f) 294, 641, 642.
rondelle(f) à denture(f) extérieure 278.
rondelle(f) à denture(f) intérieure 278.
rondelle(f) à ressort(m) 278.
rondelle(f) conique 293.
rondelle(f) de fibre(f) 300.
rondelle(f) plate 278.
**rondelles(f) 278.**
rondiste(m) 363.
**rongeur(m), mâchoire(f) 98.**
ros(m) 572.
rosace(f) 546.
rose(f) 175.
rose(f) des vents(m) 484.
rosée(f) 37.
rosette(f) 167, 289, 290.
rostre(m) 90.
rotonde(f) 190.
rotor(m) 161, 290, 437, 753, 773, 774.
rotor(m) anticouple 508.
rotule(f) 103, 122, 282.
**roue(f) 433.**
roue(f) 270, 427, 440, 727, 753, 800, 805.
roue(f) à rayons(m) 652.
roue(f) avant 147, 784.
roue(f) d'échappement(m) 706, 707.
roue(f) d'engrenage(m) 280, 575.
roue(f) d'entraînement(m) 575.
roue(f) de centre(m) 706, 707.
roue(f) de champ(m) 706.
roue(f) de poulie(f) 230.
roue(f) de pression(f) 158.
roue(f) de sécurité(f) 476.
roue(f) de support(m) 445.
roue(f) de turbine(f) 752.
roue(f) dentée 445, 573.
roue(f) folle 783.
**roue(f) Francis 754.**
**roue(f) Kaplan 754.**
roue(f) libre 448.
roue(f) motrice 147, 707.
**roue(f) Pelton 754.**
roue(f) petite moyenne 706, 707.
roue(f) pivotante 727.
roues(f) motrices 784.
rouge(m) 700, 701.
rouge(m) à lèvres(f) 366.
Rouges(m) 697.
rough(m) 676.
**rouleau(m) 304.**
rouleau(m) 231, 270, 369, 583, 702.
rouleau(m) à pâtisserie(f) 245.
rouleau(m) à vernir 582.
rouleau(m) conditionneur 158.
rouleau(m) d'encrage(m) 581.
rouleau(m) de pellicule(f) 395.
rouleau(m) principal 572.
**roulette(f) 563.**
roulette(f) 260, 383, 553, 582, 645, 788.
**roulette(f) américaine 700.**
roulette(f) de pâtissier(m) 245.
**roulette(f) française 701.**
route(f) 52, 452.
route(f) d'accès(m) 502.
route(f) secondaire 52.
**route(f), coupe(f) 450.**
ruban(m) 566, 711, 804.
ruban(m) adhésif 607.
ruban(m) blanc 618.
ruban(m) correcteur 515.
ruban(m) de caoutchouc(m) 677.
ruban(m) de tissu(m) adhésif 725.
rubis(m) 363, 706.
**ruche(f) 82.**
ruche(f) 149.
ruché(m) 349.
rue(f) 52, 184, 190.
RUE(F), COUPE(F) 186.
RUGBY(M) 606.
**rugby(m), terrain(m) 606.**
ruisseau(m) 676.
ruissellement(m) 32, 34.
russule(f) verdoyante 55.
rutabaga(m) 71.

## S

sable(m) 748, 819.
sablier(m) 244.
sablière(f) 469.
sablière(f) double 198.
**sabot(m) 104.**
sabot(m) 101, 441, 633, 656.
sabot(m) à 1 doigt(m) 99.
sabot(m) à 2 doigts(m) 99.
sabot(m) à 3 doigts(m) 99.
sabot(m) à 4 doigts(m) 99.
sabot(m) de protection(f) 783.
**sabot(m), face(f) plantaire 104.**
SABOTS(M), TYPES(M) 99.
sabre(m) 666, 794.
sabreur(m) 667.
sac(m) 536.
**sac(m) à bandoulière(f) 380.**
sac(m) à dos(m) 680.
sac(m) à provisions(f) 381.
**sac(m) accordéon(m) 380.**
sac(m) besace(f) 380.
sac(m) boîte(f) 381.
**sac(m) cartable(m) 380.**
**sac(m) de golf(m) 679.**
**sac(m) de vol(m) 382.**
sac(m) fourre-tout(m) 380, 382.
sac(m) marin(m) 381.
sac(m) polochon(m) 381.
sac(m) pour accessoires(m) 684.
**sac(m) seau(m) 381.**
sacoche(f) 448.
sacrum(m) 122, 123.
SACS(M) À MAIN(F) 380.
**sacs(m) de couchage(m) 687.**
Sagittaire(m) 13.
Sagittaire(m) (22 novembre) 820.
**saharienne(f) 338.**
saillant(m) 178.
saisie(f) des données(f) 717.
SAISONS(F), CYCLE(M) 8.
saladier(m) 238.
salamandre(f) 85.
salière(f) 238.
salle(f) 189.
salle(f) à manger 195, 460, 496, 807.
salle(f) d'embarquement(m) 505.
SALLE(F) DE BAINS(M) 292.
salle(f) de bains(m) 194, 195.
salle(f) de bal(m) 497.
salle(f) de commande(f) 746, 759.
salle(f) de commandes(f) 14.
salle(f) de contrôle(m) 16.
salle(f) de contrôle(m) des machines(f) 742.
salle(f) de prière(f) 172, 173.
salle(f) de projection(f) 16.
salle(f) de réception(f) 172, 173.
salle(f) de répétition(f) 188.
salle(f) de séjour(m) 195.
SALLE(F) DE SPECTACLE(M) 188.
salle(f) de stockage(m) du combustible(m) neuf 764.
salle(f) des cartes(f) 494.
salle(f) des gradateurs(m) 412.
salle(f) des machines(f) 496, 746, 747.
salle(f) des ordinateurs(m) 807.
salle(f) des pas(m) perdus 462.
salle(f) du treuil(m) 735.
salle(f) polyvalente 412.
salomé(m) 356.
salon(m) 195, 496.
salopette(f) 336.
**salopette(f) à bretelles(f) croisées 351.**
**salopette(f) à dos(m) montant 350.**
salsifis(m) 71.
sandale(f) 356, 791.
sandalette(f) 357.
Sandow®(m) 685, 686.
sangle(f) 428, 614, 634, 649, 651, 660, 664, 679, 777.
sangle(f) d'amortissement(m) 729.
sangle(f) de brancard(m) 653.
sangle(f) de nuque(f) 729.
sangle(f) élastique 382.
sangle(f) serre-vêtements(m) 383.
sangle(f) sous-ventrière 653.
sanglon(m) 649.
sanguine(f) 583.
**sapeur(m)-pompier(m) 777.**
saphir(m) 363.
sarcloir(m) 266.
sarment(m) 61.
sarrazin(m) 152.
sarriette(f) 74.
sas(m) 14, 493, 510.
sas(m) d'accès(m) arrière 806.
sas(m) du bâtiment(m) du réacteur(m) 758.
sas(m) du laboratoire(m) 511.
sas(m) pour équipement(m) 764.
satellite(m) 416.
**satellite(m) à défilement(m) 43.**
satellite(m) artificiel 19.
SATELLITE(M) DE TÉLÉDÉTECTION(F) 48.
**satellite(m) géostationnaire 42.**
SATELLITE(M) MÉTÉOROLOGIQUE 42.
**satellite(m) Radarsat 49.**
**satellites(m) 4.**
SATELLITES(M) DE TÉLÉCOMMUNICATIONS(F) 418.
**satellites(m) de télécommunications(f), exemples(m) 418.**
satin(m) 576.
Saturne 5.
saucière(f) 238.
sauge(f) 74.
saumon(m) d'aile(f) 638.
saupoudreuse(f) 246.
**saut(m) à la perche(f) 657.**
saut(m) à la perche(f) 655.
**saut(m) en hauteur(f) 657.**
saut(m) en hauteur(f) 654.
sauterelle(f) 77, 733.
**sauteur(m) 635.**
sauteuse(f) 249.
sautoir(m) 361.
sautoir(m), longueur(f) opéra(m) 361.
savane(f) 45.

Les termes en **caractères gras** renvoient à une illustration, ceux en CAPITALES indiquent un titre.

saveur(f) acide 143.
saveur(f) amère 143.
saveur(f) salée 143.
saveur(f) sucrée 143.
saxhorn(m) 551.
**saxophone(m) 548.**
saxophone(m) 548.
scanneur(m) 526.
scanneur(m) à hyperfréquences(f) 43.
scanneur(m) de radiations(f) terrestres 43.
SCAPHANDRE(M) SPATIAL 512.
scapulaire(f) 110.
scarole(f) 73.
**scène(f) 189.**
scène(f) 188.
**scie(f) à chaîne(f) 272.**
scie(f) à grecquer 578.
**scie(f) à métaux(m) 277.**
scie(f) à métaux(m) 299.
**scie(f) circulaire 284.**
scie(f) d'élagage(m) 269.
scie(f) de camping(m) 690.
**scie(f) égoïne 277.**
scion(m) 670.
sclérotique(f) 140.
score(m) doublé 698.
score(m) triplé 698.
Scorpion(m) 13.
Scorpion(m) (24 octobre) 820.
scorsonère(f) 71.
scotie(f) 166, 167.
scrotum(m) 116, 127.
sculpture(f) 147, 586.
SCULPTURE(F) SUR BOIS(M) 586.
sculptures(f) 433.
seau(m) isotherme 251.
sébile(f) de remboursement(m) 422.
sécateur(m) 269.
**séchage(m) 829.**
**sèche-cheveux(m) 370.**
**sèche-linge(m) électrique 259.**
sécher à plat 829.
sécher par culbutage(m) à basse température(f) 829.
sécher par culbutage(m) à moyenne ou haute température(f) 829.
séchoir(m) d'épreuves(f) 399.
second arbitre(m) 613.
second juge(m) de ligne(f) 603.
second renfort(m) 800.
seconde nageoire(f) dorsale 86.
seconde(f) 537, 667, 830.
secondeur(m) au centre(m) 603, 605.
secondeur(m) extérieur droit 603, 605.
secondeur(m) extérieur gauche 603, 605.
seconds violons(m) 556.
secrétaire(m) 226, 612, 626.
secteur(m) maintenance(f) 415.
section(f) de conduit(m) 205.
section(f) raffinerie(f) 738.
section(f) tubulaire 738.
segment(m) 432, 434.
segment(m) abdominal 78.
segment(m) de loin 376.
segment(m) de près 376.
seigle(m) 152.
SEIN(M) 129.
sein(m) 116, 118.
SÉISME(M) 23.
seizième(m) de soupir(m) 538.
séjour(m) 685.
sélecteur(m) 214.
sélecteur(m) d'enceintes(f) 402.
sélecteur(m) de bandes(f) 403.
sélecteur(m) de contrôle(m) audio 413.
sélecteur(m) de contrôle(m) vidéo 413.
sélecteur(m) de coupe(f) 374.
sélecteur(m) de fonctions(f) 391.
sélecteur(m) de micro(m) 547.
sélecteur(m) de niveau(m) d'eau(f) 258.
sélecteur(m) de points(m) 561.
sélecteur(m) de programme(m) 555.
sélecteur(m) de régime(m) 271.
sélecteur(m) de rythme(m) 555.
sélecteur(m) de stations(f) 402, 408.
sélecteur(m) de température(f) 253, 258, 259, 370.
sélecteur(m) de vitesse(f) 251, 370, 404.
sélecteur(m) de vitesses(f) 443, 444.
sélecteur(m) de voix(f) 555.
sélecteur(m) télé(f)/vidéo(f) 411.
sélecteur(m) vidéo auxiliaire 413.
sélecteurs(m) de fonctions(f) 420.
sélecteurs(m) de mode(m) 408.
sélection(f) des canaux(m) 411.
**selle(f) 649.**
selle(f) 445, 446, 648, 651, 661, 664.
selle(f) biplace 443.
selle(f) de rail(m) 466.
sellette(f) 586, 636, 653.
sellette(f) d'attelage(m) 440.
sémaphore(m) 464.
**semelle(f) 358.**
semelle(f) 198, 199, 256, 277, 284, 325, 633, 640, 641, 644, 678.
semelle(f) antidérapante 350.
semelle(f) d'usure(f) 353, 355.
semelle(f) de chargeur(m) 797.
semelle(f) du battant(m) 572.
semelle(f) intercalaire 352.
semelle(f) pivotante 282.
SEMER 158.
**semer 154.**
semi-rectangulaire 687.
**semi-remorque(f) 441.**
semi-remorque(f) 440, 742.
**semi-remorque(f) citerne(f) 742.**
**semi-remorque(f) plate-forme(f) 441.**
semoir(m) à main(f) 268.
**semoir(m) en lignes(f) 158.**
semoir(m) en lignes(f) 154.
senestre(f) 818.
SENS(M) DE L'ODORAT(M) 142.
SENS(M) DU GOÛT(M) 142.
senseur(m) d'équilibrage(m) des blancs(m) 409.
senseur(m) stellaire 16.
sensibilité(f) du film(m) 391, 396.
sep(m) 156.
sépale(m) 60, 62, 64.
séparateur(m) 216, 439, 742, 758.
séparateur(m) d'eau(f) 734.
séparateur(m) de gaz(m) 738.
séparateur(m) liquide(m)/gaz(m) 439.
séparation(f) lanceur(m)/satellite(m) 419.
séparation(f)-classeur(m) 378.
septième(f) 537.
septime(f) 667.
septum(m) interventriculaire 125.
septum(m) lucidum 134.
séquence(f) 695.
**séquence(f) de manipulation(f) du combustible(m) 764.**
sérac(m) 26.
serfouette(f) 266.
sergé(m) 576.
**seringue(f) 726.**
seringue(f) pour lavage(m) de cavités(f) 726.
serpe(f) 269.
Serpent(m) 11, 13.
**serpent(m) à sonnettes(f) 97.**
**serpent(m) venimeux, tête(f) 96.**
serpentin(m) 255, 635.
serpentin(m) de l'évaporateur(m) 214.
serpentin(m) du condenseur(m) 214.
serpette(f) 269.
serre(f) 111, 149.
**serre-joint(m) 282.**
serre-joint(m) 575.
serre-livres(m) 517.
serre-poignet(m) 615.
serre-tête(m) 406, 408, 615, 642, 729, 730.
**serre-tête(m) antibruit 729.**
SERRURE(F) 289, 290.
serrure(f) 202, 225, 289, 380, 383, 429.
serrure(f) à clé(f) 378.
serrure(f) à combinaison(f) 378.
**serrure(f) à mortaiser 290.**
serrure(f) de porte(f) 427.
**serrure(f) tubulaire 290.**
sertissage(m) 799.
sertissure(f) 364.
serveur(m) 613, 614, 616, 618.
**service(m) à fondue(f) 248.**
service(m) d'entretien(m) 453.
service(m) de colis(m) 462.
**serviette(f) 378.**
servomoteur(m) 814.
seuil(m) 202.
seuil(m) de déversoir(m) 746.
**sextant(m) 484.**
Sextant(m) 13.
sextuor(m) 558.
shekel(m) 832.
short(m) 336, 351, 600, 656.
short(m) boxeur(m) 353.
si(m) 537.
siège(m) 220, 223, 293, 294, 428, 584, 639, 649, 652, 727.
siège(m) coulissant 664.
siège(m) double 477.
siège(m) du commandant(m) 500.
siège(m) du copilote(m) 500.
siège(m) éjectable 813.
siège(m) réglable 460.
siège(m) simple 477.
**siège(m)-baquet(m) 428.**
SIÈGES(M) 222.
sifflet(m) 252.
signal(m) de position(f) d'aiguille(f) 467.
signal(m) lumineux 539.
signal(m) sonore 539.
signalisation(f) lumineuse 826, 827.
SIGNALISATION(F) MARITIME 486.
SIGNALISATION(F) ROUTIÈRE 824, 826, 828.
**signes(m) d'air(m) 820.**
**signes(m) d'eau(f) 820.**
**signes(m) de feu(m) 820.**
SIGNES(M) DE PONCTUATION(F) 832.
**signes(m) de terre(f) 820.**
SIGNES(M) DIACRITIQUES 832.
SIGNES(M) DU ZODIAQUE(M) 820.
silencieux(m) 735.
silex(m) 795.
**silique(f), coupe(f) 67.**
sill(m) 24.
sillet(m) 544, 546, 547.
sillon(m) antérieur 139.
sillon(m) concentrique 404.
sillon(m) de départ(m) 404.
sillon(m) de sortie(f) 404.
sillon(m) médian 143.
sillon(m) naso-labial 141.
sillon(m) terminal 143.
silo(m) de chargement(m) 734.
silo(m)-couloir(m) 149.
silo(m)-tour(f) 149.
silos(m) 490.
simple torsade(f) 281.
simulateur(m) d'escalier(m) 664.
sinople(m) 819.
sinus(m) 315.
sinus(m) frontal 141.
sinus(m) latéral inférieur 61.
sinus(m) latéral supérieur 61.
sinus(m) palléal 95.
sinus(m) pétiolaire 61.
sinus(m) sphénoïdal 141.
siphon(m) 24, 215, 293, 296, 301.
sismogramme(m) 714.
sismographe(m) horizontal 714.
sixain(m) 700, 701.
sixte(f) 537, 667.
ski(m) 445, 641.
SKI(M) ALPIN 640.
**ski(m) de figure(f) 633.**
SKI(M) DE FOND(M) 642.
**ski(m) de fond(m) 642.**
ski(m) de fond(m) 642.
ski(m) de saut(m) 633.
**ski(m) de slalom(m) 633.**
**ski(m) de tourisme(m) 633.**
SKI(M) NAUTIQUE 633.
**skieur(m) alpin 640.**
**skieuse(f) de fond(m) 642.**
skiff(m) 632.
skip(m) 736.
**skis(m) nautiques, types(m) 633.**
slip(m) 347.
slip(m) de bain(m) 353.
**slip(m) ouvert 325.**
**snooker(m) 673.**
soc(m) 156.
socle(m) 40, 204, 236, 250, 252, 283, 404, 453, 579, 707, 708, 712, 714, 774.
socle(m) fixe 282.
socle(m)-chargeur(m) 260.
socque(m) 357.
socquette(f) 344.
soie(f) 239, 242, 291, 374, 670.
soie(f) dentaire 373.
soies(f) 304.
soigneur(m) 669.
sol(m) 537, 750.
sol(m) naturel 450.
sole(f) 104.
soléaire(m) 120.
SOLEIL(M) 6.
Soleil(m) 4, 8.
SOLEIL(M), ÉCLIPSE(F) 8.
**Soleil(m), structure(f) 6.**
soleret(m) 792.
solin(m) 205.
solive(f) 200.
solive(f) de plafond(m) 198.
solive(f) de plancher(m) 198, 199.
solive(f) de rive(f) 198, 199.
solstice(m) d'été(m) 8.
solstice(m) d'hiver(m) 8.
sommation(f) 830.
sommet(m) 27.
sommier(m) 174, 540, 543.
sommier(m) tapissier(m) 224.
sonar(m) de coque(f) 809.
**sonde(f) 485.**
sonde(f) spatiale 19.
sonde(f) thermique 253.
**sondeur(m) à éclats(m) 485.**
sonnerie(f) de passage(m) à niveau(m) 471.
sonnette(f) 97.
**sorbetière(f) 251.**
sorgho(m) 152.
sortie(f) 82, 452.
sortie(f) d'air(m) chaud 204, 207, 438.
sortie(f) d'eau(f) chaude 208.
sortie(f) de l'eau(f) de refroidissement(m) du condenseur(m) 759.
sortie(f) de la vapeur(f) 760, 761, 762, 763.
sortie(f) de la vapeur(f) des séparateurs(m) 758.
sortie(f) de piste(f) 505.
sortie(f) de piste(f) à grande vitesse(f) 502.
sortie(f) des originaux(m) 421.
sortie(f) du caloporteur(m) 768.
sortie(f) du reflux(m) du condenseur(m) 759.
soubassement(m) 225.
**souche(f) 59.**
souche(f) 197.
SOUDAGE(M) 305, 306.
**soudage(m) à l'arc(m) 305.**
**soudage(m) bout(m) à bout(m) 307.**
**soudage(m) oxyacétylénique 306.**
SOUDAGE(M), ÉQUIPEMENT(M) DE PROTECTION(F) 308.
soudure(f) 307.
soufflante(f) 501, 760.
soufflerie(f) 543.
soufflet(m) 378, 380, 399, 536, 543.
souffleuse(f) 162.
**souffleuse(f) de fourrage(m) 162.**
souffleuse(f) de fourrage(m) 155.
soulier(m) à la poulaine(f) 318.
soulier(m) à talon(m) 318.
soupape(f) 248, 543, 735.
soupape(f) à air(m) 304.
soupape(f) à pression(f) et dépression(f) 741.
soupape(f) d'admission(f) 434, 436, 635.
soupape(f) d'arrivée(f) d'air(m) 590.
soupape(f) d'échappement(m) 435, 436, 438.
soupape(f) d'évacuation(f) 551, 710.
soupape(f) de gonflage(m) 627.
soupape(f) de purge(f) 627.
soupape(f) de réglage(m) du fluide(m) 304.
soupape(f) de sureté(f) 209.
soupape(f) de sûreté(f) 297, 766.
soupape(f) expiratoire 730.
soupape(f) inspiratoire 730.
soupière(f) 238.
soupir(m) 538.
source(f) alimentaire fondamentale 31.
sources(f) de pollution(f) 34.
sourcil(m) 140.
sourcils(m) 107.
sourdine(f) 551.
**souris(f) 530.**
souris(f) 526, 527.
sous-épineux(m) 121.
sous-fondation(f) 451.
sous-gorge(m) 649.
sous-main(m) 520.
SOUS-MARIN(M) 806.
sous-pied(m) 336.
sous-plancher(m) 198, 199, 200.
**sous-sol(m) 190.**
sous-sol(m) 197.
sous-vêtement(m) d'isolation(f) 512.
sous-vêtement(m) de contrôle(m) thermique 512.
**sous-vêtements(m) 325, 345, 346.**
soustraction(f) 523, 830.
soustraction(f) en mémoire(f) 523.
soute(f) 510.
soute(f) à bagages(m) 492, 508.
soute(f) à eau(f) 469.
soute(f) d'équipement(m) technique 415.

Les termes en **caractères gras** renvoient à une illustration, ceux en CAPITALES indiquent un titre.

soute(f) des bobines(f) de câbles(m) 415.
**soutien-gorge(m) 346.**
soutien-gorge(m) balconnet(m) 347.
soutien-gorge(m) corbeille(f) 346.
spadice(m) 60.
spatule(f) 244, 581, 589, 633, 640, 642.
spatulée 56.
spécifications(f) techniques 433.
spectromètre(m) 717.
spectromètre(m) à ultraviolet(m) 43.
spencer(m) 338.
**spermatozoïde(m) 127.**
sphère(f) céleste 3.
sphère(f) d'hélium(m) 509.
sphère(f) de verre(m) 40.
sphère(f) terrestre 3.
sphincter(m) anal 131.
spicule(m) 6.
spiral(m) 706.
spirale(f) 276, 398.
spire(f) 94.
splénius(m) de la tête(f) 121.
spores(f) 55.
spot(m) 235.
spot(m) à pince(f) 235.
SQUASH(M) 616.
**squash(m), balle(f) 616.**
**squash(m), raquette(f) 616.**
**squash(m), terrain(m) 616.**
SQUELETTE(M) 122.
**squelette(m), cheval(m) 102.**
stabilisateur(m) 499, 508, 639, 684, 780, 785, 786, 812.
stabilisateur(m) à triple plan(m) vertical 498.
stabilisateur(m) de roulis(m) 496.
stabilo(m) 636.
**stade(m) 654.**
stade(m) 185.
stade(m) final de déploiement(m) 419.
stalactite(f) 24.
stalagmite(f) 24.
station(f) d'émission(f) 722.
**station(f) de métro(m) 474.**
station(f) de pompage(m) 740.
station(f) de pompage(m) intermédiaire 740.
station(f) de pompage(m) principale 740.
station(f) de réception(f) 722.
station(f) locale 416.
**station(f) météorologique 38.**
STATION(F)-SERVICE(M) 453.
**station(f)-service(m) 453.**
stationata(f) 647.
stationnement(m) 190, 193.
stator(m) 290, 753.
stators(m) extérieurs 501.
stators(m) intérieurs 501.
steeple(m) 655.
steppe(f) 45.
sterno-cléido-mastoïdien(m) 120.
sternum(m) 102, 122.
**stéthoscope(m) 726.**
stigmate(m) 60, 66, 78, 79.
stimulateur(m) de gencives(f) 373.
stipule(f) 56.
stockage(m) des missiles(m) 808.
stop(m) 106.
**store(m) à enroulement(m) automatique 231.**
store(m) à enroulement(m) manuel 231.
store(m) bateau(m) 231.
**store(m) vénitien 231.**
strato-cumulus(m) 44.
stratosphère(f) 19.
stratus(m) 44.
**structure(f) 203.**
structure(f) 450.
**structure(f) du Soleil(m) 6.**
structure(f) du support(m) 48.
**structure(f) du tissu(m) 566.**
structure(f) tubulaire 487.
structure(m) métallique 463.
studio(m) 407.
STUDIO(M), RADIO(F) 407.
style(m) 60, 62, 63, 64, 67, 706.
STYLES(M) D'ARCHITECTURE(F) 166.
stylet(m) 389, 794.
**stylo(m)-bille(f) 389.**
stylo(m)-bille(f) 515.
**stylo(m)-plume(f) 389.**
stylo(m)-plume(f) 515.
stylobate(m) 166, 168.
sublimation(f) 34.
substance(f) blanche 135.
substance(f) corticale 132.
substance(f) grise 135.
substance(f) médullaire 132.
subtropical humide 45.
subtropical sec 45.
suceur(m) à tapis(m) et planchers(m) 260.
suceur(m) plat 260.
suceur(m) triangulaire à tissus(m) 260.
sucrier(m) 238.
sud(m) 488.
sud(m)-est(m) 488.
sud(m)-ouest(m) 488.
sulky(m) 652.
superposition(f) d'originaux(m) 532.
superstructure(f) 486.
support(m) 40, 230, 231, 232, 248, 370, 397, 552, 574, 619, 787.
support(m) à bagages(m) 445.
support(m) ajustable 521.
support(m) d'entrave(f) 652.
support(m) d'extrémité(f) 230.
support(m) de fixation(f) 230, 234, 720.
support(m) de lisse(f) 471.
support(m) de plafond(m) 230.
support(m) de plaquette(f) 376.
support(m) de pouce(m) 549.
support(m) de sphère(f) 40.
support(m) de tension(f) 569.
support(m) du filament(m) 233.
support(m) du rouleau(m) 573.
support(m) mural 230.
support-papier(m) 525.
**supports(m) 589.**
surandouiller(m) 105.
surbaissé 174.
surface(f) absorbante 772.
surface(f) de but(m) 601, 612.
surface(f) de coin(m) 601.
surface(f) de combat(m) 668.
surface(f) de cuisson(f) 253, 255.
surface(f) de frappe(f) 596.
surface(f) de glace(f) 620.
surface(f) de jeu(m) 619, 682.
surface(f) de l'eau(f) 487, 624.
surface(f) de la peau(f) 137.
surface(f) de réparation(f) 601.
surface(f) de résine(f) 405.
surface(f) de sécurité(f) 668.
surface(f) encrée 580.
surface(f) gravée 404.
surface(f) isolante 528.
surface(f) mouillée 580.
surface(f) pressée 405.
surface(f) réfléchissante 770.
surhaussé 174.
surimpression(f) 391.
surligneur(m) 515.
surliure(f) 691.
suroît(m) 329.
surpiqûre(f) 323, 350, 352, 355.
**survêtement(m) 352.**
suspendre pour sécher 829.
suspendre pour sécher sans essorer 829.
suspension(f) 236, 477.
suspension(f) à la Cardan 485.
suspente(f) 456.
suspentes(f) 636.
suspentes(f) de nacelle(f) 634.
suture(f) 67.
symbole(m) 702.
SYMBOLES(M) D'USAGE(M) COURANT 822.
SYMBOLES(M) DE SÉCURITÉ(F) 821.
SYMBOLES(M) DES NUAGES 44.
**symboles(m) divers(m) 831.**
SYMBOLES(M) MÉTÉOROLOGIQUES INTERNATIONAUX 39.
SYMBOLES(M) SCIENTIFIQUES USUELS 830.
**symboles(m), matières(f) dangereuses 821.**
**symboles(m), protection(f) 821.**
symphyse(f) pubienne 127, 128.
synapse(f) 135.
synapse(m) 135.
**synthétiseur(m) 555.**
système(m) audio 430.
système(m) d'ancrage(m) 661.
**système(m) d'échappement(m) 439.**
SYSTÈME(M) DE BASE(F) 528, 530.
système(m) de climatisation(f) 415.
système(m) de dépotage(m) 742.
système(m) de fixation(f) 735.
système(m) de lentilles(f) 719.
système(m) de lubrification(f) 469.
système(m) de pointage(m) fin 16.
système(m) de remplissage(m) et de vidange(f) 492.
système(m) de verrouillage(m) 260.
système(m) filtre(m) 385.
système(m) hydraulique 787.
SYSTÈME(M) NERVEUX 133, 134.
**système(m) nerveux central 134.**
**système(m) nerveux périphérique 133.**
système(m) racinaire 57, 61.
système(m) radar(m) 813.
**système(m) rotary 737.**
SYSTÈME(M) ROUTIER 450, 452.
SYSTÈME(M) SOLAIRE 4.

## T

T.G.V. 458.
tabac(m) 384.
tabatière(f) 197.
TABLE(F) 219.
**table(f) 674.**
table(f) 363, 578, 581, 583.
**table(f) à abattants(m) 219.**
**table(f) à dessin(m) 591.**
**table(f) à rallonges(f) 219.**
table(f) d'alimentation(f) 162.
table(f) d'harmonie(f) 540, 544, 545, 546.
**table(f) d'imprimante(f) 521.**
**table(f) d'ordinateur(m) 521.**
table(f) de production(f) 413.
table(f) de rotation(f) 737.
table(f) de roulement(m) 466.
TABLE(F) DE ROULETTE 700.
table(f) du sommier(m) 543.
**table(f), tennis 619.**
**tableau(m) américain des mises(f) 700.**
tableau(m) d'affichage(m) des vols(m) 505.
**tableau(m) de bord(m) 430, 445.**
tableau(m) de bord(m) 442.
**tableau(m) de commande(f) 257, 532.**
tableau(m) de commande(f) 214, 253, 255, 258, 259, 532.
tableau(m) de commandes(f) 717.
**tableau(m) de distribution(f) 312.**
tableau(m) de distribution(f) 757.
tableau(m) des scores(m) 698.
**tableau(m) français des mises(f) 701.**
tableau(m) horaire 463.
tableau(m) indicateur(m) 651.
tableau(m) marqueur(m) 683.
tables(f) gigognes 219.
**tables(f), principaux types(m) 219.**
tablette(f) 204, 226, 302.
tablette(f) de verre(m) 254.
tablette(f) graphique 526.
tablette(f) porte-outil(m) 302.
tablier(m) 161, 454, 455, 456, 669, 787.
**tablier(m)-blouse(f) 337.**
tablinum(m) 170.
tabouret(m) 222, 669.
tabouret(m)-bar(m) 222.
tabouret(m)-escabeau(m) 302.
tabulateur(m) 524.
tabulateur(m) décimal 524.
tache(f) 6.
tache(f) jaune 140.
tachymètre(m) 445.
taie(f) d'oreiller(m) 224.
taillant(m) 734.
taille(f) 117, 119.
taille(f) baguette(f) 362.
taille(f) brillant(m) 362.
taille(f) cabochon(m) 362.
**taille(f) d'un diamant(m) 363.**
**taille(f) des pierres(f) 362.**
taille(f) émeraude(f) 362.
taille(f) en ciseaux(m) 362.
taille(f) en escalier(m) 362.
taille(f) en goutte(f) 362.
taille(f) en poire(f) 362.
taille(f) en rose(f) 362.
taille(f) en table(f) 362.
taille(f) française 362.
taille(f) huit facettes(f) 362.
taille(f) marquise(f) 362.
taille(f) ovale 362.
**taille-bordures(m) 271.**
taille-crayon(m) 515, 516.
**taille-haies(m) 268.**
**tailleur(m) 331.**
taloche(f) 291.
talon(m) 104, 117, 119, 156, 242, 277, 325, 352, 354, 376, 385, 433, 544, 546, 562, 568, 596, 609, 615, 641, 642, 643, 644, 670, 671, 675, 678.
talon(m) d'appui(m) 250, 256.
talonnette(f) de dessus(m) 354.
talonneur(m) 606.
talonnière(f) 633, 640, 641, 642, 643.
talus(m) 451.
talus(m) continental 22, 29.
tam-tam(m) 552.
tambour(m) 167, 231, 259, 432, 484, 571, 670, 671, 707, 711, 714.
tambour(m) d'entraînement(m) 390.
**tambour(m) de basque(m) 554.**
tambourin(m) 329.
tamis(m) 615.
tamis(m) à farine(f) 245.
tamis(m) vibrant 737.
tampon(m) 581.
tampon(m) encreur 516.
**tandem(m) 338.**
**tapis(m) 668.**
tapis(m) 669, 675, 682.
tapis(m) amont 748.
tapis(m) de selle(f) 648, 651.
tapis(m) de sol(m) cousu 685, 686.
tapis(m) drainant 748.
tapis(m) roulant 504.
taquet(m) 628, 630.
taquet(m) coinceur 630.
taquet(m) d'amarrage(m) 492.
taquet(m) de verrouillage(m) 529.
**tarière(f) motorisée 270.**
tarlatane(f) 582.
tarse(m) 78, 80, 103, 108, 122.
tasse(f) 688.
tasse(f) à café(m) 238.
tasse(f) à thé(m) 238.
tassette(f) 792.
Taureau(m) 11.
Taureau(m) (20 avril) 820.
té(m) 301, 677.
té(m) de base(f) 205.
technicien(m) aiguilleur(m) 412, 415.
tectrice(f) primaire 110.
tectrice(f) sous-caudale 109.
tectrice(f) sus-alaire 108.
tectrice(f) sus-caudale 109.
teddy(m) 345.
tégument(m) 152.
tégument(m) de la graine(f) 63.
**télécommande(f) 411.**
télécommande(f) 397.
**télécommunications(f) par ligne(f) téléphonique 417.**
TÉLÉCOMMUNICATIONS(F) PAR SATELLITE(M) 417.
**télécopieur(m) 421.**
télécopieur(m) 417.
TÉLÉDIFFUSION(F) PAR SATELLITE(M) 416.
téléinformatique(f) 417.
téléobjectif(m) 392.
téléphone(m) 822.
téléphone(m) cellulaire 417.
téléphone(m) cellulaire portatif 422.
**téléphone(m) public 422.**
TÉLÉPHONE(M), COMMUNICATION(F) 420, 422.
téléport(m) 417.
TÉLESCOPE(M) 720.
**télescope(m) 14.**
télescope(m) 14, 42.
TÉLESCOPE(M) SPATIAL HUBBLE 16.
**télescope(m), coupe(f) 720.**
télésouffleur(m) 414.
**téléviseur(m) 410.**
téléviseur(m) 401.
TÉLÉVISION(F) 410, 412, 414.
**télex(m) 421.**
télex(m) 417.
telson(m) 91.
témoin(m) d'alimentation(f) 529.
témoin(m) d'ouverture(f) de porte(f) 431.
témoin(m) de bas niveau(m) de carburant(m) 431.
témoin(m) de ceinture(f) de sécurité(f) 431.
témoin(m) de charge(f) 431.
témoin(m) de clignotants(m) 431, 445.
témoin(m) de l'amorce(f) du film(m) 390.
témoin(m) de niveau(m) d'huile(f) 431.
témoin(m) de phare(m) 445.

Les termes en **caractères gras** renvoient à une illustration, ceux en CAPITALES indiquent un titre.

témoin(m) de position(f) neutre 445.
témoin(m) de pression(f) d'huile(f) 445.
témoin(m) des feux(m) de route(f) 431.
témoin(m) du retardateur(m) 391.
tempe(f) 116.
température(f) 210.
température(f) ambiante 213, 705.
température(f) de l'air(m) 38.
température(f) désirée 213, 705.
température(f) du point(m) de rosée(f) 38.
**température(f), mesure(f) 41.**
tempête(f) de sable(m) ou de poussière(f) 39.
tempête(f) tropicale 39.
TEMPLE(M) GREC 168.
**temple(m) grec, plan(m) 169.**
templet(m) 573, 578.
temporal(m) 122.
tenaille(f) 179.
tendance(f) barométrique 38.
tendeur(m) 661, 685.
tendeur(m) de timbre(m) 553.
tendon(m) 107.
TENNIS(M) 614.
tennis(m) 355.
TENNIS(M) DE TABLE(F) 619.
**tennis(m), balle(f) 615.**
**tennis(m), filet(m) 614.**
**tennis(m), raquette(f) 615.**
**tennis(m), terrain(m) 614.**
tenon(m) 376, 385.
tenseur(m) du fascia lata(m) 120.
**tensiomètre(m) 710.**
tentacule(m) oculaire 83.
tentacule(m) tactile 83.
**tente(f) canadienne 686.**
**tente(f) deux places(f) 685.**
tente(f) dôme(m) 686.
**tente(f) familiale 685.**
tente(f) grange(f) 686.
tente(f) igloo(m) 686.
tente(f) individuelle 686.
tente(f) intérieure 685, 686.
tente(f) rectangulaire 686.
**tentes(f), principaux types(m) 686.**
tentoir(m) 572.
TENUE(F) D'EXERCICE(M) 352.
**tenue(f) d'exercice(m) 351.**
térébenthine(f) 592.
**termes(m) familiers 62, 63, 64, 65.**
**termes(m) techniques 62, 63, 64, 65.**
terminaison(f) nerveuse 136.
**terminal(m) 421.**
terminal(m) à céréales(f) 490.
terminal(m) à conteneurs(m) 491.
**terminal(m) de télécommunication(f) 422.**
terminal(m) de vrac(m) 490.
terminal(m) pétrolier 491.
terrain(m) de fondation(f) 748.
terrain(m) naturel 733.
terrasse(f) 193, 263, 505.
terrasse(f) extérieure 497.
terrassement(m) 450.
Terre(f) 4, 8.
TERRE(F), STRUCTURE(F) DE LA 22.
terre-plein(m) 179, 184, 186.
terre-plein(m) central 452.
terril(m) 733, 734.
testicule(m) 127.
**têtard(m) 84.**
**tête(f) 107, 112.**
tête(f) 9, 78, 79, 80, 83, 117, 119, 124, 127, 275, 276, 279, 283, 373, 374, 384, 385, 386, 544, 546, 547, 561, 567, 570, 579, 607, 615, 618, 645, 658, 670, 674, 677, 681, 756, 804.
tête(f) à sens(m) unique 276.
tête(f) amont(m) 493.
tête(f) aval(m) 493.
tête(f) avant du cylindre(m) récupérateur 802.
tête(f) basculante 250.
tête(f) bombée 276.
tête(f) creuse 276.
tête(f) cruciforme 276.
tête(f) d'aspiration(f) 216.
**tête(f) d'attelage(m) 471.**
tête(f) d'attelage(m) 147, 156, 157, 158, 159, 162, 449, 469.
tête(f) d'impression(f) 524, 531.
tête(f) d'injection(f) 737.
tête(f) de coupe(f) 306.
tête(f) de dormant(m) 203.
tête(f) de frappe(f) 275.
tête(f) de l'humérus(m) 123.
tête(f) de lecture(f) 404.
tête(f) de lecture(f)/écriture(f) 529.
tête(f) de lit(m) 224.
tête(f) de marteau(m) 681.
tête(f) de mât(m) 631.
tête(f) de métal(m) 658.
tête(f) de puits(m) 734, 740.
tête(f) de rotor(m) 508.
tête(f) de scion(m) 670.
tête(f) diffusante 396.
tête(f) du fémur(m) 123.
tête(f) du vérin(m) de levage(m) 787.
tête(f) flottante 374.
tête(f) froncée 229.
tête(f) panoramique 393.
tête(f) plate 276.
tête(f) plissée 229.
tête(f) ronde 276.
**tête(f), chauve-souris(f) 112.**
**tête(f), oiseau(m) 109.**
**têtes(f), types(m) 229.**
têtière(f) 289, 290, 649.
texte(m) 524.
théière(f) 238.
**théodolite(m) 713.**
théodolite(m) 41.
thermocontact(m) 438.
thermocouple(m) 297.
**thermomètre(m) 705.**
thermomètre(m) 627, 635, 741.
thermomètre(m) à maxima(m) 41.
thermomètre(m) à minima(m) 41.
thermomètre(m) à viande(f) 244.
**thermomètre(m) bimétallique 705.**
**thermomètre(m) médical 705.**
thermosphère(f) 19.
thermostat(m) 210, 214, 252, 297.
**thermostat(m) d'ambiance(f) 213, 705.**
thorax(m) 78, 79, 80, 116, 118.
thym(m) 74.
tibia(m) 78, 80, 103, 108, 112, 122.
tierce(f) 537, 667.
tierceron(m) 177.
tige(f) 57, 70, 72, 214, 247, 275, 276, 294, 295, 373, 385, 386, 539, 562, 567, 568, 573, 641, 642, 644, 705, 707.
tige(f) carrée d'entraînement(m) 737.
tige(f) de forage(m) 737.
tige(f) de manœuvre(f) 796.
tige(f) de pendule(m) 539.
tige(f) de selle(f) 446.
tige(f) du poil(m) 136.
tige(f) filetée 279.
tige(f) pour col(m) 364.
tilde(m) 832.
**timbale(f) 553.**
timbales(f) 557.
timbre(m) 384, 792.
timbre(m) caoutchouc(m) 516.
timbre(m) dateur 516.
timon(m) 158, 159, 162, 449.
tipi(m) 165.
TIR(M) À L'ARC(M) 684.
tirant(m) 553, 786.
tirant(m) de registre(m) 543.
tirant(m) de réglage(m) 322.
tirant(m) des cordes(f) 669.
**tire-bouchon(m) 625.**
tire-bouchon(m) 688.
tire-bouchon(m) à levier(m) 244.
tire-bouchon(m) de sommelier(m) 244.
tire-bourre(m) 801.
tire-joint(m) 291.
tire-racine(m) 268.
tire-veille(m) 631.
tiret(m) 832.
tirette(f) 566, 571.
tireur(m) au but(m) 611.
tiroir(m) 219, 226, 255.
**tiroir(m) de fichier(m) 517.**
tisonnier(m) 205.
TISSAGE(M) 572, 574, 576.
**tissage(m), accessoires(m) 573, 575.**
**tissage(m), schéma(m) de principe(m) 576.**
tissu(m) adipeux 129, 136.
tissu(m) brodé 571.
tissu(m) conjonctif 137.
tissu(m) du vêtement(m) 565.
**tissus(m) de soutien(m) 565.**
Titan 5.
**toge(f) 315.**
toile(f) 231, 375, 397, 576, 589.
toile(f) de fond(m) 188.
toile(f) de saut(m) 659.
toilettes(f) 461.
toilettes(f) pour dames(f) 822.
toilettes(f) pour hommes(m) 822.
toit(m) 82, 171, 197, 205, 470.
toit(m) à deux croupes(f) 182.
toit(m) à l'impériale(f) 183.
toit(m) à la Mansard 183.
toit(m) à pignon(m) 182.
toit(m) à quatre versants(m) 183.
toit(m) à tourelle(f) à pans(m) 183.
toit(m) avec lanterneau(m) 182.
toit(m) de la couche(f) 733.
toit(m) de protection(f) 787.
toit(m) en appentis(m) 182.
toit(m) en carène(f) 182.
toit(m) en coupole(f) 183.
toit(m) en dôme(m) 183.
toit(m) en flèche(f) 183.
toit(m) en pavillon(m) 183.
toit(m) en pente(f) 182.
toit(m) en poivrière(f) 183.
toit(m) en rotonde(f) 183.
toit(m) en shed(m) 182.
toit(m) flottant 741.
toit(m) ouvrant 427.
toit(m) plat 182.
TOITS(M) 182.
toiture(f) 82.
tôle(f) pare-gouttes(m) 741.
tomate(f) 69.
tombant(m) 341.
tombolo(m) 30.
ton(m) de mât(m) 479.
tondeuse(f) 369, 374.
**tondeuse(f) à moteur(m) 271.**
**tondeuse(f) mécanique 271.**
tong(m) 357.
topaze(f) 363.
topinambour(m) 71.
toque(f) 329.
torche(f) 738.
tore(m) 166, 167.
toron(m) 692.
torpille(f) 807.
torrent(m) 27.
**tortue(f) 97.**
totalisateur(m) journalier 431.
Toucan(m) 13.
touche(f) 535, 536, 540, 541, 543, 544, 547.
touche(f) d'effacement(m) 530.
touche(f) d'envoi(m) 530.
touche(f) de commande(f) 530.
touche(f) de composition(f) automatique 421.
touche(f) de correction(f) 421, 569.
touche(f) de décimale(f) 523.
touche(f) de démarrage(m) 530.
touche(f) de double zéro(m) 523.
touche(f) de modulation(f) 402.
touche(f) de pédalier(m) 542.
touche(f) de présélection(f) 402.
touche(f) de résultat(m) 523.
touche(f) de retour(m) 530.
touche(f) de service(m) 530.
touche(f) de tabulateur(m) 530.
touche(f) fixe 711.
touche(f) fixe-majuscules(f) 524.
touche(f) fixe-majuscules(m) 530.
touche(f) majuscule(f) 530.
touche(f) mémoire(f) 402, 405.
touche(f) mobile 711.
touche(f) multifonctionnelle 523.
touche(f) numérique 523.
touche(f) plus(m)-égalité(f) 523.
touche(f) programmable 530.
touche(f)-majuscules(f) 524.
TOUCHER(M) 136.
touches(f) de commande(f) 422.
touches(f) de directivité(f) 530.
touches(f) de fonctions(f) 422, 709.
touches(f) de répétition(f) 405.
touches(f) de variation(f) 569.
toundra(f) 45.
toupet(m) 100.
**toupie(f) 283.**
toupie(f) 251.
tour(f) 176, 486, 770, 771, 773, 774, 786.
Tour(f) 696.
tour(f) à bureaux(m) 184, 190.
tour(f) d'angle(m) 180.
tour(f) d'extraction(f) 735, 736.
tour(f) d'habitation(f) 185, 187.
tour(f) de contrôle(m) 502, 810.
tour(f) de flanquement(m) 180.
tour(f) de forage(m) 737, 738, 740.
tour(f) de fractionnement(m) 744.
tour(f) de guidage(m) 457.
tour(f) de sauvetage(m) 509.
tour(f) du plongeoir(m) 624.
**tour(m) à pied(m) 584.**
tour(m) de coquille(f) 83.
tour(m) de cou(m) 324.
tour(m) de spire(f) 94.
tour(m) de tête(f) 729.
tour(m) embryonnaire 94.
tourelle(f) 180, 257, 780, 785, 809.
tourelle(f) mobile 805.
tourelle(f) porte-objectifs(m) 718.
tourillon(m) 675, 800.
tourmaline(f) 363.
**tournage(m) 584.**
tournant(m) de club-house(m) 651.
tournette(f) 584.
**tournevis(m) 276.**
tournevis(m) 688.
**tournevis(m) à spirale(f) 276.**
tournevis(m) cruciforme 688.
tourniquet(m) 701.
tourniquet(m) d'accès(m) 474.
tourniquet(m) de sortie(f) 474.
tournure(f) 316.
traçage(m) 586.
traceur(m) 527.
trachée(f) 130.
traçoir(m) 281.
tracteur(m) 440, 507, 742, 782.
tracteur(m) à chenilles(f) 783.
TRACTEUR(M) AGRICOLE 147.
tracteur(m) de piste(f) 506.
**tracteur(m) routier 440.**
tracteur(m)-remorqueur(m) 784.
tractus(m) olfactif 142.
tragus(m) 112, 139.
train(m) 462.
TRAIN(M) À GRANDE VITESSE(F) 458.
train(m) d'atterrissage(m) avant 498, 813.
train(m) d'atterrissage(m) principal 499, 812.
train(m) de banlieue(f) 464.
**train(m) routier 440.**
traîneau(m) 264, 643.
trait(m) de mise(f) au jeu(m) 604.
traitement(m) chimique 745.
traitement(m) de l'information(f) 722.
trame(f) 566, 572, 574.
**trampoline(f) 659.**
tranchant(m) 239, 242, 369, 564.
tranché 818.
tranche(f) de gouttière(f) 577.
tranche(f) de queue(f) 577.
tranche(f) de tête(f) 577.
tranchée(f) 733.
tranchefile(f) 577.
TRANSBORDEUR(M) 494.
transbordeur(m) 491, 505, 507.
**transcription(f) des ondes(f) sismiques 714.**
transept(m) 177.
transformateur(m) 209, 235, 747, 757, 758, 771.
transformateur(m) principal 458.
transformation(f) de l'eau(f) en vapeur(f) 766.
transmission(f) 258.
transmission(f) de l'image(f) 717.
transmission(f) de la chaleur(f) à l'eau(f) 766.
transmission(f) du courant(m) induit 714.
transmission(f) du mouvement(m) au rotor(m) 755.
transmission(f) funiculaire 467.
transmission(f) hertzienne 416.
transmission(f) par câble(m) 416.
transpalette(f) manuel 788.
transpiration(f) 35.
transplantoir(m) 268.
**transport(m) de l'électricité(f) 757.**
transport(m) de l'électricité(f) 767.
transport(m) de l'électricité(f) à haute tension(f) 755.
transport(m) de l'énergie(f) à la tension(f) de l'alternateur(m) 755.
transport(m) maritime 735.
transport(m) par taxi(m) 822.
transport(m) routier 491.
transport(m) vers les usagers(m) 755.
transversale(f) pleine 700, 701.
trapèze(m) 120, 121, 633, 637.
**trapèze(m) de figure(f) 633.**
**trapèzes(m), types(m) 633.**
trapillon(m) 188.
trappe(f) acoustique 412.

travaux(m) 826, 827.
travée(f) centrale 456.
travée(f) latérale 456.
travée(f) levante 457.
travers-banc(m) 736.
traverse(f) 178, 219, 225, 466, 535, 572, 574, 578, 728, 756, 757.
traverse(f) arrière 645.
traverse(f) avant 645.
traverse(f) d'extrémité(f) inférieure 470.
traverse(f) d'extrémité(f) supérieure 470.
traverse(f) de chargement(m) 743.
traverse(f) inférieure 202, 225.
traverse(f) intermédiaire 202.
traverse(f) médiane 223.
traverse(f) supérieure 202, 223, 225.
traverse(f) supérieure d'ouvrant(m) 203.
traversée(f) 757.
traversée(f) de transformateur(m) 746, 747.
traversin(m) 224.
trèfle(m) 175, 695.
treillis(m) 263, 401.
treillis(m) de contreflambage(m) 756.
treillis(m) de protection(f) 406.
tréma(m) 832.
trémie(f) 158, 162.
tremplin(m) 659.
tremplin(m) de 1 m 624.
tremplin(m) de 3 m 624.
**trench(m) 319.**
trépan(m) 737.
**trépied(m) 393.**
trépied(m) 397, 415, 539, 552, 721.
trépied(m) de caméra(f) 414.
trépied(m) de perche(f) 414.
trépointe(f) 355.
tréteau(m) 219.
treuil(m) 14.
treuil(m) d'amarrage(m) 743.
treuil(m) de forage(m) 737.
treuil(m) de levage(m) 786.
**triangle(m) 554.**
Triangle(m) 11.
triangle(m) 556, 674.
Triangle(m) austral 13.
tribord(m) 488, 489, 497.
tribune(f) des juges(m) 651.
tribune(f) populaire 651.
triceps(m) brachial 121.
triclinium(m) 171.
tricorne(m) 318.
TRICOT(M) 567.
TRICOTS(M) 326.
trifoliée 56.
triglyphe(m) 167.
trille(m) 538.
trilobé 174.
tringle(f) 433.
tringle(f) d'écartement(m) 467.
tringle(f) de commande(f) 467.
tringle(f) de pédale(f) 540.
tringle(f) de tension(f) 553.
tringle(f) double 230.
**tringle(f) extensible 230.**
tringle(f) métallique 517.
tringle(f) simple 230.
**tringle(f)-barre(f) 230.**
**tringle(f)-rail(m) 230.**
trio(m) 558.
tripe(f) 384.
triple croche(f) 538.
triple(m) 646.
triplure(f) 565.
tripode(m) de stabilisation(f) 507.
Triton 5.
trochanter(m) 78, 80.
trochure(f) 105.
trois-portes(f) 425.
troisième but(m) 597.
troisième étage(m) 509.
troisième joueur(m) 620.
troisième phalange(f) 103.
troisième-but(m) 597.
trombone(m) 550.
trombones(m) 515, 556.
trompe(f) 79.
trompe(f) d'Eustache 139, 141.
trompe(f) de Fallope 128.
trompes(f) de Fallope 128.
**trompette(f) 550.**
trompette(f) 550.
trompettes(f) 556.
tronc(m) 59, 61, 117, 119.
tronc(m) cœliaque 124, 132.
**tronc(m), coupe(f) transversale 59.**
tronçon(m) 756.
trop-plein(m) 215, 292, 293, 297, 399.
tropique(m) du Cancer(m) 3, 47.
tropique(m) du Capricorne(m) 3, 47.
troposphère(f) 19.
trot(m) 101.
trotteur(m) 356.
trotteuse(f) 706.
trottoir(m) 186.
trou(m) 583, 676.
trou(m) central 404.
trou(m) d'homme(m) 741, 742.
trou(m) de l'embout(m) 385.
trou(m) du souffleur(m) 188.
trou(m)-repère(m) 529.
**trousse(f) de manucure(f) 365.**
TROUSSE(F) DE SECOURS(M) 725.
trousse(f) de toilette(f) 382.
troussequin(m) 649.
**truelle(f) de maçon(m) 291.**
truelle(f) de plâtrier(m) 291.
truffe(f) 55, 107.
truie(f) 151.
trumeau(m) 175.
truqueur(m) numérique 413.
tuba(m) 551, 557, 627.
tubage(m) de production(f)/expédition(f) 738.
tubage(m) de surface(f) 740.
tube(m) 232, 370, 588, 710, 718, 719, 720, 721, 800, 803, 804.
tube(m) A 300.
tube(m) B 300.
tube(m) capillaire 705.
tube(m) conducteur 738.
tube(m) d'ajustement(m) 659, 661.
tube(m) d'alimentation(f) en air(m) 777.
tube(m) d'arrivée(f) 296.
tube(m) d'ensemencement(m) 158.
tube(m) d'orientation(f) des lames(f) 231.
tube(m) de bord(m) d'attaque(f) 637.
tube(m) de circulation(f) 768.
tube(m) de déchargement(m) 161.
tube(m) de direction(f) 447.
tube(m) de force(f) 765.
tube(m) de poussée(f) 389.
tube(m) de remplissage(m) de la cuvette(f) 293.
tube(m) de remplissage(m) du réservoir(m) 293.
tube(m) de résonance(f) 554.
tube(m) de selle(f) 446.
tube(m) droit 260.
tube(m) en Y(m) 726.
tube(m) flexible 726.
**tube(m) fluorescent 232.**
tube(m) fluorescent 233.
tube(m) horizontal 446.
tube(m) lance-torpilles(m) 807.
tube(m) oblique 447.
tube(m) porte-oculaire(m) 718, 721.
tube(m) transversal 637.
**tube(m)-image(f) 410.**
tubulure(f) d'admission(f) 434, 437.
tubulure(f) d'échappement(m) 437.
Tudor 174.
tuile(f) 169, 170, 286, 511.
tulipe(f) 247.
**tuner(m) 400, 402.**
tunique(f) 70, 337, 791.
tunnel(m) 474.
tunnel(m) de communication(f) 510.
turban(m) 329.
turbine(f) 753, 758.
turbine(f) d'entraînement(m) 438.
turbine(f) du compresseur(m) 438, 501.
turbines(f) motrices 501.
turbo-alternateur(m) 771, 806.
turboréacteur(m) 499, 812.
TURBORÉACTEUR(M) À DOUBLE FLUX(M) 501.
turion(m) 72.
turquoise(f) 363.
tuteur(m) 263.
tuyau(m) 306, 385, 543, 780.
**tuyau(m) à anche(f) 542.**
**tuyau(m) à bouche(f) 542.**
tuyau(m) arrière 439.
tuyau(m) d'air(m) 627.
tuyau(m) d'arrosage(m) 265.
tuyau(m) d'aspiration(f) 778.
tuyau(m) d'eau(f) chaude 297.
tuyau(m) d'eau(f) froide 297.
tuyau(m) d'échappement(m) 438, 439, 783.
tuyau(m) d'ensilage(m) 162.
tuyau(m) d'évacuation(f) 258, 298.
tuyau(m) d'insufflation(f) 536.
tuyau(m) de chute(f) 215, 293, 298.
tuyau(m) de refoulement(m) 778.
tuyau(m) de vidange(f) 257, 258, 298.
tuyau(m) du ventilateur(m) 162.
tuyau(m) flexible 260, 735.
tuyau(m) perforé 265.
tuyau(m) souple d'arrivée(f) 298.
tuyauterie(f) 543.
tuyauterie(f) de sortie(f) de la vapeur(f) des séparateurs(m) 759.
tuyauterie(f) de vapeur(f) primaire 759.
tuyère(f) 492, 508, 509, 510.
tuyère(f) d'échappement(m) 501.
tuyère(f) d'éjection(f) 812.
tympan(m) 84, 97, 166, 168, 175.
type(m) de carburant(m) 453.
type(m) de la masse(f) d'air(m) 38.
type(m) de nuage(m) bas 38.
type(m) de nuage(m) élevé 38.
type(m) de nuage(m) moyen 38.
**types(m) de têtes(f) 276.**
TYPES(M) DE VOITURES(F) 460.

## U

unisson(m) 537.
unité(f) d'extraction(f) par solvant(m) 744.
unité(f) de disque(m) compact 527.
unité(f) vidéo 527.
UNITÉS(F) MONÉTAIRES, EXEMPLES(M) 832.
Uranus 5.
uretère(m) 132.
urètre(m) 128, 129, 132.
urètre(m) pénien 127.
uropode(m) 91.
usine(f) 752.
usine(f) à asphalte(m) 745.
usine(f) de traitement(m) 735.
usine(f) des lubrifiants(m) 745.
**usine(f) marémotrice 752.**
**usine(f) marémotrice, coupe(f) 752.**
usine(f) pétrochimique 744.
**ustensiles(m) de campeur(m) 688.**
USTENSILES(M) DE CUISINE(F) 242, 244, 246.
**ustensiles(m) divers 246.**
**ustensiles(m), jeu(m) d' 244.**
utérus(m) 128, 129.
utiliser un chlorure(m) décolorant suivant les indications(f) 829.

## V

vache(f) 151.
vacuole(f) 115.
vagin(m) 128, 129.
VAGUE(F) 30.
vague(f) d'oscillation(f) 30.
vague(f) de translation(f) 30.
vague(f) déferlante 30.
vair(m) 819.
vaisseau(m) capillaire 137.
vaisseau(m) sanguin 136.
vaisseaux(m) sanguins 112.
VAISSELLE(F) 238.
Valet(m) 695.
valet(m) 718.
**valeur(f) des notes(f) 538.**
valeur(f) des segments(m) 698.
**valeur(f) des silences(m) 538.**
validation(f) 525.
**valise(f) fin(f) de semaine(f) 383.**
**valise(f) pullman(m) 383.**
vallée(f) 27.
valve(f) 67, 95, 447.
valve(f) de l'aorte(f) 125.
valve(f) de réglage(m) 208.
valve(f) du tronc(m) pulmonaire 125.
**valve(f) gauche, coquille(f) 95.**
valvule(f) mitrale 125.
valvule(f) tricuspide 125.
vanne(f) 746, 747, 752.
vanne(f) d'arrêt(m) de la turbine(f) 758.
vanne(f) d'arrosage(m) 759.
vanne(f) de production(f) 740.
vanne(f) fourreau(m) 753.
vanne(f) maîtresse 740.
vantail(m) 225.
vapeur(f) à basse pression(f) 758.
vaporisateur(m) 256, 264.
vaporiseur(m) 210.
variomètre(m) 635.
variomètre(m) électrique 639.
variomètre(m) mécanique 639.
vase(m) d'expansion(f) 208, 772.
vaste(m) externe du membre(m) inférieur 120, 121.
vaste(m) interne du membre(m) inférieur 120.
veau(m) 151.
vedette(f) 809.
véhicule(m) de service(m) technique 506.
véhicule(m) spatial autonome 512.
véhicule(m) tout-terrain(m) 425.
VÉHICULES(M) D'INCENDIE(M) 778, 780.
veine(f) axillaire 126.
veine(f) basilique 126.
veine(f) cave inférieure 124, 125, 126, 132.
veine(f) cave supérieure 124, 125, 126, 130.
veine(f) céphalique 126.
veine(f) fémorale 126.
veine(f) iliaque 124.
veine(f) iliaque commune 132.
veine(f) jugulaire externe 126.
veine(f) jugulaire interne 126.
veine(f) mésentrique supérieure 126.
veine(f) porte 124, 126.
veine(f) pulmonaire 126.
veine(f) pulmonaire droite 125.
veine(f) pulmonaire gauche 125.
veine(f) rénale 126, 132.
veine(f) saphène interne 126.
veine(f) sous-clavière 126.
veine(f) sus-hépatique 124.
**veines(f) 126.**
**vélo(m) d'exercice(m) 664.**
vélum(m) 80.
**vent(m) 38.**
vent(m) 629.
vent(m) arrière 629.
vent(m) de travers(m) 629.
vent(m) debout 629.
**vent(m), mesure(f) de la direction(f) 41.**
**vent(m), mesure(f) de la vitesse(f) 41.**
ventail(m) 792.
ventilateur(m) 161, 162, 207, 209, 213, 259, 434, 438, 528.
ventilateur(m) de l'évaporateur(m) 214.
ventilateur(m) de moteur(m) diesel 468.
**ventilateur(m) de plafond(m) 214.**
ventilateur(m) de sustentation(f) 492.
ventilateur(m) des radiateurs(m) 469.
ventilateur(m) du condenseur(m) 214.
ventilateur(m) hélicoïde 212.
ventilateur(m) principal 734.
ventilation(f) 772.
ventilation(f) de la cabine(f) 639.
ventouse(f) 85, 299.
ventre(m) 101, 116, 118.
ventricule(m) droit 124, 125.
ventricule(m) gauche 124, 125.
venturi(m) 804.
Vénus 4.
véraison(f) 61.
verge(f) 127, 483.
verger(m) 149.
vergette(f) 543.
verglas(m) 37.
vergue(f) 478.
vérificateur(m) de circuit(m) 310.
vérificateur(m) de continuité(f) 310.
vérificateur(m) de haute tension(f) 310.
vérificateur(m) de prise(f) de courant(m) 310.
**vérificateur(m) de tension(f) 310.**
vérification(f) de la profondeur(f) de champ(m) 391.
vérin(m) 784.
vérin(m) de commande(f) de volet(m) 812.
vérin(m) de défonceuse(f) 783.
vérin(m) de direction(f) 784.
vérin(m) de dressage(m) 780, 786.
vérin(m) de la flèche(f) 782, 785.
vérin(m) de levage(m) de la lame(f) 783.
vérin(m) du bras(m) 782, 785.

Les termes en **caractères gras** renvoient à une illustration, ceux en CAPITALES indiquent un titre.

vérin(m) du bras(m) de levage(m) 782.
vérin(m) du godet(m) 782, 785.
vérin(m) du godet(m) rétro 782.
vérin(m) hydraulique 147, 449, 788.
vernier(m) 484, 708.
vernis(m) 592.
verre(m) 376.
verre(m) à bordeaux(m) 237.
verre(m) à bourgogne(m) 237.
verre(m) à cocktail(m) 237.
verre(m) à cognac(m) 237.
verre(m) à eau(f) 237.
verre(m) à gin(m) 237.
verre(m) à liqueur(f) 237.
verre(m) à porto(m) 237.
verre(m) à vin(m) blanc 237.
verre(m) à vin(m) d'Alsace 237.
verre(m) à whisky(m) 237.
**verre(m) bifocal 376.**
verre(m) de visée(f) 390.
VERRES(M) 237.
verrière(f) 190, 195, 462, 638, 813.
verrou(m) 530, 562.
verrou(m) de barre(f) d'attelage(m) 803.
verrou(m) de chargeur(m) 795.
verrou(m) de sûreté(f) 796.
verrou(m) glaciaire 26.
verrouillage(m) 260.
versant(m) 27.
Verseau(m) 13.
Verseau(m) (20 janvier) 820.
verseuse(f) 247.
versoir(m) 156.
vert(m) 676.
vert(m) d'entraînement(m) 676.
vertèbre(f) cervicale (7) 123.
vertèbre(f) dorsale (12) 123.
**vertèbre(f) lombaire 135.**
vertèbre(f) lombaire (5) 123.
vertèbres(f) cervicales 102.
vertèbres(f) coccygiennes 103.
vertèbres(f) dorsales 102.
vertèbres(f) lombaires 103.
vertèbres(f) sacrées 103.
vésicule(f) biliaire 97, 131.
vésicule(f) de pinocytose(f) 115.
vésicule(f) séminale 127.
vessie(f) 89, 127, 128, 132.
vessie(f) natatoire 89.
veste(f) 315, 331, 667, 668.
veste(f) de pêche(f) 672.
**veste(f) droite 322.**
**vestes(f) 338.**
vestiaire(m) 194.
vestiaire(m) de bureau(m) 522.
vestiaire(m) des mineurs(m) 735.
vestiaire(m) du personnel(m) 461.
vestibule(m) 139, 170, 194.
**veston(m) croisé 322.**
**vêtement(m) d'exercice(m) 353.**
vêtement(m) ignifuge et hydrofuge 777.
vêtement(m) isothermique 627.
VÊTEMENTS(M) D'ENFANT(M) 349, 350.
VÊTEMENTS(M) D'HOMME(M) 319, 320, 322, 324.
VÊTEMENTS(M) DE FEMME(F) 330, 332, 334, 336, 338, 340, 342, 344, 346, 348.
**vêtements(m) de nuit(f) 348.**
**vêtements(m), pêche(f) 672.**
vexille(m) 110.
viaduc(m) 454.
viande(f) 33.
vide(m) 14.
vide-poches(m) 429.
Vierge(f) 11, 13.
Vierge(f) (23 août) 820.
vigie(f) 502.
VIGNE(F) 61.
**vilebrequin(m) 281.**
vilebrequin(m) 434, 436.
villa(f) 187.
**violon(m) 544.**
violon(m) 545.
**violon(m), famille(f) 545.**
violoncelle(m) 545.
violoncelles(m) 557.
virage(m) à droite(f) 826, 827.
virage(m) de brasse(f) 622.
virage(m) de papillon(m) 623.
virage(m)-culbute(f) 622, 623.
virgule(f) 832.
virole(f) 304, 675.
virole(f) femelle 670.
virole(f) mâle 670.
**vis(f) 276.**
vis(f) 544.
**vis(f) à glace(f) 681.**
vis(f) à glace(f) 680.
vis(f) à grain(m) 161.
vis(f) à otons(m) 161.
vis(f) calante 709, 713.
vis(f) centrale 579.
vis(f) d'alimentation(f) 160, 162.
vis(f) de blocage(m) (azimut(m)) 720, 721.
vis(f) de blocage(m) (latitude(f)) 720, 721.
vis(f) de fixation(f) 393.
vis(f) de nivellement(m) 40.
vis(f) de pince-aiguille(m) 562.
vis(f) de pression(f) 581, 583.
vis(f) de réglage(m) 278, 306.
vis(f) de réglage(m) de grand débit(m) 712.
vis(f) de réglage(m) de hauteur(f) 641.
vis(f) de réglage(m) de libération(f) 641.
vis(f) de réglage(m) de petit débit(m) 712.
vis(f) de réglage(m) du condenseur(m) 718.
vis(f) de réglage(m) du niveau(m) 40.
vis(f) de serrage(m) 282.
vis(f) de support(m) inférieure 40.
vis(f) de support(m) supérieure 40.
vis(f) de tension(f) 552.
vis(f) macrométrique 718.
vis(f) micrométrique 484, 711, 718.
vis(f) sans fin(f) 575.
visage(m) 116.
viseur(m) 390, 713.
viseur(m) de caméra(f) 414.
viseur(m) électronique 409.
viseur(m) périscopique 805.
visière(f) 328, 329, 443, 471, 642, 729, 777, 792.
visière(f) antisolaire 512.
**visualisation(f) des ondes(f) sismiques 714.**
visualisation(f) du seuil(m) d'alarme(f) 485.
vitrage(m) 486.
vitrail(m) 175.
vitre(f) 768, 769.
vitre(f) protectrice 410.
vitrine(f) 227.
**voie(f) 476.**
voie(f) 474.
voie(f) à sens(m) unique 824, 825.
voie(f) d'accélération(f) 452.
voie(f) de banlieue(f) 464.
voie(f) de butte(f) 465.
voie(f) de circulation(f) 452, 502.
voie(f) de circulation(f) des locomotives(f) 465.
voie(f) de décélération(f) 452.
voie(f) de dépassement(m) 452.
voie(f) de fond(m) 736.
voie(f) de service(m) 464, 502.
voie(f) de sortie(f) 465.
voie(f) de tête(f) 736.
voie(f) de transport(m) 733.
voie(f) de tri(m) primaire 465.
voie(f) de tri(m) secondaire 465.
VOIE(F) FERRÉE 466.
**voie(f) ferrée 466.**
voie(f) ferrée 184, 463, 735.
voie(f) ferrée bord(m) à quai(m) 491.
Voie(f) lactée 11.
voie(f) latérale 452.
voie(f) pour véhicules(m) lents 452.
voies(f) principales 452.
voilage(m) 229.
VOILE(F) 628, 630.
voile(f) 631, 636, 773.
voile(f) aurique 482.
voile(f) bermudienne 482.
voile(f) carrée 482.
voile(f) d'étai(m) de flèche(f) 480.
voile(f) d'étai(m) de grand perroquet(m) arrière 480.
voile(f) d'étai(m) de hune(f) arrière 480.
voile(f) de flèche(f) 480.
voile(f) latine 482.
voile(m) 433, 670.
voile(m) du palais(m) 141, 142.
Voiles(f) 13.
VOILES(F), TYPES(M) 482.
**voilure(f) 480.**
voilure(f) 627, 637.
voilure(f) delta(m) 499.
voilure(f) droite 499.
voilure(f) en flèche(f) 499.
voilure(f) trapézoïdale 499.
VOILURES(F), TYPES(M) 499.
**voiture(f) 477.**
voiture(f) sport(m) 425.
**voiture(f)-coach(m) 460.**
**voiture(f)-lit(m) 460.**
**voiture(f)-restaurant(m) 460.**
**voiturette(f) de golf(m) électrique 679.**
vol(m) 625.
VOL(M) À VOILE(F) 638.
VOL(M) LIBRE 637.
**volant(m) 618.**
volant(m) 147, 224, 228, 430, 435, 561, 579, 584.
volant(m) d'inertie(f) 664.
volant(m) de frein(m) à main(f) 470.
volant(m) de manche(m) 500.
volant(m) de manœuvre(f) 778.
VOLCAN(M) 25.
volcan(m) 23.
volcan(m) au repos(m) 24.
**volcan(m) en éruption(f) 25.**
volée(f) 201, 800.
volet(m) 511, 529, 772.
volet(m) d'air(m) 441.
volet(m) de bord(m) d'attaque(f) 812.
volet(m) de bord(m) de fuite(f) 498, 812.
volet(m) de contrôle(m) thermique 43.
volet(m) transparent 379.
volets(m) d'intérieur(m) 231.
VOLLEYBALL(M) 613.
**volleyball(m), ballon(m) 613.**
**volleyball(m), filet(m) 613.**
**volleyball(m), terrain(m) 613.**
**vols(m) 624.**
voltigeur(m) de centre(m) 597.
voltigeur(m) droit 597.
voltigeur(m) gauche 597.
volute(f) 166, 167, 220, 544.
volve(f) 55.
voussure(f) 175.
**voûte(f) 177.**
voûte(f) de projection(f) 16.
voûte(f) du palais(m) 141, 142.
voyant(m) conique 486, 488.
voyant(m) de charge(f) 374.
voyant(m) de mise(f) en circuit(m) 420.
voyant(m) de mise(f) en ondes(f) 407.
voyant(m) de réception(f) de messages(m) 420.
voyant(m) de réponse(f) automatique 420.
voyant(m) lumineux 247, 252, 255, 256, 257, 370, 585.
voyants(m) 531.
voyants(m) de contrôle(m) 405.
vrille(f) 61.
VUE(F) 140.
**vue(f) antérieure 122.**
**vue(f) arrière 147.**
**vue(f) avant 147.**
**vue(f) d'ensemble(m) 289.**
**vue(f) dorsale 95.**
**vue(f) en plongée(f) 444.**
**vue(f) extérieure 712.**
**vue(f) latérale 442.**
**vue(f) plongeante 171.**
**vue(f) postérieure 123, 129.**
vulve(f) 118, 128.
vumètres(m) 407.
vumètres(m) audio 413.

## W

**w.c.(m) 293.**
w.c.(m) 195, 215, 292.
WAGON(M) 470.
wagon(m) 464.
wagon(m) à bestiaux(m) 472.
wagon(m) à copeaux(m) 472.
**wagon(m) couvert 470.**
wagon(m) couvert 472.
wagon(m) de queue(f) 473.
wagon(m) plat 473.
wagon(m) plat à parois(f) de bout(m) 473.
wagon(m) plat surbaissé 473.
wagon(m) porte-automobiles(m) 473.
wagon(m) porte-conteneurs(m) 473.
wagon(m) rail(m)-route(f) 473.
wagon(m) réfrigérant 472.
**wagon(m)-citerne(f) 743.**
wagon(m)-citerne(f) 472.
wagon(m)-tombereau(m) 473.
wagon(m)-tombereau(m) couvert 472.
wagon(m)-trémie(f) 472.
wagon(m)-trémie(f) à minerai(m) 472.
WAGONS(M), TYPES(M) 472.
WATER-POLO(M) 626.
**water-polo(m), ballon(m) 626.**
**water-polo(m), but(m) 626.**
**water-polo(m), surface(f) de jeu(m) 626.**
WATTHEUREMÈTRE(M) 712.
**wattheuremètre(m), mécanisme(m) 712.**
wigwam(m) 165.
winch(m) 630.
wishbone(m) 631.
**wok(m) 248.**
wok(m) 248.

**xylophone(m) 554.**
xylophone(m) 556.

## Y

yen(m) 832.
yourte(f) 165.

## Z

zénith(m) 16.
zéro(m) 700, 701.
zeste(m) 65, 66.
zone(f) centrale 611.
zone(f) d'attaque(f) 608, 613.
zone(f) d'essai(m) des réacteurs(m) 811.
zone(f) de boule(f) morte 682.
zone(f) de but(m) 604, 608, 611.
zone(f) de chargement(m) 764.
zone(f) de chute(f) 655, 657.
zone(f) de convection(f) 6.
zone(f) de danger(m) 668.
zone(f) de défense(f) 608, 611, 613.
zone(f) de lavage(m) des wagons(m) 465.
zone(f) de manœuvre(f) 16.
zone(f) de précipitation(f) 38.
zone(f) de radiation(f) 6.
zone(f) de réception(f) 465.
zone(f) de retrait(m) des bagages(m) 504.
zone(f) de service(m) 613, 617.
zone(f) de service(m) droite 616.
zone(f) de service(m) gauche 616.
zone(f) de triage(m) 465.
zone(f) libre 613.
zone(f) neutre 603, 605, 608.
zone(f) réservée 610.
zone(f) scolaire 826, 827.
zoom(m) 414.

Les termes en **caractères gras** renvoient à une illustration, ceux en CAPITALES indiquent un titre.

# GERMAN INDEX

# A

a 537.
Abakus(m) 166, 167.
Abbaupfeiler(m) 736.
Abblendlicht(n) 429.
Abblendschalter(m) 444.
Abdampfleitung(f) 758.
Abdampfleitungen(f) 759.
Abdeckhaube(f) 284, 404.
Abdeckkappe(f) 386.
Abdeckung(f) 208, 213, 401, 532, 705, 712.
Abendhandschuh(m), langer 327.
Abfackelung(f) 738.
Abfahrtzeiten(f) 463.
Abflugwartehalle(f) 505.
Abfluß(m) 215.
Abfluß(m), oberirdischer 32, 34.
Abfluß(m), unterirdischer 32, 35.
Abflußkreis(m) 215.
Abfrageapparat(m) 422.
Abgas(n) 297, 501.
Abgase(n) 436.
Abgaseintritt(m) 438.
Abgasleitschaufeln(f) 501.
Abgasleitung(f) 508.
Abgasrohr(n) 209, 438.
**Abgasturbolader(m) 438.**
Abhalter(m) 448.
Abhörlautsprecher(m) 407, 415.
Abisolierer(m) 311.
**Abisolierzange(f) 311.**
Abklingbecken(n) 758, 764, 765.
Abkoppelvorrichtung(f) 470.
**Abladegebläse(n) 162.**
Abladegebläse(n) 155.
Ablage(f) 302, 532.
Ablagebrett(n) 302, 591.
Ablaßschraube(f) 710.
Ablaßventil(n) 741.
Ablaufberg(m) 465.
Ablaufrohr(n) 293, 298.
Ablaufschlauch(m) 257, 258, 298.
Ablaufstellwerk(n) 465.
Ablenkkanal(m) 746.
Abnäher(m) 565.
abnehmender Mond(m) 7.
Abreißkalender(m) 518.
Abrollbahn(f) 505.
Absatz(m) 352, 354, 644.
Absatzoberflecken(m) 354.
Absatzplatte(f) 643.
Absatzschuh(m) 318.
Absatzstopper(m) 645.
Absatzteil(n) 641.
Abschalter(m) 747.
Abschlagplatz(m) 676.
Abschleppstange(f) 506.
Abschlußkappe(f) 670.
Abschlußplatte(f) 765.
Abschlußprofil(n) 231.
Abschlußring(m) 670, 671.
Abschlußtafel(f) 521.
Abschlußwand(f) 621.
Abseihkelle(f) 244.
Abseihlöffel(m) 244.
Abseilhaken(m) 681.
Absorber(m) 768.
Absperrgitter(n) 82.
Absperrventil(n) 215, 293, 296, 298, 306.
Abspielraum(m) 620.
Abspieltaste(f) 411.
Absprungholz(n) beim Dreisprung(m) 654.
Absprungholz(n) für Weitsprung(m) 655.
Absprunglinie(f) beim Dreisprung(m) 654.
Abstandstück(n) 727.
Abstandszünder(m) 814.
Abstellplatz(m) 193, 503.
Abstellrost(n) 254.
Abstellstütze(f) 156.
Abstimmtasten(f) 410.
Abstoßsäge(f) 644.
Abstrakte(f) 543.
Abteilklammer(f) 369.
Abtransport(m) per Schiff(n) 735.
Abwasser(n) 216.
Abwasser-T-Stück(n) 298.
Abwasserkanal(m) 186.
Abwehrschild(n) 609.
Abwehrspieler(m), linker 613.
Abwehrspieler(m), mittlerer 613.
**Abwurf(m) 682.**
Abwurf(m) 682.
Abwurfstelle(f) 682.
Abzug(m) 780, 793, 795, 796, 797, 798, 799, 804.
Abzugbügel(m) 795, 797, 798, 799.
Abzugsleine(f) 802.
Abzugstange(f) 793.
Abzweig(m) 45° 301.
Abzweigkanal(m) 206.
Abzweigleitung(f) 215.
ABZWEIGUNGEN(F) 298.
Accent(m) aigu 832.
Accent(m) circonflexe 832.
Accent(m) grave 832.
Acetylenflasche(f) 306.
Acetylenventil(n) 306.
Achse(f) 373, 645.
Achselhöhle(f) 116, 118.
Achselknospe(f) 57.
**Achselkrücke(f) 728.**
Achselnerv(m) 133.
Achselstück(n) 316.
Achselstütze(f) 728.
Achselvene(f) 126.
Achsgetriebe(n) 468.
Achtelmeileneinlauf(m) 651.
Achtelnote(f) 538.
Achtelpause(f) 538.
Achter(m) 632.
Achterschiff(n) 13.
Achtkant(m) 362.
Achtknoten(m) 691.
Adamsapfel(m) 116.
Adapter(m) 374, 399.
Addiertaste(f) 523.
Addition(f) 830.
Additionstaste(f) 523.
Aderhaut(f) 140.
Adler(m) 11, 819.
aerodynamische Bremse(f) 774.
Afrika(n) 21.
After(m) 89, 92, 127, 128, 131.
Afterfeder(f) 110.
Afterflosse(f) 87.
Afterfurche(f) 117, 119.
Afterfüße(m) 91.
Afterkralle(f) 106.
Afterkrallenballen(m) 106.
Afterschließmuskel(m) 131.
Aggregat(n), irreguläres 37.
Ahle(f) 688.
Ähre(f) 60.
Ährenbrot(n) 153.
Akanthusblatt(n) 167, 220.
**Akkord(m) 539.**
**Akkordeon(n) 536.**
**Akku-Mini-Staubsauger(m) 260.**
Akroterion(n) 167, 168.
Akrylharz(m), transparenter 405.
Aktenablage(f), fahrbare 521.
Aktenbox(f) 517.
**Aktenkoffer(m) 378.**
Aktenmappe(f) 518.
Aktenordner(m) 519.
Aktenschrank(m) 520.
**Aktentasche(f) 378, 380.**
Aktuator(m) 814.
Akustik-Decke(f) 189.
Alarmschwellenwert-Anzeige(f) 485.
Alarmschwellenwert-Einstellung(f) 485.
Alhidade(f) 41, 484, 713.
Alhidadenebene(f) 713.
Alkohol(m) 485.
Alkoholkolben(m) 705.
Alkoholsäule(f) 705.
Allee(f) 52.
alphanumerisches Tastenfeld(n) 530.
Altar(m) 13.
**altazimutale Montierung(f) 15.**
Altokumulus(m) 44.
Altostratus(m) 44.
Altschlüssel(m) 537.
Altweiberknoten(m) 691.
Aluminiumschicht(f), reflektierende 405.
Alveolarknochen(m) 144.
Alveolenwand(f) 144.
am Wind(m) 629.
AM-Antenne(f) 400.
Amboß(m) 138, 798.
Ameise(f) 77.
amerikanisches Maisbrot(n) 153.
amerikanisches Weißbrot(n) 153.
Amethyst(m) 363.
Ampel(f) 263.
AMPHIBIEN(F) 84.
**Amphibien(f), wichtigste 85.**
Ampulle(f) 725.
An-/Auskontrollampe(f) 420.
Analfuß(m) 78.
**Analoguhr(f) 706.**
Ananas(f) 68.
**Anatomie(f) 88.**
Änderungslinie(f) 565.
Andromeda(f) 11.
Andruckplatte(f) 390.
Anemometer(n) 41.
Anfänger(m) 174.
Anfängerparcours(m) 646.
Anführungszeichen(n) 832.
Anführungszeichen(n), halbe 832.
Angaberaum(m) 616.
Angel(f) 239, 242, 291.
**Angelbekleidung(f) 672.**
**Angelhaken(m) 671.**
Angelhaken(m) 670.
Angelhaken(m) mit Vorfach(n) 672.
Angelwurzel(f) 242.
Anglerweste(f) 672.
Angriff(m) auf den Menschen(m) 35.
Angriff(m) auf die Natur(f) 35.
Angriffsfeldspieler(m), linker 612.
Angriffsfeldspieler(m), rechter 612.
Angriffslinie(f) 613.
Angriffsperiskop(n) 807.
Angriffsspieler(m), linker 603, 610.
Angriffsspieler(m), mittlerer 610.
Angriffsspieler(m), rechter 603, 610.
Angriffszone(f) 608, 613.
**Anhängemähwerk(n) 158.**
Anhängemähwerk(n) 154.
Anhängemaul(n) 158, 159, 162.
**Anhänger(m) 364.**
Anhänger(m) 361, 440.
Anhängerkupplung(f) 449.
Anhöhe(f) 770.
Anik-E(m) 418.
ANKER(M) 483.
Anker(m) 656.
**Ankerarten(f) 483.**
Ankerbolzen(m) 432.
Ankerhand(f) 483.
Ankerkette(f) 486.
Ankerketten(f) 738.
Ankerklüse(f) 495, 497.
Ankerrad(n) 706.
Ankerspitze(f) 483.
Anlage(f) 156.
**Anlage(f) für Außenaufstellung(f) 212.**
**Anlage(f) für Innenaufstellung(f) 213.**
Anlaßbatterie(f) 468.
Anlasser(m) 271, 272.
Anlaufhülse(f) 283.
Anlaufstrecke(f) 654, 655, 657, 683.
Anlegeeinrichtung(f) 578.
Anlegeleiter(f) 303.
annähernd gleich 830.
Annahmelinie(f) 617.
Annahmemaschine(f) 764.
Anorak(m) 353, 680.
**Anrufbeantworter(m) 420.**
Ansagekassette(f) 420.
Ansatz(m) 279.
Ansatzrohr(n) 260.
Ansatzsäge(f) 578.
Ansaugen(n) 436, 437.
Ansauggitter(n) 370.
Ansaugkanal(m) 436.
Ansaugstutzen(m) 216.
Anschlag(m) 630, 632, 711.
Anschlagführung(f) 285.
Anschluß(m) 230, 255.
Anschluß(m) für Gummischlauch(m) 735.
Anschlußbolzen(m) 439.
Anschlußbuchse(f) 547.
Anschlußbuchse(f) für Kopfhörer(m) 555.
Anschlußkabel(n) 406.
Anschlußkasten(m) 769.
Anschlußklemme(f) 309.
Anschlußleitung(f) 215.
Anschlußpol(m), negativer 439.
Anschlußpol(m), positiver 439.
Anschlußtafel(f) 407.
Anschreiber(m) 610, 613, 666.
Anschriftentafel(f) 471.
**Ansicht(f) 193.**
Anspielpunkt(m) 608.
Anspielpunkt(m), mittlerer 608.
**Ansteckknadeln(f) 364.**
Anstoßlinie(f) 674.
Anstoßpunkt(m) 601, 674.
Anstoßraum(m) 674.
Antarktis(f) 20.
Antenne(f) 16, 43, 78, 79, 80, 81, 91, 408, 427, 498, 508, 613, 805, 810.
Antenne(f) für die Linienzugbeeinflussung(f) 459.
Antenne(f), rotierende 722.
Antennula(f) 90.
Anti-Rutschfuß(m) 302.
Antiklinale(f) 737.
Antiseptikum(n) 725.
Antiskating-Vorrichtung(f) 404.
Antrieb(m) 158, 471.
Antriebsmodul(m) 418.
Antriebsrad(n) 147, 445, 783.
Antriebsräder(n) 784.
Antriebsriemen(m) 434.
Antriebswalze(f) 581.
Antriebswelle(f) 251.
Antriebswerk(n) 706, 707, 737.
Antriebswerke(n) 806.
Antrittspfosten(m) 201.
Antrittsstufe(f) 201.
Anzeige(f) 523, 708, 709.
Anzeige(f) "Sicherheitsgurte anlegen" 431.
Anzeigeeinheit(f) 627.
Anzeigefläche(f) 654.
Anzeigen(f) 405.
Anzeigenadel(f) 396.
Anzeigeskala(f) 485, 705, 709, 710.
Anzug(m), einteiliger 643.
Anzugring(m) 650.
**Anzünder(m) 307.**
Aorta(f) 125, 130.
Aorta(f), absteigende 124.
Aorta(f), aufsteigende 124.
Aorta(f), ventrale 88.
Aortenbogen(m) 124, 125, 126.
Aortenklappe(f) 125.
Aperturblende(f) 717.
Apex(m) 83, 94.
**Apfel(m) 64.**
Apfel(m) 64.
Apogäum(n) 419.
Apogäum-Motor(m) 419.
Apotheke(f) 822.
Aprikose(f) 63.
Aquamarin(m) 363.
**Aquarellfarbe(f) 588.**
Aquarius 820.
Äquator(m) 3, 47.
äquivalent 830.
**Arbeiterin(f) 80.**
Arbeiterin(f) 81.
Arbeitsbrett(n) 302.
Arbeitsdruckmesser(m) 306.
Arbeitsgalerie(f) 188.
Arbeitskittel(m) 337.
**Arbeitsleuchte(f) 234.**
**Arbeitsplatz(m) 521.**
Arbeitsspeichermodul(n) 528.
Arbeitsstiefel(m) 355.
Arbeitstisch(m) 285.
Arbeitsturbinen(f) 501.
Archipel(m) 51.
Architrav(m) 166, 168.
Archivolte(f) 175.
Arenberg-Parkett(n) 200.
Aries 820.
Arkade(f) 176.
Arkaden(f) 172, 173.
ARKEBUSE(F) 795.
Arktis(f) 20.
Arm(m) 100, 117, 119, 157, 234, 483, 561, 727.
Arm(m), oberer 793.
Arm(m), unterer 793.
**Armaturenbrett(n) 430.**
Armausschnitt(m) 325.
Armband(n) 364.
**Armbänder(n) 364.**
Armbeuger(m) 120.
ARMBRUST(F) 793.
**Armbrust(f) 793.**
Armdecken(f), große 110.
Armdecken(f), kleine 110.
Armdecken(f), mittlere 110.
Ärmel(m) 318, 322.
Ärmel(m), angeschnittener 339.
Ärmel(m), eingesetzter 324, 326.
**Ärmelarten(f) 339, 340.**
Ärmelaufschlag(m) 667.
Ärmellasche(f) 319.
Ärmelpuff(m) 318.
Ärmelschlitz(m) 324, 339.
Armgeflecht(n) 133.
Armhaltung(f) 625.
Armhebel(m) 668.
Armkachel(f) 792.
Armlehne(f) 220.
ARMLEHNSTUHL(M) 220.
**Armlehnstühle(m) 220.**
Armpolster(n) 609.
Armreif(m) 364.
Armschutz(m) 684.

**Fettgedruckte** Wörter beziehen sich auf eine Illustration; Wörter in GROSSBUCHSTABEN sind Überschriften.

Armschützer(m) 602.
Armschwingen(f) 110.
Armstrecker(m), dreiköpfiger 121.
Armstrecker(m), zweiköpfiger 120.
Armstütze(f) 220, 428, 429, 727.
Arpeggio(n) 539.
**Arterien(f) 126.**
Artischocke(f) 69.
Arzt(m) 669.
Asche(f) 386.
Asche(f), vulkanische 25.
**Aschenbecher(m) 386.**
Ascheschicht(f) 25.
Asien(n) 21.
Asphalt(m) 745.
Asphalt-Destillationsanlage(f) 745.
Asphaltschindel(f) 286.
Aspirin(n) 725.
Ass(n) 695.
**Ast(m) 58.**
Ast(m) 59, 110.
Äste(m) 59.
Asteroidengürtel(m) 4.
Asthenosphäre(f) 22.
Astragal(m) 167.
Astschere(f) 269.
Atemloch(n) 83.
Atemlöcher(n) 792.
Atemluftzufuhrschlauch(m) 777.
ATEMSCHUTZ(M) 730.
Atemschutz(m) 821.
**Atemschutzmaske(f), leichte 730.**
Atemschutzsystem(n), geschlossenes 777.
Atlantischer Ozean(m) 20.
Atlas(m) 102, 123.
Atlasbindung(f) 576.
Atmosphäre(f) 22, 31.
Atoll(n) 28.
Atrium(n) 170.
ätzend 821.
Aubergine(f) 69.
Aufbereitungsanlage(f) 735.
Aufbewahrungsfach(n) 397.
AUFBEWAHRUNGSMÖBEL(N) 225, 226.
Aufblasteil(n) 627.
Aufblasventil(n) 627.
Aufdruck(m) 350.
Auffahrgleis(n) 465.
Auffahrt(f) 184, 452, 456.
Auffanggefäß(n) 40.
Auffangschüssel(f) 255.
Aufgaberaum(m) 613.
Aufgeber(m) 613, 618.
Aufhängeband(n) 140.
Aufhängefeder(f) 707.
Aufhängeöse(f) 370.
Aufhängepunkt(m) 637.
Aufhänger(m) 326, 397.
Aufhängung(f) 230, 501, 553.
Aufheizer(m) 758.
Auflagetisch(m) 578.
Auflaufförmchen(n) 238.
**Auflieger(m) 441.**
Auflieger(m) 440.
Auflösungszeichen(n) 538.
Aufnahme-Taste(f) 403.
Aufnahmebecken(n) 764.
Aufnahmeeinstellungstasten(f) 409.
Aufnahmefläche(f) 772.
Aufnahmekammer(f) 717.
Aufnahmelicht(n) 407.
Aufnahmeregler(m) 402.
Aufnahmetaste(f) 411.
Aufnahmezeitanzeige(f) 407.
Aufreißband(n) 384.
Aufreißer(m) 783.
Aufreißerspitze(f) 783.
Aufreißerzahn(m) 783.
Aufreißerzylinder(m) 783.
Aufsatz(m) 248.
Aufsatzstück(n) 536.
Aufschlag(m) 315, 323.
Aufschlagbereich(m) 617.
Aufschlagbox(f) 617.
Aufschlagboxlinie(f) 617.
Aufschläger(m) 614, 616.
Aufschlagfeld(n) für das Doppelspiel 618.
Aufschlagfeld(n) für das Einzelspiel 618.
Aufschlagfeld(n), linkes 614, 616.
Aufschlagfeld(n), rechtes 614, 616.
Aufschlaglinie(f) 614, 616, 617.
Aufschlaglinie(f), hintere 618.
Aufschlaglinie(f), mittlere 614.
Aufschlaglinie(f), vordere 618.
Aufschlagrichter(m) 614, 618.
Aufschnitt(m) 542.
Aufsetzbacke(f) 684.
Aufsetzen(n) 682.
Aufsetzzonenmarkierungen(f) 505.
Aufsichtsingenieur(in(f))(m) 412, 415.
aufspringender Winkel(m) 178.
Aufsteckbürste(f) 373.
Aufsteckdüse(f) 373.
Aufsteckschuh(m) 393.
Aufstellmaschine(f) 683.
Aufstellpunkt(m) 675.
**Aufstellung(f) 683.**
Aufstieg(m) 147.
Auftriebsausgleich(m) 627.
Aufwickelkern(m) 403.
**Aufzeichnung(f) seismischer Wellen(f) 714.**
Aufzeichnungsgerät(n) 40.
Aufzeichnungskassette(f) 420.
Aufzeichnungstaste(f) 420.
Aufzug(m) 15, 188, 190, 736, 764, 811.
Aufzugseil(n) 786.
Aufzugsmechanismus(m) 707.
Aufzugsrad(n) 706.
**Augapfel(m) 140.**
Augapfel(m) 84.
**Auge(n) 140.**
Auge(n) 83, 90, 96, 97, 107, 118, 275, 369, 649, 681, 695, 803.
**Augen-Make-up(n) 367.**
Augenbraue(f) 140.
Augenbrauenpinzette(f) 365.
Augenbrauenstift(m) 367.
Augenkammer(f), hintere 140.
Augenkammer(f), vordere 140.
Augenlid(n) 97.
Augenlid(n), oberes 84, 107.
Augenlid(n), unteres 84, 107.
Augenmuskel(m), äußerer gerader 140.
Augenmuskel(m), medialer gerader 140.
Augenring(m) 109.
Augenringmuskel(m) 120.
AUGENSCHUTZ(M) 729.
Augenschutz(m) 821.
Augenstreif(m) 109.
Augenträger(m) 83.
Augsproß(m) 105.
Ausatemventil(n) 730.
Ausatmen(n) 622.
Ausbeinmesser(n) 242.
Ausbereich(m) 682.
**Ausbruchstätigkeit(f), Vulkan(m) 25.**
Ausdehnungsgefäß(n) 208.
Ausdehnungskammer(f) 485, 705.
Ausdehnungsmembran(f) 485.
Ausfahrgleis(n) 465.
Ausfahrt(f) 452.
Ausfahrtsspur(f) 452.
Ausfallpforte(f) 179.
Ausflugloch(n) 82.
Ausführungsgang(m), Schweißdrüse(f) 136.
**Ausgabegeräte(n) 527.**
Ausgangsmonitor(m) 413, 415.
Ausgangsposition(f) 625.
Ausgangssperre(f) 474.
Ausgußreiniger(m) 299.
Ausklapparretierung(f) 302.
Ausklinkhebel(m) 639.
Auskratzer(m) 385.
Auslaßkanal(m) 437.
Auslaßrohr(n) 742.
Auslaßventil(n) 435, 436, 438.
Auslauf(m) 149, 294, 295.
Auslaufgarnitur(f) 296.
Auslaufleitung(f) 216.
Auslaufrille(f) 404.
Auslaufrohr(n) 161, 747.
Auslaufschütz(m) 492.
Ausleger(m) 632, 782, 785, 786.
Ausleger(m), beweglicher 506.
**Auslegerbrücke(f) 454.**
Auslegerseil(n) 786.
Auslegerzylinder(m) 782, 785.
Auslinie(f) 606.
Auslöseknopf(m) 375.
Auslösepuppe(f) 541.
Auslöser(m) 391.
Auslöser(m), pneumatischer 393.
Auspuff(m) 147.
**Auspuffanlage(f) 439.**
Auspuffkanal(m) 436.
Auspuffkrümmer(m) 435, 438, 439.
Auspuffrohr(n) 440, 443, 444, 783, 784.
Auspuffrohr(n), hinteres 439.
Auspuffrohr(n), vorderes 439.
Ausrichtknopf(m) 713.
Ausrichtkopfblockierung(f) 713.
Ausrichtkopfebene(f) 713.
Ausrichtschraube(f) 709, 713.
Ausrufezeichen(n) 832.
**Ausrüstung(f) 681.**
Ausrüstung(f), technische 415.
Ausrüstungsspind(m) 412, 415.
Aussägen(n) 586.
Ausschalter(m) 272.
Ausschaltrille(f) 404.
Ausscheider(m) 742.
Ausschnitt(m) 565.
Ausschnitt(m), drapierter 343.
Ausschnitt(m), halsnaher 350.
Ausschnitt(m), runder 343.
Ausschnitt(m), viereckiger 343.
**Ausschnitte(m) 343.**
**Außenansicht(f) 712.**
AUSSENANSICHT(F) EINES HAUSES(N) 196.
Außenbrett(n) 697.
Außenfeldspieler(m), linker 597.
Außenfeldspieler(m), mittlerer 597.
Außenfeldspieler(m), rechter 597.
Außenkelch(m) 62.
Außenklüver(m) 481.
Außenknauf(m) 290.
Außenkreis(m) 620.
Außenleuchte(f) 196.
Außenlippe(f) 94.
Außenrohr(n), druckfestes 765.
Außenschicht(f) 596.
Außensichel(f), Große 668.
Außensteckhülse(f) 670.
Außensteg(m) 577.
Außentank(m) 510.
Außentasche(f) 378, 382.
äußere Kuppelhülle(f) 14.
äußerer Hausflur(m) 170.
Aussparung(f) für Magnetköpfe(m) 403.
**Ausstattung(f) 581, 582, 583, 589.**
Ausstechformen(f) 245.
Ausstellungsregal(n) 522.
Aussteuerung(f), manuelle 403.
Ausstoßen(n) 436, 437.
Ausstreichmesser(n) 585.
Ausströmmantel(m) 753.
Austauschring(m) 14.
**Auster(f) 92.**
Auster(f) 93.
Austerngabel(f) 240.
Austernmesser(n) 242.
Austernseitling(m) 55.
Australien(n) 21.
Austrittsdüse(f) 501.
Austrittskante(f) 498.
Auswerfer(m) 784.
Auswurf-Taste(f) 403.
Auswurfrohr(n) 162.
Auswurftaste(f) 250.
Auszahlungselement(n), elektrisches 702.
Auszahlungshebel(m) 702.
Auszahlungsschale(f) 702.
Ausziehbein(n) 219.
**Ausziehleiter(f) 302.**
**Ausziehtisch(m) 219.**
Auszug(m) 219.
AUTO(N) 425, 426, 428, 430, 432, 434, 438.
Auto-Manualumschalter(m) 310.
Autobahn(f) 52, 184, 452.
AUTOBAHNKREUZ(N) 452.
**Autobahnkreuz(n) 450.**
Autobahnnummer(f) 52.
Autocoat(m) 330.
Autofocus-Schalter(m) 397.
Autofocus-Umschalter(m) 391.
**Autogenschweißen(n) 306.**
**Autohandschuh(m) 327.**
Automat(m) für Umsteigekarten(f) 475.
Autopilot(m) 814.
Autoreverse-Taste(f) 408.
Autotransportwagen(m) 473.
Autowaschanlage(f) 453.
Avocado(f) 68.
Axialrippe(f) 94.
Axialverdichterschaufel(f) 501.
Axis(f) 123.
Axon(n) 135.
Azimutalprojektion(f) 50.
Azimutfeineinstellung(f) 720, 721.
Azimutfesteller(m) 721.
Azimutfeststeller(m) 720.

## B

B(n) 538.
Baby-Doll(n) 348.
Bach(m) 676.
Back(f) 495, 497.
Back-Line(f) 620.
Backblech(n) 245.
Backbordseite(f) 488, 489, 497.
Backe(f) 106, 280, 376.
Backe(f), bewegliche 279, 282.
Backe(f), feste 279, 282.
Backe(f), gekrümmte 278.
Backe(f), gerade 278.
Backen(f) 276, 280, 281, 311.
Backen(m) 642.
Backenfutter(n) 276, 280, 281.
Backenfutterschlüssel(m) 281.
Backenriemen(m) 649.
Backenzahn(m), erster vorderer 144.
Backenzahn(m), zweiter vorderer 144.
Backenzähne(m), vordere 144.
BACKGAMMON(N) 697.
**Backgerät(n) 245.**
Backofen(m) 255.
Backofenschalter(m) 255.
Bad(n) 194, 195.
Badeanzug(m) 353.
Badehose(f) 353.
Badekappe(f), blaue 626.
Badekappe(f), weiße 626.
Bademantel(m) 348.
**Badetuch(n) 349.**
Badewanne(f) 194, 215, 292.
BADEZIMMER(N) 292.
BADMINTON(N) 618.
**Badmintonplatz(m) 618.**
**Badmintonschläger(m) 618.**
Baggerlöffel(m) 785.
Baggerstiel(m) 782, 785.
Baggerstielzylinder(m) 782, 785.
Baguette(n) 153.
Baguetteform(f) 362.
**Bahn(f) 683.**
Bahn(f) 275, 621, 655.
Bahne(f) 375.
Bahnende(n) 622.
Bahnenplissee(n) 335.
Bahnenrock(m) 334.
Bahngleise(n) 735.
BAHNHOF(M) 462, 464.
Bahnhof(m) 52, 184.
Bahnhofshalle(f) 462.
Bahnmarkierung(f) 656.
Bahnnummer(f) 621.
Bahnseil(n) 621.
Bahnsteig(m) 462, 464, 475, 504.
Bahnsteigkante(f) 462, 475.
Bahnsteigüberdachung(f) 464.
Bahnübergang(m) 464, 828.
**Bahnübergang(m), schienengleicher 471.**
Bahnzeitnehmer(m) 621.
Bailey-Brücke(f) 457.
Bajonettfassung(f) 232.
Bakelitgehäuse(n) 804.
**Balalaika(f) 535.**
Balancegewicht(n) 404.
Balanceregler(m) 402.
Balg(m) 536, 543.
Balgen(m) 399.
Balgenverschluß(m) 536.
Balken(m) 134, 168, 170, 659, 708.
Balken(m), hinterer 708.
Balken(m), vorderer 708.
**Balkenbrücke(f) 454.**
**Balkenbrücken(f) 454.**
Balkenspiralgalaxie(f) 9.
**Balkenwaage(f) 708.**
Ball(m) 598.
Ball(m), blauer 673.
Ball(m), brauner 673.
Ball(m), gelber 673.
Ball(m), grüner 673.
Ball(m), rosa 673.
Ball(m), roter 673.
Ball(m), schwarzer 673.
Bälle(m) rote 673.
Balleisen(n), gerades 587.
Ballen(m) 104.
Ballerinaschuh(m) 356.
Balljunge(m) 614.
Ballon(m) 634.
**Ballonvorhang(m) 229.**
Balustrade(f) 194.
Banane(f) 68.
Band(n) 566, 571, 613, 800, 804.
Band(n), erhabenes 577.
Band(n), weißes 618, 619.

**Fettgedruckte** Wörter beziehen sich auf eine Illustration; Wörter in GROSSBUCHSTABEN sind Überschriften.

Bandage(f) 648, 662, 669.
Bändchen(n) 541.
Bande(f) 608.
Banderole(f) 384.
Bandführung(f) 403.
BANDIT(M), EINARMIGER 702.
Bandring(m) 364.
Bändsel(n) 692.
Bandsortenschalter(m) 403.
Bandsperre(f) 711.
**Banjo(n) 535.**
Bank(f) 222, 663, 733.
Bankett(n) 451.
Bankhöhe(f) 733.
Bar(f) 697.
Barbakane(f) 180.
Baren(m) 582.
Bärenhüter(m) 11.
Barhocker(m) 222.
Bärlatsch(m) 792.
Barograph(m) 41.
**Barometer(n) 710.**
Barometerskalen(f) 710.
Baronstange(f) 545.
Barrenholm(m), hölzerner 661.
Bart(m) 72.
Bartregion(f) 109.
Basalschicht(f) 136.
Basaltschale(f) 22.
BASEBALL(M) 595, 596.
**Baseball(m) 596.**
**Baseball(m) im Querschnitt 596.**
Basilikum(n) 74.
Basis(f) 166, 410, 656.
Basis(f) der Stuhllehne(f) 220.
Baskenmütze(f) 329.
**Basketball(m) 610.**
BASKETBALLSPIEL(N) 610.
Baß-Tonabnehmer(m) 547.
Baßfalle(f) 412.
Baßklarinette(f) 556.
Baßlautsprecher(m) 16.
Baßregister(n) 536.
Baßregler(m) 402.
Baßschlüssel(m) 537.
Baßsteg(m) 540.
Baßtastatur(f) 536.
Baßtrommel(f) 552, 557.
Bast(m) 59.
Bateau-Kragen(m) 343.
**Batterie(f) 439.**
Batterie(f) 393, 409, 528, 769, 777, 814.
Batterie-Radiator(m) 49.
Batterieauswurfschalter(m) 409.
Batteriekasten(m) 441.
Batterieladekontrolleuchte(f) 431.
Batteriemodule(m) 43.
Bauch(m) 101, 108, 116, 118.
Bauchaorta(f) 126, 132.
Bauchfell(n) 127, 128.
Bauchflosse(f) 86.
Bauchfuß(m) 78.
Bauchgurt(m) 651, 653.
Bauchhöhle(f) 127, 128.
Bauchmuskel(m), äußerer Schräger 120.
Bauchmuskel(m), äußerer schräger 121.
Bauchmuskel(m), gerader 120.
Bauchpanzer(m) 96.
Bauchreifen(m) 792.
Bauchschuppe(f) 97.
Bauchspeicheldrüse(f) 131.
Bauer(m) 696.
Bauernbrot(n) 153.
BAUERNHOF(M) 148.
**Baum(m) 59.**
Baum(m) 628, 649.
BAUM(M), AUFBAU(M) 59.
Baum(m), ausfahrbarer 786.
BAUMATERIALIEN(N) 286, 288.
**Baumaterialien(n) 286.**
Bäume(m) 676.
Baumhippe(f) 269.
Baumsäge(f) 269.
Baumschere(f) 269.
**Baumstamm(m) 288.**
Baumstamm(m) 288.
**Baumstamm(m), Querschnitt(m) 59.**
**Baumvogel(m) 111.**
Bauschärmel(m) 340.
Bauschaumisolierung(f) 287.
Bauschmuskel(m) 121.
Baustelle(f) 826, 827.
BAUSTILE(M) 166.
Bayonett(n), aufgepflanztes 794.
Bayonettanschluß(m) 392.
Becher(m) 13, 238.
Becken(n) 216, 552, 554, 557, 752.
Becken(n) für schadhafte Brennelemente(n) 764.
Becken(n), oberes 552.
Becken(n), unteres 552.
Beckengrund(m) 626.
Beckengurt(m) 428.
Beckenseite(f) 752.
bedeckte Säule(f) 37.
**Bedeckungsgrad(m) 39.**
**Bedienblende(f) 257.**
Bedienblende(f) 253, 255, 258, 259.
Bedienhebel(m) 787, 788.
Bedienkonsole(f) 779.
Bedienpult(n) 717.
Bedienungselement(n) für Objektbewegung(f) 717.
Bedienungshebel(m) 162.
Bedienungshebel(m) für Verschlußblock(m) 802.
**Bedienungskonsole(f) 532.**
Bedienungskonsole(f) 532.
Bedienungsschnur(f) 230.
Bedienungstasten(f) 421, 422.
**Beere(f), Querschnitt(m) 62.**
**Beerenarten(f) 62.**
BEERENOBST(N) 62.
Beete(f), rote 71.
**Beetpflug(n) 156.**
Beetpflug(n) 154.
Befehlstaste(f) 530.
befestigte Umfassungsmauer(f) 172.
Befestigungsclip(m) 711.
Befestigungshebel(m) 235.
Befestigungsriemen(m) 645, 777.
Befestigungsschiene(f) 718.
Befestigungssystem(m) 661.
Befeuchter(m) 516.
begrenzte Zone(f) 610.
Begrenzungseinsatz(m) 517.
Begrenzungskreis(m) 610.
Begrenzungsleuchte(f) 429, 441.
Begrenzungslinie(f), äußere 616.
Begrenzungslinie(f), rückwärtige 618.
Behälter(m) 40, 162, 250, 304, 511.
Behälter(m) mit Gießer(m) 251.
Behandlung(f), chemische 745.
Beifahrer-Fußraste(f) 444.
Beifahrerfußraste(f) 443.
Beil(n) 690.
Beilagscheibe(f) 278, 294.
**Beilagscheiben(f) 278.**
Bein(n) 97, 117, 119, 219, 220, 325, 553, 619, 659.
Beinarbeit(f) beim Brustschwimmen(n) 622.
Beinarbeit(f) beim Butterflyschwimmstil(m) 623.
Beinarbeit(f) beim Kraulen(n) 622.
Beinausschnitt(m), elastischer 325.
Beincurler(m) 663.
Beinhaltung(f) 625.
Beinklemme(f) 393.
Beinpolster(n) 609.
Beinröhre(f) 792.
Beinstreckerzug(m) 663.
Beitel(m) 581.
Belederung(f) 632.
Beleuchter(in(f))(m) 412.
Beleuchtung(f) 189, 368, 412, 500.
Beleuchtungsanlage(f) 412, 414.
Beleuchtungskopf(m) 399.
Beleuchtungsspiegel(m) 713.
Belichtungs-Schaltuhr(f) 399.
Belichtungseinstellung(f) 391.
Belichtungskorrekturknopf(m) 391.
**Belichtungsmesser(m) 396.**
Belichtungsmesser(m) 391.
Belichtungswert(m) 396.
Belichtungszeitskala(f) 396.
Belüftungsgitter(n) 197.
Belüftungsschlitz(m) 257.
Benzin(n) 745.
Benzintankverschluß(m) 444.
Bereichsumschalter(m) 310.
Bereitschaftsanzeige(f) 370, 420.
BERG(M) 27.
Bergehalde(f) 733, 734.
Bergère(f) 220.
Bergfried(m) 181.
Berghang(m) 27.
Bergkette(f) 7.
Bergschrund(m) 26.
BERGSTEIGEN(N) 680.
**Bergsteiger(m) 680.**
Bergsteigerspaten(m) 680.
Bergsteigerstiefel(m) 680.
Beringmeer(n) 21.
Berme(f) 748.
Bermudashorts(f) 336.
Berthe(f) 342.
Berührung(f) 697.
Besan(m) 480.
Besan-Bramstagsegel(n) 480.
Besan-Stengestagsegel(n) 480.
Besanbaum(m) 478.
Besanmast(m) 478.
Besantoppsegel(n) 480.
Besatzungsunterkünfte(f) 494.
Beschichtung(f) 619.
Beschichtung(f), nichtreflektierende 768.
Beschickungsbereich(m) 764.
Beschickungsmaschine(f) 759, 760, 761, 764.
**Beschläge(m) 630.**
Beschleunigungsspur(f) 452.
Besen(m) 205.
Bespannung(f) 615, 645, 675.
Besteckkorb(m) 257.
Bestückung(f) 284.
Besucherterrasse(f) 505.
Betonauslauf(m) 741.
Betonblock(m) 286.
Betonmantel(m) 760, 761, 762, 763.
Betonmauer(f) 772.
**Betonnte Fahrwasser(n) 488.**
BETONNUNGSSYSTEM(N) 488.
Betonsockel(m) 714.
Betriebsanzeigen(f) 410.
Betriebsbremse(f) 468.
Betriebsebene(f) 752.
Betriebseinstellung(f) 408.
Betriebsraum(m) 172, 173.
BETT(N) 224.
**Bett(n) mit Matratze(f) 687.**
Bettuch(n) 224.
**Bettwäsche(f) 224.**
Bettwäsche(f) 460.
Beutel(m) 380.
Beutelklammern(f) 515.
**Beuteltasche(f) 381.**
Beuteltasche(f) 380.
Bewegungsenergie(f) 755.
**BH(m) 346.**
**Biber(m) 98.**
Bidet(n) 292.
**Bienenstock(m) 82.**
Bienenstock(m) 149.
Bierkrug(m) 237.
**Bifokalglas(n) 376.**
**Bilderwascher(m) 399.**
Bildkontrolle(f) 412, 415.
Bildplatte(f) 527.
Bildplattenlaufwerk(n) 527.
Bildregie(f) 412.
**Bildröhre(f) 410.**
Bildschirm(m) 410, 526, 527.
**Bildschirmeinheit(f) 529.**
Bildsucher(m) 390, 409, 414.
Bildsucher(m), elektronischer 409.
Bildtechniker(in(f))(m) 412, 415.
**Bildträger(m) 589.**
**Billardqueue(m) 675.**
**Billardtisch(m) 674.**
Billettasche(f) 322.
BILLIARD(N) 673.
**Bimetall-Thermometer(n) 705.**
Bimetallfeder(f) 705.
Bimsstein-Korrekturstift(m) 583.
Binde(f), elastische 725.
Bindebogen(m) 539.
Bindegewebe(n) 137.
Bindehaut(f) 140.
Bindeteil(n) 324.
Bindung(f) 633.
Binnenklüver(m) 481.
Binnenraum(m) 179.
BINOKULARMIKROSKOP(N) 718.
Binsenstengel(m) 389.
**Biologie(f) 831.**
**Biosphäre(f), Struktur(f) 31.**
Birne(f) 64.
Birnkernform(f) 362.
Biß(m) 385.
Blank(n) 695.
Blasebalg(m) 687.
Blasebalgtasche(f) 338, 339.
BLASINSTRUMENTE(N) 548, 550.
Blaspfeife(f) 536.
**Blatt(n) 56.**
Blatt(n) 57, 72, 214, 277, 284, 291, 304, 369, 548, 564, 609, 619, 627, 632, 754.
Blattachsel(f) 56.
Blattader(f) 56.
Blattansatz(m) 56.
**Blätter(n) 549.**
**Blätter(n), einfache 56.**
**Blätter(n), zusammengesetzte 56.**
BLATTFORMEN(F) 56.
**Blattformen(f) 58.**
**Blattgemüse(n) 73.**
Blattgrund(m) 57.
**Blattrand(m) 56.**
Blattrand(m) 57.
Blattscheide(f) 56, 70.
Blattschraube(f) 548.
Blattstecher(m) 573.
Blattstiel(m) 56.
Blattstieleinschnitt(m) 61.
blau 819.
Blaulicht(n) 781.
Blaustrahl(m) 410.
Blazer(m) 331, 338.
**Blechbläser(m) 550.**
Blechverkleidung(f) 204.
Bleigürtel(m) 627.
Bleikopf(m) 542.
Bleikugel(f) 804.
Bleistift(m) 389, 515.
Bleistiftband(n) 229.
Bleistiftsspitzer(m) 515, 516.
Blende(f) 255, 258, 259, 383, 390, 396.
Blendeneinsteller(m) 717.
Blendenring(m) 392.
Blendenskala(f) 392, 396.
Blendgläser(n) 484.
Blendrahmen(m) 203.
Blendrahmen(m), oben 203.
Blinddarm(m) 131.
blinder Fleck(m) 140.
Blindschacht(m) 736.
**Blinker(m) 672.**
Blinkeranzeige(f) 430.
Blinkerkontrolleuchte(f) 445.
Blinkleuchte(f) 429, 442, 443, 444.
Blinklicht(n) 471.
Blinklichtkontrolle(f) 431.
Blitz(m) 36.
Blitzableiter(m) 197, 747, 757.
Blitzbirne(f) 393.
Blitzkontakt(m) 391.
Blitzröhre(f) 393.
Blitzwürfel(m) 393.
Block(m) 656.
Blockdeckel(m) 439.
Blockkasten(m) 439.
Blöße(f) 667.
Blumenbeet(n) 263.
Blumenkelle(f) 268.
Blumenkohl(m) 69.
Blumenkrone(f) 60.
Blumenrabatte(f) 263.
Bluse(f), klassische 337.
**Blusenarten(f) 337.**
**Blutdruckmeßgerät(n) 710.**
Blüte(f) 57, 61.
BLÜTE(F), AUFBAU(M) 60.
Blütenblatt(n) 60.
Blütenboden(m) 60, 62.
**Blütengemüse(n) 69.**
Blütenkelch(m) 60.
Blütenknospe(f) 57.
**Blütenstände(m) 60.**
Blütenstiel(m) 60, 61.
Blutgefäß(n) 136.
Blutgefäße(n) 112.
BLUTKREISLAUF(M) 124, 126.
**Blutkreislauf(m), Schema(n) 124.**
Bö(f) 39.
BOBSCHLITTEN(M) 643.
Bock(m) 586.
Böckchen(n) 553.
Bockkran(m) 746, 747.
**Bockmühle(f) 773.**
Boden(m) 252, 486, 616, 617, 799.
Boden(m), eingenähter 685, 686.
Boden(m), gewachsener 450.
Boden-Luft-Flugkörper(m) 814.
Boden-Unterwasser-Flugkörper(m) 809, 814.
Bodenablauf(m) 215.
Bodenanlaßgerät(n) 506.
**Bodenausrüstung(f) 506.**
BODENBEARBEITUNG(F) 154.
Bodendüse(f) 260.
Bodengesims(m) 800.
Bodenlinie(f) 621.
Bodenplättchen(n) 546.
Bodenplatte(f) 553, 719.
Bodenstöpsel(m) 804.
Bodenstromgerät(n) 506.
**Bodyshirt(n) 337.**
Bodysuit(m) 345.
BOGEN(M) 174, 793.
**Bogen(m) 544, 793.**
Bogen(m) 14, 206, 455, 549, 577, 793.
Bogen(m), dreiteiliger 455.

**Fettgedruckte** Wörter beziehen sich auf eine Illustration; Wörter in GROSSBUCHSTABEN sind Überschriften.

Bogen(m), gelenkloser 455.
Bogen(m), moderner 793.
Bogen(m), zweiteiliger 455.
Bogenansatz(m) 544.
Bogenarm(m) 684.
**Bogenarten(f) 455.**
**Bogenbrücke(f) 455.**
**Bogenbrücken(f) 455.**
Bogenfeld(n) 175.
**Bogenformen(f) 174.**
Bogengang(m), äußerer 139.
Bogengang(m), hinterer 139.
Bogengang(m), oberer 139.
Bogensäge(f) 690.
BOGENSCHIESSEN(N) 684.
Bogenschutz(m) 549.
**Bogenschütze(m) 684.**
Bogensehne(f) 684, 793.
**Bogenstaudamm(m) 750.**
Bohne(f), grüne 69.
Bohnen(f), dicke 72.
Bohnenkraut(n) 74.
**Bohranlage(f) 737.**
Bohranlage(f) vor der Meeresküste(f) 740.
**Bohren(n) vor der Meeresküste(f) 739.**
Bohrer(m) 280.
Bohrerstellung(f) 624.
Bohrfutter(n) 283.
Bohrgestänge(n) 737.
**Bohrhammer(m) 734.**
**Bohrinsel(f) 738.**
Bohrkopf(m) 734, 737.
Bohrkörper(m) 281.
Bohrkragen(m) 737.
**Bohrmaschine(f), elektrische 280.**
Bohrschiff(n) 739.
Bohrschnecke(f) 270.
Bohrstange(f) 734.
Bohrtisch(m) 283.
Bohrturm(m) 737, 738, 740.
**Bohrwinde(f) 281.**
Bolero(m) 338.
Bollwerk(n) 179.
Bolzen(m) 282, 793.
Bolzenmutter(f) 466.
Bomben(f), vulkanische 25.
Boot(m) 354.
Boot(n) ohne Fahrt(f) 629.
Bordeauxglas(n) 237.
Bördelgerät(n) 299.
**Bördelverbindung(f) 300.**
Bordinstrumente(n) 635.
Bordkran(m) 811.
Bordküche(f) 498.
Bordstein(m) 186.
Bordunpfeife(f) 536.
Boretsch(m) 74.
Borke(f) 59.
Borste(f) 373, 374.
Borsten(f) 304.
Böschung(f) 193, 451.
Bottich(m) 257.
Bottichrand(m) 258.
BOULE(N) UND PETANQUE(N) 682.
Boulekugel(f) 682.
Boulevard(m) 52, 184.
BOWLING(N) 683.
**Bowlingkugel(f) 683.**
Box(f) 373.
BOXEN(N) 669.
Boxer(m) 669.
Boxershorts(f) 325.
**Boxhandschuhe(m) 669.**
Boxtasche(f) 381.
Brachacker(m) 148.
Bramstenge(f) 479.
BRANDBEKÄMPFUNG(F) 777.
Brandungspfeiler(m) 30.
Brandungstor(n) 30.
Bratentopf(m) 249.
Bräter(m) 248.
**Bratpfanne(f) 688.**
Bratpfanne(f) 249.
Bratsche(f) 545.
Bratschen(f) 556.
Brauchdampf(m) 767.
Brauenbürstchen(n) 367.
Brause(f) 265.
Brausenkopf(m) 292, 296.
Brauseschlauch(m) 292, 296.
Brecheisen(n) 780.
Brecher(m) 30.
Breitengrad(m) 3.
**Breitengrade(m) 47.**
Breitengradskala(f) 40.
Breitenkreis(m) 47.
Breithalter(m) 573.
Bremsbacke(f) 432.
Bremsbelag(m) 432.
Bremse(f) 664, 670, 727.
Bremse(f), einstellbare 671.
Bremser(m) 643.
Bremsgriff(m) 447.
Bremshebel(m) 445.
Bremsklappe(f) 638, 812.
Bremsklappenhebel(m) 639.
Bremsklotz(m) 506.
Bremsleine(f) 636.
Bremsleuchte(f) 429.
Bremspedal(n) 430, 444.
Bremssattel(m) 432, 442.
Bremsscheibe(f) 432.
Bremsschlauch(m) 432.
Bremsträger(m) 432.
Bremstrommel(f) 432.
Bremswagen(m) 473.
Bremszug(m) 447.
**Brennelement(n) 765.**
Brennelement(n) 761, 765.
Brennelemente(n), Abgabeöffnung(f) für verbrauchte 764.
Brennelemente(n), Aufbewahrung(f) schadhafter 764.
Brennelemente(n), Becken(n) für schadhafte 764.
Brennelemente(n), Füllöffnung(f) für neue 764.
Brennelemente(n), Lagerraum(m) für neue 764.
Brennelemente(n), Tonnen(f) mit schadhaften 764.
**Brennelementebeschickung(f) 764.**
**Brennen(n) 585.**
Brenner(m) 209, 248, 634, 635, 689.
Brennerhebel(m) 306.
Brennholzstauraum(m) 204.
**Brennofen(m), elektrischer 585.**
Brennraum(m) 204, 209, 585.
Brennsockel(m) 689.
Brennspiritus(m) 745.
Brennstab(m) 765.
Brennstoff(m) 760, 761, 762, 763, 766.
Brennstoffregelung(f) 501.
Brennstofftablette(f) 765.
Brennstoffventile(n) 500.
**Brett(n) 288.**
Brett(n) 288, 631.
Brieföffner(m) 515.
Brieftasche(f) 379.
Briefwaage(f) 516.
Brigantine(f) 482.
Brigg(f) 482.
**Brillantschliff(m) 363.**
BRILLE(F) 376.
**Brille(f), Teile 376.**
**Brillenarten(f), wichtigste 377.**
Brillenetui(n) 379.
Briolettform(f) 362.
Broccoli(m) 69.
Bronchie(f), rechte 130.
Brosche(f) 364.
BROT(N) 153.
Brothalter(m) 252.
Brotmesser(n) 242.
Bruchstein(m) 286.
Brücke(f) 52, 134, 230, 491, 650, 719, 810.
Brücke(n) 376.
BRÜCKEN(F), BEWEGLICHE 457.
BRÜCKEN(F), STARRE 454, 456.
Brunnen(m) für rituelle Waschungen(f) 172, 173.
Brunnenkresse(f) 73.
BRUST(F) 129.
Brust(f) 100, 108, 116, 118.
Brustbaum(m) 572.
Brustbein(n) 102, 122.
Brustbeine(n) 90.
Brustdrüse(f) 129.
Brustflosse(f) 86.
Brustkopf(m) 281.
Brustkorb(m) 116, 118.
Brustleistentasche(f) 322.
Brustmuskel(m), großer 120.
Brustriemen(m) 653.
Brustschutz(m) 595, 602, 684.
**Brustschwimmen(n) 622.**
Bruststück(n) 792.
Brusttasche(f) 320, 324.
Brüstungsriegel(m) 198.
Brustwarze(f) 116, 118, 129.
Brustwehr(f) 179.
Brustwirbel(m) 102.
Brustwirbel(m) (12) 123.
Brutraum(m) 82.
Brutzwiebel(f) 70.
Bube(m) 695.
Bubikragen(m) 341.
**Buch(n), gebundenes 577.**
Bücherstütze(f) 517.
Buchrücken(m) 579.
**Buchrückenbearbeitung(f) 579.**
**Buchrückenpresse(f) 579.**
Buchse(f) 400.
Buchsenhalter(m) 309.
Büchsenöffner(m) 244.
Bucht(f) 7, 51.
Buchweizen(m) 152.
Büfett(n) 227.
Bug(m) 497, 498, 628, 631.
Bügel(m) 281, 376, 406, 544, 649, 793.
Bügel(m), verstellbarer 277.
Bügelanschlag(m) 376.
Bügelbug(m) 376.
Bügelende(n) 376.
Bügelfalte(f) 323.
Bügelhebel(m) 798.
Bügelheck(n) 256.
Bügelhorn(n) 550.
bügeln 829.
**Bügeln(n) 829.**
Bügelriemen(m) 649.
**Bügelsäge(f) 277.**
Bügelsäge(f) 299.
Bügelsohle(f) 256.
Bügelspannmechanismus(m) 671.
Bügeltritt(m) 470.
Bugfahrwerk(n) 498, 813.
Bugladeklappe(f) 494.
**Bugleuchten(f) 429.**
Bugspriet(m) 479.
Bugstrahler(m) 497.
Bugtür(f) 493.
Bugwulst(f) 497.
**Bühne(f) 189.**
Bühne(f) 188.
Bull's eye(n) 698.
Bull(m), äußerer 698.
Bullauge(n) 496.
Bulldozer(m) 733.
Bund(m) 320, 546, 547.
Bund(m) mit Druckknöpfen(m) 350.
Bund(m), elastischer 321.
Bund(n) 72.
Bundbalken(m) 199.
Bündchen(n) 325.
Bündel(n) 756.
Bundesstaat(m) 51.
Bundverlängerung(f) 323.
Bunker(m) 676.
Bunkeröl(n) 745.
Bunting(n) 817.
Buntstifte(m) 588.
BURG(F) 180.
Burg(f) 180.
Bürgersteig(m) 186.
Burggraben(m) 181.
Burghof(m) 180.
Burgunderglas(n) 237.
Büro(n) 462.
BÜRO(N), AUTOMATISIERTES 526.
Bürodrehstuhl(m) 521.
BÜROGEBÄUDE(N) 190.
Bürogebäude(n) 185, 491.
Bürohochhaus(n) 184.
Büroklammern(f) 515.
BÜROMÖBEL(N) 520, 522.
Büroturm(m) 190.
Bürstchen(n) für Webeffekt(m) 568.
Bürste(f) 260, 373.
Bürste(f) mit Stangen(f) 646, 647.
Bürzel(m) 109.
Bus(m) 190.
Bushaltestelle(f) 186.
Busmodul(n) 49.
Büstenhalter(m), trägerloser 346.
Büstenschale(f) 346.
**butangasbetriebene Geräte(n) 689.**
Butangastank(m) 386.
Butterdose(f) 238.
Butterfach(n) 254.
Butterfly(m) 663.
**Butterflyschwimmstil(m) 623.**
Butterflywende(f) 623.
Buttermesser(n) 239.
Butterroller(m) 242.
Button-down-Kragen(m) 324.

## C

c 537.
**Caban(m) 330.**
Cabochonschliff(m) 362.
Cabriole-Bein(n) 220.
Cafeteria(f) 822.
Callisto(m) 4.
Camisol(n) 345.
CAMPING(N) 685, 686, 690.
CAMPINGAUSRÜSTUNG(F) 688.
**Campingausrüstung(f) 690.**
Cancer 820.
Candlepin(m) 683.
Cañon(m), untermeerischer 29.
**Cape(n) 331.**
Capricornus 820.
**Caprihose(f) 336.**
Caraco(m) 316.
Carapax(m) 91.
Carré(n) 700, 701.
Cashewkern(m) 66.
Cassiopeia(f) 11.
CD-Fach(n) 405.
CD-Lesegerät(n) 527.
CD-ROM-Laufwerk(n) 526.
**CD-Spieler(m) 405.**
CD-Spieler(m) 400, 407, 408.
CD-Tasten(f) 408.
Cedille(f) 832.
Cello(n) 545.
Cellos(n) 557.
Celsiusskala(f) 705.
Cent(m) 832.
Centre(m) 603, 605.
Centre(m), linker 606.
Centre(m), rechter 606.
Chamäleon(n) 13.
Chantilly-Parkett(n) 200.
Charlestonmaschine(f) 552.
Charon(m) 5.
Chaton(m) 364.
Check-in-Schalter(m) 504.
Checkliste(f) 512.
Chefschreibtisch(m) 520.
**Chemie(f) 831.**
Chemischer Ofen(m) 13.
Cheval(n) 700, 701.
Cheval(n), zwei Kolonnen(f) 700.
Chicorée(m/f) 73.
Chiffoniere(f) 226.
Chinakohl(m) 73.
Chinesenkragen(m) 342.
Chinesisches Meer(n) 21.
Chirimoya(f) 68.
chloren 829.
Chloroplast(m) 115.
Chokerkette(f) 361.
Chor(m) 177.
Chorhaupt(n) 177.
Chorscheitelkapelle(f) 177.
Chorumgang(m) 177.
Chromatin(n) 115.
Chromosphäre(f) 6.
Cine-Skala(f) 396.
CITY(F) 184.
Climber(m) 664.
Clip(m) 389.
Clubsessel(m) 221.
Coach-Box(f) 597.
COCKPIT(N) 500.
**Cockpit(n) 639.**
Cockpit(n) 498, 510, 628.
Cocktailbar(f) 227.
Cocktailglas(n) 237.
Code-Taste(f) 524.
Coeur-Dekolleté(n) 343.
Collegering(m) 364.
**Compact Disc(f) 405.**
Compact Disc(f) 408.
Compluvium(n) 170, 171.
**Compound-Bogen(m) 684.**
Computerbildschirm(m) 512.
Computerraum(m) 807.
**Computertisch(m) 521.**
Concorde(f) 19.
Condylus(m) femoris lateralis 123.
Condylus(m) femoris medialis 123.
**Container(m) 470.**
Container(m) 495.
Containerbrücke(f) 490.
Containerflachwagen(m) 473.
Containerlaschsystem(m) 495.
CONTAINERSCHIFF(N) 494.
Containerschiff(n) 490.
Containerterminal(m) 491.
Cool tip(m) 370.
Copyright(n) 831.
Cornerback(m), linker 603, 605.

Cornerback(m), rechter 603, 605.
Corona(f) radiata 128.
Costalschild(m) 97.
**Cotardie(f) 316.**
Cottage(n) 187.
Coudé-Okular(n) 721.
Coupé(n) 425.
Cowper-Drüse(f) 127.
Crêpe-Pfanne(f) 249.
CRICKET(N) 598.
**Cricketball(m) 598.**
Cricketschuh(m) 598.
**Cricketspieler(m) 598.**
Crochetwinkel(m) 322, 341.
Croissant(n) 153.
Cubiculum(n) 170.
CURLING(N) 620.
**Curlingbesen(m) 620.**
**Curlingstein(m) 620.**
Curlingstein(m) 620.
Curryklemme(f) 630.

## D

d 537.
Dach(n) 82, 171, 197, 205, 427, 470, 733.
Dach(n) mit Firstlaterne(f) 182.
Dachbodenklappleiter(f) 303.
Dachentlüfter(m) 215.
DÄCHER 182.
Dachfenster(n) 194, 197.
Dachluke(f) 449.
Dachrestaurant(n) 185.
Dachrinne(f) 197.
**Dachstuhl(m) 199.**
Dachziegel(m) 286.
Dackelohrkragen(m) 341.
Dame(f) 695, 696.
Damenflanke(f) 696.
DAMENKLEIDUNG(F) 330, 332, 334, 336, 338, 340, 342, 344, 346, 348.
Damm(m) 543, 746.
Dammbrust(f) 748.
Dammkragen(m) 750.
Dammkrone(f) 746, 748, 749.
Dammsockel(m) 748.
Dampf(m) 767.
Dampfauslaß(m) 760, 761, 762, 763.
**Dampfbügeleisen(n) 256.**
Dampfdruck(m) 767.
Dämpfer(m) 541, 551, 616.
Dämpferarm(m) 541.
Dämpferpralleiste(f) 541.
Dampfgenerator(m) 759, 761, 762, 766, 767, 771, 806.
Dampfgeneratorraum(m), Kühler(m) für 759.
**Dampfkochtopf(m) 248.**
Dämpfung(f), magnetische 708.
dänisches Roggenbrot(n) 153.
Darm(m) 88, 92, 97, 124.
Darmbein(n) 103, 122.
**Dartscheibe(f) 698.**
DARTSPIEL(N) 698.
Datenanfang(m) 405.
Datenbus(m) 528, 531.
Datendisplay(n) 421.
Dateneingabe(f) 555.
Datenmonitor(m) 391.
Datensichtgerät(n) 421, 422.
Datenspeicherung(f) 717.
Datenverarbeitung(f) 722.
Datierungsnagel(f) 466.
Dattel(f) 63.
Datumstempel(m) 516.
Daumen(m) 112, 137, 327, 596.
Daumenauflage(f) 549.
Daumenfittich(m) 110.
Daumenring(m) 550.
Daumenteil(m) 726.
Daunendecke(f) 224.
Davit(m) 478.
Dechsel(f) 587.
Deckblatt(n) 66, 384.
Deckblatt(n), äußeres 70.
Deckbrücke(f) 455.
Decke(f) 205, 224, 450, 616, 617.
Deckel(m) 247, 248, 251, 252, 253, 256, 258, 295, 386, 398, 585, 590, 719, 796.
Deckelbügel(m) 585.
Deckelhalter(m), magnetischer 256.
Deckelknopf(m) 250.
Deckenbalken(m) 198, 199, 200.
Deckendurchführung(f) 205.
Deckendurchlaß(m) 207.
Deckenleuchte(f) 236.
Deckenträger(m) 230.
**Deckenventilator(m) 214.**
Deckfeder(f) 108.
Deckleiste(f) 203.
Deckung(f), linke 610.
Deckung(f), rechte 610.
Defensive-End(m), linker 603, 605.
Defensive-End(m), rechter 603, 605.
Defensive-Tackle(m), linker 603, 605.
Defensive-Tackle(m), rechter 603, 605.
Deflektor(m) 210.
Degen(m) 666.
Degenfechter(m) 667.
Dehnungsfuge(f) 466.
Deichkrone(f) 752.
Deimos(m) 4.
Deklination(f) 3.
Deklinationsachse(f) 14, 720, 721.
**Dekolletés(n) 343.**
DEKORATIONEN(F) 228.
Dekorationsaufzug(m) 188.
Delle(f) 677.
Delphin(m) 11.
Deltaflügel(m) 499.
Deltamuskel(m) 120.
Dendrit(m) 135.
Dendrit(m), räumlicher 36.
Denkmal(n) 52.
Dessertgabel(f) 240.
Dessertlöffel(m) 241.
Dessertmesser(n) 239.
Deutsche Mark(f) 832.
deutsches Roggenbrot(n) 153.
Dezimal-Tabuliertaste(f) 524.
**Dia(n) 397.**
Dia(n) 397.
Diagonalreifen(m) 433.
Diagonalstrebe(f) 756.
Diamagazin(n) 397.
Diamant(m) 363.
Diapositiv(n) 397.
**Diaprojektor(m) 397.**
Diarähmchen(n) 397.
Diawahl(f) 397.
Diawechsel(m) 397.
Dichtemesser(m) 439.
Dichtring(m) 741.
Dichtung(f) 294, 295, 300.
Dichtung(f), magnetische 254.
Dichtungsmutter(f) 294.
Dichtungsring(m) 257.
Dichtungsschleier(m) 748, 749.
Dichtverschluß(m) 689.
**Dickdarm(m) 131.**
Dickdarm(m), absteigender 131.
Dickdarm(m), aufsteigender 131.
Dickdarm(m), querverlaufender 131.
DICKEMESSUNG(F) 711.
Diechling(m) 792.
Diele(f) 194, 200.
Dieselkraftstoff(m) 745.
**Dieselmotor(m) 437.**
Dieselmotor(m) 469, 493, 495, 782, 783, 785.
Dieselmotoren(m) 809.
Dieselmotorlüfter(m) 468.
Dieseltriebwerk(n) 492.
Diffusionskalotte(f) 396.
Diffusoren(m) 501.
Digitalanzeige(f) 310, 709, 710.
Digitalisierungsunterlage(f) 526.
**Digitaluhr(f) 706.**
Dill(m) 74.
Dimmerschalter(m) 309.
Diode(f) 391, 769.
Dioxid(n) 33.
Dirigent(in(f)) (m) 556.
Dirndl-BH(m) 347.
Disc-Kamera(f) 395.
Diskantregister(n) 536.
Diskantsteg(m) 540.
Diskanttastatur(f) 536.
Diskette(f) 526, 529.
Diskettenalufwerk(n), Anschluß(m) für 528.
Diskettenlaufwerk(n) 526, 528, 555.
**Diskus(m) 658.**
Diskuswerfen(n) 654.
Display(n) 396, 409, 411, 420, 422.
Displayanzeige(f) 500.
Displaybeleuchtungstaste(f) 396.
Displayeinstellung(f) 420.
Distanzstück(n) 765.
Division(f) 830.
Divisionstaste(f) 523.
Dock(n) 490.
Dokumente(n) 421.
Dokumentenablage(f) 517.
Dokumentenmappe(f) 519.
Dolch(m) 794.
Dolde(f) 60.
Doldentraube(f) 60.
Doline(f) 24.
Dollar(m) 832.
Dolle(f) 632.
**Dom(m) 176.**
DOM(M), GOTISCHER 176.
**Dom(m), Grundriß(m) 177.**
DOMINO(N) 695.
Doppel-B(n) 538.
Doppel-Null-Taste(f) 523.
Doppelblank(n) 695.
Doppelblatt(n) 549.
Doppelbogen(m) 301.
Doppeldeck-Flachpalette(f) 787.
Doppelhaus(n) 187.
Doppelklappbrücke(f) 457.
Doppelkombination(f) 646.
Doppelkreuz(n) 538.
Doppelkurve(f) 826, 827.
**Doppelmanschette(f) 339.**
Doppeloxer(m) 646, 647.
Doppelpunkt(m) 832.
Doppelringschlüssel(m) 279.
Doppelschlag(m) 538.
Doppelsitz(m) 443, 477.
Doppelspiel(n) 614, 618.
Doppelstander(m) 817.
Doppelstander(m) mit Zunge(f) 817.
doppelt gesägt 56.
Doppelverglasung(f) 772.
Doppelwimpel(m) 817.
Dopplerwürfel(m) 697.
**dorische Säulenordnung(f) 167.**
Dorn(m) 323, 385, 566, 573, 575, 681.
Dornablage(f) 516.
Dornfortsatz(m) 135.
Dose(f) 398.
**Dosenöffner(m) 256.**
Dosenöffner(m) 688.
Dosierteller(m) 162.
Dotterhaut(n) 109.
Double zero(n) 700.
Double(m) 698.
Double-zero(n) 700.
Doublette(f) 695.
Douglasscher Raum(m) 128.
Douze dernier(n) (25 bis 36) 700, 701.
Douze milieu(n) (13 bis 24) 700, 701.
Douze premier(n) (1 bis 12) 700, 701.
Drache(m) 11.
DRACHENFLIEGEN(N) 637.
Drachme(f) 832.
Draggen(m) 483.
Draht(m) 663, 714.
Drahtauslöser(m) 393.
Drahtbesen(m) 250.
Drahtbürste(f) 368.
Drahtschlinge(f) 681.
Drahtschneider(m) 311.
Drahtzug(m) 467.
Drainage-Decke(f) 748.
Drainage-Schicht(f) 748.
**Draufsicht(f) 171, 444.**
Drehanschlußleitung(f) 370.
**Drehbohrverfahren(f) 737.**
**Drehbrücke(f) 457.**
Drehdüse(f) 264.
**Drehen(n) 584.**
Drehflügel(m) nach außen 203.
Drehflügel(m) nach innen 203.
Drehflügeltür(f) 195, 202.
**Drehgestell(n) 476.**
Drehgestell(n) 458, 468.
Drehgestell-Rahmen(m) 468.
Drehgestellflachwagen(m) 473.
**Drehgestellkastenwagen(m) 470.**
Drehgestellkastenwagen(m) 472.
Drehgriff(m) 281.
Drehkartei(f) 516.
Drehknopf(m) 670, 671, 737.
Drehkranz(m) 457, 702, 785.
Drehkreuz(n) 581, 701.
Drehkuppel(f) 14.
**Drehleiterfahrzeug(n) 780.**
Drehmomentwandler(m) 258.
**Drehscheibe(f) 584.**
Drehscheibe(f) 250, 701, 712, 780.
Drehschiene(f) 14, 584.
Drehschwengel(m) 793.
Drehsessel(m) 520.
Drehspiegel(m) 368.
Drehstromgenerator(m) 771.
Drehteller(m) 584.
Drehtisch(m) 737.
**Drehwalze(f) 714.**
Drehzahl-Einstellung(f) 404.
Drehzahlmesser(m) 431, 445.
Drehzapfen(m) 311.
Drei-Zehenhuf(m) 99.
Dreieck(n) 11, 674.
Dreieckfenster(n) 427.
Dreiecksgruppe(f) 139.
Dreiecktuch(n) 725.
Dreifachkombination(f) 646.
Dreifachleitwerk(n) 498.
Dreifuß(m) 539.
Dreifußständer(m) 552.
Dreipaß(m) 175.
Dreipunktbock(m) 156.
Dreispitz(m) 318.
Dreisprung(m) 654.
Dreiviertelarm(m) 339.
Dreivierteltakt(m) 537.
Dreivierteltasche(f) 381.
dreizählig 56.
Dreschkorb(m) 161.
Dreschtrommel(f) 160.
Dreschwerk(n) 161.
Drilling(m) 695.
Drillingshaken(m) 672.
**Drillmaschine(f) 158.**
Drillmaschine(f) 154.
**Drillschraubenzieher(m) 276.**
dritter Rang(m) 189.
Dritter(m) 620.
Drohne(f) 81.
Drosselvene(f), äußere 126.
Drosselvene(f), innere 126.
Druck(m) 580.
Druckabzug(m) 304.
Druckanzeiger(m) 627.
Druckbleistift(m) 389, 515.
Druckbogen(m) 581.
Druckeinsteller(m) 561.
DRUCKEN(N) 580.
**Drucker(m) 421.**
Drücker(m) 397, 550.
Druckeranschluß(m) 528.
Drückerschalter(m) 268.
Druckerteil(n) 523.
**Druckertisch(m) 521.**
Druckerzeuger(m) 761.
Druckgasförderanlage(f) 738.
Druckkammer(f) 763.
Druckkessel(m) 762.
**Druckknopf(m) 566.**
Druckknopf(m) 290, 321, 327, 389, 542.
Druckknopfleiste(f) 321, 350.
Druckkopf(m) 531.
Druckkopfantrieb(m) 531.
Drucklager(n) 753.
Druckluft(f) 453.
Druckluft-Bohrknecht(m) 734.
Druckluftflasche(f) 627, 777.
Druckmechanik(f) 389.
Druckmesser(m) 740.
Druckmeßgerät(n) 710.
DRUCKMESSUNG(F) 710.
Druckminderer(m) 627.
Druckmotiv(n) 350.
**Druckregler(m) 306.**
Druckregler(m) 306, 373, 777.
Druckregulierung(f) 627.
Druckrohr(n) 389.
Druckrolle(f) 158.
Druckschalter(m) 284.
Druckstab(m) 291.
Drückstange(f) 663.
Drucksteg(m) 540.
Drucktaste 250.
Drucktaste(f) 257.
Drucktendenz(f) 38.
Drucktisch(m) 581, 583.
Druckventil(n) 735.
Druckverschluß(m) 379.
Druckverstärkerpumpanlage(f) 740.
Druckwasser(n) 755, 761, 762.
**Druckwasserreaktor(m) 762.**
Druckzahnrädchen(n) 256.
Duckpin(m) 683.
**Dudelsack(m) 536.**
**Dufflecoat(m) 320.**
Düne(f) 30.
Düne(f), komplexe 46.
Dünenzug(m) 46.
Düngemittel(n) 32.
DÜNGEN(N) 156.
**Düngen(n) des Bodens(m) 154.**
Düngerstreuer(m) 270.
**Dungstreuer(m) 156.**
Dungstreuer(m) 154.
dunkles Roggenbrot(n) 153.
**Dünndarm(m) 131.**
Dunst(m) 37, 39.
**Dunstabzugshaube(f) 255.**
Duo(n) 558.
Durchflußrohr(n) 768.
Durchführung(f) 757.

Durchgangsprüfer(m) 310.
Durchgangstülle(f) 312.
Durchgrifftasche(f) 331.
Durchladegriff(m) 796.
Durchlaufträger(m) 454.
Durchschlag(m) 243.
Durchschnitt(m) 830.
Durchziehschnur(f) 320.
Durchzug(m) 229.
Durchzugsöffnung(f) 209.
Dusche(f) 194.
Duschkabine(f) 292.
Düse(f) 209, 264, 291, 304, 306, 509, 510, 590, 812.
Düsen(f) 245.
Düsenflugzeugbenzin(n) 745.
Düsenkappe(f) 590.
Düsenreiniger(m) 307.
Düsenstrahlablenkfläche(f) 810.
Düsentriebwerke(n) 811.
Duty-free-Shop(m) 505.
Dynamo(m) 446.

## E

e 537.
Ebene(f) 51.
ebener Spiegel(m) 14.
Echinus(m) 167.
Echo(n) 722.
**Echolot(n) 485.**
echter Reizker(m) 55.
Eckballfahne(f) 601.
Eckbeschlag(m) 470.
Eckbogen(m) 601.
Ecke(f) 577, 608, 669.
Eckfahne(f) 607.
Eckhocker(m) 669.
Eckholz(n) 682.
Eckpfosten(m) 198.
Eckpolster(n) 669.
**Eckrohrzange(f) 278.**
Ecksäule(f) 470.
Eckschrank(m) 227.
Eckstrebe(f) 104.
Eckstück(n) 383.
Eckturm(m) 180.
Eckzahn(m) 98, 144.
Eckzähne(m) eines Walrosses(n) 99.
Edelgas(n) 232, 233.
**Edelsteine(m) 362, 363.**
Editsearch-Tasten(f) 409.
Effiliermesser(n) 369.
**Effilierschere(f) 369.**
EGGEN(N) DES BODENS(M) 157.
**Eggen(n) des Bodens(m) 154.**
Ehering(m) 364.
**Ei(n) 109, 128.**
Ei(n) 82.
Eichel(f) 127.
Eidechse(f) 11.
Eier(n) 84, 89.
Eierfach(n) 254.
Eierschneider(m) 246.
Eierstock(m) 128, 129.
Eieruhr(f) 244.
eiförmig 56.
Eigelb(n) 109.
Eigentumswohnungen(f) 187.
Eileiter(m) 128.
Eileiterampulle(f) 129.
Eileiterenge(f) 129.
Eileitertrichter(m) 129.
Ein- und Auslaufschütz(m) 492.
Ein-/Ausschalter(m) 216, 234, 247, 256, 260, 305, 368, 370, 373, 374, 391, 396, 397, 406, 485.
Ein-Zehenhuf(m) 99.
Ein/Aus 408.
Ein/Aus/Lautstärke(f) 408.
Einatemventil(n) 730.
Einatmen(n) 622.
Einbahnstraße(f) 824, 825.
**Einbandleder(n) 579.**
Einbauwaschtisch(m) 292.
**Einbinden(n) 579.**
Einblicklupe(f) 717.
Einbuchtung(f), vordere 139.
Einer(m) 632.
Einfachdeck-Flachpalette(f) 787.
einfache Falte(f) 323.
Einfädler(m) 563.
Einfahrgleis(n) 465.
Einfahröffnung(f) 787.
Einfahrt(f) 452.
Einfamilienhaus(n) 187.
Einfaßband(n) 328.
Einfassung(f) 263, 354.
Einfassung(f), seitliche 204.
Einfeldbrücke(f) 454.
Einflugloch(n) 82.
Einfüllöffnung(f) 256.
Einfüllschacht(m) 251.
Einfüllschlacht(m) 251.
Einfüllstutzen(m) 271, 741.
Eingabe-Löschtaste(f) 523.
**Eingabegeräte(n) 526.**
Eingabetaste(f) 530.
Eingang(m) 173, 474, 685, 686.
Eingangsbereich(m) 415.
Eingangsbuchse(f) 310.
Eingangshalle(f) 190, 504.
Eingangsmonitore(m) 413.
Eingangsschalter(m) 402.
Eingangssperre(f) 474.
eingeschnittenes Satteldach(n) 183.
Eingeweideschlagader(f) 124, 132.
Einhand-Mischbatterie(f) 296.
Einhand-Rohrzange(f) 299.
Einhängefeld(n) 454.
Einhängeleiter(f) 303.
Einheit(f), mobile 416.
Einkaufstasche(f) 381.
**Einladungen(f) 667.**
Einlage(f) 384, 544, 546, 565.
Einlaßkanal(m) 437.
Einlaßtor(n) 753.
Einlaßventil(n) 434, 436.
Einlaufkanal(m) 493.
Einlaufrille(f) 404.
Einlaufsteuerring(m) 753.
**Einlegesohle(f) 358.**
Einmündung(f) 824.
Einpersonenzelt(n) 686.
**Einreiher(m) 322.**
Einreißhaken(m) 780.
**Einsägen(n) 578.**
Einsatz(m) 382, 383, 735.
Einschalter(m) 259.
Einschalttaste(f) 420.
Einschnitt(m), oberer seitlicher 61.
Einschnitt(m), unterer seitlicher 61.
Einspangenschuh(m) 356.
Einspritzdüse(f) 434, 437.
Einspritzung(f) 437.
Einstechhebel(m) 256.
**Einsteckschloß(n) 290.**
Einstecktuch(n) 322.
Einsteigegriff(m) 477.
Einsteigestation(f) 503.
Einsteigetreppe(f) 508.
Einstellanzeige(f) 641.
Einstellhebel(m) 158.
Einstellkerbe(f) 641.
Einstellrad(n) 428.
Einstellspanner(m) 645.
Einstelltasten(f) 531.
Einstellung(f) 406.
Einstellung(f), hohe 829.
Einstellung(f), horizontale 529.
Einstellung(f), mittlere 829.
Einstellung(f), niedrige 829.
Einstellung(f), vertikale 529.
Einstellungen(f) löschen 532.
Einstellungsposition(f) zur Sonne(f) 419.
Einstellventil(n) 304.
Einstichkasten(m) 657.
Einstieg(m) 627.
Einstiegschacht(m) 736.
Einstiegsloch(n) 24.
Einstiegsluke(f) 510.
Einstiegstür(f) 461, 477.
Eintauchmoment(m) 625.
**Eintauchstellungen(f) 624.**
Einteilung(f) 378.
Eintrittskante(f) 499.
Einwärtsdreher(m), runder 120.
Einweg-Brennstoffflasche(f) 307.
Einwegbrennstoffflasche(f) 299.
Einwegkamera(f) 394.
Einwegrasierer(m) 374.
**Einzel-Spielfeld(n), internationales 616.**
Einzelgefahrenzeichen(n) 489.
Einzelsitz(m) 477.
Einzelspiel(n) 614, 618.
Einziehdraht(m) 311.
Einzugsschnecke(f) 160.
Einzugswalze(f) 162.
Einzugtaste(f) 524.
Eipochierer(m) 249.
Eis(n) 34.
Eisautomat(m) 453.
**Eisbahn(f) 620.**
Eisbehälter(m) 251.
**Eisen(n) 678.**
Eisen(n) 3 678.
Eisen(n) 4 678.
Eisen(n) 5 678.
Eisen(n) 6 678.
Eisen(n) 7 678.
Eisen(n) 8 678.
Eisen(n) 9 678.
Eisen(n) mit zwei schrägen Seiten(f) 587.
Eisen(n), gebogenes 587.
Eisen(n), gerades 587.
Eisenbahn(f) 52, 184.
EISENBAHN-OBERBAU(M) 466.
**Eisenschläger(m) 677.**
Eisenträger(m) 463.
eiserner Vorhang(m) 188.
Eisfeld(n) 620.
**Eisfläche(f) 608.**
Eishaken(m) 680.
EISHOCKEY(N) 608.
**Eishockeyschläger(m) 609.**
**Eishockeyschlittschuh(m) 644.**
**Eishockeyspieler(m) 609.**
Eishutfeh(n) 819.
Eiskappe(f) 45.
Eiskörnchen(n) 37.
**Eiskunstlaufstiefel(m) 644.**
EISLAUFEN(N) 644.
**Eismaschine(f) 251.**
**Eispickel(m) 681.**
Eispickel(m) 680.
Eisportionierer(m) 246.
Eisregen(m) 39.
Eisschraube(f) 680.
**Eisschraube(f), hohle 681.**
Eissproß(m) 105.
Eiswürfelschale(f) 254.
Eiweiß(n) 109.
Ekliptik(f) 3, 419.
elastische Schürze(f) 493.
Elch(m) 105.
Elefant(m), Stoßzähne(f) 99.
**elektrische Heckenschere(f) 268.**
ELEKTRISCHE SCHREIBMASCHINE(F) 524.
ELEKTRIZITÄT(F) 309, 310, 312, 746, 748, 750, 752, 754, 756.
Elektrizität(f) 755.
Elektrizitätsraum(m) 806.
Elektrode(f) 232, 305.
Elektrodenhalter(m) 305.
Elektrodenkabel(n) 305.
Elektroelement(n) 585.
Elektroflorett(n) 666.
**Elektroherd(m) 255.**
**Elektroinstallateurwerkzeuge(n) 310, 311.**
**Elektrokonvektor(m) 210.**
Elektrometer(n) 666.
Elektromotor(m) 209, 268, 271, 438.
**Elektronenblitz(m) 393.**
**Elektronenkanone(f) 410.**
Elektronenkanone(f) 410, 717.
ELEKTRONENMIKROSKOP(N) 717.
**Elektronenmikroskop(n) 717.**
Elektronenstrahl(m) 410, 717.
Elektronenstrahljustierung(f) 717.
**Elektrorasierer(m) 374.**
**Elektroschweißen(n) 305.**
Elektrovariometer(n) 639.
Elektroweste(f) 667.
Element(n) 830.
Elfmeterpunkt(m) 601.
Ellbogen(m) 100, 106, 112, 117, 119.
Ellbogenhöcker(m) 102.
Ellbogenpolster(n) 602, 609.
Elle(f) 102, 122.
**Ellenbogenkandare(f) 650.**
Ellennerv(m) 133.
Ellenseite(f), Handbeuger(m) 120, 121.
Ellenseite(f), Handstrecker(m) 121.
elliptische Galaxie(f) 9.
Elsaßglas(n) 237.
Elternschlafzimmer(n) 194.
Emaillierung(f) 297.
Emblem(n) 817.
Embryonalgewinde(n) 94.
Empfänger(m) 15.
Empfängerstation(f) 722.
Empfangsantenne(f) 418.
Empfangsauge(n) 410.
Empfangsgleise(n) 465.
Empfangshalle(f) 172, 173.
Empfangsteil(n) 408.
en prison 700, 701.
Endableitung(f) 757.
Endaufzweigung(f) 135.
Endbande(f) 674.
Endbronchiole(f) 130.
Ende(n) 641, 642, 643.
Ende(n), hinteres 95, 277.
Ende(n), vorderes 95.
Endfaden(m) 134.
Endglied(n) 123.
Endivie(f), glatte 73.
Endivie(f), krause 73.
Endkante(f) 636, 637.
Endklammer(f) 566.
Endknopf(m) 230.
Endknospe(f) 57.
Endlappen(m) 61.
Endlinie(f) 604, 610, 611, 613, 619.
Endlosperlenkette(f) 361.
Endmoräne(f) 27.
Endokarp(n) 63, 64.
endoplasmatisches Retikulum(n) 115.
Endplatte(f), motorische 134.
Endrohr(n) 439.
Endstück(n) 127, 384, 633, 674, 765.
Endteil(n) 324.
Endträger(m) 230.
Endwindung(f) 94.
Endzone(f) 604.
**Energiesparlampe(f) 233.**
**Engländer(m) 279.**
englischer Stock(m) 728.
englisches Weißbrot(n) 153.
Englischhorn(n) 548.
Englischhörner(n) 557.
Ente(f) 150.
Entfaltung(f) der Sonnenzellenausleger(m) 48.
Entfaltung(f), volle 419.
Entfaltungsmechanismus(m) 49.
ENTFERNUNGSMESSUNG(F) 711.
Entfernungsskala(f) 392.
Entgasungsbohrung(f) 439.
Entklammerer(m) 515.
Entladungsröhre(f) 232.
Entleerungsschlauch(m) 258.
Entleerungsventil(n) 297.
Entlüfter(m) 214, 298.
Entlüftung(f) 304.
Entlüftungskreis(m) 215.
Entlüftungsventil(n) 208, 741, 743.
Entriegelungshebel(m) 428.
Entriegelungstaste(f) 260.
**Entsafter(m) 251.**
Entschärfer(m) 805.
Entsorgungsbecken(n) 758, 764.
Entspannhebel(m) 278.
Entsteiner(m) 246.
Entwickler(m) 399.
**Entwicklungsbäder(n) 399.**
**Entwicklungstrommel(f) 398.**
Epizentrum(n) 23.
Equalizer(m) 400.
Erbse(f) 67.
Erbsen(f), grüne 72.
**Erbsenschote(f) 67.**
Erdanschluß(m) 312.
ERDATMOSPHÄRE(F), PROFIL(N) 19.
ERDBEBEN(N) 23.
**Erdbeere(f), Querschnitt(m) 62.**
**Erdbohrer(m) 270.**
Erde(f) 4, 8.
ERDE(F), STRUKTUR(F) 22.
Erdgas(n) 737.
**Erdgeschoß(n) 194.**
Erdgeschoß(n) 197.
Erdkruste(f) 22, 23.
ERDKRUSTE(F), SCHNITT(M) 22.
Erdkugel(f) 3.
ERDKUGEL(F), KOORDINATENSYSTEM(N) 3.
Erdleitung(f) 312, 757.
Erdleitungsspitze(f) 756.
Erdnuß(f) 66.
Erdoberfläche(f) 733.
ERDÖL(N) 737, 738, 740, 742, 744.
Erdöl(n) 737, 744.
**Erdöleruptionskranz(m) 740.**
Erdöleruptionskranz(m) 738, 740.
Erdölterminal(n) 740.
Erdreich(n) 750.
Erdsatellit(m), künstlicher 19.
Erdsensor(m) 42, 43, 49.
Erdstrahlungsscanner(m) 43.
Erdstrahlungssensor(m) 43.
Erdung(f) 400, 741.
Erdungsdraht(m) 312.
Erdungsklemme(f) 309.
Erdungsstift(m) 309.
**Erdzeichen 820.**
Erhebung(f) 566.
Erhöhen(n)/Absenken(n) 396.
Erkerfenster(n) 197.
ERNTEN(N) 159, 160, 162.
**Ernten(n) 155.**
Ersatzelektromotor(m) 806.
Erste Hilfe(f) 822.

**Fettgedruckte** Wörter beziehen sich auf eine Illustration; Wörter in GROSSBUCHSTABEN sind Überschriften.

Erste-Hilfe-Anleitung(f) 725.
ERSTE-HILFE-KASTEN(M) 725.
erster Rang(m) 189.
erster Raum(m) 610.
**erster Stock(m) 194.**
erster Stock(m) 196.
Eruptionsdüse(f) 740.
Eruptivgesteine(n) 23.
erweiterter Zeichensatz(m), Taste(f) für 530.
Erweiterungskartei(f) 517.
Erz(n) 733.
Erzgang(m) 736.
Escudo(m) 832.
Espadrille(f) 357.
**Espresso-Maschine(f) 247.**
**eßbare Schnecken 83.**
**Eßbesteck(n) 688.**
Eßkastanie(f) 66.
Eßlöffel(m) 241.
Eßzimmer(n) 195.
Estragon(m) 74.
Et-Zeichen(n) 831.
Etagenbogen(m) 301.
Etikettenfenster(n) 517.
Etui(n) 365, 523.
**Etui(n) für Rechner(m) und Scheckheft(n) 379.**
Etuirock(m) 334.
Eurasien(n) 21.
Europa(f) 4.
Europa(n) 21.
Europäische Verrechnungseinheit(f) 832.
Eustachische Röhre(f) 139, 141.
**Eutelsat II(m) 418.**
Euthynterie(f) 166, 168.
ewiger Schnee(m) 27.
Excavatio(f) vesicouterina 128.
Exkretionsöffnung(f) 83.
Exokarp(n) 62, 63, 64.
Exosphäre(f) 19.
Expander(m) 665.
Expansionsgefäß(n) 772.
explosionsgefährlich 821.
Exportpipeline(f) 738.
Exportsteigsystem(n) 738.

# F

f 537.
F-1 Triebwerk(n) 509.
**Facetten(f) 363.**
Facettenauge(n) 79, 80, 81.
Fach(n) 226, 379, 701.
Fach(n) für Molkereiprodukte(n) 254.
Fächergerüst(n) 773.
Fächerkorb(m) 399.
Fächerpinsel(m) 366, 589.
**Fächerschrägseile(n) 456.**
Fachwerkbogen(m) 455.
Fackeln(f) 6.
Faden(m) 692.
Fadenabschneider(m) 562.
Fadenauge(n) 573.
Fadenführung(f) 569.
Fadenhebel(m) 561.
Fadenkreuz(n) 718.
Fadenleitöse(f) 561, 562.
Fagott(n) 548.
Fagotte(n) 557.
Fähnchen(n) 38.
**Fahne(f) 817.**
Fahne(f) 110, 606.
Fahne(f) mit Schwenkel(m) 817.
Fahne(f), blaue 626.
Fahne(f), rechteckige 817.
Fahne(f), rote 626, 668.
Fahne(f), viereckige 817.
Fahne(f), weiße 626.
Fahnenband(n) 817.
**Fahnenformen(f) 817.**
Fahrbahn(f) 186, 450, 454, 455, 456.
Fahrbahn(f), unebene 826, 827.
Fahrbahn(f), verengte 826, 827.
Fahrbahnmarkierung(f) 452.
Fahrbalken(m) 476.
FÄHRE(F) 494.
Fähre(f) 457.
Fahrenheitskala(f) 705.
Fahrer(m) 652.
Fahrerstand(m) 805.
Fahrgastanlage(f) 491.
Fahrgestell(n) 800, 802.
Fahrkartenkontrolle(f) 463, 474.
Fahrkartenkontrolleur(m) 463.
**Fahrkran(m) 786.**
Fahrmotor(m) 458.
Fahrplan(m) 462.
FAHRRAD(N) 446, 448.
**Fahrtrage(f) 726.**
Fahrtrichtung(f) 824, 825.
Fahrtrichtungsanzeige(f) 475.
Fahrwassermitte(f) 489.
Fahrwerkhebel(m) 500.
**Fahrzeugbeleuchtung(f) 429.**
Fairway(n) 676.
Fakultät(f) 830.
Fall(m) 341, 480.
Fall-out(n) 35.
Falle(f) 289, 290.
Falleitung(f) 746, 747, 752.
Fallrohr(n) 158.
Fallschirm(m) 510, 812.
FALLSCHIRMSPRINGEN(N) 635.
**Fallschirmspringer(m) 635.**
Fallstrang(m) 215.
Falte(f), abgesteppte 335.
Falte(f), einfache 335.
Falte(f), eingelegte 228.
**Faltenarten(f) 228, 335.**
Faltfeldbett(n) 687.
Faltfenster(n) 203.
Faltgrill(m) 690.
Faltkegeldach(n) 183.
Falttür(f) 194, 202.
Faltverschluß(m) 799.
Falz(f) 577.
Falz(m) 203.
Falzbein(n) 577.
**Familienzelt(n) 685.**
Fanfare(f) 440.
Fangen(n) 697.
**Fänger(m) 595.**
Fänger(m) 541, 597.
Fanghandschuh(m) 595, 609.
Fangseil(n) 811.
**Fangzubehör(n) 672.**
Fanion(m) 817.
Farbabbrennervorsatz(m) 307.
Farbanzeige(f) 569.
Farbbandkassette(f) 531.
Farbbehälter(m) 590.
**Farbbeispiele(n) 819.**
Farbe(f) 581.
Farbeinstellung(f) 532.
**Farben(f) 695.**
Farbfernsehkamera(f) 512.
Farbfilter(m) 392, 410.
Farbmasse(f) 389.
**Farbroller(m) 304.**
Farbspray(m) 590.
**Farbstein(m) 581.**
Farbtafel(f) 592.
Farbwalze(f) 581.
Faserwurzel(f) 57, 59.
**Fassade(f) 175.**
Fassonübertritt(m) 341.
Fassung(f) 309, 364.
**Fassungen(f) 376.**
Faszie(f) 166.
Fausthandschuh(m) 308.
Fäustling(m) 327.
**Fechtbahn(f) 666.**
**Fechter(m) 667.**
Fechthandschuh(m) 667.
Fechthose(f) 667.
Fechtjacke(f) 667.
Fechtmaske(f) 667.
Fechtschuh(m) 667.
FECHTSPORT(M) 666.
**Fechtwaffen(f) 666.**
Feder(f) 234, 258, 278, 290, 294, 375, 389, 659, 714, 804.
**Federball(m) 618.**
Federflügel(m) 276.
Federgehäuse(n) 230.
Federhaus(n) 706.
Federkranz(m) 618.
Federring(m) 278.
**Federstange(f) 665.**
Federung(f) 477.
Federverbindung(f) 702.
**Federwaage(f) 709.**
Feile(f) 688.
Feineinstellung(f) 708.
Feinnachführungssystem(n) 16.
Feinregler(m) für Dateneingabe(f) 555.
Feintrieb(m) 718.
**Feld(n) 599.**
Feld(n) 697.
Feld(n), langes 800.
Feld(n), linkes 597.
Feld(n), magnetisches 410.
Feld(n), mittleres 456.
Feld(n), rechtes 597.
Feld(n), schwarzes 696.
Feld(n), weißes 696.
Feldflasche(f) 690.
**Feldhäckseler(m) 162.**
Feldhäckseler(m) 155.
Feldlinse(f) 718.
Feldlinseneinstellung(f) 718.
Feldrichter(m) 605.
Feldsalat(m) 73.
Feldschiedsrichter(m) 612.
Feldseite(f), Spieler(m) der 599.
Feldspieler(m), zurückgezogener linker 612.
Feldspieler(m), zurückgezogener rechter 612.
Feldweg(m) 676.
Felge(f) 147, 433, 442, 447.
Felgenbremse(f), hintere 446.
Felgenbremse(f), vordere 447.
Felgenhorn(n) 433.
Fell(n) 107, 554.
Fellmütze(f) 328.
Felsen(m) 7, 30.
Felsenbecken(n) 26.
Femurkopf(m) 123.
**Fenchel(m) 72.**
FENSTER(N) 203.
Fenster(n) 194, 195, 429, 477, 498, 631.
Fensterbrett(n) 203.
Fensterhebel(m) 429.
Fensterladen(m) 203.
**Fenstertypen(m) 203.**
Fensterüberdachung(f) 685.
FENSTERZUBEHÖR(N) 230.
**Fernbedienung(f) 411.**
Fernbedienung(f) 397.
Fernbedienungssensor(m) 405.
Fernlicht(n) 429.
Fernlichtanzeige(f) 430, 431.
Fernlichtkontrolleuchte(f) 445.
Fernmeldeantenne(f) 494.
FERNMELDESATELLITEN(M) 418.
Fernmeldeschaltbrett(n) 500.
**Fernmeldeterminal(n) 422.**
Fernrohr(n) 484, 713.
**Fernsehapparat(m) 410.**
FERNSEHEN(N) 410, 412, 414.
Fernsehgerät(n) 401.
Fernteil(n) 376.
Ferse(f) 117, 119, 325.
Fersenautomatik(f) 641.
Fersenbein(n) 123.
Fersenbeinhöcker(m) 103.
Fersenhalter(m) 354.
Fersenplatte(f) 642.
Fersenrand(m) 352.
Fersenriemen(m) 356.
Fersenstütze(f) 640, 727.
Fessel(f) 101.
Fesselbein(n) 103, 107.
Festabstandmarkierung(f) 505.
**Festdachtank(m) 741.**
Festmachwinsch(m) 743.
Festplattenbus(m) 528.
**Festplattenlaufwerk(n) 529.**
Festplattenlaufwerk(n) 526, 528.
Festplattform(f) 739.
Feststeller(m) 230.
Feststeller(m) für Säule(f) 393.
Feststellgriff(m) für Hochkantstellung(f) 393.
Feststellgriff(m) für Kameraplattform(f) 393.
Feststellgriff(m) für Panoramadrehung(f) 393.
Feststellknopf(m) 280.
Feststellring(m) 276.
Feststellschraube(f) 284, 711.
Feststellspitze(f) 552.
Feststellvorrichtung(f) 230.
Feststoffrakete(f) 510.
Festungswall(m) 178.
Fett-Tröpfchen(n) 115.
Fettauffangschale(f) 253.
Fette(n) 745.
Fettgewebe(n) 129, 136.
Fettgießer(m) 246.
feucht - kurzer Sommer(m) 45.
feucht - langer Sommer(m) 45.
feuchte Subtropen(f) 45.
Feuchtigkeitsauslaß(m) 259.
Feuerbock(m) 205.
Feuerdämpfer(m) 796.
feuerhemmendes Element(n) 198.
Feuerlöscher(m) 823.
**Feuerschutzhelm(m) 777.**
Feuerschutzhelm(m) 777.
Feuerstätte(f) 204.
Feuerstein(m) 307, 791, 795.
FEUERWEHRAUTO(N) 778, 780.
Feuerwehrbeil(n) 781.
**Feuerwehrmann(m) 777.**
Feuerzange(f) 205.
**Feuerzeichen(n) 820.**
Fiale(f) 176, 181.
Fibel(f) 315.
**Fieberthermometer(n) 705.**
fiederteilig 56.
**Figuren(f) 696.**
**Figurenhantel(f) 633.**
**Figurenski(m) 633.**
Filament(n) 6.
Filiermesser(n) 242.
Filigrangewinde(n) 711.
Film(m) 390.
Filmanfang(m), Markierung(f) 390.
Filmaufnahmegerät(n) 527.
Filmaufrollspule(f) 390.
Filmdiskette(f) 395.
**Filme(m) 395.**
Filmempfindlichkeit(f) 391, 396.
Filmkassette(f) 395.
Filmlasche(f) 395.
Filmrückspulung(f) 390.
Filmtransporteinstellung(f) 391.
Filter(m) 207, 247, 252, 255, 296, 385, 772.
Filterabdeckung(f) 730.
Filterspitze(f) 384.
filum(n) terminale 134.
**Filzhut(m) 328.**
Filzhut(m) 329.
Filzstift(m) 588.
**Finger(m) 137.**
Finger(m) 84, 327, 596.
Finger(m), kleiner 137.
Fingerbeere(f) 137.
Fingerendglied(n) 137.
Fingerhut(m) 563.
Fingernagel(m) 137.
Fingernerv(m) 133.
Fingerrand(m) 726.
Fingerstrecker(m), gemeinsamer 121.
Finne(f) 579.
**Finsternisarten(f) 8.**
Firn(m) 26.
Firnis(m) 592.
Firstpfette(f) 198.
FISCH(M) 86, 88.
Fischaugenobjektiv(n) 392.
Fische(m) 11, 820.
Fischerknoten(m) 691.
Fischgabel(f) 240.
Fischgrätenmuster(n) 200.
Fischgrätenparkett(n) 200.
**Fischkochtopf(m) 248.**
Fischkorb(m) 672.
Fischmesser(n) 239.
Fischplatte(f) 238.
Fischschupper(m) 688.
FITNESSGERÄTE(N) 663, 664.
**Fittings(n) 301.**
Fixativ(n) 592.
Fixierbad(n) 399.
Fixiertaste(f) 525.
Flachbett(n) 561.
Flachbogen(m) 174.
Flachdach(n) 182.
Flächenleuchte(f) 414.
Flachfeile(f) 277.
Flachform(f) 580.
**Flachkollektor(m) 768.**
Flachpalettenwagen(m) 788.
Flachpinsel(m) 589.
Flachsilo(m) 149.
**Flachwebstuhl(m) 572.**
Flachwurzel(f) 59.
Flammenregulierung(f) 386.
Flanke(f) 101, 108, 179, 281.
Flanke(f), linke 818.
Flanke(f), rechte 818.
Flanker(m) 605.
Flare(m) 6.
Flaschendruckmesser(m) 306.
Flaschenöffner(m) 244, 688.
Flaschenwagen(m) 306.
Flechten(n) 692.
Fleck(m), blinder 140.
Fleck(m), gelber 140.
FLEDERMAUS(F) 112.
**Fledermaus(f), Kopf(m) 112.**
Fledermausärmel(m) 339.
Fleisch(n) 33.
Fleisch- und Wurstfach(n) 254.
Fleischfresser(m) 31, 33.
**Fleischfressergebiß(n) 98.**
FLEISCHIGE FRÜCHTE(F) 65.
Fleischthermometer(n) 244.
Fleischwolf(m) 243.
Fliege(f) 13, 77, 324.
Fliegender Fisch(m) 13.
Fliegenfenster(n) 685.

**Fettgedruckte** Wörter beziehen sich auf eine Illustration; Wörter in GROSSBUCHSTABEN sind Überschriften.

Fliegenpilz(m) 55.
**Fliegenrolle(f) 670.**
**Fliegenrute(f) 670.**
Fliegenschnur(f) 670.
Flieger(m) 481.
Fliese(f) 263, 286.
**Floppy-Disk(f) 529.**
Florett(n) 666.
Florettfechten(n) 666.
Florettfechter(m) 667.
Florin(m) 832.
Flosse(f) 627, 812, 814.
Flossenleitwerk(n) 498.
Flossenstrahl(m) 86.
Flug(m) 625.
Flugabwehrrakete(f) 808.
Flugbremshebel(m) 500.
Flugbrettchen(n) 82.
Flugdaten(n) 500.
Flugdeck(n) 810.
**Flugdrachen(m) 637.**
**Flügel(m) 110.**
Flügel(m) 78, 108, 112, 203, 556, 637, 638, 670, 773, 807, 812.
Flügel(m), stabiler 814.
Flügelader(f) 79.
Flügelangreifer(m) 611.
Flügelkasten(m) 812.
Flügelklappe(f), hintere 812.
Flügelmutter(f) 279.
Flügelrahmen(m) 203.
Flügelspieler(m), linker 607.
Flügelspieler(m), rechter 606, 607.
Flügelspitze(f) 637, 638.
Flügeltasche(f) 323.
Flügelverteidiger(m) 611.
Flügelwurzel(f) 498.
Fluggastbrücke(f) 503.
Fluggasttreppe(f), bewegliche 507.
FLUGHAFEN(M) 502, 504, 506.
Flughafen(m) 52.
Flughaut(f) 112.
Fluginformationsanzeige(f) 505.
FLUGKÖRPER(M) 814.
**Flugkörper(m) 814.**
**Flugkörper(m), wichtigste 814.**
Flugkörperabwehr(f) 808.
Fluglochschieber(m) 82.
Flugnavigationsvorrichtung(f) 810.
Flugrechner(m) 500.
Flugseite(f) 817.
Flugtasche(f) 382.
Flugzeug(n) 722.
FLUGZEUGTRÄGER(M) 810.
Flugzeugwartungshalle(f) 503.
Flunke(f) 483.
Flur(m) 194.
Flusensieb(n) 258.
Flush(m) 695.
Fluß(m) 51, 52.
Fluß(m) Eridanus(m) 13.
flüssiger Eyeliner(m) 367.
Flüssigkeit(f), antiseptische 725.
**Flüssigkeitskompaß(m) 484, 485.**
Flüssigsauerstofftank(m) 509.
Flüssigwasserstofftank(m) 509.
Flußkrebs(m) 90.
Flußmündung(f) 30, 51.
Fluten(n) 493.
Fly-Half(m) 606.
FM-Antenne(f) 400.
Fock(f) 481.
Fockmast(m) 479.
Fokuseinstelltaste(f), manuelle 397.
**Fön(m) 370.**
**Fondue-Set(n) 248.**
Fonduegabel(f) 240.
Fonduetopf(m) 248.
Föngehäuse(n) 370.
Foot-Line(f) 620.
**Football(m), kanadischer 605.**
FOOTBALL(N) 602, 604.
**Football(n) 602.**
**Footballspieler(m) 602.**
Foramen(n) caecum 143.
Förderband(n) 504, 733, 735.
Fördergebäude(n) 735.
Fördergerüst(n) 734.
Förderkorbstockwerk(n) 736.
Förderkübel(m) 736.
Förderplattform(f) 740.
Förderschacht(m) 736.
Fördersteigsystem(n) 738.
Förderturm(m) 735.
Förderwagen(m) 463.
Form(f), hochstehende 580.
Form(f), ovale 362.
Form(f), tiefliegende 580.
Formatbegrenzung(f), äußere 578.
Formsignal(n) 464.
Fortepedal(n) 540, 555.
Fortführungspunkte(m) 832.
Fortgeschrittenenparcours(m) 646.
**Fotoapparate(m) 394, 395.**
FOTOGRAFIE(F) 390, 392, 394, 396, 398.
FOTOKOPIERER(M) 532.
Fotozelle(f) 393.
Foullinie(f) 597, 683.
Foyer(n) 189.
Frachtempfang(m) 505.
Frachtraum(m) 499.
Frachtversand(m) 505.
Fragezeichen(n) 832.
Fraktionierturm(m) 744.
Franc(m) 832.
**Francisturbine(f) 754.**
Franse(f) 318.
Fransen(f) 229.
französisches Weißbrot(n) 153.
FREGATTE(F) 808.
**Freiballon(m) 634.**
FREIBALLONSPORT(M) 634.
Freifahrtschlitz(m) 188.
Freihand-Dekoration(f) 229.
Freilauf(m) 448.
**Freileitung(f) 757.**
Freiluftterrasse(f) 497.
Freiraum(m) 613.
Freisaiten(f) 535.
Freiwange(f) 201.
Freiwurfbahn(f) 610.
Freiwurflinie(f) 610, 612.
French-cut(m) 362.
Frequenzanzeige(f), digitale 402.
Fresko(n) 170.
Friedhof(m) 52.
Fries(m) 166, 168, 225.
Frischluftzufuhr(f) 639.
Frischwasserwagen(m) 506.
Frisierbürste(f), flache 368.
**Friteuse(f) 252.**
Fritierkorb(m) 252.
Front(f), stationäre 39.
Frontalzacken(m) 680.
**Fronten(f) 39.**
Frontgewicht(n) 147.
**Frosch(m) 84.**
Frosch(m) 544.
**Frosch(m), Lebenszyklus(m) 84.**
Fruchtbecher(m) 66.
Fruchtbildung(f) 61.
Fruchtblatt(n) 67.
FRÜCHTE(F), FLEISCHIGE 62.
Fruchtfach(n) 65.
Fruchtfleisch(n) 62, 63, 64, 65.
**Fruchtgemüse(n) 69.**
Fruchtholz(n) 61.
Fruchtkapsel(f) 67.
**Fruchtkapsel(f), Querschnitt(m) 67.**
Fruchtknoten(m) 60.
Fruchtknotenfach(n) 64.
**Fruchtschote(f), Längsschnitt(m) 67.**
Fruchtwand(f) 65, 66.
Frühling(m) 8.
Frühlingsäquinoktium(n) 3, 8.
Frühlingszwiebel(f) 70.
**Fuchsschwanz(m) 277.**
Fugendüse(f) 260.
Fugenkelle(f) 291.
Fühlerputzer(m) 80.
Führerhaus(n) 785.
Führerkabine(f) 782, 783, 784, 785.
Führerpult(n) 468.
Führerraum(m) 508.
Führerstand(m) 459, 468.
Fuhrmann(m) 11.
Führungsgriff(m) 283, 284.
Führungshebel(m) 283.
Führungsnut(f) 285.
Führungsrille(f) 641.
Führungsring(m) 670.
Führungsring(m), erster 671.
Führungsrolle(f) 403.
Führungsschiene(f) 428, 476, 517, 568.
Führungsschienenantrieb(m) 529.
Führungsständer(m) 787, 788.
Führungsturm(m) 457.
Full House(n) 695.
Füllanzeige(f), automatische 741.
Füllanzeigeschwimmer(m) 741.
Fullback(m) 603, 605, 606.
Füllen(n) 11.
**Füllfederhalter(m) 389.**
Füllfederhalter(m) 515.
Füllmenge(f) 453.
Fülloch(n) 804.
Füllrohr(n) 293.
Fülltür(f) 204.
Füllung(f) 202.
Fumarole(f) 24.
**Fundament(n) 199.**
Fundament(n) 198, 199, 751.
Fundamentklotz(m) 751.
Fundamentstreifen(m) 198, 199.
Fundamenttafel(f) 543.
Fundbüro(n) 823.
fünf Nummern(f) 700.
Fünferpin(m) 683.
Fungerät(n) 639.
Funiculus(m) 62.
Funkantenne(f) 494, 495, 497, 742, 807.
Funken(m) 436.
Funkenstrecke(f) 439.
Funkmast(m) 738.
Funktionsanzeige(f) 555.
Funktionsschalter(m) 402.
Funktionstaste(f) 699.
Funktionstasten(f) 421, 422, 530, 709.
Funktionswähler(m) 214, 420.
Funkübertragungssystem(n) 512.
Furche(f) 105.
Fuß(m) 78, 80, 83, 112, 116, 117, 118, 119, 224, 225, 236, 264, 283, 325, 350, 397, 542, 545, 574, 579, 631, 718, 817.
Fußablage(f) 727.
**Fußarten(f) 111.**
Fußbalken(m) 198, 199.
FUSSBALL(M) 600.
**Fußball(m) 600.**
Fußballschuh(m) 600.
**Fußballspieler(m) 600.**
Fußboden(m) 205.
Fußbohrung(f) 542.
Füße(m) voraus 624.
Fusselfilter(m) 259.
Fußende(n) 224.
Fußfessel(f) 652.
Fußfesselriemen(m) 652.
Fußgänger(m) 828.
Fußgängerbrücke(f) 464, 475.
Fußgängerüberweg(m) 186, 826, 827.
Fußgelenk(n) 106.
Fußgelenksgewicht(n) 665.
Fußgestell(n) 223.
Fußgewölbearterie(f) 126.
Fußholz(n) 202.
Fußnagelschere(f) 365.
Fußpferd(n) 478.
Fußrand(m) 818.
Fußraste(f), vordere 443, 444.
Fußriemen(m) 664.
Fußrückenarterie(f) 126.
Fußschlaufe(f) 631.
FUSSSCHUTZ(M) 730.
Fußsteg(m) 577.
Fußstelle(f) 818.
Fußstück(n) 579.
Fußstütze(f) 584, 656, 664.
Fußtritt(m) 542.
Fußwurzel(f) 103.
Fußwurzelknochen(m) 122.
Futter(n) 322, 324, 352, 354, 378, 565, 644.
Futteral(n) 375.
Futtergetreide(n) 149.
**Futterstoffe(m) 565.**

## G

g 537.
**Gabel(f) 240.**
Gabel(f) 105, 375, 688, 707, 721, 787.
Gabel-Ringschlüssel(m) 279.
Gabelbaum(m) 631.
Gabeln(f) 787, 788.
Gabelschlüssel(m) 279.
**Gabelstapler(m) 787.**
Gabelstaplertasche(f) 470.
**Gabeltypen(m) 240.**
Gaffel(f) 478.
Gaffelsegel(n) 482.
Gaitau(n) 481.
Gaitau(n) des Besans(m) 480.
GALAXIE(F) 9.
Galerie(f) 175, 486, 773.
Gallenblase(f) 97, 131.
Galopp(m) 101.
**Galopprennbahn(f) mit Tribüne(f) 651.**
GALOPPRENNEN(N) 651.
Ganasche(f) 100.
Gang(m) 25.
**Gangarten(f) 101, 696.**
Ganglion(n), symphatisches 135.
Gangway(f) 742.
Gans(f) 150.
Ganymed(m) 4.
ganzrandig 56.
Garage(f) 196.
Garagenzufahrt(f) 196.
Garderobe(f) 189, 194, 522.
Garderobenständer(m) 522.
**Gardinenschiene(f) 230.**
**Gardinenstange(f) 230.**
Gardinenstange(f), einläufige 230.
Gardinenstange(f), zweiläufige 230.
**Gardinentypen(m) 228.**
Garn(n) 692.
Garnball(m) 596.
Garnele(f) 90.
Garnführer(m) 569.
Garnhalter(m) 569.
Garnierspritze(f) 245.
Garnrollenstift(m) 561.
Garnspannungseinheit(f) 569.
Garnstange(f) 569.
Garten(m) 171.
Garten-Sauerampfer(m) 73.
**Gartenfräse(f) 272.**
GARTENGERÄT(N) 264, 266, 268, 270, 272.
Gartenhäuschen(n) 263.
Gartenkürbis(m) 69.
Gartenschlauch(m) 265.
Gartenspritze(f) 265.
Gartenteich(m) 263.
Gartenweg(m) 263.
Gas(n) 34, 35, 232, 744.
Gasabscheider(m) 738.
Gasbehälter(m) 689.
Gasbrenner(m) 297.
Gasbrenner(m), einflammiger 689.
**Gasbrenner(m), zweiflammiger 689.**
**Gasfeuerzeug(n) 386.**
Gashebel(m) 272, 444, 500.
Gaskolben(m) 796.
Gasleitung(f) 186.
**Gasmaske(f) 730.**
Gasöl(n) 744.
Gaspedal(n) 430.
Gasrohr(n) 297.
Gasschweif(m) 9.
Gasse(f) 614, 618, 683.
Gasstromregulierung(f) 689.
Gasventil(n) 297.
**Gaswarmwasserbereiter(m) 297.**
Gaszug(m) 270, 271.
Gatter(n) 646, 647.
Gaumen(m), harter 141, 142.
Gaumen(m), weicher 141, 142.
Gaumenbogen(m), forderer 142.
Gaumenmandel(f) 143.
Gebälk(n) 166, 168, 202.
Gebärmutter(f) 128, 129.
Gebärmutterhals(m) 128.
Gebäude(n), öffentliches 52.
GEBÄUDEPLANUNG(F) 193, 195.
Gebetshalle(f) 172, 173.
Gebirgsbach(m) 27.
Gebirgskette(f) 23, 51.
Gebirgsmasse(f) 51.
Gebiß(n) 650.
**Gebiß(n), menschliches 144.**
GEBISSARTEN(F) 98.
Gebißriemen(m) 649.
GEBISSTÜCKARTEN(F) 650.
Gebläse(n) 161, 162, 207, 209, 214, 259, 543, 760.
Gebläsemotor(m) 207.
Gebläserohr(n) 162.
geboren 831.
**gebräuchliche Bezeichnungen(f) 62, 63, 64, 65.**
gebuchtet 56.
Gedankenstrich(m) 832.
gedeckter Weg(m) 178.
gedeckter Wehrgang(m) 180.
Gedrängehalbspieler(m) 606.
Gefahrenbereich(m) 668.
Gefahrenstelle(f) 488.
Gefälle(n) 826, 827.
Gefechtskopf(m) 814.
Geflügelschere(f) 246.
Gefrierfach(n) 254.
Gegenausleger(m) 786.
Gegenauslegerballast(m) 786.
Gegenfänger(m) 541.
gegengedrehter Teil(m) 42.
Gegengewicht(n) 15, 457, 471, 784, 785, 786.
Gegenleiste(f) 139.

Gegenlichtblende(f) 392, 409, 484.
Gegenmutter(f) 40.
Gegensprechanlage(f) 477.
Gegenverkehr(m) 824, 825.
Gehäuse(n) 82, 83, 211, 214, 233, 252, 256, 258, 259, 271, 280, 305, 310, 374, 403, 406, 410, 422, 485, 486, 540, 643, 702, 705, 706, 707, 710, 711.
Gehäuseabdeckung(f) 525.
Gehäuseverstärkung(f) 702.
Gehfalte(f) 335.
Gehgestell(n) 728.
GEHHILFEN(F) 728.
Gehirn(n) 88.
**Gehkrücke(f) 728.**
GEHÖR(N) 138.
Gehörgang(m) 138, 139.
**Gehörknöchelchen(n) 138.**
Gehörknöchelchen(n) 139.
Gehörnerv(m) 139.
GEHÖRSCHUTZ(M) 729.
Gehörschutz(m) 821.
Gehrungsanschlag(m) 285.
Gehstock(m) 728.
**Geigenfamilie(f) 545.**
Geißfuß(m) 581.
gekerbt 56.
Gekrösearterie(f), obere 132.
Gekrösearterie(f), untere 132.
Gekröseschlagader(f), obere 126.
Geländer(n) 201, 454.
Geländerstab(m) 201.
Geländewagen(m) 425.
Gelatinekapsel(f) 725.
gelber Fleck(m) 140.
Geldbetrag(m) 453.
Geldrückgabe(f) 422.
Geldwechsel(m) 823.
Gelenk(n) 354, 431, 641, 785.
Gelenkhöcker(m) 123.
Gelenkschäkel(m) 630.
**gemäßigte Klimate(n) 45.**
Gemini 820.
GEMÜSE(N) 69, 70, 71, 72, 73.
Gemüse(n) 33.
Gemüsebürste(f) 246.
Gemüsedünster(m) 249.
Gemüsegarten(m) 148.
Gemüsezwiebel(f) 70.
Generator(m) 468, 753, 755, 758, 767.
Generatoreinheit(f) 747.
Generatorspannungsübertragung(f) 755.
Genicklasche(f) 729.
Genickstück(n) 649.
**Geometrie(f) 830.**
GEPÄCK(N) 382.
Gepäckablage(f) 461.
Gepäckanhänger(m) 383, 507.
Gepäckaufbewahrung(f) 462.
Gepäckausgabe(f) 504.
Gepäckcontainer(m) 492.
Gepäckförderer(m) 507.
Gepäckgummi(n) 382.
Gepäckraum(m) 458, 461, 508.
**Gepäckroller(m) 382.**
Gepäckschließfächer(n) 463.
Gepäckträger(m) 445, 446, 449.
Gerade(f), hintere 651.
Gerade(f): Pfosten(m) mit Stange(f) 646.
Geradseite(f) 743.
Geräteanschluß(m) 374.
Gerätefach(n) 458.
Geräteraum(m), allgemeiner 412.
Geräteschuppen(m) 148.
Geräteteil(m) 16.
GERÄTETURNEN(N) 659, 660.
Geräuschdämpfer(m) 735.
Gerste(f) 152.
Gerstenkornmuster(n) 567.
GERUCHSSINN(M) 141, 142.
Geruchsverschluß(m) 215, 293, 296.
Gerüstträger(m) 756.
gesägt 56.
Gesäß(n) 117, 119, 127, 128.
Gesäßmuskel(m), großer 121.
Gesäßnerv(m) 133.
Gesäßtasche(f) 323.
Geschäftsbuch(n) 518.
Geschäftshaus(n) 185.
GESCHIRR(N) 238.
Geschirr(n) 572.
**Geschirrspülmaschine(f) 257, 298.**
Geschirrspülmaschine(f) 298.
Geschirrwagen(m) 255.
Geschlechtsöffnung(f) 83.
GESCHLECHTSORGANE(N), MÄNNLICHE 127.
GESCHLECHTSORGANE(N), WEIBLICHE 128, 129.
Geschmack(m), bitterer 143.
Geschmack(m), salziger 143.
Geschmack(m), saurer 143.
Geschmack(m), süßer 143.
**Geschmacksempfindungen(f) 143.**
GESCHMACKSSINN(M) 142.
Geschoß(n) 801.
Geschoß(n), panzerbrechendes 804.
**Geschoßzubehör(n) 801.**
GESCHÜTZ(N), RÜCKSTOSSFREIES 804.
Geschützrohr(n) 805.
Geschützturm(m) 809.
Geschwindigkeitsanzeige(f) 639.
Geschwindigkeitsregelung(f) 250, 251, 561.
Geschwindigkeitsregler(m) 271.
Gesicht(n) 116.
Gesichtsmaske(f) 602, 643.
Gesichtsnerv(m) 139.
Gesichtsschutz(m) 308, 777.
Gesichtsschutz(m), geschlossener 777.
Gesichtsschutzmaske(f) 609.
Gesichtsstück(n) 730.
Gesims(n) 196, 202.
gespalten 818.
Gestänge(n) 685.
gestanztes Loch(n) 353.
Gestein(n), undurchdringliches 737.
Gestell(n) 302, 726.
gestelzter Bogen(m) 174.
gestorben 831.
geteilt 818.
Getränkeautomat(m) 453.
Getreidesilo(m) 490.
GETREIDESORTEN(F) 152.
Getriebe(n) 258, 495.
geviert 818.
Gewände(n) 175.
Gewebe(n) 634.
Gewebe-Einstellskala(f) 256.
**Gewebestruktur(f) 566.**
**Gewehr(n) 798.**
GEWEHR(N), AUTOMATISCHES 796.
Gewicht(n) 658, 665, 707, 708, 709.
Gewicht(n), feststehendes 539.
Gewichte(n) 663.
GEWICHTHEBEN(N) 662.
**Gewichtheber(m) 662.**
Gewichthebergürtel(m) 662.
Gewichtheberschuh(m) 662.
Gewichtsausgleicher(m) 802.
**Gewichtsstaudamm(m) 749.**
gewimpert 56.
Gewinde(n) 94, 276, 294, 675.
Gewindekappe(f) 301.
Gewindeschaft(m) 279.
Gewindeschneider(m) 299.
Gewinnkombination(f) 702.
Gewitter(n) 39.
Gewitter(n), starkes 39.
**Gewölbe(n) 177.**
Gewölbekörper(m) 134.
Geysir(m) 25.
gezähnter Rand(m) 95.
**Gezeitenkraftwerk(n) 752.**
Giebeldreieck(n) 166, 168, 707.
Giebelseite(f) 197.
Giebelständer(m) 198.
Gießbrause(f) 264.
**Gießkanne(f) 265.**
Gießpistole(f) 264.
Gift(n) 821.
Gift-Leitfurche(f) 96.
Giftdrüse(f) 96.
Giftkanal(m) 96.
**Giftpilz(m) 55.**
**Giftschlange(f), Kopf(m) 96.**
Giftzahn(m) 96.
Gipfel(m) 27.
Gipsbinden(f) 725.
Gipsschlinge(f) 585.
Giraffe(f) 11.
Giraffe(f), Hörner(n) 99.
**Gitarre(f), akustische 546.**
**Gitarre(f), elektrische 547.**
Gitter(n) 168, 214, 410, 536.
**Gitterboxpalette(f) 787.**
Gittereinsatz(m) 248.
Glacis(n) 178.
Glanzschicht(f) 136.
Glas(n) 376, 689.
Glasabdeckung(f) 768, 769.
Glasdach(n) 190, 195.
GLÄSER(N) 237.
Glasgehäuse(n) 709.
Glashaube(f) 484.
Glaskolben(m) 247.
Glaskörper(m) 140.
Glaskugel(f) 40.
Glasmalerei(f) 175.
Glasplatte(f) 254.
Glasscheibe(f) 718.
Glasüberdachung(f) 462.
Glattstrick(m) 567.
gleich 830.
gleich oder größer als 830.
gleich oder kleiner als 830.
Gleichtaste(f) 523.
**Gleis(n) 476.**
Gleis(n) 463, 474.
Gleise(n) 471.
Gleiskette(f) 783.
Gleiskettenschlepper(m) 783.
Gleiskreuzung(f) 464.
Gleisnummer(f) 462.
Gleitflieger(m) 636.
Gleitfuge(f) 278.
**Gleitschirm(m) 636.**
GLEITSCHIRMFLIEGEN(N) 636.
Gleitschuh(m) 284.
Gleitschutz(m) 641.
Gleitstuhl(m) 467.
GLETSCHER(M) 26.
Gletscherspalte(f) 26.
Gletscherzunge(f) 26.
Gliederpuppe(f) 592.
Gliedmaßen(f), obere 124.
Gliedmaßen(f), untere 124.
Glimmlampe(f) 310.
Glocke(f) 666.
Glockendach(n) 183.
Glockendichtung(f) 293.
Glockenstube(f) 175, 176.
Glockenturm(m) 175.
Glottis(f) 96, 142.
Glücksrad(n) 702.
Glühbirne(f) 310, 769.
Glühfaden(m) 232.
**Glühlampe(f) 232.**
Glühlampe(f) 486.
Gnomon(m) 706.
GO(N) 697.
Gobelinbindung(f) 576.
Gold(n) 819.
Golf(m) 51.
**Golfball(m) 677.**
Golfhandschuh(m) 679.
**Golfplatz(m) 676.**
**Golfschläger(m) 677, 678.**
Golfschuh(m) 679.
GOLFSPIEL(N) 676, 678.
**Golftasche(f) 679.**
Golfwagen(m) 679.
**Golfwagen(m), elektrischer 679.**
Golgi-Apparat(m) 115.
**Gondel(f) 635.**
Gondel(f) 634.
Gondelhaltegriff(m) 635.
Gonfalon(m) 817.
Gong(m) 554, 557.
GOTHISCHER DOM(M) 175.
GOTISCHER DOM(M) 176.
**Gouache(f) 588.**
Graben(m) 178, 451, 682, 733.
Grabgabel(f) 266.
Grabschaufel(f) 266.
Grabstichel(m) 13.
Grad(m) 830.
Grad(m) Celsius 705.
Grad(m) Fahrenheit 705.
Gradbogen(m) 484.
Gradeinteilung(f) 719.
**Gradnetz(n) 47.**
Grahambrot(n) 153.
Granat(m) 363.
Granatapfel(m) 68.
Granitschale(f) 22.
Granne(f) 152.
Granulation(f) 6.
Grapefruit(f) 65.
Grapefruitmesser(n) 242.
Graphit(m) 760.
Graphitstift(m) 389.
Graphosfeder(f) 589.
Grasfang(m) 271.
Grat(m) 27, 167.
graue Substanz(f) 135.
Graviernadel(f) 583.
Gravurplatte(f) 364.
Greifer(m) 562.
Greifzirkel(m) 583.
Grenze(f), innere 51.
GRIECHISCHER TEMPEL(M) 168.
**griechischer Tempel(m), Grundriß(m) 169.**
griechisches Brot(n) 153.
Griessäule(f) 156.
Griff(m) 204, 224, 239, 240, 255, 265, 270, 271, 272, 277, 278, 279, 284, 291, 304, 306, 310, 370, 373, 374, 375, 378, 380, 382, 383, 461, 544, 563, 564, 566, 570, 573, 579, 596, 598, 607, 615, 619, 620, 632, 640, 643, 665, 666, 670, 677, 679, 684, 688, 728, 735.
Griff(m), ausziehbarer 378.
Griff(m), isolierter 310, 311.
Griff(m), zusätzlicher 280.
**Griffbeispiele(n) 668.**
Griffbrett(n) 535, 544, 547.
Griffel(m) 60, 67.
Griffelbein(n) 102.
Griffhebel(m) für S-Bogen(m) 548.
Griffkamm(m) 368.
**Grifftechniken(f) 619.**
Griffteil(n) 675.
Griffzeitnehmer(m) 668.
**Grill(m) 253.**
Grillfläche(f) 253.
Grindel(m) 156.
Grobregler(m) für Dateneingabe(f) 555.
Grobspanplatte(f) 288.
Grobtrieb(m) 718.
Grönlandsee(f) 20.
Groß-Oberbramsegel(n) 481.
Groß-Obermarsegel(n) 481.
Groß-Royalsegel(n) 481.
Groß-Unterbramsegel(n) 481.
Groß-Untermarsegel(n) 481.
Große Außensichel(f) 668.
Große Innensichel(f) 668.
größer als 830.
Großer Bär(m) 11.
Großer Hund(m) 13.
Großformatkamera(f) 394.
Großhirn(n) 134.
Großmast(m) 479.
Großrad(n) 727.
**Großraumwagen(m) 460.**
Großschot(f) 628.
Großsegel(n) 481.
**Großtonne(f) 487.**
**Grubber(m) 157.**
**Grube(f) 736.**
Grube(f) 683.
**Grube(f), offene 733.**
Grubenorgan(n) 96.
grün 819.
**Grün(n) 682.**
Grünanlage(f) 184, 190.
GRUNDBAUTEILE(N) 528, 530.
**Grundbindungen(f) 576.**
Grundgestein(n) 714.
Grundglied(n) 123.
Grundierung(f), flüssige 366.
Grundlinie(f) 614.
Grundlinienrichter(m) 614.
Grundmoräne(f) 26.
Grundplatte(f) 40, 399, 404, 641, 712, 803.
Grundring(m) 753.
Grundstücksgrenze(f) 193.
Grundwasserspiegel(m) 24.
Grünkohl(m) 73.
Grünstrahl(m) 410.
Guard(m), linker 603, 605.
Guard(m), rechter 603, 605.
Guave(f) 68.
Guckloch(n) 471.
Guidon(m) 817.
Gummiband(n) 224, 323.
Gummieinsatz(m) 677.
**Gummigebiß(n) 650.**
**Gummihöschen(n) 349.**
Gummikappe(f) 728.
Gummimatte(f) 404.
Gummipfropfen(m) 726.
Gummiring(m) 296.
Gummischlauch(m) 298, 726, 735.
Gummischutz(m) 652.
Gummispannring(m) 685, 686.
Gummistiefel(m) 777.
Gummistöpsel(m) 302.
Gurke(f) 69.
Gurt(m) 668.
Gurtbogen(m) 177.
**Gürtel(m) 323.**
Gürtel(m) 319.
Gürtelband(n) 323.
Gürtellage(f) 433.
Gürtelschlaufe(f) 319, 323, 688.
Gürtelschnalle(f) 323.
Gürtelspitze(f) 323.
Gurtrohrzange(f) 299.
Gurtschließe(f) 428.
Gurtschnalle(f) 649.

**Fettgedruckte** Wörter beziehen sich auf eine Illustration; Wörter in GROSSBUCHSTABEN sind Überschriften.

Gurtstrippe(f) 649.
Gurtwerk(n) 627, 635, 636, 637.
Gußerker(m) 181.
**Gußlochreihe(f) 181.**
Gußlochreihe(f) 180.
Gußrad(n) 440.
Gutenberg-Diskontinuität(f) 22.
Güterbahnhof(m) 464.
GÜTERWAGEN(M) 472.
Güterwagen(m) 464.
Güterwagen(m), offener 473.
Gutta(f) 167.
Guyot(m) 28.
Gymnastikhose(f) ohne Fuß(m) 353.

## H

h 537.
Haar(n) 117, 119, 136, 544.
Haar(n) der Berenike(f) 11.
Haaraufrichter(m) 136.
Haarbalg(m) 136.
**Haarbürsten(f) 368.**
Haarclip(m) 369.
Haarklemme(f) 369.
Haarliftkamm(m) 368.
HAARPFLEGE(F) 368, 370.
Haarschaft(m) 136.
Haarschneidekamm(m) 368.
Haarschneider(m) 369.
**Haarschneideschere(f) 369.**
Haarspange(f) 369.
Haarstecker(m) 369.
**Haarzubehör(n) 369.**
Haarzwiebel(f) 136.
Hack(m) 620.
Hackrahmen(m) 154.
HAFEN(M) 490.
Hafenbahn(f) 491.
Hafenfähre(f) 491.
Hafenzollamt(n) 491.
Hafer(m) 152.
Haferwurz(f) 71.
Haftgurtband(n) 349.
Haftscheibe(f) 85.
Hagel(m) 37.
Hagelschauer(m) 39.
Hagelschnur(f) 109.
Hahn(m) 150, 795.
**Häkelnadel(f) 567.**
**Haken(m) 566.**
Haken(m) 230, 310, 566, 567, 568, 674, 681, 709, 711, 726, 786.
Hakenbogen(m) 671.
Hakenbogentiefe(f) 671.
Hakengurt(m) 777.
Hakenhalteöse(f) 670.
Hakenhalter(m) 680.
Hakeninnenweite(f) 671.
Hakenleiter(f) 781.
Hakenlöser(m) 672.
Hakenspitze(f) 671.
Hakenverriegelung(f) 203.
Hakler(m) 606.
Halbbrille(f) 377.
**Halbedelsteine(m) 363.**
halber Wind(m) 629.
**Halbgeschoß(n) 194.**
Halbgeschoß(n) 195.
Halbinsel(f) 51.
Halbkreis(m) 610.
Halbmond(m) 179.
Halbmond(m) (erstes Viertel(n)) 6.
Halbmond(m) (letztes Viertel(n)) 7.
Halbmumienschlafsack(m) 687.
Halbschale(f) 346.
Halbschatten(m) 8.
Halbsehnenmuskel(m) 121.
Halbseite(f) 787.
Halbspieler(m) 597.
Halbstiefel(m) 354.
Halbtaucher(m) 739.
Halfback(m) 605.
Halfback(m), linker 603.
Halfback(m), rechter 603.
Halm(m) 369, 564.
Halmteiler(m) 160.
Hals(m) 57, 97, 100, 117, 118, 119, 127, 144, 240, 241, 410, 483, 544, 545, 546, 547, 570, 579, 615, 631, 661, 678.
Halsausschnitt(n) 325.
Halsberge(f) 792.
Halskette(f) in Matineelänge(f) 361.
Halskette(f) in Opernlänge(f) 361.
Halskette(f), mehrreihig 361.
**Halsketten(f) 361.**
Halskrause(f) 318, 341.
Halsring(m) 167.
Halsschlagader(f) 126.
Halsschutz(m) 595, 609.
Halstalje(f) 628.
Halsumklammerung(f) 668.
Halswirbel(m) 102.
Halswirbel(m) (7) 123.
Haltebügel(m) 727.
Haltegriff(m) 779.
Haltegriff(m), vorderer 804.
Haltegriffe(m) 668.
Haltemutter(f) 670, 671.
Halter(m) 232.
Halteriemen(m) 652.
Halterung 447.
Halterung(f) 709, 735.
Halterung(f) für die Registrierkarten(f) 40.
Halterungsschraube(f), obere 40.
Halterungsschraube(f), untere 40.
Haltestange(f) 440, 449.
**Hammer(m) 658.**
Hammer(m) 138, 264, 275, 311, 540, 541, 797, 798, 799.
**Hammer(m) mit runder Bahn(f) 275.**
**Hammer(m) zum Rundklopfen(n) 579.**
Hammerbahn(f) 579.
Hammerfilz(m) 541.
Hammergriff(m) 658.
Hammerkopf(m) 658, 681.
Hammerleiste(f) 540.
Hammernuß(f) 541.
Hammerruheleiste(f) 541.
Hammerstiel(m) 541.
Hammerwerfen(n) 654.
**Hand(f) 137.**
Hand(f) 117, 119.
Hand- und Maschinenwäsche(f) 829.
Handapparat(m) 420, 422.
HANDBALL(M) 612.
**Handball(m) 612.**
Handbeuger(m) der Ellenseite(f) 120, 121.
Handblasebalg(m) 710.
**Handbohrer(m) 280.**
Handbrause(f) 292.
Handbremshebel(m) 430.
Handbremsrad(n) 470.
HANDBUCHBINDEREI(F) 577, 578.
Handdecken(f), große 110.
Handdecken(f), mittlere 110.
Handebremsehebel(m) 470.
**Handfeuerlöscher(m) 780.**
Handfläche(f) 137, 596.
handförmig 56.
Handgabel(f) 268.
Handgelenk(n) 112, 117, 119, 137.
Handgelenkpolster(n) 602.
Handgelenksgewicht(n) 665.
HANDGRANATE(F) 804.
Handgriff(m) 250, 251, 252, 253, 254, 256, 260, 294, 295, 793.
**Handkreissäge(f) 284.**
Handkultivator(m) 266.
Handkurbel(f) 441, 583.
**Handlampe(f) 310.**
Handlauf(m) 201.
Handlöser(m) 641.
Handmuskeltrainer(m) 665.
Handrad(n) 561, 802.
**Handrasenmäher(m) 271.**
**Handrührgerät(n) 250.**
Handschild(n) 308.
Handschlaufe(f) 640, 642, 666, 681.
**Handschuh(m) 596.**
Handschuh(m) 512, 598, 609, 635, 642, 643, 680.
HANDSCHUHE(M) 327.
Handschuhkasten(m) 430.
Handschutz(m) 268, 796.
Handschwingen(f) 110.
**Handspulgerät(n) 575.**
Handstand(m) 624.
**Handstandsprung(m) 625.**
Handstange(f) 470, 477.
Handstrecker(m) der Ellenseite(f) 121.
Handstrecker(m), kurzer 121.
Handstrecker(m), langer 121.
HANDTASCHEN(F) 380.
Handteil(n) 666.
Handtuchhalter(m) 292.
**Handwaage(f) 708.**
Handwagen(m) 788.
Handwäsche(f) 829.
Handwurzel(f) 596.
Handwurzelknochen(m) 122.
Hang(m) 451.
Hängeärmel(m) 316.
**Hängebrücke(f) 456.**
Hängegletscher(m) 26.
Hängeisolator(m) 756.
Hängekartei(f) 520.
Hängeleinen(f) 636.
Hängeleuchte(f) 236.
Hängemappe(f) 518.
Hanger(m) 478.
Hänger(m) 456.
Hängesäule(f) 199, 225.
Hängesprengwerkbrücke(f) 455.
**Hantel(f) 663, 665.**
Hantel(f) 633.
**Hantelarten(f) 633.**
Hantelgriff(m) 633.
Hantelstange(f) 662, 663.
**Harfe(f) 545.**
Harfen(f) 556.
Harmonikatür(f) 202.
Harnblase(f) 89, 127, 128, 132.
Harnleiter(m) 129, 132.
Harnröhre(f) 127, 128, 132.
Harnröhrengang(m) 127.
HARNSYSTEM(N) 132.
Harpune(f) 627.
hart am Wind(m) 629.
Hartfaserplatte(f) 289.
Hase(m) 13.
Haselnuß(f) 66.
**Haselnuß(f), Längsschnitt(m) 66.**
Haspe(f) 383.
Haspel(f) 158, 160.
Haspelrohr(n) 160.
Häubchen(n) 577.
Haube(f) 260, 440.
HAUBITZE(F), MODERNE 802.
Haue(f) 681.
Hauer(m) eines Warzenschweins(n) 99.
Hauptabschnitt(m) 700, 701.
Hauptanschluß(m) 757.
Hauptanzeige(f) 500.
Hauptapsis(f) 177.
Hauptband(n) 645.
Hauptbolzen(m) 471.
Hauptdampfleitungen(f) 759.
Hauptdampfverteiler(m) 759.
Hauptdeck(n) 743, 811.
Haupteinfüllstutzen(m) 741.
Haupteingang(m) 190, 194.
Hauptelektromotor(m) 806.
Hauptfahrwasser(n) 489.
Hauptfahrwerk(n) 499, 812.
Hauptfallschirm(m) 635.
Hauptgleis(n) 464.
Hauptgriff(m) 280.
Hauptlinienrichter(m) 603.
Hauptluftbehälter(m) 469.
Hauptlüfter(m) 734.
Hauptmannloch(n) 743.
Hauptrad(m) 707.
Hauptrand(m) 818.
Hauptreflexspiegel(m) 390.
Hauptringentlüfter(m) 215.
Hauptschalter(m) 312, 757.
Hauptschieber(m) 740.
Hauptschiedsrichter(m) 597.
Hauptschlitten(m) 568.
Hauptschlot(m) 25.
Hauptschwert(n) 631.
Hauptschwerteinzug(m) 631.
Hauptsegel(n) 628.
Hauptsicherung(f) 312.
Hauptsparren(m) 199.
Hauptspiegel(m) 14, 720.
**Hauptspielzüge(m) 697.**
Hauptspuren(f) 452.
Hauptstadt(f) 51.
Hauptstandbein(n) 756.
Hauptständer(m) 443.
Hauptstiel(m) 61.
Haupttragegurt(m) 636.
Haupttransformator(m) 458.
Haupttribüne(f) 651.
Haupttriebwerk(n) 511.
Hauptverteilleitung(f) 206.
Hauptvorhang(m) 188, 189.
Hauptvorschaumonitor(m) 413.
Hauptwurzel(f) 57.
Hauptzeitnehmer(m) 621.
Haus(n) 193, 620.
Hausbaum(m) 773.
HÄUSERFORMEN(F) IN DER STADT 187.
Hausfrauenknoten(m) 691.
HAUSHALTSGERÄTE(N) 250, 252, 254, 256, 257, 258, 260.
Hauskleid(n) 333.
**Haustür(f) 202.**
**Hauszelt(n) 686.**
**Haut(f) 136.**
Haut(f) 62, 63, 84, 134.
Hautoberfläche(f) 137.
Hebeglied(n) 541.
Hebegriff(m) 803.
Hebel(m) 252, 278, 284, 296, 365, 444, 453, 583, 590, 702.
Hebel-Korkenzieher(m) 244.
Heber(m) 785.
Hebestück(n) 737.
Hebewerk(n) 737.
Hechtsprungstellung(f) 624.
Heck(n) 250, 496, 499, 631.
Hecke(f) 263.
Heckenschere(f) 269.
**Heckleuchten(f) 429.**
Heckrotor(m) 508.
Hecksporn(m) 508.
Heft(n) 276.
Heft(n), halbes 242.
**Heften(n) 578.**
Hefter(m) 515, 519.
Heftklammern(f) 515.
**Heftlade(f) 578.**
Heftpflaster(n) 725.
Heidelbeere(f) 62.
Heidelbeere(f), amerikanische 62.
**Heimtrainer(m) 664.**
Heißluft(f) 501.
Heißluftaustritt(m) 204.
Heißring(m) 483.
Heizelement(n) 207, 257, 259, 305, 585.
Heizer(m) 771.
Heizfläche(f) 370.
Heizflächen(f) 209.
Heizkörper(m) 208.
Heizlüfter(m) 211.
Heizöl(n) 745.
Heizspirale(f) 255, 635.
Heizstrahler(m) 211, 689.
HEIZUNG(F) 204, 206, 208, 210, 212.
Heizung(f) 494.
Heizungsgitter(n) 477.
Heizventil(n) 635.
Heliostatanordnung(f) 770, 771.
Heliumsphäre(f) 509.
Helixschwanz(m) 139.
Helligkeitsregelung(f) 512.
Helligkeitsregler(m) 529.
**Helm(m) 792.**
Helm(m) 512, 791, 792.
Helmbusch(m) 791.
Helmdach(n) 183.
Helmglocke(f) 792.
Helmlampe(f) 680.
**Hemd(n) 324.**
Hemd(n) 656.
Hemdblusenärmel(m) 340.
Hemdblusenkleid(n) 333.
Hemdblusenkragen(m) 341.
Hemdchen(n) 349.
Hemdhose(f) 325.
Hemisphäre(f), nördliche 47.
Hemisphäre(f), östliche 47.
Hemisphäre(f), südliche 47.
Hemisphäre(f), westliche 47.
**Hemisphären(f) 47.**
Hemmrad(n) 706, 707.
Hemmungslappen(m) 707.
Henne(f) 150.
Hennin(m) 318.
Hepad(m) 42.
HERALDIK(F) 817, 818.
Herausarbeiten(n) 586.
Herbst(m) 8.
Herbstäquinoktium(n) 8.
Herd(m) 23.
Herdkante(f) 255.
Herdtiefe(f) 23.
Hering(m) 685, 686.
Heringsschlaufe(f) 685, 686.
Herkules(m) 11.
Hermelin(m) 819.
**Heroldsbilder(n) 818.**
Herrenhalbschuh(m) 354.
HERRENKLEIDUNG(F) 319, 320, 322, 324.
Herrenring(m) 364.
Herrentasche(f) 380.
Hertz-Wellen(f) 416.
**Herz(n) 125.**
Herz(n) 88, 92, 97, 130, 615, 695.
Herzbeutel(m) 130.
herzförmig 56.
Herzkammer(f), linke 124, 125.
Herzkammer(f), rechte 124, 125.
Herzmuschel(f) 93.
Herzstelle(f) 818.

**Fettgedruckte** Wörter beziehen sich auf eine Illustration; Wörter in GROSSBUCHSTABEN sind Überschriften.

Herzstück(n) 467, 471.
Heuboden(m) 148.
Heuschrecke(f) 77.
Hexenstich(m) 571.
Hi.-Taste(f) 396.
HIEBWAFFEN(F) 794.
Hilfslinie(f) 537.
**Hilfsmittel(n) 592.**
Hilfsprojektor(m) 16.
Hilfsschiff(n) 739.
Hilfsschwert(n) 631.
**Himbeere(f), Querschnitt(m) 62.**
Himmel(m) mit vereinzelten Wolken(f) 39.
Himmel(m), bedeckter 39.
Himmel(m), bewölkter 39.
Himmel(m), heiterer 39.
Himmel(m), stark bewölkter 39.
**Himmel(m), stürmischer 36.**
Himmel(m), wolkenloser 39.
Himmelsäquator(m) 3.
Himmelskugel(f) 3.
HIMMELSKUGEL(F), KOORDINATENSYSTEM(N) 3.
Himmelsmeridian(m) 3.
Himmelsnordpol(m) 3.
Himmelssüdpol(m) 3.
Hindernislaufhürde(f) 656.
**Hinteransicht(f) 147.**
**Hinterbein(n) 78.**
Hinterbein(n) 79, 81, 84, 85, 223.
**Hinterbein(n) (Innenseite(f)) 81.**
Hinterbindung(f) 633.
Hinterbühne(f) 188, 189.
Hinterdeckel(m) 577.
hintere Begrenzungslinie(f) 666.
hinteres Gehäuse(n) 16.
Hinterfeld(n) 617.
Hinterflügel(m) 79, 81.
Hinterhauptbein(n) 123.
Hinterhauptmuskel(m) 121.
Hinterkante(f) 638.
Hinterkappe(f) 352.
**Hinterkipper(m) 785.**
Hinterleib(m) 78, 79, 81.
Hinterleib(n) 91.
Hinterleibssegment(n) 78.
Hinterpartie(f) 670.
Hinterrohr(n) 446.
Hinterteil(n) 645.
Hinterwand(f) 616, 617.
Hinterzehe(f) 108, 111.
Hinterzwiesel(f) 649.
Hippe(f) 269.
Hirnanhangsdrüse(f) 134.
Hirnholzende(n) 288.
Hirnnerven(m) 133.
**Hirscharten(f) 105.**
HIRSCHE(M), FAMILIE(F) 105.
**Hirschgeweih(n) 105.**
Hirse(f) 152.
Hitzeschild(n) 510.
**Hobel(m) 277.**
Hobeleisen(n) 277.
Hobelschar(f) 784.
Hobelzahn(m) 272.
Hoch-/Tiefstelltaste(f) 525.
**Hochdruck(m) 580.**
Hochdruckdampfeinlaß(m) 758.
Hochdruckgebiet(n) 38.
**Hochdruckpresse(f) 159.**
Hochdruckpresse(f) 155.
HOCHDRUCKVERFAHREN(N) 581.
Hochebene(f) 27.
Hochgeschwindigkeitsparcours(m) 646.
HOCHGESCHWINDIGKEITSZUG(M) 458.
Hochhaus(n) 185.
**Hochlandklimate(n) 45.**
Hochlandklimate(n) 45.
Hochsilo(m) 149.
Hochspannungsleitung(f) 755.
Hochspannungsleitung(f), Anschluß(m) für 757.
**Hochspannungsmast(m) 756.**
Hochspannungsprüfer(m) 310.
**Hochsprung(m) 657.**
Hochsprung(m) 654.
Hochtöner(m) 401.
Hochtonlautsprecher(m) 16.
**Hochwebstuhl(m) 574.**
Hocker(m) 222.
Hockey(m) 698.
HOCKEY(N) 607.
**Hockeyball(m) 607.**
Hoden(m) 127.
Hodensack(m) 116, 127.
Hof(m) 148.
Hog-Line(f) 620.
Höhen-Tonabnehmer(m) 547.
Höheneinstellhebel(m) 803.
Höheneinstellung(f) 718.
Höhenfeineinstellung(f) 720, 721.
Höhenfeintrieb(m) 713.
Höhenfeststeller(m) 720, 721.
Höhenflosse(f) 499, 508, 639.
Höhenkaltfront(f) 39.
Höhenkontrolle(f) 399.
Höhenmesser(m) 635, 639.
Höhenregler(m) 402.
Höhenruder(n) 499, 639.
Höhenskala(f) 19, 399.
Höhensucher(m) 810.
Höhenverstellfuß(m) 397.
Höhenverstellschraube(f) 641.
Höhenverstellskala(f) 284.
Höhenverstellung(f) 659, 661, 664.
Höhenwarmfront(f) 39.
Hohlbeitel(m) 587.
HÖHLE(F) 24.
Höhle(f) 30.
Hohleisen(n), gebogenes 587.
Hohleisen(n), gerades 581, 587.
Höhlenraum(m), trockenliegender 24.
Hohlhandmuskel(m), kurzer 120.
Hohlhandmuskel(m), langer 120.
Hohlladungsgeschoß(n) 801.
Hohlvene(f), obere 124, 125, 126, 130.
Hohlvene(f), untere 124, 125, 126, 132.
Holm(m) 302, 385, 498, 728.
Holm(m), oberer 659.
Holm(m), unterer 659.
**Holz(n) 288, 678.**
Holz(n) 1 678.
Holz(n) 3 678.
Holz(n) 5 678.
**Holzblasinstrumente(n) 548.**
Holzboden(m) 635.
**Holzhammer(m) 275.**
Holzleibung(f) 203.
**Holzschläger(m) 677.**
Holzschnitt(m) 581.
HOLZSCHNITZEREI(F) 586.
Holzstock(m) 581.
Holzträger(m) 205.
**Holzunterbau(m) 200.**
**Holzwerkstoffe(m) 288, 289.**
HONIGBIENE(F) 80, 82.
Honigmelone(f) 69.
Honigraum(m) 82.
Honigzelle(f) 82.
Höraufsatz(m) 726.
Hörer(m) 420.
Horizontalseismograph(m) 714.
Horizontspiegel(m) 484.
Horn(n) 364, 631.
HORNARTEN(F) 99.
Hornhaut(f) 140.
Hornschicht(f) 136.
Hornschnabel(m) 97.
Hornschuppe(f) 111.
Hornsohle(f) 104.
Hornstrahl(m) 104.
Hornwand(f) 104.
Horsd'oeuvre-Schale(f) 238.
**Hose(f) 323.**
Hose(f) 101, 353, 595, 600, 602, 609, 662, 668, 791.
Hose(f), kurze 351.
**Hosenarten(f) 336.**
**Hosenbluse(f) 337.**
Hosenbund(m) 323.
Hosenrock(m) 334.
Hosenschlitz(m) 323.
**Hosenträger(m) 323.**
Hotel(n) 185.
Hotelreservierungsschalter(m) 504.
**Houppelande(f) 317.**
Hubarm(m) 782.
Hubarmzylinder(m) 782.
HUBBLE RAUMTELESKOP(N) 16.
**Hubblesche Klassifikation(f) 9.**
**Hubbrücke(f) 457.**
Hubel(m) 584.
Hubgebläse(n) 492, 493.
Hubkette(f) 787.
Hubplattform(f) 739.
HUBSCHRAUBER(M) 508.
Hubschrauber(m) 808.
Hubschrauberhangar(m) 808.
Hubschrauberlandeplattform(f) 808.
Hubschrauberlandeplatz(m) 738.
Hubstreben(m) 147.
Hubvorrichtung(f) 786.
Hubwerk(n) 157.
Hubwinde(f) 786.
Hubzylinder(m) 780, 786.
**Huf(m) 104.**
Huf(m) 101.
**Huf(m), Unterseite(f) 104.**
HUFARTEN(F) 99.
Hufbein(n) 103.
**Hufeisen(n) 104.**
Hufeisen(n) 104, 364.
Hufeisenbogen(m) 174.
Hufeisenmontierung(f) 14.
Hüft-Becken-Nerv(m) 133.
Hüft-Leisten-Nerv(m) 133.
Hüftarterie(f), gemeinsame 126, 132.
Hüftarterie(f), innere 124, 126, 132.
Hüfte(f) 78, 80, 117, 119.
Hüftlochnerv(m) 133.
Hüftnerv(m) 133.
Hüftpolster(n) 602.
Hüftstelle(f), linke 818.
Hüftstelle(f), rechte 818.
Hüftvene(f), gemeinsame 132.
Hüftvene(f), innere 124.
Hüftwurf(m) 668.
Hügel(m) 27.
Hühnerstall(m) 148.
**Hülle(f) 66.**
Hülle(f) 529, 634, 677, 688.
Hülse(f) 72, 798.
Hülse(f), äußere 309.
Hülsenauswurf(m) 796.
**Hülsenfrucht(f), Längsschnitt(m) 67.**
**Hülsenfrüchte(f) 72.**
Hülsenschraube(f) 290.
Humeruskopf(m) 123.
**Hummer(m) 90.**
HUND(M) 106.
**Hund(m), Vorderpfote(f) 106.**
Hupe(f) 430, 444.
Hürde(f) 656.
**Hürden(f) 647.**
Hürdenlauf(m) 655.
Hut(m) 55.
Hutband(n) 328.
Hütchen(n) 485.
Hutmutter(f) 279.
Hütte(f) 165.
Hydrant(m) 186.
Hydrantenanschluß(m) 778, 779.
Hydrantenschlüssel(m) 779.
Hydraulik(f) 787.
Hydraulik-Heber(m) 449.
**Hydraulik-Hochlöffelbagger(m) 785.**
Hydraulikanschluß(m) 158.
Hydraulikkupplung(f) 147.
Hydraulikschlauch(m) 156, 157.
Hydraulikzylinder(m) 147, 784, 788.
Hydrosphäre(f) 31.
hydrostatische Lagerung(f) 14.
Hygrograph(m) 41.
**Hygrometer(n) 210.**

## I

Identifikationsnummer(f), technische 405.
identisch 830.
Identitätsband(n) 364.
Iglu(m) 165.
Igluzelt(n), aufklappbares 686.
Imagesetter(m) 527.
Impair(n) 700, 701.
Impluvium(n) 170, 171.
**Impulsregner(m) 264.**
Inbound-Linie(f) 604.
Incisura(f) intertragica 139.
Inder(m) 13.
Indexöffnung(f) 529.
Indexspiegel(m) 484.
Indikator(m) 710.
Indischer Ozean(m) 21.
indisches Fladenbrot(n) 153.
indisches Naanbrot(n) 153.
Induktionsspule(f) 406.
Industrie(f), petrochemische 744.
Infiltration(f) 34.
Information(f) 823.
Informationsschalter(m) 504.
Infrarot-Zielsuchkopf(m) 814.
Infrarotsensor(m) 43.
Inhalt 2.
Inhaltsverzeichnis 1.
Innenbeleuchtung(f) 477.
Innenbrett(n) 697.
Innendichtschicht(f) 433.
Innenfeld(n) 597.
Innenfeldspieler(m), linker 607.
Innenfläche(f) 327.
Innenhof(m) 172, 173.
Innenknauf(m) 290.
Innenkreis(m) 620.
Innenläden(m) 231.
Innenlippe(f) 94.
Innenohr(n) 138.
Innenputz(m) 199.
Innensichel(f), Große 668.
Innensteckhülse(f) 670.
Innenstiefel(m) 641, 645.
Innentasche(f) 383.
Innentür(f) 254.
Innenzelt(n) 685, 686.
innere Grabenböschung(f) 178.
innere Kuppelhülle(f) 14.
INSEKTEN(N) 77.
Insektenfresser(m) 31, 111.
Insel(f) 51, 452.
Inside-Linebacker(m) 603.
**Installationswerkzeuge(n) 299.**
INSTRUMENTALGRUPPIERUNGEN(F) 558.
Instrumente(f), wissenschaftliche 511.
Instrumente(n) 16, 445.
INSTRUMENTE(N), ELEKTRONISCHE 555.
Instrumenteneinheit(f) 509.
Instrumentenpalette(f) 511.
Instrumentenplattform(f) 43.
**Instrumententafel(f) 431, 445.**
Instrumententafel(f) 430, 442.
Integral(n) 830.
Intelsat VII(m) 418.
Interkostalnerv(m) 133.
INTERNATIONALE WETTERSYMBOLE(N) 39.
**Intervalle(n) 537.**
Intrusivgesteine(n) 23.
Io(f) 4.
Ionisationsclip(m) 233.
**ionische Säulenordnung(f) 166.**
Iris(f) 140.
irisches Brot(n) 153.
irreguläres Aggregat(n) 37.
Isba(f) 165.
Isobare(f) 38.
Isolator(m) 439, 757.
Isolierabdeckung(f) 528.
Isolierhülse(f) 309.
Isoliermaterial(n) 257, 741.
**Isoliermaterialien(n) 287.**
Isolierschichten(f) 512.
Isolierstoff(m) 199, 200.
Isolierung(f) 297, 768.
Isoseiste(f) 23.

## J

J-2 Triebwerk(n) 509.
Jabot(n) 342.
Jacke(f) 331, 668.
**Jacken(f) 338.**
Jackpot-Kasten(m) 702.
Jackpot-Leitung(f) 702.
Jagdhunde(m) 11.
**Jagdkappe(f) 328.**
JAGDWAFFEN(F) 798.
Jahresring(m) 59.
JAHRESZEITEN(F) 8.
Jakobsmuschel(f) 93.
**Jalousie(f) 231.**
Jalousie(f) 203, 214.
Jalousiefenster(n) 203.
Jalousieschweller(m) 542.
Japanpinsel(m) 589.
Jazzband(f) 558.
Jazzbesen(m) 553.
Jeans(f) 336.
Jocharm(m) 535.
Jochbein(n) 122.
Jockey(m) 651.
**Joggingschuh(m) 352.**
Johannisbeere(f) 62.
Johannisbeere(f), schwarz 62.
Joker(m) 695.
Joystick(m) 526.
jüdisches Weißbrot(n) 153.
JUDO(N) 668.
**Judoanzug(m) 668.**
Judokämpfer(m) 668.
Jungfrau(f) 11, 13, 820.
Jupiter(m) 4.
Jurte(f) 165.
Justaucorps(m) 315.
Justierring(m) 374.

**Fettgedruckte** Wörter beziehen sich auf eine Illustration; Wörter in GROSSBUCHSTABEN sind Überschriften.

## K

K-Gerüst(n) 756.
Kabel(n) 260, 268, 271, 280, 310, 406, 408, 414, 666.
Kabelabisolierer(m) 311.
Kabeldurchführung(f) 312.
Kabelmantel(m) 280, 283, 305.
Kabelnetz(n) 416.
Kabelrolle(f) 666.
Kabelschacht(m) 186.
Kabeltrommel(f) 415.
Kabeltülle(f) 311.
Kabelversteifung(f) 256.
Kabelverteiler(m) 416.
Kabine(f) 147, 160, 496.
Kabinenhaube(f) 813.
Kabriolett(n) 425.
Kachel(f) 511.
Kaffeehausgardine(f) 228.
Kaffeekanne(f) 688.
Kaffeelöffel(m) 241.
**Kaffeemaschine(f) 247.**
KAFFEEMASCHINEN(F) 247.
**Kaffeemühle(f) 256.**
Kai(m) 490.
Kairampe(f) 490.
Kaiserdach(n) 183.
Kaiserling(m) 55.
Kaki(f) 68.
Kaktusfeige(f) 68.
Kalb(n) 151.
Kaltbuchse(f) 401.
Kältemittelbehälter(m) 212.
Kältemittelleitung(f) 213.
Kaltfront(f) am Boden(m) 39.
Kaltluft(f) 501.
Kaltluftzuleitung(f) 438.
Kaltnadel(f) 582.
Kaltwasserkreis(m) 215.
Kaltwassersteigleitung(f) 215.
Kaltwasserzulauf(m) 293, 296, 297, 298.
Kambium(n) 59.
**Kamera(f) 414.**
Kamera(f) 16, 412, 414.
**Kamera(f), Rückseite(f) 390.**
Kamera-Dolly(m) 414.
Kamera-Steckfeld(n) 412.
Kameragehäuse(n) 391.
Kameraplattform(f) 393.
Kameraschraube(f) 393.
**Kamin(m) 204, 205.**
Kamin(m) 195, 197.
Kaminabdeckung(f) 205.
Kaminabdichtung(f) 205.
Kaminanschluß(m) 204.
Kaminaufsatz(m) 197.
**Kaminbesteck(n) 205.**
Kamineinfassung(f) 204, 205.
Kaminsims(m) 204.
Kamm(m) 27, 30, 574.
**Kämme(m) 368.**
Kammer(f) 736.
Kammerscheidewand(f) 125.
Kammerton(m) A 539.
Kammerwasser(n) 140.
Kammlade(f) 572.
Kammuschel(f) 93.
Kampfbereich(m) 668.
Kämpfer(m) 174.
KAMPFFLUGZEUG(N) 812.
Kampfmesser(n) 794.
Kampfrichter(m) 666, 668, 669.
Kampfrichtertribüne(f) 651.
Kanal(m), linker 401.
Kanal(m), rechter 401.
Kanalabschnitt(m) 206.
Kanalisation(f) 215, 216.
KANALSCHLEUSE(F) 492.
Kanalschleuse(f) 490.
Kanalsohle(f) 492.
Kanalsuchtasten(f) 411.
Kanapee(n) 221.
**Kandare(f) 650.**
Kandare(f) 648, 649.
**Kandare(f), einfache 650.**
Kandarenkette(f) 649.
Kandarenzügel(m) 649.
Kanne(f) 247.
Kannelüre(f) 166, 167.
KANONE(F) AUS DEM 17. JAHRHUNDERT(N) 800.
Kante(f) 281, 719.
Kantenfläche(f) 288.
Kantenstecher(m) 266.
Kantholz(n) 572.
Kanüle(f) 726.
Kanülenansatz(m) 726.
Kanzel(f) 638.
Kanzellösehebel(m) 639.
Kap(n) 51.
Kapazitätsanzeige(f) 374.
Kapelle(f) 181.
Kapillargefäß(n) 137.
Kapillarröhrchen(n) 705.
Kapitalband(n) 577.
Kapitänssitz(m) 500.
Kapitell(n) 166.
**Kaplanturbine(f) 754.**
Käppchen(n) 328.
Kappe(f) 301, 309, 389, 398, 644.
Kappe(f), äußere 354.
Kapsel(f) 725.
**Kapsel(f), Längsschnitt(m) 67.**
Kapselfinger(m) 562.
Kapuze(f) 320, 349, 680.
Kapuze(f) mit Zugband(n) 351.
Kapuzenmuskel(m) 120, 121.
**Kapuzenmütze(f) 329.**
Kar(n) 7, 26.
**Karabiner(m) 681.**
Karabiner(m) 672.
Karabinerhaken(m) 630, 680.
Karaffe(f) 237.
**Karambolagebillard(n) 673.**
Kardanring(m) 485.
**Kardinalseezeichen(n) 488.**
Kardone(f) 72.
Karibisches Meer(n) 20.
Karo(n) 695.
**Karosserie(f) 426.**
Karotte(f) 71.
Karpalballen(m) 106.
Karrosserie(f) 449.
Kartätsche(f) 801.
Karte(f), höchste 695.
**Karte(f), politische 51.**
Karteikarten(f) 517.
Karteikasten(m) 517.
Karteiregister(n) 518.
**Karteischubfach(n) 517.**
**Kartennetzentwürfe(m) 50.**
Kartenraum(m) 494.
Kartenschlitz(m) 422.
KARTENSPIELE(N) 695.
Kartoffel(f) 71.
Kartoffelschüssel(f) 238.
Kartoffelstampfer(m) 244.
KARTOGRAPHIE(F) 47, 50, 52.
Kartreppe(f) 26.
Kartusche(f) 291, 295, 730.
**Kartuschendichtung(f) 295.**
Kartuschenkolben(m) 295.
**Kartuschenpistole(f) 291.**
Käsemesser(n) 239.
Kaserne(f) 179.
Kaspisches Meer(n) 21.
Kasse(f) 453.
**Kassette(f) 403.**
Kassette(f) 408, 526.
Kassettenauswurfschalter(m) 409, 411.
Kassettenband(n) 403.
**Kassettendeck(n) 403.**
Kassettendeck(n) 400, 407.
Kassettendecktasten(f) 408.
Kassettenfach(n) 403.
Kassettenfilm(m) 395.
Kassettenlaufwerk(n) 526.
Kassettenlift(m) 409, 411.
Kassettenteil(n) 408.
Kastagnetten(f) 554, 556.
Kastanie(f) 100.
Kasten(m) 539.
Kasteneisen(n) 587.
Kastenwagen(m), langer 472.
Katalysator(m) 439.
Katapult(n) 810.
Kathedrale(f) 184.
KATZE(F) 107.
Katze(f) 178.
**Katze(f), Kopf(m) 107.**
**Kaulquappe(f) 84.**
Kaumuskel(m) 120.
Kegel(m) 24, 251.
Kegeldach(n) 183.
Kegelprojektion(f) 50.
Kegelzahnrad(n) 280.
Kehldeckel(m) 130, 142, 143.
Kehle(f) 108, 542.
Kehlkopf(m) 130, 142.
Kehlriemen(m) 649.
Keil(m) 277, 327, 378, 380, 542, 800.
Keilbeinhöhle(f) 141.
Keilhebel(m) 277.
Keilriemen(m) 258, 434.
Keilstein(m) 174.
Keim(m) 152.
Keimblatt(n) 57.
Keimpflanze(f) 70.
Keimscheibe(f) 109.
Kelch(m) 62, 67.
Kelchblatt(n) 60, 62.
Kelimbindung(f) mit wechselnden Wenden(f) 576.
Kelimbindung(f), senkrechte 576.
Keller(m) 197.
Kellerfalte(f) 335.
Kellerfenster(n) 197.
Kellnerbesteck(n) 244.
Kennplakette(f) 712.
Kennzeichnung(f) 433.
Kepheus(m) 11.
**Keramikdichtung(f) 295.**
Kerbe(f) 674, 708.
Kerbel(m) 74.
Kern(m) 6, 9, 62, 63, 64, 65, 72, 542, 677, 692, 798.
Kern(m), äußerer 22.
Kern(m), innerer 22.
KERNENERGIE(F) 758, 760, 762, 764, 766.
**Kernenergie(f), Stromerzeugung(f) aus 766.**
**Kernfrucht(f), Querschnitt(m) 64.**
Kerngehäuse(n) 64.
Kernholz(n) 59.
**Kernkraftwerk(n) 758.**
Kernmembran(f) 115.
KERNOBST(N) 64.
**Kernobstsorten(f) 64.**
**Kernreaktor(m) 765.**
Kernreaktorraum(m) 806.
Kernschatten(m) 8.
Kernspalte(f) 542.
Kerosin(n) 744.
Kerosintank(m) 509.
**Kessel(m) 209.**
Kessel(m) 206, 208, 484, 553.
**Kessel(m), elektrischer 207.**
**Kesselpauke(f) 553.**
**Kesselstaubsauger(m) 260.**
Kesselwagen(m) 472.
Ketsch(f) 482.
Kettbaum(m) 573.
Kette(f) 293, 445, 446, 448, 573, 574, 661, 707.
Kettenantrieb(m) 156.
Kettenblatt(n), großes 448.
Kettenblatt(n), kleines 448.
Kettenblattumwerfer(m) 446, 448.
Kettenbremse(f) 272.
Kettenführung(f) 448.
Kettenlaufwerkrahmen(m) 783.
Kettenplatte(f) 805.
Kettenrad(n) 805.
Kettenrohrzange(f) 299.
**Kettensäge(f) 272.**
Kettenschuh(m) 805.
Kettenstich(m) 571.
Kettfaden(m) 576.
Keule(f) 106.
Keulenärmel(m) 340.
Kfz(n) 828.
Kibla(f) 173.
Kichererbsen(f) 72.
Kieferfüße(m) 90.
Kiefernnadeln(f) 58.
Kiel(m) 633.
Kielbogen(m) 174.
Kieldach(n) 182.
Kielfeder(f) 389.
Kielstange(f) 637.
**Kiemen(f) 87.**
Kiemen(f) 88, 92.
Kiemen(f), äußere 84.
Kiemenbogen(m), oberer 87.
Kiemenbogen(m), unterer 87.
Kiemendeckel(m) 84, 86.
Kiemenfaden(m) 87.
Kiemenreuse(f) 87.
Kies(m) 199, 216.
Kilometerzähler(m) 431.
Kimme(f) 795, 796, 797, 798, 804.
Kimono(m) 348.
Kimonoärmel(m) 340.
KINDERKLEIDUNG(F) 349, 350.
Kinn(n) 108, 118.
Kinnkette(f) 650.
Kinnkettenhaken(m) 650.
Kinnreff(n) 792.
Kinnriemen(m) 602, 777.
Kinnschutz(m) 443, 777.
Kinnstütze(f) 544.
Kino(n) 496.
Kiosk(m) 453.
Kippermulde(f) 785.
Kipphebel(m) 727.
Kirche(f) 185.
Kirschband(n) 229.
Kirsche(f) 63.
Kirsorfalte(f) 228.
Kissen(n) 570, 588.
Kissen(n), kleines 224.
**Kittelbluse(f) 337.**
Kiwi(f) 68.
Klaffmuschel(f) 93.
Klammer(f) 230.
Klammern(f), eckige 832.
Klammern(f), runde 832.
Klampe(f) 628, 630.
Klangfarbenregler(m) 547.
Klangprozessor(m) 528.
**Klappbrücke(f) 457.**
Klappe(f) 95, 219, 277, 322, 549.
Klappe(f), hintere 511.
**Klappe(f), linke 95.**
Klappendrücker(m) 549.
Klappenhebel(m) 500.
Klappenheber(m), hydraulischer 812.
Klappenschutz(m) 549.
Klappenstiel(m) 549.
Klappentasche(f) 320, 322, 339.
**Klapperschlange(f) 97.**
**Klappmessersprung(m) 625.**
Klappspaten(m) 690.
Klappstufe(f) 449.
Klappstuhl(m) 223.
**Klapptisch(m) 219.**
Klarinette(f) 548.
Klarinetten(f) 556.
Klarsichtfenster(n) 379.
Klarsichtscheibe(f) 445.
Klarspülmittelgeber(m) 257.
Klaue(f) 78, 80, 91, 112, 275.
Klaviaturboden(m) 540.
**Klavier(n) 540.**
**Klaviermechanik(f) 541.**
Klebeband(n) 607.
Klebeetiketten(n) 518.
Klebefilmspender(m) 516.
Klebestift(m) 515.
Klebstoff(m) 200.
**Kleeblatt(n) 452.**
Kleeblatt(n) 450.
Kleeblattbogen(m) 174.
**Kleid(n) mit flachem Reifrock(m) 317.**
**Kleid(n) mit Krinolinenrock(m) 318.**
**Kleid(n) mit Turnüre(f) 316.**
Kleid(n), mit angesetztem Schoß(m) 332.
**Kleiderarten(f) 332.**
Kleiderhaken(m) 522.
Kleiderrock(m) 333.
**Kleidersack(m) 382.**
**Kleiderschrank(m) 225.**
Kleiderschrank(m) 195, 226, 522.
Kleiderschutz(m) 727.
Kleiderstoff(m) 565.
Kleidung(f), feuer- und wasserfeste 777.
Kleine Wasserschlange(f) 13.
kleiner als 830.
Kleiner Bär(m) 11.
kleiner Finger(m) 137.
kleiner Hüftnerv(m) 133.
Kleiner Hund(m) 11.
Kleiner Löwe(m) 11.
Kleinfingerhaken(m) 551.
Kleinhirn(n) 134.
Klemmbacke(f) 365.
Klemmbrett(n) 519.
Klemmbügel(m) 370.
Klemme(f), verstellbare 234.
Klemmhefter(m) 519.
**Klemmschlaufe(f) 681.**
Klemmschlaufe(f) 680.
Klemmschraube(f), obere 40.
Klemmschraube(f), untere 40.
Klemmspot(m) 235.
Klemmtasche(f) 381.
Klettergürtel(m) 680.
**Kletterhaken(m) 681.**
Kletterhose(f) 680.
Kletterpflanze(f) 263.
Kliff(n) 23, 30.
KLIMAANLAGE(F) 214.
Klimaanlage(f) 415, 449, 494.
Klimagerät(n) 506.
KLIMATE(N) DER WELT(F) 45.
**Klimate(n), gemäßigte 45.**
**Klimate(n), subarktische 45.**
Klimate(n), subarktische 45.
**Klimate(n), subtropische 45.**
**Klimate(n), tropische 45.**
Klinge(f) 239, 242, 276, 374, 666.

**Fettgedruckte** Wörter beziehen sich auf eine Illustration; Wörter in GROSSBUCHSTABEN sind Überschriften.

Klinge(f), große 688.
Klinge(f), isolierte 310.
Klinge(f), kleine 688.
Klinge(f), zweischneidige 374.
Klingenkassette(f) 374.
Klingenmitte(f) 666.
Klingenschwäche(f) 666.
Klingenstärke(f) 666.
Klingenstopper 369.
Klinke(f) 573.
Klinkenstecker(m) 406.
Klips(m) 323, 361.
Klistierspritze(f) 726.
Klitoris(f) 128.
**Klöppel(m) 570.**
Klöppel(m) 570.
Klöppelbrief(m) 570.
**Klöppelkissen(n) 570.**
KLÖPPELSPITZE(F) 570.
Klosettbecken(n) 293.
Klosettbrille(f) 293.
Klosettdeckel(m) 293.
Klotz(m) 787.
Klubhaus(n) 651, 676.
Klubhauskurve(f) 651.
Klüver(m) 628.
Knarre(f) 670.
Knäuel(n) 575.
Knauf(m) 219, 596, 609, 615, 666.
Knebel(m) 650, 817.
**Knebelbolzen(m) 276.**
**Knebeltrense(f) 650.**
Knebelverschluß(m) 320.
Kneifer(m) 377.
Knethaken(m) 250.
Knie(n) 100, 106, 116, 118.
Kniebuckel(m) 792.
Kniebundhose(f) 336.
Kniehose(f) 315, 317.
Kniemanschette(f) 653.
Kniemanschettenhalter(m) 653.
Kniepolster(n) 602, 609.
Kniescheibe(f) 101, 103, 122.
Knieschützer(m) 595.
Kniestrumpf(m) 325, 344, 642, 667.
Knipsbörse(f) 379.
Knoblauch(m) 70.
Knoblauchpresse(f) 243.
Knöchel(m) 116, 118.
Knöchelsocke(f) 325.
Knolle(f) 72.
Knollenblätterpilz(m) 55.
**Knollengemüse(n) 71.**
Knopf(m) 231, 232, 324, 326, 536, 800.
Knöpfe(m), gelochte 566.
Knopflasche(f) 323.
Knopfleiste(f) 324, 326.
Knopfleiste(f), verdeckte 330, 351.
Knopfloch(n) 319.
Knorrenmuskel(m) 121.
Knötchenstich(m), französischer 571.
**Knötchenstiche(m) 571.**
KNOTEN(M) 691, 692.
Knoten(m) 576, 756.
Knoter(m) 159.
Ko-Prozessor(m) 528.
Köcher(m) 684.
KOCHGERÄTE(N) 248.
**Kochgeschirr(n) 688.**
Kochmesser(n) 242.
Kochplatte(f) 255.
Kochstelle(f) 255.
Kochtopf(m) 688.
Köderlauncher(m) 809.
**Koffer(m) 383.**
**Koffer-Sattelanhänger(m) 441.**
Kofferraum(m) 427.
Kognakschwenker(m) 237.
Kohl(m) 73.
Kohle(f) 588.
KOHLEBERGWERK(N) 733, 734, 736.
Kohlendioxid(n) 760.
Kohlendioxidkühlgas(n) 760.
**Kohlendioxidreaktor(m) 760.**
Kohlenschaufel(f) 205.
Kohlrabi(m) 71.
Kohlrübe(f) 71.
Kokosnuß(f) 66.
Kolben(m) 60, 72, 232, 233, 432, 435, 436, 437, 438, 562, 797.
Kolbenantrieb(m) 159.
Kolbenhals(m) 798.
Kolbenring(m) 434.
Kolbenschaft(f) 434.
Kollaterale(f) 135.
**Kollegmappe(f) 378.**
Kollektor(m) 753.
Koller(m) 319.
Kolonne(f) 700, 701.
Koma(f) 9.
Kombihacke(f) 266.
**Kombihammer(m) 681.**
Kombihammer(m) 680.
Kombipumpe(f) 687.
Kombiwagen(m) 425.
**Kombizange(f) 278, 311.**
Kombüse(f) 807.
KOMET(M) 9.
Komma(n) 832.
Kommandantenstand(m) 805.
Kommandoantenne(f), ferngesteuerte 49.
Kommandobrücke(f) 493.
Kommandokapsel(f) 509.
Kommandoturms(m) 807.
Kommastellen(f) 523.
Kommataste(f) 523.
Kommode(f) 226.
KOMMUNIKATION(F), TELEFONISCHE 420, 422.
Kommunikationsmodul(m) 418.
Kompass(m) 639.
Kompaßrose(f) 484, 719.
Kompressor(m) 212.
Kompressor(m) für Klimaanlage(f) 435.
Koncha(f) 139.
Kondensatauslaß(m) 759.
Kondensateinlaß(m) 759.
Kondensation(f) 35.
Kondensationskammer(f) 758.
Kondensator(m) 758, 771.
Kondensator(m) für Außenaufstellung(f) 212.
Kondensatorkühlwasserauslaß(m) 759.
Kondensatorkühlwasserbecken(n) 763.
Kondensatorkühlwassereinlaß(m) 759.
Kondensor(m) 717, 718.
Kondensoreinstellung(f) 718.
Kondensorhöhenverstellung(f) 718.
Kondenssammler(m) 210.
Konditionierer(m) 158.
Konfiguration(f), zusammengefaltete 48.
Kongreßzentrum(n) 184.
König(m) 695, 696.
Königin(f) 81.
Königsflanke(f) 696.
KONSTELLATIONEN(F) DER NÖRDLICHEN HALBKUGEL(F) 10.
KONSTELLATIONEN(F) DER SÜDLICHEN HALBKUGEL(F) 12.
**Konstruktion(f) 203.**
KONSTRUKTION(F) EINES HAUSES(N) 198.
Konsument(m) 417.
Kontakt(m) 233.
Kontaktkopiergerät(n) 398.
Kontergarde(f) 179.
Kontermutter(f) 296.
Kontinent(m) 29.
kontinental-trocken - halbtrocken 45.
kontinental-trocken - trocken 45.
Kontinentalfuß(m) 29.
Kontinentalhang(m) 22, 29.
**Kontinentalklimate(n) 45.**
**Kontinentalrand(m) 29.**
Kontinentalschelf(m) 22, 29.
KONTINENTE(M), KONFIGURATION(F) 20.
Kontrabaß(m) 545.
Kontrabasse(m) 557.
Kontrafagotte(n) 556.
Kontrasteinstellung(f) 532.
Kontrastregler(m) 529.
Kontreskarpe(f) 178.
Kontrollampe(f) 370.
Kontrollbildschirm(m) 717.
Kontrolleuchte(f) 247, 252, 255, 256, 257, 585.
Kontrollgerät(n) 699.
Kontrollkonsole(f) 683.
Kontrollmonitor(m) 413.
Kontrollmonitore(m) 412, 413, 415.
Kontrollmutter(f) 40.
Kontrollraum(m) 502, 806.
Kontrollturm(m) 502, 810.
Kontrolluhr(f) 413, 415.
**Konturfeder(f) 110.**
Konvektionszone(f) 6.
**Konvektor(m) 211.**
Konvektor(m) 208.
KOORDINATENSYSTEM(N) DER ERDKUGEL(F) 3.
KOORDINATENSYSTEM(N) DER HIMMELSKUGEL(F) 3.
Köperbindung(f) 576.
**Kopf(m) 109.**
Kopf(m) 9, 78, 79, 80, 83, 117, 119, 124, 127, 275, 276, 279, 283, 373, 374, 386, 453, 544, 561, 567, 570, 579, 615, 670, 677, 681.
**Kopf(m) der Katze(f) 107.**
Kopf(m) voraus 624.
**Kopfarten(f) 276.**
Kopfautomatik(f) 640, 641.
Kopfband(n) 729, 730.
KOPFBEDECKUNGEN(F) 328.
Kopfbruststück(n) 90.
Kopfbügel(m) 408.
Köpfchen(n) 60.
**Köpfchentypen(m) 229.**
Kopfende(n) 224.
KOPFHÖRER(M) 406.
Kopfhörer(m) 408.
Kopfhörerbuchse(f) 402, 408.
Kopfhörerstecker(m) 408.
Kopfkissen(n) 224.
Kopfkissenbezug(m) 224.
Kopfkissenschonbezug(m) 224.
Kopfnicker(m) 120.
Kopfprofil(n) 231.
Kopfriegel(m) 202.
Kopfsalat(m) 73.
**Kopfschiene(f) 230.**
KOPFSCHUTZ(M) 729.
Kopfseite(f) 736.
**Kopfsprung(m) rückwärts 625.**
**Kopfsprung(m) vorwärts 625.**
Kopfstab(m) 653.
Kopfsteg(m) 577.
Kopfstrecke(f) 736.
Kopfstütze(f) 428.
Kopfteil(m) 201, 328, 329.
Kopfwurf(m) 668.
Kopienablage(f) 532.
Kopienanzahl(f) 532.
Kopienausgabemodus(m) 532.
Kopieren(n), beidseitiges 532.
Kopierkontrolle(f) 532.
**Kopierrad(m) 563.**
Kopilotensitz(m) 500.
Koppel-Kipptaste(f) 542.
Koppen(m) 236.
**Korb(m) 610.**
Korb(m) 257, 610.
Korbbrett(n) 610.
Korbhaltetrossen(f) 634.
Korbring(m) 610.
Korbstich(m) 567.
Korbtragerohr(n) 635.
Kordel(f) 229.
Kordgriff(m) 658.
Koriander(m) 74.
**korinthische Säulenordnung(f) 167.**
Korkball(m) 596.
Korkenzieher(m) 688.
Korkspitze(f) 618.
Korn(n) 795, 797, 798, 799, 804.
Kornelevator(m) 161.
Körnerfresser(m) 111.
Körnerschicht(f) 136.
Kornett(n) 550, 556.
Kornhalter(m) mit Korn(n) 796.
Kornschnecke(f) 161.
Korntank(m) 160.
Korona(f) 6.
Körper(m) 143, 542, 670.
KÖRPER(M), MENSCHLICHER 116, 118.
Körperchen(n), Ruffinisches 136.
Körperchen(n), Vater-Pacinische 136.
Körperpolster(n) 609.
Körpertemperaturregelung(f) 512.
Korpus(m) 546, 549, 645, 658.
Korpus(m), birnenförmiger 535.
Korpus(m), dreieckiger 535.
Korpus(m), massiver 547.
Korpus(m), runder 535.
Korrekturflüssigkeit(f) 515.
Korrekturstreifen(m) 515.
Korrekturtaste(f) 569.
Korrekturtriebwerk(n) 49.
Korselett(n) 347.
Korsett(n) 346.
Kosakenmütze(f) 328.
**Kosmetikkoffer(m) 382.**
**Kostüm(n) 331.**
KOSTÜME(F), HISTORISCHE 318.
KOSTÜME(N), HISTORISCHE 315, 316.
Köte(f) 101.
Kötengelenk(n) 101.
Kotflügel(m) 147, 426, 440.
Krabbe(f) 90.
Krafträder(n) 828.
Kraftstoff-Luft-Gemisch(n) 436.
Kraftstoffanzeige(f) 431.
Kraftstoffbehälter(m) 468.
Kraftstoffreserveanzeige(f) 431.
Kraftstoffschlauch(m) 509.
Kraftstofftank(m) 272, 440, 442.
**Kraftübertragung(f) 448.**
**Kraftwerk(n) 752.**
Kraftwerk(n) 746, 752.
Kraftwerksgebäude(n) 764.
**Kragen(m) 341.**
Kragen(m) 319, 322, 324, 546, 547.
Kragen(m), drapierter 343.
**Kragen(m), gespreizter 324.**
Kragen(m), kleiner 318.
Kragen(m), transformabler 319.
**Kragenarten(f) 341, 342.**
Kragenecke(f) 341.
Kragenklammer(f) 364.
Kragenspitze(f) 324.
Kragenstäbchen(n) 324.
Kragensteg(m) 341.
Kragstein(m) 180, 181, 204.
Kragträger(m) 454.
Krähenfußstich(m) 571.
Krail(m) 267.
Kralle(f) 97, 106, 107, 108, 111, 268.
**Kralle(f), ausgestreckte 107.**
**Kralle(f), eingezogene 107.**
Krallenbein(n) 107.
Kran(m) 14, 738.
Kranbahn(f) 786.
Kranführerkabine(f) 786.
Kranich(m) 13.
Krankenhaus(n) 822.
Krankentrage(f) 726.
Kranzgesims(n) 166, 168.
Kranzprofil(n) 225.
Krappe(f) 364.
Krater(m) 7, 25, 733.
**Kraulen(n) 622.**
Kräuselfalte(f) 337.
Kräuselrock(m) 335.
Krausstrick(m) 567.
KRÄUTER(N) 74.
**Krawatte(f) 324.**
Krawattenklemme(f) 364.
Krawattennadel(f) 364.
Krawattenschal(m) 324.
Krebs(m) 11, 820.
**Krebse(m), eßbare 90.**
KREBSTIERE(N) 90.
**Kreditkartenetui(n) 379.**
Kreditkartenfach(n) 379.
Kreide(f) 675.
**Kreiskolbenmotor(m) 437.**
Kreislauf(m), elektrischer 233.
**Kreisregner(m) 264.**
**Kreissägeblatt(n) 284.**
Kreisverkehr(m) 52.
Kremaster(m) 78.
Krempe(f) 328, 329.
Kreolen(f) 361.
Krepis(f) 166, 168, 169.
Kreuz(n) 483, 538, 695, 818.
Kreuz(n) des Südens(m) 13.
Kreuz-Bramstagsegel(n) 480.
Kreuz-Royalbrasse(f) 480.
Kreuz-Royalstagsegel(n) 480.
Kreuz-Stengestagsegel(n) 480.
Kreuzaussteifung(f) 198.
Kreuzbein(n) 122, 123.
Kreuzbeinwirbel(m) 103.
Kreuzgeflecht(n) 133.
Kreuzhacke(f) 267.
Kreuzknoten(m) 691.
Kreuzkopf(m) 787.
Kreuzmast(m) 478.
Kreuzrippe(f) 177.
Kreuzschlitzschraubenzieher(m) 688.
Kreuzsegel(n) 480.
**Kreuzstiche(m) 571.**
Kreuztisch(m) 718.
Kreuztischeinstellung(f) 718.
Kriechstrombarriere(f) 439.
**Krieger(m), gallischer 791.**
**Krinolinenrock(m) 318.**
Kristalltropfen(m) 236.
Kronbein(n) 103, 107.
Krone(f) 59, 101, 105, 144, 239, 242, 363, 545, 706, 832.
Kronenblock(m) 737.
Kronenende(n) 105.
**Kronleuchter(m) 236.**
**Kröte(f) 85.**
Krummdarm(m) 131.
Krümmling(m) 201.
Kruppe(f) 101, 661.
Kübel(m) 263.
Küche(f) 171, 195.
Kuchenform(f) 245.
Kuchenform(f), flache 245.

**Fettgedruckte** Wörter beziehen sich auf eine Illustration; Wörter in GROSSBUCHSTABEN sind Überschriften.

**Küchenmaschine(f) 251.**
**Küchenmesser(n) 242.**
Kuchenpinsel(m) 245.
Kuchenrad(n) 245.
**Küchenset(n) 244.**
Küchenspalter(m) 242.
Küchenuhr(f) 244.
KÜCHENUTENSILIEN(N) 242, 244, 246.
Küchenwaage(f) 244.
Küchenwagen(m) 507.
Kufe(f) 445, 508, 643, 644.
Kufe(f), hintere 643.
Kufe(f), vordere 643.
Kugel(f) 530, 683, 795, 798.
Kugelaggregat(n) 294.
**Kugeldichtung(f) 294.**
Kugelhalterung(f) 40, 530.
Kugelmechanik(f) 389.
**Kugeln(f) 658.**
Kugelrücklaufkasten(m) 683.
**Kugelschreiber(m) 389.**
Kugelschreiber(m) 515.
Kugelstoßen(n) 655.
Kugelträger(m) 683.
Kuh(f) 151.
Kühl- und Heizbatterie(f) 213.
Kühlaggregat(n) 441.
Kühlbox(f) 690.
**Kühler(m) 438.**
Kühler(m) 771.
Kühler(m) für Dampfgeneratorraum(m) 759.
Kühlerblock(m) 438.
Kühlergrill(m) 426, 440.
Kühlergruppe(f) 469.
Kühlerverschlußdeckel(m) 438.
Kühlfach(n) 254.
Kühlgebläse(n) 528.
Kühlhaus(n) 491.
Kühlmantel(m) 796.
Kühlmittel(n) 760, 761, 762, 763, 766.
Kühlmittel(n), heißes 771.
Kühlmittel(n), kaltes 771.
Kühlmittelauslaß(m) 768.
Kühlmitteleinlaß(m) 768.
**Kühlschrank(m) 254.**
Kühlung(f) 744.
Kühlwagen(m) 472.
Kühlwasserschlauch(m) 438.
Kühlwassertank(m) 759, 766.
Kühlwasserventil(n) 759.
Kühlwasserventilator(m) 469.
Kuhstall(m) 149.
Kuhstek(m) 691.
Küken(n) 150.
Kulette(f) 363.
Kulissen(f) 189.
Kultbild(n), Standort(m) 169.
Kulturbeutel(m) 382.
Kumquat(f) 65.
Kumulonimbus(m) 44.
Kumulus(m) 44.
**Kunstfliege(f) 670.**
Kunstschwamm(m) 367.
KUNSTSPRINGEN(N) 624.
Kunststoff(m) 301.
Kunststoffisolator(m) 312.
Kupfer(n) 301.
Kupferplatte(f) 582.
Kuppe(f) 675.
Kuppel(f) 486.
Kuppel(f) des Mihrab(m) 173.
Kuppelantrieb(m) 14.
Kuppeldach(n) 183.
Kuppelspaltabdeckung(f) 14.
Kuppelzelt(n) 686.
Kuppenring(m) 675.
Kupplung(f) 778.
Kupplungsbolzen(m) 754.
Kupplungsbügel(m) 469.
Kupplungsgehäuse(n) 444.
Kupplungshebel(m) 272, 442, 444.
**Kupplungskopf(m) 471.**
Kupplungskopf(m) 147.
Kupplungsmaul(n) 156, 157.
Kupplungspedal(n) 430.
Küraß(m) 791.
Kurbel(f) 265, 280, 448, 671.
Kurbel(f) für Säule(f) 393.
Kurbelgehäuse(n) 436.
Kurbelwelle(f) 434, 436.
Kürbis(m) 69.
Kursbuchtafeln(f) 463.
**Kurse(m) 629.**
Kursstrich(m) 485.
Kurtine(f) 178, 180.
Kurve(f) 651.
Kurzhandschuh(m) 327.
Kurzschwert(n) 791.
Kurzsocke(f) 344.
Kuskustopf(m) 249.
KÜSTENFORMEN(F), TYPISCHE 30.
Kuttenkragen(m) 342.

## L

Label(n) 404.
Laboratorium(n) 15.
Laborleuchte(f) 398.
Laboruhr(f) 398.
Lade-Anschlußbuchse(f) 260.
Ladeband(n) 733.
Ladebaum(m) 742, 743.
Ladebucht(f) 510.
Ladefläche(f) 156, 441.
Ladegerät(n) für Paletten(f) und Container(m) 507.
Ladekennziffer-Plakette(f) 743.
Ladeklappen(f) 510.
Ladekontrollampe(f) 374.
Ladeluftkühler(m) 438.
Lademast(m) 743.
Laden(m) 98, 170.
Ladenbahn(f) 572.
Ladenpassage(f) 190.
Laderampe(f) 190.
Laderampe(f), klappbare 494.
Ladeschaufel(f) 801.
Ladestock(m) 795, 801.
Ladung(f) 799.
Lafettenwand(f) 800.
Laffe(f) 241.
Lage(f) 678.
**Lageplan(m) 193.**
Lagergang(m) 24.
Lagergestell(n) 764.
Lagerraster(n) 765.
Lagertank(m) 744.
Lagerzapfen(m) 800.
Lagune(f) 30.
Laibung(f) 174.
Lakkolith(m) 25.
Lamelle(f) 55, 231.
Lamm(n) 150.
Lammfelljacke(f) 321.
**Lampe(f) 689.**
Lampe(f) 471, 718.
LAMPEN(F) 232, 234, 236.
**Lampenfassung(f) 309.**
Lampenreihe(f) 235.
Land(n) 51.
Landebereich(m) 655.
Landedeck(n) 811.
Landefenster(n) 508.
Landeklappe(f) 498.
Landenge(f) 51.
Landeradar(n) 811.
Landescheinwerfer(m) 508.
Landhausgardine(f) 228.
landschaftlich schöne Strecke(f) 52.
**Landschaftskarte(f) 51.**
Landspitze(f) 30.
Landung(f) 736.
Landzunge(f) 30.
Längengrad(m) 3.
**Längengrade(m) 47.**
LÄNGENMESSUNG(F) 711.
Längenpfosten(m) 651.
Längenverstellung(f) 728.
Langhaarschneider(m) 374.
Langhandschuh(m) 327.
Langlauf-Rattenfallbindung(f) 642.
**Langläufer (in(f))(m) 642.**
Langlaufschuh(m) 642.
**Langlaufski(m) 642.**
Langlaufski(m) 642.
**Längsachsenwindturbine(f) 774.**
Längsdünen(f) 46.
Längsfaden(m) 565, 566.
Längslatte(f) 637.
Längsriegel(m) 198.
Längsschneidemaschine(f) 398.
Längsschott(n) 742.
Längsträger(m), unterer 470.
LANGSTRECKEN-DÜSENFLUGZEUG(N) 498.
Languste(f) 91.
Langustine(f) 91.
Lanze(f) 791.
Lanzettbogen(m) 174.
lanzettlich 56.
Lapislazuli(m) 363.
Lappen(m) 111.
Lappen(m), oberer seitlicher 61.
Lappen(m), unterer seitlicher 61.
Lärche(f) 58.
Larve(f) 82.
Lasche(f) 320, 378, 379.
Laschenbolzen(m) 466.
Laserdrucker(m) 527.
Laserstrahl(m) 405.
LASTENFORTBEWEGUNG(F) 786, 788.
LASTKRAFTFAHRZEUGE(N) 440.
Lateinersegel(n) 482.
Lateralzeichen(n) 489.
Laterne(f) 263, 486, 487.
Latissimuszug(m) 663.
Latrinen(f) 171.
Latte(f) 571, 626, 631, 646.
Lattengitter(n) 286.
Lattenzaun(m) 263.
Latz(m) 667.
Lätzchen(n) 349, 350, 351.
Latzenstab(m) 574.
**Latzhose(f) 350, 351.**
Latzhose(f) 336.
Laub(n) 59.
**Laubfrosch(m) 85.**
Laubwerk(n) 220.
Lauch(m) 70.
Lauf(m) 108, 599, 796.
**Lauf(m), gezogener 798.**
**Lauf(m), glatter 799.**
Laufbahn(f) 654.
Laufbein(n) 78.
Laufblatt(n) 752, 753, 754.
Laufbrett(n) 469.
Läufer(m) 696, 697, 753.
Läufer(m), halbrechter 607.
Lauffläche(f) 433, 466.
Laufgewicht(n) 539, 708.
Laufkatze(f) 457, 786.
Laufkatzenrolle(f) 786.
**Laufkran(m) 786.**
Laufkran(m) 747.
Laufrad(n) 583.
Laufrad(n), pneubereiftes 476, 477.
Laufrolle(f) 530, 805.
Laufschiene(f) 786, 798.
Laufschuh(m) 656.
Laufsohle(f) 353, 355, 640.
Laufwagen(m) 230.
Laugenbehälter(m) 258.
Lautsprecher(m) 408, 412, 413, 420, 485, 500, 779.
**Lautsprecherbox(f) 401.**
Lautsprecherschalter(m) 402.
Lautstärkeregler(m) 402, 408, 411, 420, 422, 512, 547, 555.
Lautstärkeregler(m) für den Hörer(m) 420.
Lautstärkeregler(m) für den Rufton(m) 420.
Lavaschicht(f) 25.
Lavastrom(m) 25.
LCD-Anzeige(f) 706.
Lead(m) 620.
Lebenserhaltungssystem(n) 512.
Leber(f) 88, 97, 124, 131.
Lebervene(f) 124.
LED-Pegelanzeige(f) 403.
Lederhaut(f) 137, 598.
Lederschutz(m) 690.
Lederstrippe(f) 323.
Ledertuch(n) 358.
Lederwalze(f) 582.
LEDERWAREN(F) 378.
Leerdarm(m) 131.
Leermenge(f) 830.
Leertaste(f) 525, 530.
Left-Wing(m) 606.
Lefzen(f) 106.
**Legionär(m), römischer 791.**
Legwarmer(m) 353.
Lehmkern(m) 748.
Lehnstuhl(m) 220.
leicht entzündlich 821.
LEICHTATHLETIK(F) 654, 656, 658.
Leichtbelastungseinstellschraube(f) 712.
Leier(f) 11.
Leine(f) 817.
Leinöl(n) 592.
Leinwand(f) 397, 589.
Leinwandbindung(f) 576.
Leinwandkasten(m) 397.
Leiste(f) 116, 118, 578.
Leistendurchlaß(m) 207.
Leistentasche(f) 322.
Leistungskabel(n) 312.
Leistungsschalter(m) 212.
Leitblech(n) 271.
Leiter(f) 449, 487, 493, 741, 785.
Leiterbaum(m), ausfahrbarer 780.
Leitergerüst(n) 303.
Leiterkordel(f) 231.
LEITERN(F) 302.
Leiterstrahlrohr(n) 781.
Leitöse(f) 630.
Leitrad(n), pneubereiftes 477.
Leitschaufeln(f), äußere 501.
Leitschaufeln(f), innere 501.
Leitung(f) 420.
Leitwerk(n) 499, 638, 746.
LEITWERKSFORMEN(F) 498.
Leitwerksträger(m) 508.
Leitwerkstütze(f) 507.
Lende(f) 101, 117, 119.
Lendengeflecht(n) 133.
Lendenpolster(n) 602.
**Lendenwirbel(m) 135.**
Lendenwirbel(m) 103.
Lendenwirbel(m) (5) 123.
Lenkachse(f) 788.
Lenker(m) 445.
Lenkergriff(m) 442.
Lenkerschaft(m) 447.
Lenkhebel(m) 788.
Lenkholm(m) 270, 272.
Lenkrad(n) 147, 430.
Lenkrolle(f) 260.
Lenkstange(f) 447, 637, 664.
Lenkzylinder(m) 784.
Leo 820.
Leseleuchte(f) 234.
Leuchtanzeige(f) 529.
Leuchtanzeigen(f) 531.
leuchtende Nachtwolke(f) 19.
Leuchtfeuer(n) 489.
**Leuchtfeuerkennung(f) 489.**
Leuchtpult(n) 398.
Leuchtstift(m) 515.
**Leuchtstoffröhre(f) 232.**
Leuchtstoffröhre(f) 233.
Leuchtstreifen(m) 730, 777.
**Leuchtturm(m) 486.**
Leuchtturm(m) 491.
**Leuchtturmlampe(f) 486.**
Leukoplast(m) 115.
Libelle(f) 77.
Libero(m) 601.
Libra 820.
Licht(n) 720, 721.
Lichterscheinung(f) 489.
Lichtmaschine(f) 434.
Lichtregelanlage(f) 412.
Lichtsensor(m) 390.
Lichtwertskala(f) 396.
Lichtzeichenanlage(f) 826, 827.
**Lidschatten(m) 367.**
Liebstöckel(m/n) 74.
Lieferanteneinfahrt(f) 190.
Liegestuhl(m) 223.
Ligament(n), elastisches 107.
Likörglas(n) 237.
Lilie(f) 819.
Limonadenlöffel(m) 241.
Limousine(f), viertürige 425.
lineal 56.
Lineal(n) 578, 591, 688.
Linebacker(m), äußerer 603.
Linebacker(m), mittlerer 603, 605.
Linie(f), blaue 608.
Linie(f), kurze 617.
Linienrichter(m) 601, 603, 606, 608, 612, 613, 614, 618.
Linienrichter(m), erster 605.
Linienrichter(m), zweiter 605, 613.
**Liniensystem(n) 537.**
links 189.
Linksaußen(m) 601.
Linksaußen-Linebacker(m) 605.
Linse(f) 140, 390, 392.
Linse(f), bikonkave 722.
Linse(f), bikonvexe 722.
Linse(f), konkave 722.
Linse(f), konkavkonvexe 722.
Linse(f), konvexe 722.
Linse(f), konvexkonkave 722.
Linse(f), plankonkave 722.
Linse(f), plankonvexe 722.
LINSEN(F) 722.
Linsen(f) 72.
Linsen(f), elektronenoptische 717.
LINSENFERNROHR(N) 721.
**Linsenfernrohr(n) 721.**
linsenförmige Galaxie(f) 9.
Linsenkopf(m) mit Schlitz(m) 276.
Linsensystem(n) 719.
Lippe(f) 100, 107, 630.
**Lippen-Make-up(n) 366.**
Lippenkonturenstift(m) 366.
**Lippenpfeife(f) 542.**
Lippenpinsel(m) 366.
Lippenstift(m) 366.
Lippentaster(m) 79, 81, 92.
Lira(f) 832.

**Fettgedruckte** Wörter beziehen sich auf eine Illustration; Wörter in GROSSBUCHSTABEN sind Überschriften.

LITHOGRAPHIE(F) 583.
**Lithographie(f) 580.**
Lithographiestein(m) 583.
Lithokreide(f) 583.
Lithosphäre(f) 31.
Lithostift(m) 583.
Litschi(f) 68.
Litze(f) 375.
**Litzen(f) 573.**
Litzen(f) 572, 574.
Litzenstab(m) 574.
Loch(n) 583, 676.
Loch(n), gestanztes 323, 355.
LOCHBILLARD(N) 674.
**Lochbillard(n) 673.**
Locher(m) 516.
Lochrohr(n) 216.
Lochschlitten(m) 568.
Lock-Forward(m) 606.
**Lockenbürste(f) 370.**
Lockenbürste(f) 370.
Lockennadel(f) 369.
**Lockenstab(m) 370.**
**Lockenwickler(m) 369.**
**Löffel(m) 241.**
Löffel(m) 672, 688.
Löffeleisen(n) 587.
**Löffeltypen(m) 241.**
Loge(f) 189.
Lokomotive(f) 459.
LOKOMOTIVE(F), DIESELELEKTRISCHE 468.
Lokschuppen(m) 464.
Lokverkehrsgleis(n) 465.
Longdrinkglas(n) 237.
Lorbeer(m) 74.
Lorgnette(f) 377.
Löschmittelbehälter(m) 780.
Löschtaste(f) 405, 420, 523, 530.
Löseeinstellschraube(f) 641.
Lot(n) 307.
LÖTEN(N) 305, 306, 308.
Lötkolben(m) 305.
**Lötlampe(f) 299, 307.**
**Lötpistole(f) 305.**
Lötspitze(f) 305.
Lounge(f) 496.
**Löwe(m) 98.**
Löwe(m) 11, 820.
Löwe(m), schreitender 819.
Löwenzahn(m) 73.
Luchs(m) 11.
Luer-Lock-Spitze(f) 726.
Luffaschwamm(m) 367.
Luft(f) 437.
Luft(f), kalte 772.
Luft(f), warme 772.
Luft-Boden-Flugkörper(m) 814.
Luft-Luft-Flugkörper(m) 813, 814.
Luftansaugrohr(n) 493.
Luftaustritt(m) 735.
Luftaustrittsöffnung(f) 211, 370.
Luftaustrittsschlitz(m) 260.
**Luftbefeuchter(m) 210.**
**Luftbetankung(f) 813.**
Luftbetankungsausleger(m) 813.
Luftdatenrechner(m) 500.
Luftdruck(m) 38.
Luftdruck(m) in Meereshöhe(f) 38.
**Luftdruck(m), Messung(f) 41.**
Luftdruckänderung(f) 38.
Luftdruckanschluß(m) 304.
Luftdruckkammer(f) 806.
**Luftdurchlässe(m) 207.**
Luftdüse(f) 430.
Lufteinlaß(m) 304, 443, 445, 449, 493.
Lufteinlauf(m) 508.
Lufteintritt(m) 14, 501.
Lüfter(m) 434, 438.
Lüfterkopf(m) 486.
Luftfahrt(f) 417.
Luftfeuchtigkeit(f) 34, 210.
**Luftfeuchtigkeit(f), Messung(f) 41.**
Luftfilter(m) 210, 469, 783.
Luftfilter(n) 272.
Luftkammer(f) 109.
LUFTKISSENFAHRZEUG(N) 492.
Luftklappe(f) 441.
Luftloch(n) 385, 389.
Luftmasse(f) 38.
Luftmatratze(f) 687.
Luftpolster(n) 352.
Luftpresser(m) 458, 469.
Luftpropeller(m) 492.
Luftpumpe(f) 446.
Luftreiniger(m) 210.
Luftröhre(f) 130.
Luftschlauch(m) 590, 627, 734.
Luftschleuse(f) 14, 511.
Luftschleuse(f) des Reaktorgebäudes(n) 758.
Luftspalt(m) 14, 772.
Luftsprudler(m) 294, 295.
Luftstrom(m) 590.
Luftstromrichtdüse(f) 370.
Luftstromschalter(m) 370.
Lufttemperatur(f) 38.
Lüftung(f) 477, 772.
Lüftungsziegel(m) 196.
Luftventil(n) 304, 590.
LUFTWEGE(M) 130.
**Luftzeichen(n) 820.**
Luftzielsuchradar(n) 809, 811.
Luftzufuhrregler(m) 204.
Luke(f) 805.
Lunge(f) 97.
Lunge(f), linke 124, 130.
Lunge(f), rechte 124, 130.
Lungenarterie(f) 126, 130.
Lungenarterienstamm(m) 125.
Lungenmittellappen(m) 130.
Lungenoberlappen(m) 130.
Lungenunterlappen(m) 130.
Lungenvene(f) 126.
Lungenvene(f), linke 125.
Lungenvene(f), rechte 125.
Luntenstock(m) 801.
Lunula(f) 95.
Lupe(f) 688.
**Lyra(f) 535.**
Lysosom(n) 115.

## M

Machete(f) 794.
Magazin(n) 188, 795, 796, 797.
Magazinabschluß(m) 797.
Magazinbalg(m) 543.
Magazinhalter(m) 795, 797.
Magen(m) 88, 92, 97, 124, 131.
Magenstütze(f) 346.
Magma(n) 25, 28.
Magmakammer(f) 25.
Magnet(m) 406, 485, 563, 714.
Magnetaufhängung(f) 712.
Magnetband(n) 527.
Magnetbandlaufwerk(n) 527.
Magnetbandmaschine(f) 407.
MAGNETKOMPASS(M) 719.
Magnetnadel(f) 719.
Magnetometer(n) 42.
**Mähdrescher(m) 160.**
Mähdrescher(m) 155.
MÄHEN(N) 158.
**Mähen(n) 154.**
**Mahlzahn(m) 144.**
Mahlzahn(m), erster 144.
Mahlzahn(m), zweiter 144.
Mahlzähne(m) 144.
Mähne(f) 100.
Mais(m) 152.
MAKE-UP(N) 366.
**Make-up(n) 366.**
Makro-Einstelltaste(f) 409.
**Mal(n) 599.**
Mal(n) 599.
Mal(n), drittes 597.
Mal(n), erstes 597.
Mal(n), zweites 597.
MALEN(N) 590, 592.
MALEN(N) UND ZEICHNEN(N) 588.
MALERBEDARF(M) 304.
Malerstaffelei(f) 13.
Malpappe(f) 589.
Malspachtel(m) 589.
Malspieler(m), dritter 597.
Malspieler(m), erster 597.
Malspieler(m), zweiter 597.
Malstock(m) 591.
Mandarine(f) 65.
Mandel(f) 66, 142.
**Mandoline(f) 535.**
Mango(f) 63.
**Mangold(m) 72.**
MANIKÜRE(F) 365.
Manipulatorarm(m), ferngesteuerter 510.
männlich 831.
männliche Blütenstände(m) 58.
Mannloch(n) 741, 742.
**Mannschaft(f), angreifende 603, 605.**
**Mannschaft(f), verteidigende 603, 605.**
Mannschaftsbank(f) 626.
Mannschaftstrikot(n) 595.
Mannschaftszelt(n) 686.
Manometer(n) 741.
Manöver-Triebwerk(n) 511.
Manövriereinheit(f), bemannte 512.
Manque(n) (1 bis 18) 700, 701.
Mansarddach(n) 183.
Manschette(f) 324, 609, 663, 681.
Manschette(f), aufblasbare 710.
Manschette(f), obere 641.
Manschettenknopf(m) 339.
**Mantel(m) 320.**
Mantel(m) 331, 692, 798, 804.
Mantel(m), dreiviertellanger 321.
Mantel(m), oberer 22.
Mantel(m), unterer 22.
**Mantelarten(f) 330.**
Mantelblech(n) 741.
Mantelkleid(n) 332.
Mantellinie(f) 95.
Mantelmauer(f) 181.
Mantelrand(m) 92.
Mantelstromführung(f) 501.
Manual(n) 543.
Manual(n) für das Hauptwerk(n) 542.
Manual(n) für das Oberwerk(n) 542.
Manual(n) für das Rückpositiv(n) 542.
Manuale(n) 542.
Manuell-/Automatikeinstellung(f) 585.
Marcato-Zeichen(n) 539.
Marconikutter(m) 482.
Marginalschild(m) 96.
Marienkäfer(m) 77.
Marine-Dieselkraftstoff(m) 745.
maritim 45.
Mark(n) 59, 132.
Mark(n), verlängertes 134.
Markenname(m) 384.
Marker(m) 389, 588.
Markierungslinie(f) 719.
Markierungspunkt(m) 565.
Markscheide(f) 135.
Markstrahlen(m) 59.
Mars(m) 4.
Marsstenge(f) 479.
Martinshorn(n) 779.
Mascara(f), flüssige 367.
Mascarabürstchen(n) 367.
**Mascarastein(m) 367.**
Maschen(f) 619.
Maschenanschlag(m) 567.
Maschenprobe(f) 567.
Maschinengewehr(n) 805.
MASCHINENGEWEHR(N), LEICHTES 796.
Maschinenhalle(f) 746, 747.
Maschinenhaus(n) 734.
MASCHINENPISTOLE(F) 795.
Maschinenraum(m) 496, 742, 806.
Maserung(f) 288.
Maske(f) 595, 627.
Maskendichtung(f) 730.
Massagespitze(f) 373.
Maßband(n) 563, 711.
Masse(f) 312, 714.
Masseelektrode(f) 439.
Massekabel(n) 305.
Massengut-Terminal(m) 490.
Massestück(n) 721.
Maßwerk(n) 175.
Mast(m) 471, 628, 631.
Mastdarm(m) 127, 128, 131.
Mastfenster(n) 756.
Mastfuß(m) 756.
Mastkörper(m) 756.
Mastlager(n) 631.
Mastoberteil(n) 756.
Mastspitze(f) 631.
Masttasche(f) 631.
Masttraverse(f) 756.
Matchbeutel(m) 381.
Materialschleuse(f) 764.
**Mathematik(f) 830.**
Matratze(f) 224.
Matratzenauflage(f) 224.
Matrosenbluse(f) 337.
Matrosenkragen(m) 342.
**Matte(f) 668.**
Matte(f) 682.
Mattenisolierung(f) 287.
Mattscheibe(f) 390.
Mauer(f) 646, 647.
Mauer(f) mit Stangen(f) 646, 647.
Mauerturm(m) 180.
Mauertürmchen(n) 180.
Mauerwerk(n) 199.
Maul(n) 100.
**Maultrommel(f) 536.**
MAUREREI(F) 291.
Maurerhammer(m) 291.
**Maurerkelle(f) 291.**
**Maus(f) 530.**
Maus(f) 526, 527.
Maximumthermometer(n) 41.
**Mechanismus(m) 712.**
Medaillon(n) 361.
mediane Zungenfurche(f) 143.
mediterrane Subtropen(f) 45.
Meer(n) 7, 51, 752.
Meerenge(f) 51.
MEERESGRUND(M) 28.
Meeresseite(f) 752.
Meeresspiegel(m) 22, 28.
Meerrettich(m) 71.
Mehlsieb(n) 245.
Mehrfeldbrücke(f) 454.
Mehrschichtsperrholz(n) 288.
Mehrzweckleiter(f) 303.
**Mehrzweckzange(f) 311.**
Meissnersches Tastkörperchen(n) 136.
Meldungsanzeige(f) 532.
Melodiepfeife(f) 536.
Melodiesaiten(f) 535.
Melone(f) 328.
Membrane(f) 401, 406.
Menügabel(f) 240.
Menümesser(n) 239.
Meridian(m), östlicher 47.
Meridian(m), westlicher 47.
Meridianlinie(f) 719.
**Merkmale(n), topographische 28.**
Merkur(m) 4.
Mesokarp(n) 62, 63, 64, 65.
Mesosphäre(f) 19.
Mesothorax(m) 78.
**Meßband(n) 711.**
Meßbecher(m) 244.
Meßbügel(m) 711.
**Messen(n) 244.**
**Messer(n) 239.**
Messer(n) 256, 268, 271, 272, 311, 581, 587, 688, 690.
Messer(n) aus Feuerstein(m) 791.
Messer(n), festgestelltes 578.
Messerbalken(m) 158, 160.
Messerbayonett(n) 794.
Messerscheide(f) 93.
Messerschutz(m) 250.
**Messertypen(m) 239, 242.**
Messingkörper(m) 294, 295, 296.
MESSINSTRUMENTE(N), METEOROLOGISCHE 40.
Meßkabel(n) 310.
Meßkabine(f) 15.
Meßkreisel(m) 814.
Meßlöffel(m) 244.
Meßrohr(n) 40.
Meßspeicher(m) 310.
Meßspindel(f) 711.
Meßspitze(f) 310.
Meßtaste(f) 396.
Meßtrommel(f) 711.
MESSUNG(F) SEISMISCHER WELLEN(F) 714.
**Metall(n) 819.**
Metall(n) A 307.
Metall(n) B 307.
Metallaufsatz(m) 689.
Metalle(n) 33.
Metallfeder(f), römische 389.
Metallkontaktgitter(n) 768.
Metallkopf(m) 658.
Metallrahmen(m) 540.
Metallspannreifen(m) 553.
Metallverbindung(f) 287.
Metallwinkel(m) 275.
metamorphe Gesteine(n) 23.
Metathorax(m) 78.
**Meteore(m) 39.**
METEOROLOGIE(F) 38.
METEOROLOGISCHE MESSINSTRUMENTE(N) 40.
Metope(f) 167.
**Metronom(n) 539.**
**Michigan-Schneeschuh(m) 645.**
**Mieder(n) 346.**
Mieder(n) 317.
Miederhose(f) 346.
Miesmuschel(f) 93.
Mihrab(m) 173.
Mikrofon(m) zum Studio(n) 413.
Mikrofon(n) 407, 414, 420, 639.
Mikrofon(n), eingebautes 409.
MIKROFON(N), ELEKTRODYNAMISCHES 406.
Mikrofon-Fahrspinne(f) 414.
Mikrofonausleger(m) 412, 414.
Mikrometerknopf(m) 713.
**Mikrometerschraube(f) 711.**
Mikrometerschraube(f) 484.
Mikroprozessor(m) 528.
Mikroskopokular(n) 713.
**Mikrowellengerät(n) 253.**

**Fettgedruckte** Wörter beziehen sich auf eine Illustration; Wörter in GROSSBUCHSTABEN sind Überschriften.

Mikrowellenscanner(m) 43.
Mikrowellenschüssel(f) 415.
Mikrowellensender(m) 415.
Milchbrot(n) 153.
Milchgang(m) 129.
Milchkammer(f) 149.
Milchkännchen(n) 238.
Milchstraße(f) 11.
Milz(f) 88, 124.
Minarett(n) 172, 173.
Minbar(m) 173.
Mine(f) 389.
**Mini-Diskette(f) 529.**
Minibus(m) 425.
Minimumthermometer(n) 41.
Minislip(m) 325.
Minusbereich(m) 768.
Minuskontakt(m) 768, 769.
Minusplatte(f) 439.
Minuspolbrücke(f) 439.
Minute(f) 830.
Minutenzeiger(m) 706, 707.
Minze(f) 74.
**Mischbatterie(f) 294, 295.**
Mischkammer(f) 206, 207, 306.
Mischpult(n) 407.
Mischwasserkanal(m) 186.
Mispel(f) 64.
mit dem Wind(m) 629.
Mithörtaste(f) 420.
Mitnehmerrippe(f) 259.
Mitnehmerstange(f) 737.
Mitochondrium(n) 115.
Mitralklappe(f) 125.
Mittelamerika(n) 20.
Mittelarmnerv(m) 133.
Mittelbein(n) 79, 80.
**Mittelbein(n) (Außenseite(f)) 80.**
Mitteldrittel(n) 611.
Mittelelektrode(f) 439.
Mittelfahne(f) 601.
Mittelfeld(n) 597, 617.
Mittelfeldangriffsspieler(m) 612.
Mittelfeldspieler(m) 601, 607, 611.
Mittelfeldspieler(m), linker 607.
Mittelfeldspieler(m), rechter 607.
Mittelfeldspieler(m), zurückgezogener 612.
Mittelfinger(m) 137.
Mittelformatkamera(f) SLR(6 x 6) 395.
Mittelfüllung(f) 202.
Mittelfuß(m) 80, 101.
Mittelfußknochen(m) 103, 122.
Mittelgang(m) 460.
Mittelglied(n) 107, 122, 123, 137.
Mittelhandknochen(m) 122.
Mittelkielschwein(n) 743.
Mittelkonsole(f) 430.
Mittelkreis(m) 601, 610, 611.
Mittellage-Tonabnehmer(m) 547.
Mittellinie(f) 601, 604, 606, 607, 608, 610, 612, 616, 618, 619, 620, 626, 666, 682.
Mittelloch(n) 404.
Mittelmeer(n) 21.
Mittelmoräne(f) 26.
Mittelohr(n) 138.
Mittelpunkt(m) 674, 697.
Mittelrippe(f) 56, 67.
Mittelsäule(f) 236, 427, 774.
Mittelschiff(n) 173, 177.
Mittelspannungsleitung(f) 757.
Mittelsproß(m) 105.
Mittelspur(f) 452.
Mittelsteg(m) 346.
Mittelstreifen(m) 184, 186, 452, 614.
Mittelstück(n) 127, 384.
Mittelstürmer(m) 601, 607.
Mitteltasche(f) 674.
Mittelteil(n) 756.
Mitteltöner(m) 401.
Mitteltonlautsprecher(m) 16.
Mitteltorus(m) 167.
**Mittelwagen(m) 477.**
Mittelwagen(m) 458, 476.
Mittelzeichen(n) 614.
**Mixer(m) 250.**
Mode-Taste(f) 525.
Modellierhölzer(n) 585.
Modellierscheibe(f) 584.
**Modellierschere(f) 369.**
Modem(n) 526.
Modemanschluß(m) 528.
Moderator(m) 760, 761, 762, 763, 766.
Moderatorfilz(m) 540.
Moderatorpedal(n) 540.
Moderatortank(m) 761.
Modillon(n) 167.
Modulationsrad(n) 555.
Modus-Taste(f) 402.
**Mohn(m) 67.**
Mohorovicic-Diskontinuität(f) 22.
Mohrenkopfform(f) 245.
Mokassin(m) 355.
Mokkatasse(f) 238.
Molar(m) 98.
Molkereiprodukte(n) 33.
MOND(M) 7.
Mond(m) 4, 8, 819.
**Mond(m), Oberflächenformationen(f) 7.**
Mondbahn(f) 8.
**Monde(m) 4.**
MONDFINSTERNIS(F) 8.
Mondlandeeinheit(f) 509.
MONDPHASEN(F) 6.
Mondphasenzeiger(m) 707.
Mondsichel(f) (abnehmender Mond(m)) 7.
Mondsichel(f) (zunehmender Mond(m)) 6.
Monitor(m) 699.
Monitoranschluß(m) 528.
Mono-Stereo-Taste(f) 402.
Monokel(n) 377.
Monomatic-Schloß(n) 383.
**Monoski(m) 633.**
Monster(m) 605.
Morchel(m) 55.
Mordent(m) 538.
**Morphologie(f) 86, 100, 106, 108.**
MÖRSER(M) 803.
**Mörser(m) 803.**
Mörser(m) 243.
**Mörser(m), moderner 803.**
Mosaik(n) 171.
Mosaikparkett(n) 200.
MOSCHEE(F) 172.
**Moschee(f), Grundriß(m) 173.**
**Motor(m) 438.**
Motor(m) 147, 161, 214, 257, 258, 259, 270, 271, 272, 283, 284, 442, 737, 784, 787, 805.
Motorbeiboot(n) 809.
Motorblock(m) 250, 251, 256, 260, 373, 435.
Motorgehäuse(n) 272.
Motorhaube(f) 426.
MOTORRAD(N) 442, 444.
**Motorrasenmäher(m) 271.**
MOTORTYPEN(M) 436.
Mouche(f) 684.
Mount Everest(m) 19.
Muffe(f) 301.
Mufflon(m), Hörner(n) 99.
Mufftasche(f) 321, 330, 339, 381.
Mulde(f) 270.
**Müllschlucker(m) 296.**
Müllschlucker(m) 296.
Mullverband(m) 725.
Multifunktionsantenne(f) 807.
Multifunktionstaste(f) 523.
**Multimeter(n) 310.**
Multiplikation(f) 830.
Multiplikationstaste(f) 523.
**Multitrainer(m) 663.**
Mumienschlafsack(m) 687.
**Mund(m) 142.**
Mund(m) 83, 84, 92, 118.
Munddusche(f) 373.
Mundharmonika(f) 536.
Mundhöhle(f) 130, 131.
Mundrohr(n) 550.
Mundschutz(m) 669.
Mundspeicheldrüse(f) 131.
Mundstück(n) 548, 550, 627.
Mundstückaufnahme(f) 550.
Mündung(f) 94, 797, 798, 799, 800, 803.
**Mundwerkzeuge(n) 81.**
Mundwinkel(m) 142.
Munitionsbehälter(m) 805.
Münzeinwurf(m) 422, 702.
Münzleitung(f) 702.
Münzrückgabe(f) 702.
Muschel(f) 220.
Musculus(m) bulbospongiosus 127.
Museum(n) 185.
MUSIKINSTRUMENTE(N), TRADITIONELLE 535, 536.
MUSIKNOTATION(F) 537, 538.
Musikregie(f) 412.
Musiksalon(m) 497.
MUSIKZUBEHÖR(N) 539.
Muskelblock(m) 89.
Muskeleindruck(m) 95.
Muskelfaser(f) 134.
MUSKELN(M) 120.
Muster(n) 586.
Mutter(f) 278, 279, 300.
Mutterband(n), breites 129.
Mutterband(n), rundes 129.
Mutulus(m) 167.
Mütze(f) 627.
Mützenschirm(m) 328, 329.
Myzel(n) 55.

## N

Nabe(f) 447, 727, 754, 774.
Nabel(m) 116, 118.
Nabel(m), oberer 110.
Nabel(m), unterer 110.
Nabelstrang(m) 67.
Nabenabdeckung(f) 754.
Nachführsensor(m) 16.
Nachfüllmine(f) 389.
Nachfüllrohr(n) 293.
Nachrichten(f), ausdrucken 421.
Nachrichten(f), senden und empfangen 421.
Nachrichtenanzeige(f) 420.
NACHRICHTENSATELLIT(M) 417.
Nachthemd(n) 348.
**Nachtwäsche(f) 348.**
Nacken(m) 108, 117, 119.
Nackenfeder(f) 670.
Nackenrolle(f) 224.
Nackenrolle(f), große 224.
Nackenschutz(m) 777.
**Nadel(f) 562.**
Nadel(f) 36, 561, 562, 563, 590.
NADELBAUM(M) 58.
**Nadelbett(n) 568.**
Nadelbett(n) 568.
Nadelbettrille(f) 568.
**Nadeldrucker(m) 531.**
Nadeldrucker(m) 527.
Nadelfuß(m) 568.
Nadelhalter(m) 562.
Nadelhalterschraube(f) 562.
**Nadelkissen(n) 563.**
Nadelklemmschraube(f) 590.
Nadelpositionswähler(m) 561.
**Nadelriemen(m) 632.**
Nadelstange(f) 562.
Nadelwerkzeug(n) 585.
**Nagel(m) 275.**
Nagel(m) 104.
Nagelbett(n) 137.
Nagelfeile(f) 365.
Nagelfeile(f), klappbare 365.
Nagelhautentferner(m) 365.
Nagelhautschaber(m) 365.
Nagelhautschere(f) 365.
Nagelhautschieber(m) 365.
**Nagelknipser(m) 365.**
Nagelkörper(m) 137.
Nagelloch(n) 104.
Nagelmöndchen(n) 137.
**Nagelnecessaire(n) 365.**
**Nagelpflegezubehör(n) 365.**
Nagelreiniger(m) 365.
Nagelschere(f) 365.
Nageltasche(f) 137.
Nagelweißstift(m) 365.
Nagelwurzel(f) 137.
Nagelzange(f) 365.
Nagelzieher(m) 688.
**Nagetiergebiß(n) 98.**
NÄHEN(N) 561, 562, 564, 566.
Nahlinse(f) 392.
**Nähmaschine(f) 561.**
Nährichtungseinsteller(m) 561.
**Nahrungskette(f) 31.**
Nahrungsmittelquelle(f), primäre 31.
Naht(f) 67, 94, 327, 352, 355, 384.
Nähte(f) 596.
Nahteil(n) 376.
Nahtlinie(f) 565.
Nahttasche(f) 330, 339.
Nahtzugabe(f) 565.
Name(m) der Station(f) 474.
Naos(m) 169.
Napfschnecke(f) 83.
Narbe(f) 60, 66.
Naris(f) 141.
Nase(f) 100, 118, 277, 637, 638, 792.
**Nase(f), äußere 141.**
Nasen-Bartschere(f) 365.
Nasenbein(n) 141.
Nasenblatt(n) 112.
Nasenflügel(m) 141.
**Nasenhöhle(f) 141.**
Nasenhöhle(f) 130.
Nasenklappe(f) 812.
Nasenknorpel(m), großer 141.
Nasenloch(n) 84, 96, 109.
Nasenmuschel(f), mittlere 141.
Nasenmuschel(f), obere 141.
Nasenmuschel(f), untere 141.
Nasenöffnung(f) 86.
Nasenrachenraum(m) 141.
Nasenriemen(m) 649.
Nasenrücken(m) 141.
Nasenscheidewandknorpel(m) 141.
Nasenschleimhaut(f) 142.
Nasenschoner(m) 651.
Nasenspiegel(m) 107.
Nasenspitze(f) 141.
Nasenwurzel(f) 141.
Nashorn(n), Hörner(n) 99.
Naßkammer(f) 763.
Nationalpark(m) 52.
Naturschwamm(m) 367.
Navette(f) 362.
Navigationsanzeige(f) 500.
NAVIGATIONSINSTRUMENTE(N) 484.
Navigationsperiskop(n) 807.
**Neapolitanische Tropfkanne(f) 247.**
Nebel(m) 37, 39.
Nebelleuchte(f) 429.
Nebelscheinwerfer(m) 440.
Nebeneinfüllstutzen(m) 741.
Nebenfahrwasser(n) 489.
Nebengleis(n) 464.
Nebenniere(f) 132.
Nebenstraße(f) 52.
negativ geladen 831.
Negativ(n) 399.
**Negativhalter(m) 399.**
Negativhalter(m) 399.
Negligé(n) 348.
Nehrung(f) 30.
Neigung(f) 748.
Nektarine(f) 63.
Neptun(m) 5.
Nerv(m) 136.
Nervenendigung(f) 136.
Nervenfaser(f) 136.
Nervengeflecht(n) 144.
NERVENSYSTEM(N) 133, 134.
**Nervensystem(n), peripheres 133.**
**Nervensystem(n), zentrales 134.**
Nervus(m) cutaneus femoris lateralis 133.
**Netz(n) 613, 614, 618.**
Netz(n) 13, 596, 610, 612, 613, 614, 618, 619, 626.
Netz-/Lichtschalter(m) 561.
Netzanschluß(n) 408.
NETZBALLSPIEL(N) 611.
**Netzballspiel(n) 611.**
Netzband(n) 614.
Netzhalter(m) 619.
Netzhaut(f) 140.
Netzkabel(n) 256, 370, 374.
Netzkontrollampe(f) 420.
Netzplan(m) 474.
Netzrichter(m) 614.
Netzschalter(m) 402, 405, 410, 411, 420, 529, 555.
Netzspieler(m), linker 613.
Netzspieler(m), mittlerer 613.
Netzspieler(m), rechter 613.
Netzstrumpf(m) 344.
Netzteil(n) 528.
Netzwerkanschluß(m) 528.
Netzwerkkommunikation(f) 527.
Neumond(m) 6.
Neuralfortsatz(m) 89.
Neuron(n), motorisches 135.
Neuron(n), peripher-sensorisches 135.
Neuron(n), sensibles 134.
**Neuronenkette(f) 135.**
Neutralanzeigelicht(n) 445.
neutrale Zone(f) 603, 605, 608.
nicht angebbar (z.B. wegen Nebel(m)) 39.
nicht identisch 830.
nicht waschen 829.
Nickhaut(f) 107.
Niederdruckdampf(m) 758.
Niederdruckverdichtung(f) 501.
Niederschlag(m) 34, 35.
Niederschlag(m), saurer 32, 33, 35.
NIEDERSCHLÄGE(M) 36.
Niederschlagsgebiet(n) 38.
**Niederschlagsschreiber(m) 40.**
Niedrigspannungsleitung(f) 757.
Niere(f) 89, 97, 124.
Niere(f), linke 132.
Niere(f), rechte 132.
Nierenarterie(f) 126, 132.
Nierenbecken(n) 132.

**Fettgedruckte** Wörter beziehen sich auf eine Illustration; Wörter in GROSSBUCHSTABEN sind Überschriften.

nierenförmig 56.
Nierenhilus(m) 132.
Nierenkelch(m) 132.
Nierenpapille(f) 132.
Nierenvene(f) 126, 132.
Niet(m) 242, 278, 304.
Nimbostratus(m) 44.
Nippel(m) 301.
Nivellierfuß(m) 257, 258, 259.
Nivellierschraube(f) 40.
Nocke(f) 684, 793.
Nockenpunkt(m) 684.
Nockenring(m) 281.
Nockenwelle(f) 434.
Noir(n) 700, 701.
Nonius(m) 484.
Nordamerika(n) 20.
Norden(m) 488.
nördliche Halbkugel(f) 3.
NÖRDLICHE HALBKUGEL(F), KONSTELLATIONEN(F) 10.
Nördliche Krone(f) 11.
Nördliche Wasserschlange(f) 11.
nördlicher Polarkreis(m) 3.
Nordosten(m) 488.
Nordpol(m) 3.
Nordpolarmeer(n) 21.
Nordsee(f) 21.
Nordwesten(m) 488.
Normalwaschgang(m) 829.
Notation(f) 696.
Notbremse(f) 477.
Note(f), ganze 538.
Note(f), halbe 538.
Notenablage(f) 539, 542, 555.
Notenlinie(f) 537.
**Notenschlüssel(m) 537.**
**Notenständer(m) 539.**
**Notenwerte(m) 538.**
NOTFALLAUSRÜSTUNG(F) 726.
Notizblock(m) 518.
Notlaufschiene(f) 476.
Notregulierung(f) 627.
Notschalter(m) 444.
Nuchalschild(m) 97.
Nudelholz(n) 245.
Nudelmaschine(f) 243.
Nukleolus(m) 115, 128.
Null-Leiter(m) 757.
Nulleiter(m) 312.
Nulleitersammelschiene(f) 312.
Nulleiterverbinder(m) 312.
Nullmeridian(m) 47.
Numerierstempel(m) 516.
numerisches Tastenfeld(n) 530.
Nummer-8-Forward(m) 606.
Nummernschildbeleuchtung(f) 429.
Nummerntasten(f) 421.
Nuß(f) 793.
NÜSS(F) 66.
**Nußarten(f) 66.**
Nußknacker(m) 243.
Nüster(f) 100.
Nut(f) 201.
Nutzgarten(m) 193.
Nutzlast(f) 509.
Nutzlastmodul(n) 49.
Nutzleiter(f) 303.
NUTZVIEH(N) 150.
Nylonschnur(f) 271.

## O

O-Ring(m) 294, 295.
Oase(f) 46.
Oberarmarterie(f) 126.
Oberarmbein(n) 102.
Oberarmknochen(m) 122.
Oberarmschiene(f) 792.
Oberarmspeichenmuskel(m) 120, 121.
**Oberbau(m) 466.**
Oberbeleuchter(in(f))(m) 412.
Oberbühne(f) 188.
Oberdeck(n) 498, 741.
obere Tasche(f) 675.
Obereck(n), linkes 818.
Obereck(n), rechtes 818.
oberer Anzug(m) 650.
Oberfläche(f) 619.
Oberfläche(f), befeuchtete 580.
Oberfläche(f), farbige 580.
**Oberflächenformationen(f) des Mondes(m) 7.**
Oberflächenisolierung(f) 510.
**Oberfräser(m) 283.**
Obergestein(n) 733.
Obergurt(m) 455.
Oberhaut(f) 137.
Oberkante(f) 619.
Oberkiefer(m) 81, 86, 90, 122, 141.
Oberkiefer(m), beweglicher 96.
Oberkiefer(m), vorderer 86.
Oberkieferknochen(m) 144.
Oberleiter(f) 781.
Oberleitung(f) 459.
Oberlenker(m) 147.
Oberlicht(n) 188.
Oberlid(n) 140.
Oberlippe(f) 81, 142, 542.
Obermesser(n) 578.
Obermesserhebel(m) 578.
Oberpartie(f) 670.
Oberrohr(n) 446.
Oberschale(f) 443, 645.
Oberschenkel(m) 103, 117, 119, 127, 128, 203.
Oberschenkelanzieher(m), großer 121.
Oberschenkelanzieher(m), langer 120.
Oberschenkelknochen(m) 122.
Oberschenkelnerv(m) 133.
Oberschenkelpolster(n) 602.
Oberschenkelschlagader(f) 126.
Oberschenkelvene(f) 126.
Oberschnabel(m) 109.
Oberschwanzdecken(f) 109.
Oberschwelle(f) 202.
Oberstützmauer(f) 748.
Oberteilhauptfacette(f) 363.
Obertor(n) 493.
Oberwalze(f) 581.
Oberwasser(n) 746.
Oberwasserdecke(f) 748.
Oberwassermauer(f) 749.
Objektiv(n) 391, 392, 396, 397, 718, 719, 721.
Objektivanschluß(m) 390.
Objektivauswurf(m) 391.
**Objektive(n) 392.**
Objektivlinse(f) 405.
Objektivrevolver(m) 718.
Objektivschutzdeckel(m) 392.
**Objektivzubehör(n) 392.**
Objektklammer(f) 718.
Objekttisch(m) 717, 718.
Obmann(m) 666.
Oboe(f) 548.
Oboen(f) 557.
Obst- und Gemüseschale(f) 254.
Obstbaum(m) 149.
Obstgarten(m) 149.
Ochse(m) 151.
Ockerstift(m), roter 583.
Ofen(m) 770.
**Ofen(m), langsam brennender 204.**
**öffentlicher Fernsprecher(m) 422.**
Officemesser(n) 242.
Offiziellenbank(f) 608.
Offizierskabine(f) 497.
Offiziersquartiere(n) 807, 808.
**Öffnen(n) 244.**
Öffnung(f) 282, 327.
Ohr(n) 107, 112, 116, 223.
Öhr(n) 562, 563.
Ohr(n), äußeres 138.
Ohrdecken(f) 109.
Ohrgehänge(n) 361.
Ohrklappe(f) 112.
Ohrkrempe(f) 139.
Ohrläppchen(n) 139.
**Ohrmuschel(f) 139.**
Ohrmuschel(f) 138, 406.
Ohrmuschelhöcker(m) 139.
Ohrmuschelwindung(f) 139.
**Ohrringe(m) 361.**
Ohrringe(m) mit Schraubverschluß(m) 361.
Ohrschützer(m) 328, 729.
Ohrstecker(m) 361.
Ohrstöpsel(m) 726.
Okklusion(f) 39.
ÖKOLOGIE(F) 31, 32, 34.
Okraschote(f) 69.
Oktav-Einladung(f) 667.
Oktave(f) 537.
Oktavmechanik(f) 548.
Okular(n) 390, 396, 409, 718, 719, 720, 721.
Okularträger(m) 721.
Okulartubus(m) 718.
Ölablaßschraube(f) 434.
Ölbehälter(m) 734.
**Ölbrenner(m) 209.**
Öldruckkontrolleuchte(f) 445.
Öldruckwarnleuchte(f) 431.
Olekranon(n) 123.
Ölfarbe(f) 588.
ölgefüllter Heizkörper(m) 211.
Olive(f) 63.
**Olivenkopftrense(f) 650.**
Öllöschbrücke(f) 491.
Ölpastell(n) 588.
Ölpumpe(f) 209.
Ölstein(m) 582.
Ölsumpf(m) 272.
Ölverarbeitungsbereich(m) 738.
Ölwanne(f) 434.
Ölwannendichtung(f) 434.
Ölzufuhr(f) 209.
On-Deck-Kreis(m) 597.
Opal(m) 363.
Operationszentrale(f) 807.
Opernglas(n) 377.
Opferanode(f) 297.
Opisthodomos(m) 169.
**Orange(f) 65.**
Orange(f) 65.
Orchestergraben(m) 188.
Orchestersitz(m) 188.
Ordnungsgleise(n) 465.
Oregano(m) 74.
ORGEL(F) 542.
**Orgelmechanik(f) 543.**
**Orgelspieltisch(m) 542.**
Orientierungseinlage(f) 546, 547.
Oriflamme(f) 817.
Originaleinzug(m) 421.
Originalrückführung(f) 421.
Orion(m) 11, 13.
Orkan(m) 39.
Ort(n) 818.
Ortsstation(f) 416.
Öse(f) 353, 381, 569, 671.
Öse(f) für Schulterriemen(m) 390.
Öse(f), gerade 566.
Öse(f), runde 566.
**Ösen(f) 566.**
Ösenknopf(m) 566.
Ösenverbindung(f) 658.
Osten(m) 488.
Östliches Kardinalzeichen(n) 489.
Oszillationswelle(f) 30.
Oszillograph-/Oszilloskopmonitor(m) 413.
Otolith(m) 88.
**Ottomotor(m) 434.**
Overall(m) 336, 351.
Overall(m), einteiliger 635.
Overcheck(m) 653.
Overknee-Strumpf(m) 344.
Oxer(m) 646.
Ozean(m) 7, 35, 51.
Ozeanien(n) 21.
**ozeanischer Rücken(m) 28.**
Ozon(n) 19.

## P

paarig gefiedert 56.
Paarlaufhantel(f) 633.
Packplatte(f) 383.
Packriemen(m) 383.
Packung(f) 294.
Pagenkäppi(n) 329.
Pagodenärmel(m) 340.
Pahlstek(m) 691.
Pahlstek(m), doppelter 691.
Pahlstek(m), laufender 691.
Pair(n) 700, 701.
Paketannahme(f) 462.
Palette(f) 244, 787.
Palette(f) mit Stecker(m) 592.
Palette(f) mit Vertiefungen(f) 592.
Paletten(f) 507.
Palettenhubwagen(m) 788.
**Palettenhubwagen(m), hydraulischer 788.**
Palettmesser(n) 589.
Palisade(f) 181.
Pallialsinus(m) 95.
Palmenhain(m) 46.
Palmette(f) 220.
Panamahut(m) 328.
Panel(n) 229.
Panflöte(f) 536.
Panoramafenster(n) 190, 460.
Panoramakopf(m) 393.
Pantoffel(m) 355.
Pantolette(f) 357.
Panty-Korselett(n) 347.
PANZER(M) 805.
**Panzer(m) 96.**
Panzer(m) 805.
Panzerabwehrflugkörper(m) 814.
PANZERFAUST(F) 804.
Panzerhandschuh(m) 792.
Panzerplatte(f) 805.
Panzerschnur(f) 422.
Panzerschurz(m) 792.
Panzerturm(m) 805.
Papaya(f) 68.
Papier(n) 384, 580, 589.
Papierablage(f) 521.
Papierablagen(f) 532.
Papierclip(m) 515.
Papiereinschubfach(n) 532.
Papierfänger(m) 521.
Papierfreigabehebel(m) 525, 531.
Papierführung(f) 421, 531.
Papierführungsstachel(m) 531.
Papierführungsstange(f) 531.
Papierhalter(m) 524.
Papierhalterollen(f) 531.
Papierklammer(f) 531.
Papierlösehebel(m) 525.
Papierstütze(f) 525.
Papiervorschubtaste(f) 523.
Papierzufuhr(f) 521.
Papillarmuskel(m) 125.
Papille(f) 136.
**Pappschere(f) 578.**
Paprika(m) 69.
Parabeldüne(f) 46.
Parabolantenne(f) 415.
parabolischer Reflektor(m) 15.
Parabolspiegel(m) 770.
Paradiesvogel(m) 13.
Paraffine(n) 745.
parallel 830.
Parallelanschlag(m) 284, 285.
**Parallelbarren(m) 661.**
Paranuß(f) 66.
Pärchen(n), ein 695.
Pärchen(n), zwei 695.
Pardune(f) 479.
parietale Pleura(f) 130.
Park(m) 52, 184.
**Parka(m) 321.**
Parkdeck(n) 190.
PARKETTBODEN(M) 200.
Parkettboden(m) 199.
**Parkettboden(m) auf Holzunterbau(m) 200.**
**Parkettboden(m) auf Zementestrich(m) 200.**
**Parkettmuster(n) 200.**
Parkplatz(m) 185, 464, 491, 504.
Parterre(n) 189.
partielle Finsternis(f) 8.
Partlow-Diagramm(n) 441.
Paspel(f) 349.
Paspeltasche(f) 326, 339.
Pass(m) 27.
PASSAGIERDAMPFER(M) 496.
Passagierkabine(f) 493, 494, 495.
Passagierraum(m) 499, 508.
Passagierraum(m) 1. Klasse(f) 498.
**Passagierterminal(m) 504.**
Passagierterminal(m) 503.
Passagiertransferfahrzeug(n) 505, 507.
Passe(n) (19 bis 36) 700, 701.
Paßgang(m) 101.
Paßkontrolle(f) 505.
Pastell(n) 588.
Pastinake(f) 71.
Patentanker(m) 483.
Patentrand(m) 326.
Patera(f) 220.
Patisson-Kürbis(m) 69.
**Patrone(f) 798, 799.**
Patrone(f) 797.
**Patronenfilm(m) 395.**
Patronenkammer(f) 390, 795, 796.
Patronensicherung(f) 312.
Patte(f) 322.
Pattentasche(f), schräge 330.
Pauken(f) 557.
Pausche(f) 649, 661.
**Pauschenpferd(n) 661.**
Pause(f) 539, 831.
Pause(f), ganze 538.
Pause(f), halbe 538.
Pause-Taste(f) 403.
**Pausenzeichen(n) 538.**
Pausetaste(f) 411.
Pavillondach(n) 183.
Pazifischer Ozean(m) 20.
Pecannuß(f) 66.
Pedal(n) 446, 448, 545, 552, 553, 664.
Pedal(n) zur Verstellung(f) 591.
Pedalhaken(m) 446.
Pedalklaviatur(f) 542.
Pedalstange(f) 540.
Pedaltaste(f) 542.
**Pedometer(n) 711.**
Pegasus(m) 11.
Pegelanzeige(f), digitale 407.
Pegeltongenerator(m) 407.

**Fettgedruckte** Wörter beziehen sich auf eine Illustration; Wörter in GROSSBUCHSTABEN sind Überschriften.

Peildeck(n) 494, 495, 497.
**Pelerine(f) 330.**
Pelerine(f) 330.
**Pelham-Kandare(f) 650.**
**Peltonturbine(f) 754.**
**Pelzwerk(n) 819.**
Penalty-Linie(f) 612.
Pendel(n) 539, 707.
Pendelaufhängung(f) 714.
Pendelstab(m) 707.
Pendelzug(m) 504.
Pendlerzug(m) 464.
Penholdergriff(m) 619.
Penis(m) 116, 127.
Pentaprisma(n) 390.
Peperoni(f) 69.
**Peplos(m) 315.**
Perforierung(f) 327, 395.
Pergola(f) 263.
Perikarp(n) 65.
Peripheriegeräte(n), Anschluß(m) für 528.
Peristyl(n) 168, 169, 171.
**Perkulator(m) 247.**
Perle(f) 105.
Perlen(f) 105.
Perlmutterwolke(f) 19.
Perlrippen(f) 567.
Perlzwiebel(f) 70.
Peroxyd(n) 725.
Perseus(m) 11.
**Personalcomputer(m) 528.**
Personalcomputer(m) 526.
Personalschließfach(n) 461.
Personenbahnhof(m) 464.
**Personenwaage(f) 709.**
PERSONENZÜGE(M) 460.
Peseta(f) 832.
Pestizide(n) 32.
Petanquekugel(f) 682.
Petersilie(f) 74.
Petrochemikalien(f) 745.
Petroleum(n) 745.
Pfahl(m) 818.
Pfahlbau(m) 165.
Pfahlwurzel(f) 59.
Pfanndeckel(m) 795.
Pfanne(f) 795.
Pfannenwender(m) 244.
Pfau(m) 13.
Pfefferstreuer(m) 238.
**Pfeife(f) 385.**
Pfeife(f) 252, 543.
**Pfeife(f), Querschnitt 385.**
**Pfeifenbesteck(n) 385.**
Pfeifenkopf(m) 385.
Pfeifenmundstück(n) 385.
Pfeifenputzer(m) 385.
Pfeifenrastbrett(n) 543.
Pfeifenständer(m) 385.
Pfeifenstock(m) 543.
Pfeifenwerk(n) 543.
**Pfeil(m) 684.**
Pfeil(m) 11, 38, 793.
Pfeiler(m) 175, 176, 454, 455, 464.
Pfeilerfundament(n) 456.
Pfeilflügel(m) 499.
pfeilförmig 56.
Pfeilspitze(f) 684, 791.
Pfeilstütze(f) 684.
PFERD(N) 100, 102, 104.
**Pferd(n) 98.**
Pferd(n) 661, 696.
Pfifferling(m) 55.
**Pfirsich(m) 63.**
Pfirsich(m) 63.
PFLANZE(F), AUFBAU(M) 57.
Pflanzenfresser(m) 31, 33.
**Pflanzenfressergebiß(n) 98.**
PFLANZENZELLE(F) 115.
Pflanzholz(n) 268.
Pflanzlochstecher(m) 268.
Pflanzschnur(f) 268.
Pflaume(f) 63.
Pfluganker(m) 483.
PFLÜGEN(N) 156.
**Pflügen(n) des Bodens(m) 154.**
Pflugrahmen(m) 156.
Pfortader(f) 124, 126.
Pfosten(m) 198, 572, 613, 614, 618, 626.
Pfosten(m) mit Latte(f) 646, 647.
Pfosten(m) mit Stange(f) 647.
Pfropf(m) 799, 801.
Pfund(n) 832.
Phase(f) 757.
Philtrum(n) 141.
Phobos(m) 4.
Phönix(m) 13.
Phosphorschicht(f) 232.
Photosphäre(f) 6.
Photozellenspiegel(m) 486, 487.
Pi(n) 830.
**Piano(n), elektronisches 555.**
Pianopedal(n) 540, 555.
Picknick(n) 823.
Pickup(m) 159, 162, 425.
Piedmont-Gletscher(m) 27.
Pier(f) 739.
Pik(n) 695.
Pikkoloflöte(f) 548, 557.
Pilot(m) 637.
Pilote(f) 541.
PILZ(M) 55.
**Pilz(m), Aufbau(m) 55.**
**Pilz(m), tödlich giftiger 55.**
Pilzanker(m) 483.
Pilzfaden(m) 55.
Pin(m) 683.
Pinie(f) 58.
Pinienkern(m) 58, 66.
Pinne(f) 484, 485, 539, 590, 628, 719.
Pinocytosebläschen(n) 115.
**Pins(m), verschiedene 683.**
Pinsel(m) 582, 589.
Pinzette(f) 725.
Pipeline(f) 740.
Pipeline(f), überirdische 740.
Pisces 820.
Pistazie(f) 66.
Pisten-Mittelliniemarkierungen(f) 504.
Pistenbezeichnungsmarkierung(f) 504.
Pistenrandmarkierungen(f) 504.
PISTOLE(F) 797.
Pistolengriff(m) 280, 304, 305, 795, 796, 799.
Pit(n) 405.
Pitching-Wedge(n) 678.
Pittabrot(n) 153.
Pittabrot(n) mit Sesam(m) 153.
Planenwagen(m) 472.
PLANETARIUM(N) 16.
Planetarium(n) 184.
Planetariumsprojektor(m) 16.
**Planeten(m) 4.**
**Planeten(m), Umlaufbahnen(f) 4.**
Planfilm(m) 395.
**Planierraupe(f) 783.**
Planierschaufel(f) 783.
Planierschild(n) 783.
Plasmabrücke(f) 115.
Plastikhülse(f) 799.
Plateau(n) 51.
Platine(f) 528.
Plättchen(n) 36.
Platte(f) 238, 253, 393, 529, 554, 589.
**Platten(f) ausrollen 584.**
Plattenantrieb(m) 529.
Plattengitter(n) 439.
Plattenhalter(m) 582.
**Plattenheizkörper(m) 208.**
Plattenisolierung(f) 287.
Plattenscheider(m) 439.
**Plattenspieler(m) 404.**
Plattenspieler(m) 400, 407.
Plattenstift(m) 404, 540.
Plattenteller(m) 404.
Plattform(f) 302, 621.
Plattsehnenmuskel(m) 121.
**Plattstiche(m) 571.**
Platz(m) für Wohnwagen(m) 823.
Play-Taste(f) 403.
Plazierungsrichter(m) 621.
Plein(n) 700, 701.
Plektron(n) 535.
Pleuelstange(f) 434, 436.
Pleura(f), parietale 130.
Pleurahöhle(f) 130.
Plinthe(f) 707.
Plotter(m) 527.
Pluderhose(f) 316.
plus oder minus 830.
Plusbereich(m) 768.
Pluskontakt(m) 768, 769.
Plusplatte(f) 439.
Pluspolbrücke(f) 439.
Pluto(m) 5.
PN-Übertragung(f) 768.
Pocket-Instamatic Kamera(f) 395.
Podest(n) 14, 201, 292.
Podium(n) 556.
**Pokerblätter(n), normale 695.**
Pokerwürfel(m) 699.
Polachse(f) 14.
Polarisationsfilter(m) 392.
**Polarklimate(n) 45.**
Polarkreis(m), nördlicher 47.
Polarlicht(n) 19.
Polarstern(m) 11.
Polartundra(f) 45.
Polierstahl(m) 582.
Polizei(f) 822.
Pollenbürste(f) 80, 81.
Pollenkamm(m) 81.
Pollenkörbchen(n) 81.
Pollenschieber(m) 81.
Pollenzange(f) 81.
Pollenzelle(f) 82.
Poller(m) 743.
Polohemd(n) 337, 615.
Polokleid(n) 333.
Polokragen(m) 342.
Polster(n) 598.
Polsterauflage(f) 726.
Polsterdüse(f) 260.
Polstersofa(n) 221.
Polsterung(f) 406, 635.
Polzwinge(f) 305.
Poncho(m) 331.
Ponton(m) 457, 738.
**Pontonbrücke(f) 457.**
**Pool(n) 673.**
Poop(f) 478.
Pore(f) 67, 115, 136.
Porro-Prismensystem(n) 719.
Portal(n) 172, 175, 177.
Portalbrücke(f) 455.
Portalkuppel(f) 172, 173.
Portalrahmen(m) 455.
Posaune(f) 550.
Posaunen(f) 556.
Positionsleuchte(f) 459.
Positionslicht(n) 493, 499, 508.
positiv geladen 831.
Potentialspule(f) 712.
Poterne(f) 181.
Präger(m) 516.
Prägung(f) 586.
Prallblech(n) 742.
Prämolar(m) 98.
Präputialtasche(f) 101, 106.
Prärie(f) 51.
**Präzisionswaage(f) 709.**
Preis(m) 453.
Preis(m) pro Einheit(f) 709.
Preiselbeere(f) 62.
Prellbock(m) 464.
Preßbalken(m) 578, 579.
**Pressen(n) 579.**
**Preßfilterkanne(f) 247.**
Presskammer(f) 159.
**Preßluftbohrer(m) 735.**
Preßplatte(f) 579.
Preßspindel(f) 581, 583.
Prim-Einladung(f) 667.
Primärfokus(m) 14.
Primärfokuskabine(f) 14, 15.
**Primärkonsumenten(m) 31.**
Primärspiegel(m) 16.
Prime(f) 537.
Prinzeßkleid(n) 332.
Prinzeßnaht(f) 345.
PRISMENFERNGLAS(N) 719.
Probebühne(f) 188.
Probenkammer(f) 717.
Profil(n) 433.
Programmbereich(m) 405.
Programmiertasten(f) 411.
Programmwähler(m) 257, 258, 259.
Programmwahlschalter(m) 555.
Programmwählscheibe(f) 391.
Programmwahltasten(f) 411.
**Projektile(n) 801.**
Projektionskuppel(f) 16.
**Projektionswand(f) 397.**
Promenadendeck(n) 496.
Pronaos(m) 168, 169.
Prop-Forward(m) 606.
Propanflasche(f) 449.
**propangasbetriebene Geräte(n) 689.**
Propeller(m) 160.
Propellerummantelung(f) 492.
Prospekt(m) 188.
Prostata(f) 127.
Prothorax(m) 78.
Protokollant(m) 621, 626.
Protuberanz(f) 6.
Provinz(f) 51.
Prozent(n) 830.
Prozenttaste(f) 523.
Prüflampe(f) 310.
Psychrometer(n) 41.
**Puck(m) 608.**
Pudelmütze(f) 329.
**Puder(m), gepreßter 366.**
Puder(m), loser 366.
Puderdose(f) 366.
Puderkissen(n) 366.
Puderpinsel(m) 366.
**Puderrouge(n) 366.**
Puff(m) 222.
Puffärmel(m) 340.
Puffertank(m) 740.
Pullman-Limousine(f) 425.
PULLOVER(M) 326.
Pullover(m), kragenloser 326.
Pullunder(m) 326.
Pulmonalklappe(f) 125.
Pulpa(f) 144.
Pulpahöhle(f) 144.
Pulpete(f) 543.
Pultdach(n) 182.
Pulverhorn(n) 795.
Pulverkammer(f) 801.
Pulvino(m) 750.
Pumpe(f) 257, 258, 689, 761, 762, 771.
Pumpengriff(m) 291.
Pumpenmotor(m) 216.
Pumpenraum(m) 742.
Pumpensumpf(m) 216.
Pumpernickel(m) 153.
**Pumplöschfahrzeug(n) 778.**
Pumps(m) 356.
Pumpstation(f) 740.
Pumpstation(f), zentrale 740.
Punkt(m) 832.
Punkt(m), schwacher 697.
Punktauge(n) 78, 80, 81.
Punktball(m), weißer 673.
Punktbrenner(m) 299, 307.
Punktekonsole(f) 683.
Punktetabelle(f) 698.
Punktezähler(m) 668.
Pupille(f) 107, 140.
Pupille(f), senkrechte 96.
**Puppe(f) 78.**
Puppe(f) 82.
purpur 819.
Purpursaum(m) 315.
Pushup-Griff(m) 664.
**Putter(m) 677.**
Putter(m) 678.
Puttergrün(n) 676.
Putzkelle(f) 291.
Putzsporn(m) 80.
Pygalschild(m) 96.
Pylon(m) 456, 499.
pylorische Blindsäcke(m) 88.
Pyramidendach(n) 183.

## Q

Quadratwurzel(f) 830.
Quadratwurzeltaste(f) 523.
Quart-Einladung(f) 667.
Quarte(f) 537.
Quarterback(m) 603, 605.
Quarterdeck(n) 496.
Quartett(n) 558.
Quartier(n) 352, 354.
**Quarzmetronom(n) 539.**
Quecksilber(n) 232.
Quecksilberbarometer(n) 41.
Quecksilberkolben(m) 705.
Quecksilbersäule(f) 705.
**Quellwolken(f) 44.**
Querbalken(m) 574.
Querbehang(m) 228.
Querdünen(f) 46.
Querfaden(m) 566.
Querflöte(f) 548.
Querflöten(f) 556.
Querfortsatz(m) 135.
Querholz(n) 223, 572, 599.
Querjoch(n) 535.
Querleiste(f) 225, 578.
Querleiste(f), hintere 645.
Querleiste(f), vordere 645.
Querriegel(m) 202.
Querruder(n) 498, 511, 638.
Querschiff(n) 177.
Querschlag(m) 736.
**Querschnitt 702.**
Querschott(n) 742.
Querstange(f) 637.
Querstrebe(f) 727, 756.
Querstrich(m) 832.
Querstrich(m), ganzer 38.
Querstrich(m), halber 38.
Querstück(n) 219, 728.
Querträger(m), oberer 470.
Querträger(m), unterer 470.
Quetschfuß(m) 232.
**Quetschverschraubung(f) 300.**
Quetschverschraubung(f) 296.
Quicheform(f) 245.
Quint-Einladung(f) 667.
Quinte(f) 537.
Quintett(n) 558.
Quitte(f) 64.

**Fettgedruckte** Wörter beziehen sich auf eine Illustration; Wörter in GROSSBUCHSTABEN sind Überschriften.

# R

Rabe(m) 13.
Rachen(m) 130, 131.
Rachenenge(f) 142.
**Racquetball(m) 617.**
**Racquetballschläger(m) 617.**
RACQUETBALLSPIEL(N) 617.
**Rad(n) 433.**
Rad(n) 270, 427, 583, 800.
Rad-Schneeschläger(m) 245.
RADAR(N) 722.
Radar(n) 493, 494, 495, 497.
Radar(n) zur Luftüberwachung(f) 810.
Radar(n) zur Zielverfolgung(f) 809.
Radarabwehrflugkörper(m) 814.
Radaranlage(f) 813.
Radarantenne(f) 48, 49, 807, 812.
Radarmast(m) 742.
Radarrekflektor(m) 487.
**Radarsat(m) 49.**
Radbefestigungsbolzen(m) 432.
Radbremszylinder(m) 432.
Rädchen(n) 563.
Radfahrer(m) 828.
**Radialgürtelreifen(m) 433.**
Radialkapelle(f) 177.
Radialkarkasse(f) 433.
Radialreifen(m) 433.
Radialschubdüse(f) 42.
Radiatoren(m) 510.
Radiergummi(m) 515.
Radiergummihalter(m) 515.
Radierstift(m) 515.
Radieschen(n) 71.
Radio-/Kassettengerät(n) 430.
radioaktiv 821.
Radiometer(f) 42.
Radiometer(n) 43.
**Radiorecorder(m) mit CD-Spieler(m) 408.**
RADIOTELESKOP(N) 15.
Radiowelle(f) 15.
Radkappe(f) 427.
**Radlader(m) 782.**
Radlenker(m) 467.
Radom(n) 813.
Radsatzgetriebe(n) 468.
Radschüssel(f) 433.
Radtraktor(m) 782.
**Raffgardine(f) 229.**
Raffinerie(f) 740.
**Raffinerieerzeugnisse(n) 744.**
Raffrollo(n) 231.
Raglanärmel(m) 319, 330, 340, 350.
**Raglanmantel(m) 330.**
Raglantasche(f) 319, 339.
Rah(f) 478.
Rähmchen(n) 82.
**Rahmen(m) 198, 571.**
Rahmen(m) 156, 157, 159, 204, 225, 272, 282, 355, 378, 382, 383, 443, 484, 536, 554, 572, 583, 615, 645, 659, 660, 675, 768, 769, 785, 787, 788.
Rahmen(m), obenliegender 784.
Rahmen(m), senkrechter 574.
Rahmenleiste(f) 225.
Rahmenspant(m) 743.
Rahsegel(n) 482.
RAKETE(F) 509.
Raketenantrieb(m) 814.
Raketendepot(n) 808.
Raketenschiene(f) 813.
Raketenwerfer(m) 811.
RAM-Modul(n) 528.
Rammschutzleiste(f) 441.
Rampe(f) 168, 452, 733.
Rampenlicht(n) 188.
Rand(m) 376, 627, 658, 701.
Rand(m), äußerer 104.
Rand(m), innerer 104.
Rand, freier 137.
Randkontrolltaste(f) 525.
Randlösetaste(f) 524.
RANGIERBAHNHOF(M) 465.
Ranviersche Schnürring(m) 135.
Rapier(n) 794.
Rasen(m) 193, 263.
Rasenbesen(m) 267.
**Rasentrimmer(m) 271.**
RASIERER(M) 374.
**Rasierer(m), zweischneidiger 374.**
**Rasiermesser(n) 374.**
**Rasierpinsel(m) 374.**
Raspel(f) 587.
Rassel(f) 97.
Raste(f) 656.
Rasterleiste(f) 254.
Rasthebel(m) 272.
Rastplatz(m) 52, 823.
Raststätte(f) 52.
Ratsche(f) 276, 281.
Ratschenringschlüssel(m) 279.
**Raubvogel(m) 111.**
Raubvogel(m) 111.
Rauch(m) 39.
Rauchabsauger(m) 805.
Rauchbombe(f) 805.
**Räucherapparat(m) 582.**
RAUCHERBEDARF(M) 384, 386.
Rauchklappe(f) 204.
Rauchmantel(m) 204.
Rauh(n) 676.
Rauhreif(m) 37.
Raum(m), abgedunkelter 412.
Raum(m), erster 610.
Raum(m), zweiter 610.
RAUMANZUG(M) 512.
raumer Wind(m) 629.
RAUMFÄHRE(F) 510.
**Raumfähre(f) 510.**
Raumfähre(f) 510.
**Raumklimaanlage(f) 214.**
Raumlaboratorium(n) 511.
räumlicher Dendrit(m) 36.
Raumsonde(f) 19.
Raumteiler(m) 685.
**Raumthermostat(m) 213, 705.**
**Raupe(f) 78.**
Raupenschere(f) mit Teleskopstiel(m) 269.
Raute(f) 451.
Rautenspitze(f) 225.
Reaktion(f), reversible 831.
Reaktionsrichtung(f) 831.
Reaktionstriebwerk(n) 43.
Reaktor(m) 759, 764, 766, 806.
Reaktorgebäude(n) 759, 765.
Reaktorgebäude(n), Luftschleuse(f) des 758.
Reaktorkern(m) 760, 762, 763.
Reaktorkessel(m) 765.
Reaktortank(m) 763.
REBE(F) 61.
**Rebstock(m) 61.**
Récamiere(f) 221.
Rechen(m) 267, 747, 752.
Rechenbalken(m) 159.
Rechenscheibe(f) 396.
RECHNER(M) 523.
Rechteckflügel(m) 499.
Rechteckschlafsack(m) 687.
rechts 189.
Rechtsaußen(m) 601.
Rechtsaußen-Linebacker(m) 605.
Rechtschreibkorrekturtaste(f) 524.
Rechtskurve(f) 826, 827.
**Reck(n) 660.**
Recksäule(f) 660.
Reckstange(f) 660.
Redingote(f) 331.
Reduziermuffenippel(m) 301.
Reffband(n) 480.
Reffbänsel(n) 480.
Reflektionsfläche(f) 770.
Reflektor(m) 310, 419.
Reformieranlage(f), katalytische 744.
Regelgerät(n) 297.
Regelung(f) des Lebenserhaltungssystems(n) 512.
Regen(m) 36.
Regen(m) mit Unterbrechungen(f) 39.
Regen(m), anhaltender 39.
Regenbogen(m) 36.
**Regenfall(m), Messung(f) 40.**
**Regenhut(m) 329.**
Regenleiste(f) 427.
**Regenmantel(m) 319.**
**Regenmesser(m), selbstschreibender 40.**
Regenrohr(n) 197.
Regenschauer(m) 39.
Regenschirmhalter(m) 679.
Regentropfen(m) 36.
Regenwald(m), tropischer 45.
Regenwasserabfluß(m) 186.
Regieassistent(in(f))(m) 412.
Regiepult(n) 407, 413.
**Regieraum(m) 413.**
Regieraum(m) 14, 16, 407, 412, 415.
Regiestuhl(m) 220.
Registerleiste(f) 543.
Registerschleife(f) 543.
Registerzug(m) 542, 543.
Registriereinheit(f) 712.
Registriereinlagen(f) 519.
Registrierkarten(f), Halterung(f) 40.
Registrierpapier(n) 714.
**Registrierung(f) seismischer Wellen(f) 714.**
Regler(m) 252.
Reglerventil(n) 689.
Regnerschlauch(m) 265.
Regulierhebel(m) 430.
Regulierklappe(f) 206.
Regulierventil(n) 208.
Reh(n) 105.
Reibe(f) 243.
Reibebrett(f) 291.
Reibefläche(f) 307, 386.
Reiber(m) 583.
Reibergehäuse(n) 583.
Reif- und Frostgraupel(f) 37.
**Reife(f), Stufen(f) 61.**
**Reifen(m) 433.**
Reifen(m) 440, 447.
Reifenflanke(f) 433.
Reifeprozeß(m) 61.
**Reifrock(m), flacher 317.**
Reihe(f) 373.
Reihenanzeige(f) 569.
Reihenhaus(n) 187.
Reihenzähler(m) 568.
Reinigungsbürste(f) 374.
Reinigungsmittelgeber(m) 257.
Reinigungsöffnung(f) 215, 296.
Reis(m) 152.
**Reisetasche(f) 382.**
Reisezug(m) 462.
Reißbahn(f) 634.
**Reißbrett(n) 591.**
**Reißen(n), zweiarmiges 662.**
Reißnägel(m) 515.
Reißschenkelschutz(m) 783.
**Reißverschluß(m) 566.**
Reißverschluß(m) 321, 350, 365, 382, 685.
Reißverschlußlinie(f) 565.
Reißzahn(m) 98.
REITEN(N) 646, 648.
**Reiter(m) 648.**
Reiter(m) 518.
Reiter(m), durchsichtiger 518.
Reitgerte(f) 648, 651.
Reithandschuh(m) 648.
Reithelm(m) 648.
Reithose(f) 648.
Reitjacke(f) 648.
Reitkappe(f) 651.
Reitstiefel(m) 648.
Rektaszension(f) 3.
Rektaszensionsachse(f) 720, 721.
Rennhaken(m) 448.
RENNRODEL(M) 643.
Rentier(n) 105.
Reparaturwerkstatt(f) 453.
REPTIL(N) 96.
Reserve-Fahrtmesser(m) 500.
Reserve-Fluglageanzeige(f) 500.
Reserve-Höhenmesser(m) 500.
Reservefallschirm(m) 635.
Reservepapier(n) 532.
Reset-Taste(f) 530.
Resonanzboden(m) 540.
Resonanzdecke(f) 535, 544, 545, 546.
Resonanzfell(n) 553.
Resonanzkörper(m) 545.
Resonanzröhren(f) 554.
Restaurant(n) 190, 494, 822.
Retardiermagnet(m) 712.
Retikulum(n), endoplasmatisches 115.
Rettungsboot(n) 478, 494, 496, 738.
Rettungsfloß(m) 492.
Rettungsring(m) 495.
Rettungsschiff(n) 739.
Rettungssystem(n) 637.
Rettungsturm(m) 509.
Revers(n) 322, 341.
Revers(n), abfallendes 319, 320.
Revers(n), steigendes 322.
Revisionsöffnung(f) 205, 216.
Revisionstür(f) 207.
REVOLVER(M) 797.
Rhabarber(m) 72.
Rhesusfaktor(m) negativ 831.
Rhesusfaktor(m) positiv 831.
Rhythmuswahlschalter(m) 555.
Ribosom(n) 115.
Richtaufsatz(m) 803.
Richtkurbel(f) 803.
Richtschacht(m) 736.
Richtschütze(m), Stand(m) des 805.
Richtung(f) Mekka 173.
Richtungsanzeiger(m) 441.
Richtungsbezeichnung(f) 488.
Richtungsgleis(n) 465.
Richtungstasten(f) 530.
Riechbahn(f) 142.
Riechkapsel(f) 88.
Riechlappen(m) 142.
Riechnerv(m) 88, 142.
Riegel(m) 253, 257, 289, 290, 319.
**Riemen(m) 632.**
Riemen(m) 596, 660, 662.
Riemenantrieb(m) 492.
**Riemenarten(f) 632.**
Riemenmuskel(m) 121.
Riemenscheibe(f) 434.
Riementriebabdeckung(f) 283.
Riet(n) 572.
Riffelfeile(f) 587.
Rift(n) 28.
Rigg-Stahlseil(n) 637.
Rigipsplatte(f) 286.
Rigipsplatte(f), ebene 286.
Rille(f) 578, 598, 678.
Rinde(f) 132.
**Ring(m) 669.**
Ring(m) 55, 230, 374, 483, 551, 566, 660, 681, 706, 754.
Ring(m), dioptrischer 486.
Ring(m), erster 800.
Ring(m), zweiter 800.
Ringablage(f) 518.
Ringbrennkammer(f) 501.
Ringbuch(n) 519.
Ringbuchkalender(m) 518.
**Ringe(m) 364, 660.**
Ringentlüfter(m) 215.
Ringfinger(m) 137.
ringförmige Finsternis(f) 8.
Ringmutter(f) 300.
Ringpfosten(m) 669.
Ringschlüssel(m) 279.
Ringstraße(f) 52.
Ringstufe(f) 669.
Ringumgebung(f) 669.
Ringumrandung(f) 669.
Ringverschluß(m) 512.
Ringzugang(m) 753.
Rinne(f) 562, 683, 793.
Rippe(f) 72, 97, 102, 129, 210.
Rippe(f), frei endigende 122.
Rippe(f), freie(3) 123.
Rippen(f) 122.
Rippenbündchen(n) 350.
Rippenbündchen(n), gerades 325.
Rippenpolster(n) 602.
Ritzel(n) 707.
**Roberval-Waage(f) 708.**
Rock(m) 331, 615.
Rock(m), gerader 334.
Rockabrunder(m) 564.
**Rockarten(f) 334.**
Rodehacke(f) 267.
Rodel(m) 643.
Roggen(m) 152.
Roggenbrot(n) mit Kümmel(m) 153.
Roggenknäckebrot(n) 153.
Rohöl(n) 744.
**Rohölpipeline(f) 740.**
Rohr(n) 296, 397, 795, 796, 797, 798, 799, 800, 801, 802, 803, 804.
Rohr(n) A 300.
Rohr(n) B 300.
Rohrabschneider(m) 299.
Rohrabschnitt(m) 205.
Röhrbein(n) 102.
Rohrblatt(n) 549.
Röhre(f) 247, 705.
Rohrende(n) 300.
Röhrenfassung(f) 233.
Röhrenglocken(f) 554, 556.
Röhrenkessel(m) 744.
Rohrfahrteingang(m) 740.
Rohrfeder(f) 389.
Rohrführung(f) mit Verstellmöglichkeit(f) 659, 661.
Rohrquerstrebe(f) 738.
Rohrrücklauf(m) 802.
Rohrschelle(f) 216.
Rohrstück(n) 726.
Rohrstütze(f) 487.
Rohrturbine(f) 752.
Rohrummantelung(f) 287.
Rohrverschraubung(f) 301.
Rohrverteilerstück(n) 738.
Rollbahn(f) 502, 811.
Rollbahnmarkierung(f) 503.
Rolle(f) 230, 383, 553, 583, 645, 684, 788.
Rolle(f), gekehlte 123.
Rolle(f), obere 572.
Rollenfuß(m) 670, 671.
Rollenhaltepartie(f) 671.
Rollenhalterung(f) 670, 671.
Rollenleiter(f) 303.
Rollfilm(m) 395.

**Fettgedruckte** Wörter beziehen sich auf eine Illustration; Wörter in GROSSBUCHSTABEN sind Überschriften.

Rollgabelschlüssel(m) 299.
Rollkloben(m) 793.
Rollkragen(m) 338, 342, 642.
Rollkragenpullover(m) 326.
Rollkugel(f) 526.
Rollmechanismus(m) 231.
**Rollo(n) 231.**
Rollo-Fallstab(m) 231.
Rollostoff(m) 231.
Rollring(m) 293.
ROLLSCHUH(M) 645.
Rollschweller(m) 542.
ROLLSTUHL(M) 727.
Rollstuhl(m) 461.
Rollstuhlfahrer(m) 822.
Rolltreppe(f) 189, 190, 474.
ROM-Modul(n) 528.
Romagna-Salat(m) 73.
Römerpantolette(f) 357.
RÖMISCHES WOHNHAUS(N) 170.
Rondiste(f) 363.
Rondistenfacette(f), obere 363.
Rondistenfacette(f), untere 363.
Rose(f) 105.
Rosenkohl(m) 73.
Rosennerv(m), großer 133.
Rosenschliff(m) 362.
Rosenstock(m) 105.
Rosenvene(f), große 126.
Rosette(f) 167, 175, 289, 290, 294, 295.
Rosmarin(m) 74.
Rösselsprung(m) 696.
Rost(m) 255.
Rostrum(n) 90.
rot 819.
Rot(n) 697.
Rotationsschiene(f) 15.
Rotes Meer(n) 21.
Rotor(m) 161, 290, 753, 755, 773, 774.
Rotorblatt(n) 508, 774.
Rotorkopf(m) 508.
Rotormast(m) 508.
Rotornabe(f) 508.
Rotstrahl(m) 410.
Rotunde(f) 190.
Rouge(n) 700, 701.
Rougepinsel(m) 366.
Roulette(f) 582.
**Roulette(n), amerikanisches 700.**
**Roulette(n), französisches 701.**
Roulettekessel(m) 701.
Roulettekugel(f) 701.
**Roulettespielplan(m), amerikanischer 700.**
**Roulettespielplan(m), französischer 701.**
ROULETTESPIELTISCH(M) 700.
Royal Flush(m) 695.
Royalstenge(f) 479.
Rübe(f) 71.
Rübenhacke(f) 266.
Rubin(m) 363.
**Rückansicht(f) 95, 121, 123, 129.**
Rücken(m) 101, 106, 108, 117, 119, 174, 239, 240, 241, 242, 277, 322, 386, 577.
**Rücken(m), ozeanischer 28.**
Rückenflosse(f), erste 86.
Rückenflosse(f), zweite 86.
Rückengürtel(m) 330.
Rückenlage(f) 621.
Rückenlasche(f) 653.
Rückenlehne(f) 220, 223, 428, 445, 727.
Rückenmark(n) 89, 134, 135.
Rückenmarkshaut(f), harte 134, 135.
Rückenmittelschlitz(m) 322.
Rückenmuskel(m), breiter 121.
Rückenpanzer(m) 96.
Rückenpolster(n) 653.
Rückenschlitz(m), seitlicher 322.
**Rückenschwimmen(n) 623.**
Rückenspange(f) 322.
Rückenteil(n), verstellbares 726.
Rückenverstärkung(f) 644.
Rückfahrscheinwerfer(m) 429.
Rückfeld(n) 614.
Rückfeldrichter(m) 605.
Rückfeldschiedsrichter(m) 603.
Rückgrat(n) 670.
Rückholfeder(f) 432.
Rücklagenstütze(f) 641.
Rücklauf(m) 208, 831.
Rücklauf-Taste(f) 403.
Rücklaufboden(m) 161.
Rücklauftaste(f) 408, 420.
Rücklaufverschraubung(f) 208.
Rücklicht(n) 441, 446.
Rückruftaste(f) 396.
Rucksack(m) 680.
Rückschläger(m) 614, 616, 618.
Rückschlaghinderer(m) 795, 798, 799.
Rückschlagventil(n) 216.
**Rückseite(f) 363.**
**Rücksitzbank(f) 428.**
Rückspiegel(m) 430, 442.
**Rücksprungpalette(f) 787.**
Rückspulknopf(m) 391.
Rückspultaste(f) 411.
Rückstellknopf(m) 706, 711.
Rückstelltaste(f) 403, 411, 421.
Rückstrahler(m) 441, 445, 446.
rückwärts 624.
Rückwurflinie(f) 599.
Ruder(n) 492, 496, 511, 664, 742, 814.
Ruder(n), oberes 806.
Ruderblatt(n) 628.
**Ruderboote(n) 632.**
**Rudergerät(n) 664.**
RUDERN(N) 632.
**Rudern(n) 632.**
Ruf(m), nächster 422.
Ruffinisches Körperchen(n) 136.
Rufnummernregister(n) 420.
Rufnummernregister(n) für automatische Wahl(f) 420.
RUGBY(N) 606.
**Rugbyball(m) 606.**
**Rührbesen(m) 250.**
Rührbesen(m) 250.
Rührschüssel(f) 250.
Rührschüsseln(f) 245.
Rührwerk(n) 258.
Rumpf(m) 117, 119, 445, 499, 628, 639, 698.
Rumpfleitwerk(n) 498.
Rumpfsonar(m) 809.
rund 56.
Rundblickperiskop(n) 805.
**Rundbogen(m) 174.**
Rundbürste(f) 368.
runde Bahn(f) 275.
Rundeisen(n) 581.
RUNDFUNK(M): SPRECHERRAUM(M) UND REGIERAUM(M) 407.
**Rundfunkempfänger(m) 400, 402.**
Rundfunknetz(n), privates 416.
Rundkopf(m) mit Schlitz(m) 276.
Rundmuskel(m), großer 121.
Rundmuskel(m), kleiner 121.
Rundstricknadel(f) 567.
Rungentasche(f) 441.
Rüschen(f) 349.
**Rüschenhöschen(n) 349.**
Rüschenstrumpfhose(f) 349.
Rüssel(m) 79.
russischer Pumpernickel(m) 153.
RÜSTUNG(F) 792.
Rutengriff(m) 671.
Rutenschwellkörper(m) 127.
Rutsche(f) 736.

## S

S-Bahn(f) 464.
S-Band Antenne(f) 43.
S-Band hochbündelnde Antenne(f) 42.
S-Band Rundstrahlantenne(f) 42.
S-Bogen(m) 548.
Saal(m) 496.
Saatgutbehälter(m) 158.
Säbel(m) 666, 794.
Säbel- und Degenfechten(n) 666.
Säbelfechter(m) 667.
Sackkarren(m) 788.
SÄEN(N) 158.
**Säen(n) 154.**
**Safarijacke(f) 338.**
Safety(m), linker 603.
Safety(m), rechter 603.
Safetyback(m), linker 605.
Safetyback(m), rechter 605.
Sägeblatt(n) 277, 285.
Sägeblatthöhenverstellung(f) 285.
Sägekette(f) 272.
**Sagittalschnitt(m) 127, 128, 129, 142.**
Sagittarius 820.
Sähkelle(f) 268.
Saite(f) 541, 544, 545.
Saitenaufhängung(f) 547.
Saitenbezug(m) 540.
Saitenhalter(m) 544.
SAITENINSTRUMENTE(N) 544, 546.
Salamander(m) 85.
Salatgabel(f) 240.
Salatschale(f) 238.
Salatschleuder(f) 243.
Salatschüssel(f) 238.
Salatteller(m) 238.
Salbei(m) 74.
Saling(f) 478, 628.
**Salto(m) 625.**
Saltostellung(f) 624.
Salzsee(m) 46.
Salzstreuer(m) 238.
Salzsumpf(m) 30.
Samen(m) 62, 63, 64, 65, 66, 67.
Samenanlage(f) 60.
Samenbläschen(n) 127.
Samenleiter(m) 127.
Samenmantel(m) 63.
Samenschale(f) 152.
Samenstrang(m) 127.
**Sammellinsen(f) 722.**
Sammelrohr(n) 162.
Sammelschiene(f) 747.
Sammeltrichter(m) 40.
Samtkropfband(n) 361.
Sand(m) 748.
Sand- oder Staubsturm(m) 39.
Sand-Wedge(n) 678.
Sandale(f) 357, 791.
Sandalette(f) 356.
Sandbank(f) 30.
Sandblattfeilen(f) 365.
Sandinsel(f) 30.
Sandkasten(m) 469.
Sandwüste(f) 46.
SANITÄRINSTALLATION(F) 292, 294, 296, 298, 299, 300.
SANITÄRINSTALLATIONSSYSTEM(N) 215.
Saphir(m) 363.
Sarong(m) 334.
Satellit(m) 416, 419.
SATELLIT(M), ERDERKENNUNGSGEODÄTISCHER 48.
**Satellit(m), geostationärer 42.**
**Satellit(m), polarumlaufender 43.**
**Satelliten(m) 418.**
**Satelliten(m), Umlaufbahn(f) 43.**
Satelliten-Direktempfang(m) 416.
**Sattel(m) 649.**
Sattel(m) 320, 324, 337, 397, 446, 544, 546, 547, 648, 651, 661.
Satteldach(n) 182.
Sattelgurt(m) 649.
Sattelkupplung(f) 440.
Sattelplatz(m) 651.
Sattelpolster(n) 649.
Sattelrock(m) 334.
**Sattelschlepper(m) 440.**
Sattelstütze(f) 446.
Satteltasche(f) 448.
Satteltuch(n) 651.
**Sattelzug(m) 440.**
Saturn(m) 5.
Satztische(m) 219.
SATZZEICHEN(N) 832.
Sau(f) 151.
Sauciere(f) 238.
Sauerstoffdruck-Stelleinrichtung(f) 512.
Sauerstoffflasche(f) 306.
Sauerstoffventil(n) 306.
Sauerstoffzufuhranzeige(f) 639.
Sauerstoffzufuhrregler(m) 639.
Saugarm(m) 784.
Saugpinsel(m) 260.
Saugrohr(n) 260, 434, 747, 753, 778, 784.
**Saugzubehör(n) 260.**
Säule(f) 24, 36, 166, 168, 169, 393, 399, 455, 573, 574, 578, 579, 621.
Säule(f), bedeckte 37.
**Säulenordnung(f), dorische 167.**
**Säulenordnung(f), ionische 166.**
**Säulenordnung(f), korinthische 167.**
Saum(m) 231, 565, 598.
Saummaß(n) 563.
Saumrand(m) 104.
Savanne(f), tropische 45.
Saxhorn(n) 551.
**Saxophon(n) 548.**
Saxophon(n) 548.
Scanner(m) 526.
Schaber(m) 582.
Schabracke(f) 229.
SCHACH(N) 696.
**Schachbrett(n) 696.**
Schachtelfalte(f) 228.
Schachtfördergerüst(n) 736.
Schachtgebäude(n) 734.
Schachtsumpf(m) 736.
Schädel(m) 88, 102, 116, 134.
**Schadstoffbelastung(f) im Boden(m) 32.**
**Schadstoffbelastung(f) im Wasser(n) 32.**
Schaf(n) 150.
Schaffnertisch(m) 461.
Schafstall(m) 149.
Schaft(m) 110, 166, 275, 276, 281, 483, 562, 567, 568, 573, 609, 615, 632, 652, 658, 675, 677, 684, 698, 773.
Schaftführung(f) 653.
Schaftstiefel(m) 357.
Schäftung(f) 798, 799.
Schäkelband(n) 483.
Schale(f) 64, 65, 66, 92, 109, 383.
SCHALE(F), EINKLAPPIGE 94.
Schale(f), obere 641.
Schale(f), untere 641.
SCHALE(F), ZWEIKLAPPIGE 95.
Schalenhaut(f) 109.
**Schalensitz(m) 428.**
Schäler(m) 242.
Schälfurnier(n) 288.
Schalkragen(m) 341.
Schallbecher(m) 542.
Schallbecherstütze(f) 549.
Schallbrett(n) 175.
Schalldämpfer(m) 439.
Schalloch(n) 544.
**Schallplatte(f) 404.**
Schallrille(f) 404.
Schallrose(f) 546.
Schalotte(f) 70.
Schalter(m) 254, 255, 280, 283, 285, 309.
Schalter(m), einpoliger 312.
Schalter(m), zweipoliger 312.
Schalterabdeckplatte(f) 309.
Schalthebel(m) 430, 447, 448.
Schaltpedal(n) 443, 444.
Schaltpult(n) 16.
Schalttafel(f) 210, 214.
Schaltuhr(f) 255.
Schaltung(f), elektronische 233.
Schaltzug(m) 448.
Schambein(n) 116, 118.
Schamhügel(m) 128.
Schamlippe(f), große 128, 129.
Schamlippe(f), kleine 128, 129.
Schamotteplatte(f) 204.
Schamottestein(m) 204.
Schanzkleid(n) 478.
Schar(n) 156.
**Schärbaum(m) 575.**
Schardrehkranz(m) 784.
Schardrehvorrichtung(f) 784.
Scharfeinsteller(m) 399.
Scharfeinstellung(f) 409, 720, 721.
Schärfentiefenknopf(m) 391.
Schärfentiefenskala(f) 392.
Scharfsteller(m) 399.
Scharfstellrad(n), zentrales 719.
Scharfstellring(m) 719.
Scharhubvorrichtung(f) 784.
Scharnier 202.
Scharnier(n) 203, 225, 253, 257, 378, 382, 404, 429, 443, 585, 719.
Scharwachturm(m) 178, 181.
Schatten(m) 706.
Schaufel(f) 640, 642, 681, 782.
Schaufel(f), hintere 782.
Schaufelarm(m) 782.
Schaufelblatt(n) 753.
Schaufelbolzengelenk(n) 782.
Schaufellader(m) 782.
Schaufelradbagger(m) 733.
Schaufelzahn(m) 782, 785.
Schaufelzylinder(m) 782, 785.
Schaufelzylinder(m), hinterer 782.
Schaukelstuhl(m) 221, 223.
Schaum(m) 30.
Schaumanzeiger(m) 743.
Schaumgummiisolierung(f) 287.
Schaumgummimatratze(f) 687.
Schaumgummipolsterung(f) 729.
Scheckheft(n) 379.
Scheckhülle(f) 379.
Scheibe(f) 157, 203, 583, 663.
**Scheiben(f) 251.**
**Scheibenbremse(f) 432.**
Scheibenbremse(f) 442.
**Scheibenegge(f) 157.**
Scheibenegge(f) 154.
**Scheibengardine(f) 228.**
Scheibenkopf(m) 584.
Scheibensech(m) 156.

Scheibensechhalter(m) 156.
Scheibenwaschdüse(f) 426.
**Scheibenwischer(m) 431.**
Scheibenwischer(m) 426.
Scheibenwischerhebel(m) 430.
Scheide(f) 55, 128, 129, 281, 283, 690.
Scheide(f), Schwannsche 135.
Scheidewand(f) 65, 66, 67, 141.
Scheinfach(n) 379.
Scheintasche(f) 379.
Scheinwerfer(m) 147, 426, 440, 442, 444, 445, 447, 459, 469, 778, 780, 805.
Scheinwerferraum(m) 486.
Scheitel(m) 109.
Scheitelbein(n) 123.
Scheitelpunkt(m) 625.
Scheitelrippe(f) 177.
Scheitelstück(n) 792.
Schekel(m) 832.
Schelle(f) 40, 554.
Schenkel(m) 78, 80, 101, 104, 108, 671.
Schenkelbein(n) 123.
Schenkelbindenspanner(m) 120.
Schenkelhals(m) 123.
Schenkelmuskel(m), äußerer 120, 121.
Schenkelmuskel(m), gerader 120.
Schenkelmuskel(m), innerer 120.
Schenkelmuskel(m), zweiköpfiger 121.
Schenkelring(m) 78, 80.
**Schere(f) 564.**
Schere(f) 90, 688, 725.
Scherenaufhängung(f) 414.
Scherenblatt(n), gekerbtes 369.
Scherenbrille(f) 377.
Scherenleuchte(f) 234.
Scherenschliff(m) 362.
Scherenstromabnehmer(m) 458.
Scherkopf(m) 374.
Scherkopfhalter(m) 374.
Scheuerleiste(f) 433, 449.
Scheuklappe(f) 653.
Scheune(f) 148.
Schiebedach(n) 427.
Schiebedeckel(m) 484.
Schiebefenster(n), horizontales 203.
Schiebefenster(n), vertikales 203.
Schiebegriff(m) 568, 727.
Schiebeleiter(f) 781.
Schiebeöffnung(f) 709.
Schiebeplatte(f) 561, 562.
Schieber(m) 375, 566, 585, 747, 797.
Schieberad(n) 727.
Schiebetür(f) 202, 292.
Schiedsrichter(m) 599, 601, 606, 608, 610, 611, 614, 618, 621, 626, 668, 669.
Schiedsrichter(m), erster 603, 605, 613.
Schiedsrichter(m), zweiter 603, 605, 613.
Schienbein(n) 122.
Schienbeinarterie(f), vordere 126.
Schienbeinmuskel(m), vorderer 120.
Schienbeinnerv(m) 133.
Schienbeinpolster(n) 609.
Schienbeinschützer(m) 595, 600.
**Schiene(f) 466.**
Schiene(f) 78, 80, 230, 235, 257, 466, 568, 643, 656.
Schienen(f) 725.
Schienenfuß(m) 466.
Schienenkopf(m) 466.
Schienenlasche(f) 466.
Schienenräumer(m) 459, 469.
Schienensteg(m) 466.
**Schienenstoß(m) 466.**
Schießgrube(f) 179.
Schießscharte(f) 179, 181.
**Schiffsanker(m) 483.**
Schiffskiel(m) 13.
Schiffsschraube(f) 742.
Schiffssegel(n) 13.
Schild(m) 579, 791.
Schild(n) 242, 729.
Schildbogen(m) 177.
Schildchen(n) 95.
schildförmig 56.
Schildhaupt(n) 818.
Schildhubzylinder(m) 783.
**Schildkröte(f) 97.**
**Schildplätze(m) 818.**
Schindel(f) 286.
Schinkenmesser(n) 242.
SCHIRM(M) 375.
**Schirm(m) 375.**
Schirm(m) 234, 236, 471, 636.
Schirmfeder(f) 110.
**Schirmmütze(f) 328.**
Schirmsegment(n) 636.
Schirmständer(m) 375.
Schirmwinde(f) 575.
**Schlafanzug(m) 350.**
Schlafanzug(m) 348, 351.
**Schlafanzug(m), zweiteilig 350.**
Schläfe(f) 116.
Schläfenbein(n) 122.
Schlafkabine(f) 440.
Schlafplatz(m) 460.
Schlafraum(m) 685.
Schlafsack(m) mit Rettungssystem(n) 637.
**Schlafsäcke(m) 687.**
**Schlafwagen(m) 460.**
Schlafwagenabteil(n) 460.
Schlafzimmer(n) 194, 195.
Schlagbereich(m) 596.
Schlagbohrer(m) 734.
Schlagbolzen(m) 796, 804.
Schlagbolzenmechanismus(m) 796.
Schlagbolzenschaft(m) 802.
**Schläger(m) 596, 607.**
Schläger(m) 595.
Schlägerabdeckung(f) 679.
Schlägerblatt(n) 607.
Schlagfell(n) 552, 553.
Schlagfläche(f) 677.
Schlaghandschuh(m) 595.
**Schlagholz(n) 598.**
Schlagholz(n) 598.
Schlaghose(f) 336.
SCHLAGINSTRUMENTE(N) 552, 554.
Schlagmal(n) 597.
Schlagmallinie(f) 599.
**Schlagmann(m) 595.**
Schlagmann(m) 597, 599.
Schlagmannshelm(m) 595.
Schlagrad(n) 579.
Schlagschutz(m) 547, 617.
Schlammgrube(f) 737.
Schlammpumpe(f) 737.
Schlammpumpenschlauch(m) 737.
Schlange(f) 11, 13.
**Schlangenbohrer(m) 281.**
Schlangenbohrer(m) 281.
Schlangenträger(m) 11, 13.
Schlankmuskel(m) 121.
Schlauch(m) 260, 306, 710, 780.
Schlauchdüse(f) 265.
Schlauchkleid(n) 332.
Schlauchkupplung(f) 264, 265.
Schlauchleitung(f) 778.
**Schlauchwagen(m) 265.**
Schlaufe(f) 324, 365, 452.
Schlegel(m) 552, 553, 581, 586.
Schleier(m) 670.
Schleife(f) 328.
Schleifenkragen(m) 342.
**Schleifscheibe(f) 583.**
Schlepper(m) 506, 507.
Schleppseil(n) 633.
Schleppstange(f) 803.
Schleudergefahr(f) 826, 827.
Schleudersitz(m) 813.
Schleuse(f) 752.
Schleusenkammer(f) 493.
Schleusenwand(f) 492.
Schließblech(n) 290.
Schließfrucht(f) 66.
Schließklappe(f) 772.
Schließmuskel(m) 92.
Schließzylinder(m) 290.
**Schliffformen(f) 362.**
Schlingerwand(f) 509.
**Schlingstiche(m) 571.**
**Schlitten(m) 568.**
Schlitten(m) 630.
Schlitteneinstellung(f) 569.
Schlittschuh(m) 609.
Schlittschuhschoner(m) 644.
Schlitz(m) 240, 252, 276, 325, 350, 578.
Schlitzverschluß(m) 390.
SCHLOSS(N) 289, 290.
Schloß(n) 225, 289, 369, 374, 380, 383, 448, 564.
Schloßband(n) 95.
Schloßband(n), elastisches 92.
Schloßband(n), Lage(f) 95.
Schloßbrett(n) 202.
Schloßzahn(m) 95.
Schlucht(f) 24.
Schluckloch(n) 24.
Schlüssel(m) 290, 539.
Schlüsselbein(n) 122.
Schlüsselbeinarterie(f) 126.
Schlüsselbeinvene(f) 126.
Schlüsseletui(n) 379.
Schlüsselloch(n) 290.
Schlüsselschild(n) 289.
Schlüsselschloß(n) 378.
Schlußleuchte(f) 147, 429, 443, 444.
Schlußstein(m) 174, 177.
Schmelz(m) 144.
**Schmelzschweißen(n) 307.**
Schmelzwasser(n) 27.
SCHMETTERLING(M) 78.
**Schmetterling(m) 79.**
Schmierknopf(m) 735.
Schmiermittelraffinerie(f) 745.
Schmieröle(n) 745.
Schmiersystem(n) 469.
Schmirgelsäckchen(n) 563.
Schmorpfanne(f) 249.
SCHMUCK(M) 361, 362, 364.
Schmutzfänger(m) 427, 440, 441.
SCHMUTZWASSERHEBEANLAGE(F) 216.
Schnabel(m) 108, 792.
**Schnabelarten(f) 111.**
Schnabelschuh(m) 318.
**Schnalle(f) 566.**
Schnalle(f) 319, 323, 380.
Schnallenabdeckung(f) 649.
Schnappschloß(n) 378, 380.
Schnarrsaite(f) 553.
Schnarrsaitenspanner(m) 553.
Schnauze(f) 84, 106, 107.
SCHNECKE(F) 83.
**Schnecke(f) 83.**
Schnecke(f) 139, 544.
Schnecke(f), einfache 281.
**Schnecken, eßbare 83.**
Schneckenpfännchen(n) 246.
Schneckenzange(f) 246.
Schnee(m) 34.
Schnee(m) mit Unterbrechungen(f) 39.
Schnee(m), anhaltender 39.
Schnee(m), ewiger 27.
**Schneeanzug(m) 351.**
Schneebesen(m) 245.
**Schneefall(m), Messung(f) 41.**
Schneegamaschen(f) 680.
**Schneekristalle(m), Klassifikation(f) 36.**
Schneemesser(m) 41.
**Schneemobil(n) 445.**
Schneeregen(m) 39.
Schneesack(m) 349.
Schneeschauer(m) 39.
SCHNEESCHUH(M) 645.
Schneetreiben(n), leichtes 39.
Schneetreiben(n), starkes 39.
Schneiddüse(f) 306.
Schneide(f) 239, 242, 276, 369, 564, 644.
Schneidedraht(m) 584.
**Schneideeinsatz(m) 306.**
**Schneiden(n) 578.**
Schneiderärmel(m) 340.
Schneiderbüste(f) 564.
Schneiderkragen(m) 330, 341.
Schneidermuskel(m) 120.
Schneidezahn(m) 98.
Schneidezahn(m), äußerer 144.
Schneidezahn(m), mittlerer 144.
Schneidezähne(m) 144.
Schneidkante(f) 783, 784.
Schneidklinge(f) 256.
Schneidmesser(n) 250, 251.
Schneidring(m) 300.
Schneidwerk(n) 161.
Schneidzylinder(m) 271.
Schnellabrollbahn(f) 502.
Schnellaufschlittschuh(m) 644.
Schnellhefter(m) 519.
Schnellkupplungssystem(n) 393.
Schnellstraße(f) 452.
Schnellvorlauf-Taste(f) 403.
Schnellvorlauftaste(f) 408.
Schnittführung(f) 578.
Schnittlauch(m) 70.
Schnittlinie(f) 565.
**Schnittmuster(n) 565.**
Schnitzbankschraube(f) 586.
**Schnitzeisen(n) 587.**
Schnitzen(n) 586.
Schnorchel(m) 627.
Schnur(f) 578.
Schnur(f) am Tritt(m) 572.
Schnürband(n) 596.
Schnürboden(m) 188.
Schnurfangbügel(m) 671.
Schnurfeststeller(m) 231.
Schnürhaken(m) 644.
Schnurlaufröllchen(n) 671.
Schnürloch(n) 354.
Schnürlochteil(n) 354.
Schnüröse(f) 644.
Schnurrhaare(n) 107.
Schnürschuh(m) 355.
Schnürsenkel(m) 352, 354, 644, 669.
Schnürsenkelende(n) 352, 354.
Schnurspanner(m) 230.
Schnurversteller(m) 231.
Schnurwelle(f) 230.
Schollenmuskel(m) 120.
Schoner(m) 482.
Schonwaschgang(m) 829.
Schöpflöffel(m) 244.
Schöpfteil(m) 241.
Schornstein(m) 197, 494, 496.
Schoß(m) 324, 337.
Schößling(m) 57, 59.
Schoßrock(m) 317.
Schote(f) 67.
Schotstek(m), doppelter 691.
Schotstek(m), einfacher 691.
Schottenrock(m) 335.
Schotter(m) 466.
Schotterfläche(f) 27.
schräg zum Fadenlauf(m) 566.
Schräge(f) 726.
Schrägförderer(m) 160.
Schrägfördererkette(f) 160.
Schräggeison(m) 168.
Schrägheckmodell(n) 425.
Schrägmaß(n) 713.
schrägrechts geteilt 818.
**Schrägseilbrücke(f) 456.**
**Schrägseile(n), parallele 456.**
Schrägseilverankerung(f) 456.
Schrägstellungsvorrichtung(f) 284.
Schrank(m) 522.
Schranke(f) 471.
Schrankteil(n) 226.
**Schrapper(m) 784.**
Schratten(m) 24.
**Schraube(f) 276, 625.**
Schraube(f) 278, 290, 495, 496, 544, 806.
Schrauben(f) 808.
**Schraubenbolzen(m) 279.**
**Schraubenbolzen(m) mit Ansatz(m) 279.**
Schraubenfeder(f) 469.
Schraubenwelle(f) 492, 495.
**Schraubenzieher(m) 276.**
Schraubenzieher(m) 276, 688.
Schraubfassung(f) 232.
Schraubfeder(f) 681.
Schraubklemme(f) 312.
Schraubschäkel(m) 630.
**Schraubstock(m) 282.**
Schraubstollen(m) 600.
Schreib-/Lesekopf(m) 529.
SCHREIBGERÄTE(N) 389.
Schreibkopf(m) 524.
Schreibmappe(f) 378.
SCHREIBMASCHINE(F), ELEKTRISCHE 524.
Schreibpinsel(m) 389.
Schreibplatte(f), herausklappbare 226.
Schreibschutz(m) 529.
Schreibschutzöffnung(f) 529.
Schreibspitze(f) 714.
Schreibtisch-Videogerät(n) 527.
Schreibtischleuchte(f) 234.
Schreibunterlage(f) 520.
SCHREIBWAREN(F) 515, 516, 518.
SCHREINEREI(F) 275, 276, 278, 280, 282, 284.
Schriftführer(m) 612.
Schriftgrößenskala(f) 524.
Schritt(m) 101, 325, 337.
**Schritte(m) 586.**
Schrittlängeneinstellung(f) 711.
Schrot(m) 799.
**Schrotflinte(f) 799.**
Schub(m) 455.
Schubdüse(f) 512.
**Schubkarre(f) 270.**
Schubkurbelverschluß(m) 802.
Schublade(f) 219, 226.
Schubladenelement(n), fahrbares 521.
Schubrahmen(m) 783.
**Schubrechwender(m) 159.**
Schubrechwender(m) 155.
Schuh(m) 627.
Schuh(m) mit Stoßplatten(f) 602.
**Schuhbürste(f) 358.**
Schuhbürste(f) 358.
Schuhcreme(f) 358.
SCHUHE(M) 354, 356, 358.
**Schuhlöffel(m) 358.**
**Schuhputzzeug(n) 358.**
**Schuhspanner(m) 358.**
**Schuhständer(m) 358.**

**Fettgedruckte** Wörter beziehen sich auf eine Illustration; Wörter in GROSSBUCHSTABEN sind Überschriften.

**Schuhtypen(m), wichtigste 354, 355, 356.**
Schule(f) 826, 827.
Schulter(f) 100, 106, 116, 118, 545, 670.
Schulterblatt(n) 102, 117, 119, 122, 123.
Schulterblattgräte(f) 123.
Schulterfeder(f) 110.
Schultergurt(m) 428, 679.
Schulterhöhe(f) 123.
Schulterklappe(f) 319.
Schulterpolster(n) 602, 609.
Schulterriemen(m) 375, 380, 382.
Schulterstütze(f) 796, 804.
**Schultertasche(f) 380.**
Schulterwurf(m), einarmiger 668.
Schuppe(f) 87, 96, 97.
Schuppen(m) 193.
Schürfkübel(m) 784.
Schürhaken(m) 205.
Schürzenfinger(m) 493.
Schuß(m) 572, 574.
Schüssel(f) 251.
Schußfaden(m) 576.
Schußkreis(m) 607.
Schüttelbörse(f) 379.
Schüttelsieb(n) 737.
Schüttgutwagen(m) 472.
Schüttung(f) 451.
Schüttungsisolierung(f) 287.
**Schutzausrüstung(f) 602.**
Schutzbezug(m) 224.
Schutzblech(n) 445, 446.
Schutzblech(n), vorderes 442.
Schutzbrille(f) 308, 635, 729.
Schutzdach(n) 787.
Schütze(m) 13, 820.
Schutzgehäuse(n) 271.
Schutzgeländer(n) 468.
Schutzgitter(n) 310.
Schutzglas(n) 410.
Schutzhandschuhe(m) 821.
Schutzhaube(f) 285.
**Schutzhelm(m) 443, 729.**
Schutzhelm(m) 448, 602, 609, 635, 636, 821.
Schutzkäfig(m) 654.
Schutzkante(f) 383.
Schutzkappe(f) 718, 726.
Schutzkasten(m) für Kegelräder(n) 470.
Schutzklappe(f) 16.
Schutzkorsett(n) 609.
Schutzmaske(f) 729.
**Schutzmaßnahmen(f) 821.**
Schutzpolster(n) 659.
Schutzring(m) 255.
Schutzschicht(f) 512.
Schutzschirm(m) 308.
Schutzschuhe(m) 821.
Schutzumrandung(f) 698.
Schwamm(m) 801.
**Schwämme(m) 367.**
Schwammstäbchen(n) 367.
Schwan(m) 11.
Schwanenhals(m) 784.
Schwannsche Scheide(f) 135.
Schwanz(m) 91, 96, 97, 101, 106, 107, 112, 127, 579, 670.
Schwanzfächer(m) 91.
Schwanzfeder(f) 109.
Schwanzflosse(f) 87.
Schwanzflughaut(f) 112.
Schwanzwirbel(m) 103.
Schwarte(f) 288.
schwarz 819.
Schwarz(n) 696.
Schwarzes Meer(n) 21.
Schwarzwurzel(f) 71.
**Schwebebalken(m) 659.**
**Schwebefähre(f) 457.**
Schwein(n) 151.
Schweinestall(m) 149.
Schweißband(n) 615.
Schweißblatt(n) 649.
**Schweißbrenner(m) 306.**
Schweißbrenner(m) 306, 307.
Schweißdrüse(f), apokrine 136.
Schweißdrüse(f), Ausführungsgang(m) 136.
Schweißdrüse(f), ekkrine 136.
Schweißeinsatz(m) 306.
SCHWEISSEN(N) 305, 306, 308.
Schweißerhandschuh(m) 308.
Schweißfuge(f) 307.
Schweißstab(m) 307.
Schweißtransformator(m) 305.
**schweizer Offiziersmesser(n) 688.**
Schwelle(f) 198, 199, 202, 466.
Schwellenmarkierungen(f) 505.
Schwellenschraube(f) 466.
Schwenkarm(m) 250.
Schwenkbrückenstand(m) 785.
Schwenkflügel(m) 499.
Schwenkkopf(m) 282.
Schwenklade(f) 573.
Schwenksockel(m) 282.
Schwenkverschluß(m) 282.
Schwenkverstellung(f) 285.
Schwerbehinderte(m) 822.
SCHWERFAHRZEUGE(N) 782, 784.
SCHWERMASCHINEN(F) 785.
Schweröl(n) 744.
Schwert(n) 272, 628.
Schwert(n), beidhändiges 794.
Schwertfisch(m) 13.
Schwerwasser(n) unter Druck(m) 761.
Schwerwasser(n), kaltes 761.
Schwerwasseranreicherung(f) 759.
**Schwerwasserreaktor(m) 761.**
Schwimmbecken(n) 621, 626, 772.
Schwimmblase(f) 89.
Schwimmdach(n) 741.
**Schwimmdachtank(m) 741.**
SCHWIMMEN(N) 621, 622.
Schwimmer(m) 216, 293, 485, 672, 803.
Schwimmerventil(n) 293.
Schwimmfuß(m) 84.
Schwimmhaut(f) 84, 111.
Schwimmhautzeh(m) 111.
Schwimmholz(n) 626.
Schwimmkörper(m) 486.
Schwimmkran(m) 490.
Schwimmlappenzeh(m) 111.
Schwimmschlamm(m) 216.
**Schwimmstile(m) 622.**
**Schwinger(m) 485.**
Schwingflügel(m) 203.
Schwinghebel(m) 435.
schwingungsdämpfender Bügelgriff(m) 272.
Schwingungsdämpfer(m) 258.
Schwungholen(n) 682.
Schwungrad(n) 435, 584, 664.
Scorpius 820.
**Scrimmage(n) 603, 605.**
Scrimmagelinie(f) 603, 605.
Sech(m) 158.
Sechserpasch(m) 695.
Sechskantmutter(f) 439.
Sechskantstopfen(m) 301.
Sechzehntelnote(f) 538.
Sechzehntelpause(f) 538.
Second-Einladung(f) 667.
Sedimentgesteine(n) 23.
See(m) 7, 27, 51.
See-See-Flugkörper(m) 809.
SEEZEICHEN(N) 486.
Seezielflugkörper(m) 814.
**Segel(n) 480.**
Segel(n) 631.
**Segelboot(n) 628.**
SEGELFLIEGEN(N) 638.
**Segelflugzeug(n) 638.**
Segelkleid(n) 628.
Segellatte(f) 628, 631.
Segeln(n) mit halbem Wind(m) 629.
SEGELSPORT(M) 628, 630.
Segelstange(f) 773.
Segeltasche(f) 628, 631.
Segeltuchbespannung(f) 773.
Segeltuchboden(m) 669.
SEGELTYPEN(M) 482.
Segerkegel(m) 585.
Segmentpunktzahl(f) 698.
Sehenswürdigkeit(f) 52.
Sehne(f) 107.
Sehnenschützer(m) 644.
Sehnerv(m) 140.
Sehnervkreuzung(f) 134.
Sehschlitz(m) 792.
SEHVERMÖGEN(N) 140.
Seifenbecher(m) 374.
Seifenschale(f) 292.
Seil(n) 302, 457, 669, 680, 692.
**Seil(n), gedrehtes 692.**
**Seil(n), geflochtenes 692.**
Seile(n) 456.
Seilverspannung(f) 669.
Seilzug(m) 302.
seismische Welle(f) 23.
SEISMISCHE WELLEN(F) 714.
Seismogramm(n) 714.
Seite(f) 239, 479, 579.
Seite(f), linke 288.
Seite(f), rechte 288.
**Seitenansicht(f) 363, 442.**
Seitenauslinie(f) 601.
Seitenband(n),vertikales 613.
Seitenfeintrieb(m) 713.
Seitenfenster(n) 427.
Seitenflosse(f) 499, 508, 639.
Seitengriff(m) 280, 429.
Seitenkapelle(f) 176.
Seitenklemme(f) 713.
Seitenlinie(f) 87, 604, 606, 607, 610, 611, 612, 613, 619, 620.
Seitenlinie(f) für das Doppelspiel 614, 618.
Seitenlinie(f) für das Einzelspiel 614, 618.
Seitenlinienrichter(m) 605.
Seitenmoräne(f) 27.
Seitenöffnung(f) 456.
Seitenruder(n) 499, 639, 812.
Seitenruderpedal(n) 639.
Seitenschiff(n) 177.
Seitenschlot(m) 25.
Seitenschwinge(f) 572.
Seitenspiegel(m) 368, 426, 440, 444.
Seitenspiegelverstellhebel(n) 429.
Seitensprossen(f) 470.
Seitenspur(f) 452.
Seitenständer(m) 443.
Seitensteg(m) 376.
Seitenstollen(m) 736.
Seitenstück(n) 223.
Seitentasche(f) 679.
Seitenteil(n) 319, 787.
Seitenverkleidung(f) 427.
Seitenverstellhebel(m) 277.
Seitenwand(f) 104, 441, 470, 616, 617, 621.
Seitenwandlinie(f) 616.
Seitenwurzel(f) 57.
Sekretär(m) 226.
Sektkelch(m) 237.
Sektschale(f) 237.
Sekundant(m) 669.
Sekundärfokuskabine(f) 15.
**Sekundärkonsumenten(m) 31.**
Sekundärspiegel(m) 15, 16, 390.
Sekunde(f) 537, 830.
Sekundenzeiger(m) 706, 707.
Selbstauslöser(m) 391.
Selbstauslöser-Lichtsignal(n) 391.
Selbstentladetankwagen(m) 472.
Selbststeueranlage(f) 500.
Sellerie(f) 71.
Semikolon(n) 832.
Sendeantenne(f) 418.
Sendeimpuls(m) 722.
Sendeleiter(in(f))(m) 412, 415.
Sendereinstellung(f) 402, 408.
Sendersuchlauf(m), automatischer 402.
Sendung(f) auf Hertz-Wellen(f) 416.
**Senf(m) 67.**
Senkkopf(m) mit Imbus(m) 276.
Senkkopf(m) mit Kreuzschlitz(m) 276.
Senkkopf(m) mit Schlitz(m) 276.
Senkrechte(f) 830.
Sense(f) 267.
Sensor(m) 253.
Sensor(m), biomedizinischer 512.
Sensorhülse(f) 253.
Sepalum(n) 64.
Septim-Einladung(f) 667.
Septime(f) 537.
Septum(n) pellucidum 134.
Sequenzerregler(m) 555.
Serac(m) 26.
Service-Bereich(m) 453.
Servierwagen(m) 219.
Sesambein(n) 102.
Setzholz(n) 225.
Setzstufe(f) 201.
**Sextant(m) 484.**
Sextant(m) 13.
Sexte(f) 537.
Sextett(n) 558.
Shadow-Taste(f) 396.
Shake-Hands-Griff(m) 619.
Sheddach(n) 182.
Shortline(f) 616.
Shorts(f) 336, 353.
Shot(f) 480.
Sichel(f) 269.
Sicheldüne(f) 46.
Sicherheitsbereich(m) 668.
**Sicherheitsbindung(f) 641.**
Sicherheitsfilter(m), roter 399.
Sicherheitsgriff(m) 271.
Sicherheitsgurt(m) 428.
Sicherheitshinweisschild(n) 280.
Sicherheitsholm(m) 302.
Sicherheitshülle(f) 765, 766.
Sicherheitskontrolle(f) 504.
Sicherheitsleiste(f) 254.
Sicherheitsnadel(f) 566.
**Sicherheitsohrenschützer(m) 729.**
Sicherheitsriemen(m) 512, 617.
**Sicherheitsschuh(m) 730.**
Sicherheitsstreichholz(n) 386.
Sicherheitsstreifen(m) 475.
Sicherheitstank(m) 761.
Sicherheitsthermostat(n) 259.
Sicherheitsventil(n) 209, 248, 297, 766.
SICHERHEITSWESTE(F) 730.
Sicherung(f) 757, 769, 796.
**Sicherungen(f) 312.**
Sicherungsabschnitt(m) 757.
Sicherungskappe(f) 804.
**Sicherungskasten(m) 312.**
Sicherungskette(f) 449.
Sicherungsknopf(m) 429.
Sicherungskopf(m) 276.
Sicherungsscheibe(f) 278.
Sicherungsstift(m) 780.
Sicherungsträger(m) 757.
Sicherungszieher(m) 311.
**Sichtbarmachung(f) seismischer Wellen(f) 714.**
Sichtfenster(n) 253, 255, 399, 510.
Sichtlinie(f) 719.
Sickeranlage(f) 216.
Sickerrohr(n) 199.
Sieb(n) 161, 243, 251.
Siebbein(f), Siebplatte(f) 141.
**Sieben(n) 243.**
Siebplatte(f) des Siebbeins(m) 141.
Siedewasser(n) 763.
**Siedewasserreaktor(m) 763.**
Sigmoid(n) 131.
Signal(n), akkustisches 539.
Signal(n), optisches 539.
Signalbrücke(f) 464.
Signalhorn(n) 468.
Signalleiste(f) 779.
Signalschirm(m) 471.
Signatur(f) 577.
Silber(n) 819.
SILBERBESTECK(N) 239, 240.
SILIEREN(N) 162.
**Silieren(n) 155.**
Silos(m) 490.
Sima(f) 166.
SINFONIEORCHESTER(N) 556.
Sinkblei(n) 672.
Sinkschlamm(m) 216.
**Sinnesimpuls(m) 135.**
SINNESORGANE(N) 136, 138, 140, 141.
Sinnesrezeptor(m) 134.
Sinus(m) 315.
Siphon(m) 24.
Siphonalkanal(m) 94.
Siphonwinkel(m) 301.
Sitz(m) 220, 223, 292, 428, 584, 636, 639, 649, 652, 664, 727.
Sitz(m), freilaufender 664.
Sitz(m), verstellbarer 460.
Sitzbank(f) 222, 428, 445, 475.
Sitzbein(n) 123.
SITZMÖBEL(N) 222.
Sitzrohr(n) 446.
Sitzsack(m) 222.
Sixt-Einladung(f) 667.
Skala(f) 285, 705, 708, 711, 719, 726.
skandinavisches Knäckebrot(n) 153.
SKELETT(N) 122.
**Skelett(n) 102.**
Skelettbürste(f) 368.
Ski(m) 641.
Skianzug(m) 640, 642.
Skibremse(f) 640, 641.
Skibrille(f) 640.
Skihandschuhe(m) 640.
SKILANGLAUF(M) 642.
SKILAUFEN(N), ALPINES 640.
**Skiläufer(m), alpiner 640.**
Skimütze(f) 640, 642.
Skip(m) 620.
Skispitze(f) 642.
**Skistiefel(m) 641.**
Skistiefel(m) 640.
Skistock(m) 640, 642.
Sklera(f) 140.
Skorpion(m) 13, 820.
Skript-Assistent(in(f))(m) 412.
**Skull(n) 632.**
**Skullboote(n) 632.**
SKULLEN(N) 632.
**Skullen(n) 632.**
**Slalomski(m) 633.**

**Fettgedruckte** Wörter beziehen sich auf eine Illustration; Wörter in GROSSBUCHSTABEN sind Überschriften.

Slingpumps(m) 356.
**Slip(m) 325.**
Slip(m) 346, 347.
Slipper(m) 355.
Slipstek(m) 691.
Slotback(m) 605.
Smaragd(m) 363.
Smaragdschliff(m) 362.
Smokstich(m) 571.
SNOOKER(N) 674.
**Snooker(n) 673.**
Söckchen(n) 344.
Socke(f) 344, 602, 615.
**Sockel(m) 190.**
Sockel(m) 40, 190, 204, 232, 233, 236, 368, 404, 453, 471, 545, 661, 708, 774.
Sockel(m), fester 282.
Sockel(m), rutschfester 661.
Sockelbreite(f) 756.
Sockelleiste(f) 199, 201.
Sockelplatte(f) 713.
Sockelprofil(n) 225.
**Socken(f) 325.**
Sofa(n) 221.
Soffitte(f) 188, 189.
Sofortbildkamera(f) 394.
Sohle(f) 277, 325, 641, 644, 678, 736.
Sohlenballen(m) 106, 107.
Sohlenspanner(m) 121.
Sohlenstrecke(f) 736.
Sojabohnen(f) 72.
Sojasprossen(m) 72.
**Solarhaus(n) 772.**
Solarreflektoren(m) 418.
Solarschild(n) 512.
**Solarzelle(f) 768.**
Solarzelle(f) 523, 769.
Solarzellen(f) 42.
Solarzellenfläche(f) 42.
Solarzellenfläche(f), Steuerung(f) 42.
Solarzellenprofil(n) 769.
**Solarzellensystem(n) 769.**
Solitärring(m) 364.
Solltemperatur(f) 213.
Solvent-Extraktionsanlage(f) 744.
Sommer(m) 8.
Sommersonnenwende(f) 8.
Sonderfunktionstasten(f) 569.
Sonderzeichen(n) 489.
SONNE(F) 6.
Sonne(f) 4, 8.
**Sonne(f), Struktur(f) 6.**
Sonnenblende(f) 430, 449, 721.
Sonnenbrille(f) 377.
Sonnendeck(n) 497.
SONNENENERGIE(F) 768, 770, 772.
**Sonnenenergie(f) 771.**
SONNENFINSTERNIS(F) 8.
Sonnenfleck(m) 6.
Sonnenkollektor(m) 772.
**Sonnenofen(m) 770.**
**Sonnenschein(m), Messung(f) 40.**
**Sonnenscheinautograph(m) 40.**
Sonnenschutzschirm(m) 42.
Sonnensegel(n) 16.
Sonnensensor(m) 42, 43, 49.
Sonnenstrahl(m), reflektierter 770, 771.
Sonnenstrahlung(f) 768, 769, 770, 771, 772.
SONNENSYSTEM(N) 4.
**Sonnenuhr(f) 706.**
Sonnenzellenausleger(m) 48, 418, 419.
Sonnenzellenausleger(m), entfaltete 48.
Sorghum(n) 152.
Sortierablagen(f), automatische 532.
Souffleurkasten(m) 188.
**Spachtel(m) 304.**
Spachtel(m) 581.
Spaghettizange(f) 246.
Spalier(n) 263.
Spalierbogen(m) 263.
Spalt(m) 65.
Spangang(m) 281.
Spange(f) 319.
Spannbeton(m) 286.
Spannbettuch(n) 224.
Spanndraht(m) 641.
**Spanneinrichtung(f) 562, 569.**
Spanneinrichtung(f) 561.
**Spanner(m) 228.**
Spanner(m) 661, 685.
Spannfeder(f) 562, 569, 665.
Spannfutter(n) 735.
Spanngriff(m) 282.
Spannhandgriff(m) 572.
Spannhebel(m) 285, 804.
Spannkabel(n) 684, 774.
Spannkabelhalter(m) 684.
Spannmast(m) 637.
Spannrad(n) 706, 707, 783.
Spannscheibe(f) 562, 569.
Spannschraube(f) 277, 553.
Spannstich(m), langer und kurzer 571.
Spannung(f), elektrische 821.
Spannungseinsteller(m) 562, 568, 569.
Spannungserhöhung(f) 755, 767.
**Spannungsprüfer(m) 310.**
Spannungsreduzierung(f) 755.
Spannungssammelschiene(f) 312.
Spannungsstift(m) 309.
Spanplatte(f) 289.
**Spargel(m) 72.**
Sparren(m) 198, 818.
spatelförmig 56.
Spaten(m) 266, 803.
**Spatenriemen(m) 632.**
Spazierstock(m) 375.
Speer(m) 791.
**Speere(m) 658.**
Speerspitze(f) 658.
Speerwurf(m) 654.
Speiche(f) 102, 122, 447.
Speichennerv(m) 133.
Speichenrad(n) 652.
Speichenseite(f), Handstrecker(m) 121.
Speicheranzeigetaste(f) 523.
Speichererweiterungsanschluß(m) 528.
**Speichergeräte(n) 526.**
Speicherlöschtaste(f) 396, 523.
Speichertaste(f) 396, 402, 405, 420, 523.
Speisekabel(n) 312.
Speisekammer(f) 195.
Speisekopf(m) 759.
**Speisepilze(m) 55.**
Speiseraum(m) 460, 807.
Speiseröhre(f) 88, 92, 97, 130, 131, 142.
Speisesaal(m) 496.
**Speisewagen(m) 460.**
Speisewasser(n) 760, 761, 762, 763.
Speisewasserbehälter(m) 469.
Spektrometer(m) 717.
Spenzer(m) 338.
**Sperma(n) 127.**
Sperrad(n) 573, 707.
Sperrdrehknopf(m) 711.
Sperre(f) 186, 462.
Sperrengeschoß(n) 474.
Sperrholzschichten(f) 288.
Sperrklinke(f) 281.
Sperrstift(m) 706, 707.
Spezialflachwagen(m) 473.
Spiegel(m) 292, 382, 430, 512, 719.
**Spiegel(m), beleuchteter 368.**
**Spiegelreflexkamera(f) 390.**
**Spiegelreflexkamera(f), einäugige 391.**
Spiegelreflexkamera(f), einäugige 394.
Spiegelreflexkamera(f), zweiäugige 394.
SPIEGELTELESKOP(N) 720.
**Spiegelteleskop(n) 720.**
Spiel(n) 831.
Spielanzug(m) 351.
Spielball(m) 673.
Spielball(m), weißer 673.
**Spielbereich(m) 626, 698.**
**Spielbrett(n) 697.**
Spielcassette(f) 699.
Spieler(m) 626.
Spieler(m) der Feldseite(f) 599.
Spielerbank(f) 597, 604, 608, 610, 612, 613.
Spielernummer(f) 602.
**Spielertrense(f) 650.**
**Spielfeld(n) 597, 599, 601, 606, 607, 610, 611, 612, 613, 617.**
Spielfeld(n) 599.
**Spielfeld(n) für amerikanisches Football(n) 604.**
**Spielfeld(n) für kanadisches Football(n) 604.**
Spielfläche(f) 619.
Spielraumeinstellung(f) 718.
Spielventil(n) 543.
Spierentonne(f) 487, 489.
Spike(m) 680.
Spikulen(f) 6.
Spinalganglion(n) 135.
Spinalnerv(m) 135.
Spinat(m) 73.
Spindel(f) 94, 290, 294, 575, 579, 707, 712.
Spindelfalte(f) 94.
SPINNE(F) 77.
Spinne(f) 77.
Spinnerschachtel(f) 672.
**Spinnrolle(f), offene 671.**
**Spinnrute(f) 671.**
Spiralarm(m) 9.
Spiralbindung(f) 670.
**Spiralbohrer(m) 281.**
Spirale(f) 299, 398, 801.
Spiralfeder(f) 706.
Spiralgalaxie(f) 9.
Spiralgehäuse(n) 753.
Spiralkneter(m) 250.
Spiralringbuch(n) 519.
Spiralskulptur(f) 94.
Spiralspindel(f) 276.
**Spiralwülste(f) rollen 584.**
Spitzbogen(m) 174.
Spitze(f) 27, 57, 72, 143, 144, 239, 240, 241, 242, 256, 275, 277, 291, 325, 375, 384, 389, 479, 501, 544, 562, 567, 633, 640, 644, 645, 670, 678, 681, 698, 798, 817.
**Spitzenhandschuh(m), fingerloser 327.**
Spitzenkopf(m) 666.
Spitzenvolant(n) 317.
spitzes Dekolleté(n) 343.
Spitzsegel(n) 482.
Spitztonne(f) 487, 489.
Spitzzange(f) 311.
**Spleiß(m) 692.**
Splint(m) 290.
Splintholz(n) 59.
Split-End(m) 603, 605.
Spoiler(m) 442.
Spore(f) 648.
Sporen(f) 55.
Sporn(m) 80, 112.
SPORTFISCHEREI(F) 670, 672.
Sporthalle(f) 496.
Sporthemd(n), ärmelloses 662.
Sporthose(f) 656.
SPORTKLEIDUNG(F) 352.
**Sportkleidung(f) 353.**
Sportplatz(m) 496.
**Sportset(n) 351.**
Sportwagen(m) 425.
Spot(m) 235.
Spotlight(n) 414.
**Spotmeter(m) 396.**
Sprachanzeigetaste(f) 422.
Spray(m) 256.
Sprayregler(m) 256.
**Sprecher- und Regieräume(m) 412.**
Sprecherpult(n) 407.
Sprecherraum(m) 407.
Sprechmuschel(f) 420.
Spreite(f) 57.
Spreizdübel(m) 276.
Sprengkapsel(f) 804.
Sprengladung(f) 804.
Sprengring(m) 672.
**Springeinrichtungen(f) 624.**
Springerstiefel(m) 635.
Springform(f) 245.
Springglocke(f) 653.
Springseil(n) 665.
Sprinkler(m) 766.
Spritzbeutel(m) 245.
Spritzblech(m) 741.
**Spritze(f) 726.**
Spritzenkolben(m) 726.
Spritzenkörper(m) 726.
Spritzkanälchen(n) 127.
Spritzlappen(m) 441.
**Spritzpistole(f) 304, 590.**
Sproß(m), unterirdischer 70.
Sprosse(f) 202, 203, 223, 302.
Sprossenarretierung(f) 302.
**Sprossengemüse(n) 72.**
Sprüharm(m) 257.
Sprühflasche(f) 264.
Sprühknopf(m) 256.
Sprühregen(m) mit Unterbrechungen(f) 39.
Sprühregen(m), anhaltender 39.
Sprungbein(n) 123.
Sprungbrett(n) 659.
Sprungfeder(f) 231.
Sprungfederrahmen(m) 224.
**Sprungfiguren(f) 624.**
Sprunggelenk(n) 101, 106.
Sprungkissen(n) 657.
Sprunglatte(f) 657.
Sprungpferd(n) 659.
Sprungski(m) 633.
Sprungständer(m) 657.
Sprungtuch(n) 659.
Sprungturm(m) 624.
Spülarm(m) 293.
Spule(f) 110, 561, 562, 573, 670, 671.
**Spüle(f) 296.**
Spüle(f) 296.
Spüle(f) mit Doppelablauf(m) 215.
Spulengestell(n) 575.
**Spulenkapsel(f) 562.**
Spuler(m) 561.
**Spulgerät(n), elektrisches 575.**
Spülhebel(m) 293.
Spülkasten(m) 292.
Spülkastendeckel(m) 293.
Spulrad(n) 575.
Spundbayonett(n) 794.
Spur(f), rechte 452.
Spurkranzrad(n) 476.
Spurnummer(f) 405.
Spurstange(f) 467.
Spursuchtasten(f) 405.
SQUASH(N) 616.
**Squashball(m) 616.**
**Squashschläger(m) 616.**
Staatsgrenze(f) 51.
Stab(m) 232, 263, 346, 539, 598, 599, 657.
Stabbogenbrücke(f) 455.
Stäbchenplatte(f) 288.
Stäbchenrollo(n) 231.
**Stabhochsprung(m) 657.**
Stabhochsprung(m) 655.
Stabilisator(m) 636, 684, 788.
Stabilisierungsflosse(f) 496, 509, 812.
**Stabmixer(m) 250.**
Stabparkett(n) 200.
Stabparkett(n) im verlorenen Verband(m) 200.
Stabplatte(f) 288.
Stabwerk(n) 773.
Stachel(m) 81.
Stachelbeere(f) 62.
Stachelzellenschicht(f) 136.
**Stadion(n) 654.**
Stadion(n) 185.
Stadt(f) 51.
Stadtgrenze(f) 52.
**Stadtplan(m) 52.**
Stadttasche(f) 380.
Stadtteil(m) 52.
Stadtteilgrenze(f) 52.
Staffelei(f) 591.
Stag(n) 479.
Stagsegel-Stag(n) 479.
Stahl(m) 286, 301, 795.
Stahlbeton(m) 286.
Stahlfeder(f) 795.
Stahlkante(f) 640.
Stahlkappe(f) 730.
Stahlschreibfeder(f) 389.
Stahlspitze(f) 375.
Stahlstab(m) 554.
Stalagmit(m) 24.
Stalaktit(m) 24.
Stall(m) 651.
Stamen(n) 64.
Stamm(m) 59, 61.
Stampfstag(n) 479.
Stand(m) 341.
**Standardobjektiv(n) 392.**
Standbagger(m) 733.
Standbein(n) 441.
Ständer(m) 40, 199, 248, 250, 283, 370, 382, 552, 561, 585, 659.
**Ständerbohrmaschine(f) 283.**
Standhahnzange(f) 299.
Standleuchte(f) 236.
Standrohr(n) 298, 738.
Standsockel(m) 714.
Standtom(n) 553.
**Standuhr(f) 707.**
Stange(f) 72, 105, 214, 230, 375, 384, 544, 663, 817.
Stange(f), einfache 230.
Stangen(f) 646.
Stangenkugel(f) 801.
**Stangensellerie(m/f) 72.**
Stapelstühle(m) 223.
Stärke(f) 152.
Stärkekörnchen(n) 115.
**Start(m) beim Rückenschwimmen(n) 623.**
**Start(m) in die Umlaufbahn(f) 419.**
Start(m) und Ziel(n) 646.
Start(m)/Pause(f) 405.
**Start- und Landebahn(f) 504.**
Start-Taste(f) 532.
**Startblock(m) 621, 656.**
Startblock(m) 621.
Starter(m) 621.
Startergriff(m) 272.
Starterzug(m) 270.
Startknopf(m) 706.

**Fettgedruckte** Wörter beziehen sich auf eine Illustration; Wörter in GROSSBUCHSTABEN sind Überschriften.

Startlinie(f) 655, 656, 666.
Startnummer(f) 653, 656.
**Startpositionen(f) 624.**
Startsprung(m) 622.
Startstange(f) 621.
Starttaste(f) 421.
Starttaste(f) für Strickmuster(n) 569.
Startumlaufbahn(f) 48.
Startwand(f) 621.
Stationskreis(m) 38.
**Stationsmodell(n) 38.**
Stationsspeichertaste(f) 402.
**Stativ(n) 393.**
Stativ(n) 397, 415, 718, 721.
Stativablage(f) 721.
Stator(m) 290, 753.
Staub(m) 34, 35.
Staubbehälter(m) 260.
Staubbeutel(m) 60.
Staubblatt(n) 60.
Staubfaden(m) 60.
Staubschweif(m) 9.
Staufach(n) 778, 780.
Stauraum(m) 440, 449.
Stausee(m) 746, 747, 748, 749, 750, 751.
Steakmesser(n) 239.
Stecher(m) 570.
Steckdose(f) 449.
Steckdose(f), dreipolige 309.
Steckdosenprüfer(m) 310.
**Stecker(m) 309.**
Stecker(m) 280, 400, 401, 406, 485, 592.
**Stecker(m), dreipoliger 309.**
Stecknadel(f) 563.
**Steg(m) 674.**
Steg(m) 166, 167, 180, 223, 336, 376, 544, 546.
**Steghose(f) 336.**
Stegplättchen(n) 376.
Stegschlaufe(f) 633.
Stegspangenschuh(m) 356.
Stegstütze(f) 376.
Stehbordkragen(m) 342.
**Stehleiter(f) 302.**
STEHLEITERN(F) 302.
Steigbügel(m) 138, 648, 793.
**Steigeisen(n) 358.**
Steigeisenriemen(m) 680.
Steigleitung(f) 215.
Steigleitung(f), Rücklauf(m) 208.
Steigleitung(f), Vorlauf(m) 208.
Steigradmechanismus(m) 539.
Steigrohr(n) 740.
Steigrohrkopf(m) 740.
Steigrohrventil(n) 740.
Steigung(f) 201.
Steigungseinstellung(f) 508.
steiles Satteldach(n) 182.
Steilhang(m) 27.
Steilwandzelt(n) 686.
Stein(m) 63, 364, 706.
Stein(m), schwarzer 697.
Stein(m), weißer 697.
Steinbock(m) 13, 820.
**Steindruckpresse(f) 583.**
Steine(m) 697.
Steinfaustkeil(m), polierter 791.
**Steinfrucht(f), Querschnitt(m) 63.**
Steinfrüchtchen(n) 62.
Steingarten(m) 263.
STEINOBST(N) 63.
**Steinobstsorten(f) 63.**
Steinpilz(m) 55.
Steinschlag(m) 826, 827.
Steinschlaghelm(m) 680.
**Steinschloß(n) 795.**
Steinwüste(f) 46.
Steißbein(n) 122.
Stellhebel(m) 467.
Stellring(m) 264.
Stellschraube(f) 278, 279, 282, 306, 311, 552.
Stellstange(f) 467.
Stellwarte(f) 189.
Stellwerk(n) 464.
Stemmeisen(n) 275.
Stemmtornische(f) 493.
Stempel(m) 60, 516.
Stempelkissen(n) 516.
Stempelträger(m) 516.
Stengel(m) 57.
**Stengelgemüse(n) 72.**
Stengelglied(n) 57.
Steppe(f) 45.
Stereokamera(f) 395.
Stereotaste(f) 408.
Stern(m) 36, 819.
**Sternanis(m) 67.**
Sternchen(n) 832.
Sternscheibe(f) 157.
Sternschnuppe(f) 19.
STERNWARTE(F) 14.
**Sternwarte(f) 14.**
Stert(m) 773.
**Stethoskop(n) 726.**
Steuerbordseite(f) 488, 489, 497.
Steuerbordtiefenruder(n) 806.
Steuerbügel(m) 637.
Steuereinheit(f) 699.
Steuerfeder(f) 698.
Steuerfedern(f) 684.
Steuerhebel(m) 735.
Steuerknüppel(m) 500, 508, 639.
Steuerkopf(m) 447.
Steuermann(m) 643.
Steuermarke(f) 384.
Steuerpult(n) 500.
Steuerrad(n) 500.
Steuerstab(m) 760, 761, 762, 763.
Steuerungstaste(f) 530.
Steuerzentrale(f) 746, 759.
Steven(m) 479.
Stichbreitenwähler(m) 561.
Stichlängenwähler(m) 561.
Stichplatte(f) 561.
STICHWAFFEN(F) 794.
Stichwähler(m) 561.
Sticker(m) 364.
STICKEREI(F) 571.
Stickrahmen(m), runder 571.
**Stickstiche(m) 571.**
Stickstoff(m), flüssiger 717.
Stiefel(m) 356, 542, 644, 645.
Stiefelette(f), knöchelhohe 357.
**Stiefelknecht(m) 358.**
Stiel(m) 55, 62, 63, 64, 70, 72, 241, 275, 674, 681.
Stielgrund(m) 72.
Stielkamm(m) 368.
Stielkasserolle(f) 249.
Stier(m) 11, 820.
Stift(m) 232, 233, 309.
Stift(m) mit rundem Ende(n) 231.
Stifthalter(m) 378, 379.
Stiftsockel(m) 232.
Stigma(n) 78, 79.
Stilett(n) 794.
Stillwasserspiegel(m) 30.
Stilus(m) 389.
Stimmanzeiger(m) 553.
Stimmband(n) 130.
Stimmeinrichtung(f) 553.
Stimmenwahlschalter(m) 555.
Stimmgabel(f) 539.
Stimmkrücke(f) 542.
Stimmnagel(m) 540.
Stimmstock(m) 540.
Stimmwirbel(m) 545, 547.
Stimmzug(m) 551.
Stirn(f) 109, 116, 120, 277, 792.
Stirnband(n) 615, 642.
Stirnbande(f) 675.
Stirnbein(n) 122.
Stirnhöhle(f) 141.
Stirnriemen(m) 649.
Stirnschopf(m) 100.
Stirntür(f) 470.
Stirnwand(f) 441, 785.
Stirnwandabdeckung(f) 426.
Stirnwandflachwagen(m) 473.
Stirnwandleiter(f) 470.
Stirnzahnrad(n) 280.
Stirnziegel(m) 169.
STOCK(M) 375.
Stock(m) 304, 483.
Stock(m), orthopädischer 728.
Stock(m), vierfüßiger 728.
Stockanker(m) 483.
**Stöcke(m) 728.**
Stöcke(m) 553.
Stockgriff(m) 642.
**Stockpresse(f) 579.**
Stockschaft(m) 642.
**Stockschirm(m) 375.**
Stockseite(f) 817.
Stockspitze(f) 643.
Stockteller(m) 641, 642.
Stockwerk(n) 773.
Stoff(m), bestickter 571.
Stoffbruch(m) 565.
**Stoffdrücker(m) 562.**
Stoffdrücker(m) 561, 562.
Stoffdrückerstange(f) 562.
Stoffstreifen(m) 571.
Stollen(m) 147, 353, 598, 656.
Stollenschuh(m) 595.
Stop(m) 106, 570, 831.
Stop-Taste(f) 403, 532.
Stopfer(m) 251, 385.
Stoppbad(n) 399.
Stoppknopf(m) 706.
**Stoppuhr(f) 706.**
Stöpselsicherung(f) 312.
Stoptaste(f) 405, 411, 420.
Störklappe(f) 498.
Stoßball(m), roter 673.
Stoßdämpfer(m) 445.
Stoßdämpfer(m), hinterer 443.
Stößel(m) 243.
**Stoßen(n), zweiarmiges mit Ausfallschritt(m) 662.**
Stoßfänger(m) 426, 440.
Stoßfängerverkleidung(f) 426.
Stoßleiste(f) 260.
Stoßstange(f) 445.
STOSSZÄHNE(M) 99.
Stoßzähne(m) eines Elefanten(m) 99.
Stoßzunge(f) 541.
Stoßzungenschraubenfeder(f) 541.
Strafbank(f) 608.
Strafraum(m) 601.
Strafraumbogen(m) 601.
Strafraumlinie(f) 601.
Strahlbein(n) 102.
Strahler(m) 777.
Strahlgrube(f), mittlere 104.
Strahlgrube(f), seitliche 104.
Strahlrohr(n) 778.
Strahlstörer(m) 264.
Strahlungszone(f) 6.
Strähnenkamm(m) 368.
Straight Flush(m) 695.
Strampelhöschen(n) 349.
Strand(m) 23, 30.
Strandschnecke(f) 83.
Strang(m) 631.
**Straße(f) 450.**
Straße(f) 52, 184, 190, 695.
Straße(f) für den Abtransport(m) 733.
STRASSE(F), QUERSCHNITT(M) 186.
STRASSENBAU(M) 450.
Straßendamm(m) 450.
Straßengüterverkehr(m) 491.
**Straßenhobel(m) 784.**
**Straßenkarte(f) 52.**
Straßenlaterne(f) 185, 186, 235.
Straßennummer(f) 52.
Straßenschuh(m) 356.
Stratokumulus(m) 44.
Stratosphäre(f) 19.
Stratus(m) 44.
Strauch(m) 263.
Streb(m) 733, 736.
Strebe(f) 198, 199, 553.
Strebebogen(m) 175, 176.
Streben(m), hinterer 446.
Strebepfeiler(m) 176.
Strecke(f), landschaftlich schöne 52.
Strecke(f), zurückgelegte 711.
Streckenplakette(f) 743.
Streichbaum(m) 573.
Streichblech(n) 156.
**Streichbürste(f) 304.**
Streichholz(n) 386.
**Streichholzheftchen(n) 386.**
**Streichholzschachtel(f) 386.**
Streuer(m) 246.
Streuwerk(n) 156.
Strickabstreifer(m) 568.
Strickabstreiferknopf(m) 568.
Strickarttasten(f) 569.
STRICKEN(N) 567.
**Strickhemd(n) 326.**
**Strickjacke(f) 326.**
Strickjacke(f) 326.
Strickjacke(f) mit V-Ausschnitt(m) 338.
Strickleiter(f) 303.
STRICKMASCHINE(F) 568.
Strickmaß(n) 567.
**Strickmuster(n) 567.**
Strickmusterspeicherung(f) 569.
Strickmütze(f) 329.
**Stricknadeln(f) 567.**
Strohhut(m) 328.
Strohverteiler(m) 161.
Stromabgabe(f) an Verbraucher(m) 755.
Stromabnehmer(m) 476.
Stromanschluß(m) 207, 213, 441.
Stromanschluß(m), wasserbeständiger 216.
Stromanschlußkabel(n) 449.
Stromanschlußpunkt(m) 757.
**Stromerzeugung(f) 755, 771.**
Stromerzeugung(f) 755, 767.
**Stromerzeugung(f) aus Kernenergie(f) 766.**
Stromerzeugungsabschnitt(m) 752.
Stromfortleitung(f) 767.
Stromführung(f) 746, 747.
**Stromgenerator(m) 753.**
Stromkreis(m) 312.
Stromnetz(n) 755, 771.
Stromschiene(f) 476.
**Stromschienenleuchte(f) 235.**
Stromspule(f) 712.
**Stromtransport(m) 757.**
Strömung(f) 493.
Strömungs-T(n) 301.
Strömungssicherung(f) 297.
Stromunterbrecher(m) 312.
Stromverbrauchernummer(f) 712.
Stromversorgungskabel(n) 186.
Stromverteiler(m) 415.
Stromweiterleitung(f) 714.
STROMZÄHLER(M) 712.
Stromzähler(m) 757.
**Struktur(f) der Sonne(f) 6.**
Struktur(f), stützende 48.
Strumpf(m) 344, 347.
**Strümpfe(m) 344.**
Strumpfhalter(m) 347.
Strumpfhaltergürtel(m) 347.
Strumpfhose(f) 344.
Studio-Kommandoanlage(f) 413.
**Studioebene(f) 414.**
Studioebene(f) 412.
Studiopersonal(n) 412.
Stufe(f) 201, 302.
Stufe(f), dritte 509.
Stufe(f), erste 509.
Stufe(f), zweite 509.
**Stufenbarren(m) 659.**
Stufenrock(m) 334.
STUHL(M) 223.
**Stuhltypen(m) 223.**
Stulp(m) 289, 290.
Stulpe(f) 327.
Stulpenhandschuh(m) 327.
Stummaufnahme-Taste(f) 403.
Stummel(m) 386, 670.
**Stumpf(m) 59.**
**Stumpftonne(f) 486.**
Stumpftonne(f) 489.
Stundenwinkelantrieb(m) 14.
Stundenzeiger(m) 707.
Sturm(m), tropischer 39.
Stürmer(m), linker 608.
Stürmer(m), rechter 608.
Sturmlampe(f) 690.
Sturmspitze(f) 608.
Sturz(m) 204.
Sturzhelm(m) 643.
Stützarm(m) 786.
Stützausleger(m) 780.
Stütze(f) 270, 471, 495, 661, 720, 757.
Stützen(f) der Pfeifenrastbretter(n) 543.
Stutzen(m) 595.
Stützfuß(m) 441, 449.
Stützpfeiler(m) 751.
**Stützpfeilerstaudamm(m) 751.**
Stützpunkt(m) 624.
Stützring(m) 15, 753.
Stylobat(m) 166, 168.
Stylus(m) 62, 63, 64.
**subarktische Klimate(n) 45.**
subarktische Klimate(n) 45.
Sublimation(f) 34.
Substanz(f), graue 135.
Substanz(f), weiße 135.
**Substanzen(f), gefährliche 821.**
Subtraktion(f) 830.
Subtraktionstaste(f) 523.
Subtropen(f), feuchte 45.
Subtropen(f), mediterrane 45.
Subtropen(f), trockene 45.
**subtropische Klimate(n) 45.**
Such- und Rettungsantennen(f) 43.
Sucharm(m) 529.
Sucher(m) 720, 721.
Sucherkamera(f) 394.
Südamerika(n) 20.
Süden(m) 488.
SÜDFRÜCHTE(F) 68.
**Südfrüchte(f) 68.**
südliche Halbkugel(f) 3.
SÜDLICHE HALBKUGEL(F), KONSTELLATIONEN(F) 12.
Südliche Krone(f) 13.
Südliche Wasserschlange(f) 13.
Südlicher Fisch(m) 13.
südlicher Polarkreis(m) 3.
Südliches Dreieck(n) 13.
Südliches Kardinalseezeichen(n) 489.
Südosten(m) 488.

**Fettgedruckte** Wörter beziehen sich auf eine Illustration; Wörter in GROSSBUCHSTABEN sind Überschriften.

Südpol(m) 3.
Südwesten(m) 488.
Südwester(m) 329.
Sulcus(m) terminalis 143.
**Sulky(m) 652.**
Sulky(m) 652.
Summe(f) 709, 830.
Super-Weitwinkelobjektiv(n) 392.
Suppenlöffel(m) 241.
Suppenschale(f) 238.
Suppenteller(m) 238.
Suppenterrine(f) 238.
Suppentopf(m) 249.
SURFBRETT(N) 631.
Suspensorium(n) 602, 609.
Süßkartoffel(f) 71.
Süßweinglas(n) 237.
Sweatshirt(n) 352.
Sweatshirt(n) mit Kapuze(f) 352.
Sweeping-Line(f) 620.
Swimmingpool(m) 496.
Symbol(n) 702.
SYMBOLE(N) IN DEN WISSENSCHAFTEN(F) 830.
SYMBOLE(N), METEOROLOGISCHE 44.
Symphyse(f) 127, 128.
Synapse(f) 135.
**Synthesizer(m) 555.**
**Systembausteine(m) 400.**
Systemschalter(m) 555.

## T

T-Leitwerk(n) 498.
T-Shirt Kleid(n) 351.
T-Stück(n) 298.
Tab-Taste(f) 530.
Tabak(m) 384.
Tabakkammer(f) 385.
Tabaksbeutel(m) 385.
Tablette(f) 725.
Tablinum(n) 170.
Tabulatoreinstelltaste(f) 525.
Tabulatorsetztaste(f) 525.
Tabuliertaste(f) 524.
Tachometer(m) 431, 445.
Tachometer(n) 664.
Tackle(m), linker 605.
Tackle(m), rechter 605.
Tafel(f) 363.
Tafelberg(m) 46.
Tafelfacette(f) 363.
Tafelschliff(m) 362.
Tageskilometerzähler(m) 431.
Tagzeichen(n) 486, 487.
**Tagzeichen(n) (region(f) B) 489.**
Taille(f) 117, 119.
Taillenabnäher(m) 320.
**Takelage(f) 478.**
TAKELUNG(F) 482.
Takling(m), einfacher 691.
**Taktarten(f) 537.**
Taktkennung(f) 489.
Taktstrich(m) 537.
Tal(n) 27, 30.
Talgdrüse(f) 136.
Tambour(m) 167.
**Tamburin(n) 554.**
Tampon(m) 581.
Tank(m) 742, 743.
**Tankanhänger(m) 743.**
Tankanlage(f) 740.
Tankaufsatz(m) 742.
Tankdeckel(m) 440.
**Tanker(m) 742.**
Tanker(m) 491.
Tankerflugzeug(n) 813.
Tankklappe(f) 427.
**Tanklastzug(m) 742.**
Tankluke(f) 743.
TANKSTELLE(F) 453.
**Tankstelle(f) 453.**
Tankstelle(f) 823.
Tankwagen(m) 506.
Tankwall(m) 741.
Tankwand(f) 742.
Tannennadeln(f) 58.
Tarlatan(m) 582.
Tasche(f) 358, 378, 673.
Tasche(f), aufgesetzte 320, 322, 339, 350.
Tasche(f), eingesetzte 339.
Tasche(f), falsche 330.
Tasche(f), senkrechte 316.
**Taschenarten(f) 339.**
**Taschenlampe(f) 777.**
**Taschenrechner(m) 523.**
Taschenrechner(m) 379.
**Taschenschirm(m) 375.**
Taschenträger(m) 679.
Tasse(f) 238, 688.
**Tastatur(f) 530.**
Tastatur(f) 422, 526, 527, 540, 555.
Tastatur(f), alphanumerische 422.
Tastatur(f), numerische 422.
Tastaturablage(f), verstellbare 521.
Tastaturanschluß(m) 528.
Taste(f) 530, 536, 540, 541, 543.
Taste(f) für Mittelwerte(m) 396.
Tasten(f) 420, 422.
Tastenfeld(n), alphanumerisches 530.
Tastenfeld(n), numerisches 530, 709.
TASTENINSTRUMENTE(N) 540.
Tastentelefon(n) 422.
Tastkörperchen(n), Meissnersches 136.
TASTSINN(M) 136.
tatsächliche Temperatur(f) 213.
Tau(m) 37.
Tau(n) 660.
Taube(f) 13.
Taubesfestigung(f) 492.
Täubling(m), grasgrüner 55.
Tauchanzug(m) 627.
TAUCHEN(N) 627.
**Taucher(m) 627.**
Taucherhandschuh(m) 627.
Taupunkttemperatur(f) 38.
Taurus 820.
TAUWERK(N) 692.
Taxi(n) 822.
**Techniken(f), andere 576.**
**Techniken(f), wichtigste 588.**
Teddy(m) 345.
Tee(n) 620, 677.
Tee-Ei(n) 246.
Teekanne(f) 238.
Teelöffel(m) 241.
Teerpappe(f) 286.
Teil(m) über Wasser(n) 486.
Teil(m), flacher 567.
**Teile(n) 220, 223, 224.**
**Teile(n) des Ohrs(n) 138.**
**Teile(n) des Schuhs(m) 354.**
Teilmenge(f), echte 830.
**Teilungsbeispiele(n) 818.**
Teilungsnaht(f) 322.
Telefax-Gerät(n) 417.
**Telefaxgerät(n) 421.**
Telefon(n) 413, 822.
Telefon(n), drahtloses 422.
**Telefonapparat(m) 420.**
Telefonapparat(m) 415, 417.
**Telefonarten(f) 422.**
Telefonkabel(n) 186.
Telefonnetz(n) 417.
Telefonnummernverzeichnis(n) 516.
TELEKOMMUNIKATION(F) 417.
Telekommunikation(f) 417.
Telekommunikation(f) für den Straßenverkehr(m) 417.
Telekommunikation(f) über Computer(m) 417.
Telekommunikation(f), industrielle 417.
Telekommunikation(f), maritime 417.
Telekommunikation(f), militärische 417.
Telekommunikationsantenne(f) 497, 809, 810.
**Telekommunikationstechnik(f) über das Telefonnetz(n) 417.**
Telekommunkation(f), persönliche 417.
Telekonverter(m) 392.
Teleobjektiv(n) 392.
Teleport(m) 417.
**Teleskop(n) 14.**
Teleskop(n) 14, 42.
Teleskopbein(n) 393.
Teleskopgabel(f) 442.
Teleskoptragebein(n) 726.
**Telex(n) 421.**
Telex(n) 417.
Telezoom-Taste(f) 409.
Teller(m) 236, 688.
Teller(m), flacher 238.
Teller(m), kleiner 238.
Telson(n) 91.
TEMPEL(M), GRIECHISCHER 168.
Temperatur(f) 210.
Temperatur(f), gewünschte 705.
**Temperatur(f), Messung(f) 41.**
Temperatur(f), mittlere bis hohe 829.
Temperatur(f), niedrige 829.
Temperatur(f), tatsächliche 705.
Temperaturanzeige(f) 431.
Temperatureinsteller(m) 585.
TEMPERATURMESSUNG(F) 705.
Temperaturregler(m) 209, 213, 252, 254, 256, 297, 705.
Temperaturregler(m), abziehbarer 253.
Temperaturschalter(m) 370.
Temperaturskala(f) 19.
Temperaturskalen(f) 710.
Temperaturwähler(m) 253, 258, 259.
Temporegler(m) 555.
Temposkala(f) 539.
TENNIS(N) 614.
**Tennisball(m) 615.**
**Tennisplatz(m) 614.**
**Tennisschläger(m) 615.**
Tennisschuh(m) 355, 615.
**Tennisspielerin(f) 615.**
Tentakel(m), große 83.
Tentakel(m), kleiner 83.
Teppichmuschel(f) 93.
Teppichschiffchen(n) 574.
**Terminal(n) 421.**
Terminkalender(m) 518.
Terpentin(n) 592.
Terrasse(f) 193, 263.
Terrassentür(f) 195.
**Tertiärkonsumenten(m) 31.**
Terz(f) 537.
Terz-Einladung(f) 667.
Testbereich(m) für Düsentriebwerke(n) 811.
Testbild(n) 414.
Textablesetafel(f) 414.
Textanzeige(f) 524.
TEXTILPFLEGE(F) 829.
Textmarker(m) 515.
Texttaste(f) 524.
THEATER(N) 188.
**Theodolit(m) 713.**
Theodolit(m) 41.
Thermoelement(n) 297.
Thermoelementkabel(n) 297.
**Thermometer(n) 705, 710.**
Thermometer(n) 209, 627, 635, 741.
Thermoschalter(m) 438.
Thermosflasche(f) 690.
Thermosphäre(f) 19.
Thermostat(m) 210, 214, 252, 297.
Thorax(m) 78, 79, 80, 116, 118.
Thymian(m) 74.
Ticketschalter(m) 504.
**Tiefdruck(m) 580.**
Tiefdruckgebiet(n) 38.
TIEFDRUCKVERFAHREN(N) 582.
Tiefenanschlag(m) 283.
Tiefeneinstellung(f) 283.
Tiefenmesser(m) 627.
Tiefenskala(f) 485.
Tiefenverstellschraube(f) 277.
Tiefladewagen(m) 473.
Tiefräumer(m) 782.
Tiefräumerbedienteil(n) 782.
**Tiefsee-Ebene(f) 29.**
Tiefsee-Ebene(f) 29.
Tiefseeberg(m) 29.
Tiefseeboden(m) 22.
Tiefseegraben(m) 28.
Tiefseehügel(m) 29.
Tieftöner(m) 401.
Tierceron(m) 177.
TIERISCHE ZELLE(F) 115.
TIERKREISZEICHEN(N) 820.
Tight-End(m) 603, 605.
Tilde(f) 832.
Timer(m) 664.
Tinte(f) 588.
Tintenraum(m) 389.
Tipi(n) 165.
TISCH(M) 219.
Tisch(m) 578.
Tischfeststellschraube(f) 283.
**Tischkreissäge(f) 285.**
Tischleuchte(f) 236.
Tischplatte(f) 219.
**Tischrechner(m) 523.**
**Tischrührgerät(n) 250.**
TISCHTENNIS(N) 619.
Tischtennisball(m) 619.
**Tischtennisplatte(f) 619.**
**Tischtennisschläger(m) 619.**
**Tischtypen(f) 219.**
Tischverlängerung(f) 285.
Titan(m) 5.
TL-Triebwerk(n) 499.
**Toaster(m) 252.**
**Toga(f) 315.**
**Toilette(f) 293.**
Toilette(f) 195, 215, 292, 461.
Toiletten(f) (Damen(f)) 822.
Toiletten(f) (Herren(m)) 822.
Toilettenpapierhalter(m) 292.
Toilettenwagen(m) 506.
Tomate(f) 69.
Tomtom(n) 552.
Ton V.U.Meter(m) 413.
Ton-/Bild-Vorschaueinheit(f) 413.
Tonabnehmer(m) 404.
Tonabnehmer-Wahlschalter(m) 547.
Tonabnehmersystem(n) 404.
Tonarm(m) 404.
Tonarmheber(m) 404.
Tonarmstütze(f) 404.
Tonartvorzeichen(n) 538.
Tonbandgerät(n), digitales 407.
**Tonerzeugung(f) 543.**
Tonhöhenrad(n) 555.
**Tonleiter(f) 537.**
Tonnen(f) mit schadhaften Brennelementen(n) 764.
Tonnenstein(m) 486.
Tonregiepult(n) 412, 415.
Tonregieraum(m) 412, 415.
Tontechniker(in(f))(m) 412, 415.
Tonvormischung(f) 413.
TONWIEDERGABESYSTEM(N) 400, 402, 404.
TONWIEDERGABESYSTEME(N), TRAGBARE 408.
Topas(m) 363.
TÖPFEREI(F) 584.
Topfhut(m) 329.
Topinambur(m/f) 71.
**topographische Merkmale(n) 28.**
Topplicht(n) 495.
Toppnant(f) 478.
Toppzeichen(n) 486, 488.
Toprückstand(m) 744.
Toque(f) 329.
**Tor(n) 626.**
Tor(n) 490, 601, 604, 606, 607, 608, 612, 626.
Torangreifer(m) 611.
Torbereich(m) 606.
Tordrittel(n) 611.
Torhüter(m) 612, 626.
Torhütermarkierung(f) 612.
Torkreis(m) 611.
Torlinie(f) 604, 606, 607, 608, 612, 626.
Torpedo(m) 807.
Torpedoraum(m) 807.
Torpedorohr(n) 807.
Torpfosten(m) 604, 611.
Torraum(m) 601, 608, 612.
Torraumlinie(f) 612.
Torrichter(m) 608, 626.
Torschütze(m) 611.
Torselett(n) 347.
Torus(m) 166, 167.
Torverteidiger(m) 611.
Torwächter(m) 599.
**Torwart(m) 609.**
Torwart(m) 601, 607, 608, 611.
Torwartschläger(m) 609.
totale Finsternis(f) 8.
Totalisator(m) 651.
Toupierkamm(m) 368.
Trab(m) 101.
TRABRENNSPORT(M) 652.
Trachte(f) 104.
Trachtenwand(f) 104.
Track(m) 404.
TRADITIONELLE WOHNHÄUSER(N) 165.
Trageband(n) 729.
Tragebügel(m) 408.
Tragegriff(m) 796.
Träger(m) 198, 231, 346, 644, 738, 756, 787.
Träger(m) mit Knopf(m) 351.
Träger(m), runder 230.
Träger(m), verstellbarer 350.
**Trägerhemd(n) 325.**
Trägerhemd(n) 353.
Trägerhemdchen(n) 351.
Trageriemen(m) 730.
Trägerkleid(n) 332.
Trägerrakete(f) 419.
Tragetasche(f) 381.
Tragflügel(m) 499, 511.
Tragflügel(m), hinterer 495.
Tragflügel(m), teilgetauchter 495.
Tragflügel(m), vorderer 495.
TRAGFLÜGELFORMEN(F) 499.
TRAGFLÜGELSCHIFF(N) 495.
Tragkabel(n) 456.
Tragsäule(f) 738.
Tragschicht(f), obere 451.
Tragschicht(f), untere 451.
Tragsegel(n) 637.
Tragus(m) 139.
Trainer(m) 669.
**Trainingsanzug(m) 352.**
Trainingshose(f) 352.
TRAKTOR(M) 147.

**Fettgedruckte** Wörter beziehen sich auf eine Illustration; Wörter in GROSSBUCHSTABEN sind Überschriften.

Traktormotor(m) 784.
**Trampolin(n) 659.**
Tranchiergabel(f) 242.
Tranchiermesser(n) 242.
Tränenkanal(m) 140.
Transform-Verwerfung(f) 28.
Transformator(m) 235, 747, 757, 758, 771.
Transitlagerschuppen(m) 490.
Translationswelle(f) 30.
Transpiration(f) 35.
Transporteur(m) 562.
Transporträdchen(n) 390.
Transportschiene(f) 390.
Transportwalze(f) 390.
Transversale pleine(f) 700, 701.
Transversale simple(f) 700, 701.
Trapez-Form(f) 332.
Trapezflügel(m) 499.
**Traube(f) 61.**
Traube(f) 60.
**Traveller(m) 630.**
Traveller(m) 628.
Traverse(f) 178, 219, 757.
Treble(m) 698.
Trefferanzeige(f) 666.
**Trefflächen(f) 667.**
Treibanker(m) 483.
Treibhaus(n) 149.
Treibladung(f) 798.
Treibstoff-Füllstandanzeige(f) 512.
Treibstoffart(f) 453.
Treibstofftank(m) 508, 805, 812.
Treibstoffzufuhrleitungen(f) 635.
**Trenchcoat(m) 319.**
Trennstab(m) 574.
Trennwand(f) 216, 520.
**Trense(f) 650.**
Trense(f) 649.
Trensenzügel(m) 649.
TREPPE(F) 201.
Treppe(f) 194, 474, 773.
Treppe(f) zum Halbgeschoß(n) 195.
Treppenabsatz(m) 194.
Treppenaufgang(m) 741.
Treppenhaus(n) 194.
Treppenlauf(m) 201.
Treppenschliff(m) 362.
Treppenvorbau(m) 196.
Tressenstich(m) 571.
Tretlager(n) 448.
**Tretplatte(f) 561.**
**Triangel(m) 554.**
Triangel(m) 556.
**Tribüne(f) 651.**
Trichter(m) 243, 410, 549, 551.
Trickmischer(m) 413.
Triclinium(n) 171.
Trieb(m) 61.
Triebdrehgestell(n) 459.
Triebwagen(m) 476, 477.
Triebwerke(n) 510.
Triebwerklufteinlauf(m) 813.
Trift(f) 746.
Triglyphe(f) 167.
Trikot(n) 353, 600, 602.
Trikuspidalklappe(f) 125.
Triller(m) 538.
Trinkwasserleitung(f) 186.
Trio(n) 558.
Triplebar(f) 646, 647.
Triton(m) 5.
Tritt(m) 302, 572.
Trittbrett(n) 445, 778.
Trittfläche(f) 649.
Tritthocker(m) 222, 302.
**Trittleiter(f) 302.**
Trittlöser(m) 573.
Trittstufe(f) 201, 440.
Trizepszug(m) 663.
Trochilus(m) 166, 167.
Trockendock(n) 490.
trockene Subtropen(f) 45.
TROCKENFRÜCHTE(F) 66, 67.
Trockenschrank(m) 398.
Trockenseite(f) 748.
Trockenständer(m) 399.
**Trocknen(n) 243, 829.**
Trocknen(n) 829.
Troddel(f) 229.
Trog(m) 38.
**Trombe-Wand(f) 772.**
Trombe-Wand(f) 772.
Trommel(f) 231, 258, 259, 265, 484, 707, 797.
**Trommel(f), kleine 553.**
Trommel(f), kleine 552, 557.
**Trommelbremse(f) 432.**
Trommelfell(n) 84, 97, 139.
**Trommeln(f) 552.**
**Trompete(f) 550.**
Trompete(f) 451, 550.
Trompeten(f) 556.
tropfnaß hängen 829.
**tropische Klimate(n) 45.**
tropische Savanne(f) 45.
tropischer Regenwald(m) 45.
tropischer Sturm(m) 39.
Troposphäre(f) 19.
Trosse(f) 692.
Trüffel(f) 55.
Trugdolde(f), eingliedrige 60.
Trugdolde(f), zweigliedrige 60.
Truhe(f) 226.
Truthahn(m) 150.
Tuba(f) 551, 557.
Tube(f) 588.
Tubus(m) 16, 718, 719, 720, 721.
Tubusträger(m) 718.
Tudorbogen(m) 174.
Tukan(m) 13.
Tülle(f) 247, 252.
Tüllenbayonett(n) 794.
Tunika(f) 337, 791.
Tunikakleid(n) 333.
Tunnel(m) 474.
Tunnelsohle(f) 476.
TÜR(F) 202.
Tür(f) 225, 253, 254, 259, 427, 449, 498, 617.
Tür(f), automatische 504.
Turban(m) 329.
Turbine(f) 753, 758, 767.
Turbinenabschaltventil(n) 758.
Turbinendrehung(f) 755.
Turbinengebäude(n) 758.
Turbinenläufer(m) 752.
Turbinenrad(n) 438.
Turbinenummantelung(f) 753.
Turbinenwasserabfluß(m) 755.
Turbinenwelle(f) 767.
Turboalternator(m) 806.
Turboluftstrahltriebwerk(n) 812.
Turboverdichter(m) 501.
Turboverdichterwelle(f) 501.
Türfach(n) 254.
**Türformen(f) 202.**
Türführungsschiene(f) 470.
Türfüllung(f) 225.
Türgriff(m) 289, 427.
Türinnenschale(f) 429.
Türkis(m) 363.
Türknopf(m) 202.
Turm(m) 176, 486, 696, 770, 771, 773, 774, 786, 807.
Turmalin(m) 363.
**Turmkran(m) 786.**
Turmmast(m) 786.
Turmspitze(f) 175.
**Turnüre(f) 316.**
Turnüre(f) 316.
Türöffnungshebel(m) 429.
Türpfosten(m) 202.
Türsäule(f) 471.
Türschloß(n) 202, 259, 427, 429.
Türstopper(m) 254.
Türsturz(m) 175.
Türtasche(f) 429.
Türverkleidung(f) 429.
Türzapfen(m) 202.
Tusche(f), lithographische 583.
TV-Einstellung(f) 411.
TV-Netzschalter(m) 411.
TV/Video-Taste(f) 411.
**Twinset(n) 338.**
Tympanon(n) 166, 168.
Typenschild(n) 280.

## U

U-BAHN(F) 474, 476.
U-Bahn(f) 190.
U-Bahn-Netzplan(m) 475, 477.
U-Bahn-Schild(n) 474.
**U-Bahn-Station(f) 474.**
**U-Bahn-Zug(m) 476.**
U-Bahn-Zug(m) 474.
Überbau(m) 457.
Überbehang(m) 229.
Überdach(n) 685, 686.
Überdruckventil(n) 248, 627.
Überfallrinne(f) 746.
Überfangstich(m), orientalischer 571.
Überfangstich(m), rumänischer 571.
**Überfangstiche(m) 571.**
Überführung(f) 452, 454.
**Übergänge(m) 301.**
Überholen(n) verboten 825.
Überholrollbahn(f) 502.
Überholspur(f) 452.
Überholverbot(n) 824.
Überkehr(f) 161.
Überkopfleitung(f) 756.
Überkopfschaltbrett(n) 500.
Überlappanzeige(f) 532.
Überlauf(m) 215, 292, 293, 297.
Überlaufkrone(f) 746.
Überlaufschutz(m) 257.
Überlaufstutzen(m) 399.
Überlauftor(n) 746.
Überlaufwehr(n) 746.
Überleitungstunnel(m) 764.
Überschlag(m) 380.
**Überseekoffer(m) 383.**
Übersetzungsgehäuse(n) 671.
**Übersicht(f) 289.**
Überstand(m) 201.
Überströmschlitz(m) 436.
**Übertageabbau(m) 733.**
Übertageanlage(f) 736.
**Übertageanlagen(f) 734.**
Überträger(m) 485.
Übertragungnsnetz(n), öffentliches 416.
**Übertragungsgeräte(n) 526.**
Übertragungskabel(n) 485.
ÜBERTRAGUNGSSATELLITENTECHNIK(F) 416.
Übertragungsstation(f) 722.
ÜBERTRAGUNGSWAGEN(M) 415.
Überwachungsradar(n) 809, 810.
Überwurfmutter(f) 296.
Überziehschuh(m) 355.
Übungsgrün(n) 676.
Übungsplatz(m) 178.
Ufer(n) 30, 752.
**Uferdamm(m) 748.**
UHF-Antenne(f) 42.
Uhr(f) 407, 714.
**Uhr(f), mechanische 706.**
Uhrband(n) 706.
Uhrenmeister(m) 610.
**Uhrwerk(n), zuggetriebenes 707.**
Ultraviolett-Spektrometer(n) 43.
Umfangsverbindung(f) 750.
Umgehungsstraße(f) 52.
**Umhängetasche(f) mit Dehnfalte(f) 380.**
Umhängetasche(f) mit Reißverschluß(m) 380.
Umkehrsystem(n) 718.
Umkleideraum(m) 735.
Umladeabschnitt(m) 743.
**Umlaufbahn(f) 419, 510.**
Umlaufbahn(f), anvisierte 48.
Umlaufbahn(f), geostationäre 43.
Umlaufbahn(f), polare 43.
**Umlaufbahn(f), Satelliten(m) 43.**
**Umlaufbahnen(f) der Planeten(m) 4.**
Umlaufgehäuse(n) 747.
Umlaut(m) 832.
Umlenkspiegel(m) 720.
Umlenkstern(m) 272.
Umluft(f) 206, 207.
Umrechnungsskala(f) 396.
Umrißleuchte(f) 440.
Umschaltfeststelltaste(f) 524, 530.
Umschalttaste(f) 524.
Umschalttasten(f) 530.
Umschaltvorrichtung(f) 212.
Umschlag(m) 315, 341.
Umspannwerk(n) 752.
Umwälzpumpe(f) 208, 763, 772.
Umwerfer(m), hinterer 446, 448.
unbewegter Deich(m) 752.
unendlich 830.
ungesäuertes Brot(n) 153.
ungleich 830.
Universaltreppe(f) 507.
Unkrautstecher(m) 268.
unpaarig gefiedert 56.
unregelmäßige Galaxie(f) 9.
Unteranzug(m) 512.
Unterarm(m) 106, 112, 117, 119.
Unterarmmappe(f) 378.
Unterarmschiene(f) 792.
Unterarmstütze(f) 728.
Unterbau(m) 450, 737.
Unterblock(m) des Flaschenzuges(m) 737.
Unterboden(m) 198, 199, 200.
Unterbrechung(f) 489.
Unterbrett(n) 543.
Unterbruststäbchen(n) 347.
Unterdeck(n) 741.
untere Tasche(f) 674.
Untereck(n), linkes 818.
Untereck(n), rechtes 818.
unterer Anzug(m) 650.
Unterfach(n) 379.
Unterfahrschutz(m) 441.
Unterfangkescher(m) 672.
Unterführung(f) 454, 464.
Unterfutter(n) 565.
**Untergeschoß(n) 190.**
Untergrätenmuskel(m) 121.
Untergurt(m) 455.
Unterhaut(f) 137.
Unterhemd(n) 595.
Unterhose(f), lange 325.
unterirdisches Gerinne(n) 24.
Unterkante(f) 609.
Unterkiefer(m) 78, 80, 81, 86, 102, 122.
Unterkleid(n) 345.
Unterlagsplatte(f) 466.
Unterlenker(m) 147.
Unterlid(n) 140.
Unterlippe(f) 142, 542.
Untermast(m) 478.
untermeerischer Cañon(m) 29.
Unterrock(m) 345.
Unterrohr(n) 447.
Untersattel(m) 544.
Unterschenkel(m) 103, 112.
Unterschnabel(m) 109.
Unterschwanzdecken(f) 109.
UNTERSEEBOOT(N) 806.
Unterseite(f) 633.
Unterstock(m) 375.
Unterstützmauer(f) 748.
Unterteil(n) 363.
Unterteilhauptfacette(f) 363.
Untertor(n) 492.
Untervorhang(m) 229.
**Unterwäsche(f) 325, 345, 346.**
Unterwasser(n) 746, 747, 749, 750.
Unterwasserkamera(f) 394.
Unterwassermauer(f) 749.
Unterwasserpipeline(f) 740.
Uran(n), angereichertes 762, 763.
Uran(n), nichtangereichertes 760, 761.
Uranbrennstoff(m), Spaltung(f) des 766.
Uranus(m) 5.
Urogenital-Öffnung(f) 89.
Ursprungskegel(m) 135.
**Utensilien(n) 246.**

## V

V-Ausschnitt(m) 322, 326, 343.
V.U.-Meter(n) 407.
Vakuole(f) 115.
**Vakuum-Kaffeemaschine(f) 247.**
Vakuumdestillation(f) 744.
Vakuumkammer(f) 710, 717.
Vakuumpumpe(f) 717.
Vakuumrohr(n) 717.
Variometer(n) 635.
Variometer(n), mechanisches 639.
Vater-Pacinische Körperchen(n) 136.
VAUBAN-FESTUNG(F) 178.
VCR-Einstellung(f) 411.
VCR-Netzschalter(m) 411.
VCR-Tasten(f) 411.
Vena(f) cephalica 126.
Vene(f), königliche 126.
**Venen(f) 126.**
Ventil(n) 293, 447, 550, 634.
Ventilator(m) 212, 213, 214.
Ventilatormotor(m) 214.
Ventilatorregler(m) 214.
Ventilbüchse(f) 550.
Ventilfeder(f) 434, 543.
Ventilsitz(m) 293, 294.
Ventilsitzzange(f) 299.
Ventilteller(m) 294.
Ventilzug(m), dritter 551.
Ventilzug(m), erster 550.
Ventilzug(m), zweiter 550.
Venturidüse(f) 804.
Venus(f) 4.
Venusmuschel(f) 93.
Verankerung(f) 456.
Verbindung(f) 389, 697.
Verbindung(f) des Ventilations- und Kühlsystems(n) 512.
Verbindung(f), fertige 692.
**Verbindungen(f), mechanische 300.**
Verbindungsast(m) 135.
Verbindungsclip(m) 726.
Verbindungsdraht(m) 312, 658.
Verbindungshülse(f) 678.
Verbindungskabel(n) 400, 530, 561, 585.
Verbindungspunkt(m) 757.

**Fettgedruckte** Wörter beziehen sich auf eine Illustration; Wörter in GROSSBUCHSTABEN sind Überschriften.

Verbindungsstück(n) 406.
Verbindungstunnel(m) 510.
Verbot(n) der Einfahrt(f) 824, 825.
Verbot(n) für Fahrzeuge(n) 826, 827.
Verbrennen(n) 436.
Verbrennung(f) 436, 437, 501.
Verbrennungsraum(m) 434, 438.
Verdampfer(m) 210.
Verdampferkörpermantel(m) 759.
Verdampferschlangen(f) 214.
Verdampfungsgitter(n) 210.
Verdauungsdrüse(f) 92.
VERDAUUNGSSYSTEM(N) 131.
Verdichten(n) 436, 437.
Verdichterrad(n) 438.
Verdichterturbine(f) 501.
Verdichtung(f) 501.
Verdunkelung(f) 489.
Verdunstung(f) 34, 35.
Veredelungsmesser(n) 269.
Vereinigung(f) 830.
Verengung(f) 705.
Vergaser(m) 442.
**Vergrößerer(m) 399.**
Vergrößerungsobjektiv(n) 399.
Vergrößerungsrahmen(m) 398.
Verkaufsstand(m) 475.
Verkehrsampel(f) 186.
Verkehrsinsel(f) 184.
VERKEHRSZEICHEN(N) 824, 826, 828.
**Verkehrszeichen(n), internationale 825, 827, 828.**
**Verkehrszeichen(n), nordamerikanische 824, 826, 828.**
Verkleidung(f) 198, 209, 297, 442.
**Verkleidungsmaterialien(n) 286.**
Verkleinern(n)/Vergrößern(n) 532.
Verklicker(m) 628.
Verkürzungsstek(m) 691.
Verlobungsring(m) 364.
Verminderung(f) des Strahlendiameters(m) 717.
Versailles-Parkett(n) 200.
Verschlagwagen(m) 472.
Verschluß(m) 260, 351, 529, 641.
Verschlußband(n), oberes 641.
Verschlußblock(m) 802.
**Verschlüsse(m) 566.**
Verschlußhebel(m) 471.
Verschlußring(m) 397, 802.
Verschlußstück(n) 798, 799.
**Verschmutzung(f), atmosphärische 34.**
Verschmutzung(f), industrielle 32, 33.
Verschmutzung(f), landwirtschaftliche 32.
Verschmutzungsquellen(f) 34.
**Verschraubung(f) 300.**
Verschraubung(f) 300.
Verschraubungsmutter(f) 300.
verschreibungspflichtig 831.
Versenker(m) 281.
**Versetzungszeichen(n) 538.**
VERSITZGRUBE(F) 216.
Versorgungsbereich(m) 503.
Versorgungskapsel(f) 509.
Versorgungsmodul(m) 418.
Versorgungsstraße(m) 502.
Verspannung(f) 660.
**Verstärker(m) 402.**
Verstärker(m) 714.
**Verstärker-Rückseite(f) 400.**
Verstärkerregler(m) 485.
**Verstärkung(f) seismischer Wellen(f) 714.**
Verstärkungsrippe(f) 785.
Verstärkungsschwelle(f) 729.
Verstärkungsstrebe(f) 756.
Versteifungsrippe(f) 498.
Versteller(m) 323.
Verstellnut(f) 278.
Verstellschraube(f) 539.
Verstellspindel(f) 159.
Verstrebung(f) 774.
Vertäfelung(f), obere 787.
Vertäfelung(f), untere 787.
Vertebralschild(m) 97.
Verteidiger(m) 601.
Verteidiger(m), linker 607, 608.
Verteidiger(m), rechter 601, 607, 608.
Verteidigungsdrittel(n) 611.
Verteidigungszone(f) 608, 613.
Verteiler(m) 450.
Verteilerdose(f) 471.
Verteilerkasten(m) 757.
Verteilerschleife(f) 757.
Verteilung(f) durch Kabelnetz(n) 416.
Vertiefung(f) 566.
**Vertikalachsenwindturbine(f) 774.**
Vertikulator(m) 266.
Verwaltungsgebäude(n) 752.
Verwerfung(f) 23.
Verziehnaht(f) 324.
**Verzierungen(f) 538.**
Vestibularnerv(m) 139.
VHF-Antenne(f) 808.
Viadukt(m) 454.
Vibratohebel(m) 547.
Video-Kreuzschiene(f) 413.
Video-Recorder(m) 401.
Video-Switcher(m) 412, 413, 415.
Videobedientasten(f) 409.
Videofilmdiskette(f) 395.
VIDEOKAMERA(F) 409.
Videokamera(f) 395, 526.
**Videorecorder(m) 411.**
Videorekorder(m) 526.
Videoschalttafel(f) 415.
VIDEOSPIELSYSTEM(N) 699.
Vier-Zehenhuf(m) 99.
Viereck(n) 577.
Viereckregner(m) 264.
Vierer(m) mit Steuermann(m) 632.
Vierer(m) ohne Steuermann(m) 632.
Vierkantstift(m) 231.
Vierkantstopfen(m) 301.
Vierling(m) 695.
VIERMASTBARK(F) 478, 480.
**Viertaktmotor(m) 436.**
Viertelnote(f) 538.
Viertelpause(f) 538.
Viertelstab(m) 199.
Vierundsechzigstelnote(f) 538.
Vierundsechzigstelpause(f) 538.
Vierung(f) 176, 177.
Vierungsturm(m) 176.
Viervierteltakt(m) 537.
Vinyl-Laufsohle(f) 350.
Vinylisolierung(f) 287.
**Violine(f) 544.**
Violine(f) 545.
Violinen(f), erste 556.
Violinen(f), zweite 556.
Violinschlüssel(m) 537.
Virgo 820.
Visier(n) 443, 642, 684, 719, 730, 792.
Visiergestell(n) 595.
Vitrine(f) 227.
Vitrinenschrank(m) 227.
VOGEL(M) 108, 110.
Volant(m) 228.
Volant(n) 224.
voll und bei 629.
**Vollachsel-Unterkleid(n) 345.**
Vollbelastungseinstellschraube(f) 712.
Vollbrillantschliff(m) 362.
**Volleyball(m) 613.**
VOLLEYBALLSPIEL(N) 613.
Vollgeschoß(n) 801.
Vollgummirad(n) 788.
Vollkornbrot(n) 153.
Vollmessingstange(f) 230.
Vollmond(m) 7.
Vollreife(f) 61.
Volute(f) 166, 167, 220.
Vor- und Rücklauf(m) 405.
Vor-Oberbramsegel(n) 481.
Vor-Obermarsegel(n) 481.
Vor-Royalsegel(n) 481.
Vor-Unterbramsegel(n) 481.
Vor-Untermarssegel(n) 481.
Vorbramsaling(f) 479.
Vorbühne(f) 188.
Vordach(n) 685.
Vordachrille(f) 449.
Vorderachse(f) 784.
**Vorderansicht(f) 120, 122, 147.**
Vorderbein(n) 79, 80, 84, 223.
**Vorderbein(n) (Außenseite(f)) 80.**
Vorderbindung(f) 633.
Vorderblatt(n) 353, 355.
Vorderbremse(f) 444.
Vorderdeckel(m) 577.
Vordereckpin(m) 683.
Vorderfeld(n) 614, 617.
Vorderfläche(f) 386.
Vorderflug(m) 792.
Vorderflügel(m) 79, 81.
Vorderfußwurzel(f) 102.
Vordergabel(f) 447.
Vorderkante(f) 636, 638.
Vorderkappe(f), perforierte 355.
**Vorderlade-Geschütz(n) 800.**
**Vorderladung(f) 801.**
Vordermast(m) 743.
**Vorderpfote(f) des Hundes(m) 106.**
Vorderrad(n) 147, 727, 784.
Vorderschaft(m) 798.
Vorderschürze(f) 792.
**Vorderseite(f) 363.**
Vorderseite(f) 179, 322, 324.
Vorderstangentasche(f) 637.
Vorderteil(n) 324, 352, 354.
Vorderwand(f) 616, 617.
Vorderzeug(n) 648.
Vorderzwiesel(m) 649.
Vorfach(n) 672.
Vorfach(n), Angelhaken(m) mit 672.
Vorfahrt(f) 824, 825.
Vorfahrt(f) gewähren 824.
Vorfeld(n) 502.
Vorflügel(m) 499.
Vorfußbindung(f) 642.
Vorfußgummi(n) 633.
Vorfußplatte(f) 642.
Vorfußriemen(m) 633.
Vorhafenwand(f) 492.
**Vorhang(m) 229.**
Vorhang(m) 414.
**Vorhang(m), loser 228.**
Vorhaut(f) 127.
Vorhof(m) 139, 453.
Vorhof(m), linker 124, 125.
Vorhof(m), rechter 124, 125.
Vorholer(m) 802.
Vorholervorderteil(n) 802.
Vorlauf(m) 208, 831.
Vorlauftaste(f) 420.
Vorläutewerk(n) 471.
Vorliek(n) 631.
Vororte(m) 52.
Vorraum(m) 461.
Vorsatzblatt(n) 577.
Vorschaumonitor(m) 415.
Vorschaumonitore(m) 413.
Vorschlag(m) 538.
Vorschneider(m) 281.
Vorsegelschot(n) 628.
Vorsprung(m) 27.
Vorspultaste(f) 411.
Vorstag(m) 628.
Vorstenge-Stagsegel(n) 481.
Vorstopper(m) 601.
Vortasche(f) 381.
vorwärts 624.
vorwärts/rückwärts 272.
Vorzeichentaste(f) 523.
VULKAN(M) 25.
Vulkan(m) 23.
**Vulkan(m) mit Ausbruchstätigkeit(f) 25.**
Vulkan(m), untätiger 24.
vulkanische Asche(f) 25.
vulkanische Bomben(f) 25.
vulkanische Insel(f) 28.
Vulva(f) 118, 128.

## W

Waage(f) 13, 820.
**Waage(f), elektronische 709.**
Waagebalken(m) 541.
Waagschale(f) 708, 709.
Waagschalenhaken(m) 708.
Wabe(f) 82.
**Wabenausschnitt(m) 82.**
Wache(f) 180.
Wachhäuschen(n) 178.
Wachskerze(f), dünne 582.
Wade(f) 117, 119.
Wadenbein(n) 122.
Wadenbeinmuskel(m), kurzer 121.
Wadenbeinmuskel(m), langer 120.
Wadenbeinnerv(m), gemeinsamer 133.
Wadenbeinnerv(m), oberflächlicher 133.
Wadenbeinnerv(m), tiefer 133.
Wadennerv(m) 133.
Wadenstrumpf(m) 325.
**Waffe(f), Teile der 666.**
**Waffeleisen(n) 253.**
WAFFEN(F) IN DER RÖMERZEIT(F) 791.
WAFFEN(F) IN DER STEINZEIT(F) 791.
WAGEN(M) 470.
Wagen(m) 162, 630, 645.
**Wagenanzug(m) 350.**
Wagenausbesserungshalle(f) 465.
Wagendeck(n) 494.
Wagenlaufschild(n) 471.
Wagenradhut(m) 329.
Wagenrücklauftaste(f) 525.
**Wagentür(f) 429.**
WAGENTYPEN(M) 460.
**Wagentypen(m) 425.**
Wagenübergang(m) 461.
WÄHRUNGSABKÜRZUNGEN(F) 832.
Walboot(n) 482.
Wald(m) 27, 52.
Waldhorn(n) 551.
Waldhörner(n) 557.
Walfisch(m) 11, 13.
**Walkman(m)® mit Radioteil(n) 408.**
Walmdach(n) 182.
Walnuß(f) 66.
**Walnuß(f), Längsschnitt(m) 66.**
Walroß(n), Eckzähne(m) 99.
Walze(f) 270, 304, 524, 531, 714.
Walze(f), drehbare 570.
Walzenbefestigung(f) 304.
Walzendrehknopf(m) 525, 531.
Wams(n) 316.
Wand(f) 7.
Wand-Untergurt(m) 441.
**Wandauslaufventil(n) 294.**
Wanddurchlaß(m) 207.
Wandlaterne(f) 235.
Wandleuchte(f) 234.
Wandpfosten(m) 199.
Wandträger(m) 230.
Wandwange(f) 201.
Wange(f) 118, 275, 670.
Wanne(f) 304.
Wannenfüll- und Brausegarnitur(f) 215.
Want(f) 479, 628.
Wantenspanner(m) 630.
Wapitihirsch(m) 105.
Wappen(n) 596.
**Wappenzeichen(n) 819.**
Warenbaum(m) 572.
Warencode(m) 709.
Warenzeichen(n), eingetragenes 831.
Wärmeabgabe(f) an Wasser(n) 766.
Wärmeabstrahler(m) 42.
Wärmedämmung(f) 209.
Wärmedeflektorscheibe(f) 232.
Wärmeerzeugung(f) 766.
Wärmejalousie(f) 43.
**Wärmepumpe(f) 212.**
Wärmepumpe(f) 759.
Wärmetauscher(m) 16, 209, 214, 760, 772.
Warmfront(f) am Boden(m) 39.
Warmhalteplatte(f) 247.
Warmluftauslaß(m) 438.
Warmluftaustritt(m) 206, 207.
Warmluftklappe(f) 204.
**Warmluftsystem(n) mit Zwangsumlauf(m) 206.**
Warmwasseraustritt(m) 297.
Warmwasserbereiter(m) 215.
**Warmwasserheizung(f) mit Zwangsumlauf(m) 208.**
Warmwasserkreis(m) 215.
Warmwassersteigleitung(f) 215.
Warmwasserzulauf(m) 296, 298.
WARN- UND GEBOTSZEICHEN(N) 821.
Warnanzeige(f) 500.
Warnblinklicht(n) 498.
Warngerät(n) 777.
Warnkreuz(n) 471.
Warnleuchte(f) "Tür offen" 431.
Warnleuchten(f) 431.
Warnlinie(f) beim Florettfechten(n) 666.
Warnlinie(f) beim Säbel- und Degenfechten(n) 666.
Wartebereichmarkierung(f) 504.
Wartehäuschen(n) 186.
Wartungsfahrzeug(n) 506.
Wartungskasten(m) 757.
Wartungsschacht(m) 16.
Warzenhaut(f) 85.
Warzenhof(m) 129.
Warzenschwein(n), Hauer(m) 99.
Waschbecken(n) 215, 292.
**Waschen(n) 829.**
Wascherarm(m) 257.
**Wäschetrockner(m) 259.**
Wäschetrockner(m) 829.
Waschküche(f) 194.
**Waschmaschine(f) 258, 298.**
Waschmaschine(f) 215, 298.
Waschplatte(f) 465.
Wasser(n) 485, 762, 763, 767.
Wasser(n) verdampft 766.
Wasser(n), schweres 761.
Wasser(n), sicherstes 488.
Wasser(n), Wärmeabgabe(f) an 766.
Wasser, handwarm 829.
Wasserablauf(m) 399.
Wasserabscheider(m) 734.
Wasserbadtopf(m) 249.
**Wasserball(m) 626.**
WASSERBALLSPIEL(N) 626.
Wasserbehälter(m) 210, 247, 373.

Wasserdruckanzeiger(m) 778.
Wassereinlaß(m) 747.
Wasserfall(m) 27.
Wasserflasche(f) 447.
Wasserglas(n) 237.
Wassergraben(m) 646, 647.
Wasserhahn(m) 292, 778.
Wasserheizkessel(m) 772.
Wasserhindernis(n) 676.
Wasserkanister(m) 690.
Wasserkanone(f) 778.
**Wasserkessel(m) 252.**
Wasserklappe(f) 551.
**Wasserkraftwerk(n) 746, 747.**
**Wasserkreislauf(m) 34.**
Wasserkrug(m) 238.
Wasserlinie(f) 487.
Wassermann(m) 13, 820.
Wassermelone(f) 69.
Wasseroberfläche(f) 624.
**Wasserpumpenzange(f) 278.**
Wasserschlauch(m) 257, 734.
**Wasserski(m) 633.**
WASSERSKI(N) 633.
Wasserstand(m) 210, 247, 755.
Wasserstand(m), höherer 493.
Wasserstand(m), niedrigerer 493.
Wasserstandsanzeiger(m) 256.
Wasserstandsregler(m) 258.
Wassertrense(f) 650.
Wasserturm(m) 465.
Wässerungswanne(f) 399.
Wasserversorgung(f), öffentliche 772.
**Wasservogel(m) 111.**
Wasservogel(m) 111.
Wasservorrat(m) 755.
Wasservorratstank(m) 772.
Wasserwaage(f) 291.
Wasserzähler(m) 215.
**Wasserzeichen(n) 820.**
Wasserzufluß(m) 399.
Wasserzulauf(m) 295.
Wassily-Stuhl(m) 221.
Watstiefel(m) 672.
Wattestäbchen(n) 725.
Wattetupfer(m) 725.
Watvogel(m) 111.
WEBEN(N) 572, 574, 576.
Webkante(f) 566.
Webmustereinstellung(f) 568.
Webnadel(f) 573.
**Webprinzip(n), Schaubild(n) 576.**
**Webschütz(m) 573.**
Wechsel(m) 198.
Wechselanzeige(f) 621.
Wechselraum(m) 612.
Wehrgang(m) 181.
Wehrmauer(f) 180.
weiblich 831.
weibliche Blütenstände(m) 58.
Weiche(f) 464.
**Weiche(f), fernbediente 467.**
**Weiche(f), handbediente 467.**
Weichenantrieb(m) 467.
Weichensignal(n) 467.
Weichenzunge(f) 467.
Weichstrahl(m) 87.
WEICHTIER(N) 92.
**Weichtiere(n), eßbare 93.**
Weideland(n) 148.
Weidenholz(n) 598.
Weidenkorb(m) 635.
**Weinblatt(n) 61.**
Weinblatt(n) 73.
Weinranke(f) 61.
**Weintraube(f) 62.**
Weintraube(f) 61, 62.
Weiselwiege(f) 82.
Weisheitszahn(m) 144.
Weiß(n) 696, 697.
Weißabgleichsensor(m) 409.
weiße Linie(f) 104.
weiße Substanz(f) 135.
Weißes Feuer(n) 488.
Weißkohl(m) 73.
Weißweinglas(n) 237.
**Weitere Symbole(n) 831.**
Weitsprung(m) 655.
Weitwinkelobjektiv(n) 392.
Weizen(m) 152.
**Weizenkorn(n) 152.**
Wellärmchen(n) 543.
Wellbrett(n) 543.
WELLE(F) 30.
Welle(f) 231, 584, 705, 753, 773, 808.
Wellenbasis(f) 30.
Wellenbereichseinstellung(f) 402.
Wellenhöhe(f) 30.
Wellenhose(f) 742.
Wellenlänge(f) 30.
Wellenleiter(m) 415.
Wellenmauer(f) 748.
Wellhornschnecke(f) 83.
Wende(f) 622, 623.
Wende(f) beim Brustschwimmen(n) 622.
Wendeflügel(m) 203.
Wendehebel(m) 639.
Wendekreis(m) des Krebses(m) 3, 47.
Wendekreis(m) des Steinbocks(m) 3, 47.
Wendelhalter(m) 233.
Wendeltreppe(f) 741.
Wenden(n) 824.
Wenden(n) verboten 825.
Wenderichter(m) 621.
Wenderohr(n) 231.
Wendestab(m) 231.
Wendewand(f) 621.
Wendezeiger(m) 639.
Werbetafel(f) 474, 477.
Werfer(m) 597, 599.
Werftkran(m) 490.
**Werkzeug(n) 584, 585, 690.**
WERKZEUGE(N) 275, 276, 278, 280, 282, 284.
**Werkzeuge(n) 587.**
Werkzeugfutter(n) 283.
Werkzeughalter(m) 512.
**Weste(f) 322.**
Weste(f) 315, 317, 338.
**Westen(f) 338.**
Westen(m) 488.
Westliches Kardinalseezeichen(n) 489.
**Wetterhütte(f) 41.**
**Wetterkarte(f) 38.**
Wetterlage(f), gegenwärtige 38.
Wetterradar(m) 498.
WETTERSATELLIT(M) 42.
Wetterschenkel(m) 202, 203.
WETTERSYMBOLE(N), INTERNATIONALE 39.
**Wettkampfbecken(n) 621.**
**Wettkampfparcours(m) 646.**
Wetzstahl(m) 242.
Whipping(n) 678.
Whiskybecher(m) 237.
Wickelbluse(f) 337.
Wickelkleid(n) 333.
Wickelrock(m) 334.
Wickler(m) 369.
Wicklung(f) 670.
Widder(m) 11, 820.
Widerhaken(m) 671.
Widerlager(m) 174, 176.
Widerlager(n) 454, 455, 456.
Widerrist(m) 100, 106.
Widerstand(m), hydraulischer 664.
Widerstandseinstellung(f) 664.
Wiedergabetaste(f) 408, 411, 420.
Wiederholungstasten(f) 405.
Wiederholungszeichen(n) 537.
wiederverwertbar 831.
wiederverwertet 831.
Wiege(f) 720, 721, 802.
Wiegeetikett(n) 709.
Wiegefläche(f) 709.
WIEGEN(N) 708.
Wiegestahl(m) 582.
Wiener Brot(n) 153.
Wiese(f) 149.
Wigwam(m) 165.
Wildwechsel(m) 828.
Wimpel(m) 817.
Wimper(f) 140.
Wimperg(m) 175.
Wimpern(f) 107.
Wimpernkämmchen(n) 367.
Wimpernzange(f) 367.
**Wind(m) 38.**
Wind(m) 629.
Wind(m) querab 629.
Wind(m), raumer 629.
Wind(m), Wirkung(f) 35.
Windabweiser(m) 440.
Windanzeiger(m) 628.
Winde(f) 793.
Windel(f) 349.
Windelhöschen(n) 349.
WINDENERGIE(F) 773, 774.
Windfahne(f) 41.
Windgeschwindigkeit(f) 38.
**Windjacke(f) 320, 321.**
Windkanal(m) 543.
Windlade(f) 543.
**Windmühle(f) 773.**
Windmühlenkappe(f) 773.
Windrichtung(f) 38.
**Windrichtung(f), Messung(f) 41.**
Windsack(m) 536, 817.
Windschutz(m) 14, 406, 634.
Windschutzscheibe(f) 426, 440, 442, 498, 500.
**Windstärke(f), Messung(f) 41.**
Windstärkefiederchen(n) 38.
Windstille(f) 38.
Windung(f) 83, 94.
Windzuleitung(f) 543.
Wing-Forward(m) 606.
Winglet(n) 499.
Winkel(m) 301.
Winkel(m) 45° 301.
Winkel(m), rechter 830.
Winkel(m), spitzer 830.
Winkel(m), stumpfer 830.
Winkelmesser(m) 713.
WINKELMESSUNG(F) 713.
Winkeltisch(m) 521.
Winsch(f) 630.
Winter(m) 8.
Wintersonnenwende(f) 8.
Wipfel(m) 59.
Wirbel(m) 95, 544, 546, 672.
Wirbelkasten(m) 544.
Wirbelkörper(m) 135.
Wirbelsäule(f) 89, 122, 134.
Wischblatt(n) 431.
Wischerachse(f) 431.
Wischerarm(m) 431.
Wischgummi(m) 431.
**wissenschaftliche Bezeichnungen(f) 62, 63, 64, 65.**
**Wochenendkoffer(m) 383.**
Wohnblock(m) 187.
Wohnhaus(n) 148.
WOHNHAUS(N), RÖMISCHES 170.
WOHNHÄUSER(N), TRADITIONELLE 165.
Wohnküche(f) 195.
**Wohnmobil(n) 449.**
Wohnraum(m) 685.
WOHNWAGEN(M) 449.
**Wohnwagen(m) 449.**
Wohnwagen(m) 823.
Wohnzimmer(n) 195.
Woilach(m) 648.
Wok(m) 248.
**Wok-Set(n) 248.**
**Wolfram-Halogenlampe(f) 233.**
Wolframwendel(f) 233.
Wolfssproß(m) 105.
Wolke(f) 36.
WOLKEN(F) 44.
Wolken(f), Art(f) der hohen 38.
Wolken(f), Art(f) der mittelhohen 38.
Wolken(f), Art(f) der tiefen 38.
**Wolken(f), hohe 44.**
**Wolken(f), mittelhohe 44.**
**Wolken(f), tiefe 44.**
**Wolkenhöhe(f), Messung(f) 41.**
Wolkenhöhenmesser(m) 41.
Wolkenkratzer(m) 185.
Wortkorrekturtaste(f) 525.
Wulst(f) 743.
Wulst(m) 433.
Wulstkern(m) 433.
Wundauflage(f), sterile 725.
**Wurfbeispiele(n) 668.**
WÜRFEL(M) 699.
Würfel(m) 697.
Würfel(m), gewöhnlicher 699.
Würfelbecher(m) 697.
Würfelmusterparkett(n) 200.
**Wurfgeräte(n) 658.**
Wurfhöhe(f) 597.
Wurfkreis(m) 654, 655.
Wurflinie(f) 599.
Wurflinienknoten(m) 691.
Wurfmal(n) 597.
**Wurfpfeil(m) 698.**
Wurmfortsatz(m) 131.
Wurzel(f) 70, 143, 144, 240.
Wurzel(f), hintere 135.
Wurzel(f), motorische 135.
Wurzel(f), sensorische 135.
Wurzel(f), vordere 135.
**Wurzelgemüse(n) 71.**
Wurzelhaare(n) 57.
Wurzelhaarzone(f) 59.
Wurzelhaube(f) 57.
Wurzelhaut(f) 144.
Wurzelkanal(m) 144.
Wurzelsystem(n) 57, 61.
WÜSTE(F) 46.
Wüste(f) 45.

## X

X-Band-Antenne(f) 49.
**Xylophon(n) 554.**
Xylophon(n) 556.

## Y

Y-Schlauch(m) 726.
Y-Verbindungsstück(n) 779.
Yardlinie(f) 604.
Yen(m) 832.
Ysop(m) 74.

## Z

Zahl(f) 701.
Zahlenschloß(n) 378.
Zählwerk(n) 403.
Zahn(m) 96, 268, 277, 284, 369.
Zahnbacke(f) 278.
Zahnbein(n) 144.
Zahnbogen(m) 802.
Zahnbogen(m), oberer 142.
Zahnbogen(m), unterer 142.
**Zahnbürste(f) 373.**
Zahnbürste(f) 373.
**Zahnbürste(f), elektrische 373.**
ZÄHNE(M) 144.
Zähne(m) 566.
Zahnfleisch(n) 142, 144.
Zahnpasta(f) 373.
ZAHNPFLEGE(F) 373.
Zahnrad(n) 575.
Zahnrädchen(n) 386.
Zahnscheibe(f) 278.
Zahnschnitt(m) 166, 167.
Zahnseide(f) 373.
Zahnwurzelkanalöffnung(f) 144.
Zange(f) 198, 246.
Zangenwerk(n) 179.
Zäpfchen(n) 141, 142.
Zapfen(m) 58, 225, 385, 571, 575.
Zapfenloch(n) 385.
Zapfhahn(m) 453.
**Zapfsäule(f) 453.**
Zapfsäule(f) 453.
Zapfschlauch(m) 453.
Zapfwelle(f) 156, 159, 162.
Zapfwellenstummel(m) 147.
Zarge(f) 219, 220, 223, 544, 546.
**Zaumzeug(n) 649.**
Zaumzeug(n) 653.
Zaun(m) 148.
Zeh(m) 104, 106, 116, 118.
Zehe(f) 111.
Zehe(f), dritte 108.
Zehe(f), vierte 108.
Zehe(f), zweite 108.
Zehenaufzug(m) 104.
Zehenballen(m) 106, 107.
Zehenendglied(n) 122.
Zehengrundglied(n) 122.
Zehenloch(n) 645.
Zehenschützer(m) 595, 730.
Zehenstrecker(m), kurzer 120.
Zehenstrecker(m), langer 120.
Zehenwand(f) 104.
Zehnerpin(m) 683.
Zehntelsekundenzeiger(m) 706.
**Zeichen(n) 539.**
ZEICHEN(N), ALLGEMEINE 822.
ZEICHEN(N), DIAKRITISCHE 832.
Zeichenkorrekturtaste(f) 525.
Zeichenmaschine(f) 591.
ZEICHNEN(N) 590, 592.
Zeichnen(n) 586.
Zeigefinger(m) 137.
Zeiger(m) 213, 705, 708, 709, 710.
Zeitlupe(f) 411.
ZEITMESSUNG(F) 706.
Zeitnehmer(m) 610, 612, 626, 666, 668, 669.
Zeitnehmer(m), zweiter 626.
Zeitschalter(m) 253.
Zeituhr(f) 252, 430, 585.
Zelle(f) 79, 82, 754, 774.
ZELLE(F), TIERISCHE 115.
Zelle(f), verdeckelte 82.
Zellenring(m) 754.
Zellfunktelefon(n) 417.
Zellfunktelefon(n), mobiles 422.
Zellkern(m) 115, 128, 135.
Zellkörper(m) 135.
Zellwand(f) 115.
**Zeltarten(f) 686.**
Zelte(n) 823.

**Fettgedruckte** Wörter beziehen sich auf eine Illustration; Wörter in GROSSBUCHSTABEN sind Überschriften.

Zelten(n) 823.
Zeltplatz(m) 823.
Zeltspannleine(f) 685.
Zeltstange(f) 686.
Zeltwand(f) 685.
Zement(m) 144.
Zementestrich(m) 200.
Zenit(m) 16.
Zenith S-Band-Antenne(f) 49.
Zentaur(m) 13.
Zentrale(f) 15.
**zentrales Nervensystem(n) 134.**
Zentriereinstellung(f) 529.
Zentrierspitze(f) 281.
Zentriertaste(f) 524.
Zentriol(n) 115.
**Zerkleinern(n) 243.**
zerlappte Projektion(f) 50.
Zero(n) 700, 701.
**Zerreiben(n) 243.**
Zerstäuber(m) 741.
Zerstäuberstift(m) 264.
**Zerstreuungslinsen(f) 722.**
ZETTEN(N) UND WENDEN(N) 159.
**Zetten(n) und Wenden(n) 155.**
Zeugenberg(m) 24, 46.
Zickzackschere(f) 564.
Ziege(f) 150.
Ziegel(m) 169, 170.
Ziegelstein(m) 286.
Ziegelstein(m), feuerfester 585.
Ziehbügel(m) 726.
Ziehhacke(f) 266.
Ziehharmonikafach(f) 378.
Ziel(n) 646.
Zielbahnhof(m) 463.
Zielbälle(m) 673.
ZIELFERNROHR(N) 718.
Zielfernrohr(n) 798.
Zielgebiet(n) 770.
Zielgerade(f) 651.
Zielkugel(f) 682.
Ziellinie(f) 651, 654, 683.
Zielpfosten(m) 654.
**Zielscheibe(f) 684.**
Zier-Steppnaht(f) 323, 350.
Zierbaum(m) 148, 263.
Zierborte(f) 349.
ZIERGARTEN(M) 263.
Ziergarten(m) 193.
Ziernaht(f) 327.
Ziffernblatt(n) 706, 707, 712.
Zifferntaste(f) 523.
**Zigarette(f) 384.**
**Zigarettenpackung(f) 384.**
Zigarettenpapier(n) 384.
Zigarettenspitze(f) 384.
**Zigarre(f) 384.**
Zikade(f) 77.
Ziliarkörper(m) 140.
**Zimmermannshammer(m) 275.**
Zinke(f) 157, 158, 159, 160, 162, 240.
Zinne(f) 181.
Zinnenkranz(m) 181.
Zinnenlücke(f) 181.
Zirbeldrüse(f) 134.
Zirkel(m) 13.
Zirrostratus(m) 44.
Zirrus(m) 44.
Zirruskumulus(m) 44.
**Zither(f) 535.**
Zitrone(f) 65.
Zitronenpresse(f) 243.
Zitronenschaber(m) 242.
**Zitrusfrucht(f), Querschnitt(m) 65.**
ZITRUSFRÜCHTE(F) 65.
**Zitrusfrüchte(f) 65.**
**Zitruspresse(f) 251.**
Zollkontrolle(f) 505.
Zona(f) pellucida 128.
Zone(f), begrenzte 610.
Zone(f), neutrale 603, 605, 608.
Zoomobjektiv(n) 392, 409, 414.
Zopfmuster(n) 567.
Zopfstich(m) 571.
**Zubehör(n) 358, 448, 563, 564, 573, 575, 586, 591, 592, 672.**
Zubehör(n) 563.
**Zubehör(n), fotografisches 393.**
Zubehörfach(n) 568.
Zubehörschuh(m) 391, 409.
Zubehörtasche(f) 684.
Zucchini(f) 69.
Zuchtchampignon(m) 55.
Zuckerdose(f) 238.
Zuckererbsen(f) 72.
**Zuckermais(m) 72.**
Zuckermelone(f) 69.
Zufahrt(f) 193.
Zufahrtsstraße(f) 502.
Zug(m), diagonaler 696.
Zug(m), horizontaler 696.
Zug(m), vertikaler 696.
Zugang(m) 747.
Zugang(m) zum Gleis(n) 463.
Zugangschacht(m) 752.
Zugbrücke(f) 180.
Zügel(m) 109, 651.
Zügelring(m) 650.
Zugentlastungsklemme(f) 309.
Zugfeder(f) 431.
Zuggriff(m) 397.
Zugküche(f) 460.
Zugmaschine(f) 440, 742.
Zugpendel(n) 147.
Zugrichter(m) 621.
Zugriemen(m) 383.
Zugriffsöffnung(f) 529.
Zugrohr(n) 158, 159, 162.
Zugsattelzapfen(m) 441.
Zugschnur(f) 231, 381.
Zugschublade(f) 226.
Zugstange(f) 803.
Zugstangenverschluß(m) 803.
Zugvorhang(m) 229.
Zugwagen(m) 230.
Zulauf(m) 296.
Zulaufverteiler(m) 216.
Zuleitungsdraht(m) 232.
Zuluft(f) 209.
Zuluftkanal(m) 213.
Zündanlage(f) 501.
Zündelektroden(f) 209.
Zünden(n) 436, 437.
Zündergehäuse(n) 804.
Zündgasleitung(f) 297.
Zündhütchen(n) 798, 799.
Zündkabel(n) 435.
**Zündkerze(f) 439.**
Zündkerze(f) 271, 435, 437.
Zündkerzendichtring(m) 439.
Zündkerzengehäuse(n) 439.
Zündknopf(m) 297.
Zündladung(f) 804.
Zündloch(n) 800, 801.
Zündmechanismus(m) 804.
Zündschalter(m) 444, 445.
Zündschloß(n) 430.
Zündschlüssel(m) 271.
Zündtransformator(m) 209.
Zündversteller(m) 435.
Zündverteiler(m) 435.
zunehmender Mond(m) 6.
Zunge(f) 81, 88, 131, 142, 352, 354, 536, 542, 568, 641, 644.
Zunge(f), gespaltene 96.
Zungenmandel(f) 143.
**Zungennadel(f) 568.**
Zungennadel(f) 569.
Zungenpapille(f) 143.
**Zungenpfeife(f) 542.**
Zungenraglan(m) 340.
**Zungenrücken(m) 143.**
Zungenscheide(f) 96.
Zurückhalter(m) 228, 229.
**Zusammentragen(n) 577.**
Zusatzgetriebegehäuse(n) 501.
**Zusatzheizung(f) 211.**
zusätzlicher Video-Switcher(m) 413.
Zusatzsteckdose(f) 310.
Zusatzstecker(m) 255.
Zusatztank(m) 441.
Zuschauergrenze(f) 597.
Zuschauerraum(m) 16, 189.
Zustreicher(m) 158.
Zuwachsstreifen(m) 83, 95.
**Zwangsumlauf(m) 206, 208.**
zwei Dutzend(n) geteilt 701.
Zwei-Zehenhuf(m) 99.
Zweibein(n) 796, 803.
Zweier(m) 632.
Zweier(m) mit Steuermann(m) 632.
Zweier(m) ohne Steuermann(m) 632.
Zweig(m) 57, 59.
Zweihalbetakt(m) 537.
Zweikanalton(m) 413.
**Zweipersonenzelt(n) 685.**
**Zweireiher(m) 322.**
zweireihig 319.
Zweisitzer(m) 221.
Zweispitz(m) 318.
ZWEISTROMTRIEBWERK(N) 501.
**Zweitaktmotor(m) 436.**
zweiter Raum(m) 610.
Zweiter(m) 620.
Zweiunddreißigstelnote(f) 538.
Zweiunddreißigstelpause(f) 538.
Zwerchfell(n) 130.
Zwickel(m) 174, 486.
**Zwiebel(f) 70.**
**Zwiebelgemüse(n) 70.**
Zwillinge(m) 11, 820.
Zwillingswadenmuskel(m) 120, 121.
**Zwinge(f) 282.**
Zwinge(f) 575.
Zwinger(m) 181.
Zwischenfutter(n) 565.
Zwischenknochenmuskel(m) 120.
Zwischenrad(n) 445.
Zwischenraum(m) 537.
Zwischenschiene(f) 467.
Zwischensohle(f) 352.
Zwischensummentaste(f) 523.
Zwölffingerdarm(m) 131.
Zyclorama(n) 414.
Zylinder(m) 291, 295, 328, 370, 436.
**Zylinderdruckpresse(f) 581.**
Zylindergehäuse(n) 290.
Zylinderkopfdeckel(m) 435.
Zylinderprojektion(f) 50.
**Zylinderschloß(n) 290.**
Zypressennadeln(f) 58.
Zytoplasma(n) 115, 128.
Zytoplasmamembran(f) 115.

**Fettgedruckte** Wörter beziehen sich auf eine Illustration; Wörter in GROSSBUCHSTABEN sind Überschriften.

# SPANISH INDEX

# A

a buen viento(m) 629.
a un largo(m) 629.
ábaco(m) 166, 167.
abdomen 108.
abdomen(m) 78, 79, 81, 91, 116, 118.
abdomen(m), recto(m) del 120.
ABEJA(F) 80.
ABEJA(F) DE COLMENA(F) 82.
abertura(f) 671.
abertura(f) con aletilla(f) 324.
abertura(f) de escape(m) 735.
abertura(f) de llenado(m) 493.
abertura(f) de llenado(m) y vaciado(m) 493.
abertura(f) del diafragma(m) 717.
abertura(f) para el brazo(m) 331.
abertura(f) para el cambio(m) de gases(m) 717.
abertura(f) para el sonido(m) 544.
abertura(f) para horquilla(f) de montacargas(m) 470.
abertura(f) trasera central 322.
abertura(f) trasera lateral 322.
aberturas(f) para los nudillos(m) 327.
ABONADO(M) 156.
**abonado(m) 154.**
abrazadera(f) 230, 309, 383, 575, 630, 720, 721.
abrazadera(f) inferior 40.
abrazadera(f) para el papel(m) 531.
abrazadera(f) superior 40.
abrebotellas(m) 244, 688.
abrecartas(f) 515.
**abrelatas(m) 256.**
abrelatas(m) 244, 688.
ABREVIACIONES(M) DE MONEDAS(F), EJEMPLOS 832.
**abrigo(m) 320.**
abrigo(m) 331.
**abrigo(m) con esclavina(f) 330.**
**abrigo(m) corto 330.**
abrigo(m) cruzado 331.
abrigo(m) de jugadores(m) 597.
abrigo(m) de tres cuartos 321.
**abrigos(m) y chaquetas(f) 330.**
ábside(m) 177.
abuhardillado 183.
acabado(m) 586, 692.
acampanado 336.
**acanalador(m) 283.**
acantilado(m) 23, 27, 30.
acceso(m) a los andenes(m) 463.
acceso(m) para minusválidos(m) 822.
**accesorios(m) 260, 358, 448, 563, 573, 575, 586, 591, 592, 672.**
accesorios(m) 684.
ACCESORIOS(M) DE GOLF(M) 676.
**accesorios(m) fotográficos 393.**
ACCESORIOS(M) MUSICALES 539.
**accesorios(m) para cerrar 566.**
**accesorios(m) para el peinado(m) 369.**
**accesorios(m), objetivos(m) 392.**
**accidentales(m) 538.**
acción(f) del viento(m) 35.
acción(f) sobre el ser(m) humano 35.
acción(f) sobre la naturaleza(f) 35.
accionador(m) de presión(f) del oxígeno(m) 512.
acedera(f) 73.
aceite(m) de linaza(f) 592.
aceitera(f) 734.
aceites(m) lubricantes 745.
aceituna(f) 63.
acelerador(m) 272, 444.
**acelga(f) 72.**
acento(m) 539.
acento(m) agudo 832.
acento(m) circunflejo 832.
acento(m) grave 832.
acera(f) 186.
acero(m) 286.
achicoria(f) 73.
aciculada 56.
**acondicionador(m) de aire(m) 214.**
acoplamiento(m) de pedal(m) 542.
acorazonada 56.
**acorde(m) 539.**
**acordeón(m) 536.**
acromión(m) 123.
acrotera(f) 167, 168.
**actinómetro(m) 40.**
actuador(m) 814.
**acuarela(f) y aguazo(m) 588.**
Acuario 13.
Acuario, el Aguador (20 de enero) 820.
acumulación(f) baja de nieve(f) liviana 39.
acumulación(f) baja de nieve(f) pesada 39.
acumulador(m) 769, 777.
adaptador(m) 399.
adaptador(m) al ojo(m) 409.
adaptador(m) de enchufes(m) 374.
adarve(m) cubierto 180.
adición(f) en la memoria(f) 523.
adintelado(m) 174.
admiración(f) 832.
admisión(f) 436, 437.
**adornos(m) 538.**
aduana(f) 491, 505.
aductor(m) del muslo(m) 120.
aductor(m) mayor 121.
AERODESLIZADOR(M) 495.
**aerodeslizador(m) 637.**
AERODESLIZADOR(M) (HOVERCRAFT(M)) 492.
aerofreno(m) 812.
aeroplano(m) 722.
AEROPUERTO(M) 502, 504, 506.
aeropuerto(m) 52.
afilador(m) 242.
afinación(f) 553.
afinador(m) 542.
Africa(f) 21.
afuste(m) 802.
agavilladora(f) 159.
agenda(f) 378, 518.
agenda(f) de caja(f) 518.
agitador(m) de aspas(f) 258.
aglomerado(m) 288.
agua(f) a presión(f) 755.
**agua(f) a presión(f), reactor(m) 762.**
**agua(f) caliente a presión(f), sistema(m) de 208.**
agua(f) de alimentación(f) 763.
agua(f) de deshielo(m) 27.
**agua(f) hirviente, reactor(m) 763.**
agua(f) pesada a presión(f) 761.
agua(f) pesada de enfriamiento(m) 761.
**agua(f) pesada, reactor(m) 761.**
**agua(f), signos(m) 820.**
agua(f)/alcohol(m) 485.
aguacate(m) 68.
aguamarina(f) 363.
aguanieve(f) 39.
aguarrás(m) 592.
aguas(f) seguras 488.
**aguazo(m) y acuarela(f) 588.**
aguijón(m) 81.
Aguila 11.
aguila(f) 819.
**aguja(f) 562.**
aguja(f) 36, 175, 467, 561, 562, 563, 705, 710, 726.
aguja(f) circular 567.
**aguja(f) con lengüeta(f) 568.**
aguja(f) con lengüeta(f) 569.
aguja(f) de cambio(m) 464.
**aguja(f) de control(m) a larga distancia(f) 467.**
aguja(f) de décimas(f) de segundo(m) 706.
aguja(f) del transepto(m) 176.
aguja(f) imantada 719.
aguja(f) indicadora 213, 396.
agujas(f) del abeto(m) 58.
agujas(f) del pino(m) 58.
**agujas(f) para tejer 567.**
**agujas(f), variedades(f) 58.**
agujero(m) 583.
agujero(m) apical 144.
agujero(m) ciego 143, 312.
ahogadero(m) 649.
**ahumador(m) 582.**
aire(m) 437.
AIRE(M) ACONDICIONADO 214.
aire(m) acondicionado 449.
aire(m) acondicionado de tierra(f) 506.
aire(m) caliente 501, 772.
**aire(m) caliente a presión(f), sistema(m) de 206.**
aire(m) comprimido 590.
aire(m) frío 501, 772.
**aire(m), signos(m) 820.**
aislador(m) 439, 757.
aislador(m) de suspensión(f) 756.
aislamiento(m) 209.
aislante(m) 257, 297, 768.
aislante(m) a granel 287.
aislante(m) de cera(f) 293.
aislante(m) de esponja(f) 287.
aislante(m) de espuma(f) 287.
aislante(m) metálico 287.
aislante(m) plástico 312.
aislante(m) premoldeado 287.
aislante(m) vinílico 287.
ajedrea(f) 74.
AJEDREZ(M) 696.
**ajedrez(m), tablero(m) 696.**
ají(m) 69.
ajo(m) 70.
ajustador(m) de altura(f) 641.
ajustador(m) de desenganche(m) automático 641.
ajustador(m) de la bota(f) 641.
ajustador(m) de ranilla(f) 277.
ajuste(f) de imagen(f) 527.
ajuste(m) 525.
ajuste(m) de altura(f) 664.
ajuste(m) de avance(m) del papel(m) 531.
ajuste(m) de elevación(f) 718.
ajuste(m) de la altura(f) del condensador(m) 718.
ajuste(m) de la lente(m) de campo(m) 718.
ajuste(m) de la llama(f) 386.
ajuste(m) de la velocidad(f) del obturador(m) 396.
ajuste(m) de la visualización(f) 420.
ajuste(m) de profundidad(f) 283.
ajuste(m) de resistencia(f) 664.
ajuste(m) del tabulador(m) 525.
ajuste(m) fino de la altura(f) 720, 721.
ajuste(m) fino del acimut(m) 720, 721.
**ala(f) 110.**
ala(f) 78, 108, 328, 329, 380, 499, 511, 637, 638, 670, 812.
ala(f) de la nariz(f) 107.
ala(f) de popa(f) 495.
ala(f) del cuarto(m) 352, 354.
ala(f) delantera 79, 81.
ala(f) delta 637.
ala(f) en delta 499.
ala(f) en flecha(f) 499.
ala(f) recta 499.
ala(f) trapezoidal 499.
ala(f) trasera 79, 81.
ala(f) variable 499.
ala(m) cerrado 603, 605.
ala(m) defensivo derecho 603, 605.
ala(m) defensivo izquierdo 603, 605.
ala(m) delantero 606.
álabe(m) 753.
alamar(m) 320.
alambre(m) 714.
alambre(m) de corriente(f) 232.
alambre(m) del reborde(m) 433.
alambre(m) en tubo(m) 311.
alambre(m) para cortar 584.
alarma(f) 777.
alarma(f) sonora 485.
alas(f) 112.
**alas(f), tarima(f) 787.**
ALAS(F),DIFERENTES FORMAS(F) 499.
albahaca(f) 74.
albanega(f) 174.
ALBAÑIL(M), HERRAMIENTAS(F) DE 291.
albaricoque(m) 63.
albornoz(m) 348.
albúmina(f) 109.
albura(f) 59.
alcachofa(f) 69.
alcachofa(f) de la ducha(f) 292.
alcachofa(f) para verduras(f) 249.
alcantarilla(f) 186.
alcantarilla(f) principal 186.
alce(m) 105.
alcohol(m) para friccionar 725.
aldaba(f) 383.
alerce(m) 58.
alero(m) 611.
alero(m) defensivo 611.
alero(m) derecho 610.
alero(m) izquierdo 610.
alerón(m) 498, 511, 638.
alerón(m) de hipersustentación(f) 812.
alerón(m) estabilizador 636.
aleta(f) 127, 210, 259, 499, 508, 627, 812.
aleta(f) abdominal 86.
aleta(f) anal 87.
aleta(f) caudal 87.
aleta(f) de fuselaje(m) 511.
aleta(f) de la nariz(f) 141.
aleta(f) de penetración(f) superficial 495.
aleta(f) de proa(f) 495.
aleta(f) del borde(m) de fuga(f) 498.
aleta(f) dorsal anterior 86.
aleta(f) dorsal posterior 86.
aleta(f) estabilizador(m) 633.
aleta(f) estabilizadora 496.
aleta(f) fija 814.
aleta(f) hipersustentadora 499.
aleta(f) pectoral 86.
aletilla(f) 324, 326, 339.
alféizar(m) 175, 198, 203.
alfil(m) 696.
alfiler(m) 369, 563.
alfiler(m) de corbata(f) 364.
alfiler(m) imperdible 566.
**alfileres(m) 364.**
**alfiletero(m) 563.**
algodón(m) absorbente 725.
alianza(f) 364.
alicates(m) 311.
**alicates(m) de electricista(m) 311.**
**alicates(m) de extensión(f) 278.**
**alicates(m) de pivote(m) móvil 278.**
**alicates(m) de presión(f) 278.**
alicates(m) para cutícula(f) 365.
alidada(f) 41, 484.
alidada(f) móvil 713.
alimentación(f) de agua(f) 760, 761, 762.
alimentador(m) 532.
**alimentos(m), contaminación(f) en el agua(f) 32.**
**alimentos(m), contaminación(f) en la tierra(f) 32.**
aliviadero(m) 746.
alma(f) 466, 801.
almacén(m) 170.
almacén(m) de combustible(m) nuevo 764.
**almacenamiento(m) de información(f), unidades(f) 526.**
almeja(f) 93.
almeja(f) de concha(f) dura 93.
almena(f) 179, 181.
almendra(f) 63, 66.
almidón(m) 152.
almidón(m), glóbulo(m) de 115.
almocafre(m) 266.
almohada(f) 224.
**almohadilla(f) 570.**
almohadilla(f) 570.
almohadilla(f) digitalizada 526.
alpargata(f) 357.
ALPINISMO(M) 680.
**alpinista(m) 680.**
ALTA VELOCIDAD(F), TREN(M) 458.
Altar 13.
**altavoz(m) 401.**
altavoz(m) 408, 420, 500.
altavoz(m) de comunicación(f) 477.
altavoz(m) para altas frecuencias(f) 401.
altavoz(m) para bajas frecuencias(f) 401.
altavoz(m) para frecuencias(f) intermedias 401.
altavoz(m) para frecuencias(f) medias 16.
alternador(m) 434, 468.
alternador(m) de la turbina(f) 771.
alternador(m) de turbina(f) 806.
altímetro(m) 635, 639.
altímetro(m) de emergencia(f) 500.
alto 824, 825.
alto voltaje(m) 821.
alto(m) de caña(f) 641.
altocúmulos(m) 44.
altostratos(m) 44.
altura(f) 817.
altura(f) de la ola(f) 30.
**altura(f) de las nubes(f), medición(f) 41.**
altura(f) de salto(m) 625.
altura(f) del antepecho(m) 733.
altura(f) del escalón(m) 201.
altura(f) máxima 826, 827.
álula(f) 110.
alvéolo(m) dental 144.
alza(f) 82, 544, 684, 795, 796, 798, 804.
alzada(f) 341.
amanita(f) de las moscas(f) 55.
amanita(f) real 55.
amantillo(m) 478.
amantillo(m) de botavara(f) 478.
**amapola(f) 67.**
amarra(f) 743.
amarre(m) 570, 630.
amatista(f) 363.
América(f) Central 20.
América(f) del Norte 20.
América(f) del Sur 20.
americana(f) 338.

Los términos en **negrita** corresponden a una ilustración; los que aparecen en MAYÚSCULAS indican un título.

**americano, enchufe(m) de tipo(m) 309.**
ametralladora(f) 805.
amígdala(f) 142.
amígdala(f) lingual 143.
amígdala(f) palatina 143.
amortiguador(m) 443, 445.
amortiguador(m) de fieltro(m) 540.
ampliación(f) del voltaje(m) 767.
**ampliadora(f) 399.**
**amplificación(f) de ondas(f) sísmicas 714.**
**amplificador(m) 402.**
amplificador(m) 714.
amplificador(m) de voltaje(m) 755.
**amplificador(m), parte(f) trasera 400.**
ampolla(f) de la trompa(f) uterina 129.
ampolla(f) de vidrio(m) 232.
ampolleta(f) 725.
amurada(f) 478.
anaquel(m) 226, 254.
**anatomía(f) 88.**
ANATOMÍA(F) DE UN ÁRBOL(M) 59.
**anatomía(f) de un hongo(m) 55.**
ANATOMÍA(F) DE UNA FLOR(F) 60.
ANATOMÍA(F) DE UNA PLANTA(F) 57.
anchura(f) de la base(f) 756.
ANCLA(F) 483.
ancla(f) de arado(m) 483.
**ancla(f) de buque(m) 483.**
ancla(f) de cepo(m) 483.
ancla(f) de hongo(m) 483.
ancla(f) flotante 483.
ancla(f) sin cepo(m) 483.
anclaje(m) 456.
**anclas(f), tipos(m) 483.**
anclote(m) 483.
ancóneo(m) 121.
áncora(f) 707.
andador(m) 728.
andamio(m) sobre ruedas(f) 303.
andén(m) 464, 475, 504.
andén(m) de pasajeros(m) 462.
Andrómeda 11.
anemómetro(m) 41, 639.
ANFIBIOS(M) 84.
**anfibios(m) comunes 85.**
ángel(m) de la muerte(f) 55.
ángulo(m) agudo 830.
ángulo(m) horario 14.
ángulo(m) obtuso 830.
ángulo(m) recto 830.
ángulo(m) saliente 178.
ÁNGULOS(M), MEDICIÓN(F) 713.
Anik-E 418.
anilla(f) 230, 660, 706, 709.
anilla(f) de la tuerca(f) 300.
anilla(f) de sujeción(f) 670.
anilla(f) del cordón(m) 229.
anilla(f) guía(f) 670.
anilla(f) para lanzamiento(m) largo 671.
anillas(f) para flexiones(f) 664.
**anillas(m) 660.**
anillo(m) 55, 230, 290, 374, 375, 393, 434, 551, 681, 754.
anillo(m) balancín 485.
anillo(m) de ajuste(m) 276, 304, 548.
anillo(m) de ajuste(m) del enfoque(m) 392.
anillo(m) de articulación(f) 672.
anillo(m) de bloqueo(m) 802.
anillo(m) de carrillera(f) 650.
anillo(m) de cierre(m) 397.
anillo(m) de compromiso(m) 364.
anillo(m) de crecimiento(m) 59.
anillo(m) de enfoque(m) 719.
anillo(m) de graduación(f) 364.
anillo(m) de gravedad(f) 483.
anillo(m) de las riendas(f) 650.
anillo(m) de quijada(f) 650.
anillo(m) de retención(f) 216, 295.
anillo(m) de unión del casco(m) 512.
anillo(m) dióptrico 486.
anillo(m) distribuidor 753.
anillo(m) inferior 753.
anillo(m) movible 14.
anillo(m) ocular 109.
anillo(m) regulador 753.
anillo(m) sellador 741.
anillo(m) sujetador de la empaquetadura(f) 294.
**anillos(m) 364.**
ANIMALES(M) DE LA GRANJA(F) 150.
**anís(m) estrellado 67.**
ano(m) 89, 92, 127, 128, 131.
AÑO(M), ESTACIONES(F) 8.
ánodo(m) 297.
anorak(m) 353.
anotador(m) 610, 621, 668.
Antártida(f) 20.
antebrazo(m) 106, 117, 119.
**antebrazo(m), muleta(f) 728.**
antefijas(f) de la cumbrera(f) 169.
antehélix(m) 139.
antena(f) 16, 43, 78, 79, 80, 81, 91, 408, 427, 498, 508, 613, 805, 810.
antena(f) AM 400.
antena(f) cenit(m) de banda S(f) 49.
antena(f) de banda S(f) 43.
antena(f) de banda S(f) de alta ganancia(f) 42.
antena(f) de banda X(f) 49.
antena(f) de comunicaciones(f) 810.
antena(f) de control(m) a larga distancia(f) 49.
antena(f) de emisión(f) 418.
antena(f) de emisión(f) \ recepción(f) 418.
antena(f) de radar(m) 807, 812.
antena(f) de radio(f) 742, 807.
antena(f) de radio(m) 494, 495, 497, 738.
antena(f) de telecomunicaciones(f) 494, 497, 809.
antena(f) del radar(m) 48.
antena(f) FM 400.
antena(f) múltiple 807.
antena(f) omnidireccional de banda S(f) 42.
antena(f) parabólica 415.
antena(f) regulable 722.
antena(f) UHF 42.
antena(f) VHF 808.
antenas(f) de exploración(f) y rescate(m) 43.
anténula(f) 90.
anteojera(f) 653.
anteojo(m) buscador 720, 721.
anteojo(m) telescópico 484.
anteojos(m) de seguridad(f) 729.
anteojos(m) protectores 308, 729.
antepecho(m) 733.
antepista(f) 683.
antera(f) 60.
anticlinal(m) 737.
antiséptico(m) 725.
antitrago(m) 139.
anulación(f) de la memoria(f) 523.
**anzuelo(m) 671.**
anzuelo(m) 670, 672.
aorta(f) 125, 130.
aorta(f) abdominal 126, 132.
aorta(f) ascendente 124.
aorta(f) descendente 124.
aorta(f) ventral 88.
aorta(f), cayado(m) de la 124, 125, 126.
aovada 56.
apagador(m) 541.
aparador(m) 227, 520.
aparador(m) de escritorio(m) 521.
aparato(m) de navegación(f) aérea 810.
aparato(m) de respiración(f)autónomo 777.
APARATO(M) RESPIRATORIO 130.
APARATOS(M) DE EJERCICIOS(M) 663, 664.
**aparejo(m) 672.**
aparejo(m) de juanete(m) de estay(m) 480.
aparejo(m) de mastelero(m) de estay(m) 480.
**aparejos(m), arboladura(f) 478.**
APAREJOS(M), TIPOS(M) 482.
apéndice(m) 131.
apéndice(m) nasal 112.
**apéndices(m) bucales 81.**
apéndices(m) torácicos 90.
apertura(f) terminal 94.
apertura(f) urogenital 89.
ápice(m) 83, 94, 143, 144.
**apio(m) 72.**
apio(m) nabo 71.
aplanadora(f) 583.
aplicador(m) de esponja(f) 367.
aplicadores(m) de algodón(m) 725.
aplique(m) 234.
apófosis(f) espinosa 135.
apófosis(f) transversa 135.
apogeo(m) de encendido(m) del motor(m) 419.
apogeo(m) de la trayectoria(f) 419.
apoyador(m) 603.
apoyador(m) central 605.
apoyador(m) exterior 603.
apoyador(m) externo derecho 605.
apoyador(m) externo izquierdo 605.
apoyador(m) interior 603.
apoyatura(f) 538.
apoyo(m) de la base(f) 750.
apoyo(m) de la sordina(f) 541.
apoyo(m) del macillo(m) 540, 541.
apoyo(m) del pulgar(m) 726.
apoyo(m) para el mentón(m) 544.
apoyo(m) para el pie(m) 642.
**apuesta(f) americana, distribución(f) 700.**
apuesta(f) de cinco números(m) 700.
apuesta(f) de dos docenas(f) sobre dos columnas(f) 701.
apuesta(f) en cuadro(m) 700, 701.
**apuesta(f) francesa, distribución(f) 701.**
apuesta(f) libre 700, 701.
apuesta(f) sobre dos columnas(f) 700.
apuntador(m) electrónico 414.
apuntalamiento(m) 181.
aquenio(m) 62, 66.
ARADO(M) 156.
**arado(m) 154.**
**arado(m) de vertedera(f) 156.**
arado(m) de vertedera(f) 154.
araña(f) 77.
**araña(f) de luces(f) 236.**
arándano(m) 62.
arándano(m) agrio 62.
arandela(f) 236, 255, 294, 641, 642.
arandela(f) de presión(f) común 278.
arandela(f) de presión(f) con dientes(m) externos 278.
arandela(f) de presión(f) con dientes(m) internos 278.
arandela(f) simple 278.
**arandelas(f) 278.**
árbitro(m) 599, 601, 603, 605, 606, 608, 610, 618, 621, 669.
árbitro(m) auxiliar 612.
árbitro(m) de base(f) meta(f) 597.
árbitro(m) de la defensa(f) 603.
árbitro(m) principal 612, 626.
**árbol(m) 59.**
árbol(m) 712, 753.
**árbol(m) de conexiones(f) 740.**
árbol(m) de conexiones(f) 738, 740.
árbol(m) de la hélice(f) 495.
árbol(m) de levas(f) 434.
árbol(m) de transmisión(f) 508.
árbol(m) del turbocompresor(m) 501.
árbol(m) frutal 149.
árbol(m) ornamental 148, 263.
ÁRBOL(M), ANATOMÍA(F) DE UN 59.
**arboladura(f) y aparejos(m) 478.**
árboles(m) 676.
arborización(f) terminal 135.
arbotante(m) 175, 176, 632.
arbusto(m) 263.
ARCABUZ(M) 795.
arcada(f) 176.
arcada(f) arterial 126.
arcadas(f) sombreadas 172, 173.
arcén(m) 451.
archipielago(m) 51.
archivador(m) colgante 518.
archivador(m) de fichas(f) 517.
archivador(m) lateral 520.
archivador(m) movible 521.
archivador(m) movible con cajones(m) 521.
**archivador(m), gaveta(f) 517.**
archivo(m) acordeón 517.
arcilla(f) de modelar 584.
ARCO(M) 174.
**arco(m) 544, 793.**
arco(m) 14, 281, 455, 793.
arco(m) branquial inferior 87.
arco(m) branquial superior 87.
**arco(m) de competición(f) 684.**
arco(m) de dos articulaciones(f) 455.
arco(m) de elevación 802.
arco(m) de entramado(m) 455.
**arco(m) de medio punto(m) 174.**
arco(m) de tres articulaciones(f) 455.
arco(m) dentario inferior 142.
arco(m) dentario superior 142.
arco(m) fijo 455.
arco(m) iris 36.
arco(m) moderno 793.
arco(m) natural 30.
arco(m) tensor 553.
**arco(m), presa(f) 750.**
**arco(m), puente(m) 455.**
ARCOS(M) Y BALLESTA(F) 793.
**arcos(m), tipos(m) 174.**
**arcos(m), variedades(f) 455.**
área(f) de caída(f) 655.
área(f) de combate(m) 668.
área(f) de descanso(m) 52.
área(f) de gol(m) 612.
área(f) de lixiviación(f) 216.
área(f) de peligro(m) 668.
área(f) de pénalty(m) 601, 607.
área(f) de seguridad(f) 668.
área(f) de servicio(m) 52, 617.
área(f) de trilla(f) 161.
área(f) derecha de recepción(f) de servicio(m) 616.
área(f) grabada 405.
área(f) izquierda de recepción(f) de servicio(m) 616.
área(f) pequeña 601.
área(f)de procesamiento(m) del petróleo 738.
área(m) de control(m) de la cámara(f) 415.
área(m) de mantenimiento(m) 415.
**áreas(f) válidas de tocado(m) 667.**
arena(f) 748.
arenera(f) 469.
areola(f) 129.
arganeo(m) 483.
argolla(f) de izar 483.
argolla(f) de remolque(m) 803.
argolla(f) para tirar 726.
Aries 11.
Aries, el Carnero (21 de marzo) 820.
arista(f) 167.
ARMADURA(F) 792.
armadura(f) 538, 685.
**armadura(f) del techo(m) 199.**
**armario(m) 225.**
armario(m) 522.
armario(m) de secado(m) de negativos(m) 398.
armario(m) de vajilla(f) 227.
armario(m) del lavabo(m) 292.
armario(m) empotrado 194.
armario(m) para el personal(m) 461.
**armas(f) 666.**
ARMAS(F) CORTANTES Y DE ESTOCADA(F) 794.
**armazón(m) 198.**
armazón(m) 157, 204, 209, 225, 235, 256, 258, 259, 302, 304, 382, 554, 572, 635, 768, 773.
armazón(m) de la máscara(f) 595.
armazón(m) de metal(m) 540.
armazón(m) del quemador(m) 689.
armiño(m) 819.
armónica(f) 536.
arnés(m) 635, 636, 637.
**arneses(m) para trotones(m) 652.**
aro(m) 376, 610, 649.
aro(m) de impulso(m) 727.
**arpa(f) 545.**
arpas(f) 556.
arpegio(m) 539.
arpón(m) submarino 627.
**arquero(m) 684.**
arquitrabe(m) 166, 168.
arranque(m) 272.
arriate(m) 263.
arroz(m) 152.
arteria(f) axilar 126.
arteria(f) braquial 126.
arteria(f) carótida primitiva 126.
arteria(f) femoral 126.
arteria(f) ilíaca(f) común 126, 132.
arteria(f) ilíaca(f) interna 124, 126, 132.
arteria(f) mesentérica inferior 132.
arteria(f) mesentérica superior 126, 132.
arteria(f) pulmonar 125, 126, 130.
arteria(f) renal 126, 132.
arteria(f) subclavia 126.
arteria(f) tibial anterior 126.
Artico(m) 20.
articulación(f) 431, 670, 675.
ARTÍCULOS(M) DE ESCRITORIO(M) 515, 516, 518.
arzón(m) 649, 661.
arzón(m) de amarre(m) 637.
as(m) 695.
as(m) de guía(f) 691.
as(m) de guía(f) de eslinga(f) doble 691.
asa(f) 204, 224, 250, 251, 252, 253, 254, 255, 256, 260, 265, 277, 283, 284, 378, 380, 382, 383, 408, 643, 671.
asa(f) de la barquilla(f) 635.
asa(f) de levantamiento(m) 803.
asa(f) extensible 378.
asadores(m) 248.
ascensión(f) recta 3.

Los términos en **negrita** corresponden a una ilustración; los que aparecen en MAYÚSCULAS indican un título.

ascensor(m) 15, 190, 811.
ascensor(m) para el decorado(m) 188.
asfalto(m) 745.
Asia(f) 21.
asidera(f) 429, 440, 449.
asidera(f) de la rienda(f) 652.
asidero(m) 461, 468, 728, 779.
asidero(m) horizontal 470.
asidero(m) lateral 477.
asidero(m) vertical 477.
asiento(m) 220, 223, 292, 293, 428, 445, 450, 584, 639, 652, 664, 727.
asiento(m) ajustable 460.
asiento(m) de corredera(f) 664.
asiento(m) de eyección(f) 813.
asiento(m) de la válvula(f) 294.
asiento(m) del capitán(m) 500.
asiento(m) del comandante(m) 805.
asiento(m) del copiloto(m) 500.
asiento(m) del piloto(m) 805.
asiento(m) del tapón(m) 293.
asiento(m) del teclado(m) 540.
asiento(m) doble 477.
asiento(m) individual 477.
**asiento(m) reclinable 428.**
**asiento(m) trasero 428.**
ASIENTOS(M) 222.
asistente(m) del guionista(m) 412.
aspa(f) 214, 773, 774.
aspillera(f) 181.
**aspirador(m) 260.**
aspirador(m) de aire(m) 209.
**aspirador(m) manual 260.**
aspirina(f) 725.
asta(f) 105, 385, 698, 817.
astada 56.
astenosfera(f) 22.
asterisco(m) 832.
astil(m) 708.
**astil(m), balanza(f) 708.**
astrágalo(m) 123, 167, 800.
atacador(m) 801.
atacante(m) 611.
**ataque(m) 603, 605.**
**aterrizaje(m) y despegue(m), pista(f) 504.**
ATHLETISMO(M) DE CAMPO(M) Y PISTA(F) 658.
atizador(m) 205.
atlas(m) 102, 123.
ATLETISMO(M) DE CAMPO(M) Y PISTA(F) 656.
ATMÓSFERA TERRESTRE, CORTE(M) 19.
atmósfera(f) 22, 31.
atolón(m) 28.
**atril(m) 539.**
atril(m) 542, 555.
atrio(m) 170.
aurícula(f) 81.
aurícula(f) derecha 124, 125.
aurícula(f) izquierda 124, 125.
auricular(m) 406, 420, 422, 726.
AURICULARES(M) 406.
auriculares(m) 408.
aurora(f) boreal 19.
Australia(f) 21.
autobús(m) 190.
autodefensa(f) antimisil 808.
**automático(m) 566.**
AUTOMÓVIL(M) 425, 426, 428, 430, 432, 434, 438.
autopista(f) 52, 184, 452.
AUXILIARES(M) ORTOPÉDICOS PARA CAMINAR 728.
AUXILIOS(M), BOTIQUÍN(M) PRIMEROS 725.
avambrazo(m) 792.
**avancarga(f), cañón(m) 800.**
avance rápido 831.
avance(m) rápido 411.
Ave del Paraíso 13.
AVE(F) 108, 110.
ave(f) acuática 111.
ave(f) de rapiña 111.
ave(f) granívora 111.
ave(f) insectívora 111.
ave(f) zancuda 111.
avellana(f) 66.
**avellana(f), corte(m) de una 66.**
avellanadora(f) de tubos(m) 299.
avena(f) 152.
avenida(f) 52, 184.
**aventador(m) de forraje(m) 162.**
aventador(m) de frorraje(m) 155.
**aves(f) acuáticas 111.**
**aves(f) de rapiña 111.**
**aves(f) trepadoras 111.**
AVIÓN(M) DE COMBATE(M) 812.
avión(m) nodriza(f) 813.
AVIÓN(M) TURBORREACTOR DE PASAJEROS(M) 498.
axila(f) 116, 118.
axila(f) de la hoja(f) 56.
axiómetro(m) 628.
axis(m) 123.
axón(m) 135.
ayudante(m) del cronometrador(m) 626.
azada(f) 266.
azada(f) de doble filo(m) 266.
azadón(m) 267.
azadón(m) rotatorio 157.
azucarero(m) 238.
azuela(f) para desbastar 587.
azur(m) 819.

## B

babera(f) 792.
babero(m) 349.
babilla(f) 101.
babor(m) 488, 489, 497.
BACKGAMMON(M) 697.
badén(m) 827.
BÁDMINTON(M) 618.
baguette(f) 362.
bahía(f) 7, 51.
bajada(f) de aguas(f) 197.
bajada(f) pronunciada 826, 827.
bajo 343.
bala(f) 795, 798, 801.
bala(f) antitanque 804.
bala(f) con perdigones(m) 801.
bala(f) de barra(f) 801.
bala(f) de plomo(m) 804.
bala(f) sólida 801.
**balalaika(f) 535.**
balancín(m) 230, 435.
**balanza(f) de astil(m) 708.**
**balanza(f) de precisión(f) 709.**
**balanza(f) de Roberval 708.**
balanza(f) para cartas(f) 516.
balasto(m) 466.
balaustrada(f) 194.
balaustre(m) 201.
balcón(m) 189, 486.
baldosa(f) 263, 286.
Ballena 11, 13.
ballena(f) 324.
ballenera(f) 482.
**ballesta(f) 793.**
BALLESTA(F) Y ARCOS(M) 793.
**balón(m) 600, 611, 626.**
**balón(m) de baloncesto(m) 610.**
**balón(m) de balonmano(m) 612.**
**balón(m) de fútbol(m) americano 602.**
BALÓN(M) VOLEA 613.
**balón(m) volea 613.**
BALONCESTO(M) 610.
BALONCESTO(M) DE MUJERES(F) 611.
BALONMANO(M) 612.
balsa(f) salvavidas 492.
balso(m) 691.
bambalinas(f) 188.
banco(f) 222.
banco(m) 222, 475, 663.
banco(m) de arena(f) 30.
banco(m) escalera(f) 222.
banda(f) 479, 601, 604, 607, 610, 611, 612, 613, 618, 636.
banda(f) acolchada 406.
banda(f) central 700.
banda(f) de ajuste(m) 406, 408.
banda(f) de arquitrabe(m) 166.
banda(f) de cabeza(f) 642.
banda(f) de carga(f) 733.
banda(f) de desgarre(m) 634.
banda(f) de goma(f) 674.
banda(f) de identificación(f) técnica 405.
banda(f) de jazz(m) 558.
banda(f) de la cabecera(f) 675.
banda(f) de placa(f) negativa 439.
banda(f) de placa(f) positiva 439.
banda(f) de rodamiento(m) 147.
banda(f) de suspensión(f) 729.
banda(f) de tensión(f) 40.
banda(f) de ventilación(f) 798.
banda(f) elástica 323.
banda(f) grabada 404.
banda(f) lateral de la red(f) 613.
banda(f) lateral protectora 441.
banda(f) para dobles(m) 614.
banda(f) protectora 433, 441.
banda(f) reflectora 730, 777.
banda(f) transportadora 733, 735.
bandeja(f) 210, 383.
bandeja(f) de arrastre(m) de la producción(f) 532.
bandeja(f) de correspondencia(f) 517.
bandeja(f) de pago(m) 702.
bandeja(f) de pintura(f) 304.
bandeja(f) para canapés(m) 238.
bandeja(f) para cosméticos(m) 382.
bandeja(f) para cubitos(m) de hielo(m) 254.
bandeja(f) para el papel(m) 521.
bandeja(f) para herramientas(f) 302.
bandeja(f) para hornear galletas(f) 245.
bandeja(f) para recoger el papel(m) 521.
bandejas(f) para el papel(m) 532.
bandera roja(f) 668.
bandera(f) 606.
bandera(f) azul 626.
bandera(f) blanca 626.
bandera(f) con Schwenkel 817.
bandera(f) cuadrada 817.
bandera(f) de dos puntas(f) 817.
bandera(f) de dos puntas(f) y lengua(f) 817.
bandera(f) rectangular 817.
bandera(f) roja 626.
**bandera(f), partes(f) 817.**
**banderas(f), formas(f) 817.**
banderín(m) 817.
banderín(m) de córner(m) 601.
banderín(m) de esquina(f) 607.
banderín(m) doble 817.
banderola(f) 817.
bandolera(f) 375, 380, 382.
bañera(f) 194, 215, 292, 628.
**banjo(m) 535.**
baño(m) 195.
baño(m) de fijación(f) 399.
baño(m) de pare(m) 399.
baño(m) de revelado(m) 399.
**baño(m), báscula(f) 709.**
**baños(m) de revelado(m) 399.**
banquillo(m) 669.
banquillo(m) de castigo 608.
banquillo(m) de jugadores(m) 604, 612, 613.
banquillo(m) de los jugadores(m) 608, 610.
banquillo(m) del entrenador(m) 597.
banquillo(m) del equipo(m) 626.
BARAJA(F) 695.
baranda(f) 675.
barandilla(f) 201, 302, 457.
barba(f) 110, 385.
barbacana(f) 180.
barbada(f) 649.
barbecho(m) 148.
barbilla(f) 110, 671.
barbiquejo(m) 479.
barbote(m) 792.
BARCO(M) DE VELA(F) DE CUATRO PALOS(M) 478, 480.
barco(m) perforador 739.
**barco(m) petrolero 742.**
barjana(f) 46.
barniz(m) 592.
barógrafo(m) 41.
barómetro(m) de mercurio(m) 41.
**barómetro(m)/termómetro(m) 710.**
**barquilla(f) 635.**
barquilla(f) 634.
barquilla(f) de mimbre(m) 635.
**barquillero(m) eléctrico 253.**
barra(f) 30, 104, 156, 230, 271, 376, 446, 554, 602, 633, 659, 662, 663, 665, 697, 705.
barra(f) acanalada 230.
barra(f) alta 659.
barra(f) antivibración 272.
barra(f) baja 659.
barra(f) colectora 747.
barra(f) colectora de información(f) 528, 531.
barra(f) colectora del disco(m) duro 528.
barra(f) de acero(m) 660.
barra(f) de arrastre(m) 784.
barra(f) de compás(m) 537.
**barra(f) de cortina(f) 230.**
barra(f) de cuchillas(f) 160.
barra(f) de dirección(f) 637.
**barra(f) de equilibrio(m) 659.**
**barra(f) de escotas(f) 630.**
barra(f) de extensión(f) de piernas(f) 663.
barra(f) de flexión(f) de piernas(f) 663.
barra(f) de la aguja(f) 562.
barra(f) de madera(f) 661.
barra(f) de maniobra(f) 162.
barra(f) de operación(f) 796.
barra(f) de pan(m) 153.
barra(f) de percusión(f) 780.
barra(f) de rastrillos(m) 159.
barra(f) de remolque(m) 158, 159, 162, 449, 506.
barra(f) de repetición(f) 537.
barra(f) de salida(f) de espalda(f) 621.
**barra(f) de torsión(f) 665.**
barra(f) de tracción(f) 803.
barra(f) de triceps(m) 663.
barra(f) de varilla(f) doble 230.
barra(f) de varilla(f) simple 230.
barra(f) del prensatelas(m) 562.
barra(f) deslizable 568.
barra(f) diluida al agua(f) 583.
barra(f) espaciadora 525, 530.
barra(f) estabilizadora 788.
**barra(f) fija 660.**
barra(f) guía(f) 272.
barra(f) inferior 231.
barra(f) lateral 663.
barra(f) lisa 230.
barra(f) ómnibus de carga(f) 312.
barra(f) ómnibus neutra/a tierra(f) 312.
barra(f) sujetadora 553.
barra(f) tensora 569.
barra(f) transversal 637.
**barras(f) asimétricas 659.**
**barras(f) paralelas 661.**
barrena(f) 734, 735, 737.
barrera(f) 462.
barrera(f) del paso(m) a nivel(m) 471.
**barriquete(m) 583.**
basamento(m) 166, 168.
**báscula(f) de baño(m) 709.**
báscula(f) de cocina(f) 244.
**báscula(f) electrónica 709.**
**báscula(f) romana 708.**
base(f) 72, 166, 236, 252, 277, 283, 368, 404, 410, 453, 466, 471, 578, 579, 661, 708, 712, 774, 817.
base(f) de cemento(m) 200, 714.
**base(f) de cemento(m), parqué(m) sobre 200.**
base(f) de la bombilla(f) 486.
base(f) de la espiga(f) 294.
base(f) de la ola(f) 30.
base(f) de lanzamiento(m) 597.
base(f) del cargador(m) 797.
base(f) del hogar(m) 204.
base(f) del plato(m) 404.
base(f) del respaldo(m) 220.
base(f) del telescopio(m) 14.
base(f) del tubo(m) 232.
base(f) exterior 697.
base(f) fija 282.
base(f) giratoria 282.
base(f) interior 697.
base(f) líquida 366.
base(f) meta(f) 597.
base(m) del tronco(m) 59.
**bastidor(m) 571.**
bastidor(m) 282, 378, 443, 484, 583, 660.
**bastidor(m) de coser 578.**
bastidor(m) de los rodillos(m) 783.
bastidores(m) 189.
bastión(m) 179.
bastón(m) 375.
bastón(m) cuadrangular 728.
bastón(m) de esquí(m) 640, 642.
**bastón(m) del jugador(m) 609.**
bastón(m) del portero(m) 609.
bastón(m) inglés 728.
bastón(m) ligero 375.
bastón(m) ortopédico 728.
bastón(m) para caminar 728.
**bastones(m) 677, 728.**
BASTONES(M) Y PARAGUAS(M) 375.
basurero(m) 733, 734.
batán(m) 572.
batata(f) 71.
**bate(m) 596.**
bate(m) 595.
batea(f) 226.
**bateador(m) 595.**
bateador(m) 597, 599.
**batería(f) 439.**
batería(f) 468, 528, 814.
batidor(m) 156, 245.
batidor(m) mecánico 245.
**batidora(f) 250.**
**batidora(f) de brazo(m) 250.**
**batidora(f) de mano(f) 250.**
**batidora(f) de mesa(f) 250.**
batiente(m) 203.
batímetro(m) (medidor(m)) de profundidad(f) 627.
**baúl(m) 383.**
baúl(m) 226.

bauprés(m) 479.
baya(f) 105.
**baya(f), corte(m) de una 62.**
BAYAS(F), FRUTOS(M) CARNOSOS 62.
**bayas(f), principales variedades(f) 62.**
bayoneta(f) con empuñadura(f) 794.
bayoneta(f) de cubo(m) 794.
bayoneta(f) de mango(m) 794.
bayoneta(f) integral 794.
bazo(m) 88, 124.
BAZUCA(F) 804.
becuadro(m) 538.
BÉISBOL(M) 595, 596.
**béisbol(m) 596.**
belfo(m) 100.
belfos(m) 106.
bemol(m) 538.
berberecho(m) 93.
**berbiquí(m) 281.**
berenjena(f) 69.
bergantín(m) 482.
bergantín(m) goleta(f) 482.
berma(f) 748.
bermudas(m) 336.
berro(m) 73.
Berta 342.
**besuguera(f) 248.**
betún(m) 358.
bíceps(m) braquial 120.
bíceps(m) crural 121.
BICICLETA(F) 446, 448.
**bicicleta(f) estática 664.**
bicornio(m) 318.
bidé(m) 292.
bidentada 56.
biela(f) 434, 436.
bigotes(m) 107.
BILLAR(M) 673.
**billar(m) inglés 673.**
BILLAR(M) INGLÉS Y SNOOKER(M) 674.
billetera(f) 379.
binóculos(m) de tijera(f) 377.
**biología(f) 831.**
biombo(m) 520.
biombo(m) para soldar 308.
**biosfera(f), estructura(f) 31.**
**bióxido(m) de carbono(m), reactor(m) 760.**
bípode(m) 796, 803.
**birimbao(m) 536.**
bisagra(f) 202, 203, 225, 253, 257, 378, 382, 404, 429, 585, 719.
bisel(m) 542, 726.
bita(f) 743.
bizna(f) 66.
blanca(f) 695, 697.
blanca(f) doble 695.
blanca(m) (itad(f)) 538.
blancas(f) 696.
**blanco(m) 684.**
blanco(m) 698.
blastodisco(m) 109.
blindaje(m) 805.
bloque(m) 542, 656.
bloque(m) corredizo 476.
bloque(m) de cierre(m) de la recámara(f) 798, 802.
bloque(m) de cierre(m) de recámara(f) 799.
bloque(m) de contención(f) 765.
bloque(m) de hormigón(m) 286.
bloque(m) de madera(f) grabado 581.
bloque(m) de madera(f) para grabar 581.
bloque(m) de salida(f) 656.
bloque(m) del motor(m) 435.
bloqueo(m) de los cimientos(m) 751.
bloqueo(m) del ajuste(m) de la altura(f) 720, 721.
bloqueo(m) del ajuste(m) del acimut(m) 720, 721.
blusa(f) caracó 316.
blusa(f) cruzada 337.
**blusas(f) 337.**
**blusón(m) 337.**
blusón(m) con aletilla(f) 337.
bob(m) 643.
bobina(f) 670, 671, 714.
bobina(f) de corriente(f) 712.
bobina(f) de tensión(f) 712.
bobina(f) móvil 406.
**bobinas(f) 562.**
BOBSLEIGH(M) 643.
**boca(f) 142.**
boca(f) 83, 84, 92, 118, 282, 542, 650, 797, 798, 799, 800, 803.
boca(f) de acceso(m) 186, 741, 742, 743.
boca(f) de agua(f) 778, 779.
boca(f) de agua(f) para incendios(m) 186.
boca(f) de agua(f), llave(f) 779.
boca(f) de agua(f), separador(m) 779.
boca(f) de aspiración(f) de aire(m) 493.
boca(f) de pozo(m) 736.
boca(f) del tanque(m) de combustible(m) 271.
boca(f) para la manguera(f) 264.
bocado(m) 648.
**bocado(m) acodado 650.**
**bocado(m) acodado elástico 650.**
**bocado(m) articulado 650.**
bocado(m) articulado 650.
**bocado(m) con la barbada(f) 650.**
**bocado(m) corredizo 650.**
**bocado(m) de codo(m) militar 650.**
**bocado(m) de quijada(f) acodado 650.**
**bocado(m) ovoide acodado 650.**
BOCADOS(M) 650.
bocal(m) 548.
bocel(m) 166, 167.
bocel(m) intermedio 167.
bocha(f) 682.
bocina(f) 779.
bocina(f) de aire(m) 440.
bodega(f) de contenedores(m) 495.
bodega(f) de equipaje(m) 499, 508.
body(m) 353.
bogie(m) 645.
boina(f) 329.
bol(m) 251.
bol(m) mezclador 250.
bol(m) para ensalada(f) 238.
bol(m) para sopa(f) 238.
**bola(f) 683.**
bola(f) 275, 294, 682, 683.
bola(f) amarilla 673.
bola(f) azul 673.
bola(f) blanca 673.
bola(f) café 673.
bola(f) de corcho(m) 596.
bola(f) de hilo(m) 596.
bola(f) de marfil(m) 701.
bola(f) de rastreo(m) 526.
bola(f) de rodamiento(m) 389.
bola(f) negra 673.
bola(f) pinta 673.
bola(f) roja 673.
bola(f) rosa 673.
bola(f) verde 673.
bolas(f) numeradas 673.
bolas(f) rojas 673.
**bolera(f) en el césped(m) 682.**
bolero(m) 338.
bolero(m) con botones(m) 338.
boles(m) para batir 245.
boleto(m) 55.
boliche(m) 682.
**bolígrafo(m) 389.**
bolígrafo(m) 515.
**bolillo(m) 570.**
bolillo(m) 570.
bolina(f) 629.
bolo(m) 683.
bolo(m) chico 683.
bolo(m) cilíndrico 683.
bolo(m) delantero 683.
bolo(m) pequeño 683.
**bolos(m), disposición(f) de los 683.**
BOLOS(M), JUEGO(M) DE 683.
**bolos(m), tipos(m) de 683.**
bolsa(f) 448.
**bolsa(f) de cordones(m) 381.**
bolsa(f) de cuero(m) 523.
**bolsa(f) de golf(m) 679.**
bolsa(f) de paja(f) 380.
bolsa(f) de parche(m) con cartera(f) 339.
**bolsa(f) para trajes(m) 382.**
bolsa(f) portabebé(m) 349.
BOLSAS(F) DE MANO(F) 380.
bolsillo(m) 326, 378, 673, 674, 675, 679.
bolsillo(m) con cartera(f) 320, 322.
bolsillo(m) de fuelle(m) 338.
bolsillo(m) de ojal(m) 321, 322, 330.
bolsillo(m) de parche(m) 320, 322, 350.
bolsillo(m) de ribete(m) 322.
bolsillo(m) de ribete(m) ancho 319, 330.
bolsillo(m) del cambio(m) 322.
bolsillo(m) delantero 323, 378.
bolsillo(m) disimulado 330, 339.
bolsillo(m) exterior 381, 382.
bolsillo(m) lateral 429.
bolsillo(m) secreto 379.
bolsillo(m) simulado 330.
bolsillo(m) superior 320, 324.
bolsillo(m) trasero 323.
bolsillo(m) vertical 316.
**bolsillo(m), calculadora(f) 523.**
**bolsillo(m), tipos(m) de 339.**
bolsita(f) de cordones(m) 380.
**bolso(m) 380.**
**bolso(m) clásico 380.**
**bolso(m) de acordeón(m) 380.**
bolso(m) de la compra(f) 381.
bolso(m) de vestir 381.
**bolso(m) de viaje(m) 382.**
bolso(m) de viaje(m) 381.
bolso(m) interior 383.
bolso(m) manguito(m) 381.
bomba(f) 257, 258, 689, 761, 762.
bomba(f) de aire(m) 446.
bomba(f) de aire(m) comprimido 627.
bomba(f) de circulación(f) 208, 763, 772.
bomba(f) de desagüe(m) 771.
bomba(f) de petróleo(m) 209.
bomba(f) para lodos(m) 737.
BOMBA(F) TIPO(M) PEDESTAL(M) PARA SUMIDERO(M) 216.
bomba(f) transportadora de calor(m) 759.
**bomba(f), camión(m) 778.**
bombachos(m) 336.
bombardino(m) 551.
bombas(f) volcánicas 25.
**bombero(m) 777.**
**bombero(m), casco(m) 777.**
bombero(m), hacha(f) 781.
BOMBEROS(M), COCHE(M) 778, 780.
bombilla(f) 233, 310.
bombilla(f) de bayoneta(f) 232.
bombilla(f) de flash(m) 393.
bombilla(f) de rosca(f) 232.
**bombilla(f) económica 233.**
**bombilla(f) incandescente 232.**
bombilla(f) incandescente 486.
bombilla(f) reflectora 777.
bombo(m) 552, 557.
bombona(f) de gas(m) 299, 307, 689.
boquilla(f) 209, 264, 265, 291, 301, 304, 306, 384, 385, 548, 550, 627, 778.
boquilla(f) de corte(m) 306.
boquilla(f) de llenado(m) 256.
boquilla(f) de reducir 301.
boquilla(f) de reducir con cabeza(f) hexagonal 301.
boquilla(f) del soplete(m) 299, 307.
boquilla(f) para concentrar la llama(f) 307.
boquilla(f) para expandir la llama(f) 307.
boquilla(f) para pisos(m) y alfombras(f) 260.
boquilla(f) para tapicería(f) 260.
boquilla(f) pulverizadora 264.
boquilla(f) reducidora 746, 747.
boquilla(f) reducidora(f) 757.
boquilla(f) rinconera 260.
boquilla(f) rociadora 741.
BORDADO(M) 571.
bordado(m) plano 571.
**bordados(m) planos 571.**
borde(m) 57, 255, 627.
borde(m) crenulado 95.
borde(m) de ataque(m) 499, 636, 638.
borde(m) de fuga(f) 498.
borde(m) de la cubeta(f) 258.
borde(m) de la punta(f) 281.
borde(m) de salida(f) 636, 638.
borde(m) del andén(m) 462, 475.
borde(m) del lomo(m) 281.
borde(m) del manto(m) 92.
borde(m) externo 104.
borde(m) interno 104.
borde(m) marginal 638.
**bordes(m), podadora(f) 271.**
bordillo(m) 263.
borla(f) 229, 231, 366.
borne(m) 439.
borne(m) de enlace(m) 312.
borne(m) negativo 439.
borne(m) positivo 439.
borraja(f) 74.
borrasca(f) 39.
borrén(m) 649.
borrén(m) trasero 649.
bosque(m) 27.
bosques(m) 52.
bota(f) 356, 600, 609, 627, 635, 640, 642, 644, 645.
bota(f) alpina 680.
bota(f) de la aleta(f) 627.
bota(f) de la corona(f) del casco(m) 653.
bota(f) de medio muslo(m) 357.
bota(f) de montar 648.
bota(f) de salto(m) 644.
**bota(f) de seguridad(f) 730.**
bota(f) de trabajo(m) 355.
bota(f) del pie(m) delantero 633.
bota(f) interior 641, 645.
botafuego(m) 801.
botaguas(f) 202, 203, 205.
botalón(m) 628.
botas(f) altas 672.
botas(f) de caucho(m) 777.
**botas(f) para esquiar 641.**
botavara(f) 478, 628, 631.
botavara(f) de cangreja(f) 478.
bote(m) de a ocho (con timonel(m)) 632.
bote(m) salvavidas 478, 494, 496, 738.
botella(f) 447.
botín(m) 357.
botina(f) 354.
BOTIQUÍN(M) DE PRIMEROS AUXILIOS(M) 725.
botón(m) 232, 324, 326, 530, 536, 544, 666.
botón(m) de acercamiento(m) 409.
botón(m) de acoplamiento(m) 542.
botón(m) de ajuste(m) fino 718.
botón(m) de ajuste(m) grueso 718.
botón(m) de apagado(m) 272.
botón(m) de avance(m) rápido 403, 411, 420.
botón(m) de bloqueo(m) 711.
botón(m) de cierre(m) 260.
botón(m) de control(m) 255.
botón(m) de control(m) del compartimiento(m) del disco(m) 405.
botón(m) de encendido(m) 402, 410, 420.
botón(m) de encendido(m) TV 411.
botón(m) de encendido(m) VCR 411.
botón(m) de enfoque(m) 720, 721.
botón(m) de enfoque(m) manual 397.
botón(m) de expulsión(f) 403.
botón(m) de eyección(f) de la casete(f) 409.
botón(m) de fantasía(f) 566.
botón(m) de fijación(f) del nivel(m) principal 713.
botón(m) de fuerte luminosidad(f) 396.
botón(m) de funcionamiento(m) 408, 699.
botón(m) de funcionamiento(m) del zoom(m) 409.
botón(m) de grabación(f) 411, 420.
botón(m) de grabación(f) silenciosa 403.
botón(m) de iluminación(f) de la pantalla(f) 396.
botón(m) de inicio(m) de grabación(f) 403.
botón(m) de inicio(m) de marcha(f) 706.
botón(m) de inicio(m) del contador(m) 706, 711.
botón(m) de la culata(f) 800.
botón(m) de la llave(f) 549.
botón(m) de la memoria(f) 405.
botón(m) de lectura(f) 411.
botón(m) de llamado(m) de memoria(f) 396.
botón(m) de luminosidad(f) media 396.
botón(m) de madera(f) 320.
botón(m) de medición(f) 396.
botón(m) de memoria(f) 396, 402, 420.
botón(m) de nivel(m) de grabación(f) 403.
botón(m) de parada(f) 706.
botón(m) de pare(m) 411.
botón(m) de paro(m) 403, 411, 420.
botón(m) de pausa(f) 403.
botón(m) de presión(f) 375, 389, 397.
botón(m) de puntada(f) 561.
botón(m) de rebobinado(m) 403, 408, 411, 420.
botón(m) de rebobinado(m) automático 408.
botón(m) de rebobinado(m) rápido 408.
botón(m) de registro(m) 542.
botón(m) de reproducción(f) 403, 420.
botón(m) de seguridad(f) 297.

Los términos en **negrita** corresponden a una ilustración; los que aparecen en MAYÚSCULAS indican un título.

botón(m) de selección(f) de lengua(f) 422.
botón(m) de sintonización(f) 408.
botón(m) de sombra(f) 396.
botón(m) de velocidades(f) 250.
botón(m) de visionamiento(m) preliminar de profundidad(f) de campo(m) 391.
botón(m) de visualización(f) del nivel(m) de alarma(f) 485.
botón(m) del contador(m) a cero 411.
botón(m) del contador(m) a ceros(m) 403.
botón(m) del horno(m) 255.
botón(m) del seguro(m) 429.
botón(m) del vaporizador(m) 256.
botón(m) liberador de la película(f) 391.
botón(m) liberador(m) del objetivo(m) 391.
botón(m) para ajustar la imágen(f) horizontalmente 713.
botón(m) para ajustar la imágen(f) verticalmente 713.
botón(m) para borrar 420.
botón(m) para buscar las pistas(f) 405.
botón(m) para cancelar la memoria(f) 396.
botón(m) para fijar la temperatura(f) 705.
botón(m) para parar y borrar 405.
botón(m) para sacar la pila(f) 409.
botón(m) seleccionador de temperatura(f) 370.
botón(m) seleccionador de velocidad(f) 370.
botón(m) selector 257.
botón(m) TV video(m) 411.
botonadura(f) cruzada 319.
botones de montaje(m) y búsqueda(f) 409.
botones(m) comunes 566.
botones(m) de ajuste(m) 411.
botones(m) de ajuste(m) del rodaje(m) 409.
botones(m) de ajuste(m) del visor(m) 409.
botones(m) de control(m) 531.
botones(m) para buscar canales(m) 411.
botones(m) para buscar los canales(m) 411.
botones(m) para editar la voz(f) 555.
**bóveda(f) 177.**
bóveda(f) de proyección(f) 16.
bóveda(f) del salpicadero(m) 426.
bóveda(f) palatina 141, 142.
boxeador(m) 669.
BOXEO(M) 669.
**boya(f) cilíndrica 486.**
boya(f) cónica 487, 489.
boya(f) de pértiga(f) 489.
**boya(f) de plano(m) focal elevado 487.**
boya(f) torre(f) 489.
boya(f) torre(m) 487.
BOYAS(F) MARITIMAS, SISTEMA(M) 488.
**boyas(f), regiones(f) 488.**
Boyero 11.
bráctea(f) 66.
brafonera(f) 792.
bragas(f) 346.
**bragas(f) de hule(m) 349.**
bragueta(f) 323, 325, 350.
bramador(m) 543.
**branquias(f) 87.**
branquias(f) 88, 92.
branquias(f) externas 84.
branquiespinas(f) 87.
braquial(m) anterior 120.
brazalete(m) de identificación(f) 364.
brazalete(m) neumático 710.
brazalete(m) tubular 364.
**brazaletes(m) 364.**
brazas(f) de sobrejuanete(m) de mesana(f) 480.
brazo(m) 100, 117, 119, 157, 220, 234, 264, 270, 327, 369, 431, 483, 535, 561, 568, 718, 727, 782, 785.
brazo(m) actuador 529.
brazo(m) de arrastre(m) 784.
brazo(m) de control(m) a larga distancia(f) 510.
brazo(m) de la sierra(f) 272.
brazo(m) de presión(f) 282.
brazo(m) de suspensión(f) 258.
brazo(m) del cojinete(m) 376.
brazo(m) del panel(m) solar 42.
brazo(m) del raspador(m) 583.
brazo(m) delantero 708.
brazo(m) elástico 684.
brazo(m) elevador 283.
brazo(m) espiral 9.
brazo(m) extensible 585.
brazo(m) fonocaptor 404.
brazo(m) levantador 782.
brazo(m) metálico 264.
brazo(m) telescópico 786.
brazo(m) trasero 708.
**brida(f) 649.**
brida(f) 653.
brida(f) de unión(f) 486.
brillante(m) 362.
brisa(f) leve 38.
broca(f) 280, 734.
broca(f) avellanadora 281.
**broca(f) común 281.**
**broca(f) salomónica de canal(m) ancho 281.**
broca(f) salomónica de canal(m) angosto 281.
**brocha(f) 304.**
brocha(f) 152, 366, 589.
brocha(f) aplicadora de rubor(m) 366.
**brocha(f) de afeitar 374.**
brocha(f) en forma(f) de abanico(m) 366.
broche(m) 302, 364, 378, 380.
broche(m) automático 379.
broche(m) de presión(f) 321, 327.
broches(m) de la pierna(f) 350.
broches(m) de presión(f) 350.
broches(m) delanteros 350.
brócoli(m) 69.
bronquio(m) derecho 130.
bronquiolo(m) terminal 130.
brote(m) 57, 61.
brotes(m) de soja(f) 72.
Brújula 13.
brújula(f) 639.
**brújula(f) líquida 484.**
**brújula(f) líquida, corte(m) transversal 485.**
BRÚJULA(F) MAGNÉTICA 719.
bruñidor(m) 582.
bruñidor(m) con rascador(m) 587.
bruza(f) 582.
buccino(m) 83.
**buceador(m) 627.**
BUCEO(M) 627.
buey(m) 151.
bufete(m) 226.
buhardilla(f) 197.
**bujía(f) 439.**
bujía(f) 271, 435, 437.
bulbillo(m) 70.
bulbo(m) 72, 743, 752.
bulbo(m) olfativo 88.
bulbo(m) olfatorio 142.
bulbo(m) piloso 136.
bulbo(m) raquídeo 134.
**bulbo(m), corte(m) de un 70.**
**bulbos(m) 70.**
bulevar(m) 52.
**bulldozer(m) 783.**
buque(m) cisterna(f) 491.
buque(m) portacontenedores 490.
BUQUE(M) TRASATLÁNTICO 496.
**buque(m), ancla(f) 483.**
burda(f) 479.
Buril 13.
buril(m) 581.
**burra(f) 674.**
buscador(m) de altura(f) 810.
busco(m) 493.
butaca(f) 221.
buzo(m) 680.

## C

caballerizas(f) 651.
Caballeros(m), Servicios(m) 822.
Caballete del pintor 13.
caballete(m) 141, 198, 591.
caballete(m) portapoleas 737.
Caballito 11.
CABALLO(M) 100, 102, 104.
**caballo(m) 98.**
caballo(m) 661, 696.
**caballo(m) de arzón(m) 661.**
CABALLOS(M), CARRERA(F) DE 651.
cabecera(f) 224, 577.
Cabellera de Berenice 11.
cabellera(f) 9.
**cabeza(f) 107, 109.**
cabeza(f) 9, 78, 79, 80, 83, 117, 119, 124, 127, 242, 275, 276, 279, 288, 374, 384, 386, 466, 544, 546, 547, 561, 567, 570, 579, 615, 645, 661, 670, 674, 677, 681.
cabeza(f) de empalme(m) 147, 156, 158, 159, 162, 469.
cabeza(f) de emplame(m) 157.
**cabeza(f) de enganche(m) 471.**
cabeza(f) de la caja(f) de iluminación(f) 399.
cabeza(f) de la torre(f) 756.
cabeza(f) de la tubería(f) 740.
cabeza(f) de lectura(f) \ escritura(f) 529.
cabeza(f) de mástil(m) 631.
cabeza(f) de metal(m) 658.
cabeza(f) del fémur(m) 123.
cabeza(f) del húmero(m) 123.
cabeza(f) del martillo(m) 658, 681.
**cabeza(f) del murciélago(m) 112.**
cabeza(f) delantera del cilindro(m) de recuperación(f) 802.
cabeza(f) dirigida por rayos(m) infrarrojos 814.
cabeza(f) flotante 374.
cabeza(f) hexagonal 373.
cabeza(f) impresora 531.
cabeza(f) móvil 250.
cabeza(f) panorámica 393.
CABEZA(F), PROTECCIÓN(F) 729.
**cabeza(f), tipos(m) de 276.**
cabezada(f) 577, 649.
cabezal(m) 198, 224, 239.
cabezuela(f) 60.
cabina(f) 147, 160, 445, 508, 782, 783, 784, 785.
cabina(f) de clase(f) turista 499.
cabina(f) de control(m) 16, 786.
cabina(f) de la torre(f) de control(m) 502.
cabina(f) de mando(m) 493, 498, 508, 510.
cabina(f) de pasajeros(m) 494, 495.
cabina(f) de primera clase(f) 498.
cabina(f) del maquinista(m) 459, 468.
**cabina(f) del piloto(m) 639.**
cabina(f) del revisor(m) de billetes(m) 474.
cabina(f) en el foco(m) primario 14.
cabina(f) giratoria 785.
cabina(f) para dormir 440.
**cabinas(f) de control(m), estudio(m) de televisión(f) 412.**
CABLE(M) 692.
cable(m) 268, 271, 310, 406, 408, 585, 658, 660, 663, 684, 692.
cable(m) a tierra(f) 312.
cable(m) con funda(f) metálica 422.
cable(m) de acero(m) 681.
cable(m) de alimentación(f) de 240 voltios 312.
cable(m) de alumbrado(m) 449.
cable(m) de arranque(m) 270.
cable(m) de arrastre(m) 633.
cable(m) de bujía(f) 435.
cable(m) de conexión(f) 406, 530.
cable(m) de control(m) 270.
cable(m) de corriente(f) 280, 305, 370, 374.
cable(m) de corriente(f) de la aguja(f) 467.
cable(m) de dirección(f) 684.
cable(m) de elevación(f) 786.
cable(m) de enlace(m) 312.
cable(m) de frenado(m) 811.
cable(m) de tierra(f) 305.
cable(m) de transmisión(f) 485.
cable(m) del acelerador(m) 271.
cable(m) del auricular(m) 420.
cable(m) del cambio(m) 448.
cable(m) del esgrimidor(m) 666.
cable(m) del freno(m) 447.
cable(m) distribuidor 416.
cable(m) eléctrico 186.
cable(m) giratorio 370.
cable(m) neutro 312.
cable(m) portador 456.
cable(m) principal 312.
cable(m) principal neutro 312.
**cable(m) torcido 692.**
**cable(m) trenzado 692.**
cables(m) 414.
cables(m) conectores 400.
cables(m) de anclaje(m) 738.
cables(m) de baja tensión(f) 757.
cables(m) de conexión(f) 757.
cables(m) de suministro(m) 757.
cables(m) de tensión(f) mediana 757.
cabo(m) 51, 536, 670, 692.
cabo(m) del macillo(m) 541.
cabra(f) 150.
cabrestante(m) 541.
cabrio(m) 198.
cabujón(m) 362.
cacahuete(m) 66.
cacerola(f) 249.
cacerola(f) para baño(m) de María 249.
cacerola(f) para fondue(f) 248.
cacerola(f) refractaria 249.
cadena(f) 272, 448, 661, 707.
**cadena(f) alimenticia 31.**
cadena(f) de amarre(m) 486.
cadena(f) de dunas(f) 46.
cadena(f) de elevación(f) 787.
cadena(f) de montañas(f) 51.
cadena(f) de seguridad(f) 449.
cadena(f) de transmisión(f) 156, 158, 446.
**cadena(f), sierra(f) 272.**
**cadena(f), transmisión(f) 448.**
cadeneta(f) 571.
cadenilla(f) de la barbada(f) 650.
cadenita(f) del tapón(m) 293.
cadera(f) 117, 119.
cafetera(f) 247, 688.
**cafetera(f) de émbolo(m) 247.**
**cafetera(f) de filtro(m) automática 247.**
**cafetera(f) de infusión(f) 247.**
**cafetera(f) italiana 247.**
**cafetera(f) napolitana 247.**
CAFETERAS(F) 247.
cafetería(f) 822.
caída de proa(f) 631.
caída(f) 341.
caída(f) de popa(f) 631, 637.
caireles(m) 650.
caja(f) 40, 270, 271, 280, 305, 310, 374, 385, 391, 406, 410, 422, 453, 485, 486, 539, 540, 546, 671, 702, 705, 707, 710, 711.
caja(f) archivo(m) 517.
caja(f) basculante 785.
caja(f) circular 535.
caja(f) de accesorios(m) 568.
caja(f) de caracol(m) 747.
**caja(f) de cerillas(f) 386.**
caja(f) de combustión(f) 501.
caja(f) de compresión(f) 159.
caja(f) de conexiones(f) 309, 412.
caja(f) de distribución(f) 216.
caja(f) de empalmes(m) 471.
caja(f) de engranajes(m) 495, 501, 583.
caja(f) de la batería(f) 439.
caja(f) de la pantalla(f) 397.
caja(f) de pesca(f) 672.
caja(f) de servicio(m) 757.
caja(f) de sonido(m) 545.
caja(f) del acumulador(m) 441.
caja(f) del aire(m) 543.
caja(f) del cerrojo(m) 795, 796.
caja(f) del cilindro(m) 290.
caja(f) del motor(m) 272.
caja(f) del ventilador(m) 370.
caja(f) espiral 753.
caja(f) fuerte 702.
caja(f) harmónica 540.
caja(f) luminosa 398.
caja(f) media pera(f) 535.
caja(f) neumática 543.
caja(f) orza(f) de quilla(f) 631.
caja(f) para el césped(m) 271.
caja(f) para la ceniza(f) 204.
caja(f) sonora 535, 544, 545, 546.
caja(f) superior 231.
caja(f) terminal 769.
caja(f) tipo(m) remolque(m) 440.
**caja(f) tipo(m) semirremolque(m) 441.**
caja(f) tipo(m) semirremolque(m) 440.
caja(f) triangular 535.
**caja(f), tarima(f) 787.**
caja(f)de acuarelas(f) 588.
cajetín(m) 290.
**cajetín(m) de fusibles(m) 312.**
cajita(f) reguladora 297.
cajo(m) 577.
cajón(m) 156, 219, 226, 255.
cajón(m) de batir 657.
cajón(m) de servicio(m) 616, 617.
cajón(m) del plano(m) de sustentación(f) 812.
cajón(m) para carnes(f) 254.
calabacín(m) 69.
calabaza(f) amarilla 69.
calabaza(f) común 69.
cálamo(m) egipcio 389.
calandria(f) 759.

Los términos en **negrita** corresponden a una ilustración; los que aparecen en MAYÚSCULAS indican un título.

calapié(m) 446, 448.
calcáneo(m) 103, 123.
calcar(m) 112.
calce(m) 800.
calceta(f) 344.
calcetin(m) 615.
calcetín(m) 344.
calcetín(m) con tirante(m) 595.
calcetín(m) largo 344.
**calcetines(m) 325.**
calculadora(f) 379.
**calculadora(f) con impresora(f) 523.**
**calculadora(f) de bolsillo(m) 523.**
CALCULADORAS(F) 523.
**caldera(f) 209.**
caldera(f) 208, 771.
calderón(m) 539.
CALEFACCIÓN(F) 204, 206, 208, 210, 212.
**calefacción(f) auxiliar 211.**
**calefacción(f) eléctrica 207.**
calendario(m) de escritorio(m) 518.
calendario(m) de pared(f) 518.
calentador(m) 635, 689.
calentador(m) de aceite(m) 211.
calentador(m) de agua(f) 215.
**calentador(m) de gas(m) 297.**
**calentador(m) de petróleo(m) 209.**
calentador(m) de pierna(f) 353.
calentador(m) eléctrico 211.
calentador(m) tubular 744.
calibrador(m) 432, 583.
calibrador(m) del freno(m) 442.
calículo(m) 62.
caliptra(f) 57.
Calixto 4.
cáliz(m) 60, 62, 67.
cáliz(m) renal 132.
calle(f) 52, 184, 190, 621, 655, 656, 682.
CALLE(F), VISTA(F) TRANSVERSAL DE UNA 186.
calma(f) 38.
calza(f) de descarga(f) 753.
calzada(f) 186, 450.
CALZADO(M) 356, 358.
**calzado(m), tipos(m) de 356.**
**calzador(m) 358.**
calzas(f) 315, 317.
calzo(m) de la rueda(f) 506.
calzón(m) 667.
**calzón(m) de volantes(m) 349.**
**calzoncillos(m) 325.**
calzoncillos(m) 325.
calzoncillos(m) largos 325.
CAMA(F) 224.
cama(f) 578, 659.
**cama(f) elástica 659.**
**cama(f), coche(m) 460.**
Camaleón 13.
**cámara(f) 414.**
cámara(f) 16, 412, 414, 736.
cámara(f) anterior 140.
cámara(f) anular de combustión(f) 501.
cámara(f) de aire(m) 109, 298, 352, 772.
cámara(f) de bolsillo(m) 395.
cámara(f) de combustión(f) 209, 434, 438.
cámara(f) de compresión(f) 806.
cámara(f) de disco(m) 395.
cámara(f) de enfoque(m) 394.
cámara(f) de expansión(f) 705.
cámara(f) de fotografía(f) 717.
cámara(f) de incubación(f) 82.
cámara(f) de la esclusa(f) 493.
cámara(f) de la pólvora(f) 801.
cámara(f) de magma(m) 25.
cámara(f) de mezcla(f) 306.
cámara(f) de salida(f) 746, 747, 749, 750.
cámara(f) de televisión(f) de color(m) 512.
cámara(f) de vacío(m) 14, 717.
CÁMARA(F) DE VÍDEO(M) 409.
cámara(f) de vídeo(m) 526.
cámara(f) de video(m) fijo 395.
cámara(f) desechable 394.
cámara(f) estereofotogramétrica 395.
cámara(f) frigorífica 491.
cámara(f) lenta 411.
cámara(f) para el cartucho(m) de la película(f) 390.
cámara(f) para la muestra(f) 717.
cámara(f) Polaroid Land 394.
cámara(f) posterior 140.
cámara(f) principal de vapor(m) 759.
cámara(f) pulpar 144.
cámara(f) reflex con objetivo(m) simple 394.
**cámara(f) réflex de un objetivo(m) 391.**
**cámara(f) reflex, corte(m) transversal 390.**
cámara(f) rígida de 35 mm 512.
cámara(f) submarina 394.
cámara(f) tipo(m) réflex con dos objetivos(m) 394.
**cámara(f), parte(f) trasera 390.**
**cámaras(f) fotográficas, diferentes tipos(m) 395.**
**cámaras(m) fijas 394.**
camarín(m) 189.
camarote(m) 496.
camarote(m) del capitán(m) 497.
camarotes(m) de la tripulación(f) 494.
camarotes(m) de los oficiales(m) 807, 808.
cambiador(m) de piñones(m) 446, 448.
cambiador(m) de platos(m) 446, 448.
**cambiador(m) manual de vía(f) 467.**
cambio(m) automático de bandejas(f) 532.
cambio(m) de presión(f) 38.
cambium(m) 59.
cambocadura(f) 649.
cambrillón(m) 352.
**camilla(f) 726.**
camilla(f) 726.
camino(m) de arrastrre(m) 733.
camino(m) de ronda(f) 181.
camino(m) de ronda(f) cubierto 178.
camino(m) resbaladizo 826, 827.
**camión(m) basculante 785.**
**camión(m) bomba(f) 778.**
**camión(m) cisterna(f) 742.**
camión(m) cisterna(f) de agua(f) potable 506.
camión(m) cisterna(f) de combustible(m) 506.
camión(m) de aprovisionamiento(m) 507.
**camión(m) de escalelera(f) telescópica 780.**
camión(m) sanitario 506.
**camión(m) tractor(m) 440.**
camión(m) tractor(m) 440.
**camión(m) tractor(m) con doble caja(f) 440.**
CAMIONES(M) 440.
camioneta(f) 425.
camioneta(f) con canastilla(f) telescópica 506.
camioneta(f) cubierta 425.
camioneta(f) de mantenimiento(m) de aviones(m) 506.
**camisa(f) 324, 337.**
camisa(f) 181.
camisa(f) de pistón(m) 434.
camisera clásica 337.
camisera(f) 340.
camisero 341.
camisero(m) 333.
**camiseta(f) 325.**
camiseta(f) 337, 349, 351, 353, 595, 656.
camiseta(f) de chándal(m) 352.
camiseta(f) de chándal(m) con capucha(f) 352.
camiseta(f) de cuerpo(m) entero 351.
camiseta(f) de equipo(m) 600.
camiseta(f) interior 595.
camiseta(f) sin mangas(f) 662.
camisola(f) 345.
camisón(m) 348.
camisón(m) corto 348.
**campana(f) 255.**
campana(f) 204.
campana(f) de aviso(m) de cruce(m) 471.
campanario(m) 175, 176.
campanas(f) tubulares 554, 556.
CAMPING(M) 685, 686, 690.
camping(m) gas(m) 689.
**campo(m) 597, 599, 601.**
**campo(m) de golf(m) 676.**
**campo(m) de juego(m) 606, 607.**
**campo(m) de juego(m) de fútbol(m) americano 604.**
**campo(m) de juego(m) de fútbol(m) canadiense 604.**
campo(m) magnético 410.
CAMPO(M) Y PISTA(F), ATHLETISMO(M) DE 658.
CAMPO(M) Y PISTA(F), ATLETISMO(M) DE 654, 656.
Can Mayor 13.
Can Menor 11.
caña(f) 101, 389, 483, 542, 641, 645, 671, 798, 800.
caña(f) del timón(m) 628.
**caña(f) para lanzar 671.**
**caña(f) para mosca(f) 670.**
caña(f) simple 549.
canal(m) 281, 683, 701, 741, 793.
canal(m) de ajuste(m) 278.
canal(m) de arrastre(m) del papel(m) 521.
canal(m) de carga(f) 752.
canal(m) de derivación(f) 746.
canal(m) de descarga(f) 747.
canal(m) de escurrimiento(m) 427.
canal(m) del aliviadero(m) 746.
canal(m) del sifón(m) 94.
canal(m) del veneno(m) 96.
canal(m) derecho 401.
canal(m) izquierdo 401.
canal(m) principal 489.
canal(m) secundario 489.
canal(m) transportador 764.
CANAL(M), ESCLUSA(F) 492.
canalización(f) de vacío(m) 717.
canalón(m) 105, 197.
**cañas(f) 549.**
**canasta(f) 610.**
canasta(f) 596, 610.
canastilla(f) 252, 257.
canastilla(f) para cubiertos(m) 257.
Cáncer 11.
Cáncer, el Cangrejo (22 de junio) 820.
**cancha(f) 610, 611, 612, 613, 614, 617, 618.**
cancha(f) de fondo(m) 614.
cancha(f) del fondo(m) 617.
cancha(f) delantera 617.
**cancha(f) internacional de individuales(m) 616.**
candado(m) para bicicleta(f) 448.
candaliza(f) 480.
candil(m) coronal 105.
candil(m) frontal 105.
candilejas 188.
cañería(f) 215, 296.
cañería(f) de desagüe(m) 216.
cañería(f) del desagüe(m) 215.
cañería(f) metálica para agua(f) 312.
cañería(f) perforada 216.
CAÑERÍAS(F) 215.
cañerías(f) 635.
canesú(m) 324, 337, 345.
cangilón(m) 754.
cangilón(m) trasero 782.
cangreja(f) de popa(f) 480.
cangreja(f) mayor popel 480.
cangrejo(m) 90.
canilla(f) 561, 562.
caño(m) 542.
**caño(m) del órgano(m) 542.**
cañon(m) 385.
cañón(m) 110, 698, 795, 796, 797, 798, 799, 802, 804, 805.
**cañón(m) de avancarga(f) 800.**
**cañón(m) de avancarga(f), corte(m) transversal 801.**
cañón(m) de chimenea(f) 197.
**cañón(m) de electrones(m) 410.**
cañón(m) de electrones(m) 410, 717.
cañón(m) de la presión(f) 543.
CAÑÓN(M) DEL SIGLO(M) XVII 800.
cañón(m) lanzaagua 778.
cañón(m) submarino 29.
cañonera(f) 179.
cañonería(f) 543.
canotier(m) 328.
cantarela(f) 55.
cantidad(f) de copias(f) 532.
cantilever(m) 454, 750.
cantimplora(f) 690.
canto(m) 277, 288, 640, 643, 644, 658.
canto(m) de la cabeza(f) 577.
canto(m) de la cara(f) 577.
canto(m) del pie(m) 577.
cantón(m) diestro de la punta(f) 818.
cantón(m) diestro del jefe(m) 818.
cantón(m) siniestro de la punta(f) 818.
cantón(m) siniestro del jefe(m) 818.
cantonera(f) 577, 798, 799.
**capa(f) 331.**
capa(f) basáltica 22.
capa(f) basilar 136.
capa(f) córnea 105, 136.
capa(f) cortical 132.
capa(f) de aluminio(m) 405.
capa(f) de desagüe(m) 748.
capa(f) del casco(m) 433.
capa(f) granita 22.
capa(f) granular 136.
capa(f) protectora 512.
**caparazón(m) 96.**
caparazón(m) 91.
capas(f) aislantes 512.
caperuza(f) 297, 627.
capilla(f) 181.
capilla(f) axial 177.
capilla(f) lateral 176.
capilla(f) radial 177.
capital(f) 51.
capitán(m) 620, 643.
capitel(m) 166.
capó(m) 426, 440.
caponera(f) 179.
Capricornio 13.
Capricornio, la Cabra (22 de diciembre) 820.
cápsula(f) 725.
cápsula(f) de gelatina(f) 725.
**cápsula(f), corte(m) de una 67.**
captador(m) de luz(f) 409.
captura(f) 697.
capucha(f) 320.
capucha(f) de ventilación(f) 486.
capucha(f) giratoria 773.
capuchón(m) 205, 349, 392, 398, 409, 484.
capuchón(m) con cordón(m) 351.
capuchón(m) de bastones(m) 679.
capuchón(m) de la chimenea(f) 197.
capuchón(m) de plástico(m) 311.
capuchón(m) de protección(f) 718.
capullo(m) 57.
caqui(m) 68.
cara(f) 116, 239, 275, 288, 579, 619, 677.
**cara(f) inferior 363.**
**cara(f) superior 363.**
caracol(m) marino común 83.
**caracol(m) terrestre 83.**
**carambola(f) 673.**
caramillo(m) 536, 548.
CARAVANA(F) 449.
CARBÓN(M), MINA(F) 736.
CARBÓN(M), MINA(F) SUBTERRÁNEA 734.
CARBÓN(M), MINAS(F) 733.
carboncillo(m) 588.
carbonera(f) de carga(f) 734.
carburador(m) 442.
carcaj(m) 684.
cardo(m) 72.
careta(f) 308, 730.
careta(f) de esgrima(f) 667.
careta(f) de mano(f) 308.
carga(f) 389.
carga(f) de perdigones(m) 799.
**carga(f) del reactor(m) nuclear 765.**
carga(f) útil 509.
cargador(m) 260, 795, 796, 797.
cargador(m) de contenedores(m) y plataformas(f) 507.
cargador(m) delantero 782.
cargadora(f) de combustible(m) 759.
**cargadora(f), retroexcavadora(f) 782.**
**cargas(f), ejemplos(m) 819.**
CARGUERO(M) PORTACONTENEDORES 494.
caribú(m) 105.
carne(f) 33.
carnicero(m) 98.
**carnívoro(m), mandíbula(f) 98.**
carnívoros(m) 31, 33.
Carón 5.
carpeta(f) 520.
carpeta(f) con guardas(f) 519.
carpeta(f) con mecanismo(m) de presión(f) 519.
carpeta(f) de archivo(m) 518.
carpeta(f) de argollas(f) 519.
carpeta(f) de broches(m) 519.
carpeta(f) de costilla(f) de resorte(m) 519.
carpeta(f) de espiral(f) 519.
carpeta(f) de tornillos(m) 519.
carpo(m) 102, 122.
carrera(f) 599.
carrera(f) de aprendices(m) 646.
CARRERAS(F) DE TROTONES(M) 652.
carrete(m) 265, 570.
**carrete(m) de bobina(f) fija 671.**
carrete(m) de cinta(f) adhesiva 516.

Los términos en **negrita** corresponden a una ilustración; los que aparecen en MAYÚSCULAS indican un título.

carrete(m) de rebobinado(m) 390.
carrete(m) del cable(m) 666.
**carrete(m) giratorio 670.**
carrete(m) receptor de la cinta(f) 403.
carrete(m) recogedor 158.
carretera(f) 52, 452.
carretera(f) de acceso(m) 502.
carretera(f) de circunvalación(f) 52.
carretera(f) secundaria 52.
**carretera(f), vista(f) transversal 450.**
**carreteras(f), mapa 52.**
CARRETERAS(F), SISTEMA(M) 450, 452.
**carretilla(f) 270.**
carretilla(f) 468, 788.
carretilla(f) del motor(m) 459.
carretilla(f) hidráulica 788.
**carretilla(f) para manguera(f) 265.**
**carretilla(f) y vía(f) 476.**
carril(m) 476.
carril(m) de adelantamiento(m) 452.
carril(m) de desaceleración(f) 452.
carril(m) de tránsito(m) 452.
carríl(m) guía(f) de la película(f) 390.
carril(m) para el tope(m) de ingletes(m) 285.
carrillo(m) 670.
carrito(m) de golf(m) 679.
**carrito(m) portamaletas(m) 382.**
carro(m) 230, 630.
carro(m) de encaje(m) 568.
**carro(m) de golf(m) eléctrico 679.**
carro(m) portaequipaje 463.
carro(m) principal deslizante 568.
**carrocería(f) 426.**
carrocería(f) 445, 449.
**carrocerías(f), tipos(m) 425.**
carrusel(m) 397.
**carta(f) del tiempo(m) 38.**
cartas(f) altas 695.
cartel(m) comercial 477.
cárter(m) 434, 436.
**cartera(f) 378.**
**cartera(f) de fondo(m) plegable 378.**
cartera(f) portadocumentos(m) 378.
**carterita(f) de cerillas(f) 386.**
cartílago(m) de la aleta(f) 141.
CARTOGRAFÍA(F) 47, 50, 52.
cartón(m) 589.
cartón(m) de cigarrillos(m) 384.
cartucho(m) 291, 295, 404, 730, 797.
**cartucho(m) de escopeta(f) 799.**
cartucho(m) de la cinta(f) grabadora(f) 407.
**cartucho(m) de la película(f) 395.**
cartucho(m) de la película(f) 395.
cartucho(m) de película(f) 527.
**cartucho(m) de rifle(m) 798.**
cartucho(m) para la cinta(f) 531.
carúncula(f) lagrimal 140.
casa(f) 193, 620.
casa(f) club(m) 676.
casa(f) de cambio(m) 823.
casa(f) de campo(m) 187.
casa(f) de habitación(f) 148.
**casa(f) rodante 449.**
CASA(F) ROMANA 170.
**casa(f) solar 772.**
CASA(F), ESTRUCTURA(F) DE 198.
CASA(F), EXTERIOR(M) DE UNA 196.
casaca(f) 315, 648.
casas(f) en serie(f) 187.
casas(f) gemelas 187.
casas(f) independientes 187.
cascabel(m) 97, 554.
cascada(f) 27.
cascanueces(m) 243.
**cáscara(f) 66.**
cáscara(f) 66, 152.
cascarón(m) 109.
**casco(m) 104.**
casco(m) 101, 443, 512, 602, 609, 628, 635, 680, 741, 777, 791.
**casco(m) de bombero(m) 777.**
casco(m) de salto(m) 636.
**casco(m) de seguridad(f) 729.**
casco(m) del bateador(m) 595.
**casco(m) protector 443.**
casco(m) protector 448, 643.
**casco(m), superficie(f) plantar del 104.**
casero 333.
**caseta(f) de instrumentos(m) meteorológicos 41.**
casete(f) 526.
**casete(m) 403.**
casete(m) 408.
casete(m) de juego(m) 699.
casi igual a 830.
casilla(f) 577.
casilla(f) del dinero(m) 702.
casillas(f) de consigna(f) automática 463.
Casiopea 11.
**casquete(m) 636.**
casquete(m) 294, 295, 328, 636.
casquete(m) de la palanca(f) 295.
casquete(m) de seguridad(f) 804.
casquete(m) del distribuidor(m) 435.
casquillo(m) 232, 233, 309, 675, 798.
casquillo(m) de la empuñadura(f) 281.
cassette(m) con saludo(m) 420.
cassette(m) para grabar los mensajes(m) 420.
castaña(m) 66.
castañuelas(f) 554, 556.
castillete(m) de extracción(f) 736.
CASTILLO(M) 180.
castillo(m) 180.
castillo(m) de proa(f) 495, 497.
**castor(m) 98.**
catapulta(f) 810.
**catedral(f) 176.**
catedral(f) 184.
CATEDRAL(F) GÓTICA 175, 176.
**catedral(f), plano(m) 177.**
catre(m) desmontable 687.
caucho(m) central 677.
cauda(f) helicis 139.
cavidad(f) abdominal 127, 128.
cavidad(f) bucal 130, 131.
cavidad(f) nasal 96.
cavidad(f) paleal 95.
cavidad(f) pleural 130.
cavidad(m) nasal 130.
cayado(m) de la aorta(f) 124.
CAZA(F), ARMAS(F) 798.
**cazadora(f) 320, 321, 338.**
cazoleta(f) 385, 590, 795, 800, 801.
cazonete(m) 817.
cebada(f) 152.
cebador(m) 795, 804.
cebolla(f) 70.
cebolla(f) verde 70.
cebollín(m) 70.
cebollino(m) 70.
ceda el paso(m) 824, 825.
cedazo(m) 243.
cedilla(f) 832.
cefalotórax(m) 90.
Cefeo 11.
ceja(f) 140, 540.
cejilla(f) 544, 546, 547.
celada(f) 792.
celcés(m) 479.
celda(f) 79.
celda(f) fotoeléctrica 393.
celda(f) solar 769.
**celda(f) solar(f) 768.**
celdilla(f) 65, 82.
celdilla(f) de la miel(f) 82.
celdilla(f) del polen(m) 82.
celdilla(f) operculada 82.
celdilla(f) sellada 82.
cellisca(f) 37.
celosía(f) veneciana 203.
CÉLULA(F) ANIMAL 115.
célula(f) solar 523.
CÉLULA(F) VEGETAL 115.
células(f) solares 42.
cementerio(m) 52.
cemento(m) 144.
cenefa(f) con flecos(m) 229.
**cenefas(f), tipos(m) de 228.**
**cenicero(m) 386.**
cenit(m) 16.
ceniza(f) 386.
Centauro 13.
centavo(m) 832.
centeno(m) 152.
central(f) hidroeléctrica 746.
**central(f) hidroeléctrica, corte(m) transversal 747.**
**central(f) maremotriz 752.**
**central(f) nuclear 758.**
central(m) 603, 612.
centriolo(m) 115.
centro(m) 605, 608, 611, 697.
centro(m) de congresos(m) 184.
centro(m) de la cancha(f) 617.
centro(m) de la punta(f) 818.
CENTRO(M) DE UNA CIUDAD(F) 184.
centro(m) del blanco(m) 684.
centro(m) del campo(m) 601, 606, 607.
centro(m) del jefe(m) 818.
centro(m) delantero 607.
centro(m) derecho 606.
centro(m) izquierdo 606.
**cepillo(m) 277.**
cepillo(m) 80, 81, 358, 373.
cepillo(m) aplicador de rímel(m) 367.
cepillo(m) con base(f) de goma(f) 368.
cepillo(m) de dientes(m) 373.
**cepillo(m) de dientes(m) eléctrico 373.**
cepillo(m) de púas(f) 368.
**cepillo(m) eléctrico 370.**
cepillo(m) metálico 368.
cepillo(m) para cejas(f) y pestañas(f) 367.
cepillo(m) para pisos(m) 260.
cepillo(m) para verduras(f) 246.
cepillo(m) redondo 368.
cepillo(m) rizador 370.
cepillo(m)-plumero(m) 260.
**cepillos(m) 368.**
cepo(m) 483.
CERÁMICA(F) 584.
cerca(f) 148.
cercado(m) 149.
cercado(m) para entrenar los caballos(m) 651.
cerda(f) 151, 373.
cerdas(f) 304, 374.
cerdo(m) 151.
CEREALES(M), PRINCIPALES TIPOS(M) 152.
cerebelo(m) 134.
cerebro(m) 88, 134.
cereza(f) 63.
cerilla(f) 386.
cerillas(f) de seguridad(f) 386.
cero(m) 700, 701.
cerradura(f) 202, 225, 289, 378, 383, 427, 429.
cerradura(f) de combinación(f) 378.
**cerradura(f) de pomo(m) con seguro(m) 290.**
**cerradura(f) embutida 290.**
CERRAJERÍA(F) 289, 290.
cerrojo(m) 569.
cerros(m) 819.
CÉRVIDOS(M) 105.
**cérvidos(m), principales 105.**
cerviz(f) 108.
césped(m) 193, 263, 676.
cesta(f) de pescador(m) 672.
cestillo(m) 81.
chabola(f) 165.
chafaldete(m) 481.
chalaza(f) 109.
**chaleco(m) 322.**
chaleco(m) 315, 317, 338.
chaleco(m) de pescador(m) 672.
chaleco(m) de punto(m) 326.
CHALECO(M) DE SEGURIDAD(F) 730.
**chalecos(m), jerseys(m) y chaquetas(f) 338.**
chalote(m) 70.
chambrana(f) 203.
champiñón(m) (Agaricus campestris) 55.
chancleta(f) 357.
chanclo(m) 357.
chanclo(m) de goma(f) 355.
chapa(f) 289.
chapa(f) de madera(f) 288.
chapetón(m) 220.
chapka(f) 328.
**chaqueta(f) 322.**
chaqueta(f) 331.
chaqueta(f) blanca de esgrima(f) 667.
**chaqueta(f) cruzada 322.**
chaqueta(f) de punto(m) 326.
chaquetón(m) 330, 331.
**chaquetón(m) marinero 330.**
chasis(m) 156, 157, 159, 272, 383, 726, 785, 787, 788.
chasis(m) de empuje(m) 783.
chasis(m) de la carretilla(f) 468.
chasis(m) delantero 784.
chesterfield(m) 221.
cheurón(m) 818.
chifonier(m) 226.
**chimenea(f) 204, 205.**
chimenea(f) 195, 197, 209, 494, 496, 585.
chimenea(f) de evacuación(f) 736.
chimenea(f) lateral 25.
chimenea(f) principal 25.
chimenea(f), conexión(f) de la 204.
**chimenea(f), utensilios(m) para la 205.**
chinchetas(f) 515.
chino 342.
chirimoya(f) 68.
chirivía(f) 71.
chispa(f) 436.
chistera(f) 328.
**chorrillo(m), sembradora(f) 158.**
choza(f) indígena 165.
chubasco(m) 39.
chubasco(m) de nieve(f) 39.
chumalera(f) giratoria 632.
**ciclo(m) hidrológico 34.**
ciclorama(m) 414.
ciego(m) 131.
ciego(m) pilórico 88.
**cielo(m) abierto, excavación(f) 733.**
**cielo(m) abierto, mina(f) 733.**
**cielo(m) turbulento 36.**
cierre(m) 380, 685.
cierre(m) de polea(f) 793.
cierre(m) de rosca(f) 681.
ciervo(m) de Virginia 105.
cigala(f) 90, 91.
cigarra(f) 77.
**cigarrillo(m) 384.**
cigüeñal(m) 434, 436.
cilantro(m) 74.
ciliada 56.
cilindro(m) 290, 295, 436, 707, 726, 784.
cilindro(m) de corte(m) 271.
cilindro(m) de dirección(f) 784.
cilindro(m) de elevación(f) del zanco(m) 783.
cilindro(m) de freno(m) 432.
cilindro(m) de recuperación(f) 802.
cilindro(m) de rotación(f) 570.
cilindro(m) del brazo(m) 782, 785.
cilindro(m) del brazo(m) levantador 782.
cilindro(m) del cangilón(m) trasero 782.
cilindro(m) del cucharón(m) 782, 785.
cilindro(m) del elevador(m) 782, 785.
cilindro(m) del elevador(m) de la pala(f) 783.
cilindro(m) del gas(m) 796.
cilindro(m) elevador 780, 786.
cilindro(m) externo 753.
cilindro(m) hidráulico 147, 788.
cilindro(m) inferior 581.
cilindro(m) interno 753.
cilindro(m) neumático 734.
cilindro(m) recogedor 159, 162.
cilindro(m) superior 581.
cima(f) 27, 59.
cima(f) bípara 60.
cima(f) unípara 60.
cimacio(m) 166.
cimentación(f) 199.
cimiento(m) del pilón 456.
**cimientos(m) 199.**
cimientos(m) 751.
cimientos(m) del dique(m) 748.
cincel(m) de rincón(m) 581.
cincha(f) 649, 651.
cincha(f) de la limonera(f) 653.
ciñendo el viento(m) 629.
cinta(f) 328, 566, 571, 607, 618, 619, 669, 711, 729, 730, 804.
cinta(f) adhesiva 725.
cinta(f) aislante para tubería(f) 287.
cinta(f) central 614.
cinta(f) de grabación(f) 403.
cinta(f) de la red(f) 613, 614.
cinta(f) digital grabadora(f) 407.
**cinta(f) métrica 711.**
cinta(f) métrica 563.
cinta(f) para el sudor(m) 615.
cinta(f) transportadora 504.
cintura(f) 117, 119, 354, 756.
**cinturón(m) 323.**
cinturón(m) 319, 363, 433, 662.
cinturón(m) de alpinista(m) 680.
cinturón(m) de hombros 428.
cinturón(m) de seguridad(f) 428.
cinturón(m) lastrado 627.
cinturón(m) trasero(m) 330.
**cinturones(m), neumático(m) radial 433.**
circo(m) 7.
circo(m) glaciar 26.
circuito(m) de 120 voltios 312.
circuito(m) de 240 voltios 312.
circuito(m) de agua(f) caliente 215.
circuito(m) de agua(f) fría 215.
circuito(m) de desagüe(m) 215.
circuito(m) de ventilación(f) 215.
circuito(m) eléctrico 233.
circuito(m) impreso 528.
CIRCULACIÓN(F) SANGUÍNEA 124, 126.
circular 250.

Los términos en **negrita** corresponden a una ilustración; los que aparecen en MAYÚSCULAS indican un título.

círculo(m) 25 698.
círculo(m) central 601, 610, 611, 620.
círculo(m) de canasta(f) 611.
círculo(m) de espera(f) 597.
círculo(m) de la estación(f) 38.
círculo(m) de lanzamiento(m) 654, 655.
círculo(m) de reanudación(f) del juego(m) 608.
círculo(m) de saque(m) inicial 608.
círculo(m) doble 698.
círculo(m) exterior 620.
círculo(m) polar antártico 3.
círculo(m) polar ártico 3, 47.
círculo(m) triple 698.
cirrocúmulos(m) 44.
cirros(m) 44.
cirrostratos(m) 44.
ciruela(f) 63.
Cisne 11.
cisterna(f) del retrete(m) 292.
**cisterna(f), camión(m) 742.**
**cisterna(f), vagón(m) 743.**
**cítara(f) 535.**
citoplasma(m) 115, 128.
**cítrico(m), corte(m) de un 65.**
CÍTRICOS(M), FRUTOS(M) CARNOSOS 65.
**cítricos(m), principales variedades(f) 65.**
ciudad(f) 51.
CIUDAD(F), CENTRO(M) 184.
**cizalla(f) 578.**
clarín(m) 550.
clarinete(m) 548.
clarinete(m) bajo 556.
clarinetes(m) 556.
**clasificación(f) de Hubble 9.**
clasificador(m) de fuelle(m) 378.
clave(f) 174, 177.
clave(f) de do 537.
clave(f) de fa 537.
clave(f) de sol 537.
**clave(f), modelo(m) 38.**
clavera(f) 104.
**claves(f) 537.**
clavícula(f) 122.
clavija(f) 540, 544, 545, 546, 780.
clavija(f) de afinación(f) 547.
clavija(f) de tensión(f) 552.
clavija(f) hendida 290.
clavijero(m) 540, 544.
**clavo(m) 275.**
clavo(m) 104, 680.
clavo(m) fechador 466.
claxon(m) 444.
claxón(m) 430.
**climas(f) de alta montaña(f) 45.**
**climas(f) subárticos 45.**
**climas(m) continentales 45.**
climas(m) de alta montaña(f) 45.
CLIMAS(M) DEL MUNDO(M) 45.
**climas(m) polares 45.**
climas(m) subárticos 45.
**climas(m) subtropicales 45.**
**climas(m) templados 45.**
**climas(m) tropicales 45.**
clip(m) 230.
clip(m) de ajuste(m) 233.
clítoris(m) 128.
cloroplasto(m) 115.
cobertera(f) inferior de la cola(f) 109.
cobertera(f) superior de la cola(f) 109.
coberteras(f) 108.
coberteras(f) grandes 110.
coberteras(f) medias 110.
coberteras(f) pequeñas 110.
coberteras(f) primarias 110.
coberteras(f) primarias medias 110.
cobertizo(m) 148, 193, 263.
cobertizo(m) de la parada(f) 186.
cobertizo(m) del andén(m) 464.
cobertizo(m) para ovejas(f) 149.
**cocción(f) 585.**
cóccix(m) 122.
COCHE(M) DE BOMBEROS(M) 778, 780.
coche(m) familiar 425.
Cochero 11.
**cocina(f) 689.**
cocina(f) 171, 195, 460, 807.
cocina(f) de a bordo(m) 498.
**cocina(f) eléctrica 255.**
cocina(f) pequeña 195.
COCINA(F), UTENSILIOS(M) DE 242, 244, 246, 248.
**cocina(f), utensilios(m) de 688.**
cóclea(f) 139.
coco(m) 66.
codal(m) 792.
codaste(m) 742.
codera(f) 602, 609.
código(m) 524.
código(m) del producto(m) 709.
codillo(m) 100, 106.
codo(m) 106, 112, 117, 119, 206, 376.
codo(m) de 45 grados(m) 301.
codo(m) de 90 grados(m) 301.
cofia(f) cónica 318.
COHETE(M) 509.
cohetes(m) impulsores 510.
cojín(m) 224.
cojín(m) para sellos(m) 516.
cojinete(m) 106, 376, 468.
cojinete(m) carpal 106.
cojinete(m) de rodamiento(m) 753.
cojinete(m) digital 106, 107.
cojinete(m) estéril de gasa(f) 725.
cojinete(m) móvil 631.
cojinete(m) palmar 106.
cojinete(m) plantar 107.
col(f) de China(f) 73.
col(f) rizada 73.
cola(f) 91, 96, 97, 101, 106, 107, 112, 200, 499, 579, 641, 642, 643, 645, 670.
cola(f) de polvo(m) 9.
cola(f) gaseosa 9.
colador(m) 251, 296.
COLAS(F), TIPOS(M) 498.
colchón(m) 657, 726.
colchón(m) aislante 687.
colchón(m) de aire(m) 687.
colchón(m) de espuma(f) 687.
colchón(m) de muelles(m) 224.
colchoneta(f) 657.
**colchonetas(f) y camas(f) 687.**
colector(m) 40, 741, 753.
colector(m) de grasa(f) 253.
colector(m) solar 772.
**colector(m) solar plano 768.**
coles(f) de Bruselas 73.
colgante(m) 236.
coliflor(f) 69.
colilla(f) 386.
colina(f) 27, 770.
colina(f) abisal 29.
colinabo(m) 71.
collar(m) 304.
collar(m) cortafuego 205.
collar(m) de 5 hilos(m) 361.
collar(m) de perforación(f) 737.
collar(m) de una vuelta(f) 361.
**collares(m) 361.**
collarín(m) 205, 279, 283, 663.
collarino(m) 167.
colleja(f) 73.
**colmena(f) 82.**
colmena(f) 149.
colmillo(m) 96, 98, 144.
colmillos(m) de elefante(m) 99.
colmillos(m) de jabalí(m) verrugoso 99.
colmillos(m) de morsa(f) 99.
COLMILOS(M): TIPOS(M) MÁS COMUNES 99.
colon(m) ascendente 131.
colon(m) descendente 131.
colon(m) sigmoideo 131.
colon(m) transverso 131.
color(m) 695.
color(m) vaporizado 590.
**colores(m), ejemplos(m) 819.**
columela(f) 94.
columna(f) 24, 36, 166, 168, 169, 236, 399, 455, 545, 561, 700, 701.
columna(f) central 393, 774.
columna(f) con capuchon(m) 37.
columna(f) de alcohol(m) 705.
columna(f) de control(m) 500.
columna(f) de mercurio(m) 705.
columna(f) de soporte(m) 738.
**columna(f) de tensión(f) 562.**
columna(f) vertebral 89, 122, 134.
coma(f) 832.
COMBATE(M), AVIÓN(M) 812.
**combinación(f) 345.**
combinación(f) con sostén(m) 345.
combinación(f) ganadora 702.
combustible(m) 761, 766.
**combustible(m) en vuelo(m),reaprovisionamiento(m) 813.**
combustible(m) fallido envasado 764.
combustible(m) para aviones(m) 745.
**combustible(m), elemento(m) cargador 765.**
combustible(m): uranio(m) enriquecido 762, 763.
combustible(m): uranio(m) natural 760, 761.
combustión(f) 436, 437, 501.
comedor(m) 195, 460, 496, 807.
**comedor(m), vagón(m) 460.**
COMETA(M) 9.
comienzo(m) de lectura(f) 405.
comillas(f) 832.
comillas(f) sencillas 832.
comisura(f) labial 142.
comodín(m) 695.
compartimento(m) para almacenamiento(m) 449.
compartimento(m) para el casete(m) 411.
compartimento(m) para el equipo(m) 458.
compartimento(m) para equipaje(m) 458.
compartimento(m) para la casete(f) 409.
compartimentos(m) 82.
compartimiento(m) 701.
compartimiento(m) de almacenamiento(m) 778, 780.
compartimiento(m) de pasajeros(m) 493.
compartimiento(m) del cable(m) de la batería(f) 415.
compartimiento(m) del casete(m) 403.
compartimiento(m) del equipo(m) técnico 415.
compartimiento(m) para almacenamiento(m) 397.
compartimiento(m) para el disco(m) 405.
compartimiento(m) para mantequilla(f) 254.
compartimiento(m) para queso(m) y crema(f) 254.
**compás(m) 537.**
compás(m) del volumen(m) 413.
compensador(m) de flotación(f) 627.
compensador(m) gráfico de sintonización(f) 400.
**complejo(m) hidroeléctrico 746.**
completamente nublado 39.
complexo(m) mayor 121.
compluvio(m) 170, 171.
**componentes(m) 400.**
COMPONENTES(M) BÁSICOS 528, 530.
compresión(f) 436, 437, 501.
compresión(f)/admisión(f) 436.
compresor(m) 212, 517, 761.
compresor(m) centrífugo 501.
compresor(m) de aire(m) 469.
compresor(m) de la turbina(f) 501.
compresor(m) del aire(m) acondicionado 435.
compuerta(f) 490, 747, 752.
compuerta(f) de llenado(m) 493.
compuerta(f) de toma(f) 753.
compuerta(f) del aliviadero 746.
compuerta(f) del tanque(m) 743.
compuerta(f) inferior 492.
computador(m) de gestión(f) de vuelo(m) 500.
computador(m) de vuelo(m) 500.
común fruncida 340.
comunicación(f) por computador(m) 417.
COMUNICACIÓN(F) POR SATÉLITE DE TRANSMISIÓN(F) 416.
**comunicación(f), unidades(f) 526.**
comunicaciones(f) aéreas 417.
comunicaciones(f) industriales 417.
comunicaciones(f) marítimas 417.
comunicaciones(f) militares 417.
comunicaciones(f) personales 417.
COMUNICACIONES(F) POR TELÉFONO(M) 420, 422.
comunicaciones(f) terrestres 417.
**comunicaciones(f), terminal(m) 422.**
con aletilla(f) 342.
con chorrera(f) 342.
con hombrera(f) 340.
concentrador(m) de aire(m) 370.
concha(f) 83, 92, 139, 220, 553.
CONCHA(F) BIVALVA 95.
concha(f) del apuntador(m) 188.
CONCHA(F) UNIVALVA 94.
Concorde(m) 19.
CONCURSO(M) DE SALTOS(M), EQUITACIÓN(F) 646.
concurso(m) de velocidad(f) 646.
concurso(m) profesional 646.
condensación(f) 35.
condensador(m) 717, 718, 758, 771.
cóndilo(m) externo 123.
cóndilo(m) interno 123.
condominios(m) 187.
conducto(m) 590.
conducto(m) de aire(m) caliente 259.
conducto(m) de aire(m) comprimido 590.
conducto(m) de desviación(f) 501.
conducto(m) de distribución(f) vertical 206.
conducto(m) de monedas(f) 702.
conducto(m) de salida(f) de aire(m) 501.
conducto(m) deferente 127.
conducto(m) del aire(m) 543.
conducto(m) del veneno(m) 96.
conducto(m) eyaculador 127.
conducto(m) galactófero 129.
conducto(m) principal 206.
conducto(m) principal de gas(m) 186.
conducto(m) radicular 144.
conducto(m) secundario 206.
conducto(m) semicircular lateral 139.
conducto(m) semicircular posterior 139.
conducto(m) semicircular superior 139.
conducto(m) sudorífero 136.
conductor(m) 652.
conductor(m) de fase(f) 757.
conductor(m) neutral 757.
conductor(m) transversal 161.
conector(m) 300, 312, 406, 778.
conector(m) de expansión(f) 528.
conector(m) de línea(f) cargada 757.
conector(m) de salida(f) 547.
conector(m) del desagüe(m) 215.
conector(m) en T del desagüe(m) 298.
conexión(f) 697, 756, 757.
conexión(f) a tierra(f) 757.
**conexión(f) aérea 757.**
conexión(f) de seguridad(f) del traje(m) 512.
conexión(f) eléctrica 207, 213.
conexión(f) eléctrica a tierra(f) 741.
conexión(f) en T 301.
conexión(f) en U 301.
conexión(f) en Y 301.
conexión(f) para el módem(m) 528.
conexión(f) para el teclado(m) 528.
conexión(f) para el vídeo(m) 528.
conexión(f) para la impresora(f) 528.
conexión(f) para la manguera(f) de aire(m) 304.
conexión(f) para la red(f) 528.
conexión(f) para unidad(f) de disco(m) 528.
conexión(f) para unidades(f) periféricas 528.
**conexiones(f) 301.**
conexiones(f) 441.
**conexiones(f) de transición(f) 301.**
**conexiones(f) mecánicas 300.**
**conexiones(f), árbol(m) 740.**
CONEXIONES(F), FONTANERÍA(F) 298.
confidente(m) 221.
configuración(f) de almacenamiento(m) 48.
CONFIGURACIÓN(F) DEL LITORAL(M) 30.
**configuración(f) topográfica 28.**
conformación(f) 692.
congelador(m) incorporado 254.
cónico 183.
CONÍFERA(F) 58.
conjuntiva(f) 140.
conjunto(m) de la colmena(f) 82.
conjunto(m) de montañas(f) 51.
**conjunto(m) deportivo 351.**
conjunto(m) vacío 830.
CONJUNTOS(M) INSTRUMENTALES, EJEMPLOS(M) 558.
conmutador(m) de intensidad(f) 309.
connector(m) en T 298.
cono(m) 24, 410.
cono(m) de admisión(f) 501.
cono(m) de penumbra(f) 8.
cono(m) de sombra(f) 8.
cono(m) femenino 58.
cono(m) masculino 58.
cono(m) pirométrico 585.
conopial(m) 174.
consejero(m) de producción(f) 412.
consejeros(m) musicales 412.
consigna(f) 462.
**consola(f) 542.**
consola(f) 545.

Los términos en **negrita** corresponden a una ilustración; los que aparecen en MAYÚSCULAS indican un título.

consola(f) central 430.
consola(f) de control(m) 500.
consola(f) de la unidad(f) de vídeo(m) 527.
consola(f) de sonido(m) 407, 412, 415.
consola(f) para el sistema(m) de vacío(m) 717.
CONSTELACIONES(F) DEL HEMISFERIO(M) AUSTRAL 12.
CONSTELACIONES(F) EN EL HEMISFERIO(M) BOREAL 10.
CONSTRUCCIÓN(F), MATERIALES(M) DE 286, 288.
consumidor(m) 417.
**consumidores(m) primarios 31.**
**consumidores(m) secundarios 31.**
**consumidores(m) terciarios 31.**
contacto(m) 233, 697.
contacto(m) con conexión(f) a tierra(f) 216.
contacto(m) del patín(m) 391.
contacto(m) negativo 768, 769.
contacto(m) positivo 768, 769.
contador(m) 403, 711.
contador(m) de pasadas(f) 568.
contaminación(f) agrícola 32.
**contaminación(f) atmosférica 34.**
**contaminación(f) de alimentos(m) en el agua(f) 32.**
**contaminación(f) de alimentos(m) en la tierra(f) 32.**
contaminación(f) industrial 32, 33.
**contenedor(m) 470.**
contenedor(m) 495, 784.
contenido en 830.
contera(f) 375, 383, 397, 670, 678.
contera(f) de caucho(m) 728.
**contestadora(f) automática 420.**
continental seco-árido 45.
continental seco-semiárido 45.
continente(m) 29.
CONTINENTES(M), CONFIGURACIÓN(F) 20.
contorno(m) del cuello(m) 324.
contrabajo(m) 545.
contrabajos(m) 557.
contrachapado(m) 288.
contrachapado(m) múltiple 288.
contraescalón(m) 201.
contraescarpa(f) 178.
contrafagot(m) 556.
contrafoque(m) 481.
contrafuerte(m) 176, 352, 454, 455, 456, 641, 644.
contrafuerte(m) del talón(m) 354.
contraguardia(f) 179.
contrahilo(m) de la tela(f) 566.
contrahoja(f) 277.
contrapeso(m) 15, 147, 404, 457, 471, 721, 784, 785, 786.
contrapiso(m) 198, 199, 200.
contrapluma(f) 786.
contraquilla(f) 743.
contraventana(f) 203.
**control(m) a larga distancia(f) 411.**
control(m) a larga distancia(f) 397.
**control(m) a larga distancia(f), aguja(f) 467.**
control(m) de agudos(m) 402.
control(m) de alimentador(m) de oxígeno(m) 639.
control(m) de altura(f) 399.
control(m) de balance(m) 402.
control(m) de billetes(m) 463.
control(m) de brillo(m) 529.
control(m) de centrado(m) 529.
control(m) de color(m) 532.
control(m) de combustible(m) 501.
control(m) de contraste(m) 529, 532.
control(m) de elevación(f) de la caja(f) de iluminación(f) 399.
control(m) de entrada(f) de información(f) fina 555.
control(m) de entrada(f) de información(f) rápida 555.
control(m) de fotocopias(f) 532.
control(m) de ganancia(f) 485.
control(m) de grabación(f) 402.
control(m) de graves(m) 402.
control(m) de la calefacción(f) 430.
control(m) de la entrada(f) de aire(m) 204.
control(m) de la plataforma(f) corrediza 718.
control(m) de oxígeno(m) 306.
control(m) de pasaportes(m) 505.
control(m) de posición(f) de la muestra(f) 717.
control(m) de presión(f) 373.
**control(m) de producción(f), sala(f) 413.**
control(m) de secuencias(f) 555.
control(m) de seguridad(f) 504.
control(m) de sintonización(f) 408.
control(m) de sonido(m) 412.
control(m) de temperatura 213.
control(m) de temperatura(f) 209, 256, 297, 585.
control(m) de velocidad(f) 271.
control(m) de volumen(m) 408, 411, 422, 547, 555.
control(m) de volumen(m) de la campana(f) 420.
control(m) de volumen(m) del auricular(m) 420.
control(m) del espejo(m) retrovisor exterior 429.
control(m) del margen(m) 525.
control(m) del nivel(m) de alarma(f) 485.
control(m) del sintetizador(m) 402.
control(m) del sonido(m) 547.
control(m) del sonido(m) estereofónico 413.
control(m) del tiempo(m) 555.
control(m) del vaporizador(m) 256.
control(m) del vector(m) de vibraciones(f) 413.
control(m) del ventilador(m) 214.
control(m) del volumen(m) 402, 420.
control(m) eléctrico de pago(m) 702.
control(m) estereo 408.
control(m) horizontal 529.
control(m) mecánico de agujas(f) 467.
control(m) vertical 529.
controles(m) de intensidad(f) de la pantalla(f) del ordenador(m) 512.
controles(m) de la casete(f) de vídeo(m) 409.
controles(m) de la retroexcavadora(f) 782.
controles(m) de sintonización(f) 410.
controles(m) de volumen(m) de comunicaciones(f) 512.
controles(m) del lector(m) de casetes(m) 408.
controles(m) del lector(m) de discos(m) compactos 408.
controles(m) del piloto(m) automático 500.
controles(m) del sistema(m) de soporte(m) vital 512.
controles(m) VCR 411.
**controles(m), tablero(m) 532.**
conversión(f) del agua(f) en vapor(m) 766.
convertidor(m) catalítico 439.
convertidor(m) de tensión(f) 258.
COORDENADAS(F) ASTRONÓMICAS 3.
COORDENADAS(F) GEOGRÁFICAS 3.
copa(f) 59, 328, 329, 346.
copa(f) de cava(f) 237.
copa(f) de champaña(m) 237.
copa(f) de cóctel(m) 237.
copa(f) de coñac(m) 237.
copa(f) de vino(m) blanco 237.
copa(f) para agua(f) 237.
copa(f) para licores(m) 237.
copa(f) para oporto(m) 237.
copa(f) para vino(m) de Alsacia 237.
copa(f) para vinos(m) de Borgoña 237.
copa(f) para vinos(m) de Burdeos 237.
copete(m) 100, 670.
copias(f) anverso(m)/reverso(m) 532.
copo(m) de nieve(f) 37.
coprocesador(m) 528.
copyright (derechos(m) de autor(m)) 831.
coquina(f) 93.
**corazón(m) 125.**
corazón(m) 64, 88, 92, 97, 130, 695, 818.
**corbata(f) 324.**
corbata(f) inglesa 324.
corchea(f) (octavo(m)) 538.
corchete(m) 644.
corchete(m) de presión(f) 321.
**corchetes(m) 566.**
corchetes(m) 832.
corcho(m) 618.
cordaje(m) 615, 645.
cordal(m) 544.
corderas(f) 621.
cordero(m) 150.
cordillera(f) 7, 23.
cordón(m) 229, 230, 231, 256, 260, 320, 352, 354, 381, 596, 644, 692.
cordón(m) del pedal(m) 572.
cordón(m) espermático 127.
**cordón(m) para espirales(f) 584.**
cordones(m) de listones(m) 231.
corimbo(m) 60.
**corintio, orden(m) 167.**
**cornamenta(f) 105.**
córnea(f) 140.
córner(m) 601.
corneta(f) 817.
cornete(m) inferior 141.
cornete(m) medio 141.
cornete(m) superior 141.
cornetín(m) 550, 556.
cornisa(f) 166, 168, 196, 202, 225.
cornisa(f) inclinada 168.
corno(m) francés 551.
corno(m) inglés 548.
cornos(m) franceses 557.
cornos(m) ingleses 557.
coro(m) 177.
coroides(m) 140.
corola(f) 60.
Corona Austral 13.
Corona Boreal 11.
corona(f) 6, 101, 144, 363, 545, 553, 590, 706, 832.
corona(f) externa de la cadena(f) 448.
corona(f) interna de la cadena(f) 448.
corona(f) radiata 128.
corona(f) rotatoria 784.
corpiño(m) 345.
corral(m) 148.
correa(f) 365, 383, 428, 631, 645, 649, 660, 662, 679, 706, 777.
correa(f) con broche(m) 375.
correa(f) de ajuste(m) 641.
correa(f) de amortiguación(f) 636.
correa(f) de barbilla(f) 602.
correa(f) de crampones(m) 680.
correa(f) de distribución(f) 434.
correa(f) de la cincha(f) 649.
correa(f) de la manga(f) 319.
correa(f) de muñeca(f) 681.
correa(f) de retención(f) 383.
correa(f) de seguridad(f) 512, 617.
correa(f) de transmisión(f) 492.
correa(f) del casco(m) 777.
correa(f) del tambor(m) 258.
correa(f) del ventilador(m) 434.
correa(f) para el cuello(m) 729.
correa(f) para el pie(m) 633.
correa(f) para escalera(f) y manguera(f) 777.
correa(f) para herramientas(f) 512.
correa(f) para la mano(f) 640, 642.
correa(f) principal de sustentación(f) 636.
correas(f) 730.
correas(f) de los aparatos(m) de buceo(m) 627.
corrección(f) de caracteres(m) 525.
corrección(f) de palabras(f) 525.
corrector(m) de ortografía(f) 524.
corredera(f) 230, 543, 566.
corredera(f) con enganches(m) 230.
corredera(f) de afinamiento(m) 551.
corredera(f) de ajuste(m) 323.
corredera(f) de la guía(f) 285.
corredor(m) 188.
corredor(m) de enlace(m) 461.
corredor(m) de poder(m) 603, 605.
corredor(m) derecho 603.
corredor(m) izquierdo 603.
corredor(m) ligero 605.
corredor(m) telescópico 503.
corriente(f) subterránea 24, 32.
corrosivo 821.
corsé(m) de cintura(f) de avispa(f) 347.
corta sencilla 339.
**cortacésped(m) 271.**
**cortacésped(m) eléctrico 271.**
cortador(m) de alambre(m) 311.
cortador(m) de huevos(m) duros 246.
cortafuego(m) 198.
cortahilos(m) 562.
cortapastas(m) 245.
**cortasetos(m) eléctrico 268.**
cortatubos(m) 299.
**cortaúñas(m) 365.**
cortavientos(m) 14.
**corte(m) de un bulbo(m) 70.**
**corte(m) de un diamante(m) 363.**
**corte(m) de un folículo(m) 67.**
**corte(m) de un fruto(m) carnoso con hueso(m) 63.**
**corte(m) de un fruto(m) carnoso con semillas(f) 64.**
**corte(m) de un panal(m) 82.**
corte(m) princesa(f) 332.
**corte(m) sagital 127, 128, 129, 142.**
**corte(m) transversal 702.**
**corte(m) transversal de la pelota(f) 596.**
**corte(m) transversal de un tronco(m) 59.**
**corte(m) transversal de una pipa(f) 385.**
**corte(m) transversal de una pistola(f) de pintar 590.**
**corte(m), riel(m) 466.**
corteza(f) 65.
corteza(f) terrestre 22, 23.
CORTEZA(F) TERRESTRE, CORTE(M) 22.
corteza(m) 59.
**cortina(f) 229.**
cortina(f) 178, 220, 229, 414.
**cortina(f) abombada 229.**
cortina(f) de inyecciones(f) 748, 749.
**cortina(f) de riel(m) 230.**
**cortina(f) de ventana(f) 228.**
**cortina(f) suelta corrediza 228.**
**cortina(f) sujeta de doble barra(f) 228.**
cortinas(f) corredizas 229.
**cortinas(f) cruzadas 229.**
**cortinas(f), tipos(m) de 228.**
corvejón(m) 101, 106.
COSECHA(F) 159, 160, 162.
**cosecha(f) 155.**
cosechadora(f) de forraje(m) 155.
**cosechadora(f) trilladora(f) 160.**
cosechadora(f) trilladora(f) 155.
**cosechera(f) de forraje(m) 162.**
**coser, máquina(f) de 561.**
**cosido(m) 577.**
costa(f) 30.
costado(m) 433, 579, 787.
costero(m) 288.
costilla(f) 97, 102, 129, 670.
costilla(f) axial 94.
costilla(f) de encastre(m) 498.
costilla(f) espiral 94.
costilla(f) falsa (3) 123.
costillar(m) 584.
costillas(f) 122.
COSTURA(F) 561, 562, 564, 566.
costura(f) 322, 327, 355, 384, 596, 598.
costura(f) de corte(m) princesa(f) 345.
costura(f) invisible 324.
**costura(f), accesorios(m) de 564.**
cota(f) de malla(f) 792.
cotiledón(m) 57.
cotillo(m) 275.
cotufa(f) 71.
Cowper, glándula(f) de 127.
coxa(f) 78, 80.
cráneo(m) 88, 102, 116, 134.
Cráter 13.
cráter(m) 7, 25, 733.
creciente(m) 6, 819.
**cremallera(f) 566.**
cremallera(f) 280, 321, 350, 351, 365, 382.
cremallera(f) de fijación(f) 718.
cremáster(m) 78.
crépida(f) 166, 168, 169.
cresta(f) 27, 30.
cresta(f) de la presa(f) 746.
cresta(f) del aliviadero(m) 746.
crestón(m) 792.
criba(m) 161.
CRICKET(M) 598.
**cricket(m), jugador(m) de 598.**
**cricket(m), pelota(f) de 598.**
crin(f) 100, 544.
**crisálida(f) 78.**
crisálida(f) 82.
cristal(m) 768, 769.
CRISTALERÍA(F) 237.
**cristales(m) de nieve(f), clasificación(f) 36.**
cristales(m) irregulares 37.
cristalino(m) 140.
croissant(m) 153.
cromatina(f) 115.
cromosfera(f) 6.
cronometrador(m) 610, 612, 626, 666, 668, 669.
cronometrador(m) de calle(f) 621.
cronometrador(m) de presas(f) 668.
**cronómetro(m) 706.**
cronómetro(m) 407.
cruce(m) 467.
cruce(m) con preferencia(f) 825.
cruce(m) de animales(m) salvajes 828.
cruce(m) del eclipse(m) 419.

Los términos en **negrita** corresponden a una ilustración; los que aparecen en MAYÚSCULAS indican un título.

crucero(m) 176, 177.
crucero(m) del transepto(m) 177.
cruceta(f) 628.
cruceta(f) de cabeza(f) 787.
CRUSTÁCEO(M) 90.
**crustáceos(m) comestibles comunes 90.**
Cruz del Sur 13.
cruz(f) 100, 106, 483, 818.
cruzada 334.
cruzado 333.
cuaderna(f) 743, 785.
cuadernillo(m) 577.
cuadrado 343.
cuadrante(m) 705, 706, 712.
cuadrante(m) calculador 396.
cuadro(m) 674.
cuadro(m) de bateo(m) 596.
cuadro(m) de saque(m) 614.
cuadro(m) de servicio(m) de dobles(m) 618.
cuadro(m) de servicio(m) de individuales(m) 618.
cuadro(m) de temperaturas(f) 256.
cuarta(f) 105, 537, 667.
cuartel(m) de la guardia(f) 178, 180.
cuarteles(m) 179.
cuarteto(m) 558.
cuartilla(f) 101.
cuarto hueso(m) metacarpiano 112.
cuarto(m) 104, 352, 354.
cuarto(m) creciente 6.
cuarto(m) de baño(m) 194, 195.
CUARTO(M) DE BAÑO(M), FONTANERÍA 292.
cuarto(m) de estar 195, 685.
cuarto(m) de lavado(m) 194.
cuarto(m) de servicio(m) 172, 173.
cuarto(m) menguante 7.
**cuarzo(m), metrónomo(m) 539.**
CUATRO PALOS(M), BARCO(M) DE VELA(F) 478, 480.
cuatro tiempos(m), motor(m) 436.
CUBERTERÍA(F) 239, 240.
**cubertería(f) 688.**
cubeta(f) 258, 398.
cubeta(f) congeladora 251.
cubeta(f) de alcohol(m) 705.
cubeta(f) de lavado(m) 257.
cubeta(f) de mercurio(m) 705.
**cubeta(f) para lavar impresiones(f) 399.**
cubeta(f) para verdura(f) 254.
cubículo(m) 170.
cubículo(m) de la ducha(f) 292.
**cubierta(f) 579.**
cubierta(f) 211, 214, 251, 255, 309, 403, 485, 496, 529, 796, 804.
cubierta(f) de aterrizaje(m) 811.
cubierta(f) de control(m) 699.
cubierta(f) de la aguja(f) 404.
cubierta(f) de la cabina(f) 638.
cubierta(f) de popa(f) 496.
cubierta(f) de seguridad(f) 271.
cubierta(f) de tejas(f) 169.
cubierta(f) de vidrio(m) 254.
cubierta(f) de vuelo(m) 810.
cubierta(f) del cubo(m) 754.
cubierta(f) del embrague(m) 444.
cubierta(f) del mecanismo(m) 774.
cubierta(f) del mecanismo(m) del freno(m) 470.
cubierta(f) deslizable 484.
cubierta(f) exterior de la cúpula(f) 14.
cubierta(f) frontal 577.
cubierta(f) inferior 741.
cubierta(f) interior de la bóveda(f) 14.
cubierta(f) para automóviles(m) 494.
cubierta(f) posterior 577.
cubierta(f) principal 743, 811.
cubierta(f) protectora 785.
cubierta(f) superior 498, 741.
cubierta(f) superior de la turbina(f) 753.
cubierta(f) térmica 510.
cubilete(m) 697.
cubital(m) anterior 120, 121.
cubital(m) posterior 121.
cúbito(m) 102, 122.
cubo(m) 727, 754, 774.
cubo(m) de flash(m) 393.
cubo(m) de la escalera(f) 194.
cubo(m) del rotor(m) 508.
cubrecazoleta(f) 795.
cubrellama(m) 796.
**cuchara(f) 241, 672.**
cuchara(f) 241, 587, 672, 688.
cuchara(f) de mesa(f) 241.
cuchara(f) para café(m) 241.
cuchara(f) para helado(m) 241.
cuchara(f) para postre(m) 241.
cuchara(f) para servir helado(m) 246.
cuchara(f) para sopa(f) 241.
cuchara(f) para té(m) 241.
cucharas(f) para medir 244.
**cucharas(f), tipos(m) de 241.**
cucharón(m) 244, 782, 801.
cucharón(m) excavador 785.
cuchilla(f) 158, 250, 251, 256, 268, 271, 311, 369, 609.
cuchilla(f) de corte(m) 783, 784.
cuchilla(f) de disco(m) 156.
cuchilla(f) fija 578.
cuchilla(f) móvil 578.
cuchilla(f) para delimitar el césped(m) 266.
cuchilla(f) para moldear 365.
cuchillas(f) para batir 250.
**cuchillas(f), tipos(m) de 587.**
**cuchillo(m) 239.**
cuchillo(m) 688, 690.
**cuchillo(m) de cocina(f) 242.**
cuchillo(m) de combate(m) 794.
cuchillo(m) de contornear 581, 587.
cuchillo(m) de mesa(f) 239.
cuchillo(m) de pedernal(m) 791.
cuchillo(m) de trinchar 242.
cuchillo(m) paleta(f) 589.
cuchillo(m) para carne(f) 239.
cuchillo(m) para desbastar 585.
cuchillo(m) para mantequilla(f) 239.
cuchillo(m) para pescado(m) 239.
cuchillo(m) para postre(m) 239.
cuchillo(m) para queso(m) 239.
**cuchillos(m) de cocina(f), tipos(m) de 242.**
**cuchillos(m), tipos(m) de 239.**
cuelgue al aire(m) libre después de escurrir 829.
cuelgue sin exprimir, dando forma(f) a mano(f) 829.
**cuello(m) 341.**
cuello(m) 57, 97, 100, 117, 118, 119, 127, 144, 240, 241, 306, 319, 322, 324, 325, 410, 678.
cuello(m) con botones(m) 324.
cuello(m) de cisne(m) 201.
cuello(m) de doble vista(f) 319.
cuello(m) de ganso(m) 784.
cuello(m) de Holanda 318.
cuello(m) de pico(m) 326.
**cuello(m) del remo(m) 632.**
cuello(m) del remo(m) 632.
cuello(m) del útero(m) 128.
cuello(m) en V 322.
cuello(m) hechura(f) sastre(m) 330.
**cuello(m) italiano 324.**
cuello(m) redondo 350.
**cuellos(m) 341, 342.**
cuenca(f) 26.
**cuenca(f) oceánica 29.**
cuenco(m) 241.
cuenco(m) de queso(m) blando 238.
cuentakilómetros(m) 431.
cuentalitros(m) 453.
cuerda(f) 541, 544, 545, 665, 669, 684, 706, 793.
cuerda(f) de disparo(m) 802.
cuerda(f) de elevación(f) 302.
cuerda(f) inferior 455.
cuerda(f) maestra 645.
cuerda(f) para el cosido(m) 578.
cuerda(f) superior 455.
cuerda(f) vocal 130.
CUERDA(F), INSTRUMENTOS(M) 544, 546.
cuerdas(f) 540, 553.
cuerdas(f) de acompañamiento(m) 535.
cuerdas(f) de suspensión(f) 636.
cuerdas(f) melódicas 535.
cuerdas(f) para eslálom(m) 633.
cuerno(m) 364.
cuernos(m) 83.
cuernos(m) de carnero(m) 99.
cuernos(m) de jirafa(f) 99.
cuernos(m) de rinoceronte(m) 99.
CUERNOS(M): TIPOS(M) MÁS COMUNES 99.
cuero(m) 323.
cuerpo(m) 252, 281, 294, 295, 384, 549, 645, 658, 666, 670, 711.
cuerpo(m) calloso 134.
cuerpo(m) cavernoso 127.
cuerpo(m) celular 135.
cuerpo(m) de baquelita(f) 804.
cuerpo(m) de la torre(f) 756.
cuerpo(m) de la uña(f) 137.
cuerpo(m) del fórnix(m) 134.
cuerpo(m) metálico de la bujía(f) 439.
cuerpo(m) sólido 547.
cuerpo(m) vertebral 135.
cuerpos(m) de Nissl 135.
Cuervo 13.
culata(f) 363, 549, 795, 796, 797, 798, 799.
culata(f) de los cilindros(m) 435.
culata(f) de succión(f) 216.
culote(m) 798, 799, 804.
**cultivador(m) 157.**
cultivador(m) 154.
cultivador(m) de mano(f) 268.
**cultivadora(f) 272.**
CULTIVO(M) DEL SUELO(M), PASOS(M) 154.
cumulonimbos(m) 44.
cúmulos(m) 44.
**cuña(f) 681.**
cuña(f) 277, 542, 802.
cuneta(f) 451, 682.
cúpula(f) 66, 183, 486.
cúpula(f) de la carlinga(f) 813.
cúpula(f) del Mihrab(m) 173.
cúpula(f) del pórtico(m) 172, 173.
cúpula(f) giratoria 14.
cureña(f) 793, 800.
curitas(f) 725.
CURLING(M) 620.
**curling(m), escobas(f) de 620.**
**curling(m), piedra(f) de 620.**
curva(f) 452, 671.
curva(f) a la derecha(f) 826, 827.
curva(f) del club(m) 651.
curva(f) doble 826, 827.
curva(f) lejana 651.
curva(f) para carrera(f) steeplechase(m) 655.
curvada 587.
cúter(m) Marconi 482.

## D

dado(m) 697.
dado(m) común 699.
dado(m) de póquer(m) 699.
dado(m) doble 697.
DADOS(M) 699.
daga(f) 794.
dama(f) 697.
**dardo(m) 698.**
DARDOS(M), JUEGO(M) 698.
dátil(m) 63.
de acero(m) a plástico(m) 301.
de aguja(f) 183.
de arco(m) conopial 182.
de aspas(f) 250.
de camiseta(f) 333.
de campana(f) 332, 334.
de carnicero(m) 242.
de chal(m) 341.
de cobre(m) a acero(m) 301.
de cobre(m) a plástico(m) 301.
de corazón(m) 343.
de cuatro aguas(f) 182.
de cuatro aguas(f) con canalera(f) 183.
de cuatro cuartos(m) 537.
de cuatro pezuñas(f) 99.
de cúpula(f) 183.
de dos aguas(f) 182.
de dos mitades(f) 537.
de dos pezuñas(f) 99.
de fuelle(m) 339.
de gancho(m) 250.
de globo(m) 340.
de herradura(f) 174.
de jamón(m) 340.
de lazo(m) 342.
de linternilla(f) 182.
de manguito(m) 339.
de momia(f) 687.
de murciélago(m) 339.
de ojal(m) 343.
de ojal(m) con ribete(m) 339.
de ojal(m) de sastre(m) 339.
de ojiva(f) lanceolada 174.
de pabellón(m) 183.
de pagoda(f) 340.
de parche(m) 339.
de pico(m) 343.
de piezas(f) 334.
de rotonda(f) 183.
de talle(m) largo 332.
de torrecilla(f) 183.
de tortuga(f) 338, 342.
de tres cuartos(m) 537.
de tres pezuñas(f) 99.
de una pezuña(f) 99.
de verano(m) 332.
de vertiente(f) simple 182.
de volantes(m) 334, 341.
deambulatorio(m) 177.
declinación(f) 3.
dedal(m) 563.
**dedo(m) 137.**
dedo(m) 84, 111, 327, 596, 681.
dedo(m) anular 137.
dedo(m) de pata(f) lobulada 111.
dedo(m) de pata(f) palmípeda 111.
dedo(m) del corazón(m) 137.
dedo(m) del pie(m) 118.
dedo(m) externo 108.
dedo(m) índice 137.
dedo(m) interno 108.
dedo(m) medio 108.
dedo(m) meñique 137.
dedo(m) palmeado 84.
dedo(m) posterior 108, 111.
dedos(m) del pie(m), extensor(m) común de los 120.
dedos(m), extensor(m) común de los 121.
**defensa(f) 603, 605.**
defensa(f) 611.
defensa(f) de cierre(m) 606.
defensa(m) central 601.
defensa(m) central izquierdo 607.
defensa(m) derecho 601, 608.
defensa(m) izquierdo 601, 608.
defensa(m) lateral derecho 607.
defensa(m) lateral izquierdo 607.
deflector(m) 210, 216, 264, 271, 742.
deflector(m) de viento(m) 440.
deflector(m) de viento(m) de los aviones(m) 810.
deflector(m) del tanque(m) de oxígeno(m) liquido 509.
Deimos 4.
delantero(m) 322, 324, 606.
delantero(m) central 613.
delantero(m) centro 601.
delantero(m) derecho 613.
delantero(m) izquierdo 613.
delantero(m) número 8 606.
Delfín 11.
delineador(m) 367.
delineador(m) de labios(m) 366.
deltoides(m) 120.
demarcación(f) 698.
dendrita(f) 135.
dendrita(f) espacial 36.
dentada 56.
**dentadura(f) humana 144.**
dentículo(m) 166, 167.
dentífrico(m) 373.
dentina(f) 144.
deportivo(m) 425.
depósito de polvo(m) 260.
depósito(m) de aceite(m) 272.
depósito(m) de agua(f) 247, 469.
depósito(m) de aire(m) comprimido 469.
depósito(m) de combustible(m) 468, 812.
depósito(m) de contenedores(m) 491.
depósito(m) de gas(m) 386.
depósito(m) de grano(m) 161.
depósito(m) de lodos(m) 737.
depósito(m) de mercancía(f) en tránsito(m) 490.
depósito(m) de misiles(m) 808.
depósito(m) de municiones(f) 805.
depósito(m) de pintura(f) 304.
depósito(m) del agua(f) 373.
depósito(m) del combustible(m) 508, 805.
depósito(m) del grano(m) 160.
depósito(m) externo de combustible(m) 510.
depósito(m) para el decorado(m) 188.
depósitos(m) 511.
depresión(f) barométrica 38.
derecha(f) del actor(m) 189.
derecha(f) del espectador(m) 189.
derecho(m) 567.
derivación(f) de toma(f) de aire(m) 215.
dermis(f) 137.
derrubios(m) 24.
desagüe(m) 215, 292.
desagüe(m) de la turbina(f) 755.
desagüe(m) principal 215.
desatrancador(m) 299.
desbastador(m) 369.
desbastador(m) de cutícula(f) 365.
desbaste(m) 586.
descamador(m) 688.
descansabrazos(m) 727.

Los términos en **negrita** corresponden a una ilustración; los que aparecen en MAYÚSCULAS indican un título.

descanso(m) del macillo(m) 541.
descanso(m) del pie(m) 727.
descapotable(m) 425.
descompresor(m) 627.
desenganchador(m) 291.
desenganchador(m) manual 641.
desértico 45.
desfiladero(m) 24.
deshuesador(m) de frutas(f) 246.
DESIERTO(M) 46.
desierto(m) arenoso 46.
desierto(m) rocoso 46.
desigual a 830.
desnivel(m) 193.
despachador(m) de hojas(f) de afeitar 374.
despacho(m) de camareros(m) 461.
despejado 39.
despensa(f) 195.
desplantador(m) 268.
despliegue(m) completo 419.
despliegue(m) de la antena(f) del radar(m) 49.
despliegue(m) del panel solar 419.
despliegue(m) del panel(m) solar 48.
despliegue(m) del reflector(m) del este(m) 419.
destacador(m) 515.
destilador(m) para asfalto(m) 745.
destinos(m) 463.
destorcedor(m) 672.
**destornillador(m) 276.**
destornillador(m) 688.
destornillador(m) de cruceta(f) 688.
**destornillador(m) de trinquete(m) 276.**
desviación(f) 301.
desyerbador(m) 268.
**detección(f) de ondas(f) sísmicas 714.**
detector(m) de alta tensión(f) 310.
detector(m) de continuidad(f) 310.
**detector(m) de tensión(f) 310.**
detonador(m) 804.
devanadera(f) 575.
**devanador(m) 575.**
devanador(m) 671.
**devanador(m) de bobinas(f) 575.**
devolución(f) de monedas(f) 422.
devolución(f) de monedas(f) rechazadas 702.
devolvedor(m) 683.
diablo(m) 306.
diadema(f) 729.
diafragma(m) 130, 401, 406.
diafragma(m) de expansión 485.
diafragma(m) de iris(m) 390.
diafragma(m) de vacío(m) 435.
diagonal(f) 832.
diagonal(m) 756.
**diagrama(m) de la circulación(f) 124.**
**diagramas(m) de tejidos(m) 576.**
diamante(m) 363, 451, 597, 695.
**diamante(m), corte(m) 363.**
**diana(f) 698.**
diapasón(m) 539, 544, 547, 707.
**diapositiva(f) 397.**
diapositiva(f) 397.
**diapositivas(f), proyector(m) 397.**
diastema(f) 98.
dibujo(m) 350, 570.
dibujo(m) de la superficie(f) de rodadura(f) 433.
DIBUJO(M) Y PINTURA(F) 588, 590, 592.
diente(m) 96, 158, 159, 160, 162, 240, 268, 277, 284, 369, 445, 785.
diente(m) de cucharón(m) 782.
diente(m) de la charnela(f) 95.
diente(m) de león(m) 73.
diente(m) del zanco(m) 783.
DIENTES(M) 144.
dientes(m) 566, 644.
dientes(m) de la leva(f) 562.
**dientes(m), cepillo(m) de 373.**
diéresis(f) 832.
diésel(m) 745.
diésel(m) para barcos 745.
difusor(m) 396.
DIGESTIVO, APARATO(M) 131.
**dijes(m) 364.**
dínamo(f) 446.
**dinamómetro(m) 709.**
dintel(m) 175, 202, 204.
diodo(m) 769.
dióxido(m) 33.
dique(m) 25, 490.
**dique(m) de machones(m), corte(m) transversal 751.**
dique(m) de operación(f) 752.
**dique(m) de terraplén(m), corte(m) transversal 748.**
dique(m) inerte 752.
dique(m) seco 490.
dirección(f) 465, 831.
dirección(f) de la Meca(f) 173.
dirección(f) de los puntos(m) 488.
**dirección(f) del viento(m),medición(f) 41.**
dirección(f) obligatoria 824, 825.
dirección(f) y velocidad(f) del viento(m) 38.
dirección(m) del viento(m) 38.
directorio(m) telefónico 516.
**disco(m) 251, 284, 404, 608, 658.**
disco(m) 157, 284, 285, 432, 433, 529, 583, 663, 712.
**disco(m) compacto 405.**
disco(m) compacto 408.
**disco(m) compacto, lector(m) 405.**
disco(m) de ajuste(m) de ascención(f) recta 720, 721.
disco(m) de ajuste(m) de declinación(f) 720, 721.
disco(m) de articulación(f) 440.
disco(m) de caucho(m) 404.
disco(m) de tensión(f) 562, 569.
disco(m) desviador de calor(m) 232.
**disco(m) duro, unidad(f) 529.**
**disco(m) flexible 529.**
**disco(m) flexible pequeño 529.**
disco(m) giratorio 250.
disco(m) microondas(f) 415.
disco(m) óptico 527.
disco(m) tapador 158.
disco(m) y martillo(m) (lanzamiento(m)) 654.
**disco(m), freno(m) 432.**
discontinuidad(f) de Mohorovicic 22.
discontinuidad(m) de Gutenberg 22.
**discos(m), pulverizador(m) 157.**
diseño(m) 586.
diskette(m) 526.
disparador(m) 264, 780.
disparador(m) de cable(m) 393.
disparador(m) de pago(m) 702.
disparador(m) de señuelo(m) 809.
disparador(m) neumático 393.
**disparo(m), accesorios(m) 801.**
disposición(f) de los bolos(m) 683.
dispositivo(m) antideslizante 404.
dispositivo(m) de protección(f) 549.
dispositivo(m) para enmarcar 578.
distancia(f) recorrida 711.
DISTANCIA(F), MEDICIÓN(F) 711.
distribución(f) al consumidor(m) 755.
distribución(f) por redes(f) de cable(m) 416.
distribuidor(m) de calor(m) 209.
distribuidora(f) de billetes(m) de transferencia(f) 475.
distrito(m) 52.
**divisiones(f) de los escudos(m) 818.**
divisores(m) 519.
do(C) 537.
doble 646.
**doble caja(f), camión(m) tractor(m) 440.**
doble caña(f) 549.
doble cero(m) 700.
**doble filo(m), tijeras(f) para entresacar 369.**
doble fuelle(m) 536.
doble techo(m) 685.
doble toldo(m) 686.
doble vía(f) 824, 825.
doble(m) bemol 538.
doble(m) cero 700.
doble(m) sostenido 538.
doblez(m) 341, 565.
doblez(m) hacia el interior(m) 799.
doceava costilla(f) 122.
docena(f) (1 a 12) 700, 701.
docena(f) (13 a 24) 700, 701.
docena(f) (25 a 36) 700, 701.
dólar(m) 832.
DOMINÓ(M) 695.
domo(m) de vidrio(m) 484.
**dórico, orden(m) 167.**
dormitorio(m) 194, 195, 460, 685.
dormitorio(m) principal 194.
**dorsal(f) oceánica 28.**
dorsal(m) ancho 121.
dorso(m) 143, 288, 793.
dorso(m) del pie(m), arteria(f) del 126.
dos pares(m) 695.
dos puntos(m) 832.
**dos tiempos(m), motor(m) 436.**
dos(m) doble 695.
dosel(m) 229.
dosel(m) fruncido 229.
dosel(m) plisado 229.
dosel(m) plisado de canotillo(m) 229.
doselera(f) 228.
**doseles(m), tipos(m) de 229.**
Douglas, saco(m) de 128.
dovela(f) 174.
dovelaje(m) 175.
dracma(m) 832.
Dragón 11.
drapeado 343.
driver(m), palo(m) núm. 1 678.
driza(f) 480, 817.
drupéolo(m) 62.
ducha(f) 194.
ducha(f) de teléfono(m) 292.
ducha(f) y bañera(f) 215.
duna(f) 30.
duna(f) compleja 46.
duna(f) parabólica 46.
dunas(f) longitudinales 46.
dunas(f) paralelas 46.
dúo(m) 558.
duodeno(m) 131.
duramadre(f) 134, 135.
duramen(m) 59.

## E

eclipse(m) anular 8.
ECLIPSE(M) DE LUNA(F) 8.
ECLIPSE(M) DE SOL(M) 8.
eclipse(m) parcial 8.
eclipse(m) total 8.
écliptica(f) 3.
eclisa(f) 466.
eco(m) 722.
ECOLOGÍA(F) 31, 32, 34.
ecuador(m) 3, 47.
ecuador(m) celeste 3.
EDAD(F) DE PIEDRA(F), ARMAS(F) 791.
edificio(m) 766.
edificio(m) comercial 185.
edificio(m) de apartamentos(m) 185, 187.
edificio(m) de la administración(f) 752.
edificio(m) de la turbina(f) 758.
EDIFICIO(M) DE OFICINAS(F) 190.
edificio(m) de oficinas(f) 184, 185.
edificio(m) del reactor(m) 759, 765.
edificio(m) público 52.
edredón(m) 224.
efectos(m) especiales video\digital 413.
efluvio(m) 216.
eje(m) 251, 290, 374, 468, 564, 575, 584, 645, 707, 808.
eje(m) de cuchillas(f) 156.
eje(m) de declinación(f) 14.
eje(m) de dirección(f) 788.
eje(m) de la rueda(f) 447.
eje(m) de las aspas(f) 773.
eje(m) de tiro(m) 802.
eje(m) de toma(f) de fuerza(f) 156, 159, 162.
eje(m) del cepillo(m) 373.
eje(m) del pedal(m) 448.
eje(m) delantero 784.
**eje(m) horizontal, turbina(f) de viento(m) 774.**
eje(m) polar 14.
eje(m) propulsor 492.
**eje(m) vertical, turbina(f) de viento(m) 774.**
el agua(f) de un lago(m) o de un río(m) enfría el vapor(m) utilizado 767.
el agua(f) regresa al generador(m) de vapor(m) 767.
el cuatro 632.
el cuatro con timonel(m) 632.
el dos 632.
el dos con timonel(m) 632.
el galope(m) 101.
EL OÍDO(M) 138.
EL OLFATO(M) 141.
el paso(m) 101.
el paso(m) de andadura(f) 101.
el refrigerante(m) transfiere el calor(m) al generador(m) de vapor(m) 766.
el trote(m) 101.
el vapor(m) se condensa en agua(f) 767.
elástico(m) 224, 382.
ELECTRICIDAD(F) 309, 310, 312, 746, 748, 750, 752, 754, 756.
**electricidad(f), transmisión(f) 757.**
**electricista(m), herramientas(f) de 310, 311.**
electrodo(m) 232, 305.
electrodo(m) central 439.
electrodo(m) de masa(f) 439.
ELECTRODOMÉSTICOS, APARATOS(M) 250, 252, 254, 256, 257, 258, 260.
electrodos(m) 233.
electrodos(m) de encendido(m) 209.
**electrones(m), cañón(m) 410.**
ELECTRONES(M), MICROSCOPIO(M) 717.
elemento(m) calorífero 207, 209.
**elemento(m) cargador de combustible(m) 765.**
elemento(m) cargador de combustible(m) 765.
elemento(m) horizontal 756.
elemento(m) negativo 831.
elemento(m) positivo 831.
ELEMENTOS(M) BÁSICOS DE UN PLANO(M) 195.
**elevación(f) 193.**
elevación(f) continental 29.
elevador(m) 160, 161, 764, 782.
elevador(m) del brazo(m) 404.
elevador(m) telescópico 780.
embalse(m) 746, 748, 749, 750, 751, 752.
embalse(m) de la presa(f) 747.
embarcación(f) de emergencia(f) 739.
emblema(m) 596, 817.
embocadura(f) del cable(m) 256.
émbolo(m) 159, 726.
embrague(m) de espacios(m) 525.
embudo(m) 243.
embutidor(m) 251.
**empacadora(f) de heno(m) 159.**
empacadora(f) de heno(m) 155.
empalizada(f) 181, 263, 646, 647.
**empalmadura(f) 692.**
**empalme(m) de rieles(m) 466.**
empalme(m) hidráulico 147.
empaque(m) 741.
empaquetadura(f) 294.
empate(m) de la boquilla(f) 550.
empeine(m) 325.
empella(f) 353, 355.
empujacutículas(m) 365.
empuje(m) 455.
empuñaderas(f) 665.
empuñadura(f) 281, 375, 596, 615, 633, 658, 665, 666, 670, 677, 679, 684, 793, 796, 798, 799.
empuñadura(f) del carro(m) 568.
empuñadura(f) delantera 804.
**empuñaduras(f) para esquí(m) 633.**
**empuñaduras(f) para esquí(m) de figuras(f) 633.**
en escalera(f) 362.
en espiral(f) 250.
en flor(f) 61.
en pendiente(f) 182.
en prisión(f) 700, 701.
en tijera(f) 362.
ENCAJE(M) DE BOLILLOS(M) 570.
encañado(m) 263.
**encendedor(m) 307, 386.**
encendido(m) 271.
encendido(m) \ apagado 408.
encendido(m) \ apagado(m) \ volumen(m) 408.
**enceradora(f) 358.**
enchufe(m) 255, 280, 309, 310, 400, 401, 406, 408, 485, 561, 585.
enchufe(m) con control(m) de tiempo(m) 255.
enchufe(m) de recarga(f) 374.
enchufe(m) del termómetro(m) 253.
enchufe(m) hembra(f) 400.
enchufe(m) para auriculares(m) 408.
enchufe(m) y selector(m) desmontables 253.
encía(f) 142, 144.
ENCUADERNACIÓN(F) ARTÍSTICA 578.
ENCUADERNACIÓN(F) ARTÍSTICA(F) 577.
**encuadernación(f) en rústica 578.**
endocarpio(m) 63, 64.
eneldo(m) 74.
ENERGÍA(F) EÓLICA 773, 774.
ENERGÍA(F) NUCLEAR 758, 760, 762, 764, 766.
**energía(f) nuclear, producción(f) de electricidad(f) 766.**
ENERGÍA(F) SOLAR 768, 770, 772.

Los términos en **negrita** corresponden a una ilustración; los que aparecen en MAYÚSCULAS indican un título.

**energía(f) solar, producción(f) de electricidad(f) 771.**
enfoque(m) de cerca 376.
enfoque(m) de lejos 376.
enfriador(m) 438.
enfriador(m) de la cámara(f) del generador(m) de vapor(m) 759.
enganche(m) 566.
enganche(m) de conducto(m) 590.
enganche(m) del remolque(m) 449.
**enganche(m), cabeza(f) 471.**
engaste(m) 364.
engranaje(m) 573, 575, 702.
engranaje(m) de avance(m) 256.
engrasador(m) 246.
enhebrador(m) 563.
enramada(f) 263.
enredadera(f) 263.
enrejado(m) 747.
enriquecimiento(m) del agua(f) pesada 759.
ensaladera(f) 238.
**ensamblaje(m) a espiga(f) 578.**
**ensamblaje(m) abocinado 300.**
**ensamblaje(m) por compresión(f) 300.**
ensamble(m) hembra(f) 670.
ensamble(m) macho(m) 670.
ENSILAJE(M) 162.
**ensilaje(m) 155.**
entablado(m) 198, 199.
entablamento(m) 166, 168, 202.
entarimado(m) 669.
**entarimado(m) sobre estructura(f) de madera(f) 200.**
entera 56.
entintado(m) 580.
entrada(f) 82, 195, 452, 625, 787.
entrada(f) de admisión(f) de combustible(m) 764.
entrada(f) de agua(f) 295, 747.
entrada(f) de agua(f) fría 297.
entrada(f) de aire(m) 445, 501, 508.
entrada(f) de aire(m) frío 438.
entrada(f) de cabeza(f) 624.
entrada(f) de campo(m) 407.
**entrada(f) de información(f), unidades(f) 526.**
entrada(f) de la contracorriente(f) 759.
entrada(f) de la estación(f) 474.
entrada(f) de pie(m) 624.
entrada(f) del agua(f) de enfriamiento(m) del condensador(m) 759.
entrada(f) del coche(m) 193, 196.
entrada(f) del refrigerante(m) 768.
entrada(f) del residuo(m) de combustible(m) 764.
entrada(f) del suministro(m) 757.
entrada(f) para audífonos(m) 402.
entrada(f) para auriculares(m) 555.
entrada(f) para entregas(f) 190.
entrada(f) para mercancía(f) 190.
entrada(f) principal 190, 194.
**entradas(f) al agua(f) 624.**
entre(m) 830.
entrecejo(m) 106.
entrediente(m) 240.
entrega(f) de equipaje(m) 504.
entrega(f) del grano(m) 161.
entrenador(m) 669.
entrenudo(m) 57.
entrepaño(m) 225, 302.
entrepaño(m) horizontal 202.
entrepaño(m) vertical 202.
entrepierna(f) 325, 337.
entrepiso(m) 474.
**entresuelo(m) 194.**
entresuelo(m) 195.
entretela(f) de abrigo(m) 565.
entretela(f) de armado(m) 565.
entretela(f) de refuerzo(m) 565.
envasado(m) del residuo(m) de combustible(m) 764.
envergue(m) de rizo(m) 480.
envoltura(f) 634.
envoltura(f) de tabaco(m) de hoja(f) 384.
envoltura(f) metálica 297.
epicarpio(m) 62, 63, 64.
epicentro(m) 23.
epicóndilo(m) 123.
epidermis(f) 137.
epiglotis(f) 130, 142, 143.
epitroclea(f) 123.
equilibrio(m) 624.
equino(m) 167.
equinoccio(m) de otoño(m) 8.
equinoccio(m) de primavera(f) 3, 8.
EQUIPAJE(M) 382.
**equipo(m) 581, 582, 583, 589, 681.**
equipo(m) de climatización(f) 494.
**equipo(m) de gas(m) 689.**
**equipo(m) de protección(f) 602.**
**equipo(m) de soldadura(f) autógena 306.**
**equipo(m) de soldadura(f) eléctrica 305.**
equipo(m) de soporte 415.
equipo(m) de soporte(m) 415.
**equipo(m) de tierra(f) 506.**
EQUIPO(M) ESTEREOFÓNICO 400, 402, 404.
equipo(m) marcador electrónico 666.
EQUIPO(M) PARA ACAMPAR 688.
**equipo(m) para acampar 690.**
equipo(m) receptor 599.
EQUITACIÓN(F) 648.
EQUITACIÓN(F): CONCURSO(M) DE SALTOS(M) 646.
equivalente a 830.
Eridano 13.
erupción(f) 6.
**erupción(f),volcan(m) 25.**
es paralelo a 830.
escabel(m) 222.
**escala(f) 537.**
escala(f) 711, 719, 726.
escala(f) Celsius 705.
escala(f) de abertura(f) 396.
escala(f) de abertura(f) del diafragma(m) 392.
escala(f) de ajuste(m) 524.
escala(f) de altitud(f) 19.
escala(f) de altura(f) 284.
escala(f) de ampliación(f) 399.
escala(f) de distancia(f) 392.
escala(f) de duración(f) de la exposición(f) 396.
escala(f) de imágenes(f) por segundo(m) 396.
escala(f) de inclinación(f) 284.
escala(f) de latitud(f) 40.
escala(f) de lectura(f) 396.
escala(f) de nonio 484.
escala(f) de profundidad(f) 485.
escala(f) de profundidad(f) de campo(m) de visión(f) 392.
escala(f) de temperaturas(f) 19, 705.
escala(f) de tiempo(m) 539.
escala(f) de transferencia(f) 396.
escala(f) Fahrenheit 705.
escala(f) graduada 708, 709.
escalas(f) barométricas 710.
escalas(f) de temperatura(f) 710.
ESCALERA(F) 201.
escalera(f) 664, 669, 695, 741, 773.
escalera(f) común 303.
escalera(f) con boquilla(f) telescópica 781.
escalera(f) de caracol(m) 741.
escalera(f) de color(m) 695.
escalera(f) de cuerda(f) 303.
**escalera(f) de extensión(f) 302.**
escalera(f) de gancho(m) 303.
escalera(f) de ganchos(m) 781.
escalera(f) de guardilla(f) 303.
**escalera(f) de plataforma(f) 302.**
escalera(f) de recolección(f) de fruta(f) 303.
**escalera(f) de tijera(f) 302.**
escalera(f) del entresuelo(m) 195.
escalera(f) eléctrica 189, 190.
escalera(f) mecánica 474.
escalera(f) para usos(m) múltiples 303.
escalera(f) real 695.
escalera(f) rodante 303.
escalera(f) telescópica 781.
**escalera(f) telescópica, camión(m) 780.**
escalera(f) y manguera(f), correa(f) 777.
escaleras(f) 194, 474.
ESCALERAS(F) DE MANO(F) 302.
escalerilla(f) 302, 449, 487, 493, 741, 785.
escalerilla(f) de estribo(m) 470.
escalerilla(f) lateral 469, 470.
escalerilla(f) rodante 507.
escalerilla(f) transportable 507.
escalfador(m) de huevos(m) 249.
escalinata(f) 196.
escalón(m) 201, 440.
escalón(m) retráctil 449.
escalón(m) rocoso 26.
escama(f) 87, 96, 97, 111.
escama(f) ventral 97.
escandalosa(f) 480.
escape(m) 436, 437, 501.
**escape(m), sistema(m) 439.**
escapulares(m) 110.
escaque(m) blanco 696.
escaque(m) negro 696.
escarcela(f) 792.
escarcha(f) 37.
escardillo(m) 266.
escarola(f) 73.
escarola(f) rizada 73.
escarpa(f) 178.
escarpe(m) 792.
escarpia(f) 466.
escarpín(m) 792.
escarpín(m) con correa(f) 356.
**escena(f) 189.**
escenario(m) 188.
esclavina(f) 330.
esclerótica(f) 140.
esclusa(f) 752.
esclusa(f) científica de aire(m) 511.
esclusa(f) de aire(m) 14.
esclusa(f) de aire(m) del edificio(m) del reactor(m) 758.
ESCLUSA(F) DE CANAL(M) 492.
esclusa(f) de canal(m) 490.
esclusa(f) de materiales(m) 764.
escobilla(f) 205.
escobilla(f) limpiadora 374.
escobilla(f) metálica 553.
escobillas(f) 385.
escobillón(m) 801.
escocesa 335.
escocia(f) 166, 167.
escolta(m) derecho 610.
escolta(m) izquierdo 610.
**escopeta(f) 799.**
**escopeta(f), cartucho(m) 799.**
escoplo(m) 275, 581, 587.
escoplo(m) de acanalar 587.
escoplo(m) redondo 587.
Escorpio, el Escorpión (24 de octubre) 820.
Escorpión 13.
escorzonera(f) 71.
escota(f) foque(m) 628.
escota(f) mayor 628.
escota(m) 480.
escotadura(f) 544.
escotadura(f) intertrágica 139.
escote(m) 341.
escotera(f) 628, 630.
escotero(m) 628.
**escotes(m) 343.**
escotilla(f) 510, 805.
escotillones(m) 188.
escritorio(m) 226.
escritorio(m) de ejecutivo 520.
**escritorio(m) de secretaria(f) 521.**
ESCRITORIO(M), ARTÍCULOS(M) 515, 516, 518.
escroto(m) 116, 127.
escuadra(f) 275.
escudo(m) 609, 791, 832.
escudo(m) acuartelado 818.
escudo(m) cortado 818.
escudo(m) partido 818.
escudo(m) tronchado 818.
escurridera(f) 244.
escurridor(m) 243.
**escurridores(m) y coladores(m) 243.**
escurrimiento(m) subterráneo 35.
escurrimiento(m) superficial 32, 34.
esfera(f) 530, 707, 708.
esfera(f) celeste 3.
esfera(f) de control(m) de la modalidad(f) 391.
esfera(f) de helio(m) 509.
esfera(f) de té(m) 246.
esfera(f) de vidrio(m) 40.
esfera(f) graduada 710, 719.
esfera(f) lunar 707.
esfera(f) terrestre 3.
esfínter(m) anal 131.
ESGRIMA(F) 666.
eslabón(m) 795.
eslabón(m) de compresión(f) 147.
eslabón(m) de corte(m) 272.
eslabón(m) de levantamiento(m) 147.
eslabón(m) giratorio 737.
esmalte(m) 144.
esmeralda(f) 362, 363.
esmeril(m) 386, 563.
esófago(m) 88, 92, 97, 130, 131, 142.
espacio(m) 537.
espacio(m) de almacenamiento(m) 461.
espacio(m) de expansión(f) 466.
espacio(m) interior 254.
espacio(m) para almacenamiento(m) 440.
espacio(m) para la chispa(f) 439.
espada(f) 666, 695, 791.
espada(f) de dos manos(f) 794.
espádice(m) 60.
espadín(m) 794.
espalda(f) 117, 119, 322.
espaldar(m) 96.
espaldarón(m) 792.
esparavel(m) 291.
esparcidor(m) de paja(f) 161.
esparcidora(f) de abono(m) 270.
esparcidora(f) de estiércol(m) 154.
**esparcidora(m) de estiércol(m) 156.**
**espárrago(m) 72.**
espátula(f) 244, 581, 589.
espatulada 56.
espátulas(f) de modelar 585.
especificaciones(f) técnicas(f) 433.
espectrómetro(m) 717.
espectrómetro(m) de rayos(m) ultravioleta 43.
espejo(m) 292, 382, 442, 444, 719, 770.
espejo(m) de cortesía(f) 430.
espejo(m) de lectura(f) 512.
espejo(m) doble giratorio 368.
espejo(m) iluminador 713.
espejo(m) lateral 368, 426, 440.
**espejo(m) luminoso 368.**
espejo(m) mayor(m) 484.
espejo(m) menor 484.
espejo(m) parabólico 770.
espejo(m) plano 14, 720.
espejo(m) primario 14, 16.
espejo(m) principal 720.
espejo(m) reflector central 390.
espejo(m) retrovisor 430.
espejo(m) secundario 16, 390.
espejuelo(m) 100.
**espermatozoide(m) 127.**
ESPESOR(M), MEDICIÓN 711.
espículas(f) 6.
espiga(f) 60, 225, 239, 242, 291, 376, 432, 571, 575.
espiga(f) de punta(f) cuadrada 231.
espiga(f) de punta(f) redonda 231.
espiga(f) del cartucho(m) 295.
espina(f) del omóplato(m) 123.
espinaca(f) 73.
espinapez(m) 200.
espinillera(f) 595, 600, 609.
espira(f) 83.
espira(f) corporal 94.
espiral(f) 94, 276, 398.
espiral(f) de corte(m) 281.
espiral(f) embrionaria 94.
espiral(m) 706.
espiral(m) de separación(f) 404.
espiras(f) 94.
esplenio(m) 121.
espoleta(f) 804.
espoleta(f) de proximidad(f) 814.
espolón(m) 80, 101, 106, 156, 281, 552, 803.
espolvoreador(m) 246.
esponja(f) natural 367.
esponja(f) sintética 367.
esponja(f) vegetal 367.
**esponjas(f) 367.**
esporas(f) 55.
espuela(f) 648.
espuma(f) 30, 216.
espumadera(f) 244.
ESQUELETO(M) 122.
**esqueleto(m) 102.**
esquí(m) 445, 641.
ESQUÍ(M) ACUÁTICO 633.
ESQUÍ(M) ALPINO 640.
**esquí(m) de campo(m) traviesa 642.**
esquí(m) de campo(m) traviesa 642.
**esquí(m) de eslálom(m) 633.**
**esquí(m) de figuras(f) 633.**
ESQUÍ(M) DE FONDO(M) 642.
esquí(m) de salto(m) 633.
**esquí(m) normal 633.**
**esquiador(m) alpino 640.**
**esquiadora(f) de campo(m) traviesa 642.**
esquina(f) 470, 608.
esquina(f) de calle(f) 682.
esquinera(f) 470.
esquinero(m) derecho 603, 605.
esquinero(m) izquierdo 603, 605.
estabilizador(m) 485, 509, 684, 786, 802, 812, 814.
estabilizador(m) de dirección(f) 639.

Los términos en **negrita** corresponden a una ilustración; los que aparecen en MAYÚSCULAS indican un título.

estabilizador(m) horizontal 508, 639.
establo(m) 149.
estaca(f) 385, 479.
estación(f) central de bombeo(m) 740.
estación(f) de carga(f) 464.
ESTACIÓN(F) DE FERROCARRIL(M) 462, 464.
estación(f) de ferrocarril(m) 464.
estación(f) de intercomunicación(f) 413.
**estación(f) de metro(m) 474.**
ESTACIÓN(F) DE SERVICIO(M) 453.
**estación(f) de servicio(m) 453.**
estación(f) de transmisión(f) 722.
estación(f) del ferrocarril(m) 52.
estación(f) local 416.
estación(f) receptora 722.
**estación(f), metro(m) 474.**
estación(m) de ferrocarril(m) 184.
estacionamiento(m) 185, 193, 464, 491, 504.
ESTACIONES(F) DEL AÑO(M) 8.
**estadio(m) 654.**
estadio(m) 185.
estado(m) 51.
estado(m) actual del tiempo(m) 38.
estalactita(f) 24.
estalagmita(f) 24.
estambre(m) 60, 64.
estanque(m) 263.
estante(m) para revistas(f) 522.
estaquilla(f) 685, 686.
estator(m) 290.
estatores(m) externos 501.
estatores(m) internos 501.
estay(m) 479.
estay(m) de proa(f) 628.
este(m) 488.
estepario 45.
esterilla(f) de lanzamiento(m) 682.
esternocleidomastoideo(m) 120.
esternón(m) 102, 122.
**estetoscopio(m) 726.**
**estiercol(m), esparcidora(f) 156.**
estigma(f) 60.
estigma(m) 66, 78, 79.
estilete(m) 794.
estilo(m) 60, 62, 63, 64, 67, 389, 706.
**estilo(m) de crol(m) 622.**
**estilo(m) de espalda(f) 623.**
**estilo(m) de mariposa(f) 623.**
**estilo(m) de pecho(m) 622.**
estilóbato(m) 166, 168.
**estilográfica(f) 389.**
estilográfica(f) 515.
ESTILOS(M) ARQUITECTÓNICOS 166.
estimulador(m) de encias(f) 373.
estípite(m) 55.
estípula(f) 56.
ESTOCADA(F), ARMAS(F) CORTANTES 794.
estómago(m) 88, 92, 97, 124, 131.
estrado(m) del director(m) 556.
estragón(m) 74.
estrangulación(f) 668.
estrato(m) de cenizas(f) 25.
estrato(m) de lava(f) 25.
estrato(m) lúcido 136.
estratocúmulos(m) 44.
estratos(m) 44.
estratosfera(f) 19.
estrechamiento(m) 705.
estrechamiento(m) del camino(m) 826, 827.
estrecho(m) 51.
Estrella Polar 11.
estrella(f) 36, 819.
estrella(f) fugaz 19.
estría(f) 166, 167.
estribera(f) 793.
estribo(m) 82, 138, 176, 445, 508, 584, 648.
estribo(m) trasero 778.
estribor(m) 488, 489, 497.
**estructura(f) 203.**
estructura(f) 536.
estructura(f) de base(f) 14.
estructura(f) de cola(f) 508.
**estructura(f) de la biosfera(f) 31.**
**estructura(f) de madera(f), entarimado(m) sobre 200.**
estructura(f) de soporte(m) 15, 48.
estructura(f) del ala(f) 498.
estructura(f) en K 756.
estructura(f) inferior 737.
estructura(f) tubular 487, 738.
estrucutra(f) de metal(m) 463.
estuario(m) 30, 51.
estuche(m) 358, 365, 706, 711.
**estuche(m) de manicura(f) 365.**
estuche(m) de tocador(m) 382.
**estudio(m) 414.**
estudio(m) 407, 412.
ESTUDIO(M) DE RADIO(M) Y SALA(F) DE CONTROL(M) 407.
**estudio(m) de televisión(f) y cabinas(f) de control(m) 412.**
**estufa(f) de leña(f) a fuego(m) lento 204.**
**etapas(f) 586.**
etiqueta(f) 383, 404.
etiquetas(f) adhesivas 518.
Eurasia(f) 21.
Europa 4.
Europa(f) 21.
**europeo, enchufe(m) de tipo(m) 309.**
Eustaquio, trompa(f) de 139, 141.
**Eutelsat II 418.**
evaporación(f) 34, 35.
**excavación(f) a cielo(m) abierto 733.**
excavadora(f) de rueda(f) de cangilones(m) 733.
exhalación(f) 622.
exosfera(f) 19.
expedición(f) de carga(f) 505.
explanada(f) 178.
explorador(m) de microondas(f) 43.
explorador(m) de radiaciones(f) de la tierra(f) 43.
explorador(m) óptico 526.
explosión(f) 436.
explosivo 821.
explosivo(m) 798, 799, 804.
exprimelimones(m) 243.
exprimidor(m) 251.
**exprimidor(m) de cítricos(m) 251.**
extensión(f) 219, 439.
extensión(f) de la mesa(f) 285.
extensión(f) plegable 219.
extensor(m) 375.
exterior(m) 597.
EXTERIOR(M) DE UNA CASA(F) 196.
exterior(m) derecho 597.
exterior(m) izquierdo 597.
**extinguidor(m) portátil 780.**
extintor(m) de incendios(m) 823.
extractor(m) de fusibles(m) 311.
extractor(m) de humo(m) 805.
extremidad(f) delantera 84.
extremidad(f) posterior 84, 85.
extremo(m) 376.
extremo(m) abocinado 300.
extremo(m) anterior 95.
extremo(m) del brazo(m) 272.
extremo(m) derecho 601, 606, 607, 608, 612.
extremo(m) izquierdo 601, 606, 608, 612.
extremo(m) libre 137.
extremo(m) posterior 95.
eyector(m) 784.
eyector(m) de las varillas(f) 250.
eyector(m) del protector(m) de cabina(f) 639.

## F

fa(f) 537.
faceta(f) bisel (8) 363.
faceta(f) de estrella(f) (8) 363.
faceta(f) de pabellón(m) 363.
faceta(f) inferior del contorno(m) 363.
faceta(f) superior del contorno(m) 363.
**fachada(f) 175.**
**facsímil(m) 421.**
facsímil(m) 417.
factor(m) RH negativo 831.
factor(m) RH positivo 831.
factorial 830.
fáculas(f) 6.
fagot(m) 548.
fagotes(m) 557.
**faja(f) 346.**
faja(f) con liguero(m) 346.
faja(f) con sostén(m) 347.
faja(f) corsé(m) 347.
falange(f) 107, 122, 123.
falangeta(f) 103, 107, 122, 123, 137.
falangina(f) 103, 107, 122, 123, 137.
falda(f) 331.
falda(f) de tubo(m) 334.
falda(f) pantalón(m) 334.
**falda(f), tipos(m) de 334.**
falda(m) 615.
faldar(m) 792.
faldón(m) 224, 337.
faldón(m) de la camisa(f) 324.
faldón(m) delantero 324.
faldón(m) flexible 493.
faldón(m) trasero 324.
faldoncillo(m) 649.
falla(f) 23, 28.
Falopio, istmo(m) de la trompa(f) de 129.
Falopio, pabellón(m) de la trompa(f) de 129.
Falopio, trompa(f) de 128.
falsa escuadra(f) 713.
falso almohadón(m) 224.
falso doblez(m) 349.
falso(m) registro(m) 543.
falso(m) secreto(m) 543.
falta(f) (1 a 18) 700, 701.
farallón(m) 30.
faringe(f) 130, 131.
farmacia(f) 822.
faro(f) delantero 147.
faro(m) 491, 805.
faro(m) de destello(m) 781.
faro(m) delantero 426, 440, 442, 444, 445, 459, 469.
**faro(m) marítimo 486.**
faro(m) reflector 778, 780.
**faro(m), linterna(f) 486.**
farol(m) 185, 186, 235, 263.
farola(f) 235.
**faros(m) 429.**
**faros(m) delanteros 429.**
faros(m) traseros 147.
fascia lata(f), tensor(m) de la 120.
FASES(F) DE LA LUNA(F) 6.
fechador(m) 516.
femenino(m) 831.
FEMENINOS, ÓRGANOS(M) GENITALES 128, 129.
fémur(m) 78, 80, 103, 122.
fémur(m), cabeza(f) del 123.
fémur(m), cuello(m) del 123.
Fénix 13.
**fenómenos(m) atmosféricos 39.**
ferrocarril(m) del muelle(m) 491.
FERROCARRIL(M), ESTACIÓN(F) 462, 464.
FERROCARRIL(M), TALLERES(M) 465.
fertilizantes(m) 32.
festón(m) colgado 229.
festoneada 56.
fiador(m) 666, 685.
fiador(m) elástico 685, 686.
fibra(f) 692.
fibra(f) muscular 134.
fibra(f) nerviosa 136.
fíbula(f) 122, 315.
fichas(f) 517.
fichero(m) giratorio 516.
fiel(m) 708, 709.
fieltro(m) 581.
figura(f) en relieve(m) 580.
figura(f) plana 580.
fijación(f) 633.
**fijación(f) de seguridad(f) del esquí(m) 641.**
fijación(f) para el pie(m) 642.
fijador(m) 592.
fijador(m) de carrete(m) 671.
fijador(m) de la ratonera(f) 642.
filamento(m) 6, 60, 232, 233.
filamento(m) branquial 87.
filamento(m) de tungsteno(m) 233.
filete(m) 167, 544, 546.
filetero(m) 242.
filmadora(f) 527.
filo(m) 239, 242, 369, 564.
**filo(m) simple, tijeras(f) para entresacar 369.**
filtro(m) 207, 247, 252, 255, 294, 295, 384, 385, 484, 772.
filtro(m) de aire(m) 210, 272, 469, 783.
filtro(m) de color(m) 392.
filtro(m) de focalización(f) 390.
filtro(m) de pelusa(f) 258, 259.
filtro(m) de polarización(f) 392.
filtro(m) rojo(m)de la luz(f) inactínica 399.
filtro(m) selector del color(m) 410.
filum(m) terminal 134.
filum(m) terminal interno 134.
firme(m) 450.
flanco(m) 108, 179.
flanco(m) diestro 818.
flanco(m) siniestro 818.
flanqueador(m) derecho 605.
flanqueador(m) izquierdo 605.
**flash(m) electrónico 393.**
flauta(f) 548.
flautas(f) traverseras 556.
**flecha(f) 684.**
flecha(f) 214, 684, 793.
flecha(f) indicadora de la dirección(f) del viento(m) 38.
flor(f) 57, 579.
flor(f) de lis(f) 819.
FLOR(F), ANATOMÍA(F) DE UNA 60.
florete(m) 666.
florete(m) eléctrico 666.
**floretista(m) 667.**
florín(m) 832.
flotador(m) 216, 293, 485, 672, 803.
flotador(m) de la portería(f) 626.
flotador(m) del medidor(m) 741.
flujo(m) 493.
Fobos 4.
foco(m) 235.
foco(m) de proa(f) 497.
foco(m) primario 14.
fofoque(m) 481.
fogón(m) 204.
foliador(m) 516.
folículo(m) 67.
folículo(m) piloso 136.
**folículo(m), corte(m) 67.**
follaje(m) 59, 220.
fondo(m) de la piscina(f) 626.
fondo(m) de la señal(f) 471.
fondo(m) del escenario(m) 188, 189.
fonolocalización(f) activa 402.
FONTANERÍA(F) 294, 296, 299, 300.
**fontanero(m), herramientas(f) de 299.**
foque(m) 481, 628.
**formas(f) de asir la paleta(f) 619.**
formato(m) mediano SLR (6x6) 395.
fórnix(m), cuerpo(m) del 134.
**forraje(m), aventador(m) 162.**
**forraje(m), cosechera(f) 162.**
forro(m) 322, 324, 352, 354, 378, 565, 596, 644, 649, 692.
forro(m) de cuero(m) 598.
forro(m) de la lengua(f) 96.
**forro(m) y entretelas(f) 565.**
**forros(m), ejemplos(m) 819.**
FORTIFICACIÓN(F) DE VAUBAN 178.
fosa(f) abisal 28.
fosa(f) de almacenamiento(m) de residuos(m) de combustible(m) 758.
fosa(f) de combustible(m) fallido 764.
fosa(f) de descarga(f) de residuos(m) de combustible(m) 758.
fosa(f) de desechos(m) 765.
fosa(f) de desechos(m) de combustible(m) 764.
fosa(f) de recepción(f) 764.
fosa(f) descarga de residuos(m) de combustible(m) 764.
FOSA(F) SÉPTICA 216.
fosa(f) triangular 139.
**fosas(f) nasales 141.**
foso(m) 178, 181.
foso(m) de la orquesta(f) 188.
foso(m) de recepción(f) 683.
FOTOCOPIADORA(F) 532.
FOTOGRAFÍA(F) 390, 392, 394, 396, 398.
**fotómetro(m) 396.**
**fotómetro(m) electrónico 396.**
fotosfera(f) 6.
fototipo(m) 397.
FRAGATA(F) 808.
**frambuesa(f), corte(m) de una 62.**
francés 362.
**Francis, turbina(f) 754.**
franco(m) 832.
franja(f) del faldón(m) 493.
fregadero(m) 296.
**fregadero(m) con triturador(m) de basura(f) 296.**
fregadero(m) doble 215.
**freidora(f) 252.**
freno(m) 641, 649, 664, 670, 671, 727.
freno(m) aerodinámico 774.
**freno(m) de disco(m) 432.**
freno(m) de disco(m) 442.
freno(m) de emergencia(f) 477.
freno(m) de la cadena(f) 272.
freno(m) de mano(f) 430.
**freno(m) de quijada(f) acodado 650.**
**freno(m) de tambor(m) 432.**
freno(m) del esquí(m) 640.
freno(m) delantero 447.
freno(m) dinámico 468.
freno(m) trasero 446, 645.
frenos(m) 498.

Los términos en **negrita** corresponden a una ilustración; los que aparecen en MAYÚSCULAS indican un título.

frente(f) 109, 116, 179.
frente(m) cálido de superficie(f) 39.
frente(m) cálido en las alturas(f) 39.
frente(m) de corte(m) 733, 736.
frente(m) estacionario 39.
frente(m) frío de superficie(f) 39.
frente(m) frío en las alturas(f) 39.
frente(m) ocluido 39.
**frentes(m) 39.**
**fresa(f), corte(m) de una 62.**
fresco(m) 170.
**frigorífico(m) 254.**
friso(m) 166, 168, 225.
frontal(m) 120, 122, 792.
frontalera(f) 649.
frontera(f) interna 51.
frontera(f) internacional 51.
frontis(m) 617.
frontón(m) 166, 168, 707.
frotador(m) 307, 582.
frotador(m) de fósforo(m) 386.
fructificación(f) 61.
fruncida 335.
fruncido(m) 337.
FRUTAS(F) TROPICALES 68.
**frutas(f) tropicales, principales variedades(f) 68.**
**fruto(m) carnoso con hueso(m), corte(m) de un 63.**
**fruto(m) carnoso con semillas(f), corte(m) de un 64.**
**frutos(m) 69.**
FRUTOS(M) CARNOSOS CON HUESO(M) 63.
**frutos(m) carnosos con hueso(m), principales variedades(f) 63.**
FRUTOS(M) CARNOSOS CON SEMILLAS(F) 64.
**frutos(m) carnosos con semillas(f), principales variedades(f) 64.**
FRUTOS(M) CARNOSOS: BAYAS(F) 62.
FRUTOS(M) CARNOSOS: CÍTRICOS(M) 65.
**frutos(m) secos, principales variedades(f) 66.**
FRUTOS(M) SECOS: DEHISCENTES 67.
FRUTOS(M) SECOS: OLEAGINOSOS 66.
**fuego(m), signos(m) 820.**
fuelle(m) 378, 380, 399, 543.
fuente(f) básica de alimento(m) 31.
fuente(f) de servir 238.
fuente(f) de verdura(f) 238.
fuente(f) para abluciones(f) 172, 173.
fuente(f) para pescado(m) 238.
fuentes(f) de contaminación(f) 34.
**fuerza(f) del viento(m), medición(f) 41.**
fulcro(m) 541.
full 695.
fulminante(m) 798, 799.
FUMAR, ACCESORIOS(M) PARA 384, 386.
fumarola(f) 24.
funcionamiento(m) 411.
funda(f) 375, 688, 690.
funda(f) de almohada(f) 224.
funda(f) de colchón(m) 224.
funda(f) de cuero(m) 690.
funda(f) de la almohada(f) 224.
funda(f) de mástil(m) 631.
funda(f) del sable(m) 628, 631.
funda(f) para gafas(f) 379.
funda(f) protectora de la cuchilla(f) 644.
funda(f) telescópica 283.
funículo(m) 62, 67.
**furgón(m) 470.**
furgón(m) de cola(f) 473.
fusa(f) (treintaidosavo(m)) 538.
fuselaje(m) 499, 639.
fusible(m) 757, 769.
fusible(m) de bayoneta(f) 312.
fusible(m) de cartucho(m) 312.
fusible(m) de rosca(f) 312.
fusible(m) de seguridad(f) a tierra(f) 312.
**fusibles(m) 312.**
FUSIL(M) AMETRALLADOR 796.
FUSIL(M) AUTOMÁTICO 796.
FUSIL(M) SIN RETROCESO 804.
fusta(f) 648, 651.
fuste(m) 166, 658.
fuste(m) del bastón(m) 642.
FÚTBOL(M) 600.
FÚTBOL(M) AMERICANO 602, 604.
**futbolista(m/f) 600.**

## G

gabinete(m) para papelería(f) 522.
GABINETES(M) Y ARMARIOS(M) 225, 226.
gablete(m) 175.
gafa(f) 376.
GAFAS(F) 376.
gafas(f) 627, 635.
gafas(f) de esquí(m) 640.
gafas(f) de sol(m) 377.
**gafas(f): partes(f) 376.**
**gaita(f) 536.**
gajo(m) 65.
GALAXIA(F) 9.
galaxia(f) elíptica 9.
galaxia(f) espiral 9.
galaxia(f) espiral con barras(f) 9.
galaxia(f) irregular 9.
galaxia(f) lenticular 9.
galería(f) 175, 189.
galería(f) de acceso(m) 736, 747.
galería(f) de arrastre(m) 736.
galería(f) seca 24.
galería(f) superior 736.
galería(f) transversal 736.
galería(m) inferior 736.
galleta(f) de centeno(m) 153.
galleta(f) escandinava 153.
gallina(f) 150.
gallinero(m) 148.
gallo(m) 150.
gama(f) de colores(m) 592.
gamba(f) 90.
gamuza(f) 358.
**ganchillo(m) 567.**
gancho(m) 230, 310, 397, 567, 568, 709, 711, 786.
gancho(m) de la barbada(f) 650.
gancho(m) de tracción(f) 726, 737.
gancho(m) del meñique(m) 551.
gancho(m) del pulgar(m) 549, 550.
gancho(m) del remolque(m) 147.
gancho(m) para cuerda(f) 492.
gancho(m) para el platillo(m) 708.
ganchos(m) peinadores 573.
ganchos(m), escalera(f) 781.
ganglio(m) espinal 135.
ganglio(m) simpático 135.
Ganimedes 4.
ganso(m) 150.
garabato(m) 267.
garagantilla(f) de terciopelo(m) 361.
garaje(m) 196.
garbanzos(m) 72.
garganta(f) 108, 615, 671.
gargantilla(f) 361.
garita(f) 178, 181.
garra(f) 106, 111, 579.
garrafa(f) 237.
garrafita(f) 237.
garrote(m) 160.
garrucha(f) montacarga 786.
gas refrigerante de bióxido de carbono 760.
gas(m) 34, 35, 737, 744.
gas(m) inerte 232, 233.
gases(m) quemados 436.
gasolina(f) 744, 745.
gasolina(f) pesada 744.
**gasolina(f), motor(m) 434.**
gasolinera(f) 823.
**gasterópodos(m) comestibles 83.**
gatillo(m) 268, 291, 304, 793, 795, 796, 797, 798, 799, 804.
gatillo(m) de seguridad(f) 272.
GATO(M) DOMÉSTICO 107.
gato(m) hidráulico 449.
gato(m) hidráulico del alerón(m) de curvatura(f) 812.
**gaveta(f) de archivador(m) 517.**
gavia(f) inferior proel 481.
gavia(f) mayor alta 481.
gavia(f) mayor baja 481.
gavia(f) proel alta 481.
géiser(m) 25.
gemelos(m) 120, 121, 339.
gemelos(m) de teatro(m) 377.
Géminis 11.
Géminis, los Gemelos (21 de mayo) 820.
generador(m) 753, 758.
generador(m) de aire(m) caliente 206.
generador(m) de vapor(m) 759, 761, 762, 771, 806.
generador(m) principal de tono(m) 407.
**geometría(f) 830.**
germen(m) 152.
GIMNASIA(F) 659, 660.
gimnasio(m) 496.
GLACIAR(M) 26.
glaciar(m) de piedemonte(m) 27.
glaciar(m) suspendido 26.
glande(m) 127.
glándula(f) de veneno(m) 96.
glándula(f) digestiva 92.
glándula(f) mamaria 129.
glándula(f) sebácea 136.
glándula(f) sudorípara apocrina 136.
glándula(f) sudorípara ecrina 136.
glándula(f) suprarrenal 132.
glándula(m) pineal 134.
glándulas(f) salivales 131.
globo(m) 634, 689.
**globo(m) aerostático 634.**
**globo(m) ocular 140.**
globo(m) ocular 84.
glóbulo(m) de almidón(m) 115.
glóbulo(m) de grasa(f) 115.
glorieta(f) 450.
glotis(f) 96, 142.
glúteo(m) mayor 121.
GO(SUN-TSE) 697.
gol(m) 604, 606.
gola(f) 667, 792.
goleta(f) 482.
GOLF(M) 678.
**golf(m), pelota(f) de 677.**
golfo(m) 51.
Golgi, aparato(m) de 115.
goma(f) 515.
goma(f) de sujeción(f) del talón(m) 633.
gonfalón(m) 817.
gong(m) 554, 557.
gorguera(f) 318.
**gorra(f) 328.**
gorra(f) 648, 651.
gorra(f) de cuartel(m) 328.
**gorra(f) noruega 328.**
gorro(m) 642.
gorro(m) azul 626.
gorro(m) blanco 626.
gorro(m) de esquí(m) 640.
gorro(m) de punto(m) 329.
gorrón(m) 800.
gorroverde(m) 55.
gota(f) 167, 236, 362.
gota(f) de lluvia(f) 36.
GÓTICA, CATEDRAL(F) 175.
grabación(f) 411.
**grabadora(f) y tocacintas(m) 403.**
grabadora(f) y tocacintas(m) 400, 407.
grado(m) 830.
grado(m) de rotación(f) 814.
grados(m) C 705.
grados(m) F 705.
graficador(m) 527.
gráfico(m) de lineas(f) 407.
gran angular(m) 392.
gran roncón(m) 536.
granada(f) 68.
GRANADA(F) DE MANO(F) 804.
granate(m) 363.
graneador(m) para el grabado(m) al humo(m) 582.
granero(m) 148.
granizada(f) 39.
granizo(m) 37.
GRANJA(F) 148.
GRANJA(F),ANIMALES(M) 150.
grano(m) 72.
**grano(m) de trigo(m),corte 152.**
granos(m) de arroz(m) 6.
grapadora(f) 515.
grapas(f) 515.
grasa(f), glóbulo(m) de 115.
grasas(f) 745.
grava(f) 199, 216.
greba(f) 792.
green(m) de entrenamiento(m) 676.
gregüescos(m) 316.
grieta(f) 26.
**grifo(m) 294.**
grifo(m) 292.
**grifo(m) de bola(f) 294.**
**grifo(m) de cartucho(m) 295.**
grifo(m) de cocina(f) de tres vías(f) 296.
**grifo(m) de disco(m) 295.**
grillete(m) 630.
grillete(m) de resorte(m) 630.
grosella(f) 62.
grosella(f) espinosa 62.
grosella(f) negra 62.
grúa(f) 14, 738, 743.
grúa(f) de caballete(m) 746, 747.
grúa(f) de la plataforma(f) 811.
grúa(f) de muelle(m) 490.
**grúa(f) de pórtico(m) 786.**
grúa(f) de puente(m) 747.
grúa(f) flotante 490.
**grúa(f) móvil(m) 786.**
**grúa(f) torre(f) 786.**
Grulla 13.
grupa(f) 101, 661.
grupeto(m) 538.
grupo(m) de cola(f) 638.
grupo(m) electrógeno 506.
grupo(m) motor(m) 458.
GRUTA(F) 24.
guadaña(f) 267.
gualdera(f) 201, 800, 803.
gualdera(f) de contén(m) 201.
guante(m) 512, 598, 609, 635, 642, 643, 648.
guante(m) a la muñeca(f) 327.
guante(m) corto 327.
guante(m) de bateo(m) 595.
guante(m) de brazo(m) largo 327.
guante(m) de buceo(m) 627.
guante(m) de esgrima(f) 667.
guante(m) de esquí(m) 640.
guante(m) de golf(m) 679.
**guante(m) de recogida(f) 596.**
guante(m) del portero(m) 609.
guante(m) del receptor(m) 595.
**guante(m) para conducir 327.**
guantelete(m) 792.
guantera(f) 430.
GUANTES(M) 327.
guantes(m) 308.
**guantes(m) de boxeo(m) 669.**
guarda(f) 242, 577.
guarda(f) de protección(f) superior 787.
guarda(f) del disco(m) 285.
guarda(f) fija del disco(m) 284.
guarda(f) móvil del disco(m) 284.
guardabarros(m) 147, 426, 427, 440, 441, 446.
guardabarros(m) delantero 442.
guardacaptores(m) 547.
guardafrenos(m) 643.
**guardainfante(m) 317.**
guardamano(m) 796.
guardamonte(m) 795, 797, 798, 799.
guardanieve(m) 445.
guardarropa(m) 195, 226.
guardarropa(m) de los mineros(m) 735.
guardia(m) derecho 603, 605.
guardia(m) izquierdo 603, 605.
guarnición(f) 186, 219, 223, 383, 641, 666.
guayaba(f) 68.
gubia(f) 581, 587.
**guerrero(m) galo 791.**
guía(f) 568, 630, 738, 797.
guía(f) corrediza 470.
guía(f) de corte(m) 284, 285.
guía(f) de enganche(m) 459.
guía(f) de escotas(f) 630.
guía(f) de la cadena(f) 448.
guía(f) de la onda(f) 415.
guía(f) de la punta(f) 670, 671.
guía(f) de tensión(f) 569.
guía(f) del papel(m) 421, 531.
guía(f) del prensapapel(m) 531.
guía(f) externa para enmarcar 578.
guía(f) para enmarcar 578.
guía(f) para la cinta(f) 403.
guía(m/f) 814.
guiahilos(m) 561, 562, 569.
guías(f) de archivo(m) 518.
guías(f) en T 498.
guías(f) normales 498.
**guillotina(f) 578.**
guillotina(f) 398.
guión(m) 632.
guión(m) largo 832.
**guisante(m) 67.**
guisante(m) 67.
guisantes(m) 72.
**guitarra(f) clásica 546.**
**guitarra(f) eléctrica 547.**
gules(m) 819.
GUSTO(M), EL OLFATO(M) Y EL 142.

## H

habas(f) 72.
habitación(f) lacustre 165.
hacha(f) 690.
hacha(f) de bombero(m) 781.
hacha(f) de cocinero(m) 242.

Los términos en **negrita** corresponden a una ilustración; los que aparecen en MAYÚSCULAS indican un título.

hacha(f) de piedra(f) pulida 791.
**haltera(f) 663.**
HALTEROFILIA(F) 662.
hamada(f) 46.
hangar(m) de helicóptero(m) 808.
hangar(m) de mantenimiento(m) 503.
haz(m) 756.
haz(m) azul 410.
haz(m) de electrones(m) 410, 717.
haz(m) rojo 410.
haz(m) verde 410.
**hebilla(f) 566.**
hebilla(f) 319, 323, 380, 428, 641.
hebilla(f) de ajuste(m) 645.
hebilla(f) niveladora 231.
hechura(f) de sastre(m) 341.
hechura(f) sastre(m) 340.
**heladera(f) 251.**
hélice(f) 495, 496, 742, 806.
hélice(f) bimetálica 705.
hélice(f) propulsora 492.
hélices(f) 808.
HELICÓPTERO(M) 508.
helicóptero(m) 808.
helipuerto(m) 738.
hélix(m) 139.
hembra(f) 566.
HEMISFERIO(M) AUSTRAL, CONSTELACIONES(F) 12.
HEMISFERIO(M) BOREAL, CONSTELACIONES(F) 10.
hemisferio(m) Norte 3, 47.
hemisferio(m) occidental 47.
hemisferio(m) oriental 47.
hemisferio(m) Sur 3, 47.
**hemisferios(m) 47.**
hendidura(f) 28, 578.
**henificación(f) 155.**
HENIFICACIÓN(M) 159.
henil(m) 148.
HERÁLDICA(F) 817, 818.
**herbívoro(m), mandíbula(f) de 98.**
herbívoros(m) 31, 33.
Hércules 11.
**herradura(f) 104.**
herradura(f) 104, 364.
herraje(m) 383.
herraje(m) de la esquina(f) 470.
**herramientas(f) 584, 585, 690.**
**herramientas(f) de electricista(m) 310.**
**herramientas(f) de fontanero(m) 299.**
HERRAMIENTAS(F) PARA PINTAR 304.
HERRAMIENTAS(F) Y MÁQUINAS(F) 264, 266, 268, 270, 272.
HERRAMIENTAS(F), CARPINTERÍA(F) 275, 276, 278, 280, 282, 284.
**herramientas(f), tipos de 587.**
herrete(m) 352, 354.
**hervidor(m) de silbato(m) 252.**
hexagonal(m) 439.
Hidra 11, 13.
Hidra macho 13.
hidrosfera(f) 31.
hielo(m) 34.
hielos(m) perpetuos 45.
hierbabuena(f) 74.
HIERBAS(F) AROMÁTICAS 74.
**hierro(m) 678.**
hierro(m) para soldar 305.
**hierros(m) y palos(m) 678.**
hifa(f) 55.
hígado(m) 88, 97, 124, 131.
HIGIENE(F) DENTAL 373.
higo chumbo(m) 68.
higrógrafo(m) 41.
**higrómetro(m) 210.**
hijuela(f) 672.
hilera(f) 373.
hilio(m) renal 132.
hilo(m) 692.
hilo(m) de la tela(f) 566.
hilo(m) de nilón(m) 271.
hilo(m) de trama(f) 576.
hilo(m) de urdimbre(f) 576.
**hinojo(m) 72.**
hipocentro(m) 23.
hipófisis(f) 134.
hisopo(m) 74.
hocico(m) 106, 107.
HOCKEY(M) SOBRE HIELO 608.
HOCKEY(M) SOBRE HIERBA(F) 607.
**hockey(m), pelota(f) de 607.**
hogar(m) 204.
**hoja(f) 56.**
hoja(f) 57, 70, 72, 239, 242, 276, 277, 291, 304, 369, 374.
hoja(f) corta 688.
hoja(f) de acanto(m) 167, 220.
hoja(f) de afeitar 374.
hoja(f) de cuchilla(f) 644.
hoja(f) de la película(f) 395.
hoja(f) de lámina(f) diamantada 286.
hoja(f) de las tijeras(f) 564.
hoja(f) de parra(f) 73.
hoja(f) de yeso(m) liso 286.
hoja(f) del faldón(m) lateral 649.
hoja(f) larga 688.
hojas(f) carnosas 70.
**hojas(f) compuestas 56.**
hojas(f) escamadas del ciprés(m) 58.
**hojas(f) simples 56.**
HOMBRE(M), ROPA(F) DE 319, 320, 322, 324.
hombrera(f) 316, 319, 545, 602, 609, 804.
hombrillo(m) 320.
hombro(m) 116, 118, 615, 670.
hondón(m) 649.
**hongo mortal 55.**
HONGO(M) 55.
**hongo(m) venenoso 55.**
**hongo(m), anatomía(f) de un 55.**
**hongos(m) comestibles 55.**
horarios(m) 463.
horca(f) 266.
**horma(f) 358.**
hormiga(f) 77.
hormigón(m) armado 286.
hormigón(m) precomprimido 286.
**hornear, utensilios(m) para 245.**
Horno 13.
horno(m) 255, 770.
**horno(m) de microondas(f) 253.**
**horno(m) eléctrico 585.**
**horno(m) solar 770.**
horquilla(f) 105, 327, 369, 447, 721, 787.
horquilla(f) de mano(f) 268.
horquilla(f) telescópica 442.
horquilla(f) trasera 446.
**horquilla(f), montacargas(m) 787.**
horquillas(f) 787, 788.
HORTALIZAS(F) 69, 70, 71, 72, 73.
hospital(m) 822.
hotel(m) 185.
hoyo(m) 24, 405.
hoyuelo(m) 677.
hoz(f) 269.
**Hubble, clasificación(f) 9.**
HUBBLE, TELESCOPIO(M) ESPACIAL 16.
**huecograbado(m) 580.**
huelgo(m) de ajuste(m) 718.
huella(f) 201.
huerta(f) 149.
huerto(m) 148, 193.
**huesecillos(m) auditivos 138.**
huesecillos(m) auditivos 139.
hueso(m) 63.
hueso(m) alveolar 144.
hueso(m) ilíaco(m) 122.
hueso(m) maxilar 144.
hueso(m) nasal 141.
hueso(m) pómulo(m) 122.
hueva(f) 89.
huevera(f) 254.
**huevo(m) 109, 128.**
huevo(m) 82.
huevos(m) 84.
HUMANO, CUERPO(M) 116, 118.
humedad(f) del aire(m) 210.
humedad(f) en el aire(m) 34.
**humedad(f), medición(f) 41.**
húmedo de verano(m) corto 45.
húmedo de verano(m) largo 45.
húmero(m) 102, 122.
húmero(m), cabeza(f) del 123.
**humidificador(m) 210.**
humo(m) 39.
humor(m) acuoso 140.
humor(m) vítreo 140.
huracán(m) 39.
husillo(m) 579, 711.
huso(m) 294, 573, 575.

## I

idéntico a 830.
iglesia(f) 185.
iglú(m) 165.
igual a 830.
igual o mayor que 830.
igual o menor que 830.
ijar(m) 101.
íleon(m) 131.
iluminación(f) 368.
iluminación(f) de la placa(f) de matrícula(f) 429.
imagen(f) impresa 580.
imagen(f) tallada 580.
imán(m) 254, 406, 485, 563, 714.
imán(m) frenador 712.
impar(m) 700, 701.
imparipinada 56.
imperial 183.
IMPERIO(M) ROMANO, ARMAS(F) 791.
**impermeable(m) 319.**
impertinentes(m) 377.
impluvio(m) 170, 171.
imposta(f) 174.
imposta(f) principal 177.
**impresión litográfica 580.**
IMPRESIÓN(F) 580.
impresión(f) de mensajes 421.
impresión(f) del músculo(m) 95.
IMPRESIÓN(F) EN HUECOGRABADO(M) 582.
IMPRESIÓN(F) EN RELIEVE(M) 581.
**impresión(f) en relieve(m) 580.**
impresión(f) paleal 95.
**impresiones(f), cubeta(f) para lavar 399.**
**impresora(f) 421.**
impresora(f) 523.
impresora(f) láser 527.
**impresora(f) matriz 531.**
impresora(f) matriz 527.
**impresora(f), calculadora(f) 523.**
**impresora(f), mesa(f) 521.**
impulso(m) de lanzamiento(m) 682.
impulso(m) electromagnético 722.
**impulso(m) nervioso 135.**
**impulso(m), irrigador(m) 264.**
incendios(m), manguera(f) 778.
INCENDIOS(M), PREVENCIÓN(F) 777.
incisivo(m) 98.
incisivo(m) central 144.
incisivo(m) lateral 144.
incisivos(m) 144.
indicador(m) 518, 710.
indicador(m) de ajuste(m) 641.
indicador(m) de emergencia(f) de inclinación(f) 500.
indicador(m) de emergencia(f) de velocidad(f) 500.
indicador(m) de encendido(m) 529.
indicador(m) de hora(f) de salida(f) 463.
indicador(m) de la mitad(f) 525.
indicador(m) de llamadas(f) 420.
indicador(m) de luz(f) larga 445.
indicador(m) de nivel(m) de gasolina(f) 431.
indicador(m) de número(m) de andén(m) 462.
indicador(m) de recarga(f) 374.
indicador(m) de respuesta(f) automática 420.
indicador(m) de temperatura(f) 370, 431.
indicador(m) de tiempo(m) 391.
indicador(m) de velocidad(f) 391.
indicador(m) de viraje(m) 639.
indicador(m) del cuadrante(m) 485.
indicador(m) del importe(m) total(m) 453.
indicador(m) del precio(m) por litro(m)/galón(m) 453.
indicador(m) digital 709, 710.
indicador(m) digital de frecuencia(f) 402.
indicador(m) luminoso 709.
indicador(m) neutro 445.
indicador(m) para viraje(m) en nado(m) de espalda(f) 621.
indicador(m) principal de la película(f) 390.
indicador(m) transparente 518.
indicadores(m) 405, 410.
índice(m) 529.
índice(m) de teléfonos(m) 420.
índices(m) de exposición(f) 396.
Indio 13.
industría(f) petroquímica 744.
infiltración(f) 34.
infinito(m) 830.
inflador(m) 687.
inflamable 821.
**inflorescencias(f) 69.**
**inflorescencias(f), variedades(f) 60.**
información(f) 823.
**información(f), unidades(f) de salida(f) 527.**
infraestructura(f) 451, 529.
infraspinoso(m) 121.
ingle(f) 116, 118.
inhalación(f) 622.
injección(f)/explosión(f) 437.
injector(m) de combustible(m) 437.
insecticidas(m) 32.
insectívoros(m) 31.
INSECTOS(M) Y ARAÑA(F) 77.
instrumento(m) para alinear el jardín(m) 268.
instrumentos(m) 635.
instrumentos(m) científicos 16, 511.
instrumentos(m) de inmersión(f) 627.
**instrumentos(m) de madera(f), familia(f) 548.**
**instrumentos(m) de manicura(f) 365.**
INSTRUMENTOS(M) DE MEDICIÓN(F) METEOROLÓGICA 40.
**instrumentos(m) del salpicadero(m) 431.**
INSTRUMENTOS(M) ELECTRÓNICOS 555.
INSTRUMENTOS(M) MUSICALES TRADICIONALES 535, 536.
INSTRUMENTOS(M) PARA ESCRIBIR 389.
**instrumentos(m)meteorológicos, caseta(f) 41.**
integral 830.
Intelsat VII 418.
intercambiador(m) de calor(m) 760, 772.
**intercambios(m), principales tipos(m) 450.**
interior(m) derecho 601, 607, 612.
interior(m) izquierdo 601, 607, 612.
intermitente(m) 429, 431, 441, 442, 443, 444, 445.
interóseos(m) del pie(m) 120.
interrogación(f) 832.
interruptor(m) 234, 235, 247, 254, 256, 259, 260, 280, 283, 285, 305, 309, 368, 370, 373, 374, 405, 411, 444, 485, 529, 555.
interruptor(m) automático 212, 747.
interruptor(m) automático bipolar 312.
interruptor(m) automático principal 312.
interruptor(m) automático unipolar 312.
interruptor(m) de arranque(m) automático 216.
interruptor(m) de emergencia(f) 444.
interruptor(m) de encendido(m) 430, 444, 445.
interruptor(m) de encendido(m)/apagado(m) 391, 397, 406.
interruptor(m) de expulsión(f) 411.
interruptor(m) de focalización(f) automática 397.
interruptor(m) de gatillo(m) 284.
interruptor(m) de la puerta(f) 259.
interruptor(m) del limpiaparabrisas(m) 430.
interruptor(m) luminoso 561.
interruptor(m) para el vídeo(m) auxiliar 413.
interruptor(m) para la producción(f) de vídeo(m) 413.
interruptor(m) principal 757.
intersección(f) 830.
intervalo(m) 489.
**intervalos(m) 537.**
intestino(m) 88, 92, 97, 124.
**intestino(m) delgado 131.**
**intestino(m) grueso 131.**
intradós(m) 174.
invernadero(m) 149.
invertido(m) 476.
invierno(m) 8.
inyector(m) 434.
inyector(m) de píldoras(f) 765.
inyector(m) unitario de alimentación(f) 765.
Io 4.
ippon-seoi-nage (proyección(f)) por encima del hombro(m) con una mano(f) 668.
iris(m) 140.
**iron(m) 677.**
iron(m) núm.3 678.
iron(m) núm.4 678.
iron(m) núm.5 678.
iron(m) núm.6 678.
iron(m) núm.7 678.
iron(m) núm.8 678.
irrigador(m) bucal 373.
**irrigador(m) de impulso(m) 264.**
**irrigador(m) giratorio 264.**

irrigador(m) oscilante 264.
isba(f) 165.
isla(f) 51, 452.
isla(f) de arena(f) 30.
isla(f) volcánica 28.
isobara(f) 38.
isquión(m) 123.
istmo(m) 51.
istmo(m) de las fauces(f) 142.

## J

**jabalina(f) 658.**
jabalina(f) 791.
jaboncillo(m) litográfico 583.
jabonera(f) 292, 374.
jamba(f) 202, 204.
JARDÍN(M) 263.
jardín(m) 171, 193.
jardín(m) de rocas(f) 263.
jardín(m) público 190.
jareta(f) 231.
jarra(f) para agua(f) 238.
jarra(f) para café(m) 238.
jarra(m) para cerveza(f) 237.
jarrita(f) de la leche(f) 238.
jaula(f) de extracción(f) 736.
jaula(f) de protección(f) 654.
jefe(m) 818.
jefe(m) de cronometradores(m) 621.
**jeringa(f) 726.**
jeringa(f) de irrigación(f) 726.
jeringa(f) de Luer-Lock 726.
jersey(m) 602.
jersey(m) abierto de cuello(m) en V 338.
jersey(m) de cuello(m) de cisne(m) 642.
jersey(m) de cuello(m) de tortuga(f) 326.
**jersey(m) de cuello(m) en V 326.**
jersey(m) de cuello(m) redondo 326.
JERSEYS(M) 326.
**jerseys(m) combinados 338.**
**jinete(m) 648.**
Jirafa 11.
jirafa(f) 414.
jirafa(f) del micrófono(m) 412.
jockey club(m) 651.
jockey(m) 651.
**jónico, orden(m) 166.**
jota(f) 695.
JOYERÍA(F) 361, 362, 364.
juanete(m) de mesana(f) de estay(m) 480.
juanete(m) de proa(f) alto 481.
juanete(m) de proa(f) bajo 481.
juanete(m) mayor bajo 481.
juanete(m) mayor proel alto 481.
jubón(m) 316.
judías(f) verdes 69.
JUDO(M) 668.
**judoka(m) 668.**
judoka(m) neutral 668.
JUEGO(M) DE DARDOS(M) 698.
juego(m) de mesas(f) 219.
**juego(m) de utensilios(m) 244.**
juego(m) extenso de caracteres(m) 530.
**juego(m) limpiabotas(m) 358.**
**juego(m) para fondue(f) 248.**
**juego(m), área(f) 698.**
juez(m) 603, 605, 611, 666, 668, 669.
juez(m) de brazado(m) 621.
juez(m) de campo(m) 605.
juez(m) de faltas(f) de pie(m) 614.
juez(m) de gol(m) 608, 626.
juez(m) de línea(f) 601, 603, 605, 606, 608, 613, 614, 618.
juez(m) de llegada(f) 621.
juez(m) de red(f) 614.
juez(m) de salida(f) 621.
juez(m) de servicio(m) 614, 618.
juez(m) de silla(f) 614.
juez(m) de viraje(m) 621.
**jugador(m) 602, 609.**
jugador(m) 626, 697.
jugador(m) con el servicio(m) 614.
**jugador(m) de cricket(m) 598.**
jugador(m) de primera base(f) 597.
jugador(m) de saque(m) 613, 616, 618.
jugador(m) de segunda base(f) 597.
jugador(m) de tercera base(f) 597.
jugador(m) exterior central 597.
jugador(m) exterior derecho 597.
jugador(m) exterior izquierdo 597.
jugador(m) medio 597.
junta(f) 257, 300, 439, 768.
junta(f) de goma(f) 296.
junta(f) del anillo(m) 294, 295.
junta(f) del cárter(m) 434.
Júpiter 4.

## K

**Kaplan, turbina(f) 754.**
kimono(m) 340, 348, 668.
kiosco(m) 453, 475.
kiwi(m) 68.

## L

la flecha(f) de la turbina(f) hace girar el generador(m) 767.
**la hoja(f) según su borde(m) 56.**
LA HOJA(F) SEGÚN SU LIMBO(M) 56.
la presión(f) del vapor(m) impulsa las turbinas(f) 767.
LA VISTA(F) 140.
la(A) 537.
labio(m) 100, 107.
labio(m) córneo 97.
labio(m) externo 94.
labio(m) inferior 142, 542.
labio(m) interno 94.
labio(m) mayor 128, 129.
labio(m) menor 128, 129.
labio(m) superior 81, 142, 542.
laboratorio(m) 15.
laboratorio(m) alto 15.
laboratorio(m) espacial 511.
lacolito(m) 25.
ladera(f) 27.
lado(m) de la dama(f) 696.
lado(m) del mar(m) 752.
lado(m) del rey(m) 696.
lado(m) hacia el embalse(m) 752.
ladrillo(m) 286.
ladrillo(m) refractario 204, 585.
ladrillos(m) refractarios 204.
Lagarto 11.
lago(m) 7, 27, 51.
laguna(f) 30.
laguna(f) salada 46.
lama(f) 773.
lámina(f) aislante 528.
lámina(f) cribosa del etmoides(m) 141.
lámina(f) de presión(f) 390.
lámina(f) lateral 104.
lámina(f) medial 104.
lámina(f) superior 525.
**láminas(f) y tableros(m) 289.**
laminillas(f) 55.
lámpara de pinza(f) 235.
lámpara indicadora de tocado(m) 666.
lámpara(f) 233, 477, 718.
**lámpara(f) ajustable 234.**
lámpara(f) de cabecera(f) 234.
lámpara(f) de escritorio(m) 234.
lámpara(f) de mesa(f) 236.
lámpara(f) de neón(m) 310.
lámpara(f) de petróleo(m) 690.
lámpara(f) de pie(m) 236.
lámpara(f) de prueba(f) de neón(m) 310.
lámpara(f) de techo(m) 236.
lámpara(f) del casco(m) 680.
**lámpara(f) halógena 233.**
lámpara(f) incandescente 769.
lámpara(f) orientable de pared(f) 234.
LÁMPARAS(F) 232, 234, 236.
lámparas(f) en serie(f) 235.
lanceolada 56.
lancha(f) de motor(m) 809.
**langosta(f) 90.**
langosta(f) marina 91.
lanilla(f) 817.
lanza(f) 791.
**lanzadera(f) 573.**
lanzadera(f) 510, 571, 574.
lanzadera(f) plana 573.
lanzado(m) desigual 571.
lanzador(m) 597, 599.
lanzador(m) de bombas(f) fumígenas 805.
**lanzamiento(m) 682.**
lanzamiento(m) 682.
lanzamiento(m) de jabalina(f) 654.
lanzamiento(m) de peso(m) 655.
**lanzamientos(m) 658.**
lanzamisiles(m) 811.
lapa(f) 83.
lapiaz(m) 24.
lápices(m) de colores(m) 588.
lapislázuli(m) 363.
lápiz(m) 389, 515.
lápiz(m) adhesivo 515.
lápiz(m) blanco para uñas(f) 365.
lápiz(m) borrador(m) 515.
lápiz(m) corrector de ocre(m) rojo 583.
lápiz(m) corrector de piedra(f) pómez 583.
lápiz(m) de cejas(f) 367.
lápiz(m) de grafito(m) 389.
lápiz(m) labial 366.
lápiz(m) litográfico 583.
**larga distancia(f), control(m) 411.**
LARGA DISTANCIA(F),SATÉLITE(M) DE DETECCIÓN(F) 48.
largo(m) a media pantorrilla(f) 325.
largo(m) al tobillo(m) 325.
largo(m) ejecutivo 325.
larguerillo(m) 787.
larguero(f) central 202.
larguero(m) 203, 223, 302, 498, 626, 773.
larguero(m) de la bisagra(f) 202, 225.
larguero(m) de la cerradura(f) 202.
larguero(m) del marco(m) 225.
larguero(m) inferior 470.
laringe(f) 130, 142.
larva(f) 82.
lasca(f) doble 691.
latiguillo(m) 649.
latitud(f) 3.
laurel(m) 74.
lava(f) 25.
lavabo(m) 215, 292.
**lavado(m) 829.**
lavado(m) de automóviles(m) 453.
**lavadora(f) 258, 298.**
lavadora(f) 215, 298.
**lavavajillas(m) 257.**
lávese a mano(f) con agua(f) tibia 829.
lávese en lavadora(f) con agua(f) caliente en el ciclo(m) para ropa(f) delicada 829.
lávese en lavadora(f) con agua(f) caliente, en el ciclo(m) normal 829.
lávese en lavadora(f) con agua(f) muy caliente, en el ciclo(m) normal 829.
lávese en lavadora(f) con agua(f) tibia en el ciclo(m) para ropa(f) delicada 829.
laya(f) 266.
lazo(m) 228, 328.
Lebreles 11.
lecho(m) 492.
lecho(m) de agujas(f) 568.
LECHO(M) MARINO 28.
lecho(m) oceánico 22.
lecho(m) ungular 137.
lechuga(f) francesa 73.
lechuga(f) romana 73.
lector(m) de casetes(m) 408.
**lector(m) de casetes(m) personal,radio AM \ FM 408.**
lector(m) de CD-ROM 526.
**lector(m) de disco(m) compacto 405.**
lector(m) de disco(m) compacto 407.
lector(m) de discos(m) compactos 408.
lector(m) de tarjetas(f) 422.
lectura(f)/pausa(f) 405.
**legionario(m) romano 791.**
**legumbre(f), corte(m) de una 67.**
**legumbres(f) 72.**
legumbres(f) 33.
**lencería(f) 348.**
lencería(f) 460.
**lengua(f) 143.**
lengua(f) 81, 88, 131, 142.
lengua(f) bífida 96.
lengua(f) glaciar 26.
lengüeta(f) 319, 352, 354, 378, 379, 542, 562, 566, 568, 641, 644.
lengüeta(f) ajustable del talle(m) 322.
lengüeta(f) de cuero(m) 323.
lengüeta(f) de la caña(f) 536.
lengüeta(f) protectora 529.
**lengüeta(f), tubo(m) 542.**
lente(f) 376.
**lente(f) bifocal 376.**
lente(f) convexo-plana 722.
lente(f) de ampliación(f) 399.
lente(f) de campo(m) 718.
lente(f) zoom(m) 409.
lente(m) de 180 grados(m) 392.
lente(m) de acercamiento(m) 392.
lentejas(f) 72.
LENTES(F) 722.
lentes(f) bicóncavas 722.
lentes(f) biconvexas 722.
lentes(f) cóncavas 722.
lentes(f) cóncavo-planas 722.
**lentes(f) convergentes 722.**
lentes(f) convexas 722.
lentes(f) de enfoque(m) 717.
lentes(f) de imágen(f) recta 718.
**lentes(f) divergentes 722.**
Leo 11.
Leo, el León (23 de julio) 820.
León Menor 11.
**león(m) 98.**
león(m) rampante 819.
letrero(m) de número(m) de vías(f) 471.
letrinas(f) 171.
leucoplasto(m) 115.
leva(f) 281, 573.
**levantador(m) de pesas(f) 662.**
levita(f) 317.
libélula(f) 77.
líber(m) 59.
liberador(m) del cable(m) de remolque(m) 639.
liberador(m) del margen(m) 524.
liberador(m) del seguro(m) 278.
Libra 13.
libra(f) 832.
Libra, la Balanza (23 de septiembre) 820.
libreta(f) 518.
**libro(m) encuadernado 577.**
**licuadora(f) 251.**
líder(m) 620.
Liebre 13.
lienzo(m) 589.
**lienzos(m) 589.**
liga(f) 347.
ligadura(f) 539.
ligamento(m) 95.
ligamento(m) alveolo-dentario 144.
ligamento(m) ancho del útero(m) 129.
ligamento(m) de nudos(m) 576.
ligamento(m) de rayas(f) 576.
ligamento(m) elástico 92, 107.
ligamento(m) entrecruzado 576.
ligamento(m) redondo del útero(m) 129.
ligamento(m) suspensorio 140.
ligamento(m) vertical 576.
ligamento(m), posición(f) del 95.
**ligamentos(m) textiles básicos 576.**
ligeramente nublado 39.
liguero(m) 347.
ligústico(m) 74.
lima(f) 277, 587, 688.
lima(f) de uñas(f) 365.
limbo(m) 484.
limbo(m) de la palma(f) 104.
límite(m) de distrito(m) 52.
límite(m) de la ciudad(f) 52.
límite(m) de salida(f) del portero(m) 612.
limón(m) 65.
limonera(f) 652.
limpiador(m) 431.
limpiador(m) de antenas(f) 80.
limpiador(m) de boquillas(f) 307.
limpiador(m) de uñas(f) 365.
**limpiaparabrisas(m) 431.**
limpiaparabrisas(m) 426.
Lince 11.
lindero(m) 193.
línea de caída(f) 341.
línea lateral(f) de individuales(m) 614.
línea(f) 537, 700, 701.
línea(f) azul 608.
línea(f) central 601, 612, 620, 682.
línea(f) central de servicio(m) 614.
línea(f) de 2 metros(m) 626.
línea(f) de 4 metros(m) 626.
línea(f) de aceleración(f) 452.
línea(f) de área(f) de penalty(m) 601.
línea(f) de ataque(m) 613.
línea(f) de banda(f) 606, 619, 620.
línea(f) de barrido(m) 620.
línea(f) de caja(f) de servicio(m) 617.
línea(f) de carrera(f) 599.
línea(f) de corte(m) 565.
línea(f) de costura(f) 565.
línea(f) de crecimiento(m) 83, 95.
línea(f) de cuadro(m) 674.
línea(f) de devolución(f) 599.
línea(f) de disputa(f) 605.
línea(f) de dobles(m) 614.
línea(f) de falta(f) 597.
línea(f) de fe(f) 485.
línea(f) de flotación(f) 487.

Los términos en **negrita** corresponden a una ilustración; los que aparecen en MAYÚSCULAS indican un título.

línea(f) de fondo 619.
línea(f) de fondo(m) 604, 606, 610, 613, 614, 618, 620.
línea(f) de gol(m) 604, 606, 608, 612.
línea(f) de juego(m) 620.
línea(f) de lanzamiento(m) 683.
línea(f) de llegada(f) 651.
línea(f) de los 10 metros(m) 606.
línea(f) de los 15 metros(m) 606.
línea(f) de los 22 metros(m) 606.
línea(f) de los 22,9 metros(m) 607.
línea(f) de los 5 metros(m) 606.
línea(f) de melé(m) 603.
línea(f) de meta(f) 607, 611, 626.
línea(f) de pénalty(m) 612.
línea(f) de pista(f) 503.
línea(f) de puesta(f) en guardia(f) 666.
línea(f) de puesta(f) en guardia(f) de florete(m) 666.
línea(f) de puesta(f) en guardia(f) de sable(m) y espada(f) 666.
línea(f) de recepción(f) de servicio(m) 617.
línea(f) de referencia(f) 719.
línea(f) de salida(f) 620, 621, 655, 656.
línea(f) de seguridad(f) 475.
línea(f) de servicio(m) 614, 616, 617.
línea(f) de servicio(m) corto 618.
línea(f) de servicio(m) largo 618.
línea(f) de tiro(m) 683.
línea(f) de tiro(m) libre 610, 612.
línea(f) de triple salto(m) 654.
línea(f) de visión(f) 719.
línea(f) del área(f) de gol(m) 612.
línea(f) del centro(m) 666.
línea(f) del dobladillo(m) 565.
línea(f) del fondo(m) de la piscina(f) 621.
línea(f) del medio campo(m) 626.
línea(f) del rastrillo(m) 599.
línea(f) divisoria central 616, 618, 619.
línea(f) férrea 52.
línea(f) isosísmica 23.
línea(f) lateral 87, 452, 616.
línea(f) lateral de dobles(m) 618.
línea(f) lateral de individuales(m) 618.
línea(f) límite(m) de inicio(m) de jugada(f) 604.
línea(f) límite(m) de salida(f) 666.
línea(f) media 604, 607, 608, 610.
línea(f) meridiana 719.
línea(f) para modificaciones(f) 565.
línea(f) pintada 452.
línea(f) superior 616.
línea(f) suplementaria 537.
**líneas(f) de latitud(f) 47.**
**líneas(f) de longitud(f) 47.**
líneas(f) principales 452.
**linterna(f) 689.**
linterna(f) 486.
**linterna(f) del faro(m) 486.**
**linterna(f) movible 310.**
liquido(m) corrector 515.
liquido(m) de enfriamiento(m) y ventilación(f) del traje(m) 512.
**líquidos(m) accesorios 592.**
Lira 11.
**lira(f) 535.**
lira(f) 832.
lisosoma(m) 115.
lista(f) de procedimientos(m) 512.
lista(f) superciliar 109.
listel(m) 166.
listón(m) 231, 657.
listón(m) de madera(f) 571.
litchi(m) 68.
litera(f) 460.
LITOGRAFÍA(F) 583.
LITORAL(M), CONFIGURACIÓN(F) 30.
litosfera(f) 31.
**lizos(m) 573.**
lizos(m) 572, 574.
llana(f) 291.
llanta(f) 147, 433, 442, 447.
llanta(f) maciza 788.
llanta(f) neumática de tracción(f) 476, 477.
llanta(f) neumática guía(f) 476, 477.
llanura(f) 51.
**llanura(f) abisal 29.**
llanura(f) abisal 29.
llave(f) 290, 294, 539, 549, 550.
llave(f) ajustable 299.
llave(f) combinada 279.
llave(f) de asientos(m) de válvula(f) 299.
llave(f) de boca(f) de agua(f) 779.
llave(f) de cadena(f) 299.
llave(f) de cincho(m) 299.
llave(f) de estrías(f) abierta 279.
llave(f) de estrías(f) común 279.
llave(f) de estrías(f) hexagonal 279.
llave(f) de gas(m) 297.
llave(f) de paso(m) 215, 293, 296, 298.
llave(f) de tuercas(f) española 279.
llave(f) del bocal(m) 548.
llave(f) del mandril(m) 281.
**llave(f) inglesa 279.**
llave(f) inglesa 299.
llave(f) para agua(f) 551.
llave(f) pico(m) de ganso(m) 299.
llavero(m) 379.
**llaves(f), ejemplos(m) de 668.**
llegada(f) 646, 654.
llovizna(f) continua 39.
llovizna(f) intermitente 39.
lluvia(f) 36.
lluvia(f) continua 39.
lluvia(f) helada 39.
lluvia(f) intermitente 39.
**lluvia(f),medición(f) 40.**
lobulada 56.
lóbulo(m) 111, 139, 141.
lóbulo(m) inferior 130.
lóbulo(m) lateral inferior 61.
lóbulo(m) lateral superior 61.
lóbulo(m) medio 130.
lóbulo(m) superior 130.
lóbulo(m) terminal 61.
locomotora(f) 459.
LOCOMOTORA(F) DIÉSEL ELÉCTRICA 468.
lóculo(m) 64.
lomera(f) 653.
lomo(m) 101, 106, 108, 239, 240, 241, 242, 577, 579.
lomo(m) con canal(m) 281.
lomo(m) de maniobra(f) 465.
lomo(m) del libro(m) 579.
lona(f) 669, 773.
lona(f) de separación(f) 685.
longitud(f) 3.
longitud(f) de la ola(f) 30.
LONGITUD(F), MEDICIÓN(F) 711.
loriga(f) 791.
**los pasos(m) 101.**
lubrificador(m) 735.
lucernas(f) del campanario(m) 175.
luces(f) de advertencia(f) 431.
luces(f) de emergencia(f) 779.
luces(f) de frente 189.
luces(f) indicadoras 531.
**luces(f) traseras 429.**
luces(f) traseras 147.
luchadero(m) 632.
lugar(m) para la leña(f) 204.
LUGE(M) 643.
lumbrera(f) de admisión(f) 436.
lumbrera(f) de escape(m) 436.
lumbrera(f) de transferencia(f) 436.
LUNA(F) 7.
Luna(f) 4, 8.
Luna(f) llena 7.
Luna(f) nueva 6.
LUNA(F), ECLIPSE(M) 8.
LUNA(F), FASES(F) 6.
**lunas(f), planetas(m) 4.**
luneta(f) 189.
luneta(f) preferente 188.
lúnula(f) 137.
lúnula(m) 95.
lupa(f) 688.
lupa(f)de focalización(f) 399.
luz(f) 486, 487, 489, 500, 720, 721.
luz(f) anticolisión 498.
luz(f) antiniebla 429, 440.
luz(f) blanca 488.
luz(f) de advertencia(f) de emisión(f) 407.
luz(f) de advertencia(f) de la gasolina(f) 431.
luz(f) de advertencia(f) de puerta(f) abierta 431.
luz(f) de advertencia(f) del aceite(m) 431.
luz(f) de advertencia(f) del alternador(m) 431.
luz(f) de advertencia(f) del cinturón(m) de seguridad(f) 431.
luz(f) de aterrizaje(m) 508.
luz(f) de cruce(m) 429.
luz(f) de encendido(m) 374, 420.
luz(f) de encendido(m) \ apagado(m) 420.
luz(f) de freno(m) 429.
luz(f) de la barrera(f) 471.
luz(f) de marcha(f) atrás 429.
luz(f) de navegación(f) 493, 499, 508.
luz(f) de posición(f) 429, 459.
luz(f) de tope(m) 495.
luz(f) delantera 447.
luz(f) exterior 196.
luz(f) inactínica 398.
luz(f) indicadora de la presión(f) del aceite(m) 445.
luz(f) indicadora de luz(f) larga 431.
luz(f) intermitente 471.
luz(f) larga 429.
luz(f) lateral 440, 441.
luz(f) piloto(m) 370.
**luz(f) solar, medición(f) 40.**
luz(f) trasera 429, 441, 443, 444, 446.
luz(m) de posición(f) 429.

## M

maceta(f) 263.
maceta(f) colgante 263.
machete(m) 794.
macho(m) 566.
machón(m) 751.
**machones(m), dique(m) 751.**
macillo(m) 540, 541.
macillo(m) de fieltro(m) 541.
macizo(m) de flores(f) 263.
mácula(f) lútea 140.
**madera(f) 288, 677.**
madera(f) núm.3 678.
madera(f) núm.5 678.
MADERA(F), PISOS(M) DE 200.
maderamen(m) que soporta el tejado(m) 168.
maduración(f) completa 61.
**maduración(f), etapas(f) 61.**
magma(m) 25, 28.
magnetómetro(m) 42.
**maíz(m) 72.**
maíz(m) 152.
maíz(m) forrajero 149.
**maleta(f) clásica 383.**
**maleta(f) de fin(m) de semana(f) 383.**
maletero(m) 427.
**maletín(m) 378.**
maletín(m) 382.
maleza(f) 676.
malla(f) 619.
mallas(f) con volantes(m) 349.
Malpighi, estrato(m) de 136.
**mameluco(m) 350.**
**mamelucos(m) 350.**
**mamelucos(m) de dos piezas(f) 350.**
mampara(f) de contención(f) 441.
mancha(f) solar 6.
manchas(f) auriculares 109.
mandarina(f) 65.
mandíbula(f) 78, 80, 81, 86.
**mandíbula(f) de carnívoro(m) 98.**
**mandíbula(f) de roedor(m) 98.**
mandíbula(f) inferior 102, 109.
mandíbula(f) superior 109.
mando(m) de control(m) del carro(m) 569.
mando(m) del freno(m) aerodinámico 639.
MANDO(M), PUENTE(M) 500.
**mandolina(f) 535.**
mandril(m) 276, 280, 281, 283, 735.
manecilla(f) de las horas(f) 707.
**manejo(m) del combustible(m), secuencia(f) 764.**
manga(f) 318, 322, 667, 817.
manga(f) colgante 316.
manga(f) corta 318.
manga(f) de aislamiento(m) 309.
manga(f) de distribución(f) 213.
manga(f) de volante(m) 317.
manga(f) empotrada 324, 326.
manga(f) flotante 316.
manga(f) ranglán 319, 330, 340, 350.
manga(f) y boquillas(f) 245.
**manga(f), tipos(m) de 339, 340.**
mango(m) 63, 239, 240, 241, 242, 272, 275, 276, 277, 278, 279, 280, 281, 282, 291, 304, 305, 306, 310, 370, 373, 374, 544, 563, 564, 579, 598, 607, 609, 615, 619, 620, 658, 671, 674, 675, 677, 681, 688, 735.
mango(m) aislado 310.
mango(m) aislante 311.
mango(m) auxiliar 280.
mango(m) posterior 671.
manguera(f) 260, 265, 292, 296, 298, 306, 438, 780.
manguera(f) de abastecimiento(m) en vuelo(m) 813.
manguera(f) de aire(m) 734.
manguera(f) de alimentación(f) 257.
manguera(f) de conexión(f) 735.
manguera(f) de desagüe(m) 257, 258, 298.
manguera(f) de incendios(m) 778.
manguera(f) de inyección(f) de lodo(m) 737.
manguera(f) de líquido(m) para frenos(m) 432.
manguera(f) de llenado(m) 399.
manguera(f) de riego(m) 265.
manguera(f) de servicio(m) 453.
manguera(f) de succión(f) 778.
manguera(f) de vaciado(m) 258, 399.
manguera(f) del rebosadero(m) 293.
manguera(f) flexible 735.
manguera(f) hidráulica 156, 157, 158.
manguera(f) para agua(f) 734.
**manguera(f), carretilla(f) 265.**
manguito(m) 663.
manguito(m) de enfriamiento(m) 796.
MANICURA(F) 365.
**manicura(f), estuche(m) 365.**
**manicura(f), instrumentos(m) 365.**
manija(f) en cruz(f) 701.
manillar(m) 270, 442, 445, 447, 664.
manipulador(m) de documentos(m) 532.
maniquí(m) 564, 592.
manivela(f) 280, 393, 448, 573, 583, 670, 671, 793.
manivela(f) de dirección(f) 803.
manivela(f) de elevación(f) 802, 803.
manivela(f) de elevación(f) de patas(f) 441.
manivela(f) de la ventanilla(f) 429.
manivela(f) del carrete(m) 265.
**mano(f) 137.**
mano(f) 117, 119.
MANO(F), GRANADA(F) 804.
mano(m) 243.
manojo(m) 72.
manómetro(m) 209, 627, 710, 740, 741, 778.
manómetro(m) del soplete(m) 306.
manómetro(m) del tanque(m) 306.
manopla(f) 327, 680.
manoplas(f) 308.
**manos(f) de póquer(m) 695.**
manta(f) 224.
manta(f) de la silla(f) 648.
mantenimiento(m) 453.
mantequera(f) 238.
manto(m) 204.
manto(m) externo 22.
manto(m) interno 22.
manual(m) 543.
manual(m) de primeros auxilios(m) 725.
manubrio(m) 630.
**manzana(f) 64.**
manzana(f) 64.
Mao 342.
mapa(f) 483.
**mapa(m) de carreteras(f) 52.**
mapa(m) de la ruta(f) 474.
mapa(m) de ruta(f) 477.
mapa(m) de rutas(f) 475.
**mapa(m) físico 51.**
**mapa(m) político 51.**
**mapa(m) urbano 52.**
**mapa(m), proyecciones(f) 50.**
MAQUILLAJE(M) 366.
**maquillaje(m) facial 366.**
**maquillaje(m) labial 366.**
**maquillaje(m) para ojos(m) 367.**
máquina de picar carne(f) 243.
MÁQUINA DE TRICOTAR 568.
máquina(f) abastecedora de combustible(m) 759.
máquina(f) cargadora de combustible(m) 761, 764.
máquina(f) de descarga(f) 764.
máquina(f) de dibujar con guía(f) 591.
MÁQUINA(F) DE ESCRIBIR ELECTRÓNICA 524.
máquina(f) de soldar eléctrica 305.
máquina(f) expendedora de bebidas(f) 453.
**máquina(f) lavaplatos(m) 298.**
máquina(f) lavaplatos(m) 298.
máquina(f) para hacer pasta(f) italiana 243.
MAQUINARIA(F) PESADA 785.
MÁQUINAS(F), HERRAMIENTAS(F) 264, 266, 268, 270, 272.
**maquinilla(f) de afeitar 374.**
**maquinilla(f) de afeitar eléctrica 374.**
maquinilla(f) desechable 374.

maquinilla(f) para cortar el cabello(m) 369.
mar(m) 7, 51.
mar(m) abierto 752.
mar(m) Caribe 20.
mar(m) Caspio 21.
mar(m) de Bering 21.
mar(m) de Groenlandia 20.
mar(m) de la China(f) Meridional 21.
mar(m) del Norte 21.
mar(m) Mediterráneo 21.
mar(m) Negro 21.
mar(m) Rojo 21.
marca(f) central 614, 620.
marca(f) de posición(f) 547.
marca(f) de posisición(f) 546.
marca(f) de tope(m) 486, 488.
marca(f) registrada 384, 831.
**marcador(m) 563.**
marcador(m) 389, 515, 588, 666, 683.
marcador(m) automático 420.
marcador(m) de temperatura(f) 705.
marcador(m) del dobladillo(m) 564.
marchapié(m) 478.
marco(m) 573, 615, 617, 645, 659, 769, 832.
marco(m) ajustable 277.
marco(m) vertical 574.
marcos(m) 572.
margarita(f) 691.
marginadora(f) 398.
mariconera(f) 380.
marinera 337.
marinero 342.
MARIPOSA(F) 78.
**mariposa(f) 79.**
mariposa(f) de resorte(m) 276.
mariquita(f) 77.
marítimo 45.
marquesa(f) 362.
Marte 4.
**martillo(m) 658.**
martillo(m) 138, 311, 795.
martillo(m) de albañil(m) 291.
**martillo(m) de bola(f) 275.**
martillo(m) de carpintero(m) 275.
**martillo(m) de encuadernador(m) 579.**
**martillo(m) de uña(f) 275.**
martillo(m) mixto 680.
**martillo(m) neumático 735.**
**martillo(m) para hielo(m) 681.**
martinete(m) 541.
más(m) 830.
más(m) o menos(m) 830.
masa(f) de aire(m) 38.
masa(f) inerte 714.
máscara(f) 595, 777.
**máscara(f) de gas(m) 730.**
**máscara(f) para el polvo(m) 730.**
mascarilla(f) 730.
masculino(m) 831.
MASCULINOS, ÓRGANOS(M) GENITALES 127.
masetero(m) 120.
mastelero(m) 479.
mastelero(m) de juanete(m) 479.
mastelero(m) de mesana(f) de estay(m) 480.
mastelero(m) de sobrejuanete(m) 479.
mástil(m) 508, 544, 546, 547, 628, 631, 637, 787, 788.
**matacán(m) 181.**
matacán(m) 180.
**matemáticas(f) 830.**
materia(f) gris 135.
material(m) aislante 199, 200.
material(m) impermeable 349.
**materiales(m) aislantes 287.**
**materiales(m) básicos 286.**
**materiales(m) de revestimiento(m) 286.**
**materiales(m) peligrosos 821.**
MATERIALES(M), MANEJO(M) 786, 788.
matraca(f) 281, 670.
matriz(f) ungular 137.
maxilar(m) 86, 90, 141.
maxilar(m) inferior 122.
maxilar(m) separable 96.
maxilar(m) superior 81, 122.
maxilípedos(m) 90.
mayor que 830.
maza(f) 553, 581, 675.
**mazo(m) 275.**
mazo(m) 586.
mazorca(m) 72.
meato(m) auditivo 138, 139.
meato(m) urinario 127.
**mecanismo(m) 712.**
mecanismo(m) asistido de descarga(f) 796.
mecanismo(m) de avance(m) y cambio(m) de la diapositiva(f) 397.
mecanismo(m) de carga(f) del combustible(m) 760.
mecanismo(m) de control 699.
mecanismo(m) de cuerda(f) 707.
mecanismo(m) de despliegue(m) 49.
mecanismo(m) de disparo(m) 804.
mecanismo(m) de elevación(f) de la pala(f) 784.
mecanismo(m) de empuje(m) 389.
mecanismo(m) de enrollado(m) 231.
mecanismo(m) de escape(m) 539.
mecanismo(m) de indicación del disco(m) 285.
mecanismo(m) de la barrera(f) 471.
mecanismo(m) de la palanca(f) 541.
mecanismo(m) de retroceso(m) y cambio(m) de la diapositiva(f) 397.
mecanismo(m) de reversión(f) 212.
mecanismo(m) de rotación(f) de la cuchilla(f) 784.
**mecanismo(m) del reloj(m) de pesas(f) 707.**
mecanismo(m) elevador del disco(m) 285.
mecanismo(m) para las octavas(f) 548.
mecedora(f) 221, 223.
media bota(f) 354.
media combinación(f) 345.
media luna(f) 377.
media(f) 602, 667.
media(f) alta 642.
media(f) tres-cuartos 344.
medialuna(f) 179.
mediana(f) 186.
**medias(f) 344.**
medias(f) 344, 347.
medias(f) de malla(f) 344.
MEDICIÓN(F) METEREÓLOGICA, INSTRUMENTOS 40.
médico(m) 669.
medidor(m) 757.
medidor(m) automático 741.
medidor(m) de agua(f) 215, 439.
medidor(m) de altos niveles(m) de frecuencia(f) 403.
medio de melé(m) 606.
medio lado(m) 787.
medio nublado 39.
medio punta(f) 607.
**medio punto(m), arco(m) 174.**
medio(m) alejado 606.
medio(m) central 607.
medio(m) derecho 601.
medio(m) izquierdo 601.
**medir, utensilios(m) para 244.**
médula(f) 59, 132.
médula(f) espinal 89, 134, 135.
Meissner, corpúsculo(m) de 136.
mejilla(f) 118.
mejillón(m) 93.
**melé(m) 603.**
**melé(m) en el fútbol(m) canadiense 605.**
**melocotón(m) 63.**
melocotón(m) 63.
melón(m) 69.
melón(m) chino 69.
membrana(f) 65, 84.
membrana(f) celulósica 115.
membrana(f) del ala(f) 112.
membrana(f) del cascarón(m) 109.
membrana(f) del tímpano(m) 139.
membrana(f) interdigital 111.
membrana(f) interfemoral 112.
membrana(f) nuclear 115.
membrana(f) vitelina 109.
membrillo(m) 64.
memoria(f) de tipos(m) de puntos(m) 569.
menguante(m) 7.
menisco(m) convergente 722.
menisco(m) divergente 722.
menor que 830.
menos(m) 830.
ménsula(f) 204.
mentón(m) 108, 118.
menudillo(m) 101.
Mercurio 4.
mercurio(m) 232.
meridiana(f) 221.
meridiano(m) celeste 3.
meridiano(m) occidental 47.
meridiano(m) oriental 47.
meridiano(m) principal 47.
merlón(m) 181.
MESA(F) 219.
**mesa(f) 619, 674.**
mesa(f) 28, 283, 285.
mesa(f) alimentadora 162.
mesa(f) arbitral 608.
**mesa(f) de hojas(f) abatibles 219.**
**mesa(f) de la impresora(f) 521.**
MESA(F) DE LA RULETA(F) 700.
mesa(f) de producción(f) 413.
**mesa(f) del ordenador(m) 521.**
**mesa(f) plegable 219.**
mesa(f) rotatoria 737.
MESA(F), VAJILLA(F) Y SERVICIO(M) DE 238.
**mesas(f), tipos(m) de 219.**
meseta(f) 27, 51.
mesita(f) de servicio(m) 219.
mesocarpio(m) 62, 63, 64, 65.
mesosfera(f) 19.
mesotórax(m) 78.
metacarpo(m) 102, 107, 122.
metales(m) 33.
**metales(m), ejemplos(m) 819.**
**metales(m), familia(f) 550.**
**metamórfosis(f) de la rana(f) 84.**
metatarso(m) 80, 103, 122.
metatórax(m) 78.
METEOROLOGÍA(F) 38.
metopa(f) 167.
metralla(f) 801.
METRALLETA(F) 795.
METRO(M) 474, 476.
metro(m) 190.
**metrónomo(m) 539.**
**metrónomo(m) de cuarzo(m) 539.**
mezcla(f) de aire(m) y combustible(m) 436.
MEZQUITA(F) 172.
**mezquita(f), plano 173.**
mi(E) 537.
micelio(m) 55.
micrófono(m) 407, 414, 420, 639.
micrófono(m) de intercomunicación(f) 413.
MICRÓFONO(M) ELECTRODINÁMICO 406.
micrófono(m) integrado 409.
**micrómetro(m) 711.**
microprocesador(m) 528.
MICROSCOPIO(M) BINOCULAR 718.
MICROSCOPIO(M) DE ELECTRONES 717.
**microscopio(m) de electrones(m), elementos(m) 717.**
**microscopio(m) de electrones, corte(m) transversal 717.**
miembro(m) inferior 124.
miembro(m) superior 124.
Mihrab(m) 173.
mijo(m) 152.
**mina(f) subterránea 736.**
minarete(m) 172, 173.
MINAS(F) DE CARBÓN(M) 733.
Minbar(m) 173.
mineral(m) 733.
minutero(m) 706, 707.
minutero(m) para huevos(m) pasados por agua(f) 244.
minuto(m) 830.
mira(f) 684, 797, 803.
mira(f) del tirador(m) 805.
mira(f) periscópica 805.
mira(f) telescópica 798.
mirador(m) 197, 505.
mirilla(f) 471.
misil(m) aire(m) aire(m) 813, 814.
misil(m) aire(m) tierra(f) 814.
misil(m) antiaéreo 808.
misil(m) antibuques 814.
misil(m) antiradar 814.
misil(m) antisubmarino 809, 814.
misil(m) antitanque 814.
misil(m) mar(m) a mar(m) 809.
misil(m) tierra(f) aire(m) 814.
**misil(m), estructura(f) 814.**
**misiles(m), principales tipos(m) 814.**
mitocondrio(m) 115.
**mitón(m) sin dedos(m) 327.**
mízcalo(m) (Lactarius deliciosus) 55.
mocasín(m) 355.
mochila(f) 680.
modalidad(f) 525.
**modalidad(f) arranque(m) 662.**
**modalidad(f) con impulso(m) en dos tiempos(m) 662.**
modalidad(f) de avance(m) de la película(f) 391.
modalidad(f) de exposición(f) 391.
modalidad(f) de exposición(f) múltiple 391.
modalidad(f) de producción(f) de copia(f) 532.
modalidad(f) sintetizador(m) 402.
modalidad(f) TV 411.
modalidad(f) VCR 411.
**modelo(m) de clave(f) 38.**
módem(m) 526.
moderador(m) 459, 766.
moderador(m): agua(f) natural 762, 763.
moderador(m): agua(f) pesada 761.
moderador(m): grafito(m) 760.
modillón(m) 167, 180, 181.
módulo(m) de acceso(m) a la memoria(f) RAM 528.
módulo(m) de comunicación(f) 418.
módulo(m) de conexión(f) 528.
módulo(m) de la barra(f) colectora 49.
módulo(m) de lectura de memoria(f) ROM unicamente 528.
módulo(m) de mando(m) 509.
módulo(m) de propulsión(f) 418.
módulo(m) de servicio(m) 418, 509.
módulo(m) del equipo(m) 49.
módulo(m) lunar 509.
módulo(m) para liberar el gas(m) 738.
módulos(m) de batería(f) 43.
molar(m) 98.
**molar(m), corte(m) transversal de un 144.**
molares(m) 144.
molde(m) 584.
molde(m) acanalado 245.
molde(m) para bizcocho(m) 245.
molde(m) para magdalenas(f) 245.
molde(m) para tartas(f) 245.
molde(m) redondo con muelles(m) 245.
moldes(m) de pastas(f) 245.
moldura(f) 199, 433.
moldura(f) lateral 427.
moldura(f) protectora 449.
moldura(f) superior 619.
molinete(m) 160, 773.
**molinillo(m) de café(m) 256.**
**molino(m) de plataforma(f) giratoria 773.**
**molino(m) de viento(m) 773.**
MOLUSCO(M) 92.
MOLUSCO(M) GASTERÓPODO 83.
**moluscos(m) comestibles 93.**
moneda(f) de la Comunidad(f) Europea 832.
monedero(m) 379, 381.
monitor(m) 422.
monitor(m) de efectos(m) videodigitales 413.
monitor(m) de la producción(f) técnica 413.
monitor(m) de producción(f) 415.
monitor(m) de salida(f) 413.
monitor(m) de sonido(m) 407, 413, 415.
monitor(m) de vídeo(m) 526, 527.
monitor(m) de visualización(f) previa 415.
monitor(m) del sonido(m) 412.
**monitor(m) del vídeo(m) 529.**
monitor(m) principal de visualización(f) previa 413.
monitores(m) de entrada(f) 413.
monitores(m) de visualización(f) previa 413.
mono(m) 336.
**mono(m) de tirantes cruzados atrás 351.**
monóculo(m) 377.
montacargas(m) 736, 786.
**montacargas(m) de horquilla(f) 787.**
**montacargas(m) hidráulico de tarima(f) 788.**
montado 242.
montadura(f) 364.
MONTAÑA(F) 27.
**montaña(f) alta, climas(m) 45.**
montante(m) 156, 198, 353, 572, 574, 578, 579, 644, 659, 728.
montante(m) central 203, 225, 427.
montante(m) del muro(m) 199.
montante(m) esquinero 198.
montante(m) vertical 203.
monte(m) de Venus 128.

Los términos en **negrita** corresponden a una ilustración; los que aparecen en MAYÚSCULAS indican un título.

Monte(m) Everest 19.
montes(m) marinos 29.
**montura(f) 376.**
**montura(f) acimutal 15.**
montura(f) de bayoneta(f) 392.
montura(f) de cartón(m) 397.
montura(f) de herradura(f) 14.
montura(f) de la hebilla(f) 323.
montura(f) del objetivo(m) 390.
monumento(m) 52.
mordaza(f) 276, 278, 280, 281, 283, 311, 365.
mordaza(f) curva 278.
mordaza(f) fija 279, 282.
mordaza(f) móvil 279, 282.
mordaza(f) recta 278.
mordente(m) 538.
**morfología(f) 86, 100, 106, 108.**
morilla(f) (Morchella esculenta) 55.
morillos(m) 205.
morral(m) 380.
morrena(f) central 26.
morrena(f) de fondo(m) 26.
morrena(f) lateral 27.
morrena(f) terminal 27.
morro(m) 498, 638.
mortero(m) 243, 484.
**mortero(m) del siglo(m) XVII 803.**
**mortero(m) moderno 803.**
MORTEROS(M) 803.
mosaico(m) 171.
Mosca 13.
mosca(f) 77, 675.
**mosca(f) artificial 670.**
mosca(f) central 674.
mosca(f) de la línea(f) de cuadro(m) 674.
mosca(f) superior 675.
**mosquetón(m) 681.**
mosquetón(m) 630, 672, 680.
**mostaza(f) 67.**
mostrador(m) 504.
MOTOCICLETA(F) 442, 444.
motor(m) 147, 161, 214, 250, 251, 256, 257, 258, 259, 260, 270, 271, 272, 283, 284, 373, 442, 737, 784, 787, 805.
motor(m) a reacción(f) 43.
motor(m) de arranque(m) 271.
**motor(m) de cuatro tiempos(m) 436.**
**motor(m) de dos tiempos(m) 436.**
motor(m) de elevación(f) diésel 493.
**motor(m) de gasolina(f) 434.**
motor(m) de la bomba(f) 216.
motor(m) de propulsión(f) diésel 492.
motor(m) del brazo(m) actuador 529.
motor(m) del disco(m) 529.
motor(m) del proyectil 814.
motor(m) del ventilador(m) 207, 214.
**motor(m) diésel 437.**
motor(m) diésel 469, 495, 782, 783, 785.
motor(m) eléctrico 209, 268, 271, 438.
motor(m) eléctrico de emergencia(f) 806.
motor(m) eléctrico principal 806.
**motor(m) rotatorio 437.**
**motor(m) turbo compresor 438.**
motores(m) 510.
motores(m) diésel 809.
motores(m) principales 511.
**motores(m), tipos(m) 436.**
movimiento(m) diagonal 696.
movimiento(m) en ángulo(m) 696.
movimiento(m) horizontal 696.
movimiento(m) vertical 696.
**movimientos(m) principales 697.**
**movimientos(m), tipos(m) 696.**
mucosa(f) olfatoria 142.
mueble(m) bar(m) 227.
muela(f) del juicio(m) 144.
muelle(m) 290, 490, 659, 726.
muelle(m) para cargar mercancía(f) 190.
muelle(m) para inflar y desinflar 687.
muelle(m) saliente 739.
muerte(f) 831.
muesca(f) 322, 341, 674, 684, 708, 793.
muesca(f) de protección(f) 529.
muescas(f) 578.
muestra(f) 567.
MUJER(F), ROPA(F) DE 330, 332, 334, 336, 338, 340, 342, 344, 346, 348.
**muleta(f) de antebrazo(m) 728.**
**muleta(f) de sobaco(m) 728.**
múltiple 738.
múltiple(m) de admisión(f) 434, 437.
múltiple(m) de escape(m) 435, 437, 438, 439.
MUNDO(M), CLIMAS(M) 45.
muñeca(f) 112, 117, 119, 137.
muñequera(f) 602, 609, 615, 662.
muñón(m) 105.
muralla(f) 178, 180.
MURCIÉLAGO(M) 112.
muro(m) 7, 646, 647, 685.
muro(m) con barras(f) 646.
muro(m) de abordaje(m) 492.
muro(m) de cimentación(f) 198.
muro(m) de encauzamiento(m) 746.
muro(m) de la Qibla(f) 173.
muro(m) de ladrillos(m) 199.
muro(m) de rebote(m) 616.
muro(m) fortificado 172.
muro(m) lateral 492.
muro(m) térmico 42.
musarola(f) 651.
músculo recto externo 140.
músculo recto interno 140.
músculo(m) aductor 92.
músculo(m) erector del pelo 136.
músculo(m) papilar 125.
MÚSCULOS(M) 120.
museo(m) 185.
muserola(f) 649.
muslera(f) 602.
muslo(m) 101, 106, 108, 117, 119, 127, 128.
muslo(m), aductor(m) del 120.
muy nublado 39.

## N

nabo(m) 71.
nabo(m) sueco 71.
nacimiento(m) 831.
nalga(f) 117, 119, 127, 128.
naos(m) 169.
**naranja(f) 65.**
naranja(f) 65.
naranja(f) china 65.
**nariz(f) 141.**
nariz(f) 118, 798.
nariz(f), aleta(f) de la 141.
nariz(f), ventana(f) de la 141.
nasal(m) 792.
nasofaringe(f) 141.
NATACIÓN(F) 621, 622.
**natación(f), estilos(m) de 622.**
navaja(f) 93.
**navaja(f) de barbero(m) 374.**
navaja(f) de injertar 269.
navaja(f) jardinera 269.
navaja(f) para entresacar 369.
**navaja(f) tipo(m) suizo 688.**
nave(f) 177.
nave(f) central 173.
nave(f) de carga(f) 510.
nave(f) lateral 177.
NAVEGACIÓN(F), APARATOS(M) 484.
neblina(f) 37, 39.
**neceser(m) 382.**
nectarina(f) 63.
negativo(m) 399.
negra(f) 700.
negra(f) (cuarto(m)) 538.
negras(f) 696.
negro(m) 701.
Neptuno 5.
nervadura(f) central 67.
nervadura(f) principal 56.
nervadura(f) secundaria 56.
nervio(m) 79, 136, 577.
nervio(m) abdominogenital mayor 133.
nervio(m) abdominogenital menor 133.
nervio(m) auditivo 139.
nervio(m) ciático mayor 133.
nervio(m) ciático menor 133.
nervio(m) ciático popliteo externo 133.
nervio(m) ciático poplíteo interno 133.
nervio(m) circunflejo 133.
nervio(m) crural 133.
nervio(m) cubital 133.
nervio(m) de vela(f) estay(m) 479.
nervio(m) diagonal 177.
nervio(m) digital 133.
nervio(m) facial 139.
nervio(m) femorocutáneo 133.
nervio(m) glúteo 133.
nervio(m) intercostal 133.
nervio(m) mediano 133.
nervio(m) musculocutáneo de la pierna(f) 133.
nervio(m) obturador 133.
nervio(m) olfativo 88.
nervio(m) olfatorio 142.
nervio(m) óptico 140.
nervio(m) radial 133.
nervio(m) raquídeo 135.
nervio(m) safeno externo 133.
nervio(m) safeno interno 133.
nervio(m) secundario 177.
nervio(m) tibial anterior 133.
nervio(m) transversal 177.
nervio(m) vestibular 139.
nervios(m) craneales 133.
NERVIOSO, SISTEMA(M) 133, 134.
**neumático(m) 433.**
neumático(m) 440, 447.
neumático(m) de capas(f) al sesgo(m) 433.
neumático(m) radial 433.
**neumático(m) radial con cinturones(m) 433.**
neumostoma(m) 83.
neuroespina(f) 89.
neurona(f) motriz 135.
neurona(f) sensorial 134.
**neuronas(f), encadenamiento(m) de 135.**
**nevadas(f),medición(f) 41.**
nevera(f) 453, 690.
neviza(f) incipiente 26.
niblick(m), hierro(m) núm. 9 678.
niebla(f) 37, 39.
nieve(f) 34.
nieve(f) continua 39.
nieve(f) intermitente 39.
nieves(f) perpetuas 27.
nimbostratos(m) 44.
NIÑOS(M), ROPA(F) DE 349, 350.
níspero(m) 64.
Nissl, cuerpos(m) de 135.
nivel(m) 736.
nivel(m) de agua(f) 210, 247.
nivel(m) de aire(m) 291.
nivel(m) de equilibrio(m) del agua(f) 30.
nivel(m) del agua(f) 256.
nivel(m) del mar(m) 22, 28.
nivel(m) freático 24.
nivel(m) inferior 493.
nivel(m) superior 493.
**nivel(m), paso(m) 471.**
nivelación(f) principal 713.
nivelador(m) 277.
nivelador(m) de la alidada(f) 713.
nivelador(m) principal 713.
**niveladora(f) 784.**
nivómetro(m) 41.
no es idéntico a 830.
no es paralelo a 830.
no pertenece a 830.
no se lave 829.
no use lejía(f) de cloro(m) 829.
no use plancha(f) 829.
nódulo(m) 756.
nombre(m) de la estación(f) 474.
nonio(m) 708.
noreste(m) 488.
noroeste(m) 488.
norte(m) 488.
notación(f) del ajedrez(m) 696.
NOTACIÓN(F) MUSICAL 537.
NOTACIÓN(F) MUSICAL(F) 538.
**notas(f) musicales, valores(m) 538.**
nube(f) 36.
nube(f) alta 38.
nube(f) baja 38.
nube(f) de cenizas(f) 25.
nube(f) media 38.
nube(f) nacarada 19.
nube(f) noctiluciente 19.
NUBES(F) 44.
**nubes(f) altas 44.**
**nubes(f) bajas 44.**
**nubes(f) de desarrollo(m) vertical 44.**
nubes(f) dispersas 39.
**nubes(f) medias 44.**
**nubosidad(f) 39.**
nuca(f) 117, 119.
núcleo(m) 6, 9, 115, 128, 135, 677, 692, 798.
núcleo(m) de greda(f) 748.
núcleo(m) del reactor(m) 760, 762, 763.
núcleo(m) exterior 22.
núcleo(m) interior 22.
nucléolo(m) 115, 128.
nudo(m) 57.
nudo(m) de dos cotes(m) 691.
nudo(m) de guía(m) 691.
nudo(m) de pescador(m) 691.
nudo(m) de rizo(m) 691.
nudo(m) de tejedor(m) 691.
nudo(m) llano 691.
NUDOS(M) 691.
NUDOS(M) NÁUTICOS 692.
nuez(f) 66, 116, 793.
nuez(f) de la India(f) 66.
nuez(f) del Brasil(m) 66.
nuez(f) verde 66.
**nuez(f), corte(m) de una 66.**
número(m) 701.
número(m) de calle(f) 621.
número(m) de decimales 523.
número(m) de la autopista(f) 52.
número(m) de la carretera(f) 52.
número(m) de pista(f) 405.
número(m) de salida(f) 653.
número(m) del consumidor(m) 712.
número(m) dorsal 656.

## O

o-uchi-gari (gran siega(f)) interior 668.
oasis(m) 46.
obenque(m) 479, 628.
obi (cinta(f)) 668.
obispillo(m) 109.
objetivo(m) 390, 391, 392, 396, 397, 405, 718, 719, 721.
**objetivo(m) normal 392.**
objetivo(m) normal 392.
**objetivo(m), cámara(f) reflex 391.**
**objetivos(m) 392.**
**objetivos(m) y accesorios(m) 392.**
oblicuo(m) mayor 120.
oblicuo(m) mayor del abdomen(m) 121.
oboe(m) 548.
oboes(m) 557.
**obra(f) muerta 630.**
obras(f) 826, 827.
**obrera(f) 80.**
obrera(f) 81.
obscurecido por contaminación(f) 39.
**observatorio(m) 14.**
OBSERVATORIO(M) ASTRONÓMICO 14.
obstáculo(m) 697.
**obstáculos(m) 647.**
obturador(m) 529, 680.
obturador(m) de cortina(f) 390.
obturador(m) de la cúpula(f) 14.
obturador(m) para la circulación(f) del aire(m) 772.
OBÚS(M) MODERNO 802.
occidental 619.
occipital(m) 121, 123.
Oceanía(f) 21.
océano(m) 7, 35, 51.
océano(m) Atlántico 20.
océano(m) Glacial Artico 21.
océano(m) Indico 21.
océano(m) Pacífico 20.
ocelo(m) 78, 80, 81.
ocho facetas(f) 362.
octava(f) 537, 667.
ocular(m) 390, 396, 718, 719, 720, 721.
ocular(m) acodado 721.
**odómetro(m) 711.**
odómetro(m) 431.
oeste(m) 488.
oficina(f) 453, 462, 465.
OFICINA(F) AUTOMATIZADA, CONFIGURACIÓN(F) DEL SISTEMA(M) 526.
oficina(f) de objetos(m) perdidos 823.
oficina(f) de reservas(f) de hotel(m) 504.
oficina(f) del puerto(m) 491.
OFICINA(F), MUEBLES(M) 520, 522.
OFICINAS(F), EDIFICIO(M) 190.
Ofiuco 13.
oído(m) interno 138.
oído(m) medio 138.
**oído(m), partes(f) del 138.**
OÍDOS(M), PROTECCÍON(F) 729.
oidos(m), protector(m) 729.
ojal(m) 319, 381, 573, 644.
ojete(m) 230, 323, 671.
ojete(m) para la correa(f) del cuello(m) 390.
ojillo(m) 353, 354.
ojiva(f) 814.
ojival(m) 174.
**ojo(m) 140.**
ojo(m) 83, 90, 96, 97, 107, 118, 275, 290, 369, 562, 563, 564, 566, 649, 681.
ojo(m) compuesto 79, 80, 81.

Los términos en **negrita** corresponden a una ilustración; los que aparecen en MAYÚSCULAS indican un título.

ojo(m) de buey(m) 496.
ojo(m) de pez(m) 392.
**ojos(m), maquillaje(m) 367.**
OJOS(M), PROTECCIÓN(F) 729.
okra(f) 69.
OLA(F) 30.
ola(f) de oscilación(f) 30.
ola(f) de translación(f) 30.
OLEAGINOSOS, FRUTOS(M) SECOS 66.
olécrano(m) 102, 123.
óleo(m) 588.
oleoducto(m) 740.
oleoducto(m) de salida(f) 738.
oleoducto(m) de superficie(f) 740.
**oleoducto(m) para petróleo(m) crudo 740.**
oleoducto(m) submarino 740.
OLFATO(M), EL GUSTO(M) Y EL 142.
olla(f) 249, 688.
**olla(f) a presión(f) 248.**
olla(f) para alcuzcuz(m) 249.
ombligo(m) 116, 118.
ombligo(m) inferior 110.
ombligo(m) superior 110.
omoplato(m) 102.
omóplato(m) 117, 119, 122, 123.
omóplato(m), espina(f) del 123.
onda(f) radioeléctrica 15.
onda(f) sísmica 23.
**ondas(f) sísmicas, amplificación(f) 714.**
**ondas(f) sísmicas, detección(f) 714.**
ONDAS(F) SÍSMICAS, MEDICIÓN(F) 714.
**ondas(f) sísmicas, transcripción(f) 714.**
ópalo(m) 363.
operación(f) rápida 405.
operador(m) del reloj(m) de 30 segundos(m) 610.
operador(m) técnico de video(m) 412, 415.
opérculo(m) 84, 86.
opistodemo(m) 169.
orbicular 56.
orbicular(m) 120.
órbita(f) de lanzamiento(m) 48.
**órbita(f) de los satélites(m) 43.**
órbita(f) designada 48.
órbita(f) geoestacionaria 43.
órbita(f) lunar 8.
órbita(f) polar 43.
**órbita(f) polar, satélite(m) 43.**
**órbita(f), puesta(f) 419.**
**órbita(f), transbordador(m) espacial 510.**
**órbitas(f) de los planetas(m) 4.**
**orden(m) corintio 167.**
**orden(m) dórico 167.**
**orden(m) jónico 166.**
ordenador(m) personal 526.
orégano(m) 74.
oreja(f) 107, 112, 116, 138, 223, 354.
**oreja(f), pabellón(m) de la 139.**
oreja(f), pabellón(m) de la 138.
orejera(f) 328, 406.
**orejera(f) de seguridad(f) 729.**
ÓRGANO(M) ELECTRONEUMÁTICO 542.
**órgano(m), caño(m) 542.**
**órgano(m), mecanismo(m) 543.**
oriental 619.
orificio(m) 389.
orificio(m) central 404.
orificio(m) de carga(f) 804.
orificio(m) de entrada(f) de aire(m) 304.
orificio(m) del pie(m) 542.
orificio(m) genital 83.
orificio(m) intestinal 83.
orificio(m) nasal 84, 86, 96, 100, 109.
oriflama(f) 817.
orilla(f) 181, 752.
orillo(m) 566.
Orión 11, 13.
orla(f) 318.
orla(f) de púrpura(f) 315.
orla(f) decorativa 349.
oro(m) 819.
ORQUESTA(F) SINFÓNICA 556.
**oruga(f) 78.**
oruga(f) 783.
orza(f) de popa(f) 631.
orza(f) de quilla(f) 628, 631.
orzada(f) 629.
Osa Mayor 11.
Osa Menor 11.
oscuridad(f) 489.
osoto-gari (gran siega(f)) exterior 668.
**ostra(f) 92.**
ostra(f) 93.
otero(m) 46.
otolito(m) 88.
otoño(m) 8.
otra posición(f) 525.
**otros ligamentos(m) textiles 576.**
**otros signos(m) 539.**
**outriggers(m) 632.**
oval 362.
ovario(m) 60, 128, 129.
oveja(f) 150.
óvulo(m) 60.
óxer(m) de barras(f) 646, 647.
ozono(m) 19.

# P

pabellón(m) 363, 549, 551.
**pabellón(m) de la oreja(f) 139.**
pacana(f) 66.
Pacini, corpúscula(f) de 136.
país(m) 51.
**paja(f), empacadora(f) 159.**
pajarita(f) 324.
**pala(f) 598.**
pala(f) 205, 266, 598, 607, 632, 640, 680, 681, 783, 784, 803.
pala(f) del rotor(m) 508.
pala(f) del stick(m) 609.
pala(f) del timón(m) 628.
pala(f) del ventilador(m) de sustentación(f) 492.
**pala(f) hidráulica 785.**
pala(f) mecánica 733.
pala(f) plegable 690.
paladar(m), velo(m) del 141.
palanca(f) 252, 294, 295, 296, 365, 370, 453, 549, 702, 798.
palanca(f) conmutadora de puntos(m) 568.
palanca(f) corrediza selectora(f) de diapositivas(f) 397.
palanca(f) de 1 m 624.
palanca(f) de 10 m 624.
palanca(f) de 3 m 624.
palanca(f) de 5 m 624.
palanca(f) de 7,5 m 624.
palanca(f) de accionamiento(m) de la recámara(f) 802.
palanca(f) de aflojar el papel(m) 525.
palanca(f) de alimentador(m) de oxígeno(m) 639.
palanca(f) de armar(f) 804.
palanca(f) de arranque(m) 272.
palanca(f) de avance(m)/marcha(f) atrás 272.
palanca(f) de cambio(m) de velocidades(f) 430, 443.
palanca(f) de cierre(m) 257, 471.
palanca(f) de compensación(f) 572.
palanca(f) de control(m) 735.
palanca(f) de dirección(f) 788.
palanca(f) de elevación(f) 147.
palanca(f) de enrrollado(m) del freno(m) de mano(f) 470.
palanca(f) de espaciamiento(m) de los discos(m) 158.
palanca(f) de fijación(f) del venturi(m) 804.
palanca(f) de freno(m) 500.
palanca(f) de la cisterna(f) 293.
palanca(f) de la cuchilla(f) 578.
palanca(f) de la cuña(f) 277.
palanca(f) de la sordina(f) 541.
palanca(f) de los alerones(m) de hipersustentación(f) 500.
palanca(f) de luces(f) y de cambio(m) de dirección(f) 430.
palanca(f) de mando(m) 508, 526, 639.
palanca(f) de maniobra(f) de la aguja(f) 467.
palanca(f) de maniobras(f) 787, 788.
palanca(f) de perforación(f) 256.
palanca(f) de presión(f) 583.
palanca(f) de seguridad(f) 271.
palanca(f) de vibración(f) 547.
palanca(f) de viraje(m) 639.
palanca(f) del cambio(m) de velocidades(f) 447, 448.
palanca(f) del cerrojo(m) 796.
palanca(f) del cucharón(m) 782.
palanca(f) del deslizador(m) 428.
palanca(f) del embrague(m) 272, 442, 444.
palanca(f) del freno(m) 445, 447.
palanca(f) del freno(m) delantero 444.
palanca(f) del tapón(m) 293.
palanca(f) del tren(m) de aterrizaje delantero 500.
palanca(f) estabilizadora 727.
palanca(f) para graduar la altura(f) 157, 159.
palanca(f) para liberar el sujetapapel(m) 525.
palanca(f) principal 590.
palanca(f) retractora de la guarda(f) móvil 284.
palco(m) 189.
paleta(f) 244, 619, 754.
paleta(f) con huecos(m) para pintura(f) 592.
paleta(f) con tarrito(m) 592.
**paleta(f) de albañil(m) 291.**
paleta(f) de la turbina(f) 753.
paleta(f) de relleno(m) 291.
paleta(f) del rotor(m) 752, 754.
paletas(f) de compresión(f) 501.
paletas(f) de la turbina(f) 753.
paletas(f) del escape(m) 501.
paletilla(f) 100, 106.
palillo(m) 385, 552.
palillos(m) 553.
palma(f) 104, 105, 137, 327, 596, 627.
palmar(m) 46.
palmar(m) mayor 120.
palmar(m) menor 120.
palmaticompuesta 56.
palmeta(f) 220.
**palo(m) 678.**
palo(m) 818.
palo(m) de la tienda(f) 686.
palo(m) de mesana(f) 478.
palo(m) de trinquete(m) 479, 743.
palo(m) macho 478.
palo(m) mayor 479.
palo(m) popel(m) 478.
Paloma 13.
palpo(m) labial 79, 81, 92.
pamela(f) 329.
PAN(M) 153.
pan(m) alemán de centeno(m) 153.
pan(m) americano de maíz(m) 153.
pan(m) ázimo 153.
pan(m) blanco americano de molde(m) 153.
pan(m) campesino 153.
pan(m) danés de centeno(m) 153.
pan(m) de centeno(m) con semillas(f) de alcaravea(f) 153.
pan(m) de centeno(m) negro 153.
pan(m) de flor(f) 153.
pan(m) de pita(f) 153.
pan(m) de pita(f) con semillas(f) de ajonjolí(m) 153.
pan(m) espiga(f) 153.
pan(m) francés 153.
pan(m) griego 153.
pan(m) indio chapatí 153.
pan(m) indio naan 153.
pan(m) integral 153.
pan(m) integral de molde(m) 153.
pan(m) irlandés 153.
pan(m) judío hallah 153.
pan(m) negro 153.
pan(m) negro ruso 153.
pan(m) vienés 153.
panal(m) 82.
pañal(m) 349.
panamá(m) 328.
páncreas(m) 131.
**pandereta(f) 554.**
panecillo(m) 153.
panel(m) 521.
panel(m) de acceso(m) 207.
panel(m) de celdas(f) solares 769.
panel(m) de conexión(f) del video(m) 415.
panel(m) de conexiones(f) eléctricas 415.
panel(m) de control(m) 415.
panel(m) de controles(m) 253, 391.
panel(m) de la puerta(f) 429.
panel(m) de la vela(f) 628.
panel(m) de listones(m) 288.
**panel(m) de mandos(m) 257.**
panel(m) de mandos(m) 255, 258, 259.
panel(m) de monitores(m) 412, 413.
panel(m) de publicidad(f) 474.
panel(m) de separación(f) 383.
panel(m) fotovoltaico 486, 487.
panel(m) frontal 441.
panel(m) laminado 288.
panel(m) lateral 441, 470.
panel(m) protector 727.
panel(m) radiador 510.
panel(m) retenedor de frecuencias(f) bajas 412.
panel(m) solar 16, 42, 48, 418.
panel(m) solar extendido 48.
paneles(m) de comunicación(f) 500.
paño(m) lateral 319.
pantalla(f) 233, 234, 236, 397, 410, 421, 523, 524, 699.
pantalla(f) de alarma(f) de motor y tripulación(f) 500.
pantalla(f) de colores(m) 569.
pantalla(f) de control(m) 717.
pantalla(f) de funciones(f) 555.
pantalla(f) de los sistemas(m) 500.
pantalla(f) de navegación(f) 500.
**pantalla(f) de proyección(f) 397.**
pantalla(f) del contador(m) de pasadas(f) 569.
pantalla(f) principal de vuelo(m) 500.
**pantalla(f), tubo(m) 410.**
pantalón(m) 595, 602, 609, 656, 662, 668, 680.
**pantalón(m) con tirantes(m) 350.**
pantalón(m) corto 336, 351.
pantalón(m) de boxeo(m) 353.
pantalón(m) de peto(m) 349.
**pantalones(m) 323, 336.**
pantalones(m) 353, 600, 791.
pantalones(m) de chándal(m) 352.
pantalones(m) de montar 648.
**pantalones(m) de tubo(m) 336.**
**pantiblusa(f) 337.**
pantifaja(f) 346.
pantimedias(f) 344.
pantógrafo(m) 458.
pantorrilla(f) 117, 119.
pantufla(f) 355.
pañuelo(m) de bolsillo(m) 322.
papaya(f) 68.
papel(m) 384, 580, 589, 714.
papel(m) corrector 515.
papel(m) de brea(f) 286.
papel(m) de fumar 384.
papel(m) de reserva(f) 532.
papila(f) 136.
papila(f) óptica 140.
papila(f) renal 132.
papilas(f) linguales 143.
**paquete(m) de cigarrillos(m) 384.**
paquete(m) de placas(f) fotográficas 395.
par(m) 199, 700, 701.
par(m) térmico 297.
para deshuesar 242.
para jamón(m) 242.
**para moler y rallar 243.**
para ostras(f) 242.
para pan(m) 242.
para pomelos(m) 242.
parabrisas(m) 426, 440, 442, 445, 498, 500.
paracaídas(f) 812.
paracaídas(f) auxiliar 510.
paracaídas(f) principal 635.
paracaídas(f) ventral 635.
PARACAIDISMO(M) 635.
**paracaidista(m/f) 635.**
parachoques(m) 426, 440, 441, 445.
parada(f) de autobús(m) 186.
parafinas(f) 745.
**paraguas(m) 375.**
**paraguas(m) de bastón(m) 375.**
**paraguas(m) plegable 375.**
paragüero(m) 375.
paralelo(m) 47.
paramento(m) de aguas(f) contenidas 749.
paramento(m) de aguas(f) corrientes 749.
parapeto(m) 454.
parapeto(m) contra olas(f) 748.
pararrayos(m) 197, 747, 757.
parasol(m) 42, 430, 449.
parche(m) 283, 554.
parche(m) inferior 553.
parche(m) superior 552, 553.
pared(f) 104, 736.
pared(f) celulósica 115.
pared(f) de fondo(m) 621.
pared(f) de hormigón(m) 772.
pared(f) de rebote(m) 617.
**pared(f) de Trombe 772.**
pared(f) de Trombe 772.
pared(f) de viraje(m) 621, 622.
pared(f) del tanque(m) 742.
pared(f) frontal 616.

Los términos en **negrita** corresponden a una ilustración; los que aparecen en MAYÚSCULAS indican un título.

pared(f) lateral 104, 616, 617, 621, 743.
pared(f) transversal de contención(f) 742.
paréntesis(m) 832.
parietal(m) 123.
paripinada 56.
**parka(m) 321.**
parka(m) 680.
paro(m) 532, 831.
párpado(m) 97.
párpado(m) inferior 84, 107, 140.
párpado(m) interno 107.
párpado(m) superior 84, 107, 140.
parque(m) 52, 184.
parqué(m) 200.
parqué(m) alternado a la inglesa 200.
parqué(m) Arenberg 200.
parqué(m) Chantilly 200.
parqué(m) de cestería(f) 200.
parqué(m) entretejido 200.
parqué(m) espinapez(m) 200.
parque(m) nacional 52.
**parqué(m) sobre base(f) de cemento(m) 200.**
parqué(m) sobrepuesto 200.
parqué(m) Versailles 200.
**parqué(m), tipos(m) de 200.**
parrilla(f) 253, 254.
parrilla(f) estabilizadora 689.
parrilla(f) plegable 690.
parte(f) plana 567.
parte(f) superior 302.
parteluz(m) 175, 203.
**partes(f) 220, 223, 224.**
**partes(f) de un zapato(m) 354.**
**partes(f) del arma(f) 666.**
**partes(f) del oído(m) 138.**
**particiones(f), ejemplos(m) 818.**
partida(f) 701.
partido(m) 700.
pasa(f) (19 a 36) 700, 701.
pasador(m) 289, 290, 323, 369, 566.
pasaje(m) subterráneo 464.
PASAJEROS(M), AVIÓN(M) TURBORREACTOR 498.
**pasajeros(m), terminal(m) 504.**
PASAJEROS(M), VAGONES(M) 460.
pasamanos(m) 201, 254.
**pasamontañas(m) 329.**
pasapuré(m) 244.
pasarela(f) 180, 742.
pasarela(f) superior 475.
paseo(m) 263.
pasillo(m) 194, 773.
pasillo(m) central 460.
paso(m) 27.
**paso(m) a nivel(m) 471.**
paso(m) a nivel(m) 464, 828.
paso(m) de la energía(f) hacia la red(f) de transmisión(f) 755.
paso(m) de peatones(m) 186, 826, 827.
paso(m) elevado 454.
paso(m) inferior 454.
pastel(m) 588.
pastel(m) de óleo(m) 588.
pastilla(f) de fricción(f) 432.
pata(f) 97, 112, 219, 223, 224, 225, 232, 233, 270, 309, 553, 574, 659, 671, 681.
pata(f) anal 78.
pata(f) curvada 220.
pata(f) de ajuste(m) de altura(f) 397.
pata(f) de conexión(f) a tierra(f) 309.
pata(f) de gallo(m) 571.
pata(f) de la mesa(f) 619.
pata(f) de soporte(m) 156, 449.
pata(f) delantera 79, 80, 223.
**pata(f) delantera (superficie(f) exterior) 80.**
pata(f) media 79, 80.
**pata(f) media (superficie(f) exterior) 80.**
pata(f) móvil 219.
**pata(f) posterior 78.**
pata(f) posterior 79.
pata(f) principal 756.
pata(f) soporte 441.
pata(f) telescópica 393, 726.
pata(f) torácica 78.
pata(f) trasera 81, 223.
**pata(f) trasera (superficie(f) interior) 81.**
pata(f) ventosa 78.
patada(f) de crol(m) 622.
patada(f) de mariposa(f) 623.
patada(f) de rana(f) 622.
patas(f) de ganso(m) 634.
PATAS(F) DE UNGULADOS(M): TIPOS(M) MÁS COMUNES 99.
**patas(f), principales tipos(m) de 111.**
patata(f) 71.
patilla(f) 376.
patín(m) 609, 643.
patín(m) de aterrizaje(m) 508.
patín(m) de cola(f) 508.
patín(m) de deslizamiento(m) 467.
**patín(m) de hockey(m) 644.**
patín(m) de oruga(f) 805.
patín(m) de retroceso(m) 802.
PATÍN(M) DE RUEDAS(F) 645.
patín(m) de velocidad(f) 644.
patín(m) delantero 643.
patín(m) para accesorios(m) 391, 409.
**patín(m) para figuras(f) 644.**
patín(m) trasero 643.
PATINAJE(M) 644.
patio(m) 172, 173, 263.
patio(m) de armas(f) 178, 180.
patio(m) de clasificación(f) 465.
patio(m) de lavado(m) de vagones(m) 465.
patio(m) de recepción(f) 465.
patio(m) de tanques(m) 740.
pato(m) 150.
**patrón(m) 565.**
patrón(m) de prueba(f) 414.
pausa(f) 831.
pausa(f) \ imagen(f) fija 411.
pauta(f) A 539.
pavimento(m) 450, 451.
Pavo 13.
pavo(m) 150.
pecho(m) 100, 116, 118.
pechuga(f) 108.
pecíolo(m) 56.
pectén(m) 81.
pectoral(m) 602, 663.
pectoral(m) mayor 120.
pedal(m) 446, 448, 545, 552, 553, 572, 664.
pedal(m) crescendo 542.
pedal(m) de ajuste(m) 591.
pedal(m) de amortiguación(f) 540.
pedal(m) de cambio(m) de velocidades(f) 444.
pedal(m) de expresión(f) 542.
pedal(m) de la sordina(f) 540, 555.
pedal(m) de los bajos(m) 555.
pedal(m) de los frenos(m) 430.
pedal(m) de velocidad(f) 561.
pedal(m) del acelerador(m) 430.
pedal(m) del embrague(m) 430.
pedal(m) del freno(m) 573.
pedal(m) del freno(m) trasero 444.
pedal(m) del timón(m) de mando(m) 639.
pedal(m) delantero 443, 444.
**pedal(m) eléctrico 561.**
pedal(m) suave 540.
pedal(m) trasero 443, 444.
pedalero(m) 542.
**pedernal(m) 795.**
pedernal(m) 307, 795.
pedestal(m) 236, 283, 545, 656.
pedestal(m) de la cámara(f) 414.
pedio(m) 120.
pedúnculo(m) 60, 61, 62, 63, 64.
Pegaso 11.
PEINADO(M) 368, 370.
**peinado(m), accesorios(m) 369.**
peinazo(m) 225.
peinazo(m) de la cerradura(f) 202.
peinazo(m) inferior 202, 223, 225.
peinazo(m) superior 202, 223, 225.
peine(m) 572.
peine(m) combinado(m) 368.
peine(m) de mango(m) 368.
peine(m) de peluquero(m) 368.
peine(m) de tapicería(f) 574.
peine(m) metálico 368.
peine(m) para desenredar 368.
peine(m) tenedor(m) 368.
peine(m) y cuchilla(f) 374.
**peines(m) 368.**
pelacables(m) 311.
pelapatatas(m) 242.
peldaño(m) 147, 302.
peldaño(m) inferior 470.
pelele(m) 351.
película(f) 390.
película(f) de disco(m) 395.
película(f) de disco(m) para video(m) fijo 395.
**películas(f) 395.**
peligro(m) 488.
pelillo(m) 670.
pelo(m) 117, 119, 136.
pelos(m) absorbentes 57.
pelos(m) absorbentes, zona(f) de 59.
pelota(f) 598.
**pelota(f) de cricket(m) 598.**
**pelota(f) de golf(m) 677.**
**pelota(f) de golf(m), corte(m) transversal de una 677.**
**pelota(f) de hockey(m) 607.**
pelota(f) de ping pong(m) 619.
**pelota(f) de raquetbol(m) 617.**
**pelota(f) de squash(m) 616.**
**pelota(f) de tenis(m) 615.**
**pelota(f), corte(m) transversal de la 596.**
peltada 56.
**Pelton, turbina(f) 754.**
**peluquero(m), tijeras(f) 369.**
pelusa(f) de maíz(m) 72.
pelvis(f) 103.
pelvis(f) renal 132.
penacho(m) 109, 791.
penacho(m) de plumas(f) 618.
pendiente(m) 361.
**pendientes(m) 361.**
pendientes(m) 361.
pendientes(m) de aro(m) 361.
pendientes(m) de clip(m) 361.
pendientes(m) de espiga(f) 361.
pendientes(m) de tornillo(m) 361.
pendolón(m) 199.
pendón(m) 817.
péndulo(m) 539, 707.
**péndulo(m), reloj(m) 707.**
pene(m) 116, 127.
península(f) 51.
**pentagrama(f) 537.**
peón(m) 696.
pepino(m) 69.
pepita(f) 62, 64, 65.
**peplo(m) 315.**
pera(f) 64, 362.
pera(f) de goma(f) 726.
pera(f) de goma(f) para inyectar aire(m) 710.
peraltado(m) 174.
percha(f) 620.
perchero(m) 522.
perchero(m) de pared(f) 522.
perchero(m) de pie 522.
**percolador(m) 247.**
percusión(f), barra(f) 780.
PERCUSIÓN(F), INSTRUMENTOS(M) 552, 554.
percutor(m) 797, 798, 799, 804.
perejil(m) 74.
**perfil(m) 363.**
perforación(f) 353, 395.
**perforación(f) marina 739.**
**perforación(f), torre(f) 737.**
perforaciones(f) 327, 355.
perforadora(f) 516.
pérgola(f) 263.
pericardio(m) 130.
pericarpio(m) 65, 66.
perifollo(m) 74.
perilla(f) 202, 277, 280, 284.
perilla(f) de registro(m) 543.
perilla(f) del rodillo(m) 531.
periodo(m) 489.
perioplo(m) 104.
periscopio(m) de ataque(m) 807.
periscopio(m) de navegación(f) 807.
peristilo(m) 168, 169, 171.
peritoneo(m) 127, 128.
perlas(f) 105.
**perno(m) 279.**
perno(m) 278, 282, 290.
**perno(m) con collarín(m) 279.**
perno(m) de acoplamiento(m) 754.
perno(m) de articulación(f) del cucharón(m) 782.
perno(m) de expansión(f) 276.
perno(m) de fijación(f) 432.
perno(m) de la bisagra(f) 785.
perno(m) de la eclisa(f) 466.
perno(m) difusor 264.
perno(m) maestro 441.
**perno(m) para falso plafón(m) 276.**
peroné(m) 102.
peroneo(m) lateral corto 121.
peroneo(m) lateral largo 120.
peróxido(m) 725.
perpendicular 830.
PERRO(M) 106.
**perro(m), pata(f) delantera 106.**
Perseo 11.
persiana(f) enrollable 231.
**persiana(f) enrollable automática 231.**
**persiana(f) veneciana 231.**
persianas(f) romana 231.
personal(m) suplementario de producción(f) 412.
pertenece a 830.
pértiga(f) 657.
pértiga(f) de inclinación(f) 231.
pesa(f) 707, 708.
pesa(f) corrediza 708.
**pesas(f) 665.**
pesas(f) 663, 665.
pesas(f) para muñecas(f) y tobillos(m) 665.
PESCA(F) 670, 672.
**pescador(m), vestido(m) de 672.**
**pescadores(m) 336.**
pescante(m) 478, 742, 786.
pescuezo(m) 678.
peseta(f) 832.
**peso(m) 658.**
peso(m) 658, 709.
peso(m) corredizo 539.
PESO(M), MEDICIÓN(F) 708.
pespunte(m) 571.
pespunteado(m) 352.
pestaña(f) 104, 140, 330, 565.
pestaña(f) de arrojo(m) 726.
pestaña(f) de la llanta(f) 433.
pestañas(f) 107.
pestillo(m) 203, 289, 290.
pestillo(m) de resorte(m) 375.
pétalo(m) 60.
PETANCA(F) Y BOLOS(M) 682.
petifoque(m) 481.
peto(m) 317, 350, 351, 595, 602, 609, 792.
peto(m) metálico 667.
petral(m) 653.
PETRÓLEO(M) 737, 738, 740, 742, 744.
petróleo(m) 737, 745.
petróleo(m) crudo 744.
**petróleo(m) crudo, oleoducto(m) 740.**
petróleo(m) diáfano 744.
petróleo(m) para calderas(f) 745.
petróleo(m) para calefacción(f) 745.
Pez Austral 13.
Pez Dorado 13.
Pez Volador 13.
PEZ(M) 86, 88.
pezón(m) 116, 118, 129.
pi 830.
piano(m) 556.
**piano(m) electrónico 555.**
**piano(m) vertical 540.**
**piano(m) vertical, mecanismo(m) 541.**
pica(f) 780.
picacho(m) 27.
picaporte(m) 289.
pichi(m) 333.
pico(m) 27, 108, 267, 681.
pico(m) de loro(m) 483.
pico(m) del zanco(m) 783.
pico(m) muesca(f) 565.
pícolo(m) 548, 557.
**picos(m) (de aves) (f), principales tipos(m) de 111.**
pie(m) 40, 83, 116, 117, 118, 119, 232, 250, 350, 542, 545, 670, 718.
pie(m) ajustable 257, 258, 259.
pie(m) de la cama(f) 224.
pie(m) de la torre(f) 756.
pie(m) de montura(f) 393.
pie(m) de voluta(f) 220.
pie(m) del electrodo(m) 232.
pie(m) del talud(m) 748.
pie(m) derecho 198.
pie(m), dedo(m) del 116, 118.
piedra(f) 286, 364.
piedra(f) blanca 697.
piedra(f) de aceite(m) 582.
**piedra(f) de curling(m) 620.**
piedra(f) litográfica 583.
piedra(f) negra 697.
**piedras(f) preciosas 363.**
**piedras(f) preciosas, tallas(f) 362.**
**piedras(f) semipreciosas 363.**
**piel(f) 136.**
piel(f) 62, 63, 64, 65, 84, 107, 134.
**piel(f) para encuadernar 579.**
piel(f) verrugosa 85.
PIEL(F), ARTÍCULOS(M) DE 378.
pierna(f) 101, 117, 119, 325.
pierna(f) elástica 325.
PIES(M), PROTECCIÓN(F) 730.
pieza(f) aerodinámica 442.

Los términos en **negrita** corresponden a una ilustración; los que aparecen en MAYÚSCULAS indican un título.

pieza(f) automática del talón(m) 640, 641.
pieza(f) de sujeción(f) de la punta(f) del pie(m) 640.
pieza(f) de talón(m) 642, 643.
**piezas(f) 696.**
**piezas(f) honorables, ejemplos(m) 818.**
pijama(m) 348, 351.
pijama(m) de una pieza(f) 325.
pila(f) 393, 409.
pilar(m) 174, 175, 176, 454, 455, 621, 714, 736.
pilar(m) anterior del velo(m) del paladar(m) 142.
píldora(f) de combustible(m) 765.
pilón(m) 456.
pilón(m) de los tirantes(m) 456.
pilón(m) del turborreactor(m) 499.
pilón(m) guía(m) 457.
piloto(m) 247, 252, 255, 256, 257, 585, 637.
piloto(m) de planeador(m) 636.
pimentera(f) 238.
pimiento(m) morrón 69.
piña(f) 58, 68.
pináculo(m) 176, 181.
pinatífida 56.
pincel(m) 389, 589.
pincel(m) de repostería(f) 245.
pincel(m) para labios(m) 366.
pincel(m) plano 589.
pinchador(m) 516.
PING PONG(M) 619.
**ping pong(m), paleta(f) de 619.**
pino(m) piñonero 58.
piñón(m) 58, 66, 280, 707.
piñón(m) de la rueda(f) de la película(f) 390.
piñón(m) libre 448.
PINTURA(F) Y DIBUJO(M) 590.
pinza(f) 90, 91, 320, 323, 370, 389, 515, 582, 711.
pinza(f) de conexión(f) a tierra(f) 305.
pinza(f) del electrodo(m) 305.
pinza(f) para el cabello(m) 369.
pinza(f) para rizar 369.
**pinza(f) rizadora 370.**
pinza(f) tibiotarsiana 81.
pinzas(f) 565, 725.
**pinzas(f) multiuso 311.**
pinzas(f) para depilar cejas(f) 365.
**pinzas(f) pelacables 311.**
pinzas(f) pelacables 311.
pinzas(f) verticales 565.
**piolet(m) 681.**
piolet(m) 680.
**pipa(f) 385.**
**pipa(f), accesorios(m) para la 385.**
**pipa(f), corte(m) transversal de una 385.**
pisacorbatas(m) 364.
piscina(f) 496, 621, 626, 772.
**piscina(f) olímpica 621.**
piscina(f) para enfriamiento(m) del condensador(m) 763.
Piscis 11.
Piscis, los peces (19 de febrero) 820.
piso(m) 205, 616, 617, 773.
piso(m) cosido 685, 686.
piso(m) de duela(f) 200.
piso(m) de madera(f) 199.
piso(m) de operaciones(f) 752.
pisón(m) 385.
**pista(f) 608, 620, 683.**
pista(f) 620, 676, 682, 811.
**pista(f) de aterrizaje(m) y despegue(m) 504.**
pista(f) de carreras(f) 654.
pista(f) de enlace(m) 502.
**pista(f) de esgrima(f) 666.**
pista(f) de estacionamiento(m) 502.
pista(f) de hielo(m) 620.
pista(f) de impulso(m) 655, 657.
pista(f) de lanzamiento(m) 654.
pista(f) de maniobras(f) 502.
**pista(f) para prueba(f) de obstáculos(m) 646.**
pistacho(m) 66.
pistilo(m) 60.
PISTOLA(F) 797.
pistola(f) 291.
**pistola(f) de pintar 304, 590.**
pistola(f) del surtidor(m) 453.
**pistola(f) para calafateo(m) 291.**
**pistola(f) para soldar 305.**
pistola(f) pulverizadora 264.
pistolete(m) 795, 796.
pistón(m) 432, 435, 436, 438, 550.
**pitón(m) 681.**
pitón(m) de rosca(f) 680.
pitón(m) para el descenso(m) 681.
**pitón(m) para hielo(m) 681.**
pitorro(m) 247.
pívot(m) 610.
pivote(m) 311, 369, 404, 484, 485, 539, 590, 612, 641, 658, 719.
pivote(m) de la rótula(f) 471.
pivote(m) móvil 278.
placa(f) 255, 295, 296, 393.
placa(f) antifricción 641.
placa(f) base(f) 40, 641.
placa(f) blindada 805.
placa(f) calcárea 95.
placa(f) corrediza (cubrecanilla(f)) 562.
placa(f) corrediza de la canilla(f) 561.
placa(f) costal 97.
placa(f) de absorción(f) 768.
placa(f) de advertencias(f) 280.
placa(f) de agujas(f) 568.
placa(f) de amarre(m) 661.
placa(f) de asiento(m) 466.
placa(f) de base(f) 561.
placa(f) de cobre(m) 582.
placa(f) de especificaciones(f) 280.
placa(f) de fijación(f) 713.
placa(f) de freno(m) 641.
placa(f) de identificación(f) 364.
placa(f) de instalación(f) 233.
placa(f) de la aguja(f) 561.
placa(f) de la culata(f) 802.
placa(f) de la nuca(f) 97.
placa(f) del cojinete(m) 376.
placa(f) del interruptor(m) 309.
placa(f) indicadora 712.
placa(f) marginal 96.
placa(f) metálica A 307.
placa(f) metálica B 307.
placa(f) motriz 134.
placa(f) negativa 439.
placa(f) para fusibles(m) 757.
placa(f) positiva 439.
placa(f) supracaudal 96.
placa(f) térmica 247.
placa(f) terminal 765.
placa(f) vertebral 97.
plafón(m) 236.
plana 587.
**plancha(f) 253.**
plancha(f) 253, 256.
**plancha(f) de entintado(m) 581.**
plancha(f) de muelles(m) 659.
**plancha(f) de vapor(m) 256.**
PLANCHA(F) DE WINDSURF(M) 631.
plancha(f) superior 253.
**planchado(m) 829.**
PLANEADOR(M) 636.
**planeador(m) 638.**
PLANETARIO(M) 16.
planetario(m) 184.
**planetas(m) y lunas(f) 4.**
**planetas(m), orbitas(f) 4.**
planicie(f) 51.
planicie(f) fluvio-glaciar 27.
plano con orejas(f) 341.
plano tipo(m) Peter Pan 341.
plano(m) 182.
plano(m) de deriva(f) 499.
**plano(m) de la catedral(f) 177.**
**plano(m) de la mezquita(f) 173.**
PLANO(M) DE UNA CASA 193.
**plano(m) del templo(m) griego 169.**
**plano(m) del terreno 193.**
**plano(m) focal elevado, boyas(f) 487.**
plano(m) horizontal 499.
plano(m) vertical 499.
PLANO(M), ELEMENTOS(M) BÁSICOS DE UN 195.
planta(f) 325.
**planta(f) alta 194.**
planta(f) alta 196.
**planta(f) baja 194.**
planta(f) baja 197.
planta(f) de bombeo(m) 740.
planta(f) de lubricantes(m) 745.
planta(f) de reforma(f) catalítica 744.
planta(f) de tratamiento(m) 735.
**planta(f) exterior 734.**
planta(f) intermedia de refuerzo(m) 740.
planta(f) maremotriz 752.
**planta(f) maremotriz, corte(m) transversal 752.**
PLANTA(F), ANATOMÍA(F) DE UNA 57.
plantador(m) 268.
plantador(m) de bulbos(m) 268.
plantar(m) delgado 121.
**plantilla(f) 358.**
plantilla(f) de arcilla(f) 748.
plantilla(f) de desagüe(m) 748.
plaquita(f) de hielo(m) 36.
plasmodesma(m) 115.
plástico(m) transparente 379.
plásticos(m) transparentes 379.
plastrón(m) 96.
plata(f) 819.
**plataforma(f) 441.**
plataforma(f) 302, 393, 441, 451, 457, 473, 709, 714, 787.
plataforma(f) continental 22, 29.
plataforma(f) de carga(f) 736.
plataforma(f) de corte(m) 158.
plataforma(f) de instrumentos(m) 43, 511.
plataforma(f) de jaula(f) 736.
plataforma(f) de lanzamiento(m) 597.
plataforma(f) de piso(m) bajo 473.
**plataforma(f) de producción(f) 738.**
plataforma(f) de producción(f) 740.
plataforma(f) de vuelo(m) del helicóptero(m) 808.
plataforma(f) elevadora 188.
plataforma(f) fija 739.
plataforma(f) giratoria 780.
**plataforma(f) giratoria, molino(m) 773.**
plataforma(f) hidráulica 788.
plataforma(f) inferior 787.
plataforma(f) montada en gatos(m) mecánicos 739.
plataforma(f) móvil 788.
plataforma(f) para transportar vagones(m) 473.
plataforma(f) semisumergida 739.
plátano(m) 68.
platillo(m) 552, 708, 709.
platillo(m) charleston 552.
platillo(m) inferior 552.
platillo(m) superior 552.
platillos(m) 554, 557.
platina(f) 583, 717, 718.
platina(f) mecánica 718.
plato(m) 404, 584, 688, 701.
plato(m) ajustable 521.
plato(m) de retroceso(m) 432.
plato(m) giratorio 282, 785.
plato(m) llano 238.
plato(m) para caracoles(m) 246.
plato(m) para ensalada(f) 238.
plato(m) para pan(m) y mantequilla(f) 238.
plato(m) sopero 238.
playa(f) 23, 30.
plaza(f) de la culata(f) 800.
plegadera(f) 577.
plegador(m) de urdimbre(f) 573.
plegador(m) del tejido(m) 572.
plegador(m) posterior 573.
pleno(m) 206, 207.
pleópodos(m) 91.
pleura(f) parietal 130.
plexo(m) braquial 133.
plexo(m) lumbar 133.
plexo(m) nervioso 144.
plexo(m) sacro 133.
pliego(m) 577.
pliegue(m) 315.
pliegue(m) anal 117, 119.
pliegue(m) de cajón(m) 228.
pliegue(m) de cajón(m) invertido 228.
pliegue(m) de la columela(f) 94.
pliegue(m) de pinza(f) 228.
**pliegue(m), tipos de 335.**
plisada 335.
plomo(m) 486, 672.
**pluma(f) 110.**
pluma(f) 785.
pluma(f) de ave(f) 389.
pluma(f) de caña(f) 389.
pluma(f) de dirección(f) 684.
pluma(f) metálica 389.
pluma(f) metálica romana 389.
plumafuente(f) 589.
plumas(f) timoneras 109.
plumón(m) 110.
Plutón 5.
**pluviómetro(m) 40.**
**pluviómetro(m) de lectura(f) directa 40.**
pocilga(f) 149.
podadera(f) 269.
podadera(f) de árboles(m) 269.
**podadora(f) de bordes(m) 271.**
podio(m) 190.
**podio(m) de salida(f) 621.**
podio(m) de salida(f) 621.
**podio(m) y basamento(m) 190.**
podón(m) 269.
polaina(f) 652, 680.
polea(f) 230, 302, 434, 684, 793.
polea(f) de transmisión(f) 575.
polea(f) del montacargas(m) 786.
polea(f) tensora 230.
poleas(f) de tensión(f) 448.
policía(f) 822.
polipasto(m) 737.
polisón(m) 316.
pollito(m) 150.
**polo(m) 326.**
polo(m) 615.
polo(m) Norte 3.
polo(m) Norte celeste 3.
polo(m) Sur 3.
polo(m) Sur celeste 3.
polvera(f) 366.
polvo(m) 34, 35.
**polvo(m) compacto 366.**
polvos(m) sueltos 366.
poma(f) 543.
pomo(m) 219, 609, 666.
pomo(m) exterior 290.
pomo(m) interior 290.
poncho(m) 331.
pontón(m) 457, 738.
**pontones(m), puente(m) 457.**
**pool(m) 673.**
Popa 13.
popa(f) 478, 496, 631.
póquer(m) 695.
**póquer(m), manos(f) 695.**
por lo ancho(m) 629.
por(m) 830.
porcentaje(m) 830.
poro(m) 67, 115, 136.
portaaguja(m) 562.
portaagujas(m) 726.
PORTAAVIONES(M) 810.
portabobinas(m) 575.
portabolsa(f) 679.
portabotellas(m) 447.
portacanilla(m) 562.
portacarrete(m) 561, 670, 671.
**portachequera(f) con calculadora(f) 379.**
portaequipajes(m) 445, 446, 449, 492.
portafusible(m) 757.
portagomas(m) 515.
portahorquilla(m) 787.
portal(m) 175, 455.
**portalámparas(m) 309.**
portaleños(m) 205.
portaminas(m) 389, 515.
portamonedas(m) 379.
**portanegativos(m) 399.**
portanegativos(m) 399.
portaobjetivo(m) rotatorio 718.
portaobjetos(m) 718.
portaocular(m) 721.
portaparaguas(m) 679.
portapasaportes(m) 379.
portapipas(m) 385.
portapitones(m) 680.
portaplumas(m) 378, 379.
portarrollos(m) de papel(m) higiénico 292.
portasellos(m) 516.
portatubo(m) 718.
portaviento(m) 536.
**portería(f) 626.**
portería(f) 601, 607, 608, 612, 626.
**portero(m) 609.**
portero(m) 601, 607, 608, 611, 612, 626.
portero(m) del equipo(m) receptor 599.
pórtico(m) 172, 177.
pórtico(m) de tirantes(m) 756.
posición(f) A - derecho 624.
posición(f) B - hacer la carpa(f) 624.
posición(f) C - cuerpo(m) encogido 624.
posición(f) de la cremallera(f) 565.
**posición(f) de lanzamiento(m), transbordador(m) espacial 510.**
posición(f) de las piernas(f) 625.
posición(f) de los brazos(m) 625.
posición(f) de salida(f) 625.
**posición(f) de salida(f) de espalda(f) 623.**
posición(f) del documento(m) para enviar 421.
posición(f) del haz(m) de electrones(m) 717.
posición(f) del ligamento(m) 95.
posición(f) respecto al sol(m) 419.
**posiciones(f) 667.**
**posiciones(f) de salto(m) 624.**

Los términos en **negrita** corresponden a una ilustración; los que aparecen en MAYÚSCULAS indican un título.

poste(m) 201, 464, 471, 604, 613, 618, 626, 669.
poste(m) con tablas(f) 646.
poste(m) de canasta(f) 611.
poste(m) de dobles(m) 614.
poste(m) de individuales(m) 614.
poste(m) de la grúa(f) 743.
poste(m) de llegada(f) 654.
poste(m) de salto(m) 657.
poste(m) del asiento(m) 446.
poste(m) del radar(m) 742.
**poste(m) extensible, taladro(m) 734.**
poste(m) indicador 651.
postigos(m) interiores 231.
poterna(f) 179, 181.
potro(m) 659.
pozo(m) 763.
pozo(m) ciego(m) 736.
pozo(m) de acceso(m) 752.
pozo(m) de extracción(f) 736.
pozo(m) marino 740.
pozo(m) principal 734.
pozo(m) seco 763.
pradera(f) 149.
prado(m) 148.
precio(m) total 709.
precio(m) unitario 709.
precipitación(f) 34, 35.
precipitación(f) ácida 32, 33, 35.
precipitación(f) radiactiva 35.
PRECIPITACIONES(F) 36.
**precisión(f), balanza(f) 709.**
premaxilar(m) 86.
premolar(m) 98.
premolares(m) 144.
**prensa(f) 579.**
prensa(f) 578, 579.
**prensa(f) de aguafuerte(f) 581.**
**prensa(f) de cajos(m) 579.**
prensa(f) de contactos(m) 398.
**prensa(f) de tornillo(m) 579.**
**prensa(f) en C 282.**
**prensa(f) litográfica 583.**
prensapapel(m) 531.
**prensatelas(m) 562.**
prensatelas(m) 561, 562.
preparación(f) del eclipse(m) 419.
prepucio(m) 101, 106, 127.
**presa(f) 749.**
presa(f) 668, 746.
**presa(f) de arco(m), corte(m) transversal 750.**
presa(f) de brazo(m) 668.
**presa(f), corte(m) transversal 749.**
presidente(m) 666.
presilla(f) 323, 324, 688.
presilla(f) de estaquilla(f) 685, 686.
presilla(f) de la manga(f) 319.
presilla(f) del cinturón(m) 319.
presillas(f) 515.
presión(f) 663.
presión(f) barométrica 38.
presión(f) barométrica a nivel(m) del mar(m) 38.
**presión(f) del aire(m), medición(f) 41.**
PRESIÓN(F), MEDICIÓN(F) 710.
pretina(f) 320, 323.
pretina(f) con broches(m) 350.
pretina(f) elástica 321, 325.
PREVENCIÓN(F) DE INCENDIOS(M) 777.
primavera(f) 8.
primer árbitro(m) 613.
primer escalón(m) 201.
primer espacio(m) 610.
primer jugador(m) 620.
primer molar(m) 144.
primer pistón(m) móvil 550.
primer premolar(m) 144.
primer recinto(m) focal 15.
primera base(f) 597.
primera etapa(f) 509.
primera falange(f) 103.
primera vía(f) de clasificación(f) 465.
primera(f) 667.
PRIMEROS AUXILIOS(M), EQUIPO(M) 726.
primeros violines(m) 556.
**principales señales(f) de circulación(f) internacionales 827, 828.**
**principales señales(f) de circulación(f) norteamericanas 824, 825, 826, 828.**
**principales tipos(m) de intercambios(m) 450.**
**principales tipos(m) de lentes(m) 377.**
**principales variedades(f) de bayas(f) 62.**
**principales variedades(f) de frutos(m) carnosos con hueso(m) 63.**
principio(m) de la película(f) 395.
prisma(m) 390.
prisma(m) de Porro 719.
PRISMÁTICOS(M) BINOCULARES 719.
proa(f) 497, 628, 631, 637.
probador(m) de contactos(m) con tierra(f) 310.
probóscide(m) 79.
procesador(m) digital de sonido(m) 528.
procesamiento(m) de la información(f) 722.
proceso(m) de maduración(f) 61.
procesos(m) ciliares 140.
producción(f) de calor(m) 766.
producción(f) de electricidad(f) 767.
**producción(f) de electricidad(f) por energía(f) solar 771.**
producción(f) de electricidad(f) por generador(m) 755.
**producción(f) de electricidad(f) por medio de energía(f) nuclear 766.**
**producción(f) de electricidad(f), etapas(f) 755.**
**producción(f), plataforma(f) 738.**
productor(m) 412, 415.
productor(m) técnico 412, 415.
**productos(m) del refinado(m) 744.**
productos(m) lácteos 33.
productos(m) petroquímicos 745.
profundidad(f) del hipocentro(m) 23.
profundo(m) derecho 603, 605.
profundo(m) izquierdo 603, 605.
profundo(m) libre 605.
programador(m) 257, 258, 259.
prohibido acampar 823.
prohibido adelantar 824, 825.
prohibido dar vuelta(f) en U 824, 825.
prohibido el paso 825.
prohibido el paso(m) 824.
prohibido el paso(m) de bicicletas(f) 828.
prohibido el paso(m) de camiones(m) 828.
prohibido el paso(m) de motocicletas(f) 828.
prohibido el paso(m) de peatones(m) 828.
prohibido hacer comidas(f) campestres 823.
prohibido usar silla(f) de ruedas(f) 822.
pronador(m) redondo 120.
pronaos(m) 168, 169.
propulsor F-1(m) 509.
propulsor J-2(m) 509.
propulsor(m) 49, 160, 509, 510, 512.
propulsor(m) de maniobras(f) 511.
propulsor(m) de proa(f) 497.
propulsor(m) radial 42.
proscenio(m) 188.
próstata(f) 127.
protección del sistema(m) respiratorio 821.
**protección(f) 821.**
protección(f) contra el vaho(m) 721.
protección(f) contra la luz(f) 16.
protección(f) de la cabeza(f) 821.
protección(f) de las manos(f) 821.
protección(f) de los oidos(m) 821.
protección(f) de los ojos(m) 821.
protección(f) de los pies(m) 821.
protector(m) 255, 268, 319, 598, 659, 669, 698, 726.
protector(m) abdominal 609.
protector(m) bucal 669.
protector(m) de brazo(m) 684.
protector(m) de la barbilla(f) 443.
protector(m) de la correa(f) 283.
protector(m) de la culata(f) 549.
protector(m) de la garganta(f) 595.
protector(m) de oídos(m) 729.
protector(m) de ojos(m) 777.
protector(m) de piernas(f) 609.
protector(m) del brazo(m) 602, 609.
protector(m) del cable(m) 280, 283, 305.
protector(m) del cuello(m) 609, 777.
protector(m) del mentón 777.
protector(m) del motor(m) 442.
protector(m) del pie(m) 595.
protector(m) del quemador(m) 634.
protector(m) del tendón(m) 644.
protector(m) del zanco(m) 783.
protector(m) facial 609, 643.
protector(m) genital 602, 609.
protector(m) lumbar 602.
protector(m) para las costillas(f) 602.
protector(m) pectoral 684.
protector(m) solar 512.
protoneurona(f) 135.
protórax(m) 78.
protuberancia(f) 6.
provincia(f) 51.
próxima llamada(f) 422.
proyección(f) cilíndrica 50.
proyección(f) cónica 50.
proyección(f) en círculo(m) 668.
proyección(f) interrumpida 50.
proyección(f) plana 50.
proyección(f) primera de cadera(f) 668.
**proyección(f), pantalla(f) 397.**
**proyecciones(f) del mapa(m) 50.**
PROYECTILES(M) 814.
**proyectiles(m) 801.**
proyector(m) auxiliar 16.
proyector(m) de altura(f) máxima 41.
**proyector(m) de diapositivas(f) 397.**
proyector(m) de luz(f) difusa 414.
proyector(m) múltiple 16.
proyector(m) sobre el pantógrafo(m) 414.
psicrómetro(m) 41.
púa(f) 535.
púa(f) de muelle(m) 157, 272.
pubis(m) 116, 118.
puente(m) 52, 109, 230, 376, 452, 491, 544, 546, 650, 719.
**puente(m) colgante 456.**
**puente(m) de arco(m) 455.**
puente(m) de carga(f) para contenedores(m) 490.
puente(m) de ensamblaje(m) 547.
puente(m) de los altos(m) 540.
puente(m) de los bajos(m) 540.
PUENTE(M) DE MANDO(M) 500.
puente(m) de mando(m) 494, 495, 497, 810.
**puente(m) de pontones(m) 457.**
puente(m) de portal(m) 455.
puente(m) de señales(f) 464.
puente(m) de tablero(m) inferior 455.
puente(m) de tablero(m) intermedio 455.
puente(m) de tablero(m) superior 455.
**puente(m) de viga(f) 454.**
puente(m) de viga(f) de un tramo(m) 454.
puente(m) de viga(f) de varios tramos(m) 454.
puente(m) desmontable tipo(m) Bailey 457.
**puente(m) elevador 457.**
**puente(m) giratorio 457.**
puente(m) levadizo 180.
puente(m) levadizo doble 457.
**puente(m) levadizo sencillo 457.**
puente(m) peatonal 464.
**puente(m) transportador 457.**
**puente(m) voladizo 454.**
**puentes(m) de arco(m), tipos 455.**
**puentes(m) de tirantes(m) 456.**
**puentes(m) de viga(f), tipos(m) 454.**
PUENTES(M) FIJOS 454, 456.
PUENTES(M) MOVIBLES 457.
puerro(m) 70.
PUERTA(F) 202.
**puerta(f) 429.**
puerta(f) 16, 173, 225, 253, 259, 427, 449, 498, 617, 685, 686, 709.
puerta(f) a la nave(f) de carga(f) 510.
puerta(f) abatible 195.
puerta(f) automática 504.
puerta(f) convencional 202.
puerta(f) corrediza 202.
puerta(f) de acceso(m) a la rejilla(f) de las luces(f) 412.
puerta(f) de acordeón(m) 202.
**puerta(f) de entrada(f) 202.**
puerta(f) de proa(f) 493, 494.
puerta(f) del congelador(m) 254.
puerta(f) del fogón(m) 204.
puerta(f) del refrigerador(m) 254.
puerta(f) del vestíbulo(m) 461.
puerta(f) lateral 477.
puerta(f) plegable 194, 202, 292.
puerta(f) trasera 195, 470.
**puertas(f), tipos(m) de 202.**
PUERTO(M) 490.
puesta(f) en marcha(f) 532, 569.
**puesta(f) en órbita(f) 419.**
puesto(m) de bombeo(m) 453.
puesto(m) de información(f) 504.
puesto(m) de socorro(m) 822.
pujamen(m) 631.
pulgar(m) 112, 137, 327, 596.
pullman(m) de ocho plazas(f) 425.
pulmón(m) 97.
pulmón(m) derecho 124, 130.
pulmón(m) izquierdo 124, 130.
pulpa(f) 62, 63, 64, 65, 144.
pulpejo(m) 104.
pulsera(f) de dijes(m) 364.
PULVERIZACIÓN(F) 157.
**pulverización(f) 154.**
pulverizador(m) 257, 264, 265, 590.
pulverizador(m) de agua(f) 426.
**pulverizador(m) de discos(m) 157.**
pulverizador(m) de discos(m) 154.
puñal(m) 794.
puño(m) 315, 324, 596, 615, 640, 642, 666, 727.
puño(m) de amura(f) 631.
puño(m) de escota(f) 631.
puño(m) de la puerta(f) 427.
**puño(m) para gemelos(m) 339.**
punta 818.
punta grabadora(f) 714.
punta(f) 30, 57, 72, 239, 240, 241, 242, 275, 276, 277, 284, 291, 305, 323, 325, 375, 384, 389, 544, 562, 567, 633, 640, 642, 658, 671, 678, 684, 697, 698, 817.
punta(f) de caja(f) cuadrada (Robertson) 276.
punta(f) de cruz(f) (Phillips) 276.
punta(f) de diamante(m) 225.
punta(f) de flecha(f) de pedernal(m) 791.
punta(f) de hoja(f) plana 276.
punta(f) de la plancha(f) 256.
punta(f) de plástico(m) 370.
punta(f) de sujeción(f) 540.
punta(f) del ala(f) 637.
punta(f) del bastón(m) 643.
punta(f) del cuello(m) 324, 341.
punta(f) del esquí(m) 642.
punta(f) delantera 680.
punta(f) seca 582, 583.
puntal(m) 199, 553, 757.
puntal(m) derecho 606.
puntal(m) izquierdo 606.
puntal(m) trasero 773.
puntales(m) de refuerzo(m) 198.
punteo(m) 586.
puntera(f) 277, 355, 641, 644, 645.
puntera(f) protectora 730.
puntera(f) reforzada 644.
puntero(m) 719.
punto(m) 565, 695, 832.
punto(m) de apoyo(m) variable 624.
punto(m) de cambio(m) 467.
punto(m) de concentración(f) 770.
punto(m) de cruz(f) 571.
punto(m) de escapulario(m) 571.
punto(m) de espiga(f) 571.
punto(m) de inserción(f) 684.
punto(m) de interés 52.
punto(m) de malla(f) 567.
punto(m) de mira(f) 719, 795, 796, 797, 798, 799, 804.
punto(m) de montaje(m) 501.
punto(m) de musgo(m) 567.
punto(m) de nudos(m) 571.
punto(m) de ochos(m) 567.
punto(m) de pénalty(m) 601.
punto(m) de respiguilla(f) 567.
punto(m) de salida(f) 676.
punto(m) de saque(m) 608.
punto(m) y coma(f) 832.
**punto(m), tipos(m) de 567.**
**puntos(m) de cruz(f) 571.**
**puntos(m) de malla(f) 571.**
puntos(m) de montado(m) 567.
**puntos(m) de relleno(m) 571.**
**puntos(m) de relleno(m) sueltos 571.**
puntos(m) suspensivos 832.
**puntos(m), tipos(m) de 571.**
PUNTUACIÓN(F), SIGNOS(M) 832.
punzón(m) 570, 585, 688.
pupila(f) 107, 140.
pupila(f) vertical 96.
purificador(m) de aire(m) 210.
**puro(m) 384.**
púrpura(m) 819.
**putter(m) 677.**
putter(m) 678.

Los términos en **negrita** corresponden a una ilustración; los que aparecen en MAYÚSCULAS indican un título.

## Q

quarterback(m) 603, 605.
queche(m) 482.
quemador(m) 209, 248, 634, 635, 689, 738.
quemador(m) de gas(m) 297.
queroseno(m) 744, 745.
quevedos(m) 377.
quiasma(m) óptico 134.
quijada(f) 100, 106.
quijada(f) inferior 650.
quijada(f) superior 650.
quijera(f) 649.
quijote(m) 792.
Quilla 13.
quilla(f) 637.
**química(f) 831.**
quinta(f) 537, 667.
quinteto(m) 558.
quinto hueso(m) metacarpiano 112.
quinto(m) octante 6.
quitapiedras(m) 459, 469.

## R

rábano(m) 71.
rábano(m) blanco 71.
rabillo(m) 62, 63, 64.
rabiza(f) 670.
racimo(m) 60.
RADAR(M) 722.
radar(m) 493, 494, 495, 497.
radar(m) aéreo 809.
radar(m) de aterrizaje(m) 811.
radar(m) de búsqueda(f) aérea 811.
radar(m) de control(m) aéreo 810.
radar(m) de detección de blancos(m) 809.
radar(m) de navegación(f) 498.
radar(m) de vgilancia(f) de superficie(f) 809.
radar(m) de vigilancia(f) de superficie(f) 810.
**Radarsat, satélite(m) 49.**
radiación(f) solar 768, 769, 770, 771, 772.
**radiador(m) 438.**
radiador(m) 16, 208, 469.
**radiador(m) de convexión(f) 211.**
radiador(m) de la batería(f) 49.
**radiador(m) eléctrico 210.**
**radiador(m) tubular 208.**
radial(m) externo primero 121.
radial(m) externo segundo 121.
radícula(f) 57, 59.
**radio AM \ FM y lector(m) de casetes(m) personal 408.**
radio(m) 102, 112, 122, 447, 639.
radio(m) blando 87.
radio(m) espinoso 86.
radio(m) medular 59.
radioactivo 821.
**radiocasete(m) con lector(m) de disco(m) compacto 408.**
radiómetro(m) 42, 43.
RADIOTELESCOPIO(M) 15.
radomo(m) 813.
raedor(m) 582.
**raíces(f) 71.**
raíces(f) 57, 61.
raíces(f) superficiales 59.
raíz(f) 70, 143, 144, 240.
raíz(f) anterior 135.
raíz(f) cuadrada de 830.
raíz(f) de la uña 137.
raíz(f) del hélix(m) 139.
raíz(f) motriz 135.
raíz(f) posterior 135.
raíz(f) primaria 57, 59.
raíz(f) secundaria 57.
raíz(f) sensorial 135.
rallador(m) 242, 243.
**rama(f) 58.**
rama(f) 57, 59, 104, 726.
rama(f) comunicante 135.
rama(f) con fruto(m) 61.
rama(f) inferior 793.
rama(f) madre 59.
rama(f) superior 793.
ramaje(m) 59.
ramificación(f) 61.
ramificación(f) colateral 135.
ramilla(f) 59.
rampa(f) 452.
rampa(f) de acceso(m) 168, 456.
rampa(f) de transferencia(f) 452.
rampa(f) del muelle(m) 490.
rampa(f) para mercancías(f) 184.
rampa(f) plegable 494.
**rana(f) 84.**
**rana(f) arbórea 85.**
ranilla(f) 104.
ranura(f) 276, 379, 439, 562, 656.
ranura(f) de corte(m) 285.
ranura(f) de visión(f) 792.
ranura(f) del larguero(m) de la vidriera(f) 203.
ranura(f) guía(f) 598, 641.
ranura(f) para el pan(m) 252.
ranura(f) para monedas(f) 422, 702.
ranura(f) para toldo(m) 441, 449.
Ranvier, nódulo(m) de 135.
RAQUETA(F) 645.
**raqueta(f) de bádminton(m) 618.**
**raqueta(f) de raquetbol(m) 617.**
**raqueta(f) de squash(m) 616.**
**raqueta(f) de tenis(m) 615.**
RAQUETBOL(M) 617.
**raquetbol(m), pelota(f) de 617.**
raquis(m) 110.
rascacielos(m) 185.
**raspador(m) 304, 784.**
raspador(m) 385, 583, 585.
ráspano(m) 62.
rastreador(m) de estrellas(f) 16.
**rastrillo(m) 159.**
rastrillo(m) 155, 267, 599.
**rastrillo(m) con los travesaños(m) 599.**
rastrillo(m) con los travesaños(m) 598, 599.
RASURADORAS(F) 374.
**ratón(m) 530.**
ratón(m) 526, 527.
ratonera(f) 642.
raya(f) 323.
rayo(m) 36.
rayo(m) laser 405.
rayo(m) solar reflejado 770, 771.
re(D) 537.
reacción(f) 831.
reactor(m) 759, 764, 766, 806.
**reactor(m) nuclear, carga(f) 765.**
**reaprovisionamiento(m) de combustible(m) en vuelo(m) 813.**
rebajo(m) de escalón(m) 201.
rebobinado(m) 411, 831.
rebobinador(m) 561.
reborde(m) 24, 188, 189, 544, 546.
rebosadero(m) 215, 293, 746.
recalentador(m) 758.
recámara(f) 585.
recepción(f) de carga(f) 505.
recepción(f) de documentos(m) 421.
recepción(f) de equipaje(m) 504.
recepción(f) directa en la casa(f) 416.
recepción(f) y transmisión de mensajes(m) 421.
receptáculo(m) 60, 62.
receptáculo(m) del cepillo(m) 373.
**receptor(m) 595.**
receptor(m) 15, 420, 541, 597.
receptor(m) abierto 603, 605.
receptor(m) de los bajos(m) 547.
receptor(m) de los intermedios(m) 547.
receptor(m) del sonido(m) 726.
receptor(m) sensorial 134.
receptor(m) triple 547.
receta(f) médica 831.
recibidor(m) 496.
recibo(m) 709.
recipiente(m) 251.
recipiente(m) con asa(f) 250.
recipiente(m) con vertedor(m) 251.
recipiente(m) de acumulación(f) 40.
recipiente(m) de agua(f) 210.
recipiente(m) de enjuague(m) 257.
recipiente(m) de presión(f) 762.
recipiente(m) de vertido(m) 40.
recipiente(m) del detergente(m) 257.
recipiente(m) del reactor(m) 765.
recipiente(m) inferior 247.
recipiente(m) para almancenamiento(m) 764.
recipiente(m) superior 247.
recogepelotas(m) 613, 614.
recortador(m) de patillas(f) 374.
recta 334.
recta de tres cuartos(m) 339.
recta(f) de fondo(m) 651.
recto entallado 332.
recto(m) 127, 128, 131.
recto(m) anterior 120.
recto(m) del abdomen(m) 120.
recto(m) interno del muslo(m) 121.
recuadro(m) 756.
recubrimiento(m) aislante 510.
recubrimiento(m) antirreflectante 768.
recubrimiento(m) de la popa(f) 16.
recubrimiento(m) de la primera tubería(f) 740.
recuperable 831.
recuperación(f) de aire(m) 206, 207.
recuperación(f) del documento(m) enviado 421.
recuperado 831.
**red(f) 613, 614, 618.**
red(f) 610, 612, 613, 614, 618, 619, 626.
red(f) de cables(m) telefónicos 186.
red(f) de comunicación(f) 527.
red(f) de mano(f) 672.
red(f) de transmisión(f) de electricidad(f) 771.
red(f) de transmisión(f) privada 416.
red(f) nacional de transmisión(f) 416.
red(f) para el equipaje(m) 461.
red(f) telefónica 417.
**red(f) telefónica, telecomunicaciones(f) 417.**
redonda(f) (unidad(f)) 538.
**redondeo(m) 579.**
redondo 343.
redondo(m) mayor 121.
redondo(m) menor 121.
reducción(f) del diámetro(m) del haz(m) 717.
reducción(f)/ampliación(f) 532.
reductor(m) de calibre(m) 301.
reductor(m) de entrada(f) 82.
reductor(m) de flujo(m) 740.
reductor(m) de voltaje(m) 755.
**refinado(m), productos(m) 744.**
refinería(f) 740.
reflector(m) 310, 441, 445, 446.
reflector(m) del radar(m) 487.
reflector(m) orientable 414.
reflector(m) parabólico 15.
**reflector(m) portátil 777.**
reflector(m) secundario 15.
reflectores(m) solares 418.
refrigerante(m) 744, 766, 771.
refrigerante(m) caliente 771.
refrigerante(m) frío 771.
refrigerante(m): agua(f) a presión(f) 762.
refrigerante(m): agua(f) hirviente 763.
refrigerante(m): agua(f) pesada a presión(f) 761.
refrigerante(m): bióxido(m) de carbono(m) 760.
refuerzo(m) 346, 729.
refuerzo(m) de la culata(f) 800.
refuerzo(m) del talón(m) 354.
refuerzo(m) embobinado 678.
refuerzo(m) secundario 756.
**regadera(f) 265.**
regatón(m) 681.
región(f) lumbar 117, 119.
región(f) malar 109.
región(f) negativa 768.
región(f) positiva 768.
**regiones(f) de boyas(f) 488.**
registro(m) 712.
registro(m) de aire(m) caliente 206.
registro(m) de altos(m) 536.
registro(m) de cristal(m) líquido 706.
registro(m) digital 310.
registros(m) de los bajos(m) 536.
regla(f) 563, 578, 688.
regla(f) de corte(m) 285.
regla(f) de escuadra(f) 591.
regla(f) para medir puntos(m) 567.
regulador(m) 206, 541.
regulador(m) de altura(f) 659, 661.
regulador(m) de ancho de puntada(f) 561.
regulador(m) de emergencia(f) 627.
regulador(m) de entrada(f) de agua(f) 257.
regulador(m) de fluidos(m) 304.
regulador(m) de la 1ª etapa(f) de descompresión(f) 627.
regulador(m) de la 2ª etapa(f) de descompresión(f) 627.
regulador(m) de la presión(f) 543.
regulador(m) de largo(m) de puntada(f) 561.
regulador(m) de luminosidad(f) 231.
**regulador(m) de presión(f) 306.**
regulador(m) de presión(f) 248, 306, 561, 689, 777.
regulador(m) de tamaño(m) de punto(m) 562.
regulador(m) de temperatura(f) 441.
regulador(m) de tensión(f) 561, 568, 569.
reina(f) 81, 695, 696.
reja(f) 156, 310.
reja(f) de entrada(f) al pronaos(m) 168.
reja(f) metálica de contacto(m) 768.
reja(f) trilladora 160.
rejilla(f) 188, 208, 214, 248, 252, 255, 406, 410, 426, 438, 439, 536.
rejilla(f) de calefacción(f) 477.
rejilla(f) de control térmico 43.
rejilla(f) de entrada(f) de aire(m) 370.
rejilla(f) de iluminación(f) 414.
rejilla(f) de pared(f) 207.
rejilla(f) de piso(m) 207.
rejilla(f) de salida(f) 211.
rejilla(f) de salida(f) de aire(m) 370.
rejilla(f) de techo(m) 207.
rejilla(f) de vaporización(f) 210.
rejilla(f) de ventilación(f) 214, 257.
rejilla(f) del radiador(m) 440.
rejilla(f) del ventilador(m) 260.
rejilla(f) desmontable 248.
rejilla(f) protectora 401.
**rejilla(f), sistema(m) 47.**
**rejillas(f) 207.**
relicario(m) 361.
rellano(m) 201.
rellano(m) de la escalera(f) 194.
relleno exterior(m) 733.
relleno(m) alternado 571.
relleno(m) exterior 733.
reloj(m) 252, 255, 398, 407, 413, 415, 430, 664, 714.
reloj(m) automático 585.
reloj(m) de cocina(f) 244.
reloj(m) de la ampliadora(f) 399.
**reloj(m) de péndulo(m) 707.**
**reloj(m) de pesas(f), mecanismo(m) 707.**
**reloj(m) de pulsera(f) 706.**
**reloj(m) de sol(m) 706.**
**reloj(m) digital 706.**
**reloj(m) mecánico 706.**
reloj(m) programador 253.
remache(m) 242, 278.
remate(m) 201.
remate(m) en T 205.
remeras(f) primarias 110.
remeras(f) secundarias 110.
remeras(f) terciarias 110.
REMO(M) 632.
**remo(m) 632, 664.**
remo(m) 664.
remolacha(m) 71.
**remolque(m) 449.**
remolque(m) 507.
**remos(m), tipos de 632.**
**renacuajo(m) 84.**
reniforme 56.
repisa(f) 204.
repisa(f) para accesorios(m) 721.
repollo(m) 73.
repollo(m) verde 73.
reproducción(f) 831.
REPTIL(M) 96.
repuesto(m) 389.
resbaladero(m) 736.
resguardo(m) 426.
resguardo(m) de espuma(f) 729.
resguardo(m) de hormigón(m) 760, 761, 762, 763.
residuos(m) primarios 744.
resistencia(f) 255, 257, 259, 305, 585.
resonador(m) 406, 542, 554, 616.
resonador(m) de rayos(m) infrarrojos 43.
resorte(m) 230, 234, 258, 278, 294, 389, 469, 804.
resorte(m) de la válvula(f) 434.
resorte(m) de retorno(m) 432.
resorte(m) de suspensión(f) 707.
resorte(m) de tensión(f) 562, 665.
resorte(m) de válvula(f) 543.
resorte(m) del eslabón(m) 795.
resorte(m) del martinete(m) 541.
resorte(m) del sistema(m) articulado 702.
resorte(m) del tensor(m) 569.
resorte(m) espiral 231.
resorte(m) hidráulico 664.
resorte(m) tensor 431.
respaldo(m) 220, 223, 386, 428, 445, 727.
respaldo(m) reclinatorio 726.
respiradero(m) 14, 82, 196, 197, 214, 385, 443, 741.
respiradero(m) lateral 449.
restador(m) 614, 616, 618.

Los términos en **negrita** corresponden a una ilustración; los que aparecen en MAYÚSCULAS indican un título.

restaurante(m) 185, 190, 494, 822.
retén(m) 735.
retén(m) de la esfera(f) 530.
retén(m) del cargador(m) 795.
retén(m) imantado 256.
retención(f) de datos(m) 310.
retícula(f) 718.
Retículo 13.
retículo(m) endoplasmático 115.
retina(f) 140.
retoño(m) 59.
retorno(m) a la memoria(f) 523.
**retrete(m) 293.**
retrete(m) 215, 292.
retroexcavadora(f) 782.
**retroexcavadora(f) cargadora(f) 782.**
**revelado(m), baños(m) 399.**
**revelado(m), tanque(m) 398.**
revés(m) 567.
revestimiento(m) 432, 619, 635, 677, 748, 798, 799.
revestimiento(m) de fibra(f) de vidrio(m) 297.
revestimiento(m) de fósforo(m) 232.
revestimiento(m) interior 429, 433.
revisor(m) de billetes(m) 463.
REVÓLVER(M) 797.
rey(m) 695, 696.
ría(f) 646, 647, 676.
ribera(f) 750.
ribete(m) 322, 328, 352, 354.
ribosoma(m) 115.
**riel(m) 230.**
riel(m) 230, 466, 476, 786.
riel(m) corredizo 257, 630.
riel(m) de cierre(m) 467.
**riel(m) de iluminación(f) 235.**
riel(m) de lanzamiento(m) de proyectiles(m) 813.
riel(m) de retención(f) 467.
riel(m) de rodamiento(m) 786.
riel(m) de rotación(f) 15.
riel(m) deslizador 428.
riel(m) eléctrico 476.
riel(m) metálico 517.
riel(m) para las parrillas(f) 254.
**rieles(m), empalme(m) 466.**
rienda(f) 651.
rienda(f) del bocado(m) 649.
rienda(f) del freno(m) 649.
**rifle(m) 798.**
**rifle(m), cartucho(m) 798.**
rimaya(f) 26.
**rímel(m) en pasta(f) 367.**
rímel(m) líquido 367.
rincón(m) 669.
rinconera(f) 227.
**ring(m) de boxeo(m) 669.**
ringside(m) 669.
riñón(m) 89, 97, 124.
riñón(m) derecho 132.
riñón(m) izquierdo 132.
riñonera(f) 602.
riñones(m) 101.
río(m) 51, 52.
ripia(f) 286.
risco(m) 7.
**ritmo(m) de las señales(f) nocturnas 489.**
rizador(m) de mantequilla(f) 242.
rizador(m) de pestañas(f) 367.
**Roberval, balanza(f) 708.**
**robot(m) de cocina(f) 251.**
roca(f) 30.
roca(f) firme 714.
roca(f) impermeable 737.
rocas(f) ígneas 23.
rocas(f) intrusivas 23.
rocas(f) metamórficas 23.
rocas(f) sedimentarias 23.
rociador(m) 296.
rociadores(m) 766.
rocío(m) 37.
roda(f) 479.
rodamiento(m) 530, 753.
rodapié(m) 225.
rodete(m) 105.
rodilla(f) 100, 106, 116, 118.
rodillera(f) 595, 602, 609, 649, 653, 792.
**rodillo(m) 584.**
rodillo(m) 231, 245, 270, 304, 524, 531.
rodillo(m) de entrada(f) 160, 162.
**rodillo(m) de pintor(m) 304.**
rodillo(m) entintador 581.
rodillo(m) guía(f) de la película(f) 390.
rodillo(m) para barnizar 582.
rodillo(m) triturador 158.
rodillo(m)guía(f) 403.
rodrigón(m) 263.
roja(f) 697, 700.
rojo(m) 701.
rollo(m) de la película(f) 395.
rollo(m) para recubrimiento(m) impermeabilizante 287.
romero(m) 74.
rompiente(m) 30.
**ropa(f) de cama(f) 224.**
ROPA(F) DE HOMBRE(M) 319, 320, 322, 324.
ROPA(F) DE MUJER(F) 330, 332, 334, 336, 338, 340, 342, 344, 346, 348.
ROPA(F) DE NIÑOS(M) 349, 350.
ROPA(F) DEPORTIVA 352.
**ropa(f) interior 325, 345, 346.**
**ropa(f) para ejercicio(m) 353.**
ropero(m) 226.
rosa(f) de los vientos(m) 484, 719.
rosa(f) holandesa 362.
rosca(f) 276, 279, 294, 711.
roseta(f) 265, 289, 290, 546.
rosetón(m) 167, 175.
rostro(m) 90.
rotación(f) de la turbina(f) 755.
rotonda(f) 52, 190.
rotor(m) 161, 290, 437, 508, 773, 774.
rotor(m) de cola(f) 508.
rotor(m) de la turbina(f) 752.
rótula(f) 103, 122.
rótula(f) de enganche(m) 471.
rotulador(m) 516, 588.
rótulo(m) de destino(m) 743.
rótulo(m) de identificación(f) 743.
rubí(m) 363, 706.
**rubor(m) en polvo(m) 366.**
**rueda(f) 433.**
rueda(f) 270, 427, 440, 563, 583, 645, 664, 727, 788, 800, 805.
rueda(f) catalina 783.
rueda(f) central 706, 707.
rueda(f) central de enfoque(m) 719.
rueda(f) compresora 158.
rueda(f) de cadena(f) 445.
rueda(f) de cangilones(m) 754.
rueda(f) de corona(f) 707.
rueda(f) de escape(m) 706, 707.
rueda(f) de la dirección(f) 727.
rueda(f) de los segundos(m) 706.
rueda(f) de modulación(f) 555.
rueda(f) de radios(m) 652.
rueda(f) de transmisión(f) 445.
rueda(f) de trinquete(m) 706, 707.
rueda(f) de volante(m) 584.
rueda(f) delantera 147, 784.
rueda(f) giratoria 701.
rueda(f) guía(f) 783.
rueda(f) humedecedora 516.
rueda(f) libre 435.
rueda(f) media 706.
rueda(f) metálica de seguridad(f) 476.
rueda(f) motriz 147, 707, 805.
rueda(f) para ajustar el tono(m) 555.
rueda(f) para graduar el respaldo(m) 428.
ruedas(f) de tracción(f) 784.
RUEDAS(F), SILLA(F) 727.
ruedecilla(f) 260, 383, 553.
Ruffini, corpúsculo(m) de 136.
RUGBY(M) 606.
**rugby(m), balón(m) de 606.**
ruibarbo(m) 72.
**ruleta(f) americana 700.**
ruleta(f) estriada 582.
**ruleta(f) francesa 701.**
RULETA(F), MESA(F) 700.
**rulo(m) para el cabello(m) 369.**
ruta(f) circular 52.
ruta(f) de servicio(m) 502.
ruta(f) pintoresca 52.

## S

sabana(f) 45.
sábana(f) 224.
sábana(f) ajustable 224.
sabañón(m) 55.
sable(m) 628, 631, 637, 666, 794, 819.
sabor(m) agrio 143.
sabor(m) amargo 143.
sabor(m) dulce 143.
sabor(m) salado 143.
**sabores(m) 143.**
sacaanzuelos(m) 672.
**sacabotas(m) 358.**
sacacorchos(m) 244, 688.
sacacorchos(m) con brazos(m) 244.
sacapuntas(m) 515, 516.
sacatrapos(m) 801.
saco(m) de marinero(m) 381.
saco(m) de piel(f) 536.
saco(m) de pilotaje(m) 637.
saco(m) de viaje(m) 380.
saco(m) rectangular 687.
saco(m) semirrectangular 687.
saco(m) uterovesical 128.
**sacos(m) de dormir 687.**
sacro(m) 122, 123.
Saeta 11.
Sagitario 13.
Sagitario, el Arquero (22 de noviembre) 820.
sala(f) 195.
sala(f) de bombeo(m) 742.
sala(f) de cine(m) 496.
sala(f) de computación(f) 807.
sala(f) de control(m) 14, 15, 189, 407, 746, 759.
sala(f) de control(m) de la producción(f) 415.
sala(f) de control(m) de luces(f) 412.
sala(f) de control(m) de máquinas(f) de propulsión(f) 806.
sala(f) de control(m) de operaciones(f) 807.
**sala(f) de control(m) de producción(f) 413.**
sala(f) de control(m) de sonido(m) 415.
SALA(F) DE CONTROL(M), ESTUDIO(M) DE RADIO(M) 407.
sala(f) de ensayo(m) 188.
sala(f) de equipajes(m) 462.
sala(f) de espera(f) de embarque(m) 505.
sala(f) de instalaciones(f) auxiliares 412.
sala(f) de la caldera(f) nuclear 806.
sala(f) de máquinas(f) 496, 742, 746, 747, 806.
sala(f) de molinetes(m) del ancla(f) 495, 497.
sala(f) de navegación(f) 494.
sala(f) de oración(f) 172, 173.
sala(f) de producción(f) de electricidad(f) 806.
sala(f) de producción(f) y control(m) 412.
sala(f) de proyección(f) 16.
sala(f) de regulación(f) de luces 412.
sala(f) de torpedos(m) 807.
sala(f) del montacargas(m) 735.
sala(f) para el público(m) 189.
salamandra(f) 85.
salero(m) 238.
salida(f) 452.
salida(f) de agua(f) caliente 208, 296, 297.
salida(f) de agua(f) fría 296.
salida(f) de aire(m) caliente 204, 207, 438.
salida(f) de humo(m) 204.
salida(f) de la contracorriente(f) 759.
salida(f) de la pista(f) 505.
salida(f) de la pista(f) de alta velocidad(f) 502.
salida(f) de vapor(m) 760, 761, 762, 763.
salida(f) del agua(f) de enfriamiento(m) del condensador(m) 759.
salida(f) del refrigerante(m) 768.
salida(f) y llegada(f) 646.
salida(m) de la pista(f) 651.
salina(f) 30.
salón(m) de baile(m) 497.
salón(m) de pasajeros(m) 496.
**salpicadero(m) 430.**
salsera(f) 238.
salsifí(m) 71.
saltamontes(m) 77.
SALTO(M) 624.
salto(m) al frente(m) 624.
**salto(m) al frente(m) en posición(f) A 625.**
salto(m) atrás 624.
**salto(m) atrás en posición(f) A 625.**
**salto(m) de altura(f) 657.**
salto(m) de altura(f) 654.
salto(m) de cama(f) 348.
**salto(m) de pértiga(f) 657.**
salto(m) de pértiga(f) 655.
salto(m) de salida(f) 622.
**salto(m) en equilibrio(m) 625.**
**salto(m) interior en posición(f) B 625.**
**salto(m) inverso en posición(f) B 625.**
**salto(m) tirabuzón(m) en posición(f) A 625.**
**saltos(m) 624.**
salvavidas(m) 495.
salvia(f) 74.
sandalia(f) 356, 357, 791.
sandía(f) 69.
**sapo(m) 85.**
sarga(f) 576.
**sarmiento(m) 61.**
sarong(m) malayo 334.
sarta(f) 361.
**sartén(f) 688.**
sartén(f) 249.
sartén(f) honda 249.
sartén(f) para crepes(f) 249.
sartorio(m) 120.
satélite(m) 416.
satélite(m) artificial 19.
SATÉLITE(M) DE DETECCIÓN(F) A LARGA DISTANCIA(F) 48.
**satélite(m) de órbita(f) polar 43.**
SATÉLITE(M) DE TRANSMISIÓN(F), COMUNICACIÓN(F) 416.
**satélite(m) geoestacionario 42.**
SATÉLITE(M) METEOROLÓGICO 42.
**satélite(m) Radarsat 49.**
SATÉLITE(M), TELECOMUNICACIONES(F) 417.
SATÉLITES(M) DE TELECOMUNICACIONES(F) 418.
**satélites(m), ejemplos(m) 418.**
**satélites(m), órbita(f) 43.**
satén(m) 576.
Saturno 5.
**saxofón(m) 548.**
saxofón(m) 548.
Schwann, célula(f) de 135.
**secado(m) 829.**
**secador(f) manual 370.**
secadora(f) de ensalada(f) 243.
secadora(f) de pruebas(f) 399.
**secadora(f) de ropa(f) 259.**
sección(f) antirrotacional 42.
sección(f) de carga(f) del combustible(m) 764.
sección(f) de flotación(f) 486.
sección(f) del cañón(m) 205.
sección(f) frontal 730.
sección(f) para el equipo(m) 16.
sección(f) principal 701.
seco(m) 700, 701.
secretario(m) 612, 626.
seda(f) dental 373.
sedal(m) 670.
sedán(m) de cuatro puertas(f) 425.
sedimento(m) 216.
**segadora(f) 158.**
segadora(f) 154.
segmento(m) abdominal 78.
segmento(m) de marcas(f) 698.
segmento(m) intermediario 127.
segmento(m) muscular 89.
segmento(m) terminal 127.
segueta(f) 277.
seguimiento(m) de la bola(f) 682.
segunda base(f) 597.
segunda etapa(f) 509.
segunda vía(f) de clasificación(f) 465.
segunda(f) 537, 667.
segundero(m) 706.
segundo árbitro(m) 613.
segundo espacio(m) 610.
segundo hueso(m) metacarpiano 112.
segundo jugador(m) 620.
segundo molar(m) 144.
segundo pistón(m) móvil 550.
segundo premolar(m) 144.
segundo recinto(m) focal 15.
segundo refuerzo(m) 800.
segundo(m) 669, 830.
segundos violines(m) 556.
seguridad(f), anteojos(m) 729.
**seguridad(f), casco(m) 729.**
**seguridad(f), orejera(f) 729.**
SEGURIDAD(F), SÍMBOLOS(M) 821.
seguro(m) 253, 260, 278, 281, 290, 396, 796.
seguro(m) de inclinación(f) del disco(m) 284.
seguro(m) de inclinación(f) lateral 393.
seguro(m) de la barra(f) de tracción(f) 803.
seguro(m) de la base(f) 282.
seguro(m) de la columna(f) 393.
seguro(m) de la guía(f) 285.
seguro(m) de la mesa(f) 283.
seguro(m) de la plataforma(f) 393.
seguro(m) de movimiento(m) horizontal 393.
seguro(m) del brazo(m) 568.
seguro(m) del cargador(m) 797.
seguro(m) del cordón(m) 231.

Los términos en **negrita** corresponden a una ilustración; los que aparecen en MAYÚSCULAS indican un título.

seguro(m) del fuelle(m) 536.
seguro(m) del interruptor(m) 280.
seis(m) doble 695.
selección auto/manual 310.
selector automático/manual 585.
selector(m) 214, 252, 310.
selector(m) de altavoz(m) 402.
selector(m) de banda(f) 402.
selector(m) de canales(m) 411.
selector(m) de corte(m) 374.
selector(m) de emisoras(f) memorizadas 402.
selector(m) de entrada(f) 402.
selector(m) de focalización(f) 391.
selector(m) de función(f) 402.
selector(m) de la recepción(f) 547.
selector(m) de la voz(f) 555.
selector(m) de nivel(m) de agua(f) 258.
selector(m) de posición(f) de aguja(f) 561.
selector(m) de programa(m) 555.
selector(m) de puntada(f) 561.
selector(m) de temperatura(f) 253, 258, 259.
selector(m) de tipo(m) de cinta(f) 403.
selector(m) de tostado(m) 252.
selector(m) de velocidad(f) 404.
selector(m) de velocidades(f) 250, 251.
selector(m) del control(m) de vídeo(m) 413.
selector(m) del control(m) de volumen(m) 413.
selector(m) del premio(m) 702.
selector(m) del ritmo(m) 555.
selector(m) mono/estéreo 402.
selector(m) para regular el tamaño(m) de los puntos(m) 568.
selectores(m) de funciones(f) 420.
selectores(m) de modalidad(f) 408.
sello(m) de goma(f) 516.
semáforo(m) 186, 464, 826, 827.
**sembradora(f) a chorrillo(m) 158.**
sembradora(f) a chorrillo(m) 154.
sembradora(f) de mano(f) 268.
semicírculo(m) 674.
semicírculo(m) de la zona(f) de tiro(m) libre 610.
semicírculo(m) del área(f) 601.
semicorchea(f) (dieciseisavo(m)) 538.
semifusa(f) (sesentaicuatroavo(m)) 538.
semilla(f) 62, 63, 64, 65, 66, 67.
semillas(f) de soja(f) 72.
semimembranoso(m) 121.
semirremolque(m) 742.
**semirremolque(m), caja(f) tipo(m) 441.**
semitendinoso(m) 121.
señal(f) aislada de peligro(m) 489.
señal(f) cardinal del este(m) 489.
señal(f) cardinal del oeste(m) 489.
señal(f) cardinal del sur(m) 489.
señal(f) de aguas(f) seguras 489.
señal(f) de cruce(m) 471.
señal(f) de dirección(f) 475.
señal(f) de distancia(f) fija 505.
señal(f) de eje(m) de pista(f) 504.
señal(f) de identificación(f) de pista(f) 504.
señal(f) de posición(f) de la aguja(f) 467.
señal(f) de unión(m) 824.
señal(f) de zona(f) de contacto(m) de pista(f) 505.
señal(f) de zona(f) de espera(f) 504.
señal(f) del sonido(m) 539.
señal(f) diurna 486, 487.
señal(f) especial 489.
señal(f) exterior 474.
señal(f) lateral 489.
señal(f) luminosa 539.
señales de límite(m) de la pista(f) 505.
SEÑALES(F) DE CIRCULACIÓN(F) 824, 826, 828.
**señales(f) de los puntos(m) cardinales 488.**
**señales(f) diurnas (región(f) B) 489.**
señales(f) laterales de pista(f) 504.
SEÑALES(F) MARÍTIMAS 486.
**señales(f) nocturnas, ritmo(m) 489.**
SENO(M) 129.
seno(m) 30, 118, 315.
seno(m) del pecíolo(m) 61.
seno(m) esfenoidal 141.
seno(m) frontal 141.
seno(m) lateral inferior 61.
seno(m) lateral superior 61.
Señoras(f), Servicios(m) 822.
sensibilidad(f) de la película(f) 396.
sensor solar 43.
sensor(m) 42.
sensor(m) de control(m) a larga distancia(f) 410.
sensor(m) de control(m) biomédico 512.
sensor(m) de luz(f) 390.
sensor(m) de nivel(m) de combustible(m) 512.
sensor(m) de radiaciones(f) de la tierra(f) 43.
sensor(m) del control(m) a larga distancia(f) 405.
sensor(m) solar 42, 49.
sensor(m) terrestre 42, 43, 49.
sépalo(m) 60, 62, 64.
separación(f) del lanzador(m) de satélites(m) 419.
separación(f) entre bolos(m) 683.
separador(m) 160, 184, 378, 452, 727, 742, 758, 765.
separador(m) de agua(f) 734.
separador(m) de boca(f) de agua(f) 779.
separador(m) de gas(m) y líquido(m) 439.
separador(m) de petróleo(m) y gas(m) 738.
separador(m) de placas(f) 439.
separador(m) de reinas(f) 82.
separador(m) del escape(m) de vapor(m) 758.
séptima(f) 537, 667.
septum(m) 67, 141.
septum(m) lucidum 134.
seque en secadora(f) a temperatura(f) baja 829.
seque en secadora(f) a temperatura(f) de mediana a alta 829.
seque extendido sobre una toalla(f) después de escurrir 829.
sérac(m) 26.
Serpentario 11.
serpentín(m) del condensador(m) 214.
serpentines(m) de enfriamiento(m) y calefacción(f) 213.
serpentines(m) del evaporador(m) 214.
Serpiente 11, 13.
**serpiente(f) de cascabel(m) 97.**
**serpiente(f) venenosa, cabeza(f) de 96.**
serpollo(m) 61.
**serrucho(m) 277.**
servicio(m) de enlace(m) ferroviario 504.
servicio(m) de taxis(m) 822.
SERVICIO(M), ESTACIÓN(F) 453.
servicios(m) sanitarios 461.
sesamoideo(m) mayor 102.
sesamoideo(m) menor 102.
sesgo(m) 566.
seto(m) 263.
seto(m) y barra(f) 646.
sexta(f) 537, 667.
Sextante 13.
**sextante(m) 484.**
sexteto(m) 558.
shekel(m) 832.
si(B) 537.
SIEGA(F) 158.
**siega(f) 154.**
SIEMBRA(F) 158.
**siembra(f) 154.**
sien(f) 116.
**sierra(f) circular de mano(f) 284.**
**sierra(f) circular de mesa(f) 285.**
**sierra(f) de cadena(f) 272.**
sierra(f) de campo(m) 690.
sierra(f) de ensamblar 578.
sierra(f) de podar 269.
**sierra(f) para metales(m) 277.**
sierra(f) para metales(m) 299.
sifón(m) 24, 215, 296, 301.
sifón(m) de desagüe(m) 298.
sifón(m) inodoro 293.
SIGLO(M) XVII, CAÑÓN(M) 800.
**siglo(m) XVII, mortero(m) 803.**
SIGNOS(M) DE PUNTUACIÓN(F) 832.
SIGNOS(M) DEL ZODÍACO(M) 820.
SIGNOS(M) DIACRÍTICOS 832.
silbato(m) 252, 468.
silenciador(m) 439, 735.
silencio(m) de blanca(f) 538.
silencio(m) de corchea(f) 538.
silencio(m) de fusa(f) 538.
silencio(m) de negra(f) 538.
silencio(m) de redonda(f) 538.
silencio(m) de semicorchea(f) 538.
silencio(m) de semifusa(f) 538.
**silencios(m), valores(m) 538.**
**silicua(f), corte(m) de una 67.**
silla(f) 636, 648, 651, 661.
silla(f) cabriolé 220.
silla(f) cojín(m) 222.
SILLA(F) DE BRAZOS(M) 220.
**silla(f) de montar 649.**
SILLA(F) DE RUEDAS(F) 727.
silla(f) de ruedas(f) 461.
silla(f) de secretaria(f) 521.
silla(f) plegable 223.
silla(f) plegable de lona(f) 220.
silla(f) poltrona 220.
SILLA(F) SIN BRAZOS(M) 223.
silla(f) Wassily 221.
sillas(f) apilables 223.
**sillas(f) de brazos(m), principales 220.**
**sillas(f), tipos(m) de 223.**
sillín(m) 446, 648, 649, 653.
sillín(m) doble 443.
sillón(m) giratorio 520.
silo(m) 149.
silos(m) 490.
símbolo(m) 702.
**símbolos(m) 695.**
SÍMBOLOS(M) CIENTÍFICOS COMUNES 830.
SÍMBOLOS(M) METEOROLÓGICOS 44.
SÍMBOLOS(M) METEOROLÓGICOS INTERNACIONALES 39.
simulado 339.
sinapsis(f) 135.
sinápsis(f) 135.
sinfín(m) para el grano(m) 161.
sínfisis(f) púbica 127, 128.
sinople(m) 819.
**sintetizador(m) 555.**
**sintonizador(m) 400, 402.**
sintonizador(m) 408.
sirena(f) 779.
sisa(f) 325.
sismógrafo(m) horizontal 714.
sismograma(m) 714.
sistema(m) afinado de dirección(f) 16.
sistema(m) de audio(m) 430.
**sistema(m) de bomba(f) de calor(m) 212.**
sistema(m) de botones(m) 555.
SISTEMA(M) DE CARRETERAS(F) 450, 452.
**sistema(m) de celdas(f) solares 769.**
sistema(m) de disparo(m) rápido 393.
sistema(m) de elevación(f) 786.
**sistema(m) de escape(m) 439.**
sistema(m) de esclusas(f) de vaciado(m) y desagüe(m) 492.
sistema(m) de esclusas(f) de vaciado(m) y llenado(m) 492.
SISTEMA(M) DE JUEGOS(M) DE VÍDEO(M) 699.
sistema(m) de lentes(f) 719.
sistema(m) de lubricación(f) 469.
sistema(m) de rebobinado(m) de la película(f) 390.
sistema(m) de registro(m) de la información(f) 717.
**sistema(m) de rejilla(f) 47.**
sistema(m) de soporte(m) vital 512.
**sistema(m) de tensión(f) 569.**
sistema(m) de tuberia montante para sacar la producción(f) 738.
sistema(m) hidraúlico 787.
sistema(m) magnético de amortiguación(f) 708.
**sistema(m) nervioso central 134.**
**sistema(m) nervioso periférico 133.**
SISTEMA(M) RESPIRATORIO, PROTECCIÓN(F) 730.
**sistema(m) rotativo 737.**
sistema(m) rotativo de la cúpula(f) 14.
SISTEMA(M) SOLAR 4.
**skif(m) 632.**
skif(m) doble 632.
skif(m) unipersonal 632.
slip(m) 347.
**snooker(m) 673.**
SNOOKER(M) Y BILLAR(M) INGLÉS 674.
**sobaco(m), muleta(f) 728.**
sobrecincha(f) 653.
sobrecortina(f) 229.
sobreimpresión(f) del original(m) 532.
sobrejuanete(m) de mesana(f) de estay(m) 480.
sobrejuanete(m) de proa(f) 481.
sobrejuanete(m) mayor 481.
sobrenudo(m) 691.
sobrepespunte(m) 323, 327, 350.
sobrepespunteada(f) 335.
socavón(m) 30.
sofá(f) 221.
sofá(m) tipo(m) imperio 221.
sofera(f) doble 198.
soga(f) 680.
sol(G) 537.
SOL(M) 6.
Sol(m) 4, 8.
**Sol(m), estructura(f) 6.**
solapa(f) 322, 341, 386.
solapa(f) con ojal(m) 319, 320.
solapa(f) puntiaguda 322.
solárium(m) 497.
SOLDADURA(F) 305, 306.
soldadura(f) 307.
**soldadura(f) a tope(m) 307.**
SOLDADURA(F): ACCESORIOS(M) DE PROTECCIÓN(F) 308.
sóleo(m) 120.
solera(f) 199.
solera(f) inferior 198.
solera(f) interior 199.
solitario(m) 364.
solsticio(m) de invierno(m) 8.
solsticio(m) de verano(m) 8.
sombra(f) 706.
**sombra(f) de ojos(m) 367.**
sombrero(m) 55.
sombrero(m) de campana(f) 329.
**sombrero(m) de fieltro(m) 328.**
sombrero(m) de fieltro(m) 329.
sombrero(m) de hongo(m) 328.
**sombrero(m) de marinero(m) 329.**
sombrero(m) sin alas(f) 329.
SOMBREROS(M) 328.
somier(m) 224.
**sonar(m) 485.**
sonar(m) del casco(m) 809.
**sonda(f) 485.**
sonda(f) destapacaños(m) 299.
sonda(f) espacial 19.
**sonido(m), producción(f) 543.**
SONIDO(M), SISTEMAS(M) PORTÁTILES 408.
sopera(f) 238.
soplador(m) 543.
**soplete(m) 299, 307.**
soplete(m) 306.
**soplete(m) de corte(m) 306.**
**soplete(m) de soldadura(f) autógena 306.**
soporte(m) 40, 230, 231, 232, 248, 264, 284, 370, 382, 397, 399, 431, 495, 552, 585, 660, 661, 719, 720, 765, 787.
soporte(m) colgante 727.
soporte(m) de flecha(f) 684.
soporte(m) de la barrera(f) 471.
soporte(m) de la cadena(f) 446.
soporte(m) de la conexión(f) 756.
soporte(m) de la esfera(f) 40.
soporte(m) de la plataforma(f) 773.
soporte(m) de la red(f) 619.
soporte(m) de pared(f) 230.
soporte(m) de techo(m) 230.
soporte(m) del brazo(m) 220, 404.
soporte(m) del falso(m) secreto(m) 543.
soporte(m) del juego(m) de marcos(m) 573.
soporte(m) del papel(m) 525.
soporte(m) del pie(m) 656, 664.
soporte(m) del plano(m) fijo 780, 785.
soporte(m) del rótulo(m) 517.
soporte(m) lateral 443.
soporte(m) para el antebrazo(m) 728.
soporte(m) para el brazo(m) 428, 429.
soporte(m) para el equipo(m) 412.
soporte(m) para el sobaco(m) 728.
soporte(m) para la cabeza(f) 428.
soporte(m) plegable 539.
soporte(m) principal 443.
soporte(m) trípode de cola(f) 507.
sordina(f) 551.
sorgo(m) 152.
sortija(f) de sello(m) 364.
**sostén(m) 346.**
sostén(m) con talle(m) reforzado 347.
sostén(m) de escote(m) bajo 346.
sostén(m) de la traba(f) 652.
sostén(m) sin tirantes(m) 346.
sostenido(m) 538.

Los términos en **negrita** corresponden a una ilustración; los que aparecen en MAYÚSCULAS indican un título.

sótano(m) 197.
SQUASH(M) 616.
**squash(m), pelota(f) de 616.**
stand(m) de bolos(m) 683.
**stick(m) 607.**
subestación(f) 752.
sublimación(f) 34.
SUBMARINO(M) 806.
substancia(f) blanca 135.
substracción(f) de la memoria(f) 523.
subtotal(m)/sin adición(f) 523.
subtropical húmedo 45.
subtropical mediterráneo 45.
subtropical seco 45.
suburbios(m) 52.
sudadero(m) 651.
suela(f) 353, 355, 633, 644, 675.
suela(f) de hule(m) 350.
suela(f) rígida 641.
suelo(m) de madera(f) 635.
sueste(m) 329.
sujeción(f) 230.
sujeción(f) delantera 633.
sujeción(f) trasera 633.
sujetador(m) 553, 718.
sujetador(m) del hilo(m) 569.
sujetador(m) del pabellón(m) 549.
sujetalibros(m) 517.
sujetapapel(m) 524.
sulky(m) 652.
suma(f) 830.
sumidero(m) 24, 216, 736.
sumie(m) 589.
suministro(m) de agua(f) 755, 772.
superestructura(f) 486.
superficie(f) acanalada 678.
superficie(f) de absorción(f) 772.
superficie(f) de deslizamiento(m) 640.
superficie(f) de juego(m) 619.
superficie(f) de la piel(f) 137.
superficie(f) de resina(f) 405.
superficie(f) de rodadura(f) 433.
superficie(f) de rodamiento(m) 466.
superficie(f) del agua(f) 624.
superficie(f) del terreno(m) 733.
superficie(f) humedecida 580.
superficie(f) irregular 826.
**superficie(f) lunar 7.**
supinador(m) largo 120, 121.
sur(m) 488.
surco(f) medio 143.
surco(m) 678.
surco(m) concéntrico 404.
surco(m) de salida(f) 404.
surco(m) en espiral(m) 404.
surco(m) intertragohelicano 139.
surco(m) nasolabial 141.
surco(m) terminal 143.
sureste(m) 488.
suroeste(m) 488.
surtidor(m) 162, 294, 295, 296.
surtidor(m) de agua(f) 373.
**surtidor(m) de gasolina(f) 453.**
surtidor(m) de gasolina(f) 453.
surtidor(m) principal 208.
suspensión(f) 458, 477.
suspensión(f) magnética 712.
sutura(f) 67, 94.

## T

tabaco(m) 384.
tabaquera(f) 385.
tabique(m) cortafuego 741.
tabique(m) de contención(m) longitudinal 742.
tabique(m) interventricular 125.
tabique(m) nasal (vómer y cartilagonasal) 141.
**tabla(f) 288.**
tabla(f) 288, 362, 363, 589.
tabla(f) abierta 335.
tabla(f) biselada 579.
tabla(f) con argollas(f) 518.
tabla(f) con broche(m) de presión(f) 519.
tabla(f) de impulso(m) de salto(m) de longitud(f) 655.
tabla(f) de surf(m) 631.
tabla(f) de triple salto(m) 654.
tabla(f) harmónica 543.
tablas(f) 335.
**tablero(m) 445, 697.**
tablero(m) 219, 442, 454, 455, 456, 610.
tablero(m) de accesorios(m) 591.
tablero(m) de aglomerado(m) 289.
tablero(m) de aglomerado(m) con laminado(m) de plástico(m) 289.
**tablero(m) de ajedrez(m) 696.**
tablero(m) de base(f) 399.
tablero(m) de conmutadores(m) 500.
tablero(m) de control(m) 210, 214, 259, 717.
**tablero(m) de controles(m) 532.**
tablero(m) de controles(m) 16, 255, 532.
**tablero(m) de dibujo(m) 591.**
tablero(m) de distribución(f) 757.
tablero(m) de fibra(f) de madera(f) 289.
tablero(m) de fibra(f) de madera(f) perforada 289.
tablero(m) de información(f) 462, 654.
tablero(m) de instrumentos(m) 430.
tablero(m) de llegadas(f) y salidas(f) 505.
tablero(m) de luces(f) 412.
tablero(m) de mandos(m) 468.
tablero(m) de notación(f) 698.
tablero(m) de operación(f) de luces(f) 412.
tablero(m) de operaciónes(f) 779.
tablero(m) de rodillos(m) y brazos(m) 543.
tablero(m) de rótulo(m) 471.
tablero(m) de yeso(m) 286.
tablero(m) indicador 651.
tablero(m) rígido aislante 287.
**tableros(m) y láminas(f) 288, 289.**
tableta(f) 725.
tableta(f) de resonancia(f) 542.
tablillas(f) 725.
tablino(m) 170.
tablón(m) delantero 335.
tabulador(m) 524.
tabulador(m) decimal 524.
taburete(m) 222, 586.
tachuelas(f) para papel(m) 515.
tacita(f) de café(m) 238.
tacle(m) defensivo derecho 603, 605.
tacle(m) defensivo izquierdo 603, 605.
tacle(m) derecho 603, 605.
tacle(m) izquierdo 603, 605.
taco(m) 799, 801.
**taco(m) de billar(m) 675.**
**taco(m) de salida(f) 656.**
tacómetro(m) 431, 445.
tacón(m) 644.
tacos(m) 598, 656.
tacos(m) de rosca(f) 600.
TACTO(M) 136.
tafetán(m) 576.
taladro(m) 270.
**taladro(m) de mano(f) 280.**
**taladro(m) de motor(m) 270.**
taladro(m) de percusión(f) 734.
**taladro(m) de poste(m) extensible 734.**
**taladro(m) eléctrico 280.**
**taladro(m) vertical 283.**
talla(f) 586.
TALLA(F) EN MADERA(F) 586.
**tallas(f) de piedras(f) preciosas 362.**
talle(m) corto 346.
taller(m) de mantenimiento(m) 734.
taller(m) de máquinas(f) diésel 464.
taller(m) de mecánica(f) 453.
taller(m) de reparación(f) de vagones(m) 465.
TALLERES(M) DE FERROCARRIL(M) 465.
tallo(m) 57, 70, 72, 136.
tallo(m) principal 61.
tallo(m) subterráneo 70.
**tallos(m) 72.**
talón(m) 104, 117, 119, 277, 281, 325, 352, 354, 544, 546, 596, 609, 633, 670, 671, 678, 727.
talón(m) de aguja(f) 562.
talón(m) de apoyo(m) 250, 256.
talón(m) de la aguja(f) 568.
talón(m) de la hoja(f) 242.
talonario(m) de cheques(m) 379.
taloneador(m) 606.
talud(m) 451, 733.
talud(m) continental 22, 29.
talud(m) de aguas(f) abajo 748.
talud(m) de aguas(f) contenidas 748.
tam-tam(m) 552.
tambor(m) 167, 231, 258, 259, 432, 484, 552, 702, 711, 714, 797.
**tambor(m) de tirantes(m) 553.**
tambor(m) principal 572.
**tambor(m) rotativo 714.**
**tambor(m), freno(m) 432.**
**tambores(m) 552.**
tamboril(m) 553.
tamiz(m) 245.
tamiz(m) vibratorio para lodos(m) 737.
tampón(m) 581.
TANQUE(M) 805.
tanque(m) 216, 399, 689, 742, 743, 780.
tanque(m) auxiliar 441.
tanque(m) calentador de agua(f) 772.
tanque(m) de acetileno(m) 306.
tanque(m) de agua(f) 465.
tanque(m) de agua(f) de rociado(m) 759, 766.
tanque(m) de aire(m) comprimido 627, 777.
tanque(m) de almacenamiento(m) 744, 772.
tanque(m) de expansión(f) 208, 772.
tanque(m) de gas(m) propano(m) 449.
tanque(m) de hidrógeno(m) liquido 509.
tanque(m) de keroseno(m) 509.
tanque(m) de la gasolina(f) 442.
tanque(m) de oxígeno(m) 306.
tanque(m) de oxígeno(m) liquido 509.
tanque(m) de refrigeración(f) 212.
tanque(m) de regulación(f) de presión(f) 740.
**tanque(m) de revelado(m) 398.**
tanque(m) de seguridad(f) 761.
**tanque(m) de techo(m) fijo 741.**
**tanque(m) de techo(m) pontón 741.**
tanque(m) del combustible(m) 272, 440.
tanque(m) del nitrógeno(m) 717.
tanque(m) del reactor(m) 763.
tanque(m) moderador 761.
tanteador(m) 613.
tapa(f) 213, 247, 248, 251, 252, 256, 258, 260, 289, 290, 309, 354, 383, 386, 389, 398, 438, 532, 542, 543, 585, 590, 705, 712, 719, 765.
tapa(f) de la batería(f) 439.
tapa(f) de la cisterna(f) 293.
tapa(f) de medida(f) 250.
tapa(f) del filtro(m) 730.
tapa(f) del objetivo(m) 392.
tapa(f) del retrete(m) 293.
tapa(f) del tanque(m) 440.
tapa(f) del tanque(m) de gasolina(f) 427.
tapa(f) del tanque(m) de la gasolina(f) 444.
tapa(f) flotante 741.
tapa(f) superior 543.
tapa(m) guardapolvo 404.
tapacubos(m) 427.
tapete(m) 675.
tapón(m) 293, 301.
tapón(m) de registro(m) 215, 216.
tapón(m) de vaciado(m) 434.
tapón(m) del sifón(m) 296.
tapón(m) hembra(f) 301.
tapón(m) hermético 689.
tapón(m) macho(m) 301.
tarima(f) 787.
**tarima(f) con alas(f) 787.**
**tarima(f) de caja(f) 787.**
tarima(f) de plataforma(f) doble 787.
tarima(f) de plataforma(f) sencilla 787.
**tarima(f), montacargas(m) hidraúlico 788.**
tarjeta(f) de ruta(f) 471.
**tarjetero(m) 379.**
tarjetero(m) 379.
tarlatana(m) 582.
tarola(f) 557.
tarrito(m) para pincel(m) 592.
tarso(m) 78, 80, 103, 108, 122.
**tatami(m) 668.**
Tauro 11.
Tauro, el Toro (20 de abril) 820.
taza(f) 238, 293, 688.
tazas(f) para medir 244.
TEATRO(M) 188.
techo(m) 82, 171, 205, 427, 470, 616, 617.
techo(m) acústico 189.
techo(m) corredizo 427.
techo(m) de vidiro(m) 462.
techo(m) de vidrio 195.
techo(m) de vidrio(m) 190.
**techo(m) fijo, tanque(m) 741.**
**techo(m) ponton, tanque(m) 741.**
**techo(m), armadura(f) del 199.**
TECHOS(M) 182.
tecla(f) 536, 540, 541, 543.
tecla(f) correctora 569.
tecla(f) de aceptación(f) 530.
tecla(f) de adición(f) 523.
tecla(f) de arrastre(m) del papel(m) 523.
tecla(f) de cambio(m) de signo(m) 523.
tecla(f) de centrado(m) 524.
tecla(f) de corrección(f) 530.
tecla(f) de división(f) 523.
tecla(f) de doble cero(m) 523.
tecla(f) de entrada(f) 530.
tecla(f) de función(f) 530.
tecla(f) de igualdad(f) 523.
tecla(f) de iniciación(m) 421.
tecla(f) de mando(m) 530.
tecla(f) de más/igual 523.
tecla(f) de mayúsculas(f) 524, 530.
tecla(f) de multiplicación(f) 523.
tecla(f) de número(m) 523.
tecla(f) de pedal(m) 542.
tecla(f) de porcentaje(m) 523.
tecla(f) de raíz(f) cuadrada 523.
tecla(f) de regreso(m) del carro(m) 525.
tecla(f) de reinicialización(f) 421.
tecla(f) de repetición(f) 405.
tecla(f) de sangrado(m) 524.
tecla(f) de seguro(m) para las mayúsculas(f) 524.
tecla(f) de servicio(m) 530.
tecla(f) de substracción(f) 523.
tecla(f) de supresión(f) 530.
tecla(f) de tabulación(f) 530.
tecla(f) de utilización(f) múltiple 523.
tecla(f) decimal 523.
tecla(f) para limpiar la pantalla(f) 523.
tecla(f) para limpiar la pantalla(f) y de acceso 523.
tecla(f) seguro(m) de mayúsculas(f) 530.
**teclado(m) 530.**
teclado(m) 420, 422, 526, 527, 540, 555, 683.
teclado(m) alfanumérico 422, 530.
teclado(m) de funciones(f) 709.
teclado(m) de los bajos(m) 536.
teclado(m) del gran órgano(m) 542.
teclado(m) del órgano(m) de expresión(f) 542.
teclado(m) del órgano(m) positivo 542.
teclado(m) numérico 422, 530, 709.
teclado(m) triple 536.
TECLADO(M), INSTRUMENTOS(M) 540.
teclados(m) manuales 542.
teclas(f) 422.
teclas(f) conmutadoras de puntos(m) 569.
teclas(f) de control(m) 421.
teclas(f) de función(f) 421, 422.
teclas(f) de números(m) 421.
teclas(f) de operación(f) 422.
teclas(f) de selección(f) 569.
teclas(f) direccionales 530.
**técnicas principales 588.**
técnico(m) de control(m) de cámaras(f) 412.
técnico(m) de control(m) de la cámara(f) 415.
técnico(m) de luces(f) 412.
técnico(m) de sonido(m) 412, 415.
tee(m) 677.
tegumento(m) de la semilla(f) 63.
teja(f) 170, 286, 511.
teja(f) de asfalto(m) 286.
tejado(m) 197, 205.
tejado(m) en diente(m) de sierra(f) 182.
TEJIDO(M) 574.
tejido(m) adiposo 129, 136.
tejido(m) conjuntivo 137.
TEJIDO(M) DE PUNTO(M) 567.
tejido(m) subcutáneo 137.
TEJIDOS(M) 576.
**tejidos(m) 566.**
**tejidos(m), diagramas(m) de 576.**
tela(f) 565, 634.
tela(f) bordada 571.
tela(f) impermeable 375.
TELAR(M) 572.
**telar(m) de cuatro marcos(m) 572.**
**telar(m) de tapicería(f) 574.**
TELAS(F), CUIDADO(M) 829.
**telecomunicaciones(f) por red(f) telefónica 417.**
TELECOMUNICACIONES(F) POR SATÉLITE(M) 417.
TELECOMUNICACIONES(F), SATÉLITES(M) 418.
teleconvertidor(m) 392.
**teléfono(m) 420.**
teléfono(m) 413, 415, 417, 822.

Los términos en **negrita** corresponden a una ilustración; los que aparecen en MAYÚSCULAS indican un título.

teléfono(m) celular 417.
teléfono(m) celular portátil 422.
teléfono(m) de teclado(m) 422.
teléfono(m) para ejecutivo(m) 422.
**teléfono(m) público 422.**
teléfono(m) sin cable(m) 422.
TELÉFONO(M), COMUNICACIONES(F) 420, 422.
**teléfonos(m) 422.**
telémetro(m) 394.
teleobjetivo(m) 392.
teleporte(m) 417.
**telescopio(m) 14.**
telescopio(m) 14, 42, 713.
TELESCOPIO(M) ESPACIAL HUBBLE 16.
TELESCOPIO(M) REFLECTOR 720.
**telescopio(m) reflector, corte(m) transversal 720.**
TELESCOPIO(M) REFRACTOR 721.
**telescopio(m) refractor, corte(m) transversal 721.**
TELEVISIÓN(F) 410, 412, 414.
televisión(f) 401.
**televisor(m) 410.**
**télex(m) 421.**
télex(m) 417.
telón(m) de boca(f) 188, 189.
telón(m) de fondo(m) 188.
telón(m) metálico 188.
telson(m) 91.
temperatura(f) 210.
temperatura(f) ambiente 38.
temperatura(f) del punto(m) de rocío(m) 38.
temperatura(f) deseada 213.
temperatura(f) real 213, 705.
TEMPERATURA(F), MEDICIÓN(F) 705.
**temperatura(f),medición(f) 41.**
tempestad(f) 38.
templador(m) 578.
templazo(m) 573.
TEMPLO(M) GRIEGO 168.
**templo(m) griego, plano(m) 169.**
temporal(m) 122.
tenacilla(f) 78.
tenacillas(f) 246.
tenacillas(f) para caracoles(m) 246.
tenacillas(f) para espagueti(m) 246.
tenaza(f) 179.
tenazas(f) 205.
tendencia(f) barométrica 38.
tendón(m) 107.
**tenedor(m) 240.**
tenedor(m) 688.
tenedor(m) de mesa(f) 240.
tenedor(m) de trinchar 242.
tenedor(m) para ensalada(f) 240.
tenedor(m) para fondue(f) 240.
tenedor(m) para ostras(f) 240.
tenedor(m) para pescado(m) 240.
tenedor(m) para postre(m) 240.
**tenedores(m), tipos(m) de 240.**
TENIS(M) 614.
**tenis(m), pelota(f) de 615.**
**tenista(m/f) 615.**
**tensiómetro(m) 710.**
tensor(m) 630, 660, 661, 669, 671.
tensor(m) de alambre(m) 774.
tensor(m) de la fascia lata(f) 120.
tensor(m) de las cuerdas(f) 553.
tensores(m) pectorales 665.
tentáculo(m) ocular 83.
tentáculo(m) táctil 83.
**teodolito(m) 713.**
teodolito(m) 41.
tercelete(m) 177.
tercer hueso(m) metacarpiano 112.
tercer jugador(m) 620.
tercer pistón(m) móvil 551.
tercer(m) octante 7.
tercera base(f) 597.
tercera etapa(f) 509.
tercera(f) 105, 537, 667.
tercio(m) diestro 818.
tercio(m) siniestro 818.
terminación(f) nerviosa 136.
**terminal(m) 421.**
terminal(m) 309, 312, 740, 757.
terminal(m) de carga(f) 490.
**terminal(m) de comunicaciones(f) 422.**
terminal(m) de entrada(f) 310.
terminal(m) de granos(m) 490.
**terminal(m) de pasajeros(m) 504.**
terminal(m) de pasajeros(m) 491, 503.
terminal(m) de petróleo(m) 491.
terminal(m) de tierra(f) 309.
terminal(m) del control(m) a larga distancia(f) 391.
terminal(m) radial de pasajeros(m) 503.
**términos familiares 62, 63, 64, 65.**
**términos técnicos 62, 63, 64, 65.**
**termómetro(m) 705.**
termómetro(m) 627, 635, 741.
**termómetro(m) bimetálico 705.**
**termómetro(m) clínico 705.**
termómetro(m) máximo 41.
termómetro(m) mínimo 41.
termómetro(m) para carne(f) 244.
termómetro(m) para carnes(f) 253.
**termómetro(m), barómetro(m) 710.**
termos(m) 690.
termos(m) con llave(f) de servicio(m) 690.
termosfera(f) 19.
**termostato(m) 213.**
termostato(m) 210, 214, 252, 254, 297.
**termostato(m) ambiental 705.**
termostato(m) de seguridad(f) 259.
termostato(m) del ventilador(m) 438.
ternero(m) 151.
terraja(f) 299.
terraplén(m) 179, 450.
terraplén(m) de los helióstatos(m) 770, 771.
**terraplén(m), dique(m) 748.**
terraza(f) 193, 497.
TERREMOTO(M) 23.
**terreno(m) de juego(m) 599, 626.**
terreno(m) de juego(m) 599.
terreno(m) de recubrimiento 733.
testículo(m) 127.
testuz(m) 100.
tetera(f) 238.
texto(m) 524.
tibia(f) 78, 103, 112, 122.
tibia(m) 80.
tibial(m) anterior 120.
**tiempo(m), carta(f) 38.**
TIEMPO(M), MEDICIÓN(F) 706.
**tienda(f) de campaña(f) clásica 686.**
**tienda(f) de campaña(f) tamaño(m) familiar 685.**
tienda(f) interior 685, 686.
tienda(f) libre de impuestos(m) 505.
**tienda(f) para dos 685.**
tienda(f) rectangular 686.
tienda(f) tipo(m) domo(m) 686.
tienda(f) tipo(m) iglú(m) 686.
tienda(f) tipo(m) vagón(m) 686.
tienda(f) unipersonal 686.
**tiendas(f), tipos(m) de 686.**
tiento(m) 591.
Tierra(f) 4, 8.
tierra(f) apisonada 450.
**tierra(f), equipo(m) 506.**
TIERRA(F), ESTRUCTURA(F) 22.
**tierra(f), signos(m) 820.**
tijeras(f) 365, 688, 725.
**tijeras(f) con doble filo(m) para entresacar 369.**
**tijeras(f) con filo(m) simple para entresacar 369.**
**tijeras(f) de modista(f) 564.**
tijeras(f) de pedicura(f) 365.
**tijeras(f) de peluquero(m) 369.**
tijeras(f) de podar 269.
tijeras(f) de punta(f) roma 365.
tijeras(f) para aves(f) 246.
tijeras(f) para cutícula(f) 365.
tijeras(f) para podar setos(m) 269.
tijeras(f) para rematar 564.
tilde(f) 832.
**timbal(m) 553.**
timbales(m) 557.
timbre(m) 384.
**timón(m) 632.**
timón(m) 492, 496, 499, 511, 742, 812, 814.
timón(m) de buceo(m) 807.
timón(m) de control(m) 500.
timón(m) de dirección(f) 639.
timón(m) de inmersión(f) 806.
timón(m) de profundidad(f) 499, 639.
timón(m) superior 806.
tímpano(m) 84, 97, 166, 168, 175, 581.
tímpano(m), membrana(f) del 139.
tinta(f) 389, 581.
tinta(f) china 588.
tipi(m) 165.
tipo(m) cogulla(f) 342.
tipo(m) de combustible(m) 453.
**tipo(m) Michigan 645.**
**tipos(m) de bolsillo(m) 339.**
**tipos(m) de calzado(m) 354, 355.**
**tipos(m) de carrocerías(f) 425.**
**tipos(m) de eclipses(m) 8.**
**tipos(m) de esquís(m) 633.**
**tipos(m) de falda(f) 334.**
TIPOS(M) DE MANDÍBULAS(F) 98.
**tipos(m) de manga(f) 339, 340.**
TIPOS(M) DE MOTORES(M) 436.
**tipos(m) de pliegue(m) 335.**
**tipos(m) de puentes(m) de arco(m) 455.**
**tipos(m) de puentes(m) de viga(f) 454.**
**tipos(m) de punto(m) 567.**
**tipos(m) de puntos(m) 571.**
**tipos(m) de tiendas(f) 686.**
**tipos(m) de vestido(m) 332.**
tira(f) de tela(f) 571.
tira(f) para rasgar la envoltura(f) 384.
tirador(m) 397.
tirador(m) de espada(f) 667.
tirador(m) de florete(m) 667.
tirador(m) de la puerta(f) 429.
tirador(m) de sable(m) 667.
tirahilos(m) 561.
tirante(m) 198, 199, 302, 346, 456, 541.
tirante(m) ajustable 350.
tirante(m) con botones(m) 351.
tirante(m) de fijación(f) 637.
tirante(m) de la botavara(f) 631.
tirante(m) de la cabeza(f) 653.
tirante(m) de la rodillera(f) 653.
tirante(m) del pescante(m) 786.
**tirantes(m) 323.**
tirantes(m) 456.
**tirantes(m) en abanico(m) 456.**
**tirantes(m) en forma(f) de arpa(f) 456.**
**tirantes(m), puentes(m) 456.**
**tirantes(m), tambor(m) 553.**
tirilla(f) elástica 325, 326, 350.
tirita(f) Velcro® 349.
TIRO(M) AL ARCO(M) 684.
tiro(m) de aire(m) caliente 204.
tiro(m) vertical 736.
Titán 5.
tiza(f) 675.
**toalla(f) con capuchón(m) 349.**
toallero(m) 292.
tobillera(f) 344.
tobillo(m) 116, 118.
toca(f) 329.
**tocacintas(m), grabadora(f) 403.**
**tocadiscos(m) 404.**
tocadiscos(m) 400, 407.
tocadiscos(m) compacto 400.
tocador(m) 226.
**tocón(m) 59.**
toe(m) 678.
**toga(f) 315, 317.**
toldo(m) de ventana(f) 685.
toldo(m) delantero 685.
tolva(f) 158, 162.
toma(f) 265, 449.
toma(f) a tierra(f) 400.
toma(f) de agua(f) potable 186.
toma(f) de aire(m) 298, 453.
toma(f) de aire(m) del motor(m) 813.
toma(f) de aire(m) del tejado(m) 215.
toma(f) de aire(m) para el ventilador(m) de sustentación(f) 493.
toma(f) de aire(m) principal 215.
toma(f) de fuerza(f) 147.
toma(f) de gases(m) de combustión(f) 438.
toma(f) de llenado(m) 493.
toma(f) de vapor(m) a alta presión(f) 758.
toma(f) para auriculares(m) 408.
toma(f) principal de llenado(m) 741.
toma(f) secundaria 741.
tomarrizos(m) 480.
tomate(m) 69.
tómbolo(m) 30.
tomillo(m) 74.
topacio(m) 363.
tope(m) 230, 369, 375, 464, 478, 566, 632, 730.
tope(m) amortiguador 260.
tope(m) de ingletes(m) 285.
tope(m) de la escalera(f) 781.
tope(m) de la puerta(f) 254, 471.
tope(m) de profundidad(f) 283.
tope(m) del dique(m) 748, 749, 752.
tope(m) fijo 711.
tope(m) móvil 711.
tórax(m) 78, 79, 80, 116, 118.
tormenta(f) 39.
tormenta(f) de polvo(m) 39.
tormenta(f) eléctrica 39.
tormenta(f) tropical 39.
torneta(f) 584.
**tornillo(m) 276.**
tornillo(m) 279, 304, 544, 586.
tornillo(m) de ajuste(m) 234, 278, 282, 306, 311, 539, 710.
tornillo(m) de ajuste(m) de la exposición(f) 391.
tornillo(m) de ajuste(m) del condensador(m) 718.
tornillo(m) de anclaje(m) 656.
tornillo(m) de cabeza(f) achaflanada 276.
tornillo(m) de cabeza(f) plana 276.
tornillo(m) de cabeza(f) redonda 276.
tornillo(m) de caja(f) cuadrada (Robertson) 276.
tornillo(m) de cruz(f) (Phillips) 276.
tornillo(m) de fijación(f) 393.
tornillo(m) de fijación(f) horizontal 713.
tornillo(m) de la aguja(f) 562.
tornillo(m) de presión(f) 581, 583.
tornillo(m) de rebobinado(m) de la película(f) 391.
tornillo(m) de regulación(f) para carga(f) completa 712.
tornillo(m) de regulación(f) para carga(f) ligera 712.
tornillo(m) de soporte(m) inferior 40.
tornillo(m) de soporte(m) superior 40.
tornillo(m) de sujeción(f) 284.
tornillo(m) de un solo sentido(m) 276.
tornillo(m) elevador 277.
tornillo(m) guía 281.
tornillo(m) micrométrico 484, 713.
tornillo(m) nivelador 40, 709, 713.
tornillo(m) sinfín 575.
torniquete(m) de entrada(f) 474.
torniquete(m) de salida(f) 474.
**torno(m) 584.**
**torno(m) de banco(m) 282.**
torno(m) de sondeo(m) 737.
toronja(f) 65.
torpedo(m) 807.
torre(f) 176, 486, 696, 770, 771, 773, 774, 786.
**torre(f) de alta tensión(f) 756.**
torre(f) de control(m) 502, 810.
torre(f) de escape(m) 509.
torre(f) de extracción(f) 735.
torre(f) de oficinas(f) 190.
**torre(f) de perforación(f) 737.**
torre(f) de perforación(f) 737, 738, 740.
**torre(f) de saltos(m) 624.**
torre(f) de saltos(m) 624.
torre(f) de señales(f) 464.
torre(f) del homenaje(m) 181.
torre(f) del locutor(m) 407.
torre(f) del productor(m) 407.
torre(f) esquinera 180.
torre(f) flanqueante 180.
torre(f) fraccionadora 744.
**torre(f), grúa(f) 786.**
torrecilla(f) de lavado(m) 257.
torrente(m) de montaña(f) 27.
torreta(f) 180, 809.
torreta(f) de mando(m) 807.
torreta(f) giratoria 805.
**tortuga(f) 97.**
**tostador(m) 252.**
traba(f) 652, 681.
trabilla 323.
trabilla(f) 336, 370, 596, 641, 649.
trabilla(f) de suspensión(f) 326.
trabilla(f) para el pie(m) 664.
tracería(f) 175.
tracto(m) olfatorio 142.
TRACTOR(M) 147.
tractor(m) 742.
tractor(m) de avance(m) 531.
tractor(m) de orugas(f) 783.
tractor(m) de ruedas(f) 782.
tractor(m) nivelador 733.
tractor(m) remolcador 507.
tractor(m) remolque(m) 506.
tragadero(m) 24.
tragaluz(m) 194, 197.
TRAGAPERRAS(M) 702.
trago(m) 112, 139.
**traje(m) 331.**
traje(m) de baño(m) 353.
**traje(m) de entrenamiento(m) 352.**
traje(m) de esqui 640.

Los términos en **negrita** corresponden a una ilustración; los que aparecen en MAYÚSCULAS indican un título.

traje(m) de esquí(m) 642.
**traje(m) de invierno(m) con capuchón(m) 351.**
traje(m) de malla(f) 353.
traje(m) de una sola pieza(f) 643.
traje(m) de vuelo 635.
TRAJE(M) ESPACIAL 512.
traje(m) isotérmico 627.
traje(m) pantalón(m) 336, 351.
trama(f) 572, 574.
tramo(m) 201.
tramo(m) central 456.
tramo(m) de elevación(f) 457.
tramo(m) giratorio 457.
tramo(m) lateral 456.
tramo(m) suspendido 454.
trampa(f) de agua(f) 676.
trampa(f) de arena(f) 676.
trampilla(f) de freno(m) aerodinámico 638.
**transbordador espacial en órbita 510.**
TRANSBORDADOR(M) 494.
transbordador(m) 491, 505.
TRANSBORDADOR(M) ESPACIAL 510.
**transbordador(m) espacial en posición(f) de lanzamiento(m) 510.**
**transcripción(f) de ondas(f) sísmicas 714.**
transductor(m) 485.
transferencia(f) de calor(m) al agua(f) 766.
transformación(f) del trabajo(m) mecánico en electricidad(f) 755.
transformador(m) 235, 747, 757, 758, 771.
transformador(m) de ignición(f) 209.
transformador(m) principal 458.
tránsito(m) lento 452.
transmisión(f) 258.
**transmisión(f) de cadena(f) 448.**
**transmisión(f) de electricidad(f) 757.**
transmisión(f) de electricidad(f) 767.
transmisión(f) de electricidad(f) de alto voltaje(m) 755.
transmisión(f) de energía(f) al generador(m) de voltaje(m) 755.
transmisión(f) de la corriente(f) eléctrica 714.
transmisión(f) de ondas(f) Hertzianas 416.
transmisión(f) del movimiento(m) hacia el rotor(m) 755.
transmisión(f) visual 717.
transmisor(m) 420.
transmisor(m) de microondas(f) 415.
transpiración(f) 35.
transportador(m) 713.
transportador(m) de equipaje(m) 507.
transporte(m) marítimo 735.
transporte(m) terrestre 491.
trapecio(m) 120, 121, 637.
tráquea(f) 130.
trasbordador(m) 507.
trasdós(m) 174.
traslape(m) de la pretina(f) 323.
traste(m) 535, 547.
trastes(m) 546.
tratamiento(m) químico 745.
traversa(f) 178.
travesaño(f) superior 470.
travesaño(m) 198, 203, 219, 223, 302, 535, 572, 574, 578, 599, 727, 728, 756, 757, 773.
travesaño(m) de apoyo(m) 774.
travesaño(m) delantero 645.
travesaño(m) frontal 572.
travesaño(m) frontal interior 572.
travesaño(m) inferior 470.
travesaño(m) intermedio del batán(m) 572.
travesaño(m) superior de la vidriera(f) 203.
travesaño(m) superior del batán(m) 573.
travesaño(m) trasero 645.
traviesa(f) 466.
**trébol(m) 452.**
trébol(m) 450, 695.
trebolado(m) 174.
TREN(M) DE ALTA VELOCIDAD(F) 458.
tren(m) de aterrizaje(m) delantero 498, 813.
tren(m) de aterrizaje(m) principal 499, 812.
tren(m) de pasajeros(m) 462.
**tren(m) subterráneo 476.**
tren(m) subterráneo 474.
tren(m) suburbano 464.
**trenca(f) 320.**
**trepadora(f) 358.**
Triángulo 11.
Triángulo Austral 13.
**triángulo(m) 554.**
triángulo(m) 556, 674.
tribuna(f) de los jueces(m) 651.
tribuna(f) para el público(m) 651.
**tribunas(f) y pista(f) 651.**
tríceps(m) braquial 121.
triclinio(m) 171.
tricornio(m) 318.
**tricotadoras(f) 568.**
trifoliada 56.
trifolio(m) 175.
triglifo(m) 167.
trigo(m) 152.
trigo(m) sarraceno 152.
**trilladora(f), cosechadora(f) 160.**
**trinchera(f) 319.**
trinchera(f) 178.
trineo(m) 643.
**trineo(m) motorizado 445.**
trino(m) 538.
trinquete(m) 276, 481, 706, 707.
trio(m) 558.
trío(m) 695.
tripa(f) 384.
triple 646.
triple barra(f) 646.
triple de barras(f) 647.
triple plano(m) vertical 498.
**trípode(m) 393.**
trípode(m) 397, 415, 539, 552, 721.
trípode(m) jirafa(f) para el micrófono 414.
Tritón 5.
triturador(m) de ajos(m) 243.
triturador(m) de basura(f) 296.
trocánter(m) 78, 80.
trocánter(m) mayor 123.
troje(m) 149.
trole(m) 457.
**Trombe, pared(f) 772.**
trombón(m) 550.
trombones(m) 556.
trompa(f) 84.
trompa(f) de Eustaquio 141.
trompa(f) uterina, ampolla(f) de la 129.
**trompeta(f) 550.**
trompeta(f) 451, 550.
trompetas(f) 556.
tronco(m) 59, 61, 117, 119, 288.
tronco(m) celiaco 124, 132.
**tronco(m), corte(m) de un 288.**
**tronco(m), corte(m) transversal de un 59.**
tronera(f) 181.
tropical lluvioso 45.
trópico(m) de Cáncer 3, 47.
trópico(m) de Capricornio 3, 47.
troposfera(f) 19.
trufa(f) 55.
tuba(f) 551, 557.
**tubérculos(m) 71.**
tubería(f) 740.
tubería(f) ascendente 208.
tubería(f) de agua(f) caliente 215, 298.
tubería(f) de agua(f) fría 215, 293, 298.
tubería(f) de carga(f) 746, 747.
tubería(f) de conducción(f) de carburante(m) 509.
tubería(f) de escape(m) del vapor(m) 759.
tubería(f) de refrigeración 213.
tubería(f) de retorno(m) 208.
tubería(f) del caudal(m) del pozo(m) 738.
tubería(f) descendente 208.
tubería(f) para la llama(f) piloto(m) 297.
tubería(f) principal del vapor(m) 759.
tubito(m) de decoración(f) 245.
tubo ajustable(m) 728.
tubo de escape(m) 232.
tubo(m) 208, 232, 297, 369, 397, 543, 550, 588, 627, 710, 719, 800, 803, 804.
tubo(m) A 300.
tubo(m) alimentador 251.
tubo(m) articulado 431.
tubo(m) B 300.
tubo(m) binocular 718.
tubo(m) capilar 705.
tubo(m) de aire(m) 209, 370, 627, 777.
tubo(m) de ajuste(m) 659, 661.
tubo(m) de alimentación(f) 160.
tubo(m) de aspiración(f) 747, 753.
tubo(m) de circulación(f) 768.
tubo(m) de cola(f) 439.
tubo(m) de cristal(m) 705.
tubo(m) de desagüe(m) 293, 297.
tubo(m) de descarga(f) 161, 742.
tubo(m) de disparo(m) 807.
tubo(m) de drenaje(m) 199, 399.
tubo(m) de empuje(m) 389.
tubo(m) de ensilaje(m) 162.
tubo(m) de entrada(f) 251.
tubo(m) de escape(m) 147, 232, 438, 439, 440, 443, 444, 508, 783, 784, 812.
tubo(m) de extensión(f) 260.
tubo(m) de flash(m) 393.
tubo(m) de la helice(f) 492.
**tubo(m) de lengüeta(f) 542.**
tubo(m) de llenado(m) 293.
**tubo(m) de pantalla(f) 410.**
tubo(m) de par(m) térmico 297.
tubo(m) de perforación(f) 737.
tubo(m) de salida(f) 216.
tubo(m) de subida(f) del agua(f) 247.
tubo(m) de suministro(m) de agua(f) 215, 296.
tubo(m) de suministro(m) de agua(f) caliente 298.
tubo(m) de suministro(m) de gas(m) 297.
tubo(m) de suministro(m) de petróleo(m) 209.
tubo(m) de toma(f) de agua(f) 215.
tubo(m) de ventilación(f) 162.
tubo(m) del asiento(m) 446.
tubo(m) del borde(m) de ataque(m) 637.
tubo(m) del manillar(m) 447.
tubo(m) del pistón(m) 550.
tubo(m) drenaje(m)de tormenta(f) 186.
tubo(m) en Y 726.
tubo(m) expulsor de espuma(f) 743.
tubo(m) flexible 726.
**tubo(m) fluorescente 232.**
tubo(m) fluorescente 233.
tubo(m) inferior del cuadro(m) 447.
tubo(m) medidor 40.
tubo(m) para el grano(m) 158.
tubo(m) portaocular 718.
tubo(m) principal 720, 721.
tubo(m) principal de observación(f) 718.
tubo(m) rígido 260.
tubos(m) difusores 501.
Tucán 13.
Tudor 174.
tuerca(f) 278, 279, 290, 300, 466.
tuerca(f) cerrada 279.
tuerca(f) de ajuste(f) 296.
tuerca(f) de ajuste(m) 296, 300.
tuerca(f) de bloqueo(m) 711.
tuerca(f) de fijación(f) 40.
tuerca(f) de la empaquetadura(f) 294.
tuerca(f) de mariposa(f) 279.
tuerca(f) de seguridad(f) 40.
tuerca(f) de sujeción(f) 670.
tuerca(f) plana de seguridad(f) 296.
tumbona(f) 223.
tundra(f) 45.
túnel(m) 474.
túnel(m) de comunicación(f) 510.
túnel(m) de embarque(m) 503.
túnica(f) 333, 337, 791.
**túnica(f) de manga(f) larga 316.**
turbante(m) 329.
turbina(f) 753, 758.
turbina(f) de transmisión(f) 438.
**turbina(f) de viento(m) de eje(m) horizontal 774.**
**turbina(f) de viento(m) de eje(m) vertical 774.**
turbina(f) del compresor(m) 438.
**turbina(f) Francis 754.**
**turbina(f) Kaplan 754.**
**turbina(f) Pelton 754.**
turbinas(f) 747.
turbinas(f) de potencia(f) 501.
TURBOREACTOR(M) 501.
turborreactor(m) 499, 812.
turión(m) 72.
turismo(m) de dos puertas(f) 425.
turismo(m) de tres puertas(f) 425.
turmalina(f) 363.
turquesa(f) 363.

## U

uapití(m) 105.
ubicación(f) de la estatua(f) 169.
uke (defensor(m)) 668.
última(f) recta(f) 651.
umbela(f) 60.
umbo(m) 95.
umbral(m) 202.
un par(m) 695.
una vía(f) 824, 825.
uña(f) 80, 97, 104, 106, 107, 108, 112, 137, 275, 364, 483.
**uña(f) contraída 107.**
**uña(f) extendida 107.**
uñas(f) 515.
unidad de visualización de imagen(f) \ sonido 413.
unidad(f) cruciforme 498.
unidad(f) de aire(m) 506.
unidad(f) de aire(m) acondicionado 415.
unidad(f) de cartuchos(m) 527.
unidad(f) de casetes(f) 526.
unidad(f) de compresión(f) de aire(m) 458.
unidad(f) de control(m) de cámaras(f) 412.
unidad(f) de control(m) de la cámara(f) 415.
unidad(f) de control(m) de la temperatura(f) del cuerpo(m) 512.
unidad(f) de destilación(f) al vacío(m) 744.
unidad(f) de disco(m) compacto 527.
unidad(f) de disco(m) óptico 527.
unidad(f) de discos(m) 555.
unidad(f) de diskettes(m) 526.
unidad(f) de extracción(f) de solventes(m) 744.
unidad(f) de grabación(f) 40.
unidad(f) de impresión(f) 524.
unidad(f) de instrumentos(m) 509.
unidad(f) de la cabeza(f) impresora 531.
unidad(f) de medición(f) de volumen(m) 407.
**unidad(f) de pesas(f) 663.**
unidad(f) de refrigeración(f) 441.
unidad(f) del disco(m) duro 526, 528.
unidad(f) del disco(m) flexible 528.
unidad(f) del radar(m) 813.
**unidad(f) exterior 212.**
unidad(f) exterior condensadora 212.
**unidad(f) generadora 753.**
**unidad(f) interior 213.**
UNIDAD(F) MÓBIL 415.
unidad(f) móvil 416.
unidad(f) para maniobras(f) en el espacio(m) 512.
**unión(f) 300.**
unión(f) 301, 389, 830.
unión(f) de caña(f) y brazos(m) 483.
unión(f) periférica 750.
unísono(m) 537.
uranio(m) en fisión(f) 766.
Urano 5.
**urdidor(m) 575.**
urdimbre(f) 573, 574.
uréter(m) 132.
uretra(f) 127, 128, 129, 132.
uretra(f), cuerpo(m) esponjoso de la 127.
URINARIO, APARATO(M) 132.
urna(f) 709.
urópodo(m) 91.
use lejía(f) de cloro(m) siguiendo las indicaciones(f) 829.
use plancha(f) caliente 829.
use plancha(f) muy caliente 829.
use plancha(f) tibia 829.
USO(M) COMÚN, SÍMBOLOS(M) 822.
**utensilios(m) de cocina(f) 688.**
**utensilios(m) diversos 246.**
**utensilios(m) para abrir y descorchar 244.**
**utensilios(m) para hornear 245.**
**utensilios(m) para medir 244.**
útero(m) 128, 129.
UVA(F) 61.
**uva(f) 62.**
uva(f) 61, 62.
**uvas(f), racimo(m) de 61.**
úvula(f) 141, 142.

## V

vaca(f) 151.
vacío(m) barométrico 710.
vacuola(f) 115.
vagina(f) 128, 129.
VAGÓN(M) 470.
vagón(m) 162.
vagón(m) cerrado 472.
**vagón(m) cisterna(f) 743.**
vagón(m) cisterna(f) 472.

Los términos en **negrita** corresponden a una ilustración; los que aparecen en MAYÚSCULAS indican un título.

vagón(m) con cubierta(f) alquitranada 472.
vagón(m) de carga(f) 464.
vagón(m) de mercancías(f) 473.
**vagón(m) de pasajeros(m) 460, 477.**
vagón(m) de pasajeros(m) 458, 476.
vagón(m) frigorífico 472.
vagón(m) máquina(f) 476, 477.
vagón(m) para automóviles(m) 473.
vagón(m) para contenedores(m) 473.
vagón(m) para ganado(m) 472.
vagón(m) para madera(f) 472.
vagón(m) plano con retenedores(m) 473.
vagón(m) tolva(f) 472.
vagón(m) tolva(f) para minerales(m) 472.
VAGONES(M) DE CARGA(F) TIPOS(M) 472.
VAGONES(M) DE PASAJEROS(M) 460.
vaina(f) 56, 67.
vaina(f) de mielina(f) 135.
valla(f) 186, 656.
valla(f) de la carrera(f) de obstáculos(m) 656.
valla(f) de madera(f) 608.
valla(f) sobre muro(m) 647.
valla(f) sobre seto(m) 647.
valle(m) 27.
valva(f) 95.
**valva(f) izquierda 95.**
válvula(f) 447, 543, 634.
válvula(f) aórtica 125.
válvula(f) de aceleración(f) 735.
válvula(f) de acetileno(m) 306.
válvula(f) de admisión(f) 434, 436.
válvula(f) de agua(f) de rociado(m) 759.
válvula(f) de aire(m) 304, 590.
válvula(f) de aire(m) comprimido 627.
válvula(f) de ajuste(m) 304.
válvula(f) de control(m) 216, 689.
válvula(f) de desagüe(m) 297.
válvula(f) de entrada(f) 293.
válvula(f) de escape(m) 209, 435, 436, 438.
válvula(f) de exhalación(f) 730.
válvula(f) de freno(m) 306.
válvula(f) de inhalación(f) 730.
válvula(f) de la tubería(f) 740.
válvula(f) de liberación(f) de aire(m) 743.
válvula(f) de llenado(m) 741.
válvula(f) de oxígeno(m) 306.
válvula(f) de pare(m) de la turbina(f) 758.
válvula(f) de presión(f) 297.
válvula(f) de purga(f) 208.
válvula(f) de regulación(f) 208.
válvula(f) de seguridad(f) 248, 766.
válvula(f) de vaciado(m) 741.
válvula(f) del quemador(m) 635.
válvula(f) maestra 740.
válvula(f) mitral 125.
válvula(f) pulmonar 125.
válvula(f) tricúspide 125.
válvulas(f) de combustible(m) del motor(m) 500.
válvulas(f) de control(m) de combustible(m) 500.
vapor(m) a baja presión(f) 758.
vaporizador(m) 210, 256.
vaquería(f) 149.
vaqueros(m) 336.
vara(f) 544.
varal(m) de la cabeza(f) 653.
**variedades(f) de agujas(f) 58.**
**variedades(f) de arcos(m) 455.**
**variedades(f) de inflorescencias(f) 60.**
varilla(f) 346, 347, 375, 539, 567, 569, 573.
varilla(f) de acero(m) 554.
varilla(f) de batir 250.
varilla(f) de calada(f) 574.
varilla(f) de cambio(m) 467.
varilla(f) de contacto(m) 310.
varilla(f) de control(m) 760, 761, 762, 763.
varilla(f) de empuje(m) 467.
varilla(f) de lizos(m) 574.
varilla(f) de registro(m) 543.
varilla(f) de relleno(m) 307.
varilla(f) de tensión(f) 553.
varilla(f) del pedal(m) 540.
varilla(f) del péndulo(m) 539, 707.
varilla(f) rizadora 370.
varilla(f) telescópica de desenganche(m) 470.
varilla(f) tensora 574.
varillas(f) 543.
**varillas(f), tipos(m) de 250.**
variómetro(m) 635.
variómetro(m) eléctrico 639.
variómetro(m) mecánico 639.
**varios 831.**
Varolio, puente(m) de 134.
vaso(m) capilar 137.
vaso(m) corto 237.
vaso(m) largo 237.
vaso(m) sanguíneo 136.
vasos(m) sanguíneos 112.
vástago(m) 275, 276, 447, 563, 568, 674.
vástago(m) aislado 310.
vástago(m) de arrastre(m) 737.
vástago(m) de vidrio(m) 232.
vástago(m) del macillo(m) 541.
vasto(m) externo 120.
vasto(m) interno 120, 121.
VATÍMETRO(M) 712.
VAUBAN, FORTIFICACIÓN(F) 178.
vehículo(m) todo terreno(m) 425.
VEHÍCULOS(M) PESADOS 782, 784.
vejiga(f) 127, 128, 132.
vejiga(f) natatoria 89.
vejiga(f) urinaria 89.
VELA(F) 628, 630.
vela(f) 582, 631.
vela(f) Bermuda 482.
vela(f) cangreja 482.
vela(f) cuadrada 482.
vela(f) flameante 629.
vela(f) latina 482.
vela(f) mayor 628.
vela(f) mayor proel 481.
**velamen(m) 480.**
Velas 13.
**velas(f), disposiciones(f) de las 629.**
VELAS(F), TIPOS(M) 482.
**velero(m) 628.**
veleta(f) 41.
veleta(f) (grímpola) 628.
velo(m) 80, 670.
velo(m) del paladar(m) 142.
velocidad(f) de la película(f) 396.
velocidad(f) del viento(m) 38.
velocímetro(m) 431, 445, 664.
vena(f) axilar 126.
vena(f) basílica 126.
vena(f) cava inferior 124, 125, 126, 132.
vena(f) cava superior 124, 125, 126, 130.
vena(f) cefálica 126.
vena(f) femoral 126.
vena(f) hepática 124.
vena(f) iliaca o ilíaca(f) 124.
vena(f) ilíaca(f) común 132.
vena(f) mesentérica superior 126.
vena(f) porta 124, 126.
vena(f) pulmonar 126.
vena(f) pulmonar derecha 125.
vena(f) pulmonar izquierda 125.
vena(f) renal 126, 132.
vena(f) safena interna 126.
vena(f) subclavia 126.
vena(f) yugular externa 126.
vena(f) yugular interna 126.
**venas(f) y arterias(f), principales 126.**
venda(f) de gasa(f) 725.
venda(f) elástica 725.
venda(f) triangular 725.
vendaje(m) 648, 669.
veneno(m) 821.
venera(f) 93.
ventalla(f) 67.
ventalle(m) 792.
VENTANA(F) 203.
ventana(f) 194, 195, 253, 255, 399, 631.
ventana(f) basculante 203.
ventana(f) corrediza 203.
ventana(f) de acceso(m) 529.
ventana(f) de acordeón(m) 203.
ventana(f) de celosía(f) 203.
ventana(f) de dos hojas(f) 203.
ventana(f) de eyección(f) 796.
ventana(f) de guillotina(f) 203.
ventana(f) de la nariz(f) 141.
ventana(f) de la torre(f) 756.
ventana(f) de lectura(f) 403.
ventana(f) francesa 203.
ventana(f) giratoria 203.
ventana(f) panorámica 190.
ventana(f) protectora 410.
**ventana(f), tipos(m) de 203.**
ventana(f)-mosquitero(m) 685.
ventanal(m) 197.
VENTANAS(F), ACCESORIOS(M) PARA LAS 228, 230.
ventanilla(f) 427, 429, 477, 498.
ventanilla(f) de aterrizaje(m) 508.
ventanilla(f) de observación(f) 510.
ventanilla(f) de ventilación(f) del techo(m) 449.
ventanilla(f) panorámica 460.
ventanilla(f) trasera 427.
ventilación(f) 430, 772.
ventilador(m) 161, 162, 207, 209, 212, 259, 434, 438, 441, 469, 477, 501, 528.
ventilador(m) centrífugo 213.
ventilador(m) de aire(m) caliente 211.
ventilador(m) de cabina(f) 639.
ventilador(m) de césped(m) 266.
**ventilador(m) de techo(m) 214.**
ventilador(m) del condensador(m) 214.
ventilador(m) del evaporador(m) 214, 760.
ventilador(m) del motor(m) diésel 468.
ventilador(m) principal 734.
ventosa(f) 85.
ventrículo(m) derecho 124, 125.
ventrículo(m) izquierdo 124, 125.
venturi(m) 804.
Venus 4.
verano(m) 8.
**verduras(f) de hojas(f) 73.**
vereda(f) 676.
verga(f) 478.
**vértebra(f) lumbar 135.**
vértebras(f) caudales 103.
vértebras(f) cervicales 102.
vértebras(f) cervicales (7) 123.
vértebras(f) dorsales (12) 123.
vértebras(f) lumbares 103.
vértebras(f) lumbares (5) 123.
vértebras(f) sacras 103.
vértebras(f) torácicas 102.
vertedera(f) 156.
**vertedera(f), arado(m) 156.**
vertedor(m) 252.
vertical de barras(f) 646.
vertical de desviadores(m) 647.
vertical(m) de barras(f) 647.
vesícula(f) biliar 97, 131.
vesícula(f) pinocítica 115.
vesícula(f) seminal 127.
vestíbulo(m) 139, 170, 189, 190, 194, 461, 462, 504.
vestíbulo(m) de recibo(m) 172, 173.
vestido(m) abrigo 332.
vestido(m) antifuego e impermeable 777.
**vestido(m) con miriñaque(m) 318.**
**vestido(m) con polisón(m) 316.**
**vestido(m), tipos(m) de 332.**
VESTIDURAS(F) ANTIGUAS 315, 316, 318.
veta(f) 288.
Vía Láctea 11.
vía(f) 463, 474.
vía(f) de salida(f) 465.
vía(f) de tren(m) suburbano 464.
vía(f) de unión(f) 464.
VÍA(F) FÉRREA 466.
**vía(f) férrea 466.**
vía(f) férrea 184, 735.
vía(f) locomotriz 465.
vía(f) principal 464.
vía(f) subsidiaria 464.
**vía(f), cambiador(m) manual 467.**
**vía(f), carretilla(f) 476.**
viaducto(m) 454.
**vid(f), hoja(f) de la 61.**
**videograbadora(f) 411.**
videograbadora(f) 401, 526.
vidriado(m) 772.
vidriera(f) 486.
vidrio(m) 203.
vieira(f) 93.
**viento(m) 38.**
viento(m) 629, 685.
viento(m) contrario 629.
viento(m) de través 629.
viento(m) en popa(f) 629.
viento(m) en proa(f) 629.
viento(m) moderado 38.
viento(m) suave 38.
VIENTO(M), INSTRUMENTOS(M) 548, 550.
**viento(m), molino(m) 773.**
vientre(m) 101.
viga(f) 170, 188, 200.
viga(f) continua 454.
viga(f) maestra 198.
**viga(f), puente(m) 454.**
vigueta(f) del piso(m) 198, 199.
vigueta(f) del techo(m) 198.
vigueta(f) esquinera 198, 199.
viola(f) 545.
violas(f) 556.
**violín(m) 544.**
violín(m) 545.
**violines(m), familia(f) 545.**
violoncelo(m) 545.
violoncelos(m) 557.
vira(f) 355.
viraje(m) (toque(m)) con dos manos(f) 622.
viraje(m) de mariposa(f) 623.
Virgo 11, 13.
Virgo, la Virgen (23 de agosto) 820.
virotillo(m) 199.
visera(f) 328, 329, 443, 471, 642, 729, 792.
visillo(m) 228, 231.
visillos(m) recogidos 228.
visillos(m) sencillos 229.
visor(m) 390, 414, 713.
visor(m) electrónico 409.
visor(m) lateral 443.
VISOR(M) TELESCÓPICO 718.
**vista posterior 123.**
**vista(f) anterior 120, 122.**
**vista(f) dorsal 95.**
**vista(f) exterior 712.**
**vista(f) frontal 147.**
**vista(f) general 289.**
**vista(f) lateral 442.**
**vista(f) por encima 171, 444.**
**vista(f) por encima de un ordenador(m) personal 528.**
**vista(f) posterior 121, 129.**
VISTA(F) TRANSVERSAL DE UNA CALLE(F) 186.
**vista(f) transversal de una carretera(f) 450.**
**vista(f) trasera 147.**
visualización(f) 420, 422.
visualización(f) de datos(m) 421.
visualización(f) de la información(f) 396, 409, 411.
**visualización(f) de las ondas(f) sísmicas 714.**
visualización(f) de valores(m) de abertura(f) y de exposición(f) 396.
visualización(f) del mensaje 532.
vitola(f) 384.
vitrales(m) 175.
vitrina(f) 227.
VIVIENDAS(F) TRADICIONALES 165.
VIVIENDAS(F) URBANAS 187.
volador(m) 698.
**volante(m) 618.**
volante(m) 147, 228, 430, 561, 579.
volante(m) de aspas(f) 581.
volante(m) de control(m) 778.
volante(m) del freno(m) manual 470.
volantes(m) 349.
VOLCÁN(M) 25.
volcán(m) 23.
**volcán(m) en erupción(f) 25.**
volcán(m) inactivo 24.
**voltímetro(m) 310.**
volumen(m) de agua(f) 755.
voluta(f) 166, 167, 220, 544.
volva(f) 55.
vuelo(m) 625, 817.
vuelo(m) del escalón(m) 201.
VUELO(M) EN GLOBO(M) 634.
VUELO(M) LIBRE 637.
VUELO(M) SIN MOTOR(M) 638.
vuelta(f) 323.
vuelta(f) al comienzo(m) 532.
vuelta(f) de cabo(m) 691.
vuelta(f) de campana(f) 622, 623.
vuelta(f) de escota(f) 691.
vuelta(f) de escota(f) doble 691.
vulva(f) 118, 128.

## W

WATERPOLO(M) 626.
wedge(m) para arena(f) 678.
wedge(m) para rough(m) 678.
wigwam(m) 165.
**wok(m) 248.**
wok(m) 248.

## X

**xilófono(m) 554.**
xilófono(m) 556.

Los términos en **negrita** corresponden a una ilustración; los que aparecen en MAYÚSCULAS indican un título.

## Y

y 831.
yardas(f) 604.
**yelmo(m) 792.**
yelmo(m) 792.
yema(f) 70, 109, 137.
yema(f) axilar 57.
yema(f) terminal 57.
yen(m) 832.
yeyuno(m) 131.
yugo(m) 364.
yunque(m) 138.
yurta(f) 165.

## Z

zafiro(m) 363.
zaguero(m) central 613.
zaguero(m) izquierdo 613.
zamarra(f) 321.
zampoña(f) 536.
zanahoria(f) 71.
zanco(m) 783.
zángano(m) 81.
zanja(f) 733.
zapata(f) 293, 294, 295, 432, 441, 678.
zapata(f) antideslizante 302, 661.
zapata(f) de goma(f) 302.
zapata(f) de la cadena(f) 805.
zapata(f) hidrostática 14.
**zapatera(f) de alambre(m) 358.**
zapatilla(f) 598, 656, 662.
zapatilla(f) con tacos(m) 595.
zapatilla(f) de ballet(m) 356.
zapatilla(f) de tenis(m) 615.
zapatillas(f) de esgrima(f) 667.
zapato(m) a la polaca 318.
zapato(m) con tacos(m) 602.
zapato(m) de calle(f) 355, 356.
zapato(m) de cordones(m) 354.
zapato(m) de correa(f) 356.
zapato(m) de golf(m) 679.
zapato(m) de tacón(m) 318.
zapato(m) de tacón(m) alto 356.
zapato(m) de tacón(m) alto con presillas(f) 356.
zapato(m) de tenis(m) 355.
zapato(m) de vestir 355.
**zapato(m) deportivo 352.**
ZAPATOS(M) 354.
zarcillo(m) 61.
zarpa(f) 198, 199.
zócalo(m) 199, 201, 707.
zócalo(m) de la bañera(f) 292.
ZODÍACO(M), SIGNOS(M) 820.
zona(f) 610.
zona(f) central 611.
zona(f) comercial 190.
zona(f) de alta presión(f) 38.
zona(f) de anotación(f) 604.
zona(f) de asteroides(m) 4.
zona(f) de ataque(m) 608, 613.
zona(f) de atención(f) 597.
zona(f) de baja presión(f) 38.
zona(f) de cambio(m) 612.
zona(f) de circulación(f) 502.
zona(f) de comidas(f) campestres 823.
zona(f) de convección(f) 6.
zona(f) de defensa(f) 608, 613.
zona(f) de derrumbes(m) 826, 827.
zona(f) de estacionamiento(m) 503.
zona(f) de gol(m) 606.
zona(f) de la portería(f) 608.
zona(f) de pelos(m) absorbentes 59.
zona(f) de precipitación(f) 38.
zona(f) de prueba(f) de motores(m) de aviones(m) 811.
zona(f) de radiación(f) 6.
zona(f) de recreo(m) 496.
zona(f) de saque(m) derecha 614.
zona(f) de saque(m) izquierda 614.
zona(f) de servicio(m) 503, 613, 764.
zona(f) de trabajo(m) 16.
zona(f) de traspaso(m) de carga(f) 743.
zona(f) de tres segundos(m) 610.
zona(f) débil de la hoja(f) 666.
zona(f) defensiva 611.
zona(f) del hoyo(m) 676.
zona(f) escolar 826, 827.
zona(f) fuerte de la hoja(f) 666.
zona(f) libre 613.
zona(f) media 666.
zona(f) neutral 603, 605, 608.
zona(f) ofensiva 611.
zona(f) para acampar 823.
zona(f) para acampar y para caravanas(f) 823.
zona(f) para caravanas(f) 823.
zona(f) pelúcida 128.
zona(f) verde 184.
zoom(m) 392, 414.

Los términos en **negrita** corresponden a una ilustración; los que aparecen en MAYÚSCULAS indican un título.